URAL MOUNTAINS
RUSSIA
Moscow
Volga R.
Kama
Ural R.
Minsk
BELARUS
Dnieper R.
Don R.
Volga R.
KAZAKHSTAN
Kiev
Donets R.
UKRAINE
Dnieper R.
Don R.
MOLDOVA
Chişinau
Aral Sea
Tashkent
UZBEKISTAN
TAJIKISTAN
Dushanbe
Bucharest
Black Sea
CAUCASUS MOUNTAINS
Caspian Sea
GEORGIA
T'bilisi
Baku
AZERBAIJAN
ARMENIA
Yerevan
TURKMENISTAN
Ashkhabad
Ankara
TURKEY
Tehran
AFGHANISTAN
Euphrates R.
Tigris R.
Nicosia
SYRIA
CYPRUS
Beirut
Baghdad
IRAN
Sea
LEBANON
Damascus
IRAQ
ISRAEL
Amman
Jerusalem
PAKISTAN
JORDAN
Kuwait
Cairo
KUWAIT
SAUDI ARABIA
Persian Gulf
EGYPT
Nile R.
BAHRAIN
Manama
QATAR
Doha
UNITED ARAB EMIRATES
Abu Dhabi
Red
Arabian

About the Covers for the Tenth Edition of *The Western Heritage*

The different versions of *The Western Heritage,* Tenth Edition, share three different covers. Each cover juxtaposes two images that share a common theme in a manner similar to the way sources are contrasted in the new "Compare and Connect" feature found in each chapter of the text.

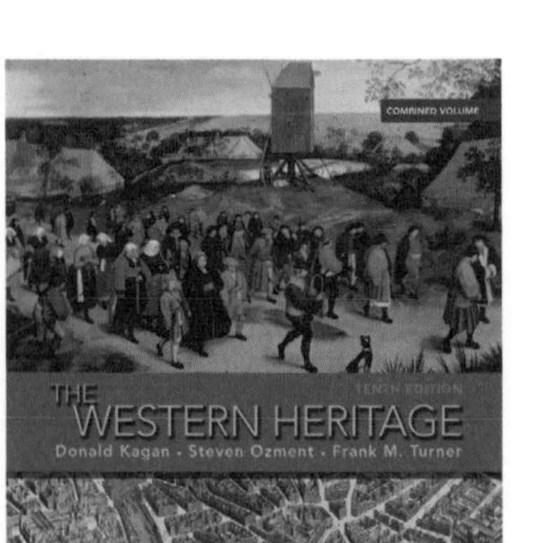

Combined Version
Since 1300
Volume B

Top: *A Wedding Procession,* by Pieter Brueghel the Younger
Bottom: Detail from a 1739 aerial view of Paris

The theme reflected in this pairing of images is urbanization. The Brueghel painting, from 1630, shows a scene from a small village where many of the residents likely knew one another. In contrast, the 1739 bird's eye view of Paris depicts a bustling European capital where residents experienced a level of anonymity common in the modern world. Scenes like the one in the Brueghel painting have become increasingly rare in the West.

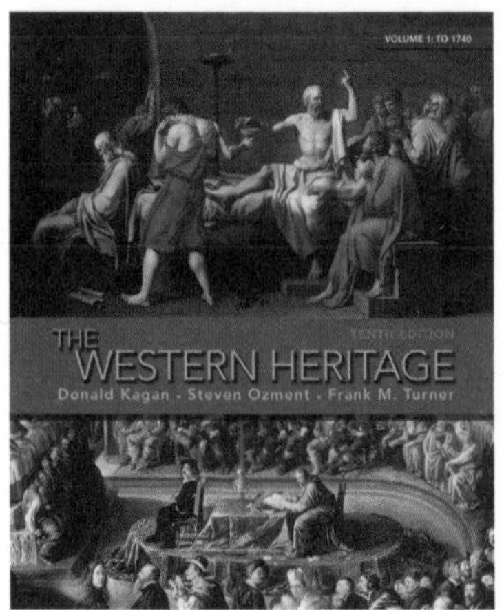

Volume 1
Volume A

Top: *The Death of Socrates,* by Jacques Louis David
Bottom: *Trial of Galileo,* anonymous

Famous trials of those who acted in defiance of the established order is the theme of this pairing of images. Socrates was tried and convicted of corrupting the youth of Athens and disbelieving in the ancestral gods. He was sentenced to death and carried out his own execution by drinking hemlock poison, as shown in this eighteenth–century depiction of the execution. Galileo was tried for and convicted of heresy by the Catholic Church in 1633 for his support for the heliocentric theory of Copernicus.

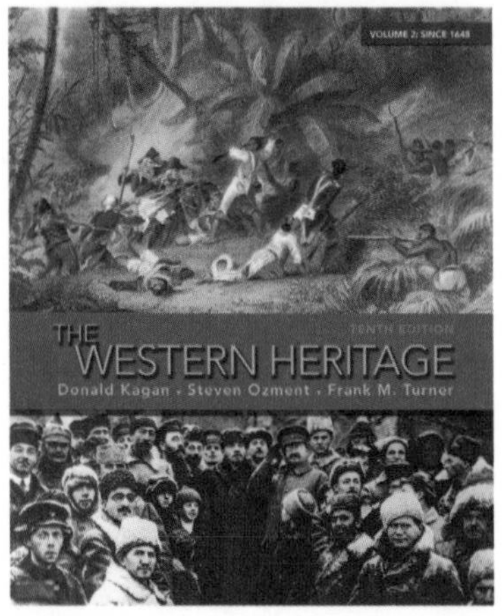

Volume 2
Volume C

Top: François-Dominique Toussaint L'Ouverture engaged in revolt against French colonial forces in Saint Dominique, Haiti.
Bottom: Lenin, Trotsky, and other members of the Bolshevik Party celebrate the third anniversary of the 1917 revolution in Russia.

The theme reflected in this pairing of images is revolution. The Haitian Revolution, led by Toussaint L'Ouverture, was the only successful slave revolt in history, establishing Haiti—originally a French colony—as the first republic ruled by people of African descent. The 1917 revolution in Russia put an end to Tsarist autocracy and led to the establishment of the Union of Soviet Socialist Republics (USSR).

The Western Heritage

Tenth Edition

Combined Volume

Donald Kagan
Yale University

Steven Ozment
Harvard University

Frank M. Turner
Yale University

Prentice Hall
Upper Saddle River London Singapore
Toronto Tokyo Sydney Hong Kong Mexico City

VP, Editorial Director: Leah Jewell
Executive Editor: Charles Cavaliere
Editorial Project Manager: Rob DeGeorge
Production Project Manager: Lynn Savino Wendel
Editorial Assistant: Lauren Aylward
Senior Managing Editor: Ann Marie McCarthy
Director of Marketing: Brandy Dawson
Senior Marketing Manager: Sue Westmoreland
Marketing Assistant: Ashley Fallon
Senior Operations Supervisor: Mary Ann Gloriande
Senior Art Director: Maria Lange
Text and Cover Designer: Liz Harasymczuk
AV Project Manager: Mirella Signoretto
Manager, Visual Research: Beth Brenzel
Manager, Rights and Permissions: Zina Arabia
Image Permission Coordinator: Michelina Viscusi
Manager, Cover Visual Research & Permissions: Karen Sanatar
Media Director: Brian Hyland
Lead Media Project Manager: Sarah Kinney
Supplements Editor: Emsal Hasan
Composition/Full-Service Project Management: Rebecca Dunn, Prepare, Inc.
Printer/Binder: Courier Kendallville
Cover Printer: Lehigh-Phoenix Color

This book was set in 10/12 Trump Mediaeval

Credits and acknowledgments borrowed from other sources and reproduced, with permission, in this textbook appear on appropriate page within text.

Cover photo credits: Private Collection/The Bridgeman Art Library (top illustration); Courtesy of the Library of Congress (bottom illustration).

Library of Congress Cataloging-in-Publication Data

Kagan, Donald
The Western Heritage / Donald Kagan, Steven Ozment, Frank M. Turner.—10th ed.
p. cm.
"Combined volume."
Includes bibliographical references and index.
ISBN 978-0-205-66072-8 (combined)—ISBN 978-0-205-69967-4 (exam)—ISBN 978-0-205-70515-3 (v. 1)—ISBN 978-0-205-70516-0 (v. 2)
ISBN 978-0-205-69978-0 (v. A)—ISBN 978-0-205-69979-7 (v. B)—ISBN 978-0-205-70514-6 (v. C)—ISBN 978-0-205-70517-7 (since 1300)
1. Civilization, Western—History—Textbooks. I. Ozment, Steven E. II. Turner, Frank M. (Frank Miller), 1994 III. Title.
CB245.K28 2010
909'.09821—dc22

2009012769

10 9 8 7 6 5 4 3 2 1

Prentice Hall
is an imprint of

www.pearsonhighered.com

Student edition ISBN 10:0-205-66072-X
ISBN 13:978-0-205-66072-8
Examination Copy ISBN 10:0-205-69967-7
ISBN 13:978-0-205-69967-4

BRIEF CONTENTS

PART 1 The Foundations of Western Civilization in the Ancient World to 400 C.E.

1 The Birth of Civilization 1
2 The Rise of Greek Civilization 33
3 Classical and Hellenistic Greece 61
4 Rome: From Republic to Empire 97
5 The Roman Empire 129

PART 2 The Middle Ages, 476 C.E.–1300 C.E.

6 Late Antiquity and the Early Middle Ages: Creating a New European Society and Culture (476–1000) 170
7 The High Middle Ages: The Rise of European Empires and States (1000–1300) 202
8 Medieval Society: Hierarchies, Towns, Universities, and Families (1000–1300) 227

PART 3 Europe in Transition, 1300–1750

9 The Late Middle Ages: Social and Political Breakdown (1300–1453) 257
10 Renaissance and Discovery 281
11 The Age of Reformation 313
12 The Age of Religious Wars 345
13 European State Consolidation in the Seventeenth and Eighteenth Centuries 371
14 New Directions in Thought and Culture in the Sixteenth and Seventeenth Centuries 407
15 Society and Economy Under the Old Regime in the Eighteenth Century 433
16 The Transatlantic Economy, Trade Wars, and Colonial Rebellion 462

PART 4 Enlightenment and Revolution, 1700–1850

17 The Age of Enlightenment: Eighteenth-Century Thought 492
18 The French Revolution 529
19 The Age of Napoleon and the Triumph of Romanticism 561
20 The Conservative Order and the Challenges of Reform (1815–1832) 593
21 Economic Advance and Social Unrest (1830–1850) 622

PART 5 Toward the Modern World, 1850–1939

22 The Age of Nation-States 661
23 The Building of European Supremacy: Society and Politics to World War I 690
24 The Birth of Modern European Thought 724
25 The Age of Western Imperialism 754
26 Alliances, War, and a Troubled Peace 798
27 The Interwar Years: The Challenge of Dictators and Depression 833

PART 6 Global Conflict, Cold War, and New Directions, 1939–2008

28 World War II 865
29 The Cold War Era, Decolonization, and the Emergence of a New Europe 902
30 The West at the Dawn of the Twenty-First Century 947

CONTENTS

Preface xxii
What Is the Western Heritage? xxix

PART 1
The Foundations of Western Civilization in the Ancient World to 400 C.E.

1 The Birth of Civilization 1

Early Humans and Their Culture 2
The Paleolithic Age 2
The Neolithic Age 3
The Bronze Age and the Birth of Civilization 4

Early Civilizations to about 1000 B.C.E 4
Mesopotamian Civilization 5
Egyptian Civilization 14

Ancient Near Eastern Empires 22
The Hittites 22
The Assyrians 22
The Second Assyrian Empire 22
The Neo-Babylonians 23

The Persian Empire 23
Cyrus the Great 23
Darius the Great 24
Government and Administration 25
Religion 26
Art and Culture 26

Palestine 27
The Canaanites and the Phoenicians 27
The Israelites 27
The Jewish Religion 28

General Outlook of Mideastern Cultures 28
Humans and Nature 29
Humans and the Gods, Law and Justice 29

Toward the Greeks and Western Thought 30

In Perspective 31

Review Questions 31

Suggested Readings 32

A Closer LOOK THE ROYAL STANDARD OF UR 8

■ ENCOUNTERING THE PAST
Divination in Ancient Mesopotamia 10

COMPARE AND CONNECT:
The Great Flood 12

2 The Rise of Greek Civilization 33

The Bronze Age on Crete and on the Mainland to about 1150 B.C.E. 34
The Minoans 34
The Mycenaeans 35

The Greek "Middle Ages" to about 750 B.C.E. 37
Greek Migrations 37
The Age of Homer 38

The *Polis* 39
Development of the Polis 39
The Hoplite Phalanx 40
The Importance of the Polis 40

Expansion of the Greek World 40
Magna Graecia 42
The Greek Colony 42
The Tyrants (ca. 700–500 B.C.E.) 43

The Major States 44
Sparta 44
Athens 46

Life in Archaic Greece 49
Society 49
Religion 50
Poetry 53

The Persian Wars 53
The Ionian Rebellion 54
The War in Greece 54

In Perspective 58

Review Questions 59

Suggested Readings 59

■ ENCOUNTERING THE PAST
Greek Athletics 51

A Closer LOOK THE TRIREME 52

COMPARE AND CONNECT:
Greek Strategy in the Persian War 56

3 Classical and Hellenistic Greece 61

Aftermath of Victory 62
The Delian League 62
The Rise of Cimon 63

The First Peloponnesian War: Athens against Sparta 63
The Breach with Sparta 63
The Division of Greece 63

Classical Greece 64
The Athenian Empire 64
Athenian Democracy 65

The Women of Athens: Social Status and Everyday Life 67
Slavery 71
Religion in Public Life 72
The Great Peloponnesian War 73
Causes 73
Strategic Stalemate 73
The Fall of Athens 74
Competition for Leadership in the Fourth Century B.C.E. 74
The Hegemony of Sparta 74
The Hegemony of Thebes: The Second Athenian Empire 75
The Culture of Classical Greece 75
The Fifth Century B.C.E. 75
The Fourth Century B.C.E. 80
Philosophy and the Crisis of the Polis 80
The Hellenistic World 86
The Macedonian Conquest 86
Alexander the Great 88
The Successors 90
Hellenistic Culture 91
Philosophy 91
Literature 93
Architecture and Sculpture 93
Mathematics and Science 93
In Perspective 95
Review Questions 95
Suggested Readings 96

■ **ENCOUNTERING THE PAST**
Going to Court in Athens **66**

COMPARE AND CONNECT
Athenian Democracy—Pro and Con **68**

A Closer LOOK **THE ERECHTHEUM: PORCH OF THE MAIDENS** **82**

4 Rome: From Republic to Empire 97

Prehistoric Italy 98
The Etruscans 98
Government 98
Religion 98
Women 99
Dominion 99
Royal Rome 99
Government 99
The Family 100
Women in Early Rome 100
Clientage 100
Patricians and Plebeians 101
The Republic 101
Constitution 101
The Conquest of Italy 103
Rome and Carthage 105
The Republic's Conquest of the Hellenistic World 108
Civilization in the Early Roman Republic 109
Religion 109
Education 111
Slavery 113
Roman Imperialism: The Late Republic 115
The Aftermath of Conquest 116
The Gracchi 116
Marius and Sulla 119
The Fall of the Republic 120
Pompey, Crassus, Caesar, and Cicero 120
The First Triumvirate 121
Julius Caesar and His Government of Rome 121
The Second Triumvirate and the Triumph of Octavian 126
In Perspective 127
Review Questions 128
Suggested Readings 128

A Closer LOOK **LICTORS** **103**

■ **ENCOUNTERING THE PAST**
Two Roman Festivals: The Saturnalia and Lupercalia **112**

COMPARE AND CONNECT
Did Caesar Want to Be King? **124**

5 The Roman Empire 129

The Augustan Principate 130
Administration 130
The Army and Defense 131
Religion and Morality 132
Civilization of the Ciceronian and Augustan Ages 132
The Late Republic 133
The Age of Augustus 133
Imperial Rome, 14 to 180 C.E. 135
The Emperors 135
The Administration of the Empire 136
Women of the Upper Classes 141
Life in Imperial Rome: The Apartment House 142
The Culture of the Early Empire 142
The Rise of Christianity 145
Jesus of Nazareth 145
Paul of Tarsus 145

Organization 147
The Persecution of Christians 147
The Emergence of Catholicism 148
Rome as a Center of the Early Church 148
The Crisis of the Third Century 148
Barbarian Invasions 149
Economic Difficulties 149
The Social Order 152
Civil Disorder 152
The Late Empire 152
The Fourth Century and Imperial Reorganization 152
The Triumph of Christianity 156
Arts and Letters in the Late Empire 160
The Preservation of Classical Culture 160
Christian Writers 160
The Problem of the Decline and Fall of the Empire in the West 161
In Perspective 162
Review Questions 162
Suggested Readings 162

A Closer LOOK SPOILS FROM JERUSALEM ON THE ARCH OF TITUS IN ROME 138
■ ENCOUNTERING THE PAST Chariot Racing 146
COMPARE AND CONNECT **Christianity in the Roman Empire—Why Did the Romans Persecute the Christians?** 150

THE WEST & THE WORLD Ancient Warfare 164

PART 2
The Middle Ages, 476 C.E.–1300 C.E.

6 Late Antiquity and the Early Middle Ages: Creating a New European Society and Culture (476–1000) 170

On the Eve of the Frankish Ascendancy 171
Germanic Migrations 172
New Western Masters 172
The Byzantine Empire 173
The Reign of Justinian 174
The Spread of Byzantine Christianity 177
Persians and Muslims 177
Islam and the Islamic World 178
Muhammad's Religion 178
Islamic Diversity 179
Islamic Empires 182
The Western Debt to Islam 182
Western Society and the Developing Christian Church 183
Monastic Culture 183
The Doctrine of Papal Primacy 184
The Religious Division of Christendom 186
The Kingdom of the Franks: From Clovis to Charlemagne 187
Governing the Franks 187
The Reign of Charlemagne (768–814) 189
Breakup of the Carolingian Kingdom 192
Feudal Society 196
Origins 196
Vassalage and the Fief 198
Daily Life and Religion 198
Fragmentation and Divided Loyalty 199
In Perspective 200
Review Questions 200
Suggested Readings 201

COMPARE AND CONNECT **The Battle of the Sexes in Christianity and Islam** 180
A Closer LOOK A MULTICULTURAL BOOK COVER 193
■ ENCOUNTERING THE PAST Medieval Cooking 197

7 The High Middle Ages: The Rise of European Empires and States (1000–1300) 202

Otto I and the Revival of the Empire 203
Unifying Germany 203
Embracing the Church 203
The Reviving Catholic Church 204
The Cluny Reform Movement 204
The Investiture Struggle: Gregory VII and Henry IV 206
The Crusades 207
The Pontificate of Innocent III (r. 1198–1216) 211
England and France: Hastings (1066) to Bouvines (1214) 215
William the Conqueror 216
Henry II 216
Eleanor of Aquitaine and Court Culture 217
Popular Rebellion and Magna Carta 217
Philip II Augustus 218
France in the Thirteenth Century: The Reign of Louis IX 220
Generosity Abroad 220
Order and Excellence at Home 220

The Hohenstaufen Empire (1152–1272) 221
Frederick I Barbarossa 221
Henry VI and the Sicilian Connection 222
Otto IV and the Welf Interregnum 223
Frederick II 223
Romanesque and Gothic Architecture 224
In Perspective 225
Review Questions 226
Suggested Readings 226

A Closer LOOK EUROPEAN EMBRACE OF A BLACK SAINT 210
COMPARE AND CONNECT Christian Jihad, Muslim Jihad 212
■ ENCOUNTERING THE PAST Pilgrimages 219

8 Medieval Society: Hierarchies, Towns, Universities, and Families (1000–1300) 227

The Traditional Order of Life 228
Nobles 228
Clergy 232
Peasants 234
Towns and Townspeople 236
The Chartering of Towns 236
The Rise of Merchants 236
Challenging the Old Lords 236
New Models of Government 238
Towns and Kings 239
Jews in Christian Society 239
Schools and Universities 239
University of Bologna 240
Cathedral Schools 242
University of Paris 242
The Curriculum 244
Philosophy and Theology 244
Women in Medieval Society 245
Image and Status 245
Life Choices 248
Working Women 248
The Lives of Children 248
Children as "Little Adults" 248
Childhood as a Special Stage 250
In Perspective 250
Review Questions 250
Suggested Readings 251

A Closer LOOK THE JOYS AND PAINS OF THE MEDIEVAL JOUST 229
■ ENCOUNTERING THE PAST Warrior Games 231
COMPARE AND CONNECT Faith and Love in the High Middle Ages 246

THE WEST & THE WORLD The Invention of Printing in China and Europe 252

PART 3
Europe in Transition, 1300–1750

9 The Late Middle Ages: Social and Political Breakdown (1300–1453) 257

The Black Death 258
Preconditions and Causes of the Plague 258
Popular Remedies 258
Social and Economic Consequences 260
New Conflicts and Opportunities 262
The Hundred Years' War and the Rise of National Sentiment 262
The Causes of the War 263
Progress of the War 265
Ecclesiastical Breakdown and Revival: The Late Medieval Church 267
The Thirteenth-Century Papacy 267
Boniface VIII and Philip the Fair 268
The Avignon Papacy (1309–1377) 272
John Wycliffe and John Huss 273
The Great Schism (1378–1417) and the Conciliar Movement to 1449 274
Medieval Russia 278
Politics and Society 278
Mongol Rule (1243–1480) 279
In Perspective 279
Review Questions 279
Suggested Readings 280

■ ENCOUNTERING THE PAST Dealing with Death 261
COMPARE AND CONNECT Who Runs the World: Priests or Princes? 270
A Closer LOOK THE ENCAMPMENT OF THE IMPERIAL ARMY 277

10 Renaissance and Discovery 281

The Renaissance in Italy (1375–1527) 282
The Italian City-State 283
Humanism 285
Renaissance Art 289
Slavery in the Renaissance 294
Italy's Political Decline: The French Invasions (1494–1527) 295
Charles VIII's March Through Italy 295
Pope Alexander VI and the Borgia Family 295
Pope Julius II 296
Niccolò Machiavelli 296

Revival of Monarchy in Northern Europe 297
France 298
Spain 298
England 299
The Holy Roman Empire 300
The Northern Renaissance 301
The Printing Press 301
Erasmus 302
Humanism and Reform 302
Voyages of Discovery and the New Empires in the West and East 303
The Portuguese Chart the Course 303
The Spanish Voyages of Columbus 305
The Spanish Empire in the New World 305
The Church in Spanish America 307
The Economy of Exploitation 308
The Impact on Europe 309
In Perspective 311
Review Questions 311
Suggested Readings 312

■ ENCOUNTERING THE PAST
The Renaissance Garden **286**
COMPARE AND CONNECT
Is the Renaissance Man a Myth? 290
A Closer LOOK LEONARDO PLOTS THE PERFECT MAN **293**

11 The Age of Reformation 313

Society and Religion 314
Social and Political Conflict 314
Popular Religious Movements and Criticisms of the Church 314
Martin Luther and German Reformation to 1525 316
Justification by Faith Alone 316
The Attack on Indulgences 318
Election of Charles V 319
Luther's Excommunication and the Diet of Worms 319
Imperial Distractions: War with France and the Turks 320
How the Reformation Spread 321
The Peasants' Revolt 321
The Reformation Elsewhere 324
Zwingli and the Swiss Reformation 324
Anabaptists and Radical Protestants 326
John Calvin and the Genevan Reformation 327
Political Consolidation of the Lutheran Reformation 329
The Diet of Augsburg 329
The Expansion of the Reformation 329
Reaction against Protestants 330
The Peace of Augsburg 330
The English Reformation to 1553 330
The Preconditions of Reform 330
The King's Affair 330
The "Reform Parliament" 331
Wives of Henry VIII 332
The King's Religious Conservatism 332
The Protestant Reformation under Edward VI 332
Catholic Reform and Counter-Reformation 333
Sources of Catholic Reform 333
Ignatius of Loyola and the Jesuits 333
The Council of Trent (1545–1563) 334
The Social Significance of the Reformation in Western Europe 335
The Revolution in Religious Practices and Institutions 336
The Reformation and Education 336
The Reformation and the Changing Role of Women 338
Family Life in Early Modern Europe 339
Later Marriages 339
Arranged Marriages 339
Family Size 339
Birth Control 339
Wet Nursing 341
Loving Families? 341
Literary Imagination in Transition 341
Miguel de Cervantes Saavedra: Rejection of Idealism 341
William Shakespeare: Dramatist of the Age 342
In Perspective 343
Review Questions 343
Suggested Readings 343

A Closer LOOK A SAINT AT PEACE IN THE GRASP OF TEMPTATION **317**
COMPARE AND CONNECT
A Raw Deal for the Common Man, or His Just Desserts? 322
■ ENCOUNTERING THE PAST
Table Manners **340**

12 The Age of Religious Wars 345

Renewed Religious Struggle 345
The French Wars of Religion (1562–1598) 346
Appeal of Calvinism 348
Catherine de Médicis and the Guises 348
The Rise to Power of Henry of Navarre 350
The Edict of Nantes 351
Imperial Spain and Philip II (r. 1556–1598) 352
Pillars of Spanish Power 352

The Revolt in the Netherlands 353
England and Spain (1553–1603) 356
Mary I (r. 1553–1558) 357
Elizabeth I (r. 1558–1603) 357
The Thirty Years' War (1618–1648) 363
Preconditions for War 363
Four Periods of War 365
The Treaty of Westphalia 368
In Perspective 368
Review Questions 370
Suggested Readings 370

A Closer LOOK BAROQUE AND PLAIN CHURCH: ARCHITECTURAL REFLECTIONS OF BELIEF 347
COMPARE AND CONNECT A Great Debate over Religious Tolerance 358
■ ENCOUNTERING THE PAST Going to the Theater 361

13 European State Consolidation in the Seventeenth and Eighteenth Centuries 371

The Netherlands: Golden Age to Decline 372
Urban Prosperity 372
Economic Decline 373
Two Models of European Political Development 374
Constitutional Crisis and Settlement in Stuart England 374
James I 374
Charles I 377
The Long Parliament and Civil War 377
Oliver Cromwell and the Puritan Republic 378
Charles II and the Restoration of the Monarchy 378
The "Glorious Revolution" 379
The Age of Walpole 380
Rise of Absolute Monarchy in France: The World of Louis XIV 381
Years of Personal Rule 381
Versailles 382
King by Divine Right 382
Louis's Early Wars 384
Louis's Repressive Religious Policies 384
Louis's Later Wars 388
France after Louis XIV 391
Central and Eastern Europe 392
Poland: Absence of Strong Central Authority 392
The Habsburg Empire and the Pragmatic Sanction 393
Prussia and the Hohenzollerns 395
Russia Enters the European Political Arena 397
The Romanov Dynasty 397
Peter the Great 397
Russian Expansion in the Baltic: The Great Northern War 398
The Ottoman Empire 401
Religious Toleration and Ottoman Government 401
The End of Ottoman Expansion 403
In Perspective 404
Review Questions 405
Suggested Readings 405

■ ENCOUNTERING THE PAST Early Controversy over Tobacco and Smoking 376
A Closer LOOK VERSAILLES 383
COMPARE AND CONNECT The Debate over the Origin and Character of Political Authority 386

14 New Directions in Thought and Culture in the Sixteenth and Seventeenth Centuries 407

The Scientific Revolution 408
Nicolaus Copernicus Rejects an Earth-Centered Universe 408
Tycho Brahe and Johannes Kepler Make New Scientific Observations 410
Galileo Galilei Argues for a Universe of Mathematical Laws 410
Isaac Newton Discovers the Laws of Gravitation 411
Philosophy Responds to Changing Science 412
Nature as Mechanism 412
Francis Bacon: The Empirical Method 412
René Descartes: The Method of Rational Deduction 414
Thomas Hobbes: Apologist for Absolute Government 415
John Locke: Defender of Moderate Liberty and Toleration 416
The New Institutions of Expanding Natural Knowledge 418
Women in the World of the Scientific Revolution 419
The New Science and Religious Faith 421
The Case of Galileo 421
Blaise Pascal: Reason and Faith 425
The English Approach to Science and Religion 425
Continuing Superstition 427
Witch Hunts and Panic 427
Village Origins 427
Influence of the Clergy 428

Who Were the Witches? 428
End of the Witch Hunts 428
Baroque Art 428
In Perspective 431
Review Questions 432
Suggested Readings 432

COMPARE AND CONNECT Descartes and Swift Debate the Scientific Enterprise 422
A Closer LOOK THE SCIENCES AND THE ARTS 426
■ ENCOUNTERING THE PAST Midwives 430

15 Society and Economy Under the Old Regime in the Eighteenth Century 433

Major Features of Life in the Old Regime 434
Maintenance of Tradition 434
Hierarchy and Privilege 434
The Aristocracy 435
Varieties of Aristocratic Privilege 435
Aristocratic Resurgence 437
The Land and Its Tillers 437
Peasants and Serfs 437
Aristocratic Domination of the Countryside: The English Game Laws 439
Family Structures and the Family Economy 439
Households 439
The Family Economy 441
Women and the Family Economy 441
Children and the World of the Family Economy 442
The Revolution in Agriculture 443
New Crops and New Methods 444
Expansion of the Population 445
The Industrial Revolution of the Eighteenth Century 448
A Revolution in Consumption 448
Industrial Leadership of Great Britain 449
New Methods of Textile Production 449
The Steam Engine 451
Iron Production 452
The Impact of the Agricultural and Industrial Revolutions on Working Women 452
The Growth of Cities 453
Patterns of Preindustrial Urbanization 453
Urban Classes 455
The Urban Riot 458
The Jewish Population: The Age of the Ghetto 458
In Perspective 459
Review Questions 461
Suggested Readings 461

A Closer LOOK AN ARISTOCRATIC COUPLE 436
COMPARE AND CONNECT Two Eighteenth-Century Writers Contemplate the Effects of Different Economic Structures 446
■ ENCOUNTERING THE PAST Water, Washing, and Bathing 456

16 The Transatlantic Economy, Trade Wars, and Colonial Rebellion 462

Periods of European Overseas Empires 463
Mercantile Empires 464
Mercantilist Goals 464
French–British Rivalry 465
The Spanish Colonial System 465
Colonial Government 466
Trade Regulation 466
Colonial Reform under the Spanish Bourbon Monarchs 466
Black African Slavery, the Plantation System, and the Atlantic Economy 469
The African Presence in the Americas 469
Slavery and the Transatlantic Economy 473
The Experience of Slavery 473
Mid-Eighteenth-Century Wars 478
The War of Jenkins's Ear 478
The War of the Austrian Succession (1740–1748) 478
The "Diplomatic Revolution" of 1756 479
The Seven Years' War (1756–1763) 480
The American Revolution and Europe 481
Resistance to the Imperial Search for Revenue 481
The Crisis and Independence 482
American Political Ideas 483
Events in Great Britain 484
Broader Impact of the American Revolution 486
In Perspective 487
Review Questions 487
Suggested Readings 488

■ ENCOUNTERING THE PAST Sugar Enters the Western Diet 471
A Closer LOOK A SUGAR PLANTATION IN THE WEST INDIES 472
COMPARE AND CONNECT The Atlantic Passage 474

THE WEST & THE WORLD The Columbian Exchange, Disease, Animals, and Agriculture 489

PART 4
Enlightenment and Revolution, 1700–1850

17 The Age of Enlightenment: Eighteenth-Century Thought 492

Formative Influences on the Enlightenment 493
Ideas of Newton and Locke 493
The Example of British Toleration and Political Stability 493
The Emergence of a Print Culture 494
The Philosophes 495
Voltaire—First among the Philosophes 497
The Enlightenment and Religion 498
Deism 498
Toleration 499
Radical Enlightenment Criticism of Christianity 499
Jewish Thinkers in the Age of Enlightenment 501
Islam in Enlightenment Thought 502
The Enlightenment and Society 504
The Encyclopedia*: Freedom and Economic Improvement* 505
Beccaria and Reform of Criminal Law 505
The Physiocrats and Economic Freedom 505
Adam Smith on Economic Growth and Social Progress 505
Political Thought of the *Philosophes* 507
Montesquieu and Spirit of the Laws 507
Rousseau: A Radical Critique of Modern Society 508
Enlightened Critics of European Empires 509
Women in the Thought and Practice of the Enlightenment 511
Rococo and Neoclassical Styles in Eighteenth-Century Art 514
Enlightened Absolutism 517
Frederick the Great of Prussia 519
Joseph II of Austria 520
Catherine the Great of Russia 524
The Partition of Poland 526
The End of the Eighteenth Century in Central and Eastern Europe 527
In Perspective 527
Review Questions 528
Suggested Readings 528

■ ENCOUNTERING THE PAST
Coffeehouses and Enlightenment 496

A Closer LOOK AN EIGHTEENTH-CENTURY ARTIST APPEALS TO THE ANCIENT WORLD 518

COMPARE AND CONNECT
Maria Theresa and Joseph II of Austria Debate Toleration 522

18 The French Revolution 529

The Crisis of the French Monarchy 530
The Monarchy Seeks New Taxes 530
Necker's Report 531
Calonne's Reform Plan and the Assembly of Notables 531
Deadlock and the Calling of the Estates General 532
The Revolution of 1789 532
The Estates General Becomes the National Assembly 532
Fall of the Bastille 534
The "Great Fear" and the Night of August 4 537
The Declaration of the Rights of Man and Citizen 537
The Parisian Women's March on Versailles 539
The Reconstruction of France 539
Political Reorganization 539
Economic Policy 541
The Civil Constitution of the Clergy 545
Counterrevolutionary Activity 545
The End of the Monarchy: A Second Revolution 546
Emergence of the Jacobins 546
The Convention and the Role of the Sans-culottes 547
Europe at War with the Revolution 548
Edmund Burke Attacks the Revolution 548
Suppression of Reform in Britain 549
The Second and Third Partitions of Poland, 1793, 1795 549
The Reign of Terror 549
War with Europe 549
The Republic Defended 551
The "Republic of Virtue" and Robespierre's Justification of Terror 553
Repression of the Society of Revolutionary Republican Women 553
De-Christianization 554
Revolutionary Tribunals 554
The End of the Terror 555
The Thermidorian Reaction 555
Establishment of the Directory 557
Removal of the Sans-culottes *from Political Life* 558
In Perspective 558
Review Questions 560
Suggested Readings 560

A Closer LOOK CHALLENGING THE FRENCH POLITICAL ORDER 536

COMPARE AND CONNECT The Declaration of the Rights of Man and Citizen Opens the Door for Disadvantaged Groups to Demand Equal Civic Rights 542

■ ENCOUNTERING THE PAST
The Metric System 544

19 The Age of Napoleon and the Triumph of Romanticism 561

The Rise of Napoleon Bonaparte 562
Early Military Victories 562
The Constitution of the Year VIII 563
The Consulate in France (1799–1804) 563
Suppressing Foreign Enemies and Domestic Opposition 563
Concordat with the Roman Catholic Church 563
The Napoleonic Code 564
Establishing a Dynasty 564
Napoleon's Empire (1804–1814) 564
Conquering an Empire 564
The Continental System 566
European Response to the Empire 568
German Nationalism and Prussian Reform 568
The Wars of Liberation 570
The Invasion of Russia 571
European Coalition 574
The Congress of Vienna and the European Settlement 574
Territorial Adjustments 575
The Hundred Days and the Quadruple Alliance 576
The Romantic Movement 577
Romantic Questioning of the Supremacy of Reason 577
Rousseau and Education 577
Kant and Reason 579
Romantic Literature 579
The English Romantic Writers 579
The German Romantic Writers 581
Romantic Art 582
The Cult of the Middle Ages and Neo-Gothicism 582
Nature and the Sublime 583
Religion in the Romantic Period 584
Methodism 586
New Directions in Continental Religion 587
Romantic Views of Nationalism and History 587
Herder and Culture 587
Hegel and History 588
Islam, the Middle East, and Romanticism 588
In Perspective 591
Review Questions 591
Suggested Readings 591

A Closer LOOK THE CORONATION OF NAPOLEON 565

■ ENCOUNTERING THE PAST
Sailors and Canned Food 567

COMPARE AND CONNECT The Experience of War in the Napoleonic Age 572

20 The Conservative Order and the Challenges of Reform (1815–1832) 593

The Challenges of Nationalism and Liberalism 594
The Emergence of Nationalism 594
Early Nineteenth-Century Political Liberalism 595
Conservative Governments: The Domestic Political Order 600
Conservative Outlooks 600
Liberalism and Nationalism Resisted in Austria and the Germanies 601
Postwar Repression in Great Britain 602
Bourbon Restoration in France 605
The Conservative International Order 606
The Congress System 606
The Spanish Revolution of 1820 607
Revolt against Ottoman Rule in the Balkans 608
The Wars of Independence in Latin America 608
Revolution in Haiti 610
Wars of Independence on the South American Continent 612
Independence in New Spain 613
Brazilian Independence 614
The Conservative Order Shaken in Europe 614
Russia: The Decembrist Revolt of 1825 614
Revolution in France (1830) 617
Belgium Becomes Independent (1830) 618
The Great Reform Bill in Britain (1832) 619
In Perspective 620
Review Questions 621
Suggested Readings 621

COMPARE AND CONNECT Mazzini and Lord Acton Debate the Political Principles of Nationalism 596

■ ENCOUNTERING THE PAST
Gymnastics and German Nationalism 604

A Closer LOOK AN ENGLISH POET APPEARS AS AN ALBANIAN 609

21 Economic Advance and Social Unrest (1830–1850) 622

Toward an Industrial Society 623
Population and Migration 623
Railways 624
The Labor Force 626
The Emergence of a Wage Labor Force 626
Working-Class Political Action: The Example of British Chartism 627
Family Structures and the Industrial Revolution 630
The Family in the Early Factory System 630
Women in the Early Industrial Revolution 632
Opportunities and Exploitation in Employment 632
Changing Expectations in the Working-Class Marriage 634
Problems of Crime and Order 634
New Police Forces 636
Prison Reform 636
Classical Economics 638
Malthus on Population 638
Ricardo on Wages 638
Government Policies Based on Classical Economics 638
Early Socialism 639
Utopian Socialism 639
Anarchism 641
Marxism 642
1848: Year of Revolutions 645
France: The Second Republic and Louis Napoleon 646
The Habsburg Empire: Nationalism Resisted 649
Italy: Republicanism Defeated 652
Germany: Liberalism Frustrated 652
In Perspective 653
Review Questions 654
Suggested Readings 654

■ ENCOUNTERING THE PAST
The Potato and the Great Hunger in Ireland 625

COMPARE AND CONNECT
Andrew Ure and John Ruskin Debate the Conditions of Factory Production 628

A Closer LOOK THE GREAT EXHIBITION IN LONDON 631

THE WEST & THE WORLD The Abolition of Slavery in the Transatlantic Economy 655

PART 5
Toward the Modern World, 1850 –1939

22 The Age of Nation-States 661

The Crimean War (1853–1856) 662
Peace Settlement and Long-Term Results 662
Reforms in the Ottoman Empire 662
Italian Unification 664
Romantic Republicans 664
Cavour's Policy 665
The New Italian State 666
German Unification 670
Bismarck 671
The Franco-Prussian War and the German Empire (1870–1871) 673
France: From Liberal Empire to the Third Republic 674
The Paris Commune 674
The Third Republic 675
The Dreyfus Affair 675
The Habsburg Empire 676
Formation of the Dual Monarchy 678
Unrest of Nationalities 678
Russia: Emancipation and Revolutionary Stirrings 680
Reforms of Alexander II 680
Revolutionaries 681
Great Britain: Toward Democracy 684
The Second Reform Act (1867) 684
Gladstone's Great Ministry (1868–1874) 684
Disraeli in Office (1874–1880) 686
The Irish Question 687
In Perspective 688
Review Questions 688
Suggested Readings 688

A Closer LOOK THE CRIMEAN WAR RECALLED 663

COMPARE AND CONNECT
Nineteenth Century Nationalism: Two Sides 668

■ ENCOUNTERING THE PAST
The Arrival of Penny Postage 685

23 The Building of European Supremacy: Society and Politics to World War I 690

Population Trends and Migration 691

The Second Industrial Revolution 691
New Industries 692
Economic Difficulties 694
The Middle Classes in Ascendancy 694
Social Distinctions within the Middle Classes 694
Late-Nineteenth-Century Urban Life 697
The Redesign of Cities 697
Urban Sanitation 698
Housing Reform and Middle-Class Values 700
Varieties of Late-Nineteenth-Century Women's Experiences 700
Women's Social Disabilities 700
New Employment Patterns for Women 702
Working-Class Women 703
Poverty and Prostitution 704
Women of the Middle Class 704
The Rise of Political Feminism 706
Jewish Emancipation 709
Differing Degrees of Citizenship 709
Broadened Opportunities 709
Labor, Socialism, and Politics to World War I 710
Trade Unionism 710
Democracy and Political Parties 711
Karl Marx and the First International 711
Great Britain: Fabianism and Early Welfare Programs 712
France: "Opportunism" Rejected 713
Germany: Social Democrats and Revisionism 713
Russia: Industrial Development and the Birth of Bolshevism 714
In Perspective 722
Review Questions 722
Suggested Readings 723

■ ENCOUNTERING THE PAST
Bicycles: Transportation, Freedom, and Sport 695
COMPARE AND CONNECT
Bernstein and Lenin Debate the Character of Tactics of European Socialism 718
A Closer LOOK BLOODY SUNDAY, ST. PETERSBURG 1905 721

24 The Birth of Modern European Thought 724

The New Reading Public 725
Advances in Primary Education 725
Reading Material for the Mass Audience 726
Science at Midcentury 726
Comte, Positivism, and the Prestige of Science 726
Darwin's Theory of Natural Selection 728
Science and Ethics 728
Christianity and the Church under Siege 729
Intellectual Skepticism 729
Conflict between Church and State 732
Areas of Religious Revival 732
The Roman Catholic Church and the Modern World 733
Islam and Late-Nineteenth-Century European Thought 734
Toward a Twentieth-Century Frame of Mind 735
Science: The Revolution in Physics 735
Rays and Radiation 736
Literature: Realism and Naturalism 737
Modernism in Literature 738
The Coming of Modern Art 739
Friedrich Nietzsche and the Revolt Against Reason 742
The Birth of Psychoanalysis 743
Retreat from Rationalism in Politics 744
Racism 745
Anti-Semitism and the Birth of Zionism 747
Women and Modern Thought 747
Anti-Feminism in Late-Century Thought 747
New Directions in Feminism 749
In Perspective 751
Review Questions 753
Suggested Readings 753

■ ENCOUNTERING THE PAST
The Birth of Science Fiction 727
COMPARE AND CONNECT
The Debate over Social Darwinism 730
A Closer LOOK CONFLICT BETWEEN CHURCH AND STATE IN GERMANY 733

25 The Age of Western Imperialism 754

The Close of the Age of Early Modern Colonization 755
The Age of British Imperial Dominance 756
The Imperialism of Free Trade 756
British Settler Colonies 757
India—The Jewel in the Crown of the British Empire 757
The "New Imperialism," 1870–1914 761
Motives for the New Imperialism 763
The Partition of Africa 768
Algeria, Tunisia, Morocco, and Libya 768

Egypt and British Strategic Concern about the Upper Nile 768
West Africa 773
The Belgian Congo 774
German Empire in Africa 775
Southern Africa 775
Russian Expansion in Mainland Asia 776
Western Powers in Asia 778
France in Asia 778
The United States' Actions in Asia and the Pacific 779
The Boxer Rebellion 780
Tools of Imperialism 782
Steamboats 782
Conquest of Tropical Diseases 782
Firearms 782
The Missionary Factor 784
Evangelical Protestant Missionaries 784
Roman Catholic Missionary Advance 785
Tensions between Missionaries and Imperial Administrators 785
Missionaries and Indigenous Religious Movements 787
Science and Imperialism 787
Botany 788
Zoology 789
Medicine 789
Anthropology 790
In Perspective 791
Review Questions 791
Suggested Readings 792

A Closer LOOK THE FRENCH IN MOROCCO 765

COMPARE AND CONNECT Two Views of Turn-of-the-Twentieth-Century Imperial Expansion 766

■ ENCOUNTERING THE PAST Submarine Cables 783

THE WEST & THE WORLD Imperialism: Ancient and Modern 793

26 Alliances, War, and a Troubled Peace 798

Emergence of the German Empire and the Alliance Systems (1873–1890) 799
Bismarck's Leadership 799
Forging the Triple Entente (1890–1907) 801
World War I 804
The Road to War (1908–1914) 804
Sarajevo and the Outbreak of War (June–August 1914) 806
Strategies and Stalemate: 1914–1917 811
The Russian Revolution 817
The Provisional Government 818
Lenin and the Bolsheviks 820
The Communist Dictatorship 820
The End of World War I 821
Germany's Last Offensive 822
The Armistice 822
The End of the Ottoman Empire 823
The Settlement at Paris 824
Obstacles the Peacemakers Faced 825
The Peace 827
World War I and Colonial Empires 829
Evaluating the Peace 830
In Perspective 831
Review Questions 832
Suggested Readings 832

COMPARE AND CONNECT The Outbreak of World War I 808

A Closer LOOK THE DEVELOPMENT OF THE ARMORED TANK 816

■ ENCOUNTERING THE PAST War Propaganda and the Movies: Charlie Chaplin 826

27 The Interwar Years: The Challenge of Dictators and Depression 833

After Versailles: Demands for Revision and Enforcement 834
Toward the Great Depression in Europe 834
Financial Tailspin 835
Problems in Agricultural Commodities 836
Depression and Government Policy in Britain and France 836
The Soviet Experiment 838
War Communism 838
The New Economic Policy 838
The Third International 839
Stalin versus Trotsky 839
The Decision for Rapid Industrialization 840
The Collectivization of Agriculture 841
The Purges 843
The Fascist Experiment in Italy 844
The Rise of Mussolini 845
The Fascists in Power 846
German Democracy and Dictatorship 847
The Weimar Republic 847

Depression and Political Deadlock 851
Hitler Comes to Power 851
Hitler's Consolidation of Power 852
Anti-Semitism and the Police State 854
Racial Ideology and the Lives of Women 855
Nazi Economic Policy 857
Trials of the Successor States in Eastern Europe 861
Economic and Ethnic Pressures 861
Poland: Democracy to Military Rule 861
Czechoslovakia: A Viable Democratic Experiment 861
Hungary: Turmoil and Authoritarianism 862
Austria: Political Turmoil and Nazi Occupation 862
Southeastern Europe: Royal Dictatorships 862
In Perspective 863
Review Questions 863
Suggested Readings 863

■ ENCOUNTERING THE PAST
Cinema of the Political Left and Right **853**

COMPARE AND CONNECT
The Soviets and the Nazis Confront the Issues of Women and the Family **858**

A Closer LOOK THE NAZI PARTY RALLY **860**

PART 6
Global Conflict, Cold War, and New Directions, 1939– 2008

28 World War II 865

Again the Road to War (1933–1939) 866
Hitler's Goals 866
Italy Attacks Ethiopia 866
Remilitarization of the Rhineland 867
The Spanish Civil War 868
Austria and Czechoslovakia 869
Munich 870
The Nazi-Soviet Pact 874
World War II (1939–1945) 874
The German Conquest of Europe 874
The Battle of Britain 875
The German Attack on Russia 876
Hitler's Plans for Europe 878
Japan and the United States Enter the War 878
The Tide Turns 879
The Defeat of Nazi Germany 883
Fall of the Japanese Empire 884
The Cost of War 885
Racism and the Holocaust 886
The Destruction of the Polish Jewish Community 887
Polish Anti-Semitism Between the Wars 887
The Nazi Assault on the Jews of Poland 889
Explanations of the Holocaust 890
The Domestic Fronts 891
Germany: From Apparent Victory to Defeat 892
France: Defeat, Collaboration, and Resistance 893
Great Britain: Organization for Victory 895
The Soviet Union: "The Great Patriotic War" 896
Preparations for Peace 897
The Atlantic Charter 897
Tehran: Agreement on a Second Front 897
Yalta 899
Potsdam 899
In Perspective 900
Review Questions 900
Suggested Readings 901

COMPARE AND CONNECT
The Munich Settlement **872**

■ ENCOUNTERING THE PAST
Rosie the Riveter and American Women in the War Effort **881**

A Closer LOOK THE VICHY REGIME IN FRANCE **894**

29 The Cold War Era, Decolonization, and the Emergence of a New Europe 902

The Emergence of the Cold War 903
Containment in American Foreign Policy 904
Soviet Domination of Eastern Europe 905
The Postwar Division of Germany 908
NATO and the Warsaw Pact 909
The Creation of the State of Israel 909
The Korean War 911
The Khrushchev Era in the Soviet Union 912
Khruschev's Domestic Policies 912
The Three Crises of 1956 914
Later Cold War Confrontations 914
The Berlin Wall 914
The Cuban Missile Crisis 915
The Brezhnev Era 916
1968: The Invasion of Czechoslovakia 916
The United States and Détente 917
The Invasion of Afghanistan 917

Communism and Solidarity in Poland 917
Relations with the Reagan Administration 918
Decolonization: The European Retreat from Empire 918
Major Areas of Colonial Withdrawal 920
India 920
Further British Retreat from Empire 922
The Turmoil of French Decolonization 922
France and Algeria 922
France and Vietnam 924
Vietnam Drawn into the Cold War 924
Direct United States Involvement 925
The Collapse of European Communism 926
Gorbachev Attempts to Reform the Soviet Union 927
1989: Revolution in Eastern Europe 929
The Collapse of the Soviet Union 930
The Yeltsin Decade 934
The Collapse of Yugoslavia and Civil War 935
Putin and the Resurgence of Russia 937
The Rise of Radical Political Islamism 940
Arab Nationalism 940
The Iranian Revolution 940
Afghanistan and Radical Islamism 941
A Transformed West 942
In Perspective 943
Review Questions 945
Suggested Readings 945

COMPARE AND CONNECT The Soviet Union and the United States Draw the Lines of the Cold War 906
■ **ENCOUNTERING THE PAST** Rock Music and Political Protest 928
A Closer LOOK COLLAPSE OF THE BERLIN WALL 932

30 The West at the Dawn of the Twenty-First Century 947

The Twentieth-Century Movement of Peoples 948
Displacement through War 948
External and Internal Migration 948
The New Muslim Population 949
European Population Trends 950
Toward a Welfare State Society 950
Christian Democratic Parties 951
The Creation of Welfare States 951
Resistance to the Expansion of the Welfare State 952
New Patterns in the Work and Expectations of Women 953
Feminism 953
More Married Women in the Workforce 953
New Work Patterns 957
Women in the New Eastern Europe 957
Transformations in Knowledge and Culture 957
Communism and Western Europe 957
Existentialism 959
Expansion of the University Population and Student Rebellion 960
The Americanization of Europe 961
A Consumer Society 962
Environmentalism 962
Art Since World War II 964
Cultural Divisions and the Cold War 964
Memory of the Holocaust 965
The Christian Heritage 966
Neo-Orthodoxy 967
Liberal Theology 967
Roman Catholic Reform 967
Late-Twentieth-Century Technology: The Arrival of the Computer 968
The Demand for Calculating Machines 969
Early Computer Technology 970
The Development of Desktop Computers 970
The Challenges of European Unification 971
Postwar Cooperation 971
The European Economic Community 972
The European Union 973
Discord over the Union 974
New American Leadership and Financial Crisis 976
In Perspective 977
Review Questions 977
Suggested Readings 977

COMPARE AND CONNECT Margaret Thatcher and Tony Blair Debate Government's Social Responsibility for Welfare 954
■ **ENCOUNTERING THE PAST** Toys from Europe Conquer the United States 963
A Closer LOOK THE COPENHAGEN OPERA HOUSE 972

THE WEST & THE WORLD Energy and the Modern World 979
Glossary G-1
Index I-1

DOCUMENTS

CHAPTER 1

Hammurabi's Law Code 11
An Assyrian Woman Writes to Her Husband, ca. 1800 B.C.E. 15
Love Poems from the New Kingdom 19

CHAPTER 2

Tyrtaeus on the Citizen Soldier 41

CHAPTER 3

Medea Bemoans the Condition of Women 71
Lysistrata Ends the War 78
Plato on the Role of Women in His Utopian Republic 85

CHAPTER 4

Rome's Treatment of Conquered Italian Cities 105
Plutarch Describes a Roman Triumph 110
Women's Uprising in Republican Rome 114
The Ruin of the Roman Family Farm and the Gracchan Reforms 117

CHAPTER 5

Daily Life in a Roman Provincial Town: Graffiti from Pompeii 140
Rome's Independent Women: Two Views 141
Juvenal on Life in Rome 144
Ammianus Marcellinus Describes the People Called Huns 157

CHAPTER 6

Salvian the Priest Compares the Romans and the Barbarians 174
The Benedictine Order Sets Its Requirements for Entrance 185

CHAPTER 7

Pope Gregory VII Asserts the Power of the Pope 206

CHAPTER 8

Thomas Aquinas Proves the Existence of God 243

CHAPTER 9

Joan of Arc Refuses to Recant Her Beliefs 268

CHAPTER 10

Christine De Pisan Instructs Women on How to Handle Their Husbands 288
A Defense of American Natives 308
Montaigne on "Cannibals" in Foreign Lands 310

CHAPTER 11

Zwingli Lists the Errors of the Roman Church 326

CHAPTER 12

Theodore Beza Defends the Right to Resist Tyranny 351

CHAPTER 13

King James I Defends Popular Recreation against the Puritans 375
Louis XIV Revokes the Edict of Nantes 389
The Great Elector Welcomes Protestant Refugees from France 396
Peter the Great Tells His Son to Acquire Military Skills 399

CHAPTER 14

Margaret Cavendish Questions the Fascination with Scientific Instruments 420
Galileo Discusses the Relationship of Science to the Bible 424
Why More Women Than Men Are Witches 429

CHAPTER 15

Manchester's Calico Printers Protest the Use of New Machinery 450
Priscilla Wakefield Demands More Occupations for Women 454
Belorussian Jews Petition Catherine the Great 460

CHAPTER 16

Buccaneers Prowl the High Seas 467
Major Cartwright Calls for the Reform of Parliament 486

CHAPTER 17

Voltaire Attacks Religious Fanaticism 500
Adam Smith Calls for Government Action to Support the Education of the Poor 506
Denis Diderot Condemns European Empires 510

Rousseau Argues for Separate Spheres for Men and Women 513
Mary Wollstonecraft Criticizes Rousseau's View of Women 515

CHAPTER 18

The Third Estate of a French City Petitions theKing 533
The National Assembly Decrees Civic Equality in France 538
Burke Denounces the Extreme Measures of the French Revolution 550
The Paris Jacobin Club Alerts the Nation to Internal Enemies of the Revolution 552
The Convention Establishes the Worship of the Supreme Being 556

CHAPTER 19

Napoleon Advises His Brother to Rule Constitutionally 569
Madame de Staël Describes the New Romantic Literature of Germany 580
Hegel Explains the Role of Great Men in History 589

CHAPTER 20

Benjamin Constant Discusses Modern Liberty 599
The German Federation Issues the Carlsbad Decrees 603

CHAPTER 21

Women Industrial Workers Explain Their Economic Situation 635
Karl Marx and Friedrich Engels Describe the Class Struggle 644
The Pan-Slavic Congress Calls for the Liberation of Slavs 651

CHAPTER 22

Émile Zola Accuses the Enemies of Dreyfus of Self-Interest and Illegal Actions 677
The People's Will Issues a Revolutionary Manifesto 683

CHAPTER 23

Paris Department Stores Expand Their Business 696
Emmeline Pankhurst Defends Militant Suffragette Tactics 708
A Russian Social Investigator Describes the Condition of Children in the Moscow Tailoring Trade 716

CHAPTER 24

Leo XIII Considers the Social Question in European Politics 735
H. S. Chamberlain Exalts the Role of Race 746
Herzl Calls for a Jewish State 748
Virginia Woolf Urges Women to Write 752

CHAPTER 25

A Chinese Official Appeals to Queen Victoria to Halt the Opium Trade 758
T. B. Macaulay Prescribes English for Indian Education 760
Winston Churchill Reports on the Power of Modern Weaponry 772
General von Trotha Demands that the Herero People Leave Their Land 776
The Russian Foreign Minister Explains the Imperatives of Expansion in Asia 779

CHAPTER 26

Bismarck Explains His Foreign Policy 802
The Outbreak of the Russian Revolution 819
An Eyewitness Account of the Bolsheviks' Seizure of Power 820

CHAPTER 27

John Maynard Keynes Calls for Government Investment to Create Employment 837
Mussolini Heaps Contempt on Political Liberalism 845
An American Diplomat Witnesses *Kristallnacht* in Leipzig 856

CHAPTER 28

Hitler Describes His Goals in Foreign Policy 867
Mass Murder at Belsen 888

CHAPTER 29

Khrushchev Denounces the Crimes of Stalin: The Secret Speech 913
Gandhi Explains His Doctrine of Nonviolence 921
Vladimir Putin Outlines a Vision of the Russian Future 939

CHAPTER 30

Simone De Beauvoir Urges Economic Freedom for Women 956
Sartre Discusses His Existentialism 960
Pope Benedict XVI Call for the Recognition of Religious Freedom as a Human Right 969
An English Business Editor Calls for Europe to Take Charge of Its Economic Future 975

MAPS

1–1 The Ancient Near East 5
1–2 The Near East and Greece about 1400 B.C.E. 16
1–3 The Achaemenid Persian Empire 24
1–4 Ancient Palestine 27
2–1 The Aegean Area in the Bronze Age 37
2–2 Greek Colonization 42
2–3 The Peloponnesus 44
2–4 Attica and Vicinity 46
2–5 The Persian Invasion of Greece 55
3–1 Classical Greece 62
3–2 The Athenian Empire about 450 B.C.E. 64
3–3 Ancient Athens 77
3–4 Alexander's Campaigns 89
3–5 The World According to Eratosthenes 94
4–1 Ancient Italy 98
4–2 The Western Mediterranean Area During the Rise of Rome 106
4–3 Roman Dominions of the Late Republic 115
4–4 The Civil Wars of the Late Roman Republic 123
5–1 The Roman Empire, 14 C.E. 132
5–2 Provinces of the Roman Empire to 117 C.E. 137
5–3 Ancient Rome 143
5–4 Divisions of the Roman Empire under Diocletian 153
5–5 The Empire's Neighbors 155
5–6 The Spread of Christianity 158
6–1 Barbarian Migrations into the West in the Fourth and Fifth Centuries 173
6–2 The Byzantine Empire at the Time of Justinian's Death 175
6–3 Muslim Conquests and Domination of the Mediterranean to about 750 C.E. 182
6–4 The Empire of Charlemagne to 814 190
6–5 The Treaty of Verdun, 843, and the Treaty of Mersen, 870 194
6–6 Viking, Islamic, and Magyar Invasions to the Eleventh Century 195
7–1 The Early Crusades 209
7–2 Germany and Italy in the Middle Ages 222
8–1 Some Medieval Trade Routes and Regional Products 237
9–1 Spread of the Black Death 259
9–2 The Hundred Years' War 264
10–1 Renaissance Italy 283
10–2 European Voyages of Discovery and the Colonial Claims of Spain and Portugal in the Fifteenth and Sixteenth Centuries 304
11–1 The Empire of Charles V 320
11–2 The Swiss Confederation 325
11–3 The Religious Situation about 1560 334
12–1 The Netherlands during the Reformation 354
12–2 Germany in 1547 363
12–3 Religious Divisions about 1600 365
12–4 The Holy Roman Empire about 1618 366
12–5 Europe in 1648 369
13–1 The First Three Wars of Louis XIV 385
13–2 Europe in 1714 390
13–3 The Austrian Habsburg Empire, 1521–1772 394
13–4 Expansion of Brandeburg-Prussia 395
13–5 The Ottoman Empire in the Late Seventeenth Century 403
16–1 Viceroyalties in Latin America in 1780 468
16–2 The Slave Trade, 1400–1860 476
16–3 North America in 1763 482
17–1 Expansion of Russia, 1689–1796 526
17–2 Partitions of Poland, 1772, 1793, and 1795 527
18–1 French Provinces and the Republic 540
19–1 The Continental System, 1806–1810 568
19–2 Napoleonic Europe in Late 1812 571
19–3 The German States after 1815 575
19–4 Europe 1815, after the Congress of Vienna 577
20–1 Latin America in 1830 611
20–2 Centers of Revolution, 1820–1831 614
21–1 European Railroads in 1850 624
21–2 Centers of Revolution in 1848–1849 645
22–1 The Unification of Italy 667
22–2 The Unification of Germany 670
22–3 Nationalities within the Habsburg Empire 679
23–1 Patterns of Global Migration, 1840–1900 692
23–2 European Industrialization, 1860–1913 693
25–1 British India, 1820 and 1856 759
25–2 Imperial Expansion in Africa to 1880 769
25–3 Partition of Africa, 1880–1914 770
25–4 Asia, 1880–1914 781
26–1 The Balkans, 1912–1913 805
26–2 The Schlieffen Plan of 1905 811

26–3 World War I in Europe 813
26–4 The Western Front, 1914–1918 814
26–5 World War I Peace Settlement in Europe and the Middle East 828
27–1 Germany's Western Frontier 850
28–1 The Spanish Civil War, 1936–1939 869
28–2 Partitions of Czechoslovakia and Poland, 1938–1939 871
28–3 Axis Europe, 1941 877
28–4 North African Campaigns, 1942–1945 880
28–5 Defeat of the Axis in Europe, 1942–1945 882
28–6 World War II in the Pacific 885
28–7 The Holocaust 887
28–8 Yalta to the Surrender 898
29–1 Territorial Changes in Europe after World War II 904
29–2 Occupied Germany and Austria 909
29–3 Major Cold War European Alliance Systems 910
29–4 Israel and Its Neighbors in 1949 911
29–5 Korea, 1950–1953 912
29–6 Decolonization Since World War II 919
29–7 Vietnam and Its Southeast Asian Neighbors 926
29–8 The Borders of Germany in the Twentieth Century 931
29–9 The Commonwealth of Independent States 934
30–1 The Growth of the European Union 973

PREFACE

Students undertaking the study of the Western heritage on the threshold of the second decade of the twenty-first century do so at a remarkable historical moment. In 2008, the United States elected its first African-American president, a Democrat backed by larger Democratic congressional majorities pledged to undertaking major new policy directions at home and abroad. Both the Western and non-Western worlds confront a changing global economy that gave birth to a financial crisis with the most serious implications for economic stability since the 1930s. The August 2008 invasion of Georgia by Russian Federation troops signaled the possibility of a move from a period of relative quietude to one of military resurgence that may bring into question numerous strategic military assumptions that prevailed for almost two decades after the collapse of the Soviet Union. The United States and Western Europe, after several years of controversial military engagement in Iraq and Afghanistan, continue efforts to reshape foreign policy with an emphasis on diplomacy instead of preemptive warfare. Christians in the northern and southern hemispheres continue to be sharply divided as they debate the character of their faith and its relationship to other faiths and the social questions of the day. A growing consensus of opinion recognizes the dangers posed by environmental change.

The authors of this volume continue to believe that the heritage of Western civilization remains a major point of departure for understanding and defining the challenges of this no longer new century. The unprecedented globalization of daily life that is a hallmark of our era has occurred largely through the spread of Western influences. From the sixteenth century onward, the West has exerted vast influences throughout the globe for both good and ill, and today's global citizens continue to live in the wake of that impact. It is the goal of this book to introduce its readers to the Western heritage, so that they may be better informed and more culturally sensitive citizens of the increasingly troubled and challenging global age. The events of recent years and the hostility that has arisen in many parts of the world to the power and influence of the West require new efforts to understand how the West sees itself and how other parts of the world see the West.

Since *The Western Heritage* first appeared, we have sought to provide our readers with a work that does justice to the richness and variety of Western civilization and its many complexities. We hope that such an understanding of the West will foster lively debate about its character, values, institutions, and global influence. Indeed, we believe such a critical outlook on their own culture has characterized the peoples of the West since the dawn of history. Through such debates we define ourselves and the values of our culture. Consequently, we welcome the debate and hope that *The Western Heritage*, Tenth Edition, can help foster an informed discussion through its history of the West's strengths and weaknesses and the controversies surrounding Western history. To further that debate, we have included a new introductory essay entitled "What Is the Western Heritage?" to introduce students to the concept of the West and to allow instructors and students to have a point of departure for debating this concept in their course of study.

We also believe that any book addressing the experience of the West must also look beyond its historical European borders. Students reading this book come from a wide variety of cultures and experiences. They live in a world of highly interconnected economies and instant communication between cultures. In this emerging multicultural society it seems both appropriate and necessary to recognize how Western civilization has throughout its history interacted with other cultures, both influencing and being influenced by them. For this reason, we have introduced in this edition a new chapter on the nineteenth-century European age of imperialism. Further examples of Western interaction with other parts of the world, such as with Islam, appear throughout the text. To further highlight the theme of cultural interaction, *The Western Heritage* includes a series of comparative essays,"The West & the World." (A more complete description follows.)

In this edition as in past editions, our goal has been to present Western civilization fairly, accurately, and in a way that does justice to this great, diverse legacy of human enterprise. History has many facets, no single one of which can alone account for the others. Any attempt to tell the story of the West from a single overarching perspective, no matter how timely, is bound to neglect or suppress some important parts of this story. Like all other authors of introductory texts, we have had to make choices, but we have attempted to provide the broadest possible introduction to Western civilization.

GOALS OF THE TEXT

Our primary goal has been to present a strong, clear, narrative account of the central developments in Western history. We have also sought to call attention to certain critical themes:

- The capacity of Western civilization, from the time of the Greeks to the present, to transform itself through self-criticism.
- The development in the West of political freedom, constitutional government, and concern for the rule of law and individual rights.
- The shifting relations among religion, society, and the state.
- The development of science and technology and their expanding impact on Western thought, social institutions, and everyday life.
- The major religious and intellectual currents that have shaped Western culture.

We believe that these themes have been fundamental in Western civilization, shaping the past and exerting a continuing influence on the present.

Flexible Presentation *The Western Heritage*, Tenth Edition, is designed to accommodate a variety of approaches to a course in Western civilization, allowing teachers to stress what is most important to them. Some teachers will ask students to read all the chapters. Others will select among them to reinforce assigned readings and lectures. We believe the documents as well as the "Encountering the Past" and "A Closer Look" features may also be adopted selectively by instructors for purposes of classroom presentation and debate and as the basis for short written assignments.

Integrated Social, Cultural, and Political History *The Western Heritage* provides one of the richest accounts of the social history of the West available today, with strong coverage of family life, the changing roles of women, and the place of the family in relation to broader economic, political, and social developments. This coverage reflects the explosive growth in social historical research in the past half-century, which has enriched virtually all areas of historical study.

We have also been told repeatedly by teachers that no matter what their own historical specialization, they believe that a political narrative gives students an effective tool to begin to understand the past. Consequently, we have sought to integrate such a strong political narrative with our treatment of the social, cultural, and intellectual factors in Western history.

We also believe that religious faith and religious institutions have been fundamental to the development of the West. No other survey text presents so full an account of the religious and intellectual development of the West. People may be political and social beings, but they are also reasoning and spiritual beings. What they think and believe are among the most important things we can know about them. Their ideas about God, society, law, gender, human nature, and the physical world have changed over the centuries and continue to change. We cannot fully grasp our own approach to the world without understanding the religious and intellectual currents of the past and how they have influenced our thoughts and conceptual categories. We seek to recognize the impact of religion in the expansion of the West, including the settlement the Americas in the sixteenth century and the role of missionaries in nineteenth-century Western imperialism.

Clarity and Accessibility Good narrative history requires clear, vigorous prose. As with earlier editions, we have paid careful attention to our writing, subjecting every paragraph to critical scrutiny. Our goal has been to make the history of the West accessible to students without compromising vocabulary or conceptual level. We hope this effort will benefit both teachers and students.

THE TENTH EDITION

New to This Edition

- We include a new introductory essay entitled "What Is the Western Heritage?" designed to introduce students to the concept of Western civilization as it has changed over the centuries and at the same to provide instructors the opportunity to debate this concept and its implications with their students.
- Each chapter includes a new feature entitled "**Compare and Connect**" that juxtaposes two or more documents in which an important question is debated or a comparison between a document and an illustration is presented. Each "Compare and Connect" feature contains three to five questions on each of the documents, one of which asks students to make connections between and among the viewpoints presented in the feature. These features are intended to encourage students to debate different points of view in class and to learn to read and evaluate differing viewpoints or to analyze documentary and visual evidence. An interactive version of this feature is available on www.myhistorylab.com

- An entirely new chapter, "The Age of Western Imperialism" (Chapter 25), provides an in-depth global overview of nineteenth-century Western imperial expansion. Topics covered in this chapter include the nineteenth-century shift in Western imperial ventures from the Americas to Africa and Asia, the significance of the British Empire, British imperial rule in India, the New Imperialism, the partition of Africa, the role of missionaries in European colonialism, the relationship of technology and science to imperialism, and international colonial rivalries.
- The new chapter on imperialism has led to a streamlining of the chapter on World War I and its aftermath as well as more extensive comments on the colonial ramifications of the peace settlement (Chapter 26).
- A single, more sharply focused chapter on the twentieth-century interwar years (Chapter 27) has replaced two longer chapters on this period.
- The two closing chapters of the book (Chapters 29 and 30) carry the narrative through important recent events such as the Russian invasion of Georgia and the collapse of financial institutions in Europe and the United States in the fall of 2008.

Features That Enliven Student Interest and Understanding

"A Closer Look" Reflecting the increased use of visual sources to interpret the Western heritage, one illustration per chapter is examined and analyzed using leader lines to point out important and historically significant details.

Examples include a Greek trireme, the cover of the Lindau Gospels, a statue of St. Maurice, and a French imperialist poster from the early twentieth century. This feature further enhances the already rich visual presentation of *The Western Heritage*. An interactive version of this feature is available on www.myhistorylab.com

"Encountering the Past" Each chapter includes an essay on a significant issue of everyday life or popular culture. These essays explore a variety of subjects, including gladiatorial bouts and medieval games, smoking in early modern Europe, and the politics of rock music in the late twentieth century. These thirty essays, each of which includes an illustration and study questions, expand *The Western Heritage*'s rich coverage of social and cultural history.

"The West & The World" In this feature, we focus on six subjects that compare Western institutions with those in other parts of the world or discuss how developments in the West have influenced other cultures. In the Tenth Edition, the essays are

Part 1:	Ancient Warfare (page 164)
Part 2:	The Invention of Printing in China and Europe (page 252)
Part 3:	The Columbian Exchange, Disease, Animals, and Agriculture (page 489)
Part 4:	The Abolition of Slavery in the Transatlantic Economy (page 655)
Part 5:	Imperialism: Ancient and Modern (page 793)
Part 6:	Energy and the Modern World (page 979)

Recent Scholarship As in previous editions, changes in this edition reflect our determination to incorporate the most recent developments in historical scholarship and the concerns of professional historians.

Maps and Illustrations To help students understand the relationship between geography and history, approximately half of the maps include relief features. One or two maps in each chapter feature interactive exercises that can be found in MyHistoryLab. All maps have been carefully edited for accuracy. The text also contains close to 500 color and black and white illustrations, many of which are new to the Tenth Edition.

Pedagogical Features This edition retains the pedagogical features of previous editions, including a list of key topics at the beginning of each chapter, glossary terms, chapter review questions, and questions accompanying the more than 200 source documents in the text. Each of these features is designed to make the text more accessible to students and to reinforce key concepts.

- **Primary-source documents,** many of which are new to this edition, acquaint students with the raw material of history and provide intimate contact with the people of the past and their concerns. Questions accompanying the source documents direct students toward important, thought-provoking issues and help them relate the documents to the material in the text. They can be used to stimulate class discussion or as topics for essays and study groups.
- **An outline, a list of key topics, and an introduction** are included in each chapter. Together these features provide a succinct overview of each chapter.
- **Chronologies** follow each major section in a chapter, listing significant events and their dates.

- **In Perspective** sections summarize the major themes of each chapter and provide a bridge to the next chapter.
- **Chapter Review Questions** help students review the material in a chapter and relate it to broader themes. These too can be used for class discussion and essay topics.
- **Suggested Readings** lists following each chapter have been updated with new titles reflecting recent scholarship.
- **Map Explorations** prompt students to engage with maps in an interactive fashion. Each Map Exploration can be found in MyHistoryLab.

A Note on Dates and Transliterations This edition of *The Western Heritage* continues the practice of using B.C.E. (before the common era) and C.E. (common era) instead of B.C. (before Christ) and A.D. (anno Domini, the year of the Lord) to designate dates. We also follow the most accurate currently accepted English transliterations of Arabic words. For example, today *Koran* has been replaced by the more accurate *Qur'an*; similarly *Muhammad* is preferable to *Mohammed* and *Muslim* to *Moslem*.

ANCILLARY INSTRUCTIONAL MATERIALS

The ancillary instructional materials that accompany *The Western Heritage*, Tenth Edition, are designed to reinforce and enliven the richness of the past and inspire students with the excitement of studying the history of Western civilization.

For Instructors

Instructor's Manual The Instructor's Manual contains chapter summaries, key points and vital concepts, and information on audiovisual resources that can be used in developing and preparing lecture presentations. (ISBN 0-205-66073-8)

Test Item File The Test Item File includes over 1,500 multiple-choice, identification, map, and essay test questions. (ISBN 0-205-66076-2)

MyTest MyTest is a browser-based test management program. The program allows instructors to select items from the Test Item File in order to create tests. It also allows for online testing. (ISBN 0-205-66075-4)

The Instructor's Resource Center (www.pearsonhighered.com) Text-specific materials, such as the Instructor's Manual and the Test Item File, are available for downloading by adopters.

For Instructors and Students

PEARSON myhistorylab **MyHistoryLab (www.myhistorylab.com)** MyHistoryLab provides students with an online package complete with the electronic textbook and numerous study aids. With several hundred primary sources, many of which are assignable and link to a gradebook, pre- and post-tests that link to a gradebook and result in individualized study plans, "Closer Look" investigations, videos and images, as well as map activities with gradable quizzes, the site offers students a unique, interactive experience that brings history to life. The comprehensive site also includes a History Bookshelf with fifty of the most commonly assigned books in history classes and a History Toolkit with tutorials and helpful links. Other features include gradable assignments and chapter review materials as well as a Test Item File.

For Students

Primary Source: Documents in Western Civilization DVD This DVD-ROM offers a rich collection of textual and visual—many never before available to a wide audience—and serves as an indispensable tool for working with sources. Extensively developed with the guidance of historians and teachers, *Primary Source: Documents in Western Civilization* includes over 800 sources in Western civilization history—from cave art, to text documents, to satellite images of Earth from space. All sources are accompanied by headnotes and focus questions and are searchable by topic, region, or theme. In addition, a built-in tutorial guides students through the process of working with documents. The DVD can be bundled with *The Western Heritage*, Tenth Edition, at no charge. Please contact your Pearson Arts and Sciences representative for ordering information (ISBN 0-13-134407-2).

A two-volume print version of *Primary Source: Documents in Western Civilization* is also available:

Primary Sources in Western Civilization, Volume 1: To 1700, Second Edition (ISBN 0-13-175583-8)
Primary Sources in Western Civilization, Volume 2: Since 1400, Second Edition (ISBN 0-13-175584-6)

Please contact your Pearson Arts and Sciences representative for ordering information.

***Lives and Legacies: Biographies in Western Civilization*, Second Edition** Extensively revised, *Lives and*

Legacies includes brief, focused biographies of sixty individuals whose lives provide insight into the key developments of Western civilization. Each biography includes an introduction, prereading questions, and suggestions for additional reading. Available in two volumes:

Lives and Legacies, Volume 1, Second Edition (ISBN 0-205-64915-7)
Lives and Legacies, Volume 2, Second Edition (ISBN 0-205-64914-9)

CourseSmart Textbooks Online This is an exciting new choice for students looking to save money. As an alternative to purchasing the print textbook, students can subscribe to the same content online and save up to 50 percent off the suggested list price of the print text. With a CourseSmart eTextbook, students can search the text, make notes online, print out reading assignments that incorporate lecture notes, and bookmark important passages for later review. For more information, or to subscribe to the Course-Smart eTextbook, visit www.coursesmart.com.

Western Civilization Study Site (www.ablongman.com/longmanwesterncivilization/) This course-based, open-access online companion provides both students and professors with links for further research as well as test questions in multiple choice, true/false, and fill-in-the-blank formats.

Penguin Classics Selected titles from the renowned Penguin Classics series can be bundled with *The Western Heritage*, Tenth Edition, for a nominal charge. Please contact your Pearson Arts and Sciences sales representative for details.

Longman Atlas of Western Civilization This 52-page atlas features carefully selected historical maps that provide comprehensive coverage for the major historical periods. Contact your Pearson Arts and Sciences representative for details. (ISBN 0-321-21626-1)

***The Prentice Hall Atlas of Western Civilization*, Second Edition** Produced in collaboration with Dorling Kindersley, the leader in cartographic publishing, the updated second edition of *The Prentice Hall Atlas of Western Civilization* applies the most innovative cartographic techniques to present Western civilization in all of its complexity and diversity. Contact your Pearson Arts and Sciences sales representative for details. (ISBN 0-13-604246-5)

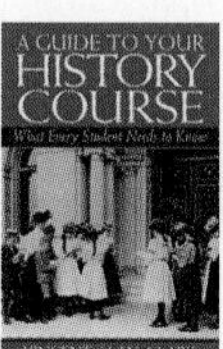

A Guide to Your History Course: What Every Student Needs to Know Written by Vincent A. Clark, this concise, spiral-bound guidebook orients students to the issues and problems they will face in the history classroom. Available at a discount when bundled with *The Western Heritage*, Tenth Edition. (ISBN 0-13-185087-3)

***A Short Guide to Writing about History*, Seventh Edition** Written by Richard Marius, late of Harvard University, and Melvin E. Page, Eastern Tennessee State University, this engaging and practical text helps students get beyond merely compiling dates and facts. Covering both brief essays and the documented resource paper, the text explores the writing and researching processes, identifies different modes of historical writing, including argument, and concludes with guidelines for improving style. (ISBN 0-205-67370-8)

Interpretations of the Western World (www.pearsoncustom.com/custom-library/interpretations-of-the-western-world) The selections in this customizable database of secondary source readings are grouped together topically so instructors can assign readings that illustrate different points of view on a given historical debate.

ACKNOWLEDGMENTS

We are grateful to the scholars and teachers whose thoughtful and often detailed comments helped shape this revision:

Mark Baker, California State University at Bakersfield
Fred Baumgartner, Virginia Tech
Jane Bishop, The Citadel, The Military College of South Carolina
Eugene Boia, Cleveland State University
Kristen Burkholder, Oklahoma State University
Joseph Byrnes, Oklahoma State University
Anthony Cardoza, Loyola University, Chicago
Marcus Cox, The Citadel, The Military College of South Carolina
Delores Davison, Foothill College
Paul Deslandes, University of Vermont
Petra DeWitt, University of Missouri, Rolla
Richard Eller, Catawaba Valley Community College
Axel Fair-Schulz, State University of New York at Potsdam
Sean Field, University of Vermont
Shannon Fogg, Missouri S&T
Stephen Gibson, Ranken Technical College
Stephanie Hallock, Harford Community College
Michael Hickey, Bloomsburg University
Anthony Heideman, Range Community College
William Hudon, Bloomsburg University
Terry Jones, Oklahoma State University
Kevin Keating, Broward Community College
Michael Khodarkovsky, Loyola University, Chicago
Martha Kinney, Suffolk County Community College
Helena Krohn, Tidewater Community College
Eugene Larson, Los Angeles Pierce College
Karl Loewenstein, University of Wisconsin at Oshkosh
Arthur Lysiak, Bloomsburg University
William Martin, University of Utah
Lisa McClain, Boise State University
Daniel Miller, University of West Florida
Eva Mo, Meridian Junior College
Michelle Mouton, University of Wisconsin at Oshkosh
Tonia Sharlach Nash, Oklahoma State University
Charles Odahl, Boise State University
Mark Orsag, Doane College
Michael Pascale, SUNY at Suffolk, Farmingdale College
Neal Pease, University of Wisconsin at Milwaukee
Norman Raiford, Greenville Technical College
Pete Rottier, Cleveland State University
Thomas Rowland, University of Wisconsin at Oshkosh
Michael Rutz, University of Wisconsin at Oshkosh
Stephen Ruzicka, University of North Carolina at Greensboro
Mark Schumann, Eastern Michigan University
Patrick Speelman, The Citadel, The Military College of South Carolina
Frank W. Thackeray, Indiana University Southeast
Daniel Trifan, Missouri Western State University
Miriam Vivian, California State University at Bakersfield
Andrew Zimmerman, George Washington University

We would like to thank the dedicated people who helped produce this new edition. Our acquisitions editor, Charles Cavaliere; our development editor, Gerald Lombardi; our project manager, Rob DeGeorge; our production liaison, Lynn Savino Wendel; Maria Lange who created the beautiful new design of this edition; Mary Ann Gloriande, our operations specialist; and Rebecca Dunn, production editor.

D.K.
S.O.
F.M.T.

ABOUT THE AUTHORS

DONALD KAGAN is Sterling Professor of History and Classics at Yale University, where he has taught since 1969. He received the A.B. degree in history from Brooklyn College, the M.A. in classics from Brown University, and the Ph.D. in history from Ohio State University. During 1958 to 1959 he studied at the American School of Classical Studies as a Fulbright Scholar. He has received three awards for undergraduate teaching at Cornell and Yale. He is the author of a history of Greek political thought, *The Great Dialogue* (1965); a four-volume history of the Peloponnesian war, *The Origins of the Peloponnesian War* (1969); *The Archidamian War* (1974); *The Peace of Nicias and the Sicilian Expedition* (1981); *The Fall of the Athenian Empire* (1987); and a biography of Pericles, *Pericles of Athens and the Birth of Democracy* (1991); *On the Origins of War* (1995) and *The Peloponnesian War* (2003). He is coauthor, with Frederick W. Kagan, of *While America Sleeps* (2000). With Brian Tierney and L. Pearce Williams, he is the editor of *Great Issues in Western Civilization*, a collection of readings. He was awarded the National Humanities Medal for 2002 and was chosen by the National Endowment for the Humanities to deliver the Jefferson Lecture in 2004.

▼

STEVEN OZMENT is McLean Professor of Ancient and Modern History at Harvard University. He has taught Western Civilization at Yale, Stanford, and Harvard. He is the author of eleven books. *The Age of Reform, 1250–1550* (1980) won the Schaff Prize and was nominated for the 1981 National Book Award. Five of his books have been selections of the History Book Club: *Magdalena and Balthasar: An Intimate Portrait of Life in Sixteenth Century Europe* (1986), *Three Behaim Boys: Growing Up in Early Modern Germany* (1990), *Protestants: The Birth of a Revolution* (1992), *The Burgermeister's Daughter: Scandal in a Sixteenth Century German Town* (1996), and *Flesh and Spirit: Private Life in Early Modern Germany* (1999). His most recent publications are *Ancestors: The Loving Family of Old Europe* (2001), *A Mighty Fortress: A New History of the German People* (2004), and "Why We Study Western Civ," *The Public Interest, 158* (2005).

▼

FRANK M. TURNER is John Hay Whitney Professor of History at Yale University and Director of the Beinecke Rare Book and Manuscript Library at Yale University, where he served as University Provost from 1988 to 1992. He received his B.A. degree at the College of William and Mary and his Ph.D. from Yale. He has received the Yale College Award for Distinguished Undergraduate Teaching. He has directed a National Endowment for the Humanities Summer Institute. His scholarly research has received the support of fellowships from the National Endowment for the Humanities and the Guggenheim Foundation and the Woodrow Wilson Center. He is the author of *Between Science and Religion: The Reaction to Scientific Naturalism in Late Victorian England* (1974), *The Greek Heritage in Victorian Britain* (1981), which received the British Council Prize of the Conference on British Studies and the Yale Press Governors Award, *Contesting Cultural Authority: Essays in Victorian Intellectual Life* (1993), and *John Henry Newman: The Challenge to Evangelical Religion* (2002). He has also contributed numerous articles to journals and has served on the editorial advisory boards of *The Journal of Modern History, Isis*, and *Victorian Studies*. He edited *The Idea of a University* by John Henry Newman (1996), *Reflections on the Revolution in France* by Edmund Burke (2003), and *Apologia Pro Vita Sua and Six Sermons* by John Henry Newman (2008). Between 1996 and 2006 he served as a Trustee of Connecticut College and between 2004 and 2008 as a member of the Connecticut Humanities Council. In 2003, Professor Turner was appointed Director of the Beinecke Rare Book and Manuscript Library at Yale University.

WHAT IS THE WESTERN HERITAGE?

This book invites students and instructors to explore the Western Heritage. What is that heritage? The Western Heritage emerges from an evolved and evolving story of human actions and interactions, peaceful and violent, that arose in the eastern Mediterranean, then spread across the western Mediterranean into northern Europe, and eventually to the American continents, and in their broadest impact, to the peoples of Africa and Asia as well.

The Western Heritage as a distinct portion of world history descends from the ancient Greeks. They saw their own political life based on open discussion of law and policy as different from that of Mesopotamia, Persia, and Egypt, where kings ruled without regard to public opinion. The Greeks invented the concept of citizenship, defining it as engagement in some form of self-government. Furthermore, through their literature and philosophy, the Greeks established the conviction, which became characteristic of the West, that reason can shape and analyze physical nature, politics, and morality.

The city of Rome, spreading its authority through military conquest across the Mediterranean world, embraced Greek literature and philosophy. Through their conquests and imposition of their law, the Romans created the Western world as a vast empire stretching from Egypt and Syria in the east to Britain in the west. Although the Roman Republic, governed by a Senate and popular political institutions, gave way after civil wars to the autocratic rule of the Roman Empire, the idea of a free republic of engaged citizens governed by public law and constitutional arrangements limiting political authority survived centuries of arbitrary rule by emperors. As in the rest of the world, the Greeks, the Romans, and virtually all other ancient peoples excluded women and slaves from political life and tolerated considerable social inequality.

In the early fourth century C.E., the Emperor Constantine reorganized the Roman Empire in two fundamental ways that reshaped the West. First, he moved the imperial capital from Rome to Constantinople (Istanbul), establishing separate emperors in the East and West. Thereafter, large portions of the Western empire became subject to the rulers of Germanic tribes. In the confusion of these times, most of the texts embodying ancient philosophy, literature, and history became lost in the West, and for centuries Western Europeans were intellectually severed from that ancient heritage, which would later be recovered in a series of renaissances, or cultural rebirths, beginning in the eighth century.

Constantine's second fateful major reshaping of the West was his recognition of Christianity as the official religion of the empire. Christianity had grown out of the ancient monotheistic religion of the Hebrew people living in ancient Palestine. With the ministry of Jesus of Nazareth and the spread of his teachings by the Apostle Paul, Christianity had established itself as one of many religions in the empire. Because Christianity was monotheistic, Constantine's official embrace of it led to the eradication of pagan polytheism. Thereafter, the West became more or less coterminous with Latin Christianity, or that portion of the Christian Church acknowledging the Bishop of Rome as its head.

As the emperors' rule broke down, bishops became the effective political rulers in many parts of Western Europe. But the Christian Church in the West never governed without negotiation or conflict with secular rulers, and religious law never replaced secular law. Nor could secular rulers govern if they ignored the influence of the church. Hence from the fourth century C.E. to the present day, rival claims to political and moral authority between ecclesiastical and political officials have characterized the West.

In the seventh century the Christian West faced a new challenge from the rise of Islam. This new monotheistic religion originating in the teachings of the prophet Muhammad arose on the Arabian Peninsula and spread through rapid conquests across North Africa and eventually into Spain, turning the Mediterranean into what one historian has termed "a Muslim lake." Between the eleventh and the thirteenth centuries, Christians attempted to reclaim the Holy Land from Muslim control in church-inspired military crusades that still resonate negatively in the Islamic world.

It was, however, in the Muslim world that most of the texts of ancient Greek and Latin learning survived and were studied, while intellectual life languished in the West. Commencing in the twelfth century, knowledge of those texts began to work its way back into Western Europe. By the fourteenth century, European thinkers redefined themselves and their intellectual ambitions by recovering the literature and science from the ancient world, reuniting Europe with its Graeco-Roman past.

From the twelfth through the eighteenth centuries, a new European political system slowly arose based on centralized monarchies characterized by large armies, navies, and bureaucracies loyal to the monarch, and by

In his painting *The School of Athens*, the great Italian Renaissance painter Raphael portrayed the ancient Greek philosopher Plato and his student, Aristotle, engaged in debate. Plato, who points to the heavens, believed in a set of ideal truths that exist in their own realm distinct from the earth. Aristotle urged that all philosophy must be in touch with lived reality and confirms this position by pointing to the earth. Such debate has characterized the intellectual, political, and social experience of the West. Indeed, the very concept of "Western Civilization" has itself been subject to debate, criticism, and change over the centuries.
© Scala/Art Resource, NY

the capacity to raise revenues. Whatever the personal ambitions of individual rulers, for the most part these monarchies recognized both the political role of local or national assemblies drawn from the propertied elites and the binding power of constitutional law on themselves. Also, in each of these monarchies, church officials and church law played important roles in public life. The monarchies, their military, and their expanding commercial economies became the basis for the extension of European and Western influence around the globe.

In the late fifteenth and early sixteenth centuries, two transforming events occurred. The first was the European discovery and conquest of the American continents, thus opening the Americas to Western institutions, religion, and economic exploitation. Over time the labor shortages of the Americas led to the forced migration of millions of Africans as slaves to the "New World." By the mid-seventeenth century, the West consequently embraced the entire transatlantic world and its multiracial societies.

Second, shortly after the American encounter, a religious schism erupted within Latin Christianity. Reformers rejecting both many medieval Christian doctrines as unbiblical and the primacy of the Pope in Rome established Protestant churches across much of northern Europe. As a consequence, for almost two centuries religious warfare between Protestants and Roman Catholics overwhelmed the continent as monarchies chose to defend one side or the other. This religious turmoil meant that the Europeans who conquered and settled the Americas carried with them particularly energized religious convictions, with Roman Catholics dominating Latin America and English Protestants most of North America.

By the late eighteenth century, the idea of the West denoted a culture increasingly dominated by two new forces. First, science arising from a new understanding of nature achieved during the sixteenth and seventeenth centuries persuaded growing numbers of the educated elite that human beings can rationally master nature for ever-expanding productive purposes improving the health and well-being of humankind. From this era to the present, the West has been associated with advances in technology, medicine, and scientific research. Second, during the eighteenth century, a drive for economic improvement that vastly increased agricultural production and then industrial manufacturing transformed economic life, especially in Western Europe and later the United States. Both of these economic developments went hand in hand with urbanization and the movement of the industrial economy into cities where the new urban populations experienced major social dislocation.

During these decades certain West European elites came to regard advances in agricultural and manufacturing economies that were based on science and tied to commercial expansion as "civilized" in contrast to cultures that lacked those characteristics. From these ideas emerged the concept of Western Civilization defined to suggest that peoples dwelling outside Europe or inside Europe east of the Elbe River were less than civilized. Whereas Europeans had once defined themselves against the rest of the world as free citizens and then later as Christians, they now defined themselves as "civilized." Europeans would carry this self-assured superiority into their nineteenth- and early twentieth-century encounters with the peoples of Asia, Africa, and the Pacific.

During the last quarter of the eighteenth century, political revolution erupted across the transatlantic world. The British colonies of North America revolted. Then revolution occurred in France and spread across much of Europe. From 1791 through 1830, the Wars of Independence liberated Latin America from its European conquerors. These revolutions created bold new modes of political life, rooting the legitimacy of the state in some form of popular government and generally written constitutions. Thereafter, despite the presence of authoritarian governments on the European continent, the idea of the West, now including the new republics of the United States and Latin America, became associated with liberal democratic governments.

Furthermore, during the nineteenth century, most major European states came to identify themselves in terms of nationality—language, history, and ethnicity—rather than loyalty to a monarch. Nationalism eventually inflamed popular opinion and unloosed unprecedented political ambition by European governments.

These ambitions led to imperialism and the creation of new overseas European empires in the late nineteenth century. For the peoples living in European-administered Asian and African colonies, the idea and reality of the West embodied foreign domination and often disadvantageous involvement in a world economy. When in 1945 the close of World War II led to a sharp decline in European imperial authority, colonial peoples around the globe challenged that authority and gained independence. These former colonial peoples, however, often still suspected the West of seeking to control them. Hence, anticolonialism like colonialism before it redefined definitions of the West far from its borders.

Late nineteenth-century nationalism and imperialism also unleashed with World War I in 1914 unprecedented military hostilities among European nations that spread around the globe, followed a quarter century later by an even greater world war. As one result of World War I, revolution occurred in Russia with the establishment of the communist Soviet Union. During the interwar years a Fascist Party seized power in Italy and a Nazi Party took control of Germany. In response to these new authoritarian regimes, West European powers and the United States identified themselves with liberal democratic constitutionalism, individual freedom, commercial capitalism, science and learning freely pursued, and religious liberty, all of which they defined as the Western Heritage. During the Cold War, conceived of as an East-West, democratic versus communist struggle that concluded with the collapse of the Soviet Union in 1991, the Western Powers led by the United States continued to embrace those values in conscious opposition to the Soviet government, which since 1945 had also dominated much of Eastern Europe.

Since 1991 the West has again become redefined in the minds of many people as a world political and economic order dominated by the United States. Europe clearly remains the West, but political leadership has moved to North America. That American domination and recent American foreign policy have led throughout the West and elsewhere to much criticism of the United States.

Such self-criticism itself embodies one of the most important and persistent parts of the Western Heritage. From the Hebrew prophets and Socrates to the critics of European imperialism, American foreign policy, social inequality, and environmental devastation, voices in the West have again and again been raised to criticize often in the most strident manner the policies of

Western governments and the thought, values, social conditions, and inequalities of Western societies.

Consequently, we study the Western Heritage not because the subject always or even primarily presents an admirable picture, but because the study of the Western Heritage like the study of all history calls us to an integrity of research, observation, and analysis that clarifies our minds and challenges our moral sensibilities. The challenge of history is the challenge of thinking, and it is to that challenge that this book invites its readers.

QUESTIONS

1. How have people in the West defined themselves in contrast with civilizations of the ancient East, and later in contrast with Islamic civilization, and still later in contrast with less economically developed regions of the world? Have people in the West historically viewed their own civilization to be superior to civilizations in other parts of the world? Why or why not?
2. How did the Emperor Constantine's adoption of Christianity as the official religion of the Roman Empire change the concept of the West? Is the presence of Christianity still a determining characteristic of the West?
3. How has the geographical location of what has been understood as the West changed over the centuries?
4. In the past two centuries Western nations established empires around the globe. How did these imperial ventures and the local resistance to them give rise to critical definitions of the West that contrasted with the definitions that had developed in Europe and the United States? How have those non-Western definitions of the West contributed to self-criticism within Western nations?
5. How useful is the concept of Western civilization in understanding today's global economy and global communications made possible by the Internet? Is the idea of Western civilization synonymous with the concept of modern civilization? Do you think the concept of the West will once again be redefined ten years from now?

To view a video of the authors discussing the Western heritage, go to www.myhistorylab.com

This depiction of the Pharaoh Tutankahmun (r. 1336–1327 B.C.E.) and his queen comes from his tomb, which was discovered in the 1920s. "King Tut" died at the age of eighteen.
Robert Frerck/Odyssey Production/Woodfin Camp & Associates

1 The Birth of Civilization

- **Early Humans and Their Culture**
  The Paleolithic Age • The Neolithic Age • The Bronze Age and the Birth of Civilization
- **Early Civilizations to about 1000 B.C.E**
  Mesopotamian Civilization • Egyptian Civilization
- **Ancient Near Eastern Empires**
  The Hittites • The Assyrians • The Second Assyrian Empire • The Neo-Babylonians
- **The Persian Empire**
  Cyrus the Great • Darius the Great • Government and Administration • Religion • Art and Culture
- **Palestine**
  The Canaanites and the Phoenicians • The Israelites • The Jewish Religion
- **General Outlook of Mideastern Cultures**
  Humans and Nature • Humans and the Gods, Law, and Justice
- **Toward the Greeks and Western Thought**
- **In Perspective**

KEY TOPICS

- The earliest history of humanity, including the beginnings of human culture in the Paleolithic Age, the agricultural revolution and the shift from food gathering to food production
- The ancient civilizations of Mesopotamia and Egypt
- The great Near Eastern empires, 1500–486 B.C.E.
- The emergence of Judaism
- The difference in outlook between ancient Near Eastern and Greek civilizations

HISTORY, IN ITS two senses—as the events of the past that make up the human experience on earth and as the written record of those events—is a subject of both interest and importance. We naturally want to know how we came to be who we are, and how the world we live in came to be what it is. But beyond its intrinsic interest, history provides crucial insight into present human behavior. To understand who we are now, we need to know the record of the past and to try to understand the people and forces that shaped it.

For hundreds of thousands of years after the human species emerged, people lived by hunting, fishing, and collecting wild plants. Only some 10,000 years ago did they learn to cultivate plants, herd animals, and make airtight pottery for storage. These discoveries transformed them from gatherers to producers and allowed them to grow in number and to lead a settled life. About 5,000 years ago humans learned how to control the waters of great river valleys, making possible much richer harvests and supporting a further increase in population. The peoples of these river valley societies created the earliest civilizations. They invented writing, which, among other things, enabled them to keep inventories of food and other resources. They discovered the secret of smelting metal to make tools and weapons of bronze far superior to the stone implements of earlier times. They came together in towns and cities, where industry and commerce flourished. Complex religions took form, and social divisions increased. Kings—considered to be representatives of the gods or to be themselves divine—emerged as rulers, assisted by priests and defended by well-organized armies.

The first of these civilizations appeared among the Sumerians before 3500 B.C.E. in the Tigris-Euphrates Valley we call Mesopotamia. From the Sumerians to the Assyrians and Babylonians, a series of peoples ruled Mesopotamia, each shaping and passing along its distinctive culture, before the region fell under the control of great foreign empires. A second early civilization emerged in the Nile Valley around 3100 B.C.E. Egyptian civilization developed a remarkably continuous pattern, in part because Egypt was largely protected from invasion by the formidable deserts surrounding the valley. The essential character of Egyptian civilization changed little for nearly 3,000 years. Influences from other areas, however, especially Nubia to the south, Syria-Palestine to the northeast, and the Aegean to the north, may be seen during many periods of Egyptian history.

By the fourteenth century B.C.E., several powerful empires had arisen and were vying for dominance in regions that included Egypt, Mesopotamia, and **Asia Minor**. Northern warrior peoples, such as the Hittites who dominated Asia Minor, conquered and ruled peoples in various areas. For two centuries, the Hittite and Egyptian Empires struggled with each other for control of Syria-Palestine. By about 1200 B.C.E., however, both these empires had collapsed. Beginning about 850 B.C.E., the Assyrians arose in northern Mesopotamia and ultimately established a mighty new empire, even invading Egypt in the early seventh century B.C.E. The Assyrians were dominant until the late seventh century B.C.E., when they fell to a combination of enemies. Their vast empire was overtaken by the Babylonians, but these people, too, would soon become only a small, though important, part of the enormous empire of Persia.

Among all these great empires nestled a people called the Israelites, who maintained a small, independent kingdom in the region between Egypt and Syria for several centuries. This kingdom ultimately fell to the Assyrians and later remained subject to other conquerors. The Israelites possessed little worldly power or wealth, but they created a powerful religion, Judaism, the first certain and lasting worship of a single god in a world of polytheism. Judaism was the seedbed of two other religions that have played a mighty role in the history of the world: Christianity and Islam. The great empires have collapsed, their power forgotten for millennia until the tools of archaeologists uncovered their remains, but the religion of the Israelites, in itself and through its offshoots, has endured as a powerful force.

▼ Early Humans and Their Culture

Scientists estimate the earth may be as many as 6 billion years old and that creatures very much like humans appeared perhaps 3 to 5 million years ago, probably in Africa. Some 1 to 2 million years ago, erect and tool-using early humans spread over much of Africa, Europe, and Asia. Our own species, ***Homo sapiens***, probably emerged some 200,000 years ago, and the earliest remains of fully modern humans date to about 90,000 years ago.

Humans, unlike other animals, are cultural beings. **Culture** may be defined as the ways of living built up by a group and passed on from one generation to another. It includes behavior such as courtship or child-rearing practices; material things such as tools, clothing, and shelter; and ideas, institutions, and beliefs. Language, apparently a uniquely human trait, lies behind our ability to create ideas and institutions and to transmit culture from one generation to another. Our flexible and dexterous hands enable us to hold and make tools and so to create the material artifacts of culture. Because culture is learned and not inherited, it permits rapid adaptation to changing conditions, making possible the spread of humanity to almost all the lands of the globe.

The Paleolithic Age

Anthropologists designate early human cultures by their tools. The earliest period—the **Paleolithic** (from Greek, "old stone")—dates from the earliest use of stone tools some 1 million years ago to about 10,000 B.C.E. During this immensely long period, people were hunters, fishers, and gatherers, but not producers, of food. They learned to make and use increasingly sophisticated tools of stone and perishable materials like wood; they learned to make and control fire; and they acquired language and the ability to use it to pass on what they had learned.

These early humans, dependent on nature for food and vulnerable to wild beasts and natural disasters, may have developed responses to the world rooted in fear of the unknown—of the uncertainties of human life or the overpowering forces of nature. Religious and magical beliefs and practices may have emerged in an effort to propitiate or coerce the superhuman forces thought to animate or direct the natural world. Evidence of religious faith and practice, as well as of magic, goes as far back as archaeology can take us. Fear or awe, exaltation, gratitude, and empathy with the natural world must all have figured in the cave art and in the ritual practices, such as burial, that we find evidenced at Paleolithic sites around the globe. The sense that there is more to the world than meets the eye—in other words, the religious response to the world—seems to be as old as humankind.

The style of life and the level of technology of the Paleolithic period could support only a sparsely settled society. If hunters were too numerous, game would not suffice. In Paleolithic times, people were subject to the same natural and ecological constraints that today maintain a balance between wolves and deer in Alaska.

Evidence from Paleolithic art and from modern hunter-gatherer societies suggests that human life in the Paleolithic Age was probably characterized by a division of labor by sex. Men engaged in hunting, fishing, making tools and weapons, and fighting against other families, clans, and tribes. Women, less mobile because of childbearing, gathered nuts, berries, and wild grains, wove baskets, and made clothing. Women gathering food probably discovered how to plant and care for seeds. This knowledge eventually made possible the development of agriculture and animal husbandry.

The Neolithic Age

Only a few Paleolithic societies made the initial shift from hunting and gathering to agriculture. Anthropologists and archaeologists disagree as to why, but however it happened, some 10,000 years ago parts of what we now call the Near East began to change from a nomadic hunter-gatherer culture to a more settled agricultural one. Because the shift to agriculture coincided with advances in stone tool technology—the development of greater precision, for example, in chipping and grinding—this period is called the **Neolithic Age** (from Greek, "new stone," the later period in the Stone Age). Productive animals, such as sheep and goats, and food crops, such as wheat and barley, were first domesticated in the mountain foothills where they already lived or grew in the wild. Once domestication had taken place, people could move to areas where these plants and animals did not occur naturally, such as the river valleys of the Near East. The invention of pottery during the Neolithic Age enabled people to store surplus foods and liquids and to transport them, as well as to cook agricultural products that were difficult to eat or digest raw. Cloth was made from flax and wool. Crops required constant care from planting to harvest, so Neolithic farmers built permanent dwellings. The earliest of these tended to be circular huts, large enough to house only one or two people and clustered in groups around a central storage place. Later people built square and rectangular family-sized houses with individual storage places and enclosures to house livestock. Houses in a Neolithic village were normally all the same size and were built on the same plan, suggesting that most Neolithic villagers had about the same level of wealth and social status. A few items, such as stones and shells, were traded long distance, but Neolithic villages tended to be self-sufficient.

Two larger Neolithic settlements do not fit this village pattern. One was found at Çatal Höyük, in a fertile agricultural region about 150 miles south of Ankara, the capital of present-day Turkey. This was a large town covering over fifteen acres, with a population probably well over 6,000 people. The houses were clustered so closely that they had no doors but were entered by ladders from the roofs. Many were decorated inside with sculptures of animal heads and horns, as well as paintings that were apparently redone regularly. Some appear to depict ritual or festive occasions involving men and women. One is the world's oldest landscape picture, showing a nearby volcano exploding. The agriculture, arts, and crafts of this town were astonishingly diversified and at a much higher level of attainment than other, smaller settlements of the period. The site of Jericho, an oasis around a spring near the Dead Sea, was occupied as early as 12,000 B.C.E. Around 8000 B.C.E., a town of eight to ten acres grew up, surrounded by a massive stone wall with at least one tower against the inner face. Although this wall may have been for defense, its use is disputed because no other Neolithic settlement has been found with fortifications. The inhabitants of Neolithic Jericho had a mixed agricultural, herding, and hunting economy and may have traded salt. They had no pottery but plastered the skulls of their dead to make realistic memorial portraits of them. These two sites show that the economy and the settlement patterns of the Neolithic period may be more complicated than many scholars have thought.

Throughout the Paleolithic Age, the human population had been small and relatively stable. The shift from food gathering to food production may not have been associated with an immediate change in population, but over time in the regions where agriculture and animal husbandry appeared, the number of human beings grew at an unprecedented rate. One reason for this is that farmers usually had larger families than hunters. Their children began to work and matured at a younger age than the children of hunters. When animals and plants were domesticated and brought to the river valleys, the relationship between human beings and nature was changed forever. People had learned to control nature, a vital prerequisite for the emergence of civilization. But farmers had to work harder and longer than hunters did, and they had to stay in one place. Herders, in contrast, often moved from place to place in search of pasture and water, returning to their villages in the spring. Some scholars refer to the dramatic changes in subsistence, settlement, technology, and population of this time as the **Neolithic Revolution**. The earliest Neolithic societies appeared in the Mideast about 8000 B.C.E., in China about 4000 B.C.E., and in India about 3600 B.C.E. Neolithic agriculture was based on wheat and barley in the Mideast, on millet and rice in China, and on corn in Mesoamerica, several millennia later.

In 1991 a discovery in the Ötztal Tyrolean Alps on the border between Italy and Austria shed new light on the Neolithic period. A tourist came upon a frozen body, which turned out to be the oldest mummified human being yet discovered. Dated to about 3300 B.C.E., it was the remains of a man between 25 and 35 years old, 5 feet 2 inches tall, weighing 110 pounds. He has been called Ötzi, the Ice Man from the place of his discovery. He had not led a peaceful life, for his nose was broken, and several of his ribs were fractured. An arrowhead in his shoulder suggests he bled to death in the ice and snow. He wore a fur robe made of the skins of mountain animals, and under it he wore a woven grass cape. His shoes were made of leather stuffed with grass. He was heavily armed for his time, carrying a dagger of flint and a bow with arrows also tipped in flint. He also carried an axe whose blade was made of copper, indicating that metallurgy was already under way. His discovery provides a vivid evidence of the beginning of the transition from the Stone Age to the Bronze Age.

Ötzi is the nickname scientists have given to the remains of the oldest mummified human body yet discovered. This reconstruction shows his probable appearance and the clothing and weapons found on and with him.
Wieslav Smetek/Stern/Black Star

The Bronze Age and the Birth of Civilization

Neolithic agricultural villages and herding cultures gradually replaced Paleolithic culture in much of the world. Then another major shift occurred, first in the plains along the Tigris and Euphrates Rivers in the region the Greeks and Romans called **Mesopotamia** (modern Iraq), later in the valley of the Nile River in Egypt, and somewhat later in India and the Yellow River basin in China. This shift was associated initially with the growth of towns alongside villages, creating a hierarchy of larger and smaller settlements in the same region. Some towns then grew into much larger urban centers and often drew population into them, so that nearby villages and towns declined. The urban centers, or cities, usually had monumental buildings, such as temples and fortifications. These were vastly larger than individual houses and could be built only by the sustained effort of hundreds and even thousands of people over many years. Elaborate representational artwork appeared, sometimes made of rare and imported materials. New technologies, such as smelting and the manufacture of metal tools and weapons, were characteristic of urban life. Commodities, like pottery and textiles that had been made in individual houses in villages, were mass produced in cities, which also were characterized by social stratification—that is, the grouping of people into classes based on factors such as control of resources, family, religious or political authority, and personal wealth. The earliest writing is also associated with the growth of cities. Writing, like representational art, was a powerful means of communicating over space and time and was probably invented to deal with urban problems of management and record keeping.

These attributes—urbanism; technological, industrial, and social change; long-distance trade; and new methods of symbolic communication—are defining characteristics of the form of human culture called **civilization**. At about the time the earliest civilizations were emerging, someone discovered how to combine tin and copper to make a stronger and more useful material—bronze. Archaeologists coined the term ***Bronze Age*** to refer to the period 3100 to 1200 B.C.E. in the Near East and eastern Mediterranean.

▼ Early Civilizations to about 1000 B.C.E.

By 4000 B.C.E., people had settled in large numbers in the river-watered lowlands of Mesopotamia and Egypt. By about 3000 B.C.E., when the invention of writing gave birth to history, urban life and the organization of society into centralized states were well established in the valleys of the Tigris and Euphrates Rivers in Mesopotamia and of the Nile River in Egypt.

Much of the population of cities consists of people who do not grow their own food, so urban life is possible only where farmers and stockbreeders can be made to produce a substantial surplus beyond their own needs. Also, some process has to be in place so this surplus can be collected and redeployed to sustain city dwellers. Efficient farming of plains alongside rivers, moreover, requires intelligent management of water resources for irrigation. In Mesopotamia, irrigation was essential, because in the south (later Babylonia), there was not enough rainfall to sustain crops. Furthermore, the rivers, fed by melting snows in Armenia, rose to flood the fields in the spring, about the time for harvest, when water was not needed. When water was needed for the autumn planting, less was available. This meant that people had to build dikes to keep the rivers from flooding the fields in the spring and had to devise means to store water for use in the autumn. The Mesopotamians became skilled at that activity early on. In Egypt, however, the Nile River flooded at the right moment for cultivation, so irrigation was simply a matter of directing the water to the fields. In Mesopotamia, villages, towns, and cities tended to be strung along natural watercourses and, eventually, manmade canal systems. Thus, control of water could be important in warfare, because an enemy could cut off water upstream of a city to force it to submit. Since the Mesopotamian plain was flat, branches of the rivers often changed their courses, and people would have to abandon their cities and move to new locations. Archeologists once believed that urban life and centralized government arose in response to the need to regulate irrigation. This theory supposed that only a strong, central authority could construct and maintain the necessary waterworks. However, archeologists have now shown that large-scale irrigation appeared only long after urban civilization had already developed, so major waterworks were a *consequence* of urbanism, not a cause of it.

Mesopotamian Civilization

The first civilization appears to have arisen in Mesopotamia. The region is divided into two ecological zones, roughly north and south of modern Baghdad. In the south (Babylonia), as noted, irrigation is vital; in the north (later Assyria), agriculture is possible with rainfall and wells. The south has high yields from irrigated lands, whereas the north has lower yields, but much more land under cultivation, so it can produce more than the south. The oldest Mesopotamian cities seem to have been founded by a people called the Sumerians during the fourth millennium B.C.E. in the land of Sumer, which is the southern half of Babylonia. By 3000 B.C.E., the Sumerian city of Uruk was the largest city in the world. (See Map 1–1.) Colonies of people from Uruk built cities and

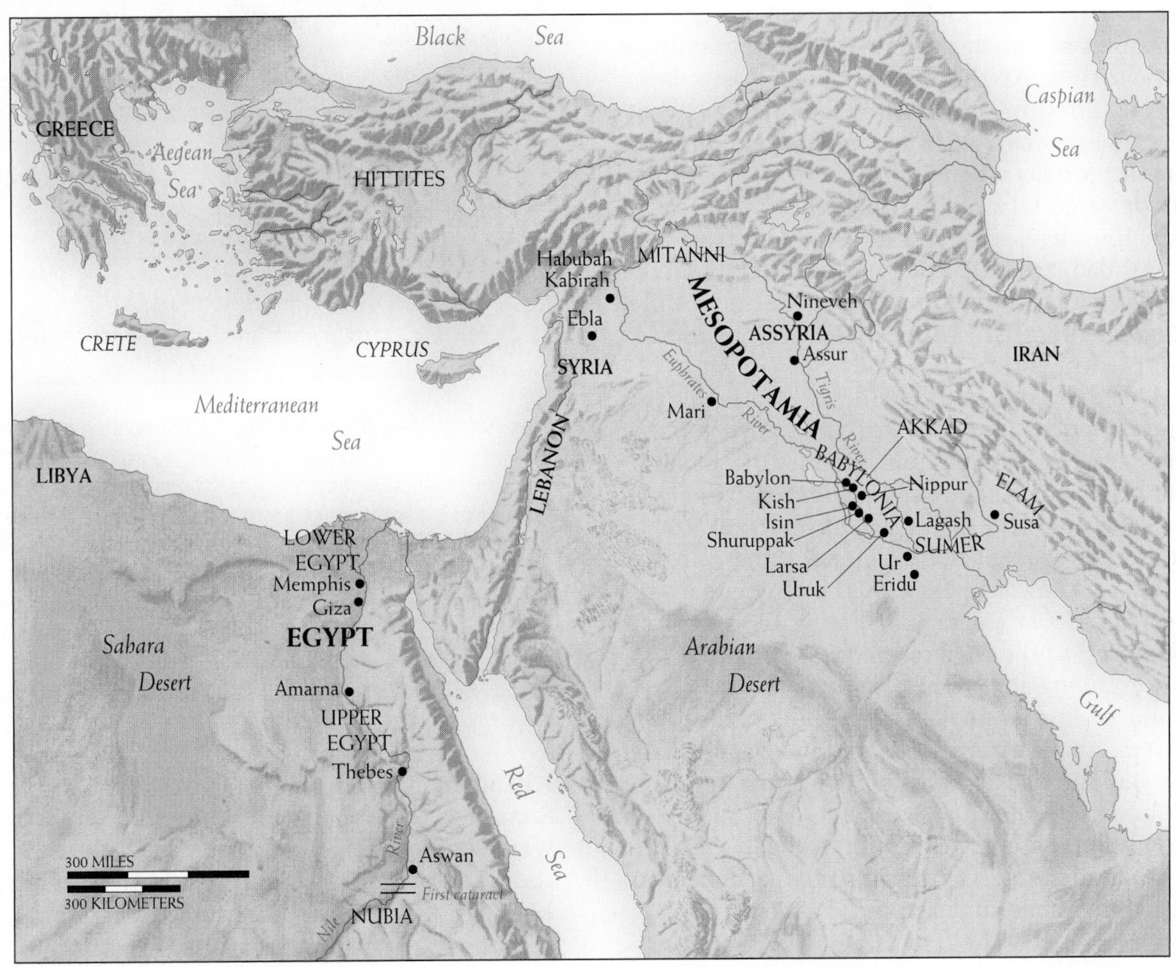

Map 1–1 **THE ANCIENT NEAR EAST** There were two ancient river valley civilizations. Egypt was united into a single state, and Mesopotamia was long divided into a number of city-states.

outposts in northern Syria and southern Anatolia. One of these, at Habubah Kabirah on the Euphrates River in Syria, was built on a regular plain on virgin ground, with strong defensive walls, but was abandoned after a few generations and never inhabited again. No one knows how the Sumerians were able to establish colonies so far from their homeland or even what their purpose was. They may have been trading centers.

From about 2800 to 2370 B.C.E., in what is called the Early Dynastic period, several Sumerian city-states, independent political units consisting of a major city and its surrounding territory, existed in southern Mesopotamia, arranged in north-south lines along the major watercourses. Among these cities were Uruk, Ur, Nippur, Shuruppak, and Lagash. Some of the city-states formed leagues among themselves that apparently had both political and religious significance. Quarrels over water and agricultural land led to incessant warfare, and in time, stronger towns and leagues conquered weaker ones and expanded to form kingdoms ruling several city-states.

Peoples who, unlike the Sumerians, mostly spoke Semitic languages (that is, languages in the same family as Arabic and Hebrew) occupied northern Mesopotamia and Syria. The Sumerian language is not related to any language known today. Many of these Semitic peoples absorbed aspects of Sumerian culture, especially writing. At the western end of this broad territory, at Ebla in northern Syria, scribes kept records using Sumerian writing and studied Sumerian word lists. In northern Babylonia, the Mesopotamians believed the large city of Kish had the first kings in history. In the far east of this territory, not far from modern Baghdad, a people known as the Akkadians established their own kingdom at a capital city called Akkade, under their first king, Sargon, who had been a servant of the king of Kish.

The Akkadians conquered all the Sumerian city-states and invaded southwestern Iran and northern Syria. This was the first empire in history, having a heartland, provinces, and an absolute ruler. It included numerous peoples, cities, languages, and cultures, as well as different ecological zones, under one rule. Sargon's name became legendary as the first great conqueror of history. His grandson, Naram-Sin, ruled from the Persian Gulf to the Mediterranean Sea, with a standardized administration, unheard-of wealth and power, and a grand style that to later Mesopotamians was a high point of their history. Naram-Sin even declared himself a god and had temples built to himself, something no Sumerian ruler had ever done. External attack and internal weakness destroyed the Akkadian Empire, but several smaller states flourished independently, notably Lagash in Sumer, under its ruler Gudea.

About 2125 B.C.E., the Sumerian city of Ur rose to dominance, and the rulers of the Third Dynasty of Ur established an empire built on the foundation of the

The Victory Stele of Naram-Sin, the Akkadian ruler, commemorates the king's campaign (c. 2230 B.C.E.) against the Lullubi, a people living in the northern Zagros Mountains, along the eastern frontier of Mesopotamia. Kings set up monuments like this one in the courtyards of temples to record their deeds. They were also left in remote corners of the empire to warn distant peoples of the death and enslavement awaiting the king's enemies (pink sandstone). Victory stele of Naram-Sin, King of Akkad, over the mountain-dwelling Lullubi, Mesopotamian, Akkadian Period, c. 2230 B.C. (pink sandstone). Louvre, Paris, France/The Bridgeman Art Library International Ltd.

Akkadian Empire, but far smaller. In this period, Sumerian culture and literature flourished. Epic poems were composed, glorifying the deeds of the ancestors of the kings of Ur. A highly centralized administration kept detailed records of agriculture, animal husbandry, commerce, and other matters. Over 100,000 of these documents have been found in the ruins of Sumerian cities. After little more than a century of prominence,

KEY EVENTS AND PEOPLE IN MESOPOTAMIAN HISTORY

ca. 3500 B.C.E.	Development of Sumerian cities, especially Uruk
ca. 2800–2370 B.C.E.	Early Dynastic period of Sumerian city-states
ca. 2370 B.C.E.	Sargon establishes Akkadian dynasty and Akkadian Empire
ca. 2125–2027 B.C.E.	Third Dynasty of Ur
ca. 2000–1800 B.C.E.	Establishment of Amorites in Mesopotamia
ca. 1792–1750 B.C.E.	Reign of Hammurabi

the kingdom of Ur disintegrated in the face of famine and invasion. From the east, the Elamites attacked the city of Ur and captured the king. From the north and west, a Semitic-speaking people, the Amorites, invaded Mesopotamia in large numbers, settling around the Sumerian cities and eventually founding their own dynasties in some of them, such as at Uruk, Babylon, Isin, and Larsa.

The fall of the Third Dynasty of Ur put an end to Sumerian rule, and the Sumerians gradually disappeared as an identifiable group. The Sumerian language survived only in writing as the learned language of Babylonia taught in schools and used by priests and scholars. So great was the respect for Sumerian that seventeen centuries after the fall of Ur, when Alexander the Great arrived in Babylon in 331 B.C.E., Sumerian was still used as a scholarly and religious language there.

For some time after the fall of Ur, there was relative peace in Babylonia under the Amorite kings of Isin, who used Sumerian at their court and considered themselves the successors of the kings of Ur. Eventually, another Amorite dynasty at the city of Larsa contested control of Babylonia, and a period of warfare began, mostly centering around attacks on strategic points on waterways. A powerful new dynasty at Babylon defeated Isin, Larsa, and other rivals and dominated Mesopotamia for nearly 300 years. Its high point was the reign of its most famous king, Hammurabi (r. ca. 1792–1750 B.C.E.), best known today for the collection of laws that bears his name. (See "Hammurabi's Law Code," page 11.) Hammurabi destroyed the great city of Mari on the Euphrates and created a kingdom embracing most of Mesopotamia.

Collections of laws existed as early as the Third Dynasty of Ur, and Hammurabi's owed much to earlier models and different legal traditions. His collection of laws, now referred to as the Code of Hammurabi, reveals a society divided by class. There were nobles, commoners, and slaves, and the law did not treat all of them equally. In general, punishments were harsh, based literally on the principle of "an eye for an eye, a tooth for a tooth," whereas Sumerian law often levied fines instead of bodily mutilation or death. Disputes over property and other complaints were heard in the first instance by local city assemblies of leading citizens and heads of families. Professional judges heard cases for a fee and held court near the city gate. In Mesopotamian trials, witnesses and written evidence had to be produced and a written verdict issued. False testimony was punishable by death. Sometimes the contesting parties would submit to an oath before the gods, on the theory that no one would risk swearing a false oath. In cases where evidence or oath could not establish the truth, the contesting parties might take an ordeal, such as being thrown into the river for the god to decide who was telling the truth. Cases of capital punishment could be appealed to the king. Hammurabi was closely concerned with the details of his kingdom, and his surviving letters often deal with minor local disputes.

About 1600 B.C.E., the Babylonian kingdom fell apart under the impact of invasions from the north by the Hittites, Hurrians, and Kassites, all non-Mesopotamian peoples.

Government From the earliest historical records, it is clear that the Sumerians were ruled by monarchs in some form. The earliest Sumerian rulers are shown in their art leading an army, killing prisoners, and making offerings to the gods. The type of rule varied at different times and places. In later Assyria, for example, the king served as chief priest; in Babylonia, the priesthood was separate from royalty. Royal princesses were sometimes appointed as priestesses of important gods. One of the most famous of these was Enheduanna, daughter of Sargon of Akkad. She is the first author in history whose writings can be identified with a real person. Although she was an Akkadian, she wrote complicated, passionate, and intensely personal poetry in the Sumerian language, in which she tells of important historical events that she experienced. In one passage, she compares the agony of writing a poem to giving birth.

The government and the temples cultivated large areas of land to support their staffs and retinue. Laborers of low social status who were given rations of raw foods and other commodities to sustain them and their families did some of the work on this land. Citizens leased some land for a share of the crop and a cash payment. These lands were carefully surveyed, and sometimes the crop could be estimated in advance. The government and temples owned large herds of sheep, goats, cattle, and donkeys. The Sumerian city-states exported wool and textiles to buy metals, such as copper, that were not available in Mesopotamia. Families and private individuals often owned their own farmland or houses in the cities, which they bought and sold as they liked.

A Closer LOOK

THE ROYAL STANDARD OF UR

THIS MYSTERIOUS OBJECT, dated about 2500 B.C.E., was found in one of the largest graves in the Royal Cemetery at Ur, a major city of the Sumerians, who created the earliest civilization in Mesopotamia, perhaps in the world.

We do not know the original function of the Standard. The archaeologist who discovered it thought that it was carried on a pole. It is made of a wooden frame carrying a mosaic of shell, red limestone, and a blue stone called lapis lazuli. It was found in damaged condition, and the present restoration is only a guess as to how it originally appeared.

The main panels are known as "War" and "Peace." "War" shows one of the earliest representations of a Sumerian army. Chariots, each pulled by four donkeys, trample enemies; infantry with cloaks carry spears; enemy soldiers are killed with axes, others are paraded naked and presented to the king who holds a spear. The "Peace" panel depicts animals, fish, and other goods brought in procession to a banquet.

British Museum, London, UK/Bridgeman Art Library

Seated figures, wearing woolen fleeces or fringed skirts, drink to the accompaniment of a musician playing a lyre.

Picture Desk, Inc./Kobal Collection

To examine this image in an interactive fashion, please go to www.myhistorylab.com

Writing and Mathematics Government, business, and scholarship required a good system of writing. The Sumerians invented the writing system now known as **cuneiform** (from the Latin *cuneus*, "wedge") because of the wedge-shaped marks they made by writing on clay tablets with a cut reed stylus. At first the writing system was sketchy, giving only a few elements of a sentence to help a reader remember something he probably already knew. Later, people thought to write whole sentences in the order in which they were to be spoken, so writing could communicate new information to a reader. The Sumerian writing system used several thousand characters, some of which stood for words and some for sounds. Some characters stood for many different sounds or words, and some sounds could be written using a choice of many different characters. The result was a writing system that was difficult to learn. Sumerian students were fond of complaining about their unfair teachers, how hard their schoolwork was, and their too-short vacations. Sumerian and Babylonian schools emphasized language and literature, accounting, legal practice, and mathematics, especially geometry, along with memorization of much abstract knowledge that had no relevance to everyday life. The ability to read and write was restricted to an elite who could afford to go to school. Success in school, however, and factors such as good family connections meant a literate Sumerian could find employment as a clerk, surveyor, teacher, diplomat, or administrator.

The Sumerians also began the development of mathematics. The earliest Sumerian records suggest that before 3000 B.C.E. people had not yet thought of the concept of "number" independently of counting specific things. Therefore, the earliest writing used different numerals for counting different things, and the numerals had no independent value. (The same sign could be 10 or 18, for example, depending on what was counted.) Once an independent concept of number was established, mathematics developed rapidly. The Sumerian system was based on the number 60 ("sexagesimal"), rather than the number 10 ("decimal"), the system in general use today. Sumerian counting survives in the modern 60-minute hour and the circle of 360 degrees. By the time of Hammurabi, the Mesopotamians were expert in many types of mathematics, including mathematical astronomy. The calendar the Mesopotamians used had twelve lunar months of thirty days each. To keep it in accordance with the solar year and the seasons, the Mesopotamians occasionally introduced a thirteenth month.

Religion The Sumerians and their successors worshiped many gods and goddesses. They were visualized in human form, with human needs and weaknesses. Most of the gods were identified with some natural phenomenon such as the sky, fresh water, or storms. They differed from humans in their greater power, sublime position in the universe, and immortality. The Mesopotamians believed the human race was created to serve the gods and to relieve the gods of the necessity of providing for themselves. The gods were considered universal, but also residing in specific places, usually one important god or goddess in each city. Mesopotamian temples were run like great households where the gods were fed lavish meals, entertained with music, and honored with devotion and ritual. There were gardens for their pleasure and bedrooms to retire to at night. The images of the gods were dressed and adorned with the finest materials. Theologians organized the gods into families and generations. Human social institutions, such as kingship, or crafts, such as carpentry, were associated with specific gods, so the boundaries between human and divine society were not always clearly drawn. Because the great gods were visualized like human rulers, remote from the common people and their concerns, the Mesopotamians imagined another more personal intercessor god who was supposed to look after a person, rather like a guardian spirit. The public festivals of the gods were important holidays, with parades, ceremonies, and special foods. People wore their best clothes and celebrated their city and its gods. The Mesopotamians were religiously tolerant and readily accepted the possibility that different people might have different gods.

The Mesopotamians had a vague and gloomy picture of the afterworld. The winged spirits of the dead were recognizable as individuals. They were confined to a dusty, dark netherworld, doomed to perpetual hunger and thirst unless someone offered them food and drink. Some spirits escaped to haunt human beings. There was no preferential treatment in the afterlife for those who had led religious or virtuous lives—everyone was in equal misery. Mesopotamian families often had a ceremony to remember and honor their dead. People were usually buried together with goods such as pottery and ornaments. In the Early Dynastic period, certain kings were buried with a large retinue of attendants, including soldiers and musicians, who apparently took poison during the funeral ceremony and were buried where they fell. But this practice soon disappeared. Children were sometimes buried under the floors of houses. Some families used burial vaults; others, large cemeteries. No tombstones or inscriptions identified the deceased. Mesopotamian religion focused on problems of this world and how to lead a good life before dying. (See "Encountering The Past: Divination in Ancient Mesopotamia," page 10.)

Religion played a large part in the literature and art of Mesopotamia. Epic poems told of the deeds of the gods, such as how the world was created and organized, of a great flood the gods sent to wipe out the human race, and of the hero-king Gilgamesh, who tried to

DIVINATION IN ANCIENT MESOPOTAMIA

DIVINATION ATTEMPTS TO foretell the future by the use of magic or occult practices. The ancient Mesopotamians put much thought and effort into discovering signs that they believed would indicate future events, interpreting the meaning of these signs, and taking steps to avert evil. Mesopotamians believed in divination the way many people today put their trust in science.

One of the earliest divination methods the Mesopotamians used involved the sacrifice of sheep and goats. Seers examined the entrails of the sacrificed animals to look for deformations that could foretell the future. Clay tablets recorded particular deformations and the historical events they had foretold. The search for omens in the entrails of sacrificial animals was especially important for Mesopotamian kings, who always performed that ceremony before undertaking important affairs of state.

But animal sacrifice was expensive. Most Mesopotamians, therefore, used other devices. They burned incense and examined the shape of the smoke that arose. They poured oil into water and studied the resulting patterns for signs. They found omens in how people answered questions or in what they overheard strangers say. They collected clay tablets—their books—that described people's appearance and what it might tell them about the future.

The heavens were another source of omens. Astrologers recorded and interpreted the movements of the stars, planets, comets, and other heavenly bodies. Mesopotamia's great progress in astronomy derived in large part from this practice. The study of dreams and of unusual births, both human and animal, was also important. Troubled dreams and monstrous offspring had frightening implications for human affairs.

All these practices derived from the belief that the gods sent omens to warn human beings. Once the omens had been interpreted, the Mesopotamians sought to avert danger with magic and prayers.

How did the Mesopotamians try to learn what would happen in the future, and what did they try to do about what they learned?

How would they explain their great interest in omens?

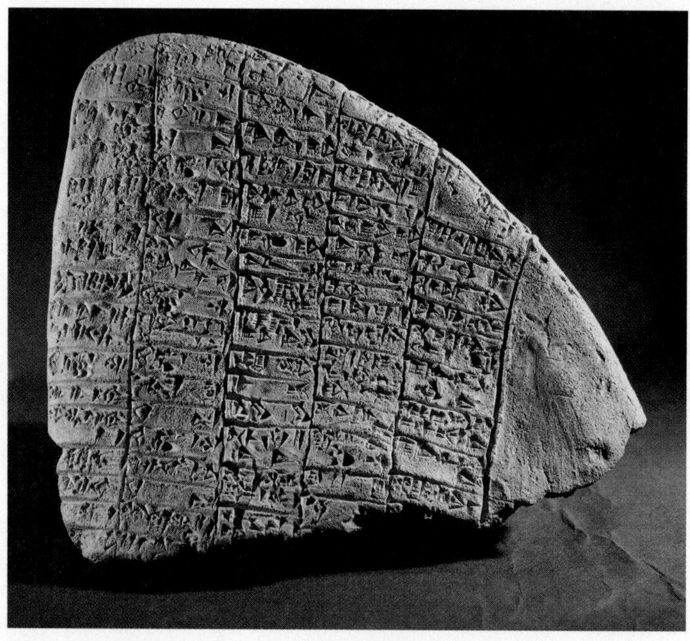

Astrological calendar. From Uruk, Mesopotamia. Astrological calendar. From Uruk, Mesopotamia. Babylonian, 1st mill. B.C.E. Museum of Oriental Antiquities, Istanbul, Turkey. Photograph © Erich Lessing/Art Resource, NY

HAMMURABI'S LAW CODE

Hammurabi (1792–1750 B.C.E.) ruled the great Babylonian Empire that stretched from the Persian Gulf to the Mediterranean Sea. Building on older Mesopotamian laws, he compiled one of the great ancient codes, the most complete collection of Babylonian laws. His legal decisions were inscribed in the Semitic Akkadian language in cuneiform script placed in Babylon's temple of Marduk. It contains 282 case laws dealing with economics (prices, tariffs, trade, and commerce), family law (marriage and divorce), criminal law (assault, theft), and civil law (slavery, debt). The stone was discovered in the ancient Persian capital of Susa in 1901 and can now be found in the Louvre in Paris.

What principles of justice underlie the cases shown here? By what rights did Hammurabi claim to declare the law?

LAWS

If a son has struck his father, they shall cut off his hand.
If a seignior has destroyed the eye of a member of the aristocracy, they shall destroy his eye.
If he has broken another seignior's bone, they shall break his bone.
If he has destroyed the eye of a commoner or broken the bone of a commoner, he shall pay one mina of silver.
If he has destroyed the eye of a seignior's slave or broken the bone of a seignior's slave, he shall pay one-half his value.
If a seignior has knocked out a tooth of a seignior of his own rank, they shall knock out his tooth.
If he has knocked out a commoner's tooth, he shall pay one-third mina of silver. . . .

EPILOGUE

I, Hammurabi, the perfect king,
was not careless (or) neglectful of the black-headed (people),
whom Enlil had presented to me,
(and) whose shepherding Marduk had committed to me;
I sought out peaceful regions for them;
I overcame grievous difficulties; . . .
With the mighty weapon which Zababa and Inanna entrusted to me,
with the insight that Enki allotted to me,
with the ability that Marduk gave me,
I rooted out the enemy above and below;
I made an end of war;
I promoted the welfare of the land;
I made the peoples rest in friendly habitations; . . .
The great gods called me,
so I became the beneficent shepherd whose scepter is righteous ...

James Pritchard, *The Ancient Near East*.

escape death by going on a fantastic journey to find the sole survivor of the great flood. (See "Compare & Connect: The Great Flood," on page 12.) There were also many literary and artistic works that were not religious in character, so we should not imagine religion dominated all aspects of the Mesopotamians' lives. Religious architecture took the form of great temple complexes in the major cities. The most imposing religious structure was the *ziggurat*, a tower in stages, sometimes with a small chamber on top. The terraces may have been planted with trees to resemble a mountain. Poetry about ziggurats often compares them to mountains, with their peaks in the sky and their roots in the netherworld, linking heaven to earth, but their precise purpose is not known. Eroded remains of many of these monumental structures still dot the Iraqi landscape. Through the Bible, they have entered Western tradition as "the tower of Babel."

COMPARE AND CONNECT

The Great Flood

STORIES OF A great deluge appeared in many cultures at various times in the ancient world. In the Mesopotamian world the earliest known story of a great flood sent by the gods to destroy mankind appeared in the Sumerian civilization. Later the story was included in the Gilgamesh epic in a Semitic language. The great flood of Noah's time appears in the book of Genesis in the Hebrew Bible.

QUESTIONS

1. **In what ways is the story from the *Epic of Gilgamesh* similar to the Story of Noah in the Hebrew Bible?**
2. **How is the account of a great flood in the Story of Noah different from that in the *Epic of Gilgamesh*?**
3. **What is the significance of the similarities and differences between the two accounts?**

I. The Babylonian Story of the Flood

The passage that follows is part of the Babylonian Epic of Gilgamesh. *An earlier independent Babylonian Story of the Flood suggested that the gods sent a flood because there were too many people on the earth. A version of this story was later combined with the* Epic of Gilgamesh, *a legendary king who became terrified of death when his best friend and companion died. After many adventures, Gilgamesh crossed the distant ocean and the "waters of death" to ask Utanapishtim, who, with his wife, was the only survivor of the great flood, the secret of eternal life. In response, Utanapishtim narrated the story of the great flood, to show that his own immortality derived from a onetime event in the past, so Gilgamesh could not share his destiny.*

Six days and seven nights
The wind continued, the deluge and windstorm levelled the land.
When the seventh day arrived,
The windstorm and deluge left off their battle,
Which had struggled, like a woman in labor.
The sea grew calm, the tempest stilled, the deluge ceased.
I looked at the weather, stillness reigned,
And the whole human race had turned into clay.
The landscape was flat as a rooftop.
I opened the hatch, sunlight fell upon my face.
Falling to my knees, I sat down weeping,
Tears running down my face.
I looked at the edges of the world, the borders of the sea,
At twelve times sixty double leagues the periphery emerged.
The boat had come to rest on Mount Nimush,
Mount Nimush held the boat fast, not letting it move.
One day, a second day Mount Nimush held the boat fast, not letting it move.
A third day, a fourth day Mount Nimush held the boat fast, not letting it move.
A fifth day, a sixth day Mount Nimush held the boat fast, not letting it move.
When the seventh day arrived,
I brought out a dove and set it free.
The dove went off and returned,
No landing place came to its view, so it turned back.
I brought out a swallow and set it free,
The swallow went off and returned,
No landing space came to its view, so it turned back.
I brought out a raven and set it free.
The raven went off and saw the ebbing of the waters.
It ate, preened, left droppings, did not turn back.
I released all to the four directions,
I brought out an offering and offered it to the four directions.
I set up an incense burner on the summit of the mountain,
I arranged seven and seven cult vessels,
I heaped reeds, cedar, and myrtle in their bowls.
The gods smelled the savor,
The gods smelled the sweet savor,
The gods crowded round the sacrificer like flies.
As soon as the Belet-ili arrived,
She held up the great fly-ornaments that Anu had made in his ardor:

The Flood Tablet (Tablet XI), which relates part of the *Epic of Gilgamesh*. The eleventh tablet describes the meeting of Gilgamesh and Utanapishtim who, along with his wife, survived a great flood that destroyed the rest of humankind. Art Resource/The British Museum Great Court Ltd. © Copyright The British Museum

'O ye gods, as surely as I shall not forget these lapis pendants on my neck,
'I shall be mindful of these days and not forget, not ever!
'The gods should come to the incense burner,
'But Enlil should not come to the incense burner,
'For he, irrationally, brought on the flood,
'And marked my people for destruction!'
As soon as Enlil arrived,
He saw the boat, Enlil flew into a rage,
He was filled with fury at the gods:
'Who came through alive? No man was to survive destruction!'
Ninurta made ready to speak,
Said to the valiant Enlil:
'Who but Ea could contrive such a thing?
'For Ea alone knows every artifice.'
Ea made ready to speak,
Said to the valiant Enlil:
'You, O valiant one, are the wisest of the gods,
'How could you, irrationally, have brought on the flood?
'Punish the wrong-doer for his wrong-doing,
'Punish the transgressor for his transgression,
'But be lenient, lest he be cut off,
'Bear with him, lest he [. . .].
'Instead of your bringing on a flood,
'Let the lion rise up to diminish the human race!
'Instead of your bringing on a flood,
'Let the wolf rise up to diminish the human race!
'Instead of your bringing on a flood,
'Let famine rise up to wreak havoc in the land!
'Instead of your bringing on a flood,
'Let pestilence rise up to wreak havoc in the land!
'It was not I who disclosed the secret of the great gods,
'I made Atrahasis have a dream and so he heard the secret of the gods.
'Now then, make some plan for him.'
Then Enlil came up into the boat,
Leading me by the hand, he brought me up too.
He brought my wife up and had her kneel beside me.
He touched our brows, stood between us to bless us:
'Hitherto Utanapishtim has been a human being,
'Now Utanapishtim and his wife shall become like us gods.
'Utanapishtim shall dwell far distant at the source of the rivers.'

Source: "The Babylonian Story of the Flood" from *The Babylonian Epic of Gilgamesh*, in *The Epic of Gilgamesh*, trans. by Benjamin R. Foster. Copyright © 2001 by W.W. Norton & Company. Used by permission of W.W. Norton & Company, Inc.

II. Noah's Flood—Genesis 7.11–9.11

In the six hundredth year of Noah's life, in the second month, on the seventeenth day of the month, on that day all the fountains of the great deep burst forth, and the windows of the heavens were opened. The rain fell on the earth forty days and forty nights. . . .

At the end of forty days Noah opened the window of the ark that he had made and sent out the raven; and it went to and fro until the waters were dried up from the earth. Then he sent out the dove from him, to see if the waters had subsided from the face of the ground; but the dove found no place to set its foot, and it returned to him to the ark, for the waters were still on the face of the whole earth. So he put out his hand and took it and brought it into the ark with him. He waited another seven days, and again he sent out the dove from the ark; and the dove came back to him in the evening, and there in its beak was a freshly plucked olive leaf; so Noah knew that the waters had subsided from the earth. Then he waited another seven days, and sent out the dove; and it did not return to him any more. . . .

Then God said to Noah and to his sons with him, "As for me, I am establishing my covenant with you and your descendants after you, and with every living creature that is with you, the birds, the domestic animals, and every animal of the earth with you, as many as came out of the ark." I establish my covenant with you, that never again shall all flesh be cut off by the waters of a flood, and never again shall there be a flood to destroy the earth."

Society Hundreds of thousands of cuneiform texts from the early third millennium B.C.E. until the third century B.C.E. give us a detailed picture of how peoples in ancient Mesopotamia conducted their lives and of the social conditions in which they lived. From the time of Hammurabi, for example, there are many royal letters to and from the various rulers of the age, letters from the king to his subordinates, administrative records from many different cities, and numerous letters and documents belonging to private families.

Categorizing the laws of Hammurabi according to the aspects of life with which they deal reveals much about Babylonian life in his time. The third largest category of laws deals with commerce, relating to such issues as contracts, debts, rates of interest, security, and default. Business documents of Hammurabi's time show how people invested their money in land, moneylending, government contracts, and international trade. Some of these laws regulate professionals, such as builders, judges, and surgeons. The second largest category of laws deals with land tenure, especially land given by the king to soldiers and marines in return for their service. The letters of Hammurabi that deal with land tenure show he was concerned to uphold the individual rights of landholders against powerful officials who tried to take their land from them. The largest category of laws relates to the family and its maintenance and protection, including marriage, inheritance, and adoption.

Parents usually arranged marriages, and betrothal was followed by the signing of a marriage contract. The bride usually left her own family to join her husband's. The husband-to-be could make a bridal payment, and the father of the bride-to-be provided a dowry for his daughter in money, land, or objects. A marriage started out monogamous, but a husband whose wife was childless or sickly could take a second wife. Sometimes husbands also sired children from domestic slave women. Women could possess their own property and do business on their own. Women divorced by their husbands without good cause could get their dowry back. A woman seeking divorce could also recover her dowry if her husband could not convict her of wrongdoing. A married woman's place was thought to be in the home, but hundreds of letters between wives and husbands show them as equal partners in the ventures of life. (See "An Assyrian Woman Writes to Her Husband, ca. 1800 B.C.E.") Single women who were not part of families could set up in business on their own, often as tavern owners or moneylenders, or could be associated with temples, sometimes working as midwives and wet nurses, or taking care of orphaned children.

Slavery: Chattel Slaves and Debt Slaves There were two main types of slavery in Mesopotamia: chattel and debt slavery. Chattel slaves were bought like any other piece of property and had no legal rights. They had to wear their hair in a certain way and were sometimes branded or tattooed on their hands. They were often non-Mesopotamians bought from slave merchants. Prisoners of war could also be enslaved. Chattel slaves were expensive luxuries during most of Mesopotamian history. They were used in domestic service rather than in production, such as fieldwork. A wealthy household might have five or six slaves, male and female.

Debt slavery was more common than chattel slavery. Rates of interest were high, as much as 33.3 percent, so people often defaulted on loans. One reason the interest rates were so high was that the government periodically canceled certain types of debts, debt slavery, and obligations, so lenders ran the risk of losing their money. If debtors had pledged themselves or members of their families as surety for a loan, they became the slave of the creditor; their labor went to pay the interest on the loan. Debt slaves could not be sold but could redeem their freedom by paying off the loan. True chattel slavery did not become common until the Neo-Babylonian period (612–539 B.C.E.).

Although laws against fugitive slaves or slaves who denied their masters were harsh—the Code of Hammurabi permits the death penalty for anyone who sheltered or helped a runaway slave to escape—Mesopotamian slavery appears enlightened compared with other slave systems in history. Slaves were generally of the same people as their masters. They had been enslaved because of misfortune from which their masters were not immune, and they generally labored alongside them. Slaves could engage in business and, with certain restrictions, hold property. They could marry free men or women, and the resulting children would normally be free. A slave who acquired the means could buy his or her freedom. Children of a slave by a master might be allowed to share his property after his death. Nevertheless, slaves were property, subject to an owner's will and had little legal protection.

Egyptian Civilization

As Mesopotamian civilization arose in the valley of the Tigris and Euphrates, another great civilization emerged in Egypt, centered on the Nile River. From its sources in Lake Victoria and the Ethiopian highlands, the Nile flows north some 4,000 miles to the Mediterranean. Ancient Egypt included the 750-mile stretch of smooth, navigable river from Aswan to the sea. South of Aswan the river's course is interrupted by several cataracts—rocky areas of rapids and whirlpools.

The Egyptians recognized two sets of geographical divisions in their country. **Upper** (southern) **Egypt** consisted of the narrow valley of the Nile. **Lower** (northern)

AN ASSYRIAN WOMAN WRITES TO HER HUSBAND, CA. 1800 B.C.E.

The wives of early Assyrian businessmen were often active in their husbands' business affairs. They made extra money for themselves by having slave girls weave textiles that the husbands then sold on business trips. Their letters are one of the largest groups of women's records from the ancient world. The woman writing this letter, Taram-Kubi, complains of her husband's selfishness and points out all the matters she has worked on during his absence on business.

What functions did this woman perform on behalf of the family? How do you judge her real power in regard to her husband? On what evidence do you base that judgment? What does this document reveal about the place of women in Assyrian society?

You wrote to me saying, "You'll need to safeguard the bracelets and rings which are there so they'll be available [to buy] food." In fact, you sent [the man] Ilum-bani a half pound of gold! Which are the bracelets you left me? When you left, you didn't leave me an ounce of silver, you picked the house clean and took away everything! After you left, there was a severe famine in the city. Not so much as a quart of grain did you leave me, I always had to buy grain for our food. Besides that, I paid the assessment for the divine icon (?); in fact, I paid for my part in full. Besides that, I paid over to the Town Hall the grain owed [the man] Atata. What is the extravagance you keep writing to me about? There is nothing for us to eat—we're the ones being extravagant? I picked up whatever I had to hand and sent it to you—today I'm living in an empty house. It's high time you sent me the money realized on my weavings, in silver, from what you have to hand, so I can buy ten quarts of grain!

Trans. by Benjamin R. Foster, 1999.

Egypt referred to the broad triangular area, named by the Greeks after their letter "delta," formed by the Nile as it branches out to empty into the Mediterranean. (See Map 1–2.) They also made a distinction between what they termed the "black land," the dark fertile fields along the Nile, and the "red land," the desert cliffs and plateaus bordering the valley.

The Nile alone made agriculture possible in Egypt's desert environment. Each year the rains of central Africa caused the river to rise over its floodplain, cresting in September and October. In places the plain extends several miles on either side; elsewhere the cliffs slope down to the water's edge. When the floodwaters receded, they left a rich layer of organically fertile silt. The construction and maintenance of canals, dams, and irrigation ditches to control the river's water, together with careful planning and organization of planting and harvesting, produced an agricultural prosperity unmatched in the ancient world.

The Nile served as the major highway connecting Upper and Lower Egypt. There was also a network of desert roads running north and south, as well as routes across the eastern desert to the Sinai and the Red Sea. Other tracks led to oases in the western desert. Thanks to geography and climate, Egypt was more isolated and enjoyed far more security than Mesopotamia. This security, along with the predictable flood calendar, gave Egyptian civilization a more optimistic outlook than the civilizations of the Tigris and Euphrates, which were more prone to storms, flash floods, and invasions.

The 3,000-year span of ancient Egyptian history is traditionally divided into thirty-one royal dynasties, from the first, said to have been founded by Menes, the king who originally united Upper and Lower Egypt, to the last, established by Alexander the Great, who conquered Egypt in 332 B.C.E. (as we see in Chapter 3). Ptolemy, one of Alexander's generals, founded the Ptolemaic Dynasty, whose last ruler was Cleopatra. In 30 B.C.E., the Romans defeated Egypt, effectively ending the independent existence of a civilization that had lasted three millennia.

The unification of Upper and Lower Egypt was vital, for it meant the entire river valley could benefit from an unimpeded distribution of resources. Three times in its history, Egypt experienced a century or more of political and social disintegration, known as Intermediate Periods. During these eras, rival dynasties often set up separate power bases in Upper and Lower Egypt until a strong leader reunified the land.

The Old Kingdom (2700–2200 B.C.E.) The Old Kingdom represents the culmination of the cultural and historical developments of the Early Dynastic period. For over four hundred years, Egypt enjoyed internal stability and great prosperity. During this period, the **pharaoh** (the term comes from the Egyptian for "great house," much as we use "White House" to refer to the president) was a king who was also a god. From his capital at Memphis, the god-king administered Egypt according to set principles, prime among them being *maat*, an ideal of order, justice, and truth. In return for the king's building and maintaining temples, the gods preserved the equilibrium of the state and en-

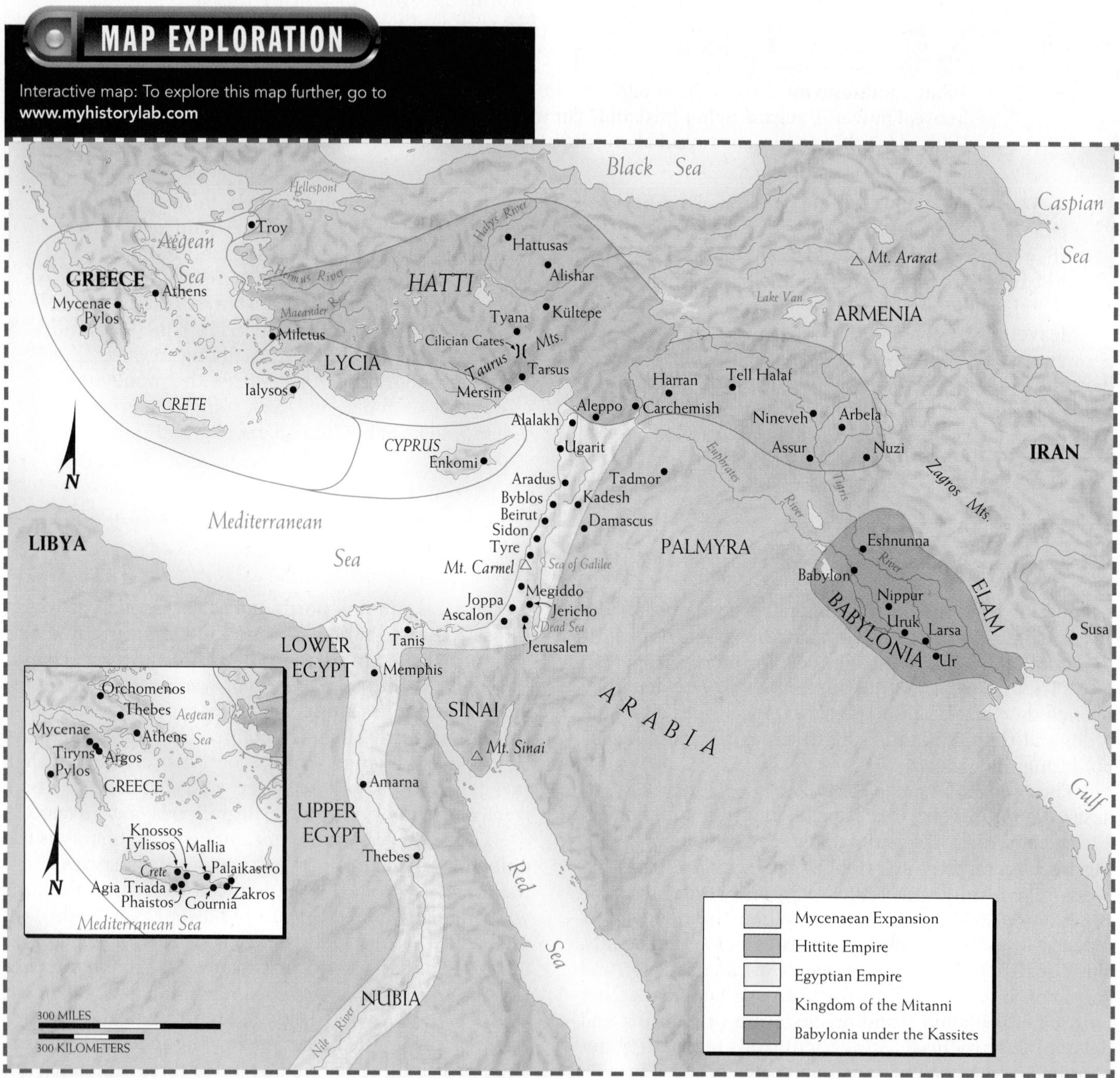

Map 1–2 **THE NEAR EAST AND GREECE ABOUT 1400 B.C.E.** About 1400 B.C.E., the Near East was divided among four empires. Egypt extended south to Nubia and north through Palestine and Phoenicia. The Kassites ruled in Mesopotamia, the Hittites in Asia Minor, and the Mitannians in Assyrian lands. In the Aegean, the Mycenaean kingdoms were at their height.

MAJOR PERIODS IN ANCIENT EGYPTIAN HISTORY (DYNASTIES IN ROMAN NUMERALS)

3100–2700 B.C.E.	Early Dynastic Period (I–II)
2700–2200 B.C.E.	Old Kingdom (III–VI)
2200–2052 B.C.E.	First Intermediate Period (VII–XI)
2052–1630 B.C.E.	Middle Kingdom (XII–XIII)
1630–1550 B.C.E.	Second Intermediate Period (XIV–XVII)
1550–1075 B.C.E.	New Kingdom (XVIII–XX)

sured the king's continuing power, which was absolute. Since the king was obligated to act infallibly in a benign and beneficent manner, the welfare of the people of Egypt was automatically guaranteed and safeguarded.

Nothing better illustrates the nature of Old Kingdom royal power than the pyramids built as pharaonic tombs. Beginning in the Early Dynastic period, kings constructed increasingly elaborate burial complexes in Upper Egypt. Djoser, a Third Dynasty king, was the first to erect a monumental six-step pyramid of hard stone. Subsequent pharaohs built other stepped pyramids until Snefru, the founder of the Fourth Dynasty, converted a stepped to a true pyramid over the course of putting up three monuments.

His son Khufu (Cheops in the Greek version of his name) chose the desert plateau of Giza, south of Memphis, as the site for the largest pyramid ever constructed. Its dimensions are prodigious: 481 feet high, 756 feet long on each side, and its base covering 13.1 acres. The pyramid is made of 2.3 million stone blocks averaging 2.5 tons each. It is also a geometrical wonder, deviating from absolutely level and square only by the most minute measurements using the latest modern devices. Khufu's successors, Khafre (Chephren) and Menkaure (Mycerinus), built equally perfect pyramids at Giza, and together, the three constitute one of the most extraordinary achievements in human history. Khafre also built the huge composite creature, part lion and part human, that the Greeks named the Sphinx. Recent research has shown that the Sphinx played a crucial role in the solar cult aspects of the pyramid complex.

The pyramids are remarkable not only for the great technical skill they demonstrate, but also for the concentration of resources they represent. They are evidence that the pharaohs controlled vast wealth and had the power to focus and organize enormous human effort over the years it took to build each pyramid. They also provide a visible indication of the nature of the Egyptian state: The pyramids, like the pharaohs, tower above the land; the low tombs at their base, like the officials buried there, seem to huddle in relative unimportance.

Originally, the pyramids and their associated cult buildings contained statuary, offerings, and all the pharaoh needed for the afterlife. Despite great precautions and ingenious concealment methods, tomb robbers took nearly everything, leaving little for modern archeologists to recover. Several full-size wooden boats have been found, however, still in their own graves at the base of the pyramids, ready for the pharaoh's journeys in the next world. Recent excavations have uncovered remains of the large town built to house the thousands of pyramid builders, including the farmers who worked at Giza during the annual flooding of their fields.

Numerous officials, both members of the royal family and nonroyal men of ability, aided the god-kings. The highest office was the *vizier* (a modern term from Arabic). Central offices dealing with granaries, surveys, assessments, taxes, and salaries administered the land. Water management was local rather than on a national level. Upper and Lower Egypt were divided into ***nomes***, or districts, each governed by a *nomarch*, or governor, and his local officials. The kings could also appoint royal officials to oversee groups of nomes or to supervise pharaonic landholdings throughout Egypt.

The Great Sphinx has the body of a lion and the head of a man. It was carved at Giza in the reign of the Pharaoh Khafre (c. 2570–2544 B.C.E.). SEF/Art Resource, NY

The First Intermediate Period and Middle Kingdom (2200–1786 B.C.E.) Toward the end of the Old Kingdom, for a combination of political and economic reasons, absolute pharaonic power waned as the nomarchs and other officials became more independent and influential. About 2200 B.C.E., the Old Kingdom collapsed and gave way to the decentralization and disorder of the First Intermediate Period, which lasted until about 2052 B.C.E. Eventually, the kings of Dynasty 11, based in Thebes in Upper Egypt, defeated the rival Dynasty 10, based in a city south of Giza.

Amunemhet I, the founder of Dynasty 12 and the Middle Kingdom, probably began his career as a successful vizier under an Eleventh Dynasty king. After reuniting Upper and Lower Egypt, he turned his attention to making three important and long-lasting administrative changes. First, he moved his royal residence from Thebes to a brand-new town, just south of the old capital at Memphis, signaling a fresh start rooted in past glories. Second, he reorganized the nome structure by more clearly defining the nomarchs' duties to the state, granting them some local autonomy within the royal structure. Third, he established a co-regency system to smooth transitions from one reign to another.

Amunemhet I and the other Middle Kingdom pharaohs sought to evoke the past by building pyramid complexes like those of the later Old Kingdom rulers. Yet the events of the First Intermediate Period had irrevocably changed the nature of Egyptian kingship. Gone was the absolute, distant god-king; the king was now more directly concerned with his people. In art, instead of the supremely confident faces of the Old Kingdom pharaohs, the Middle Kingdom rulers seem thoughtful, careworn, and brooding.

Egypt's relations with its neighbors became more aggressive during the Middle Kingdom. To the south, royal fortresses were built to control Nubia and the growing trade in African resources. To the north and east, Syria and Palestine increasingly came under Egyptian influence, even as fortifications sought to prevent settlers from the Levant from moving into the Delta.

The Second Intermediate Period and the New Kingdom (1630–1075 B.C.E.) For some unknown reason, during Dynasty 13, the kingship changed hands rapidly and the western Delta established itself as an independent Dynasty 14, ushering in the Second Intermediate Period. The eastern Delta, with its expanding Asiatic populations, came under the control of the Hyksos (Dynasty 15) and minor Asiatic kings (Dynasty 16). Meanwhile, the Dynasty 13 kings left their northern capital and regrouped in Thebes (Dynasty 17).

Though much later sources describe the Hyksos ("chief of foreign lands" in Egyptian) as ruthless invaders from parts unknown, they were almost certainly Amorites from the Levant, part of the gradual infiltration of the Delta during the Middle Kingdom. Ongoing excavations at the Hyksos capital of Avaris in the eastern Delta have revealed architecture, pottery, and other goods consistent with that cultural background. After nearly a century of rule, the Hyksos were expelled, a process begun by Kamose, the last king of Dynasty 17, and completed by his brother Ahmose, the first king of the Eighteenth Dynasty and the founder of the New Kingdom.

During Dynasty 18, Egypt pursued foreign expansion with renewed vigor. Military expeditions reached as far north as the Euphrates in Syria, with frequent campaigns in the Levant. To the south, major Egyptian temples were built in the Sudan, almost 1,300 miles from Memphis. Egypt's economic and political power was at its height.

Egypt's position was reflected in the unprecedented luxury and cosmopolitanism of the royal court and in the ambitious palace and temple projects undertaken throughout the country. Perhaps to foil tomb robbers, the Dynasty 18 pharaohs were the first to cut their tombs deep into the rock cliffs of a desolate valley in Thebes, known today as the Valley of the Kings. To date, only one intact royal tomb has been discovered there, that of the young Dynasty 18 king Tutankhamun, and even it had been disturbed shortly after his death. The thousands of goods buried with him, many of them marvels of craftsmanship, give an idea of Egypt's material wealth during this period.

Following the premature death of Tutankhamun in 1323 B.C.E., a military commander named Horemheb assumed the kingship, which passed in turn to his own army commander, Ramses I. The pharaohs Ramessides of Dynasty 19 undertook numerous monumental projects, among them Ramses II's rock-cut temples at Abu Simbel, south of the First Cataract, which had to be moved to a higher location when the Aswan High Dam was built in the 1960s. There and elsewhere, Ramses II left textual and pictorial accounts of his battle in 1285 B.C.E. against the Hittites at Kadesh on the Orontes in Syria. Sixteen years later, the Egyptians and Hittites signed a formal peace treaty, forging an alliance against an increasingly volatile political situation in the Mideast and eastern Mediterranean during the thirteenth century B.C.E.

Merneptah, one of the hundred offspring of Ramses II, held off a hostile Libyan attack, as well as incursions by the Sea Peoples, a loose coalition of Mediterranean raiders who seem to have provoked and taken advantage of unsettled conditions. One of Merneptah's inscriptions commemorating his military triumphs contains the first known mention of Israel.

Despite his efforts, by the end of Dynasty 20, Egypt's period of imperial glory had passed. The next

LOVE POEMS FROM THE NEW KINGDOM

Numerous love poems from ancient Egypt reveal the Egyptians' love of life through their frank sensuality.

How does the girl in the first poem propose to escape the supervision of her parents? What ails the young man in the second poem?

SHE: Love, how I'd love to slip down to the pond,
bathe with you close by on the bank.
Just for you I'd wear my new Memphis swimsuit,
made of sheer linen, fit for a queen—
Come see how it looks in the water!
Couldn't I coax you to wade in with me? Let the
cool creep slowly around us?
Then I'd dive deep down and come up for you
dripping,
Let you fill your eyes with the little red fish that
I'd catch.
And I'd say, standing there tall in the shallows:
Look at my fish, love, how it lies in my hand,
How my fingers caress it, slip down its sides . . .
But then I'd say softer, eyes bright with your
seeing:
A gift, love. No words.
Come closer and look, it's all me.
HE: I think I'll go home and lie very still, feigning
terminal illness.
Then the neighbors will all troop over to stare, my
love, perhaps, among them.
How she'll smile while the specialists snarl in
their teeth!—
she perfectly well knows what ails me.

"Love, how I'd love to slip down to the pond" and "I think I'll go home and lie very still," from *Love Songs of the New Kingdom*, trans. from the Ancient Egyptian by John L. Foster, copyright © 1969, 1970, 1971, 1972, 1973, 1974 by John L. Foster. By permission of the University of Texas Press.

thousand years witnessed a Third Intermediate Period, a Saite Renaissance, Persian domination, conquest by Alexander the Great, the Ptolemaic period, and finally, defeat at the hands of Octavian in 30 B.C.E.

Language and Literature Writing first appears in Egypt about 3000 B.C.E. Although the impetus for the first Egyptian writing probably came from Mesopotamia, the Egyptians may have invented it on their own. The writing system, dubbed **hieroglyphics** ("sacred carvings") by the Greeks, was highly sophisticated, involving hundreds of picture signs that remained relatively constant in the way they were rendered for over 3,000 years. Many of them formed a syllabary of one, two, or three consonantal sounds; some conveyed a word's meaning or category, either independently or added to the end of the word. Texts were usually written horizontally from right to left, but could be written from left to right, as well as vertically from top to bottom in both horizontal directions. A cursive version of hieroglyphics was used for business documents and literary texts, which were penned rapidly in black and red ink. The Egyptian language, part of the Afro-Asiatic (or Hamito-Semitic) family, evolved through several stages—Old, Middle, and Late Egyptian, Demotic, and Coptic—thus giving it a history of continuous recorded use well into the medieval period.

Egyptian literature includes narratives, myths, books of instruction in wisdom, letters, religious texts, and poetry, written on papyri, limestone flakes, and postherds. (See "Love Poems from the New Kingdom.") Unfortunately only a small fraction of this enormous literature has survived, and many texts are incomplete. Though they surely existed, we have no epics or dramas from ancient Egypt. Such nonliterary documents as lists of kings, autobiographies in tombs, wine jar labels, judicial records, astronomical observations, and medical and other scientific texts are invaluable for our understanding of Egyptian history and civilization.

Religion: Gods and Temples Egyptian religion encompasses a multitude of concepts that often seem mutually contradictory to us. Three separate explanations for the origin of the universe were formulated, each based in the philosophical traditions of a venerable

Seated Egyptian scribe, height 21 feet (53 cm) painted limestone, fifth dynasty, c. 2510–2460 B.C.E. One of the hallmarks of the early river valley civilizations was the development of writing. Ancient Egyptian scribes had to undergo rigorous training but were rewarded with a position of respect and privilege. "Seated Scribe" from Saqqara, Egypt. 5th Dynasty, c. 2510–2460 B.C.E. Painted limestone, height 21' (53 cm). Musee du Louvre, Paris. Bridgeman-Giraudon/Art Resource, NY

Egyptian city. The cosmogony of Heliopolis, north of Memphis, held that the creator sun god Atum (also identified as Re) emerged from the darkness of a vast sea to stand upon a primeval mound, containing within himself the life force of the gods he was to create. At Memphis, it was the god Ptah who created the other gods by uttering their names. Further south, at Hermopolis, eight male and female entities within a primordial slime suddenly exploded, and the energy that resulted created the sun and Atum, from which the rest came.

The Egyptian gods, or pantheon, similarly defy neat categorization, in part because of the common tendency to combine the character and function of one or more gods. Amun, one of the eight entities in the Hermopolitan cosmogony, provides a good example. Thebes, Amun's cult center, rose to prominence in the Middle Kingdom. In the New Kingdom, Amun was elevated above his seven cohorts and took on aspects of the sun god Re to become Amun-Re.

Not surprisingly in a nearly rainless land, solar cults and mythologies were highly developed. Much thought was devoted to conceptualizing what happened as the sun god made his perilous way through the underworld in the night hours between sunset and sunrise. Three long texts trace Re's journey as he vanquishes immense snakes and other foes.

The Eighteenth Dynasty was one of several periods during which solar cults were in ascendancy. Early in his reign, Amunhotep IV promoted a single, previously minor aspect of the sun, the Aten ("disk") above Re himself and the rest of the gods. He declared that the Aten was the creator god who brought life to humankind and all living beings, with himself and his queen Nefertiti the sole mediators between the Aten and the people. For religious and political reasons still imperfectly understood, he went further, changing his name to Akhenaten ("the effective spirit of the Aten"), building a new capital called Akhetaten ("the horizon of the Aten") near Amarma north of Thebes, and chiseling out the name of Amun from inscriptions everywhere. Shortly after his death, Amarna was abandoned and partially razed. A large diplomatic archive of tablets written in Akkadian was left at the site, which give us a vivid, if one-sided, picture of the political correspondence of the day. During the reigns of Akhenaten's successors, Tutankhamun (born Tutankhaten) and Horemheb, Amun was restored to his former position, and Akhenaten's monuments were defaced and even demolished.

In representations, Egyptian gods have human bodies, possess human or animal heads, and wear crowns, celestial disks, or thorns. The lone exception is the Aten, made nearly abstract by Akhenaten, who altered its image to a plain disk with solar rays ending in small hands holding the hieroglyphic sign for life to the nostrils of Akhenaten and Nefertiti. The gods were thought to reside in their cult centers, where, from the New Kingdom on, increasingly ostentatious temples were built, staffed by full-time priests. At Thebes, for instance, successive kings enlarged the great Karnak temple complex dedicated to Amun for over 2,000 years. Though the ordinary person could not enter a temple precinct, great festivals took place for all to see. During Amun's major festival of Opet, the statue of the god traveled in a divine boat along the Nile, whose banks were thronged with spectators.

Worship and the Afterlife For most Egyptians, worship took place at small local shrines. They left offerings to the chosen gods, as well as votive inscriptions with simple prayers. Private houses often had niches containing busts for ancestor worship and statues of household deities. The Egyptians strongly believed in the power of magic, dreams, and oracles, and they possessed a wide variety of amulets to ward off evil.

The Egyptians thought the afterlife was full of dangers, which could be overcome by magical means, among them the spells in the *Book of the Dead*. The goals were to join and be identified with the gods, espe-

The Egyptians believed in the possibility of life after death through the god Osiris. Aspects of each person's life had to be tested by forty-two assessor-gods before the person could be presented to Osiris. In the scene from a papyrus manuscript of the *Book of the Dead*, the deceased and his wife (on the left) watch the scales of justice weighing his heart (on the left side of the scales) against the feather of truth. The jackal-headed god Anubis also watches the scales, and the ibis-headed god Thoth keeps the record. British Museum, London, UK/The Bridgeman Art Library International Ltd.

cially Osiris, or to sail in the "boat of millions." Originally only the king could hope to enjoy immortality with the gods, but gradually this became available to all. Since the Egyptians believed the preservation of the body was essential for continued existence in the afterlife, early on they developed mummification, a process that took seventy days by the New Kingdom. How lavishly tombs were prepared and decorated varied over the course of Egyptian history and in accordance with the wealth of a family. A high-ranking Dynasty 18 official, for example, typically had a Theban rock-cut tomb of several rooms embellished with scenes from daily life and funerary texts, as well as provisions and equipment for the afterlife, statuettes of workers, and a place for descendants to leave offerings.

Women in Egyptian Society It is difficult to assess the position of women in Egyptian society, because our pictorial and textual evidence comes almost entirely from male sources. Women's prime roles were connected with the management of the household. They could not hold office, go to scribal schools, or become artisans. Nevertheless, women could own and control property, sue for divorce, and, at least in theory, enjoy equal legal protection.

Royal women often wielded considerable influence, particularly in the Eighteenth Dynasty. The most remarkable was Hatshepsut, daughter of Thutmosis I and widow of Thutmosis II, who ruled as pharaoh for nearly twenty years. Many Egyptian queens held the title "god's wife of Amun," a power base of great importance.

In art, royal and nonroyal women are conventionally shown smaller than their husbands or sons (see illustration). Yet it is probably of greater significance that they are so frequently depicted in such a wide variety of contexts. Much care was lavished on details of their gestures, clothing, and hairstyles. With their husbands, they attend banquets, boat in the papyrus marshes, make and receive offerings, and supervise the myriad affairs of daily life.

Slaves Slaves did not become numerous in Egypt until the growth of Egyptian imperial power in the Middle Kingdom (2052–1786 B.C.E.). During that period, black Africans from Nubia to the south and Asians from the east were captured in war and brought back to Egypt as slaves. The great period of Egyptian imperial expansion, the New Kingdom (1550–1075 B.C.E.), vastly increased the number of slaves and captives in Egypt. Sometimes an entire people was enslaved, as the Bible says the Hebrews were.

Slaves in Egypt performed many tasks. They labored in the fields with the peasants, in the shops of artisans, and as domestic servants. Others worked as policemen and soldiers. Many slaves labored to erect the great temples, obelisks, and other huge monuments of Egypt's imperial age. As in Mesopotamia, slaves were branded for identification and to help prevent their escape. Slaves could be freed in Egypt, but manumission seems to have been rare. Nonetheless, former slaves were not set apart and could expect to be assimilated into the mass of the population.

▼ Ancient Near Eastern Empires

In the time of Dynasty 18 in Egypt, new groups of peoples had established themselves in the Near East: the Kassites in Babylonia, the Hittites in Asia Minor, and the Mitannians in northern Syria and Mesopotamia. (See Map 1–2, page 16.) The Kassites and Mitannians were warrior peoples who ruled as a minority over more civilized folk and absorbed their culture. The Hittites established a kingdom of their own and forged an empire that lasted some two hundred years.

The Hittites

The Hittites were an Indo-European people, speaking a language related to Greek and Sanskrit. By about 1500 B.C.E., they established a strong, centralized government with a capital at Hattusas (near Ankara, the capital of modern Turkey). Between 1400 and 1200 B.C.E., they emerged as a leading military power in the Mideast and contested Egypt's ambitions to control Palestine and Syria. This struggle culminated in a great battle between the Egyptian and Hittite armies at Kadesh in northern Syria (1285 B.C.E.) and ended as a standoff. The Hittites adopted Mesopotamian writing and many aspects of Mesopotamian culture, especially through the Hurrian peoples of northern Syria and southern Anatolia. Their extensive historical records are the first to mention the Greeks, whom the Hittites called Ahhiyawa (the Achaeans of Homer). The Hittite kingdom disappeared by 1200 B.C.E., swept away in the general invasions and collapse of the Mideastern nation-states at that time. Successors to the empire, called the Neo-Hittite states, flourished in southern Asia Minor and northern Syria until the Assyrians destroyed them in the first millennium B.C.E.

The government of the Hittites was different from that of Mesopotamia in that Hittite kings did not claim to be divine or even to be the chosen representatives of the gods. In the early period, a council of nobles limited the king's power, and the assembled army had to ratify his succession to the throne.

The Discovery of Iron An important technological change took place in northern Anatolia, somewhat earlier than the creation of the Hittite kingdom, but perhaps within its region. This was the discovery of how to smelt iron and the decision to use it to manufacture weapons and tools in preference to copper or bronze. Archaeologists refer to the period after 1100 B.C.E. as the Iron Age.

The Assyrians

The Assyrians were originally a people living in Assur, a city in northern Mesopotamia on the Tigris River. They spoke a Semitic language closely related to Babylonian. They had a proud, independent culture heavily influenced by Babylonia. Assur had been an early center for trade but emerged as a political power during the fourteenth century B.C.E. The first Assyrian Empire spread north and west but was brought to an end in the general collapse of Near Eastern states at the end of the second millennium. A people called the Arameans, a Semitic nomadic and agricultural people originally from northern Syria who spoke a language called Aramaic, invaded Assyria. Aramaic is still used in parts of the Near East and is one of the languages of medieval Jewish and Mideastern Christian culture.

The Second Assyrian Empire

After 1000 B.C.E., the Assyrians began a second period of expansion, and by 665 B.C.E., they controlled all of Mesopotamia, much of southern Asia Minor, Syria, Palestine, and Egypt to its southern frontier. They succeeded, thanks to a large, well-disciplined army and a society that valued military skills. Some Assyrian kings boasted of their atrocities, so their names inspired terror throughout the Near East. They constructed magnificent palaces at Nineveh and Nimrud (near modern Mosul, Iraq), surrounded by parks and gardens. The walls of the reception rooms and hallways were decorated with stone reliefs and inscriptions proclaiming the power and conquests of the king.

The Assyrians organized their empire into provinces with governors, military garrisons, and administration for taxation, communications, and intelligence. Important officers were assigned large areas of land throughout the empire, and agricultural colonies were set up in key regions to store up supplies for military actions beyond the frontiers. Vassal kings had to send tribute and delegations to the Assyrian capital every year. Tens of thousands of people were forcibly displaced from their homes and resettled in other areas of the empire, partly to populate sparsely inhabited regions, partly to diminish resistance to Assyrian rule. People of the kingdom of Israel, which the Assyrians invaded and destroyed, were among them.

Relief, Israel, tenth–sixth century: Judean exiles carrying provisions. Detail of the Assyrian conquest of the Jewish fortified town of Lachish (battle 701 B.C.). Relief, Israel, 10th-6th Century: Judean exiles carrying provisions. Detail of the Assyrian conquest of the Jewish fortified town of Lachish (battle 701 BC). Part of a relief from the palace of Sennacherib at Nineveh, Mesopotamia (Iraq). British Museum, London, Great Britain. Copyright Erich Lessing/Art Resource, NY

The empire became too large to govern efficiently. The last years of Assyria are obscure, but civil war apparently divided the country. The Medes, a powerful people from western and central Iran, had been expanding across the Iranian plateau. They were feared for their cavalry and archers, against which traditional Mideastern armies were ineffective. The Medes attacked Assyria and were joined by the Babylonians, who had always been restive under Assyrian rule, under the leadership of a general named Nebuchadnezzar. They eventually destroyed the Assyrian cities, including Nineveh in 612 B.C.E., so thoroughly that Assyria never recovered. The ruins of the great Assyrian palaces lay untouched until archaeologists began to explore them in the nineteenth century.

The Neo-Babylonians

The Medes did not follow up on their conquests, so Nebuchadnezzar took over much of the Assyrian Empire. Under him and his successors, Babylon grew into one of the greatest cities of the world. The Greek traveler Herodotus described its wonders, including its great temples, fortification walls, boulevards, parks, and palaces, to a Greek readership that had never seen the like. Babylon prospered as a center of world trade, linking Egypt, India, Iran, and Syria-Palestine by land and sea routes. For centuries, an astronomical center at Babylon kept detailed records of observations that were the longest-running chronicle of the ancient world. Nebuchadnezzar's dynasty did not last long, and the government passed to various men in rapid succession. The last independent king of Babylon set up a second capital in the Arabian desert and tried to force the Babylonians to honor the Moon-god above all other gods. He allowed dishonest or incompetent speculators to lease huge areas of temple land for their personal profit. These policies proved unpopular—some said that the king was insane—and many Babylonians may have welcomed the Persian conquest that came in 539 B.C.E. After that, Babylonia began another, even more prosperous phase of its history as one of the most important provinces of another great Eastern empire, that of the Persians.

▼ The Persian Empire

The great Persian Empire arose in the region now called Iran. The ancestors of the people who would rule it spoke a language from the Aryan branch of the family of Indo-European languages, related to the Greek spoken by the Hellenic peoples and the Latin of the Romans. The most important collections of tribes among them were the Medes and the Persians, peoples so similar in language and customs that the Greeks used both names interchangeably.

The Medes were the first Iranian people to organize their tribes into a union. They were aggressive enough to build a force that challenged the great empires of Mesopotamia. With the help of the ruler of Babylon, they defeated the mighty Assyrian Empire in 612 B.C.E. Until the middle of the sixth century, the Persians were subordinate to the Medes, but when Cyrus II (called the Great) became King of the Persians (r. 559–530 B.C.E.), their positions were reversed. About 550 B.C.E., Cyrus captured the capital at Ecbatana and united the Medes and Persians under his own rule.

Cyrus the Great

Cyrus quickly expanded his power. The territory he inherited from the Medes touched on Lydia, ruled by the rich and powerful king Croesus. Croesus controlled

MAP EXPLORATION

Interactive map: To explore this map further, go to **www.myhistorylab.com**

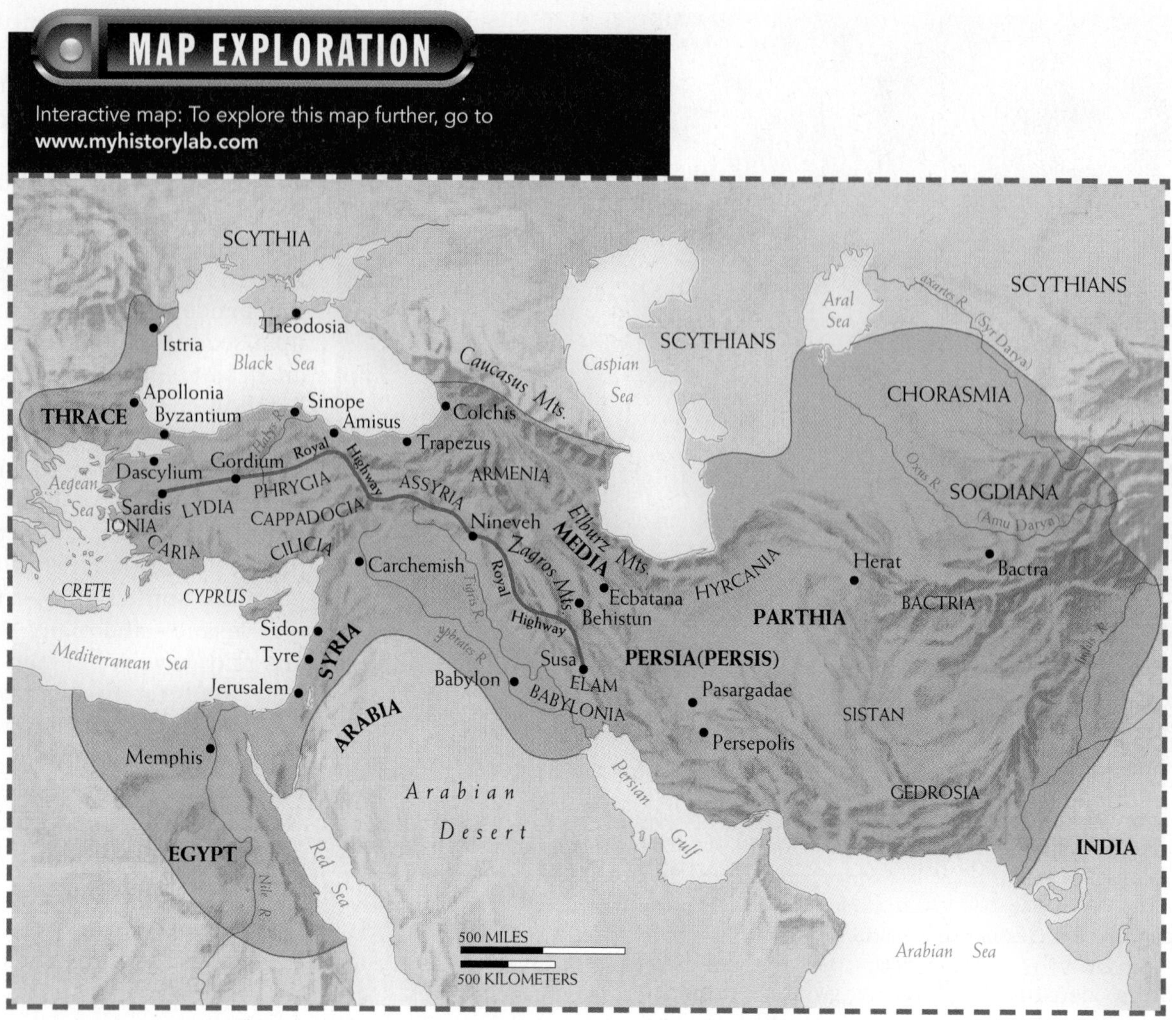

Map 1–3 **THE ACHAEMENID PERSIAN EMPIRE** The empire created by Cyrus had reached its fullest extent under Darius when Persia attacked Greece in 490 B.C.E. It extended from India to the Aegean, and even into Europe, encompassing the lands formerly ruled by Egyptians, Hittites, Babylonians, and Assyrians.

western Asia Minor, having conquered the Greek cities of the coast about 560 B.C.E. Made confident by his victories, by alliances with Egypt and Babylon, and by what he thought was a favorable signal from the Greek oracle of Apollo at Delphi, he invaded Persian territory in 546 B.C.E. Cyrus achieved a decisive victory, capturing Croesus and his capital city of Sardis. By 539 B.C.E. he had conquered the Greek cities and extended his power as far to the east as the Indus valley and modern Afghanistan.

In that same year he captured Babylon. Because its last king was unpopular, Cyrus was greeted not as a conqueror, but as a liberator. On the cylinder on which was inscribed his version of events, he claimed that the Babylonian god Marduk had "got him into his city Babylon without fighting or battle."[1]

Unlike the harsh Babylonian and Assyrian conquerors who preceded him, Cyrus pursued a policy of toleration and restoration. He did not impose the Persian religion but claimed to rule by the favor of the Babylonian god. Instead of deporting defeated peoples from their native lands and destroying their cities, he rebuilt their cities and allowed the exiles to return. The conquest of the Babylonian Empire had brought Palestine under Persian rule, so Cyrus permitted the Hebrews, taken into captivity by King Nebuchadnezzar in 586 B.C.E., to return to their native land of **Judah**. This policy, followed by his successors, was effective but not as gentle as it might seem. Wherever they ruled, Cyrus and his successors demanded tribute from their subjects and military service, enforcing these requirements strictly and sometimes brutally.

Darius the Great

Cyrus's son Cambyses succeeded to the throne in 529 B.C.E. His great achievement was the conquest of Egypt, establishing it as a satrapy (province) that ran as far west

[1]"The Cyrus Cylinder," in D. Winton Thomas, *Documents from Old Testament Times* (New York: Harper and Row, 1961), p. 92.

Persian nobles pay homage to King Darius in this relief from the treasury at the Persian capital of Persepolis. Darius is seated on the throne; his son and successor Xerxes stands behind him. Darius and Xerxes are carved in larger scale to indicate their royal status. Oriental Institute Museum, University of Chicago

as Libya and as far south as Ethiopia. The Persians ruled, as the Bible puts it, "from India to Ethiopia, one hundred and twenty-seven provinces" (Esther 1:1). (See Map 1–3.) On Cambyses's death in 522 B.C.E., a civil war roiled much of the Persian Empire. Darius emerged as the new emperor in 521 B.C.E.

On a great rock hundreds of feet in the air near the mountain Iranian village of Behistun, Darius had carved an inscription in three languages, Babylonian, Old Persian, and Elamite, all in the cuneiform script. They boasted of his victories and the greatness of his rule and, discovered almost two thousand years later, greatly helped scholars decipher all three languages. Darius's long and prosperous reign lasted until 486 B.C.E., during which he brought the empire to its greatest extent. To the east he added new conquests in northern India. In the west he sought to conquer the nomadic people called Scythians who roamed around the Black Sea. For this purpose he crossed into Europe over the Hellespont (Dardanelles) to the Danube River and beyond, taking possession of Thrace and Macedonia on the fringes of the Greek mainland. In 499 B.C.E., the Ionian Greeks of western Asia Minor rebelled, launching the wars between Greeks and Persians that would not end until two decades later. (See Chapter 2.)

Government and Administration

Like the Mesopotamian kingdoms, the Persian Empire was a hereditary monarchy that claimed divine sanction from the god Ahura Mazda. The ruler's title was *Shahanshah*, "king of kings." In theory all the land and the peoples in the empire belonged to him as absolute monarch, and he demanded tribute and service for the use of his property. In practice he depended on the advice and administrative service of aristocratic courtiers, ministers, and provincial governors, the satraps. He was expected, as Ahura Mazda's chosen representative, to rule with justice, in accordance with established custom and the precedents in the Law of the Medes and Persians. Still, the king ruled as a semi-divine autocrat; anyone approaching him prostrated himself as before a god who could demand their wealth, labor, and military service and had the power of life and death. The Greeks would see him as the model of a despot or tyrant who regarded his people as slaves.

The empire was divided into twenty-nine satrapies. The satraps were allowed considerable autonomy. They ruled over civil affairs and commanded the army in war, but the king exercised several means of control. In each satrapy he appointed a secretary and a military commander. He also chose inspectors called "the eyes and ears of the king" who traveled throughout the empire reporting on what they learned in each satrapy. Their travels and those of royal couriers were made swifter and easier by a system of excellent royal roads. The royal postal system was served by a kind of "pony express" that placed men mounted on fast horses at stations along the way. It normally took three months to travel the 1,500 miles from Sardis in Lydia to the Persian capital at Susa. The royal postal service made the trip in less than two weeks. Ruling over a vast empire whose people spoke countless different languages, the Persians did not try to impose their own, but instead adopted Aramaic, the most common language of Middle-Eastern commerce, as the imperial tongue. This practical decision simplified both civil and military administration.

Medes and Persians made up the core of the army. The best of them served in the 10,000 Immortals, while an additional 4,000 composed the Great King's bodyguard, divided equally between infantry and cavalry. Royal schools trained aristocratic Median and Persian boys as military officers and imperial administrators. The officers commanded not only the Iranian troops but also drafted large numbers of subject armies when needed. A large Persian army, such as the one that invaded Greece in 480 B.C.E., included hundreds of thousands of non-Iranian soldiers organized by ethnic group, each dressed in its own uniforms, taking orders from Iranian officers.

Religion

Persia's religion was different from that of its neighbors and subjects. Its roots lay in the Indo-European traditions of the Vedic religion that Aryan peoples brought into India about 1500 B.C.E. Their religious practices included animal sacrifices and a reverence for fire. Although the religion was polytheistic, its chief god Ahura Mazda, the "Wise Lord," demanded an unusual emphasis on a stern ethical code. It took a new turn with the appearance of Zarathushtra, a Mede whom the Greeks called Zoroaster, perhaps as early as 1000 B.C.E., as tradition states, although some scholars place him about 600 B.C.E. He was a great religious prophet and teacher who changed the traditional Aryan worship.

Zarathushtra's reform made Ahura Mazda the only god, dismissing the others as demons not to be worshipped but fought. There would be no more polytheism and no sacrifices. The old sacrificial fire was converted into a symbol of goodness and light. Zarathushtra insisted that the people should reject the "Lie" (*druj*) and speak only the "Truth" (*asha*), portraying life as an unending struggle between two great forces, Ahura Mazda, the creator and only god, representing goodness and light, and Ahriman, a demon, representing darkness and evil. He urged human beings to fight for the good, in the expectation that the good would be rewarded with glory and the evil punished with suffering.

Traditions and legends about Zarathustra as well as law, liturgy, and the teachings of the prophet are contained in the *Avesta*, the sacred book of the Persians. By the middle of the sixth century B.C.E., Zoroastrianism had become the chief religion of the Persians. On the great inscribed monument at Behistun, Darius the Great paid public homage to the god of Zarathustra and his teachings: "On this account Ahura Mazda brought me help . . . because I was not wicked, nor was I a liar, nor was I a tyrant, neither I nor any of my line. I have ruled according to righteousness."[2]

[2]J. H. Breasted, *Ancient Times: A History of the Early World*, 2nd ed. (Boston: Ginn & Co., 1935), p. 277.

KEY EVENTS IN THE HISTORY OF ANCIENT NEAR EASTERN EMPIRES

ca. 1400–1200 B.C.E.	Hittite Empire
ca. 1100 B.C.E.	Rise of Assyrian power
732–722 B.C.E.	Assyrian conquest of Syria-Palestine
671 B.C.E.	Assyrian conquest of Egypt
612 B.C.E.	Destruction of Assyrian capital at Nineveh
612–539 B.C.E.	Neo-Babylonian (Chaldean) Empire
550 B.C.E.	Cyrus the Great unites Persians and Medes
546 B.C.E.	Persia conquers Lydia
521–486 B.C.E.	Reign of Darius the Great

Art and Culture

The Persians learned much from the people they encountered and those they conquered, especially from Mesopotamia and Egypt, but they shaped it to fit comfortably on a Persian base. A good example is to be found in their system of writing. They adapted the Aramaic alphabet of the Semites to create a Persian alphabet and used the cuneiform symbols of Babylon to write the Old Persian language they spoke. They borrowed their calendar from Egypt.

Persian art and architecture contain similar elements of talents and styles borrowed from other societies and blended with Persian traditions to serve Persian purposes. In describing, with justifiable pride, the construction of his palace at Susa, Darius says:

> The cedar timber—a mountain by name Lebanon—from there it was brought . . . the yaka-timber was brought from Gandara and from Carmania. The gold was brought from Sardis and from Bactria . . . the precious stone lapis-lazuli and carnelian . . . was brought from Sogdiana. The . . . turquoise from Chorasmia. . . . The silver and ebony . . . from Egypt . . . the ornamentation from Ionia . . . the ivory . . . from Ethiopia and from Sind and from Arachosia. . . . The stone-cutters who wrought the stone, those were Ionians and Sardians. The goldsmiths . . . were Medes and Egyptians. The men who wrought the wood, those were Sardians and Egyptians. The men who wrought the baked brick, those were Babylonians. The men who adorned the wall, those were Medes and Egyptians.[3]

Probably the most magnificent of Persian remains are those of the Royal Palace at Persepolis, built by Darius and his successor Xerxes (r. 485–465 B.C.E.). Its foundation is a high platform supported on three sides by a stone wall 20 or 30 feet high. This was reached by a grand stairway whose sides are covered with carvings.

The complex contained the Hall of a Hundred Columns where the kings did their judicial duties. Better than any other tangible objects, the columns,

[3]T. Cuyler Young, Jr., "Iran, ancient," *Ecyclopaedia Britannica Online*.

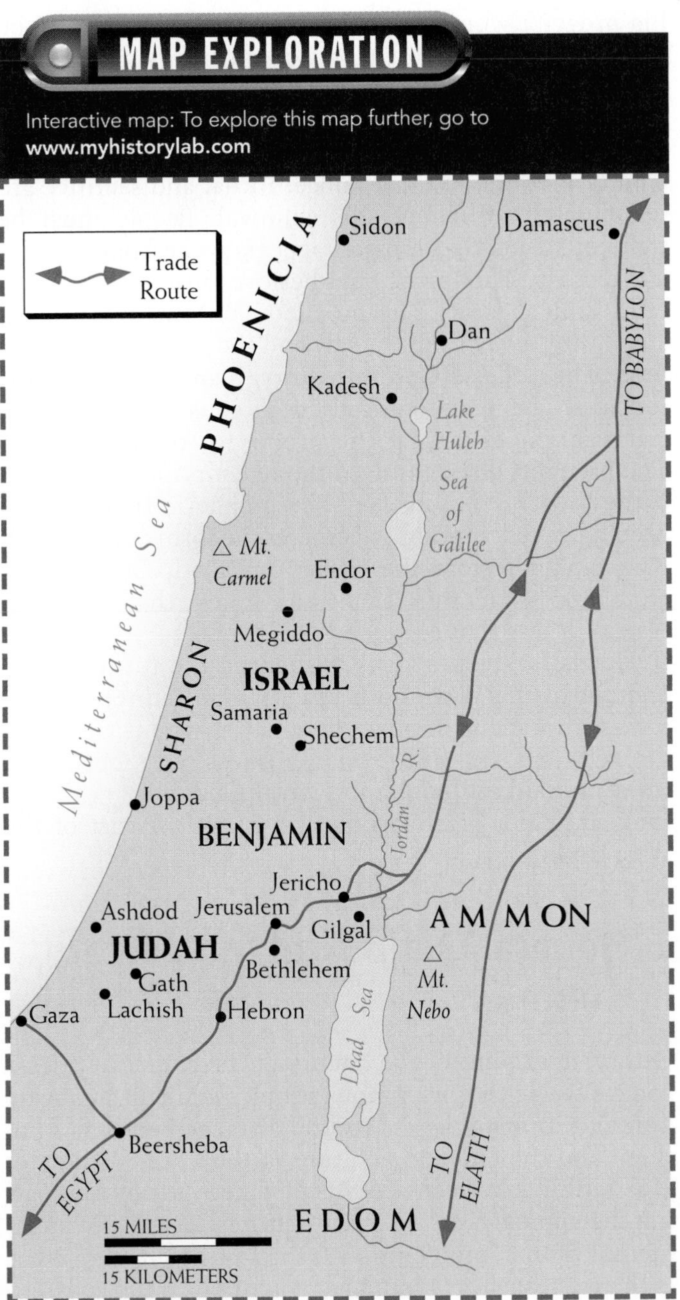

Map 1–4 **ANCIENT PALESTINE** The Hebrews established a unified kingdom under Kings David and Solomon in the tenth century B.C.E. After Solomon, the kingdom was divided into Israel in the north and Judah, with its capital, Jerusalem, in the south. North of Israel were the great commercial cities of Phoenicia, Tyre, and Sidon.

stairway, and the gateway with winged bulls reveal the grandeur of the ancient Persian Empire.

▼ Palestine

None of the powerful kingdoms of the ancient Near East had as much influence on the future of Western civilization as the small stretch of land between Syria and Egypt, the land called Palestine for much of its history. The three great religions of the modern world outside the Far East—Judaism, Christianity, and Islam—trace their origins, at least in part, to the people who arrived there a little before 1200 B.C.E. The book that recounts their experiences is the Hebrew Bible.

The Canaanites and the Phoenicians

Before the Israelites arrived in their promised land, it was inhabited by groups of people speaking a Semitic language called Canaanite. The Canaanites lived in walled cities and were farmers and seafarers. They had their own writing system, an alphabet that may have originated among people who were impressed by Egyptian writing, but wanted something much simpler to use. Instead of the hundreds of characters required to read Egyptian or cuneiform, their alphabet used between twenty and thirty characters. The Canaanites, like the other peoples of Syria-Palestine, worshipped many gods, especially gods of weather and fertility, whom they thought resided in the clouds atop the high mountains of northern Syria. The invading Israelites destroyed various Canaanite cities and holy places and may have forced some of the population to move north and west, though Canaanite and Israelite culture also intermingled.

The **Phoenicians** were the descendants of the Canaanites and other peoples of Syria-Palestine, especially those who lived along the coast. They played an important role in Mediterranean trade, sailing to ports in Cyprus, Asia Minor, Greece, Italy, France, Spain, Egypt, and North Africa, as far as Gibraltar and possibly beyond. They founded colonies throughout the Mediterranean as far west as Spain. The most famous of these colonies was Carthage, near modern Tunis in North Africa. Sitting astride the trade routes, the Phoenician cities were important sites for the transmission of culture from east to west. The Greeks, who had long forgotten their older writing system of the Bronze Age, adopted a Phoenician version of the Canaanite alphabet that is the origin of our present alphabet.

The Israelites

The history of the Israelites must be pieced together from various sources. They are mentioned only rarely in the records of their neighbors, so we must rely chiefly on their own account, the Hebrew Bible. This is not a history in our sense, but a complicated collection of historical narrative, pieces of wisdom, poetry, law, and religious witness. Scholars of an earlier time tended to discard it as a historical source, but the most recent trend is to take it seriously while using it with caution.

According to tradition, the patriarch Abraham came from Ur and wandered west to tend his flocks in the land

THE ISRAELITES

ca. 1000–961 B.C.E.	Reign of King David
ca. 961–922 B.C.E.	Reign of King Solomon
722 B.C.E.	Assyrian conquest of Israel (northern kingdom)
586 B.C.E.	Destruction of Jerusalem; fall of Judah (southern kingdom); Babylonian Captivity
539 B.C.E.	Restoration of temple; return of exiles

of the Canaanites. Some of his people settled there, and others wandered into Egypt. By the thirteenth century B.C.E., led by Moses, they had left Egypt and wandered in the desert until they reached and conquered Canaan. They established a united kingdom that reached its peak under David and Solomon in the tenth century B.C.E. The sons of Solomon could not maintain the unity of the kingdom, and it split into two parts: Israel in the north and Judah, with its capital at Jerusalem, in the south. (See Map 1–4, page 27.) The rise of the great empires brought disaster to the Israelites. The northern kingdom fell to the Assyrians in 722 B.C.E., and its people—the **ten lost tribes**—were scattered and lost forever. Only the kingdom of Judah remained. It is from this time that we may call the Israelites Jews.

In 586 B.C.E., Judah was defeated by the Neo-Babylonian king Nebuchadnezzar II. He destroyed the great temple built by Solomon and took thousands of hostages off to Babylon. When the Persians defeated Babylonia, they ended this Babylonian captivity of the Jews and allowed them to return to their homeland. After that, the area of the old kingdom of the Jews in Palestine was dominated by foreign peoples for some 2,500 years, until the establishment of the State of Israel in 1948 C.E.

The Jewish Religion

The fate of the small nation of Israel would be of little interest were it not for its unique religious achievement. The great contribution of the Jews is the development of **monotheism**—the belief in one universal God, the creator and ruler of the universe. Among the Jews, this idea may be as old as Moses, as the Jewish tradition asserts, and it certainly dates as far back as the prophets of the eighth century B.C.E. The Jewish God is neither a natural force nor like human beings or any other creatures; he is so elevated that those who believe in him may not picture him in any form. The faith of the Jews is given special strength by their belief that God made a covenant with Abraham that his progeny would be a chosen people who would be rewarded for following God's commandments and the law he revealed to Moses.

Like the teachings of Zarathushtra in Iran, Jewish religious thought included a powerful ethical element. God is a severe, but just, judge. Ritual and sacrifice are not enough to achieve his approval. People must be righteous, and God himself appears to be bound to act righteously. The Jewish prophetic tradition was a powerful ethical force. The prophets constantly criticized any falling away from the law and the path of righteousness. They placed God in history, blaming the misfortunes of the Jews on God's righteous and necessary intervention to punish the people for their misdeeds. The prophets also promised the redemption of the Jews if they repented, however. The prophetic tradition expected the redemption to come in the form of a Messiah who would restore the house of David. Christianity, emerging from this tradition, holds that Jesus of Nazareth was that Messiah.

Jewish religious ideas influenced the future development of the West, both directly and indirectly. The Jews' belief in an all-powerful creator (who is righteous himself and demands righteousness and obedience from humankind) and a universal God (who is the father and ruler of all peoples) is a critical part of the Western heritage.

▼ General Outlook of Mideastern Cultures

Our brief account of the history of the ancient Mideast so far reveals that its various peoples and cultures were different in many ways. Yet the distance between all of them and the emerging culture of the Greeks (Chapter 2) is striking. We can see this distance best by comparing the approach of the other cultures to several fundamental human problems with that of the Greeks: What is the relationship of humans to nature? To the gods? To each other? These questions involve attitudes toward religion, philosophy, science, law, politics, and government. Unlike the Greeks, the civilizations of the Mideast seem to have these features in common: Once established, they tended toward cultural uniformity and stability. Reason, though employed for practical and intellectual purposes, lacked independence from religion and the high status to challenge the most basic received ideas. The standard form of government was a monarchy; republics were unknown. Rulers were considered divine or the appointed spokesmen for divinity. Religious and political institutions and beliefs were thoroughly intertwined. Government was not subject to secular, reasoned analysis but rested on religious authority, tradition, and power. Individual freedom had no importance.

Humans and Nature

For the peoples of the Mideast, there was no simple separation between humans and nature or even between animate creatures and inanimate objects. Humanity was part of a natural continuum, and all things partook of life and spirit. These peoples imagined that gods more or less in the shape of humans ruled a world that was irregular and unpredictable, subject to divine whims. The gods were capricious because nature seemed capricious.

A Babylonian story of creation makes it clear that humanity's function is merely to serve the gods. The creator Marduk says,

I shall compact blood, I shall cause bones to be,
I shall make stand a human being, let "Man" be its name.
I shall create humankind,
They shall bear the gods' burden that those may rest.[4]

In a world ruled by powerful deities of this kind, human existence was precarious. Disasters that we would think human in origin, the Mesopotamians saw as the product of divine will. Thus, a Babylonian text depicts the destruction of the city of Ur by invading Elamites as the work of the gods, carried out by the storm god Enlil:

Enlil called the storm.
The people mourn.
Exhilarating winds he took from the land.
The people mourn.
Good winds he took away from Sumer.
The people mourn.
He summoned evil winds.
The people mourn.
Entrusted them to Kingaluda, tender of storms.
He called the storm that will annihilate the land.
The people mourn.
He called disastrous winds.
The people mourn.
Enlil—choosing Gibil as his helper—
Called the (great) hurricane of heaven.
The people mourn.[5]

Both the Egyptian and the Babylonian versions of the destruction of humankind clearly show human vulnerability in the face of divine powers. In one Egyptian tale, Re, the god who had created humans, decided to destroy them because they were plotting evil against him. He sent the goddess Sekhmet to accomplish the deed, and she was resting in the midst of her task, having enjoyed the work and wading in a sea of blood, when Re changed his mind. He ordered 7,000 barrels of blood-colored beer poured in Sekhmet's path. She quickly became too drunk to continue the slaughter and thus humanity was preserved. In the Babylonian story of the flood, the motive for the destruction of humanity is given as follows:

The land had grown numerous, the peoples had increased,
The land was bellowing like a bull.
The god was disturbed by their uproar,
The god Enlil heard their clamor.
He said to the great gods,
"The clamor of mankind has become burdensome to me,
"I am losing sleep to their uproar!"[6]

Utanapishtim and his wife survived because he was friendly with Enki, the god of wisdom, who helped him to pull through by a trick.

In such a universe, humans could not hope to understand nature, much less control it. At best, they could try by magic to use uncanny forces against others. An example of this device is provided by a Mesopotamian incantation to cure sickness. The sufferer tries to use magical powers by acting out the destruction of the powers he thinks caused his illness:

As this garlic is peeled off and thrown into the fire,
[And the Fire God] burns it up with fire,
Which will not be cultivated in a garden patch,
Whose roots will not take hold in the ground,
Whose sprout will not come forth nor see the sun,
Which will not be used for the repast of god or king,
[So] may the curse, something evil, revenge, interrogation,
The sickness of my suffering, wrong-doing, crime, misdeed, sin
The sickness which is in my body, flesh, and sinews
Be peeled off like this garlic,
May [the Fire God] burn it with fire this day,
May the wicked thing go forth, that I may see light.[7]

Humans and the Gods, Law, and Justice

Human relationships to the gods were equally humble. There was no doubt that the gods could destroy human beings and might do so at any time for no good reason. Humans could—and, indeed, had to—try to win the gods over by prayers and sacrifices, but there was no guarantee of success. The gods were bound by no laws and no morality. The best behavior and the greatest devotion to the cult of the gods were no defense against the divine and cosmic caprice.

In the earliest civilizations, human relations were guided by laws, often set down in written codes. The basic question about law concerned its legitimacy: Why, apart from the lawgiver's power to coerce obedience, should anyone obey the law? For Old Kingdom Egyptians, the answer was simple: The king was bound to act

[4]Benjamin R. Foster, *From Distant Days, Myths, Tales, and Poetry of Ancient Mesopotamia* (Bethesda, MD: CDL Press, 1999), p. 38.

[5]Thorkild Jacobsen in Henri Frankfort et al., *Before Philosophy* (Baltimore: Penguin, 1949), p. 154.

[6]Foster, pp. 170–171.

[7]Foster, p. 412.

in accordance with maat, and so his laws were righteous. For the Mesopotamians, the answer was almost the same: The king was a representative of the gods, so the laws he set forth were authoritative. The prologue to the most famous legal document in antiquity, the Code of Hammurabi, makes this plain:

> I am the king who is preeminent among kings;
> my words are choice; my ability has no equal.
> By the order of Sharnash, the great judge of heaven and earth,
> may my justice prevail in the land;
> by the word of Marduk, my lord,
> may my statutes have no one to rescind them.[8]

The Hebrews introduced some important new ideas. Their unique God was capable of great anger and destruction, but he was open to persuasion and subject to morality. He was therefore more predictable and comforting, for all the terror of his wrath. The biblical version of the flood story, for instance, reveals the great difference between the Hebrew God and the Babylonian deities. The Hebrew God was powerful and wrathful, but he was not arbitrary. He chose to destroy his creatures for their moral failures:

> the wickedness of man was great in the earth, and that every imagination of the thought of his heart was evil continually . . . the earth was corrupt in God's sight and the earth was filled with violence.[9]

When he repented and wanted to save someone, he chose Noah because "Noah was a righteous man, blameless in his generation."[10]

The biblical story of Sodom and Gomorrah shows that God was bound by his own definition of righteousness. He had chosen to destroy these wicked cities but felt obliged by his covenant to inform Abraham first.[11] Abraham called on God to abide by his own moral principles, and God saw Abraham's point.

Such a world offers the possibility of order in the universe and on this earth. There is also the possibility of justice among human beings, for the Hebrew God had provided his people with law. Through his prophet Moses, he had provided humans with regulations that would enable them to live in peace and justice. If they would abide by the law and live upright lives, they and their descendants could expect happy and prosperous lives. This idea was different from the uncertainty of the Babylonian view, but like it and its Egyptian partner, it left no doubt of the certainty of the divine. Cosmic order, human survival, and justice all depended on God.

[8]James B. Pritchard, *Ancient Near Eastern Texts Related to the Old Testament*, 3rd ed. (Princeton: Princeton University Press, 1969), p. 164.

[9]Genesis 6:5, 6:11.

[10]Genesis 6:9.

[11]Genesis 18:20–33.

▼ Toward the Greeks and Western Thought

Greek thought offered different approaches and answers to many of the concerns we have been discussing. Calling attention to some of those differences will help convey the distinctive outlook of the Greeks and the later cultures within Western civilization that have drawn heavily on Greek influence.

Greek ideas had much in common with the ideas of earlier peoples. The Greek gods had most of the characteristics of the Mesopotamian deities. Magic and incantations played a part in the lives of most Greeks, and Greek law, like that of earlier peoples, was usually connected with divinity. Many, if not most, Greeks in the ancient world must have lived their lives with notions similar to those other peoples held. The surprising thing is that some Greeks developed ideas that were strikingly different and, in so doing, set part of humankind on an entirely new path.

As early as the sixth century B.C.E., some Greeks living in the Ionian cities of Asia Minor raised questions and suggested answers about the nature of the world that produced an intellectual revolution. In their speculations, they made guesses that were completely naturalistic and made no reference to supernatural powers. One historian of Greek thought, discussing the views of Thales, the first Greek philosopher, put the case particularly well:

> In one of the Babylonian legends it says: "All the lands were sea . . . Marduk bound a rush mat upon the face of the waters, he made dirt and piled it beside the rush mat." What Thales did was to leave Marduk out. He, too, said that everything was once water. But he thought that earth and everything else had been formed out of water by a natural process, like the silting up of the Delta of the Nile. . . . It is an admirable beginning, the whole point of which is that it gathers into a coherent picture a number of observed facts without letting Marduk in.[12]

By putting the question of the world's origin in a naturalistic form, Thales, in the sixth century B.C.E., may have begun the unreservedly rational investigation of the universe and, in so doing, initiated both philosophy and science.

The same relentlessly rational approach was used even in regard to the gods themselves. In the same century as Thales, Xenophanes of Colophon expressed the opinion that humans think of the gods as resembling themselves, that, like themselves, they were born, that they wear clothes like theirs, and that they have voices and bodies like theirs. If oxen, horses, and lions had hands and could paint like humans, Xenophanes argued, they would paint gods in their own image; the oxen would draw gods like oxen and the horses like horses. Thus, Africans believed in flat-nosed, black-faced gods,

[12]Benjamin Farrington, *Greek Science* (London: Penguin, 1953), p. 37.

and the Thracians in gods with blue eyes and red hair.[13] In the fifth century B.C.E., Protagoras of Abdera went so far toward agnosticism as to say, "About the gods I can have no knowledge either that they are or that they are not or what is their nature."[14]

This rationalistic, skeptical way of thinking carried over into practical matters. The school of medicine led by Hippocrates of Cos (about 400 B.C.E.) attempted to understand, diagnose, and cure disease without any attention to supernatural forces. One of the Hippocratics wrote, of the mysterious disease epilepsy:

> It seems to me that the disease is no more divine than any other. It has a natural cause, just as other diseases have. Men think it divine merely because they do not understand it. But if they called everything divine which they do not understand, why, there would be no end of divine things.[15]

By the fifth century B.C.E., the historian Thucydides could analyze and explain human behavior completely in terms of human nature and chance, leaving no place for the gods or supernatural forces.

The same absence of divine or supernatural forces characterized Greek views of law and justice. Most Greeks, of course, liked to think that, in a vague way, law came ultimately from the gods. In practice, however, and especially in the democratic states, they knew that laws were made by humans and should be obeyed because they represented the expressed consent of the citizens. Law, according to the fourth-century B.C.E. statesman Demosthenes, is "a general covenant of the whole State, in accordance with which all men in that State ought to regulate their lives."[16]

In Perspective

The statement of the following ideas, so different from any that came before the Greeks, opens the discussion of most of the issues that appear in the long history of Western civilization and that remain major concerns in the modern world. What is the nature of the universe, and how can it be controlled? Are there divine powers, and if so, what is humanity's relationship to them? Are law and justice human, divine, or both? What is the place in human society of freedom, obedience, and reverence? These and many other matters were either first considered or first elaborated on by the Greeks.

The Greeks' sharp departure from the thinking of earlier cultures marked the beginning of the unusual experience that we call Western civilization. Nonetheless, they built on a foundation of lore that people in the Near East had painstakingly accumulated. From ancient Mesopotamia and Egypt, they borrowed important knowledge and skills in mathematics, astronomy, art, and literature. From Phoenicia, they learned the art of writing. The discontinuities, however, are more striking than the continuities.

Hereditary monarchies, often elevated by the aura of divinity, ruled the great civilizations of the river valleys. Powerful priesthoods presented yet another bastion of privilege that stood between the ordinary person and the knowledge and opportunity needed for freedom and autonomy. Religion was an integral part of the world of the ancient Near East, in the kingdoms and city-states of Palestine, Phoenicia, and Syria, just as in the great empires of Egypt, Mesopotamia, and Persia. The secular, reasoned questioning that sought to understand the world in which people lived—that sought explanations in the natural order of things rather than in the supernatural acts of the gods—was not characteristic of the older cultures. Nor would it appear in similar societies at other times in other parts of the world. The new way of looking at things was uniquely the product of the Greeks. We now need to see why they raised fundamental questions in the way that they did.

Review Questions

1. How would you define "history"? What different academic disciplines do historians rely on, and why is the study of history important?
2. How was life during the Paleolithic Age different from that in the Neolithic Age? What advancements in agriculture and human development had taken place by the end of the Neolithic era? Is it valid to speak of a Neolithic Revolution?
3. What were the political and intellectual outlooks of the civilizations of Egypt and Mesopotamia? How did geography influence the religious outlooks of these two civilizations?
4. To what extent did the Hebrew faith bind the Jews politically? Why was the concept of monotheism so radical for Near Eastern civilizations?
5. How did the Assyrian Empire differ from that of the Hittites or Egyptians? Why did the Assyrian Empire ultimately fail to survive? Why was the Persian Empire so successful? What were the main teachings of Zarathustra? How did his concept of the divine compare to that of the Jews?
6. In what ways did Greek thought develop along different lines from that of Near Eastern civilizations? What new questions about human society did the Greeks ask?

[13]Henri Frankfort et al., *Before Philosophy* (Baltimore: Penguin, 1949), pp. 14–16.

[14]Hermann Diels, *Fragmente der Vorsokratiker*, 5th ed., ed. by Walter Krantz (Berlin: Weidmann, 1934–1938), Frg. 4.

[15]Diels, Frgs. 14–16.

[16]Demosthenes, *Against Aristogeiton* 16.

SUGGESTED READINGS

C. Aldred, *The Egyptians* (1998). Probably the best one-volume history of the subject.

P. Briant, *From Cyrus to Alexander: A History of the Persian Empire* (2002). A scholarly account of ancient Persia with greater knowledge of the Persian evidence than is usual.

T. Bryce, *The Kingdom of the Hittites* (1998). A fine new account.

M. Ehrenberg, *Women in Prehistory* (1989). Discusses the role of women in early times.

B. M. Fagan, *People of the Earth: An Introduction to World Prehistory*, 11th ed. (2003). A narrative account of human prehistory up to the earliest civilizations.

W. W. Hallo and W. K. Simpson, *The Ancient Near East: A History*, rev. ed. (1998). A fine survey of Egyptian and Mesopotamian history.

A. Kamm, *The Israelites: An Introduction* (1999). A brief, excellent, and accessible account.

R. Matthews, *Archaeology of Mesopotamia: Theories and Approaches* (2003). A fascinating investigation of the theories, methods, approaches, and history of Mesopotamian archaeology from its origins in the nineteenth century up to the present day.

J. B. Pritchard, ed., *Ancient Near Eastern Texts Relating to the Old Testament* (1969). A good collection of documents in translation with useful introductory material.

R. Rudgley, *The Lost Civilizations of the Stone Age* (1999). A bold new interpretation that claims that many elements of civilization were already present in the Stone Age.

H. W. F. Saggs, *Babylonians* (1995). A general account of ancient Mesopotamia by an expert scholar.

I. Shaw, ed., *The Oxford History of Ancient Egypt* (2000). An up-to-date survey by leading scholars.

W. K. Simpson et al., *The Literature of Ancient Egypt: An Anthology of Stories, Instructions, Stelae, Autobiographies, and Poetry* (2003). A fine collection of writings from ancient Egypt.

D. C. Snell, *Life in the Ancient Near East, 3100–332 B.C.E.* (1997). A social history with emphasis on culture and daily life.

In 1972, this striking bronze statue was found off the coast of Riace, southern Italy. Possibly a votive statue from the sanctuary of Delphi in Greece, it may have been the work of the sculptor Phidias (ca. 490–430 B.C.E.). Erich Lessing/Art Resource, N.Y.

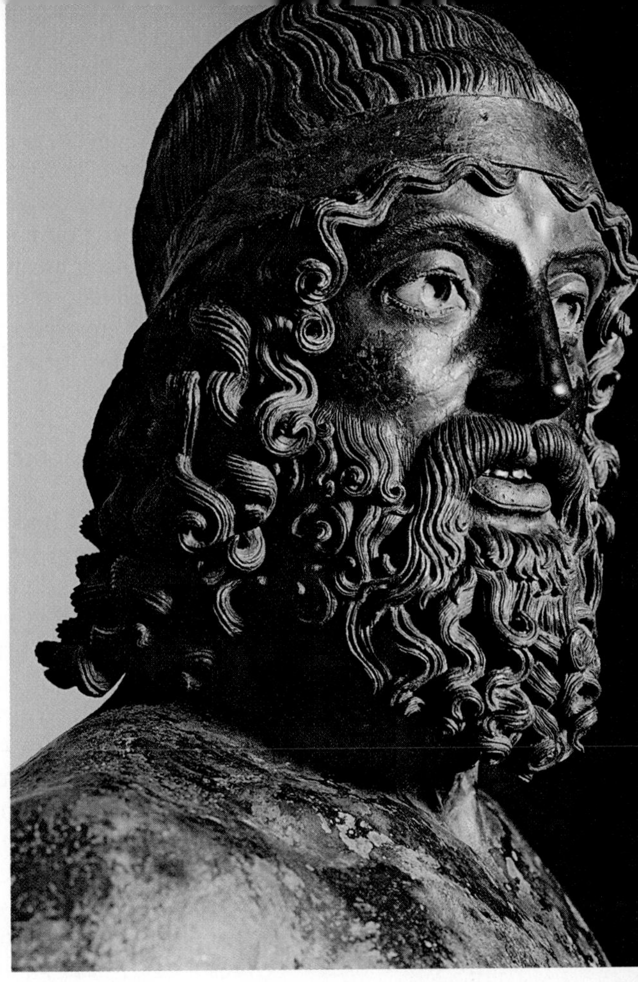

2

The Rise of Greek Civilization

▼ **The Bronze Age on Crete and on the Mainland to about 1150 B.C.E.**
The Minoans • The Mycenaeans

▼ **The Greek "Middle Ages" to about 750 B.C.E.**
Greek Migrations • The Age of Homer

▼ **The *Polis***
Development of the *Polis* • The *Hoplite* Phalanx • The Importance of the *Polis*

▼ **Expansion of the Greek World**
Magna Graecia • The Greek Colony • The Tyrants (about 700–500 B.C.E.)

▼ **The Major States**
Sparta • Athens

▼ **Life in Archaic Greece**
Society • Religion • Poetry

▼ **The Persian Wars**
The Ionian Rebellion • The War in Greece

▼ **In Perspective**

KEY TOPICS

- **The Bronze Age civilizations that ruled the Aegean area before the development of Hellenic civilization**
- **The rise, development, and expansion of the *polis*, the characteristic political unit of Hellenic Greece**
- **The early history of Sparta and Athens**
- **The wars between the Greeks and the Persians**

ABOUT 2000 B.C.E., Greek-speaking peoples settled the lands surrounding the Aegean Sea and established a style of life and formed a set of ideas, values, and institutions that spread far beyond the Aegean corner of the Mediterranean Sea. Preserved and adapted by the Romans, Greek culture powerfully influenced the society of western Europe in the Middle Ages and dominated the Byzantine Empire in the same period. It would ultimately spread across Europe and cross the Atlantic to the Western Hemisphere.

At some time in their history, the Greeks of the ancient world founded cities on every shore of the Mediterranean Sea. Pushing on through the Dardanelles, they placed many settlements on the coasts of the Black Sea in southern Russia and as far east as the approaches to the Caucasus Mountains. The center of Greek life, however, has always been the Aegean Sea and the islands in and around it. This location at the eastern end of the Mediterranean soon put the Greeks in touch with the more advanced civilizations of Mesopotamia, Egypt, Asia Minor, and Syria-Palestine.

The Greeks acknowledged the influence of these predecessors. A character in one of Plato's dialogues says, "Whatever the Greeks have acquired from foreigners they have, in the end, turned into something finer."[1] This is a proud statement, but it also shows that the Greeks were aware of how much they had learned from other civilizations.

The Bronze Age Minoan culture of Crete contributed to Greek civilization; and the mainland Mycenaean culture, which conquered Minoan Crete, contributed even more. Both these cultures, however, had more in common with the cultures of the Near East than with the new Hellenic culture established by the Greeks in the centuries after the end of the Bronze Age in the twelfth century B.C.E.

The rugged geography of the Greek peninsula and its nearby islands isolated the Greeks of the early Iron Age from their richer and more culturally advanced neighbors, shaping, in part, their way of life and permitting them to develop that way of life on their own. The aristocratic world of the "Greek Dark Ages" (1150–750 B.C.E.) produced impressive artistic achievements, especially in the development of painted pottery and most magnificently, in the epic poems of Homer. In the eighth century B.C.E., social, economic, and military changes profoundly influenced the organization of Greek political life; the Greek city-state, the *polis*, came into being and thereafter dominated the cultural development of the Greek people.

This change came in the midst of turmoil, for the pressure of a growing population led many Greeks to leave home and establish colonies far away. Those who remained often fell into political conflict, from which tyrannies sometimes emerged. These tyrannies, however, were transitory, and the Greek cities emerged from them as self-governing polities, usually ruled by an oligarchy, broad or narrow. The two most important states, Athens and Sparta, developed in different directions. Sparta formed a mixed constitution in which a small part of the population dominated the vast majority, and Athens developed the world's first democracy.

▼ The Bronze Age on Crete and on the Mainland to about 1150 B.C.E.

The Bronze Age civilizations in the region the Greeks would rule arose on the island of Crete, on the islands of the Aegean, and on the mainland of Greece. Crete was the site of the earliest Bronze Age settlements, and modern scholars have called the civilization that arose there **Minoan**, after Minos, the legendary king of Crete. A later Bronze Age civilization was centered at the mainland site of Mycenae and is called **Mycenaean**.

[1]Plato, *Epinomis* 987 d.

The Minoans

With Greece to the north, Egypt to the south, and Asia to the east, Crete was a cultural bridge between the older civilizations and the new one of the Greeks. The Bronze Age came to Crete not long after 3000 B.C.E., and the Minoan civilization, which powerfully influenced the islands of the Aegean and the mainland of Greece, arose in the third and second millennia B.C.E.

Scholars have established links between stratigraphic layers at archaeological sites on Crete and specific styles of pottery and other artifacts found in the layers. On this basis they have divided the Bronze Age on Crete into three major periods—Early, Middle, and Late Minoan—with some subdivisions. Dates for Bronze Age settlements on the Greek mainland, for which the term *Helladic* is used, are derived from the same chronological scheme.

During the Middle and Late Minoan periods in the cities of eastern and central Crete, a civilization developed that was new and unique in its character and beauty. Its most striking creations are the palaces uncovered at such sites as Phaestus, Haghia Triada, and, most important, Cnossus. Each of these palaces was built around a central court surrounded by a labyrinth of rooms. Some sections of the palace at Cnossus were four stories high. The basement contained many storage rooms for oil and grain, apparently paid as taxes to the king. The main and upper floors contained living quarters, and workshops for making pottery and jewelry. There were sitting rooms and even bathrooms, to which water was piped through excellent plumbing. Lovely columns, which tapered downward, supported the ceilings, and many of the walls carried murals showing landscapes and seascapes, festivals, and sports. The palace design and the paintings show the influence of Syria, Asia Minor, and Egypt, but the style and quality are unique to Crete.

In contrast to the Mycenaean cities on the mainland of Greece, Minoan palaces and settlements lacked strong defensive walls. This evidence that the Minoans built without defense in mind has raised questions and encouraged speculation. Some scholars, pointing also to evidence that Minoan religion was more matriarchal than the patriarchal religion of the Mycenaeans and their Greek descendants, have argued that the civilizations of Crete, perhaps reflecting the importance of women, were inherently more tranquil and pacific than others. An earlier and different explanation for the absence of fortifications was that the protection provided by the sea made them unnecessary. The evidence is not strong enough to support either explanation, and the mystery remains.

Along with palaces, paintings, pottery, jewelry, and other valuable objects, excavations have revealed clay writing tablets like those found in Mesopotamia. The tablets, preserved accidentally when a great fire that destroyed the royal palace at Cnossus hardened them, have three distinct kinds of writing on them: a kind of picture writing called *hieroglyphic*, and two different linear scripts called Linear A and Linear B. The languages of the two other scripts remain unknown, but Linear B proved to be an early form of Greek. The contents of the tablets, primarily inventories, reveal an organization centered on the palace and ruled by a king who was supported by an extensive bureaucracy that kept remarkably detailed records.

This sort of organization is typical of early civilizations in the Near East, but as we shall see, is nothing like that of the Greeks after the Bronze Age. Yet the inventories were written in a form of Greek. If they controlled Crete throughout the Bronze Age, why should Minoans, who were not Greek, have written in a language not their own? This question raises the larger one of what the relationship was between Crete and the Greek mainland in the Bronze Age and leads us to an examination of mainland culture.

The Mycenaeans

In the third millennium B.C.E.—the Early Helladic Period—most of the Greek mainland, including many of the sites of later Greek cities, was settled by people who used metal, built some impressive houses, and traded with Crete and the islands of the Aegean. The names they gave to places, names that were sometimes preserved by later invaders, make it clear they were not Greeks and they spoke a language that was not Indo-European (the language family to which Greek belongs).

Not long after the year 2000 B.C.E., many of these Early Helladic sites were destroyed by fire, some were abandoned, and still others appear to have yielded peacefully to an invading people. These signs of invasion probably signal the arrival of the Greeks.

All over Greece, there was a smooth transition between the Middle and Late Helladic periods. The invaders succeeded in establishing control of the entire mainland. The shaft graves cut into the rock at the royal palace-fortress of Mycenae show that they prospered and sometimes became rich. At Mycenae, the richest finds come from the period after 1600 B.C.E. The city's wealth and power reached their peak during this time, and the culture of the whole mainland during the Late Helladic Period goes by the name *Mycenaean*.

The presence of the Greek Linear B tablets at Cnossus suggests that Greek invaders also established themselves in Crete, and there is good reason to believe that at the height of Mycenaean power (1400–1200 B.C.E.), Crete was part of the Mycenaean world. Although their dating is still controversial, the Linear B tablets at Cnossus seem to belong to Late Minoan III. Thus, what is called the great "palace period" at Cnossus would have followed an invasion by Mycenaeans in 1400 B.C.E. These Greek invaders ruled Crete until the end of the Bronze Age.

Mycenaean Culture The excavation of Mycenae, Pylos, and other Mycenaean sites reveals a culture influenced by, but different from, the Minoan culture. Mycenae and Pylos, like Cnossus, were built some distance from the sea, but defense against attack was foremost in the minds of the founders of the Mycenaean cities. Both Mycenae and Pylos were built on hills in a position commanding the neighboring territory. The Mycenaean people were warriors, as their art, architecture, and weapons reveal. The success of their campaigns and the defense of their territory required strong central authority, and all available evidence shows that the kings provided it. Their palaces, in which the royal family and its retainers lived, were located within the walls; most of the population lived outside the walls. As on Crete, paintings usually covered the palace walls, but instead of peaceful landscapes and games, the Mycenaean murals depicted scenes of war and boar hunting.

About 1500 B.C.E., the already impressive shaft graves were abandoned in favor of *tholos* tombs. These large, beehivelike chambers were built of enormous well-cut and fitted stones and were approached by an unroofed passage (*dromos*) cut horizontally into the side of the hill. The lintel block alone of one of these tombs weighs over one hundred tons. Only a strong king whose wealth was great, whose power was unquestioned, and who commanded the labor of many people could undertake such a project. His wealth probably came from plundering raids, piracy, and trade. Some of this trade went westward to Italy and Sicily, but most of it was with the islands of the Aegean, the coastal towns of Asia Minor, and the cities of Syria, Egypt, and Crete. The Mycenaeans sent pottery, olive oil, and animal hides in exchange for jewels and other luxuries.

This statuette of a female with a snake in each of her hands is thought to represent either the Minoan snake goddess herself or one of her priestesses performing a religious ritual. It was found on Crete and dates from around 1600 B.C.E. Max Alexander/Dorling Kindersley © Archaeological Receipts Fund (TAP)

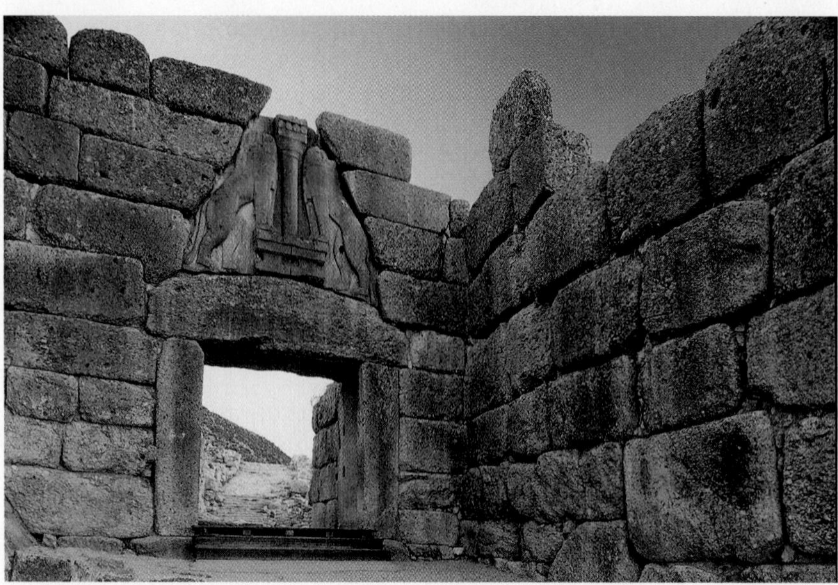

The citadel of Mycenae, a major center of the Greek civilization of the Bronze Age, was built of enormously heavy stones. The lion gate at its entrance was built in the thirteenth century B.C.E. Joe Cornish/Dorling Kindersley © Archaeological Receipts Fund (TAP)

Tablets containing the Mycenaean Linear B writing have been found all over the mainland; the largest and most useful collection was found at Pylos. These tablets reveal a world similar to the one the records at Cnossus show. The king, whose title was *wanax*, held a royal domain, appointed officials, commanded servants, and kept a close record of what he owned and what was owed to him. This evidence confirms all the rest; the Mycenaean world was made up of several independent, powerful, and well-organized monarchies.

The Rise and Fall of Mycenaean Power At the height of their power (1400–1200 B.C.E.), the Mycenaeans were prosperous and active. They enlarged their cities, expanded their trade, and even established commercial colonies in the East. The archives of the Hittite kings of Asia Minor mention them. Egyptian records name them as marauders of the Nile Delta. Sometime about 1250 B.C.E., they probably sacked Troy, on the coast of northwestern Asia Minor, giving rise to the epic poems of Homer—the *Iliad* and the *Odyssey*. (See Map 2–1.) Around 1200 B.C.E., however, the Mycenaean world showed signs of trouble, and by 1100 B.C.E., it was gone. Its palaces were destroyed, many of its cities were abandoned, and its art, way of life, and system of writing were buried and forgotten.

What happened? Some recent scholars, noting evidence that the Aegean island of Thera (modern Santorini) suffered a massive volcanic explosion in the middle to late second millennium B.C.E., have suggested that this natural disaster was responsible. According to one version of this theory, the explosion occurred around 1400 B.C.E., blackening and poisoning the air for miles around and sending a monstrous tidal wave that destroyed the great palace at Cnossus and, with it, Minoan culture. According to another version, the explosion took place about 1200 B.C.E., destroying Bronze Age culture throughout the Aegean. This second version conveniently accounts for the end of both Minoan and Mycenaean civilizations in a single blow, but the evidence does not support it. The Mycenaean towns were not destroyed all at once; many fell around 1200 B.C.E., but some flourished for another century, and the Athens of the period was never destroyed or abandoned. No theory of natural disaster can account for this pattern, leaving us to seek less dramatic explanations for the end of Mycenaean civilization.

The Dorian Invasion Some scholars have suggested that piratical sea raiders destroyed Pylos and, perhaps, other sites on the mainland. The Greeks themselves believed in a legend that told of the Dorians, a rude people from the north who spoke a Greek dialect different from that of the Mycenaean peoples. According to the legend, the Dorians joined with one of the Greek tribes, the Heraclidae, in an attack on the southern Greek peninsula of Peloponnesus, which was repulsed. One hundred years later, they returned and gained full control. Recent historians have identified this legend of "the return of the Heraclidae" with a Dorian invasion.

Archaeology has not provided material evidence of whether there was a single Dorian invasion or a series of them, and it is impossible as yet to say with any certainty what happened at the end of the Bronze Age in the Aegean. The chances are good, however, that Mycenaean civilization ended gradually over the century between 1200 B.C.E. and 1100 B.C.E. Its end may have been the result of internal conflicts among the Mycenaean kings combined with continuous pressure from outsiders, who raided, infiltrated, and eventually dominated Greece and its neighboring islands. There is reason to believe that Mycenaean society suffered internal weaknesses due to its organization around the centralized control of military force and agricultural production. This rigid organization may have deprived it of flexibility and vitality, leaving it vulnerable to outside challengers. In any case, Cnossus, Mycenae, and Pylos were abandoned, their secrets to be kept for over 3,000 years.

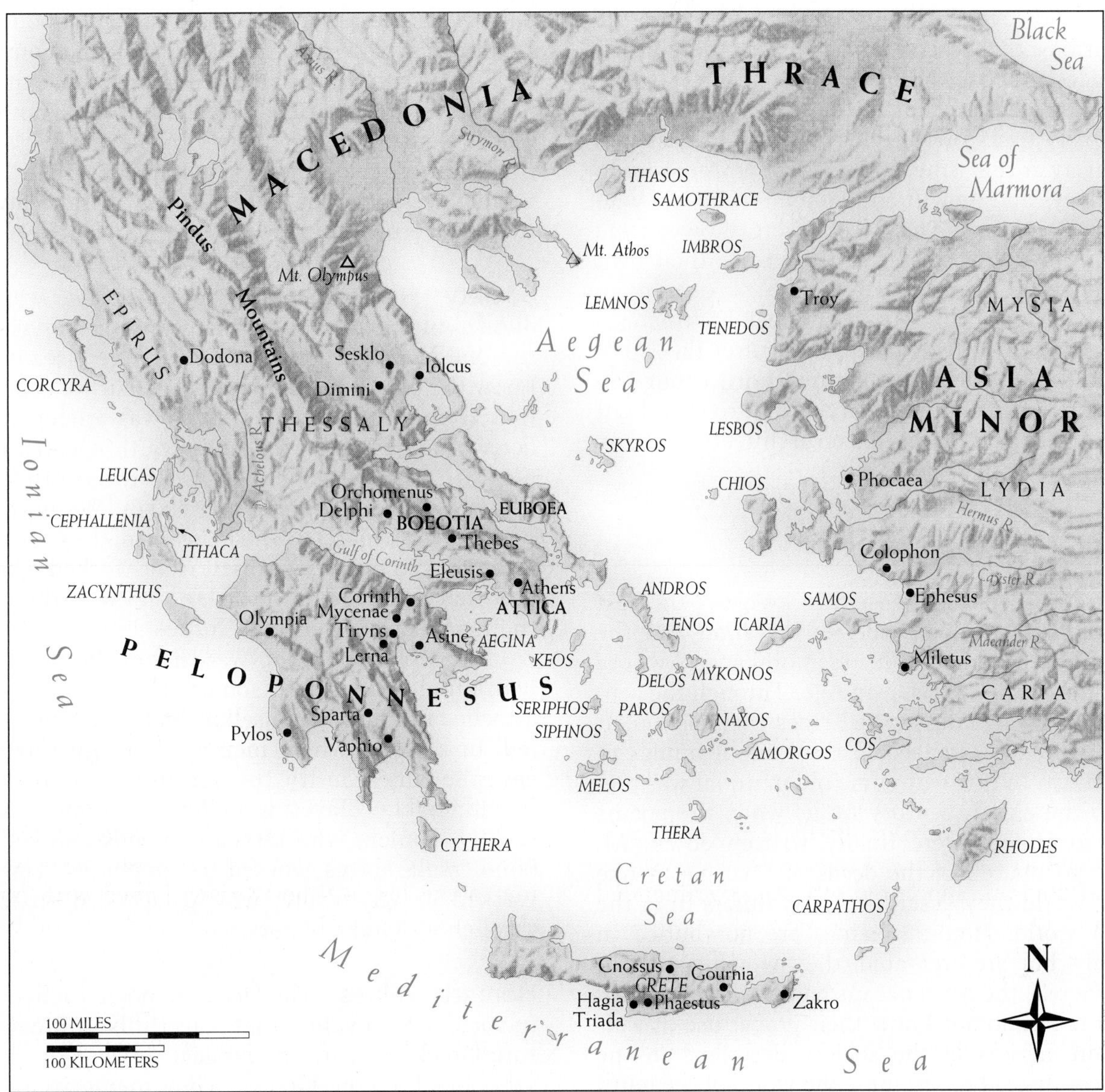

Map 2–1 **THE AEGEAN AREA IN THE BRONZE AGE** The Bronze Age in the Aegean area lasted from about 1900 to about 1100 B.C.E. Its culture on Crete is called Minoan and was at its height about 1900–1400 B.C.E. Bronze Age Helladic culture on the mainland flourished from about 1600–1200 B.C.E.

▼ The Greek "Middle Ages" to about 750 B.C.E.

The immediate effects of the Dorian invasion were disastrous for the inhabitants of the Mycenaean world. The palaces and the kings and bureaucrats who managed them were destroyed. The wealth and organization that had supported the artists and merchants were likewise swept away by a barbarous people who did not have the knowledge or social organization to maintain them. Many villages were abandoned and never resettled. Some of their inhabitants probably turned to a nomadic life, and many perished. The chaos resulting from the collapse of the rigidly controlled palace culture produced severe depopulation and widespread poverty that lasted for a long time.

Greek Migrations

Another result of the invasion was the spread of the Greek people eastward from the mainland to the Aegean islands and the coast of Asia Minor. The Dorians themselves, after occupying most of the Peloponnesus, occupied the southern Aegean islands and the southern part of the Anatolian coast.

These migrations made the Aegean a Greek lake. The fall of the advanced Minoan and Mycenaean civilizations, however, virtually ended trade with the old civilizations of the Near East; nor was there much internal trade among the different parts of Greece. The Greeks were forced to turn inward, and each community was left largely to its own devices. The Near East was also in disarray at this time, and no great power arose to impose its ways and its will on the helpless people who lived about the Aegean. The Greeks were allowed time to recover from their disaster and to create their own unique style of life.

Our knowledge of this period in Greek history rests on limited sources. Writing disappeared after the fall of Mycenae, and no new script appeared until about 750 B.C.E., so we have no contemporary author to shed light on the period. Excavation reveals no architecture, sculpture, or painting until after 750 B.C.E.

The Age of Homer

For a picture of society in these "Dark Ages," the best source is Homer. His epic poems, the ***Iliad*** and the ***Odyssey***, emerged from a tradition of oral poetry whose roots extend into the Mycenaean Age. Through the centuries bards had sung tales of the heroes who had fought at Troy, using verse arranged in rhythmic formulas to aid the memory. In this way some old material was preserved into the eighth century B.C.E., when the poems attributed to Homer were finally written down. Although the poems tell of the deeds of Mycenaean Age heroes, the world they describe clearly differs from the Mycenaean world. Homer's heroes are not buried in *tholos* tombs but are cremated; they worship gods in temples, whereas the Mycenaeans had no temples; they have chariots but do not know their proper use in warfare. Certain aspects of the society described in the poems appear instead to resemble the world of the tenth and ninth centuries B.C.E., and other aspects appear to belong to the poet's own time, when population was growing at a swift pace and prosperity was returning, thanks to changes in Greek agriculture, society, and government.

Government In the Homeric poems, the power of the kings is much less than that of the Mycenaean rulers. Homeric kings had to consult a council of nobles before they made important decisions. The nobles felt free to discuss matters in vigorous language and in opposition to the king's wishes. In the *Iliad*, Achilles does not hesitate to address Agamemnon, the "most kingly" commander of the Trojan expedition, in these words: "you with a dog's face and a deer's heart." Such language may have been impolite, but it was not treasonous. The king could ignore the council's advice, but it was risky for him to do so.

Only noblemen had the right to speak in council, but the common people could not be entirely ignored. If a king planned a war or a major change of policy during a campaign, he would not fail to call the common soldiers to an assembly; they could listen and express their feelings by acclamation, though they could not take part in the debate. Homer shows that even in these early times the Greeks, unlike their predecessors and contemporaries, practiced some forms of limited constitutional government.

Society Homeric society, nevertheless, was sharply divided into classes, the most important division being the one between nobles and everyone else. We do not know the origin of this distinction, but we cannot doubt that at this time Greek society was aristocratic. Birth determined noble status, and wealth usually accompanied it. Below the nobles were three other classes: *thetes*, landless laborers, and slaves. We do not know whether the *thetes* owned the land they worked outright (and so were free to sell it) or worked a hereditary plot that belonged to their clan (and was, therefore, not theirs to dispose of as they chose).

The worst condition was that of the free, but landless, hired agricultural laborer. The slave, at least, was attached to a family household and so was protected and fed. In a world where membership in a settled group gave the only security, the free laborers were desperately vulnerable. Slaves were few in number and were mostly women, who served as maids and concubines. Some male slaves worked as shepherds. Few, if any, worked in agriculture, which depended on free labor throughout Greek history.

Homeric Values The Homeric poems reflect an aristocratic code of values that powerfully influenced all future Greek thought. In classical times, Homer was the schoolbook of the Greeks. They memorized his texts, settled diplomatic disputes by citing passages in them, and emulated the behavior and cherished the values they found in them. Those values were physical prowess; courage; fierce protection of one's family, friends, property; and, above all, personal honor and reputation. Speed of foot, strength, and, most of all, excellence at fighting make a man great, and all these attributes promote personal honor. Achilles, the great hero of the *Iliad*, refuses to fight in battle, allowing his fellow Greeks to be slain and almost defeated, because Agamemnon has wounded his honor by taking away his battle prize. He returns not out of a sense of duty to the army, but to avenge the death of his dear friend Patroclus. Odysseus, the hero of the *Odyssey*, returning home after his wanderings, ruthlessly kills the many suitors who had, in his long absence, sought to marry his wife Penelope; they had dishonored him by consuming his wealth, wooing Penelope, and scorning his son.

The highest virtue in Homeric society was ***arete***—manliness, courage in the most general sense, and the excellence proper to a hero. This quality was best revealed in a contest, or *agon*. Homeric battles are not primarily group combats, but a series of individual contests between great champions. One of the prime forms of entertainment is the athletic contest, and such a contest celebrates the funeral of Patroclus.

The central ethical idea in Homer can be found in the instructions that Achilles' father gives him when he sends him off to fight at Troy: "Always be the best and distinguished above others." The father of another Homeric hero has given his son exactly the same orders and has added to them the injunction: "Do not bring shame on the family of your fathers who were by far the best in Ephyre and in wide Lycia." Here in a nutshell we have the chief values of the aristocrats of Homer's world: to vie for individual supremacy in *arete* and to defend and increase the honor of the family. These would remain prominent aristocratic values long after Homeric society was only a memory.

Women in Homeric Society In the world described by Homer, the role of women was chiefly to bear and raise children, but the wives of the heroes also had a respected position, presiding over the household, overseeing the servants, and safeguarding the family property. They were prized for their beauty, constancy, and skill at weaving. All these fine qualities are combined in Penelope, the wife of Odysseus, probably the ideal Homeric woman. For the twenty years of her husband's absence, she put off the many suitors who sought to marry her and take his place, remained faithful to him, preserved his property, and protected the future of their son. Far different was the reputation of Agamemnon's wife, Clytemnestra, who betrayed her husband while he was off fighting at Troy and murdered him on his return. Homer contrasts her with the virtuous Penelope in a passage that reveals a streak of hostility to women that can be found throughout the ancient history of the Greeks:

> Not so did the daughter of Tyndareus fashion her evil deeds, when she killed her wedded lord, and a song of loathing will be hers among men, to make evil the reputation of womankind, even for those whose acts are virtuous.[2]

Unlike Greek women in later centuries, the women of the higher class depicted in Homer are seen moving freely about their communities in town and country. They have a place alongside their husbands at the banquets in the great halls and take part in the conversation. In the *Odyssey*'s land of Phaeacia, admittedly a kind of fairyland, the wise queen Arete can decide the fate of suppliants and sometimes is asked to settle disputes even between men. A good marriage is seen as essential, admirable, and desirable. The shipwrecked Odysseus tries to win the sympathy of Arete's young daughter by wishing for her "all that you desire in your heart":

> A husband and a home and the accompanying unity of mind and feeling
> Which is so desirable, for there is nothing nobler or better than this,
> When two people, who think alike, keep house
> As man and wife; causing pain to their enemies,
> And joy to their well-wishers, as they themselves know best.[3]

▼ The *Polis*

The characteristic Greek institution was the ***polis*** (plural ***poleis***). The common translation of that word as "city-state" is misleading, for it says both too much and too little. All Greek *poleis* began as little more than agricultural villages or towns, and many stayed that way, so the word "city" is inappropriate. All of them were states, in the sense of being independent political units, but they were much more than that. The *polis* was thought of as a community of relatives; all its citizens, who were theoretically descended from a common ancestor, belonged to subgroups, such as fighting brotherhoods or *phratries*, clans, and tribes, and worshipped the gods in common ceremonies.

Aristotle argued that the *polis* was a natural growth and the human being was by nature "an animal who lives in a *polis*." Humans alone have the power of speech and from it derive the ability to distinguish good from bad and right from wrong, "and the sharing of these things is what makes a household and a *polis*." Therefore, humans who are incapable of sharing these things or who are so self-sufficient that they have no need of them are not humans at all, but either wild beasts or gods. Without law and justice, human beings are the worst and most dangerous of the animals. With them, humans can be the best, and justice exists only in the *polis*. These high claims were made in the fourth century B.C.E., hundreds of years after the *polis* came into existence, but they accurately reflect an attitude that was present from the first.

Development of the *Polis*

Originally the word *polis* referred only to a citadel—an elevated, defensible rock to which the farmers of the neighboring area could retreat in case of attack. The **Acropolis** in Athens and the hill called Acrocorinth in Corinth are examples. For some time, such high places and the adjacent farms made up the *polis*. The towns grew gradually and without planning, as their narrow, winding, and disorderly streets show. For centuries they had no walls. Unlike the city-states of the Near East, they were not placed for commercial convenience on

[2]Homer, *Odyssey* 24.199–202, trans. by Richmond Lattimore (Chicago: University of Chicago Press, 1965).

[3]Homer, *Odyssey* 6.181–185, in *Ancient Greece*, trans. by M. Dillon and L. Garland (London and New York: Routledge, 2000).

rivers or the sea. Nor did they grow up around a temple to serve the needs of priests and to benefit from the needs of worshippers. The availability of farmland and of a natural fortress determined their location. They were placed either well inland or far enough away from the sea to avoid piratical raids. Only later and gradually did the ***agora***—a marketplace and civic center—appear within the *polis*. The *agora* was to become the heart of the Greeks' remarkable social life, distinguished by conversation and argument carried on in the open air.

Some *poleis* probably came into existence early in the eighth century B.C.E. The institution was certainly common by the middle of the century, for all the colonies that were established by the Greeks in the years after 750 B.C.E. took the form of the *polis*. Once the new institution had been fully established, true monarchy disappeared. Vestigial kings survived in some places, but they were almost always only ceremonial figures without power. The original form of the *polis* was an aristocratic republic dominated by the nobility through its council of nobles and its monopoly of the magistracies.

Just as the *polis* emerged from sources within Greek society after the Bronze Age, striking changes also appeared in the creation and decoration of Greek pottery.

About 750 B.C.E., coincident with the development of the *polis*, the Greeks borrowed a writing system from one of the Semitic scripts and added vowels to create the first true alphabet. This new Greek alphabet was easier to learn than any earlier writing system, leading to much wider literacy.

The *Hoplite* Phalanx

A new military technique was crucial to the development of the *polis*. In earlier times, small troops of cavalry and individual "champions" who first threw their spears and then came to close quarters with swords may have borne the brunt of fighting. Toward the end of the eighth century B.C.E., however, the ***hoplite* phalanx** came into being and remained the basis of Greek warfare thereafter.

The *hoplite* was a heavily armed infantryman who fought with a spear and a large shield. Most scholars believe that these soldiers were formed into a phalanx in close order, usually at least eight ranks deep, although some argue for a looser formation. As long as the *hoplites* fought bravely and held their ground, there would be few casualties and no defeat, but if they gave way, the result was usually a rout. All depended on the discipline, strength, and courage of the individual soldier. At its best, the phalanx could withstand cavalry charges and defeat infantries not as well protected or disciplined. Until defeated by the Roman legion, it was the dominant military force in the eastern Mediterranean.

The usual *hoplite* battle in Greece was between the armies of two *poleis* quarreling over land. One army invaded the territory of the other when the crops were almost ready for harvest. The defending army had to protect its fields. If the army was beaten, its fields were captured or destroyed and its people might starve. In every way, the phalanx was a communal effort that relied not on the extraordinary actions of the individual, but on the courage of a considerable portion of the citizenry. This style of fighting produced a single, decisive battle that reduced the time lost in fighting other kinds of warfare; it spared the houses, livestock, and other capital of the farmer-soldiers who made up the phalanx, and it also reduced the number of casualties. It perfectly suited the farmer-soldier-citizen, who was the backbone of the *polis*, and, by keeping wars short and limiting their destructiveness and expense, it helped the *polis* prosper. (See "Tyrtaeus on the Citizen Soldier.")

The phalanx and the *polis* arose together, and both heralded the decline of the kings. The phalanx, however, was not made up only of aristocrats. Most of the *hoplites* were farmers working small holdings. The immediate beneficiaries of the royal decline were the aristocrats, but because the existence of the *polis* depended on small farmers, their wishes could not long be wholly ignored. The rise of the *hoplite* phalanx created a bond between the aristocrats and the yeomen family farmers who fought in it. This bond helps explain why class conflicts were muted for some time. It also guaranteed, however, that the aristocrats, who dominated at first, would not always be unchallenged.

The Importance of the *Polis*

The Greeks looked to the *polis* for peace, order, prosperity, and honor in their lifetime. They counted on it to preserve their memory and to honor their descendants after death. Some of them came to see it not only as a ruler, but also as the molder of its citizens. Knowing this, we can understand the pride and scorn that underlie the comparison the poet Phocylides made between the Greek state and the capital of the powerful Assyrian Empire: "A little *polis* living orderly in a high place is stronger than a block-headed Nineveh."

▼ Expansion of the Greek World

From the middle of the eighth century B.C.E. until well into the sixth century B.C.E., the Greeks vastly expanded their territory, their wealth, and their contacts with other peoples. A burst of colonizing activity placed *poleis* from Spain to the Black Sea. A century earlier, a few Greeks had established trading posts in Syria. There they had learned new techniques in the arts and crafts and much more from the older civilizations of the Near East.

TYRTAEUS ON THE CITIZEN SOLDIER

The military organization of citizen soldiers for the defense of the polis *and the idea of the* polis *itself that permeated Greek political thought found echoes in Greek poetry. A major example is this part of a poem by Tyrtaeus, who wrote in Sparta about 625* B.C.E.

How do the values expressed in this poem compare with those esteemed in the epic of Homer? Why, according to Tyrtaeus, is the Spartan soldier right and wise to risk his life by showing courage in battle?

I would not say anything for a man nor take account of him
for any speed of his feet or wrestling skill he might have,
not if he had the size of a Cyclops and strength to go with it,
not if he could outrun Bóreas, the North Wind of Thrace,
not if he were more handsome and gracefully formed than Tithónos,
or had more riches than Midas had, or Kinyras too,
not if he were more of a king than Tantalid Pelops,
or had the power of speech and persuasion Adrastos had,
not if he had all splendors except for a fighting spirit.
For no man ever proves himself a good man in war
unless he can endure to face the blood and the slaughter,
go close against the enemy and fight with his hands.
Here is courage, mankind's finest possession, here is
the noblest prize that a young man can endeavor to win,
and it is a good thing his city and all the people share with him
when a man plants his feet and stands in the foremost spears
relentlessly, all thought of foul flight completely forgotten,
and has well trained his heart to be steadfast and to endure,
and with words encourages the man who is stationed beside him.
Here is a man who proves himself to be valiant in war.
With a sudden rush he turns to flight the rugged battalions
of the enemy, and sustains the beating waves of assault.
And he who so falls among the champions and loses his sweet life,
so blessing with honor his city, his father, and all his people,
with wounds in his chest, where the spear that he was facing has transfixed
that massive guard of his shield, and gone through his breastplate as well,
why, such a man is lamented alike by the young and the elders,
and all his city goes into mourning and grieves for his loss.
His tomb is pointed to with pride, and so are his children,
and his children's children, and afterward all the race that is his.
His shining glory is never forgotten, his name is remembered,
and he becomes an immortal, though he lies under the ground.
when one who was a brave man has been killed by the furious War God
standing his ground and fighting hard for his children and land.
But if he escapes the doom of death, the destroyer of bodies,
and wins his battle, and bright renown for the work of his spear,
all men give place to him alike, the youth and the elders,
and much joy comes his way before he goes down to the dead.
Aging he has reputation among his citizens. No one
tries to interfere with his honors or all he deserves,
all men withdraw before his presence, and yield their seats to him,
and youth, and the men of his age, and even those older than he.
Thus a man should endeavor to reach this high place of courage
with all his heart, and, so trying, never be backward in war.

From *Greek Lyrics*, trans. by Richmond Lattimore, pp. 14–15, 1960. Reprinted by permission of The University of Chicago Press.

Magna Graecia

Syria and its neighboring territory were too strong to penetrate, so the Greeks settled the southern coast of Macedonia. This region was sparsely settled, and the natives were not well enough organized to resist the Greek colonists. Southern Italy and eastern Sicily were even more inviting areas. Before long, there were so many Greek colonies in Italy and Sicily that the Romans called the whole region ***Magna Graecia***, "Great Greece." The Greeks also put colonies in Spain and southern France. In the seventh century B.C.E., Greek colonists settled the coasts of the northeastern Mediterranean, the Black Sea, and the straits connecting them. About the same time, they established settlements on the eastern part of the North African coast. The Greeks now had outposts throughout the Mediterranean world. (See Map 2–2.)

The Greek Colony

The Greeks did not lightly leave home to join a colony. The voyage by sea was dangerous and uncomfortable, and at the end of it were uncertainty and danger. Only powerful pressures like overpopulation and hunger for land drove thousands from their homes to establish new *poleis*.

The colony, although sponsored by the mother city, was established for the good of the colonists rather than for the benefit of those they left behind. The colonists tended to divide the land they settled into equal shares, reflecting an egalitarian tendency inherent in the ethical system of the yeoman farmers in the mother cities. They often copied their home constitution, worshipped the same gods as the people of the mother city at the same festivals in the same way, and carried on a busy trade with the mother city. Most colonies, though independent, were friendly with their mother cities. Each might ask the other for aid in time of trouble and expect to receive a friendly hearing, although neither was obligated to help the other.

The Athenians had colonies of this typical kind but introduced innovations during their imperial period (478–404 B.C.E.). At one point they began to treat all the colonies of their empire as though they were Athenian

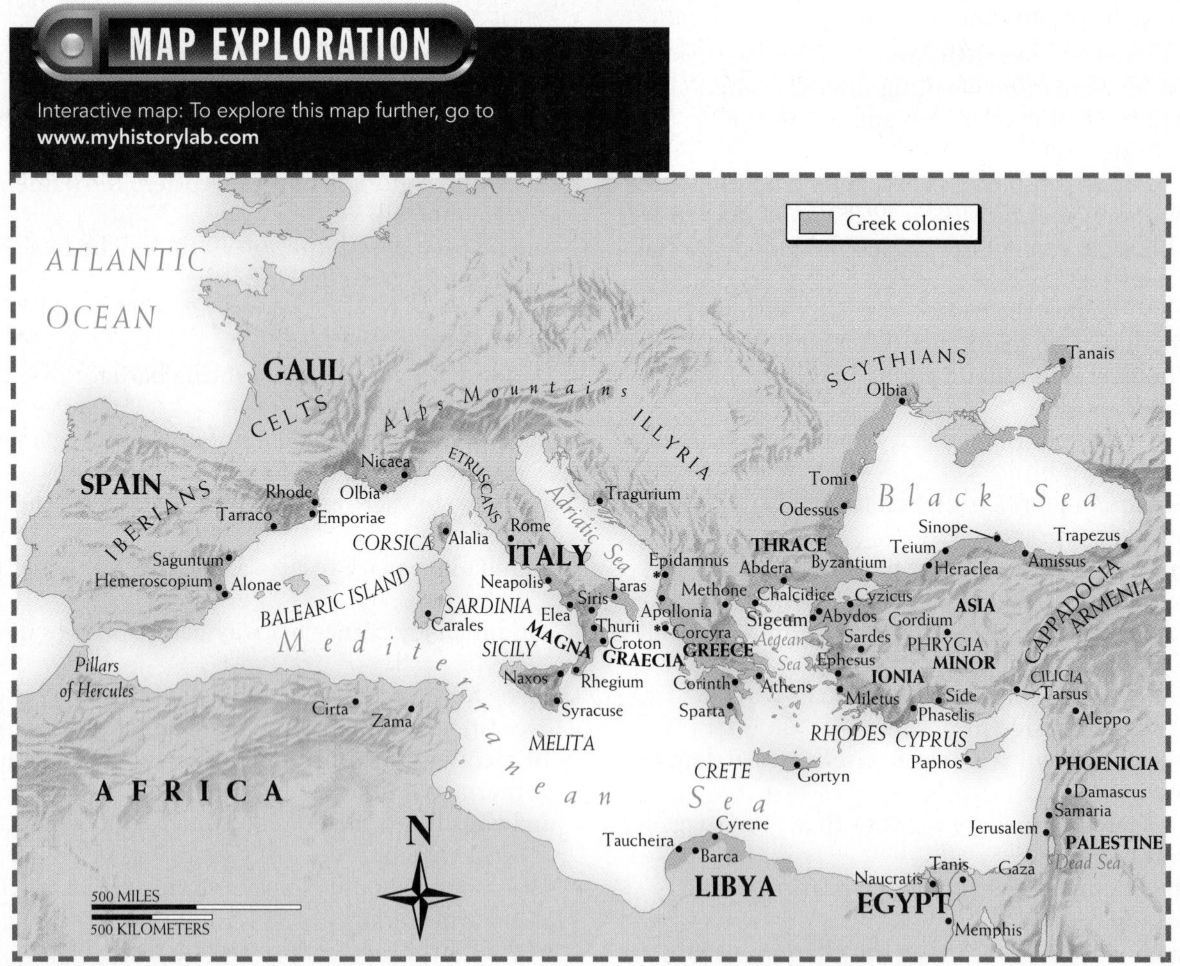

Map 2–2 **GREEK COLONIZATION** The height of Greek colonization was between about 750 and 550 B.C.E. Greek colonies stretched from the Mediterranean coasts of Spain and Gaul (modern France) in the west to the Black Sea and Asia Minor in the east.

settlements, requiring them to bring an offering of a cow and a suit of armor to the Great Panathenaic festival, just like true Athenian colonies. The goal may have been to cloak imperial rule in the more friendly garb of colonial family attachment.

The best known exception to the rule of friendly relations between colony and mother city was the case of Corinth and its colony Corcyra, which quarreled and fought for more than two centuries. Thucydides tells of a fateful conflict between them that played a major role in causing the Peloponnesian War.

Colonization had a powerful influence on Greek life. By relieving the pressure of a growing population, it provided a safety valve that allowed the *poleis* to escape civil wars. By confronting the Greeks with the differences between themselves and the new peoples they met, colonization gave them a sense of cultural identity and fostered a **Panhellenic** ("all-Greek") spirit that led to the establishment of common religious festivals. The most important ones were at Olympia, Delphi, Corinth, and Nemea.

Colonization also encouraged trade and industry. The influx of new wealth from abroad and the increased demand for goods from the homeland stimulated a more intensive use of the land and an emphasis on crops for export, chiefly the olive and the wine grape. The manufacture of pottery, tools, weapons, and fine artistic metalwork, as well as perfumed oil, the soap of the ancient Mediterranean world, was likewise encouraged. New opportunities allowed some men, sometimes outside the nobility, to become wealthy and important. The new rich became a troublesome element in the aristocratic *poleis*, for, although increasingly important in the life of their states, the ruling aristocrats barred them from political power, religious privileges, and social acceptance. These conditions soon created a crisis in many states.

The Tyrants (about 700–500 B.C.E.)

In some cities—perhaps only a small percentage of the more than 1,000 Greek *poleis*—the crisis produced by new economic and social conditions led to or intensified factional divisions within the ruling aristocracy. Between 700 and 500 B.C.E., the result was often the establishment of a tyranny.

The Rise of Tyranny

A tyrant was a monarch who had gained power in an unorthodox or unconstitutional, but not necessarily wicked, way and who exercised a strong one-man rule that might well be beneficent and popular.

The founding tyrant was usually a member of the ruling aristocracy who either had a personal grievance or led an unsuccessful faction. He often rose to power because of his military ability and support from the *hoplites*. He generally had the support of the politically powerless group of the newly wealthy and of the poor farmers. When he took power, he often expelled many of his aristocratic opponents and divided at least some of their land among his supporters. He pleased his commercial and industrial supporters by destroying the privileges of the old aristocracy and by fostering trade and colonization.

The tyrants presided over a period of population growth that saw an increase especially in the number of city dwellers. They responded with a program of public works that included the improvement of drainage systems, care for the water supply, the construction and organization of marketplaces, the building and strengthening of city walls, and the erection of temples. They introduced new local festivals and elaborated the old ones. They patronized the arts, supporting poets and artisans with gratifying results. All this activity contributed to the tyrant's popularity, to the prosperity of his city, and to his self-esteem.

In most cases, the tyrant's rule was secured by a personal bodyguard and by mercenary soldiers. An armed citizenry, necessary for an aggressive foreign policy, would have been dangerous, so the tyrants usually sought peaceful alliances with other tyrants abroad and avoided war.

The End of the Tyrants

By the end of the sixth century B.C.E., tyranny had disappeared from the Greek states and did not return in the same form or for the same reasons. The last tyrants were universally hated for their cruelty and repression. They left bitter memories in their own states and became objects of fear and hatred everywhere.

Besides the outrages individual tyrants committed, the very concept of tyranny was inimical to the idea of the *polis*. The notion of the *polis* as a community to which every member must be responsible, the connection of justice with that community, and the natural aristocratic hatred of monarchy all made tyranny seem alien and offensive. The rule of a tyrant, however beneficent,

CHRONOLOGY OF THE RISE OF GREECE

ca. 2900–1150 B.C.E.	Minoan period
ca. 1900 B.C.E.	Probable date of the arrival of the Greeks on the mainland
ca. 1600–1150 B.C.E.	Mycenaean period
ca. 1250 B.C.E.	Sack of Troy (?)
ca. 1200–1150 B.C.E.	Destruction of Mycenaean centers in Greece
ca. 1100–750 B.C.E.	"Greek Dark Ages"
ca. 750–600 B.C.E.	Major period of Greek colonization
ca. 750 B.C.E.	Probable date when Homer flourished
ca. 700 B.C.E.	Probable date when Hesiod flourished
ca. 700–500 B.C.E.	Major period of Greek tyranny

was arbitrary and unpredictable. Tyranny came into being in defiance of tradition and law, and the tyrant governed without either. He was not answerable in any way to his fellow citizens.

From a longer perspective, however, the tyrants made important contributions to the development of Greek civilization. They encouraged economic changes that helped secure the future prosperity of Greece. They increased communication with the rest of the Mediterranean world and cultivated crafts and technology, as well as arts and literature. Most important of all, they broke the grip of the aristocracy and put the productive powers of the most active and talented of its citizens fully at the service of the *polis*.

▼ The Major States

Generalization about the *polis* becomes difficult not long after its appearance, for although the states had much in common, some of them developed in unique ways. Sparta and Athens, which became the two most powerful Greek states, had especially unusual histories.

Sparta

At first Sparta—located on the **Peloponnesus**, the southern peninsula of Greece—seems not to have been strikingly different from other *poleis*. About 725 B.C.E., however, the pressure of population and land hunger led the Spartans to launch a war of conquest against their western neighbor, Messenia. (See Map 2–3.) The First Messenian War gave the Spartans as much land as they would ever need. The reduction of the Messenians to the status of serfs, or **Helots**, meant the Spartans did not even need to work the land that supported them.

The turning point in Spartan history came about 650 B.C.E., when, in the Second Messenian War, the Helots rebelled with the help of Argos and other Peloponnesian cities. The war was long and bitter and at one point threatened the existence of Sparta. After they had suppressed the revolt, the Spartans were forced to reconsider their way of life. They could not expect to keep down the Helots, who outnumbered them perhaps ten to one, and still maintain the old free and easy habits typical of most Greeks. Faced with the choice of making drastic changes and sacrifices or abandoning their con-

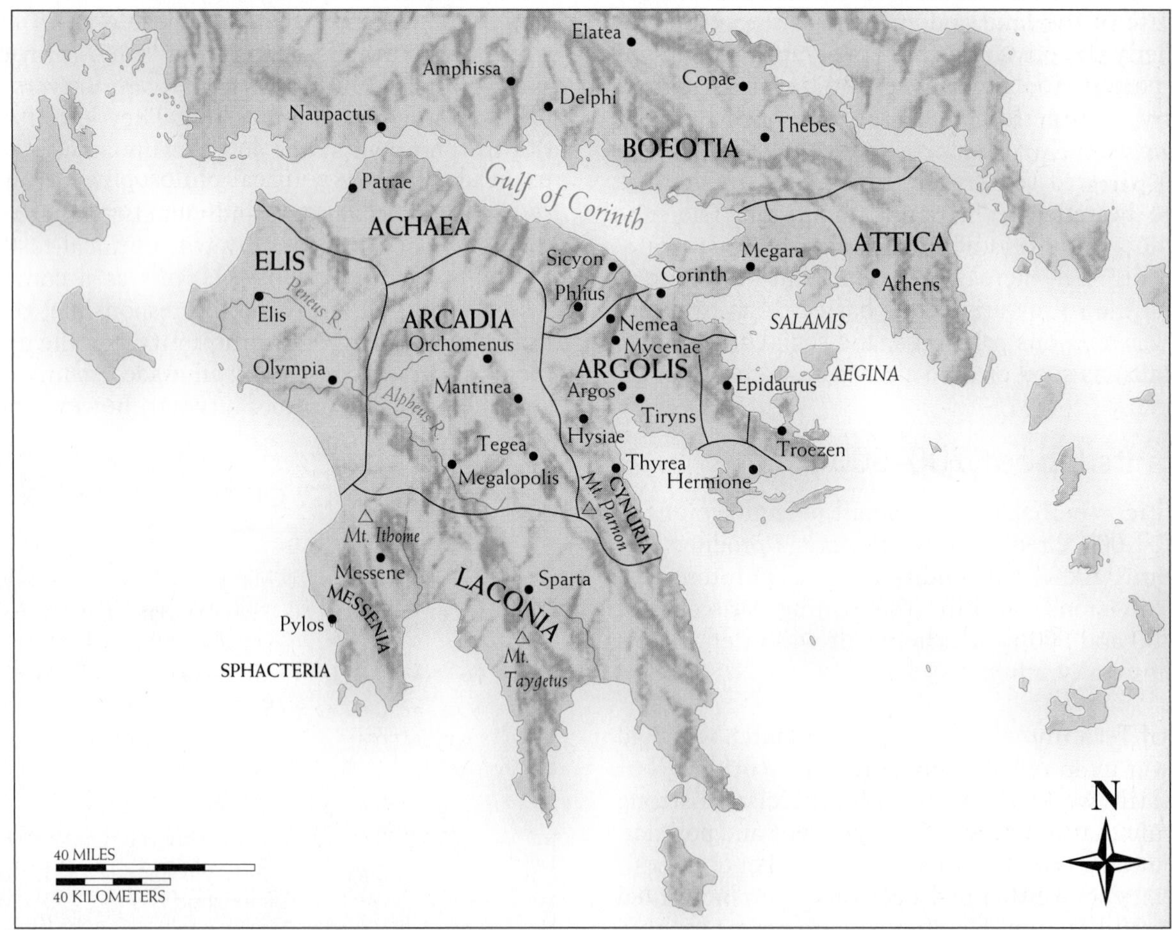

Map 2–3 **THE PELOPONNESUS** Sparta's region, Laconia, was in the Peloponnesus. Most nearby states were members of the Peloponnesian League under Sparta's leadership.

trol of Messenia, the Spartans chose to turn their city forever after into a military academy and camp.

Spartan Society The new system that emerged late in the sixth century B.C.E. exerted control over each Spartan from birth, when officials of the state decided which infants were physically fit to survive. At the age of seven, the Spartan boy was taken from his mother and turned over to young instructors. He was trained in athletics and the military arts and taught to endure privation, to bear physical pain, and to live off the country, by theft if necessary. At twenty, the Spartan youth was enrolled in the army, where he lived in barracks with his companions until the age of thirty. Marriage was permitted, but a strange sort of marriage it was, for the Spartan male could visit his wife only infrequently and by stealth. At thirty, he became a full citizen, an "equal." He took his meals at a public mess in the company of fifteen comrades. His own plot of land, worked by Helots, provided his food, a simple diet without much meat or wine. Military service was required until the age of sixty; only then could the Spartan retire to his home and family.

This educational program extended to women, too, although they were not given military training. Like males, female infants were examined for fitness to survive. Girls were given gymnastic training, were permitted greater freedom of movement than among other Greeks, and were equally indoctrinated with the idea of service to Sparta.

The entire system was designed to change the natural feelings of devotion to family and children into a more powerful commitment to the *polis*. Privacy, luxury, and even comfort were sacrificed to the purpose of producing soldiers whose physical powers, training, and discipline made them the best in the world. Nothing that might turn the mind away from duty was permitted. The very use of coins was forbidden lest it corrupt the desires of Spartans. Neither family nor money was allowed to interfere with the only ambition permitted to a Spartan male: to win glory and the respect of his peers by bravery in war.

Spartan Government The Spartan constitution was mixed, containing elements of monarchy, oligarchy, and democracy. There were two kings, whose power was limited by law and also by the rivalry that usually existed between the two royal houses. The origins and explanation of this unusual dual kingship are unknown, but both kings ruled together in Sparta and exercised equal powers. Their functions were chiefly religious and military. A Spartan army rarely left home without a king in command.

A council of elders, consisting of twenty-eight men over the age of sixty, elected for life, and the kings, represented the oligarchic element. These elders had important judicial functions, sitting as a court in cases involving the kings. They also were consulted before any proposal was put before the assembly of Spartan citizens. In a traditional society like Sparta's, they must have had considerable influence.

The Spartan assembly consisted of all males over thirty. This was thought to be the democratic element in the constitution, but its membership included only a small percentage of the entire population. Theoretically, they were the final authority, but in practice, only magistrates, elders, and kings participated in debate, and voting was usually by acclamation. Therefore, the assembly's real function was to ratify decisions already made or to decide between positions favored by the leading figures. Sparta also had a unique institution, the board of *ephors*. This consisted of five men elected annually by the assembly. Originally, boards of *ephors* appear to have been intended to check the power of the kings, but gradually they gained other important functions. They controlled foreign policy, oversaw the generalship of the kings on campaign, presided at the assembly, and guarded against rebellions by the Helots.

The whole system was remarkable both for how it combined participation by the citizenry with significant checks on its power and for its unmatched stability. Most Greeks admired the Spartan state for these qualities and also for its ability to mold citizens so thoroughly to an ideal. Many political philosophers, from Plato to modern times, have based utopian schemes on a version of Sparta's constitution and educational system.

The Peloponnesian League By about 550 B.C.E., the Spartan system was well established, and its limitations were plain. Suppression of the Helots required all the effort and energy that Sparta had. The Spartans could expand no further, but they could not allow unruly independent neighbors to cause unrest that might inflame the Helots.

When the Spartans defeated Tegea, their northern neighbor, they imposed an unusual peace. Instead of taking away land and subjugating the defeated state, Sparta left the Tegeans their land and their freedom. In exchange, they required the Tegeans to follow the Spartan lead in foreign affairs and to supply a fixed number of soldiers to Sparta on demand. This became the model for Spartan relations with the other states in the Peloponnesus. Soon Sparta was the leader of an alliance that included every Peloponnesian state but Argos; modern scholars have named this alliance the Peloponnesian League. It provided Sparta with security and made it the most powerful *polis* in Hellenic history. By 500 B.C.E., Sparta and the league had given the Greeks a force capable of facing mighty threats from abroad.

Athens

Athens—located in **Attica**—was slow to come into prominence and to join in the new activities that were changing the more advanced states. The reasons were several: Athens was not situated on the most favored trade routes of the eighth and seventh centuries B.C.E.; its large area (about 1,000 square miles) allowed population growth without great pressure; and the many villages and districts within this territory were not fully united into a single *polis* until the seventh century B.C.E. (See Map 2–4.)

Aristocratic Rule In the seventh century B.C.E., Athens was a typical aristocratic *polis*. Its people were divided into four tribes and into several clans and brotherhoods (*phratries*). The aristocrats held the most land and the best land, and dominated religious and political life. There was no written law, and powerful nobles rendered decisions on the basis of tradition and, most likely, self-interest. The **Areopagus**, a council of nobles deriving its name from the hill where it held its sessions, governed the state. Annually the council elected nine magistrates, called *archons*, who joined the Areopagus after their year in office. Because the *archons* served for only a year, were checked by their colleagues, and looked forward to a lifetime as members of the Areopagus, the aristocratic Areopagus, not the *archons*, was the true master of the state.

Pressure for Change In the seventh century B.C.E., the peaceful life of Athens was disturbed, in part by quarrels within the nobility and in part by the beginnings of an agrarian crisis. In 632 B.C.E., a nobleman named Cylon attempted a coup to establish himself as tyrant. He was thwarted, but the unrest continued.

In 621 B.C.E., a man named Draco was given special authority to codify and publish laws for the first time. In later years Draco's penalties were thought to be harsh—hence the saying that his laws were written in blood. (We still speak of unusually harsh penalties as Draconian.) Draco's work was probably limited to laws concerning homicide and was aimed at ending blood feuds between clans, but it set an important precedent: The publication of laws strengthened the hand of the state against the local power of the nobles.

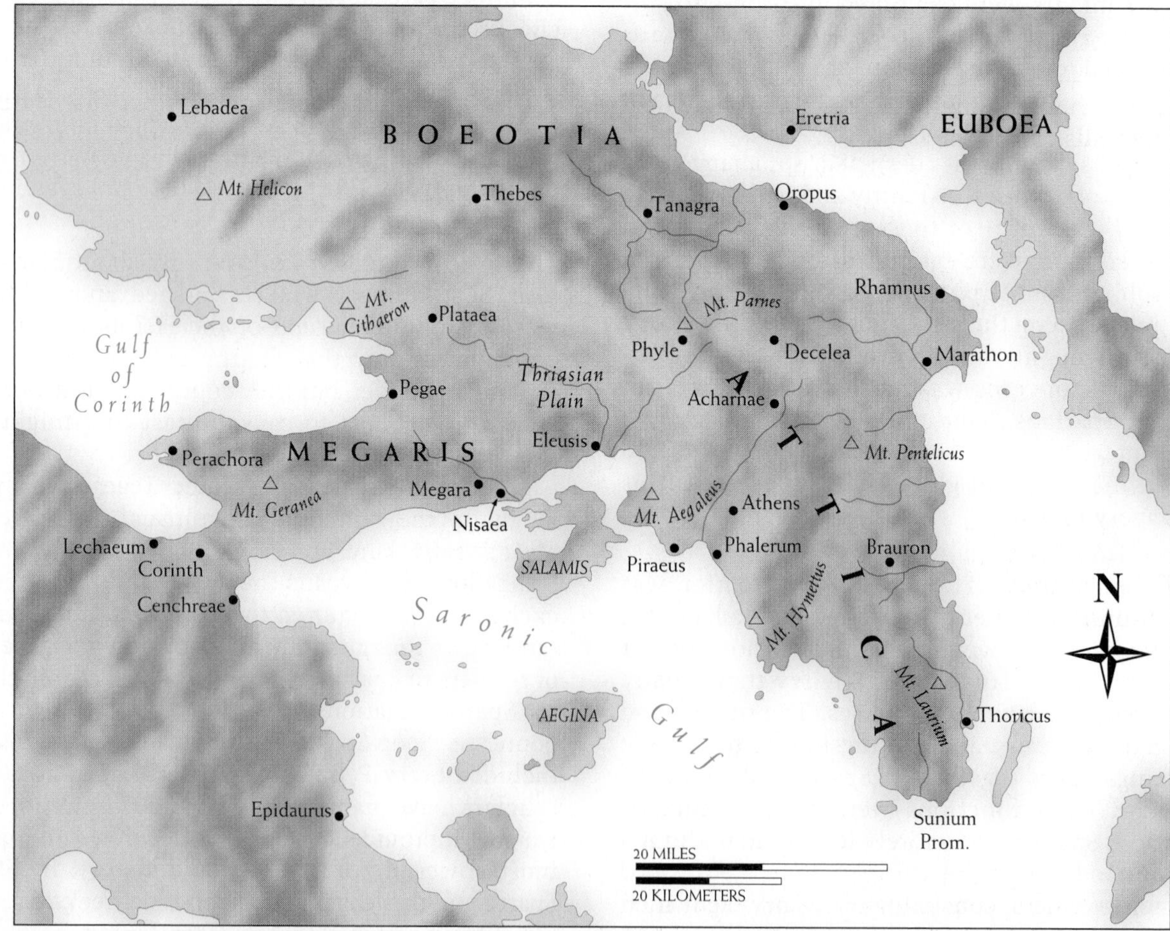

Map 2–4 **ATTICA AND VICINITY** Citizens of all towns in Attica were also citizens of Athens.

The root of Athens's troubles was agricultural. Many Athenians worked family farms, from which they obtained most of their living. It appears that they planted wheat, the staple crop, year after year without rotating fields or using enough fertilizer. Shifting to more intensive agricultural techniques and to the planting of fruit and olive trees and grapevines required capital, leading the less successful farmers to acquire excessive debt. To survive, some farmers had to borrow from wealthy neighbors to get through the year. In return, they promised one sixth of the next year's crop. The deposit of an inscribed stone on the entailed farms marked the arrangement. As their troubles persisted, debtors had to pledge their wives, their children, and themselves as surety for new loans. Inevitably, many Athenians defaulted and were enslaved. Some were even sold abroad. Revolutionary pressures grew among the poor, who began to demand the abolition of debt and a redistribution of the land.

Reforms of Solon In the year 594 B.C.E., as tradition has it, the Athenians elected Solon as the only *archon*, with extraordinary powers to legislate and revise the constitution. Immediately, he attacked the agrarian problem by canceling current debts and forbidding future loans secured by the person of the borrower. He helped bring back many Athenians enslaved abroad and freed those in Athens enslaved for debt. This program was called the "shaking off of burdens." It did not, however, solve the fundamental economic problem, and Solon did not redistribute the land.

In the short run, therefore, Solon did resolve the economic crisis, but his other economic actions had profound success in the long run. He forbade the export of wheat and encouraged that of olive oil. This policy had the initial effect of making wheat more available in Attica and encouraging the cultivation of olive oil (used in the ancient world not only as a food, but as soap and as fuel for lamps) and wine as cash crops. By the fifth century B.C.E., the cultivation of cash crops had become so profitable that much Athenian land was diverted from grain production, and Athens became dependent on imported wheat. Solon also changed the Athenian standards of weights and measures to conform with those of Corinth and Euboea and the cities of the east. This change also encouraged commerce and turned Athens in the direction that would lead it to great prosperity in the fifth century B.C.E. Solon also encouraged industry by offering citizenship to foreign artisans, and the development of the outstanding Attic pottery of the sixth century reflects his success.

Solon also changed the constitution. Citizenship had previously been the privilege of all male adults whose fathers were citizens; to their number he added those immigrants who were tradesmen and merchants. All these Athenian citizens were divided into four classes on the basis of wealth, measured by annual agricultural production. The two highest classes alone could hold the *archonship*, the chief magistracy in Athens, and sit on the Areopagus.

Men of the third class were allowed to serve as *hoplites*. They could be elected to a council of 400 chosen by all the citizens, 100 from each tribe. Solon seems to have meant this council to serve as a check on the Areopagus and to prepare any business that needed to be put before the traditional assembly of all adult male citizens. The *thetes* made up the last class. They voted in the assembly for the *archons* and the council members and on any other business brought before them by the *archons* and the council. They also sat on a new popular court established by Solon. This new court was recognized as a court of appeal, and by the fifth century B.C.E., almost all cases came before it. In Solon's Athens, as everywhere in the world before the twentieth century, women took no part in the political or judicial process.

Pisistratus the Tyrant Solon's efforts to avoid factional strife failed. Within a few years contention reached such a degree that no *archons* could be chosen. Out of this turmoil emerged the first Athenian tyranny. Pisistratus, a nobleman, leader of a faction, and military hero, briefly seized power in 560 B.C.E. and again in 556 B.C.E., but each time his support was inadequate, and he was driven out. At last, in 546 B.C.E., he came back at the head of a mercenary army from abroad and established a successful tyranny. It lasted beyond his death, in 527 B.C.E., until the expulsion of his son Hippias in 510 B.C.E.

In many respects, Pisistratus resembled the other Greek tyrants. His rule rested on the force provided by mercenary soldiers. He engaged in great programs of public works, urban improvement, and religious piety. Temples were built, and religious centers were expanded and improved. Poets and artists were supported to add cultural luster to the court of the tyrant.

Pisistratus sought to increase the power of the central government at the expense of the nobles. The newly introduced festival of the god Dionysus and the improved and expanded Great Panathenaic festival helped fix attention on the capital city, as did the new temples and the reconstruction of the *agora* as the center of public life. Circuit judges were sent out into the country to hear cases, weakening the power of the local barons. All this time Pisistratus made no formal change in the Solonian constitution. The assembly, councils, and courts met; the magistrates and councils were elected. Pisistratus merely saw to it that his supporters dominated these bodies. The intended effect was to blunt the sharp edge of tyranny with the appearance of a constitutional government, and it worked. The rule of Pisistratus was remembered as popular and mild. The unintended effect was to give the Athenians more experience in the procedures of self-government and a growing taste for it.

Aristogeiton and Harmodius were Athenian aristocrats slain in 514 B.C.E. after assassinating Hipparchus, brother of the tyrant Hippias. After the overthrow of the son of Pisistratus in 510 B.C.E., the Athenians erected a statue to honor their memory. This is a Roman copy. Aristogeiton and Harmodius of Athens ("The Tyrant Slayers"). Roman copy of Greek original. Museo Archeologico Nazionale, Naples, Italy. Photograph © Scala/Art Resource, NY

Spartan Intervention Pisistratus was succeeded by his oldest son, Hippias, who followed his father's ways at first. In 514 B.C.E., however, his brother Hipparchus was murdered as a result of a private quarrel. Hippias became nervous, suspicious, and harsh. The Alcmaeonids, one of the noble clans that Hippias and Hipparchus had exiled, won favor with the influential oracle at Delphi and used its support to persuade Sparta to attack the Athenian tyranny. Led by their ambitious king, Cleomenes I, the Spartans marched into Athenian territory in 510 B.C.E. and deposed Hippias, who went into exile to the Persian court. The tyranny was over.

The Spartans must have hoped to leave Athens in friendly hands, and indeed Cleomenes' friend Isagoras, a rival of the Alcmaeonids, held the leading position in Athens after the withdrawal of the Spartan army. Isagoras, however, faced competitors, chief among them Clisthenes of the restored Alcmaeonid clan. Clisthenes lost out in the initial political struggle among the noble factions. Isagoras seems then to have tried to restore a version of the pre-Solonian aristocratic state. As part of his plan, he removed from the citizen lists those whom Solon or Pisistratus had added and any others thought to have a doubtful claim.

Clisthenes then took an unprecedented action—he turned to the people for political support and won it with a program of great popular appeal. In response, Isagoras called in the Spartans again; Cleomenes arrived and allowed Isagoras to expel Clisthenes and many of his supporters. But the fire of Athenian political consciousness, ignited by Solon and kept alive under Pisistratus, had been fanned into flames by the popular appeal of Clisthenes. The people refused to tolerate an aristocratic restoration and drove out the Spartans and Isagoras with them. Clisthenes and his allies returned, ready to put their program into effect.

Clisthenes, the Founder of Democracy A central aim of Clisthenes' reforms was to diminish the influence of traditional localities and regions in Athenian life, for these were an important source of power for the nobility and of factions in the state. He immediately restored to citizenship those Athenians who had supported him whom Isagoras had disenfranchised, and he added new citizens to the rolls. In 508 B.C.E., he made the *deme*, the equivalent of a small town in the country or a ward in the city, the basic unit of civic life. The ***deme*** was a purely political unit that elected its own officers. The distribution of *demes* in each tribe guaranteed that no region would dominate any of them. Because the tribes had common religious activities and fought as regimental units, the new organization also increased devotion to the *polis* and diminished regional divisions and personal loyalty to local barons.

A new council of 500 replaced the Solonian council of 400. The council's main responsibility was to prepare legislation for the assembly to discuss, but it also had important financial duties and received foreign emissaries. Final authority in all things rested with the assembly of all adult male Athenian citizens. Debate in the assembly was free and open; any Athenian could submit legislation, offer amendments, or argue the merits of any question. In practice, political leaders did most of the talking. We may imagine that in the early days the council had more authority than it did after the Athenians became more confident in their new self-government.

It is fair to call Clisthenes the father of Athenian democracy. He did not alter the property qualifications of Solon, but his enlargement of the citizen rolls, his

KEY EVENTS IN THE EARLY HISTORY OF SPARTA AND ATHENS

ca. 725–710 B.C.E.	First Messenian War
ca. 650–625 B.C.E.	Second Messenian War
632 B.C.E.	Cylon tries to establish a tyranny at Athens
621 B.C.E.	Draco publishes legal code at Athens
594 B.C.E.	Solon institutes reforms at Athens
ca. 560–550 B.C.E.	Sparta defeats Tegea: Beginning of Peloponnesian League
546–527 B.C.E.	Pisistratus reigns as tyrant at Athens (main period)
510 B.C.E.	Hippias, son of Pisistratus, deposed as tyrant of Athens
ca. 508–501 B.C.E.	Clisthenes institutes reforms at Athens

diminution of the power of the aristocrats, and his elevation of the role of the assembly, with its effective and manageable council, all give him a firm claim to that title.

As a result of the work of Solon, Pisistratus, and Clisthenes, Athens entered the fifth century B.C.E. well on the way to prosperity and democracy. It was much more centralized and united than it had been, and it was ready to take its place among the major states that would lead the defense of Greece against the dangers that lay ahead.

Greek houses had no running water. This scene painted ca. 520 B.C.E. shows five women carrying water home from a fountain. "Hydria (water jug)." Greek, Archaic period, ca. 520 B.C. Attributed to the Priam Painter. Greece, Athens. Ceramic, black-figure, H: 0.53 m diam (with handles): 0.37 m. William Francis Warden Fund. © Museum of Fine Arts, Boston. Accession #61.195

▼ Life in Archaic Greece

Society

As the "Dark Ages" ended, the features that would distinguish Greek society thereafter took shape. The artisan and the merchant grew more important as contact with the non-Hellenic world became easier. Most people, however, continued to make their living from the land. Wealthy aristocrats with large estates, powerful households, families, and clans led different lives from those of the poorer countryfolk and the independent farmers who had smaller and less fertile fields.

Farmers Ordinary country people rarely leave a written record of their thoughts or activities, and we have no such record from ancient Greece. The poet Hesiod (ca. 700 B.C.E.), however, was certainly no aristocrat. He presented himself as a small farmer, and his *Works and Days* gives some idea of the life of such a farmer. The crops included grain—chiefly barley, but also wheat; grapes for making wine; olives for food and oil; green vegetables, especially the bean; and some fruit. Sheep and goats provided milk and cheese. The Homeric heroes had great herds of cattle and ate lots of meat, but by Hesiod's time land fertile enough to provide fodder for cattle was needed to grow grain. He and small farmers like him tasted meat chiefly from sacrificial animals at festivals.

These farmers worked hard to make a living. Although Hesiod had the help of oxen and mules and one or two hired helpers for occasional labor, his life was one of continuous toil. The hardest work came in October, at the start of the rainy season, the time for the first plowing. The plow was light and easily broken, and the work of forcing the iron tip into the earth was backbreaking, even with the help of a team of oxen. For the less fortunate farmer, the cry of the crane that announced the time of year to plow "bites the heart of the man without oxen." Autumn and winter were the time for cutting wood, building wagons, and making tools. Late winter was the time to tend to the vines, May was the time to harvest the grain, July to winnow and store it. Only at the height of summer's heat did Hesiod allow for rest, but when September came, it was time to harvest the grapes. As soon as that task was done the cycle started again. The work went on under the burning sun and in the freezing cold.

Hesiod wrote nothing of pleasure or entertainment, but his poetry displays an excitement and pride that reveals the new hopes of a rural population more dynamic and confident than we know of anywhere else in the ancient world. Less austere farmers than Hesiod gathered at the blacksmith's shop for warmth and companionship in winter, and even he must have taken part in religious rites and festivals that were accompanied by some kind of entertainment. Nonetheless, the lives of yeoman farmers were certainly hard and their pleasures few.

Aristocrats Most aristocrats were rich enough to employ many hired laborers, sometimes sharecroppers, and sometimes even slaves, to work their extensive lands. They could therefore enjoy leisure for other activities. The center of aristocratic social life was the drinking party, or ***symposium***. This activity was not a mere drinking bout meant to remove inhibitions and produce oblivion. The Greeks, in fact, almost always mixed their wine with water, and one of the goals of the participants was to drink as much as the others without becoming drunk.

The *symposium* was a carefully organized occasion, with a "king" chosen to set the order of events and to determine that night's mixture of wine and water. Only men took part; they ate and drank as they reclined on couches along the walls of the room. The sessions began with prayers and libations to the gods. Usually there were games, such as dice or *kottabos*, in which wine was flicked from the cups at different targets. Sometimes dancing girls or flute girls offered entertainment. Frequently the aristocratic participants provided their own amusements with songs, poetry, or even philosophical disputes. Characteristically, these took the form of contests, with some kind of prize for the winner, for aristocratic values continued to emphasize competition and the need to excel, whatever the arena.

This aspect of aristocratic life appears in the athletic contests that became widespread early in the sixth century. The games included running events; the long jump; the discus and javelin throws; the pentathlon, which included all of these; boxing; wrestling; and the chariot race. Only the rich could afford to raise, train, and race horses, so the chariot race was a special preserve of aristocracy. The nobility also especially favored wrestling, and the *palaestra*, or fields, where they practiced became an important social center for the aristocracy. The contrast between the hard, drab life of the farmers and the leisured and lively one of the aristocrats could hardly have been greater. (See "Encountering the Past: Greek Athletics.")

Religion

Like most ancient peoples, the Greeks were **polytheists**, and religion played an important part in their lives. Much of Greek art and literature was closely connected with religion, as was the life of the *polis* in general.

Olympian Gods The Greek pantheon consisted of the twelve gods who lived on Mount Olympus. These were

- Zeus, the father of the gods
- Hera, his wife

Zeus's siblings:

- Poseidon, his brother, god of the seas and earthquakes
- Hestia, his sister, goddess of the hearth
- Demeter, his sister, goddess of agriculture and marriage

and Zeus's children:

- Aphrodite, goddess of love and beauty
- Apollo, god of the sun, music, poetry, and prophecy
- Ares, god of war
- Artemis, goddess of the moon and the hunt
- Athena, goddess of wisdom and the arts
- Hephaestus, god of fire and metallurgy
- Hermes, messenger of the gods, connected with commerce and cunning

These gods were seen as behaving much like mortals, with all the foibles of humans, except they were superhuman in these as well as in their strength and immortality. In contrast, Zeus, at least, was seen as a source of human justice, and even the Olympians were understood to be subordinate to the Fates. Each *polis* had one of the Olympians as its guardian deity and worshipped that god in its own special way, but all the gods were Panhellenic. In the eighth and seventh centuries B.C.E., common shrines were established at Olympia for the worship of Zeus, at Delphi for Apollo, at the Isthmus of Corinth for Poseidon, and at Nemea once again for Zeus. Each held athletic contests in honor of its deity, to which all Greeks were invited and for which a sacred truce was declared.

Immortality and Morality Besides the Olympians, the Greeks also worshipped countless lesser deities connected with local shrines. They even worshipped human heroes, real or legendary, who had accomplished great deeds and had earned immortality and divine status. The worship of these deities was not a very emotional experience. It was a matter of offering prayer, libations, and gifts in return for protection and favors from the god during the lifetime of the worshipper. The average human had no hope of immortality, and these devotions involved little moral teaching.

Most Greeks seem to have held to the commonsense notion that justice lay in paying one's debts. They thought that civic virtue consisted of worshipping the

GREEK ATHLETICS

ATHLETIC CONTESTS WERE central to life in ancient Greece. From the mythical world portrayed in the eighth century B.C.E. in Homer's *Iliad* and *Odyssey* almost until the fall of the Roman Empire in the late fifth century C.E., organized athletic games were the focus of attention not only for the competitors and spectators but throughout the Hellenic world. Victors won praise and everlasting fame in the verses of great poets like Pindar (ca. 522–ca. 440 B.C.E.) and received extraordinary honors from their native cities.

The games were part of religious festivals held all over the Greek lands. The gods—Zeus, Apollo, Poseidon—were thought to enjoy the same pleasures as mortals and so to delight in contests that tested physical excellence. The most famous and prestigious were the Olympic games, held every four years in honor of Zeus at Olympia, which were said to have begun in 776 B.C.E.

Team games were of little interest to the Greeks, who preferred contests among individuals, where each man—and all the contestants were males—could demonstrate his individual excellence. By the fifth century B.C.E., the athletes competed in the nude and anointed their bodies with oil. Running events included the stadium run, a sprint of about 200 meters that carried the most prestige of all; a run of twice that distance; a distance race of about 4,800 meters; and a race in armor. Field events consisted of the long jump, and the discus and javelin throws. Combat sports included wrestling, boxing, and the *pankration*; a kind of no-holds-barred contest that forbade gouging and biting but permitted just about anything else, including kicking and breaking of fingers.

The prizes for victors were wreaths or crowns of olive, laurel, pine leaves, or wild celery. The common conception that ancient Greek athletes were pure amateurs competing merely for laurel wreaths and honors is, however, an oversimplification. The cities of the victors were free to add more tangible rewards. In Athens, Olympic winners were honored with free meals at the town hall for life. Many festivals—but not the Olympics—also awarded cash prizes, some worth far more than the annual salary of a working man. Victors could earn wealth as well as glory.

What kinds of contests made up Greek athletics?

What were the incentives for Greek athletes?

A foot race, probably a sprint, at the Panathenaic Games in Athens, ca. 580 B.C.E. National Archives and Records Administration

A Closer LOOK

THE TRIREME

THE TRIREME WAS the warship that dominated naval warfare in the Mediterranean in the fifth and fourth centuries B.C.E. The naval battles of the Persian Wars and the Peloponnesian War were fought between fleets of triremes—light, fast, and maneuverable ships powered by oars. This is a picture of the *Olympias*, a modern reconstruction of an ancient trireme, commissioned by the Greek navy.

The trireme was propelled by 170 rowers in three tiers along each side of the vessel: 31 in the top tier, 27 in the middle, and 27 in the bottom. It was about 120 feet long and 18 feet wide, with a hull that was made of a thin shell of planks joined edge-to-edge and then stiffened by a keel and light transverse ribs. The mast supported a sail that could help propel the ship when the wind was favorable. During battle, however, the mast was taken down, and the trireme maneuvered by oars alone.

After the Persian Wars, the Athenians built the largest and best navy in the ancient Mediterranean, developing the trireme to its highest level of skill and efficiency.

The principal armament of the trireme was a bronze-clad ram, which extended from the keel at or below the waterline and was designed to pierce the light hulls of enemy warships. The ship also carried spearmen and bowmen who sometimes attacked enemy crews and could be landed like today's marines to fight on shore.

To examine this image in an interactive fashion, please go to www.myhistorylab.com

PEARSON myhistorylab

state deities in the traditional way, performing required public services, and fighting in defense of the state. To them, private morality meant to do good to one's friends and harm to one's enemies.

The Cult of Delphian Apollo In the sixth century B.C.E., the influence of the cult of Apollo at Delphi and of his oracle there became great. The oracle was the most important of several that helped satisfy the human craving for a clue to the future. The priests of Apollo preached moderation; the two famous sayings identified with Apollo: "Know thyself" and "Nothing in excess" exemplified their advice. Humans needed self-control (*sophrosynē*). Its opposite was arrogance (***hubris***), brought on by excessive wealth or good fortune. *Hubris* led to moral blindness and, finally, to divine vengeance. This theme of moderation and the dire consequences of its absence was central to Greek popular morality and appears frequently in Greek literature.

The Cult of Dionysus and the Orphic Cult The somewhat cold religion of the Olympian gods and of the cult of Apollo did little to assuage human fears or satisfy human hopes and passions. For these needs, the Greeks turned to other deities and rites. Of these deities, the most popular was Dionysus, a god of nature and fertility, of the grapevine, drunkenness, and sexual abandon. In some of his rites, this god was followed by *maenads*, female devotees who cavorted by night, ate raw flesh, and were reputed to tear to pieces any creature they came across.

The Orphic cult, named after its supposed founder, the mythical poet Orpheus, provided its followers with more hope than did the worship of the twelve Olympians. Cult followers are thought to have refused to kill animals or eat their flesh and to have believed in the transmigration of souls, which offered the prospect of some form of life after death.

This Attic cup from the fifth century B.C.E. shows the two great poets from the island of Lesbos, Sappho (right) and Alcaeus.
Hirmer Fotoarchiv

Poetry

The poetry of the sixth century B.C.E. also reflected the great changes sweeping through the Greek world. The lyric style—poetry meant to be sung, either by a chorus or by one person—predominated. Sappho of Lesbos, Anacreon of Teos, and Simonides of Cos composed personal poetry, often relating the pleasure and agony of love. Alcaeus of Mytilene, an aristocrat driven from his city by a tyrant, wrote bitter invective.

Perhaps the most interesting poet of the century from a political point of view was Theognis of Megara. He was an aristocrat who lived through a tyranny, an unusually chaotic and violent democracy, and an oligarchy that restored order but ended the rule of the old aristocracy. Theognis was the spokesperson for the old, defeated aristocracy of birth. He divided everyone into two classes, the noble and the base; the former were the good, the latter bad. Those nobly born must associate only with others like themselves if they were to preserve their virtue; if they mingled with the base, they became base. Those born base, however, could never become noble. Only nobles could aspire to virtue and possessed the critical moral and intellectual qualities—respect or honor and judgment. These qualities could not be taught; they were innate. Even so, they had to be carefully guarded against corruption by wealth or by mingling with the base. Intermarriage between the noble and the base was especially condemned. These were the ideas of the unreconstructed nobility, whose power had been destroyed or reduced in most Greek states by this time. Such ideas remained alive in aristocratic hearts throughout the next century and greatly influenced later thinkers, Plato among them.

▼ The Persian Wars

The Greeks' period of fortunate isolation and freedom ended in the sixth century B.C.E. They had established colonies along most of the coast of Asia Minor from as early as the eleventh century B.C.E. The colonies maintained friendly relations with the mainland but developed a flourishing economic and cultural life independent of their mother cities and of their eastern neighbors. In the middle of the sixth century B.C.E., however, these Greek cities of Asia Minor came under the control of Lydia and its king, Croesus (ca. 560–546 B.C.E.). Lydian rule seems not to have been harsh, but the Persian conquest of Lydia in 546 B.C.E. brought a less pleasant subjugation. (See Chapter 1.)

The Ionian Rebellion

The Ionian Greeks (those living on the central part of the west coast of Asia Minor and nearby islands) had been moving toward democracy and were not pleased to find themselves under the monarchical rule of Persia. That rule, however, was not overly burdensome at first. The Persians required their subjects to pay tribute and to serve in the Persian army. They ruled the Greek cities through local individuals, who governed their cities as "tyrants." Most of the tyrants, however, were not harsh, the Persian tribute was not excessive, and the Greeks enjoyed general prosperity. Neither the death of the Persian king Cyrus the Great fighting on a distant frontier in 530 B.C.E., nor the suicide of his successor Cambyses, nor the civil war that followed it in 522–521 B.C.E. produced any disturbance in the Greek cities. When Darius emerged as Great King in 521 B.C.E., he found **Ionia** perfectly obedient.

The private troubles of the ambitious tyrant of Miletus, Aristagoras, ended this calm. He had urged a Persian expedition against the island of Naxos; when it failed, he feared the consequences and organized the Ionian rebellion of 499 B.C.E. To gain support, he overthrew the tyrannies and proclaimed democratic constitutions. Then he turned to the mainland states for help, petitioning first Sparta, the most powerful Greek state. The Spartans, however, would have none of Aristagoras's promises of easy victory and great wealth. They had no close ties with the Ionians and no national interest in the region. Furthermore, the thought of leaving their homeland undefended against the Helots while their army was far off terrified them.

Aristagoras next sought help from the Athenians, who were related to the Ionians and had close ties of religion and tradition with them. Besides, Hippias, the deposed tyrant of Athens, was an honored guest at the court of Darius, who had already made it plain that he favored the tyrant's restoration. The Persians, moreover, controlled both sides of the Hellespont, the route to the grain fields beyond the Black Sea that were increasingly vital to Athens. Perhaps some Athenians already feared that a Persian attempt to conquer the Greek mainland was only a matter of time. The Athenian assembly agreed to send a fleet of twenty ships to help the rebels. The Athenian expedition was strengthened by five ships from Eretria in Euboea, which participated out of gratitude for past favors.

In 498 B.C.E., the Athenians and their allies made a surprise attack on Sardis, the old capital of Lydia and now the seat of the *satrap*, and burned it. This action caused the revolt to spread throughout the Greek cities of Asia Minor outside Ionia, but the Ionians could not follow it up. The Athenians withdrew and took no further part. Gradually the Persians reimposed their will. In 495 B.C.E., they defeated the Ionian fleet at Lade, and in the next year they wiped out Miletus. The Ionian rebellion was over.

The War in Greece

In 490 B.C.E., the Persians launched an expedition directly across the Aegean to punish Eretria and Athens, to restore Hippias, and to gain control of the Aegean Sea. (See Map 2–5.) They landed their infantry and cavalry forces first at Naxos, destroying it for its successful resistance in 499 B.C.E. Then they destroyed Eretria and deported its people deep into the interior of Persia.

Marathon Rather than submit and accept the restoration of the hated tyranny of Hippias, the Athenians chose to resist the Persian forces bearing down on them and risk the same fate that had just befallen Eretria. Miltiades, an Athenian who had fled from Persian service, led the city's army to confront the Persians at Marathon. There some 10,000 Athenians, and the Plataeans defeated two or three times their number, killing thousands of the enemy while losing only 192 of their own men.

A Persian victory at Marathon would have destroyed Athenian freedom and led to the conquest of all the mainland Greeks. The greatest achievements of Greek culture, most of which lay in the future, would never have occurred. But the Athenians won a decisive victory, instilling them with a sense of confidence and pride in their *polis*, their unique form of government, and themselves.

The Great Invasion Internal troubles prevented the Persians from taking swift revenge for their loss at Marathon. Almost ten years elapsed before Darius's successor, Xerxes, in 481 B.C.E., gathered an army of at least 150,000 men and a navy of more than 600 ships to conquer Greece. In Athens, Themistocles, who favored making Athens into a naval power, had become the leading politician. During his *archonship* in 493 B.C.E., Athens had already built a fortified port at Piraeus. A decade later the Athenians came upon a rich vein of silver in the state mines, and Themistocles persuaded them to use the profits to increase their fleet. By 480 B.C.E., Athens had over two hundred ships, the backbone of a navy that was to defeat the Persians.

Of the hundreds of Greek states, only thirty-one—led by Sparta, Athens, Corinth, and Aegina—were willing to fight as the Persian army gathered south of the Hellespont. In the spring of 480 B.C.E., Xerxes launched his invasion. The Persian strategy was to march into Greece, destroy Athens, defeat the Greek army, and add the Greeks to the number of Persian subjects. The huge Persian army needed to keep in touch with the fleet for supplies. If the Greeks could defeat the Persian navy, the army could not remain in Greece long. Themistocles

Map 2–5 **THE PERSIAN INVASION OF GREECE** This map traces the route taken by the Persian king Xerxes in his invasion of Greece in 480 B.C.E. The gray arrows show movements of Xerxes' army, the purple arrows show movements of his navy, and the green arrows show movements of the Greek army and navy.

knew that the Aegean was subject to sudden devastating storms. His strategy was to delay the Persian army and then to bring on the kind of naval battle he might hope to win. (See "Compare & Connect: Greek Strategy in the Persian War," on page 56.)

Severe storms wrecked many Persian ships while the Greek fleet waited safely in a protected harbor. Then Xerxes attacked Thermopylae, and for two days the Greeks butchered his best troops without serious loss to themselves. On the third day, however, a traitor

COMPARE AND CONNECT Greek Strategy in the Persian War

IN THE SUMMER of 480 B.C.E., Xerxes, Great King of Persia, took an enormous invading army into Greece. During the previous year those Greeks who meant to resist met to plan a defense. After abandoning an attempt to make a stand at Tempe in Thessaly, they fell back to central Greece, at Thermopylae on land and Artemisium at sea. Herodotus is our main source and his account of the Greek strategy is not clear. How did the Greeks hope to check the Persians? Did they hope to stop them for good at Thermopylae, or was the idea to force a sea battle at Artemisium? Were both the army and the fleet intended only to fight holding actions until the Athenians fled to Salamis and the Peloponnesus? Scholars have long argued these questions, which have been sharpened by the discovery of the "Themistocles Decree," an inscription from the third century B.C.E. which purports to be an Athenian decree passed in 480 B.C.E. before the Battle of Artemisium. The authenticity of the decree is still in question, but if it reflects a reliable tradition, it must influence our view in important ways.

QUESTIONS

1. **In Herodotus' account what is the state of the Athenian preparation?**
2. **What light does it reflect on the original Greek strategy for the war?**
3. **Was the Themistocles Decree passed before or after the battle at Thermopylae? What light does this decree shed on Greek strategy?**
4. **How do the two documents compare?**
5. **Are they incompatible?**

I. The Account of Herodotus

In this passage Herodotus describes Athens after the Greek defeat at Thermopylae.

Meanwhile, the Grecian fleet, which had left Artemisium, proceeded to Salamis, at the request of the Athenians, and there cast anchor. The Athenians had begged them to take up this position, in order that they might convey their women and children out of Attica, and further might deliberate upon the course which it now behooved them to follow. Disappointed in the hopes which they had previously entertained, they were about to hold a council concerning the present posture of their affairs. For they had looked to see the Peloponnesians drawn up in full force to resist the enemy in Boeotia, but found nothing of what they had expected; nay, they learnt that the Greeks of those parts, only concerning themselves about their own safety, were building a wall across the Isthmus, and intended to guard the Peloponnese, and let the rest of Greece take its chance. These tidings caused them to make the request whereof I spoke, that the combined fleet should anchor at Salamis.

So while the rest of the fleet lay to off this island, the Athenians cast anchor along their own coast. Immediately upon their arrival, proclamation was made, that every Athenian should save his children and household as he best could; whereupon some sent their families to Aegina, some to Salamis, but the greater number to Troezen. This removal was made with all possible haste, partly from a desire to obey the advice of the oracle, but still more for another reason. The Athenians say they have in their acropolis a huge serpent which lives in the temple, and is the guardian of the whole place. Nor do they only say this, but, as if the serpent really dwelt there, every month they lay out its food, which consists of a honey-cake. Up to this time the honey-cake had always been consumed; but now it lay untouched. So the priestess told the people what had happened; whereupon they left Athens the more readily, since they believed that the goddess had abandoned the citadel.

Source: Herodotus, *Histories* 8.40.41, trans. by George Rawlinson.

II. The Themistocles Decree

THE GODS

Resolved by the Council and the People

Themistocles, son of Neokles, of Phrearroi, made the motion:

To entrust the city to Athena the Mistress of Athens and to all the other Gods to guard and defend from the Barbarian for the sake of the land. The Athenians themselves and the foreigners who live in Athens are to send their children and women to safety in Troizen, their protector being Pittheus, the founding hero of the land. They are to send the old men and their movable possessions to safety on Salamis. The treasurers and priestesses are to remain on the acropolis guarding the property of the gods.

All the other Athenians and foreigners of military age are to embark on the 200 ships that are ready and defend against the Barbarian for the sake of their own freedom and that of the rest of the Greeks along with the Lakedaimonians, the Korinthians, the Aiginetans, and all others who wish to share the danger.

The generals are to appoint, starting tomorrow, 200 trierarchs [captains], one to a ship, from among those who have land and house in Athens and legitimate children and who are not older than fifty; to these men the ships are to be assigned by lot. They are to enlist marines, 10 to each ship, from men between the ages of twenty and thirty, and four archers. They are to distribute the servicemen [the marines and archers] by lot at the same time as they assign the trierarchs to the ships by lot. The generals are to write up the rest ship by ship on white boards, (taking) the Athenians from the lexiarchic registers, the foreigners from those registered with the polemarch. They are to write them up assigning them by divisions, 200 of about one hundred (men) each, and to write above each division the name of the trireme and of the trierarch and the servicemen, so that they may know on which trireme each division is to embark. When all the divisions have been composed and allotted to the triremes, the Council and the generals are to man all the 200 ships, after sacrificing a placatory offering to Zeus the Almighty and Athena and Nike and Poseidon the Securer.

When the ships have been manned, with 100 of them they are to meet the enemy at Artemision in Euboia, and with the other 100 they are to lie off Salamis and the coast of Attica and keep guard over the land. In order that all Athenians may be united in their defense against the Barbarian those who have been sent into exile for ten years are to go to Salamis and to stay there until the People come to some decision about them, while those who have been deprived of citizen rights are to have their rights restored . . .

Source: "Waiting for the Barbarian," *Greece and Rome*, second series, 8 trans. by Michael H. Jameson (Oxford, 1961), pp. 5–18. By permission of the Oxford University Press.

The Greek League, founded specifically to resist this Persian invasion, met at Corinth as the Persians were ready to cross the Hellespont. They chose Sparta as leader and first confronted the Persians at Thermopylae, the "hot gates," on land and off Artemisium at sea. The opening between the mountains and the sea at Thermopylae was so narrow that a small army could hold it against a much larger one. The Spartans sent their king, Leonidas, with 300 of their own citizens and enough allies to make a total of about 9,000.

A Greek *hoplite* attacks a Persian soldier. The contrast between the Greek's metal body armor, large shield, and long spear and the Persian's cloth and leather garments indicates one reason the Greeks won. This Attic vase was found on Rhodes and dates from ca. 475 B.C.E. Greek. Vase, Red-figured. Attic. ca. 480–470 B.C. Neck amphora, Nolan type. Side 1: "Greek warrior attacking a Persian." Said to be from Rhodes. Terracotta. H. 13-11/16 in. The Metropolitan Museum of Art, Rogers Fund, 1906. (06.1021.117) Photograph © 1986 The Metropolitan Museum of Art

THE GREEK WARS AGAINST PERSIA

ca. 560–546 B.C.E.	Greek cities of Asia Minor conquered by Croesus of Lydia
546 B.C.E.	Cyrus of Persia conquers Lydia and gains control of Greek cities
499–494 B.C.E.	Greek cities rebel (Ionian rebellion)
490 B.C.E.	Battle of Marathon
480–479 B.C.E.	Xerxes' invasion of Greece
480 B.C.E.	Battles of Thermopylae, Artemisium, and Salamis
479 B.C.E.	Battles of Plataea and Mycale

showed the Persians a mountain trail that permitted them to come on the Greeks from behind. Many allies escaped, but Leonidas and his 300 Spartans all died fighting. At about the same time, the Greek and Persian fleets fought an indecisive battle at Artemisium. The fall of Thermopylae, however, forced the Greek navy to withdraw.

After Thermopylae, the Persian army moved into Attica and burned Athens. If an inscription discovered in 1959 is authentic, Themistocles had foreseen this possibility before Thermopylae, and the Athenians had begun to evacuate their homeland before they sent their fleet north to fight at Artemisium.

Defeating the Persians A sea battle in the narrow waters to the east of the island of Salamis, to which the Greek fleet withdrew after the battle at Artemisium, decided the fate of Greece. The Peloponnesians were reluctant to confront the Persian fleet at this spot, but Themistocles persuaded them to stay by threatening to resettle all the Athenians in Italy. The Spartans knew that they and the other Greeks could not hope to win without the aid of the Athenians. Because the Greek ships were fewer, slower, and less maneuverable than those of the Persians, the Greeks put soldiers on their ships and relied chiefly on hand-to-hand combat. In the ensuing battle the Persians lost more than half their ships and retreated to Asia with a good part of their army, but the danger was not over yet.

The Persian general Mardonius spent the winter in central Greece, and in the spring he unsuccessfully tried to win the Athenians away from the Greek League. The Spartan regent, Pausanias, then led the largest Greek army up to that time to confront Mardonius in Boeotia. At Plataea, in the summer of 479 B.C.E., the Persians suffered a decisive defeat. Mardonius died in battle, and his army fled.

Meanwhile the Ionian Greeks urged King Leotychidas, the Spartan commander of the fleet, to fight the Persian fleet. At Mycale, on the coast of Samos, Leotychidas destroyed the Persian camp and its fleet. The Persians fled the Aegean and Ionia. For the moment, at least, the Persian threat was gone.

In Perspective

Hellenic civilization, that unique cultural experience at the root of Western civilization, has powerfully influenced the peoples of the modern world. It was itself influenced by the great Bronze Age civilization of Crete called Minoan and emerged from the collapse of the Bronze Age civilization on the Greek mainland called Mycenaean. These earlier Aegean civilizations more closely resembled other early civilizations in Egypt, Mesopotamia, Syria-Palestine, and elsewhere than the Hellenic civilization that sprang from them. They had highly developed cities; a system of writing; a strong, centralized monarchical government with tightly organized, large bureaucracies; hierarchical social systems; professional standing armies; and a regular system of taxation to support it all. To a greater or lesser degree, these early civilizations tended toward cultural stability—changing little over time—and uniformity—all sharing many structural features. The striking thing about the emergence of the Hellenic civilization is its sharp departure from this pattern.

The collapse of the Mycenaean world produced a harsh material and cultural decline for the Greeks. Small farm villages replaced cities. Trade all but ended, and communication among the Greeks themselves and between them and other peoples was sharply curtailed. The art of writing was lost for more than three centuries. During this "Dark Age," the rest of the world ignored the Greeks—poor, few in number, isolated, and illiterate—and left them alone to develop their own society and the matrix of Hellenic civilization.

During the three-and-a-half centuries from about 1100 to 750 B.C.E., the Greeks set the foundations for their great achievements. The crucial unit in the new Greek way of life was the *polis*, the Hellenic city-state. There were hundreds of them, and each evoked a kind of loyalty and attachment by its citizens that made the idea of dissolving one's own *polis* into a larger unit unthinkable. The result was a dynamic, many-faceted, competitive, sometimes chaotic world in which rivalry for excellence and victory had the highest value. This agonistic, or competitive, quality marks Greek life throughout its history. Its negative aspect was constant warfare among the states. Its positive side was an extraordinary achievement in literature and art; competition, sometimes formal and organized, spurred on poets and artists.

Kings had been swept away with the Mycenaean world, and the *poleis* were republics. Since the Greeks were so poor, the differences in wealth among them were relatively small. Therefore, class distinctions were less marked and important than in other civilizations. The introduction of a new mode of fighting, the *hoplite* phalanx, had further leveling effects, for it placed the safety of the state in the hands of the average farmer. Armies were made up of citizen-soldiers, who were not paid and who returned to their farms after a campaign. As a result, a relatively large portion of the people shared political control, and participation in political life was highly valued. There was no bureaucracy, for there were no kings and not much economic surplus to support bureaucrats. Most states imposed no regular taxation. There was no separate caste of priests and little concern with life after death. In this varied, dynamic, secular, and remarkably free context, speculative natural philosophy arose based on observation and reason, the root of modern natural science and philosophy.

Contact with the rest of the world increased trade and wealth and brought in valuable new information and ideas. Egyptian and Near Eastern models that were always adapted and changed, rather than copied, powerfully shaped Greek art. Changes often produced social and economic strain, leading to the overthrow of traditional aristocratic regimes by tyrants. But monarchic rule was anathema to the Greeks, and these regimes were temporary. In Athens, the destruction of the tyranny brought the world's first democracy. Sparta, in contrast, developed a uniquely stable government that avoided tyranny and impressed the other Greeks.

The Greeks' time of independent development, untroubled by external forces, ended in the sixth century, when Persia conquered the Greek cities of Asia Minor. When the Persian kings tried to conquer the Greek mainland, however, the leading states managed to put their quarrels aside and unite against the common enemy. Their determination to preserve their freedom carried them to victory over tremendous odds.

REVIEW QUESTIONS

1. How did the later Bronze Age Mycenaean civilization differ from the Minoan civilization of Crete in political organization, art motifs, and military posture?
2. What are the most important historical sources for the Minoan and Mycenaean civilizations? What is Linear B, and what problems does it raise for the reconstruction of Bronze Age history? How valuable are the Homeric epics as sources of early Greek history?
3. What was a *polis*? What role did geography play in its development, and why did the Greeks consider it a unique and valuable institution?
4. What were the fundamental political, social, and economic institutions of Athens and Sparta in about 500 B.C.E.? Why did Sparta develop its unique form of government?
5. What were the main stages in the transformation of Athens from an aristocratic state to a democracy between 600 and 500 B.C.E.? In what ways did Draco, Solon, Pisistratus, and Clisthenes each contribute to the process?
6. Why did the Greeks and Persians go to war in 490 and 480 B.C.E.? Why did the Persians want to conquer Greece? Why were the Greeks able to defeat the Persians and how did they benefit from the victory?

SUGGESTED READINGS

E. K. Anhalt, *Solon the Singer*. A fine study of the Athenian poet-politician.

W. Burkert, *The Orientalizing Revolution: Near Eastern Influence on Greek Culture in the Early Archaic Age* (1992). A study of the Eastern impact on Greek literature and religion from 750 to 650 B.C.E.

J. Chadwick, *The Mycenaean World* (1976). A readable account by an author who helped decipher Mycenaean writing.

R. Drews, *The Coming of the Greeks* (1988). A fine study of the arrival of the Greeks as part of the movement of Indo-European peoples.

J. V. A. Fine, *The Ancient Greeks* (1983). An excellent survey that discusses historical problems and the evidence that gives rise to them.

M. I. Finley, *World of Odysseus*, rev. ed. (1965). A fascinating attempt to reconstruct Homeric society.

V. D. Hanson, *The Other Greeks* (1995). A revolutionary account of the invention of the family farm by the Greeks and the central role of agrarianism in shaping the Greek city-state.

V. D. Hanson, *The Western Way of War* (1989). A brilliant and lively discussion of the rise and character of the *hoplite* phalanx and its influence on Greek society.

J. M. Hurwit, *The Art and Culture of Early Greece* (1985). A fascinating study of the art of early Greece in its literary and cultural context.

W. K. Lacey, *The Family in Ancient Greece* (1984).

P. B. Manville, *The Origins of Citizenship in Ancient Athens* (1990). An examination of the origins of citizenship in the time of Solon of Athens.

J. F. McGlew, *Tyranny and Political Culture in Ancient Greece* (1993). A study of tyranny and its effect on Greek political tradition.

S. G. Miller, *Ancient Greek Athletics* (2004). The best available account.

R. Osborne, *Greece in the Making, 1200–479 B.C.* (1996). An up-to-date, well-illustrated account of early Greek history.

S. Price, *Religions of the Ancient Greeks* (1999). A valuable survey from early times through the fifth century B.C.E.

R. Sallares, *The Ecology of the Ancient Greek World* (1991). A valuable study of the Greeks and their environment.

D. M. Schaps, *Economic Rights of Women in Ancient Greece* (1981).

B. Strauss, *The Battle of Salamis: The Naval Encounter That Saved Greece—and Western Civilization* (2004). A lively account of the great Persian invasion of Greece.

C. G. Thomas and C. Conant, *Citadel to City-State: The Transformation of Greece, 1200–700 B.C.E.* (1999). A good account of Greece's emergence from the Dark Ages into the world of the *polis*.

H. van Wees, *Greek Warfare: Myths and Realities* (2004). An account of Greek fighting that challenges traditional understandings.

For additional learning resources related to this chapter, please go to www.myhistorylab.com

PEARSON myhistorylab

The Winged Victory of Samothrace. This is one of the great masterpieces of Hellenistic sculpture. It appears to be the work of the Rhodian sculptor Pythokritos, about 200 B.C.E. The statue stood in the sanctuary of the Great Gods on the Aegean island of Samothrace on a base made in the shape of a ship's prow. The goddess is seen as landing on the ship to crown its victorious commander and crew. The Nike of Samothrace, goddess of victory. Marble figure (190 B.C.E.) from Rhodos, Greece. Height 328 cm, MA 2369, Louvre, Dpt. des Antiquités Grecques/Romaines, Paris, France. Photograph © Erich Lessing/Art Resource, NY

3

Classical and Hellenistic Greece

▼ Aftermath of Victory
The Delian League • The Rise of Cimon

▼ The First Peloponnesian War: Athens Against Sparta
The Breach with Sparta • The Division of Greece

▼ Classical Greece
The Athenian Empire • Athenian Democracy • The Women of Athens: Legal Status and Everyday Life • Slavery • Religion in Public Life

▼ The Great Peloponnesian War
Causes • Strategic Stalemate • The Fall of Athens

▼ Competition for Leadership in the Fourth Century B.C.E.
The Hegemony of Sparta • The Hegemony of Thebes: The Second Athenian Empire

▼ The Culture of Classical Greece
The Fifth Century B.C.E. • The Fourth Century B.C.E. • Philosophy and the Crisis of the *Polis*

▼ The Hellenistic World
The Macedonian Conquest • Alexander the Great • The Successors

▼ Hellenistic Culture
Philosophy • Literature • Architecture and Sculpture • Mathematics and Science

▼ In Perspective

KEY TOPICS

- **The Peloponnesian War and the struggle between Athens and Sparta**
- **Democracy and empire in fifth-century B.C.E. Athens**
- **Culture and society in Classical Greece**
- **The struggle for dominance in Greece after the Peloponnesian War**
- **The Hellenistic world**

THE GREEKS' REMARKABLE victory over the Persians in 480–479 B.C.E. won them another period of freedom and autonomy. They used this time to carry their political and cultural achievement to its height. In Athens, especially, it produced a great sense of confidence and ambition.

Spartan withdrawal from active leadership against the Persians left a vacuum that was filled by the Delian League, which soon turned into the Athenian Empire. At the same time as it tightened its hold over the Greek cities in and around the

Aegean Sea, Athens developed an extraordinarily democratic constitution at home. Fears and jealousies of this new kind of state and empire created a split in the Greek world that led to major wars impoverishing Greece and leaving it vulnerable to conquest. In 338 B.C.E., Philip of Macedon conquered the Greek states, putting an end to the age of the *polis*.

▼ Aftermath of Victory

The unity of the Greeks had shown strain even in the life-and-death struggle against the Persians. Within two years of the Persian retreat, it gave way almost completely and yielded to a division of the Greek world into two spheres of influence, dominated by Sparta and Athens. The need of the Ionian Greeks to obtain and defend their freedom from Persia and the desire of many Greeks to gain revenge and financial reparation for the Persian attack brought on the split. (See Map 3–1.)

The Delian League

Sparta had led the Greeks to victory, and it was natural to look to the Spartans to continue the campaign against Persia. But Sparta was ill-suited to the task, which required both a long-term commitment far from the Peloponnesus and continuous naval action.

Athens had become the leading naval power in Greece, and the same motives that led the Athenians to support the Ionian revolt prompted them to try to drive the Persians from the Aegean and the Hellespont. The Ionians were at least as eager for the Athenians to take the helm as the Athenians were to accept the responsibility and opportunity.

In the winter of 478–477 B.C.E., the islanders and the Greeks from the coast of Asia Minor and other Greek cities on the Aegean met with the Athenians on the sacred island of Delos and swore oaths of alliance. As a symbol that the alliance was meant to be permanent, they dropped lumps of iron into the sea; the alliance was to hold until these lumps of iron rose to the surface. The aims of this new **Delian League** were to free

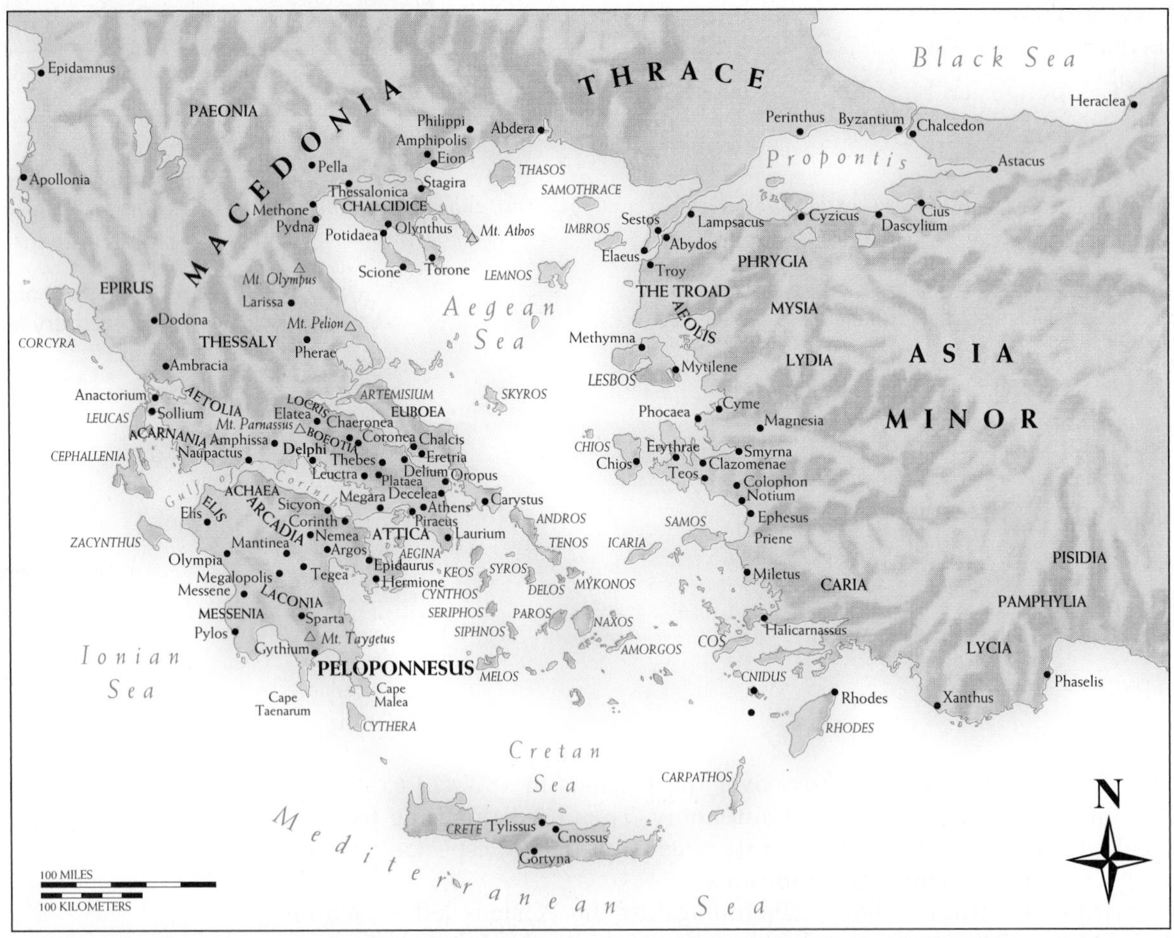

Map 3–1 **CLASSICAL GREECE** Greece in the Classical period (ca. 480–338 B.C.E.) centered on the Aegean Sea. Although there were important Greek settlements in Italy, Sicily, and all around the Black Sea, the area shown in this general reference map embraced the vast majority of Greek states.

those Greeks who were under Persian rule, to protect all against a Persian return, and to obtain compensation from the Persians by attacking their lands and taking booty. An assembly in which each state, including Athens, had one vote was supposed to determine league policy. Athens, however, was clearly designated the leader.

From the first, the league was remarkably successful. The Persians were driven from Europe and the Hellespont, and the Aegean was cleared of pirates. Some states were forced into the league or were prevented from leaving. The members approved coercion because it was necessary for the common safety. In 467 B.C.E., a great victory at the Eurymedon River in Asia Minor routed the Persians and added several cities to the league.

The Rise of Cimon

Cimon, son of Miltiades, the hero of Marathon, became the leading Athenian soldier and statesman soon after the war with Persia. A coalition of his enemies drove Themistocles from power. Ironically, the author of the Greek victory over Persia of 480 B.C.E. was exiled and ended his days at the court of the Persian king. Cimon, who was to dominate Athenian politics for almost two decades, pursued a policy of aggressive attacks on Persia and friendly relations with Sparta. In domestic affairs Cimon was conservative. He accepted the democratic constitution of Clisthenes, which appears to have become somewhat more limited after the Persian War. Defending this constitution and his interventionist foreign policy, Cimon led the Athenians and the Delian League to victory after victory, and his own popularity grew with his successes.

▾ The First Peloponnesian War: Athens Against Sparta

In 465 B.C.E., the island of Thasos rebelled from the Delian League, and Cimon put it down after a siege of more than two years. The Thasian revolt is the first recorded instance in which Athenian interests alone seemed to determine league policy, a significant step in the league's evolution into the Athenian Empire.

When Cimon returned to Athens from Thasos, he was charged with taking bribes for having refrained from conquering Macedonia, although conquering Macedonia had not been part of his assignment. He was acquitted; the trial was only a device by which his political opponents tried to reduce his influence. Their program at home was to undo the gains made by the Areopagus and bring about further democratic changes. In foreign policy, Cimon's enemies wanted to break with Sparta and contest its claim to leadership over the Greeks. They intended at least to establish the independence of Athens and its alliance. The head of this faction was Ephialtes. His supporter, and the person chosen to be the public prosecutor of Cimon, was Pericles, a member of a distinguished Athenian family. He was still young, and his defeat in court did not do lasting damage to his career.

The Breach with Sparta

When the Thasians began their rebellion, they asked Sparta to invade Athens the next spring, and the *ephors*, the annual magistrates responsible for Sparta's foreign policy, agreed. An earthquake, however, accompanied by a rebellion of the Helots that threatened the survival of Sparta, prevented the invasion. The Spartans asked their allies, the Athenians among them, for help, and Cimon persuaded the Athenians to send it. This policy was disastrous for Cimon and his faction. While Cimon was in the Peloponnesus helping the Spartans, Ephialtes stripped the Areopagus of almost all its power. The Spartans, meanwhile, fearing "the boldness and revolutionary spirit of the Athenians," ultimately sent them home. In 462 B.C.E., Ephialtes was assassinated, and Pericles replaced him as leader of the democratic faction. In the spring of 461 B.C.E., Cimon was ostracized, and Athens made an alliance with Argos, Sparta's traditional enemy. Almost overnight, Cimon's domestic and foreign policies had been overturned.

The Division of Greece

The new regime at Athens, led by Pericles and the democratic faction, was confident and ambitious. When Megara, getting the worst of a border dispute with Corinth, withdrew from the Peloponnesian League, the Athenians accepted the Megarians as allies. This alliance gave Athens a great strategic advantage, for Megara barred the way from the Peloponnesus to Athens. Sparta, however, resented the defection of Megara to Athens, leading to the outbreak of the first of the **Peloponnesian Wars**, the first phase in a protracted struggle between Athens and Sparta. The Athenians conquered Aegina and gained control of Boeotia. At this moment Athens was supreme and apparently invulnerable, controlling the states on its borders and dominating the sea. (See Map 3–2, page 64.)

About 455 B.C.E., however, the tide turned. A disastrous defeat met an Athenian fleet that had gone to aid an Egyptian rebellion against Persia. The great loss of men, ships, and prestige caused rebellions in the empire, forcing Athens to make a truce in Greece to subdue its allies in the Aegean. In 449 B.C.E., the Athenians ended the war against Persia.

In 446 B.C.E., the war on the Greek mainland broke out again. Rebellions in Boeotia and Megara removed

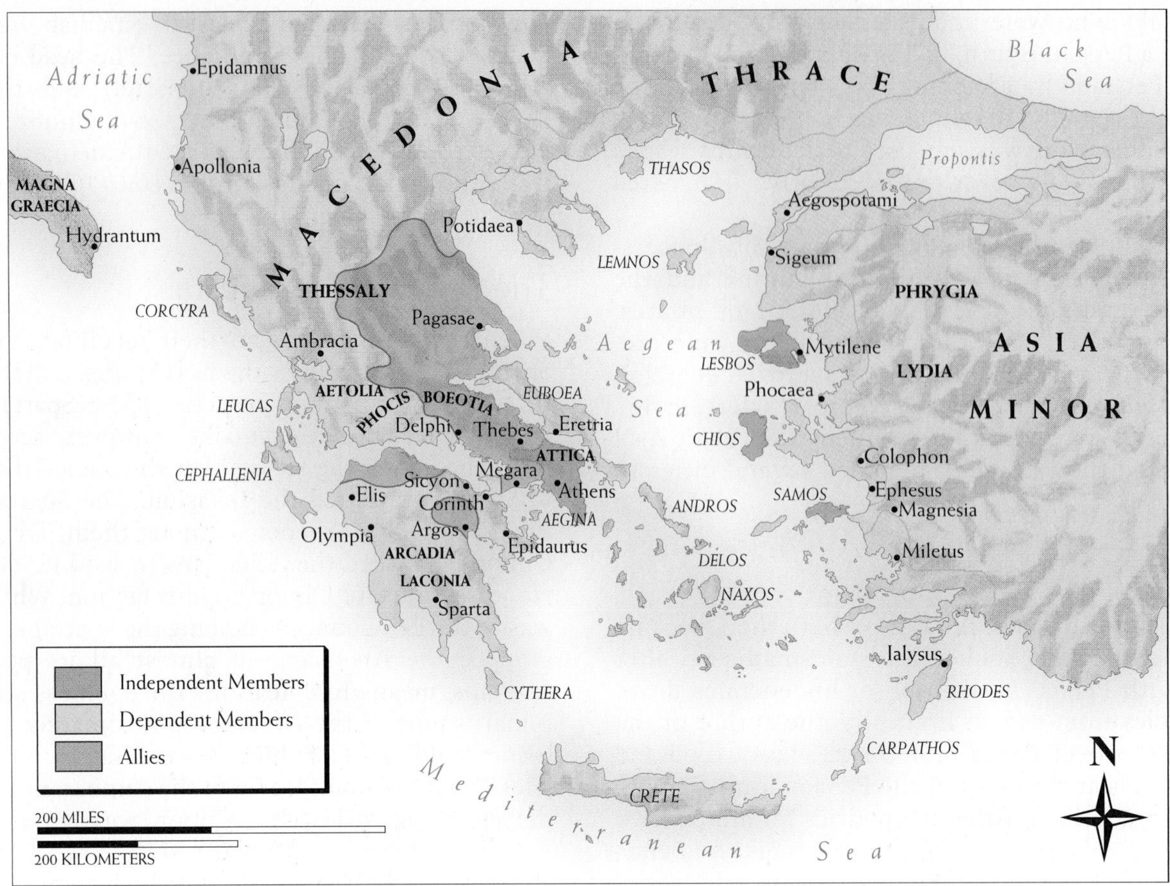

Map 3–2 **THE ATHENIAN EMPIRE ABOUT 450 B.C.E.** The Athenian Empire at its fullest extent shortly before 450 B.C.E. We see Athens and the independent states that provided manned ships for the imperial fleet but paid no tribute; dependent states that paid tribute; and states allied to, but not actually in, the empire.

Athens's land defenses and brought a Spartan invasion. Rather than fight, Pericles, the commander of the Athenian army, agreed to a peace of thirty years by the terms of which he abandoned all Athenian possessions on the Greek mainland outside of Attica. In return, the Spartans gave formal recognition to the Athenian Empire. From then on, Greece was divided into two power blocs: Sparta with its alliance on the mainland, and Athens ruling its empire in the Aegean.

▼ Classical Greece

The Athenian Empire

After the Egyptian disaster, the Athenians moved the Delian League's treasury to Athens and began to keep one sixtieth of the annual revenues for themselves. Because of the peace with Persia, there seemed no further reason for the allies to pay tribute, so the Athenians were compelled to find a new justification for their empire. They called for a Panhellenic congress to meet at Athens to discuss rebuilding the temples the Persians had destroyed and to consider how to maintain freedom of the seas. When Sparta's reluctance to participate prevented the congress, Athens felt free to continue to collect funds from the allies, both to maintain its navy and to rebuild the Athenian temples. Athenian propaganda suggested that henceforth the allies would be treated as colonies and Athens as their mother city, the whole to be held together by good feeling and common religious observances.

There is little reason, however, to believe the allies were taken in or were truly content with their lot. Nothing could cloak the fact that Athens was becoming the master and its allies mere subjects. By 445 B.C.E., when the Thirty Years' Peace gave formal recognition to an Athenian Empire, only Chios, Lesbos, and Samos were autonomous and provided ships. All the other states paid tribute. The change from alliance to empire came about because of the pressure of war and rebellion and largely because the allies were unwilling to see to their own defense. Although the empire had many friends among the lower classes and the democratic politicians in the subject cities, it was seen more and more as a tyranny. Athenian prosperity and security, however, had come to depend on the empire, and the Athenians were determined to defend it.

An Athenian silver four-drachma coin (*tetradrachm*) from the fifth century B.C.E. (440–430 B.C.E.). On the front (left) is the profile of Athena and on the back (right) is her symbol of wisdom, the owl. The silver from which the coins were struck came chiefly from the state mines at Sunium in southern Attica. Hirmer Fotoarchiv

Athenian Democracy

Even as the Athenians were tightening their control over their empire, they were expanding democracy at home. Under the leadership of Pericles, they evolved the freest government the world had yet seen.

Democratic Legislation Legislation was passed making the *hoplite* class eligible for the *archonship*, and, in practice, no one was thereafter prevented from serving in this office on the basis of his property class. Pericles himself proposed a law introducing pay for jury members, opening that important duty to the poor. Circuit judges were reintroduced, a policy making swift impartial justice available even to the poorest residents in the countryside.

Finally, Pericles himself introduced a bill limiting citizenship to those who had two citizen parents. From a modern perspective this measure might be seen as a step away from democracy, and, in fact, it would have barred Cimon and one of Pericles's ancestors. In Greek terms, however, it was natural. Democracy was defined as the privilege of those who held citizenship, making citizenship a valuable commodity. Limiting it increased its value. Thus, the bill must have won a large majority. Women, resident aliens, and slaves were also denied participation in government in all the Greek states.

How Did the Democracy Work? Within the citizen body, the extent of Athenian democracy was remarkable. The popular assembly—a collection of the people, not their representatives—had to approve every decision of the state. Every judicial decision was subject to appeal to a popular court of not fewer than 51 and as many as 1,501 citizens, chosen from an annual panel of jurors widely representative of the Athenian population. (See Encountering the Past, "Going to Court in Athens," page 66.) Most officials were selected by lot without regard to class. The main elected officials, such as the ten generals (the generalship was an office that had both political and military significance) and the imperial treasurers, were usually nobles and almost always rich men, but the people were free to choose otherwise. All public officials were subject to scrutiny before taking office

KEY EVENTS IN ATHENIAN HISTORY BETWEEN THE PERSIAN WAR AND THE GREAT PELOPONNESIAN WAR

478–477 B.C.E.	Delian League founded
ca. 474–462 B.C.E.	Cimon leading politician
467 B.C.E.	Victory over Persians at Eurymedon River
465–463 B.C.E.	Rebellion of Thasos
462 B.C.E.	Ephialtes murdered; Pericles rises to leadership
461 B.C.E.	Cimon ostracized
461 B.C.E.	Reform of Areopagus
ca. 460 B.C.E.	First Peloponnesian War begins
454 B.C.E.	Athens defeated in Egypt; crisis in the Delian League
449 B.C.E.	Peace with Persia
445 B.C.E.	Thirty Years' Peace ends First Peloponnesian War

ENCOUNTERING THE *Past*

GOING TO COURT IN ATHENS

THE ATHENIANS PLACED the administration of justice directly into the hands of their fellow citizens, including the poorest ones. Each year 6,000 Athenian males, between a quarter and a fifth of the citizen body, signed on to a panel. (Because women were not considered citizens, they were not allowed to sit on juries or sue in the courts.) From this panel on any given day, jurors were assigned to specific courts and cases. The usual size of a jury was 501, although there were juries of from 51 to as many as 1,501 members.

Unlike in a modern American court, there was no public prosecutor, no lawyers at all, and no judge. The jury was everything. Private citizens registered complaints and argued their own cases. In deciding fundamental matters of justice and fairness, the Athenian democrat put little faith in experts.

In the courtroom the plaintiff and defendant would each present his case for himself, rebut his opponent, cite the relevant laws and precedents, produce witnesses, and sum up. No trial lasted more than a day. The jury did not deliberate but just voted by secret ballot. A simple majority decided the verdict. If a penalty was called for and not prescribed by law (as few were), the plaintiff proposed one penalty, and the defendant a different one. The jury voted to choose one of these but could not propose any other. Normally, this process led both sides to suggest moderate penalties, for an unreasonable suggestion would alienate the jury. To further deter frivolous lawsuits, the plaintiff had to pay a large fine if he did not win a stated percentage of the jurors' votes.

The Athenian system of justice had obvious flaws. Decisions could be quirky and unpredictable because they were unchecked by precedent. Juries could be prejudiced, and the jurors had no defense except their own intelligence and knowledge against speakers who cited laws incorrectly and distorted history. Speeches—unhampered by rules of evidence and relevance, and without the discipline judges impose—could be fanciful, false, and deceptive.

For all its flaws, however, the Athenian system was simple, speedy, open, and easily understood by the citizens. It counted, as always, on the common sense of the ordinary Athenian and contained provisions aimed at producing moderate penalties and deterring unreasonable lawsuits. No legal technicalities or experts came between the citizens and their laws.

What were the advantages and disadvantages of the Athenian justice system?

Do you think it would lead to fair and just results?

Water-clock and Jury Ballots. Participants in an Athenian trial could speak for only a limited time. A water-clock (Clepsydra) like this kept the time. In front of it are two ballots used by the jurors to vote in favor of the plaintiff or the defendant. Picture Desk/The Art Archive/Agora Museum Athens/Dagli Orti and could be called to account or to be removed from office during their tenure. They were held to compulsory examination and accounting at the end of their term. There was no standing army, no police force, open or secret, and no way to coerce the people.

Pericles was elected to the generalship fifteen years in a row and thirty times in all, not because he was a dictator, but because he was a persuasive speaker, a skillful politician, a respected military leader, an acknowledged patriot, and patently incorruptible. When he lost the people's confidence, they did not hesitate to depose him from office. In 443 B.C.E., however, he stood at the height of his power. The defeat of the Athenian fleet in the Egyptian campaign and the failure of Athens's continental campaigns had persuaded him to favor a conservative policy, seeking to retain the empire in the Aegean and live at peace with the Spartans. It was in this direction that he led Athens's imperial democracy in the years after the First Peloponnesian War. (See "Compare & Connect: Athenian Democracy—Pro and Con," on page 68.)

The Women of Athens: Legal Status and Everyday Life

Men dominated Greek society, as in most other societies all over the world throughout history. This was true of the democratic city of Athens in the great days of Pericles, in the fifth century B.C.E., no less than of any other Greek city. The actual position of women in classical Athens, however, has been the subject of much controversy.

The bulk of the evidence, coming from the law, from philosophical and moral writings, and from information about the conditions of daily life and the organization of society, shows that women were excluded from most aspects of public life. They could not vote, could not take part in the political assemblies, could not hold public office, and could not take any direct part in politics. Since Athens was one of the few places in the ancient world where male citizens of all classes had these public responsibilities and opportunities, the exclusion of women was all the more significant.

The same sources show that in the private aspects of life women were always under the control of a male guardian—a father, a husband, or some other male relative. Women married young, usually between age twelve and eighteen, whereas their husbands were typically over thirty. In many ways, women's relationships with men were similar to father-daughter relationships. Marriages were arranged; women normally had no choice of husband, and male relatives controlled their doweries. To obtain a divorce, women needed the approval of a male relative who was willing to serve as guardian after the dissolution of the marriage. In case of divorce, the dowry returned with the woman, but her father or the appropriate male relative controlled it.

The main function and responsibility of a respectable Athenian woman of a citizen family was to

The Acropolis was both the religious and civic center of Athens. In its final form it is the work of Pericles and his successors in the late fifth century B.C.E. This photograph shows the Parthenon and to its left the Erechtheum. Meredith Pillon, Greek National Tourism Organization

COMPARE AND CONNECT

Athenian Democracy—Pro and Con

THE FIRST DEMOCRACY in the world's history appeared in Athens at the end of the sixth century B.C.E. By the middle of the fifth century B.C.E. the Athenian constitution had broadened to give all adult males participation in all aspects of government.

Although most Greek states remained oligarchic, some adopted the Athenian model and became democratic, but democracy was harshly criticized by members of the upper classes, traditionalists, and philosophers. In the following documents Pericles, the most famous Athenian political leader, and an anonymous pamphleteer present contrasting evaluations of the Athenian democracy.

QUESTIONS

1. **What virtues does Pericles find in the Athenian constitution?**
2. **Against what criticisms is he defending it?**
3. **What are the author's objections to democracy?**
4. **How would a defender of the Athenian constitution and way of life meet his complaints?**
5. **To what extent do these descriptions agree?**
6. **How do they disagree?**

I. Pericles' Funeral Oration

In 431 B.C.E., the first year of the Peloponnesian War, Pericles delivered a speech to honor and commemorate the Athenian soldiers who died in the fighting. A key part of it was the praise of the Athenian democratic constitution which, he argued, justified the sacrifice they had made.

Our constitution does not copy the laws of neighbouring states; we are rather a pattern to others than imitators ourselves. Its administration favours the many instead of the few; this is why it is called a democracy. If we look to the laws, they afford equal justice to all in their private differences; if to social standing, advancement in public life falls to reputation for capacity, class considerations not being allowed to interfere with merit; nor again does poverty bar the way, if a man is able to serve the state, he is not hindered by the obscurity of his condition. The freedom which we enjoy in our government extends also to our ordinary life. There, far from exercising a jealous surveillance over each other, we do not feel called upon to be angry with our neighbour for doing what he likes, or even to indulge in those injurious looks which cannot fail to be offensive, although they inflict no positive penalty. But all this ease in our private relations does not make us lawless as citizens. Against this fear is our chief safeguard, teaching us to obey the magistrates and the laws, particularly such as regard the protection of the injured, whether they are actually on the statute book, or belong to that code which, although unwritten, yet cannot be broken without acknowledged disgrace.

Source: Thucydides, *The Peloponnesian War* 2.37, trans. by Richard Crawley, New York, Random House, 1951.

II. Athenian Democracy: An Unfriendly View

The following selection comes from an anonymous pamphlet thought to have been written in the midst of the Peloponnesian War. Because it has come down to us among the works of Xenophon, but cannot be his work, it is sometimes called "The Constitution of the Athenians" by Pseudo-Xenophon. It is also common to refer to the unknown author as "The Old Oligarch"—although neither his age nor his purpose is known—because of the obviously antidemocratic tone of the work. Such opinions were common among members of the upper classes in Athens late in the fifth century B.C.E. and thereafter.

Now, in discussing the Athenian constitution, I cannot commend their present method of running the state, because in choosing it they preferred that the masses should do better than the respectable citizens; this, then, is my reason for not commending it. Since, however, they have made this choice, I will demonstrate how well they preserve their constitution and handle the other affairs for which the rest of the Greeks criticize them.

Again, some people are surprised at the fact that in all fields they give more power to the masses, the poor, and the common people than they do to the respectable elements of society, but it will become clear that they preserve the democracy by doing precisely this. When the poor, the ordinary people, and the lower classes flourish and increase in numbers, then the power of the democracy will be increased; if, however, the rich and the respectable flourish, the democrats increase the strength of their opponents. Throughout the world the aristocracy are opposed to democracy, for they are naturally least liable to loss of self-control and injustice and most meticulous in their regard for what is respectable, whereas the masses display extreme ignorance, indiscipline, and wickedness, for poverty gives them a tendency towards the ignoble, and in some cases the lack of money leads to their being uneducated and ignorant.

It may be objected that they ought not to grant each and every man the right of speaking in the Ekklesia and serving on the Boule, but only the ablest and best of them; however, in this also they are acting in their own best interests by allowing the mob also a voice. If none but the respectable spoke in the Ekklesia and the Boule, the result would benefit that class and harm the masses; as it is, anyone who wishes rises and speaks, and as a member of the mob he discovers what is to his own advantage and that of those like him.

But someone may say: "How could such a man find out what was advantageous to himself and the common people?" The Athenians realize that this man, despite his ignorance and badness, brings them more advantage because he is well-disposed to them than the ill-disposed, respectable man would, despite his virtue and wisdom. Such practices do not produce the best city, but they are the best way of preserving democracy. For the common people do not wish to be deprived of their rights in an admirably governed city, but to be free and to rule the city; they are not disturbed by inferior laws, for the common people get their strength and freedom from what you define as inferior laws.

Source: *Aristotle and Xenophon on Democracy and Oligarchy*, trans. with introductions and commentary by J. M. Moore (Berkeley and Los Angeles: University of California Press, 1975), pp. 37–38.

Pericles (ca. 495–429 B.C.E.) was the leading statesman of Athens for much of the fifth century. This is a Roman copy in marble of the Greek bronze bust that was probably cast in the last decade of Pericles' life. Library of Congress produce male heirs for the ***oikos***, or household, of her husband. If, however, her father's *oikos* lacked a male heir, the daughter became an *epikleros*, the "heiress" to the family property. In that case, she was required by law to marry a relative on her father's side to produce the desired male offspring. In the Athenian way of thinking, one household "lent" a woman to another for bearing and raising a male heir to continue the existence of the *oikos*.

Because the pure and legitimate lineage of the offspring was important, women were carefully segregated from men outside the family and were confined to the women's quarters in the house. Men might seek sexual gratification outside the house with prostitutes of high or low style, frequently recruited from abroad. Respectable women stayed home to raise the children, cook, weave cloth, and oversee the management of the household. The only public function of women—an important one—was in the various rituals and festivals of the state religion. Apart from these activities, Athenian women were expected to remain at home out of sight, quiet, and unnoticed. Pericles told the widows and mothers of the Athenian men who died in the first year of the Peloponnesian War only this: "Your great glory is not to fall short of your natural character, and the greatest glory of women is to be least talked about by men, whether for good or bad."

The picture of the legal status of women derived from these sources is largely accurate. It does not fit well, however, with other evidence from mythology, from pictorial art, and from the tragedies and comedies by the great Athenian dramatists. These often show women as central characters and powerful figures in both the public and the private spheres, suggesting that Athenian women may have played a more complex role than their legal status suggests. In Aeschylus's tragedy *Agamemnon*, for example, Clytemnestra arranges the murder of her royal husband and establishes the tyranny of her lover, whom she dominates.

As a famous speech in Euripides' tragedy *Medea* makes clear, we are left with an apparent contradiction. In this speech, Medea paints a bleak picture of the subjugation of women as dictated by their legal status. (See "Medea Bemoans the Condition of Women.") Yet Medea, as Euripides depicted her, is a powerful figure who negotiates with kings. She is the central character in a tragedy bearing her name, produced at state expense before most of the Athenian population and written by one of Athens's greatest poets and dramatists. She is a cause of terror to the audience and, at the same time, an object of their pity and sympathy as a victim of injustice. She is certainly not, what Pericles recommended in his *Funeral Oration*, "least talked about by men, whether for good or for bad." It is also important to remember that she is a foreigner with magical powers, by no means a typical Athenian woman.

An Exceptional Woman: Aspasia Pericles' life did not conform to his own prescription. After divorcing his first wife, he entered a liaison that was unique in his time, to a woman who was, in her own way, as remarkable as the great Athenian leader. His companion was Aspasia, a young woman who had left her native Miletus and come to live in Athens. The ancient writers refer to her as a *hetaira*, a kind of high-class courtesan who provided men with both erotic and other kinds of entertainment. She clearly had a keen and lively intellect and may well have been trained in the latest ideas and techniques of discussion in her native city, the home of the Greek Enlightenment. Socrates thought it was worth his time to talk with her in the company of his followers and friends. In the dialogue *Menexenus*, Plato jokingly gives her credit for writing Pericles' speeches, including the *Funeral Oration.* There should be no doubt that both Pericles and the men in his circle took her seriously.

Aspasia represented something completely different from Athenian women. She was not a child, not a sheltered and repressed creature confined to the narrow world of slave women, children, and female relatives, but a beautiful, independent, brilliantly witty young woman capable of holding her own in conversation with the best minds in Greece and of discussing and illuminating any question with her husband. There can be no doubt that Pericles loved her passionately. He took her into his house, and whether or not they were formally and legally married, he treated her as his one and only beloved wife. Each morning when he left home and every evening when he returned, he embraced her and kissed her tenderly, by no means the ordinary greeting between an Athenian man and woman.

For an Athenian to consort with courtesans was normal—to take one into his house and treat her as a concubine, perhaps only a little less so. What was shocking and, to many, offensive, was to treat such a woman, a foreigner, as a wife, to lavish such affection on her as few Athenian wives enjoyed, to involve her regularly in conversation with other men, and to discuss important matters with her and treat her opinions with respect. The scandal was immense, and the comic poets made the most of it. Enemies claimed that Pericles was enslaved to a foreign woman who was using her hold over him for political purposes of her own. The Samian War, which arose over a quarrel between Aspasia's native Miletus and Samos, intensified these allegations, for the story spread that Pericles had launched the war at her bidding. After Pericles' death, Aristophanes would pick up these old charges and work them around comically to blame Aspasia for the Peloponnesian War as well.

To some degree, the reality of women's lives in ancient Greece must have depended on their social and

MEDEA BEMOANS THE CONDITION OF WOMEN

In 431 B.C.E., Euripides (ca. 485–406 B.C.E.) presented his play Medea *at the Festival of Dionysus in Athens. The heroine is a foreign woman who has unusual powers. Her description of the condition of women in the speech that follows, however, appears to be an accurate representation of the condition of women in fifth-century B.C.E. Athens.*

Apart from participation in politics, how did the lives of men and women differ in ancient Athens? How well or badly did that aspect of Athenian society suit the needs of the Athenian people and the state in the Classical Age? Since men had a dominant position in the state, and the state managed and financed the presentation of tragedies, how do you explain the sympathetic account of the condition of women Euripides puts into the mouth of Medea?

Of all things which are living and can form a judgment
We women are the most unfortunate creatures.
Firstly, with an excess of wealth it is required
For us to buy a husband and take for our bodies
A master; for not to take one is even worse.
And now the question is serious whether we take
A good or bad one; for there is no easy escape
For a woman, nor can she say no to her marriage.
She arrives among new modes of behavior and manners,
And needs prophetic power, unless she has learned at home,
How best to manage him who shares the bed with her.
And if we work out all this well and carefully,
And the husband lives with us and lightly bears his yoke,
Then life is enviable. If not, I'd rather die.
A man, when he's tired of the company in his home,
Goes out of the house and puts an end to his boredom
And turns to a friend or companion of his own age.
But we are forced to keep our eyes on one alone.
What they say of us is that we have a peaceful time
Living at home, while they do the fighting in war.
How wrong they are! I would very much rather stand
Three times in the front of battle than bear one child.

From Euripides, *Medea in Four Tragedies*, trans. by Rex Warner, copyright © 1955, The Bodley Head.

economic status. Poorer women necessarily worked hard at household as well as agricultural tasks and in shops. They also fetched water from the wells and fountains, and both vase paintings and literature show women gathering and chatting at these places. Aristotle asks "How would it be possible to prevent the wives of the poor from going out of doors?"[1] Women of the better classes, however, had no such duties or opportunities. They were more easily and closely supervised. Our knowledge of the experience of women, however, comes from limited sources that do not always agree. Different scholars arrive at conflicting pictures by emphasizing one kind of a source rather than another. Although the legal subordination of women cannot be doubted, the reality of their place in Greek society remains a lively topic of debate.

Slavery

The Greeks had some form of slavery from the earliest times, but true chattel slavery was initially rare. The most common forms of bondage were different kinds of serfdom in relatively backward areas such as Crete, Thessaly, and Sparta. As noted in Chapter 2, the Spartans

[1] Aristotle, *Politics* 1300a.

conquered the natives of their region and reduced them to the status of Helots, subjects who belonged to the Spartan state and worked the land for their Spartan masters. Another early form of bondage involving a severe, but rarely permanent, loss of freedom resulted from default in debt. In Athens, however, at about 600 B.C.E., such bondsmen, called *hektemoroi*, were sold outside their native land as true slaves until the reforms of Solon put an end to debt bondage entirely.

True chattel slavery began to increase about 500 B.C.E. and remained important to Greek society thereafter. The main sources of slaves were war captives and the captives of pirates. Like the Chinese, Egyptians, and many other peoples, the Greeks regarded foreigners as inferior, and most slaves working for the Greeks were foreigners. Greeks sometimes enslaved Greeks, but not to serve in their home territories.

The chief occupation of the Greeks, as of most of the world before our century, was agriculture. Most Greek farmers worked small holdings too poor to support even one slave, but some had one or two slaves to work alongside them. The upper classes had larger farms that were let out to free tenant farmers or were worked by slaves, generally under an overseer who was himself a slave. Large landowners generally did not have a single great estate but possessed several smaller farms scattered about the *polis.* This arrangement did not encourage the amassing of great numbers of agricultural slaves such as those who would later work the cotton and sugar plantations of the New World. Industry, however, was different.

Larger numbers of slaves labored in industry, especially in mining. Nicias, a wealthy Athenian of the fifth century B.C.E., owned a thousand slaves he rented to a mining contractor for profit, but this is by far the largest number known. Most manufacturing was on a small scale, with shops using one, two, or a handful of slaves. Slaves worked as craftsmen in almost every trade, and, like agricultural slaves on small farms, they worked alongside their masters. Many slaves were domestic servants or shepherds. Publicly held slaves served as policemen, prison attendants, clerks, and secretaries.

The number of slaves in ancient Greece and their importance to Greek society are the subjects of controversy. We have no useful figures of the absolute number of slaves or their percentage of the free population in the classical period (fifth and fourth centuries B.C.E.), and estimates range from 20,000 to 100,000. Accepting the mean between the extremes, 60,000, and estimating the free population at its height at about 40,000 households, would yield a figure of fewer than two slaves per family. Estimates suggest that only a quarter to a third of free Athenians owned any slaves at all.

Some historians have noted that in the American South during the period before the Civil War—where slaves made up less than one third of the total population and three quarters of free Southerners had no slaves—the proportion of slaves to free citizens was similar to that of ancient Athens. Because slavery was so important to the economy of the South, these historians suggest, it may have been equally important and similarly oppressive in ancient Athens. This argument has several problems.[2] First, in the cotton states of the American South before the Civil War, a single cash crop, well suited for exploitation by large groups of slaves, dominated the economy and society. In Athens, in contrast, the economy was mixed, the crops varied, and the land and its distribution were poorly suited to massive slavery.

Different, too, was the likelihood that a slave would become free. Americans rarely freed their slaves, but in Greece liberation was common. The most famous example is that of the Athenian slave Pasion, who began as a bank clerk, earned his freedom, became Athens's richest banker, and was awarded Athenian citizenship. Such cases were certainly rare, but gaining one's freedom was not.

It is important also to distinguish the American South, where skin color separated slaves from their masters, from the different society of classical Athens. Southern masters were increasingly hostile to freeing slaves and afraid of slave rebellions, but in Athens slaves walked the streets with such ease that it offended class-conscious Athenians.

Even more remarkable, the Athenians sometimes considered freeing all their slaves. In 406 B.C.E., when their city was facing defeat in the Peloponnesian War, they freed all slaves of military age and granted citizenship to those who rowed the ships that won the battle of Arginusae. Twice more at crucial moments, similar proposals were made, although without success.

Religion in Public Life

In Athens, as in the other Greek states, religion was more a civic than a private matter. Participation in the rituals of the state religion was not a matter of faith, but of patriotism and good citizenship. In its most basic form, it had little to do with morality. Over time poets and philosophers put forth ethical and moral ideas that among other peoples, like the Hebrews and Persians, were the work of religious prophets and basic to their religious beliefs. Greek religion, however, emphasized not moral conduct to orthodox belief, but the faithful practice of rituals meant to win the favor of the gods. To fail

[2] M. I. Finley, "Was Greek Civilization Based on Slave Labor?," *Historia* 8 (1959), p. 151.

to carry out these duties or to attack the gods in any way were seen as blows against the state and were severely punished.

Famous examples of such blasphemies and their punishment occurred late in the fifth and early in the fourth centuries B.C.E. In 415, some men mutilated the statues of Hermes found on every street in Athens. Others were accused of mocking the sacred mysteries of the worship of the goddesses Demeter and Persephone. Suspicions arose at once that the purpose of these sacrilegious acts was to overthrow the Athenian democracy, and the perpetrators were put to death. In 399 B.C.E., the philosopher Socrates was convicted of not honoring the state's gods and of introducing new divinities, and he was also put to death. This was connected with the further charge of corrupting the youths, both acts believed to do harm to the well-being of Athens. In ancient Greece there was no thought of separating religion from civic and political life.

▼ The Great Peloponnesian War

During the first decade after the Thirty Years' Peace of 445 B.C.E., the willingness of each side to respect the new arrangements was tested and not found wanting. About 435 B.C.E., however, a dispute in a remote and unimportant part of the Greek world ignited a long and disastrous war that shook the foundations of Greek civilization.

Causes

The spark that ignited the conflict was a civil war at Epidamnus, a Corcyraean colony on the Adriatic. This civil war caused a quarrel between Corcyra (modern Corfu) and its mother city and traditional enemy, Corinth, an ally of Sparta. The Corcyraean fleet was second in size only to that of Athens, and the Athenians feared that its capture by Corinth would threaten Athenian security. As a result, they made an alliance with the previously neutral Corcyra, angering Corinth and leading to a series of crises in 433–432 B.C.E. that threatened to bring the Athenian Empire into conflict with the Peloponnesian League.

In the summer of 432 B.C.E., the Spartans met to consider the grievances of their allies. Persuaded, chiefly by the Corinthians, that Athens was an insatiably aggressive power seeking to enslave all the Greeks, they voted for war. The treaty of 445 B.C.E. specifically provided that all differences be submitted to arbitration, and Athens repeatedly offered to arbitrate any question. Pericles insisted that the Athenians refuse to yield to threats or commands and to uphold the treaty and the arbitration clause. Sparta refused to arbitrate, and in the spring of 431 B.C.E., its army marched into Attica, the Athenian homeland.

THE GREAT PELOPONNESIAN WAR

435 B.C.E.	Civil war at Epidamnus
432 B.C.E.	Sparta declares war on Athens
431 B.C.E.	Peloponnesian invasion of Athens
421 B.C.E.	Peace of Nicias
415–413 B.C.E.	Athenian invasion of Sicily
405 B.C.E.	Battle of Aegospotami
404 B.C.E.	Athens surrenders

Strategic Stalemate

The Spartan strategy was traditional: to invade the enemy's country and threaten the crops, forcing the enemy to defend them in a *hoplite* battle. Such a battle the Spartans were sure to win because they had the better army and they outnumbered the Athenians at least two to one. Any ordinary *polis* would have yielded or fought and lost. Athens, however, had an enormous navy, an annual income from the empire, a vast reserve fund, and long walls that connected the fortified city with the fortified port of Piraeus.

The Athenians' strategy was to allow devastation of their own land to prove that Spartan invasions could not hurt Athens. At the same time, the Athenians launched seaborne raids on the Peloponnesian coast to hurt Sparta's allies. Pericles expected that within a year or two—three at most—the Peloponnesians would become discouraged and make peace, having learned their lesson. If the Peloponnesians held out, Athenian resources were inadequate to continue for more than four or five years without raising the tribute in the empire and running an unacceptable risk of rebellion.

The plan required restraint and the leadership only a Pericles could provide. In 429 B.C.E., however, after a devastating plague and a political crisis that had challenged his authority, Pericles died. After his death, no dominant leader emerged to hold the Athenians to a consistent policy. Two factions vied for influence: One, led by Nicias, wanted to continue the defensive policy, and the other, led by Cleon, preferred a more aggressive strategy. In 425 B.C.E., the aggressive faction was able to win a victory that changed the course of the war. Four hundred Spartans surrendered. Sparta offered peace at once to get them back.

The great victory and the prestige it brought Athens made it safe to raise the imperial tribute, without which Athens could not continue to fight. The Athenians indeed wanted to continue, for the Spartan peace offer gave no adequate guarantee of Athenian security.

In 424 B.C.E., the Athenians undertook a more aggressive policy. They sought to make Athens safe by conquering Megara and Boeotia. Both attempts failed, and defeat helped discredit the aggressive policy, leading to a truce in 423 B.C.E. Meanwhile, Sparta's ablest general, Brasidas, took a small army to Thrace and Macedonia. He captured Amphipolis, the most important Athenian colony in the region. Thucydides was in charge of the Athenian fleet in those waters and was held responsible for the city's loss. He was exiled and was thereby given the time and opportunity to write his famous history of the Great Peloponnesian War. In 422 B.C.E., Cleon led an expedition to undo the work of Brasidas. At Amphipolis, both he and Brasidas died in battle. The removal of these two leaders of the aggressive factions in their respective cities paved the way for the Peace of Nicias, named for its chief negotiator, which was ratified in the spring of 421 B.C.E.

The Fall of Athens

The peace, officially supposed to last fifty years and, with a few exceptions, guarantee the status quo, was in fact fragile. Neither side carried out all its commitments, and several of Sparta's allies refused ratification. In 415 B.C.E., Alcibiades persuaded the Athenians to attack Sicily to bring it under Athenian control. This ambitious and unnecessary undertaking ended in disaster in 413 B.C.E., when the entire expedition was destroyed. The Athenians lost some 200 ships, about 4,500 of their own men, and almost ten times as many allies. It shook Athens's prestige, reduced its power, provoked rebellions, and brought the wealth and power of Persia into the war on Sparta's side.

It is remarkable that the Athenians could continue fighting despite the disaster. They survived a brief oligarchic coup in 411 B.C.E. and won several important victories at sea as the war shifted to the Aegean. Their allies rebelled, however, and Persia paid for fleets to sustain them. Athenian financial resources shrank and finally disappeared. When its fleet was caught napping and was destroyed at Aegospotami in 405 B.C.E., Athens could not build another. The Spartans, under Lysander, a clever and ambitious general who was responsible for obtaining Persian support, cut off the food supply through the Hellespont, and the Athenians were starved into submission. In 404 B.C.E., they surrendered unconditionally; the city walls were dismantled, Athens was permitted no fleet, and the empire was gone. The Great Peloponnesian War was over.

▼ Competition for Leadership in the Fourth Century B.C.E.

Athens's defeat did not bring domination to the Spartans. Instead, the period from 404 B.C.E. until the Macedonian conquest of Greece in 338 B.C.E. was a time of intense rivalry among the Greek cities, each seeking to achieve leadership and control over the others. Sparta, a recovered Athens, and a newly powerful Thebes were the main competitors in a struggle that ultimately weakened all the Greeks and left them vulnerable to outside influence and control.

The Hegemony of Sparta

The collapse of the Athenian Empire created a vacuum of power in the Aegean and opened the way for Spartan leadership or hegemony. Fulfilling the contract that had brought them the funds to win the war, the Spartans handed the Greek cities of Asia Minor back to Persia. Under the leadership of Lysander, the Spartans made a mockery of their promise to free the Greeks by stepping into the imperial role of Athens in the cities along the European coast and the islands of the Aegean. In most of the cities, Lysander installed a board of ten local oligarchs loyal to him and supported them with a Spartan garrison. Tribute brought in an annual revenue almost as great as that the Athenians had collected.

Limited population, the Helot problem, and traditional conservatism all made Sparta a less than ideal state to rule a maritime empire. The increasing arrogance of Sparta's policies alienated some of its allies, especially Thebes and Corinth. In 404 B.C.E., Lysander installed an oligarchic government in Athens, and its leaders' outrageous behavior earned them the title "Thirty Tyrants." Democratic exiles took refuge in Thebes and Corinth and raised an army to challenge the oligarchy. Sparta's conservative king, Pausanias, replaced Lysander, arranging a peaceful settlement and, ultimately, the restoration of democracy. Thereafter, Athenian foreign policy remained under Spartan control, but otherwise Athens was free.

In 405 B.C.E., Darius II of Persia died and was succeeded by Artaxerxes II. His younger brother, Cyrus, received Spartan help in recruiting a Greek mercenary army to help him contest the throne. The Greeks marched inland as far as Mesopotamia, where they defeated the Persians at Cunaxa in 401 B.C.E., but Cyrus was killed in the battle. The Greeks were able to march back to the Black Sea and safety; their success revealed the potential weakness of the Persian Empire.

The Greeks of Asia Minor had supported Cyrus and were now afraid of Artaxerxes' revenge. The Spartans accepted their request for aid and sent an army into Asia, attracted by the prospect of prestige, power, and money. In 396 B.C.E., the command of Sparta's army was given to a new king, Agesilaus, who dominated Sparta until his death in 360 B.C.E. His consistent advocacy of aggressive policies that provided him with opportunities to display his bravery in battle may have been motivated by a psychological need to compensate for his physical lameness and his disputed claim to the throne.

Agesilaus collected much booty and frightened the Persians. They sent a messenger with money and promises of further support to friendly factions in all of the Greek states likely to help them against Sparta. By 395 B.C.E., Thebes was able to organize an alliance that included Argos, Corinth, and a resurgent Athens. The result was the Corinthian War (395–387 B.C.E.), which put an end to Sparta's Asian adventure. In 394 B.C.E., the Persian fleet destroyed Sparta's maritime empire. Meanwhile, the Athenians rebuilt their walls, enlarged their navy, and even recovered some of their lost empire in the Aegean. The war ended when the exhausted Greek states accepted a peace dictated by the Great King of Persia.

The Persians, frightened now by the recovery of Athens, turned the management of Greece over to Sparta. Agesilaus broke up all alliances except the Peloponnesian League. He used or threatened to use the Spartan army to interfere in other *poleis* and put friends of Sparta in power within them. Sparta reached a new level of lawless arrogance in 382 B.C.E., when it seized Thebes during peacetime without warning or pretext. In 379 B.C.E., a Spartan army made a similar attempt on Athens. That action persuaded the Athenians to join with Thebes, which had rebelled from Sparta a few months earlier, to wage war on the Spartans.

In 371 B.C.E., the Thebans, led by their great generals Pelopidas and Epaminondas, defeated the Spartans at Leuctra. The Thebans encouraged the Arcadian cities of the central Peloponnesus to form a league, freed the Helots, and helped them found a city of their own. They deprived Sparta of much of its farmland and of the people who worked it and hemmed Sparta in with hostile neighbors. Sparta's population had shrunk so it could put fewer than 2,000 men into the field at Leuctra. Its aggressive policies had led to ruin. The Theban victory brought the end of Sparta as a power of the first rank.

The Hegemony of Thebes: The Second Athenian Empire

Thebes's power after its victory at Leuctra lay in its democratic constitution, its control over Boeotia, and its two outstanding and popular generals. One of these generals, Pelopidas, died in a successful attempt to gain control of Thessaly. The other, Epaminondas, made Thebes dominant over all of Greece north of Athens and the Corinthian Gulf and challenged the reborn Athenian Empire in the Aegean. All this activity provoked resistance, and by 362 B.C.E., Thebes faced a Peloponnesian coalition as well as Athens. Epaminondas, once again leading a Boeotian army into the Peloponnesus, confronted this coalition at the Battle of Mantinea. His army was victorious, but Epaminondas himself was killed, and Theban dominance died with him.

The Second Athenian Confederation, which Athens had organized in 378 B.C.E., was aimed at resisting Spartan aggression in the Aegean. Its constitution avoided the abuses of the Delian League, but the Athenians soon began to repeat them anyway. This time, however, they did not have the power to put down resistance. When the collapse of Sparta and Thebes and the restraint of Persia removed any reason for voluntary membership, Athens's allies revolted. By 355 B.C.E., Athens had to abandon most of the empire. After two centuries of almost continuous warfare, the Greeks returned to the chaotic disorganization that characterized the time before the founding of the Peloponnesian League.

▼ The Culture of Classical Greece

The repulse of the Persian invasion released a flood of creative activity in Greece that was rarely, if ever, matched anywhere at any time. The century and a half between the Persian retreat and the conquest of Greece by Philip of Macedon (479–338 B.C.E.) produced achievements of such quality as to justify the designation of that era as the Classical Period. Ironically, we often use the term *classical* to suggest calm and serenity, but the word that best describes Greek life, thought, art, and literature in this period is *tension*.

The Fifth Century B.C.E.

Two sources of tension contributed to the artistic outpouring of fifth-century B.C.E. Greece. One arose from the conflict between the Greeks' pride in their accomplishments and their concern that overreaching would bring retribution. Friction among the *poleis* intensified during this period as Athens and Sparta gathered most of them into two competing and menacing blocs. The victory over the Persians brought a sense of exultation in the capacity of humans to accomplish great things and a sense of confidence in the divine justice that had brought low the arrogant pride of Xerxes. But the Greeks recognized that Xerxes' fate awaited all those who reached too far, creating a sense of unease. The

This storage jar (amphora), made about 540 B.C.E., is attributed to the anonymous Athenian master artist called the Amasis painter. It shows Dionysus, the god of wine, revelry, and fertility with two of his ecstatic female worshippers called maenads.
Cliche Bibliotheque Nationale de France—Paris

second source of tension was the conflict between the soaring hopes and achievements of individuals and the claims and limits their fellow citizens in the *polis* put on them. These tensions were felt throughout Greece. They had the most spectacular consequences, however, in Athens in its Golden Age, the time between the Persian and the Peloponnesian wars.

Attic Tragedy Nothing reflects Athens's concerns better than Attic tragedy, which emerged as a major form of Greek poetry in the fifth century B.C.E. The tragedies were presented in a contest as part of the public religious observations in honor of the god Dionysus. The festivals in which they were shown were civic occasions.

Each poet who wished to compete submitted his work to the *archon.* Each offered three tragedies (which might or might not have a common subject) and a satyr play, or comic choral dialogue with Dionysus, to close. The three best competitors were each awarded three actors and a chorus. The state paid the actors. The state selected a wealthy citizen to provide the chorus as *choregos*, for the Athenians had no direct taxation to support such activities. Most of the tragedies were performed in the theater of Dionysus on the south side of the Acropolis, and as many as 30,000 Athenians could attend. A jury of Athenians chosen by lot voted prizes and honors to the best author, actor, and *choregos.*

Attic tragedy served as a forum in which the poets raised vital issues of the day, enabling the Athenian audience to think about them in a serious, yet exciting, context. On rare occasions, the subject of a play might be a contemporary or historic event, but almost always it was chosen from mythology. Until late in the century, the tragedies always dealt solemnly with difficult questions of religion, politics, ethics, morality, or some combination of these. The plays of the dramatists Aeschylus and Sophocles, for example, follow this pattern. The plays of Euripides, written toward the end of the century, are less solemn and more concerned with individual psychology.

Old Comedy Comedy was introduced into the Dionysian festival early in the fifth century B.C.E. Cratinus, Eupolis, and the great master of the genre called Old Comedy, Aristophanes (ca. 450–385 B.C.E.), the only one from whom we have complete plays, wrote political comedies. They were filled with scathing invective and satire against such contemporary figures as Pericles, Cleon, Socrates, and Euripides. (See "Lysistrata Ends the War," page 78.)

Architecture and Sculpture The great architectural achievements of Periclean Athens, as much as Athenian tragedy, illustrate the magnificent results of the union and tension between religious and civic responsibilities, on the one hand, and the transcendent genius of the individual artist, on the other. Beginning in 448 B.C.E. and continuing to the outbreak of the Great Peloponnesian War, Pericles undertook a great building program on the Acropolis. (See Map 3–3.) The income from the empire paid for it. The new buildings included temples to honor the city's gods and a fitting gateway to the temples. Pericles' main purpose seems to have been to represent visually the greatness and power of Athens, by emphasizing intellectual and artistic achievement—civilization rather than military and naval power. It was as though these buildings were tangible proof of Pericles' claim that Athens was "the school of Hellas"—that is, the intellectual center of all Greece.

Philosophy The tragic dramas, architecture, and sculpture of the fifth century B.C.E. all indicate an extraordinary concern with human beings—their capacities, their limits, their nature, and their place in the universe. The same concern is clear in the development of philosophy.

To be sure, some philosophers continued the speculation about the nature of the cosmos (as opposed to human nature) that began with Thales in the sixth century B.C.E. Parmenides of Elea and his pupil Zeno, in opposition to the earlier philosopher Heraclitus, argued that change was only an illusion of the senses.

MAP EXPLORATION

Interactive map: To explore this map further, go to **www.myhistorylab.com**

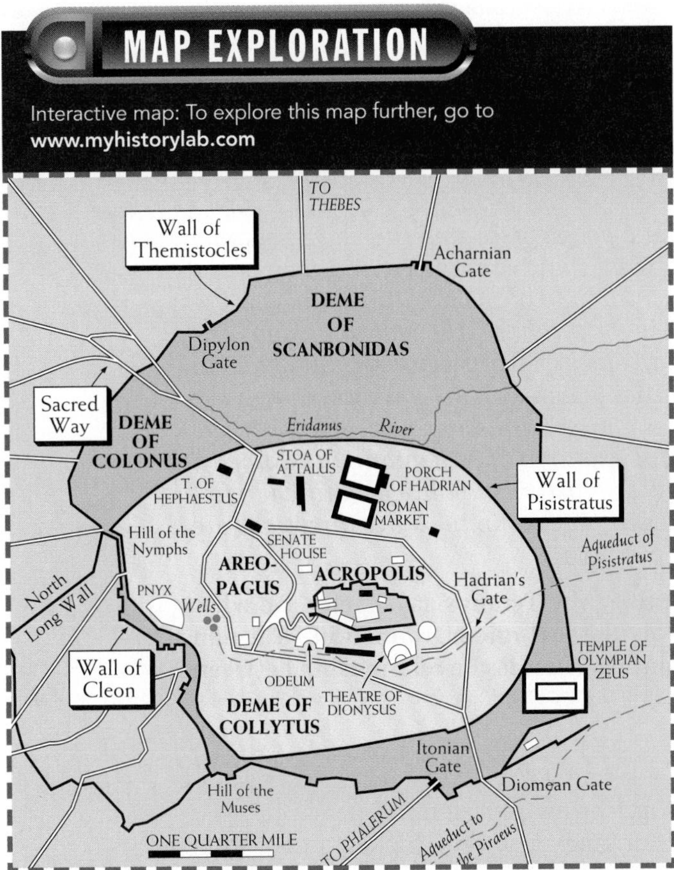

Map 3–3 **ANCIENT ATHENS** This sketch locates some of the major features of the ancient city of Athens that have been excavated and are visible today. It includes monuments ranging in age from the earliest times to the period of the Roman Empire. The geographical relation of the Acropolis to the rest of the city is apparent, as is that of the Agora, the Areopagus (where the early council of aristocrats met), and the Pnyx (site of assembly for the larger, more democratic meetings of the entire people).

Reason and reflection showed that reality was fixed and unchanging, because it seemed evident that nothing could be created out of nothingness. Empedocles of Acragas further advanced such fundamental speculations by identifying four basic elements: fire, water, earth, and air. Like Parmenides, he thought that reality was permanent, but he thought it was not immobile; two primary forces, he contended, love and strife—or, as we might say, attraction and repulsion—moved the four elements.

Empedocles' theory is clearly a step on the road to the **atomist** theory of Leucippus of Miletus and Democritus of Abdera. According to this theory, the world consists of innumerable tiny, solid, indivisible, and unchangeable particles—or "atoms"—that move about in the void. The size of the atoms and the arrangements they form when joined produce the secondary qualities that our senses perceive, such as color and shape. These secondary qualities are merely conventional—the result of human interpretation and agreement—unlike the atoms themselves, which are natural.

Previous to the atomists, Anaxagoras of Clazomenae, an older contemporary and a friend of Pericles, had spoken of tiny fundamental particles called *seeds*, which were put together on a rational basis by a force called *nous*, or "mind." Anaxagoras was thus suggesting a distinction between matter and mind. The atomists, however, regarded "soul," or mind, as material and believed purely physical laws guided everything. In these conflicting positions, we have the beginning of the enduring philosophical debate between materialism and idealism.

These speculations were of interest to few people, and in fact, most Greeks were suspicious of them. A group of professional teachers who emerged in the mid-fifth century began a far more influential debate. Called *Sophists*, they traveled about and received pay for teaching such practical techniques of persuasion as rhetoric, dialectic, and argumentation. (Persuasive

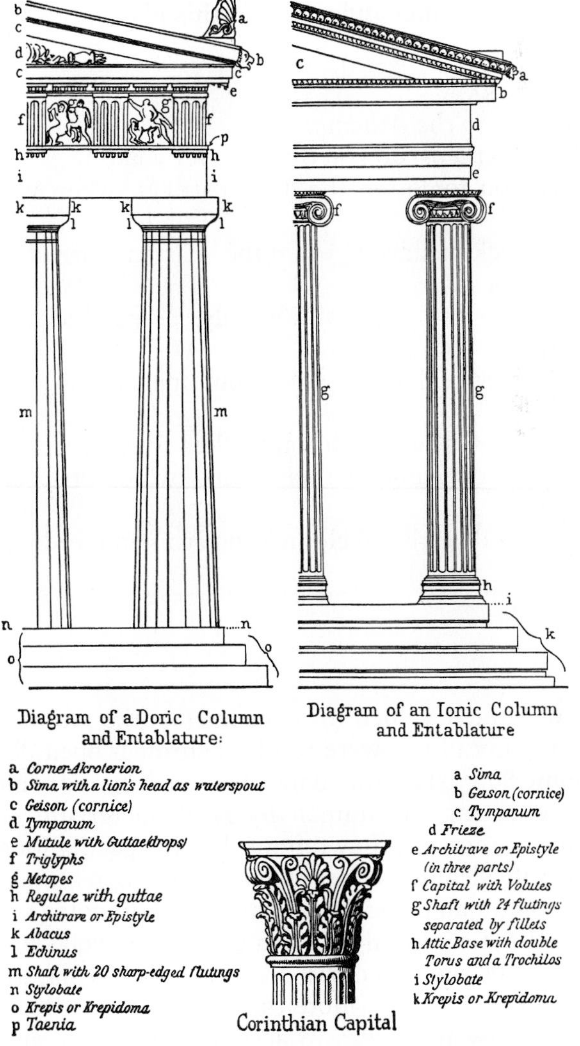

The three orders of Greek architecture, Doric, Ionic, and Corinthian, have had an enduring impact on Western architecture.

LYSISTRATA ENDS THE WAR

Aristophanes, the greatest of the Athenian comic poets, presented the play Lysistrata *in 411 B.C.E., two decades into the Great Peloponnesian War. The central idea of the plot is that the women of Athens, led by Lysistrata, tired of the privations the war imposed, decide to take matters into their own hands and bring the war to an end. The device they employ is to get the women on both sides to deny their marital favors to their husbands, a kind of sexual strike that quickly achieves its purpose. Before the following passage, Lysistrata has set the terms the Spartans must accept. Next she turns to the Athenians. The play is a masterful example of Athenian Old Comedy, which was almost always full of contemporary and historical political satirical references and sexual puns and jokes. The references to "Peace" in the stage directions are to an actor playing the goddess Peace.*

To what historic event does the passage concerning "the Tyrant's days" refer? To what does the "Promontory of Pylos" refer? What was the real role of women in Athenian political life, and what does the play tell us about it? What is the relationship between humor and reality in this play?

LYSISTRATA
(Turning to the Athenians)
Men of Athens, do you think I'll let you off?
Have you forgotten the Tyrant's days, when you wore
the smock of slavery, when the Spartans turned to the spear,
cut down the pride of Thessaly, despatched the friends
of tyranny, and dispossessed your oppressors?
Recall:
On that great day, your only allies were Spartans;
your liberty came at their hands, which stripped away
your servile garb and clothed you again in Freedom!

SPARTAN
(Indicating Lysistrata)
Hain't never seed no higher type of woman.

KINESIAS
(Indicating Peace)
Never saw one I wanted so much to top.

LYSISTRATA
(Oblivious to the byplay, addressing both groups)
With such a history of mutual benefits conferred
and received, why are you fighting? Stop this wickedness!
Come to terms with each other! What prevents you?

SPARTAN
We'd a heap sight druther make Peace, if we was indemnified with a plumb strategic location.

skills were much valued in democracies like Athens, where so many issues were resolved through open debate.) Some Sophists claimed to teach wisdom and even virtue. Reflecting the human focus characteristic of fifth-century thought, they refrained from speculations about the physical universe, instead applying reasoned analysis to human beliefs and institutions. In doing so, they identified a central problem of human social life and the life of the *polis*: the conflict between nature and custom, or law. The more traditional among them argued that law itself was in accord with nature and was of divine origin, a view that fortified the traditional beliefs of the *polis*.

Others argued, however, that laws were merely the result of convention—an agreement among people—and not in accord with nature. The laws could not pretend to be a positive moral force but merely had the negative function of preventing people from harming each other. The most extreme Sophists argued that law was contrary to nature, a trick whereby the weak control the strong. Critias, an Athenian oligarch and one of the more extreme Sophists, even said that some clever person had invented the gods themselves to deter people from doing what they wished. Such ideas attacked the theoretical foundations of the *polis* and helped provoke the philosophical responses of Plato and Aristotle in the next century.

(Pointing at Peace's rear)
We'll take thet butte.

LYSISTRATA
Butte?

SPARTAN
The Promontory of Pylos—Sparta's Back Door.
We've missed it fer a turrible spell.
(Reaching)
Hev to keep our
hand in.

KINESIAS
(Pushing him away)
The price is too high—you'll never take that!

LYSISTRATA
Oh, let them have it.

KINESIAS
What room will we have left
for maneuvers?

LYSISTRATA
Demand another spot in exchange.

KINESIAS
(Surveying Peace like a map as he addresses the Spartan)
Then you hand over to us—uh, let me see—
let's try Thessaly . . .
(Indicating the relevant portions of Peace)
First of all, Easy Mountain . . .
then the Maniac Gulf behind it . . .
and down to Megara for the legs . . .

SPARTAN
You cain't take all of thet! Yore plumb
out of yore mind!

LYSISTRATA
(To Kinesias)
Don't argue. Let the legs go.
(Kinesias nods. A pause, general smiles of agreement)

KINESIAS
(Doffing his cloak)
I feel an urgent desire to plow a few furrows.

SPARTAN
(Doffing his cloak)
Hit's time to work a few loads of fertilizer in.

LYSISTRATA
Conclude the treaty and the simple life is yours.
If such is your decision, convene your councils,
and then deliberate the matter with your allies.

KINESIAS
Deliberate? Allies?
We're over-extended already!
Wouldn't every ally approve of our position—
Union Now?

SPARTAN
I know I kin speak for ourn?

KINESIAS
And I for ours
They're just a bunch of gigolos.

LYSISTRATA
I heartily approve.
Now first attend to your purification,
then we, the women, will welcome you to the Citadel
and treat you to all the delights of a home-cooked banquet.
Then you'll exchange your oaths and pledge your faith,
and every man of you will take his wife
and depart for home.

Aristophanes, *Lysistrata*, trans. by Douglass Parker, in *Four Comedies by Aristophanes*, ed. by W. Arrowsmith (Ann Arbor: University of Michigan Press, 1969), pp. 79–81. Reprinted by permission of the University of Michigan Press.

History The first prose literature in the form of history was Herodotus's account of the Persian War. "The father of history," as he has been deservedly called, was born shortly before the outbreak of the war. His account goes far beyond all previous chronicles, genealogies, and geographical studies and attempts to explain human actions and to draw instruction from them.

Although his work was completed about 425 B.C.E. and shows a few traces of Sophist influence, its spirit is that of an earlier time. Herodotus accepted the evidence of legends and oracles, although not uncritically, and often explained human events in terms of divine intervention. Human arrogance and divine vengeance are key forces that help explain the defeat of Croesus by Cyrus, as well as Xerxes' defeat by the Greeks. Yet the *History* is typical of its time in celebrating the crucial role of human intelligence as exemplified by Miltiades at Marathon and Themistocles at Salamis. Nor was Herodotus unaware of the importance of institutions. His pride in the superiority of the Greek *polis*, in the discipline it inspired in its citizen soldiers, and in the superiority of the Greeks' voluntary obedience to law over the Persians' fear of punishment is unmistakable.

Thucydides, the historian of the Peloponnesian War, was born about 460 B.C.E. and died a few years after the end of the Great Peloponnesian War. He was very much a product of the late fifth century B.C.E. His work, which was influenced by the secular, human-centered, skeptical rationalism of the Sophists, also reflects the scientific attitude of the school of medicine named for his contemporary, Hippocrates of Cos.

The Hippocratic school, known for its pioneering work in medicine and scientific theory, emphasized an approach to the understanding, diagnosis, and treatment of disease that combined careful observation with reason. In the same way, Thucydides took pains to achieve factual accuracy and tried to use his evidence to discover meaningful patterns of human behavior. He believed human nature was essentially unchanging, so a wise person equipped with the understanding history provided might accurately foresee events and thus help to guide them. He believed, however, that only a few had the ability to understand history and to put its lessons to good use. He thought that the intervention of chance, which played a great role in human affairs, could foil even the wisest. Thucydides focused his interest on politics, and in that area his assumptions about human nature do not seem unwarranted. His work has proved to be, as he hoped, "a possession forever." Its description of the terrible civil war between the two basic kinds of *poleis* is a final and fitting example of the tension that was the source of both the greatness and the decline of Classical Greece.

The Fourth Century B.C.E.

Historians often speak of the Peloponnesian War as the crisis of the *polis* and of the fourth century B.C.E. as the period of its decline. The war did bring powerfully important changes: the impoverishment of some Greek cities and, with it, an intensification of class conflict; the development of professionalism in the army; and demographic shifts that sometimes reduced the citizen population and increased the numbers of resident aliens. The Greeks of the fourth century B.C.E. did not know, however, that their traditional way of life was on the verge of destruction. Still, thinkers recognized that they lived in a time of troubles, and they responded in various ways. Some looked to the past and tried to shore up the weakened structure of the *polis*; others tended toward despair and looked for new solutions; and still others averted their gaze from the public arena altogether. All of these responses are apparent in the literature, philosophy, and art of the period.

Drama The tendency of some to turn away from the life of the *polis* and inward to everyday life, the family, and their own individuality is apparent in the poetry of the fourth century B.C.E. A new genre, called Middle Comedy, replaced the political subjects and personal invective of the Old Comedy with a comic-realistic depiction of daily life, plots of intrigue, and a mild satire of domestic situations. Significantly, the role of the chorus, which in some way represented the *polis*, was diminished quite a bit. These trends all continued and were carried even further in the New Comedy. Its leading playwright, Menander (342–291 B.C.E.), completely abandoned mythological subjects in favor of domestic tragicomedy. His gentle satire of the foibles of ordinary people and his tales of lovers temporarily thwarted before a happy and proper ending would not be unfamiliar to viewers of modern situation comedies.

Tragedy faded as a robust and original form. It became common to revive the great plays of the previous century. No tragedies written in the fourth century B.C.E. have been preserved. The plays of Euripides, which rarely won first prize when first produced for Dionysian festival competitions, became increasingly popular in the fourth century and after. Euripides was less interested in cosmic confrontations of conflicting principles than in the psychology and behavior of individual human beings. Some of his late plays, in fact, are less like the tragedies of Aeschylus and Sophocles than forerunners of later forms such as the New Comedy. Plays like *Helena*, *Andromeda*, and *Iphigenia in Tauris* are more like fairy tales, tales of adventure, or love stories than tragedies.

Sculpture The same movement away from the grand, the ideal, and the general, and toward the ordinary, the real, and the individual is apparent in the development of Greek sculpture. To see these developments, one has only to compare the statue of the striding god from Artemisium (ca. 460 B.C.E.), thought to be either Zeus on the point of releasing a thunderbolt or Poseidon about to throw his trident, or the Doryphoros of Polycleitus (ca. 450–440 B.C.E.) with the Hermes of Praxiteles (ca. 340–330 B.C.E.) or the Apoxyomenos attributed to Lysippus (ca. 330 B.C.E.).

Philosophy and the Crisis of the *Polis*

Socrates Probably the most complicated response to the crisis of the *polis* may be found in the life and teachings of Socrates (469–399 B.C.E.). Because he wrote nothing, our knowledge of him comes chiefly from his disciples Plato and Xenophon and from later tradition. Although as a young man he was interested in speculations about the physical world, he later turned to the investigation of ethics and morality; as the Roman writer and statesman Cicero put it, he brought philosophy down from the heavens. Socrates was committed to the search for truth and for the knowledge about human affairs that he believed reason could discover. His method was to question and cross-examine men, particularly those reputed to know something, such as craftsmen, poets, and politicians.

The result was always the same. Those Socrates questioned might have technical information and skills

The theater at Epidaurus was built in the fourth century B.C.E. The city contained the Sanctuary of Asclepius, a god of healing, and drew many visitors who packed the theater at religious festivals. Hirmer Fotoarchiv

but seldom had any knowledge of the fundamental principles of human behavior. It is understandable that Athenians so exposed should be angry with their examiner, and it is not surprising they thought Socrates was undermining the beliefs and values of the *polis.* Socrates' unconcealed contempt for democracy, which seemingly relied on ignorant amateurs to make important political decisions without any certain knowledge, created further hostility. Moreover, his insistence on the primacy of his own individualism and his determination to pursue philosophy even against the wishes of his fellow citizens reinforced this hostility and the prejudice that went with it.

But Socrates, unlike the Sophists, did not accept pay for his teaching; he professed ignorance and denied that he taught at all. His individualism, moreover, was unlike the worldly hedonism of some of the Sophists. It was not wealth or pleasure or power that he urged people to seek, but "the greatest improvement of the soul." Unlike the more radical Sophists, he also denied that the *polis* and its laws were merely conventional. He thought, on the contrary, that they had a legitimate claim on the citizen, and he proved it in the most convincing fashion.

In 399 B.C.E., an Athenian jury condemned him to death on the charges of bringing new gods into the city and of corrupting the youth. His dialectical inquiries had angered many important people. His criticism of democracy must have been viewed with suspicion, especially since Critias and Charmides, who were members of the Thirty Tyrants, and the traitor Alcibiades, who had gone over to the Spartans, had been among his disciples. He was given a chance to escape but, as Plato's *Crito* tells us, he refused to do so because of his veneration of the laws. Socrates' career set the stage for later responses to the travail of the *polis.* He recognized its difficulties and criticized its shortcomings, and he turned away from an active political life, but he did not abandon the idea of the *polis.* He fought as a soldier in its defense, obeyed its laws, and sought to put its values on a sound foundation by reason.

The Cynics One branch of Socratic thought—the concern with personal morality and one's own soul, the disdain of worldly pleasure and wealth, and the withdrawal from political life—was developed and then distorted almost beyond recognition by the **Cynic School**. Antisthenes (ca. 455–360 B.C.E.), a follower of Socrates, is said

A Closer LOOK

THE ERECHTHEUM: PORCH OF THE MAIDENS

THE ERECHTHEUM, LOCATED on the north side of the Acropolis of Athens, was a temple to the goddess Athena in her oldest form as Athena Polias, the protector of the city. It was built between 421 and 407 B.C.E., probably to replace an older temple the Persians had destroyed in 480.

The new temple included the sites of some of the most ancient and holy relics of the Athenians: a small olive wood statue of Athena Polias; the tombs of Cecrops and Erechtheus, legendary early kings of Athens; the marks of the sea god Poseidon's trident; and the salt water well (the "salt sea") that legend said resulted from Poseidon's strike. In the courtyard, according to the myth, Athena caused an olive tree to grow when she was contesting Poseidon for the honor of being the patron divinity of Athens. Poseidon created a salt-water spring on the Acropolis, but Athena's olive tree won over the judges, and she was victorious. Sculpture in the west pediment of the Parthenon depicted this contest.

Within the foundations the sacred snake of the temple, which represented the spirit of Cecrops and whose well-being was thought essential for the safety of the city, was thought to live. The priestesses of Athena fed the snake honey cakes. The snake's occasional refusal to eat the cakes was considered a disastrous omen.

Roy Rainford/Robert Harding/Getty Images

On the north side, there is another large porch with columns, and on the south, the famous "porch of the maidens," with six draped female figures (Caryatids) used instead of a column as a support. Lord Elgin, an early nineteenth-century British ambassador to the Ottoman Empire, removed one of the Caryatids and sent it to Britain to decorate his Scottish mansion. It was later sold to the British Museum (along with other sculptures plundered from the Parthenon). Today the five original Caryatids are displayed in helium-filled glass cases in the Acropolis Museum and have been replaced on the temple by exact replicas.

Steve Allen/Getty Images, Inc.—Brand × Pictures

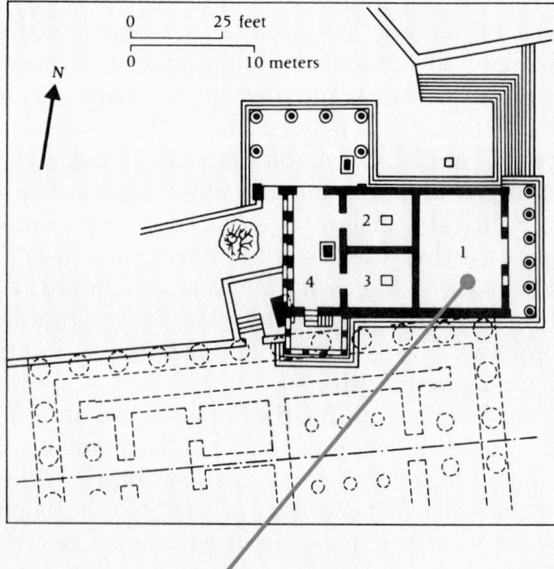

To examine this image in an interactive fashion, please go to www.myhistorylab.com

myhistorylab

The need to preserve the many sacred precincts likely explains the complex design. The main structure consists of four compartments, the largest being the east cella, with an Ionic portico on its east end.

to have been its founder, but its most famous exemplar was Diogenes of Sinope (ca. 400–325 B.C.E.). Because Socrates disparaged wealth and worldly comfort, Diogenes wore rags and lived in a tub. He performed shameful acts in public and made his living by begging to show his rejection of convention. He believed happiness lay in satisfying natural needs in the simplest and most direct way; because actions to this end, being natural, could not be indecent, they could and should be done publicly.

Socrates questioned the theoretical basis for popular religious beliefs; the Cynics, in contrast, ridiculed all religious observances. As Plato said, Diogenes was Socrates gone mad. Beyond that, the way of the Cynics contradicted important Socratic beliefs. Socrates, unlike traditional aristocrats such as Theognis, believed virtue was a matter not of birth, but of knowledge and that people do wrong only through ignorance of what is virtuous. The Cynics, in contrast, believed "virtue is an affair of deeds and does not need a store of words and learning."[3] Wisdom and happiness come from pursuing the proper style of life, not from philosophy.

The Cynics moved even further away from Socrates by abandoning the concept of the *polis* entirely. When Diogenes was asked about his citizenship, he answered he was *kosmopolites*, a citizen of the world. The Cynics plainly had turned away from the past, and their views anticipated those of the Hellenistic Age.

The striding god from Artemisium is a bronze statue dating from about 460 B.C.E. It was found in the sea near Artemisium, the northern tip of the large Greek island of Euboea, and is now on display in the Athens Archaeological Museum. Exactly whom he represents is not known. Some have thought him to be Poseidon holding a trident; others believe he is Zeus hurling a thunderbolt. In either case, he is a splendid representative of the early Classical period of Greek sculpture. National Archaeological Museum, Athens

Plato Plato (429–347 B.C.E.) was by far the most important of Socrates' associates and is a perfect example of the pupil who becomes greater than his master. He was the first systematic philosopher and therefore the first to place political ideas in their full philosophical context. He was also a writer of genius, leaving us twenty-six philosophical discussions. Almost all are in the form of dialogues, which somehow make the examination of difficult and complicated philosophical problems seem dramatic and entertaining. Plato came from a noble Athenian family, and he looked forward to an active political career until the excesses of the Thirty Tyrants and the execution of Socrates discouraged him from that pursuit. Twice he made trips to Sicily in the hope of producing a model state at Syracuse under the tyrants Dionysius I and II, but without success.

In 386 B.C.E., he founded the Academy, a center of philosophical investigation and a school for training statesmen and citizens. It had a powerful impact on Greek thought and lasted until the emperor Justinian closed it in the sixth century C.E.

Like Socrates, Plato firmly believed in the *polis* and its values. Its virtues were order, harmony, and justice, and one of its main objects was to produce good people. Like his master, and unlike the radical Sophists, Plato thought the *polis* was in accord with nature. He accepted Socrates' doctrine of the identity of virtue and knowledge. He made it plain what that knowledge was: *episteme*—science—a body of true and unchanging wisdom open to only a few philosophers, whose training, character, and intellect allowed them to see reality. Only such people were qualified to rule; they would prefer the life of pure contemplation, but would accept their responsibility and take their turn as philosopher kings. The training of such an individual required a specialization of function and a subordination of that individual to the community even greater than that at Sparta. This specialization would lead to Plato's definition of justice: Each person should do only that one thing to which his or her nature is best suited. (See "Plato on the Role of Women in His Utopian Republic," page 85.)

Plato understood that the *polis* of his day suffered from terrible internal stress, class struggle, and factional divisions. His solution, however, was not that of some Greeks—that is, conquest and resulting economic prosperity. For Plato, the answer was in moral and political reform. The way to harmony was to destroy the causes

[3] Diogenes Laertius, *Life of Antisthenes* 6.11.

of strife: private property, the family—anything, in short, that stood between the individual citizen and devotion to the *polis*.

Concern for the redemption of the *polis* was at the heart of Plato's system of philosophy. He began by asking the traditional questions: What is a good man, and how is he made? The goodness of a human being belonged to moral philosophy, and when goodness became a function of the state, it became political philosophy. Because goodness depended on knowledge of the good, it required a theory of knowledge and an investigation of what kind of knowledge goodness required. The answer must be metaphysical and so required a full examination of metaphysics. Even when the philosopher knew the good, however, the question remained how the state could bring its citizens to the necessary comprehension of that knowledge. The answer required a theory of education. Even purely logical and metaphysical questions, therefore, were subordinate to the overriding political questions. In this way, Plato's need to find a satisfactory foundation for the beleaguered *polis* contributed to the birth of systematic philosophy.

Aristotle Aristotle (384–322 B.C.E.) was a pupil of Plato's and owed much to the thought of his master, but his different experience and cast of mind led him in new directions. He was born at Stagirus, the son of the court doctor of neighboring Macedon. As a young man, he went to Athens to study at the Academy, where he stayed until Plato's death. Then he joined a Platonic colony at Assos in Asia Minor, and from there he moved to Mytilene. In both places he did research in marine biology, and biological interests played a large part in all his thoughts. In 342 B.C.E., Philip, the king of Macedon, appointed him tutor to his son, the young Alexander. (See "The Hellenistic World," page 86.)

In 336 B.C.E., Aristotle returned to Athens, where he founded his own school, the Lyceum, or the Peripatos, as it was also called because of the covered walk within it. In later years its members were called *Peripatetics.* On the death of Alexander in 323 B.C.E., the Athenians rebelled against the Macedonian rule, and Aristotle found it wise to leave. He died the following year.

Unlike the Academy, the members of the Lyceum took little interest in mathematics and were concerned with gathering, ordering, and analyzing all human knowledge. Aristotle wrote dialogues on the Platonic model, but none survive. He and his students also prepared many collections of information to serve as the basis for scientific works. Of these, only the *Constitution of the Athenians*, one of 158 constitutional treatises, remains. Almost all of what we possess is in the form of philosophical and scientific studies, whose loose organization and style suggest they were lecture notes. The range of subjects treated is astonishing, including logic, physics, astronomy, biology, ethics, rhetoric, literary criticism, and politics.

In each field, the method is the same. Aristotle began with observation of the empirical evidence, which in some cases was physical and in others was common opinion. To this body of information, he applied reason and discovered inconsistencies or difficulties. To deal with these, he introduced metaphysical principles to explain the problems or to reconcile the inconsistencies.

His view on all subjects, like Plato's, was teleological; that is, both Plato and Aristotle recognized purposes apart from and greater than the will of the individual human being. Plato's purposes, however, were contained in ideas, or forms that were transcendental concepts outside the experience of most people. For Aristotle, the purposes of most things were easily inferred by observation of their behavior in the world. Aristotle's most striking characteristics are his moderation and his common sense. His epistemology finds room for both reason and experience; his metaphysics gives meaning and reality to both mind and body; his ethics aims at the good life, which is the contemplative life, but recognizes the necessity for moderate wealth, comfort, and pleasure.

All these qualities are evident in Aristotle's political thought. Like Plato, he opposed the Sophists' assertion that the *polis* was contrary to nature and the result of mere convention. His response was to apply to politics the teleology he saw in all nature. In his view, matter existed to achieve an end, and it developed until it achieved its form, which was its end. There was constant development from matter to form, from potential to actual. Therefore, human primitive instincts could be seen as the matter out of which the human's potential as a political being could be realized. The *polis* made individuals self-sufficient and allowed the full realization of their potentiality. It was therefore natural.

It was also the highest point in the evolution of the social institutions that serve the human need to continue the species—marriage, household, village, and, finally, *polis.* For Aristotle, the purpose of the *polis* was neither economic nor military, but moral. According to Aristotle, "The end of the state is the good life" (*Politics* 1280b), the life lived "for the sake of noble actions" (1281a), a life of virtue and morality.

Characteristically, Aristotle was less interested in the best state—the utopia that required philosophers to rule it—than in the best state that was practically possible, one that would combine justice with stability. The constitution for that state he called *politeia*, not the best constitution, but the next best, the one most suited to, and most possible, for most states. Its quality was moderation, and it naturally gave power to neither the rich nor the poor, but to the middle class, which must also be the most numerous. The middle class possessed many virtues; because of its moderate wealth, it was free of the arrogance of the rich and the malice of the poor. For this reason, it was the most stable class.

PLATO ON THE ROLE OF WOMEN IN HIS UTOPIAN REPUBLIC

The Greek invention of reasoned intellectual analysis of all things led the philosopher Plato to consider the problem of justice, which is the subject of his most famous dialogue, the Republic. This leads him to sketch out a utopian state in which justice may be found and where the most radical arrangements may be necessary. These include the equality of the sexes and the destruction of the family in favor of the practice of men having wives and children in common. In the following excerpts, he argues for the fundamental equality of men and women and that women are no less appropriate as Guardians—leaders of the state—than men.

Why does Plato treat men and women the same? What objections could be raised to that practice? Would that policy, even if appropriate in Plato's utopia, also be suitable to conditions in the real world of classical Athens? In the world of today?

"If, then, we use the women for the same things as the men, they must also be taught the same things."

"Yes."

"Now music and gymnastics were given to the men."

"Yes."

"Then these two arts, and what has to do with war, must be assigned to the women also, and they must be used in the same ways."

"On the basis of what you say," he said, "it's likely."

"Perhaps," I said, "compared to what is habitual, many of the things now being said would look ridiculous if they were to be done as is said."

"Indeed they would," he said.

"Well," I said, "since we've started to speak, we mustn't be afraid of all the jokes—of whatever kind—the wits might make if such a change took place in gymnastics, in music and, not the least, in the bearing of arms and the riding of horses."

"Then," I said, "if either the class of men or that of women show its superiority in some art or other practice, then we'll say that that art must be assigned to it. But if they look as though they differ in this alone, that the female bears and the male mounts, we'll assert that it has not thereby yet been proved that a woman differs from a man with respect to what we're talking about; rather, we'll still suppose that our guardians and their women must practice the same things."

"And rightly," he said.

"Therefore, my friend, there is no practice of a city's governors which belongs to woman because she's woman, or to man because he's man; but the natures are scattered alike among both animals; and woman participates according to nature in all practices, and man in all, but in all of them woman is weaker than man."

"Certainly."

"So, shall we assign all of them to men and none to women?"

"How could we?"

"For I suppose there is, as we shall assert, one woman apt at medicine and another not, one woman apt at music and another unmusical by nature."

"Of course."

"And isn't there then also one apt at gymnastics and at war, and another unwarlike and no lover of gymnastics?"

"I suppose so."

"And what about this? Is there a lover of wisdom and a hater of wisdom? And one who is spirited and another without spirit?"

"Yes, there are these too."

"There is, therefore, one woman fit for guarding and another not, or wasn't it a nature of this sort we also selected for the men fit for guarding?"

"Certainly, that was it."

The stability of the constitution also came from its being a mixed constitution, blending in some way the laws of democracy and of oligarchy. Aristotle's scheme was unique because of its realism and the breadth of its vision. All the political thinkers of the fourth century B.C.E. recognized the *polis* was in danger, and all hoped to save it. All recognized the economic and social troubles that threatened it. Isocrates, a contemporary of Plato and Aristotle, urged a program of imperial conquest as a cure for poverty and revolution. Plato saw the folly of solving a political and moral problem by purely economic means and resorted to the creation of utopias. Aristotle combined the practical analysis of political and economic realities with the moral and political purposes of the traditional defenders of the *polis.* The result was a passionate confidence in the virtues of moderation and of the middle class, and the proposal of a constitution that would give it power. It is ironic that the ablest defense of the *polis* came soon before its demise.

▼ The Hellenistic World

The term *Hellenistic* was coined in the nineteenth century to describe the period of three centuries during which Greek culture spread far from its homeland to Egypt and deep into Asia. The new civilization formed in this expansion was a mixture of Greek and Near Eastern elements, although the degree of mixture varied from time to time and place to place. The Hellenistic world was larger than the world of Classical Greece, and its major political units were much larger than the city-states, though these persisted in different forms. The new political and cultural order had its roots in the rise to power of a Macedonian dynasty that conquered Greece and the Persian Empire in two generations.

The Macedonian Conquest

The quarrels among the Greeks brought on defeat and conquest by a new power that suddenly rose to eminence in the fourth century B.C.E.: the kingdom of Macedon. The Macedonians inhabited the land to the north of Thessaly (see Map 3–1, page 62), and through the centuries they had unknowingly served the vital purpose of protecting the Greek states from the barbarian tribes further to the north.

By Greek standards, Macedon was a backward, semibarbaric land. It had no *poleis* and was ruled loosely by a king in a rather Homeric fashion. He was chosen partly on the basis of descent, but the acclamation of the army gathered in assembly was required to make him legitimate. Quarrels between pretenders to the throne and even murder to secure it were not uncommon. A council of nobles checked the royal power and could reject a weak or incompetent king. Hampered by constant wars with the barbarians, internal strife, loose organization, and lack of money, Macedon played no great part in Greek affairs up to the fourth century B.C.E.

The Macedonians were of the same stock as the Greeks and spoke a Greek dialect, and the nobles, at least, thought of themselves as Greeks. The kings claimed descent from Heracles and the royal house of Argos. They tried to bring Greek culture into their court and won acceptance at the Olympic games. If a king could be found to unify this nation, it was bound to play a greater part in Greek affairs.

Philip of Macedon That king was Philip II (r. 359–336 B.C.E.), who, although still under thirty, took advantage of his appointment as regent to overthrow his infant nephew and make himself king. Like many of his predecessors, he admired Greek culture. Between 367 and 364 B.C.E., he had been a hostage in Thebes, where he learned much about Greek politics and warfare from Epaminondas. His talents for war and diplomacy and his boundless ambition made him the ablest king in Macedonian history. Using both diplomatic and military means, he pacified the tribes on his frontiers and strengthened his own hold on the throne. Then he began to undermine Athenian control of the northern Aegean. He took Amphipolis, which gave him control of gold and silver mines. The income allowed him to found new cities, to bribe

This freestanding statue of the *Charioteer of Delphi* is one of the few full-scale bronze sculptures that survive from the fifth century B.C.E. Polyzalos, the tyrant of the Greek city of Gela in Sicily, dedicated it after winning a victory in the chariot race in the Pythian games, either in 478 or 474. The games were held at the sacred shrine of the god Apollo at Delphi, and the statue was placed within the god's sanctuary, not far from Apollo's temple. The Charioteer of Delphi. Dedicated by Polyzalos of Gela for a victory either in 478 or 474 B.C.E. Greek (Classical). Bronze, H: 180 cm. Archaelogical Museum, Delphi, Greece. Photograph politicians in foreign towns, and to reorganize his army into the finest fighting force in the world.

The Macedonian Army Philip put to good use what he had learned in Thebes and combined it with the advantages afforded by Macedonian society and tradition. His genius created a versatile and powerful army that was at once national and professional, unlike the amateur armies of citizen-soldiers who fought for the individual *poleis.*

The infantry was drawn from among Macedonian farmers and the frequently rebellious Macedonian hill people. In time, these two elements were integrated to form a loyal and effective national force. Infantrymen were armed with thirteen-foot pikes instead of the more common nine-foot pikes and stood in a more open phalanx formation than the *hoplite* phalanx of the *poleis.* The effectiveness of this formation depended more on the skillful use of the pike than the weight of the charge. In Macedonian tactics, the role of the phalanx was not to be the decisive force, but to hold the enemy until a massed cavalry charge could strike a winning blow on the flank or into a gap. The cavalry was made up of Macedonian nobles and clan leaders, called Companions, who lived closely with the king and developed a special loyalty to him.

Philip also employed mercenaries who knew the latest tactics used by mobile light-armed Greek troops and were familiar with the most sophisticated siege machinery known to the Greeks. With these mercenaries, and with draft forces from among his allies, he could expand on his native Macedonian army of as many as 40,000 men.

The Invasion of Greece So armed, Philip turned south toward central Greece. Since 355 B.C.E., the Phocians had been fighting against Thebes and Thessaly. Philip gladly accepted the request of the Thessalians to be their general, defeated Phocis, and treacherously took control of Thessaly. Swiftly he turned northward again to Thrace and gained domination over the northern Aegean coast and the European side of the straits to the Black Sea. This conquest threatened the vital interests of Athens, which still had a formidable fleet of three hundred ships.

The Athens of 350 B.C.E. was not the Athens of Pericles. It had neither imperial revenue nor allies to share the burden of war, and its own population was smaller than in the fifth century. The Athenians, therefore, were reluctant to go on expeditions themselves or even to send out mercenary armies under Athenian generals, for they had to be paid out of taxes or contributions from Athenian citizens.

The leading spokesman against these tendencies and the cautious foreign policy that went with them was Demosthenes (384–322 B.C.E.), one of the greatest orators in Greek history. He was convinced that Philip was a dangerous enemy to Athens and the other Greeks. He spent most of his career urging the Athenians to resist Philip's encroachments. He was right, for beginning in 349 B.C.E., Philip attacked several cities in northern and central Greece and firmly planted Macedonian power in those regions. The king of "barbarian" Macedon was elected president of the Pythian Games at Delphi, and the Athenians were forced to concur in the election.

In these difficult times it was Athens's misfortune not to have the kind of consistent political leadership that Cimon or Pericles had offered a century earlier. Many, perhaps most, Athenians accepted Demosthenes' view of Philip, but few were willing to run the risks and make the sacrifices necessary to stop him. Others, like Eubulus, an outstanding financial official and conservative political leader, favored a cautious policy of cooperation with Philip in the hope that his aims were limited and were no real threat to Athens.

Not all Athenians feared Philip. Isocrates (436–338 B.C.E.), the head of an important rhetorical and philosophical school in Athens, looked to him to provide the unity and leadership needed for a Panhellenic campaign against Persia. He and other orators had long urged such a campaign. They saw the conquest of Asia Minor as the solution to the economic, social, and political problems that had brought poverty and civil war to the Greek cities ever since the Peloponnesian War. Finally, there seem to have been some Athenians who were in the pay of Philip, for he used money lavishly to win support.

The years between 346 B.C.E. and 340 B.C.E. were spent in diplomatic maneuvering, each side trying to win useful allies. At last, Philip attacked Perinthus and Byzantium, the lifeline of Athenian commerce; in 340 B.C.E., he besieged both cities and declared war. The Athenian fleet saved both, and so in the following year, Philip marched into Greece. Demosthenes performed wonders in rallying the Athenians and winning Thebes over to the Athenian side. In 338 B.C.E., however, Philip defeated the allied forces at Chaeronea in Boeotia. The decisive blow in this great battle was a cavalry charge led by Alexander, the eighteen-year-old son of Philip.

The Macedonian Government of Greece The Macedonian settlement of Greek affairs was not as harsh as many had feared, although in some cities the friends of Macedon came to power and killed or exiled their enemies. Demosthenes remained free to engage in politics. Athens was spared from attack on the condition that it give up what was left of its empire and follow the lead of Macedon. The rest of Greece was arranged so as to remove all dangers to Philip's rule. To guarantee his security, Philip placed garrisons at Thebes, Chalcis, and Corinth.

In 338 B.C.E., Philip called a meeting of the Greek states to form the federal League of Corinth. The constitution of the league provided for autonomy, freedom from tribute and garrisons, and suppression of piracy and civil war. The league delegates would make foreign policy in theory without consulting their home governments or Philip. All this was a facade; not only was Philip of Macedon president of the league, but he was also its ruler. The defeat at Chaeronea ended Greek freedom and autonomy. Although it maintained its form and way of life for some time, the *polis* had lost control of its own affairs and the special conditions that had made it unique.

Philip did not choose Corinth as the seat of his new confederacy simply from convenience or by accident. It was at Corinth that the Greeks had gathered to resist a Persian invasion almost 150 years earlier. And it was there in 337 B.C.E. that Philip announced his intention to invade Persia in a war of liberation and revenge, as leader of the new league. In the spring of 336 B.C.E., however, as he prepared to begin the campaign, Philip was assassinated.

In 1977, a mound was excavated at the Macedonian village of Vergina. The structures revealed and the extraordinarily rich finds associated with them have led many scholars to conclude this is the royal tomb of Philip II, and the evidence seems persuasive. Philip certainly deserved so distinguished a resting place. He found Macedon a disunited kingdom of semibarbarians, despised and exploited by the Greeks. He left it a united kingdom, master and leader of the Greeks, rich, powerful, and ready to undertake the invasion of Asia.

Alexander the Great

Philip's first son, Alexander III (356–323 B.C.E.), later called Alexander the Great, succeeded his father at the age of twenty. The young king also inherited his father's daring plans to conquer Persia.

The Conquest of the Persian Empire The Persian Empire was vast and its resources enormous. The usurper Cyrus and his Greek mercenaries, however, had shown it to be vulnerable when they penetrated deep into its interior in the fourth century B.C.E. Its size and disparate nature made it hard to control and exploit. Its rulers faced constant troubles on its far-flung frontiers and intrigues within the royal palace. Throughout the fourth century, they had used Greek mercenaries to suppress uprisings. At the time of Philip II's death in 336 B.C.E., a new and inexperienced king, Darius III, was ruling Persia. Yet with a navy that dominated the sea, a huge army, and vast wealth, it remained a formidable opponent.

In 334 B.C.E., Alexander crossed the Hellespont into Asia. His army consisted of about 30,000 infantry and 5,000 cavalry; he had no navy and little money. These facts determined his early strategy—he must seek quick and decisive battles to gain money and supplies from the conquered territory, and he must move along the coast to neutralize the Persian navy by depriving it of ports. Memnon, the commander of the Persian navy, recommended the perfect strategy against this plan: to retreat, to scorch the earth and deprive Alexander of supplies, to avoid battles, to use guerrilla tactics, and to stir up rebellion in Greece. He was ignored. The Persians preferred to stand and fight; their pride and courage were greater than their wisdom.

Alexander met the Persian forces of Asia Minor at the Granicus River, where he won a smashing victory in characteristic style. (See Map 3–4.) He led a cavalry charge across the river into the teeth of the enemy on the opposite bank. He almost lost his life in the process, but he won the devotion of his soldiers. That victory left the coast of Asia Minor open. Alexander captured the coastal cities, thus denying them to the Persian fleet.

In 333 B.C.E., Alexander marched inland to Syria, where he met the main Persian army under King Darius at Issus. Alexander himself led the cavalry charge that broke the Persian line and sent Darius fleeing into central Asia Minor. He continued along the coast and captured previously impregnable Tyre after a long and ingenious siege, putting an end to the threat of the Persian navy. He took Egypt with little trouble and was greeted as liberator, pharaoh, and son of Re (an Egyptian god whose Greek equivalent was Zeus). At Tyre, Darius sent Alexander a peace offer, yielding his entire empire west of the Euphrates River and his daughter in exchange for an alliance and an end to the invasion. But Alexander aimed at conquering the whole empire and probably whatever lay beyond.

In the spring of 331 B.C.E., Alexander marched into Mesopotamia. At Gaugamela, near the ancient Assyrian city of Nineveh, he met Darius, ready for a last stand. Once again, Alexander's tactical genius and personal leadership carried the day. The Persians were broken, and Darius fled once more. Alexander entered Babylon, again hailed as liberator and king.

THE RISE OF MACEDON

359–336 B.C.E.	Reign of Philip II
338 B.C.E.	Battle of Chaeronea; Philip conquers Greece
338 B.C.E.	Founding of League of Corinth
336–323 B.C.E.	Reign of Alexander III (the Great)
334 B.C.E.	Alexander invades Asia
333 B.C.E.	Battle of Issus
331 B.C.E.	Battle of Gaugamela
330 B.C.E.	Fall of Persepolis
327 B.C.E.	Alexander reaches Indus Valley
323 B.C.E.	Death of Alexander

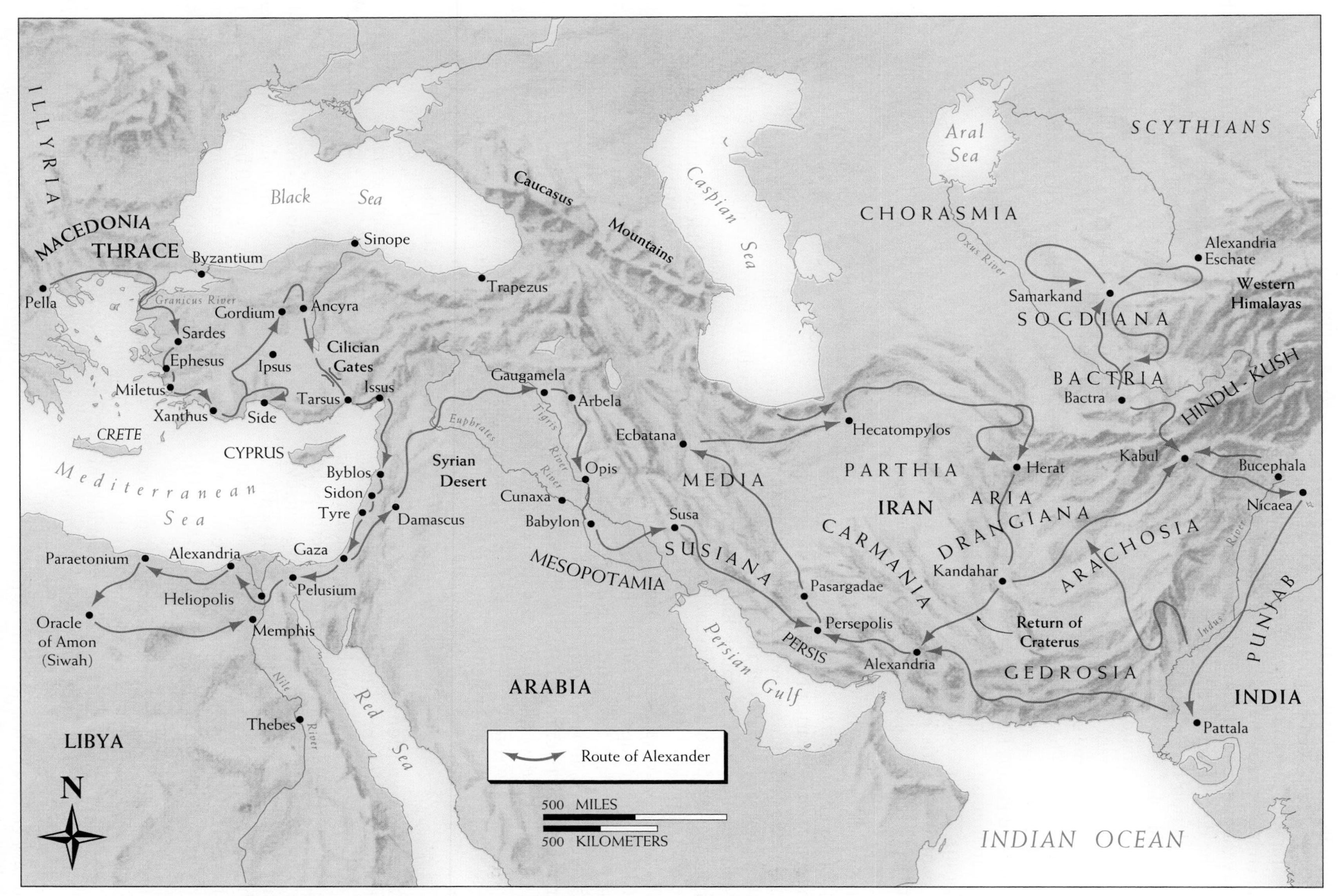

Map 3–4 **Alexander's Campaigns** The route taken by Alexander the Great in his conquest of the Persian Empire, 334 to 323 B.C.E. Starting from the Macedonian capital at Pella, he reached the Indus Valley before being turned back by his own restive troops. He died of fever in Mesopotamia.

In January of 330 B.C.E., he came to Persepolis, the Persian capital, which held splendid palaces and the royal treasury. This bonanza ended his financial troubles and put a vast sum of money into circulation, with economic consequences that lasted for centuries. After a stay of several months, Alexander burned Persepolis to dramatize the destruction of the native Persian dynasty and the completion of Hellenic revenge for the earlier Persian invasion of Greece.

The new regime could not be secure while Darius lived, so Alexander pursued him eastward. Just south of the Caspian Sea, he came on the corpse of Darius, killed by his relative Bessus. The Persian nobles around Darius had lost faith in him and had joined in the plot. The murder removed Darius from Alexander's path, but now he had to catch Bessus, who proclaimed himself successor to Darius. The pursuit of Bessus (who was soon caught), combined with his own great curiosity and longing to go to the most distant places, took Alexander to the frontier of India.

Near Samarkand, in the land of the Scythians, he founded Alexandria Eschate ("Furthest Alexandria"), one of the many cities bearing his name that he founded as he traveled. As part of his grand scheme of amalgamation and conquest, he married the Bactrian princess Roxane and enrolled 30,000 young Bactrians into his army. These were to be trained and sent back to the center of the empire for later use.

In 327 B.C.E., Alexander took his army through the Khyber Pass in an attempt to conquer the lands around the Indus River (modern Pakistan). He reduced the king of these lands, Porus, to vassalage but pushed on in the hope of reaching the river called Ocean that the Greeks believed encircled the world. Finally, his weary men refused to go on. By the spring of 324 B.C.E., the army was back at the Persian Gulf and celebrated in the Macedonian style, with a wild spree of drinking.

The Death of Alexander Alexander was filled with plans for the future: for the consolidation and organization of his empire; for geographical exploration; for building new cities, roads, and harbors; and perhaps for further conquests in the west. There is even some evidence that he asked to be deified and worshipped as a god, although we cannot be sure if he really did so or why. In June 323 B.C.E., however, he was overcome by a fever and died in Babylon at the age of thirty-three. His memory has never faded, and he soon became the subject of myth, legend, and romance. From the beginning, estimates of him have varied. Some have seen in him a man of grand and noble vision who transcended the narrow limits of Greek and Macedonian ethnocentrism and sought to realize the solidarity of humankind in a great world state. Others have seen him as a calculating despot, given to drunken brawls, brutality, and murder.

The truth is probably somewhere in between. Alexander was one of the greatest generals the world has seen; he never lost a battle or failed in a siege, and with a modest army he conquered a vast empire. He had rare organizational talents, and his plan for creating a multinational empire was the only intelligent way to consolidate his conquests. He established many new cities—seventy, according to tradition—mostly along trade routes. These cities encouraged commerce and prosperity and introduced Hellenic civilization into new areas. It is hard to know if even Alexander could have held together the vast new empire he had created, but his death proved that only he would have had a chance to succeed.

The Successors

Nobody was prepared for Alexander's sudden death, and a weak succession further complicated affairs: Roxane's unborn child and Alexander's weak-minded half brother. His able and loyal Macedonian generals at first hoped to preserve the empire for the Macedonian royal house, and to this end they appointed themselves governors of the various provinces of the empire. The conflicting ambitions of these strong-willed men, however, led to prolonged warfare among them. In these conflicts three of the original number were killed, and all of the direct members of the Macedonian royal house were either executed or murdered. With the murder of Roxane and her son in 310 B.C.E., there was no longer any focus for the enormous empire; and in 306 and 305 B.C.E., the surviving governors proclaimed themselves kings of their various holdings.

Three of these Macedonian generals founded dynasties of significance in the spread of Hellenistic culture:

- Ptolemy I, 367–283 B.C.E.; founder of Dynasty 31 in Egypt, the Ptolemies, of whom Cleopatra, who died in 30 B.C.E., was the last
- Seleucus I, 358–280 B.C.E.; founder of the Seleucid Dynasty in Mesopotamia
- Antigonus I, 382–301 B.C.E.; founder of the Antigonid Dynasty in Asia Minor and Macedon

For the first seventy-five years or so after the death of Alexander, the world ruled by his successors enjoyed considerable prosperity. The vast sums of money that he and they put into circulation greatly increased the level of economic activity. The opportunities for service and profit in the East attracted many Greeks and relieved their native cities of some of the pressure of the poor. The opening of vast new territories to Greek trade, the increased demand for Greek products, and the new availability of desired goods, as well as the conscious policies of the Hellenistic kings, all helped the growth of commerce.

The new prosperity, however, was not evenly distributed. The urban Greeks, the Macedonians, and the

One of the masterpieces of Hellenistic sculpture, the *Laocoön*. This is a Roman copy. According to legend, Laocoön was a priest who warned the Trojans not to take the Greeks' wooden horse within their city. This sculpture depicts his punishment. Great serpents sent by the goddess Athena, who was on the side of the Greeks, devoured Laocoön and his sons before the horrified people of Troy. Direzione Generale Musei Vaticani

Hellenized natives who made up the upper and middle classes lived in comfort and even luxury, but the rural native peasants did not. Unlike the independent men who owned and worked the relatively small and equal lots of the *polis* in earlier times, Hellenistic farmers were reduced to subordinate, dependent peasant status, working on large plantations of decreasing efficiency. During prosperous times these distinctions were bearable, although even then there was tension between the two groups. After a while, however, the costs of continuing wars, inflation, and a gradual lessening of the positive effects of the introduction of Persian wealth all led to economic crisis. The kings bore down heavily on the middle classes, who were skilled at avoiding their responsibilities, however. The pressure on the peasants and the city laborers became great too, and they responded by slowing down their work and even by striking. In Greece, economic pressures brought clashes between rich and poor, demands for the abolition of debt and the redistribution of land, and even, on occasion, civil war.

These internal divisions, along with international wars, weakened the capacity of the Hellenistic kingdoms to resist outside attack. By the middle of the second century B.C.E., they had all, except for Egypt, succumbed to an expanding Italian power, Rome. The two centuries between Alexander and the Roman conquest, however, were of great and lasting importance. They saw the entire eastern Mediterranean coast, Greece, Egypt, Mesopotamia, and the old Persian Empire formed into a single political, economic, and cultural unit.

▼ Hellenistic Culture

The career of Alexander the Great marked a significant turning point in Greek thought as it was represented in literature, philosophy, religion, and art. His conquests and the establishment of the successor kingdoms put an end to the central role of the *polis* in Greek life and thought. Some scholars disagree about the end of the *polis*, denying that Philip's victory at Chaeronea marked its demise. They point to the persistence of *poleis* throughout the Hellenistic period and even see a continuation of them in the Roman *municipia.* These were, however, only a shadow of the vital reality that had been the true *polis.*

Deprived of control of their foreign affairs, and with a foreign monarch determining their important internal arrangements, the post-Classical cities lost the political freedom that was basic to the old outlook. They were cities, perhaps—in a sense, even city-states—but not *poleis.* As time passed, they changed from sovereign states to municipal towns merged into military empires. Never again in antiquity would there be either a serious attack on or defense of the *polis*, for its importance was gone. For the most part, the Greeks after Alexander turned away from political solutions for their problems. Instead, they sought personal responses to their hopes and fears, particularly in religion, philosophy, and magic. The confident, sometimes arrogant, humanism of the fifth century B.C.E. gave way to a kind of resignation to fate, a recognition of helplessness before forces too great for humans to manage.

Philosophy

These developments are noticeable in the changes that overtook the established schools of philosophy as well as in the emergence of two new and influential groups of philosophers: the Epicureans and the Stoics. Athens's position as the center of philosophical studies was reinforced, for the Academy and the Lyceum continued in operation, and the new schools were also located in Athens. The Lyceum turned gradually away from the universal investigations of its founder, Aristotle, even from his scientific interests, to become a center chiefly of literary and especially historical studies.

The Academy turned even further away from its tradition. It adopted the systematic Skepticism of Pyrrho of Elis. Under the leadership of Arcesilaus and Carneades, the Skeptics of the Academy became skilled at pointing out fallacies and weaknesses in the philosophies of the rival schools. They thought that nothing could be known and so consoled themselves and their followers by suggesting that nothing mattered. It was easy for them, therefore, to accept conventional morality and the world as it was. The Cynics, of course, continued to denounce convention and to advocate the crude life in accordance with nature, which some of them practiced publicly to the shock and outrage of respectable citizens. Neither Skepticism nor Cynicism had much appeal to the middle-class city dweller of the third century B.C.E., who sought some basis for choosing a way of life now that the *polis* no longer provided one ready-made.

The Epicureans Epicurus of Athens (342–271 B.C.E.) formulated a new teaching, embodied in the school he founded in his native city in 306 B.C.E. His philosophy conformed to the mood of the times in that its goal was not knowledge, but human happiness, which he believed a style of life based on reason could achieve. He took sense perception to be the basis of all human knowledge. The reality and reliability of sense perception rested on the acceptance of the physical universe described by the atomists, Democritus and Leucippus. The **Epicureans** proclaimed atoms were continually falling through the void and giving off images that were in direct contact with the senses. These falling atoms could swerve in an arbitrary, unpredictable way to produce the combinations seen in the world.

Epicurus thereby removed an element of determinism that existed in the Democritean system. When a person died, the atoms that composed the body dispersed, so the person had no further existence or perception and therefore nothing to fear after death. Epicurus believed the gods existed, but that they took no interest in human affairs. This belief amounted to a practical atheism, and Epicureans were often thought to be atheists.

The purpose of Epicurean physics was to liberate people from their fear of death, of the gods, and of all nonmaterial or supernatural powers. Epicurean ethics were hedonistic, that is, based on the acceptance of pleasure as true happiness. But pleasure for Epicurus was chiefly negative: the absence of pain and trouble. The goal of the Epicureans was *ataraxia*, the condition of being undisturbed, without trouble, pain, or responsibility. Ideally, a man should have enough means to allow him to withdraw from the world and avoid business and public life. Epicurus even advised against marriage and children. He preached a life of genteel, restrained selfishness that might appeal to intellectual men of means but was not calculated to be widely attractive.

The Stoics Soon after Epicurus began teaching in his garden in Athens, Zeno of Citium in Cyprus (335–263 B.C.E.) established the **Stoic** school. It derived its name from the *stoa poikile*, or painted portico, in the Athenian *agora*, where Zeno and his disciples walked and talked beginning about 300 B.C.E. From then until about the middle of the second century B.C.E., Zeno and his successors preached a philosophy that owed a good deal to Socrates, by way of the Cynics. It was also fed by a stream of Eastern thought. Zeno, of course, came from Phoenician Cyprus; Chrysippus, one of his successors, came from Cilicia in southern Asia Minor; and other early Stoics came from such places as Carthage, Tarsus, and Babylon.

Like the Epicureans, the Stoics sought the happiness of the individual. Quite unlike them, the Stoics proposed a philosophy almost indistinguishable from religion. They believed humans must live in harmony within themselves and with nature; for the Stoics, God and nature were the same. The guiding principle in nature was divine reason (***Logos***), or fire. Every human had a spark of this divinity, and after death it returned to the eternal divine spirit. From time to time the world was destroyed by fire, from which a new world arose.

The aim of humans, and the definition of human happiness, was the virtuous life: a life lived in accordance with natural law, "when all actions promote the harmony of the spirit dwelling in the individual man with the will of him who orders the universe."[4] To live such a life required the knowledge only the wise possessed. They knew what was good, what was evil, and what was neither, but "indifferent." According to the Stoics, good and evil were dispositions of the mind or soul: prudence, justice, courage, temperance, and so on, were good, whereas folly, injustice, cowardice, and the like, were evil. Life, health, pleasure, beauty, strength, wealth, and so on, were neutral—morally indifferent—for they did not contribute either to happiness or to misery. Human misery came from an irrational mental contraction—from passion, which was a disease of the soul. The wise sought *apatheia*, or freedom from passion, because passion arose from things that were morally indifferent.

Politically, the Stoics fit well into the new world. They thought of it as a single *polis* in which all people were children of the same God. Although they did not forbid political activity, and many Stoics took part in political life, withdrawal was obviously preferable

[4] Diogenes Laertius, *Life of Antisthenes* 6.11.

because the usual subjects of political argument were indifferent. Because the Stoics strove for inner harmony of the individual, their aim was a life lived in accordance with the divine will, their attitude fatalistic, and their goal a form of apathy. They fit in well with the reality of post-Alexandrian life. In fact, Stoicism facilitated the task of creating a new political system that relied not on the active participation of the governed, but merely on their docile submission.

Literature

Hellenistic literature reflects the new intellectual currents, the new conditions of literary life, and the new institutions created in that period. The center of literary production in the third and second centuries B.C.E. was the new city of Alexandria in Egypt. There the Ptolemies, the monarchs of Egypt during that time, founded the museum—a great research institute where royal funds supported scientists and scholars—and the library, which contained almost half a million papyrus scrolls.

The library contained much of the great body of past Greek literature, most of which has since been lost. The Alexandrian scholars made copies of what they judged to be the best works. They edited and criticized these works from the point of view of language, form, and content, and wrote biographies of the authors. Their work is responsible for the preservation of most of what remains to us of ancient literature. While some of their work is dry, petty, quarrelsome, and simply foolish, at its best, it is full of learning and perception.

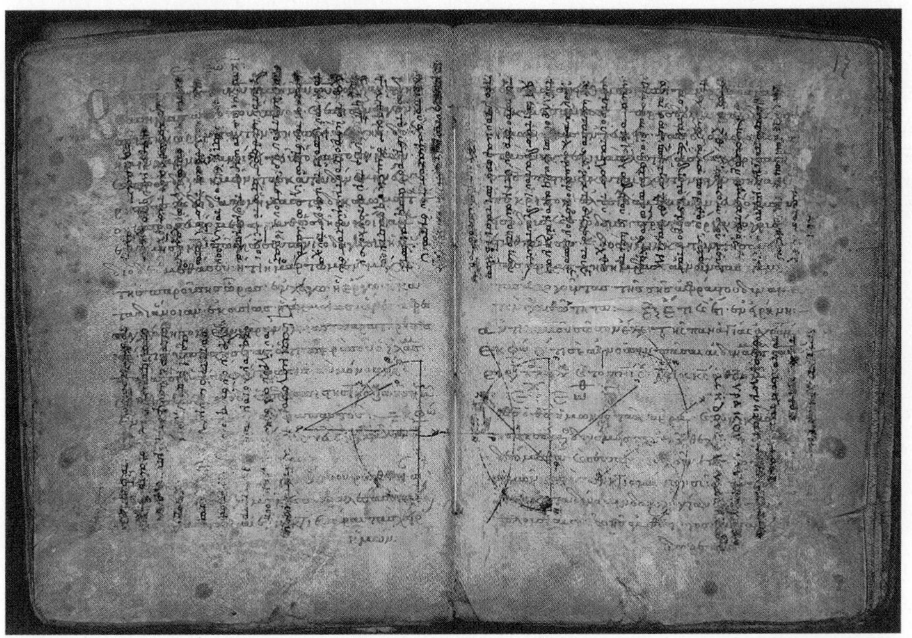

A page from *On Floating Bodies*. Archimedes' work was covered over by a tenth-century manuscript, but ultraviolet radiation reveals the original text and drawings underneath. © 2004 Christie's Images, Inc.

The scholarly atmosphere of Alexandria naturally gave rise to work in history and chronology. Eratosthenes (ca. 275–195 B.C.E.) established a chronology of important events dating from the Trojan War, and others undertook similar tasks. Contemporaries of Alexander, such as Ptolemy I, Aristobulus, and Nearchus, wrote what were apparently sober and essentially factual accounts of his career. We know most of the work of Hellenistic historians only in fragments that later writers cited. It seems, in general, to have emphasized sensational and biographical detail over the kind of rigorous, impersonal analysis that marked the work of Thucydides.

Architecture and Sculpture

The advent of the Hellenistic monarchies greatly increased the opportunities open to architects and sculptors. Money was plentiful, rulers sought outlets for conspicuous display, new cities needed to be built and beautified, and the well-to-do wanted objects of art. The new cities were usually laid out on the grid plan introduced in the fifth century B.C.E. by Hippodamus of Miletus. Temples were built on the classical model, and the covered portico, or *stoa*, became a popular addition to the *agoras* of the Hellenistic towns.

Reflecting the cosmopolitan nature of the Hellenistic world, leading sculptors accepted commissions wherever they were attractive. The result was a certain uniformity of style, although Alexandria, Rhodes, and the kingdom of Pergamum in Asia Minor developed their own distinctive characteristics. For the most part, Hellenistic sculpture moved away from the balanced tension and idealism of the fifth century B.C.E. toward the sentimental, emotional, and realistic mode of the fourth century B.C.E. These qualities are readily apparent in the marble statue called the Laocoon, carved at Rhodes in the second century B.C.E. and afterward taken to Rome.

Mathematics and Science

Among the most spectacular and remarkable intellectual developments of the Hellenistic age were those that came in mathematics and science. The burst of activity in these subjects drew their inspiration from several sources. The stimulation and organization provided by the work of Plato and Aristotle should not be ignored. Alexander's interest in science, evidenced by the scientists he took with him on his expedition and the aid he gave them in collecting data provided further impetus.

The expansion of Greek horizons geographically and the consequent contacts with Egyptian and Babylonian knowledge were also helpful. Finally, the patronage of the Ptolemies and the opportunity for many scientists to work with one another at the museum at Alexandria provided a unique opportunity for scientific work. The work the Alexandrians did formed the greater part of the scientific knowledge available to the Western world until the scientific revolution of the sixteenth and seventeenth centuries C.E.

Euclid's *Elements* (written early in the third century B.C.E.) remained the textbook of plane and solid geometry until recent times. Archimedes of Syracuse (ca. 287–212 B.C.E.) made further progress in geometry, established the theory of the lever in mechanics, and invented hydrostatics.

These advances in mathematics, once they were applied to the Babylonian astronomical tables available to the Hellenistic world, spurred great progress in astronomy. As early as the fourth century B.C.E., Heraclides of Pontus (ca. 390–310 B.C.E.) had argued that Mercury and Venus circulate around the sun and not Earth. He appears to have made other suggestions leading to a **heliocentric theory** of the universe. Most scholars, however, give credit for that theory to Aristarchus of Samos (ca. 310–230 B.C.E.), who asserted that the sun, along with the other fixed stars, did not move and that Earth revolved around the sun in a circular orbit and rotated on its axis while doing so. The heliocentric theory ran contrary not only to the traditional view codified by Aristotle, but also to what seemed to be common sense.

Hellenistic technology was not up to proving the theory, and, of course, the planetary orbits are not circular. The heliocentric theory did not, therefore, take hold. Hipparchus of Nicea (b. ca. 190 B.C.E.) constructed a model of the universe on the geocentric theory; his ingenious and complicated model did a good job of accounting for the movements of the sun, the moon, and the planets. Ptolemy of Alexandria (second century C.E.) improved Hipparchus's system, which remained dominant until the work of Copernicus, in the sixteenth century C.E.

Hellenistic scientists mapped the earth as well as the sky. Eratosthenes of Cyrene (ca. 275–195 B.C.E.) calculated the circumference of Earth to within about two hundred miles. He wrote a treatise on geography based on mathematical and physical reasoning and the reports of travelers. Despite the new data that were available to later geographers, Eratosthenes' map was in many ways more accurate than the one Ptolemy of Alexandria constructed, which became standard in the Middle Ages. (See Map 3–5.)

The Hellenistic Age contributed little to the life sciences, such as biology, zoology, and medicine. Even the

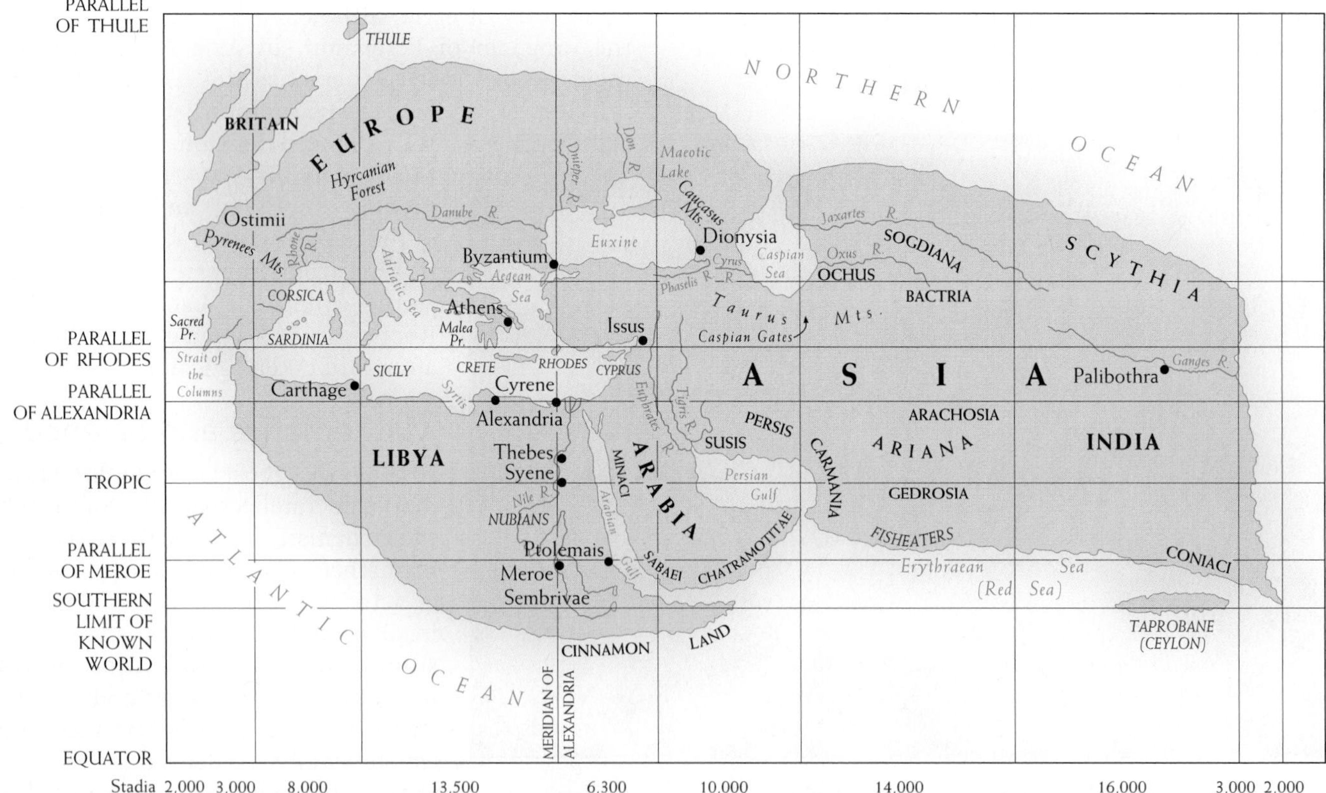

Map 3–5 **THE WORLD ACCORDING TO ERATOSTHENES** Eratosthenes of Alexandria (ca. 275–195 B.C.E.) was a Hellenistic geographer. His map, reconstructed here, was remarkably accurate for its time. The world was divided by lines of "latitude" and "longitude," thus anticipating our global divisions.

sciences that had such impressive achievements to show in the third century B.C.E. made little progress thereafter. In fact, to some extent, there was a retreat from science. Astrology and magic became subjects of great interest as scientific advance lagged.

In Perspective

The Classical Age of Greece was a period of unparalleled achievement. Whereas monarchical, hierarchical, command societies continued to characterize the rest of the world, in Athens democracy was carried as far as it would go before modern times. Although Athenian citizenship was limited to adult males of native parentage, citizens were granted full and active participation in every decision of the state without regard to wealth or class. Democracy disappeared late in the fourth century B.C.E. with the end of Greek autonomy. When it returned in the modern world more than two millennia later, it was broader, but shallower. Democratic citizenship did not again imply the active, direct participation of every citizen in the government of the state.

It was in this democratic, imperial Athens that the greatest artistic, literary, and philosophical achievements of Classical Greece took place. Analytical, secular history, tragedy and comedy, the philosophical dialogue, an organized system of logic, and the logical philosophical treatise were among the achievements of the Classical Age. The tradition of rational, secular speculation in natural philosophy and science was carried forward, but more attention was devoted to human questions in medicine and ethical and political philosophy. A naturalistic style of art evolved that showed human beings first as they ideally might look and then as they really looked, an approach that dominated Greek and Roman art until the late stages of the Roman Empire. This naturalistic style had a powerful effect on the Italian Renaissance and, through it, the modern world.

These Hellenic developments, it should be clear, diverge sharply from the experience of previous cultures and of contemporary ones in the rest of the world. To a great degree, they sprang from the unique political experience of the Greeks, based on the independent city-states. That unique experience and the Classical period ended with the Macedonian conquest, which introduced the Hellenistic Age and ultimately made the Greeks subject to, or part of, a great national state or empire.

The Hellenistic Age speaks to us less fully and vividly than that of Classical Greece, chiefly because it had no historian to compare with Herodotus and Thucydides. We lack the clear picture that a continuous, rich, lively, and meaningful narrative provides. This deficiency should not obscure the great achievements of the age. Its literature, art, scholarship, and science deserve attention in their own right.

The Hellenistic Age did perform a vital civilizing function. It spread Greek culture over a remarkably wide area and made a significant and lasting impression on much of it. Greek culture also adjusted to its new surroundings, unifying and simplifying its cultural cargo to make it more accessible to outsiders. The various Greek dialects gave way to a version of the Attic tongue, the koine, or common language.

In the same way, the scholarship of Alexandria established canons of literary excellence and the scholarly tools with which to make the great treasures of Greek culture understandable to later generations. The syncretism of thought and belief introduced in this period also made understanding and accord more likely among different peoples. When the Romans came into contact with Hellenism, it powerfully impressed them. When they conquered the Hellenistic world, they became, as their poet Horace said, captives of its culture.

REVIEW QUESTIONS

1. How was the Delian League transformed into the Athenian Empire during the fifth century B.C.E.? Did the empire offer any advantages to its subjects? Why was there such resistance to Athenian efforts to unify the Greek world in the fifth and fourth centuries B.C.E.?
2. Why did Athens and Sparta come to blows in the Great Peloponnesian War? What was each side's strategy for victory? Why did Sparta win the war?
3. Give examples from art, literature, and philosophy of the tension that characterized Greek life and thought in the Classical Age. How does Hellenistic art differ from that of the Classical Age?
4. Between 431 and 362 B.C.E., why did Athens, Sparta, and Thebes each fail to impose hegemony over the city-states of Greece? What does your analysis tell you about the components of successful rule?
5. How and why did Philip II conquer Greece between 359 and 338 B.C.E.? How was he able to turn Macedon into a formidable military and political power? Why was Athens unable to defend itself against Macedon? Where does more of the credit for Philip's success lie—in Macedon's strength or in the weakness of the Greek city-states?
6. What were the major consequences of Alexander's death? What did he achieve? Was he a conscious promoter of Greek civilization or just an egomaniac drunk with the lust of conquest?

SUGGESTED READINGS

J. Buckler, *Aegean Greece in the Fourth Century BC* (2003). A political, diplomatic, and military history of the Aegean Greeks of the fourth century B.C.E.

W. Burkert, *Greek Religion* (1985). A fine general study.

P. Cartledge, *Alexander the Great: The Hunt for a New Past* (2004). A learned and lively biography.

P. Cartledge, *Spartan Reflections* (2001). A collection of valuable essays by a leading scholar of ancient Sparta.

G. Cawkwell, *Philip of Macedon* (1978). A brief but learned account of Philip's career.

Y. Garlan, *Slavery in Ancient Greece* (1988). An up-to-date survey.

R. Garland, *Daily Life of the Ancient Greeks* (1998). A good account of the way the Greeks lived.

P. Green, *From Alexander to Actium* (1990). A brilliant synthesis of the Hellenistic period.

P. Green, *The Greco-Persian War* (1996). A lively account by a fine scholar with a keen feeling for the terrain.

E. S. Gruen, *Heritage and Hellenism: The Reinvention of Jewish Tradition* (1998). A fine account of the interaction between Jews and Greeks in Hellenistic times.

C. D. Hamilton, *Agesilaus and the Failure of Spartan Hegemony* (1991). An excellent biography of the king who was the central figure in Sparta during its domination in the fourth century B.C.E.

R. Just, *Women in Athenian Law and Life* (1988). A good study of the place of women in Athenian life.

D. Kagan, *The Peloponnesian War* (2003). An analytic narrative of the great war between Athens and Sparta.

D. Kagan, *Pericles of Athens and the Birth of Athenian Democracy* (1991). An account of the life and times of the great Athenian statesman.

B. M. W. Knox, *The Heroic Temper: Studies in Sophoclean Tragedy* (1964). A brilliant analysis of tragic heroism.

D. M. Lewis, *Sparta and Persia* (1977). A valuable discussion of relations between Sparta and Persia in the fifth and fourth centuries B.C.E.

C. B. Patterson, *The Family in Greek History* (1998). An interesting interpretation of the relationship between family and state in ancient Greece.

J. J. Pollitt, *Art and Experience in Classical Greece* (1972). A scholarly and entertaining study of the relationship between art and history in Classical Greece, with excellent illustrations.

J. J. Pollitt, *Art in the Hellenistic Age* (1986). An extraordinary analysis that places the art in its historical and intellectual context.

R. W. Sharples, *Stoics, Epicureans, and Sceptics. An Introduction to Hellenistic Philosophy* (1996). A brief and useful introduction.

B. S. Strauss, *Athens after the Peloponnesian War* (1987). An excellent discussion of Athens's recovery and of the nature of Athenian society and politics in the fourth century B.C.E.

I. Worthington, *Demosthenes, Statesman and Orator* (2000). A useful collection of essays on the career and importance of the Athenian political leader.

For additional learning resources related to this chapter, please go to www.myhistorylab.com

PEARSON myhistorylab

The Pont du Gard, an aqueduct and bridge, was built in the first century B.C.E. in southern France in Rome's first province beyond the Alps. Walter S. Clark/Photo Researchers, Inc.

4 Rome: From Republic to Empire

▼ **Prehistoric Italy**

▼ **The Etruscans**
Government • Religion • Women • Dominion

▼ **Royal Rome**
Government • The Family • Women in Early Rome • Clientage • Patricians and Plebeians

▼ **The Republic**
Constitution • The Conquest of Italy • Rome and Carthage • The Republic's Conquest of the Hellenistic World

▼ **Civilization in the Early Roman Republic**
Religion • Education • Slavery

▼ **Roman Imperialism: The Late Republic**
The Aftermath of Conquest • The Gracchi • Marius and Sulla

▼ **The Fall of the Republic**
Pompey, Crassus, Caesar, and Cicero • The First Triumvirate • Julius Caesar and His Government of Rome • The Second Triumvirate and the Triumph of Octavian

▼ **In Perspective**

KEY TOPICS

- **The emergence of the Roman Republic**
- **The development of the republican constitution**
- **Roman expansion and imperialism**
- **The character of Roman society in the republican era**
- **The fall of the republic**

THE ACHIEVEMENT OF the Romans was one of the most remarkable in human history. The descendants of the inhabitants of a small village in central Italy, they came eventually to rule the entire Italian peninsula, then the entire Mediterranean coastline. They conquered most of the Near East and, finally, much of continental Europe. They ruled this vast empire under a single government that provided considerable peace and prosperity for centuries. Never before the Romans nor since has that area been united, and rarely, if ever, has it enjoyed a stable peace. But

Rome's legacy was not merely military excellence and political organization. The Romans adopted and transformed the intellectual and cultural achievements of the Greeks and combined them with their own outlook and historical experience. The resulting Graeco-Roman tradition in literature, philosophy, and art provided the core of learning for the Middle Ages and pointed the way to the new paths taken in the Renaissance. It remains at the heart of Western civilization to this day.

▾ Prehistoric Italy

The culture of Italy developed late. Paleolithic settlements gave way to the Neolithic mode of life only around 2500 B.C.E. The Bronze Age came around 1500 B.C.E. About 1000 B.C.E., bands of new arrivals—warlike peoples speaking a set of closely related languages we call *Italic*—began to infiltrate Italy from across the Adriatic Sea and around its northern end. These invaders cremated their dead and put the ashes in tombs stocked with weapons and armor. Their bronzework was of a higher quality than that of the people they displaced, and they were soon making weapons, armor, and tools of iron. By 800 B.C.E., they had occupied the highland pastures of the Apennines, and within a short time, they began to challenge the earlier settlers for control of the tempting western plains. It would be the descendants of these tough mountain people—Umbrians, Sabines, Samnites, and Latins—together with others soon to arrive—Etruscans, Greeks, and Celts—who would shape the future of Italy.

▾ The Etruscans

The **Etruscans** exerted the most powerful external influence on the Romans. Their civilization arose in Etruria (now Tuscany), west of the Apennines between the Arno and Tiber Rivers, about 800 B.C.E. (See Map 4–1.) Since antiquity their origin has been debated, some arguing that they were indigenous and others that they came from the east. The evidence does not permit any certainty, and scholarship today focuses on the formation of a people rather than its origins.

Government

The Etruscans brought civilization with them. Their settlements were self-governing, fortified city-states, of which twelve formed a loose religious confederation. At first, kings ruled these cities, but they were replaced by an agrarian aristocracy, which ruled through a council and elected annual magistrates. The Etruscans were a military ruling class that exploited the native Italians (the predecessors of the later Italic speakers), who worked the Etruscans' land and mines and served as infantry in Etruscan armies. This aristocracy accumulated wealth through agriculture, industry, piracy, and commerce with the Carthaginians and the Greeks.

Religion

The Etruscans' influence on the Romans was greatest in religion. They imagined a world filled with gods and spirits, many of them evil. To deal with such demons, the Etruscans developed complicated rituals and powerful priesthoods. Divination by sacrifice and omens in

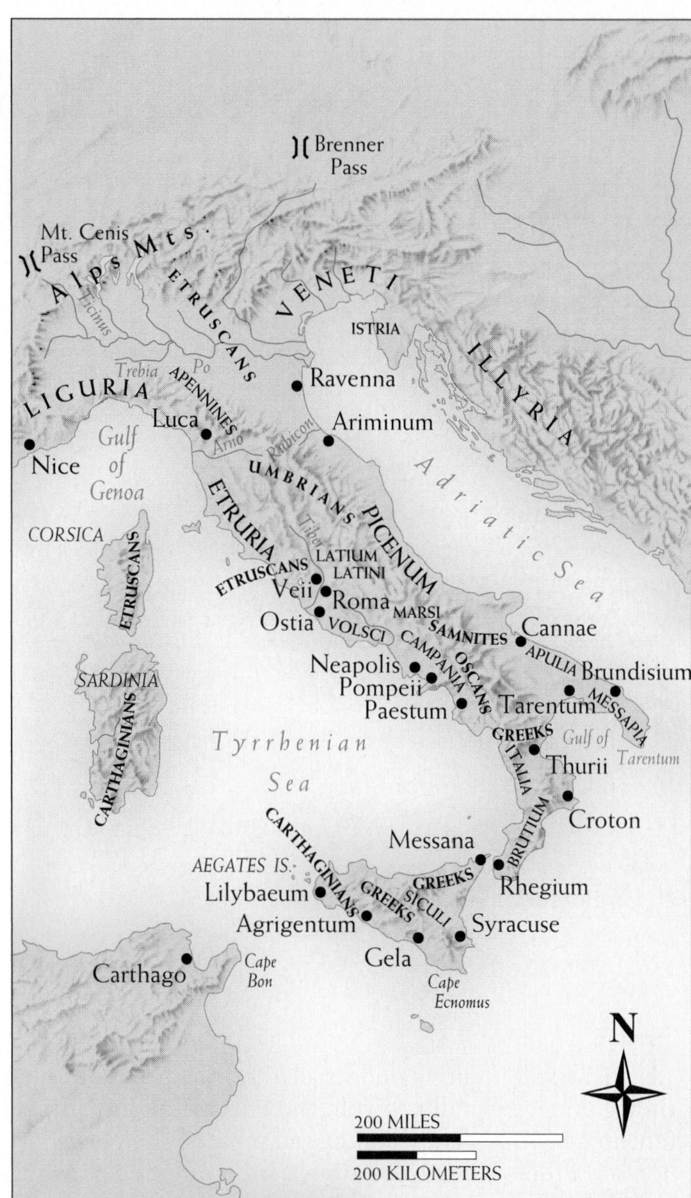

Map 4–1 **ANCIENT ITALY** This map of ancient Italy and its neighbors before the expansion of Rome shows major cities and towns as well as several geographical regions and the locations of some of the Italic and non-Italic peoples.

nature helped discover the divine will, and careful attention to precise rituals directed by priests helped please the gods. After a while the Etruscans, influenced by the Greeks, worshipped gods in the shape of humans and built temples for them.

Women

Etruscan women had a more significant role in family and society than did Greek women in the world of the *polis*. Etruscan wives appeared in public, in religious festivals, and at public banquets together with their husbands. Many of them were literate, and women both took part in athletic contests and watched them as spectators alongside men. Inscriptions on tombs and paintings on coffins mention both father and mother of the deceased and often show husbands and wives together in respectful and loving attitudes.

Dominion

The Etruscan aristocracy remained aggressive and skillful in the use of horses and war chariots. In the seventh and sixth centuries B.C.E., they expanded their power in Italy and across the sea to Corsica and Elba. They conquered **Latium** (a region that included the small town of Rome) and Campania, where they became neighbors of the Greeks of Naples. In the north, they got as far as the Po Valley. Small bands led by Etruscan chieftains who did not work in concert and would not necessarily aid one another in distress carried out these conquests. As a result, the conquests outside Etruria were not firmly based and did not last long.

Etruscan power reached its height some time before 500 B.C.E. and then rapidly declined. About 400 B.C.E., Celtic peoples from the area the Romans called **Gaul** (modern France) broke into the Po Valley and drove out the Etruscans. They settled this land so firmly that the Romans thereafter called it *Cisalpine Gaul* (Gaul on this side of the Alps). Eventually, even the Etruscan heartland in Etruria lost its independence and was incorporated into Roman Italy. The Etruscan language was forgotten, and Etruscan culture gradually became only a memory, but its influence on the Romans remained.

▼ Royal Rome

Rome was an unimportant town in Latium until the Etruscans conquered it, but its location—fifteen miles from the mouth of the Tiber River at the point at which hills made further navigation impossible—gave it advantages over its Latin neighbors. The island in the Tiber southwest of the Capitoline Hill made the river fordable, so Rome was naturally a center for communication and trade, both east-west and north-south.

This elaborate Etruscan coffin was discovered in a tomb at Cerveteri in the Italian region of Tuscany, the heart of ancient Etruria. It has been dated to about 520 B.C.E. Made of terra cotta, it shows wife and husband reclining affectionately together.
Sarcophagus of a Couple. Etruscan, 6th B.C.E. Terracotta. H: 114 cm. Louvre, Paris, France. Copyright Erich Lessing/Art Resource, NY

Government

In the sixth century B.C.E., Rome came under Etruscan control. Led by Etruscan kings, the Roman army, equipped and organized like the Greek phalanx, gained control of most of Latium. An effective political and social order that gave extraordinary power to the ruling figures in both public and private life made this success possible. To their kings the Romans gave the awesome power of ***imperium***—the right to issue commands and to enforce them by fines, arrests, and corporal, or even capital, punishment. Although it tended apparently to remain in the same family, kingship was elective. The Roman Senate had to approve the candidate for the office, and a vote of the people gathered in an assembly formally granted the *imperium*. A basic characteristic of later Roman government—the granting of great power to executive officers contingent on the approval of the Senate and, ultimately, the people—was already apparent in this structure. The same word is at the root of *imperator*, a military title, the source of our word *emperor*, that would eventually become the title of Rome's rulers. The union of military and political power would be a major theme in the transformation of the Roman Republic into a monarchical empire.

In theory and law, the king was the commander of the army, the chief priest, and the supreme judge. He could make decisions in foreign affairs, call out the army, lead it in battle, and impose discipline on his troops, all by virtue of his *imperium*. In practice, the royal power was much more limited.

The Senate was the second branch of the early Roman government. According to tradition, it originated when Romulus, Rome's legendary first king, chose one hundred of Rome's leading men to advise him. The number of senators ultimately rose to three hundred, where it stayed through most of the history of the republic. Ostensibly, the Senate had neither executive nor legislative power; it met only when the king summoned it to advise him. In reality its authority was great, for the senators, like the king, served for life. The Senate, therefore, had continuity and experience, and its members were the most powerful men in the state. It could not be lightly ignored.

The third branch of government, the curiate assembly, was made up of all citizens, as divided into thirty groups. (In early Rome, citizenship required descent from Roman parents on both sides.) The assembly met only when the king summoned it; he determined the agenda, made proposals, and recognized other speakers, if any. Usually, the assembly was called to listen and approve. Voting was not by head, but by group; a majority within each group determined its vote, and the majority vote of the groups determined decisions. Group voting would be typical of all future forms of Roman assembly.

The Family

The center of Roman life was the family. At its head stood the father, whose power and authority within the family resembled those of the king within the state. Over his children, the father held broad powers analogous to *imperium* in the state; he had the right to sell his children into slavery, and he even had the power of life and death over them. Over his wife, he had less power; he could not sell or kill her. In practice, consultation within the family, public opinion, and, most of all, tradition limited his power to dispose of his children. The father was the chief priest of the family. He led it in daily prayers to the dead, which reflected the ancestor worship central to the Roman family and state.

Women in Early Rome

Early Roman society was hierarchical and dominated by males. Throughout her life, a woman was under the control of some adult male. Before her marriage it was her father, afterward her husband or, when neither was available, a guardian chosen from one of their male relatives. One of them had to approve her right to buy or sell property or make contracts. Roman law gave control of a woman from father to husband by the right of *manus* (hand). This was conferred by one of two formal marriage ceremonies that were typical in early Rome. Over time, however, a third form of marriage became popular that left the power of *manus* in the hands of the woman's father, even after her marriage. This kind of union was similar to what we would call common-law marriage, in which a woman could stay out of her husband's control of her and her dowry by absenting herself from her husband's home for at least three consecutive nights each year. This gave her greater rights of inheritance in her father's family and greater independence in her marriage.

In early Rome, marriage with *manus* was most common, but women of the upper classes had a position of influence and respect greater than the classical Greeks had and more like what appears to have been true of the Etruscans. Just as the husband was *paterfamilias*, the wife was *materfamilias*. She was mistress within the home, controlling access to the storerooms, keeping the accounts, and supervising the slaves and the raising of the children. She also was part of the family council and a respected adviser on all questions concerning the family. Divorce was difficult and rare, limited to a few specific transgressions by the wife, one of which was drunkenness. Even when divorced for cause, the wife retained her dowry.

Busts of a Roman couple from the period of the Republic. Although some have identified the individuals as Cato the Younger and his daughter Porcia, no solid evidence confirms this claim. Bust of Cato and Porcia. Roman sculpture. Vatican Museums, Vatican State. Photograph © Scala/Art Resource, NY

Clientage

Clientage was one of Rome's most important institutions. The client was "an inferior entrusted, by custom or by himself, to the protection of a stranger more powerful than he, and rendering certain services and observances in return for this protection."[1] The Romans spoke of a client as being in the *fides*, or trust, of his patron, and so the relationship always had moral implications. The patron provided his client with protection, both physical and legal. He gave him economic assistance in the form of a land grant, the opportunity to work as a tenant farmer or a laborer on the patron's land, or simply handouts. In return, the client would fight for his patron, work his land, and support him politically. Public opinion and tradition reinforced these mutual obligations. When early custom was codified in the mid-fifth century B.C.E., one of the twelve tablets of laws announced, "Let the patron who has defrauded his client be accursed."

In the early history of Rome, patrons were rich and powerful, whereas clients were poor and weak, but as time passed, rich and powerful members of the upper classes became clients of even more powerful men, chiefly for political purposes. Because the client-patron relationship was hereditary and sanctioned by religion and custom, it played an important part in the life of the Roman Republic.

Patricians and Plebeians

In the royal period, a class distinction based on birth divided Roman society in two. The wealthy **patrician** upper class held a monopoly of power and influence. Its members alone could conduct state religious ceremonies, sit in the Senate, or hold office. They formed a closed caste by forbidding marriage outside their own group.

The **plebeian** lower class must have consisted originally of poor, dependent small farmers, laborers, and artisans, the clients of the nobility. As Rome and its population grew, families that were rich, but outside the charmed circle of patricians, grew wealthy. From early times, therefore, there were rich plebeians, and incompetence and bad luck must have produced some poor patricians. The line between the classes and the monopoly of privileges remained firm, nevertheless, and the struggle of the plebeians to gain equality occupied more than two centuries of republican history.

▼ The Republic

Roman tradition tells us that the outrageous behavior of the last kings led the noble families to revolt in 509 B.C.E., bringing the monarchy to a sudden close and leading to the creation of the Roman Republic.

[1] E. Badian, *Foreign Clientelae* (264–70 B.C.E.), Clarendon Press (Oxford, 1958), p. 1.

Constitution

The Consuls The Roman constitution was an unwritten accumulation of laws and customs. The Romans were a conservative people and were never willing to deprive their chief magistrates of the great powers the monarchs had exercised. They elected two patricians to the office of consul and endowed them with *imperium*. Two financial officials called *quaestors*, whose number ultimately reached eight, assisted them. Like the kings, the **consuls** led the army, had religious duties, and served as judges. They retained the visible symbols of royalty—the purple robe, the ivory chair, and the *lictors* (minor officials), who accompanied them bearing rods and axe. The power of the consuls, however, was limited legally and institutionally as well as by custom.

The power of the consulship was granted not for life, but only for a year. Each consul could prevent any action by his colleague simply by saying no to his proposal, and the consuls shared their religious powers with others. Even the *imperium* was limited. Although the consuls had full powers of life and death while leading an army, within the sacred boundary of the city of Rome, the citizens had the right to appeal all cases involving capital punishment to the popular assembly. Besides, after their one year in office, the consuls would spend the rest of their lives as members of the Senate. It was a reckless consul who failed to ask the advice of the Senate or to follow it when there was general agreement.

The many checks on consular action tended to prevent initiative, swift action, and change, but this was just what a conservative, traditional, aristocratic republic wanted. Only in the military sphere did divided counsel and a short term of office create important problems. The Romans tried to get around the difficulties by sending only one consul into the field or, when this was impossible, allowing each consul sole command on alternate days. In serious crises, the consuls, with the advice of the Senate, could appoint a *dictator* to the command and could retire in his favor. The *dictator*'s term of office was limited to six months, but his own *imperium* was valid both inside and outside the city without appeal.

These devices worked well enough in the early years of the republic, when Rome's battles were near home. Longer wars and more sophisticated opponents, however, revealed the system's weaknesses and required significant changes. Long campaigns prompted the invention of the **proconsulship** in 325 B.C.E., whereby the term of a consul serving in the field was extended. This innovation contained the seeds of many troubles for the constitution.

The creation of the office of *praetor* also helped provide commanders for Rome's many campaigns. The basic function of the *praetors* was judicial, but they also had *imperium* and served as generals. *Praetors'* terms were also for one year. By the end of the republic, there were eight *praetors*, whose annual terms, like the consuls', could be extended for military commands when necessary.

At first, the consuls identified citizens and classified them according to age and property. After the middle of the fifth century B.C.E., this job was delegated to a new office, that of ***censor***. The Senate elected two *censors* every five years. They conducted a census and drew up the citizen rolls. Their task was not just clerical; the classification of the citizens fixed taxation and status, so the *censors* had to be men of fine reputation, former consuls. They soon acquired additional powers. By the fourth century B.C.E., they compiled the roll of senators and could strike senators from that roll not only for financial but also for moral reasons. As the prestige of the office grew, it became the ultimate prize of a Roman political career.

The Senate and the Assembly With the end of the monarchy, the Senate became the single continuous, deliberative body in the Roman state, greatly increasing its influence and power. Its members were prominent patricians, often leaders of clans and patrons of many clients. The Senate soon gained control of the state's finances and of foreign policy. Neither magistrates nor popular assemblies could lightly ignore its formal advice.

The most important assembly in the early republic was the *centuriate assembly*, which was, in a sense, the Roman army acting in a political capacity. Its basic unit was the *century*, theoretically one hundred fighting men classified according to their weapons, armor, and equipment. Because each man equipped himself, this meant the organization was by classes according to wealth.

Voting was by *century* and proceeded in order of classification from the cavalry down. The assembly elected the consuls and several other magistrates, voted on bills put before it, made decisions of war and peace, and also served as the court of appeal against decisions of the magistrates affecting the life or property of a citizen. In theory, the assembly had final authority, but the Senate exercised great, if informal, influence.

The Struggle of the Orders The laws and constitution of the early republic gave to the patricians almost a monopoly of power and privilege. Plebeians were barred from public office, from priesthoods, and from other public religious offices. They could not serve as judges and could not even know the law, for there was no published legal code. The only law was traditional practice, and that existed only in the minds and actions of patrician magistrates. Plebeians were subject to the *imperium* but could not exercise its power. They were not allowed to marry patricians. When Rome gained new land by conquest, patrician magistrates distributed it in a way that favored patricians. The patricians dominated the assemblies and the Senate. The plebeians undertook a campaign to achieve political, legal, and social equality, and this attempt, which succeeded after two centuries of intermittent effort, is called the *Struggle of the Orders*.

The most important source of plebeian success was the need for their military service. According to tradition, the plebeians, angered by patrician resistance to their demands, withdrew from the city and camped on the Sacred Mount. There they formed a plebeian tribal assembly and elected plebeian **tribunes** to protect them from the arbitrary power of the magistrates. They declared the tribune inviolate and sacrosanct; anyone laying violent hands on him was accursed and liable to death without trial. By extension of his right to protect the plebeians, the tribune gained the power to veto any action of a magistrate or any bill in a Roman assembly or the Senate. The plebeian assembly voted by tribe, and a vote of the assembly was binding on plebeians. They tried to make their decisions binding on all Romans, but could not do so until 287 B.C.E.

Next, the plebeians obtained access to the laws, when early Roman custom in all its harshness and simplicity was codified in the Twelve Tables around 450 B.C.E. In 445 B.C.E., plebeians gained the right to marry patricians. The main prize, the consulship, the patricians did not yield easily. Not until 367 B.C.E. did legislation—the Licinian-Sextian Laws—provide that at least one consul could be a plebeian. Before long, plebeians held other offices—even the dictatorship and the censorship. In 300 B.C.E., they were admitted to the most important priesthoods, the last religious barrier to equality. In 287 B.C.E., the plebeians completed their triumph. They once again withdrew from the city and secured the passage of a law whereby decisions of the plebeian assembly bound all Romans and did not require the approval of the Senate.

It might seem that the Roman aristocracy had given way under the pressure of the lower class. Yet the victory of the plebeians did not bring democracy. An aristocracy based strictly on birth had given way to an aristocracy more subtle, but no less restricted, based on

THE RISE OF THE PLEBEIANS TO EQUALITY IN ROME

509 B.C.E.	Kings expelled; republic founded
450–449 B.C.E.	Laws of the Twelve Tables published
445 B.C.E.	Plebeians gain right of marriage with patricians
367 B.C.E.	Licinian-Sextian Laws open consulship to plebeians
300 B.C.E.	Plebeians attain chief priesthoods
287 B.C.E.	Laws passed by Plebeian Assembly made binding on all Romans

A Closer LOOK

LICTORS

THE LICTORS WERE attendants of the Roman magistrates who held the power of *imperium*, the right to command. In republican times these magistrates were the consuls, praetors, and proconsuls. The lictors were men from the lower classes—some were even former slaves. They constantly attended the magistrates when the latter appeared in public. The lictors cleared a magistrate's way in crowds, and summoned, arrested, and punished offenders for him. They also served as their magistrate's house guard.

The axe carried by the man on the left is a symbol of the magistrate's power, when he was acting as a military commander outside the city, to put a Roman citizen to death.

Alinari/Art Resource, NY

The bundle of sticks, called *fasces*, the other two lictors carry indicates the magistrates' right to employ corporal punishment, but their bindings symbolize the right of citizens not on military duty not to be punished without a trial.

The traditional dress of a lictor was a toga when in Rome, and a red coat called a *sagum* when outside the city or when taking part in a triumph.

To examine this image in an interactive fashion, please go to www.myhistorylab.com

myhistorylab

a combination of wealth and birth. A relatively small group of rich and powerful families, both patrician and plebeian, known as *nobiles*, attained the highest offices in the state. The significant distinction was no longer between patrician and plebeian but between the *nobiles* and everyone else.

The absence of the secret ballot in the assemblies enabled the *nobiles* to control most decisions and elections through intimidation and bribery. The leading families constantly competed with one another for office, power, and prestige, but they often combined in marriage and less formal alliances to keep the political plums within their own group. In the century from 233 to 133 B.C.E., for instance, twenty-six families provided 80 percent of the consuls, and only ten families accounted for almost 50 percent. These same families dominated the Senate, whose power became ever greater. Rome's success brought the Senate prestige, increased control of policy, and increased confidence in its capacity to rule. The end of the Struggle of the Orders brought domestic peace under a republican constitution dominated by a capable, if narrow, senatorial aristocracy. This outcome satisfied most Romans outside the ruling group, because Rome conquered Italy and brought many benefits to its citizens.

The Conquest of Italy

Not long after the fall of the monarchy in 509 B.C.E., a coalition of Romans, Latins, and Italian Greeks drove the Etruscans out of Latium for good. Throughout the fifth century B.C.E., the powerful Etruscan city of Veii, only twelve miles north of the Tiber River, raided Roman territory. After a hard struggle and a long siege, the Romans took Veii in 392 B.C.E., more than doubling the size of Rome.

Roman policy toward defeated enemies used both the carrot and the stick. When the Romans made friendly alliances with some, they gained new soldiers for their army. When they treated others more harshly by annexing their land, they achieved a similar end. Service in the Roman army was based on property, and the distribution to poor Romans of conquered land made soldiers of previously useless men. It also gave the poor a stake in Rome and reduced the pressure against its aristocratic regime. The long siege of Veii kept soldiers from their farms during the campaign. From that time on, the Romans paid their soldiers, thus giving their army greater flexibility and a more professional quality.

Gallic Invasion and Roman Reaction At the beginning of the fourth century B.C.E., a disaster struck. In 387 B.C.E., the Gauls, barbaric Celtic tribes from across the Alps, defeated the Roman army and burned Rome. The Gauls sought plunder, not conquest, so they extorted a ransom from the Romans and returned to the north. Rome's power appeared to be wiped out.

By about 350 B.C.E., however, the Romans were more dominant than ever. Their success in turning back new Gallic raids added to their power and prestige. As the Romans tightened their grip on Latium, the Latins became resentful. In 340 B.C.E., they demanded independence from Rome or full equality and launched a war of independence that lasted until 338 B.C.E. The victorious Romans dissolved the Latin League, and their treatment of the defeated opponents provided a model for the settlement of Italy.

Roman Policy Toward the Conquered The Romans did not destroy any of the Latin cities or their people, nor did they treat them all alike. Some near Rome received full Roman citizenship. Others farther away gained municipal status, which gave them the private rights of intermarriage and commerce with Romans, but not the public rights of voting and holding office in Rome. They retained the rights of local self-government and could obtain full Roman citizenship if they moved to Rome. They followed Rome in foreign policy and provided soldiers to serve in the Roman legions. (See "Rome's Treatment of Conquered Italian Cities.")

Still other states became allies of Rome on the basis of treaties, which differed from city to city. Some were given the private rights of intermarriage and commerce with Romans, and some were not; the allied states were always forbidden to exercise these rights with one another. Some, but not all, were allowed local autonomy. Land was taken from some, but not from others, nor was the percentage taken always the same. All the allies supplied troops to the army, in which they fought in auxiliary battalions under Roman officers, but they did not pay taxes to Rome.

On some of the conquered land, the Romans placed colonies, permanent settlements of veteran soldiers in the territory of recently defeated enemies. The colonists retained their Roman citizenship and enjoyed home rule; in return for the land they had been given, they were a kind of permanent garrison to deter or suppress rebellion. These colonies were usually connected to Rome by a network of military roads built as straight as possible and so durable that some are used even today. The roads guaranteed that a Roman army could swiftly reinforce an embattled colony or put down an uprising in any weather.

The Roman settlement of Latium reveals even more clearly than before the principles by which Rome was able to conquer and dominate Italy. The excellent army and the diplomatic skill that allowed Rome to separate its enemies help explain its conquests. The reputation for harsh punishment of rebels, and the sure promise that such punishment would be delivered, was made unmistakably clear: Both the colonies and military roads help explain the reluctance to revolt. But the positive side, represented by Rome's organization of the defeated states, is at least as important. The Romans did not regard the status given each newly conquered city as permanent. They held out to loyal allies the prospect of improving their status—even of achieving the ultimate prize, full Roman citizenship. In so doing, the Romans gave their allies a stake in Rome's future success and a sense of being colleagues, though subordinate ones, rather than subjects. The result, in general, was that most of Rome's allies remained loyal even when put to the severest test.

Defeated Samnites The next great challenge to Roman arms came in a series of wars with a tough mountain people of the southern Apennines, the Samnites. Some of Rome's allies rebelled, and soon the Etruscans and Gauls joined in the war against Rome. But most of

ROMAN EXPANSION IN ITALY

392 B.C.E.	Fall of Veii; Etruscans defeated
387 B.C.E.	Gauls burn Rome
338 B.C.E.	Latin League defeated
295 B.C.E.	Battle of Sentinum; Samnites and allies defeated
275 B.C.E.	Pyrrhus driven from Italy
265 B.C.E.	Rome rules Italy south of the Po River

ROME'S TREATMENT OF CONQUERED ITALIAN CITIES

Titus Livius (59 B.C.E.–17 C.E.), called Livy in English-speaking countries, wrote a history of Rome from its origins until his own time. In the following excerpt from it he describes the kind of settlement they imposed on various Italian cities after crushing their revolt in the years 340–338 B.C.E.

What principles and purposes underlay Rome's treatment of the different cities? What purposes were intended in settling Roman colonists among them?

The principal members of the senate applauded the consul's statement on the business on the whole; but said that, as the states were differently circumstanced, their plan might be readily adjusted and determined according to the desert of each, if they should put the question regarding each state specifically. The question was therefore so put regarding each separately and a decree passed. To the people of Lanuvium the right of citizenship was granted, and the exercise of their religious rights was restored to them with this provision, that the temple and grove of Juno Sospita should be common between the Lanuvian burghers and the Roman people. The peoples of Aricia, Nomentum, and Pedum were admitted into the number of citizens on the same terms as the Lanuvians. To the Tusculans the rights of citizenship which they already possessed were continued; no public penalty was imposed and the crime of rebellion was visited on its few instigators. On the people of Velitrae, Roman citizens of long standing, measures of great severity were inflicted because they had so often rebelled; their walls were razed, and their senate deported and ordered to dwell on the other side of the Tiber; any individual who should be caught on the hither side of the river should be fined one thousand asses, and the person who had apprehended him should not discharge his prisoner from confinement until the money was paid down. Into the lands of the senators colonists were sent; by their addition Velitrae recovered its former populous appearance.

From *History of Rome by Livy*, trans. by D. Spillan et al. (New York: American Book Company, n.d.). Vol. 1, p. 561, 1896.

the allies remained loyal. In 295 B.C.E., at Sentinum, the Romans defeated an Italian coalition, and by 280 B.C.E., they were masters of central Italy. Their power extended from the Po Valley south to Apulia and Lucania.

Now the Romans were in direct contact with the Greek cities of southern Italy. Roman intervention in a quarrel between Greek cities brought them face to face with Pyrrhus, king of Epirus. Pyrrhus, probably the best general of his time, commanded a well-disciplined and experienced mercenary army, which he hired out for profit, and a new weapon: twenty war elephants. He defeated the Romans twice but suffered many casualties. When one of his officers rejoiced at the victory, Pyrrhus told him, "If we win one more battle against the Romans, we shall be completely ruined." This "Pyrrhic victory" led him to withdraw to Sicily in 275 B.C.E. The Greek cities that had hired him were forced to join the Roman confederation. By 265 B.C.E., Rome ruled all Italy as far north as the Po River, an area of 47,200 square miles. The year after the defeat of Pyrrhus, Ptolemy Philadelphus, king of Egypt, sent a message of congratulations to establish friendly relations with Rome. This act recognized Rome's new status as a power in the Hellenistic world.

Rome and Carthage

The conquest of southern Italy brought the Romans face to face with the great naval power of the western Mediterranean, Carthage. (See Map 4–2, page 106.) Late in the ninth century B.C.E., the Phoenician city of Tyre had planted a colony on the coast of northern Africa near modern Tunis, calling it the New City, or Carthage. In the sixth century B.C.E., the conquest of Phoenicia by the Assyrians and the Persians left Carthage independent and free to exploit its advantageous

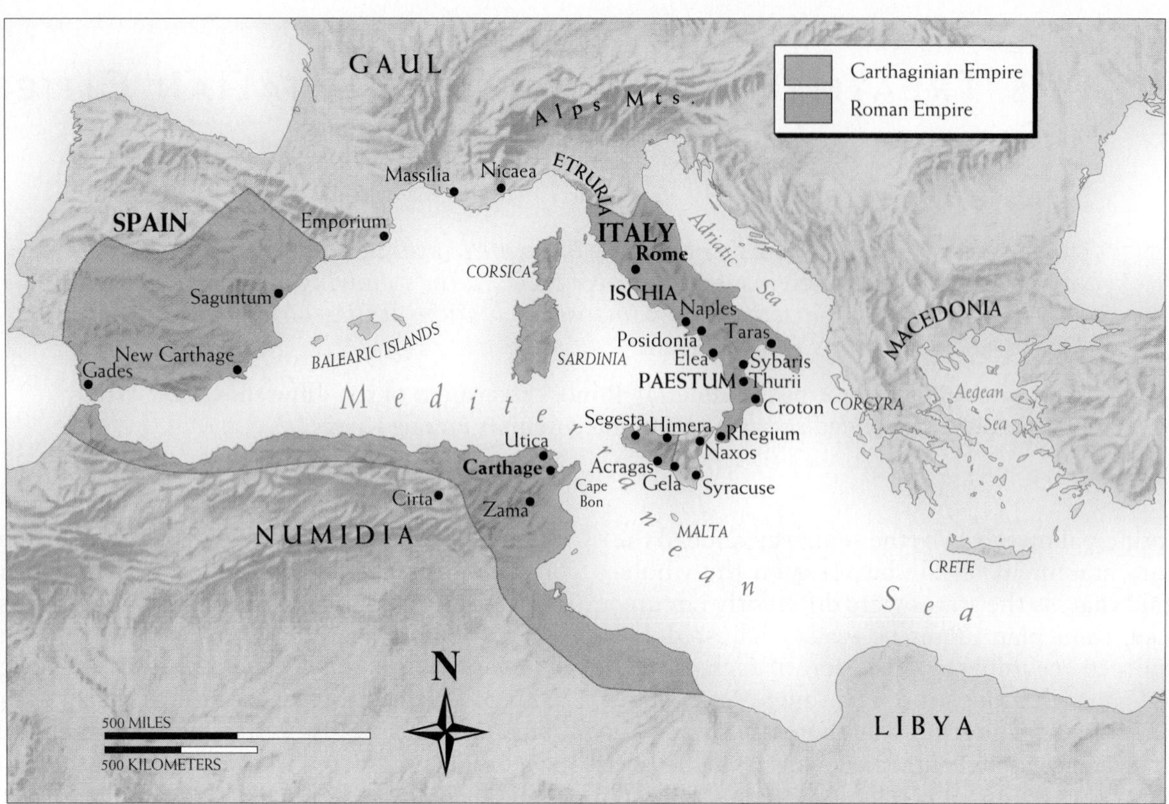

Map 4–2 **THE WESTERN MEDITERRANEAN AREA DURING THE RISE OF ROME** This map covers the theater of conflict between the growing Roman dominions and those of Carthage in the third century B.C.E. The Carthaginian Empire stretched westward from the city (in modern Tunisia) along the North African coast and into southern Spain.

situation. The city was located on a defensible site and commanded an excellent harbor that encouraged commerce. The coastal plain grew abundant grains, fruits, and vegetables. An inland plain allowed sheepherding. The Phoenician settlers conquered the native inhabitants and used them to work the land.

Beginning in the sixth century B.C.E., the Carthaginians expanded their domain to include the coast of northern Africa west beyond the Straits of Gibraltar and eastward into Libya. Overseas, they came to control the southern part of Spain, Sardinia, Corsica, Malta, the Balearic Islands, and western Sicily. The people of these territories, though originally allies, were all reduced to subjection like the natives of the Carthaginian home territory. They all served in the Carthaginian army or navy and paid tribute. Carthage also profited greatly from the mines of Spain and from an absolute monopoly of trade imposed on the western Mediterranean.

An attack by Hiero, tyrant of Syracuse, on the Sicilian city of Messana just across from Italy, first caused trouble between Rome and Carthage. Messana had been seized by a group of Italian mercenary soldiers who called themselves *Mamertines*, the sons of the war god Mars. When Hiero defeated the Mamertines, some of them called on the Carthaginians to help save their city. Carthage agreed and sent a garrison, for the Carthaginians wanted to prevent Syracuse from dominating the straits. One Mamertine faction, however, fearing that Carthage might take undue advantage of the opportunity, asked Rome for help.

In 264 B.C.E., the request came to the Senate. Because a Punic garrison (the Romans called the Carthaginians *Phoenicians*; in Latin the word is *Poeni* or *Puni*—hence the adjective *Punic*) was in place at Messana, any intervention would be not against Syracuse, but against the mighty empire of Carthage. Unless Rome intervened, however, Carthage would gain control of all Sicily and the straits. The assembly voted to send an army to Messana and expelled the Punic garrison. The First **Punic War** was on.

The First Punic War (264–241 B.C.E.) The war in Sicily soon settled into a stalemate until the Romans built a fleet to cut off supplies to the besieged Carthaginian cities at the western end of Sicily. When Carthage sent its own fleet to raise the siege, the Romans destroyed it. In 241 B.C.E., Carthage signed a treaty giving up Sicily and the islands between Italy and Sicily; it also agreed to pay a war indemnity in ten annual installments. Neither side was to attack the allies of the other. The peace was realistic and not unduly harsh; Rome had earned Sicily, and Carthage could well afford

Rome became a naval power late in its history to defeat Carthage in the First Punic War (264–241 B.C.E.). This sculpture in low relief shows a Roman ship, propelled by oars, with both ram and soldiers, ready either to ram or board an enemy ship. A Roman Warship. Direzione Generale Musei Vaticani

the indemnity. If it had been carried out in good faith, it might have brought lasting peace.

A rebellion, however, broke out in Carthage among the mercenaries, newly recruited from Sicily, who now demanded their pay. In 238 B.C.E., while Carthage was still preoccupied with the rebellion, Rome seized Sardinia and Corsica and demanded that Carthage pay an additional indemnity. This was a harsh and cynical action by the Romans; even the historian Polybius, a great champion of Rome, could find no justification for it. It undid the calming effects of the peace of 241 B.C.E. without preventing the Carthaginians from recovering their strength to seek vengeance in the future.

The conquest of overseas territory presented the Romans with new administrative problems. Instead of following the policy they had pursued in Italy, they made Sicily a province and Sardinia and Corsica another. It became common to extend the term of the governors of these provinces beyond a year. The governors were unchecked by colleagues and exercised full *imperium*. New magistracies, in effect, were thus created free of the limits put on the power of officials in Rome.

The new populations were neither Roman citizens nor allies; they were subjects who did not serve in the army but paid tribute instead. The old practice of extending citizenship and, with it, loyalty to Rome thus stopped at the borders of Italy. Rome collected taxes on these subjects by "farming" them out at auction to the highest bidder. At first, the tax collectors were natives from the same province. Later they were Roman allies and, finally, Roman citizens below senatorial rank who could become powerful and wealthy by squeezing the provincials hard. These innovations were the basis for Rome's imperial organization in the future. In time, they strained the constitution and traditions and threatened the existence of the republic.

After the First Punic War, campaigns against the Gauls and across the Adriatic distracted Rome. Meanwhile Hamilcar Barca, the Carthaginian governor of Spain from 237 B.C.E. until his death in 229 B.C.E., was leading Carthage on the road to recovery. Hamilcar sought to build a Punic Empire in Spain. He improved the ports and the commerce conducted in them, exploited the mines, gained control of the hinterland, won over many of the conquered tribes, and built a strong and disciplined army.

Hamilcar's successor, his son-in-law Hasdrubal, pursued the same policies. His success alarmed the Romans. They imposed a treaty in which he promised not to take an army north across the Ebro River in Spain, although Punic expansion in Spain was well south of that river at the time. Though the agreement appeared to put Rome in the position of giving orders to an inferior, it benefited both sides equally. If the Carthaginians accepted the limit of the Ebro on their expansion in Spain, the Romans would not interfere with that expansion.

The Second Punic War (218–202 B.C.E.) On Hasdrubal's assassination in 221 B.C.E., the army chose as his successor Hannibal, son of Hamilcar Barca. Hannibal was at that time twenty-five years old. He quickly consolidated and extended the Punic Empire in Spain. A few years before his accession, Rome had received an offer of alliance from the people of Saguntum, a Spanish town about one hundred miles south of the Ebro. The Romans accepted the friendship and the responsibilities

THE PUNIC WARS

264–241 B.C.E.	First Punic War
238 B.C.E.	Rome seizes Sardinia and Corsica
221 B.C.E.	Hannibal takes command of Punic army in Spain
218–202 B.C.E.	Second Punic War
216 B.C.E.	Battle of Cannae
209 B.C.E.	Scipio takes New Carthage
202 B.C.E.	Battle of Zama
149–146 B.C.E.	Third Punic War
146 B.C.E.	Destruction of Carthage

it entailed, despite the Ebro treaty. At first, Hannibal avoided any action against Saguntum, but the Saguntines, confident of Rome's protection, began to interfere with some of the Spanish tribes allied with Hannibal. When the Romans sent an embassy to Hannibal warning him to let Saguntum alone and repeating the injunction not to cross the Ebro, he ignored the warning and captured the town. The Romans sent an ultimatum to Carthage demanding the surrender of Hannibal. Carthage refused, and Rome declared war in 218 B.C.E.

Between the close of the First Punic War and the outbreak of the Second, Rome had repeatedly provoked Carthage, taking Sardinia in 238 B.C.E. and interfering in Spain, but had not prevented Carthage from building a powerful and dangerous empire in Spain. Hannibal saw to it that the Romans paid the price for these blunders. By September 218 B.C.E., he was across the Alps, in Italy and among the friendly Gauls.

Hannibal defeated the Romans at the Ticinus River and crushed the joint consular armies at the Trebia River. In 217 B.C.E., he outmaneuvered and trapped another army at Lake Trasimene. The key to success, however, would be defection by Rome's allies. Hannibal released Italian prisoners without harm or ransom and moved his army south of Rome to encourage rebellion. But the allies remained firm.

Sobered by their defeats, the Romans elected Quintus Fabius Maximus dictator. His strategy was to avoid battle while harassing Hannibal's army. He would fight only when his army had recovered and then only on favorable ground.

In 216 B.C.E., Hannibal marched to Cannae in Apulia to tempt the Romans, under different generals, into another open fight. They sent off an army of some 80,000 men to meet him. Almost the entire Roman army was wiped out. It was the worst defeat in Roman history. Rome's prestige was shattered, and most of its allies in southern Italy, as well as Syracuse in Sicily, went over to Hannibal. For more than a decade, no Roman army would dare face Hannibal in the field.

Hannibal, however, had neither the numbers nor the supplies to besiege walled cities, nor did he have the equipment to take them by assault. The Romans appointed Publius Cornelius Scipio (237–183 B.C.E.), later called Africanus, to the command in Spain with proconsular *imperium*. Scipio was not yet twenty-five and had held no high office. But he was a general almost as talented as Hannibal. Within a few years, young Scipio had conquered all of Spain and had deprived Hannibal of any hope of help from that region.

In 204 B.C.E., Scipio landed in Africa and forced the Carthaginians to accept a peace, the main clause of which was the withdrawal of Hannibal and his army from Italy. Hannibal had won every battle but lost the war, for he had not counted on the determination of Rome and the loyalty of its allies. Hannibal's return inspired Carthage to break the peace and to risk all in battle. In 202 B.C.E., Scipio and Hannibal faced each other at the Battle of Zama. The generalship of Scipio and the desertion of Hannibal's mercenaries gave the victory to Rome. The new peace terms reduced Carthage to the status of a dependent ally of Rome. The Second Punic War ended the Carthaginian command of the western Mediterranean and Carthage's term as a great power. Rome ruled the seas and the entire Mediterranean coast from Italy westward.

The Republic's Conquest of the Hellenistic World

The East By the middle of the third century B.C.E., the eastern Mediterranean had reached a condition of stability based on a balance of power among the three great Hellenistic kingdoms that allowed an established place even for lesser states. Two aggressive monarchs: Philip V of Macedon (221–179 B.C.E.) and Antiochus III of the Seleucid kingdom (223–187 B.C.E.) threatened this equilibrium, however. Philip and Antiochus moved swiftly, the latter against Syria and Palestine, the former against cities in the Aegean, in the Hellespontine region, and on the coast of Asia Minor.

The threat that a more powerful Macedon might pose to Rome's friends and, perhaps, even to Italy persuaded the Romans to intervene. Philip had already attempted to meddle in Roman affairs when he formed an alliance with Carthage during the Second Punic War, provoking a conflict known as the First Macedonian War (215–205 B.C.E.). In 200 B.C.E., in an action that began the Second Macedonian War, the Romans sent an ultimatum to Philip ordering him not to attack any Greek city and to pay reparations to Pergamum. These orders were meant to provoke, not avoid, war, and Philip refused to obey. Two years later the Romans sent out a talented young general, Flamininus, who demanded that Philip withdraw from Greece entirely. In 197 B.C.E., with Greek support, Flamininus defeated Philip at Cynoscephalae,

ROMAN ENGAGEMENT OVERSEAS

215–205 B.C.E.	First Macedonian War
200–197 B.C.E.	Second Macedonian War
196 B.C.E.	Proclamation of Greek freedom by Flamininus at Corinth
189 B.C.E.	Battle of Magnesia; Antiochus defeated in Asia Minor
172–168 B.C.E.	Third Macedonian War
168 B.C.E.	Battle of Pydna
154–133 B.C.E.	Roman wars in Spain
134 B.C.E.	Numantia taken

ending the war. The Greek cities freed from Philip were made autonomous, and in 196 B.C.E., Flamininus proclaimed the freedom of the Greeks.

Soon after the Romans withdrew from Greece, they came into conflict with Antiochus, who was expanding his power in Asia and on the European side of the Hellespont. On the pretext of freeing the Greeks from Roman domination, he landed an army on the Greek mainland. The Romans routed Antiochus at Thermopylae and quickly drove him from Greece. In 189 B.C.E., they crushed his army at Magnesia in Asia Minor. The peace of Apamia in the next year deprived Antiochus of his elephants and his navy and imposed a huge indemnity on him. Once again, the Romans took no territory for themselves and left several Greek cities in Asia free. They regarded Greece, and now Asia Minor, as a kind of protectorate in which they could intervene or not as they chose.

This relatively mild policy was destined to end as the stern and businesslike policies of the conservative *censor* Cato gained favor in Rome. A new harshness was to be applied to allies and bystanders, as well as to defeated opponents.

In 179 B.C.E., Perseus succeeded Philip V as king of Macedon. He tried to gain popularity in Greece by favoring the democratic and revolutionary forces in the cities. The Romans, troubled by his threat to stability, launched the Third Macedonian War (172–168 B.C.E.), and in 168 B.C.E. Aemilius Paulus defeated Perseus at Pydna. (See "Plutarch Describes a Roman Triumph," page 110.) The peace that followed this war, reflecting the changed attitude at Rome, was harsh. It divided Macedon into four separate republics, whose citizens were forbidden to intermarry or even to do business across the new national boundaries. Anti-Roman factions in the Greek cities were punished severely.

When Aemilius Paulus returned from his victory, he celebrated for three days by parading the spoils of war, royal prisoners, and great wealth through the streets of Rome. The public treasury benefited to such a degree that the direct property tax on Roman citizens was abolished. Part of the booty went to the general and part to his soldiers. New motives were thereby introduced into Roman foreign policy, or, perhaps, old motives were given new prominence. Foreign campaigns could bring profit to the state, rewards to the army, and wealth, fame, honor, and political power to the general.

The West Harsh as the Romans had become toward the Greeks, they treated the people of the Iberian Peninsula (Spain and Portugal), whom they considered barbarians, even worse. They committed dreadful atrocities, lied, cheated, and broke treaties to exploit and pacify the natives, who fought back fiercely in guerrilla style. From 154 to 133 B.C.E., the fighting waxed, and it became hard to recruit Roman soldiers to participate in the increasingly ugly war. At last, in 134 B.C.E., Scipio Aemilianus took the key city of Numantia by siege and burned it to the ground. This put an end to the war in Spain.

Roman treatment of Carthage was no better. Although Carthage lived up to its treaty with Rome faithfully and posed no threat, some Romans refused to abandon their hatred of the traditional enemy. Cato is said to have ended all his speeches in the Senate with the same sentence: "Ceterum censeo delendam esse Carthaginem" ("Besides, I think that Carthage must be destroyed"). At last the Romans took advantage of a technical breach of the peace to destroy Carthage. In 146 B.C.E., Scipio Aemilianus took the city, plowed up its land, and put salt in the furrows as a symbol of the permanent abandonment of the site. The Romans incorporated it as the province of Africa, one of six Roman provinces, including Sicily, Sardinia-Corsica, Macedonia, Hither Spain, and Further Spain.

▼ Civilization in the Early Roman Republic

Close and continued association with the Greeks of the Hellenistic world wrought important changes in the Roman style of life and thought. The Roman attitude toward the Greeks ranged from admiration for their culture and history to contempt for their constant squabbling, their commercial practices, and their weakness. Conservatives such as Cato might speak contemptuously of the Greeks as "Greeklings" (*Graeculi*), but even he learned Greek and absorbed Greek culture.

Before long, the education of the Roman upper classes was bilingual. Young Roman nobles studied Greek rhetoric, literature, and sometimes philosophy. These studies even affected education and the Latin language. As early as the third century B.C.E., Livius Andronicus, a liberated Greek slave, translated the *Odyssey* into Latin. It became a primer for young Romans and put Latin on the road to becoming a literary language.

Religion

The Greeks influenced Roman religion almost from the beginning. The Romans identified their own gods with Greek equivalents and incorporated Greek mythology into their own. Mostly, however, Roman religious practice remained simple and Italian, until the third century B.C.E. brought important new influences from the East.

Traditional Religion and Character In early Rome the family stood at the center of religious observance, and gods of the household and farm were most important. The *Lares* protected the family property, the *Penates* guarded what was inside the household. The *Genius* protected the life of the family. In the early days, before they were

PLUTARCH DESCRIBES A ROMAN TRIUMPH

In 168 B.C.E., L. Aemilius Paulus defeated King Perseus in the Battle of Pydna, bringing an end to the Third Macedonian War. For his great achievement, the Senate granted Paulus the right to celebrate a triumph, the great honorific procession granted only for extraordinary victories and that all Roman generals sought. The Greek historian. Plutarch (ca. 46–ca. 120 C.E.), who wrote a famous collection of biographies of eminent Greeks and Romans, described Paulus's triumph.

How do you explain the particular elements displayed on each day of the triumph? What purposes do you think a triumph served? What does this account tell us about Roman values? How are they different from the values Americans cherish today? Are there any similarities?

The people erected scaffolds in the forum, in the circuses, as they call their buildings for horse races, and in all other parts of the city where they could best behold the show. The spectators were clad in white garments; all the temples were open, and full of garlands and perfumes; the ways were cleared and kept open by numerous officers, who drove back all who crowded into or ran across the main avenue. This triumph lasted three days. On the first, which was scarcely long enough for the sight, were to be seen the statues, pictures, and colossal images which were taken from the enemy, drawn upon two hundred and fifty chariots. On the second was carried in a great many wagons the finest and richest armour of the Macedonians, both of brass and steel, all newly polished and glittering; the pieces of which were piled up and arranged purposely with the greatest art, so as to seem to be tumbled in heaps carelessly and by chance.

On the third day, early in the morning, first came the trumpeters, who did not sound as they were wont in a procession or solemn entry, but such a charge as the Romans use when they encourage the soldiers to fight. Next followed young men wearing frocks with ornamented borders, who led to the sacrifice a hundred and twenty stalled oxen, with their horns gilded, and their heads adorned with ribbons and garlands; and with these were boys that carried basins for libation, of silver and gold.

After his children and their attendants came Perseus himself, clad all in black, and wearing the boots of his country, and looking like one altogether stunned and deprived of reason, through the greatness of his misfortunes. Next followed a great company of his friends and familiars, whose countenances were disfigured with grief, and who let the spectators see, by their tears and their continual looking upon Perseus, that it was his fortune they so much lamented, and that they were regardless of their own.

After these were carried four hundred crowns, all made of gold, sent from the cities by their respective deputations to Aemilius, in honour of his victory. Then he himself came, seated on a chariot magnificently adorned (a man well worthy to be looked at, even without these ensigns of power), dressed in a robe of purple, interwoven with gold, and holding a laurel branch in his right hand. All the army, in like manner, with boughs of laurel in their hands, divided into their bands and companies, followed the chariot of their commander; some singing verses, according to the usual custom, mingled with raillery; others, songs of triumph and the praise of Aemilius' deeds; who, indeed, was admired and accounted happy by all men, and unenvied by every one that was good; except so far as it seems the province of some god to lessen that happiness which is too great and inordinate, and so to mingle the affairs of human life that no one should be entirely free and exempt from calamities; but, as we read in Homer, that those should think themselves truly blessed whom fortune has given an equal share of good and evil.

From Plutarch, "Aemilius Paulus," in *Lives of the Noble Grecians and Romans*, trans. by John Dryden, rev. by A. H. Clough (New York: Random House, n.d.), pp. 340–341.

influenced by the Etruscans and Greeks, Roman religion knew little of mythology: Their gods were impersonal forces, *numina*, rather than deities in human or superhuman form. To win their favor and protection the Romans developed a detailed and rigid set of rituals that used ceremony as a kind of magical bargain with which they could win and bind the benevolence of divinity. Their image of an afterlife was vague and insubstantial. Rome had no priestly caste, so the father *(paterfamilias)* was the family's priest. In the same way, in the Republic, the head of the state's board of chief priests, *the pontifex maximus*, was elected by the popular assembly. Morality played little role in Roman religion but, since failure to perform the necessary rites correctly could bring harm on the entire state, everyone had to participate in religious observance as a civic duty and evidence of patriotism. (See "Encountering the Past, Two Roman Festivals," page 112.)

In 205 B.C.E., the Senate approved the public worship of Cybele, the Great Mother goddess from Phrygia in Asia Minor. Hers was a fertility cult accompanied by ecstatic, frenzied, and sensual rites that so outraged conservative Romans that they soon banned the cult. Similarly, the Senate banned the worship of Dionysus, or Bacchus, in 186 B.C.E. In the second century B.C.E., interest in Babylonian astrology also grew, and the Senate's attempt in 139 B.C.E. to expel the "Chaldaeans," as the astrologers were called, did not prevent the continued influence of their superstition.

Education

Education in the early republic reflected the limited, conservative, and practical nature of that community of plain farmers and soldiers. Education was entirely the responsibility of the family, the father teaching his own son at home. It is not clear whether in these early times girls received any education, though they certainly did later on. The boys learned to read, write, calculate, and how to farm. They memorized the laws of the Twelve Tables, learned how to perform religious rites, heard stories of the great deeds of early Roman history and particularly those of their ancestors, and engaged in the physical training appropriate for potential soldiers. This course of study was practical, vocational, and moral; it aimed to make the boys moral, pious, patriotic, law abiding, and respectful of tradition.

Hellenized Education In the third century B.C.E., the Romans came into contact with the Greeks of southern Italy, and this contact changed Roman education. Greek teachers introduced the study of language, literature, and philosophy, as well as the idea of a liberal education, or what the Romans called ***humanitas***, the root of our concept of the humanities. The aim of education changed from the mastery of practical, vocational skills to an emphasis on broad intellectual training, critical thinking, an interest in ideas, and the development of a well-rounded person.

The new emphasis required students to learn Greek, for Rome did not yet have a literature of its own. Hereafter, educated Romans were expected to be bilingual. Schools were established in which a teacher, called a *grammaticus*, taught students the Greek language and its literature, especially the poets and particularly Homer. After the completion of this elementary education, Roman boys of the upper classes studied rhetoric—the art of speaking and writing well. For the Greeks, rhetoric was less important than philosophy. The more practical Romans took to it avidly, however, for it was of great use in legal disputes and political life.

Some Romans were attracted to Greek literature and philosophy. Scipio Aemilianus, the man who finally defeated and destroyed Carthage, surrounded himself and his friends with such Greek thinkers as the historian Polybius and the philosopher Panaetius.

Equally outstanding Romans, such as Cato the Elder, were more conservative and opposed the new learning on the grounds that it would weaken Roman moral fiber. On more than one occasion they passed laws expelling philosophers and teachers of rhetoric. But these attempts to go back to older ways failed. The new education suited the needs of the Romans of the second century B.C.E. They found themselves changing from a rural to an urban society and were being thrust into the sophisticated world of Hellenistic Greeks.

By the last century of the Roman Republic, the new Hellenized education had become dominant. Latin literature had come into being and, along with Latin translations of Greek poets, formed part of the course of study. But Roman gentlemen still were expected to be bilingual, and Greek language and literature were still central to the curriculum. Many schools were established. The number of educated people grew.

This carved relief from the second century C.E. shows a schoolmaster and his pupils. The pupil at the right is arriving late. Rheinisches Landesmuseum, Trier, Germany. Alinari/Art Resource, NY

ENCOUNTERING THE *Past*

TWO ROMAN FESTIVALS: THE SATURNALIA AND LUPERCALIA

THE ROMANS LOVED festivals, and their calendar contained many of them. The most famous celebrations were the Lupercalia, on February 15, and the Saturnalia, which took place from December 17 to 24. Both festivals were so popular that Christianity later adopted them under different names for its own religious calendar.

The Saturnalia celebrated Saturn, an agricultural god. (Our Saturday is named after him.) During this festival all public and private business gave way to feasting, gambling, wild dancing, and the kind of revelry that still occurs today during Mardi Gras in cities like New Orleans and Rio de Janeiro.

During the Saturnalia, masters permitted slaves to say and do what they liked; moral restrictions were eased; and Romans exchanged presents. Rather than try to abolish the Saturnalia, Christianity established December 25th as the birth date of Jesus, and the irrepressible Roman holiday, including the giving of presents, parties, and elaborate meals, became the celebration of Christmas.

The Lupercalia was dedicated, in part, to Faunus, the ancient Italian god of the countryside. Worshipped as the bringer of fertility to fields and flocks, Faunus was typically represented in art as half man, half goat and was associated with merriment like the Greek god Pan.

On the day of the Lupercalia, young male priests called Luperci sacrificed goats and a dog to Faunus. The Luperci then ran naked around the city, striking any woman who came near them with a thong cut from the skins of the sacrificed goats to render her fertile. Women who had not conceived or who wanted more children made sure that the Luperci struck them. It was at the Lupercalia of 44 B.C.E that the consul Marcus Antonius (Shakespeare's Mark Antony) offered a royal crown to Julius Caesar. In 494 C.E., the Christian church converted the festival into the Feast of the Purification of the Virgin Mary.

Why do you think the Romans loved these festivals?
Why might the Christian Church have chosen to adapt pagan customs instead of trying to abolish them?

This is a bronze statuette of the ancient Italian rural deity Faunus, whom the Romans identified with the Greek god Pan. Christi Graham and Nick Nicholls © The British Museum

In the late republic, Roman education, though still entirely private, became more formal and organized. From the ages of seven to twelve, boys went to elementary school accompanied by a Greek slave called a *paedagogus* (hence our term *pedagogue*), who looked after their physical well-being and their manners and improved their ability in Greek conversation. At school the boys learned to read and write, using a wax tablet and a stylus, and to do simple arithmetic with an abacus and pebbles (*calculi*). Discipline was harsh and corporal punishment frequent. From twelve to sixteen, boys went to a higher school, where the *grammaticus* provided a liberal education, using Greek and Latin literature as his subject matter. He also taught dialectic, arithmetic, geometry, astronomy, and music. Sometimes he included the elements of rhetoric, especially for those boys who would not go on to a higher education.

At sixteen, some boys went on to advanced study in rhetoric. The instructors were usually Greek. They trained their charges by studying models of fine speech of the past and by having them write, memorize, and declaim speeches suitable for different occasions. Sometimes the serious student attached himself to some famous public speaker to learn what he could. Sometimes a rich Roman would support a Greek philosopher in his own home. His son could converse with the philosopher and acquire the learning and polished thought necessary for the fully cultured gentleman. Some, like the great orator Cicero, undertook what we might call postgraduate study by traveling abroad to study with great teachers of rhetoric and philosophy in the Greek world.

This style of education broadened the Romans' understanding through the careful study of a foreign language and culture. It made them a part of the older and wider culture of the Hellenistic world, a world they had come to dominate and needed to understand.

Education for Women Though the evidence is limited, we can be sure that girls of the upper classes received an education equivalent at least to the early stages of a boy's education. They were probably taught by tutors at home rather than going to school, as was increasingly the fashion among boys in the late republic. Young women did not study with philosophers and rhetoricians, for they were usually married by the age at which the men were pursuing their higher education. Still, some women continued their education and became prose writers or poets. By the first century C.E., there were apparently enough learned women to provoke the complaints of a crotchety and conservative satirist:

> Still more exasperating is the woman who begs as soon as she sits down to dinner, to discourse on poets and poetry, comparing Virgil with Homer; professors, critics, lawyers, auctioneers—even another woman—can't get a word in. She rattles on at such a rate that you'd think that all the pots and pans in the kitchen were crashing to the floor or that every bell in town was clanging. All by herself she makes as much noise as some primitive tribe chasing away an eclipse. She should learn the philosopher's lesson: "moderation is necessary even for intellectuals." And, if she still wants to appear educated and eloquent, let her dress as a man, sacrifice to men's gods and bathe in the men's baths. Wives shouldn't try to be public speakers; they shouldn't use rhetorical devices; they shouldn't read all the classics—there should be some things women don't understand. I myself cannot understand a woman who can quote the rules of grammar and never make a mistake and cites obscure, long-forgotten poets—as if men cared about such things. If she has to correct somebody let her correct her girl friends and leave her husband alone.[2] (See also "Women's Uprising in Republican Rome," page 114.)

Slavery

Like most ancient peoples, the Romans had slaves from early in their history, but among the shepherds and family farmers of early Rome, they were relatively few. Slavery became a basic element in the Roman economy and society only during the second century B.C.E., after the Romans had conquered most of the lands bordering the Mediterranean. In the time between the beginning of Rome's first war against Carthage (264 B.C.E.) and the conquest of Spain (133 B.C.E.), the Romans enslaved some 250,000 prisoners of war, greatly increasing the availability of slave labor and reducing its price. Many slaves worked as domestic servants, feeding the growing appetite for luxury of the Roman upper class; at the other end of the spectrum, many worked in the mines of Spain and Sardinia. Some worked as artisans in small factories and shops or as public clerks. Slaves were permitted to marry, and they produced sizable families. As in Greece, domestic slaves and those used in crafts and commerce could earn money, keep it, and, in some cases, use it to purchase their own freedom. *Manumission* (the freeing of slaves) was common among the Romans. After a time, a considerable proportion of the Roman people included freedmen who had been slaves themselves or whose ancestors had been bondsmen. It was not uncommon to see the son or grandson of a slave become wealthy as a freedman and the slave himself or his son become a Roman citizen.

The unique development in the Roman world was the emergence of an agricultural system that employed and depended on a vast number of slaves. By the time of Jesus, there were between 2 and 3 million slaves in Italy, about 35 to 40 percent of the total population, most of them part of great slave gangs that worked the vast plantations the Romans called ***latifundia***. The life of Rome's agricultural slaves appears to have been much harder than that of other Roman slaves and of slaves in other ancient societies, with the possible exception of slaves working in

[2]Juvenal, *Satires* 6.434–456, trans. by Roger Killian, Richard Lynch, Robert J. Rowland, and John Sims, cited by Sarah B. Pomeroy in *Goddesses, Whores, Wives, and Slaves* (New York: Schocken Books, 1975), p. 172.

WOMEN'S UPRISING IN REPUBLICAN ROME

In 195 B.C.E., Roman women staged a rare public political protest when they demanded the repeal of a law passed two decades earlier during the Second Punic War, which they believed limited their rights unfairly. Livy (59 B.C.E.–17 C.E.) describes the affair and the response of the traditionalist Marcus Porcius Cato (234–149 B.C.E.).

Why did the women complain? How did they try to achieve their goals? Which of Cato's objections to their behavior do you think were most important? Since women did not vote or sit in assemblies, why did the affair end as it did?

Amid the anxieties of great wars, either scarce finished or soon to come, an incident occurred, trivial to relate, but which, by reason of the passions it aroused, developed into a violent contention. [Two] tribunes of the people, proposed to the assembly the abrogation of the Oppian law. The tribune Gaius Oppius had carried this law in the heat of the Punic War, . . . that no woman should possess more than half an ounce of gold or wear a parti-coloured garment or ride in a carriage in the City or in a town within a mile thereof, except on the occasion of a religious festival . . . . [T]he Capitoline was filled with crowds of supporters and opponents of the ill. The matrons could not be kept at home by . . . their husbands' orders, but blocked all the streets and approaches to the Forum, begging the men as they came down to the Forum that, in the prosperous condition of the state, when the private fortunes of all men were daily increasing, they should allow the woman too to have their former distinctions restored. The crowd of women grew larger day by day; for they were now coming in from the towns and rural districts. Soon they dared even to approach and appeal to the consuls, the praetors, and the other officials, but one consul, at least, they found adamant, Marcus Porcius Cato, who spoke thus in favour of the law whose repeal was being urged:

"If each of us, citizens, had determined to assert his rights and dignity as a husband with 'respect to his own spouse,' we should have less trouble with the sex as a whole; as it is, our liberty, destroyed at home by female violence, even here in the Forum is crushed and trodden underfoot, and because we have not kept them individually under control, we dread them collectively . . . . But from no class is there not the greatest danger if you permit them meetings . . . and secret consultations.

"I should have said, 'What sort of practice is this, of running out into the streets and blocking the roads and speaking to other women's husbands? Could you not have made the same requests, each of your own husband, at home? And yet, not even at home, if modesty would keep matrons within the limits of their proper rights, did it become you to concern yourselves with the question of what laws should be adopted in this place or repealed.' Our ancestors permitted no woman to conduct even personal business without a guardian to intervene in her behalf; they wished them to be under the control of fathers, brothers, husbands; we (Heaven help us!) allow them now even to interfere in public affairs, yes, and to visit the Forum and our informal and formal sessions. Give loose rein to their uncontrollable nature and to this untamed creature and expect that they will themselves set bounds to their licence; unless you act, this is the least of the things enjoined upon women by custom or law and to which they submit with a feeling of injustice. It is complete liberty or, rather, if we wish to speak the truth, complete licence that they desire.

"If they win in this, what will they not attempt? Review all the laws with which your forefathers restrained their licence and made them subject to their husbands; even with all these bonds you can scarcely control them. What of this? If you suffer them to seize these bonds one by one and wrench themselves free and finally to be placed on a parity with their husbands, do you think that you will be able to endure them? The moment they begin to be your equals, they will be your superiors."

The next day an even greater crowd of women appeared in public, and all of them in a body beset the doors of those tribunes, who were vetoing their colleagues' proposal, and they did not desist until the threat of veto was withdrawn by the tribunes. After that there was no question that all the tribes would vote to repeal the law. The law was repealed twenty years after it was passed.

From *Livy*, trans. by Evan T. Stage (Cambridge, MA: Harvard University Press, 1935), XXXIV, i–iii; viii, pp. 413–419, 439.

mines. *Latifundia* owners sought maximum profits and treated their slaves simply as means to that end. The slaves often worked in chains, were oppressed by brutal foremen, and lived in underground prisons.

Such harsh treatment led to serious slave rebellions of a kind we do not hear of in other ancient societies. A rebellion in Sicily in 134 B.C.E. kept the island in turmoil for more than two years, and the rebellion of the gladiators led by Spartacus in 73 B.C.E. produced an army of 70,000 slaves that repeatedly defeated the Roman legions and overran southern Italy before it was brutally crushed.

Slavery retained its economic and social importance in the first century of the imperial period, but its centrality began to decline in the second. The institution was never abolished, nor did it disappear while the Roman Empire lasted, but over time it became less important. The reasons for this decline are rather obscure. A rise in the cost of slaves and a consequent reduction in their economic value seem to have been factors. More important, it appears, was a general economic decline that permitted increasing pressure on the free lower classes. More and more they were employed as *coloni*—tenant farmers—tied by imperial law to the land they worked, ostensibly free, but bonded and obligated. Over centuries, these increasingly serf-like *coloni* replaced most agricultural slave labor. Pockets of slave labor remained as late as the eighth century C.E., but the system of ancient slavery had essentially been replaced by the time the Roman Empire fell in the West.

▼ Roman Imperialism: The Late Republic

Rome's expansion in Italy and overseas was accomplished without a grand general plan. (See Map 4–3.) The Romans gained the new territories as a result of wars

Map 4–3 **ROMAN DOMINIONS OF THE LATE REPUBLIC** The Roman Republic's conquest of Mediterranean lands—and beyond—until the death of Julius Caesar is shown here. Areas conquered before Tiberius Gracchus (ca. 133 B.C.E.) are distinguished from later ones and from client areas owing allegiance to Rome.

that they believed were either defensive or preventive. Their foreign policy was aimed at providing security for Rome on Rome's terms, but these terms were often unacceptable to other nations and led to continued conflict. Whether intended or not, Rome's expansion brought the Romans an empire and, with it, power, wealth, and responsibilities. The need to govern an empire beyond the seas would severely test the republican constitution that had served Rome well during its years as a city-state and that had been well adapted to the mastery of Italy. Roman society and the Roman character had maintained their integrity through the period of expansion in Italy, but the temptations and strains the wealth and the complicated problems of an overseas empire presented would test them.

The Aftermath of Conquest

War and expansion changed the economic, social, and political life of Italy. Before the Punic Wars, most Italians owned their own farms, which provided the greater part of the family's needs. Some families owned larger holdings, but their lands chiefly grew grain, and they used the labor of clients, tenants, and hired workers rather than slaves. Fourteen years of fighting in the Second Punic War did terrible damage to Italian farmland. Many veterans returning from the wars found it impossible or unprofitable to go back to their farms. Some moved to Rome, where they could find work as laborers, but most stayed in the country as tenant farmers or hired hands. Often, the wealthy converted the abandoned land into *latifundia* for growing cash crops—grain, olives, and grapes for wine—or into cattle ranches.

The upper classes had plenty of capital to operate these estates because of profits from the war and from exploiting the provinces. Land was cheap, and so was slave labor. By fair means and foul, large landholders obtained great quantities of public land and forced small farmers from it. These changes separated the people of Rome and Italy more sharply into rich and poor, landed and landless, privileged and deprived. The result was political, social, and, ultimately, constitutional conflict that threatened the existence of the republic.

This wall painting from the first century B.C.E. comes from the villa of Publius Fannius Synistor at Pompeii and shows a woman playing a cithera. Roman. Paintings. Pompeian, Boscoreale. 1st Century B.C. "Lady Playing the Cithara." Wall painting from the east wall of large room in the villa of Publius Fannius Synistor. Fresco on lime plaster. H. 6 ft. 1 1/2 in. W. 6 ft. 1 1/2 in. (187 × 187 cm.) The Metropolitan Museum of Art, Rogers Fund, 1903. (03.14.5) Photograph © 1986 The Metropolitan Museum of Art

The Gracchi

By the middle of the second century B.C.E., the problems caused by Rome's rapid expansion troubled perceptive Roman nobles. The fall in status of peasant farmers made it harder to recruit soldiers and came to present a political threat as well. The patron's traditional control over his clients was weakened when they fled from their land. Even those former landowners who worked on the land of their patrons as tenants or hired hands were less reliable. The introduction of the secret ballot in the 130s B.C.E. made them even more independent.

Tiberius Gracchus In 133 B.C.E., Tiberius Gracchus tried to solve these problems. He became tribune for 133 B.C.E. on a program of land reform; some of the most powerful members of the Roman aristocracy helped him draft the bill. They meant it to be a moderate attempt at solving Rome's problems. The bill's target was public land that had been acquired and held illegally, some of it for many years. The bill allowed holders of this land to retain as many as five hundred iugera (approximately 320 acres), but the state would reclaim

THE RUIN OF THE ROMAN FAMILY FARM AND THE GRACCHAN REFORMS

The independent family farm was the backbone both of the Greek polis *and of the early Roman Republic. Rome's conquests, the long wars that kept the citizen-soldier away from his farm, and the availability of great numbers of slaves at a low price, however, badly undercut the traditional way of farming and with it the foundations of republican society. In the following passage, Plutarch describes the process of agricultural change and the response to it of the reformer Tiberius Gracchus, tribune in 133 B.C.E.*

Why did Roman farmers face troubles? What were the social and political consequences of the changes in agricultural life? What solution did Tiberius Gracchus propose? Why, besides selfishness and greed, did people oppose his plan?

Of the territory which the Romans won in war from their neighbours, a part they sold, and a part they made common land, and assigned it for occupation to the poor and indigent among the citizens, on payment of a small rent into the public treasury. And when the rich began to offer larger rents and drove out the poor, a law was enacted forbidding the holding by one person of more than five hundred [iugera] of land. For a short time this enactment gave a check to the rapacity of the rich, and was of assistance to the poor, who remained in their places on the land which they had rented and occupied the allotment which each had held from the outset. But later on the neighbouring rich men, by means of fictitious personages, transferred these rentals to themselves, and finally held most of the land openly in their own names. Then the poor, who had been ejected from their land, no longer showed themselves eager for military service, and neglected the bringing up of children, so that soon all Italy was conscious of a dearth of freemen, and was filled with gangs of foreign slaves, by whose aid the rich cultivated their estates, from which they had driven away the free citizens.

And it is thought that a law dealing with injustice and rapacity so great was never drawn up in milder and gentler terms. For men who ought to have been punished for their disobedience and to have surrendered with payment of a fine the land which they were illegally enjoying, these men it merely ordered to abandon their injust acquisitions upon being paid their value, and to admit into ownership of them such citizens as needed assistance. But although the rectification of the wrong was so considerate, the people were satisfied to let bygones be bygones if they could be secure from such wrong in the future; the men of wealth and substance, however, were led by their greed to hate the law, and by their wrath and contentiousness to hate the lawgiver, and tried to dissuade the people by alleging that Tiberius was introducing a re-distribution of land for the confusion of the body politic, and was stirring up a general revolution.

From Plutarch, "Tiberius Gracchus," in *Lives* 8–9, Vol. 10, trans. by Bernadotte Perrin and William Heinemann (London and New York: G. P. Putnam's Sons, 1921), pp. 159–167.

anything over that and redistribute it in small lots to the poor, who would pay a small rent to the state and could not sell what they had received.

The bill aroused great hostility. Its passage would hurt many senators who held vast estates. Others thought it would be a bad precedent to allow any interference with property rights, even if they involved illegally held public land. Still others feared the political gains that Tiberius and his associates would make if the beneficiaries of their law were properly grateful to its drafters. (See "The Ruin of the Roman Family Farm and the Gracchan Reforms.")

When Tiberius put the bill before the tribal assembly, one of the tribunes, M. Octavius, interposed his veto. Tiberius went to the Senate to discuss his proposal, but the senators continued their opposition. Tiberius now had to choose between dropping the matter and undertaking a revolutionary course. Unwilling to give up, he put his bill before the tribal assembly again. Again Octavius vetoed. So Tiberius, strongly supported by the people, had Octavius removed from office, violating the constitution. The assembly's removal of a magistrate implied a fundamental shift of power from the Senate to the people. If the assembly could pass laws the Senate opposed and a tribune vetoed, and if they could remove magistrates, then Rome would become a democracy like Athens instead of a traditional oligarchy. At this point, many of Tiberius's senatorial allies deserted him.

Tiberius proposed a second bill, harsher than the first and more appealing to the people, for he had given up hope of conciliating the Senate. This bill, which passed the assembly, provided for a commission to carry it out. When King Attalus of Pergamum died and left his kingdom to Rome, Tiberius proposed using the Pergamene revenue to finance the commission. This proposal challenged the Senate's control both of finances and of foreign affairs. Hereafter there could be no compromise: Either Tiberius or the Roman constitution must go under.

Tiberius understood the danger he would face if he stepped down from the tribunate, so he announced his candidacy for a second successive term, striking another blow at tradition. His opponents feared he might go on to hold office indefinitely, to dominate Rome in what appeared to them a demagogic tyranny. They concentrated their fire on the constitutional issue, the deposition of the tribune. They appear to have had some success, for many of Tiberius's supporters did not come out to vote. At the elections a riot broke out, and a mob of senators and their clients killed Tiberius and some three hundred of his followers and threw their bodies into the Tiber River. The Senate had put down the threat to its rule, but at the price of the first internal bloodshed in Roman political history.

The tribunate of Tiberius Gracchus changed Roman politics. Heretofore Roman political struggles had generally been struggles for honor and reputation between great families or coalitions of such families. Fundamental issues were rarely at stake. The revolutionary proposals of Tiberius, however, and the senatorial resort to bloodshed created a new situation. Tiberius's use of the tribunate to challenge senatorial rule encouraged imitation despite his failure. From then on, Romans could pursue a political career that was not based solely on influence within the aristocracy; pressure from the people might be an effective substitute. In the last century of the republic, politicians who sought such backing were called ***populares***, whereas those who supported the traditional role of the Senate were called ***optimates***, or "the best men."

These groups were not political parties with formal programs and party discipline, but they were more than merely vehicles for the political ambitions of unorthodox politicians. Fundamental questions—such as those about land reform, the treatment of the Italian allies, the power of the assemblies versus the power of the Senate, and other problems—divided the Roman people, from the time of Tiberius Gracchus to the fall of the republic. Some popular leaders, of course, were cynical self-seekers who used the issues only for their own ambitions. Some few may have been sincere advocates of a principled position. Most, no doubt, were a mixture of the two, like most politicians in most times.

Gaius Gracchus The tribunate of Gaius Gracchus (brother of Tiberius) was much more dangerous than that of Tiberius. All the tribunes of 123 B.C.E. were his supporters, so there could be no veto, and a recent law permitted the reelection of tribunes. Gaius's program appealed to a variety of groups. First, he revived the agrarian commission, which had been allowed to lapse. Because there was not enough good public land left to meet the demand, he proposed to establish new colonies: two in Italy and one on the old site of Carthage. Among other popular acts, he put through a law stabilizing the price of grain in Rome, which involved building granaries to guarantee an adequate supply.

Gaius broke new ground in appealing to the equestrian order in his struggle against the Senate. The **equestrians** (so called because they served in the Roman cavalry) were neither peasants nor senators. Some were businesspeople who supplied goods and services to the Roman state and collected its taxes. Almost continuous warfare and the need for tax collection in the provinces had made many of them rich. Most of the time, these wealthy men had the same outlook as the Senate; generally, they used their profits to purchase land and to try to reach senatorial rank themselves. Still, they had a special interest in Roman expansion and in the exploitation of the provinces. In the late second century B.C.E., they developed a clear sense of group interest and exerted political influence.

In 129 B.C.E., Pergamum became the new province of Asia. Gaius put through a law turning over to the equestrian order the privilege of collecting its revenue. He also barred senators from serving as jurors on the courts that tried provincial governors charged with extortion. The combination was a wonderful gift for wealthy equestrian businessmen, who were now free to squeeze profits out of the rich province of Asia without much fear of interference from the governors. The results for Roman provincial administration were bad, but the immediate political consequences for Gaius were excellent. The equestrians were now given reality as a class; as a political unit they might be set against the Senate or be formed into a coalition to serve Gaius's purposes.

Gaius easily won reelection as tribune for 122 B.C.E. He aimed at giving citizenship to the Italians, both to resolve their dissatisfaction and to add them to his political coalition. But the common people did not want to share the advantages of Roman citizenship. The Senate seized on this proposal to drive a wedge between Gaius and his supporters.

The Romans did not reelect Gaius for 121 B.C.E., leaving him vulnerable to his enemies. A hostile consul provoked an incident that led to violence. The Senate invented an extreme decree ordering the consuls to see to it that no harm came to the republic; in effect, this decree established martial law. Gaius was hunted down and killed, and a senatorial court condemned and put to death some 3,000 of his followers without any trial.

Marius and Sulla

For the moment, the senatorial oligarchy had fought off the challenge to its traditional position. Before long, it faced more serious dangers arising from troubles abroad. The first grew out of a dispute over the succession to the throne of Numidia, a client kingdom of Rome's near Carthage.

Marius and the Jugurthine War The victory of Jugurtha, who became king of Numidia, and his massacre of Roman and Italian businessmen in the province, gained Roman attention. Although the Senate was reluctant to become involved, pressure from the equestrians and the people forced the declaration of what became known as the Jugurthine War in 111 B.C.E.

As the war dragged on, the people, sometimes with good reason, suspected the Senate of taking bribes from Jugurtha. They elected C. Marius (157–86 B.C.E.) to the consulship for 107 B.C.E. The assembly, usurping the role of the Senate, assigned him to Numidia. This action was significant in several ways. Marius was a *novus homo*, a "new man"—that is, the first in the history of his family to reach the consulship. Although a wealthy equestrian, he had been born in the town of Arpinum and was outside the closed circle of the old Roman aristocracy. His earlier career had won him a reputation as an outstanding soldier and a political maverick.

Marius quickly defeated Jugurtha, but Jugurtha escaped, and guerrilla warfare continued. Finally, Marius's subordinate, L. Cornelius Sulla (138–78 B.C.E.), trapped Jugurtha and brought the war to an end. Marius celebrated the victory, but Sulla, an ambitious though impoverished descendant of an old Roman family, resented being cheated of the credit he thought he deserved. Rumors credited Sulla with the victory and diminished Marius's role. Thus were the seeds planted for a mutual hostility that would last until Marius's death.

While the Romans were fighting Jugurtha, a far greater danger threatened Rome from the north. In 105 B.C.E., two barbaric tribes, the Cimbri and the Teutones, had come down the Rhone Valley and crushed a Roman army at Arausio (Orange) in southern France. When these tribes threatened again, the Romans elected Marius to his second consulship to meet the danger. He served five consecutive terms until 100 B.C.E., when the crisis was over.

While the barbarians were occupied elsewhere, Marius used the time to make important changes in the army. He began using volunteers for the army, mostly the dispossessed farmers and rural proletarians whose problems the Gracchi had not solved. They enlisted for a long term of service and looked on the army not as an unwelcome duty, but as an opportunity and a career. They became semiprofessional clients of their general and sought guaranteed food, clothing, shelter, and booty from victories. They came to expect a piece of land as a form of mustering-out pay, or veteran's bonus, when they retired.

Volunteers were most likely to enlist with a man who was a capable soldier and influential enough to obtain what he needed for them. They looked to him rather than to the state for their rewards. He, however, had to obtain these favors from the Senate if he was to maintain his power and reputation. Marius's innovation created both the opportunity and the necessity for military leaders to gain enough power to challenge civilian authority. The promise of rewards won these leaders the personal loyalty of their troops, and that loyalty allowed them to frighten the Senate into granting their demands.

The Wars against the Italians (90–88 B.C.E.) For a decade Rome avoided serious troubles, but in that time the Senate took no action to deal with Italian discontent. The Italians were excluded from the land bill for Marius's veterans. Their discontent caused the Senate to expel all Italians from Rome in 95 B.C.E. Four years later, the tribune M. Livius Drusus put forward a bill to enfranchise the Italians. Drusus seems to have been a sincere aristocratic reformer, but he was assassinated in 90 B.C.E. Frustrated, the Italians revolted and established a separate confederation with its own capital and coinage.

Employing the traditional device of divide and conquer, the Romans immediately offered citizenship to those cities that remained loyal and soon made the same offer to the rebels if they laid down their arms. Even then, hard fighting was needed to put down the uprising, but by 88 B.C.E., the war against the allies was over. All the Italians became Roman citizens with the protections that citizenship offered. However, they retained local self-government and a dedication to their own municipalities that made Italy flourish. The passage of time blurred the distinction between Romans and Italians and forged them into a single nation.

Sulla's Dictatorship During the war against the allies, Sulla had performed well. He was elected consul for 88 B.C.E. and was given command of the war against Mithridates, who was leading a major rebellion in Asia. At this point, the seventy-year-old Marius emerged from obscurity and sought the command for himself. With popular and equestrian support, he got the assembly to transfer the command to him. Sulla, defending the rights of the Senate and his own interests, marched his army against Rome. This was the first time a Roman general had used his army against fellow citizens. Marius and his friends fled, and Sulla regained the command. No sooner had he left again for Asia, than Marius joined with the consul Cinna and seized Rome. He outlawed Sulla and massacred the senatorial opposition. Marius died soon after his election to a seventh consulship, for 86 B.C.E.

Cinna now was the chief man at Rome. Supported by Marius's men, he held the consulship from 87 to 84 B.C.E. His future depended on Sulla's fortunes in the East.

By 85 B.C.E., Sulla had driven Mithridates from Greece and had crossed over to Asia Minor. Eager to regain control of Rome, he negotiated a compromise peace. In 83 B.C.E., he returned to Italy and fought a civil war that lasted for more than a year. Sulla won and drove the followers of Marius from Italy. He had himself appointed dictator, not in the traditional sense, but to remake the state.

Sulla's first step was to wipe out the opposition. The names of those proscribed were posted in public. As outlaws, anyone could kill them and receive a reward. Sulla proscribed not only political opponents, but also his personal enemies and men whose only crime was their wealth. With the proceeds from the confiscations, Sulla rewarded his veterans, perhaps as many as 100,000 men, and thereby built a solid base of support.

Sulla had enough power to make himself the permanent ruler of Rome. He was traditional enough to want to restore senatorial government, but reformed so as to prevent the misfortunes of the past. To deal with the decimation of the Senate caused by the proscriptions and the civil war, he enrolled three hundred new members, many of them from the equestrian order and the upper classes of the Italian cities. The office of tribune, which the Gracchi had used to attack senatorial rule, was made into a political dead end.

Sulla's most valuable reforms improved the quality of the courts and the entire legal system. He created new courts to deal with specified crimes, bringing the number of courts to eight. Because both judge and jurors were senators, the courts, too, enhanced senatorial power. These actions were the most permanent of Sulla's reforms, laying the foundation for Roman criminal law.

Sulla retired to a life of ease and luxury in 79 B.C.E. He could not, however, undo the effect of his own example—that of a general using the loyalty of his own troops to take power and to massacre his opponents, as well as innocent men. These actions proved to be more significant than his constitutional arrangements.

▼ The Fall of the Republic

Within a year of Sulla's death, his constitution came under assault. To deal with an armed threat to its powers, the Senate violated the very procedures meant to defend them.

Pompey, Crassus, Caesar, and Cicero

The Senate gave the command of the army to Pompey (106–48 B.C.E.), who was only twenty-eight and had never been elected to a magistracy. Then, when Sertorius, a Marian general, resisted senatorial control, the Senate appointed Pompey proconsul in Spain in 77 B.C.E. These actions ignored Sulla's rigid rules for office holding, which had been meant to guarantee experienced, loyal, and safe commanders. In 71 B.C.E., Pompey returned to Rome with new glory, having put down the rebellion of Sertorius. In 73 B.C.E., the Senate made another extraordinary appointment to put down a great slave rebellion led by the gladiator Spartacus. Marcus Licinius Crassus, a rich and ambitious senator, received powers that gave him command of almost all of Italy. Together with the newly returned Pompey, he crushed the rebellion in 71 B.C.E. Extraordinary commands of this sort proved to be the ruin of the republic.

Crassus and Pompey were ambitious men whom the Senate feared. Both demanded special honors and election to the consulship for the year 70 B.C.E. Pompey was legally ineligible because he had never gone through the strict course of offices Sulla's constitution prescribed, and Crassus needed Pompey's help. They joined forces, though they disliked and were jealous of each other. They gained popular support by promising to restore the full powers of the tribunes, which Sulla had curtailed, and they gained equestrian backing by promising to restore equestrians to the extortion court juries. They both won election and repealed most of Sulla's constitution. This opened the way for further attacks on senatorial control and for collaboration between ambitious generals and demagogic tribunes.

In 67 B.C.E., a special law gave Pompey *imperium* for three years over the entire Mediterranean and fifty miles in from the coast. It also gave him the power to raise troops and money to rid the area of pirates. The assembly passed the law over senatorial opposition, and in three months Pompey cleared the seas of piracy. Meanwhile, a new war had broken out with Mithridates. In 66 B.C.E., the assembly transferred the command to Pompey, giving him unprecedented powers. He held *imperium* over all Asia, with the right to make war and peace at will. His *imperium* was superior to that of any proconsul in the field.

Once again, Pompey justified his appointment. He defeated Mithridates and drove him to suicide. By 62 B.C.E., he had extended Rome's frontier to the Euphrates River and had organized the territories of Asia so well that his arrangements remained the basis of Roman rule well into the imperial period. When Pompey returned to Rome in 62 B.C.E., he had more power, prestige, and popular support than any Roman in history. The Senate and his personal enemies had reason to fear he might emulate Sulla and establish his own rule.

Rome had not been quiet in Pompey's absence. Crassus was the foremost among those who had reason to fear Pompey's return. Although rich and influential, Crassus did not have the confidence of the Senate, a firm political base of his own, or the kind of military glory needed to rival Pompey. During the 60s B.C.E., therefore, he allied himself with various popular leaders.

The ablest of these men was Gaius Julius Caesar (100–44 B.C.E.). He was a descendant of an old, but politically obscure, patrician family that claimed descent from the kings and even from the goddess Venus. Despite this noble lineage, Caesar was connected to the popular party through his aunt, the wife of Marius, and through his own wife, Cornelia, the daughter of Cinna. Caesar was an ambitious young politician whose daring and rhetorical skill made him a valuable ally in winning the discontented of every class to the cause of the *populares*. Though Crassus was the senior partner, each needed the other to achieve what both wanted: significant military commands with which to build a reputation, a political following, and a military force to compete with Pompey's.

The chief opposition to Crassus's candidates for the consulship for 63 B.C.E. came from Cicero (106–43 B.C.E.), a *novus homo*, from Marius's hometown of Arpinum. He had made a spectacular name as the leading lawyer in Rome. Cicero, though he came from outside the senatorial aristocracy, was no *popularis*. His program was to preserve the republic against demagogues and ambitious generals by making the government more liberal. He wanted to unite the stable elements of the state—the Senate and the equestrians—in a harmony of the orders. This program did not appeal to the senatorial oligarchy, but the Senate preferred Cicero to Catiline, a dangerous and popular politician thought to be linked with Crassus. Cicero and Antonius were elected consuls for 63 B.C.E., with Catiline running third.

Cicero soon learned of a plot hatched by Catiline. Catiline had run in the previous election on a platform of cancellation of debts; this appealed to discontented elements in general, but especially to the heavily indebted nobles and their many clients. Made desperate by defeat, Catiline planned to stir up rebellions around Italy, to cause confusion in the city, and to take it by force. Quick action by Cicero defeated Catiline.

The First Triumvirate

Toward the end of 62 B.C.E., Pompey landed at Brundisium. Surprisingly, he disbanded his army, celebrated a great triumph, and returned to private life. He had delayed his return in the hope of finding Italy in such a state as to justify his keeping the army and dominating the scene. Cicero's quick suppression of Catiline prevented his plan. Pompey, therefore, had either to act illegally or to lay down his arms. Because he had not thought of monarchy or revolution, but merely wanted to be recognized and treated as the greatest Roman, he chose the latter course.

Pompey had achieved amazing things for Rome and simply wanted the Senate to approve his excellent arrangements in the East and to make land allotments to his veterans. His demands were far from unreasonable, and a prudent Senate would have granted them and tried to employ his power in defense of the constitution. But the Senate was jealous and fearful of overmighty individuals and refused his requests. Pompey was driven to an alliance with his natural enemies, Crassus and Caesar, because the Senate blocked what all three wanted.

In 60 B.C.E., Caesar returned to Rome from his governorship of Spain. He wanted to celebrate a triumph, the great victory procession that the Senate granted certain generals to honor especially great achievements, and to run for consul. The law did not allow him to do both, however, requiring him to stay outside the city with his army but demanding that he canvass for votes personally within the city. He asked for a special dispensation, but the Senate refused. Caesar then performed a political miracle. He reconciled Crassus with Pompey and gained the support of both for his own ambitions. So was born the First Triumvirate, an informal agreement among three Roman politicians, each seeking his private goals, which further undermined the republic.

Julius Caesar and His Government of Rome

Though he was forced to forgo his triumph, Caesar was elected to the consulship for 59 B.C.E. His fellow consul was M. Calpernius Bibulus, the son-in-law of Cato and a conservative hostile to Caesar and the other *populares*. Caesar did not hesitate to override his colleague. The triumvirs' program was quickly enacted. Caesar got the extraordinary command that would give him a chance to earn the glory and power with which to rival Pompey: the governorship of Illyricum and Gaul for five years. A land bill settled Pompey's veterans comfortably, and his eastern settlement was ratified. Crassus, much of whose influence came from his position as champion of the equestrians, won for them a great windfall by having the government renegotiate a tax contract in their favor. To guarantee themselves against any reversal of these actions, the triumvirs continued their informal but effective collaboration, arranging for the election of friendly consuls and the departure of potential opponents.

A bust of Julius Caesar. Bust of Julius Caesar (100–44 B.C.E.). Roman statesman. Museo Archeologico Nazionale, Naples, Italy. Photograph © Scala/Art Resource, NY

Caesar was now free to seek the military success he craved. His province included Cisalpine Gaul in the Po Valley (by now occupied by many Italian settlers as well as Gauls) and Narbonese Gaul beyond the Alps (modern Provence).

Relying first on the excellent quality of his army and the experience of his officers and then on his own growing military ability, Caesar made great progress. By 56 B.C.E., he had conquered most of Gaul, but he had not yet consolidated his victories firmly. He therefore sought an extension of his command, but quarrels between Crassus and Pompey so weakened the Triumvirate that the Senate was prepared to order Caesar's recall.

To prevent the dissolution of his base of power, Caesar persuaded Crassus and Pompey to meet with him at Luca in northern Italy to renew the coalition. They agreed that Caesar would get another five-year command in Gaul, and Crassus and Pompey would be consuls again in 55 B.C.E. After that, they would each receive an army and a five-year command. Caesar was free to return to Gaul and finish the job. The capture of Alesia in 51 B.C.E. marked the end of the serious Gallic resistance and of Gallic liberty. For Caesar, it brought the wealth, fame, and military power he wanted. He commanded thirteen loyal legions, a match for his enemies as well as for his allies.

By the time Caesar was ready to return to Rome, the Triumvirate had dissolved and a crisis was at hand. At Carrhae, in 53 B.C.E., Crassus died trying to conquer the Parthians, successors to the Persian Empire. His death broke one link between Pompey and Caesar. The death of Caesar's daughter Julia, who had been Pompey's wife, dissolved another.

As Caesar's star rose, Pompey became jealous and fearful. He did not leave Rome but governed his province through a subordinate. In the late 50s B.C.E., political rioting at Rome caused the Senate to appoint Pompey sole consul. This grant of unprecedented power and responsibility brought Pompey closer to the senatorial aristocracy in mutual fear of, and hostility to, Caesar. The Senate wanted to bring Caesar back to Rome as a private citizen after his proconsular command expired. He would then be open to attack for past illegalities. Caesar tried to avoid the trap by asking permission to stand for the consulship in absentia.

Early in January of 49 B.C.E., the more extreme faction in the Senate had its way. It ordered Pompey to defend the state and Caesar to lay down his command by a specified day. For Caesar, this meant exile or death, so he ordered his legions to cross the Rubicon River, the boundary of his province. (See Map 4–4.) This action started a civil war. In 45 B.C.E., Caesar defeated the last forces of his enemies under Pompey's sons at Munda in Spain. The war was over, and Caesar, in Shakespeare's words, bestrode "the narrow world like a Colossus."

From the beginning of the civil war until his death in 44 B.C.E., Caesar spent less than a year and a half in Rome, and many of his actions were attempts to deal with immediate problems between campaigns. His innovations generally sought to make rational and orderly what was traditional and chaotic. An excellent example is Caesar's reform of the calendar. By 46 B.C.E., it was 80 days ahead of the proper season, because the official year was lunar, containing only 355 days. Using the best scientific advice, Caesar instituted a new calendar, now known as the **Julian Calendar**: With minor changes by Pope Gregory XIII in the sixteenth century, it is the calendar in use today.

Another general tendency of his reforms in the political area was the elevation of the role of Italians and even provincials at the expense of the old Roman families, most of whom were his political enemies. He raised the number of senators to nine hundred and filled the Senate's depleted ranks with Italians and even Gauls. He was free with grants of Roman citizenship, giving the franchise to Cisalpine Gaul as a whole and to many individuals of various regions.

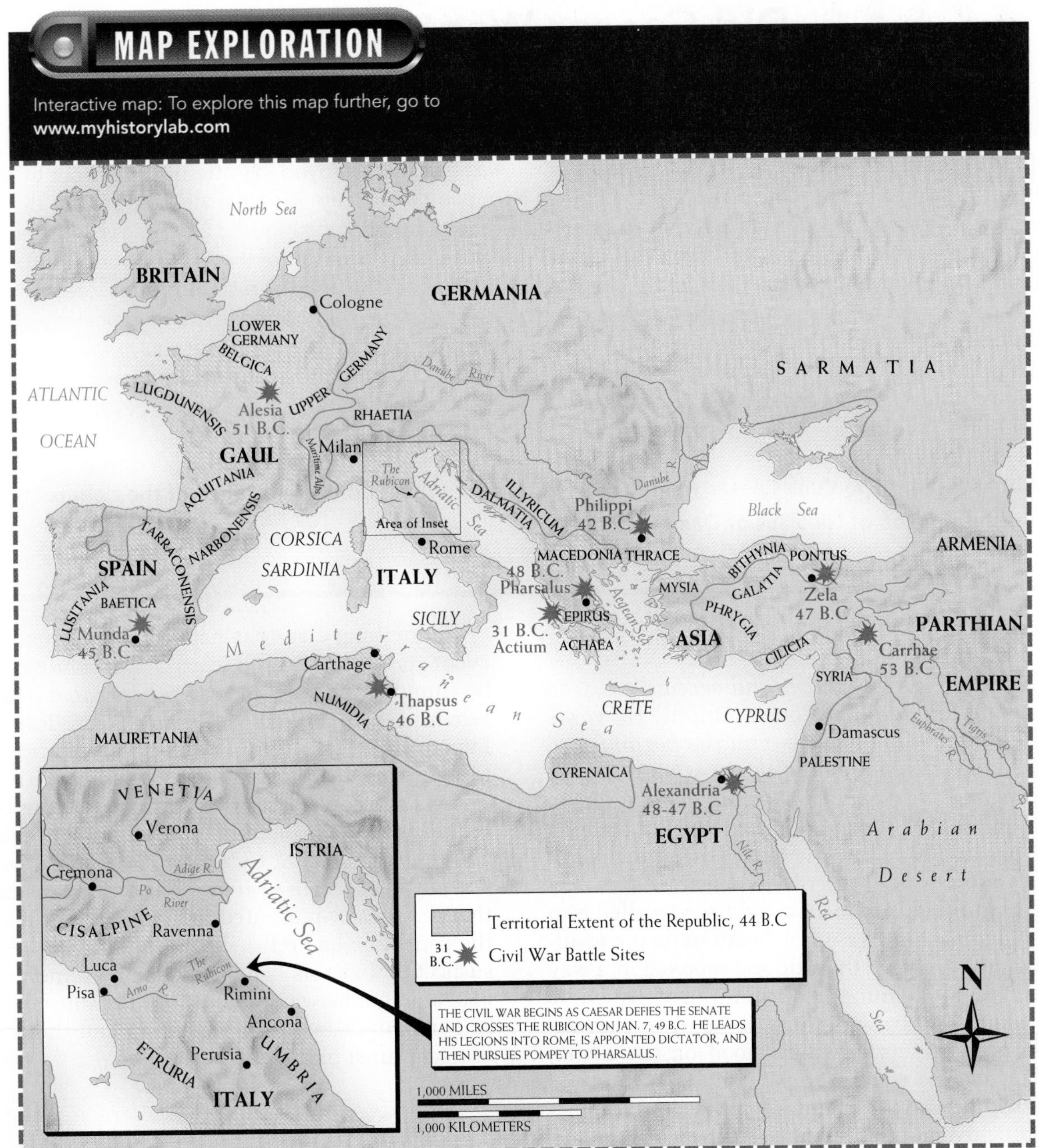

Map 4–4 **THE CIVIL WARS OF THE LATE ROMAN REPUBLIC** This map shows the extent of the territory controlled by Rome at the time of Caesar's death and the sites of the major battles of the civil wars of the late republic.

Caesar made few changes in the government of Rome. The Senate continued to play its role, in theory. But its increased size, its packing with supporters of Caesar, and his own monopoly of military power made the whole thing a sham. He treated the Senate as his creature, sometimes with disdain. His legal position rested on several powers. In 46 B.C.E., he was appointed dictator for ten years, and in the next year he was appointed for life. He also held the consulship, the immunity of a tribune (although, being a patrician, he had never been a tribune), the chief priesthood of the state, and a new position, prefect of morals, which gave him the censorial power. Usurping the elective power of the assemblies, he even named the magistrates for the next few years, because he expected to be away in the East.

The enemies of Caesar were quick to accuse him of aiming at monarchy. (See "Compare & Connect: Did Caesar Want to Be King?," page 124.) A conspiracy under the leadership of Gaius Cassius Longinus and Marcus Junius Brutus included some sixty senators.

COMPARE AND CONNECT Did Caesar Want to Be King?

AFTER THE RETIREMENT and death of Sulla, his constitution was quickly destroyed, his attempt to restore the rule of the Senate proven a failure. The remaining years of the Roman Republic were occupied with a struggle among dynasts and senatorial factions to achieve dominance. From 49 to 46 B.C.E. Caesar and Pompey fought a great civil war that ended in total defeat for Pompey and the senatorial forces. Caesar was unchallenged master of the Roman world. His problem was to invent a system of government that would avoid the pitfalls of divided rule and yet rest upon widespread popular support. From antiquity to the present time, men have argued that his solution was nothing less than monarchy pure and simple. Others have denied that this was his goal. The question cannot be settled, for Caesar was assassinated before he could put his plans into practice, yet it is important to consider the problem both because of its intrinsic interest and because it represents a significant stage in the transition from republic to empire.

QUESTIONS

1. **What does Cassius Dio think Caesar wanted?**
2. **What is the opinion of Nicolaus of Damascus?**
3. **What is the significance of the debate?**

I. Cassius Dio

Cassius Dio was a Greek of the third century C.E. who became a senator under the Roman Empire. He wrote an eighty-book history of Rome from the beginning to 229 C.E. Here he tells the story of the growing suspicion among his enemies and the plots arising among them.

When he had reached this point, the conduct of the men plotting against him became no longer doubtful, and in order to embitter even his best friends against him they did their best to traduce the man and finally called him "king,"—a name which was often heard in their consultations. When he refused the title and rebuked in a way those that so saluted him, yet did nothing by which he could be thought to be really displeased at it, they secretly adorned his statue, which stood on the rostra, with a diadem. And when Gaius Epidius Marullus and Lucius Cassetius Flavus, tribunes, took it down, he became thoroughly angry, although they uttered no insulting word and furthermore spoke well of him before the people as not desiring anything of the sort. At this time, though vexed, he remained quiet; subsequently, however, when he was riding in from Albanum, some men again called him king, and he said that his name was not king but Caesar: then when those tribunes brought suit against the first man that termed him king, he no longer restrained his wrath but showed evident irritation, as if these officials were actually aiming at the stability of his government. . . .

Something else that happened not long after these events proved still more clearly that while pretendedly he shunned the title, in reality he desired to assume it. When he had entered the Forum at the festival of the Lupercalia . . . Antony with his fellow priests saluted him as king and surrounding his brows with a diadem said: "The people gives this to you through my hands." He answered that Jupiter alone was king of the Romans and sent the diadem to him to the Capitol, yet he was not angry and caused it to be inscribed in the records that the royalty presented to him by the people through the consul he had refused to receive. It was accordingly suspected that this had been done by some prearranged plan and that he was anxious for the name but wished to be somehow compelled to take it, and the consequent hatred against him was intense.

Source: CassiusDio, 44.8–11, trans. by H. B. Foster, pp. 414–417, Cambridge, MA, Harvard University Press, 1961.

II. Nicolaus of Damascus

Nicolaus was born to a distinguished Greek family in the first century B.C. He served as adviser and court historian to Herod the Great of Judea. In addition to the biography of the young Augustus, from which the following selection is taken, he wrote dramas, philosophical works, and a multivolume history of the world.

Such was the people's talk at that time. Later, in the course of the winter, a festival was held in Rome, called Lupercalia, in which old and young men together take part in a procession, naked except for a girdle, and anointed, railing at those whom they meet and striking them with pieces of goat's hide. When this festival came on Marcus Antonius was chosen director. He proceeded through the Forum, as was the custom, and the rest of the throng followed him. Caesar was sitting in a golden chair on the Rostra, wearing a purple toga. At first Licinius advanced toward him carrying a laurel wreath, though inside it a diadem was plainly visible. He mounted up, pushed up by his colleagues (for the place from which Caesar was accustomed to address the assembly was high), and set the diadem down before Caesar's feet. Amid the cheers of the crowd he placed it on Caesar's head. Thereupon Caesar called Lepidus, the master of horse, to ward him off, but Lepidus hesitated. In the meanwhile Cassius Longinus, one of the conspirators, pretending to be really well disposed toward Caesar so that he might the more readily escape suspicion, hurriedly removed the diadem and placed it in Caesar's lap. Publius Casca was also with him. While Caesar kept rejecting it, and among the shouts of the people, Antonius suddenly rushed up, naked and anointed, just as he was in the procession, and placed it on his head. But Caesar snatched it off, and threw it into the crowd. Those who were standing at some distance applauded this action, but those who were near at hand clamored that he should accept it and not repel the people's favor. Various individuals held different views of the matter. Some were angry, thinking it an indication of power out of place in a democracy; others, thinking to court favor, approved; still others spread the report that Antonius had acted as he did not without Caesar's connivance. There were many who were quite willing that Caesar be made king openly. All sorts of talk began to go through the crowd. When Antonius crowned Caesar a second time, the people shouted in chorus, 'Hail, King,' but Caesar still refusing the crown, ordered it to be taken to the temple of Capitolme Jupiter, saying that it was more appropriate there. Again the same people applauded as before. There is told another story, that Antonius acted thus wishing to ingratiate himself with Caesar, and at the same time was cherishing the hope of being adopted as his son. Finally, he embraced Caesar and gave the crown to some of the men standing near to place it on the head of the statue of Caesar which was near by. This they did. Of all the occurrences of that time this was not the least influential in hastening the action of the conspirators, for it proved to their very eyes the truth of the suspicions they entertained.

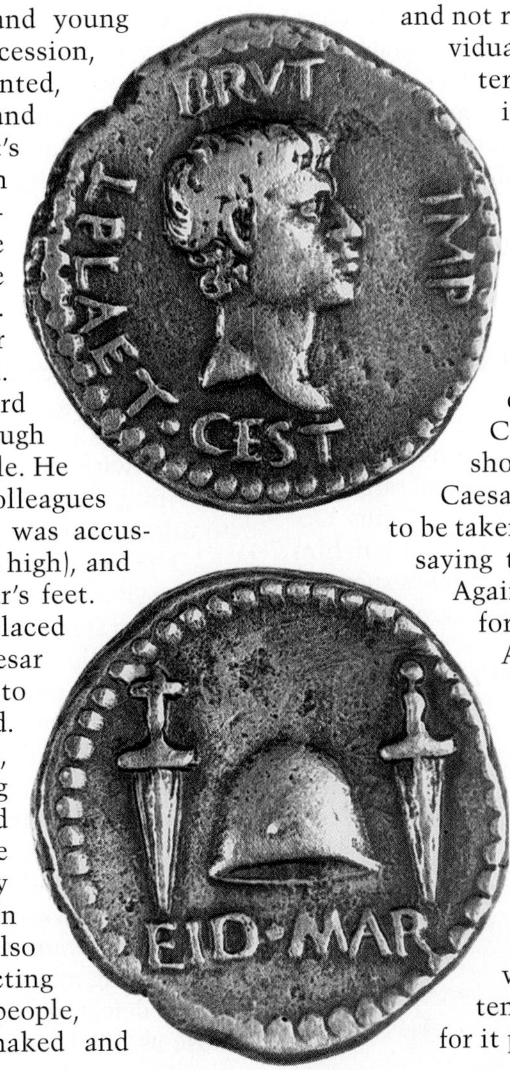

A profile of Brutus, one of Caesar's assassins, appeared on this silver coin. The reverse shows a cap of liberty between two daggers and reads "Ides of March." Getty Images, Inc–Liaison

Source: Nicolaus of Damascus, *Life of Augustus*, 19–22, trans. by Clayton M. Hall (Menascha, WI: George Banta, 1923), p. 41. Reprinted by permission of Clayton M. Hall.

On 15 March 44 B.C.E., Caesar entered the Senate, characteristically without a bodyguard, and was stabbed to death. The assassins regarded themselves as heroic tyrannicides but did not have a clear plan of action to follow the tyrant's death. No doubt they simply expected the republic to be restored in the old way, but things had gone too far for that. There followed instead thirteen more years of civil war, at the end of which the republic received its final burial.

The Second Triumvirate and the Triumph of Octavian

Caesar had had legions of followers, and he had a capable successor in Mark Antony. But the dictator had named his eighteen-year-old grandnephew, Gaius Octavius (63 B.C.E.–14 C.E.), as his heir and had left him three quarters of his vast wealth. To everyone's surprise, the sickly and inexperienced young man came to Rome to claim his legacy. He gathered an army, won the support of many of Caesar's veterans, and became a figure of importance—the future **Augustus**.

THE FALL OF THE ROMAN REPUBLIC

133 B.C.E.	Tribunate of Tiberius Gracchus
123–122 B.C.E.	Tribunate of Gaius Gracchus
111–105 B.C.E.	Jugurthine War
104–100 B.C.E.	Consecutive consulships of Marius
90–88 B.C.E.	War against the Italian allies
88 B.C.E.	Sulla's march on Rome
82 B.C.E.	Sulla assumes dictatorship
71 B.C.E.	Crassus crushes rebellion of Spartacus
71 B.C.E.	Pompey defeats Sertorius in Spain
70 B.C.E.	Consulship of Crassus and Pompey
60 B.C.E.	Formation of First Triumvirate
58–50 B.C.E.	Caesar in Gaul
53 B.C.E.	Crassus killed in Battle of Carrhae
49 B.C.E.	Caesar crosses Rubicon; civil war begins
48 B.C.E.	Pompey defeated at Pharsalus; killed in Egypt
46–44 B.C.E.	Caesar's dictatorship
45 B.C.E.	End of civil war
43 B.C.E.	Formation of Second Triumvirate
42 B.C.E.	Triumvirs defeat Brutus and Cassius at Philippi
31 B.C.E.	Octavian and Agrippa defeat Antony at Actium

At first, the Senate tried to use Octavius against Antony, but when the conservatives rejected his request for the consulship, Octavius broke with them. Following Sulla's grim precedent, he took his army and marched on Rome. There he finally assumed his adopted name, C. Julius Caesar Octavianus. Modern historians refer to him at this stage in his career as Octavian, although he insisted on being called Caesar. In August 43 B.C.E., he became consul and declared the assassins of Caesar outlaws. Brutus and Cassius had an army of their own, so Octavian made a pact with Mark Antony and M. Aemilius Lepidus, a Caesarean governor of the western provinces. They took control of Rome and had themselves appointed "triumvirs to put the republic in order," with great powers. This was the Second Triumvirate, and unlike the first, it was legally empowered to rule almost dictatorially.

The need to pay their troops, their own greed, and the passion that always emerges in civil wars led the triumvirs to start a wave of proscriptions that outdid even those of Sulla. In 42 B.C.E., the triumviral army defeated Brutus and Cassius at Philippi in Macedonia, and the last hope of republican restoration died with the tyrannicides. Each of the triumvirs received a command. The junior partner, Lepidus, was given Africa, Antony took the rich and inviting East, and Octavian got the West and the many troubles that went with it.

Octavian had to fight a war against Sextus, the son of Pompey, who held Sicily. He also had to settle 100,000 veterans in Italy, confiscating much property and making many enemies. Helped by his friend Agrippa, he defeated Sextus Pompey in 36 B.C.E. Among his close associates was Maecenas, who served him as adviser and diplomatic agent. Maecenas helped manage the delicate relations with Antony and Lepidus, but perhaps equally important was his role as a patron of the arts. Among his clients were the poets Vergil and Horace, both of whom did important work for Octavian. They painted him as a restorer of Roman values, as a man of ancient Roman lineage and of traditional Roman virtues, and as the culmination of Roman destiny. More and more he was identified with Italy and the West, as well as with order, justice, and virtue.

Meanwhile Antony was in the East, chiefly at Alexandria with Cleopatra, the queen of Egypt. In 36 B.C.E., he attacked Parthia, with disastrous results. Octavian had promised to send troops to support Antony's Parthian campaign but never sent them. Antony was forced to depend on the East for support, and this meant reliance on Cleopatra. Octavian understood the advantage of representing himself as the champion of the West, Italy, and Rome. Meanwhile he represented Antony as the man of the East and the dupe of Cleopatra, her tool in establishing Alexandria as the center of an empire and herself as its ruler. Such propaganda made it easier for Caesareans to abandon Antony in favor of the young heir of Caesar. It did not help Antony's cause that he agreed to a public festival at Alexandria in 34 B.C.E., where he and Cleopatra sat on golden thrones. She was proclaimed "Queen of Kings," her son by Julius Caesar was named "King of Kings," and her other children received parts of the Roman Empire.

By 32 B.C.E., all pretense of cooperation ended. Octavian and Antony each tried to put the best face on what was essentially a struggle for power. Lepidus had been put aside some years earlier. Antony sought senatorial support and promised to restore the republican constitution. Octavian seized and published what was alleged to be the will of Antony, revealing his gifts of provinces to the children of Cleopatra. This caused the conflict to take the form of East against West, Rome against Alexandria.

In 31 B.C.E., the matter was settled at Actium in western Greece. Agrippa, Octavian's best general, cut off the enemy by land and sea, forcing and winning a naval battle. Octavian pursued Antony and Cleopatra to Alexandria, where both committed suicide. The civil wars were over, and at the age of thirty-two, Octavian was absolute master of the Mediterranean world. His power was enormous, but he had to restore peace, prosperity, and confidence. All of these required establishing a constitution that would reflect the new realities without offending unduly the traditional republican prejudices that still had so firm a grip on Rome and Italy.

In Perspective

The history of the Roman Republic was almost as sharp a departure from the common experiences of ancient civilizations as that of the Greek city-states. A monarchy in its earliest known form, Rome not long thereafter expelled its king and established an aristocratic republic somewhat like the *poleis* of the Greek "Dark Ages." But unlike the Greeks, the Romans continued to be in touch with foreign neighbors, including the far more civilized urban monarchies of the Etruscans. Nonetheless, the Romans clung to their republican institutions. For a long time the Romans remained a nation of farmers and herdsmen, to whom trade was relatively unimportant, especially outside of Italy.

Over time, the caste distinctions between patricians and plebeians were replaced by distinctions based on wealth and, even more important, aristocracy, wherein the significant distinction was between noble families, who held the highest elected offices in the state, and those outside the nobility. The Roman Republic from the first found itself engaged in almost continuous warfare with its neighbors—either in defense of its own territory, in fights over disputed territory, or in defense of other cities or states who were friends and allies of Rome.

Both internally and in their foreign relations, the Romans were a legalistic people, placing great importance on traditional behavior encoded into laws. Although backed by the powerful authority of the magistrates at home and the potent Roman army abroad, the laws were based on experience, common sense, and equity. Roman law aimed at stability and fairness, and it succeeded well enough that few people who lived under it wanted to do away with it. It lived on and grew during the imperial period and beyond. During the European Middle Ages, it played an important part in the revival of the West and continued to exert an influence into modern times.

The force of Roman arms, the high quality of Roman roads and bridges, and the pragmatic character of Roman law helped create something unique: an empire ruled by a republic, first a large one on land that included all of Italy and later one that commanded the shores of the entire Mediterranean and extended far inland in many places. Rome controlled an area that bears comparison with some of the empires of the East. It acquired that territory, wealth, and power in a state managed by annual magistrates elected by the male Roman citizens and by an aristocratic Senate, which had to take notice of popular assemblies and a published, impersonal code of law. It achieved its greatness with an army of citizens and allies, without a monarchy or a regular bureaucracy.

The temptations and responsibilities of governing a vast and rich empire, however, finally proved too much for the republican constitution. Trade grew, and with it a class of merchants and financiers—equestrians—that was neither aristocratic nor agricultural, but increasingly powerful. The influx of masses of slaves captured in war undermined the small farmers who had been the backbone of the Roman state and its army. As many of them were forced to leave their farms, they moved to the cities, chiefly to Rome, where they had no productive role. Conscripted armies of farmers serving relatively short terms gave way to volunteer armies of landless men serving as professionals and expecting to be rewarded for their services with gifts of land or money. The generals of these armies were not annual magistrates whom the Senate and the constitution controlled, but ambitious military leaders seeking glory and political advantage.

The result was civil war and the destruction of the republic. The conquest of a vast empire moved the Romans away from their unusual historical traditions toward the more familiar path of an empire that older rulers in Egypt and Mesopotamia had trodden.

REVIEW QUESTIONS

1. How did the institutions of family and clientage and the establishment of patrician and plebeian classes contribute to the stability of the early Roman Republic? How important were education and slavery to the success of the republic?
2. What was the Struggle of the Orders? How did plebeians get what they wanted? How was Roman society different after the struggle ended?
3. How was Rome able to conquer and control Italy? In their relations with Greece and Asia Minor in the second century B.C.E., were the Romans looking for security? Wealth? Power? Fame?
4. Why did the Romans and the Carthaginians clash in the First and Second Punic Wars? Could the wars have been avoided? How did Rome benefit from its victory over Carthage? What problems did this victory create?
5. What social, economic, and political problems did Italy have in the second century B.C.E.? What were the main proposals of Tiberius and Gaius Gracchus? What questions about Roman society did they raise? Why did the proposals fail?
6. What problems plagued the Roman Republic in its last century? What caused these problems and how did the Romans try to solve them? To what extent was the republic destroyed by ambitious generals who loved power more than Rome itself?

SUGGESTED READINGS

G. Barker and T. Rasmussen, *The Etruscans* (2000). A valuable new study of a mysterious people.

R. Baumann, *Women and Politics in Ancient Rome* (1995). A study of the role of women in Roman public life.

A. H. Bernstein, *Tiberius Sempronius Gracchus: Tradition and Apostasy* (1978). An interpretation of Tiberius's place in Roman politics.

T. J. Cornell, *The Beginnings of Rome: Italy and Rome from the Bronze Age to the Punic Wars* (1995). A fine new study of early Rome.

T. Cornell and J. Matthews, *Atlas of the Roman World* (1982). Presents a comprehensive view of the Roman world in its physical and cultural setting.

J-M. David, *The Roman Conquest of Italy* (1997). A good analysis of how Rome united Italy.

E. S. Gruen, *The Hellenistic World and the Coming of Rome* (1984). A new interpretation of Rome's conquest of the eastern Mediterranean.

W. V. Harris, *War and Imperialism in Republican Rome, 327–70 B.C.E.* (1975). An analysis of Roman attitudes and intentions concerning imperial expansion and war.

T. Holland, *Rubicon: The Last Years of the Roman Republic* (2004). A lively account of the fall of the republic.

S. Lancel, *Carthage, A History* (1995). A good account of Rome's great competitor.

H. Mouritsen, *Plebs and Politics in the Late Roman Republic* (2001). A new study of Roman republican politics and the place of the common people in them.

J. Powell and J. Patterson, *Cicero the Advocate* (2004). A careful study of the Roman statesman's legal career.

H. H. Scullard, *A History of the Roman World 753–146 B.C.E.*, 4th ed. (1980). An unusually fine narrative history with useful critical notes.

For additional learning resources related to this chapter, please go to www.myhistorylab.com

PEARSON myhistorylab

This statue of Emperor Augustus (r. 27 B.C.E.–14 C.E.), now in the Vatican, stood in the villa of Augustus's wife Livia. The figures on the elaborate breastplate are all of symbolic significance. At the top, for example, Dawn in her chariot brings in a new day under the protective mantle of the sky god; in the center, Tiberius, Augustus's future successor, accepts the return of captured Roman army standards from a barbarian prince; and at the bottom, Mother Earth offers a horn of plenty. Vatican Museums & Galleries, Vatican City/Superstock

5

The Roman Empire

▼ **The Augustan Principate**
Administration • The Army and Defense • Religion and Morality

▼ **Civilization of the Ciceronian and Augustan Ages**
The Late Republic • The Age of Augustus

▼ **Imperial Rome, 14 to 180 C.E.**
The Emperors • The Administration of the Empire • Women of the Upper Classes • Life in Imperial Rome: The Apartment House • The Culture of the Early Empire

▼ **The Rise of Christianity**
Jesus of Nazareth • Paul of Tarsus • Organization • The Persecution of Christians • The Emergence of Catholicism • Rome as a Center of the Early Church

▼ **The Crisis of the Third Century**
Barbarian Invasions • Economic Difficulties • The Social Order • Civil Disorder

▼ **The Late Empire**
The Fourth Century and Imperial Reorganization • The Triumph of Christianity

▼ **Arts and Letters in the Late Empire**
The Preservation of Classical Culture • Christian Writers

▼ **The Problem of the Decline and Fall of the Empire in the West**

▼ **In Perspective**

KEY TOPICS

- **The Augustan constitution**
- **The organization and government of the Roman Empire**
- **Culture and civilization from the late republic through the imperial period**
- **The early history of Christianity**
- **The decline and fall of Rome in the West**

THE VICTORY OF Augustus put an end to the deadly period of civil strife that had begun with the murder of Tiberius Gracchus. The establishment of a monarchy, at first concealed in republican forms but gradually more obvious, brought a long period of peace. Rome's unquestioned control of the entire Mediterranean permitted the growth of trade and a prosperity in the first two centuries of the Roman Empire not to be equaled for more than a millennium.

Management of the empire outside Italy became more benign and efficient. With shared citizenship, the provinces usually accepted Roman rule readily and even enthusiastically. Latin became the official language of the western part of the empire and Greek the official language in the east. This permitted the growth and spread of a common culture, today called *classical civilization*, throughout the empire. The same conditions fostered a great outburst of activity and excellence in the arts. The loss of political freedom, however, brought a decline in the vitality of the great Roman genre of rhetoric.

Christianity emerged in the first century C.E. as one of many competing Eastern cults. It continued to spread and attract converts, winning toleration and finally dominance in the fourth century. The world of imperial Rome powerfully shaped Christianity, which absorbed and used classical culture even while fighting it.

The third century C.E. brought serious attacks on Rome's frontiers, causing political and economic chaos. For a time, such emperors as Diocletian (r. 284–305) and Constantine (r. 306–337) instituted heroic measures to restore order. Their solutions involved increased centralization, militarization, and attempts to control every aspect of life. The emperors became more exalted and remote, the people increasingly burdened with heavy taxes even as the loss of economic freedom reduced their ability to pay. At last a new wave of barbarian attacks proved irresistible, and the Roman Empire in the West ended in the second half of the fifth century.

▼ The Augustan Principate

If the problems facing Octavian after the Battle of Actium in 31 B.C.E. were great, so were his resources for addressing them. He was the master of a vast military force, the only one in the Roman world, and he had loyal and capable assistants. Of enormous importance was the rich treasury of Egypt, which Octavian treated as his personal property. The people of Italy were eager for an end to civil war and a return to peace, order, and prosperity. In exchange for these, most people were prepared to accept a considerable abandonment of republican practices and to give power to an able ruler. The memory of Julius Caesar's fate, however, was still fresh in Octavian's mind. Its lesson was that it was dangerous to flaunt unprecedented powers and to disregard all republican traditions.

Octavian did not create his constitutional solution at a single stroke. It developed gradually as he tried new devices to fit his perception of changing conditions. Behind all the republican trappings and the apparent sharing of authority with the Senate, the government of Octavian, like that of his successors, was a monarchy. All real power, both civil and military, lay with the ruler—whether he was called by the unofficial title of *princeps*, or "first citizen," like Octavian, the founder of the regime, or *imperator*, "emperor," like those who followed. During the civil war Octavian's powers came from his triumviral status, whose dubious legality and unrepublican character were an embarrassment. From 31 B.C.E. on, he held the consulship each year, but this circumstance was neither strictly legal nor satisfactory.

On 13 January 27 B.C.E., Octavian put forward a new plan in dramatic style, coming before the Senate to give up all his powers and provinces. In what was surely a rehearsed response, the Senate begged him to reconsider. At last he agreed to accept the provinces of Spain, Gaul, and Syria with proconsular power for military command and to retain the consulship in Rome. The other provinces would be governed by the Senate as before. Because the provinces he retained were border provinces that contained twenty of Rome's twenty-six legions, his true power was undiminished. The Senate, however, responded with almost hysterical gratitude, voting him many honors. Among them was the semireligious title Augustus, which implied veneration, majesty, and holiness. From this time on, historians speak of Rome's first emperor as Augustus and of his regime as the *Principate*. This would have pleased him, for it helps conceal the novel, unrepublican nature of the regime and the naked power on which it rested.

In 23 B.C.E., Augustus resigned his consulship and held that office only rarely thereafter. Instead, he was voted two powers that were to be the base of his rule thenceforth: the proconsular *imperium maius* and the *tribunician power*. The former made his proconsular power greater than that of any other proconsul and permitted him to exercise it even within the city of Rome. The latter gave him the right to conduct public business in the assemblies and the Senate, gave him the power of the veto, the *tribunician sacrosanctity* (immunity from arrest and punishment), and a connection with the Roman popular tradition. Thereafter, with only minor changes, Augustus's powers remained those conferred by the settlement of 23 B.C.E.

Administration

Augustus made important changes in the government of Rome, Italy, and the provinces. Most of his reforms reduced inefficiency and corruption, ended the danger to peace and order from ambitious individuals, and lessened the distinction between Romans and Italians, senators and equestrians. The assemblies lost their significance as a working part of the constitution, and the Senate took on most of the functions of the assemblies. Augustus purged the old Senate of undesirable members and fixed its number at six hundred. He recruited its members from wealthy men of good character, who entered after serving as lesser magistrates. Augustus controlled the elections and ensured that promising young men, whatever their origin, served the state as administrators and provincial governors. In this way, many equestrians and Italians who had no connection with the Roman aristocracy entered the Senate. For

This scene from Augustus's Ara Pacis, the Altar of Peace, in Rome shows the general Marcus Agrippa (63–12 B.C.E.) in procession with the imperial family. Agrippa was a powerful deputy, close friend, and son-in-law of Augustus. He was chiefly responsible for the victory over Mark Antony at the Battle of Actium in 31 B.C.E. Museum of the Ara Pacis, Rome, Italy

all his power, Augustus was always careful to treat the Senate with respect and honor.

Augustus divided Rome into regions and wards with elected local officials. He gave the city, with its rickety wooden tenements, its first public fire department and police force. He carefully controlled grain distribution to the poor and created organizations to provide an adequate water supply. The Augustan period was one of great prosperity, based on the wealth brought in by the conquest of Egypt, on the great increase in commerce and industry made possible by general peace, on a vast program of public works, and on the revival of small farming by Augustus's resettled veterans.

The union of political and military power in the hands of the *princeps* enabled him to install rational, efficient, and stable government in the provinces for the first time. The emperor, in effect, chose the governors, removed the incompetent or rapacious, and allowed the effective ones to keep their provinces for longer periods. Also, he allowed much greater local autonomy, giving considerable responsibility to the upper classes in the provincial cities and towns and to the tribal leaders in less civilized areas.

The Army and Defense

The main external problem facing Augustus—and one that haunted all his successors—was the northern frontier. (See Map 5–1 on page 132.) Rome needed to pacify the regions to the north and the northeast of Italy and to find defensible frontiers against the recurring waves of barbarians. Augustus's plan was to push forward into central Europe to create the shortest possible defensive line. The eastern part of the plan succeeded, and the campaign in the West started well. In 9 C.E., however, the German tribal leader Herrmann, or Arminius, as the Romans called him, ambushed and destroyed three Roman legions, and the aged Augustus abandoned the campaign, leaving a problem of border defense that bedeviled his successors.

Under Augustus, the armed forces achieved professional status. Enlistment, chiefly by Italians, was for twenty years, but the pay was good, with occasional bonuses and the promise of a pension on retirement in the form of money or a plot of land. Together with the auxiliaries from the provinces, these forces formed a

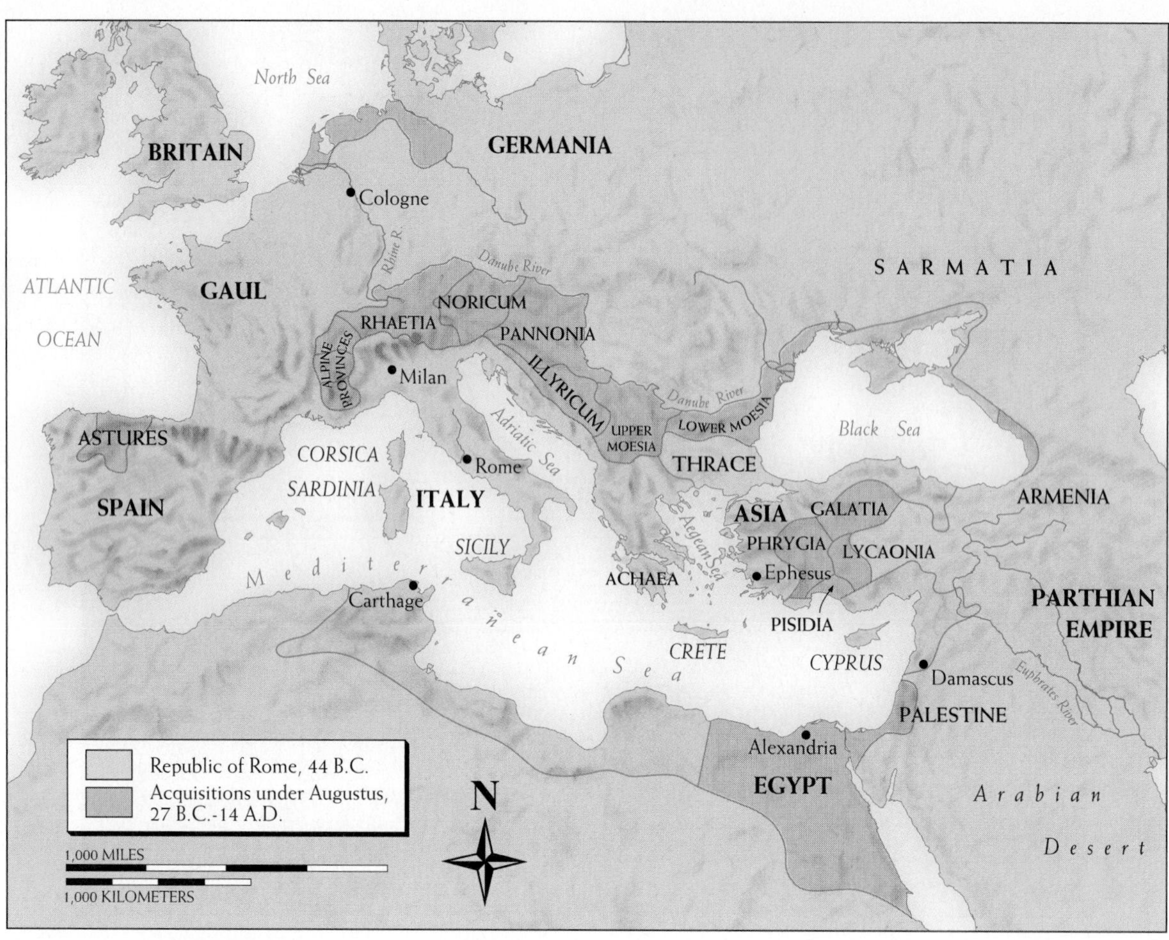

Map 5–1 **THE ROMAN EMPIRE, 14 C.E.** This map shows the growth of the empire under Augustus and its extent at his death.

frontier army of about 300,000 men. In normal times, this was barely enough to hold the line.

The army permanently based in the provinces brought Roman culture to the natives. The soldiers spread their language and customs, often marrying local women and settling down in the area of their service. They attracted merchants, as new towns and cities that grew into centers of Roman civilization grew up around the military camps. As time passed, the provincials on the frontiers became Roman citizens who helped strengthen Rome's defenses against the barbarians outside.

Religion and Morality

A century of political strife and civil war had undermined many of the foundations of traditional Roman society. To repair the damage, Augustus sought to preserve and restore the traditional values of the family and religion in Rome and Italy. He introduced laws curbing adultery and divorce and encouraging early marriage and the procreation of legitimate children. He set an example of austere behavior in his own household and even banished his daughter, Julia, whose immoral behavior had become public knowledge.

Augustus worked at restoring the dignity of formal Roman religion, building many temples, reviving old cults, and invigorating the priestly colleges. He banned the worship of newly introduced foreign gods. Writers he patronized, such as Vergil, pointed out his family's legendary connection with Venus. During his lifetime he did not accept divine honors, though he was deified after his death. As with Julius Caesar, a state cult was dedicated to his worship.

▼ Civilization of the Ciceronian and Augustan Ages

The high point of Roman culture came in the last century of the republic and during the Principate of Augustus. Both periods reflected the dominant influence of Greek culture, especially its Hellenistic mode. Upper-class Romans were educated in Greek rhetoric, philosophy, and literature, which also served as the models for Roman writers and artists. Yet in spirit and sometimes in form, the art and writing of both periods show uniquely Roman qualities, though each in different ways.

The Late Republic

Cicero The towering literary figure of the late republic was Cicero (106–43 B.C.E.). He is most famous for the orations he delivered in the law courts and in the Senate. Together with a considerable body of his private letters, these orations provide us with a clearer and fuller insight into his mind than into that of any other figure in antiquity. We see the political life of his period largely through his eyes. He also wrote treatises on rhetoric, ethics, and politics that put Greek philosophical ideas into Latin terminology and at the same time changed them to suit Roman conditions and values.

Cicero's own views provide support for his moderate and conservative practicality. He believed in a world governed by divine and natural law that human reason could perceive and human institutions reflect. He looked to law, custom, and tradition to produce both stability and liberty. His literary style, as well as his values and ideas, were an important legacy for the Middle Ages and, reinterpreted, for the Renaissance. He was killed at the order of Mark Antony, whose political opponent he had been during the civil wars after the death of Julius Caesar.

History The last century of the republic produced some historical writing, much of which is lost to us. Sallust (86–35 B.C.E.) wrote a history of the years 78 to 67 B.C.E., but only a few fragments remain to remind us of his reputation as the greatest of republican historians. His surviving work consists of two pamphlets on the Jugurthine War and on the conspiracy of Catiline of 63 B.C.E. They reveal his Caesarean and antisenatorial prejudices and the stylistic influence of Thucydides.

Julius Caesar wrote important treatises on the Gallic and civil wars. They are not fully rounded historical accounts, but chiefly military narratives written from Caesar's point of view and to enhance his repuation. Their objective manner (Caesar always referred to himself in the third person) and their direct, simple, and vigorous style make them persuasive even today. They must have been most effective with the citizens of Rome who were their immediate audience.

Law The period from the Gracchi to the fall of the republic was important in the development of Roman law. Before that time, Roman law was essentially national and had developed chiefly by juridical decisions, case by case. Contact with foreign peoples and the influence of Greek ideas, however, forced a change. From the last century of the republic on, the edicts of the *praetors* had increasing importance in developing the Roman legal code. They interpreted and even changed and added to existing law. Quite early, the edicts of the magistrates who dealt with foreigners developed the idea of the ***jus gentium***, or "law of peoples," as opposed to that arising strictly from the experience of the Romans. In the first century B.C.E., the influence of Greek thought made the idea of *jus gentium* identical with that of the ***jus naturae***, or "natural law," taught by the Stoics. It was this view of a world ruled by divine reason that Cicero enshrined in his treatise on the law, *De Legibus*.

Poetry The time of Cicero was also the period of two of Rome's greatest poets, Lucretius and Catullus, each representing a different aspect of Rome's poetic tradition. The Hellenistic poets and literary theorists saw two functions for the poet: entertainer and teacher. They thought the best poet combined both roles, and the Romans adopted the same view. When Naevius and Ennius wrote epics on Roman history, they combined historical and moral instruction with pleasure. Lucretius (ca. 99–55 B.C.E.) pursued a similar path in his epic poem *De Rerum Natura* (*On the Nature of the World*). In it, he set forth the scientific and philosophical ideas of Epicurus and Democritus with the zeal of a missionary trying to save society from fear and superstition. He knew his doctrine might be bitter medicine to the reader: "That is why I have tried to administer it to you in the dulcet strain of poesy, coated with the sweet honey of the Muses."[1]

Catullus (ca. 84–54 B.C.E.) was a thoroughly different kind of poet. He wrote poems that were personal—even autobiographical. Imitating the Alexandrians, he wrote short poems filled with learned allusions to mythology, but he far surpassed his models in intensity of feeling. He wrote of the joys and pains of love, he hurled invective at important contemporaries like Julius Caesar, and he amused himself in witty poetic exchanges with others. He offered no moral lessons and was not interested in Rome's glorious history and in contemporary politics. In a sense, he is an example of the proud, independent, pleasure-seeking nobleman who characterized part of the aristocracy at the end of the republic.

The Age of Augustus

The spirit of the Augustan Age, the Golden Age of Roman literature, was different, reflecting the new conditions of society. The old aristocratic order, with its independent nobles following their own particular interests, was gone. So was the world of poets of the lower orders, receiving patronage from individual aristocrats. Under Augustus, all patronage flowed from the *princeps*, usually through his chief cultural adviser, Maecenas.

The major poets of this time, Vergil and Horace, had lost their property during the civil wars. The patronage of the *princeps* allowed them the leisure and the security to write poetry, but it also made them dependent on him and limited their freedom of expression. They wrote on subjects that were useful for his policies and

[1]Lucretius, *De Rerum Natura*, lines 931 ff.

glorified him and his family. These poets were not mere propagandists, however. It seems clear that mostly they believed in the virtues of Augustus and his reign and sang its praises with some degree of sincerity. Because they were poets of genius, they were also able to maintain a measure of independence in their work.

Vergil Vergil (70–19 B.C.E.) was the most important of the Augustan poets. His first important works, the *Eclogues*, or *Bucolics*, are pastoral idylls in a somewhat artificial mode. The subject of the *Georgics*, however, was suggested to Vergil by Maecenas. The model here was the early Greek poet Hesiod's *Works and Days* (see Chapter 2), but Vergil's poem pays homage to the heroic human effort to forge order and social complexity out of a hostile and sometimes brutal natural environment. It was also a hymn to the cults, traditions, and greatness of Italy.

All this served the purpose of glorifying Augustus's resettlement of the veterans of the civil wars on Italian farms and his elevation of Italy to special status in the empire. Vergil's greatest work is the *Aeneid*, a long national epic that placed the history of Rome in the great tradition of the Greeks and the Trojan War. Its hero, the Trojan warrior Aeneas, personifies the ideal Roman qualities of duty, responsibility, serious purpose, and patriotism. As the Romans' equivalent of Homer, Vergil glorified not the personal honor and excellence of the Greek epic heroes, but the civic greatness, peace, and prosperity that Augustus and the Julian family had given to imperial Rome.

This mosaic found in Tunisia shows the poet Vergil reading from his Aeneid to the Muses of Epic and Tragedy. Roger Wood/CORBIS/Bettmann

Horace Horace (65–8 B.C.E.) was the son of a freedman and fought on the republican side until its defeat at Philippi. The patronage of Maecenas and the attractions of the Augustan reforms won him over to the Augustan side. His *Satires* are genial and humorous. His *Odes*, which are ingenious in their adaptation of Greek meters to the requirements of Latin verse, best reveal his great skills as a lyric poet. Two of the *Odes* are directly in praise of Augustus, and many of them glorify the new Augustan order, the imperial family, and the empire.

Propertius Sextus Propertius lived in Rome in the second half of the first century B.C.E., a contemporary of Vergil and Horace. Like them, he was part of the poetic circle around Augustus's friend Maecenas. He wrote witty and graceful elegies.

Ovid The career of Ovid (43 B.C.E.–18 C.E.) reveals the darker side of Augustan influence on the arts. He wrote light and entertaining love elegies that reveal the sophistication and the loose sexual code of a notorious sector of the Roman aristocracy whose values and amusements were contrary to the seriousness and family-centered life Augustus was trying to foster. Ovid's *Ars Amatoria*, a poetic textbook on the art of seduction, angered Augustus and was partly responsible for the poet's exile in 8 C.E. Ovid tried to recover favor, especially with his *Fasti*, a poetic treatment of Roman religious festivals, but to no avail. His most popular work is the *Metamorphoses*, a kind of mythological epic that turns Greek myths into charming stories in a graceful and lively style. Ovid's fame did not fade with his exile and death, but his fate was an effective warning to later poets.

History The achievements of Augustus, his emphasis on tradition, and the continuity of his regime with the glorious history of Rome encouraged both historical and antiquarian prose works. Some Augustan writers wrote scholarly treatises on history and geography in Greek. By far the most important and influential prose writer of the time, however, was Livy (59 B.C.E.–17 C.E.), an Italian from Padua. His *History of Rome* was written in Latin and treated the period from the legendary origins of Rome until 9 B.C.E. Only a fourth of his work is extant; of the rest we have only pitifully brief summaries. He based his history on earlier accounts and made no effort at original research. His great achievement was to tell the story of Rome in a continuous and impressive narrative. Its purpose was moral, and he set up historical models as examples of good and bad behavior and, above all, patriotism. He glorified Rome's greatness and connected it with Rome's past, as Augustus tried to do.

Architecture and Sculpture Augustus was as great a patron of the visual arts as he was of literature. His building program beautified Rome, glorified his reign, and contributed to the general prosperity and his own popularity. He filled the Campus Martius with beautiful new buildings, theaters, baths, and basilicas; the Roman Forum was rebuilt, and Augustus built a forum of his own. At its heart was the temple of Mars the Avenger, which commemorated Augustus's victory and the greatness of his ancestors. On Rome's Palatine Hill, he built a splendid temple to his patron god, Apollo, to further his religious policy.

The Greek classical style, which aimed at serenity and the ideal type, influenced most of the building. The same features were visible in the portrait sculpture of Augustus and his family. The greatest monument of the age is the *Ara Pacis*, or "Altar of Peace," dedicated in 9 B.C.E. Part of it shows a procession in which Augustus and his family appear to move forward, followed in order by the magistrates, the Senate, and the people of Rome. There is no better symbol of the new order.

▾ Imperial Rome, 14 to 180 C.E.

The central problem for Augustus's successors was the position of the ruler and his relationship to the ruled. Augustus tried to cloak the monarchical nature of his government, but his successors soon abandoned all pretense. The ruler came to be called *imperator*—from which comes our word "emperor"—as well as Caesar. The latter title signified connection with the imperial house, and the former indicated the military power on which everything was based.

The Emperors

Because Augustus was ostensibly only the "first citizen" of a restored republic and the Senate and the people theoretically voted him his powers, he could not legally name his successor. In fact, however, he plainly designated his heirs by lavishing favors on them and by giving them a share in the imperial power and responsibility. Tiberius (r. 14–37 C.E.),[2] his immediate successor, was at first embarrassed by the ambiguity of his new role, but soon the monarchical and hereditary nature of the regime became clear. Gaius (Caligula, r. 37–41 C.E.), Claudius (r. 41–54 C.E.), and Nero (r. 54–68 C.E.) were all descended from either Augustus or his wife, Livia, and all were elevated because of that fact.

Gaius Caesar Germanicus succeeded Tiberius in 37 at the age of twenty-five. When he was a boy, the soldiers of his father's legions gave him the nickname Caligula (little boot), which stayed with him for the rest of his life. Recovered from a severe illness that struck him soon after becoming emperor, he launched a series of wild, tyrannical actions. He restored the use of trials for treason that had darkened the reign of Tiberius and was vicious and cruel. He claimed to be divine even while alive and was thought to aim at a despotic monarchy like that of the Ptolemies in Egypt. Caligula spent the large amount of money in the state treasury and tried to get more by seizing the property of wealthy Romans. He was widely thought to be insane.

In 41 C.E., the naked military basis of imperial rule was revealed when the Praetorian Guard, having assassinated Caligula, dragged the lame, stammering, and frightened Claudius from behind a curtain and made him emperor. In 68 C.E., the frontier legions learned what the historian Tacitus (ca. 55–120) called "the secret of Empire . . . that an emperor could be made elsewhere than at Rome." Nero's incompetence and unpopularity, and especially his inability to control his armies, led to a serious rebellion in Gaul in 68 C.E. The year 69 saw four different emperors assume power in quick succession as different Roman armies took turns placing their commanders on the throne.

Vespasian (r. 69–79 C.E.) emerged victorious from the chaos, and his sons, Titus (r. 79–81 C.E.) and Domitian (r. 81–96 C.E.), carried forward his line, the Flavian dynasty. Vespasian, a tough soldier from the Italian middle class, was the first emperor who did not come from the old Roman nobility. A good administrator and a hardheaded realist of rough wit, he resisted all attempts by flatterers to find noble ancestors for him. On his deathbed he is said to have ridiculed the practice of deifying emperors by saying, "Alas, I think I am becoming a god."

RULERS OF THE EARLY EMPIRE

27 B.C.E.–14 C.E.	Augustus
The Julio-Claudian Dynasty	
14–37 C.E.	Tiberius
37–41 C.E.	Gaius (Caligula)
41–54 C.E.	Claudius
54–68 C.E.	Nero
69 C.E.	Year of the Four Emperors
The Flavian Dynasty	
69–79 C.E.	Vespasian
79–81 C.E.	Titus
81–96 C.E.	Domitian
The "Good Emperors"	
96–98 C.E.	Nerva
98–117 C.E.	Trajan
117–138 C.E.	Hadrian
138–161 C.E.	Antoninus Pius
161–180 C.E.	Marcus Aurelius

[2]Dates for emperors give the years of their reigns, indicated by "r."

Marcus Aurelius, emperor of Rome from 161 to 180 C.E., was one of the five "good emperors" who brought a period of relative peace and prosperity to the empire. This is the only Roman bronze equestrian statue that has survived. Capitoline Museums, Rome, Italy/Canali PhotoBank, Milan/Superstock

The assassination of Domitian put an end to the Flavian dynasty. Because Domitian had no close relative who had been designated as successor, the Senate put Nerva (r. 96–98 C.E.) on the throne to avoid chaos. He was the first of the five "good emperors," who included Trajan (r. 98–117 C.E.), Hadrian (r. 117–138 C.E.), Antoninus Pius (r. 138–161 C.E.), and Marcus Aurelius (r. 161–180 C.E.). Until Marcus Aurelius, none of these emperors had sons, so they each followed the example set by Nerva of adopting an able senator and establishing him as successor. This rare solution to the problem of monarchical succession was, therefore, only a historical accident. The result, nonetheless, was almost a century of peaceful succession and competent rule, which ended when Marcus Aurelius allowed his incompetent son, Commodus (r. 180–192 C.E.), to succeed him, with unfortunate results.

The genius of the Augustan settlement lay in its capacity to enlist the active cooperation of the upper classes and their effective organ, the Senate. The election of magistrates was taken from the assemblies and given to the Senate, which became the major center for legislation and exercised important judicial functions. This semblance of power persuaded some contemporaries and even some modern scholars that Augustus had established a *dyarchy*—a system of joint rule by *princeps* and Senate. That was never true.

The hollowness of the senatorial role became more apparent as time passed. Some emperors, like Vespasian, took pains to maintain, increase, and display the prestige and dignity of the Senate. Others, like Caligula, Nero, and Domitian, degraded the Senate and paraded their own despotic power. But from the first, the Senate's powers were illusory. The emperors controlled magisterial elections, and the Senate's legislative function quickly degenerated into mere assent to what the emperor or his representatives put before it. The true function of the Senate was to be a legislative and administrative extension of the emperor's rule.

Real opposition to the imperial rule sometimes took the form of plots against the life of the emperor. Plots and the suspicion of plots led to repression, the use of spies and paid informers, book burning, and executions. The opposition consisted chiefly of senators who looked back to republican liberty for their class and who found justification in the Greek and Roman traditions of tyrannicide as well as in the precepts of Stoicism. Plots and repression were most common under Nero and Domitian. From Nerva to Marcus Aurelius, however, the emperors, without yielding any power, again learned to enlist the cooperation of the upper class by courteous and modest deportment.

The Administration of the Empire

The provinces flourished economically and generally accepted Roman rule easily. (See Map 5–2.) In the eastern provinces, the emperor was worshipped as a god; even in Italy, most emperors were deified after their death as long as the imperial cult established by Augustus continued. Imperial policy usually combined an attempt to unify the empire and its various peoples with a respect for local customs and differences. Roman citizenship was spread ever more widely, and by 212 C.E., almost every free inhabitant of the empire was a citizen. Latin became the language of the western provinces. Although the East remained essentially Greek in language and culture, even it adopted many aspects of Roman life. The spread of ***Romanitas***, or "Roman-ness," was more than nominal, for senators and even emperors began to be drawn from provincial families.

Local Municipalities From an administrative and cultural standpoint, the empire was a collection of cities and towns and had little to do with the countryside. Roman policy during the Principate was to raise urban centers to the status of Roman municipalities, with the rights and privileges attached to them. A typical municipal charter left much responsibility in the hands of local councils and

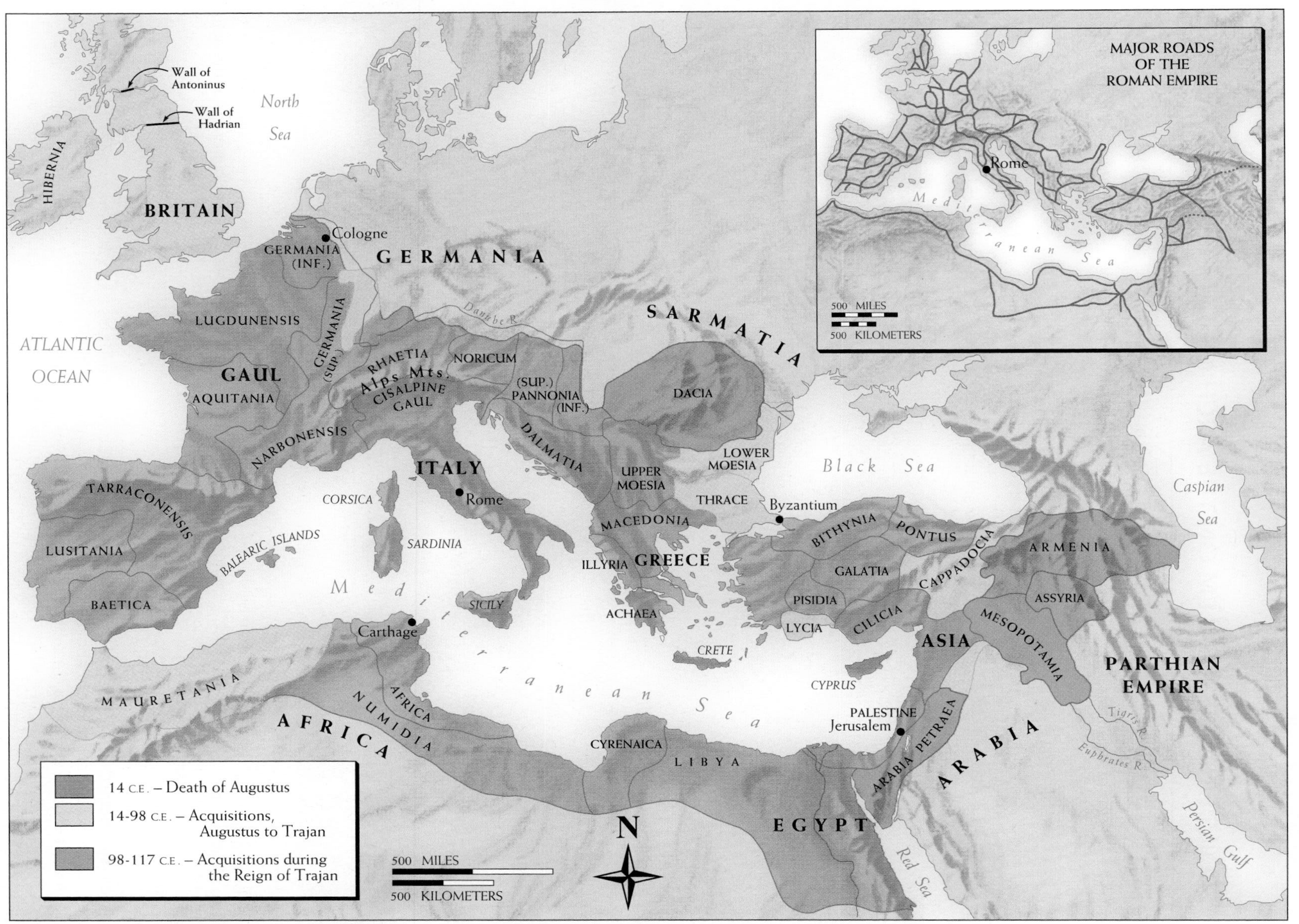

Map 5–2 **PROVINCES OF THE ROMAN EMPIRE TO 117 C.E.** The growth of the empire to its greatest extent is here shown in three stages—at the death of Augustus in 14 C.E., at the death of Nerva in 98, and at the death of Trajan in 117. The division into provinces is also shown. The insert shows the main roads that tied the far-flung empire together.

A Closer LOOK

SPOILS FROM JERUSALEM ON THE ARCH OF TITUS IN ROME

THE ARCH OF the Emperor Titus (r. 79–81 C.E.) stands at the highest point of the ancient Sacred Way that leads to the Roman Forum. It commemorates Titus's conquest of Judea, which ended the Jewish Wars (66–70 C.E.).

Carved on one of the internal faces of the passageway is a scene showing the triumphal procession with the booty from the Temple at Jerusalem—the sacred Menorah, the Table of the Shewbread shown at an angle, and the silver trumpets that called the Jews to celebrate the holy days of Rosh Hashanah.

Scala/Art Resource, NY

The bearers of the booty wear laurel crowns and those carrying the candlestick have pillows on their shoulders. Placards in the background explain the spoils and the victories Titus won. These few figures, standing for hundreds in the actual procession, move toward the carved arch at the right.

To examine this image in an interactive fashion, please go to www.myhistorylab.com

PEARSON myhistorylab

Flavius Josephus, a first-century C.E. historian and eyewitness to the event, described Titus's triumph: "The spoils in general were borne in promiscuous heaps; but conspicuous above all stood out those captured in the Temple at Jerusalem. These consisted of a golden table, many talents in weight, and a lampstand, likewise made of gold, but constructed on a different pattern from those we use in ordinary life. Affixed to a pedestal was a central shaft, from which there extended slender branches, arranged trident-fashion, a wrought lamp being attached to the extremity of each branch; of these there were seven, indicating the honor paid to the number among the Jews. After these, and last of all the spoils, was carried a copy of the Jewish Law."
(*The Jewish War* 7.148–50).

The largest city of the ancient region of Tripolitania, Leptis Magna was located 62 miles southeast of Tripoli on the Mediterranean coast of Libya in North Africa. In its heyday, it was one of the richest cities in the Roman Empire, and it contains some of the finest remains of Roman architecture. The city was lavishly rebuilt by the Emperor Septimius Severus (r. 193–211 C.E.), who was born at Leptis in 146 C.E.
Peter Wilson/Rough Guides DK

magistrates elected from the local aristocracy. Moreover, the holding of a magistracy, and later a seat on the council, carried Roman citizenship with it. Therefore, the Romans enlisted the upper classes of the provinces in their own government, spread Roman law and culture, and won the loyalty of the influential people. (For a glimpse into the lives of ordinary people, see "Daily Life in a Roman Provincial Town: Graffiti from Pompeii," page 140.)

There were exceptions to this picture of success. The Jews found their religion incompatible with Roman demands and were savagely repressed when they rebelled in 66–70, 115–117, and 132–135 C.E. In Egypt, the Romans exploited the peasants with exceptional ruthlessness and did not pursue a policy of urbanization.

As the efficiency of the bureaucracy grew, so did the number and scope of its functions and therefore its size. The emperors came to take a broader view of their responsibilities for the welfare of their subjects than before. Nerva conceived and Trajan introduced the *alimenta*, a program of public assistance for the children of the poor. More and more the emperors intervened when municipalities got into difficulties, usually financial, sending imperial troubleshooters to deal with problems. The importance and autonomy of the municipalities shrank as the central administration took a greater part in local affairs. The provincial aristocracy came to regard public service in its own cities as a burden rather than an opportunity. The price paid for the increased efficiency that centralized control offered was the loss of the vitality of the cities throughout the empire.

The success of Roman civilization also came at great cost to the farmers who lived outside of Italy. Taxes, rents, mandatory gifts, and military service drew capital away from the countryside to the cities on a scale not previously seen in the Graeco-Roman world. More and more the rich life of the urban elite came at the expense of millions of previously stable farmers.

Foreign Policy Augustus's successors, for the most part, accepted his conservative and defensive foreign policy. Trajan was the first emperor to take the offensive in a sustained way. Between 101 and 106 C.E., he crossed the Danube and, after hard fighting, established the new province of Dacia between the Danube and the Carpathian Mountains. He was tempted, no doubt, by its gold mines, but he probably was also pursuing a new general strategy: to defend the empire more aggressively by driving wedges into the territory of threatening barbarians. The same strategy dictated the invasion of the Parthian Empire in the East (113–117 C.E.). Trajan's early success was astonishing, and he established three new provinces in Armenia, Assyria, and Mesopotamia. But his lines were overextended. Rebellions sprang up, and the campaign crumbled. Trajan was forced to retreat, and he died before getting back to Rome.

Hadrian's reign marked an important shift in Rome's frontier policy. Heretofore, Rome had been on the offensive against the barbarians. Although the Romans rarely gained new territory, they launched frequent attacks to chastise and pacify troublesome tribes. Hadrian hardened the Roman defenses, building a stone wall in the south of Scotland and a wooden one across the Rhine-Danube triangle.

The Roman defense became rigid, and initiative passed to the barbarians. Marcus Aurelius was compelled to spend most of his reign resisting dangerous attacks in the East and on the Danube frontier.

Agriculture: The Decline of Slavery and the Rise of the *Coloni* The defense of its frontiers put enormous pressure on the human and financial resources of the empire, but the effect of these pressures was not immediately felt. The empire generally experienced considerable economic growth well into the reigns of the "good emperors." Internal peace and efficient administration benefited agriculture as well as trade and industry. Farming and trade developed together as political conditions made it easier to sell farm products at a distance.

Small farms continued to exist, but the large estate, managed by an absentee owner and growing cash

DAILY LIFE IN A ROMAN PROVINCIAL TOWN: GRAFFITI FROM POMPEII

On the walls of the houses of Pompeii, buried and preserved by the eruption of Mount Vesuvius in 79 C.E., many scribblings give us an idea of what the life of ordinary people was like.

How do these graffiti differ from those one sees in a modern American city? What do they reveal about the similarities and differences between the ordinary people of ancient Rome and the people of today? How would you account for the differences?

I

Twenty pairs of gladiators of Decimus Lucretius Satrius Valens, lifetime flamen of Nero son of Caesar Augustus, and ten pairs of gladiators of Decimus Lucretius Valens, his son, will fight at Pompeii on April 8, 9, 10, 11, 12. There will be a full card of wild beast combats, and awnings [for the spectators]. Aemilius Celer [painted this sign], all alone in the moonlight.

II

Market days: Saturday in Pompeii, Sunday in Nuceria, Monday in Atella, Tuesday in Nola, Wednesday in Cumae, Thursday in Puteoli, Friday in Rome.

III

Pleasure says: "You can get a drink here for an as [a few cents], a better drink for two, Falernian for four."

IV

A copper pot is missing from this shop. 65 sesterces reward if anybody brings it back, 20 sesterces if he reveals the thief so we can get our property back.

V

The weaver Successus loves the innkeeper's slave girl, Iris by name. She doesn't care for him, but he begs her to take pity on him. Written by his rival. So long.

[Answer by the rival:] Just because you're bursting with envy, don't pick on a handsomer man, a lady-killer and a gallant.

[Answer by the first writer:] There's nothing more to say or write. You love Iris, who doesn't care for you.

VI

Take your lewd looks and flirting eyes off another man's wife, and show some decency on your face!

VII

Anybody in love, come here. I want to break Venus' ribs with a club and cripple the goddess' loins. If she can pierce my tender breast, why can't I break her head with a club?

VIII

I write at Love's dictation and Cupid's instruction;
But damn it! I don't want to be a god without you.

IX

[A prostitute's sign:] I am yours for 2 asses cash.

Excerpt from N. Lewis and M. Reinhold, *Roman Civilization*, Vol. 2 (New York: Columbia University Press, 1955). Reprinted by permission of Columbia University Press.

ROME'S INDEPENDENT WOMEN: TWO VIEWS

In the last years of the republic and into the transition to the empire, Roman writers begin to describe what might be called the "new woman." These women are pictured as wearing makeup, dressing and behaving shamelessly, and engaging in adulterous affairs. Perhaps the most shocking of their practices was to engage in sexual activity, but to refuse to have children. The following passages reveal two different approaches to the newly popular means of birth control. The first comes from Soranus, a doctor who practiced in Rome late in the first century C.E. *The second comes from Ovid's poems about love.*

According to the doctors, when might abortion and contraception be appropriate? What reasons do they have for their opinions? What arguments does Ovid make against the use of abortion? How do these ancient arguments compare with modern ones?

SORANUS

For one party [of doctors] banishes abortives, citing the testimony of Hippocrates who says: "I will give to no one an abortive"; moreover, because it is the specific task of medicine to guard and preserve what has been engendered by nature. The other party prescribes abortives, but with discrimination, that is, they do not prescribe them when a person wishes to destroy the embryo because of adultery or out of consideration for youthful beauty; but only to prevent subsequent danger in parturition if the uterus is small and not capable of accommodating the complete development, or if the uterus at its orifice has knobbly swellings and fissures, or if some similar difficulty is involved. And they say the same about contraceptives as well, and we too agree with them.

OVID

She who first began the practice of tearing out her tender progeny deserved to die in her own warfare. Can it be that, to be free of the flaw of stretchmarks, you have to scatter the tragic sands of carnage? Why will you subject your womb to the weapons of abortion and give dread poisons to the unborn? The tigress lurking in Armenia does no such thing, nor does the lioness dare destroy her young. Yet tender girls do so—though not with impunity; often she who kills what is in her womb dies herself.

Soranus, *Gynecology* 1.19.60 in O. Temkin, *Soranus: Gynecology* (Baltimore: Johns Hopkins Press, 1956).

Ovid, *Amores* 2.14.5–9, 27–28, 35–38, trans. by Natalie Kampen in E. Fantham, E. P. Foley, N. B. Kampen, S. B. Pomeroy and H. A. Shapiro, *Women in the Classical World* (New York: Oxford University Press 1994), pp. 301–302.

crops, dominated agriculture. At first, as in the republican period, slaves mostly worked these estates, but in the first century, this began to change. Economic pressures forced many of the free lower classes to become tenant farmers, or *coloni*, and eventually the *coloni* replaced slaves as the mainstay of agricultural labor. Typically, these sharecroppers paid rent in labor or in kind, though sometimes they made cash payments. Eventually, they were tied to the land they worked, much as were the manorial serfs of the Middle Ages. Whatever its social costs, the system was economically efficient, however, and contributed to the general prosperity.

Women of the Upper Classes

By the late years of the Roman republic, women of the upper classes had achieved a considerable independence and influence. Some of them had become wealthy through inheritance and they were well educated. Women conducted literary salons and took part in literary groups. Marriage without the husband's right of *manus* became common, and some women conducted their sexual lives as freely as men. (See "Rome's Independent Women: Two Views.") The notorious Clodia, from one of Rome's noblest and most powerful families, is described as conducting many affairs, the most famous with the poet Catullus, who reviles her even as he describes the pangs of his love. Such women were reluctant to have children and increasingly employed contraception and abortion to avoid childbirth.

During the Principate, Augustus's daughter and granddaughter, both named Julia, were the subject of scandal and they were punished for adultery. Augustus tried to restore Rome to an earlier ideal of decency and family integrity that reduced the power and sexual freedom of women. He also introduced legislation to encourage the procreation of children, but the new laws seem to have had little effect. In the first imperial century, several powerful women played an important, if unofficial, political role. Augustus's wife Livia had great influence during his reign, and he honored her with the title Augusta in his will. Even in the reign of her son (and Augustus's stepson) Tiberius, she exercised great influence. It was said that he fled Rome to live in Capri in order to escape her domination. The Emperor Claudius's wife Messalina took part in a plot to overthrow him. The Elder Agrippina, wife of the general Germanicus, was active in opposition to Tiberius, and her daughter, also called Agrippina, helped bring her son Nero to the throne. In later centuries, women were permitted to make wills and inherit from children. At the turn of the first century, the Emperor Domitian freed women from the need for guardianship.

Life in Imperial Rome: The Apartment House

The civilization of the Roman Empire depended on the vitality of its cities. The typical city had about 20,000 inhabitants, and perhaps only three or four had a population of more than 75,000. The population of Rome, however, was certainly greater than 500,000, perhaps more than a million. People coming to Rome for the first time found it overwhelming and its size, bustle, and noise either thrilled or horrified them. The rich lived in elegant homes called *domūs*. These were single-storied houses with plenty of space, an open central courtyard, and rooms designed for specific and different purposes, such as dining, sitting, or sleeping, in privacy and relative quiet. Though only a small portion of Rome's population lived in them, *domūs* took up as much as a third of the city's space. Public space for temples, markets, baths, gymnasiums, theaters, forums, and governmental buildings took up another quarter of Rome's territory.

This left less than half of Rome's area to house the mass of its inhabitants, who were squeezed into multiple dwellings that grew increasingly tall. Most Romans during the imperial period lived in apartment buildings called ***insulae***, or "islands," that rose to a height of five or six stories and sometimes even more. The most famous of them, the Insula of Febiala, seems to have "towered above the Rome of the Antonines like a skyscraper."[3]

These buildings were divided into separate apartments (*cenicula*) of undifferentiated rooms, the same plan on each floor. The apartments were cramped and uncomfortable. They had neither central heating nor open fireplaces; heat and fire for cooking came from small portable stoves. The apartments were hot in summer, cold in winter, and stuffy and smoky when the stoves were lit. There was no plumbing, so tenants needed to go into the streets to wells or fountains for water and to public baths and latrines, or to less regulated places. The higher up one lived, the more difficult were these trips, so chamber pots and commodes were kept in the rooms. These receptacles were emptied into vats on the staircase landings or in the alleys outside; on occasion, the contents, and even the containers, were tossed out the window. Roman satirists complained of the discomforts and dangers of walking the streets beneath such windows. Roman law tried to find ways to assign responsibilities for the injuries done to dignity and person.

Despite these difficulties, the attractions of the city and the shortage of space caused rents to rise, making life in the *insulae* buildings expensive, uncomfortable, and dangerous. The houses were lightly built of concrete and brick and were far too high for the limited area of their foundations, and so they often collapsed. Laws limiting the height of buildings were not always obeyed and did not, in any case, always prevent disaster. The satirist Juvenal did not exaggerate much when he wrote, "We inhabit a city held up chiefly by slats, for that is how the landlord patches up the cracks in the old wall, telling the tenants to sleep peacefully under the ruin that hangs over their heads." (See "Juvenal on Life in Rome," page 144.)

Even more serious was the threat of fire. Wooden beams supported the floors, and torches, candles, and oil lamps lit the rooms and braziers heated them. Fires broke out easily and, without running water, they usually led to disaster.

When we compare these apartments with the attractive public places in the city, we can understand why the Romans spent most of their time out of doors.

The Culture of the Early Empire

The years from 14 to 180 C.E. were a time of general prosperity and a flourishing material and artistic culture, but one not so brilliant and original as in the Age of Augustus.

Literature In Latin literature, the period between the death of Augustus and the time of Marcus Aurelius is known as the Silver Age. As the name implies,

[3]J. Carcopino, *Daily Life in Ancient Rome* (New Haven, CT: Yale University Press, 1940), p. 26.

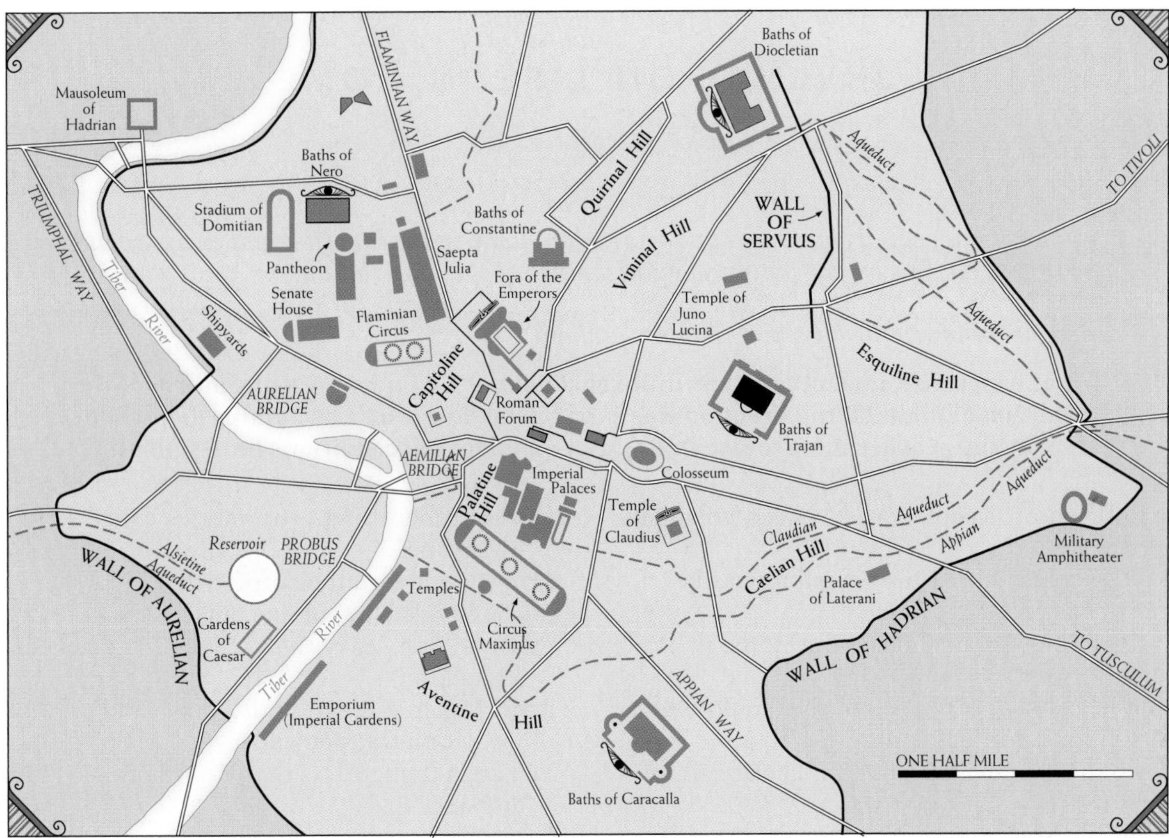

Map 5–3 **ANCIENT ROME** This map of Rome during the late empire shows the seven hills on and around which the city was built, as well as the major walls, bridges, and other public sites and buildings.

this age produced work of high quality although probably less high than in the Augustan era. In contrast to the hopeful, positive optimists of the Augustans, the writers of the Silver Age were gloomy, negative, and pessimistic. In the works of the former period, praise of the emperor, his achievements, and the world abounds; in the latter, criticism and satire lurk everywhere. Some of the most important writers of the Silver Age came from the Stoic opposition and reflected its hostility to the growing power and personal excesses of the emperors.

The writers of the second century C.E. appear to have turned away from contemporary affairs and even recent history. Historical writing was about remote periods so there would be less danger of irritating imperial sensibilities. Scholarship was encouraged, but we hear little of poetry, especially that dealing with dangerous subjects. In the third century C.E., romances written in Greek became popular and offer further evidence of the tendency of writers of the time to seek and offer escape from contemporary realities.

Architecture The main contribution of the Romans lay in two new kinds of buildings—the great public bath and a new freestanding kind of amphitheater—and in the advances in engineering that made these large structures possible. While keeping the basic post-and-lintel construction used by the Greeks, the Romans added to it the principle of the semicircular arch, borrowed from the Etruscans. They also made good use of concrete, a building material the Hellenistic Greeks first used and the Romans fully developed. The arch, combined with the post and lintel, produced the great Colosseum built by the Flavian emperors. When used internally in the form of vaults and domes, the arch permitted great buildings like the baths, of which the most famous and best preserved are those of the later emperors Caracalla (r. 211–217) and Diocletian (r. 284–305). (See Map 5–3.)

One of Rome's most famous buildings, the Pantheon, begun by Augustus's friend Agrippa and rebuilt by Hadrian, combined all these elements. Its portico of Corinthian columns is of Greek origin, but its rotunda of brick-faced concrete with its domed ceiling and relieving arches is thoroughly Roman. The new engineering also made possible the construction of more mundane, but useful, structures like bridges and aqueducts.

Society Seen from the harsh perspective of human history, the first two centuries of the Roman Empire deserve their reputation of a "golden age." One of the dark sides of Roman society, at least since the third century B.C.E., had been its increasing addiction to the brutal

JUVENAL ON LIFE IN ROME

The satirical poet Juvenal lived and worked in Rome in the late first and early second centuries C.E. His poems present a vivid picture of the material and cultural world of the Romans of his time. In the following passages, he tells of the discomforts and dangers of life in the city, both indoors and out.

What dangers awaited pedestrians in Juvenal's Rome? Who had responsibility for the condition of Rome? If the situation was as bad as he says, why was nothing done about it? Why did people choose to live in Rome at all under the conditions he describes?

Who, in Praeneste's cool, or the wooded Volsinian uplands,
Who, on Tivoli's heights, or a small town like Gabii, say,
Fears the collapse of his house? But Rome is supported on pipestems,
Matchsticks; it's cheaper, so, for the landlord to shore up his ruins,
Patch up the old cracked walls, and notify all the tenants
They can sleep secure, though the beams are in ruins above them.
No, the place to live is out there, where no cry of Fire!
Sounds the alarm of the night, with a neighbor yelling for water,
Moving his chattels and goods, and the whole third story is smoking.

Look at other things, the various dangers of nighttime.
How high it is to the cornice that breaks, and a chunk beats my brains out,
Or some slob heaves a jar, broken or cracked, from a window.
Bang! It comes down with a crash and proves its weight on the sidewalk.
You are a thoughtless fool, unmindful of sudden disaster,
If you don't make your will before you go out to have dinner.
There are as many deaths in the night as there are open windows
Where you pass by; if you're wise, you will pray, in your wretched devotions,
People may be content with no more than emptying slop jars.

From Juvenal, *The Satires of Juvenal*, trans. by Rolfe Humphries. Copyright © 1958 Indiana University Press, pp. 40, 43. Reprinted by permission of Indiana University Press.

contests involving gladiators. By the end of the first century C.E., emperors regularly appealed to this barbaric entertainment as a way of winning the acclaim of their people. On broader fronts in Roman society, by the second century C.E., troubles were brewing that foreshadowed the difficult times ahead. The literary efforts of the time reveal a flight from the present, from reality, and from the public realm to the past, to romance, and to private pursuits. Some of the same aspects may be seen in everyday life, especially in the decline of vitality in the local government.

In the first century C.E., members of the upper classes vied with one another for election to municipal office and for the honor of doing service to their communities. By the second century C.E., the emperors had to intervene to correct abuses in local affairs and even to force unwilling members of the ruling classes to accept public office. Magistrates and council members were held personally and collectively responsible for the revenues due. Some magistrates even fled to avoid their office, a practice that became widespread in later centuries.

These difficulties reflected more basic problems. The prosperity that the end of civil war and the influx of wealth from the East brought could not sustain itself beyond the first half of the second century C.E. Population also appears to have declined for reasons that remain mysterious. The cost of government kept rising. The emperors were required to maintain a standing army, minimal in size, but costly, to keep the people in Rome happy with "bread and circuses," to pay for an increasingly numerous bureaucracy, and to wage expensive wars to defend the frontiers against dangerous and determined barbarian enemies. The ever-increasing need for money compelled the emperors to raise taxes, to press hard on their subjects, and to bring on inflation by debasing the coinage. These elements brought about the desperate crises that ultimately destroyed the empire.

▾ The Rise of Christianity

Christianity emerged, spread, survived, and ultimately conquered the Roman Empire despite its origin among poor people from an unimportant and remote province of the empire. Christianity faced the hostility of the established religious institutions of its native Judea. It also had to compete against the official cults of Rome and the highly sophisticated philosophies of the educated classes and against such other "**mystery**" **religions** as the cults of Mithra, Isis, and Osiris. The Christians also faced the opposition of the imperial government and formal persecution. Yet Christianity achieved toleration and finally exclusive command as the official religion of the empire.

Jesus of Nazareth

An attempt to understand this amazing outcome must begin with the story of Jesus of Nazareth. The most important evidence about his life is in the Gospel accounts, all of them written well after his death. The earliest, by Mark, is dated about 70 C.E. and the latest, by John, about 100 C.E. They are not, moreover, attempts at simply describing the life of Jesus with historical accuracy. Rather, they are statements of faith by true believers. The authors of the Gospels believed Jesus was the son of God and that he had come into the world to redeem humanity and to bring immortality to those who believed in him and followed his way. To the Gospel writers, Jesus' resurrection was striking proof of his teachings. At the same time, the Gospels regard Jesus as a figure in history, and they recount events in his life as well as his sayings.

There is no reason to doubt that Jesus was born in the province of Judea in the time of Augustus and that he was a most effective teacher in the tradition of the prophets. This tradition promised the coming of a **Messiah** (in Greek, *christos*—so Jesus Christ means "Jesus the Messiah"), the redeemer who would make Israel triumph over its enemies and establish the kingdom of God on earth. In fact, Jesus seems to have insisted the Messiah would not establish an earthly kingdom but would bring an end to the world as human beings knew it at the Day of Judgment. On that day, God would reward the righteous with immortality and happiness in heaven and condemn the wicked to eternal suffering in hell. Until then (a day his followers believed would come soon), Jesus taught the faithful to abandon sin and worldly concerns; to follow him and his way; to follow the moral code described in the Sermon on the Mount, which preached love, charity, and humility; and to believe in him and his divine mission.

Jesus won a considerable following, especially among the poor, which caused great suspicion among the upper classes. His novel message and his criticism of the religious practices connected with the temple at Jerusalem and its priests provoked the hostility of the religious establishment. A misunderstanding of the movement made it easy to convince the Roman governor, Pontius Pilate, that Jesus and his followers might be dangerous revolutionaries. He was put to death in Jerusalem by the cruel and degrading device of crucifixion, probably in 30 C.E. His followers believed he was resurrected on the third day after his death, and that belief became a critical element in the religion they propagated throughout the Roman Empire and beyond.

The new belief spread quickly to the Jewish communities of Syria and Asia Minor. It might, however, have had only a short life as a despised Jewish heresy were it not for the conversion and career of Paul.

Paul of Tarsus

Paul was born Saul, a citizen of the Cilician city of Tarsus in Asia Minor. He had been trained in Hellenistic culture and was a Roman citizen. But he was also a zealous member of the Jewish sect known as the **Pharisees**, the group that was most strict in its adherence to Jewish law. He took part in the persecution of the early Christians until his own conversion outside Damascus about 35 C.E., after which he changed his name from Saul to Paul.

The great problem facing the early Christians was to resolve their relationship to Judaism. If the new faith was a version of Judaism, then it must adhere to the Jewish law and seek converts only among Jews. James, called the brother of Jesus, was a conservative who held to that view, whereas the Hellenist Jews tended to see Christianity as a new and universal religion. To force all converts to follow Jewish law would have been fatal to the growth of the new sect. Jewish law's many technicalities and dietary prohibitions were strange to Gentiles, and the necessity of circumcision—a frightening, painful, and dangerous operation for adults—would have been a tremendous deterrent to conversion. Paul supported the position of the Hellenists and soon won many converts among the Gentiles. After some conflict within the sect, Paul won out. Consequently, the "apostle to the Gentiles" deserves recognition as a crucial contributor to the success of Christianity.

Paul believed that the followers of Jesus should be *evangelists* (messengers), to spread the gospel, or "good news," of God's gracious gift. He taught that Jesus would soon return for the Day of Judgment, and that all who would, should believe in him and accept his way.

ENCOUNTERING THE *Past*

CHARIOT RACING

FROM THEIR EARLIEST history the Romans enjoyed watching chariot races. As early as the period of the kings (seventh and sixth centuries B.C.E.), they built chariot racecourses, which they called "circuses" because of their curved or circular shape. Of these, the most famous, and one of the earliest, was the Circus Maximus ("largest"). Over the centuries politicians of the republic and, later, emperors of Rome, used the structures to provide such other free entertainments for the Roman public as trick riding displays and exhibitions and hunts of wild animals, but the chariot races were the most popular.

Spectators watched the races in tiers of seats along the two parallel sides of the course, which came together as a semicircle at one end. At the other end were stations called *carceres*, or barriers, for the chariots. Down the center of the course ran a fence that separated the two lanes for about two-thirds of the way, and at each end was a post around which the chariots had to make their turns. The races consisted of seven laps, the last one ending in a dash down the final straightaway. The full distance of a race in the Circus Maximus has been estimated at about 2.7 miles.

The earliest races may have been run for fun by rich aristocrats competing for glory, but the first written evidence shows the sport in the hands of racing companies called *factiones* who supplied the horses, chariots, and professional drivers. These companies were distinguished by their colors: At first there was only one red and one white company; later blue, green, purple, and gold *factiones* joined the competition. Each stable gained great numbers of fanatical supporters who bet large sums of money on the races. All kinds of devices were used to win. Horses were drugged; drivers were bribed or even poisoned when they refused a bribe.

Although various numbers of horses were used to pull the chariots at different times, the *quadriga*, or four-horse team, was the most common. The horse on the far left was the most important, because turns were made to the left and that horse's quick response was critical to the team's safety and success. As many as twelve chariots could compete in a race. Because of the short stretches, sharp turns, and crowded track, sheer speed was less important than strength, courage, and endurance. The races were dangerous to horse and rider, and the risk of collisions, falls, injury, and death appears to have provided the chief thrills to the Roman audience.

Why did Romans go to see the chariot races? Why did politicians and emperors sponsor them?

Romans bet heavily on the kind of chariot races shown on this low relief and were fanatically attached to their favorite riders and stables.

Faith in Jesus as the Christ was necessary, but not sufficient, for salvation, nor could good deeds alone achieve it. That final blessing of salvation was a gift of God's grace that would be granted to all who asked for it.

Organization

Paul and the other apostles did their work well. The new religion spread throughout the Roman Empire and even beyond its borders. It had its greatest success in the cities and among the poor and uneducated. The rites of the early communities appear to have been simple and few. Baptism by water removed original sin and permitted participation in the community and its activities. The central ritual was a common meal called the ***agape***, or "love feast," followed by the ceremony of the ***Eucharist***, or "thanksgiving," a celebration of the Lord's Supper in which unleavened bread was eaten and unfermented wine was drunk. There were also prayers, hymns, or readings from the Gospels.

Not all the early Christians were poor, and the rich provided for the poor at the common meals. The sense of common love fostered in these ways focused the community's attention on the needs of the weak, the sick, the unfortunate, and the unprotected. This concern gave the early Christian communities a warmth and a human appeal that stood in marked contrast to the coldness and impersonality of the pagan cults. No less attractive were the promise of salvation, the importance to God of each human soul, and the spiritual equality of all in the new faith. As Paul put it, "There is neither Jew nor Greek, there is neither slave nor free, there is neither male nor female; for you are all one in Christ Jesus."[4]

The future of Christianity depended on its communities finding an organization that would preserve unity within the group and help protect it against enemies outside. At first, the churches had little formal organization. Soon, it appears, affairs were placed in the hands of boards of prebytersor "elders," and **deacons**, or "those who serve." By the second century C.E., as their numbers grew, the Christians of each city tended to accept the authority and leadership of **bishops** (*episkopoi*, or "overseers"). The congregations elected bishops to lead them in worship and to supervise funds. As time passed, the bishops extended their authority over the Christian communities in outlying towns and the countryside. The power and almost monarchical authority of the bishops were soon enhanced by the doctrine of **Apostolic Succession**, which asserted that ordination passed on the powers Jesus had given his original disciples from bishop to bishop.

The bishops kept in touch with one another, maintained communications between different Christian communities, and prevented doctrinal and sectarian splintering, which would have destroyed Christian unity. They maintained internal discipline and dealt with the civil authorities. After a time they began the practice of coming together in councils to settle difficult questions, to establish orthodox opinion, and even to expel as **heretics** those who would not accept it. It is unlikely that Christianity could have survived the travails of its early years without such strong internal organization and government.

[4]Galatians 3:28, Revised Standard Version of the Bible.

This second-century statue in the Lateran Museum in Rome shows Jesus as the biblical Good Shepherd. "The Good Shepherd," marble, Height: as restored cm 99, as preserved cm 55, head cm 15.5. Late 3rd century A.D. Vatican Musuems, Pio-Christian Museum, Inv. 28590. Courtesy of the Vatican Museums

The Persecution of Christians

The new faith soon incurred the distrust of the pagan world and of the imperial government. At first, Christians were thought of as a Jewish sect and were therefore protected by Roman law. It soon became clear, however, that they were different, both mysterious and dangerous. They denied the existence of the pagan gods and so were accused of atheism. Their refusal to worship the emperor was judged treasonous. Because they kept mostly to themselves, took no part in civic affairs, engaged in secret rites, and had an organized network of local associations, they were misunderstood and suspected. The love feasts were erroneously reported to be scenes of sexual scandal. The alarming doctrine of the actual presence of Jesus' body in the Eucharist was distorted into an accusation of cannibalism.

The privacy and secrecy of Christian life and worship ran counter to a traditional Roman dislike of any private association, especially any of a religious nature. Christians thus earned the reputation of being "haters of humanity." Claudius expelled them from Rome, and Nero tried to make them scapegoats for the great fire that struck the city in 64 C.E. By the end of the first century, "the name alone"—that is, simple membership in the Christian community—was a crime.

But, for the most part, the Roman government did not take the initiative in attacking Christians in the first two centuries. When one governor sought instructions for dealing with the Christians, the emperor Trajan urged moderation. Christians were not to be sought out, anonymous accusations were to be disregarded, and anyone denounced could be acquitted merely by renouncing Christ and sacrificing to the emperor. (See "Compare & Connect: Christianity in the Roman Empire—Why Did the Romans Persecute the Christians?" on page 150.) Unfortunately, no true Christian could meet the conditions, and so there were martyrdoms.

Mobs, not the government, started most persecutions in this period, however. Though they lived quiet, inoffensive lives, some Christians must have seemed unbearably smug and self-righteous. Unlike the tolerant, easygoing pagans, who were generally willing to accept the new gods of foreign people and add them to the pantheon, the Christians denied the reality of the pagan gods. They proclaimed the unique rightness of their own way and looked forward to their own salvation and the damnation of nonbelievers. It is not surprising, therefore, that pagans disliked these strange and unsocial people, tended to blame misfortunes on them, and, in extreme cases, turned to violence. But even this adversity had its uses. It weeded out the weaklings among the Christians and brought greater unity to those who remained faithful. It also provided the Church with martyrs around whom legends could grow that would inspire still greater devotion and dedication.

The Emergence of Catholicism

Division within the Christian Church may have been an even greater threat to its existence than persecution from outside. Most Christians never accepted complex, intellectualized opinions but held to what even then were traditional, simple, conservative beliefs. This body of majority opinion, considered to be universal, or catholic, was enshrined by the church that came to be called Catholic. The Catholic Church's doctrines were deemed **orthodox**, that is, "holding the right opinions," whereas those holding contrary opinions were heretics.

The need to combat heretics, however, compelled the orthodox to formulate their own views more clearly and firmly. By the end of the second century C.E., an orthodox canon included the Old Testament, the Gospels, and the Epistles of Paul, among other writings. The process of creating a standard set of holy books was not completed for at least two more centuries, but a vitally important start had been made. The orthodox declared the Catholic Church itself to be the depository of Christian teaching and the bishops to be its receivers. They also drew up a **creed** or brief statements of faith to which true Christians should adhere.

In the first century, all that was required of one to be a Christian was to be baptized, to partake of the Eucharist, and to call Jesus the Lord. By the end of the second century, an orthodox Christian—that is, a member of the Catholic Church—was required to accept its creed, its canon of holy writings, and the authority of the bishops. The loose structure of the apostolic church had given way to an organized body with recognized leaders able to define its faith and to exclude those who did not accept it. Whatever the shortcomings of this development, it provided the clarity, unity, and discipline needed for survival.

Rome as a Center of the Early Church

During this same period, the church in Rome came to have special prominence. As the center of communications and the capital of the empire, Rome had natural advantages. After the Roman destruction of Jerusalem in 135 C.E., no other city had any convincing claim to primacy in the church. Besides having the largest single congregation of Christians, Rome also benefited from the tradition that Jesus' apostles Peter and Paul were martyred there.

Peter, moreover, was thought to be the first bishop of Rome. The Gospel of Matthew (16:18) reported Jesus' statement to Peter: "Thou art Peter [in Greek, *Petros*] and upon this rock [in Greek, *petra*] I will build my church." Eastern Christians might later point out that Peter had been the leader of the Christian community at Antioch before he went to Rome. But in the second century, the church at Antioch, along with the other Christian churches of Asia Minor, was fading in influence, and by 200 C.E., Rome was the most important center of Christianity. Because of the city's early influence and because of the Petrine doctrine derived from the Gospel of Matthew, later bishops of Rome claimed supremacy in the Catholic Church. But as the era of the "good emperors" came to a close, this controversy was far in the future.

▼ The Crisis of the Third Century

Dio Cassius, a historian of the third century C.E., described the Roman Empire after the death of Marcus Aurelius as declining from "a kingdom of gold into one of iron and rust." Although we have seen that the gold contained more than a little impurity, there is no reason to quarrel with Dio's assessment of his own time. Commodus (r. 180–192 C.E.), the son of Marcus Aurelius, proved the wisdom of the "good emperors" in selecting their successors for their talents rather than for family ties. Commodus was incompetent and autocratic. He reduced the respect in which the imperial office was held, and his assassination brought the return of civil war.

Barbarian Invasions

The pressure on Rome's frontiers reached massive proportions in the third century. In the East, a new power threatened the frontiers. In the third century B.C.E., the Parthians had made the Iranians independent of the Hellenistic kings and had established an empire of their own on the old foundations of the Persian Empire. Roman attempts to conquer them had failed, but as late as 198 C.E., the Romans could reach and destroy the Parthian capital and bring at least northern Mesopotamia under their rule.

In 224 C.E., however, a new Iranian dynasty, the Sassanians, seized control from the Parthians and brought new vitality to Persia. They soon recovered Mesopotamia in 260 C.E. and humiliated the Romans by taking the emperor Valerian (r. 253–260) prisoner; he died in captivity.

On the western and northern frontiers, the pressure came not from a well-organized rival empire, but from an ever-increasing number of German tribes. Though the Germans had been in contact with the Romans at least since the second century B.C.E., civilization had not much affected them. The men did no agricultural work, but confined their activities to hunting, drinking, and fighting. They were organized on a family basis by clans, hundreds, and tribes. Their leaders were chiefs, usually from a royal family, elected by the assembly of fighting men. The king was surrounded by a collection of warriors, whom the Romans called his *comitatus*. Always eager for plunder, these tough barbarians were attracted by the civilized delights they knew existed beyond the frontier of the Rhine and Danube Rivers.

The most aggressive of the Germans in the third century C.E. were the Goths. Centuries earlier they had wandered from their ancestral home near the Baltic Sea into southern Russia. In the 220s and 230s C.E., they began to put pressure on the Danube frontier. By about 250 C.E., they were able to penetrate the empire and overrun the Balkans. The need to meet this threat and the one the Persian Sassanids posed in the East made the Romans weaken their western frontiers, and other Germanic peoples—the Franks and the Alemanni—broke through in those regions. There was danger that Rome would be unable to meet this challenge.

The unprecedentedly numerous and simultaneous attacks, no doubt, caused Rome's perils but its internal weakness encouraged these attacks. The Roman army was not what it had been in its best days. By the second century C.E., it was made up mostly of romanized provincials. The pressure on the frontiers and epidemics of plague in the time of Marcus Aurelius forced the emperor to conscript slaves, gladiators, barbarians, and brigands. The training and discipline with which the Romans had conquered the Mediterranean world had declined. The Romans also failed to respond to the new conditions of constant pressure on all the frontiers. A strong, mobile reserve that could meet a threat in one place without causing a weakness elsewhere might have helped, but no such unit was created.

Septimius Severus (r. 193–211 C.E.) and his successors transformed the character of the Roman army. Septimius was a military usurper who owed everything to the support of his soldiers. He meant to establish a family dynasty, in contrast to the policy of the "good emperors" of the second century. He was prepared to make Rome into an undisguised military monarchy. Septimius drew recruits for the army increasingly from peasants of the less civilized provinces.

Economic Difficulties

These changes were a response to the great financial needs the barbarian attacks caused. Inflation had forced Commodus to raise the soldiers' pay. Yet the Severan emperors had to double it to keep up with prices, which increased the imperial budget by as much as 25 percent. To raise money, the emperors invented new taxes, debased the coinage, and even sold the palace furniture. But it was still hard to recruit troops. The new style of military life Septimius introduced—with its laxer discipline, more pleasant duties, and greater opportunity for advancement, not only in the army, but also in Roman society—was needed to attract men into the army. The policy proved effective for a short time but could not prevent the chaos of the late third century.

The same forces that caused problems for the army damaged society at large. The shortage of workers for the large farms, which had all but wiped out the independent family farm, reduced agricultural production. Distracted by external threats, the emperors were less able to preserve domestic peace. Piracy, brigandage, and the neglect of roads and harbors hampered trade. So, too, did the debasement of the coinage and the inflation in general. Imperial taxation and confiscations of the property of the rich removed badly needed capital from productive use.

More and more, the government had to demand services that had been given gladly in the past. Because the empire lived hand to mouth, with no significant reserve fund and no system of credit financing, the emperors had to compel the people to provide food, supplies, money, and labor. The upper classes in the cities were made to serve as administrators without pay and to meet deficits in revenue out of their own pockets. Sometimes these

Christianity in the Roman Empire—Why Did the Romans Persecute the Christians?

THE RISE OF Christianity and its spread throughout the Mediterranean presented a serious problem to the magistrates of the Roman Empire. Like most other pagans, the Romans were tolerant of most religious beliefs. Persecution on religious grounds was unusual among the Romans. The Christians, however, were very different from votaries of Isis, Mithra, Magna Mater, even from the Jews. The Romans did, in fact, persecute the Christians with varying degrees of severity. The following passages shed light on the character of and reasons for these persecutions.

QUESTIONS

1. **Why did Nero blame the Christians?**
2. **On what grounds did Pliny punish the Christians?**
3. **What was the reaction of Trajan?**
4. **How did the approach of the two emperors compare?**

I. The Persecution by Nero

In 64 C.E. a terrible fire broke out in Rome that destroyed a good part of the city. Here the historian Tacitus tells us how the Emperor Nero dealt with its aftermath.

The next thing was to seek means of propitiating the gods, and recourse was had to the Sibylline books, by the direction of which prayers were offered to Vulcanus, Ceres, and Proserpina. Juno, too, was entreated by the matrons, first, in the Capitol, then on the nearest part of the coast, whence water was procured to sprinkle the fane and image of the goddess. And there were sacred banquets and nightly vigils celebrated by married women. But all human efforts, all the lavish gifts of the emperor, and the propitiations of the gods, did not banish the sinister belief that the conflagration was the result of an order. Consequently, to get rid of the report, Nero fastened the guilt and inflicted the most exquisite tortures on a class hated for their abominations, called Christians by the populace. Christus, from whom the name had its origin, suffered the extreme penalty during the reign of Tiberius at the hands of one of our procurators, Pontius Pilatus, and a most mischievous superstition, thus checked for the moment, again broke out not only in Judaea, the first source of the evil, but even in Rome, where all things hideous and shameful from every part of the world find their centre and become popular. Accordingly, an arrest was first made of all who pleaded guilty; then, upon their information, an immense multitude was convicted, not so much of the crime of firing the city, as of hatred against mankind. Mockery of every sort was added to their deaths. Covered with the skins of beasts, they were torn by dogs and perished, or were nailed to crosses, or were doomed to the flames and burnt, to serve as a nightly illumination, when daylight had expired.

Nero offered his gardens for the spectacle, and was exhibiting a show in the circus, while he mingled with the people in the dress of a charioteer or stood aloft on a car. Hence, even for criminals who deserved extreme and exemplary punishment, there arose a feeling of compassion; for it was not, as it seemed, for the public good, but to glut one man's cruelty, that they were being destroyed.

Source: Tacitus, *Annals* 15. 44, trans. by A. J. Church and W. J. Brodribb, Modern Library, N.Y., 1942.

II. The Emperor Trajan and the Christians

Pliny the Younger was governor of the Roman province of Bithynia in Asia Minor about 112 C.E. Confronted by problems caused by Christians, he wrote to the Emperor Trajan to report his policies and to ask for advice. The following exchange between governor and empire provides evidence of the challenge Christianity posed to Rome and the Roman response.

TO THE EMPEROR TRAJAN

Having never been present at any trials of the Christians, I am unacquainted with the method and limits to be observed either in examining or punishing them.

In the meanwhile, the method I have observed towards those who have been denounced to me as Christians is this: I interrogated them whether they were Christians; if they confessed it, I repeated the question twice again, adding the threat of capital punishment; if they still persevered, I ordered them to be executed. For whatever the nature of their creed might be, I could at least feel no doubt that contumacy and inflexible obstinacy deserved chastisement. There were others also possessed with the same infatuation, but being citizens of Rome, I directed them to be carried thither. . . .

TRAJAN TO PLINY

The method you have pursued, my dear Pliny, in sifting the cases of those denounced to you as Christians is extremely proper. It is not possible to lay down any general rule which can be applied as the fixed standard in all cases of this nature. No search should be made for these people, when they are denounced and found guilty they must be punished; with the restriction, however, that when the party denies himself to be a Christian, and shall give proof that he is not (that is, by adoring our Gods he shall be pardoned on the ground of repentance even though he may have formerly incurred suspicion). Informations without the accuser's name subscribed must not be admitted in evidence against anyone, as it is introducing a very dangerous precedent, and by no means agreeable to the spirit of the age.

Source: From Pliny the Younger, *Letters*, trans. by W. Melmoth, rev. by W. M. Hutchinson (London: William Heinemann, Ltd; Cambridge, MA: Harvard University Press, 1925).

Thrown to the lions in 275 C.E. by the Romans for refusing to recant his Christian beliefs, St. Mamai is an important martyr in the iconography of Georgia, a Caucasian kingdom that embraced Christianity early in the fourth century. This gilded silver medallion, made in Georgia in the eleventh century, depicts the saint astride a lion while he bears a cross in one hand, symbolizing his triumphant victory over death and ignorance. Kekelidze Institute, Tblisi, Georgia. Courtesy of the Library of Congress demands caused provincial rebellions, as in Egypt and Gaul. More typically, they caused peasants and even town administrators to flee to escape their burdens. All these difficulties weakened Rome's economic strength when it was most needed.

The Social Order

The new conditions caused important changes in the social order. Hostile emperors and economic losses decimated the Senate and the traditional ruling class. Men coming up through the army took their places. The whole state began to take on an increasingly military appearance. Distinctions among the classes by dress had been traditional since the republic; in the third and fourth centuries C.E., the people's everyday clothing became a kind of uniform that precisely revealed status. Titles were assigned to ranks in society as to ranks in the army. The most important distinction was the one Septimius Severus formally established, which drew a sharp line between the ***honestiores*** (senators, equestrians, the municipal aristocracy, and the soldiers) and the lower classes, or ***humiliores***. Septimius gave the *honestiores* a privileged position before the law. They were given lighter punishments, could not be tortured, and alone had the right of appeal to the emperor.

As time passed, it became more difficult to move from the lower order to the higher, another example of the growing rigidity of the late Roman Empire. Peasants were tied to their lands, artisans to their crafts, soldiers to the army, merchants and shipowners to the needs of the state, and citizens of the municipal upper class to the collection and payment of increasingly burdensome taxes. Freedom and private initiative gave way before the needs of the state and its ever-expanding control of its citizens.

Civil Disorder

Commodus was killed on the last day of 192 C.E. The succeeding year was similar to the year 69. Three emperors ruled in swift succession, Septimius Severus emerging, as we have seen, to establish firm rule and a dynasty. The murder of Alexander Severus, the last of the dynasty, in 235 C.E., brought on a half century of internal anarchy and foreign invasion.

The empire seemed on the point of collapse. But the two conspirators who overthrew and succeeded the emperor Gallienus (r. 253–268) proved to be able soldiers. Claudius II Gothicus (268–270 C.E.) and Aurelian (270–275 C.E.) drove back the barbarians and stamped out internal disorder. The soldiers who followed Aurelian on the throne were good fighters who made significant changes in Rome's system of defense. Around Rome, Athens, and other cities, they built heavy walls that could resist barbarian attack. They drew back their best troops from the frontiers, relying chiefly on a newly organized heavy cavalry and a mobile army near the emperor's own residence.

Hereafter, mercenaries, who came from among the least civilized provincials and even from among the Germans, largely made up the army. The officers gave personal loyalty to the emperor rather than to the empire. These officers became a foreign, hereditary caste of aristocrats that increasingly supplied high administrators and even emperors. In effect, the Roman people hired an army of mercenaries, who were only technically Roman, to protect them.

▼ The Late Empire

During the fourth and fifth centuries, the Romans strove to meet the many challenges, internal and external, that threatened the survival of their empire. Growing pressure from barbarian tribes pushing against its frontier intensified the empire's tendency to smother individuality, freedom, and initiative, in favor of an intrusive and autocratic centralized monarchy. Economic and military weakness increased, and it became even harder to keep the vast empire together. Hard and dangerous times may well have helped the rise of Christianity, encouraging people to turn away from the troubles of this world to be concerned about the next.

The Fourth Century and Imperial Reorganization

The period from Diocletian (r. 284–305 C.E.) to Constantine (r. 306–337 C.E.) was one of reconstruction and reorganization after a time of civil war and turmoil. Diocletian was from Illyria (the former Yugoslavia of the twentieth century). A man of undistinguished birth, he rose to the throne through the ranks of the army. He knew that the job of defending and governing the entire empire was too great for one individual.

Diocletian therefore decreed the introduction of the **tetrarchy**, the rule of the empire by four men with power divided territorially. (See Map 5–4.) He allotted the provinces of Thrace, Asia, and Egypt to himself. His co-emperor, Maximian, shared with him the title of Augustus and governed Italy, Africa, and Spain. In addition, two men were given the subordinate title of Caesar: Galerius, who was in charge of the Danube frontier and the Balkans, and Constantius, who governed Britain and Gaul. This arrangement not only afforded a good solution to the military problem but also provided for a peaceful succession.

Diocletian was the senior Augustus, but each tetrarch was supreme in his own sphere. The Caesars were recognized as successors to each half of the empire, and marriages to daughters of the Augusti enhanced their loyalty. It was a return, in a way, to the precedent of the

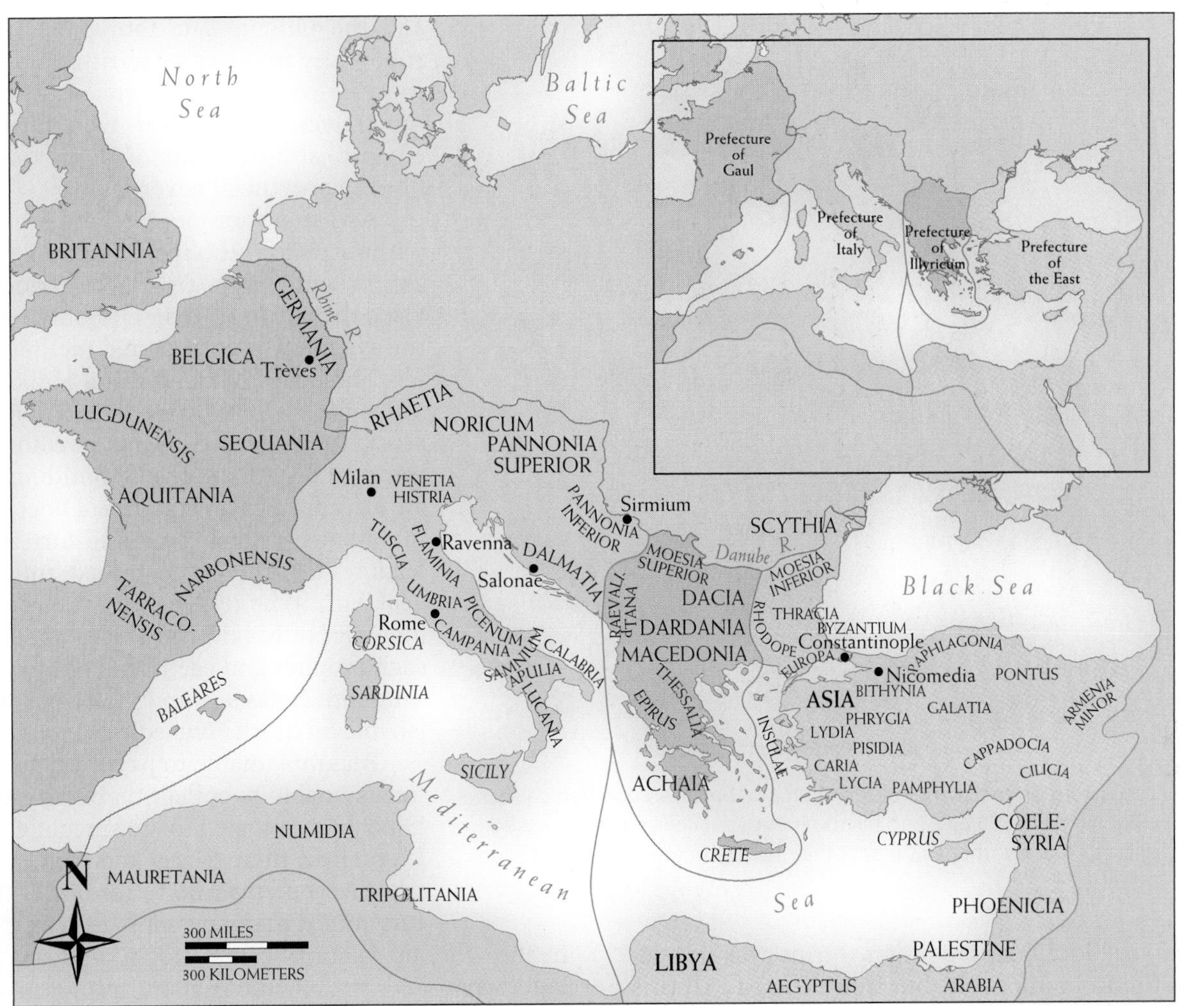

Map 5–4 **DIVISIONS OF THE ROMAN EMPIRE UNDER DIOCLETIAN** Diocletian divided the sprawling empire into four prefectures for more effective government and defense. The inset map shows their boundaries, and the larger map gives some details of regions and provinces. The major division between the East and the West was along the line running south between Pannonia and Moesia.

"good emperors" of 96 to 180 C.E., who chose their successors from the ranks of the ablest men. It seemed to promise orderly and peaceful transitions instead of assassinations, chaos, and civil war.

Each man established his residence and capital at a place convenient for frontier defense, and none chose Rome. The effective capital of Italy became the northern city of Milan. Diocletian beautified Rome by constructing his monumental baths, but he visited the city only once and made his own capital at Nicomedia in Asia Minor. This was another step in the long leveling process that had reduced the eminence of Rome and Italy. It was also evidence of the growing importance of the East.

In 305 C.E., Diocletian retired and compelled his co-emperor to do the same. But his plan for a smooth succession failed. In 310, there were five Augusti and no Caesars. Out of this chaos, Constantine, son of Constantius, produced order. In 324, he defeated his last opponent and made himself sole emperor, uniting the empire once again; he reigned until 337. Mostly, Constantine carried forward the policies of Diocletian. He supported Christianity, however, which Diocletian had tried to suppress.

Development of Autocracy Diocletian and Constantine carried the development of the imperial office toward **autocracy** to the extreme. The emperor ruled by decree, consulting only a few high officials whom he himself appointed. The Senate had no role whatever, and the elimination of all distinctions between senator and equestrian further diminished its dignity.

The emperor was a remote figure surrounded by carefully chosen high officials. He lived in a great palace and was almost unapproachable. Those admitted to his presence had to prostrate themselves before him and kiss the hem of his robe, which was purple and had golden threads woven through it. The emperor was addressed

This porphyry sculpture on the corner of the church of San Marco in Venice shows Emperor Diocletian (r. 284–305 C.E.) and his three imperial colleagues. Dressed for battle, they clasp one another to express their mutual solidarity. John Heseltine © Dorling Kindersley

as *dominus*, or "lord," and his right to rule was not derived from the Roman people, but from heaven. All this remoteness and ceremony had a double purpose: to enhance the dignity of the emperor and to safeguard him against assassination.

Constantine erected the new city of Constantinople on the site of ancient Byzantium on the Bosporus, which leads to both the Aegean and Black Seas. He made it the new capital of the empire. Its strategic location was excellent for protecting the eastern and Danubian frontiers, and, surrounded on three sides by water, it was easily defended. This location also made it easier to carry forward the policies that fostered autocracy and Christianity. Rome was full of tradition, the center of senatorial and even republican memories, and of pagan worship. Constantinople was free from both, and its dedication in 330 C.E. marked the beginning of a new era. Until its fall to the Turks in 1453, it served as a bastion of civilization, the preserver of classical culture, a bulwark against barbarian attack, and the greatest city in Christendom.

A civilian bureaucracy, carefully separated from the military to reduce the chances of rebellion by anyone combining the two kinds of power, carried out the autocratic rule of the emperors. Below the emperor's court, the most important officials were the *praetorian* prefects, each of whom administered one of the four major areas into which the empire was divided: Gaul, Italy, Illyricum, and the Orient. The four prefectures were subdivided into twelve territorial units called *dioceses*, each under a vicar subordinate to the prefect. The dioceses were further divided into almost a hundred provinces, each under a provincial governor.

A vast system of spies and secret police, without whom the increasingly rigid organization could not be trusted to perform, supervised the entire system. Despite these efforts, the system was corrupt and inefficient.

The cost of maintaining a 400,000-man army, as well as the vast civilian bureaucracy, the expensive imperial court, and the imperial taste for splendid buildings strained an already weak economy. Diocletian's attempts to establish a reliable currency failed, leading instead to increased inflation. To deal with it, he resorted to price control with his Edict of Maximum Prices in 301 C.E. For each product and each kind of labor, a maximum price was set, and violations were punishable by death. The edict still failed.

Peasants unable to pay their taxes and officials unable to collect them tried to escape. Diocletian resorted to stern regimentation to keep all in their places and at the service of the government. The terror of the third century forced many peasants to seek protection in the *villa*, or "country estate," of a large and powerful landowner and to become tenant farmers. As social boundaries hardened, these *coloni* and their descendants became increasingly tied to their estates.

The Arch of Constantine. Built in 315 C.E., it represents a transition between classical and medieval, pagan and Christian. Many of the sculptures incorporated in it were taken from earlier works dating to the first and second centuries. Others, contemporary with the arch, reflect new, less refined style. Scala/Art Resource, NY

REIGNS OF SELECTED LATE EMPIRE RULERS (ALL DATES ARE C.E.)

180–192	Commodus
193–211	Septimius Severus
222–235	Alexander Severus
249–251	Decius
253–259	Valerian
259 (253)–268	Gallienus
268–270	Claudius II Gothicus
270–275	Aurelian
284–305	Diocletian
306–337	Constantine (sole emperor after 324)
337–361	Constantius II
361–363	Julian the Apostate
364–375	Valentinian I
364–378	Valens
379–395	Theodosius I

Division of the Empire The peace and unity Constantine established did not last long. Constantius II (r. 337–361 C.E.) won the struggle for succession after his death. Constantius's death, in turn, left the empire to his young cousin Julian (r. 361–363 C.E.), whom Christians called the Apostate because of his attempt to stamp out Christianity and restore paganism. Julian undertook a campaign against Persia to put a Roman on the throne of the Sassanids and end the Persian menace once and for all. He penetrated deep into Persia but was killed in battle. His death ended the expedition and the pagan revival.

The Germans in the West took advantage of the eastern campaign to attack along the Rhine and upper Danube Rivers. In addition, even greater trouble was brewing along the middle and upper Danube. (See Map 5–5.) The eastern Goths, known as the Ostrogoths, occupied that territory. They were being pushed hard by their western cousins, the Visigoths, who in turn had been driven from their home in the Ukraine by the fierce Huns, a nomadic people from central Asia. (See "Ammianus Marcellinus Describes the People Called Huns," page 157.)

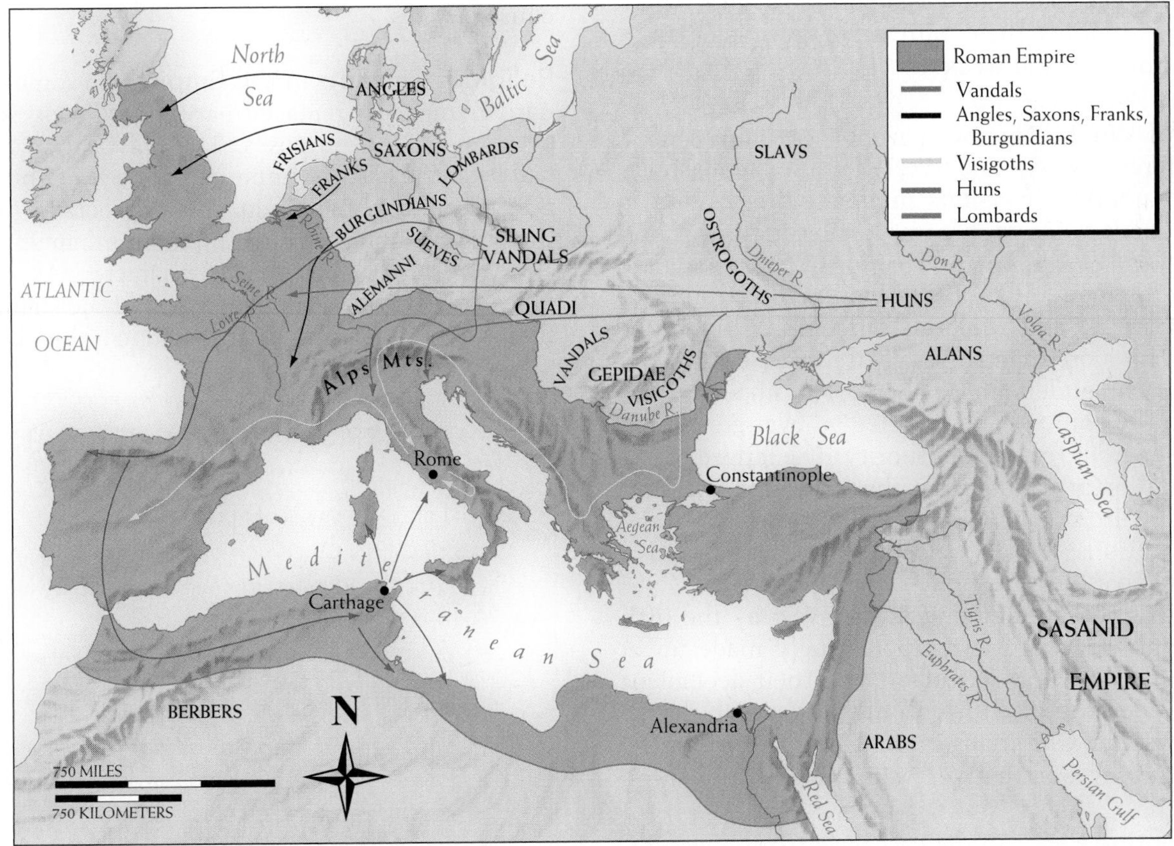

Map 5–5 **THE EMPIRE'S NEIGHBORS** In the fourth century the Roman Empire was nearly surrounded by ever more threatening neighbors. The map shows who these so-called barbarians were and where they lived before their armed contact with the Romans.

The emperor Valentinian I (r. 364–375 C.E.) saw he could not defend the empire alone and appointed his brother Valens (r. 364–378 C.E.) as co-ruler. Valentinian made his own headquarters at Milan and spent the rest of his life fighting and defeating the Franks and the Alemanni in the West. Valens was given control of the East. The empire was once again divided in two. The two emperors maintained their own courts, and the halves of the empire became increasingly separate and different. Latin was the language of the West and Greek of the East.

In 376, the Visigoths, pursued by the Huns, won rights of settlement and material assistance within the empire from the eastern emperor Valens (r. 364–378) in exchange for defending the eastern frontier as *foederati*, or special allies of the empire. The Visigoths, however, did not keep their bargain with the Romans and plundered the Balkan provinces. Nor did the Romans comply. They treated the Visigoths cruelly, even forcing them to trade their children for dogs to eat. Valens attacked the Goths and died, along with most of his army, at Adrianople in Thrace in 378. Theodosius I (r. 379–395 C.E.), an able and experienced general, was named co-ruler in the East. By a combination of military and diplomatic skills, he pacified the Goths, giving them land and autonomy and enrolling many of them in his army. He made important military reforms, putting greater emphasis on the cavalry. Theodosius tried to unify the empire again, but his death in 395 left it divided and weak.

The Rural West The two parts of the empire went their different ways. The West became increasingly rural as barbarian invasions intensified. The *villa*, a fortified country estate, became the basic unit of life. There, *coloni* gave their services to the local magnate in return for economic assistance and protection from both barbarians and imperial officials. Many cities shrank to no more than tiny walled fortresses ruled by military commanders and bishops. The upper classes moved to the country and asserted an ever-greater independence from imperial authority. The failure of the central authority to maintain the roads and the constant danger from bands of robbers curtailed trade and communications, forcing greater self-reliance and a more primitive lifestyle.

The new world emerging in the West by the fifth century and afterwards was increasingly made up of isolated units of rural aristocrats and their dependent laborers. The only institution providing a high degree of unity was the Christian Church. The pattern for the early Middle Ages in the West was already formed.

The Byzantine East In the East the situation was different. Constantinople became the center of a vital and flourishing culture we call *Byzantine* that lasted until the fifteenth century. Because of its defensible location, the skill of its emperors, and the firmness and strength of its base in Asia Minor, it could deflect and repulse barbarian attacks. A strong navy allowed commerce to flourish in the eastern Mediterranean and, in good times, far beyond. Cities continued to prosper, and the emperors made their will good over the nobles in the countryside. The civilization of the Byzantine Empire was a unique combination of classical culture, the Christian religion, Roman law, and Eastern artistic influences. (See Chapter 6.)

While barbarians overran the West, the Roman Empire, in altered form, persisted in the East. While Rome shrank to an insignificant ecclesiastical town, Constantinople flourished as the seat of the empire, the "New Rome." Indeed, the Byzantines even called themselves "Romans." When we contemplate the decline and fall of the Roman Empire in the fourth and fifth centuries, we are speaking only of the West. A form of classical culture persisted in the Byzantine East for a thousand years more.

The Triumph of Christianity

The rise of Christianity to dominance in the empire was closely connected with the political and cultural experience of the third and fourth centuries. Political chaos and decentralization had religious and cultural consequences.

Religious Currents in the Empire In some provinces, native languages replaced Latin and Greek, sometimes even for official purposes. The classical tradition that had been the basis of imperial life became the exclusive possession of a small, educated aristocracy. In religion, the public cults had grown up in an urban environment and were largely political in character. As the importance of the cities diminished, so did the significance of their gods. People might still take comfort in the wor-

THE TRIUMPH OF CHRISTIANITY

ca. 4 B.C.E.	Jesus of Nazareth born
ca. 30 C.E.	Crucifixion of Jesus
64 C.E.	Fire at Rome: persecution by Nero
ca. 70–100 C.E.	Gospels written
ca. 250–260 C.E.	Severe persecutions by Decius and Valerian
303 C.E.	Persecution by Diocletian
311 C.E.	Galerius issues Edict of Toleration
312 C.E.	Battle of Milvian Bridge; conversion of Constantine to Christianity
325 C.E.	Council of Nicaea
395 C.E.	Christianity becomes official religion of Roman Empire

AMMIANUS MARCELLINUS DESCRIBES THE PEOPLE CALLED HUNS

Ammianus Marcellinus was born about 330 C.E. in Syria, where Greek was the language of his well-to-do family. After a military career, he lived in Rome and wrote an encyclopedic Latin history of the empire, covering the years 96 to 378 C.E., giving special emphasis to the difficulties of the fourth century. Here he describes the Huns, one of the barbarous peoples pressing on the frontiers. Like most Romans, he was appalled by these nomadic peoples. His account combines observation, hearsay, and prejudice, and it is not always easy to separate facts from fantasy.

How did the culture of the Huns differ from that of the Romans? How did their way of life give them an advantage against Rome? How was it disadvantageous? Which of the writer's statements do you think are factual?

The people called Huns, barely mentioned in ancient records, live beyond the sea of Azof, on the border of the Frozen Ocean, and are a race savage beyond all parallel. At the very moment of birth the cheeks of their infant children are deeply marked by an iron, in order that the hair, instead of growing at the proper season on their faces, may be hindered by the scars; accordingly the Huns grow up without beards, and without any beauty. They all have closely knit and strong limbs and plump necks; they are of great size, and low legged, so that you might fancy them two-legged beasts or the stout figures which are hewn out in a rude manner with an ax on the posts at the end of bridges.

They are certainly in the shape of men, however uncouth, and are so hardy that they neither require fire nor well-flavored food, but live on the roots of such herbs as they get in the fields, or on the half-raw flesh of any animal, which they merely warm rapidly by placing it between their own thighs and the backs of their horses.

They never shelter themselves under roofed houses, but avoid them, as people ordinarily avoid sepulchers as things not fit for common use. Nor is there even to be found among them a cabin thatched with reeds; but they wander about, roaming over the mountains and the woods, and accustom themselves to bear frost and hunger and thirst from their very cradles. . . .

There is not a person in the whole nation who cannot remain on his horse day and night. On horseback they buy and sell, they take their meat and drink, and there they recline on the narrow neck of their steed, and yield to sleep so deep as to indulge in every variety of dream.

And when any deliberation is to take place on any weighty matter, they all hold their common council on horseback. They are not under kingly authority, but are contented with the irregular government of their chiefs, and under their lead they force their way through all obstacles.

From Ammianus Marcellinus, *Res Gestae*, trans. by C. D. Yonge (London: George Bell and Son, 1862), pp. 312–314.

ship of the friendly, intimate deities of family, field, hearth, storehouse, and craft, but these gods were too petty to serve their needs in a confused and frightening world. The only universal worship was of the emperor, but he was far off, and obeisance to his cult was more a political than a religious act.

In the troubled fourth and fifth centuries, people sought powerful, personal deities who would bring them safety and prosperity in this world and immortality in the next. Paganism was open and tolerant. Many people worshipped new deities alongside the old and even intertwined elements of several to form a new amalgam by the device called **syncretism**.

Manichaeism was an especially potent rival of Christianity. Named for its founder, Mani, a Persian who lived in the third century C.E., this movement contained aspects of various religious traditions, including Zoroastrianism from Persia and both Judaism and Christianity. The Manichaeans pictured a world in which light and darkness, good and evil, were constantly at war. Good was spiritual and evil was material. Because human beings were made of matter, their bodies were a prison of evil and darkness, but they also contained an element of light and good. The "Father of Goodness" had sent Mani, among other prophets, to free humanity and gain its salvation. To achieve salvation, humans must want to reach the realm of light and abandon all physical desires. Manichaeans led an ascetic life and practiced a simple worship guided by a well-organized church. The movement reached its greatest strength in the fourth and fifth centuries, and some of its central ideas persisted into the Middle Ages.

Christianity had something in common with these cults and answered many of the same needs their devotees felt. None of them, however, attained Christianity's universality, and none appears to have given the early Christians as much competition as the ancient philosophies or the state religion.

Imperial Persecution By the third century, Christianity had taken firm hold in the eastern provinces and in Italy. It had not made much headway in the West, however. (See Map 5–6.) Christian apologists pointed out that Christians were good citizens who differed from others only in not worshipping the public gods. Until the middle of the third century, the emperors tacitly accepted this view, without granting official toleration. As times became bad and the Christians became more numerous and visible, that policy changed. Popular opinion blamed disasters, natural and military, on the Christians.

About 250, the emperor Decius (r. 249–251 C.E.) invoked the aid of the gods in his war against the Goths and required all citizens to worship the state gods publicly. True Christians could not obey, and Decius started a major persecution. Many Christians—even some bishops—yielded to threats and torture, but others held out and were killed. Valerian (r. 253–260 C.E.) resumed the persecutions, partly to confiscate the wealth of rich Christians. His successors, however, found other matters more pressing, and the persecution lapsed until the end of the century.

By the time of Diocletian, the increasing number of Christians included high officials. But hostility to the Christians had also grown on every level. Diocletian was not generous toward unorthodox intellectual or religious movements. His own effort to bolster imperial power with the aura of divinity boded ill for the church, and in 303 he launched the most serious persecution inflicted on the Christians in the Roman Empire. He confiscated church property and destroyed churches and their sacred books. He deprived upper-class Christians of public office and judicial rights, imprisoned clergy, and enslaved Christians of the lower classes. He fined anyone refusing to sacrifice to the public gods. A final decree required public sacrifices

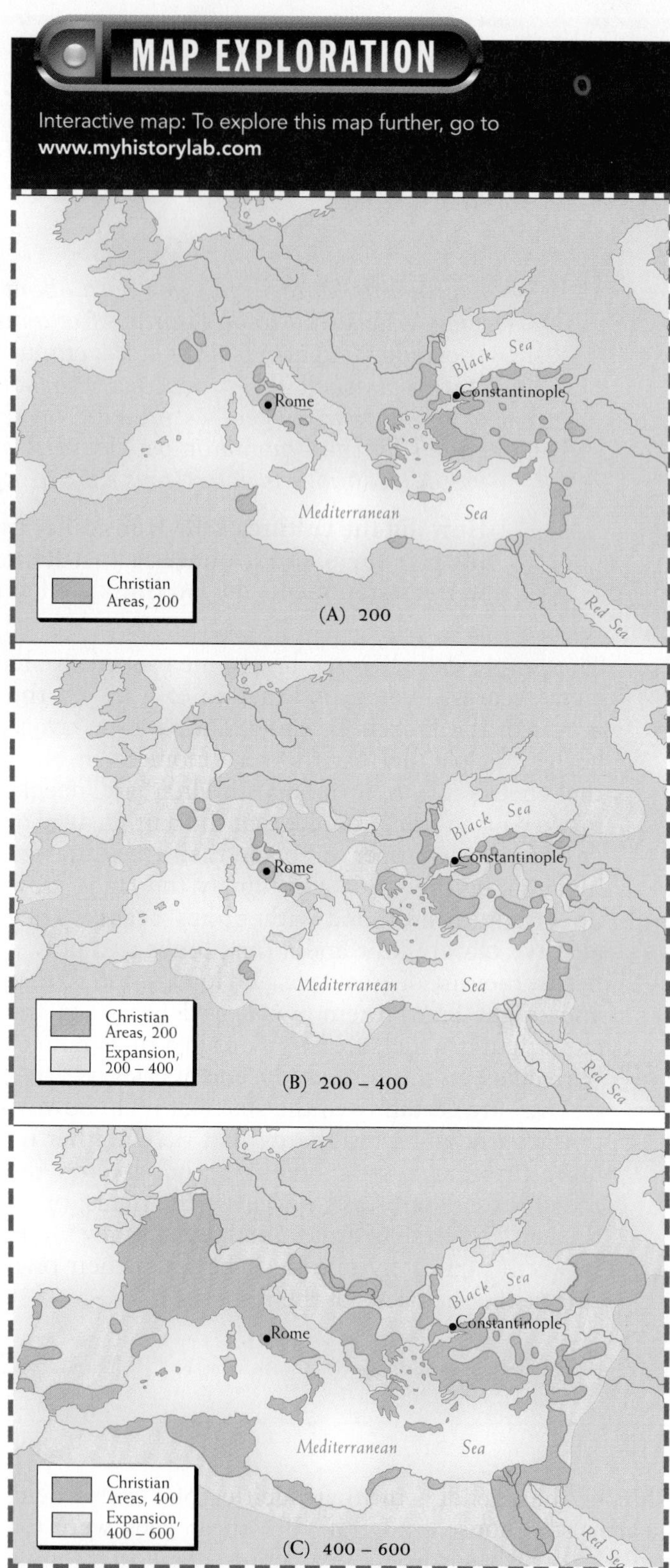

Map 5–6 **THE SPREAD OF CHRISTIANITY** Christianity grew swiftly in the third, fourth, fifth, and sixth centuries—especially after the conversion of the emperors in the fourth century. By 600, on the eve of the birth of the new religion of Islam, Christianity was dominant throughout the Mediterranean world and most of western Europe.

and libations. The persecution horrified many pagans, and the plight and the demeanor of the martyrs aroused pity and sympathy.

Ancient states could not carry out a program of terror with the thoroughness of modern totalitarian governments, so the Christians and their church survived to enjoy what they must have considered a miraculous change of fortune. In 311, Galerius, who had been one of the most vigorous persecutors, was influenced, perhaps by his Christian wife, to issue the Edict of Toleration, permitting Christian worship.

The victory of Constantine and his emergence as sole ruler of the empire changed the condition of Christianity from a precariously tolerated sect to the religion the emperor favored. This put it on the path to becoming the official and only legal religion in the empire.

Emergence of Christianity as the State Religion

The sons of Constantine continued to favor the new religion, but the succession of Julian the Apostate in 360 posed a new threat. He was a devotee of traditional classical pagan culture and, as a believer in **Neoplatonism**, an opponent of Christianity. Neoplatonism was a religious philosophy, or a philosophical religion, whose connection with Platonic teachings was distant. Its chief formulator was Plotinus (205–270 C.E.), who tried to combine classical and rational philosophical speculation with the mystical spirit of his time. Plotinus's successors were bitter critics of Christianity, and their views influenced Julian. Though he refrained from persecution, he tried to undo the work of Constantine by withdrawing the privileges of the church, removing Christians from high offices, and introducing a new form of pagan worship. His reign, however, was short, and his work did not last.

In 394, Theodosius forbade the celebration of pagan cults and abolished the pagan religious calendar. At his death, Christianity was the official religion of the Roman Empire.

The establishment of Christianity as the state religion did not put an end to the troubles of the Christians and their church; instead, it created new ones and complicated some old ones. The favored position of the church attracted converts for the wrong reasons and diluted the moral excellence and spiritual fervor of its adherents. The problem of the relationship between church and state arose, presenting the possibility that religion would become subordinate to the state, as it had been in the classical world and in earlier civilizations. In the East, that largely happened.

In the West, the weakness of the emperors permitted church leaders to exercise remarkable independence. In 390, Ambrose, bishop of Milan, excommunicated Theodosius I for a massacre he had carried out, and the emperor did penance. This act provided an important precedent for future assertions of the church's autonomy and authority, but it did not end secular interference and influence in the church.

Arianism and the Council of Nicaea Internal divisions proved to be even more troubling as new heresies emerged. Because they threatened the unity of an empire that was now Christian, they inevitably involved the emperor and the powers of the state. Before long, the world would see Christians persecuting other Christians with a zeal at least as great as the most fanatical pagans had displayed against them.

Among the many controversial views that arose, the most important and the most threatening was **Arianism**. A priest named Arius of Alexandria (ca. 280–336 C.E.) founded it. The issue creating difficulty was the relation of God the Father to God the Son. Arius argued that Jesus was a created being, unlike God the Father. He was, therefore, not made of the substance of God and was not eternal. "The Son has a beginning," he said, "but God is without beginning." For Arius, Jesus was neither fully man nor fully God, but something in between. Arius's view did away with the mysterious concept of the Trinity, the difficult doctrine that holds that God is three persons (the Father, the Son, and the Holy Spirit) and also one in substance and essence.

The Arian concept appeared simple, rational, and philosophically acceptable. To its ablest opponent, Athanasius, however, it had serious shortcomings. Athanasius (ca. 293–373 C.E.), later bishop of Alexandria, saw the Arian view as an impediment to any acceptable theory of salvation, to him the most important religious question. He adhered to the old Greek idea of salvation as involving the change of sinful mortality into divine immortality through the gift of "life." Only if Jesus were both fully human and fully God could the transformation of humanity to divinity have taken place in him and be transmitted by him to his disciples. "Christ was made man," he said, "that we might be made divine."

To deal with the controversy, Constantine called a council of Christian bishops at Nicaea, not far from Constantinople, in 325. For the emperor the question was essentially political, but for the disputants salvation was at stake. At Nicaea, Athanasius's view won out, became orthodox, and was embodied in the Nicene Creed. But Arianism persisted and spread. Some later emperors were either Arians or sympathetic to that view. Some of the most successful missionaries to the barbarians were Arians; as a result, many of the German tribes that overran the empire were Arians. The Christian emperors hoped to bring unity to their increasingly decentralized realms by imposing a single religion. Over time it did prove to be a unifying force, but it also introduced divisions where none had existed before.

▼ Arts and Letters in the Late Empire

The art and literature of the late empire reflect the confluence of pagan and Christian ideas and traditions and the conflict between them. Much of the literature is polemical and much of the art is propaganda.

A military revolution led by provincials whose origins were in the lower classes saved the empire from the chaos of the third century. They brought with them the fresh winds of cultural change, which blew out not only the dust of classical culture, but much of its substance as well. Yet the new ruling class was not interested in leveling; it wanted instead to establish itself as a new aristocracy. It thought of itself as effecting a great restoration rather than a revolution and sought to restore classical culture and absorb it. The comfort of Christianity tempered the confusion and uncertainty of the times. But the new ruling class also sought order and stability—ethical, literary, and artistic—in the classical tradition.

The Preservation of Classical Culture

One of the main needs and accomplishments of this period was the preservation of classical culture. Ways were discovered to make it available and useful to the newly arrived ruling class. Works of the great classical authors were reproduced in many copies and were transferred from perishable and inconvenient papyrus rolls to sturdier codices, bound volumes that were as easy to use as modern books. Scholars also digested long works like Livy's *History of Rome* into shorter versions, wrote learned commentaries, and compiled grammars. Original works by pagan writers of the late empire were neither numerous nor especially distinguished.

Christian Writers

The late empire, however, did see a great outpouring of Christian writings, including many examples of Christian apologetics, in poetry and prose, and sermons, hymns, and biblical commentaries. Christianity could also boast important scholars. Jerome (348–420 C.E.),

This late-Roman ivory plaque shows a scene from Christ's Passion. The art of the late empire was transitional between the classical past and the medieval future. Crucifixion, carving, c. 420 A.D. (ivory). British Museum, London, UK/Bridgeman Art Library

thoroughly trained in classical Latin literature and rhetoric, produced a revised version of the Bible in Latin. Commonly called the **Vulgate**, it became the Bible the Catholic Church used. Probably the most important eastern scholar was Eusebius of Caesarea (ca. 260–340 C.E.). He wrote apologetics, an idealized biography of Constantine, and a valuable chronology of important events in the past. His most important contribution, however, was his *Ecclesiastical History*, an attempt to set forth the Christian view of history. He saw all of history as the working out of God's will. History, therefore, had a purpose and a direction, and Constantine's victory and the subsequent unity of empire and church were its culmination.

The closeness and also the complexity of the relationship between classical pagan culture and that of the Christianity of the late empire are nowhere better displayed than in the career and writings of Augustine (354–430 C.E.), bishop of Hippo in North Africa. He was born at Carthage and was trained as a teacher of rhetoric. His father was a pagan, but his mother was a Christian, and hers was ultimately the stronger influence. He passed through several intellectual way stations—skepticism and Neoplatonism among others—before his conversion to Christianity. His training and skill in pagan rhetoric and philosophy made him peerless among his contemporaries as a defender of Christianity and as a theologian.

His greatest works are his *Confessions*, an autobiography describing the road to his conversion, and *The City of God*. The latter was a response to the pagan charge that the abandonment of the old gods and the advent of Christianity caused the Visigoths' sack of Rome in 410. The optimistic view some Christians held that God's will worked its way in history and was easily comprehensible needed further support in the face of this calamity. Augustine sought to separate the fate of Christianity from that of the Roman Empire. He contrasted the secular world, the City of Man, with the spiritual, the City of God. The former was selfish, the latter unselfish; the former evil, the latter good.

Augustine argued that history was moving forward, in the spiritual sense, to the Day of Judgment, but there was no reason to expect improvement before then in the secular sphere. The fall of Rome was neither surprising nor important. All states, even a Christian Rome, were part of the City of Man and were therefore corrupt and mortal. Only the City of God was immortal, and it, consisting of all the saints on earth and in heaven, was untouched by earthly calamities.

Though the *Confessions* and *The City of God* are Augustine's most famous works, they emphasize only a part of his thought. His treatises *On the Trinity* and *On Christian Education* reveal the great skill with which he supported Christian belief with the learning, logic, and philosophy of the pagan classics. Augustine believed faith is essential and primary (a thoroughly Christian view), but it is not a substitute for reason (the foundation of classical thought). Instead, faith is the starting point for, and liberator of, human reason, which continues to be the means by which people can understand what faith reveals. His writings constantly reveal the presence of both Christian faith and pagan reason, as well as the tension between them, a legacy he left to the Middle Ages.

▼ The Problem of the Decline and Fall of the Empire in the West

Whether important to Augustine or not, the massive barbarian invasions of the fifth century put an end to effective imperial government in the West. For centuries people have speculated about the causes of the collapse of the ancient world. Every kind of reason has been put forward, and some suggestions seem to have nothing to do with reason at all. Exhaustion of the soil, plague, climatic change, and even poisoning by lead water pipes have been suggested as reasons for Rome's decline in population, vigor, and the capacity to defend itself. Some blame the slavery and a resulting failure to make advances in science and technology. Others blame excessive government interference in the economic life of the empire and still others the destruction of the urban middle class, the carrier of classical culture.

A simpler and more obvious explanation might begin with the observation that the growth of so mighty an empire as Rome's was by no means inevitable. Rome's greatness had come from conquests that provided the Romans with the means to expand still further, until there were not enough Romans to conquer and govern any more peoples and territory. When pressure from outsiders grew, the Romans lacked the resources to advance and defeat the enemy as in the past. The tenacity and success of their resistance for so long were remarkable. Without new conquests to provide the immense wealth needed to defend and maintain internal prosperity, the Romans finally yielded to unprecedented onslaughts by fierce and numerous attackers.

To blame the ancients and slavery for the failure to produce an industrial and economic revolution like that of the later Western world (one capable of producing wealth without taking it from another) is to stand the problem on its head. No one yet has a satisfactory explanation for those revolutions. So it is improper to blame any institution or society for not achieving what has been achieved only once in human history. Perhaps we would do well to think of the problem as did Edward

Gibbon, the author of the great eighteenth-century study of Rome's collapse and transformation:

> The decline of Rome was the natural and inevitable effect of immoderate greatness. Prosperity ripened the principle of decay; the cause of the destruction multiplied with the extent of conquest; and, as soon as time or accident had removed the artificial supports, the stupendous fabric yielded to the pressure of its own weight. The story of the ruin is simple and obvious; and instead of inquiring why the Roman Empire was destroyed, we should rather be surprised that it had subsisted so long.[5]

In Perspective

Out of the civil wars and chaos that brought down the republic, Augustus brought unity, peace, order, and prosperity. As a result, he was regarded with almost religious awe and attained more military and political power than any Roman before him. He ruled firmly, but with moderation. He tried to limit military adventures and the costs they incurred. His public works encouraged trade and communications. He tried to restore and invigorate the old civic pride, and in this he had much success. He was less successful in promoting private morality based on family values. He patronized the arts to beautify Rome and glorify his reign. On his death, Augustus was able to pass on the regime to his family, the Julio-Claudians.

For almost two hundred years, with a few brief interruptions, the empire was generally prosperous, peaceful, and well run. But problems grew. Management of the many responsibilities the government assumed required the growth of a large bureaucracy that placed a heavy and increasing burden on the treasury, required higher taxes, and stifled both civic spirit and private enterprise. Pressure from barbarians on the frontiers required a large standing army, which led to further taxation.

In the late empire, Rome's rulers resorted to many devices for dealing with their problems. More and more, the emperors' rule and their safety depended on the loyalty of the army, so they courted the soldiers' favor with gifts. This only increased the burden of taxes; the rich and powerful found ways to avoid their obligations, increasing the load on everyone else. The government's control over the lives of its people became ever greater and the society more rigid as people tried to flee to escape the crushing load of taxes. Expedients were tried, including inflating the currency, fixing farmers to the soil as serfs or *coloni*, building walls to keep the barbarians out, and bribing barbarian tribes to fight for Rome against other barbarians. Ultimately, all these measures failed. The Roman Empire in the west fell, leaving disunity, insecurity, disorder, and poverty. Like similar empires in the ancient world, it had been unable to sustain its "immoderate greatness."

[5]Edward Gibbon, *The History of the Decline and Fall of the Roman Empire*, 2nd ed., Vol. 4, ed. by J. B. Bury McThuen & Co. (London: 1909), pp. 173–174.

Review Questions

1. What solutions did Augustus provide for the political problems that had plagued the Roman Republic? Why was the Roman population willing to accept Augustus as head of the state?
2. How was the Roman Empire organized and why did it function smoothly? What role did the emperor play in maintaining political stability?
3. How did the literature in the Golden Age of Augustus differ from that of the Silver Age during the first and second centuries C.E.? How did the poetry of Vergil and Horace contribute to Augustus's rule?
4. Why did the Roman authorities persecute Christians? What were the more important reasons for Christianity's success?
5. What political, social, and economic problems beset Rome in the third and fourth centuries C.E.? How did Diocletian and Constantine deal with them? Were they effective in stemming the tide of decline and disintegration in the Roman Empire? What problems were they unable to solve?
6. What theories have scholars advanced to explain the decline and fall of the Roman Empire. What are the difficulties involved in explaining the fall? What explanation would you give?

Suggested Readings

W. Ball, *Rome in the East* (2000). A study of the eastern parts of the empire and how they interacted with the West.

A. A. Barrett, *Livia: First Lady of Imperial Rome* (2004). Biography of Augustus's powerful and controversial wife.

P. Brown, *The Rise of Western Christendom: Triumph and Diversity, 200–1000*, 2nd ed. (2003). A vivid picture of the spread of Christianity by a master of the field.

A. Ferrill, *The Fall of the Roman Empire, The Military Explanation* (1986). An interpretation that emphasizes the decline in the quality of the Roman army.

K. Galinsky, *Augustan Culture* (1996). A work that integrates art, literature, and politics.

E. Gibbon, *The History of the Decline and Fall of the Roman Empire*, 7 vols., ed. by J. B. Bury, 2nd ed. (1909–1914). A masterwork of the English language.

D. Johnston, *Roman Law in Context* (2000). Places Rome's law in the context of its economy and society.

D. Kagan, ed., *The End of the Roman Empire: Decline or Transformation*? 3rd ed. (1992). A collection of essays on the problems of the decline and fall of the Roman Empire.

C. Kelly, *Ruling the Later Roman Empire* (2004). A study of the complexities of Roman government in the last centuries of the empire.

J. Lendon, *Empire of Honour: The Art of Government in the Roman World* (1997). A brilliant study that reveals how an aristocratic code of honor led the upper classes to cooperate in Roman rule.

R. W. Mathison, *Roman Aristocrats in Barbarian Gaul: Strategies for Survival* (1993). An unusual slant on the late empire.

S. Mattern, *Rome and the Enemy: Imperial Strategy in the Principate* (1999). A study of Rome's foreign and imperial policy under the Principate.

F. G. B. Millar, *The Emperor in the Roman World, 31 B.C.–A.D. 337* (1977). A study of Roman imperial government.

H. M. D. Parker, *A History of the Roman World from A.D. 138 to 337* (1969). A good survey.

D. S. Potter, *The Roman Empire at Bay: A.D. 180–395* (2004). An account of the challenges to Rome in the third and fourth centuries and how the Romans tried to meet them.

M. I. Rostovtzeff, *Social and Economic History of the Roman Empire*, 2nd ed. (1957). A masterpiece whose main thesis is much disputed.

V. Rudich, *Political Dissidence under Nero, The Price of Dissimulation* (1993). A brilliant exposition of the lives and thoughts of political dissidents in the early empire.

G. E. M. de Ste. Croix, *The Class Struggle in the Ancient World* (1981). An ambitious interpretation of all of classical civilization from a Marxist perspective.

R. Syme, *The Roman Revolution* (1960). A brilliant study of Augustus, his supporters, and their rise to power.

For additional learning resources related to this chapter, please go to www.myhistorylab.com

PEARSON myhistorylab

THE WEST & THE WORLD

Ancient Warfare

The Causes of War

WAR HAS BEEN a persistent part of human experience since before the birth of civilization.[1] Organized warfare goes back to the Stone Age. There may be evidence of it as early as the late Paleolithic Age, but clearly it was a significant human activity by the Neolithic Age. The earliest civilizations of Egypt and Mesopotamia added powerful new elements to the character of warfare and were from the first occupied with war, as were later Bronze and Iron Age cultures all over the world.

The earliest literary work in the Western tradition, Homer's *Iliad*, describes a long, bitter war and the men who fought it. The Rigvedic hymns of the ancient culture of India tell of the warrior god Indra, who smashes the fortifications of his enemies. The earliest civilizations of China were established by armies armed with spears, composite bows, and war chariots. The evidence is plentiful that war is one of the oldest and most continuous activities of the human species.

Ancient philosophers like Plato and Aristotle took all this for granted. They believed men (they never thought of women in this context) were naturally acquisitive and aggressive, and that governments and laws existed to curb those tendencies. The ancient Greeks, wracked as they were by perpetual war, were eager to investigate its causes. Thucydides, writing at the end of the fifth century B.C.E., set forth with great care the quarrels between the Athenians and the Peloponnesians and told why they broke their treaty: "so that no one may ever have to seek the cause that led to the outbreak of so great a war among the Greeks." He provided a profound and helpful understanding of the causes of wars and of the motives of human beings in going to war. He understood war as the armed competition for power, but he thought that unusually wise and capable leaders could limit their own fears and desires—and those of their people—and could choose to gain and defend only so much power as was needed for their purposes.

In this struggle for power, whether for a rational sufficiency or in the insatiable drive for all the power there is, Thucydides found that people go to war out of "fear, honor, and interest."[2] That trio of motives is illuminating in understanding the origins of wars throughout history. That fear and interest should move states to war will not surprise the modern reader, but that concern for honor should do so may seem strange. If we take honor to mean "fame," "glory," "renown," or "splendor," it may appear applicable to the premodern world alone. If, however, we understand its significance as "deference," "esteem," "just due," "regard," "respect," or "prestige," we will find it an important motive of nations in the modern world as well.

Wars are made by human beings who may choose different courses of action. Sometimes the decisions are made by a single individual or a small group, sometimes by a very large number. Their choices are always limited and affected by circumstances, and the closer they come to the outbreak of a war, the more limited the choices seem. Those who decide to make war always think they have good reason to fight. Although impersonal forces play a role, and the reasons publicly given are not necessarily the true ones, the reasons must be taken seriously, for "the conflicts between states which have usually led to war have normally arisen, not from any irrational and emotional drives, but from almost a superabundance of analytic rationality. . . . [I]n general men have fought during the past two hundred years neither because they are aggressive nor because they are acquisitive animals, but because they are reasoning ones: because they discern, or believe that they can discern, dangers before they become immediate, and thus the possibility of threats before they are made."[3]

At any time in history, there has been widespread agreement that some things are desirable and worth fighting for. Liberty, autonomy, the freedom to exercise one's religion, and the search for wealth have been among the most common through the ages. Fear of their opposites—slavery, subordination, religious suppression, and poverty—have probably been even greater causes of wars. All of them, however, depend on power, for the distribution of power determines who can and cannot impose his or her will on others. In one sense, there is no single cause

[1] Arther Ferrill, *The Origins of War* (London, Thames and Hudson, 1985), p. 13, says "organized warfare appeared at least by the end of the Paleolithic Age," but Richard A. Gabriel argues that true warfare did not come until the Bronze Age and the invention of the state and the social structure that came with it. No one, however, doubts that war is at least as old as civilization.

[2] 1.75.3.

[3] Michael Howard, *The Lessons of History* (Yale University Press, New Haven, 1991), p. 81.

of war, but a myriad. But in another sense, there is only one cause: Wars have rarely happened by accident or because of honest misunderstandings; most of them have resulted from calculations about power, which is valued because it can provide security, reputation, and material advantage.

In the sixth century B.C.E., the Greek philosopher Heracleitus observed that "war is the father of all things." In 1968, Will and Ariel Durant calculated that, in the previous 3,421 years, only 268 were free of war. There have been none since, suggesting, in that respect, that little has changed in more than three millennia. The reasons that have led to war in the past seem not to have disappeared.

Human beings, organized into nations and states, continue to compete for a limited supply of desirable things, to seek honor and advantage, and to fear others. All too often, the result has been war.

War and Technology

The conduct of war is shaped at the deepest level by the character of the societies involved, their values, their needs, and their organization, but from the first, technology has played a vital role. Weapons and other necessities of war are the product of technological development, and war and technology have had a mutually stimulating effect from the earliest times as new technologies have helped shape the character of war, and the needs of armies have provoked technological advance.

FORTRESS WALLS

Jericho, built about 7000 B.C.E. in the Neolithic Age, already reveals the importance of warfare and the development of technology to deal with it. Jericho is surrounded by a stone wall 700 yards around, 10 feet thick, and 13 feet high, protected by a moat 10 feet deep and 30 feet wide. This barrier made the town a powerful fortress that could be defeated only by an enemy who could besiege it long enough to starve it out. Nobody would have undertaken the expense and effort to build such a structure unless war was a relatively common danger. Not too many years after the rise of civilization in Mesopotamia (ca. 3000 B.C.E.), fortified Sumerian cities appeared in the south. A thousand years later, the pharaohs of Dynasty 12 in Egypt devised a strategic defense system of fortresses on their southern frontier with Nubia. In early China, the towns had no walls because the surrounding plains lacked both trees and stone. During the Shang dynasty (ca. 1766–1050 B.C.E.), however, towns with walls made of beaten earth appeared. Once the techniques needed to build fortresses strong enough to withstand attack were mastered, kingdoms could expand into empires that could defend their conquered lands.

The history of warfare and military technology is a story of continued change caused by a permanent competition between defense and offense. In time, construction of fortified strongholds provoked new devices and techniques for besieging them. Excavations in Egypt

This mound marks the ancient city of Jericho. Thought by some to be the earliest Neolithic site in the Near East, it sprang up around an oasis about 7000 B.C.E. The thick stone walls and moat that surround it show it was meant to be a fortress that could resist sieges, affirming that warfare was common at least as early as the construction of this city. © Zev Radovan, Jerusalem, Israel and Mesopotamia have uncovered scaling ladders, battering rams, siege towers (some of them mobile), and mines burrowing under fortress walls. Catapults capable of hurling stones against an enemy's walls appear in Greece in the fourth century B.C.E.; the weapon was brought to greater perfection and power by the Romans centuries later. Alexander the Great and some of his Hellenistic successors became skillful at storming fortified cities with the aid of such technology, but throughout ancient history, success against a fortified place usually came as a result of starvation and surrender after a long siege. Not until the invention of gunpowder and powerful cannons did offensive technology overcome the defensive strength of fortification.

ARMY AGAINST ARMY

A different kind of warfare, of army against army in the open field, appeared as early as the Stone Age. Scholars disagree as to whether it came in the Paleolithic Age or emerged in Neolithic times, but we know that warriors used such weapons as wooden or stone clubs, spears and axes with sharpened stone heads, and simple bows with stone-tipped arrows. The discovery of metallurgy brought the Bronze Age to Mesopotamia, perhaps as early as 3500 B.C.E., providing armies with weapons that were sharper and sturdier than stone and with body armor and helmets that brought greater safety to warriors. The Mesopotamian rulers already had wealth, a sizable population, a civilized organization, and substantial fortress walls. Now, with bronze weapons, Mesopotamian rulers could expand their empires far beyond their early frontiers. When, not much later, the Bronze Age came to Egypt, its rulers, too, used the new technology to expand and defend their wealthy kingdom.

THE CHARIOT AND THE BOW

The next great revolution in warfare occurred with the inventions of the chariot and the composite bow. When these came together by about 1800 B.C.E., their users swept all before them, conquering both Egypt and Mesopotamia. The chariot was a light vehicle, a platform on two wheels pulled by a team of two or four horses that could move swiftly on a battlefield. It was strong enough to hold two men—a driver and a warrior—as it sped along on an open field. The wheels were of wood—not solid, but with spokes and a hub—and were attached to an axle; building them required great skill and experience. The warrior on the chariot wielded a new weapon: the composite bow, more powerful by far than anything that had come before it. Made of thin strips of wood glued together and fastened with animal tendons and horn, the bow was short and easy to use from a moving chariot. It could shoot a light arrow accurately for 300 yards and penetrate the armor of the day at about 100. A man on a chariot on a flat enough field, using a composite bow with a quiver full of light arrows, could devastate an army of foot soldiers. "Circling at a distance of 100 or 200 yards from the herds of unarmored foot soldiers, a chariot crew—one to drive, one to shoot—might have transfixed six men a minute. Ten minutes' work by ten chariots would cause 500 casualties or more."[4]

For several centuries, beginning about 1800 B.C.E., peoples from the north using such weapons smashed into Mesopotamia and conquered the kingdoms they attacked. In India, the Aryans, who also spoke an Indo-European language, smashed the indigenous Indus civilization. In Egypt, the Hyksos, speakers of a Semitic language, conquered the northern kingdom. In China, the chariot-riding Shang dynasty established an aristocratic rule based on the new weapons. In Europe, the Mycenaean Greeks used chariots, although it is not clear if they had the composite bow and used the tactics that had brought such great success elsewhere.

The most sophisticated users of ancient military technology before Alexander the Great were the Assyrians. They had a wide range of devices for siege warfare and took them along on all their campaigns. As always, new weapons made of new materials with new techniques do not in themselves constitute a revolution in military affairs. To use them effectively, armies require organizations that can devise appropriate operational plans and train their soldiers in the needed skills and discipline.

The Assyrian annals suggest that by the eighth century B.C.E., their kings had turned their chariot forces into "a weapon of shock and terror, manipulated by the driver to charge at breakneck speed behind a team of perfectly schooled horses and used by the archer as a platform from which to launch a hail of arrows; squadrons of chariots, their drivers trained to act in mutual support, might have clashed much as armored vehicles have done in our time, success going to the side that could disable the larger opposing number, while the footmen unlucky or foolhardy enough to stand in their way would have been scattered like chaff."[5]

MOUNTED CAVALRY

In 612 B.C.E., the great Assyrian Empire fell before a coalition of opponents, but it had already been weakened by enemies who commanded a new military technique: mounted cavalry. Ironically, the Assyrians themselves may have been the first to develop the critical skills of riding astride a horse while keeping both hands free to shoot with a bow. The first peoples to use

[4]John Keegan, *A History of Warfare* (New York: Vintage Books, 1993), p. 166.
[5]Ibid., pp. 176–177.

This mosaic was found on a wall of the House of the Faun at Pompei. It is believed to be a copy of a painting by Philoxelus of Emtrea in the fourth century B.C.E. Alexander is the mounted hatless man on the left and King Darius wears a headdress as he stands on a chariot on the right. Battle between Alexander the Great and King Dareios. House of the Faun, Pompeii VI 12, 2 Inv. 10020. Museo Archelogico Nazionale, Naples, Italy. Photograph © Erich Lessing/Art Resource, NY

the new cavalry technology to great effect were nomads from the steppes of northern Eurasia. About 690 B.C.E., a people the Greeks called Cimmerians flooded into Asia Minor on their warhorses, shaking the established order. Later in that century they were followed by another group of steppe nomads called the Scythians, who came from the Altay mountains in central Asia. The Scythians overthrew the Cimmerians and then joined with more settled peoples in the battles that destroyed the Assyrian Empire. This was the beginning of a series of attacks by horse-riding nomads from the steppes against the settled lands to their south that lasted for two millennia. In China no clear evidence exists for such attacks before the fourth century B.C.E., but it is possible that attacks from Mongolia and nearby areas may have brought down the western Chou dynasty in 771 B.C.E.

In the Middle East, the Babylonian Empire had succeeded the Assyrian but was soon replaced by the Persian Empire. The Persians had no other way of preventing the nomads' devastating raids than to pay other nomads to defend their frontiers, and the Chinese emperors did the same. The Chinese also developed a cavalry that carried the crossbow, more powerful than the composite bow. Another device for defending against the invaders was the Great Wall of China, built during the Ch'in dynasty (256–206 B.C.E.) and designed to keep the ravaging horsemen out. But this, too, proved ineffective. Despite endless perturbations of the political and military relationships between grassland and plowland, peoples of the steppe enjoyed a consistent advantage because of their superior mobility and the cheapness of their military equipment. This produced a pattern of recurrent nomad conquests of civilized lands.[6]

IRON-WIELDING WARRIORS

Even as the chariot and the warhorse were having so great an impact on the nature of ancient warfare, a far more fundamental revolution in military affairs was under way. Bronze is an alloy of copper and tin, but the latter is a rather rare metal, so it was expensive. Horses also were costly to keep, so warfare that depended on bronze weapons and horses was necessarily limited to a relatively

[6]William H. McNeill, *The Pursuit of Power* (Chicago: University of Chicago Press, 1982), p. 16.

The Great Wall of China was originally built during the Ch'in dynasty (256–206 B.C.E.), but what we see today is the wall as it was completely rebuilt during the Ming dynasty (1368–1644 C.E.). Paolo Koch/Photo Researchers, Inc.

small number of men. About 1400 B.C.E., however, in Asia Minor, someone discovered the technique of working iron to give it an edge so hard and durable that tools and weapons made of it were clearly superior to those of bronze. Iron, moreover, is far more abundant than the components of bronze, easier to work with, and much less expensive. For the first time, it became possible for common people to own and use metal. Now a much larger part of the population could own arms and armor, and "[o]rdinary farmers and herdsmen thereby achieved a new formidability in battle, and the narrowly aristocratic structure of society characteristic of the chariot age altered abruptly. A more democratic era dawned as iron-wielding invaders overthrew ruling elites that had based their power on a monopoly of chariotry."[7]

Within two centuries, the new technology spread over the Middle East and into Europe. A new round of invasions by iron-wielding warriors swept away kingdoms and empires and brought new peoples to power. The Assyrians, combining the bureaucratic organizational skills of Mesopotamian civilization with a warrior spirit and an ability to assimilate new techniques, achieved control of their own region with the aid of iron weapons, but many indigenous rulers of civilized lands were subdued or swept away. In Europe, a Greek-speaking people we call the Mycenaeans had ruled the Greek peninsula and the Aegean Sea with a Bronze Age civilization similar to those of the Middle East. Between 1200 B.C.E. and 1100 B.C.E., however, the Mycenaeans were overthrown by a new wave of Greeks with iron weapons who obliterated the old civilization and brought a new culture based on new ways of fighting.

THE SHIELD AND THE PHALANX

The heart of this new Greek civilization, which is called *Hellenic*, was the city-state, or *polis*, hundreds of which came into being toward the end of the eighth century B.C.E. (See Chapter 2.) Their armies consisted of independent yeoman farmers who produced enough wealth to supply their own iron weapons and body armor, made cheap enough by the revolution in metallurgy. But again, these would have been of little value without organizational change. Now, a new way of warfare, which made infantry the dominant fighting force on land for centuries, permitted an alliance of poor Greek states to defeat the mighty and wealthy Persian Empire. The soldiers, wearing helmets, body armor,

[7]Ibid., p. 12.

and a heavy, large round shield for protection, carried short iron swords but used iron-tipped wooden pikes as their chief weapon. Arrayed in compact blocks called *phalanxes*, usually eight men deep, these freemen, well disciplined and highly motivated, defeated lesser infantries, archers, and cavalry. Adapted by the Macedonians under King Philip II and his son Alexander the Great, the *hoplite* phalanx remained the dominant infantry force until it was defeated by the Roman legion in the second century B.C.E.

TRIREME WARFARE

The Greeks also achieved supremacy at sea by improving an existing technological innovation and providing it with an effective operational plan. Oared galleys were known at Cyprus as early as about 1000 B.C.E., and the Phoenicians improved their speed and maneuverability by superimposing a second and then a third bank of rowers over the first to produce a ship the Greeks called a *trireme.* The Greeks added outriggers for the top rowers, and it is possible this permitted their rowers to use the full power of their strongest leg muscles by sliding back and forth as they rowed. At first, the main mode of *trireme* warfare was for one ship to come alongside another, grapple it, and send marines to board the enemy ship. In time, however, the Greeks placed a strong ram at the prow of each ship and learned how to row with great bursts of speed and to make sharp turns that allowed them to ram and disable their opponents by striking them in the side or rear. With such ships and tactics, the Greek *triremes* repeatedly sank fleets of the Egyptians and Phoenicians who rowed for the Persian Empire, thus gaining complete naval mastery.

The Macedonians came to dominate the Greek world, to conquer the Persian Empire, and to rule its successor states in the Hellenistic period (323–31 B.C.E.), but technological innovation in military affairs played only a small part in their success. Military victories came chiefly from the quality of their leaders, the number, spirit, and discipline of their troops, and the ability to combine infantry, cavalry, and light-armed troops to win battles. Alexander's engineers also brought unprecedented skill to the use of siege weapons.

ROMAN LEGIONS

The armies of the Roman Republic defeated Macedon in a series of wars in the third and second centuries B.C.E. and brought the entire Mediterranean world under Roman sway by the end of the second century. This conquest was achieved almost entirely by the power of the infantry. In time, the Roman army moved from the phalanx formation to a looser, more open order of battle based on the legion, which was divided into smaller, self-sufficient units. The Romans abandoned the pike as the chief infantry weapon, using instead the *pilum*, a heavy iron javelin that was thrown to cause disarray in the enemy line and permit the Romans to use their short double-edged swords at close quarters. In the imperial period, beginning especially in the third century of our era, nomadic barbarian tribes began applying the severe pressure on Rome's frontiers that would ultimately bring down the empire. Like the Chinese, the Romans built walls in some places to ease the burden of defending their extensive borders. In the empire's last years, the Romans began to use heavily armored horses ridden by knights in heavy armor, carrying lances and capable of charging an enemy with great force and effect. These armored cavalrymen, called *cataphracts* in Greek, would develop into a major new system of fighting in the Western Middle Ages, but they were too few to take a significant role in the final, futile defense of the empire.

How early is the evidence for warfare among human beings? What did Thucydides think war was about? For what purposes did he think people went to war? Is war a rational or irrational action? Can you think of any good reason for fighting a war? How did war and technology affect one another in the ancient world?

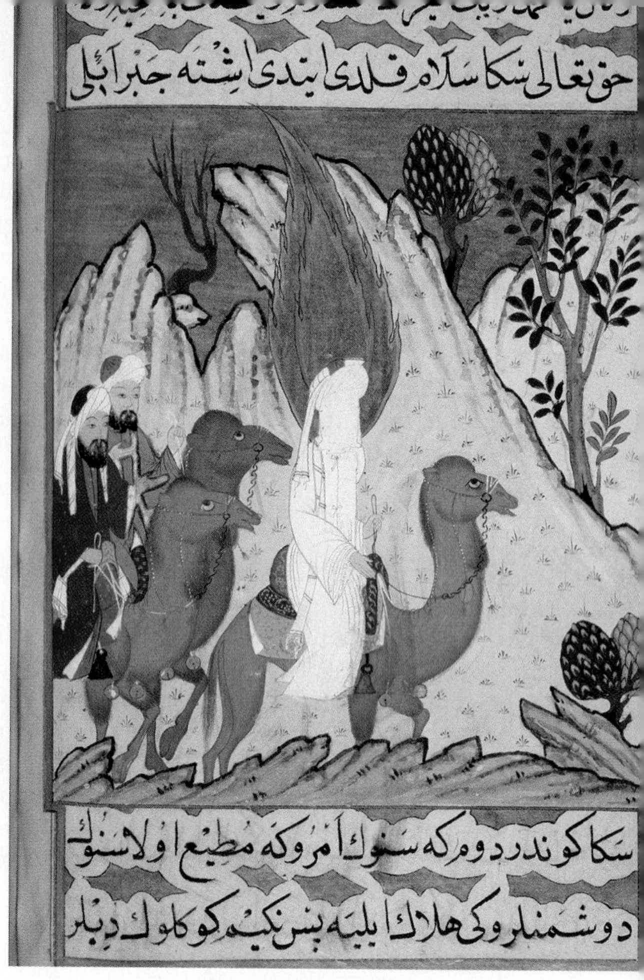

This illustration from a fourteenth-century "Life of the Prophet" shows Muhammad's family: his daughter Fatima, her husband Ali, and Muhammad's father-in-law Abu Bakr traveling together. Muhammad himself is not shown because like God he cannot be portrayed in Islamic art. Hence, whenever Muslims travel, Muhammad is in their midst but cannot be seen with the naked eye. The New York Public Library/Art Resource, NY

6 Late Antiquity and the Early Middle Ages: Creating a New European Society and Culture (476–1000)

▼ **On the Eve of the Frankish Ascendancy**
Germanic Migrations • New Western Masters

▼ **The Byzantine Empire**
The Reign of Justinian • The Spread of Byzantine Christianity • Persians and Muslims

▼ **Islam and the Islamic World**
Muhammad's Religion • Islamic Diversity • Islamic Empires • The Western Debt to Islam

▼ **Western Society and the Developing Christian Church**
Monastic Culture • The Doctrine of Papal Primacy • The Religious Division of Christendom

▼ **The Kingdom of the Franks: From Clovis to Charlemagne**
Governing the Franks • The Reign of Charlemagne (768–814) • Breakup of the Carolingian Kingdom

▼ **Feudal Society**
Origins • Vassalage and the Fief • Daily Life and Religion • Fragmentation and Divided Loyalty

▼ **In Perspective**

KEY TOPICS

- The collapse of the Western Roman Empire and the resulting fusion of Roman and Germanic culture
- The Byzantine and Islamic empires and their impact on the West
- The role of the church in Western society during the early Middle Ages
- The political and economic features of Europe under the Franks
- The characteristics of feudal society

SCHOLARS INCREASINGLY VIEW the six centuries between 250 C.E. and 800 C.E. as a single world bounded by the Roman and Sassanian (Persian) empires, spreading from Rome to Baghdad. Embracing Late Antiquity and the early Middle Ages, this epoch saw the Western and Eastern (Byzantine) Empires of Rome alternately decline and recover, separate and mingle, while never succumbing culturally to barbarian and Muslim invaders. In the East, Rome's provinces were deeply penetrated by an enduring Iranian dynasty, the Sassanians, who came to power in Persia and Mesopotamia in the third century C.E., overthrowing the Parthians and creating a powerful empire. In doing so, they laid a sure foundation for a later Muslim empire in the Middle East. During the reign of the Sassanid king Khosro I Anushirvan (r. 530–579), a contemporary of the Byzantine emperor Justinian (r. 527–565), this new Persian Empire, like its Byzantine counterpart, attained its cultural and military peak. But decades of warfare exhausted both empires, and by the mid-eighth century, the Arab conquests had extended Muslim influence across the Middle East and North Africa into Europe and eventually as far as northern Spain.

Meanwhile, in Western Europe, the Merovingian and Carolingian Franks were weaving their own Germanic barbarian heritage together with Judeo-Christian religion, Roman language and law, and Greco-Byzantine administration and culture to create a Western civilization of their own. The reign of Charlemagne (r. 768–814) saw a modest renaissance of classical antiquity. The peculiar Western social and political forms that emerged at this time—the manor and feudalism—not only coped with unprecedented chaos, but proved also to be fertile seedbeds from which distinctive Western political institutions were in time to grow.

Late Antiquity The centuries before and after the fall of Rome (476) were thus a vibrant period of self-discovery and self-definition for all of the above peoples. Many scholars have called this period—between the end of the ancient world and the birth of the Middle Ages—**Late Antiquity** (250–800 C.E.). It witnessed a new appropriation of ancient history by Jews, Christians, Muslims, and pagan Germanic and eastern tribes, each of which competed for their roots in the past (from which they drew authority) and their place in the future (where they would exercise power). In the process, each appropriated the best features of the other. The Jews had long adopted the attractive myths of the ancient Mesopotamians and the Christians the biblical prophecies of the Jews, while the Muslims subordinated both the Jewish and Christian scriptures to God's final, seventh-century revelations to Muhammad, the last of the prophets. The Christian Franks, the most eclectic and enterprising of all, claimed ancestors among the ancient Trojans of Greek myth and Homer's *Iliad.* (See Chapter 2.)

In Late Antiquity, these various peoples and their religions borrowed from and bumped into each other for several centuries, as the ancient world evolved into the medieval. In government, religion, and language, as well as geography, the Christian West ultimately grew apart from the Byzantine East and the Islamic Arab world. Although divided by states and cultures that became increasingly rigid and competitive over time, the world these peoples inhabited between 250 C.E. and 800 C.E. was also a cohesive one, a world together as well as a world moving apart.

▼ On the Eve of the Frankish Ascendancy

As we have already seen, by the late third century, the Roman Empire had become too large for a single emperor to govern and was beginning to fail. (See Chapter 5.) The emperor Diocletian (r. 284–305) tried to strengthen the empire by dividing it between himself and a coemperor. The result was a dual empire with an eastern and a western half, each with its own emperor and, eventually, imperial bureaucracy and army. A critical shift of the empire's resources and orientation to the eastern half accompanied these changes. In 284, Diocletian moved to Nicomedia (in modern Turkey), where he remained until the last two years of his reign. As imperial rule weakened in the West and strengthened in the East, it also became increasingly autocratic.

Diocletian's reign was followed by factional strife. His eventual successor, Constantine the Great (r. 306–337), briefly reunited the empire by conquest (his three sons and their successors would divide it again) and ruled as sole emperor of the eastern and western halves after 324. In that year, he moved the capital of the empire from Rome to Byzantium, an ancient Greek city that stood at the crossroads of the major sea and land routes between Europe and Asia Minor. Here, Constantine built the new city of Constantinople, which he dedicated in 330. As the imperial residence and the new administrative center of the empire, Constantinople gradually became a "new Rome." The "old" Rome, suffering from internal political and religious quarrels and geographically distant from the crucial military fronts in Syria and along the Danube River, declined in importance. The city of Rome and the Western empire were already in decline in the late third and fourth centuries, well before the barbarian invasions in the West began. Milan in northern Italy had replaced Rome as the imperial residence in 286. In 402, the seat of Western government would be moved to another northern Italian city, Ravenna, a seaport on the Adriatic that was protected on the landward side by impenetrable marshes. When the barbarian invasions of non-Roman Germanic and eastern peoples began in the late fourth century, the West was in political and economic disarray, and imperial power and prestige had shifted decisively to Constantinople and the East.

Germanic Migrations

The German tribes did not burst in on the West all of a sudden. They were at first a token and benign presence on the fringes of the empire and even within it. Before the massive migrations from the north and the east, Roman and Germanic cultures had commingled peacefully for centuries. The Romans had "imported" barbarians as servants, slaves, and soldiers. Barbarian soldiers commanded Roman legions.

Beginning in 376 with a great influx of Visigoths, or "west Goths," into the empire, this peaceful coexistence ended. The Visigoths, accomplished horsemen and fierce warriors, were themselves pushed into the empire by the emergence of a notoriously violent people, the Huns, from what is now Mongolia. The Visigoths ultimately reached southern Gaul and Spain. Soon to be Christianized, they won rights of settlement and material assistance within the empire from the Eastern emperor Valens (r. 364–378) in exchange for defending the eastern frontier as ***foederati***, or the emperor's "special" allies. Instead of the promised assistance, however, the Visigoths received harsh treatment from their new allies. After repeated conflicts, the Visigoths rebelled and overwhelmed Valens at the Battle of Adrianople in 378. (See Chapter 5.)

Thereafter, the Romans passively permitted the settlement of barbarians within the heart of the Western empire. The Vandals crossed the Rhine in 406 and within three decades gained control of northwest Africa and much of the Mediterranean. The Burgundians, who came on the heels of the Vandals, settled in Gaul. Most important for subsequent Western history were the Franks, who settled northern and central Gaul, some along the seacoast (the Salian Franks) and others along the Rhine, Seine, and Loire Rivers (the Ripuarian Franks).

Why was there so little Roman resistance to these Germanic tribes, whose numbers—at most 100,000 people in the largest of them—were comparatively small? The invaders were successful because they came in rapid succession upon a badly overextended Western empire divided politically by ambitious military commanders and weakened by decades of famine, pestilence, and overtaxation. By the second half of the fourth century, Roman frontiers had become too vast to manage. Efforts to do so by "barbarizing" the Roman army, that is, by recruiting many peasants into it and by making the Germanic tribes key Roman allies, only weakened it further. The Eastern empire retained enough wealth and vitality to field new armies or to buy off the invaders. The Western empire, in contrast, succumbed not only because of moral decay and materialism, but also because of a combination of military rivalry, political mismanagement, disease, and sheer poverty.

New Western Masters

In the early fifth century, Italy and the "eternal city" of Rome suffered devastating blows. In 410 the Visigoths, under Alaric (ca. 370–410), sacked Rome. In 452 the Huns, led by Attila—the "scourge of God"—invaded Italy. Rome was sacked still again, in 455—this time by the Vandals.

By the mid-fifth century, power in Western Europe had passed decisively from the hands of the Roman emperors to those of barbarian chieftains. In 476, the traditional date historians give for the fall of the Roman Empire, the barbarian Odovacer (ca. 434–493) deposed the last Western emperor Romulus Augustulus. The Eastern emperor Zeno (r. 474–491) recognized Odovacer's authority in the West, and Odovacer acknowledged Zeno as sole emperor, contenting himself to serve as Zeno's Western viceroy. In a later coup in 493, Theodoric (ca. 454–526), king of the Ostrogoths, or "east Goths," replaced Odovacer. Theodoric then governed with the full acceptance of the Roman people, the emperor in Constantinople, and the Christian Church.

By the end of the fifth century, the barbarians from west and east had saturated the Western empire. The Ostrogoths settled in Italy, the Franks in northern Gaul, the Burgundians in Provence, the Visigoths in southern Gaul and Spain, the Vandals in Africa and the western Mediterranean, and the Angles and Saxons in England. (See Map 6–1.)

These barbarian military victories did not, however, obliterate Roman culture; Western Europe's new masters were willing to learn from the people they had conquered. They admired Roman culture and had no desire to destroy it. Except in Britain and northern Gaul, Roman law, Roman government, and Latin, the Roman language, coexisted with the new Germanic institutions. In Italy under Theodoric, tribal custom gradually gave way to Roman law. Only the Vandals and the pagan Anglo-Saxons—and, after 466, the Visigoths—refused to profess at least titular obedience to the emperor in Constantinople.

The Visigoths, the Ostrogoths, and the Vandals had entered the West as Christians, which helped them accommodate to Roman culture. They were, however,

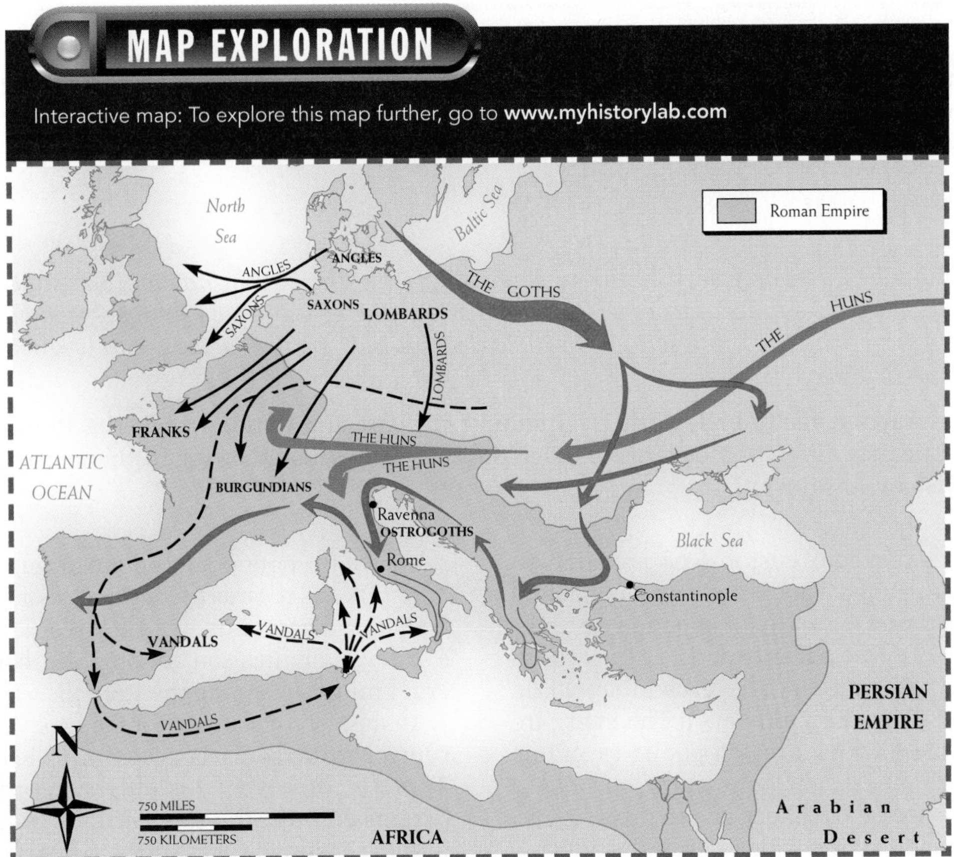

Map 6–1 **BARBARIAN MIGRATIONS INTO THE WEST IN THE FOURTH AND FIFTH CENTURIES** The forceful intrusion of Germanic and non-Germanic barbarians into the Roman Empire from the last quarter of the fourth century through the fifth century made for a constantly changing pattern of movement and relations. The map shows the major routes taken by the usually unwelcome newcomers and the areas most deeply affected by the main groups.

Arians, followers of a version of Christianity that had been condemned as heresy at the **Council of Nicaea** in 325. Later, around 500, the Franks, who had settled in Gaul, would convert to the Nicene, or "Catholic," form of Christianity supported by the bishops of Rome. As we will see, the Franks ultimately dominated most of Western Europe, helping convert the Goths and other barbarians to Roman Christianity.

All things considered, a gradual interpenetration of two strong cultures—a creative tension—marked the period of the Germanic migrations. The stronger culture was the Roman, and it became dominant in a later fusion. Despite Western military defeat, the Goths and the Franks became far more romanized than the Romans were germanized. Latin language, Nicene Catholic Christianity, and eventually Roman law and government were to triumph in the West during the Middle Ages.

▼ The Byzantine Empire

As the Roman Empire in the West succumbed to Germanic and other barbarian invasions, imperial power shifted to the eastern part of the Roman Empire, whose center was the city of Constantinople or Byzantium (modern-day Istanbul). It remained the sole imperial capital until the eighth century, when Charlemagne revived the Western empire and reclaimed its imperial title. In historical usage, the term *Byzantine* indicates the Hellenistic Greek, Roman, and Judaic monotheistic elements that distinguish the culture of the East from the Latin West.

Between 324 and 1453, the Byzantine Empire passed from an early period of expansion and splendor to a time of sustained contraction and splintering and finally ended in catastrophic defeat. Historians divide its history into three distinct periods:

SALVIAN THE PRIEST COMPARES THE ROMANS AND THE BARBARIANS

Salvian, a Christian priest writing around 440, found the barbarians morally superior to the Romans—indeed, truer to Roman virtues than the Romans themselves, whose failings were all the more serious because they, unlike the barbarians, had knowledge of Christianity.

Does Salvian really believe the Germanic tribes are more moral than the Romans? Does he use different standards to judge the two groups? Is he trying to shame the Romans, and if so, why?

In what respects can our customs be preferred to those of the Goths and Vandals, or even compared with them? And first, to speak of affection and mutual charity, . . . almost all barbarians, at least those who are of one race and kin, love each other, while the Romans persecute each other. . . . The many are oppressed by the few, who regard public exactions as their own peculiar right, who carry on private traffic under the guise of collecting the taxes. . . . So the poor are despoiled, the widows sigh, the orphans are oppressed, until many of them, born of families not obscure, and liberally educated, flee to our enemies that they may no longer suffer the oppression of public persecution. They doubtless seek Roman humanity among the barbarians, because they cannot bear barbarian inhumanity among the Romans. And although they differ from the people to whom they flee in manner and in language; although they are unlike as regards the fetid odor of the barbarians' bodies and garments, yet they would rather endure a foreign civilization among the barbarians than cruel injustice among the Romans.

It is urged that if we Romans are wicked and corrupt, that the barbarians commit the same sins. . . . There is, however, this difference, that if the barbarians commit the same crimes as we, yet we sin more grieviously. . . . All the barbarians . . . are pagans or heretics. The Saxon race is cruel, the Franks are faithless . . . the Huns are unchaste—in short there is vice in the life of all the barbarian peoples. But are their offenses as serious as [those of Christians]? Is the unchastity of the Hun so criminal as ours? Is the faithlessness of the Frank so blameworthy as ours?

From *Of God's Government,* in James Harvey Robinson, *Readings in European History,* Vol. 1 (Boston: Athenaeum, 1904), pp. 28–30.

1. From the rebuilding of Byzantium as Constantinople in 324 to the beginning of the Arab expansion and the spread of Islam in 632
2. From 632 to the conquest of Asia Minor by the Seljuk Turks in 1071, or, as some prefer, to the fall of Constantinople to the Western Crusaders in 1204
3. From 1071, or 1204, to the fall of Constantinople to the Ottoman Turks in 1453, the end of the empire in the East

The Reign of Justinian

In terms of territory, political power, and cultural achievement, the first period of Byzantine history (324–632) was far the greater. (See Map 6–2.) Its pinnacle was the reign of Emperor Justinian (r. 527–565) and his like-minded wife, Empress Theodora (d. 548). A strongman ruler who expected all his subjects, clergy and laity, high and low, to submit absolutely to his hierarchical control, Justinian spent, built, and destroyed on a grand scale. Theodora, the daughter of a circus bear trainer, had been an entertainer in her youth and, if Justinian's tell-all court historian, Procopius, is believed, a prostitute as well. Whatever her background, she possessed an intelligence and toughness that matched and might even have exceeded that of her husband. Theodora was a true co-ruler. In 532, after massive tax riots—the so-called Nika Revolt, named after the rebel's cry of "victory" (in Greek *Nika*)—rocked Constantinople threatening its

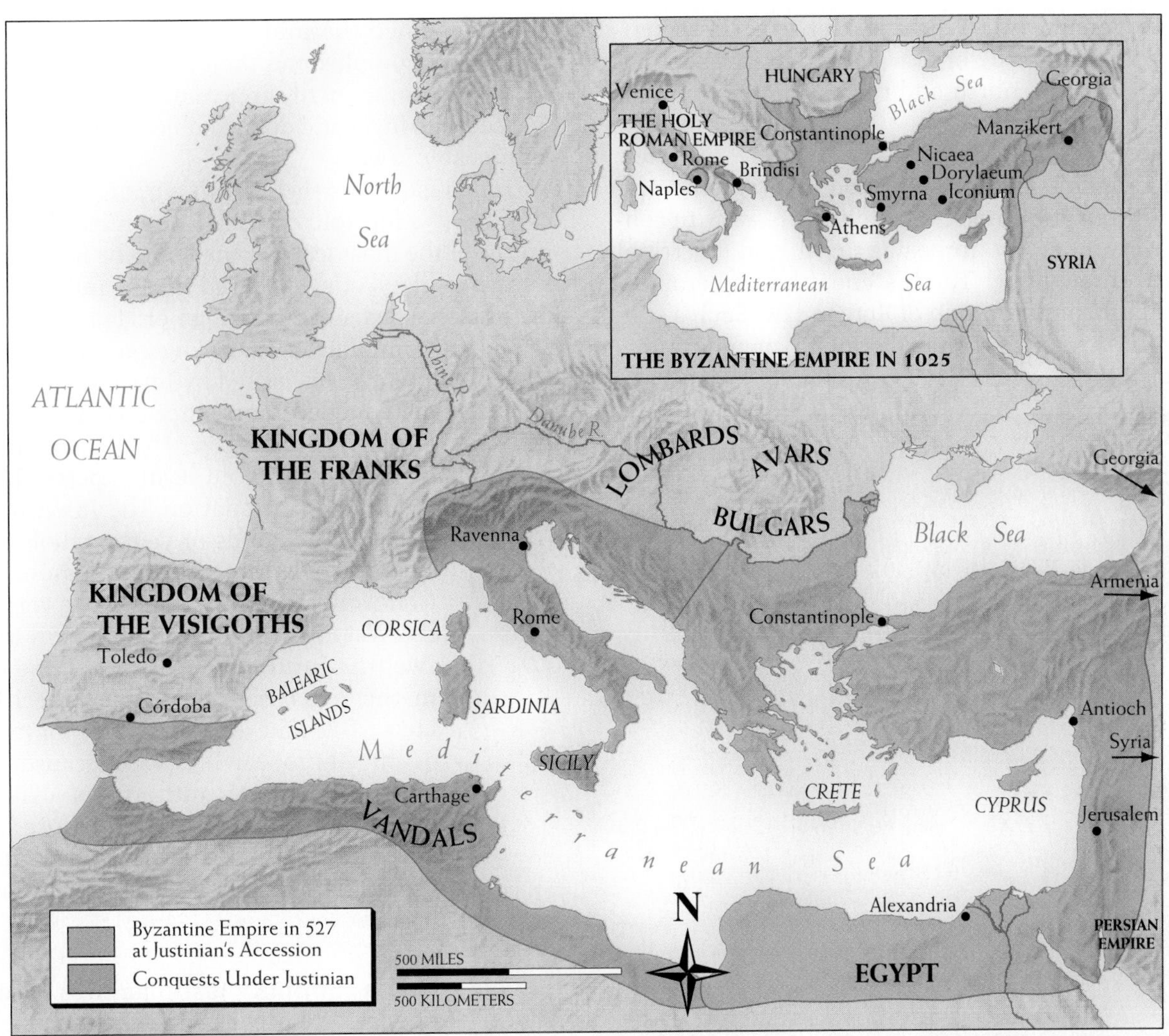

Map 6–2 **THE BYZANTINE EMPIRE AT THE TIME OF JUSTINIAN'S DEATH** The inset shows the empire in 1025, before its losses to the Seljuk Turks.

destruction and the end of Justinian's reign, a panicked emperor contemplated abdication and flight. Theodora insisted that he reestablish his authority, which he did by ordering a bloodbath that left tens of thousands of protesters dead.

Cities During Justinian's thirty-eight-year reign, the empire's strength lay in its more than 1,500 cities. Constantinople, with perhaps 350,000 inhabitants, was the largest city and the cultural crossroads of Asian and European civilizations. The dominant provincial cities had populations of 50,000. A fifth-century record suggests the size and splendor of Constantinople at its peak: 5 imperial and 9 princely palaces; 8 public and 153 private baths; 4 public forums; 5 granaries; 2 theaters; 1 hippodrome; 322 streets; 4,388 substantial houses; 52 porticoes; 20 public and 120 private bakeries; and 14 churches.[1] The most popular entertainments were the theater, where, according to clerical critics, nudity and immorality were on display, and the chariot races at the Hippodrome.

Between the fourth and fifth centuries, urban councils of roughly two hundred members, known as *Decurions,* all local, wealthy landowners, governed the cities. Being the intellectual and economic elite of the empire, they were heavily taxed, which did not make them the emperor's most docile or loyal servants. By the sixth century, fidelity to the throne had become the coin of the realm, and special governors, lay and clerical, chosen from the landholding classes, replaced the *decurion* councils as more reliable instruments of the

[1]Cyril Mango, *Byzantium: The Empire of New Rome* (New York: Charles Scribner's Sons, 1980), p. 88.

emperor's sovereign will. As the sixth and seventh centuries saw the beginning of new barbarian invasions of the empire from the north and the east, such political tightening was imperative.

Law The imperial goal—as reflected in Justinian's policy of "one God, one empire, one religion"—was to centralize government by imposing legal and doctrinal conformity throughout. To this end, the emperor ordered a collation and revision of Roman law. Such a codification was long overdue because an enormous number of legal decrees, often contradictory, had been piling up since the mid-second century, as the empire grew more complex and then more Christian and imperial rule became increasingly autocratic. What Justinian wanted was loyal and docile subjects guided by clear and enforceable laws.

The result was the *Corpus Juris Civilis,* or "body of civil law," a fourfold compilation undertaken by a committee of the most learned lawyers. The first compilation, known as the *Code,* appeared in 533 and revised imperial edicts issued since the reign of Hadrian (r. 117–138). A second compilation, the *Novellae,* or "new things," presented the decrees issued by Justinian and his immediate predecessors since 534. The third compilation, the *Digest,* gathered the major opinions of the old legal experts. The goal of the fourth compilation, the *Institutes,* was to put into the hands of young scholars a practical textbook that drew its lessons from the *Code* and the *Digest.* The *Code* was taught in the West by Irnerius at Bologna in Italy in the twelfth century (see Chapter 8), and beginning in the Renaissance (see Chapter 10), Justinian's *Code* laid the foundation for most subsequent European law. Because bringing subjects under the authority of a single sovereign was the fundamental feature of Roman law, rulers seeking to centralize their states especially benefited from Justinian's legal legacy.

Built during the reign of Justinian, Hagia Sophia (Church of Holy Wisdom) is a masterpiece of Byzantine and world architecture. After the Turkish conquest of Constantinople in 1453, Hagia Sophia was transformed into a mosque with four minarets, still visible today. Turkish Tourism and Information Office

Hagia Sophia Justinian was also a great builder. At his command and expense, fortifications, churches, monasteries, and palaces arose across the empire. His most famous and enduring monument in stone is the Church of Hagia Sophia (Holy Wisdom) completed in Constantinople in 537. Its key feature is a massive dome, 112 feet in diameter, which together with the church's many other windows, and open spaces, floods the nave with light and gives the interior a remarkable airiness and luminosity.

Reconquest in the West Justinian sought to reconquer the imperial provinces lost to the barbarians in the West. Beginning in 533, his armies overran the Vandal kingdom in North Africa and Sicily, the Ostrogothic kingdom in Italy, and part of Spain. But the price paid in blood and treasure was enormous, particularly in Italy, where prolonged resistance by the Ostrogoths did not end until 554. By Justinian's death, his empire was financially exhausted, and plague had ravaged the population of Constantinople and much of the East. Although Byzantine rule survived in Sicily and parts of southern Italy until the eleventh century, most of Justinian's Western and North African conquests were soon lost to Lombard invaders from north of the Alps and to the Muslim Arabs.

The Spread of Byzantine Christianity

In the late sixth and seventh centuries, nomadic, pagan tribes of Avars, Slavs, and Bulgars invaded and occupied the Balkan provinces of the eastern empire, threatening a "dark age" there. More than once, these fierce raiders menaced Constantinople itself. Yet after almost two centuries of intermittent warfare, the Slavs and Bulgars eventually converted to Eastern Orthodoxy or Byzantine Christianity. Hoping to build a cultural-linguistic firewall against menacing Franks from the West who had conquered the Avars and were attempting to convert his people to Roman Catholicism in Latin, a language they did not understand, the Slav Duke Rastislav of Moravia turned in the ninth century to Constantinople for help. In response, the emperor sent two learned missionaries to convert the Moravians: the brothers, priests, and future saints Constantine, later known as Cyril, and Methodius. In Moravia, the two created a new, Greek-based alphabet, which permitted the Slavs to create their own written language. That language gave the Christian gospels and Byzantine theology a lasting Slavic home. Later, after the Bulgars conquered and absorbed many of the Slavs, that alphabet was elevated to a broader script known as Cyrillic after St. Cyril. Known today as Old Church Slavonic, it has ever since been the international Slavic language through which Byzantine Christianity penetrated eastern Europe: Bohemia, much of the Balkans, Ukraine, and Kievan Russia. In prior centuries, the Byzantines had given Goths, Armenians, and Syrians similar native tools for accessing Byzantine culture and religion.

Persians and Muslims

During the reign of Emperor Heraclius (r. 610–641), the Byzantine Empire took a decidedly Eastern, as opposed to a Western Roman, direction. Heraclius spent his entire reign resisting Persian and Islamic invasions, the former successfully, the latter in vain. In 628 he defeated the Persian Sassanid king Chosroes and took back one of Western Christendom's great lost relics: a piece of Christ's Cross that Chosroes had carried off when he captured Jerusalem in 614. After 632, however, Islamic armies overran much of the empire, directly attacking Constantinople for the first time in the mid-670s. Not until Leo III of the Isaurian dynasty (r. 717–740) did the Byzantines succeed in repelling Arab armies and regaining most of Asia Minor, having lost forever Syria, Egypt, and North Africa. The setback was traumatic and forced a major restructuring of the diminished empire, creating a new system of provincial government under the direct authority of imperial generals. A major break with the old governance of the empire by local elites, the new system made possible a more disciplined and flexible use of military power in time of crisis. In the tenth century, a reinvigorated Byzantium went on the offensive, pushing back the Muslims in Armenia and northern Syria and conquering the Bulgar kingdom in the Balkans.

But like Justinian's conquests in the sixth century, these may have overtaxed the empire's strength; and in the eleventh century, Byzantine fortunes rapidly reversed. After inflicting a devastating defeat on the Byzantine

Empress Theodora and her attendants. The union of political and spiritual authority in the person of the empress is shown by the depiction on Theodora's mantle of three magi carrying gifts to the Virgin and Jesus. The Court of Empress Theodora. Byzantine early Christian mosaic. San Vitale, Ravenna, Italy Photograph © Scala/Art Resource, NY army at Manzikert in Armenia in 1071, Muslim Seljuk Turks overran most of Asia Minor, from which the Byzantines had drawn most of their tax revenue and troops. The empire never fully recovered, yet its end—which came when the Seljuks' cousins, the Ottoman Turks, captured Constantinople in 1453—was still almost four centuries away. In 1092, after two decades of steady Turkish advance, the Eastern emperor Alexius I Comnenus (r. 1081–1118) called for Western aid, which helped spark the First Crusade. It also heightened tensions between Latin West and Greek East and exposed the riches of Constantinople to predatory Western eyes. A century later (1204), the Fourth Crusade was diverted from Jerusalem to Constantinople, not, however, to rescue the city, but rather to inflict more damage on it and on the Byzantine Empire than all previous non-Christian invaders had done before. (See Chapter 7.) When the Byzantines eventually recovered the city in 1261, Byzantine power was a shadow of its former self, the empire was impoverished, and the Turks had become a constant threat.

▼ Islam and the Islamic World

A new drama began to unfold in the sixth century with the awakening of a rival far more dangerous to the West than the German tribes: the new faith of **Islam**. By the time of Muhammad's death (632), Islamic armies were beginning to absorb the attention and the resources of the emperors in Constantinople and the rulers in the West.

At first, the Muslims were both open and cautious. They borrowed and integrated elements of Persian and Greek culture into their own. The new religion of Islam adopted elements of Christian, Jewish, and Arab pagan religious beliefs and practices. Muslims tolerated religious minorities within the territories they conquered as long as those minorities recognized Islamic political rule, refrained from trying to convert Muslims, and paid their taxes. Nonetheless, the Muslims were keen to protect the purity and integrity of Islamic religion, language, and law from any corrupting foreign influence. Over time and after increased conflict with Eastern and Western Christians, this protective tendency grew stronger. Despite significant contacts and exchanges, Islamic culture did not take root as creatively in the West as barbarian and Byzantine cultures did, leaving Islam a strange and threatening religion to many Westerners.

Muhammad's Religion

Muhammad (570–632), an orphan, was raised by a family of modest means. As a youth, he worked as a merchant's assistant, traveling the major trade routes. When he was twenty-five, he married a wealthy widow from the city of Mecca, the religious and commercial center of Arabia. Thereafter, himself a wealthy man, he became a kind of social activist, criticizing Meccan materialism, paganism, and unjust treatment of the poor and needy. At about age forty, a deep religious experience heightened his commitment to reform and it transformed his life. He began to receive revelations from the angel Gabriel, who recited God's word to him at irregular intervals. These revelations were collected after his death into the Islamic holy book, the **Qur'an** (literally, a "reciting"), which his followers compiled between 650 and 651. The basic message Muhammad received was a summons to all Arabs to submit to God's will. Followers of Muhammad's religion came to be called *Muslim* ("submissive" or "surrendering"); *Islam* itself, means "submission."

The message was not a new one. A long line of Jewish prophets going back to Noah had reiterated it. According to Muslims, however, this line ended with Muhammad, who, as the last of God's chosen prophets, became "the Prophet." The Qur'an also recognized Jesus Christ as a prophet but denied that he was God's co-eternal and co-equal son. Like Judaism, Islam was a monotheistic and theocentric religion, not a trinitarian one like Christianity.

Mecca was a major pagan pilgrimage site (the ***Ka'ba***, which became Islam's holiest shrine, housed a sacred black meteorite that was originally a pagan object of worship). Muhammad's condemnation of idolatry and immorality threatened the trade that flowed from the pilgrims, enraging the merchants of the city. Persecuted for their attacks on traditional religion, Muhammad and his followers fled Mecca in 622 for Medina, 240 miles to the north. This event came to be known as the ***Hegira*** ("flight") and marks the beginning of the Islamic calendar.

In Medina, Muhammad organized his forces and drew throngs of devoted followers. He raided caravans going back and forth to Mecca. He also had his first conflicts with Medina's Jews, who were involved in trade with Mecca. By 624, he was able to conquer Mecca and make it the center of the new religion.

During these years the basic rules of Islamic practice evolved. True Muslims were expected (1) to be honest and modest in all their dealings and behavior; (2) to be unquestionably loyal to the Islamic community; (3) to abstain from pork and alcohol at all times; (4) to wash and pray facing Mecca five times a day; (5) to contribute to the support of the poor and needy; (6) to fast during daylight hours for one month each year; and (7) to make a pilgrimage to Mecca and visit the *Ka'ba* at least once in a lifetime. The last requirement reflects the degree to which Islam was an assimilationist religion: it "Islamicized" a major pagan religious practice.

Islam also permitted Muslim men to have up to four wives—provided they treated them all justly and gave each equal attention—and as many concubines as they wished. A husband could divorce a wife with a simple declaration, whereas, to divorce her husband, a wife had to show good cause before a religious judge. A wife was expected to be totally loyal and devoted to her husband and was allowed to show her face to no man but him. (See "Compare & Connect: The Battle of the Sexes in Christianity and Islam," page 180.)

In contrast to Christianity, Islam drew no rigid distinction between the clergy and the laity. A lay scholarly elite developed, however, and held moral authority within Islamic society in domestic and religious matters. This elite, known as the ***ulema***, or "persons with correct knowledge," served a social function similar to that of a professional priesthood or rabbinate. Its members were men of great piety and obvious learning whose opinions came to have the force of law in Muslim society. They also saw that Muslim rulers adhered to the letter of the Qur'an.

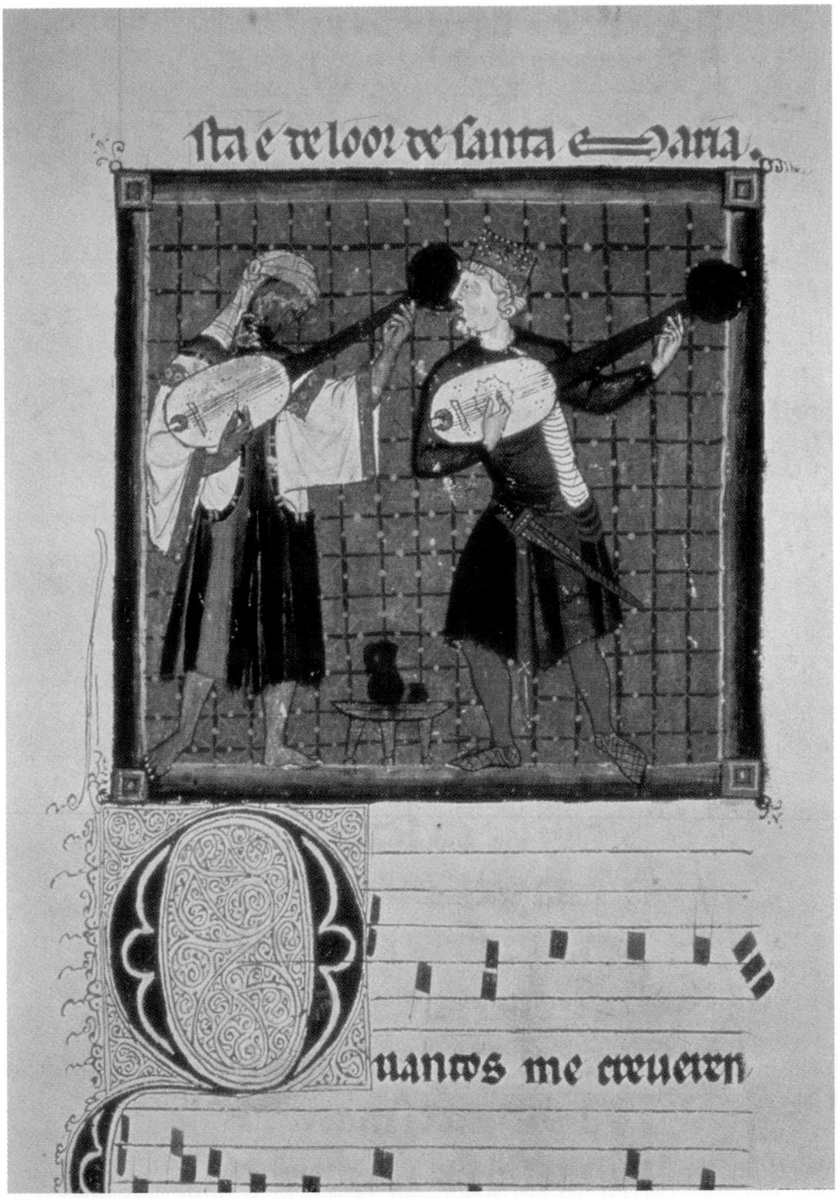

A Muslim and a Christian play the *ud* or lute together, from a thirteenth-century *Book of Chants* in the Escorial Monastery of Madrid. Medieval Europe was deeply influenced by Arab–Islamic culture, transmitted particularly through Spain. Some of the many works in Arabic on musical theory were translated into Latin and Hebrew, but the main influence on music came from the arts of singing and playing spread by minstrels. A Moor and a Christian playing the lute, miniature in a book of music from the "Cantigas" of Alphonso X "the Wise" (1221–1284). Thirteenth century (manuscript). Monastero de El Excorial, El Escorial, Spain/index/Bridgeman Art Library

Islamic Diversity

The success of Islam lay in its ability to unify and inspire tribal Arabs and other non-Jewish and non-Christian people. Islam also appealed to Arab pride, for it deemed Muhammad to be history's major religious figure and his followers to be God's chosen people.

As early as the seventh century, however, disputes arose among Muslims over the nature of Islamic society and authority within it that left permanent divisions. Disagreement over the true line of succession to Muhammad—the **caliphate**—was one source of discord. Another disagreement related to this was over doctrinal issues involving the extent to which Islam was an inclusive religion, open to sinners as well as to the virtuous. Several groups emerged from these disputes. The most radical was the Kharijites, whose leaders seceded from the camp of the caliph Ali (656–661) because Ali compromised with his enemies on a matter of principle. Righteous and judgmental, the Kharijites wanted all but the most rigorously virtuous Muslims excluded from the community of the faithful. In 661, a Kharijite assassinated Ali.

Another, more influential group was the **Shi'a**, or "partisans of Ali" (*Shi'at Ali*). The Shi'a looked on Ali and his descendants as the rightful successors of Muhammad not only by virtue of kinship, but also by the expressed will of the Prophet himself. To the Shi'a, Ali's assassination revealed the most basic truth of a devout Muslim life: A true *imam*, or "ruler," must expect to suffer unjustly even unto death in the world, and so, too, must his followers. A distinctive theology of martyrdom has ever since been a mark of Shi'a teaching. And the Shi'a, until modern times, have been an embattled minority within mainstream Islamic society.

A third group, which has been dominant for most of Islamic history, was the majority centrist **Sunnis** (followers of **sunna**, or "tradition"). Sunnis have always put loyalty to the community of Islam above all else and have spurned the exclusivism and purism of the Kharijites and the Shi'a.

COMPARE AND CONNECT

The Battle of the Sexes in Christianity and Islam

IN EARLY CHRISTIANITY man and woman were viewed as one and the same offspring, Eve born of Adam, for which reason they were forever after drawn irresistibly to one another. What one did to the other, one also did to oneself, so tightly were they bound. And that bond between husband and wife made their relationship all the more caring and charitable.

Muhammad's role as a husband was by all accounts exemplary: a spouse who dealt shrewdly and fairly with his wives, a splendid model for his followers. In the teaching of the *Qur'an*, all conflict between husband and wife was to be resolved by talking and, that failing, by the husband's departure from the marital bed. Heeding the example of the Prophet and the teaching of the *Qur'an*, devout Muslim men viewed a husband's hitting a wife as a last resort in his disciplining of her. Yet, when a wife flagrantly disobeyed (*nashiz*) her husband, or, much worse, was unfaithful to him, hitting often became the husband's and society's first response.

QUESTIONS

1. **How does the marriage bond differ in the Christian and Muslim faiths? What does it mean to Christians to say that husband and wife are one flesh? Is that also the way spouses are perceived in Islam?**
2. **How successful is male discipline of self and of wife in Islam? Is Christian marriage too egalitarian, and hence more vulnerable to failure?**
3. **If marriage is a mirror of a religion, what does it reveal Christianity and Islam to be?**

I. Christian Marriage

St. John Chrysostom (347–407) elaborated the relationship between Christian spouses in his Homily on Christian Spouses: *"Wives, be subject to your husbands, as to the Lord . . . Husbands, love your wives as Christ loved the Church." (Ephesians 5:22–25)*

There is no relationship between human beings so close as that of husband and wife, if they are united as they ought to be . . . God did not fashion woman independently from man . . . nor did He enable woman to bear children without man . . . He made the one man Adam to be the origin of all mankind, both male and female, and made it impossible for men and women to be self-sufficient [without one another] . . .

The love of husband and wife is [thus] the force that wields society together . . . Why else would [God] say, "Wives, be subject to your husbands?" Because when harmony prevails, the children are raised well, the household is kept in order . . . and great benefits, both for families and for states result . . .

Having seen the amount of obedience necessary, hear now about the amount of love that is needed. [If] you want your wife to be obedient to you . . . then be responsible for the same providential care of her as Christ has for the Church. Even if you see her belittling you, or despising and mocking you . . . subject her to yourself through affection, kindness, and your great regard for her . . . One's partner for life, the mother of one's children, the source of one's every joy, should never be fettered with fear and threats, but with love and patience . . . What sort of satisfaction could a husband have, if he lives with his wife as if she were a slave and not a woman [there] by her own free will. [So] suffer anything for her sake, but never disgrace her, for Christ never did this with the Church . . .

A wife should never nag her husband [saying] "You lazy coward, you have no ambition! Look at our relatives and neighbors; they have plenty of money. Their wives have far more than I do." Let no wife say any such thing; she is her husband's body, and it is not for her to dictate to her head, but rather to submit and obey . . . Likewise, if a husband has a wife who behaves this way, he must never exercise his authority by insulting and abusing her.

Source: Don S. Browning et al., *Sex, Marriage, and Family in World Religions* (New York: Columbia University Press), pp. 106–108.

Muslims are enjoined to live by the divine law, or *Shari'a*, and have a right to have disputes settled by an arbiter of the *Shari'a*. Here we see a husband complaining about his wife before the state-appointed judge, or *qadi*. The wife, backed up by two other women, points an accusing finger at the husband. In such cases, the first duty of the *qadi*, who should be a learned person of faith, is to try to effect a reconciliation before the husband divorces his wife, or the wife herself seeks a divorce. Bibliothèque Nationale de France, Paris

II. Muslim Marriage

Chroniclers Abu Hamid Al-Ghazali (1058–1111), Ihya'U-lum, 2:34–35 (eleventh century C.E.) elaborate the teaching of Qur'an 4:34: "Men are the protectors and maintainers of women because God has given [men] more strength . . . and because they support [women] from their means."

Treating women well and bearing their ill treatment [is] required for marriage . . . God said, "keep them good company." [Among] the last things the Messenger [Muhammad] recommended was to take care of your slaves. Do not burden them with things beyond their capacity, and observe God's exhortations relating to your wives, for they are like slaves in your hands. You took them in trust from God and made them your wives by His words . . .

One should know that treating one's wife well does not only mean not harming her; it also means to endure ill treatment and be patient when she gets angry and loses her temper, a [method] the Messenger used to forgive his wives who argued with him and turned away from him for the whole day . . .

'A'ishah [a wife of the Prophet] once got angry and said to the Prophet . . . "You, who claims to be the Prophet of God!" The Messenger of God smiled and tolerated her in the spirit of forgiveness and generosity . . . It is believed that the first love story in Islam was that of Prophet Muhammad and 'A'ishah. The Prophet used to say to his other wives: "Do not upset me by saying bad things about 'A'ishah, for she is the only woman in whose company I have received the revelation [of God]! Anas [Ibn Malik, a ninth-century chronicler] reported that the Prophet was the most compassionate person in matters concerning women and children . . .

Respond to [as he did to women's] harshness by teasing, joking, and kidding them, for it is certain this softens women's hearts. The Prophet said, "The people with the most perfect faith are those with the best ethics and those who are the kindest toward their families." Umar [a companion of the Prophet and the second caliph of Islam] once said: "One should always be like a child with his family, but when they need him they should find [in him] a man."

Source: Browning, *Sex, Marriage, and Family*, pp. 190–91, 194–95.

Islamic Empires

Under Muhammad's first three successors—the caliphs Abu Bakr (r. 632–634), Umar (r. 634–644), and Uthman (r. 644–655)—Islam expanded by conquest throughout the southern and eastern Mediterranean, into territories mostly still held today by Islamic states. In the eighth century, Muslim armies occupied parts of Spain in the West and of India in the East, producing a truly vast empire. (See Map 6–3.) The capital of this empire moved, first, from Mecca to Damascus in Syria, and then, in 750, to Baghdad in Iraq after the Abbasid dynasty replaced the Umayyads in a struggle for the caliphate. Thereafter, the huge Muslim Empire gradually broke up into separate states, some with their own line of caliphs claiming to be the true successors of Muhammad.

The early Muslim conquests would not have been so rapid and thorough had the contemporary Byzantine and Persian empires not been exhausted by decades of war. The Muslims struck at both empires in the 630s, completely overrunning the Persian Empire by 651. Most of the inhabitants in Byzantine Syria and Palestine, although Christian, were Semites like the Arabs. Any religious unity they felt with the Byzantine Greeks may have been offset by hatred of the Byzantine army of occupation and by resentment of Constantinople's efforts to impose Greek "orthodox" beliefs on the Monophysite churches of Egypt and Syria. As a result, many Egyptian and Syrian Christians, hoping for deliverance from Byzantine oppression, appear to have welcomed the Islamic conquerors.

Although Islam gained converts from among the Christians in the Near East, North Africa, and Spain, its efforts to invade northern Europe were rebuffed. The ruler of the Franks, Charles Martel, defeated a raiding party of Arabs on the western frontier of Europe at Poitiers (today in central France) in 732. This victory and the failure to capture Constantinople ended any Arab effort to expand into Western or Central Europe.

The Western Debt to Islam

Arab invasions and their presence in the Mediterranean area during the early Middle Ages contributed both directly and indirectly to the formation of Western Europe. They did so indirectly by driving Western Europeans back onto their native tribal and inherited Judeo-Christian, Greco-Roman, and Byzantine resources, from which they created a Western culture of their own. Also, by diverting the attention and energies of the Byzantine Empire during the formative centuries, the Arabs may have prevented it from expanding into and reconquering Western Europe. That allowed two Germanic peoples to gain ascendancy: first, the Franks and then the Lombards, who invaded Italy in the sixth century and settled in the Po valley around the city of Milan.

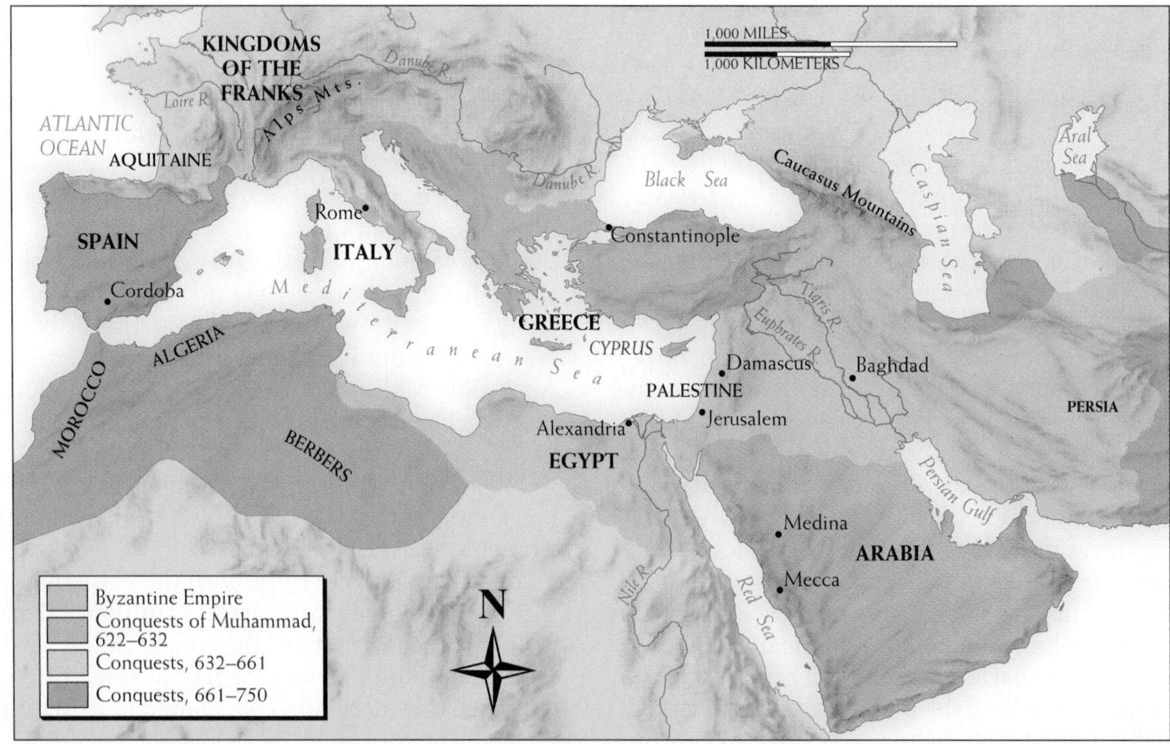

Map 6–3 **MUSLIM CONQUESTS AND DOMINATION OF THE MEDITERRANEAN TO ABOUT 750 C.E.** The rapid spread of Islam (both as a religion and as a political-military power) is shown here. Within 125 years of Muhammad's rise, Muslims came to dominate Spain and all areas south and east of the Mediterranean.

Despite the hostility of the Christian West to the Islamic world, there was nonetheless much creative interchange between these two different cultures, and the West profited greatly and directly from it. At this time, Arab civilizations were the more advanced, enjoying their golden age, and they had much to teach a toddling West. Between the eighth and tenth centuries, Cordoba, the capital of Muslim Spain, was a model multicultural city embracing Arabs, Berbers from North Africa, Christian converts to Islam, and Jews. Cordoba was a conduit for the finest Arabian tableware, leather, silks, dyes, aromatic ointments, and perfumes into the West. The Arabs taught Western farmers how to irrigate fields and Western artisans how to tan leather and refine silk. The West also gained from its contacts with Arabic scholars. Thanks to the skills of Islamic scholars, ancient Greek works on astronomy, mathematics, and medicine became available in Latin translation to Westerners. Down to the sixteenth century, the basic gynecological and child-care manuals guiding the work of Western midwives and physicians were compilations made by the Baghdad physician Al-Razi (Rhazes), the philosopher and physician Ibn-Sina (Avicenna) (980–1037), and Ibn Rushd (known in the West as Averröes, 1126–1198), who was also Islam's greatest authority on Aristotle. Jewish scholars also thrived amid the intellectual culture Islamic scholars created. The greatest of them all, Moses Maimonides (1135–1204), wrote in both Arabic and Hebrew. The medieval Arabs also gave the West one of its most popular books: *The Arabian Nights*, poetic folk tales that are still read and imitated in the West.

▼ Western Society and the Developing Christian Church

Facing barbarian invasions from the north and east and a strong Islamic presence in the Mediterranean, the West found itself in decline during the fifth and sixth centuries. As trade waned, cities rapidly fell on hard times, depriving the West of centers for the exchange of goods and ideas that might enable it to look and live beyond itself.

In the seventh century, the Byzantine emperors, their hands full with the Islamic threat in the East, were unable to assert themselves in the West, leaving most of the region to the Franks and the Lombards. As a result, Western Europeans now had to rely on their native Greco-Roman, Judeo-Christian, and barbarian heritages as they put together a distinctive culture of their own. As Western shipping declined in the Mediterranean, urban populations that otherwise would have engaged in trade-related work left the cities for the countryside in ever greater numbers. There they found the employment and protection they sought on the estates of the great landholders, who, for their part, needed laborers and welcomed the new emigrants. (See "Feudal Society," page 196.)

While these social changes were occurring, one institution remained firmly entrenched and increasingly powerful within the declining cities of the waning Roman Empire: the Christian church. The church had long modeled its own structure on that of the imperial Roman administration. Like the imperial government, church government was centralized and hierarchical. Strategically placed "generals" (bishops) in European cities looked for spiritual direction to their leader, the bishop of Rome. As the Western empire crumbled, Roman governors withdrew and populations emigrated to the countryside, where the resulting vacuum of authority was filled by local bishops and cathedral chapters. The local cathedral became the center of urban life and the local bishop the highest authority for those who remained in the cities. In Rome, on a larger and more fateful scale, the pope took control of the city as the Western emperors gradually departed and died out. Left to its own devices, Western Europe soon discovered that the Christian church was its best repository of Roman administrative skills and classical culture.

Challenged by Rome's decline to become a major political force, the Christian church survived the period of Germanic and Islamic invasions as a somewhat spiritually weakened and compromised institution. Yet it remained a potent civilizing and unifying force. It had a religious message of providential purpose and individual worth that could give solace and meaning to life at its worst. It had a ritual of baptism and a creed, or statement of belief, that united people beyond the traditional barriers of social class, education, and gender. Alone in the West, the church retained an effective hierarchical administration, scattered throughout the old empire, staffed by the best educated minds in Europe and centered in emperor-less Rome.

Monastic Culture

Throughout late antiquity the Christian church gained the services of growing numbers of monks, who were not only loyal to its mission, but also objects of great popular respect. Monastic culture proved again and again to be the peculiar strength of the church during the Middle Ages.

The first monks were hermits who had withdrawn from society to pursue a more perfect way of life. Inspired by the Christian ideals, they led a life of complete self-denial in imitation of Christ. The popularity of monasticism began to grow as Roman persecution of Christians waned and Christianity became the favored religion of the empire during the fourth century. **Monasticism** replaced martyrdom as the most perfect way to imitate Christ and to confess one's faith.

Christians came to view monastic life—embracing, as it did, the biblical "counsels of perfection" (chastity, poverty, and obedience)—as the purest form of religious practice, going beyond the baptism and creed that identified ordinary believers. This view evolved during the Middle Ages into a belief in the general superiority of the clergy and in the church's mission over the laity and the state. That belief served the papacy in later confrontations with secular rulers.

Anthony of Egypt (ca. 251–356), the father of hermit monasticism, was inspired by Jesus' command in the Gospels to the rich young ruler: "If you will be perfect, sell all that you have, give it to the poor, and follow me" (Matthew 19:21). Anthony went into the desert to pray and work, setting an example followed by hundreds in Egypt, Syria, and Palestine in the fourth and fifth centuries.

Hermit monasticism was soon joined by the development of communal monasticism. In the first quarter of the fourth century, Pachomius (ca. 286–346) organized monks in southern Egypt into a highly regimented community in which monks shared a life of labor, order, and discipline enforced by a strict penal code. Such monastic communities grew to contain a thousand or more inhabitants. They were little "cities of God," trying to separate themselves from the collapsing Roman and the nominal Christian world. Basil the Great (329–379) popularized communal monasticism throughout the East, providing a less severe rule than Pachomius, one that directed monks into such worldly services as caring for orphans, widows, and the infirm in surrounding communities.

Athanasius (ca. 293–373) and Martin of Tours (ca. 315–399) introduced monasticism to the West. The teachings of John Cassian (ca. 360–435) and Jerome (ca. 340–420) then helped shape the basic values and practices of Western monasticism. The great organizer of Western monasticism, however, was Benedict of Nursia (ca. 480–547). In 529, he established a monastery at Monte Cassino, in Italy, founding the form of monasticism—Benedictine—that bears his name and quickly came to dominate in the West. It eventually replaced an Irish, non-Benedictine monasticism that was common until the 600s in the British Isles and Gaul.

Benedict wrote *Rule for Monasteries,* a sophisticated and comprehensive plan for every activity of the monks, even detailing the manner in which they were to sleep. His *Rule* opposed the severities of earlier monasticism that tortured the body and anguished the mind. Benedict insisted on good food and even some wine, adequate clothing, and proper amounts of sleep and relaxation. Periods of devotion (about four hours each day) were set aside for the "work of God." That is, regular prayers, liturgical activities, and study alternated with manual labor (farming). This program permitted not a moment's idleness and carefully nurtured the religious, intellectual, and physical well-being of the cloistered monks. The monastery was directed by an abbot, whose command the monks had to obey unquestioningly. (See "The Benedictine Order Sets Its Requirements for Entrance.")

Individual Benedictine monasteries remained autonomous until the later Middle Ages, when the Benedictines became a unified order of the church. During the early Middle Ages, Benedictine missionaries Christianized both England and Germany. Their disciplined organization and devotion to hard work made the Benedictines an economic and political power as well as a spiritual force wherever they settled.

The Doctrine of Papal Primacy

Constantine and his successors, especially the Eastern emperors, ruled religious life with an iron hand and consistently looked on the church as little more than a department of the state. Such political assumption of spiritual power involved the emperor directly in the church's affairs, allowing him to play the theologian and to summon councils to resolve its doctrinal quarrels. At first, state control of religion was also the rule in the West. Most of the early popes were mediocre and not very influential. To increase their influence, in the fifth and sixth centuries, they took advantage of imperial weakness and distraction to develop a new defense: the powerful weaponry of papal primacy. This doctrine raised the Roman pope, or pontiff, to unassailable supremacy within the church when it came to defining church doctrine. It also put him in a position to make important secular claims, paving the way to repeated conflicts between church and state, pope and emperor, throughout the Middle Ages.

Papal primacy was first asserted as a response to the decline of imperial Rome. It was also a response to the claims of the patriarchs of the Eastern church, who, after imperial power was transferred to Constantinople, looked on the bishop of Rome as an equal, but no superior. In 381, the ecumenical Council of Constantinople declared the bishop of Constantinople to be of first rank after the bishop of Rome "because Constantinople is the new Rome." In 451, the ecumenical Council of Chalcedon recognized Constantinople as having the same religious primacy in the East as Rome had possessed in the West. By the mid-sixth century, the bishop of Constantinople described himself in his correspondence as a "universal" patriarch.

Roman pontiffs, understandably jealous of such claims and resentful of the political interference of Eastern emperors, launched a counteroffensive. Pope Damasus I (r. 366–384)[2] took the first of several major steps in the rise of the Roman church when he declared a Roman "**apostolic**" **primacy**. Pointing to Jesus' words to Peter in the Gospel of Matthew (16:18) ("Thou art Peter, and upon this rock I will build my church"), he claimed himself and all other popes to be Peter's direct successors as the unique "rock" on which the Christian church was built. Pope Leo I (r. 440–461) took still another fateful

[2]Dates after popes' names are the years of each reign.

THE BENEDICTINE ORDER SETS ITS REQUIREMENTS FOR ENTRANCE

The religious life had great appeal in a time of political and social uncertainty. Entrance into a monastery was not, however, escapism. Much was demanded of the new monk, both during and after his probationary period, which is described here. Benedict's contribution was to prescribe a balanced blend of religious, physical, and intellectual activities within a well-structured community.

Why did the religious life have such great appeal at this time in history? Were there materialistic as well as spiritual reasons for entering a cloister? What are Benedict's reasons for not allowing a monk to change his mind and leave the cloister, once vows have been taken?

When anyone is newly come for the reformation of his life, let him not be granted an easy entrance, but, as the Apostle says, "Test the spirits to see whether they are from God." If the newcomer, therefore, perseveres in his knocking, and if it is seen after four or five days that he bears patiently the harsh treatment offered him and the difficulty of admission, and that he persists in his petition, then let entrance be granted him, and let him stay in the guest house for a few days.

After that let him live in the novitiate, where the novices study, eat, and sleep. A senior shall be assigned to them who is skilled in winning souls, to watch over them with the utmost care. Let him examine whether the novice is truly seeking God, and whether he is zealous for the Work of God, for obedience and for humiliations. Let the novice be told all the hard and rugged ways by which the journey to God is made.

If he promises stability and perseverance, then at the end of two months let this Rule be read through to him, and let him be addressed thus: "Here is the law under which you wish to fight. If you can observe it, enter; if you cannot, you are free to depart." If he still stands firm, let him be taken to the above-mentioned novitiate and again tested in all patience. And after the lapse of six months let the Rule be read to him, that he may know on what he is entering. And if he still remains firm, after four months let the same Rule be read to him again.

Then, having deliberated with himself, if he promises to keep it in its entirety and to observe everything that is commanded him, let him be received into the community. But let him understand that, according to the law of the Rule, from that day forward he may not leave the monastery nor withdraw his neck from under the yoke of the Rule which he was free to refuse or to accept during that prolonged deliberation.

Leonard J. Doyle, *St. Benedict's Rule for Monasteries* (Collegeville, MN: Liturgical Press, 1948), pp. 79–80.

step by assuming the title ***pontifex maximus***, or "supreme priest." He further proclaimed himself to be endowed with a "plentitude of power," thereby establishing the supremacy of the bishop of Rome over all other bishops. During Leo's reign, an imperial decree recognized his exclusive jurisdiction over the Western church. At the end of the fifth century, Pope Gelasius I (r. 492–496) proclaimed the authority of the clergy to be "more weighty" than the power of kings, because priests had charge of divine affairs and the means of salvation.

Events as well as ideology favored the papacy. As barbarian and Islamic invasions isolated the West by diverting the attention of the Byzantine empire, they also prevented both emperors and the Eastern patriarchs from interfering in the affairs of the Western church. Islam may even be said to have "saved" the Western church from Eastern domination. At the same time, the Franks became a new political ally of the church. Eastern episcopal competition with Rome ended as bishopric after bishopric fell to Islamic armies in the East. The power of the exarch of Ravenna—the Byzantine emperor's viceroy in the West—was eclipsed in the late sixth century by invading Lombards who conquered most of Italy. Thanks to Frankish prodding, the Lombards became Nicene Christians loyal to Rome and a new counterweight to Eastern power and influence in the West. In an unprecedented act, Pope Gregory I, "the Great" (r. 590–604), instead of looking for protection to the emperor in Constantinople, negotiated an independent peace treaty with the Lombards.

The Religious Division of Christendom

In both East and West, religious belief alternately served and undermined imperial political unity. Since the fifth century, the patriarch of Constantinople had blessed Byzantine emperors in that city (the "second Rome"), attesting the close ties between rulers and the Eastern church. In 391, Christianity became the official faith of the Eastern empire, while all other religions and sects were deemed "demented and insane."[3] Between the fourth and sixth centuries, the patriarchs of Constantinople, Alexandria, Antioch, and Jerusalem received generous endowments of land and gold from rich, pious donors, empowering the church to act as the state's welfare agency.

While Orthodox Christianity was the religion that mattered most, it was not the only religion in the empire with a significant following. Nor did Byzantine rulers view religion as merely a political tool. From time to time, Christian heresies also received imperial support. Moreover, with imperial encouragement, Christianity absorbed pagan religious practices and beliefs that were too deeply rooted in rural and urban cultures to be eradicated, thus turning local gods and their shrines into Christian saints and holy places. (See Encountering the Past, "Two Roman Festivals" in Chapter 4, page 112.)

The empire was also home, albeit inhospitably, to large numbers of Jews. Pagan Romans viewed Jews as narrow, dogmatic, and intolerant but tolerated Judaism as an ancient and acceptable form of worship. When Rome adopted Christianity, Jews continued to have legal protection as long as they did not attempt to convert Christians, build new synagogues, or try to hold certain official positions or enter some professions. Whereas the emperor most intent on religious conformity within the empire, Justinian, encouraged Jews to convert voluntarily, later emperors commanded them to be baptized and gave them tax breaks as incentives to become Christians. However, neither persuasion nor coercion succeeded in converting the empire's Jews.

The differences between Eastern and Western Christianity grew to be no less irreconcilable than those between Christians and Jews. One issue even divided Justinian and his wife Theodora. Whereas Justinian remained

A ninth-century Byzantine manuscript shows an iconoclast whiting out an image of Christ. The Iconoclastic Controversy was an important factor in the division of Christendom into separate Latin and Greek branches. State Historical Museum, Moscow

strictly orthodox in his Christian beliefs, Theodora supported a divisive Eastern teaching that the Council of Chalcedon in 451 had condemned as a heresy, namely, that Christ had a single, immortal nature and was not both eternal God and mortal man in one and the same person. In reaction to the Monophysite controversy, orthodox Christianity became even more determined to protect the sovereignty of God. This concern is apparent in Byzantine art, which portrays Christ as impassive and transcendent, as united in his personhood with God, not as a suffering mortal man. In the sixth century, despite imperial persecution, the Monophysites became a separate church in the East where many Christians still today adhere to it.

A similar dispute appeared in Eastern debates over the relationship among the members of the Trinity, specifically whether the Holy Spirit proceeded only from the Father, as the Nicene-Constantinopolitan Creed taught, or from the Father and the Son (*filioque* in Latin), an idea that became increasingly popular in the West and was eventually adopted by the Western church and inserted into its creed. These disputes, which appear trivial and are almost unintelligible to many people today, seemed vitally important to many Christians at the time. Eastern theologians argued that adding *filioque* to the creed not

[3]Mango, *Byzantium*, p. 88.

only diminished God's majesty by seeming to subordinate the Holy Spirit but also weakened a core Christian belief—the divine unity and dignity of all three persons of the Trinity. Some perceive here a hidden political concern, important in the East. By protecting the unity and majesty of God the Father, Eastern theology also safeguarded the unity and majesty of the emperor himself, from whom all power on earth was believed properly to flow. The idea of a divisible Godhead, no matter how abstract and subtle, was unacceptable to Eastern Christians and the imperial government because it also suggested the divisibility of imperial power, not a tenet for an emperor who closely associated himself with God.

Another major rift between the Christian East and West was over the veneration of images in worship. In 726, Emperor Leo III (r. 717–741) forbade the use of images and icons that portrayed Christ, the Virgin Mary, and the saints throughout Christendom. As their veneration had been commonplace for centuries, the decree came as a shock, especially to the West where it was rejected as heresy. **Iconoclasm**, as the change in policy was called, may have been a pretext to close monasteries and seize their lands because monks were among the most zealous defenders of the veneration of images. On the other hand, the emperor may have wished to accommodate Muslim sensitivities at a time when he was at war with the Arabs (Islam strictly forbade image worship). Be that as it may, the emperor's decree drove the popes into the camp of the Franks, where they found in Charlemagne an effective protector against the Byzantine world. (See page 000.) Although images were eventually restored in the Eastern churches, many masterpieces were lost during a near century of theology-inspired destruction.

A third difference between East and West was the Eastern emperors' pretension to absolute sovereignty, both secular and religious. Expressing their sense of sacred mission, the emperors presented themselves in the trappings of holiness and directly interfered in matters of church and religion, what is called **Caesaropapism**, or the emperor acting as if he were pope as well as caesar. To a degree unknown in the West, Eastern emperors appointed and manipulated the clergy, convening church councils and enforcing church decrees. By comparison, the West nurtured a distinction between church and state that became visible in the eleventh century.

The Eastern church also rejected several disputed requirements of Roman Christianity. It denied the existence of Purgatory, permitted lay divorce and remarriage, allowed priests, but not bishops, to marry, and conducted religious services in the languages that people in a given locality actually spoke (the so-called "vernacular" languages) instead of Greek and Latin. In these matters Eastern Christians gained opportunities and rights that Christians in the West would not enjoy, and then only in part, until the Protestant Reformation in the sixteenth century. (See Chapter 11.)

Having piled up over the centuries, these various differences ultimately resulted in a schism between the two churches in 1054. In that year a Western envoy of the pope, Cardinal Humbertus, visited the Patriarch of Constantinople, Michael Cerularius, in the hope of overcoming the differences that divided Christendom. The patriarch was not, however, welcoming. Relations between the two men quickly deteriorated, and cardinal and patriarch engaged in mutual recriminations and insults. Before leaving the city, Humbertus left a bull of excommunication on the altar of Hagia Sophia. In response, the patriarch proclaimed all Western popes to have been heretics since the sixth century! Nine hundred and eleven years would pass before this breach was repaired. In a belated ecumenical gesture in 1965, a Roman pope met with the patriarch of Constantinople to revoke the mutual condemnations of 1054.

▼ The Kingdom of the Franks: From Clovis to Charlemagne

A warrior chieftain, Clovis (ca. 466–511), who converted to Catholic Christianity around 496, founded the first Frankish dynasty, the Merovingians, named for Merovich, an early leader of one branch of the Franks. Clovis and his successors united the Salian and Ripuarian Franks, subdued the Arian Burgundians and Visigoths, and established the kingdom of the Franks within ancient Gaul, making the Franks and the Merovingian kings a significant force in Western Europe. The Franks themselves occupied a broad belt of territory that extended throughout modern France, Belgium, the Netherlands, and western Germany, and their loyalties remained strictly tribal and local.

Governing the Franks

In attempting to govern this sprawling kingdom, the Merovingians encountered what proved to be the most persistent problem of medieval political history—the competing claims of the "one" and the "many." On the one hand, the king struggled for a centralized government and transregional loyalty, and on the other, powerful local magnates strove to preserve their regional autonomy and traditions.

The Merovingian kings addressed this problem by making pacts with the landed nobility and by creating the royal office of counts. The counts were men without possessions to whom the king gave great lands in the expectation that they would be, as the landed aristocrats often were not, loyal officers of the kingdom. Like local aristocrats, however, the Merovingian counts also let their immediate self-interest gain the upper hand. Once established in office for a period of time, they, too, became territorial rulers in their own right, so the

Frankish kingdom progressively fragmented into independent regions and tiny principalities. The Frankish custom of dividing the kingdom equally among the king's legitimate male heirs furthered this tendency.

Rather than purchasing allegiance and unity within the kingdom, the Merovingian largess simply occasioned the rise of competing magnates and petty tyrants, who became laws unto themselves within their regions. By the seventh century, the Frankish king was king in title only and had no effective executive power. Real power came to be concentrated in the office of the "mayor of the palace," spokesperson at the king's court for the great landowners of the three regions into which the Frankish kingdom was divided: Neustria, Austrasia, and Burgundy. Through this office, the Carolingian dynasty rose to power.

The Carolingians controlled the office of the mayor of the palace from the ascent to that post of Pepin I of Austrasia (d. 639) until 751, when, with the enterprising connivance of the pope, they simply seized the Frankish crown. Pepin II (d. 714) ruled in fact, if not in title, over the Frankish kingdom. His illegitimate son, Charles Martel ("the Hammer," d. 741), created a great cavalry by bestowing lands known as **benefices**, or **fiefs**, on powerful noblemen. In return, they agreed to be ready to serve as the king's army. It was such an army that defeated the Muslims at Poitiers in 732.

MAJOR POLITICAL AND RELIGIOUS DEVELOPMENTS OF THE EARLY MIDDLE AGES

313	Emperor Constantine issues the Edict of Milan
325	Council of Nicaea defines Christian doctrine
451	Council of Chalcedon further defines Christian doctrine
451–453	Europe invaded by the Huns under Attila
476	Odovacer deposes Western emperor and rules as king of the Romans
489–493	Theodoric establishes kingdom of Ostrogoths in Italy
529	Benedict founds monastery at Monte Cassino
533	Justinian codifies Roman law
533–554	Byzantines reconquer parts of the Western Empire
622	Muhammad's flight from Mecca (Hegira)
711	Muslim invasion of Spain
732	Charles Martel defeats Muslims at Poitiers
754	Pope Stephen II and Pepin III ally

The fiefs so generously bestowed by Charles Martel to create his army came in large part from landed property he usurped from the church. His alliance with the landed aristocracy in this grand manner permitted the Carolingians to have some measure of political success where the Merovingians had failed. The Carolingians created counts almost entirely from among the same landed nobility from which the Carolingians themselves had risen. The Merovingians, in contrast, had tried to compete directly with these great aristocrats by raising landless men to power. By playing to strength rather than challenging it, the Carolingians strengthened themselves, at least for the short term. The church, by this time dependent on the protection of the Franks against the Eastern emperor and the Lombards, could only suffer the loss of its lands in silence. Later, although they never returned them, the Franks partially compensated the church for these lands.

The Frankish Church The church came to play a large and enterprising role in the Frankish government. By Carolingian times, monasteries were a dominant force. Their intellectual achievements made them respected centers of culture. Their religious teaching and example imposed order on surrounding populations. Their relics and rituals made them magical shrines to which pilgrims came in great numbers. Also, thanks to their many gifts and internal discipline and industry, many had become profitable farms and landed estates, their abbots rich and powerful magnates. Already in Merovingian times, the higher clergy were employed along with counts as royal agents.

It was the policy of the Carolingians, perfected by Charles Martel and his successor, Pepin III ("the Short," d. 768), to use the church to pacify conquered neighboring tribes—Frisians, Thüringians, Bavarians, and especially the Franks' archenemies, the Saxons. Conversion to Nicene Christianity became an integral part of the successful annexation of conquered lands and people. The cavalry broke their bodies while the clergy won their hearts and minds. The Anglo-Saxon missionary Saint Boniface (born Wynfrith; 680?–754) was the most important cleric to serve Carolingian kings in this way. Christian bishops in missionary districts and elsewhere became lords, appointed by and subject to the king. In this ominous integration of secular and religious policy lay the seeds of the later investiture controversy of the eleventh and twelfth centuries. (See Chapter 7.)

The church served more than Carolingian territorial expansion. Pope Zacharias (r. 741–752) also sanctioned Pepin the Short's termination of the Merovingian dynasty and supported the Carolingian accession to outright kingship of the Franks. With the pope's public blessing, Pepin was proclaimed king by the nobility in council in 751; the last of the Merovingians, the puppet king Childeric III, was hustled off to a monastery and dynastic oblivion. According to legend, Saint Boniface first anointed Pepin, thereby investing Frankish rule from the start with a certain holiness.

Zacharias's successor, Pope Stephen II (r. 752–757), did not let Pepin forget the favor of his predecessor. In 753, when the Lombards besieged Rome, Pope Stephen crossed the Alps and appealed directly to Pepin to cast out the invaders and to guarantee papal claims to central Italy, largely dominated at this time by the Eastern emperor. As already noted, in 754 during the controversy over icons, the Franks and the church formed an alliance against the Lombards and the Eastern emperor. Carolingian kings became the protectors of the Catholic Church and thereby "kings by the grace of God." Pepin gained the title *patricius Romanorum,* "patrician of the Romans," a title first borne by the ruling families of Rome and heretofore applied to the representative of the Eastern emperor. In 755, the Franks defeated the Lombards and gave the pope the lands surrounding Rome, creating what came to be known as the **Papal States**.

In this period a fraudulent document appeared—the *Donation of Constantine* (written between 750 and 800)—that was enterprisingly designed to remind the Franks of the church's importance as the heir of Rome. Many believed it to be genuine until it was definitely exposed as a forgery in the fifteenth century by the humanist Lorenzo Valla. (See Chapter 10.)

The papacy had looked to the Franks for an ally strong enough to protect it from the Eastern emperors. It is an irony of history that the church found in the Carolingian dynasty a Western imperial government that drew almost as slight a boundary between state and church and between secular and religious policy as did Eastern emperors. Although Carolingian patronage was eminently preferable to Eastern domination for the popes, it proved in its own way to be no less constraining.

Interior of the Palace Chapel of Charlemagne, Aachen. French Government Tourist Office

The Reign of Charlemagne (768–814)

Charlemagne, the son of Pepin the Short, continued the role of his father as papal protector in Italy and his policy of territorial conquest in the north. After decisively defeating King Desiderius and the Lombards of northern Italy in 774, Charlemagne took upon himself the title "King of the Lombards." He widened the frontiers of his kingdom further by subjugating surrounding pagan tribes, foremost among them the Saxons, whom the Franks brutally Christianized and dispersed in small groups throughout Frankish lands. The Muslims were chased beyond the Pyrenees, and the Avars (a tribe related to the Huns) were practically annihilated, bringing the Danubian plains into the Frankish orbit.

By the time of his death on January 28, 814, Charlemagne's kingdom embraced modern France, Belgium, Holland, Switzerland, almost the whole of western Germany, much of Italy, a portion of Spain, and the island of Corsica. (See Map 6–4, on page 190.)

The New Empire Encouraged by his ambitious advisers, Charlemagne came to harbor imperial designs. He desired to be not only king of all the Franks but a universal emperor as well. He had his sacred palace city, Aachen (in French, Aix-la-Chapelle) near the modern border between Germany and France, constructed in imitation of the courts of the ancient Roman and contemporary Eastern emperors. Although he permitted the church its independence, he looked after it with a

Map 6–4 **THE EMPIRE OF CHARLEMAGNE TO 814** Building on the successes of his predecessors, Charlemagne greatly increased the Frankish domains. Such traditional enemies as the Saxons and the Lombards fell under his sway.

paternalism almost as great as that of any Eastern emperor. He used the church, above all, to promote social stability and hierarchical order throughout the kingdom—as an aid in the creation of a great Frankish Christian Empire. Frankish Christians were ceremoniously baptized, professed the Nicene Creed (with the *filioque* clause), and learned in church to revere Charlemagne.

The formation of a distinctive Carolingian Christendom was made clear in the 790s, when Charlemagne issued the so-called *Libri Carolini.* These documents attacked the Second Council of Nicaea, which, in what was actually a friendly gesture to the West, had met in 787 to formulate a new, more accommodating position for the Eastern church on the use of images. "No compromise" was Charlemagne's message to the East.

Charlemagne fulfilled his imperial pretensions on Christmas Day, 800, when Pope Leo III (r. 795–816) crowned him emperor in Rome. This event began what would come to be known as the **Holy Roman Empire**, a revival of the old Roman Empire in the West, based in Germany after 870.

In 799, Pope Leo III had been imprisoned by the Roman aristocracy but escaped to the protection of Charlemagne, who restored him as pope. The fateful coronation of Charlemagne was thus, in part, an effort by the pope to enhance the church's stature and to gain some leverage over this powerful king. It was, however, no papal **coup d'état**; Charlemagne's control over the church remained as strong after as before the event. If the coronation benefited the church, as it certainly did, it also served Charlemagne's purposes.

Before his coronation, Charlemagne had been a minor Western potentate in the eyes of Eastern emperors. After the coronation, Eastern emperors reluctantly recognized his new imperial dignity, and Charlemagne even found it necessary to disclaim ambitions to rule as emperor over the East.

The New Emperor Charlemagne stood a majestic six feet three and a half inches tall—a fact confirmed when his tomb was opened and exact measurements of his remains were taken in 1861. He was restless, ever ready for a hunt. Informal and gregarious, he insisted on the presence of friends even when he bathed. He was widely known for his practical jokes, lusty good humor, and warm hospitality. Aachen was a festive palace city to which people and gifts came from all over the world. In 802, Charlemagne even received from the caliph of Baghdad, Harun-al-Rashid, a white elephant, whose transport across the Alps was as great a wonder as the creature itself.

Charlemagne had five official wives in succession, as well as many mistresses and concubines, and he sired numerous children. This connubial variety created special problems. His oldest son by his first marriage, Pepin, jealous of the attention shown by his father to the sons of his second wife and fearing the loss of paternal favor, joined noble enemies in a conspiracy against his father. He spent the rest of his life in confinement in a monastery after the plot was exposed.

Problems of Government Charlemagne governed his kingdom through counts, of whom there were perhaps as many as 250, strategically located within the administrative districts into which the kingdom was divided. Carolingian counts tended to be local magnates who possessed the armed might and the self-interest to enforce the will of a generous king. Counts had three main duties: to maintain a local army loyal to the king, to collect tribute and dues, and to administer justice throughout their districts.

This last responsibility a count undertook through a district law court known as the *mallus.* The *mallus* received testimony from witnesses familiar with the parties involved in a dispute or criminal case, much as a modern court does. Through such testimony, it sought to discover the character and believability of each side. On occasion, in difficult cases where the testimony was insufficient to determine guilt or innocence, recourse would be taken to judicial duels or to a variety of "divine" tests or ordeals. Among these was the length of time it took a defendant's hand to heal after immersion in boiling water. In another, a defendant was thrown with his hands and feet bound into a river or pond that a priest had blessed. If he floated, he was pronounced guilty, because the pure water had obviously rejected him; if, however, the water received him and he sank, he was deemed innocent and quickly retrieved.

In such ordeals God was believed to render a verdict. Once guilt had been made clear to the *mallus,* either by testimony or by ordeal, it assessed a monetary compensation to be paid to the injured party. This most popular way of settling grievances usually ended hostilities between individuals and families.

As in Merovingian times, many counts used their official position and new judicial powers to their own advantage and became little despots within their districts. As the strong became stronger, they also became more independent. They began to look on the land grants with which they were paid as hereditary possessions rather than generous royal donations—a development that began to fragment Charlemagne's kingdom. Charlemagne tried to oversee his overseers and improve local justice by creating special royal envoys. Known as ***missi dominici***, these were lay and clerical agents (counts, archbishops, and bishops) who made annual visits to districts other than their own. Yet their impact was marginal. Permanent provincial governors, bearing the title of prefect, duke, or margrave, were created in what was still another attempt to supervise the counts and organize the outlying regions of the kingdom. Yet as these governors became established in their areas, they proved no less corruptible than the others.

Charlemagne never solved the problem of creating a loyal bureaucracy. Ecclesiastical agents proved no better than secular ones in this regard. Landowning bishops had not only the same responsibilities, but also the same secular lifestyles and aspirations as the royal counts. Save for their attendance to the liturgy and to church prayers, they were largely indistinguishable from the lay nobility. *Capitularies,* or royal decrees, discouraged the more outrageous behavior of the clergy. However, Charlemagne also sensed, and rightly so as the Gregorian reform of the eleventh century would prove, that the emergence of a distinctive, reform-minded class of ecclesiastical landowners would be a danger to royal government. He purposefully treated his bishops as he treated his counts, that is, as vassals who served at the king's pleasure.

To be a Christian in this period was more a matter of ritual and doctrine (being baptized and reciting the creed) than of following rules for ethical behavior and social service. Both clergy and laity were more concerned with contests over the most basic kinds of social protections than with more elevated ethical issues. An important legislative achievement of Charlemagne's reign, for example, was to give a free vassal the right to break his oath of loyalty to his lord if the lord tried to kill him, reduce him to an unfree serf, withhold promised protection in time of need, or seduce his wife.

Alcuin and the Carolingian Renaissance Charlemagne accumulated great wealth in the form of loot and land from conquered tribes. He used part of this booty to attract Europe's best scholars to Aachen, where they developed court culture and education. By making scholarship materially as well as intellectually rewarding, Charlemagne attracted such scholars as Theodulf of Orleans, Angilbert, his own biographer Einhard, and the renowned Anglo-Saxon master Alcuin of York

(735–804). In 782, at almost fifty years of age, Alcuin became director of the king's palace school. He brought classical and Christian learning to Aachen in schools run by the monasteries. Alcuin was handsomely rewarded for his efforts with several monastic estates, including that of Saint Martin of Tours, the wealthiest in the kingdom.

Although Charlemagne also appreciated learning for its own sake, his grand palace school was not created simply for the love of classical scholarship. Charlemagne wanted to upgrade the administrative skills of the clerics and officials who staffed the royal bureaucracy. By preparing the sons of the nobility to run the religious and secular offices of the realm, court scholarship served kingdom building. The school provided basic instruction in the seven liberal arts, with special concentration on grammar, logic, rhetoric, and the basic mathematical arts. It therefore provided training in reading, writing, speaking, sound reasoning, and counting—the basic tools of bureaucracy.

Among the results of this intellectual activity was the appearance of a more accurate Latin in official documents and the development of a clear style of handwriting known as *Carolingian minuscule.* By making reading both easier and more pleasurable, Carolingian minuscule helped lay the foundations of subsequent Latin scholarship. It also increased lay literacy.

A modest renaissance of antiquity occurred in the palace school as scholars collected and preserved ancient manuscripts for a more curious posterity. Alcuin worked on a correct text of the Bible and made editions of the works of Gregory the Great and the monastic *Rule* of Saint Benedict. These scholarly activities aimed at concrete reforms and helped bring uniformity to church law and liturgy, educate the clergy, and improve monastic morals. Through personal correspondence and visitations, Alcuin created a genuine, if limited, community of scholars and clerics at court. He did much to infuse the highest administrative levels with a sense of comradeship and common purpose.

Breakup of the Carolingian Kingdom

In his last years, an ailing Charlemagne knew his empire was ungovernable. The seeds of dissolution lay in regionalism, that is, the determination of each region, no matter how small, to look first—and often only—to its own self-interest. Despite his skill and resolve, Charlemagne's realm became too fragmented among powerful regional magnates. Although they were his vassals, they were also landholders and lords in their own right. They knew their sovereignty lessened as Charlemagne's increased, and accordingly they became reluctant royal servants. In feudal society, a direct relationship existed between physical proximity to authority and loyalty to authority. Local people obeyed local lords more readily than they obeyed a glorious, but distant, king.

Charlemagne had been forced to recognize and even to enhance the power of regional magnates to gain needed financial and military support. But as in the Merovingian kingdom, the tail came increasingly also to wag the dog in the Carolingian.

Louis the Pious The Carolingian kings did not give up easily, however. Charlemagne's only surviving son and successor was Louis the Pious (r. 814–840), so-called because of his close alliance with the church and his promotion of puritanical reforms. Before his death, Charlemagne secured the imperial succession for Louis by raising him to "co-emperor" in a grand public ceremony. After Charlemagne's death, Louis no longer referred to himself as king of the Franks. He bore instead the single title of emperor. The assumption of this title reflected not only the Carolingian pretense to be an imperial dynasty, but also Louis's determination to unify his kingdom and raise its people above mere regional and tribal loyalties.

Unfortunately, Louis's own fertility joined with Salic, or Frankish, law and custom to prevent the attainment of this high goal. Louis had three sons by his first wife. According to Salic law, a ruler partitioned his kingdom equally among his surviving sons (Salic law forbade women to inherit the throne). Louis, who saw himself as an emperor and no mere king, recognized that a tripartite kingdom would hardly be an empire and acted early in his reign, in 817, to break this legal tradition. This he did by making his eldest son, Lothar (d. 855), co-regent and sole imperial heir by royal decree. To Lothar's brothers he gave important, but much lesser, *appanages*, or assigned hereditary lands; Pepin (d. 838) became king of Aquitaine, and Louis "the German" (d. 876) became king of Bavaria, over the eastern Franks.

In 823, Louis's second wife, Judith of Bavaria, bore him a fourth son, Charles, later called "the Bald" (d. 877). Mindful of Frankish law and custom, and determined her son should receive more than just a nominal inheritance, the queen incited the brothers Pepin and Louis against Lothar, who fled for refuge to the pope. More important, Judith was instrumental in persuading Louis to adhere to tradition and divide the kingdom equally among his four living sons. As their stepmother and the young Charles rose in their father's favor, the three brothers, fearing still further reversals, decided to act against their father. Supported by the pope, they joined forces and defeated their father in a battle near Colmar in 833.

As the bestower of crowns on emperors, the pope had an important stake in the preservation of the revived Western empire and the imperial title. Louis's belated agreement to an equal partition of his kingdom threatened to weaken the pope as well as the royal family. Therefore, the pope condemned Louis and restored Lothar to his original inheritance. But Lothar's regained

A Closer LOOK

A MULTICULTURAL BOOK COVER

CAROLINGIAN EDUCATION, ART, and architecture served royal efforts to unify the kingdom by fusing inherited Celtic-Germanic and Greco-Roman-Byzantine cultures. Charlemagne, his son, and grandsons decorated their churches with a variety of art forms, among them illuminated manuscripts, such as the bejeweled metalwork that became the binding of the *Lindau Gospels* (c. 870).

Art Resource/The Pierpont Morgan Library

Precious stones are set on tiny pedestals to maximize the luster illuminating the crucified Christ from the gold background.

The Christ seen here reflects early Christian art and Byzantine theology, which did not endow divinity with human suffering. So impassive is this Christ that he seems almost to smile on the cross. However, the surrounding panels show the angels in heaven and Christ's followers on earth writhing with grief.

To examine this image in an interactive fashion, please go to www.myhistorylab.com

imperial dignity only stirred anew the resentments of his brothers, including his stepbrother, Charles, who joined in renewed warfare against him.

The Treaty of Verdun and Its Aftermath In 843, with the Treaty of Verdun, peace finally came to the surviving heirs of Louis the Pious. (Pepin had died in 838.) But this agreement also brought about the disaster that Louis had originally feared. The great Carolingian Empire was divided into three equal parts. Lothar received a middle section, known as Lotharingia, which embraced roughly modern Holland, Belgium, Switzerland, Alsace-Lorraine, and Italy. Charles the Bald acquired the western part of the kingdom, or roughly modern France. And Louis the German took the eastern part, or roughly modern Germany. (See Map 6–5.)

Although Lothar retained the imperial title, the universal empire of Charlemagne and Louis the Pious ceased to exist after Verdun. Not until the sixteenth century, with the election in 1519 of Charles I of Spain as Holy Roman Emperor Charles V (see Chapter 11), would the Western world again see a kingdom as vast as Charlemagne's.

The Treaty of Verdun proved to be only the beginning of Carolingian fragmentation. When Lothar died in 855, his middle kingdom was divided equally among his three surviving sons, the eldest of whom, Louis II, retained Italy and the imperial title. This partition of the partition sealed the dissolution of the great empire of Charlemagne. Henceforth, Western Europe saw an eastern and a western Frankish kingdom—roughly Germany and France—at war over parts of the middle kingdom, a contest that continued into modern times.

In Italy the demise of the Carolingian emperors enhanced for the moment the power of the popes, who had become adept at filling vacuums. The popes were now strong enough to excommunicate weak emperors and override their wishes. In a major church crackdown on the polygyny of the Germans, Pope Nicholas I (r. 858–867) excommunicated Lothar II for divorcing his wife. After the death of the childless emperor Louis II in 875, Pope John VIII (r. 872–882) installed Charles the Bald as emperor against the express last wishes of Louis II.

When Charles the Bald died in 877, both the papal and the imperial thrones suffered defeat. They became pawns in the hands of powerful Italian and German magnates, respectively. The last Carolingian emperor died in 911. This internal political breakdown of the empire and the papacy coincided with new barbarian attacks. Neither pope nor emperor knew dignity and power again until a new Western imperial dynasty—the Saxons—attained dominance during the reign of Otto I (r. 962–973).

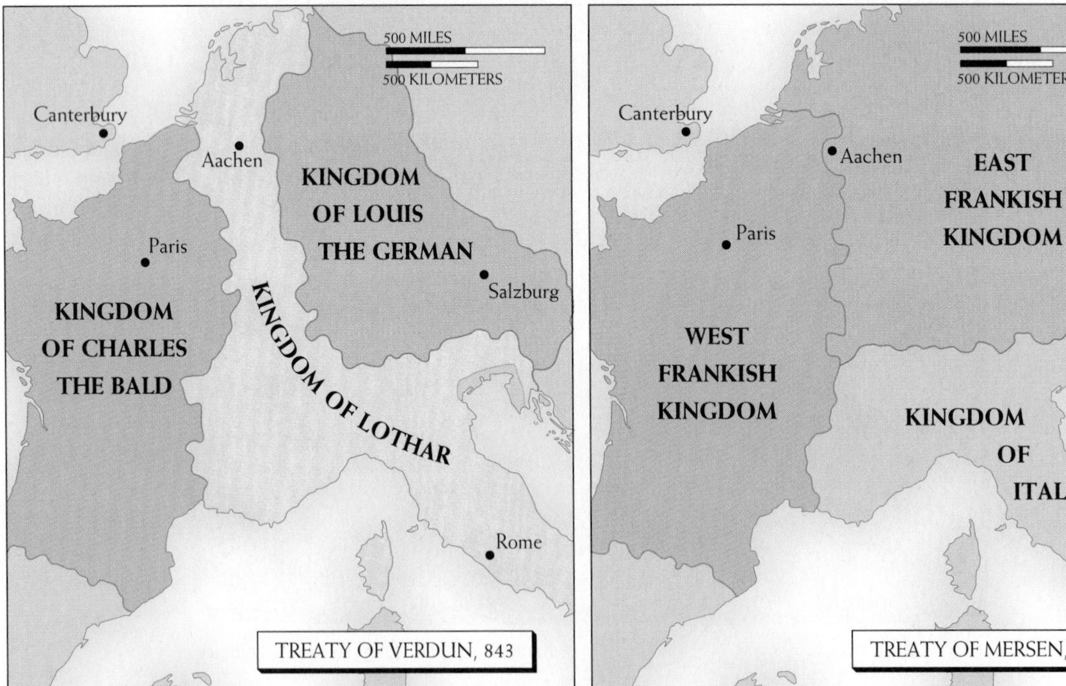

Map 6–5 **THE TREATY OF VERDUN, 843, AND THE TREATY OF MERSEN, 870** The Treaty of Verdun divided the kingdom of Louis the Pious among his three feuding children: Charles the Bald, Lothar, and Louis the German. After Lothar's death in 855, his lands and titles were divided among his three sons: Louis, Charles, and Lothar II. When Lothar II, who had received his father's northern kingdom, died in 870, Charles the Bald and Louis the German claimed the middle kingdom and divided it between themselves in the Treaty of Mersen.

Vikings, Magyars, and Muslims It is especially at this juncture in European history—the last quarter of the ninth and the first half of the tenth century—that we may speak with some justification of a "dark age." The late ninth and tenth centuries saw successive waves of Normans (North-men), better known as Vikings, from Scandinavia, **Magyars**, or Hungarians, the great horsemen from the eastern plains, and Muslims from the south. (See Map 6–6.) The political breakdown of the Carolingian Empire coincided with these new external threats, both probably set off by overpopulation and famine in northern and eastern Europe. The exploits of the Scandinavian peoples, or Vikings, who visited Europe, alternately as gregarious traders and savage raiders, have been preserved in Sagas and they reveal a cultural world filled with mythical gods and spirits. Taking to the sea in rugged longboats of doubled-hulled construction, they terrified their neighbors to the south, invading and occupying English and European coastal and river towns. In the 880s, the Vikings even penetrated to Aachen and besieged Paris.

In the ninth century, the Vikings turned York in northern England into a major trading post for their woolens, jewelry, and ornamental wares. Erik the Red made it to Greenland, and his son, Leif Erikson wintered in Newfoundland and may even have reached New England five hundred years before Columbus. In the eleventh century, Christian conversions and the English defeat of the Danes and Norwegians effectively restricted the Vikings to their Scandinavian homelands.

Magyars, the ancestors of the modern Hungarians, swept into Western Europe from the eastern plains, while Muslims made incursions across the Mediterranean from North Africa. The Franks built fortified towns and castles in strategic locations, and when they could, they bought off the invaders with grants of land and payments of silver. In the resulting turmoil, local populations became more dependent than ever on local strongmen for life, limb, and livelihood—the essential precondition for the maturation of feudal society.

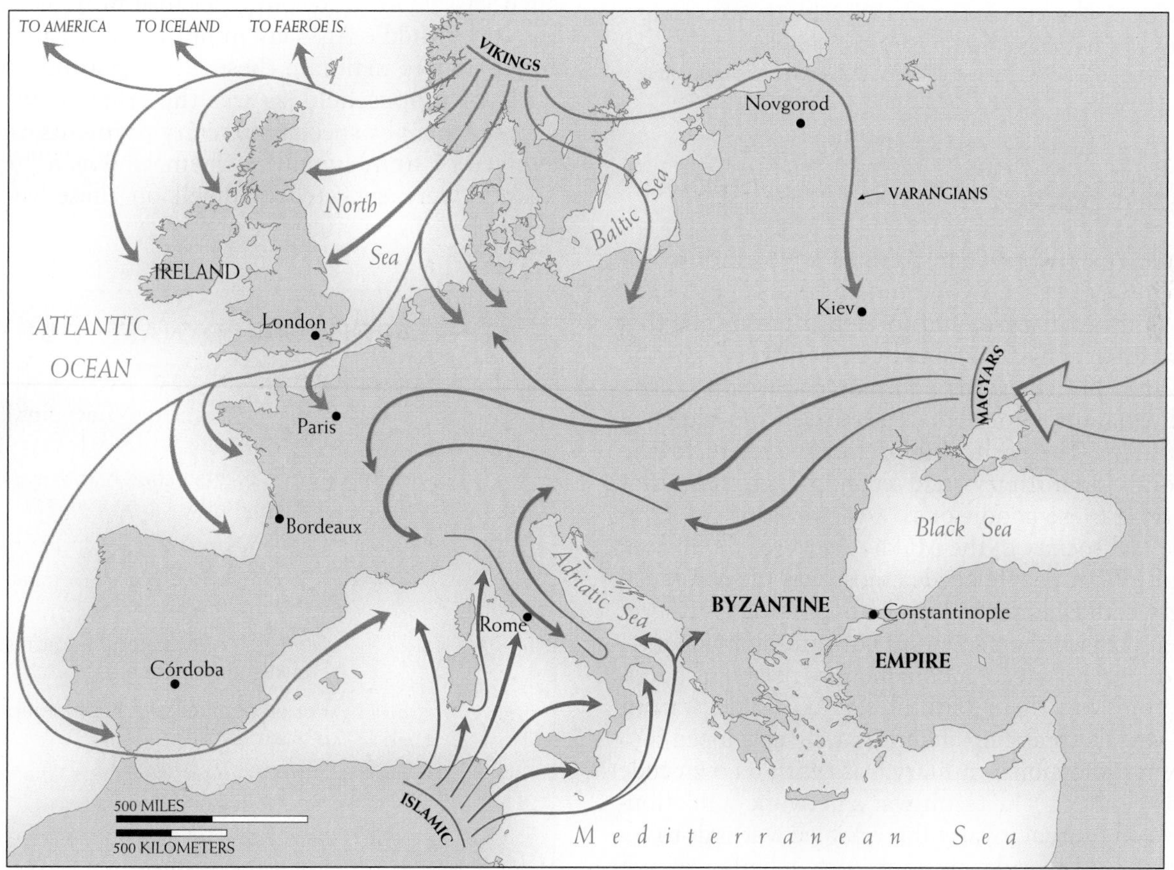

Map 6–6 **VIKING, ISLAMIC, AND MAGYAR INVASIONS TO THE ELEVENTH CENTURY** Western Europe was sorely beset by new waves of outsiders from the ninth to the eleventh centuries. From north, east, and south, a stream of invading Vikings, Magyars, and Muslims brought the West at times to near collapse and, of course, gravely affected institutions within Europe.

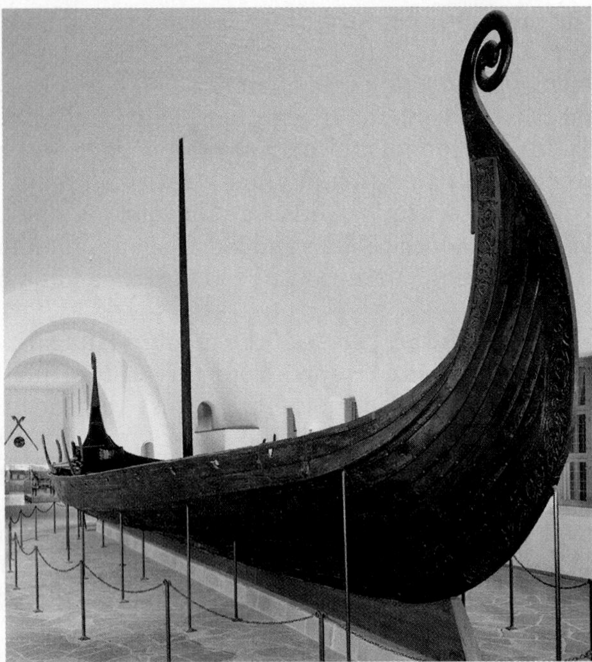

This seventy-five-foot-long Viking burial ship from the early ninth century is decorated with beastly figures. It bore a dead queen, her servant, and assorted sacrificed animals to the afterlife. The bodies of the passengers were confined within a burial cabin at mid-ship surrounded with a treasure trove of jewels and tapestries. Dorling Kindersley Media Library. Universitets Oldsaksamling © Dorling Kindersley

▼ Feudal Society

The Middle Ages were characterized by a chronic absence of effective central government and the constant threat of famine, disease, and foreign invasion. In this state of affairs, the weaker sought the protection of the stronger, and the true lords and masters became those who could guarantee immediate security from violence and starvation. The term ***feudal society*** refers to the social, political, military, and economic system that emerged from these conditions.

The feudal society of the Middle Ages was dominated by warlords. What people needed most was the assurance that others could be depended on in time of dire need. Lesser men pledged themselves to powerful individuals—warlords or princes—recognizing them as personal superiors and promising them faithful service. Large warrior groups of vassals sprang up and ultimately developed into a prominent professional military class with its own code of knightly conduct. The result was a network of relationships based on mutual loyalty that enabled warlords to acquire armies and to rule over territory, whether or not they owned land or had a royal title. The emergence of these extensive military organizations—warlords and their groups of professional military vassals—was an adaptation to the absence of strong central government and the predominance of a noncommercial, rural economy.

Origins

Following the modern authority on the subject, the late French historian Marc Bloch, historians distinguish the cruder forms of feudal government that evolved during the early Middle Ages from the sophisticated institutional arrangements by which princes and kings consolidated their territories and established royal rule during the High Middle Ages (the so-called second feudal age).

The origins of feudal government can be found in the divisions and conflicts of Merovingian society. In the sixth and seventh centuries, it became customary for individual freemen who did not already belong to families or groups that could protect them to place themselves under the protection of more powerful freemen. In this way the latter built up armies and became local magnates, and the former solved the problem of simple survival. Freemen who so entrusted themselves to others came to be described as **vassals**, *vassi* or "those who serve," from which evolved the term *vassalage,* meaning the placement of oneself in the personal service of another who promises protection in return.

Landed nobles, like kings, tried to acquire as many such vassals as they could, because military strength in the early Middle Ages lay in numbers. Because it proved impossible to maintain these growing armies within the lord's own household (as was the original custom) or to support them by special monetary payments, the practice evolved of simply granting them land as a "tenement." Vassals were expected to dwell on these *benefices,* or

THE CAROLINGIAN DYNASTY (751–987)

751	Pepin III "the Short" becomes king of the Franks
755	Franks protect church against Lombards and create the Papal States
768–814	Charlemagne rules as king of the Franks
774	Charlemagne defeats Lombards in northern Italy
ca. 775	*Donation of Constantine* protests Frankish domination of church
800	Pope Leo III crowns Charlemagne emperor
814–840	Louis the Pious succeeds Charlemagne as emperor
843	Treaty of Verdun partitions the Carolingian Empire
911	Death of last Carolingian emperor
962	Saxons under Otto I firmly established as successors to Carolingians in Germany

ENCOUNTERING THE *Past*

MEDIEVAL COOKING

THE MENUS OF medieval Europeans seem, at first glance, similar to those of modern Europeans. As early as the twelfth century, the Italians were stuffing pasta and calling it ravioli and the French and the English baking meat pies and custards. Yet much in the medieval kitchen would be bizarre to a modern diner.

First, the priorities of the medieval cook were not those of a modern chef. Both artist and scientist, the medieval cook worried more about being "humorally" correct than about cooking food that tasted good. Medieval medical theory traced illness to imbalances among the four bodily humors (blood, black bile, yellow bile, and phlegm), each of which was generated by digested food and believed to contribute heat and moisture to the body. For instance, an excess of blood (considered hot and wet) would lead to a sanguine, or hot and wet, illness, whereas an excess of black bile might cause cold and dry suffering. The medieval cook had to choose ingredients that would maintain proper temperature and moisture levels in the diner by balancing the amounts of humors digested food would produce. The bad cook was thus one whose food caused humoral excess and illness. The bad cook added piquant spices to a roasted meat, causing a feverish abundance of hot and dry bile, whereas the good cook modulated hot spices with cold and wet seasonings, such as rosewater, to keep bile levels acceptable.

The medieval cook also attempted to delight the eye with extravagant and whimsical presentations, a passion inherited from the Romans. A simple recipe might add unusual colorings to gruel; more complex ones aimed for the surprising and even grotesque. An egg custard, for example, might be shaped into a giant egg, or cooked pieces of a chicken might be stuffed back into the feathered skin from which they had come and sewn shut. The bird would then be presented to the admiring diners in its natural state. Although such masterpieces were more available to a rich man than to a poor laborer, the village festivals of the rural poor could also inspire cooks to displays of food artistry. These folksy attempts to dress up food often took on the tone of a practical joke: One cookbook suggested sprinkling an animal's dried blood over stewed meat to make the diner believe the meat was raw or maggoty.[4]

Another characteristic of the poor person's diet was the absence of vegetables. Medieval peasants prized meat so highly that they scorned the greens growing around them. Most Europeans seem to have survived on a diet of mush and bread porridge, whipped together by boiling bread or meal in milk and coloring it with saffron, supplemented by an occasional egg. When meat was available, the country cook typically chopped it up, encased it within a thick pastry shell, and baked it under coals. Here, all in one, was the forerunner of the modern oven, the antecedent of the dessert pie, and the ancestor of modern dumplings and stuffed pastas.

Sources: *Food in the Middle Ages: A Book of Essays,* ed. by Melitta Weiss Adamson (New York: Greenwood Press, 1995); *Regional Cuisines of Medieval Europe: A Book of Essays,* ed. by Melitta Weiss Adamson (New York: Routledge, 2002); Terrence Scully, *The Art of Cookery in the Middle Ages* (Woodbridge, England: Boydell Press, 1995).

How were bad medieval cooks believed to make a diner ill? Give three examples of how a good medieval chef might please the diner.

[Top] The Lord of the Manor Dining. [Bottom] Kitchen Scene; Chopping Meat. From *The Luttrell Psalter*, by permission of The British Library (1000102.021).

[4]Melitta Weiss Adamson, "The Games Cooks Play," in *Food in the Middle Ages,* (New York: Greenwood Press, 1995), p. 184.

fiefs, and maintain horses, armor, and weapons in good order. Originally, vassals therefore were little more than gangs-in-waiting.

Vassalage and the Fief

Vassalage involved "fealty" to the lord. To swear **fealty** was to promise to refrain from any action that might in any way threaten the lord's well-being and to perform personal services for him on his request. Chief among the expected services was military duty as a mounted knight. This could involve a variety of activities: a short or long military expedition, escort duty, standing castle guard, or placing his own fortress at the lord's disposal, if the vassal had one. Continuous bargaining and bickering occurred over the terms of service. Limitations were placed on the number of days a lord could require services from a vassal. In France in the eleventh century, about forty days of service a year were considered sufficient. It also became possible for vassals to buy their way out of military service by a monetary payment, known as **scutage**. The lord, in turn, could use this payment to hire mercenaries, who often proved more efficient than contract-conscious vassals.

Beyond military duty, the vassal was also expected to advise his lord upon request and to sit as a member of his court when it was in session. The vassal also owed his lord financial assistance when his lord was in obvious need or distress, for example, if he were captured and needed to be ransomed or when he was outfitting himself for a crusade or a major military campaign. Also, gifts of money might be expected when the lord's daughters married or when his sons became knights.

Beginning with the reign of Louis the Pious (r. 814–840), bishops and abbots swore fealty to the king and received their offices from him as a *benefice.* The king formally "invested" these clerics in their offices during a special ceremony in which he presented them with a ring and a staff, the symbols of high spiritual office. Earlier, Louis's Frankish predecessors had confiscated church lands with only modest and belated compensation to the church. This practice was long a sore point with the church, and lay investiture of the clergy provoked a serious confrontation of church and state in the late tenth and eleventh centuries. At that time, reform-minded clergy rebelled against what they then believed to be a kind of involuntary clerical vassalage. Even reform-minded clerics, however, welcomed the king's grants of land and power to the clergy.

The lord's obligations to his vassals were specific. First, he was obligated to protect the vassal from physical harm and to stand as his advocate in public court. After fealty was sworn and homage paid, the lord provided for the vassal's physical maintenance by the bestowal of a *benefice,* or fief. The fief was simply the physical or material wherewithal to meet the vassal's military and other obligations. It could take the form of liquid wealth, as well as the more common grant of real property. There were so-called money fiefs, which empowered a vassal to receive regular payments from the lord's treasury. Such fiefs created potential conflicts because they made it possible for a nobleman in one land to acquire vassals among the nobility in another. Normally, the fief consisted of a landed estate of anywhere from a few to several thousand acres. It could also take the form of a castle.

In Carolingian times a *benefice,* or fief, varied in size from one or more small villas to several *mansi,* agricultural holdings of twenty-five to forty-eight acres. The king's vassals are known to have received benefices of at least 30 and as many as 200 such *mansi,* truly a vast estate. Royal vassalage with a *benefice* understandably came to be widely sought by the highest classes of Carolingian society. As a royal policy, however, it ultimately proved deadly to the king. Although Carolingian kings jealously guarded their rights over property granted in *benefice* to vassals, resident vassals could dispose of their *benefices* as they pleased. Vassals of the king, strengthened by his donations, in turn created their own vassals. These, in turn, created still further vassals of their own—vassals of vassals of vassals—in a pyramiding effect that fragmented land and authority from the highest to the lowest levels by the late ninth century.

Daily Life and Religion

The Humble Carolingian Manor The agrarian economy of the early Middle Ages was organized and controlled through village farms known as **manors**. On these, peasants labored as tenants for a lord, that is, a more powerful landowner who allotted them land and tenements in exchange for their services and a portion of their crops. The part of the land tended for the lord was the ***demesne***, on average about one quarter to one third of the arable land. All crops grown there were harvested for the lord. The manor also included common meadows for grazing animals and forests reserved exclusively for the lord to hunt in.

Peasants were treated according to their personal status and the size of their tenements. A freeman, that is, a peasant with his own modest *allodial,* or hereditary property (property free from the claims of an overlord), became a serf by surrendering his property to a greater landowner—a lord—in exchange for protection and assistance. The freeman received his land back from the lord with a clear definition of his economic and legal rights. Although the land was no longer his property, he had full possession and use of it, and the number of services and amount of goods he was to supply to the lord were carefully spelled out.

Peasants who entered the service of a lord with little real property (perhaps only a few farm implements and animals) ended up as unfree serfs. Such serfs were far more vulnerable to the lord's demands, often spending up to three days a week working the lord's fields. Peasants who had nothing to offer a lord except their hands had the lowest status and were the least protected from excessive demands on their labor.

All classes of serfs were subject to various dues in kind: firewood in return for cutting the lord's wood, sheep for being allowed to graze their sheep on the lord's land, and the like. Thus the lord, who, for his part, furnished shacks and small plots of land from his vast domain, had at his disposal an army of servants of varying status who provided him with everything from eggs to boots. Weak serfs often fled to monasteries rather than continue their servitude. That many serfs were discontented is reflected in the high number of recorded escapes. An astrological calendar from the period even marks the days most favorable for escaping. Escaped serfs roamed as beggars and vagabonds, searching for better masters.

By the time of Charlemagne, the moldboard plow and the three-field system of land cultivation were coming into use. The **moldboard plow** cut deep into the soil, turning it to form a ridge, which provided a natural drainage system and permitted the deep planting of seeds. This made cultivation possible in the regions north of the Mediterranean, where soils were dense and waterlogged from heavy precipitation. The **three-field system** alternated fallow with planted fields each year, and this increased the amount of cultivated land by leaving only one third fallow in a given year. It also better adjusted crops to seasons. In fall, one field was planted with winter crops of wheat or rye, to be harvested in early summer. In late spring, a second field was planted with summer crops of oats, barley, and beans. The third field was left fallow, to be planted in its turn with winter and summer crops. The new summer crops, especially beans, restored nitrogen to the soil and helped increase yields. (See "Encountering the Past: Medieval Cooking," page 197.)

These developments made possible what has been called the "expansion of Europe within Europe." They permitted the old lands formerly occupied by barbarians to be cultivated and filled with farms and towns. This, in turn, led to major population growth in the north and ultimately a shift of political power from the Mediterranean to northern Europe.

The Cure of Carolingian Souls The lower clergy lived among, and were drawn from, peasant ranks. They fared hardly better than peasants in Carolingian times. As owners of the churches on their lands, the lords had the right to raise chosen serfs to the post of parish priest, placing them in charge of the churches on the lords' estates. Church law directed a lord to set a serf free before he entered the clergy. Lords, however, were reluctant to do this and risk thereby a possible later challenge to their jurisdiction over the ecclesiastical property with which the serf, as priest, was invested. Lords preferred a "serf priest," one who not only said the Mass on Sundays and holidays, but who also continued to serve his lord during the week, waiting on the lord's table and tending his steeds. Like Charlemagne with his bishops, Frankish lords cultivated a docile parish clergy.

The ordinary people looked to religion for comfort and consolation. They especially associated religion with the major Christian holidays and festivals, such as Christmas and Easter. They baptized their children, attended mass, tried to learn the Lord's Prayer and the Apostles' Creed, and received the last rites from the priest as death approached. This was all probably done with more awe and simple faith than understanding. Because local priests on the manors were no better educated than their congregations, religious instruction in the meaning of Christian doctrine and practice remained at a bare minimum. The church sponsored street dramas in accordance with the church calendar. These were designed to teach onlookers the highlights of the Bible and church history and to instill basic Christian moral values.

People understandably became particularly attached in this period to the more tangible veneration of saints and relics. The Virgin Mary was also widely revered, although a true cult of Mary would not develop until the eleventh and twelfth centuries. Religious devotion to saints has been compared to subjection to powerful lords in the secular world. Both the saint and the lord were protectors whose honor the serfs were bound to defend and whose help in time of need they hoped to receive. Veneration of saints was also rooted in old tribal customs, to which the common folk were still attached. Indeed, Charlemagne enforced laws against witchcraft, sorcery, and the ritual sacrifice of animals by monks.

But religion also had an intrinsic appeal and special meaning to the masses of medieval men and women who found themselves burdened, fearful, and with little hope of material betterment on this side of eternity. Charlemagne shared many of the religious beliefs of his ordinary subjects. He collected and venerated relics, made pilgrimages to Rome, and frequented the Church of Saint Mary in Aachen several times a day. In his last will and testament, he directed that all but a fraction of his great treasure be spent to endow masses and prayers for his departed soul.

Fragmentation and Divided Loyalty

In addition to the fragmentation brought about by the multiplication of vassalage, effective occupation of land led gradually to claims of hereditary possession. Hereditary possession became a legally recognized principle in the ninth century and laid the basis for claims to real ownership. Fiefs given as royal donations became hereditary possessions and, over time, sometimes even the real property of the possessor.

Further, vassal obligations increased in still another way as enterprising freemen sought to accumulate as much land as possible. One man could become a vassal to several different lords. This development led in the ninth century to the "liege lord"—the one master the vassal must obey even against his other masters, should a direct conflict arise among them.

The problem of loyalty was reflected both in the literature of the period, with its praise of the virtues of honor and fidelity and in the ceremonial development of the very act of commendation by which a freeman became a vassal. In the mid-eighth century, an oath of fealty highlighted the ceremony. A vassal reinforced his promise of fidelity to the lord by swearing a special oath with his hand on a sacred relic or the Bible. In the tenth and eleventh centuries, paying homage to the lord involved not only swearing such an oath, but also placing the vassal's hands between the lord's and sealing the ceremony with a kiss.

As the centuries passed, personal loyalty and service became secondary to the acquisition of property. In developments that signaled the waning of feudal society in the tenth century, the fief came to overshadow fealty, the *benefice* became more important than vassalage, and freemen would swear allegiance to the highest bidder.

Feudal arrangements nonetheless provided stability throughout the early Middle Ages and aided the difficult process of political centralization during the High Middle Ages (c. 1000–1300). The genius of feudal government lay in its adaptability. Contracts of different kinds could be made with almost anybody, as circumstances required. The process embraced a wide spectrum of people, from the king at the top to the lowliest vassal in the remotest part of the kingdom. The foundations of the modern nation-state would emerge in France and England from the fine tuning of essentially feudal arrangements as kings sought to adapt their goal of centralized government to the reality of local power and control.

In Perspective

The centuries between 476 and 1000 saw both the decline of classical civilization and the birth of a new European civilization in the regions of what had been the Western Roman Empire. Beginning in the fifth century, barbarian invasions separated Western Europe culturally from much of its classical past. Although some important works and concepts survived from antiquity and the Church preserved major features of Roman government, the West would be recovering its classical heritage for centuries in "renaissances" that stretched into the sixteenth century. Out of the mixture of barbarian and surviving or recovered classical culture, a distinct Western culture was born. Aided and abetted by the Church, the Franks created a new imperial tradition and shaped basic Western political and social institutions for centuries to come.

The early Middle Ages also saw the emergence of a rift between Eastern and Western Christianity. Evolving from the initial division of the Roman Empire into eastern and western parts, this rift resulted in bitter conflict between popes and patriarchs.

During this period, the capital of the Byzantine Empire, Constantinople, far exceeded in population and culture any city of the West. Serving both as a buffer against Persian, Arab, and Turkish invasions of the West and as a major repository of classical learning and science for Western scholars, the Byzantine Empire did much to make possible the development of Western Europe as a distinctive political and cultural entity. Another cultural and religious rival of the West, Islam, also saw its golden age during these same centuries. Like the Byzantine world, the Muslim world preserved ancient scholarship and, especially through Muslim Spain, retransmitted it to the West. But despite examples of coexistence and even friendship, the cultures of the Western and Muslim worlds were too different and their people too estranged and suspicious of one another for them to become good neighbors.

The early Middle Ages were not centuries of great ambition in the West. It was a time when modest foundations were laid. Despite a semicommon religious culture, Western society remained more primitive and fragmented than probably anywhere else in the contemporary world. Two distinctive social institutions developed in response to these conditions: the manor and feudal bonds. The manor ensured that all would be fed and cared for; feudal bonds provided protection from outside predators. Western people were concerned primarily to satisfy basic needs; great cultural ambition would come later.

Review Questions

1. What role did the church play in the West after the fall of the Roman Empire? Why did Christianity split into Eastern and Western branches?
2. What role did the nobility play during Charlemagne's rule? Why did Charlemagne encourage learning at his court? How could the Carolingian renaissance have been dangerous to Charlemagne's rule? Why did his empire break apart?
3. How and why was the history of the eastern half of the Roman empire so different from that of the western half? What role did emperors play in the Eastern Church?
4. What were the tenets of Islam, and how were the Muslims suddenly able to build an empire? How did Islamic civilization influence Western Europe?
5. How and why did feudal society begin? What were the essential ingredients of feudalism? How easy do you think it would be for modern society to slip back into a feudal pattern?

SUGGESTED READINGS

K. Armstrong, *Muhammad: A Biography of the Prophet* (1992). Substantial popular biography.

G. Barraclough, *The Origins of Modern Germany* (1963). Originally published in 1946 and still the best survey of medieval Germany.

R. Bartlett, *The Making of Europe* (1993). How migration and colonization created Europe.

G. W. Bowersock et al., *Interpreting Late Antiquity: Essays on the Postclassical World* (2001). Introductory essays presenting a unified interpretation of the centuries between 250 C.E. and 800 C.E.

P. Brown, *Augustine of Hippo: A Biography* (1967). Late antiquity seen through the biography of its greatest Christian thinker.

P. Brown et al. (eds.), *The Rise of Western Christendom: Triumph and Diversity* (1997). Sweeping, detailed summary.

Virginia Burrus, ed., *A Peoples' History of Christianity, II* (2005). Substantial and accessible.

R. Collins, *Charlemagne* (1998). Latest biography.

J. W. Currier, *Clovis, King of the Franks* (1997). Biography of founder of first Frankish dynasty.

F. L. Ganshof, *Feudalism* (1964). The most profound brief analysis of the subject.

P. Godman et al., eds., *Charlemagne's Heir: New Perspectives on Louis the Pious (814–40)* (1990). Latest research on the king whose divided kingdom set the boundaries of modern Europe.

S. Guthrie, *Arab Social Life in the Middle Ages* (1995). How Arab society holds itself together.

A. Hourani, *A History of the Arab Peoples* (1991). Comprehensive with overviews of the origins and early history of Islam.

B. Lewis, *The Middle East: A Brief History of the Last 2,000 Years* (1995). An authoritative overview.

R. McKitterick, ed., *Carolingian Culture: Emulation and Innovation* (1994). The culture from which western Europe was born.

R. J. Morrissey, *Charlemagne and France: A 1000 Years of Mythology* (2002). The European argument over who owns Charlemagne.

P. Riche, *The Carolingians: A Family Who Forged Europe* (1993). Readable account of the dynasty from start to finish.

P. Sawyer, *Kings and Vikings: Scandinavia and Europe A.D. 700–1100* (1994). Raiding Vikings and their impact on Europe.

W. Walther, *Woman in Islam* (1981). One hour spent with this book teaches more about the social import of Islam than days spent with others.

For additional learning resources related to this chapter, please go to www.myhistorylab.com

PEARSON myhistorylab

In medieval Europe, the traditional geocentric or earth-centered universe was usually depicted by concentric circles. In this popular German work on natural history, medicine, and science, Konrad von Megenberg (1309–1374) depicted the universe in a most unusual but effective manner. The seven known planets are contained within straight horizontal bands that separate the earth, below, from heaven, populated by the saints, above. Konrad von Megenberg. *Buch der Natur* (Book of Nature). Augsburg: Johannes Bämler, 1481. Rosenwald Collection. Courtesy of the Library of Congress. Rare Book and Special Collections Division.

7

The High Middle Ages: The Rise of European Empires and States (1000–1300)

▼ **Otto I and the Revival of the Empire**
Unifying Germany • Embracing the Church

▼ **The Reviving Catholic Church**
The Cluny Reform Movement • The Investiture Struggle: Gregory VII and Henry IV • The Crusades • The Pontificate of Innocent III (r. 1198–1216)

▼ **England and France: Hastings (1066) to Bouvines (1214)**
William the Conqueror • Henry II • Eleanor of Aquitaine and Court Culture • Popular Rebellion and Magna Carta • Philip II Augustus

▼ **France in the Thirteenth Century: The Reign of Louis IX**
Generosity Abroad • Order and Excellence at Home

▼ **The Hohenstaufen Empire (1152–1272)**
Frederick I Barbarossa • Henry VI and the Sicilian Connection • Otto IV and the Welf Interregnum • Frederick II • Romanesque and Gothic Architecture

▼ **In Perspective**

KEY TOPICS

- **The revival of the Holy Roman Empire by a new German dynasty, the Saxons**
- **The emergence of a great reform movement in the church and the church's successful challenge to political domination by kings and emperors**
- **The development of strong national monarchies in England and France**
- **The fragmentation of Germany in the wake of a centuries-long struggle between the emperors of the Hohenstaufen dynasty and the papacy**

THE HIGH MIDDLE Ages mark a period of political expansion and consolidation and of intellectual flowering and synthesis. The noted medievalist Joseph Strayer called it the age that saw "the full development of all the potentialities of medieval civilization."[1] Some even argue that as far as the development of Western institutions

[1]Joseph Strayer, *Western History in the Middle Ages—A Short History* (New York: Appleton-Century-Crofts, 1955).

is concerned, this was a more creative period than the later Italian Renaissance and the German Reformation.

The High Middle Ages saw the borders of Western Europe largely secured against foreign invaders. Although intermittent Muslim aggression continued well into the sixteenth century, fear of assault from without diminished. On the contrary, a striking change occurred during the late eleventh and the twelfth centuries. Western Europe, which had for so long been the prey of outsiders, became, through the Crusades and foreign trade, the feared hunter within both the eastern Byzantine and the Muslim worlds.

During the High Middle Ages, "national" monarchies emerged. Rulers in England and France successfully adapted feudal principles of government to create newly centralized political realms. At the same time, parliaments and popular assemblies emerged to secure the rights and customs of the privileged many—the nobility, the clergy, and propertied townspeople—against the desires of kings. In the process, the foundations of modern European states were laid. The Holy Roman Empire, however, proved the great exception to this centralizing trend: Despite a revival of the empire under the Ottonians (Otto I, the most powerful member of the Saxon imperial dynasty, and his immediate successors, Otto II and Otto III), the events of these centuries left it weak and fragmented until modern times.

The High Middle Ages also saw the Latin, or Western, church establish itself in concept and law as a spiritual authority independent of monarchical secular government, thus sowing the seeds of the distinctive Western separation of church and state. During the **investiture controversy**, a confrontation between popes and emperors that began in the late eleventh century and lasted through the twelfth, a reformed papacy overcame its long subservience to the Carolingian and Ottonian kings. In this struggle over the authority of rulers to designate bishops and other high clergy and to invest them with their symbols of authority, the papacy, under Gregory VII and his immediate successors, won out. It did so, however, by becoming itself a monarchy among the world's emerging monarchies, preparing the way for still more dangerous confrontations between popes and monarchs in the later Middle Ages. Some religious reformers later saw in the Gregorian papacy of the High Middle Ages the fall of the church from its spiritual mission as well as a declaration of its independence from secular power.

▼ Otto I and the Revival of the Empire

The fortunes of both the old empire and the papacy began to revive after the dark period of the late ninth century and the early tenth century. In 918, the Saxon Henry I ("the Fowler," d. 936), the strongest of the German dukes, became the first non-Frankish king of Germany.

Unifying Germany

Henry rebuilt royal power by forcibly combining the duchies of Swabia, Bavaria, Saxony, Franconia, and Lotharingia. He secured imperial borders by checking the invasions of the Hungarians and the Danes. Although much smaller than Charlemagne's empire, the German kingdom Henry created placed his son and successor Otto I (r. 936–973) in a strong territorial position.

The able Otto maneuvered his own kin into positions of power in Bavaria, Swabia, and Franconia. He refused to recognize each duchy as an independent hereditary entity, as the nobility increasingly expected, treating each instead as a subordinate member of a unified kingdom. In a truly imperial gesture in 951, he invaded Italy and proclaimed himself its king. In 955, he won his most magnificent victory by defeating the Hungarians at Lechfeld. That victory secured German borders against new barbarian attacks, further unified the German duchies, and earned Otto the well-deserved title "the Great." In defining the boundaries of Western Europe, Otto's conquest was comparable to Charles Martel's earlier triumph over the Saracens at Poitiers in 732.

Embracing the Church

As part of a careful rebuilding program, Otto, following the example of his predecessors, enlisted the church. Bishops and abbots—men who possessed a sense of universal empire, yet because they did not marry, could not found competitive dynasties—were made princes and agents of the king. Because these clergy, as royal bureaucrats, received great landholdings and immunity from local counts and dukes, they also found such vassalage to the king attractive. The medieval church did not become a great territorial power reluctantly. It appreciated the blessings of receiving while teaching the blessedness of giving.

In 961, Otto, who had long aspired to the imperial crown, responded to a call for help from Pope John XII (r. 955–964), who was then being bullied by an Italian enemy of the German king, Berengar of Friuli. In recompense for this rescue, Pope John crowned Otto emperor on February 2, 962. Otto, for his part, recognized the existence of the Papal States and proclaimed himself their special protector. Over time, such close cooperation between emperor and pope put the church more than ever under royal control. Its bishops and abbots became Otto's appointees and bureaucrats, and the pope reigned in Rome under the protection of the emperor's sword.

Pope John belatedly recognized the royal web in which the church was becoming entangled and joined the Italian opposition to the new emperor. This turnabout brought Otto's swift revenge. An ecclesiastical synod over which Otto presided deposed Pope John and proclaimed that henceforth no pope could take office without first swearing an oath of allegiance to the emperor. Under Otto I, popes ruled at the emperor's pleasure.

As these events reflect, Otto had shifted the royal focus from Germany to Italy. His successors—Otto II (r. 973–983) and Otto III (r. 983–1002)—became so preoccupied with running the affairs of Italy that their German base began to disintegrate, sacrificed to imperial dreams. They might have learned a lesson from the contemporary Capetian kings, the successor dynasty to the Carolingians in France. Those kings, perhaps more by circumstance than by design, pursued a different course than the Ottonians. They mended local fences and concentrated their limited resources on securing the royal domain, never neglecting it for the lure of foreign adventure.

The Ottonians, in contrast, reached far beyond their grasp when they tried to subdue Italy. As the briefly revived empire began to crumble in the first quarter of the eleventh century, the church, long unhappy with Carolingian and Ottonian domination, prepared to declare its independence and exact its own vengeance.

▼ The Reviving Catholic Church

During the late ninth and early tenth centuries, the clergy had become tools of kings and magnates, and the papacy a toy of Italian nobles. The Ottonians made bishops their servile princes and likewise dominated the papacy. The church was about to gain renewed respect and authority, however, thanks not only to the failing fortunes of the overextended Ottonian empire, but also to a new, determined force for reform within the church itself.

The Cluny Reform Movement

The great monastery in Cluny in east-central France gave birth to a monastic reform movement that won the support of secular lords and German kings. Here began the real Christianization of Europe. Surface belief and lip service to Christian values appear now to have penetrated more deeply into the lives of rulers and the laity, as both new, successful reform movements and the growth of heresy attest. This development enabled the church to challenge royal authority at both the episcopal and papal levels.

The reformers of Cluny were aided by widespread popular respect for the church that found expression in lay religious fervor and generous baronial patronage of religious houses. One reason so many people admired clerics and monks was that the church was medieval society's most democratic institution as far as lay participation was concerned. In the Middle Ages any man could theoretically rise to the position of pope, who was supposed to be elected by "the people and the clergy." All people were candidates for the church's grace and salvation. The church promised a better life to come to the great mass of ordinary people, who found the present one brutish and without hope.

Since the fall of the Roman Empire, popular support for the church had been especially inspired by the example set by monks. Monasteries provided an important alternative way of life for the religiously earnest in an age when most people had very few options. Monks remained the least secularized and most spiritual of the church's clergy. Their cultural achievements were widely admired, their relics and rituals were considered magical, and their high religious ideals and sacrifices were imitated by the laity.

The tenth and eleventh centuries saw an unprecedented boom in the construction of monasteries. William the Pious, duke of Aquitaine, founded Cluny in 910. It was a Benedictine monastery devoted to the strictest observance of Saint Benedict's *Rule for Monasteries,* with a special emphasis on liturgical purity. Although the reformers who emerged at Cluny were loosely organized and their demands not always consistent, they shared a determination to maintain a spiritual church. They absolutely rejected the subservience of the clergy, especially that of the German bishops, to royal authority. They taught that the pope in Rome was sole ruler over all the clergy.

No local secular rulers, the Cluniacs asserted, could have any control over their monasteries. And they further denounced the sins of the flesh of the "secular" parish clergy, who maintained concubines in a relationship akin to marriage. The Cluny reformers thus resolved to free the clergy from both kings and "wives"—to create an independent and chaste clergy. The church alone was to be the clergy's lord and spouse. Thus, the distinctive Western separation of church and state, and the celibacy of the Catholic clergy, both of which continue today, had their definitive origins in the Cluny reform movement.

Cluny rapidly became a center from which reformers were dispatched to other monasteries throughout France and Italy. Under its aggressive abbots, especially Saint Odo (r. 926–946), it grew to embrace almost fifteen hundred dependent cloisters, each devoted to monastic and church reform. In the latter half of the eleventh century, the Cluny reformers reached the summit of their influence when the papacy itself embraced their reform program.

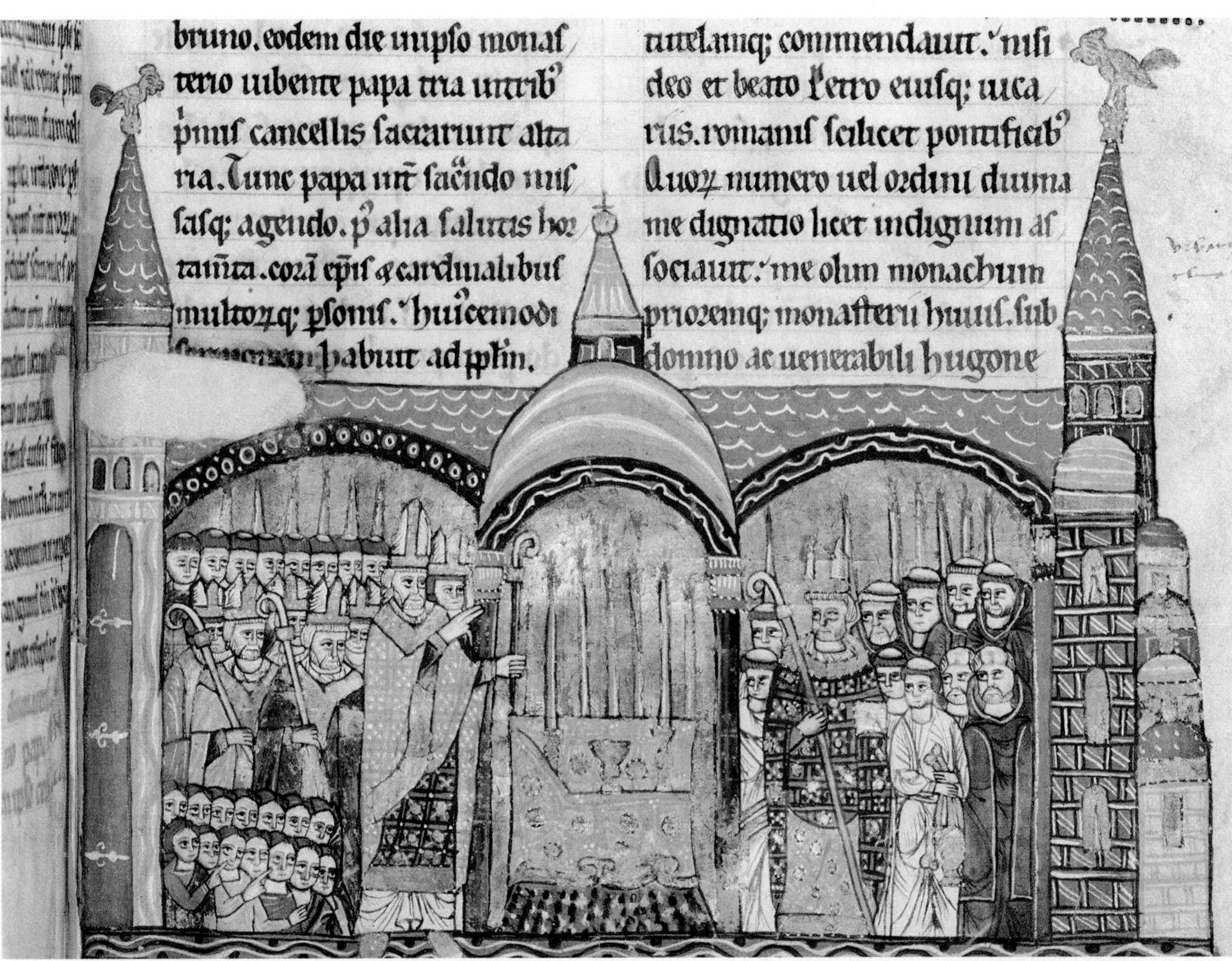

The consecration of the Abbey of Cluny by Pope Urban II from a twelfth-century manuscript. Bibliotheque Nationale Paris/Picture Desk, Inc./Kobal Collection

In the late ninth and early tenth centuries the proclamation of a series of church decrees, called the Peace of God, reflected the influence of the Cluny movement. Emerging from a cooperative venture between the clergy and the higher nobility, these decrees tried to lessen the endemic warfare of medieval society by threatening excommunication for all who, at any time, harmed members of such vulnerable groups as women, peasants, merchants, and the clergy. The Peace of God was subsequently reinforced by the Truce of God, a church order proclaiming that all men must abstain from violence and warfare during a certain part of each week (eventually from Wednesday night to Monday morning) and in all holy seasons.

Popes devoted to reforms like those urged by Cluny came to power during the reign of Emperor Henry III (r. 1039–1056). Pope Leo IX (r. 1049–1054) promoted regional synods to oppose *simony* (the selling of spiritual things, especially church offices) and clerical marriage (celibacy was not strictly enforced among the secular clergy until after the eleventh century). He also placed Cluniacs in key administrative posts in Rome. Imperial influence over the papacy, however, was still strong during Henry III's reign and provided a counterweight to the great aristocratic families that manipulated the elections of popes for their own gain. Before Leo IX's papacy, Henry had deposed three such popes, each a pawn of a Roman noble faction, and had installed a German bishop of his own choosing who ruled as Pope Clement II (r. 1046–1047).

Such high-handed practices ended soon after Henry III's death. During the turbulent minority of his successor, Henry IV (r. 1056–1106), reform popes began to assert themselves more openly. Pope Stephen IX (1057–1058) reigned without imperial ratification, contrary to the earlier declaration of Otto I. To prevent local factional control of papal elections, Pope Nicholas II (1059–1061) decreed in 1059 that a body of high church officials and advisers, known as the College of Cardinals, would henceforth choose the pope, establishing the procedures for papal succession that the Catholic Church still follows. With this action, the papacy declared its full independence from both local Italian and distant royal interference. Rulers continued nevertheless to have considerable indirect influence on the election of popes.

POPE GREGORY VII ASSERTS THE POWER OF THE POPE

Church reformers of the High Middle Ages vigorously asserted the power of the pope within the church and his rights against emperors and all others who might encroach on papal jurisdiction. Here is a statement of the basic principles of the Gregorian reformers, known as the Dictatus Papae *("The Sayings of the Pope"), which is attributed to Pope Gregory VII (1073–1085).*

In defining his powers as pope, on what authority does Pope Gregory base his authority? How many of his assertions are historically verifiable by actual events in church history? Can any of them be illustrated from Chapters 6 and 7? Compare Gregory's statements on papal power with those of Marsilius of Padua.

That the Roman Church was founded by God alone.
That the Roman Pontiff alone is rightly to be called universal.
That the Pope may depose the absent.
That for him alone it is lawful to enact new laws according to the needs of the time, to assemble together new congregations, to make an abbey of a canonry; and . . . to divide a rich bishopric and unite the poor ones.
That he alone may use the imperial insignia.
That the Pope is the only one whose feet are to be kissed by all princes.
That his name alone is to be recited in churches.
That his title is unique in the world.
That he may depose emperors.
That he may transfer bishops, if necessary, from one See to another.
That no synod may be called a general one without his order.
That no chapter or book may be regarded as canonical without his authority.
That no sentence of his may be retracted by any one; and that he, alone of all, can retract it.
That he himself may be judged by no one.
That the Roman Church has never erred, nor ever, by the witness of Scripture, shall err to all eternity.
That the Pope may absolve subjects of unjust men from their fealty.

From *Church and State through the Centuries: A Collection of Historic Documents,* trans. and ed. by S. Z. Ehler and John B. Morrall (New York: Biblo and Tannen, 1967), pp. 43–44. Reprinted by permission of Biblio-Moser Book Publishers.

Pope Nicholas II also embraced Cluny's strictures against simony and clerical concubinage and even struck his own political alliances with the Normans in Sicily and with France and Tuscany. His successor, Pope Alexander II (r. 1061–1073), was elected solely by the College of Cardinals, although not without a struggle.

The Investiture Struggle: Gregory VII and Henry IV

Alexander's successor was Pope Gregory VII (r. 1073–1085), a fierce advocate of Cluny's reforms who had entered the papal bureaucracy a quarter of a century earlier during the pontificate of Leo IX. (See "Pope Gregory VII Asserts the Power of the Pope.") It was he who put the church's declaration of independence to the test. Cluniacs had repeatedly inveighed against simony. Cardinal Humbert, a prominent reformer, argued that lay investiture of the clergy—that is, the appointment of bishops and other church officials by secular officials and rulers—was the worst form of this evil practice. In 1075, Pope Gregory embraced these arguments and condemned, under penalty of **excommunication**, lay investiture of clergy at any level. He had primarily in mind the emperor's well-established custom of installing bishops by presenting them with the ring and staff that symbolized the episcopal office.

After Gregory's ruling, emperors were no more able to install bishops than they were to install popes. As popes were elected by the College of Cardinals and were not raised up by kings or nobles, so bishops would henceforth be installed in their offices by high ecclesiastical authority empowered by the pope. The spiritual origins and allegiance of the episcopal office was thereby made clear.

Gregory's prohibition came as a jolt to royal authority. Since the days of Charlemagne, emperors had routinely passed out bishoprics to favored clergy. Bishops, who received royal estates, were the emperors' appointees and servants of the state. Henry IV's Carolingian and Ottonian predecessors had carefully nurtured the theocratic character of the empire in both concept and administrative bureaucracy. The church and religion had become integral parts of government.

Now the emperor, Henry IV, suddenly found himself ordered to secularize the empire by drawing a distinct line between the spheres of temporal and spiritual—royal and ecclesiastical—authority and jurisdiction. But if his key administrators were no longer to be his own carefully chosen and sworn servants, then was not his kingdom in jeopardy? Henry considered Gregory's action a direct challenge to his authority. The territorial princes, however, eager to see the emperor weakened, were quick to see the advantages of Gregory's ruling. If a weak emperor could not gain a bishop's ear, then a strong prince might, thus bringing the offices of the church into his orbit of power. In the hope of gaining an advantage over both the emperor and the clergy in their territory, the princes fully supported Gregory's edict.

The lines of battle were quickly drawn. Henry assembled his loyal German bishops at Worms in January 1076 and had them proclaim their independence from Gregory. Gregory promptly responded with the church's heavy artillery: He excommunicated Henry and absolved all of Henry's subjects from loyalty to him. This turn of events delighted the German princes, and Henry found himself facing a general revolt led by the duchy of Saxony. He had no recourse but to come to terms with Gregory. In a famous scene, Henry prostrated himself outside Gregory's castle retreat at Canossa on January 25, 1077. There he reportedly stood barefoot in the snow off and on for three days before the pope agreed to absolve him.

Papal power had at this moment reached a pinnacle. But Gregory's power, as he must have known when he restored Henry to power, was soon to be challenged.

Henry regrouped his forces, regained much of his power within the empire, and soon acted as if the humiliation at Canossa had never occurred. In March 1080, Gregory excommunicated Henry once again, but this time the action was ineffectual. (Historically, repeated excommunications of the same individual have proved to have diminishing returns.) In 1084, Henry, absolutely dominant, installed his own antipope, Clement III, and forced Gregory into exile, where he died the following year. It appeared as if the old practice of kings controlling popes had been restored—with a vengeance. Clement, however, was never recognized within the church, and Gregory's followers, who retained wide popular support, later regained power.

The settlement of the investiture controversy came in 1122 with the Concordat of Worms. Emperor Henry V (r. 1106–1125), having early abandoned his predecessors' practice of nominating popes and raising up antipopes, formally renounced his power to invest bishops with ring and staff. In exchange, Pope Calixtus II (r. 1119–1124) recognized the emperor's right to be present and to invest bishops with fiefs before and after their investment with ring and staff by the church. The old church-state back-scratching in this way continued, but now on different terms. The clergy received their offices and attendant religious powers solely from ecclesiastical authority and no longer from kings and emperors. Rulers continued to bestow lands and worldly goods on high clergy in the hope of influencing them. The Concordat of Worms thus made the clergy more independent, but not necessarily less worldly.

The Gregorian party may have won the independence of the clergy, but the price it paid was division among the feudal forces within the empire. The pope made himself strong by making imperial authority weak. In the end, those who profited most from the investiture controversy were the German princes.

The new Gregorian fence between temporal and spiritual power did not prevent kings and popes from being good neighbors if each was willing. Succeeding centuries, however, proved the aspirations of kings to be too often in conflict with those of popes for peaceful coexistence to endure. The most bitter clash between church and state was still to come. It would occur during the late thirteenth and early fourteenth centuries in the confrontation between Pope Boniface VIII and King Philip IV of France. (See Chapter 9.)

The Crusades

If an index of popular piety and support for the pope in the High Middle Ages is needed, the **Crusades** amply provide it. What the Cluny reform was to the clergy, the Crusades to the Holy Land were to the laity: an outlet for the heightened religious zeal, much of it fanatical, of the late eleventh and twelfth centuries.

Late in the eleventh century, the Byzantine Empire was under severe pressure from the Seljuk Turks, and the Eastern emperor, Alexius I Comnenus (r. 1081–1118), appealed for Western aid. At the Council of Clermont in 1095, Pope Urban II (r. 1088–1099) responded positively to that appeal, setting the First Crusade in motion. (See "Compare & Connect: Christian Jihad, Muslim Jihad," page 212.) This event has puzzled some historians, because the First Crusade was a risky venture. Yet the pope, the nobility, and Western society at large had much to gain by removing large numbers of nobility temporarily from Europe.

Too many idle, restless noble youths spent too great a part of their lives feuding with each other and raiding other people's lands. The pope saw that peace and tranquility might more easily be gained at home by sending these quarrelsome aristocrats abroad, 100,000 of whom marched off with the First Crusade. The nobility, in turn, saw that fortunes could be made in foreign wars. That was especially true for the younger sons of noblemen, who, in an age of growing population and shrinking landed wealth, saw in crusading the opportunity to become landowners. Pope Urban may well have believed that the Crusade would reconcile and reunite Western and Eastern Christianity.

Religion was not the only motive inspiring the Crusaders; hot blood and greed were no less strong. But unlike the later Crusades, which were undertaken for mercenary reasons, the early Crusades were inspired by genuine religious piety and carefully orchestrated by a revived papacy. Popes promised the first Crusaders a plenary indulgence should they die in battle. That was a complete remission of the temporal punishment due them for unrepented mortal sins, and hence a release from suffering for them in purgatory. In addition to this spiritual reward, the prospect of a Holy War against the Muslim infidel also propelled the Crusaders. Also, the sheer romance of a pilgrimage to the Holy Land played a role. All these motives combined to make the First Crusade a Christian success.

En route the Crusaders also began a general cleansing of Christendom that would intensify during the thirteenth-century papacy of Pope Innocent III. Accompanied by the new mendicant orders of Dominicans and Franciscans, Christian knights attempted to rid Europe of Jews as well as Muslims. Along the Crusaders' routes, especially in the Rhineland, Jewish communities were subjected to pogroms.

The First Victory The Eastern emperor welcomed Western aid against advancing Islamic armies. However, the Crusaders had not assembled merely to defend Europe's outermost borders against Muslim aggression. Their goal was to rescue the holy city of Jerusalem, which had been in the hands of the Muslims since the seventh century. To this end, three great armies—tens of thousands of Crusaders—gathered in France, Germany, and Italy and, taking different routes, reassembled in Constantinople in 1097. (See Map 7–1.)

The convergence of these spirited soldiers on the Eastern capital was a cultural shock that deepened antipathy toward the West. The Eastern emperor suspected their motives, and the common people, whose villages they plundered and suppressed, did not consider them to be Christian brothers in a common cause. Nonetheless, the Crusaders accomplished what no Byzantine army had been able to do. They soundly defeated one Muslim army after another in a steady advance toward Jerusalem, which they captured on July 15, 1099. The Crusaders owed their victory to superior military discipline and weaponry and were also helped by the deep political divisions within the Islamic world that prevented a unified Muslim resistance.

The victorious Crusaders divided conquered territories into the feudal states of Jerusalem, Edessa, and Antioch, which were apportioned to them as fiefs from the pope. Godfrey of Bouillon, leader of the French-German army, and after him his brother Baldwin, ruled over the kingdom of Jerusalem. The Crusaders, however, remained small islands within a great sea of Muslims, who looked on the Western invaders as savages to be slain or driven out. Once settled in the Holy Land, the Crusaders found themselves increasingly on the defensive. Now an occupying rather than a conquering army, they became obsessed with fortification, building castles and forts throughout the Holy Land, the ruins of which can still be seen today.

Once secure within their new enclaves, the Crusaders ceased to live off the land, as they had done since departing Europe, and increasingly relied on imports from home. As they developed the economic resources of their new possessions, the once fierce warriors were transformed into international traders and businessmen. The Knights Templar, originally a military-religious order, remade themselves into castle stewards and escorts for Western pilgrims going to and from the Holy Land. Through such endeavors, they became rich, ending up as wealthy bankers and moneylenders.

The Second and Third Crusades Native resistance broke the Crusaders' resolve around mid-century, and the forty-year-plus Latin presence in the East began to crumble. Edessa fell to Islamic armies in 1144. A Second Crusade, preached by Christendom's most eminent religious leader, the Cistercian monk Bernard of Clairvaux (1091–1153), attempted a rescue but met with dismal failure. In October 1187, Saladin (1138–1193), king of Egypt and Syria, reconquered Jerusalem. Save for a brief interlude in the thirteenth century, the holiest of cities remained thereafter in Islamic hands until the twentieth century.

THE CRUSADES

1095	Pope Urban II launches the First Crusade
1099	The Crusaders take Jerusalem
1147–1149	The Second Crusade
1187	Jerusalem retaken by the Muslims
1189–1192	Third Crusade
1202–1204	Fourth Crusade

MAP EXPLORATION

Interactive Map: To explore this map further, go to www.myhistorylab.com

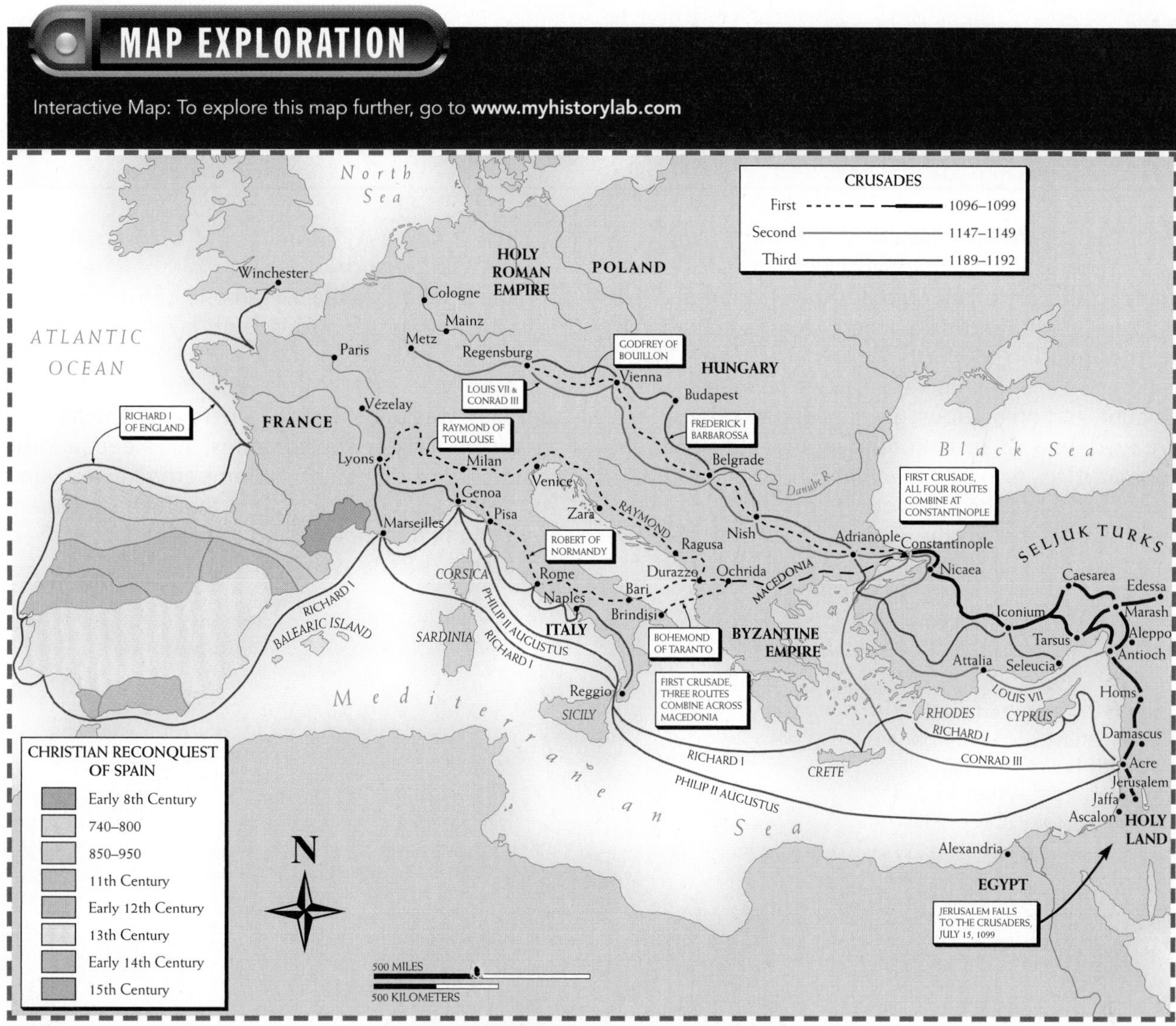

Map 7–1 **THE EARLY CRUSADES** Routes and several leaders of the Crusades during the first century of the movement are shown. The names on this map do not exhaust the list of great nobles who went on the First Crusade. The even showier array of monarchs of the Second and Third Crusades still left the Crusades, on balance, ineffective in achieving their goals.

A Third Crusade in the twelfth century (1189–1192) attempted yet another rescue, led by the most powerful Western rulers: Hohenstaufen emperor Frederick Barbarossa, Richard the Lion-Hearted, the king of England, and Philip Augustus, the king of France. It became instead a tragicomic commentary on the passing of the original crusading spirit. Frederick Barbarossa drowned while fording a small stream, the Saleph River, near the end of his journey across Asia Minor. Richard the Lion-Hearted and Philip Augustus reached Palestine, only to shatter the Crusaders' unity and chances of victory by their intense personal rivalry. Philip Augustus returned to France and made war on Richard's continental territories. Richard, in turn, fell captive to the Emperor Henry VI while returning to England.

The English paid a handsome ransom for their adventurous king's release. Popular resentment of taxes levied for that ransom became part of the background of the revolt against the English monarchy that led to royal recognition of English freedoms in the Magna Carta of 1215.

The long-term results of the first three Crusades had little to do with their original purpose. Politically and religiously they were a failure. The Holy Land reverted as firmly as ever to Muslim hands. The Crusades had, however, been a safety valve for violence-prone Europeans. More importantly, they stimulated Western trade with the East, as Venetian, Pisan, and Genoan merchants followed the Crusaders across Byzantium to lucrative new markets. The need to resupply the

A Closer LOOK

EUROPEANS EMBRACE A BLACK SAINT

ST. MAURICE, PATRON saint of Magdeburg, Germany, was a third-century Egyptian Christian, who commanded the Egyptian legion of the Roman army in Gaul. In 286 C.E. he and his soldiers were executed for impiety after refusing to worship the Roman gods. Maurice's cult began in 515, and he became a favorite saint of Charlemagne and other pious, warring German kings.

Portrayed as a white man for centuries, St. Maurice first appeared as a black man in the mid-thirteenth century. In the era of the Crusades, rulers had their eyes on new possessions in the Orient, and an Eastern-looking patron saint (Maurice) seemed the perfect talisman as Western merchants and armies ventured forth to trade and conquer. At this time, artists also began to paint as a black man one of the three Magi who visited baby Jesus on his birthday. The name Maurice was close to the German word for black dye ("Mauro") and later Moors ("Mohren"). Progressively, the third-century saint was transformed into a black African. By the fifteenth and sixteenth centuries, his head adorned the coats-of-arms of leading Nuremberg families who traded in the Near East, among them the Tuchers, Nuremberg's great cloth merchants, and Albrecht Dürer, Germany's most famous Renaissance artist.

Note the exaggerated black African features, which Europeans apparently believed would win them more trust as they traded with and occupied Eastern lands.

Note also the simple suit of chain mail and the simplicity of the saint himself, which suggest that a living model, instead of the usual glorification of a saintly figure, may have posed for this realistic-looking hero.

Constantin Beyer

To examine this image in an interactive fashion, please go to www.myhistorylab.com

PEARSON myhistorylab

Crusaders sail towards the Holy Land, from a twelfth-century gilded silver and enamel panel from the Pala d'Oro in the Basilica of St. Mark, Venice. The city-state of Venice, with its dominance of eastern Mediterranean shipping, profited enormously from the Crusades. Picture Desk, Inc./Kobal Collection

Christian settlements in the Near East also created new trade routes and reopened old ones long closed by Islamic supremacy over the Mediterranean.

The Fourth Crusade It is a commentary on both the degeneration of the original crusading ideal and the Crusaders' true historical importance that a Fourth Crusade transformed itself into a piratical, commercial venture controlled by the Venetians. In 1202, 30,000 Crusaders arrived in Venice to set sail for Egypt. When they could not pay the price of transport, the Venetians negotiated an alternative venture: the conquest of Zara, a rival Christian port on the Adriatic. As a shocked world watched, the Crusaders obliged the Venetians. Zara, however, proved to be only their first digression; in 1204, they beseiged, captured, and sacked Constantinople itself.

This stunning event brought Venice new lands and maritime rights that assured its domination of the eastern Mediterranean. Constantinople was now the center for Western trade throughout the Near East. Although its capture embarrased Pope Innocent III, the papacy was soon sharing the spoils, gleeful at the prospect of extending Roman Christianity to the East. A confidant of the pope became patriarch of Constantinople and launched a mission to win the Greeks and the Slavs to the Roman Church. Western control of Constantinople continued until 1261, when eastern emperor Michael Paleologus (r. 1261–1282), helped by the Genoese, who envied their Venetian rival's windfall in the East, finally recaptured the city. This fifty-seven-year occupation of Constantinople did nothing to heal the political and religious divisions between East and West.

The Pontificate of Innocent III (r. 1198–1216)

Pope Innocent III was a papal monarch in the Gregorian tradition of papal independence from secular domination. He proclaimed and practiced as none before him the doctrine of the plenitude of papal power. In a famous statement, he likened the relationship of the pope to the emperor—or the church to the state—to that of the sun to the moon. As the moon received its light from the sun, so the emperor received his brilliance (that is, his crown) from the hand of the pope—an allusion to the famous precedent set on Christmas Day, 800, when Pope Leo III crowned Charlemagne.

Although this pretentious theory greatly exceeded Innocent's ability to practice it, he and his successors did not hesitate to act on the ambitions it reflected. When Philip II, the king of France, tried unlawfully to annul his marriage, Innocent placed France under interdict, suspending all church services save baptism and the last rites. The same punishment befell England with even greater force when King John refused to accept Innocent's nominee for archbishop of Canterbury. Later in the chapter it will be shown how Innocent also intervened frequently and forcefully in the political affairs of the Holy Roman Empire.

The New Papal Monarchy Innocent made the papacy a great secular power, with financial resources and a bureaucracy equal to those of contemporary monarchs. During his reign the papacy transformed itself, in effect, into an efficient ecclesio-commercial complex, which reformers would attack throughout the later Middle Ages. Innocent consolidated and expanded ecclesiastical taxes on the laity, the chief of which was "Peter's pence." In England, that tax, long a levy on all but the poorest houses, became a lump-sum payment by the English crown during Innocent's reign. Innocent also imposed an income tax of 2.5 percent on the clergy. *Annates* (the payment of a portion or all of the first year's income received by the holder of a new *benefice*) and fees for the *pallium* (an archbishop's symbol of office) became especially favored revenue-gathering devices.

Innocent also reserved to the pope the absolution of many sins and religious crimes, requiring those desirous of pardons or exemptions to bargain directly with Rome. It was a measure of the degree to which the papacy had embraced the new money economy, since it now employed Lombard merchants and bankers to collect the growing papal revenues.

Christian Jihad, Muslim Jihad

ON NOVEMBER 26, 1095, Pope Urban II summoned the First Crusade to the Holy Land, its mission to take back Jerusalem from the Muslims. In a seeming propaganda and smear campaign, Urban depicted Muslims as savages. Roughly four years later, July 15, 1099, Western Crusaders captured the holy city with overwhelming force and untold carnage.

Eighty-eight years later, October 2, 1187, the fabled Sultan of Egypt and Syria, Saladin, returned Jerusalem to the Muslim fold by defeating the Third Crusade. During his march to Jerusalem, he massacred captured members of the Christian military-religious orders of the Knights Templar and the Hospitallers, who were escorts and protectors of Christians journeying back and forth to the Holy Land.

QUESTIONS

1. **Were the Christian Crusades, as the pope argued, a legitimate reclamation of the Christian Holy Land, or a preemptive Christian jihad?**
2. **Did Saladin's counteroffensive have stronger legal and moral grounds?**
3. **What role did religion play in the behavior of both sides?**

I. Pope Urban II (r. 1088–1099) Preaches the First Crusade

When Pope Urban II summoned the First Crusade in a sermon at the Council of Clermont on November 26, 1095, he painted a savage picture of the Muslims who controlled Jerusalem. Urban also promised the Crusaders, who responded by the tens of thousands, remission of their unrepented sins and assurance of heaven. Robert the Monk is one of four witnesses who has left us a summary of the sermon.

From the confines of Jerusalem and the city of Constantinople a horrible tale has gone forth and very frequently has been brought to our ears, namely, that a race from the kingdom of the Persians [that is, the Seljuk Turks], an accursed race, a race utterly alienated from God, a generation forsooth which has not directed its heart and has not entrusted its spirit to God, has invaded the lands of those Christians and has depopulated them by the sword, pillage and fire; it has led away a part of the captives into its own country, and a part it has destroyed by cruel tortures; it has either entirely destroyed the churches of God or appropriated them for the rites of its own religion. They destroy the altars, after having defiled them with their uncleanness. They circumcise the Christians, and the blood of the circumcision they either spread upon the altars or pour into the vases of the baptismal font. When they wish to torture people by a base death, they perforate their navels, and dragging forth the extremity of the intestines, bind it to a stake; then with flogging they lead the victim around until the viscera having gushed forth, the victim falls prostrate upon the ground. Others they bind to a post and pierce with arrows. Others they compel to extend their necks and then, attacking them with naked swords, attempt to cut through the neck with a single blow. What shall I say of the abominable rape of the women? The kingdom of the Greeks is now dismembered by them and deprived of territory so vast in extent that it can not be traversed in a march of two months. On whom therefore is the labor of avenging these wrongs and of recovering this territory incumbent, if not upon you? . . .

Jerusalem is the navel of the world; the land is fruitful above others, like another paradise of delights. This the Redeemer of the human race has made illustrious by His advent, has beautified by residence, has consecrated by suffering, has redeemed by death, has glorified by burial. This royal city, therefore, situated at the centre of the world, is now held captive by His enemies, and is in subjection to those who do not know God, to the worship of the heathens. She seeks therefore and desires to be liberated, and does not cease to implore you to come to her aid. From you especially she asks succor, because, as we have already said, God has conferred upon you above all nations great glory in arms.

Accordingly undertake this journey for the remission of your sins, with the assurance of the imperishable glory of the kingdom of heaven.

Source: Translations and reprints from *Original Sources of European History*, Vol. 1 (Philadelphia: Department of History, University of Pennsylvania, 1910), pp. 5–7.

II. Saladin (r. 1174–1193) Defeats the Third Crusade: The Report of an Eyewitness

[En route to liberating Jerusalem] Saladin sought out the Templars and Hospitallers . . . saying: 'I shall purify the land of these two impure races.' He ordered them to be beheaded, choosing to have them dead rather than in prison. With him [were] scholars and sufis [mystics] . . . devout men and ascetics, each begging to kill one of them . . . Saladin, his face joyful, sat on his dais [while] the unbelievers [Christians] showed black despair . . . There were some who slashed and cut [the Christians] cleanly, and were thanked for it. Some refused and failed to act . . . I [the eye-witness] saw the man who laughed scornfully as he slaughtered [the Christians] . . . How much praise he won! [How great] the eternal rewards he secured by the blood he had shed . . .! How many ills did he cure by the ills he brought upon a Templar . . .! I saw how he killed unbelief to give life to Islam, and destroyed polytheism [i.e. Trinitarian Christianity] to build monotheism . . .

[Later, during the conquest of Jerusalem] the Franks [i.e. Crusaders] saw how violently the Muslims attacked [and] decided to ask for safe-conduct out of the city [agreeing to] hand Jerusalem over to Saladin . . . A deputation . . . asked for terms, but . . . Saladin refused to grant [them]. 'We shall deal with you,' he said, 'just as you dealt with the population of Jerusalem when you took it [from us] in 1099, with murder and enslavement and other such savageries . . .! Despairing of this approach, [one of the city's Christian leaders] said: 'Know, O Sultan, that there are many of us in this city . . . At the moment we are fighting [against you] half-hearted in the hope to be spared by you as you have spared others—this because of our horror of death and our love of life. However, if we see that death is inevitable . . . we shall kill our children and our wives, burn our possessions, so as not to leave you with . . . a single man or woman to enslave [and we will also raze the city]. Saladin took counsel with his advisers [and] agreed to give the Franks assurances of safety on the understanding that each man, rich and poor alike [would pay] the appropriate ransom.

Source: From "Chronicles of Imad Ad-Din and Ibn Al-Athir," in Francesco Gabrieli, ed. and trans., *Arab Historians of the Crusades* (Routledge & Kegan Paul: London, 1957), pp. 138–140; Carole Hillenbrand, *The Crusades: Islamic Perspectives* (Chicago: Fitzroy Dearborn Publishers, 1999), p. 554.

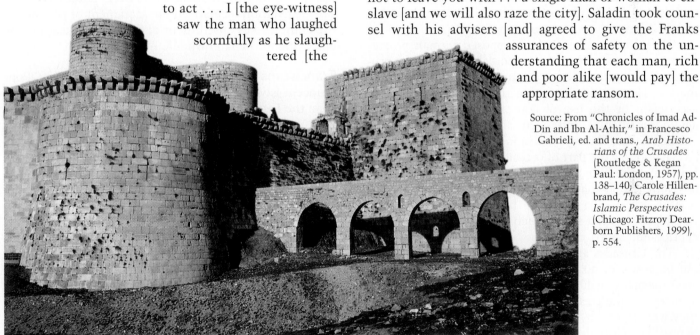

Krak des Chavaliers served as the headquarters of the Knights of St. John (Hospitallers) during the Crusades. This fortress is among the most notable surviving examples of medieval military architecture. Dorling Kindersley Media Library/Alistar Duncan © Dorling Kindersley

Crusades in France and the East Innocent's predilection for power politics also expressed itself in his use of the Crusade, the traditional weapon of the church against Islam, to suppress internal dissent and heresy. Heresy had grown under the influence of native religious reform movements that tried, often naively, to disassociate the church from the growing materialism of the age and to keep it pure of political scheming. Heresy also stemmed from anticlericalism fed by real clerical abuses that the laity could see for themselves, such as immorality, greed, and poor pastoral service.

The idealism of these movements was too extreme for the papacy. In 1209, Innocent launched a Crusade against the **Albigensians**, also known as Cathars, or "pure ones." These advocates of an ascetic, dualist religion were concentrated in the area of Albi in Languedoc in southern France, but they also had adherents among the laity in Italy and Spain. The Albigensians generally sought a pure and simple religious life, claiming to follow the model of the apostles of Jesus in the New Testament. Yet they denied the Old Testament and its God of wrath, as well as God's incarnation in Jesus Christ; despite certain Christian-influenced ideas, they were non-Christians. Their idea of a church was an invisible spiritual force, not a real-world institution.

The more radical Cathars opposed human procreation, because to reproduce corporeal bodies was to prolong the imprisonment of immortal souls in dying matter. They avoided it either through extreme sexual asceticism or the use of contraceptives (sponges and acidic ointments) and even abortion. The Cathars' strong dualism, however, also justified latitude in sexual behavior on the part of ordinary believers, this in the belief that the flesh and the spirit were so fundamentally different that it mattered little what the former did. It was in opposition to such beliefs that the church developed its strict social teachings condemning contraception and abortion.

The Crusades against the Albigensians were carried out by powerful noblemen from northern France. These great magnates, led by Simon de Montfort, were as much attracted by the great wealth of the area of Languedoc as they were moved by a Christian conscience to stamp out heresy. The Crusades also allowed the northerners to extend their political power into the south. This resulted in a succession of massacres and ended with a special Crusade led by King Louis VIII of France from 1225 to 1226, which destroyed the Albigensians as a political entity. Pope Gregory IX (r. 1227–1241) introduced the **Inquisition** into the region to complete the work of the Crusaders. This institution, a formal tribunal to detect and punish heresy, had been in use by the church since the mid-twelfth century as a way for bishops to maintain diocesan discipline. During Innocent's pontificate it became centralized in the papacy. Papal legates were dispatched to chosen regions to conduct interrogations, trials, and executions.

The Fourth Lateran Council Under Innocent's direction, the Fourth Lateran Council met in 1215 to formalize church discipline throughout the hierarchy, from pope to parish priest. The council enacted many important landmarks in ecclesiastical legislation. It gave full dogmatic sanction to the controversial doctrine of **transubstantiation**, according to which the bread and wine of the Lord's Supper become the true body and blood of Christ when consecrated by a priest in the sacrament of the Eucharist. This doctrine has been part of Catholic teaching ever since. It reflects the influence of the Cluniac monks and those of a new order, the Cistercians. During the twelfth century, these orders made the adoration of the Virgin Mary (the patron saint of the Cistercians) and the worship of Christ in the Eucharist the centerpieces of a reformed, christocentric piety. The doctrine of transubstantiation is an expression of the popularity of this piety. It also enhanced the power and authority of the clergy, because it specified that only they could perform the miracle of the Eucharist.

In addition, the council made annual confession and Easter communion mandatory for every adult Christian. This legislation formalized the sacrament of penance as the church's key instrument of religious education and discipline in the later Middle Ages.

Franciscans and Dominicans During his reign, Pope Innocent gave official sanction to two new monastic orders: the Franciscans and the Dominicans. No other action of the pope had more of an effect on spiritual life. Unlike other regular clergy, the members of these mendicant orders, known as *friars,* did not confine themselves to the cloister. They went out into the world to preach the church's mission and to combat heresy, begging or working to support themselves (hence the term *mendicant*).

Lay interest in spiritual devotion, especially among urban women, was particularly intense at the turn of the twelfth century. In addition to the heretical Albigensians, there were movements of **Waldensians**, Beguines, and Beghards, each of which stressed biblical simplicity in religion and a life of poverty in imitation of Christ. Such movements were especially active in Italy and France. Their heterodox teachings—teachings that, although not necessarily heretical, nonetheless challenged church orthodoxy—and the critical frame of mind they promoted caused the pope deep concern. Innocent feared they would inspire lay piety to turn militantly against the church. The Franciscan and Dominican orders, however, emerged from the same background of intense religiosity. By sanctioning them and thus keeping their followers within the confines of church organization, the pope provided a response to heterodox piety as well as an answer to lay criticism of the worldliness of the papal monarchy.

The Franciscan order was founded by Saint Francis of Assisi (1182–1226), the son of a rich Italian cloth merchant, who became disaffected with wealth and urged his followers to live a life of extreme poverty. Pope Innocent recognized the order in 1210, and its official rule was approved in 1223. The Dominican order, the Order of Preachers, was founded by Saint Dominic (1170–1221), a well-educated Spanish cleric, and was sanctioned in 1216. Both orders received special privileges from the pope and were solely under his jurisdiction. This special relationship with Rome gave the friars an independence from local clerical authority that bred resentment among some secular clergy.

Pope Gregory IX (r. 1227–1241) canonized Saint Francis only two years after Francis's death—a fitting honor for Francis and a stroke of genius by the pope. By bringing the age's most popular religious figure, one who had even miraculously received the *stigmata* (bleeding wounds like those of the crucified Jesus), so emphatically within the confines of the church, he enhanced papal authority over lay piety.

Two years after the canonization, however, Gregory canceled Saint Francis's own *Testament* as an authoritative rule for the Franciscan order. He did so because he found it to be an impractical guide for the order and because the unconventional nomadic life of strict poverty it advocated conflicted with papal plans to enlist the order as an arm of church policy. Most Franciscans themselves, under the leadership of moderates like Saint Bonaventure, general of the order between 1257 and 1274, also came to doubt the wisdom of extreme asceticism. During the thirteenth century, the main branch of the order progressively complied with papal wishes. In the fourteenth century, the pope condemned a radical branch, the Spiritual Franciscans, extreme followers of Saint Francis who considered him almost a new Messiah. In his condemnation, the pope declared absolute poverty a fictitious ideal that not even Christ endorsed.

The Dominicans, a less factious order, combated doctrinal error through visitations and preaching. They conformed new convents of **Beguines** (lay religious sisterhoods of single lay women in the Netherlands and Belgium; see Chapter 8) to the church's teaching, led the church's campaign against heretics in southern France, and staffed the offices of the Inquisition after Pope Gregory centralized it in 1223. The great Dominican theologian Thomas Aquinas (d. 1274) was canonized in 1322 for his efforts to synthesize faith and reason in an enduring definitive statement of Catholic belief. (See Chapter 8.)

Dominicans (top), and Franciscans (bottom). Unlike the other religious orders, the Dominicans and Franciscans did not live in cloisters but wandered about preaching and combating heresy. They depended for support on their own labor and the kindness of the laity. Cliche Bibliothèque Nationale de France, Paris

The Dominicans and the Franciscans strengthened the church among the laity. Through the institution of so-called Third Orders, they provided ordinary men and women the opportunity to affiliate with the monastic life and pursue the high religious ideals of poverty, obedience, and chastity while remaining laypeople. Laity who joined such orders were known as **Tertiaries**. Such organizations helped keep lay piety orthodox and within the church during a period of heightened religiosity.

▼ England and France: Hastings (1066) to Bouvines (1214)

In 1066, the death of the childless Anglo-Saxon ruler Edward the Confessor (so named because of his reputation for piety) occasioned the most important change in English political life. Edward's mother was a Norman, giving the duke of Normandy a competitive, if not the best, hereditary claim to the English throne. Before his death, Edward, who was not a strong ruler, acknowledged that claim and even directed that his throne be given to William, the reigning duke of Normandy (d. 1087). Yet the Anglo-Saxon assembly, which customarily bestowed the royal power, had a mind of its own and vetoed Edward's last wishes, choosing instead Harold Godwinsson. This action triggered the swift conquest of England by the powerful Normans. William's forces defeated Harold's army at Hastings on October 14, 1066. Within weeks of the invasion William was crowned king of England in Westminster Abbey, both by right of heredity and by right of conquest.

William the Conqueror

Thereafter, William embarked on a twenty-year conquest that eventually made all of England his domain. Every landholder, whether large or small, was henceforth his vassal, holding land legally as a fief from the king. William organized his new English nation shrewdly. He established a strong monarchy whose power was not fragmented by independent territorial princes. He kept the Anglo-Saxon tax system and the practice of court writs (legal warnings) as a flexible form of central control over localities. And he took care not to destroy the Anglo-Saxon quasi-democratic tradition of frequent "parleying"—that is, the holding of conferences between the king and lesser powers who had vested interests in royal decisions.

The practice of parleying had been initially nurtured by Alfred the Great (r. 871–899). A strong and willful king who had forcibly unified England, Alfred cherished the advice of his councilors in the making of laws. His example was respected and emulated by Canute (r. 1016–1035), the Dane who restored order and brought unity to England after the civil wars that had engulfed the land during the reign of the incompetent Ethelred II (r. 978–1016). The new Norman king, William, although he thoroughly subjugated his noble vassals to the crown, maintained the tradition of parleying by consulting with them regularly about decisions of state. The result was a unique blending of the "one" and the "many," a balance between monarchical and parliamentary elements that has ever since been a feature of English government—although the English Parliament as we know it today did not formally develop as an institution until the late thirteenth century.

For administration and taxation purposes William commissioned a county-by-county survey of his new realm, a detailed accounting known as the ***Domesday Book*** (1080–1086). The title of the book may reflect the thoroughness and finality of the survey. As none would escape the doomsday judgment of God, so no property was overlooked by William's assessors.

Henry II

William's son, Henry I (r. 1100–1135), died without a male heir, throwing England into virtual anarchy until the accession of Henry II (r. 1154–1189). Son of the count of Anjou and Matilda, daughter of Henry I, Henry mounted the throne as head of the new Plantagenet dynasty, the family name of the Angevin (or Anjouan) line of kings who ruled England until the death of Richard III in 1485. Henry tried to recapture the efficiency and stability of his grandfather's regime, but in the process he steered the English monarchy rapidly toward an oppressive rule. Thanks to his inheritance from his father (Anjou) and his marriage to Eleanor of Aquitaine (ca. 1122–1204), Henry brought to the throne virtually the entire west coast of France.

The union with Eleanor created the Angevin, or English-French, Empire. Eleanor married Henry while

The *Battle of Hastings*. Detail of the *Bayeux Tapestry*, c. 1073–1083. Wool embroidery on linen, height 20" (50.7 cm). Centre Guillaume Le Conquerant. Detail of the Bayeux Tapestry-XIth century. By special permission of the City of Bayeux

THE GROWING POWER AND INFLUENCE OF THE CHURCH

910	Cluny founded by William the Pious
1059	Pope Nicholas II establishes College of Cardinals
1075	Pope Gregory VII condemns lay investiture of clergy under penalty of excommunication
1076	Emperor Henry IV excommunicated by Pope Gregory VII for defying ban on lay investiture
1077	Henry IV begs for and receives papal absolution in Canossa
1084	Henry IV installs an antipope and forces Gregory VII into exile
1095	Pope Urban II preaches the First Crusade at the Council of Clermont
1122	Concordat of Worms between Emperor Henry V and Pope Calixtus II ends investiture controversy
1209	Pope Innocent III launches Albigensian Crusade in southern France; excommunicates King John of England
1210	Pope Innocent III recognizes the Franciscan order
1215	Fourth Lateran Council sanctions doctrine of transubstantiation and mandates annual confession by all adult Christians

he was still the count of Anjou and not yet king of England. The marriage occurred eight weeks after the annulment of Eleanor's fifteen-year marriage to the ascetic French king Louis VII in March 1152. Although the annulment was granted on grounds of consanguinity (blood relationship), the true reason for the dissolution of the marriage was Louis's suspicion of her infidelity. According to rumor, Eleanor had been intimate with a cousin. The annulment was costly to Louis, who lost Aquitaine along with his wife. Eleanor and Henry had eight children, five of them sons, among them the future kings Richard the Lion-Hearted and John.

In addition to gaining control of most of the coast of France, Henry also conquered part of Ireland and made the king of Scotland his vassal. Louis VII saw a mortal threat to France in this English expansion. He responded by adopting what came to be a permanent French policy of containment and expulsion of the English from their continental holdings in France. This policy succeeded in the mid-fifteenth century, when English power on the Continent collapsed after the Hundred Years' War. (See Chapter 9.)

Eleanor of Aquitaine and Court Culture

Eleanor of Aquitaine was a powerful influence on both politics and culture in twelfth-century France and England. She accompanied her first husband, King Louis VII, on the Second Crusade, becoming an example for women of lesser stature, who were also then venturing in increasing numbers into war and business and other areas previously considered the province of men. After marrying Henry, she settled in Angers, the chief town of Anjou, where she sponsored troubadours and poets at her lively court. There the troubadour Bernart de Ventadorn composed in Eleanor's honor many of the most popular love songs of high medieval aristocratic society. Eleanor spent the years 1154 to 1170 as Henry's queen in England. She separated from Henry in 1170, partly because of his public philandering and cruel treatment of her, and took revenge on him by joining ex-husband Louis VII in provoking Henry's three surviving sons, who were unhappy with their inheritance, into an unsuccessful rebellion against their father in 1173. From 1179 until his death in 1189, Henry kept Eleanor under mild house arrest to prevent any further such mischief from her.

After her separation from Henry in 1170 and until her confinement in England, Eleanor lived in Poitiers with her daughter Marie, the countess of Champagne, and the two made the court of Poitiers a famous center for the literature of courtly love. This genre, with its thinly veiled eroticism, has been viewed as an attack on medieval ascetic values. Be that as it may, it was certainly a commentary on contemporary domestic life within the aristocracy. The troubadours hardly promoted promiscuity at court—the code of chivalry that guided relations between lords and their vassals condemned the seduction of the wife of one's lord as the most heinous offense, punishable in some places by castration or execution (or both). Rather, the troubadours, in a frank and entertaining way, satirized carnal love or depicted it with tragic irony, while praising the ennobling power of friendly, or "courteous," love. The most famous courtly literature was that of Chrétien de Troyes, whose stories of King Arthur and the Knights of the Round Table recounted the tragic story of Sir Lancelot's secret and illicit love for Arthur's wife, Guinevere.

Popular Rebellion and Magna Carta

As Henry II acquired new lands abroad, he became more autocratic at home. He forced his will on the clergy in the Constitutions of Clarendon (1164). These measures limited judicial appeals to Rome, subjected the clergy to the civil courts, and gave the king control over the election of bishops. The result was strong political resistance from both the nobility and the clergy. The archbishop of Canterbury, Thomas à Becket (1118?–1170), once Henry's compliant chancellor, broke openly with the king and fled to Louis VII. Becket's subsequent assassination in 1170 and his canonization by Pope Alexander III in 1172 helped focus popular resentment against the king's heavy-handed tactics. Two hundred years later, Geoffrey Chaucer, writing in an age made cynical by the Black Death and the Hundred Years' War, had the pilgrims of his *Canterbury Tales* journey to the shrine of Thomas à Becket. (See "Encountering the Past: Pilgrimages.")

Under Henry's successors, the brothers Richard I, the Lion-Hearted (r. 1189–1199), and John (r. 1199–1216), new burdensome taxation in support of unnecessary foreign Crusades and a failing war with France turned resistance into outright rebellion. In 1209, Pope Innocent III, in a dispute with King John over the pope's choice for archbishop of Canterbury, excommunicated the king and placed England under interdict. To extricate himself and keep his throne, John had to make humiliating concessions, even declaring England a fief of the pope. The last straw for the English, however, was the defeat of the king's forces by the French at Bouvines in 1214. With the full support of the clergy and the townspeople, English barons revolted against John. The popular rebellion ended with the king's grudging recognition of **Magna Carta**, or "Great Charter," in 1215.

The Magna Carta put limits on autocratic behavior of the kind exhibited by the Norman kings and Plantagenet kings. It also secured the rights of the privileged against the monarchy. In Magna Carta the privileged preserved their right to be represented at the highest levels of government in important matters like taxation. The monarchy, however, was also preserved and kept strong. This balancing act, which gave power to both sides, had always been the ideal of feudal government.

Political accident had more to do with Magna Carta than political genius. Nevertheless, the English did manage to avoid both a dissolution of the monarchy by the nobility and the abridgment of the rights of the nobility by the monarchy. Although King John continued to resist the Magna Carta in every way, and succeeding kings ignored it, Magna Carta nonetheless became a cornerstone of modern English law.

A depiction of the murder of Saint Thomas à Becket in Canterbury Cathedral.
From the *Playfair Book of Hours*. The Murder of Saint Thomas Beckett. Playfair Book of Hours. Ms. L. 475–1918, fol. 176. French (Rouen), late 15th c. (CT9892). Victoria and Albert Museum, London, Great Britain/Art Resource, NY

Philip II Augustus

The English struggle in the High Middle Ages had been to secure the rights of the privileged many, not the authority of the king. (The Plantagenets had unbroken rule in the male line from 1154–1485.) The French, by contrast, faced the opposite problem. In 987, noblemen chose Hugh Capet to succeed the last Carolingian ruler, replacing the Carolingian dynasty with the Capetian, a third Frankish dynasty that ruled France for twelve generations, until 1328. For two centuries thereafter, until the reign of Philip II Augustus (r. 1180–1223), powerful feudal princes contested Capetian rule, burying the principle of election.

During this period, after a rash attempt to challenge the more powerful French nobility before they had enough strength to do so, the Capetian kings concentrated their limited resources on securing the royal domain, their uncontested territory around Paris and the Ile-de-France to the northeast. Aggressively exercising their feudal rights,

PILGRIMAGES

A MEDIEVAL PILGRIMAGE WAS both a spiritual and a social event, and everyone, from king to peasant, might join it. For penitent Christians, a priest might impose a pilgrimage as a temporal "satisfaction" for their sins, a pious act that canceled the punishment that God meted out to sinners. Because travel to faraway shrines required self-sacrifice and posed dangers, the church considered pilgrimages especially pleasing to God. The pilgrims' destination was always the shrine and often the tomb of a saint, before whose remains and relics pilgrims gained both forgiveness for sins and the saint's friendship and protection. Saints' "bones" and the waters from springs, wells, and streams at the site were believed to cure the ills of body and mind, so pilgrims also came in search of miracles. Infertile women believed a pilgrimage could "open their womb," and parents took ill or crippled children on pilgrimage to beg for a cure. Some parents even carried dead infants, in desperate hope the saint would move God to restore their children's lives.[2]

The three great pilgrimage tombs were those of St. Peter in Rome, St. James in Santiago de Compostela in northern Spain, and Jesus in Jerusalem. Businesses sprang up along the pilgrim trails and at the shrines, providing transportation, shelter, and emergency services. Manuscript "guidebooks" described the routes to the shrines. For example, a mid-twelfth-century guide told pilgrims headed for Santiago de Compostela what to expect in southwestern France:

> This is a desolate region . . . there is no bread, wine, meat, fish, water, or springs; villages are rare here. The sandy and flat land abounds none the less in honey, millet, panic-grass (fodder), and wild boars. If you . . . cross in summertime, guard your face diligently from the enormous flies [wasps and horseflies] that abound there. And if you do not watch your feet . . . you will rapidly sink up to the knees in the sea-sand.[3]

Pilgrimages were also often group "outings" that medieval people must have found diverting as well as edifying. Most pilgrims traveled with bands of friends, relatives, or neighbors. In the fourteenth century, the English poet Geoffrey Chaucer (ca. 1345–1400) wrote a famous work *The Canterbury Tales* about a group of pilgrims who were traveling to the shrine of St. Thomas à Becket (1118–1170), the martyred archbishop of Canterbury, and passed the time telling each other amusing stories.

Because the shrines were usually in or near great churches, pilgrimages also gave the best history and architecture lessons available in the Middle Ages. Thus, in Canterbury Cathedral, pilgrims could venerate Becket's relics, which were housed in a glittering jewel-encrusted shrine, and learn about the conflict that had led to the archbishop's murder in that same cathedral by the knights of King Henry II (r. 1154–1189).

Sources: Klaus Arnold, *Kind und Gesellschaft in Mittelalter und Renaissance* (MartinLurz, Munich Paderborn, 1980), pp. 30–31; Georges Duby, *The Age of the Cathedrals*, trans. by E. Levieux and B. Thompson (Chicago: University of Chicago Press, 1981), pp. 50–51; H. W. Janson and A. F. Janson, *History of Art* (New York: Prentice Hall, 1997), pp. 386–387; Compton Reeves, *Pleasures and Pastimes in Medieval England* (Oxford: Oxford University Press, 1998), pp. 174–175, 180.

List three reasons why people went on pilgrimages. Name the three great tombs to which pilgrims journeyed in the Middle Ages.

A thirteenth-century stained glass window depicts pilgrims traveling to Canterbury Cathedral. © Archivo Iconografico, S.A./CORBIS

[2]Klaus Arnold, *Kind und Gesellschaft in Mittelalter und Renaissance* (Munich: Paderborn, 1980), pp. 30–31.
[3]H. W. Janson and A. F. Janson, *History of Art* (New York: Prentice Hall, 1997), pp. 386–387.

French kings, especially after 1100, gained near absolute obedience from the noblemen in this area and established a solid base of power. By the reign of Philip II Augustus, Paris had become the center of French government and culture, and the Capetian dynasty a secure hereditary monarchy. Thereafter, the kings of France could impose their will on the French nobles, who were always in law, if not in political fact, the king's sworn vassals.

In an indirect way the Norman conquest of England helped stir France to unity and made it possible for the Capetian kings to establish a truly national monarchy. The duke of Normandy, who after 1066 was master of the whole of England, was also among the vassals of the French king in Paris. Capetian kings understandably watched with alarm as the power of their Norman vassal grew. Other powerful vassals of the king also watched with alarm. King Louis VI, the Fat (r. 1108–1137), entered an alliance with Flanders, traditionally a Norman enemy. King Louis VII (r. 1137–1180), assisted by a brilliant minister, Suger, abbot of St. Denis and famous for his patronage of Gothic architecture, found allies in the great northern French cities and used their wealth to build a royal army.

When he succeeded Louis VII as king, Philip II Augustus inherited financial resources and a skilled bureaucracy that put him in a strong position. He was able to resist the competition of the French nobility and the clergy and to focus on the contest with the English king. Confronted at the same time with an internal and an international struggle, he proved successful in both. His armies occupied all the English king's territories on the French coast except for Aquitaine. As a showdown with the English neared on the continent, however, Holy Roman Emperor Otto IV (r. 1198–1215) entered the fray on the side of the English, and the French found themselves assailed from both east and west. But when the international armies finally clashed at Bouvines in Flanders on July 27, 1214, in what history records as the first great European battle, the French won handily over the opposing Anglo-Flemish-German army. This victory unified France politically around the monarchy and thereby laid the foundation for French ascendancy in the later Middle Ages. The defeat so weakened Otto IV that he fell from power in Germany. (It also, as we have seen, sparked the rebellion in England that forced King John to accept Magna Carta.)

▼ France in the Thirteenth Century: The Reign of Louis IX

If Innocent III realized the fondest ambitions of medieval popes, Louis IX (r. 1226–1270), the grandson of Philip Augustus, embodied the medieval view of the perfect ruler. Coming to power after the French victory at Bouvines (1214), Louis inherited a unified and secure kingdom. Although he was endowed with a moral character that far exceeded that of his royal and papal contemporaries, he was also at times prey to naïveté. Not beset by the problems of sheer survival, and a reformer at heart, Louis found himself free to concentrate on what medieval people believed to be the business of civilization.

Generosity Abroad

Magnanimity in politics is not always a sign of strength, and Louis could be very magnanimous. Although in a strong position during negotiations for the Treaty of Paris (1259), which momentarily settled the dispute between France and England, he refused to take advantage of it to drive the English from their French possessions. Had he done so and ruthlessly confiscated English territories on the French coast, he might have lessened, if not averted altogether, the conflict underlying the Hundred Years' War, which began in the fourteenth century. Instead he surrendered disputed territory on the borders of Gascony to the English king, Henry III, and confirmed Henry's possession of the duchy of Aquitaine.

Although he occasionally chastised popes for their crude political ambitions, Louis remained neutral during the long struggle between the German Hohenstaufen emperor Frederick II and the papacy and his neutrality worked to the pope's advantage. Louis also remained neutral when his brother, Charles of Anjou, intervened in Italy and Sicily against the Hohenstaufens, again to the pope's advantage. Urged on by the pope and his noble supporters, Charles was crowned king of Sicily in Rome, and his subsequent defeat of the son and grandson of Frederick II ended the Hohenstaufen dynasty. For such service to the church, both by action and by inaction, the Capetian kings of the thirteenth century received many papal favors.

Order and Excellence at Home

Louis's greatest achievements lay at home. The efficient French bureaucracy, which his predecessors had used to exploit their subjects, became under Louis an instrument of order and fair play in local government. He sent forth royal commissioners (*enquêteurs*), reminiscent of Charlemagne's far less successful *missi dominici.* Their mission was to monitor the royal officials responsible for local governmental administration (especially the *baillis* and *prévôts,* whose offices had been created by his predecessor, Philip Augustus) and to ensure that justice would truly be meted out to all. These royal ambassadors were received as genuine tribunes of the people. Louis further abolished private wars and serfdom within his royal domain. He gave his subjects the judicial right of appeal from local to higher courts and made the tax system, by medieval standards, more equitable. The French people came to associate their king with justice; consequently, national feeling, the glue of nationhood, grew strong during his reign.

Respected by the kings of Europe and possessed of far greater moral authority than the pope, Louis became an arbiter among the world's powers. During his reign French society and culture became an example to all of Europe, a pattern that would continue into the modern period. Northern France became the showcase of monastic reform, chivalry, and Gothic art and architecture. Louis's reign also coincided with the golden age of Scholasticism, which saw the convergence of Europe's greatest thinkers on Paris, among them Saint Thomas Aquinas and Saint Bonaventure. (See Chapter 8.)

Louis's perfection remained, however, that of a medieval king. Like his father, Louis VIII (r. 1223–1226), who had taken part in the Albigensian Crusade, Louis was something of a religious fanatic. He sponsored the French Inquisition. He led two French Crusades against the Muslims, which, although inspired by the purest religious motives, proved to be personal disasters. During the first (1248–1254), Louis was captured and had to be ransomed out of Egypt. He died of a fever during the second in 1270. It was especially for this selfless, but also useless, service on behalf of the church that Louis later received the rare honor of sainthood. Probably not coincidentally, the church bestowed this honor when it was under pressure from a more powerful and less than "most Christian" French king, the ruthless Philip IV, "the Fair" (r. 1285–1314). (See Chapter 9.)

▼ The Hohenstaufen Empire (1152–1272)

During the twelfth and thirteenth centuries, stable governments developed in both England and France. In England Magna Carta balanced the rights of the nobility against the authority of the kings, and in France the reign of Philip II Augustus secured the authority of the king over the competitive claims of the nobility. During the reign of Louis IX, the French exercised international influence over politics and culture. The story within the Holy Roman Empire, which embraced Germany, Burgundy, and northern Italy by the mid-thirteenth century, was different. (See Map 7–2, page 222.) There, primarily because of the efforts of the Hohenstaufen dynasty to extend imperial power into southern Italy, disunity and blood feuding remained the order of the day for two centuries. It left as a legacy the fragmentation of Germany until the nineteenth century.

Frederick I Barbarossa

The investiture struggle had earlier weakened imperial authority. After the Concordat of Worms, the German princes were the supreme lay powers within the rich ecclesiastical territories and held a dominant influence over the appointment of the church's bishops.

The power of the emperor promised to return, however, with the accession to the throne of Frederick I Barbarossa (r. 1152–1190) of the Hohenstaufen dynasty, the strongest line of emperors yet to succeed the Ottonians. This new dynasty not only reestablished imperial authority but also started a new, deadlier phase in the contest between popes and emperors. Never have kings and popes despised and persecuted one another more than during the Hohenstaufen dynasty.

Frederick I confronted powerful feudal princes in Germany and Lombardy and a pope in Rome who still looked on the emperor as his creature. However, the incessant strife among the princes and the turmoil caused by the papacy's pretensions to great political power alienated many people. Such popular sentiment presented Frederick with an opportunity to recover imperial authority and he was shrewd enough to take advantage of it. Frederick especially took advantage of the contemporary revival of Roman law, which served him on two fronts. On one hand, it praised centralized authority, that of king or emperor, against the nobility; on the other, it stressed the secular origins of imperial power against the tradition of Roman election of the emperor and papal coronation of him, thus reducing papal involvement to a minimum.

From his base in Switzerland, Frederick attempted to hold his empire together by invoking feudal bonds. He was relatively successful in Germany, thanks largely to the fall from power and exile in 1180 of his strongest German rival, Henry the Lion (d. 1195), the duke of Saxony. Although he could not defeat the many German duchies, Frederick never missed an opportunity to remind each German ruler of his prescribed duties as one who held his land legally as a fief of the emperor. The Capetian kings of France had used the same tactic when they faced superior forces of the nobility.

Italian popes proved to be the greatest obstacle to Frederick's plans to revive his empire. In 1155, he restored Pope Adrian IV (r. 1154–1159) to power in Rome after a religious revolutionary had taken control of the city. For his efforts, Frederick won a coveted papal coronation—and strictly on his terms, not on those of the pope. Despite fierce resistance to him in Italy, led by Milan, the door to Italy had opened, and an imperial assembly sanctioned his claims to Italian lands.

As this challenge to royal authority was occurring, Cardinal Roland, a skilled lawyer, became Pope Alexander III (r. 1159–1181). In a clever effort to strengthen the papacy against growing imperial influence, the new pope had, while still a cardinal, negotiated an alliance between the papacy and the Norman kingdom of Sicily. Knowing him to be a capable foe, Frederick opposed his election as pope and backed a rival candidate after the election in a futile effort to undo it. Frederick now found himself at war with the pope, Milan, and Sicily.

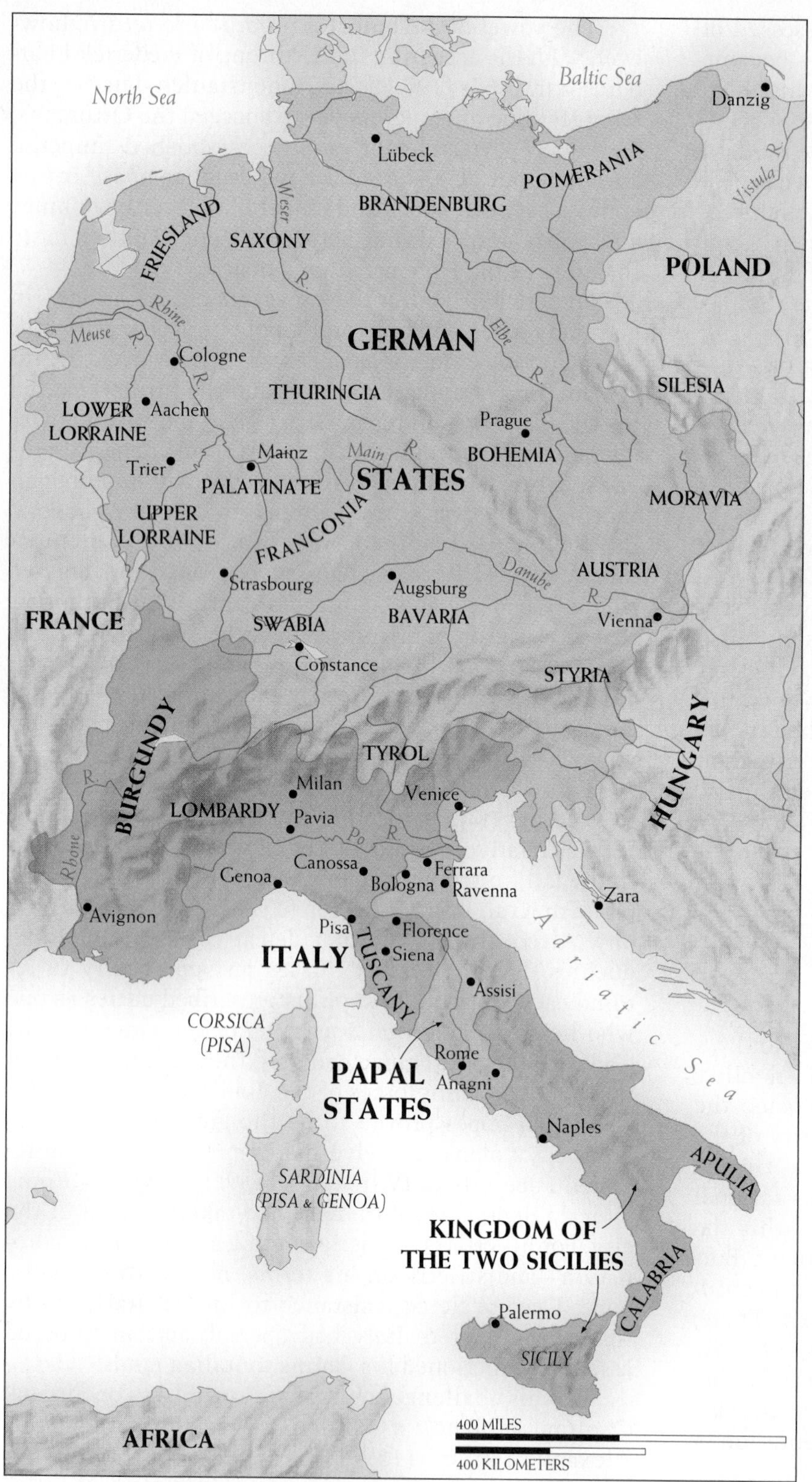

Map 7–2 **GERMANY AND ITALY IN THE MIDDLE AGES** Medieval Germany and Italy were divided lands. The Holy Roman Empire (Germany) embraced hundreds of independent territories that the emperor ruled only in name. The papacy controlled the Rome area and tried to enforce its will on Romagna. Under the Hohenstaufens (mid-twelfth to mid-thirteenth centuries), internal German divisions and papal conflict reached new heights; German rulers sought to extend their power to southern Italy and Sicily.

By 1167, the combined forces of the north Italian communes had driven Frederick back into Germany, and a decade later, in 1176, Italian forces soundly defeated his armies at Legnano. In the Peace of Constance in 1183, which ended the hostilities, Frederick recognized the claims of the Lombard cities to full rights of self-rule, a great blow to his imperial plans.

Henry VI and the Sicilian Connection

Frederick's reign thus ended with stalemate in Germany and defeat in Italy. At his death in 1190, he was not a ruler equal in stature to the kings of England and France. After the Peace of Constance, he seems to have accepted the reality of the empire's division among the feudal princes of Germany. However, in the last years of his reign he seized an opportunity to gain control of Sicily, then still a papal ally, and form a new territorial base of power for future emperors. The opportunity arose when the Norman ruler of the kingdom of Sicily, William II (r. 1166–1189), sought an alliance with Frederick that would free him to pursue a scheme to conquer Constantinople. In 1186, a fateful marriage occurred between Frederick's son, the future Henry VI (r. 1190–1197), and Constance, the eventual heiress to the kingdom of Sicily, which promised to change the balance of imperial-papal power.

It proved, however, to be but another well-laid plan that went astray. The Sicilian kingdom became a fatal distraction for succeeding Hohenstaufen kings, tempting them to sacrifice their traditional territorial base in northern Europe to dreams of imperialism. Equally disastrous for the Hohenstaufens, the union of the empire with Sicily left Rome encircled, ensuring even greater emmity from a papacy already thoroughly distrustful of the emperor.

When Henry VI became emperor in 1190, he thus faced a hostile papacy, German princes more defiant than ever of the emperor, and an England whose adventurous king, Richard the Lion-Hearted, plotted against Henry VI with the old Hohenstaufen enemy, the exiled duke of Saxony, Henry the Lion.

It was into these circumstances that the future Emperor Frederick II was born in 1194. Heretofore the German princes had not recognized birth alone as qualifying one for the imperial throne, although the offspring of the emperor did have the inside track. To ensure baby Frederick's succession and stabilize his monarchy, Henry campaigned vigorously for recognition of the principle of hereditary succession. He won many German princes to his side by granting them what he asked for himself and his son: full hereditary rights to their own fiefs. Not surprisingly, the encircled papacy strongly opposed hereditary succession and joined dissident German princes against Henry.

Otto IV and the Welf Interregnum

Henry died in September 1197, leaving his son Frederick a ward of the pope. Henry's brother succeeded him as German king, but the Welf family, who were German rivals of the Hohenstaufens, put forth their own candidate, whom the English supported. The French, beginning a series of interventions in German affairs, stuck with the Hohenstaufens. The papacy supported first one side and then the other, depending on which seemed most to threaten it. The struggle for power threw Germany into anarchy and civil war.

The Welf candidate, Otto of Brunswick, outlasted his rival and was crowned Otto IV by his followers in Aachen in 1198, thereafter winning general recognition in Germany. In October 1209, Pope Innocent III (r. 1198–1216) boldly meddled in German politics by crowning Otto emperor in Rome. Playing one German dynasty against the other in an evident attempt to curb imperial power in Italy, while fully restoring papal power there, the pope had badly underestimated the ambition of the new German emperor. After his papal coronation, Otto proceeded to attack Sicily, an old imperial policy threatening to Rome. Four months after crowning Otto emperor, Pope Innocent excommunicated him.

MAJOR POLITICAL EVENTS OF THE HIGH MIDDLE AGES

955	Otto I defeats Hungarians at Lechfeld, securing Europe's eastern border
1066	Normans win the Battle of Hastings and assume English rule
1152	Frederick I Barbarossa becomes first Hohenstaufen emperor; reestablishes imperial authority
1154	Henry II assumes the English throne as the first Plantagenet or Angevin king
1164	Henry II forces the Constitutions of Clarendon on the English clergy
1170	Henry II's defiant archbishop, Thomas à Becket, assassinated
1176	Papal and other Italian armies defeat Frederick I at Legnano
1194	Birth of future Hohenstaufen ruler Frederick II, who becomes a ward of the pope
1198	Welf interregnum in the empire begins under Otto IV
1212	Frederick II crowned emperor in Mainz with papal, French, and German support
1214	French armies under Philip II Augustus defeat combined English and German forces at Bouvines in the first major European battle
1215	English barons revolt against King John and force the king's recognition of Magna Carta
1227	Frederick II excommunicated for the first of four times by the pope; conflict between Hohenstaufen dynasty and papacy begins
1250	Frederick II dies, having been defeated by the German princes with papal support
1257	German princes establish their own electoral college to elect future emperors

Frederick II

Casting about for a counterweight to the treacherous Otto, the pope joined with the French, who had remained loyal to the Hohenstaufens. His new ally, French king Philip Augustus, impressed on Innocent that a solution to their mutual problem with Otto IV lay near at hand in the person of Innocent's ward: Frederick of Sicily, son of the late Hohenstaufen emperor Henry VI, who had now come of age. Unlike Otto, the young Frederick had an immediate hereditary claim to the imperial throne. In December 1212, with papal, French, and German support, Frederick was crowned king of the Romans in the German city of Mainz. Within a year and a half, Philip Augustus ended the reign of Otto IV on the battlefield of Bouvines, and three years later (1215), Frederick II was crowned emperor again, this time in the sacred imperial city of Aachen.

During his reign, Frederick effectively turned dreams of a unified Germany into a nightmare of disunity, assuring German fragmentation into modern times. Raised Sicilian and dreading travel beyond the Alps, Frederick spent only nine of his thirty-eight years as emperor in Germany, and six of those were before 1218. Although he pursued his royal interests in Germany, he did so mostly through representatives, seeming to desire only the imperial title for himself and his sons, and willing to give the German princes whatever they wanted to secure it. It was this eager compliance with their demands that laid the foundation for six centuries of German division. In 1220, he recognized the jurisdictional claims of the ecclesiastical princes of Germany, and twelve years later (1232) he extended the same recognition to the secular princes.

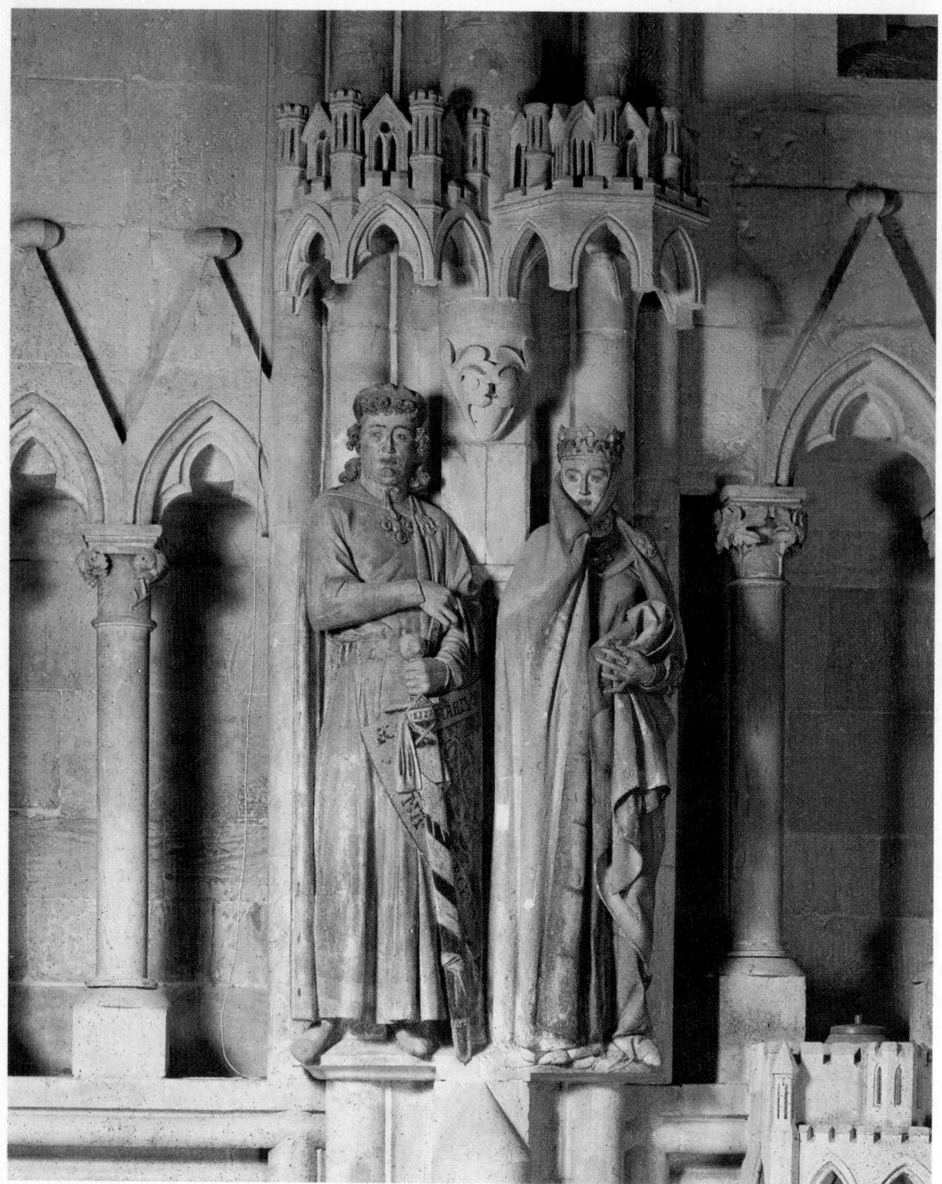

Ekkehard and Uta, ca. 1240–50. This famous noble pair founded Naumburg Cathedral in Germany in the middle of the thirteenth century and are exemplary studies of medieval nobility. © Achim Bednorz, Koln

Frederick's concessions amounted to an abdication of imperial power in Germany. Some view them as a kind of German Magna Carta in that they secured the rights of the German nobility for the forseeable future. But unlike the king of England within his realm, Frederick did little to secure the rights of the emperor in Germany. Whereas Magna Carta had the long-term consequence of promoting a balance of power between king and parliament, Frederick made the German princes little emperors within their respective realms. Centuries of petty absolutism, not parliamentary government, were the result.

Frederick's relations with the pope were equally disastrous, leading to his excommunication on four different occasions—the first in 1227 for refusing to finish a crusade he had begun at the pope's request. He was also determined to control Lombardy and Sicily, a policy that was anathema to the pope. The papacy came to view Frederick as the Antichrist, the biblical beast of the Apocalypse, whose persecution of the faithful signaled the end of the world.

The papacy won the long struggle that ensued, although its victory was arguably a Pyrrhic one. During this bitter contest, Pope Innocent IV (r. 1243–1254) launched the church into European politics on a massive scale, a policy that left the church vulnerable to criticism from both religious reformers and royal apologists. Pope Innocent organized the German princes against Frederick, who—thanks to Frederick's grand concessions—were a superior force and able to gain full control of Germany by the 1240s.

When Frederick died in 1250, the German monarchy died with him. The princes established their own informal electoral college in 1257, which thereafter controlled the succession. Through this institution, which the emperor recognized in 1356, the "king of the Romans" became a puppet of the princes, and one with firmly attached strings. The princes elected him directly, and his offspring had no hereditary right to succeed him. The last male Hohenstaufen was executed in 1268.

Independent princes henceforth controlled Germany while the imperial kingdom in Italy fell to local Italian magnates. The connection between Germany and Sicily ended forever, and the papal monarchy emerged as one of Europe's most formidable powers, soon to enter its most costly conflict of the Middle Ages with the new French and English monarchies. Internal division and the absence of a representative system of government persisted in Germany for six centuries. Even after Chancellor Bismarck created a new German empire in 1871, the legacy of the Hohenstaufen dynasty's defeat was still visible until the end of World War I.

Romanesque and Gothic Architecture

The High Middle Ages witnessed the peak of Romanesque art and the transition to the Gothic. Romanesque literally means "like Rome," and the art

Transept, Cathedral of St. James Santiago de Compostela. Achim Bednorz/© Achim Bednorz, Koln

Salisbury Cathedral, England. © Christopher Cormack/CORBIS.

and architecture of the High Middle Ages embraced the classical style of ancient Rome. Romanesque churches are fortress-like. Rounded arches, thick stone walls, and heavy columns support their vaults or ceilings. In the early Middle Ages this architecture expressed the church's role as a refuge for the faithful and a new world power. Developed under the Carolingians and Ottonians, the Romanesque attained its perfection and predominated between 1050 and 1200.

Appearing first in mid-twelfth-century France, Gothic art and architecture evolved directly from the Romanesque. The term *Gothic* implies barbaric (although, in fact, Gothic art was not related in any way to the ancient Goths), and critics initially used it to condemn the new style. Gothic architecture, however, quickly silenced its critics. Its distinctive features are a ribbed, crisscrossed ceiling, with pointed arches in place of rounded ones, a clever construction technique that allows Gothic churches to soar far above their Romanesque predecessors. The greater weight on the walls was off-loaded by exterior "flying" buttresses built directly into them. With the walls thus shored up, they could be filled with wide expanses of stained glass windows that flooded the churches with colored light.

In Perspective

With its borders finally secured, Western Europe was free to develop its political institutions and cultural forms during the High Middle Ages. The map of Europe as we know it today began to take shape. England and France can be seen forming into modern nation-states, but within Germany and the Holy Roman Empire the story was different. There, imperial rule first revived (under the Ottonians) and then collapsed totally (under the Hohenstaufens). The consequences for Germany were ominous: Thereafter, it became Europe's most fractured land. On a local level, however, an effective organization of society from noble to serf emerged throughout Western Europe.

The major disruption of the period was an unprecedented conflict between former allies, church and state. During the investiture struggle and the period of the Crusades, the church became a powerful monarchy in its own right. For the first time, it competed with secular states on the latter's own terms, dethroning emperors, kings, and princes by excommunication and interdict. In doing so, it inadvertently laid the foundation for the Western doctrine of the separation of church and state.

Having succeeded so brilliantly in defending its spiritual authority against rulers, popes ventured boldly into the realm of secular politics as well, especially during the pontificates of Innocent III and Innocent IV. As the sad story of the Hohenstaufen dynasty attests, the popes had remarkable, if short-lived, success there also. But the church was to pay dearly for its successes, both spiritually and politically. Secularization of the papacy during the High Middle Ages left it vulnerable to the attacks of a new breed of unforgiving religious reformers, and the powerful monarchs of the later Middle Ages were to subject it to bold and vengeful bullying.

REVIEW QUESTIONS

1. How was the Saxon king Otto I able to consolidate political rule over the various German duchies and use the church to his advantage? Does he deserve the title "the Great"?
2. What were the main reasons for the Cluny reform movement? Why did it succeed? How did this reform movement influence the subsequent history of the medieval church?
3. Why did Pope Gregory VII and King Henry IV conflict over the issue of lay investiture? What was the outcome of the struggle? What did each side have at stake and how did the struggle affect the emperor's power in Germany?
4. The eighteenth-century French intellectual Voltaire said the Holy Roman Empire was neither holy, nor Roman, nor an empire. What did he mean? Do you agree with him?
5. What major development in western and eastern Europe encouraged the emergence of the Crusades? Why did the Crusaders fail to establish lasting political and religious control over the Holy Land? What were the political, religious, and economic results of the Crusades? Which do you consider most important and why?
6. What were some of the factors preventing German consolidation under the Hohenstaufens? Why did Germany remain in feudal chaos while France and England eventually coalesced into reasonably strong states?

SUGGESTED READINGS

J. W. Baldwin, *The Government of Philip Augustus* (1986). The standard work.

S. Flanagan, *Hildegard of Bingen, 1098–1179: A Visionary Life* (1998). Latest biography of a powerful religious woman.

S. D. Goitein, *Letters of Medieval Jewish Traders* (1973). Rare first-person accounts.

E. M. Hallam, *Capetian France 987–1328* (1980). Good on politics and heretics.

J. C. Holt, *Magna Carta*, 2nd ed. (1992). Succeeding generations interpret the famous document.

K. Leyser, *Medieval Germany and Its Neighbors, 900–1250* (1982). Basic and authoritative.

H. E. Mayer, *The Crusades*, trans. by John Gilligham (1972). The best one-volume account.

W. Melczer, *The Pilgrim's Guide to Santiago de Compostela* (1993). Do's and dont's, and what the medieval pilgrim might expect along the way.

C. Moriarity, ed., *The Voice of the Middle Ages: In Personal Letters, 1100–1500* (1989). Rare first-person accounts.

J. B. Morrall, *Political Thought in Medieval Times* (1962). Readable, elucidating account.

J. Riley-Smith, *The Oxford Illustrated History of the Crusades* (1995). Sweeping account.

C. Tyerman, *Fighting for Christendom* (2004). Brief and accessible.

For additional learning resources related to this chapter, please go to www.myhistorylab.com

PEARSON myhistorylab

The livelihood of towns and castles depended on the labor of peasants in surrounding villages. Here a peasant family collects the September grape harvest from a vineyard outside a fortified castle in France in preparation for making wine. The Granger Collection

8

Medieval Society: Hierarchies, Towns, Universities, and Families (1000–1300)

▼ **The Traditional Order of Life**
Nobles • Clergy • Peasants

▼ **Towns and Townspeople**
The Chartering of Towns • The Rise of Merchants • Challenging the Old Lords • New Models of Government • Towns and Kings • Jews in Christian Society

▼ **Schools and Universities**
University of Bologna • Cathedral Schools • University of Paris • The Curriculum • Philosophy and Theology

▼ **Women in Medieval Society**
Image and Status • Life Choices • Working Women

▼ **The Lives of Children**
Children as "Little Adults" • Childhood as a Special Stage

▼ **In Perspective**

KEY TOPICS

- The major groups composing medieval society
- The rise of towns and a new merchant class
- The founding of universities and educational curricula
- How women and children fared in the Middle Ages

BETWEEN THE TENTH and twelfth centuries, European agricultural production steadily improved, due to a warming climate and improved technology. With increased food supplies came something of a population explosion by the eleventh century. The recovery of the countryside, in turn, stimulated new migration into and trade with the long-dormant towns. Old towns revived and new ones arose. A rich and complex fabric of life developed, closely integrating town and countryside and allowing civilization to flourish in the twelfth and thirteenth centuries as it had not done in the West since the Roman Empire. Beginning with the Crusades, trade with distant towns and foreign lands also revived. With the rise of towns, a new merchant class, the ancestors of modern capitalists, came into being. Enormous numbers of skilled artisans and day workers, especially in the cloth-making industries, were the foundation of the new urban wealth.

Urban culture and education also flourished. The revival of trade with the East and contacts with Muslim intellectuals, particularly in Spain, made possible the recovery of ancient scholarship and science. Unlike the comparative dabbling in antiquity during Carolingian times, the twelfth century enjoyed a true renaissance of classical learning. Schools and curricula also broadened beyond the clergy during the twelfth century to educate lay men and some women, thereby greatly increasing literacy among laypeople and their role in government and culture.

In the mid-twelfth century in France, Gothic architecture began to replace the plain and ponderous Romanesque style preferred by fortress Europe during the vulnerable early Middle Ages. Its new grace and beauty—soaring arches, bold flying buttresses, dazzling light, and stained glass—were a testament to the vitality of humankind as well as to the glory of God in this unique period of human achievement.

▼ The Traditional Order of Life

In the art and literature of the Middle Ages, three basic social groups were represented: those who fought as mounted knights (the landed nobility), those who prayed (the clergy), and those who labored in fields and shops (the peasantry and village artisans). After the revival of towns in the eleventh century, a fourth social group emerged: long-distance traders and merchants. Like the peasantry, they also labored, but in ways strange to the traditional groups. They were freemen who often possessed great wealth, yet unlike the nobility and the clergy, they owned no land, and unlike the peasantry, they did not toil in fields and shops. Their rise to power caused an important crack in the old social order, for they drew behind them the leadership of the urban artisan groups that the new urban industries that grew up in the wake of the revival of trade had created. During the late Middle Ages, these new "middling classes" firmly established themselves, and their numbers have been enlarging ever since.

Nobles

As a distinctive social group, not all nobles were originally great men with large hereditary lands. Many rose from the ranks of feudal vassals or warrior knights. The successful vassal attained a special social and legal status based on his landed wealth (accumulated fiefs), his exercise of authority over others, and his distinctive social customs—all of which set him apart from others in medieval society. By the late Middle Ages, a distinguishable higher and lower nobility living in both town and country had evolved. The higher were the great landowners and territorial magnates, who had long been the dominant powers in their regions, while the lower were comprised of petty landlords, descendants of minor knights, newly rich merchants able to buy country estates, and wealthy farmers patiently risen from ancestral serfdom.

It was a special mark of the nobility that they lived off the labor of others. Basically lords of manors, the nobility of the early and High Middle Ages neither tilled the soil like the peasantry nor engaged in the commerce of merchants—activities considered beneath their dignity. The nobleman resided in a country mansion or, if he was particularly wealthy, a castle. Personal preference drew him to the countryside as much as the fact that his fiefs were usually rural manors.

Warriors Arms were the nobleman's profession; to wage war was his sole occupation and reason for living. In the eighth century, the adoption of stirrups made mounted warriors, or cavalry, indispensable to a successful army (stirrups permitted the rider to strike a blow without falling off the horse). Good horses (and a warrior needed several) and the accompanying armor and weaponry of horse warfare were expensive. Thus only those with means could pursue the life of a cavalryman. The nobleman's fief gave him the means to acquire the expensive military equipment that his rank required. He maintained that enviable position as he had gained it, by fighting for his chief.

The nobility accordingly celebrated the physical strength, courage, and constant activity of warfare. Warring gave them both new riches and an opportunity to gain honor and glory. Knights were paid a share in the plunder of victory, and in war everything became fair game. Special war wagons, designed to collect and transport booty, followed them into battle. Sadness greeted periods of peace, as they meant economic stagnation and boredom. Whereas the peasants and the townspeople counted peace the condition of their occupational success, the nobility despised it as unnatural to their profession.

They looked down on the peasantry as cowards who ran and hid during war. They held urban merchants, who amassed wealth by business methods strange to feudal society, in equal contempt, which increased as the affluence and political power of the townspeople grew. The nobility possessed as strong a sense of superiority over these "unwarlike" people as the clergy did over the general run of the laity.

A Closer LOOK

THE JOYS AND PAINS OF THE MEDIEVAL JOUST

THIS SCENE FROM a manuscript from c. 1300–1340 idealizes medieval noblewomen and the medieval joust. Revived in the late Middle Ages, jousts were frequently held in peacetime. They kept the warring skills of noblemen sharp and became popular entertainment. Only the nobility were legally allowed to joust, but over time, uncommon wealth enabled a persistent commoner to qualify.

Although jousts often led to mayhem and death, the intent was not to inflict bodily harm on one's opponent. To that end, the lances had blunt ends and the goal was to knock the crests or helmut ornamentation off the opponent's head. These crests, like body armor and shields, displayed the nobleman's valued coat-of-arms.

The helmet was especially designed to protect the face, while providing a thin window for visibility.

Missing from the illustration are the musicians and trumpeters who provided the hoopla that accompanied a joust. Also not depicted here are the nonparticipant knights who rode about on their chargers with noblewomen sitting sidesaddle at their backs with one hand firmly around the rider's waist, much as motorcycle couples do today.

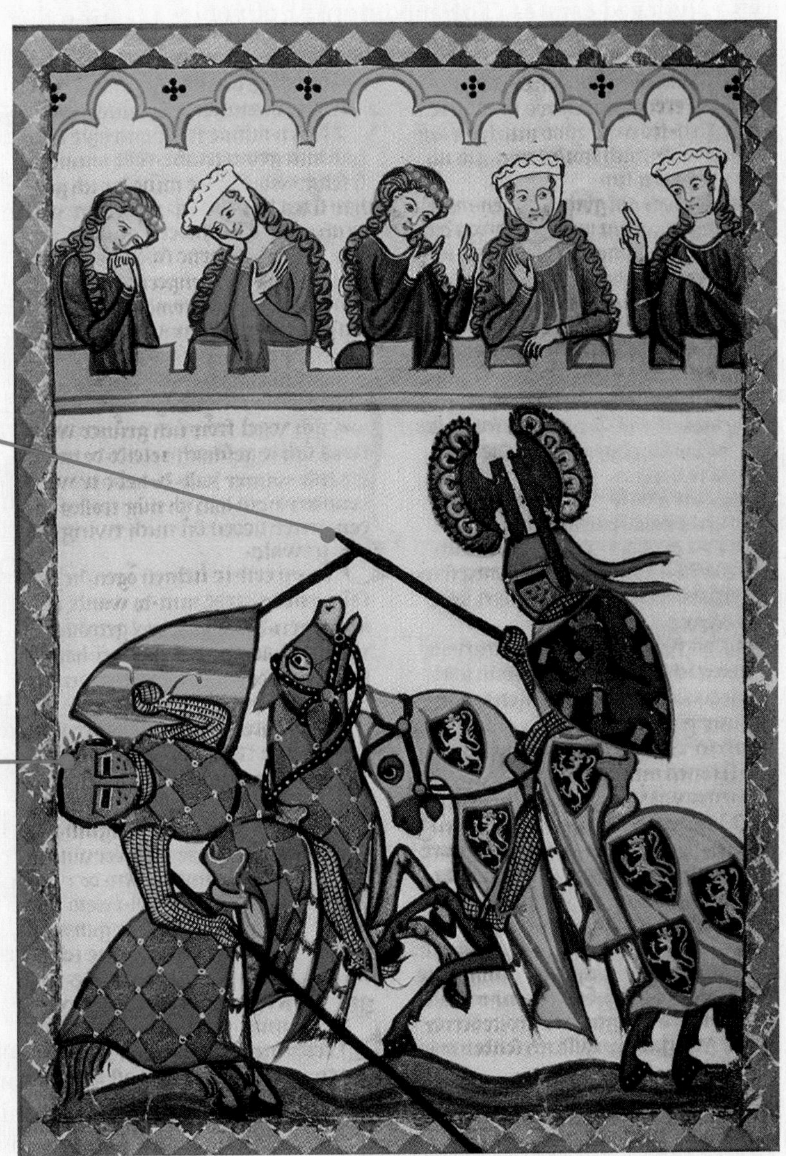

Universitatsbibliothek Heidelberg.

To examine this image in an interactive fashion, please go to www.myhistorylab.com

PEARSON myhistorylab

Knighthood The nobleman nurtured his sense of distinctiveness within medieval society by the chivalric ritual of dubbing to knighthood. This ceremonial entrance into the noble class became almost a religious sacrament. A bath of purification, confession, communion, and a prayer vigil preceded the ceremony. Thereafter, the priest blessed the knight's standard, lance, and sword. As prayers were chanted, the priest girded the knight with his sword and presented him his shield, enlisting him as much in the defense of the church as in the service of his lord. Dubbing raised the nobleman to a state as sacred in his sphere as clerical ordination made the priest in his. The comparison is legitimate: The clergy and the nobility were medieval society's privileged estates. The appointment of noblemen to high ecclesiastical office and their eager participation in the church's Crusades had strong ideological and social underpinnings as well as economic and political motives.

In the twelfth century, knighthood was legally restricted to men of high birth. This circumscription of noble ranks came in reaction to the growing wealth, political power, and successful social climbing of newly rich townspeople (mostly merchants), who formed a new urban patriciate that was increasingly competitive with the lower nobility. Kings remained free, however, to raise up knights at will and did not shrink from increasing royal revenues by selling noble titles to wealthy merchants. But the law was building fences—fortunately, with gates—between town and countryside in the High Middle Ages.

Sportsmen In peacetime, the nobility had two favorite amusements: hunting and tournaments. Where they could, noblemen progressively monopolized the rights to game, forbidding commoners from hunting in their "lord's'" forests. This practice built resentment among common people to the level of revolt. Free game, fishing, and access to wood were basic demands in the petitions of grievance and the revolts of the peasantry throughout the High and later Middle Ages.

Tournaments also sowed seeds of social disruption, but more within the ranks of the nobility itself. They were designed not only to keep men fit for war, but also to provide the excitement of war without the maiming and killing of prized vassals. But as regions competed fiercely with one another for victory and glory, even mock battles with blunted weapons proved to be deadly. Often, tournaments got out of hand, ending with bloodshed and animosity among the combatants. (The intense emotions and occasional violence that accompany interregional soccer in Europe today may be seen as a survival of this kind of rivalry.) The church came to oppose tournaments as occasions of pagan revelry and senseless violence. Kings and princes also turned against them as sources of division within their realms. Henry II of England proscribed them in the twelfth century. They did not end in France until the mid-sixteenth century, after Henry II of France was mortally wounded by a shaft through his visor during a tournament celebrating his daughter's marriage. (See "Encountering the Past: Warrior Games.")

Courtly Love From the repeated assemblies in the courts of barons and kings, set codes of social conduct, or "courtesy," developed in noble circles. With the French leading the way, mannered behavior and court etiquette became almost as important as expertise on the battlefield. Knights became literate gentlemen, and lyric poets sang and moralized at court. The cultivation of a code of behavior and a special literature to eulogize it was not unrelated to problems within the social life of the nobility. Noblemen were notorious philanderers; their illegitimate children mingled openly with their legitimate offspring in their houses. The advent of courtesy was, in part, an effort to reform this situation.

Although the poetry of courtly love was sprinkled with frank eroticism and the beloved in these epics were married women pursued by those to whom they were not married, the poet usually recommended love at a distance, unconsummated by sexual intercourse. It was love without touching, a kind of sex without sex, and only as such was it ennobling. Court poets depicted those who succumbed to illicit carnal love as reaping at least as much suffering as joy.

Social Divisions No medieval social group was absolutely uniform—not the nobility, the clergy, the townspeople, or even the peasantry. Not only was the nobility a class apart; it also had strong social divisions within its own ranks. Noblemen formed a broad spectrum—from minor vassals without subordinate vassals to mighty barons, the principal vassals of a king or prince, who had many vassals of their own. Dignity and status within the nobility were directly related to the exercise of authority over others; a chief with many vassals obviously far excelled the small country nobleman who served another and was lord over none but himself.

Even among the domestic servants of the nobility, a social hierarchy developed according to assigned manorial duties. Although peasants in the eyes of the law, the chief stewards—charged with overseeing the operation of the lord's manor and the care and education of the noble children—became powerful "lords" within their "domains." Some freemen found the status of the steward enviable enough to surrender their own freedom and become domestic servants in the hope of attaining it. In time, the superiority of the higher ranks of domestic servants won legal recognition as medieval law adjusted to acknowledge the privileges of wealth and power at whatever level they appeared.

ENCOUNTERING THE *Past*

WARRIOR GAMES

IN THE MIDDLE Ages, the nobility—the warrior class—dominated society, and their favorite games grew out of their work, which was fighting. Boys of the warrior class learned to ride early. Some boys received horses and daggers at age two! At fourteen, they were given a man's sword and thereafter engaged in sports that prepared them for battle.

During the Middle Ages those war-preparing activities evolved into mock combats called *tournaments*. In peacetime, the warrior class continued to divert itself by such games amid a constant stream of poems, songs, and art that glorified war.

Peasants, townspeople, and clergy also engaged in warlike games and sports. Peasants and townspeople attended tournaments and imitated what they saw there; their children's toys (homemade lances, shields, and pikes) and games (mock combats, sheriffs and outlaws) reflected the tournament's influence.

Although there were famous clerical sportsmen and warriors, the clergy's "penchant for violence" was largely vicarious. The *Bayeaux Tapestry* (1070–1082), over two thirds of a football field long, with seventy-two scenes of blood-dripping medieval hunts and battles, was the brainstorm of a bishop, Odo of Bayeaux (ca. 1036–1097), half brother of William the Conqueror (r. 1066–1087). The aristocratic women who wove such tapestries might ride to the hunt and "ooh" and "ah" at tournaments but remained spectators, not participants, in the violent pastimes of the nobility.

More reflective of the contemplative life of the religious and of noblewomen were the indoor board games played in manor houses and cloisters. Two of many such games were "Tick, Tack, Toe" and "Fox and the Geese." The object of the latter game was to fill, or capture, the most holes, or spaces (geese), in the board with pebbles or fruit stones. Men and women of leisure, clerical and lay, also played chess and backgammon.

By the late fifteenth century, when changes in warfare had reduced the role of the mounted knight in battle, tournaments, like less bellicose games, were held for their own sake, merely as pastimes. At fairs, the horse races and mock combats of the tournament were now spread among ball games (early versions of rugby, soccer, and football), animal acts, puppet shows, juggling, and the like. Pieter Breughel's *Children's Games* (1560) depicts boys and girls engaged in seventy-eight different games. Some of them, such as jousting and wrestling, are adapted from the war preparation activities of the European nobility. Yet others are the kind of games children, like knights in earlier centuries preparing for real war, invented to escape boredom and idleness—hoops, leapfrog, blind man's bluff, marbles, golf, stilts, masquerades, tug-of-war, and jacks.

Source: John Marshall Carter, *Medieval Games: Sports and Recreations in Feudal Society* (New York: Greenwood Press, 1992), pp. 25, 30–33, 34, 69; ibid., "The Ludic Life of the Medieval Peasant: A Pictorial Essay," *Arete* III (1986): 169–187; J. T. Micklethwaite, "On the Indoor Games of School Boys in the Middle Ages," *Archeological Journal* (1892), pp. 319–328; Carter, "Ludic Life," p. 177; Steven Ozment, *Ancestors: The Loving Family in Old Europe* (Cambridge, MA: Harvard University Press, 2001), pp. 71–72.

Why did the medieval nobility play warlike games?

How did medieval women and children participate in these pastimes?

Breughel, *Children's Games.* Pieter the Elder Brueghel (1525–1569), "Children's Games," 1560. Oil on oakwood, 118 × 161 cm. Kunsthistoriches Museum, Vienna, Austria. Photo copyright Erich Lessing/Art Resource, NY

Lovers playing chess on an ivory mirror back, ca. 1300.
The Bridgeman Art Library International

In the late Middle Ages, the landed nobility suffered a steep economic and political decline. Climatic changes and agricultural failures created large famines, and the great plague (see Chapter 9) brought unprecedented population loss. Changing military tactics occasioned by the use of infantry and heavy artillery during the Hundred Years' War made the noble cavalry nearly obsolete. Also, the alliance of wealthy towns with kings challenged the nobility within their own domains. A waning of the landed nobility occurred after the fourteenth century when the effective possession of land and wealth counted more than lineage for membership in the highest social class. Still a shrinking nobility continued to dominate society down to the nineteenth century, and they have been with us ever since.

Clergy

Unlike the nobility and the peasantry, the clergy was an open estate. Although the clerical hierarchy reflected the social classes from which the clergy came, one was still a cleric by religious training and ordination, not by the circumstances of birth or military prowess.

Regular and Secular Clerics

There were two basic types of clerical vocation: the regular clergy and the secular clergy. The **regular clergy** was made up of the orders of monks who lived according to a special ascetic rule (*regula*) in cloisters separated from the world. They were the spiritual elite among the clergy, and theirs was not a way of life lightly entered. Canon law required that a man be at least twenty-one years old before making a final profession of the monastic vows of poverty, chastity, and obedience. The monks' personal sacrifices and high religious ideals made them much respected in high medieval society. This popularity was a major factor in the success of the Cluny reform movement and of the Crusades of the eleventh and twelfth centuries. (See Chapter 7.) The Crusades provided laypeople with a way to participate in the admired life of asceticism and prayer; in such holy pilgrimages they could imitate the suffering and perhaps even the death of Jesus, as the monks imitated his suffering and death by retreat from the world and severe self-denial.

Many monks (and also nuns, who increasingly embraced the vows of poverty, obedience, and chastity without a clerical rank) secluded themselves altogether. The regular clergy, however, were never completely cut off from the secular world. They maintained frequent contact with the laity through such charitable activities as feeding the destitute and tending the sick, through liberal arts instruction in monastic schools, through special pastoral commissions from the pope, and as supplemental preachers and confessors in parish churches during Lent and other peak religious seasons. It became the mark of the Dominican and Franciscan friars to live a common life according to a special rule and still to be active in a worldly ministry. Some monks, because of their learning and rhetorical skills, even rose to prominence as secretaries and private confessors to kings and queens.

The **secular clergy**, those who lived and worked directly among the laity in the world (*saeculum*), formed a vast hierarchy. At the top were the high prelates—the wealthy cardinals, archbishops, and bishops, who were drawn almost exclusively from the nobility—and below them the urban priests, the cathedral canons, and the court clerks. Finally, there was the great mass of poor parish priests, who were neither financially nor intellectually far above the common people they served. (The basic educational requirement was an ability to say the mass.) Until the Gregorian reform in the eleventh century, parish priests lived with women in a relationship akin to marriage, and the communities they served

Monks and nuns play a bat-and-ball game. Bodleian Library, University of Oxford

accepted their concubines and children. Because of their relative poverty, priests often took second jobs as teachers, artisans, or farmers. Their parishioners also accepted and even admired this practice.

New Orders One of the results of the Gregorian reform was the creation of new religious orders aspiring to a life of poverty and self-sacrifice in imitation of Christ and the first apostles. The more important were the Canons Regular (founded 1050–1100), the Carthusians (founded 1084), the Cistercians (founded 1098), and the Praemonstratensians (founded 1121). Carthusians, Cistercians, and Praemonstratensians practiced extreme austerity in their quest to recapture the pure religious life of the early church.

Strictest of them all were the Carthusians. Members lived in isolation and fasted three days a week. They also devoted themselves to long periods of silence and even self-flagellation in their quest for perfect self-denial and conformity to Christ.

The Cistercians (from Citeaux in Burgundy) were a reform wing of the Benedictine order and were known as the "white monks," a reference to their all-white attire, symbolic of apostolic purity. (The Praemonstratensians also wore white.) They hoped to avoid the materialistic influences of urban society and maintain uncorrupted the original *Rule* of Saint Benedict, which their leaders believed Cluny was compromising. The Cistercians accordingly stressed anew the inner life and spiritual goals of monasticism. They located their houses in remote areas and denied themselves worldly comforts and distractions. Remarkably successful, the order could count three hundred chapter houses within a century of its founding, and many others imitated its more austere spirituality.

The Canons Regular were independent groups of secular clergy (and also earnest laity) who, in addition to serving laity in the world, adopted the *Rule* of Saint Augustine (a monastic guide dating from around the year 500) and practiced the ascetic virtues of regular clerics. There were monks who renounced exclusive withdrawal from the world. There were also priests who renounced exclusive involvement in it. By merging the life of the cloister with traditional clerical duties, the Canons Regular foreshadowed the mendicant friars of the thirteenth century—the Dominicans and the Franciscans, who combined the ascetic ideals of the cloister with an active ministry in the world.

The monasteries and nunneries of the established orders recruited candidates from among wealthy social groups. Crowding in these convents and the absence of patronage gave rise in the thirteenth century to lay satellite convents known as Beguine houses. These convents housed religiously earnest single women from the upper and middle social strata. In the German city of Cologne, one hundred such houses were established between 1250 and 1350, each with eight to twelve "sisters." Several of these convents fell prey to heresy. The church made the new religious orders of Dominicans and Franciscans responsible for "regularizing" such convents.

Prominence of the Clergy The clergy constituted a far greater proportion of medieval society than modern society. Estimates suggest that 1.5 percent of fourteenth-century Europe was in clerical garb. The clergy were concentrated in urban areas, especially in towns with universities and cathedrals, where, in addition to studying, they found work in a wide variety of religious services. Late-fourteenth-century England had one cleric for every seventy laypeople, and in counties with a cathedral or a university, the proportion rose to one cleric for every fifty laypeople.[1] In large university towns, the clergy might exceed 10 percent of the population.

Despite the moonlighting of poorer parish priests, the clergy as a whole, like the nobility, lived on the labor of others. Their income came from the regular collection of tithes and church taxes according to an elaborate system that evolved in the High and later Middle Ages. The church was, of course, a major landowner and regularly collected rents and fees. Monastic communities and high prelates amassed great fortunes; there was a popular saying that monastery granaries were always full. The immense secular power attached to high clerical posts can be seen in the intensity of the investiture struggle. (See Chapter 7.)

For most of the Middle Ages, the clergy were the "first estate," and theology was the queen of the sciences. How did the clergy achieve such prominence? Much of it was self-proclaimed. However, there was also popular respect and reverence for the clergy's role as a mediator between God and humanity. The priest brought the very Son of God down to earth when he celebrated the sacrament of the Eucharist; his absolution released penitents from punishment for mortal sin. It was improper for mere laypeople to sit in judgment on such a priest.

Theologians elaborated the distinction between the clergy and the laity to the clergy's benefit. The belief in the superior status of the clergy underlay the evolution of clerical privileges and immunities in both person and property. Secular rulers were not supposed to tax the clergy, who were holy persons, without special permission from the ecclesiastical authorities. Clerical crimes were under the jurisdiction of special ecclesiastical courts, not the secular courts. Because churches and monasteries were deemed holy places, they, too, were free from secular taxation and legal jurisdiction. Hunted criminals, lay and clerical, regularly sought asylum within them, disrupting the normal processes of law

[1]Denys Hay, *Europe in the Fourteenth and Fifteenth Centuries*, 2nd ed. (New York: Holt, Rinehart, 1966), pp. 58–59.

In this image of rustic labors, peasants clear ground, mow fields, plant seed, harvest grain, shear sheep, stomp grapes, and slaughter hogs, among other chores, while the lord of the manor hunts with his falcon in the fields as they work. The Labors of the 12 Months. Pietro de Crescenzi, Le Rustican. Ms.340/603. France, c.1460. Location: Musée Condé, Chantilly, France. Giraudon/Art Resource, NY

and order. When city officials violated this privilege, ecclesiastical authorities threatened excommunication and interdict. People feared this suspension of the church's sacraments, including Christian burial, almost as much as they feared the criminals to whom the church gave asylum.

By the late Middle Ages, townspeople increasingly resented the special immunities of the clergy. They complained that the clergy had greater privileges, yet fewer responsibilities, than all others who lived within the town walls. An early-sixteenth-century lampoon reflected what had by then become a widespread sentiment:

Priests, monks, and nuns
Are but a burden to the earth.
They have decided
That they will not become citizens.
That's why they're so greedy—
They stand firm against our city
And will swear no allegiance to it.
And we hear their fine excuses:
"It would cause us much toil and trouble
Should we pledge our troth as burghers."[2]

[2]Cited by S. Ozment, *The Reformation in the Cities* (New Haven, CT: Yale University Press, 1975), p. 36.

The separation of church and state and the distinction between the clergy and the laity have persisted into modern times. After the fifteenth century, however, the clergy ceased to be the superior class they had been for so much of the Middle Ages. In both Protestant and Catholic lands, governments progressively subjected them to the basic responsibilities of citizenship.

Peasants

The largest and lowest social group in medieval society was the one on whose labor the welfare of all the others depended: the agrarian peasantry. Many peasants lived on and worked the manors of the nobility, the primitive cells of rural social life. All were to one degree or another dependent on their lords and were considered to be their property. The manor in Frankish times was a plot of land within a village, ranging from twelve to seventy-five acres in size, assigned to a certain member by a settled tribe or clan. This member and his family became lords of the land, and those who came to dwell there formed a smaller, self-sufficient community within a larger village. In the early Middle Ages, such manors consisted of the dwellings of the lord and his family, the huts of the peasants, agricultural sheds, and fields.

The Duties of Tenancy The landowner or lord of the manor required a certain amount of produce (grain, eggs, and the like) and a certain number of services from the peasant families that came to dwell on and farm his land. The tenants were free to divide the labor as they wished and could keep what goods remained after the lord's levies were met. A powerful lord might own many such manors. Kings later based their military and tax assessments on the number of manors a vassal landlord owned. No set rules governed the size of manors. There were manors of a hundred acres or fewer and some of several thousand or more.

There were both servile and free manors. The tenants of the latter had originally been freemen known as *coloni.* (See Chapter 5.) Original inhabitants of the territory and petty landowners, they swapped their small possessions for a guarantee of security from a more powerful lord, who came in this way to possess their land. Unlike the pure serfdom of the servile manors, whose tenants had no original claim to a part of the land, the tenancy obligations on free manors tended to be limited, and the tenants' rights more carefully defined. It was a milder serfdom. Tenants of servile manors were, by comparison, far more vulnerable to the whims of their landlords. These two types of manors tended, however, to merge. The most common situation was the manor on which tenants of greater and lesser degrees of servitude dwelt together, their services to the lord defined by their personal status and local custom. In many regions free, self-governing peasant communities existed without any overlords and tenancy obligations.

The lord held both judicial and police powers. He owned and operated the machines that processed crops into food and drink. Marc Bloch, a modern authority on manorial society, has vividly depicted the duties of tenancy:

> On certain days the tenant brings the lord's steward perhaps a few small silver coins or, more often, sheaves of grain harvested on his fields, chickens from his farmyard, cakes of wax from his beehives or from the swarms of the neighboring forest. At other times he works on the arable or the meadows of the demesne [the lord's plot of land in the manorial fields, between one-third and one-half of that available]. Or else we find him carting casks of wine or sacks of grain on behalf of the master to distant residences. His is the labour which repairs the walls or moats of the castle. If the master has guests the peasant strips his own bed to provide the necessary extra bedclothes. When the hunting season comes round, he feeds the pack. If war breaks out he does duty as a foot soldier or orderly, under the leadership of the reeve of the village.[3]

The lord also had the right to subject his tenants to exactions known as **banalities**. He could, for example, force them to breed their cows with his bull and to pay for the privilege, to grind their bread grains in his mill, to bake their bread in his oven, to make their wine in his wine press, to buy their beer from his brewery, and even to surrender to him the tongues or other choice parts of all animals slaughtered on his lands. The lord also collected a serf's best animal as an inheritance tax. Without the lord's permission, serfs could neither travel nor marry outside the manor in which they served.

The Life of a Serf Exploited as the serfs may appear to have been from a modern point of view, their status was far from chattel slavery. It was to the lord's advantage to keep his serfs healthy and happy; his welfare, like theirs, depended on a successful harvest. Serfs had their own dwellings and modest strips of land and lived by the produce of their own labor and organization. They could market for their own profit what surpluses might remain after the harvest. They were free to choose their spouses within the local village, although they needed the lord's permission to marry a wife or husband from another village. Serfs could pass their property (their dwellings and field strips) and worldly goods on to their children.

[3]Marc Bloch, *Feudal Society*, trans. by L. A. Manyon (Chicago: University of Chicago Press, 1968), p. 250.

Peasants lived in timber-framed huts. Except for the higher domestic servants, they seldom ventured far beyond their own villages. The local priest often was their window on the world, and church festivals were their major communal entertainment.

Despite the social distinctions between free and servile serfs—and, within these groups, between those who owned plows and oxen and those who possessed only hoes—the common dependence on the soil forced close cooperation. The ratio of seed to grain yield was consistently poor; about two bushels of seed were required to produce six to ten bushels of grain in good times. There was rarely an abundance of bread and ale, the staple peasant foods. Two important American crops, potatoes and corn (maize), were unknown in Europe until the sixteenth century. Pork was the major source of protein, and every peasant household had its pigs. At slaughter time a family might also receive a little tough beef. Basically, however, everyone depended on the grain crops. When they failed or fell short, peasants went hungry unless their lord had surplus stores he was willing to share.

Changes in the Manor Two basic changes occurred in the evolution of the manor from the early to the later Middle Ages. The first was its fragmentation and the rise to dominance of the single-family holding. Such technological advances as the collar harness (ca. 800), the horseshoe (ca. 900), and the three-field system of crop rotation facilitated this development by making it easier for small family units to support themselves. As the lords parceled out their land to new tenants, their own plots became progressively smaller. This increase in tenants and decrease in the lord's fields brought about a corresponding reduction in the labor services exacted from the tenants. Also, the bringing of new fields into production increased individual holdings and modified labor services. In France, by the reign of Louis IX (r. 1226–1270), only a few days of labor a year were required, whereas in the time of Charlemagne (r. 768–814) peasants had worked the lords' fields several days a week.

As the single-family unit replaced the clan as the basic nuclear group, assessments of goods and services fell on individual fields and households, no longer on manors as a whole. Family farms replaced manorial units. The peasants' carefully nurtured communal life made possible a family's retention of its land and dwelling after the death of the head of the household. In this way, land and property remained in the possession of a single family from generation to generation.

The second change in the evolution of the manor was the conversion of the serf's dues into money payments, a change brought about by the revival of trade and the rise of the towns. This development, completed by the thirteenth century, permitted serfs to hold their land as rent-paying tenants and to overcome their servile status.

Although tenants thereby gained more freedom, they were not necessarily better off materially. Whereas servile workers could have counted on the benevolent assistance of their landlords in hard times, rent-paying workers were left, by and large, to their own devices. Their independence caused some landlords to treat them with indifference and even resentment.

Lands and properties that generations of peasants had occupied as their own were always under the threat of the lord's claim to a prior right of inheritance and even outright usurpation. As their *demesnes* declined, the lords were increasingly tempted to encroach on such traditionally common lands. The peasantry fiercely resisted such efforts, instinctively clinging to the little they had. In many regions they organized to gain a voice in the choice of petty rural officials.

By the mid-fourteenth century, a declining nobility in England and France, faced with the ravages of the great plague and the Hundred Years' War, tried to turn back the historical clock by increasing taxes on the peasantry and restricting their migration into the cities. The peasantry responded with armed revolts. These revolts became the rural equivalents of the organization of medieval cities in sworn communes to protect their self-interests against powerful territorial rulers. The revolts of the agrarian peasantry, like those of the urban proletariat, were brutally crushed. They stand out at the end of the Middle Ages as violent testimony to the breakup of medieval society. As growing national sentiment would break its political unity and heretical movements would end its nominal religious unity, peasant revolts revealed the absence of medieval social unity.

▾ Towns and Townspeople

In the eleventh and twelfth centuries, towns held only about 5 percent of western Europe's population. By comparison to modern towns, they were small. Of Germany's 3,000 towns, for example, 2,800 had populations under 1,000. Only fifteen German towns exceeded 10,000. The largest, Cologne, had 30,000. In England, only London had more than 10,000. Paris was larger than London, but not by much. The largest European towns were in Italy; Florence approached 100,000 and Milan was not far behind. Italian towns were not feudally chartered, which accounts for their greater political independence. In the Middle Ages and now, cities and towns were where the action was. There one might find the whole of medieval society, including its most creative segments.

The Chartering of Towns

Feudal lords, both lay and clerical, originally dominated towns. The lords created the towns by granting charters to those who would agree to live and work within them. The charters guaranteed their safety and gave inhabitants a degree of independence unknown on the land. The purpose was originally to concentrate skilled laborers who could manufacture the finished goods lords and bishops wanted. In this way, manorial society actually created its urban challenger and weakened itself. Because the nobility longed for finished goods and luxuries from faraway places, noblemen prodded their serfs to become skilled craftspeople. By the eleventh century, skilled serfs began to pay their manorial dues in manufactured goods, rather than in field labor, eggs, chickens, and beans, as they had earlier done. In return for a fixed rent and proper subservience, serfs were also encouraged to move to the towns. There they gained special rights and privileges from the charters.

As towns grew and beckoned, serfs fled the countryside with their skills going directly to the new urban centers. There they found the freedom and profits that might lift an industrious craftsperson into higher social ranks. As this migration of serfs to the towns accelerated, the lords in the countryside offered them more favorable terms of tenure to keep them on the land. But serfs could not easily be kept down on the farms after they had discovered the opportunities of town life. In this way, the growth of towns improved the lot of serfs generally.

The Rise of Merchants

Not only did rural society give the towns their craftspeople and day laborers, the first merchants themselves may also have been enterprising serfs. Not a few long-distance traders were men who had nothing to lose and everything to gain by the enormous risks of foreign trade. They traveled together in armed caravans and convoys, buying goods and products as cheaply as possible at the source, and selling them for all they could get in Western ports. (See Map 8–1.)

At first, traditional social groups—nobility, clergy, and peasantry—considered the merchants an oddity. As late as the fifteenth century, we find the landed nobility still snubbing the urban patriciate. Such snobbery never died out among the older landed nobility, who looked down on the traders as men of poor breeding and character possessed of money they did not properly earn or deserve. Over time the powerful grew to respect the merchants, and the weak to imitate them, because wherever the merchants went, they left a trail of wealth behind.

Challenging the Old Lords

As they grew in wealth and numbers, merchants formed their own protective associations and were soon challenging traditional seigneurial authority. They especially wanted to end the tolls and tariffs regional authorities

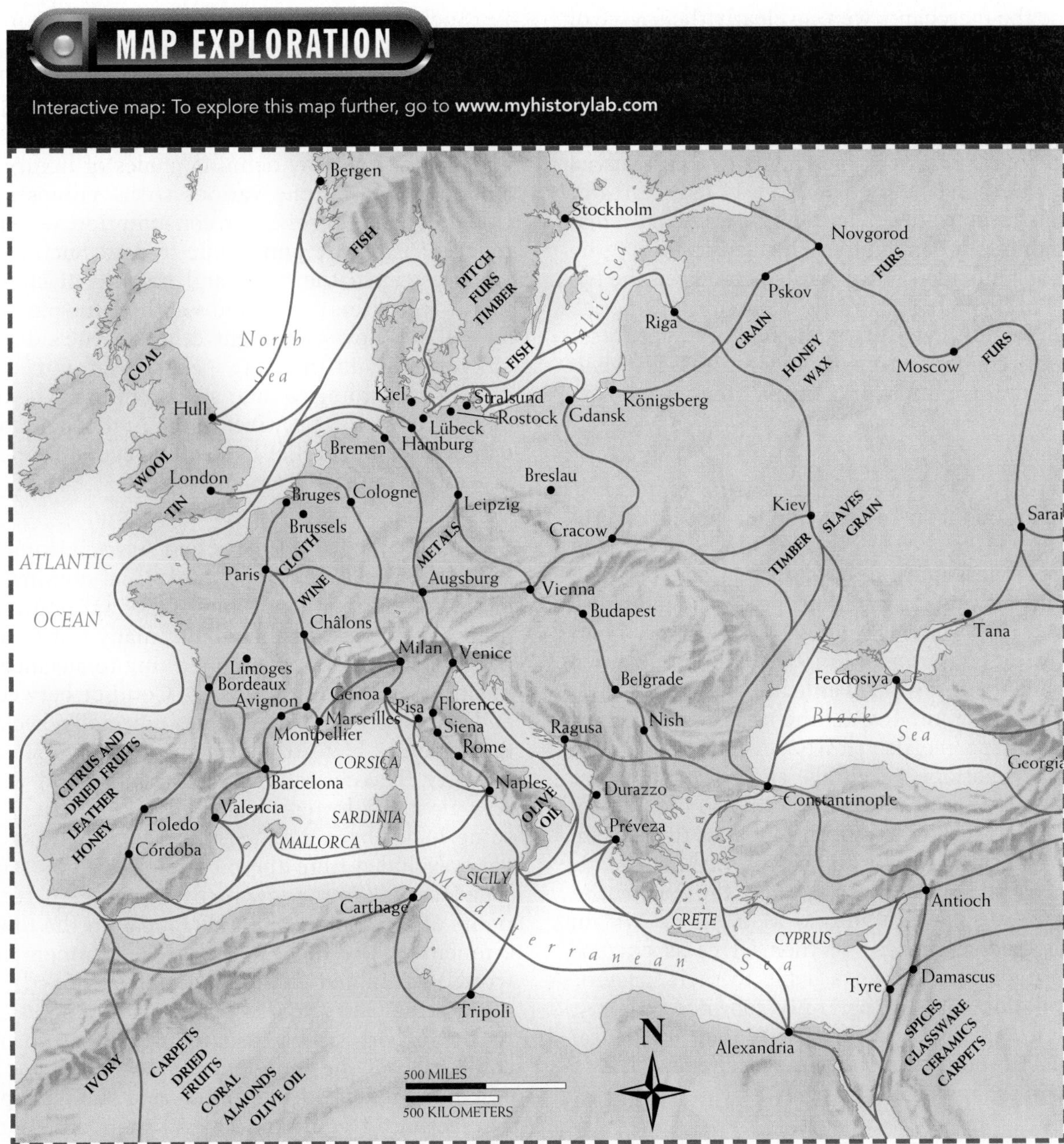

Map 8–1 **SOME MEDIEVAL TRADE ROUTES AND REGIONAL PRODUCTS** The map shows some of the channels that came to be used in interregional commerce as well as the products traded by particular regions.

imposed on the surrounding countryside. Such regulations hampered the flow of commerce on which both merchant and craftsperson in the growing urban export industries depended. Wherever merchants settled in large numbers, they challenged the tolls, tariffs, and other petty restrictions on trade. Merchant guilds or protective associations also sprang up in the eleventh century and were followed in the twelfth century by those of craftspeople (drapers, haberdashers, furriers, hosiers, goldsmiths). Both quickly found themselves in conflict with the norms of a comparatively static agricultural society.

Merchants and craftspeople needed simple and uniform laws and a fluid government sympathetic to their new forms of business activity—not the fortress mentality of the lords of the countryside. The result was a struggle with the old nobility within and outside the towns. This conflict led towns in the High and later Middle Ages to form their own independent communes and to ally themselves with kings against the nobility in the countryside, a development that eventually rearranged the centers of power in medieval Europe and dissolved classic feudal government.

Because the merchants were so clearly the engine of the urban economy, small shopkeepers and artisans identified more with them than with the aloof royal lords and bishops who were the chartered town's original masters. Most townspeople found that the development of urban life to benefit merchants also best served their own interests. The merchants' way led to greater commercial freedom, fewer barriers to trade and business, and a more fluid urban life. The lesser nobility (the small knights) outside the towns also embraced the opportunities of the new mercantile economy. During the eleventh and twelfth centuries, the burgher upper class increased its economic strength and successfully challenged the old urban lords for control of the towns.

New Models of Government

With urban autonomy came new models of self-government. Around 1100, the old urban nobility and the new burgher upper class merged. It was a marriage between those wealthy by birth (inherited property) and those who made their fortunes in long-distance trade. From this new ruling class was born the aristocratic town council, which henceforth governed towns.

Enriching and complicating the situation, small artisans and craftspeople also slowly developed their own protective associations, or **guilds**, and began to gain a voice in government. The towns' ability to provide opportunities for the "little person" created the slogan, "Town air brings freedom." In the countryside the air one breathed still belonged to the lord of the land, but in the towns residents were treated as freemen. Within town walls, people thought of themselves as citizens with basic rights, not subjects liable to their masters' whim. Economic hardship certainly continued to exist among the lower urban groups, despite their basic legal and political freedoms, but social mobility was at least a possibility in the towns.

Keeping People in Their Places Traditional measures of success had great appeal within the towns. Despite their economic independence, the wealthiest urban groups admired and imitated the lifestyle of the old landed nobility. Although the latter treated the urban patriciate with disdain, successful merchants longed to live the noble, knightly life. They wanted coats of arms, castles, country estates, and the life of a gentleman or a lady on a great manor. This became particularly true in the later Middle Ages, when reliable bills of exchange and international regulation of trade, together with the maturation of merchant firms, allowed merchants to conduct their business by mail. Then only the young apprentices did a lot of traveling, to learn the business from the ground up. When merchants became rich enough to do so, they took their fortunes to the countryside.

Such social climbing disturbed city councils, and when merchants departed for the countryside, towns often lost out economically. A need to be socially distinguished and distinct pervaded urban society. The merchants were just the tip of the iceberg. Towns tried to control this need by defining grades of luxury in dress and residence for the various social groups and vocations. Overly conspicuous consumption was a kind of indecent exposure punishable by law. Such sumptuary laws restricted the types and amount of clothing one might wear (the length and width of fur pieces, for example) and how one might decorate one's dwelling architecturally. In this way, people were forced to dress and live according to their station in life. The intention of such laws was positive: to maintain social order and dampen social conflict by keeping everyone clearly and peacefully in their place.

Social Conflict and Protective Associations (Guilds)

Despite unified resistance to external domination, medieval towns were not internally harmonious social units. They were a collection of many selfish and competitive communities, each seeking to advance its own business and family interests. Conflict between haves and have-nots was inevitable, especially because medieval towns had little concept of social and economic equality. Theoretically, poor artisans could work their way up from lower social and vocational levels, and some lucky ones did. Yet those who had not done so were excluded from the city council. Only families of long standing in the town who owned property had full rights of citizenship and a direct say in the town's government at the highest levels. Government, in other words, was inbred and aristocratic.

Conflict also existed between the poorest workers in the export trades (usually the weavers and wool combers) and the economically better off and socially ascending independent workers and small shopkeepers. The better-off workers also had their differences with the merchants, whose export trade often brought competitive foreign goods into the city, so independent workers and small shopkeepers organized to restrict foreign trade to a minimum and corner the local market in certain items.

Over time, the formation of artisan guilds gave workers in the trades a direct voice in government. Ironically, the long-term effect of this gain limited the social mobility of the poorest artisans. The guilds gained representation on city councils, where, to discourage imports, they used their power to enforce quality standards and fair prices on local businesses. These actions tightly restricted guild membership, squeezing out poorer artisans and tradesmen. As a result, lesser merchants and artisans found their opportunities progressively limited. So rigid and exclusive did the dominant guilds become that they often stifled their own creativity and inflamed the journeymen whom they excluded from their ranks. Unrepresented artisans and craftspeople constituted a true urban proletariat prevented by law from forming their own guilds or entering existing ones. The efforts by guild-dominated governments to protect local craftspeople and industries tended to narrow trade and depress the economy for all.

Towns and Kings

By providing kings with the resources they needed to curb factious noblemen, towns became a major force in the transition from feudal societies to national governments. In many places kings and towns formally allied against the traditional lords of the land. A notable exception to this general development is England, where the towns joined with the barons against the oppressive monarchy of King John (r. 1199–1216), becoming part of the parliamentary opposition to the crown. But by the fifteenth century, kings and towns had also joined forces in England, so much so that Henry VII's (r. 1485–1509) support of towns brought him the title, the "burgher king."

Towns attracted kings and emperors for obvious reasons. They were a ready source of educated bureaucrats and lawyers who knew Roman law, the ultimate tool for running kingdoms and empires. Kings could also find money in the towns in great quantity, enabling them to hire their own armies instead of relying on the nobility. Towns had the human, financial, and technological resources to empower kings. By such alliances, towns won royal political recognition and guarantees for their constitutions. This proved somewhat easier to do in the stronger coastal areas than inland, where urban life remained less vigorous and territorial government was on the rise. In France, towns were integrated early into royal government. In Germany, they fell under ever tighter control by the princes. In Italy, uniquely, towns dominated the surrounding countryside, becoming genuine city-states during the Renaissance.

It was also in the towns' interest to have a strong monarch as their protector against despotic local lords and princes, who were always eager to integrate or engulf the towns within their expanding territories. Unlike a local magnate, a king tended to remain at a distance, allowing towns to exercise their precious autonomy. A king was thus the more desirable overlord. It was also an advantage for a town to conduct its long-distance trade in the name of a powerful monarch. This gave predators pause and improved official cooperation along the way. Such alliances profited both sides—kings and towns.

Between the eleventh and fourteenth centuries, towns had considerable freedom and autonomy. As in Roman times, they again became the flourishing centers of Western civilization. But after the fourteenth century, and even earlier in France and England, the towns, like the church before them, were steadily bent to the political will of kings and princes in most places. By the seventeenth century, few towns would be truly autonomous. Most had been integrated thoroughly into the larger purposes of the "state."

Jews in Christian Society

The major urban centers, particularly in France and Germany, attracted many Jews during the late twelfth and thirteenth centuries. Jews gathered there both by choice and for safety in the increasingly hostile Christian world. Mutually wary of one another, Christians and Jews limited direct contact with one another to exchanges between their merchants and scholars. The church expressly forbade Jews from hiring Christians in their businesses and from holding any public authority over them. Jews freely conducted their own small businesses, catering to private clients, both Christian and Jewish. The wealthier Jews became bankers to kings and popes. Jewish intellectual and religious culture, always elaborate and sophisticated, both dazzled and threatened Christians who viewed it from outside. These various factors—the separateness of Jews, their exceptional economic power, and their rich cultural strength—contributed to envy, suspicion, and distrust among many Christians, whose religious teaching held Jews responsible for the death of Christ.

Between the late twelfth and fourteenth centuries, Jews were exiled from France and persecuted elsewhere. Two factors lay behind this unprecedented surge in anti-Jewish sentiment. The first was a desire by kings to confiscate Jewish wealth and property and to eliminate the Jews as economic competitors with the monarchy. In the fourteenth century, French kings acted similarly against a wealthy Christian military order known as the Knights Templar. (See Chapters 7 and 9.) The church's increasing political vulnerability to the new dynastic monarchies also contributed to the surge in anti-Jewish sentiment. Faced with the loss of its political power, the church became more determined than ever to maintain its spiritual hegemony. Beginning with the Crusades and the creation of new mendicant orders, the church reasserted its claims to spiritual sovereignty over Europe, instigating campaigns against dissenters, heretics, witches, Jews, and infidels at home and abroad.

▼ Schools and Universities

In the twelfth century, Byzantine and Spanish Islamic scholars made it possible for the works of Aristotle on logic, the mathematical and astronomical writings of Euclid and Ptolemy, the basic works of Greek physicians and Arab mathematicians, and the larger texts of Roman law to circulate among Western scholars. Islamic scholars preserved these works and wrote extensive, thought-provoking commentaries on them, which were

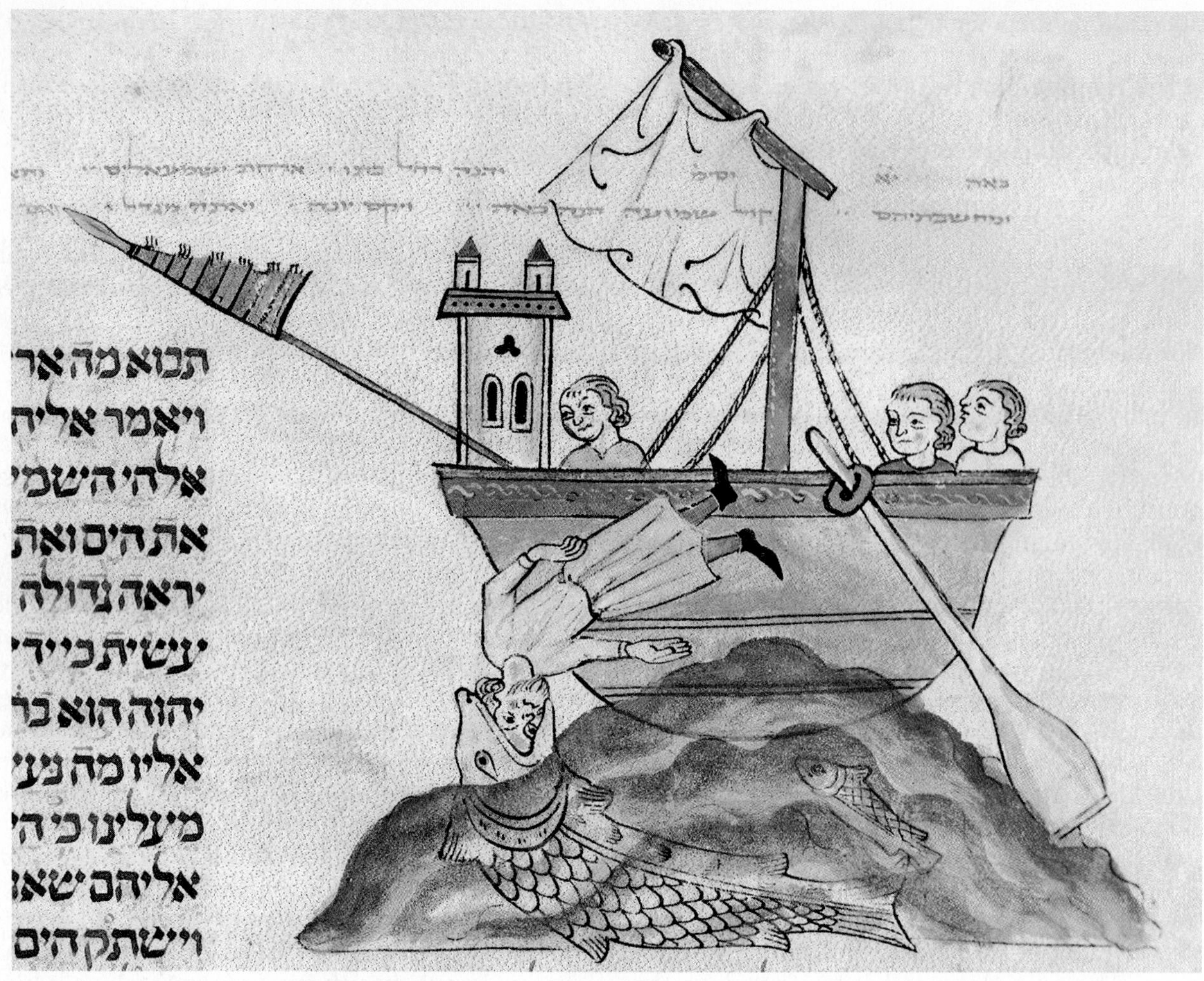

Jonah is swallowed by a great fish in a scene from a thirteenth-century Hebrew Torah from Portugal, an example of the rich Jewish heritage of medieval Iberia. Instituto da Biblioteca Nacional, Lisbon, Portugal/The Bridgeman Art Library

translated into Latin and made available to Western scholars and students. This renaissance of ancient knowledge produced an intellectual ferment that gave rise to Western universities.

University of Bologna

The first important Western university, established by Emperor Frederick I Barbarossa in 1158, was in Bologna. There we find the first formal organizations of students and masters and the first degree programs—the institutional foundations of the modern university. Originally, the term *university* meant simply a corporation of individuals (students and masters) who joined for their mutual protection from overarching episcopal authority (the local bishop oversaw the university) and from the local townspeople. Because townspeople then looked on students as foreigners without civil rights, such protective unions were necessary. They followed the model of an urban trade guild.

Bolognese students also "unionized" to guarantee fair rents and prices from their often reluctant hosts. And students demanded regular, high-quality teaching from their masters. In Italy, students actually hired their own teachers, set pay scales, and drew up desired lecture topics. Masters who did not keep their promises or live up to student expectations were boycotted. Price gouging by townspeople was met with the threat to move the university to another town. This could be done rather easily, because the university was not yet tied to a fixed physical plant. Students and masters moved freely from town to town as they chose. Such mobility gave them a unique independence from their surroundings.

Masters also formed their own protective associations and established procedures and standards for certification to teach within their ranks. The first academic degree was a certificate that licensed one to teach, a *licentia docendi.* It granted graduates in the liberal arts program—the program basic to all higher learning—as well as those in the higher professional sciences of med-

In this medieval school scene, a teacher and his wife, with switches, teach children their music lessons. German Information Center

icine, theology, and law, "the right to teach anywhere" (*ius ibique docendi*).

Bologna was famous for the revival of Roman law. During the Frankish era and later, from the seventh to the eleventh centuries, only the most rudimentary manuals of Roman law had survived. With the growth of trade and towns in the late eleventh century, Western scholars had come into contact with the larger and more important parts of the *Corpus juris civilis* of Justinian, which had been lost during the intervening centuries. (See Chapter 6.) The study and dissemination of this recovered material was now undertaken in Bologna under the direction of Irnerius, a scholar who flourished in the early twelfth century. He and his students made authoritative commentaries, or *glosses,* on existing laws, based on their newly broadened knowledge of the *Corpus juris civilis.* Around 1140, a monk named Gratian, also a resident in Bologna, created the standard legal text in church, or canon, law, the *Concordance of Discordant Canons,* known simply as Gratian's *Decretum.*

As Bologna was the model for southern European universities (those of Spain, Italy, and southern France) and the study of law, so Paris became the model for northern European universities and the study of theology.

Oxford and Cambridge in England, and (much later) Heidelberg in Germany were among its imitators. All these universities required a foundation in the liberal arts for advanced study in the higher sciences of medicine, theology, and law. The **liberal arts** program consisted of the *trivium* (grammar, rhetoric, and logic) and the *quadrivium* (arithmetic, geometry, astronomy, and music), the language arts and the mathematical arts.

In this engraving, a teacher at the University of Paris leads fellow scholars in a discussion. As shown here, all of the students wore the scholar's cap and gown. CORBIS/Bettmann

Cathedral Schools

Before the emergence of universities, the liberal arts were taught in cathedral and monastery schools to train the clergy. By the late eleventh and twelfth centuries, cathedral schools also began to provide lectures for nonclerical students, broadening their curricula to include training for purely secular vocations. In 1179, a papal decree obliged cathedrals to provide teachers at no cost for laity who wanted to learn.

After 1200, increasing numbers of future notaries and merchants who had no particular interest in becoming priests, but who needed Latin and related intellectual disciplines to fill their secular positions, studied side by side with aspiring priests in cathedral and monastery schools. By the thirteenth century, the demand for secretaries and notaries in growing urban and territorial governments and for literate personnel in the expanding merchant firms gave rise to schools for secular vocational preparation. With the appearance of these schools, the church began to lose its monopoly on higher education.

The most famous of the cathedral schools were those of Rheims and Chartres in France. Chartres won fame under the direction of such distinguished teachers as Fulbert, Saint Ivo, and Saint Bernard of Chartres (not to be confused with the more famous Saint Bernard of Clairvaux). Gerbert, later Pope Sylvester II (r. 999–1003), guided Rheims to greatness in the last quarter of the tenth century. Gerbert was filled with enthusiasm for knowledge and promoted both logical and rhetorical studies. He did much to raise the study of logic to preeminence within the liberal arts, despite his own preference for rhetoric.

University of Paris

The University of Paris grew institutionally out of the cathedral school of Notre Dame, among others. King Philip Augustus and Pope Innocent III gave the new university its charter in 1200. At Paris the college, or house system, originated. At first, a college was just a hospice providing room and board for poor students who could not rent rooms in town. But the educational life of the university quickly expanded into fixed structures and began to thrive on sure endowments.

In Paris, the most famous college was the Sorbonne, founded for theology students around 1257 by Robert de Sorbon, chaplain to

THOMAS AQUINAS PROVES THE EXISTENCE OF GOD

People in the Middle Ages saw continuity between Earth and heaven, the world of the living and the world of the dead. Intellectuals believed that reason and revelation, although different, were nonetheless connected. So reasoned argument could prove some of what the Bible revealed to faith. Thomas Aquinas, perhaps the greatest medieval theologian explicating orthodox Christian belief, here states his famous five arguments for the existence of God, which he believed any rational person would agree with.

Are these arguments persuasive? Which is the most persuasive, which is the least? Are they basically the same argument?

Is there a God?

REPLY: There are five ways in which one can prove that there is a God.

The FIRST . . . is based on change. Some things . . . are certainly in process of change: this we plainly see. Now anything in the process of change is being changed by something else. . . . Hence one is bound to arrive at some first cause of change not itself being changed by anything, and this is what everybody understands by God.

The SECOND way is based on the nature of causation. In the observable world causes are found to be ordered in series. . . . Such a series must however stop somewhere. . . . One is therefore forced to suppose some first cause, to which everyone gives the name "God."

The THIRD way is based on what need not be and on what must be. . . . Some . . . things . . . can be, but need not be for we find them springing up and dying away . . . Now everything cannot be like this [for then we must conclude that] once upon a time there was nothing. But if that were true there would be nothing even now, because some thing that does not exist can only be brought into being by something already existing. . . . One is forced therefore to suppose something which must be . . . [and] is itself the cause that other things must be.

The FOURTH way is based on the gradation observed in things. Some things are found to be more good, more true, more noble . . . and other things less [so]. But such comparative terms describe varying degrees of approximation to a superlative . . . [something that is] the truest and best and most noble of things. . . . There is something, therefore, which causes in all other things their being, their goodness, and whatever other perfection they have. And this we call "God."

The FIFTH way is based on the guidedness of nature. An orderedness of actions to an end is observed in all bodies obeying natural laws . . .; they truly tend to a goal and do not merely hit it by accident. . . . Everything in nature, therefore, is directed to its goal by someone with intelligence, and this we call "God."

Thomas Aquinas, *Summa Theologiae*, 1st ed. by Thomas Gilby (New York: Image Books, 1969), pp. 67–70.

the king. In Oxford and Cambridge, the colleges became the basic unit of student life and were indistinguishable from the university proper. By the end of the Middle Ages, such colleges tied universities to physical plants and fixed foundations. Their mobility was also forevermore restricted, as were their earlier autonomy and freedom.

As a group, Parisian students had power and prestige. They enjoyed royal protections and privileges that were denied to ordinary citizens. Many Parisian students were well-to-do, many of whom were spoiled and petulant. They did not endear themselves to the townspeople, whom they considered inferior. The city's ordinances show that townspeople sometimes let their resentments lead to violence against students. City law forbade the beating of students. Only those students who had clearly committed serious crimes could be imprisoned. Only in self-defense might a citizen strike a student. Citizens had to testify against anyone seen abusing a student. University laws also required teachers to be carefully examined before being licensed to teach.

The Curriculum

Before the "renaissance" of the twelfth century, when many Greek and Arabic texts became available to Western scholars and students in Latin translations, the education available within cathedral and monastery schools had been limited. Students learned grammar, rhetoric, and elementary geometry and astronomy. They had the classical Latin grammars of Donatus and Priscian, Saint Augustine's treatise *On Christian Doctrine,* and Cassiodorus's treatise *On Divine and Secular Learning.* The writings of Boethius provided instruction in arithmetic and music and preserved the small body of Aristotle's works on logic then known in the West. After the textual finds of the early twelfth century, Western scholars possessed the whole of Aristotle's logic, the astronomy of Ptolemy, the writings of Euclid, and many Latin classics. By the mid-thirteenth century, almost all of Aristotle's works circulated in the West.

In the High Middle Ages, the learning process was basic. The assumption was that truth already existed; one did not have to go out and find it. Truth only had to be organized, elucidated, and defended. Such conviction made logic and dialectic the focus of education. Students wrote commentaries on authoritative texts, especially those of Aristotle and the Church Fathers. This method of study, based on logic and dialectic, was known as **Scholasticism**. It reigned supreme in all the faculties—in law and medicine as well as in philosophy and theology. Students read the traditional authorities in their field, formed short summaries of their teaching, disputed them with their peers, and then drew conclusions. Logic and dialectic dominated training in the arts because they were the tools that disciplined knowledge and thought. *Dialectic* is negative logical inquiry, the art of discovering a truth by finding the contradictions in arguments against it. Although seemingly abstract and boring, the reading and harmonizing of learned authorities in direct debate and disputation exhilarated students.

Few books existed for students and those available were expensive hand-copied works. Students could not leisurely master a subject in the quiet of a library as they do today. Instead they had to learn it in lecture, discussion, and debate. This required memorization and the ability to think on one's feet. Rhetoric, or persuasive argument, was the ultimate goal, an ability to eloquently defend the knowledge one had gained by logic and dialectic. Successful students became virtual encyclopedias.

Philosophy and Theology

Scholastics quarreled over the proper relationship between philosophy, by which they meant almost exclusively the writings of Aristotle, and theology, which they believed to be a "science" based on divine revelation. The problem between philosophy and theology arose because, in Christian eyes, Aristotle's writings contained heresy. Islamic commentators on Aristotle heightened the problem by embracing those heresies as true. Aristotle, for example, taught the eternality of the world, which called into question the Judeo-Christian teaching that God created the world in time, as the book of Genesis said. Aristotle also taught that intellect, or mind, was ultimately one, a seeming denial of human individuality and hence of Christian teaching about individual responsibility and personal immortality. Church authorities wanted the works of Aristotle and other ancient authorities to be submissive handmaidens to Christian truth.

Abelard When philosophers and theologians applied the logic and metaphysics of Aristotle to the interpretation of Christian revelation, many believed it posed a mortal threat to biblical truth and church authority. Few philosophers and theologians gained greater notoriety for such wrongful interpretation of the Scriptures than Peter Abelard (1079–1142). Possibly the brightest logician and dialectician of the High Middle Ages, Abelard was the first European scholar to gain a large student audience. No one promoted the new Aristotelian learning more boldly than he, nor did any other pay more dearly for it: Abelard ended his life not as an academic superstar, but in a monastery. His bold subjection of church teaching to Aristotelian logic and dialectic made him many powerful enemies at a time when there was no tenure to protect genius and free speech in schools and universities. Accused of multiple transgressions of church doctrine, he recounted in an autobiography the "calamities" that had befallen him over a lifetime because of his boldness.

His critics especially condemned him for his subjective interpretations of Scripture. He likened the trinitarian bonds among God the Father, the Son, and the Holy Spirit to sworn documents and covenants made among people. Rather than a God-begotten cosmic ransom of humankind from the Devil, Christ's crucifixion, he argued, redeemed Christians by virtue of its impact on their hearts and minds when they heard the story. Abelard's ethical teaching stressed intent over deed: The motives of the doer made an act good or evil, not the act itself. Inner feelings were thus more important for receiving divine forgiveness than the church's sacrament of penance administered by a priest.

Abelard's native genius and youthful disrespect for seniority and tradition gained him powerful enemies in high places. He gave those enemies the opportunity to strike him down when, in Paris, where he became Master of Students at Notre Dame, he seduced a bright, seventeen-year-old niece of a powerful canon, who hired him to be her tutor in his home. Her name was Héloïse and their passionate affair ended in public scandal, with Héloïse pregnant. Unable to marry officially (university teachers then had to be single and celibate), they wed secretly and placed their illegitimate child with Abelard's sister to raise. Intent on punishing Abelard and ending his career, the enraged uncle exposed their secret marriage and hired men to castrate Abelard.

In the aftermath of those terrible events, the lovers entered cloisters nearby Paris: Héloïse at Argentueil, Abelard at St. Denis. She continued to love Abelard and relive their passion in her mind, while Abelard became a self-condemning recluse, assuring Héloïse in his letters to her that his "love" had only been wretched desire. The famous philosopher ended his life as a platitudinous monk. In 1121, a church synod ordered all his writings to be burned. Another synod in 1140 condemned nineteen propositions from his philosophical and theological works as heresy. Retracting his teaching, Abelard lived out the remaining two years of his life in an obscure priory near Chalons. As for Héloïse, she lived another twenty years and gained renown for her positive efforts to reform the rules for the cloistered life of women, under which she had suffered. Their story is a revelation of both private and public life in the Middle Ages. It also shows how a powerful and demanding culture could shape and coerce universal human feelings.

A fourteenth-century English manuscript shows women at their daily tasks: carrying jugs of milk from the sheep pen, feeding the chickens, carding and spinning wool. By permission of The British Library

▾ Women in Medieval Society

The image and the reality of medieval women are two different things. Male Christian clergy, whose ideal was a celibate life of chastity, poverty, and obedience, strongly influenced the image. Drawing on the Bible and classical medical, philosophical, and legal traditions predating Christianity, Christian thinkers depicted women as physically, mentally, and morally weaker than men.

On the basis of such assumptions, the religious life was led to be superior to marriage, and virgins and celibate widows were praised over wives. A wife was to be subject and obedient to her husband, who, as the stronger of the two, had a duty to protect and discipline her. This image of medieval woman suggests two basic options: to become either a subjugated housewife or a confined nun. In reality, most medieval women were neither.

Image and Status

Both within and outside Christianity, this image of women was contradicted. In chivalric romances and courtly love literature of the twelfth and thirteenth centuries, as in the contemporaneous cult of the Virgin Mary, women were put on pedestals and treated as superior to men in purity. If the church harbored misogynist sentiments, it also condemned them, as in the case of the late thirteenth century *Romance of the Rose* and other popular bawdy literature.

The learned churchman Peter Lombard (1100–1169), whose *Four Books of the Sentences* every theological student annotated, asked why Eve had been created from Adam's rib rather than from his head or his feet? The answer: God took Eve from Adam's side because she was meant neither to rule over man, nor to be man's slave, but rather to stand squarely at his side, as his companion and partner in mutual aid and trust. By such

COMPARE AND CONNECT

Faith and Love in the High Middle Ages

SEPARATE AND APART in their respective cloisters, Abelard and Héloïse performed a lengthy postmortem on their tragic love affair in letters to one another. Therein, they show their open wounds and share completely different assessments of where their love led them. Unhappy in the cloister, Héloïse had only regret for what they had lost, while Abelard, having found his true self in the cloister, looked back on their relationship only with shame.

QUESTIONS

1. **Did the expectations of contemporary religion and culture contribute to the tragedy of their love?**
2. **Did they have only themselves to blame?**
3. **Which of the two better understood the situation? Who, in the end, was the stronger?**

I. Héloïse to Abelard

Why, after our conversion [and entrance into the cloisters], which you alone decreed, am I fallen into such neglect and oblivion that I am neither refreshed by your presence, nor comforted by a letter in your absence . . . When I was enjoying carnal pleasures with you, many were uncertain whether I did so from love or from desire. Now the end [result] shows the spirit [in which I acted]. I have forbidden myself all pleasures so that I might obey your will. I have reserved nothing for myself, save this one thing: to be entirely yours . . .

When we enjoyed the delights of love . . . we were spared divine wrath. But when we corrected the unlawful with the lawful [by marriage] and covered the filth of fornication with the honesty of marriage, the wrath of the Lord vehemently fell upon us . . . For men taken in the most flagrant adultery what you suffered [castration] would have been a proper punishment. But what others might merit by adultery, you incurred by a [proper] marriage. What an adulteress brings to her lover, your own wife brought to you! And this did not happen when we were still indulging our old pleasures, but when we were separated and living chaste lives apart . . .

So sweet to me were those delights of lovers that they can neither displease me nor pass from my memory. Whatever I am doing, they always come to mind. Not even when I am asleep do they spare me . . . [At] Mass, when prayer ought to be pure, the memory of those delights thoroughly captivate my wretched soul rather than heed my prayers. And although I ought to lament what I have done, I sigh rather for what I now have to forgo. Not only the things that we did, but the places and the times in which we did them are so fixed with you in my mind that I reenact them all . . . At times the thoughts of my mind are betrayed by the very motions of my body . . . 'O wretched person that I am, who shall deliver me from this body of death?' Would that I might truthfully add what follows: 'I thank God through Jesus Christ our Lord.'

II. Abelard to Héloïse

Héloïse, my lust sacrificed our bodies to such great infamy that no reverence for honor, nor for God, or for the days of our Lord's passion, or for any solemn thing whatsoever could I be stopped from wallowing in that filth . . . [and although you resisted] I made you consent. Wherefore most justly . . . of that part of my body have I been diminished wherein was the seat of my lust . . . God truly loved you [Héloïse], not I. My love . . . was lust, not love. I satisfied my wretched desires in you . . . So weep for your Savior, not for your seducer, for your Redeemer, not for your defiler, for the Lord who died for you, not for me, his servant, who is now truly free for the first time . . .

O how detestable a loss [it would have been] if, given over to carnal pleasure, you were to bring forth a few children . . . for the world, when you are now delivered of a numerous progeny [i.e. the young nuns who are Héloïse's wards in the cloister]. Nor would you then be more than a woman, you who now transcend even men, and have turned the curse of Eve into the blessing of Mary [by your chastity in the cloister]. O how indecent it would be for those holy hands of yours, which now turn the pages of sacred books, to serve the obscenities of womanly cares.

Source: *The Letters of Abelard and Heloise*, trans. by C. K. Scott Moncrieff (1942), pp. 59–61, 78, 81, 97–98, 100, 103.

Adam and Eve were not cast out of the Garden of Eden because of their sexual lust for one another but rather for their disobedience to God in eating the forbidden fruit from the Tree of Knowledge of Good and Evil. St. Augustine who, like Abelard, was known to exhibit a certain weakness for the charms of the opposite sex, taught that before their Fall, Adam and Eve had complete control over their libidos as opposed to their libidos having complete control over them. Their minds and hearts filled only with thoughts of God when, without any shame or self-indulgence, they engaged in sexual intercourse. Abelard and Heloise's sexual lust and shame serve as a commentary on fallen humankind, tracing back to Adam and Eve. This medieval depiction of Adam and Eve is courtesy of the Library of Congress, Rare Book and Special Collections Division insistence on the spiritual equality of men and women and their shared responsibility in marriage, the church to this extent also helped protect the dignity of women.

Germanic law treated women better than Roman law had done, recognizing basic rights that forbade their treatment as chattel. Unlike Roman women, who as teens married men much older than themselves, German women married husbands of similar age. Another practice unknown to the Romans was the groom's conveyance of a portion, or dowry (*dos*), to his bride, which became her own in the event of his death. All major Germanic law codes recognized the economic freedom of women: their right to inherit, administer, dispose of, and confer property and wealth on their children. They could also press charges in court against men for bodily injury and rape, whose punishment, depending on the circumstances, ranged from fines, flogging, and banishment to blinding, castration, and death.

Life Choices

The nunnery was an option for single women from the higher social classes. Entrance required a dowry and could be almost as expensive as a wedding, although usually cheaper. Within the nunnery, a woman could rise to a position of leadership as an abbess or a mother superior, exercising authority denied her in much of secular life. The nunneries of the established religious orders remained under male supervision, however, so that even abbesses had to answer to higher male authority.

In the ninth century, under the influence of Christianity, the Carolingians made monogamous marriage official policy. Heretofore they had practiced polygamy and concubinage and permitted divorce. The result was both a boon and a burden to women. On one hand, wives gained greater dignity and legal security. On the other hand, a wife's labor as household manager and bearer of children greatly increased. And the Carolingian wife was now also the sole object of her husband's wrath and pleasure. Such demands clearly took their toll. The mortality rates of Frankish women increased and their longevity decreased after the ninth century. Under such conditions, the cloister became an appealing refuge for women. However, the number of women in cloisters was never large. In late medieval England, no more than 3,500 women entered the cloister.

Working Women

Most medieval women were neither housewives nor nuns, but workers like their husbands. The evidence suggests that their husbands respected and loved them, perhaps because they worked shoulder to shoulder with them in running the household and home-based businesses. Between the ages of ten and fifteen, girls were apprenticed and gained trade skills much as did boys. If they married, they often continued their trade, operating their bake or dress shops next to their husbands' businesses, or becoming assistants and partners in the shops of their husbands. Women appeared in virtually every "blue-collar" trade, from butcher to goldsmith, but mostly worked in the food and clothing industries. Women belonged to guilds, just like men, and they became craft masters. By the fifteenth century, townswomen increasingly had the opportunity to go to school and gain at least vernacular literacy.

Although women did not have as wide a range of vocations as men, the latter's vocational destinies were also fixed. Womens gender, however, excluded them from the learned professions of scholarship, medicine, and law. Women's freedom of movement within a profession was more often regulated than a man's and their wages for the same work were not as great. Still, women remained as prominent and as creative a part of workaday medieval society as men. Rare was the medieval woman who considered herself merely a wife.

▼ The Lives of Children

The image of medieval children and the reality of their lives were also two different things. Until recently, historians were inclined to believe that parents were emotionally distant from their children during the Middle Ages. Evidence of low esteem for children comes from a variety of sources.

Children as "Little Adults"

Some historians maintain that medieval art and sculpture rarely portray children as being different from adults. If, pictorially, children and adults look alike, does that mean that people in the Middle Ages were unaware that childhood was a separate period of life requiring special care and treatment? High infant and child mortality also existed, which, one theorizes, could only have discouraged parents from making a deep emotional investment in their children. Could a parent be deeply attached to a child who had a 30 to 50 percent chance of dying before age five?

During the Middle Ages, children also assumed adult responsibilities early in life. The children of peasants labored in the fields alongside their parents as soon as they could physically manage the work. Urban artisans and burghers sent their children out of their homes into apprenticeships in various crafts and trades be-

A scene of children at play, illustrating popular pastimes, toys and games: catching butterflies, spinning tops, toddling in a walker. Such scenes document the recognition of a child's world. The Bridgeman Art Library International

tween the ages of eight and twelve. Could loving parents remove a child from the home at so tender an age? The canonical age for marriage, which was twelve for girls and fourteen for boys, is also evidence that children were expected to grow up fast, although few (mostly royalty) actually married at these ages.

The practice of infanticide is another striking suggestion of low esteem for children in ancient and early medieval times. According to the Roman historian Tacitus (ca. 55–120), the Romans exposed unwanted children, especially girls, at birth to regulate family size. The surviving children appear to have been given plenty of attention and affection. The Germanic tribes of medieval Europe, by contrast, had large families but tended to neglect their children by comparison to the Romans. Infanticide, particularly of girls, continued to be practiced in the early Middle Ages, if its condemnation in penance books and by church synods is any measure. The church also forbade parents to sleep with infants and small children, less they suffocate them either by accident or design.

Among the German tribes, one paid a much lower compensatory fine (*wergild*) for injury to a child than to an adult—only one fifth of that for injuring an adult. The *wergild* for injury to a female child under fifteen was one half that for injury to a male child—an indication that female children were the least esteemed members of German tribal society. Mothers appear also to have nursed boys longer than they did girls, which favored boys' health and survival. A woman's *wergild*, however, increased eightfold between infancy and her childbearing years.[4]

[4]David Herlihy, "Medieval Children," in *Essays on Medieval Civilization*, ed. by B. K. Lackner and K. R. Phelp (Austin: University of Texas Press, 1978), pp. 109–131.

Childhood as a Special Stage

Despite such evidence of parental distance and neglect, there is another side to the story. Since the early Middle Ages, physicians and theologians had understood childhood to be a distinct and special stage of life. Isidore (560–636), bishop of Seville and a leading intellectual authority throughout the Middle Ages, distinguished six ages of life, the first four of which were infancy, childhood, adolescence, and youth.

According to the medical authorities, infancy proper extended from birth to anywhere between six months and two years and covered the period of speechlessness and suckling. The period thereafter, until age seven, was considered a higher level of infancy, marked by the beginning of a child's ability to speak and his or her weaning. At seven, when a child could think, act decisively, and speak clearly, childhood proper began. At this point a child could be reasoned with, profit from regular discipline, and begin to learn vocational skills. At seven a child was ready for schooling, private tutoring, or apprenticeship in a chosen craft or trade. Until physical growth was complete, which could extend to twenty-one years of age, the child or youth remained legally under the guardianship of parents or a surrogate authority.

There is evidence that high infant and child mortality, rather than distancing parents from their children, actually made them all the more precious to them. The medical authorities most respected during the Middle Ages—Hippocrates, Galen, and Soranus of Ephesus—dealt at length with postnatal care and childhood diseases. Both in learned and in popular medicine, sensible as well as fanciful cures existed for the leading killers of children (diarrhea, worms, pneumonia, and fever). When infants and children died, medieval parents can be found grieving as pitiably as modern parents do. In the art and literature of the Middle Ages, we find mothers baptizing dead infants and children, even carrying them to pilgrim shrines in the hope of miraculous revival. Examples also exist of parental mental illness and suicide brought on by the death of a child.[5]

Clear evidence of special attention being paid to children may be seen in children's toys and aids (walkers and potty chairs). Medieval authorities on child rearing widely condemned child abuse and urged moderation in disciplining and punishing children. In church art and drama, parents were urged to love their children as Mary loved Jesus. Early apprenticeships may also be seen as an expression of parental love and concern. In the Middle Ages, no parental responsibility was greater than that of equipping a child for useful and gainful work. Certainly, by the High Middle Ages if not earlier, children were widely viewed as special creatures with their own needs and rights.

[5]Klaus Arnold, *Kind und Gesellschaft in Mittelater und Renaissance*, (Paderborn, Germany: 1980), pp. 31–37.

In Perspective

During the High Middle Ages, the growth of Mediterranean trade revived old cities and caused the creation of new ones. The Crusades aided and abetted this development. Italian cities especially flourished during the late eleventh and twelfth centuries. Venice dominated Mediterranean trade and extended its political and economic influence throughout the Near East. It had its own safe ports as far away as Syria. As cities grew in population and became rich from successful trade, a new social group, the long-distance traders, rose to prominence. By marriage and political organization, these merchant families organized themselves into an unstoppable force. They successfully challenged the old nobility in and around the cities. A new elite of merchants gained control of city governments almost everywhere. They brought with them a policy of open trade and the blessings and problems of nascent capitalism. Artisans and small shopkeepers at the lower end of the economic spectrum aspired to follow their example, as new opportunities opened for all. The seeds of social conflict and of urban class struggle had been sown.

One positive result of the new wealth of towns was the patronage of education and culture, which was given an emphasis not experienced since Roman times. Western Europe's first universities appeared in the eleventh century, and universities steadily expanded over the next four centuries. There were twenty by 1300. Not only did Scholasticism flourish, but a new literature, art, and architecture reflected both a new human vitality and the reshaping of society and politics. For all of this, Western Europeans had no one to thank so much as the new class of merchants, whose greed, daring, and ambition made it all possible.

REVIEW QUESTIONS

1. How did the responsibilities of the nobility differ from those of the clergy and the peasantry during the High Middle Ages? What did each social class contribute to the stability of society?
2. What led to the revival of trade and the growth of towns in the twelfth century? What political and social conditions were essential for a revival of trade? How did towns change medieval society?

3. What were the strengths and weaknesses of higher education during the Middle Ages? What subjects made up the university curriculum?
4. What was the Scholastic program and method of study? Who were the main critics of Scholasticism and what were their complaints?
5. How would you assess the position of women in Germanic law and Roman law? What were the options and responsibilities for women in each social class? Were children viewed as small adults? What are our best sources for the study of parent–child relations?

SUGGESTED READINGS

E. Amt, ed., *Women's Lives in Medieval Europe: A Sourcebook* (1993). Outstanding collection of sources.

P. Aries, *Centuries of Childhood: A Social History of Family Life* (1962). Influential pioneer effort on the subject.

J. W. Baldwin, *The Scholastic Culture of the Middle Ages: 1000–1300* (1971). Good brief synthesis.

M. Black, *The Medieval Cookbook* (1992). Dishing it up in the Middle Ages.

M. T. Clanchy, *Abelard: A Medieval Life* (1998). The biography of the famous philosopher and seducer of Héloïse.

L. Grane, *Peter Abelard: Philosophy and Christianity in the Middle Ages* (1970).

B. A. Hanawalt, *Growing Up in Medieval London* (1993). Positive portrayal of parental and societal treatment of children.

D. Herlihy, *Women, Family, and Society in Medieval Europe: Historical Essays, 1978–91* (1995). A major historian's collected essays.

A. Hopkins, *Knights* (1990). Europe's warriors and models.

D. Krueger, ed., *Byzantine Christianity* (2006). A people's history of Christianity.

E. Male, *The Gothic Image: Religious Art in France in the Thirteenth Century* (1913). An enduring classic.

L. De Mause, ed., *The History of Childhood* (1974). Substantial essays on the inner as well as the material lives of children.

R. I. Moore, *The Formation of a Persecuting Society: Power and Deviance in Western Europe, 950–1250* (1987). A sympathetic look at heresy and dissent.

J. T. Noonan, *Contraception: A History of Its Treatment by the Catholic Theologians and Canonists* (1967). Fascinating account of medieval theologians' take on sex.

S. Ozment, *Ancestors: The Loving Family in Old Europe* (2001). A sympathetic look at families past.

S. Shahar, *The Fourth Estate: A History of Women in the Middle Ages* (1983). A comprehensive survey, making clear the great variety of women's work.

For additional learning resources related to this chapter, please go to www.myhistorylab.com

PEARSON myhistorylab

THE WEST & THE WORLD

The Invention of Printing in China and Europe

THE ABILITY TO put information and ideas on paper and to circulate them widely in multiple identical copies has been credited in the West with the rise of humanism, the Protestant Reformation, the modern state, and the scientific revolution. In truth, the message preceded the machinery: It was a preexisting desire to rule more effectively and to shape and control the course of events that brought the printing press into existence in both China and Europe. Before there was printing, rulers, religious leaders, and merchants longed to disperse their laws, scriptures, and wares more widely and efficiently among their subjects, followers, and customers.

To create the skilled agents and bureaucrats, leaders of state, church, and business cooperated in the sponsorship of schools and education, which spurred the growth of reading and writing among the middle and upper urban classes. Literacy, in turn, fueled the desire for easily accessible and reliable information. Literacy came more slowly to the lower social classes, because authorities feared too much knowledge in the hands of the uneducated or poorly educated would only fan the fires of discontent. To the many who remained illiterate after the invention of printing, information was conveyed carefully in oral and pictorial form. Printed official statements were designed to be read to, as well as read by, people; and religious leaders put images and pictures in the hands of simple folk, hoping to content them with saints and charms.

Resources and Technology: Paper and Ink

Among the indispensable materials of the print revolution were sizable supplies of durable, inexpensive paper and a reliable ink. As early as the Shang period (1766–1122 B.C.E.), a water-based soot and gum ink was used across Asia. (Europe would not have such an ink until the early Middle Ages.) Also in the Shang period, official seals and stamps used to authenticate documents were made by carving bronze, jade, ivory, gold, and stone in a reverse direction (that is, in a mirror form, to prevent the print from appearing backward).

Similar seals appeared in ancient Mesopotamia and Egypt, but only for religious use—not for the affairs of daily secular life. Later, more easily carved clay or wax seals reproduced characters on silk or bamboo surfaces.

Silk in the East and parchment in the West had been early, but very expensive, print media. Bamboo and wood were cheaper, but neither was suited to large-scale printing.

A step forward occurred in the second century B.C.E. when the Chinese invented a crude paper from hemp fibers, which was previously used only for wrappings. Three centuries later (105 C.E.), an imperial eunuch named Ts'ia Lun combined tree bark, hemp, rags, and old fishnets into a superior and reliable paper. A better blend of mulberry bark, fishnets, and natural fibers became the standard paper mixture. By the Tang period (618–907), high-quality paper manufacturing had become a major industry.

In the eighth century, the improved Chinese recipe began to make its way west, after Chinese prisoners taught their Arab captors how to make paper. By the ninth century, Samarkand in Russian Turkestan had become the leading supplier of paper in the East. A century later, Baghdad and Damascus shipped fine paper to Egypt and Europe. Italy became a major Western manufacturer in the thirteenth century followed by Nuremberg, Germany, in the late fourteenth.

Early Printing Techniques

By the seventh century C.E., multiple copies of the *Confucian Scriptures* were made by taking paper rubbings from stone and metal engravings, a direct prelude to block printing. At this time in the West, the arts of engraving, and particularly of coin casting (by hammering hot alloy on an anvil that bore a carved design), took the first steps toward printing with movable type.

The invention of printing occurred much earlier in the East than in the West. The Chinese invented *block printing* (that is, printing with carved wooden blocks) in the eighth century, almost six hundred years before the technique appeared in Europe (1395). The Chinese also far outpaced the West in printing with *movable type* (that is, with individual characters or letters that could

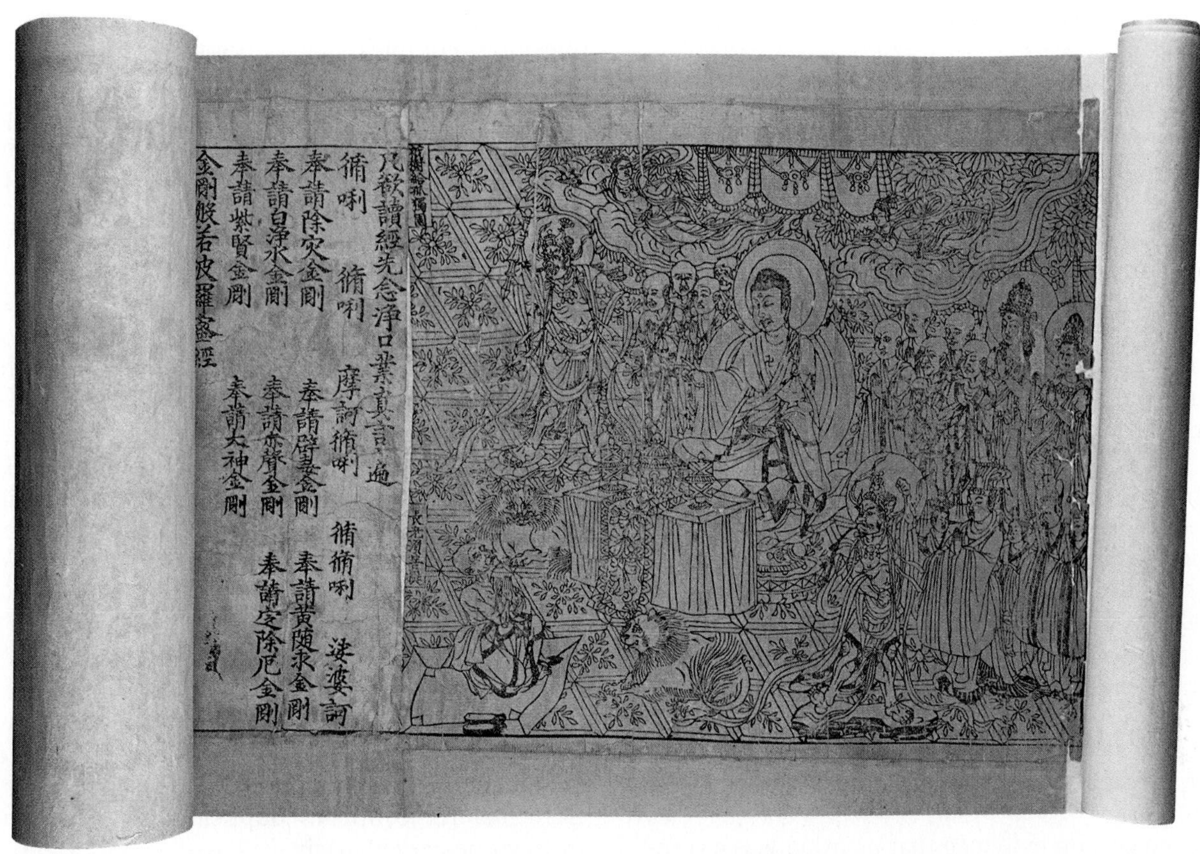

The Diamond Sutra. This Chinese translation of a Sanskrit Buddhist work was printed in 868 and found at Dunhuang. It is the earliest dated piece of block printing yet discovered. Dorling Kindersley Media Library. The image depicts the frontispiece to the world's earliest dated printed book, the Chinese translation of the Buddhist text the Diamond Sutra. This consists of a scroll, over sixteen feet long, made up of a long series of printed pages. Printed in China in 868 C.E., it was found in the Dunhuang Caves in 1907, in the North Western province of Gansu. Image taken from The Diamond Sutra. Originally published/produced in China, 11th May, 868. (c) British Library Board. All Rights Reserved (Picture number 1022251.611). © Dorling Kindersley.

be arranged by hand to make a page)—a technique invented by Pi Scheng in the 1040s, four hundred years before Johann Gutenberg set up the first Western press in Mainz, Germany (around 1450).

Block printing used hard wood (preferably from pear or jujube trees), whose surface was glazed with a filler (glue, wax, or clay). A paper copy of what one wanted to duplicate (be it a drawn image, a written sentence, or both) was placed face down on a wet glaze covering the block and the characters cut into it. The process accommodated any artistic style while allowing text and illustration to coexist harmoniously on a page. Once carved, the block was inked and mild pressure applied, allowing a great many copies to be made before it wore out.

The first movable type was ceramic. The printer set each character or piece in an iron form and arranged them on an iron baking plate filled with heated resin and wax, which, when cooled, created a tight page. After the print run was finished, the plate was heated again to melt the wax and free the type for new settings. Ceramic and later metal type was fragile and left uneven impressions, and metal type was expensive as well and did not hold water-based Chinese inks.

Carved wooden type did not have these problems and therefore became the preferred tool. Set in a wooden frame and tightened with wooden wedges, the readied page was inked up and an impression made, just as in printing with carved wooden blocks. Cutting a complete set of type or font required much time and effort because of the complexity and enormity of Chinese script. To do the latter justice, a busy press required 10,000 individual characters, and that number could increase several-fold, depending on the project.

Printing Comes of Age

In 952, after a quarter century of preparation, a standardized Chinese text, unblemished by any scribal errors, was printed for the first time on a large scale. That text, the *Confucian Classics,* was an epochal event in the history of printing. The main reading of the elite, these famous scrolls became the basis of the entry exam for a government office. In awakening people to the power of printing, the *Confucian Classics* may be compared to the publication of Gutenberg's Latin Bible.

The Sung period (960–1278) saw the first sustained flowering of block printing. Still today among the Chinese the phrase "Sung style" connotes high quality. Three monumental publications stand out: the *Standard Histories* of previous Chinese dynasties, serially appearing between 994 and 1063; the *Buddhist Scriptures* in scrolls up to sixty feet and longer, requiring 130,000 carved wooden blocks (971–983); and the *Daoist Scriptures* (early eleventh century). For the literate, but not necessarily highly educated, numerous how-to books on medical, botanical, and agricultural topics became available. Printed paper money also appeared for the first time in copper-poor Szechwan during the Sung.

There is no certain evidence that printing was a complete gift of the Far East to the West. Although some scholars believe Chinese block printing accompanied playing cards through the Islamic world and into Europe, the actual connecting links have not yet been demonstrated. So although there was a definite paper trail from East to West, Europe appears to have developed its own inks and invented its own block and movable type printing presses independently.[1]

Indeed in the East and the West, different writing systems would favor distinct forms of printing. In China, carved wooden blocks suited an ideographic script that required a seemingly boundless number of characters. Each ideograph, or character, expressed a complete concept. In contrast, European writing was based on a very small phonetic alphabet. Each letter could express meaning only when connected to other letters, forming words. For such a system, movable metal type worked far better than carved wooden blocks. So although China mastered movable type printing earlier than the West, the enormous number of characters required by the Chinese language made movable type impractical.

Ironically, the simpler machinery of block printing did greater justice to China's more intricate and complex script, whereas Europe's far simpler script required the more complex machinery of movable type. Today the Chinese still face the problem of storing and retrieving their rich language in digitized form, "the space-age equivalent of movable type." In telecommunications, they prefer faxes, "the modern-day equivalent of the block print."[2]

Society and Printing

In neither the East nor the West do the availability of essential material resources (wood, ink, and paper) and the development of new technologies sufficiently explain the advent of printing. Cultural and emotional factors played an equally large role. In China, the religious and moral demands of Buddhists, Taoists, and Confucians lay behind the invention of block printing. For Buddhists, copying and disseminating their sacred writings had always been a traditional path of salvation. Taoists, who wanted to hang protective charms or seals around their necks, printed sacred messages blessed by their priests that were up to four inches wide. These were apparently the first block prints. Confucianists, too, lobbied for standardized printed copies of their texts, which they had for centuries duplicated by crude rubbings from stone-carved originals.

In Europe, the major religious orders (Augustinians, Dominicans, and Franciscans) and popular lay religious movements (Waldensians, Lollards, and Hussites) joined with humanists to promote the printing of standardized, orthodox editions of the Bible and other religious writings. As the numbers of literate laity steadily grew, the demand for cheap, practical reading material (calendars, newssheets, and how-to pamphlets) also rapidly increased. By 1500, fifty years after Gutenberg's invention, two hundred printing presses operated throughout Europe, sixty of them in German cities. Just as in China, the large print runs of the new presses tended to be religious or moral subjects in the early years: Latin Bibles and religious books, indulgences and Protestant pamphlets, along with decorated playing cards often bearing moral messages.

With the printing press came the first copyright laws. Knowledge had previously been considered "free." The great majority of medieval scholars and writers were clergy, who lived by the church or other patronage and whose knowledge was deemed a gift of God to be shared freely with all. After the printing press, however, a new sense of intellectual property emerged. In Europe, primitive protective laws took the form of a ruler's "privilege," by

[1]Carter, *Invention of Printing in China*, pp. 143, 150, 182.

[2]Twitchett, *Printing and Publishing in Medieval China*, p. 86.

A European Printshop. This sixteenth-century woodcut shows typesetting and printing underway in an early printshop. Printing made it possible to reproduce exactly and in quantity both text and illustrations, leading to the distribution of scientific and technical information on a scale unimaginable in the pre-print world. Courtesy of the Library of Congress

which a ruler pledged to punish the pirating of a particular work within his or her realm over a limited period of time. Such measures had clear limits: More than half of the books published during the first century of print in the West were pirated editions, a situation that would not change significantly until the eighteenth century.

Government censorship laws also ran apace with the growth of printing. The clergy of Cologne, Germany, issued the first prohibition of heretical books in 1479. In 1485, the church banned the works of the heretics John Wycliffe and John Huss throughout Europe, and two years later the pope promulgated the first bull against any and all books "harmful to the faith." In 1521, Emperor Charles V banned Martin Luther's works throughout the Holy Roman Empire, along with their author. In 1527, the first publisher was hanged for printing a banned book of Luther's. And in 1559, the pope established the *Index of Forbidden Books,* which still exists.

Printing stimulated numerous new ancillary trades. In addition to the proliferation of bookstores and the rise of traveling booksellers, who carried flyers from town to town promoting particular works, there were new specialized stationery shops, ink and inkstone stores, bookshelf and reading-table makers, and businesses manufacturing brushes and other printing tools. The new print industry also brought social and economic upheaval to city and countryside when, like modern corporations relocating factories to underdeveloped countries, it went in search of cheaper labor by moving presses out of guild-dominated cities and into the freer marketplace of the countryside.

For society's authorities, the new numbers of literate citizens and subjects made changes and reforms both easier and more difficult. As a tool of propaganda, the printing press remained a two-edged sword. On the one hand, it gave authorities the means to propagandize more effectively than ever. On the other hand, the new literate public found itself in an unprecedented position to recognize deceit, challenge tradition, and expose injustice.

Sources: Thomas F. Carter, *The Invention of Printing in China and Its Spread Westward* (1928); Elisabeth L. Eisensrein, *The Printing Press as an Agent of Change,* I–II (1979); Rudolf Hirsch, *Printing, Selling and Reading 1450–1550* (Wiesbaden: Harrassowitz, 1967); Constance R. Miller, *Technical and Cultural Prerequisites for the Invention of Printing in China and the West* (Chinese Materials Center, 1983). Denis Twitchett, *Printing and Publishing in Medieval China* (New York: Frederic C. Beil, 1983).

Why did the invention of printing occur earlier in the East than in the West? Did the West inherit all of its knowledge of printing from the East? What are the differences between the Chinese and European writing systems? What problems do these systems create for printing? Why might one Chinese scholar prefer to send another Chinese scholar a fax rather than an e-mail? What was the impact of printing on Chinese and European societies?

A procession of flagellants at Tournai in Flanders in 1349, marching with the crucified Christ and scourging themselves in imitation of his suffering. © ARPL/HIP/The Image Works

9

The Late Middle Ages: Social and Political Breakdown (1300–1453)

▼ **The Black Death**

Preconditions and Causes of the Plague • Popular Remedies • Social and Economic Consequences • New Conflicts and Opportunities

▼ **The Hundred Years' War and the Rise of National Sentiment**

The Causes of the War • Progress of the War

▼ **Ecclesiastical Breakdown and Revival: The Late Medieval Church**

The Thirteenth-Century Papacy • Boniface VIII and Philip the Fair • The Avignon Papacy (1309–1377) • John Wycliffe and John Huss • The Great Schism (1378–1417) and the Conciliar Movement to 1449

▼ **Medieval Russia**

Politics and Society • Mongol Rule (1243–1480)

▼ **In Perspective**

KEY TOPICS

- **The effects of the bubonic plague on population and society**
- **The Hundred Years' War between England and France**
- **The growing power of secular rulers over the papacy**
- **Schism, heresy, and reform of the church**

THE LATE MIDDLE Ages saw almost unprecedented political, social, and ecclesiastical calamity. Bubonic plague, known to contemporaries as the Black Death, swept over almost all of Europe between 1348 and 1350 leaving as much as two fifths of the population dead and transforming many pious Christians into believers in the omnipotence of death. France and England grappled with each other in a bitter conflict known as the Hundred Years' War (1337–1453), an exercise in seemingly willful self-destruction that was made even more terrible in its later stages by the introduction of gunpowder and the invention of heavy artillery. A schism emerged within the church, which lasted thirty-nine years (1378–1417) and led, by 1409, to the election of three competing popes and colleges of cardinals. In 1453, the Turks marched seemingly invincibly through Constantinople and toward the West. As their political and religious institutions buckled, disease, bandits, and wolves ravaged their cities, and Islamic armies gathered at their borders, Europeans beheld what seemed to be the imminent total collapse of Western civilization.

It was against this background that such scholars as Marsilius of Padua, William of Ockham, and Lorenzo Valla produced lasting criticisms of medieval assumptions about the nature of God, humankind, and society. Kings worked through parliaments and clergy through councils to limit the pope's temporal power. The notion, derived from Roman law, that a secular ruler is accountable to the body he or she governs had already found expression in documents like the Magna Carta. It came increasingly to carry the force of accepted principle, and conciliarists, who advocated the judicial superiority of church councils over popes, now sought to extend it to papal accountability to the church.

Viewed in terms of their three great calamities—war, plague, and schism—the fourteenth and fifteenth centuries were years in which politics resisted wisdom, nature strained mercy, and the church was less than faithful to its flock.

▾ The Black Death

The virulent plague known as the Black Death struck fourteenth-century Europe when it was already suffering from overpopulation and malnutrition.

Preconditions and Causes of the Plague

In the fourteenth century, nine tenths of the population worked the land. The three-field system of crop production increased the amount of arable land and with it the food supply. As that supply grew, however, so did the population. It is estimated that Europe's population doubled between the years 1000 and 1300 and began thereafter to outstrip food production. There were now more people than there was food to feed them or jobs to employ them, and the average European faced the probability of extreme hunger at least once during his or her expected thirty-five-year life span.

Between 1315 and 1317, crop failures produced the greatest famine of the Middle Ages. Densely populated urban areas such as the industrial towns of the Netherlands suffered greatly. Decades of overpopulation, economic depression, famine, and bad health progressively weakened Europe's population and made it highly vulnerable to a virulent bubonic plague that struck with full force in 1348.

The **Black Death**, so called by contemporaries because of the way it discolored the body, followed the trade routes from Asia into Europe. Rats, or more precisely, the fleas the rats bore, on ships from the Black Sea area most likely brought it to Western Europe. Appearing in Constantinople in 1346 and Sicily in late 1347, it entered Europe through the ports of Venice, Genoa, and Pisa in 1348. From there it swept rapidly through Spain and southern France and into northern Europe. Areas that lay outside the major trade routes, like Bohemia, appear to have remained virtually unaffected. Bubonic plague made numerous reappearances in succeeding decades. (See Map 9–1.)

Popular Remedies

The plague often reached a victim's lungs during the course of the disease. From the lungs, the victim's sneezing and wheezing spread it from person to person. Physicians had little understanding of these processes, so even the most rudimentary preventive measures against the disease were lacking. Contemporaries could neither explain the plague nor defend themselves against it. To them, the Black Death was a catastrophe with no apparent explanation and against which there was no known defense. Throughout much of Western Europe, it inspired an obsession with death and dying and a deep pessimism that endured long after the plague years. (See "Encountering the Past: Dealing with Death," page 261.)

Popular wisdom held that a corruption in the atmosphere caused the disease. Some blamed poisonous fumes released by earthquakes. Many wore aromatic amulets as a remedy. According to the contemporary observations of Giovanni Boccaccio, an Italian who recorded the reactions in his *Decameron* (1353), some sought a remedy in moderation and a temperate life, others gave themselves over entirely to their passions (sexual promiscuity ran high within the stricken areas), and still others, "the most sound, perhaps, in judgment," chose flight and seclusion as the best medicine.

One extreme reaction was processions of flagellants, religious fanatics who beat themselves in ritual penance, believing such action would bring divine intervention. The terror the flagellants created—and their dirty, bleeding bodies may have spread the disease—became so socially disruptive and threatening that the church finally outlawed such processions.

In some places, Jews were cast as scapegoats. Centuries of Christian propaganda had bred hatred toward Jews, as had their role as society's moneylenders. Pogroms occurred in several cities, sometimes incited by the flagellants.

MAP EXPLORATION

Interactive map: To explore this map further, go to **www.myhistorylab.com**

Map 9–1 **SPREAD OF THE BLACK DEATH** Apparently introduced by seaborne rats from Black Sea areas where plague-infested rodents had long been known, the Black Death brought huge human, social, and economic consequences. One of the lower estimates of Europeans dying is 25 million. The map charts the plague's spread in the mid-fourteenth century. Generally following trade routes, the plague reached Scandinavia by 1350, and some believe it then went on to Iceland and even Greenland. Areas off the main trade routes were largely spared.

The Prince of the World, a sandstone sculpture, vividly portrays the transitory nature of life. When viewers look behind the attractive young prince, they discover his beauty to be only skin deep. His body, like every human body, is filled with death, here symbolized by worms and flesh-eating frogs. A serpect spirals up his left leg and enters his back, an allusion to the biblical teaching that the wages of sin are death. Stadt Nürnberg

Social and Economic Consequences

Whole villages vanished in the wake of the plague. Among the social and economic consequences of such high depopulation were a shrunken labor supply and a decline in the value of the estates of the nobility.

Farms Decline As the number of farm laborers decreased, wages increased and those of skilled artisans soared. Many serfs chose to commute their labor services into money payments and pursue more interesting and rewarding jobs in skilled craft industries in the cities. Agricultural prices fell because of waning demand, and the price of luxury and manufactured goods—the work of skilled artisans—rose. The noble landholders suffered the greatest decline in power. They were forced to pay more for finished products and for farm labor, while receiving a smaller return on their agricultural produce. Everywhere rents declined after the plague.

Peasants Revolt To recoup their losses, some landowners converted arable land to sheep pasture, substituting more profitable wool production for labor-intensive grains. Others abandoned the farms, leasing them to the highest bidder. Landowners also sought to reverse their misfortune by new repressive legislation that forced peasants to stay on their farms while freezing their wages at low levels. In 1351, the English Parliament passed a Statute of Laborers, which limited wages to pre-plague levels and restricted the ability of peasants to leave their masters' land. Opposition to such legislation sparked the English peasants' revolt in 1381. In France the direct tax on the peasantry, the ***taille***, was increased, and opposition to it helped ignite the French peasant uprising known as the Jacquerie.

Cities Rebound Although the plague hit urban populations hard, the cities and their skilled industries came in time to prosper from its effects. Cities had always protected their own interests, passing legislation as they grew to regulate competition from rural areas and to control immigration. After the plague, the reach of such laws extended beyond the cities to include the surrounding lands of nobles and landlords, many of whom now peacefully integrated into urban life.

The omnipresence of death also whetted the appetite for goods that only skilled industries could produce. Expensive clothes and jewelry, furs from the north, and silks from the south were in great demand in

DEALING WITH DEATH

DEATH WAS ALL too familiar in the late Middle Ages, and not just in the time of the plague, when both princes and the simple folk buried their children in the same communal pits. In popular art and literature, the living and the dead embraced in the "Dance of Death," reminding rich and poor, young and old, of their mortality. In the fourteenth century, death divided the Middle Ages from the Renaissance: On one side of the divide was an overpopulated medieval society devastated by the four horsemen of the Apocalypse, while on the other side, a newly disciplined Renaissance society learned to forestall famine, plague, war, and conquest, by abstinence, late marriage, birth control, and diplomacy.

Yet death rates in the past were three times those of the modern West and life expectancy only half as long. Life was a progressive dying, and death a promise of everlasting life. In sixteenth-century Florence, fully a third of newborns died in infancy. In seventeenth-century England, infant mortality was 2 percent on the day of birth, 4 percent at the first week, 9 percent by the first month, and 13 percent at the end of the first year. Almost everyone by their teens and adulthood suffered from some chronic illness (tuberculosis), debilitating condition (arthritis, gout), or life-threatening infection (streptococci) that pitted them in a personal battle with death.

In Renaissance Italy, Lorenzo de' Medici, duke of Urbino (d. 1519), was plagued with leg ulcers and syphilis in his early twenties. At twenty-five, he received a head wound that was treated by trephination, or by boring holes in his skull. He also developed an abscessed foot that never healed. At twenty-six, he fell prey to chills, fever, diarrhea, vomiting, joint pains, and anorexia, and was dead at twenty-seven. His physicians identified the cause of death as a catarrhal phlegm, or tuberculosis, that caused "suffocation of the heart."

In Reformation Germany, at thirty-nine, Elector Frederick III the Wise of Saxony (d. 1525), Luther's protector, spent the last year of his life enclosed in his favorite residence. When his strength permitted, he rolled about the castle on a specially made stool with wheels. Cursed with kidney stones, he died from a septic infection and kidney failure when the stones became too many and too large to pass through his urethra. An autopsy discovered stones "almost two finger joints long and spiked."

Those who suffered from such afflictions found themselves, in the words of a sixteenth-century merchant, "between God and the physicians," a precarious position for the chronically ill in any age. The clergy and the physicians profited greatly from the age's great mortality. People feared both dying and dying out of God's grace. Together, the physician and the priest prepared the way to a good temporal death, while the priest guided the dead through purgatory and into heaven, assisted by the laity's purchase of indulgences and commemorative masses. Like the physicians' bleedings and herbal remedies, the church's sacraments and commemorations both exploited and eased the feared passage into eternity that every Christian soul had to make.

A caricature of physicians (early sixteenth century). A physician carries a uroscope (for collecting and examining urine); discolored urine signaled an immediate need for bleeding. The physician/surgeon wears surgical shoes and his assistant carries a flail—a comment on the risks of medical services. Hacker Art Books Inc.

Source: Bruce Gordon and Peter Marshall, eds. *The Place of the Dead: Death and Remembrance in Late Medieval and Early Modern Europe* (Cambridge: Cambridge University Press, 2008), chaps. 2, 14; Ann C. Carmichael, "The Health Status of Florentines in the Fifteenth Century," in M. Tetel et al., eds. *Life and Death in Fifteenth-Century Florence* (Durham: Duke University Press, 1989), chap. 3.

How do illness and death shape history and culture?

How effective were the physicians and the clergy in the face of everyday afflictions? Why did people bother with them?

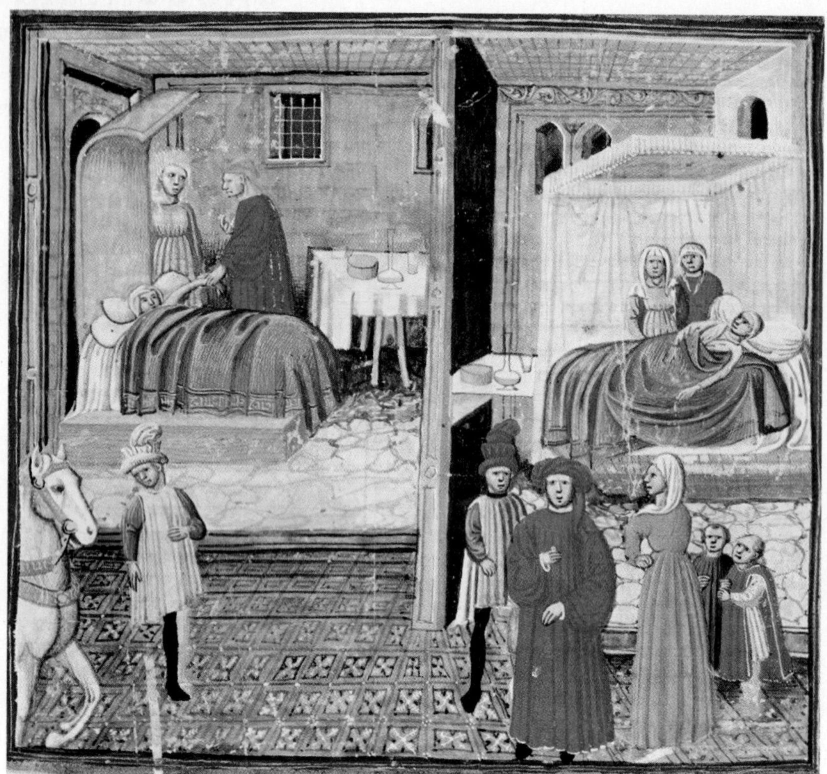

This illustration from the *Canon of Medicine* by the Persian physician and philosopher Avicenna (980–1037), whose Arabic name was Ibn Sina, shows him visiting the homes of rich patients. In the High Middle Ages, the *Canon of Medicine* was the standard medical textbook in the Middle East and Europe.
Biblioteca Universitaria, Bologna, Italy. Scala/Art Resource, NY

the decades after the plague. Initially this new demand could not be met. The basic unit of urban industry, the master and his apprentices (usually one or two), purposely kept its numbers low, jealously guarding its privileges. The first wave of plague turned this already restricted supply of skilled artisans into a shortage almost overnight. As a result, the prices of manufactured and luxury items rose to new heights, which, in turn, encouraged workers to migrate from the countryside to the city and learn the skills of artisans. Townspeople profited coming and going. As wealth poured into the cities and per capita income rose, the prices of agricultural products from the countryside, now less in demand, declined.

The church also gained and lost. It suffered as a landholder and was politically weakened, yet it also received new revenues from the vastly increased demand for religious services for the dead and the dying, along with new gifts and bequests.

New Conflicts and Opportunities

By increasing the importance of skilled artisans, the plague contributed to new social conflicts within the cities. The economic and political power of local artisans and trade guilds grew steadily in the late Middle Ages, along with the demand for their goods and services. The merchant and patrician classes found it increasingly difficult to maintain their traditional dominance and grudgingly gave guild masters a voice in city government. As the guilds won political power, they encouraged restrictive legislation to protect local industries. The restrictions, in turn, caused conflict between master artisans, who wanted to keep their numbers low and expand their industries at a snail's pace, and the many journeymen, who were eager to rise to the rank of master. To the long-existing conflict between the guilds and the ruling urban patriciate was now added one within the guilds themselves.

Also, after 1350, the results of the plague put two traditional "containers" of monarchy—the landed nobility and the church—on the defensive. Kings now exploited growing national sentiment in an effort to centralize their governments and economies. At the same time, the battles of the Hundred Years' War demonstrated the military superiority of paid professional armies over the traditional noble cavalry, thus bringing the latter's future role into question. The plague also killed many members of the clergy—perhaps one third of the German clergy fell victim as they dutifully ministered to the sick and dying. This reduction in clerical ranks occurred in the same century that saw the pope move from Rome to Avignon in southeast France (1309–1377) and the Great Schism (1378–1417) divide the Church into warring factions.

▼ The Hundred Years' War and the Rise of National Sentiment

Medieval governments were by no means all-powerful and secure. The rivalry of petty lords kept localities in turmoil, and dynastic rivalries could plunge entire lands into war, especially when power was being transferred to a new ruler—and woe to the ruling dynasty that failed to produce a male heir.

To field the armies and collect the revenues that made their existence possible, late medieval rulers depended on carefully negotiated alliances among a wide range of lesser powers. Like kings and queens in earlier centuries, they, too, practiced the art of feudal government, but on a grander scale and with greater sophistication. To maintain the order they required, the Norman kings of England and the Capetian kings of France fine-tuned traditional feudal relationships by stressing the duties of lesser to higher powers and the unquestioning loyalty noble vassals owed to the king. The result was a degree of centralized royal power unseen before in these lands and a growing national consciousness that together equipped both France and England for international warfare.

The Causes of the War

The conflict that came to be known as the Hundred Years' War began in May 1337 and lasted until October 1453. The English king Edward III (r. 1327–1377), the grandson of Philip the Fair of France (r. 1285–1314), may have started the war by asserting a claim to the French throne after the French king Charles IV (r. 1322–1328), the last of Philip the Fair's surviving sons, died without a male heir. The French barons had no intention of placing the then fifteen-year-old Edward on the French throne. They chose instead the first cousin of Charles IV, Philip VI of Valois (r. 1328–1350), the first of a new French dynasty that would rule into the sixteenth century.

But there was, of course, more to the war than just an English king's assertion of a claim to the French throne. England and France were then emergent territorial powers in too close proximity to one another. Edward was actually a vassal of Philip VI, holding several sizable French territories as fiefs from the king of France, a relationship that went back to the days of the Norman conquest. English possession of any French land was repugnant to the French because it threatened the royal policy of centralization. England and France also quarreled over control of Flanders, which, although a French fief, was subject to political influence from England because its principal industry, the manufacture of cloth, depended on supplies of imported English wool. Compounding these frictions was a long history of prejudice and animosity between the French and English people, who constantly confronted one another on the high seas and in ports. Taken together, these various factors made the Hundred Years' War a struggle for national identity as well as for control of territory.

French Weakness France had three times the population of England, was far the wealthier of the two countries, and fought on its own soil. Yet, for most of the conflict, until after 1415, the major battles ended in often stunning English victories. (See Map 9–2, page 264.) The primary reason for these French failures was internal disunity caused by endemic social conflicts. Unlike England, fourteenth-century France was still struggling to make the transition from a splintered feudal society to a centralized "modern" state.

Desperate to raise money for the war, French kings resorted to such financial policies as depreciating the currency and borrowing heavily from Italian bankers, which aggravated internal conflicts. In 1355, in a bid to secure funds, the king turned to the **Estates General**, a representative council of townspeople, clergy, and nobles. Although it levied taxes at the king's request, its independent members also exploited the king's plight to broaden their own regional sovereignty, thereby deepening territorial divisions.

France's defeats also reflected English military superiority. The English infantry was more disciplined than the French, and English archers carried a formidable weapon, the longbow, capable of firing six arrows a minute with enough force to pierce an inch of wood or the armor of a knight at two hundred yards.

Edward III pays homage to his feudal lord Philip VI of France. Legally, Edward was a vassal of the king of France. Archives Snark International/Art Resource, NY

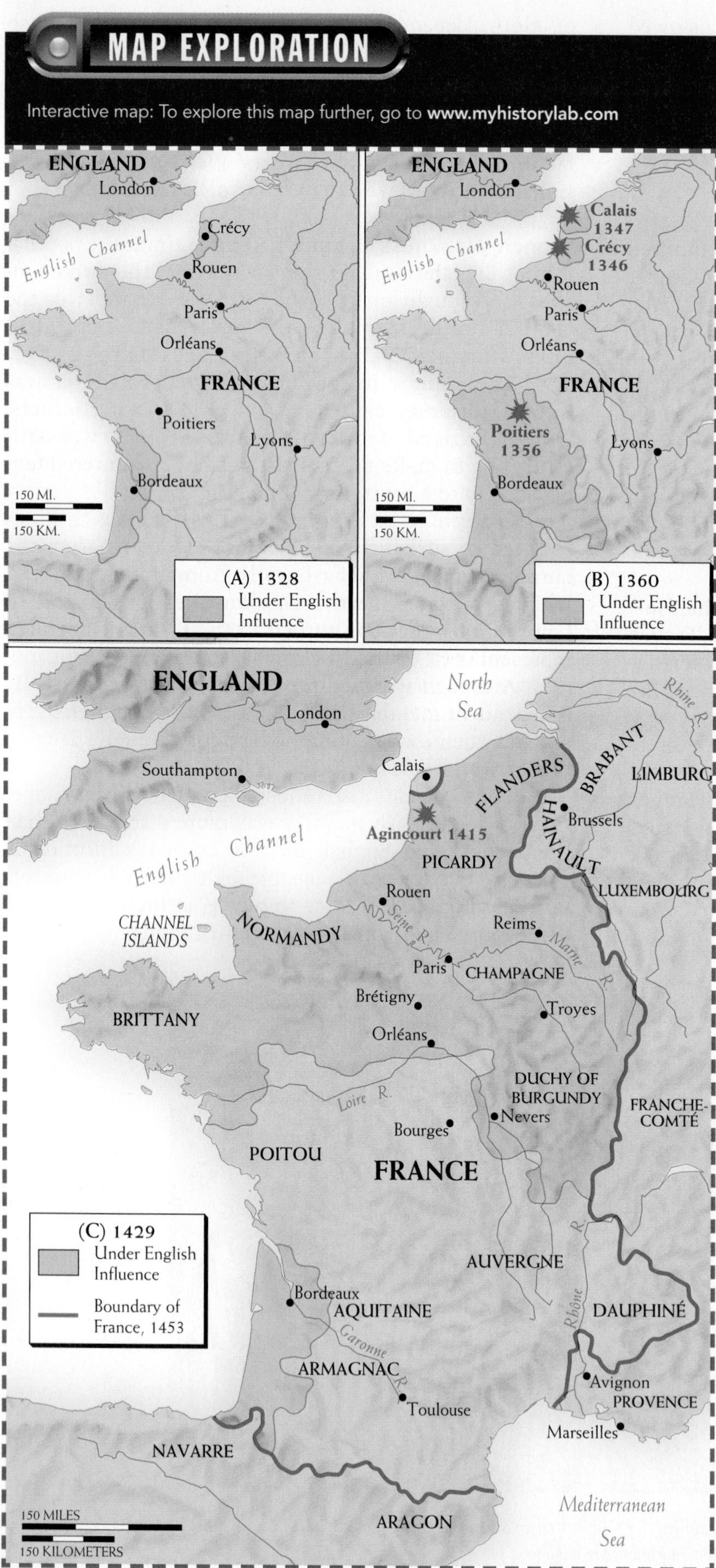

Map 9–2 **THE HUNDRED YEARS' WAR** The Hundred Years' War went on intermittently from the late 1330s until 1453. These maps show the remarkable English territorial gains up to the sudden and decisive turning of the tide of battle in favor of the French by the forces of Joan of Arc in 1429.

Finally, French weakness during the Hundred Years' War was due, in no small degree, to the comparative mediocrity of its royal leadership. English kings were far shrewder.

Progress of the War

The war had three major stages of development, each ending with a seemingly decisive victory by one or the other side.

The Conflict During the Reign of Edward III In the first stage of the war, Edward embargoed English wool to Flanders, sparking urban rebellions by merchants and the trade guilds. Inspired by a rich merchant, Jacob van Artevelde, the Flemish cities, led by Ghent, revolted against the French and in 1340 signed an alliance with England acknowledging Edward as king of France. On June 23 of that same year, in the first great battle of the war, Edward defeated the French fleet in the Bay of Sluys, but his subsequent effort to invade France by way of Flanders failed.

In 1346, Edward attacked Normandy and, after a series of easy victories that culminated at the Battle of Crécy, seized the port of Calais (which the English would retain until 1558). Exhaustion of both sides and the onset of the Black Death forced a truce in late 1347, as the war entered a brief lull. In 1356, near Poitiers, the English won their greatest victory, routing France's noble cavalry and taking the French king, John II the Good (r. 1350–1364), captive back to England. A complete breakdown of political order in France followed.

Power in France now lay with the Estates General. Led by the powerful merchants of Paris under Etienne Marcel, that body took advantage of royal weakness, demanding and receiving rights similar to those the Magna Carta had granted to the English privileged classes. Yet, unlike the English Parliament, which represented the interests of a comparatively unified English nobility, the French Estates General was too divided to be an instrument for effective government.

To secure their rights, the French privileged classes forced the peasantry to pay ever-increasing taxes and to repair their war-damaged properties without compensation. This bullying became more than the peasants could bear, and they rose up in several regions in a series of bloody rebellions known as the **Jacquerie** in 1358 (after the peasant revolutionary popularly known as Jacques Bonhomme, or "simple Jack"). The nobility quickly put down the revolt, matching the rebels atrocity for atrocity.

On May 9, 1360, another milestone of the war was reached when England forced the Peace of Brétigny-Calais on the French. This agreement declared an end to Edward's vassalage to the king of France and affirmed his sovereignty over English territories in France (including Gascony, Guyenne, Poitou, and Calais). France also agreed to pay a ransom of 3 million gold crowns to win King John the Good's release. In return, Edward simply renounced his claim to the French throne.

Such a partition was unrealistic, and sober observers on both sides knew it could not last. France struck back in the late 1360s and, by the time of Edward's death in 1377, had beaten the English back to coastal enclaves and the territory around Bordeaux.

French Defeat and the Treaty of Troyes After Edward's death the English war effort lessened, partly because of domestic problems within England. During the reign of Richard II (r. 1377–1399), England had its own version of the Jacquerie. In June 1381, long-oppressed peasants and artisans joined in a great revolt of the underprivileged classes under the leadership of John Ball, a secular priest, and Wat Tyler, a journeyman. As in France, the revolt was brutally crushed within the year, but it left the country divided for decades.

England recommenced the war under Henry V (r. 1413–1422), who took advantage of internal French turmoil created by the rise to power of the duchy of Burgundy. With France deeply divided, Henry V struck hard in Normandy. Happy to see the rest of France besieged, the Burgundians foolishly watched from the sidelines while Henry's army routed the French at Agincourt on October 25, 1415. In the years thereafter, belatedly recognizing that the defeat of France would leave them easy prey for the English, the Burgundians closed ranks with French royal forces. The renewed French unity, loose as it was, promised to bring eventual victory over the English, but it was shattered in September 1419 when the duke of Burgundy was assassinated. The duke's son and heir, determined to avenge his father's death, joined forces with the English.

France now became Henry V's for the taking—at least in the short run. The Treaty of Troyes in 1420 disinherited the legitimate heir to the French throne and proclaimed Henry V the successor to the French king, Charles VI. When Henry and Charles died within months of one another in 1422, the infant Henry VI of England was proclaimed in Paris to be king of both France and England. The dream of Edward III that had set the war in motion—to make the ruler of England the ruler also of France—seemed to have been realized.

The son of Charles VI went into retreat in Bourges, where, on the death of his father, he became Charles VII to most of the French people, who ignored the Treaty of Troyes. Displaying unprecedented national feeling inspired by the remarkable Joan of Arc, they soon rallied to his cause and united in an ultimately victorious coalition.

Joan of Arc and the War's Conclusion Joan of Arc (1412–1431), a peasant from Domrémy in Lorraine in eastern France, presented herself to Charles VII in March

A contemporary portrait of Joan of Arc (1412–1431). Anonymous, 15th century. "Joan of Arc." Franco-Flemish miniature. Archives Nationales, Paris, France. Photograph copyright Bridgeman-Giraudon/Art Resource, NY

1429, declaring that the King of Heaven had called her to deliver besieged Orléans from the English. Charles was skeptical, but being in retreat from what seemed to be a hopeless war, he was also willing to try anything to reverse French fortunes. The deliverance of Orléans, a city key to the control of the territory south of the Loire River, would be a godsend. Charles's desperation overcame his skepticism, and he gave Joan his leave.

Circumstances worked perfectly to her advantage. The English force, already exhausted by a six-month siege, was at the point of withdrawal when Joan arrived with fresh French troops. After repulsing the English from Orléans, the French enjoyed a succession of victories they popularly attributed to Joan. She did deserve much of this credit, but not because she was a military genius. She rather gave the French something military experts could not: an enraged sense of national identity and destiny.

Within a few months of the liberation of Orléans, Charles VII received his crown in Rheims, ending the nine-year "disinheritance" prescribed by the Treaty of Troyes. The king now forgot his liberator as quickly as he had embraced her. When the Burgundians captured Joan in May 1430, he might have secured her release but did little to help her. The Burgundians and the English wanted her publicly discredited, believing this would also discredit Charles VII and demoralize French resistance. She was turned over to the Inquisition in English-held Rouen. The inquisitors there broke the courageous "Maid of Orléans" after ten weeks of interrogation, and she was executed as a relapsed heretic on May 30, 1431. Twenty-five years later, in 1456, Charles reopened her trial, as the French state and church moved to get on history's side. She was now declared innocent of all the charges against her. In 1920, the Roman Catholic Church declared her a saint.

In 1435, the duke of Burgundy made peace with Charles, allowing France to force the English back. By 1453, when the war ended, the English held only their coastal enclave of Calais.

The Hundred Years' War, with sixty-eight years of nominal peace and forty-four of hot war, had lasting political and social consequences. It devastated France, but it also awakened French nationalism and hastened

THE HUNDRED YEARS' WAR (1337–1453)

1340	English victory at Bay of Sluys
1346	English victory at Crécy and seizure of Calais
1347	Black Death strikes
1356	English victory at Poitiers
1358	Jacquerie disrupts France
1360	Peace of Brétigny-Calais recognizes English holdings in France
1381	English peasants revolt
1415	English victory at Agincourt
1420	Treaty of Troyes recognizes the English king as heir to the French throne
1422	Henry VI proclaimed king of both England and France
1429	Joan of Arc leads French to victory at Orléans
1431	Joan of Arc executed as a heretic
1453	War ends; English retain only Calais

the transition there from a feudal monarchy to a centralized state. It saw Burgundy become a major European political power. It also encouraged the English, in response to the seesawing allegiance of the Netherlands throughout the conflict, to develop their own clothing industry and foreign markets. In both France and England, the burden of the on-again, off-again war fell most heavily on the peasantry, who were forced to support it with taxes and services.

▼ Ecclesiastical Breakdown and Revival: The Late Medieval Church

At first glance, the popes may appear to have been in a favorable position in the latter thirteenth century. Frederick II had been vanquished and imperial pressure on Rome had been removed. (See Chapter 8.) The French king, Louis IX, was an enthusiastic supporter of the church, as evidenced by his two disastrous Crusades, which won him sainthood. Although it lasted only seven years, a reunion of the Eastern church with Rome was proclaimed by the Council of Lyons in 1274, when the Western church took advantage of Byzantine emperor Michael VII Palaeologus's (r. 1261–1282) request for aid against the Turks. But despite these positive events, the church's position was less favorable than it appeared.

The Thirteenth-Century Papacy

As early as the reign of Pope Innocent III (r. 1198–1216), when papal power reached its height, there were ominous developments. Innocent had elaborated the doctrine of papal **plenitude of power** and on that authority had declared saints, disposed of *benefices,* and created a centralized papal monarchy with a clearly political mission. Innocent's transformation of the papacy into a great secular power weakened the church spiritually even as it strengthened it politically. Thereafter, the church as a papal monarchy increasingly parted company with the church as the "body of the faithful." It was against this perceived "papal church" and in the name of the "true Christian church" that both reformers and heretics protested until the Protestant Reformation.

What Innocent began, his successors perfected. Under Urban IV (r. 1261–1264), the papacy established its own law court, the *Rota Romana,* which tightened and centralized the church's legal proceedings. The latter half of the thirteenth century saw an elaboration of the system of clerical taxation; what had begun in the twelfth century as an emergency measure to raise funds for the Crusades became a fixed institution. In the same period, papal power to determine appointments to many major and minor church offices—the "reservation of *benefices*"—was greatly broadened. The thirteenth-century papacy became a powerful political institution governed by its own law and courts, serviced by an efficient international bureaucracy, and preoccupied with secular goals.

Papal centralization of the church undermined both diocesan authority and popular support. Rome's interests, not local needs, came to control church appointments, policies, and discipline. Discontented lower clergy appealed to the higher authority of Rome against the discipline of local bishops. In the second half of the thirteenth century, bishops and abbots protested such undercutting of their power. To its critics, the church in Rome was hardly more than a legalized, "fiscalized," bureaucratic institution. As early as the late twelfth century, heretical movements of Cathars and Waldensians had appealed to the biblical ideal of simplicity and separation from the world. Other reformers who were unquestionably loyal to the church, such as Saint Francis of Assisi, also protested perceived materialism in official religion.

Political Fragmentation More than internal religious disunity was undermining the thirteenth-century church. The demise of imperial power meant the papacy in Rome was no longer the leader of anti-imperial (Guelf, or propapal) sentiment in Italy. Instead of being the center of Italian resistance to the emperor, popes now found themselves on the defensive against their old allies. That was the ironic price the papacy paid to vanquish the Hohenstaufens.

Rulers with a stake in Italian politics now directed the intrigue formerly aimed at the emperor toward the College of Cardinals. For example, Charles of Anjou, the French king of Naples and Sicily (r. 1266–1285), managed to create a French-Sicilian faction within the college. Such efforts to control the decisions of the college led Pope Gregory X (r. 1271–1276) to establish the practice of sequestering the cardinals immediately upon the death of the pope. The purpose of this so-called conclave of cardinals was to minimize political influence on the election of new popes, but the college became so politicized that it proved to be of little avail.

In 1294, such a conclave, in frustration after a deadlock of more than two years, chose a saintly, but inept, hermit as Pope Celestine V. Celestine abdicated under suspicious circumstances after only a few weeks in office. He also died under suspicious circumstances; his successor's critics later argued that the powers behind the papal throne had murdered him to ensure the survival of the papal office. Celestine's tragicomic reign shocked the Cardinals into electing his opposite, Pope Boniface VIII (r. 1294–1303), a nobleman and a skilled politician. His pontificate, however, would mark the beginning of the end of papal pretensions to great-power status.

JOAN OF ARC REFUSES TO RECANT HER BELIEFS

Joan of Arc, threatened with torture, refused to recant her beliefs and instead defended the instructions she had received from the voices that spoke to her. Here is a part of her self-defense from the contemporary trial record.

Do the judges appear to have made up their minds about Joan in advance? How does this judicial process, which was based on intensive interrogation of the accused, differ from a trial today? Why was Joan deemed heretical and not insane when she acknowledged hearing voices?

On Wednesday, May 9th of the same year [1431], Joan was brought into the great tower of the castle of Rouen before us the said judges and in the presence of the reverend father, lord abbot of St. Cormeille de Compiegne, of masters Jean de Châtillon and Guillaume Erart, doctors of sacred theology, of André Marguerie and Nicolas de Venderos, archdeacons of the church of Rouen, of William Haiton, bachelor of theology, Aubert Morel, licentiate in canon law, Nicolas Loiseleur, canon of the cathedral of Rouen, and master Jean Massieu.

And Joan was required and admonished to speak the truth on many different points contained in her trial which she had denied or to which she had given false replies, whereas we possessed certain information, proofs, and vehement presumptions upon them. Many of the points were read and explained to her, and she was told that if she did not confess them truthfully she would be put to the torture, the instruments of which were shown to her all ready in the tower. There were also present by our instruction men ready to put her to the torture in order to restore her to the way and knowledge of truth, and by this means to procure the salvation of her body and soul which by her lying inventions she exposed to such grave perils.

To which the said Joan answered in this manner: "Truly if you were to tear me limb from limb and separate my soul from my body, I would not tell you anything more and if I did say anything, I should afterwards declare that you had compelled me to say it by force." Then she said that on Holy Cross Day last she received comfort from St. Gabriel, she firmly believes it was St. Gabriel. She knew by her voices whether she should submit to the Church, since the clergy were pressing her hard to submit. Her voices told her that if she desired Our Lord to aid her, she must wait upon Him in all her doings. She said that Our Lord has always been the master of her doings, and the Enemy never had power over them. She asked her voices if she would be burned and they answered that she must wait upon God, and He would aid her.

W. P. Barrett, *The Trial of Jeanne D'Arc* (New York: Gotham House, 1932), pp. 303–304.

Boniface VIII and Philip the Fair

Boniface came to rule when England and France were maturing as nation-states. In England, a long tradition of consultation between the king and powerful members of English society evolved into formal parliaments during the reigns of Henry III (r. 1216–1272) and Edward I (r. 1272–1307), and these meetings helped create a unified kingdom. The reign of the French king Philip IV the Fair (r. 1285–1314) saw France become an efficient, centralized monarchy. Philip was no Saint Louis, but a ruthless politician. He was determined to end England's continental holdings, control wealthy Flanders, and establish French hegemony within the Holy Roman Empire.

Boniface had the further misfortune of bringing to the papal throne memories of the way earlier popes had brought kings and emperors to their knees. Painfully he was to discover that the papal monarchy of the early thirteenth century was no match for the new political powers of the late thirteenth century.

The Royal Challenge to Papal Authority France and England were on the brink of all-out war when Boniface became pope in 1294. Only Edward I's preoccupation with rebellion in Scotland, which the French encouraged, prevented him from invading France and starting the Hundred Years' War a half century earlier than it did start. As both countries mobilized for war, they used the pretext of preparing for a Crusade to tax the clergy heavily. In 1215, Pope Innocent III had decreed that the clergy were to pay no taxes to rulers without papal consent. Viewing English and French taxation of the clergy as an assault on traditional clerical rights, Boniface took a strong stand against it. On February 5, 1296, he issued a bull, *Clericis laicos*, which forbade lay taxation of the clergy without papal approval and revoked all previous papal dispensations in this regard.

In England, Edward I retaliated by denying the clergy the right to be heard in royal court, in effect removing from them the protection of the king. But Philip the Fair struck back with a vengeance: In August 1296, he forbade the exportation of money from France to Rome, thereby denying the papacy the revenues it needed to operate. Boniface had no choice but to come to terms quickly with Philip. He conceded Philip the right to tax the French clergy "during an emergency," and, not coincidentally, he canonized Louis IX in the same year.

Boniface was then also under siege by powerful Italian enemies, whom Philip did not fail to patronize. A noble family (the Colonnas), rivals of Boniface's family (the Gaetani) and radical followers of Saint Francis of Assisi (the Spiritual Franciscans), were seeking to invalidate Boniface's election as pope on the grounds that Celestine V had been forced to resign the office. Charges of heresy, simony, and even the murder of Celestine were hurled against Boniface.

Boniface's fortunes appeared to revive in 1300, a "Jubilee year." During such a year, all Catholics who visited Rome and fulfilled certain conditions had the penalties for their unrepented sins remitted. Tens of thousands of pilgrims flocked to Rome, and Boniface, heady with this display of popular religiosity, reinserted himself into international politics. He championed Scottish resistance to England, for which he received a firm rebuke from an outraged Edward I and from Parliament.

But once again a confrontation with the king of France proved the more costly. Philip seemed to be eager for another fight with the pope. He arrested Boniface's Parisian legate, Bernard Saisset, the bishop of Pamiers and also a powerful secular lord, whose independence Philip had opposed. Accused of heresy and treason, Saisset was tried and convicted in the king's court. Thereafter, Philip demanded that Boniface recognize the process against Saisset, something Boniface could do only if he was prepared to surrender his jurisdiction over the French episcopate. Boniface could not sidestep this challenge, and he acted swiftly to champion Saisset as a defender of clerical political independence within France. He demanded Saisset's unconditional release, revoked all previous agreements with Philip regarding clerical taxation, and ordered the French bishops to convene in Rome within a year. A bull, *Ausculta fili*, or "Listen, My Son," was sent to Philip

Pope Boniface VIII (r. 1294–1303), depicted here, opposed the taxation of the clergy by the kings of France and England and issued one of the strongest declarations of papal authority over rulers, the bull *Unam Sanctam*. This statue is in the Museo Civico, Bologna, Italy. Statue of Pope Boniface VIII. Museo Civico, Bologna. Scala/Art Resource, NY

COMPARE AND CONNECT

Who Runs the World: Priests or Princes?

IN ONE OF the boldest papal bulls in the history of Christianity, Pope Boniface VIII declared the temporal authority of rulers to be subject to papal authority. Behind that ideology lay a long, bitter dispute between the papacy and the kings of France and England. Despite the strained scholastic arguments from each side's apologists, the issue was paramount and kingdoms were at stake. The debaters were Giles of Rome, a philosopher and papal adviser, and John of Paris, a French Dominican and Aristotle expert. Quoting ecclesiastical authorities, Giles defended a papal theocracy, while John made the royal case for secular authority.

QUESTIONS

1. **Are the arguments pro and con logical and transparent?**
2. **How is history invoked to support their positions?**
3. **Which of the two seems to have the better authorities behind his arguments?**

I. Giles of Rome, *On Ecclesiastical Power* (1301)

Hugh of St. Victor . . . declares that the spiritual power has to institute the earthly power and to judge it if it has not been good . . . We can clearly prove from the order of the universe that the church is set above nations and kingdoms [Jeremias 1:10] . . . It is the law of divinity that the lowest are led to the highest through intermediaries . . . At Romans 13 . . . the Apostle, having said that there is no power except from God, immediately added: "And those that are, are ordained of God." If then there are two swords [governments], one spiritual, the other temporal, as can be gathered from the words of the Gospel, "Behold, here are two swords" (Luke 22:38), [to which] the Lord at once added, "It is enough" because these two swords suffice for the church, [then] it follows that these two swords, these two powers and authorities, are [both] from God, since there is no power except from God. But, therefore they must be rightly ordered since, what is from God must be ordered. [And] they would not be so ordered unless one sword was led by the other and one was under the other since, as Dionysius said, the law of divinity which God gave to all created things requires this . . . Therefore the temporal sword, as being inferior, is led by the spiritual sword, as being superior, and the one is set below the other as an inferior below a superior.

It may be said that kings and princes ought to be subject spiritually but not temporally . . . But those who speak thus have not grasped the force of the argument. For if kings and princes were only spiritually subject to the church, one sword would not be below the other, nor temporalities below spiritualities; there would be no order in the powers, the lowest would not be led to the highest through intermediaries. If they *are* ordered, the temporal sword must be below the spiritual, and [royal] kingdoms below the vicar of Christ, and that by law . . . [then] the vicar of Christ must hold dominion over temporal affairs.

II. John of Paris, *Treatise on Royal and Papal Power* (1302–1303)

It is easy to see which is first in dignity, the kingship or the priesthood . . . A kingdom is ordered to this end, that an assembled multitude may live virtuously . . . and it is further ordered to a higher end which is the enjoyment of God; and responsibility for this end belongs to Christ, whose ministers and vicars are the priests. Therefore, the priestly power is of greater dignity than the secular and this is commonly conceded . . .

But if the priest is greater in himself than the prince and is greater in dignity, it does not follow that he is greater in all respects. For the lesser secular power is not related to the greater spiritual power as having its origin from it or being derived from it as the power of a proconsul is related to that of the emperor, which is greater in all respects since the power of the former is derived from the latter. The relationship is rather like that of a head of a household to a general of armies, since one is not derived from the other but both from a superior power. And so the secular power is greater than the spiritual in some things, namely in temporal affairs, and in such affairs it is not subject to the spiritual power in any way because it does not have its origin from it, but rather both have their origin immediately from the one supreme power, namely, the divine. Accordingly the inferior power is not subject to the superior in all things, but only in those where the supreme power has subordinated it to the greater. [For example] a teacher of literature or an instructor in morals directs the members of a household to a very noble end: the knowledge of truth. [That] end is more noble than [that] of a doctor who is concerned with a lower end, namely, the health of bodies. But who would say therefore that the doctor should be subjected to the teacher in preparing his medicines . . .? Therefore, the priest is greater than the prince in spiritual affairs and, on the other hand, the prince is greater in temporal affairs.

Source: Brian Tierney, *The Crisis of Church and State 1050–1300* (Toronto: Toronto University Press, 1996) pp. 198–199 [Giles of Rome], 209–209 [John of Paris].

Papal ring: gold with an engraving on each side and set with a square stone.
Dorling Kindersley Media Library. Geoff Dann © The British Museum

in December 1301, pointedly informing him that "God has set popes over kings and kingdoms."

Unam Sanctam (1302) Philip unleashed a ruthless antipapal campaign. Two royal apologists, Pierre Dubois and John of Paris, refuted papal claims to the right to intervene in temporal matters. Increasingly placed on the defensive, Boniface made a last-ditch stand against state control of national churches. On November 18, 1302, he issued the bull *Unam Sanctam*. This famous statement of papal power declared that temporal authority was "subject" to the spiritual power of the church. On its face a bold assertion, *Unam Sanctam* was, in truth, the desperate act of a besieged papacy. (See "Compare & Connect: Who Runs the World: Priests or Princes?" pages 270–271.)

After *Unam Sanctam*, the French and the Colonnas moved against Boniface with force. Philip's chief minister, Guillaume de Nogaret, denounced Boniface to the French clergy as a heretic and common criminal. In mid-August 1303, his army surprised the pope at his retreat in Anagni, beat him up, and almost executed him before an aroused populace returned him safely to Rome. The ordeal, however, proved to be too much, and Boniface died in October 1303.

Boniface's immediate successor, Benedict XI (r. 1303–1304), excommunicated Nogaret for his deed, but there was to be no lasting papal retaliation. Benedict's successor, Clement V (r. 1305–1314), was forced into French subservience. A former archbishop of Bordeaux, Clement declared that *Unam Sanctam* should not be understood as in any way diminishing French royal authority. He released Nogaret from excommunication and pliantly condemned the Knights Templars, whose treasure Philip thereafter seized.

In 1309, Clement moved the papal court to Avignon, an imperial city on the southeastern border of France. Situated on land that belonged to the pope, the city maintained its independence from the French king. In 1311, Clement made it his permanent residence, to escape both a Rome ridden with strife after the confrontation between Boniface and Philip and further pressure from Philip. There the papacy would remain until 1377.

After Boniface's humiliation, popes never again seriously threatened kings and emperors, despite continuing papal excommunications and political intrigue. The relationship between church and state now tilted in favor of the state, and the control of religion fell into the hands of powerful monarchies. Ecclesiastical authority would become subordinate to larger secular political policies.

The Avignon Papacy (1309–1377)

The Avignon papacy was in appearance, although not always in fact, under strong French influence. Under Clement V, the French dominated the College of Cardinals, testing the papacy's agility both politically and economically. Finding itself cut off from its Roman estates, the papacy had to innovate to get needed funds. Clement expanded papal taxes, especially the practice of collecting *annates*, the first year's revenue of a church office, or *benefice*, bestowed by the pope. Clement VI (r. 1342–1352) began the practice of selling *indulgences*, or pardons, for unrepented sins. To make the purchase of indulgences more compelling, church doctrine on purgatory—a place of punishment where souls would atone for venial sins—also developed enterprisingly during this period. By the fifteenth century, the church had extended indulgences to cover the souls of people already dead, allowing the living to buy a reduced sentence in purgatory for their deceased loved ones. Such practices contributed to the Avignon papacy's reputation for materialism and political scheming and gave reformers new ammunition.

Pope John XXII Pope John XXII (r. 1316–1334), the most powerful Avignon pope, tried to restore papal independence and to return to Italy. This goal led him into war with the Visconti, the powerful ruling family of Milan, and a costly contest with Emperor Louis IV (r. 1314–1347). John had challenged Louis's election as emperor in 1314 in favor of the rival Habsburg candidate. The result was a minor replay of the confrontation between Philip the Fair and Boniface VIII. When John obstinately and without legal justification refused to recognize Louis's election, the emperor declared him deposed and put in his place an antipope. As Philip the Fair had also done, Louis enlisted the support of the Spiritual Franciscans, whose views on absolute poverty John had condemned as heretical. Two outstanding pamphleteers wrote lasting tracts for the royal cause: William of Ockham, whom John excommunicated in 1328, and Marsilius of Padua (ca. 1290–1342), whose teaching John declared heretical in 1327.

In his *Defender of Peace* (1324), Marsilius of Padua stressed the independent origins and autonomy of secular government. Clergy were subjected to the strictest apostolic ideals and confined to purely spiritual functions, and all power of coercive judgment was denied the pope. Marsilius argued that spiritual crimes must await an eternal punishment. Transgressions of divine law, over which the pope had jurisdiction, were to be punished in the next life, not in the present one, unless the secular ruler declared a divine law also a secular law. This assertion directly challenged the power of the pope to excommunicate rulers and place countries under interdict. The *Defender of Peace* depicted the pope as a subordinate member of a society over which the emperor ruled supreme and in which temporal peace was the highest good.

John XXII made the papacy a sophisticated international agency and adroitly adjusted it to the growing European money economy. The more the **Curia**, or papal court, mastered the latter, however, the more vulnerable it became to criticism. Under John's successor, Benedict

XII (r. 1334–1342), the papacy became entrenched in Avignon. Seemingly forgetting Rome altogether, Benedict began to build the great Palace of the Popes and attempted to reform both papal government and the religious life. His high-living French successor, Clement VI (r, 1342–1352), placed papal policy in lockstep with the French. In this period the cardinals became barely more than lobbyists for policies their secular patrons favored.

National Opposition to the Avignon Papacy As Avignon's fiscal tentacles probed new areas, monarchies took strong action to protect their interests. The latter half of the fourteenth century saw legislation restricting papal jurisdiction and taxation in France, England, and Germany. In England, where the Avignon papacy was identified with the French enemy after the outbreak of the Hundred Years' War, Parliament passed statutes that restricted payments and appeals to Rome and the pope's power to make high ecclesiastical appointments several times between 1351 and 1393.

In France, the so-called Gallican, or French, liberties regulated ecclesiastical appointments and taxation. These national rights over religion had long been exercised in fact, and the church legally acknowledged them in the *Pragmatic Sanction of Bourges* in 1438. This agreement recognized the right of the French church to elect its own clergy without papal interference, prohibited the payment of *annates* to Rome, and limited the right of appeals from French courts to the Curia in Rome. In German and Swiss cities in the fourteenth and fifteenth centuries, local governments also limited and even overturned traditional clerical privileges and immunities.

John Wycliffe and John Huss

The popular lay religious movements that most successfully assailed the late medieval church were the **Lollards** in England and the **Hussites** in Bohemia. The Lollards looked to the writings of John Wycliffe (d. 1384) to justify their demands, while moderate and extreme Hussites turned to those of John Huss (d. 1415), although both Wycliffe and Huss would have disclaimed the extremists who revolted in their names.

A portrayal of John Huss as he was led to the stake at Constance. After his execution, his bones and ashes were scattered in the Rhine River to prevent his followers from claiming them as relics. This pen-and-ink drawing is from Ulrich von Richenthal's *Chronicle of the Council of Constance* (ca. 1450). CORBIS/Bettmann

Wycliffe was an Oxford theologian and a philosopher of high standing. His work initially served the anticlerical policies of the English government. He became within England what William of Ockham and Marsilius of Padua had been for Emperor Louis IV: a major intellectual spokesman for the rights of royalty against the secular pretensions of popes. After 1350, English kings greatly reduced the power of the Avignon papacy to make ecclesiastical appointments and to collect taxes within England, a position that Wycliffe strongly supported. His views on clerical poverty followed original Franciscan ideals and, more by accident than by design, gave justification to government restriction and even confiscation of church properties within England. Wycliffe argued that the clergy "ought to be content with food and clothing."

Wycliffe also maintained that personal merit, not rank and office, was the true basis of religious authority. This was a dangerous teaching, because it raised allegedly pious laypeople above allegedly corrupt ecclesiastics, regardless of the latter's official stature. It thus threatened secular as well as ecclesiastical dominion and jurisdiction. At his posthumous condemnation by the pope, Wycliffe was accused of the ancient heresy of **Donatism**—the teaching that the efficacy of the church's sacraments did not only lie in their true performance but also depended on the moral character of the clergy who administered them. Wycliffe also anticipated certain Protestant criticisms of the medieval church by challenging papal infallibility, the sale of indulgences, the authority of Scripture, and the dogma of transubstantiation.

The Lollards, English advocates of Wycliffe's teaching, like the Waldensians, preached in the vernacular, disseminated translations of Holy Scripture, and championed clerical poverty. At first, they came from every social class. Lollards were especially prominent among the groups that had something tangible to gain from confiscating clerical properties (the nobility and the gentry) or that had suffered most under the current church system (the lower clergy and the poor people). After the English peasants' revolt in 1381, an uprising filled with egalitarian notions that could find support in Wycliffe's teaching, Lollardy was officially viewed as subversive. Opposed by an alliance of church and crown, it became a capital offense in England by 1401.

Heresy was less easily brought to heel in Bohemia, where it coalesced with a strong national movement. The University of Prague, founded in 1348, became the center for both Czech nationalism and a religious reform movement. The latter began within the bounds of orthodoxy. It was led by local intellectuals and preachers, the most famous of whom was John Huss, the rector of the university after 1403.

The Czech reformers supported vernacular translations of the Bible and were critical of traditional ceremonies and allegedly superstitious practices, particularly those relating to the sacrament of the Eucharist. They advocated lay communion with cup as well as bread, which was traditionally reserved only for the clergy as a sign of the clergy's spiritual superiority over the laity. Hussites taught that bread and wine remained bread and wine after priestly consecration, and they questioned the validity of sacraments performed by priests in mortal sin.

Wycliffe's teaching appears early to have influenced the movement. Regular traffic between England and Bohemia had existed since the marriage in 1381 of Anne of Bohemia to King Richard II. Czech students studied at Oxford and returned with Wycliffe's writings.

Huss became the leader of the pro-Wycliffe faction at the University of Prague. In 1410, his activities brought about his excommunication, and Prague was placed under papal interdict. In 1414, Huss won an audience with the newly assembled Council of Constance. He journeyed to the council eagerly under a safe-conduct pass from Emperor Sigismund (r. 1410–1437), naïvely believing he would convince his strongest critics of the truth of his teaching. Within weeks of his arrival in early November 1414, he was accused of heresy and imprisoned. He died at the stake on July 6, 1415, and was followed there less than a year later by his colleague Jerome of Prague.

The reaction in Bohemia to the execution of these national heroes was fierce revolt. Militant Hussites, the Taborites, set out to transform Bohemia by force into a religious and social paradise under the military leadership of John Ziska. After a decade of belligerent protest, the Hussites won significant religious reforms and control over the Bohemian church from the Council of Basel.

The Great Schism (1378–1417) and the Conciliar Movement to 1449

Pope Gregory XI (r. 1370–1378) reestablished the papacy in Rome in January 1377, ending what had come to be known as the "Babylonian Captivity" of the church in Avignon, a reference to the biblical bondage of the Israelites. The return to Rome proved to be short lived, however.

Urban VI and Clement VII On Gregory's death, the cardinals, in Rome, elected an Italian archbishop as Pope Urban VI (r. 1378–1389), who immediately announced his intention to reform the Curia. The cardinals, most of whom were French, responded by calling for the return of the papacy to Avignon. The French king, Charles V (r. 1364–1380), wanting to keep the papacy within the sphere of French influence, lent his support to what came to be known as the **Great Schism**.

On September 20, 1378, five months after Urban's election, thirteen cardinals, all but one of whom was French, formed their own conclave and elected Pope

Clement VII (r. 1378–1397), a cousin of the French king. They insisted they had voted for Urban in fear of their lives, surrounded by a Roman mob demanding the election of an Italian pope. Be that as it may, the papacy now became a "two-headed thing" and a scandal to Christendom. Allegiance to the two papal courts divided along political lines. England and its allies (the Holy Roman Empire, Hungary, Bohemia, and Poland) acknowledged Urban VI, whereas France and those in its orbit (Naples, Scotland, Castile, and Aragon) supported Clement VII. Subsequent church history has, however, recognized the Roman line of popes as legitimate.

Two approaches were initially taken to end the schism. One tried to win the mutual cession of both popes, thereby clearing the way for the election of a new pope. The other sought to secure the resignation

Justice in the late Middle Ages. Depicted are the most common forms of corporal and capital punishment in Europe in the late Middle Ages and the Renaissance. At top: burning, hanging, drowning. At center: blinding, quartering, the wheel, cutting of hair (a mark of great shame for a freeman). At bottom: thrashing, decapitation, amputation of hand (for thieves). Herzog August Bibliothek of the one in favor of the other. Both approaches proved fruitless. Each pope considered himself fully legitimate, and too much was at stake for either to make a magnanimous concession. One way remained: the deposition of both popes by a special council of the church.

Conciliar Theory of Church Government Legally, only a pope could convene a church council, but the competing popes were not inclined to summon a council they knew would depose them. Also, the deposition of a legitimate pope against his will by a council of the church was as serious as the deposition of a monarch by a representative assembly.

The correctness of a conciliar deposition of a pope was thus debated a full thirty years before any direct action was taken. Advocates of **conciliar theory** sought to fashion a church in which a representative council could effectively regulate the actions of the pope. The conciliarists defined the church as the whole body of the faithful, of which the elected head, the pope, was only one part. And the pope's sole purpose was to maintain the unity and well-being of the church—something the schismatic popes were far from doing. The conciliarists further argued that a council of the church acted with greater authority than the pope alone. In the eyes of the pope(s), such a concept of the church threatened both its political and its religious unity.

The Council of Pisa (1409–1410) On the basis of the arguments of the conciliarists, cardinals representing both popes convened a council on their own authority in Pisa in 1409, deposed both the Roman and the Avignon popes, and elected a new pope, Alexander V. To the council's consternation, neither pope accepted its action, and Christendom suddenly faced the spectacle of three contending popes. Although most of Latin Christendom accepted Alexander and his Pisan successor John XXIII (r. 1410–1415), the popes of Rome and Avignon refused to step down.

The Council of Constance (1414–1417) The intolerable situation ended when Emperor Sigismund prevailed on John XXIII to summon a new council in Constance in 1414, which the Roman pope Gregory XII also recognized. In a famous declaration entitled *Sacrosancta*, the council asserted its supremacy and elected a new pope, Martin V (r. 1417–1431), after the three contending popes had either resigned or been deposed. The council then made provisions for regular meetings of church councils, within five, then seven, and thereafter every ten years.

The Council of Basel (r. 1431–1449) Conciliar government of the church peaked at the Council of Basel, when the council directly negotiated church doctrine with heretics. In 1432, the Hussites of Bohemia presented the *Four Articles of Prague* to the council as a basis for negotiations. This document contained requests for (1) giving the laity the Eucharist with cup as well as bread; (2) free, itinerant preaching; (3) the exclusion of the clergy from holding secular offices and owning property; and (4) just punishment of clergy who commit mortal sins.

In November 1433, an agreement among the emperor, the council, and the Hussites gave the Bohemians jurisdiction over their church similar to what the French and the English held. Three of the four Prague articles were conceded: communion with cup, free preaching by ordained clergy, and similar punishment of clergy and laity for mortal sins.

The end of the Hussite wars and the new reform legislation curtailing the pope's powers of appointment and taxation were the high points of the Council of Basel and ominous signs of what lay ahead for the church. The exercise of such power by a council did not please the pope, and in 1438, he upstaged the Council of Basel by negotiating a reunion with the Eastern church. Although the agreement, signed in Florence in 1439, was short lived, it restored papal prestige and signaled the demise of the conciliar movement. Having overreached itself, the Council of Basel collapsed in 1449. A decade later, Pope Pius II (r. 1458–1464) issued the papal bull *Execrabilis* (1460) condemning appeals to councils as "erroneous and abominable" and "completely null and void."

Consequences A major consequence of the conciliar movement was the devolving of greater religious responsibility onto the laity and secular governments. Without effective papal authority and leadership, secular control of national or territorial churches increased. Kings asserted their power over the church in England and France. In German, Swiss, and Italian cities, magistrates and city councils reformed and regulated religious life. The High Renaissance could not reverse this development. On the contrary, as the papacy became a limited, Italian territorial regime, national control of the church ran apace. Perceived as just one among several Italian states, the Papal States could now be opposed as much on the grounds of "national" policy as for religious reasons.

A Closer LOOK

THE ENCAMPMENT OF THE IMPERIAL ARMY

THIS FIFTEENTH-CENTURY scene, drawn by a skilled and imaginative artist, depicts an imperial Habsburg army. Because every army marches on its stomach, the wagons carrying provisions make up the inner circle, which is protected by a wider circle of war wagons.

The cavalry is either mustering for a foray or returning from one.

A face appears to be looking out of a window on the scene below. Could this be a crude depiction of God gazing down from the heavens? Or is it the artist's signature? Most likely it is graffiti added later by an opportunist seeking a bit of fame.

The provision wagons are empty because the tents, weapons, clothing, food, and cooking pots they carry have been unloaded. In the middle, standing around the towering black and gold Habsburg flag, are the commanders, their staff, and perhaps the emperor himself (speaking to a rider).

Kunstsammlungen der Fursten zu Waldburg-Wolfegg

Armed soldiers man a gate as scouts enter with a captive whose hands are bound. To the right of the gate, a mother with two small children and another beggar seek alms.

Workers and soldiers play games of cards and dice, while outside the barrier is danger, death, and desolation: Wolves gnaw at dead horses.

To examine this image in an interactive fashion, please go to www.myhistorylab.com

PEARSON myhistorylab

▼ Medieval Russia

In the late tenth century, Prince Vladimir of Kiev (r. 980–1015), then Russia's dominant city, received delegations of Muslims, Roman Catholics, Jews, and Greek Orthodox Christians, each of which hoped to persuade the Russians to embrace their religion. Vladimir chose Greek Orthodoxy, which became the religion of Russia, adding strong cultural bonds to the close commercial ties that had long linked Russia to the Byzantine Empire.

Politics and Society

Vladimir's successor, Yaroslav the Wise (r. 1016–1054), developed Kiev into a magnificent political and cultural center, with architecture rivaling that of Constantinople. He also pursued contacts with the West in an unsuccessful effort to counter the political influence of the Byzantine emperors. After his death, rivalry among their princes slowly divided Russians into three cultural groups: the Great Russians, the White Russians, and the Little Russians (Ukrainians). Autonomous principalities also challenged Kiev's dominance, and it became just one of several national centers. Government in the principalities combined monarchy (the prince), aristocracy (the prince's council of noblemen), and democracy (a popular assembly of all free adult males). The broadest social division was between freemen and slaves. Freemen included the clergy, army officers, **boyars** (wealthy landowners), townspeople, and peasants. Slaves were mostly prisoners of war. Debtors working off their debts made up a large, semifree, group.

Genghis Khan holding an audience. This Persian miniature shows the great conqueror and founder of the Mongol empire with members of his army and entourage as well as an apparent supplicant (lower right). Picture Desk, Inc./Kobal Collection

Mongol Rule (1243–1480)

In the thirteenth century, Mongol, or Tatar, armies swept through China, much of the Islamic world, and Russia. These were steppe peoples with strongholds in the south, whence they raided the north, devastating Russia and compelling the obedience of Moscow for a while. Ghengis Khan (1155–1227) invaded Russia in 1223, and Kiev fell to his grandson Batu Khan in 1240. Russian cities became dependent, tribute-paying principalities of the segment of the Mongol Empire known as the *Golden Horde* (the Tatar words for the color of Batu Khan's tent). Geographically, the Golden Horde included the steppe region of what is today southern Russia and its capital at Sarai on the lower Volga. The conquerors stationed their own officials in all the principal Russian towns to oversee taxation and the conscription of Russians into Tatar armies. The Mongols filled their harems with Russian women and sold Russians who resisted into slavery in foreign lands. Russian women—under the influence of Islam, which became the religion of the Golden Horde—began to wear veils and lead more secluded lives. This forced integration of Mongol and Russian created further cultural divisions between Russia and the West. The Mongols, however, left Russian political and religious institutions largely intact and, thanks to their far-flung trade, brought most Russians greater prosperity. Princes of Moscow collected tribute for their overlords and grew wealthy under Mongol rule. As that rule weakened, the Moscow princes took control of the territory surrounding the city in what was called "the gathering of the Russian Land." Gradually the principality of Moscow expanded through land purchases, colonization, and conquest. In 1380, Grand Duke Dimitri of Moscow (r. 1350–1389) defeated Tatar forces at Kulikov Meadow, a victory that marked the beginning of the decline of the Mongol hegemony. Another century would pass, however, before Ivan III, the Great (d. 1505), would bring all of northern Russia under Moscow's control and end Mongol rule (1480). Moscow replaced Kiev as the political and religious center of Russia. After Constantinople fell to the Turks in 1453, the city became, in Russian eyes, the "third Rome."

In Perspective

Plague, war, and schism convulsed much of late medieval Europe throughout the fourteenth and into the fifteenth centuries. Two fifths of the population, particularly along the major trade routes, died from plague in the fourteenth century. War and famine continued to take untold numbers after the plague had passed. Revolts erupted in town and countryside as ordinary people attempted to defend their traditional communal rights and privileges against the new autocratic territorial regimes. Even God's house seemed to be in shambles in 1409, when three popes came to rule simultaneously.

There is, however, another side to the late Middle Ages. By the end of the fifteenth century, the population losses were rapidly being made up. Between 1300 and 1500, education had become far more accessible, especially to lay people. The number of universities increased from twenty to seventy, and the rise in the number of residential colleges was even more impressive, especially in France, where sixty-three were built. The fourteenth century saw the birth of humanism, and the fifteenth century gave us the printing press. Most impressive were the artistic and cultural achievements of the Italian Renaissance during the fifteenth century. The later Middle Ages were thus a period of growth and creativity, as well as one of waning and decline.

REVIEW QUESTIONS

1. What were the underlying and precipitating causes of the Hundred Years' War? What advantages did each side have? Why were the French finally able to drive the English almost entirely out of France?
2. What were the causes of the Black Death, and why did it spread so quickly throughout Western Europe? Where was it most virulent? How did it affect European society? How important do you think disease is in changing the course of history?
3. Why did Pope Boniface VIII quarrel with King Philip the Fair? Why was Boniface so impotent in the conflict? How had political conditions changed since the reign of Pope Innocent III in the late twelfth century, and what did that mean for the papacy?
4. How did the church change from 1200 to 1450? What was its response to the growing power of monarchs? How great an influence did the church have on secular events?
5. What was the Avignon papacy, and why did it occur? How did it affect the papacy? What relationship did it have to the Great Schism? How did the church become divided and how was it reunited? Why was the conciliar movement a setback for the papacy?
6. Why were kings in the late thirteenth and early fourteenth centuries able to control the church more than the church could control the kings? How did kings attack the church during this period?

SUGGESTED READINGS

C. Allmand, *The Hundred Years' War: England and France at War, c. 1300–c. 1450* (1988). Overview of the war's development and consequences.

P. R. Backscheider et al., eds., *A Journal of the Plague Year* (1992). The Black Death at ground level.

R. Barber, ed., *The Pastons: Letters of a Family in the War of the Roses* (1984). Rare revelations of English family life in an age of crisis.

E. H. Gillett et al., *Life and Times of John Huss: The Bohemian Reformation of the Fifteenth Century* (2001). The latest biography.

J. Huizinga, *The Waning of the Middle Ages: A Study of the Forms of Life, Thought, and Art in France and the Netherlands in the Dawn of the Renaissance* (1924). Exaggerated but engrossing study of mentality at the end of the Middle Ages.

P. Kahn et al., *Secret History of the Mongols: The Origins of Ghingis Kahn* (1998). Introduction to the greatest Mongol ruler.

S. Ozment, *The Age of Reform, 1250–1550* (1980). Highlights of late medieval intellectual and religious history.

E. Perroy, *The Hundred Years' War*, trans. by W. B. Wells (1965). Still the most comprehensive one-volume account.

M. Spinka, *John Huss's Concept of the Church* (1966). Lucid account of Hussite theology.

W. R. Trask, ed. and trans., *Joan of Arc in Her Own Words* (1996). Joan's interrogation and self-defense.

P. Ziegler, *The Black Death* (1969). Highly readable account.

For additional learning resources related to this chapter, please go to www.myhistorylab.com

PEARSON myhistorylab

The Renaissance celebrated human beauty and dignity. Here the Flemish painter Rogier van der Weyden (1400–1464) portrays an ordinary woman more perfectly on canvas than she could ever have appeared in life. Rogier van der Weyden (Netherlandish, 1399.1400–1464), "Portrait of a Lady." 1460. .370 × .270 (14 1/16 × 10 5/8) framed: .609 × .533 × .114 (24 × 21 × 4 1/2). Photo: Bob Grove. Andrew W. Mellon Collection. Photograph © Board of Trustees, National Gallery of Art, Washington, DC

10

Renaissance and Discovery

▼ **The Renaissance in Italy (1375–1527)**
The Italian City-State • Humanism • Renaissance Art • Slavery in the Renaissance

▼ **Italy's Political Decline: The French Invasions (1494–1527)**
Charles VIII's March Through Italy • Pope Alexander VI and the Borgia Family • Pope Julius II • Niccolò Machiavelli

▼ **Revival of Monarchy in Northern Europe**
France • Spain • England • The Holy Roman Empire

▼ **The Northern Renaissance**
The Printing Press • Erasmus • Humanism and Reform

▼ **Voyages of Discovery and the New Empires in the West and East**
The Portuguese Chart the Course • The Spanish Voyages of Columbus • The Spanish Empire in the New World • The Church in Spanish America • The Economy of Exploitation • The Impact on Europe

▼ **In Perspective**

KEY TOPICS

- **The politics, culture, and art of the Italian Renaissance**
- **Political struggle and foreign intervention in Italy**
- **The powerful new monarchies of northern Europe**
- **The thought and culture of the northern Renaissance**

IF THE LATE Middle Ages saw unprecedented chaos, it also witnessed a rebirth that would continue into the seventeenth century. Two modern Dutch scholars have employed the same word (*Herfsttij*, or "harvesttide") with different connotations to describe the period. Johan Huizinga has used the word to mean a "waning" or "decline," and Heiko Oberman has used it to mean a "harvest." If something was dying away, some ripe fruit was also being gathered and seed grain was being sown. The late Middle Ages was a time of creative fragmentation.

By the late fifteenth century, Europe was recovering well from two of the three crises of the late Middle Ages: the demographic and the political. The great losses in population were being replenished, and able monarchs and rulers were imposing a new political order. However, a solution to the religious crisis would have to await the Reformation and Counter-Reformation of the sixteenth century.

Although the opposite would be true in the sixteenth and seventeenth centuries, the city-states of Italy survived the century and a half between 1300 and 1450 better than the territorial states of northern Europe. This was due to Italy's strategic location between East and West and its lucrative Eurasian trade. Great wealth gave rulers and merchants the ability to work their will on both society and culture. They became patrons of government, education, and the arts, always as much for their own self-aggrandizement as out of benevolence, for whether a patron was a family, a firm, a government, or the church, endowments enhanced their reputation and power. The result of such patronage was a cultural Renaissance in Italian cities unmatched elsewhere.

With the fall of Constantinople to the Turks in 1453, Italy's once unlimited trading empire began to shrink. City-state soon turned against city-state, and by the 1490s, French armies invaded Italy. Within a quarter century, Italy's great Renaissance had peaked.

The fifteenth century also saw an unprecedented scholarly renaissance. Italian and northern humanists made a full recovery of classical knowledge and languages and set in motion educational reforms and cultural changes that would spread throughout Europe in the fifteenth and sixteenth centuries. In the process the Italian humanists invented, for all practical purposes, critical historical scholarship, while exploiting a new fifteenth-century invention, the "divine art" of printing with movable type.

In this period the vernacular—the local language—began to take its place alongside Latin, the international language, as a widely used literary and political means of communication. In addition, European states progressively superseded the church as the community of highest allegiance, as patriotism and incipient nationalism seized hearts and minds as strongly as religion. Nations henceforth "transcended" themselves not by journeys to Rome, but by competitive voyages to the Far East and the Americas, as the age of global exploration opened.

For Europe, the late fifteenth and sixteenth centuries were a period of unprecedented expansion and experimentation. Permanent colonies were established within the Americas, and the exploitation of the New World's human and mineral resources began. Imported American gold and silver spurred scientific invention and a new weapons industry. The new bullion also helped create the international traffic in African slaves as rival African tribes eagerly sold their captives to the Portuguese. Transported in ever-increasing numbers, these slaves worked the mines and plantations of the New World as replacements for American natives, whose population declined precipitously following the conquest.

The period also saw social engineering and political planning on a large scale, as newly centralized governments began to put long-range economic policies into practice, a development that came to be called mercantilism.

▼ The Renaissance in Italy (1375–1527)

A nineteenth-century Swiss historian famously described the Renaissance as the "prototype of the modern world." In his *Civilization of the Renaissance in Italy* (1860), Jacob Burckhardt argued that the revival of ancient learning in fourteenth- and fifteenth-century Italy gave rise to new secular and scientific values. This was the period in which people began to adopt a rational and statistical approach to reality and to rediscover the worth and creativity of the individual. The result, in Burckhardt's words, was the gradual release of the "full, whole nature of man."

Most scholars today find Burckhardt's description exaggerated and accuse him of overlooking the continuity between the Middle Ages and the Renaissance. His critics especially point to the still strongly Christian character of Renaissance humanism. Earlier "renaissances," such as that of the twelfth century, had also seen the revival of the ancient classics, new interest in the Latin language and Greek science, and an appreciation of the worth and creativity of individuals.

Despite the exaggeration and bias of Burckhardt's portrayal, most scholars agree that the **Renaissance** (which means "rebirth" in French) was a time of transition from medieval to modern times. Medieval Europe, especially before the twelfth century, had been a fragmented feudal society with an agricultural economy, and the church largely dominated its thought and culture. Renaissance Europe, especially after the fourteenth century, was characterized by growing national consciousness and political centralization, an urban economy based on organized commerce and capitalism, and growing lay and secular control of thought and culture, including religion.

Italy between 1375 and 1527, a century and a half of cultural creativity, most strikingly reveals the distinctive features of the Renaissance. Two events coincide with the beginning of this period: the deaths of Petrarch, considered the "father" of humanism, in 1374 and that of Giovanni Boccaccio, author of the *Decameron,* in 1375. Thereafter, Florentine humanist culture spread throughout Italy and into northern Europe. Scholars have coined the term *civic humanism* to describe this apparent coalescence of humanism and civic reform.

This creative expansion, however, appeared to reach an abrupt end in 1527, when Spanish-imperial soldiers looted and torched Rome, recalling Rome's sacking by the Visigoths and Vandals in antiquity. At this time, French king Francis I and the Holy Roman Emperor Charles V had made Italy the battleground for their mutual dynastic claims to Burgundy and parts of Italy. Pope Clement VIII (r. 1523–1534) had incurred the emperor's wrath by taking the side of the French. However, the infamous sack of Rome in 1527 appears to have been less the result of a breach of papal loyalty than of the anger and boredom of

Spanish-imperial soldiers poorly provisioned and paid by the emperor. Their looting and sacking have since marked the beginning of the end of the cultured Italian Renaissance.

The Italian City-State

Renaissance society first took distinctive shape within the merchant cities of late medieval Italy. Italy had always had a cultural advantage over the rest of Europe because its geography made it the natural gateway between East and West. Venice, Genoa, and Pisa had traded uninterruptedly with the Near East throughout the Middle Ages, maintaining vibrant urban societies by virtue of such trade. When commerce revived on a large scale in the eleventh century, Italian merchants had quickly mastered the business skills of organization, bookkeeping, scouting new markets, and securing monopolies. During the thirteenth and fourteenth centuries, trade-rich cities became powerful city-states, dominating the political and economic life of the surrounding countryside. By the fifteenth century, the great Italian cities were the bankers for much of Europe.

Growth of City-States The endemic warfare between pope and emperor and the Guelf (propapal) and Ghibelline (proimperial) factions assisted the growth of Italian cities and urban culture. Either of these factions might successfully have subdued the cities had they permitted each other to concentrate on doing so. Instead, they chose to weaken one another, which strengthened the merchant oligarchies of the cities. Unlike the great cities of northern Europe, which kings and territorial princes dominated, the great Italian cities remained free to expand on their own. Becoming independent states, they absorbed the surrounding countryside, assimilating the local nobility in a unique urban meld of old and new rich. Five such major competitive states evolved: the duchy of Milan the republics of Florence and Venice, the Papal States, and the kingdom of Naples. (See Map 10–1.)

Social strife and competition for political power became so intense within the cities that most evolved into despotisms just to survive. A notable exception was Venice, which was ruled by a successful merchant oligarchy. The Venetian government operated through a patrician senate of three hundred members and a ruthless judicial body. The latter, known as the Council of Ten, was quick to anticipate and suppress all rival groups.

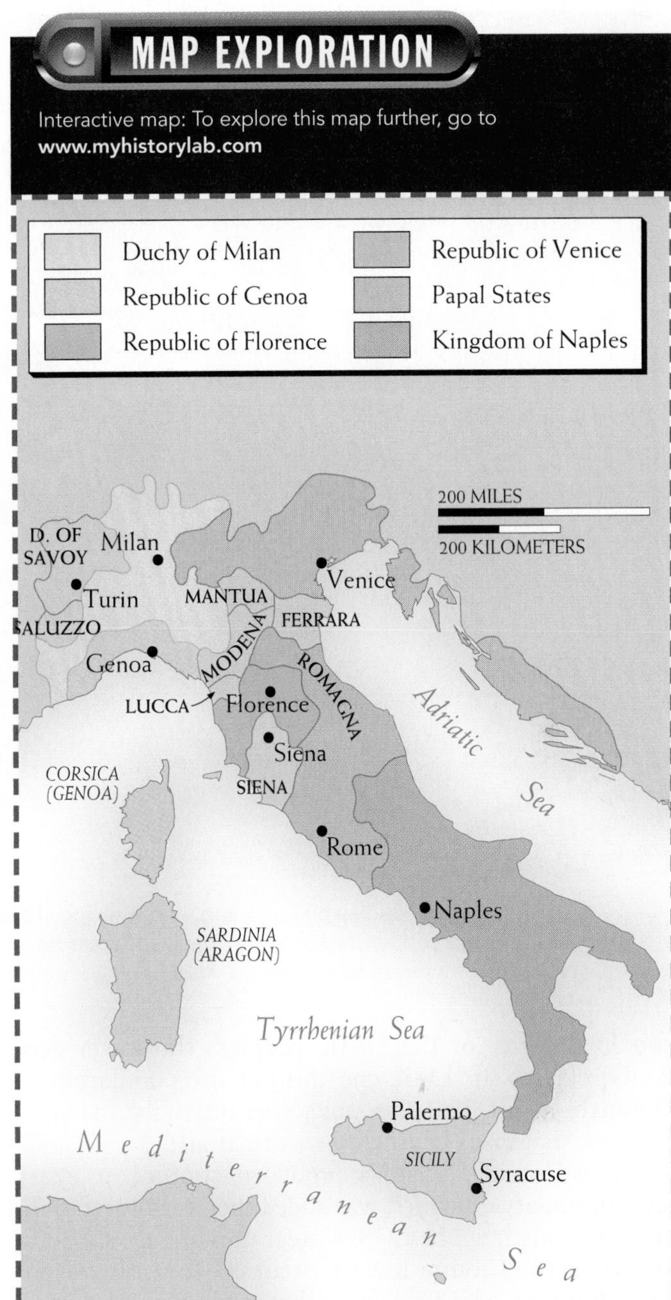

Map 10–1 **RENAISSANCE ITALY** The city-states of Renaissance Italy were self-contained principalities whose internal strife was monitored by their despots and whose external aggression was long successfully controlled by treaty.

Social Class and Conflict Florence was the most striking example of social division and anarchy. Four distinguishable social groups existed within the city. There was the old rich, or *grandi,* the nobles and merchants who traditionally ruled the city. The emergent newly rich merchant class, capitalists and bankers known as the *popolo grosso,* or "fat people," formed a second group. In the late thirteenth and early fourteenth centuries, they began to challenge the old rich for political powers. Then there were the middle-burgher ranks of guild masters, shop owners, and professionals, the smaller businesspeople who, in Florence, as elsewhere, tended to side with the new rich against the conservative policies of the old rich. Finally, there was the

Florentine women doing needlework, spinning, and weaving. These activities took up much of a woman's time and contributed to the elegance of dress for which Florentine men and women were famed. Palazzo Schifanoia, Ferrara. Alinari/Art Resource, NY

popolo minuto, or the "little people," the lower economic classes. In 1457, one third of the population of Florence, about 30,000 people, was officially listed as paupers, that is, as having no wealth at all.

These social divisions produced conflict at every level of society, to which was added the ever-present fear of foreign intrigue. In 1378, a great uprising of the poor, known as the Ciompi Revolt, occurred. It resulted from a combination of three factors that made life unbearable for those at the bottom of society: the feuding between the old rich and the new rich; the social anarchy created when the Black Death cut the city's population almost in half; and the collapse of the great banking houses of Bardi and Peruzzi, which left the poor more vulnerable than ever. The Ciompi Revolt established a chaotic four-year reign of power by the lower Florentine classes. True stability did not return to Florence until the ascent to power of the Florentine banker and statesman, Cosimo de' Medici (1389–1464) in 1434.

Despotism and Diplomacy Cosimo de' Medici was the wealthiest Florentine and a natural statesman. He controlled the city internally from behind the scenes, manipulating the constitution and influencing elections. A council, first of six and later of eight members, known as the *Signoria,* governed the city. These men were chosen from the most powerful guilds, namely, those representing the major clothing industries (cloth, wool, fur, and silk) and such other groups as bankers, judges, and doctors. Through informal, cordial relations with the electors, Cosimo was able to keep councilors loyal to him in the *Signoria.* From his position as the head of the Office of Public Debt, he favored congenial factions. His grandson, Lorenzo the Magnificent (1449–1492; r. 1478–1492), ruled Florence in almost totalitarian fashion during the last, chaotic quarter of the fifteenth century. The assassination of his brother in 1478 by a rival family, the Pazzi, who had long plotted with the pope against the Medicis, made Lorenzo a cautious and determined ruler.

Despotism elsewhere was even less subtle. To prevent internal social conflict and foreign intrigue from paralyzing their cities, the dominant groups cooperated to install hired strongmen, or despots. Known as a *podestà,* the despot's sole purpose was to maintain law and order. He held executive, military, and judicial authority, and his mandate was direct and simple: to permit, by whatever means required, the normal flow of business activity without which neither the old rich and new rich, nor the poor of a city, could long survive, much less prosper. Because despots could not count on the loyalty of the divided populace, they operated through mercenary armies obtained through military brokers known as ***condottieri***.

It was a hazardous job. Not only was a despot subject to dismissal by the oligarchies that hired him, he was also a popular object of assassination attempts. The spoils of success, however, were great. In Milan, it was as despots that the Visconti family came to power in 1278 and the Sforza family in 1450, both ruling without constitutional restraints or serious political competition.

Mercifully, the political turbulence and warfare of the times also gave birth to the art of diplomacy. Through their diplomats, the various city-states stayed abreast of foreign military developments and, when shrewd enough, gained power and advantage over their enemies without actually going to war. Most city-states established resident embassies in the fifteenth century for that very purpose. Their ambassadors not only represented them in ceremonies and at negotiations, they also became their watchful eyes and ears at rival courts.

Whether within the comparatively tranquil republic of Venice, the strong-arm democracy of Florence, or the undisguised despotism of Milan, the disciplined Italian city proved a congenial climate for an unprecedented flowering of thought and culture. Italian Renaissance culture was promoted as vigorously by despots as by republicans and as enthusiastically by secularized popes as by the more spiritually minded. Such widespread support occurred because the main requirement for patronage of the arts and letters was the one thing that Italian cities of the High Renaissance had in abundance: great wealth.

Humanism

Scholars still debate the meaning of the term *humanism.* Some see the Italian Renaissance as Burckhardt did, as the birth of modernity, driven by an un-Christian philosophy that stressed the dignity of humankind, individualism, and secular values. Others argue that the humanists were actually the champions of Catholic Christianity, opposing the pagan teaching of Aristotle and the Scholasticism his writings nurtured. For still others, humanism was a neutral form of historical scholarship adopted to promote above all a sense of civic responsibility and political liberty.

A leading scholar, Paul O. Kristeller, accused all of the above of dealing more with the secondary effects of humanism than with its essence. Humanism was not a philosophy or a value system, but an educational program built on rhetoric and scholarship for their own sake.

Each of these definitions has some truth. **Humanism** was the scholarly study of the Latin and Greek classics and of the ancient Church Fathers, both for its own sake and in the hope of reviving respected ancient norms and values. Humanists advocated the ***studia humanitatis***, a liberal arts program of study embracing grammar, rhetoric, poetry, history, politics, and moral philosophy. Not only were these subjects considered a joy in themselves, they also celebrated the dignity of humankind and prepared people for a life of virtuous action. The Florentine Leonardo Bruni (ca. 1370–1444) first gave the name *humanitas,* or "humanity," to the learning that resulted from such scholarly pursuits. Bruni was a star student of Manuel Chrysoloras (ca. 1355–1415), the Byzantine scholar who opened the world of Greek scholarship to Italian humanists when he taught at Florence between 1397 and 1403.

The first humanists were orators and poets. They wrote original literature in both classical and vernacular languages, inspired by and modeled on the newly discovered works of the ancients. They also taught rhetoric within the universities. When humanists were not employed as teachers of rhetoric, princely and papal courts sought their talents as secretaries, speechwriters, and diplomats.

The study of classical and Christian antiquity had existed before the Italian Renaissance. There were memorable recoveries of ancient civilization during the Carolingian renaissance of the ninth century, within the cathedral school of Chartres in the twelfth century, during the great Aristotelian revival in Paris in the thirteenth century, and among the Augustinians in the early fourteenth century. These precedents, however, only partially compare with the achievements of the Italian Renaissance of the fourteenth and fifteenth centuries. The latter was far more secular and lay-dominated, had much broader interests, was blessed with far more recovered manuscripts, and its scholars possessed far superior technical skills than those who had delivered the earlier "rebirths" of antiquity.

Unlike their Scholastic rivals, humanists were less bound to recent tradition; nor did they focus all their attention on summarizing and comparing the views of recognized authorities. Their most respected sources were classical and biblical, not medieval philosophers and theologians. Avidly searching out manuscript collections, Italian humanists made the full riches of Greek and Latin antiquity available to contemporary scholars. So great was their achievement that there is a kernel of truth in their assertion that the period between themselves and classical civilization was a "dark middle age."

Petrarch, Dante, and Boccaccio Francesco Petrarch (1304–1374) was the "father of humanism." He left the legal profession to pursue letters and poetry. Most of his life was spent in and around Avignon. He was involved in a popular revolt in Rome (1347–1349) and, in his later years, he served the Visconti family in Milan.

Petrarch celebrated ancient Rome in his *Letters to the Ancient Dead,* fancied personal letters to Cicero, Livy, Vergil, and Horace. He also wrote a Latin epic poem (*Africa,* a poetic historical tribute to the Roman general Scipio Africanus) and biographies of famous Roman men (*Lives of Illustrious Men*). His most famous contemporary work was a collection of highly introspective love sonnets to a certain Laura, a married woman he admired romantically from a safe distance.

His critical textual studies, elitism, and contempt for the learning of the Scholastics were features many later humanists also shared. As with many later humanists, Classical and Christian values coexist uneasily in his work. Medieval Christian values can be seen in his imagined dialogues with Saint Augustine and in tracts he wrote to defend the personal immortality of the soul against the Aristotelians.

Petrarch was, however, far more secular in orientation than his famous near-contemporary Dante

THE RENAISSANCE GARDEN

IN THE MIDDLE Ages and early Renaissance, few possessions were as prized, or as vital, as a garden. Within that enclosed space grew both ornamental and medicinal flowers and herbs. The more common kitchen garden existed in every manor, castle, monastery, guildhall, and small household. In addition to their large, elaborate gardens, the rich also had orchards and vineyards to grow the fruit from which they made sweet drinks and wine. Behind their shops and guildhalls, apothecaries and barber-surgeons cultivated the curative flowers and herbs from which they concocted the medicines of their trades. Beyond manor and guildhall walls, small householders and cottagers hoed the small, narrow plots behind their houses in which they grew the basic herbs and vegetables of their diet. Although the grandeur and variety of a garden reflected the prestige of its owner, every garden's main purpose was to serve the immediate needs of the household.

Versatility and pungency distinguished the most popular flowers and herbs. The violet was admired for its beauty, fragrance, and utility. Medieval people put violets in baths, oils, and syrups, prizing its soft scent and healing power as well as its ability to color, flavor, and garnish dishes. Nonetheless, subtlety and delicacy were not as important to the medieval palate as they are to ours. An herb or flower was only as good as its impact on the senses. Potent scents and flavors were loved for their ability to bring an otherwise starchy and lackluster meal to life. Fruit, although it was the main ingredient for sweet drinks, rarely appeared on a medieval plate, and vegetables were only slightly more common. Cabbage, lentils, peas, beans, onions, leeks, beets, and parsnips were the most often served vegetables at the medieval table, made palatable by heavy application of the sharpest and bitterest spices.

A wealthy man oversees apple picking at harvest time in a fifteenth-century French orchard. In the town below, individual house gardens can be seen. Protective fences, made of woven sticks, keep out predatory animals. In the right foreground, a boar can be seen overturning an apple barrel. The British Library

Beyond its practical function as a source of food and medicine, the medieval garden was a space of social and religious significance. In Christian history, gardens represented sacred places on earth. During the Middle Ages and early Renaissance, it was not the sprawling paradise of the Garden of Eden that captured the imagination, but rather the closed garden of the Bible's Song of Songs (4:12): "A garden enclosed is my sister, my spouse; a spring shut up, a fountain sealed." Such sensuous imagery symbolized the soul's union with God, Christ's union with the Catholic Church, and the bond of love between a man and a woman.

Although enclosed behind walls, fences, or hedges to protect them as vital food sources, gardens were also the private places of dreamers and lovers. Pleasure gardens bloomed around the homes of the wealthy. There, amid grottoes and fountains, lovers breathed the warm scents of roses and lilies and pursued the romantic trysts popularized in court poetry. The stories of courtly love were cautionary as well as titillating, for as the catechism reminded every medieval Christian, the garden was also a place of temptation and lost innocence.

What kinds of gardens existed in the Middle Ages and early Renaissance? How did religion give meaning to gardens?

Teresa McClean, *Medieval English Gardens* (New York: Viking Press, 1980), pp. 64, 133; Marilyn Stokstad and Jerry Stannard, *Gardens of the Middle Ages* (Lawrence, KS: Spencer Museum, 1983), pp. 19–21, 61.

Alighieri (1265–1321), whose *Vita Nuova* and *Divine Comedy* form, with Petrarch's sonnets, the cornerstones of Italian vernacular literature. Petrarch's student and friend Giovanni Boccaccio (1313–1375) was also a pioneer of humanist studies. His *Decameron*—one hundred often bawdy tales told by three men and seven women in a safe country retreat away from the plague that ravaged Florence in 1348 (see Chapter 9)—is both a stinging social commentary (it exposes sexual and economic misconduct) and a sympathetic look at human behavior. An avid collector of manuscripts, Boccaccio also assembled an encyclopedia of Greek and Roman mythology.

Educational Reforms and Goals Humanists delighted in taking their mastery of ancient languages directly to the past, refusing to be slaves to later tradition. Such an attitude not only made them innovative educators, but also kept them constantly in search of new sources of information. In the search, they assembled magnificent manuscript collections, treating them as potent medicines for the ills of contemporary society, and capable of enlightening the minds of any who would immerse themselves in them.

The goal of humanist studies was wisdom eloquently spoken, both knowledge of the good and the ability to move others to desire it. Learning was not meant to remain abstract and unpracticed. "It is better to will the good than to know the truth," Petrarch taught, and it became a motto of many later humanists, who, like Petrarch, believed learning ennobled people. Pietro Paolo Vergerio (1349–1420), the author of the most influential Renaissance tract on education (*On the Morals That Befit a Free Man*), left a classic summary of the humanist concept of a liberal education:

> We call those studies liberal which are worthy of a free man; those studies by which we attain and practice virtue and wisdom; that education which calls forth, trains, and develops those highest gifts of body and mind which ennoble men and which are rightly judged to rank next in dignity to virtue only, for to a vulgar temper, gain and pleasure are the one aim of existence, to a lofty nature, moral worth and fame.[1]

The ideal of a useful education and well-rounded people inspired far-reaching reforms in traditional education. The Roman orator Quintilian's (ca. 35–100) *Education of the Orator*, the complete text of which was discovered in 1416, became the basic classical guide for the humanist revision of the traditional curriculum. Vittorino da Feltre (d. 1446) exemplified the ideals of humanist teaching. Not only did he have his students read the difficult works of Pliny, Ptolemy, Terence, Plautus, Livy, and Plutarch, he also subjected them to vigorous physical exercise and games. Still another contemporary educator, Guarino da Verona (d. 1460), the rector of the new University of Ferrara and another student of Greek scholar Manuel Chrysoloras, streamlined the study of classical languages.

Despite the grinding scholarly process of acquiring ancient knowledge, humanistic studies were not confined to the classroom. As Baldassare Castiglione's (1478–1529) *Book of the Courtier* illustrates, the rediscovered knowledge of the past was both a model and a challenge to the present. Written as a practical guide for the nobility at the court of Urbino, a small duchy in central Italy, it embodies the highest ideals of Italian humanism. The successful courtier is said to be one who knows how to integrate knowledge of ancient languages and history with athletic, military, and musical skills, while at the same time practicing good manners and exhibiting a high moral character.

Privileged, educated noblewomen also promoted the new education and culture at royal courts. Among them was Christine de Pisan (1363?–1434), the Italian-born daughter of the physician and astrologer of French king Charles V. She became an expert in classical, French, and Italian languages and literature. Married at fifteen and the widowed mother of three at twenty-seven, she wrote lyric poetry to support herself and was much read throughout the courts of Europe. Her most famous work, *The Treasure of the City of Ladies,* is a chronicle of the accomplishments of the great women of history. (See "Christine de Pisan Instructs Women on How to Handle Their Husbands," page 288.)

The Florentine "Academy" and the Revival of Platonism Of all the important recoveries of the past made during the Italian Renaissance, none stands out more than the revival of Greek studies—especially the works of Plato—in fifteenth-century Florence. Many factors combined to bring this revival about. A foundation, already mentioned above, was laid in 1397 when the city invited Manuel Chrysoloras to come from Constantinople to promote Greek learning. A half century later (1439), the ecumenical Council of Ferrara-Florence, convened to negotiate the reunion of the Eastern and Western churches, opened the door for many Greek scholars and manuscripts to pour into the West. After the fall of Constantinople to the Turks in 1453, many Greek scholars fled to Florence for refuge. This was the background against which the Florentine Platonic Academy evolved under the patronage of Cosimo de' Medici and the supervision of Marsilio Ficino (1433–1499) and Pico della Mirandola (1463–1494).

Renaissance thinkers were especially attracted to the Platonic tradition and to those Church Fathers who tried to synthesize Platonic philosophy with Christian teaching. The so-called Florentine Academy was actually not a formal school, but an informal gathering of influential Florentine humanists devoted to the revival of the works of Plato and the Neoplatonists: Plotinus, Proclus,

[1]Cited by De Lamar Jensen, *Renaissance Europe: Age of Recovery and Reconciliation* (Lexington, MA: D. C. Health, 1981), p. 111.

CHRISTINE DE PISAN INSTRUCTS WOMEN ON HOW TO HANDLE THEIR HUSBANDS

Renowned Renaissance noblewoman Christine de Pisan has the modern reputation of being perhaps the first feminist, and her book, The Treasure of the City of Ladies *(also known as* The Book of Three Virtues*), has been described as the Renaissance woman's survival manual. Here she gives advice to the wives of artisans.*

How does Christine de Pisan's image of husband and wife compare with other medieval views? Would the church question her advice? As a noblewoman commenting on the married life of artisans, does her high social standing influence her advice? Would she give similar advice to women of her own social class?

All wives of artisans should be very painstaking and diligent if they wish to have the necessities of life. They should encourage their husbands or their workmen to get to work early in the morning and work until late. . . . [And] the wife herself should [also] be involved in the work to the extent that she knows all about it, so that she may know how to oversee his workers if her husband is absent, and to reprove them if they do not do well. . . . And when customers come to her husband and try to drive a hard bargain, she ought to warn him solicitously to take care that he does not make a bad deal. She should advise him to be chary of giving too much credit if he does not know precisely where and to whom it is going, for in this way many come to poverty. . . .

Christine de Pisan, who has the modern reputation of being the first European feminist, presents her internationally famous book *The Treasure of the City of Ladies*, also known as *The Book of Three Virtues*, to Isabella of Bavaria amid her ladies in waiting. Historical Picture Archive/CORBIS/Bettmann

In addition, she ought to keep her husband's love as much as she can, to this end: that he will stay at home more willingly and that he may not have any reason to join the foolish crowds of other young men in taverns and indulge in unnecessary and extravagant expense, as many tradesmen do, especially in Paris. By treating him kindly she should protect him as well as she can from this. It is said that three things drive a man from his home: a quarrelsome wife, a smoking fireplace, and a leaking roof. She too ought to stay at home gladly and not go off every day traipsing hither and yon gossiping with the neighbours and visiting her chums to find out what everyone is doing. That is done by slovenly housewives roaming about the town in groups. Nor should she go off on these pilgrimages got up for no good reason and involving a lot of needless expense.

From *The Treasure of the City of Ladies* by Christine de Pisan, trans. by Sarah Lawson (New York: Penguin, 1985), pp. 167–168.

Porphyry, and Dionysius the Areopagite. To this end, Ficino edited and published the complete works of Plato.

The appeal of **Platonism** lay in its flattering view of human nature. It distinguished between an eternal sphere of being and the perishable world in which humans actually lived. Human reason was believed to have preexisted in this pristine world and still to commune with it, a theory supported by human knowledge of eternal mathematical and moral truths.

Strong Platonic influence is evident in Pico's *Oration on the Dignity of Man,* perhaps the most famous Renaissance statement on the nature of humankind. (See "Compare & Connect: Is the "Renaissance Man" a Myth?" page 290.) Pico wrote the *Oration* as an introduction to his pretentious collection of nine hundred theses. Published in Rome in December 1486, the theses were intended to serve as the basis for a public debate on all of life's important topics. The *Oration* drew on Platonic teaching to depict humans as the only creatures in the world who possessed the freedom to be whatever they chose, able at will to rise to the height of angels or just as quickly to wallow with pigs.

Critical Work of the Humanists: Lorenzo Valla

Because they were guided by scholarly ideals of philological accuracy and historical truth, the humanists could become critics of tradition even when that was not their intention. Dispassionate critical scholarship shook long-standing foundations, not the least of which were those of the medieval church.

The work of Lorenzo Valla (1406–1457), author of the standard Renaissance text on Latin philology, the *Elegances of the Latin Language* (1444), reveals the explosive character of the new learning. Although a good Catholic, Valla became a hero to later Protestant reformers. His popularity among them stemmed from his exposé of the *Donation of Constantine* (see Chapter 6) and his defense of predestination against the advocates of free will.

The fraudulent *Donation,* written in the eighth century, purported to be a grant of vast territories that the Roman emperor Constantine (r. 307–337) donated to the pope. Valla did not intend the exposé of the *Donation* to have the devastating force that Protestants later attributed to it. He only proved in a careful, scholarly way what others had long suspected. Using textual analysis and historical logic, Valla demonstrated that the document was filled with anachronistic terms, such as *fief,* and contained information that could not have existed in a fourth-century document. In the same dispassionate way, he also pointed out errors in the Latin Vulgate, still the authorized version of the Bible for the Western church.

Such discoveries did not make Valla any less loyal to the church, nor did they prevent his faithful fulfillment of the office of apostolic secretary in Rome under Pope Nicholas V (r. 1447–1455). Nonetheless, historical humanistic criticism of this type also served those less loyal to the medieval church. Young humanists formed the first identifiable group of Martin Luther's supporters.

Civic Humanism

A basic humanist criticism of Scholastic education was that much of its content was useless. Education, humanists believed, should promote individual virtue and public service, hence the designation, **civic humanism**. The most striking examples of this were found in Florence, where three humanists served as chancellors of the city: Coluccio Salutati (1331–1406), Leonardo Bruni (ca. 1370–1444), and Poggio Bracciolini (1380–1459). Each used his rhetorical skills to rally the Florentines against the aggression of Naples and Milan. Bruni and Poggio wrote adulatory histories of the city. Another accomplished humanist scholar, Leon Battista Alberti (1402–1472), was a noted Florentine architect and builder. However, many modern scholars doubt that humanistic scholarship really accounted for such civic activity and rather view the three famous humanist chancellors of Florence as men who simply wanted to exercise power.

Toward the end of the Renaissance, many humanists became cliquish and snobbish, an intellectual elite more concerned with narrow scholarly interests and writing pure, classical Latin than with revitalizing civic and social life. In reaction to this elitist trend, the humanist historians Niccolò Machiavelli (1469–1527) and Francesco Guicciardini (1483–1540) wrote in Italian and made contemporary history their primary source and subject matter. Here, arguably, we can see the two sides of humanism: deep scholarship and practical politics.

Renaissance Art

In Renaissance Italy, as in Reformation Europe, the values and interests of the laity were no longer subordinated to those of the clergy. In education, culture, and religion, the laity assumed a leading role and established models for the clergy to emulate. This development was due in part to the church's loss of international power during the great crises of the late Middle Ages. The rise of national sentiment and the emergence of national bureaucracies staffed by laymen, not clerics, and the rapid growth of lay education over the fourteenth and fifteenth centuries also encouraged it. Medieval Christian values were adjusted to a more this-worldly spirit.

This new perspective on life is prominent in the painting and sculpture of the High Renaissance (1450–1527), when art and sculpture reached their full maturity. Whereas medieval art tended to be abstract and formulaic, Renaissance art emphatically embraced the natural world and human emotions. Renaissance artists gave their works a rational, even mathematical, order—perfect symmetry and proportionality reflecting a belief in the harmony of the universe.

COMPARE AND CONNECT

Is the "Renaissance Man" a Myth?

AS SEVERAL ILLUSTRATIONS in this chapter attest, the great artists of the Renaissance (Raphael, Leonardo da Vinci, Albrecht Dürer) romanticized their human subjects and made them larger than life. Not only was the iconic "Renaissance man" perfectly proportioned physically, he was also effective in what he undertook, endowed with the divine freedom and power to be and to do whatever he chose.

QUESTIONS

1. **Who or what are Pico's and Dürer's glorified humans? Is the vaunted "Renaissance Man" real or fictional?**
2. **What is one to make of an era fixated on the perfect body and mind?**
3. **Is Martin Luther's rejoinder (the bondage of the human will) truer to life, or religious misanthropy?**

I. Pico della Mirandola, *Oration on the Dignity of Man* (ca. 1486)

One of the most eloquent descriptions of the Renaissance image of human beings comes from the Italian humanist Pico della Mirandola (1463–1494). In his famed Oration on the Dignity of Man *(ca. 1486), Pico describes humans as free to become whatever they choose.*

Pico's "Renaissance Man" stands in stark contrast to the devout Christian pilgrim of the Middle Ages. The latter found himself always at the crossroads of heaven and hell, in constant fear of sin, death, and the devil, regularly confessing his sins and receiving forgiveness in an unending penitential cycle. Had the Middle Ages misjudged human nature? Was there a great transformation in human nature between the Middle Ages and the Renaissance?

The best of artisans [God] ordained that that creature (man) to whom He had been able to give nothing proper to himself should have joint possession of whatever had been peculiar to each of the different kinds of being. He therefore took man as a creature of indeterminate nature and, assigning him a place in the middle of the world, addressed him thus: "Neither a fixed abode nor a form that is thine alone nor any function peculiar to thyself have we given thee, Adam, to the end that according to thy longing and according to thy judgment thou mayest have and possess what abode, what form, and what functions thou thyself shalt desire. The nature of all other beings is limited and constrained within the bounds of laws prescribed by Us. Thou, constrained by no limits, in accordance with thine own free will, in whose hand We have placed thee, shall ordain for thyself the limits of thy nature. We have set thee at the world's center that thou mayest from thence more easily observe whatever is in the world. We have made thee neither of heaven nor of earth, neither mortal nor immortal, so that with freedom of choice and with honor, as though the maker and molder of thyself, thou mayest fashion thyself in whatever shape thou shalt prefer. Thou shalt have the power to degenerate into the lower forms of life, which are brutish. Thou shalt have the power, out of thy soul's judgment, to be reborn into the higher forms, which are divine." O supreme generosity of God the Father, O highest and most marvelous felicity of man! To him it is granted to have whatever he chooses, to be whatever he wills.

Source: Giovanni Pico della Mirandola, *Oration on the Dignity of Man,* in *The Renaissance Philosophy of Man,* ed. by E. Cassirer et al. (Chicago: Phoenix Books, 1961), pp. 224–225.

II. Albrecht Dürer

In 1500, Albrecht Dürer, then 28, painted the most famous self-portrait of the European Renaissance and Reformation, one that celebrated his own beauty and genius by imposing his face on a portrayal of Christ, a work of art that has been called "the birth of the modern artist."

Fourteen years later (1514), on the occasion of his mother's death, Dürer engraved another famous image of himself, only now as a man in deep depression, or melancholy, his mind darkened and his creativity throttled.

In this self-portrait he is neither effective nor handsome, much less heroic and divine, not a self-portrait of a Renaissance man.

Albrecht Dürer (1471–1528). *Self-portrait at Age 28 with Fur Coat.* 1500. Oil on wood, 67 × 49 cm. Alte Pinakothek, Munich, Germany. Photograph © Scala/Art Resource, NY

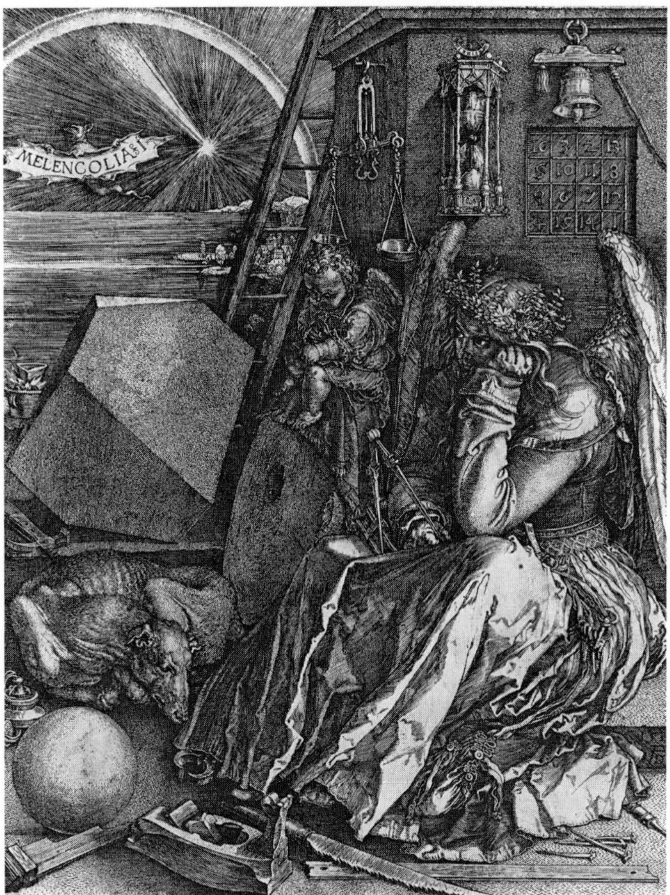

Albrecht Dürer. *Melencolia I.* 1514. Engraving. 23.8 × 18.9 cm. Courtesy of the Library of Congress.

III. Martin Luther, *The Bondage of the Will* (1525)

The greater challenge to the Renaissance man came from Martin Luther, who met his "Pico" in the northern humanist Desiderius Erasmus. Like Pico, Erasmus, flying in the face of Reformation theology, conceived free will to be "a power of the human will by which a man may apply himself to those things that lead to eternal salvation, or turn away from the same." Of such thinking, Luther made short-shift.

It is in the highest degree wholesome and necessary for a Christian to know whether or not his will has anything to do in matters pertaining to salvation . . . We need to have in mind a clear-cut distinction between God's power and ours and God's work and ours, if we would live a godly life . . . The will, be it God's or man's, does what it does, good or bad, under no compulsion, but just as it wants or pleases, as if totally free . . . Wise men know what experience of life proves, that no man's purposes ever go forward as planned, but events overtake all men contrary to their expectation. . . Who among us always lives and behaves as he should? But duty and doctrine are not therefore condemned, rather they condemn us.

God has promised His grace to the humbled, that is, to those who mourn over and despair of themselves. But a man cannot be thoroughly humbled till he realizes that his salvation is utterly beyond his own powers, counsels, efforts, will and works, and depends absolutely on the will, counsel, pleasure, and work of Another: GOD ALONE. As long as he is persuaded that he can make even the smallest contribution to his salvation, he . . . does not utterly despair of himself, and so is not humbled before God, but plans for himself a position, an occasion, a work, which shall bring him final salvation. But he who [no longer] doubts that his destiny depends entirely only on the will of God . . . waits for God to work in him, and such a man is very near to grace for his salvation. So if we want to drop this term ("free will") altogether, which would be the safest and most Christian thing to do, we may, still in good faith, teach people to use it to credit man with 'free will' in respect not of what is above him, but of what is below him . . . However, with regard to God and in all that bears on salvation or damnation, he has no 'free will' but is a captive, prisoner and bond-slave, either to the will of God, or to the will of Satan.

Source: Martin Luther, *On the Bondage of the Will*, ed. by J. I Packer and O. R. Johnston (Westwood, NJ: Fleming H. Fevell Co., 1957), pp. 79, 81, 83, 87, 100, 104, 107, 137.

Combining the painterly qualities of all the Renaissance masters, Raphael created scenes of tender beauty and subjects sublime in both flesh and spirit. Musée du Louvre, Paris/Giraudon, Paris/SuperStock

Renaissance artists were helped by the development of new technical skills during the fifteenth century. In addition to the availability of oil paints, two special techniques gave them an edge: the use of shading to enhance naturalness (**chiaroscuro**) and the adjustment of the size of figures to give the viewer a feeling of continuity with the painting (*linear perspective*). These techniques enabled the artist to portray space realistically and to paint a more natural world. The result, compared to their flat Byzantine and Gothic counterparts, was a three-dimensional canvas filled with energy and life.

Giotto (1266–1336), the father of Renaissance painting, signaled the new direction. An admirer of Saint Francis of Assisi, whose love of nature he shared, Giotto painted a more natural world. Though still filled with religious seriousness, his work was no longer an abstract and unnatural depiction of the world. The painter Masaccio (1401–1428) and the sculptor Donatello (1386–1466) also portrayed the world around them literally and naturally. The great masters of the High Renaissance, Leonardo da Vinci (1452–1519), Raphael (1483–1520), and Michelangelo Buonarroti (1475–1564), reached the heights of such painting.

Leonardo da Vinci A true master of many skills, Leonardo exhibited the Renaissance ideal of the universal person. One of the greatest painters of all time, he also advised Italian princes and the French king Francis I (r. 1515–1547) on military engineering. He advocated scientific experimentation, dissected corpses to learn anatomy, and was a self-taught botanist. His inventive mind foresaw such modern machines as airplanes and submarines. The variety of his interests was so great that it could shorten his attention span. His great skill in conveying inner moods through complex facial expression is apparent not only in his most famous painting, the *Mona Lisa,* but in his self-portrait as well.

Raphael A man of great kindness and a painter of great sensitivity, Raphael was loved by his contemporaries as much for his person as for his work. He is most famous for his tender madonnas and the great fresco in the Vatican, *The School of Athens,* a virtually perfect example of Renaissance technique. It depicts Plato and Aristotle surrounded by other great philosophers and scientists of antiquity who bear the features of Raphael's famous contemporaries.

Michelangelo The melancholy genius Michelangelo also excelled in a variety of arts and crafts. His eighteen-foot sculpture of David, which long stood majestically in the great square of Florence, is a perfect example of Renaissance devotion to harmony, symmetry, and proportion, all serving the glorification of the human form. Four different popes commissioned works by Michelangelo. The frescoes in the Vatican's Sistine Chapel are the most famous, painted during the pontificate of Pope Julius II (r. 1503–1513), who also set Michelangelo to work on his own magnificent tomb. The Sistine frescoes originally covered 10,000 square feet and involved 343 figures, over half of which exceeded ten feet in height, but it is their originality and perfection as works of art that impress one most. This labor of love and piety took four years to complete.

His later works are more complex and suggest deep personal changes. They mark, artistically and philosophically, the passing of High Renaissance painting and the advent of a new style known as **mannerism**, which reached its peak in the late sixteenth and early seventeenth centuries. A reaction to the simplicity and symmetry of High Renaissance art, which also had a parallel in contemporary music and literature, mannerism made room for the strange and the abnormal, giving freer reign to the individual perceptions and feelings of the artist, who now felt free to paint, compose, or write in a "mannered," or "affected," way. Tintoretto (d. 1594) and El Greco (d. 1614) are mannerism's supreme representatives.

A Closer LOOK

LEONARDO PLOTS THE PERFECT MAN

VITRUVIAN MAN BY Leonardo da Vinci, c. 1490. The name "Vitruvian" is taken from that of a first-century C.E. Roman architect and engineer, Marcus Pollio Vitruvius, who used squares and circles to demonstrate the human body's symmetry and proportionality. According to Vitruvius:

And just as the human body yields a circular outline, so too a square figure may be found from it. For if we measure the distance from the soles of the feet to the top of the head, and then apply that measure to the outstretched arms, the breadth will be found to be the same as the height.

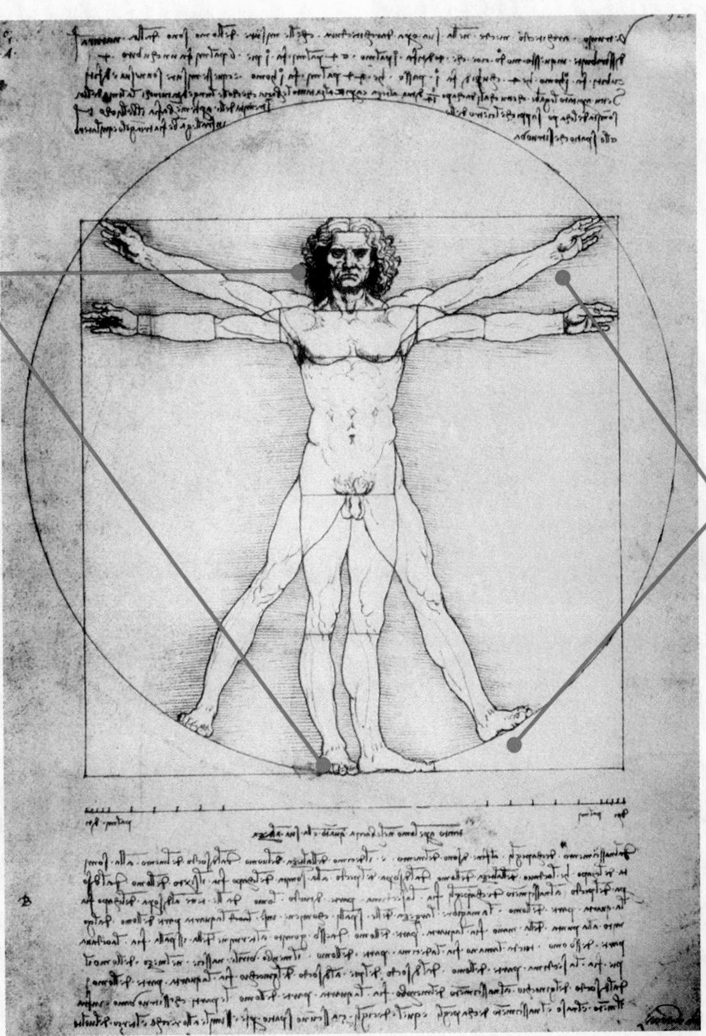

CORBIS/Bettmann

If a man be placed flat on his back, with his hands and feet extended, and a pair of compasses centered at his navel, the fingers and toes of his two hands and feet will touch the circumference of a circle described therefrom.

Leonardo, like most artists of his time, shared this classical ideal of human perfection even in his gloomiest etchings and paintings. With few exceptions, the great painters of the age wanted to portray men and women in a more than human beauty and glory. Even the rabbits of the German painter Albrecht Dürer, who shared this ideal, were superior to any rabbit one might see in the wild.

To examine this image in an interactive fashion, please go to www.myhistorylab.com

PEARSON myhistorylab

Marilyn Stokstad and David Cateforis, *Art History* (New York: Pearson, 2005), p. 651.

Michelangelo's Scene from the Last Judgment. The High Italian Renaissance obsession with the beefy, pumped up, heroic body finds expression in this detail of a fresco in Michelangelo's rendering of the *Last Judgment* in the Sistine Chapel. Nippon Television Network Corporation

MAJOR POLITICAL EVENTS OF THE ITALIAN RENAISSANCE (1375–1527)

1378–1382	The Ciompi Revolt in Florence
1434	Medici rule in Florence established by Cosimo de' Medici
1454–1455	Treaty of Lodi allies Milan, Naples, and Florence (in effect until 1494)
1494	Charles VIII of France invades Italy
1494–1498	Savonarola controls Florence
1495	League of Venice unites Venice, Milan, the Papal States, the Holy Roman Empire, and Spain against France
1499	Louis XII invades Milan (the second French invasion of Italy)
1500	The Borgias conquer Romagna
1512–1513	The Holy League (Pope Julius II, Ferdinand of Aragon, Emperor Maximilian, and Venice) defeats the French
1513	Machiavelli writes *The Prince*
1515	Francis I leads the third French invasion of Italy
1516	Concordat of Bologna between France and the papacy
1527	Sack of Rome by imperial soldiers

Slavery in the Renaissance

Throughout Renaissance Italy, slavery flourished as extravagantly as art and culture. A thriving western slave market existed as early as the twelfth century, when the Spanish sold Muslim slaves captured in raids and war to wealthy Italians and other buyers. Contemporaries looked on such slavery as a merciful act, since their captors would otherwise have killed the captives. In addition to widespread household or domestic slavery, collective plantation slavery, following East Asian models, also developed in the eastern Mediterranean during the High Middle Ages. In the savannas of Sudan and the Venetian estates on the islands of Cyprus and Crete, gangs of slaves cut sugarcane, setting the model for later slave plantations in the Mediterranean and the New World.

After the Black Death (1348–1350) reduced the supply of laborers everywhere in Western Europe, the demand for slaves soared. Slaves were imported from Africa, the Balkans, Constantinople, Cyprus, Crete, and the lands surrounding the Black Sea. Taken randomly from conquered people, they consisted of many races: Tatars, Circassians, Greeks, Russians, Georgians, and Iranians as well as Asians and Africans. According to one source, "By the end of the fourteenth century, there was hardly a well-to-do household in Tuscany without at least one slave: brides brought them [to their marriages] as part of their dowry, doctors accepted them from their patients in lieu of fees—and it was not unusual to find them even in the service of a priest."[2]

Owners had complete dominion over their slaves; in Italian law, this meant the "[power] to have, hold, sell, alienate, exchange, enjoy, rent or unrent, dispose of in [their] will[s], judge soul and body, and do with in perpetuity whatsoever may please [them] and [their] heirs and no man may gainsay [them]."[3] A strong, young, healthy slave cost the equivalent of the wages paid a free servant over several years. Considering the lifetime of free service thereafter, slaves were well worth the price.

[2]Iris Origo, *The Merchant of Prato: Francesco di Marco Datini, 1335–1410* (New York: David Godine, 1986), pp. 90–91.

[3]Origo, *The Merchant of Prato*, p. 209.

Tatars and Africans appear to have been the worst treated, but as in ancient Greece and Rome, slaves at this time were generally accepted as family members and integrated into households. Not a few women slaves became mothers of their masters' children. Fathers often adopted children of such unions and raised them as their legitimate heirs. It was also in the interest of their owners to keep slaves healthy and happy; otherwise they would be of little use and even become a threat. Slaves nonetheless remained a foreign and suspected presence in Italian society; they were, as all knew, uprooted and resentful people.

▼ Italy's Political Decline: The French Invasions (1494–1527)

As a land of autonomous city-states, Italy had always relied on internal cooperation for its peace and safety from foreign invasion—especially by the Turks. Such cooperation was maintained during the second half of the fifteenth century, thanks to a political alliance known as the Treaty of Lodi (1454–1455). Its terms brought Milan and Naples, long traditional enemies, into the alliance with Florence. These three stood together for decades against Venice, which frequently joined the Papal States to maintain an internal balance of power. However, when a foreign enemy threatened Italy, the five states could also present a united front.

Around 1490, after the rise to power of the Milanese despot Ludovico il Moro, hostilities between Milan and Naples resumed. The peace that the Treaty of Lodi made possible ended in 1494 when Naples, supported by Florence and the Borgia Pope Alexander VI (r. 1492–1503), threatened Milan. Ludovico made a fatal response to these new political alignments: He appealed to the French for aid. French kings had ruled Naples from 1266 to 1442 before being driven out by Duke Alfonso of Sicily. Breaking a wise Italian rule, Ludovico invited the French to reenter Italy and revive their dynastic claim to Naples. In his haste to check rival Naples, Ludovico did not recognize sufficiently that France also had dynastic claims to Milan. Nor did he foresee how insatiable the French appetite for new territory would become once French armies had crossed the Alps and encamped in Italy.

Charles VIII's March Through Italy

The French king Louis XI had resisted the temptation to invade Italy while nonetheless keeping French dynastic claims in Italy alive. His successor, Charles VIII (r. 1483–1498), an eager youth in his twenties, responded to Ludovico's call with lightning speed. Within five months, he had crossed the Alps (August 1494) and raced as conqueror through Florence and the Papal States into Naples. As Charles approached Florence, its Florentine ruler, Piero de' Medici, who was allied with Naples against Milan, tried to placate the French king by handing over Pisa and other Florentine possessions. Such appeasement only brought about Piero's exile by a citizenry that was being revolutionized by a radical Dominican preacher named Girolamo Savonarola (1452–1498). Savonarola convinced the fearful Florentines that the French king's arrival was a long-delayed and fully justified divine vengeance on their immorality.

That allowed Charles to enter Florence without resistance. Between Savonarola's fatal flattery and the payment of a large ransom, the city escaped destruction. After Charles's departure, Savonarola exercised virtual rule over Florence for four years. In the end, the Florentines proved not to be the stuff theocracies are made of. Savonarola's moral rigor and antipapal policies made it impossible for him to survive indefinitely in Italy. After the Italian cities reunited and ousted the French invader, whom Savonarola had praised as a godsend, Savonarola's days were numbered. In May 1498, he was imprisoned and executed.

Charles's lightning march through Italy also struck terror in non-Italian hearts. Ferdinand of Aragon (r. 1479–1516), who had hoped to expand his own possessions in Italy from his base in Sicily, now found himself vulnerable to a French-Italian axis. In response he created a new counteralliance—the League of Venice. Formed in March 1495, the League brought Venice, the Papal States, and Emperor Maximilian I (r. 1493–1519) together with Ferdinand against the French. The stage was now set for a conflict between France and Spain that would not end until 1559.

Ludovico il Moro meanwhile recognized that he had sown the wind. Having desired a French invasion only as long as it weakened his enemies, he now saw a whirlwind of events he had himself created threaten Milan. In reaction, he joined the League of Venice, which was now strong enough to send Charles into retreat and to end the menace he posed to Italy.

Pope Alexander VI and the Borgia Family

The French returned to Italy under Charles's successor, Louis XII (r. 1498–1515). This time a new Italian ally, the Borgia pope, Alexander VI, assisted them. Probably the most corrupt pope who ever sat on the papal throne, he openly promoted the political careers of Cesare and Lucrezia Borgia, the children he had had before he became pope. He placed papal policy in tandem with the efforts of his powerful family to secure a political base in Romagna in north central Italy.

In Romagna, several principalities had fallen away from the church during the Avignon papacy. Venice, the pope's ally within the League of Venice, continued to contest the Papal States for their loyalty. Seeing that a French alliance would allow him to reestablish control over the region, Alexander took steps to secure French favor. He annulled Louis XII's marriage to Charles VIII's sister so Louis could marry Charles's widow, Anne of Brittany—a popular political move designed to keep Brittany French. The pope also bestowed a cardinal's hat on the archbishop of Rouen, Louis's favorite cleric. Most important, Alexander agreed to abandon the League of Venice, a withdrawal of support that made the league too weak to resist a French reconquest of Milan. In exchange, Cesare Borgia received the sister of the king of Navarre, Charlotte d'Albret, in marriage, a union that enhanced Borgia military strength. Cesare also received land grants from Louis XII and the promise of French military aid in Romagna.

All in all it was a scandalous trade-off, but one that made it possible for both the French king and the pope to realize their ambitions within Italy. Louis invaded Milan in August 1499. Ludovico il Moro, who had originally opened the Pandora's box of French invasion, spent his last years languishing in a French prison. In 1500, Louis and Ferdinand of Aragon divided Naples between them, and the pope and Cesare Borgia conquered the cities of Romagna without opposition. Alexander's victorious son was given the title "duke of Romagna."

Pope Julius II

Cardinal Giuliano della Rovere, a strong opponent of the Borgia family, succeeded Alexander VI as Pope Julius II (r. 1503–1513). He suppressed the Borgias and placed their newly conquered lands in Romagna under papal jurisdiction. Julius raised the Renaissance papacy to its peak of military prowess and diplomatic intrigue, gaining him the title of "warrior pope." Shocked, as were other contemporaries, by this thoroughly secular papacy, the humanist Erasmus (1466?–1536), who had witnessed in disbelief a bullfight in the papal palace during a visit to Rome, wrote a popular anonymous satire entitled *Julius Excluded from Heaven.* This humorous account purported to describe the pope's unsuccessful efforts to convince Saint Peter that he was worthy of admission to heaven.

Assisted by his powerful allies, Pope Julius drove the Venetians out of Romagna in 1509 and fully secured the Papal States. Having realized this long-sought papal goal, Julius turned to the second major undertaking of his pontificate: ridding Italy of his former ally, the French invader. Julius, Ferdinand of Aragon, and Venice formed a second Holy League in October 1511 and were joined by Emperor Maximilian I and the Swiss. In 1512, the league had the French in full retreat, and the Swiss defeated them in 1513 at Novara.

The French were nothing if not persistent. They invaded Italy a third time under Louis's successor, Francis I (r. 1515–1547). This time French armies massacred Swiss soldiers of the Holy League at Marignano in September 1515, avenging the earlier defeat at Novara. The victory won the Concordat of Bologna from the pope in August 1516, an agreement that gave the French king control over the French clergy in exchange for French recognition of the pope's superiority over church councils and his right to collect annates in France. This concordat helped keep France Catholic after the outbreak of the Protestant Reformation, but the new French entry into Italy set the stage for the first of four major wars with Spain in the first half of the sixteenth century: the Habsburg-Valois wars, none of which France won.

Niccolò Machiavelli

The foreign invasions made a shambles of Italy. The same period that saw Italy's cultural peak in the work of Leonardo, Raphael, and Michelangelo also witnessed Italy's political tragedy. One who watched as French, Spanish, and German armies wreaked havoc on Italy was Niccolò Machiavelli (1469–1527). The more he saw, the more convinced he became that Italian political unity and independence were ends that justified any means.

A humanist and a careful student of ancient Rome, Machiavelli was impressed by the way Roman rulers and citizens had then defended their homeland. They possessed *virtù,* the ability to act decisively and heroically for the good of their country. Stories of ancient Roman patriotism and self-sacrifice were Machiavelli's favorites, and he lamented the absence of such traits among his compatriots. Such romanticizing of the Roman past exaggerated both ancient virtue and contemporary failings. His Florentine contemporary, Francesco Guicciardini (1483–1540), a more sober historian less given to idealizing antiquity, wrote truer chronicles of Florentine and Italian history.

Machiavelli also held republican ideals, which he did not want to see vanish from Italy. He believed a strong and determined people could struggle successfully with fortune. He scolded the Italian people for the self-destruction their own internal feuding was causing. He wanted an end to that behavior above all, so a reunited Italy could drive all foreign armies out.

His fellow citizens were not up to such a challenge. The juxtaposition of what Machiavelli believed the ancient Romans had been, with the failure of his contemporaries to attain such high ideals, made him the famous cynic whose name—in the epithet "Machiavellian"—has become synonymous with ruthless political expediency. Only a strongman, he concluded, could impose order on so divided and selfish a people; the salvation of Italy required, for the present, cunning dictators.

Santi di Tito's portrait of Machiavelli, perhaps the most famous Italian political theorist, who advised Renaissance princes to practice artful deception and inspire fear in their subjects if they wished to be successful. Scala/Art Resource, NY

It has been argued that Machiavelli wrote *The Prince* in 1513 as a cynical satire on the way rulers actually do behave and not as a serious recommendation of unprincipled despotic rule. To take his advocacy of tyranny literally, it is argued, contradicts both his earlier works and his own strong family tradition of republican service. But Machiavelli seems to have been in earnest when he advised rulers to discover the advantages of fraud and brutality, at least as a temporary means to the higher end of a unified Italy. He apparently hoped to see a strong ruler emerge from the Medici family, which had captured the papacy in 1513 with the pontificate of Leo X (r. 1513–1521). At the same time, the Medici family retained control over the powerful territorial state of Florence. The situation was similar to that of Machiavelli's hero Cesare Borgia and his father Pope Alexander VI, who had earlier brought factious Romagna to heel by combining secular family goals with religious policy. *The Prince* was pointedly dedicated to Lorenzo de' Medici, duke of Urbino and grandson of Lorenzo the Magnificent.

Whatever Machiavelli's hopes may have been, the Medicis were not destined to be Italy's deliverers. The second Medici pope, Clement VII (r. 1523–1534), watched helplessly as the army of Emperor Charles V sacked Rome in 1527, also the year of Machiavelli's death.

▼ Revival of Monarchy in Northern Europe

After 1450, the emergence of truly sovereign rulers set in motion a shift from divided feudal monarchy to unified national monarchies. Dynastic and chivalric ideals of feudal monarchy did not, however, vanish. Territorial princes remained on the scene and representative bodies persisted and even grew in influence. Still, in the late fifteenth and early sixteenth centuries, the old problem of the one and the many was now progressively decided in favor of national monarchs.

The feudal monarchy of the High Middle Ages was characterized by the division of the basic powers of government between the king and his semiautonomous vassals. The nobility and the towns then acted with varying degrees of unity and success through evolving representative assemblies, such as the English Parliament, the French Estates General, and the Spanish *Cortés,* to thwart the centralization of royal power into a united nation. But after the Hundred Years' War and the Great Schism in the church, the nobility and the clergy were in decline and less able to block growing national monarchies.

The increasingly important towns now began to ally with the king. Loyal, business-wise townspeople, not the nobility and the clergy, increasingly staffed royal offices and became the king's lawyers, bookkeepers, military tacticians, and foreign diplomats. This new alliance between king and town broke the bonds of feudal society and made possible the rise of sovereign states.

In a sovereign state, the powers of taxation, war making, and law enforcement no longer belong to semiautonomous vassals but are concentrated in the monarch and exercised by his or her chosen agents. Taxes, wars, and laws become national, rather than merely regional, matters. Only as monarchs became able to act independently of the nobility and representative assemblies could they overcome the decentralization that impeded nation building. Ferdinand and Isabella of Spain rarely called the *Cortés* into session. The French Estates General met irregularly, mostly in time of crisis, but was never essential to royal governance. Henry VII (r. 1485–1509) of England managed to raise revenues without going begging to Parliament, which had voted him customs revenues for life in 1485. Brilliant theorists, from Marsilius of Padua in the fourteenth century to Machiavelli in the fifteenth to Jean Bodin (1530–1596) in the sixteenth, emphatically defended the sovereign rights of monarchy.

The many were, of course, never totally subjugated to the one. But in the last half of the fifteenth century, rulers demonstrated that the law was their creature. They appointed civil servants whose vision was no longer merely local or regional. In Castile they were the *corregidores,* in England the justices of the peace, and in France bailiffs operating through well-drilled lieutenants. These royal ministers and agents could become closely attached to the localities they administered in the ruler's name, and regions were able to secure congenial royal appointments. Throughout England, for example, local magnates served as representatives of the Tudor dynasty that seized the throne in 1485. Nonetheless, these new executives remained royal executives, bureaucrats whose outlook was now "national" and whose loyalty was to the "state."

Monarchies also began to create standing national armies in the fifteenth century. The noble cavalry receded as the infantry and the artillery became the backbone of royal armies. Mercenary soldiers were recruited from Switzerland and Germany to form the major part of the "king's army." Professional soldiers who fought for pay and booty proved far more efficient than feudal vassals who fought simply for honor's sake. Monarchs who failed to meet their payrolls, however, now faced a new danger of mutiny and banditry by foreign troops.

The growing cost of warfare in the fifteenth and sixteenth centuries increased the monarch's need for new national sources of income. The great obstacle was the stubborn belief of the highest social classes that they were immune from government taxation. The nobility guarded their properties and traditional rights and despised taxation as an insult and a humiliation. Royal revenues accordingly had to grow at the expense of those least able to resist and least able to pay.

The monarchs had several options when it came to raising money. As feudal lords, they could collect rents from their royal domains. They could also levy national taxes on basic food and clothing, such as the salt tax (***gabelle***) in France and the 10 percent sales tax (*alcabala*) on commercial transactions in Spain. The rulers could also levy direct taxes on the peasantry, which they did through agreeable representative assemblies of the privileged classes in which the peasantry did not sit. The *taille,* which the French kings independently determined from year to year after the Estates General was suspended in 1484, was such a tax. Innovative fund-raising devices in the fifteenth century included the sale of public offices and the issuance of high-interest government bonds. Rulers still did not levy taxes on the powerful nobility, but instead, they borrowed from rich nobles and the great bankers of Italy and Germany. In money matters, the privileged classes remained as much the kings' creditors and competitors as their subjects.

France

Charles VII (r. 1422–1461) was a king made great by those who served him. His ministers created a permanent professional army, which—thanks initially to the inspiration of Joan of Arc—drove the English out of France. In addition, the enterprise of an independent merchant banker named Jacques Coeur helped develop a strong economy, diplomatic corps, and national administration during Charles's reign. These sturdy tools in turn enabled Charles's son and successor, the ruthless Louis XI (r. 1461–1483), to make France a great power.

French nation building had two political cornerstones in the fifteenth century. The first was the collapse of the English Empire in France following the Hundred Years' War. The second was the defeat of Charles the Bold (r. 1467–1477) and his duchy of Burgundy. Perhaps Europe's strongest political power in the mid-fifteenth century, Burgundy aspired to dwarf both France and the Holy Roman Empire as the leader of a dominant middle kingdom, which it might have done had not the continental powers joined to prevent it. When Charles the Bold died in defeat in a battle at Nancy in 1477, the dream of a Burgundian Empire died with him. Louis XI and Habsburg emperor Maximilian I divided the conquered Burgundian lands between them, with the treaty-wise Habsburgs getting the better part. The dissolution of Burgundy ended its constant intrigue against the French king and left Louis XI free to secure the monarchy. Between the newly acquired Burgundian lands and his own inheritance the king was able to end his reign with a kingdom almost twice the size of that he had inherited. Louis successfully harnessed the nobility, expanded the trade and industry that Jacques Cœur so carefully had nurtured, created a national postal system, and even established a lucrative silk industry.

A strong nation is a two-edged sword. Because Louis's successors inherited a secure and efficient government, they felt free to pursue what proved ultimately to be a bad foreign policy. Conquests in Italy in the 1490s and a long series of losing wars with the Habsburgs in the first half of the sixteenth century left France, by the mid-sixteenth century, once again a defeated nation almost as divided as it had been during the Hundred Years' War.

Spain

Both Castile and Aragon had been poorly ruled and divided kingdoms in the mid-fifteenth century, but the union of Isabella of Castile (r. 1474–1504) and Ferdinand of Aragon (r. 1479–1516) changed that situation. The two future sovereigns married in 1469, despite strong protests from neighboring Portugal and France, both of which foresaw the formidable European power the marriage would create. Castile was by far the richer and more populous of the two, having an estimated 5 million inhabitants to Aragon's population of under 1 million. Castile was also distinguished by its lucrative sheep-farming industry, run by a government-backed organization called the *Mesta,* another example of a developing centralized economic planning. Although the marriage of Ferdinand and Isabella dynastically united the two kingdoms, they remained constitutionally separated. Each retained its respective government agencies—separate laws, armies, coinage, and taxation—and cultural traditions.

Ferdinand and Isabella could do together what neither was able to accomplish alone: subdue their realms, secure their borders, venture abroad militarily, and Christianize the whole of Spain. Between 1482 and 1492 they conquered the Moors in Granada. Naples became a Spanish possession in 1504. By 1512, Ferdinand had secured his northern borders by conquering the kingdom of Navarre. Internally, the Spanish king and queen won the allegiance of the *Hermandad,* a powerful league of cities and towns that served them against stubborn noble landowners. The crown also extended its authority over the wealthy chivalric orders, further limiting the power of the nobility.

Spain had long been remarkable among European lands as a place where three religions—Islam, Judaism, and Christianity—coexisted with a certain degree of toleration. That toleration was to end dramatically under Ferdinand and Isabella, who made Spain the prime exemplar of state-controlled religion.

Ferdinand and Isabella exercised almost total control over the Spanish church as they placed religion in the service of national unity. They appointed the higher clergy and the officers of the Inquisition. The latter, run by Tomás de Torquemada (d. 1498), Isabella's confessor, was a key national agency established in 1479 to monitor the activity of converted Jews (*conversos*) and Muslims (*Moriscos*) in Spain. In 1492, the Jews were exiled and their properties confiscated. In 1502, nonconverting Moors in Granada were driven into exile by Cardinal Francisco Jiménez de Cisneros (1437–1517), under whom Spanish spiritual life was successfully conformed. This was a major reason why Spain remained a loyal Catholic country throughout the sixteenth century and provided a secure base of operation for the European Counter-Reformation.

Despite a certain internal narrowness, Ferdinand and Isabella were rulers with wide horizons. They contracted anti-French marriage alliances that came to determine a large part of European history in the sixteenth century. In 1496, their eldest daughter, Joanna, later known as "the Mad," married Archduke Philip, the son of Emperor Maximilian I. The fruit of this union, Charles I, was the first to rule over a united Spain; because of his inheritance and election as emperor in 1519, his empire almost equaled in size that of Charlemagne. A second daughter, Catherine of Aragon, wed Arthur, the son of the English king Henry VII. After Arthur's premature death, she was betrothed to his brother, the future King Henry VIII (r. 1509–1547), whom she married eight years later, in 1509. The failure of this marriage became the key factor in the emergence of the Anglican church and the English Reformation.

The new power of Spain was also revealed in Ferdinand and Isabella's promotion of overseas exploration. They sponsored the Genoese adventurer Christopher Columbus (1451–1506), who arrived at the islands of the Caribbean while sailing west in search of a shorter route to the spice markets of the Far East. This patronage led to the creation of the Spanish Empire in Mexico and Peru, whose gold and silver mines helped make Spain Europe's dominant power in the sixteenth century.

England

The latter half of the fifteenth century was a period of especially difficult political trial for the English. Following the Hundred Years' War, civil warfare broke out between two rival branches of the royal family: the House of York and the House of Lancaster. The roots of the war lay in succession irregularities after the forced deposition of the erratic king Richard II (r. 1377–1399). This conflict, known to us today as the Wars of the Roses (because York's symbol, according to legend, was a white rose and Lancaster's a red rose), kept England in turmoil from 1455 to 1485.

The duke of York and his supporters in the prosperous southern towns challenged the Lancastrian monarchy of Henry VI (r. 1422–1461). In 1461, Edward IV (r. 1461–1483), son of the duke of York, seized power and instituted a strong-arm rule that lasted more than twenty years; it was only briefly interrupted, in 1470–1471, by Henry VI's short-lived restoration. Assisted by able ministers, Edward effectively increased the power and finances of the monarchy.

His brother, Richard III (r. 1483–1485), usurped the throne from Edward's son, and after Richard's death, the new Tudor dynasty portrayed him as an unprincipled villain who had also murdered Edward's sons in the Tower of London to secure his hold on the throne. Shakespeare's *Richard III* is the best-known version of this characterization—unjust according to some. Be that as it may, Richard's reign saw the growth of support for the exiled Lancastrian Henry Tudor, who returned to England to defeat Richard on Bosworth Field in August 1485.

Henry Tudor ruled as Henry VII (r. 1485–1509), the first of the new Tudor dynasty that would dominate England throughout the sixteenth century. To bring the rival royal families together and to make the hereditary claim of his offspring to the throne uncontestable, Henry married Edward IV's daughter, Elizabeth of York.

He succeeded in disciplining the English nobility through a special instrument of the royal will known as the Court of Star Chamber. Created with the sanction of Parliament in 1487, the court was intended to end the perversion of English justice by "over-mighty subjects," that is, powerful nobles who used intimidation and bribery to win favorable verdicts in court cases. In the Court of Star Chamber, the king's councilors sat as judges, and such tactics did not sway them. The result was a more equitable court system.

It was also a court more amenable to the royal will. Henry shrewdly used English law to further the ends of the monarchy. He managed to confiscate lands and fortunes of nobles with such success that he was able to govern without dependence on Parliament for royal funds, always a cornerstone of a strong monarchy. In these ways, Henry began to shape a monarchy that would develop into one of early modern Europe's most exemplary governments during the reign of his granddaughter, Elizabeth I (r. 1558–1603).

This portrait of Katharina, by Albrecht Dürer, provides evidence of African slavery in Europe during the sixteenth century. Katharina was in the service of one João Bradao, a Portuguese economic minister living in Antwerp, then the financial center of Europe. Dürer became friends with Bradao during his stay in the Low Countries in the winter of 1520–1521. Albrecht Dürer (1471–1528), *Portrait of the Moorish Woman Katharina*. Drawing. Uffizi Florence, Italy. Photograph © Foto Marburg/Art Resource, NY

The Holy Roman Empire

Germany and Italy were the striking exceptions to the steady development of politically centralized lands in the last half of the fifteenth century. Unlike England, France, and Spain, the Holy Roman Empire saw the many thoroughly repulse the one. In Germany, territorial rulers and cities resisted every effort at national consolidation and unity. As in Carolingian times, rulers continued to partition their kingdoms, however small, among their sons. By the late fifteenth century, Germany was hopelessly divided into some three hundred autonomous political entities.

The princes and the cities did work together to create the machinery of law and order, if not of union, within the divided empire. Emperor Charles IV (r. 1346–1378) and the major German territorial rulers reached an agreement in 1356 known as the **Golden Bull**. It established a seven-member electoral college consisting of the archbishops of Mainz, Trier, and Cologne; the duke of Saxony; the margrave of Brandenburg; the count Palatine; and the king of Bohemia. This group also functioned as an administrative body. They elected the emperor and, in cooperation with him, provided what transregional unity and administration existed.

The figure of the emperor gave the empire a single ruler in law if not in fact. The conditions of his rule and the extent of his powers over his subjects, especially the seven electors, were renegotiated with every imperial election. Therefore, the rights of the many (the princes) were always balanced against the power of the one (the emperor).

In the fifteenth century, an effort was made to control incessant feuding by the creation of an imperial diet known as the *Reichstag*. This was a national assembly of the seven electors, the nonelectoral princes, and representatives from the sixty-five imperial free cities. The cities were the weakest of the three bodies represented in the diet. During such an assembly in Worms in 1495, the members won from Emperor Maximilian I an imperial ban on private warfare, the creation of a Supreme Court of Justice to enforce internal peace, and an imperial Council of Regency to coordinate imperial and internal German policy. The emperor only grudgingly conceded the latter because it gave the princes a share in executive power.

These reforms were still a poor substitute for true national unity. In the sixteenth and seventeenth centuries, the territorial princes became virtually sovereign rulers in their various domains. Such disunity aided religious dissent and conflict. It was in the cities and territories of still feudal, fractionalized, backward Germany that the Protestant Reformation broke out in the sixteenth century.

▼ The Northern Renaissance

The scholarly works of northern humanists created a climate favorable to religious and educational reforms on the eve of the Reformation. Northern humanism was initially stimulated by the importation of Italian learning through such varied intermediaries as students who had studied in Italy, merchants who traded there, and the Brothers of the Common Life. This last was an influential lay religious movement that began in the Netherlands and permitted men and women to live a shared religious life without making formal vows of poverty, chastity, and obedience.

The northern humanists, however, developed their own distinctive culture. They tended to come from more diverse social backgrounds and to be more devoted to religious reforms than their Italian counterparts. They were also more willing to write for lay audiences as well as for a narrow intelligentsia. Thanks to the invention of printing with movable type, it became possible for humanists to convey their educational ideals to laypeople and clerics alike. Printing gave new power and influence to elites in both church and state, who now could popularize their viewpoints freely and widely.

The printing press made possible the diffusion of Renaissance learning, but no book stimulated thought more at this time than did the Bible. With Gutenberg's publication of a printed Bible in 1454, scholars gained access to a dependable, standardized text, so Scripture could be discussed and debated as never before.

The Printing Press

A variety of forces converged in the fourteenth and fifteenth centuries to give rise to the invention of the printing press. Since the days of Charlemagne, kings and princes had encouraged schools and literacy to help provide educated bureaucrats to staff the offices of their kingdoms. Without people who could read, think critically, and write reliable reports, no kingdom, large or small, could be properly governed. By the fifteenth century, a new literate lay public had been created, thanks to the enormous expansion of schools and universities during the late Middle Ages.

The invention of a cheap way to manufacture paper also helped make books economical and broaden their content. Manuscript books had been inscribed on vellum, a cumbersome and expensive medium (170 calfskins or 300 sheepskins were required to make a single vellum Bible.) Single-sheet woodcuts had long been printed. The process involved carving words and pictures on a block of wood, inking it, and then stamping out as many copies as possible before the wood deteriorated. The end product was much like a cheap modern poster.

In response to the demand for books that the expansion of lay education and literacy created, Johann Gutenberg (d. 1468) invented printing with movable type in the mid-fifteenth century in the German city of Mainz, the center of printing for the whole of Western Europe. Thereafter, books were rapidly and handsomely produced on topics both profound and practical and were intended for ordinary lay readers, scholars, and clerics alike. Especially popular in the early decades of print were books of piety and religion, calendars and almanacs, and how-to books (for example, on childrearing, making brandies and liquors, curing animals, and farming).

The new technology proved enormously profitable to printers, whose numbers exploded. By 1500, within just fifty years of Gutenberg's press, printing presses operated in at least sixty German cities and in more than two hundred cities throughout Europe. The printing press was a boon to the careers of humanists, who now gained international audiences.

Literacy deeply affected people everywhere, nurturing self-esteem and a critical frame of mind. By standardizing texts, the print revolution made anyone who could read an instant authority. Rulers in church and state now had to deal with a less credulous and less docile laity. Print was also a powerful tool for political and religious propaganda. Kings could now indoctrinate people as never before, and clergymen found themselves able to mass-produce both indulgences and pamphlets. (See "The West & The World: The Invention of Printing in China and Europe," on page 252.)

Erasmus

The far-reaching influence of Desiderius Erasmus (1466?–1536), the most famous northern humanist, illustrates the impact of the printing press. Through his printed works, Erasmus gained fame both as an educational and as a religious reformer. A lifelong Catholic, Erasmus, through his life and work, made clear that many loyal Catholics wanted major reforms in the church long before the Reformation made them a reality.

When patronage was scarce (authors received no royalties and had to rely on private patrons for their livelihood), Erasmus earned his living by tutoring well-to-do youths. He prepared short Latin dialogues for his students, intended to teach them how to speak and live well, inculcating good manners and language by internalizing what they read.

These dialogues were entitled *Colloquies.* In consecutive editions, they grew in number and length, including anticlerical dialogues and satires on religious dogmatism and superstition. Erasmus also collected ancient and contemporary proverbs, which appeared under the title *Adages.* Beginning with 800 examples, the final edition included more than 5,000. Among the locutions the *Adages* popularized are such common expressions as "Leave no stone unturned" and "Where there is smoke, there is fire."

Erasmus aspired to unite classical ideals of humanity and civic virtue with the Christian ideals of love and piety. He believed disciplined study of the classics and the Bible, if begun early enough, was the best way to reform individuals and society. He summarized his own beliefs with the phrase *philosophia Christi,* a simple, ethical piety in imitation of Christ. He set this ideal in stark contrast to what he believed to be the dogmatic, ceremonial, and bullying religious practices of the later Middle Ages. What most offended him about the Scholastics, both the old authorities of the Middle Ages and the new Protestant ones, was their letting dogma and argument overshadow Christian piety and practice.

Erasmus was a true idealist, who expected more from people than the age's theologians believed them capable of doing. To promote what he deemed to be the essence of Christianity, he made ancient Christian sources available in their original versions, believing that if people would only imbibe the pure sources of the faith, they would recover the moral and religious health the New Testament promises. To this end, Erasmus edited the works of the Church Fathers and produced a Greek edition of the New Testament (1516), later adding a new Latin translation of the latter (1519). Martin Luther used both of those works when he translated the New Testament into German in 1522.

These various enterprises did not please the church authorities. They remained unhappy with Erasmus's "improvements" on the Vulgate, Christendom's Bible for over a thousand years, and his popular anticlerical writings. At one point in the mid-sixteenth century, all of Erasmus's works were on the church's *Index of Forbidden Books.* Luther also condemned Erasmus for his views on the freedom of human will. Still, Erasmus's works put sturdy tools of reform in the hands of both Protestant and Catholic reformers. Already in the 1520s, there was a popular saying: "Erasmus laid the egg that Luther hatched."

Humanism and Reform

In Germany, England, France, and Spain, humanism stirred both educational and religious reform.

Germany Rudolf Agricola (1443–1485), the "father of German humanism," spent ten years in Italy and introduced Italian learning to Germany when he returned. Conrad Celtis (d. 1508), the first German poet laureate, and Ulrich von Hutten (1488–1523), a fiery knight, gave German humanism a nationalist coloring hostile to non-German cultures, particularly Roman culture. Von Hutten especially illustrates the union of humanism, German nationalism, and Luther's religious reform. A poet who admired Erasmus, he attacked indulgences and published an edition of Valla's exposé of the *Donation of Constantine.* He died in 1523, the victim of a hopeless knights' revolt against the princes.

The controversy that brought von Hutten onto the historical stage and unified reform-minded German humanists was the Reuchlin affair. Johann Reuchlin (1455–1522) was Europe's foremost Christian authority on Hebrew and Jewish learning. He wrote the first reliable Hebrew grammar by a Christian scholar and was attracted to Jewish mysticism. Around 1506, supported by the Dominican order in Cologne, a Christian who had converted from Judaism began a movement to suppress Jewish writings. When this man, whose name was Pfefferkorn, attacked Reuchlin, many German humanists, in the name of academic freedom and good scholarship—not for any pro-Jewish sentiment—rushed to Reuchlin's defense. The controversy lasted for years and produced one of the great satires of the period, the *Letters of Obscure Men* (1515), a merciless satire of monks and Scholastics to which von Hutten contributed. When Martin Luther came under attack in 1517 for his famous ninety-five theses against indulgences, many German humanists saw a repetition of the Scholastic attack on Reuchlin and rushed to his side.

England Italian learning came to England by way of English scholars and merchants and visiting Italian prelates. Lectures by William Grocyn (d. 1519) and Thomas Linacre (d. 1524) at Oxford and those of Erasmus at Cambridge marked the scholarly maturation of English humanism. John Colet (1467–1519), dean of Saint Paul's Cathedral, patronized humanist studies for the young and promoted religious reform.

Thomas More (1478–1535), a close friend of Erasmus, is the best-known English humanist. His *Utopia* (1516), a conservative criticism of contemporary society, rivals the plays of Shakespeare as the most read sixteenth-century English work. *Utopia* depicted an imaginary society based on reason and tolerance that overcame social and political injustice by holding all property and goods in common and requiring everyone to earn their bread by their own work.

More became one of Henry VIII's most trusted diplomats. His repudiation of the Act of Supremacy (1534), which made the king of England head of the English church in place of the pope (see Chapter 11), and his refusal to recognize the king's marriage to Anne Boleyn, however, led to his execution in July 1535. Although More remained Catholic, humanism in England, as also in Germany, helped prepare the way for the English Reformation.

France The French invasions of Italy made it possible for Italian learning to penetrate France, stirring both educational and religious reform. Guillaume Budé (1468–1540), an accomplished Greek scholar, and Jacques Lefèvre d'Etaples (1454–1536), a biblical authority, were the leaders of French humanism. Lefèvre's scholarly works exemplified the new critical scholarship and influenced Martin Luther. Guillaume Briçonnet (1470–1533), the bishop of Meaux, and Marguerite d'Angoulême (1492–1549), sister of King Francis I, the future queen of Navarre, and a successful spiritual writer in her own right, cultivated a generation of young reform-minded humanists. The future Protestant reformer John Calvin was a product of this native reform circle.

Spain Whereas in England, France, and Germany humanism prepared the way for Protestant reforms, in Spain it entered the service of the Catholic Church. Here the key figure was Francisco Jiménez de Cisneros (1437–1517), a confessor to Queen Isabella and, after 1508, the "Grand Inquisitor"—a position that allowed him to enforce the strictest religious orthodoxy. Jiménez founded the University of Alcalá near Madrid in 1509, printed a Greek edition of the New Testament, and translated many religious tracts designed to reform clerical life and better direct lay piety. His great achievement, taking fifteen years to complete, was the *Complutensian Polyglot Bible,* a six-volume work that placed the Hebrew, Greek, and Latin versions of the Bible in parallel columns. Such scholarly projects and internal church reforms joined with the repressive measures of Ferdinand and Isabella to keep Spain strictly Catholic throughout the Age of Reformation.

▼ Voyages of Discovery and the New Empires in the West and East

The discovery of the Americas dramatically expanded the horizons of Europeans, both geographically and intellectually. Knowledge of the New World's inhabitants and the exploitation of its mineral and human wealth set new cultural and economic forces in motion throughout Western Europe.

Beginning with the voyages of the Portuguese and Spanish in the fifteenth century, commercial supremacy progressively shifted from the Mediterranean and Baltic seas to the Atlantic seaboard, setting the stage for global expansion. (See Map 10–2, page 304.)

The Portuguese Chart the Course

Seventy-seven years before Columbus, who sailed under the flag of Spain, set foot in the Americas, Prince Henry "the Navigator" (1394–1460), brother of the king of Portugal, captured the North African Muslim city of Ceuta. His motives were mercenary and religious, both a quest for gold and spices and the pious work of saving the souls of Muslims and pagans who had no knowledge of Christ. Thus began the Portuguese exploration of the African coast, first in search of gold and slaves, and then by century's end, of a sea route around Africa to Asia's spice markets. Pepper and cloves topped the list of spices, as they both preserved and enhanced the dull diet of most Europeans. Initially the catch of raiders, African slaves were soon taken by Portuguese traders in direct commerce with tribal chiefs, who readily swapped captives for horses, grain, and finished goods (cloth and brassware). Over the second half of the fifteenth century, Portuguese ships delivered 150,000 slaves to Europe.

Before there was a sea route to the East, Europeans could only get spices through the Venetians, who bought or bartered them from Muslim merchants in Egypt and the Ottoman Empire. The Portuguese resolved to beat this powerful Venetian-Muslim monopoly by sailing directly to the source. Overland routes to India and China had long existed, but their transit had become too difficult and unprofitable by the fifteenth century. The route by sea posed a different obstacle and risk: fear of the unknown, making the first voyages of exploration slow and tentative. Venturing down the African coast, the

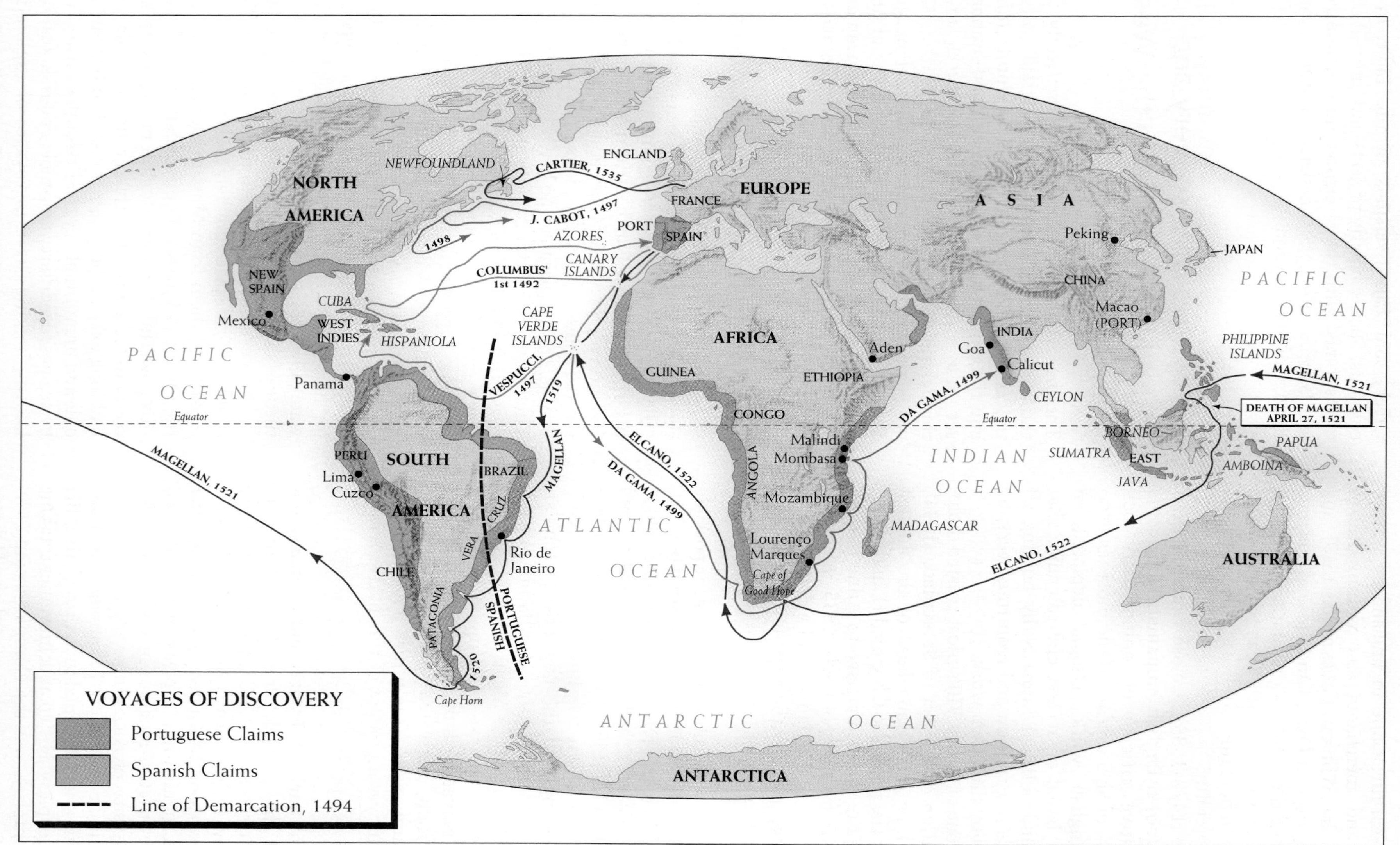

Map 10–2 **European Voyages of Discovery and the Colonial Claims of Spain and Portugal in the Fifteenth and Sixteenth Centuries** The map dramatizes Europe's global expansion in the fifteenth and sixteenth centuries.

Portuguese ships were turned out into the deep ocean by every protruding cape, and the farther out they sailed to round them, the greater the sailors' fear that the winds would not return them to land. Each cape rounded became a victory and a lesson, giving the crews the skills they needed to cross the oceans to the Americas and East Asia.

In addition to spice markets, the voyagers also gained new allies against Western Europe's archenemies, the Muslims. In 1455, a self-interested pope granted the Portuguese explorers all the spoils of war—land, goods, and slaves—from the coast of Guinea in West Africa to the Indies in East Asia. The church expected exploration to lead to mass conversions, a Christian coup as well as a mercantile advantage. The explorers also kept an eye out for a legendary Eastern Christian ruler known as Prester John.

Bartholomew Dias (ca. 1450–1500) pioneered the eastern Portuguese Empire after safely rounding the Cape of Good Hope at the tip of Africa in 1487. A decade later, in 1498, Vasco da Gama (1469–1525) stood on the shores of India. When he returned to Portugal, he carried a cargo of spices worth sixty times the cost of the voyage. Later, the Portuguese established colonies in Goa and Calcutta on the coast of India, whence they challenged the Arabs and the Venetians for control of the spice trade.

The Portuguese had concentrated their explorations on the Indian Ocean. The Spanish turned west, believing they could find a shorter route to the East Indies by sailing across the Atlantic. Instead, Christopher Columbus (1451–1506) discovered the Americas.

The Spanish Voyages of Columbus

Thirty-three days after departing the Canary Islands, on October 12, 1492, Columbus landed in San Salvador (Watlings Island) in the eastern Bahamas. Thinking he was in the East Indies, he mistook his first landfall as an outer island of Japan. The error was understandable given the information he relied on, namely, Marco Polo's thirteenth-century account of his years in China and Martin Behaim's spherical map of the presumed world. That map showed only ocean and Cipangu (Japan) between the west coast of Europe and the east coast of Asia. (See Martin Behaim's map, page 306.) Not until his third voyage to the Caribbean in 1498 did Columbus realize that Cuba was not Japan and South America was not China.

Naked, friendly natives met Columbus and his crew on the beaches of the New World. They were Taino Indians, who spoke a variant of a language known as Arawak. Believing the island on which he landed to be the East Indies, Columbus called these people Indians, a name that stuck with Europeans even after they realized he had actually discovered a new continent. The natives' generosity amazed Columbus, as they freely gave his men all the corn, yams, and sexual favors they desired. "They never say no," Columbus marveled. He also observed how easily the Spanish could enslave them.

On the heels of Columbus, Amerigo Vespucci (1451–1512), after whom America is named, and Ferdinand Magellan (1480–1521) explored the coastline of South America. Their travels proved that the new lands Columbus had discovered were an entirely unknown continent that opened on the still greater Pacific Ocean. Magellan, who was continuing the search for a westward route to the Indies, made it all the way around South America and across the Pacific to the Philippines, where he was killed in a skirmish with the inhabitants. The remnants of his squadron eventually sailed on to Spain, making them the first sailors to circumnavigate the globe.

Intended and Unintended Consequences Columbus's first voyage marked the beginning of more than three centuries of a vast Spanish empire in the Americas. What began as voyages of discovery became expeditions of conquest, not unlike the warfare Christian Aragon and Castile waged against Islamic Moors. Those wars had just ended in 1492, and their conclusion imbued the early Spanish explorers with a zeal for conquering and converting non-Christian peoples.

Much to the benefit of Spain, the voyages of discovery created Europe's largest and longest surviving trading bloc and spurred other European countries to undertake their own colonial ventures. The wealth extracted from its American possessions financed Spain's commanding role in the religious and political wars of the sixteenth and seventeenth centuries, while fueling a Europe-wide economic expansion.

European expansion also had a profound biological impact. Europeans introduced numerous new species of fruits, vegetables, and animals into the Americas and brought American species back to Europe. European expansion also spread European diseases. Vast numbers of Native Americans died from measles and smallpox epidemics, while Europeans died from a virulent form of syphilis that may have originated in the Americas.

For the Native Americans, the voyages of discovery were the beginning of a long history of conquest, disease, and slave labor they could neither evade nor survive. In both South and North America, Spanish rule left a lasting imprint of Roman Catholicism, economic dependency, and hierarchical social structure, all still visible today. (See Chapter 18.)

The Spanish Empire in the New World

When the first Spanish explorers arrived, the Aztec Empire dominated Mesoamerica, which stretches from Central Mexico to Guatemala, and the Inca Empire dominated Andean South America. Both were rich, and their conquest promised the Spanish the possibility of acquiring large quantities of gold.

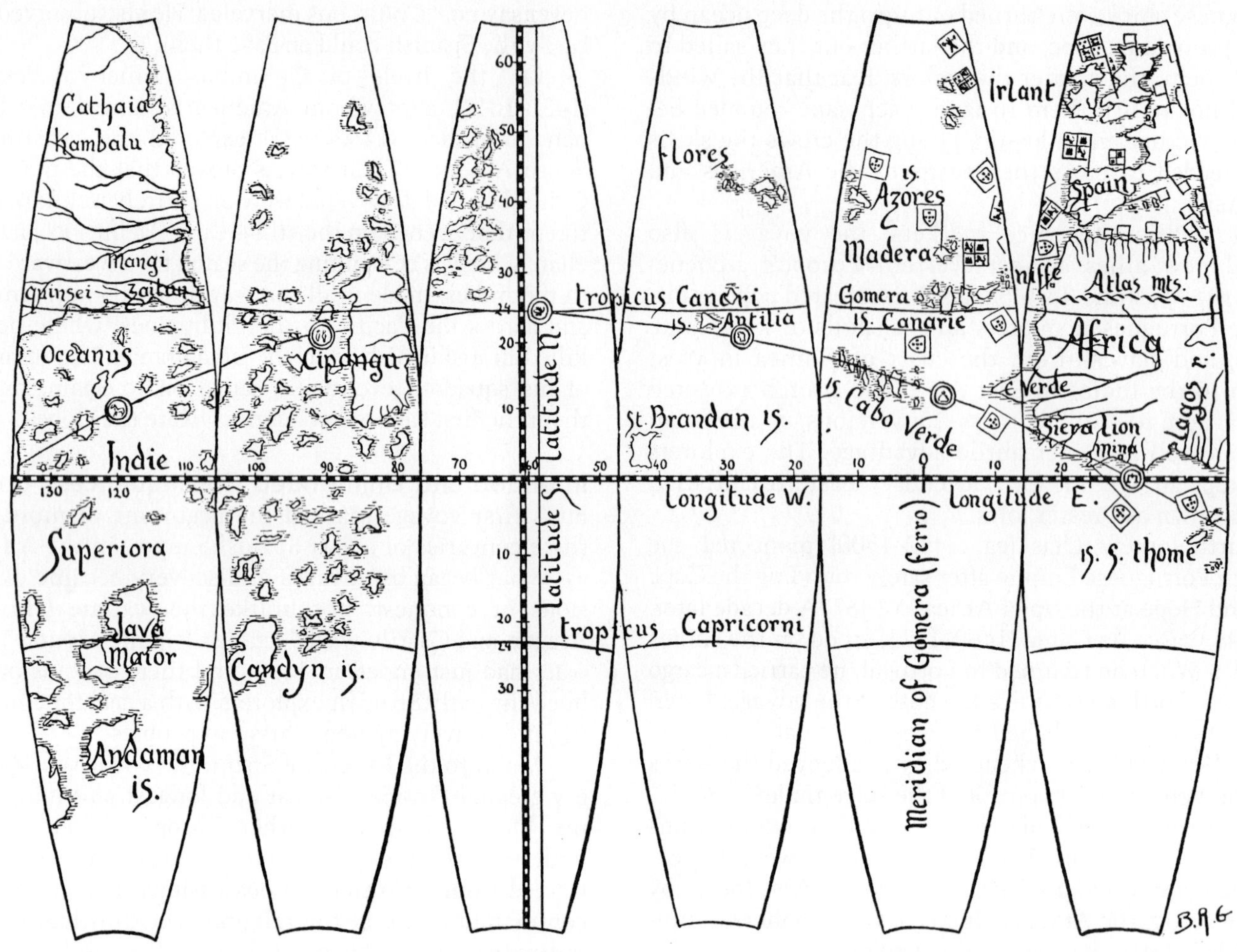

What Columbus knew of the world in 1492 was contained in this map by the Nuremberg geographer Martin Behaim, creator of the first spherical globe of the earth. The ocean section of Behaim's globe is reproduced here. Departing the Canary Islands (in the second section from the right), Columbus expected his first major landfall to be Japan (Cipangu, in the second section from the left). When he landed at San Salvador, he thought he was on the outer island of Japan. Thus, when he arrived in Cuba, he thought he was in Japan. From *Admiral of the Ocean Sea* by Samuel Eliot Morison. Copyright © 1942 by Samuel Eliot Morison; Copyright © renewed 1970 by Samuel Eliot Morison. By permission of Little, Brown and Company, (Inc.)

The Aztecs in Mexico The forebears of the Aztecs had arrived in the Valley of Mexico early in the twelfth century, where they lived as a subservient people. In 1428, however, they began a period of imperial expansion. By the time of Spanish conquest, the Aztecs ruled almost all of central Mexico from their capital Tenochtitlán (modern-day Mexico City). The Aztecs demanded heavy tribute in goods and labor from their subjects and, believing the gods must literally be fed with human blood to guarantee sunshine and fertility, they also took thousands of captives each year for human sacrifice. These policies bred resentment and fear among the subject peoples.

In 1519, Hernán Cortés (1485–1547) landed in Mexico with about five hundred men and a few horses. He opened communication with Moctezuma II (1466–1520), the Aztec emperor. Moctezuma may initially have believed Cortés to be the god Quetzalcoatl, who, according to legend, had been driven away centuries earlier but had promised to return. Whatever the reason, Moctezuma hesitated to confront Cortés, attempting at first to appease him with gold, which only whetted Spanish appetites. Cortés forged alliances with the Aztecs' subject peoples, most importantly, with Tlaxcala, an independent state and traditional enemy of the Aztecs. His forces then marched on Tenochtitlán, where Moctezuma welcomed him. Cortés soon seized Moctezuma, who died in unexplained circumstances. The Aztecs' wary acceptance of the Spaniards turned to open hostility. The Spaniards were driven from Tenochtitlán and were nearly wiped out, but they returned and laid siege to the city. The Aztecs, under their last ruler, Cuauhtemoc (ca. 1495–1525), resisted fiercely but were finally defeated in 1521. Cortés razed Tenochtitlán, building his own capital over its ruins, and proclaimed the Aztec Empire to be New Spain.

Armored Spanish soldiers, under the command of Pedro de Alvarado (d. 1541) and bearing crossbows, engage unprotected and crudely armed Aztecs, who are nonetheless portrayed as larger than life by Spanish artist Diego Duran (sixteenth century). Codex Duran: Pedro de Alvarado (c. 1485–1541), companion-at-arms of Hernando Cortés (1845–1547) besieged by Aztec warriors (vellum) by Diego Duran (16th Century), Codex Duran, Historia De Las Indias (16th century). Biblioteca Nacional, Madrid, Spain. The Bridgeman Art Library International Ltd.

The Incas in Peru The second great Native American civilization the Spanish conquered was that of the Incas in the highlands of Peru. Like the Aztecs, the Incas also began to expand rapidly in the fifteenth century and, by the time of the Spanish conquest, controlled an enormous empire. Unlike the Aztecs, who extracted tribute from their subject peoples, the Incas compelled their subjects to work for the state on a regular basis.

In 1532, largely inspired by Cortés's example in Mexico, Francisco Pizarro (c. 1478–1541) landed on the western coast of South America with about two hundred men to take on the Inca Empire. Pizarro lured Atahualpa (ca. 1500–1533), the Inca ruler, into a conference and then seized him, killing hundreds of Atahualpa's followers in the process. The imprisoned Atahualpa tried to ransom himself with a hoard of gold, but instead of releasing him, Pizarro executed him in 1533. The Spaniards then captured Cuzco, the Inca capital, but Inca resistance did not end until the 1570s.

The conquests of Mexico and Peru are among the most dramatic and brutal events in modern history. Small military forces armed with advanced weapons subdued, in a remarkably brief time, two powerful peoples. The spread of European diseases, especially smallpox, among the Native Americans also aided the conquest. But beyond the drama and bloodshed, these conquests, as well as those of other Native American peoples, marked a fundamental turning point. Whole civilizations with long histories and enormous social, architectural, and technological achievements were destroyed. Native American cultures endured, accommodating themselves to European dominance, but there was never any doubt about which culture had the upper hand. In that sense, the Spanish conquests of the early sixteenth century marked the beginning of the transformation of South America into Latin America.

The Church in Spanish America

Roman Catholic priests had accompanied the earliest explorers and the conquerors of the Native Americans. Steeped with the social and religious ideals of Christian humanism, these first clergy members believed they could foster Erasmus's concept of the "philosophy of Christ" in the New World. They were filled with zeal not only to convert the inhabitants to Christianity, but also to bring to them European learning and civilization.

Tension, however, existed between the early Spanish conquerors and the mendicant friars who sought to minister to the Native Americans. Without conquest, the church could not convert the Native Americans, but the priests often deplored the harsh conditions imposed on the native peoples. By far the most effective and outspoken clerical critic of the Spanish conquerors was Bartolomé de Las Casas (1474–1566), a Dominican. He contended that conquest was not necessary for conversion. One result of his campaign was new royal regulations to protect the Indians after 1550.

Another result of Las Casas's criticism was the emergence of the "Black Legend," according to which all Spanish treatment of the Native Americans was unprincipled and inhumane. (See "A Defense of American Natives," page 308.) Those who created this view of Spanish behavior drew heavily on Las Casas's writings. Although substantially true, the "Black Legend" exaggerated the case against Spain. Certainly the rulers of the native empires—as the Aztec demands for sacrificial victims attest—had often themselves been exceedingly cruel to their subjects.

By the end of the sixteenth century, the church in Spanish America had become largely an institution upholding the colonial status quo. Although individual priests defended the communal rights of Indian peoples, the colonial church prospered as the Spanish elite prospered by exploiting the resources and peoples of the New World. The church became a great landowner through crown grants and bequests from Catholics who died in the New World. The monasteries took on an economic as well as a spiritual life of their own. Whatever its concern for the spiritual welfare of the Native Americans, the church remained one of the indications that Spanish

A Defense of American Natives

Bartolomé de Las Casas (1474–1566), a Dominican missionary to the New World, describes the native people of the islands of the Caribbean and their systematic slaughter by the Spanish.

Is Las Casas romanticizing the American natives? Does he truly respect their native culture and beliefs?

This infinite multitude of people was so created by God that they were without fraud . . . or malice. . . . Toward the Spaniards whom they serve, patient, meek, and peaceful, [they] lay aside all contentious and tumultuous thoughts, and live without any hatred or desire of revenge. The people are most delicate and tender, enjoying such a feeble constitution of body as does not permit them to endure labour. . . . The[ir] nation [the West Indies] is very poor and indigent, possessing little, and by reason that they gape not after temporal goods, [being] neither proud nor ambitious. Their diet is such that the most holy hermit cannot feed more sparingly in the wildernesse. They go naked . . . and a poor shag mantle . . . is their greatest and their warmest covering. They lie upon mats; only those who have larger fortunes lie upon a kind of net which is tied at the four corners and so fasten'd to the roof, which the Indians in their natural language call *Hamecks* [hammocks]. They are of a very apprehensive and docile wit, and capable of all good learning, and very apt to receive our Religion, which when they have but once tasted [it], they are carried [off] with a very ardent and zealous desire to make further progress in it; so that I have heard divers Spaniards confess that they had nothing else to hinder them from enjoying heaven, but the ignorance of the true God.

To these quiet Lambs, endued with such blessed qualities, came the Spaniards like most cruel Tygres, Wolves, and Lions . . . for these forty years, minding nothing else but the slaughter of these unfortunate wretches . . . [whom] they have so cruelly and inhumanely butchered, [so] that of three millions of people which Hispaniola [modern Haiti and the Dominican Republic] itself did contain, there are left remaining alive scarce three hundred persons. And the island of Cuba . . . lies wholly desert, untilled and ruined. The islands of St. John and Jamaica lie waste and desolate. The Lycayan islands neighboring to the north upon Cuba and Hispaniola . . . are now totally unpeopled and destroyed; the inhabitants thereof amounting to above 500,000 souls, partly killed, and partly forced away to work in other places. . . . Other islands there were near the island of St. John, more than thirty in number, which were totally made desert. All which islands . . . lie now altogether solitary without any people or inhabitant.

Bartolomé de Las Casas, *The Tears of the Indians*, trans. by John Phillips (1656), from reprint of original edition (Stanford, CA: Academic Reprints, n.d.), pp. 2–4.

America was a conquered world. Those who spoke for the church did not challenge Spanish domination or any but the most extreme modes of Spanish economic exploitation. By the end of the colonial era in the late eighteenth century, the Roman Catholic Church had become one of the most conservative forces in Latin America.

The Economy of Exploitation

From the beginning, both the Native Americans and their lands were drawn into the Atlantic economy and the world of competitive European commercialism. For the Indians of Latin America and, somewhat later, the black peoples of Africa, that drive for gain meant forced labor.

The colonial economy of Latin America had three major components: mining, agriculture, and shipping. Each involved labor, servitude, and the intertwining of the New World economy with that of Spain.

Mining The early ***conquistadores***, or "conquerors," were primarily interested in gold, but by the mid-sixteenth century, silver mining provided the chief source of metallic wealth. The great mining centers were Potosí in Peru and somewhat smaller sites in northern Mexico. The Spanish crown received one fifth (the *quinto*) of all mining revenues. For this reason, the crown maintained a monopoly over the production and sale of mercury, required in the silver-smelting process. Exploring for silver continued throughout the colonial era. Its production by forced labor for the benefit of Spaniards and the Spanish crown epitomized the wholly extractive economy that stood at the foundation of colonial life.

Agriculture The major rural and agricultural institution of the Spanish colonies was the ***hacienda***, a large landed estate owned by persons originally born in Spain (*peninsulares*) or persons of Spanish descent born in America (*creoles*). Laborers on the *hacienda* were usually subject in some legal way to the owner and were rarely free to move from working for one landowner to another.

The *hacienda* economy produced two major products: foodstuffs for mining areas and urban centers and leather goods used in mining machinery. Both farming and ranching were subordinate to the mining economy.

In the West Indies, the basic agricultural unit was the plantation. In Cuba, Hispaniola, Puerto Rico, and other islands, the labor of black slaves from Africa produced sugar to supply an almost insatiable demand for the product in Europe.

A final major area of economic activity in the Spanish colonies was urban service occupations, including government offices, the legal profession, and shipping. Those who worked in these occupations were either *peninsulares* or *creoles,* with the former dominating more often than not.

Labor Servitude All of this extractive and exploitive economic activity required labor, and the Spanish in the New World decided early that the native population would supply it. A series of social devices was used to draw them into the new economic life the Spanish imposed.

The first of these was the ***encomienda***, a formal grant of the right to the labor of a specific number of Indians, usually a few hundred, but sometimes thousands, for a particular period of time. The *encomienda* was in decline by the mid-sixteenth century because the Spanish monarchs feared its holders might become too powerful. There were also humanitarian objections to this particular kind of exploitation of the Indians.

The passing of the *encomienda* led to a new arrangement of labor servitude: the *repartimiento.* This device required adult male Indians to devote a certain number of days of labor annually to Spanish economic enterprises. In the mines of Peru, the *repartimiento* was known as the *mita,* the Inca term for their labor tax. *Repartimiento* service was often harsh, and some Indians did not survive their stint. The limitation on labor time led some Spanish managers to abuse their workers on the assumption that fresh workers would soon replace them.

The eventual shortage of workers and the crown's pressure against extreme versions of forced labor led to the use of free labor. The freedom, however, was more in appearance than reality. Free Indian laborers were required to purchase goods from the landowner or mine owner, to whom they became forever indebted. This form of exploitation, known as *debt peonage,* continued in Latin America long after the nineteenth-century wars of liberation.

Black slavery was the final mode of forced or subservient labor in the New World. Both the Spanish and the Portuguese had earlier used African slaves in Europe. The sugar plantations of the West Indies and Brazil now became the major center of black slavery.

The conquest, the forced labor of the economy of exploitation, and the introduction of European diseases had devastating demographic consequences for the Native Americans. For centuries, Europeans had lived in a far more complex human and animal environment than Native Americans did. They had frequent contact with different ethnic and racial groups and with a variety of domestic animals. Such interaction helped them develop strong immune systems that enabled them to survive measles, smallpox, and typhoid. Native Americans, by contrast, grew up in a simpler and more sterile environment and were defenseless against these diseases. Within a generation, the native population of New Spain (Mexico) was reduced to an estimated 8 percent of its numbers, from 25 million to 2 million.

The Impact on Europe

Among contemporary European intellectuals, Columbus's discovery increased skepticism about the wisdom of the ancients. If traditional knowledge about the world had been so wrong geographically, how trustworthy was it on other matters? For many, Columbus's discovery demonstrated the folly of relying on any fixed body of presumed authoritative knowledge. Both in Europe and in the New World, there were those who condemned the explorers' treatment of American natives, as more was learned about their cruelty. (See "Montaigne on 'Cannibals' in Foreign Lands," page 310.) Three centuries later, however, on the third centenary of Columbus's discovery (1792), the great thinkers of the age lionized Columbus for having opened up new possibilities for civilization and morality. By establishing new commercial contacts among different peoples of the world, Columbus was said to have made cooperation, civility, and peace among them indispensable. Enlightenment thinkers drew parallels between the discovery of America and the invention of the printing press—both portrayed as world-historical events opening new eras in communication and globalization, an early multicultural experiment.[4]

[4]Cf. Anthony Pagden, "The Impact of the New World on the Old: The History of an Idea," *Renaissance and Modern Studies* 30 (1986): pp. 1–11.

MONTAIGNE ON "CANNIBALS" IN FOREIGN LANDS

The French philosopher Michel de Montaigne (1533–1592) had seen a Brazilian native in Rouen in 1562, who was alleged to be a cannibal. The experience gave rise to an essay on the subject of what constitutes a "savage." Montaigne concluded that no people on earth were more barbarous than Europeans, who take natives of other lands captive.

Is Montaigne romanticizing the New World natives? Is he being too hard on Europeans? Had the Aztecs or Incas had the ability to discover and occupy Europe, would they have enslaved and exploited Europeans?

Now, to return to my subject, I think there is nothing barbarous and savage in that nation [Brazil], from what I have been told . . . Each man calls barbarism whatever is not his own practice; for indeed it seems we have no other test of truth and reason than the example and pattern of the opinions and customs of the country we live in. There [we] always [find] the perfect religion, the perfect government, the perfect and accomplished manners in all things. Those [foreign] people are wild, just as we call wild the fruits that Nature has produced by herself and in her normal course; where really it is those that we have changed artificially and led astray from the common order that we should rather call wild. The former retain alive and vigorous their genuine virtues and properties, which we have debased in the latter by adapting them to gratify our corrupted taste. And yet for all that, the savor and delicacy of some uncultivated fruits of those countries is quite as excellent, even to our taste, as that of our own. It is not reasonable that [our human] art should win the place of honor over our great and powerful mother Nature. We have so overloaded the beauty and richness of her works by our inventions that we have quite smothered her. Yet wherever her purity shines forth, she wonderfully puts to shame our vain and frivolous attempts: "Ivy comes readier without our care;/In lonely caves the arbutus grows more fair;/No art with artless bird song can compare."[1] All our efforts cannot even succeed in reproducing the nest of the tiniest little bird, its contexture, its beauty and convenience; or even the web of the puny spider. All things, says Plato,[2] are produced by nature, by fortune, or by art; the greatest and most beautiful by one or the other of the first two, the least and most imperfect by the last.

These nations, then, seem to me "barbarous" in this sense, that they have been fashioned very little by the human mind, and are still very close to their original naturalness. The laws of nature still rule them, very little corrupted by ours; and they are in such a state of purity that I am sometimes vexed that they were unknown earlier, in the days when there were men able to judge them better than we.

[1]Propertius 1.11.10.
[2]Laws 10.

From *The Complete Essays of Montaigne,* trans. by Donald M. Frame (Stanford, CA: Stanford University Press, 1958), pp. 153–154.

On the material side, the influx of spices and precious metals into Europe from the new Portuguese and Spanish Empires was a mixed blessing. It contributed to a steady rise in prices during the sixteenth century that created an inflation rate estimated at 2 percent a year. The new supply of bullion from the Americas joined with enlarged European production to increase greatly the amount of coinage in circulation, and this increase, in turn, fed inflation. Fortunately, the increase in prices was by and large spread over a long period and was not sudden. Prices doubled in Spain by 1550, quadrupled by 1600. In Luther's Wittenberg in Germany, the cost of basic food and clothing increased almost 100 percent between 1519 and 1540. Generally, wages and rents remained well behind the rise in prices.

The new wealth enabled governments and private entrepreneurs to sponsor basic research and expansion in the printing, shipping, mining, textile, and weapons industries. There is also evidence of large-scale government planning in such ventures as the French silk industry and the Habsburg-Fugger development of mines in Austria and Hungary.

In the thirteenth and fourteenth centuries, capitalist institutions and practices had already begun to develop in the rich Italian cities (for example, the Florentine banking houses of Bardi and Peruzzi). Those who owned the means of production, either privately or corporately, were clearly distinguished from the workers who operated them. Wherever possible, entrepreneurs created monopolies in basic goods. High interest was charged on loans—actual, if not legal, usury. The "capitalist" virtues of thrift, industry, and orderly planning were everywhere in evidence—all intended to permit the free and efficient accumulation of wealth.

The late fifteenth and the sixteenth centuries saw the maturation of this type of capitalism together with its attendant social problems. The Medicis of Florence grew rich as bankers of the pope, as did the Fuggers of Augsburg, who bankrolled Habsburg rulers. The Fuggers lent Charles I of Spain more than 500,000 florins to buy his election as the Holy Roman Emperor in 1519 and boasted they had created the emperor. The new wealth and industrial expansion also raised the expectations of the poor and the ambitious and heightened the reactionary tendencies of the wealthy. This effect, in turn, aggravated the traditional social divisions between the clergy and the laity, the urban patriciate and the guilds, and the landed nobility and the agrarian peasantry.

These divisions indirectly prepared the way for the Reformation as well, by making many people critical of traditional institutions and open to new ideas—especially those that seemed to promise greater freedom and a chance at a better life.

In Perspective

As it recovered from national wars during the late Middle Ages, Europe saw the establishment of permanent centralized states and regional governments. The foundations of modern France, Spain, England, Germany, and Italy were laid at this time. As rulers imposed their will on regions outside their immediate domains, the "one" progressively took control of the "many," and previously divided lands came together as nations.

Thanks to the work of Byzantine and Islamic scholars, ancient Greek science and scholarship found its way into the West in these centuries. Europeans had been separated from their classical cultural heritage for almost eight centuries. No other world civilization had experienced such a disjunction from its cultural past. The discovery of classical civilization occasioned a rebirth of intellectual and artistic activity in both southern and northern Europe. One result was the splendor of the Italian Renaissance, whose scholarship, painting, and sculpture remain among Western Europe's most impressive achievements.

Ancient learning was not the only discovery of the era. New political unity spurred both royal greed and national ambition. By the late fifteenth century, Europeans were in a position to venture far away to the shores of Africa, the southern and eastern coasts of Asia, and the New World of the Americas. European discovery was not the only outcome of these voyages: The exploitation of the peoples and lands of the New World revealed a dark side of Western civilization. Some penalties were paid even then. The influx of New World gold and silver created new human and economic problems on the European mainland. Some Europeans even began to question their civilization's traditional values.

Review Questions

1. What was Jacob Burckhardt's interpretation of the Renaissance? What criticisms have been leveled against it? What did the term mean in the context of fifteenth- and sixteenth-century Italy?
2. How would you define Renaissance humanism? In what ways was the Renaissance a break with the Middle Ages, and in what ways did it owe its existence to medieval civilization?
3. Who were some of the famous literary and artistic figures of the Italian Renaissance? What did they have in common that might be described as "the spirit of the Renaissance"?
4. Why did the French invade Italy in 1494? How did this event trigger Italy's political decline? How did the actions of Pope Julius II and the ideas of Niccolò Machiavelli signify a new era in Italian civilization?
5. A common assumption is that creative work proceeds best in periods of calm and peace. Given the combination of political instability and cultural productivity in Renaissance Italy, do you think this assumption is valid?
6. How did the Renaissance in the north differ from the Italian Renaissance? In what ways was Erasmus the embodiment of the northern Renaissance?
7. What factors led to the voyages of discovery? Why were the Portuguese interested in finding a route to the East? Why did Columbus sail west across the Atlantic in 1492?

SUGGESTED READINGS

D. Abulafia, *The Discovery of Mankind: Atlantic Encounters in the Age of Columbus* (2008). The latest telling of the European invasion of the New World.

L. B. Alberti, *The Family in Renaissance Florence*, trans. by R. N. Watkins (1962). A contemporary humanist, who never married, explains how a family should behave.

K. Atchity, ed., *The Renaissance Reader* (1996). The Renaissance in its own words.

H. Baron, *The Crisis of the Early Italian Renaissance*, Vols. 1 and 2 (1966). A major work on the civic dimension of Italian humanism.

G. A. Brucker, *Giovanni and Lusanna: Love and Marriage in Renaissance Florence* (1986). Love in the Renaissance shown to be more Bergman than Fellini.

J. Burckhardt, *The Civilization of the Renaissance in Italy* (1958). Modern edition of an old nineteenth-century classic that still has as many defenders as detractors.

R. E. Conrad, *Children of God's Fire: A Documentary History of Black Slavery in Brazil* (1983). Not for the squeamish.

L. Hanke, *Bartholomé de Las Casas: An Interpretation of His Life and Writings* (1951). Biography of the great Dominican critic of Spanish exploitation of Native Americans.

J. Hankins, *Plato in the Renaissance* (1992). A magisterial study of how Plato was read and interpreted by Renaissance scholars.

D. Herlihy and C. Klapisch-Zuber, *Tuscans and Their Families* (1985). Important work based on unique demographic data that give the reader a new appreciation of quantitative history.

J. C. Hutchison, *Albrecht Dürer: A Biography* (1990).

L. Martines, *Power and Imagination: City States in Renaissance Italy* (1980). Stimulating account of cultural and political history.

S. E. Morrison, *Admiral of the Ocean Sea: A Life of Christopher Columbus* (1946). Still the best Columbus read.

E. Panofsky, *Meaning in the Visual Arts* (1955). Eloquent treatment of Renaissance art.

J. H. Parry, *The Age of Reconnaissance* (1964). A comprehensive account of exploration in the years 1450 to 1650.

I. A. Richter, ed., *The Notebooks of Leonardo da Vinci* (1985). The master in his own words.

A. Wheatcroft, *The Habsburgs* (1995). The dynasty that ruled the center of late medieval and early modern Europe.

C. C. Willard, *Christine de Pizan* (1984). Demonstration of what an educated woman could accomplish in the Renaissance.

For additional learning resources related to this chapter, please go to www.myhistorylab.com

Painted on the eve of the Reformation, Matthias Grunewald's (ca. 1480–1528) *Crucifixion* shows a Christ who takes all the sins of the world into his own body, as his mother, Mary Magdalene, and John the Baptist share the pain of his afflictions. Musée Unterlinden, Colmar, France/SuperStock

11

The Age of Reformation

▼ **Society and Religion**

Social and Political Conflict • Popular Religious Movements and Criticism of the Church

▼ **Martin Luther and German Reformation to 1525**

Justification by Faith Alone • The Attack on Indulgences • Election of Charles V • Luther's Excommunication and the Diet of Worms • Imperial Distractions: War with France and the Turks • How the Reformation Spread • The Peasants' Revolt

▼ **The Reformation Elsewhere**

Zwingli and the Swiss Reformation • Anabaptists and Radical Protestants • John Calvin and the Genevan Reformation

▼ **Political Consolidation of the Lutheran Reformation**

The Diet of Augsburg • The Expansion of the Reformation • Reaction Against Protestants • The Peace of Augsburg

▼ **The English Reformation to 1553**

The Preconditions of Reform • The King's Affair • The "Reformation Parliament" • Wives of Henry VIII • The King's Religious Conservatism • The Protestant Reformation under Edward VI

▼ **Catholic Reform and Counter-Reformation**

Sources of Catholic Reform • Ignatius of Loyola and the Jesuits • The Council of Trent (1545–1563)

▼ **The Social Significance of the Reformation in Western Europe**

The Revolution in Religious Practices and Institutions • The Reformation and Education • The Reformation and the Changing Role of Women

▼ **Family Life in Early Modern Europe**

Later Marriages • Arranged Marriages • Family Size • Birth Control • Wet Nursing • Loving Families?

▼ **Literary Imagination in Transition**

Miguel de Cervantes Saavedra: Rejection of Idealism • William Shakespeare: Dramatist of the Age

▼ **In Perspective**

KEY TOPICS

- The social and religious background of the Reformation
- Martin Luther's challenge to the church and the course of the Reformation in Germany
- The Reformation in Switzerland, France, and England
- Transitions in family life between medieval and modern times

IN THE SECOND decade of the sixteenth century, a long-building, powerful religious movement began in Saxony in Germany and spread rapidly throughout northern Europe, deeply affecting society and politics, as well as the spiritual lives of men and women. Attacking what they believed to be burdensome superstitions that robbed people of both their money and their peace of mind, Protestant reformers led a broad revolt against the medieval church. In a short time, hundreds of thousands of people from all social classes set aside the beliefs of centuries and adopted a more simplified religious practice.

The Protestant Reformation challenged aspects of the Renaissance, especially its tendency to follow classical sources in glorifying human nature and its loyalty to traditional religion. Protestants were more impressed by the human potential for evil than by the inclination to do good. They encouraged parents, teachers, and magistrates to be firm disciplinarians, but they also embraced many Renaissance values, especially educational reforms and the training of students in ancient languages. Like the Italian humanists, the Protestant reformers prized the tools that allowed them to go directly to the original sources. For the reformers, however, this meant the study of the Hebrew and Greek scriptures, enabling them to root their challenges to traditional authority and institutions in biblical antiquity.

▼ Society and Religion

The Protestant **Reformation** occurred at a time of sharp conflict between the emerging nation-states of Europe bent on conformity and centralization within their realms and the self-governing towns and villages long accustomed to running their own affairs. Since the late fourteenth century, the territorial ruler's law and custom had progressively overridden local law and custom almost everywhere. The towns remained keenly sensitive to the loss of traditional rights and freedoms. Many townspeople and village folk perceived in the religious revolt an ally in their struggle to remain politically free and independent.

Social and Political Conflict

The Reformation broke out first in the free imperial cities of Germany and Switzerland, and the basic tenets of Lutheran and Zwinglian Protestantism remained visible in subsequent Protestant movements. There were about sixty-five free imperial cities, each a small kingdom unto itself. Most had Protestant movements but with mixed success and duration. Some quickly turned Protestant and remained so. Some were Protestant only for a short time. Still others developed mixed confessions. Frowning on sectarianism and aggressive proselytizing, they made it possible for Catholics and Protestants to live side by side with appropriate barriers between them.

A seeming life-and-death struggle with higher princely or royal authority was not the only conflict late medieval cities were experiencing. They also coped with deep social and political divisions. Certain groups favored the Reformation more than others. In many places, guilds whose members were economically prospering and socially rising were in the forefront of the Reformation. The printers' guild is a prominent example. Its members were literate, sophisticated about the world, and belonged to a rapidly growing industry. They also had an economic stake in fanning religious conflict with Protestant propaganda, which many, of course, also sincerely believed. Guilds with a history of opposition to reigning governmental authority also stood out among early Protestant supporters, regardless of education level. Evidence also suggests that people who felt pushed around and bullied by either local or distant authority—a guild by an autocratic local government, or a city or region by a powerful prince or king—often perceived an ally in the Protestant movement.

Social and political experience naturally influenced religious change in town and countryside. A Protestant sermon or pamphlet praising religious freedom seemed directly relevant, for example, to the townspeople of German and Swiss cities who faced incorporation into the territory of a powerful local prince, who looked on them as his subjects rather than as free citizens. When Martin Luther and his followers, who wrote, preached, and sang about a priesthood of all believers, scorned the authority of ecclesiastical landlords and ridiculed papal laws as arbitrary human inventions, they touched political as well as religious nerves. This was also true in the villages and in the towns. Like city dwellers, the peasants on the land also heard in the Protestant sermon and pamphlet a promise of political liberation, even a degree of social betterment. More than the townspeople, the peasants found their traditional liberties—from fishing and hunting rights to representation at local diets—progressively being chipped away by the secular and ecclesiastical landlords of the age.

Popular Religious Movements and Criticism of the Church

The Protestant Reformation could also not have occurred without the monumental challenges to the medieval church during its "exile" in Avignon, the Great Schism, the Conciliar period, and the Renaissance papacy. For sizable numbers of people in future Protestant lands, the medieval church had ceased to provide a viable foundation for religious piety. Many intellectuals and laypeople felt a sense of spiritual crisis. At the Diet of Worms in 1521 (see page 320), the German nobility presented the emperor with a list of 102 "oppressive [church] burdens and abuses" said to be corrupting the care of German souls. Between the secular pretensions of the papacy and the dry teaching of Scholastic theologians, laity and clerics alike began to seek a more heartfelt, idealistic, and—often, in the eyes of the pope—heretical religious piety. The late Middle Ages were marked by independent lay and clerical efforts to reform local religious practice and by widespread experimentation with new religious forms.

A variety of factors contributed to the growing lay criticism of the church. Urban laypeople were increasingly knowledgeable about the world around them and about the rulers who controlled their lives. They traveled widely—as soldiers, pilgrims, explorers, and traders. New postal systems and the printing press increased the information at their disposal. A new age of books and libraries raised literacy and heightened curiosity. Laypeople were able to shape the cultural life of their communities.

From the Albigensians, Waldensians, Beguines, and Beghards in the thirteenth century to the Lollards and Hussites in the fifteenth, lay religious movements shared a common goal of religious simplicity in the imitation of Jesus. Almost everywhere, the laity was inspired by ideals of apostolic poverty in religion. A simple religion of love and self-sacrifice like that of Jesus and the first disciples seemed to be the ideal. To that end, the laity sought a more egalitarian church—one that gave the members as well as the head of the church a voice—and also a more spiritual church—one that lived manifestly according to its New Testament model.

The Modern Devotion One of the more constructive lay religious movements in northern Europe on the eve of the Reformation was that of the Brothers of the Common Life, also known as the Modern Devotion, a kind of boarding school for reform-minded laity. The brothers fostered religious life outside formal church offices and apart from formal religious vows—a lay religious life of prayer and study without surrendering the world. Centered at Zwolle and Deventer in the Netherlands, the brother and (less numerous) sister houses of the Modern Devotion spread rapidly throughout northern Europe and influenced parts of southern Europe as well. In these houses clerics and laity shared a common life, stressing individual piety and practical religion. Lay members were not expected to take special religious vows or to wear a special religious dress, nor did they abandon their ordinary secular vocations.

The brothers were also educators. They worked as copyists, sponsored many religious and some classical publications, ran hospices for poor students, and conducted schools for the young—especially boys preparing for the priesthood or a monastic vocation. As youths, the future philosopher Nicholas of Cusa, the humanist and Hebraist Johannes Reuchlin, and Desiderius Erasmus, the proclaimed "prince of the humanists," were looked after by these brothers. Erasmus later formulated his own "philosophy of Christ" after what he had learned there. Thomas à Kempis (d. 1471) summarized the philosophy of the brothers in what became the most popular religious book of the period, the *Imitation of Christ*. This semimystical guide to the inner life was intended primarily for monks and nuns but was also widely read by laity who wanted to pursue the ascetic life.

The Modern Devotion has been seen as the source of humanist, Protestant, and Catholic reform movements in the sixteenth century. Some scholars, however, believe it represented an individualistic approach to religion, indifferent and even hostile to the sacramental piety of the church and papal authority. It was, in truth, a conservative movement. The brothers retained the old clerical doctrines and values but placed them within the new framework of an active common life. Their practices clearly met a need for a more personal piety and a more informed religious life. Their movement appeared at a time when the laity was demanding good preaching in the **vernacular** and taking the initiative to endow special funds for preaching in cities and towns to ensure it.

Lay Control over Religious Life On the eve of the Reformation, Rome's international network of church offices, which had unified Europe religiously during the Middle Ages, was falling apart in many areas. This collapse was hurried along by a growing sense of regional identity, an increasingly competent local secular administration, and a newly emerging nationalism. The long-entrenched *benefice* system of the medieval church had permitted important ecclesiastical posts to be sold to the highest bidders and had often failed to enforce the requirement that priests and bishops had to live in their parishes and dioceses. Such a system threatened a vibrant, lay spiritual life. The substitutes hired by nonresident holders of *benefices* frequently lived elsewhere, preferably in Rome. They milked the revenues of their offices, performed their clerical chores mechanically, if they did them at all, and had neither firsthand knowledge of, nor much sympathy for, local spiritual needs and problems. Rare was the late medieval German town that did not have complaints about the maladministration, concubinage, or financial greed of its clergy—especially the higher clergy (bishops, abbots, and prelates).

Communities loudly protested the financial and spiritual abuses of the medieval church long before Luther published his famous summary of economic grievances in a treatise entitled *Address to the Christian Nobility of the German Nation* (1520). The sale of indulgences, in particular, had been repeatedly attacked before Luther came on the scene. On the eve of the Reformation, this practice had expanded to permit people to buy release from time in purgatory for both themselves and their deceased loved ones. Rulers and magistrates had little objection to their sale and might even encourage it, as long as a generous portion of the income the sales generated remained in the local coffers. Yet when an indulgence was offered primarily for the benefit of distant interests, as with the sale of indulgences to raise money for a new Saint Peter's basilica in Rome that Luther protested, resistance arose also for strictly financial reasons: their sale drained away local revenues.

The sale of indulgences would not end until rulers found new ways to profit from religion and the laity discovered more effective remedies for religious anxiety. The Reformation provided the former by sanctioning the secular dissolution of monasteries and the confiscation of ecclesiastical properties. It promised the latter in its new theology of justification by faith in God and a life of self-sacrificial service to one's neighbor.

City governments also undertook to improve local religious life on the eve of the Reformation by endowing preacherships. These positions, supported by *benefices,* made possible the hiring of well-trained pastors who provided regular preaching and pastoral care beyond the performance of the Mass. These preacherships often became platforms for Protestants.

Magistrates also carefully restricted the growth of ecclesiastical properties and clerical privileges. During the Middle Ages, canon and civil law had recognized special clerical rights in both property and person. Because they were holy places of "sacral peace" and asylum, churches and monasteries were exempted from the taxes and laws that affected others. Law also deemed it inappropriate for holy persons (clergy) to burden themselves with such "dirty jobs" as military service, compulsory labor, standing watch at city gates, and other ordinary civic obligations. Nor was it thought right that the laity should sit in judgment on those who were their shepherds and intermediaries with God. The clergy, accordingly, came to enjoy an immunity from the jurisdiction of civil courts.

Already on the eve of the Reformation, measures were passed to restrict these clerical privileges and to end their abuses. Governments grew tired of church interference in what to them were strictly secular political spheres of competence and authority. Secular authorities accordingly began to scrutinize the church's acquisition of new properties, finding ways to get around its right of asylum when it interrupted the administration of justice, and generally bringing the clergy under local tax codes.

▼ Martin Luther and the German Reformation to 1525

Unlike England and France, late medieval Germany lacked the political unity to enforce "national" religious reforms during the late Middle Ages. There were no lasting Statutes of Provisors and Praemunire, as in England, nor a Pragmatic Sanction of Bourges, as in France, limiting papal jurisdiction and taxation on a national scale. What had happened on a unified national level in England and France occurred only locally and piecemeal within German territories and towns. As popular resentment of clerical immunities and ecclesiastical abuses spread among German cities and towns, an unorganized "national" opposition to Rome formed. German humanists had long given voice to such criticism, and by 1517 it was pervasive enough to provide a solid foundation for Martin Luther's protest of indulgences and the theology that legitimated them.

The son of a successful Thüringian miner, Luther (1483–1546) was educated in Mansfeld, Magdeburg (where the Brothers of the Common Life had been his teachers) and Eisenach. Between 1501 and 1505, he attended the University of Erfurt, where the nominalist teachings of William of Ockham and Gabriel Biel (d. 1495) prevailed. (See Chapter 8.) After receiving his master-of-arts degree in 1505, Luther registered with the law faculty in accordance with his parents' wishes. But he never began the study of law. To the disappointment of his family, he instead entered the Order of the Hermits of Saint Augustine in Erfurt on July 17, 1505. That decision had apparently been building for some time and was resolved during a lightning storm in which a young Luther, terrified and crying out to Saint Anne for assistance (she was the patron saint of travelers in distress), promised to enter a monastery if he escaped death.

Ordained in 1507, Luther pursued a traditional course of study. In 1510, he journeyed to Rome on the business of his order, finding there justification for the many criticisms of the church he had heard in Germany. In 1511, he moved to the Augustinian monastery in Wittenberg, where he earned his doctorate in theology in 1512, thereafter, to become a leader within the monastery, the new university, and the spiritual life of the city.

Justification by Faith Alone

Luther was especially plagued by the disproportion between his own sense of sinfulness and the perfect righteousness God required for salvation, according to traditional church teaching. Luther came to despise the phrase "righteousness of God," because it demanded of him a perfection neither he nor any other human being could attain. His insight into the meaning of "justification by faith alone" (*sola fide*) was a gradual process between 1513 and 1518. The righteousness that God demands, he concluded, did not result from charitable acts and religious ceremonies but was given in full measure to any and all who believe in and trust Jesus Christ as their perfect righteousness satisfying to God.

The medieval church had always taught that salvation was a joint venture, a combination of divine mercy and human good works, what God alone could do and what man was expected to do in return. Luther also believed that faith without charitable service to one's neighbor was dead. The Christian did not fulfill all the due obligations of a Christian life by simply saying, "I believe," and thereafter did as he pleased. The issue was not whether good works should be done, but how those works should be regarded. It was unbiblical, Luther argued, to treat works as contributing to one's eternal salvation, something only an almighty God could bestow. He also believed that the church's conditioning of salvation on

A SAINT AT PEACE IN THE GRASP OF TEMPTATION

MARTIN SCHONGAUER (c. 1430–1491), the best engraver in the Upper Rhine, portrays the devil's temptation of St. Anthony in the wilderness as a robust physical attack by demons rather than the traditional melancholic introspection.

Unlike the saint, the demons look perplexed and disbelieving, as their every thrust fails to penetrate.

Although the demons are all over him, Anthony remains untouched. The artist's remarkably distinct lines keep saint and demons apart, reinforcing the saint's inner peace and serenity.

National Gallery of Art, Washington, DC

This rendering of faith as serenity amid the most brutal assault anticipates Martin Luther's great hymn of the Reformation: "A Mighty Fortress Is Our God," in which it is said that "one little word" (belief in Christ) slays the devil and his minions.

To examine this image in an interactive fashion, please go to www.myhistorylab.com

PEARSON myhistorylab

good works left many Christians only counting their merits and demerits, unable to act selflessly, and struggling to maintain inner peace of mind.

Good works were expected over a lifetime, Luther taught, but not because they earned salvation. The believer who is bound to Christ by faith already possesses God's perfect righteousness. It is this knowledge of faith that sets narcissistic souls free to serve their neighbors selflessly. Such service is ethical, not soteriological—a good work, not a saving work. Inspired by the security faith conveys, such works belong to one's neighbor, who needs help, not to God in heaven, who has everything. God is pleased when those who believe in him do good works, and he expects his people always to do them, but he does not take those works into account when he is merciful and bestows eternal life, which would make God a puppet of man.

The Attack on Indulgences

An **indulgence** was a remission of the temporal penalty imposed on penitents by priests as a "work of satisfaction" for their confessed mortal sins. According to medieval theology, after the priest absolved a penitent of guilt for sin, the penitent still remained under an eternal penalty, a punishment God justly imposed. Priestly absolution, however, was said to transform this eternal penalty into a temporal penalty, a manageable "work of satisfaction" a penitent might perform here and now by prayers, fasting, almsgiving, retreats, and/or pilgrimages. Penitents who defaulted on such prescribed works of satisfaction could expect to suffer for them in purgatory for an indefinite period of time before entering heaven.

Indulgences were originally given to Crusaders who could not complete their penances because they had fallen in battle. By the late Middle Ages, indulgences had become an aid to laypeople made genuinely anxious by their fear of a future suffering in purgatory for neglected penances or unrepented sins. In 1343, Pope Clement VI (r. 1342–1352) proclaimed the existence of a "treasury of merit," an infinite reservoir of good works in the church's possession that could be dispensed at the pope's discretion. On the basis of this alleged treasury, the church sold "letters of indulgence," which made good on the works of satisfaction owed by penitents. In 1476, Pope Sixtus IV (r. 1471–1484) extended indulgences to the unrepented sins of all Christians in purgatory.

By Luther's time, indulgences were regularly dispensed for small cash payments, modest sums that were regarded as a good work of almsgiving. Indulgence preachers presented them to the laity as remitting not only their own future punishments, but also those of dead relatives presumed still to be suffering in purgatory.

In 1517, Pope Leo X (r. 1513–1521) revived a plenary Jubilee Indulgence that had first been issued by Pope Julius II (r. 1503–1513), the proceeds of which were to rebuild St. Peter's Basilica in Rome. Such an indulgence promised for-

A contemporary caricature depicts John Tetzel, the famous indulgence preacher. The last lines of the jingle read, "As soon as gold in the basin rings, right then the soul to Heaven springs." It was Tetzel's preaching that spurred Luther to publish his ninety-five theses. Courtesy Stiftung Luthergedenkstaten in Sachsen-Anhalt/Lutherhalle, Wittenberg giveness of all outstanding unrepented sins upon the completion of certain acts. That indulgence was subsequently preached on the borders of Saxony in the territories of the future Archbishop Albrecht of Mainz, who was much in need of revenues because of the large debts he had incurred to gain a papal dispensation to hold three ecclesiastical appointments at one and the same time.

The selling of the indulgence became a joint venture by Albrecht, the Augsburg banking house of Fugger, and Pope Leo X, with half the proceeds going to the pope and half to Albrecht and his creditors. The famous indulgence preacher John Tetzel (d. 1519) was enlisted to preach the indulgence in Albrecht's territories. A seasoned professional, he knew how to stir ordinary people to action. As he exhorted on one occasion,

> Don't you hear the voices of your dead parents and other relatives crying out, "Have mercy on us, for we suffer great punishment and pain. From this you could release us with a few alms. . . . We have created you, fed you, cared for you, and left you our temporal goods. Why do you treat us so cruelly and leave us to suffer in the flames, when it takes only a little to save us?"[1]

When Luther posted his ninety-five theses against indulgences on the door of Castle Church in Wittenberg (October 31, 1517), he protested especially the impression Tetzel created that indulgences remitted sins and released unrepentant sinners from punishment in purgatory. Luther believed these claims went far beyond the traditional practice and seemed to make salvation something that could be bought and sold.

Election of Charles V

The ninety-five theses were embraced by Nuremberg humanists, who translated and widely circulated them. This made Luther a central figure in an already organized national German cultural movement against foreign influence and competition, particularly on the part of the Italians. In October, he was summoned before the general of the Dominican order in Augsburg to answer for his criticism of the church. Yet as sanctions were being prepared against him, Emperor Maximilian I died (January 12, 1519)—a fortunate event for the budding Reformation, because it turned attention away from heresy in Saxony to the contest for a new emperor.

In that contest, the pope backed the French king, Francis I. However, Charles I of Spain, a youth of nineteen, successfully succeeded his grandfather as Emperor Charles V. (See Map 11–1, page 320.) Charles was blessed by both the long tradition of the Habsburg imperial rule and a massive Fugger campaign chest that secured the votes of the seven imperial **electors**. The most prominent among the seven was Frederick the Wise, Luther's lord and protector. Frederick took great pride in his new University of Wittenberg, and he was not about to let any harm come to his famous court preacher.

In exchange for their votes, the electors wrung new concessions from the Spanish favorable to the Germans. Before becoming emperor, Charles I agreed to revive the German-based Imperial Supreme Court and the Council of Regency and also promised to consult with a diet of the empire on all major domestic and foreign affairs affecting the empire. These measures also helped the development of the Reformation by preventing unilateral imperial action against the Germans.

Luther's Excommunication and the Diet of Worms

In the same month in which Charles was elected emperor, Luther debated the Ingolstadt professor John Eck in Leipzig (June 27, 1519). During this contest, Luther challenged the infallibility of the pope and the inerrancy of church councils, appealing, for the first time, to the

In 1520, Luther's first portrait, shown here, depicted him as a tough, steely-eyed monk. Afraid that this portrayal might convey defiance rather than reform to Emperor Charles V, Elector Frederick the Wise of Saxony, Luther's protector, ordered court painter Lucas Cranach to soften the image. The result was a Luther placed within a traditional monk's niche reading an open Bible, a reformer, unlike the one depicted here, who was prepared to listen as well as to instruct. Martin Luther as a monk, 1521. © Foto Marburg/Art Resource, NY

[1]*Die Reformation in Augenzeugen berichten*, ed. by Helmar Junghaus (Düsseldorf: Karl Rauch Verlag, 1967), p. 44.

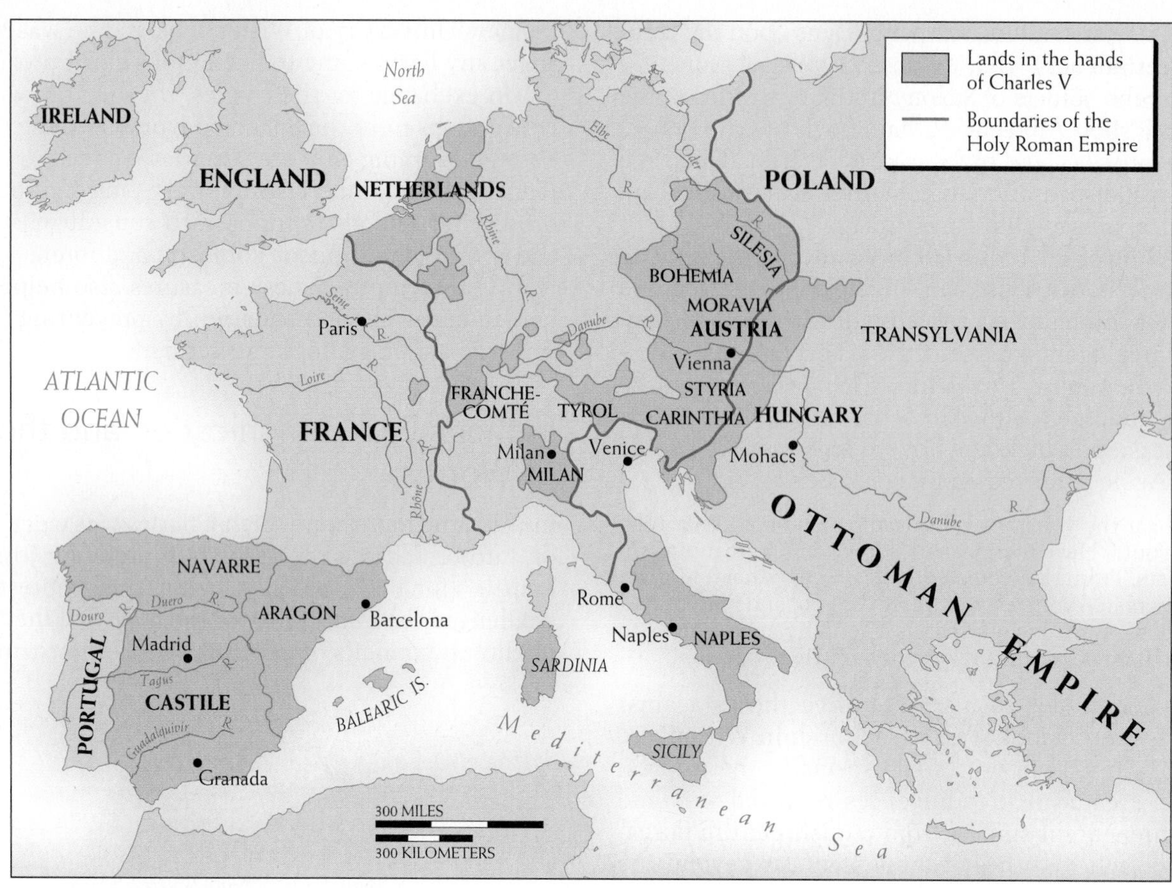

Map 11–1 **THE EMPIRE OF CHARLES V** Dynastic marriages and simple chance concentrated into Charles's hands rule over the lands shown here, plus Spain's overseas possessions. Crowns and titles rained down on him; his election in 1519 as emperor gave him new distractions and responsibilities.

sovereign authority of Scripture alone. He burned all his bridges to the old church when he further defended certain teachings of John Huss, who had been condemned to death for heresy at the Council of Constance.

In 1520, Luther signaled his new direction with three famous pamphlets. The *Address to the Christian Nobility of the German Nation* urged the German princes to force reforms on the Roman church, especially to curtail its political and economic power in Germany. The *Babylonian Captivity of the Church* attacked the traditional seven sacraments, arguing that only two, baptism and the Eucharist, were unquestionably biblical, and it exalted the authority of Scripture, church councils, and secular princes over that of the pope. The eloquent *Freedom of a Christian* summarized the new teaching of salvation by faith alone.

On June 15, 1520, Leo's papal bull *Exsurge Domine* ("Arise, O Lord") condemned Luther for heresy and gave him sixty days to retract. The final bull of excommunication was issued on January 3, 1521.

In April 1521, Luther presented his views before the Diet of Worms, over which the newly elected Emperor Charles V presided. Ordered to recant, Luther declared that to do so would be to act against Scripture, reason, and his conscience. On May 26, 1521, he was placed under the imperial ban, which made him an "outlaw" to secular as well as religious authority. For his own protection, friends disguised and hid him in Wartburg Castle at the instruction of Elector Frederick. There, he spent almost a year, from April 1521 to March 1522. During his stay, he translated the New Testament into German using Erasmus's new Greek text and Latin translation, while overseeing by correspondence the first steps of the Reformation in Wittenberg.

Imperial Distractions: War with France and the Turks

The Reformation was greatly helped in these early years by the emperor's war with France and the advance of the Ottoman Turks into eastern Europe. Against both adversaries Charles V, who remained a Spanish king with dynastic responsibilities in Spain and Austria, needed loyal German troops, to which end he sought friendly relations with the German princes. Between 1521 and 1559, Spain (the Habsburg dynasty) and France (the Valois dynasty) fought four major wars over disputed territories within Italy and along their respective borders.

Thus preoccupied, the emperor agreed through his representatives at the German Diet of Speyer (1526) that each German territory was free to enforce the Edict of Worms (1521) against Luther "so as to be able to answer in good conscience to God and the emperor." That concession in effect gave the German princes, who five years earlier had refused to publish the emperor's condemnation of Luther, territorial sovereignty in religious matters. It also bought the Reformation time to put down deep roots in Germany and Switzerland. In addition, Speyer proved to be a true precedent for the final settlement of the religious conflict in the empire. Later, the Peace of Augsburg (1555) would enshrine regional princely control over religion in imperial law.

How the Reformation Spread

In the late 1520s and 1530s, the Reformation passed from the free hands of the theologians and pamphleteers into the firmer ones of the magistrates and princes. In many cities, the latter quickly mandated new religious reforms. Many rulers had themselves worked for decades to bring about basic church reforms, and they welcomed Lutheran preachers as new allies. Reform now ceased to be merely slogans and was transformed into laws all townspeople had to obey.

The elector of Saxony and the prince of Hesse, the two most powerful German Protestant rulers, led the politicization of religious reform within their territories. Like the urban magistrates, the German princes recognized the political and economic opportunities offered them by the demise of the Roman Catholic Church in their lands. Soon they were pushing Protestant faith and politics onto their neighbors. In the 1530s, German Protestant lands formed a powerful defensive alliance, the Schmaldkaldic League, and prepared for war with the Catholic emperor.

The Peasants' Revolt

In its first decade, the Reformation suffered more from internal division than from imperial interference. By 1525, Luther had become almost as much an object of protest within Germany as was the pope. Original allies, sympathizers, and fellow travelers increasingly declared their independence from Wittenberg.

Like the German humanists, the German peasantry also had at first believed Luther to be an ally. Since the late fifteenth century, the peasantry had opposed the efforts of their secular and ecclesiastical lords to override their traditional laws and customs and to subject them to new territorial regulations and taxes. Peasant leaders, several of whom had been Lutherans, saw in Luther's teaching about Christian freedom and his criticism of monastic landowners a point of view close to their own. They openly solicited

The punishment of a peasant leader in a village near Heilbronn. After the defeat of rebellious peasants in and around the city of Heilbronn, Jacob Rorbach, a well-to-do peasant leader from a nearby village, was tied to a stake and slowly roasted to death.
Courtesy of the Library of Congress

Luther's support of their alleged "Christian" political and economic rights, including a revolutionary demand of release from serfdom.

Luther had initially sympathized with the peasants, condemning the tyranny of the princes and urging them to meet the just demands of the peasants. Lutheran pamphleteers made Karsthans (Hans with a hoe), the burly, hard-working peasant who earned his bread by the sweat of his brow, a model of the honest life God wanted all people to live. The Lutherans, however, were not social revolutionaries and they saw no hope for their movement if it became intertwined with a peasant revolution. When the peasants revolted against their landlords in 1524–1525, invoking Luther's name, Luther predictably condemned them as "un-Christian" and urged the princes to crush the revolt mercilessly. Tens of thousands of peasants (estimates run between 70,000 and 100,000) died by the time the revolt was suppressed.

For Luther, the freedom of the Christian lay in inner spiritual release from guilt and anxiety, not in revolutionary politics. Had the reformers joined the peasants' revolt, Luther would have contradicted his own teaching and likely shared the fate of former Lutherans who died as leaders of peasant revolts. In that scenario the

COMPARE AND CONNECT

A Raw Deal for the Common Man, or His Just Desserts?

BEGINNING IN THE late fifteenth century, German feudal lords, both secular and ecclesiastical, increased labor and crop quotas on their peasant tenants, while restricting their freedoms and overriding their customary laws as well. In 1525 massive revolts occurred in southern Germany, in what became the largest social uprising before the French Revolution. Among those responding directly to the revolt were two highly respected authorities: Wittenberg theologian Martin Luther and Nuremberg artist Albrecht Dürer.

QUESTIONS

1. **What is there in Luther's religious teaching that might have led the peasants to think he would support their revolt? What personal interest might he have had in turning them his way? What does he advise them to do to address their grievances properly?**
2. **Does Dürer's 1527 sketch of a "Memorial to the Peasants' Revolt," depicting a peasant sitting atop a chicken coop with a sword thrust through his back, suggest a greater sympathy for the peasants? Or can it be read as agreement with Luther that the peasants received their just desserts for rebelling against lawful authority?**
3. **Does Dürer's monument support or condemn the rebellious peasants?**

I. Martin Luther, *An Admonition to Peace* (1525)

ON STOPPING THE WAR

This matter is great and perilous, concerning both the kingdom of God and the kingdom of the world; if this rebellion gets the upper hand, both kingdoms will be destroyed and there will be neither world government nor Word of God; there will rather result the permanent destruction of all of Germany, therefore, it is necessary . . . to speak boldly . . . Since there is nothing Christian on either side and nothing Christian is at issue between you . . . let yourselves be advised and attack these matters with justice, not with force or strife, and do not start an endless bloodshed in Germany!

We have no one on earth to thank for this mischievous rebellion, except you lords and princes, especially you blind bishops and mad priests and monks . . . In your government you do nothing but flay and rob your subjects in order that you may lead a life of splendor and pride, until the poor common folk can bear it no longer . . .

[As for] the peasants, they must take the name and title of a people who fight because they will not and ought not endure wrong or evil, according to the teaching of nature. You should have that name, and let the name of Christ alone . . . [As for your so-called 'Christian' demands for] freedom of game, birds, fish, wood, forests, labor services, tithes, imposts, excises, and release from the death tax, these I leave to the lawyers, for they are things that do not concern a Christian who is a martyr on this earth . . . Let the name of Christian alone and act in some other name, as men and women who want human and natural rights.

Sources: *A Sincere Admonition to Peace*, cited by Ozment, *Age of Reform*, p. 283 [first paragraph]; cited by Steven Ozment, *The Age of Reform* (New Haven, CT:, Yale University Press, 1980), pp. 280–282, [second and third paragraphs].

II. Martin Luther, *Against the Robbing and Murdering Peasants* (1525)

FINAL WORDS

[The princes] should have no mercy on obstinate, hardened, blinded peasants who refuse to listen to reason. Let everyone, as he is able, strike, hew, stab, and slay, as though among mad dogs, so that by doing so he may show mercy to those [non-rebelling peasants] who have been ruined, put to flight, and led astray by these rebelling peasants [so that] peace and safety may return . . .

Source: Ozment, *The Age of Reform*, p. 284.

III. *An Open Letter Concerning the Hard Book Against the Peasants* (1525)

FINAL WORDS

Suppose I were to break into a man's house, rape his wife and daughters, break open his coffers, take his money, set a sword to his breast and say: 'If you will not put up with this, I shall run you through, for you are a godless wretch.' Then if a crowd gathered and were about to kill me for doing this, or if the judge ordered my head off, suppose I were to cry out: 'But Christ teaches that you are to be merciful and not kill me.' What would people say then? Well, that is exactly what my peasants and their advocates are doing now. The kingdom of this world is nothing else than the servant of God's wrath upon the wicked and it is a real precursor of hell and everlasting death. It should not be merciful, but strict, severe, and wrathful in the fulfillment of its works and duty. Its tool is not a wreath or roses or a flower of love, but a naked sword.

From the start I had two fears. If the peasants became lords, the devil would become abbot; if these tyrants became lords, the devil's dam would become abbess. Therefore I wanted to do two things: quiet the peasants and instruct the lords. The peasants were unwilling, and now they have their reward. The lords will not hear, and they shall have their reward also.

Sources: An Open Letter Concerning the Hard Book Against the peasants, cited by Ozment, Age of Reform, p. 286-287 [first paragraph]; Ozment, *The Age of Reform*, p. 287, [second and third paragraph].

IV. Albrecht Dürer, *Memorial to the Peasants' Revolt* (1527)

Dürer's "Memorial to the Peasants," drawn in 1527, the year before his death, appeared in a book devoted to 'perspective in art.' Fearing that Protestant iconoclasm (destruction of icons) and the coming of religious wars would remove decorative art from the churches, his book was to be a primer for artists who in the aftermath of such destruction would have to learn the art of painting all over again. The sketch shows a peasant sitting atop a chicken coop with a sword thrust through his back, the classic iconography of betrayal.

At this time Dürer's peers, friends, and associates condemned the Peasants' Revolt as strongly as Luther. During the war Dürer painted portraits of the Fuggers, the great merchant family the peasants despised, and also Margrave Casimir of Brandenburg-Ansbach, a brutal slayer of peasants and Anabaptists. Within this context might Dürer's slain rebellious peasant, like Luther's, have gotten his just due?

Source: Joseph Leo Koerner, *The Moment of Self-Portraiture in Renaissance Art* (Chicago: Chicago University Press, 1993), p. 235.

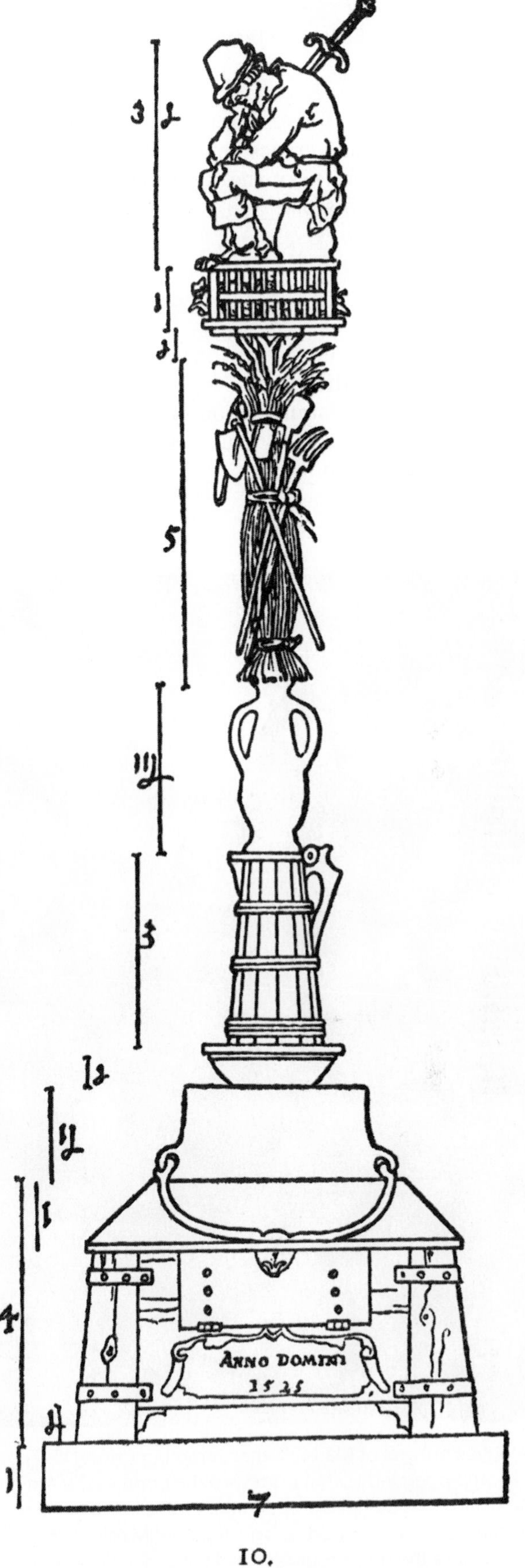

10.

The caption reads: "He who wants to commemorate his victory over the rebellious peasants might use to that end a structure such as I portray here." Illustration from Jane Campbell Hutchinson, *Albrecht Dürer: A Biography* (Princeton, NJ: Princeton University Press, 1990)

German Reformation would not have survived beyond the 1520s. Still, many critics believe that Luther's decision ended the promise of the Reformation as a social and moral force in history.

▼ The Reformation Elsewhere

Although the German Reformation was the first, Switzerland and France had their own independent church reform movements almost simultaneously with Germany's. From them developed new churches as prominent and lasting as the Lutheran.

A Catholic Portrayal of Martin Luther Tempting Christ (1547). Reformation propaganda often portrayed the pope as the Antichrist or the devil. Here Catholic propaganda turns the tables on the Protestant reformers by portraying a figure of Martin Luther as the devil (note the monstrous feet and tail under his academic robes). Re-creating the biblical scene of Christ being tempted by the devil in the wilderness, the figure of Luther asks Christ to transform stone into bread, to which temptation Christ responds by saying that humans do not live by bread alone. Versucung Christi, 1547, Gemälde, Bonn, Rheinisches Landesmuseum, Inv. Nr. 58.3

Zwingli and the Swiss Reformation

Switzerland was a loose confederacy of thirteen autonomous *cantons*, or states, and their allied areas. (See Map 11–2.) Some cantons became Protestant, some remained Catholic, and a few others managed to effect a compromise. There were two main preconditions of the Swiss Reformation. First was the growth of national sentiment occasioned by popular opposition to foreign mercenary service. (Providing mercenaries for Europe's warring nations was a major source of Switzerland's livelihood.) Second was a desire for church reform that had persisted in Switzerland since the councils of Constance (1414–1417) and Basel (1431–1449).

The Reformation in Zurich Ulrich Zwingli (1484–1531), the leader of the Swiss Reformation, had been humanistically educated. He credited Erasmus over Luther with having set him on the path to reform. He served as a chaplain with Swiss mercenaries who were on the losing side in the disastrous Battle of Marignano in Italy in 1515. Thereafter he became an eloquent critic of Swiss mercenary service, believing it threatened both the political sovereignty and the moral fiber of the Swiss confederacy. By 1518, Zwingli was also widely known for his opposition to the sale of indulgences and to religious superstition.

In 1519, he competed for the post of people's priest in the main church of Zurich. His candidacy was initially questioned after he acknowledged fornicating with a barber's daughter, who had since delivered a child. Zwingli successfully minimized the affair, claiming the woman in question had been a skilled seducer, and denying any paternity as she had had affairs with other men as well. Zwingli's conduct was not so scandalous to contemporaries, who sympathized with the plight of a celibate clergy. One of Zwingli's first acts as a reformer was to petition for an end to clerical celibacy and for the right of clergy legally to marry, a practice accepted in all Protestant lands.

From his new position as people's priest in Zurich, Zwingli engineered the Swiss Reformation. In March 1522, he was party to the breaking of the Lenten fast—then an act of protest analogous to burning one's national flag today. Zwingli's reform guideline was simple and effective: Whatever lacked literal support in Scripture was to be neither believed nor practiced. As had also happened with Luther, that test soon raised questions about such honored traditional teachings and practices as fasting, transubstantiation, the worship of saints, pilgrimages, purgatory, clerical celibacy, and certain sacraments. A disputation held on January 29, 1523, concluded with the city government's sanction of Zwingli's Scripture test. (See "Zwingli Lists the Errors of the Roman Church," page 326.) Thereafter Zurich became the center of the Swiss Reformation. The new regime imposed a harsh discipline that made the city one of the first examples of puritanical Protestantism.

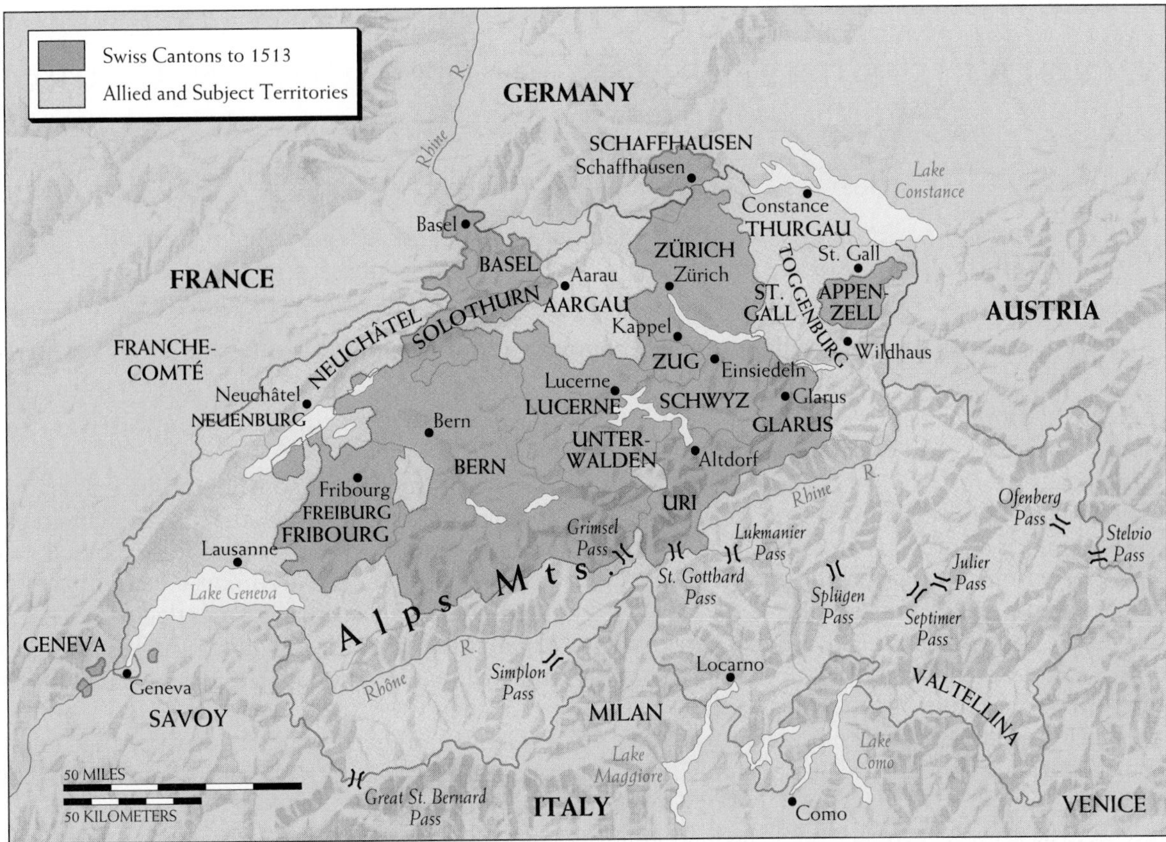

Map 11–2 **THE SWISS CONFEDERATION** Although nominally still a part of the Holy Roman Empire, Switzerland grew from a loose defensive union of the central "forest cantons" in the thirteenth century into a fiercely independent association of regions with different languages, histories, and, finally, religions.

The Marburg Colloquy Landgrave Philip of Hesse (1504–1567) sought to unite Swiss and German Protestants in a mutual defense pact. However, Luther's and Zwingli's bitter theological differences, especially over the nature of Christ's presence in the Eucharist, spoiled his efforts. Zwingli favored a symbolic interpretation of Christ's words, "This is my body." Christ, he argued, was spiritually, not bodily, present in the bread and wine of the Eucharist. Luther, to the contrary, insisted that Christ's human nature was such that it shared the properties of his divine nature. Hence, where Christ was spiritually present, he could also be bodily present, for such was his special human nature. Luther wanted no part of an abstract, spiritualized Christ, while Zwingli feared Luther was still mired in medieval sacramental theology.

Philip of Hesse brought the two Protestant leaders together in his castle in Marburg in early October 1529, to work out their differences. However, the effort proved to be in vain. Luther left thinking Zwingli a dangerous fanatic, forevermore to paint him black. Although cooperation between the two Protestant sides did not cease altogether, the disagreement splintered the Protestant movement theologically and politically. Separate defense leagues formed, and semi-Zwinglian theological views came to be embodied in the non-Lutheran *Tetrapolitan Confession* prepared by the Strasbourg reformers Martin Bucer and Caspar Hedio in 1530.

Swiss Civil Wars As the Swiss cantons divided themselves between Protestantism and Catholicism, civil wars erupted. There were two major battles, both at Kappel, one in June 1529 and a second in October 1531. The first ended in a Protestant victory, which forced the Catholic cantons to break their foreign alliances and to recognize the rights of Swiss Protestants. After the second battle, Zwingli lay wounded on the battlefield, and when discovered, he was unceremoniously executed, his remains thereafter hacked into pieces and scattered to the four winds so his followers would have no relics to console and inspire them. The subsequent treaty confirmed the right of each canton to determine its own religion. Heinrich Bullinger (1504–1575), Zwingli's protégé and later son-in-law, became the new leader of the Swiss Reformation and guided its development into an established religion, eventually to merge with Calvinism.

ZWINGLI LISTS THE ERRORS OF THE ROMAN CHURCH

Prior to the first Zurich Disputation (1523), which effectually introduced the Protestant Reformation in Zurich, the reformer Zwingli prepared such a summary of the errors of the Roman Church known as the Sixty-Seven Articles. *Here are some of them.*

How do Zwingli's basic religious views compare with those of Martin Luther?

All who consider other teachings equal to or higher than the Gospel err, and they do not know what the Gospel is.

In the faith rests our salvation, and in unbelief our damnation; for all truth is clear in Christ.

In the Gospel one learns that human doctrines and decrees do not aid in salvation.

That Christ, having sacrificed himself once, is to eternity a certain and valid sacrifice for the sins of all faithful, wherefrom it follows that the Mass is not a sacrifice, but is a remembrance of the sacrifice and assurance of the salvation which Christ has given us.

That God desires to give us all things in his name, whence it follows that outside of this life we need no [intercession of the saints or any] mediator except himself.

That no Christian is bound to do those things which God has not decreed, therefore one may eat at all times all food, where from one learns that the decree about cheese and butter is a Roman swindle.

That no special person can impose the ban upon anyone, but the Church, that is, the congregation of those among whom the one to be banned dwells, together with their watchman, i.e., the pastor.

All that the spiritual so-called state [i.e., the papal church] claims to have of power and protection belongs to the lay [i.e., the secular magistracy], if they wish to be Christians.

Greater offence I know not than that one does not allow priests to have wives, but permits them to hire prostitutes.

Christ has borne all our pains and labor. Hence whoever assigns to works of penance what belongs to Christ errs and slanders God.

The true divine Scriptures know naught about purgatory after this life.

The Scriptures know no priests except those who proclaim the word of God.

Ulrich Zwingli (1484–1531), *Selected Works*, ed. by Samuel M. Jackson (Philadelphia: University of Pennsylvania Press, 1972), pp. 111–117.

Anabaptists and Radical Protestants

The moderate pace and seemingly low ethical results of the Lutheran and Zwinglian reformations discontented many people, among them some of the original followers of Luther and Zwingli. These were devout fundamentalist Protestants who desired a more rapid and thorough implementation of Apostolic Christianity. They accused the reform movements that went before them of having gone only halfway. The most important of these radical groups were the **Anabaptists**, the sixteenth-century ancestors of the modern Mennonites and Amish. The Anabaptists were especially distinguished by their rejection of infant baptism and their insistence on only adult baptism, as was the case with Jesus, who was baptized as an adult. (The term *Anabaptism* derives from the Greek word meaning "to rebaptize.") Only a thoughtful consenting adult, able to understand the Scriptures and what the biblical way of life required, could enter the covenant of faith.

Although Luther and Zwingli also taught that believers must believe for themselves (Luther called it the "priesthood of all believers"), they retained the historical practice of infant baptism, despite the absence of any clear biblical mandate. They argued that the congregation "believed for the infant," stood in his or her place, and pledged to raise the baptized infant in the faith. Here, the communal nature and responsibility of the church was deemed to be more basic to Christianity than the radical individualism the Anabaptists asserted.

Conrad Grebel and the Swiss Brethren Conrad Grebel (1498–1526), with whom Anabaptism originated, performed the first adult rebaptism in Zurich in January 1525. Initially a co-worker of Zwingli's and an even greater biblical literalist, Grebel broke openly with him.

In a religious disputation in October 1523, Zwingli supported the city government's plea for a peaceful, gradual removal of resented traditional religious practices—not the rush to perfection the Anabaptists demand.

The alternative of the Swiss Brethren, as Grebel's group came to be called, was embodied in the *Schleitheim Confession* of 1527. This document distinguished Anabaptists not only by their practice of adult baptism, but also by their pacifism, refusal to swear oaths, and nonparticipation in the offices of secular government. By both choice and coercion, Anabaptists physically separated from established society to form a more perfect communion modeled on the first Christians. Because of the close connection between religious and civic life in the sixteenth century, the political authorities also viewed such separatism as a threat to basic social bonds, even as a form of sedition.

The Anabaptist Reign in Münster At first, Anabaptism drew adherents from all social classes. As Lutherans and Zwinglians joined with Catholics in opposition and persecuted them within the cities, however, a more rural, agrarian class came to make up the great majority of Anabaptists. In 1529, rebaptism became a capital offense within the Holy Roman Empire. At least 1,000 and perhaps as many as 5,000 men and women were executed for rebaptizing themselves as adults between 1525 and 1618.

Brutal measures were universally applied against nonconformists after Anabaptist extremists came to power in the German city of Münster in 1534–1535. Led by two Dutch emigrants, a baker, Jan Matthys of Haarlem, and a tailor, Jan Beukelsz of Leiden, the Anabaptists in Münster forced Lutherans and Catholics in the city either to convert or to emigrate. After their departure, the city was blockaded by besieging armies. Under such pressures, Münster was transformed into an Old Testament theocracy, replete with charismatic leaders and the practice of polygamy. The latter was implemented as a measure of social control to deal with the many recently widowed and deserted women left behind in the city. Women opposed to the practice were allowed to leave polygymous marriages.

These developments shocked the outside world, and Protestant and Catholic armies united to crush the radicals. The skeletons of their leaders long hung in public view as a warning to all who would so offend traditional Christian sensitivities. After this episode, moderate, pacifistic Anabaptism became the norm among most nonconformists. Menno Simons (1496–1561), the founder of the Mennonites, set an example of non-provocative separatist Anabaptism, which became the historical form in which Anabaptist sects survived down to the present.

Spiritualists Another diverse and highly individualistic group of Protestant dissenters was the Spiritualists. These were mostly isolated individuals distinguished by their disdain for external, institutional religion. They believed the only religious authority was the Spirit of God, which spoke not in some past revelation, but here and now in the heart and mind of every listening individual. Among them were several renegade Lutherans. Thomas Müntzer (d. 1525), who had close contacts with Anabaptist leaders in Germany and Switzerland, died as a leader of a peasants' revolt in Frankenhausen, Germany. Sebastian Franck (d. 1541), a critic of all dogmatic religion, proclaimed the religious autonomy and freedom of every individual soul. Caspar Schwenckfeld (d. 1561) was a prolific writer and wanderer after whom the Schwenckfeldian Church is named.

Antitrinitarians A final group of persecuted radical Protestants also destined for prominence in the modern world was the Antitrinitarians. These were exponents of a commonsense, rational, and ethical religion. Prominent among them were the Spaniard Michael Servetus (1511–1553), executed in 1553 in Geneva at the encouragement of John Calvin for "blasphemies against the Holy Trinity." The Italians, Lelio (d. 1562) and Faustus Sozzini (d. 1604), the founders of Socinianism, also stand out. These thinkers were the strongest opponents of Calvinism, especially its belief in original sin and **predestination**, and have a deserved reputation as defenders of religious toleration.

John Calvin and the Genevan Reformation

In the second half of the sixteenth century, Calvinism replaced Lutheranism as the dominant Protestant force in Europe. Calvinism was the religious ideology that inspired or accompanied massive political resistance in France, the Netherlands, and Scotland. During the reign of Elector Frederick III (r. 1559–1576) Calvinism established itself within the geographical region of the Palatinate, the German state in the Rhineland in which the Thirty Years' War, the worst of the wars of religion, would break out in 1618. Calvinists believed strongly in both divine predestination and the individual's responsibility to reorder society according to God's plan. They were determined to transform society so men and women lived their lives externally as they professed to believe internally and were presumably destined to live eternally.

The namesake of Calvinism and its perfect embodiment, John Calvin (1509–1564), was born into a well-to-do French family, the son of the secretary to the bishop of Noyon. At age twelve, he received church *benefices* that financed the best possible education at Parisian colleges and a law degree. In the 1520s, he identified with the French reform party. Although he would finally reject this group as ineffectual compromisers, its members contributed much to his intellectual preparation as a religious reformer.

A portrait of the young John Calvin. Bibliothèque Publique et Universitaire, Geneva

It was probably in the spring of 1534 that Calvin experienced that conversion to Protestantism by which he said his "long stubborn heart" was "made teachable" by God. His own hard experience became a personal model of reform by which he would measure the recalcitrant citizenry of Geneva. His mature theology stressed the sovereignty of God's will over all creation and the necessity of humankind's conformity to it. In May 1534, he dramatically surrendered the *benefices* that had educated him and joined the budding Reformation in Geneva.

Political Revolt and Religious Reform in Geneva Whereas in Saxony religious reform paved the way for a political revolution against the emperor, in Geneva a political revolution against the local prince-bishop laid the foundation for the religious change. Genevans revolted against their resident prince-bishop in the late 1520s, and the city council assumed his legal and political powers in 1527.

In late 1533, the Protestant city of Bern dispatched two reformers to Geneva: Guillaume Farel (1489–1565) and Antoine Froment (1508–1581). In the summer of 1535, after much internal turmoil, the Protestants triumphed, and the traditional Mass and other religious practices were removed. On May 21, 1536, Geneva voted officially to adopt the Reformation: "to live according to the Gospel and the Word of God . . . without any more Masses, statues, idols, or other papal abuses."

Calvin arrived in Geneva after these events, in July 1536. He was actually en route to a scholarly refuge in Strasbourg, in flight from the persecution of Protestants in France, when warring between France and Spain forced him to turn sharply south to Geneva. Farel persuaded him to stay in the city and assist the Reformation, threatening Calvin with divine vengeance if he turned away from this task.

Calvin drew up articles for the governance of the new church, as well as a catechism to guide and discipline the people. Both were presented for approval to the city councils in early 1537. Because of the strong measures they proposed to govern Geneva's moral life, many suspected the reformers were intent on creating a "new papacy." Opponents feared Calvin and Farel were going too far too fast. Geneva's powerful Protestant ally, Bern, which had adopted a more moderate Protestant reform, pressured Geneva's magistrates to restore traditional religious ceremonies and holidays that Calvin and Farel had abolished. When the reformers opposed these actions, they were exiled from the city.

Calvin went to Strasbourg, a model Protestant city, where he became pastor to French exiles and wrote biblical commentaries. He also produced a second edition of his masterful *Institutes of the Christian Religion*, which many consider the definitive theological statement of the Protestant faith. Most importantly, he learned from the Strasbourg reformer Martin Bucer how to achieve his goals.

Calvin's Geneva In 1540, Geneva elected officials both favorable to Calvin and determined to establish full Genevan political and religious independence from Bern. They knew Calvin would be a valuable ally in that undertaking and invited him to return. This he did in September 1540, never to leave the city again. Within months of his return, the city implemented new ecclesiastical ordinances that provided for cooperation between the magistrates and the clergy in matters of internal discipline.

Following the Strasbourg model, the Genevan Church was organized into four offices: (1) pastors, of whom there were five; (2) teachers or doctors to instruct the populace in, and to defend, true doctrine; (3) elders, a group of twelve laypeople chosen by and from the Genevan councils and empowered to "oversee the life of everybody"; and (4) deacons to dispense church goods and services to the poor and the sick.

The controversial doctrine of predestination was at the center of Calvin's theology as justification by faith was at Luther's. Both doctrines have been criticized,

Luther's for seeming to deny the believer's need to do good works and Calvin's for seeming to deny the existence of human free will. Luther believed works were a mark of a true Christian, even though they did not make him such or save him. Calvin did not discuss predestination until the end of his great theological work, the *Institutes of the Christian Religion*. Explaining why he delayed its discussion, he described predestination as a doctrine only for mature Christians. Whereas it offended nonbelievers, true Christians might take consolation from it. For true believers, predestination recognized that the world and all who dwell in it are in God's hands from eternity to eternity, regardless of all else. When the world seems utterly godless and the devil to be its only lord, the true Christian takes consolation from the knowledge that his present life and future destiny are determined irrevocably by a loving and ever-lasting God. By believing that, and living as the Bible instructed them to do, Calvinists found consoling, presumptive evidence that they were among God's elect.

Possessed of such assurance, Calvinists turned their energies to transforming society spiritually and morally. Faith, Calvin taught, did not sit idly in the mind but conformed one's every action to God's law. The "elect" should at least live in a manifestly God-pleasing way if they are truly God's "elect." In the attempted realization of that goal, Calvin spared no effort. The consistory, or Geneva's regulatory court, became his instrument of power. Composed of the elders and the pastors and presided over by one of the city's chief magistrates that body implemented the strictest moral discipline.

Among the personal conflicts in Geneva that gave Calvin the reputation of a stern moralist, none proved more damaging than his role in the capture and execution in 1553 of the Spanish physician and amateur theologian Michael Servetus, who had already been condemned by the Inquisition for heresy. He died at the stake in Protestant Geneva for denying the doctrine of the Trinity, a subject on which he had written a book scandalous to church authorities.

After 1555, Geneva became home to thousands of exiled Protestants who had been driven out of France, England, and Scotland. Refugees numbering more than 5,000, most of them utterly loyal to Calvin, made up more than one third of Geneva's population. All of Geneva's magistrates were now devout Calvinists, greatly strengthening Calvin's position in the city.

To the thousands of persecuted Protestants who flocked to Geneva in mid-century, the city was a beacon and a refuge, Europe's only free city. During Calvin's lifetime, Geneva also gained the reputation of being a "woman's paradise" because its laws severely punished men who beat their wives, behavior deemed unbefitting a true Calvinist Christian.

▼ Political Consolidation of the Lutheran Reformation

By 1530, the Reformation was in Europe to stay. It would, however, take several decades and major attempts to eradicate it, before all would recognize this fact. With the political triumph of Lutheranism in the empire by the 1550s, Protestant movements elsewhere gained a new lease on life.

The Diet of Augsburg

Charles V devoted most of his first decade as emperor to the pursuit of politics and military campaigns outside the empire, particularly in Spain and Italy. In 1530, he returned to the empire to direct the Diet of Augsburg. This assembly of Protestant and Catholic representatives had been called to address the growing religious division within the empire in the wake of the Reformation's success. With its terms dictated by the Catholic emperor, the diet adjourned with a blunt and unrealistic order to all Lutherans to revert to Catholicism.

The Reformation was by this time too firmly established for that to occur. In February 1531, the Lutherans responded with the formation of their own defensive alliance, the Schmalkaldic League. The league took as its banner the **Augsburg Confession**, a moderate statement of Protestant beliefs that had been spurned by the emperor at the Diet of Augsburg. In 1538, Luther drew up a more strongly worded Protestant confession known as the *Schmalkaldic Articles*. Under the leadership of Landgrave Philip of Hesse and Elector John Frederick of Saxony, the league achieved a stalemate with the emperor, who was again distracted by renewed war with France and the ever-resilient Turks.

The Expansion of the Reformation

In the 1530s, German Lutherans formed regional consistories, judicial bodies composed of theologians and lawyers, which oversaw and administered the new Protestant churches and replaced the old Catholic episcopates. Educational reforms provided for compulsory primary education, schools for girls, a humanist revision of the traditional curriculum, and instruction of the laity in the new religion.

The Reformation also entrenched itself elsewhere. Introduced into Denmark by King Christian II (r. 1513–1523), Lutheranism thrived there under Frederick I (r. 1523–1533), who joined the Schmalkaldic League. Under Christian III (r. 1536–1559), Lutheranism became the official state religion.

In Sweden, King Gustavus Vasa (r. 1523–1560), supported by a Swedish nobility greedy for church lands, embraced Lutheranism, confiscated church property, and subjected the clergy to royal authority at the Diet of Vesteras (1527).

In politically splintered Poland, Lutherans, Anabaptists, Calvinists, and even Antitrinitarians found room to practice their beliefs. Primarily because of the absence of a central political authority, Poland became a model of religious pluralism and toleration in the second half of the sixteenth century.

Reaction Against Protestants

Charles V made abortive efforts in 1540–1541 to enforce a compromise between Protestants and Catholics. As these and other conciliar efforts failed, he turned to a military solution. In 1547, imperial armies crushed the Protestant Schmalkaldic League, defeating and capturing John Frederick of Saxony and Philip of Hesse.

The emperor established puppet rulers in Saxony and Hesse and issued an imperial law mandating that Protestants everywhere readopt old Catholic beliefs and practices. Protestants were granted a few cosmetic concessions, for example, clerical marriage (with papal approval of individual cases) and communion in both bread and wine. Many Protestant leaders went into exile. In Germany, the city of Magdeburg became a refuge for persecuted Protestants and the center of Lutheran resistance.

The Peace of Augsburg

The Reformation was too entrenched by 1547 to be ended even by brute force. Maurice of Saxony, handpicked by Charles V to rule Saxony, had recognized the inevitable and shifted his allegiance to the Lutherans. Confronted by fierce resistance and weary from three decades of war, the emperor was forced to relent. After a defeat by Protestant armies in 1552, Charles reinstated the Protestant leaders and guaranteed Lutherans religious freedoms in the Peace of Passau (August 1552). With this declaration, he effectively surrendered his lifelong quest for European religious unity.

The Peace of Augsburg in September 1555 made the division of Christendom permanent. This agreement recognized in law what had already been well established in practice: *Cuius regio, eius religio,* meaning the ruler of a land would determine its religion. Lutherans were permitted to retain all church lands forcibly seized before 1552. An "ecclesiastical reservation" was added, however, that was intended to prevent high Catholic prelates who converted to Protestantism from taking their lands, titles, and privileges with them. People discontented with the religion of their region were permitted to migrate to another.

The Peace of Augsburg did not extend official recognition to Calvinism and Anabaptism as legal forms of Christian belief and practice. Anabaptists had long adjusted to such exclusion by forming their own separatist communities. Calvinists, however, were not separatists. They remained determined to secure the right to worship publicly as they pleased, and to shape society according to their own religious convictions. While Anabaptists retreated and Lutherans enjoyed the security of an established religion, Calvinists organized to lead national revolutions throughout northern Europe in the second half of the sixteenth century.

▼ The English Reformation to 1553

Late medieval England had a well-earned reputation for maintaining the rights of the crown against the pope. Edward I (r. 1272–1307) had rejected efforts by Pope Boniface VIII to prevent secular taxation of the clergy. Statutes of Provisors and Praemunire passed in the mid-fourteenth century laid a foundation for curtailing payments and judicial appeals to Rome rejecting papal appointments in England. Lollardy, humanism, and widespread anticlerical sentiments prepared the way for Protestant ideas, which entered England in the early sixteenth century.

The Preconditions of Reform

In the early 1520s, future English reformers met in Cambridge to discuss Lutheran writings smuggled into England by merchants and scholars. One of these future reformers was William Tyndale (ca. 1492–1536), who translated the New Testament into English in 1524–1525 while in Germany. Printed in Cologne and Worms, Tyndale's New Testament began to circulate in England in 1526.

Cardinal Thomas Wolsey (ca. 1475–1530), the chief minister of King Henry VIII (r. 1509–1547), and Sir Thomas More (1478–1535), Wolsey's successor, guided royal opposition to incipient English Protestantism. The king himself defended the seven sacraments against Luther, receiving as a reward the title "Defender of the Faith" from Pope Leo X. Following Luther's intemperate reply to Henry's amateur theological attack, More wrote a lengthy *Response to Luther* in 1523.

The King's Affair

Lollardy and humanism may have provided some native seeds for religious reform, but it was Henry's unhappy marriage to Catherine of Aragon (d. 1536) and obsession to get a male heir that broke the soil and allowed the seeds to take root. In 1509, Henry had married Catherine, the daughter of Ferdinand and Isabella of Spain and the aunt of Emperor Charles V. By 1527, the union had produced only one surviving child, a daughter, Mary. Although women could inherit the throne, Henry fretted over the political consequences of leaving only a female heir. In this period, people believed it unnatural for women to rule over men. At best a woman ruler foreshadowed a contested reign, at worst turmoil and revolution. By the end of the century, Elizabeth's strong rule would expose such fears as greatly exaggerated.

Henry came even to believe that God had cursed his union with Catherine, who had many miscarriages and stillbirths. The reason lay in Catherine's previous marriage to Henry's brother Arthur. After Arthur's premature death, Henry's father, Henry VII, betrothed her to Henry to keep the English alliance with Spain intact. The two were wed in 1509, a few days before Henry VIII received his crown. Because marriage to the wife of one's brother was prohibited by both canon and biblical law (see Leviticus 18:16, 20:21), the marriage had required a special dispensation from Pope Julius II.

By 1527, Henry was also thoroughly enamored of Anne Boleyn, one of Catherine's ladies-in-waiting. He determined to put Catherine aside and take Anne as his wife. This he could not do in Catholic England, however, without a papal annulment of the marriage to Catherine. Therein lay a special problem. 1527 was also the year when imperial soldiers fighting in Italy mutinied and sacked Rome. Pope Clement VII was then a prisoner of Emperor Charles V, who also happened to be Catherine's nephew, and he was not about to encourage the pope to annul the royal marriage. Even if such coercion had not existed, it would have been virtually impossible for the pope to grant an annulment of a marriage that not only had survived for eighteen years but had also been made possible in the first place by a special papal dispensation.

Cardinal Wolsey, who aspired to become pope, was placed in charge of securing the royal annulment. Lord Chancellor since 1515 and papal legate-at-large since 1518, Wolsey had long been Henry's heavy and the object of much popular resentment. When he failed to secure the annulment through no fault of his own, he was dismissed in disgrace in 1529. Thomas Cranmer (1489–1556) and Thomas Cromwell (1485–1540), both of whom harbored Lutheran sympathies, thereafter became the king's closest advisers. Finding the way to a papal annulment closed, Henry's new advisers struck a different course: Why not simply declare the king supreme in English spiritual affairs as he was in English temporal affairs? Then the king could settle the king's affair himself.

The "Reformation Parliament"

In 1529, Parliament convened for what would be a seven-year session that earned it the title of the "Reformation Parliament." During this period, it passed a flood of legislation that harassed, and finally placed royal reins on, the clergy. In so doing, it established a precedent that would remain a feature of English government: Whenever fundamental changes are made in religion, the monarch must consult with and work through Parliament. In January 1531, the Convocation (a legislative assembly representing the English clergy) publicly recognized Henry as head of the church in England "as far as the law of Christ allows." In 1532, Parliament published official grievances against the church, ranging from alleged indifference to the needs of the laity to an excessive number of religious holidays. In the same year, Parliament passed the Submission of the Clergy, which effectively placed canon law under royal control and thereby the clergy under royal jurisdiction.

Hans Holbein the Younger (1497–1543) was the most famous portrait painter of the Reformation. Here he portrays a seemingly almighty Henry VIII. © Scala / Art Resource

In January 1533, Henry wed the pregnant Anne Boleyn, with Thomas Cranmer officiating. In February 1533, Parliament made the king the highest court of appeal for all English subjects. In March 1533, Cranmer became archbishop of Canterbury and led the Convocation in invalidating the king's marriage to Catherine. In 1534, Parliament ended all payments by the English clergy and laity to Rome and gave Henry sole jurisdiction over high ecclesiastical appointments. The Act of Succession in the same year made Anne Boleyn's children legitimate heirs to the throne, and the **Act of Supremacy** declared Henry "the only supreme head in earth of the Church of England."

When Thomas More and John Fisher, bishop of Rochester, refused to recognize the Act of Succession and the Act of Supremacy, Henry had them executed, making clear his determination to have his way regardless of the cost. In 1536 and 1538, Parliament dissolved England's monasteries and nunneries.

Wives of Henry VIII

Henry's domestic life lacked the consistency of his political life. In 1536, Anne Boleyn was executed for alleged treason and adultery, and her daughter Elizabeth, like Elizabeth's half sister Mary before her, was declared illegitimate by her father. Henry had four more marriages. His third wife, Jane Seymour, died in 1537 shortly after giving birth to the future Edward VI. Henry wed Anne of Cleves sight unseen on the advice of Cromwell, the purpose being to create by the marriage an alliance with the Protestant princes of Germany. Neither the alliance nor the marriage proved worth the trouble; the marriage was annulled by Parliament, and Cromwell was dismissed and executed. Catherine Howard, Henry's fifth wife, was beheaded for adultery in 1542. His last wife, Catherine Parr, a patron of humanists and reformers, for whom Henry was the third husband, survived him to marry still a fourth time—obviously she was a match for the English king.

The King's Religious Conservatism

Henry's boldness in politics and domestic affairs did not extend to religion. True, because of Henry's actions, the pope had ceased to be head of the English church and English Bibles were placed in English churches, but despite the break with Rome, Henry remained decidedly conservative in his religious beliefs. With the Ten Articles of 1536, he made only mild concessions to Protestant tenets. Otherwise Catholic doctrine was maintained in a country filled with Protestant sentiment. Despite his many wives and amorous adventures, Henry forbade the English clergy to marry and threatened to execute clergy who were caught twice in concubinage.

Angered by the growing popularity of Protestant views, even among his chief advisers, Henry struck directly at them in the Six Articles of 1539. These reaffirmed transubstantiation, denied the Eucharistic cup to the laity, declared celibate vows inviolable, provided for private Masses, and ordered the continuation of oral confession. Protestants referred to the articles as the "whip with six stings," a clear warning from the king that religious reform would not race ahead in England during his reign. Although William Tyndale's English New Testament grew into the Coverdale Bible (1535) and the Great Bible (1539), and the latter was mandated for every English parish, England had to await Henry's death before it could become a genuinely Protestant country.

The Protestant Reformation under Edward VI

When Henry died in 1547, his son and successor, Edward VI (d. 1553), was only ten years old. Edward reigned under the successive regencies of Edward Seymour, who became the duke of Somerset (1547–1550), and the earl of Warwick, who became known as the duke of Northumberland (1550–1553). During this time, England enacted Protestant Reformation. The new king and Somerset cor-

MAIN EVENTS OF THE ENGLISH REFORMATION

1529	Reformation Parliament convenes
1532	Parliament passes the Submission of the Clergy
1533	Henry VIII weds Anne Boleyn; Convocation invalidates marriage to Catherine of Aragon
1534	Act of Succession makes Anne Boleyn's children legitimate heirs to the English throne
1534	Act of Supremacy declares Henry VIII "the only supreme head of the Church of England"
1535	Thomas More executed for opposition to Acts of Succession and Supremacy
1535	Publication of Coverdale Bible
1539	Henry VIII imposes the Six Articles
1547	Edward VI succeeds to the throne under protectorships of Somerset and Northumberland
1549	First Act of Uniformity imposes *Book of Common Prayer* on English churches
1553–1558	Mary Tudor restores Catholic doctrine
1558–1603	Elizabeth I fashions an Anglican religious settlement

responded directly with John Calvin. During Somerset's regency, Henry's Six Articles and laws against Protestant heresy were repealed, and clerical marriage and communion with cup were sanctioned.

In 1547, the chantries, places where endowed Masses had traditionally been said for the dead, were dissolved. In 1549, the Act of Uniformity imposed Thomas Cranmer's *Book of Common Prayer* on all English churches. Images and altars were removed from the churches in 1550. After Charles V's victory over the German princes in 1547, German Protestant leaders had fled to England for refuge. Several of these refugees, with Martin Bucer prominent among them, now directly assisted the completion of the English Reformation.

The Second Act of Uniformity, passed in 1552, imposed a revised *Book of Common Prayer* on all English churches. A forty-two-article confession of faith, also written by Thomas Cranmer, set forth a moderate Protestant doctrine. It taught justification by faith and the supremacy of Holy Scripture, denied transubstantiation (although not the real presence), and recognized only two sacraments.

All these changes were short-lived, however. In 1553, Catherine of Aragon's daughter succeeded Edward (who had died in his teens) to the throne as Mary I (d. 1558) and restored Catholic doctrine and practice with a single-mindedness rivaling that of her father. It was not until the reign of Anne Boleyn's daughter, Elizabeth I (r. 1558–1603), that England worked out a lasting religious settlement.

▾ Catholic Reform and Counter-Reformation

The Protestant Reformation did not take the medieval church completely by surprise. There were many internal criticisms and efforts at reform before there was a Counter-Reformation in reaction to Protestant successes.

Sources of Catholic Reform

Before the Reformation began, ambitious proposals had been made for church reform. But sixteenth-century popes, ever mindful of how the councils of Constance and Basel had stripped the pope of his traditional powers, squelched such efforts to change the laws and institutions of the church.

Despite such papal foot-dragging, the old church was not without its reformers. Many new religious orders also sprang up in the sixteenth century to lead a broad revival of piety within the church. The first of these orders was the Theatines, founded in 1524 to groom devout and reform-minded leaders at the higher levels of the church hierarchy. One of the co-founders was Bishop Gian Pietro Carafa, who would be Pope Paul IV (r. 1555–1559). Another new order, whose mission pointed in the opposite direction, was the Capuchins. Recognized by the pope in 1528, they sought to return to the original ideals of Saint Francis and became popular among the ordinary people to whom they directed their ministry. The Somaschi, who became active in the mid-1520s, and the Barnabites, founded in 1530, worked to repair the moral, spiritual, and physical damage done to people in war-torn Italy.

For women, there was the influential new order of Ursulines. Founded in 1535, it established convents in Italy and France for the religious education of girls from all social classes. Another new order, the Oratorians, officially recognized in 1575, was an elite group of clerics devoted to the promotion of religious literature and church music. Among their members was the great hymnist and musician Giovanni Perluigi da Palestrina (1526–1594).

In addition to these lay and clerical movements, the mystical piety of medieval monasticism was revived and popularized by two Spanish mystics, Saint Teresa of Avila (1515–1582) and Saint John of the Cross (1542–1591).

Ignatius of Loyola and the Jesuits

Of the various reform groups, none was more instrumental in the success of the Counter-Reformation than the Society of Jesus, the new order of Jesuits. Organized by Ignatius of Loyola in the 1530s, the church recognized it in 1540. The society grew within a century from its original ten members to more than 15,000 members scattered throughout the world, with thriving missions in India, Japan, and the Americas.

The founder of the Jesuits, Ignatius of Loyola (1491–1556), was a heroic figure. A dashing courtier and *soldiero* in his youth, he began his spiritual pilgrimage in 1521 after he had been seriously wounded during a battle with the French. During a lengthy and painful convalescence, he passed the time by reading Christian classics. So impressed was he with the heroic self-sacrifice of the church's saints and their methods of overcoming mental anguish and pain that he underwent a profound religious conversion. Henceforth, he, too, would serve the church as a soldier of Christ.

After recuperating, Ignatius applied the lessons he had learned during his convalescence to a program of religious and moral self-discipline that came to be embodied in the *Spiritual Exercises.* This psychologically perceptive devotional guide contained mental and emotional exercises designed to teach one absolute spiritual self-mastery over one's feelings. It taught that a person could shape his or her own behavior—even create a new religious self—through disciplined study and regular practice.

Whereas in Jesuit eyes Protestants had distinguished themselves by disobedience and religious

MAP EXPLORATION

Interactive map: To explore this map further, go to **www.myhistorylab.com**

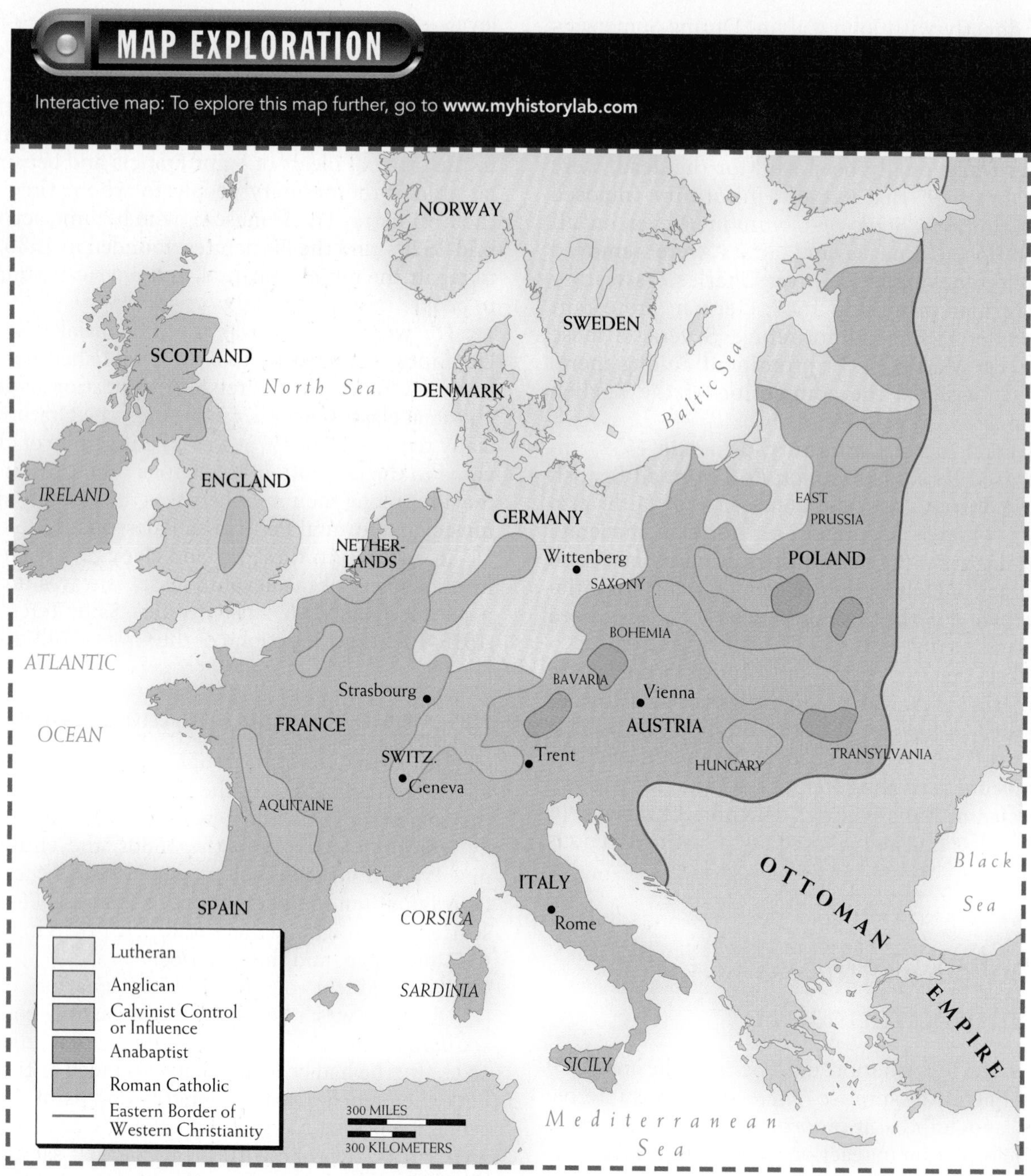

Map 11–3 **THE RELIGIOUS SITUATION ABOUT 1560** By 1560, Luther, Zwingli, and Loyola were dead, Calvin was near the end of his life, the English break from Rome was complete, and the last session of the Council of Trent was about to assemble. This map shows "religious geography" of western Europe at the time.

innovation, the exercises of Ignatius were intended to teach good Catholics to deny themselves and submit without question to higher church authority and spiritual direction. Perfect discipline and self-control were the essential conditions of such obedience. To these were added the enthusiasm of traditional spirituality and mysticism and uncompromising loyalty to the church's cause. This potent combination helped counter the Reformation and win many Protestants back to the Catholic fold, especially in Austria and parts of Germany. (See Map 11–3.)

The Council of Trent (1545–1563)

The broad success of the Reformation and the insistence of the Emperor Charles V forced Pope Paul III (r. 1534–1549) to call a general council of the church to reassert church doctrine. In anticipation, the pope appointed a reform commission, chaired by Caspar Contarini (1483–1542), a leading liberal theologian. His report, presented to the pope in February 1537, was so critical of the fiscal practices and simony of the papal Curia that Paul attempted unsuccessfully to suppress its publication, while Protestants circulated it as justification of their criticism.

The long-delayed council of the church met in 1545 in the imperial city of Trent in northern Italy. There were three sessions, spread over eighteen years, with long interruptions due to war, plague, and imperial and papal politics. The council met from 1545 to 1547, from 1551 to 1552, and from 1562 to 1563, a period that spanned the reigns of four different popes.

Unlike the general councils of the fifteenth century, Trent was strictly under the pope's control, with high Italian prelates prominent in the proceedings. At its final session in 1562, more than three quarters of the council fathers were Italians. Voting was limited to the high levels of the clergy; university theologians, the lower clergy, and the laity did not share in the council's decisions.

The council's most important reforms concerned internal church discipline. Steps were taken to curtail the selling of church offices and other religious goods. Many bishops who resided in Rome were forced to move to their dioceses. Trent strengthened the authority of local bishops so they could effectively discipline popular religious practices. The bishops were also subjected to new rules that required them to be highly visible by preaching regularly and conducting annual visitations of their diocesan parishes. Parish priests were required to be neatly dressed, better educated, strictly celibate, and active among their parishioners. To train priests, Trent also called for a seminary in every diocese.

Not a single doctrinal concession was made to the Protestants, however. Instead, the Council of Trent reaffirmed the traditional Scholastic education of the clergy; the role of good works in salvation; the authority of tradition; the seven sacraments; transubstantiation; the withholding of the Eucharistic cup from the laity; clerical celibacy; purgatory; the veneration of saints, relics, and sacred images; and indulgences. The council resolved medieval Scholastic quarrels in favor of the theology of Saint Thomas Aquinas, further enhancing his authority within the church. Thereafter, the church offered its strongest resistance to groups like the Jansenists, who endorsed the medieval Augustinian tradition, a source of alternative Catholic, as well as many Protestant, doctrines.

Rulers initially resisted Trent's reform decrees, fearing a revival of papal political power and new confessional conflicts within their lands. Over time, however, and with the pope's assurances that religious reforms were his sole intent, the new legislation took hold, and parish life revived under a devout and better trained clergy.

▼ The Social Significance of the Reformation in Western Europe

The Lutheran, Zwinglian, and Calvinist reformers all sought to work within the framework of reigning political power. Luther, Zwingli, and Calvin saw themselves and their followers as subject to definite civic responsibilities and obligations. Their political conservatism has led scholars to characterize them as "magisterial reformers," meaning not only that they were the leaders of the major Protestant movements, but also that they succeeded by the force of the magistrate's sword. Some have argued that this willingness to resort to coercion led the reformers to compromise their principles. They themselves, however, never contemplated reform outside or against the societies of which they were

PROTESTANT REFORMATION AND CATHOLIC REFORM ON THE CONTINENT

1517	Luther posts ninety-five theses against indulgences
1519	Charles I of Spain elected Holy Roman Emperor (as Charles V)
1519	Luther challenges authority of pope and inerrancy of church councils at Leipzig Debate
1521	Papal bull excommunicates Luther for heresy
1521	Diet of Worms condemns Luther
1521–1522	Luther translates the New Testament into German
1524–1525	Peasants' revolt in Germany
1527	The *Schleitheim Confession* of the Anabaptists
1529	Marburg Colloquy between Luther and Zwingli
1530	Diet of Augsburg fails to settle religious differences
1531	Formation of Protestant Schmalkaldic League
1534–1535	Anabaptists assume political power in Münster
1536	Calvin arrives in Geneva
1540	Jesuits, founded by Ignatius of Loyola, recognized as order by pope
1546	Luther dies
1547	Armies of Charles V crush Schmalkaldic League
1555	Peace of Augsburg recognizes rights of Lutherans to worship as they please
1545–1563	Council of Trent institutes reforms and responds to the Reformation

members. They wanted reform to take shape within reigning laws and institutions. They thus remained highly sensitive to what was politically and socially possible in their age. Some scholars believe the reformers were so cautious that they changed late medieval society very little and actually encouraged acceptance of the sociopolitical status quo.

The Revolution in Religious Practices and Institutions

The Reformation may have been politically conservative, but by the end of the sixteenth century, it had brought about radical changes in traditional religious practices and institutions in those lands where it succeeded.

Religion in Fifteenth-Century Life In the fifteenth century, on the streets of the great cities of Europe that later turned Protestant (for example, Zurich, Strasbourg, Nuremberg, and Geneva), the clergy and the religious were everywhere. They made up six to eight percent of the urban population, and they exercised considerable political as well as spiritual power. They legislated and taxed, they tried cases in special church courts, and they enforced their laws with threats of excommunication.

The church calendar regulated daily life. About one third of the year was given over to some kind of religious observance or celebration. There were frequent periods of fasting. On almost a hundred days out of the year, a pious Christian could not, without special dispensation, eat eggs, butter, animal fat, or meat.

Monasteries, and especially nunneries, were prominent and influential institutions. The children of society's most powerful citizens resided there. Local aristocrats identified with particular churches and chapels, whose walls recorded their lineage and proclaimed their generosity. On the streets, friars begged alms from passersby. In the churches, the Mass and liturgy were read entirely in Latin. Images of saints were regularly displayed, and on certain holidays their relics were paraded about and venerated.

Local religious shrines enjoyed a booming business. Pilgrims gathered there by the hundreds—even thousands—many sick and dying, all in search of a cure or a miracle, but also for diversion and entertainment. Several times during the year, special preachers arrived in the city to sell letters of indulgence.

Many clergy walked the streets with concubines and children, although they were sworn to celibacy and forbidden to marry. The church tolerated such relationships upon payment of penitential fines.

People everywhere complained about the clergy's exemption from taxation and also often from the civil criminal code. People also grumbled about having to support church offices whose occupants actually lived and worked elsewhere, turning the cure of souls over to poorly trained and paid substitutes. Townspeople expressed concern that the church had too much influence over education and culture.

Religion in Sixteenth-Century Life In these same cities, after the Reformation had firmly established itself, few changes in politics and society were evident. The same aristocratic families governed as before, and the rich generally got richer and the poor poorer. Overall numbers of clergy fell by two thirds, and religious holidays shrank by one third. Cloisters were nearly gone, and many that remained were transformed into hospices for the sick and poor or into educational institutions, their endowments turned over to these new purposes. A few cloisters remained for devout old monks and nuns who could not be pensioned off or lacked families and friends to care for them. These remaining cloisters died out with their present inhabitants, since no new religious were allowed to enter.

The churches, were reduced in number by at least one third, and worship was conducted almost completely in the vernacular. In some, particularly those in Zwinglian cities, the walls were stripped bare and whitewashed to make sure the congregation meditated only on God's word. The laity observed no obligatory fasts. Indulgence preachers no longer appeared. Local shrines were closed down, and anyone found openly venerating saints, relics, and images was subject to fine and punishment.

Copies of Luther's translation of the New Testament (1522) or, more often, excerpts from it could be found in private homes, and the new clergy encouraged meditation on the Bible. The clergy could marry, and most did. They paid taxes and were punished for their crimes in civil courts. Committees composed of roughly equal numbers of laity and clergy, over whose decisions secular magistrates had the last word, regulated domestic moral life.

Not all Protestant clergy remained enthusiastic about this new lay authority in religion. And the laity was also ambivalent about certain aspects of the Reformation. Over half of the original converts returned to the Catholic fold before the end of the sixteenth century. Whereas one half of Europe could be counted in the Protestant camp in the mid-sixteenth century, only one fifth would be there by the mid-seventeenth century.[2]

The Reformation and Education

Another major cultural achievement of the Reformation was its implementation of many of the educational reforms of humanism in new Protestant schools and universities. Many Protestant reformers in Germany, France,

[2]Geoffrey Parker, *Europe in Crisis, 1598–1648* (Ithaca, NY: Cornell University Press, 1979), p. 50.

and England were humanists. And even when their views on church doctrine and human nature separated them from the humanist movement, the Protestant reformers continued to share a common opposition to Scholasticism and a belief in the unity of wisdom, eloquence, and action. The humanist program of studies, providing the language skills to deal authoritatively with original sources, proved to be a more appropriate tool for the elaboration of Protestant doctrine than it did for Scholastic dialectic, which remained ascendant in the Counter-Reformation.

The Catholic counter-reformers recognized the close connections between humanism and the Reformation. Ignatius of Loyola observed how the new learning had been embraced by and served the Protestant cause. In his *Spiritual Exercises,* he insisted that when the Bible and the Church Fathers were read directly, they be read under the guidance of the authoritative Scholastic theologians: Peter Lombard, Bonaventure, and Thomas Aquinas. Aquinas especially, Ignatius argued, being "of more recent date," had the clearest understanding of what Scripture and the Fathers meant and, therefore, he should guide the study of the past.

When, in August 1518, Philip Melanchthon (1497–1560), "the praeceptor of Germany," a young humanist and professor of Greek, arrived at the University of Wittenberg, his first act was to reform the curriculum on the humanist model. In his inaugural address, entitled *On Improving the Studies of the Young,* Melanchthon presented himself as a defender of good letters and classical studies against "barbarians who practice barbarous arts." By the latter, he meant the Scholastic theologians of the later Middle Ages, whose methods of seeking to reconcile the views of conflicting authorities by disputation had, he believed, undermined both good

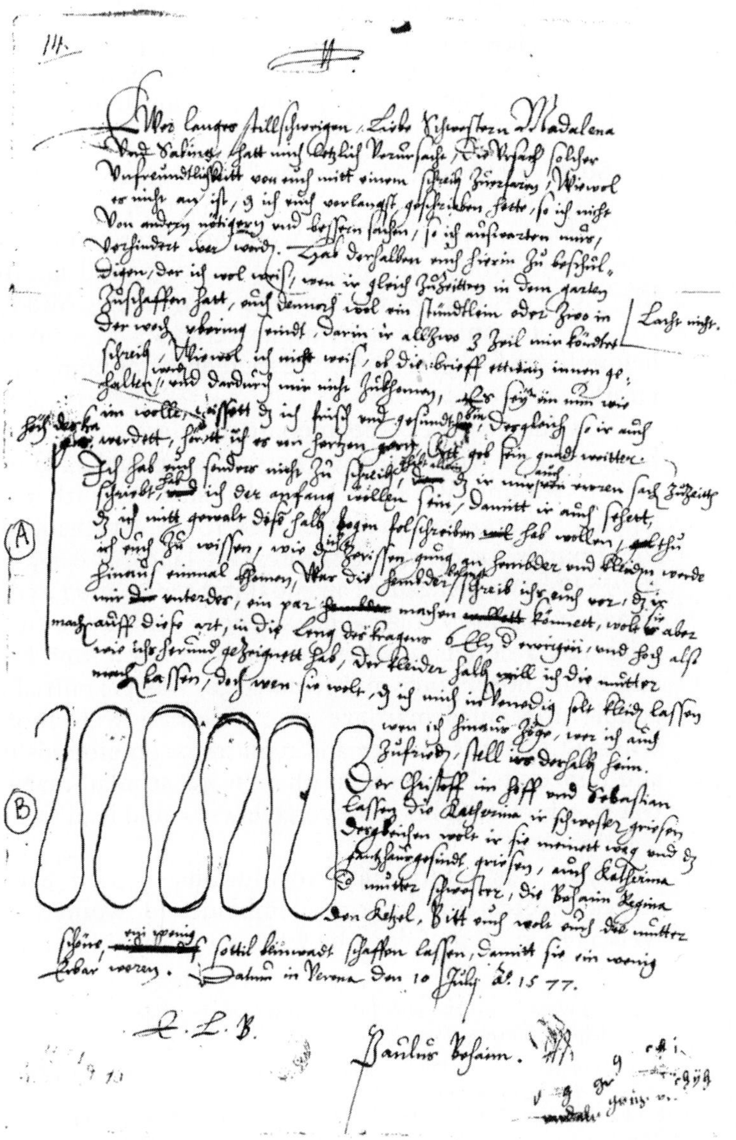

Brothers and Sisters. While away from home at law school in Padua, Italy, nineteen-year-old Paul Behaim, Jr., wrote in July 1577 to his older sisters Magdalena (twenty-two) and Sabina (twenty-one) to complain about the infrequency of their writing to him. Typical of sibling relations in every age, the letter is affectionate and joking. The sisters were then at home with their widowed mother and busy with the many chores of the self-sufficient sixteenth-century domestic household—especially, at this time of the year, gardening. Because of their alleged neglect Paul teasingly tells them they must now do "penance" by making him two new shirts, as his were embarrassingly tattered. He indicated in the left margin the exact collar length (A) and style (B) he wishes the shirts to be. Sewing for the household was another regular domestic chore for burgher and patrician women not working in trades outside the home. But Magdalena and Sabina went even further to "cover" their brother: They also allowed him to receive income (to be repaid in the future) from their own paternal inheritances so he might finish his legal education, on the successful completion of which the whole family depended for its future success. German National Museum, Nuremberg, Germany, Behaim-Archiv Fasz, 106 letters and sound biblical doctrine. Melanchthon saw Scholastic dominance in the universities as breeding contempt for the Greek language and learning and encouraging neglect of the study of mathematics, sacred studies, and oratory. He urged the careful study of history, poetry, and other humanist disciplines.

Together, Luther and Melanchthon restructured the University of Wittenberg's curriculum. Commentaries on Lombard's *Sentences* were dropped, as was canon law. Straightforward historical study replaced old Scholastic lectures on Aristotle. Students read primary sources directly, rather than by way of accepted Scholastic commentators. Candidates for theological degrees defended the new doctrine on the basis of their own study of the Bible. New chairs of Greek and Hebrew were created.

In Geneva, John Calvin and his successor, Theodore Beza, founded the Genevan Academy, which later evolved into the University of Geneva. That institution, created primarily to train Calvinist ministers, pursued ideals similar to those set forth by Luther and Melanchthon. Calvinist refugees who studied there later carried Protestant educational reforms to France, Scotland, England, and the New World. Through such efforts, many educated people acquired a working knowledge of Greek and Hebrew in the sixteenth and seventeenth centuries.

Some famous contemporaries decried what they saw as a narrowing of the original humanist program as Protestants took it over. Erasmus, for example, came to fear the Reformation as a threat to the liberal arts and good learning. Sebastian Franck pointed to parallels between Luther's and Zwingli's debates over Christ's presence in the Eucharist and such old Scholastic disputations as that over the Immaculate Conception of the Virgin.

Humanist culture and learning nonetheless remained indebted to the Reformation. The Protestant endorsement of the humanist program of studies remained as significant for the humanist movement as the latter had been for the Reformation. Protestant schools and universities consolidated and preserved for the modern world many of the basic pedagogical achievements of humanism. There, the *studia humanitatis,* although often as little more than a handmaiden to theological doctrine, found a permanent home, one that remained hospitable even in the heyday of conservative Protestantism.

The Reformation and the Changing Role of Women

The Protestant reformers favored clerical marriage and opposed monasticism and the celibate life. From this position, they challenged the medieval tendency alternately to degrade women as temptresses (following the model of Eve) and to exalt them as virgins (following the model of Mary). Protestants opposed the popular anti-woman and antimarriage literature of the Middle Ages. They praised woman in her own right, but especially in her biblical vocation as mother and housewife. Although wives remained subject to their husbands, new laws gave them greater security and protection.

Relief of sexual frustration and a remedy for fornication were prominent in Protestant arguments for universal marriage. But the reformers also viewed their wives as indispensable companions in their work, and this not solely because they took domestic cares off their husbands' minds. Luther, who married in 1525 at the age of forty-two, wrote the following of women:

> Imagine what it would be like without women. The home, cities, economic life, and government would virtually disappear. Men cannot do without women. Even if it were possible for men to beget and bear children, they still could not do without women.[3]

John Calvin wrote this at the death of his wife:

> I have been bereaved of the best companion of my life, of one who, had it been so ordered, would not only have been the willing sharer of my indigence, but even of my death. During her life she was the faithful helper of my ministry.[4]

Such tributes were intended to counter Catholic criticism of clerical marriage as a distraction of the clergy from their ministry. They were an expression of the high value Protestants placed on marriage and family life. In opposition to the celibate ideal of the Middle Ages, Protestants stressed, as no religious movement before them had ever done, the sacredness of home and family.

The ideal of the companionate marriage—that is, of husband and wife as co-workers in a special God-ordained community of the family, sharing authority equally within the household—led to an expansion of the grounds for divorce in Protestant lands as early as the 1520s. Women gained an equal right with men to divorce and remarry in good conscience—unlike the situation in Catholicism, where only a separation from bed and table, not divorce and remarriage, was permitted a couple in a failed marriage. The reformers were more willing to permit divorce and remarriage on grounds of adultery and abandonment than were secular magistrates, who feared liberal divorce laws would lead to social upheaval.

Typical of reforms and revolutions in their early stages, Protestant doctrines emboldened women as well as men. Renegade nuns wrote exposés of the nun-

[3]*Luther's Works*, Vol. 54: *Table Talk*, ed. and trans. by Theodore G. Tappert (Philadelphia: Fortress Press, 1967), p. 161.

[4]*Letters of John Calvin*, Vol. 2, trans. by J. Bonnet (Edinburgh: T. Constable, 1858), p. 216; E. G. Schwiebert, *Luther and His Times* (St. Louis, MO: Concordia, 1950), pp. 226–227, 266–268, 581–602; Steven Ozment, *Protestants: The Birth of a Revolution* (New York: Doubleday, 1992), pp. 17, 154, 159–162.

nery in the name of Christian freedom and justification by faith, declaring the nunnery was no special woman's place at all and that supervisory male clergy (who alone could hear the nuns' confessions and administer sacraments to them) made their lives as unpleasant and burdensome as any abusive husband. Women in the higher classes, who enjoyed new social and political freedoms during the Renaissance, found in Protestant theology a religious complement to their greater independence in other walks of life. Some cloistered noblewomen, however, protested the closing of nunneries, arguing that the cloister provided them a more interesting and independent way of life than they would have known in the secular world.

Because Protestants wanted women to become pious housewives, they encouraged the education of girls to literacy in the vernacular, with the expectation that they would thereafter model their lives on the Bible. However, women also found biblical passages that made clear their equality to men in the presence of God. Education also gave some women roles as independent authors on behalf of the Reformation. Although small advances from a modern perspective, these were also steps toward the emancipation of women.

▼ Family Life in Early Modern Europe

Changes in the timing and duration of marriage, family size, and infant and child care suggest that family life was under a variety of social and economic pressures in the sixteenth and seventeenth centuries.

Later Marriages

Between 1500 and 1800, men and women in Western Europe married at later ages than they had in previous centuries: men in their mid- to late-twenties, and women in their early- to mid-twenties. The canonical, or church-sanctioned, age for marriage remained fourteen for men and twelve for women. The church also recognized as valid free, private exchanges of vows between a man and a woman for whom no impediment to marriage existed. After the Reformation, which condemned such clandestine unions, both Protestants and Catholics required parental consent and public vows in church before a marriage could be deemed fully licit.

Late marriage in the West reflected the difficulty couples had supporting themselves independently. It simply took the average couple a longer time than before to prepare themselves materially for marriage. In the sixteenth century, one in five women never married, and these, combined with the estimated 15 percent who were unmarried widows, constituted a large unmarried female population. A later marriage was also a shorter marriage; in an age when few people lived into their sixties, couples who married in their thirties spent less time together than couples who married in their twenties. Also, because women who bore children for the first time at advanced ages had higher mortality rates, late marriage meant more frequent remarriage for men. As the rapid growth of orphanages and foundling homes between 1600 and 1800 makes clear, delayed marriage increased premarital sex and the number of illegitimate children.

Arranged Marriages

Marriage tended to be "arranged" in the sense that the parents met and discussed the terms of the marriage before the prospective bride and bridegroom became directly party to the preparations. The wealth and social standing of the bride and the bridegroom, however, were not the only things considered when youth married. By the fifteenth century, it was usual for the future bride and bridegroom to have known each other and to have had some prior relationship. Also, parents respected the couple's emotional feeling for one another. Parents did not force total strangers to live together, and children had a legal right to resist a coerced marriage, which was by definition invalid. The best marriage was one desired by both the bride and groom and their families.

Family Size

The Western European family was conjugal, or nuclear, consisting of a father and a mother and two to four children who survived into adulthood. This nuclear family lived within a larger household, including in-laws, servants, laborers, and boarders. The average husband and wife had six to seven children, a new birth about every two years. Of these, an estimated one third died by age five, and one half by their teens. Rare was the family, at any social level, that did not experience child death.

Birth Control

Artificial birth control (sponges, acidic ointments) has existed since antiquity. The church's condemnation of *coitus interruptus* (male withdrawal before ejaculation) during the thirteenth and fourteenth centuries suggests the existence of a contraceptive mentality, that is, a conscious, regular effort at birth control. Early birth control measures, when applied, were not very effective, and for both historical and moral reasons, the church opposed them. According to Saint Thomas Aquinas, a moral act

ENCOUNTERING THE *Past*

TABLE MANNERS

PLEASURE AT TABLE in the sixteenth century was considered a matter of self-control. The well-dressed table taught the lessons of life as well as offered its bread. Neatness and order showed respect, respect ensured attentiveness, and attentiveness made for learning. The union of pleasure and discipline at mealtime was believed to inculcate in the young the traits that would keep them free and safe in an unforgiving world. Here is how Hans Sachs, a sixteenth-century father, expected children to behave:

Listen you children who are going to table.
Wash your hands and cut your nails.
Do not sit at the head of the table;
This is reserved for the father of the house.
Do not commence eating until a blessing has been said.
Dine in God's name
And permit the eldest to begin first.
Proceed in a disciplined manner.
Do not snort or smack like a pig.
Do not reach violently for bread,
Lest you may knock over a glass.
Do not cut bread on your chest,
Or conceal pieces of bread or pastry under your hands.
Do not tear pieces for your plate with your teeth.
Do not stir food around on your plate
Or linger over it.
Do not fill your spoon too full.

A Family Meal. In Max Geisberg, *The German Single-Leaf Woodcuts, III: 1500–1550*, rev. and ed. by W. L. Strauss (New York: Hacker Art Books, 1974). Used by permission of Hacker Art Books.

Rushing through your meal is bad manners.
Do not reach for more food
While your mouth is still full,
Nor talk with your mouth full.
Be moderate; do not fall upon your plate like an animal.
Be the last to cut your meat and break your fish.
Chew your food with your mouth closed.
Do not lick the corners of your mouth like a dog.
Do not hover greedily over your food.
Wipe your mouth before you drink,
So that you do not grease up your wine.
Drink politely and avoid coughing into your cup.
Do not belch or cry out.
With drink be most prudent.
Sit smartly, undisturbed, humble . . .
Do not stare at a person
As if you were watching him eat.
Do not elbow the person sitting next to you.
Sit up straight; be a model of gracefulness.
Do not rock back and forth on the bench,
Lest you let loose a stink.
Do not kick your feet under the table.
Guard yourself against all shameful
Words, gossip, ridicule, and laughter . . .
If sexual play occurs at table,
Pretend you do not see it.
Never start a quarrel,
Quarreling at table is most despicable.
Say nothing that might offend another.
Do not blow your nose
Or do other shocking things.
Do not pick your nose.
If you must pick your teeth, be discreet about it.
Never scratch your head
(This goes for girls and women too);
Or fish out lice.
Let no one wipe his mouth on the table cloth,
Or lay his head in his hands.
Do not lean back against the wall
Until the meal is finished.
Silently praise and thank God
For the food he has graciously provided. . . .

Source: Trans. by S. Ozment, from S. Ozment, *When Fathers Ruled: Family Life in Reformation Europe* (Cambridge, MA: Harvard University Press, 1983), pp. 142–43.

How do table manners prepare a child for life? Has table etiquette changed since the sixteenth century?

must aid and abet, never frustrate, nature's goal, and the natural end of sex was the birth of children and their godly rearing within the bounds of holy matrimony and the community of the church.

Wet Nursing

The church allied with the physicians of early modern Europe on another intimate family matter. Both condemned women who hired wet nurses to suckle their newborn children. The practice was popular among upper-class women and reflected their social standing. It appears to have increased the risk of infant mortality by exposing infants to a strange and shared milk supply from women who were often not as healthy as the infants' own mothers and lived under less sanitary conditions. Nursing was distasteful to some upper-class women, whose husbands also preferred that they not do it. Among women, vanity and convenience appear to have been motives for hiring a wet nurse, while for husbands, even more was at stake. Because the church forbade lactating women from indulging in sexual intercourse, a nursing wife could become a reluctant lover. Nursing also had a contraceptive effect (about 75 percent effective). Some women prolonged nursing their children to delay a new pregnancy, and some husbands cooperated in this form of family planning. For other husbands, however, especially noblemen and royalty who desired an abundance of male heirs, nursing seemed to rob them of offspring and jeopardize their patrimony—hence their support of hired wet nurses.

Loving Families?

The traditional Western European family had features that seem cold and distant. Children between the ages of eight and thirteen were routinely sent from their homes into apprenticeships, school, or employment in the homes and businesses of relatives, friends, and occasionally strangers. The emotional ties between spouses also seem to have been as tenuous as those between parents and children. Widowers and widows often married again within a few months of their spouses' deaths, and marriages with extreme difference in age between partners suggest limited affection.

In response to modern-day criticism, an early modern parent might well have asked: "What greater love can parents have for their children than to equip them well for a worldly vocation?" A well-apprenticed child was a self-supporting child, and hence a child with a future. In light of the comparatively primitive living conditions, contemporaries also appreciated the purely utilitarian and humane side of marriage and understood when widowers and widows quickly remarried. Marriages with extreme disparity in age, however, were no more the norm in early modern Europe than the practice of wet nursing, and they received just as much criticism and ridicule.

▼ Literary Imagination in Transition

Alongside the political and cultural changes brought about by the new religious systems of the Reformation (Lutheranism, Calvinism, and Puritanism) and Catholic Reform, medieval outlooks and religious values continued to be debated, embraced, and rejected into the seventeenth century. Major literary figures of the post-Reformation period had elements of both the old and the new in their own new transitional works. Two who stand out are Miguel de Cervantes Saavedra (1547–1616), writing in still deeply Catholic Spain, and William Shakespeare (1564–1616), who wrote in newly Anglican England.

Miguel de Cervantes Saavedra: Rejection of Idealism

Spanish literature of the sixteenth and seventeenth centuries reflects the peculiar religious and political history of Spain in this period. Traditional Catholic teaching was a major influence on Spanish life. Since the joint reign of Ferdinand and Isabella (1479–1504), the church had received the unqualified support of the reigning political power. Although there was religious reform in Spain, and genuine Protestant groups were persecuted for "Lutheranism," a Protestant Reformation never occurred there, thanks largely to the entrenched power of the church and the Inquisition.

A second influence on Spanish literature was the aggressive piety of Spanish rulers. Their intertwining of Catholic piety and political power underlay a third influence: preoccupation with medieval chivalric virtues, in particular, questions of honor and loyalty. The novels and plays of the period almost invariably focus on a special test of character, bordering on the heroic, that threatens honor and reputation. In this regard, Spanish literature remained more Catholic and medieval than that of England and France, where major Protestant movements had occurred. Two of the most important Spanish writers of this period became priests (the dramatists Lope de Vega and Pedro Calderón de la Barca). The writer generally acknowledged to be Spain's greatest, Cervantes, was preoccupied in his work with the strengths and weaknesses of traditional religious idealism.

Cervantes (1547–1616) had only a smattering of formal education. He educated himself by wide reading in popular literature and immersion in the "school of life." As a young man, he worked in Rome for a Spanish cardinal. As a soldier, he was decorated for gallantry in the Battle of Lepanto against the Turks (1571). He also spent five years as a slave in Algiers after his ship was pirated in 1575. Later, while working as a tax collector, he was imprisoned several times for padding his accounts, and it was in prison that he began, in 1603, to write his most famous work, *Don Quixote.*

The first part of *Don Quixote* appeared in 1605. The intent of this work seems to have been to satirize the chivalric romances then popular in Spain. But Cervantes could not conceal his deep affection for the character he created as an object of ridicule. The work is satire only on the surface and appeals as much to philosophers and theologians as to students of Spanish literature. Cervantes presented Don Quixote as a none-too-stable middle-aged man. Driven mad by reading too many chivalric romances, he had come to believe he was an aspiring knight who had to prove his worthiness by brave deeds. To this end, he donned a rusty suit of armor and chose for his inspiration an unworthy peasant girl (Dulcinea), whom he fancied to be a noble lady to whom he could, with honor, dedicate his life.

Don Quixote's foil—Sancho Panza, a clever, worldly wise peasant who serves as Quixote's squire—watches with bemused skepticism as his lord does battle with a windmill (which he has mistaken for a dragon) and repeatedly makes a fool of himself as he gallops across the countryside. The story ends tragically with Don Quixote's humiliating defeat at the hand of a well-meaning friend who, disguised as a knight, bested Quixote in combat and forced him to renounce his quest for knighthood. Don Quixote did not, however, come to his senses but rather returned to his village to die a brokenhearted old man.

Throughout the novel, Cervantes juxtaposes the down-to-earth realism of Sancho Panza with the old-fashioned religious idealism of Don Quixote. The reader perceives that Cervantes admired the one as much as the other and meant to portray both as representing attitudes necessary for a happy life.

William Shakespeare: Dramatist of the Age

There is much less factual knowledge about Shakespeare (1564–1616) than we would expect of the greatest playwright in the English language. He married at the early age of eighteen, in 1582, and he and his wife, Anne Hathaway, were the parents of three children (including twins) by 1585. He apparently worked as a schoolteacher for a time and in this capacity gained his broad knowledge of Renaissance literature. His own reading and enthusiasm for the learning of his day are manifest in the many literary allusions that appear in his plays.

Shakespeare lived the life of a country gentleman. There is none of the Puritan distress over worldliness in his work. He took the new commercialism and the bawdy pleasures of the Elizabethan Age in stride and with amusement. He was a radical neither in politics nor religion. The few allusions in his works to the Puritans seem more critical than complimentary.

That Shakespeare was interested in politics is apparent from his historical plays and the references to contemporary political events that fill all his plays. He viewed government through the character of the individual ruler, whether Richard III or Elizabeth Tudor, rather than in terms of ideal systems or social goals. By modern standards, he was a political conservative, accepting the social rankings and the power structure of his day and demonstrating unquestioned patriotism.

Shakespeare knew the theater as one who participated in every phase of its life—as a playwright, an actor, and part owner of a theater. He was a member and principal writer of a famous company of actors known as the King's Men. Between 1590 and 1610, many of his plays were performed at court, where he moved with comfort and received enthusiastic royal patronage.

Elizabethan drama was already a distinctive form when Shakespeare began writing. Unlike French drama of the seventeenth century, which was dominated by classical models, English drama developed in the sixteenth and seventeenth centuries as a blending of many forms: classical comedies and tragedies, medieval morality plays, and contemporary Italian short stories.

Two contemporaries, Thomas Kyd and Christopher Marlowe, influenced Shakespeare's tragedies. Kyd (1558–1594) wrote the first dramatic version of *Hamlet.* The tragedies of Marlowe (1564–1593) set a model for character, poetry, and style that only Shakespeare among the English playwrights of the period surpassed. Shakespeare synthesized the best past and current achievements. A keen student of human motivation and passion, he had a unique talent for getting into people's minds.

Shakespeare wrote histories, comedies, and tragedies. *Richard III* (1593), an early play, stands out among the histories, although some scholars view the picture it presents of Richard as an unprincipled villain as "Tudor propaganda." Shakespeare's comedies, although not attaining the heights of his tragedies, surpass his history plays in originality.

Shakespeare's tragedies are considered his unique achievement. Four of these were written within a three-year period: *Hamlet* (1603), *Othello* (1604), *King Lear* (1605), and *Macbeth* (1606). The most original of the tragedies, *Romeo and Juliet* (1597), transformed an old popular story into a moving drama of "star-cross'd lovers." Both Romeo and Juliet, denied a marriage by their warring families, die tragic deaths. Romeo, believing Juliet to be dead when she has merely taken a sleeping potion, poisons himself. When Juliet awakes to find Romeo dead, she kills herself with his dagger.

Shakespeare's works struck universal human themes, many of which were deeply rooted in contemporary religious traditions. His plays were immensely popular with both the playgoers and the play readers of Elizabethan England. Still today, the works of no other dramatist from his age are performed in theaters or on film more regularly than his.

In Perspective

During the early Middle Ages, Christendom had been divided into Western and Eastern churches with irreconcilable theological differences. When, in 1517, Martin Luther posted ninety-five theses questioning the selling of indulgences and the traditional sacrament of penance that lay behind them, he created a division within Western Christendom itself—an internal division between Protestants and Catholics.

The Lutheran protest came at a time of political and social discontent with the church. Not only princes and magistrates but many ordinary people as well resented traditional clerical rights and privileges. The clergy were exempted from many secular laws and taxes while remaining powerful landowners whose personal lifestyles were not all that different from those of the laity. Spiritual and secular protest combined to make the Protestant Reformation a successful assault on the old church. In town after town and region after region within Protestant lands, the major institutions and practices of traditional piety were transformed.

It soon became clear, however, that the division would not stop with the Lutherans. Making Scripture the only arbiter in religion had opened a Pandora's box. People proved to have different ideas about what Scripture taught. Indeed, there seemed to be as many points of view as there were readers. Rapidly, the Reformation created Lutheran, Zwinglian, Anabaptist, Spiritualist, Calvinist, and Anglican versions of biblical religion—a splintering of Protestantism that has endured and increased until today.

Catholics had been pursuing reform before the Reformation broke out in Germany, although without papal enthusiasm and certainly not along clear Protestant lines. When major reforms finally came in the Catholic Church around the mid-sixteenth century, they were doctrinally reactionary, but administratively and spiritually flexible. The church enforced strict obedience and conformity to its teaching, but it also provided the laity with a better educated and disciplined clergy. For laity who wanted a deeper and more individual piety, experimentation with proven spiritual practices was now permitted. By century's end, such measures had countered, and in some areas even spectacularly reversed, Protestant gains.

After the Reformation, pluralism steadily became a fact of Western religious life. It did so at first only by sheer force, since no one religious body was then prepared to concede the validity of alternative Christian beliefs and practices. During the sixteenth and seventeenth centuries, only those groups that fought doggedly for their faith gained the right to practice it freely. Despite these struggles, religious pluralism endured. Never again would there be only a Catholic Christian Church in Europe.

REVIEW QUESTIONS

1. What problems in the church contributed to the Protestant Reformation? Why was the church unable to suppress dissent as it had earlier?
2. What were the basic similarities and differences between the ideas of Luther and Zwingli? Between Luther and Calvin? How did the differences tend to affect the success of the Protestant movement?
3. Why did the Reformation begin in Germany? What political factors contributed to its success there as opposed to in France, Spain, or Italy?
4. What was the Catholic Counter-Reformation? What reforms did the Council of Trent introduce? Was the Protestant Reformation healthy for the Catholic Church?
5. Why did Henry VIII break with Rome? Was the "new" church he established really Protestant? How did the English church change under his successors?
6. How did the Reformation affect women in the sixteenth and seventeenth centuries? How did relations between men and women, family size, and child care change during this period?

SUGGESTED READINGS

H. Bloom, *Shakespeare: The Invention of the Human* (1998). An analysis of the greatest writer in the English language.

T. A. Brady, Jr. ed., *Handbook of European History: Late Middle Ages, Renaissance, Reformation* (1995). Essays summarizing recent research on aspects of the Reformation.

P. Collinson, *The Reformation* (2004). Portrays the Reformation as creating religious pluralism and civil liberty despite itself.

E. Duffy, *The Stripping of the Altars: Traditional Religion in England, 1400–1580* (1992). Strongest of recent arguments that popular piety survived the Reformation in England.

M. Duran, *Cervantes* (1974). Detailed biography.

B. S. Gregory, *Salvation at Stake: Christian Martyrdom in Early Modern Europe* (1999). Massive, enthralling study of religion.

R. Houlbrooke, *English Family Life, 1450–1716. An Anthology from Diaries* (1988). A rich collection of documents illustrating family relationships.

J. C. Hutchison, *Albrecht Dürer: A Biography* (1990). An art historian chronicles both the life and work of the artist.

H. Jedin, *A History of the Council of Trent*, Vols. 1 and 2 (1957–1961). Still the gold standard.

P. Johnston and R. W. Scribner, *The Reformation in Germany and Switzerland* (1993). Reformation from the bottom up.

D. MacColloch, *The Reformation* (2004). Finds old Catholics and non-Protestant Evangelicals to be the forerunners of modern religion.

H. A. Oberman, *Luther: Man between God and the Devil* (1989). Perhaps the best account of Luther's life, by a Dutch master.

J. O'Malley, *The First Jesuits* (1993). Detailed account of the creation of the Society of Jesus and its original purposes.

S. Ozment, *The Age of Reform, 1250–1550: An Intellectual and Religious History of Late Medieval and Reformation Europe* (1980). A broad survey of major religious ideas and beliefs.

B. Roberts, *Through the Keyhole: Dutch Child-Rearing Practices in the 17th and 18th Centuries* (1998). A study of three elite families.

Q. Skinner, *The Foundations of Modern Political Thought II: The Age of Reformation* (1978). A comprehensive survey that treats every political thinker and tract.

D. Starkey, *Elizabeth: The Struggle for the Throne* (2000). Complex, riveting account by a sympathetic historian.

L. Stone, *The Family, Sex, and Marriage in England 1500–1800* (1977). Controversial but enduring in many respects.

G. Strauss, ed. and trans., *Manifestations of Discontent in Germany on the Eve of the Reformation* (1971). Rich collection of both rural and urban sources.

F. Wendel, *Calvin: The Origins and Development of His Religious Thought*, trans. by P. Mairet (1963). The best treatment of Calvin's theology.

H. Wunder, *He Is the Sun, She Is the Moon: A History of Women in Early Modern Germany* (1998). A model of gender history.

For additional learning resources related to this chapter, please go to www.myhistorylab.com

PEARSON myhistorylab

The massacre of worshipping Protestants at Vassy, France (March 1, 1562), which began the French wars of religion. An engraving by an unidentified seventeenth-century artist. The Granger Collection

12

The Age of Religious Wars

▼ **Renewed Religious Struggle**

▼ **The French Wars of Religion (1562–1598)**
Appeal of Calvinism • Catherine de Médicis and the Guises • The Rise to Power of Henry of Navarre • The Edict of Nantes

▼ **Imperial Spain and Philip II (r. 1556–1598)**
Pillars of Spanish Power • The Revolt in the Netherlands

▼ **England and Spain (1553–1603)**
Mary I (r. 1553–1558) • Elizabeth I (r. 1558–1603)

▼ **The Thirty Years' War (1618–1648)**
Preconditions for War • Four Periods of War • The Treaty of Westphalia

▼ **In Perspective**

KEY TOPICS

- **The war between Calvinists and Catholics in France**
- **The Spanish occupation of the Netherlands**
- **The struggle for supremacy between England and Spain**
- **The devastation of central Europe during the Thirty Years' War**

THE LATE SIXTEENTH and the first half of the seventeenth centuries are described as the Age of Religious Wars because of the bloody conflict of Protestants and Catholics across Europe. Both genuine religious conflict and bitter dynastic rivalries fueled the wars. In France, the Netherlands, England, and Scotland in the second half of the sixteenth century, Calvinists fought Catholic rulers for the right to govern their own territories and to practice their chosen religion openly. In the first half of the seventeenth century, Lutherans, Calvinists, and Catholics marched against one another in central and northern Europe during the Thirty Years' War. By the mid-seventeenth century, English Puritans had successfully revolted against the Stuart monarchy and the Anglican Church. (See Chapter 13.)

▼ Renewed Religious Struggle

During the first half of the sixteenth century, religious conflict had been confined to central Europe and was primarily a struggle by Lutherans and Zwinglians to secure rights and freedoms for themselves. In the second half of the century, the focus shifted to Western Europe—to France, the Netherlands, England, and Scotland—and became a struggle by Calvinists for recognition. After the Peace of Augsburg (1555) and acceptance of the principle that a region's ruler determined its religion (*cuius regio, eius religio*), Lutheranism became a legal religion in the Holy Roman Empire. The Peace of Augsburg did not, however, extend recognition to non-Lutheran Protestants. Anabaptists and other sectarians continued to be scorned as heretics and anarchists, and Calvinists were not strong enough to gain legal standing.

Outside the empire, the struggle for religious freedom had intensified in most countries. After the Council of Trent adjourned in 1563, Catholics began a Jesuit-led international counteroffensive against Protestants. At the time of John Calvin's death in 1564, Geneva had become both a refuge for Europe's persecuted Protestants and an international school for Protestant resistance, producing leaders equal to the new Catholic challenge.

Genevan Calvinism and Catholicism as revived by the Council of Trent were two equally dogmatic, aggressive, and irreconcilable church systems. Calvinists may have looked like "new papists" to critics when they dominated cities like Geneva. Yet when, as minorities, they found their civil and religious rights denied, they became firebrands and revolutionaries. Calvinism adopted an organization that magnified regional and local religious authority. Boards of **presbyters**, or elders, represented the individual congregations of Calvinists, directly shaping policy.

By contrast, the **Counter-Reformation** sponsored a centralized episcopal church system hierarchically arranged from pope to parish priest and stressing unquestioning obedience to the person at the top. The high clergy—the pope and his bishops—not the synods of local churches, were supreme. Calvinism proved attractive to proponents of political decentralization who opposed such hierarchical rule, in principle, whereas the Roman Catholic Church, an institution also devoted to one head and one law, found absolute monarchy congenial.

The opposition between the two religions may be seen in their respective art and architecture. The Catholic Counter-Reformation found the baroque style congenial. A successor to mannerism, **baroque** presented life in a grandiose, three-dimensional display of raw energy. The great baroque artists Peter Paul Rubens (1571–1640) and Gianlorenzo Bernini (1598–1680) were Catholics. By contrast, the works of prominent Protestant artists were restrained, as can be seen in the gentle, searching portraits of the Dutch Mennonite, Rembrandt van Rijn (1606–1669). (See the juxtaposition of Bavarian Catholic and Palatine Calvinist churches.)

As religious wars engulfed Europe, the intellectuals perceived the wisdom of religious pluralism and toleration more quickly than did the politicians. A new skepticism, relativism, and individualism in religion became respectable in the sixteenth and seventeenth centuries. (See Chapter 14.) Sebastian Castellio's (1515–1563) pithy censure of John Calvin for his role in the execution of the Antitrinitarian Michael Servetus summarized a growing sentiment: "To kill a man is not to defend a doctrine, but to kill a man."[1] The French essayist Michel de Montaigne (1533–1592) asked in scorn of the dogmatic mind, "What do I know?" The Lutheran Valentin Weigel (1533–1588), surveying a half century of religious strife in Germany, advised people to look within themselves for religious truth and no longer to churches and creeds.

Such skeptical views gained currency in larger political circles only at the cost of painful experience. Religious strife and civil war were best held in check where rulers tended to subordinate theological doctrine to political unity, urging tolerance, moderation, and compromise—even indifference—in religious matters. Rulers of this kind came to be known as ***politiques***, and the most successful among them was Elizabeth I of England. By contrast, Mary I of England, Philip II of Spain, and Oliver Cromwell, all of whom took their religion with the utmost seriousness and refused any compromise, did not, in the end, achieve their political goals.

The wars of religion were both internal national conflicts and truly international wars. Catholic and Protestant subjects struggled against one another for control of the crown of France, the Netherlands, and England. The Catholic governments of France and Spain conspired and finally sent armies against Protestant regimes in England and the Netherlands. The outbreak of the Thirty Years' War in 1618 made the international dimension of the religious conflict especially clear; before it ended in 1648, the war drew every major European nation directly or indirectly into its deadly net.

▼ The French Wars of Religion (1562–1598)

French Protestants are known as **Huguenots**, a term derived from Besançon Hugues, the leader of Geneva's political revolt against the House of Savoy in the 1520s, which had been a prelude to that city's Calvinist Reformation. Huguenots were already under surveillance in France in the early 1520s when Lutheran writings and doctrines began to circulate in Paris. The capture of the French king Francis I by the forces of Emperor Charles V at the Battle of Pavia in 1525 provided a motive for the first wave of Protestant persecution in France. The French government hoped thereby to pacify the Habsburg victor, a fierce opponent of German Protestants, and to win their king's swift release.

A second major crackdown came a decade later. When Protestants plastered Paris and other cities with anti-Catholic placards on October 18, 1534, mass arrests

[1]*Contra libellum Calvini* (N.P., 1562), p. E2a.

A Closer LOOK

BAROQUE AND PLAIN CHURCH: ARCHITECTURAL REFLECTIONS OF BELIEF

CONTRAST AN eighteenth-century Catholic baroque church in Ottobeuren, Bavaria, and a seventeenth-century Calvinist plain church in the Palatinate. The Catholic church pops with sculptures, paintings, and ornamentation, while the Calvinist church has been stripped of every possible decoration.

Decorated altars dominate the interior of the Catholic church and make the sacrifice of the Eucharist in the Mass the center of worship. The intent is to inspire worshippers to self-transcendence.

Vanni/Art Resource, NY

The open Bible and raised pulpit dominate the Protestant church. The intent is to keep worshippers' attention on God's word and their own immortal souls and to prevent any form of decoration from distracting them.

German National Museum, Nuremberg, Germany

To examine this image in an interactive fashion, please go to www.myhistorylab.com

of suspected Protestants followed. The government retaliation drove John Calvin and other members of the French reform party into exile. In 1540, the Edict of Fontainebleau subjected French Protestants to the Inquisition. Henry II (r. 1547–1559) established new measures against Protestants in the Edict of Chateaubriand in 1551. Save for a few brief interludes, the French monarchy remained a staunch foe of the Protestants until the ascension to the throne of Henry IV of Navarre in 1589.

The Habsburg-Valois wars (see Chapter 11) had ended with the Treaty of Cateau-Cambrésis in 1559, after which Europe experienced a moment of peace. The same year, however, marked the beginning of internal French conflict and a shift of the European balance of power away from France to Spain. The shift began with an accident. During a tournament held to celebrate the marriage of his thirteen-year-old daughter to Philip II, the son of Charles V and heir to the Spanish Habsburg lands, the French king, Henry II, was mortally wounded when a lance pierced his visor. This unforeseen event brought to the throne his sickly fifteen-year-old son, Francis II, who died after reigning only a year (1559–1560). With the monarchy weakened, three powerful families saw their chance to control France and began to compete for the young king's ear: the Bourbons, whose power lay in the south and west; the Montmorency-Chatillons, who controlled the center of France; and the strongest among them, the Guises, who were dominant in eastern France.

The Guises had little trouble establishing firm control over the young king. Francis, duke of Guise, had been Henry II's general and his brothers, Charles and Louis, were cardinals of the church. Mary Stuart, Queen of Scots, the eighteen-year-old widow of Francis II, was their niece. Throughout the latter half of the sixteenth century, the name "Guise" remained interchangeable with militant, reactionary Catholicism.

The Bourbon and Montmorency-Chatillon families, in contrast, developed strong Huguenot sympathies, largely for political reasons. The Bourbon Louis I, prince of Condé (d. 1569), and the Montmorency-Chatillon admiral Gaspard de Coligny (1519–1572) became the political leaders of the French Protestant resistance. They collaborated early in an abortive plot to kidnap Francis II from his Guise advisers in the Conspiracy of Amboise in 1560. Calvin, who considered such tactics a disgrace to the Reformation, condemned this conspiracy.

Appeal of Calvinism

Often for different reasons, ambitious aristocrats and discontented townspeople joined Calvinist churches in opposing the Guise-dominated French monarchy. In 1561, more than 2,000 Huguenot congregations existed throughout France. Yet Huguenots were a majority of the population in only two regions: Dauphiné and Languedoc. Although they made up only about one fifteenth of the population, Huguenots held important geographic areas and were heavily represented among the more powerful segments of French society. A good two fifths of the French aristocracy became Huguenots. Many apparently hoped to establish within France a principle of territorial sovereignty akin to what the Peace of Augsburg had secured within the Holy Roman Empire. Calvinism thus served the forces of political decentralization.

John Calvin and Theodore Beza sought to advance their cause by currying favor with powerful aristocrats. Beza converted Jeanne d'Albert, the mother of the future Henry IV. The prince of Condé was apparently converted in 1558 under the influence of his Calvinist wife. For many aristocrats—Condé probably among them—Calvinist religious convictions proved useful to their political goals.

The military organization of Condé and Coligny progressively merged with the religious organization of the French Huguenot churches, creating a potent combination that benefited both political and religious dissidents. Calvinism justified and inspired political resistance, while the resistance made Calvinism a viable religion in Catholic France. Each side had much to gain from the other. The confluence of secular and religious motives, although beneficial to aristocratic resistance and the Calvinist religion alike, cast suspicion on the religious appeal of Calvinism. Clearly, religious conviction was neither the only, nor always the main, reason for becoming a Calvinist in France in the second half of the sixteenth century.

Catherine de Médicis and the Guises

Following Francis II's death in 1560, the queen mother, Catherine de Médicis (1519–1589) became regent for her minor son, Charles IX (r. 1560–1574). At a meeting in Poissy, she tried unsuccessfully to reconcile the Protestant and Catholic factions. Fearing the power and guile of the Guises, Catherine, whose first concern was always to preserve the monarchy, sought allies among the Protestants. In 1562, after conversations with Beza and Coligny, she issued the January Edict, which granted Protestants freedom to worship publicly outside towns—although only privately within them—and to hold synods. In March 1562, this royal toleration came to an abrupt end when the duke of Guise surprised a Protestant congregation at Vassy in Champagne and massacred many worshippers. That event marked the beginning of the French wars of religion.

Had Condé and the Huguenot armies rushed immediately to the queen's side after this attack, Protestants might well have secured an alliance with the crown. The queen mother's fear of Guise power was great. Condé's hesitation, however, placed the young king and the

Catherine de Médicis (1519–1589) exercised power in France during the reigns of her three sons, Francis II (r. 1559–1560), Charles IX (r. 1560–1574), and Henry III (r. 1574–1589). Getty Images, Inc.–Liaison

queen mother, against their deepest wishes, under firm Guise control. Cooperation with the Guises became the only alternative to capitulation to the Protestants.

The Peace of Saint-Germain-en-Laye During the first French war of religion, fought between April 1562 and March 1563, the duke of Guise was assassinated. It was a measure of the international character of the struggle in France that troops from Hesse and the Palatinate fought alongside the Huguenots. A brief resumption of hostilities in 1567–1568 was followed by the bloodiest of all the conflicts, between September 1568 and August 1570. In this period, Condé was killed, and Huguenot leadership passed to Coligny. This was actually a blessing in disguise for the Protestants, because Coligny was far the better military strategist. In the peace of Saint-Germain-en-Laye (1570), which ended the third war, the crown, acknowledging the power of the Protestant nobility, granted the Huguenots religious freedoms within their territories and the right to fortify their cities.

Perpetually caught between fanatical Huguenot and Guise extremes, Queen Catherine had always sought to balance one side against the other. Like the Guises, she wanted a Catholic France, but she feared a Guise-dominated monarchy. After the Peace of Saint-Germain-en-Laye, the crown tilted manifestly toward the Bourbon faction and the Huguenots, and Coligny became Charles IX's most trusted adviser. Unknown to the king, Catherine began to plot with the Guises against the ascendant Protestants. As she had earlier sought Protestant support when Guise power threatened to subdue the monarchy, she now sought Guise support as Protestant influence grew.

There was reason for Catherine to fear Coligny's hold on the king. Louis of Nassau, the leader of Protestant resistance to Philip II in the Netherlands, had gained Coligny's ear. Coligny used his influence to win the king of France over to a planned French invasion of the Netherlands to support the Dutch Protestants. This would have placed France squarely on a collision course with mighty Spain. Catherine recognized far better than her son that France stood little chance in such a contest. News of the stunning Spanish victory over the Turks at Lepanto in October 1571 had sobered Catherine and her advisors.

The Saint Bartholomew's Day Massacre When Catherine lent her support to the infamous Saint Bartholomew's Day Massacre of Protestants, she did so out of a far less reasoned judgment. Her decision appears to have been made in near panic. On August 22, 1572, four days after the Huguenot Henry of Navarre had married the king's sister, Marguerite of Valois—still another sign of growing Protestant power—Coligny was struck down, although not killed, by an assassin's bullet. Catherine had apparently been party to this Guise plot to eliminate Coligny. After its failure, she feared both the king's reaction to her complicity with the Guises and Coligny's response. Catherine convinced Charles that a Huguenot coup was afoot, inspired by Coligny, and that only the swift execution of Protestant leaders could save the crown from a Protestant attack on Paris.

On Saint Bartholomew's Day, August 24, 1572, Coligny and 3,000 fellow Huguenots were butchered in Paris. Within three days coordinated attacks across France killed an estimated 20,000 Huguenots. It is a date that has ever since lived in infamy for Protestants.

Pope Gregory XIII and Philip II of Spain reportedly greeted the news of the Protestant massacre with special religious celebrations. Philip had good reason to rejoice. By throwing France into civil war, the massacre ended any planned French opposition to his efforts to subdue his rebellious subjects in the Netherlands. But the massacre of thousands of Protestants also gave the discerning Catholic world cause for new alarm. The event changed the nature of the struggle between Protestants and Catholics both within and beyond the borders of France. It was thereafter no longer an internal contest between Guise and Bourbon factions for French political influence, nor was it simply a Huguenot campaign to win basic religious freedoms. Henceforth, in Protestant eyes, it became an international struggle for sheer survival against an adversary whose cruelty justified any means of resistance.

Protestant Resistance Theory Only as Protestants faced suppression and sure defeat did they begin to sanction active political resistance. At first, they tried to practice the biblical precept of obedient subjection to worldly authority (Romans 13:1). Luther had only grudgingly approved resistance to the emperor after the Diet of Augsburg in 1530. In 1550, Lutherans in Magdeburg had published an influential defense of the right of lower authorities to oppose the emperor's order that all Lutherans return to the Catholic fold.

Calvin, who never faced the specter of total political defeat after his return to Geneva in September 1540, had always condemned willful disobedience and rebellion against lawfully constituted governments as un-Christian. Yet he also taught that lower magistrates, as part of the lawfully constituted government, had the right and duty to oppose tyrannical higher authority.

The exiled Scots reformer John Knox (1513–1572), who had seen Mary of Guise, the Regent of Scotland, and Mary I of England crush his cause, laid the groundwork for later Calvinist resistance. In his famous *First Blast of the Trumpet against the Terrible Regiment of Women* (1558), he declared that the removal of a heathen tyrant was not only permissible, but also a Christian duty. He had the Catholic queen of England in mind.

After the great massacre of French Protestants on Saint Bartholomew's Day 1572, Calvinists everywhere came to appreciate the need for an active defense of their religious rights. Classical Huguenot theories of resistance appeared in three major works of the 1570s. The first was the *Franco-Gallia* of François Hotman (1573), a humanist argument that the representative Estates General of France historically held higher authority than the French king. The second was Theodore Beza's *On the Right of Magistrates over Their Subjects* (1574), which, going beyond Calvin's views, justified the correction and even the overthrow of tyrannical rulers by lower authorities. (See "Theodore Beza Defends the Right to Resist Tyranny.") Finally, Philippe du Plessis Mornay's *Defense of Liberty against Tyrants* (1579) admonished princes, nobles, and magistrates beneath the king, as guardians of the rights of the body politic, to take up arms against tyranny in other lands.

The Rise to Power of Henry of Navarre

Henry III (r. 1574–1589) was the last of Henry II's sons to wear the French crown. He found the monarchy wedged between a radical Catholic League, formed in 1576 by Henry of Guise, and vengeful Huguenots. Neither group would have been reluctant to assassinate a ruler they considered heretical and a tyrant. Like the queen mother, Henry sought to steer a middle course. In this effort, he received support from a growing body of neutral Catholics and Huguenots, who put the political survival of France above its religious unity. Such *politiques* were prepared to compromise religious creeds to save the nation.

The Peace of Beaulieu in May 1576 granted the Huguenots almost complete religious and civil freedom. France, however, was not ready then for such sweeping toleration. Within seven months of the Peace, the Catholic League forced Henry to return to the illusory quest for absolute religious unity in France. In October 1577, the king truncated the Peace of Beaulieu and once again limited areas of permitted Huguenot worship. Thereafter, Huguenot and Catholic factions returned to their accustomed anarchical military solutions. The Protestants were led by Henry of Navarre, a legal heir to the French throne by virtue of his descent in a direct male line from St. Louis IX (d. 1270).

In the mid-1580s, the Catholic League, with Spanish support, became dominant in Paris. In what came to be known as the Day of the Barricades, Henry III attempted to rout the league with a surprise attack in 1588. The effort failed, and the king had to flee Paris. Forced by his weakened position into unkingly guerrilla tactics, and also emboldened by news of the English victory over the Spanish Armada in 1588, Henry had both the duke and the cardinal of Guise assassinated. These murders sent France reeling once again. Led by still another Guise brother, the Catholic League reacted with a fury that matched the earlier Huguenot response to the Massacre of Saint Bartholomew's Day. The king was now forced to strike an alliance with the Protestant Henry of Navarre in April 1589.

As the two Henrys prepared to attack the Guise stronghold of Paris, however, an enraged Dominican friar killed Henry III. Thereupon, the Bourbon Huguenot Henry of Navarre succeeded the childless Valois king to the French throne as Henry IV (r. 1589–1610). Pope Sixtus V and Philip II were aghast at the sudden prospect of a Protestant France. They had always wanted France to be religiously Catholic and politically weak, and they now acted to achieve that end. Spain rushed troops to support the besieged Catholic League. Philip II apparently even hoped to place his eldest daughter, Isabella, the granddaughter of Henry II and Catherine de Médicis, on the French throne.

Direct Spanish intervention in the affairs of France seemed only to strengthen Henry IV's grasp on the crown. The French people viewed his right to hereditary succession more seriously than his Protestantism. Henry was also widely liked. Notoriously informal in dress and manner—which made him especially popular with the soldiers—Henry also had the wit and charm to neutralize the strongest enemy in a face-to-face confrontation. He came to the throne as a *politique*, long weary with religious

THEODORE BEZA DEFENDS THE RIGHT TO RESIST TYRANNY

One of the oldest problems in political and social theory has been that of knowing when resistance to repression in matters of conscience is justified. Since Luther's day, Protestant reformers, although accused by their Catholic critics of fomenting social division and revolution, had urged their followers to strict obedience to established political authority. After the 1572 massacre of Saint Bartholomew's Day, however, Protestant pampheteers urged Protestants to resist tyrants and persecutors with armed force. Here, in 1574, Theodore Beza points out the obligation of rulers to their subjects and the latter's right to resist rulers who fail to meet the conditions of their office.

It is apparent that there is a mutual obligation between the king and the officers of a kingdom; that the government of the kingdom is not in the hands of the king in its entirety, but only the sovereign degree; that each of the officers has a share in accord with his degree; and that there are definite conditions on either side. If these conditions are not observed by the inferior officers, it is the part of the sovereign to dismiss and punish them. . . . If the king, hereditary or elective, clearly goes back on the conditions without which he would not have been recognized and acknowledged, can there be any doubt that the lesser magistrates of the kingdom, of the cities, and of the provinces, the administration of which they have received from the sovereignty itself, are free of their oath, at least to the extent that they are entitled to resist flagrant oppression of the realm which they swore to defend and protect according to their office and their particular jurisdiction? . . .

We must now speak of the third class of subjects, which though admittedly subject to the sovereign in a certain respect, is, in another respect, and in cases of necessity the protector of the rights of the sovereignty itself, and is established to hold the sovereign to his duty, and even, if need be, to constrain and punish him. . . . The people is prior to all the magistrates, and does not exist for them, but they for it. . . . Whenever law and equity prevailed, nations neither created nor accepted kings except upon definite conditions. From this it follows that when kings flagrantly violate these terms, these who have the power to give them their authority have no less power to deprive them of it.

Hotman, Beza, and Mornay, trans. and ed. by Julian H. Franklin, *Constitutionalism and Resistance in the Sixteenth Century: Three Treatises* (New York: Pegasus, 1969), pp. 111–114.

strife and fully prepared to place political peace above absolute religious unity. He believed a royal policy of tolerant Catholicism would be the best way to achieve such peace. On July 25, 1593, he publicly abandoned the Protestant faith and embraced the traditional and majority religion of his country. "Paris is worth a Mass," he is reported to have said.

It was, in fact, a decision he had made only after a long period of personal agonizing. The Huguenots were horrified, and Pope Clement VIII was skeptical of Henry's sincerity, but most of the French church and people, having known internal strife too long, rallied to his side. By 1596, the Catholic League was dispersed, its ties with Spain were broken, and the wars of religion in France, to all intents, had ground to a close.

The Edict of Nantes

On April 13, 1598, Henry IV's famous Edict of Nantes proclaimed a formal religious settlement. The following month, on May 2, 1598, the Treaty of Vervins ended hostilities between France and Spain.

In 1591, Henry IV had already assured the Huguenots of at least qualified religious freedoms. The Edict of Nantes made good that promise. It recognized minority religious rights within what was to remain an officially Catholic country. This religious truce—and it was never more than that—granted the Huguenots, who by this time numbered well over a million, freedom of public worship, the right of assembly, admission to public offices and universities, and permission to maintain

Henry IV of France (r. 1589–1610) on horseback, painted in 1594. Réunion des Musées Nationaux/Art Resource, NY

fortified towns. They were to exercise most of the new freedoms, however, within their own towns and territories. Concession of the right to fortify their towns revealed the continuing distrust between French Protestants and Catholics. As significant as it was, the edict only transformed a long hot war between irreconcilable enemies into a long cold war. To its critics, it had only created a state within a state.

A Catholic fanatic assassinated Henry IV in May 1610. Although he is best remembered for the Edict of Nantes, Henry IV's political and economic policies were equally important. They laid the foundations for the transformation of France into the absolute state it would become under Cardinal Richelieu and Louis XIV. (See Chapter 13.) Ironically, in pursuit of the political and religious unity that had escaped Henry IV, Louis XIV, calling for "one king, one law, one faith," would revoke the Edict of Nantes in 1685, an action that forced France and Europe to learn again by bitter experience the hard lessons of the wars of religion.

▼ Imperial Spain and Philip II (r. 1556–1598)

Pillars of Spanish Power

Until the English defeated the mighty Spanish Armada in 1588, no one person stood larger in the second half of the sixteenth century than Philip II of Spain. Philip was heir to the intensely Catholic and militarily supreme western Habsburg kingdom. His father, Charles V, had given the eastern Habsburg lands of Austria, Bohemia, and Hungary to Philip's uncle, the emperor Ferdinand I (r. 1558–1564). These lands, together with the imperial title, remained in the possession of the Austrian branch of the family until 1918.

New World Riches Populous and wealthy Castile gave Philip a solid home base. The regular arrival in Seville of bullion from the Spanish colonies in the New World provided additional wealth. In the 1540s, great silver mines had been opened in Potosí in present-day Bolivia and in Zacatecas in Mexico. These provided the great sums needed to pay the king's bankers and mercenaries. He nonetheless never managed to erase the debts his father left or to finance his own foreign adventures fully. He later contributed to the bankruptcy of the Fuggers when, at the end of his life, he defaulted on his enormous debts.

Increased Population The new American wealth brought dramatic social change to the peoples of Europe during the second half of the sixteenth century. As Europe became richer, it was also becoming more populous. In the economically and politically active towns of France, England, and the Netherlands, populations had tripled and quadrupled by the early seventeenth century. Europe's population exceeded 70 million by 1600.

The combination of increased wealth and population triggered inflation. A steady 2-percent-a-year rise in prices in much of Europe had serious cumulative effects by the mid-sixteenth century. There were more people and more coinage in circulation than before, but less food and fewer jobs; wages stagnated while prices doubled and tripled in much of Europe.

MAIN EVENTS OF THE FRENCH WARS OF RELIGION

1559	Treaty of Cateau-Cambrésis ends Habsburg-Valois wars
1559	Francis II succeeds to French throne under regency of his mother, Catherine de Médicis
1560	Conspiracy of Amboise fails
1562	Protestant worshippers massacred at Vassy in Champagne by the duke of Guise
1572	The Saint Bartholomew's Day Massacre leaves thousands of Protestants dead
1589	Assassination of Henry III brings the Huguenot Henry of Navarre to throne as Henry IV
1593	Henry IV embraces Catholicism
1598	Henry IV grants Huguenots religious and civil freedoms in the Edict of Nantes
1610	Henry IV assassinated

This was especially the case in Spain. Because the new wealth was concentrated in the hands of a few, the traditional gap between the haves—the propertied, privileged, and educated classes—and the have-nots widened. Nowhere did the unprivileged suffer more than in Spain, where the Castilian peasantry, the backbone of Philip II's great empire, became the most heavily taxed people of Europe. Those whose labor contributed most to making possible Spanish hegemony in Europe in the second half of the sixteenth century prospered least from it.

Efficient Bureaucracy and Military A subjugated peasantry and wealth from the New World were not the only pillars of Spanish strength. Philip II shrewdly organized the lesser nobility into a loyal and efficient national bureaucracy. A reclusive man, he managed his kingdom by pen and paper rather than by personal presence. He was also a learned and pious Catholic, although some popes suspected he used religion as much for political as for devotional purposes. That he was a generous patron of the arts and culture can be seen in his unique retreat outside Madrid, the Escorial, a combination palace, church, tomb, and monastery. Philip also knew personal sorrows: His mad and treacherous son, Don Carlos, died under suspicious circumstances in 1568—some contemporaries suspected that Philip had him quietly executed—only three months before the death of his queen.

Supremacy in the Mediterranean During the first half of Philip's reign, attention focused almost exclusively on the Mediterranean and the Turkish threat. By history, geography, and choice, Spain had traditionally been Catholic Europe's champion against Islam. During the 1560s, the Turks advanced deep into Austria, and their fleets dominated the Mediterranean. Between 1568 and 1570, armies under Philip's half brother, Don John of Austria (1547–1578), the illegitimate son of Charles V, suppressed and dispersed the Moors in Granada.

In May 1571, a Holy League of Spain, Venice, Genoa, and the pope, again under Don John's command, formed to check Turkish belligerence in the Mediterranean. In the largest naval battle of the sixteenth century, Don John's fleet engaged the Ottoman navy under Ali Pasha off Lepanto in the Gulf of Corinth on October 7, 1571. Before the engagement ended, over a third of the Turkish fleet had been sunk or captured, and 30,000 Turks had died. However, the resilient Ottomans still maintained their base in Cyprus and would soon rebuild their fleet and regain control of the eastern Mediterranean. For the moment, however, the Mediterranean belonged to Spain, and the Europeans were left to fight each other. Philip's armies also suppressed resistance in neighboring Portugal, when Philip inherited the throne of that kingdom in 1580. The union with Portugal not only enhanced Spanish sea power, but it also brought Portugal's overseas empire in Africa, India, and Brazil into the Spanish orbit.

The Revolt in the Netherlands

The spectacular Spanish military success in southern Europe was not repeated in northern Europe. When Philip attempted to impose his will within the Netherlands and on England and France, he learned the lessons of defeat. The resistance of the Netherlands especially proved the undoing of Spanish dreams of world empire. (See Map 12–1, page 354.)

Cardinal Granvelle The Netherlands was the richest area not only of Philip's Hapsburg kingdom, but of Europe as well. In 1559, Philip departed the Netherlands for Spain, never again to return. His half sister, Margaret of Parma, assisted by a special council of state, became regent in his place. The council was headed by the extremely able Antoine Perrenot (1517–1586), known after 1561 as Cardinal Granvelle, who hoped to check Protestant gains by internal church reforms. He planned to break down the traditional local autonomy of the seventeen Netherlands provinces by stages and establish in its place a centralized royal government directed from Madrid. A politically docile and religiously uniform country was the goal.

The merchant towns of the Netherlands were, however, Europe's most independent; many, like magnificent Antwerp, were also Calvinist strongholds. By tradition and habit, the people of the Netherlands were far more disposed to variety and toleration than to obedient conformity and hierarchical order. Two members of the council of state led a stubborn opposition to the

Map 12–1 **THE NETHERLANDS DURING THE REFORMATION** The northern and southern provinces of the Netherlands. The former, the United Provinces, were mostly Protestant in the second half of the sixteenth century; the southern Spanish Netherlands made peace with Spain and remained largely Catholic.

Spanish overlords, who now attempted to reimpose their traditional rule with a vengeance. They were the Count of Egmont (1522–1568) and William of Nassau, the Prince of Orange (1533–1584), known as "the Silent" because of his small circle of confidants.

Like other successful rulers in this period, William of Orange placed the political autonomy and well-being of the Netherlands above religious creeds. He personally was successively a confessed Catholic, Lutheran, and Calvinist. In 1561, he married Anne of Saxony, the daughter of the Lutheran elector Maurice and the granddaughter of the late landgrave Philip of Hesse. He maintained his Catholic practices until 1567, the year he turned Lutheran. After the Saint Bartholomew's Day Massacre (1572), Orange (as he was called) became an avowed Calvinist.

In 1561, Cardinal Granvelle proceeded with his planned ecclesiastical reorganization of the Netherlands. It was intended to tighten the control of the Catholic hierarchy over the country and to accelerate its consolidation as a Spanish ward. Organizing the Dutch nobility in opposition, Orange and Egmont succeeded in gaining Granvelle's removal from office in 1564. Aristocratic control of the country after Granvelle's departure, however, proved woefully inefficient. Popular unrest grew, especially among urban artisans, who joined the congregations of radical Calvinist preachers in large numbers.

The Compromise The year 1564 also saw the first fusion of political and religious opposition to Regent Margaret's government. This opposition resulted from Philip II's unwise insistence on trying to enforce the decrees of the Council of Trent throughout the Netherlands. William of Orange's younger brother, Louis of Nassau, who had been raised a Lutheran, led the opposition with support from the Calvinist-inclined lesser nobility and townspeople. A national covenant called the *Compromise* was drawn up, a solemn pledge to resist the decrees of Trent and the Inquisition. Grievances were loudly and persistently voiced. When Regent Margaret's government spurned the protesters as "beggars" in 1566, Calvinists rioted throughout the country. Louis called for aid from French Huguenots and German Lutherans, and a full-scale rebellion against the Spanish regency appeared imminent.

The Duke of Alba The rebellion failed to materialize, however, because the higher nobility of the Netherlands would not support it. Their shock at Calvinist iconoclasm and anarchy was as great as their resentment of Granvelle's more subtle repression. Philip, determined to make an example of the Protestant rebels, dispatched the duke of Alba to suppress the revolt. His army of 10,000 journeyed northward from Milan in 1567 in a show of combined Spanish and papal might. A special tribunal, known to the Spanish as the Council of Troubles and among the Netherlanders as the Council of Blood, reigned over the land. Before Alba's reign of terror ended, the counts of Egmont and Horn and several thousand suspected heretics were publicly executed.

The Spanish levied new taxes, forcing the Netherlands to pay for the suppression of its own revolt. One, the "tenth penny," a 10 percent sales tax, met such resistance from merchants and artisans that it could not be collected in some areas even after reduction to 3 percent. Combined persecution and taxation sent tens of thousands fleeing from the Netherlands during Alba's six-year rule, a man more hated than Granvelle or the radical Calvinists had ever been.

Resistance and Unification William of Orange was an exile in Germany during these turbulent years. He now emerged as the leader of a broad movement for the independence of the Netherlands from Spain. The northern, Calvinist-inclined provinces of Holland, Zeeland, and Utrecht, of which Orange was the *Stadholder*, or governor, became his base. As in France, political resistance in the Netherlands gained both organization and inspiration by merging with Calvinism.

The early victories of the resistance attest to the popular character of the revolt. A case in point is the capture of the port city of Brill by the "Sea Beggars," an international group of anti-Spanish exiles and criminals, among them many Englishmen. William of Orange did not hesitate to enlist their services. Their brazen piracy, however, had forced Queen Elizabeth to disassociate herself from them and to bar their ships from English ports. In 1572, the Beggars captured Brill and other seaports in Zeeland and Holland. Mixing with the native population, they quickly sparked rebellions against Alba in town after town and spread

The Milch Cow, a sixteenth-century satirical painting depicting the Netherlands as a cow in whom all the great powers of Europe have an interest. Elizabeth of England is feeding her (England had long-standing commercial ties with Flanders); Philip II of Spain is attempting to ride her (Spain was trying to reassert its control over the entire area); William of Orange is trying to milk her (he was the leader of the anti-Spanish rebellion); and the king of France holds her tail (France hoped to profit from the rebellion at Spain's expense). The "Milch Cow." Rijksmuseum, Amsterdam the resistance southward. In 1574, the people of Leiden heroically resisted a long Spanish siege. The Dutch opened the dikes and flooded their country to repulse the hated Spanish. The faltering Alba had by that time ceded power to Don Luis de Requesens, who replaced him as commander of the Spanish forces in the Netherlands in November 1573.

The Pacification of Ghent The greatest atrocity of the war came after Requesens's death in 1576. Spanish mercenaries, leaderless and unpaid, ran amok in Antwerp on November 4, 1576, leaving 7,000 people dead in the streets. The event came to be known as the Spanish Fury.

These atrocities accomplished in just four days what neither religion nor patriotism had previously been able to do. The ten largely Catholic southern provinces (what is roughly modern Belgium) now came together with the seven largely Protestant northern provinces (what is roughly the modern Netherlands) in unified opposition to Spain. This union, known as the Pacification of Ghent, was accomplished on November 8, 1576. It declared internal regional sovereignty in matters of religion, a key clause that permitted political cooperation among the signatories, who were not agreed over religion. It was a Netherlands version of the territorial settlement of religious differences brought about in the Holy Roman Empire in 1555 by the Peace of Augsburg. Four provinces initially held out, but they soon made the resistance unanimous by joining the all-embracing Union of Brussels in January 1577. For the next two years, the Spanish faced a unified and determined Netherlands.

Don John, the victor over the Turks at Lepanto in 1571, had taken command of Spanish land forces in November 1576. He now experienced his first defeat. Confronted by unified Netherlands' resistance, he signed the humiliating Perpetual Edict in February 1577, which provided for the removal of all Spanish troops from the Netherlands within twenty days. The withdrawal gave the country to William of Orange and effectively ended, for the time being, whatever plans Philip may have had for using the Netherlands as a staging area for an invasion of England.

The Union of Arras and the Union of Utrecht The Spanish, however, were nothing if not persistent. Don John and Alexander Farnese of Parma, the Regent Margaret's son, revived Spanish power in the southern provinces, where fear of Calvinist extremism had moved the leaders to break the Union of Brussels. In January 1579, the southern provinces formed the Union of Arras and soon made peace with Spain. These provinces later served the cause of the Counter-Reformation. The northern provinces responded by forming the Union of Utrecht.

Netherlands Independence Seizing what now appeared to be a last opportunity to break the back of Netherlands' resistance, Philip II declared William of Orange an outlaw and placed a bounty of 25,000 crowns on his head. The act predictably stiffened the resistance of the northern provinces. In a famous defiant speech to the Estates General of Holland in December 1580, known as the Apology, Orange publicly denounced Philip as a heathen tyrant whom the Netherlands need no longer obey.

On July 22, 1581, the member provinces of the Union of Utrecht met in The Hague and formally declared Philip no longer their ruler. They turned instead to the French duke of Alençon, the youngest son of Catherine de Médicis. The southern provinces had also earlier looked to him as a possible middle way between Spanish and Calvinist overlordship. All the northern provinces save Holland and Zeeland (which distrusted him almost as much as they did Philip II) accepted Alençon as their "sovereign" but with the clear understanding that he would be only a titular ruler. Yet Alençon, an ambitious failure, saw this as his one chance at greatness. When he rashly attempted to take actual control of the provinces in 1583, he was deposed and returned to France.

Spanish efforts to reconquer the Netherlands continued into the 1580s. William of Orange, assassinated in July 1584, was succeeded by his seventeen-year-old son, Maurice (1567–1625), who, with the assistance of England and France, continued the Dutch resistance. Fortunately for the Netherlands, Philip II began now to meddle directly in French and English affairs. He signed a secret treaty with the Guises (the Treaty of Joinville in December 1584) and sent armies under Alexander Farnese into France in 1590. Hostilities with the English, who openly aided the Dutch rebels, also increased. Gradually, they built to a climax in 1588, when Philip's great Armada was defeated in the English Channel.

These new fronts overextended Spain's resources, thus strengthening the Netherlands. Spanish preoccupation with France and England now permitted the northern provinces to drive out all Spanish soldiers by 1593. In 1596, France and England formally recognized their independence. Peace was not, however, concluded with Spain until 1609, when the Twelve Years' Truce gave the northern provinces virtual independence. Full recognition came with the Peace of Westphalia in 1648.

▼ England and Spain (1553–1603)

Before Edward VI died in 1553, he agreed to a device to make Lady Jane Grey, the teenage daughter of a powerful Protestant nobleman and the granddaughter, on her mother's side, of Henry VIII's younger sister Mary, his successor in place of the Catholic Mary Tudor

(r. 1553–1558). Yet popular support for the principle of hereditary monarchy was too strong to deprive Mary of her rightful rule. Uprisings in London and elsewhere led to Jane Grey's removal from the throne within days of her crowning, and she was eventually beheaded.

Mary I (r. 1553–1558)

Once enthroned, Mary proceeded to act even beyond the worst fears of the Protestants. In 1554, she entered a highly unpopular political marriage with Philip (later Philip II) of Spain, a symbol of militant Catholicism to English Protestants. At his direction, she pursued a foreign policy that in 1558 cost England its last enclave on the Continent, Calais.

Mary's domestic measures were equally shocking to the English people and even more divisive. During her reign, Parliament repealed the Protestant statutes of Edward and reverted to the Catholic religious practice of her father, Henry VIII. The great Protestant leaders of the Edwardian Age—John Hooper, Hugh Latimer, and Thomas Cranmer—were executed for heresy. Hundreds of Protestants either joined them in martyrdom (287 were burned at the stake during Mary's reign) or fled to the Continent. These "Marian exiles" settled in Germany and Switzerland, especially in Frankfurt, Strasbourg, and Geneva. (John Knox, the future leader of the Reformation in Scotland, was prominent among them.) There they waited for the time when a Protestant counteroffensive could be launched in their homelands. They were also exposed to Protestant religious beliefs more radical than any set forth during Edward VI's reign. Many of these exiles later held positions in the Church of England during Elizabeth I's reign.

Portrait of Mary I (r. 1553–1558), Queen of England. Queen Mary I, 1554 (oil on panel) by Sir Anthonis Mor (Antonio Moro) (1517/20 - 76/7). Prado, Madrid, Spain/Bridgeman Art Library

Elizabeth I (r. 1558–1603)

Mary's successor was her half sister, Elizabeth I, the daughter of Henry VIII and Anne Boleyn. Elizabeth had remarkable and enduring successes in both domestic and foreign policy. Assisted by a shrewd adviser, Sir William Cecil (1520–1598), she built a true kingdom on the ruins of Mary's reign. Between 1559 and 1603, she and Cecil guided a religious settlement through Parliament that prevented religious differences from tearing England apart in the sixteenth century. A ruler who subordinated religious to political unity, Elizabeth merged a centralized episcopal system that she firmly controlled with broadly defined Protestant doctrine and traditional Catholic ritual. The resulting Anglican Church contained inflexible religious extremes for decades.

In 1559, an Act of Supremacy passed Parliament, repealing all the anti-Protestant legislation of Mary Tudor and asserting Elizabeth's right as "supreme governor" over both spiritual and temporal affairs. In the same year, the Act of Uniformity mandated for every English parish a revised version of the second *Book of Common Prayer* (1552). In 1563, the issuance of the **Thirty-Nine Articles**, a revision of Thomas Cranmer's original forty-two, made a moderate Protestantism the official religion within the Church of England.

Catholic and Protestant Extremists Elizabeth hoped to avoid both Catholic and Protestant extremism by pursuing a middle way. Her first archbishop of Canterbury, Matthew Parker (d. 1575), represented this ideal. Elizabeth could not prevent the emergence of subversive Catholic and Protestant zealots, however. When she ascended the throne, Catholics were in the majority in England. The extremists among them, encouraged by the Jesuits, plotted against her. The Spanish, piqued both by Elizabeth's Protestant sympathies and by her refusal to take Philip II's hand in marriage, encouraged and later directly assisted Catholic radicals. Elizabeth deliberately remained unmarried throughout her reign, using the possibility of a royal marriage to her diplomatic advantage.

Catholic extremists hoped eventually to replace Elizabeth with Mary Stuart, Queen of Scots. Unlike Elizabeth, who had been declared illegitimate during the reign of her father, Mary Stuart had an unblemished

COMPARE AND CONNECT

A Great Debate Over Religious Tolerance

ON OCTOBER 27, 1553, the Spanish physician and amateur theologian Michael Servetus died at the stake in Geneva for alleged "blasphemies against the Holy Trinity." A bold and confident man, he had also incurred the wrath of Rome before badgering John Calvin in Geneva on theological issues. In the wake of Sevetus's execution, Calvin was much criticized for fighting heresy with capital punishment. In 1544, he came to his own defense in a tract entitled *Defense of the Orthodox Faith in the Holy Trinity Against the Monstrous Errors of Michael Servetus of Spain*. Thereafter, Sebastian Castellio, an accomplished humanist and former rector of the *college* in Geneva, whom Calvin had driven out of the city years earlier, began a series of writings against Calvin. One of his titles, *Whether Heretics Should Be Punished By the Sword of the Magistrates*, was an anonymous anthology on religious toleration that included a supporting excerpt from John Calvin himself! Writing over the years under several pseudonyms, Castellio excerpted statements from Calvin's works and put them in a sustained "debate" with his own liberal point of view.

QUESTIONS

1. **Why does Calvin believe that heresy deserves capital punishment?**
2. **What are Castellio's best rebuttal arguments?**
3. **Why does Castellio write under pseudonyms?**

I

CALVIN: Kings are duty bound to defend the doctrine of piety.

CASTELLIO: [Yes, but] to kill a man is not to defend doctrine, but rather to kill a man . . .

CALVIN: What of today? The majority of people have lost all sense of shame and openly mock God. They burst as boldly into God's awesome mysteries as pigs poke their snouts into costly storehouses.

CASTELLIO: Calvin appears to be criticizing himself. For truly the awesome mysteries of God are the Trinity, predestination, and election. But this man [Calvin] speaks so assuredly about these matters that one would think he was in Paradise. So thorny is his own teaching about the Trinity . . . that by his own curiosity he weakens and makes doubtful the consciences of the simple. He has taught so crudely about predestination that innumerable men have been seduced into a security as great as that which existed before the Flood . . .
Tell me, in brief, what you think about predestination.

CALVIN: I have been taught the following about predestination: All men are not created in an equal state. Rather in eternity, God, by inevitable decree, determined in advance those whom he would save and those whom he would damn to destruction. Those whom he has deemed worthy of salvation have been chosen by his mercy without consideration of their worthiness. And those given damnation, he shuts off from life by a just and irreprehensible, albeit incomprehensible, judgment.

CASTELLIO: So you maintain that certain men are created by God already marked for damnation so that they cannot be saved?

CALVIN: Precisely.

CASTELLIO: But what if they *should* obey God? Would they not then be saved?

CALVIN: They would then be saved. However, they are not able to obey God, because God excludes them from the knowledge of his name and the spirit of his justification so that they can and will do only evil and are inclined only to every kind of sin.

CASTELLIO: Hence, they have that inclination [to sin] from God's creation and predestination?

CALVIN: They have it so, just as surely as God has created the wolf with the inclination to eat sheep!

CASTELLIO: Therefore they have been damned and rejected by God even before they existed?

CALVIN: Exactly.

CASTELLIO: But are they not damned for their sins?

CALVIN: Indeed so. Those who were destined to that [damned] lot are completely worthy of it.

CASTELLIO: When were they worthy of it?

CALVIN: When they were destined to it?

CASTELLIO: Then they have 'been' before they 'are'. Do you see what you are saying?!

CALVIN: I don't understand.

CASTELLIO: If they were worthy, then they 'were.' For to be worthy is to be. And if you concede that they have been damned before they are, then they have 'been' before they were.

CALVIN: God elects the foolish things of the world to confound the wise.

CASTELLIO: Calvin and his kind reject the foolish things of the world so that they may exalt the wise [themselves]. Hence, they admit hardly anyone into . . . their circle who is not accomplished in sciences and languages . . . If Christ himself came to them, he would certainly be turned away if he spoke no Latin . . .

[But] Christ wishes to be judged by common sense and refers the matters of the gospel to human judgment . . . He would never have employed such analogies had he wished to deprive us of our common sense. And who would have believed him had he taught things repugnant to nature and contradictory to human experience . . .? What kind of master would he have been, had he said to the woman who cried out to him and washed his feet with her hair: "O woman, whatever your sin, it was done by God's decree!

Source: Steven Ozment, *Mysticism and Dissent: Religious Ideology and Social Protest in the Sixteenth Century* (New Haven, CT: Yale University Press), pp. 171–179.

Queen Elizabeth I of England (r. 1558–1603) served as an example of religious tolerance during her reign. Despite her Protestant sympathies, she steered clear of both Catholic and Protestant extremism and, despite proven cases of Catholic treason and even attempted regicide, she executed fewer Catholics during her forty-five years on the throne than Mary Tudor had executed Protestants during her brief five-year reign. Courtesy of the Library of Congress, Rare Book and Special Collections Division

An idealized likeness of Elizabeth Tudor when she was a princess, attributed to Flemish court painter L. B. Teerling, ca. 1551. The painting shows her blazing red hair and alludes to her learning by the addition of books. UNKNOWN, formerly attributed to William Scrots. Elizabeth I, when Princess (1533–1603). The Royal Collection © 2002, Her Majesty Queen Elizabeth II

claim to the throne by way of her grandmother Margaret, the sister of Henry VIII. Elizabeth acted swiftly against Catholic assassination plots, rarely letting her emotions override her political instincts. Despite proven cases of Catholic treason and even attempted regicide, she executed fewer Catholics during her forty-five years on the throne than Mary Tudor had executed Protestants during her brief five-year reign.

Elizabeth showed little mercy, however, to any who threatened the unity of her rule. She dealt cautiously with the Puritans, who were Protestants working within the national church to "purify" it of every vestige of "popery" and to make its Protestant doctrine more precise. The Puritans had two special grievances against her reign:

1. The retention of Catholic ceremony and vestments within the Church of England, which made it appear to the casual observer that no Reformation had occurred
2. The continuation of the episcopal system of church governance, which conceived the English church to be theologically the true successor to Rome, while placing it politically under the firm hand of the queen and her compliant archbishop

Sixteenth-century Puritans were not true separatists. They enjoyed popular support and were led by widely respected men like Thomas Cartwright (d. 1603). They worked through Parliament to create an alternative national church of semiautonomous congregations governed by representative presbyteries (hence, **Presbyterians**), following the model of Calvin and Geneva. Elizabeth dealt firmly, but subtly, with them, conceding nothing that lessened the hierarchical unity of the Church of England and her control over it.

The more extreme Puritans wanted every congregation to be autonomous, a law unto itself, with neither higher episcopal nor presbyterian control. They came to be known as **Congregationalists**. Elizabeth and her second archbishop of Canterbury, John Whitgift (d. 1604), refused to tolerate this group, whose views on independence they found patently subversive. The Conventicle Act of 1593 gave such separatists the option either to conform to the practices of the Church of England or face exile or death.

Deterioration of Relations with Spain A series of events led inexorably to war between England and Spain, despite the sincere desires of both Philip II and Elizabeth to avoid a confrontation. In 1567, the Spanish duke of Alba marched his mighty army into the Netherlands, which was, from the English point of view, simply a convenient staging area for a Spanish invasion of England. Pope Pius V (r. 1566–1572), who favored a military conquest of Protestant England, "excommunicated" Elizabeth for heresy in 1570. This mischievous act encouraged both internal resistance and international intrigue against the queen. Two years later, as noted earlier, the piratical sea beggars, many of whom were Englishmen, occupied the port of Brill in the Netherlands and aroused the surrounding countryside against the Spanish.

Following Don John's demonstration of Spain's awesome sea power at Lepanto in 1571, England signed a mutual defense pact with France. Also in the 1570s, Elizabeth's famous seamen John Hawkins (1532–1595) and Sir Francis Drake (1545?–1596) began to prey regularly on Spanish shipping in the Americas. Drake's circumnavigation of the globe between 1577 and 1580 was one in a series of dramatic demonstrations of English ascendancy on the high seas.

After the Saint Bartholomew's Day Massacre, Elizabeth was the only protector of Protestants in France and the Netherlands. In 1585, she signed the Treaty of Nonsuch, which provided English soldiers and cavalry to the

GOING TO THE THEATER

THE MODERN ENGLISH stage play originated in the religious dramas that educated and entertained medieval Europeans for centuries before Shakespeare's birth in 1564. Teaching a lesson as well as telling a suspenseful story, these dramas were known as *morality plays* and typically were presented in the countryside by roving bands of players under church supervision. The medieval theater usually consisted of a small circular field for the actors, ringed by earthen mounds for the spectators. The circular stage was divided into four quadrants, each with its own tent at the four points of the compass: heaven at the east, evil at the north, worldly rulers at the west, and good characters at the south.

Each player emerged from his tent in turn to speak his lines, then went back in to await his next appearance. This format was a way of shifting scenes and a forerunner of the custom in modern theaters of ending a scene by lowering a curtain.

In England in the fifteenth century, as the urban population grew, ambitious promoters moved their productions into the courtyards of inns. London, the seat of the royal court, became the center of English theatrical life.

This sheltered, urban setting gave theater companies several advantages. Audiences were larger, and the inns could be easily renovated to provide permanent stages and more complex sets. The enclosed courtyards also made it easier to keep out nonpaying crashers, the greatest enemies of the new showmen—capitalists who produced and often wrote the plays and had to make a living from them.

Several of London's more scrupulous clergymen decried another advantage of the combined inn and theater—the opportunity it gave for sexual license. By the sixteenth century, the allegorical moralizing of the medieval country theater had evolved into the ribald, worldly entertainment of the London stage. Going to the theater was now more like being part of a festival than listening to a sermon. The workmen and young women who comprised much of the audience found it convenient to hire rooms in which they might romance one another during or after the performance.

London's theater world reached full maturity in the late sixteenth and early seventeenth centuries. The Rose and The Globe theaters, where many of Shakespeare's plays were presented, were built in the 1590s on the south bank of the River Thames, reachable only by water taxis. During Shakespeare's heyday, some 40,000 waterboys were said to ferry customers to these theaters. Performances by troupes of adult males or boys (women were banned from the stage) were often rowdy affairs, the crowds egged on both by the witty repartee on stage and the food and beer sold in the pit.

What were the basic elements and purpose of the medieval stage, and what was carried over from it to the Elizabethan theater?

Sources: E. K. Chambers, *The Elizabethan Stage*, Vols. I–IV (Oxford: Oxford University Press, 1923); Lawrence M. Clopper, *Drama, Play, and Game: English Festive Culture in the Medieval and Early Modern Period* (Chicago: Chicago University Press, 2001); F. E. Halliday, *Shakespeare in His Age* (New York: Duckworth, 1956).

A seventeenth-century sketch of the Swan Theater, which stood near Shakespeare's Globe Theater on the south bank of the Thames. The Bridgeman Art Library

Netherlands. Funds that had previously been funneled covertly to support Henry of Navarre's army in France now flowed openly.

Mary, Queen of Scots These events made a tinderbox of English–Spanish relations. The spark that finally touched it off was Elizabeth's execution of Mary, Queen of Scots (1542–1587).

Mary Stuart was the daughter of King James V of Scotland and Mary of Guise and had resided in France from the time she was six years old. This thoroughly French and Catholic queen had returned to Scotland after the death of her husband, the French king Francis II, in 1561. There she found a successful, fervent Protestant Reformation legally sanctioned the year before by the Treaty of Edinburgh (1560). As hereditary heir to the throne of Scotland, Mary remained queen by divine and human right and the Protestants who controlled her realm did not intimidate her. She established an international French court culture, the gaiety and sophistication of which impressed many Protestant nobles whose religion often made their lives exceedingly dour.

The ever-vigilant Scottish reformer John Knox watched Mary closely. He fumed publicly and always with effect against the queen's private Mass and other Catholic practices, which Scottish law made a capital offense for everyone else. Knox won support in his role of watchdog from Elizabeth and Cecil. Elizabeth personally despised Knox and never forgave him for writing the *First Blast of the Trumpet against the Terrible Regiment of Women*, a work aimed at provoking a revolt against Mary Tudor but, unfortunately for Knox, published in the year of Elizabeth's ascent to the throne. Elizabeth and Cecil tolerated Knox because they knew he would never permit Scotland to succumb to young Mary's French and Catholic ways.

In 1568, a public scandal forced Mary's abdication and flight to her cousin Elizabeth in England. Mary's reputed lover, the earl of Bothwell, was, with cause, suspected of having killed her legal husband, Lord Darnley. When a packed court acquitted Bothwell, he subsequently married Mary. The outraged reaction from Protestant nobles forced Mary to surrender the throne to her one-year-old son, the future James VI of Scotland and, later, Elizabeth's successor as King James I of England. Because of Mary's clear claim to the English throne, she was an international symbol of a possible Catholic England and consumed by the desire to be England's queen. For this reason, her presence in England, where she resided under house arrest for nineteen years, was a constant discomfort to Elizabeth.

In 1583, Elizabeth's vigilant secretary, Sir Francis Walsingham, uncovered a plot against Elizabeth involving the Spanish ambassador Bernardino de Mendoza. After Mendoza's deportation in January 1584, popular antipathy toward Spain and support for Protestant resistance in France and the Netherlands became massive throughout England.

In 1586, Walsingham uncovered still another plot against Elizabeth, the so-called Babington plot, after Anthony Babington, who was caught seeking Spanish support for an attempt on the queen's life. This time he had uncontestable proof of Mary's complicity. Elizabeth believed the execution of a sovereign, even a dethroned sovereign, weakened royalty everywhere. She was also aware of the outcry that Mary's execution would create throughout the Catholic world, and she sincerely wanted peace with English Catholics. Yet she really had no choice in the matter and consented to Mary's execution, which took place on February 18, 1587. This event dashed all Catholic hopes for a bloodless reconversion of Protestant England. After the execution of the Catholic queen of Scotland, Pope Sixtus V (r. 1585–1590), who feared Spanish domination almost as much as he abhorred English Protestantism, could no longer withhold public support for a Spanish invasion of England. Philip II ordered his Armada to make ready.

The Armada In the spring of 1587, Sir Francis Drake shelled the port of Cádiz, inflicting heavy damages on Spanish ships and stores and interrupting Spain's war preparations. After "singeing the beard of Spain's king," as he put it, Drake raided the coast of Portugal, further incapacitating the Spanish. These strikes forced the Spanish to postpone their invasion of England until 1588.

On May 30 of that year, 130 ships bearing 25,000 sailors and soldiers under the command of the duke of Medina-Sidonia set sail for England. In the end, however, the English won a stunning victory. The invasion barges that were to transport Spanish soldiers from the galleons onto English shores were prevented from leaving Calais and Dunkirk. The swifter English and Netherlands' ships, helped by what came to be known as an "English wind," dispersed the waiting Spanish fleet, over one third of which never returned to Spain.

The news of the Armada's defeat gave heart to Protestant resistance everywhere. Although Spain continued to win impressive victories in the 1590s, it never fully recovered. Spanish soldiers faced unified and inspired French, English, and Dutch armies. By the time of Philip's death on September 13, 1598, his forces had been rebuffed on all fronts. His seventeenth-century successors were all inferior leaders who never knew responsibilities equal to his, nor did Spain ever again know such imperial grandeur. The French soon dominated the Continent, and in the New World the Dutch and the English whittled away at Spain's overseas empire.

Elizabeth died on March 23, 1603, leaving behind her a strong nation poised to expand into a global empire.

▼ The Thirty Years' War (1618–1648)

The Thirty Years' War in the Holy Roman Empire was the last and most destructive of the wars of religion. Religious and political differences had long set Catholics against Protestants and Calvinists against Lutherans. What made the Thirty Years' War so devastating was the entrenched hatred of the various sides and their seeming determination to sacrifice all for their religious beliefs. When the hostilities ended in 1648, the peace terms shaped the map of northern Europe much as we know it today.

Preconditions for War

Fragmented Germany In the second half of the sixteenth century, Germany was an almost ungovernable land of about 360 autonomous political entities. (See Map 12–2.) There were independent secular principalities

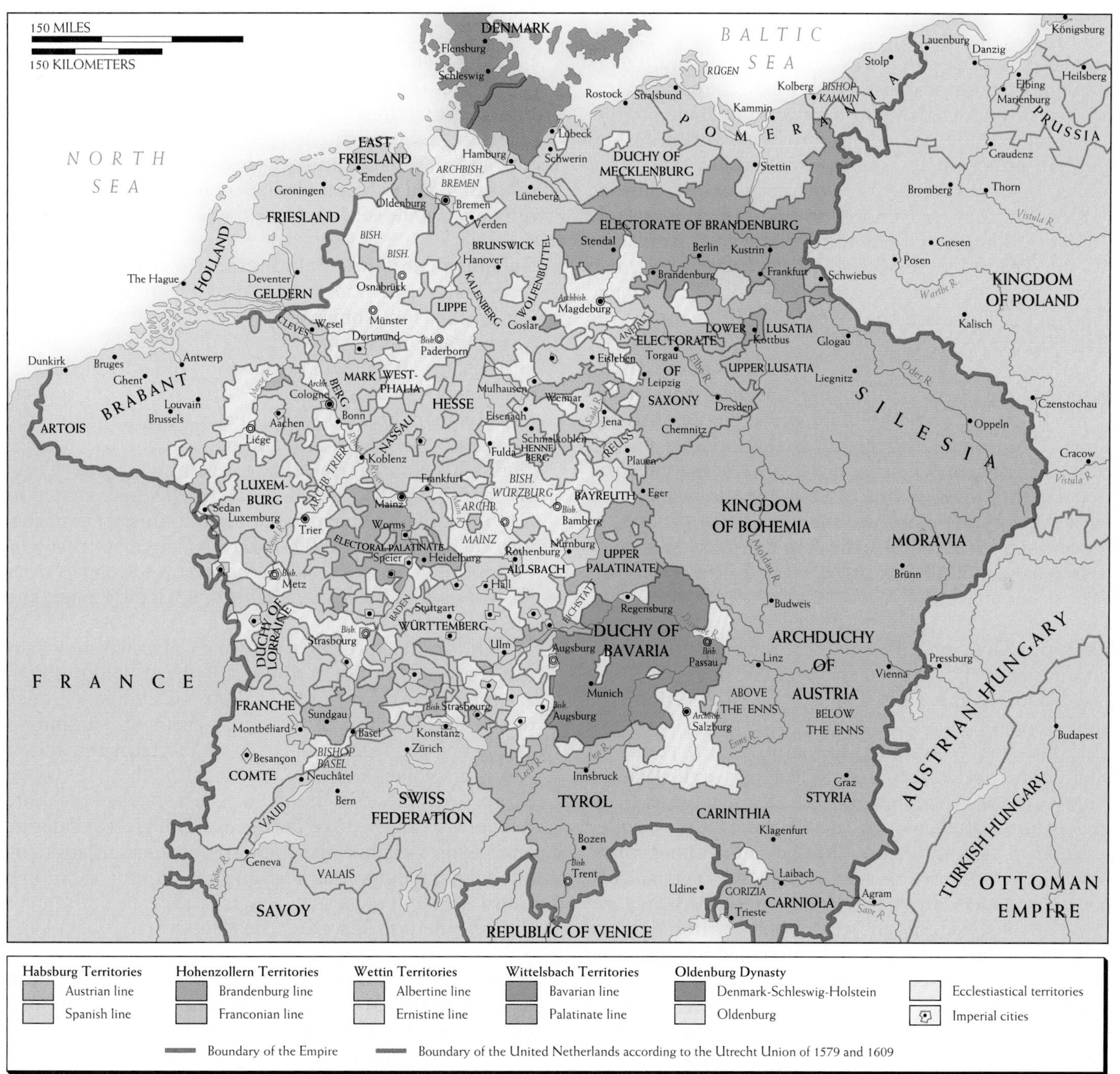

Map 12–2 **GERMANY IN 1547** Mid-sixteenth-century Germany was an almost ungovernable land of about 360 autonomous political entities. Originally "Map of Germany Showing Its Great Division/Fragmentation in the 16th Century" from Hajo Holborn, *A History of Germany: The Reformation*, Copyright © 1982 by Princeton University Press. Reprinted by permission of Princeton University Press.

(duchies, landgraviates, and marches), ecclesiastical principalities (archbishoprics, bishoprics, and abbeys), numerous free cities, and knights ruling small areas from castles. The Peace of Augsburg (1555) had given each of them significant sovereignty within its own borders. Each levied its own tolls and tariffs and coined its own money, which made land travel and trade between the various regions difficult to impossible. Many of these little lands also had great-power pretensions. As the seventeenth century opened, Germany was decentralized and fragmented; it was not a unified nation like Spain, England, or even strife-filled France.

Because of its central location, Germany had always been Europe's highway for merchants and traders going north, south, east, and west. Europe's rulers pressed in on Germany both because of trade and because some held lands or legal privileges within certain German principalities. German princes, in their turn, looked to import and export markets beyond German borders and opposed efforts to consolidate the Holy Roman Empire, lest their territorial rights, confirmed by the Peace of Augsburg, be overturned. German princes were not loath to turn to Catholic France or to the kings of Denmark and Sweden for allies against the Habsburg emperor.

After the Council of Trent, Protestants in the empire suspected the existence of an imperial and papal conspiracy to re-create the Catholic Europe of pre-Reformation times. The imperial diet, which the German princes controlled, demanded strict observance of the constitutional rights of Germans, as set forth in agreements with the emperor since the mid-fourteenth century. In the late sixteenth century, the emperor ruled only to the degree to which he was prepared to use force of arms against his subjects.

Religious Division Religious conflict accentuated the international and internal political divisions. (See Map 12–3.) During this period, the population within the Holy Roman Empire was about equally divided between Catholics and Protestants, the latter having perhaps a slight numerical edge by 1600. The terms of the Peace of Augsburg had attempted to freeze the territorial holdings of the Lutherans and the Catholics (the so-called *ecclesiastical reservation*). In the intervening years, however, the Lutherans had gained and kept political control in some Catholic areas, as had the Catholics in a few previously Lutheran areas. Such territorial reversals, or the threat of them, only increased the suspicion and antipathy between the two sides.

The Lutherans had been far more successful in securing their rights to worship in Catholic lands than the Catholics had been in securing such rights in Lutheran lands. The Catholic rulers, who were in a weakened position after the Reformation, had made, but resented, concessions to Protestant communities within their territories. With the passage of time, they demanded that all ecclesiastical princes, electors, archbishops, bishops, and abbots who had deserted the Catholic for the Protestant side be immediately deprived of their religious offices and that their ecclesiastical holdings be promptly returned to Catholic control in accordance with the ecclesiastical reservation. However, the Lutherans and, even more so, the Calvinists in the Palatinate ignored this stipulation at every opportunity.

There was also religious strife in the empire between liberal and conservative Lutherans and between Lutherans and the growing numbers of Calvinists. The last half of the sixteenth century was a time of warring Protestant factions within German universities. And in addition to the heightened religious strife, a new scientific and material culture was becoming ascendant in intellectual and political circles, increasing the anxiety of religious people of all persuasions.

Calvinism and the Palatinate As elsewhere in Europe, Calvinism was the political and religious leaven within the Holy Roman Empire on the eve of the Thirty Years' War. Unrecognized as a legal religion by the Peace of Augsburg, it gained a strong foothold within the empire when Frederick III (r. 1559–1576), a devout convert to Calvinism, became Elector Palatine (ruler within the Palatinate; see Map 12–3) and made it the official religion of his domain. Heidelberg became a German Geneva in the 1560s: both a great intellectual center of Calvinism and a staging area for Calvinist penetration into the empire. By 1609, Palatine Calvinists headed a Protestant defensive alliance that received support from Spain's sixteenth-century enemies: England, France, and the Netherlands.

The Lutherans came to fear the Calvinists almost as much as they did the Catholics. By their bold missionary forays into the empire, Palatine Calvinists seemed to the Lutherans to threaten the Peace of Augsburg—and hence the legal foundation of the Lutheran states. Also, outspoken Calvinist criticism of the doctrine of Christ's real presence in the Eucharist shocked the more religiously conservative Lutherans. The Elector Palatine once expressed his disbelief in transubstantiation by publicly shredding the host and mocking it as a "fine God." To Lutherans, such religious disrespect disgraced the Reformation as well as the elector.

Maximilian of Bavaria and the Catholic League If the Calvinists were active within the Holy Roman Empire, so also were their Catholic counterparts, the Jesuits. Staunchly Catholic Bavaria, supported by Spain, became militarily and ideologically for the Counter-Reformation what the Palatinate was for

Map 12–3 **RELIGIOUS DIVISIONS ABOUT 1600** By 1600, few could seriously expect Christians to return to a uniform religious allegiance. In Spain and southern Italy, Catholicism remained relatively unchallenged, but note the existence elsewhere of large religious minorities, both Catholic and Protestant.

Protestantism. From Bavaria, the Jesuits launched successful missions throughout the empire, winning such major cities as Strasbourg and Osnabrück back to the Catholic fold by 1600. In 1609, Maximilian I, duke of Bavaria (r. 1597–1651), organized a Catholic league to counter a new Protestant alliance that had been formed in the same year under the leadership of Calvinist Elector Palatine, Frederick IV (r. 1583–1610). When the league fielded a great army under the command of Count Johann von Tilly, the stage was set, both internally and internationally, for the worst of the religious wars, the Thirty Years' War. (See Map 12–4, page 366.)

Four Periods of War

The war went through four distinguishable periods. During its course, it drew in every major Western European nation—at least diplomatically and financially if not by direct military intervention. The four periods were the Bohemian (1618–1625); the Danish (1625–1629); the Swedish (1630–1635); and the Swedish-French (1635–1648).

The Bohemian Period The war broke out in Bohemia after the ascent to the Bohemian throne in 1618 of the Habsburg Ferdinand, archduke of Styria, who was

Map 12–4 **THE HOLY ROMAN EMPIRE ABOUT 1618** On the eve of the Thirty Years' War, the Holy Roman Empire was politically and religiously fragmented, as revealed by this somewhat simplified map. Lutherans dominated the north and Catholics the south; Calvinists controlled the United Provinces and the Palatinate and were important in Switzerland and Brandenburg.

also heir to the imperial throne. Educated by the Jesuits and a fervent Catholic, Ferdinand was determined to restore the traditional faith to the eastern Habsburg lands (Austria, Bohemia, and Hungary).

No sooner had Ferdinand become king of Bohemia than he revoked the religious freedoms of Bohemian Protestants. In force since 1575, these freedoms had even been recently broadened by Emperor Rudolf II (r. 1576–1612) in his Letter of Majesty in 1609. The Protestant nobility in Prague responded to Ferdinand's act in May 1618 by throwing his regents out the window of the royal palace. The event has ever since been known as the "defenestration of Prague." (The three officials fell fifty feet into a dry moat that, fortunately, was padded with manure, which cushioned their fall and spared their lives.) In the following year Ferdinand became Holy Roman Emperor as Ferdinand II (r. 1619–1637), by the unanimous vote of the seven electors. The Bohemians, however, defiantly deposed him in Prague and declared the Calvinist elector Palatine, Frederick V (r. 1616–1623), their king.

What had begun as a revolt of the Protestant nobility against an unpopular king of Bohemia escalated into

Bohemian protesters throw three of Emperor Ferdinand II's agents out of windows at Hradschin Castle in Prague to protest his revocation of Protestant freedoms. Bildarchiv Preussischer Kulturbesitz/Art Resource, NY

an international war. Spain sent troops to Ferdinand, who found more motivated allies in Maximilian of Bavaria and the Lutheran elector John George I of Saxony (r. 1611–1656). The latter had their own agendas. Maximilian wanted to wrest the electoral title from his distant Palatine cousin, while John George saw a sure route to territorial gain by joining in an easy victory over the weaker elector Palatine. This was not the only time politics and greed would overshadow religion during the long conflict, although Lutheran-Calvinist religious animosity also overrode a common Protestantism.

Ferdinand's army under Tilly routed Frederick V's troops at the Battle of White Mountain in 1620. By 1622, Ferdinand had not only subdued and re-Catholicized Bohemia but conquered the Palatinate as well. Meanwhile, Maximilian of Bavaria pressed the conflict into northwestern Germany, laying claim to land as he went.

The Danish Period These events raised new fears that a reconquest and re-Catholicization of the empire now loomed, which was precisely Ferdinand II's design. The Lutheran king Christian IV (r. 1588–1648) of Denmark, who already held territory within the empire as the duke of Holstein, was eager to extend Danish influence over the coastal towns of the North Sea. With English, French, and Dutch encouragement, he picked up the Protestant banner of resistance, opening the Danish period of the conflict (1625–1629). Entering Germany with his army in 1626, he was, however, quickly humiliated by Maximilian and forced to retreat into Denmark.

As military success made Maximilian stronger and an untrustworthy ally, Emperor Ferdinand sought a more pliant tool for his policies in Albrecht of Wallenstein (1583–1634), a powerful mercenary. Another opportunistic Protestant, Wallenstein had gained a great deal of territory by joining Ferdinand during the conquest of Bohemia. A brilliant and ruthless military strategist, Wallenstein carried Ferdinand's campaign into Denmark. By 1628, he commanded a crack army of more than 100,000 men and also became a law unto himself, completely outside of the emperor's control.

Wallenstein, however, had so broken Protestant resistance that Ferdinand could issue the Edict of Restitution in 1629, reasserting the Catholic safeguards of the Peace of Augsburg (1555). It reaffirmed the illegality of Calvinism—a completely unrealistic move by 1629—and it ordered the return of all church lands the Lutherans had acquired since 1552, an equally unrealistic goal despite its legal basis. Compliance would have involved the return of no fewer than sixteen bishoprics and twenty-eight cities and towns to Catholic allegiance. The new edict struck panic in the hearts of Protestants and Habsburg opponents everywhere.

The Swedish Period Gustavus Adolphus II of Sweden (r. 1611–1632), a deeply pious king of a unified Lutheran nation, became the new leader of Protestant forces within the empire, opening the Swedish period of the war (1630–1635). He was controlled by two interested bystanders: (1) the French minister Cardinal Richelieu (1585–1642), whose foreign policy was to protect

French interests by keeping the Habsburg armies tied down in Germany, and (2) the Dutch, who had not forgotten Spanish Habsburg rule in the sixteenth century. In alliance with the electors of Brandenburg and Saxony, the Swedish king won a smashing victory at Breitenfeld in 1630—one that reversed the course of the war so dramatically that it has been regarded as the most decisive engagement of the long conflict.

One of the reasons for the overwhelming Swedish victory at Breitenfeld was the military genius of Gustavus Adolphus. The Swedish king brought a new mobility to warfare by having both his infantry and his cavalry employ fire-and-charge tactics. At six deep, his infantry squares were smaller than the traditional ones, yet he filled them with equal numbers of musketeers and pikemen. His cavalry also alternated pistol shots with charges with the sword. His artillery was lighter and more mobile in battle. Each unit of his army—infantry, cavalry, and artillery—had both defensive and offensive capability and could quickly change from one to the other.

Gustavus Adolphus died at the hands of Wallenstein's forces during the Battle of Lützen (November 1632)—a costly engagement for both sides that created a brief standstill. Ferdinand had long resented Wallenstein's independence, although he was the major factor in imperial success. In 1634, Ferdinand had Wallenstein assassinated. By that time, not only had the great general served his purpose for the emperor, but, ever opportunistic, he was openly trying to strike bargains with the Protestants for his services. The episode is a telling commentary on this war without honor. Despite the deep religious motivations, greed and political gain were the real forces at work in the Thirty Years' War. Even allies that owed one another their success were not above treating each other as mortal enemies.

In the Peace of Prague in 1635, the German Protestant states, led by Saxony, reached a compromise with Ferdinand. France and the Netherlands, however, continued to support Sweden. Desiring to maximize their investment in the war, they refused to join the agreement. Their resistance to settlement plunged the war into its fourth and most devastating phase.

The Swedish-French Period The French openly entered the war in 1635, sending men and munitions as well as financial subsidies. Thereafter, the war dragged on for thirteen years, with French, Swedish, and Spanish soldiers looting the length and breadth of Germany—warring, it seemed, simply for the sake of warfare itself. The Germans, long weary of the devastation, were too disunited to repulse the foreign armies; they simply suffered. By the time peace talks began at Münster and Osnabrück in Westphalia in 1644, the war had killed an estimated one third of the German population. It has been called the worst European catastrophe since the Black Death of the fourteenth century.

The Treaty of Westphalia

The Treaty of Westphalia in 1648 ended all hostilities within the Holy Roman Empire. It was the first general peace in Europe after a war unprecedented for its number of warring parties. (See Map 12–5.) Written not in Latin, but in French, henceforth to become the international diplomatic language, the treaty rescinded Ferdinand's Edict of Restitution and reasserted the major feature of the religious settlement of the Peace of Augsburg ninety-three years earlier: The ruler of a land determines the official religion of that land. The treaty also gave the Calvinists their long-sought legal recognition. The independence of the Swiss Confederacy and the United Provinces of the Netherlands, long recognized in fact, was now proclaimed in law. Bavaria became an elector state, Brandenburg-Prussia emerged as the most powerful northern German state, and the other German princes became supreme over their principalities. Yet, as guarantors of the treaty, Sweden and France found many opportunities to meddle in German affairs until the century's end—France for reasons of considerable territorial gain. Because the treaty broadened the legal status of Protestantism, the pope opposed it altogether, but he had no power to prevent it.

France and Spain remained at war outside the empire until 1659, when French victories forced the humiliating Treaty of the Pyrenees on the Spanish. Thereafter France became Europe's dominant power, and Habsburg Spain never recovered. (See Chapter 13.)

By confirming the territorial sovereignty of Germany's many political entities, the Treaty of Westphalia perpetuated German division and political weakness into the modern period. Only two German states attained any international significance during the seventeenth century: Austria and Brandenburg-Prussia. The petty regionalism within the empire also reflected on a small scale the drift of larger European politics. In the seventeenth century, distinctive nation-states, each with their own political, cultural, and religious identity, reached maturity and firmly established the competitive nationalism of the modern world.

In Perspective

Religion and politics played major roles in each of the great conflicts of the Age of Religious Wars—the internal struggle in France, Spain's unsuccessful effort to subdue the Netherlands, England's successful resistance to Spain, and the intervention of virtually every major European power in the hapless Holy Roman Empire during the first half of the seventeenth century. Each conflict involved parties and armies of different religious persuasions in a life-or-death political struggle.

MAP EXPLORATION

Interactive map: To explore this map further, go to **www.myhistorylab.com**

Map 12–5 **EUROPE IN 1648** At the end of the Thirty Years' War, Spain still had extensive possessions. Austria and Brandenburg-Prussia were rising powers, the independence of the United Provinces and Switzerland was recognized, and Sweden had footholds in northern Germany.

The wars ended with the recognition of minority religious rights and a guarantee of the traditional boundaries of political sovereignty. In France, the Edict of Nantes (1598) brought peace by granting Huguenots basic religious and civil freedoms and by recognizing their towns and territories. With the departure of the Spanish, peace and sovereignty also came to the Netherlands, guaranteed initially by the Twelve Years' Truce (1609) and secured fully by the Peace of Westphalia (1648). The conflict between England and Spain ended with the removal of the Spanish threat to English sovereignty in politics and religion, which resulted from the execution of Mary, Queen of Scots (1587) and the English victory over the Armada (1588). In the Holy Roman Empire, peace came with the reaffirmation of the political principle of the Peace of Augsburg (1555), as the Peace of Westphalia brought the Thirty Years' War to an end by again recognizing the sovereignty of rulers within their lands and their right to determine the religious beliefs of their subjects. Europe at mid-century had real, if brief, peace.

REVIEW QUESTIONS

1. How did politics shape the religious positions of the French leaders? What led to the Saint Bartholomew's Day Massacre, and what did it achieve?
2. How did Spain gain a position of dominance in the sixteenth century? What were Philip II's successes and failures?
3. Henry of Navarre (Henry IV of France), Elizabeth I, and William of Orange were all *politiques*. What does that term mean and why does it apply to these three rulers?
4. What led to the establishment of the Anglican Church in England? Why did Mary I fail? What was Elizabeth I's settlement, and why was it difficult to impose on England? Who were her detractors and what were their criticisms?
5. Why was the Thirty Years' War fought? Was politics or religion more important in determining the outcome of the war? What were the main terms of the Treaty of Westphalia in 1648?
6. Why has the Thirty Years' War been called the outstanding example in European history of meaningless conflict? Was it really such? Were the results worth the cost of the war?

SUGGESTED READINGS

F. Braudel, *The Mediterranean and the Mediterranean World in the Age of Philip the Second*, Vols. 1 and 2 (1976). Widely acclaimed "big picture" by a master historian.

N. Z. Davis, *Society and Culture in Early Modern France* (1975). Essays on popular culture.

R. Dunn, *The Age of Religious Wars, 1559–1689* (1979). Excellent brief survey of every major conflict.

J. H. Franklin, ed. and trans., *Constitutionalism and Resistance in the Sixteenth Century: Three Treatises by Hotman, Beza, and Mornay* (1969). Three defenders of the right to resist tyranny.

J. Guy, *Tudor England* (1990). The standard history and a good synthesis of recent scholarship.

D. Loades, *Mary Tudor* (1989). Authoritative and good storytelling.

G. Mattingly, *The Armada* (1959). A masterpiece resembling a novel in style.

J. E. Neale, *The Age of Catherine de Médicis* (1962). Short, concise summary.

A. Soman, ed., *The Massacre of St. Bartholomew's Day: Reappraisals and Documents* (1974). Essays from an international symposium on the anniversary of the massacre.

C. Wedgwood, *William the Silent* (1944). Eloquent political biography of William of Orange.

A. B. Weir, *The Life of Elizabeth I* (1998). Detailed portrayal of a successful ruler.

J. Wormald, *Mary, Queen of Scots: A Study in Failure* (1991). Mary portrayed as out of touch with her country and her times.

Peter the Great (r. 1682–1725), seeking to make Russia a military power after West European models reorganized the country's political, social, and economic structures. He also radically changed the relationship of the Russian Church to the Russian state. His reign saw Russia enter fully into European power politics. *The Apotheosis of Tsar Peter the Great 1672–1725* by unknown artist, 1710. Historical Museum, Moscow, Russia/E.T. Archive

13

European State Consolidation in the Seventeenth and Eighteenth Centuries

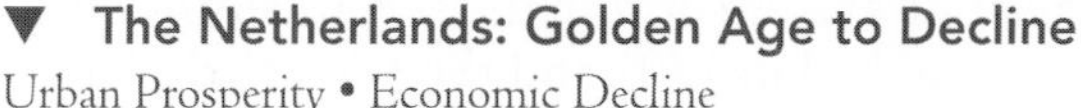

▼ **The Netherlands: Golden Age to Decline**
Urban Prosperity • Economic Decline

▼ **Two Models of European Political Development**

▼ **Constitutional Crisis and Settlement in Stuart England**
James I • Charles I • The Long Parliament and Civil War • Oliver Cromwell and the Puritan Republic • Charles II and the Restoration of the Monarchy • The "Glorious Revolution" • The Age of Walpole

▼ **Rise of Absolute Monarchy in France: The World of Louis XIV**
Years of Personal Rule • Versailles • King by Divine Right • Louis's Early Wars • Louis's Repressive Religious Policies • Louis's Later Wars • France After Louis XIV

▼ **Central and Eastern Europe**
Poland: Absence of Strong Central Authority • The Habsburg Empire and the Pragmatic Sanction • Prussia and the Hohenzollerns

▼ **Russia Enters the European Political Arena**
The Romanov Dynasty • Peter the Great • Russian Expansion in the Baltic: The Great Northern War

▼ **The Ottoman Empire**
Religious Toleration and Ottoman Government • The End of Ottoman Expansion

▼ **In Perspective**

KEY TOPICS

- **The Dutch Golden Age**
- **The divergent political paths of Britain and France: Parliamentary supremacy and royal absolutism**
- **Poland's failure to establish a strong central government**
- **The Habsburg efforts to preserve their holdings**
- **The emergence of Prussia and Russia as major powers**
- **Power and decline of the Ottoman Empire**

BETWEEN THE EARLY seventeenth and the mid-twentieth centuries, no region so dominated other parts of the world politically, militarily, and economically as Europe. Such had not been the case before that date and would not be the case after World War II. However, for approximately three and a half centuries, Europe became the chief driving force in one world historical development after another. This era of European dominance, which appears quite temporary in the larger scope of history, also coincided with a shift in power within Europe itself from the Mediterranean, where Spain and Portugal had taken the lead in the conquest and early exploitation of the Americas, to the states of northwest and later north-central Europe.

During the seventeenth and early eighteenth centuries, certain states in northern Europe organized themselves politically so as to be able to dominate Europe and later to influence and even govern other large areas of the world through military might and economic strength. Even within the region of northern Europe, there occurred a sorting out of influence among political states with some successfully establishing long-term positions of dominance and others passing from the scene after relatively brief periods of either military or economic strength.

By the mid-eighteenth century, five major states had come to dominate European politics and would continue to do so until at least World War I. They were Great Britain, France, Austria, Prussia, and Russia. Through their military strength, economic development, and, in some cases, colonial empires, they would affect virtually every other world civilization. Within Europe, these states established their dominance at the expense of Spain, Portugal, the United Provinces of the Netherlands, Poland, Sweden, and the Ottoman Empire. Equally essential to their rise was the weakness of the Holy Roman Empire after the Peace of Westphalia (1648).

In western Europe, Britain and France emerged as the dominant powers. This development represented a shift of influence away from Spain and the United Netherlands. Both of the latter countries had been powerful and important during the sixteenth and seventeenth centuries, but they became politically and militarily marginal during the eighteenth century. Neither, however, disappeared from the map, and both retained considerable economic vitality and influence. Spanish power declined after the War of the Spanish Succession. The case of the Netherlands was more complicated.

▼ The Netherlands: Golden Age to Decline

The seven provinces that became the United Provinces of the Netherlands emerged as a nation after revolting against Spain in 1572. During the seventeenth century, the Dutch engaged in a series of naval wars with England. Then, in 1672, the armies of Louis XIV invaded the Netherlands. Prince William III of Orange (1650–1702), the grandson of William the Silent (1533–1584) and the hereditary chief executive, or *stadtholder*, of Holland, the most important of the provinces, rallied the Dutch and eventually led the entire European coalition against France. As a part of that strategy, he answered the invitation of Protestant English aristocrats in 1688 to assume, along with his wife Mary, the English throne.

During both the seventeenth and eighteenth centuries, the political and economic life of the Netherlands differed from that of the rest of Europe. The other major nations pursued paths toward strong central government, generally under monarchies, as with France, or in the case of England, under a strong parliamentary system. By contrast, the Netherlands was formally a republic. Each of the provinces retained considerable authority, and the central government, embodied in the States General that met in the Hague, exercised its authority through a kind of ongoing negotiation with the provinces. Prosperous and populous Holland dominated the States General. The Dutch deeply distrusted monarchy and the ambitions of the House of Orange. Nonetheless, when confronted with major military challenges, the Dutch would permit the House of Orange and, most notably, William III to assume dominant leadership. These political arrangements proved highly resilient and allowed the republic to establish itself permanently in the European state system during the seventeenth century. When William died in 1702 and the wars with France ended in 1714, the Dutch reverted to their republican structures.

Although the provinces making up the Netherlands were traditionally identified with the Protestant cause in Europe, toleration marked Dutch religious life. The Calvinist Reformed Church was the official church of the nation, but it was not an established church. There was always a significant number of Roman Catholics and Protestants who did not belong to the Reformed Church. The country also became a haven for Jews. Consequently, while governments in other European states attempted to impose a single religion on their people or tore themselves apart in religious conflict, in the Netherlands peoples of differing religious faiths lived together peacefully.

Urban Prosperity

Beyond the climate of religious toleration, what most amazed seventeenth-century contemporaries about the Dutch Republic was its economic prosperity. Its remarkable economic achievement was built on the foundations of high urban consolidation, transformed agriculture, extensive trade and finance, and an overseas commercial empire.

In the Netherlands, more people lived in cities than in any other area of Europe. Key transformations in Dutch farming that served as the model for the rest of Europe made this urban transformation possible. During the seventeenth century, the Dutch drained and reclaimed land from the sea, which they used for highly profitable farming. Because Dutch shipping provided a steady supply of cheap grain, Dutch farmers themselves could produce more profitable dairy products and beef and cultivate cash products such as tulip bulbs.

Dutch fishermen dominated the market for herring and supplied much of the continent's dried fish. The Dutch also supplied textiles to many parts of Europe. Dutch ships appeared in harbors all over the continent, with their captains purchasing goods that they then transported and resold at a profit to other nations. The overseas trades also supported a vast shipbuilding and ship supply industry. The most advanced financial system of the day supported all of this trade, commerce, and manufacturing.

The final foundation of Dutch prosperity was a seaborne empire. Dutch traders established a major presence in East Asia, particularly in spice-producing areas of Java, the Moluccas, and Sri Lanka. The vehicle for this penetration was the Dutch East India Company (chartered in 1602). The company eventually displaced Portuguese dominance in the spice trade of East Asia and for many years prevented English traders from establishing a major presence there. Initially, the Dutch had only wanted commercial dominance of the spice trade, but in time, they moved toward producing the spices themselves, which required them to control many of the islands that now constitute Indonesia. The Netherlands remained the colonial master of this region until after World War II.

Economic Decline

The decline in political influence of the United Provinces of the Netherlands occurred in the eighteenth century. After the death of William III of Britain in 1702, the provinces prevented the emergence of another strong *stadtholder*. Unified political leadership therefore vanished. Naval supremacy slowly but steadily passed to the British. The fishing industry declined, and the Dutch lost their technological superiority in shipbuilding. Countries between which Dutch ships had once carried goods now traded directly with each other.

Similar stagnation overtook the Dutch domestic industries. The disunity of the provinces hastened this economic decline and prevented action that might have halted it.

What saved the United Provinces from becoming completely insignificant in European affairs was their continued financial dominance. Well past the middle of the eighteenth century, Dutch banks continued to finance European trade, and the Amsterdam stock exchange remained an important financial institution.

The technologically advanced fleet of the Dutch East India Company, shown here at anchor in Amsterdam, linked the Netherlands' economy with that of southeast Asia. Andries van Eertvelt (1590–1652), *The Return to Amsterdam of the Fleet of the Dutch East India Company in 1599*. Oil on copper. Johnny van Haeften Gallery, London, UK. The Bridgeman Art Library

▼ Two Models of European Political Development

The United Netherlands, like Venice and the Swiss cantons, was a republic governed without a monarch. Elsewhere in Europe monarchy of two fundamentally different patterns predominated in response to the military challenges of international conflict.

The two models became known as *parliamentary monarchy* and ***political absolutism***. England embodied the first, and France, the second. Neither model was inevitable for either country, but each resulted from the historical developments and political personalities that molded each nation during the seventeenth century.

The political forces that led to the creation of these two models had arisen from military concerns. During the second half of the sixteenth century, changes in military organization, weapons, and tactics sharply increased the cost of warfare. Because their traditional sources of income could not finance these growing expenses, in addition to the other costs of government, monarchs sought new revenues. Only monarchies that succeeded in building a secure financial base that was not deeply dependent on the support of noble estates, diets, or assemblies achieved absolute rule. The French monarchy succeeded in this effort, whereas the English monarchy failed. That success and failure led to the two models of government—*absolutism* in France and ***parliamentary monarchy*** in England—that shaped subsequent political development in Europe.

The divergent developments of England and France in the seventeenth century would have surprised most people in 1600. It was not inevitable that the English monarchy would have to govern through Parliament or that the French monarchy would avoid dealing with national political institutions that could significantly limit its authority. The Stuart kings of England aspired to the autocracy Louis XIV achieved, and some English political philosophers eloquently defended the ***divine right of kings*** and absolute rule. At the beginning of the seventeenth century, the English monarchy was strong. Queen Elizabeth, after a reign of almost forty-five years (1558–1603), was much revered. Parliament met only when the monarch summoned it to provide financial support. France, however, was emerging from the turmoil of its religious wars. The strife of that conflict had torn French society apart. The monarchy was relatively weak. Henry IV, who had become king in 1589, pursued a policy of religious toleration. The French nobles had significant military forces at their disposal and in the middle of the seventeenth century rebelled against the king. These conditions would change dramatically in both nations by the late seventeenth century.

▼ Constitutional Crisis and Settlement in Stuart England

James I

In 1603 James VI, the son of Mary Stuart, Queen of Scots, who had been King of Scotland since 1567, succeeded without opposition or incident the childless Elizabeth I as James I of England. He also inherited a large royal debt and a fiercely divided church. A strong believer in the divine right of kings, he expected to rule with a minimum of consultation beyond his own royal court.

Parliament met only when the monarch summoned it, which James hoped to do rarely. In place of parliamentarily approved revenues, James developed other sources of income, largely by levying new custom duties known as *impositions*. Members of Parliament regarded this as an affront to their authority over the royal purse, but they did not seek a serious confrontation. Rather, throughout James's reign they wrangled and negotiated.

The religious problem also festered under James. Since the days of Elizabeth, **Puritans** within the Church of England had sought to eliminate elaborate religious ceremonies and replace the hierarchical episcopal system of church governance under bishops appointed by the king with a more representative Presbyterian form like that of the Calvinist churches in Scotland and on the Continent. At the Hampton Court Conference of January 1604, James rebuffed the Puritans and firmly declared his intention to maintain and even enhance the Anglican episcopacy. Thereafter, both sides had deep suspicions of the other. (See "King James I Defends Popular Recreation against the Puritans.")

Religious dissenters began to leave England. In 1620, Puritan separatists founded Plymouth Colony on Cape Cod Bay in North America, preferring flight from England to Anglican conformity. Later in the 1620s, a larger, better financed group of Puritans left England to found the Massachusetts Bay Colony. In each case, the colonists believed that reformation would or could not go far enough in England and that only in America could they worship freely and organize a truly reformed church.

James's court became a center of scandal and corruption. He governed by favorites, of whom the most influential was the duke of Buckingham, whom rumor made the king's homosexual lover. Buckingham controlled royal patronage and openly sold peerages and titles to the highest bidders—a practice that angered the nobility because it cheapened their rank. There had always been court favorites, but seldom before had a single person so controlled access to the monarch.

James's foreign policy roused further opposition and doubt about his Protestant loyalty. In 1604, he concluded a much-needed peace with Spain, England's longtime adversary. The war had been ruinously ex-

KING JAMES I DEFENDS POPULAR RECREATION AGAINST THE PURITANS

The English Puritans believed in strict observance of the Sabbath, disapproving any sports, games, or general social conviviality on Sunday. James I thought these strictures prevented many Roman Catholics from joining the Church of England. In 1618, he ordered the clergy of the Church of England to read the Book of Sports from their pulpits. In this declaration, he permitted people to engage in certain sports and games after church services. His hope was to allow innocent recreations on Sunday while encouraging people to attend the Church of England. Despite the king's good intentions, the order offended the Puritans. The clergy resisted his order and he had to withdraw it.

What motives of state might have led James I to issue this declaration? How does he attempt to make it favorable to the Church of England? Why might so many clergy have refused to read this statement to their congregations?

With our own ears we heard the general complaint of our people, that they were barred from all lawful recreation and exercise upon the Sunday's afternoon, after the ending of all divine service, which cannot but produce two evils: the one the hindering of the conversion of many [Roman Catholic subjects], whom their priests will take occasion hereby to vex, persuading them that no honest mirth or recreation is lawful or tolerable in our religion, which cannot but breed a great discontentment in our people's hearts, especially as such as are peradventure upon the point of turning [to the Church of England]: the other inconvenience is, that this prohibition barreth the common and meaner sort of people from using such exercises as may make their bodies more able for war, when we or our successors shall have occasion to use them; and in place thereof sets up filthy tipplings and drunkenness, and breeds a number of idle and discontented speeches in their ale-houses. For when shall the common people have leave to exercise, if not upon the Sundays and holy days, seeing they must apply their labor and win their living in all working days? . . .

[A]s for our good people's lawful recreation, our pleasure likewise is, that after the end of divine service our good people be not disturbed, . . . or discouraged from any lawful recreation, such as dancing, either men or women; archery for men, leaping, vaulting, or any other such harmless recreation, or from having of Hay-games, Whitsun-ales, and Morris-dances; and the setting up of May-poles and other sports therewith used; . . . but withal we do here account still as prohibited all unlawful games to be used upon Sundays only, as bear and bull-baitings . . . and at all times in the meaner sort of people by law prohibited, bowling.

And likewise we bar from this benefit and liberty all such known as recusants [Roman Catholics], either men or women, as will abstain from coming to church or divine service, being therefore unworthy of any lawful recreation after the said service, that will not first come to the church and serve God; prohibiting in like sort the said recreations to any that, though [they] conform in religion [i.e., members of the Church of England], are not present in the church at the service of God, before their going to the said recreations.

From Henry Bettenson, ed., *Documents of the Christian Church*, 2nd ed. (London: Oxford University Press, 1963), pp. 400–403. By permission of Oxford University Press.

pensive, but his subjects considered the peace a sign of pro-Catholic sentiment. James's unsuccessful attempt to relax penal laws against Catholics further increased suspicions, as did his wise hesitancy in 1618 to rush English troops to the aid of German Protestants at the outbreak of the Thirty Years' War. His failed efforts to arrange a marriage between his son Charles and a Spanish princess, and then Charles's marriage in 1625 to Henrietta Marie, the Catholic daughter of Henry IV of France, further increased religious concern. In 1624,

ENCOUNTERING THE *Past*

EARLY CONTROVERSY OVER TOBACCO AND SMOKING

SMOKING TODAY IS widely condemned throughout the West, but the controversy over tobacco goes back to the earliest European encounter with the plant, which was native to the Americas.

Christopher Columbus on his first voyage in 1492 saw Native Americans smoking tobacco. Later, the first Spanish missionaries associated smoking with pagan religious practices and tried to stop Native Americans from using tobacco. Once tobacco reached Europe in the late sixteenth century, more opposition to smoking arose (although—ironically—some physicians thought it might cure diseases of the lungs and internal organs). As early as 1610, Sir Francis Bacon (1561–1626) noted that smokers found it difficult to stop smoking. The Christian clergy throughout Europe denounced smoking as immoral, and Muslim clerics condemned the practice as contrary to Islam when it spread to the Ottoman Empire. Nonetheless, smoking tobacco in pipes became popular.

The chief British critic of the new practice was none other than King James I (r. 1603–1625). While he defended Sunday sports against Puritan critics who believed any amusements on the Sabbath were sinful, he detested smoking. In 1604, he published his *Counterblaste to Tobacco* in which he declared, "Have you not reason then to be ashamed, and to forbear this filthy novelty . . .? In your abuse thereof sinning against God, harming yourselves in person . . . and taking thereby the marks . . . of vanity upon you. . . . A custom loathsome to the eye, hateful to the nose, harmful to the brain, dangerous to the lungs, and the black stinking fume thereof, nearest resembling the horrible Stygian smoke of the pit that is bottomless."[1]

To discourage smoking, James's government put a high tax on tobacco. Yet when a brisk trade in smuggled tobacco developed, the government decided to lower the tax to a level where people would not seek to evade it. In 1614, James created a royal monopoly to import tobacco into England, which created a steady government revenue that the increasingly unpopular king badly needed. James, like governments to the present day, may also have regarded this policy as a tax on sin. By 1619, James approved the incorporation of a company of clay pipe makers in London, and 40,000 pounds of tobacco arrived from Virginia the next year. Other European governments would also find tobacco a significant source of tax revenue. Often they would tax tobacco and at the same time attempt to regulate its use, especially among the young.

Which groups in Europe in the sixteenth and seventeenth centuries opposed the habit of smoking tobacco?

Why did the English government under King James I modify its opposition to tobacco?

[1]*A Counterblaste to Tobacco* (1604), reprinted by the Rodale Press, London, 1954, p. 36.

Practically from the moment of its introduction into Europe tobacco smoking was controversial. Here a court jester is portrayed as exhaling rabbits from a pipe as three pipe-smoking gentlemen look on.

shortly before James's death, England again went to war against Spain, largely in response to parliamentary pressures.

Charles I

Parliament had favored the war with Spain but would not adequately finance it because its members distrusted the monarchy. Unable to gain adequate funds from Parliament, Charles I (r. 1625–1649), like his father, resorted to extraparliamentary measures. These included levying new tariffs and duties, attempting to collect discontinued taxes, and subjecting English property owners to a so-called forced loan (a tax theoretically to be repaid) and then imprisoning those who refused to pay. All these actions, as well as quartering troops in private homes, challenged local political influence of nobles and landowners.

Engraved for
RAYMOND's
History of England
King CHARLES the FIRST in the HOUSE of COMMONS, demanding
the FIVE impeached MEMBERS to be delivered up to his AUTHORITY.

One of the key moments in the conflict between Charles I and Parliament occurred in January 1642 when Charles personally arrived at the House of Commons intent on arresting five members who had been responsible for opposing him. They had already escaped. Thereafter Charles departed London to raise his army. The event was subsequently often portrayed in English art. The present illustration is from an eighteenth-century engraving.
The Granger Collection, New York

When Parliament met in 1628, its members would grant new funds only if Charles recognized the Petition of Right. This document required that henceforth there should be no forced loans or taxation without the consent of Parliament, that no freeman should be imprisoned without due cause, and that troops should not be billeted in private homes. Charles agreed to the petition, but whether he would keep his word was doubtful. The next year after further disputes, Charles dissolved Parliament and did not recall it until 1640.

Years of Personal Rule To conserve his limited resources, Charles made peace with France in 1629 and Spain in 1630, again rousing fears that he was too friendly to Roman Catholic powers. To allow Charles to rule without renegotiating financial arrangements with Parliament, his chief adviser Thomas Wentworth (1593–1641; after 1640, earl of Strafford), imposed strict efficiency and administrative centralization in the government and exploited every legal fund-raising device, enforcing previously neglected laws and extending existing taxes into new areas.

Charles might have ruled indefinitely without Parliament had not his religious policies provoked war with Scotland. James I had allowed a wide variety of religious observances in England, Scotland, and Ireland; by contrast, Charles hoped to impose religious conformity at least within England and Scotland. In 1637, Charles and his high-church Archbishop William Laud (1573–1645), against the opposition of both the English Puritans and the Presbyterian Scots, tried to impose on Scotland the English episcopal system and a prayer book almost identical to the Anglican Book of Common Prayer.

The Scots rebelled, and Charles, with insufficient resources for war, was forced in 1640 to call Parliament. It refused even to consider funds for war until the king agreed to redress a long list of political and religious grievances. The king, in response, immediately dissolved that Parliament—hence its name, the Short Parliament (April–May 1640). When the Scots defeated an English army at the Battle of Newburn in the summer of 1640, Charles reconvened Parliament—this time on its terms—for a long and fateful duration.

The Long Parliament and Civil War

The landowners and the merchant classes represented in Parliament had long resented the king's financial measures and paternalistic rule. The Puritans in Parliament resented his religious policies and distrusted the influence of his Roman Catholic wife. What became known as the Long Parliament (1640–1660) thus acted with widespread support and general unanimity when it convened in November 1640.

The House of Commons impeached both Strafford and Laud. Both were executed—Strafford in 1641, Laud in 1645. Parliament abolished the courts that had enforced royal policy and prohibited the levying of new taxes without its consent. Finally, Parliament resolved that no more than three years should elapse between its meetings and that the king could not dissolve it without its own consent.

Parliament, however, was sharply divided over religion. Both moderate Puritans (the Presbyterians) and more extreme Puritans (the Independents) wanted to abolish bishops and the Book of Common Prayer. Yet religious conservatives in both houses of Parliament were determined to preserve the Church of England in its current form.

These divisions intensified in October 1641, when Parliament was asked to raise funds for an army to suppress the rebellion in Scotland. Charles's opponents argued that he could not be trusted with an army and that Parliament should become the commander-in-chief of English armed forces. In January 1642, Charles invaded Parliament, intending to arrest certain of his opponents, but they escaped. The king then left London and began to raise an army. Shocked, a majority of the House of Commons passed the Militia Ordinance, which gave Parliament authority to raise an army of its own. The die was now cast. For the next four years (1642–1646), civil war engulfed England with the king's supporters known as Cavaliers and the parliamentary opposition as Roundheads.

Oliver Cromwell and the Puritan Republic

Two factors led finally to Parliament's victory. The first was an alliance with Scotland in 1643 that committed Parliament to a Presbyterian system of church government. The second was the reorganization of the parliamentary army under Oliver Cromwell (1599–1658), a country squire of iron discipline and strong, independent religious sentiment. Cromwell and his "godly men" were willing to tolerate an established majority church, but only if it permitted Protestant dissenters to worship outside it.

Defeated militarily by June 1645, Charles for the next several years tried to take advantage of divisions within Parliament, but Cromwell and his army foiled him. Members who might have been sympathetic to the monarch were expelled from Parliament in December 1648. After a trial by a special court, Charles was executed on January 30, 1649, as a public criminal. Parliament then abolished the monarchy, the House of Lords, and the Anglican Church.

From 1649 to 1660, England became officially a Puritan republic, although Cromwell dominated it. His army brutally conquered Scotland and Ireland, where his radically Protestant army carried out numerous atrocities against Irish Catholics. As a national leader, however, Cromwell, proved to be no politician. When in 1653, the House of Commons wanted to disband his expensive army of 50,000 men, Cromwell instead disbanded Parliament. He ruled thereafter as Lord Protector.

Oliver Cromwell's New Model Army defeated the royalists in the English Civil War. After the execution of Charles I in 1649, Cromwell dominated the short-lived English republic, conquered Ireland and Scotland, and ruled as Lord Protector from 1653 until his death in 1658. Dorling Kindersley Media Library. The Wallace Collection, London

Cromwell's military dictatorship, however, proved no more effective than Charles's rule and became just as harsh and hated. People deeply resented his Puritan prohibitions of drunkenness, theatergoing, and dancing. Political liberty vanished in the name of religious conformity. When Cromwell died in 1658, the English were ready by 1660 to restore both the Anglican Church and the monarchy.

Charles II and the Restoration of the Monarchy

After negotiations with the army, Charles II (r. 1660–1685) returned to England amid great rejoicing. A man of considerable charm and political skill, Charles set a refreshing new tone after eleven years of somber Puritanism. England returned to the status quo of 1642, with a hereditary monarch, a Parliament of Lords and Commons that met only when the king summoned it, and the Anglican Church, with its bishops and prayer book, supreme in religion.

The king, however, had secret Catholic sympathies and favored religious toleration. He wanted to allow loyal Catholics and Puritans to worship freely. Yet ultraroyalists in Parliament between 1661 and 1665, through a series of laws known as the Clarendon Code, excluded

ENGLAND IN THE SEVENTEENTH CENTURY

1603	James VI of Scotland becomes James I of England
1604	Hampton Court conference
1611	Publication of the authorized, or King James, version of the English Bible
1625	Charles I becomes English monarch
1628	Petition of Right
1629	Charles I dissolves Parliament and embarks on eleven years of personal rule
1640	April–May, Short Parliament; November, Long Parliament convenes
1642	Outbreak of the Civil War
1645	Charles I defeated at Naseby
1648	Pride's Purge
1649	Charles I executed
1649–1660	Various attempts at a Puritan Commonwealth
1660	Charles II restored to the English throne
1670	Secret Treaty of Dover between France and England
1672	Parliament passes the Test Act
1678	Popish Plot
1685	James II becomes king of England
1688	"Glorious Revolution"
1689	William and Mary proclaimed English monarchs
1701	Acts of Settlement provides for Hanoverian succession
1702–1714	Reign of Queen Anne, the last of the Stuarts
1707	Act of Union between England and Scotland
1713	Treaty of Utrecht ends the War of the Spanish Succession
1714	George I becomes king of Great Britain and establishes the Hanoverian dynasty
1721–1742	Robert Walpole dominates British politics
1727	George II becomes king of Great Britain

Roman Catholics, Presbyterians, and Independents from the official religious and political life of the nation.

In 1670 by the Treaty of Dover, England and France formally allied against the Dutch, their chief commercial competitor. In a secret portion of this treaty, Charles pledged to announce his conversion to Catholicism as soon as conditions in England permitted this to happen. In return for this announcement (which Charles never made), Louis XIV promised to pay Charles a substantial subsidy. In an attempt to unite the English people behind the war with Holland, and as a sign of good faith to Louis XIV, Charles issued a Declaration of Indulgence in 1672, suspending all laws against Roman Catholics and non-Anglican Protestants. Parliament refused to fund the war, however, until Charles rescinded the measure. After he did so, Parliament passed the Test Act requiring all civil and military officials of the crown to swear an oath against the doctrine of transubstantiation—which no loyal Roman Catholic could honestly do. Parliament had aimed the Test Act largely at the king's brother, James, duke of York, heir to the throne and a recent, devout convert to Catholicism.

In 1678, a notorious liar named Titus Oates swore before a magistrate that Charles's Catholic wife, through her physician, was plotting with Jesuits and Irishmen to kill the king so James could assume the throne. Parliament believed Oates. In the ensuing hysteria, known as the Popish Plot, several innocent people were tried and executed. Riding the crest of anti-Catholic sentiment and led by the earl of Shaftesbury (1621–1683), opposition members of Parliament, called Whigs, made an unsuccessful effort to exclude James from succession to the throne.

More suspicious than ever of Parliament, Charles II turned again to increased customs duties and the assistance of Louis XIV for extra income. By these means, he was able to rule from 1681 to 1685 without recalling Parliament. In those years, Charles drove Shaftesbury into exile, executed several Whig leaders for treason, and bullied local corporations into electing members of Parliament submissive to the royal will. When Charles died in 1685 (after a deathbed conversion to Catholicism), he left James the prospect of a Parliament filled with royal friends.

The "Glorious Revolution"

When James II (r. 1685–1688) became king, he immediately demanded the repeal of the Test Act. When Parliament balked, he dissolved it and proceeded to appoint Catholics to high positions in both his court and the army. In 1687, he issued another Declaration of Indulgence suspending all religious tests and permitting free worship. In June 1688, James imprisoned seven Anglican bishops who had refused to publicize his suspension of laws against the Catholics. Each of these actions represented a direct royal attack on the local authority of nobles, landowners, the church, and other corporate bodies whose members believed they possessed particular legal privileges. James not only sought to aid his fellow Roman Catholics but also to pursue absolutist policies similar to those of Louis XIV whom he deeply admired.

The English had hoped that James would be succeeded by Mary (r. 1689–1694), his Protestant eldest daughter. She was the wife of William III of Orange, the leader of European opposition to Louis XIV. But on June 20, James II's Catholic second wife gave birth to a son. There was now a Catholic male heir to the throne. The Parliamentary opposition invited William to invade

England to preserve its "traditional liberties," that is, the Anglican Church and parliamentary government.

William of Orange arrived with his army in November 1688 and was received with considerable popular support. James fled to France, and Parliament, in 1689, proclaimed William III and Mary II the new monarchs, thus completing the "**Glorious Revolution**." William and Mary, in turn, recognized a Bill of Rights that limited the powers of the monarchy and guaranteed the civil liberties of the English privileged classes. Henceforth, England's monarchs would be subject to law and would rule by the consent of Parliament, which was to be called into session every three years. The Bill of Rights also prohibited Roman Catholics from occupying the English throne. The Toleration Act of 1689 permitted worship by all Protestants and outlawed only Roman Catholics and those who denied the Christian doctrine of the Trinity. It did not, however, extend full political rights to persons outside the Church of England.

As will be seen more fully in the next chapter, in 1690 John Locke published his *Second Treatise of Civil Government*, which defended the idea that government resided in the consent of the governed. This view directly opposed Tory support for absolutism as well as absolutist political thought on the continent. (See "Compare & Connect: The Debate over the Origin and Character of Political Authority," pages 386–387.)

The Revolution of 1688 has traditionally been seen as a relatively peaceful event. Recent scholarship, however, has disclosed considerable resistance in both Scotland and Ireland, which resulted in significant loss of life. Conversely events in England itself now appear driven not only by the long recognized actions of the political elite, but also by a genuinely popular resistance to James II. Furthermore, the political results of the revolution went well beyond the assertion of parliamentary authority. In one area of government policy after another the reign of William and Mary marked important new departures for Britain. These included not only the aforementioned embrace of moderate religious toleration, but also a turn to policies favoring more modern economic activity resembling that of the Netherlands and a redirection of foreign policy toward direct opposition to France whereas both Charles II and James II had sought to imitate French absolutism and to pursue close relationships with Louis XIV.

The parliamentary measure closing this century of strife was the Act of Settlement (1701), which provided for the English crown to go to the Protestant House of Hanover in Germany if Queen Anne (r. 1702–1714), the second daughter of James II and the heir to the childless William III, died without issue. Thus, at Anne's death in 1714, the Elector of Hanover became King George I of Great Britain (r. 1714–1727) since England and Scotland had been combined in an Act of Union in 1707.

Sir Robert Walpole (1676–1745), far left, is shown talking with the Speaker of the House of Commons. Walpole, who dominated British political life from 1721 to 1742, is considered the first prime minister of Britain. Mansell/TimePix/Getty Images, Inc.

The Age of Walpole

George I almost immediately confronted a challenge to his title. James Edward Stuart (1688–1766), the Catholic son of James II, landed in Scotland in December 1715, but met defeat less than two months later.

Despite the victory over the Stuart pretender, the political situation after 1715 remained in flux until Sir Robert Walpole (1676–1745) took over the helm of government. Walpole's ascendancy from 1721 to 1742 was based on royal support, his ability to handle the House of Commons, and his control of government patronage. Walpole maintained peace abroad and promoted the status quo at home. Britain's foreign trade spread from New England to India. Because the central government refrained from interfering with the local political influence of nobles and other landowners, they were willing to serve as local government administrators, judges, and military commanders, and to collect and pay the taxes to support a powerful military force, particularly a strong navy. As a result, Great Britain became not only a European power of the first order but eventually a world power as well.

The power of the British monarchs and their ministers had real limits. Parliament could not wholly ignore popular pressure. Even with the extensive use of patronage, many members of Parliament maintained independent views. Newspapers and public debate flourished. Free speech could be exercised, as could freedom of association. There was no large standing army. There existed significant religious toleration. Walpole's enemies could and did openly oppose his policies, which would not have been possible on the Continent. Consequently, the English state combined considerable military power with both religious and political liberty. British political life became the model for all progressive Europeans who questioned the absolutist political developments of the Continent. Furthermore, many of the political values that had emerged in the British Isles during the seventeenth century also took deep root among their North American colonies.

▼ Rise of Absolute Monarchy in France: The World of Louis XIV

Historians once portrayed Louis XIV's reign (r. 1643–1715) as a time when the French monarchy exerted far-reaching, direct control of the nation at all levels. A somewhat different picture has now emerged.

The French monarchy, which had faced numerous challenges from strong, well-armed nobles and discontented Protestants during the first half of the seventeenth century, only gradually achieved the firm authority for which it became renowned later in the century. The groundwork for Louis XIV's absolutism had been laid by two powerful chief ministers, Cardinal Richelieu (1585–1642) under Louis XIII (r. 1610–1643), and then by Cardinal Mazarin (1602–1661). Both Richelieu and Mazarin attempted to impose direct royal administration on France. Richelieu had also circumscribed many of the political privileges Henry IV had extended to French Protestants in the Edict of Nantes (1598). The centralizing policies of Richelieu and then of Mazarin, however, finally provoked a series of widespread rebellions among French nobles between 1649 and 1652 known as the ***Fronde*** (after the slingshots used by street boys).

Though unsuccessful, these rebellions convinced Louis XIV and his advisors that heavy-handed policies could endanger the throne. Thereafter Louis would concentrate unprecedented authority in the monarchy, but he would be more subtle than his predecessors. His genius was to make the monarchy the most important and powerful political institution in France while also assuring the nobles and other wealthy groups of their social standing and influence on the local level. Rather than destroying existing local social and political institutions, Louis largely worked through them. Nevertheless, the king was clearly the senior partner in the relationship.

Years of Personal Rule

On the death of Mazarin in 1661, Louis XIV assumed personal control of the government at the age of twenty-three. He appointed no single chief minister. Rebellious nobles would now be challenging the king directly; they could not claim to be resisting only a bad minister.

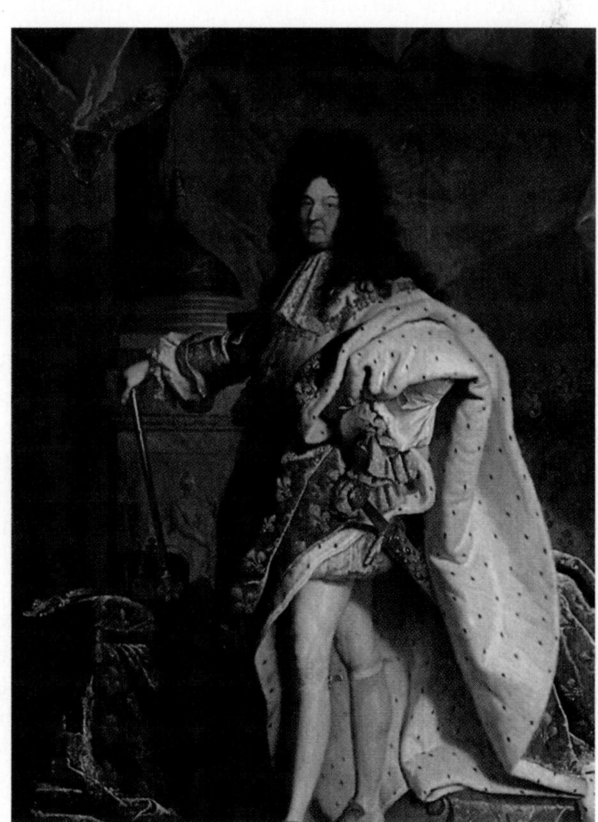

Louis XIV of France came to symbolize absolute monarchy though such government was not as absolute as the term implied. This state portrait was intended to convey the grandeur of the king and of his authority. The portrait was brought into royal council meetings when the king himself was absent. Hyacinthe Rigaud (1659–1743), *Portrait of Louis XIV*. Louvre, Paris, France. Dorling Kindersley Media Library/Max Alexander. © Dorling Kindersley, courtesy of l'Etablissement public du musée et du domaine national de Versailles

Louis devoted enormous personal energy to his political tasks. He ruled through councils that controlled foreign affairs, the army, domestic administration, and economic regulations. Each day he spent hours with the ministers of these councils, whom he chose from families long in royal service or from among people just beginning to rise in the social structure. Unlike the more ancient noble families, the latter had no real or potential power bases in the provinces and depended solely on the king for their standing in both government and society.

Louis made sure, however, that the nobility and other major social groups would benefit from the growth of his own authority. Although he controlled foreign affairs and limited the influence of noble institutions on the monarchy, he never tried to abolish those institutions or limit their local authority. The crown, for example, usually conferred informally with regional judicial bodies, called ***parlements***, before making rulings that would affect them. Likewise, the crown would rarely enact economic regulations without consulting local opinion. Louis did, however, clash with the Parlement of Paris, which had the right to register royal laws. In 1673, he curtailed its power by requiring it to register laws before raising any questions about them. Many regional parlements and other authorities, however, had long resented the power of that Parisian body and thus supported the monarch.

Versailles

Louis and his advisors became masters of propaganda and political image creation. Louis never missed an opportunity to impress the grandeur of his crown on the French people but most especially on the French nobility. He did so by the manipulation of symbols. For example, when the *dauphin* (the heir to the French throne) was born in 1662, Louis appeared for the celebration dressed as a Roman emperor. He also dominated the nobility by demonstrating that he could outspend them and create a greater social display than the strongest nobles in the land.

The central element of the image of the monarchy was the palace of Versailles, which, when completed, was the largest secular structure in Europe. More than any other monarch of the day, Louis XIV used the physical setting of his court to exert political control. Versailles, built between 1676 and 1708 on the outskirts of Paris, became Louis's permanent residence after 1682. It was a temple to royalty, designed and decorated to proclaim the glory of the Sun King, as Louis was known. A spectacular estate with magnificent fountains and gardens, it housed thousands of the more important nobles, royal officials, and servants. The stables alone could hold 12,000 horses. Some nobles paid for their own residence at the palace, thus depleting their resources; others required royal patronage to remain in residence. In either case they became dependent on the monarch. Although it consumed over half Louis's annual revenues, Versailles paid significant political dividends.

Because Louis ruled personally, he was himself the chief source of favors and patronage in France. To emphasize his prominence, he organized life at court around every aspect of his own daily routine. Elaborate etiquette governed every detail of life at Versailles. Moments near the king were important to most court nobles because they were effectively excluded from the real business of government. The king's rising and dressing were times of rare intimacy, when nobles could whisper their special requests in his ear. Fortunate nobles held his night candle when he went to his bed.

Some nobles, of course, avoided Versailles. They managed their estates and cultivated their local influence. Many others were simply too poor to cut a figure at court. All the nobility understood, however, that Louis, unlike Richelieu and Mazarin, would not threaten their local social standing. Louis supported France's traditional social structure and the social privileges of the nobility. Yet even the most powerful nobles knew they could strike only a modest figure when compared to the Sun King.

King by Divine Right

An important source for Louis's concept of royal authority was his devout tutor, the political theorist Bishop Jacques-Bénigne Bossuet (1627–1704). Bossuet defended what he called the "divine right of kings" and cited examples of Old Testament rulers divinely appointed by and answerable only to God. Medieval popes had insisted that only God could judge a pope; so Bossuet argued that only God could judge the king. Although kings might be duty bound to reflect God's will in their rule, yet as God's regents on earth they could not be bound to the dictates of mere nobles and parliaments. Such assumptions lay behind Louis XIV's alleged declaration: *"L'êtat, c'est moi"* ("I am the state"). (See "Compare & Connect: The Debate over the Origin and Character of Political Authority," pages 386–387.)

Despite these claims, Louis's rule did not exert the oppressive control over the daily lives of his subjects that police states would do in the nineteenth and twentieth centuries. His absolutism functioned primarily in the classic areas of European state action—the making of war and peace, the regulation of religion, and the oversight of economic activity. Even at the height of his power, local institutions, some controlled by townspeople and others by nobles, retained their administrative authority. The king and his ministers supported the social and financial privileges of these local elites. In contrast to the Stuart kings of England, however, Louis firmly prevented them from interfering with his authority on the national level. This system would endure until a financial crisis demoralized the French monarchy in the 1780s.

A Closer LOOK

VERSAILLES

LOUIS XIV CONSTRUCTED his great palace at Versailles, as painted here in 1668 by Pierre Patel the Elder (1605–1676), to demonstrate the new centralized power he sought to embody in the French monarchy.

The outer wings, extending from the front of the central structure, housed governmental offices.

The central building is the hunting lodge his father Louis XIII had built earlier in the century. Its interior and that of the wings added to it were decorated with themes from mythology presenting Louis XIV as the "Sun King" around whom all his kingdom revolved.

The gardens and ponds behind the main structure were the sites of elaborate entertainment, concerts, and fireworks.

Pierre Patel, *Perspective View of Versailles*. Chateaux de Versailles et de Trianon, Versailles, France. Photo copyright Bridgeman-Giraudon/ Art Resource, NY

To examine this image in an interactive fashion, please go to www.myhistorylab.com

PEARSON myhistorylab

Louis's Early Wars

By the late 1660s, France was superior to any other European nation in population, administrative bureaucracy, army, and national unity. Because of the economic policies of Jean-Baptiste Colbert (1619–1683), his most brilliant minister, Louis could afford to raise and maintain a large and powerful army. His enemies and some later historians claimed that Louis wished to dominate all of Europe, but it would appear that his chief military and foreign policy goal was to achieve secure international boundaries for France. He was particularly concerned to secure its northern borders along the Spanish Netherlands, the Franche-Comté, Alsace, and Lorraine from which foreign armies had invaded France and could easily do so again. Louis was also determined to frustrate Habsburg ambitions that endangered France and, as part of that goal, sought to secure his southern borders toward Spain. Whether reacting to external events or pursuing his own ambitions, Louis's pursuit of French interests threatened and terrified neighboring states and led them to form coalitions against France.

FRANCE FROM LOUIS XIV TO CARDINAL FLEURY

1643	Louis ascends the French throne at the age of five
1643–1661	Cardinal Mazarin directs the French government
1648	Peace of Westphalia
1649–1652	The *Fronde* revolt
1653	The pope declares Jansenism a heresy
1660	Papal ban on Jansenists enforced in France
1661	Louis commences personal rule
1667–1668	War of Devolution
1670	Secret Treaty of Dover between France and Great Britain
1672–1679	French war against the Netherlands
1685	Louis revokes the Edict of Nantes
1688–1697	War of the League of Augsburg
1701	Outbreak of the War of the Spanish Succession
1713	Treaty of Utrecht between France and Great Britain
1714	Treaty of Rastatt between France and the Empire and Holland
1715	Death of Louis XIV
1715–1720	Regency of the duke of Orléans in France
1720	Mississippi Bubble bursts in France
1726–1743	Cardinal Fleury serves as Louis XV's chief minister

The early wars of Louis XIV included conflicts with Spain and the United Netherlands. The first was the War of the Devolution in which Louis supported the alleged right of his first wife, Marie Thérèse, to inherit the Spanish Netherlands. He contended that through complex legal arrangements they should have "devolved" upon her, hence the name of the war. In 1667, Louis's armies invaded Flanders and the Franche-Comté. He was repulsed by the Triple Alliance of England, Sweden, and the United Provinces. By the Treaty of Aix-la-Chapelle (1668), he gained control of certain towns bordering the Spanish Netherlands. (See Map 13–1.)

In 1670, with the secret Treaty of Dover, England and France became allies against the Dutch. Louis invaded the Netherlands again in 1672. The Prince of Orange, the future William III of England, forged an alliance with the Holy Roman Emperor, Spain, Lorraine, and Brandenburg against Louis, now regarded as a menace to the whole of western Europe, Catholic and Protestant alike. The war ended inconclusively with the Peace of Nijmwegen, signed with different parties in successive years (1678, 1679). France gained more territory, including the Franche-Comté.

Louis's Repressive Religious Policies

Like Richelieu before him, Louis believed that political unity and stability required religious conformity. To that end he carried out repressive actions against both Roman Catholics and Protestants.

Suppression of the Jansenists The French crown and the French Roman Catholic church had long jealously guarded their ecclesiastical independence or "Gallican Liberties" from papal authority in Rome. However, after the conversion to Roman Catholicism of Henry IV in 1593, the Jesuits, fiercely loyal to the authority of the Pope, had monopolized the education of French upper-class men, and their devout students promoted the religious reforms and doctrines of the Council of Trent. As a measure of their success, Jesuits served as confessors to Henry IV, Louis XIII, and Louis XIV.

A Roman Catholic religious movement known as ***Jansenism*** arose in the 1630s in opposition to the theology and the political influence of the Jesuits. Jansenists adhered to the teachings of St. Augustine (354–430) that had also influenced many Protestant doctrines. Serious and uncompromising, they particularly opposed Jesuit teachings about free will. They believed with Augustine that original sin had so corrupted humankind that individuals could by their own effort do nothing good nor contribute anything to their own salvation. The namesake of the movement, Cornelius Jansen (d. 1638), was a Flemish theologian and the bishop of Ypres. His posthumously published *Augustinus* (1640) assailed Jesuit teaching on grace and salvation as morally lax.

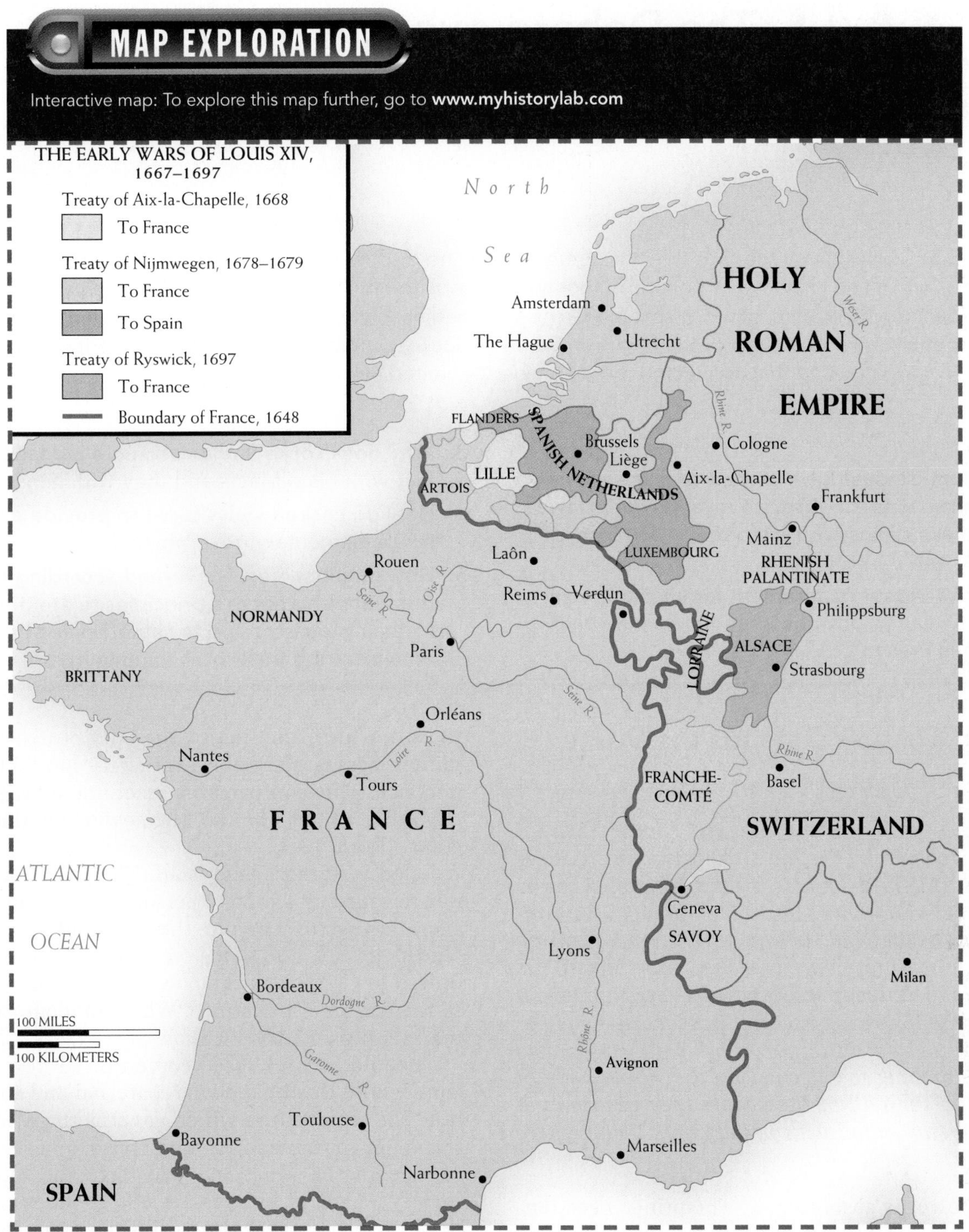

Map 13–1 **THE FIRST THREE WARS OF LOUIS XIV** This map shows the territorial changes resulting from Louis XIV's first three major wars (1667–1697).

Jansenism made considerable progress among prominent families in Paris. They were opposed to the Jesuits and supported Jansenist religious communities such as the convent at Port-Royal outside Paris. Jansenists, whose Augustinian theology resembled Calvinism, were known to live extremely pious and morally austere lives. In these respects, though firm Roman Catholics, they resembled English Puritans. Also, like the Puritans, the Jansenists became associated with opposition to royal authority, and families of Jansenist sympathies had been involved in the *Fronde*.

COMPARE AND CONNECT The Debate over the Origin and Character of Political Authority

DURING THE SECOND half of the seventeenth century a profound dispute occurred among European political philosophers over the origin and character of political authority. Some political philosophers, here illustrated by the French bishop Jacques-Bénigne Bossuet, contended that monarchs governed absolutely by virtue of authority derived from God. Other philosophers, here illustrated by the English writer John Locke, contended that political authority originated in the consent of the governed and that such authority was inherently limited in its scope.

QUESTIONS

1. **Why might Bossuet have wished to make such extravagant claims for absolute royal power? How might these claims be transferred to any form of government?**
2. **How does Bossuet's argument for absolute royal authority lead also to the need for a single uniform religion in France?**
3. **Why does Locke find an absolute monarch in conflict with his subjects and they with him?**
4. **How do Locke's views serve to provide a foundation for parliamentary government?**
5. **How might subjects governed according to Bossuet's and Locke's principles relate differently to their monarchs and to the officials of monarchs administering their local communities?**

I. Bishop Bossuet Defends the Divine Right of Kings

The revolutions of the seventeenth century caused many to fear anarchy far more than tyranny, among them the influential French bishop Jacques-Bénigne Bossuet (1627–1704), the leader of French Catholicism in the second half of the seventeenth century. Louis XIV made him court preacher and tutor to his son, for whom Bossuet wrote a celebrated universal history. In the following excerpt, Bossuet defends the divine right and absolute power of kings. He depicts kings as embracing in their person the whole body of the state and the will of the people they govern and, as such, as being immune from judgment by any mere mortal.

The royal power is absolute. . . . The prince need render account of his acts to no one. "I counsel thee to keep the king's commandment, and that in regard of the oath of God. Be not hasty to go out of his sight; stand not on an evil thing for he doeth whatsoever pleaseth him. Where the word of a king is, there is power; and who may say unto him, What doest thou? Whoso keepeth the commandment shall feel no evil thing" [Eccles. 8:2–5]. Without this absolute authority the king could neither do good nor repress evil. It is necessary that his power be such that no one can hope to escape him, and finally, the only protection of individuals against the public authority should be their innocence. This confirms the teaching of St. Paul: "Wilt thou then not be afraid of the power? Do that which is good" [Rom. 13:3].

God is infinite, God is all. The prince, as prince, is not regarded as a private person: he is a public personage, all the state is in him; the will of all the people is included in his. As all perfection and all strength are united in God, so all the power of individuals is united in the person of the prince. What grandeur that a single man should embody so much! . . .

Behold an immense people united in a single person; behold this holy power, paternal and absolute; behold the secret cause which governs the whole body of the state, contained in a single head: you see the image of God in the king, and you have the idea of royal majesty. God is holiness itself, goodness itself, and power itself. In these things lies the majesty of God. In the image of these things lies the majesty of the prince.

Source: From *Politics Drawn from the Very Words of Holy Scripture*, as quoted in James Harvey Robinson, ed., *Readings in European History*, Vol. 2 (Boston: Athenaeum, 1906), pp. 275–276.

II. John Locke Denounces the Idea of Absolute Monarchy

John Locke (1632–1704) was the most important English philosopher of the late seventeenth century. As will be seen in Chapter 14 he wrote on a wide variety of subjects including both political philosophy and religious toleration. In 1690 he published his second Treatise of Civil Government. *In this work he defended limitations on government and rooted political authority in the consent of the governed. He drafted the treatise in the late 1670s in response to Tory assertions of absolute monarchy set forth by supporters of Charles II. The treatise was published in the wake of the Revolution of 1688 and was read at the time as a justification of that event. Locke's thought would almost a century later influence the American Declaration of Independence. In the passages below Locke explains that under absolute monarchy citizens must submit to an authority from which they can make no appeal. Consequently, there is a necessary conflict between citizens and the absolute monarchy. It was to escape such conflict and to secure property and liberty that human beings had left the state of nature to found civil society.*

Man being born . . . with a title to perfect freedom, and an uncontrolled enjoyment of all the rights and privileges of the law of nature, equally with any other man, or number of men in the world, hath by nature a power, not only to preserve his property, that is, his life, liberty and estate, against the injuries and attempts of other men; but to judge of, and punish the breaches of that law in others, as he is persuaded the offence deserve . . . [T]here and there only is political society, where every one of the members hath quitted this natural power, resigned it up into the hands of the community in all cases that excludes him not from appealing for protection to the law established by it. And thus all private judgment of every particular member being excluded, the community comes to be umpire, by settled standing rules, indifferent, and the same to all parties; and by men having authority from the community, for the execution of those rules, decides all the differences that may happen between any members of that society concerning any matter of right . . .

Whenever therefore any number of men are so united into one society, as to quit every one his executive power of the law of nature, and to resign it to the public, there and there only is a political, or civil society. . . .

Hence it is evident, that absolute monarchy, which by some men is counted the only government in the world, is indeed inconsistent with civil society, and so can be no form of civil government at all; for the end of civil society, being to avoid, and remedy those inconveniencies of the state of nature, which necessarily follow from every man's being judge in his own case, by setting up a known authority, to which every one of that society may appeal upon any injury received, or controversy that may arise, and which every one of the society ought to obey; whereever any persons are, who have not such an authority to appeal to, for the decision of any difference between them, there those persons are still in the state of nature; and so is every absolute prince, in respect of those who are under his dominion.

For he being supposed to have all, both legislative and executive power in himself alone, there is no judge to be found, no appeal lies open to any one, who may fairly, and indifferently, and with authority decide, and from whose decision relief and redress may be expected of any injury or inconveniency, that may be suffered from the prince, or by his order: so that such a man, however intitled, czar, or grand seignior, or how you please, is as much in the state of nature, with all under his dominion, as he is with the rest of mankind: for where-ever any two men are, who have no standing rule, and common judge to appeal to on earth, for the determination of controversies of right betwixt them, there they are still in the state of nature, and under all the inconveniencies of it . . .

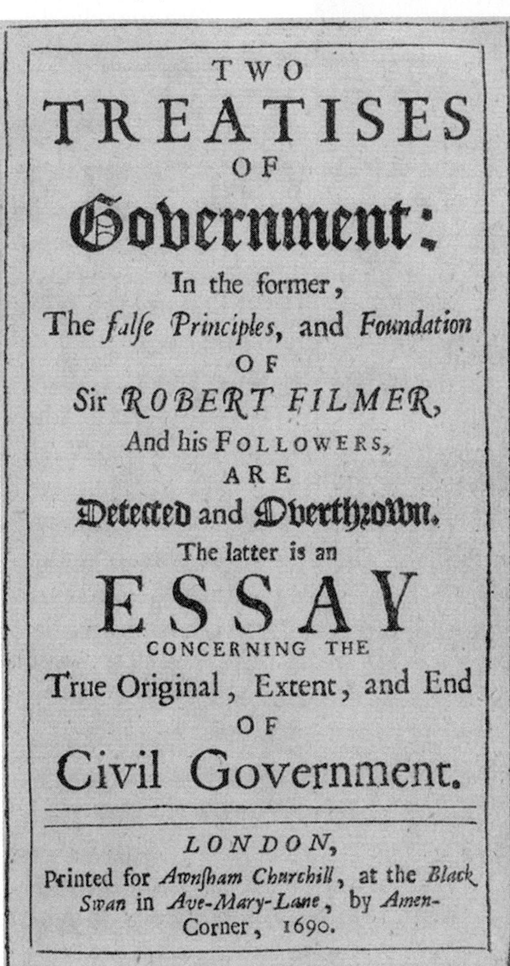
TWO
TREATISES
OF
Government:
In the former,
The *false Principles*, and *Foundation*
OF
Sir ROBERT FILMER,
And his FOLLOWERS,
ARE
Detected and Overthrown.
The latter is an
ESSAY
CONCERNING THE
True Original, Extent, and End
OF
Civil Government.

LONDON,
Printed for *Awnsham Churchill*, at the *Black Swan* in *Ave-Mary-Lane*, by *Amen-Corner*, 1690.

Title page from *Two Treatises of Government* by John Locke, London, 1690. Courtesy of the Library of Congress (Rosenwald Collection, Rare Book and Special Collections Division)

Source: John Locke, *Of Civil Government*, paragraphs 87, 89, 90, 91 in *Two Treatises of Government*, a new ed. (London: 1824), pp. 179–183.

Françoise d'Aubigne, Madame de Maintenon (1635–1719), a mistress to Louis XIV, secretly married him after his first wife's death. The deeply pious Maintenon influenced Louis's policy to make Roman Catholicism France's only religion. Pierre Mignard (1612–1695), *Portrait of Francoise d'Aubigne, Marquise de Maintenon (1635–1719), mistress and second wife of Louis XIV*, c. 1694. Oil on canvas, 128 × 97 cm. Inv.: MV 3637. Chateaux de Versailles et de Trianon, Versailles. Bridgeman-Giraudon/Art Resource, NY

On May 31, 1653, Pope Innocent X declared heretical five Jansenist theological propositions on grace and salvation. In 1656, the pope banned Jansen's *Augustinus*. In 1660, Louis permitted the papal bull banning Jansenism to be enforced in France. He also eventually closed down the Port-Royal community. Thereafter, Jansenists either retracted their views or went underground. In 1713, Pope Clement XI issued the bull *Unigenitus*, which again extensively condemned Jansenist teaching. The now aged Louis XIV ordered the French church to accept the bull despite internal ecclesiastical opposition.

The theological issues surrounding Jansenism were complex. By persecuting the Jansenists, however, Louis XIV turned his back on the long tradition of protecting the Gallican Liberties of the French Church and fostered within the French Church a core of opposition to royal authority. This had long-term political significance. During the eighteenth century after the death of Louis XIV, the Parlement of Paris and other French judicial bodies would reassert their authority in opposition to the monarchy. These courts were sympathetic to the Jansenists because of their common resistance to royal authority. Jansenism, because of its austere morality, then also came to embody a set of religious and moral values that contrasted with what eighteenth-century public opinion saw as the corruption of the mid-eighteenth-century French royal court.

Revocation of the Edict of Nantes After the Edict of Nantes in 1598, relations between the Catholic majority (nine tenths of the French population) and the Protestant minority had remained hostile. There were about 1.75 million Huguenots in France in the 1660s (out of an overall population of around 18 million), but their numbers were declining. The French Catholic church had long supported their persecution as both pious and patriotic.

After the Peace of Nijmwegen, Louis launched a methodical campaign against the Huguenots in an effort to unify France religiously. He was also influenced in this policy by his mistress who became his second wife Madame de Maintenon (1635–1719), a deeply pious Catholic who drew Louis toward a much more devout religious observance. Louis hounded Huguenots out of public life, banning them from government office and excluding them from such professions as printing and medicine. He used financial incentives to encourage them to convert to Catholicism. In 1681, he bullied them by quartering troops in their towns. Finally, in October 1685, Louis revoked the Edict of Nantes, and extensive religious repression followed. Protestant churches and schools were closed, Protestant ministers exiled, nonconverting laity were condemned to be galley slaves, and Protestant children were baptized by Catholic priests. (See "Louis XIV Revokes the Edict of Nantes.")

The revocation was a major blunder. Henceforth, Protestants across Europe considered Louis a fanatic who must be resisted at all costs. More than a quarter million people, many of whom were highly skilled, left France. They formed new communities abroad and joined the resistance to Louis in England, Germany, Holland, and the New World. As a result of the revocation of the Edict of Nantes and the ongoing persecution of Jansenists, France became a symbol of religious repression in contrast to England's reputation for moderate, if not complete, religious toleration.

Louis's Later Wars

The League of Augsburg and the Nine Years' War After the Treaty of Nijmwegen in 1678–1679, Louis maintained his army at full strength and restlessly probed beyond his borders. In 1681 his forces occupied the free city of Strasbourg on the Rhine River, prompting new defensive coalitions to form against him. One of these, the League of Augsburg, grew to include England, Spain, Sweden, the United Provinces, and the major German states. It also had the support of the

LOUIS XIV REVOKES THE EDICT OF NANTES

Believing a country could not be governed by one king and one law unless it was also under one religious system, Louis XIV stunned much of Europe in October 1685, by revoking the Edict of Nantes, which had protected the religious freedoms and civil rights of French Protestants since 1598. Years of serious, often violent, persecution of French Protestants followed this revocation. Consequently, after 1685 in the minds of many Europeans political absolutism was associated with intolerance and religious persecution. Paradoxically, Pope Innocent XI (1676–1689) opposed Louis XIV's revocation of the Edict of Nantes because he understood that this act and other aspects of Louis's ecclesiastical policy were intended as political measures to allow his government to dominate the Roman Catholic Church in France.

Compare this document to the one on page 396 in which the elector of Brandenburg welcomes displaced French Protestants into his domains.

What specific actions does this declaration order against Protestants? Does it offer any incentives for Protestants to convert to Catholicism? How does this declaration compare with the English Test Act?

Art. 1. Know that we . . . with our certain knowledge, full power and royal authority, have by this present, perpetual and irrevocable edict, suppressed and revoked the edict of the aforesaid king our grandfather, given at Nantes in the month of April, 1598, in all its extent . . . together with all the concessions made by [this] and other edicts, declarations, and decrees, to the people of the so-called Reformed religion, of whatever nature they be . . . and in consequence we desire . . . that all the temples of the people of the aforesaid so-called Reformed religion situated in our kingdom . . . should be demolished forthwith.

Art. 2. We forbid our subjects of the so-called Reformed religion to assemble any more for public worship of the above-mentioned religion. . . .

Art. 3. We likewise forbid all lords, of whatever rank they may be, to carry out heretical services in houses and fiefs . . . the penalty for . . . the said worship being confiscation of their body and possessions.

Art. 4. We order all ministers of the aforesaid so-called Reformed religion who do not wish to be converted and to embrace the Catholic, Apostolic, and Roman religion, to depart from our kingdom and the lands subject to us within fifteen days from the publication of our present edict . . . on pain of the galleys.

Art. 5. We desire that those among the said [Reformed] ministers who shall be converted [to the Catholic religion] shall continue to enjoy during their life, and their wives shall enjoy after their death as long as they remain widows, the same exemptions from taxation and billeting of soldiers, which they enjoyed while they fulfilled the function of ministers. . . .

Art. 8. With regard to children who shall be born to those of the aforesaid so-called Reformed religion, we desire that they be baptized by their parish priests. We command the fathers and mothers to send them to the churches for that purpose, on penalty of a fine of 500 livres or more if they fail to do so; and afterwards, the children shall be brought up in the Catholic, Apostolic, and Roman religion. . . .

Art. 10. All our subjects of the so-called Reformed religion, with their wives and children, are to be strongly and repeatedly prohibited from leaving our aforesaid kingdom . . . or of taking out . . . their possessions and effects. . . .

The members of the so-called Reformed religion, while awaiting God's pleasure to enlighten them like the others, can live in the towns and districts of our kingdom . . . and continue their occupation there, and enjoy their possessions . . . on condition . . . that they do not make public profession of [their religion].

S. Z. Ehler and John B. Morrall, eds. and trans., *Church and State Through the Centuries: A Collection of Historic Documents* (New York: Biblo and Tannen, 1967), pp. 209–213. Reprinted by permission of Biblo and Tannen Booksellers and Publishers.

Map 13–2 **EUROPE IN 1714** The War of the Spanish Succession ended a year before the death of Louis XIV. The Bourbons had secured the Spanish throne, but Spain had forfeited its possessions in Flanders and Italy.

Habsburg emperor Leopold I (r. 1658–1705). Between 1689 and 1697, the League and France battled each other in the Nine Years' War, while England and France struggled to control North America.

The Peace of Ryswick, signed in September 1697, which ended the war, secured Holland's borders and thwarted Louis's expansion into Germany.

War of the Spanish Succession On November 1, 1700, the last Habsburg king of Spain, Charles II (r. 1665–1700), died without direct heirs. Before his death, negotiations had begun among the nations involved to partition his inheritance in a way that would preserve the existing balance of power. Charles II, however, left his entire inheritance to Louis's grandson Philip of Anjou, who became Philip V of Spain (r. 1700–1746).

Spain and the vast trade with its American empire appeared to have fallen to France. In September 1701, England, Holland, and the Holy Roman Empire formed the Grand Alliance to preserve the balance of power by once and for all securing Flanders as a neutral barrier between Holland and France and by gaining for the emperor, who was also a Habsburg, his fair share of the Spanish inheritance. Louis soon increased the political stakes by recognizing the Stuart claim to the English throne.

In 1701 the War of the Spanish Succession (1701–1714) began, and it soon enveloped western Europe. France for the first time in Louis's reign went to war with inadequate finances, a poorly equipped army, and mediocre generals. The English, in contrast, had advanced weaponry (flintlock rifles, paper cartridges, and ring bayonets) and superior tactics (thin, maneuverable troop columns rather than the traditional deep ones). John Churchill, the Duke of Marlborough (1650–1722), bested Louis's soldiers in every major engagement, although French arms triumphed in Spain. After 1709 the war became a bloody stalemate.

France finally made peace with England at Utrecht in July 1713, and with Holland and the emperor at Rastatt in March 1714. Philip V remained king of Spain, but England got Gibraltar and the island of Minorca, making it a Mediterranean power. (See Map 13–2.) Louis also recognized the right of the House of Hanover to the English throne.

The impending collapse of John Law's bank triggered a financial panic throughout France. Desperate investors, such as those shown here in the city of Rennes, sought to exchange their paper currency for gold and silver before the banks' supply of precious metals was exhausted. Collection Musée de Bretagne, Rennes

France After Louis XIV

Despite its military reverses in the War of the Spanish Succession, France remained a great power. It was less strong in 1715 than in 1680, but it still possessed the largest European population, an advanced, if troubled, economy, and the administrative structure bequeathed it by Louis XIV. Moreover, even if France and its resources had been drained by the last of Louis's wars, the other major states of Europe were similarly debilitated.

Louis XIV was succeeded by his five-year-old great-grandson Louis XV (r. 1715–1774). The young boy's uncle, the duke of Orléans, became regent and remained so until his death in 1720. The regency, marked by financial and moral scandals, further undermined the faltering prestige of the monarchy.

John Law and the Mississippi Bubble The duke of Orléans was a gambler, and for a time he turned over the financial management of the kingdom to John Law (1671–1729), a Scottish mathematician and fellow gambler. Law believed an increase in the paper-money supply would stimulate France's economic recovery. With the permission of the regent, he established a bank in Paris that issued paper money. Law then organized a monopoly, called the Mississippi Company, on trading privileges with the French colony of Louisiana in North America.

The Mississippi Company also took over the management of the French national debt. The company issued shares of its own stock in exchange for government bonds, which had fallen sharply in value. To redeem large quantities of bonds, Law encouraged speculation in the Mississippi Company stock. In 1719, the price of the stock rose handsomely. Smart investors, however, took their profits by selling their stock in exchange for paper money from Law's bank, which they then sought to exchange for gold. The bank, however, lacked enough gold to redeem all the paper money brought to it.

In February 1720, all gold payments were halted in France. Soon thereafter, Law himself fled the country. The Mississippi Bubble, as the affair was called, had burst. The fiasco brought disgrace on the government that had sponsored Law. The Mississippi Company was later reorganized and functioned profitably, but fear of paper money and speculation marked French economic life for decades.

Renewed Authority of the Parlements The duke of Orléans made a second decision that also lessened the power of the monarchy. He attempted to draw the French nobility once again into the decision-making processes of the government. He set up a system of councils on which nobles were to serve along with bureaucrats. The years of idle noble domestication at Versailles, however, had worked too well, and the nobility seemed to lack both the talent and the desire to govern. The experiment failed. Despite this failure, the great French nobles did not surrender their ancient ambition to assert their rights, privileges, and local influence over those of the monarchy. The chief feature of eighteenth-century French political life was the attempt of the nobility to use its authority to limit the power of the monarchy. The most effective instrument in this process was the previously mentioned *parlements*, or courts dominated by the nobility.

The duke of Orléans reversed the previously noted policy of Louis XIV and formally approved the reinstitution of the full power of the Parlement of Paris to allow

Under Louis XV (r. 1715–1774) France suffered major defeats in Europe and around the world and lost most of its North American empire. Louis himself was an ineffective ruler, and during his reign, the monarchy encountered numerous challenges from the French aristocracy. CORBIS/Bettmann

or disallow laws. Moreover, throughout the eighteenth century that and other local *parlements* also succeeded in identifying their authority and resistance to the monarchy with wider public opinion. This situation meant that until the revolution in 1789, the *parlements* became natural centers not only for aristocratic, but also for popular resistance to royal authority. In a vast transformation from the days of Louis XIV, the *parlements* rather than the monarchy would come to be seen as more nearly representing the nation.

By 1726, the general political direction of the nation had come under the authority of Cardinal Fleury (1653–1743). He worked to maintain the authority of the monarchy, including ongoing repression of the Jansenists, while continuing to preserve the local interests of the French nobility. Like Walpole in Britain, he pursued economic prosperity at home and peace abroad. Again like Walpole, after 1740, Fleury could not prevent France from entering a worldwide colonial conflict. (See Chapter 17.)

▼ Central and Eastern Europe

Central and eastern Europe were economically much less advanced than western Europe. Except for the Baltic ports, the economy was agrarian. There were fewer cities and many more large estates worked by serfs. The states in this region did not possess overseas empires; nor did they engage in extensive overseas trade of any kind, except for supplying grain to western Europe—grain, more often than not, carried on western European ships.

During the sixteenth and early seventeenth centuries, the political authorities in this region, which lay largely east of the Elbe River, were weak. The almost constant warfare of the seventeenth century had led to a habit of temporary and shifting political loyalties with princes and aristocracies of small states refusing to subordinate themselves to central monarchical authorities.

During the last half of the seventeenth century, however, three strong dynasties, whose rulers aspired to the absolutism then being constructed in France, emerged in central and eastern Europe. After the Peace of Westphalia in 1648, the Austrian Habsburgs recognized the basic weakness of the position of the Holy Roman Emperor and started to consolidate their power outside Germany. At the same time, Prussia under the Hohenzollern dynasty emerged as a factor in north German politics and as a major challenger to the Habsburg domination of Germany. Most important, Russia under the Romanov dynasty at the opening of the eighteenth century became a military and naval power of the first order. These three monarchies would dominate central and eastern Europe until the close of World War I in 1918. By contrast, Poland during the eighteenth century became the single most conspicuous example in Europe of a land that failed to establish a viable centralized government.

Poland: Absence of Strong Central Authority

In no other part of Europe was the failure to maintain a competitive political position as complete as in Poland. In 1683 King John III Sobieski (r. 1674–1696) had led a Polish army to rescue Vienna from a Turkish siege. Following that spectacular effort, however, Poland became a byword for the dangers of aristocratic independence.

The Polish monarchy was elective, but the deep distrust and divisions among the nobility usually prevented their electing a king from among themselves. Sobieski was a notable exception. Most of the Polish monarchs were foreigners and the tools of foreign powers. The Polish nobles did have a central legislative body called the ***Sejm***, or diet. It included only nobles and specifically excluded representatives from corporate bodies, such as the towns. The diet, however, had a practice known as the *liberum veto*, whereby the staunch opposition of any single member, who might have been bribed by a foreign power, could require the body to disband. Such opposition, termed "exploding the diet," was most often the work of a group of dissatisfied nobles rather than of one person. Nonetheless, the requirement of unanimity was a major stumbling block

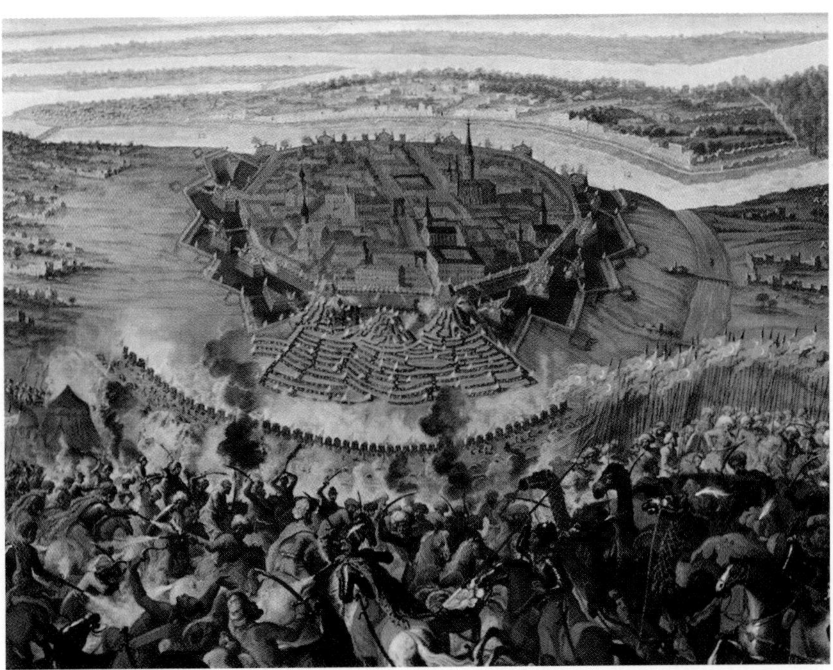

In 1683 the Ottomans laid siege to Vienna. Only the arrival of Polish forces under King John III Sobieski (r. 1674–1696) saved the Habsburg capital. Dagli Orti/Picture Desk, Inc./Kobal Collection

to effective government. The price of this noble liberty would eventually be the disappearance of Poland from the map of Europe in the late eighteenth century.

The Habsburg Empire and the Pragmatic Sanction

The close of the Thirty Years' War marked a fundamental turning point in the history of the Austrian Habsburgs. Previously, in alliance with their Spanish cousins, they had hoped to bring all of Germany under their control and back to the Catholic fold. In this they had failed, and the decline of Spanish power meant that the Austrian Habsburgs were on their own. (See Map 13–3, page 394.)

After 1648, the Habsburg family retained a firm hold on the title of Holy Roman Emperor, but the power of the emperor depended less on the force of arms than on the cooperation he could elicit from the various political bodies in the empire. These included large German units (such as Saxony, Hanover, Bavaria, and Brandenburg) and scores of small German cities, bishoprics, principalities, and territories of independent knights. While establishing their new dominance among the German states, the Habsburgs also began to consolidate their power and influence within their hereditary possessions outside the Holy Roman Empire, which included the Crown of Saint Wenceslas, encompassing the kingdom of Bohemia (in the modern Czech Republic) and the duchies of Moravia and Silesia; and the Crown of Saint Stephen, which ruled Hungary, Croatia, and Transylvania. Much of Hungary was only liberated from the Turks at the end of the seventeenth century (1699).

Through the Treaty of Rastatt in 1714, the Habsburgs further extended their domains, receiving the former Spanish (thereafter Austrian) Netherlands and Lombardy in northern Italy. Thereafter, the Habsburgs' power and influence would be based primarily on their territories outside of Germany.

In each of their many territories the Habsburgs ruled by virtue of a different title—king, archduke, duke—and they needed the cooperation of the local nobility, which was not always forthcoming. They repeatedly had to bargain with nobles in one part of Europe to maintain their position in another. Their domains were so geographically diverse and the people who lived in them of so many different languages and customs that almost no grounds existed on which to unify them politically. Even Roman Catholicism proved ineffective as a common bond, particularly in Hungary, where many Magyar nobles were Calvinist and seemed ever ready to rebel. Over the years the Habsburg rulers established various central councils to chart common policies for their far-flung domains. Virtually all of these bodies, however, dealt with only a portion of the Habsburg holdings.

Despite these internal difficulties, Leopold I (r. 1658–1705) managed to resist the advances of the

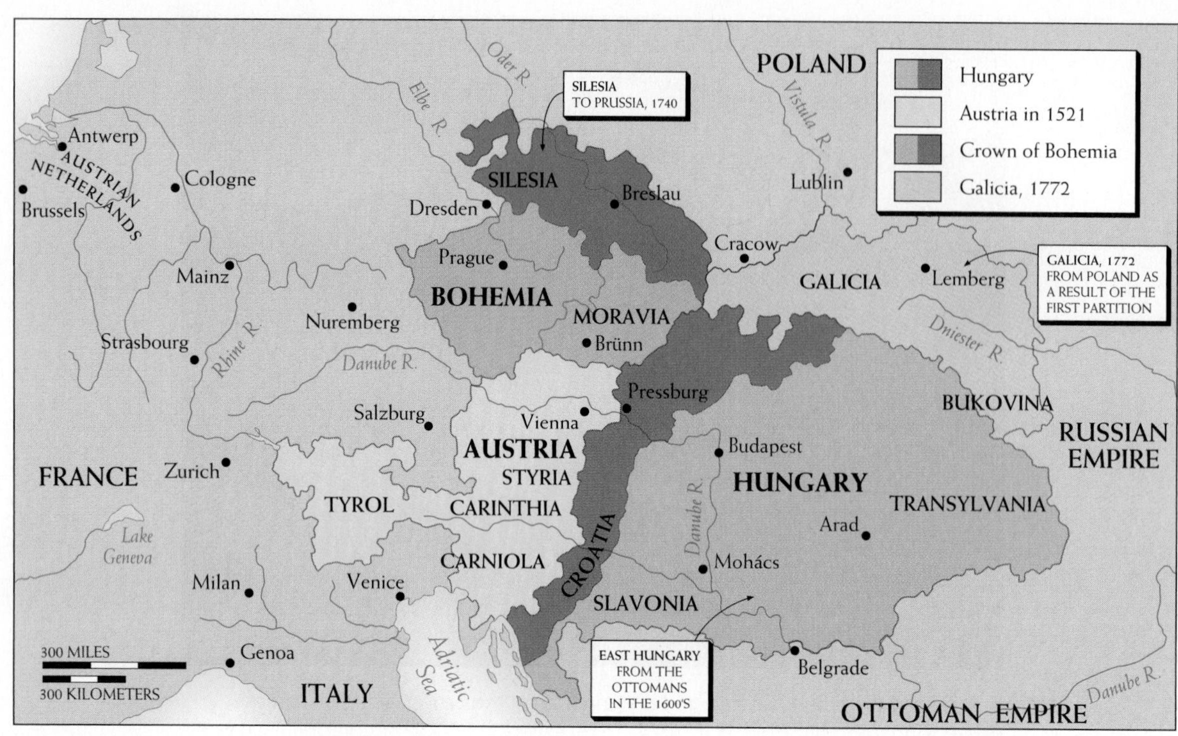

Map 13–3 **THE AUSTRIAN HABSBURG EMPIRE, 1521–1772** The empire had three main units—Austria, Bohemia, and Hungary. Expansion was mainly eastward: eastern Hungary from the Ottomans (seventeenth century) and Galicia from Poland (1772). Meantime, Silesia was lost after 1740, but the Habsburgs remained Holy Roman Emperors.

Ottoman Empire into central Europe, which included a siege of Vienna in 1683, and to thwart the aggression of Louis XIV. He achieved Ottoman recognition of his sovereignty over Hungary in 1699 and extended his territorial holdings over much of the Balkan Peninsula and western Romania. These conquests allowed the Habsburgs to hope to develop Mediterranean trade through the port of Trieste on the northern coast of the Adriatic Sea and helped compensate for their loss of effective power over the Holy Roman Empire. Strength in the East gave them greater political leverage in Germany. Joseph I (r. 1705–1711) continued Leopold's policies.

When Charles VI (r. 1711–1740) succeeded Joseph, a new problem was added to the chronic one of territorial diversity. He had no male heir, and there was only the weakest of precedents for a female ruler of the Habsburg domains. Charles feared that on his death the Austrian Habsburg lands might fall prey to the surrounding powers, as had those of the Spanish Habsburgs in 1700. He was determined to prevent that disaster and to provide his domains with the semblance of legal unity. To those ends, he devoted most of his reign to seeking the approval of his family, the estates of his realms, and the major foreign powers for a document called the ***Pragmatic Sanction***.

This instrument provided the legal basis for a single line of inheritance within the Habsburg dynasty through Charles VI's daughter Maria Theresa (r. 1740–1780). Other members of the Habsburg family recognized her as the rightful heir. After extracting various concessions from Charles, the nobles of the various Habsburg domains and the other European rulers also recognized her. Consequently, when Charles VI died in October 1740, he believed that he had secured legal unity for the Habsburg Empire and a safe succession for

AUSTRIA AND PRUSSIA IN THE LATE SEVENTEENTH AND EARLY EIGHTEENTH CENTURIES

1640–1688	Reign of Frederick William, the Great Elector
1658–1705	Leopold I rules Austria and resists the Turkish invasions
1683	Turkish siege of Vienna
1688–1713	Reign of Frederick I of Prussia
1699	Peace treaty between Turks and Habsburgs
1711–1740	Charles VI rules Austria and secures agreement to the Pragmatic Sanction
1713–1740	Frederick William I builds up the military power of Prussia
1740	Maria Theresa succeeds to the Habsburg throne
1740	Frederick II violates the Pragmatic Sanction by invading Silesia

his daughter. He had indeed established a permanent line of succession and the basis for future legal bonds within the Habsburg holdings. Despite the Pragmatic Sanction, however, his failure to provide his daughter with a strong army or a full treasury left her inheritance open to foreign aggression. Less than two months after his death, the fragility of the foreign agreements became apparent. In December 1740, Frederick II of Prussia invaded the Habsburg province of Silesia in eastern Germany. Maria Theresa had to fight for her inheritance.

Prussia and the Hohenzollerns

The rise of Prussia occurred within the German power vacuum created by the Peace of Westphalia. It is the story of the extraordinary Hohenzollern family, which had ruled Brandenburg since 1417. Through inheritance the family had acquired the duchy of Cleves, and the counties of Mark and Ravensburg in 1614, East Prussia in 1618, and Pomerania in 1648. (See Map 13–4.) Except for Pomerania, none of these lands shared a border with Brandenburg. East Prussia lay inside Poland and outside the authority of the Holy Roman Emperor. All of the territories lacked good natural resources, and many of them were devastated during the Thirty Years' War. Still, by the late seventeenth century, the geographically scattered Hohenzollern holdings represented a block of territory within the Holy Roman Empire, second in size only to that of the Habsburgs.

The person who began to forge these areas into a modern state was Frederick William (r. 1640–1688), who became known as the Great Elector. He established himself and his successors as the central uniting power by breaking the local noble estates, organizing a royal bureaucracy, and building a strong army. (See "The Great Elector Welcomes Protestant Refugees from France," page 396.)

Between 1655 and 1660, Sweden and Poland fought each other across the Great Elector's holdings in Pomerania and East Prussia. Frederick William had neither an adequate army nor the tax revenues to confront this threat. In 1655, the Brandenburg estates refused to grant him new taxes; however, he proceeded to collect them by military force. In 1659, a different grant of taxes, originally made in 1653, elapsed; Frederick William continued to collect them as well as those he had imposed by his own authority. He used the money to build an army, which allowed him to continue to enforce his will without the approval of the nobility. Similar coercion took place against the nobles in his other territories.

There was, however, a political and social trade-off between the Elector and his various nobles. In exchange for their obedience to the Hohenzollerns, the ***Junkers***, or German noble landlords, received the right to demand obedience from their serfs. Frederick William also tended to choose as the local administrators of the tax structure men who would normally have been members of the

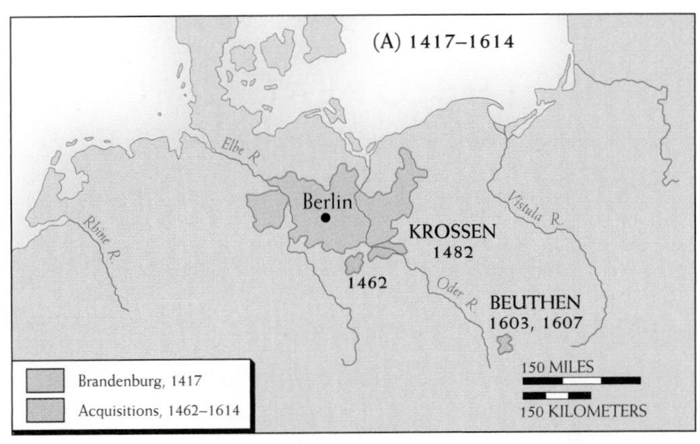

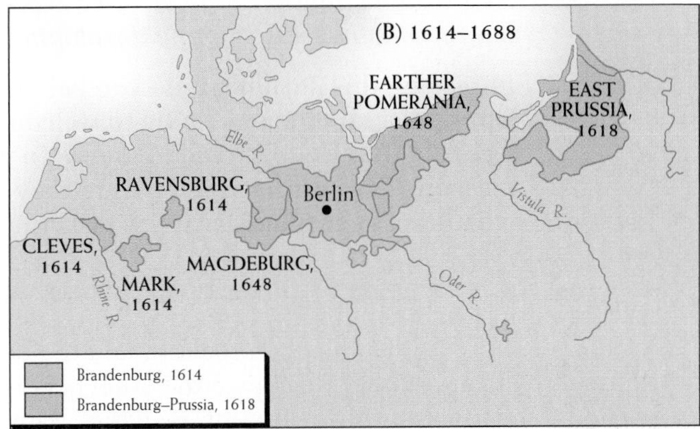

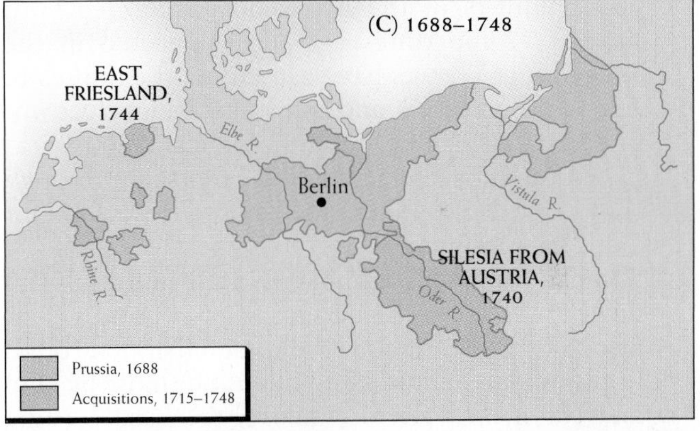

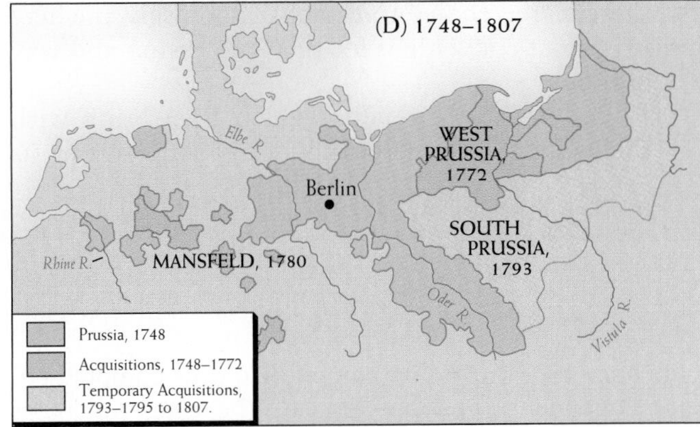

Map 13–4 **EXPANSION OF BRANDEBURG-PRUSSIA** In the seventeenth century Brandenburg-Prussia expanded mainly by acquiring dynastic titles in geographically separated lands. In the eighteenth century it expanded through aggression to the east, seizing Silesia in 1740 and various parts of Poland in 1772, 1793, and 1795.

THE GREAT ELECTOR WELCOMES PROTESTANT REFUGEES FROM FRANCE

The Hohenzollern dynasty of Brandenburg–Prussia pursued a policy of religious toleration. The family itself was Calvinist, whereas most of its subjects were Lutherans. When Louis XIV of France revoked the Edict of Nantes in 1685, Frederick William, the Great Elector, seized the opportunity to invite French Protestants into his realms. As his proclamation indicates, he wanted to attract persons with productive skills who could aid the economic development of his domains.

In reading this document, do you believe religious or economic concerns more nearly led the elector of Brandenburg to welcome the French Protestants? What specific privileges did the elector extend to them? To what extent were these privileges a welcoming measure, and to what extent were they inducements to emigrate to Brandenburg? In what kind of economic activity does the elector expect the French refugees to engage?

We, Friedrich Wilhelm, by Grace of God Margrave of Brandenburg . . . Do hereby proclaim and make known to all and sundry that since the cruel persecutions and rigorous ill-treatment in which Our co-religionists of the Evangelical-Reformed faith have for some time past been subjected in the Kingdom of France, have caused many families to remove themselves and to betake themselves out of the said Kingdom into other lands, We now . . . have been moved graciously to offer them through this Edict . . . a secure and free refuge in all Our Lands and Provinces. . . .

Since Our Lands are not only well and amply endowed with all things necessary to support life, but also very well-suited to the reestablishment of all kinds of manufactures and trade and traffic by land and water, We permit, indeed, to those settling therein free choice to establish themselves where it is most convenient for their profession and way of living. . . .

The personal property which they bring with them, including merchandise and other wares, is to be totally exempt from any taxes, customs dues, licenses, or other imposts of any description, and not detained in any way. . . .

As soon as these Our French co-religionists of the Evangelical-Reformed faith have settled in any town or village, they shall be admitted to the domiciliary rights and craft freedoms customary there, gratis and without payments of any fee; and shall be entitled to the benefits, rights, and privileges enjoyed by Our other, native, subjects, residing there. . . .

Not only are those who wish to establish manufacture of cloth, stuffs, hats, or other objects in which they are skilled to enjoy all necessary freedoms, privileges and facilities, but also provision is to be made for them to be assisted and helped as far as possible with money and anything else which they need to realize their intention. . . .

Those who settle in the country and wish to maintain themselves by agriculture are to be given a certain plot of land to bring under cultivation and provided with whatever they need to establish themselves initially. . . .

From C. A. Macartney, ed., *The Habsburg and Hohenzollern Dynasties in the Seventeenth and Eighteenth Centuries* (New York: Walker, 1970), pp. 270–273.

noble branch of the old parliament. He thus co-opted potential opponents into his service. The taxes fell most heavily on the backs of the peasants and the urban classes. As the years passed, *Junkers* increasingly dominated the army officer corps, and this situation became even more pronounced during the eighteenth century. All officials and army officers took an oath of loyalty directly to the Elector. The army and the Elector thus came to embody the otherwise absent unity of the state. The army made Prussia a valuable potential ally.

Yet even with the considerable accomplishments of the Great Elector, the house of Hohenzollern did not possess a crown. The achievement of a royal title was one of the few state-building accomplishments of Frederick I (r. 1688–1713). This son of the Great Elector was the least "Prussian" of his family during these crucial years. He built palaces, founded Halle University (1694), patronized the arts, and lived luxuriously. In the War of the Spanish Succession, he put his army at the disposal of the Habsburg Holy Roman Emperor Leopold I. In exchange, the emperor permitted Frederick to assume the title of "King in Prussia" in 1701.

His successor, Frederick William I (r. 1713–1740), was both the most eccentric monarch to rule the Hohenzollern domains and one of the most effective. He organized the bureaucracy along military lines. The discipline that he applied to the army was fanatical. The Prussian military grew from about 39,000 in 1713 to over 80,000 in 1740, making it the third or fourth largest army in Europe. Prussia's population, in contrast, ranked thirteenth in size. Separate laws applied to the army and to civilians. Laws, customs, and royal attention made the officer corps the highest social class of the state. Military service thus attracted the sons of *Junkers*. In this fashion the army, the *Junker* nobility, and the monarchy became forged into a single political entity. Military priorities and values dominated Prussian government, society, and daily life as in no other state in Europe. It has often been said that whereas other states possessed armies, the Prussian army possessed its state.

Although Frederick William I built the best army in Europe, he avoided conflict. His army was a symbol of Prussian power and unity, not an instrument for foreign adventures or aggression. At his death in 1740, he passed to his son Frederick II later known as Frederick the Great (r. 1740–1786), this superb military machine, but not the wisdom to refrain from using it. Almost immediately on coming to the throne, Frederick II upset the Pragmatic Sanction and invaded Silesia. He thus crystallized the Austrian-Prussian rivalry for the control of Germany that would dominate central European affairs for over a century.

▼ Russia Enters the European Political Arena

The emergence of Russia in the late seventeenth century as an active European power was a wholly new factor in European politics. Previously, Russia had been considered part of Europe only by courtesy. Before 1673, it did not send permanent ambassadors to western Europe, though it had sent various diplomatic missions since the fifteenth century. Geographically and politically, it lay on the periphery. Hemmed in by Sweden on the Baltic and by the Ottoman Empire on the Black Sea, Russia had no warm-water ports. Its chief outlet for trade to the West was Archangel on the White Sea, which was ice free for only part of the year.

The Romanov Dynasty

The reign of Ivan IV (r. 1533–1584), later known as Ivan the Terrible, had commenced well but ended badly. About midway in his reign he underwent a personality change that led him to move from a program of sensible reform of law, government, and the army toward violent personal tyranny. A period known as the "Time of Troubles" followed upon his death. In 1613, hoping to end the uncertainty, an assembly of nobles elected as tsar a seventeen-year-old boy named Michael Romanov (r. 1613–1645). Thus began the dynasty that ruled Russia until 1917.

Michael Romanov and his two successors, Aleksei (r. 1654–1676) and Theodore II (r. 1676–1682), brought stability and modest bureaucratic centralization to Russia. The country remained, however, weak and impoverished. After years of turmoil, the *boyars*, the old nobility, still largely controlled the bureaucracy. Furthermore, the government and the tsars faced the danger of mutiny from the *streltsy*, or guards of the Moscow garrison.

Peter the Great

In 1682, another boy—ten years old at the time—ascended the fragile Russian throne as co-ruler with his half brother. His name was Peter (r. 1682–1725), and Russia would never be the same after him. He and the sickly Ivan V had come to power on the shoulders of the *streltsy*, who expected to be rewarded for their support. Violence and bloodshed had surrounded the disputed succession. Matters became even more confused when the boys' sister, Sophia, was named regent. Peter's followers overthrew her in 1689. From that date onward, Peter ruled personally, although in theory he shared the crown until Ivan died in 1696. The dangers and turmoil of his youth convinced Peter of two things: First, the power of the tsar must be made secure from the jealousy of the *boyars* and the greed of the *streltsy*; second, Russian military power must be increased. In both respects, he self-consciously resembled Louis XIV of France, who had experienced the turmoil of the *Fronde* during his youth and resolved to establish a strong monarchy safe from the nobility and defended by a powerful army.

Northwestern Europe, particularly the military resources of the maritime powers, fascinated Peter I, who eventually became known as Peter the Great. In 1697, he made a famous visit in transparent disguise to western Europe. There he dined and talked with the great and the powerful, who considered this almost seven-foot-tall ruler crude. He spent his happiest moments on the trip inspecting shipyards, docks, and the manufacture of military hardware in England and the Netherlands. An imitator of the first order, Peter returned to Moscow determined to copy what he had seen abroad, for he knew warfare would be necessary to make Russia a great power. Yet he understood his goal would require him to confront the long-standing power and traditions of the Russian nobles.

Taming the *Streltsy* and *Boyars* In 1698, while Peter was abroad, the *streltsy* had rebelled. On his return, Peter brutally suppressed the revolt with private tortures and public executions, in which Peter's own ministers took part. Approximately a thousand of the rebels were put to death, and their corpses remained on public display to discourage disloyalty.

The new military establishment that Peter built would serve the tsar and not itself. He introduced effective and ruthless policies of conscription, drafting an unprecedented 130,000 soldiers during the first decade of the eighteenth century and almost 300,000 troops by the end of his reign. He had adopted policies for the officer corps and general military discipline patterned on those of West European armies.

Peter also made a sustained attack on the *boyars* and their attachment to traditional Russian culture. After his European journey, he personally shaved the long beards of the court *boyars* and sheared off the customary long hand-covering sleeves of their shirts and coats, which had made them the butt of jokes among other European courts. Peter became highly skilled at balancing one group off against another while never completely excluding any as he set about to organize Russian government and military forces along the lines of the more powerful European states.

Developing a Navy In the mid-1690s, Peter oversaw the construction of ships to protect his interests in the Black Sea against the Ottoman Empire. In 1695, he began a war with the Ottomans and captured Azov on the Black Sea in 1696.[1] Part of the reason for Peter's trip to western Europe in 1697 was to learn how to build still better warships, this time for combat on the Baltic. The construction of a Baltic fleet was essential in Peter's struggles with Sweden that over the years accounted for many of his major steps toward westernizing his realm.

Russian Expansion in the Baltic: The Great Northern War

Following the end of the Thirty Years' War in 1648, Sweden had consolidated its control of the Baltic, thus preventing Russian possession of a port on that sea and permitting Polish and German access to the sea only on Swedish terms. The Swedes also had one of the better armies in Europe. Sweden's economy, however, based primarily on the export of iron, was not strong enough to ensure continued political success.

In 1697, Charles XII (r. 1697–1718) came to the Swedish throne. He was headstrong, to say the least, and perhaps insane. In 1700, Peter the Great began a drive to the west against Swedish territory to gain a foothold on the Baltic. In the resulting Great Northern War (1700–1721), Charles XII led a vigorous and often brilliant campaign, defeating the Russians at the Battle of Narva (1700). As the conflict dragged on, however, Peter was able to strengthen his forces. By 1709, he decisively defeated the Swedes at the Battle of Poltava in Ukraine. Thereafter, the Swedes could maintain only a holding action against their enemies. Charles himself sought refuge in Turkey and did not return to Sweden until 1714. He was killed under uncertain circumstances four years later while fighting the Danes in Norway. When the Great Northern War came to a close in 1721, the Peace of Nystad confirmed the Russian conquest of Estonia, Livonia, and part of Finland. Henceforth, Russia possessed ice-free ports and a permanent influence on European affairs.

Founding St. Petersburg At one point, the domestic and foreign policies of Peter the Great intersected. This was at the site on the Gulf of Finland where he founded his new capital city of St. Petersburg in 1703. There he built government structures and compelled the *boyars* to construct town houses. He thus imitated those European monarchs who had copied Louis XIV by constructing smaller versions of Versailles. The founding of St. Petersburg went beyond establishing a central imperial court, however; it symbolized a new Western orientation of Russia and Peter's determination to hold his position on the Baltic coast. Moreover, he and his successors employed architects from western Europe for many of the most prominent buildings in and around the city. Consequently, St. Petersburg looked different from the old capital Moscow and other Russian cities.

The Case of Peter's Son Aleksei Peter's son Aleksei had been born to his first wife whom he had divorced in 1698. Peter was jealous of the young man, who had never demonstrated strong intelligence or ambition. (See "Peter the Great Tells His Son to Acquire Military Skills," page 399.) By 1716, Peter was becoming convinced that his opponents looked to Aleksei as a focus for their possible sedition while Russia remained at war with Sweden. There was some truth to these concerns because the next year Aleksei went to Vienna where he attempted to enter into a vague conspiracy with the Habsburg emperor Charles VI. Compromised by this trip, Aleksei then returned to Russia surrounded by rumors and suspicions.

Peter, who was investigating official corruption, realized his son might become a rallying point for those he accused. Early in 1718, when Aleksei reappeared in St. Petersburg, the tsar began to look into his son's

[1]Although Peter had to return Azov to the Ottomans in 1711, its recapture became a goal of Russian foreign policy. See Chapter 18.

PETER THE GREAT TELLS HIS SON TO ACQUIRE MILITARY SKILLS

Enormous hostility existed between Peter the Great and his son Aleksei. Peter believed his son was not prepared to inherit the throne. In October 1715, he composed a long letter to Aleksei in which he berated him for refusing to take military matters seriously. The letter indicates how an early eighteenth-century ruler saw the conduct of warfare as a fundamental part of the role of a monarch. Peter also points to Louis XIV of France as a role model. Peter and Aleksei did not reach an agreement. Aleksei died under mysterious circumstances in 1718, with Peter possibly responsible for his death.

How did Peter use the recent war with Sweden to argue for the necessity of his son acquiring military skills? What concept of leadership does Peter attempt to communicate to his son? Why did Peter see military prowess as the most important ability in a ruler?

You cannot be ignorant of what is known to all the world, to what degree our people groaned under the oppression of the Swede before the beginning of the present war. . . . You know what it has cost us in the beginning of this war . . . to make ourselves experienced in the art of war, and to put a stop to those advantages which our implacable enemies obtained over us. . . .

But you even will not so much as hear warlike exercises mentioned: though it was by them that we broke through that obscurity in which we were involved, and that we make ourselves known to nations, whose esteem we share at present.

I do not exhort you to make war without lawful reasons: I only desire you to apply yourself to learn the art of it: for it is impossible to govern well without knowing the rules and discipline of it, was it for no other end than for the defense of the country. . . .

You mistake, if you think it is enough for a prince to have good generals to act under his order. Everyone looks upon the head; they study its inclinations and conform themselves to them: all the world own this. . . .

You have no inclination to learn war. You do not apply yourself to it, and consequently you will never learn it: And how then can you command others, and judge of the reward which those deserve who do their duty, or punish others who fail of it? You will do nothing, nor judge of anything but by the assent and help of others, like a young bird that holds up his bill to be fed. . . .

If you think there are some, whose affairs do not fail of success, though they do not go to war themselves; it is true: But they do not go themselves, yet they have an inclination for it, and understand it.

For instance, the late King of France did not always take the field in person; but it is known to what degree he loved war, and what glorious exploits he performed in it, which make his campaigns to be called the theatre and school of the world. His inclinations were not confined solely to military affairs, he also loved mechanics, manufacture and other establishment, which rendered his kingdom more flourishing than any other whatsoever.

From Friedrich C. Weber, *The Present State of Russia* (London, 1722), 2, pp. 97–100; P. F. Riley, *The Global Experience*, 3rd ed., Vol. 2, © 1998. Reprinted by permission of Prentice Hall, Inc., Upper Saddle River, NJ.

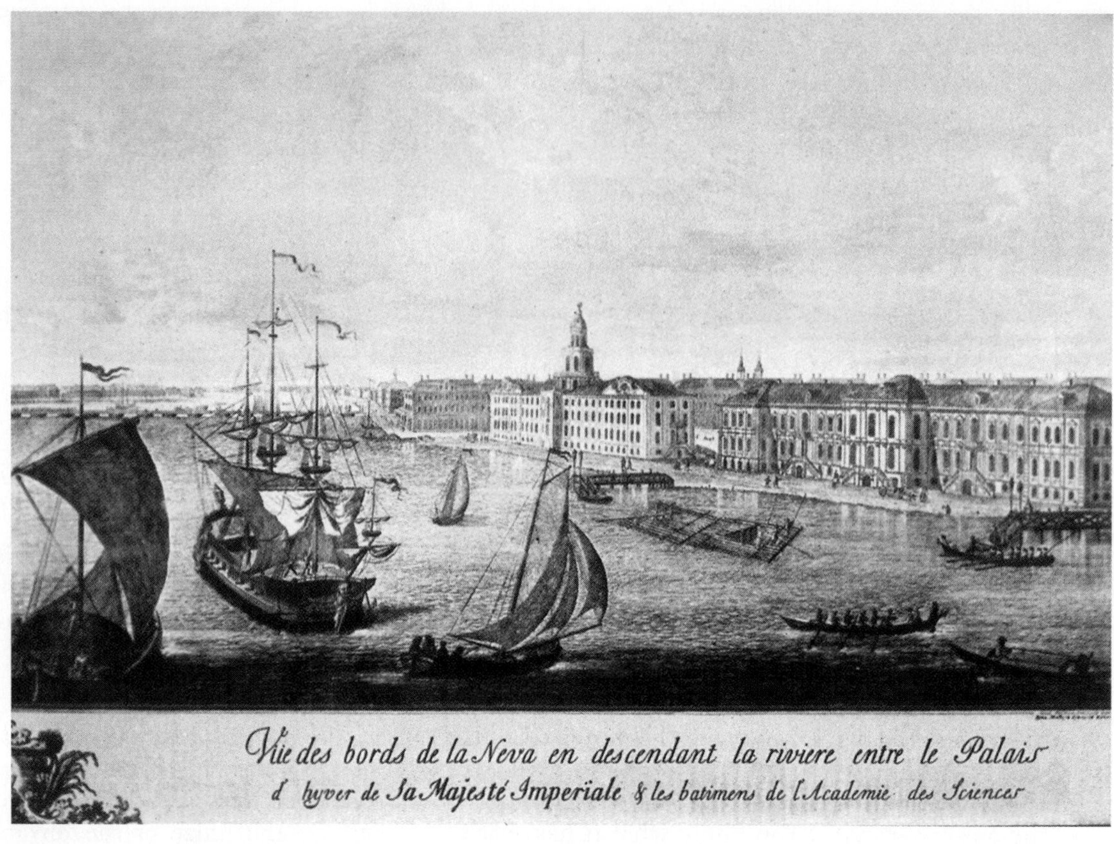

Vüe des bords de la Neva en descendant la riviere entre le Palais
d'hyver de Sa Majesté Imperiale & les batimens de l'Academie des Sciences

Peter the Great built St. Petersburg on the Gulf of Finland to provide Russia with better contact with western Europe. He moved Russia's capital there from Moscow in 1712. This is an eighteenth-century view of the city. The Granger Collection

RISE OF RUSSIAN POWER

1533–1584	Reign of Ivan the Terrible
1584–1613	"Time of Troubles"
1613	Michael Romanov becomes tsar
1682	Peter the Great, age ten, becomes tsar
1689	Peter assumes personal rule
1696	Russia captures Azov on the Black Sea from the Turks
1697	European tour of Peter the Great
1698	Peter returns to Russia to put down the revolt of the *streltsy*
1700	The Great Northern War opens between Russia and Sweden; Russia defeated at Narva by Swedish army of Charles XII
1703	St. Petersburg founded
1709	Russia defeats Sweden at the Battle of Poltava
1718	Charles XII of Sweden dies
1718	Aleksei, son of Peter the Great, dies in prison under mysterious circumstances
1721	Peace of Nystad ends the Great Northern War
1721	Peter establishes a synod for the Russian church
1722	Peter issues the Table of Ranks
1725	Peter dies, leaving an uncertain succession

relationships with Charles VI. Peter discovered that had Aleksei and Charles VI succeeded in organizing a conspiracy, many Russian nobles, officials, and churchmen might have joined them. During this six-month investigation, Peter personally interrogated Aleksei, who was eventually condemned to death and died under mysterious circumstances on June 26, 1718.

Reforms of Peter the Great's Final Years The interrogations surrounding Aleksei had revealed greater degrees of court opposition than Peter had suspected. Recognizing he could not eliminate his opponents the way he had attacked the *streltsy* in 1698, Peter undertook radical administrative reforms designed to bring the nobility and the Russian Orthodox Church more closely under the authority of persons loyal to the tsar.

Administrative Colleges In December 1717, while his son was returning to Russia, Peter reorganized his domestic administration to sustain his own personal authority and to fight rampant corruption. To achieve this goal, Peter looked to Swedish institutions called *colleges*—bureaus of several persons operating according to written instructions rather than departments headed by a single minister. He created eight of these colleges to oversee matters such as the collection of taxes, foreign relations, war, and economic affairs. Each college was to receive advice from a foreigner. Peter divided the members of these colleges between nobles and persons he was certain would be personally loyal to himself.

Table of Ranks Peter made another major administrative reform with important consequences when in 1722 he published a **Table of Ranks**, which was intended to draw the nobility into state service. That table equated a person's social position and privileges with his rank in the bureaucracy or the military, rather than with his lineage among the traditional landed nobility, many of whom continued to resent the changes Peter had introduced into Russia. Peter thus made the social standing of individual *boyars* a function of their willingness to serve the central state.

Achieving Secular Control of the Church Peter also moved to suppress the independence of the Russian Orthodox Church where some bishops and clergy had displayed sympathy for the tsar's son. In 1721, Peter simply abolished the position of *patriarch*, the bishop who had been head of the church. In its place he established a government department called the *Holy Synod*, which consisted of several bishops headed by a layman, called the *procurator general*. This body would govern the church in accordance with the tsar's secular requirements. This ecclesiastical reorganization was the most radical transformation of a traditional institution in Peter's reign.

For all the numerous decisive actions Peter had taken since 1718, he still had not settled on a successor. Consequently, when he died in 1725, there was no clear line of succession to the throne. For more than thirty years, soldiers and nobles again determined who ruled Russia. Peter had laid the foundations of a modern Russia, but not the foundations of a stable state.

▼ The Ottoman Empire

On the southeastern borders of Europe and surrounding the southern and eastern shores of the Mediterranean Sea lay the Ottoman Empire. Throughout the sixteenth and seventeenth centuries, Europeans had found themselves in frequent conflict with this empire in the Mediterranean, the Balkans, around the Black Sea, along the borders of Russia, and as far west as Vienna. As Ottoman authority gradually receded during the eighteenth century, the European states on the empire's borders sought to extend their own influence at its expense.

Now that it no longer exists, it is difficult to realize the enormous importance and geographical magnitude of the Ottoman Empire, although its final demise has affected Europe and the United States since the outbreak of the First World War. Governing a remarkably diverse collection of peoples that ranged from Baghdad eastward across the Arabian peninsula, Anatolia, the Balkan peninsula, and across North Africa from Egypt to Algiers, the **Ottoman Empire** was the largest and most stable political entity to arise in or near Europe following the collapse of the Roman Empire. (See Map 13–5, page 403.) It had achieved this power between the eleventh and early sixteenth centuries as Ottoman tribes migrated eastward from the steppes of Asia. In 1453, they conquered Constantinople, thus putting an end to the Byzantine Empire.

Religious Toleration and Ottoman Government

The Ottoman Empire was the dominant political power in the Muslim world after 1516, when it administered the holy cities of Mecca and Medina as well as Jerusalem, and arranged the safety of Muslim pilgrimages to Mecca. Yet its population was exceedingly diverse ethnically, linguistically, and religiously with significant numbers of Orthodox and Roman Catholic Christians and, after the late fifteenth century, thousands of Jews from Spain.

The Ottomans extended far more religious toleration to their subjects than existed anywhere in Europe. The Ottoman sultans governed their empire through units, called **millets**, of officially recognized religious communities. Various laws and regulations applied to the persons who belonged to a particular millet rather than to a particular administrative territory. Non-Islamic persons in the empire, known as *dhimmis*, or followers of religions tolerated by law, could practice their religion and manage their internal community affairs through their own religious officials but were second-class citizens generally unable to rise in the service of the empire. *Dhimmis* paid a special poll tax (*jizyah*), could not serve in the military, and were prohibited from wearing certain colors. Their residences and places of worship could not be as large as those of Muslims. Over the years, however, they often attained economic success because they possessed the highest level of commercial skills in the empire. Because the Ottomans discouraged their various peoples from interacting with each other, the Islamic population rarely acquired these and other skills from their non-Islamic neighbors. Thus, for example, when the Ottomans negotiated with European powers, their Greek subjects almost invariably served as the interpreters.

The Ottoman dynasty also kept itself separated from the most powerful families of the empire by recruiting military leaders and administrative officers from groups whom the sultans believed would be personally loyal to them. For example, through a practice known as the *devshirme*, the Ottomans, until the end of the seventeenth century, recruited their most elite troops from Christian communities usually in the Balkans. Christian boys so recruited were raised as

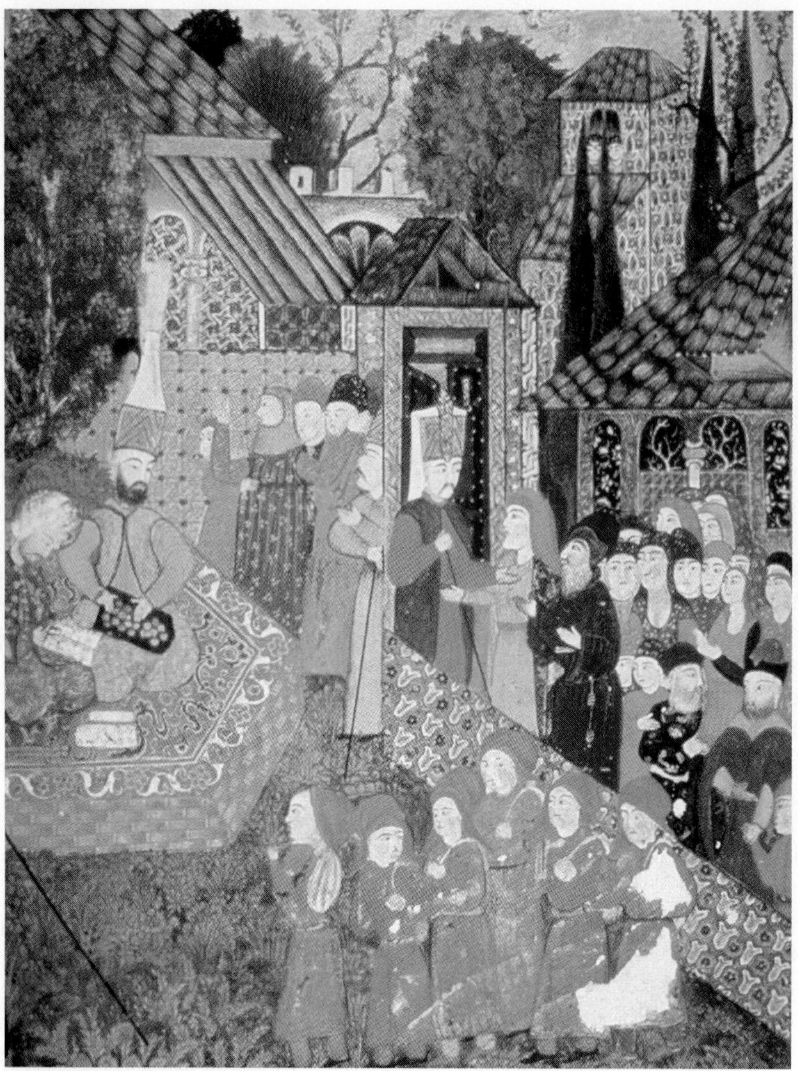

An Ottoman portrayal of the *Devshirme*. This miniature painting from about 1558 depicts the recruiting of young Christian children for the Sultan's elite Janissary corps. Arifi, "Suleymanname," Topkapi Palace Museum, II 1517, fol. 31b, photograph courtesy of Talat Halman.

Muslims and organized into elite military units, the most famous of which were infantry troops called *Janissaries.* It was thought these troops would be extremely loyal to the sultan and the state because they owed their life and status to the sultan. As a result of this policy, entry into the elite military organizations and advancement in the administrative structures of the empire remained generally closed to the native Islamic population and most especially to members of the most elite Islamic families. Instead, in addition to the army, thousands of persons usually from the outer regions of the empire, who were technically slaves of the sultan, filled government posts and achieved major political influence and status. Thus, in contrast to Europe, few people from the socially leading families gained military, administrative, or political experience in the central institutions of the empire but remained primarily linked to local government in provincial cities. Paradoxically, many people in the Ottoman Empire believed it was better to be a favored slave of the sultan than a free subject.

The Role of the Ulama Again in contrast to the longstanding tension between church and state in Europe, Islamic religious authorities played a significant and enduring role in the political, legal, and administrative life of the Ottoman Empire. The dynasty saw itself as one of the chief protectors of Islamic law (*Shari'a*) and

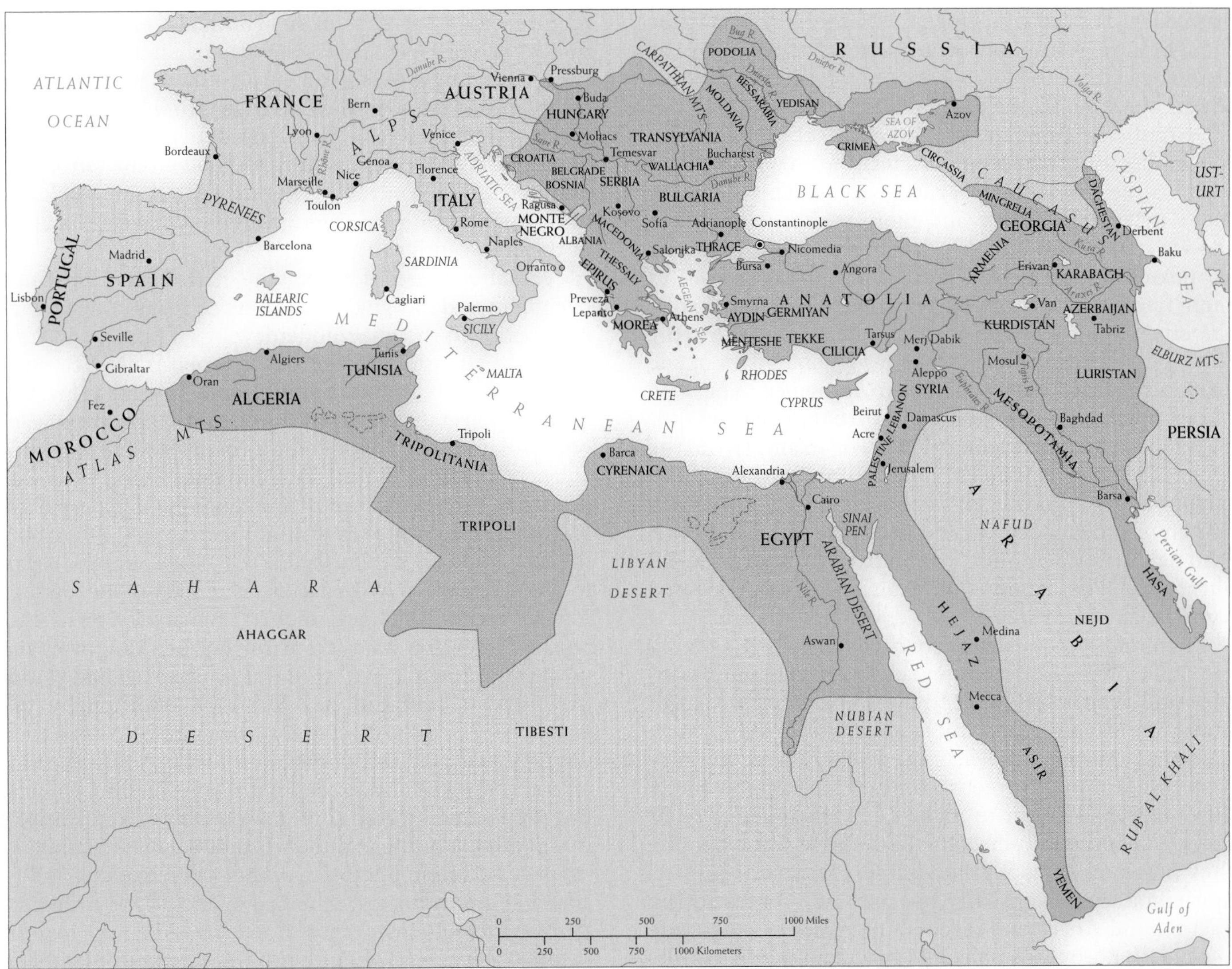

Map 13–5 **THE OTTOMAN EMPIRE IN THE LATE SEVENTEENTH CENTURY** By the 1680s the Ottoman Empire had reached its maximum extent, but the Ottoman failure to capture Vienna in 1683 marked the beginning of a long and inexorable decline that ended with the empire's collapse after World War I.

the Sunni traditions of Islam as well as its holy places. Islamic scholars, or *Ulama*, dominated not only Ottoman religious institutions, but also schools and courts of law. There essentially existed a trade-off between Ottoman political and religious authorities. The sultan and his administrative officials would consult these Islamic scholars for advice with regard to how their policies and the behavior of their subjects accorded with Islamic law and the Qur'an. In turn, the Ulama would support the Ottoman state while the latter deferred to their judgments. This situation would prove a key factor in the fate of the Ottoman Empire. From the late seventeenth century onward, the Ulama urged the sultans to conform to traditional life even as the empire confronted a rapidly changing and modernizing Europe. The Janissaries also resisted changes that might undermine their own privileged status.

The End of Ottoman Expansion

From the fifteenth century onward, the Ottoman Empire had tried to push further westward into Europe. Even after its naval defeat in 1571 at the Battle of Lepanto, the empire retained control of the eastern Mediterranean and the lands bordering it. Still determined to move toward the west, the Ottomans made their deepest military invasion into Europe in 1683, when they unsuccessfully besieged Vienna. Although that defeat proved to be decisive, many observers at the time thought it the result only of an overreach of power by the Ottomans rather than as a symptom of a deeper decline, which was actually the case.

Gradually, from the seventeenth century onward, the authority of the grand vizier, the major political figure after the sultan, began to grow. This development meant that more and more authority lay with the administrative and military bureaucracy. Rivalries for power among army leaders and nobles, as well as their flagrant efforts to enrich themselves, weakened the effectiveness of the government. About the same time local elites in the various provincial cities of the empire began to assert their own influence. They did not as much reject imperial authority but instead quietly renegotiated its conditions. For example, in the outer European provinces, such as Transylvania, Wallachia, and Moldavia (all parts of modern Romania), the empire depended on the goodwill of local rulers, who paid tribute but never submitted fully to imperial authority. The same was true in Egypt, Algeria, Tunisia, and elsewhere.

External factors also accounted for both the blocking of Ottoman expansion in the late seventeenth century and then its slow decline thereafter. During the European Middle Ages, the Islamic world had far outdistanced Europe in learning, science, and military prowess. From the fifteenth century onward, however, Europeans had begun to make rapid advances in technology, wealth, and scientific knowledge. For example, they designed ships for the difficult waters of the Atlantic and thus eventually opened trade routes to the East around Africa and reached the Americas. As trade expanded, Europeans achieved new commercial skills, founded trading posts in South Asia, established the plantation economies and precious metal mines of the Americas, and became much wealthier. By the seventeenth century, Europeans, particularly the Dutch and Portuguese, imported directly from Asia or America commodities such as spices, sugar, and coffee that they had previously acquired through the Ottoman Empire. By sailing around the Cape of Good Hope in Africa, the Europeans literally circumnavigated the Middle East, which could not match the quantity of raw goods and commodities available in South Asia. During the same decades, Europeans developed greater military and naval power and new weapons.

The Ottoman defeats at Lepanto and Vienna had occurred at the outer limits of their expansion. Then, however, during the 1690s, the Ottomans unsuccessfully fought a league of European states including Austria, Venice, Malta, Poland, and Tuscany, joined by Russia, which, as we have already seen, was emerging as a new aggressive power to the north. In early 1699, the defeated Ottomans negotiated the Treaty of Carlowitz, which required them to surrender significant territory lying not at the edges, but at the heart of their empire in Europe, including most of Hungary, to the Habsburgs. This treaty meant not only the loss of territory but also of the revenue the Ottomans had long drawn from those regions. From this time onward, Russia and the Ottomans would duel for control of regions around the Black Sea with Russia achieving ever greater success by the close of the eighteenth century.

Despite these defeats, the Ottomans remained deeply inward looking, continuing to regard themselves as superior to the once underdeveloped European West. Virtually no works of the new European science were translated into Arabic or Ottoman Turkish. Few Ottoman subjects traveled in Europe. The Ottoman leaders, isolated from both their own leading Muslim subjects and from Europe, failed to understand what was occurring far beyond their immediate borders, especially European advances in military technology. When during the eighteenth century the Ottoman Empire began to recognize the new situation, it tended to borrow European technology and import foreign advisers, thus failing to develop its own infrastructure. Moreover, the powerful influence of the Ulama worked against imitation of Christian Europe. Although traditionally opposed to significant interaction with non-Muslims, they did eventually allow non-Muslim teachers into the empire and approved alliances with non-Muslim powers. But the Ulama limited such relationships. For example, in the middle of the eighteenth century, the Ulama persuaded the sultan to close a school of technology and to abandon a printing press he had opened. This influence by Muslim religious teachers occurred just as governments, such as that of Peter the Great, and secular intellectuals across Europe, through the influence of the Enlightenment (see Chapter 17), were increasingly diminishing the influence of the Christian churches in political and economic affairs. Consequently, European intellectuals began to view the once feared Ottoman Empire as a declining power and Islam as a backward-looking religion.

In Perspective

By the second quarter of the eighteenth century, the major European powers were not yet nation-states in which the citizens felt themselves united by a shared sense of community, culture, language, and history. Rather, they were monarchies in which the personality of the ruler and the personal relationships of the great noble families continued to exercise considerable influence over public affairs. The monarchs, except in Great Britain, had generally succeeded in making their power greater than that of the nobility. The power of the aristocracy and its capacity to resist or obstruct the policies of the monarch were not destroyed, however.

In Britain, of course, the nobility had tamed the monarchy, but even there tension between nobles and monarchs would continue throughout the rest of the century.

In foreign affairs, the new arrangement of military and diplomatic power established early in the century prepared the way for two long conflicts. The first was a commercial rivalry for trade and the overseas empire between France and Great Britain. During the reign of Louis XIV, these two nations had collided over the French bid for dominance in Europe. During the eighteenth century, they would duel for control of commerce on other continents. The second arena of warfare would arise in central Europe, where Austria and Prussia fought for the leadership of the German states.

Behind these international conflicts and the domestic rivalry of monarchs and nobles, however, the society of eighteenth-century Europe began to change. The character and the structures of the societies over which the monarchs ruled were beginning to take on some features associated with the modern age. These economic and social developments would eventually transform the life of Europe to a degree beside which the state building of the early eighteenth-century monarchs paled. Parallel to that economic advance, Europeans came to have new knowledge and understanding of nature.

REVIEW QUESTIONS

1. What were the sources of Dutch prosperity and why did the Netherlands decline in the eighteenth century? Why did England and France develop different systems of government and religious policies?
2. Why did the English king and Parliament quarrel in the 1640s? What were the most important issues behind the war between them, and who bears more responsibility for it? What was the Glorious Revolution, and why did it take place? What role did religion play in seventeenth-century English politics? Do you think the victory of Parliament over the monarchy in England inevitable?
3. Why did France become an absolute monarchy? How did Louis XIV consolidate his monarchy? What limits were there on his authority? What was Louis's religious policy? What were the goals of his foreign policy? How did he use ceremony and his royal court to strengthen his authority? What features of French government might Europeans outside of France have feared?
4. How were the Hohenzollerns able to forge their diverse landholdings into the state of Prussia? Who were the major personalities involved in this process and what were their individual contributions? Why was the military so important in Prussia? What major problems did the Habsburgs face and how did they seek to resolve them? Which family, the Hohenzollerns or the Habsburgs, was more successful and why?
5. How and why did Russia emerge as a great power but Poland did not? How were Peter the Great's domestic reforms related to his military ambitions? What were his methods of reform? How did family conflict influence his later policies? Was Peter a successful ruler? In what respects might one regard Peter as an imitator of Louis XIV?
6. What were the strengths and weaknesses of the Ottoman Empire? How did the Ottomans deal with religious minorities? Why did the Empire discourage interaction between its subjects and people from Europe? How did its failure to adapt to modern technology undermine its power?

SUGGESTED READINGS

W. Beik, *Louis XIV and Absolutism: A Brief Study with Documents* (2000). An excellent collection by a major scholar of absolutism.

T. Blanning, *The Pursuit of Glory: Europe 1648–1815* (2007). The best recent synthesis of the emergence of the modern European state system.

J. Brewer, *The Sinews of Power: War, Money and the English State, 1688–1783* (1989). An important study of the financial basis of English power.

P. Burke, *The Fabrication of Louis XIV* (1992). Examines how Louis XIV used art to forge his public image.

C. Clark, *The Rise and Downfall of Prussia 1600–1947* (2006). A stunning survey.

P. Collinson, *The Religion of Protestants: The Church in English Society, 1559–1625* (1982). Remains the best introduction to Puritanism.

R. Cust, *Charles I* (2007). The definitive biography.

N. Davis, *God's Playground: A History of Poland: The Origins to 1795* (2005). The recent revision of a classic survey.

J. De Vries and A. van der Woude, *The First Modern Economy* (1997). Compares Holland to other European nations.

P. G. Dwyer, *The Rise of Prussia 1700–1830* (2002). An excellent collection of essays.

S. Faroqhi, *The Ottoman Empire and the World Around It* (2006). Emphasizes the various interactions of the empire with both Asian and European powers.

R. I. Frost, *The Northern Wars: War, State and Society in Northeastern Europe, 1558–1721* (2000). A survey of an often neglected subject.

D. Goffman, *The Ottoman Empire and Early Modern Europe* (2002). An accessible introduction to a complex subject.

T. Harris, *Restoration: Charles II and His Kingdom, 1660–1685* (2006). A major exploration of the tumultuous years of the restoration of the English monarchy after the civil war.

L. Hughes, *Russia in the Age of Peter the Great* (2000). A major overview of the history and society of Peter's time.

C. Imber, *The Ottoman Empire, 1300–1650: The Structure of Power* (2003). A sweeping analysis based on a broad range of sources.

C. J. Ingrao, *The Habsburg Monarchy, 1618–1815* (2000). The best recent survey.

J. I. Israel, *The Dutch Republic: Its Rise, Greatness, and Fall, 1477–1806* (1995). The major work of the subject.

M. Kishlansky, *A Monarchy Transformed: Britain, 1603–1714* (1996). An important overview.

J. A. Lynn, *The Wars of Louis XIV* (1999). The best recent treatment.

J. Lukowski and H. Zawadzki, *A Concise History of Poland* (2006). A straightforward survey.

D. McKay, *The Great Elector: Frederick William of Brandenburg–Prussia* (2001). An account of the origins of Prussian power.

P. K. Monod, *The Power of Kings: Monarchy and Religion in Europe, 1589–1715* (1999). An important and innovative examination of the roots of royal authority as early modern Europe became modern Europe.

G. Parker, *The Military Revolution: Military Innovation and the Rise of the West (1500–1800)* (1988). A classic work on the impact of military matters on the emergence of centralized monarchies.

H. Phillips, *Church and Culture in Seventeenth-Century France* (1997). A clear examination of the major religious issues confronting France and their relationship to the larger culture.

S. Pincus, *England's Glorious Revolution 1688–1689: A Brief History with Documents* (2005). A useful collection by an outstanding historian of the subject.

G. Treasure, *Louis XIV* (2001). The best, most accessible recent study.

For additional learning resources related to this chapter, please go to www.myhistorylab.com

PEARSON myhistorylab

The great Dutch artist Rembrandt van Rijn (1606–1669) recorded the contemporary life of the United Provinces of the Netherlands during its golden age. The new sciences including medicine made much progress in the Netherlands, which was a center for publishing and instrument making and known for its religious toleration. *The Anatomy Lesson of Dr. Tulp* (1632) presents the dissection of a cadaver of an executed criminal by the noted Dutch physician Dr. Nicolass Tulp who stands on the right surrounded by other members of the Amsterdam guild of surgeons. Such dissections were a controversial part of new emerging medical education with only one a year permitted in Amsterdam. The dramatic use of light and darkness is characteristic of the painting of the baroque style.
Rembrandt van Rijn (1606–1669). *The Anatomy Lesson of Dr. Tulp.* Mauritshuis, The Hague, The Netherlands. SCALA/Art Resource, NY

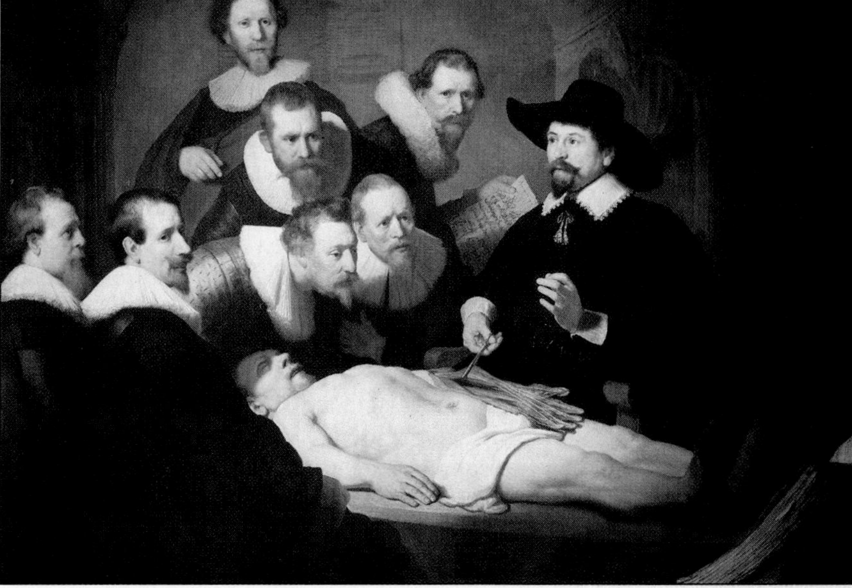

14

New Directions in Thought and Culture in the Sixteenth and Seventeenth Centuries

▼ **The Scientific Revolution**
Nicolaus Copernicus Rejects an Earth-Centered Universe • Tycho Brahe and Johannes Kepler Make New Scientific Observations • Galileo Galilei Argues for a Universe of Mathematical Laws • Isaac Newton Discovers the Laws of Gravitation

▼ **Philosophy Responds to Changing Science**
Nature as Mechanism • Francis Bacon: The Empirical Method • René Descartes: The Method of Rational Deduction • Thomas Hobbes: Apologist for Absolute Government • John Locke: Defender of Moderate Liberty and Toleration

▼ **The New Institutions of Expanding Natural Knowledge**

▼ **Women in the World of the Scientific Revolution**

▼ **The New Science and Religious Faith**
The Case of Galileo • Blaise Pascal: Reason and Faith • The English Approach to Science and Religion

▼ **Continuing Superstition**
Witch Hunts and Panic • Village Origins • Influence of the Clergy • Who Were the Witches? • End of the Witch Hunts

▼ **Baroque Art**

▼ **In Perspective**

KEY TOPICS

- The astronomical theories of Copernicus, Brahe, Kepler, Galileo, and Newton and the emergence of the scientific worldview
- Impact of the new science on philosophy
- Social setting of early modern science
- Women and the scientific revolution
- Approaches to science and religion
- Witchcraft and witch hunts

THE SIXTEENTH AND seventeenth centuries witnessed a sweeping change in the scientific view of the universe. An earth-centered picture gave way to one in which the earth was only another planet orbiting about the sun. The sun itself became one of millions of stars. This transformation of humankind's perception of its place in the larger scheme of things led to a profound rethinking of moral and religious matters, as well as of scientific theory. Faith and reason needed new modes of reconciliation, as did faith and science. The new ideas and methods of science, usually termed *natural philosophy* at the time, challenged those modes of thought associated with late medieval times: Scholasticism and Aristotelian philosophy.

The impact of the new science that explored the realm of the stars through the newly invented telescope and the world of microorganisms through the newly invented microscope must be viewed in the context of two other factors that simultaneously challenged traditional modes of European thought and culture in the sixteenth and seventeenth centuries. The first of these was the Reformation, which permanently divided the religious unity of central and western Europe and fostered decades of warfare and theological dispute. Although by no means a complete break with medieval thought, the theology of the Reformation did question many ideas associated with medieval Christianity and society. The second factor was the cultural impact of Europe's encounter with the New World of the Americas. The interaction with the Americas meant that Europeans directly or indirectly acquired knowledge of new peoples, plants, and animals wholly different from their own and about which Europeans in neither ancient nor medieval times had any information. Consequently, new uncertainties and unfamiliar vistas confronted many Europeans as they considered their souls, geographical knowledge, and physical nature.

Side by side with this new knowledge and science, however, came a new wave of superstition and persecution. The changing world of religion, politics, and knowledge also created profound fear and anxiety among both the simple and the learned, resulting in the worst witch hunts in European history.

▼ The Scientific Revolution

The process that established the new view of the universe is normally termed the ***scientific revolution***. The revolution-in-science metaphor must be used carefully, however. Not everything associated with the "new" science was necessarily new. Sixteenth- and seventeenth-century natural philosophers were often reexamining and rethinking theories and data from the ancient world and the late Middle Ages. Moreover, the word *revolution* normally denotes rapid, collective political change involving many people. The scientific revolution was not rapid. It was a complex movement with many false starts and brilliant people suggesting wrong as well as useful ideas. Nor did it involve more than a few hundred people who labored in widely separated studies and crude laboratories located in Poland, Italy, Denmark, Bohemia, France, and Great Britain. Furthermore, the achievements of the new science were not simply the function of isolated brilliant scientific minds. The leading figures of the scientific revolution often drew on the aid of artisans and craftspeople to help them construct new instruments for experimentation and to carry out those experiments. Thus, the scientific revolution involved older knowledge as well as new discoveries. Additionally, because the practice of science involves social activity as well as knowledge, the revolution also saw the establishment of new social institutions to support the emerging scientific enterprise.

Natural knowledge was only in the process of becoming science as we know it today during the era of the scientific revolution. In fact the word *scientist*, which was only coined in the 1830s, did not yet exist in the seventeenth century, nor did anything resembling the modern scientific career. Individuals devoted to natural philosophy might work in universities or in the court of a prince or even in their own homes and workshops. Only in the second half of the seventeenth century did formal societies and academies devoted to the pursuit of natural philosophy come into existence. Even then the entire process of the pursuit of natural knowledge was a largely informal one.

Yet by the close of the seventeenth century, the new scientific concepts and the methods of their construction were so impressive that they set the standard for assessing the validity of knowledge in the Western world. From the early seventeenth century through the end of the twentieth century, science achieved greater cultural authority in the Western world than any other form of intellectual activity, and the authority and application of scientific knowledge became one of the defining characteristics of modern Western civilization.

Although new knowledge emerged in many areas during the sixteenth and seventeenth centuries, including medicine, chemistry, and natural history, the scientific achievements that most captured the learned imagination and persuaded people of the cultural power of natural knowledge were those that occurred in astronomy.

Nicolaus Copernicus Rejects an Earth-Centered Universe

Nicolaus Copernicus (1473–1543) was a Polish priest and an astronomer who enjoyed a high reputation during his life, but who was not known for strikingly original or unorthodox thought. He had been educated first at the University of Kraków in Poland and later in Italy. In 1543, the year of his death, Copernicus published *On the Revolutions of the Heavenly Spheres*, which has been described as "a revolution-making rather than a revolutionary text."[1] What Copernicus did was to provide an intellectual springboard for a complete criticism of the then-dominant view of the position of the earth in the universe. He had undertaken this task to help the papacy reform the calendar, so that it could correctly calculate the date for Easter based on a more accurate understanding of astronomy.

The Ptolemaic System In Copernicus's time, the standard explanation of the place of the earth in the heavens combined the mathematical astronomy of Ptolemy, contained in his work entitled the *Almagest* (150 C.E.), with the physical cosmology of Aristotle. Over the centuries, commentators on Ptolemy's work had developed several alternative **Ptolemaic systems**, on the basis of which they made mathematical calculations relating to astronomy. Most of these writers assumed the earth was the center of the universe, an outlook known as *geocentrism*. Drawing on Aristotle, these commentators assumed that above the earth lay a series of concentric spheres, probably fluid in character, one of which contained the moon, another the sun, and still others the planets and the stars. At the outer regions of these spheres lay the realm of God and the angels. The earth had to be the center because of its heaviness. The stars and the other heavenly bodies had to be enclosed in the spheres so they could move, since nothing could move unless something was actually moving it. The state of rest was presumed to be natural; motion required explanation. This was the astronomy found in such works as Dante's *Divine Comedy*.

The Ptolemaic model gave rise to many problems, which had long been recognized. The most important was the observed motions of the planets. At certain times the planets appeared to be going backwards. The Ptolemaic model accounted for these motions primarily through epicycles. The planet moved uniformly about a small circle (an *epicycle*), and the center of the epicycle moved uniformly about a larger circle (called a *deferent*), with the earth at or near its center. The combination of these two motions, as viewed from the earth, was meant to replicate the changing planetary positions among the fixed stars—and did so to a high degree of accuracy. The circles employed in Ptolemaic systems were not meant to represent the actual paths of anything; that is, they were not orbits. Rather, they were the components of purely mathematical models meant to predict planetary positions. Other intellectual, but nonobservational, difficulties related to the immense speed at which the spheres had to move around the earth. To say the least, the Ptolemaic systems were cluttered. They were effective, however, as long as one assumed Aristotelian physics to be correct.

[1]Thomas S. Kuhn, *The Copernican Revolution: Planetary Astronomy in the Development of Western Thought* (New York: Vintage, 1959), p. 135.

Copernicus's Universe Copernicus's *On the Revolutions of the Heavenly Spheres* challenged the Ptolemaic picture in the most conservative manner possible. He adopted many elements of the Ptolemaic model, but transferred them to a *heliocentric* (sun-centered) model, which assumed the earth moved about the sun in a circle. Copernicus's model, which retained epicycles, was actually no more accurate than Ptolemy's. However, Copernicus could claim certain advantages over the ancient model. In particular, the epicycles were smaller. The retrograde motion of the planets was now explained as a result of an optical illusion that arose because people were observing them from earth, which was itself moving. Furthermore, Copernicus argued that the farther planets were from the sun, the longer they took to revolve around it. The length of these individual revolutions made it easier to determine the order of the planets, how they ranked in terms of distance from the sun.

The repositioning of the earth had not been Copernicus's goal. Rather, he appears to have set out to achieve new intelligibility and mathematical elegance in astronomy by rejecting Aristotle's cosmology and by removing the earth from the center of the universe. His system was no more accurate than the existing ones for predicting the location of the planets. He had used no new evidence. The major impact of his work was to provide another way of confronting some of the difficulties inherent in Ptolemaic astronomy. The Copernican system did not immediately replace the old astronomy, but it allowed other people who were also discontented with the

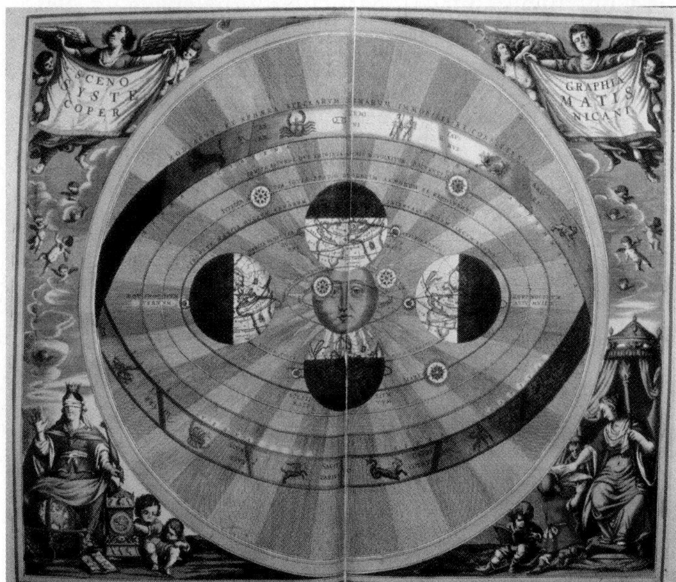

This 1543 map of the heavens based on the writings of Nicholas Copernicus shows the earth and the other planets moving about the sun. Until well into the 1600s, however, astronomers continued to debate whether the sun revolved around the earth.
British Library, London, UK/Bridgeman Art Library

Ptolemaic view to think in new directions. Indeed, for at least a century, only a minority of natural philosophers and astronomers embraced the Copernican system.

Tycho Brahe and Johannes Kepler Make New Scientific Observations

The Danish astronomer Tycho Brahe (1546–1601) took the next major step toward the conception of a sun-centered system. He did not embrace Copernicus's view of the universe and actually spent most of his life advocating an earth-centered system. He suggested that Mercury and Venus revolved around the sun, but that the moon, the sun, and the other planets revolved around the earth. In pursuit of his own theory, Brahe constructed scientific instruments with which he made more extensive naked-eye observations of the planets than anyone else had ever done. His labors produced a vast body of astronomical data from which his successors could work.

When Brahe died, his assistant, Johannes Kepler (1571–1630), a German astronomer, took possession of these tables. Kepler was a convinced Copernican and a more consistently rigorous advocate of a heliocentric model than Copernicus himself had been. Like Copernicus, Kepler was deeply influenced by Renaissance Neoplatonism, which held the sun in special honor. In keeping with this outlook, Kepler was determined to find in Brahe's numbers mathematical harmonies that would support a sun-centered universe. After much work, Kepler discovered that to keep the sun at the center of things, he must abandon the circular components of Copernicus's model, particularly the epicycles. Based on the mathematical relationships that emerged from his study of Brahe's observations, Kepler set forth the first astronomical model that actually portrayed motion—that is, the path of the planets—and those orbits were elliptical, not circular. Kepler published his findings in his 1609 book entitled *The New Astronomy*. He had used Copernicus's sun-centered universe and Brahe's empirical data to solve the problem of planetary motion.

Kepler had also defined a new problem. None of the available theories could explain why the planetary orbits were elliptical or, for that matter, why planetary motion was orbital at all rather than simply moving off along a tangent. That solution awaited the work of Sir Isaac Newton.

Galileo Galilei Argues for a Universe of Mathematical Laws

From Copernicus to Brahe to Kepler, there had been little new information about the heavens that might not have been known to Ptolemy. In 1609, however, the same year that Kepler published *The New Astronomy*, an Italian mathematician and natural philosopher named Galileo Galilei (1564–1642) first turned a telescope on the heavens. Using that recently invented Dutch instrument, he saw stars where none had been known to exist, mountains on the moon, spots moving across the sun, and moons orbiting Jupiter. The heavens were far more complex than anyone had suspected. These discoveries, with some work, could have been accommodated into the Ptolemaic model. Such accommodation would, however, have required a highly technical understanding of Ptolemaic astronomy. Galileo knew that few people who controlled patronage possessed such complex knowledge. Consequently, in the *Starry Messenger* (1610) and *Letters on Sunspots* (1613), he used his considerable rhetorical skills to argue that his newly observed physical evidence, particularly the phases of Venus, required a Copernican interpretation of the heavens.

Galileo's career illustrates that the forging of the new science involved more than just presenting arguments and evidence. In 1610, he had left the University

Galileo Galilei achieved a Europeanwide reputation as a mathematician, instrument maker, and astronomer. His use of the telescope revealed sights of objects in the heavens never previously viewed by human beings. His writings in defense of the Copernican system became increasingly controversial and eventually led to his condemnation by Roman Catholic authorities. Justus Sustermans (1597–1681), "Portrait of Galileo Galilei." Galleria Palatina, Palazzo Pitti, Florence, Italy. Nimatallah/Art Resource, NY.

of Padua for Florence, where he became the philosopher and mathematician to the Grand Duke of Tuscany, who was a Medici. Galileo was now pursuing natural philosophy in a princely court and had become dependent on princely patronage. To win such support both for his continued work and for his theories, he named the moons of Jupiter after the Medicis. As a natural philosopher working with the new telescope, he had literally presented recently discovered heavenly bodies to his patron. By his political skills and his excellent prose, he had transformed himself into a high-profile advocate of Copernicanism. Galileo's problems with the Roman Catholic Church (see page 424), arose from both his ideas and his flair for self-advertisement.

Galileo not only popularized the Copernican system, but he also articulated the concept of a universe subject to mathematical laws. More than any other writer of the century, he argued that nature displayed mathematical regularity in its most minute details.

> Philosophy is written in that great book which ever lies before our eyes—I mean the universe—but we cannot understand it if we do not first learn the language and grasp the symbols in which it is written. This book is written in the mathematical language, and the symbols are triangles, circles, and other geometrical figures, without whose help it is impossible to comprehend a single word of it; without which one wanders through a dark labyrinth.[2]

The universe was rational; however, its rationality was not that of medieval scholastic logic, but of mathematics. Copernicus had thought that the heavens conformed to mathematical regularity; Galileo saw this regularity throughout physical nature.

A world of quantities was replacing one of qualities. All aspects of the world—including color, beauty, and taste—would increasingly be described in terms of the mathematical relationships among quantities. Mathematical models would eventually be applied even to social relations. The new natural philosophy portrayed nature as cold, rational, mathematical, and mechanistic. What was real and lasting was what was mathematically measurable. For many people, the power of the mathematical arguments that appeared irrefutable proved more persuasive than the new information from physical observation that produced so much controversy. Few intellectual shifts have wrought such momentous changes for Western civilization.

Isaac Newton Discovers the Laws of Gravitation

The question that continued to perplex seventeenth-century scientists who accepted the theories of Copernicus, Kepler, and Galileo was how the planets and other heavenly bodies moved in an orderly fashion. The Ptolemaic and Aristotelian answer had been the spheres and a universe arranged in the order of the heaviness of its parts. Many unsatisfactory theories had been set forth to deal with the question. It was this issue of planetary motion that the Englishman Isaac Newton (1642–1727) addressed and, in so doing, established a basis for physics that endured for more than two centuries.

In 1687, Newton published *The Mathematical Principles of Natural Philosophy*, better known by its Latin title of *Principia Mathematica*. Much of the research and thinking for this great work had taken place more than fifteen years earlier. Galileo's mathematical bias permeated Newton's thought, as did his view that inertia applied to bodies both at rest and in motion. Newton reasoned that the planets and all other physical objects in the universe moved through mutual attraction, or gravity. Every object in the universe affected every other object through gravity. The attraction of gravity explained why the planets moved in an orderly, rather than a chaotic, manner. Newton had found that "the force of gravity towards the whole planet did arise from and was compounded of the forces of

Sir Isaac Newton's experiments dealing with light passing through a prism became a model for writers praising the experimental method. CORBIS/Bettmann

[2]Quoted in E. A. Burtt, *The Metaphysical Foundations of Modern Physical Science* (Garden City, NY: Anchor-Doubleday, 1954), p. 75.

gravity towards all its parts, and towards every one part was in the inverse proportion of the squares of the distances from the part."[3] Newton demonstrated this relationship mathematically; he made no attempt to explain the nature of gravity itself.

Newton was a mathematical genius, but he also upheld the importance of empirical data and observation. Like Francis Bacon, he believed in empiricism—that one must observe phenomena before attempting to explain them. The final test of any theory or hypothesis for him was whether it described what was actually observed. Newton was a great opponent of the rationalism of the French philosopher René Descartes (see page 414), which he believed included insufficient guards against error. Consequently, as Newton's own theory of universal gravitation became increasingly accepted, so, too, was Baconian empiricism.

▼ Philosophy Responds to Changing Science

The revolution in scientific thought contributed directly to a major reexamination of Western philosophy. Several of the most important figures in the scientific revolution, such as Bacon and Descartes, were also philosophers discontented with the scholastic heritage. Bacon stressed the importance of empirical research. Descartes attempted to find certainty through the exploration of his own thinking processes. Newton's interests likewise extended to philosophy; he wrote broadly on many topics, including scientific method and theology.

Nature as Mechanism

If a single idea informed all of these philosophers, though in different ways, it was the idea of *mechanism*. The proponents of the new science sought to explain the world in terms of mechanical metaphors, or the language of machinery. The image to which many of them turned was that of the clock. Johannes Kepler once wrote, "I am much occupied with the investigation of the physical causes. My aim in this is to show that the machine of the universe is not similar to a divine animated being, but similar to a clock."[4] Nature conceived as machinery removed much of the mystery of the world and the previous assumption of the presence of divine purpose in nature. The qualities that seemed to inhere in matter came to be understood as the result of mechanical arrangement. Some writers came to understand God as a kind of divine watchmaker or mechanic who had arranged the world as a machine that would thereafter function automatically. The drive to a mechanical understanding of nature also meant that the language of science and of natural philosophy would become largely that of mathematics. The emphasis that Galileo had placed on mathematics spread to other areas of thought.

This new mode of thinking transformed physical nature from a realm in which Europeans looked for symbolic or sacramental meaning related to the divine into a realm where they looked for utility or usefulness. Previously, philosophers had often believed a correct understanding of the natural order would reveal divine mysteries or knowledge relating to sacred history. Henceforth, they would tend to see knowledge of nature as revealing nothing beyond itself—nothing about divine purposes for the life of humankind on earth. Natural knowledge became the path toward the physical improvement of human beings through their ability to command and manipulate the processes of nature. Many people associated with the new science also believed such knowledge would strengthen the power of their monarchs.

Francis Bacon: The Empirical Method

Bacon (1561–1626) was an Englishman of almost universal accomplishment. He was a lawyer, a high royal official, and the author of histories, moral essays, and philosophical discourses. Traditionally, he has been regarded as the father of **empiricism** and of experimentation in science. Much of this reputation was actually unearned. Bacon was not a natural philosopher, except in the most amateur fashion. His real accomplishment was setting an intellectual tone and helping create a climate conducive to scientific work.

In books such as *The Advancement of Learning* (1605), the *Novum Organum* (1620), and *The New Atlantis* (1627), Bacon attacked the scholastic belief that most truth had already been discovered and only required explanation, as well as the scholastic reverence for authority in intellectual life. He believed scholastic thinkers paid too much attention to tradition and to the knowledge of the ancients. He urged contemporaries to strike out on their own in search of a new understanding of nature. He wanted seventeenth-century Europeans to have confidence in themselves and their own abilities rather than in the people and methods of the past. Bacon was one of the first major European writers to champion innovation and change.

Bacon believed that human knowledge should produce useful results—deeds rather than words. In particular, knowledge of nature should be enlisted to improve

[3]Quoted in A. Rupert Hall, *From Galileo to Newton, 1630–1720* (London: Fontana, 1970), p. 300.

[4]Quoted in Steven Shapin, *The Scientific Revolution* (Chicago: University of Chicago Press, 1996), p. 33.

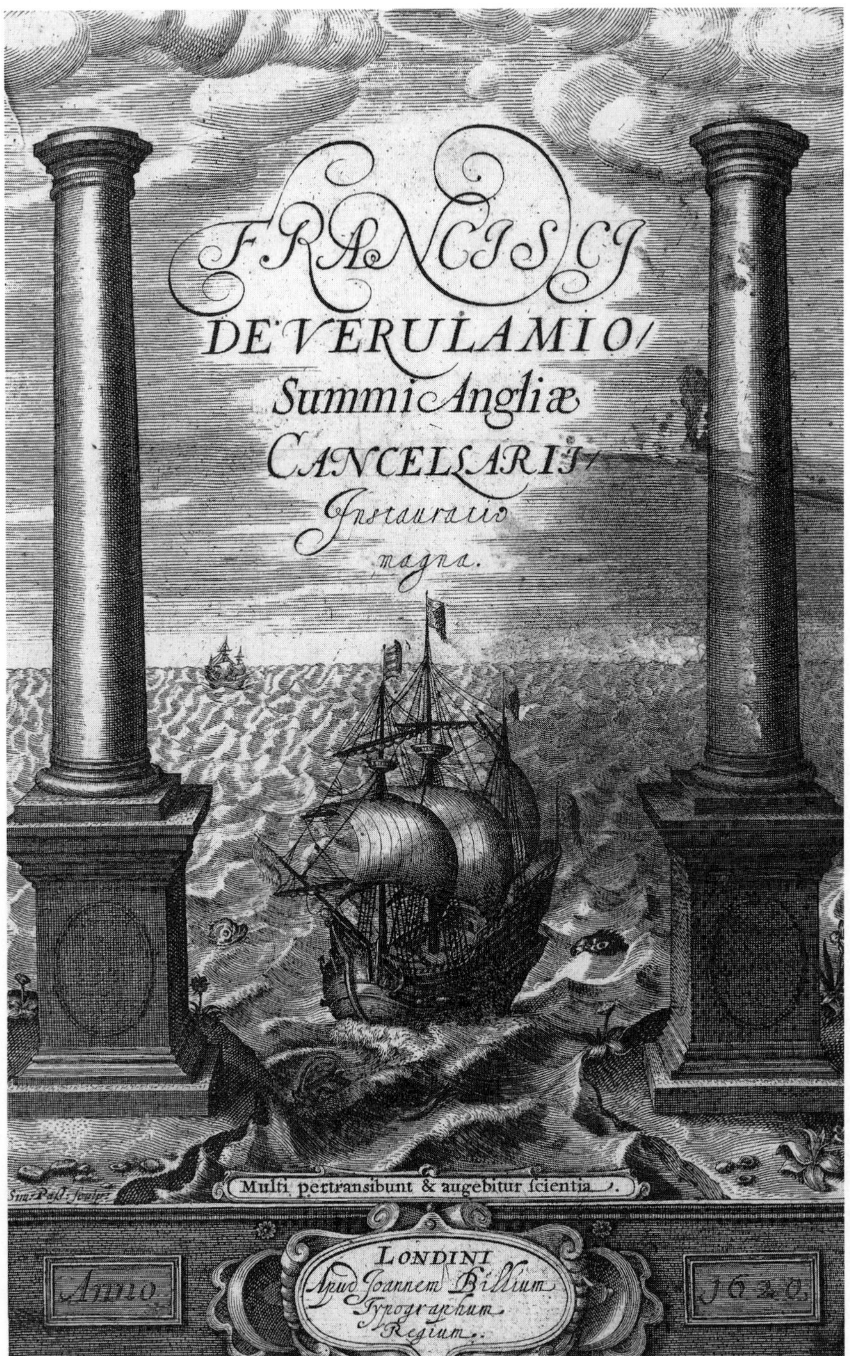

Published in 1620, *Novum Organum* ("new organ or instrument") by Francis Bacon is one of the most important works of the scientific revolution. In this and other works Bacon attacked the long-held belief that most truth had already been discovered. This allegorical image, from the frontispiece of *Novum Organum*, shows a ship striking out for unknown territories, seeking, as did Bacon, for a new understanding of the natural world. The ship is flanked by the mythical pillars of Hercules that stand at the point where the Mediterranean meets the Atlantic—the realm of the unknown and unexplored. Courtesy of the Library of Congress

the human condition. These goals required modifying or abandoning scholastic modes of learning and thinking. Bacon contended, "The [scholastic] logic now in use serves more to fix and give stability to the errors which have their foundation in commonly received notions than to help the search after truth."[5] Scholastic philosophers could not escape from their syllogisms to examine the foundations of their thought and intellectual presuppositions. Bacon urged that philosophers and investigators of nature examine the evidence of their senses before constructing logical speculations. In a famous passage, he divided all philosophers into "men of experiment and men of dogmas" and then observed,

> The men of experiment are like the ant, they only collect and use; the reasoners resemble spiders, who make cobwebs out of their own substance. But the bee takes a middle course: it gathers its material from the flowers of the garden and of the field, but transforms and digests it by a power of its own. Not unlike this is the true business of philosophy.[6]

By directing natural philosophy toward an examination of empirical evidence, Bacon hoped it would achieve new knowledge and thus new capabilities for humankind.

Bacon boldly compared himself with Columbus, plotting a new route to intellectual discovery. The comparison is significant, because it displays the consciousness of a changing world that appears so often in writers of the late sixteenth and early seventeenth centuries. They were rejecting the past not from simple contempt or arrogance, but rather from a firm understanding that the world was much more complicated than their medieval forebearers had thought. Neither Europe nor European thought could remain self-contained. Like the new worlds on the globe, new worlds of the mind were also emerging.

Most of the people in Bacon's day, including the intellectuals influenced by humanism, thought that the best era of human history lay in antiquity. Bacon dissented vigorously from that view. He looked to a future of material improvement achieved through the empirical examination of nature. His own theory of induction from empirical evidence was unsystematic, but his insistence on appealing to experience influenced others whose methods were more productive. He and others of his outlook received almost daily support from the reports not only of European explorers, but also of ordinary seamen who now sailed all over the world and could describe wondrous

[5]Quoted in Franklin Baumer, *Main Currents of Western Thought*, 4th ed. (New Haven, CT: Yale University Press, 1978), p. 281.

[6]Quoted in Baumer, *Main Currents of Western Thought*, p. 288.

cultures, as well as plants and animals, unknown to the European ancients.

Bacon believed that expanding natural knowledge had a practical purpose and its goal was human improvement. Some scientific investigation does have this character. Much pure research does not. Bacon, however, linked science and material progress in the public mind. This was a powerful idea that still influences Western civilization. It has made science and those who can appeal to the authority of science major forces for change and innovation. Thus, although not making any major scientific contribution himself, Bacon directed investigators of nature to a new method and a new purpose. As a person actively associated with politics, Bacon also believed the pursuit of new knowledge would increase the power of governments and monarchies. Again, his thought in this area opened the way for the eventual strong links between governments and the scientific enterprise.

René Descartes: The Method of Rational Deduction

Descartes (1596–1650) was a gifted mathematician who invented analytic geometry. His most important contribution, however, was to develop a scientific method that relied more on deduction—reasoning from general principle to arrive at specific facts—than empirical observation and induction.

In 1637, he published his *Discourse on Method*, in which he rejected scholastic philosophy and education and advocated thought founded on a mathematical model. (See "Compare & Connect: Descartes and Swift Debate the Scientific Enterprise," pages 422–423.) The work appeared in French rather than in Latin because Descartes wanted it to have wide circulation and application. In the *Discourse*, he began by saying he would doubt everything except those propositions about which he could have clear and distinct ideas. This approach rejected all forms of intellectual authority, except the conviction of his own reason. Descartes concluded that he could not doubt his own act of thinking and his own existence. From this base, he proceeded to deduce the existence of God. The presence of God was important to Descartes because God guaranteed the correctness of clear and distinct ideas. Since God was not a deceiver, the ideas of God-given reason could not be false.

On the basis of such an analysis, Descartes concluded that human reason could fully comprehend the world. He divided existing things into two basic categories: thinking things and things occupying space—mind and body, respectively. Thinking was the defining quality of the mind, and extension (the property by which things occupy space) was the defining quality of material bodies. Human reason could grasp and understand the world of extension, which became the realm of the natural philosopher. That world had no place for spirits, divinity, or anything nonmaterial. Descartes separated mind from body to banish nonmaterial matters from the realm of scientific speculation and analysis. Reason was to be applied only to the mechanical realm of matter or to the exploration of itself.

Descartes's emphasis on deduction, rational speculation, and internal reflection by the mind, all of which he explored more fully in his *Meditations* of 1641, have influenced philosophers from his time to the present. His deductive methodology, however, eventually lost favor to **scientific induction**, whereby scientists draw generalizations derived from and test hypotheses against empirical observations.

Queen Christina of Sweden (r. 1632–1654), shown here with the French philosopher and scientist René Descartes, was one of many women from the elite classes interested in the new science. In 1649 she invited Descartes to live at her court in Stockholm, but he died a few months after moving to Sweden. Pierre-Louis the Younger Dumesnil (1698–1781), *Christina of Sweden (1626–89) and her Court: detail of the Queen and René Descartes (1596–1650) at the Table.* Oil on canvas. Chateau de Versailles, France/Bridgeman Art Library

Thomas Hobbes: Apologist for Absolute Government

Nowhere did the impact of the methods of the new science so deeply affect political thought as in the thought of Thomas Hobbes (1588–1679), the most original political philosopher of the seventeenth century.

An urbane and much-traveled man, Hobbes enthusiastically supported the new scientific movement. During the 1630s, he visited Paris, where he came to know Descartes, and Italy, where he spent time with Galileo. He took special interest in the works of William Harvey (1578–1657), who was famous for his discovery of the circulation of blood through the body. Hobbes was also a superb classicist. His earliest published work was the first English translation of Thucydides' *History of the Peloponnesian War* and is still being reprinted today. Part of Hobbes's dark view of human nature would appear to derive from Thucydides' historical analysis.

Hobbes had written works of political philosophy before the English Civil War, but the turmoil of that struggle led him in 1651 to publish his influential work *Leviathan*. His aim was to provide a rigorous philosophical justification for a strong central political authority. Hobbes portrayed human beings and society in a thoroughly materialistic and mechanical way. He traced all psychological processes to bare sensation and regarded all human motivations as egoistical, intended to increase pleasure and minimize pain. According to his analysis, human reasoning penetrated to no deeper reality or wisdom than those physical sensations. Consequently, for Hobbes, unlike both previous Christian and ancient philosophers, human beings exist only to meet the needs of daily life, not for higher spiritual ends or for any larger moral purpose. Only a sovereign commonwealth established by a contract between the ruler and the ruled could enable human beings to meet those needs by limiting the free exercise of the natural human pursuit of self-interest with all its potential for conflict.

According to Hobbes human beings in their natural state are inclined to a "perpetual and restless desire" for power. Because all people want and, in their natural state, possess a natural right to everything, their equality breeds enmity, competition, diffidence, and perpetual quarreling—"a war of every man against every man," as Hobbes put it in a famous summary.

> In such condition there is no place for industry, because the fruit thereof is uncertain; and consequently no culture of the Earth; no navigation nor use of the commodities that may be imported by sea; no commodious building; no instruments of moving and removing such things as require much force; no knowledge of the face of the Earth; no account of time; no arts; no letters; no society; and, which is worst of all, continual fear and danger of violent death; and the life of man solitary, poor, nasty, brutish, and short.[7]

The famous title page illustration for Hobbes's *Leviathan*. The ruler is pictured as absolute lord of his lands, but note that the ruler incorporates the mass of individuals whose self-interests are best served by their willing consent to accept him and cooperate with him. Courtesy of the Library of Congress

As seen in this passage, Hobbes, contrary to Aristotle and Christian thinkers like Thomas Aquinas (1225–1274), rejected the view that human beings are naturally sociable. Rather, they are self-centered creatures who lack a master. Thus, whereas earlier and later philosophers saw the original human state as a paradise from which humankind had fallen, Hobbes saw it as a state of natural, inevitable conflict in which neither safety, security, nor any final authority existed. Human beings in this state of nature were constantly haunted by fear of destruction and death.

Human beings escaped this terrible state of nature, according to Hobbes, only by entering into a particular kind of political contract according to which they agreed

[7]Thomas Hobbes, *Leviathan*, Parts I and II, ed. by H. W. Schneider (Indianapolis: Bobbs-Merrill, 1958), pp. 86, 106–107.

to live in a commonwealth tightly ruled by a recognized sovereign. This contract obliged every person, for the sake of peace and self-defense, to agree to set aside personal rights to all things and to be content with as much liberty against others as he or she would allow others against himself or herself. All agreed to live according to a secularized version of the golden rule, "Do not that to another which you would not have done to yourself."[8]

Because, however, words and promises are insufficient to guarantee this agreement, the contract also established the coercive use of force by the sovereign to compel compliance. Believing the dangers of anarchy to be always greater than those of tyranny, Hobbes thought that rulers should be absolute and unlimited in their power, once established as authority. Hobbes's political philosophy has no room for protest in the name of individual conscience or for individual appeal to some other legitimate authority beyond the sovereign. In a reply to critics of his position on sovereign authority, Hobbes pointed out the alternative:

> The greatest [unhappiness] that in any form of government can possibly happen to the people in general is scarce sensible in respect of the miseries and horrible calamities that accompany a civil war or that dissolute condition of masterless men, without subjection to laws and a coercive power to tie their hands from rapine and revenge.[9]

The specific structure of this absolute government was not of enormous concern to Hobbes. He believed absolute authority might be lodged in either a monarch or a legislative body, but once that person or body had been granted authority, there existed no argument for appeal. For all practical purposes, obedience to the Hobbesian sovereign was absolute.

Hobbes's argument for an absolute political authority that could assure order aroused sharp opposition. Monarchists objected to his willingness to assign sovereign authority to a legislature. Republicans rejected his willingness to accept a monarchical authority. Many Christian writers, including those who supported the divine right of kings, furiously criticized his materialist arguments for an absolute political authority. Other Christian writers attacked his refusal to recognize the authority of either God or the church as standing beside or above his secular sovereign. The religious critique of Hobbes meant that his thought had little immediate practical impact, but his ideas influenced philosophical literature from the late seventeenth century onward.

John Locke: Defender of Moderate Liberty and Toleration

Locke (1632–1704) proved to be the most influential philosophical and political thinker of the seventeenth century. Although he was less original than Hobbes, his political writings became a major source of criticism of absolutism and provided a foundation for later liberal political philosophy in both Europe and America. His philosophical works dealing with human knowledge became the most important work of psychology for the eighteenth century.

Locke's family had Puritan sympathies, and during the English Civil War his father had fought for the parliamentary forces against the Stuart monarchy. Although a highly intellectual person who was well read in all the major seventeenth-century natural philosophers, Locke became deeply involved with the tumultuous politics of the English Restoration period. He was a close associate of Anthony Ashley Cooper, the earl of Shaftesbury (1621–1683), considered by his contemporaries to be a radical in both religion and politics. Shaftesbury organized an unsuccessful rebellion against Charles II in 1682, after which both he and Locke, who lived with him, were forced to flee to Holland.

During his years of association with Shaftesbury and the opposition to Charles II, Locke wrote two treatises on government that were eventually published in 1690. In the first of these, he rejected arguments for absolute gov-

John Locke (1632–1704), defender of the rights of the people against rulers who think their power absolute. *John Locke (1632–1704).* By courtesy of the National Portrait Gallery, London

[8]Hobbes, *Leviathan*, Parts I and II, p. 130.

[9]Hobbes, *Leviathan*, Parts I and II, p. 152.

ernment that based political authority on the patriarchal model of fathers ruling over a family. After the publication of this treatise, no major political philosopher again appealed to the patriarchal model. In that regard, though not widely read today, Locke's *First Treatise of Government* proved enormously important by clearing the philosophical decks, so to speak, of a long-standing traditional argument that could not stand up to rigorous analysis.

In his *Second Treatise of Government*, Locke presented an extended argument for a government that must necessarily be both responsible for and responsive to the concerns of the governed. Locke portrayed the natural human state as one of perfect freedom and equality in which everyone enjoyed, in an unregulated fashion, the natural rights of life, liberty, and property. Locke, contrary to Hobbes, regarded human beings in their natural state as creatures of reason and basic goodwill rather than of uncontrolled passion and selfishness. For Locke, human beings possess a strong capacity for dwelling more or less peacefully in society before they enter a political contract. What they experience in the state of nature is not a state of war, but a condition of competition and modest conflict that requires a political authority to sort out problems rather than to impose sovereign authority. They enter into the contract to form political society to secure and preserve the rights, liberty, and property that they already possess prior to the existence of political authority. In this respect, government exists to protect the best achievements and liberty of the state of nature, not to overcome them. Thus, by its very foundation, Locke's government is one of limited authority. (See "John Locke Denounces the Idea of Absolute Monarchy" in the previous chapter, page 387).

The conflict that Hobbes believed characterized the state of nature emerged for Locke only when rulers failed to preserve people's natural freedom and attempted to enslave them by absolute rule. The relationship between rulers and the governed is that of trust, and if the rulers betray that trust, the governed have the right to replace them. In this regard, Locke's position resembled that of Thomas Aquinas, who also permitted rebellion when government violated laws of nature.

In his *Letter Concerning Toleration* (1689), Locke used the premises of the as yet unpublished *Second Treatise* to defend extensive religious toleration among Christians, which he saw as an answer to the destructive religious conflict of the past two centuries. To make his case for toleration, Locke claimed that each individual was required to work out his or her own religious salvation and these efforts might lead various people to join different religious groups. For its part, government existed by its very nature to preserve property, not to make religious decisions for its citizens. Governments that attempted to impose religious uniformity thus misunderstood their real purpose. Moreover, government-imposed religious uniformity could not achieve real religious ends, because assent to religious truth must be freely given by the individual's conscience rather than by force. Consequently, Locke urged a wide degree of religious toleration among differing voluntary Christian groups. He did not, however, extend toleration to Roman Catholics, whom he believed to have given allegiance to a foreign prince (i.e., the pope), to non-Christians, or to atheists, whom he believed could not be trusted to keep their word. Despite these limitations, Locke's *Letter Concerning Toleration* established a powerful foundation for the future extension of toleration, religious liberty, and the separation of church and state. His vision of such expansive toleration was partially realized in England after 1688 and most fully in the United States after the American Revolution.

Finally, just as Newton had set forth laws of astronomy and gravitation, Locke hoped to elucidate the basic structures of human thought. He did so in the most immediately influential of his books, his *Essay Concerning Human Understanding* (1690), which became the major work of European psychology during the eighteenth century. There, Locke portrayed a person's mind at birth as a blank tablet whose content would be determined by sense experience. His vision of the mind has been aptly compared to an early version of behaviorism. It was a reformer's psychology, which contended that the human condition could be improved by changing the environment.

Locke's view of psychology rejected the Christian understanding of original sin, yet he believed his psychology had preserved religious knowledge. He thought such knowledge came through divine revelation in Scripture and also from the conclusions that human reason could draw from observing nature. He hoped this

MAJOR WORKS OF THE SCIENTIFIC REVOLUTION

1543	*On the Revolutions of the Heavenly Spheres* (Copernicus)
1605	*The Advancement of Learning* (Bacon)
1609	*The New Astronomy* (Kepler)
1610	*The Starry Messenger* (Galileo)
1620	*Novum Organum* (Bacon)
1632	*Dialogue on the Two Chief World Systems* (Galileo)
1637	*Discourse on Method* (Descartes)
1651	*Leviathan* (Hobbes)
1687	*Principia Mathematica* (Newton)
1689	*Letter Concerning Toleration* (Locke)
1690	*An Essay Concerning Human Understanding* (Locke)
1690	*Treatises of Government* (Locke)

interpretation of religious knowledge would prevent human beings from falling into what he regarded as fanaticism arising from the claims of alleged private revelations and irrationality arising from superstition. For Locke, reason and revelation were compatible and together could sustain a moderate religious faith that would avoid religious conflict.

▼ The New Institutions of Expanding Natural Knowledge

One of the most fundamental features of the expansion of science was the emerging idea that *genuinely new knowledge* about nature and humankind could be discovered. In the late Middle Ages, the recovery of Aristotle and the rise of humanistic learning looked back to the ancients to rediscover the kind of knowledge that later Europeans needed. Luther and other Reformers had seen themselves as recovering a better understanding of the original Christian message. By contrast, the proponents of the new natural knowledge and the new philosophy sought to pursue what Bacon called the advancement of learning. New knowledge would be continuously created. This outlook required new institutions.

The expansion of natural knowledge had powerful social implications. Both the new science and the philosophical outlook associated with it opposed Scholasticism and Aristotelianism. These were not simply disembodied philosophical outlooks, but ways of approaching the world of knowledge most scholars in the universities of the day still believed in. Such scholars had a clear, vested interest in preserving those traditional outlooks. As they saw it, they were defending the ancients against the moderns. Not surprisingly, the advanced thinkers of the seventeenth century often criticized the universities. For example, in his *Discourse on Method*, Descartes was highly critical of the education he had received. Hobbes filled the *Leviathan* with caustic remarks about the kind of learning then dominating schools and universities, and Locke advocated educational reform.

Some of the criticism of universities was exaggerated. Medical faculties, on the whole, welcomed the advancement of learning in their fields of study. Most of the natural philosophers had themselves received their education at universities. Moreover, however slowly new ideas might penetrate universities, the expanding world of natural knowledge would be taught to future generations. With that diffusion of science into the universities came new supporters of scientific knowledge beyond the small group of natural philosophers themselves. Universities also provided much of the physical and financial support for teaching and investigating natural philosophy and employed many scientists, the most important of whom was Newton himself. University support of science did, however, vary according to country, with the Italian universities being far more supportive than the French.

Yet because of the reluctance of universities to rapidly assimilate the new science, its pioneers quickly understood that they required a framework for cooperating and sharing of information that went beyond existing intellectual institutions. Consequently, they and their supporters established what have been termed "institutions of sharing" that allowed information and ideas associated with the new science to be gathered, exchanged, and debated.[10] The most famous of these institutions was the Royal Society of London, founded in 1660, whose members consciously saw themselves as following the path Bacon had laid out almost a half century earlier. The Royal Society had been preceded by the Academy of Experiments in Florence in 1657 and was followed by the French Academy of Science in 1666. Germany only slowly overcame the destruction of the Thirty Years' War, and the Berlin Academy of Science was not founded until 1700. In addition to these major institutions, the new science was discussed and experiments were carried out in many local societies and academies.

These societies met regularly to hear papers and observe experiments. One of the reasons many early experiments achieved

Colbert was Louis XIV's most influential minister. He sought to expand the economic life of France and to associate the monarchy with the emerging new science from which he hoped might flow new inventions and productive technology. Here he is portrayed presenting members of the French Academy of Science to the monarch. On the founding of the French Academy. Henri Testelin (1616–1695). (after Le Brun). Minister of Finance Colbert presenting the members of the Royal Academy of Science (founded in 1667) to Louis XIV. Study for a tapestry. Photo: Gerard Blot. Chateaux de Versailles et de Trianon, Versailles, France. Reunion des Musées Nationaux/Art Resource, NY

[10]Lewis Pyenson and Susan Sheets-Pyenson, *Servants of Nature: A History of Scientific Institutions, Enterprises, and Sensibilities* (New York: W. W. Norton, 1999), p. 75.

credibility was that they had been observed by persons of social respectability who belonged to one or more of the societies and who, because of their social standing, were presumed to be truthful witnesses of what they had observed. These groups also published information relating to natural philosophy and often organized libraries for their members. Perhaps most important, they attempted to separate the discussion and exploration of natural philosophy from the religious and political conflicts of the day. They intended science to exemplify an arena for the polite exchange of ideas and for civil disagreement and debate. This particular function of science as fostering civility became one of its major attractions.

The activities of the societies also constituted a kind of crossroads between their own members always drawn from the literate classes, and people outside the elite classes, whose skills and practical knowledge might be important for advancing the new science. The latter included craftspeople who could manufacture scientific instruments, sailors whose travels had taken them to foreign parts and who might report on the plants and animals they had seen there, and workers who had practical knowledge of problems in the countryside. In this respect, the expansion of the European economy and the drive toward empires contributed to the growth of the scientific endeavor by bringing back to Europe specimens and experiences that required classification, analysis, and observation.

In good Baconian fashion, the members of the societies presented science as an enterprise that could aid the goals of government and the growth of the economy. For example, mathematicians portrayed themselves as being useful for solving surveying and other engineering problems and for improving armaments. Furthermore, people who had ideas for improving production, navigation, or military artillery might seek the support of the associated societies. In the English context, these people became known as *projectors* and were often regarded as people simply eager to sell their often improbable ideas to the highest bidder. Nonetheless, their activities brought the new science and technology before a wider public. (See "Compare & Connect: Descartes and Swift Debate the Scientific Enterprise" pages 422–423.)

The work, publications, and interaction of the scientific societies with both the government and private business established a distinct role and presence for scientific knowledge in European social life. By 1700, that presence was relatively modest, but it would grow steadily during the coming decades. The groups associated with the new science saw themselves as championing modern practical achievements of applied knowledge and urging religious toleration, mutual forbearance, and political liberty. Such people would form the social base for the eighteenth-century movement known as the **Enlightenment**.

▼ Women in the World of the Scientific Revolution

The absence of women in the emergence of the new science of the seventeenth century has been a matter of much historical speculation. What characteristics of early modern European intellectual and cultural life worked against extensive contributions by women? Why have we heard so little of the activity by women that did actually occur in regard to the new science?

The same factors that had long excluded women from participating in most intellectual life continued to exclude them from working in the emerging natural philosophy. Traditionally, the institutions of European intellectual life had all but excluded women. Both monasteries and universities had been institutions associated with celibate male clerical culture. Except for a few exceptions in Italy, women had not been admitted to either medieval or early modern European universities; they would continue to be excluded from them until the end of the nineteenth century. Women could and did exercise influence over princely courts where natural philosophers, such as Galileo, sought patronage, but they usually did not determine those patronage decisions or benefit from them. Queen Christina of Sweden (r. 1632–1654), who brought René Descartes to Stockholm to provide the regulations for a new science

Margaret Cavendish, who wrote widely on scientific subjects, was the most accomplished woman associated with the new science in seventeenth-century England. ImageWorks/Mary Evans Picture Library Ltd.

academy, was an exception. When various scientific societies were founded, women were not admitted to membership. In that regard, there were virtually no social spaces that might have permitted women to pursue science easily.

Yet a few isolated women from two different social settings did manage to engage in the new scientific activity—noblewomen and women from the artisan class. In both cases, they could do so only through their husbands or male relatives.

The social standing of certain noblewomen allowed them to command the attention of ambitious natural philosophers who were part of their husband's social circle. Margaret Cavendish (1623–1673) actually made significant contributions to the scientific literature of the day. As a girl she had been privately tutored and become widely read. Her marriage to the duke of Newcastle introduced her into a circle of natural philosophers. She understood the new science, quarreled with the ideas of Descartes and Hobbes, and criticized the Royal Society for being more interested in novel scientific instruments than in solving practical problems. Her most important works were *Observations Upon Experimental Philosophy* (1666) and *Grounds of Natural Philosophy* (1668). She was the only woman in the seventeenth century to be allowed to visit a meeting of the Royal Society of London. (See "Margaret Cavendish Questions the Fascination with Scientific Instruments.")

MARGARET CAVENDISH QUESTIONS THE FASCINATION WITH SCIENTIFIC INSTRUMENTS

Margaret Cavendish, duchess of Newcastle, was the most scientifically informed woman of seventeenth-century England. She read widely in natural philosophy and had many acquaintances who were involved in the new science. Although she was enthusiastic about the promise of science, she also frequently criticized some of its leading proponents, including Descartes and Hobbes. She was skeptical of the activities of the newly established Royal Society of London, which she was once permitted to visit. She believed some of its members had become overly enthusiastic about experimentation and new scientific instruments for their own sakes and had begun to ignore the practical questions that she thought science should address. In this respect, her criticism of the Royal Society and its experiments is a Baconian one. She thought the society had replaced scholastic speculation with experimental speculation and that both kinds of speculation ignored important problems of immediate utility.

Why might Margaret Cavendish think that the experiments which were reported about new optical instruments dealt with superficial wonders? Why does she contrast experimental philosophy with the beneficial arts? Do you find a feminist perspective in her comparison of the men of the Royal Society with boys playing with bubbles?

Art has intoxicated so many men's brains, and wholly imployed their thoughts and bodily actions about phaenomena, or the exterior figure of objects, as all better Arts and Studies are laid aside. ... But though there be numerous Books written of the wonder of these [experimental optical] Glasses, yet I cannot perceive any such; at best, they are but superficial wonders, as I may call them. But could Experimental Philosophers find out more beneficial Arts then our Fore-fathers have done, either for the better increase of Vegetables and brute Animals to nourish our bodies, or better and commodious contrivances in the Art of Architecture to build us houses, or for the advancing of trade and traffick . . . it would not only be worth their labour, but of as much praise as could be given to them: But, as Boys that play with watry Bubbles . . . are worthy of reproof rather than praise, for wasting their time with useless sports; so those that addict themselves to unprofitable Arts, spend more time than they reap benefit thereby.

From Margaret Cavendish, *Observations Upon Experimental Philosophy*, to which is added, *The Description of a New Blazing World* (London, 1666), pp. 10–11, as quoted in Anna Battigelli, *Margaret Cavendish and the Exiles of the Mind* (Lexington: University of Kentucky Press, 1998), p. 94.

Women associated with artisan crafts actually achieved greater freedom to pursue the new sciences than did noblewomen. Traditionally, women had worked in artisan workshops, often with their husbands, and might take over the business when their spouse died. In Germany, much study of astronomy occurred in these settings, with women assisting their fathers or husbands. One German female astronomer, Maria Cunitz, published a book on astronomy that many people thought her husband had written until he added a preface supporting her sole authorship. Elisabetha and Johannes Hevelius constituted a wife-and-husband astronomical team, as did Maria Winkelmann and her husband Gottfried Kirch. In each case, the wife served as the assistant to an artisan astronomer. Although Winkelmann discovered a comet in 1702, it was not until 1930 that the discovery was ascribed to her rather than to her husband. Nonetheless, contemporary philosophers did recognize her abilities and understanding of astronomy. Winkelmann had worked jointly with her husband who was the official astronomer of the Berlin Academy of Sciences and was responsible for an official calendar the academy published. When her husband died in 1710, Winkelmann applied for permission to continue the work, basing her application for the post on the guild's tradition of allowing women to continue their husbands' work, in this case the completion of observations required to create an accurate calendar. After much debate, the academy formally rejected her application on the grounds of her gender, although its members knew of her ability and previous accomplishments. Years later, she returned to the Berlin Academy as an assistant to her son, who had been appointed astronomer. Again, the academy insisted that she leave, forcing her to abandon astronomy. She died in 1720.

Such policies of exclusion, however, did not altogether prevent women from acquiring knowledge about scientific endeavors. Margaret Cavendish had composed a *Description of a New World, Called the Blazing World* (1666) to introduce women to the new science. Other examples of scientific writings for a female audience were Bernard de Fontenelle's *Conversations on the Plurality of Worlds* and Francesco Algarotti's *Newtonianism for Ladies* (1737). During the 1730s, Emilie du Châtelet (1706–1749) aided Voltaire in his composition of an important French popularization of Newton's science. Her knowledge of mathematics was more extensive than his and crucial to his completing his book. She also translated Newton's *Principia* into French, an accomplishment made possible only by her exceptional understanding of advanced mathematics.

Still, with few exceptions, women were barred from science and medicine until the late nineteenth century, and not until the twentieth century did they enter these fields in significant numbers. Not only did the institutions of science exclude them, but also, the ideas associated with medical practice, philosophy, and biology suggested that women and their minds were essentially different from, and inferior to, men. By the early eighteenth century, despite isolated precedents of women pursuing natural knowledge, reading scientific literature, and engaging socially with natural philosophers, it had become a fundamental assumption of European intellectual life that the pursuit of knowledge about nature was a male vocation.

▼ The New Science and Religious Faith

For many contemporaries, the new science posed a potential challenge to religion. Three major issues were at stake. First, certain theories and discoveries did not agree with biblical statements about the heavens. Second, who would decide conflicts between religion and science—church authorities or the natural philosophers? Finally, for many religious thinkers, the new science seemed to replace a universe of spiritual meaning and significance with a purely materialistic one. Yet most of the natural philosophers genuinely saw their work as supporting religious belief by contributing to a deeper knowledge of the divine. Their efforts and those of their supporters to reconcile faith and the new science constituted a fundamental factor in the spread of science and its widespread acceptance in educated European circles. The process was not an easy one.

The Case of Galileo

The condemnation of Galileo by Roman Catholic authorities in 1633 is the single most famous incident of conflict between modern science and religious institutions. For centuries it was interpreted as exemplifying the forces of religion smothering scientific knowledge. More recent research has modified that picture.

The condemnation of Copernicanism and of Galileo occurred at a particularly difficult moment in the history of the Roman Catholic Church. In response to Protestant emphasis on private interpretation of Scripture, the Council of Trent (1545–1563) had stated that only the church itself possessed the authority to interpret the Bible. Furthermore, after the Council, the Roman Catholic Church had adopted a more literalist mode of reading the Bible in response to the Protestant emphasis on the authority of Scripture. Galileo's championing of Copernicanism took place in this particular climate of opinion and practice when the Roman Catholic Church, on the one hand, could not surrender the interpretation of the Bible to a layman and, on the other, had difficulty moving beyond a literal reading of the Bible, lest the Protestants accuse it of abandoning Scripture.

In a *Letter to the Grand Duchess Christina* (1615), Galileo, as a layman, had published his own views about how scripture should be interpreted to accommodate the new science. (See "Galileo Discusses the Relationship of Science to the Bible," page 424.) To certain

COMPARE AND CONNECT

Descartes and Swift Debate the Scientific Enterprise

THROUGHOUT THE SEVENTEENTH and eighteenth centuries various writers asserted that the growth of natural knowledge held the promise of improving the human situation. Others, who did not dispute the truth or correctness of the new natural knowledge, nonetheless questioned whether it could actually improve the human situation. In these two documents the French philosopher René Descartes upholds the former position while many decades later the English satirist Jonathan Swift questions the usefulness of the new natural knowledge pursued by the Royal Society of London and by implication by other European scientific academies.

QUESTIONS

1. **How does Descartes compare the usefulness of science with previous speculative philosophy?**
2. **What, if any, limits does he place on the extension of scientific knowledge?**
3. **Why might Swift have so emphasized what he saw as the impracticality of science?**
4. **How might Swift's presentation be seen as manifesting jealousy of a literary figure toward the growing influence of science?**
5. **How does Swift's passage serve as an effort to refute the promise of science championed by Bacon and Descartes?**

I. Descartes Explores the Promise of Expanding Natural Knowledge

In 1637, Descartes published his Discourse on Method. *He wrote against what he believed to be the useless speculations of scholastic philosophy. He championed the careful investigation of physical nature on the grounds that it would expand the scope of human knowledge beyond anything previously achieved and, in doing so, make human beings the masters of nature. This passage contains much of the broad intellectual and cultural argument that led to the ever-growing influence and authority of science from the seventeenth century onward.*

My speculations were indeed truly pleasing to me; but I recognize that other men have theirs, which perhaps please them even more. As soon, however, as I had acquired some general notions regarding physics, and on beginning to make trial of them in various special difficulties had observed how far they can carry us and how much they differ from the principles hitherto employed, I believed that I could not keep them hidden without grievously sinning against the law which lays us under obligation to promote, as far as in us lies, the general good of all mankind. For they led me to see that it is possible to obtain knowledge highly useful in life, and that in place of the speculative philosophy taught in the Schools we can have a practical philosophy, by means of which, knowing the force and the actions of fire, water, air, and of the stars, of the heavens, and of all the bodies that surround us—knowing them as distinctly as we know the various crafts of the artisans—we may in the same fashion employ them in all the uses for which they are suited, thus rendering ourselves the masters and possessors of nature. This is to be desired, not only with a view to the invention of an infinity of arts by which we would be enabled to enjoy without heavy labor the fruits of the earth and all its conveniences, but above all for the preservation of health, which is, without doubt, of all blessings in this life, the first of all goods and the foundation on which the others rest. For the mind is so dependent on the temper and disposition of the bodily organisms that if any means can ever be found to render men wiser and more capable than they have hitherto been, I believe that it is in the science of medicine that the means must be sought. . . . With no wish to depreciate it, I am yet sure there is no one, even of those engaged in the profession, who does not admit that all we know is almost nothing in comparison with what remains to be discovered; and that we could be freed from innumerable maladies, both of body and of mind, and even perhaps from the infirmities of age, if we had sufficient knowledge of their causes and of the remedies provided by nature.

Source: From René Descartes, *Discourse on Method,* in Norman Kemp Smith, ed., *Descartes's Philosophical Writings* (New York: The Modern Library, 1958), pp. 130–131. Reprinted by permission of Macmillan Press Ltd.

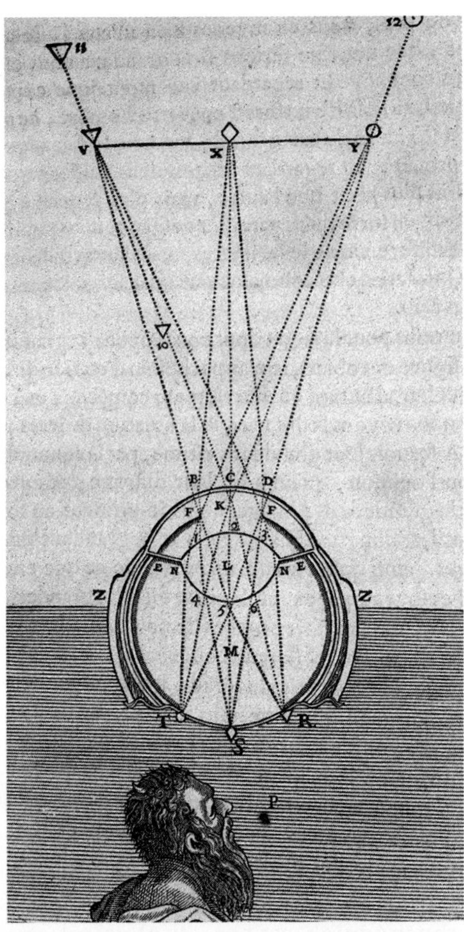

An illustration from *Discourse on Method* by René Descartes (1637). Courtesy of the Library of Congress

II. Jonathan Swift Satirizes Scientific Societies

Swift, the greatest author of English satire in the eighteenth century, was a deeply pessimistic person who thought much of the promise held forth for scientific enterprise would never be realized. In the Third Voyage of Gulliver's Travels, *published in 1726, Swift portrays Gulliver as visiting the land of Lagardo where he encounters a learned academy filled with scholars pursuing outlandish projects. Swift lists the efforts of a whole series of Projectors each of which is more impractical than the next. This passage in which Swift pillories the various people who hoped to received patronage for project from persons associated with the Royal Society of London remains one of the most famous satires of science in the English language. That Swift wrote it is a testimony to the cultural authority that science had achieved by the early eighteenth century.*

Gulliver reports a conversation he encountered while visiting Lagardo:

"The Sum of his Discourse was to this Effect. That about Forty Years ago, certain Persons went up to *Laputa*, either upon Business or Diversion; and after five Months Continuance, came back with a very little Smattering in Mathematics, but full of Volatile Spirits acquired in that Airy Region. That these Persons upon their Return, began to dislike the Management of every Thing below; and fell into Schemes of putting all Arts, Sciences, Languages, and Mechanics upon a new Foot. To this End they procured a Royal Patent for erecting an Academy of *Projectors* in *Lagado*; And the Humour prevailed so strongly among the People, that there is not a Town of any Consequence in the Kingdom without such an Academy. In these Colleges, the Professors contrive new Rules and Methods of Agriculture and Building, and new Instruments and Tools for all Trades and Manufactures, whereby, as they undertake, one Man shall do the Work of Ten; a Palace may be built in a Week, of Materials so durable as to last for ever without repairing. All the Fruits of the Earth shall come to Maturity at whatever Season we think fit to chuse; and increase an Hundred Fold more than they do at present; with innumerable other happy Proposals. The only Inconvenience is, that none of these Projects are yet brought to Perfection; and in the mean time, the whole Country lies miserably waste, the Houses in Ruins, and the People without Food or Cloaths. By all which, instead of being discouraged they are Fifty Times more violently bent upon prosecuting their Schemes, driven equally on by Hope and Depair. . . ."

Gulliver then reports what he found occurring in the rooms of an academy in Lagardo:

"The first Man I saw . . . had been Eight Years upon a Project for extracting Sun-Beams out of Cucumbers, which were to be put into Vials hermetically sealed, and let out to warm the Air in raw inclement Summers. . . .

"I saw another at work to calcine ice into Gunpowder . . .

"There was another most ingenius Architect who had contrived a new Method for building Houses, by beginning at the Roof, and working downwards to the Foundation. . . .

In another Apartment I was highly pleased with a Projector, who had found a Device of plowing the Ground with Hogs, to save the Charges of Plows, Cattle, and Labour. The Method is this: In an Acre of Ground you bury at six Inches Distance, and eight deep, a quantity of Acorns, Dates, Chesnuts, and other Masts or Vegetables whereof these Animals are fondest; then you drive six Hundred or more of them into the Field, where in a few Days they will root up the whole Ground in search of their Food, and make it fit for sowing, at the same time manuring it with their Dung. It is true, upon Experiment they found the Charge and Trouble very great, and they had little or no Crop. However, it is not doubted that this Invention may be capable of great Improvement."

Source: Jonathan Swift, *Gulliver's Travels*, Part III, chaps. iv and v (New York: The Heritage Press, 1960), pp. 193–194, 197–199.

GALILEO DISCUSSES THE RELATIONSHIP OF SCIENCE TO THE BIBLE

The religious authorities were often critical of the discoveries and theories of sixteenth- and seventeenth-century science. For years before his condemnation by the Roman Catholic Church in 1633, Galileo had contended that scientific theory and religious piety were compatible. In his Letter to the Grand Duchess Christina *(of Tuscany), written in 1615, he argued that God had revealed truth in both the Bible and physical nature and that the truth of physical nature did not contradict the Bible if the latter were properly understood. Galileo encountered difficulties regarding this letter because it represented a layman telling church authorities how to read the Bible.*

Is Galileo's argument based on science or theology? Did the church believe that nature was as much a revelation of God as the Bible was? As Galileo describes them, which is the surer revelation of God, nature or the Bible? Why might the pope reject Galileo's argument?

The reason produced for condemning the opinion that the Earth moves and the sun stands still is that in many places in the Bible one may read that the sun moves and the Earth stands still. . . .

With regard to this argument, I think in the first place that it is very pious to say and prudent to affirm that the holy Bible can never speak untruth—whenever its true meaning is understood. But I believe nobody will deny that it is often very abstruse, and may say things which are quite different from what its bare words signify. . . .

This being granted, I think that in discussions of physical problems we ought to begin not from the authority of scriptural passages, but from sense experiences and necessary demonstrations; for the holy Bible and the phenomena of nature proceed alike from the divine Word, the former as the dictate of the Holy Ghost and the latter as the observant executrix of God's commands. It is necessary for the Bible, in order to be accommodated to the understanding of every man, to speak many things which appear to differ from the absolute truth so far as the bare meaning of the words is concerned. But Nature, on the other hand, is inexorable and immutable; she never transgresses the laws imposed upon her, or cares a whit whether her abstruse reasons and methods of operation are understandable to men. For that reason it appears that nothing physical which sense-experience sets before our eyes, or which necessary demonstrations prove to us, ought to be called in question (much less condemned) upon the testimony of biblical passages which may have some different meaning beneath their words. For the Bible is not chained in every expression to conditions as strict as those which govern all physical effects; nor is God any less excellently revealed in Nature's actions than in the sacred statements of the Bible. . . .

From this I do not mean to infer that we need not have an extraordinary esteem for the passages of holy Scripture. On the contrary, having arrived at any certainties in physics, we ought to utilize these as the most appropriate aids in the true exposition of the Bible and in the investigation of those meanings which are necessarily contained therein for these must be concordant with demonstrated truths. I should judge the authority of the Bible was designed to persuade men of those articles and propositions which, surpassing all human reasoning, could not be made credible by science, or by any other means than through the very mouth of the Holy Spirit. . . .

But I do not feel obliged to believe that the same God who has endowed us with senses, reason, and intellect has intended to forgo their use and by some other means to give us knowledge which we can attain by them.

Roman Catholic authorities, his actions resembled those of a Protestant who looked to himself rather than the church to understand the Bible. In 1615 and 1616, he visited Rome and discussed his views openly and aggressively. In early 1616, however, the Roman Catholic Inquisition formally censured Copernicus's views, placing *On the Revolutions of the Heavenly Spheres* in the Index of Prohibited Books. The ground for the condemnation was Copernicus's disagreement with the literal word of the Bible and the biblical interpretations of the Church Fathers. It should be recalled that at the time fully satisfactory empirical evidence to support Copernicus did not yet exist, even in Galileo's mind.

Galileo, who was not on trial in 1616, was formally informed of the condemnation of Copernicanism. Exactly what agreement he and the Roman Catholic authorities reached as to what he would be permitted to write about Copernicanism remains unclear. It appears that he agreed not to advocate that Copernican astronomy was actually physically true, but only to suggest that it could be true in theory.

In 1623, however, a Florentine acquaintance of Galileo's was elected as Pope Urban VIII. He gave Galileo permission to resume discussing the Copernican system, which he did in *Dialogue on the Two Chief World Systems* (1632). The book clearly was designed to defend the physical truthfulness of Copernicanism. Moreover, the voices in the dialogue favoring the older system appeared slow-witted—and those voices presented the views of Pope Urban. Feeling humiliated and betrayed, the pope ordered an investigation of Galileo's book. The actual issue in Galileo's trial of 1633 was whether he had disobeyed the mandate of 1616, and he was held to have done so even though the exact nature of that mandate was less than certain. Galileo was condemned, required to renounce his views, and placed under the equivalent of house arrest in his home near Florence for the last nine years of his life.

Although much more complicated than a simple case of a conflict between science and religion, the condemnation of Galileo cast a long and troubled shadow over the relationship of the emerging new science and the authority of the Roman Catholic Church. The controversy continued into the late twentieth century, when Pope John Paul II formally ordered the reassessment of the Galileo case. In 1992, the Roman Catholic Church admitted that errors had occurred, particularly in the biblical interpretation of Pope Urban VIII's advisers.

Blaise Pascal: Reason and Faith

Blaise Pascal (1623–1662), a French mathematician and a physical scientist who surrendered his wealth to pursue an austere, self-disciplined life, made one of the most influential efforts to reconcile faith and the new science. He aspired to write a work that would refute both dogmatism (which he saw epitomized by the Jesuits) and skepticism. Pascal considered the Jesuits' casuistry (i.e., arguments designed to minimize and excuse sinful acts) a distortion of Christian teaching. He rejected the skeptics of his age because they either denied religion altogether (atheists) or accepted it only as it conformed to reason (deists). He never produced a definitive refutation of the two sides. Rather, he formulated his views on these matters in piecemeal fashion in a provocative collection of reflections on humankind and religion published posthumously under the title *Pensées (Thoughts)*.

Pascal allied himself with the Jansenists, seventeenth-century Catholic opponents of the Jesuits. (See Chapter 13.) His sister was a member of the Jansenist convent of Port-Royal, near Paris. The Jansenists shared with the Calvinists Saint Augustine's belief in human beings' total sinfulness, their eternal predestination to heaven or hell by God, and their complete dependence on faith and grace for knowledge of God and salvation.

Pascal believed that in religious matters, only the reasons of the heart and a "leap of faith" could prevail. For him, religion was not the domain of reason and science. He saw two essential truths in the Christian religion: A loving God exists, and human beings, because they are corrupt by nature, are utterly unworthy of God. He believed the atheists and the deists of his age had overestimated reason. To Pascal, reason itself was too weak to resolve the problems of human nature and destiny. Ultimately, reason should drive those who truly heeded it to faith in God and reliance on divine grace.

Pascal made a famous wager with the skeptics. It is a better bet, he argued, to believe God exists and to stake everything on his promised mercy than not to do so. This is because, if God does exist, the believer will gain everything, whereas, should God prove not to exist, comparatively little will have been lost by having believed in him.

Convinced that belief in God improved life psychologically and disciplined it morally (regardless of whether God proved in the end to exist), Pascal worked to strengthen traditional religious belief. He urged his contemporaries to seek self-understanding by "learned ignorance" and to discover humankind's greatness by recognizing its misery. He hoped thereby to counter what he believed to be the false optimism of the new rationalism and science.

The English Approach to Science and Religion

Francis Bacon established a key framework for reconciling science and religion that long influenced the English-speaking world. He argued there were two books of divine revelation: the Bible and nature. In studying nature, the natural philosopher could achieve a deeper knowledge of things divine, just as could the theologian studying the Bible. Because both books of revelation shared the same author, they must be compatible. Whatever discord might first appear between science and

A Closer LOOK

THE SCIENCES AND THE ARTS

PAINTERS DURING THE seventeenth century were keenly aware that they lived in an age of expanding knowledge of nature and of the world. Adriaen Stalbent (1589–1662) portrayed this close interrelationship of *The Sciences and the Arts*. Across Europe various societies were founded to study the expanding realm of natural knowledge. As in this painting, women only were rarely admitted to the meetings of these societies or to the rooms where the new natural knowledge was pursued or discussed.

The paintings on the wall illustrate the great masters of the day, some of whom drew on ancient mythological themes, others biblical scenes, and still others contemporary landscapes. Sophisticated viewers would have been able to identify each painting and its artist. The themes from the Bible and ancient mythology here are intended to contrast with the symbols of modern knowledge displayed elsewhere in the room.

On the red, covered table stands an astronomical instrument that natural philosophers used to illustrate the theories of Copernicus, Kepler, and Galileo.

On the table on the right stands a globe and volumes of maps that allow observers to trace the explorations of the Americas and other parts of the non-European world.

Adriaen Stalbent (1589–1662), *The Sciences and the Arts*. Wood, 93 × 114 cm. Inv. 1405. Museo del Prado, Madrid, Spain. Photograph © Erich Lessing, Art Resource, NY

To examine this image in an interactive fashion, please go to www.myhistorylab.com

myhistorylab

religion must eventually be reconciled. Natural theology based on a scientific understanding of the natural order would thus support theology derived from Scripture.

Later in the seventeenth century, with the work of Newton, the natural universe became a realm of law and regularity. Most natural philosophers were devout people who saw in the new picture of physical nature a new picture of God. The Creator of this rational, lawful nature must also be rational. To study nature was to come to a better understanding of that Creator. Science and religious faith were not only compatible, but also mutually supportive. As Newton wrote, "The main Business of Natural Philosophy is to argue from Phaenomena without feigning Hypothesis, and to deduce Causes from Effects, till we come to the very first Cause, which certainly is not mechanical."[11]

The religious thought associated with such deducing of religious conclusions from nature became known as *physico-theology*. This reconciliation of faith and science allowed the new physics and astronomy to spread rapidly. At the very time when Europeans were finally tiring of the wars of religion, the new science provided the basis for a view of God that might lead away from irrational disputes and wars over religious doctrine. Faith in a rational God encouraged faith in the rationality of human beings and in their capacity to improve their lot once liberated from the traditions of the past. The scientific revolution provided the great model for the desirability of change and of criticism of inherited views.

Finally, the new science and the technological and economic innovations associated with its culture came again, especially among English thinkers, to be interpreted as part of a divine plan. By the late seventeenth century, natural philosophy and its practical achievements had become associated in the public mind with consumption and the market economy. Writers such as the Englishman John Ray in *The Wisdom of God Manifested in His Works of Creation* (1690) argued it was evident that God had placed human beings in the world to understand it and then, having understood it, to turn it to productive practical use through rationality. Scientific advance and economic enterprise came to be interpreted in the public mind as the fulfillment of God's plan: Human beings were meant to improve the world. This outlook provided a religious justification for the processes of economic improvement that would characterize much of eighteenth-century Western Europe.

▼ Continuing Superstition

Despite the great optimism among certain European thinkers associated with the new ideas in science and philosophy, traditional beliefs and fears long retained their hold on Western culture. During the sixteenth and seventeenth centuries, many Europeans remained preoccupied with sin, death, and the devil. Religious people, including many among the learned and many who were sympathetic to the emerging scientific ideas, continued to believe in the power of magic and the occult. Until the end of the seventeenth century, almost all Europeans in one way or another believed in the power of demons.

[11]Quoted in Baumer, *Main Currents of Western Thought*, p. 323.

Witch Hunts and Panic

Nowhere is the dark side of early modern thought and culture more strikingly visible than in the witch hunts and panics that erupted in almost every Western land. Between 1400 and 1700, courts sentenced an estimated 70,000 to 100,000 people to death for harmful magic (*maleficium*) and diabolical witchcraft. In addition to inflicting harm on their neighbors, witches were said to attend mass meetings known as *sabbats*, to which they were believed to fly. They were also accused of indulging in sexual orgies with the devil, who appeared in animal form, most often as a he-goat. Still other charges against them were cannibalism—particularly the devouring of small Christian children—and a variety of ritual acts and practices, often sexual in nature, that denied or perverted Christian beliefs.

Why did witch panics occur in the sixteenth and early seventeenth centuries? The disruptions created by religious division and warfare were major factors. (The peak years of the religious wars were also those of the witch hunts.) Some argue that the Reformation spurred the panics by taking away the traditional defenses against the devil and demons, thus compelling societies to protect themselves preemptively by searching out and executing witches. Political consolidation by secular governments and the papacy played an even greater role, as both aggressively conformed their respective realms in an attempt to eliminate competition for the loyalty of their subjects.

Village Origins

The roots of belief in witches are found in both popular and elite culture. In village societies, feared and respected "cunning folk" helped people cope with natural disasters and disabilities by magical means. For local people, these were important services that kept village life moving forward in times of calamity. The possession of magical powers, for good or ill, made one an important person within village society. Those who were most in need of security and influence, particularly old, impoverished single or widowed women, often made claims to such authority. In village society witch beliefs may also have been a way to defy urban Christian society's attempts to impose its orthodox beliefs, laws, and institutions on the countryside. Under church persecution local fertility cults, whose semipagan practices were intended to ensure good harvests, acquired the features of diabolical witchcraft.

Influence of the Clergy

Popular belief in magical power was the essential foundation of the witch hunts. Had ordinary people not believed that "gifted persons" could help or harm by magical means, and had they not been willing to accuse them, the hunts would never have occurred; however, the contribution of Christian theologians was equally great. When the church expanded into areas where its power and influence were small, it encountered semipagan cultures rich in folkloric beliefs and practices that predated Christianity. There, it clashed with the cunning men and women, who were respected spiritual authorities in their local communities, the folk equivalents of Christian priests. The Christian clergy also practiced high magic. They could transform bread and wine into the body and blood of Christ (the sacrament of the Eucharist) and eternal penalties for sin into temporal ones (the sacrament of Penance or Confession). They also claimed the power to cast out demons who possessed the faithful.

In the late thirteenth century, the church declared its magic to be the only true magic. Since such powers were not innate to humans, the theologians reasoned, they must come either from God or from the devil. Those from God were properly exercised within and by the church. Any who practiced magic outside and against the church did so on behalf of the devil. From such reasoning grew allegations of "pacts" between nonpriestly magicians and Satan. Attacking accused witches became a way for the church to extend its spiritual hegemony.

In working its will, the church had an important ally in the princes of the age, who were also attempting to extend and consolidate their authority over villages and towns within their lands. As the church sought to supplant folk magic with church magic, the princes sought to supplant customary laws with Roman law. Here the stage was set for a one-sided conflict. Witch trials became one of the ways church and state realized their overlapping goals. To identify, try, and execute witches was a demonstration of absolute spiritual and political authority over a village or a town.

Who Were the Witches?

Roughly 80 percent of the victims of witch hunts were women, most single and aged over forty. This has suggested to some that misogyny fueled the witch hunts. Inspired by male hatred and sexual fear of strong women, and occurring at a time when women were breaking out from under male control, witch hunts were a conspiracy of males against females.

A perhaps better argument holds that women were targeted in higher numbers for more commonsensical reasons. (See "Why More Women Than Men Are Witches.") Three groups of women appear especially to have drawn the witch-hunters' attention. The first was widows, who, living alone in the world after the deaths of their husbands, were often dependent on help from others, unhappy, and known to strike out. A second group was midwives, whose work made them unpopular when mothers and newborns died during childbirth. (See "Encountering the Past: Midwives," page 430.) Surviving family members remembered those deaths. Finally, there were women healers and herbalists, who were targeted because their work gave them a moral and spiritual authority over people whom the church wished to reserve for its priests. These women found themselves on the front lines in disproportionate numbers when the church declared war on those who practiced magic without its special blessing. Social position, vocation, and influence, not gender per se, put old, single women in harm's way. Nowhere do we find women being randomly rounded up for burning. The witch hunts targeted specific women.

End of the Witch Hunts

Several factors helped end the witch hunts. One was the emergence of a more scientific point of view. In the seventeenth century, mind and matter came to be viewed as two independent realities, making it harder to believe that thoughts in the mind or words on the lips could alter physical things. A witch's curse was mere words. With advances in medicine, the rise of insurance companies, and the availability of lawyers, people gained greater physical security against the physical afflictions and natural calamities that drove the witch panics. Finally, the witch hunts began to get out of hand. Tortured witches, when asked whom they saw at witches' sabbats, sometimes alleged having seen leading townspeople there, and even the judges themselves! At this point the trials ceased to serve the interests of those conducting them, becoming dysfunctional and threatening anarchy as well.

▼ Baroque Art

Art historians use the term *baroque* to denote the style associated with seventeenth-century painting, sculpture, and architecture. As with other terms used in art history, the word *baroque* covers a variety of related styles that developed during the century and moved in different directions in different countries. Baroque painters depicted their subjects in a thoroughly naturalistic, rather than an idealized, manner. This faithfulness to nature paralleled the interest in natural knowledge associated with the rise of the new science and the deeper understanding of human anatomy that was achieved during this period. These painters, the most famous of whom was Michelangelo Caravaggio (1573–1610), also were devoted to picturing

WHY MORE WOMEN THAN MEN ARE WITCHES

A classic of misogyny, The Hammer of Witches *(1486), written by two Dominican monks, Heinrich Krämer and Jacob Sprenger, was sanctioned by Pope Innocent VIII as an official guide to the church's detection and punishment of witches. Here, Krämer and Sprenger explain why they believe most witches are women rather than men.*

Why would two Dominican monks say such things about women? What are the biblical passages that they believe justify them? Do their descriptions have any basis in the actual behavior of women in that age? What is the rivalry between married and unmarried people that they refer to?

Why are there more superstitious women than men? The first [reason] is that they are more credulous; and since the chief aim of the devil is to corrupt faith, therefore he rather attacks them. . . . The second reason is that women are naturally more impressionable and ready to receive the influence of a disembodied spirit. . . . The third reason is that they have slippery tongues and are unable to conceal from their fellow-women those things which by evil arts they know; and since they are weak, they find an easy and secret manner of vindicating themselves by witchcraft. . . . [Therefore] since women are feebler both in mind and body, it is not surprising that they should come more under the spell of witchcraft. For as regards intellect, or the understanding of spiritual things, they seem to be of a different nature from men, a fact which is vouched for by the logic of the authorities, backed by various examples from the Scriptures. . . . .

But the natural reason [for woman's proclivity to witchcraft] is that she is more carnal than a man, as is clear from her many carnal abominations. And it should be noted that there was a defect in the formation of the first woman, since she was formed from a bent rib, that is, a rib of the breast, which is bent as it were in a contrary direction to a man. And since through this defect she is an imperfect animal, she always deceives. . . . .

As to her other mental quality, her natural will, when she hates someone whom she formerly loved, then she seethes with anger and impatience in her whole soul, just as the tides of the sea are always heaving and boiling. . . . .

Truly the most powerful cause which contributes to the increase of witches is the woeful rivalry between married folk and unmarried women and men. This [jealousy or rivalry exists] even among holy women, so what must it be among the others . . . ?

Just as through the first defect in their intelligence women are more prone [than men] to abjure the faith, so through their second defect of inordinate affections and passions they search for, brood over, and inflict various vengeances, either by witchcraft or by some other means. Wherefore it is no wonder that so great a number of witches exist in this sex. . . . [Indeed, witchcraft] is better called the heresy of witches than of wizards, since the name is taken from the more powerful party [that is, the greater number, who are women]. Blessed be the Highest who has so far preserved the male sex from so great a crime.

From *Malleus Maleficarum*, trans. by Montague Summers (Bungay, Suffolk, UK: John Rodker, 1928), pp. 41–47. Reprinted by permission.

sharp contrasts between light and darkness, which created dramatic scenes in their painting. Consequently both baroque painting and sculpture have been seen as theatrical and intending to draw the observer into an emotional involvement with the subject that is being portrayed.

The work of Baroque artists served both religious and secular ends. Baroque painters, especially in Roman Catholic countries, often portrayed scenes from the Bible and from the lives of saints intended to instruct the observer in religious truths. Artists used the same style of painting, however, to present objects and scenes of everyday life in new realistic detail. Such was the case with Dutch painters of still lifes who portrayed all manner of elaborate foodstuffs as well as with artists

ENCOUNTERING THE *Past*

MIDWIVES

ALTHOUGH WOMEN IN early modern Europe generally found themselves excluded from the world of the new science, midwives across Europe oversaw the delivery of children until well into the eighteenth century. Often known as *wise women* because of their knowledge and medical skills, midwives were among the few women who carried out independent economic and public roles.

Midwifery was a trade, often pursued by elderly or widowed women of the lower social classes, for which women apprenticed for several years. In the 1630s, the Hôtel Dieu, a public hospital near Paris, set up a basic course for training midwives. Unlike other skilled workers and tradesmen, however, midwives were not allowed to organize guilds or associations to protect their trade, pass on their skills, and stabilize their incomes. Instead, civil or church authorities, who were invariably men, licensed midwives and often appointed upper-class women, known as honorable women, to supervise them.

Personal respectability and respect for the privacy of the women they attended were essential qualities for successful midwives. They were present at some of the most private moments in the lives of women and their families and were expected not to gossip about family secrets. Furthermore, women from all social classes feared that if their attending midwives were not of good character their own babies might be stillborn or imperfectly formed. Careless or incompetent midwives who injured mother or child could lose their license.

Midwives also performed important religious and civic functions at births. In emergencies they could baptize a frail newborn. They also often registered births and were officially required both to discourage abortion and infanticide and to report those activities when they occurred to the authorities. The respectability of midwives also gave them legal standing to testify to a child's legitimacy or illegitimacy.

Midwifery was one of numerous skills and occupations associated with women in early modern Europe that men took over during the eighteenth century. (See Chapter 16.) Male medical practitioners claimed to possess better training, which was available to them in medical schools, and more professional knowledge about delivering children. Over time, civil and medical authorities began to demand that people who delivered children be trained as doctors in medical schools, which women were not allowed to attend until well into the nineteenth century. In particular, the use of forceps by male surgeons to deliver a child involved a level of training unavailable to women. Yet even as medical professionalization became entrenched, midwives continued to provide their services to the poor and rural populations of Europe.

Linda Schiebinger, *The Mind Has No Sex? Women in the Origins of Modern Science* (Cambridge, MA: Harvard University Press, 1989); Hilary Marland, ed., *The Art of Midwifery: Early Modern Midwives in Europe* (London: Routledge, 1993).

What types of women became midwives in early modern Europe? How did the authorities regulate the practice of midwifery?

Why did male professionals gradually replace midwives in delivering babies?

Until well into the eighteenth century, midwives oversaw the delivery of most children in Europe. CORBIS

Bernini designed the elaborate Baldacchino that stands under the dome of St. Peter's Basilica. It is one of the major examples of baroque interior decoration. Scala/Art Resource, NY

such Louis LeNain (1593–1648) who painted scenes of French peasant life (see Chapter 15, page 440).

Baroque art became associated, rightly or wrongly, with both Roman Catholicism and absolutist politics. Baroque art first emerged in papal Rome. Gian Lorenzo Bernini's work (1598–1680) in St. Peter's Basilica there was the most famous example of baroque decoration. At the direction of Pope Urban VIII (r. 1623–1644), during whose reign Galileo was condemned, Bernini designed and oversaw the construction of the great tabernacle that stands beneath the church's towering dome and directly over the space where St. Peter is said to be buried. Behind the tabernacle, Bernini also designed a monument to papal authority with the chair of St. Peter resting on the shoulders of four of the church fathers. In front of the cathedral, he designed the two vast colonnades that he said symbolized the arms of the church reaching out to the world. In the church of Santa Maria de la Vittoria in Rome, Bernini created the dramatic sculpture of the Spanish mystic St. Teresa of Avila (1515–1582), depicting her in religious ecstasy.

The association of baroque art with Roman Catholicism had its counterpart in the secular world. Charles I (r. 1625–1649) of England during the 1630s when he ruled as an all-but absolute monarch without calling Parliament employed the Roman Catholic Flemish artist Peter Paul Rubens (1577–1640) to decorate the ceiling of the Banqueting Hall at his palace in London with paintings commemorating his father James I (r. 1603–1625). Rubens was the leading religious painter of the Catholic Reformation. Charles's employment of him fed Puritan suspicions that the king harbored Roman Catholic sympathies. Consequently, it was not by coincidence that Charles I was led to his execution in 1649 through the Rubens-decorated Banqueting Hall to his death on the scaffold erected outside.

The most elaborate baroque monument to political absolutism was Louis XIV's palace at Versailles. (See Chapter 13.) The exterior of the palace was classical in its restrained design. Room after room on the interior, however, was decorated with vast, dramatic paintings and murals presenting Louis as the Sun King. The Hall of Mirrors, which runs across the entire rear of the palace, allowed for a glittering and elaborate play of light whose purpose was to reflect the power of the monarch. In the gardens of Versailles fountains depicted mythical gods as if they had come to pay court or to amuse the Sun King. Monarchs across Europe, Protestant as well as Catholic, who hoped to imitate Louis's absolutism in their own domains, erected similar, if smaller, palaces filled with elaborate decoration. Baroque architecture dominated the capitals of the rulers of the smaller German states as well as the imperial court of the Habsburgs in Vienna.

In Perspective

The scientific revolution and the thought of writers whose work was contemporaneous with it mark a major turning point in the history of Western culture and eventually had a worldwide impact. The scientific and political ideas of the late sixteenth and seventeenth centuries gradually overturned many of the most fundamental premises of the medieval worldview. The sun replaced the earth as the center of the solar system. The solar system itself came to be viewed as one of many possible systems in the universe. The new knowledge of the physical universe gave rise to challenges to the authority of the church and Scripture. Mathematics began to replace theology and metaphysics as the tool for understanding nature.

Parallel to these developments and sometimes related to them, political thought became much less concerned with religious issues. Hobbes's theory of political obligation made virtually no reference to God. Locke's theories about politics recognized God, but paid little attention to Scripture. He also championed greater freedom of religious and political expression. Locke's ideas about psychology emphasized the influence of environment on human character and action. All of these new ideas gradually displaced or reshaped theological and religious modes of thought and placed humankind and life on earth at the center of Western thinking. Intellectuals in the West consequently developed greater self-confidence in their own capacity to shape the world and their own lives.

None of this change came easily, however. The new science and enlightenment were accompanied by new anxieties that were reflected in a growing preoccupation with sin, death, and the devil. The worst expression of this preoccupation was a succession of witch hunts and trials that took the lives of as many as 100,000 people between 1400 and 1700.

Review Questions

1. What did Copernicus, Brahe, Kepler, Galileo, and Newton each contribute to the scientific revolution? Which do you think made the most important contributions and why? What did Francis Bacon contribute to the foundation of scientific thought?
2. How would you define the term *scientific revolution*? In what ways was it truly revolutionary? Which is more enduring, a political revolution or an intellectual one?
3. What were the differences between the political philosophies of Thomas Hobbes and John Locke? How did each view human nature? Would you rather live under a government designed by Hobbes or by Locke? Why?
4. Why were women unable to participate fully in the new science? How did family relationships help some women become involved in the advance of natural philosophy?
5. Why did the Catholic Church condemn Galileo? How did Pascal seek to reconcile faith and reason? How did English natural theology support economic expansion?
6. How do you explain the phenomena of witchcraft and witch hunts in an age of scientific enlightenment? Why did the witch panics occur in the late sixteenth and early seventeenth centuries? How might the Reformation have contributed to them?

Suggested Readings

R. Ashcraft, *Revolutionary Politics and Locke's Two Treatises of Government* (1986). A major study emphasizing the radical side of Locke's thought.

J. Barry, M. Hester, and G. Roberts, eds., *Witchcraft in Early Modern Europe: Studies in Culture and Belief* (1998). A collection of recent essays.

M. Biagioli, *Galileo Courtier: The Practice of Science in the Culture of Absolutism* (1993). A major revisionist work.

J. A. Conner, *Kepler's Witch: An Astronomer's Discovery of Cosmic Order Amid Religious War, Political Intrigue, and the Heresy Trial of His Mother* (2005). Fascinating account of Kepler's effort to vindicate his mother against charges of witchcraft.

P. Dear, *Revolutionizing the Sciences: European Knowledge and Its Ambitions, 1500–1700* (2001). A broad-ranging study of both the ideas and institutions of the new science.

M. Feingold, *The Newtonian Moment: Isaac Newton and the Making of Modern Culture* (2004). A superb, well-illustrated volume.

S. Gaukroger, *The Emergence of a Scientific Culture: Science and the Shaping of Modernity* (2007). A challenging book exploring the differing understanding of natural knowledge in early modern European culture.

S. Gaukroger, *Francis Bacon and the Transformation of Early-Modern Philosophy* (2001). An excellent, accessible introduction.

J. Gleik, *Isaac Newton* (2003). Highly accessible to the general reader.

I. Harris, *The Mind of John Locke: A Study of Political Theory in Its Intellectual Setting* (1994). The most comprehensive recent treatment.

J. L. Heilbron, *The Sun in the Church: Cathedrals as Solar Observatories* (2000). Explores uses made of Roman Catholic cathedrals to make astronomical observations.

K. J. Howell, *God's Two Books: Copernican Cosmology and Biblical Interpretation in Early Modern Science* (2002). The clearest discussion of this important subject.

L. Jardine, *Ingenious Pursuits: Building the Scientific Revolution* (1999). A lively exploration of the interface of personalities, new knowledge, and English society.

A. C. Kors and E. Peters, eds., *European Witchcraft, 1100–1700* (1972). Classics of witch belief.

T. S. Kuhn, *The Copernican Revolution: Planetary Astronomy in the Development of Western Thought* (1957). Remains the classic work.

B. Levack, *The Witch Hunt in Early Modern Europe* (1986). Lucid survey.

P. Machamer, ed., *The Cambridge Companion to Galileo* (1998). Essays that aid the understanding of the entire spectrum of the new science.

J. Marshall, *John Locke, Toleration and Early Enlightenment Culture* (2006). A magisterial and challenging survey of the background of seventeenth-century arguments for and against toleration.

J. R. Martin, *Baroque* (1977). A classic introduction to Baroque art.

M. Osler, *Rethinking the Scientific Revolution* (2000). A collection of revisionist essays particularly exploring issues of the interrelationship of the new science and religion.

R. Popkin, *The History of Scepticism: From Savonarola to Bayle* (2003). A classic study of the fear of loss of intellectual certainty.

L. Pyenson and S. Sheets-Pyenson, *Servants of Nature: A History of Scientific Institutions, Enterprises, and Sensibilities* (1999). A history of the settings in which the creation and diffusion of scientific knowledge have occurred.

J. Repcheck, *Copernicus' Secret: How the Scientific Revolution Began* (2007). A highly accessible biography of Copernicus.

L. Schiebinger, *The Mind Has No Sex? Women in the Origins of Modern Science* (1989). A major study of the subject.

S. Shapin, *The Scientific Revolution* (1996). A readable brief introduction.

W. R. Shea and M. Artigas, *Galileo in Rome: The Rise and Fall of a Troublesome Genius* (2003). Argues that Galileo in part brought about his own condemnation.

T. Sorell, *The Cambridge Companion to Hobbes* (1994). Excellent essays on the major themes of Hobbes's thought.

R. S. Westfall, *The Construction of Modern Science: Mechanisms and Mechanics* (1971). A classic work.

For additional learning resources related to this chapter, please go to www.myhistorylab.com

During the eighteenth century farm women normally worked in the home and performed such tasks as churning butter as well as caring for children. As time passed tasks such as making butter were mechanized and women were displaced from such work. Francis Wheatley (RA) (1747–1801) *Morning*, signed and dated 1799, oil on canvas, 17½ × 21½ in. (44.5 × 54.5 cm), Yale Center for British Art, Paul Mellon Collection, USA/Bridgeman Art Library (B1977.14.120)

15

Society and Economy Under the Old Regime in the Eighteenth Century

▼ **Major Features of Life in the Old Regime**
Maintenance of Tradition • Hierarchy and Privilege

▼ **The Aristocracy**
Varieties of Aristocratic Privilege • Aristocratic Resurgence

▼ **The Land and Its Tillers**
Peasants and Serfs • Aristocratic Domination of the Countryside: The English Game Laws

▼ **Family Structures and the Family Economy**
Households • The Family Economy • Women and the Family Economy • Children and the World of the Family Economy

▼ **The Revolution in Agriculture**
New Crops and New Methods • Expansion of the Population

▼ **The Industrial Revolution of the Eighteenth Century**
A Revolution in Consumption • Industrial Leadership of Great Britain • New Methods of Textile Production • The Steam Engine • Iron Production • The Impact of the Agricultural and Industrial Revolutions on Working Women

▼ **The Growth of Cities**
Patterns of Preindustrial Urbanization • Urban Classes • The Urban Riot

▼ **The Jewish Population: The Age of the Ghetto**

▼ **In Perspective**

KEY TOPICS

- The varied privileges and powers of Europe's aristocracies in the Old Regime and their efforts to increase their wealth
- The plight of rural peasants
- Family structure and family economy
- The transformation of Europe's economy by the Agricultural and Industrial Revolutions
- Urban growth and the social tensions that accompanied it
- The strains on the institutions of the Old Regime brought about by social change

DURING THE FRENCH Revolution and the turmoil that upheaval spawned, it became customary to refer to the patterns of social, political, and economic relationships that had existed in France before 1789 as the *ancien régime*, or the **Old Regime**. The term has come to be applied generally to the life and institutions of pre-revolutionary Europe. Politically, on the continent, though not in Great Britain, it meant the rule of theoretically absolute monarchies with growing bureaucracies and aristocratically led armies. Economically, a scarcity of food, the predominance of agriculture, slow transport, a low level of iron production, comparatively unsophisticated financial institutions, and, in some cases, competitive commercial overseas empires characterized the Old Regime. Socially, men and women living during the period saw themselves less as individuals than as members of distinct corporate bodies that possessed certain privileges or rights as a group.

Tradition, hierarchy, a corporate feeling, and privilege were the chief social characteristics of the Old Regime. Yet it was by no means a static society. Change and innovation were fermenting in its midst. Farming became more commercialized, and both food production and the size of the population increased. The early stages of the Industrial Revolution made more consumer goods available, and domestic consumption expanded throughout the century. The colonies in the Americas provided strong demand for European goods and manufactures. Merchants in seaports and other cities were expanding their businesses. By preparing their states for war, European governments put new demands on the resources and the economic organizations of their nations. The spirit of rationality that had been so important to the scientific revolution of the seventeenth century continued to manifest itself in the economic life of the eighteenth century. The Old Regime itself fostered the changes that eventually transformed it into a different kind of society.

▼ Major Features of Life in the Old Regime

Socially, pre-revolutionary Europe was based on (1) aristocratic elites possessing a wide variety of inherited legal privileges; (2) established churches intimately related to the state and the aristocracy; (3) an urban labor force usually organized into guilds; and (4) a rural peasantry subject to high taxes and feudal dues. Of course, the men and women living during this period did not know it was the Old Regime. Most of them earned their livelihoods and passed their lives as their forebearers had done for generations before them and as they expected their children to do after them.

Maintenance of Tradition

During the eighteenth century, the past weighed more heavily on people's minds than did the future. Few persons outside the government bureaucracies, the expanding merchant groups, and the movement for reform called the Enlightenment (see Chapter 17) considered change or innovation desirable. This was especially true of social relationships. Both nobles and peasants, for different reasons, repeatedly called for the restoration of traditional, or customary, rights. The nobles asserted what they considered their ancient rights against the intrusion of the expanding monarchical bureaucracies. The peasants, through petitions and revolts, called for the revival or the maintenance of the customary manorial rights that allowed them access to particular lands, courts, or grievance procedures.

Except for the early industrial development in Britain and the accompanying expansion of personal consumption, the eighteenth-century economy was also predominantly traditional. The quality and quantity of the grain harvest remained the most important fact of life for most of the population and the gravest concern for governments.

Hierarchy and Privilege

Closely related to this traditional social and economic outlook was the hierarchical structure of the society. The medieval sense of rank and degree not only persisted, but also became more rigid during the century. In several continental cities, sumptuary laws regulating the dress of the different classes remained on the books. These laws forbade persons in one class or occupation from wearing clothes like those worn by their social superiors. The laws, which sought to make the social hierarchy easily visible, were largely ineffective by this time. What really enforced the hierarchy was the corporate nature of social relationships.

Each state or society was considered a community composed of numerous smaller communities. Eighteenth-century Europeans did not enjoy what Americans regard as "individual rights." Instead, a person enjoyed such rights and privileges as were guaranteed to the particular communities or groups of which she or he was a part. The "community" might include the village, the municipality, the nobility, the church, the guild, a university, or the parish. In turn, each of these bodies enjoyed certain privileges, some great and some small. The privileges might involve exemption from taxation or from some especially humiliating punishment, the right to practice a trade or craft, the right of one's children to pursue a particular occupation, or, for the church, the right to collect the tithe.

▼ The Aristocracy

The eighteenth century was the great age of the aristocracy. The nobility constituted approximately 1 to 5 percent of the population of any given country. Yet in every country, it was the single wealthiest sector of the population, had the widest degree of social, political, and economic power, and set the tone of polite society. In most countries, the nobility had their own separate house in the parliament, estates, or diet. Only nobles had any kind of representation in Hungary and Poland. Land continued to provide the aristocracy with its largest source of income, but aristocrats did not merely own estates: Their influence was felt throughout social and economic life. In much of Europe, however, manual labor was regarded as beneath a noble. In Spain, it was assumed that even the poorer nobles would lead lives of idleness. In other nations, however, the nobility often fostered economic innovation and embraced the commercial spirit. Such willingness to change helped protect the nobility's wealth and, in both Great Britain and France, gave them common interest with the commercial classes who were also eager to see the economy grow and protect their property.

Varieties of Aristocratic Privilege

To be an aristocrat was a matter of birth and legal privilege. This much the aristocracy had in common across the Continent. In almost every other respect, they differed markedly from country to country.

British Nobility The smallest, wealthiest, best defined, and most socially responsible aristocracy resided in Great Britain. It consisted of about four hundred families, and the eldest male members of each family sat in the House of Lords. Through the corruptions of the electoral system, these families also controlled many seats in the House of Commons. The estates of the British nobility ranged from a few thousand to 50,000 acres, from which they received rents. The nobles owned about one fourth of all the arable land in the country. Increasingly, the British aristocracy invested its wealth in commerce, canals, urban real estate, mines, and even industrial ventures. Because only the eldest son inherited the title (called a "peerage"), the right to sit in the House of Lords, and the land, younger sons moved into commerce, the army, the professions, and the church. British landowners in both houses of Parliament levied taxes and also paid them. They had few significant legal privileges, but their direct or indirect control of local government gave them immense political power and social influence. The aristocracy dominated the society and politics of the English counties. Their country houses, many of which were built in the eighteenth century, were the centers of local society.

French Nobility The situation of the continental nobilities was less clear-cut. In France, the approximately 400,000 nobles were divided between nobles "of the sword," or those whose nobility was derived from military service, and those "of the robe," who had acquired their titles either by serving in the bureaucracy or by having purchased them. The two groups had quarreled in the past but often cooperated during the eighteenth century to defend their common privileges.

The French nobles were also divided between those who held office or favor with the royal court at Versailles and those who did not. The court nobility reaped the immense wealth that could be gained from holding high office. The nobles' hold on such offices intensified during the century. By the late 1780s, appointments to the church, the army, and the bureaucracy, as well as other profitable positions, tended to go to the nobles already established in court circles. Whereas these well-connected aristocrats were rich, the provincial nobility, called *hobereaux*, were often little better off than wealthy peasants.

Despite differences in rank, origin, and wealth, certain hereditary privileges set all French aristocrats apart from the rest of society. They were exempt from many taxes. For example, most French nobles did not pay the *taille*, or land tax, the basic tax of the Old Regime. The nobles were technically liable for payment of the ***vingtième***, or the "twentieth," which resembled an income tax, but they rarely had to pay it in full. The nobles were not liable for the royal ***corvées***, or forced labor on public works, which fell on the peasants. In addition to these exemptions, French nobles could collect feudal dues from their tenants and enjoyed exclusive hunting and fishing privileges.

Eastern European Nobilities East of the Elbe River, the character of the nobility became even more complicated and repressive. Throughout the area, the military traditions of the aristocracy remained important. In Poland, there were thousands of nobles, or *szlachta*, who were entirely exempt from taxes after 1741. Until 1768, these Polish aristocrats possessed the right of life and death over their serfs. Most of the Polish nobility were relatively poor. A few rich nobles who had immense estates exercised political power in the fragile Polish state.

In Austria and Hungary, the nobility continued to possess broad judicial powers over the peasantry through their manorial courts. They also enjoyed various degrees of exemption from taxation. The wealthiest of them, Prince Esterhazy of Hungary, owned 10 million acres of land.

In Prussia, after the accession of Frederick the Great in 1740, the position of the Junker nobles became much stronger. Frederick's various wars required their full support. He drew his officers almost wholly from the Junker

A Closer LOOK

AN ARISTOCRATIC COUPLE

PORTRAITS, SUCH AS this one of the English landowner, *Robert Andrews and His Wife*, by Thomas Gainsborough (1728–1788), contain many clues to the aristocratic dominance of landed society.

Andrews's gun and dog indicate his exclusive right to hunt game on his land.

His wife's sitting against the expanse of his landed estate suggests the character of their legal relationship, whereby he could have controlled her property, which would have thus become an extension of his.

The market price of the wheat raised on his estate (known in England as corn) would have been protected by various import laws enacted by the English Parliament whose membership was dominated by landowners such as Andrews himself.

To examine this image in an interactive fashion, please go to www.myhistorylab.com

PEARSON myhistorylab

class. Nobles also increasingly made up the bureaucracy. As in other parts of eastern Europe, the Prussian nobles had extensive judicial authority over the serfs.

In Russia, the eighteenth century saw what amounted to the creation of the nobility. Peter the Great's (r. 1682–1725) linking of state service and noble social status through the Table of Ranks (1722) established among Russian nobles a self-conscious class identity that had not previously existed. Thereafter, they were determined to resist compulsory state service. In 1736, Empress Anna (r. 1730–1740) reduced such service to twenty-five years. In 1762, Peter III (r. 1762) exempted the greatest nobles entirely from compulsory service. In 1785, in the Charter of the Nobility, Catherine the Great (r. 1762–1796) legally defined the rights and privileges of noble men and women in exchange for the assurance that the nobility would serve the state voluntarily. Noble privileges included the right of transmitting noble status to a nobleman's wife and children, the judicial protection of noble rights and property, considerable power over the serfs, and exemption from personal taxes.

Aristocratic Resurgence

The Russian Charter of the Nobility constituted one aspect of the broader European-wide development termed the ***aristocratic resurgence***. This was the nobility's reaction to the threat to their social position and privileges that they felt from the expanding power of the monarchies. This resurgence took several forms in the eighteenth century.

First, all nobilities tried to preserve their exclusiveness by making it more difficult to become a noble. Second, they pushed to reserve appointments to the officer corps of the armies, the senior posts in the bureaucracies and government ministries, and the upper ranks of the church exclusively for nobles. By doing this, they hoped to resist the encroaching power of the monarchies.

Third, the nobles attempted to use the authority of existing aristocratically controlled institutions against the power of the monarchies. These institutions included the British Parliament, the French courts, or *parlements*, and the local aristocratic estates and provincial diets in Germany and the Habsburg Empire.

Fourth, the nobility sought to improve its financial position by gaining further exemptions from taxation or by collecting higher rents or long-forgotten feudal dues from the peasantry. The nobility tried to shore up its position by various appeals to traditional and often ancient privileges that had lapsed over time. This aristocratic challenge to the monarchies was a fundamental political fact of the day and a potentially disruptive one.

▼ The Land and Its Tillers

Land was the economic basis of eighteenth-century life and the foundation of the status and power of the nobility. Well over three fourths of all Europeans lived in the country, and few of them ever traveled more than a few miles from their birthplace. Except for the nobility and the wealthier nonaristocratic landowners, most people who dwelled on the land were poor, and in many regions, desperately poor. They lived in various states of economic and social dependency, exploitation, and vulnerability. (See "Two Eighteenth-Century Writers Contemplate the Effects of Different Economic Structures," pages 446–447.)

Peasants and Serfs

Rural social dependency related directly to the land. The nature of the dependency differed sharply for free peasants, such as English tenants and most French cultivators, and for the serfs of Germany, Austria, and Russia, who were legally bound to a particular plot of land and a particular lord. Yet everywhere, the class that owned most of the land also controlled the local government and the courts. For example, in Great Britain, all farmers and smaller tenants had the legal rights of English citizens. The justices of the peace, however, who presided over the county courts and who could call out the local militia, were always substantial landowners, as were the members of Parliament, who made the laws. In eastern Europe, the landowners presided over the manorial courts. On the Continent, the burden of taxation fell on the tillers of the soil.

Obligations of Peasants The power of the landlord increased as one moved across Europe from west to east. Most French peasants owned some land, but there were a few serfs in eastern France. Nearly all French peasants were subject to certain feudal dues, called *banalités.* These included the required use-for-payment of the lord's, or **seigneur's**, mill to grind grain and his oven to bake bread. The seigneur could also require a certain number of days each year of the peasant's labor. This practice of forced labor was termed the *corvée.* Because French peasants rarely possessed enough land to support their families, they had to rent more land from the seigneur and were also subject to feudal dues attached to those plots. In Prussia and Austria, despite attempts by the monarchies late in the century to improve the lot of the serfs, the landlords continued to exercise almost complete control over them. In many of the Habsburg lands, law and custom required the serfs to provide service, or ***robot***, to the lords.

Serfs were worst off in Russia. There, nobles reckoned their wealth by the number of "souls," or male serfs, they owned rather than the size of their acreage. Russian landlords, in effect, regarded serfs merely as economic commodities. They could demand as many as six days a week of labor, known as *barshchina*, from the serfs. Like Prussian and Austrian landlords, they enjoyed the right to punish their serfs. On their own authority, Russian landlords could even exile a serf to Siberia. Serfs had no legal recourse against the orders and whims of their lords. There was little difference between Russian serfdom and slavery.

In southeastern Europe, where the Ottoman Empire held sway, peasants were free, though landlords tried to

Eighteenth-century France had some of the best roads in the world, but they were often built with forced labor. French peasants were required to work part of each year on such projects. This system, called the *corvée*, was not abolished until the French Revolution in 1789. Joseph Vernet, *Construction of a Road*. Louvre, Paris, France. Bridgeman-Giraudon/Art Resource, NY

exert authority in every way. The domain of the landlords was termed a *çift*. The landlord was often an absentee who managed the estate through an overseer. During the seventeenth and eighteenth centuries, these landlords, like those elsewhere in Europe, often became more commercially oriented and turned to the production of crops, such as cotton, vegetables, potatoes, and maize, that they could sell in the market.

A scarcity of labor rather than the recognition of their legal rights supported the independence of the southeastern European peasants. A peasant might migrate from one landlord to another. Because the second landlord needed the peasant's labor, he had no reason to return him to the original landlord. During the seventeenth and eighteenth centuries, however, disorder originating in Constantinople (now Istanbul), the capital, spilled over into the Balkan Peninsula. In this climate, landlords increased their authority by offering their peasants protection from bandits or rebels who might destroy peasant villages. As in medieval times, the manor house or armed enclosure of a local landlord became the peasants' refuge. These landlords also owned all the housing and tools the peasants needed to work the land and also furnished their seed grain. Consequently, despite legal independence, Balkan peasants under the Ottoman Empire became largely dependent on the landlords, though never to the extent of serfs in eastern Europe or Russia.

Peasant Rebellions The Russian monarchy itself contributed to the further degradation of the serfs. Peter the Great gave whole villages to favored nobles. Later in the century, Catherine the Great confirmed the authority of the nobles over their serfs in exchange for the landowners' political cooperation. Russia experienced vast peasant unrest, with well over fifty peasant revolts between 1762 and 1769. These culminated in Pugachev's Rebellion between 1773 and 1775, when Emelyan Pugachev (1726–1775) promised the serfs land of their own and freedom from their lords. All of southern Russia was in turmoil until the government brutally suppressed the rebellion. Thereafter, any thought of improving the condition of the serfs was set aside for a generation.

Pugachev's was the largest peasant uprising of the eighteenth century, but smaller peasant revolts or disturbances took place in Bohemia in 1775, in Transylvania in 1784, in Moravia in 1786, and in Austria in 1789. There were almost no revolts in Western Europe, but England experienced many rural riots. Rural rebellions were violent, but the peasants and serfs normally directed their wrath against property rather than per-

Emelyan Pugachev (1726–1775) led the largest peasant revolt in Russian history. In this contemporary propaganda picture he is shown in chains. An inscription in Russian and German was printed below the picture decrying the evils of revolution and insurrection. Bildarchiv Preussischer Kulturbesitz sons. The rebels usually sought to reassert traditional or customary rights against practices that they perceived as innovations. Their targets were carefully chosen and included unfair pricing, onerous new or increased feudal dues, changes in methods of payment or land use, unjust officials, or extraordinarily brutal overseers and landlords. Peasant revolts were thus conservative in nature.

Aristocratic Domination of the Countryside: The English Game Laws

One of the clearest examples of aristocratic domination of the countryside and of aristocratic manipulation of the law to its own advantage was the English legislation on hunting.

Between 1671 and 1831, English landowners had the exclusive legal right to hunt game animals, including, in particular, hares, partridges, pheasants, and moor fowl. Similar legislation covered other animals such as deer, the killing of which by an unauthorized person became a capital offense in the eighteenth century. By law, only persons owning a particular amount of landed property could hunt these animals. Excluded from the right to hunt were all persons renting land, wealthy city merchants who did not own land, and poor people in cities, villages, and the countryside. The poor were excluded because the elite believed that allowing them to enjoy the sport of hunting would undermine their work habits. The city merchants were excluded because the landed gentry in Parliament wanted to demonstrate visibly and legally the superiority of landed wealth over commercial wealth. Thus, the various game laws upheld the superior status of the aristocracy and the landed gentry.

The game laws were a prime example of legislation related directly to economic and social status. The gentry who benefited from the laws and whose parliamentary representatives had passed them also served as the local justices of the peace who enforced the laws and punished their violation. The justices of the peace could levy fines and even have poachers impressed into the army. Gentry could also take civil legal action against wealthier poachers, such as rich farmers who rented land, and thus saddle them with immense legal fees. The gentry also employed gamekeepers to protect game from poachers. The gamekeepers were known to kill the dogs belonging to people suspected of poaching. By the middle of the century, gamekeepers had devised guns to shoot poachers who tripped their hidden levers.

A small industry arose to circumvent the game laws, however. Many poor people living either on an estate or in a nearby village would kill game for food. They believed the game actually belonged to the community, and this poaching increased during hard times. Poaching was thus one way for the poor to find food.

Even more important was the black market in game animals that the demand in the cities for this kind of luxury meat sustained. This created the possibility of poaching for profit, and indeed, poaching technically meant stealing or killing game for sale. Local people from both the countryside and the villages would steal the game and then sell it to intermediaries called *higglers*. Later, coachmen took over this function. The higglers and the coachmen would smuggle the game into the cities, where poulterers would sell it at a premium price. Everyone involved made a bit of money along the way. During the second half of the century, English aristocrats began to construct large game preserves. The rural poor, who had lost their rights to communal land as a result of its enclosure by the large landowners, resented these preserves, which soon became hunting grounds to organized gangs of poachers.

Penalties against poaching increased in the 1790s after the outbreak of the French Revolution, but so did the amount of poaching as the economic hardships increased. Britain's participation in the wars of the era put a greater burden on poor people as the demand for food in English cities grew along with their population. By the 1820s, both landowners and reformers called for a change in the law. In 1831, Parliament rewrote the game laws, retaining the landowners' possession of the game, but permitting them to allow other people to hunt it. Poaching continued, but the exclusive right of the landed classes to hunt game had ended.

▼ Family Structures and the Family Economy

In preindustrial Europe, the household was the basic unit of production and consumption. Few productive establishments employed more than a handful of people not belonging to the family of the owner, and those rare exceptions were in cities. Most Europeans, however, lived in rural areas. There, as well as in small towns and cities, the household mode of organization predominated on farms, in artisans' workshops, and in small merchants' shops. With that mode of economic organization, there developed what is known as the **family economy**. Its structure, as described here, had prevailed over most of Europe for centuries.

Households

What was a household in the preindustrial Europe of the Old Regime? There were two basic models, one characterizing northwestern Europe and the other eastern Europe.

Northwestern Europe In northwestern Europe, the household almost invariably consisted of a married couple, their children through their early teenage

During the seventeenth century the French Le Nain brothers painted scenes of French peasant life. Although the images softened many of the harsh realities of peasant existence, the clothing and the interiors were based on actual models and convey the character of the life of better-off French peasants whose lives would have continued very much the same into the eighteenth century. Erich Lessing/Art Resource, NY

years, and their servants. Except for the few wealthy people, households usually consisted of not more than five or six members. Furthermore, in these households, more than two generations of a family rarely lived under the same roof. High mortality and late marriage prevented a formation of families of three generations or more. In other words, grandparents rarely lived in the same household as their grandchildren, and families consisted of parents and children. The family structure of northwestern Europe was thus nuclear rather than extended.

Historians used to assume that before industrialization Europeans lived in extended familial settings, with several generations living together in a household. Demographic investigation has now sharply reversed this picture. Children lived with their parents only until their early teens. Then they normally left home, usually to enter the workforce of young servants who lived and worked in another household. A child of a skilled artisan might remain with his or her parents to learn a valuable skill; but only rarely would more than one child do so, because children earned more working outside the home.

Those young men and women who had left home would eventually marry and form their own independent households. This practice of moving away from home is known as *neolocalism.* These young people married relatively late. Men were usually over twenty-six, and women over twenty-three. The new couple usually had children as soon after marriage as possible. Frequently, the woman was already pregnant at marriage. Family and community pressure often compelled the man to marry her. In any case, premarital sexual relations were common. The new couple would soon employ a servant, who, together with their growing children, would undertake whatever form of livelihood the household used to support itself.

The word *servant* in this context does not refer to someone looking after the needs of wealthy people. Rather, in preindustrial Europe, a servant was a person—either male or female—who was hired, often under a clear contract, to work for the head of the household in exchange for room, board, and wages. The servant was usually young and by no means always socially inferior to his or her employer. Normally, the servant was an integral part of the household and ate with the family.

Young men and women became servants when their labor was no longer needed in their parents' household or when they could earn more money for their family outside the parental household. Being a servant for several years—often as many as eight or ten years—allowed young people to acquire the productive skills and the monetary savings necessary to begin their own household. These years spent as servants largely account for the late age of marriage in northwestern Europe.

Eastern Europe As one moved eastward across the Continent, the structure of the household and the pattern of marriage changed. In eastern Europe, both men and women usually married before the age of twenty. Consequently, children were born to much younger parents. Often—especially among Russian serfs—wives were older than their husbands. Eastern European households were generally larger than those in the West. Frequently a rural Russian household consisted of more than nine, and possibly more than twenty, members, with three or perhaps even four generations of the same family living together. Early marriage made this situation more likely. In Russia, marrying involved not starting a new household, but remaining in and expanding one already established.

The landholding structure in eastern Europe accounts, at least in part, for these patterns of marriage and the family. The lords of the manor who owned land wanted to ensure that it would be cultivated, so they could receive their rents. Thus, in Poland, for example, landlords might forbid marriage between their own serfs and those from another estate. They might also require widows and widowers to remarry to assure adequate labor for a particular plot of land. Polish landlords also frowned on the hiring of free laborers—the equivalent of servants in the West—to help cultivate land. The landlords preferred to use other serfs. This practice inhibited the formation of independent households. In Russia, landlords ordered the families of young people in their villages to arrange marriages within a short set time. These lords discouraged single-generation family households because the death or serious illness of one person in such a household might mean the land assigned to it would go out of cultivation.

The Family Economy

Throughout Europe, most people worked within the family economy. That is to say, the household was the basic unit of production and consumption. Almost everyone lived within a household of some kind because it was virtually impossible for ordinary people to support themselves independently. Indeed, except for members of religious orders, people living outside a household were viewed with great suspicion. They were considered potentially criminal, disruptive, or at least dependent on the charity of others. Everywhere beggars met deep hostility.

Depending on their ages and skills, everyone in the household worked. The need to survive poor harvests or economic slumps meant that no one could be idle. Within this family economy, all goods and income produced went to the benefit of the household rather than to the individual family member. On a farm, much of the effort went directly into raising food or producing other agricultural goods that could be exchanged for food. Few Western Europeans, however, had enough land to support their household from farming alone. Thus, one or more family members might work elsewhere and send wages home; for example, the father and older children might work as harvesters, fishermen, or engage in other labor either in the neighborhood or farther from home. If the father was such a migrant worker, his wife and their younger children would have to work the family farm. This was not an uncommon pattern.

The family economy also dominated the life of skilled urban artisans. The father was usually the chief artisan. He normally employed one or more servants but would expect his children to work in the enterprise also. He usually trained his eldest child in the trade. His wife often sold his wares or opened a small shop of her own. Wives of merchants also frequently ran their husbands' businesses, especially when the husband traveled to purchase new goods. In any case, everyone in the family was involved. If business was poor, family members would look for employment elsewhere—not to support themselves as individuals, but to ensure the survival of the family unit.

In Western Europe, the death of a father often brought disaster to the household. The continuing economic life of the family usually depended on his land or skills. The widow might take on the farm or the business, or his children might do so. The widow usually sought to remarry quickly to restore the labor and skills of a male to the household and to prevent herself from becoming dependent on relatives or charity.

The high mortality rate of the time meant that many households were reconstituted second-family groups that included stepchildren. Because of the advanced age of the widow or economic hard times, however, some households might simply dissolve. The widow became dependent on charity or relatives. The children became similarly dependent or entered the workforce as servants earlier than they would have otherwise. In other cases, the situation could be so desperate that they would resort to crime or to begging. The personal, emotional, and economic vulnerability of the family cannot be overemphasized.

In Eastern Europe, the family economy functioned in the context of serfdom and landlord domination. Peasants clearly thought in terms of their families and expanding the land available for cultivation. The village structure may have mitigated the pressures of the family economy, as did the multigenerational family. Dependence on the available land was the chief fact of life. There were many fewer artisan and merchant households, and there was far less geographical mobility than in Western Europe.

Women and the Family Economy

The family economy established many of the chief constraints on the lives and personal experiences of women in preindustrial society. Most of the historical research that has been undertaken on this subject relates to Western Europe. There, a woman's life experience was largely the function of her capacity to establish and maintain a household. For women, marriage was an economic necessity, as well as an institution that fulfilled sexual and psychological needs. Outside a household, a woman's life was vulnerable and precarious. Some women became economically independent, but they were the exception. Normally, unless she were an aristocrat or a member of a religious order, a woman probably could not support herself solely by her own efforts. Consequently, a woman devoted much of her life first to maintaining her parents' household and then to devising some means of getting her own household to live in as an adult. Bearing and rearing children were usually subordinate to these goals.

By the age of seven, a girl would have begun to help with the household work. On a farm, this might mean looking after chickens, watering the animals, or carrying food to the adults working the land. In an urban artisan's household, she would do light work, perhaps cleaning or carrying, and later sewing or weaving. The girl would remain in her parents' home as long as she made a real contribution to the family enterprise or as long as her labor elsewhere was not more remunerative to the family.

An artisan's daughter might not leave home until marriage, because at home she could learn increasingly valuable skills associated with the trade. The situation was different for the much larger number of girls growing up on farms. Their parents and brothers could often do all the necessary farm work, and a girl's labor at home quickly became of little value to her family. She would then leave home, usually between the age of twelve and fourteen years. She might take up residence on another farm, but more likely she would migrate to a nearby town or city. She would rarely travel more than thirty miles from her parents' household. She would then normally become a servant, once again living in a household, but this time in the household of an employer. Having left home, the young woman's chief goal was to accumulate enough capital for a dowry. Her savings would make her eligible for marriage, because they would allow her to make the necessary contribution to form a household with her husband. Marriage within the family economy was a joint economic undertaking, and the wife was expected to make an immediate contribution of capital to establish the household. A young woman might well work for ten years or more to accumulate a dowry. This practice meant that marriage was usually postponed until her mid- to late twenties.

Within marriage, earning enough money or producing enough farm goods to ensure an adequate food supply dominated women's concerns. Domestic duties, childbearing, and child rearing were subordinate to economic pressures. Consequently, couples tried to limit the number of children they had, usually through the practice of *coitus interruptus*, the withdrawal of the male before ejaculation.

The work of married women differed markedly between city and country and was in many ways a function of their husbands' occupations. If the peasant household had enough land to support itself, the wife spent much of her time literally carrying things for her husband—water, food, seed, harvested grain, and the like. Such landholdings, however, were few. If the husband had to do work besides farming, such as fishing or migrant labor, the wife might actually be in charge of the farm and do the plowing, planting, and harvesting. In the city, the wife of an artisan or a merchant might be in charge of the household finances and help manage the business. When her husband died, she might take over the business and perhaps hire an artisan. Finally, if economic disaster struck the family, it was usually the wife who organized what Olwen Hufton has called the "economy of expedients,"[1] within which family members might be sent off to find work elsewhere or even to beg in the streets.

Despite all this economic activity, women found many occupations and professions closed to them because they were female. They labored with less education than men, because in such a society women at all levels of life consistently found fewer opportunities for education than did men. They often received lower wages than men for the same work. The mechanization of agriculture and the textile industries, which will be discussed later in this chapter, made these disabilities worse.

Children and the World of the Family Economy

For women of all social ranks, childbirth meant fear and vulnerability. Contagious diseases endangered both mother and child. Puerperal fever was frequent, as were other infections from unsterilized medical instruments. Not all midwives were skillful practitioners. Furthermore, most mothers gave birth in conditions of immense poverty and wretched housing. Assuming both mother and child survived, the mother might nurse the infant, but often the child would be sent to a wet nurse. The wealthy may have done this for convenience, but economic necessity dictated it for the poor. The structures and customs of the family economy did not permit a woman to devote herself entirely to rearing a child. The wet-nursing industry was well organized, with urban children being frequently transported to wet nurses in the country, where they would remain for months or even years.

The birth of a child was not always welcome. The child might represent another economic burden on an already hard-pressed household, or it might be illegitimate. The number of illegitimate births seems to have increased during the eighteenth century, possibly because increased migration of the population led to fleeting romances.

[1]Olwen Hufton, "Women and the Family Economy in Eighteenth-Century France," *French Historical Studies* 9 (1976), p. 19.

Through at least the end of the seventeenth century, unwanted or illegitimate births could lead to infanticide, especially among the poor. The parents might smother the infant or expose it to the elements. These practices were one result of both the ignorance and the prejudice surrounding contraception.

The late seventeenth and the early eighteenth centuries saw a new interest in preserving the lives of abandoned children. Although foundling hospitals established to care for abandoned children had existed before, their size and number expanded during these years. Two of the most famous were the Paris Foundling Hospital (1670) and the London Foundling Hospital (1739). Such hospitals cared for thousands of children, and the demand for their services increased during the eighteenth century. For example, early in the century, an average of 1,700 children a year were admitted to the Paris Foundling Hospital. In the peak year of 1772, however, that number rose to 7,676 children. Not all of those children came from Paris. Many had been brought to the city from the provinces, where local foundling homes and hospitals were overburdened. The London Foundling Hospital lacked the income to deal with all the children brought to it. In the middle of the eighteenth century, the hospital found itself compelled to choose children for admission by a lottery system.

Sadness and tragedy surrounded abandoned children. Most of them were illegitimate infants from across the social spectrum. Many, however, were left with the foundling hospitals because their parents could not support them. There was a close relationship between rising food prices and increasing numbers of abandoned children in Paris. Parents would sometimes leave personal tokens or saints' medals on the abandoned baby in the vain hope they might one day be able to reclaim the child. Few children were reclaimed. Leaving a child at a foundling hospital did not guarantee its survival. In Paris, only about 10 percent of all abandoned children lived to the age of ten.

Despite all of these perils of early childhood, children did grow up and come of age across Europe. The world of the child may not have received the kind of attention it does today, but during the eighteenth century, the seeds of that modern sensibility were sown. Particularly among the upper classes, new interest arose in educating children. In most areas, education remained firmly in the hands of the churches. As economic skills became more demanding, literacy became more valuable, and literacy rates rose during the century. Yet most Europeans remained illiterate. Not until the late nineteenth century was the world of childhood inextricably linked to the process of education. Then children would be reared to become members of a national citizenry. In the Old Regime, they were reared to make their contribution to the economy of their parents' family and then to set up their own households.

▼ The Revolution in Agriculture

Thus far, this chapter has examined those groups that sought stability and that, except for certain members of the nobility, resisted change. Other groups, however, wished to pursue significant new directions in social and economic life. The remainder of the chapter considers those forces and developments that would transform European life during the next century. These developments first appeared in agriculture.

The main goal of traditional peasant society was a stability that would ensure the local food supply. Despite differences in rural customs across Europe, the tillers resisted changes that might endanger the sure supply of food, which they generally believed traditional methods of cultivation would provide. The food supply was never certain, and the farther east one traveled, the more uncertain it became. Failure of the harvest meant not only hardship, but also death from either outright starvation or malnutrition. People living in the countryside often had more difficulty finding food than did city dwellers, whose local government usually stored reserve supplies of grain.

Poor harvests also played havoc with prices. Smaller supplies or larger demand raised grain prices. Even small increases in the cost of food could exert heavy pressure on peasant or artisan families. If prices increased sharply, many of those families fell back on poor relief from their local government or the church.

Historians now believe that during the eighteenth century bread prices slowly but steadily rose, spurred largely by population growth. Since bread was their main food, this inflation put pressure on the poor. Prices rose faster than urban wages and brought no appreciable advantage to the small peasant producer. However, the

The English agricultural improver Jethro Tull devised this seed drill, which increased wheat crops by planting seed deep in the soil rather than just casting it randomly on the surface. Image Works/Mary Evans Picture Library Ltd.

rise in grain prices benefited landowners and those wealthier peasants who had surplus grain to sell.

The rising grain prices gave landlords an opportunity to improve their incomes and lifestyle. To achieve those ends, landlords in Western Europe began a series of innovations in farm production that became known as the **Agricultural Revolution**. Landlords commercialized agriculture and thereby challenged the traditional peasant ways of production. Peasant revolts and disturbances often resulted. The governments of Europe, hungry for new taxes and dependent on the goodwill of the nobility, used their armies and militias to smash peasants who defended traditional practices.

New Crops and New Methods

The drive to improve agricultural production began during the sixteenth and seventeenth centuries in the Low Countries, where the pressures of the growing population and the shortage of land required changes in cultivation. Dutch landlords and farmers devised better ways to build dikes and to drain land, so they could farm more land. They also experimented with new crops, such as clover and turnips, that would increase the supply of animal fodder and restore the soil. These improvements became so famous that early in the seventeenth century English landlords hired Cornelius Vermuyden, a Dutch engineer, to drain thousands of acres of land around Cambridge.

English landlords provided the most striking examples of eighteenth-century agricultural improvement. They originated almost no genuinely new farming methods, but they popularized ideas developed in the previous century either in the Low Countries or in England. Some of these landlords and agricultural innovators became famous. For example, Jethro Tull (1674–1741) was willing to conduct experiments himself and to finance the experiments of others. Many of his ideas, such as the rejection of manure as fertilizer, were wrong. Others, however, such as using iron plows to turn the earth more deeply and planting wheat by a drill rather than by just casting seeds, were excellent. His methods permitted land to be cultivated for longer periods without having to leave it fallow.

Charles "Turnip" Townsend (1674–1738) encouraged other important innovations. He learned from the Dutch how to cultivate sandy soil with fertilizers. He also instituted crop rotation, using wheat, turnips, barley, and clover. This new system of rotation replaced the fallow field with one sown with a crop that both restored nutrients to the soil and supplied animal fodder. The additional fodder meant that more livestock could be raised. These fodders allowed animals to be fed during the winter and assured a year-round supply of meat. The larger number of animals increased the quantity of manure available as fertilizer for the grain crops. Consequently, in the long run, both animals and human beings had more food.

A third British agricultural improver was Robert Bakewell (1725–1795), who pioneered new methods of animal breeding that produced more and better animals and more milk and meat. These and other innovations received widespread discussion in the works of Arthur Young (1741–1820), who edited the *Annals of Agriculture*. In 1793, he became secretary of the British Board of Agriculture. Young traveled widely across Europe, and his books are among the most important documents of life during the late eighteenth century.

Enclosure Replaces Open-Field Method Many of the agricultural innovations, which were adopted only slowly, were incompatible with the existing organization of land in England. Small cultivators who lived in village communities still farmed most of the soil. Each farmer tilled an assortment of unconnected strips. The two- or three-field systems of rotation left large portions of land fallow and unproductive each year. Animals grazed on the common land in the summer and on the stubble of the harvest in the winter. Until at least the mid-eighteenth century, the whole community decided what crops to plant. The entire system discouraged improvement and favored the poorer farmers, who needed the common land and stubble fields for their animals. The village method precluded expanding pastureland to raise more animals that would, in turn, produce more manure for fertilizer. Thus, the methods of traditional production aimed at a steady, but not a growing, supply of food.

In 1700, approximately half the arable land in England was farmed by this open-field method. By the second half of the century, the rising price of wheat encouraged landlords to consolidate or enclose their lands to increase production. The **enclosures** were intended to use land more rationally and to achieve greater commercial profits. The process involved the fencing of common lands, the reclamation of previously untilled waste, and the transformation of strips into block fields. These procedures brought turmoil to the economic and social life of the countryside. Riots often ensued.

Because many English farmers either owned their strips or rented them in a manner that amounted to ownership, the larger landlords usually resorted to parliamentary acts to legalize the enclosure of the land, which they owned but rented to the farmers. Because the large landowners controlled Parliament, such measures passed easily. Between 1761 and 1792, almost 500,000 acres were enclosed through acts of Parliament, compared with 75,000 acres between 1727 and 1760. In 1801, a general enclosure act streamlined the process.

The enclosures were controversial at the time and have remained so among historians. They permitted the extension of both farming and innovation and thus increased food production on larger agricultural units. They also disrupted small traditional communities; they forced off the land independent farmers, who had needed the common pasturage, and poor cottage dwellers, who had lived on the reclaimed wasteland. The enclosures, however, did not depopulate the countryside. In some counties where the enclosures took place, the population increased. New soil had come into production, and services that supported farming also expanded.

The enclosures did not create the labor force for the British Industrial Revolution. What the enclosures most conspicuously displayed was the introduction of the entrepreneurial or capitalistic attitude of the urban merchant into the countryside. This commercialization of agriculture, which spread from Britain slowly across the Continent during the next century, strained the paternal relationship between the governing and governed classes. Previously, landlords had often looked after the welfare of the lower orders through price controls or waivers of rent during hard times. As the landlords became increasingly concerned about profits, they began to leave the peasants to the mercy of the marketplace.

Limited Improvements in Eastern Europe Improving agriculture tended to characterize farm production west of the Elbe River. Dutch farming was efficient. In France, despite the efforts of the government to improve agriculture, enclosures were restricted. Yet many people in France wanted to improve agricultural methods. These new procedures benefited the ruling classes because better agriculture increased their incomes and assured a larger food supply, which discouraged social unrest. (See "Compare & Connect: Two Eighteenth-Century Writers Contemplate the Effects of Different Economic Structures," pages 446–447.)

In Prussia, Austria, Poland, and Russia, agricultural improvement was limited. Nothing in the relationship of the serfs to their lords encouraged innovation. In eastern Europe, the chief method of increasing production was to bring previously untilled lands under the plow. The landlords or their agents, and not the villages, normally directed farm management. By extending tillage, the great landlords sought to squeeze more labor from their serfs, rather than greater productivity from the soil. Eastern European landlords, like their western counterparts, sought to increase their profits, but they were less ambitious and successful. The only significant nutritional gain they achieved was the introduction of maize and the potato. Livestock production did not increase significantly.

Expansion of the Population

The population explosion with which the entire world must contend today had its origins in the eighteenth century. Before that time, Europe's population had experienced dramatic increases, but plagues, wars, or famine had redressed the balance. Beginning in the second quarter of the eighteenth century, the population began to increase steadily. The need to feed this population caused food prices to rise, which spurred agricultural innovation. The need to provide everyday consumer goods for the expanding numbers of people fueled the demand side of the Industrial Revolution.

In 1700, Europe's population, excluding the European provinces of the Ottoman Empire, was probably between 100 million and 120 million people. By 1800, the figures had risen to almost 190 million and by 1850, to 260 million. The population of England and Wales rose from 6 million in 1750 to more than 10 million in 1800. France grew from 18 million in 1715 to about 26 million in 1789. Russia's population increased from 19 million in 1722 to 29 million in 1766. Such extraordinary sustained growth put new demands on all resources and considerable pressure on the existing social organization.

The population expansion occurred across the Continent in both the country and the cities. Only a limited consensus exists among scholars about the causes of this growth. The death rate clearly declined. There were fewer wars and epidemics in the eighteenth century. Hygiene and sanitation also improved. Better medical knowledge and techniques, however, did not contribute much to the decline in deaths. The more important medical advances came after the initial population explosion and would not have affected it directly.

Instead, changes in the food supply itself may have allowed population growth to be sustained. Improved and expanding grain production made one contribution. Another and even more important change was the cultivation of the potato. This tuber was a product of the New World and came into widespread European production during the eighteenth century. (See "The West & The World," page 489.) On a single acre, a peasant family could grow enough potatoes to feed itself for an entire year. This more certain food supply enabled more children to survive to adulthood and rear children of their own.

The impact of the population explosion can hardly be overestimated. It created new demands for food, goods, jobs, and services. It provided a new pool of labor. Traditional modes of production and living had to be revised. More people lived in the countryside than could find employment there. Migration increased. There were also more people who might become socially and politically discontented. Because the population growth fed on itself, these pressures and demands continued to increase. The society and the social practices of the Old Regime literally outgrew their traditional bounds.

Two Eighteenth-Century Writers Contemplate the Effects of Different Economic Structures

AMONG EIGHTEENTH-CENTURY public officials and commentators there existed a broad agreement that European economic life needed to be reorganized and stimulated to achieve greater productivity and wealth. These writers also understood that different modes of productive activity resulted in very different kinds of society. In these two documents a French writer bemoans problems of French agriculture and landholding while a Scottish writer praises the wealth and good society that flow from growing commerce and refinement of both mechanical and liberal arts.

QUESTIONS

1. **Why does Turgot favor those farmers who can make investments in the land they rent from a proprietor?**
2. **What are the structures of the métayer system? Why did it lead to poor investments and lower harvests?**
3. **Why does Hume link industry and the arts?**
4. **How does he see a commercial, improving economy producing important intellectual outlooks and social skills?**
5. **What benefits to agriculture might Hume have assigned to prosperous cities, and what benefits might Turgot have seen agriculture contributing to urban life?**

I. Turgot Decries French Landholding

During the eighteenth century, many observers became keenly aware that different kinds of landholding led to different attitudes toward work and to different levels of production and wealth. Robert Jacques Turgot (1727–1781), who later became finance minister of France, analyzed these differences in an effort to reform French agriculture. He was especially concerned with arrangements that encouraged long-term investment. The métayer *system Turgot discusses was an arrangement whereby landowners had land farmed by peasants who received part of the harvest as payment for working the land, but the peasant had no long-term interest in improving the land. Virtually all observers regarded the system as inefficient.*

1. What really distinguishes the area of large-scale farming from the areas of small-scale production is that in the former areas the proprietors find farmers who provide them with a permanent revenue from the land and who buy from them the right to cultivate it for a certain number of years. These farmers undertake all the expenses of cultivation, the ploughing, the sowing and the stocking of the farm with cattle, animals and tools. They are really agricultural entrepreneurs, who possess, like the entrepreneurs in all other branches of commerce, considerable funds, which they employ in the cultivation of land. . . .

   They have not only the brawn but also the wealth to devote to agriculture. They have to work, but unlike workers, they do not have to earn their living by the sweat of their brow, but by the lucrative employment of their capital, just as the ship owners of Nantes and Bordeaux employ theirs in maritime commerce.

2. *Métayer* System The areas of small-scale farming, that is to say at least four-sevenths of the kingdom, are those where there are no agricultural entrepreneurs, where a proprietor who wishes to develop his land cannot find anyone to cultivate it except wretched peasants who have no resources other than their labor, where he is obliged to make, at his own expense, all the advances necessary for tillage, beasts, tools, sowing, even to the extent of advancing to his *métayer* the wherewithal to feed himself until the first harvest, where consequently a proprietor who did not have any property other than his estate would be obliged to allow it to lie fallow.

   After having deducted the costs of sowing and feudal dues with which the property is burdened, the proprietor shares with the *métayer* what remains of the profits, in accordance with the agreement they have concluded. The proprietor runs all the risks of harvest failure and any loss of cattle: he is the real entrepreneur. The *métayer* is nothing more than a mere workman, a farm hand to whom the proprietor surrenders a share of his profits instead of paying wages. But in his work the proprietor enjoys none of the advantages of the farmer who, working on his own behalf, works carefully and diligently; the proprietor is obliged to entrust all his advances to a man who may be negligent or a scoundrel and is answerable for nothing.

This *métayer*, accustomed to the most miserable existence and without the hope and even the desire to obtain a better living for himself, cultivates badly and neglects to employ the land for valuable and profitable production; by preference he occupies himself in cultivating those things whose growth is less troublesome and which provide him with more foodstuffs, such as buckwheat and chestnuts which do not require any attention. He does not worry very much about his livelihood; he knows that if the harvest fails, his master will be obliged to feed him in order not to see his land neglected.

Source: From *(Œuvres, et documents les concernant*, by A. M. R. Turgot, ed. by F. Schelle, 5 vols. (Paris, 1914), Vol. II, pp. 448–450; *Documents of European Economic History*, as quoted and trans. by S. Pollard and C. Holmes (Edward Arnold, 1968), pp. 38–39.

This is the detail of a 1739 map by Louis Bretez, a member of the Academy of Painting and Sculpture, showing an aerial view of the city of Paris. The primary function of the map was to reestablish Paris as the universal model of a capital city. Library of Congress

II. David Hume Praises Luxury and the Refinement of the Arts

David Hume (1711–1776) was a Scottish philosopher, historian, and economic commentator. He was deeply committed to the modernization of the Scottish and wider European economy through the growth of commerce and the fostering of improved means of mechanical production. In this essay published in 1752 he outlined the beneficial social consequence he saw resulting from commercial wealth and new mechanical inventions. He believed such economic activity not only increased riches but also produced a population capable of providing a national defense. He was quite concerned to demonstrate that luxury and the economy that fostered it would not lead to moral decay.

In times when industry and the arts flourish, men are kept in perpetual occupation, and enjoy, as their reward, the occupation itself, as well as those pleasures which are the fruit of their labour. The mind acquires new vigour; enlarges its powers and faculties; and by an assiduity in honest industry, both satisfies its natural appetites, and prevents the growth of unnatural ones, which commonly spring up, when nourished by ease and idleness. . . .

Another advantage of industry and of refinements in the mechanical arts, is, that they commonly produce some refinements in the liberal; nor can one be carried to perfection, without being accompanied, in some degree, with the other. . . .

The more these refined arts advance, the more sociable men become . . . They flock into cities; love to receive and communicate knowledge; to show their wit or their breeding; their taste in conversation or living, in clothes or furniture. Curiosity allures the wise; vanity the foolish, and pleasure both. Particular clubs and societies are everywhere formed: Both sexes meet in an easy and sociable manner: and the tempers of men, as well as their behaviour, refine apace. So that, beside the improvements which they receive from knowledge and the liberal arts, it is impossible but they must feel an encrease of humanity, from the very habit of conversing together, and contributing to each other's pleasure and entertainment. Thus *industry*, *knowledge*, and *humanity*, are linked together by an indissoluble chain, and are found, from experience as well as reason, to be peculiar to the more polished, and, what are commonly denominated, the more luxurious ages. . . .

But industry, knowledge, and humanity are not advantageous in private life alone: They diffuse their beneficial influence on the *public*, and render the government as great and flourishing as they make individuals happy and prosperous. The encrease and consumption of all the commodities . . . are advantageous to society; because . . . they are a kind of *storehouse* of labour, which, in the exigencies of state, may be turned to the public service. In a nation, where there is no demand for such superfluities, men sink into indolence, lose all enjoyment of life, and are useless to the public, which cannot maintain or support its fleets and armies, from the industry of such slothful members.

Source: David Hume, "Of Refinement in the Arts (1752)," in *Essays: Moral, Political and Literary* (Indianapolis, IN: Liberty Classics, 1985), pp. 270–272.

▾ The Industrial Revolution of the Eighteenth Century

The second half of the eighteenth century witnessed the beginning of the industrialization of the European economy. That achievement of sustained economic growth is termed the ***Industrial Revolution***. Previously, the economy of a province or a country might grow, but growth soon reached a plateau. Since the late eighteenth century, however, the economy of Europe has managed to expand at an almost uninterrupted pace. Depressions and recessions have been temporary, and even during such economic downturns, the Western economy has continued to grow.

At considerable social cost, industrialization made possible the production of more goods and services than ever before in human history. Industrialization in Europe eventually overcame the economy of scarcity. The new means of production demanded new kinds of skills, new discipline in work, and a large labor force. The goods produced met immediate consumer demand and also created new demands. In the long run, industrialization raised the standard of living and overcame the poverty that most Europeans, who lived during the eighteenth century and earlier, had taken for granted. It gave human beings greater control over nature than they had ever known before; yet by the mid-nineteenth century, industrialism would also cause new and unanticipated problems with the environment.

Consumption of all forms of consumer goods increased greatly in the eighteenth century. This engraving illustrates a shop, probably in Paris. Here women, working apparently for a woman manager, are making dresses and hats to meet the demands of the fashion trade. As the document on page 454 demonstrates, some women writers urged more such employment opportunities for women. Bildarchiv Preussischer Kulturbesitz

During the eighteenth century, people did not call these economic developments a *revolution.* That term came to be applied to the British economic phenomena only after the French Revolution. Then continental writers observed that what had taken place in Britain was the economic equivalent of the political events in France, hence an Industrial Revolution. It was revolutionary less in its speed, which was on the whole rather slow, than in its implications for the future of European society.

A Revolution in Consumption

The most familiar side of the Industrial Revolution was the invention of new machinery, the establishment of factories, and the creation of a new kind of workforce. Recent studies, however, have emphasized the demand side of the process and the vast increase in both the desire and the possibility of consuming goods and services that arose in the early eighteenth century.

The inventions of the Industrial Revolution increased the supply of consumer goods as never before in history. The supply of goods was only one side of the economic equation, however. An unprecedented demand for the humble goods of everyday life created the supply. Those goods included clothing, buttons, toys, china, furniture, rugs, kitchen utensils, candlesticks, brassware, silverware, pewterware, glassware, watches, jewelry, soap, beer, wines, and foodstuffs. It was the ever-increasing demand for these goods that sparked the ingenuity of designers and inventors. Furthermore, consumer demand seemed unlimited. (See "David Hume Praises Luxury and the Refinement of the Arts," page 447.)

Many social factors helped establish the markets for these consumer goods. During the seventeenth century, the Dutch had enjoyed enormous prosperity and had led the way in new forms of consumption. For reasons that are still not clear, during the eighteenth century, first the English and then the people on the Continent came to have more disposable income. This wealth may have resulted from the improvements in agriculture. Those incomes allowed people to buy consumer goods that previous generations had inherited or did not possess. What is key to this change in consumption is that it depended primarily on expanding the various domestic markets in Europe.

This revolution, if that is not too strong a term, in consumption was not automatic. People became persuaded that they needed or wanted new consumer goods. Often, entrepreneurs caused it to happen by developing new methods of marketing. For example, the English porcelain manufacturer

Josiah Wedgwood (1730–1795) first attempted to find customers among the royal family and the aristocracy. Once he had gained their business with luxury goods, he then produced a less expensive version of the chinaware for middle-class customers. He also used advertising, opened showrooms in London, and sent salespeople all over Britain with samples and catalogs of his wares. On the Continent, his salespeople used bilingual catalogs. There seemed to be no limit to the markets for consumer goods that social emulation on the one hand and advertising on the other could stimulate.

Furthermore, the process of change in style itself became institutionalized. New fashions and inventions were always better than old ones. If new kinds of goods could be produced, there usually was a market for them. If one product did not find a market, its failure provided a lesson for how to develop a different new product.

This expansion of consumption quietly, but steadily, challenged the social assumptions of the day. Fashion publications made all levels of society aware of new styles. Clothing fashions could be copied. Servants could begin to dress well if not luxuriously. Changes in the consumption of food and drink demanded new kinds of dishware for the home. Tea and coffee became staples. The brewing industry became fully commercialized. Those developments entailed the need for new kinds of cups and mugs and many more of them.

There would always be critics of this consumer economy. The vision of luxury and comfort it offered contrasted with the asceticism of ancient Sparta and contemporary Christian ethics. Yet, the ever-increasing consumption and production of the goods of everyday life became hallmarks of modern Western society from the eighteenth century to our own day. It would be difficult to overestimate the importance of the desire for consumer goods and the higher standard of living that they made possible in Western history after the eighteenth century. The presence and accessibility of such goods became the hallmark of a nation's prosperity. It was the absence of such consumer goods, as well as of civil liberties, that during the 1980s led to such deep discontent with the communist regimes in Eastern Europe and the former Soviet Union.

Industrial Leadership of Great Britain

Great Britain was the home of the Industrial Revolution and, until the middle of the nineteenth century, remained the industrial leader of Europe. Several factors contributed to the early start in Britain.

Great Britain took the lead in the **consumer revolution** that expanded the demand for goods that could be efficiently supplied. London was the largest city in Europe. It was the center of a world of fashion and taste to which hundreds of thousands, if not millions, of British citizens were exposed each year. In London, these people learned to want the consumer goods they saw on visits for business and pleasure. Newspapers thrived in Britain during the eighteenth century, and the advertising they printed increased consumer wants. The social structure of Britain encouraged people to imitate the lifestyles of their social superiors. It seems to have been in Britain that a world of fashion first developed that led people to want to accumulate goods. In addition to the domestic consumer demand, the British economy benefited from demand from the colonies in North America.

Britain was also the single largest free-trade area in Europe. The British had good roads and waterways without internal tolls or other trade barriers. The country had rich deposits of coal and iron ore. Its political structure was stable, and property was absolutely secure. The sound systems of banking and public credit established a stable climate for investment. Taxation in Britain was heavy, but it was efficiently and fairly collected, largely from indirect taxes. Furthermore, British taxes received legal approval through Parliament, with all social classes and all regions of the nation paying the same taxes. In contrast to the Continent, there was no pattern of privileged tax exemptions.

Finally, British society was mobile by the standards of the time. Persons who had money or could earn it could rise socially. The British aristocracy would receive into its ranks people who had amassed large fortunes. Even persons of wealth who did not join the aristocracy could enjoy their riches, receive social recognition, and exert political influence. No one of these factors preordained the British advance toward industrialism. Together, however, when added to the progressive state of British agriculture, they provided the nation with the marginal advantage to create a new mode of economic production.

New Methods of Textile Production

The industry that pioneered the Industrial Revolution and met the growing consumer demand was the production of textiles for clothing. Textile production is the key example of industrialism emerging to supply the demands of an ever-growing market for everyday goods. Furthermore, it illustrates the surprising fact that much of the earliest industrial change took place not in cities, but in the countryside.

Although the eighteenth-century economy was primarily agricultural, manufacturing also permeated rural areas. The peasant family living in a one- or two-room cottage, rather than the factory, was the basic unit of production. The same peasants who tilled the land in spring and summer often spun thread or wove textiles in the winter.

Under what is termed the ***domestic***, or putting-out, ***system of textile production***, agents of urban textile merchants took wool or other unfinished fibers to the homes of peasants, who spun it into thread. The agent then transported the thread to other peasants, who wove it into the finished product. The merchant sold the wares. In thousands of peasant cottages from Ireland to

MANCHESTER'S CALICO PRINTERS PROTEST THE USE OF NEW MACHINERY

The introduction of the new machines associated with the Industrial Revolution stirred much protest. With machines able to duplicate the skills of laborers, workers feared the loss of jobs and the resulting loss of status when their chief means of livelihood lay in their possession of those displaced and now mechanized skills. The following letter was sent anonymously to a Manchester manufacturer by English workers. It shows the outrage of those workers, the intimidation they were willing to use as threats, and their own economic fears.

How might new machines adversely affect the livelihood of workers? Did the workers have other complaints against Mr. Taylor in addition to the introduction of new machinery? How have these workers reached an agreement to protect the interests of James Hobson? How do the workers combine the threat of violent actions with claims that other actions they have taken are legal?

Mr. Taylor, If you dont discharge James Hobson from the House of Correction we will burn your House about your Ears for we have sworn to stand by one another and you must immediately give over any more Mashen Work for we are determined there shall be no more of them made use of in the Trade and it will be madness for you to contend with the Trade as we are combined by Oath to fix Prices we can afford to pay him a Guinea Week and not hurt the fund if you was to keep him there till Dumsday therefore mind you comply with the above or by God we will keep our Words with you we will make some rare Bunfires in this Countey and at your Peril to call any more Meetings mind that we will make the Mosney Pepel shake in their Shoes we are determined to destroy all Sorts of Masheens for Printing in the Kingdom for there is more hands then is work for so no more from the ingerd Gurnemen Rember we are a great number sworn nor you must not advertise the Men that you say run away from you when your il Usage was the Cause of their going we will punish you for that our Meetings are legal for we want nothing but what is honest and to work for selvs and familers and you want to starve us but it is better for you and a few more which we have marked to die then such a Number of Pore Men and their fameries to be starved.

London Gazette, 1786, p. 36, as reprinted in Douglas Hay, ed., *Albion's Fatal Tree* (New York: Pantheon Books, 1975), p. 318.

Austria, there stood a spinning wheel or a hand loom. Sometimes the spinners or weavers owned their own equipment, but more often than not by the middle of the century, the merchant capitalist owned the machinery as well as the raw material.

The domestic system of textile production was a basic feature of this family economy and would continue to be so in Britain and on the Continent well into the nineteenth century. By the mid-eighteenth century, however, production bottlenecks had developed within the domestic system. The demand for cotton textiles was growing more rapidly than production, especially in Britain, which had a large domestic and North American market for these goods. Inventors devised some of the most famous machines of the early Industrial Revolution to meet consumer demand for cotton textiles.

The Spinning Jenny Cotton textile weavers had the technical capacity to produce the quantity of fabric demanded. The spinners, however, did not have the equipment to produce as much thread as the weavers needed. John Kay's invention of the flying shuttle, which increased the productivity of the weavers, had created this imbalance during the 1730s. Thereafter, manufacturers and merchants offered prizes for the invention of a machine to eliminate this bottleneck.

About 1765, James Hargreaves (d. 1778) invented the **spinning jenny**. Initially, this machine allowed 16 spindles of thread to be spun, but by the close of the century, it could operate 120 spindles.

The Water Frame The spinning jenny broke the bottleneck between the productive capacity of the

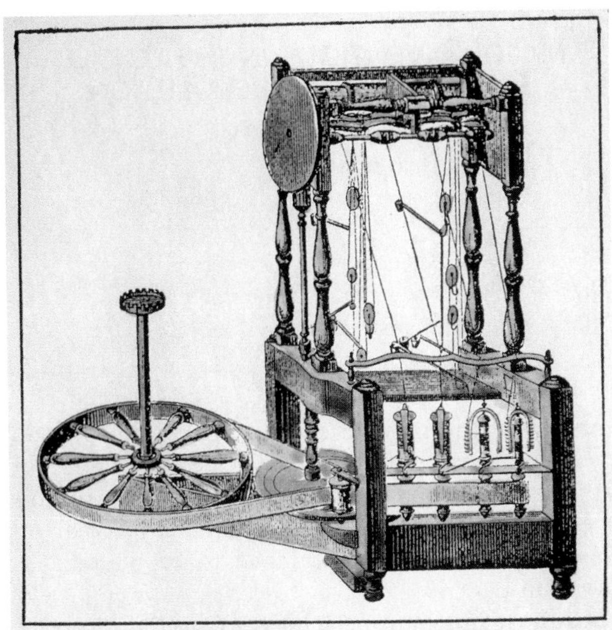

James Hargreaves's spinning jenny permitted the spinning of numerous spindles of thread on a single machine. AKG London Ltd.

spinners and the weavers, but it was still a piece of machinery used in the cottage. The invention that took cotton textile manufacture out of the home and put it into the factory was Richard Arkwright's (1732–1792) **water frame**, patented in 1769. This was a water-powered device designed to permit the production of a purely cotton fabric, rather than a cotton fabric containing linen fiber for durability. Eventually Arkwright lost his patent rights, and other manufacturers used his invention freely. As a result, many factories sprang up in the countryside near streams that provided the necessary water power. From the 1780s onward, the cotton industry could meet an ever-expanding demand. Cotton output increased by 800 percent between 1780 and 1800. By 1815, cotton composed 40 percent of the value of British domestic exports and by 1830, just over 50 percent.

The Industrial Revolution had commenced in earnest by the 1780s, but the full economic and social ramifications of this unleashing of human productive capacity were not really felt until the early nineteenth century. The expansion of industry and the incorporation of new inventions often occurred slowly. For example, Edmund Cartwright (1743–1822) invented the power loom for machine weaving in the late 1780s. Yet not until the 1830s were there more power-loom weavers than hand-loom weavers in Britain. Nor did all the social ramifications of industrialism appear immediately. The first cotton mills used water power, were located in the country, and rarely employed more than two dozen workers. Not until the late-century application of the steam engine, perfected by James Watt (1736–1819) in 1769, to run textile machinery could factories easily be located in or near urban centers. The steam engine not only vastly increased and regularized the available energy, but also made possible the combination of urbanization and industrialization.

The Steam Engine

More than any other invention, the steam engine permitted industrialization to grow on itself and to expand into one area of production after another. This machine provided for the first time in human history a steady and essentially unlimited source of inanimate power. Unlike engines powered by water or wind, the steam engine, driven by burning coal, provided a portable source of industrial power that did not fail or falter as the seasons of the year changed. Unlike human or animal power, the steam engine depended on mineral energy that never tired. Finally, the steam engine could be applied to many industrial and, eventually, transportation uses.

Thomas Newcomen (1663–1729) in the early eighteenth century had invented the first practical engine to use steam power. When the steam that had been induced into the cylinder condensed, it caused the piston of this device to fall. The Newcomen machine was large and inefficient in its use of energy because both the condenser and the cylinder were heated, and practically untransportable. Despite these problems, English mine operators used the Newcomen machines to pump water out of coal and tin mines. By the third quarter of the eighteenth century, almost a hundred Newcomen machines were operating in the mining districts of England.

During the 1760s, James Watt, a Scottish engineer and machine maker, began to experiment with a model of a Newcomen machine at the University of Glasgow. He gradually understood that separating the condenser from the piston and the cylinder would achieve much greater efficiency. In 1769, he patented his new invention, but transforming his idea into a practical application presented difficulties. His design required precise metalwork. Watt soon found a partner in Matthew Boulton (1728–1809), a successful toy and button manufacturer in Birmingham, the city with the most skilled metalworkers in Britain. Watt and Boulton, in turn, consulted with John Wilkinson (1728–1808), a cannon manufacturer, to drill the precise metal cylinders Watt's design required. In 1776, the Watt steam engine found its first commercial application pumping water from mines in Cornwall.

The use of the steam engine spread slowly because until 1800 Watt retained the exclusive patent rights. He was also reluctant to make further changes to permit the engine to operate more rapidly. Boulton eventually persuaded him to make modifications and improvements that allowed the engines to be used not only for pumping, but also for running cotton mills. By the early nineteenth century, the steam engine had become the prime mover for all industry. With its application to ships and then to wagons on iron rails, the steam engine also revolutionized transportation.

Iron Production

The manufacture of high-quality iron has been basic to modern industrial development. Iron is the chief element of all heavy industry and of land or sea transport. Most productive machinery itself is also manufactured from iron. During the early eighteenth century, British ironmakers produced somewhat less than 25,000 tons of iron annually. Three factors held back the production. First, charcoal rather than coke was used to smelt the ore. Charcoal, derived from wood, was becoming scarce as forests in Britain diminished, and it does not burn at as high a temperature as coke, derived from coal. Second, until the perfection of the steam engine, furnaces could not achieve high enough blasts. Finally, the demand for iron was limited. The elimination of the first two problems also eliminated the third.

Eventually, British ironmakers began to use coke, and the steam engine provided new power for the blast furnaces. Coke was an abundant fuel because of Britain's large coal deposits. The steam engine both improved iron production and increased the demand for iron.

In 1784, Henry Cort (1740–1800) introduced a new puddling process, that is, a new method for melting and stirring molten ore. Cort's process allowed the removal of more slag (the impurities that bubbled to the top of the molten metal) and thus the production of purer iron. Cort also developed a rolling mill that continuously shaped the still-molten metal into bars, rails, or other forms. Previously, the metal had to be pounded into these forms.

All these innovations achieved a better, more versatile, cheaper product. The demand for iron consequently grew. By the early nineteenth century, the British produced over a million tons annually. The lower cost of iron, in turn, lowered the cost of steam engines and allowed them to be used more widely.

MAJOR INVENTIONS IN THE TEXTILE-MANUFACTURING REVOLUTION

1733	John Kay's flying shuttle
1765	James Hargreaves's spinning jenny (patented 1770)
1769	James Watt's steam engine patent
1769	Richard Arkwright's water frame patent
1787	Edmund Cartwright's power loom

During the eighteenth century, most goods were produced in small workshops, such as this iron forge painted by Joseph Wright of Derby (1734–1797), or in the homes of artisans. Not until very late in the century, with the early stages of industrialization, did a few factories appear. In the small early workshops, it would not have been uncommon for the family of the owner to visit, as portrayed in this painting. *The Iron Forge*, 1772 (oil on canvas) by Joseph Wright of Derby (1734–1797). Broadlands Trust, Hampshire, UK/Bridgeman Art Library, London

The Impact of the Agricultural and Industrial Revolutions on Working Women

The transformation of agriculture and industry led to a series of seemingly modest changes that, taken collectively, diminished the importance and the role of those women already in the workforce.

Women had been an important part of traditional European agriculture. They worked in and often were permitted to glean the grain left over after the general harvest. Women also managed industries like milking and cheese production. However, primarily in Western Europe, increasing commercialization and mechanization eroded these traditional roles. Machinery operated by men displaced the work of women in the field and their skills in dairying and home industry, particularly in Britain. Even nonmechanized labor came to favor men. For example, during the late eighteenth century, heavy scythes wielded by men replaced the lighter sickles that women had used to harvest grain. Moreover, the drive to maximize profits led landlords to enclose lands and curtail customary rights like gleaning.

This transformation of farming constricted women's ability to earn their living from the land. Women came to be viewed as opponents of agricultural improvement because these improvements hurt them economically. As a result, proponents of the new agriculture often demeaned the role of women in farming and their related work. Indeed, the vast literature on agricultural improvement specifically advocated removing women from the agricultural workforce.

A similar process took place in textile manufacturing, where mechanization deprived many women of one of their most traditional means of earning income. Before mechanization thousands of women worked at spinning wheels to produce thread that hand-loom weavers, who were often their husbands, then wove. The earlier, small spinning jennies did not immediately disrupt this situation because women could use them in the loft of a home, but the larger ones required a factory setting where men often ran the machinery. As a result, most women spinners were put out of work, and those women who did move into the factory labor force performed less skilled work than men. In the long run, however, the mechanization of spinning left many other women without one of their most traditional means of earning income.

Many working women, displaced from spinning thread or from farming, slowly turned to cottage industries, such as knitting, button making, straw plaiting, bonnet making, or glove stitching, that invariably earned them less than their former occupations had. In later generations, women who earlier would have been spinners or farm workers moved directly into cottage industries. The work and skills these occupations involved were considered inferior; and because it paid so poorly, women who did this work might become prostitutes or engage in other criminal activity. Consequently, the reputations and social standing of many working women suffered.

Among women who did not work in the cottage industries, thousands became domestic servants in the homes of landed or commercial families. During the nineteenth century, such domestic service became the largest area of female employment. It was far more respectable than the cottage industries but was isolated from the technologically advanced world of factory manufacture or transport.

By the end of the eighteenth century, the work and workplaces of men and women were becoming increasingly separate and distinct. In this respect, many people, such as the English writer Priscilla Wakefield (1750–1832), believed the kinds of employment open to women had narrowed. Wakefield called for new occupations for women. (See "Priscilla Wakefield Demands More Occupations for Women," on page 454.)

This shift in female employment, or what one historian has termed "this defamation of women workers,"[2] produced several long-term results. First, women's work, whether in cottage industries or domestic service, became associated with the home rather than with places where men worked. Second, the laboring life of most women was removed from the new technologies in farming, transportation, and manufacturing. Woman's work thus appeared traditional, and people assumed women could do only such work. Third, during the nineteenth and early twentieth centuries, Europeans also assumed most women worked only to supplement a husband's income. Finally, because the work women did was considered marginal and only as supplementing a male income, men were paid much more than women. Most people associate the Industrial Revolution with factories, but for many working women, these revolutions led to a life located more in homes than ever before. Indeed, in the nineteenth century, one, though only one, motive behind efforts to restrict the hours and improve the conditions of women in factories was the belief that it was bad for them to be there in the first place. The larger picture of the relationship of the new industrial workplace to family life will be addressed in Chapter 21.

[2]Deborah Valenze, *The First Industrial Woman* (New York: Oxford University Press, 1995), p. 183.

▼ The Growth of Cities

Remarkable changes occurred in the pattern of city growth between 1500 and 1800. In 1500, within Europe (excluding Hungary and Russia) 156 cities had a population greater than 10,000. Only four of those cities—Paris, Milan, Venice, and Naples—had populations larger than 100,000. By 1800, 363 cities had 10,000 or more inhabitants, and 17 of them had populations larger than 100,000. The percentage of the European population living in urban areas had risen from just over 5 percent to just over 9 percent. A major shift in urban concentration from southern, Mediterranean Europe to the north had also occurred.

Patterns of Preindustrial Urbanization

The eighteenth century witnessed a considerable growth of towns, closely related to the tumult of the day and the revolutions with which the century closed. London grew from about 700,000 inhabitants in 1700 to almost 1 million in 1800. By the time of the French Revolution, Paris had more than 500,000 inhabitants. Berlin's population tripled during the century, reaching 170,000 in 1800. Warsaw had 30,000 inhabitants in 1730, but almost 120,000 in 1794. St. Petersburg, founded in 1703, numbered more than 250,000 inhabitants a century later. The number of smaller cities with 20,000 to 50,000 people also increased considerably. This urban growth must, however, be kept in perspective. Even in France and Great Britain, probably somewhat less than 20 percent of the population lived in cities. And the town of 10,000 inhabitants was much more common than the giant urban center.

PRISCILLA WAKEFIELD DEMANDS MORE OCCUPATIONS FOR WOMEN

At the end of the eighteenth century, Priscilla Wakefield was one of several English women writers who began to demand a wider life for women. She was concerned that women found themselves able to pursue only occupations that paid poorly. They were often excluded from work because of their alleged physical weakness. She also believed women should receive equal wages for equal work. These issues reflected a narrowing of opportunities for women that had occurred in England during the second half of the eighteenth century. As a result of the mechanization of both agriculture and the textile industry, many found traditional occupations were closing to women. Wakefield is thus addressing a general question of opportunities available to women and more recent developments. Many of the issues she raised have yet to be adequately addressed.

What arguments were used at the end of the eighteenth century to limit the kinds of employment that women might enter? Why did women receive less pay than men for similar or the same work? What occupations traditionally filled by men does Wakefield believe women might also pursue?

Another heavy discouragement to the industry of women, is the inequality of the reward of their labor, compared with that of men; an injustice which pervades every species of employment performed by both sexes.

In employments which depend on bodily strength, the distinction is just; for it cannot be pretended that the generality of women can earn as much as men, when the produce of their labor is the result of corporeal exertion; but it is a subject of great regret, that this inequality should prevail even where an equal share of skill and application is exerted. Male stay-makers, mantua-makers, and hair-dressers, are better paid than female artists of the same professions; but surely it will never be urged as an apology for this disproportion, that women are not as capable of making stays, gowns, dressing hair, and similar arts, as men; if they are not superior to them, it can only be accounted for upon this principle, that the prices they receive for their labor are not sufficient to repay them for the expense of qualifying themselves for their business; and that they sink under the mortification of being regarded as artisans of inferior estimation. . . .

Besides these employments which are commonly performed by women, and those already shown to be suitable for such persons as are above the condition of hard labor, there are some professions and trades customarily in the hands of men, which might be conveniently exercised by either sex. Watchmaking requiring more ingenuity than strength, seems peculiarly adapted to women; as do many parts of the business of stationer, particularly, ruling account books or making pens. The compounding of medicines in an apothecary's shop, requires no other talents than care and exactness; and if opening a vein occasionally be an indispensable requisite, a woman may acquire the capacity of doing it, for those of her own sex at least, without any reasonable objection. . . . Pastry and confectionery appear particularly consonant to the habits of women, though generally performed by men; perhaps the heat of the ovens, and the strength requisite to fill and empty them, may render male assistants necessary; but certain women are most eligible to mix up the ingredients, and prepare the various kinds of cakes for baking. Light turnery and toy-making depend more upon dexterity and invention than force, and are therefore suitable work for women and children. . . .

Farming, as far as respects the theory, is commensurate with the powers of the female mind: nor is the practice of inspecting agricultural processes incompatible with the delicacy of their frames if their constitution be good.

Priscilla Wakefield, *Reflections on the Present Condition of the Female Sex* (1798) (London, 1817), pp. 125–127, as quoted in Bridget Hill, ed., *Eighteenth-Century Women: An Anthology* (London: George Allen & Unwin, 1984), pp. 227–228.

These raw figures conceal significant changes that took place in how cities grew and how the population redistributed itself. The major urban development of the sixteenth century had been followed by a leveling off, and even a decline, in the seventeenth. New growth began in the early eighteenth century and accelerated during the late eighteenth and the early nineteenth centuries.

Between 1500 and 1750, major urban expansion took place within already established and generally already large cities. After 1750, the pattern changed with the birth of new cities and the rapid growth of older, smaller cities.

Growth of Capitals and Ports In particular, between 1600 and 1750, the cities that grew most vigorously were capitals and ports. This situation reflects the success of monarchical state building during those years and the consequent burgeoning of bureaucracies, armies, courts, and other groups who lived in the capitals. The growth of port cities, in turn, reflects the expansion of European overseas trade—especially, that of the Atlantic routes. Except for Manchester in England and Lyons in France, the new urban conglomerates were nonindustrial cities.

Furthermore, between 1600 and 1750, cities with populations of fewer than 40,000 inhabitants declined. These included older landlocked trading centers, medieval industrial cities, and ecclesiastical centers. They contributed less to the new political regimes, and the expansion of the putting-out system transferred production from medieval cities to the countryside because rural labor was cheaper than urban labor.

The Emergence of New Cities and the Growth of Small Towns In the mid-eighteenth century, a new pattern emerged. The rate of growth of existing large cities declined, new cities emerged, and existing smaller cities grew. Several factors were at work in the process, which Jan De Vries has termed "an urban growth from below."[3] First was the general overall population increase. Second, the early stages of the Industrial Revolution, particularly in Britain, occurred in the countryside and fostered the growth of smaller towns and cities located near factories. Factory organization itself led to new concentrations of population.

Cities also grew as a result of the new prosperity of European agriculture, even where there was little industrialization. Improved agricultural production promoted the growth of nearby market towns and other urban centers that served agriculture or allowed more prosperous farmers to have access to consumer goods and recreation. This new pattern of urban growth—new cities and the expansion of smaller existing ones—would continue into the nineteenth century.

[3]Jan De Vries, "Patterns of Urbanization in Pre-Industrial Europe, 1500–1800," in H. Schmal, ed., *Patterns of Urbanization since 1500* (London: Croom Helm, 1981), p. 103.

Urban Classes

Social divisions were as marked in eighteenth-century cities as they were in nineteenth-century industrial centers. The urban rich were often visibly segregated from the urban poor. Aristocrats and the upper middle class lived in fashionable town houses, often constructed around newly laid-out green squares. The poorest town dwellers usually congregated along the rivers. Small merchants and artisans lived above their shops. Whole families might live in a single room. Modern sanitary facilities were unknown. Pure water was rare. Cattle, pigs, goats, and other animals roamed the streets. All reports on the cities of Europe during this period emphasize both the striking grace and beauty of the dwellings of the wealthy and the dirt, filth, and stench that filled the streets. (See "Encountering the Past: Water, Washing, and Bathing," page 456.)

Poverty was not just an urban problem; it was usually worse in the countryside. In the city, however, poverty was more visible in the form of crime, prostitution, vagrancy, begging, and alcoholism. Many a young man or woman from the countryside migrated to the nearest city to seek a better life, only to discover poor housing, little food, disease, degradation, and finally death. It did not require the Industrial Revolution and the urban factories to make the cities into hellholes for the poor and the dispossessed. The full darkness of London life during the mid-century "gin age," when consumption of that liquor blinded and killed many poor people, is evident in the engravings of William Hogarth (1697–1764).

Also contrasting with the serenity of the aristocratic and upper-commercial-class lifestyle were the public executions that took place all over Europe, the breaking of men and women on instruments of torture in Paris, and the public floggings in Russia. Brutality condoned and carried out by the ruling classes was a fact of everyday life.

The Upper Classes At the top of the urban social structure stood a generally small group of nobles, large merchants, bankers, financiers, clergy, and government officials. These upper-class men controlled the political and economic affairs of the town. Normally, they constituted a self-appointed and self-electing oligarchy that governed the city through its corporation or city council. Some form of royal charter usually gave the city corporation its authority and the power to select its own members. In a few cities on the Continent, artisan guilds controlled the corporations, but generally, the local nobility and the wealthiest commercial people dominated the councils.

The Middle Class Another group in the city was the prosperous, but not always immensely wealthy, merchants, trades people, bankers, and professional people. They were the most dynamic element of the urban

WATER, WASHING, AND BATHING

BEFORE THE LATE nineteenth century, clean water was scarce in Europe. Except for the few households and institutions that had their own wells, water had to be carried from a public fountain or public well. Drought in summer and freezing in winter could lead to shortages.

Governments made little effort to provide water. Everyone assumed that people required little water for their personal use—less than 7.5 liters per day, according to one eighteenth-century commentator. (The average American uses 210 liters per day.) Commerce and agriculture used much more water than individuals: to power mills in the cloth and dye trades, and to quench the thirst of work animals and irrigate fields.

Attitudes toward personal appearance also determined the use of water. In the Middle Ages, public bathhouses were not uncommon. The appearance of the body—cleanliness—was believed to reflect the state of the soul, and townspeople and aristocrats bathed fairly often. However, during the Renaissance and the Reformation, the quality and condition of clothing, not bodily cleanliness, were thought to mirror the soul. Clean clothes also revealed a person's social status—clothes made the man and the woman.

Moreover, from the late Middle Ages through the end of the eighteenth century, etiquette and medical manuals advised people to wash only those parts of their bodies that could be seen in public—the hands, the face, the neck, and the feet. All forms of public bathing were associated with immoral behavior—public bathing meant public nudity, and prostitutes frequented bathhouses.

The switch from woolen to linen clothing accompanied the decline in bathing. By the sixteenth century, easily washable linen clothing had begun to replace woolen garments in much of Western Europe. Clean linen shirts or blouses allowed persons who had not bathed to appear clean. Possession of large quantities of freshly laundered linens was a sign of high social status.

Appearance thus became more important than bodily hygiene. Medical opinion supported these practices. Physicians believed odors or *miasma* (bad air), such as might be found in soiled linens—along with lice, fleas, and other vermin—caused disease. One should therefore change one's shirt every few days but avoid baths, which might let the bad air enter the body through the open pores. Consequently, in an age in which there were practically no personal bathtubs, thousands of shirts were washed each week, almost always by female laundresses, in every city.

Attitudes toward bathing only began to change toward the middle of the eighteenth century when writers argued that frequent bathing might lead to greater health. Large public baths, such as had been known in the ancient world and were a fixture of the Ottoman Empire, revived during the nineteenth century, and the germ theory of disease led health authorities to urge people to bathe often to rid their bodies of germs. The great water projects of the nineteenth century (see Chapter 23) would assure vast quantities of water for personal hygiene.

Source: Daniel Roche, *The Culture of Clothing: Dress and Fashion in the "Ancien Regime"* (Cambridge: Cambridge University Press, 1994); Georges Vigarello, *Concepts of Cleanliness: Changing Attitudes in France since the Middle Ages* (Cambridge: Cambridge University Press, 1988); Alain Corbin, *The Foul and the Fragrant: Odor and the French Social Imagination* (Cambridge, MA: Harvard University Press, 1988).

Why did bathing become less frequent after the late Middle Ages? How did the use of linen clothing contribute to this change?

In the eighteenth century washing linen clothing by hand was a major task of women servants. J. B. S. Chardin, *The Washerwoman*. Nationalmuseum med Prins Eugens Waldemarsudde. Photo: The National Museum of Fine Arts population and made up the middle class, or bourgeoisie. The concept of the middle class was much less clear-cut than that of the nobility. The middle class itself was and would remain diverse and divided, with persons employed in the professions often resentful of those who drew their incomes from commerce. Less wealthy members of the middle class of whatever occupation resented wealthier members who might be connected to the nobility through social or business relationships.

The middle class had less wealth than most nobles, but more than urban artisans. Middle-class people lived in the cities and towns, and their sources of income had little or nothing to do with the land. In one way or another, they all benefited from expanding trade and commerce, whether as merchants, lawyers, or small-factory owners. Theirs was a world in which earning and saving of money enabled rapid social mobility and change in lifestyle. They saw themselves as willing to put their capital and energy to work, whereas they portrayed the nobility as idle. The members of the middle class tended to be economically aggressive and socially ambitious. People often made fun of them for these characteristics and were jealous of their success. The middle class normally supported reform, change, and economic growth. They also wanted more rational regulations for trade and commerce, as did some progressive aristocrats.

The middle class was made up of people whose lives fostered the revolution in consumption. On one hand, as owners of factories and of wholesale and retail businesses, they produced and sold goods for the expanding consumer market; on the other hand, members of the middle class were among the chief consumers. It was to their homes that the vast array of new consumer goods made their way. They were also the people whose social values most fully embraced the commercial spirit. They might not enjoy the titles or privileges of the nobility, but they could enjoy material comfort and prosperity. It was this style of life that less well-off people could emulate as they sought to acquire consumer goods for themselves.

During the eighteenth century, the relationship between the middle class and the aristocracy was complicated. On one hand, the nobles, especially in England and France, increasingly embraced the commercial spirit associated with the middle class by improving their estates and investing in cities. On the other hand, wealthy members of the middle class often tried to imitate the lifestyle of the nobility by purchasing landed estates. The aspirations of the middle class for social mobility, however, conflicted with the determination of the nobles to maintain and reassert their own privileges and to protect their own wealth. Middle-class commercial figures—traders, bankers, manufacturers, and lawyers—often found their pursuit of profit and prestige blocked by the privileges of the nobility and its social exclusiveness, by the inefficiency of monarchical bureaucracies dominated by the nobility, or by aristocrats who controlled patronage and government contracts.

The bourgeoisie was not rising to challenge the nobility; rather, both were seeking to increase their existing political power and social prestige. The tensions that arose between the nobles and the middle class during the eighteenth century normally involved issues of power sharing or access to political influence, rather than clashes over values or goals associated with class.

The middle class in the cities also feared the lower urban classes as much as they envied the nobility. The lower orders were a potentially violent element in society, a threat to property, and, in their poverty, a drain on national resources. The lower classes, however, were much more varied than either the city aristocracy or the middle class cared to admit.

Artisans Shopkeepers, artisans, and wage earners were the single largest group in any city. They were grocers, butchers, fishmongers, carpenters, cabinetmakers, smiths, printers, hand-loom weavers, and tailors, to give a few examples. They had their own culture, values, and institutions. Like the peasants, they were, in many

This engraving illustrates a metalworking shop such as might have been found in almost any town of significance in Europe. Most of the people employed in the shop probably belonged to the same family. Note that two women are also working. The wife may very well have been the person in charge of keeping the accounts of the business. The two younger boys might be children of the owner or apprentices in the trade, or both. The Granger Collection, New York respects, conservative. Their economic position was vulnerable. If a poor harvest raised the price of food, their own businesses suffered. These urban classes also contributed to the revolution in consumption, however. They could buy more goods than ever before, and, to the extent their incomes permitted, many of them sought to copy the domestic consumption of the middle class.

The lives of these artisans and shopkeepers centered on their work and their neighborhoods. They usually lived near or at their place of employment. Most of them worked in shops with fewer than a half dozen other artisans. Their primary institution had historically been the guild, but by the eighteenth century, the guilds rarely exercised the influence their predecessors had in medieval or early modern Europe.

Nevertheless, the guilds were not to be ignored. They played a conservative role. Rather than seeking economic growth or innovation, they tried to preserve the jobs and skills of their members. In many countries, the guilds still determined who could pursue a craft. To lessen competition, they attempted to prevent too many people from learning a particular skill.

The guilds also provided a framework for social and economic advancement. At an early age, a boy might become an apprentice to learn a craft or trade. After several years, he would be made a journeyman. Still later, if successful and competent, he might become a master. The artisan could also receive social benefits from the guilds, including aid for his family during sickness or the promise of admission for his son. The guilds were the chief protection for artisans against the workings of the commercial market. They were particularly strong in central Europe.

The Urban Riot

The artisan class, with its generally conservative outlook, maintained a rather fine sense of social and economic justice based largely on traditional practices. If they felt that what was economically "just" had been offended, artisans frequently manifested their displeasure by rioting. The most sensitive area was the price of bread, the staple food of the poor. If a baker or a grain merchant announced a price that was considered unjustly high, a riot might well ensue. Artisan leaders would confiscate the bread or grain and sell it for what the urban crowd considered a "just price." They would then give the money paid for the grain or bread to the baker or merchant.

The danger of bread riots restrained the greed of merchants. Such disturbances represented a collective method of imposing the "just price" in place of the price the commercial marketplace set. Thus, bread and food riots, which occurred throughout Europe, were not irrational acts of screaming, hungry people, but highly ritualized social phenomena of the Old Regime and its economy of scarcity.

Other kinds of riots also characterized eighteenth-century society and politics. The riot was a way in which people who were excluded in every other way from the political processes could make their will known. Sometimes religious bigotry led to urban riots. For example, in 1753, London Protestant mobs compelled the government to withdraw an act to legalize Jewish naturalization. In 1780, the same rabidly Protestant spirit manifested itself in the Gordon riots. Lord George Gordon (1751–1793) had raised the specter of an imaginary Catholic plot after the government relieved military recruits from having to take specifically anti-Catholic oaths.

In these riots and in food riots, violence was normally directed against property rather than people. The rioters themselves were not disreputable people but usually small shopkeepers, freeholders, artisans, and wage earners. They usually wanted only to restore a traditional right or practice that seemed endangered. Nevertheless, their actions could cause considerable turmoil and destruction.

During the last half of the century, urban riots increasingly involved political ends. Though often simultaneous with economic disturbances, the political riot always had nonartisan leadership or instigators. In fact, an eighteenth-century "crowd" was often the tool of the upper classes. In Paris, the aristocratic *Parlement* often urged crowd action in its disputes with the monarchy. In Geneva, middle-class citizens supported artisan riots against the local oligarchy. In Great Britain in 1792, the government incited mobs to attack English sympathizers of the French Revolution. Such outbursts indicate that the crowd or mob had entered the European political and social arena well before the revolution in France.

▼ The Jewish Population: The Age of the Ghetto

Although the small Jewish communities of Amsterdam and other Western European cities became famous for their intellectual life and financial institutions, most European Jews lived in Eastern Europe. In the eighteenth century and thereafter, the Jewish population of Europe was concentrated in Poland, Lithuania, and Ukraine, where no fewer than 3 million Jews dwelled. Perhaps 150,000 Jews lived in the Habsburg lands, primarily Bohemia, around 1760. Fewer than 100,000 Jews lived in Germany. France had approximately 40,000 Jews. England and Holland, each had a Jewish population of fewer than 10,000. There were even smaller groups of Jews elsewhere.

In 1762, Catherine the Great of Russia specifically excluded Jews from a manifesto that welcomed foreigners to settle in Russia. She relaxed the exclusion a few years later, but Jews during her reign often felt they needed assurances of imperial protection for their livelihoods and religious practices against the ordinances of local officials. (See "Belorussian Jews Petition Catherine

During the Old Regime, European Jews were separated from non-Jews, typically in districts known as ghettos. Relegated to the least desirable section of a city or to rural villages, most lived in poverty. This watercolor painting depicts a street in Kazimlesz, the Jewish quarter of Kraków, Poland. Judaica Collection, Max Berger, Vienna, Austria. Photograph © Erich Lessing/Art Resource, NY

the Great," page 460.) After the first partition of Poland of 1772, discussed in Chapter 17, the Russian Empire included a large Jewish population, and the number of Jews in Prussia and under Austrian rule also increased.

Jews dwelled in most nations without enjoying the rights and privileges that other subjects had unless monarchs specifically granted them to Jews. Jews were regarded as a kind of resident alien whose residence might well be temporary or changed at the whim of rulers.

No matter where they dwelled, Old Regime Jews lived apart in separate communities from non-Jewish Europeans. These communities might be distinct districts of cities, known as **ghettos**, or in primarily Jewish villages in the countryside. Jews were also treated as a distinct people religiously and legally. In Poland for much of the century, they were virtually self-governing. In other areas, they lived under the burden of discriminatory legislation. Except in England, Jews could not and did not mix in the mainstream of the societies in which they dwelled. This period, which may be said to have begun with the expulsion of the Jews from Spain at the end of the fifteenth century, is known as the age of the ghetto, or separate community.

During the seventeenth century, a few Jews had helped finance the wars of major rulers. These financiers often became close to the rulers and were known as "court Jews." Perhaps the most famous was Samuel Oppenheimer (1630–1703), who helped the Habsburgs finance their struggle against the Turks and the defense of Vienna. However, these loans were often not repaid. The court Jews and their financial abilities became famous. They tended to marry among themselves.

Most European Jews, however, lived in poverty. They occupied the most undesirable sections of cities or poor villages. Some were small-time moneylenders, but most worked at the lowest occupations. Their religious beliefs, rituals, and community set them apart. Virtually all laws and social institutions kept them socially inferior to and apart from their Christian neighbors.

Under the Old Regime, it is important to emphasize that this discrimination was based on religious separateness. Jews who converted to Christianity were welcomed, even if not always warmly, into the major political and social institutions of Gentile European society. Until the last two decades of the eighteenth century, in every part of Europe, however, those Jews who remained loyal to their faith were subject to various religious, civil, and social disabilities. They could not pursue the professions freely, they often could not change residence without official permission, and they were excluded from the political structures of the nations in which they lived. Jews could be expelled from their homes, and their property could be confiscated. They could be required to listen to sermons that insulted their religion. Their children could be taken away from them and given Christian instruction. They knew their non-Jewish neighbors might suddenly turn against them and kill them.

In subsequent chapters, it will be shown how the end of the Old Regime brought major changes in the lives of European Jews and in their relationship to the larger culture.

In Perspective

Near the close of the eighteenth century, European society was on the brink of a new era. That society had remained traditional and corporate largely because of an economy of scarcity. Beginning in the eighteenth century, however, the commercial spirit and the values of the marketplace, although not new, were permitted fuller play

BELORUSSIAN JEWS PETITION CATHERINE THE GREAT

In the 1780s, through military expansion, Empress Catherine the Great of Russia (see Chapter 17) annexed Belorussia, bringing a new Jewish minority under her imperial government. In response to her decree, governing many aspects of the region's law and economy, Belorussian Jews petitioned the empress to protect certain of their traditional rights regarding the distillation and sale of spirits. They also petitioned for protection in court and for the right to retain their own traditional practices and courts for matters relating to their own community. The petition indicates how in Russia, as elsewhere in Europe, Jews were treated as a people apart. It also illustrates how Jews, like other minorities in Old Regime Europe, sought both to receive the protection of monarchies against arbitrary local officials and to maintain long-standing social practices. The document reveals the Jews' dependence on the goodwill of the non-Jewish community.

How do the petitioners attempt to appeal to long-standing custom to defend their interests? How does the petition suggest that Jewish law and practice, distinct from the rest of the society, governed Jewish social life? In the context of this petition, which non-Jewish authorities may actually or potentially influence Jewish life?

2.

According to an ancient custom, when the squires built a new village, they summoned the Jews to reside there and gave them certain privileges for several years and then permanent liberty to distill spirits, brew beer and mead, and sell these drinks. On this basis, the Jews built houses and distillation plants at considerable expense. . . . A new decree of Her Imperial Majesty . . . reserved [this right] to the squires. . . . But a decree of the governor-general of Belorussia has now forbidden the squires to farm out distillation in their villages to Jews, even if the squires want to do this. As a result, the poor Jews who built houses in small villages and promoted both this trade and distillation have been deprived of these and left completely impoverished. But until all the Jewish people are totally ruined, the Jewish merchants suffer restraints equally with the poor rural Jews, since their law obliges them to assist all who share their religious faith. They therefore request an imperial decree authorizing the squire, if he wishes, to farm out distillation to Jews in rural areas.

3.

Although, with Her Imperial Majesty's permission, Jews may be elected as officials . . . , Jews are allotted fewer votes than other people and hence no Jew can ever attain office. Consequently, Jews have no one to defend them in courts and find themselves in a desperate situation—given their fear and ignorance of Russian—in case of misfortune, even if innocent. To consummate all the good already bestowed, Jews dare to petition that an equal number of electors be required from Jews as from others (or, at least, that in matters involving Jews and non-Jews, a representative from the Jewish community hold equal rights with non-Jews, be present to accompany Jews in court, and attend the interrogation of Jews). But cases involving only Jews (except for promissory notes and debts) should be handled solely in Jewish courts, because Jews assume obligations among themselves, make agreements and conclude all kinds of deals in the Jewish language and in accordance with Jewish rites and laws (which are not known to others). Moreover, those who transgress their laws and order should be judged in Jewish courts. [Similarly, preserve intact all their customs and holidays in the spirit of their faith, as is mercifully assured in the imperial manifesto.]

than ever before in European history. The newly unleashed commercial spirit led increasingly to a conception of human beings as individuals rather than as members of communities. In particular, that spirit manifested itself in the Agricultural and Industrial Revolutions, as well as in the drive toward greater consumption. Together, those two vast changes in production overcame most of the scarcity that had haunted Europe and the West generally. The accompanying changes in landholding and production would transform the European social structure.

The expansion of population further stimululated change. More people meant more labor, more energy, and more minds contributing to the creation and solution of social difficulties. Cities had to accommodate expanding populations. Corporate groups, such as the guilds, had to confront the existence of a larger labor force. New wealth meant that birth would eventually become less and less a determining factor in social relationships, except for the social roles assigned to the two sexes. Class structure and social hierarchy remained, but the boundaries became more blurred.

Finally, the conflicting ambitions of monarchs, the nobility, and the middle class generated innovation. In the pursuit of new revenues, the monarchs interfered with the privileges of the nobles. In the name of ancient rights, the nobles attempted to secure and expand their existing social privileges. The middle class, in all of its diversity, was growing wealthier from trade, commerce, and the practice of the professions. Its members wanted social prestige and influence equal to their wealth. They resented privileges, frowned on hierarchy, and rejected tradition.

All these factors meant the society of the eighteenth century stood at the close of one era in European history and at the opening of another.

REVIEW QUESTIONS

1. What kinds of privileges separated European aristocrats from other social groups? How did their privileges and influence affect other people living in the countryside? What was the condition of serfs in central and eastern Europe?
2. How would you define the term *family economy*? How did the family economy constrain the lives of women in preindustrial Europe?
3. What caused the Agricultural Revolution? How did the English aristocracy contribute to the Agricultural Revolution? Why did peasants revolt in the eighteenth century?
4. Why did Europe's population increase in the eighteenth century? How did population growth affect consumption?
5. What was the Industrial Revolution and what caused it? Why did Great Britain take the lead in the Industrial Revolution? How did consumers contribute to the Industrial Revolution?
6. How did the distribution of population in cities and towns change? How did the lifestyle of the upper class compare to that of the middle and lower classes? What were some of the causes of urban riots?
7. Where were the largest Jewish populations in eighteenth-century Europe? What was their social and legal position? What were the sources of prejudices against Jews?

SUGGESTED READINGS

J. Blum, *Lord and Peasant in Russia from the Ninth to the Nineteenth Century* (1961). Remains a classic discussion.

J. Burnet, *Gender, Work and Wages in Industrial Revolution Britain* (2008). A major revisionist study of the wage structure for work by men and women.

P. M. Deane, *The First Industrial Revolution* (1999). A well-balanced and systematic treatment.

P. Earle, *The Making of the English Middle Class: Business, Community, and Family Life in London, 1660–1730* (1989). The most careful study of the subject.

M. W. Flinn, *The European Demographic System, 1500–1820* (1981). Remains a major summary.

E. Hobsbawm, *Industry and Empire: The Birth of the Industrial Revolution* (1999). A survey by a major historian of the subject.

K. Honeyman, *Women, Gender and Industrialization in England, 1700–1850* (2000). Emphasizes how certain work or economic roles became associated with either men or women.

O. H. Hufton, *The Poor of Eighteenth-Century France, 1750–1789* (1975). A brilliant study of poverty and the family economy.

A. Kahan, *The Plow, the Hammer, and the Knout: An Economic History of Eighteenth-Century Russia* (1985). An extensive and detailed treatment.

D. I. Kertzer and M. Barbagli, *The History of the European Family: Family Life in Early Modern Times, 1500–1709* (2001). Broad-ranging essays covering the entire Continent.

S. King and G. Timmons, *Making Sense of the Industrial Revolution: English Economy and Society, 1700–1850* (2001). Examines the Industrial Revolution through the social institutions that brought it about and were changed by it.

F. E. Manuel, *The Broken Staff: Judaism Through Christian Eyes* (1992). An important discussion of Christian interpretations of Judaism.

K. Morgan, *The Birth of Industrial Britain: Social Change, 1750–1850* (2004). A useful brief overview.

M. Overton, *Agricultural Revolution in England: The Transformation of the Agrarian Economy, 1500–1850* (1996). A highly accessible treatment.

J. R. Ruff, *Violence in Early Modern Europe 1500–1800* (2001). An excellent survey of an important and disturbing topic.

P. Stearns, *The Industrial Revolution in World History* (2007). A broad interpretive account.

D. Valenze, *The First Industrial Woman* (1995). An elegant, penetrating volume.

E. A. Wrigley, *Continuity, Chance and Change: The Character of the Industrial Revolution in England* (1994). A major conceptual reassessment.

General James Wolfe was mortally wounded during his victory over the French at Quebec in 1759. This painting by the American artist Benjamin West (1738–1820) became famous for portraying the dying Wolfe and the officers around him in poses modeled after classical statues. Getty Images Inc.—Hulton Archive Photos

16

The Transatlantic Economy, Trade Wars, and Colonial Rebellion

▼ **Periods of European Overseas Empires**

▼ **Mercantile Empires**
Mercantilist Goals • French–British Rivalry

▼ **The Spanish Colonial System**
Colonial Government • Trade Regulation • Colonial Reform under the Spanish Bourbon Monarchs

▼ **Black African Slavery, the Plantation System, and the Atlantic Economy**
The African Presence in the Americas • Slavery and the Transatlantic Economy • The Experience of Slavery

▼ **Mid-Eighteenth-Century Wars**
The War of Jenkins's Ear • The War of the Austrian Succession (1740–1748) • The "Diplomatic Revolution" of 1756 • The Seven Years' War (1756–1763)

▼ **The American Revolution and Europe**
Resistance to the Imperial Search for Revenue • The Crisis and Independence • American Political Ideas • Events in Great Britain • Broader Impact of the American Revolution

▼ **In Perspective**

KEY TOPICS

- **Europe's mercantilist empires**
- **Spain's vast colonial empire in the Americas**
- **Africa, slavery, and the transatlantic plantation economies**
- **The wars of the mid-eighteenth century in Europe and its colonies**
- **The struggle for independence in Britain's North American colonies**

THE MID-EIGHTEENTH century witnessed a renewal of European warfare on a worldwide scale. The conflict involved two separate, but interrelated, rivalries. Austria and Prussia fought for dominance in central Europe while Great Britain and France dueled for commercial and colonial supremacy. The wars were long, extensive, and costly in both effort and money. They resulted in a new balance of power on the Continent and on the high seas. Prussia emerged as a great power, and Great Britain gained a world empire.

The expense of these wars led every major European government after the Peace of Paris of 1763 to reconstruct its policies of taxation and finance. Among the results of these policies were the American Revolution, an enlightened absolutism on the Continent, a continuing financial crisis for the French monarchy, and a reform of the Spanish Empire in South America.

▼ Periods of European Overseas Empires

Since the Renaissance, European contacts with the rest of the world have gone through four distinct stages. The first was that of the European discovery, exploration, initial conquest, and settlement of the New World. This phase also witnessed the penetration of Southeast Asian markets by Portugal and the Netherlands, which established major imperial outposts and influence in the region. This period closed by the end of the seventeenth century. (See Chapter 10.)

The second era—that of the mercantile empires, which are largely the concern of this chapter—was one of colonial trade rivalry among Spain, France, and Great Britain. Although during the sixteenth and seventeenth centuries differing motives had led to the establishment of overseas European empires, by the eighteenth century they generally existed to foster trade and commerce. These commercial goals, however, often sparked intense rivalry and conflict in key imperial trouble spots. As a result, the various imperial ventures led to the creation of large navies and a series of major naval wars at the mid-century—wars that in turn became linked to warfare on the European continent. The Anglo-French side of the contest has often been compared to a second Hundred Years' War, with theaters of conflict in Europe, the Americas, West Africa, and India.

A fundamental element in these first two periods of European imperial ventures in the Americas was the presence of slavery. By the eighteenth century, the slave population of the New World consisted almost entirely of a black population that had either recently been forcibly imported from Africa or born to slaves whose forebearers had been forcibly imported from Africa. Both the forced migration of so many people from one continent to another and the mid-Atlantic **plantation economies** that such slave labor supported were unprecedented in history. The creation in the Americas of this slave-based plantation economy led directly to over three centuries of extensive involvement by Europeans and white Americans in the slave trade with Africa—particularly, with the societies of West Africa. In turn, on the American continent the slave trade created extensive communities of Africans from the Chesapeake region of Maryland and Virginia south to Brazil. The Africans brought to the American experience not only their labor, but also their languages, customs, and ethnic associations. The Atlantic economy and the societies that arose in the Americas were, consequently, the creation of both Europeans and Africans while, as a result of the Spanish conquest, Native Americans were pressed toward the margins of those societies. In this respect from the sixteenth century onward Africans became a significant factor in the forging of the Western Heritage as commodities in the slave trade that enriched western European economies and as laborers in the New World plantation economy, the wealth and products of which enriched the daily life of peoples in Europe and European settlers and their descendants in the Americas.

Finally, during the second period, both the British colonies of the North American seaboard and the Spanish colonies of Mexico and Central and South America emancipated themselves from European control. This era

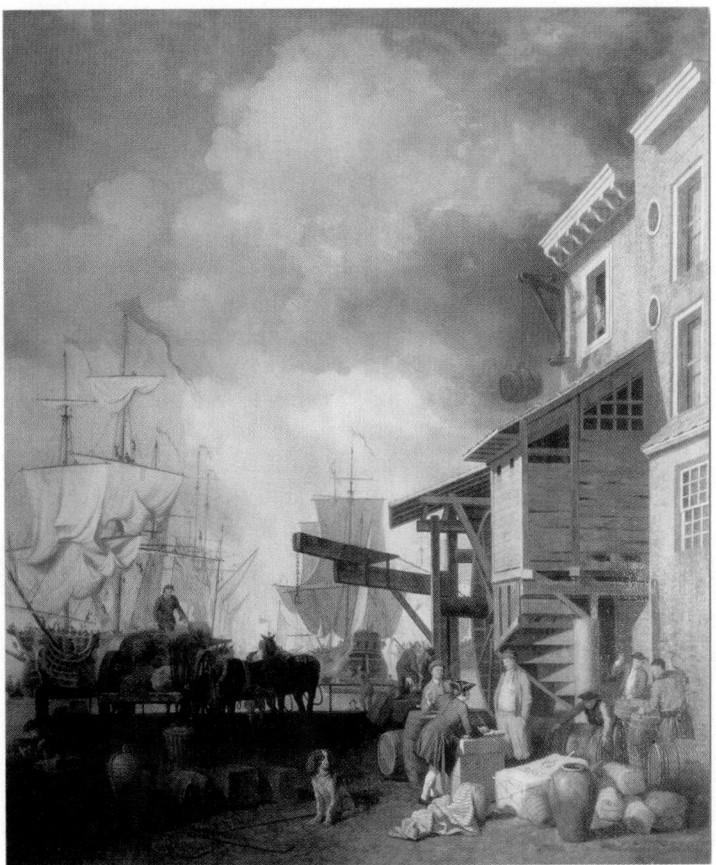

During the seventeenth and eighteenth centuries, European maritime nations established overseas empires and set up trading monopolies within them in an effort to magnify their economic strength. As this painting of the Old Custom House Quay in London suggests, trade from these empires and the tariffs imposed on it were expected to generate revenue for the home country. But behind many of the goods carried in the great sailing ships in the harbor and landed on these docks lay the labor of African slaves working on the plantations of North and South America. Samuel Scott "Old Custom House Quay" Collection. V & A Images, The Victoria and Albert Museum, London of independence, part of which is discussed in this chapter and part in Chapter 20, may be said to have closed during the 1820s. This same revolutionary era witnessed the beginning of the antislavery movement that extended through the third quarter of the nineteenth century. (See "The West and the World: The Abolition of Slavery in the Transatlantic Economy," p. 655.)

The third stage of European contact with the non-European world occurred in the nineteenth century. During that period, European governments largely turned from their involvement in the Americas and carved out new formal empires involving the direct European administration of indigenous peoples in Africa and Asia. Those nineteenth-century empires also included new areas of European settlement, such as Australia, New Zealand, South Africa, and Algeria. The bases of these empires were trade, national honor, Christian missionary enterprise, and military strategy. Unlike the previous two eras, the nineteenth-century empires were based on formally free labor forces though they still involved much harsh treatment of non-white indigenous populations. (See Chapter 25.)

The last period of the European empire occurred during the mid- and late twentieth century, with the decolonization of peoples who had previously lived under European colonial rule. (See Chapter 29.)

During the four-and-one-half centuries before decolonization, Europeans exerted political, military, and economic dominance over much of the rest of the world that was far disproportional to the geographical size or population of Europe. Europeans frequently treated other peoples as social, intellectual, economic, and racial inferiors. Europeans ravaged existing cultures because of greed, religious zeal, or political ambition. These actions are major facts of both European and world history and remain significant factors in the contemporary relationship between Europe and its former colonies, as well as between the United States and those former colonies. What allowed the Europeans initially to exert such influence and domination for so long over so much of the world was not any innate cultural superiority, but a technological supremacy related to naval power and gunpowder. Ships and guns allowed the Europeans to exercise their will almost wherever they chose.

▼ Mercantile Empires

Navies and merchant shipping were the keystones of the mercantile empires that were meant to bring profit to a nation rather than to provide areas for settlement. The Treaty of Utrecht (1713) established the boundaries of empire during the first half of the eighteenth century.

Except for Brazil, which Portugal governed, and Dutch Guiana, Spain controlled all of mainland South America. In North America, it ruled Florida, Mexico, California, and the Southwest. The Spanish also governed Central America and the islands of Cuba, Puerto Rico, Trinidad, and the eastern part of Hispaniola that is today the Dominican Republic.

The British Empire consisted of the colonies along the North Atlantic seaboard, Nova Scotia, Newfoundland, Bermuda, Jamaica, and Barbados. Britain also possessed a few trading stations on the Indian subcontinent.

The French domains covered the Saint Lawrence River valley and the Ohio and Mississippi River valleys. They included the West Indian islands of Saint Domingue (modern Haiti on the western part of Hispaniola), Guadeloupe, and Martinique, and also stations in India and on the West Coast of Africa. To the French and British merchant communities, India appeared as a vast potential market for European goods, as well as the source of calico cloth and spices that were in much demand in Europe.

The Dutch controlled Surinam, or Dutch Guiana, in South America, Cape Colony in what is today South Africa, and trading stations in West Africa, Sri Lanka, and Bengal in India. Most importantly, they also controlled the trade with Java in what is now Indonesia. The Dutch had opened these markets largely in the seventeenth century and had created a vast trading empire far larger in extent, wealth, and importance than the geographical size of the United Netherlands would have led one to expect. The Dutch had been daring sailors and they made important technological innovations in sailing.

All of these powers and the Danes also possessed numerous smaller islands in the Caribbean. In the eighteenth century, the major rivalries existed among the Spanish, the French, and the British.

Mercantilist Goals

If any formal economic theory lay behind the conduct of eighteenth-century empires, it was **mercantilism**, that practical creed of hard-headed businesspeople. The terms *mercantilism* and *mercantile system* were invented by later opponents and critics of the system whereby governments heavily regulated trade and commerce in hope of increasing national wealth. Economic writers believed this system necessary for a nation to gain a favorable trade balance of gold and silver bullion. They regarded bullion as the measure of a country's wealth, and a nation was truly wealthy only if it amassed more bullion than its rivals.

The mercantilist statesmen and traders regarded the world as an arena of scarce resources and economic limitations. Mercantilist thinking assumed that only modest levels of economic growth were possible. Such thinking predated the expansion of agricultural and later industrial productivity discussed in the previous chapter. Before such sustained economic growth began, the wealth of one nation was assumed to grow or increase largely at the direct expense of another nation. That is to say, the wealth of one state might expand only if its armies or navies conquered the domestic or colonial territory of another state and thus gained the productive capacity of that area, or if a state expanded its trading monopoly over new territory, or if, by smuggling, it could intrude on the trading monopoly of another state.

From beginning to end, the economic well-being of the home country was the primary concern of mercantilist writers. Colonies existed to provide markets and natural resources for the industries of the home country. In turn, the home country was to protect and administer the colonies. Both sides assumed the colonies were the inferior partner in the relationship. The home country and its colonies were to trade exclusively with each other. To that end, governments tried to forge trade-tight systems of national commerce through navigation laws, tariffs, bounties to encourage production, and prohibitions against trading with the subjects of other monarchs. National monopoly was the ruling principle.

Mercantilist ideas had always been neater on paper than in practice. By the early eighteenth century, mercantilist assumptions were far removed from the economic realities of the colonies. The colonial and home markets simply did not mesh. Spain could not produce enough goods for South America. Economic production in the British North American colonies challenged English manufacturing and led to British attempts to limit certain colonial industries, such as iron and hat making.

Colonists of different countries wished to trade with each other. English colonists could buy sugar more cheaply from the French West Indies than from English suppliers. The traders and merchants of one nation always hoped to break the monopoly of another. For all these reasons, the eighteenth century became what one historian many years ago termed the "golden age of smugglers."[1] Governments could not effectively control their subjects' activities. Clashes among colonists could and did bring about conflict between European governments.

French–British Rivalry

Major flash points existed between France and Britain in North America. Their colonists quarreled endlessly with each other over the coveted regions of the lower Saint Lawrence River valley, upper New England, and, later, the Ohio River valley. Other rivalries arose over fishing rights, the fur trade, and alliances with Native Americans.

The heart of the eighteenth-century colonial rivalry in the Americas, however, lay in the West Indies. These tropical islands, close to the American continents, were the jewels of empire. The West Indies plantations raised tobacco, cotton, indigo, coffee, and, above all, sugar, for which there existed huge markets in Europe. These commodities were becoming part of daily life, especially in Western Europe. They represented one aspect of those major changes in consumption that marked eighteenth-century European culture. Sugar in particular had become a staple rather than a luxury. It was used in coffee, tea, and cocoa, for making candy and preserving fruits, and in the brewing industry. There seemed no limit to its uses, no limit to consumer demand for it, and, for a time, almost no limit to the riches it might bring to plantation owners. Only slave labor allowed the profitable cultivation of these products during the seventeenth and eighteenth centuries. (See "Encountering the Past: Sugar Enters the Western Diet," page 471.)

India was another area of French–British rivalry. In India, both France and Britain traded through privileged chartered companies that enjoyed a legal monopoly. The East India Company was the English institution; the French equivalent was the *Compagnie des Indes.* The trade of India and Asia figured only marginally in the economics of early eighteenth-century empire. Nevertheless, enterprising Europeans always hoped to develop profitable commerce with India. Others regarded India as a springboard into the even larger potential market of China. The original European footholds in India were trading posts called *factories.* They existed through privileges granted by various Indian governments that in theory were themselves subject to the decaying Mughal Empire, which exercised little effective authority.

Two circumstances in the mid-eighteenth century changed this situation in India. First, the administration and government of several Indian states had decayed. Second, Joseph Dupleix (1697–1763) for the French and Robert Clive (1725–1774) for the British saw the developing power vacuum as providing opportunities for expanding the control of their respective companies. To maintain their own security and to expand their privileges, each of the two companies began in effect to take over the government of some of the regions. Each group of Europeans hoped to checkmate the other.

The Dutch maintained their extensive commercial empire further to the east in what today is Indonesia. By the eighteenth century, the other European powers more or less acknowledged Dutch predominance in that region.

▼ The Spanish Colonial System

Spanish control of its American Empire involved a system of government and a system of monopolistic trade regulation. Both were more rigid in appearance than in practice. Actual government was often informal, and the trade monopoly was frequently breached. Until the mid-eighteenth century, the primary purpose of the Spanish Empire was to supply Spain with the precious metals mined in the New World.

[1]Walter Dorn, *Competition for Empire, 1740–1763* (New York: Harper, 1940), p. 266.

Colonial Government

Because Queen Isabella of Castile (r. 1474–1504) had commissioned Columbus, the technical legal link between the New World and Spain was the crown of Castile. Its powers both at home and in America were subject to few limitations. The Castilian monarch assigned the government of America to the Council of the Indies, which, with the monarch, nominated the viceroys of New Spain (Mexico) and Peru. These viceroys served as the chief executives in the New World and carried out the laws issued by the Council of the Indies.

Each of the viceroyalties was divided into several subordinate judicial councils, known as *audiencias.* There was also a variety of local officers, the most important of which were the *corregidores,* who presided over municipal councils. All of these officers represented a vast array of patronage, which the monarchy usually bestowed on persons born in Spain. Virtually all power flowed from the top of this political structure downward; in effect, local initiative or self-government scarcely existed.

Trade Regulation

The colonial political structures functioned largely to support Spanish commercial self-interests. The *Casa de Contratación* (House of Trade) in Seville regulated all trade with the New World. Cádiz was the only port authorized for use in the American trade. The *Casa* was the most influential institution of the Spanish Empire. Its members worked closely with the *Consulado* (Merchant Guild) of Seville and other groups involved with American commerce in Cádiz.

A complicated system of trade and bullion fleets administered from Seville maintained Spain's trade monopoly. Each year, a fleet of commercial vessels (the *flota*), controlled by Seville merchants and escorted by warships, carried merchandise from Spain to a few specified ports in America, including Portobello, Veracruz, and Cartagena on the Atlantic coast. There were no authorized ports on the Pacific Coast. Areas far to the south, such as Buenos Aires on the Río de la Plata, received goods only after the shipments had been unloaded at one of the authorized ports. After selling their wares, the ships were loaded with silver and gold bullion; they usually spent the winter in heavily fortified Caribbean ports and then sailed back to Spain. The *flota* system always worked imperfectly, but trade outside it was illegal. Regulations prohibited the Spanish colonists within the American Empire from establishing direct trade with each other and from building their own shipping and commercial industry. Foreign merchants were also forbidden to breach the Spanish monopoly. Spanish ships continued to transport precious metals and coins from the Americas to Spain through the early nineteenth century. Modern day treasure hunters still occasionally discover troves of precious metal from shipwrecked vessels of the colonial Spanish Empire.

Colonial Reform under the Spanish Bourbon Monarchs

A crucial change occurred in the Spanish colonial system in the early eighteenth century. The War of the Spanish Succession (1701–1714) and the Treaty of Utrecht (1713) replaced the Spanish Habsburgs with the Bourbons of France on the Spanish throne. Philip V (r. 1700–1746) and his successors tried to use French administrative skills to reassert the imperial trade monopoly, which had decayed under the last Spanish Habsburgs, and thus to improve the domestic economy and revive Spanish power in Europe.

Under Philip V, Spanish coastal patrol vessels tried to suppress smuggling in American waters. (See "Buccaneers Prowl the High Seas.") An incident arising from this policy led to war with England in 1739, the year in which Philip established the viceroyalty of New Granada in the area that today includes Venezuela, Colombia, and Ecuador. The goal was to strengthen the royal government there.

The great mid-century wars exposed the vulnerability of the Spanish empire to naval attack and economic penetration. As an ally of France, Spain emerged as one of the defeated powers in 1763. Government circles then became convinced that the colonial system had to be reformed.

Charles III (r. 1759–1788), the most important of the imperial reformers, attempted to reassert Spain's control of the empire. Like his Bourbon predecessors, Charles emphasized royal ministers rather than councils. Thus, the role of both the Council of the Indies and the *Casa de Contratación* diminished. After 1765, Charles abolished the monopolies of Seville and Cádiz and permitted other Spanish cities to trade with America. He also opened more South American and Caribbean ports to trade and authorized commerce between Spanish ports in America. In 1776, he organized a fourth viceroyalty in the region of Río de la Plata, which included much of present-day Argentina, Uruguay, Paraguay, and Bolivia. (See Map 16–1, page 468.)

To increase the efficiency of tax collection and end bureaucratic corruption, Charles III introduced the institution of the *intendant* into the Spanish Empire. These loyal, royal bureaucrats were patterned on the domestic French *intendants* made so famous and effective as agents of French royal administration under the absolutism of Louis XIV.

The late-eighteenth-century Bourbon reforms did stimulate the imperial Spanish economy. Trade expanded and became more varied. These reforms, however, also brought the empire more fully under direct Spanish control. Many ***peninsulares*** (persons born in Spain) entered

BUCCANEERS PROWL THE HIGH SEAS

Piracy was a major problem for transatlantic trade. There was often a fine line between freewheeling buccaneering pirates operating for their own gain and privateers who in effect worked for various European governments that wanted to penetrate the commercial monopoly of the Spanish Empire. Alexander Exquemelin was a ship's surgeon who for a time plied his trade on board a pirate ship and then later settled in Holland. His account of those days emphasizes the careful code of conduct among the pirates themselves and the harshness of their behavior toward both those on ships they captured and poor farmers and fishermen whom they robbed and virtually enslaved.

How did the restrictive commercial policy of the Spanish Empire encourage piracy and privateering? Was there a code of honor among the pirates? What kinds of people may have suffered most from piracy? To what extent did pirates have any respect for individual freedom? How romantic was the real world of pirates?

When a buccaneer is going to sea he sends word to all who wish to sail with him. When all are ready, they go on board, each bringing what he needs in the way of weapons, powder, and shot.

On the ship, they first discuss where to go and get food supplies. . . . The meat is either [salted] pork or turtle. . . . Sometimes they go and plunder the Spaniards' *corrales*, which are pens where they keep perhaps a thousand head of tame hogs. The rovers. . . find the house of the farmer. . . [whom] unless he gives them as many hogs as they demand, they hang. . . without mercy. . . .

When a ship has been captured, the men decide whether the captain should keep it or not: if the prize is better than their own vessel, they take it and set fire to the other. When a ship is robbed, nobody must plunder and keep the loot to himself. Everything taken. . . must be shared. . . , without any man enjoying a penny more than his fair share. To prevent deceit, before the booty is distributed everyone has to swear an oath on the Bible that he has not kept for himself so much as the value of a sixpence. . . . And should any man be found to have made a false oath, he would be banished from the rovers, and never be allowed in their company. . . .

When they have captured a ship, the buccaneers set the prisoners on shore as soon as possible, apart from two or three whom they keep to do the cooking and other work they themselves do not care for, releasing these men after two or three years.

The rovers frequently put in for fresh supplies at some island or other, often . . . lying off the south coast of Cuba. . . . Everyone goes ashore and sets up his tent, and they take turns to go on marauding expeditions in their canoes. They take prisoner. . . poor men who catch and set turtles for a living, to provide for their wives and children. Once captured, these men have to catch turtle for the rovers as long as they remain on the island. Should the rovers intend to cruise along a coast where turtle abound, they take the fishermen along with them. The poor fellows may be compelled to stay away from their wives and families four or five years, with no news whether they are alive or dead.

Alexander O. Exquemelin, *The Buccaneers of America*, trans. by Alexis Brown (Baltimore, MD: Penguin Books, 1969), pp. 70–72.

the New World to fill new posts, which were often the most profitable jobs in the region. Expanding trade brought more Spanish merchants to Latin America. The economy remained export oriented, and their economic life was still organized to benefit Spain. As a result of these policies, the **creoles** (persons of European descent born in the Spanish colonies) came to feel they were second-class subjects. In time, their resentment would provide a major source of the discontent leading to the wars of independence in the early nineteenth century. The imperial reforms of Charles III were the Spanish equivalent of the new colonial measures the British government undertook after 1763, which, as will be seen later in this chapter, led to the American Revolution.

MAP EXPLORATION

Interactive map: To explore this map further, go to **www.myhistorylab.com**

Map 16–1 **VICEROYALTIES IN LATIN AMERICA IN 1780** The late eighteenth-century viceroyalties in Latin America display the effort of the Spanish Bourbon monarchy to establish more direct control of the colonies. They sought this control through the introduction of more royal officials and by establishing more governmental districts.

The Silver Mines of Potosí. The Spanish had discovered precious metals in their South American Empire early in the sixteenth century. The silver mines of Potosi were worked by conscripted Indian laborers under extremely harsh conditions. These mines provided Spain with a vast treasure in silver from the sixteenth through the eighteenth century. Hispanic Society of America

▼ Black African Slavery, the Plantation System, and the Atlantic Economy

Within various parts of Europe itself, slavery had existed since ancient times. Before the eighteenth century, little or no moral or religious stigma was attached to slave owning or slave trading. It had a continuous existence in the Mediterranean world, where only the sources of slaves changed over the centuries. After the conquest of Constantinople in 1453, the Ottoman Empire forbade the exportation of white slaves from regions under its control. The Portuguese then began to import African slaves into the Iberian Peninsula from the Canary Islands and West Africa. Black slaves from Africa were also not uncommon in other parts of the Mediterranean, and a few found their way into northern Europe. There they might be used as personal servants or displayed because of the novelty of their color in royal courts or in wealthy homes.

Yet, from the sixteenth century onward, first within the West Indies and the Spanish and Portuguese settlements in South America and then in the British colonies on the South Atlantic seaboard of North America, slave labor became a fundamental social and economic factor. The development of those plantation economies based on slave labor led to unprecedented interaction between the peoples of Europe and Africa and between the European settlers in the Americas and Africa. From that point onward, Africa and Africans were drawn into the Western experience as never before in history.

The African Presence in the Americas

Once they had encountered and begun to settle the New World, the Spanish and Portuguese faced a severe shortage of labor. They and most of the French and English settlers who came later had no intention of undertaking manual work themselves. At first, they used Native Americans as laborers, but during the sixteenth century as well as afterward, disease killed hundreds of thousands of the native population. As a result, labor soon became scarce. The Spanish and Portuguese then turned to the labor of imported African slaves. Settlers in the English colonies of North America during the seventeenth century turned more slowly to slavery, with the largest number coming to the Chesapeake Bay region of Virginia and Maryland and then later into the low country of the Carolinas. Which African peoples became sold into slavery during any given decade largely depended on internal African warfare and state-building. This remained the case until the end of the transatlantic slave trade in the nineteenth century.

The major sources for slaves were slave markets on the West African Coast from Senegambia to Angola. Slavery and an extensive slave trade had existed in West Africa for centuries. Just as particular social and economic conditions in Europe had led to the voyages of exploration and settlement, political and military conditions in Africa and warfare among various African nations similarly created a supply of slaves that certain African

This eighteenth-century print shows bound African captives being forced to a slaving port. It was largely African middlemen who captured slaves in the interior and marched them to the coast. North Wind Picture Archives

societies were willing to sell to Europeans. European slave traders did not confront a passive situation in West Africa over which they exercised their will by force and commerce. Rather, they encountered dynamic African societies working out their own internal historic power relationships and rivalries in which Africans sold and acquired other Africans from different regions and nations as slaves.

The West Indies, Brazil, and Sugar To grasp the full impact of the forced immigration of Africans to the Americas, we must take into account both regions and the entire picture of the transatlantic economy. Far more slaves were imported into the West Indies and Brazil than into North America. Although citizens of the United States mark the beginning of slavery in 1619 with the arrival of African slaves on a Dutch ship in Jamestown, Virginia, over a century of slave trading in the West Indies and South America had preceded that event. Indeed, by the late sixteenth century, Africans had become a major social presence in the West Indies and in the major cities of both Spanish and Portuguese South America. Their presence and influence in these regions would grow over the centuries. African labor and African immigrant slave communities were the most prominent social features of these regions, making the development of their economies and cultures what one historian has described as "a Euro-African phenomenon."[2] In these places, African slaves equaled or more generally surpassed the numbers of white European settlers in what soon constituted multiracial societies. Someone passing through the marketplace of these towns and cities would have heard a vast number of African, as well as European, languages. Although Native American labor continued to be exploited on the South American continent, it was increasingly a marginal presence in the ever-expanding African slave-based plantation economy of the Atlantic seaboard, the Caribbean, and offshore islands.

Within much of Spanish South America, the numbers of slaves declined during the late seventeenth century, and slavery became somewhat less fundamental there than elsewhere. Slavery continued to expand its influence, however, in Brazil and in the Caribbean through the spreading cultivation of sugar to meet the demand of the European market. By the close of the seventeenth century, the Caribbean islands were the world center for the production of sugar and the chief supplier for the ever-growing demand for it. The opening of new areas of cultivation and other economic enterprises required additional slaves during the eighteenth century, a period of major slave importation. The growing prosperity of sugar islands that had begun to be exploited in the late seventeenth century, as well as the new sugar, coffee, and tobacco regions of Brazil, where gold mining also required additional slaves, accounts for this increase in slave commerce and allowed higher prices to be paid for slaves. In Brazil, the West Indies, and the southern British colonies, prosperity and slavery went hand in hand.

A vast increase in the number of Africans brought as slaves to the Americas occurred during the eighteenth century, with most arriving in the Caribbean or Brazil. Early in the century, as many as 20,000 new Africans a year arrived in the West Indies as slaves. By 1725, it has been estimated that almost 90 percent of the population of Jamaica consisted of black slaves. After the midcentury, the numbers were even larger. The influx of new Africans in most areas—even in the British colonies—meant the numbers of new forced immigrants outnumbered the slaves of African descent already present.

[2]John Thornton, *Africa and the Africans in the Making of the Atlantic World, 1400–1800*, 2nd ed. (Cambridge: Cambridge University Press, 1998), p. 140.

SUGAR ENTERS THE WESTERN DIET

BEFORE THE EUROPEAN discovery of the Americas, sugar was a luxury product that only the wealthy could afford. Because it requires subtropical temperatures and heavy rainfall, sugarcane could not be grown in Europe. Sugar had to be imported, at great expense, from the Arab world or from the Spanish and Portuguese islands off the coast of Africa, which were too arid for the plant to flourish.

The Caribbean, however, is ideal for sugarcane. Columbus carried it to the New World in 1493, and within about a decade sugar was being cultivated—by slaves—on Santo Domingo.

Yet, sugar production did not begin to soar until Britain and France established themselves in the Caribbean in the seventeenth century and the demand for sugar began to grow in Europe, first slowly and then insatiably. By the eighteenth century, the small British and French islands in the Caribbean where sugar was produced by African slave labor had become some of the most valuable real estate on earth.

Whereas the North American colonies imported Caribbean molasses to make rum, Europeans desired sugar to sweeten other foods. Sugar, the largest colonial import into Britain, embodied the mercantile policy of a closed economic system. It was raised in British colonies, paid for by British exports, shipped on British ships, insured by British firms, refined in British cities, and consumed on British tables.

The voracious demand for sugar as a sweetener was tied up with three other tropical products—coffee, tea, and chocolate—that European consumers began to drink in enormous quantities in the seventeenth and eighteenth centuries. Each of these beverages is a stimulant, which helps explain their popularity, but by themselves they taste bitter. Sugar made them palatable to European consumers. The demand for sugar and these drinks became mutually reinforcing. As the markets for coffee, chocolate, and especially tea grew in England and the English colonies, so did the demand for sugar.

As the production of sugar rose, its price fell. The cheaper sugar became, the more of it Europeans consumed. By the end of the eighteenth century, tea with sugar was cheaper than beer or milk, and it had become the most popular drink among the British poor (while remaining an elegant drink for the wealthy). Moreover, because sugar had originally been a luxury item, people felt they were improving their standard of living if they consumed more of it.

During the nineteenth century, sugar consumption continued to expand, and sugar became even cheaper when free-trade policies reduced protective import duties and when the French began to manufacture it from sugar beets, which could easily be grown in Europe. Nineteenth-century Westerners developed the custom of ending a meal with dessert, food usually sweetened with sugar.

Source: Sidney Mintz, *Sweetness and Power: The Place of Sugar in Modern History* (New York: Penguin Books, 1985).

How did the colonization of the Americas affect the European demand for sugar?

Why did sugar consumption increase so rapidly in Europe during the eighteenth and nineteenth centuries?

Sugar was both raised and processed on plantations such as this one in Brazil. Library of Congress

A Closer LOOK

A SUGAR PLANTATION IN THE WEST INDIES

WEST INDIES SUGAR plantations, owned by Europeans who often stayed only long enough to make their fortunes, were located on the remarkably beautiful islands of the Caribbean that today attract thousands of tourists. Employing slave laborers imported from Africa, the sugar plantations combined agricultural production of sugarcane and the industrial processing of it into sugar for export to Europe. The latter involved slaves working with dangerous machinery often near fires and hot metal equipment used in the distillation process.

The production of sugar from the cane occurred in structures near the sugarcane fields themselves. Note the aqueducts carrying water to power some machinery.

Plantation owners generally lived on high windswept areas of their estates while slaves dwelled in quite humble housing near the areas of sugarcane cultivation or the grazing of animals used for food and sugar production.

The Granger Collection, New York

Raw sugarcane from the nearby fields was placed between the vertical crushers to extract juice to be distilled into sugar crystals elsewhere on the plantation in cauldrons over fires.

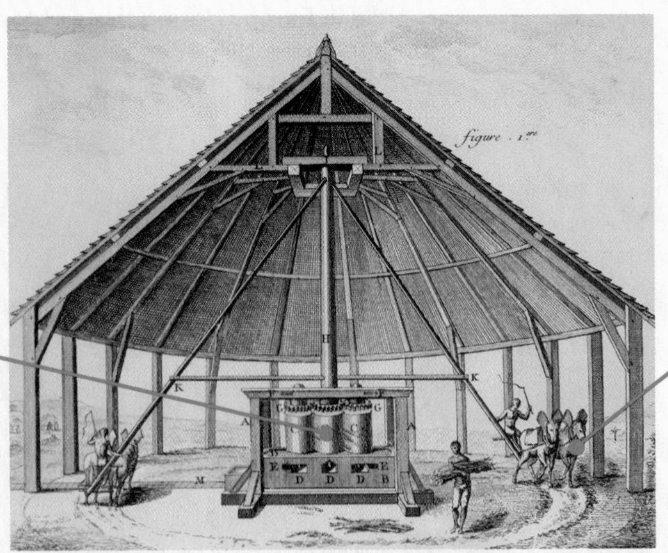

Animal power was used to move the crushers until the late eighteenth century when on some plantations steam engines replaced horses or mules.

Denis Diderot, *Encyclopedie, ou, Dictionnaire Raisonné des Sciences, des Arts et des Métiers*. Recueil de Planches, sur les Sciences. (Paris, 1762), vol. 1. Special Collections, University of Virginia Library

To examine this image in an interactive fashion, please go to www.myhistorylab.com

myhistorylab

Newly imported African slaves were needed because the fertility rate of the earlier slave population was low and the death rate high from disease, overwork, and malnutrition. The West Indies proved to be a particularly difficult region in which to secure a stable, self-reproducing slave population. The conditions for slaves there led to high rates of mortality with new slaves coming primarily from the ongoing slave trade. A similar situation prevailed in Brazil. Restocking through the slave trade meant the slave population of those areas consisted of African-born persons rather than of persons of African descent. Consequently, one of the key factors in the social life of many of the areas of American slavery during the eighteenth century was the presence of persons newly arrived from Africa, carrying with them African languages, religion, culture, and local African ethnic identities that they would infuse into the already existing slave communities. Thus, the eighteenth century witnessed an enormous new African presence throughout the Americas.

Slavery and the Transatlantic Economy

Different nations dominated the slave trade in different periods. During the sixteenth century, the Portuguese and the Spanish were most involved. The Dutch supplanted them during most of the seventeenth century. Thereafter, during the late seventeenth and eighteenth centuries, the English were the chief slave traders. French traders also participated in the trade.

Slavery touched most of the economy of the transatlantic world. (See Map 16–2, page 476.) Colonial trade followed roughly a geographic triangle. European goods—often guns—were carried to Africa to be exchanged for slaves, who were then taken to the West Indies, where they were traded for sugar and other tropical products, which were then shipped to Europe. Not all ships covered all three legs of the triangle. Another major trade pattern existed between New England and the West Indies with New England fish, rum, or lumber being traded for sugar. At various times, the prosperity of such cities as Amsterdam, Liverpool, England, and Nantes, France, rested largely on the slave trade. Cities in the British North American colonies, such as Newport, Rhode Island, profited from slavery sometimes by trading in slaves, but more often by supplying other goods to the West Indian market. All the shippers who handled cotton, tobacco, and sugar depended on slavery, though they might not have had direct contact with the institution, as did all the manufacturers and merchants who produced finished products for the consumer market.

As had been the case during previous centuries, eighteenth-century political turmoil in Africa, such as the civil wars in the Kingdom of Kongo (modern Angola and Republic of Congo), increased the supply of slaves during that period. These Kongo wars had originated in a dispute over succession to the throne in the late seventeenth century and continued into the eighteenth. Some captives were simply sold to European slave traders calling at ports along the West African coast. Other African leaders conducted slave raids, so their captives could be sold to finance the purchase of more weapons. Similar political unrest and turmoil in the Gold Coast area (modern Ghana) during the eighteenth century increased the supply of African captives to be sold into American slavery. Consequently, warfare in West Africa, often far into the interior, and the economic development of the American Atlantic seaboard were closely related.

The Experience of Slavery

The Portuguese, Spanish, Dutch, French, and English slave traders forcibly transported several million (perhaps more than 9 million; the exact numbers are disputed) Africans to the New World—the largest forced intercontinental migration in human history. During the first four centuries of settlement, far more black slaves came involuntarily to the New World than did free European settlers or European indentured servants. The conditions of slaves' passage across the Atlantic were wretched. Quarters were unspeakably cramped, food was bad, disease was rampant. Many Africans died during the crossing. (See "Compare & Connect: The Atlantic Passage," pages 474–475.) There were always more African men than women transported, so it was difficult to preserve traditional African extended family structures. During the passage and later, many Africans attempted to re-create such structures among themselves, even if they were not actually related by direct family ties.

In the Americas, the slave population was divided among new Africans recently arrived, old Africans who had lived there for some years, and creoles who were the descendants of earlier generations of African slaves. Plantation owners preferred the two latter groups, who were already accustomed to the life of slavery. They sold for higher prices. The newly arrived Africans were subjected to a process known as *seasoning*, during which they were prepared for the laborious discipline of slavery and made to understand that they were no longer free. The process might involve receiving new names, acquiring new work skills, and learning, to some extent, the local European language. Some newly arrived Africans worked in a kind of apprentice relationship to an older African slave of similar ethnic background. Other slaves were broken into slave labor through work on field gangs. Occasionally, plantation owners preferred to buy younger Africans, whom they thought might be more easily acculturated to the labor conditions of the Americas. Generally, North American

COMPARE AND CONNECT The Atlantic Passage

SLAVERY LAY AT the core of the eighteenth-century transatlantic economy. At the heart of slavery lay the forced transportation in slave ships across the Atlantic of millions of Africans to the Americas. The frightening and horrific character of the Atlantic Passage became widely known through the memoirs of sailors and slave trade captains. Later the groups who after the mid-eighteenth century sought the abolition of slavery made known the inhumanity of the passage through published attacks on the slave trade and by providing illustrations of slave ships such as that of the *Brooks*.

QUESTIONS

1. **Who are the various people described in this document who in one way or another were involved in or profited from the slave trade?**
2. **What dangers did the Africans face on the voyage?**
3. **What contemporary attitudes could have led this captain to treat and think of his human cargo simply as goods to be transported?**
4. **How might the publication of the interior compartments of a slave ship have served the cause of antislavery? How and why might this illustration of a slave ship have proved more persuasive in rousing antislavery sentiment than a prose description?**
5. **How would this illustration and the description of the Atlantic Passage have contrasted with contemporary illustrations and memoirs of victorious naval battles on the high seas?**

I. A Slave Trader Describes the Atlantic Passage

During 1693 and 1694, Captain Thomas Phillips carried slaves from Africa to Barbados on the ship Hannibal. *The financial backer of the voyage was the Royal African Company of London, which held an English crown monopoly on slave trading. Phillips sailed to the west coast of Africa, where he purchased the Africans who were sold into slavery by an African king. Then he set sail westward.*

Having bought my complement of 700 slaves, 480 men and 220 women, and finish'd all my business at Whidaw [on the Gold Coast of Africa], I took my leave of the old king and his *cappasheirs* [attendants], and parted, with many affectionate expressions on both sides, being forced to promise him that I would return again the next year, with several things he desired me to bring from England. . . . I set sail the 27th of July in the morning, accompany'd with the East-India Merchant, who had bought 650 slaves, for the Island of St. Thomas. . . from which we took our departure on August 25th and set sail for Barbadoes.

We spent in our passage from St. Thomas to Barbadoes two months eleven days, from the 25th of August to the 4th of November following: in which time there happened such sickness and mortality among my poor men and Negroes. Of the first we buried 14, and of the last 320, which was a great detriment to our voyage, the Royal African Company losing ten pounds by every slave that died, and the owners of the ship ten pounds ten shillings, being the freight agreed on to be paid by the charter-party for every Negro delivered alive ashore to the African Company's agents at Barbadoes. . . . The loss in all amounted to near 6500 pounds sterling.

The distemper which my men as well as the blacks mostly died of was the white flux, which was so violent and inveterate that no medicine would in the least check it, so that when any of our men were seized with it, we esteemed him a dead man, as he generally proved. . . .

The Negroes are so incident to [subject to] the smallpox that few ships that carry them escape without it, and sometimes it makes vast havoc and destruction among them. But tho' we had 100 at a time sick of it, and that it went thro' the ship, yet we lost not above a dozen by it. All the assistance we gave the diseased was only as much water as they desir'd to drink, and some palm-oil to anoint their sores, and they would generally recover without any other helps but what kind nature gave them. . . .

But what the smallpox spar'd, the flux swept off, to our great regret, after all our pains and care to give them their messes in due order and season, keeping their lodgings as clean and sweet as possible, and enduring so much misery and stench so long among a parcel of creatures nastier than swine, and after all our expectations to be defeated by their mortality. . . .

No gold-finders can endure so much noisome slavery as they do who carry Negroes; for those have some respite and satisfaction, but we endure twice the misery; and yet by their mortality our voyages are ruin'd, and we pine and fret ourselves to death, and take so much pains to so little purpose.

Source: From Thomas Phillips, "Journal," *A Collection of Voyages and Travels*, Vol. 6, ed. by Awnsham and John Churchill (London, 1746), as quoted in Thomas Howard, ed., *Black Voyage: Eyewitness Accounts of the Atlantic Slave Trade* (Boston: Little, Brown and Company, 1971), pp. 85–87.

II. The Slave Ship *Brookes*

This print records the main decks of the 320-ton slave ship *Brookes.*

The average space for each African destined for slavery in the Americas was 78 inches by 16 inches. The Africans were normally shackled to assure discipline and to prevent their injuring the crew. Iron shackles also prevented Africans from committing suicide on the voyage.

The ship measured 25 feet wide and 100 feet long.

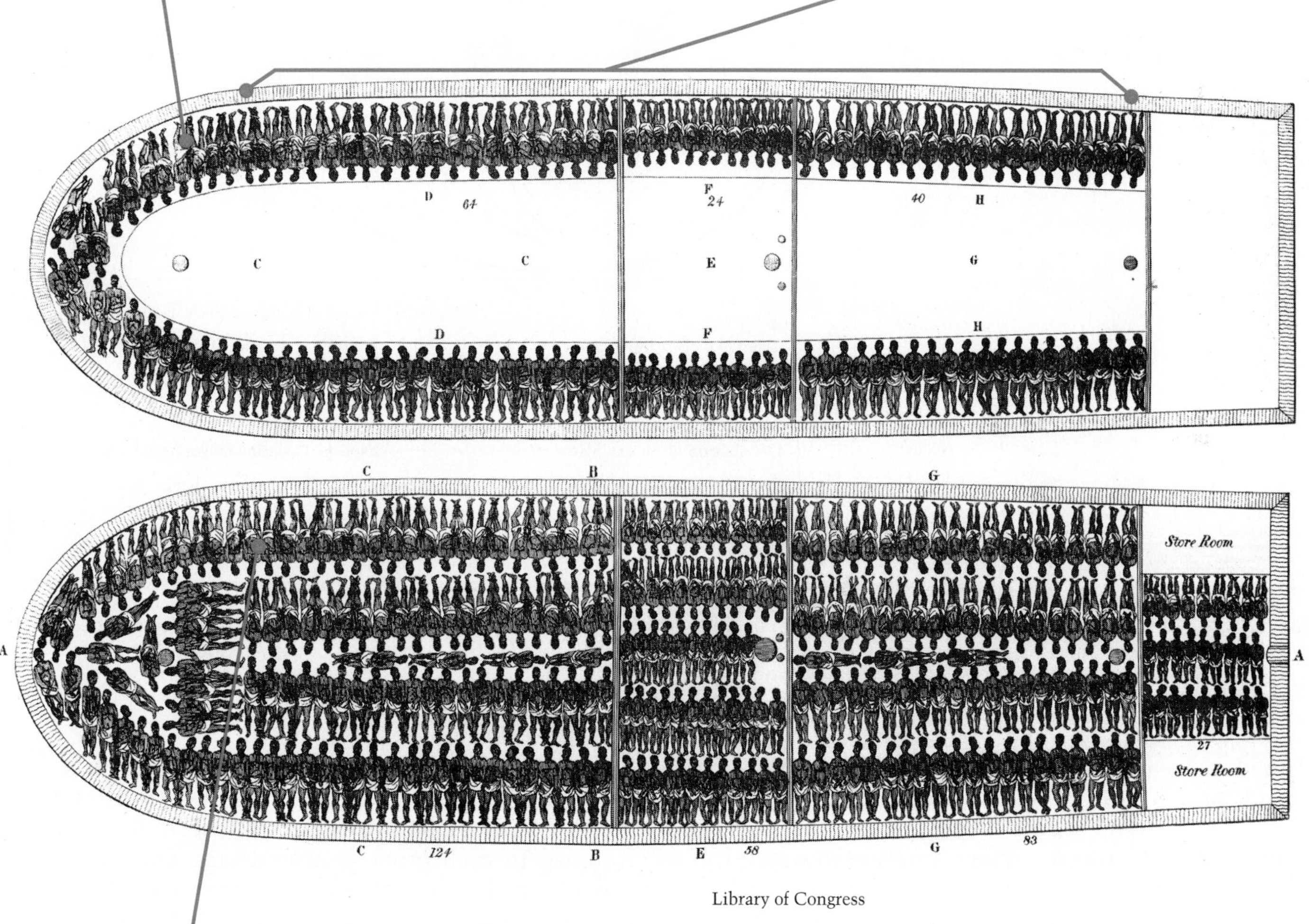

Library of Congress

Through the most inhumane use of space efficiency, 609 slaves could be crammed onboard for the nightmarish passage to America. A Parliamentary inquiry in 1788 found that the ship had been designed to carry no more than approximately 450 persons.

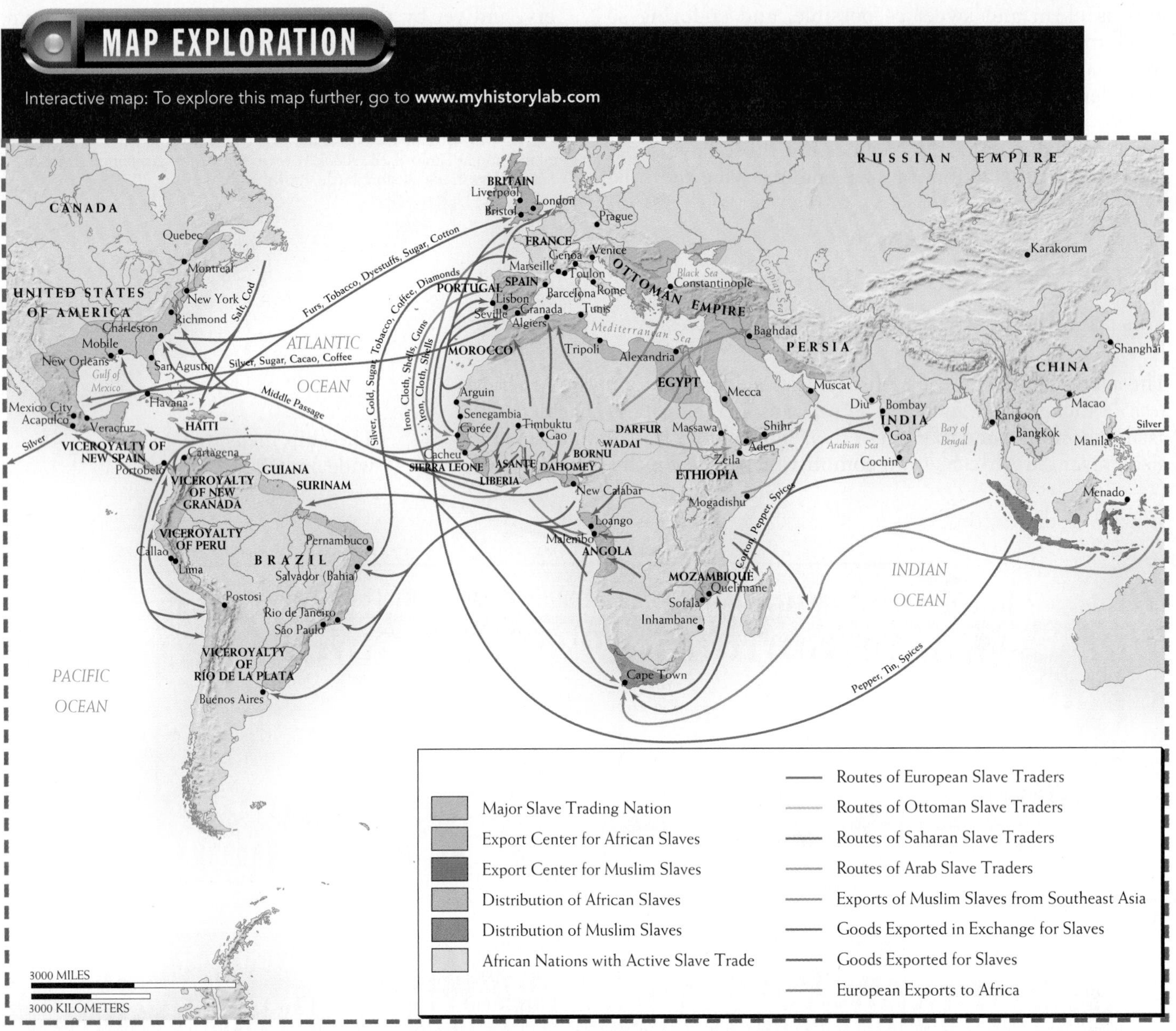

Map 16–2 **THE SLAVE TRADE, 1400–1860** Slavery is an ancient institution and complex slave-trading routes were in existence in Africa, the Middle East, and Asia for centuries, but it was the need to supply labor for the plantations of the Americas that led to the greatest movement of peoples across the face of the earth.

plantation owners were willing to purchase only such recently arrived Africans seasoned in the West Indies.

Language and Culture The plantation to which the slaves eventually arrived always lay in a more or less isolated rural setting, but its inhabitants could usually visit their counterparts on other plantations or in nearby towns on market days. Within the sharply restricted confines of slavery, the recently arrived Africans were able, at least for a time, to sustain elements of their own culture and social structures. From the West Indies southward throughout the eighteenth century, there were more people whose first language was African rather than European. For example, Coromantee was the predominant language on Jamaica. In South Carolina and on St. Domingue, most African slaves spoke Kikongo to each other. It would take more than two generations for the colonial language to dominate, and even then the result was often a dialect combining an African and a European language.

Through these languages, Africans on plantation estates could organize themselves into nations with similar, though not necessarily identical, ethnic ties to regions of West Africa. The loyalty achieved through a shared African language in the American setting created a solidarity among African slaves that was wider than what in Africa had probably been a primary loyalty to a village. These nations that the plantation experience organized and sustained also became the basis for a wide variety of religious communities among African slaves that had roots in their African experience. In this manner, some Africans maintained a loyalty to the Islamic faith of their homeland.

Many of the African nations on plantations, such as those of Brazil, organized lay religious brotherhoods that carried out various kinds of charitable work within the slave communities. In the Americas, the various African nations would elect their own kings and queens, who might preside over gatherings of the members of the nation drawn from various plantations.

Slaves on the plantations of the American South were the chattel property of their masters, and their lives were grim. Some artists sought to disguise this harsh reality by depicting the lighter moments of slave society as in this scene of slaves dancing. Getty Images Inc.—Hulton Archive Photos

The shared language of a particular African nation in the Americas enabled the slaves to communicate among themselves during revolts such as that in South Carolina in 1739, in Jamaica in the early 1760s, and, most successfully, during the Haitian Revolution of the 1790s. In the South Carolina revolt, the slave owners believed their slaves had communicated among themselves by playing African drums. In the aftermath of the revolt, the owners attempted to suppress such drum playing in the slave community.

Daily Life The living conditions of plantation slaves differed from colony to colony. Black slaves living in Portuguese areas had the fewest legal protections. In the Spanish colonies, the church attempted to provide some protection for black slaves, but devoted more effort toward the welfare of Native Americans. Slave codes were developed in the British and the French colonies during the seventeenth century, but they provided only the most limited protection to slaves while assuring dominance to their owners. Slave owners always feared a revolt, and legislation and other regulations were intended to prevent one. All slave laws favored the master rather than the slave. Slave masters were permitted to whip slaves and inflict other harsh corporal punishment. Furthermore, slaves were often forbidden to gather in large groups lest they plan a revolt. In most of these slave societies, the law did not recognize slave marriages. Legally, the children of slaves were slaves, and the owner of their parents owned them too.

The daily life of most slaves during these centuries involved hard agricultural labor, poor diet, and inadequate housing. Owners could separate slave families, or their members could be sold separately after owners died. The slaves' welfare and their lives were sacrificed to the continuing expansion of the sugar, rice, and tobacco plantations that made their owners wealthy and that produced goods for European consumers. Scholars have sometimes concluded that slaves in one area lived better than in another. Today, it is generally accepted that all the slaves in plantation societies led exposed and difficult lives with little variation among them.

Conversion to Christianity Most African slaves transported to the Americas were, like the Native Americans, eventually converted to Christianity. In the Spanish, French, and Portuguese domains, they became Roman Catholics. In the English colonies, most became Protestants of one denomination or another. Both forms of Christianity preached to slaves to accept both their slavery and a natural social hierarchy with their masters at the top.

Although organized African religion eventually disappeared in the Americas, especially in the British colonies, some African religious practices survived in muted forms, gradually separated from African religious belief. These included an African understanding of nature and the cosmos, and the belief in witches and other people with special spiritual powers, such as conjurers, healers, and voodoo practitioners. Although slaves did manage to mix Christianity with their previous African religions, their conversion to Christianity was nonetheless another example, like that of the Native Americans, of the crushing of a set of non-European cultural values in the context of the New World economies and social structures.

European Racial Attitudes The European settlers in the Americas and the slave traders also carried with them prejudices against black Africans. Many Europeans considered Africans to be savages or less than civilized. Still others looked down on them simply because they were slaves.

Both Christians and Muslims had shared these attitudes in the Mediterranean world, where slavery had existed for so long. Furthermore, many European languages and cultures attached negative connotations to the idea and image of blackness. In virtually all these plantation societies, race was an important element in keeping black slaves in subservience. Although racial thinking about slavery became important primarily in the nineteenth century, that slaves were black and masters were white was as fundamental to the system as that slaves were chattel property.

The plantations that stretched from the Middle Atlantic colonies of North America through the West Indies and into Brazil constituted a vast corridor of slave societies in which social and economic subordination was based on both involuntary servitude and race. These societies had not existed before the European discovery and exploitation of the Americas. In its complete dependence on slave labor and racial differences, this kind of society was unique in both European and world history. As already noted, its social and economic influence touched not only the plantation societies themselves, but West Africa, Western Europe, and New England as well. It existed from the sixteenth century through the late nineteenth century, when the emancipation of slaves had been completed through the slave revolt of Saint Domingue (1794), the British outlawing of the slave trade (1807), the Latin American wars of independence, the Emancipation Proclamation of 1863 and the Civil War in the United States, and the Brazilian emancipation of 1888. To the present day, every society in which plantation slavery once existed still contends with the long-term effects of that institution.

▼ Mid-Eighteenth-Century Wars

From the standpoint of international relations, the state system of the mid-eighteenth century was quite unstable and tended to lead the major states of Europe into prolonged warfare. The statesmen of the period generally assumed that warfare could further national interests. No forces or powers saw it in their interest to prevent war or maintain peace. Because professional armies and navies fought eighteenth-century wars before the French Revolution, the conflicts rarely affected civilian populations deeply. Wars did not lead to domestic political or social upheaval, and peace did not bring international stability. Consequently, nations often viewed periods of peace at the conclusion of a war simply as opportunities to recoup their strength, so that they could start fighting again to seize another nation's territory or disrupt another empire's trading monopoly.

The two fundamental areas of great power rivalry were the overseas empires and central and eastern Europe. Conflict in one of these regions repeatedly overlapped with conflict in the other, and this interaction influenced strategy and the pattern of alliances among the great powers.

The War of Jenkins's Ear

By the mid-eighteenth century, the West Indies had become a hotbed of trade rivalry and illegal smuggling. Much to British chagrin, the Spanish government took its own alleged trading monopoly seriously and maintained coastal patrols, which boarded and searched English vessels to look for contraband.

In 1731, during one such boarding operation, there was a fight, and the Spaniards cut off the ear of an English captain named Robert Jenkins. Thereafter he carried about his severed ear preserved in a jar of brandy. This incident was of little importance until 1738, when Jenkins appeared before the British Parliament, reportedly brandishing his ear as an example of Spanish atrocities to British merchants in the West Indies. The British merchant and West Indian planters lobbied Parliament to relieve Spanish intervention in their trade. Sir Robert Walpole (1676–1745), the British prime minister, could not resist these pressures. In late 1739, Britain went to war with Spain. This war might have been a relatively minor event, but because of developments in continental European politics, it became the opening encounter to a series of European wars fought across the world until 1815.

The War of the Austrian Succession (1740–1748)

In December 1740, after being king of Prussia for less than seven months, Frederick II (r. 1740–1786) seized the Austrian province of Silesia in eastern Germany. The invasion shattered the provisions of the Pragmatic Sanction (see Chapter 13) and upset the continental balance of power. The young king of Prussia had treated the House of Habsburg simply as another German state rather than as the leading power in the region. Silesia itself rounded out Prussia's possessions, and Frederick was determined to keep his ill-gotten prize.

Maria Theresa Preserves the Habsburg Empire The Prussian seizure of Silesia could have marked the opening of a general hunting season on Habsburg holdings and the beginning of revolts by Habsburg subjects. Instead, it led to new political allegiances. Maria Theresa's (r. 1740–1780) great achievement was not the reconquest of Silesia, which eluded her, but the preservation of the Habsburg Empire as a major political power.

She was then just twenty-three and had succeeded to the Habsburg realms only two months before the invasion. She won loyalty and support from her various subjects not merely through her heroism, but also by

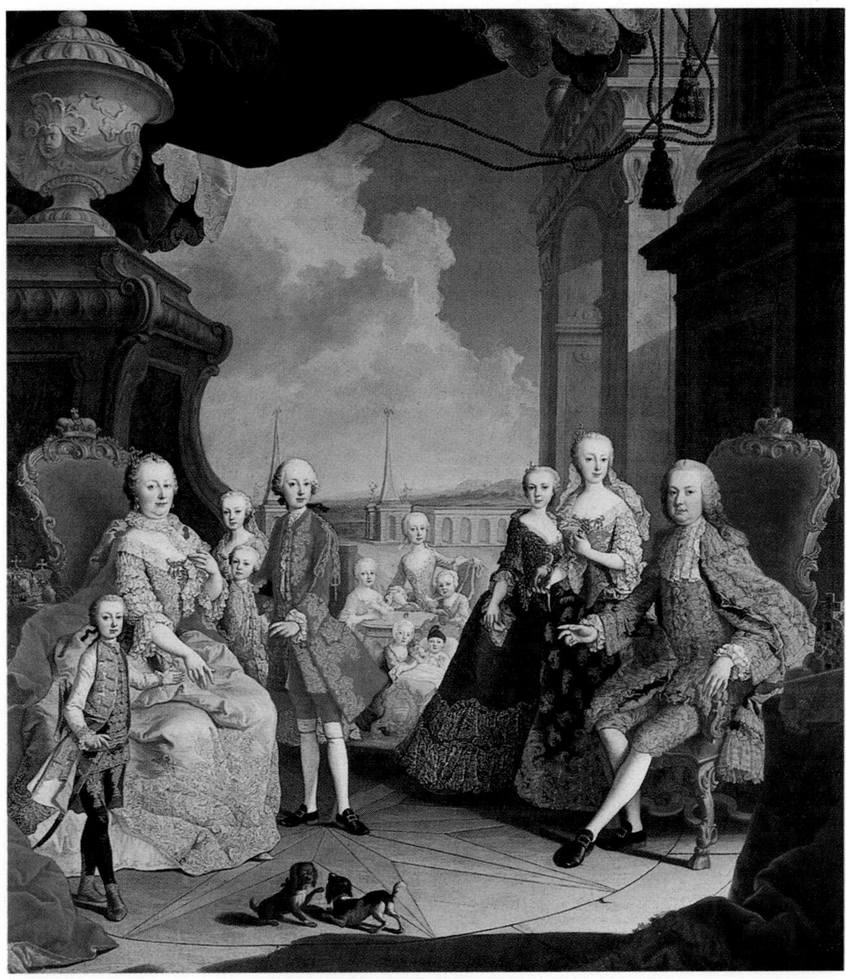

Maria Theresa of Austria provided the leadership that saved the Habsburg Empire from possible disintegration after the Prussian invasion of Silesia in 1740.
Martin van Meytens: *Kaiserin Maria Theresia mit ihrer Familie auf der Schloßterasse von Schobrunn.* Kunsthistorisches Museum, Vienna, Austria

granting new privileges to the nobility. Most significantly, the empress recognized Hungary as the most important of her crowns and promised the Magyar nobility local autonomy. She thus preserved the Habsburg state, but at considerable cost to the power of the central monarchy.

Hungary would continue to be, as it had been in the past, a particularly troublesome area in the Habsburg Empire. When the monarchy was strong and secure, it could ignore guarantees made to Hungary. When the monarchy was threatened, or when the Magyars could stir up enough opposition, the Habsburgs promised new concessions.

France Draws Great Britain into the War The war over the Austrian succession and the British–Spanish commercial conflict could have remained separate disputes. What united them was the role of France. Just as British merchant interests had pushed Sir Robert Walpole into war, aggressive court aristocrats compelled the elderly Cardinal Fleury (1653–1743), first minister of Louis XV (r. 1715–1774), to abandon his planned naval attack on British trade and instead to support the Prussian aggression against Austria, the traditional enemy of France. This was among the more fateful decisions in French history.

In the first place, aid to Prussia consolidated a new and powerful state in Germany. That new power could, and indeed later did, endanger France. Second, the French move against Austria brought Great Britain into the continental war, as Britain sought to make sure the Low Countries remained in the friendly hands of Austria, not France. In 1744, the British–French conflict expanded beyond the Continent when France supported Spain against Britain in the New World. As a result, French military and economic resources were badly divided. France could not bring sufficient strength to the colonial struggle. Having chosen to continue the old struggle with Austria, France lost the struggle for the future against Great Britain. The war ended in a stalemate in 1748 with the Treaty of Aix-la-Chapelle. Prussia retained Silesia, and Spain renewed Britain's privilege from the Treaty of Utrecht (1713) to import slaves into the Spanish colonies.

The "Diplomatic Revolution" of 1756

Although the Treaty of Aix-la-Chapelle had brought peace in Europe, France and Great Britain continued to struggle unofficially in the Ohio River valley and in upper New England. These clashes were the prelude to what is known in American history as the French and Indian War, which formally erupted in the summer of 1755.

Before war commenced again in Europe, however, a dramatic shift of alliances took place, in part, as a result of the events in North America. The British king, George II (r. 1727–1760), who was also the Elector of Hanover in Germany, thought the French might attack Hanover in response to the conflict in America. In January 1756, Britain and Prussia signed the Convention of Westminster, a defensive alliance aimed at preventing the entry of foreign troops into the German states. Whereas George II feared a French attack on Hanover, Frederick II feared an alliance of Russia and Austria. The convention meant that Great Britain, the ally of Austria since the wars of Louis XIV, had now joined forces with Austria's major eighteenth-century enemy.

Maria Theresa was despondent over this development. It delighted her foreign minister, Prince Wenzel Anton Kaunitz (1711–1794), however. He had long hoped for an alliance with France to help dismember Prussia. The Convention of Westminster made possible this alliance, which would have been unthinkable a few years earlier. France was agreeable because Frederick had not consulted with its ministers before coming to his understanding with Britain. So, in May 1756, France and Austria signed a defensive alliance. Kaunitz had succeeded in completely reversing the direction that French foreign policy had followed since the sixteenth century. France would now fight to restore Austrian supremacy in central Europe.

The Seven Years' War (1756–1763)

Once again, however, Frederick II precipitated a European war that extended into a colonial theater.

Frederick the Great Opens Hostilities In August 1756, Frederick II opened what would become the Seven Years' War by invading Saxony. Frederick considered this to be a preemptive strike against a conspiracy by Saxony, Austria, and France to destroy Prussian power. He regarded the invasion as a continuation of the defensive strategy of the Convention of Westminster. The invasion itself, however, created the very destructive alliance that Frederick feared. In the spring of 1757, France and Austria made a new alliance dedicated to the destruction of Prussia. Sweden, Russia, and many of the smaller German states joined them.

Two factors in addition to Frederick's stubborn leadership (it was after this war that he came to be called Frederick the Great) saved Prussia. First, Britain furnished considerable financial aid. Second, in 1762, Empress Elizabeth of Russia (r. 1741–1762) died. Her successor was Tsar Peter III (he was murdered the same year), whose admiration for Frederick was boundless. He immediately made peace with Prussia, thus relieving Frederick of one enemy and allowing him to hold off Austria and France. The Treaty of Hubertusburg of 1763 ended the continental conflict with no significant changes in prewar borders. Silesia remained Prussian, and Prussia clearly stood among the ranks of the great powers.

William Pitt's Strategy for Winning North America The survival of Prussia was less impressive to the rest of Europe than were the victories of Great Britain in every theater of conflict. The architect of these victories was William Pitt the Elder (1708–1778), a person of colossal ego and administrative genius. Although he had previously criticized British involvement with the Continent, once he became secretary of state in charge of the war in 1757, he pumped huge sums into the coffers of Frederick the Great. He regarded the German conflict as a way to divert French resources and attention from the colonial struggle. He later boasted of having won America on the plains of Germany.

North America was the center of Pitt's real concern. Put simply, he wanted all of North America east of the Mississippi for Great Britain, and that was what he won. He sent more than 40,000 regular English and colonial troops against the French in Canada. Never had so many soldiers been devoted to colonial warfare. He achieved unprecedented cooperation with the American colonies, whose leaders realized they might finally defeat their French neighbors.

The French government was unwilling and unable to direct similar resources against the English in America. Their military administration was corrupt, the military and political commands in Canada were divided, and France could not adequately supply its North American forces. In September 1759, on the Plains of Abraham, overlooking the valley of the Saint Lawrence River at Quebec City, the British army under James Wolfe defeated the French under Louis Joseph de Montcalm. The French Empire in Canada was ending.

Pitt's colonial vision, however, extended beyond the Saint Lawrence valley and the Great Lakes basin. The major islands of the French West Indies fell to British fleets. Income from the sale of captured sugar helped finance the British war effort. British slave interests captured the bulk of the French slave trade. Between 1755 and 1760, the value of the French colonial trade fell by more than 80 percent. In India, the British forces under the command of Robert Clive defeated France's Indian allies in 1757 at the Battle of Plassey. This victory opened the way for the eventual conquest of Bengal in northeast India and later of all of India by the British East India Company. (See Chapter 25.) Never had Great Britain or any other European power experienced such a complete worldwide military victory.

CONFLICTS OF THE MID-EIGHTEENTH CENTURY

1713	Treaty of Utrecht
1739	Outbreak of War of Jenkins's Ear between England and Spain
1740	War of the Austrian Succession commences
1748	Treaty of Aix-la-Chapelle
1756	Convention of Westminster between England and Prussia
1756	Seven Years' War opens
1757	Battle of Plassey
1759	British forces capture Quebec
1763	Treaty of Hubertusburg
1763	Treaty of Paris

This scene, painted by artist Edward Penny, shows Robert Clive receiving a sum of money from Siraj-ud-daulah, the Mughal Nawab of Bengal, for injured officers and soldiers at Plassey. Clive's victory in 1757 at the Battle of Plassey brought English domination of the Indian subcontinent for almost two centuries. Clive had won the battle largely through bribing many of the Nawab's troops and potential allies. Erich Lessing © The Trustees of the British Museum/Art Resource, NY

The Treaty of Paris of 1763 The Treaty of Paris of 1763 reflected somewhat less of a victory than Britain had won on the battlefield. Pitt was no longer in office. George III (r. 1760–1820) and Pitt had quarreled over policy, and the minister had departed. His replacement was the earl of Bute (1713–1792), a favorite of the new monarch. Bute was responsible for the peace settlement. Britain received all of Canada, the Ohio River valley, and the eastern half of the Mississippi River valley. Britain returned Pondicherry and Chandernagore in India and the West Indian sugar islands of Guadeloupe and Martinique to the French.

The Seven Years' War had been a vast worldwide conflict. Tens of thousands of soldiers and sailors had been killed or wounded. Major battles had been fought around the globe. At great internal sacrifice, Prussia had permanently wrested Silesia from Austria and had turned the Holy Roman Empire into an empty shell. Habsburg power now depended largely on the Hungarian domains. France, though still having sources of colonial income, was no longer a great colonial power. The Spanish Empire remained largely intact, but the British were still determined to penetrate its markets.

In India, the British East India Company continued to impose its own authority on the decaying indigenous governments. The ramifications of that situation would extend until the mid-twentieth century. In North America, the British government faced the task of organizing its new territories. From this time until World War II, Great Britain was a world power, not just a European one.

The quarter century of warfare also caused a long series of domestic crises among the European powers. Defeat convinced many in France of the necessity for political and administrative reform. The financial burdens of the wars had astounded all contemporaries. Every power had to increase its revenues to pay its war debt and finance its preparation for the next combat. Nowhere did this search for revenue lead to more far-ranging consequences than in the British colonies in North America.

▼ The American Revolution and Europe

The revolt of the British colonies in North America was an event in both transatlantic and European history. It marked the beginning of the end of European colonial domination of the American continents. The colonial American revolt that led eventually to revolution erupted from problems of revenue collection common to all the major powers after the Seven Years' War. The War of the American Revolution also continued the conflict between France and Great Britain. The French support of the Americans deepened the existing financial and administrative difficulties of the French monarchy.

Resistance to the Imperial Search for Revenue

After the Treaty of Paris of 1763, the British government faced two imperial problems. The first was the sheer cost of maintaining their empire, which the British felt they could no longer carry alone. The national debt had risen considerably, as had domestic taxation. Since the American colonies had been the chief beneficiaries of the conflict, the British felt it was rational for the colonies henceforth to bear part of the cost of their protection and administration. The second problem was the vast expanse of new territory in North America that the British had to organize. This included all the land from the mouth of the Saint Lawrence River to the Mississippi River, with its French settlers and, more importantly, its Native Americans. (See Map 16–3, page 482.)

The British drive for revenue began in 1764 with the passage of the Sugar Act under the ministry of George Grenville (1712–1770). The measure attempted to produce more revenue from imports into the colonies by

MAP EXPLORATION

Interactive map: To explore this map further, go to www.myhistorylab.com

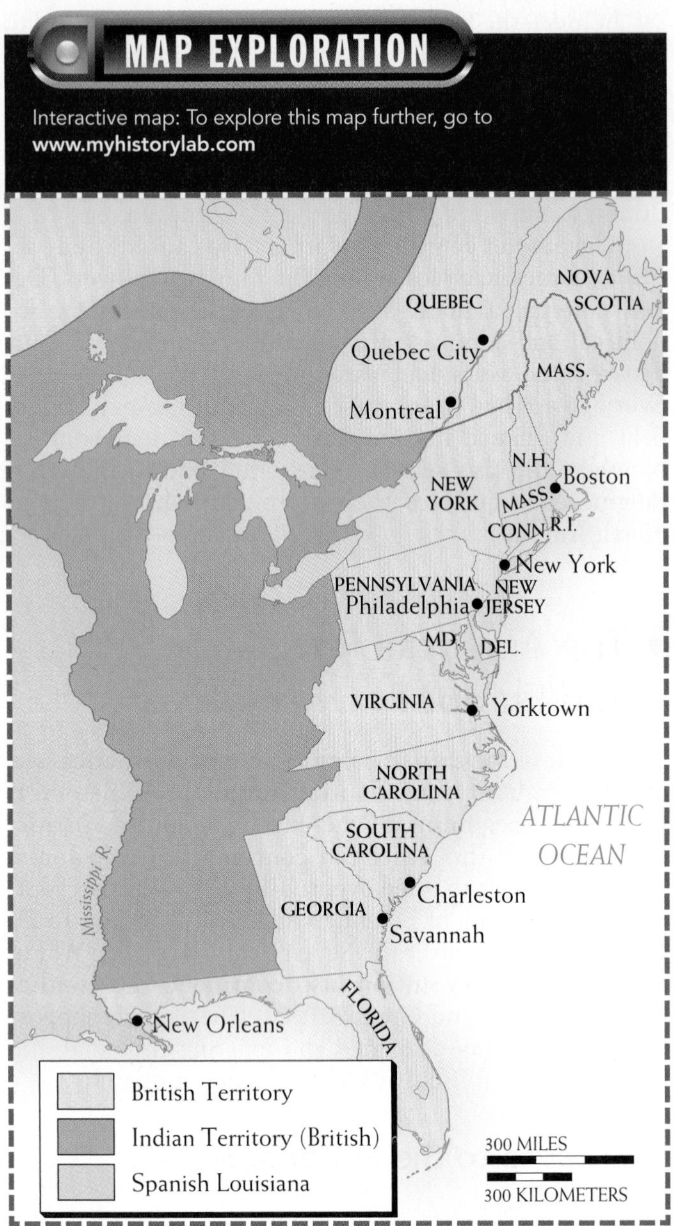

Map 16–3 **NORTH AMERICA IN 1763** In the year of the victory over France, the English colonies lay along the Atlantic seaboard. The difficulties of organizing authority over the previous French territory in Canada and west of the Appalachian Mountains would contribute to the coming of the American Revolution.

the rigorous collection of what was actually a lower tax. Smugglers who violated the law were to be tried in admiralty courts without juries. The next year, Parliament passed the Stamp Act, which put a tax on legal documents and other items such as newspapers. The British considered these taxes legal, because Parliament had approved the decision to collect them, and fair, because the money was to be spent in the colonies.

The Americans responded that they alone, through their colonial assemblies, had the right to tax themselves and that they were not represented in Parliament. Furthermore, the expenditure in the colonies of the revenue Parliament levied did not reassure the colonists. They feared that if their colonial government was financed from outside, they would lose control over it. In October 1765, the Stamp Act Congress met in America and drew up a protest to the crown. There was much disorder in the colonies, particularly in Massachusetts, roused by groups known as the Sons of Liberty. The colonists agreed to refuse to import British goods. In 1766, Parliament repealed the Stamp Act, but through the Declaratory Act said it had the power to legislate for the colonies.

The Stamp Act crisis set the pattern for the next ten years. Parliament, under the leadership of a royal minister, would approve revenue or administrative legislation. The Americans would then resist by reasoned argument, economic pressure, and violence. Then the British would repeal the legislation, and the process would begin again. Each time, tempers on both sides became more frayed and positions more irreconcilable. With each clash, the Americans more fully developed their own thinking about political liberty.

The Crisis and Independence

In 1767, Charles Townshend (1725–1767), as Chancellor of the Exchequer, the British finance minister, led Parliament to pass a series of revenue acts relating to colonial imports. The colonists again resisted. The ministry sent over its own customs agents to administer the laws. To protect these new officers, the British sent troops to Boston in 1768. The obvious tensions resulted. In March 1770, the Boston Massacre, in which British troops killed five citizens, took place. That same year, Parliament repealed all of the Townshend duties except the one on tea.

In May 1773, Parliament passed a new law relating to the sale of tea by the East India Company. The measure permitted the direct importation of tea into the American colonies. It actually lowered the price of tea while retaining the tax imposed without the colonists' consent. In some cities, the colonists refused to permit the unloading of the tea; in Boston, a shipload of tea was thrown into the harbor.

The British ministry of Lord North (1732–1792) was determined to assert the authority of Parliament over the colonies. During 1774, Parliament passed a series of laws known in American history as the **Intolerable Acts**. These measures closed the port of Boston, reorganized the government of Massachusetts, allowed troops to be quartered in private homes, and removed the trials of royal customs officials to England. The same year, the Quebec Act extended the boundaries of Quebec to include the Ohio River valley. The Americans regarded the Quebec Act as an attempt to prevent their mode of self-government from spreading beyond the Appalachian Mountains.

During these years, citizens critical of British policy had established committees of correspondence throughout the colonies. They made the various sections of the eastern seaboard aware of common problems and encouraged united action. In September 1774, these committees organized the First Continental Congress in Philadelphia. This body hoped to persuade Parliament to restore self-government in the colonies and abandon its direct supervision of colonial affairs. Conciliation, however, was not forthcoming. By April 1775, the Battles of Lexington and Concord had been fought. In June, the colonists suffered defeat at the Battle of Bunker Hill. Despite that defeat, the colonial assemblies began to meet under their own authority rather than under that of the king.

The Second Continental Congress gathered in May 1775. It still sought conciliation with Britain, but the pressure of events led it to begin to conduct the government of the colonies. By August 1775, George III had declared the colonies in rebellion. During the winter, Thomas Paine's (1737–1809) pamphlet *Common Sense* galvanized public opinion in favor of separation from Great Britain. A colonial army and navy were organized. In April 1776, the Continental Congress opened American ports to the trade of all nations. On July 4, 1776, the Continental Congress adopted the Declaration of Independence. Thereafter, the War of the American Revolution continued until 1781, when the forces of George Washington defeated those of Lord Cornwallis at Yorktown. Early in 1778, however, the war had widened into a European conflict when Benjamin Franklin (1706–1790) persuaded the French government to support the rebellion. In 1779, the Spanish also joined the war against Britain. The 1783 Treaty of Paris concluded the conflict, and the thirteen American colonies finally established their independence.

Many Americans fiercely objected to the British Parliament's attempts to tax the colonies. This print of a British tax collector being tarred and feathered warned officials of what could happen to them if they tried to collect these taxes. Philip Dawe (c. 1750–c.1785), *The Bostonians Paying the Excise-Man or Tarring & Feathering*. London, 1774. Colored Engraving. The Gilder Lehman Collection on deposit at the Pierpont Morgan Library. GL 4961.01. Photography: Joseph Zehavi. The Pierpont Morgan Library/Art Resource, NY

American Political Ideas

The political ideas of the American colonists had largely arisen out of the struggle of the seventeenth-century English aristocrats and gentry against the absolutism of the Stuart monarchs. The American colonists looked to the English Revolution of 1688 as having established many of their own fundamental political liberties, as well as those of the English. The colonists claimed that, through the measures imposed from 1763 to 1776, George III and the British Parliament were attacking those liberties and dissolving the bonds of moral and political allegiance that had formerly united the two peoples. Consequently, the colonists employed a theory that had developed to justify an aristocratic rebellion to support their own popular revolution.

These Whig political ideas, largely derived from the writings of John Locke, were, however, only a part of the English ideological heritage that affected the Americans. Throughout the eighteenth century, they had become familiar with a series of British political writers called the **Commonwealthmen**, who held republican political ideas that had their intellectual roots in the most radical thought of the Puritan revolution. During the early eighteenth century, these writers, the most influential of whom were John Trenchard (1662–1723) and Thomas Gordon (d. 1750) in *Cato's Letters* (1720–1723), had relentlessly criticized the government patronage and parliamentary management of Sir Robert Walpole and his successors. They argued that such government was corrupt and it undermined liberty. They regarded much parliamentary taxation as simply a means of financing political corruption. They also considered standing armies instruments of tyranny. In Great Britain, this republican political tradition had only a marginal impact. The writers were largely ignored because most British subjects regarded themselves as the freest people in the world. Three thousand miles away, however, colonists read the radical books and pamphlets and often accepted them at face value. The policy of Great Britain toward America following the Treaty of Paris of 1763 and certain political events in Britain had made many colonists believe the worst fears of the Commonwealthmen were coming true. All of these events coincided with the accession of George III to the throne.

Events in Great Britain

George III believed that a few powerful Whig families and the ministries they controlled had bullied and dominated his two immediate royal predecessors. George III also believed he should have ministers of his own choice and Parliament should function under royal, rather than aristocratic, management. When George appointed the Earl of Bute as his first minister after William Pitt resigned in 1761, he ignored the great Whig families that had run the country since 1715. The king sought the aid of politicians whom the Whigs hated. Moreover, he tried to use the same kind of patronage techniques Walpole developed to control of the House of Commons.

Between 1761 and 1770, George tried one minister after another, but each, in turn, failed to gain enough support from the various factions in the House of Commons. Finally, in 1770, he turned to Lord North, who remained the king's first minister until 1782. The Whig families and other political spokespersons claimed that George III was attempting to impose a tyranny. What they meant was that the king was attempting to curb the power of a particular group of the aristocracy. George III certainly was seeking to restore more royal influence to the government of Great Britain, but he was not trying to make himself a tyrant.

The Challenge of John Wilkes Then, in 1763 began the affair of John Wilkes (1725–1797). This London political radical and member of Parliament published a newspaper called *The North Briton*. In issue number 45, Wilkes strongly criticized Lord Bute's handling of the peace negotiations with France. Wilkes was arrested under the authority of a general warrant issued by the secretary of state. He pleaded the privileges of a member of Parliament and was released. The courts also later ruled that the vague kind of general warrant by which he had been arrested was illegal. The House of Commons, however, ruled that issue number 45 of *The North Briton* constituted libel, and it expelled Wilkes. He soon fled the country and was outlawed. Throughout these procedures Wilkes enjoyed widespread support.

In 1768, Wilkes returned to England and was reelected to Parliament, but the House of Commons, under the influence of George III's friends, refused to seat him. He was elected three more times. After the fourth election, the House of Commons simply ignored the results and seated the government-supported candidate. As had happened earlier, large, unruly demonstrations of shopkeepers, artisans, and small-property owners supported Wilkes as did aristocratic politicians who wished to humiliate George III. "Wilkes and Liberty" became the slogan of political radicals and many noble opponents of the monarch. Wilkes was finally seated in 1774, after having become the lord mayor of London.

The American colonists followed these developments closely. Events in Britain confirmed their fears about a monarchical and parliamentary conspiracy against liberty. The king, as their Whig friends told them, was behaving like a tyrant. The Wilkes affair displayed the arbitrary power of the monarch, the corruption of the House of Commons, and the contempt of both for popular electors. That same monarch and Parliament were attempting to overturn the traditional relationship of Great Britain to its colonies by imposing parliamentary taxes. The same government had then landed troops in Boston, changed the government of Massachusetts, and undermined the traditional right of jury trial. All of these events fulfilled too exactly the portrait of political tyranny that had developed over the years in the minds of articulate colonists.

Movement for Parliamentary Reform The political influences between America and Britain operated both ways. The colonial demand for no taxation without representation and the criticism of the adequacy of the British system of representation struck at the core of the eighteenth-century British political structure. British subjects at home who were no more directly represented in the House of Commons than were the Americans could adopt the colonial arguments. The colonial questioning of the tax-levying authority of the House of Commons was related to the protest of John Wilkes. Both the Americans and Wilkes were challenging the power of the monarch and the authority of Parliament. Moreover, both the colonial leaders and Wilkes appealed over the head of legally constituted political authorities to popular opinion and popular demonstrations. Both were protesting the power of a largely self-selected aristocratic political body. The British ministry was fully aware of these broader political implications of the American troubles.

The American colonists also demonstrated to Europe how a politically restive people in the Old Regime could fight tyranny and protect political liberty. They established revolutionary, but orderly, political bodies that could function outside the existing political framework: the congress and the convention. These began with the Stamp Act Congress of 1765 and culminated in the Constitutional Convention of 1787. The legitimacy of these congresses and conventions lay not in existing law, but in the alleged consent of the governed. This approach represented a new way to found a government.

Toward the end of the War of the American Revolution, calls for parliamentary reform arose in Britain itself. The method proposed for changing the system was the extra-legal Association Movement.

The surrender of Lord Cornwallis's British army at Yorktown, Virginia, in 1781 to American and French forces under George Washington ended Britain's hopes of suppressing the American Revolution. John Trumbull (American 1756–1843), *The Surrender of Lord Cornwallis at Yorktown, 19 October 1781*, 1787–c. 1828. Oil on canvas, 53.3 × 77.8 × 1.9 cm (21 × 30 ⅝ × ¾ in.) 1832.4. Yale University Art Gallery, Trumbull Collection

The Yorkshire Association Movement

By the close of the 1770s, many in Britain resented the mismanagement of the American war, the high taxes, and Lord North's ministry. In northern England in 1778, Christopher Wyvil (1740–1822), a landowner and retired clergyman, organized the Yorkshire Association Movement. Property owners, or freeholders, of Yorkshire met in a mass meeting to demand moderate changes in the corrupt system of parliamentary elections. They organized corresponding societies elsewhere. They intended that the association examine, and suggest reforms for, the entire government. The Association Movement was thus a popular attempt to establish an extra-legal institution to reform the government. (See "Major Cartwright Calls for the Reform of Parliament," page 486.)

The movement collapsed during the early 1780s because its supporters, unlike Wilkes and the American rebels, were not willing to appeal for broad popular support. Nonetheless, the agitation of the Association Movement provided many people with experience in political protest. Several of its younger figures lived to raise the issue of parliamentary reform after 1815.

Parliament was not insensitive to the demands of the Association Movement. In April 1780, the Commons passed a resolution that called for lessening the power of the crown. In 1782, Parliament adopted a measure for "economical" reform, which abolished some patronage at the disposal of the monarch. These actions, however, did not prevent George III from appointing a minister of his own choice. In 1783, shifts in Parliament obliged Lord North to form a ministry with Charles James Fox (1749–1806), a longtime critic of George III. The monarch was most unhappy with the arrangement.

In 1783, the king approached William Pitt the Younger (1759–1806), son of the victorious war minister, to manage the House of Commons. During the election of 1784, Pitt received immense patronage support from the crown and constructed a House of Commons favorable to the monarch. Thereafter, Pitt sought to formulate trade policies that would give his ministry broad popularity. In 1785, he attempted one measure of modest parliamentary reform. When it failed, the young prime minister, who had been only twenty-four at the time of his appointment, abandoned the cause of reform.

By the mid-1780s, George III had achieved part of what he had sought since 1761. He had reasserted the influence of the monarchy in political affairs. It proved a temporary victory, because his own mental illness, which would eventually require a regency, weakened the royal power.

EVENTS IN BRITAIN AND AMERICA RELATING TO THE AMERICAN REVOLUTION

1760	George III becomes king
1763	Treaty of Paris concludes the Seven Years' War
1763	John Wilkes publishes issue number 45 of *The North Briton*
1764	Sugar Act
1765	Stamp Act
1766	Stamp Act repealed and Declaratory Act passed
1767	Townshend Acts
1768	Parliament refuses to seat John Wilkes after his election
1770	Lord North becomes George III's chief minister
1770	Boston Massacre
1773	Boston Tea Party
1774	Intolerable Acts
1774	First Continental Congress
1775	Second Continental Congress
1776	Declaration of Independence
1778	France enters the war on the side of America
1778	Yorkshire Association Movement founded
1781	British forces surrender at Yorktown
1783	Treaty of Paris concludes War of the American Revolution

MAJOR CARTWRIGHT CALLS FOR THE REFORM OF PARLIAMENT

During the American Revolution there were many demands in England to reform Parliament. In this pamphlet of 1777, Major John Cartwright demands that many more English citizens be allowed to vote for members of the House of Commons. He also heaps contempt on the opponents of reform. Note how he declares that no political authority in Britain has the power to establish the unjust situation he describes.

What does Cartwright mean by "corruption"? How does he believe Britain has been deprived of its liberties? Why does he prefer an annual election of Parliament to elections every seven years? How does he illustrate the wrongful state of representation under the present system?

Suffering as we do, from a deep parliamentary corruption, it is no time to tamper with silly correctives, and trifle away the life of public freedom: but we must go to the bottom of the stinking sore and cleanse it thoroughly: we must once more infuse into the constitution the vivifying spirit of liberty and expel the very last dregs of this poison. *Annual parliaments* with an *equal representation of the commons* are the only specifics in this case: and they would effect a radial cure. That a house of commons, formed as ours is, should maintain septennial elections [i.e., elections every seven years], and laugh at every other idea is no wonder. The wonder is, that the British nation which, but the other day, was the greatest nation on earth, should be so easily laughed out of its liberties. . . .

Those who now claim the *exclusive* right of sending to parliament the 513 representatives for about six million souls (amongst whom are one million five hundred thousand males, *competent as electors*) consist of about two hundred and fourteen thousand persons; and 254 of these representatives are elected by 5,723. . . . Their pretended rights are many of them, derived from *royal favour*; some from antient usage and prescription; and some indeed from act of parliament; but neither the most authentic acts of royalty, nor precedent, nor prescription, nor even parliament can establish any flagrant injustice; much less can they strip one million two hundred and eighty-six thousand of an inalienable right, to vest it in a number amounting to only one-seventh of that multitude. . . .

From *Legislative Rights of the Commonality Vindicated*, by John Carwright (1740–1824), in *The English Radical Tradition*, 1763–1914 (London: Adam and Charles Black, 1966), pp. 32–33.

The cost of his years of dominance had been high, however. On both sides of the Atlantic, the issue of popular sovereignty had been widely discussed. The American colonies had been lost. Economically, this loss did not prove disastrous. British trade with America after independence actually increased.

Broader Impact of the American Revolution

The Americans—through their state constitutions, the Articles of Confederation, and the federal Constitution adopted in 1788—had demonstrated to Europe the possibility of government without kings and hereditary nobilities. They had established the example of a nation in which written documents based on popular consent and popular sovereignty—rather than on divine law, natural law, tradition, or the will of kings—were the highest political and legal authority. The political novelty of these assertions should not be ignored.

As the crisis with Britain unfolded during the 1760s and 1770s, the American colonists had come to see themselves first as preserving traditional English liberties against the tyrannical crown and corrupt Parliament and then as developing a whole new sense of liberty. By the mid-1770s, the colonists had rejected monarchical government and embraced republican political ideals. They would govern themselves through elected assemblies without any monarchical authority.

Once a constitution was adopted, they would insist on a Bill of Rights specifically protecting a whole series of civil liberties. The Americans would reject the aristocratic social hierarchy that had existed in the colonies. They would embrace democratic ideals—even if the franchise remained limited. They would assert the equality of white male citizens not only before the law, but also in ordinary social relations. They would reject social status based on birth and inheritance and assert the necessity of the liberty for all citizens to improve their social standing and economic lot by engaging in free commercial activity. They did not free their slaves, nor did they address issues of the rights of women or of Native Americans. Yet in making their revolution, the American colonists of the eighteenth century produced a society more free than any the world had ever seen and one that would eventually expand the circle of political and social liberty. In all these respects, the American Revolution was a genuinely radical movement, whose influence would widen as Americans moved across the continent and as other peoples began to question traditional modes of European government.

In Perspective

During the sixteenth and seventeenth centuries, the West European maritime powers established extensive commercial, mercantile empires in North and South America. The point of these empires was to extract wealth and to establish commercial advantage for the colonial power. Spain had the largest of these empires, but by the end of the seventeenth century, Britain and France had also each established a major American presence. As a vast plantation economy emerged, significant portions of these American empires became economically dependent on slave labor, drawn from the forced importation of Africans. Through this large slave labor force, African linguistic, social, and religious influences became major cultural factors in these regions.

During the eighteenth century, the great European powers engaged in warfare over their American empires and over their power in India. These colonial wars became entangled in dynastic wars in central and eastern Europe and resulted in worldwide mid-century European conflict.

In the New World, Britain, France, and Spain battled for commercial dominance. France and Britain also clashed in India. By the third quarter of the century, Britain had ousted France from its major holdings in North America and from any significant presence in India. Spain, though no longer a military power of the first order, had managed to maintain its vast colonial empire in Latin America and much of its monopoly over the region's trade.

On the Continent, France, Austria, and Prussia collided over conflicting territorial and dynastic ambitions. Britain used the continental wars to divert France from the colonial arena. With British aid, Prussia had emerged in 1763 as a major continental power. Austria had lost territory to Prussia, while France had accumulated a vast debt.

The mid-century conflicts, in turn, led to major changes in all the European states. Each of the monarchies needed more money and tried to govern itself more efficiently. This problem led Britain to attempt to tax the North American colonies, which led to a revolution and the colonies' independence. Already deeply in debt, the French monarchy aided the Americans, fell into a deeper financial crisis, and soon clashed sharply with the nobility as royal ministers tried to find new revenues. That clash eventually unleashed the French Revolution. Spain moved to administer its Latin American empire more efficiently, which increased revolutionary discontent in the early nineteenth century. In preparation for future wars, the rulers of Prussia, Austria, and Russia pursued a mode of activist government known as Enlightened Absolutism (see Chapter 17). In that regard, the mid-eighteenth-century wars set in motion most of the major political developments of the next half century.

REVIEW QUESTIONS

1. What were the fundamental ideas associated with mercantile theory? Did they work? Which European country was most successful in establishing a mercantile empire? Least successful? Why?
2. What were the main points of conflict between Britain and France in North America, the West Indies, and India? How did the triangles of trade function among the Americas, Europe, and Africa?
3. How was the Spanish colonial empire in the Americas organized and managed? What changes did the Bourbon monarchs institute in the Spanish Empire?
4. What was the nature of slavery in the Americas? How was it linked to the economies of the Americas, Europe, and Africa? Why was the plantation system unprecedented? How did the plantation system contribute to the inhumane treatment of slaves?
5. What were the results of the Seven Years' War? Which countries emerged in a stronger position and why?
6. How did European ideas and political developments influence the American colonists? How did their actions, in turn, influence Europe? What was the relationship between American colonial radicals and contemporary political radicals in Great Britain?

SUGGESTED READINGS

F. Anderson, *Crucible of War: The Seven Years' War and the Fate of Empire in British North America, 1754–1766* (2001). A splendid narrative account.

B. Bailyn, *The Ideological Origins of the American Revolution* (1992). An important work illustrating the role of English radical thought in the perceptions of the colonists.

C. A. Bayly, *Imperial Meridian: The British Empire and the World, 1780–1830* (1989). A major study of the empire after the loss of America.

I. Berlin, *Many Thousands Gone: The First Two Centuries of Slavery in North America* (1998). The most extensive recent treatment emphasizing the differences in the slave economy during different decades.

R. Blackburn, *The Making of New World Slavery from the Baroque to the Modern, 1492–1800* (1997). An extraordinary work.

M. A. Burkholder and L. L. Johnson, *Colonial Latin America* (2004). A standard synthesis.

L. Colley, *Britons: Forging the Nation, 1707–1837* (1992). Important discussions of the recovery from the loss of America.

D. B. Davis, *Inhuman Bondage: The Rise and Fall of Slavery in the New World* (2006). A splendid overview by a leading scholar.

D. B. Davis, *The Problem of Slavery in the Age of Revolution, 1770–1823* (1975). A major work on both European and American history.

J. Elliott, *Empires of the Atlantic: Britain and Spain in America 1492–1830* (2006). A brilliant and accessible comparative history.

J. J. Ellis, *His Excellency: George Washington* (2004). A biography that explores the entire era of the American Revolution.

R. Harms, *The Diligent: A Voyage through the Worlds of the Slave Trade* (2002). A powerful narrative of the voyage of a French slave trader.

H. S. Klein, *The Atlantic Slave Trade* (1999). A succinct synthesis based on recent literature.

P. Langford, *A Polite and Commercial People: England, 1717–1783* (1989). An excellent survey covering social history, politics, the overseas wars, and the American Revolution.

P. Maier, *American Scripture: Making the Declaration of Independence* (1997). Replaces previous works on the subject.

A. Pagden, *Lords of All the World: Ideologies of Empire in Spain, Britain, and France, 1492–1830* (1995). One of the few comparative studies of the empires during this period.

M. Rediker, *The Slave Ship: A Human History* (2007). An exploration of the harrowing experience of slave transportation across the Atlantic.

M. Rediker, *Villains of All Nations: Atlantic Pirates in the Golden Age* (2008). A serious historical treatment of the subject.

J. Thornton, *Africa and the Africans in the Making of the Atlantic World, 1400–1800*, 2nd ed. (1998). A discussion of the role of Africans in the emergence of the transatlantic economy.

J. Winik, *The Great Upheaval: America and the Birth of the Modern World, 1788–1800* (2007). Sets the founding of the American republic in a transatlantic political context.

G. S. Wood, *The American Revolution: A History* (2002). A major interpretation.

For additional learning resources related to this chapter, please go to www.myhistorylab.com

The Columbian Exchange: Disease, Animals, and Agriculture

THE EUROPEAN ENCOUNTER with the Americas produced remarkable ecological transformations that have shaped the world to the present moment. The same ships that carried Europeans and Africans to the New World also transported animals, plants, and germs that had never before appeared in the Americas. There was a similar transport back to Europe and Africa. Alfred Crosby, the leading historian of the process, has named this cross-continental flow "the Columbian exchange."

Diseases Enter the Americas

With the exception of a few ships that had gone astray or, in the case of the Vikings that had gone in search of new lands, the American continents had been biologically separated from Europe, Africa, and Asia for tens of thousands of years. In the Americas no native animals could serve as major beasts of burden except for the llama, which could not transport more than about a hundred pounds. Nor did animals constitute a major source of protein for Native Americans, whose diets consisted largely of maize, beans, peppers, yams, and potatoes. At the same time, the American continents included areas of vast grassland without grazing animals that would have transformed those plants into animal protein. Moreover, it also appears that native peoples had lived on the long-isolated American continents without experiencing major epidemics.

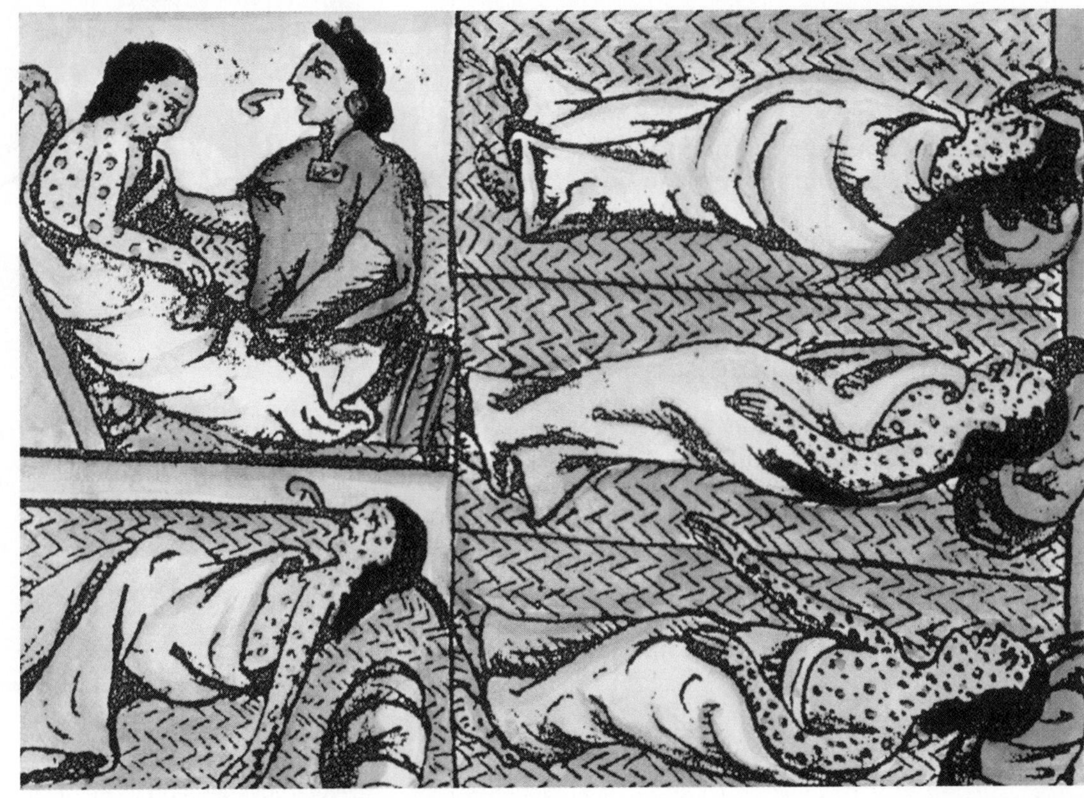

Nothing so destroyed the life of the Native Americans whom the Spanish encountered as the introduction of smallpox. With no immune defenses to this new disease, millions of Native Americans died of smallpox during the sixteenth and seventeenth centuries. The Granger Collection

By the second voyage of Columbus (1493), that picture began to change in remarkable ways. On his return voyage to Hispaniola and other islands of the Caribbean, Columbus brought a number of animals and plants that were previously unknown to the New World. The men on all his voyages and those on subsequent European voyages also carried diseases novel to the Americas.

The diseases thus transported by Europeans ultimately accounted for the conquest of the people of the Americas as much as the advanced European weaponry. Much controversy surrounds the question of the actual size of the populations of Native Americans in the Caribbean islands, Mexico, Peru, and the North Atlantic coast. All accounts present those populations as quite significant, with those of Mexico in particular numbering many millions. Yet in the first two centuries after the encounter, wherever Europeans went either as settlers or as conquerors, extremely large numbers of Native Americans died from diseases they had never before encountered. The most deadly such disease was smallpox, which destroyed millions of people. Beyond the devastation wrought by that disease, bubonic plague, typhoid, typhus, influenza, measles, chicken pox, whooping cough, malaria, and diphtheria produced deadly results in more localized epidemics. For example, an unknown disease, but quite possibly typhus, caused major losses among the Native Americans of New England between approximately 1616 and 1619.

Native Americans appear to have been highly susceptible to these diseases because, with no earlier exposure, they lacked immunity. Wherever such outbreaks are recorded, Europeans either contracted or died from them at a much lower rate than the Native Americans. These diseases would continue to victimize Native Americans at a higher rate than Americans of European descent through the end of the nineteenth century when smallpox and measles still killed large numbers of the Plains Indian peoples of North America.

Although many historical and medical questions still surround the subject, it appears almost certain that syphilis, which became a rampant venereal disease in Europe at the close of the fifteenth century and eventually spread around the globe, originated in the New World. It seems to have been an entirely new disease, spawned through a mutation when the causal agent for yaws migrated from the Americas to new climatic settings in Europe. Until the discovery of penicillin in the 1940s, syphilis remained a major concern of public health throughout the world.

Animals and Agriculture

The introduction of European livestock to the Americas quite simply revolutionized the agriculture of two continents. The most important new animals were pigs, cattle, horses, goats, and sheep. Once transported to the New World, these animals multiplied at unprecedented rates. The place where this first occurred was in the islands of the Caribbean, during the first forty years of Spanish settlement and exploitation. This situation established the foundation for the later Spanish conquest of both Mexico and Peru by providing the Spanish with strong breeds of animals, especially horses, acclimated to the Americas when they set out to conquer the mainland of South America.

The horse became first the animal of the conquest and then the animal of colonial Latin American culture. Native Americans had no experience with such large animals who would obey the will of a human rider. The mounted Spanish horseman struck fear into these people, and for good reason. After the conquest, however, the Americas from Mexico southward became the largest horse-breeding region of the world, with ranches raising thousands of animals. Horses became relatively cheap, and even Native Americans could acquire them. By the nineteenth century, the possession of horses would allow the Plains Indians of North America to resist the advance of their white conquerors.

The flourishing of pigs, cattle, and sheep allowed a vast economic exploitation of the Americas. These animals produced enormous quantities of hides and wool. Their presence in such large numbers also meant the

Within one year of Columbus's encounter with the Americas, the event had been captured in this woodcut (c. 1493). Columbus's several voyages, and those of later Europeans as well, introduced not only European warfare but also began a vast ecological exchange of plants, animals, and diseases between the Old and New Worlds. Courtesy of the Library of Congress

Americas from the sixteenth century through the present would support a diet more plentiful in animal protein than anywhere else in the world.

Europeans also brought their own plants to the New World, including peaches, oranges, grapes, melons, bananas, rice, onions, radishes, and various green vegetables. Socially, for three centuries the most significant of these was sugarcane, whose cultivation created the major demand for slavery throughout the transatlantic plantation economy. Nutritionally, European wheat would, over the course of time, allow the Americas not only to feed themselves, but also to export large amounts of grain throughout the world. This American production of wheat on the vast plains of the two continents contrasted sharply with the difficulty Europeans faced raising grain in the northern and northeastern parts of the Continent, particularly in Russia.

No significant animals from the Americas, except the turkey, actually came to be raised in Europe. The Americas did send to Europe, however, a series of plants that eventually changed the European diet: maize, potatoes, sweet potatoes, peppers, beans, manioc (tapioca), peanuts, squash, pumpkin, pineapple, cocoa, and tomatoes. All of these, to a greater or lesser degree, eventually entered the diet of Europeans and of European settlers and their descendants in the Americas. Maize and the potato, however, had the most transforming impact. Each of these two crops became a major staple in European farming, as well as in the European diet. Both crops grow rapidly, supplying food quickly and steadily if not attacked by disease. Tobacco, we should note, originated in the Americas, too.

Maize was established as a crop in Spain within thirty years of the country's encounter with the New World. A century and a half later it was commonplace in the Spanish diet, and its cultivation had spread to Italy and France. Maize produced more grain for the seed and farming effort than wheat did. Throughout Europe, maize was associated primarily with fodder for animals. As early as the eighteenth century, travelers noted the presence of polenta in the peasant diet, and other forms of maize dishes, such as fried mush, spread.

The potato established its European presence more slowly than maize. The Spanish encountered the potato only when Pizarro conquered Peru, where it was a major part of the Native American food supply. It was adopted slowly by Europeans because it needed to be raised in climates more temperate than that of Spain and the Mediterranean. It appears to have become a major peasant food in Scotland, Ireland, and parts of Germany during the eighteenth century. It became more widely cultivated elsewhere in Europe only after new strains of the plant were imported from Chile in the late nineteenth century. In the middle of the seventeenth century, Irish peasants were urged to cultivate the potato as a major source of cheap nutrition that could grow in quantity on a small plot. The food shortages arising from the wars of Louis XIV and then during the eighteenth century led farmers in northern Europe to adopt the potato for similar reasons. It was nutrient insurance against failure of the grain harvest. There is good reason to believe the cultivation of the potato was one of the major causes of the population increase in eighteenth- and nineteenth-century Europe. It was the quintessential food of the poor.

Many tragedies arose from the encounter between the people of the Americas and those of Europe, as well as from the forging of new nations and civilizations in the Americas. Yet, one of the last chapters of those tragedies to arise as a direct fallout of the Columbian exchange three centuries earlier was the Irish famine of the 1840s. Irish peasants had become almost wholly dependent on the potato as a source of food. In the middle of the 1840s, an American parasite infected the Irish potato crop. The result of the failure of the crop was the death of hundreds of thousands of Irish peasants and the migration of still more hundreds of thousands to the Americas and elsewhere in the world.

Define the Columbian exchange. What was the impact of European diseases on the Americas? Why was the impact so profound? Why could so many European crops grow well in the Americas? What was the cultural impact of animals taken from Europe to the Americas? How did food from the Americas change the diet of Europe and then later, as Europeans immigrated, the diet of the entire world?

The salon of Madame Marie Thérèse Geoffrin (1699–1777) was one of the most important Parisian gathering spots for Enlightenment writers during the middle of the eighteenth century. Well-connected women such as Madame Geoffrin were instrumental in helping the philosophes they patronized to bring their ideas to the attention of influential people in French society and politics. Chateaux de Malmaison et Bois-Preau, Rueil-Malmaison. Bridgeman-Giraudon/Art Resource, NY

17

The Age of Enlightenment: Eighteenth-Century Thought

▼ **Formative Influences on the Enlightenment**

Ideas of Newton and Locke • The Example of British Toleration and Political Stability • The Emergence of a Print Culture

▼ **The Philosophes**

Voltaire—First Among the Philosophes

▼ **The Enlightenment and Religion**

Deism • Toleration • Radical Enlightenment Criticism of Christianity • Jewish Thinkers in the Age of Enlightenment • Islam in Enlightenment Thought

▼ **The Enlightenment and Society**

The *Encyclopedia*: Freedom and Economic Improvement • Beccaria and Reform of Criminal Law • The Physiocrats and Economic Freedom • Adam Smith on Economic Growth and Social Progress

▼ **Political Thought of the Philosophes**

Montesquieu and *Spirit of the Laws* • Rousseau: A Radical Critique of Modern Society • Enlightened Critics of European Empires

▼ **Women in the Thought and Practice of the Enlightenment**

▼ **Rococo and Neoclassical Styles in Eighteenth-Century Art**

▼ **Enlightened Absolutism**

Frederick the Great of Prussia • Joseph II of Austria • Catherine the Great of Russia • The Partition of Poland • The End of the Eighteenth Century in Central and Eastern Europe

▼ **In Perspective**

KEY TOPICS

- **The intellectual and social background of the Enlightenment**
- **The philosophes of the Enlightenment and their agenda of intellectual and political reform**
- **Enlightenment writers' attitude toward religion**
- **The philosophes' political thought**
- **Efforts of "enlightened" monarchs in central and eastern Europe to increase the economic and military strength of their domains**
- **The partition of Poland by Prussia, Russia, and Austria**

DURING THE EIGHTEENTH century, the conviction began to spread throughout the expanding literate sectors of European society that economic improvement and political reform were both possible and desirable. This attitude is now commonplace, but it came into its own only after 1700. It represents one of the primary continuing intellectual inheritances from that age. The movement of people and ideas that fostered such thinking is called the Enlightenment.

Inspired by the scientific revolution and prepared to challenge traditional intellectual and ecclesiastical authority, Enlightenment writers believed that human beings can comprehend the operation of physical nature and mold it to achieve material and moral improvement, economic growth, and administrative reform. They advocated agricultural improvement, commercial society, expanding consumption, and the application of innovative rational methods to traditional social and economic practices. The rationality of the physical universe became a standard against which they measured and criticized the customs and traditions of society. In religious matters they generally advocated a policy of toleration that opposed the claims to exclusive religious privilege of state-supported established churches whether Roman Catholic or Protestant. As the criticisms of Enlightenment writers penetrated every corner of contemporary society, politics, and religious opinion, the spirit of innovation and improvement came to characterize modern Europe and Western society.

Some of the ideas and outlooks of the Enlightenment had a direct impact on rulers in central and eastern Europe. These rulers, whose policies became known by the term *enlightened absolutism*, sought to centralize their authority so as to reform their countries. They often attempted to restructure religious institutions and to sponsor economic growth. Although they frequently associated themselves with the Enlightenment, many of their military and foreign policies were in direct opposition to enlightened ideals. Nonetheless, both the Enlightenment writers and these monarchs were forces for modernization in European life.

▾ Formative Influences on the Enlightenment

The Newtonian worldview, the political stability and commercial prosperity of Great Britain after 1688, the need for administrative and economic reform in France after the wars of Louis XIV, and the consolidation of what is known as a *print culture* were the chief factors that fostered the ideas of the Enlightenment and the call for reform throughout Europe.

Ideas of Newton and Locke

Isaac Newton (1642–1727) and John Locke (1632–1704) were the major intellectual forerunners of the Enlightenment. The achievements of the Scientific Revolution from Copernicus to Newton had persuaded natural philosophers and then many other writers that traditions of thought inherited from both the ancient and medieval Christian worlds were incorrect or confused and needed to be challenged. Newton's formulation of the law of universal gravitation exemplified the newly perceived power of the human mind. Newtonian physics had portrayed a pattern of mechanical and mathematical rationality in the physical world. During the eighteenth century, thinkers from a variety of backgrounds began to apply this insight to society. If nature was rational, they reasoned, society, too, should be organized rationally. Furthermore, Newton had encouraged natural philosophers to approach the study of nature directly and to avoid metaphysics and supernaturalism. He had insisted on the use of empirical experience to check rational speculation. This emphasis on concrete experience became a key feature of Enlightenment thought.

As explained in Chapter 14, Newton's success in physics had inspired his fellow countryman John Locke to explain human psychology in terms of experience. In *An Essay Concerning Human Understanding* (1690), Locke argued that all humans enter the world a ***tabula rasa***, or blank page. Personality is the product of the sensations that impinge on an individual from the external world throughout his or her life. Thus, experience, and only experience, shapes character. This essentially behaviorist theory implied that human nature is changeable and can be molded by modifying the surrounding physical and social environment. Locke's was thus a reformer's psychology that suggested the possibility of improving the human condition. Locke's psychology also, in effect, rejected the Christian doctrine that sin permanently flawed human beings. By contrast, Locke's thought implied that human beings need not wait for the grace of God or other divine aid to better their lives. They can take charge of their own destiny.

The Example of British Toleration and Political Stability

Newton's physics and Locke's psychology provided the theoretical basis for a reformist approach to society. The domestic stability of Great Britain after the Revolution of 1688 furnished a living example of a society in which, to many contemporaries, enlightened reforms appeared to benefit everyone. England permitted religious toleration to all except Unitarians and Roman Catholics, and even they were not actively persecuted. Relative freedom of the press and free speech prevailed. The authority of the monarchy was limited, and political sovereignty resided in Parliament. The courts protected citizens from arbitrary government action. The army was small. Furthermore, the domestic economic life of Great Britain displayed far less regulation than that of France or other continental nations, and English commerce flourished. As reformist observers on the Continent noted, these liberal policies had produced neither disorder nor instability, but rather economic prosperity, political stability, and a loyal citizenry.

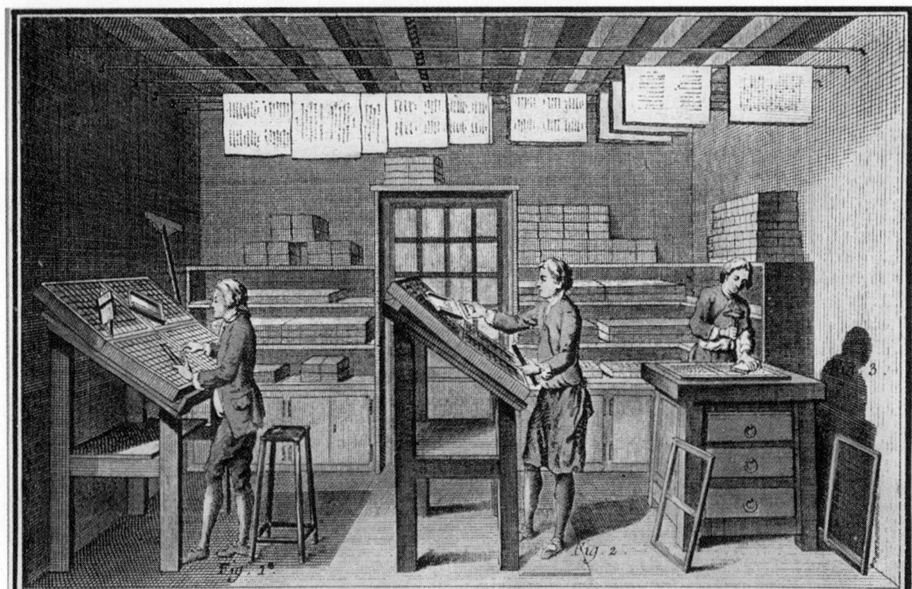

Printing shops were the productive centers for the book trade and newspaper publishing that spread the ideas of the Enlightenment. The Granger Collection

This view may have been idealized, but England was nonetheless significantly freer than any other European nation at the time. Many writers of the continental Enlightenment contrasted what they regarded as the wise, progressive features of English life with the absence of religious toleration, the extensive literary censorship, the possibility of arbitrary arrest, the overregulation of the economy, and the influence of aristocratic military values in their own nations and most particularly in France.

The Emergence of a Print Culture

The Enlightenment flourished in a *print culture*, that is, a culture in which books, journals, newspapers, and pamphlets had achieved a status of their own. In the past, print culture had deeply influenced the intellectual and religious movements associated with Renaissance humanism, the Reformation, and the Counter-Reformation. During the seventeenth century, a lively world of publication had arisen, which many governments sought to censor. During the eighteenth century, the volume of printed material—books, journals, magazines, and daily newspapers—increased sharply throughout Europe, notably in Britain. Prose came to be valued as highly as poetry, and the novel emerged as a distinct literary genre.

One of the driving forces behind this expansion of printed materials was the increase in literacy that occurred across Europe. Significantly more people especially in the urban centers of Western and central Europe could read. As a result, the printed word became the chief vehicle for communicating information and ideas and would remain so until the electronic revolution of our own day.

A growing concern with everyday life and material concerns—with secular as opposed to religious issues—accompanied this expansion of printed forms. Toward the end of the seventeenth century, half the books published in Paris were religious; by the 1780s, only about 10 percent were. Novels often came to provide the moral and social instruction that books of piety once furnished. An English journal observed unhappily in 1790: "Novels spring into existence like insects on the banks of the Nile; and, if we may be indulged in another comparison, cover the shelves of circulating libraries, as locusts crowd the fields of Asia. Their great and growing number is a serious evil; for, in general, they exhibit delusive views of human life; and while they amuse, frequently they poison the mind."[1] People may have thus criticized the moral influence of the novel but did not deny its influence.

Books were not inexpensive in the eighteenth century, but they, and the ideas they conveyed, circulated in a variety of ways to reach a broad public. Private and public libraries, as the previous quotation noted, grew in number, allowing single copies to reach many readers. Authors might also publish the same material in different formats. The English essayist, critic, and dictionary author Samuel Johnson (1709–1784), for example, published as books a collection of essays that had first appeared in newspapers or journals. The number of the latter publications also expanded throughout the century.

Within both aristocratic and middle-class society, people were increasingly expected to be familiar with books and secular ideas. Popular publications, such as *The Spectator*, begun in 1711 by Joseph Addison (1672–1719) and Richard Steele (1672–1729), fostered the value of polite conversation and the reading of books. Coffeehouses became centers for discussing writ-

[1]Quoted T. C. W. Blanning, *The Culture of Power and the Power of Culture: Old Regime Europe 1660–1789* (Oxford: Oxford University Press, 2002), p. 151.

ing and ideas. (See "Encountering the Past: Coffeehouses and Enlightenment," page 496.) The lodges of Freemasons, the meeting places for members of a movement that began in Britain and spread to the Continent, provided another site for discussing secular ideas in secular books.

The expanding market for printed matter allowed writers to earn a living from their work for the first time, making authorship an occupation. Parisian ladies who hosted fashionable salons sought out popular writers. Some writers, notably Alexander Pope (1688–1744) in England and Voltaire in France, grew wealthy, providing an example for their young colleagues. In a challenge to older aristocratic values, status for authors in this new print culture was based on merit and commercial competition, not heredity and patronage.

A division, however, soon emerged between high and low literary culture. Successful authors of the Enlightenment addressed themselves to monarchs, nobles, the upper middle classes, and professional groups, and they were read and accepted in these upper levels of society. Other aspiring authors found social and economic disappointment. They lived marginally, writing professionally for whatever newspaper or journal that would pay for their work. Many of these lesser writers grew resentful, blaming a corrupt society for their lack of success. From their anger, they often espoused radical ideas or took moderate Enlightenment ideas to radical extremes, transmitting them in this embittered form to their often lower-class audience.

An expanding, literate public and the growing influence of secular printed materials created a new and increasingly influential social force called *public opinion*. This force—the collective effect on political and social life of views circulated in print and discussed in the home, the workplace, and centers of leisure—seems not to have existed before the middle of the eighteenth century. Books and newspapers could have thousands of readers, who in effect supported the writers whose works they bought, as they discussed their ideas and circulated them widely. The writers, in turn, had to answer only to their readers. The result changed the cultural and political climate in Europe. In 1775, a new member of the French Academy declared:

> A tribunal has arisen independent of all powers and that all powers respect, that appreciates all talents, that pronounces on all people of merit. And in an enlightened century, in a century in which each citizen can speak to the entire nation by way of print, those who have a talent for instructing men and a gift for moving them—in a word, men of letters—are, amid the public dispersed, what the orators of Rome and Athens were in the middle of the public assembled.[2]

Governments could no longer operate wholly in secret or with disregard to the larger public sphere. They, as well as their critics, had to explain and discuss their views and policies openly.

Continental European governments sensed the political power of the new print culture. They regulated the book trade, censored books and newspapers, confiscated offending titles, and imprisoned offending authors. The eventual, but never in the eighteenth nor in most of the nineteenth century expansion of freedom of the press represented also an expansion of the print culture—with its independent readers, authors, and publishers—and the challenge it posed to traditional intellectual, social, and political authorities.

▾ The Philosophes

The writers and critics who flourished in the expanding print culture and who took the lead in forging the new attitudes favorable to change, championed reform, and advocated toleration were known as the **philosophes**. Not usually philosophers in a formal sense, but rather usually literary figures, economists, or historians, these figures sought rather to apply the rules of reason, criticism, and common sense to nearly all the major institutions, economic practices, and exclusivist religious policies of the day. The most famous of their number included Voltaire, Montesquieu, Diderot, D'Alembert, Rousseau, Hume, Gibbon, Smith, Lessing, and Kant.

A few of these philosophes, particularly those in Germany, were university professors. Most, however, were free agents who might be found in London coffeehouses, Edinburgh drinking spots, the salons of fashionable Parisian ladies, the country houses of reform-minded nobles, or the courts of the most powerful monarchs on the Continent. In eastern Europe, they were often royal bureaucrats. They were not an organized group; they disagreed on many issues and did not necessarily like or respect each other. Their relationship to one another and to lesser figures of the same turn of mind has been compared with that of a family, which, despite quarrels and tensions, preserves a basic unity. Another historian has portrayed the unity of the Enlightenment across many different local cultures as that of "eighteenth-century thinkers who saw themselves as members of a wider intellectual movement, dedicated to understanding and publicizing the cause of human betterment on this earth."[3]

The philosophes drew the bulk of their readership from the prosperous commercial and professional urban classes. These people as well as forward-looking aristocrats discussed the reformers' writings and ideas in local philosophical societies, Freemason lodges, and clubs. These

[2]Chrétien-Guillaume Malesherbes, as quoted in Roger Chartier, *The Cultural Origins of the French Revolution*, trans. by Lydia G. Cochran (Durham, NC: Duke University Press, 1991), pp. 30–31.

[3]Peter Gay, *The Enlightenment: An Interpretation*, Vol. 1 (New York: Knopf, 1967), p. 4; John Robertson, *The Case for the Enlightenment: Scotland and Napes 1680–1760* (Cambridge: 2005), p. 377.

ENCOUNTERING THE *Past*

COFFEEHOUSES AND ENLIGHTENMENT

THE IDEAS OF the Enlightenment not only spread through books and journals. They also took on a life of their own in public discussions in what was a new popular institution of European social life—the coffeehouse.

Coffee, originally imported into Europe from the Ottoman Empire, is the chief Turkish contribution to the Western diet. Coffeehouses had long existed in the Muslim world, encouraged by the Islamic prohibition on alcoholic drink. The first European coffeehouse appeared in Venice in the 1640s, and the first coffeehouse in Vienna opened its doors in 1683 with coffee left behind when the Turks abandoned their siege of the city.

By the middle of the eighteenth century, thousands of coffeehouses dotted European cities and towns. Customers were attracted to them in part because the coffeehouses did not serve alcoholic beverages, which made unruly behavior less likely than in taverns. (The practice of tipping began in the coffeehouses of London. The word *tips* originated as an acronym for "to insure prompt service.")

Throughout Europe, the coffeehouse provided a social arena for the open, spontaneous discussion of events, politics, literature, and ideas—but only for men (respectable women did not enter coffeehouses). By furnishing copies of newspapers and other journals, the proprietors of coffeehouses linked their customers to the growing print culture just as today's Internet cafés link customers to the World Wide Web. In London coffeehouses, members of the Royal Society and other men associated with the new science mixed with merchants and bankers. Some London coffeehouse proprietors invited learned persons to lecture, usually for a fee, on Newtonian physics, the mechanical philosophy, ethics, and the relationship of science and religion. One historian has described these lecturers as "the philosophical brotherhood of the coffeehouses."[1]

In France the philosophes, such as Voltaire, Rousseau, and Diderot, looked to the café as a place to meet other writers. By 1743, a German commented, "A coffeehouse is like a political stock exchange, where the most gallant and wittiest heads of every estate come together. They engage in wide-ranging and edifying talk, issue well-founded judgments on matters concerning the political and the scholarly world, converse sagaciously about the most secret news from all courts and states, and unveil the most hidden truths."[2]

One irony, however, should be noted about the eighteenth-century European coffeehouses. Although they provided one of the chief locations for the public discussion of the ideas of the Enlightenment, which fostered greater liberty of thought in Europe, the coffee and sugar consumed in these establishments were cultivated by slave labor on plantations in the Caribbean and Brazil. The coffeehouse was one of many institutions of European life that was connected to the transatlantic plantation slave economy.

How did coffeehouses help spread the ideas of the Enlightenment?

How was the consumption of coffee related to the transatlantic slave trade?

Business, science, religion, and politics were discussed in London coffeehouses such as this. Permission of the Trustees of the British Museum

[1]Larry Stewart, *The Rise of Public Science, Rhetoric Technology, and Natural Philosophy in Newtonian Britain, 1660–1750* (Cambridge: Cambridge University Press, 1992), p. 145.

[2]Quoted in James Van Horn Melton, *The Rise of the Public in Enlightenment Europe* (Cambridge: Cambridge University Press, 2001), p. 243.

readers had enough income to buy and the leisure to read the philosophes' works. Although the writers of the Enlightenment did not consciously champion the goals or causes of the middle class, they did provide an intellectual ferment and a major source of ideas that could be used to undermine existing social practices and political structures based on aristocratic privilege. They taught their contemporaries, including reform-minded aristocrats, how to pose pointed, critical questions. Moreover, the philosophes generally supported the expansion of trade, the improvement of agriculture and transport, and the invention of new manufacturing machinery that were transforming the society and the economy of the eighteenth century and enlarging the business and commercial classes.

The chief bond among the philosophes was their common desire to reform religion, political thought, society, government, and the economy for the sake of human liberty. As the historian Peter Gay once suggested, this goal included "freedom from arbitrary power, freedom of speech, freedom of trade, freedom to realize one's talents, freedom of aesthetic response, freedom, in a word, of moral man to make his way in the world."[4] Though challenged over the last three centuries, no other single set of ideas has done so much to shape and define the modern Western world.

Statue of Voltaire by Jean-Antoine Houdon (Théâtre Francais, Paris). Musée Lambinet, Versailles/Giraudon/Art Resource, NY

Voltaire—First Among the Philosophes

By far the most influential of the philosophes was François-Marie Arouet, known to posterity by his pen name Voltaire (1694–1778). During the 1720s, Voltaire had offended first the French monarch and then certain nobles by his politically and socially irreverent poetry and plays. He was arrested and twice briefly imprisoned, in comfortable conditions, in the Bastille, the royal prison-fortress in Paris. In 1726, to escape the wrath of a powerful aristocrat whom he had offended, Voltaire went into exile in England. There he visited its best literary circles, observed its tolerant intellectual and religious climate, relished the freedom he felt in its moderate political atmosphere, and admired its science and economic prosperity. In 1727, he also witnessed the elaborate funeral of Sir Isaac Newton. The next year Voltaire returned to France and, in 1733, published *Letters on the English*, which appeared in French the next year. The book praised the virtues of the English, especially their religious liberty, and implicitly criticized the abuses of French society. The Parlement of Paris condemned the book, and the authorities harassed Voltaire. He moved to Cirey from which, if necessary, he could easily escape France into what was then the nearby independent duchy of Lorraine. There he lived with Countess Emilie de Chatelet (1706–1749), the brilliant mathematician, discussed in Chapter 14, who became his mistress. In 1738, with her considerable help, he published *Elements of the Philosophy of Newton*, which more than any other single book popularized the thought of Isaac Newton across the continent. In 1749, Madame de Chatelet died.

Shortly thereafter, Voltaire took up residence for three years in Berlin at the court of Frederick the Great of Prussia with whom he had corresponded for several years. The residency ended unhappily with Voltaire fleeing to France. For a time he settled in Switzerland near Geneva but clashed with local conservative Calvinist clergy over his sponsoring plays in the theater in his

[4]Gay, *The Enlightenment*, p. 3.

home. Thereafter he acquired the estate of Ferney, just across the French border, but close enough to flee to Geneva should the French authorities bother him. His extremely popular plays, essays, histories, and stories along with his far-flung correspondence made him the literary dictator of Europe. For the rest of his long life, he turned the venom of his satire and sarcasm against one evil after another in French and European life.

In 1755 a huge earthquake struck Lisbon, Portugal, killing at least 60,000 people. Voltaire wrote a deeply pessimistic poem commemorating the event. Other contemporary writers questioned his pessimism arguing for a more optimistic view of life and nature. In 1759, Voltaire replied in the novel *Candide*, his still widely read satire attacking war, religious persecution, and what he considered unwarranted optimism about the human condition. Like most of the philosophes, Voltaire believed human society could and should be improved, but he was never certain that reform, if achieved, would be permanent. In that respect his thought reflected the broader pessimistic undercurrent of the Enlightenment. As his fellow philosophe Jean d'Alembert wrote, "Barbarism lasts for centuries; it seems that it is our natural element; reason and good taste are only passing."[5]

In his later years, as will be seen in the next section, Voltaire also became a major voice attacking religious persecution and advocating toleration. He died in 1778 in Paris after a triumphal return to that city, which he had not seen for decades.

▼ The Enlightenment and Religion

For many, but not all, philosophes of the eighteenth century, ecclesiastical institutions, especially in their frequently privileged position as official parts of the state, were the chief impediment to human improvement and happiness. Voltaire's cry, "Crush the Infamous Thing," summed up the attitude of a number of philosophes toward the churches and Christianity. Almost all varieties of Christianity, but especially Roman Catholicism, felt their criticism as also did both Judaism and Islam.

The critical philosophes complained that both established and non-established Christian churches hindered the pursuit of a rational life and the scientific study of humanity and nature. Both Roman Catholic and Protestant clergy taught that humans were basically depraved, becoming worthy only through divine grace. According to the doctrine of original sin—either Protestant or Catholic—meaningful improvement in human nature on earth was impossible. Religion thus turned attention away from this world to the world to come. For example, the philosophes argued that the Calvinist doctrine of predestination denied that virtuous behavior in this life could affect the fate of a person's soul after death. Mired in conflicts over obscure doctrines, the churches promoted intolerance and bigotry, inciting torture, war, and other forms of human suffering.

With this attack, the philosophes were challenging not only a set of ideas, but also some of Europe's most powerful institutions. The churches were deeply enmeshed in the power structure of the Old Regime. They owned large amounts of land and collected tithes from peasants before any secular authority collected its taxes. Most clergy were legally exempt from taxes and made only annual voluntary grants to the government. The upper clergy in most countries were relatives or clients of aristocrats. High clerics were actively involved in politics. Bishops served in the British House of Lords and on the Continent, cardinals and bishops advised rulers or were sovereign princes themselves. In Protestant countries, the leading local landowner usually appointed the parish clergyman. In Britain and on the Continent, membership in the state church conferred political and social advantages. Those who did not belong to it were often excluded from political life, the universities, and the professions. Clergy frequently provided intellectual justification for the social and political status quo, and they were active agents of religious and literary censorship.

Deism

The philosophes, although critical of many religious institutions and frequently anticlerical, did not oppose all religion. In Scotland, for example, the enlightened historian William Robertson (1721–1793) was the head of the Scottish Presbyterian Kirk. In England, Anglican clergymen did much to popularize the thought of Newton. In France, several of the leading philosophes were Catholic priests. What the philosophes sought, however, was religion without fanaticism and intolerance, a religious life that would largely substitute human reason for the authority of churches. The Newtonian worldview had convinced many writers that nature was rational. Therefore, the God who had created nature must also be rational, and the religion through which that God was worshipped should be rational. Most of them believed the life of religion and of reason could be combined, giving rise to a a broad set of ideas known as **deism**.

The title of one of the earliest deist works, *Christianity Not Mysterious* (1696) by John Toland (1670–1722), indicates the general tenor of this religious outlook. Toland and later deist writers promoted religion as a natural and rational, rather than a supernatural and mystical, phenomenon. In this respect they differed from Newton and Locke, both of whom regarded themselves as Christians (though not necessarily theologically orthodox ones). Newton believed God could interfere with the natural order, whereas the deists regarded God as a

[5]Jean Le Rond d'Alembert, *Preliminary Discourse to the Encyclopedia of Diderot*, trans. by Richard N. Schwab (Indianapolis: ITT Bobbs-Merrill Educational Publishing, 1985), p. 103.

kind of divine watchmaker who had created the mechanism of nature, set it in motion, and then departed.

The deists' informal creed had two major points. The first was a belief in the existence of God, which they thought the contemplation of nature could empirically justify, and in this respect many Protestant and Roman Catholic writers fully agreed with them. Joseph Addison's poem on the spacious firmament (1712) illustrates this idea:

The spacious firmament on high,
With all the blue ethereal sky,
And spangled heav'n, a shining frame,
Their great Original proclaim:
Th' unwearied Sun, from day to day,
Does his Creator's power display,
And publishes to every land
The work of an Almighty hand.

Because nature provided evidence of a rational God, that deity must also favor rational morality. So the second point in the deists' creed was a belief in life after death, when rewards and punishments would be meted out according to the virtue of the lives people led on this earth.

Deism, Enlightenment writers urged, was empirical, tolerant, reasonable, and capable of encouraging virtuous living. Voltaire once wrote,

> The great name of Deist, which is not sufficiently revered, is the only name one ought to take. The only gospel one ought to read is the great book of Nature, written by the hand of God and sealed with his seal. The only religion that ought to be professed is the religion of worshiping God and being a good man.[6]

Deists hoped that wide acceptance of their faith would end rivalry among the various Christian sects and with it religious fanaticism, conflict, and persecution. They also felt deism would remove the need for priests and ministers, who, in their view, were often responsible for fomenting religious differences and denominational hatred. Deistic thought led some contemporaries to believe God had revealed himself in different ways and that many religions might embody divine truth.

There was never a formal or extensive deist movement, but deist ideas spread informally throughout the culture and provided for some people a framework for a nondogmatic religious outlook. Furthermore, in England writers defending the privileges of the Church of England often ascribed deist ideas to quite orthodox English nonconformists who were serious Protestants who simply dissented from the established church. Most deist writers were strongly anticlerical and were for that reason regarded as politically radical, an association that was strengthened by the links between Unitarians and political radicalism. Christian writers often attacked the deists because of this anticlericalism and associated political radicalism and thus actually spread their ideas and may have made the movement appear more influential and pervasive than it was. In this respect, religious controversy arising from orthodox writers themselves placed new religious ideas into the public sphere as much or more than the actual publications of unorthodox authors.

[6]Quoted in J. H. Randall, *The Making of the Modern Mind*, rev. ed. (New York: Houghton Mifflin, 1940), p. 292.

Toleration

As discussed in Chapter 14, John Locke had set forth a strong argument for toleration in his *Letter Concerning Toleration* of 1689. Except in England, however, toleration generally remained the exception during most of the eighteenth century. Continuing in Locke's spirit, the philosophes presented religious toleration as a primary social condition for the virtuous life. Again Voltaire took the polemical lead in championing this cause. In 1762, the Roman Catholic political authorities in the city of Toulouse ordered the execution of a Huguenot named Jean Calas, who had been accused of murdering his son to prevent him from converting to Roman Catholicism. Calas was viciously tortured and publicly strangled without ever confessing his guilt. The confession would not have saved his life, but it would have given the Catholics good propaganda to use against Protestants.

Voltaire learned of the case only after Calas's death. He made the dead man's cause his own. In 1763, he published his *Treatise on Tolerance* and hounded the authorities for a new investigation. Finally, in 1765, the judicial decision against the unfortunate man was reversed. For Voltaire, the case illustrated the fruits of religious fanaticism and the need for rational reform of judicial processes. (See "Voltaire Attacks Religious Fanaticism," page 500.)

In 1779, the German playwright and critic Gotthold Lessing (1729–1781) wrote *Nathan the Wise*, a plea for toleration not only of different Christian groups, but also of religious faiths other than Christianity. The premise behind all of these calls for toleration was, in effect, that life on earth and human relationships should not be subordinated to religious zeal that permitted one group of people to persecute, harm, or repress other groups.

Radical Enlightenment Criticism of Christianity

Some philosophes went beyond the formulation of a rational religious alternative to Christianity and the advocacy of toleration to attack the churches and the clergy with vehemence. The Scottish philosopher David Hume (1711–1776), argued in "Of Miracles," a chapter in his *Inquiry into Human Nature* (1748), that no empirical evidence supported the belief in divine miracles central to much of Christianity. For Hume, the greatest miracle was that people believed in miracles. Voltaire repeatedly

VOLTAIRE ATTACKS RELIGIOUS FANATICISM

The chief complaint of the philosophes against Christianity was that over the course of its history it had bred a fanaticism that led people to commit crimes in the name of religion. In this passage from Voltaire's Philosophical Dictionary *(1764), he directly reminds his readers of the intolerance of the Reformation era and indirectly referred to examples of contemporary religious excesses. He argues that the philosophical spirit can overcome fanaticism and foster toleration and more humane religious behavior. Shocking many of his contemporaries, he praises the virtues of Confucianism over those of Christianity.*

What concrete examples of religious fanaticism might Voltaire have had in mind? Why does Voltaire contend that neither religion nor laws can contain religious fanaticism? Why does Voltaire admire the Chinese?

Fanaticism is to superstition what delirium is to fever and rage to anger. The man visited by ecstasies and visions, who takes dreams for realities and his fancies for prophecies, is an enthusiast; the man who supports his madness with murder is a fanatic. . . .

The most detestable example of fanaticism was that of the burghers of Paris who on St. Bartholomew's Night [1572] went about assassinating and butchering all their fellow citizens who did not go to mass, throwing them out of windows, cutting them in pieces.

Once fanaticism has corrupted a mind, the malady is almost incurable. . . . The only remedy for this epidemic malady is the philosophical spirit which, spread gradually, at last tames men's habits and prevents the disease from starting; for once the disease has made any progress, one must flee and wait for the air to clear itself. Laws and religion are not strong enough against the spiritual pest; religion, far from being healthy food for infected brains, turns to poison in them. . . .

Even the law is impotent against these attacks of rage; it is like reading a court decree to a raving maniac. These fellows are certain that the holy spirit with which they are filled is above the law, that their enthusiasm is the only law they must obey.

What can we say to a man who tells you that he would rather obey God than men, and that therefore he is sure to go to heaven for butchering you?

Ordinarily fanatics are guided by rascals, who put the dagger into their hands; these latter resemble that Old Man of the Mountain who is supposed to have made imbeciles taste the joys of paradise and who promised them an eternity of the pleasures of which he had given them a foretaste, on condition that they assassinated all those he would name to them. There is only one religion in the world that has never been sullied by fanaticism, that of the Chinese men of letters. The schools of philosophy were not only free from this pest, they were its remedy; for the effect of philosophy is to make the soul tranquil, and fanaticism is incompatible with tranquility. If our holy religion has so often been corrupted by this infernal delirium, it is the madness of men which is at fault.

Voltaire, *Philosophical Dictionary*, trans. by P. Gay (New York: Basic Books, 1962), pp. 267–269.

questioned the truthfulness of priests and the morality of the Bible. In his *Philosophical Dictionary* (1764), he humorously pointed out inconsistencies in biblical narratives and immoral acts of the biblical heroes. In *The Decline and Fall of the Roman Empire* (1776), Edward Gibbon (1737–1794), the English historian, explained the rise of Christianity in terms of natural causes rather than the influence of miracles and piety. Some of these ideas were new, but many had existed before the Enlightenment in the anti–Roman Catholic polemics of Protestant writers and were brought back into circulation by the philosophes.

A few, but actually very few, philosophes went further than criticism. Baron d'Holbach (1723–1789) and Julien Offray de La Mettrie (1709–1751) embraced positions close to atheism and materialism. Theirs was distinctly a minority position, however. Most of the philosophes sought not the abolition of religion, but its transformation into a humane force that would encourage virtuous living. In the words of the title of a work by the German philosopher Immanuel Kant (1724–1804), they sought to pursue *Religion within the Limits of Reason Alone* (1793).

Jewish Thinkers in the Age of Enlightenment

Despite their emphasis on toleration, the philosophes' criticisms of traditional religion often reflected an implicit contempt not only for Christianity but also, and sometimes more vehemently, for Judaism and, as we see later, for Islam as well. Their attack on the veracity of biblical miracles and biblical history undermined the authority of the Hebrew scriptures as well as the Christian. They often aimed their satirical barbs at personalities from the Hebrew scriptures. Some philosophes characterized Judaism as a more primitive faith than Christianity and one from which philosophical rationalism provided a path of escape. The Enlightenment view of religion thus served in some ways to further stigmatize Jews and Judaism in the eyes of non-Jewish Europeans.

Enlightenment values also, however, allowed certain Jewish intellectuals to rethink the relationship of their communities to the wider European culture from which they had largely lived apart. Two major Jewish writers—one a few decades before the opening of the Enlightenment and one toward the close—entered the larger debate over religion and the place of Jews in European life. These were Baruch Spinoza (1632–1677), who lived in the Netherlands, and Moses Mendelsohn (1729–1786), who lived in Germany. Spinoza set the example for a secularized version of Judaism, and Mendelsohn established the main outlines of an assimilationist position. Although their approaches displayed certain similarities, there were also important differences.

The new science of the mid-seventeenth century deeply influenced Spinoza, the son of a Jewish merchant of Amsterdam. Like his contemporaries, Hobbes and Descartes, he looked to the power of human reason to reconceptualize traditional thought. In that regard his thinking reflected the age of scientific revolution and looked toward the later Enlightenment.

In his *Ethics*, the most famous of his works, Spinoza so closely identified God and nature, or the spiritual and material worlds, that contemporaries condemned him. Many thought he drew God and nature too intimately into a single divine substance, leaving little room for the possibility of a distinctly divine revelation to humankind in scripture. Both Christians and Jews also believed Spinoza's near pantheistic position (the idea that God is not a distinct personality but that everything in the universe is) meant that human beings might not be personally responsible for their actions and that there could be no personal, individual immortality of the human soul after death. During his lifetime the controversial character of his writings led both Jews and Protestants to criticize him as an atheist. When he was twenty-four, his own synagogue excommunicated him, and thereafter he lived apart from the Amsterdam Jewish community.

The Dutch Jewish philosopher Baruch Spinoza was deeply influenced by the new science of the mid-seventeenth century. In his writings, Spinoza argued for rationality over traditional spiritual beliefs. Library of Congress

In his *Theologico-Political Treatise* (1670), Spinoza directly anticipated much of the religious criticism of the Enlightenment and its attacks on the power of superstition in human life. Spinoza described the origins of religion in thoroughly naturalistic terms. He believed the Hebrew Bible provided Jews with divine legislation, but not with specially revealed theological knowledge. In this respect, he was calling on both Jews and Christians to use their own reason in religious matters and to read the Bible like other ancient books. Spinoza's extensive rational and historical criticism of the biblical narratives disturbed Christian and Jewish contemporaries who saw him as a writer seeking to lead people away from all religion. He actually argued, however, that the formally organized religious institutions of both Christianity and Judaism led people away from the original teaching of scripture and encouraged them to persecute those who disagreed with the leaders of their respective churches and synagogues.

Because of Spinoza's excommunication from his synagogue, the philosophes considered him a martyr for rationality against superstition. He also symbolized Jews who, through the use of their critical reason, separated themselves from traditional Judaism and attempted to enter mainstream society to pursue a secular existence with little or no regard for their original faith. Consequently, his life and his writings, as one commentator has stated, "made it possible for defenders of the Enlightenment to advocate toleration of Jews while simultaneously holding Judaism in contempt."[7] This stance of championing toleration while condemning Judaism itself would later characterize the outlook of many non-Jewish Europeans regarding the assimilation of Jews into European civic life. It was, however, an outlook that Jewish communities themselves could not welcome without considerable modification.

Moses Mendelsohn, the leading Jewish philosopher of the eighteenth century, was known as the "Jewish Socrates." Writing almost a century after Spinoza, he also advocated the entry of Jews into modern European life. In contrast to Spinoza, however, Mendelsohn argued that a Jew could combine loyalty to Judaism with adherence to rational, Enlightenment values. Mendelsohn could hold this position in part because of the influence of Lessing's arguments for toleration. Indeed, Mendelsohn had been the chief model for Lessing's character *Nathan the Wise*.

Mendelsohn's most influential work was *Jerusalem; or, On Ecclesiastical Power and Judaism* (1783) in which he argued both for extensive religious toleration and for maintaining the religious distinction of Jewish communities. Mendelsohn urged that religious diversity within a nation did not harm loyalty to the government; therefore, governments should be religiously neutral and Jews should enjoy the same civil rights as other subjects. Then, in the spirit of the deists, he presented Judaism as one of many religious paths revealed by God. Jewish law and practice were intended for the moral benefit of Jewish communities; other religions similarly served other people. Consequently, various communities should be permitted to practice their religious faith alongside other religious groups.

Unlike Spinoza, Mendelsohn wished to advocate religious toleration while genuinely sustaining the traditional religious practices and faith of Judaism. Nevertheless, Mendelsohn believed Jewish communities should not have the right to excommunicate their members over differences in theological opinions or even if their members embraced modern secular ideas. He thus sought both toleration of Jews within European society and toleration by Jews of a wider spectrum of opinion within their own communities. His hope was that the rationalism of the Enlightenment would provide the foundation for both types of toleration. Mendelsohn thus set forth a far more extensive vision of religious toleration than had John Locke almost a century earlier. Locke had contended that while the state should tolerate many different religious communities, each should retain the right of excommunication over its members (see Chapter 14).

[7]Steven B. Smith, *Spinoza, Liberalism, and the Question of Jewish Identity* (New Haven, CT: Yale University Press, 1997), p. 166.

Islam in Enlightenment Thought

Unlike Judaism, Islam, except in the Balkan Peninsula, had few adherents in eighteenth-century Europe. Although European merchants traded with the Ottoman Empire or with those parts of South Asia where Islam prevailed, most Europeans came to know what little they did know about the Islamic world and Islam as a religion through books—the religious commentaries of Christian missionaries, histories, and the reports of travelers—that, with rare exceptions, were hostile to Islam and deeply misleading.

Islam continued to be seen as a rival to Christianity. European writers, such as Pascal in his *Pensées* (see Chapter 14), repeated what other Christian critics had said for centuries. They portrayed Islam as a false religion and Muhammad as an impostor and a false prophet because he had not performed miracles. Furthermore, they also attacked Islam as an exceptionally carnal or sexually promiscuous religion because of its teaching that heaven was a place of sensuous delights, its permission for a man to have more than one wife, Muhammad's own polygamy, and the presence of harems in the Islamic world.

Christian authors also ignored the Islamic understanding of the life and mission of Muhammad. They referred to Islam as Muhammadanism, thus implying that Muhammad was divine rather than a human being with whom God had chosen to communicate. Muslims consider the suggestion that Muhammad was divine to be blasphemous.

European universities did endow professorships to study Arabic during the seventeenth century, but these university scholars generally agreed with theological critics that Islam too often embodied religious fanaticism. Even relatively well-informed works based on knowledge of Arabic and Islamic sources, such as Barthélemy d'Herbelot's *Bibliothèque orientale* (*Oriental Library*), a reference book published in 1697, Simon Ockley's *History of the Saracens* (1718), and George Sale's introduction to the first full English translation of the Qur'an (1734), were largely hostile to their subject. All of these books continued to be reprinted and remained influential well into the nineteenth century, demonstrating how little information disinterested Europeans had about Islam.

Enlightenment philosophes spoke with two voices regarding Islam. Voltaire indicated his opinion along with that of many of his contemporaries in the title of his 1742 tragedy *Fanaticism, or Mohammed the Prophet*. Although he sometimes spoke well of the Qur'an, Voltaire declared in a later historical work, "We must suppose that Muhammed, like all enthusiasts, violently impressed by his own ideas, retailed them in good faith, fortified them with fancies, deceived himself in deceiving others, and

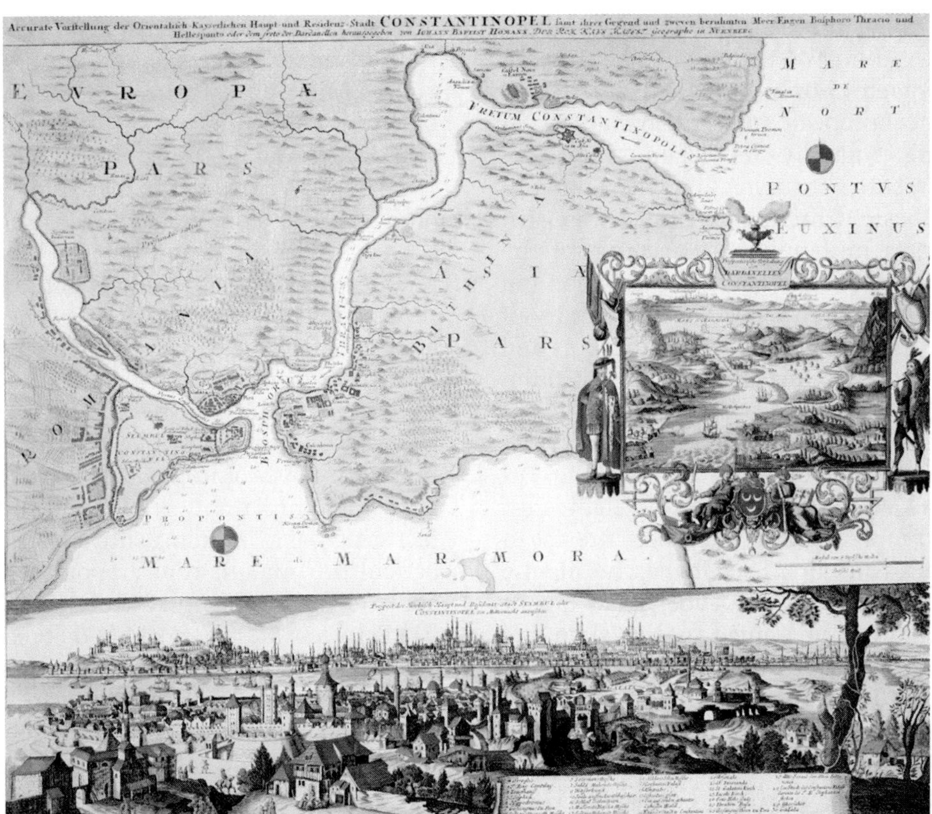

Few Europeans visited the Ottoman Empire. What little they knew about it came from reports of travelers and from illustrations such as this 1710 view of Constantinople, the empire's capital. © Historical Picture Archive/CORBIS

finally sustained with deceit a doctrine he believed to be good."[8] Thus, for Voltaire, Muhammad and Islam in general represented simply one more example of the religious fanaticism he had so often criticized among Christians.

Some Enlightenment writers, however, spoke well of the Islamic faith. The deist John Toland, who opposed prejudice against both Jews and Muslims, contended that Islam derived from early Christian writings and was thus a form of Christianity. These views so offended most of his contemporaries that Toland became known as a "Mohametan" Christian. Edward Gibbon, who blamed Christianity for contributing to the fall of the Roman Empire, wrote with respect of Muhammad's leadership and Islam's success in conquering so vast a territory in the first century of its existence. Other commentators approved of Islam's tolerance and the charitable work of Muslims.

Some philosophes criticized Islam on cultural and political grounds. In *The Persian Letters* (1721), supposedly written by two Muslim Persians visiting Europe, the young philosophe Charles de Montesquieu used Islamic culture as a foil to criticize his own European society. Yet, by the time he wrote his more influential *Spirit of the Laws* (1748), discussed more fully later in this chapter, Montesquieu associated Islamic society with the passivity that he ascribed to people subject to political despotism. Like other Europeans, Montesquieu believed the excessive influence of Islamic religious leaders prevented the Ottoman Empire from adapting itself to new advances in technology.

One of the most positive commentators on eighteenth-century Islam was a woman. Between 1716 and 1718, Lady Mary Wortley Montagu (1689–1762) lived in Istanbul with her husband, the British ambassador to Turkey. She wrote a series of letters about her experiences there that were published the year after her death. In these *Turkish Embassy Letters*, she praised much about Ottoman society and urged the English to copy the Turkish practice of vaccination against smallpox. Unlike European males, Montagu had access to the private quarters of women in Istanbul. In contrast to the constraints under which English women found themselves, she thought upper-class Turkish women were remarkably free and well treated by their husbands despite having to wear clothing that completely covered them in public. In fact, Montagu thought the anonymity these coverings bestowed allowed Turkish women to move freely about Istanbul. She also considered the magnificent Ottoman architecture better than anything in Western Europe. Montagu repeatedly criticized the misinformation that

[8]Quoted in Theodore Besterman, *Voltaire* (New York: Harcourt, Brace, & World, 1969), p. 409.

prevailed in Europe about the Ottoman Empire and declared that many of the hostile comments about Islam and Islamic morality were simply wrong.

Nevertheless, the European voices demanding fairness and expressing empathy for Islam were rare throughout the eighteenth century. As one historian has commented, "The basic Christian attitude was still what it had been for a millennium: a rejection of the claim of Muslims that Muhammad was a prophet and the Qur'an the word of God, mingled with a memory of periods of fear and conflict, and also, a few thinkers and scholars apart, with legends, usually hostile and often contemptuous."[9]

Muslims were not curious about the Christian West themselves. Only a handful of Muslims from the Ottoman Empire visited Western Europe in the eighteenth century, and no Islamic writers showed much interest in contemporary European authors. The Ulema, the Islamic religious scholars, reinforced these attitudes. They taught that God's revelations to Muhammad meant Islam had replaced Christianity as a religion and therefore there was little for Muslims to learn from Christian culture.

▾ The Enlightenment and Society

The *Encyclopedia:* Freedom and Economic Improvement

The mid-century witnessed the publication of the *Encyclopedia*, one of the greatest monuments of the Enlightenment and its most monumental undertaking in the realm of print culture. Under the heroic leadership of Denis Diderot (1713–1784) and Jean Le Rond d'Alembert (1717–1783), the first volume appeared in 1751. Eventually, numbering seventeen volumes of text and eleven of plates (illustrations), the project was completed in 1772. No other work of the Enlightenment so illustrated the movement's determination to probe life on earth rather than in the religious realm. As one writer in the *Encyclopedia* observed, "Man is the unique point to which we must refer everything, if we wish to interest and please amongst considerations the most arid and details the most dry."[10] The use of the word *man* in this passage was not simply an accident of language. Most philosophes, as we shall see later in the chapter, were thinking primarily of men, not women, when they framed their reformist ideas.

The *Encyclopedia*, in part a collective plea for freedom of expression, reached fruition only after many attempts to censor it and halt its publication. It was the product of the collective effort of more than a hundred authors, and its editors had at one time or another solicited articles from all the major French philosophes. It included the most advanced critical ideas of the time on religion, government, and philosophy. To avoid official censure, these ideas often had to be hidden in obscure articles or under the cover of irony. The *Encyclopedia* also included numerous important articles and illustrations on manufacturing, canal building, ship construction, and improved agriculture, making it an important source of knowledge about eighteenth-century social and economic life.

Between 14,000 and 16,000 copies of various editions of the *Encyclopedia* were sold before 1789. The project had been designed to secularize learning and to undermine intellectual assumptions that lingered from the Middle Ages and the Reformation. The articles on politics, ethics, and society ignored divine law and concentrated on humanity and its immediate well-being. The Encyclopedists looked to antiquity rather than to the Christian centuries for their intellectual and ethical models. For them, the future welfare of humankind lay not in pleasing God or following divine commandments, but rather in harnessing the power and resources of the earth and in living at peace with one's fellow human beings. The good life lay here and now and was to be achieved through the application of reason to human relationships. The publication of the *Encyclopedia* spread Enlightenment thought more fully over the Continent, penetrating German and Russian intellectual and political circles.

Denis Diderot was the heroic editor of the *Encylopedia* published in seventeen volumes of text and eleven of prints between 1751 and 1772. Through its pages many of the chief ideas of the Enlightenment reached a broad audience of readers. Réunion des Musées Nationaux/Art Resource, NY. Jean-Simon Berthelemy (1743-1811), "Denis Diderot" (1713–1784). Writer and Encyelopaedist. Oil on canvas, 55 x 46 cm. Inv.: P 2082. Photo: Bulloz. Musee de la Ville de Paris, Musee Carnavalet, Paris, France/Art Resource, NY

[9]A. Hourani, *Islam in European Thought* (Cambridge: Cambridge University Press, 1991), p. 136.

[10]Quoted in F. L. Baumer, *Main Currents of Western Thought*, 4th ed. (New Haven, CT: Yale University Press, 1978), p. 374.

Beccaria and Reform of Criminal Law

Although the term did not appear until later, the idea of *social science* originated with the Enlightenment. Philosophes hoped to end human cruelty by discovering social laws and making people aware of them. These concerns are most evident in the philosophes' work on law and prisons.

In 1764, Marquis Cesare Beccaria (1738–1794), an Italian aristocrat and philosophe, published *On Crimes and Punishments*, in which he applied critical analysis to the problem of making punishments both effective and just. He wanted the laws of monarchs and legislatures—that is, positive law—to conform with the rational laws of nature. He rigorously and eloquently attacked both torture and capital punishment. He thought the criminal justice system should ensure a speedy trial and certain punishment and the intent of punishment should be to deter further crime. The purpose of laws was not to impose the will of God or some other ideal of perfection, but to secure the greatest good or happiness for the greatest number of human beings. This utilitarian philosophy based on happiness in this life permeated most Enlightenment writing on practical reforms.

The Physiocrats and Economic Freedom

Economic policy was another area in which the philosophes saw existing legislation and administration preventing the operation of natural social laws. They believed mercantilist legislation (designed to protect a country's trade from external competition) and the regulation of labor by governments and guilds actually hampered the expansion of trade, manufacture, and agriculture. In France, these economic reformers were called the **physiocrats**. Their leading spokespeople were François Quesnay (1694–1774) and Pierre Dupont de Nemours (1739–1817).

The physiocrats believed the primary role of government was to protect property and to permit its owners to use it freely. They argued that agriculture was the basis on which all economic production depended. They favored the consolidation of small peasant holdings into larger, more efficient farms. Here, as elsewhere, the rationalism of the Enlightenment was closely connected to the spirit of improvement that influenced so much of eighteenth-century European economic life.

Adam Smith on Economic Growth and Social Progress

The most important economic work of the Enlightenment was Adam Smith's (1723–1790) *Inquiry into the Nature and Causes of the Wealth of Nations* (1776). Smith, who was for a time a professor at Glasgow University in Scotland, believed economic liberty was the foundation of a natural economic system. As a result, he urged that the mercantile system of England—including the navigation acts governing colonial trade, the bounties the government gave to favored merchants and industries, most tariffs, trading monopolies, and the domestic regulation of labor and manufacture—be abolished. These regulations were intended to preserve the wealth of the nation, to capture wealth from other nations, and to maximize the work available for the nation's laborers. Smith argued, however, that they hindered the expansion of wealth and production. The best way to encourage economic growth, he maintained, was to unleash individuals to pursue their own selfish economic interests. As self-interested individuals sought to enrich themselves by meeting the needs of others in the marketplace, the economy would expand. Consumers would find their wants met as manufacturers and merchants competed for their business.

Mercantilism assumed that the earth's resources were limited and scarce, so one nation could acquire wealth only at the expense of others. Smith's book challenged this assumption. He saw the resources of nature—water, air, soil, and minerals—as boundless. To him, they demanded exploitation for the enrichment and comfort of humankind. In effect, Smith was saying the nations and peoples of Europe need not be poor.

Smith is usually regarded as the founder of **laissez-faire** economic thought and policy, which favors a limited role for the government in economic life. *The Wealth of Nations* was, however, a complex book. Smith was no simple dogmatist. For example, he did not oppose all government activity in the economy. The government, he argued, should provide schools, armies, navies, and roads. It should also undertake certain commercial ventures, such as opening dangerous new trade routes that were economically desirable, but too expensive or risky for private enterprise. The public should in particular support education of those people who occupied the humbler occupations of life. (See "Adam Smith Calls for Government Action to Support the Education of the Poor," page 506.)

Within *The Wealth of Nations*, Smith, like other Scottish thinkers of the day, embraced an important theory of human social and economic development, known as the *four-stage theory*. According to this theory, human societies can be classified as hunting and gathering, pastoral or herding, agricultural, or commercial. The hunters and gatherers have little or no settled life. Pastoral societies are groups of nomads who tend their herds and develop some private property. Agricultural or farming societies are settled and have clear-cut property arrangements. Finally, the commercial state includes advanced cities, the manufacture of numerous items for wide consumption, extensive trade between cities and the countryside, as well as elaborate forms of property and financial arrangements. Smith and other Scottish writers described the passage of human society through these stages as a movement from barbarism to civilization.

ADAM SMITH CALLS FOR GOVERNMENT ACTION TO SUPPORT THE EDUCATION OF THE POOR

Adam Smith in The Wealth of Nations *had argued that the division of labor increased the productive capacity of human beings and hence economic growth and the accumulation of wealth. Smith, however, also recognized that the division of labor might over the course of time take a very heavy toll on the lives of workers involved in repetitive activities of production. In this passage he portrays that human toll and then calls for government action to provide education for the poor. He also believed that the workers should pay for part of their education so that the schoolmaster would be held accountable to paying students.*

What does Smith portray as the results of repetitive work caused by the division of labor? Why does he place so much emphasis on the mental and emotional costs? How does he see this situation as undermining civic interest? What solutions does he propose?

In the progress of the division of labour, the employment of the far greater part of those who live by labour, that is, of the great body of the people, comes to be confined to a few very simple operations, frequently to one or two. But the understandings of the greater part of men are necessarily formed by their ordinary employments. The man whose whole life is spent in performing a few simple operations, of which the effects too are, perhaps, always the same, or very nearly the same, has no occasion to exert his understanding, or to exercise his invention in finding out expedients for removing difficulties which never occur. He naturally loses, therefore, the habit of such exertion, and generally becomes as stupid and ignorant as it is possible for a human creature to become. The torpor of his mind renders him not only incapable of relishing or bear a part in any rational conversation, but of conceiving any generous, noble, or tender sentiment, and consequently of forming any just judgment concerning many even of the ordinary duties of private life. Of the great and extensive interest of his country he is altogether incapable of judging; and unless very particular pains have been taken to render him otherwise, he is equally incapable of defending his country in war. The uniformity of his stationary life naturally corrupts the courage of his mind, and makes him regard with abhorrence the irregular, uncertain, and adventurous life of a soldier. It corrupts even the activity of his body, and render him incapable of exerting his strength with vigour and perseverance, in any other employment than that to which he has been bred. His dexterity at his own particular trade seems, in this manner, to be acquired at the expence of his intellectual, social, and martial virtues. But in every improved and civilized society this is the state into which the labouring poor, that is, the great body of the people, must necessarily fall, unless government takes some pains to prevent it. . . .

The education of the common people requires . . . the attention of the public more than that of people of some rank and fortune . . . [who]are generally eighteen or nineteen years of age before they enter upon that particular business, profession, or trade by which they propose to distinguish themselves in the world. . . .

It is otherwise with the common people. They have little time to spare for education. Their parents can scarce afford to maintain them even in infancy. As soon as they are able to work, they must apply to some trade by which they can earn their subsistence. . . . but though the common people cannot . . . be so well instructed as people of some rank and fortune, the most essential parts of education, however to read, write, and account, can be acquired at so early a period of life, that the greater part even of those who are to be bred to the lowest occupations, have time to acquire them before they can be employed in those occupations. For a very small expence the public can facilitate, can encourage, and can even impose upon almost the whole body of the people, the necessity of acquiring those most essential parts of education.

Adam Smith, *An Inquiry into the Nature and Causes of the Wealth of Nations* (London: T. Nelson and Sons, 1852), pp. 327–328.

The four-stage theory implicitly evaluated the later stages of economic development and the people dwelling in them as higher, more progressive, and more civilized than the earlier ones. A social theorist using this theory could thus quickly look at a society and, on the basis of the state of its economic development and organizations, rank it in terms of the stage it had achieved. In fact, the commercial stage, the highest rank in the theory, described society as it appeared in northwestern Europe. Thus, Smith's theory allowed Europeans to look about the world and always find themselves dwelling at the highest level of human achievement. To Europeans, this outlook helped justify their economic and imperial domination of the world during the following century. They repeatedly portrayed themselves as bringing a higher level of civilization to people elsewhere who, according to the four-stage theory, lived in lower stages of human social and economic development. Europeans thus imbued with the spirit of the Enlightenment presented themselves as carrying out a civilizing mission to the rest of the world. (See Chapter 25.)

▼ Political Thought of the Philosophes

Nowhere was the philosophes' reformist agenda, as well as tensions among themselves, so apparent as in their political thought. Most philosophes were discontented with certain political features of their countries, but French philosophes were especially discontented. There, the corruption around the royal court, the blundering of the bureaucracy, the less-than-glorious mid-century wars, and the power of the church seemed to make all problems worse. Consequently, the most important political thought of the Enlightenment occurred in France. The French philosophes, however, were divided over how to solve their country's problems. Their proposed solutions spanned a wide political spectrum, from aristocratic reform to democracy to absolute monarchy.

Montesquieu and *Spirit of the Laws*

Charles Louis de Secondat, baron de Montesquieu (1689–1755), was a lawyer, a noble of the robe, and a member of a provincial *parlement*. He also belonged to the Bordeaux Academy of Science, before which he presented papers on scientific topics.

Although living comfortably within the bosom of French society, he saw the need for reform. In 1721, as already noted, he published *The Persian Letters* to satirize contemporary institutions. Behind the humor lay the cutting edge of criticism and an exposition of the cruelty and irrationality of European life. About a decade after this volume appeared, Montesquieu, like Voltaire, visited England and deeply admired English institutions.

In his most enduring work, *Spirit of the Laws* (1748), Montesquieu held up the example of the British constitution as the wisest model for regulating the power of government. Montesquieu's *Spirit of the Laws*, perhaps the single most influential book of the century, exhibits the internal tensions of the Enlightenment. In it, Montesquieu pursued an empirical method, taking illustrative examples from the political experience of both ancient and modern nations. From these, he concluded that no single set of political laws could apply to all peoples at all times and in all places. The good political life depended rather on the relationship among many political variables. Whether the best form of government for a country was a monarchy or a republic, for example, depended on that country's size, population, social and religious customs, economic structure, traditions, and climate. Only a careful examination and evaluation of these elements could reveal what mode of government would most benefit a particular people.

For France, Montesquieu favored a monarchical government tempered and limited by various intermediary institutions, including the aristocracy, the towns, and the other corporate bodies that enjoyed liberties the monarch had to respect. These corporate bodies might be said to represent segments of the general population and thus of public opinion. In France, he regarded the aristocratic courts, or *parlements*, as a major example of an intermediary association. Their role was to limit the power of the monarchy and thus to preserve the liberty of its subjects.

In championing these aristocratic bodies and the general oppositional role of the aristocracy, Montesquieu was a political conservative. He adopted this conservatism in the hope of achieving reform, however, for he believed the oppressive and inefficient absolutism of the monarchy accounted for the degradation of French life.

One of Montesquieu's most influential ideas was that of the division of power in government. For his model of a government with authority wisely separated among different branches, he took contemporary Great Britain. There, he believed, executive power resided in the king, legislative power in the Parliament, and judicial power in the courts. He thought any two branches could check and balance the power of the other. His perception of the eighteenth-century British constitution was incorrect because he failed to see how patronage and electoral corruption allowed a handful of powerful aristocrats to dominate the government. Moreover, he was also unaware of the emerging cabinet system, which was slowly making the executive power a creature of the Parliament.

Nevertheless, Montesquieu's analysis illustrated his strong belief that monarchs should be subject to constitutional limits on their power and that a separate legislature, not the monarch, should formulate laws. For this reason, although he set out to defend the political privileges of the

French aristocracy, Montesquieu's ideas have had a profound effect on the constitutional form of liberal democracies for more than two centuries.

Rousseau: A Radical Critique of Modern Society

Jean-Jacques Rousseau (1712–1778) held a different view of the exercise and reform of political power from Montesquieu's. Rousseau was a strange, isolated genius who never felt particularly comfortable with the other philosophes. His own life was troubled. He could form few close friendships. He sired numerous children, whom he abandoned to foundling hospitals. Yet perhaps more than any other writer of the mid-eighteenth century, he transcended the political thought and values of his own time. Rousseau hated the world and the society in which he lived. It seemed to him impossible for human beings living according to the commercial values of his time to achieve moral, virtuous, or sincere lives. In 1750, in his *Discourse on the Moral Effects of the Arts and Sciences*, he contended that the process of civilization and the Enlightenment had corrupted human nature. In 1755, in his *Discourse on the Origin of Inequality*, Rousseau blamed much of the evil in the world on the uneven distribution of property. He contended that human beings in a primeval state of nature had been good, but that as they eventually formed social relations and then social institutions, they had lost that goodness. Society itself was the source of human evil for Rousseau, and one manifestation of that unnatural evil was unequal distribution of property.

In both discourses, Rousseau brilliantly and directly challenged the social fabric of the day. He questioned the concepts of material and intellectual progress and the morality of a society in which commerce, industry, and the preservation of property rights were regarded as among the most important human activities. The other philosophes generally believed life would improve if people could enjoy more of the fruits of the earth or could produce more goods. Rousseau raised the more fundamental questions of what constitutes the good life and how human society can be reshaped to achieve that life. This question has haunted European social thought ever since the eighteenth century.

Among the philosophes of the Enlightenment Jean-Jacques Rousseau set forth the most democratic and egalitarian political ideas. This bust was created by the French sculptor Jean-Antoine Houdon after Rousseau's death mask. Réunion des Musées Nationaux/Art Resource, NY

Rousseau carried these same concerns into his political thought. His most extensive discussion of politics appeared in *The Social Contract* (1762). Although the book attracted little immediate attention, by the end of the century it was widely read in France. Compared with Montesquieu's *Spirit of the Laws*, *The Social Contract* is an abstract book. It does not propose specific reforms but outlines the kind of political structure that Rousseau believed would overcome the evils of contemporary politics and society.

In the tradition of John Locke, most eighteenth-century political thinkers regarded human beings as individuals and society as a collection of individuals pursuing personal, selfish goals. These writers wished to liberate individuals from the undue bonds of government. Rousseau picked up the stick from the other end. His book opens with the declaration, "All men are born free, but everywhere they are in chains."[11] The rest of the volume is a defense of the chains of a properly organized society over its members.

Rousseau suggested that society is more important than its individual members, because they are what they are only by virtue of their relationship to the larger community. Independent human beings living alone can achieve little. Through their relationship to the larger political community, they become moral creatures capable of significant action. The question then becomes: What kind of community allows people to behave morally? In his two previous discourses, Rousseau had explained that the contemporaneous European society was not such a community; it was merely an aggregate of competing individuals whose chief social goal was to preserve selfish independence despite all potential social bonds and obligations.

Rousseau envisioned a society in which each person could maintain personal freedom while behaving as a loyal member of the larger community. Drawing on the traditions of Plato and Calvin, he defined freedom as obedience to law. In his case, the law to be obeyed was that created by the general will. In a society with virtuous customs and morals in which citizens have adequate information on

[11]Jean-Jacques Rousseau, *The Social Contract and Discourses*, trans. by G. D. H. Cole (New York: Dutton, 1950), p. 3.

important issues, the concept of the general will is normally equivalent to the will of a majority of voting citizens. Democratic participation in decision making would bind the individual citizen to the community. Rousseau believed the general will, thus understood, must always be right and that to obey the general will is to be free. This argument led him to the notorious conclusion that under certain circumstances some people must be forced to be free. Rousseau's politics thus constituted a justification for radical direct democracy and for collective action against individual citizens.

Rousseau had, in effect, attacked the eighteenth-century cult of the individual and the fruits of selfishness. He stood at odds with the commercial spirit that was transforming the society in which he lived. Rousseau would have disapproved of the main thrust of Adam Smith's *Wealth of Nations*, which he may or may not have read, and would no doubt have preferred a study on the virtue of nations. Smith wanted people to be prosperous; Rousseau wanted them to be good even if being good meant they might remain poor. He saw human beings not as independent individuals, but as creatures enmeshed in necessary social relationships. He believed loyalty to the community should be encouraged. As one device to that end, he suggested a properly governed society should decree a civic religion based on the creed of deism. Such a shared religion could, he argued, help unify a society even if it had to be enforced by repressive legislation.

Rousseau had only a marginal impact on his own time. The other philosophes questioned his critique of material improvement. Aristocrats and royal ministers could hardly be expected to welcome his proposal for radical democracy. Too many people were either making or hoping to make money to appreciate his criticism of commercial values. He proved, however, to be a figure to whom later generations returned. Leading figures in the French Revolution were familiar with his writing, and he influenced writers in the nineteenth and twentieth centuries who were critical of the general tenor and direction of Western culture. Rousseau hated much about the emerging modern society in Europe, but he contributed much to modernity by exemplifying for later generations the critic who dared to question the very foundations of social thought and action.

Enlightened Critics of European Empires

Most European thinkers associated with the Enlightenment favored the extension of European empires across the world. Like the Scottish writers who embraced the four-stage theory, they believed that the extension of the political structures and economies of northwestern Europe amounted to the spread of progress and civilization. The Scottish commentators and their followers were not without their criticisms of European civilization and of excessive economic regulation in contemporary empires, but on the whole, they believed European civilization superior to that of other cultures.

A few Enlightenment voices, however, did criticize the European empires on moral grounds, especially the European conquest of the Americas, the treatment of Native Americans, and the enslavement of Africans on the two American continents. The most important of these critics were Denis Diderot and two German philosophers, Immanuel Kant and Johann Gottlieb Herder (1744–1803). (See "Denis Diderot Condemns European Empires," page 510.)

What ideas allowed these figures from the Enlightenment to criticize their empires? As Sankar Muthu has recently written, "The first and most basic idea is that human beings deserve some modicum of moral and political respect simply because of the fact that they are human."[12] In other words, the Enlightenment critics of their empires argued for a form of shared humanity that the sixteenth-century European conquerors and their successors in the Americas and in other areas of imperial conquest had ignored. Immanuel Kant wrote, "When America, the Negro countries, the Spice Islands, the Cape, and so forth were discovered, they were to them [the Europeans], countries belonging to no one, since they counted the inhabitants as *nothing*."[13] Kant, Diderot, and Herder rejected this dismissive outlook and the harsh policies that had flowed from it. They believed no single definition of human nature could be made the standard throughout the world and then used to dehumanize people whose appearance or culture differed from it.

A second of these critical ideas was the conviction that the people whom Europeans had encountered in the Americas had possessed cultures that should have been respected and understood rather than destroyed. Some Europeans in the early years of the encounter with America had argued that while the native peoples were human, their way of life was too degraded to treat them as the human equals of Europeans. In the late eighteenth century, Herder rejected such a view, "'European culture' is a mere abstraction, an empty concept. Where does or did it actually exist in its entirety? In which nation? In which period? . . . Only a misanthrope could regard European culture as the universal condition of our species. The culture of *man* is not the culture of the *European*; it manifests itself according to time and place in every people."[14] For

[12]Sankar Muthu, *Enlightenment Against Empire* (Princeton, NJ: Princeton University Press, 2003), p. 268. This section draws primarily from this excellent recent book.

[13]Quoted in Muthu, *Enlightenment Against Empire*, p. 267.

[14]Quoted in F. M. Barnard, *Self-Direction and Political Legitimacy: Rousseau and Herder* (Oxford: Clarendon Press, 1988), p. 227.

DENIS DIDEROT CONDEMNS EUROPEAN EMPIRES

Denis Diderot was one of the most prolific writers of the Enlightenment. He is most famous as the editor of the Encyclopedia. *Some of his writings were published without being directly attributed to him. Among these were his contributions to Abbé G. T. Raynal's* History of the Two Indies, *published in various editions after 1772. Diderot's contributions appear to have been made in 1780. Raynal's entire* History *was critical of the European colonial empires that had arisen since the Spanish encounter with the New World. Diderot particularly condemned the inhumane treatment of the native populations of the Americas, the greed all Europeans displayed, and the various forms of forced labor.*

What is the basis for Diderot's view that Europeans have behaved tyrannically? How does he portray the behavior of Europeans in foreign areas? What specific social results does he associate with European greed?

Let the European nations make their own judgment and give themselves the name they deserve. . . . Their explorers arrive in a region of the New World unoccupied by anyone from the Old World, and immediately bury a small strip of metal on which they have engraved these words: *This country belongs to us.* Any why does it belong to you? . . . You have no right to the natural products of the country where you land, and you claim a right over your fellow-men. Instead of recognizing this man as a brother you only see him as a slave, a beast of burden. Oh my fellow citizens! You think like that and you behave like that; and you have ideas of justice, a morality, a holy religion . . . . in common with whose whom you treat so tryannically. This reproach should especially be addressed to the Spaniards.

* * *

Beyond the Equator a man is neither English, Dutch, French, Spanish, nor Portuguese. He retains only those principles and prejudices of his native country which justify or excuse his conduct. He crawls when he is weak; he is violent when strong; he is in a hurry to acquire, in a hurry to enjoy, and capable of every crime which will lead him most quickly to his goals. He is a domestic tiger returning to the forest; the thirst for blood takes hold of him once more. This is how all the Europeans, every one of them, indistinctly, have appeared in the countries of the New World. There they have assumed a common frenzy—the thirst for gold.

* * *

The Spaniard, the first to be thrown up by the waves onto the shores of the New World, thought he had no duty to people who did not share his color, customs, or religion. He saw in them only tools for his greed, and he clapped them in irons. These weak men, not used to work, soon died in the foul air of the mines, or in other occupations which were virtually as lethal. Then people called for slaves from Africa. Their number has gone up as more land has been cultivated. The Portuguese, Dutch, English, French, Danes, all the nations, free or subjected, have without remorse sought to increase their fortune in the sweat, blood and despair of these unfortunates. What a horrible system!

From "Extracts from the Histoire des Deux Indes," "6 Principles of Colonisation" (Book 8, Chap. I; IV, 105–8), pgs. 176–177, "7 National Character at Home and Overseas" (Book 9, Chap. I; IV, 233–5), pg. 178, "14 Slavery and Liberty" (Book 11, Chap. 24, V, 275–8), pg. 178 in *Political Writings* by Denis Diderot, trans. by John Hope Mason and Robert Wokler.

Herder, human beings living in different societies possessed the capacity as human beings to develop in culturally different fashions. He thus embraced an outlook later known as cultural relativism.

A third idea, closely related to the second, was that human beings may develop distinct cultures possessing intrinsic values that cannot be compared, one to the detriment of another, because each culture possesses deep inner social and linguistic complexities that make any simple comparison impossible. Indeed, Diderot, Kant, and Herder argued that being a human includes the ability to develop a variety of distinctly different cultures.

MAJOR WORKS OF THE ENLIGHTENMENT AND THEIR PUBLICATION DATES

1670	Spinoza's *Theologico-Political Treatise*
1677	Spinoza's *Ethics* (published posthumously)
1687	Newton's *Principia Mathematica*
1690	Locke's *Essay Concerning Human Understanding*
1696	Toland's *Christianity Not Mysterious*
1721	Montesquieu's *Persian Letters*
1733	Voltaire's *Letters on the English*
1738	Voltaire's *Elements of the Philosophy of Newton*
1748	Montesquieu's *Spirit of the Laws*
1748	Hume's *Inquiry into Human Nature*, with the chapter "Of Miracles"
1750	Rousseau's *Discourse on the Moral Effects of the Arts and Sciences*
1751	First volume of the *Encyclopedia*, edited by Diderot
1755	Rousseau's *Discourse on the Origin of Inequality*
1759	Voltaire's *Candide*
1762	Rousseau's *Social Contract* and *Émile*
1763	Voltaire's *Treatise on Tolerance*
1764	Voltaire's *Philosophical Dictionary*
1764	Beccaria's *On Crimes and Punishments*
1776	Gibbon's *Decline and Fall of the Roman Empire*
1776	Smith's *Wealth of Nations*
1779	Lessing's *Nathan the Wise*
1783	Mendelsohn's *Jerusalem; or, On Ecclesiastical Power and Judaism*
1792	Wollstonecraft's *Vindication of the Rights of Woman*
1793	Kant's *Religion within the Limits of Reason Alone*

These arguments critical of empire often involved criticism of New World slavery and were part of the antislavery movement to be discussed in Chapter 20. Whereas the antislavery arguments took strong hold in both Europe and America from the late eighteenth century onward, the arguments critical of empires did not. They remained isolated from the rest of Enlightenment political thought and would not be strongly revived until new anticolonial voices were raised in Europe and the non-European world at the close of the nineteenth century.

▼ Women in the Thought and Practice of the Enlightenment

Women, especially in France, helped significantly to promote the careers of the philosophes. In Paris, the salons of women such as Marie-Thérèse Geoffrin (1699–1777), Julie de Lespinasse (1733–1776), and Claudine de Tencin (1689–1749) gave the philosophes access to useful social and political contacts and a receptive environment in which to circulate their ideas. Association with a fashionable salon brought philosophes increased social status and added luster and respectability to their ideas. Philosophes clearly enjoyed the opportunity to be the center of attention that a salon provided, and their presence at them could boost the sales of their works. The women who organized the salons were well connected to political figures who could help protect the philosophes and secure royal pensions for them. The marquise de Pompadour (1721–1764), the mistress of King Louis XV, played a key role in overcoming efforts to censor the *Encyclopedia*. She also hindered the publication of works attacking the philosophes. Other salon hostesses distributed the writings of the philosophes among their friends. Madame de Tencin promoted Montesquieu's *Spirit of the Laws* in this way.

Despite this help and support from the learned women of Paris, the philosophes were on the whole not strong feminists. Many urged better and broader education for women. They criticized the education women did receive as overly religious, and they tended to reject ascetic views of sexual relations. In general, however, they displayed traditional views toward women and advocated no radical changes in their social condition.

Montesquieu, for example, maintained, in general, that the status of women in a society was the result of climate, the political regime, culture, and women's physiology. He believed women were not naturally inferior to men and should have a wider role in society. He showed himself well aware of the kinds of personal, emotional, and sexual repression European women endured in his day. He sympathetically observed the value placed on women's appearance and the prejudice women met as they aged. In *The Persian Letters*, he included a long exchange about the repression of women in a Persian harem, condemning by implication the restrictions on women in European society. Yet Montesquieu's willingness to consider social change for women in European life had limits. Although in the *Spirit of the Laws* he indicated a belief in the equality of the sexes, he still retained a traditional view of marriage and family and expected men to dominate those institutions. Furthermore, although he supported the right of women to divorce and opposed laws that oppressed them, he upheld the ideal of female chastity.

The views about women expressed in the *Encyclopedia* were less generous than those of Montesquieu. The *Encyclopedia* suggested ways to improve women's lives, but in general, it did not emphasize that the condition of women needed reform. Almost all the contributors were men, and the editors, Diderot and d'Alembert, evidently saw no need to include many articles by women. Most of the articles that dealt with women specifically or discussed women in connection with other subjects often emphasized their physical weakness and inferiority, usually attributed to menstruation or childbearing. Some contributors favored the social equality of women, others opposed it, and still others were indifferent. The articles conveyed a general sense that women were reared to be frivolous and unconcerned with important issues. The Encyclopedists discussed women primarily within a family context—as daughters, wives, and mothers—and presented motherhood as a woman's most important occupation. On sexual behavior, the Encyclopedists upheld an unquestioned double standard.

In contrast to the articles, however, illustrations in the *Encyclopedia* showed women deeply involved in the economic activities of the day. The illustrations also portrayed the activities of lower-class and working-class women, about whom the articles had little to say.

One of the most surprising and influential analyses of the position of women came from Jean-Jacques Rousseau. This most radical of all Enlightenment political theorists urged a traditional and conservative role for women. In his novel *Émile* (1762) (discussed again in Chapter 19), he set forth a radical version of the view that men and women occupy separate spheres. He declared that women should be educated for a position subordinate to men, emphasizing especially women's function in bearing and rearing children. In his vision, there was little else for women to do but make themselves pleasing to men. He portrayed them as weaker and inferior to men in virtually all respects, except perhaps for their capacity for feeling and giving love. He excluded them from political life. Only men were to populate the world of citizenship, political action, and civic virtue. Women were relegated to the domestic sphere. (See "Rousseau Argues for Separate Spheres for Men and Women.") Many of these attitudes were not new—some have roots as ancient as Roman law—but Rousseau's powerful presentation and the influence of his other writings gave them new life in the late eighteenth century. Rousseau deeply influenced many leaders of the French Revolution, who, as shall be seen in the next chapter, often incorporated his view on gender roles in their policies.

Paradoxically, despite these views and despite his own ill treatment of the women who bore his many children, Rousseau achieved a vast following among women in the eighteenth century. He is credited with persuading thousands of upper-class women to breast-feed their own children rather than putting them out to wet nurses. One explanation for this influence is that his writings, although they did not advocate liberating women or expanding their social or economic roles, did stress the importance of their emotions. He portrayed the domestic life and the role of wife and mother as a noble and fulfilling vocation, giving middle- and upper-class women a sense that their daily occupations had a purpose. He assigned them a degree of influence in the domestic sphere that they could not have competing with men outside it.

Mary Wollstonecraft in her *Vindication of the Rights of Woman* defended equality of women with men on the grounds of men and women sharing the capacity of human reason. CORBIS/Bettmann

In 1792, in *A Vindication of the Rights of Woman*, Mary Wollstonecraft (1759–1797) brought Rousseau before the judgment of the rational Enlightenment ideal of progressive knowledge. The immediate incentive for this essay was her opposition to certain policies of the French Revolution, unfavorable to women, that Rousseau had inspired. Wollstonecraft (who, like so many women of her day, died of puerperal fever, a form of blood poisoning caused by unsanitary conditions during childbirth) accused Rousseau and others after him who upheld traditional roles for women of attempting to narrow women's vision and limit their experience. She argued that to confine women to the separate domestic sphere because of supposed limitations of their physiology was to make them the sensual slaves of men. Confined in this separate sphere, they were the victims of male tyranny, their obedience was blind, and they could never achieve their own moral or intellectual identity.

ROUSSEAU ARGUES FOR SEPARATE SPHERES FOR MEN AND WOMEN

Rousseau published Émile, *a novel about education, in 1762. In it, he made one of the strongest and most influential arguments of the eighteenth century for distinct social roles for men and women. Furthermore, he portrayed women as fundamentally subordinate to men. In the next document, Mary Wollstonecraft, a contemporary, presents a rebuttal.*

How does Rousseau move from the physical differences between men and women to an argument for distinct social roles and social spheres? What would be the proper kinds of social activities for women in Rousseau's vision? What kind of education would he think appropriate for women?

There is no parity between the two sexes in regard to the consequences of sex. The male is male only at certain moments. The female is female her whole life or at least during her whole youth. Everything constantly recalls her sex to her; and, to fulfill its functions well, she needs a constitution which corresponds to it. She needs care during her pregnancy; she needs rest at the time of childbirth; she needs a soft and sedentary life to suckle her children; she needs patience and gentleness, a zeal and an affection that nothing can rebuff in order to raise her children. She serves as the link between them and their father; she alone makes him love them and gives him the confidence to call them his own. How much tenderness and care is required to maintain the union of the whole family! And, finally, all this must come not from virtues but from tastes, or else the human species would soon be extinguished.

The strictness of the relative duties of the two sexes is not and cannot be the same. When woman complains on this score about unjust man-made inequality, she is wrong. This inequality is not a human institution—or, at least, it is the work not of prejudice but of reason. It is up to the sex that nature has charged with the bearing of children to be responsible for them to the other sex. Doubtless it is not permitted to anyone to violate his faith, and every unfaithful husband who deprives his wife of the only reward of the austere duties of her sex is an unjust and barbarous man. But the unfaithful woman does more; she dissolves the family and breaks all the bonds of nature. . . .

Once it is demonstrated that man and woman are not and ought not be constituted in the same way in either character or temperament, it follows that they ought not to have the same education. In following nature's directions, man and woman ought to act in concert, but they ought not to do the same things. The goal of their labors is common, but their labors themselves are different, and consequently so are the tastes directing them. . . .

The good constitution of children initially depends on that of their mothers. The first education of men depends on the care of women. Men's morals, their passions, their tastes, their pleasures, their very happiness also depend on women. Thus the whole education of women ought to relate to men. To please men, to be useful to them, to make herself loved and honored by them, to raise them when young, to care for them when grown, to counsel them, to console them, to make their lives agreeable and sweet—these are the duties of women at all times, and they ought to be taught from childhood. So long as one does not return to this principle, one will deviate from the goal, and all the precepts taught to women will be of no use for their happiness or for ours.

Denying good education to women would impede the progress of all humanity. With these arguments, Wollstonecraft was demanding for women the kind of liberty that male writers of the Enlightenment had been championing for men for more than a century. In doing so, she placed herself among the philosophes and broadened the agenda of the Enlightenment to include the rights of women as well as those of men. (See "Mary Wollstonecraft Criticizes Rousseau's View of Women.")

▼ Rococo and Neoclassical Styles in Eighteenth-Century Art

Two contrasting styles dominated eighteenth-century European art and architecture. The Rococo style embraced lavish, often lighthearted decoration with an emphasis on pastel colors and the play of light. Neoclassicism embodied a return to figurative and architectural models drawn from the Renaissance and the ancient world. The Rococo became associated with the aristocracies of the Old Regime while Neoclassicism recalled ancient republican values that implicitly criticized the Old Regime and, toward the end of the century, was embraced by the French Revolution and Napoleon.

Rococo architecture and decoration originated in early eighteenth-century France. After Louis XIV's death in 1715, the Regent Philippe d'Orleans (1674–1723) and the French aristocracy spent less time at Versailles and began to enjoy the diversions of Paris. There, wealthy French aristocrats built houses known as *hôtels*. Their designers compensated for the relatively small scale and nondescript exteriors of these mansions with interiors that were elaborately decorated and painted in light colors to make the rooms seem brighter and more spacious. It was in such aristocratic urban settings that fashionable Parisian hostesses held the salons the philosophes attended. Louis XV also liked Rococo art, and he had both Madame de Pompadour and other mistresses painted, sometimes in compromising poses, by Rococo artists, especially Francois Boucher (1700–1770). Consequently Rococo also became known as the Style of Louis XV, suggesting a social and political world more accommodating to the French aristocracy and less religiously austere than that of Louis XIV.

Beyond such domestic and personally intimate settings in France, the Rococo style spread across Europe and was adapted to many public buildings and churches. One of the most spectacular Rococo spaces was the Imperial Hall (*Kaisarsaal*) built in Würzburg, Bavaria, to the design of Balthasar Neumann (1687–1753) with ceilings painted with scenes from Greek mythology by the Venetian Gian Battista Tiepolo (1696–1770).

The paintings associated with Rococo art often portrayed the aristocracy, and particularly the French aristocracy, at play. Artists depicted what were known as *fêtes galantes* or scenes of elegant parties in lush gardens. The paintings showed not reality, but an idealized landscape with carefree men and women pursuing a life of leisure, romance, and seduction. Among the most prominent of such artists was Jean-Antoine Watteau (1684–1721) in

Jean-Antoine Watteau, *Embarkation for Cythera*, (1717). Oil on canvas. 129 × 194 cm. Louvre, Paris, France/ Giraudon-Bridgeman Art Library

MARY WOLLSTONECRAFT CRITICIZES ROUSSEAU'S VIEW OF WOMEN

Mary Wollstonecraft published A Vindication of the Rights of Woman *in 1792, thirty years after Rousseau's* Émile *had appeared. In this pioneering feminist work, she criticizes and rejects Rousseau's argument for distinct and separate spheres for men and women. She portrays that argument as defending the continued bondage of women to men and as hindering the wider education of the entire human race.*

What criticisms does Wollstonecraft direct against Rousseau's views? Why does Wollstonecraft emphasize a new kind of education for women?

The most perfect education . . . is such an exercise of the understanding as is best calculated to strengthen the body and form the heart. Or, in other words, to enable the individual to attain such habits of virtue as will render it independent. In fact, it is a farce to call any being virtuous whose virtues do not result from the exercise of its own reason. This was Rousseau's opinion respecting men: I extend it to women. . . .

I may be accused of arrogance; still I must declare what I firmly believe, that all the writers who have written on the subject of female education and manners from Rousseau to Dr. Gregory [a Scottish physician], have contributed to render women more artificial, weak characters, than they would otherwise have been; and, consequently, more useless members of society. . . .

Strengthen the female mind by enlarging it, and there will be an end to blind obedience; but, as blind obedience is ever sought for by power, tyrants and sensualists are in the right when they endeavour to keep women in the dark, because the former only wants slaves, and the latter a plaything. The sensualist, indeed, has been the most dangerous of tyrants, and women have been duped by their lovers, as princes by their ministers, whilst dreaming that they reigned over them. . . .

Rousseau declares that a woman should never, for a moment, feel herself independent, that she should be governed by fear to exercise her natural cunning, and made a coquettish slave in order to render her a more alluring object of desire, a sweeter companion to man, whenever he chooses to relax himself. He carries the arguments, which he pretends to draw from the indications of nature, still further, and insinuates that truth and fortitude, the cornerstones of all human virtue, should be cultivated with certain restrictions, because, with respect to the female character, obedience is the grand lesson which ought to be impressed with unrelenting rigour.

What nonsense! When will a great man arise with sufficient strength of mind to put away the fumes which pride and sensuality have thus spread over the subject! If women are by nature inferior to men, their virtues must be the same in quality, if not in degree, or virtue is a relative idea; consequently, their conduct should be founded on the same principles, and have the same aim.

Connected with man as daughters, wives, and mothers, their moral character may be estimated by their manner of fulfilling those simple duties; but the end, the grand end of their exertions should be to unfold their own faculties and acquire the dignity of conscious virtue. . . .

But avoiding . . . any direct comparison of the two sexes collectively, or frankly acknowledging the inferiority of women according to the present appearance of things, I shall only insist that men have increased that inferiority till women are almost sunk below the standard of rational creatures. Let their faculties have room to unfold, and their virtues to gain strength, and then determine where the whole sex must stand in the intellectual scale. . . .

I . . . will venture to assert, that till women are more rationally educated, the progress of human virtue and improvement in knowledge must receive continual checks. . . .

The mother, who wishes to give true dignity of character to her daughter, must, regardless of the sneers of ignorance, proceed on a plan diametrically opposite to that which Rousseau has recommended with all the deluding charms of eloquence and philosophical sophistry: for his eloquence renders absurdities plausible, and his dogmatic conclusions puzzle, without convincing, those who have not ability to refute them.

From Mary Wollstonecraft, *A Vindication of the Rights of Woman*, ed. by Carol H. Poston (New York: W.W. Norton, 1975), pp. 21, 22, 24–26, 35, 40, 41.

whose *Pilgrimage to Isle of Cithera* young lovers embark to pay homage to the goddess Venus. Other artists such as Boucher and Jean-Honoré Fragonard (1732–1806) produced works filled with female nudes and with men and women in sexually suggestive poses.

As the eighteenth century wore on, the way of life illustrated in Rococo paintings and of more popular prints produced from them convinced many people in France that the monarchy, the court, and the aristocracy were frivolous and decadent. In reality, as seen in Chapter 15, many French and European aristocrats were hardworking and disciplined, and Louis XVI, who succeeded Louis XV in 1774, was a well-intentioned, pious, and highly moral monarch. Nonetheless, the lighthearted carelessness of Rococo art increased hostility toward the political and social elites of the Old Regime.

Contemporaries, moreover, did not have to wait for the tumult of the French Revolution to view art that directly criticized the society Rococo art portrayed. The mid-eighteenth century witnessed a new admiration for the art of the ancient world. In 1755, Johann Joachim Winckelmann (1717–1768), a German archaeologist, published *Thoughts on the Imitation of Greek Works in Painting and Sculpture*, followed in 1764 by *The History of Ancient Art*. In both works he either directly or indirectly contrasted the superficiality of the Rococo with the seriousness of ancient art and architecture. His books and the simultaneous rediscovery and partial excavation of the ancient Roman cities of Pompeii and Herculaneum in southern Italy fostered the rise of *Neoclassicism* in art and architecture. This movement constituted a return to themes, topics, and styles drawn from antiquity itself and from the Renaissance appeal to antiquity.

The popularity of the city of Rome as a destination for artists and aristocratic tourists contributed to the rise of Neoclassicism. European aristocrats who came to Italy in the mid-eighteenth century on what was called "the Grand Tour" increasingly admired both the ancient and Renaissance art that was on view there and the Neoclassical works that contemporary artists were producing there. Not only did these wealthy and influential travelers purchase paintings and statues to bring home with them, but they also commissioned architects to rebuild their own houses and public buildings in Neoclassical style.

Figures in Neoclassical paintings rarely suggest movement and often seem to stand still in a kind of tableau illustrating a moral theme. These paintings were didactic rather than emotional or playful. Their

The color, the light, and the elaborate decorative details associated with Rococo style are splendidly exemplified in the Imperial Hall (Kaisarsaal) built in Würzburg, Bavaria, according to the design of Balthasar Neumann (1687–1753). Art Resource, N.Y.

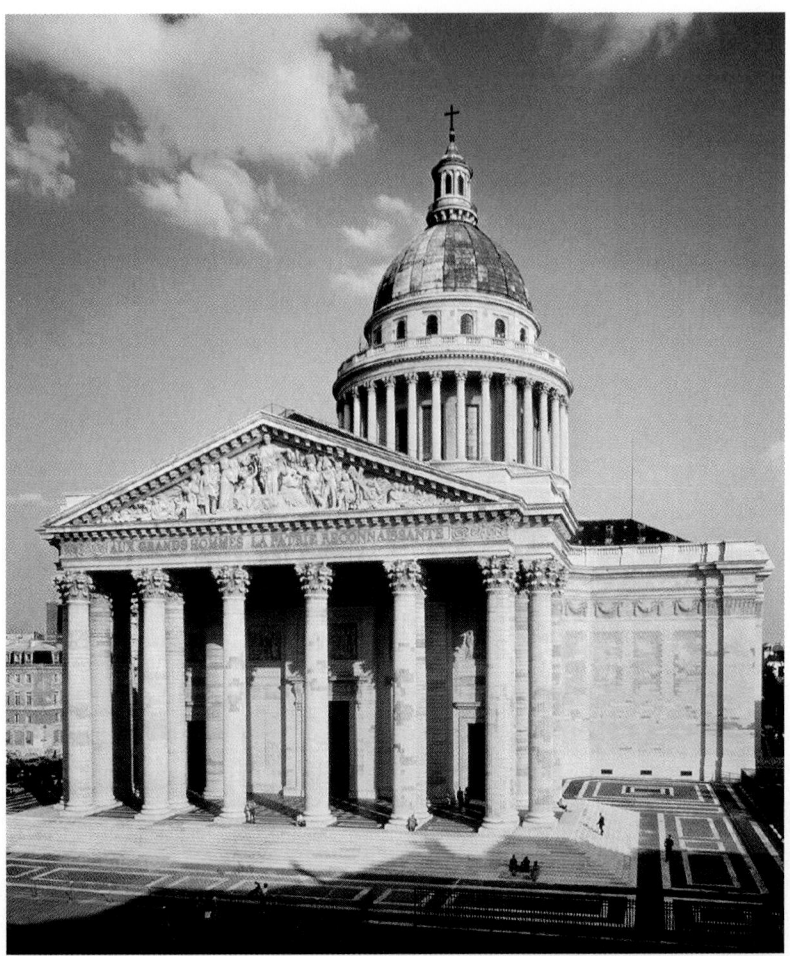

The Pantheon in Paris (construction commencing 1758) embodied the Neoclassical style used for a Jesuit church. After the French Revolution it became a national monument where famous figures of the Enlightenment and Revolution were buried. The bodies of both Voltaire and Rousseau were transferred there during the 1790s. Jacques Germain Soufflot (1713–1780), Facade of the Pantheon (formerly Church of Ste. Genevieve), 1757. Pantheon, Paris, France. © Bridgeman-Giraudon/Art Resource, NY

subject matter was usually concerned with public life or public morals, rather than depicting intimate family life, daily routine, or the leisure activity favored by Rococo painters.

Many Neoclassical painters used scenes of heroism and self-sacrifice from ancient history to draw contemporary moral and political lessons. Such scenes provided a sharp moral contrast to the works of Watteau or Boucher in which lovers seek only pleasure and escape from care.

Other Neoclassical artists intended their paintings to be a form of direct political criticism. Jacques-Louis David (1748–1825), the foremost French Neoclassical painter, used ancient republican themes in the 1780s to emphasize the corruption of French monarchical government. His *Oath of the Horatii* in 1784 illustrates a scene, derived from the ancient Roman historian Livy, of soldiers taking an oath to die for the Roman Republic. The painting also portrays the concept of separate spheres for men and women. The brothers are taking the oath to defend the republic with their lives. The women in the scene appear emotional and incapable of entering the masculine civic life of the republic. David painted many similar scenes from the ancient Roman Republic and later became an artistic champion of the French Revolution and Napoleon (who, ironically, made him a baron).

The philosophes themselves became the subjects of Neoclassical artists. The French sculptor Jean-Antoine Houdon (1741–1828) produced numerous portraits in stone of leading philosophes including Voltaire and Rousseau as well as American admirers of the Enlightenment such as Benjamin Franklin (1706–1790) and Thomas Jefferson (1743–1826). Such statues furnished a gallery of writers who had criticized the Old Regime or embodied modern republican values.

Even religious structures built in the Neoclassical style were, by the end of the century, transformed to monuments to the Enlightenment and Revolution. Modeled on its ancient pagan namesake in Rome, the Pantheon in Paris was begun in 1758 as a Jesuit church. During the French Revolution, the new government transformed it into a national monument where the remains of French heroes could be interred. Voltaire's remains were placed there in 1791 and Rousseau's in 1794.

▾ Enlightened Absolutism

Most of the philosophes favored neither Montesquieu's reformed and revived aristocracy nor Rousseau's democracy as a solution to contemporary political problems. Like other thoughtful people of the day in other stations and occupations, they looked to the existing monarchies. Because of his personal clash with aristocrats as a young writer and his general distrust of democratic ideas, Voltaire was a strong monarchist. In 1759, he published a *History of the Russian Empire under Peter the Great*, which declared, "Peter was born, and Russia was formed."[15] Voltaire and other philosophes, such as Diderot, who visited Catherine II of Russia, and the physiocrats, some of whom were ministers to Louis XV and Louis XVI, did not wish to limit the power of monarchs. Rather, they sought to use that power to rationalize economic and political structures and liberate intellectual life. Most

[15]Quoted in Larry Wolff, *Inventing Eastern Europe: The Map of Civilization on the Mind of the Enlightenment* (Palo Alto, CA: Stanford University Press, 1994), p. 200.

A Closer LOOK

AN EIGHTEENTH-CENTURY ARTIST APPEALS TO THE ANCIENT WORLD

JACQUES-LOUIS DAVID completed *The Oath of the Horatii* in 1784. Like many of his other works, it used themes from the supposedly morally austere ancient Roman Republic to criticize the political life of his own day. David intended the painting to contrast ancient civic virtue with the luxurious aristocratic culture of contemporary France.

The Horatii take an oath their father administers to protect the Roman Republic against enemies even if it means sacrificing their own lives. One of these enemies is romantically involved with one of their sisters in the right of the painting. Patriotism must be upheld over other relationships.

The sharp division of the painting with a male world on the left and a female world on the right illustrates how eighteenth-century republican thinkers, such as Rousseau, excluded women from civic life and political participation.

The sisters and mother of the Horatii weep in a separate part of the scene. The emotion of the women and their uncertain political loyalty suggest that civic virtue pertains only to men.

Jacques-Louis David, *The Oath of the Horatii.* 1784–1785.© Réunion des Musees Nationaux, Paris, France/Art Resource, NY

To examine this image in an interactive fashion, please go to www.myhistorylab.com

myhistorylab

philosophes were not opposed to power if they could find a way to use it for their own purposes or if they could profit in one way or another from their personal relationships to strong monarchs. For this reason, it is important not to see Enlightenment political thought only as a source of modern liberal outlooks.

During the last third of the century, some observers believed that several European rulers had embraced many of the reforms the philosophes advocated. Historians use the term *enlightened absolutism* for this form of monarchical government in which the central absolutist administration was strengthened and rationalized at the cost of other, lesser centers of political power, such as the aristocracy, the church, and the parliaments or diets that had survived from the Middle Ages. The monarchs most closely associated with it are Frederick II (r. 1740–1786) of Prussia, Joseph II of Austria (r. 1765–1790), and Catherine II (r. 1762–1796) of Russia. Each had complicated relationships with the community of enlightened writers.

Frederick II corresponded with the philosophes, gave Voltaire and other philosophes places at his court, and even wrote history, political tracts, literary criticism, and music. Catherine II, adept at what would later be called public relations, consciously sought to create the image of being an enlightened ruler. She read and cited the works of the philosophes, subsidized Diderot, and corresponded with Voltaire, lavishing compliments on him, all in the hope that she would receive favorable comments from them, as she indeed did. Joseph II continued numerous initiatives begun by his mother, Maria Theresa (r. 1740–1780). He imposed a series of religious, legal, and social reforms that contemporaries believed he had derived from the philosophes' suggestions.

The relationship between these rulers and the writers of the Enlightenment was, however, more complicated than these appearances suggest. The humanitarian and liberating zeal of the Enlightenment writers was only part of what motivated the policies of the rulers. Frederick II, Joseph II, and Catherine II were also determined to play major diplomatic and military roles in Europe. In no small measure, they adopted Enlightenment policies favoring the rational economic and social integration of their realms because these policies also increased their military strength and political power. As explained in Chapter 13, all the major European states had emerged from the Seven Years' War knowing they would need stronger armies for future wars and increased revenues to finance these armies. The search for new revenues and internal political support was one of the incentives prompting the "enlightened" reforms of the monarchs of Russia, Prussia, and Austria. Consequently, they and their advisers used rationality to pursue goals most philosophes admired, and also to further what some philosophes considered irrational militarism. The flattery of monarchs could bend the opinions of a philosophe. For example, Voltaire, who had written against war, could praise the military expansion of Catherine's Russia because it appeared in his mind to bring civilization to peoples he regarded as uncivilized and because he enjoyed being known as a literary confidant of the empress.

Frederick the Great of Prussia

More than any other ruler of the age, Frederick the Great of Prussia embodied enlightened absolutism. Drawing upon the accomplishments of his Hohenzollern forebearers, he forged a state that commanded the loyalty of the military, the junker nobility, the Lutheran clergy, a growing bureaucracy recruited from an educated middle class, and university professors. Because the authority of the Prussian monarchy and the military were so strong and because the nobles, bureaucracy, clergy, and professors were so loyal, Frederick had the confidence to permit a more open discussion of Enlightenment ideas and to put into effect more Enlightenment values, such as extensive religious toleration, than any other continental ruler. Consequently, in marked contrast to France, Prussians sympathetic to the Enlightenment tended to support the state rather than criticize it.

Promotion Through Merit Reflecting an important change in the European view of the ruler, Frederick frequently described himself as "the first servant of the State" contending that his own personal and dynastic interests should always be subordinate to the good of his subjects. Like earlier Hohenzollern rulers, he protected the local social and political interests of the Prussian nobility as well as their role in the army, but he also required nobles who sought positions in his well-paid bureaucracy to qualify for those jobs by merit. By 1770, a Prussian Civil Service Commission oversaw the education and examinations required for all major government appointments. Frederick thus made it clear that merit rather than privilege of birth would determine who served the Prussian state.

During his reign Frederick created few new nobles, and those persons whom he did ennoble earned their titles by merit, for having served the king and the state well. This policy of ennobling only for merit and Frederick's protecting the nobility's local social interests and leadership of the army meant that Prussia did not experience the conflicts between the aristocracy and the monarchy that troubled other eighteenth-century European states.

Frederick felt comfortable in the intellectual life of his day and personally participated in the culture of the Enlightenment. He favored the Prussian universities and allowed professors wide latitude to discuss new ideas. In turn, Prussian professors were virtually unanimous in their praise and support of Frederick.

Frederick II of Prussia became known as Frederick the Great after his victories in the Seven Years' Wars. This portrait of 1763 shows him at the time of those triumphs when he had permanently secured the position of Prussia as a major European power. He was equally interested in the economic development of Prussia. Erich Lessing/Art Resource, NY

Because the Prussian state required academic training for appointment to positions of authority, nobles attended the universities. There they studied with middle-class Prussians who were training to serve the state either as Protestant clergy or bureaucrats. Consequently, nobles, clergy, and bureaucrats in Prussia shared a similar educational background that combined a moderate exposure to Enlightenment ideas with broadly shared religious values and loyalty to the state.

Religious Toleration No single policy so associated Frederick with the Enlightenment as that of full religious toleration. Continuing the Hohenzollern policy of toleration for foreign workers who brought important skills into Prussia, Frederick allowed Catholics and Jews to settle in his predominantly Lutheran country, and he protected the Catholics living in Silesia after he conquered that province from the Habsburgs in the 1740s. (See Chapter 13.) He even stated that he would be willing to build mosques for Turks should they move into his country. His religious toleration won the strong support of philosophers, such as Immanuel Kant and Moses Mendelsohn. Frederick nonetheless tended to appoint Protestants to most key positions in the bureaucracy and army.

Administrative and Economic Reforms Frederick also ordered a new codification of Prussian law, which was completed after his death. His objective was to rationalize the existing legal system and make it more efficient, eliminating regional peculiarities, reducing aristocratic influence, abolishing torture, and limiting the number of capital crimes. The other enlightened monarchs shared this concern for legal reform, which they saw as a way to extend and strengthen royal power.

The mid-century wars had inflicted considerable economic damage on Prussia. Thereafter, Frederick used the power of the state to foster economic growth. He continued the long-standing Hohenzollern policy of importing workers from outside Prussia. He sought to develop Prussian agriculture. Under state supervision, swamps were drained, new crops introduced, and peasants encouraged and sometimes compelled to migrate where they were needed. For the first time in Prussia, potatoes and turnips became important crops. Frederick also established a land-mortgage credit association to help landowners raise money for agricultural improvements. Despite these efforts, however, most Prussians did not prosper under Frederick's reign, and the burden of taxation, reflecting his protection of the interests of the nobles, fell disproportionately on peasants and townspeople.

Joseph II of Austria

No eighteenth-century ruler so embodied rational, impersonal force as did the emperor Joseph II of Austria. He was the son of Maria Theresa and co-ruler with her from 1765 to 1780. Thereafter, he ruled alone until his death in 1790. Joseph was an austere and humorless person. During much of his life, he slept on straw and ate little but boiled beef. He prided himself on a narrow, passionless rationality, which he sought to impose by his own will on the various Habsburg domains. Despite his personal eccentricities and cold personality, Joseph II sincerely wished to improve the lot of his people. He was much less a political opportunist and cynic than either Frederick the Great of Prussia or Catherine the Great of Russia. Nonetheless, the ultimate result of his well-intentioned efforts was a series of aristocratic and peasant rebellions extending from Hungary to the Austrian Netherlands.

Centralization of Authority As explained in Chapter 13, of all the rising states of the eighteenth century, Austria was the most diverse in its people and problems. The historian Robert Palmer likened the Habsburg domains to "a vast holding company."[16] The Habsburgs never succeeded in creating either a unified administrative structure or a strong aristocratic loyalty to the dynasty. To preserve the monarchy during the War of the Austrian Succession (1740–1748), Maria Theresa had guaranteed the aristocracy considerable independence, especially in Hungary.

During and after the conflict, however, she took steps to strengthen the power of the crown outside of Hungary, building more of a bureaucracy than had previous Habsburg rulers. In Austria and Bohemia, the empress imposed a much more efficient system of tax collection that extracted funds even from the clergy and the nobles. She also established central councils to deal with governmental problems. To assure her government a supply of educated officials, she sought to bring all educational institutions into the service of the crown and expanded primary education on the local level.

Maria Theresa was concerned about the welfare of the peasants and serfs. She brought them some relief by expanding the authority of the royal bureaucracy over the local power of the nobility and limiting the amount of labor, or *robot*, landowners could demand from peasants. Her motives were less humanitarian than to assure a good pool from which to draw military recruits. In these policies and in her desire to stimulate prosperity and military strength by royal initiative, Maria Theresa anticipated the policies of her son.

Joseph II was more determined than his mother, and his projected reforms were more wide ranging. He aimed to extend his territories at the expense of Poland, Bavaria, and the Ottoman Empire. His greatest ambition, however, was to increase the authority of the Habsburg emperor over his various realms. He sought to overcome the pluralism of the Habsburg holdings by imposing central authority on areas of political and social life in which Maria Theresa had wisely chosen not to interfere.

In particular, Joseph sought to reduce Hungarian autonomy. To avoid having to guarantee Hungary's existing privileges or extend new ones at the time of his coronation, he refused to have himself crowned king of Hungary and even had the Crown of Saint Stephen, symbol of the Hungarian state, sent to the Imperial Treasury in Vienna. He reorganized local government in Hungary to increase the authority of his own officials. He also required the use of German in all governmental matters.

[16]Robert R. Palmer, *The Age of Democratic Revolution*, Vol. 1 (Princeton, NJ: Princeton University Press, 1959), p. 103.

Ecclesiastical Policies Another target of Joseph's royal absolutism was the church. Since the reign of Charles V (r. 1510–1558), the Habsburgs had been the most important dynastic champions of Roman Catholicism. Maria Theresa was devout, but she had not allowed the church to limit her authority. Although she had attempted to discourage certain of the more extreme modes of Roman Catholic popular religious piety, such as public flagellation, she was adamantly opposed to religious toleration. (See "Compare & Connect: Maria Theresa and Joseph II of Austria Debate Toleration," pages 522–523)

Joseph II was also a practicing Catholic, but based on both Enlightenment values and pragmatic politics, he favored a policy of toleration. In October 1781, Joseph extended freedom of worship to Lutherans, Calvinists, and the Greek Orthodox. They were permitted to have their own places of worship, to sponsor schools, to enter skilled trades, and to hold academic appointments and positions in the public service. Joseph also granted the right of private worship to Jews and relaxed the financial and social burdens imposed on them, though he did not give Jews full equality with other Habsburg subjects.

Above all, Joseph sought to bring the Roman Catholic Church directly under royal control. He forbade the bishops of his realms to communicate directly with the pope. Since he considered religious orders that did not run schools or hospitals to be unproductive, he dissolved more than six hundred monasteries, confiscated their lands, and used some of their revenue to found new parishes in areas where there was a shortage of priests. He also reorganized the training of priests. The emperor believed that the traditional Roman Catholic seminaries, which were run by the various dioceses, instilled in priests too great a loyalty to the papacy and too little concern for their future parishioners. They were, therefore, replaced by eight general seminaries under government supervision whose training emphasized parish duties. In effect, Joseph's policies made Roman Catholic priests the employees of the state, ending the influence of the Roman Catholic Church as an independent institution in Habsburg lands. In many respects, his ecclesiastical policies, known as *Josephinism*, prefigured those of the French Revolution.

Economic and Agrarian Reform Like Frederick of Prussia, Joseph sought to improve the economic life of his domains. He abolished many internal tariffs, encouraged road building, and improved river transport. He personally inspected farms and manufacturing districts. Joseph also reconstructed the judicial system to make laws more uniform and rational and to lessen the influence of local landlords. All of these improvements were expected to bring new unity to the state and more taxes into the imperial coffers in Vienna.

Joseph's policies toward serfdom and the land were a far-reaching extension of those Maria Theresa had

COMPARE AND CONNECT

Maria Theresa and Joseph II of Austria Debate Toleration

THE ISSUE OF religious toleration was widely debated throughout the age of Enlightenment. Many rulers feared that their domains would be overcome by religious turmoil and potential political unrest if their subjects could pursue religious freedom. The issue divided the Empress Maria Theresa and her son Joseph II who since l765 had been co-rulers of the Austrian Empire. In l777 they exchanged important letters setting forth their sharply differing views of the subject.

Joseph believed some religious toleration should be introduced into the Habsburg realms. Maria Theresa refused to consider toleration. The toleration of Protestants that is in dispute related only to Lutherans and Calvinists. Maria Theresa died in 1780; the next year Joseph issued an edict of toleration.

QUESTIONS

1. **How does Joseph define toleration, and why does Maria Theresa believe it is the same as religious indifference?**
2. **Why does Maria Theresa fear that toleration will bring about political as well as religious turmoil?**
3. **Why does Maria Theresa think that Joseph's belief in toleration has come from Joseph's acquaintance with wicked books?**

I. Joseph to Maria Theresa, July 20, 1777

It is only the word "toleration" which has caused the misunderstanding. You have taken it in quite a different meaning [from mine expressed in an earlier letter]. God preserve me from thinking it a matter of indifference whether the citizens turn Protestant or remain Catholic, still less, whether they cleave to, or at least observe, the cult which they have inherited from their fathers! I would give all I possess if all the Protestants of your states would go over to Catholicism.

The word "toleration," as I understand it, means only that I would employ any person, without distinction of religion, in purely temporal matters, allow them to own property, practice trades, be citizens, if they were qualified and if this would be of advantage to the State and its industry. Those who, unfortunately, adhere to a false faith, are far further from being converted if they remain in their own country than if they migrate into another, in which they can hear and see the convincing truths of the Catholic faith. Similarly, the undisturbed practice of their religion makes them far better subjects and causes them to avoid irreligion, which is a far greater danger to our Catholics than if one lets them see others practice their religion unimpeded.

II. Maria Theresa to Joseph, Late July 1777

Without a dominant religion? Toleration, indifference are precisely the true means of undermining everything, taking away every foundation; we others will then be the greatest losers. . . . He is no friend of humanity, as the popular phrase is, who allows everyone his own thoughts. I am speaking only in the political sense, not as a Christian, nothing is so necessary and salutary as religion. Will you allow everyone to fashion his own religion as he pleases? No fixed cult, no subordination to the Church—what will then become of us? The result will not be quiet and contentment; its outcome will be the rule of the stronger and more unhappy times like those which we have already seen. A manifesto by you to this effect can produce the utmost distress and make you responsible for many thousands of souls. And what are my own sufferings, when I see you entangled in opinions so erroneous? What is at stake is not only the welfare of the State but your own salvation. . . . Turning your eyes and ears everywhere, mingling your spirit of contradiction with the simultaneous desire to create something, you are ruining yourself and dragging the Monarchy down with you into the abyss. . . . I only wish to live so long as I can hope to descend to my ancestors with the consolation that my son will be as great, as religious as his forebearer, that he will return from his erroneous views, from those wicked books whose authors parade their cleverness at the expense of all that is most holy and most worthy of respect in the world, who want to introduce an imaginary freedom which can never exist and which degenerates into license and into complete revolution.

Source: As quoted in C. A. Macartney, ed., *The Habsburg and Hohenzollern Dynasties in the Seventeenth and Eighteenth Centuries* (New York: Walker, 1970), pp. 151–153. Reprinted by permission of Walker and Co.

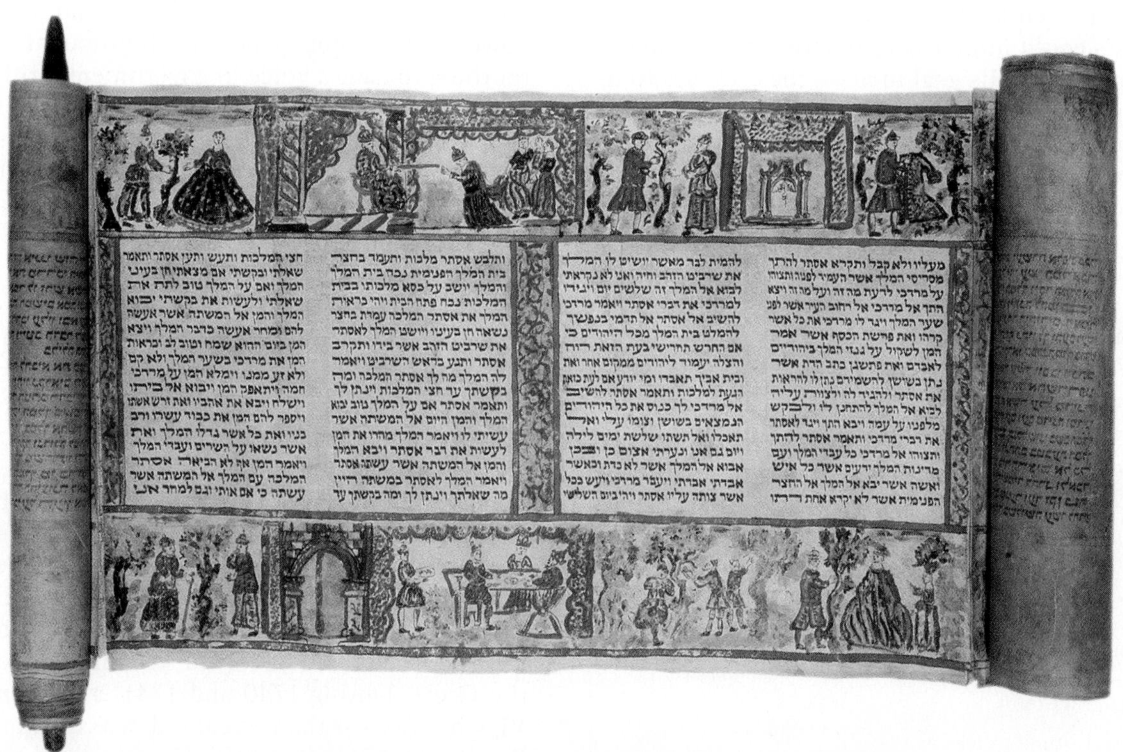

An eighteenth-century scroll of the biblical Book of Esther. According to the story, Queen Esther, who was married to King Ahasuerus of Persia, was responsible for thwarting a plan to annihilate all Jews in the Persian Empire. Unbeknownst to the king when they married, Esther, herself, was Jewish. The vizier, Haman the Agagite, devised this genocidal plan and the king ordered him to be hanged for his role in it. Courtesy of the Library of Congress initiated. During his reign, he introduced reforms that touched the very heart of the rural social structure. He did not abolish the authority of landlords over their peasants, but he did seek to make that authority more moderate and subject to the oversight of royal officials. He abolished serfdom as a legally sanctioned state of servitude. He granted peasants a wide array of personal freedoms, including the right to marry, to engage in skilled work, and to have their children learn a skill without having to secure the landlord's permission.

Joseph reformed the procedures of the manorial courts and opened avenues of appeal to royal officials. He also encouraged landlords to change land leases, so that peasants could more easily inherit land or transfer it to other peasants. His goal in all of these efforts to reduce traditional burdens on peasants was to make them more productive and industrious farmers.

Near the end of his reign, Joseph proposed a new and daring system of land taxation. He decreed in 1789 that all proprietors of the land were to be taxed regardless of social status. No longer were the peasants alone to bear the burden of taxation. He commuted *robot* into a monetary tax, only part of which was to go to the landlord, the rest reverting to the state. Angry nobles blocked the implementation of this decree, and it died with Joseph in 1790. This and other of Joseph's earlier measures, however, brought turmoil throughout the Habsburg realms. Peasants revolted over disagreements with landlords about their newly granted rights. The nobles of the various Habsburg realms protested the taxation scheme. The Magyars resisted Joseph's centralization measures in Hungary and forced him to rescind them.

Joseph was succeeded by his brother Leopold II (r. 1790–1792). Although sympathetic to Joseph's goals, Leopold was forced to repeal many of the most controversial decrees, such as that on taxation. In other areas, Leopold considered his brother's policies simply wrong. For example, he returned political and administrative power to local nobles because he thought it expedient for them to have a voice in government. Still, he did not repudiate his brother's program wholesale. He retained, in particular, Joseph's religious policies and maintained as much political centralization as he thought possible.

RUSSIA FROM PETER THE GREAT THROUGH CATHERINE THE GREAT

1725	Death of Peter the Great
1725–1727	Catherine I
1727–1730	Peter II
1730–1741	Anna
1740–1741	Ivan VI
1741–1762	Elizabeth
1762	Peter III
1762	Catherine II (the Great) becomes empress
1767	Legislative commission summoned
1769	War with Turkey begins
1773–1775	Pugachev's Rebellion
1772	First Partition of Poland
1774	Treaty of Kuchuk-Kainardji ends war with Turkey
1775	Reorganization of local government
1783	Russia annexes Crimea
1785	Catherine issues the Charter of the Nobility
1793	Second Partition of Poland
1795	Third Partition of Poland
1796	Death of Catherine the Great

Catherine the Great of Russia

Joseph II never grasped the practical necessity of forging political constituencies to support his policies. Catherine II, who had been born a German princess, but who became empress of Russia, understood only too well the fragility of the Romanov dynasty's base of power.

After the death of Peter the Great in 1725, the court nobles and the army repeatedly determined the Russian succession. As a result, the crown fell primarily into the hands of people with little talent. Peter's wife, Catherine I, ruled for two years (1725–1727) and was succeeded for three years by Peter's grandson, Peter II. In 1730, the crown devolved on Anna, a niece of Peter the Great. During 1740 and 1741, a child named Ivan VI, who was less than a year old, was the nominal ruler. Finally, in 1741, Peter the Great's daughter Elizabeth came to the throne. She held the title of empress until 1762, but her reign was not notable for new political departures or sound administration. Her court was a shambles of political and romantic intrigue. Much of the power the tsar possessed at the opening of the century had vanished.

At her death in 1762, Elizabeth was succeeded by her nephew Peter III. He was a weak ruler whom many contemporaries considered mad. He immediately exempted the nobles from compulsory military service and then rapidly made peace with Frederick the Great, for whom he held unbounded admiration. That decision probably saved Prussia from military defeat in the Seven Years' War. The one positive feature of this unbalanced creature's life was his marriage in 1745 to a young German princess born in the small duchy of Anhalt Zerbst. This was the future Catherine the Great.

For almost twenty years, Catherine lived in misery and frequent danger at the court of Elizabeth. During that

Catherine the Great ascended to the Russian throne after the murder of her husband. She tried initially to enact major reforms, but she never intended to abandon absolutism. She assured nobles of their rights and by the end of her reign had imposed press censorship. The Granger Collection

time, she befriended important nobles and read widely the books of the philosophes. She was a shrewd person whose experience in a court crawling with rumors, intrigue, and conspiracy had taught her how to survive. She exhibited neither love nor fidelity toward her demented husband. A few months after his accession as tsar, Peter was deposed and murdered with Catherine's approval, if not her aid, and she was immediately proclaimed empress.

Catherine's familiarity with the Enlightenment and the general culture of Western Europe convinced her Russia was backward and that it needed major reforms to remain a great power. She understood that any significant reform must have a wide base of political and social support, especially since she had assumed the throne through a palace coup. In 1767, she summoned a legislative commission to advise her on revising the law and government of Russia. There were more than five hundred delegates, drawn from all sectors of Russian life. Before the commission convened, Catherine issued a set of instructions, partly written by herself. They contained many ideas drawn from the political writings of the philosophes. The commission considered the instructions as well as other ideas and complaints its members raised.

Russian law, however, was not revised for more than half a century. In 1768, Catherine dismissed the commission before several of its key committees had reported. Yet the meeting had not been useless, for it had gathered a vast amount of information about the conditions of local administration and economic life throughout Russia. The inconclusive debates and the absence of programs from the delegates themselves suggested that most Russians saw no alternative to an autocratic monarchy, and Catherine had no intention of departing from absolutism.

Limited Administrative Reform Catherine carried out limited reforms on her own authority. She gave strong support to the rights and local power of the nobility. In 1775, she reorganized local government to solve problems the legislative commission had brought to light. She put most local offices in the hands of nobles rather than creating a royal bureaucracy. In 1785, Catherine issued the Charter of the Nobility, which guaranteed nobles many rights and privileges. In part, the empress had to favor the nobles because they could topple her from the throne. Moreover, Russia's educated class was too small to provide an independent bureaucracy, and the treasury could not afford an army strictly loyal to the crown. So Catherine wisely made a virtue of necessity. She strengthened the stability of her crown by making convenient friends with her nobles.

Economic Growth Part of Catherine's program was to continue the economic development begun under Peter the Great. She attempted to suppress internal barriers to trade. Exports of grain, flax, furs, and naval stores grew dramatically. She also favored the expansion of the small Russian urban middle class that was so vital to trade. Through all of these departures, Catherine tried to maintain ties of friendship and correspondence with the philosophes. She knew that if she treated them kindly, they would be sufficiently flattered to give her a progressive reputation throughout Europe.

Territorial Expansion Catherine's limited administrative reforms and her policy of economic growth had a counterpart in the diplomatic sphere. The Russian drive for warm-water ports continued. (See Map 17–1, page 526.) This goal required warfare with the Turks. In 1769, as a result of a minor Russian incursion, the Ottoman Empire declared war on Russia. The Russians responded with a series of strikingly successful military moves.

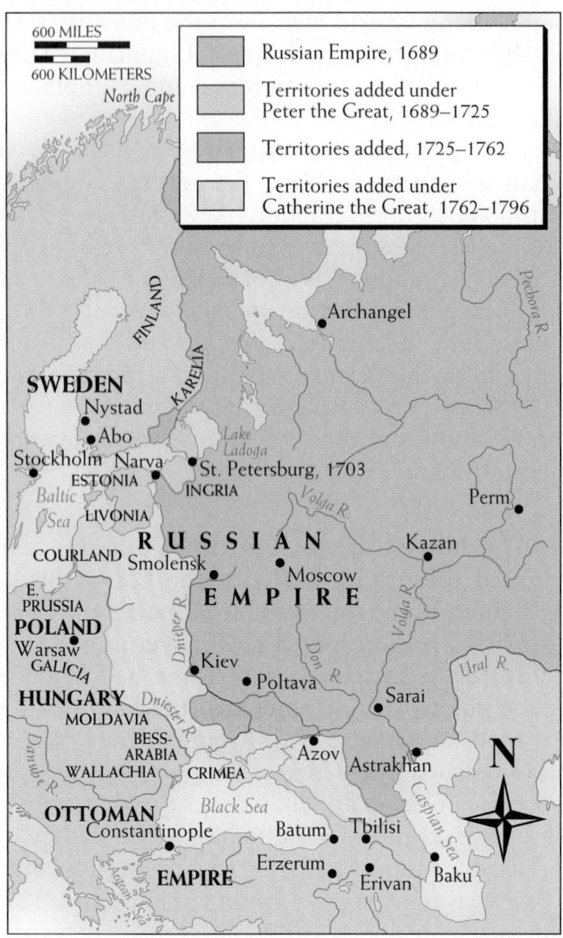

Map 17–1 **EXPANSION OF RUSSIA, 1689–1796** The overriding territorial aim of the two most powerful Russian monarchs of the eighteenth century, Peter the Great (in the first quarter of the century) and Catherine the Great (in the last half of the century), was to secure navigable outlets to the sea in both the north and the south for Russia's vast empire; hence Peter's push to the Baltic Sea and Catherine's to the Black Sea. Russia also expanded into Central Asia and Siberia during this time period.

During 1769 and 1770, the Russian fleet sailed all the way from the Baltic Sea into the eastern Mediterranean. The Russian army won several major victories that by 1771 gave Russia control of Ottoman provinces on the Danube River and the Crimean coast of the Black Sea. The conflict dragged on until 1774, when the Treaty of Kuchuk-Kainardji gave Russia a direct outlet on the Black Sea, free navigation rights in its waters, and free access through the Bosporus. Crimea became an independent state, which Catherine painlessly annexed in 1783. Finally, under this treaty Catherine, as empress of Russia, was made the protector of the Orthodox Christians living in the Ottoman Empire. In the future this would cause conflict with France whose monarch had previously been recognized as the protector of Roman Catholic Christians in the empire.

The Partition of Poland

The Russian military successes increased Catherine's domestic political support, but they made the other states of eastern Europe uneasy. These anxieties were overcome by an extraordinary division of Polish territory known as the First Partition of Poland.

The Russian victories along the Danube River were most unwelcome to Austria, which also harbored ambitions of territorial expansion in that direction. At the same time, the Ottoman Empire was pressing Prussia for aid against Russia. Frederick the Great made a proposal to Russia and Austria that would give each something it wanted, prevent conflict among the powers, and save appearances. After long, complicated secret negotiations, Russia agreed to abandon the conquered Danubian provinces. In compensation, it received a large portion of Polish territory with almost 2 million inhabitants. As a reward for remaining neutral, Prussia annexed most of the territory between East Prussia and Prussia proper. This land allowed Frederick to unite two previously separate sections of his realm. Finally, Austria took Galicia in southern Poland, with its important salt mines, and other Polish territory with more than 2.5 million inhabitants. (See Map 17–2.)

In September 1772, the helpless Polish aristocracy, paying the price for maintaining internal liberties at the expense of developing a strong central government, ratified this seizure of nearly one third of Polish territory. The loss was not necessarily fatal to Poland's continued existence, and it inspired a revival of national feeling. Attempts were made to strengthen the Polish state and reform its feeble central government, but they proved to be too little and too late. Poland was no match for its stronger, more ambitious neighbors. The partition of Poland clearly demonstrated that any nation without a strong monarchy, bureaucracy, and army could no longer compete within the European state system. It also demonstrated that the major powers in eastern Europe were prepared to settle their own rivalries at the expense of such a weak state. If Polish territory had not been available to ease tensions, international rivalries might have led to warfare among Russia, Austria, and Prussia.

As shall be seen in Chapter 18, the wars and social upheaval that followed the outbreak of the French Revolution gave Russia and Prussia an excuse to partition Poland again in 1793, and Russia, Prussia, and Austria partitioned it a third time in 1795, removing it from the map of Europe for more than a century. Each time, the great powers contended they were saving themselves, and by implication the rest of Europe, from Polish anarchy. The fact was that Poland's political weakness left it vulnerable to plunderous aggression by its more powerful neighbors.

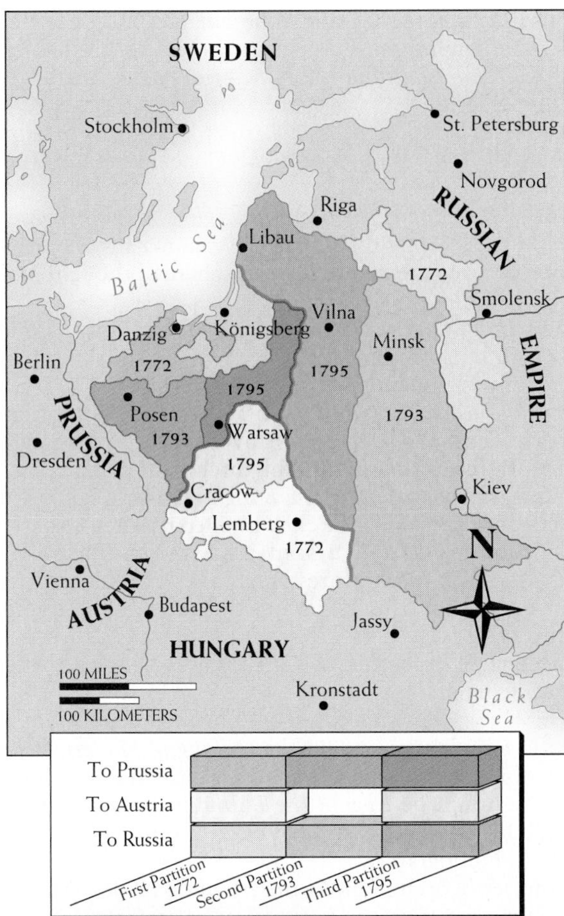

Map 17–2 **PARTITIONS OF POLAND, 1772, 1793, AND 1795.** The callous eradication of Poland from the map displayed eighteenth-century power politics at its most extreme. Poland, without a strong central government, fell victim to the strong absolute monarchies of central and eastern Europe.

The End of the Eighteenth Century in Central and Eastern Europe

During the last two decades of the eighteenth century, all three regimes based on enlightened absolutism became more conservative and politically repressive. In Prussia and Austria, the innovations of the rulers stirred resistance among the nobility. In Russia, fear of peasant unrest was the chief factor.

Frederick the Great of Prussia grew remote during his old age, leaving the aristocracy to fill important military and administrative posts. A reaction to Enlightenment ideas also set in among Prussian Lutheran writers.

In Austria, Joseph II's plans to restructure society and administration in his realms provoked growing frustration and political unrest, with the nobility calling for an end to innovation. In response, Joseph turned increasingly to censorship and his secret police.

Russia faced a peasant uprising, the Pugachev Rebellion, between 1773 and 1775, and Catherine the Great never fully recovered from the fears of social and political upheaval that it raised. Once the French Revolution broke out in 1789, the Russian empress censored books based on Enlightenment thought and sent offensive authors into Siberian exile.

By the close of the century, fear of, and hostility to, change permeated the ruling classes of central and eastern Europe. This reaction had begun before 1789, but the events in France bolstered and sustained it for almost half a century. Paradoxically, nowhere did the humanity and liberalism of the Enlightenment encounter greater rejection than in those states that had been governed by "enlightened" rulers.

In Perspective

The writers of the Enlightenment, known as *philosophes*, charted a major new path in modern European and Western thought. They operated within a print culture that made public opinion into a distinct, cultural force. Admiring Newton and the achievements of physical science, they tried to apply reason and the principles of science to the cause of social reform. They also believed that passions and feelings are essential parts of human nature. Throughout their writings they championed reasonable moderation in social life. More than any other previous group of Western thinkers, they opposed the authority of the established churches and especially of Roman Catholicism. Most of them championed some form of religious toleration. They also sought to achieve a science of society that could discover how to maximize human productivity and material happiness. The great dissenter among them was Rousseau, who also wished to reform society, but in the name of virtue rather than material happiness.

The political influence of these writers was diverse and far-reaching. The founding fathers of the American republic looked to them for political guidance, as did moderate liberal reformers throughout Europe, especially within royal bureaucracies. The autocratic rulers of eastern Europe consulted the philosophes in the hope that Enlightenment ideas might allow them to rule more efficiently. The revolutionaries in France would honor them. This diverse assortment of followers illustrates the diverse character of the philosophes themselves. It also shows that Enlightenment thought cannot be reduced to a single formula. Rather, it should be seen as an outlook that championed change and reform, giving central place to humans and their welfare on earth rather than to God and the hereafter.

REVIEW QUESTIONS

1. How did the Enlightenment change basic Western attitudes toward reform, faith, and reason? What were the major formative influences on the philosophes? How important were Voltaire and the *Encyclopedia* in the success of the Enlightenment?
2. Why did the philosophes consider organized religion to be their greatest enemy? What were the basic tenets of deism? How did Jewish writers contribute to Enlightenment thinking about religion? What are the similarities and differences between the Enlightenment evaluation of Islam and its evaluations of Christianity and Judaism?
3. What were the attitudes of the philosophes toward women? What was Rousseau's view of women? What were the separate spheres he imagined men and women occupying? What were Mary Wollstonecraft's criticisms of Rousseau's view?
4. How did the views of the mercantilists about the earth's resources differ from those of Adam Smith in his book *The Wealth of Nations*? Why might Smith be regarded as an advocate of the consumer? How did his theory of history work to the detriment of less economically advanced non-European peoples? How did some Enlightenment writers criticize European empires?
5. How did the political views of Montesquieu differ from those of Rousseau? Was Montesquieu's view of England accurate? Was Rousseau a child of the Enlightenment or its enemy? Which did Rousseau value more, the individual or society?
6. Were the enlightened monarchs true believers in the ideals of the philosophes, or was their enlightenment a mere veneer? Was their power really absolute? What motivated their reforms? What does the partition of Poland indicate about the spirit of enlightened absolutism?

SUGGESTED READINGS

D. D. Bien, *The Calas Affair: Persecution, Toleration, and Heresy in Eighteenth-Century Toulouse* (1960). The standard treatment of the famous case.

T. C. W. Blanning, *The Culture of Power and the Power of Culture: Old Regime Europe 1660–1789* (2002). A remarkable synthesis of the interaction of political power and culture in France, Prussia, and Austria.

P. Bloom, *Enlightening the World: Encyclopedie, The Book That Changed the Course of History* (2005). A lively, accessible introduction.

J. Buchan, *Crowded with Genius: The Scottish Enlightenment* (2003). A lively, accessible introduction.

L. Damrosch, *Rousseau: Restless Genius* (2007). The best recent biography.

I. De Madariaga, *Russia in the Age of Catherine the Great* (1981). The best discussion in English.

S. Feiner, *The Jewish Enlightenment* (2002). An extensive work, challenging pan-European treatment of the subject.

P. Gay, *The Enlightenment: An Interpretation*, 2 vols. (1966, 1969). A classic.

D. Goodman, *The Republic of Letters: A Cultural History of the French Enlightenment* (1994). Concentrates on the role of salons.

C. Hesse, *The Other Enlightenment: How French Women Became Modern* (2004). Explores the manner in which French women authors created their own sphere of thought and cultural activity.

J. Israel, *Enlightenment Contested: Philosophy, Modernity, and the Emancipation of Man 1670–1752* (2006). A challenging major revisionist history of the subject.

J. I. Israel, *Radical Enlightenment: Philosophy and the Making of Modernity* (2001). A controversial account of the most radical strains of thought in Enlightenment culture.

C. A. Kors, *Encyclopedia of the Enlightenment* (2002). A major reference work on all of the chief intellectual themes of the era.

J. P. Ledonne, *The Russian Empire and the World, 1700–1917* (1996). Explores the major reasons for Russian expansion from the eighteenth to the early twentieth centuries.

G. Macdonagh, *Frederick the Great* (2001). A thoughtful and accessible biography.

D. MacMahon, *Enemies of the Enlightenment: The French Counter-Enlightenment and the Making of Modernity* (2001). A fine exploration of French writers critical of the philosophes.

J. V. H. Melton, *The Rise of the Public in Enlightenment Europe* (2001). Explores the social basis of print culture with an excellent bibliography.

S. Muthu, *Enlightenment Against Empire* (2003). A challenging volume covering the critique of the empire.

R. Peason, *Voltaire Almighty: A Life in Pursuit of Freedom* (2005). An accessible biography.

R. Porter, *The Creation of the Modern World: The Untold Story of the British Enlightenment* (2000). Seeks to shift the center of the Enlightenment from France to England.

P. Riley, *The Cambridge Companion to Rousseau* (2001). Excellent accessible essays by major scholars.

E. Rothchild, *Economic Sentiments: Adam Smith, Condorcet, and the Enlightenment* (2001). A sensitive account of Smith's thought and its relationship to the social questions of the day.

J. Sheehan, *The Enlightenment Bible* (2007). Explores the Enlightenment treatment of the Bible.

S. Smith, *Spinoza, Liberalism, and the Question of Jewish Identity* (1997). A clear introduction to a challenging thinker.

A. M. Wilson, *Diderot* (1972). A splendid biography of the person behind the *Encyclopedia* and other major Enlightenment publications.

L. Wolff, *Inventing Eastern Europe: The Map of Civilization on the Mind of the Enlightenment* (1994). A remarkable study of how Enlightenment writers recast the understanding of this part of the Continent.

For additional learning resources related to this chapter, please go to www.myhistorylab.com

On July 14, 1789, crowds stormed the Bastille, a prison in Paris. This event, whose only practical effect was to free a few prisoners, marked the first time the populace of Paris redirected the course of the revolution. Anonymous, France, eighteenth century, *Siege of the Bastille, 14 July, 1789.* Musée de la Ville de Paris, Musée Carnavalet, Paris, France. Bridgeman—Giraudon/Art Resource, NY

18

The French Revolution

▼ **The Crisis of the French Monarchy**
The Monarchy Seeks New Taxes • Necker's Report • Calonne's Reform Plan and the Assembly of Notables • Deadlock and the Calling of the Estates General

▼ **The Revolution of 1789**
The Estates General Becomes the National Assembly • Fall of the Bastille • The "Great Fear" and the Night of August 4 • The Declaration of the Rights of Man and Citizen • The Parisian Women's March on Versailles

▼ **The Reconstruction of France**
Political Reorganization • Economic Policy • The Civil Constitution of the Clergy • Counterrevolutionary Activity

▼ **The End of the Monarchy: A Second Revolution**
Emergence of the Jacobins • The Convention and the Role of the *Sans-culottes*

▼ **Europe at War with the Revolution**
Edmund Burke Attacks the Revolution • Suppression of Reform in Britain • The Second and Third Partitions of Poland, 1793, 1795

▼ **The Reign of Terror**
War with Europe • The Republic Defended • The "Republic of Virtue" and Robespierre's Justification of Terror • Repression of the Society of Revolutionary Republican Women • De-Christianization • Revolutionary Tribunals • The End of the Terror

▼ **The Thermidorian Reaction**
Establishment of the Directory • Removal of the *Sans-culottes* from Political Life

▼ **In Perspective**

KEY TOPICS

- **The financial crisis that impelled the French monarchy to call the Estates General**
- **The transformation of the Estates General into the National Assembly, the Declaration of the Rights of Man and Citizen, and the reconstruction of the political and ecclesiastical institutions of France**
- **The second revolution, the end of the monarchy, and the turn to more radical reforms**
- **The war between France and the rest of Europe**
- **The Reign of Terror, the Thermidorian Reaction, and the establishment of the Directory**

IN THE SPRING of 1789 political turmoil soon resulting in revolution erupted in France. The events of that year marked the beginning of a new political order in France and eventually throughout the West. The French Revolution brought to the foreground the principles of civic equality and popular sovereignty that challenged the major political and social institutions of Europe and that in evolving forms have continued to shape and reshape Western political and social life to the present day. During the 1790s the forces the revolution unleashed would cause small-town provincial lawyers and Parisian street orators to exercise more influence over the fate of the Continent than aristocrats, royal ministers, or monarchs. Citizen armies commanded by people of low birth and filled by conscripted village youths would defeat armies composed of professional soldiers led by officers of noble birth. The king and queen of France, as well as thousands of French peasants and shopkeepers, would be executed. The existence of the Roman Catholic faith in France and indeed of Christianity itself would be challenged. Finally Europe would embark on almost a quarter century of war that would eventually extend across the continent and result in millions of casualties.

▾ The Crisis of the French Monarchy

Although the French Revolution would shatter many of the political, social, and ecclesiastical structures of Europe, its origins lay in a much more mundane problem. By the late 1780s, the French royal government could not command sufficient taxes to finance itself. The monarchy's unsuccessful search for adequate revenues led it into ongoing conflicts with aristocratic and ecclesiastical institutions. Eventually, the resulting deadlock was so complete that Louis XVI and his ministers were required to summon the French Estates General, which had not met since 1614. Once the deputies to that body gathered, a new set of issues and problems quickly emerged that led to the revolution itself. Yet, none of this would have occurred if the monarchy had not reached a state of financial crisis that meant it could no longer function within the limits and practices of existing political institutions.

The Monarchy Seeks New Taxes

The French monarchy emerged from the Seven Years' War (1756–1763) defeated, deeply in debt, and unable thereafter to put its finances on a sound basis. French support of the American revolt against Great Britain further deepened the financial difficulties of the government. On the eve of the revolution, the interest and payments on the royal debt amounted to just over one half of the entire budget. Given the economic vitality of France, the debt was neither overly large nor disproportionate to the debts of other European powers. The problem lay with the inability of the royal government to tap the nation's wealth through taxes to service and repay the debt. Paradoxically, France was a rich nation with an impoverished government.

The debt was symptomatic of the failure of the late-eighteenth-century French monarchy to come to terms with the political power of aristocratic institutions and, in particular, the *parlements*. As explained in Chapter 13, French absolutism had always involved a process of ongoing negotiation between the monarchy and local aristocratic interests. This process had become more difficult after the death of Louis XIV (r. 1643–1715) when the aristocracy had sought to reclaim parts of the influence it had lost. Nonetheless, for the first half of the century, the monarchy had retained most of its authority.

For twenty-five years after the Seven Years' War, however, a standoff occurred between the monarchy and the aristocracy, as one royal minister after another attempted to devise new tax schemes that would tap the wealth of the nobility, only to be confronted by opposition from both the *Parlement* of Paris and provincial *parlements*. Both Louis XV (r. 1715–1774) and Louis XVI (r. 1774–1792) lacked the character, resolution, and political skills to resolve the dispute. In place of a consistent policy for dealing with the growing debt and aristocratic resistance to change, the monarchy hesitated, retreated, and even lied.

In 1770, Louis XV appointed René Maupeou (1714–1792) as chancellor. The new minister was determined to break the *parlements* and increase taxes on the nobility. He abolished the *parlements* and exiled their members to different parts of the country. He then began an ambitious program to make the administration more efficient. What ultimately doomed Maupeou's policy was

Well-meaning, but weak and vacillating, Louis XVI (r. 1774–1792) stumbled from concession to concession until he finally lost all power to save his throne. Joseph Siffred Duplessis (1725–1802), *Louis XVI*. Versailles, France. Photograph copyright Bridgeman—Giraudon/Art Resource, NY

less the resistance of the nobility than the unexpected death from smallpox of Louis XV in 1774. His successor, Louis XVI, in an attempt to regain what he conceived to be popular support, dismissed Maupeou, restored all the *parlements*, and confirmed their old powers.

Although the *parlements* spoke for aristocratic interests, they appear to have enjoyed public support. By the second half of the eighteenth century, many French nobles shared with the wealthy professional and commercial classes similar economic interests and similar goals for administrative reforms that would support economic growth. Both groups regarded the lumbering institutions of monarchical absolutism as a burden. Moreover, throughout these initial and later disputes with the monarchy, the *parlements*, though completely dominated by the aristocracy, used the language of liberty and reform to defend their cause. They portrayed the monarchy as despotic—that is, as acting arbitrarily in defiance of the law. Here they drew on the ideas and arguments of many Enlightenment writers, such as Montesquieu and the physiocrats, discussed in Chapter 16.

The monarchy was unable to rally public opinion to its side because it had lost much of its moral authority. The sexually scandalous life of Louis XV was known throughout France, and the memory of his behavior lingered long after his death. Marie Antoinette (1755–1793), the wife of Louis XVI, also rightly or wrongly, gained a reputation for sexual misconduct and personal extravagance. She became the subject of numerous prurient prints and pamphlets that circulated throughout Paris and beyond. Louis XVI's own faithfulness to his queen and upright morals could not outweigh the monarchy's reputation for scandal. Furthermore, Louis XVI and his family continued to live at Versailles, rarely leaving its grounds to mix with his subjects and with the aristocracy, who now, unlike in the days of Louis XIV, often dwelled in Paris or on their estates. Hence, the French monarch stood at a distinct popular disadvantage in his clashes first with the *parlements* and later with other groupings of the aristocracy.

In all these respects, the public image and daily reality of the French monarchy were much more problematical than those of other contemporary monarchs. Frederick II of Prussia and Joseph II of Austria genuinely saw themselves, and were seen by their subjects, as patriotic servants of the state. George III of Great Britain, despite all his political difficulties, was regarded by most Britons as having a model character and as seeking the economic improvement of his nation. All three had reputations for personal frugality, and they moved frequently among the people they governed.

Necker's Report

France's successful intervention on behalf of the American colonists against the British only worsened the financial problems of Louis XVI's government. By 1781, as a result of the aid to America, its debt was larger, and its sources of revenues were unchanged. The new royal director-general of finances, Jacques Necker (1732–1804), a Swiss banker, then produced a public report in 1781 that suggested the situation was not so bad as had been feared. He argued that if the expenditures for the American war were removed, the budget was in surplus. Necker's report also revealed that a large portion of royal expenditures went to pensions for aristocrats and other royal court favorites. This revelation angered court aristocratic circles, and Necker soon left office. His financial sleight of hand, nonetheless, made it more difficult for government officials to claim a real need to raise new taxes.

Calonne's Reform Plan and the Assembly of Notables

The monarchy hobbled along until 1786. By this time, Charles Alexandre de Calonne (1734–1802) was the minister of finance. Calonne proposed to encourage internal trade, to lower some taxes, such as the *gabelle* on salt, and to transform the *corvée*, peasants' labor services on public works, into money payments. He also sought to remove internal barriers to trade and reduce government regulation of the grain trade. More importantly, Calonne wanted to introduce a new land tax that all landowners would have to pay regardless of their social status. If this tax had been imposed, the monarchy could have abandoned other indirect taxes. The government would also have had less need to seek additional taxes that required approval from the aristocratically dominated *parlements*. Calonne also intended to establish new local assemblies made up of landowners to approve land taxes; in these assemblies the voting power would have depended on the amount of land a person owned rather than on his social status. All these proposals would have undermined both the political and the social power of the French aristocracy. Other of his proposals touched the economic privileges of the French Church. These policies reflected much advanced economic and administrative thinking of the day.

The monarchy, however, had little room to maneuver. The creditors were at the door, and the treasury was nearly empty. Calonne needed public support for such bold new undertakings. In February 1787, he met with an Assembly of Notables, nominated by the royal ministry from the upper ranks of the aristocracy and the church, to seek support for his plan. The Assembly adamantly refused to give it. There was some agreement that reform and greater fairness in taxation were necessary, but the Assembly did not trust the information they had received from Calonne. In his place they called for the reappointment of Necker, who they believed had left the country in sound fiscal condition. Finally, they claimed that only the Estates General of France, a medieval institution that had not met since 1614, could consent to new taxes. The notables believed that calling the Estates General, which had been traditionally organized to allow aristocratic and church dominance, would actually allow the nobility to have a direct role in governing the country alongside the monarchy. The issue was less the nobility not wishing to reform tax structure than its determination to acquire power at the expense of the monarchy and to direct reforms itself.

Deadlock and the Calling of the Estates General

Again, Louis XVI backed off. He replaced Calonne with Étienne Charles Loménie de Brienne (1727–1794), archbishop of Toulouse and the chief opponent of Calonne at the Assembly of Notables. Once in office, Brienne found, to his astonishment, that the financial situation was as bad as his predecessor had asserted. Brienne himself now sought to reform the land tax. The *Parlement* of Paris, however, in its self-appointed role as the embodiment of public opinion, took the new position that it lacked authority to authorize the tax and that only the Estates General could do so. Shortly thereafter, Brienne appealed to the Assembly of the Clergy to approve a large subsidy to fund that part of the debt then coming due for payment. The clergy, like the *Parlement* dominated by aristocrats, not only refused the subsidy, but also reduced the voluntary contribution, or *don gratuit*, that it paid to the government in lieu of taxes.

As these unfruitful negotiations were taking place at the center of political life, local aristocratic *parlements* and estates in the provinces were making their own demands. They wanted to restore the privileges they had enjoyed during the early seventeenth century, before Richelieu and Louis XIV had crushed their independence. Furthermore, bringing the financial crisis to a new point of urgency, bankers refused in the summer of 1788 to extend necessary short-term credit to the government. Consequently, in July 1788, the king, through Brienne, agreed to convoke the Estates General the next year. Brienne resigned, and Necker replaced him. Some kind of political reform was coming, but what form it would take and how it would happen would be largely determined by the conflicts that emerged from summoning the Estates General.

▼ The Revolution of 1789

The Estates General Becomes the National Assembly

The Estates General had been called because of the political deadlock between the French monarchy and the vested interests of aristocratic institutions and the church. Almost immediately after it was summoned, however, the three groups, or estates, represented within it clashed with each other. The First Estate was the clergy, the Second Estate the nobility, and the **Third Estate** was, theoretically, everyone else in the kingdom, although its representatives were drawn primarily from wealthy members of the commercial and professional middle classes. All the representatives in the Estates General were men. During the widespread public discussions preceding the meeting of the Estates General, representatives of the Third Estate made it clear they would not permit the monarchy and the aristocracy to decide the future of the nation.

A comment by a priest, the Abbé Siéyès (1748–1836), in a pamphlet published in 1789, captures the spirit of the Third Estate's representatives: "What is the Third Estate? Everything. What has it been in the political order up to the present? Nothing. What does it ask? To become something."[1] The spokesmen for the Third Estate became more determined to assert their role less from any preexisting conflicts with the nobility than from the conflicts that emerged during the debates and electioneering for the Estates General in late 1788 and early 1789.

Debate over Organization and Voting Before the Estates General gathered, a public debate over its proper organization drew the lines of basic disagreement. The aristocracy made two important attempts to limit the influence of the Third Estate. First, a reconvened Assembly of Notables demanded that each estate have an equal number of representatives. Second, in September 1788, the *Parlement* of Paris ruled that voting in the Estates General should be conducted by order rather than by head—that is, each estate, or order, in the Estates General, rather than each individual member, should have one vote. This procedure would in all likelihood have ensured the aristocratically dominated First and Second Estates could always outvote the Third by a vote of two estates to one estate. Both moves raised doubt about the aristocracy's previously declared concern for French liberty and revealed it as a group hoping to maintain its privileged influence no matter what government reforms might be enacted. Spokesmen for the Third Estate immediately denounced the arrogant claims of the aristocracy.

In many respects the interests of the aristocracy and the most prosperous and well-educated members of the Third Estate had converged during the eighteenth century, and many nobles had married husbands and wives from the elite of the Third Estate. Yet a fundamental social distance separated the members of the two orders. Many aristocrats were much richer than members of the Third Estate, and noblemen had all but monopolized the high command in the army and navy. The Third Estate had also experienced various forms of political and

[1]Quoted in Leo Gershoy, *The French Revolution and Napoleon* (New York: Appleton-Century-Crofts, 1964), p. 102.

THE THIRD ESTATE OF A FRENCH CITY PETITIONS THE KING

In the spring of 1789 representatives to the Estates General brought to Versailles cahiers de doléances which were lists of grievances generated during the election process. *(See page 534)* *This particular* cahier *originated in Dourdan, a city in central France, and reflects the complaints of the Third Estate. The first two articles refer to the organization of the Estates General. The other articles ask the king to grant various forms of equality before the law and in taxation. Most of the* cahiers *of the Third Estate included these demands for equality.*

Which of the following petitions relate to political rights and which to economic equality? The slogan most associated with the French Revolution was "Liberty, Equality, Fraternity." Which of these petitions represents each of these values?

The order of the third estate of the City . . . of Dourdan . . . supplicates [the king] to accept the grievances, complaints, and remonstrances which it is permitted to bring to the foot of the throne, and to see therein only the expression of its zeal and the homage of its obedience.

It wishes:

1. That his subjects of the third estate, equal by such status to all other citizens, present themselves before the common father without other distinction which might degrade them.
2. That all the orders, already united by duty and common desire contribute equally to the needs of the State, also deliberate in common concerning its needs.
3. That no citizen lose his liberty except according to law: that, consequently, no one be arrested by virtue of special orders, or, if imperative circumstances necessitate such orders that the prisoner be handed over to regular courts of justice within forty-eight hours at the latest.

12. That every tax, direct or indirect, be granted only for a limited time, and that every collection beyond such term be regarded as peculation, and punished as such.

15. That every personal tax be abolished; that thus the capitation [a poll tax] and the taille [tax from which nobility and clergy were exempt] and its accessories be merged with the vingtièmes [an income tax] in a tax on land and real or nominal property.
16. That such tax be borne equally, without distinction, by all classes of citizens and by all kinds of property, even feudal . . . rights.
17. That the tax substituted for the corvée be borne by all classes of citizens equally and without distinction. That said tax, at present beyond the capacity of those who pay it and the needs to which it is destined, be reduced by at least one-half.

From John Hall Stewart, *Documentary Survey of the French Revolution*, 1st ed.,

social discrimination from the nobility. The resistance of the nobility to voting by head confirmed the suspicions and resentments of the members of the Third Estate, who tended to be well-off, but not enormously rich, lawyers. The stance of both the reconvened Assembly of Notables and the *Parlement* of Paris regarding the composition and functioning of the forthcoming Estates General meant that the elected members of the Third Estate would approach the gathering with a newly awakened profound distrust of the nobility and of the aristocratically dominated church.

Doubling the Third In the face of widespread public uproar over the aristocratic effort to dominate composition and procedures of the Estates General, the royal council eventually decided that strengthening the Third Estate would best serve the interests of the monarchy and the cause of fiscal reform. In December 1788, the council announced the Third Estate would elect twice as many representatives as either the nobles or the clergy. This so-called doubling of the Third Estate meant it could easily dominate the Estates General if voting proceeded by head rather than by order. The council correctly assumed that liberal nobles and clergy would support the Third Estate, confirming that, despite social differences, these groups shared important interests and reform goals. The method of voting had not yet been decided when the Estates General gathered at Versailles in May 1789.

The *Cahiers de Doléances* When the representatives came to the royal palace, they brought with them ***cahiers de doléances***, or lists of grievances, registered by the local electors, to be presented to the king. Many of these lists have survived and provide considerable information about the state of France on the eve of the revolution. The documents criticized government waste, indirect taxes, church taxes and corruption, and the hunting rights of the aristocracy. They included calls for periodic meetings of the Estates General, more equitable taxes, more local control of administration, unified weights and measures to facilitate trade and commerce, and a free press. The overwhelming demand of the *cahiers* was for equality of rights among the king's subjects. Yet it is also clear that the *cahiers* that originated among the nobility were not radically different from those of the Third Estate. There was broad agreement that the French government needed major reform, that greater equality in taxation and other matters was desirable, and that many aristocratic privileges must be abandoned. (See "The Third Estate of a French City Petitions the King," page 533.) The *cahiers* drawn up before May 1789 indicate that the three estates could have cooperated to reach these goals. But that conflict among the estates, rather than cooperation, was to be the case became clear almost from the moment the Estates General opened.

The Third Estate Creates the National Assembly The complaints, demands, and hopes for reform expressed in the *cahiers* could not, however, be discussed until the questions of the organization and voting in the Estates General had been decided. From the beginning, the Third Estate, whose members consisted largely of local officials, professionals, and other persons of property, refused to sit as a separate order as the king desired. For several weeks there was a standoff. Then, on June 1, the Third Estate invited the clergy and the nobles to join them in organizing a new legislative body. A few priests did so. On June 17, that body declared itself the National Assembly, and on June 19 by a narrow margin, the Second Estate voted to join the Assembly.

The Tennis Court Oath At this point, Louis XVI hoped to reassert a role in the proceedings. He intended to call a "Royal Session" of the Estates General for June 23 and closed the room where the National Assembly had been gathering. On June 20, finding themselves thus unexpectedly locked out of their usual meeting place, the National Assembly moved to a nearby indoor tennis court. There, its members took an oath to continue to sit until they had given France a constitution. This was the famous Tennis Court Oath. Louis XVI ordered the National Assembly to desist, but many clergy and nobles joined the Assembly in defiance of the royal command.

On June 27, the king, now having completely lost control of the events around him, capitulated and formally requested the First and Second Estates to meet with the National Assembly, where voting would occur by head rather than by order. The Third Estate because of the doubling of its membership had twice as many members as either of the other estates that joined them. Had nothing further occurred, the government of France would already have been transformed. Henceforth, the monarchy could govern only in cooperation with the National Assembly, and the National Assembly would not be a legislative body organized according to privileged orders. The National Assembly, which renamed itself the National Constituent Assembly because of its intention to write a new constitution, was composed of a majority of members drawn from all three orders, who shared liberal goals for the administrative, constitutional, and economic reform of the country. The revolution in France against government by privileged hereditary orders, however, rapidly extended beyond events occurring at Versailles.

Fall of the Bastille

Two new forces soon intruded on the scene. First, Louis XVI again attempted to regain the political initiative by mustering royal troops near Versailles and Paris. On the advice of Queen Marie Antoinette, his brothers, and the most conservative aristocrats at court, he seemed to be contemplating the use of force against the National Constituent Assembly. On July 11, without consulting Assembly leaders, Louis abruptly dismissed Necker, his minister of finance. Louis's gathering troops and dismissal of Necker marked the beginning of a steady, but consistently poorly executed, royal attempt to undermine the Assembly and halt the revolution. Most of the National Constituent Assembly wished to establish some form of constitutional monarchy, but from the start, Louis's refusal to cooperate thwarted that effort. The king fatally decided to throw in his lot with the conservative aristocracy against the emerging forces of reform drawn from across the social and political spectrum.

The second new factor to impose itself on the events at Versailles was the populace of Paris, which numbered more than 600,000 people. The mustering of royal troops created anxiety in the city, where throughout the winter and spring of 1789 high prices for bread, which was the staple food of the poor, had produced riots. Those Parisians who had elected representatives to the Third Estate had continued to meet after the

This painting of the Tennis Court Oath, June 20, is by Jacques-Louis David (1748–1825). In the center foreground are members of different estates joining hands in cooperation as equals. The presiding officer is Jean-Sylvain Bailly, soon to become mayor of Paris. Jacques-Louis David, *Oath of the Tennis Court, the 20th of June 1789*. Chateaux de Versailles et de Trianon, Versailles, France. Bridgeman–Giraudon/Art Resource, NY

elections. By June they were organizing a citizen militia and collecting arms. They regarded the dismissal of Necker as the opening of a royal offensive against the National Constituent Assembly and the city. They intended to protect the Assembly and the revolution had begun.

On July 14, large crowds of Parisians, most of them small shopkeepers, tradespeople, artisans, and wage earners, marched to the Bastille to get weapons for the militia. This great fortress, with ten-foot-thick walls, had once held political prisoners. Through miscalculations and ineptitude by the governor of the fortress, the troops in the Bastille fired into the crowd, killing ninety-eight people and wounding many others. Thereafter, the crowd stormed the fortress. They released the seven prisoners inside, none of whom was a political prisoner, and killed several troops and the governor.

On July 15, the militia of Paris, by then called the National Guard, offered its command to a young liberal aristocrat, the Marquis de Lafayette (1757–1834). This hero of the American Revolution gave the guard a new insignia: the red and blue stripes from the colors of the coat of arms of Paris, separated by the white stripe of the royal flag. The emblem became the revolutionary *cockade* (badge) and eventually the tricolor flag of revolutionary France.

The attack on the Bastille marked the first of many crucial *journées*, days on which the populace of Paris redirected the course of the revolution. The fall of the fortress signaled that the National Constituent Assembly alone would not decide the political future of the nation. As the news of the taking of the Bastille spread, similar disturbances took place in provincial cities. A few days later, Louis XVI again bowed to the force of events and personally visited Paris, where he wore the revolutionary *cockade* and recognized the organized electors as the legitimate government of the city. The king also recognized the National Guard and thus implicitly admitted that he lacked the military support to turn back the revolution. The citizens of Paris were, for the time being, satisfied. They also had established themselves as an independent political force with which other political groups might ally for their own purposes.

A Closer LOOK

CHALLENGING THE FRENCH POLITICAL ORDER

THIS LATE EIGHTEENTH-CENTURY cartoon satirizes the French social and political structure as the events and tensions leading up to the outbreak of the French Revolution unfolded. This image embodies the highly radical critique of the French political structure that erupted from about 1787 when the nobility and church refused to aid the financial crisis of the monarchy.

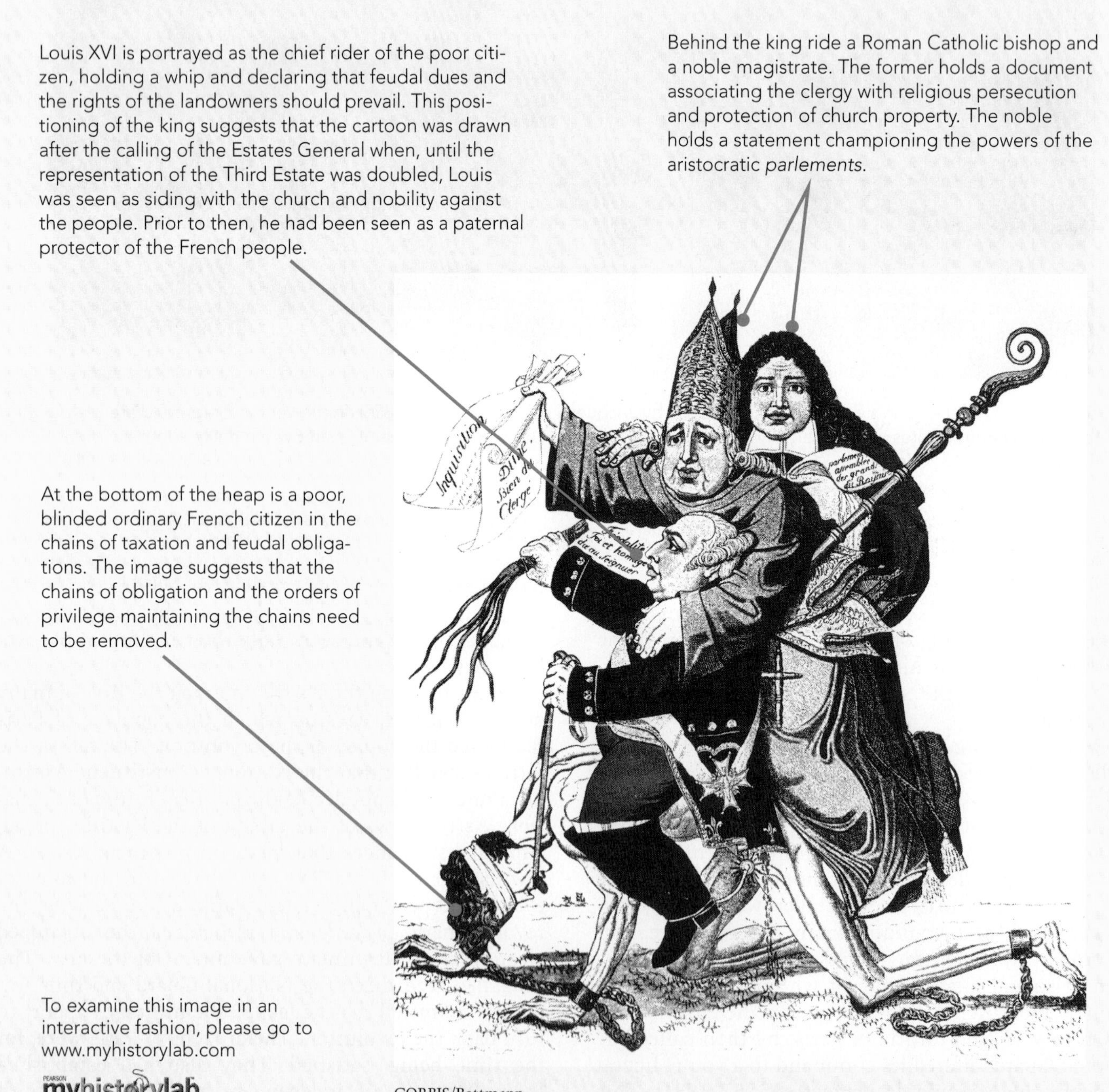

Louis XVI is portrayed as the chief rider of the poor citizen, holding a whip and declaring that feudal dues and the rights of the landowners should prevail. This positioning of the king suggests that the cartoon was drawn after the calling of the Estates General when, until the representation of the Third Estate was doubled, Louis was seen as siding with the church and nobility against the people. Prior to then, he had been seen as a paternal protector of the French people.

Behind the king ride a Roman Catholic bishop and a noble magistrate. The former holds a document associating the clergy with religious persecution and protection of church property. The noble holds a statement championing the powers of the aristocratic *parlements*.

At the bottom of the heap is a poor, blinded ordinary French citizen in the chains of taxation and feudal obligations. The image suggests that the chains of obligation and the orders of privilege maintaining the chains need to be removed.

To examine this image in an interactive fashion, please go to www.myhistorylab.com

myhistorylab

CORBIS/Bettmann

The "Great Fear" and the Night of August 4

Simultaneous with the popular urban disturbances, a movement known as the "Great Fear" swept across much of the French countryside. Rumors that royal troops would be sent into the rural districts intensified the peasant disturbances that had begun during the spring. The Great Fear saw the burning of *châteaux*, the destruction of legal records and documents, and the refusal to pay feudal dues. The peasants were determined to take possession of food supplies and land that they considered to be rightfully theirs. They were reclaiming rights and property they had lost through administrative tightening of the collection of feudal dues during the past century as well as venting their anger against the injustices of rural life. Their targets were both aristocratic and ecclesiastical landlords.

On the night of August 4, 1789, aristocrats in the National Constituent Assembly attempted to halt the spreading disorder in the countryside. By prearrangement, several liberal nobles and clerics rose in the Assembly and renounced their feudal rights, dues, and tithes. In a scene of great emotion, they surrendered hunting and fishing rights, judicial authority, and legal exemptions. These nobles and clerics gave up what they had already lost and what they could not have regained without civil war in the rural areas. Many of them later received financial compensation for their losses. Nonetheless, after the night of August 4, all French citizens were subject to the same and equal laws. Furthermore, since the sale of government offices was also abolished, the events of that night opened political and military positions, careers, and advancement to talent rather than basing them exclusively on birth or wealth. This dramatic session of the Assembly effectively abolished the major social institutions of the Old Regime and created an unforeseen situation that required a vast legal and social reconstruction of the nation. Without those renunciations, the constructive work of the National Constituent Assembly would have been much more difficult and certainly much more limited. (See "The National Assembly Decrees Civic Equality in France," page 538.)

Both the attack on the Bastille and the Great Fear displayed characteristics of the urban and rural riots that had occurred often in eighteenth-century France. Louis XVI first thought the turmoil over the Bastille was simply another bread riot. Indeed, the popular disturbances were only partly related to the events at Versailles. A deep economic downturn had struck France in 1787 and continued into 1788. The harvests for both years had been poor, and the food prices in 1789 were higher than at any time since 1703. Wages had not kept up with the rise in prices. Throughout the winter of 1788–1789, an unusually cold one, many people suffered from hunger. Wage and food riots had erupted in several cities. These economic problems fanned the fires of revolution.

The political, social, and economic grievances of many sections of the country became combined. The National Constituent Assembly could look to the popular forces as a source of strength against the king and the conservative aristocrats. When the various elements of the Assembly later quarreled among themselves, however, the resulting factions would appeal for support to the politically sophisticated and well-organized shopkeeping and artisan classes. They, in turn, would demand a price for their cooperation.

The Declaration of the Rights of Man and Citizen

In late August 1789, the National Constituent Assembly decided that before writing a new constitution, it should publish a statement of broad political principles. On August 27, the Assembly issued the Declaration of the Rights of Man and Citizen. This declaration drew on the political language of the Enlightenment and the Declaration of Rights that the state of Virginia had adopted in June 1776.

The French declaration proclaimed that all men were "born and remain free and equal in rights." The natural rights so proclaimed were "liberty, property, security, and resistance to oppression." Governments existed to protect those rights. All political sovereignty resided in the nation and its representatives. All citizens were to be equal before the law and were to be "equally admissible to all public dignities, offices, and employments, according to their capacity, and with no other distinction than that of their virtues and talents." There were to be due process of law and presumption of innocence until proof of guilt. Freedom of religion was affirmed. Taxation was to be apportioned equally according to the capacity to pay. Property constituted "an inviolable and sacred right."[2]

The Declaration of the Rights of Man and Citizen was directed in large measure against specific abuses of the old French monarchical and aristocratic regime, but it was framed in abstract universalistic language applicable to other European nations. In this respect, the ideas set forth in the declaration like those of the Protestant reformers three centuries earlier could jump across national borders and find adherents outside France. The two most powerful, universal political ideas of the declaration were civic equality and popular sovereignty. The first would challenge the legal and social inequities of European life, and the second would assert that governments must be

[2]Quoted in Georges Lefebvre, *The Coming of the French Revolution*, trans. by R. R. Palmer (Princeton, NJ: Princeton University Press, 1967), pp. 221–223.

THE NATIONAL ASSEMBLY DECREES CIVIC EQUALITY IN FRANCE

These famous decrees of August 4, 1789, in effect created civic equality in France. The special privileges previously possessed or controlled by the nobility were removed.

What institutions and privileges are included in "the feudal regime"? How do these decrees recognize that the abolition of some privileges and former tax arrangements will require new kinds of taxes and government financing to support religious, educational, and other institutions?

1. The National Assembly completely abolishes the feudal regime. It decrees that, among the rights and dues . . . all those originating in real or personal serfdom, personal servitude, and those which represent them, are abolished without indemnification; all other are declared redeemable, and that the price and mode of redemption shall be fixed by the National Assembly. . . .
2. The exclusive right to maintain pigeon-houses and dove-cotes is abolished. . . .
3. The exclusive right to hunt and to maintain unenclosed warrens is likewise abolished. . . .
4. All manorial courts are suppressed without indemnification.
5. Tithes of every description and the dues which have been substituted for [them] . . . are abolished on condition, however, that some other method be devised to provide for the expenses of divine worship, the support of the officiating clergy, the relief of the poor, repairs and rebuilding of churches and parsonages, and for all establishments, seminaries, schools, academies, asylums, communities, and other institutions, for the maintenance of which they are actually devoted. . . .
6. The sale of judicial and municipal offices shall be suppressed forthwith. . . .
7. Pecuniary privileges, personal or real, in the payment of taxes are abolished forever. . . .
8. All citizens, without distinction of birth, are eligible to any office or dignity, whether ecclesiastical, civil or military. . . .

From Frank Maloy Anderson, ed. and trans., *The Constitutions and Other Select Documents Illustrative of the History of France, 1789–1907*, 2nd ed., rev. and enl. (Minneapolis, MN: H. W. Wilson, 1908), pp. 11–13.

responsible to the governed. These two principles, in turn, could find themselves in tension with the declaration's principle of the protection of property.

It was not accidental that the Declaration of the Rights of Man and Citizen specifically applied to men and not to women. As discussed in Chapter 17, much of the political language of the Enlightenment, and especially that associated with Rousseau, separated men and women into distinct gender spheres. According to this view, which influenced legislation during the revolution, men were suited for citizenship, women for motherhood and the domestic life. Nonetheless, in the charged atmosphere of the summer of 1789, many politically active and informed Frenchwomen hoped the guarantees of the declaration would be extended to them. They were particularly concerned with property, inheritance, family, and divorce. Some people saw in the declaration a framework within which women might eventually enjoy the rights and protection of citizenship. Those hopes would be disappointed during the years of the revolution and for many decades thereafter.

Nonetheless, over the succeeding two centuries the universalist language of the Declaration of the Rights of Man and Citizen would provide an intellectual framework for bringing into the realm of active civic life many groups who were excluded in the late eighteenth century. (See "Compare & Connect: The Declaration of the Rights of Man and Citizen Opens the Door for Disadvantaged Groups to Demand Equal Civic Rights," pages. 542–543.)

The Parisian Women's March on Versailles

Louis XVI stalled before ratifying both the Declaration of the Rights of Man and Citizen and the aristocratic renunciation of feudalism. His hesitations fueled suspicions that he might again try to resort to force. Moreover, bread remained scarce and expensive. On October 5, some 7,000 Parisian women armed with pikes, guns, swords, and knives marched to Versailles demanding more bread. They milled about the palace, and many stayed the night. Intimidated, the king agreed to sanction the decrees of the Assembly. The next day he and his family appeared on a balcony before the crowd. Deeply suspicious of the monarch and believing that he must be kept under the watchful eye of the people, the Parisians demanded that Louis and his family return to Paris with them. The monarch had no real choice. On October 6, 1789, his carriage followed the crowd into the city, where he and his family settled in the old palace of the Tuileries in the heart of Paris.

The National Constituent Assembly also soon moved to Paris. Thereafter, both Paris and France remained relatively stable and peaceful until the summer of 1792. A decline in the price of bread in late 1789 helped to calm the atmosphere.

▼ The Reconstruction of France

In Paris, the National Constituent Assembly set about reorganizing France. In government, it pursued a policy of constitutional monarchy; in administration, rationalism; in economics, unregulated freedom; and in religion, anticlericalism. Throughout its proceedings and following the principles of the Declaration of the Rights of Man and Citizen, the Assembly was determined to protect property in all its forms. The Assembly sought to limit the impact on the national life of those French people who had no property or only small amounts of it. Although championing civic equality before the law, the Assembly, with the aristocrats and middle-class elite united, spurned social equality and extensive democracy. It thus charted a general course that, to a greater or lesser degree, nineteenth-century liberals across Europe would follow.

Political Reorganization

In the Constitution of 1791, the National Constituent Assembly established a constitutional monarchy. The major political authority of the nation would be a unicameral Legislative Assembly, in which all laws would

The women of Paris marched to Versailles on October 5, 1789. The following day the royal family was forced to return to Paris with them. Henceforth, the French government would function under the constant threat of mob violence. Anonymous, eighteenth century, *To Versailles, to Versailles*. The women of Paris going to Versailles, 7 October, 1789. French. Musée de la Ville de Paris, Musée Carnavalet, Paris, France. Photograph copyright Bridgeman—Giraudon/Art Resource, NY

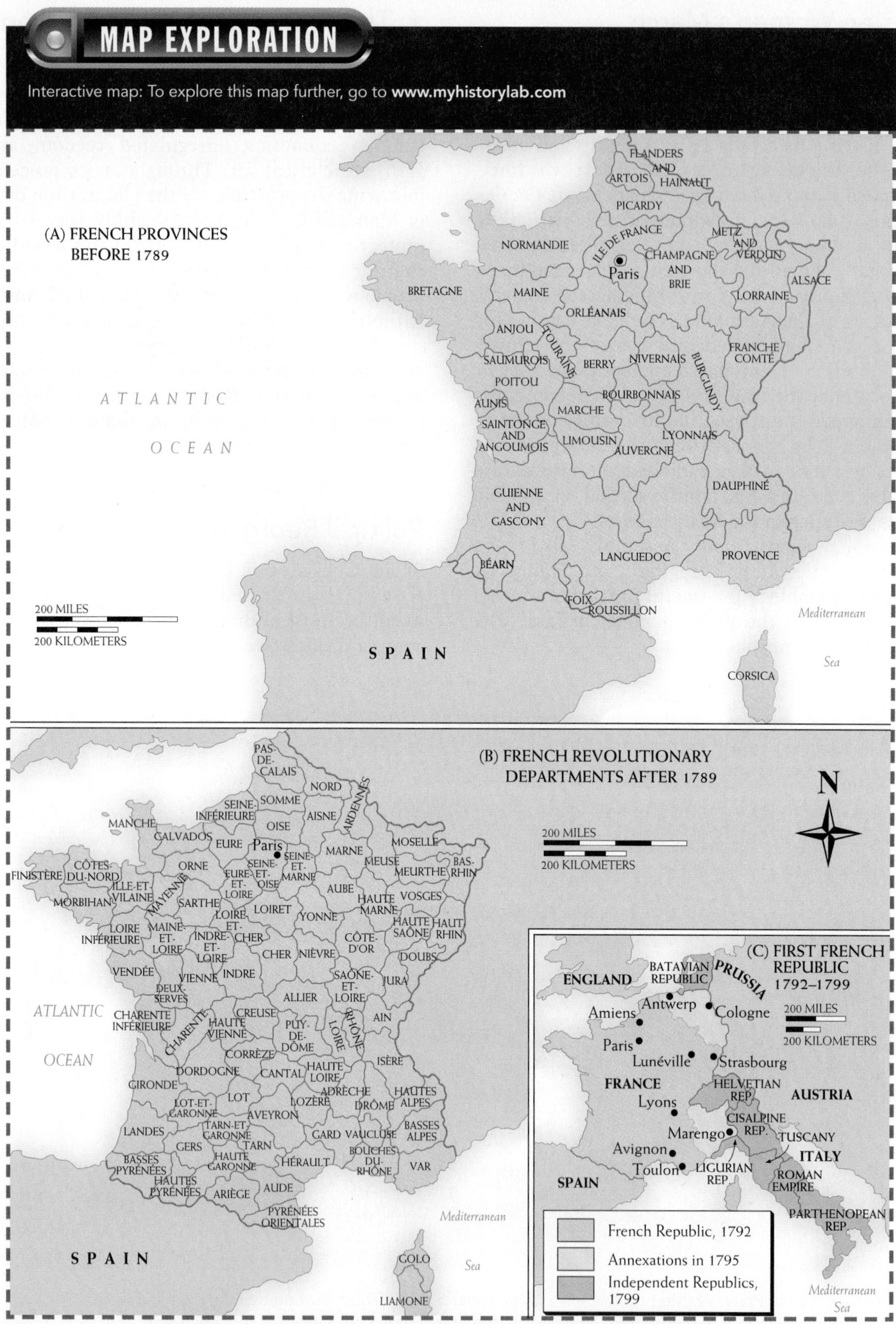

Map 18–1 **FRENCH PROVINCES AND THE REPUBLIC** In 1789, the National Constituent Assembly redrew the map of France. The ancient provinces (A) were replaced with a larger number of new, smaller departments (B). This redrawing of the map was part of the Assembly's effort to impose greater administrative rationality in France. The borders of the republic (C) changed as the French army conquered new territory.

originate. The monarch was allowed a suspensive veto that could delay, but not halt, legislation. The Assembly also had the power to make war and peace.

Active and Passive Citizens The constitution provided for an elaborate system of indirect elections to thwart direct popular pressure on the government. The citizens of France were divided into active and passive categories. Only active citizens—that is, men paying annual taxes equal to three days of local labor wages—could vote. They chose electors, who then, in turn, voted for the members of the legislature. Further property qualifications were required to serve as an elector or member of the legislature. Only about 50,000 citizens of a population of about 25 million could qualify as electors or members of the Legislative Assembly. Women could neither vote nor hold office.

These constitutional arrangements effectively transferred political power from aristocratic wealth to all forms of propertied wealth in the nation. The accumulation of wealth from land and commercial property, not hereditary privilege or the purchase of titles or offices, would open the path to political authority. These new political arrangements based on property rather than birth reflected the changes in French society over the past century and allowed more social and economic interests to have a voice in governing the nation.

Olympe de Gouges's Declaration of the Rights of Woman The laws that excluded women from voting and holding office did not pass unnoticed. In 1791, Olympe de Gouges (d. 1793), a butcher's daughter from Montauban in northwest France who became a major revolutionary radical in Paris, composed a Declaration of the Rights of Woman, which she ironically addressed to Queen Marie Antoinette. Much of the document reprinted the Declaration of the Rights of Man and Citizen, adding the word *woman* to the various original clauses. That strategy demanded that women be regarded as citizens and not merely as daughters, sisters, wives, and mothers of citizens. Olympe de Gouges further outlined rights that would permit women to own property and require men to recognize the paternity of their children. She called for equality of the sexes in marriage and improved education for women. She declared, "Women, wake up; the *tocsin* of reason is being heard throughout the whole universe; discover your rights."[3] Her declaration illustrated how the simple listing of rights in the Declaration of the Rights of Man and Citizen created a structure of universal civic expectations even for those it did not cover. The National Assembly had established a set of values against which it could itself be measured. It provided criteria for liberty, and those to whom it had not extended full liberties could demand to know why and could claim the revolution was incomplete until they too enjoyed those freedoms. (See "Compare & Connect: The Declaration of the Rights of Man and Citizen Opens the Door for Disadvantaged Groups to Demand Equal Civic Rights," pages 542–543.)

Departments Replace Provinces In reconstructing the local and judicial administration, the National Constituent Assembly applied the rational spirit of the Enlightenment. It abolished the ancient French provinces, such as Burgundy and Brittany, and established in their place eighty-three administrative units called departments, or *départements*, of generally equal size named after rivers, mountains, and other geographical features. The departments in turn were subdivided into districts, cantons, and communes. Elections for departmental and local assemblies were also indirect. This administrative reconstruction proved to be permanent. The departments still exist in twenty-first-century France. (See Map 18–1.)

All the ancient judicial courts, including the seigneurial courts and the *parlements*, were also abolished and replaced by uniform courts with elected judges and prosecutors. Procedures were simplified, and the most degrading punishments, such as branding, torture, and public flogging, were removed from the books.

Economic Policy

In economic matters, the National Constituent Assembly continued the policies Louis XVI's reformist ministers had formerly advocated. It suppressed the guilds and liberated the grain trade. The Assembly established the metric system to provide the nation with uniform weights and measures. (See "Encountering the Past: The Metric System," page 544.)

Workers' Organizations Forbidden The new policies of economic freedom and uniformity disappointed both peasants and urban workers. In 1789, the Assembly placed the burden of proof on the peasants to rid themselves of the residual feudal dues for which compensation was to be paid. On June 14, 1791, the Assembly crushed the attempts of urban workers to protect their wages by enacting the Chapelier Law, which forbade workers' associations. The Assembly saw the efforts of workers to organize in such a way as to resemble the abolished guilds of the Old Regime and thus to oppose the new values of political and social individualism, which the revolution championed. Peasants and workers were henceforth to be left to the freedom and mercy of the marketplace.

Confiscation of Church Lands While these various reforms were being put into effect, the financial crisis that had occasioned the calling of the Estates General persisted. The Assembly did not repudiate the royal debt, because it was owed to the bankers, the merchants, and the commercial traders of the Third Estate. The

[3]Quoted in Sara E. Melzer and Leslie W. Rabine, eds., *Rebel Daughters: Women and the French Revolution* (New York: Oxford University Press, 1992), p. 88.

The Declaration of the Rights of Man and Citizen Opens the Door for Disadvantaged Groups to Demand Equal Civic Rights

THE NATIONAL ASSEMBLY passed the Declaration of the Rights of Man and Citizen on August 26, 1789. The principles of the declaration were very broad and in theory could be extended beyond the domestic male French citizens to whom it applied. Within months various civically disadvantaged groups stepped forward to demand inclusion within the newly proclaimed realm of civic rights. These included free persons of color from French Caribbean colony of St. Dominque and French women. It should be noted that during the same period French Jews also asked to have the principles of religious toleration proclaimed in the Declaration of the Rights of Man and Citizen extended to themselves.

QUESTIONS

1. **How does Raymond portray himself as free but still clearly victimized by the Assembly in St. Domingue, composed only of white members?**
2. **How does Raymond invoke the principles of the Declaration of the Rights of Man and Citizen to apply pressure on the French National Assembly?**
3. **What are the specific parallels that de Gouges draws between the rights of man and the rights of woman?**
4. **How does her declaration suggest civic responsibilities for women as well as rights?**
5. **On what grounds might the same people who championed the Declaration of the Rights of Man and Citizen in 1789 deny the extension of those rights to the various groups that soon demanded inclusion under the ideals of the declaration?**

I. A Free Person of Color from St. Domingue Demands Recognition of His Status

In the spring of 1791 Julian Raymond, a free person of color from the French Caribbean colony of St. Domingue (Haiti), petitioned the French National Assembly to recognize persons such as himself as free citizens. The National Assembly did so in May 1791 but later rescinded the decree. Only in March 1792 did the Assembly firmly recognize the civic equality of such persons. The background for the request and for the confusion of the French National Assembly over the matter was the eruption of the slave revolution in Haiti, which is discussed in Chapter 20.

Remaining to this day under the oppression of the white colonists, we dare hope that we do not ask the National Assembly in vain for the rights, which it has declared, belong to every man.

In our just protests, if the troubles, the calumnies that you have witnessed until today under the legislation of white colonists, and finally, if the truths which we had the honor of presenting yesterday to the bar of the Assembly do not overcome the unjust pretensions of the white colonial legislators who want to [proceed] without our participation, we beg the Assembly not to jeopardize the little remaining liberty we have, that of being able to abandon the ground soaked with the blood of our brothers and of permitting us to flee the sharp knife of the laws they will prepare against us.

If the Assembly has decided to pass a law which lets our fate depend on twenty-nine whites [in the colonial Assembly], our decided enemies, we demand to add an amendment to the decree which would be rendered in this situation, that free men of color can emigrate with their fortunes so that they can be neither disturbed nor hindered by the whites.

Mr. President, this is the last recourse which remains for us to escape the vengeance of the white colonists who menace us for not having given up our claims to the rights which the National Assembly has declared belong to every man.

Source: As quoted in Laura Mason and Tracey Rizzo, *The French Revolution: A Document Collection* (Boston: Houghton Mifflin Company, 1999), p. 109.

This is an example of the French Revolution-era clothing worn by the *Sans-culottes* or members of the poorer classes and their leaders. The outfit is comprised of the *pantalon* (long trousers), *carmagnole* (short-skirted coat), red cap of liberty, and *sabots* (wooden shoes). Dorling Kindersley Media Library/Mark Hamilton © Dorling Kindersley

II. Olympe de Gouges Issues a Declaration of the Rights of Woman

In September 1791 Olympe de Gouges published a Declaration of the Rights of Woman that paralleled in many respects the Declaration of the Rights of Man and Citizen proclaimed two years earlier. A self-educated woman and butcher's daughter, she had written widely on a number of reform topics. Radical as she was, she remained loyal to the monarchy and was eventually executed by the revolutionary government in 1793.

Mothers, daughters, sisters [and] representatives of the nation demand to be constituted into a national assembly. . . . Consequently, the sex that is as superior in beauty as it is in courage during the sufferings of maternity recognizes and declares in the presence and under the auspices of the Supreme Being, the following Rights of Woman and of Female Citizens.

ARTICLE I

Woman is born free and lives equal to man in her rights. Social distinctions can be based only on the common utility.

ARTICLE II

The purpose of any political association is the conservation of the natural and impresciptible rights of woman and man; these rights are liberty property, security, and especially resistance to oppression. . . .

ARTICLE IV

Liberty and justice consist of restoring all that belongs to others; thus, the only limits on the exercise of the natural rights of woman are perpetual male tyranny; these limits are to be reformed by the laws of nature and reason. . . .

ARTICLE VI

The law must be the expression of the general will; all female and male citizens must contribute either personally or through their representatives to its formation; it must be the same for all: male and female citizens, being equal in the eyes of the law, must be equally admitted to all honors, positions, and public employment according to their capacity and without other distinctions besides those of their virtues and talents. . . .

ARTICLE X

No one is to be disquieted for his very basic opinions; woman has the right to mount the scaffold; she must equally have the right to mount the rostrum, provided that her demonstrations do not disturb the legally established public order. . . .

ARTICLE XIII

For the support of the public force and the expenses of administration, the contributions of woman and man are equal; she shares all the duties and all the painful tasks; therefore, she must have the same share in the distribution of positions, employment, offices, honors, and jobs. . . .

ARTICLE XVII

Property belongs to both sexes whether united or separate; for each it is an inviolable and sacred right; no one can be deprived of it, since it is the true patrimony of nature, unless the legally determined public need obviously dictates it, and then only with a just and prior indemnity.

POSTSCRIPT

Woman, wake up; the tocsin of reason is being heard throughout the whole universe; discover your rights.

Source: As quoted in Darline Gay Levy, Harriet Branson Applewhite, and Mary Durham Johnson, eds., *Women in Revolutionary Paris, 1789–1795* (Urbana: University of Illinois Press, 1980), pp. 87–96.

THE METRIC SYSTEM

MUCH ABOUT THE era of the French Revolution seems alien to us today. One French regime followed another amidst confusion, violence, and bloodshed. Yet one thing that the revolutionaries did still touches the lives of virtually all Europeans and, if the U.S. Congress has its way, will touch everyone in the United States as well. In 1795, the French revolutionary government decreed a new standard for weights and measures—the metric system.

Inspired by the rationalism of the eighteenth-century Enlightenment, the metric system was intended to bring the order and simplicity of a system based on 10 to the chaos of different weights and measures used in the various regions of prerevolutionary France. For its adherents, the republic marked the dawn of a new era in human history in which the triumph of science would replace the reign of superstition and obscurity. A new system of uniform weights and measures would also further one of the revolutionaries' political goals: centralization. With one set of weights and measures in use throughout the country, France would be closer to becoming a single "indivisible" republic.

Jean-Baptiste Delambre (1749–1822) was one of the French astronomers whose measurements of the arch of meridians formed the basis for establishing the length of the meter.
Image Works/Mary Evans Picture Library Ltd.

Astronomy, which relied on the rational application of mathematics to measure the heavens, provided the basis for the new system of distance or length. Astronomers had devised methods to measure the arch of meridians—the highest point reached by the sun—around the earth. So the revolutionary authorities took the meridian in the latitude of Paris, which is 45°, as their standard for measuring the meter. The meter was to be one ten-millionth of one quarter of that meridian. All other measurements of length were then defined as decimal fractions or multiples of the meter.

1 centimeter (cm) = 10 millimeters (mm)
1 decimeter (dm) = 10 centimeters
1 meter = 100 centimeters
1 kilometer (km) = 1,000 meters

The standard for measuring weights was the gram, which constituted the weight of a cube of pure water measuring 0.01 meter on each side. Each measure of weight was defined as a decimal fraction or multiple of a gram. So a kilogram is 1,000 grams.

The metric system was soon adopted by scientists, but in their everyday lives, the population of France clung to their old, familiar weights and measures. Change, however "rational," did not come easily and was resisted. In 1812, Napoleon, bowing to popular sentiment, brought back the old units, but in 1840, the French government reimposed the metric system. Thereafter, rationality—and convenience—triumphed, and by the close of the nineteenth century, the metric system was used throughout continental Europe and had been introduced into Latin America. In the twentieth century it was adopted throughout Asia and Africa.

Today, the United States remains the great exception. Despite efforts by scientists, engineers, and doctors, who all use the metric system in their work, people in the United States still prefer to measure in inches, feet, yards, and miles and to weigh in ounces and pounds. Perhaps without even being aware of it, they are rejecting a system introduced during the French Revolution.

Why did the French revolutionary government introduce the metric system? How did the metric system reflect the ideas of the Enlightenment? Why has most of the world accepted this system?

National Constituent Assembly had suppressed many of the old, hated indirect taxes and had substituted new land taxes, but these proved insufficient. Moreover, there were not enough officials to collect those taxes, and many people simply evaded them in the general confusion of the day. The continuing financial problem led the Assembly to take what may well have been, for the future of French life and society, its most decisive action. The Assembly decided to finance the debt by confiscating and then selling the land and property of the Roman Catholic Church in France. The results were further inflation, religious schism, and civil war. In effect, the National Constituent Assembly had opened a new chapter in the relations of church and state in Europe.

The *assignats* were government bonds that were backed by confiscated church lands. They circulated as money. When the government printed too many of them, inflation resulted and their value fell. Bildarchiv Preussischer Kulturbesitz

The *Assignats* Having chosen to plunder the church, the Assembly authorized the issuance of ***assignats***, or government bonds, in December 1789. Their value was guaranteed by the revenue to be generated from the sale of church property. Initially, a limit was set on the quantity of *assignats* to be issued. The bonds, however, proved so acceptable to the public that they began to circulate as currency. The Assembly decided to issue an ever-larger number of them to liquidate the national debt and to create a large body of new property owners with a direct stake in the revolution. Within a few months, however, the value of the *assignats* began to fall and inflation increased, putting new stress on the urban poor. Fluctuation in the worth of this currency would plague the revolutionary government throughout the 1790s.

The Civil Constitution of the Clergy

The confiscation of church lands required an ecclesiastical reconstruction. In July 1790, the National Constituent Assembly issued the Civil Constitution of the Clergy, which transformed the Roman Catholic Church in France into a branch of the secular state. This legislation reduced the number of bishoprics from 135 to 83, making one diocese for each of the new departments. It also provided for the election of pastors and bishops, who henceforth became salaried employees of the state. The Assembly, which also dissolved all religious orders in France except those that cared for the sick or ran schools, consulted neither Pope Pius VI (r. 1775–1799) nor the French clergy about these sweeping changes. The king approved the measure only with the greatest reluctance.

The Civil Constitution of the Clergy was the major blunder of the National Constituent Assembly. It embittered relations between the French church and the state, a problem that has persisted to the present day. The measure immediately created immense opposition within the French church, even from bishops who had long championed Gallican liberties over papal domination. In the face of this resistance, the Assembly unwisely ruled that all clergy must take an oath to support the Civil Constitution. Only seven bishops and a little less than half the lower clergy did so. In reprisal, the Assembly designated those clergy who had not taken the oath as "refractory" and removed them from their clerical functions.

Angry reactions were swift. Refractory priests celebrated Mass in defiance of the Assembly. In February 1791, Pope Pius condemned not only the Civil Constitution of the Clergy, but also the Declaration of the Rights of Man and Citizen. That condemnation marked the opening of a Roman Catholic offensive against the revolution and liberalism that continued throughout the nineteenth century. Within France itself, the pope's action created a crisis of conscience and political loyalty for all sincere Catholics. Religious devotion and revolutionary loyalty became incompatible for many people. French citizens were divided between those who supported the constitutional priests and those who, like the royal family, followed the refractory clergy.

Counterrevolutionary Activity

The revolution had other enemies besides the pope and devout Catholics. As it became clear that the old political and social order was undergoing fundamental and probably permanent change, many aristocrats, eventually over 16,000, left France. Known as the **émigrés**, they settled in countries near the French border, where they sought to foment counterrevolution. Among the most important of their number was the king's younger brother, the count of Artois (1757–1836). In the summer of 1791, his agents and the queen persuaded Louis XVI to attempt to flee the country.

Flight to Varennes On the night of June 20, 1791, Louis and his immediate family, disguised as servants, left Paris. They traveled as far as Varennes on their way to Metz in eastern France where a royalist military force was waiting for them. At Varennes the king was recognized, and his flight was halted. On June 24, a company of soldiers escorted the royal family back to Paris. Eventually the leaders of the National Constituent Assembly, determined to save the constitutional monarchy, announced the king had been abducted from the capital. This convenient public fiction could not cloak the reality that the king was now the chief counterrevolutionary in France and that the constitutional monarchy might not last long. Profound distrust now dominated the political scene.

Declaration of Pillnitz Two months later, on August 27, 1791, under pressure from the *émigrés*, Emperor Leopold II (r. 1790–1792) of Austria, who was the brother of Marie Antoinette, and King Frederick William II (r. 1786–1797) of Prussia issued the Declaration of Pillnitz. The two monarchs promised to intervene in France to protect the royal family and to preserve the monarchy if the other major European powers agreed. This provision rendered the declaration meaningless because, at the time, Great Britain would not have given its consent. The declaration was, however, taken seriously in France, where the revolutionaries saw the nation surrounded by aristocratic and monarchical foes seeking to undo all that had been accomplished since 1789.

In June 1791, Louis XVI and his family attempted to flee France. They were recognized in the town of Varennes, where their flight was halted and they were returned to Paris. This ended any realistic hope for a constitutional monarchy. © Bettmann/CORBIS

▾ The End of the Monarchy: A Second Revolution

The National Constituent Assembly drew to a close in September 1791, having completed its task of reconstructing the government and the administration of France. The Assembly had passed a measure that forbade any of its own members to sit in the Legislative Assembly the new constitution established. That new Assembly filled with entirely new members met on October 1 and immediately had to confront the challenges flowing from the resistance to the Civil Constitution of the Clergy, the king's flight, and the Declaration of Pillnitz.

Emergence of the Jacobins

Ever since the original gathering of the Estates General, deputies from the Third Estate had organized themselves into clubs composed of politically like-minded persons. The most famous and best organized of these clubs were the **Jacobins** because the group met in a former Dominican priory dedicated to St. Jacques (James) in Paris. The Jacobins had also established a network of local clubs throughout the provinces. They had been the most advanced political group in the National Constituent Assembly and had pressed for a republic rather than a constitutional monarchy. They drew their political language from the most radical thought of the Enlightenment, most particularly Rousseau's emphasis on equality, popular sovereignty, and civic virtue. Such thought and language became all the more effective because the events of 1789 to 1791 had destroyed the old political framework, and the old monarchical political vocabulary was less and less relevant. The rhetoric of republicanism filled that vacuum and for a time supplied the political values of the day. The flight of Louis XVI in the summer of 1791 and the Declaration of Pillnitz led to renewed demands for a republic.

Factionalism plagued the Legislative Assembly throughout its short life (1791–1792). A group of Jacobins known as the *Girondists* (because many of them came from the department of the Gironde in southwest France) assumed leadership of the Assembly.[4] They were determined to oppose the forces of counterrevolution. They passed one measure ordering the *émigrés* to return or suffer the loss of their property and another requiring the refractory clergy to support the Civil Constitution or lose their state pensions. The king vetoed both acts.

[4]The Girondists are also frequently called the Brissotins after Jacques-Pierre Brissot (1754–1793), their chief spokesperson in early 1792.

Furthermore, on April 20, 1792, the Girondists led the Legislative Assembly to declare war on Austria, by this time governed by Francis II (r. 1792–1835) and allied to Prussia. This decision launched a period of armed conflict across Western Europe that with only brief intervals of peace lasted until the final defeat of France at Waterloo in June 1815.

The Girondists believed the war would preserve the revolution from domestic enemies and bring the most advanced revolutionaries to power. Paradoxically, Louis XVI and other monarchists also favored the war. They thought the conflict would strengthen the executive power (the monarchy). The king also hoped that foreign armies might defeat French forces and restore the Old Regime. Both sides were playing a dangerously, deluded political game. The war radicalized French politics and within months led to what is usually called the second revolution, which overthrew the constitutional monarchy and established a republic.

With the outbreak of war, the country and the revolution seemed in danger. As early as March 1791, a group of women led by Pauline Léon had petitioned the Legislative Assembly for the right to bear arms and to fight to protect the revolution. Léon also wanted women to serve in the National Guard. These demands to serve, voiced in the universal language of citizenship, illustrated how the rhetoric of the revolution could be used to challenge traditional social roles and the concept of separate social spheres for men and women. Furthermore, the pressure of war raised the possibility that the nation could not meet its military needs if it honored the idea of separate spheres. Once the war began, some Frenchwomen did enlist in the army and served with distinction. Initially, the war effort went poorly. In July 1792, the duke of Brunswick, commander of the Prussian forces, issued a manifesto threatening to destroy Paris if the French royal family were harmed. This statement stiffened support for the war and increased distrust of the king.

Late in July, under radical working-class pressure, the government of Paris passed from the elected council to a committee, or *commune*, of representatives from the sections (municipal wards) of the city. Thereafter the Paris commune became an independent political force casting itself in the role of the protector of the gains of the revolution against both internal and external enemies. Its activities and forceful modes of intimidation largely accounted for the dominance of the city of Paris over many of the future directions of the revolutionary government for the next three years.

On August 10, 1792, a large crowd invaded the Tuileries palace and forced Louis XVI and Marie Antoinette to take refuge in the Legislative Assembly. The crowd fought with the royal Swiss guards. When Louis was finally able to call off the troops, several hundred of them and many Parisian citizens lay dead in the most extensive violence since the fall of the Bastille. Thereafter the royal family was imprisoned in comfortable quarters, but the king was allowed to perform none of his political functions. The recently established constitutional monarchy no longer had a monarch.

The Convention and the Role of the *Sans-culottes*

The September Massacres Early in September, the Parisian crowd again made its will felt. During the first week of the month, in what are known as the September Massacres, the Paris Commune summarily executed or murdered about 1,200 people who were in the city jails. Some of these people were aristocrats or priests, but most were simply common criminals. The crowd had assumed the prisoners were all counterrevolutionaries. News of this event along with the massacre of the Swiss guards as well as the imprisonment of the royal family spread rapidly across Europe, rousing new hostility toward the revolutionary government.

The Paris Commune then compelled the Legislative Assembly to call for the election by universal male suffrage of still another new assembly to write a democratic constitution. That body, called the **Convention** after the American Constitutional Convention of 1787, met on September 21, 1792. The previous day, the French army filled with patriotic recruits willing to die for the revolution had halted the Prussian advance at the Battle of Valmy in eastern France. Victory on the battlefield had confirmed the victory of democratic forces at home. As its first act, the Convention declared France a republic—that is, a nation governed by an elected assembly without a monarch.

Goals of the *Sans-culottes* The second revolution had been the work of Jacobins more radical than the Girondists and of the people of Paris known as the ***sans-culottes***. The name of this group means "without breeches" and derived from the long trousers that, as working people, they wore instead of aristocratic knee breeches. The *sans-culottes* were shopkeepers, artisans, wage earners, and, in a few cases, factory workers. The persistent food shortages and the revolutionary inflation reflected in the ongoing fall of the value of the *assignats* had made their difficult lives even more burdensome. The politics of the Old Regime had ignored them, and the policies of the National Constituent Assembly had left them victims of unregulated economic liberty. The government, however, required their labor and their lives if the war was to succeed. From the summer of 1792 until the summer of 1794, their attitudes, desires, and ideals were the primary factors in the internal development of the revolution.

On January 21, 1793, the Convention executed Louis XVI by guillotine. 18th century CE. "Execution of Louis XVI." Aquatint. French. Musée de la Ville de Paris, Musée Carnavalet, Paris, France. Copyright Bridgeman-Giraudon/Art Resource, NY

The *sans-culottes* generally knew what they wanted. The Parisian tradespeople and artisans sought immediate relief from food shortages and rising prices through price controls. The economic hardship of their lives made them impatient to see their demands met. They believed all people have a right to subsistence, and they resented most forms of social inequality. This attitude made them intensely hostile to the aristocracy and the original leaders of the revolution of 1789 from the Third Estate, who, they believed, simply wanted to share political power, social prestige, and economic security with the aristocracy. The *sans-culottes'* hatred of inequality did not take them so far as to demand the abolition of property. Rather, they advocated a community of small property owners who would also participate in the political nation.

In politics they were antimonarchical, strongly republican, and suspicious even of representative government. They believed the people should make the decisions of government to an extent as great as possible. In Paris, where their influence was most important, the *sans-culottes* had gained their political experience in meetings of the Paris sections. The Paris Commune organized the previous summer was their chief political vehicle and crowd action their chief instrument of action.

The Policies of the Jacobins The goals of the *sans-culottes* were not wholly compatible with those of the Jacobins, republicans who sought representative government. Jacobin hatred of the aristocracy and hereditary privilege did not extend to a general suspicion of wealth. Basically, the Jacobins favored an unregulated economy. From the time of Louis XVI's flight to Varennes onward, however, the more extreme Jacobins began to cooperate with leaders of the Parisian *sans-culottes* and the Paris Commune to overthrow the monarchy. Once the Convention began to deliberate, these Jacobins, known as the *Mountain* because their seats were high up in the assembly hall, worked with the *sans-culottes* to carry the revolution forward and to win the war. This willingness to cooperate with the forces of the popular revolution separated the Mountain from the Girondists, who were also members of the Jacobin Club.

Execution of Louis XVI By the spring of 1793, several issues had brought the Mountain and its *sans-culottes* allies to dominate the Convention and the revolution. In December 1792, Louis XVI was put on trial as mere "Citizen Capet," the original medieval name of the royal family. The Girondists looked for a way to spare his life, but the Mountain defeated the effort. An overwhelming majority convicted Louis of conspiring against the liberty of the people and the security of the state. Condemned to death by a smaller majority, he was beheaded on January 21, 1793.

The next month, the Convention declared war on Great Britain and Holland, and a month later on Spain. Soon thereafter, the Prussians renewed their offensive and drove the French out of Belgium. To make matters worse, General Dumouriez (1739–1823), the Girondist victor of Valmy, deserted to the enemy. Finally, in March 1793, a royalist revolt led by aristocratic officers and priests erupted in the Vendée in western France and roused much popular support. Thus, the revolution found itself at war with most of Europe and much of the French nation. The Girondists had led the country into the war but had been unable either to win it or to suppress the enemies of the revolution at home. The Mountain stood ready to take up the task.

▼ Europe at War with the Revolution

Initially, the rest of Europe had been ambivalent toward the revolutionary events in France. Those people who favored political reform regarded the revolution as wisely and rationally reorganizing a corrupt and inefficient government. The major foreign governments thought that the revolution meant France would cease to be an important factor in European affairs for years.

Edmund Burke Attacks the Revolution

In 1790, however, the Irish-born writer and British statesman Edmund Burke (1729–1799) argued a different position in *Reflections on the Revolution in France.* Burke condemned the reconstruction of the French administration as the application of a blind rationalism that ignored the historical realities of political development and the concrete complexities of social relations. He also forecast further turmoil as people without political experience tried to govern France, predicted the possible deaths of Louis XVI and Marie Antoinette at the hands of the revolutionaries, and forecast that the revolution would end in military despotism. As the revolutionaries proceeded to attack the church, the monarchy, and finally the rest of Europe, Burke's ideas came to have many admirers.

Thomas Paine, the hero of the American Revolution, composed *The Rights of Man* (1791–1792) in direct response to Burke and in defense of the revolutionary principles. Paine declared, "From what we now see, nothing of reform on the political world ought to be held improbable. It is an age of revolutions, in which everything may be looked for."[5] Paine's volume sold more copies at the time in England, but Burke's exercised more influence in the long run and was immediately published widely on the continent where it became a handbook of European conservatives.

By the outbreak of the war with Austria in April 1792, the other European monarchies recognized, along with Burke, the danger of both the ideas and the aggression of revolutionary France. In response, one government after another turned to repressive domestic policies. (See "Burke Denounces the Extreme Measures of the French Revolution," page 550.)

Suppression of Reform in Britain

In Great Britain, William Pitt the Younger (1759–1806), the prime minister, who had unsuccessfully supported moderate reform of Parliament during the 1780s, turned against both reform and popular movements. The government suppressed the London Corresponding Society, founded in 1792 as a working-class reform group. In Birmingham, the government sponsored mob action to drive Joseph Priestley (1733–1804), a famous chemist and a radical political thinker, out of the country. In early 1793, Pitt secured parliamentary approval for acts suspending *habeas corpus* and making the writing of certain ideas treasonable. With less success, Pitt also attempted to curb freedom of the press. All political groups who dared oppose the government faced being associated with sedition.

The Second and Third Partitions of Poland, 1793, 1795

The final two partitions of Poland, already noted in Chapter 16, occurred as a direct result of fears by the eastern powers that the principles of the French Revolution were establishing themselves in Poland. After the first partition in 1772, Polish leaders had commenced reforms to provide for a stronger state. In 1791, a group of nobles known as the Polish Patriots actually issued a new constitution that substituted a hereditary for an elective monarchy, provided for real executive authority in the monarch and his council, established a new bicameral diet, and eliminated the *liberum veto.* The Polish government also adopted equality before the law and religious toleration. Frederick William II of Prussia (r. 1786–1797) promised to defend the new Polish constitutional order because he believed that a stronger Poland was in Prussia's interest against the growing Russian power. Catherine the Great of Russia also understood that a reformed Polish state would diminish Russian influence in Poland and eastern Europe.

In April 1792, conservative Polish nobles who opposed the reforms invited Russia to restore the old order. The Russian army quickly defeated the reformist Polish forces led by Tadeusz Kosciuszko (1746–1817), a veteran of the American Revolution. In response to the Russian invasion, Frederick William II moved his troops from the west where they were confronting the French revolutionary army to his eastern frontier with Poland. That transfer of Prussian troops proved crucial to the important later French victories in the autumn of 1792. However, rather than protecting Poland as he had promised, Frederick William reached an agreement with Catherine early in 1793 to carry out a second partition of Poland. The reformed constitution was abolished, and the new Polish government remained under the influence of Russia.

In the spring of 1794, Polish officers mutinied against efforts to unite their forces with the Russian army. Kosciuszko, who had been in France and Germany since his defeat in 1792, returned to Poland to lead these troops. Initially he was successful. As the rebellion expanded, the language and symbols of the French Revolution appeared in Polish cities. Before long, Prussia, Austria, and Russia sent troops into Poland. On November 4 in the single bloodiest day of combat in the decade, Russian troops killed well over 10,000 Poles outside Warsaw. Kosciuszko ended up in a Russian prison, and the next year the three eastern powers portioned what remained of Poland among them. Polish officers and troops who escaped Poland after the last partition later fought with the armies of the French Revolution and Napoleon against the forces of the partitioning powers.

▼ The Reign of Terror

War with Europe

The French invasion of the Austrian Netherlands (Belgium) and the revolutionary reorganization of that territory in 1792 roused the rest of Europe to active hostility. In November 1792, the Convention declared it would aid

[5]Thomas Paine, *Political Writings*, rev. student ed., Bruce Kuklick, ed. (Cambridge: Cambridge University Press, 1997), p. 153.

BURKE DENOUNCES THE EXTREME MEASURES OF THE FRENCH REVOLUTION

Edmund Burke was the most important foreign critic of the French Revolution. His first critique, Reflections on the Revolution in France, *appeared in 1790. In 1796, he composed* Letters on a Regicide Peace, *which opposed a proposed peace treaty between Great Britain and revolutionary France. In that work, he summarized what he regarded as the worst evils of the revolutionary government: the execution of the king, the confiscation of property of the church and nobles, and de-Christianization* *(see page 554).*

To which of the major events in the French Revolution does Burke refer? Why, by 1796, would Burke and others have emphasized the religious policies of the revolution? Did Burke exaggerate the evils of the revolution? Who was Burke trying to persuade?

A government of the nature of that set up at our very door has never been hitherto seen, or ever imagined in Europe. . . . France, since her revolution, is under the sway of a sect, whose leaders have deliberately, at one stroke, demolished the whole body of that jurisprudence which France had pretty nearly in common with other civilized countries. . . .

Its foundation is laid in regicide, in Jacobinism, and in atheism, and it has joined to those principles a body of systematic manners, which secures their operation. . . .

I call a commonwealth regicide, which lays it down as a fixed law of nature, and a fundamental right of man, that all government, not being a democracy, is an usurpation. That all kings, as such, are usurpers; and for being kings may and ought to be put to death, with their wives, families, and adherents. That commonwealth which acts uniformly upon those principles . . . —this I call regicide by establishment.

Jacobinism is the revolt of the enterprising talents of a country against its property. When private men form themselves into associations for the purpose of destroying the pre-existing laws and institutions of their country; when they secure to themselves an army, by dividing amongst the people of no property the estates of the ancient and lawful proprietors, when a state recognizes those acts; when it does not make confiscations for crimes, but makes crimes for confiscations; when it has its principal strength, and all its resources, in such a violation of property . . . —I call this Jacobinism by establishment.

I call it atheism by establishment, when any state, as such, shall not acknowledge the existence of God as a moral governor of the world; . . . —when it shall abolish the Christian religion by a regular decree;—when it shall persecute with a cold, unrelenting, steady cruelty, by every mode of confiscation, imprisonment, exile, and death, all its ministers;—when it shall generally shut up or pull down churches; when the few buildings which remain of this kind shall be opened only for the purpose of making a profane apotheosis of monsters, whose vices and crimes have no parallel amongst men . . . When, in the place of that religion of social benevolence, and of individual self-denial, in mockery of all religion, they institute impious, blasphemous, indecent theatric rites, in honour of their vitiated, perverted reason, and erect altars to the personification of their own corrupted and bloody republic; . . . when wearied out with incessant martyrdom, and the cries of a people hungering and thristing for religion, they permit it, only as a tolerated evil—I call this atheism by establishment.

When to these establishments of regicide, of Jacobinism, and of atheism, you add the correspondent system of manners, no doubt can be left on the mind of a thinking man concerning their determined hostility to the human race.

From *The Works of the Right Honourable Edmund Burke* (London: Henry G. Bohn, 1856), 5, pp. 206–208.

all peoples who wished to cast off aristocratic and monarchical oppression. The Convention had also proclaimed the Scheldt River in the Netherlands open to the commerce of all nations and thus had violated a treaty that Great Britain had made with Austria and Holland. The British were on the point of declaring war on France over this issue when the Convention issued its own declaration of hostilities against Britain in February 1793.

By April 1793, when the Jacobins began to direct the French government, the nation was at war with Austria, Prussia, Great Britain, Spain, Sardinia, and Holland. The governments of these nations, allied in what is known as the First Coalition, were attempting to protect their social structures, political systems, and economic interests against the aggression of the revolution.

This widening of the war in the winter and spring of 1792–1793 brought new, radical political actions within France as the revolutionary government mobilized itself and the nation for the conflict. Throughout France, there was the sense that a new kind of war had erupted. In this war the major issue was not protection of national borders as such, but rather the defense of the bold new republican political and social order that had emerged since 1789. The French people understood that the achievements of the revolution were in danger. To protect those achievements, the government took extraordinary actions that touched almost every aspect of national life. Thousands of people from all walks of life including peasants, nobles, clergy, business and professional people, one-time revolutionary leaders as well as the king and queen were arbitrarily arrested and, in many cases, executed. The immediate need to protect the revolution from enemies, real or imagined, from across the spectrum of French political and social life was considered more important than the security of property or even of life. These actions to protect the revolution and silence dissent came to be known as the **Reign of Terror**. (See "The Paris Jacobin Club Alerts the Nation to Internal Enemies of the Revolution," page 552.)

The Republic Defended

To mobilize for war, the revolutionary government organized a collective executive in the form of powerful committees. These, in turn, sought to organize all French national life on a wartime footing. The result was an immense military effort dedicated both to protecting and promoting revolutionary ideals.

The Committee of Public Safety In April 1793, the Convention established a Committee of General Security and a Committee of Public Safety to carry out the executive duties of the government. The latter committee eventually enjoyed almost dictatorial power. All of the revolutionary leaders who served on the Committee of Public Safety were convinced republicans who had long opposed the more vacillating policies of the Girondists. They saw their task as saving the revolution from mortal enemies at home and abroad. They enjoyed a working political relationship with the *sans-culottes* of Paris, but this was an alliance of expediency for the committee.

The *Levée en Masse* The major problem for the Convention was to wage the war and at the same time to secure domestic support for the war effort. In early June 1793, the Parisian *sans-culottes* invaded the Convention and successfully demanded the expulsion of the Girondist members. That action further radicalized the Convention and gave the Mountain complete control. On June 22, the Convention approved a fully democratic constitution but delayed its implementation until the conclusion of the war. In fact, it was never implemented. On August 23, Lazare Carnot (1753–1823), the member of the Committee of Public Safety in charge of the military, began a mobilization for victory by issuing a ***levée en masse***, a military requisition on the entire population, conscripting males into the army and directing economic production to military purposes. The Convention decreed:

> From this moment until that in which the enemy shall have been driven from the soil of the Republic, all Frenchmen are in permanent requisition for the service of the armies.
>
> The young men shall go to battle; the married men shall forge arms and transport provisions; the women shall make tents and clothing and shall serve in the hospitals; the children shall turn old linen into lint; the aged shall betake themselves to the public places in order to arouse the courage of the warriors and preach the hatred of kings and the unity of the Republic.[6]

Following the *levée en masse*, the Convention on September 29, 1793, established a ceiling on prices in accord with *sans-culotte* demands. During these same months, the armies of the revolution also successfully crushed many of the counterrevolutionary disturbances in the provinces. Never before had Europe seen a nation organized in this way, nor one defended by a citizen army, which, by late 1794, with over a million men, had become larger than any ever organized in European history.

Other events within France astounded Europeans even more. The Reign of Terror had begun. Those months of quasi-judicial executions and murders stretching from the autumn of 1793 to the midsummer of 1794 are probably the most famous or infamous period of the revolution. They can be understood only in the context of the war on one hand and the revolutionary expectations of the Convention and the *sans-culottes* on the other.

[6]Frank Maloy Anderson, ed. and trans., *The Constitutions and Other Select Documents Illustrative of the History of France, 1789–1907*, 2nd ed., rev. and enl. (Minneapolis, MN: H. W. Wilson, 1908), pp. 184–185.

THE PARIS JACOBIN CLUB ALERTS THE NATION TO INTERNAL ENEMIES OF THE REVOLUTION

By early 1793, the revolutionary groups in Paris stood sharply divided amongst themselves. The Girondists (also known as Brissotins), who had led the nation into war, faced military reversals. General Dumouriez, a former revolutionary commander, had changed sides and was leading an army against France. At this point, on April 5, the radical Jacobin Club of Paris sent a circular to its provincial clubs, painting a dire picture of the fate of the revolution. While Dumouriez was marching against Paris, they accused members of the government and its administrators of conspiring to betray the revolution. The circular suggested that some people were cooperating with England in the war against France. The Jacobins also portrayed as counterrevolutionaries all those political figures who had opposed the execution of Louis XVI. The Paris Jacobins then called on their allies in the provinces to defend the revolution and to take vengeance against its internal enemies. The distortion of the motives of political enemies, the appeal to a possible reversal of the revolution, and the accusations of internal conspiracy served to justify the demand for justice against enemies of the revolution. The accusations embodied in this circular and the fears it sought to arouse represented the kind of thinking that informed the suspension of legal rights and due process associated with the Reign of Terror.

How did the Jacobins use the war to call for actions against their own domestic political enemies? What real and imagined forces did they see threatening the revolution? How did this circular constitute a smear campaign by one group of revolutionaries against other groups? What actions did the Jacobins seek?

Friends, we are betrayed! To arms! To arms! The terrible hour is at hand when the defenders of the *Patrie* must vanquish or bury themselves under the bloody ruins of the Republic. Frenchmen, never was your liberty in such great peril! At last our enemies have put the finishing touch to their foul perfidy, and to complete it their accomplice Dumouriez is marching on Paris. . . .

But Brothers, not all your dangers are to be found there! . . . You must be convinvced of a grievous truth! Your greatest enemies are in your midst, they direct your operations. O Vengeance !!! . . .

Yes, brothers and friends, yes, it is in the Senate that parricidal hands tear at your vitals! Yes, the counterrevolution is in the Government . . ., in the National Conventional. It is there, at the center of your security and your hope, that criminal delegates hold the threads of the web that they have woven with the horde of despots who come to butcher us! . . . It is there that a sacrilegious cabal is directed by the English court . . . and others. . . .

Let us rise! Yes, let us rise! Let us arrest all the enemies of our revolution, and all suspected persons. Let us exterminate, without pity, all conspirators, unless we wish to be exterminated ourselves. . . .

Let the departments, the districts, the municipalities, and all the popular societies unite and concur in protesting to the Convention, by dispatching thereto a veritable rain of petitions manifesting the formal wish for the immediate recall of all unfaithful members who have betrayed their duty by not wishing the death of the tyrant, and, above all, against those who have led astray so many of their colleagues. Such delegates are traitors, royalists, or fatuous men. The Republic condemns the friends of kings! . . .

Let us all unite equally to demand that the thunder or indictments be loosed against generals who are traitors to the Republic, against prevaricating ministers, against postal administrators, and against all unfaithful agents of the government. Therein lies our most salutary means of defence; but let us repel the traitors and tyrants.

The center of their conspiracy is here: it is in Paris that our perfidious enemies wish to consummate their crime. Paris, the cradle, the bulwark of liberty, is, without doubt, the place where they have sworn to annihilate the holy cause of humanity under the corpses of patriots.

The "Republic of Virtue" and Robespierre's Justification of Terror

The presence of armies closing in on the nation made it easy to dispense with legal due process. The people who sat in the Convention and those sitting on the Committee of Public Safety, however, did not see their actions simply in terms of expediency made necessary by war. They also believed they had created something new in world history, a "republic of virtue." In this republic, civic virtue largely understood in terms of Rousseau's *Social Contract*, the sacrifice of one's self and one's interest for the good of the republic, would replace selfish aristocratic and monarchical corruption. The republic of virtue manifested itself in many ways: in the renaming of streets from the egalitarian vocabulary of the revolution; in republican dress copied from that of the *sans-culottes* or the Roman Republic; in the absence of powdered wigs; in the suppression of plays and other literature that were insufficiently republican; and in a general attack against crimes, such as prostitution, that were supposedly characteristic of aristocratic society. Yet the core value of the republic of virtue in line with Rousseau's thought was the upholding of the public over the private good or the championing of the general will over individual interests. It was in the name of the public good that the Committee of Public Safety carried out the policies of the terror.

The person who embodied this republic of virtue defended by terror was Maximilien de Robespierre (1758–1794), who, by late 1793, had emerged as the dominant figure on the Committee of Public Safety. This utterly selfless revolutionary figure has remained controversial from his day to the present. From the beginning of the revolution, he had favored a republic. The Jacobin Club provided his primary forum and base of power. A shrewd and sensitive politician, Robespierre had opposed the war in 1792 because he feared it might aid the monarchy. He depended largely on the support of the *sans-culottes* of Paris, but he continued to dress as he had before the revolution in powdered wig and knee breeches. For him, the republic of virtue meant wholehearted support of the republican government, the renunciation of selfish gains from political life, and the assault on foreign and domestic enemies of the revolution. Portraying revolutionary France as endangered on all sides, he told the Convention early in 1794,

> Without, all the tyrants encircle you; within, all the friends of tyranny conspire—they will conspire until crime has been robbed of hope. We must smother the internal and external enemies of the Republic or perish with them. Now, in this situation, the first maxim of your policy ought to be to lead the people by reason and the people's enemies by terror. If the mainspring of popular government in peacetime is virtue, amid revolution it is at the same time [both] virtue and *terror*: virtue, without which terror is fatal; terror, without which virtue is impotent. Terror is nothing but prompt, severe, inflexible justice; it is therefore an emanation of virtue. It is less a special principle than a consequence of the general principle of democracy applied to our country's most pressing needs.[7]

Maximilien Robespierre (1758–1794) emerged as the most powerful revolutionary figure in 1793 and 1794, dominating the Committee of Public Safety. He considered the Terror essential for the success of the revolution. Musée des Beaux-Arts, Lille. Bridgeman—Giraudon/Art Resource, NY

Robespierre and those who supported his policies were among the first of a succession of secular ideologues of the left and the right who, in the name of humanity, would bring so much suffering to Europe in the following two centuries. The policies associated with terror in the name of republican virtue included the exclusion of women from active political life, the de-Christianization of France, and the use of revolutionary tribunals to dispense justice to alleged enemies of the republic.

Repression of the Society of Revolutionary Republican Women

Revolutionary women established their own distinct institutions during these months. In May 1793, Pauline Léon and Claire Lacombe founded the Society of Revolutionary Republican Women. Its purpose was to fight the internal enemies of the revolution. Its members saw themselves as militant citizens. Initially, the Jacobin leaders welcomed the organization. Members of the society and other women filled the galleries of the

[7]Quoted in Richard T. Bienvenu, *The Ninth of Thermidor: The Fall of Robespierre* (New York: Oxford University Press, 1968), p. 38.

Convention to hear the debates and cheer their favorite speakers. The society became increasingly radical, however. Its members sought stricter controls on the price of food and other commodities, worked to ferret out food hoarders, and brawled with working market women whom they thought to be insufficiently revolutionary. The women of the society also demanded the right to wear the revolutionary *cockade* that male citizens usually wore in their hats. By October 1793, the Jacobins in the Convention had begun to fear the turmoil the society was causing and banned all women's clubs and societies. The debates over these decrees show that the Jacobins believed the society opposed many of their economic policies, but the deputies used Rousseau's language of separate spheres for men and women to justify their exclusion of women from active political life.

There were other examples of repression of women in 1793. Olympe de Gouges, author of the Declaration of the Rights of Woman, opposed the Terror and accused Jacobins of corruption. She was guillotined in November 1793. The same year, women were formally excluded from serving in the French army and from the galleries of the Convention. The exclusion of women from public political life was part of the establishment of the Jacobin republic of virtue, because in such a republic men would be active citizens in the military and political sphere and women would be active only in the domestic sphere.

De-Christianization

The most dramatic step taken by the republic of virtue, and one that illustrates its imposition of political values to justify the Terror, was the Convention's attempt to de-Christianize France. In November 1793, the Convention proclaimed a new calendar dating from the first day of the French Republic. There were twelve months of thirty days each, with names associated with the seasons and climate. Every tenth day, rather than every seventh, was a holiday. Many of the most important events of the next few years became known by their dates on the revolutionary calendar.[8] In November 1793, the Convention decreed the Cathedral of Notre Dame in Paris to be a "Temple of Reason."

The legislature then sent trusted members, known as deputies on mission, into the provinces to enforce de-Christianization by closing churches, persecuting clergy and believers (both Roman Catholic and Protestant), occasionally forcing priests to marry, and sometimes simply by killing priests and nuns. Churches were desecrated, torn down, or used as barns or warehouses. This radical religious policy attacking both clergy and religious property roused enormous popular opposition and alienated parts of the French provinces from the revolutionary government in Paris. Robespierre personally opposed de-Christianization because he was convinced it would prove a political blunder that would erode loyalty to the republic.

Revolutionary Tribunals

The Reign of Terror manifested itself in revolutionary tribunals that the Convention established during the summer of 1793. The mandate of these tribunals, the most prominent of which was in Paris, was to try the enemies of the republic, but the definition of who was an "enemy" shifted as the months passed. It included those who might aid other European powers, those who endangered republican virtue, and, finally, good republicans who opposed the policies of the dominant faction of the government. The Terror of the revolutionary tribunals systematized and channeled the popular resentment that had manifested itself in the September Massacres of 1792. Those whom the tribunal condemned in Paris were beheaded on the guillotine, a recently invented instrument of efficient and supposedly humane execution. (The drop of the blade

On the way to her execution in 1793, Marie Antoinette was sketched from life by Jacques-Louis David as she passed his window. Jacques Louis David (1748–1825), *Marie-Antoinette brought to the guillotine (after a drawing by David who witnessed the execution)*. Pen drawing. 1793. Bibliothèque Nationale, Paris, France. Bridgeman—Giraudon/Art Resource, NY

[8]From summer to spring, the months of the revolutionary calendar were Messidor, Thermidor, Fructidor, Vendémiaire, Brumaire, Frimaire, Nivose, Pluviose, Ventose, Germinal, Floreal, and Prairial.

of the guillotine was certain to sever the head of the condemned at once, whereas beheading by axe or sword could, and often did, require multiple blows and cause unnecessary pain.) Other modes of execution, such as mass shootings and drowning, were used in the provinces.

The first victims of the Terror were Marie Antoinette, other members of the royal family, and aristocrats, who were executed in October 1793. Girondist politicians who had been prominent in the Legislative Assembly followed them. These executions took place in the same weeks that the Convention had moved against the Society of Revolutionary Republican Women, whom it had also seen as endangering Jacobin control.

In early 1794, the Terror moved to the provinces, where the deputies on mission presided over the summary execution of thousands of people, most of whom were peasants, who had allegedly supported internal opposition to the revolution. One of the most infamous incidents occurred in Nantes on the west coast of France, where several hundred people, including many priests, were simply tied to rafts and drowned in the river Loire. The victims of the Terror were now coming from every social class, including the *sans-culottes.*

The End of the Terror

Revolutionaries Turn Against Themselves In Paris during the late winter of 1794, Robespierre began to orchestrate the Terror against republican political figures of the left and right. On March 24, he secured the execution of certain extreme *sans-culottes* leaders known as the *enragés.* They had wanted further measures to regulate prices, secure social equality, and press de-Christianization. Robespierre then turned against other republicans in the Convention. Most prominent among them was Jacques Danton (1759–1794), who had provided heroic national leadership in the dark days of September 1792 and who had later served briefly on the Committee of Public Safety before Robespierre joined the group. Danton and others were accused of being insufficiently militant on the war, profiting monetarily from the revolution, and rejecting the link between politics and moral virtue. Danton was executed in April 1794. Robespierre thus exterminated the leadership of both groups that might have threatened his position. Finally, on June 10, he secured passage of the Law of 22 Prairial, which permitted the revolutionary tribunal to convict suspects without hearing substantial evidence against them. The number of executions was growing steadily.

Fall of Robespierre In May 1794, at the height of his power, Robespierre, considering the worship of "Reason" too abstract for most citizens, replaced it with the "Cult of the Supreme Being." This deistic cult reflected Rousseau's vision of a civic religion that would induce morality among citizens. (See "The Convention Establishes the Worship of the Supreme Being," page 556.) Robespierre, however, did not long preside over his new religion.

On July 26, Robespierre made an ill-tempered speech in the Convention, declaring that other leaders of the government were conspiring against him and the revolution. Similar accusations against unnamed persons had preceded his earlier attacks. No member of the Convention could now feel safe. On July 27—the Ninth of Thermidor on the revolutionary calendar—members of the Convention, by prearrangement, shouted him down when he rose to make another speech. That night Robespierre was arrested, and the next day he and approximately 80 of his supporters were executed. The revolutionary *sans-culottes* of Paris did not try to save him because he had deprived them of their chief leaders. He had also recently supported a measure to cap workers' wages. Other Jacobins turned against him because, after Danton's death, they feared they would be his next victims. Robespierre had destroyed rivals for leadership without creating supporters for himself. He had also for months tried to persuade the Paris populace that the Convention itself was harboring enemies of the revolution. Assured by the Convention that Robespierre had sought dictatorial powers, Parisians saw him as one more of those internal enemies. Robespierre was the unwitting creator of his own destruction.

▾ The Thermidorian Reaction

The fall of Robespierre might simply have been one more shift in the turbulent politics of the revolution, but instead it proved to be a major turning point. The members of the Convention used the event to reassert their authority over the executive power of Committee of Public Safety. Within a short time, the Reign of Terror, which had claimed more than 25,000 victims, came to a close. It no longer seemed necessary since the war abroad was going well and the republican forces had crushed the provincial uprisings.

This tempering of the revolution, called the **Thermidorian Reaction**, because of its association with the events of 9 Thermidor, consisted of the destruction of the machinery of terror and the establishment of a new constitutional regime. It resulted from a widespread feeling that the revolution had become too radical. In particular, it displayed a weariness of the Terror and a fear that the *sans-culottes* had become too powerful. The influence of generally wealthy middle-class and professional people soon replaced that of the *sans-culottes.*

In the weeks and months after Robespierre's execution, the Convention allowed the Girondists who had been in prison or hiding to return to their seats.

THE CONVENTION ESTABLISHES THE WORSHIP OF THE SUPREME BEING

On May 7, 1794, the Convention passed an extraordinary piece of revolutionary legislation. It established the worship of the Supreme Being as a state cult. Although the law drew on the religious ideas of deism, the point of the legislation was to provide a religious basis for the new secular French state. Pay particular attention to Article 6, which outlines the political and civic values that the Cult of the Supreme Being was supposed to nurture.

How does this declaration reflect the ideas of the Enlightenment? Why has it been seen as establishing a civil religion? What personal and social values was this religion supposed to nurture? How might this declaration have led to Burke's criticism of the policies of the revolution?

1. The French people recognize the existence of the Supreme Being and the immortality of the soul.
2. They recognize that the worship worthy of the Supreme Being is the observance of the duties of man.
3. They place in the forefront of such duties detestation of bad faith and tyranny, punishment of tyrants and traiters, succoring of unfortunates, respect of weak persons, defence of the oppressed, doing to others all the good that one can, and being just towards everyone.
4. Festivals shall be instituted to remind man of the concept of the Divinity and of the dignity of his being.
5. They shall take their names from the glorious events of our Revolution, or from the virtues most dear and most useful to man, or from the greatest benefits of nature. . . .
6. On the days of *décade*, the name given to a particular day in each month of the revolutionary calendar, it shall celebrate the following festivals:

To the Supreme Being and to nature; to the human race; to the French people; to the benefactors of humanity; to the martyrs of liberty; to liberty and equality; to the Republic; to the liberty of the world; to the love of the *Patrie* [Fatherland]; to the hatred of tyrants and traitors; to truth; to justice; to modesty; to glory and immortality; to friendship; to frugality; to courage; to good faith; to heroism; to disinterestedness; to stoicism; to love; to conjugal love; to paternal love; to maternal tenderness; to filial piety; to infancy; to youth; to manhood; to old age; to misfortune; to agriculture; to industry; to our forefathers; to posterity; to happiness.

A general amnesty freed political prisoners. The Convention restructured the Committee of Public Safety and diminished its power while repealing the notorious Law of 22 Prairial. Some, though by no means all, of the people responsible for the Terror were removed from public life. The Paris Commune was outlawed, and its leaders and deputies on mission were executed. The Paris Jacobin Club was closed, and Jacobin clubs in the provinces were forbidden to correspond with each other.

The executions of former terrorists marked the beginning of "the white terror." Throughout the country, people who had been involved in the Reign of Terror were attacked and often murdered. Jacobins were executed with little more due process than they had extended to their victims a few months earlier. The Convention itself approved some of these trials. In other cases, gangs of youths who had aristocratic connections or who had avoided serving in the army roamed the streets, beating known Jacobins. In Lyons, Toulon, and Marseilles, these so-called "bands of Jesus" dragged suspected terrorists from prisons and murdered them much as alleged royalists had been murdered during the September Massacres of 1792.

The Festival of the Supreme Being, which took place in June 1794, inaugurated Robespierre's new civic religion. Its climax occurred when a statue of Atheism was burned and another statue of Wisdom rose from the ashes. Pierre-Antoine Demachy, *Festival of the Supreme Being at the Champ de Mars on June 8, 1794.* Musée de la Ville de Paris, Musée Carnavalet, Paris, France. Bridgeman—Giraudon/Art Resource, NY

The republic of virtue gave way, if not to one of vice, at least to one of frivolous pleasures. The dress of the *sans-culottes* and the Roman Republic disappeared among the middle class and the aristocracy. New plays appeared in the theaters, and prostitutes again roamed the streets of Paris. Families of victims of the Reign of Terror gave parties in which they appeared with shaved necks, like the victims of the guillotine, and with red ribbons tied about them. Although the Convention continued to favor the Cult of the Supreme Being, it allowed Catholic services to be held. Many refractory priests returned to the country. One of the unanticipated results of the Thermidorian Reaction was a genuine revival of Catholic worship.

The Thermidorian Reaction also saw the repeal of legislation that had been passed in 1792 making divorce more equitable for women. As the passage of that measure suggests, the reaction did not extend women's rights or improve their education. The Thermidorians and their successors had seen enough attempts at political and social change. They sought to return family life to its status before the outbreak of the revolution. Political authorities and the church were determined to reestablish separate spheres for men and women and to reinforce traditional gender roles. As a result, Frenchwomen may have had less freedom after 1795 than before 1789.

Establishment of the Directory

The Thermidorian Reaction led to still another new constitution. The democratic constitution of 1793, which had never gone into effect, was abandoned. In its place, the Convention issued the Constitution of the Year III, which reflected the Thermidorian determination to reject *both* constitutional monarchy and democracy. In recognition of the danger of a legislature with only one chamber and unlimited authority, this new document provided for a legislature of two houses. Members of the upper body, or Council of Elders, were to be men over forty years of age who were either husbands or widowers. The lower Council of Five Hundred was to consist of men of at least thirty who could be either married or single. The executive body was to be a five-person Directory whom the Elders would choose from a list the Council of Five Hundred submitted. Property qualifications limited the franchise, except for soldiers, who were permitted to vote whether they had property or not.

Historically, the term *Thermidor* has come to be associated with political reaction. That association requires considerable qualification. By 1795, the political structure and society of the Old Regime in France based on rank and birth had given way permanently to a political system based on civic equality and social status based on property ownership. People who had never been allowed direct, formal access to political power had, to different degrees, been granted it. Their entrance into political life had given rise to questions of property distribution and economic regulations that could not again be ignored. Representation was an established principle of politics. Henceforth, the question before France and eventually before all of Europe would be which new groups would be permitted representation. In the *levée en masse,* the French had demonstrated to Europe the power of the secular ideal of nationhood and of the willingness of citizen soldiers to embrace self-sacrifice.

The post-Thermidorian course of the French Revolution did not undo these stunning changes in the political and social contours of Europe. What triumphed in the Constitution of the Year III was the revolution of the holders of property. For this reason the French Revolution has often been considered a victory of the bourgeoisie, or middle class. The property that won the day, however, was not industrial wealth, but the wealth stemming from commerce, the professions, and land. The largest new propertied class to emerge from the revolutionary turmoil was the peasantry, who, as a result of the destruction of aristocratic privileges, now owned their own land. Unlike peasants liberated from traditional landholding in other parts of Europe during the next century, French peasants had to pay no monetary compensation either to their former landlords or to the state.

Removal of the *Sans-culottes* from Political Life

The most decisively reactionary element in the Thermidorian Reaction and the new constitution was the removal of the *sans-culottes* from political life. With the war effort succeeding, the Convention severed its ties with the *sans-culottes.* True to their belief in an unregulated economy, the Thermidorians repealed the ceiling on prices. As a result, the winter of 1794–1795 brought the worst food shortages of the period. There were many food riots, which the Convention suppressed to prove that the era of the *sans-culottes journées* had come to a close. Royalist agents, who aimed to restore the monarchy, tried to take advantage of their discontent. On October 5, 1795—13 Vendémiaire—the sections of Paris led by the royalists rose up against the Convention. The government turned the artillery against the royalist rebels. A general named Napoleon Bonaparte (1769–1821) commanded the cannon, and with a "whiff of grapeshot," he dispersed the crowd.

By the Treaties of Basel in March and June 1795, the Convention concluded peace with Prussia and Spain. The legislators, however, feared a resurgence of both radical democrats and royalists in the upcoming elections for the Council of Five Hundred. Consequently, the Convention ruled that at least two thirds of the new legislature must have served in the Convention itself, thus rejecting the decision the National Constituent Assembly had made in 1791 when it forbade its members to be elected to the new Legislative Assembly. The Two-Thirds Law, which sought to foster continuity but also clearly favored politicians already in office, quickly undermined public faith in the new constitutional order.

The Directory faced almost immediate social unrest. During the spring of 1796 in Paris, Gracchus Babeuf (1760–1797) led the Conspiracy of Equals. He and his followers called for more radical democracy and for more equality of property. They declared at one point, "The aim of the French Revolution is to destroy inequality and to re-establish the general welfare . . . . The Revolution is not complete, because the rich monopolize all the property and govern exclusively, while the poor toil like slaves, languish in misery, and count for nothing in the state."[9] In a sense, they were correct. The Directory intended to resist any further social changes in France that might endanger property or political stability. Babeuf was arrested, tried, and executed. This minor plot became famous decades later, when European socialists attempted to find their historical roots in the French Revolution.

The suppression of the *sans-culottes,* the narrow franchise of the constitution, the Two-Thirds Law, and the Catholic royalist revival presented the Directory with challenges that it was never able to overcome. Because France remained at war with Austria and Great Britain, it needed a broader-based active loyalty than it was able to command. Instead, the Directory came to depend on the power of the army to govern France. All soldiers could vote. Moreover, within the army that the revolution had created and sustained were ambitious officers who were eager for power. As will be seen in the next chapter, the instability of the Directory, the growing role of the army, and the ambitions of its leaders held profound consequences not only for France but for the entire Western world as well.

In Perspective

The French Revolution is the central political event of modern European history. It unleashed political and social forces that shaped Europe and much of the rest of the world for the next two centuries. The revolution began with a clash between the monarchy and the nobility.

[9]Quoted in John Hall Stewart, *A Documentary Survey of the French Revolution* (New York: Macmillan, 1966), pp. 656–657.

THE FRENCH REVOLUTION

1787	
February–May	Unsuccessful negotiations with the Assembly of Notables
1788	
August 8	Louis XVI summons the Estates General
December 27	Approval of doubling of the Third Estate membership
1789	
May 5	The Estates General opens at Versailles
June 17	The Third Estate declares itself the National Assembly
June 20	The National Assembly takes the Tennis Court Oath
July 14	Fall of the Bastille in the city of Paris
Late July	The Great Fear spreads in the countryside
August 4	The nobles surrender their feudal rights at a meeting of the National Constituent Assembly
August 27	Declaration of the Rights of Man and Citizen
October 5–6	Parisian women march to Versailles and force Louis XVI and his family to return to Paris
1790	
July 12	Civil Constitution of the Clergy adopted
July 14	A new political constitution is accepted by the king
1791	
June 14	Chapelier Law
June 20–24	Louis XIV and his family attempt to flee France and are stopped at Varennes
August 27	The Declaration of Pillnitz
October 1	The Legislative Assembly meets
1792	
April 20	France declares war on Austria
August 10	The Tuileries palace is stormed, and Louis XVI takes refuge with the Legislative Assembly
September 2–7	The September Massacres
September 20	France wins the Battle of Valmy
September 21	The Convention meets, and the monarchy is abolished
1793	
January 21	King Louis XVI is executed
February 1	France declares war on Great Britain
March	Counterrevolution breaks out in the Vendée
April	The Committee of Public Safety is formed
June 22	The Constitution of 1793 is adopted but not implemented
July	Robespierre enters the Committee of Public Safety
August 23	*Levée en masse* proclaimed
September 29	Maximum prices set on food and other commodities
October 16	Queen Marie Antoinette is executed
October 30	Women's societies and clubs banned
November 10	The Cult of Reason is proclaimed; the revolutionary calendar, beginning on September 22, 1792, is adopted
1794	
March 24	Execution of the leaders of the *sans-culottes* known as the *enragés*
April 6	Execution of Danton
May 7	Cult of the Supreme Being proclaimed
June 8	Robespierre leads the celebration of the Festival of the Supreme Being
June 10	The Law of 22 Prairial is adopted
July 27	The Ninth of Thermidor and the fall of Robespierre
July 28	Robespierre is executed
August 1	Repeal of the Law of 22 Prairial
August 10	Reorganization of the Revolutionary Tribunal
November 12	Closing of Jacobin Club in Paris
1795	
May 31	Abolition of Revolutionary Tribunal
August 22	The Constitution of the Year III establishes the Directory
September 23	Two-Thirds Law adopted
1796	
May 10	Babeuf's Conspiracy of Equals
1799	
November 9	Napoleon's (8 Brumaire) coup d'état overthrows the Directory

Once the Estates General gathered, however, the traditional boundaries of eighteenth-century political life could not contain the discontent. The Third Estate, in all of its diversity, demanded real influence in government. Initially, that meant the participation of middle-class members of the Estates General, but soon the people of Paris and the peasants made their own demands known. Thereafter, popular nationalism exerted itself on French political life and the destiny of Europe.

Revolutionary legislation and popular uprisings in Paris, the countryside, and other cities transformed the social as well as the political life of the nation. Nobles surrendered traditional social privileges. The church saw its property confiscated and its operations brought under state control. For a time, there was an attempt to de-Christianize France. Vast amounts of landed property changed hands, and France became a nation of peasant landowners. Urban workers lost the protection they had enjoyed under the guilds and became more subject to the forces of the marketplace.

Violence accompanied many of the revolutionary changes. Thousands died during the Reign of Terror. France also found itself at war with virtually the rest of Europe. Resentment, fear, and a new desire for stability eventually brought the Terror to an end. That desire for stability, combined with a determination to defeat the foreign enemies of the revolution and to carry it abroad, would, in turn, work to the advantage of the army. Eventually, Napoleon Bonaparte would claim leadership in the name of stability and national glory.

REVIEW QUESTIONS

1. Why has France been called a rich nation with an impoverished government? How did the financial weaknesses of the French monarchy lay the foundations of the revolution of 1789?
2. What were Louis XVI's most serious mistakes during the French Revolution? Had he been a more able ruler, could the French Revolution have been avoided or a constitutional monarchy have succeeded? Did the revolution ultimately have little to do with the competence of the monarch?
3. How was the Estates General transformed into the National Assembly? How does the Declaration of the Rights of Man and Citizen reflect the social and political values of the eighteenth-century Enlightenment? How were France and its government reorganized in the early years of the revolution? Why has the Civil Constitution of the Clergy been called the greatest blunder of the National Assembly?
4. Why were some political factions dissatisfied with the constitutional settlement of 1791? What was the revolution of 1792 and why did it occur? Who were the *sans-culottes*, and how did they become a factor in the politics of the period? How influential were they during the Terror in particular? Why did the *sans-culottes* and the Jacobins cooperate at first? Why did that cooperation end?
5. Why did France go to war with Austria in 1792? What were the benefits and drawbacks for France of fighting an external war in the midst of a domestic political revolution?
6. What were the causes of the Terror? How did the rest of Europe react to the French Revolution and the Terror? How did events in France influence the last two partitions of Poland?
7. A motto of the French Revolution was "equality, liberty, and fraternity." How did the revolution both support and violate this motto? Did French women benefit from the revolution? Did French peasants benefit from it?

SUGGESTED READINGS

D. Andress, *The Terror: The Merciless War for Freedom in Revolutionary France* (2006). The best recent survey of the reign of terror.

N. Aston, *Christianity and Revolutionary Europe c. 1750–1830* (2002). Continent-wide survey of the impact of revolution on religion.

T. C. Blanning, *The Revolutionary Wars, 1787–1802* (1996). Essential for understanding the role of the army and the revolution.

S. Desan, *The Family on Trial in Revolutionary France* (2004). An important analysis of how the revolution impacted French domestic life.

W. Doyle, *The Oxford History of the French Revolution* (2003). A broad, complex narrative with an excellent bibliography.

A. Forrest, *Revolutionary Paris, the Provinces and the French Revolution* (2004). A clear presentation of the tensions between the center of the revolution and the provinces.

C. Hayden and W. Doyle, eds., *Robespierre* (1999). Essays evaluating Robespierre's ideas, career, and reputation.

P. Higonnet, *Goodness beyond Virtue: Jacobins During the French Revolution* (1998). An outstanding work that clearly relates political values to political actions.

D. Jordon, *The King's Trial: Louis XVI vs. the French Revolution* (1979). A gripping account of the event.

E. Kennedy, *A Cultural History of the French Revolution* (1989). An important examination of the role of the arts, schools, clubs, and intellectual institutions.

S. E. Melzer and L. W. Rabine, eds., *Rebel Daughters: Women and the French Revolution* (1997). Essays exploring the role and image of women in the revolution.

S. Neely, *A Concise History of the French Revolution* (2008). The best of the numerous brief accounts.

C. C. O'Brien, *The Great Melody: A Thematic Biography of Edmund Burke* (1992). A deeply thoughtful biography.

R. R. Palmer, *The Age of Democratic Revolution: A Political History of Europe and America, 1760–1800*, 2 vols. (1959, 1964). Still an impressive survey of the political turmoil in the transatlantic world.

M. Price, *The Road from Versailles: Louis XVI, Marie Antoinette, and the Fall of the French Monarchy* (2004). A lively narrative that brings the personalities of the king and queen into focus.

R. Scurr, *Fatal Purity: Robespierre and the French Revolution* (2007). A compelling analysis of a personality long difficult to understand.

T. Tackett, *Becoming a Revolutionary: The Deputies of the French National Assembly and the Emergence of a Revolutionary Culture (1789–1790)* (1996). The best study of the early months of the revolution.

For additional learning resources related to this chapter, please go to www.myhistorylab.com

PEARSON myhistorylab

This portrait of Napoleon on his throne by Jean Ingres (1780–1867) shows him in the splendor of an imperial monarch who embodies the total power of the state. Jean Auguste Dominique Ingres (1780–1867), *Napoleon on His Imperial Throne*, 1806. Oil on canvas, 259 × 162 cm. Musée des Beaux-Arts, Rennes. Photograph © Erich Lessing/Art Resource, NY

19

The Age of Napoleon and the Triumph of Romanticism

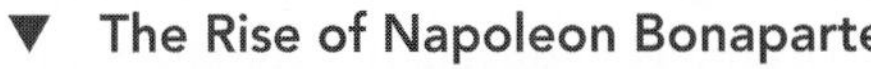

▼ **The Rise of Napoleon Bonaparte**
Early Military Victories • The Constitution of the Year VIII

▼ **The Consulate in France (1799–1804)**
Suppressing Foreign Enemies and Domestic Opposition • Concordat with the Roman Catholic Church • The Napoleonic Code • Establishing a Dynasty

▼ **Napoleon's Empire (1804–1814)**
Conquering an Empire • The Continental System

▼ **European Response to the Empire**
German Nationalism and Prussian Reform • The Wars of Liberation • The Invasion of Russia • European Coalition

▼ **The Congress of Vienna and the European Settlement**
Territorial Adjustments • The Hundred Days and the Quadruple Alliance

▼ **The Romantic Movement**

▼ **Romantic Questioning of the Supremacy of Reason**
Rousseau and Education • Kant and Reason

▼ **Romantic Literature**
The English Romantic Writers • The German Romantic Writers

▼ **Romantic Art**
The Cult of the Middle Ages and Neo-Gothicism • Nature and the Sublime

▼ **Religion in the Romantic Period**
Methodism • New Directions in Continental Religion

▼ **Romantic Views of Nationalism and History**
Herder and Culture • Hegel and History • Islam, the Middle East, and Romanticism

▼ **In Perspective**

KEY TOPICS

- **Napoleon's rise, his coronation as emperor, and his administrative reforms**
- **Napoleon's conquests, the creation of a French Empire, and Britain's enduring resistance**
- **The invasion of Russia and Napoleon's decline**
- **The reestablishment of a European order at the Congress of Vienna**
- **Romanticism and the reaction to the Enlightenment**
- **Islam and Romanticism**

BY THE LATE 1790s, the French people, especially property owners, who now included the peasants, longed for stability. The Directory was not providing it. Only the army was able to take charge of the nation as a symbol of both order and the popular values of the revolution. The most politically astute general was Napoleon Bonaparte, who had been a radical during the early revolution, a victorious commander in Italy, and a supporter of the repression of revolutionary disturbances after Thermidor.

Once in power, Napoleon consolidated many of the achievements of the revolution. He also repudiated much of it by establishing an empire. Thereafter, his ambitions drew France into wars of conquest and liberation across the Continent. For over a decade, Europe was at war, with only brief periods of armed truce. Through his conquests Napoleon spread many of the ideas and institutions of the revolution and overturned much of the old political and social order. He also provoked popular nationalism in opposition to French domination. This new force and the great alliances that opposed France eventually defeated Napoleon.

Throughout these Napoleonic years, new ideas and sensibilities, known by the term *Romanticism*, grew across Europe. Many of the ideas had originated in the eighteenth century, but they flourished in the turmoil of the French Revolution and the Napoleonic Wars. The revolution spurred the imagination of poets, painters, and philosophers. Some Romantic ideas, such as nationalism, supported the revolution; others, such as the emphasis on history and religion, opposed its values.

▾ The Rise of Napoleon Bonaparte

The chief threat to the Directory came from royalists, who hoped to restore the Bourbon monarchy by legal means. Many of the *émigrés* had returned to France. Their plans for a restoration drew support from devout Catholics and from those citizens disgusted by the excesses of the revolution. Monarchy promised stability. The spring elections of 1797 replaced most incumbents with constitutional monarchists and their sympathizers, thus giving them a majority in the national legislature.

To preserve the republic and prevent a peaceful restoration of the Bourbons, the antimonarchist Directory staged a *coup d'état* on 18 Fructidor (September 4, 1797). They put their own supporters into the legislative seats their opponents had won. They then imposed censorship and exiled some of their enemies. At the request of the Directors, Napoleon Bonaparte, the general in charge of the French invasion of Italy, had sent a subordinate to Paris to guarantee the success of the coup. In 1797, as in 1795, the army and Bonaparte had saved the day for the government installed in the wake of the Thermidorian Reaction.

Napoleon Bonaparte was born in 1769 to a poor family of lesser nobles at Ajaccio, on the Mediterranean island of Corsica. Because France had annexed Corsica in 1768, he went to French schools and, in 1785, obtained a commission as a French artillery officer. He favored the revolution and was a fiery Jacobin. In 1793, he played a leading role in recovering the port of Toulon from the British. As a reward for his service, he was appointed a brigadier general. During the Thermidorian Reaction, his defense of the new regime on 13 Vendémiaire won him a command in Italy.

Early Military Victories

By 1795, French arms and diplomacy had shattered the enemy coalition, but France's annexation of Belgium guaranteed continued fighting with Britain and Austria. The invasion of Italy aimed to deprive Austria of its rich northern Italian province of Lombardy. In a series of lightning victories, Bonaparte crushed the Austrian and Sardinian armies. On his own initiative, and against the wishes of the government in Paris, he concluded the Treaty of Campo Formio in October 1797. The treaty took Austria out of the war and crowned Napoleon's campaign with success. Before long, France dominated all of Italy and Switzerland.

In November 1797, the triumphant Bonaparte returned to Paris as a hero and to confront France's only remaining enemy, Britain. He judged it impossible to cross the Channel and invade England at that time. Instead, he chose to attack British interests through the eastern Mediterranean by capturing Egypt from the Ottoman Empire. By this strategy, he hoped to drive the British fleet from the Mediterranean, cut off British communications with India, damage British trade, and threaten the British Empire.

Napoleon easily overran Egypt, but the invasion was a failure. Admiral Horatio Nelson (1758–1805) destroyed the French fleet at Abukir on August 1, 1798. The French army was cut off from France. To make matters worse, the situation in Europe was deteriorating. The invasion of Egypt had alarmed Russia, which had its own ambitions in the Near East. The Russians, the Austrians, and the Ottomans joined Britain to form the Second Coalition against France. In 1799, the Russian and Austrian armies defeated the French in Italy and Switzerland and threatened to invade France.

Napoleon's venture into Egypt in 1798 and 1799 marked the first major Western European assault on the Ottoman Empire. It occurred less than a quarter century after Russia, under Catherine the Great, had taken control of the Crimea in the Treaty of Kuchuk-Kainardji. (See Chapter 17.) Significantly, British, not Ottoman forces, drove the French out of Egypt. As shall be seen in Chapter 22, after Napoleon's invasion, the Ottoman Empire realized that it had to reform itself if it was to resist other European encroachments.

The Constitution of the Year VIII

Economic troubles and the dangerous international situation eroded the Directory's fragile support. One of the Directors, the Abbé Siéyès (1748–1836), proposed a new constitution. The author of the pamphlet *What Is the Third Estate?* (1789) now wanted an executive body independent of the whims of electoral politics, a government based on the principle of "confidence from below, power from above." The change would require another *coup d'état* with military support. News of France's misfortunes had reached Napoleon in Egypt. Without orders and leaving his army behind, he returned to France in October 1799 to popular acclaim. Soon he joined Siéyès. On 19 Brumaire (November 10, 1799), his troops ensured the success of the coup.

Siéyès appears to have thought that Napoleon could be used and then dismissed, but he misjudged his man. The proposed constitution divided executive authority among three consuls. Bonaparte quickly pushed Siéyès aside, and in December 1799, he issued the Constitution of the Year VIII. Behind a screen of universal male suffrage that suggested democratic principles, a complicated system of checks and balances that appealed to republican theory, and a Council of State that evoked memories of Louis XIV, the new constitution established the rule of one man—the First Consul, Bonaparte. To find an appropriate historical analogy, we must go back to Caesar and Augustus in ancient Rome, and to the Greek tyrants of the sixth century B.C.E. The career of Bonaparte, however, pointed forward to the dictators of the twentieth century. He was the first modern political figure to use the rhetoric of revolution and nationalism, to back it with military force, and to combine these elements into a mighty weapon of imperial expansion in the service of his own power.

▼ The Consulate in France (1799–1804)

The **Consulate** in effect ended the revolution in France. The leading elements of the Third Estate—that is, officials, landowners, doctors, lawyers, and financiers—had achieved most of their goals by 1799. They had abolished hereditary privilege, and the careers thus opened to talent allowed them to achieve wealth, status, and security for their property. The peasants were also satisfied. They had gained the land they had always wanted and had destroyed oppressive feudal privileges. The newly established dominant classes had little or no desire to share their new privileges with the lower social orders. Bonaparte seemed just the person to give them security. When he submitted his constitution to the voters in a plebiscite, they overwhelmingly approved it.

Suppressing Foreign Enemies and Domestic Opposition

Throughout much of the 1790s, the pressures of warfare, particularly conscription, had accounted for much French internal instability. Bonaparte justified the public's confidence in himself by making peace with France's enemies. Russia had already left the Second Coalition. A campaign in Italy brought another victory over Austria at Marengo in 1800. The Treaty of Luneville early in 1801 took Austria out of the war. Britain was now alone and, in 1802, concluded the Treaty of Amiens, which brought peace to Europe.

Bonaparte also restored peace and order at home. He used generosity, flattery, and bribery to win over enemies. He issued a general amnesty and employed men from all political factions. He required only that they be loyal to him. Men who had been radicals during the Reign of Terror, or who had fled the Terror and favored constitutional monarchy, or who had been high officials under Louis XVI occupied some of the highest offices.

Bonaparte, however, ruthlessly suppressed opposition. He established a highly centralized administration in which prefects responsible to the government in Paris managed all departments. He employed secret police. He stamped out the royalist rebellion in the west and made the rule of Paris effective in Brittany and the Vendée for the first time in years.

Napoleon also used and invented opportunities to destroy his enemies. A plot on his life in 1804 provided an excuse to attack the Jacobins, though it was the work of the royalists. Also in 1804, he violated the sovereignty of the German state of Baden to seize and execute the Bourbon duke of Enghien (1772–1804). The duke was accused of participation in a royalist plot, though Bonaparte knew him to be innocent. The action was a flagrant violation of international law and of due process. Charles Maurice de Talleyrand-Périgord (1754–1838), Bonaparte's foreign minister, later termed the act "worse than a crime—a blunder" because it provoked foreign opposition. It was popular with the former Jacobins, however, for it seemed to preclude the possibility of a Bourbon restoration. The executioner of a Bourbon was not likely to restore the royal family. The execution also seems to have put an end to royalist plots.

Concordat with the Roman Catholic Church

No single set of revolutionary policies had aroused as much domestic opposition as those regarding the French Catholic Church; nor were there any other policies to which fierce supporters of the revolution seemed so attached. When the French armies had invaded Italy, they had driven Pope Pius VI (r. 1775–1799) from Rome, and he eventually died in exile in France. In 1801, to the shock and dismay of his anticlerical supporters, Napoleon concluded a concordat with Pope Pius VII (r. 1800–1823). The agreement was possible because Pius VII, before becoming pope, had written that Christianity was compatible with the ideals of equality and democracy. The concordat gave Napoleon what he most wanted. The agreement required both the refractory clergy and those who had accepted the revolution to resign. Their replacements received their spiritual investiture from the pope, but the state named the bishops and paid their salaries and the salary of one priest in each parish. In return, the church gave up its claims to its confiscated property.

The concordat declared, "Catholicism is the religion of the great majority of French citizens." This was merely a statement of fact and fell far short of what the pope had wanted: religious dominance for the Roman Catholic Church. The clergy had to swear an oath of loyalty to the state. The Organic Articles of 1802, which the government issued on its own authority without consulting the pope, established the supremacy of state over church. Similar laws were applied to the Protestant and Jewish communities, reducing still further the privileged position of the Catholic Church.

The Napoleonic Code

In 1802, a plebiscite ratified Napoleon as consul for life, and he soon produced another constitution that granted him what amounted to full power. He thereafter set about reforming and codifying French law. The result was the Civil Code of 1804, usually known as the Napoleonic Code.

The Napoleonic Code safeguarded all forms of property and tried to secure French society against internal challenges. All the privileges based on birth that the revolution had overthrown remained abolished.

The conservative attitudes toward labor and women that had emerged during the revolution also received full support. Workers' organizations remained forbidden, and workers had fewer rights than their employers. Fathers were granted extensive control over their children and husbands over their wives. However, primogeniture—the right of an eldest son to inherit most or all of his parents' property—remained abolished, and property was distributed among all children, males and females, but married women needed their husbands' consent to dispose of their own property. Divorce remained more difficult for women than for men. Before this code, French law had differed from region to region. That confused set of laws had given women opportunities to protect their interests. The universality of the Napoleonic Code ended that.

Establishing a Dynasty

In 1804, Bonaparte seized on a bomb attack on his life to make himself emperor. He argued that establishing a dynasty would make the new regime secure and make further attempts on his life useless. Another new constitution declared Napoleon Bonaparte Emperor of the French, instead of First Consul of the Republic. A plebiscite also overwhelmingly ratified this constitution.

To conclude the drama, Napoleon invited Pope Pius VII to Notre Dame to take part in the coronation. At the last minute, however, the pope agreed that Napoleon should crown himself. The emperor would not allow anyone to think his power and authority depended on the church. Henceforth, he was called Napoleon I.

▼ Napoleon's Empire (1804–1814)

Between his coronation as emperor and his final defeat at Waterloo (1815), Napoleon conquered most of Europe. France's victories changed the map of the Continent. The wars put an end to the Old Regime and its feudal trappings throughout Western Europe and forced the eastern European states to reorganize themselves to resist Napoleon's armies.

Everywhere, Napoleon's advance unleashed the powerful force of nationalism, discussed more fully in Chapter 20. His weapon was the militarily mobilized French nation, one of the achievements of the revolution. Napoleon could put 700,000 men under arms at one time, risk 100,000 troops in a single battle, endure heavy losses, and fight again. He could conscript citizen soldiers in unprecedented numbers, thanks to their loyalty to the nation and to him. No single enemy could match such resources. Even coalitions were unsuccessful, until Napoleon's mistakes led to his own defeat.

Conquering an Empire

The Peace of Amiens (1802) between France and Great Britain was merely a truce. Napoleon's unlimited ambitions shattered any hope that it might last. He sent an army to restore the rebellious colony of Haiti to French rule. This move aroused British fears that he was planning a new French empire in America, because Spain had restored Louisiana to France in 1801. More serious were his interventions in the Dutch Republic, Italy, and Switzerland and his reorganization of Germany. The Treaty of Campo Formio had required a redistribution of territories along the Rhine River, and the petty princes of the region engaged in a scramble to enlarge their holdings. Among the results were the reduction of Austrian influence and the emergence of fewer, but larger, German states in the West, all dependent on Napoleon.

British Naval Supremacy Alarmed by these developments, the British issued an ultimatum. When Napoleon ignored it, Britain declared war in May 1803. William Pitt the Younger returned to office as prime minister in 1804 and began to construct the Third Coalition. By August 1805, he had persuaded Russia

A Closer LOOK

THE CORONATION OF NAPOLEON

JACQUES-LOUIS DAVID recorded the elaborate coronation of Napoleon in a monumental painting that revealed the enormous political and religious tensions of that event, which involved the kind of ritual and ceremony associated with the monarchy of the ancient regime.

Napoleon's mother sits in a balcony-like setting and presides over her son's establishment of a new reigning dynasty in France and across Europe, through the placement of relatives on various thrones.

Napoleon is about to place a crown on the head of his wife Josephine whom he will later divorce because she and he were unable to conceive an heir for his new dynasty. He would then marry the daughter of the Habsburg emperor.

Jacques-Louis David (1748–1825), *Consecration of the Emperor Napoleon I and Coronation of Empress Josephine*, 1806–07. Louvre, Paris. Bridgeman—Giraudon/Art Resource, NY

To the right sits Pope Pius VII who observes the event but is not a real participant. Napoleon and the pope had signed a Concordat that restored much of the standing but by no means all of the prerevolutionary authority of the Roman Catholic Church in France. The pope understood that at that moment in France as well as throughout Europe his authority was largely subject to the wishes of the French emperor.

To examine this image in an interactive fashion, please go to www.myhistorylab.com

PEARSON myhistorylab

In this early-nineteenth-century cartoon, England, personified by a caricature of William Pitt, and France, personified by a caricature of Napoleon, are carving out their areas of interest around the globe. Bildarchiv Preussischer Kulturbesitz

and Austria to move once more against France. A great naval victory soon raised the fortunes of the allies. On October 21, 1805, the British admiral Lord Nelson destroyed the combined French and Spanish fleets at the Battle of Trafalgar off the Spanish coast. Nelson died in the battle, but the British lost no ships. Trafalgar ended all French hope of invading Britain and guaranteed British control of the seas for the rest of the war. (See "Encountering the Past: Sailors and Canned Food.")

Napoleonic Victories in Central Europe On land the story was different. Even before Trafalgar, Napoleon had marched to the Danube River to attack his continental enemies. In mid-October he forced an Austrian army to surrender at Ulm and occupied Vienna. On December 2, 1805, in perhaps his greatest victory, Napoleon defeated the combined Austrian and Russian forces at Austerlitz. The Treaty of Pressburg that followed won major concessions from Austria. The Austrians withdrew from Italy and left Napoleon in control of everything north of Rome. He was recognized as king of Italy.

Napoleon also made extensive political changes in Germany. In July 1806, he organized the Confederation of the Rhine, which included most of the western German princes. Their withdrawal from the Holy Roman Empire led Francis II to dissolve that ancient political body and henceforth to call himself Emperor Francis I of Austria.

Prussia, which had remained neutral up to this point, now foolishly went to war against France. Napoleon's forces quickly crushed the famous Prussian army at Jena and Auerstädt on October 14, 1806. Two weeks later, Napoleon was in Berlin. There, on November 21, he issued the Berlin Decrees, forbidding his allies from importing British goods. On June 13, 1807, Napoleon defeated the Russians at Friedland and occupied East Prussia. The French emperor was master of all Germany.

Treaty of Tilsit Unable to fight another battle and unwilling to retreat into Russia, Tsar Alexander I (r. 1801–1825) was ready to make peace. He and Napoleon met on a raft in the Niemen River while the two armies and the nervous king of Prussia watched from the bank. On July 7, 1807, they signed the Treaty of Tilsit, which confirmed France's gains. Prussia lost half its territory. Only the support of Alexander saved it from extinction. Prussia openly and Russia secretly became allies of Napoleon.

Napoleon organized conquered Europe much like the estate of a Corsican family. The great French Empire was ruled directly by the head of the clan, Napoleon. On its borders lay satellite states ruled by members of his family. His stepson ruled Italy for him, and three of his brothers and his brother-in-law were made kings of other conquered states. Napoleon denied a kingdom only to his brother Lucien, of whose wife he disapproved. The French emperor expected his relatives to take orders without question. When they failed to do so, he rebuked and even punished them. This establishment of the Napoleonic family as the collective sovereigns of Europe provoked political opposition that needed only encouragement and assistance to flare up into serious resistance.

The Continental System

After the Treaty of Tilsit, such assistance could come only from Britain, and Napoleon knew he must defeat the British before he could feel safe. Unable to compete with the British navy, he continued the economic warfare the Berlin Decrees had begun. He planned to cut off all British trade with the European continent and thus to cripple British commercial and financial power. He hoped to cause domestic unrest and drive Britain from the war. The Milan Decree of 1807 went further and attempted to stop neutral nations from trading with Britain. (See Map 19–1, page 568.)

Despite initial drops in exports and domestic unrest, the British economy survived. British control of the seas assured access to the growing markets of North and South America and of the eastern Mediterranean. At the same time, the Continental System badly hurt the European economies. Napoleon rejected advice to turn his empire into a free-trade area. Such a policy would have been both popular and helpful. Instead, his tariff policies favored France, increased the resentment of foreign merchants, and made them less willing to enforce the system and more ready to engage in smuggling. It was, in part, to prevent smuggling that Napoleon invaded Spain in 1808. The resulting peninsular campaign in Spain and Portugal helped bring on his ruin.

SAILORS AND CANNED FOOD

IN 1803, DURING the Napoleonic wars, the French navy undertook a secret experiment—provisioning a few of its naval vessels involved in long overseas voyages or blockades with food preserved by the then novel process of canning. The results were excellent: The crews thrived and the French government ordered more canned goods.

Until the discovery of canning, the chief methods for preserving food were drying, salting, pickling, smoking, fermenting, and condensing. Most of these techniques are still used, but they strongly alter the taste of food and destroy some of its nutritive value. Although vitamins were unknown in the eighteenth century, military authorities did know that something in fresh fruit and vegetables kept their men healthy. In the 1790s, the French government offered a reward to anyone who could invent a method of preserving food that would make it both nearer in taste and texture to fresh products and more nourishing for sailors and soldiers who often suffered from scurvy and malnutrition from their rations of dried bread and salted meat. The desired food would allow naval vessels to stay at sea longer without having to put into port for fresh food and armies to campaign without having to live off the land.

Nicholas Appert, a French chef, was determined to produce preserved food that would be both tasty and healthful. In 1795, he established what amounted to a small food preservation laboratory on the outskirts of Paris. He eventually discovered that if he filled glass jars with fresh vegetables, fruit, soups, or meat, added water or a sauce, sealed the jars with tight stoppers, and then cooked them in a hot water bath, the result was a tasty preserved food that lasted indefinitely as long as the jars remained sealed. Although Appert did not know it, one reason the food remained unspoiled was that his process killed any microbes in it.

Although many fine French foods are still canned in jars, the process quickly took a new turn in Great Britain where the navy as well as food producers were interested in it. Appert published a book on his method in 1810, and by 1813 an English company began canning in tins, which were less expensive and more durable than glass jars. Soon other canning companies appeared in Europe, including those that produced canned sardines. By mid-century, millions of people, particularly in Western Europe and North America, were eating canned food. By 1900, canned goods had become what they remain today—part of everyday life around the world. The basic process used in canning is still the one Appert devised in the 1790s.

Source: Sue Shephard, *Pickled, Potted, and Canned: How the Art and Science of Food Processing Changed the World* (New York: Simon & Schuster, 2000).

Nicholas Appert (1749–1841) invented canning as a way of preserving food nutritiously. Canned food could be transported over long distances without spoiling.
Private Collection/Bridgeman Art Library

What advantages did canning have over other methods of preserving food?

Why was the military interested in it?

How did canning become a part of everyday life?

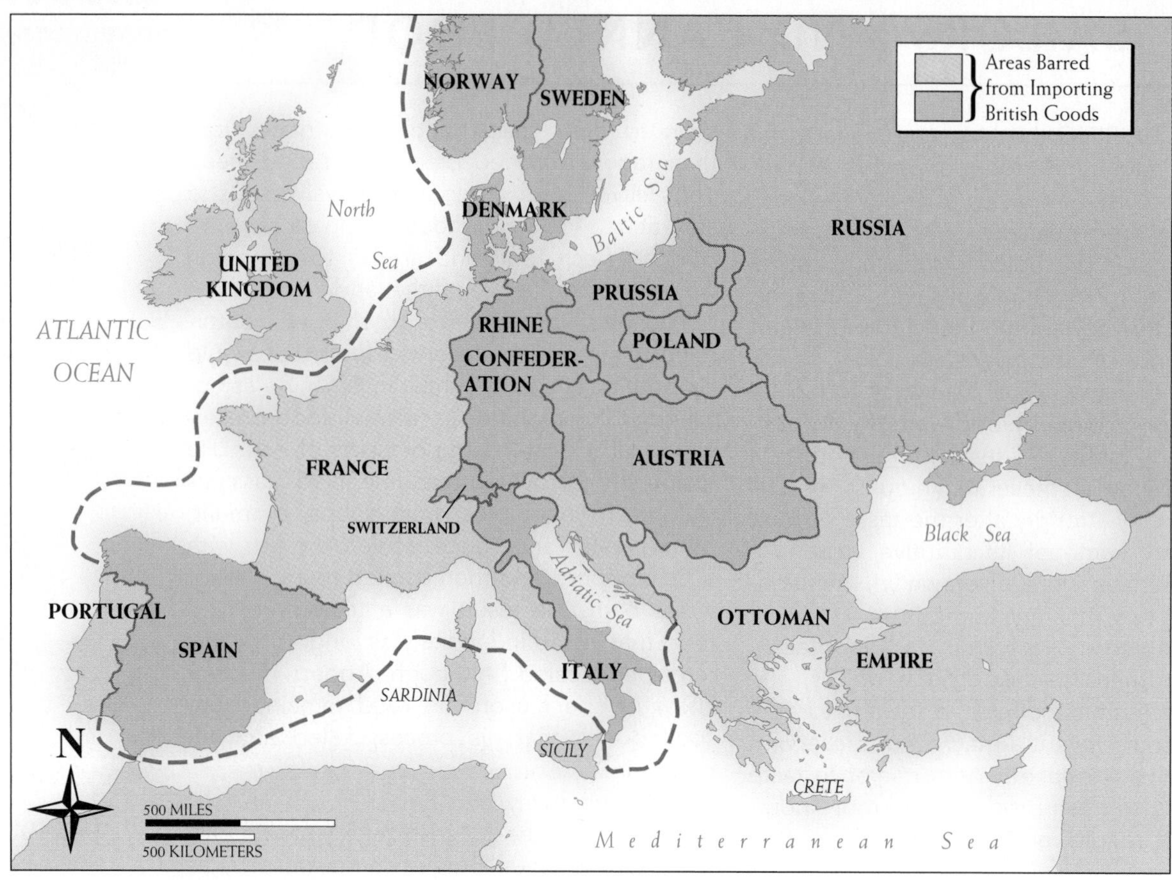

Map 19–1 **THE CONTINENTAL SYSTEM, 1806–1810** Napoleon hoped to cut off all British trade with the European continent and thereby drive the British from the war.

▼ European Response to the Empire

Wherever Napoleon ruled, he imposed the Napoleonic Code and abolished hereditary social distinctions. Feudal privileges disappeared, and the peasants were freed from serfdom and manorial dues. In the towns, the guilds and the local oligarchies that had been dominant for centuries were dissolved or deprived of their power. The established churches lost their traditional independence and were made subordinate to the state. Toleration replaced monopoly of religion by an established church. Despite these reforms, however, it was always clear that Napoleon's policies were intended first for his own glory and that of France. The Continental System demonstrated that Napoleon's rule was intended to enrich France, rather than Europe generally. Consequently, before long, the conquered states and peoples grew restive. (See "Napoleon Advises His Brother to Rule Constitutionally.")

German Nationalism and Prussian Reform

The German response to Napoleon's success was particularly interesting and important. There had never been a unified German state. The great German writers of the Enlightenment, such as Immanuel Kant and Gotthold Lessing, were neither deeply politically engaged nor nationalistic.

At the beginning of the nineteenth century, the Romantic Movement had begun to take hold. One of its basic features in Germany was the emergence of nationalism, which went through two distinct stages there. Initially, nationalistic writers emphasized the unique and admirable qualities of German culture, which, they argued, arose from the history of the German people. Such cultural nationalism prevailed until Napoleon's humiliation of Prussia at Jena in 1806.

At that point many German intellectuals began to urge resistance to Napoleon on the basis of German nationalism. The French conquest endangered the independence and achievements of all German-speaking people. Many nationalists also criticized the German

NAPOLEON ADVISES HIS BROTHER TO RULE CONSTITUTIONALLY

As Napoleon swept through Europe, he set his relatives on the thrones of various conquered kingdoms and then imposed written constitutions on them. In this letter of November 1807, Napoleon sent his brother Jerome (1784–1860) a constitution for the Kingdom of Westphalia in Germany. The letter shows how Napoleon spread the political ideas and institutions of the French Revolution across Europe. Napoleon ignored, however, the nationalistic resentment that French conquest aroused, even when that conquest brought more liberal political institutions. Such nationalism would contribute to his downfall.

What benefits does Napoleon believe his conquest and subsequent rule by his brother will bring to their new subjects? Why does he believe that these, rather than military victory, will achieve new loyalty? How does Napoleon suggest playing off the resentment of the upper classes to consolidate power? What is the relationship between having a written constitution such as Napoleon is sending his brother and the power of public opinion that he mentions toward the close of the letter?

I enclose the constitution for your Kingdom. You must faithfully observe it. I am concerned for the happiness of your subjects, not only as it affects your reputation, and my own, but also for its influence on the whole European situation.

Don't listen to those who say that your subjects are so accustomed to slavery that they will feel no gratitude for the benefits you give them. There is more intelligence in the Kingdom of Westphalia than they would have you believe; and your throne will never be firmly established except upon the trust and affection of the common people. What German opinion impatiently demands is that men of no rank, but of marked ability, shall have an equal claim upon your favour and your employment, and that every trace of serfdom, or of a feudal hierarchy between the sovereign and the lowest class of his subjects shall be done away with. The benefits of the Code Napoleon, public trial, and the introduction of juries, will be the leading features of your Government. And to tell you the truth, I count more upon their effects, for the extension and consolidation of your rule, than upon the most resounding victories. I want your subjects to enjoy a degree of liberty, equality, and prosperity hitherto unknown to the German people. . . . Such a method of government will be a stronger barrier between you and Prussia than the Elbe, the fortresses, and the protection of France. What people will want to return under the arbitrary Prussian rule, once it has tasted the benefits of a wise and liberal administration? In Germany, as in France, Italy, and Spain, people long for equality and liberalism. I have been managing the affairs of Europe long enough now to know that the burden of the privileged classes was resented everywhere. Rule constitutionally. Even if reason, and the enlightenment of the age, were not sufficient cause, it would be good policy for one in your position; and you will find that the backing of public opinion gives you a great natural advantage over the absolute kings who are your neighbors.

From J. M. Thompson, ed., *Napoleon's Letters* (London: Dent, 1954), pp. 190–191, as quoted in Maurice Hutt, ed., *Napoleon* (Englewood Cliffs, NJ: Prentice Hall, 1972), p. 34.

princes, who ruled selfishly and inefficiently and who seemed ever ready to lick Napoleon's boots. Only a people united through its language and culture could resist the French onslaught. No less important in forging a German national sentiment was the example of France itself, which had attained greatness by enlisting the active support of the entire people in the patriotic cause. Henceforth, many Germans sought to solve their internal political problems by attempting to establish a unified German state, reformed to harness the energies of the entire people.

After Tilsit, only Prussia could arouse such patriotic feelings. Elsewhere German rulers were either under Napoleon's thumb or collaborating with him. Defeated, humiliated, and diminished, Prussia continued to resist, however feebly. To Prussia fled German nationalists from other states, calling for reforms and unification that King Frederick William III (r. 1797–1840) and the Junker nobility in fact feared and hated. Reforms came about despite such opposition because the defeat at Jena had shown that the Prussian state had to change to survive.

The Prussian administrative and social reforms were the work of Baron vom Stein (1757–1831) and Prince von Hardenberg (1750–1822). Neither of these reformers intended to reduce the autocratic power of the Prussian monarch or to end the dominance of the Junkers, who formed the bulwark of the state and of the officer corps. Rather, they wanted to fight French power with their own version of the French weapons. As Hardenberg declared,

> Our objective, our guiding principle, must be a revolution in the better sense, a revolution leading directly to the great goal, the elevation of humanity through the wisdom of those in authority . . . Democratic rules of conduct in a monarchical administration, such is the formula . . . which will conform most comfortably with the spirit of the age.[1]

Although the reforms came from the top, they wrought important changes in Prussian society.

Stein's reforms broke the Junker monopoly of landholding. Serfdom was abolished. However, unlike in the western German states where all remnants of serfdom simply disappeared, in Prussia the Junkers ensured that vestiges of the system survived. Former Prussian serfs were free to leave the land if they chose, but those who stayed had to continue to perform manorial labor. They could obtain the ownership of the land they worked only if they forfeited a third of it to the lord. The result was that Junker holdings grew larger. Some peasants went to the cities to find work, others became agricultural laborers, and some did actually become small freeholding farmers. In Prussia and elsewhere, serfdom had ended, but the rise in the numbers of landless laborers created new social problems.

Military reforms sought to increase the supply of soldiers and to improve their quality. Jena had shown that an army of free patriots commanded by officers chosen on merit rather than by birth could defeat an army of serfs and mercenaries commanded by incompetent nobles. To remedy the situation, the Prussian reformers abolished inhumane military punishments, sought to inspire patriotic feelings in the soldiers, opened the officer corps to commoners, gave promotions on the basis of merit, and organized war colleges that developed new theories of strategy and tactics.

These reforms soon enabled Prussia to regain its former power. Because Napoleon strictly limited the size of its army to 42,000 men, however, Prussia could not introduce universal conscription until it broke with Napoleon in 1813. Before that date, the Prussians evaded the limit by training one group each year, putting them into the reserves, and then training a new group the same size. Prussia could thus boast an army of 270,000 by 1814.

The Wars of Liberation

Spain In Spain more than elsewhere in Europe, national resistance to France had deep social roots. Spain had achieved political unity as early as the sixteenth century. The Spanish peasants were devoted to the ruling dynasty and especially to the Roman Catholic Church. France and Spain had been allies since 1796. In 1807, however, a French army came into the Iberian Peninsula to force Portugal to abandon its traditional alliance with Britain. The army stayed in Spain to protect lines of supply and communication. Napoleon used a revolt that broke out in Madrid in 1808 as a pretext to depose the Spanish Bourbons and to place his brother Joseph (1768–1844) on the Spanish throne. Attacks on the privileges of the church increased public outrage. Many members of the upper classes were prepared to collaborate with Napoleon, but the peasants, urged on by the lower clergy and the monks, rebelled.

In Spain, Napoleon faced a new kind of warfare. Guerrilla bands cut lines of communication, killed stragglers, destroyed isolated units, and then disappeared into the mountains. The British landed an army under Sir Arthur Wellesley (1769–1852), later the duke of Wellington, to support the Spanish insurgents. Thus began the long peninsular campaign that would drain French strength from elsewhere in Europe and hasten Napoleon's eventual defeat. (See "Compare & Connect: The Experience of War in the Napoleonic Age," pages 572–573.)

Austria The French troubles in Spain encouraged the Austrians to renew the war in 1809. Since their defeat at Austerlitz, they had sought a war of revenge. The Austrians counted on Napoleon's distraction in Spain, French war weariness, and aid from other German princes. Napoleon was fully in command in France, however, and the German princes did not move. The French army marched swiftly into Austria and won the Battle of Wagram. The resulting Peace of Schönbrunn deprived Austria of much territory and 3.5 million subjects.

[1]Quoted in Geoffrey Brunn, *Europe and the French Imperium* (New York: Harper & Row, 1938), p. 174.

Another spoil of victory was the Austrian archduchess Marie Louise (1791–1847), daughter of Emperor Francis I. Napoleon's wife, Josephine de Beauharnais (1763–1814), was forty-six and had borne him no children. His dynastic ambitions, as well as the desire for a royal marriage, led him to divorce Josephine and marry the eighteen-year-old Marie Louise. Napoleon had also considered marrying the sister of Tsar Alexander, but had received a polite rebuff.

The Invasion of Russia

The failure of Napoleon's marriage negotiations with Russia emphasized the shakiness of the Franco-Russian alliance concluded at Tilsit. Russian nobles disliked the alliance because of the liberal politics of France and because the Continental System prohibited timber sales to Britain. Only French aid in gaining Constantinople could justify the alliance in their eyes, but Napoleon gave them no help against the Ottoman Empire. The organization of the Polish Duchy of Warsaw as a Napoleonic satellite on the Russian doorstep and its enlargement with Austrian territory in 1809 after the Battle of Wagram angered Alexander. Napoleon's annexation of Holland in violation of the Treaty of Tilsit, his recognition of the French marshal Bernadotte (1763–1844) as the future King Charles XIV of Sweden, and his marriage to Marie Louise further disturbed the tsar. At the end of 1810, Russia withdrew from the Continental System and began to prepare for war. (See Map 19–2.)

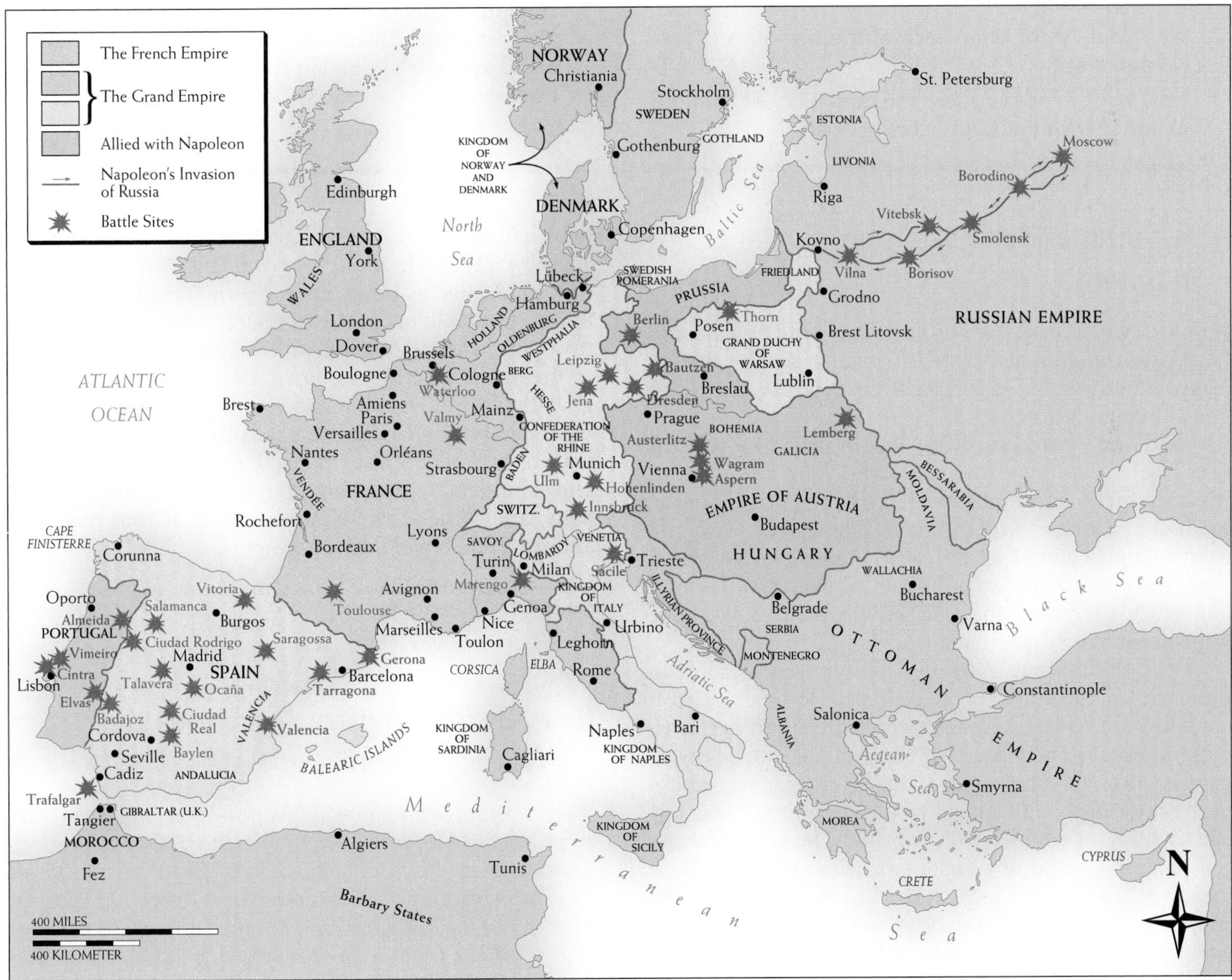

Map 19–2 **NAPOLEONIC EUROPE IN LATE 1812** By mid-1812 the areas shown in peach were incorporated into France, and most of the rest of Europe was directly controlled by or allied with Napoleon. But Russia had withdrawn from the failing Continental System, and the decline of Napoleon was about to begin.

COMPARE AND CONNECT The Experience of War in the Napoleonic Age

THE NAPOLEONIC WARS spread violence across Europe. Different participants, writers, and artists portrayed the experience of war differently. William Napier reported his own heroism in a quite matter-of-fact manner. The German poet and historian Ernest Moritz Arndt recalled moments of intense nationalistic patriotism. The Spanish painter Goya portrayed a moment of enormous brutality suffered by the Spanish at the hands of French troops.

QUESTIONS

1. **What were Napier's expectations of his men? Of his officers? Of himself?**
2. **Why does Arndt claim each of these various groups wanted war?**
3. **How does Arndt suggest the possibility of a united nation that did not yet actually exist?**
4. **How does Goya portray Spaniards as victims of harsh, unmerciful military violence?**
5. **How do Napier's memoir, Arndt's call to arms, and Goya's painting illustrate different points of view and ways of interpreting the violence of modern warfare?**

I. A Commander Recalls an Incident in Spain

William Napier, a British officer during the Napoleonic Wars and later a distinguished leader in the British army, describes his experiences in a battle that took place in Spain during 1811.

I arrived [with two companies] just in time to save Captain Dobbs, 52nd, and two men who were cut off from their regiment. The French were gathering fast about us, we could scarcely retreat, and Dobbs agreed with me that boldness would be our best chance; so we called upon the men to follow, and, jumping over a wall which had given us cover, charged the enemy with a shout which sent the nearest back. . . .

Only the two men of the 52nd followed us, and we four arrived unsupported at a second wall, close to a considerable body of French, who rallied and began to close upon us. Their fire was very violent, but the wall gave cover. I was, however, stung by the backwardness of my men, and told Dobbs I would save him or lose my life by bringing up the two companies; he entreated me not, saying I could not make two paces from the wall and live. Yet I did go back to the first wall, escaped the fire, and, reproaching the men gave them the word again, and returned to Dobbs, who was now upon the point of being taken; but again I returned alone! The soldiers had indeed crossed the wall in their front, but kept edging away to the right to avoid the heavy fire. Being now maddened by this second failure, I made another attempt, but I had not made ten paces when a shot struck my spine, and the enemy very ungenerously continued to fire at me when I was down. I escaped death by dragging myself by my hands—for my lower extremities were paralyzed—towards a small heap of stones which was in the midst of the field, and thus covering my head and shoulders. . . . However, Captain Lloyd and my company, and some of the 52nd, came up at that moment, and the French were driven away.

Source: Quoted in H. A. Bruce, *Life of Sir William Napier* (London: John Murray, 1864), 1, pp. 55–57.

II. A German Writer Describes the War of Liberation

The German resistance to Napoleon as his army retreated from Moscow in 1813 was the first time in modern German history that people from virtually all German-speaking lands cooperated together. Ernest Moritz Arndt (1769–1860) described the excitement of that moment in a passage frequently reprinted in German history textbooks for more than a century.

Fired with enthusiasm, the people rose, "with God for King and Fatherland." Among the Prussians there was only one voice, one feeling, one anger and one love, to save the Fatherland and to free Germany. . . . War, war, sounded the cry from the Carpathians to the Baltic, from the Niemen to the Elbe. War! cried the nobleman and landed proprietor who had become impoverished. War! that peasant who was driving his last horse to death. . . . War! the citizen who was growing exhausted from quartering soldiers and paying taxes. War! the widow who was sending her only son to the front. War! the young girl who, with tears of pride and pain, was leaving her betrothed. . . . Even young women, under all sorts of disguises, rushed to arms; all wanted to drill, arm themselves and fight and die for the Fatherland. . . .

The most beautiful thing about all this holy zeal and happy confusion was . . . that the one great feeling for the Fatherland, its freedom and honor, swallowed all other feelings, caused all other considerations and relationships to be forgotten.

Source: Louis L., Snyder, trans., *Documents of German History*. Copyright © 1958 by Rutgers, the State University. Reprinted by permission of Rutgers University Press.

III. Francisco Goya, *The Third of May, 1808* (painted 1814–1815)

Napoleon had begun to send troops into Spain in 1807 after the king of Spain had agreed to aid France against Portugal, which was assisting Britain. By early 1808 Spain had essentially become an occupied nation. On May 2, riots took place in Madrid between French troops, many of whom were Islamic soldiers whom Napoleon had recruited in Egypt, and Spanish civilians. In response to that resistance the French general Murat ordered the execution of numerous citizens of Madrid, which occurred the night of May 2 and 3. The events of these two days marked the opening of the Spanish effort to rid their peninsula of French rule.

After the restoration of the Spanish monarchy, Francisco Goya (1745–1828) depicted the savagery of those executions in the most memorable war painting of the Napoleonic era, The Third of May, 1808. *There is one group of humble Spaniards who have already been shot, another in the process of execution, and a third group, some of whom are hiding their eyes, who will be the next victims.*

The painting illustrates two forces of Napoleonic warfare confronting each other: the professional solider and the guerilla (a term coined during the Spanish resistance of this era). The guerilla must fight with what few resources he finds at his command and with few advanced weapons. By contrast, in this painting the well-disciplined soldiers, equipped with modern rifles, carry out the execution by the light of large technologically advanced lanterns fueled by either gas or oil with which Napoleon equipped his troops. Goya succeeds in making ordinary people and very poor clergy not only the victims, but also symbolic heroes of the national war of liberation.

Goya y Lucientes, Francisco de Goya, recorded Napoleon's troops executing Spanish guerilla fighters who had rebelled against the French occupation in *The Third of May, 1808.* Francisco de Goya, *Los fusilamientos del 3 de Mayo, 1808*. 1814. Oil on canvas, 8'60" × 11'40". © Museo Nacional del Prado, Madrid

Napoleon was determined to end the Russian military threat. He amassed an army of more than 600,000 men, including a core of Frenchmen and more than 400,000 other soldiers drawn from the rest of his empire. He intended the usual short campaign crowned by a decisive battle, but the Russians retreated before his advance. His vast superiority in numbers—the Russians had only about 160,000 troops—made it foolish for them to risk a battle. Instead they followed a "scorched-earth" policy, destroying all food and supplies as they retreated. The so-called Grand Army of Napoleon could not live off the country, and the expanse of Russia made supply lines too long to maintain. Terrible rains, fierce heat, shortages of food and water, and the courage of the Russian rear guard eroded the morale of Napoleon's army. Napoleon's advisers urged him to abandon the venture, but he feared an unsuccessful campaign would undermine his position in the empire and in France. He pinned his faith on the Russians' unwillingness to abandon Moscow without a fight.

In September 1812, Russian public opinion forced the army to give Napoleon the battle he wanted despite the canny Russian general Mikhail Kutuzov's (1745–1813) wish to let the Russian winter defeat the invader. At Borodino, not far west of Moscow, the bloodiest battle of the Napoleonic era cost the French 30,000 casualties and the Russians almost twice as many. Yet the Russian army was not destroyed. Napoleon won nothing substantial, and the battle was regarded as a defeat for him.

Fires set by the Russians soon engulfed Moscow and left Napoleon far from home with a badly diminished army lacking adequate supplies as winter came to a vast and unfriendly country. After capturing the burned city, Napoleon addressed several peace offers to Alexander, but the tsar ignored them. By October, what was left of the Grand Army was forced to retreat. By December, Napoleon realized the Russian fiasco would encourage plots against him at home. He returned to Paris, leaving the remnants of his army to struggle westward. Perhaps only 100,000 of the original 600,000 survived their ordeal.

European Coalition

Even as the news of the disaster reached the West, the final defeat of Napoleon was far from certain. He was able to put down his opponents in Paris and raise another 350,000 men. Neither the Prussians nor the Austrians were eager to risk another contest with Napoleon, and even the Russians hesitated. The Austrian foreign minister, Prince Klemens von Metternich (1773–1859), would have been glad to make a negotiated peace that would leave Napoleon on the throne of a shrunken and chastened France rather than see Russia dominate Europe. Napoleon might have negotiated a reasonable settlement had he been willing to make concessions that would have split his jealous opponents. He would not consider that solution, however. As he explained to Metternich,

> Your sovereigns born on the throne can let themselves be beaten twenty times and return to their capitals. I cannot do this because I am an upstart soldier. My domination will not survive the day when I cease to be strong, and therefore feared.[2]

In 1813, patriotic pressure and national ambition brought together the last and most powerful coalition against Napoleon. The Russians drove westward, and Prussia and then Austria joined them. Vast amounts of British money assisted them. From Spain, Wellington marched his army into France. Napoleon's new army was inexperienced and poorly equipped. His generals had lost confidence in him and were tired. The emperor himself was worn out and sick. Still, he waged a skillful campaign in central Europe and defeated the allies at Dresden. In October, however, the combined armies of the enemy decisively defeated him at Leipzig in what the Germans called the Battle of the Nations. In March 1814, the allied armies marched into Paris. A few days later, Napoleon abdicated and went into exile on the island of Elba, off the coast of central Italy. (See "The Experience of War in the Napoleonic Age," pages 572–573.)

▼ The Congress of Vienna and the European Settlement

Fear of Napoleon and hostility to his ambitions had held the victorious coalition together. As soon as he was removed, the allies pursued their separate ambitions. The key person in achieving eventual agreement among them was Robert Stewart, Viscount Castlereagh (1769–1822), the British foreign secretary. Even before the victorious armies had entered Paris, he brought about the signing of the Treaty of Chaumont on March 9, 1814. It provided for the restoration of the Bourbons to the French throne and the contraction of France to its frontiers of 1792. Even more importantly, Britain, Austria, Russia, and Prussia agreed to form a Quadruple Alliance for twenty years to preserve whatever settlement they agreed on. Remaining problems—and there were many—and final details were left for a conference to be held at Vienna.

[2]Quoted in Felix Markham, *Napoleon and the Awakening of Europe* (New York: Macmillan, 1965), pp. 115–116.

In this political cartoon of the Congress of Vienna, Tallyrand simply watches which way the wind is blowing, Castlereagh hesitates, while the monarchs of Russia, Prussia, and Austria form the dance of the Holy Alliance. The king of Saxony holds on to his crown and the republic of Geneva pays homage to the kingdom of Sardinia. Bildarchiv Preussischer Kulturbesitz

Territorial Adjustments

The Congress of Vienna assembled in September 1814, but did not conclude its work until November 1815. Although a glittering array of heads of state attended the gathering, the four great powers conducted the important work of the conference. The only full session of the congress met to ratify the arrangements the big four made. The easiest problem the great powers faced was France. All the victors agreed that no single state should be allowed to dominate Europe, and all were determined to prevent France from doing so again. The restoration of the French Bourbon monarchy, which was temporarily popular, and a nonvindictive boundary settlement were designed to keep France calm and satisfied.

The powers also strengthened the states around France's borders to serve as barriers to renewed French expansion. They established the kingdom of the Netherlands, which included Belgium and Luxembourg, in the north and added the important port of Genoa to strengthen Piedmont in the south. Prussia was given important new territories along the Rhine River to deter French aggression in the West. Austria gained full control of northern Italy to prevent a repetition of Napoleon's conquests there. As for the rest of Germany, most of Napoleon's territorial arrangements were left untouched. The venerable Holy Roman Empire, which had been dissolved in 1806, was not revived. (See Map 19–3.) In all these areas, the

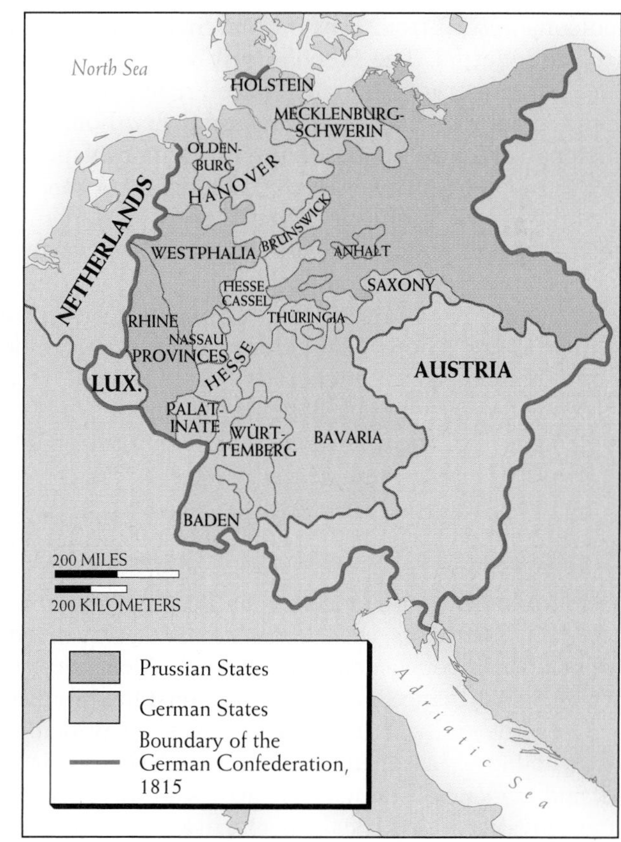

Map 19–3 **THE GERMAN STATES AFTER 1815** As noted, the German states were also recognized.

congress established the rule of legitimate monarchs and rejected any hint of the republican and democratic policies that had flowed from the French Revolution.

On these matters agreement was not difficult, but the settlement of eastern Europe sharply divided the victors. Alexander I of Russia wanted all of Poland under his rule. Prussia was willing to give it to him in return for all of Saxony, which had been allied with Napoleon. Austria, however, was unwilling to surrender its share of Poland or to see Prussian power grow or Russia penetrate deeper into central Europe. The Polish-Saxon question almost caused a new war among the victors, but defeated France provided a way out. The wily Talleyrand, now representing France at Vienna, suggested the weight of France added to that of Britain and Austria might bring Alexander to his senses. When news of a secret treaty among the three leaked out, the tsar agreed to become ruler of a smaller Poland, and Prussia settled for only part of Saxony. Thereafter, France was included as a fifth great power in all deliberations.

The Hundred Days and the Quadruple Alliance

Napoleon's return from Elba on March 1, 1815, further united the victors. The French army was still loyal to the former emperor, and many of the French people preferred his rule to that of the restored Bourbons. The coalition seemed to be dissolving in Vienna. Napoleon seized the opportunity, escaped to France, and soon regained power. He promised a liberal constitution and a peaceful foreign policy. The allies were not convinced. They declared Napoleon an outlaw (a new device under international law) and sent their armies to crush him. Wellington, with the crucial help of the Prussians under Field Marshal von Blücher (1742–1819), defeated Napoleon at Waterloo in Belgium on June 18, 1815. Napoleon again abdicated and was exiled on Saint Helena, a tiny Atlantic island off the coast of Africa, where he died in 1821.

The Hundred Days, as the period of Napoleon's return is called, frightened the great powers and made the peace settlement harsher for France. In addition to some minor territorial adjustments, the victors imposed a war indemnity and an army of occupation on France. Alexander proposed a Holy Alliance, whereby the monarchs promised to act together in accordance with Christian principles. Austria and Prussia signed, but Castlereagh thought it absurd, and England abstained. The tsar, who was then embracing mysticism, believed his proposal a valuable tool for international relations. The Holy Alliance soon became a symbol of extreme political reaction.

England, Austria, Prussia, and Russia renewed the Quadruple Alliance on November 20, 1815. Henceforth, it was as much a coalition for maintaining peace as for pursuing victory over France. A coalition for such a purpose had never existed in European diplomacy before. It represented an important new departure in European affairs. Unlike eighteenth-century diplomacy, certain powers were determined to prevent war. The statesmen at Vienna had seen the armies of the French Revolution and Napoleon overturning the political and social order of much of the Continent. Their nations had experienced unprecedented destruction and had had to raise enormous military forces. They knew war affected not just professional armies and navies, but entire civilian populations as well. They were determined to prevent any more such upheaval and destruction.

Consequently, the chief aims of the Congress of Vienna were to prevent a recurrence of the Napoleonic nightmare and to arrange a lasting peace. The leaders of Europe had learned that a treaty should secure not victory, but peace. The diplomats aimed to establish a framework for stability, rather than to punish France. The great powers sought to ensure that each of them would respect the Vienna settlement and not use force to change it.

The Congress of Vienna achieved its goals. France accepted the new situation without undue resentment, in part because the new international order recognized it as a great power. The victorious powers settled difficult problems reasonably. They established a new legal framework whereby treaties were made between states rather than between monarchs. The treaties remained in place when a monarch died. Furthermore, during the quarter century of warfare, European leaders had come to calculate the nature of political and economic power in new ways that went beyond the simple vision of gaining a favorable balance of trade that had caused so many eighteenth-century wars. They took into account their natural resources and economies, their systems of education, and the possibility that general growth in agriculture, commerce, and industry would benefit all states and not one at the expense of others.

The congress has been criticized for failing to recognize and provide for the great forces that would stir the nineteenth century—nationalism and democracy. Such criticism is inappropriate. At the time nationalist pressures were relatively rare; the general desire was for peace. The settlement, like all such agreements, aimed to solve past ills, and in that it succeeded. The statesmen at Vienna would have had to have a super-human ability to have anticipated future problems or to have yielded to forces of which they disapproved and that they believed threatened international peace and stability. The measure of the suc-

Map 19–4 **EUROPE 1815, AFTER THE CONGRESS OF VIENNA** The Congress of Vienna achieved the post-Napoleonic territorial adjustments shown on the map. The most notable arrangements dealt with areas along France's borders (the Netherlands, Prussia, Switzerland, and Piedmont) and in Poland and northern Italy.

cess of the Vienna settlement is that it remained essentially intact for almost half a century and prevented general war for a hundred years. (See Map 19–4.)

▾ The Romantic Movement

The years of the French Revolution and the conquests of Napoleon saw the emergence of a new and important intellectual movement throughout Europe. **Romanticism**, in its various manifestations, was a reaction against much of the thought of the Enlightenment. Romantic writers and artists saw the imagination or some such intuitive intellectual faculty supplementing reason as a means to perceive and understand the world. Many of them urged a revival of Christianity, so that it would once again permeate Europe as it had during the Middle Ages. Unlike the philosophes, the Romantics liked the art, literature, and architecture of medieval times. They were also deeply interested in folklore, folk songs, and fairy tales. Dreams,

NAPOLEONIC EUROPE

1797	Napoleon concludes the Treaty of Campo Formio
1798	Nelson defeats the French navy in the harbor of Abukir in Egypt
1799	Consulate established in France
1801	Concordat between France and the papacy
1802	Treaty of Amiens
1803	War renewed between France and Britain
1804	Execution of Duke d'Enghien
1804	Napoleonic Civil Code issued
1804	Napoleon crowned as emperor
1805 (October 21)	Nelson defeats French and Spanish fleet at Trafalgar
1805 (December 2)	Austerlitz
1806	Jena
1806	Continental System established by Berlin Decrees
1807	Friedland
1807	Treaty of Tilsit; Russia becomes an ally of Napoleon
1808	Beginning of Spanish resistance to Napoleonic domination
1809	Wagram
1809	Napoleon marries Archduchess Marie Louise of Austria
1812	Invasion of Russia and French defeat at Borodino
1813	Leipzig (Battle of the Nations)
1814 (March)	Treaty of Chaumont establishes Quadruple Alliance
1814 (September)	Congress of Vienna convenes
1815 (March 1)	Napoleon returns from Elba
1815 (June 18)	Waterloo
1815 (September 26)	Holy Alliance formed at Congress of Vienna
1815 (November 20)	Quadruple Alliance renewed at Congress of Vienna
1821	Napoleon dies on Saint Helena

hallucinations, sleepwalking, and other phenomena that suggested the existence of a world beyond that of empirical observation, sensory data, and discursive reasoning fascinated the Romantics.

▼ Romantic Questioning of the Supremacy of Reason

The Romantic Movement had roots in the individualism of the Renaissance, Protestant devotion and personal piety, sentimental novels of the eighteenth century, and dramatic German poetry of the **Sturm und Drang** (literally, "storm and stress") movement, which rejected the influence of French rationalism on German literature. However, two writers who were also closely related to the Enlightenment provided the immediate intellectual foundations for Romanticism: Jean-Jacques Rousseau and Immanuel Kant raised questions about whether the rationalism so dear to the philosophes was sufficient to explain human nature and be the bedrock principle for organizing human society.

Rousseau and Education

We already pointed out in Chapter 17 that Jean-Jacques Rousseau, though sharing in the reformist spirit of the Enlightenment, opposed many of its other facets. Rousseau's conviction that society and material prosperity had corrupted human nature profoundly influenced Romantic writers.

Rousseau set forth his view on how the individual could develop to lead a good and happy life uncorrupted by society in his novel *Émile* (1762), a work that was for a long time far more influential than *The Social Contract.* (See Chapter 17.) In *Émile*, Rousseau stressed the difference between children and adults. He distinguished the stages of human maturation and urged that children be raised with maximum individual freedom. Each child should be allowed to grow freely, like a plant, and to learn by trial and error what reality is and how best to deal with it. The parent or teacher would help most by providing the basic necessities of life and warding off what was manifestly harmful. Beyond that, the adult should stay completely out of the way, like a gardener who waters and weeds a garden but otherwise lets nature take its course. As noted in Chapter 17, Rousseau thought that, because of their physical differences, men and women would naturally grow into social roles with different spheres of activity.

Rousseau also thought that adults should allow the child's sentiments, as well as its reason, to flourish. To Romantic writers, this concept of human development vindicated the rights of nature over those of artificial society. They thought such a form of open education would eventually lead to a natural society. In its fully developed form, this view of life led the Romantics to value the uniqueness of each individual and to explore childhood in great detail. Like Rousseau, the Romantics saw humankind, nature, and society as organically interrelated.

Kant and Reason

Immanuel Kant (1724–1804) wrote the two greatest philosophical works of the late eighteenth century: *The Critique of Pure Reason* (1781) and *The Critique of Practical Reason* (1788). He sought to accept the rationalism of the Enlightenment and to still preserve a belief in human freedom, immortality, and the existence of God. Against Locke and other philosophers who saw knowledge rooted in sensory experience alone, Kant argued for the subjective character of human knowledge. For Kant, the human mind does not simply reflect the world around it like a passive mirror; rather, the mind actively imposes on the world of sensory experience "forms of sensibility" and "categories of understanding." The mind itself generates these categories. In other words, the human mind perceives the world as it does because of its own internal mental categories. This meant that human perceptions are as much the product of the mind's own activity as of sensory experience.

Kant found the sphere of reality that was accessible to pure reason to be limited. He believed, however, that beyond the phenomenal world of sensory experience, over which "pure reason" was master, there existed what he called the "noumenal" world. This world is a sphere of moral and aesthetic reality known by "practical reason" and conscience. Kant thought all human beings possess an innate sense of moral duty or an awareness of what he called a **categorical imperative**. This term refers to an inner command to act in every situation as one would have all other people always act in the same situation. Kant regarded the existence of this imperative of conscience as incontrovertible proof of humankind's natural freedom. On the basis of humankind's moral sense, Kant postulated the existence of God, eternal life, and future rewards and punishments. He believed that reason alone could not prove these transcendental truths. Still, he was convinced they were realities to which every reasonable person could attest.

To many Romantic writers, Kantian philosophy refuted the narrow rationality of the Enlightenment. Whether they called it "practical reason," "fancy," "imagination," "intuition," or simply "feeling," the Romantics believed that the human mind had the power to penetrate beyond the limits of largely passive human understanding as set forth by Hobbes, Locke, and Hume. Most Romantics also believed poets and artists possess these powers in abundance. Other Romantic writers appealed to the limits of human reason to set forth new religious ideas or political thought that were often at odds with Enlightenment writers.

▼ Romantic Literature

The term *Romantic* appeared in English and French literature as early as the seventeenth century. Neoclassical writers then used the word to describe literature they considered unreal, sentimental, or excessively fanciful. In the eighteenth century, the English writer Thomas Warton (1728–1790) associated Romantic literature with medieval romances. In Germany, a major center of the Romantic literary movement, Johann Gottfried Herder (1744–1803) used the terms *Romantic* and *Gothic* interchangeably. In both England and Germany, the term came to be applied to all literature that did not observe classical forms and rules and gave free play to the imagination.

As an alternative to such dependence on the classical forms, August Wilhelm von Schlegel (1767–1845) praised the "Romantic" literature of Dante, Petrarch, Boccaccio, Shakespeare, the Arthurian legends, Cervantes, and Calderón. According to Schlegel, Romantic literature was to classical literature what the organic and living were to the merely mechanical. He set forth his views in *Lectures on Dramatic Art and Literature* (1809–1811).

The Romantic Movement had peaked in Germany and England before it became a major force in France under the leadership of Madame de Staël (1766–1817) and Victor Hugo (1802–1885). (See "Madame de Staël Describes the New Romantic Literature of Germany," page 580.) So influential was the classical tradition in France that not until 1816 did a French writer openly declare himself a Romantic. That was Henri Beyle (1783–1842), who wrote under the pseudonym Stendhal. He praised Shakespeare and criticized his own countryman, the seventeenth-century classical dramatist Jean Racine (1639–1699).

The English Romantic Writers

The English Romantics believed poetry was enhanced by freely following the creative impulses of the mind. In this belief, they directly opposed Lockean psychology, which regarded the mind as a passive receptor and poetry as a mechanical exercise of "wit" following prescribed rules. For Samuel Taylor Coleridge (1772–1834), the artist's imagination was God at work in the mind. As Coleridge expressed his views, the imagination was "a repetition in the finite mind of the eternal act of creation in the infinite I AM." Poetry

MADAME DE STAËL DESCRIBES THE NEW ROMANTIC LITERATURE OF GERMANY

Anne-Louise-Germaine de Staël, known generally as Madame de Staël, was the daughter of Jacques Necker, the finance minister of Louis XVI. She was also the friend of major French political liberals and a critic of Napoleonic absolutism. More importantly for European literary life, Madame de Staël visited Germany, read the emerging German Romantic literature, and introduced it to both French- and English-speaking Europe in her book Concerning Germany *(1813). In the passage that follows, she endorses the new literature then emerging in Germany. She points to the novelty of this Romantic poetry and then relates it to a new appreciation of Christianity and the Middle Ages. The Christian features she associates with the poetry represent one strain among many of the religious revival that followed the de-Christianizing religious policies of the French Revolution.*

How does de Staël characterize the new Romantic school of poetry? Why does she contrast it with the literature that had its roots in ancient Greece and Rome? Why does she believe the new literature will continue to grow? What is the relationship of the Middle Ages to the new poetry and other examples of the fine arts touched by Romantic sensibilities?

The word *romantic* has been lately introduced in Germany, to designate that kind of poetry which is derived from the songs of the Troubadours; that which owes its birth to the union of chivalry and Christianity. If we do not admit that the empire of literature has been divided between paganism and Christianity, the north and the south, antiquity and the middle ages, chivalry and the institutions of Greece and Rome, we shall never succeed in forming a philosophical judgment of ancient and of modern taste.

Some French critics have asserted that German literature is still in its infancy; this opinion is entirely false: men who are best skilled in the knowledge of languages, and the works of the ancients, are certainly not ignorant of the defects and advantages attached to the species of literature which they either adopt or reject; but their character, their habits, and their modes of reasoning, have led them to prefer that which is founded on the recollection of chivalry, on the wonders of the middle ages, to that which has for its basis the mythology of the Greeks. The literature of romance is alone capable of further improvement, because, being rooted in our own soil, that alone can continue to grow and acquire fresh life: it expresses our religion; it recalls our history; its origin is ancient, although not of classical antiquity. Classic poetry, before it comes home to us, must pass through our recollections of paganism; that of the Germans is the Christian era of the fine arts; it employs our personal impressions to excite strong and vivid emotions; the genius by which it is inspired addresses itself immediately to our hearts; of all phantoms at once the most powerful and the most terrible. . . .

The new school maintains the same system in the fine arts as in literature, and affirms that Christianity is the source of all modern genius; the writers of this school also characterize, in a new manner, all that in Gothic architecture agrees with the religious sentiments of Christians. It does not follow however from this, that the moderns can and ought to construct Gothic churches; . . . it is only of consequence to us, in the present silence of genius, to lay aside the contempt which has been thrown on all the conceptions of the middle ages.

From Madame De Staël, *Concerning Germany* (London, John Murray, 1814) as quoted in Howard E. Hugo, ed., *The Romantic Reader* (Viking, 1957), pp. 64–66.

thus could not be considered idle play. Rather, it was the highest of human acts, humankind's self-fulfillment in a transcendental world.

Coleridge was the master of Gothic poems of the supernatural, such as "The Rime of the Ancient Mariner," which relates the story of a sailor cursed for killing an albatross. The poem treats the subject as a crime against nature and God and raises the issues of guilt, punishment, and the redemptive possibilities of humility and penance. At the end of the poem, the mariner discovers the unity and beauty of all things. Having repented, he is delivered from his awful curse, which has been symbolized by the dead albatross hung around his neck:

O happy living things! no tongue
Their beauty might declare:
A spring of love gushed from my heart,
And I blessed them unaware . . .
The self-same moment I could pray;
And from my neck so free
The Albatross fell off, and sank
Like lead into the sea.

Wordsworth William Wordsworth (1770–1850) was Coleridge's closest friend. Together they published *Lyrical Ballads* in 1798 as a manifesto of a new poetry that rejected the rules of eighteenth-century criticism. Among Wordsworth's most important later poems is his "Ode on Intimations of Immortality" (1803), written in part to console Coleridge, who was suffering a deep personal crisis. Its subject is the loss of poetic vision, something Wordsworth also felt then in himself. Nature, which he had worshipped, no longer spoke freely to him, and he feared it might never speak to him again:

There was a time when meadow, grove, and stream,
The earth, and every common sight,
To me did seem
Appareled in celestial light,
The glory and the freshness of a dream.
It is not now as it hath been of yore—
Turn whereso'er I may,
By night or day,
The things which I have seen I now can
see no more.

He had lost what he believed all human beings lose in the necessary process of maturation: their childlike vision and closeness to spiritual reality. For both Wordsworth and Coleridge, childhood was the bright period of creative imagination. Wordsworth held a theory of the soul's preexistence in a celestial state before its creation. The child, being closer in time to its eternal origin and undistracted by worldly experience, recollects the supernatural world much more easily. Aging and urban living corrupt and deaden the imagination, making one's inner feelings and the beauty of nature less important. In his book-length poem *The Prelude* (1850), Wordsworth presented a long autobiographical account of the growth of the poet's mind.

Lord Byron A true rebel among the Romantic poets was Lord Byron (1788–1824). In Britain, even most of the other Romantic writers distrusted and disliked him. He had little sympathy for their views of the imagination. Outside England, however, Byron was regarded as the embodiment of the new person the French Revolution had created. He rejected the old traditions (he was divorced and famous for his many love affairs) and championed the cause of personal liberty. Byron was outrageously skeptical and mocking, even of his own beliefs. In *Childe Harold's Pilgrimage* (1812), he created a brooding, melancholy Romantic hero. In *Don Juan* (1819), he wrote with ribald humor, acknowledged nature's cruelty as well as its beauty, and even expressed admiration for urban life.

The German Romantic Writers

Much Romantic poetry was also written on the Continent, but almost all major German Romantics wrote at least one novel. Romantic novels often were highly sentimental and borrowed material from medieval romances. The characters of Romantic novels were treated as symbols of the larger truth of life. Purely realistic description was avoided. The first German Romantic novel was Ludwig Tieck's (1773–1853) *William Lovell* (1793–1795). It contrasts the young Lovell, whose life is built on love and imagination, with those who live by cold reason alone and who thus become easy prey to unbelief, misanthropy, and egoism. As the novel rambles to its conclusion, a mixture of philosophy, materialism, and skepticism, administered to him by two women he naively loves, destroys Lovell.

Schlegel Friedrich Schlegel (1767–1845) wrote the progressive early Romantic novel *Lucinde* (1799) that attacked prejudices against women as capable of being little more than lovers and domestics. Schlegel's novel reveals the ability of the Romantics to become involved in the social issues of their day. He depicted Lucinde as the perfect friend and companion, as well as the unsurpassed lover, of the hero. Like other early Romantic novels, the work shocked contemporary morals by frankly discussing sexual activity and by describing Lucinde as equal to the male hero.

PUBLICATION DATES OF MAJOR ROMANTIC WORKS

1762	Rousseau's *Émile*
1774	Goethe's *Sorrows of Young Werther*
1781	Kant's *Critique of Pure Reason**
1788	Kant's *Critique of Practical Reason**
1798	Wordsworth and Coleridge's *Lyrical Ballads*
1799	Schlegel's *Lucinde*
1799	Schleiermacher's *Speeches on Religion to Its Cultured Despisers*
1802	Chateaubriand's *Genius of Christianity*
1806	Hegel's *Phenomenology of Mind*
1808	Goethe's *Faust*, Part I
1812	Byron's *Childe Harold's Pilgrimage*
1819	Byron's *Don Juan*
1825	Scott's *Tales of the Crusaders*
1841	Carlyle's *On Heroes and Hero-Worship*

*Kant's books were not themselves part of the Romantic Movement, but they were fundamental to later Romantic writers.

Goethe Towering above all of these German writers stood Johann Wolfgang von Goethe (1749–1832). Perhaps the greatest German writer of modern times, Goethe defies easy classification. Part of his literary production fits into the Romantic mold, and part of it was a condemnation of Romantic excesses. The book that made his early reputation was *The Sorrows of Young Werther*, published in 1774. This novel, like many in the eighteenth century, is a series of letters. The hero falls in love with Lotte, who is married to another man. The letters explore their relationship with the sentimentalism that was characteristic of the age. Eventually Werther and Lotte part, but in his grief, Werther takes his own life. This novel became popular throughout Europe. Romantic authors admired its emphasis on feeling and on living outside the bounds of polite society.

Goethe's masterpiece was *Faust*, a long dramatic poem. Part I, published in 1808, tells the story of Faust, who makes a pact with the devil—he will exchange his soul for greater knowledge than other human beings possess. As the story progresses, Faust seduces a young woman named Gretchen. She dies but is received into heaven as the grief-stricken Faust realizes he must continue to live.

In Part II, completed in 1832, Faust is taken through a series of adventures involving witches and mythological characters. At the conclusion, however, he dedicates his life, or what remains of it, to the improvement of humankind. He feels this goal will allow him to overcome the restless striving that induced him to make the pact with the devil. That new knowledge breaks the pact. Faust dies and is received by angels.

▼ Romantic Art

The art of the Romantic Era, like its poetry and philosophy, stood largely in reaction to that of the eighteenth century. Whereas the Rococo artists had looked to Renaissance models and Neo-Classical painters to the art of the ancient world, Romantic painters often portrayed scenes from medieval life. For them, the Middle Ages represented the social stability and religious reverence that was disappearing from their own era.

The Cult of the Middle Ages and Neo-Gothicism

Like many early Romantic artists, the English landscape painter John Constable (1776–1837) was politically conservative. In *Salisbury Cathedral from the Meadows*, he portrayed a stable world in which neither political turmoil nor industrial development challenged the traditional dominance of the church and the landed classes. Although the clouds and sky in the painting depict a severe storm, the works of both nature and humankind present a powerful sense of enduring order. The trees clearly have withstood this storm as they have withstood others for many years. The cathedral, built in the Middle Ages, has also stood majestically intact for centuries. Like many English conservatives of his day, Constable saw the church and the British constitution as intimately related. Religious institutions were barriers to political radicalism. In his private letters, Constable associated liberal reformers with the devil, leading some scholars to suggest that the lightning striking the back roof of the cathedral symbolizes those evil forces and that the rainbow, arching over the entire scene and giving it a sacramental nature, indicates God's blessing for the traditional order of nature and society.

Constable and other Romantics tended to idealize rural life because they believed it was connected to the medieval past and was opposed to the increasingly urban, industrializing, commercial society that was developing around them. In fact, the rural landscape and rustic society that Constable depicted in his paintings had already largely disappeared from England.

John Constable's *Salisbury Cathedral from the Meadows* displays the appeal of Romantic art to both medieval monuments and the sublime power of nature. Art Resource, NY. © The National Gallery, London

Medieval structures not only appeared in Romantic painting. The Neo-Gothic revival in architecture also dotted the European landscape with modern imitations of them. Many medieval cathedrals were restored during this era, and new churches were designed to resemble their medieval forerunners. The British Houses of Parliament built in 1836–1837 were the most famous public buildings in the Neo-Gothic style, but town halls, schools, and even railroad stations were designed to look like medieval buildings, while aristocratic country houses were rebuilt to resemble medieval castles.

The single most remarkable nineteenth-century Neo-Gothic structure was the castle of Neuschwanstein constructed between 1869 and 1886 on a mountain in southern Germany by King Ludwig II of Bavaria (r. 1864–1886). The cost of this castle, the interior of which was never completed, almost bankrupted the Bavarian monarchy.

Nature and the Sublime

Beyond their attraction to history, Romantic artists also sought to portray nature in all of its majestic power as no previous generation of European artists had ever done. Moreover, like Romantic poets, the artists of the era were drawn toward the mysterious and unruly side of nature rather than toward the rational Newtonian order that had prevailed during the Enlightenment. Their works often sought to portray what they and others termed *the sublime*—that is, subjects from nature that aroused strong emotions, such as fear, dread, and

At the castle of Neuschwanstein King Ludwig II of Bavaria erected the most extensive Neo-Gothic monument of central Europe. Josaf Beck/Getty Images, Inc.—Taxi

awe, and raised questions about whether and how much we control our lives. Painters often traveled to remote areas such as the Scottish Highlands, the mountains of Wales, or the Swiss Alps to portray unruly and dangerous scenes from nature that would immediately grip and engage the viewer's emotions.

Romantics saw nature as a set of infinite forces that overwhelmed the smallness of humankind. For example, in 1824, the German artist Caspar David Friedrich (1774–1840) in *The Polar Sea* painted the plight of a ship trapped and crushed by the force of a vast polar ice field. In direct contrast to eighteenth-century artists' portrayal of sunny Enlightenment, Friedrich also painted numerous scenes in which human beings stand shrouded in the mysterious darkness of night where moonlight and torches cast only fitful illumination.

An artist who similarly understood the power of nature but also depicted the forces of the new industrialism that was challenging them was Joseph Mallord William Turner (1775–1851) whose painting *Rain, Steam and Speed—The Great Western Railway* of 1844 illustrated the recently invented railway engine barreling through an enveloping storm. In this scene the new technology is both part of the natural world and strong enough to dominate it.

Friedrich's and Turner's paintings taken together symbolize the contradictory forces affecting Romantic artists—the sense of the power, awe, and mastery of nature coupled with the sense that the advance of industry represented a new kind of awesome human power that could challenge or even surpass the forces of nature itself.

▼ Religion in the Romantic Period

During the Middle Ages, the foundation of religion had been the authority of the church. The Reformation leaders had appealed to the authority of the Bible. Then, many Enlightenment writers attempted to derive religion from the rational nature revealed by Newtonian physics. Other Enlightenment figures attacked religion in general and Christianity in particular. Romantic religious thinkers, in contrast, sought the foundations of

Caspar David Friedrich's *The Polar Sea* illustrated the power of nature to diminish the creations of humankind as seen in the wrecked ship on the right of the painting. Kunsthalle, Hamburg, Germany/A.K.G., Berlin/SuperStock

Joseph Mallord William Turner's *Rain, Steam, and Speed—The Great Western Railway* captured the tensions many Europeans felt between their natural environment and the new technology of the industrial age. Joseph Mallord William Turner, 1775–1851, *Rain, Steam, and Speed—The Great Western Railway 1844.* Oil on canvas, 90.8 × 121.9. © The National Gallery, London religion in the inner emotions of humankind. Reacting to the anticlericalism of both the Enlightenment and the French Revolution, these thinkers also saw religious faith, experience, and institutions as central to human life. Their forerunners were the mystics of Western Christianity. One of the first great examples of a religion characterized by Romantic impulses—Methodism—arose in mid-eighteenth-century England during the Enlightenment itself and became one of the most powerful forces in transatlantic religion during the nineteenth century.

Methodism

Methodism originated in the middle of the eighteenth century as a revolt against deism and rationalism in the Church of England. The Methodist revival formed an important part of the background of English Romanticism. The leader of the Methodist movement was John Wesley (1703–1791). His mother, Susannah Wesley, who bore eighteen children, had carefully supervised his education and religious development.

While at Oxford University studying to be an Anglican priest, Wesley organized a religious group known as the Holy Club. He soon left England for missionary work in the new colony of Georgia in America, where he arrived in 1735. While he was crossing the Atlantic, a group of German Moravians on the ship deeply impressed him with their unshakable faith and confidence during a storm. Wesley, who had despaired of his life, concluded they knew far better than he the meaning of justification by faith. When he returned to England in 1738, Wesley began to worship with Moravians in London. There, in 1739, he underwent a conversion experience that he described in the words, "My heart felt strangely warmed." From that point on, he felt assured of his own salvation.

Wesley discovered he could not preach his version of Christian conversion and practical piety in Anglican church pulpits. Therefore, late in 1739, he began to preach in the open fields near the cities and towns of western England. Thousands of humble people responded to his message of repentance and good works. Soon he and his brother Charles (1707–1788), who be-

John Wesley (1703–1791) was the founder of Methodism. He emphasized the role of emotional experience in Christian conversion.
CORBIS/Bettmann

came famous for his hymns, began to organize Methodist societies. By the late eighteenth century, the Methodists had become a separate church. They ordained their own clergy and sent missionaries to America, where they eventually achieved their greatest success and influence.

Methodism stressed inward, heartfelt religion and the possibility of Christian perfection in this life. John Wesley described Christianity as "an inward principle . . . the image of God impressed on a created spirit, a fountain of peace and love springing up into everlasting life."[3] True Christians were those who were "saved in this world from all sin, from all unrighteousness . . . and now in such a sense perfect as not to commit sin and . . . freed from evil thoughts and evil tempers."[4]

Many people, weary of the dry rationalism that derived from deism, found Wesley's ideal relevant to their own lives. The Methodist preachers emphasized the role of enthusiastic, emotional experience as part of Christian conversion. After Wesley, religious revivals became highly emotional in style and content.

New Directions in Continental Religion

Similar religious developments based on feeling appeared on the Continent. After the Thermidorian Reaction, a strong Roman Catholic revival took place in France. Its followers disapproved of both the religious policy of the revolution and the anticlericalism of the Enlightenment. The most important book to express these sentiments was *The Genius of Christianity* (1802) by Viscount François René de Chateaubriand (1768–1848). In this work, which became known as the "bible of Romanticism," Chateaubriand argued that the essence of religion is "passion." The foundation of faith in the church was the emotion that its teachings and sacraments inspired in the heart of the Christian.

Against the Newtonian view of the world and of a rational God, the Romantics found God immanent in nature. No one stated the Romantic religious ideal more eloquently or with greater impact on the modern world than Friedrich Schleiermacher (1768–1834). In 1799, he published *Speeches on Religion to Its Cultured Despisers*. It was a response to Lutheran orthodoxy, on the one hand, and to Enlightenment rationalism, on the other. The advocates of both were the "cultured despisers" of real, or heartfelt, religion. According to Schleiermacher, religion was neither dogma nor a system of ethics. It was an intuition or feeling of absolute dependence on an infinite reality. Religious institutions, doctrines, and moral activity expressed that primal religious feeling only in a secondary, or indirect, way.

Although Schleiermacher considered Christianity the "religion of religions," he also believed every world religion was unique in its expression of the primal intuition of the infinite in the finite. He thus turned against the universal natural religion of the Enlightenment, which he termed "a name applied to loose, unconnected impulses," and defended the meaningfulness of the numerous world religions. Every such religion was seen to be a unique version of the emotional experience of dependence on an infinite being. In so arguing, Schleiermacher interpreted the religions of the world in the same way that other Romantic writers interpreted the variety of unique peoples and cultures.

▼ Romantic Views of Nationalism and History

A distinctive feature of Romanticism, especially in Germany, was its glorification of both the individual person and individual cultures. Behind these views lay the philosophy of German idealism, which understood the world as the creation of subjective egos. J. G. Fichte (1762–1814), an important German philosopher and nationalist, identified the individual ego with the Absolute that underlies all existing things. According to him and similar philosophers, the world is truly the creation of humankind. The world is as it is because especially strong persons conceive of it in a particular way and impose their wills on the world and other people. Napoleon served as the contemporary example of such a great person. This philosophy has ever since served to justify the glorification of great persons and their actions in overriding all opposition to their will and desires.

Herder and Culture

In addition to this philosophy, the influence of new historical studies lay behind the German glorification of individual cultures. German Romantic writers went in search of their own past in reaction to the copying of French manners in eighteenth-century Germany, the impact of the French Revolution, and the imperialism of Napoleon. An early leader in this effort was Johann Gottfried Herder (1744–1803), already discussed in Chapter 17, as a critic of European colonialism. Herder resented French cultural dominance in Germany. In 1778, he published an influential essay entitled "On the Knowing and Feelings of the Human Soul." In it, he vigorously rejected the mechanical explanation of nature so popular with Enlightenment writers. He saw human

[3]Quoted in Albert C. Outler, ed., *John Wesley: A Representative Collection of His Writings* (New York: Oxford University Press, 1964), p. 220.

[4]Outler, *John Wesley*, p. 220.

beings and societies as developing organically, like plants, over time. Human beings were different at different times and places.

Herder revived German folk culture by urging the collection and preservation of distinctive German songs and sayings. His most important followers in this work were the Grimm brothers, Jakob (1785–1863) and Wilhelm (1786–1859), famous for their collection of fairy tales. Believing each language and culture were the unique expression of a people, Herder opposed both the concept and the use of a "common" language, such as French, and "universal" institutions, such as those Napoleon had imposed on Europe. These, he believed, were forms of tyranny over the individuality of a people. Herder's writings led to a broad revival of interest in history and philosophy. Although initially directed toward identifying German origins, such work soon expanded to embrace other world cultures. Eventually the ability of the Romantic imagination to be at home in any age or culture spurred the study of non-Western religion, comparative literature, and philology.

Hegel and History

The most important philosopher of history in the Romantic period was the German Georg Wilhelm Friedrich Hegel (1770–1831). He is one of the most complicated and significant philosophers in the history of Western civilization.

Hegel believed ideas develop in an evolutionary fashion that involves conflict. At any given time, a predominant set of ideas, which he termed the **thesis**, holds sway. Conflicting ideas, which Hegel termed the **antithesis**, challenge the thesis. As these patterns of thought clash, a **synthesis** emerges that eventually becomes the new thesis. Then the process begins all over again. Periods of world history receive their character from the patterns of thought that predominate during them. (See "Hegel Explains the Role of Great Men in History.")

Several important philosophical conclusions followed from this analysis. One of the most significant was the belief that all periods of history have been of almost equal value because each was, by definition, necessary to the achievements of those that came later. Also, all cultures are valuable because each contributes to the necessary clash of values and ideas that allows humankind to develop. Hegel discussed these concepts in *The Phenomenology of Mind* (1806), *Lectures on the Philosophy of History* (1822–1831), and other works, many of which were published only after his death. During his lifetime, his ideas became widely known through his university lectures at Berlin.

Islam, the Middle East, and Romanticism

The new religious, literary, and historical sensibilities of the Romantic period modified the European understanding of both Islam and the Arab world while at the same time preserving long-standing attitudes.

The energized Christianity associated with Methodist-like forms of Protestantism, on the one hand, and Chateaubriand's emotional Roman Catholicism, on the other, renewed the traditional sense of necessary conflict between Christianity and Islam. Chateaubriand wrote a travelogue of his journey from Paris to Jerusalem in 1811. A decade later, when he was a member of the French parliament, he invoked the concept of a crusade against the Muslim world in a speech on the danger posed by the Barbary pirates of North Africa.

Indeed, the medieval Crusades against Islam fired the Romantic imagination. Nostalgic European artists painted from a Western standpoint the great moments of the Crusades including the bloody capture of Jerusalem. Stories from those conflicts filled historical novels such as *Tales of the Crusaders* (1825) by Sir Walter Scott (1771–1832). Although they presented heroic images of Muslim warriors, these paintings and novels ignored the havoc that the crusaders had visited on the peoples of the Middle East.

The general nineteenth-century association of nationalistic aspirations with Romanticism also cast the Ottoman Empire and with it Islam in an unfavorable political light. Romantic poets and intellectuals championed the cause of the Greek Revolution (see Chapter 20) and revived older charges of Ottoman despotism.

By contrast, other Romantic sensibilities induced Europeans to see the Muslim world in a more positive fashion. The Romantic emphasis on the value of literature drawn from different cultures and ages allowed many nineteenth-century European readers to enjoy the stories from *The Thousand and One Nights*, which first appeared in English in 1778 from a French translation. As poets across Europe rejected classicism in literature in favor of folk stories and fairy tales, they saw the *Arabian Nights* as mysterious and exotic. In 1859, Edward FitzGerald (1809–1883) published his highly popular translation of the *Rubáiyát of Omar Khayyám* of Nishapur, a Persian poet of the twelfth century.

Herder's and Hegel's concepts of history gave both the Arab peoples and Islam distinct roles in history. For Herder, Arab culture was one of the numerous communities that composed the human race and manifested the human spirit. The Prophet Muhammad, while giving voice to the ancient spirit of the Arab people, had drawn them from a polytheistic faith to a great monotheistic vision. For Hegel, Islam represented an important stage of

HEGEL EXPLAINS THE ROLE OF GREAT MEN IN HISTORY

Hegel believed that behind the development of human history from one period to the next lay the mind and purpose of what he termed the World-Spirit, *a concept somewhat like the Christian God. Hegel thought particular heroes from the past (such as Caesar) and in the present (such as Napoleon) were the unconscious instruments of that spirit. In this passage from his lectures on the philosophy of history, Hegel explained how these heroes could change history. All these concepts are characteristic of the Romantic belief that human beings and human history are always intimately connected with larger, spiritual forces at work in the world. The passage also reflects the widespread belief of the time that the world of civic or political action pertained to men and that of the domestic sphere belonged to women.*

How might the career of Napoleon have inspired this passage? What are the antidemocratic implications of this passage? In this passage, do great men make history or do historical developments make great men? Why do you think Hegel does not associate this power of shaping history with women as well as men? In that regard, note how he relates history with political developments rather than with those of the private social sphere.

Such are all great historical men—whose own particular aims involve those large issues which are the will of the World-Spirit. They may be called Heroes, inasmuch as they have derived their purposes and their vocation, not from the calm, regular course of things, sanctioned by the existing order, but from a concealed fount—one which has not attained to phenomenal, present existence—from that inner Spirit, still hidden beneath the surface, which, impinging on the outer world as on a shell, bursts it in pieces, because it is another kernel than that which belonged to the shell in question. They are men, therefore, who appear to draw the impulse of their life from themselves; and whose deeds have produced a condition of things and a complex of historical relations which appear to be only their interest, and their work.

Such individuals had no consciousness of the general Idea they were unfolding, while prosecuting those aims of theirs; on the contrary, they were practical, political men. But at the same time they were thinking men, who had an insight into the requirements of the time—what was ripe for development. This was the very Truth for their age, for their world; the species next in order, so to speak, and which was already formed in the womb of time. It was theirs to know this nascent principle; the necessary, directly sequent step in progress, which their world was to take; to make this their aim, and to expend their energy in promoting it. World historical men—the Heroes of an epoch—must, therefore, be recognized as its clear-sighted ones; their deeds, their words are the best of that time.

From G. W. F. Hegel, *The Philosophy of History*, trans. by J. Sibree (New York: Dover, 1956), pp. 30–31. Reprinted by permission.

When Napoleon invaded Egypt in 1799, he met stiff resistance. On July 25, however, the French won a decisive victory. This painting of that battle by Baron Antoine Gros (1771–1835) emphasizes French heroism and Muslim defeat. Such an outlook was typical of European views of Arabs and the Islamic world. Antoine Jean Gros (1771–1835). Detail, *Battle of Aboukir, July 25, 1799*, c. 1806. Oil on canvas. Chateaux de Versailles et de Trianon, Versailles, France. Bridgeman—Giraudon/Art Resource, NY

the development of the world spirit. However, Hegel believed Islam had fulfilled its role in history and no longer had any significant part to play. These outlooks, which penetrated much nineteenth-century intellectual life, made it easy for Europeans to believe that Islam could, for all practical purposes, be ignored or reduced to a spent historical force.

The British historian and social commentator Thomas Carlyle (1795–1881) attributed new, positive qualities to Muhammad himself. Carlyle disliked the Enlightenment's disparagement of religion and spiritual values. He was also drawn to German theories of history. In his book *On Heroes and Hero-Worship* (1841), Carlyle presented Muhammad as the embodiment of the hero as prophet. He repudiated the traditional Christian and general Enlightenment view of Muhammad as an impostor. (See Chapter 17.) To Carlyle, Muhammad was straightforward and sincere. Carlyle's understanding of religion was similar to Schleiermacher's, and thus in his pages, Muhammad appeared as a person who had experienced God subjectively and had communicated a sense of the divine to others. Although friendly to Muhammad from a historical standpoint, Carlyle nonetheless saw him as one of many great religious figures and not, as Muslims believed, as the last of the prophets through whom God had spoken.

The person whose actions in the long run did perhaps the most to reshape the idea of both Islam and the Middle East in the European imagination was Napoleon himself. With his Egyptian expedition of 1798, the first European military invasion of the Near East since the Crusades, the study of the Arab world became an important activity within French intellectual life. For his invasion of Egypt to succeed, Napoleon believed he must make it clear he had no intention of destroying Islam but rather sought to liberate Egypt from the military clique that governed the country in the name of the Ottoman Empire. To that end, he took with him scholars of Arabic and Islamic culture whom he urged to converse with the most educated people they could meet. Napoleon personally met with the local Islamic leaders and had all of his speeches and proclamations translated into classical Arabic. Such cultural sensitivity and the serious efforts of the French scholars to learn Arabic and study the Qur'an impressed Egyptian scholars. (When the French sought to levy new taxes, however, the Egyptians' enthusiasm waned.)

It was on this expedition that the famous Rosetta Stone was discovered. Now housed in the British Museum, it eventually led to the decipherment of ancient Egypt's hieroglyphic writing. Napoleon's scholars also published a twenty-three volume *Description of Egypt* (1809–1828), which concentrated largely on ancient Egypt. Their approach suggested the history of the Ottoman Empire needed to be related first to the larger context of Egyptian history and that Islam, although enormously important, was only part of a larger cultural story. The implication was that if Egypt and Islam were to be understood, it would be through European—if not necessarily Christian—categories of thought.

Two cultural effects in the West of Napoleon's invasion were an increase in the number of European visitors to the Middle East and a demand for architecture based on ancient Egyptian models. Perhaps the most famous example of this fad is the Washington Monument in Washington, D.C., which is modeled after ancient Egyptian obelisks.

In Perspective

Romantic ideas made a major contribution to the emergence of nationalism, which proved to be one of the strongest motivating forces of the nineteenth and twentieth centuries. The writers of the Enlightenment had generally championed a cosmopolitan outlook on the world. By contrast, the Romantic thinkers emphasized the individuality and worth of each separate people and culture. A people or a nation was defined by a common language, history, and customs and by the possession of a historical homeland. This cultural nationalism gradually became transformed into a political creed. It came to be widely believed that every people, ethnic group, or nation should constitute a separate political entity and that only when it so existed could the nation be secure in its own character.

France under the revolutionary government and Napoleon had demonstrated the power of nationhood. Other peoples came to desire similar strength and confidence. Napoleon's toppling of ancient political structures, such as the Holy Roman Empire, proved the need for new political organization in Europe. By 1815, only a few Europeans aspired to this, but as time passed, peoples from Ireland to Ukraine came to share these yearnings. The Congress of Vienna could ignore such feelings, but for the rest of the nineteenth century, as shall be seen in subsequent chapters, statesmen had to confront the growing power these feelings had unleashed.

REVIEW QUESTIONS

1. How did Napoleon rise to power? What groups supported him? What were his major domestic achievements? Did his rule fulfill or betray the French Revolution?
2. What regions made up Napoleon's realm, and what was the status of each region within it? Did his administration show foresight, or was the empire a burden he could not afford?
3. Why did Napoleon decide to invade Russia? Why did the operation fail?
4. What were the results of the Congress of Vienna? Was the Vienna settlement a success?
5. Why did Romantic writers champion feelings over reason? What questions did Rousseau and Kant raise about reason?
6. Why was poetry important to Romantic writers? How did the Romantic concept of religion differ from Reformation Protestantism and Enlightenment deism? How did Romantic ideas and sensibilities modify European ideas of Islam and the Middle East? What were the cultural results of Napoleon's invasion of Egypt?

SUGGESTED READINGS

M. H. Abrams, *The Mirror and the Lamp: Romantic Theory and the Critical Tradition* (1958). A classic on Romantic literary theory.

E. Behler, *German Romantic Literary Theory* (1993). A clear introduction to a difficult subject.

D. Bell, *The First Total War: Napoleon's Europe and the Birth of Warfare as We Know It* (2007). A consideration of the Napoleonic conflicts and the culture of warfare.

G. E. Bentley, *The Stranger from Paradise: A Biography of William Blake* (2001). Now the standard work.

N. Boyle, *Goethe* (2001). A challenging two-volume biography.

M. Broers, *Europe under Napoleon 1799–1815* (2002). Examines the subject from the standpoint of those Napoleon conquered.

T. Chapman, *Congress of Vienna: Origins, Processes, and Results* (1998). A clear introduction to the major issues.

P. Dwyer, *Napoleon: The Path to Power, 1769–1799* (2008). A major study of the subject.

P. Dwyer, *Talleyrand* (2002). A useful account of his diplomatic influence.

S. Englund, *Napoleon: A Political Life* (2004). A thoughtful recent biography.

C. Esdaile, *The Peninsular War: A New History* (2003). A narrative of the Napoleonic wars in Spain.

A. Forrest, *Napoleon's Men: The Soldiers of the Revolution and Empire* (2002). An examination of the troops rather than their commander.

H. Honour, *Romanticism* (1979). Still the best introduction to Romantic art, well illustrated.

F. Kagan, *The End of the Old Order: Napoleon and Europe, 1801–1805* (2006). A masterful narrative.

S. Körner, *Kant* (1955). A classic brief, clear introduction.

J. Lusvass, *Napoleon on the Art of War* (2001). A collection of Napoleon's own writings.

J. J. McGann and J. Soderholm, eds., *Byron and Romanticism* (2002). Essays on the poet who most embodied Romantic qualities to the people of his time.

R. Muir, *Tactics and the Experience of Battle in the Age of Napoleon* (1998). A splendid account of troops in battle.

T. Pinkard, *Hegel: A Biography* (2000). A long but accessible study.

N. Roe, *Romanticism: An Oxford Guide* (2005). A series of informative essays.

P. W. Schroeder, *The Transformation of European Politics, 1763–1848* (1994). A major synthesis of the diplomatic history of the period, emphasizing the new departures of the Congress of Vienna.

I. Woloch, *Napoleon and His Collaborators: The Making of a Dictatorship* (2001). A key study by one of the major scholars of the subject.

A. Zamoyski, *Rites of Peace: The Fall of Napoleon and the Congress of Vienna* (2007). A lively analysis and narrative.

For additional learning resources related to this chapter, please go to www.myhistorylab.com

PEARSON myhistorylab

In 1830, revolution again erupted in France as well as elsewhere on the Continent. Eugène Delacroix's *Liberty Leading the People* was the most famous image recalling that event. Note how he portrays persons from different social classes and occupations joining the revolution led by the figure of Liberty. Eugène Delacroix (1798–1863), *Liberty Leading the People*, 1830. Oil on canvas, 260 × 325 cm—RF 129. Musée du Louvre RMN Reunion des Musées Nationaux, France. Photograph © Erich Lessing/Art Resource, NY

20

The Conservative Order and the Challenges of Reform (1815–1832)

▼ **The Challenges of Nationalism and Liberalism**
The Emergence of Nationalism • Early-Nineteenth-Century Political Liberalism

▼ **Conservative Governments: The Domestic Political Order**
Conservative Outlooks • Liberalism and Nationalism Resisted in Austria and the Germanies • Postwar Repression in Great Britain • Bourbon Restoration in France

▼ **The Conservative International Order**
The Congress System • The Spanish Revolution of 1820 • Revolt Against Ottoman Rule in the Balkans

▼ **The Wars of Independence in Latin America**
Revolution in Haiti • Wars of Independence on the South American Continent • Independence in New Spain • Brazilian Independence

▼ **The Conservative Order Shaken in Europe**
Russia: The Decembrist Revolt of 1825 • Revolution in France (1830) • Belgium Becomes Independent (1830) • The Great Reform Bill in Britain (1832)

▼ **In Perspective**

KEY TOPICS

- **The challenges of nationalism and liberalism to the conservative order in the early nineteenth century**
- **The domestic and international politics of the conservative order from the Congress of Vienna through the 1820s**
- **The Wars of Independence in Latin America**
- **The revolutions of 1830 on the Continent and the passage of the Great Reform Bill in Britain**

THE CONGRESS OF Vienna was followed by a decade in which conservative political forces controlled virtually all of Europe. In the international arena, these forces sought to maintain peace and to prevent the outbreak of war that would unleash destruction and disorder. They did so through unprecedented forms of cooperation and mutual consultation. Domestically, they sought to maintain the authority of monarchies and aristocracies after the turmoil the French Revolution and Napoleon had wrought. Two sets of critics challenged this conservative order. Nationalists wished to redraw the map of Europe according to the boundaries of nationalities or ethnic groups. Liberals sought moderate political reform and freer economic markets. The goals of nationalists and liberals threatened the dominance of landed aristocracies and the rule of monarchs who governed by virtue of dynastic inheritance rather than nationality. The efforts of Europe's Latin American colonies to gain independence also challenged the status quo.

For the first fifteen years after the Congress of Vienna, the forces of conservatism were successful, except for the failure of Spain and Portugal to retain control of Latin America. In the late 1820s, however, the conservatives faced stronger challenges. Thereafter, certain major liberal goals were achieved when a revolution occurred in France in 1830 and a sweeping reform bill passed through the British Parliament in 1832. During the same period, however, Russia and other countries in eastern and central Europe continued to resist political and social change.

▾ The Challenges of Nationalism and Liberalism

Observers have frequently regarded the nineteenth century as the great age of "isms." Throughout the Western world, secular ideologies began to take hold of the learned and popular imaginations in opposition to the political and social status quo. These included nationalism, liberalism, republicanism, socialism, and communism. A noted historian once called all such words "trouble-breeding and usually thought-obscuring terms."[1] They are just if we use them as an excuse to avoid thinking or if we fail to see the variety of opinions each of them conceals.

The Emergence of Nationalism

Nationalism proved to be the single most powerful European political ideology of the nineteenth and early twentieth centuries. It has reasserted itself in present-day Europe following the collapse of communist governments in Eastern Europe and in the former Soviet Union. As a political outlook, nationalism was and is based on the relatively modern concept that a nation is composed of people who are joined together by the bonds of a common language, as well as common customs, culture, and history, and who, because of these bonds, should be administered by the same government. That is to say, nationalists in the past and the present contend that political and ethnic boundaries should coincide. Political units had not been so defined or governed earlier in European history. The idea came into its own during the late eighteenth and the early nineteenth centuries.

[1]Arthur O. Lovejoy, *The Great Chain of Being: A Study in the History of an Idea* (New York: Harper Torchbooks, 1963), p. 6.

Opposition to the Vienna Settlement Early nineteenth-century nationalism directly opposed the principle upheld at the Congress of Vienna that legitimate monarchies or dynasties, rather than ethnicity, provide the basis for political unity. Nationalists naturally protested multinational states such as the Austrian and Russian empires. They also objected to peoples of the same ethnic group, such as Germans and Italians, dwelling in political units smaller than that of the ethnic nation. Consequently, nationalists challenged both the domestic and the international order of the Vienna settlement.

Behind the concept of nationalism usually, though not always, lay the idea of popular sovereignty, since the qualities of peoples, rather than their rulers, determine a national character. This aspect of nationalism, however, frequently led to confusion or conflict because of the presence of minorities. Within many territories in which one national group has predominated, there have also existed significant minority ethnic enclaves that the majority has had every intention of governing with or without their consent. In some cases, a nationalistically conscious group would dominate in one section of a country, but people of the same ethnicity in another region would not have nationalistic aspirations. The former might then attempt to impose their aspirations on the latter.

Creating Nations In fact, it was nationalists who actually created nations in the nineteenth century. During the first half of the century, a particular, usually small, group of nationalistically minded writers or other intellectual elites, using the printed word, spread a nationalistic concept of the nation. These groups were frequently historians who chronicled a people's past, or writers and literary scholars who established a national literature by collecting and publishing earlier writings in the people's language. In effect, they gave a people a sense of their past and a literature of their own. As time passed, schoolteachers spread nationalistic ideas by imparting a nation's official language and history. These small groups of early nationalists established the cultural beliefs and political expectations on which the later mass-supported nationalism of the second half of the century would grow.

Which language to use in the schools and in government offices was always a point of contention for nationalists. In France and Italy, official versions of the national language were imposed in the schools and they replaced local dialects. In parts of Scandinavia and eastern Europe, nationalists attempted to resurrect from earlier times what they regarded as purer versions of the national language. Often, modern scholars or linguists virtually invented these resurrected languages. This process of establishing national languages led to far more linguistic uniformity in European nations than had existed before the nineteenth century. Yet even in 1850, perhaps fewer than half of the inhabitants of France spoke the official French language.

Language could become such an effective cornerstone in the foundation of nationalism thanks largely to the emergence of the print culture discussed in Chapter 17. The presence of a great many printed books, journals, magazines, and newspapers "fixed" language in a more permanent fashion than did the spoken word. This uniform language found in printed works could overcome regional spoken dialects and establish itself as dominant. In most countries, spoken and written proficiency in the official, printed language became a path to social and political advancement. The growth of a uniform language helped persuade people who had not thought of themselves as constituting a nation that in fact they were one.

Meaning of Nationhood Nationalists used a variety of arguments and metaphors to express what they meant by *nationhood*. Some argued that gathering, for example, Italians into a unified Italy or Germans into a unified Germany, thus eliminating or at least federating the petty dynastic states that governed those regions, would promote economic and administrative efficiency. Adopting a tenet from political liberalism, certain nationalist writers suggested that nations determining their own destinies resembled individuals exploiting personal talents to determine their own careers. Some nationalists claimed that nations, like biological species in the natural world, were distinct creations of God. Other nationalists claimed a place for their nations in the divine order of things. Throughout the nineteenth century, for example, Polish nationalists portrayed Poland as the suffering Christ among nations, thus implicitly suggesting that Poland, like Christ, would experience resurrection and a new life.

A significant difficulty for nationalism was, and is, determining which ethnic groups could be considered nations, with claims to territory and political autonomy. In theory, any of them could, but in reality, nationhood came to be associated with groups that were large enough to support a viable economy, that had a significant cultural history, that possessed a cultural elite that could nourish and spread the national language, and that had the military capacity to conquer other peoples or to establish and protect their own independence. Throughout the century many smaller ethnic groups claimed to fulfill these criteria, but could not effectively achieve either independence or recognition. They could and did, however, create domestic unrest within the political units they inhabited. (See "Compare & Connect: Mazzini and Lord Acton Debate the Political Principles of Nationalism," pages 596–597.)

Regions of Nationalistic Pressure During the nineteenth century, nationalists challenged the political status quo in six major areas of Europe. England had brought Ireland under direct rule in 1800, abolishing the separate Irish Parliament and allowing the Irish to elect members to the British Parliament in Westminster. Irish nationalists, however, wanted independence or at least larger measures of self-government. The "Irish problem," as it was called, would haunt British politics for the next two centuries. German nationalists sought political unity for all German-speaking peoples, challenging the multinational structure of the Austrian Empire and pitting Prussia and Austria against each other. Italian nationalists sought to unify Italian-speaking peoples on the Italian peninsula and to drive out the Austrians. Polish nationalists, targeting primarily their Russian rulers, struggled to restore Poland as an independent nation. In eastern Europe, a host of national groups, including Hungarians, Czechs, Slovenes, and others, sought either independence or formal recognition within the Austrian Empire. Finally, in southeastern Europe on the Balkan peninsula and eastward, national groups, including Serbs, Greeks, Albanians, Romanians, and Bulgarians, sought independence from Ottoman and Russian control.

Although there were never disturbances in all six areas at the same time, any one of them had the potential to erupt into turmoil for much of the nineteenth century and beyond. In each area, nationalist activity ebbed and flowed. The dominant governments often thought they needed only to repress the activity or ride it out until stability returned. Over the course of the century, however, nationalists changed the political map and political culture of Europe.

Early-Nineteenth-Century Political Liberalism

The word *liberal*, as applied to political activity, entered the European and American vocabulary during the nineteenth century. Its meaning has varied over time. Nineteenth-century European conservatives often regarded as *liberal* almost anyone or anything that challenged their own political, social, or religious values. For twenty-first-century Americans, the word *liberal* carries with it meanings and connotations that have little or nothing to do with its significance to nineteenth-century Europeans. European conservatives of the last century saw liberals as more radical than they actually were; present-day Americans often think of nineteenth-century liberals as more conservative than they were.

Political Goals Nineteenth-century liberals derived their political ideas from the writers of the Enlightenment, the example of English liberties, and the so-called principles of 1789 embodied in the French Declaration of the Rights of Man and Citizen. They sought to establish a political framework of legal equality, religious toleration, and freedom of the press. Their general goal was a political structure that would limit the arbitrary power of government against the persons and property

COMPARE AND CONNECT

Mazzini and Lord Acton Debate the Political Principles of Nationalism

NO POLITICAL FORCE in the nineteenth and twentieth centuries was stronger than nationalism. It eventually replaced loyalty to a dynasty with loyalty based on ethnic considerations. It received new standing after World War I when the self-determination of nations became one of the cornerstones of the Paris Peace treaties. Still later, former European colonies embraced this powerful idea. Yet from the earliest enunciation of the principles of nationalism the concept confronted major critics who understood its potential destructiveness. In these two documents Mazzini, the great Italian nationalist, sets forth his understanding of nationalism, and Lord Acton, the distinguished nineteenth-century English historian, points to the dangers lurking behind the ideas and realities of politics based on nationalism.

QUESTIONS

1. **What qualities of a people does Mazzini associate with nationalism?**
2. **How and why does Mazzini relate nationalism to divine purposes?**
3. **Why does Acton see the principle of nationality as dangerous to liberty?**
4. **Why does Acton see nationalism as a threat to minority groups and to democracy?**
5. **How might the connection that Mazzini draws between nationalism and divine will serve to justify the repression of minority rights that Acton feared?**

I. Mazzini Defines Nationality

In 1835 the Italian nationalist and patriot Giuseppe Mazzini (1805–1872) explained his understanding of nationalism. Note how he combines a generally democratic view of politics with a religious concept of the divine destiny of nations. Once in power, however, nationalist states in Europe and the rest of the world were often not democratic states.

The essential characteristics of a nationality are common ideas, common principles and a common purpose. A nation is an association of those who are brought together by language, by given geographical conditions or by the role assigned them by history, who acknowledge the same principles and who march together to the conquest of a single definite goal under the rule of a uniform body of law.

The life of a nation consists in harmonious activity (that is, the employment of all individual abilities and energies comprised within the association) towards this single goal. . . .

But nationality means even more than this. Nationality also consists in the share of mankind's labors which God assigns to a people. This mission is the task which a people must perform to the end that the Divine Idea shall be realized in this world; it is the work which gives a people its rights as a member of Mankind; it is the baptismal rite which endows a people with its own character and its rank in the brotherhood of nations. . . .

Nationality depends for its very existence upon its sacredness within and beyond its borders.

If nationality is to be inviolable for all, friends and foes alike, it must be regarded inside a country as holy, like a religion, and outside a country as a grave mission. It is necessary too that the ideas arising within a country grow steadily, as part of the general law of Humanity which is the source of all nationality. It is necessary that these ideas be shown to other lands in their beauty and purity, free from any alien mixture, from any slavish fears, from any skeptical hesitancy, strong and active, embracing in their evolution every aspect and manifestation of the life of the nation. These ideas, a necessary component in the order of universal destiny, must retain their originality even as they enter harmoniously into mankind's general progress.

The people must be the basis of nationality; its logically derived and vigorously applied principles its means; the strength of all its strength; the improvement of the life of all and the happiness of the greatest possible number its results; and the accomplishment of the task assigned to it by God its goal. This is what we mean by nationality.

Source: From Herbert H. Rowen, ed., *From Absolutism to Revolution, 1648–1848*, 2nd ed. © 1969. Reprinted by permission of Prentice Hall, Inc., Upper Saddle River, NJ, pp. 277–280.

II. Lord Acton Condemns Nationalism

As well as being a historian, Lord Acton (1834–1902) was an important nineteenth-century commentator on contemporary religious and political events. He was deeply concerned with the character and preservation of liberty. In his essay on "Nationality" of 1862 Lord Acton's became one of the earliest voices to warn that nationalism or what he here terms "the modern theory of nationality" could endanger liberty of both individuals and people who found themselves to be an ethnic minority within a state dominated by an different ethnic or nationalist majority. Acton's words would prove prophetic with regard to the fate of ethnic minorities within Europe for the next century. Acton also pointed out that the pursuit of nationalist goals might mean that a government would ignore the economic well-being of its peoples.

The greatest adversary of the rights of nationality is the modern theory of nationality. By making the State and the nation commensurate with each other in theory, it reduces practically to a subject condition all other nationalities that may be within the boundary. It cannot admit them to an equality with the ruling nation which constitutes the State, because the State would then cease to be national, which would be a contradiction of the principle of its existence. According, therefore, to the degree of humanity and civilization in that dominant body which claims all the rights of the community, the inferior races are exterminated, or reduced to servitude, or outlawed, or put in a condition of dependence.

If we take the establishment of liberty for the realization of moral duties to be the end of civil society, we must conclude that those states are substantially the most perfect which, like the British and Austrian Empires, include various distinct nationalities without oppressing them. Those in which no mixture of races has occurred are imperfect; and those in which its effects have disappeared are decrepit. A State which is incompetent to satisfy different races condemns itself; a State which labors to neutralize, to absorb, or to expel them, destroys its own vitality; a State which does not include them is destitute of the chief basis of self-government. The theory of nationality, therefore, is a retrograde step in history. . . .

[N]ationality does not aim either at liberty or prosperity, both of which it sacrifices to the imperative necessity of making the nation the mold and measure of the State. Its course will be marked with material as well as moral ruin, in order that a new invention may prevail over the works of God and the interests of mankind. There is no principle of change, no phrase of political speculation conceivable, more comprehensive, more subversive, or more arbitrary than this. It is a confutation of democracy, because it sets limits to the exercise of the popular will, and substitutes for it a higher principle.

Source: From John Emerich Edward Dalbert-Acton, First Baron Acton, *Essays in the History of Liberty*, ed. by J. Rufus Fears (Indianapolis, IN: Liberty Classics, 1985), pp. 431–433.

During the revolutionary months of 1848, Italian nationalists unfurled the tri-colored green, white and red Italian nationalist flag on St. Mark's Square in Venice to replace the flag of Austria, which then ruled the city. Austrian rule of Venice only ended in 1866. Dagli Orti/Picture Desk Inc., Kobal Collection of individual citizens. They generally believed the legitimacy of government emanated from the freely given consent of the governed. The popular basis of such government was to be expressed through elected representative, or parliamentary, bodies. Most importantly, free government required government ministers to be responsible to the representatives rather than to the monarch. Liberals sought to achieve these political arrangements through written constitutions. They wanted to see constitutionalism and constitutional governments installed across the Continent.

These goals may seem limited, and they were. Responsible constitutional government, however, existed nowhere in Europe in 1815. Even in Great Britain, the cabinet ministers were at least as responsible to the monarch as to the House of Commons. Conservatives were suspicious of written constitutions, associating them with the French Revolution and Napoleon's regimes. They were also certain that no written constitution could embody all the political wisdom needed to govern a state.

Those who espoused liberal political structures often were educated, relatively wealthy people, usually associated with the professions or commercial life, but who were excluded in one manner or another from the existing political processes. Because of their wealth and education, they felt their exclusion was unjustified. Liberals were often academics, members of the learned professions, and people involved in the rapidly expanding commercial and manufacturing segments of the economy. They believed in, and were products of, a career open to talent. The monarchical and aristocratic regimes, as restored after the Congress of Vienna, often failed both to recognize their new status sufficiently and to provide for their economic and professional interests.

Although liberals wanted broader political participation, they did not advocate democracy. What they wanted was to extend representation to the propertied classes. Second only to their hostility to the privileged aristocracies was their contempt for the lower, unpropertied classes. Liberals transformed the eighteenth-century concept of aristocratic liberty into a new concept of privilege based on wealth and property rather than birth. As the French liberal theorist Benjamin Constant (1767–1830) wrote in 1814,

> Those whom poverty keeps in eternal dependence are no more enlightened on public affairs than children, nor are they more interested than foreigners in national prosperity, of which they do not understand the basis and of which they enjoy the advantages only indirectly. Property alone, by giving sufficient leisure, renders a man capable of exercising his political rights.[2]

By the middle of the century, this widely shared attitude meant that throughout Europe liberals had separated themselves from both the rural peasant and the urban working class, a division that was to have important consequences.

Economic Goals The economic goals of nineteenth-century liberals also divided them from working people. The manufacturers of Great Britain, the landed and manufacturing middle class of France, and the commercial interests of Germany and Italy, following the Enlightenment ideas of Adam Smith, sought to abolish the economic restraints associated with mercantilism or the regulated economies of enlightened absolutists. They wanted to manufacture and sell goods freely. To that end, they favored the removal of international tariffs and internal barriers to trade. Economic liberals opposed the old paternalistic legislation that established wages and labor practices by government regulation or by guild privileges. They saw labor as simply one more commodity to be bought and sold freely.

Liberals wanted an economic structure in which people were at liberty to use whatever talents and property they possessed to enrich themselves. Such a structure, they contended, would produce more goods and services for everyone at lower prices and provide the basis for material progress.

Because the social and political circumstances of various countries differed, the specific programs of liberals also differed from one country to another. In Great Britain, the monarchy was already limited, and most individual liberties had been secured. With reform, Parliament could provide more nearly representative government. Links between land, commerce, and industry were in place. France also already had many structures liberals favored. The Napoleonic Code gave France a modern legal system. French liberals could justify calls for greater rights by appealing to the widely accepted "principles of 1789." As in England, representatives of the different economic interests in France had worked together. The problem for liberals in both countries was to protect civil liberties, define the respective powers of the monarch and the elected legislature, and expand the electorate moderately while avoiding democracy. (See "Benjamin Constant Discusses Modern Liberty.")

The complex political situation in German-speaking Europe was different from that in France or Britain, and German liberalism differed accordingly from its French and British counterparts. In the German states and Austria, monarchs and aristocrats offered stiffer resistance to liberal ideas, leaving German liberals with less access to direct political influence. A sharp social divide separated the aristocratic landowning classes, which filled the bureaucracies and officer corps, from the small middle-class commercial and industrial interests. Little or no precedent existed for middle-class participation in the government or the military, and there was no strong tradition of civil or individual liberty. From the time of

[2]Quoted in Frederick B. Artz, *Reaction and Revolution, 1814–1832* (New York: Harper, 1934), p. 94.

BENJAMIN CONSTANT DISCUSSES MODERN LIBERTY

In 1819, the French liberal theorist Benjamin Constant (1767–1830) delivered lectures on the character of ancient and modern liberty. In this passage, he emphasizes the close relationship of modern liberty to economic freedom and a free private life. He then ties the desire for a free private life to the need for a representative government. Modern life did not leave people enough time to make the political commitment that the ancient Greek polis *had required. Consequently, modern citizens turned over much of their political concern and activity to representatives. In this discussion Constant set forth the desire of nineteenth-century liberals to maximize private freedom and to minimize areas of life in which the government might interfere. His argument also provides a foundation for rejecting direct democracy, which he and other liberals associated with the reign of terror and with Napoleon's plebiscites.*

According to Constant, what are the ways in which a modern citizen is free of government control and interference? How does he defend a representative government? On the basis of this passage, do you believe that Constant was opposed to a democratic government?

[Modern liberty] is, for each individual, the right not to be subjected to anything but the law, not to be arrested, or detained, or put to death, or mistreated in any manner, as a result of the arbitrary will of one or several individuals. It is each man's right to express his opinions, to choose and exercise his profession, to dispose of his property and even abuse it, to come and go without obtaining permission and without having to give an account of either his motives or his itinerary. It is the right to associate with other individuals, either to confer about mutual interests or profess the cult that he and his associates prefer or simply to fill his days and hours in the manner most conforming to his inclinations and fantasies. Finally, it is each man's right to exert influence on the administration of government, either through the election of some or all of its public functionaries, or through remonstrances, petitions, and demands which authorities are more or less obliged to take into account. . . .

Just as the liberty we now require is distinct from that of the ancients, so this new liberty itself requires an organization different from that suitable for ancient liberty. For the latter, the more time and energy a man consecrated to the exercise of his political rights, the more free he believed himself to be. Given the type of liberty to which we are now susceptible, the more the exercise of our political rights leaves us time for our private interests, the more precious we find liberty to be. From this . . . stems the necessity of the representative system. The representative system is nothing else than an organization through which a nation unloads on several individuals what it cannot and will not do for itself. Poor men handle their own affairs; rich men hire managers. This is the story of ancient and modern nations. The representative system is the power of attorney given to certain men by the mass of the people who want their interests defended but who nevertheless do not always have the time to defend these interests themselves.

Constant as quoted in S. Holmes, *Benjamin Constant and the Making of Modern Liberalism* (New Haven, CT: Yale University Press, 1984), pp. 66, 74.

Martin Luther in the 1500s through Kant and Hegel in the late eighteenth century, freedom in Germany had meant conformity to a higher moral law rather than participation in politics.

Most German liberals favored a united Germany and looked either to Austria or to Prussia as the instrument of unification. As a result, they were more tolerant of a strong state and monarchical power than other liberals were. They believed that unification would lead to a freer social and political order. The monarchies in Austria and Prussia refused to cooperate with these dreams of unification, frustrating German liberals and forcing them to settle for more modest achievements, such as lowering internal trade barriers.

Relationship of Nationalism to Liberalism Nationalism was not necessarily or even logically linked to liberalism. Indeed, nationalism could be, and often was, directly opposed to liberal political values. Some nationalists wanted their own particular ethnic group to dominate minority national or ethnic groups within a particular region. This was true of the Magyars, who sought political control over non-Magyar peoples living within the historical boundaries of Hungary. Nationalists also often defined their own national group in opposition to other national groups whom they might regard as cultural inferiors or historical enemies. This darker side of nationalism would emerge starkly in the second half of the nineteenth century and would poison European political life for much of the twentieth century. Furthermore, conservative nationalists might seek political autonomy for their own ethnic group but have no intention of establishing liberal political institutions thereafter.

Nonetheless, although liberalism and nationalism were not identical, they were often compatible. By espousing representative government, civil liberties, and economic freedom, nationalist groups in one country could gain the support of liberals elsewhere in Europe who might not otherwise share their nationalist interests. Many nationalists in Germany, Italy, and much of the Austrian Empire adopted this tactic. Some nationalists took other symbolic steps to arouse sympathy. Nationalists in Greece, for example, made Athens their capital because they believed it would associate their struggle for independence with ancient Athenian democracy, which English and French liberals revered.

▼ Conservative Governments: The Domestic Political Order

Despite the challenges of liberalism and nationalism, the domestic political order that the restored conservative institutions of Europe established, particularly in Great Britain and eastern Europe, showed remarkable staying power. Not until World War I did their power and pervasive influence come to an end.

Conservative Outlooks

The major pillars of nineteenth-century **conservatism** were legitimate monarchies, landed aristocracies, and established churches. The institutions themselves were ancient, but the self-conscious alliance of throne, land, and altar was new. In the eighteenth century, these groups had often quarreled. Only the upheavals of the French Revolution and the Napoleonic era transformed them into natural, if sometimes reluctant, allies. In that sense, conservatism as an articulated outlook and set of cooperating institutions was as new a feature on the political landscape as nationalism and liberalism.

The more theoretical political and religious ideas of the conservative classes were associated with thinkers such as Edmund Burke (see Chapter 18) and Friedrich Hegel (see Chapter 19). Conservatives shared other, less formal attitudes forged by the revolutionary experience. The execution of Louis XVI at the hands of radical democrats convinced most monarchs they could trust only aristocratic governments or governments of aristocrats in alliance with the wealthiest middle-class and professional people. The European aristocracies believed that no form of genuinely representative government would protect their property and influence. All conservatives spurned the idea of a written constitution unless they were permitted to write the document themselves. Even then, some rejected the concept.

The churches equally distrusted popular movements, except their own revivals. Ecclesiastical leaders throughout the Continent regarded themselves as entrusted with the educational task of supporting the social and political status quo. They also feared and hated most of the ideas associated with the Enlightenment, because those rational concepts and reformist writings enshrined the critical spirit and undermined revealed religion.

Conservative aristocrats retained their former arrogance, but not their former privileges or their old confidence. They saw themselves as surrounded by enemies and as standing permanently on the defensive against the forces of liberalism, nationalism, and popular sovereignty. They knew that political groups that hated them could topple them. They also understood that revolution in one country could spill over into another.

All of the nations of Europe in the years immediately after 1815 confronted problems arising directly from their entering an era of peace after a quarter century of armed conflict. The war effort, with its loss of life and property and its need to organize people and resources, had distracted attention from other problems. The wartime footing had allowed all the belligerent governments to exercise firm control over their populations. War had fueled economies and had furnished vast areas of employment in armies, navies, military industries, and agriculture. The onset of peace meant citizens could raise new political issues and that economies were no longer geared to supplying military needs. Soldiers and sailors came home and looked for jobs as civilians. The vast demands of the military effort on industries subsided and caused unemployment. The young were no longer growing up in a climate of war and could think about other issues. For all of these reasons, the conservative statesmen who led every major government in 1815 confronted new pressures that would cause various degrees of domestic unrest and would lead them to resort to differing degrees of repression.

Liberalism and Nationalism Resisted in Austria and the Germanies

The early-nineteenth-century statesman who, more than any other epitomized conservatism, was the Austrian prince Metternich (1773–1859). This devoted servant of the Habsburg emperor had been, along with Britain's Viscount Castlereagh (1769–1822), the chief architect of the Vienna settlement. It was Metternich who seemed to exercise chief control over the forces of European reaction.

Dynastic Integrity of the Habsburg Empire The Austrian government could make no serious compromises with the new political forces in Europe. To no other country were the programs of liberalism and nationalism potentially more dangerous. Germans and Hungarians, as well as Poles, Czechs, Slovaks, Slovenes, Italians, Croats, and other ethnic groups, peopled the Habsburg domains. Through client governments, Austria also dominated those parts of the Italian peninsula that it did not rule directly.

For Metternich and other Austrian officials, the recognition of the political rights and aspirations of any of the various national groups would mean the probable

Prince Klemens von Metternich (1773–1859) epitomized nineteenth-century conservatism. Sir Thomas Lawrence (1769–1830), *Clemens Lothar Wenzel, Prince Metternich* (1773–1859), RCIN 404948, OM 905 WC 206. The Royal Collection © 2006, Her Majesty Queen Elizabeth II

dissolution of the empire. If Austria permitted representative government, Metternich feared the national groups would fight their battles internally at the cost of Austria's international influence.

To safeguard dynastic integrity, Austria had to dominate the newly formed German Confederation to prevent the formation of a German national state that might absorb the German-speaking heart of the empire and exclude the other realms the Habsburgs governed. The Congress of Vienna had created the German Confederation to replace the defunct Holy Roman Empire. It consisted of thirty-nine states under Austrian leadership. Each state remained more or less autonomous, but Austria was determined to prevent any movement toward constitutionalism in as many of them as possible.

Defeat of Prussian Reform An important victory for this holding policy came in Prussia in the years immediately after the Congress of Vienna. In 1815, Frederick William III (r. 1797–1840), caught up in the exhilaration that followed the War of Liberation, as Germans called the last part of their conflict with Napoleon, had promised some form of constitutional government. After stalling, he formally reneged on his pledge in 1817. Instead, he created a new Council of State, which, although it improved administrative efficiency, was responsible to him alone.

In 1819, the king moved further from reform. After a major disagreement over the organization of the army, he replaced his reform-minded ministers with hardened conservatives. On their advice, in 1823, Frederick William III established eight provincial estates, or diets. These bodies were dominated by the Junkers and exercised only an advisory function. The old bonds linking monarchy, army, and landholders in Prussia had been reestablished. The members of this alliance would oppose the threats the German nationalists posed to the conservative social and political order.

Student Nationalism and the Carlsbad Decrees To widen their bases of political support, the monarchs of three southern German states—Baden, Bavaria, and Württemberg—had granted constitutions after 1815. None of these constitutions, however, recognized popular sovereignty, and all defined political rights as the gift of the monarch. Yet in the aftermath of the defeat of Napoleon, many young Germans continued to cherish nationalist and liberal expectations.

University students who had grown up during the days of the reforms of Stein and Hardenberg and had read the writings of early German nationalists made up the most important of these groups. Many of them or their friends had fought Napoleon. When they went to the universities, they continued to dream of a united Germany. They formed *Burschenschaften*, or student associations. Like student groups today, these clubs served numerous social functions, one of which was to replace

In May 1820, Karl Sand, a German student and a member of a *Burschenschaft*, was executed for his murder of the conservative playwright August von Kotzebue the previous year. In the eyes of many young German nationalists, Sand was a political martyr.
Bildarchiv Preussischer Kulturbesitz

old provincial attachments with loyalty to the concept of a united German state. It should also be noted that these clubs were often anti-Semitic. (See "Encountering the Past: Gymnastics and German Nationalism," page 604.)

In 1817, in Jena, one such student club organized a large celebration for the fourth anniversary of the Battle of Leipzig and the tercentenary of Luther's Ninety-five Theses. There were bonfires, songs, and processions as more than five hundred people gathered for the festivities. The event made German rulers uneasy, for the student clubs included a few republicans.

Two years later, in March 1819, a student named Karl Sand, a *Burschenschaft* member, assassinated the conservative dramatist August von Kotzebue, who had ridiculed the *Burschenschaft* movement. Sand, who was tried and publicly executed, became a nationalist martyr. Although Sand had acted alone, Metternich used the incident to suppress institutions associated with liberalism.

In July 1819, Metternich persuaded the major German states to issue the Carlsbad Decrees, which dissolved the *Burschenschaften*. The decrees also provided for university inspectors and press censors. (See "The German Confederation Issues the Carlsbad Decrees.") The next year the German Confederation issued the Final Act, which limited the subjects that the constitutional chambers of Bavaria, Württemberg, and Baden could discuss. The measure also asserted the right of the monarchs to resist demands of constitutionalists. For many years thereafter, the secret police of the various German states harassed potential dissidents. In the opinion of the princes, these included almost anyone who sought even moderate social or political change.

Postwar Repression in Great Britain

The years 1819 and 1820 marked a high tide for conservative influence and repression in western as well as eastern Europe. After 1815, Great Britain experienced two years of poor harvests. At the same time, discharged sailors and soldiers and out-of-work industrial workers swelled the ranks of the unemployed.

Lord Liverpool's Ministry and Popular Unrest The Tory ministry of Lord Liverpool (1770–1828) was unprepared to deal with these problems of postwar dislocation. Instead, it sought to protect the interests of the landed and wealthy classes. In 1815, Parliament passed a Corn Law to maintain high prices for domestically produced grain (called "corn" in Britain) by levying import duties on foreign grain. The next year, Parliament replaced the income tax that only the wealthy paid with excise or sales taxes on consumer goods that both the wealthy and the poor paid. These laws continued a legislative trend that marked the abandonment by the British ruling class of its traditional role of paternalistic protector of the poor. In 1799, the Combination Acts had outlawed workers' organizations or unions. During the war, wage protection had been removed. Many in the taxpaying classes wanted to abolish the Poor Law that provided public relief for the destitute and unemployed.

THE GERMAN CONFEDERATION ISSUES THE CARLSBAD DECREES

In 1819, following Karl Sand's assassination of the playwright August von Kotzebue, the German Confederation, deeply fearful of nationalistic student activism, issued the Carlsbad Decrees under the guidance of Prince Metternich. These decrees limited the activities of German students, faculty, and publishers.

By what devices did the government attempt to replace the university discipline of students with government discipline? What kind of actions by faculty and students do these decrees forbid or discourage? How did they seek to make universities institutions of the status quo? How did all of the rules regarding universities seek to isolate students and faculty suspected of dangerous political opinions or actions? How was the censorship of newspapers to work?

REGARDING UNIVERSITY LIFE

1. There shall be appointed for each university a special representative of the ruler of each state, the said representatives to have appropriate instructions and extended powers, and they shall have their place of residence where the university is located. . . .

This representative shall enforce strictly the existing laws and disciplinary regulations; he shall observe with care the attitude shown by the university instructors in their public lectures and registered courses; and he shall, without directly interfering in scientific matters or in teaching methods, give a beneficial direction to the teaching, keeping in view the future attitude of the students. Finally, he shall give . . . attention to everything that may promote morality . . . among the students. . . .

2. The confederated governments mutually pledge themselves to eliminate from the universities or any other public educational institutions all instructors who shall have obviously proved their unfitness for the important work entrusted to them by openly deviating from their duties, or by going beyond the boundaries of their functions, or by abusing their legitimate influence over young minds, or by presenting harmful ideas hostile to public order or subverting existing governmental instructions. . . .

Any instructor who has been removed in this manner becomes ineligible for a position in any other public institution of learning in another state of the Confederation.

3. The laws that have for some time been directed against secret and unauthorized societies in the universities shall be strictly enforced. . . . The special representatives of the government are enjoined to exert great care in watching these organizations.

The governments mutually agree that all individuals who shall be shown to have maintained their membership in secret or unauthorized associations, or shall have taken membership in such associations, shall not be eligible for any public office.

4. No student who shall have been expelled from any university by virtue of a decision of the university senate ratified or initiated by the special representative . . ., shall be admitted by any other university. . . .

REGARDING THE PRESS

1. As long as this edict remains in force, no publication which appears daily, or as a serial not exceeding twenty sheets of printed matter, shall be printed in any state of the Confederation without the prior knowledge and approval of the state officials. . . .

4. Each state of the Confederation is responsible, not only to the state against which the offense is directly committed but to the entire Confederation, for any publication printed within the limits of its jurisdiction, in which the honor or security of other states is impinged upon or their constitution or administration attacked. . . .

7. When a newspaper or periodical is suppressed by a decision of the Diet, the editor of such publication may not within five years edit a similar publication in any state of the Confederation.

Quoted from P. A. G. von Meyer, *Corpus juris confoederationis Germanicae*, 2nd ed., Vol. 2 (Frankfort on Main, 1833), pp. 138 ff., as quoted and translated in Louis L. Snyder, ed., *Documents of German History* (New Brunswick, NJ: Rutgers University Press, 1958), pp. 158–160.

GYMNASTICS AND GERMAN NATIONALISM

TODAY CITIZENS TAKE great pride in the performance of their nations' athletes in the Olympics. This modern link between athletics and nationalism originated in early nineteenth-century Germany with the *Turnverein*, or gymnastic movement.

Its founder was Friedrich Ludwig Jahn (1778–1852), later known as Turnvater Jahn on the grounds that he was the father of the movement, which he described as "Love of the Fatherland through Gymnastics." He was also an innovator in gymnastic equipment, credited with inventing the parallel bars and improving the pommel vault.

Jahn became a fervent patriot when he saw the German states and particularly Prussia humiliated by Napoleon. He attacked what he regarded as foreign influences on German life, including that of German Jews. Jahn was convinced that Germans must cultivate their bodily strength to overcome external enemies. In 1811, he established an open-air gymnasium in a meadow near Berlin. The young men who attended this gymnasium and others that he soon founded throughout the German states saw themselves as an advanced nationalistic guard.

After the defeat of Napoleon in 1815, gymnastic clubs spread across Germany, fostered nationalist sentiment, and challenged the social and political status quo. The clubs embodied social equality. All members wore plain gray exercise uniforms that Jahn had designed and addressed each other with the familiar "Du." Conservatives were suspicious. They saw these early gymnastic clubs as a state within the various disunited German states. For a time Prussia banned gymnastics and sent Jahn to prison.

During the 1840s, however, the gymnastic movement revived. Germany soon had tens of thousands of adult gymnasts, and the clubs became increasingly nationalistic, often excluding Jews. After German unification in 1870, national festivals often featured gymnastic performances, and national monuments had areas for gymnastic display. Political figures from Bismarck to Hitler cultivated their links to the gymnastic societies. The connection between gymnastics and German nationalism was so strong that even liberal Germans who immigrated to the United States founded *Turnvereins* in their new homes.

Source: Liah Greenfeld, *Nationalism: Five Roads to Modernity* (Cambridge, MA: Harvard University Press, 1992), pp. 367–370; Matthew Levinger, *Enlightened Nationalism: The Transformation of Prussian Political Culture, 1806–1848* (New York: Oxford University Press, 2000); George L. Mosse, *The Nationalization of the Masses: Political Symbolism and Mass Movements in Germany from the Napoleonic Wars through the Third Reich* (New York: New American Library, 1975), p. 128.

What factors turned Jahn to nationalism?

Why did he associate nationalism with physical strength? How could the *Turnverein* movement spread easily in the Germanies?

Turnvater Jahn encouraged German gymnasts to use athletic equipment in their exercises. Here at a Bonn gymnastic festival of 1872 an athlete works out on a pommel horse, a piece of athletic equipment that predated Jahn, but the design of which he improved. Also note the athletic clothing which emphasizes egalitarian social relations among the athletes.

In light of these policies and the postwar economic downturn, it is hardly surprising that the lower social orders began to doubt the wisdom of their rulers and to demand political changes. Mass meetings called for the reform of Parliament. Reform clubs were organized. Radical newspapers, such as William Cobbett's *Political Registrar*, demanded change. In the hungry, restive agricultural and industrial workers, the government could see only images of continental *sans-culottes* ready to hang aristocrats from the nearest lamppost. Government ministers regarded radical leaders, such as Cobbett (1763–1835), Major John Cartwright (1740–1824), and Henry "Orator" Hunt (1773–1835), as demagogues who were seducing the people away from allegiance to their natural leaders.

The government's answer to the discontent was repression. In December 1816, an unruly mass meeting took place at Spa Fields near London. This disturbance gave Parliament an excuse to pass the Coercion Acts of March 1817, which temporarily suspended *habeas corpus* and extended existing laws against seditious gatherings.

"Peterloo" and the Six Acts This initial repression, in combination with improved harvests, calmed the political landscape for a time. By 1819, however, the people were restive again. In the industrial north, well-organized mass meetings demanded the reform of Parliament. The radical reform campaign culminated on August 16, 1819, with a meeting in the industrial city of Manchester at Saint Peter's Fields. Royal troops and the local militia were on hand to ensure order. As the speeches were about to begin, a local magistrate ordered the militia to move into the audience. The result was panic and death. At least eleven people in the crowd were killed; scores were injured. The event became known as the Peterloo Massacre, a phrase that drew a contemptuous comparison with Wellington's victory at Waterloo.

Peterloo had been the act of local officials, whom the Liverpool ministry felt it must support. The cabinet also decided to act once and for all to end these troubles. Most of the radical leaders were arrested and imprisoned. In December 1819, a few months after the German Carlsbad Decrees, Parliament passed a series of laws called the Six Acts, which (1) forbade large unauthorized, public meetings, (2) raised the fines for seditious libel, (3) speeded up the trials of political agitators, (4) increased newspaper taxes, (5) prohibited the training of armed groups, and (6) allowed local officials to search homes in certain disturbed counties. In effect, the Six Acts attempted to prevent radical leaders from agitating and to give the authorities new powers.

Two months after the passage of the Six Acts, the Cato Street Conspiracy was unearthed. Under the guidance of a possibly demented man named Arthur Thistlewood (1770–1820), a group of extreme radicals had plotted to blow up the entire British cabinet. The plot was foiled. The leaders were arrested and tried, and five of them were hanged. Although little more than a half-baked plot, the conspiracy helped discredit the movement for parliamentary reform.

Bourbon Restoration in France

The abdication of Napoleon in 1814 opened the way for a restoration of Bourbon rule in the homeland of the great revolution. The new king was the former count of Provence and a brother of Louis XVI. The son of the executed monarch had died in prison. Royalists had regarded the dead boy as Louis XVII, and so his

The French Bourbons were restored to the throne in 1815 but would rule only until 1830. This picture shows Louis XVIII, seated, second from left, and his brother, the count of Artois, who would become Charles X, standing on the left. Notice the bust of Henry IV in the background, placed there to associate the restored rulers with their popular late-sixteenth–early-seventeenth-century forebearer. Bildarchiv Preussischer Kulturbesitz uncle became Louis XVIII (r. 1814–1824). This fat, awkward man had become a political realist during his more than twenty years of exile. He understood he could not turn back the clock to 1789. France had undergone too many irreversible changes. Consequently, Louis XVIII agreed to become a constitutional monarch, but under a constitution of his own making called the Charter.

The Charter The Charter provided for a hereditary monarchy and a bicameral legislature. The monarch appointed the upper house, the Chamber of Peers, modeled on the British House of Lords; a narrow franchise with a high property qualification elected the lower house, the Chamber of Deputies. The Charter guaranteed most of the rights the Declaration of the Rights of Man and Citizen had enumerated. There was to be religious toleration, but Roman Catholicism was designated the official religion of the nation. Most importantly for thousands of French people at all social levels who had profited from the revolution, the Charter promised not to challenge the property rights of the current owners of land that had been confiscated from aristocrats and the church. With this provision, Louis XVIII hoped to reconcile to his regime those who had benefited from the revolution.

Ultraroyalism This moderate spirit did not penetrate deeply into the ranks of royalist supporters whose families had suffered during the revolution. Rallying around Louis's brother and heir, the count of Artois (1757–1836), those people who were more royalist than the monarch now demanded their revenge. In the months after Napoleon's final defeat at Waterloo, royalists in the south and west carried out a White Terror against former revolutionaries and supporters of the deposed emperor. The king could do little or nothing to halt this bloodbath. Similar extreme royalist sentiment could be found in the Chamber of Deputies. The ultraroyalist majority elected in 1816 proved so dangerously reactionary that the king soon dissolved the chamber. The second election returned a more moderate majority. Several years of political give-and-take followed, with the king making mild accommodations to liberals.

In February 1820, however, the duke of Berri, son of Artois and heir to the throne after his father, was murdered by a lone assassin. The ultraroyalists persuaded Louis XVIII that the murder was the result of his ministers' cooperation with liberal politicians, and the king responded with repressive measures. New electoral laws gave wealthy electors two votes. Press censorship was imposed, and people suspected of dangerous political activity were made subject to easy arrest. By 1821, the government placed secondary education under the control of the Roman Catholic bishops.

All these actions revealed the basic contradiction of the French restoration. By the early 1820s, the veneer of constitutionalism had worn away. Liberals were being driven out of politics and into a near illegal status.

▼ The Conservative International Order

At the Congress of Vienna, the major powers—Russia, Austria, Prussia, and Great Britain—had agreed to consult with each other from time to time on matters affecting Europe as a whole. Such consultation was one of the new departures in international relations the Congress achieved. The vehicle for this consultation was a series of postwar congresses, or conferences. Later, as differences arose among the powers, the consultations became more informal. This new arrangement for resolving mutual foreign policy issues was known as the ***Concert of Europe***. It prevented one nation from taking a major action in international affairs without working in concert with and obtaining the assent of the others. The initial goal of the Concert of Europe was to maintain the balance of power against new French aggression and against the military might of Russia. The Concert continued to function, however, on large and small issues until the third quarter of the century. Its goal—a novel one in European affairs—was to maintain the peace. In that respect, although the great powers sought to maintain conservative domestic governments, they were taking genuinely new steps to regulate their international relations.

The Congress System

In the years immediately after the Congress of Vienna, the new **congress system** of mutual cooperation and consultation functioned well. The first congress took place in 1818 at Aix-la-Chapelle in Germany near the border of Belgium. As a result of this gathering, the four major powers removed their troops from France, which had paid its war reparations, and readmitted France to good standing among the European nations. Despite unanimity on these decisions, the conference was not without friction. Tsar Alexander I (r. 1801–1825) suggested that the Quadruple Alliance (see Chapter 19) agree to uphold the borders and the existing governments of all European countries. Castlereagh, representing Britain, flatly rejected the proposal. He contended the Quadruple Alliance was intended only to prevent future French aggression. These disagreements appeared somewhat academic until revolutions broke out in southern Europe.

THE PERIOD OF POLITICAL REACTION

1814	French monarchy restored
1815	Russia, Austria, Prussia form Holy Alliance
1815	Russia, Austria, Prussia, and Britain renew Quadruple Alliance
1818	Congress of Aix-la-Chapelle
1819 (July)	Carlsbad Decrees
1819 (August 16)	Peterloo Massacre
1819 (December)	Great Britain passes Six Acts
1820 (January)	Spanish revolution
1820 (October)	Congress of Troppau
1821 (January)	Congress of Laibach
1821 (February)	Greek revolution
1822	Congress of Verona
1823	France helps crush Spanish revolution

The Spanish Revolution of 1820

When the Bourbon Ferdinand VII of Spain (r. 1814–1833) was placed on his throne after Napoleon's downfall, he had promised to govern according to a written constitution. Once in power, however, he ignored his pledge, dissolved the *Cortés* (the parliament), and ruled alone. In 1820, army officers who were about to be sent to suppress revolution in Spain's Latin American colonies rebelled. In March, Ferdinand once again announced he would abide by the provisions of the constitution. For the time being, the revolution had succeeded.

Almost at the same time, in July 1820, revolution erupted in Naples, where the king of the Two Sicilies quickly accepted a constitution. There were other, lesser revolts in Italy, but none of them succeeded.

These events frightened the ever-nervous Metternich. Italian disturbances were especially troubling to him. Austria hoped to dominate the peninsula to provide a buffer against the spread of revolution on its own southern flank. The other powers were divided on the best course of action. Britain opposed joint intervention in either Italy or Spain. Metternich turned to Prussia and Russia, the other members of the Holy Alliance formed in 1815, for support. The three eastern powers, along with unofficial delegations from Britain and France, met at the Congress of Troppau in late October 1820. Led by Tsar Alexander, the members of the Holy Alliance issued the Protocol of Troppau. This declaration asserted that stable governments might intervene to restore order in countries experiencing revolution. Yet even Russia hesitated to authorize Austrian intervention in Italian affairs. That decision was finally reached in January 1821 at the Congress of Laibach. Shortly thereafter, Austrian troops marched into Naples and restored the absolutist rule of the king of the Two Sicilies. From then on, Metternich attempted to foster policies that would improve the efficient administration of the various Italian governments so as to increase their support among their subjects.

The final postwar congress took place in October 1822 at Verona. Its primary purpose was to resolve the situation in Spain. Once again, Britain balked at joint action. Shortly before the meeting, Castlereagh had committed suicide. George Canning (1770–1827), the new foreign minister, was much less sympathetic to Metternich's goals. At Verona, Britain, in effect, withdrew from continental affairs. Austria, Prussia, and Russia agreed to support French intervention in Spain. In April 1823, a French army crossed the Pyrenees and within a few months suppressed the Spanish revolution. French troops remained in Spain to prop up King Ferdinand until 1827.

What did not happen in Spain, however, was as important for the new international order as what did happen. France did not use its intervention as an excuse to aggrandize its power or increase its territory. The same had been true of all the other interventions under the congress system. The great powers authorized these interventions to preserve or restore conservative regimes, not to conquer territory for themselves. Their goal was to maintain the international order established at Vienna. Such a situation stood in sharp contrast to the alliances to invade or confiscate territory that the European powers had made during the eighteenth century and the wars of the French Revolution and Napoleon. This new mode of international restraint through formal and informal consultation prevented war among the great powers until the middle of the century and averted a general European conflict until 1914. As one historian has commented, "The statesmen of the Vienna generation . . . did not so much fear war because they thought it would bring revolution as because they had learned from bitter experience that war was revolution."[3]

The Congress of Verona and the Spanish intervention had a second diplomatic result. The new British foreign minister, George Canning, was much more interested in British commerce and trade than Castlereagh had been. Thus Canning sought to prevent the extension of European reaction to Spain's colonies in Latin America, which were then in revolt (see page 608). He intended to exploit these South American revolutions to break Spain's old trading monopoly with its colonies and gain access for Britain to Latin American trade. To that end, he supported the American Monroe Doctrine in 1823, prohibiting further colonization and intervention by European powers in the Americas.

[3]Paul W. Schroeder, *The Transformation of European Politics, 1763–1848* (Oxford: Clarendon Press, 1994), p. 802.

Britain soon recognized the Spanish colonies as independent states. Through the rest of the century, British commercial interests dominated Latin America. Canning may thus be said to have brought the War of Jenkins's Ear (1739) to a successful conclusion.

Revolt Against Ottoman Rule in the Balkans

The Greek Revolution of 1821 While the powers were plotting conservative interventions in Italy and Spain, a third Mediterranean revolt erupted—in Greece. The Greek revolution became one of the most famous of the century because it attracted the support and participation of many illustrious writers. Liberals throughout Europe, who were seeing their own hopes crushed at home, imagined that the ancient Greek democracy was being reborn. Lord Byron went to fight in Greece and died there in 1824 (of cholera). Philhellenic ("pro-Greek") societies were founded in nearly every major country. The struggle was posed in the eighteenth-century Enlightenment terms of Western liberal Greek freedom against the Asian oriental despotism of the Ottoman Empire.

As discussed in Chapter 13, the Ottoman Empire had not changed its fundamental political or economic structures during the eighteenth century even as the major European states grew richer and more powerful. Ottoman weakness and instability troubled European diplomacy throughout the nineteenth century, raising what was known as "the Eastern Question": What should the European powers do about the Ottoman inability to assure political and administrative stability in its possessions in and around the eastern Mediterranean? Most of the major powers had a keen interest in those territories. Russia and Austria coveted land in the Balkans. France and Britain were concerned with the empire's commerce and with control of key naval positions in the eastern Mediterranean. Also at issue was the treatment of the Christian inhabitants of the empire and access to the Christian shrines in the Holy Land. The goals of the great powers often conflicted with the desire for independence of the many national groups in the Ottoman Empire. Yet, because the powers had little desire to strengthen the empire, they were often more sympathetic to nationalistic aspirations there than elsewhere in Europe.

These conflicting interests, as well as mutual distrust, prevented any direct intervention in Greek affairs for several years. Eventually, however, Britain, France, and Russia concluded that an independent Greece would benefit their strategic interests and would not threaten their domestic security. In 1827, they signed the Treaty of London, demanding Turkish recognition of Greek independence, and sent a joint fleet to support the Greek revolt. In 1828, Russia sent troops into the Ottoman holdings in what is today Romania, ultimately gaining control of that territory in 1829 with the Treaty of Adrianople. The treaty also stipulated the Turks would allow Britain, France, and Russia to decide the future of Greece. In 1830, a second Treaty of London declared Greece an independent kingdom. Two years later, Otto I (r. 1832–1862), the son of the king of Bavaria, was chosen to be the first king of the new Greek kingdom.

Serbian Independence The year 1830 also saw the establishment of a second independent state on the Balkan peninsula. Since the late eighteenth century, Serbia had sought independence from the Ottoman Empire. During the Napoleonic wars, its fate had been linked to Russian policy and Russian relations with the Ottoman Empire. Between 1804 and 1813, a remarkable Serbian leader, Kara George (1762–1817), had led a guerrilla war against the Ottomans. This ultimately unsuccessful revolution helped build national self-identity and attracted the interest of the great powers.

In 1815 and 1816, a new leader, Milos Obrenovitch (1780–1860), succeeded in negotiating greater administrative autonomy for some Serbian territory, but most Serbs lived outside the borders of this new entity. In 1830, the Ottoman sultan formally granted independence to Serbia, and by the late 1830s, the major powers granted it diplomatic recognition. Serbia's political structure, however, remained in doubt for many years.

In 1833, Milos, now a hereditary prince, pressured the Ottoman authorities to extend the borders of Serbia, which they did. These new boundaries persisted until 1878. Serbian leaders continued to seek additional territory, however, creating tensions with Austria. The status of minorities, particularly Muslims, within Serbian territory, was also a problem.

In the mid-1820s, Russia, which like Serbia was a Slav state and Eastern Orthodox in religion, became Serbia's formal protector. In 1856, Serbia came under the collective protection of the great powers, but the special relationship between Russia and Serbia would continue until the First World War and would play a decisive role in the outbreak of that conflict.

▼ The Wars of Independence in Latin America

The wars of the French Revolution and, more particularly, those of Napoleon sparked movements for independence from European domination throughout Latin

A Closer LOOK

AN ENGLISH POET APPEARS AS AN ALBANIAN

THE FAMOUS ENGLISH poet George Gordon, Lord Byron (1788–1824) was one of many European liberals who went to Greece to aid the cause of its independence. He died there of fever in 1824.

His portrait here in Albanian dress was intended to demonstrate his willingness to exchange Western European clothes for what many of his contemporaries would have regarded as the exotic garb of the Balkan peoples. The costume also suggested that Byron, whose personal life was regarded as scandalous, did not intend to see his cultural identity shaped solely by England.

The portrait also demonstrated that Byron, the Romantic poet, saw himself capable of embodying many different personalities.

Byron's association with liberal causes indicated that Romantic writers, who were often seen as supporting conservatism, could also embrace liberal movements.

The Granger Collection, NY

To examine this image in an interactive fashion, please go to www.myhistorylab.com

PEARSON myhistorylab

America. In less than two decades, between 1804 and 1824, France was driven from Haiti, Portugal lost control of Brazil, and Spain was forced to withdraw from all of its American empire except Cuba and Puerto Rico. Three centuries of Iberian colonial government over the South American continent ended. These wars brought to a conclusion the era of European political domination and direct economic exploitation of the American continents that had begun with the encounter between the peoples of the New World and Spain at the end of the fifteenth century. The period of transatlantic history beginning with the American Revolution and ending with the Latin American Wars of Independence thus constituted the first era of decolonization from European rule. (See Map 20–1.)

Toussaint L'Ouverture (1746–1803) began the revolt that led to Haitian independence in 1804. Library of Congress

Revolution in Haiti

Between 1791 and 1804, the French colony of Haiti achieved independence. This event was of key importance for two reasons. First, it was sparked by policies of the French Revolution overflowing into its New World Empire. Second, the Haitian Revolution demonstrated that slaves of African origins could lead a revolt against white masters and mulatto freemen. The example of the Haitian Revolution for years thereafter terrified slaveholders throughout the Americas.

The relationship between slaves and masters on Haiti had been filled with violence throughout the eighteenth century. The French colonial masters had frequently used racial divisions between black slaves and mulatto freemen to their own political advantage. Once the French Revolution had broken out in France, the French National Assembly in 1791 decreed that free property-owning mulattos on Haiti should enjoy the same rights as white plantation owners. The Colonial Assembly in Haiti resisted the orders from France.

In 1791, a full-fledged slave rebellion shook Haiti. It arose as a result of a secret conspiracy among the slaves. François-Dominique Toussaint L'Ouverture (1743?–1803), himself a former slave, quickly emerged as its leader. The rebellion involved enormous violence and loss of life on both sides. Although the slave rebellion collapsed, mulattos and free black people on Haiti, who hoped to gain the rights the French National Assembly had promised, then took up arms against the white colonial masters. French officials sent by the revolutionary government in Paris soon backed them. Slaves now came to the aid of an invading French force, and in early 1793, the French abolished slavery in Haiti.

By this time both Spain and Great Britain were attempting to intervene in Haitian events to expand their own influence in the Caribbean. Both were opposed to the end of slavery and both coveted Haiti's rich sugar-producing lands. Toussaint L'Ouverture and his force of ex-slaves again supported the French against the Spanish and the British. By 1800, his army had

MAP EXPLORATION

Interactive map: To explore this map further, go to **www.myhistorylab.com**

Map 20–1 **LATIN AMERICA IN 1830** By 1830 most of Latin America had been liberated from Europe. This map shows the initial borders of the states of the region with the dates of their independence. The United Provinces of La Plata formed the nucleus of what later became Argentina.

achieved dominance throughout the island of Hispanola. He imposed an authoritarian constitution on Haiti and made himself Governor-General for life, but he preserved formal ties with France.

The French government under Napoleon distrusted L'Ouverture and feared that his example would undermine French authority elsewhere in the Caribbean and North America. In 1802, Napoleon sent an army to Haiti and eventually captured L'Overture, who was sent back to France where he died in prison in 1803. Other Haitian military leaders of slave origin, the most important of whom was Jean-Jacques Dessalines (1758–1806), continued to resist. When Napoleon found himself again at war with Britain in 1803, he decided to abandon his American empire, selling Louisiana to the United States and withdrawing his forces from Haiti. Thus, the Haitian slave-led rebellion became the first successful assault on colonial government in Latin America. France formally recognized Haitian independence in 1804.

Wars of Independence on the South American Continent

Haiti's revolution, which involved the popular uprising of a repressed social group, proved to be the great exception in the Latin American drive for liberty from European masters. Generally speaking, on the South American continent, the Creole elite—merchants, landowners, and professional people of Spanish descent—led the movements against Spain and Portugal. Few Native Americans, black people, mestizos, mulattos, or slaves became involved in or benefited from the end of Iberian rule. Indeed, the example of the Haitian slave revolt haunted the Creoles, as did the revolts of Indians in the Andes in 1780 and 1781. The Creoles were determined that any drive for political independence from Spain and Portugal should not cause social disruption or the loss of their own privileges. In this respect, the Creole revolutionaries were not unlike American revolutionaries in the southern colonies, who wanted to reject British rule but keep their slaves, or French revolutionaries, who wanted to depose the king but not to extend liberty to the French working class.

Creole Discontent Creole discontent with Spanish colonial government had many sources. (The Brazilian situation will be discussed separately. See page 614.) Latin American merchants wanted to trade more freely within the region and with North American and European markets. They wanted commercial regulations that would benefit them rather than Spain. They had also resented increases in taxation by the Spanish crown.

Creoles resented Spanish policies that favored *peninsulares*—white people born in Spain—for political patronage, including appointments in the colonial government, church, and army. The Creoles believed the *peninsulares* secured all the best positions. Seen in this light, the royal patronage system represented another device with which Spain extracted wealth and income from America to benefit its own people in Europe rather than its colonial subjects.

Creole leaders had read the Enlightenment philosophes and regarded their reforms as potentially beneficial to the region. They were also well aware of the events and the political philosophy of the American Revolution. To transform Creole discontent into revolt against the Spanish government required more, however, than reform programs and revolutionary examples. That transforming event occurred in Europe when Napoleon invaded Portugal in 1807 and made his own brother king of Spain in 1808. The Portuguese royal family fled to Brazil and established its government there, but the Bourbon monarchy of Spain had, for the time being, been overthrown. That situation created an imperial political vacuum throughout Spanish Latin America and gave Creole leaders both the opportunity and the necessity to act.

The Creole elite feared a liberal Napoleonic monarchy in Spain would attempt to impose reforms in Latin America that would harm their economic and social interests. They also feared a French-controlled Spain would try to drain the region of the wealth and resources Napoleon needed for his wars. To protect their interests and to seize the opportunity to direct their own political destiny, between 1808 and 1810 Creole *juntas*, or political committees, claimed the right to govern different regions of Latin America. Many of them insincerely declared they were ruling in the name of the deposed Spanish Bourbon monarch Ferdinand VII. After the establishment of these local *juntas*, Spain never effectively reestablished its authority in South America, although it would take ten years or more of politically and economically exhausting warfare before Latin American independence became permanent. The establishment of the *juntas* also ended the privileges of the *peninsulares*, whose welfare had always depended on the favors of the Spanish crown. Creoles now took over positions in the government and army.

San Martín in Río de la Plata The vast size of Latin America, its geographical barriers, its distinct regional differences, and the absence of an even marginally integrated economy meant there would be several different paths to independence. The first region to assert itself was the Río de la Plata, or modern Argentina. The center of revolt was the city of Buenos Aires, whose citizens, as early as 1806, had fought off a British invasion and thus had learned they could protect themselves rather than have to rely on Spain. In 1810, the *junta* in Buenos Aires not only thrust off Spanish authority, but also sent forces into Paraguay and Uruguay to liberate them from Spain. These armies were defeated, but Spain nevertheless lost control of both areas. Paraguay asserted its own independence. Brazil took over Uruguay.

These early defeats did not discourage the Buenos Aires government, which determined to liberate Peru, the stronghold of royalist power and loyalty on the continent. By 1817, José de San Martín (1778–1850), the leading general of the Río de la Plata forces, led an army in a daring march over the Andes Mountains and occupied Santiago in Chile, where the Chilean independence leader Bernardo O'Higgins (1778–1842) was established as the supreme dictator. From Santiago, San Martín organized a fleet that, in 1820, carried his army by sea to Peru. The next year, San Martín drove royalist forces from Lima and became Protector of Peru.

Simón Bolívar's Liberation of Venezuela While the army of San Martín had been liberating the southern portion of the continent, Simón Bolívar (1783–1830) had been pursuing a similar task in the north. Bolívar had been involved in the organization of a liberating *junta* in Caracas, Venezuela, in 1810. He was a firm advocate of both independence and a republic. Between 1811 and 1814, civil war broke out throughout Venezuela as both royalists, on one hand, and slaves and *llaneros* (Venezuelan cowboys), on the other, challenged the authority of the republican government. Bolívar had to go into exile first in Colombia and then in Jamaica. In 1816, with help from Haiti, he returned to the continent. He first captured Bogotá, capital of New Granada (including modern Colombia, Bolivia, and Ecuador), to secure a base for an attack on Venezuela. The tactic worked. By the summer of 1821, Bolívar's forces captured Caracas, and he was named president.

A year later, in July 1822, the armies of Bolívar and San Martín joined as they moved to liberate Quito, the capital of what is today Ecuador. At a famous meeting in Guayaquil, the two liberators sharply disagreed about the future political structure of Latin America. San Martín believed the peoples of the region required monarchies; Bolívar maintained his republicanism. Not long after the meeting, San Martín quietly retired from public life and went into exile in Europe. Meanwhile, Bolívar deliberately allowed the political situation in Peru to fall into confusion, and in 1823, he sent in troops to establish his control. On December 9, 1824, at the Battle of Ayacucho, the liberating army crushed the main Spanish royalist forces. This battle marked the end of Spain's effort to retain its South American empire.

Simón Bolívar. Bolívar was the liberator of much of Latin America. He inclined toward a policy of political liberalism.

Independence in New Spain

The drive for independence in New Spain, which included present-day Mexico as well as Texas, California, and the rest of the southwest United States, illustrates better than in any other region the socially conservative outcome of the Latin American colonial revolutions. As elsewhere, a local governing *junta* was organized in 1808. Before it had undertaken any significant measures, however, a Creole priest, Miguel Hidalgo y Costilla (1753–1811) in 1810, issued a call for rebellion to the Indians in his parish. They and other repressed groups of black and mestizo urban and rural workers responded. Father Hidalgo set forth a program of social reform, including hints of changes in landholding. Soon he stood at the head of a loosely organized group of 80,000 followers, who captured several major cities and then marched on Mexico City. Hidalgo's forces and the royalist army that opposed them committed many atrocities. In July 1811, the revolutionary priest was captured and executed. Leadership of his movement then fell to José María Morelos y Pavón (1765–1815), a mestizo priest. Far more radical than Hidalgo, he called for an end to forced labor and for substantial land reforms. He was executed in 1815, ending five years of popular uprising.

The uprising and its demand for fundamental social reforms united all conservative political groups in Mexico, both Creole and Spanish. These groups opposed any kind of reform that might diminish their privileges. In 1820, however, an unexpected challenge arose to their recently achieved security. As already discussed, the revolution in Spain had forced Ferdinand VII to accept a liberal constitution. Conservative Mexicans feared the new liberal monarchy would attempt to impose liberal reforms on Mexico. Therefore, for the most conservative of reasons, they rallied behind a former royalist general, Augustín de Iturbide (1783–1824), who declared Mexico independent of Spain in 1821. Shortly thereafter, Iturbide was declared emperor. His own regime did not last long, but he had created an independent Mexico, governed by groups determined to resist significant social reform.

Brazilian Independence

Brazilian independence, in contrast to that of Spanish Latin America, came relatively simply and peacefully. As already noted, the Portuguese royal family, along with several thousand government officials and members of the court, fled to Brazil in 1807. Their arrival immediately transformed Rio de Janeiro into a royal city. The prince regent João addressed many of the local complaints, equivalent to those of the Spanish Creoles, by, for example, taking measures that expanded trade. In 1815, he made Brazil a kingdom, which meant it was no longer to be regarded merely as a colony of Portugal. This change was in many respects long overdue, since Brazil was far larger and more prosperous than Portugal itself. Then, in 1820, a revolution occurred in Portugal, and its leaders demanded João's return to Lisbon. They also demanded the return of Brazil to colonial status. João, who had become King João VI in 1816 (r. 1816–1826), returned to Portugal but left his son Dom Pedro as regent in Brazil and encouraged him to be sympathetic to the political aspirations of the Brazilians. In September 1822, Dom Pedro embraced the cause of Brazilian independence against the recolonizing efforts of Portugal. By the end of the year, he had become emperor of an independent Brazil, which remained a monarchy under his son and successor Dom Pedro II (r. 1831–1889) until 1889. Thus, in contrast to virtually all other nations of Latin America, Brazil achieved independence in a way that left no real dispute as to where the center of political authority lay.

Two other factors aided the peaceful transition to independence in Brazil. First, the political and social elite of Brazil wanted to avoid the destruction that the wars of independence had unleashed in the Spanish American Empire. Second, these leaders had every intention of preserving slavery. The wars of independence elsewhere had generally led to the abolition of slavery or moved the new states closer to abolishing it. Warfare in Brazil might have caused social turmoil with similar consequences.

▼ The Conservative Order Shaken in Europe

During the first half of the 1820s, the restored conservative order had, in general, successfully resisted the forces of liberalism. The two exceptions to this success, the Greek Revolution and the Latin American wars of independence, both occurred on the periphery of the European world. Beginning in the mid-1820s, however, the conservative governments of Russia, France, and Great Britain faced new political discontent. (See Map 20–2.) In Russia the result was suppression, in France revolution, and in Britain, accommodation. Belgium emerged as a newly indepent state.

Russia: The Decembrist Revolt of 1825

Tsar Alexander I had come to the throne in 1801 after a palace coup against his father, Tsar Paul (r. 1796–1801). After flirting with Enlightenment ideas, Alexander

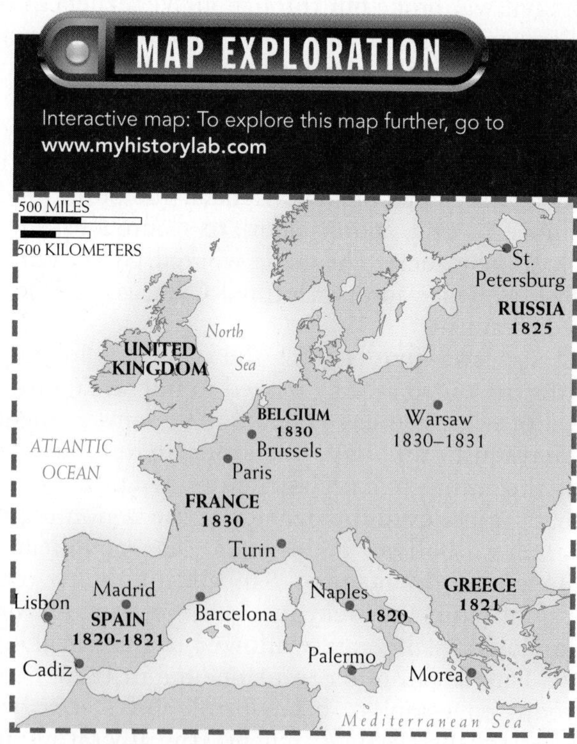

Map 20–2 **CENTERS OF REVOLUTION, 1820–1831** The conservative order imposed by the great powers in post-Napoleonic Europe was challenged by various uprisings and revolutions, beginning in 1820–1821 in Spain, Naples, and Greece and spreading to Russia, Poland, France, and Belgium later in the decade.

turned permanently away from reform. Both at home and abroad, he took the lead in suppressing liberalism and nationalism. There would be no significant challenge to tsarist autocracy until his death.

Unrest in the Army As Russian forces drove Napoleon's army across Europe and then occupied defeated France, many Russian officers were exposed to the ideas of the French Revolution and the Enlightenment. Some of them, realizing how economically backward and politically stifled their own nation remained, developed reformist sympathies. Unable to express themselves openly because of Alexander's repressive policies, they formed secret societies. One of these, the Southern Society, led by an officer named Pestel, advocated representative government and the abolition of serfdom. Pestel himself even favored limited independence for Poland and democracy. Another secret society, the Northern Society, was more moderate. It favored constitutional monarchy and the abolition of serfdom but wanted to protect the interests of the aristocracy. Both societies were small and often in conflict with each other. They agreed only that Russia's government must change. Sometime during 1825, they apparently decided to carry out a *coup d'état* in 1826.

Dynastic Crisis In late November 1825, Tsar Alexander I died unexpectedly. His death created two crises. The first was dynastic. Alexander had no direct heir. His brother Constantine (1779–1831), the next in line to the throne and at the time the commander of Russian forces in occupied Poland, had married a woman who was not of royal blood. He had thus excluded himself from the throne and was more than willing to renounce any claim to it. Through a series of secret instructions made public only after his death, Alexander had named his younger brother, Nicholas (r. 1825–1855), as the new tsar.

Once Alexander was dead, the legality of these instructions became uncertain. Constantine acknowledged Nicholas as tsar, and Nicholas acknowledged Constantine. This family muddle continued for about three weeks, during which, to the astonishment of all Europe, Russia actually had no ruler. Then, in early December, the army command told Nicholas about a conspiracy among certain officers. Able to wait no longer, Nicholas had himself declared tsar, much to the delight of the by-now-exasperated Constantine.

The second crisis then unfolded. Junior officers had indeed plotted to rally the troops under their command to the cause of reform. On December 26, 1825, the army was to take the oath of allegiance to Nicholas, who was less popular than Constantine and regarded as more conservative. Most regiments took the oath, but the Moscow regiment, whose chief officers, surprisingly, were not secret society members, marched into the Senate Square in Saint Petersburg and refused to swear allegiance. Instead, they called for a constitution and Constantine as tsar. Attempts to settle the situation peacefully failed. Late in the afternoon, Nicholas ordered the cavalry and the artillery to attack the insurgents. More than sixty people were killed. Early in 1826, Nicholas himself presided over the commission that investigated the Decembrist Revolt and the secret army societies. Five of the plotters were executed, and more than a hundred others were exiled to Siberia.

Although the Decembrist Revolt failed completely, it was the first rebellion in modern Russian history whose instigators had had specific political goals. They wanted a constitutional government and the abolition of serfdom. As the century passed, the political martyrdom of the Decembrists came to symbolize the yearnings of the never numerous Russian liberals.

The Autocracy of Nicholas I Although Nicholas was neither an ignorant nor a bigoted reactionary, he came to symbolize the most extreme form of nineteenth-century autocracy. He knew economic growth and social improvement in Russia required reform, but he was afraid of change. In 1842, he told his State Council, "There is no doubt that serfdom, in its present form, is a flagrant evil which everyone realizes, yet to attempt to remedy it now would be, of course, an evil more disastrous."[4] To remove serfdom would necessarily, in his view, have undermined the nobles' support of the tsar. So Nicholas turned his back on this and practically all other reforms. Literary and political censorship and a widespread system of surveillance by secret police flourished throughout his reign. There was little attempt to forge even an efficient and honest administration. Nicholas's only significant reform was a codification of Russian law, published in 1833.

Official Nationality In place of reform, Nicholas and his closest advisers embraced a program called Official Nationality. Presiding over this program was Count S. S. Uvarov, minister of education from 1833 to 1849. Its slogan, published repeatedly in government documents, newspapers, journals, and schoolbooks, was "Orthodoxy, Autocracy, and Nationalism." The Russian Orthodox church was to provide the basis for morality, education, and intellectual life. The church, which, since the days of Peter the Great, had been an arm of the secular government, controlled the schools and universities. Young Russians were taught to accept their place in life and to spurn social mobility.

Autocracy meant the unrestrained power of the tsar as the only authority that could hold the vast expanse of

[4]Quoted in Michael T. Florinsky, *Russia: A History and an Interpretation*, Vol. 2 (New York: Macmillan, 1953), p. 755.

When the Moscow regiment refused to swear allegiance to Nicholas, he ordered the cavalry and artillery to attack them. Although a total failure, the Decembrist Revolt came to symbolize the yearnings of all Russian liberals in the nineteenth century for a constitutional government. *The Insurrection of the Decembrists at Senate Square, St. Petersburg on 14th December, 1825* (w/c on paper) by Russian School (nineteenth century). Private Collection/Archives Charmet/Bridgeman Art Library

Russia and its peoples together. Political writers stressed that only under the autocracy of Peter the Great, Catherine the Great, and Alexander I had Russia prospered and exerted a major influence on world affairs.

Through the glorification of Russian nationality, Russians were urged to see their religion, language, and customs as a source of perennial wisdom that separated them from the moral corruption and political turmoil of the West. This program alienated serious Russian intellectuals from the tsarist government.

Revolt and Repression in Poland Nicholas I was also extremely conservative in foreign affairs, as became apparent in Poland in the 1830s. Most of Poland, which had been partitioned in the late eighteenth century and ceased to exist as an independent state, remained under Russian domination after the Congress of Vienna but was granted a constitutional government with a parliament, called the diet, that had limited powers. Under this arrangement, the tsar also reigned as king of Poland. Both Alexander and Nicholas delegated their brother, the Grand Duke Constantine, to run Poland's government. Although both tsars frequently infringed on the constitution and quarreled with the Polish diet, this arrangement held through the 1820s. Nevertheless, Polish nationalists continued to agitate for change.

In late November 1830, after news of the French and Belgian revolutions of that summer had reached Poland, a small insurrection of soldiers and students broke out in Warsaw. Disturbances soon spread throughout the country. On December 18, the Polish diet declared the revolution a nationalist movement. Early the next month, the diet deposed Nicholas as king of Poland. The tsar sent troops into the country and suppressed the revolt. In February 1832, Nicholas issued the Organic Statute, declaring Poland to be an integral part of the Russian Empire. Although this statute guaranteed certain Polish liberties, in practice, the Russian government systematically ignored them. The Polish uprising had confirmed the tsar's worst fears. Henceforth Russia and Nicholas became the gendarme of Europe, ever ready to provide troops to suppress liberal and nationalist movements.

Revolution in France (1830)

The Polish revolt was the most distant of several disturbances that flowed from the overthrow of the Bourbon dynasty in France during July 1830. When Louis XVIII had died in 1824, his brother, the count of Artois, the leader of the ultraroyalist faction, succeeded him as Charles X (r. 1824–1830). The new king was a firm believer in rule by divine right.

The Reactionary Policies of Charles X Charles X's first action was to have the Chamber of Deputies in 1824 and 1825 indemnify aristocrats who had lost their lands in the revolution. He did this by lowering the interest rates on government bonds to create a fund to pay an annual sum to the survivors of the *émigrés* who had forfeited land. Middle-class bondholders, who had lost income, resented this measure. Charles also restored the rule of primogeniture, whereby only the eldest son of an aristocrat inherited the family domains. To support the Roman Catholic Church, he enacted a law that punished sacrilege with imprisonment or death. Liberals disapproved of all these measures.

In the elections of 1827, the liberals gained enough seats in the Chamber of Deputies to compel the king to compromise. He appointed a less conservative ministry. Laws against the press were eased as was government dominance of education. Liberals, however, wanted a genuinely constitutional regime and remained unsatisfied. In 1829, the king replaced his moderate ministry with an ultraroyalist cabinet headed by the Prince de Polignac (1780–1847). The opposition, in desperation, opened negotiations with the liberal Orléans branch of the royal family.

The July Revolution In 1830, Charles X called for new elections, in which the liberals scored a stunning victory. Instead of accepting the new Chamber of Deputies, the king and his ministers decided to attempt a royalist seizure of power. In June and July 1830, Polignac sent a naval expedition against Algiers, which was nominally under Ottoman rule but had in fact become a pirate state whose ships preyed on the merchant vessels of all nations. News of the capture of Algiers and the founding of a French Empire in North Africa reached Paris on July 9. Taking advantage of the euphoria this victory created, Charles issued the Four Ordinances on July 25, 1830, staging what amounted to a royal *coup d'état*. These ordinances restricted freedom of the press, dissolved the recently elected Chamber of Deputies, limited the franchise to the wealthiest people in the country, and called for new elections.

The Four Ordinances provoked swift and decisive popular reaction. Liberal newspapers called on the nation to reject the monarch's actions. The workers of Paris, burdened since 1827 by an economic downturn, erected barricades in the streets. The king called out troops, and although more than 1,800 people died during the ensuing battles, the army was not able to gain control of Paris.

On August 2, Charles X abdicated and went into exile in England. The Chamber of Deputies named a new min-

On July 5, 1830, French forces captured Algiers, which France would continue to rule until 1962. Note how this drawing contrasts the power and modernity of the French conquerors with the almost medieval appearance of the Algerian defenses. Roger Viollet/Getty Images, Inc.—Liaison istry composed of constitutional monarchists. In an act that finally ended the rule of the Bourbon dynasty, it also proclaimed Louis Philippe (r. 1830–1848), the duke d'Orléans, the new king instead of the Count de Chambord, the infant grandson of Charles X in whose favor Charles had abdicated.

In the Revolution of 1830, the liberals of the Chamber of Deputies had filled a power vacuum the Paris uprising and the failure of effective royal action had created. Had Charles X provided himself with sufficient troops in Paris, the outcome could have been different. Moreover, had the liberals, who favored a constitutional monarchy, not acted quickly, the workers and shopkeepers of Paris might have attempted to form a republic. By seizing the moment, the middle class, the bureaucrats, and the moderate aristocratic liberals overthrew the restoration monarchy and still avoided a republic. These liberals feared a new popular revolution such as the one that had swept France in 1792. They had no desire for another *sans-culotte* republic. A fundamental political and social tension thus underlay the new monarchy. The revolution had succeeded thanks to a temporary alliance between hard-pressed laborers and the prosperous middle class, but these two groups soon realized that their basic goals were different.

Monarchy under Louis Philippe Politically, the **July Monarchy**, as the new regime was called, was more liberal than the restoration government. Louis Philippe was called the "king of the French" rather than "king of France." The tricolor flag of the revolution replaced the white flag of the Bourbons. The new constitution was regarded as a right of the people rather than as a concession of the monarch. Catholicism became the religion of a majority of the people rather than "the official religion." The new government was strongly anticlerical. Censorship was abolished. The franchise became wider but remained restricted. The king had to cooperate with the Chamber of Deputies; he could not dispense with laws on his own authority.

Socially, however, the Revolution of 1830 proved conservative. The hereditary peerage was abolished in 1831, but the everyday economic, political, and social influence of the landed oligarchy continued. Money was the path to power and influence in the government. There was much corruption.

Most importantly, the liberal monarchy displayed little or no sympathy for the lower and working classes. In 1830, the workers of Paris had called for the protection of jobs, better wages, and the preservation of the traditional crafts, rather than for the usual goals of political liberalism. The government of Louis Philippe ignored their demands and their plight. The laboring classes of Paris and the provincial cities seemed just one more possible source of disorder. In late 1831, troops suppressed a workers' revolt in Lyons. In July 1832, an uprising occurred in Paris during the funeral of a popular Napoleonic general. Again the government called out troops, and more than eight hundred people were killed or wounded. In 1834, a large strike by silk workers in Lyons was crushed. Such discontent might be smothered for a time, but unless the government addressed the social and economic conditions that created it, new turmoil would eventually erupt.

The new French government of 1830 was only too happy to retain the control of the city of Algiers that Charles X had achieved less than a month before his overthrow. The occupation of Algeria gave French merchants in Marseilles new economic ties to North Africa. Moreover, the French quickly dismantled the structures of the Ottoman government that had survived in Algeria and set out to conquer and administer the interior of the country, which was larger than France itself and where Ottoman rule had never penetrated. By the 1850s, the French had extended their rule, after constant warfare against Muslim tribesmen, as far as the northern Sahara desert. France now had a vast new empire, and French citizens and other Europeans also began to settle in Algeria in large numbers, especially in the cities. In the second half of the nineteenth century, the French government came to regard Algeria, despite its overwhelmingly Muslim population, as not a colony but an integral part of France itself. This was to have serious repercussions after World War II when a pro-independence movement developed among Muslim Algerians.

Belgium Becomes Independent (1830)

The July Revolution in Paris sent sparks to other political tinder on the Continent. The revolutionary fires first flared in neighboring Belgium. The former Austrian Netherlands, Belgium had been merged with the kingdom of Holland in 1815. The two countries differed in language, religion, and economy, however, and the Belgian upper classes never reconciled themselves to Dutch rule.

On August 25, 1830, disturbances broke out in Brussels after the performance of an opera about a rebellion in Naples against Spanish rule. To end the rioting, the municipal authorities and people from the propertied classes formed a provisional national government. When compromise between the Belgians and the Dutch failed, King William I of Holland (r. 1815–1840) sent troops and ships against Belgium. By November 10, 1830, the Dutch had been defeated. A national congress then wrote a liberal Belgian constitution, which was issued in 1831.

Although the major powers saw the revolution in Belgium as upsetting the boundaries the Congress of Vienna had established, they were not inclined to intervene to reverse it. Russia was preoccupied with the Polish revolt. Prussia and the other German states were suppressing small uprisings in their own domains. The Austrians were busy putting down disturbances in Italy. France under Louis Philippe hoped to dominate an independent Belgium. Britain could tolerate a liberal Belgium, as long as it was free of foreign domination.

In December 1830, Lord Palmerston (1784–1865), the British foreign minister, persuaded representatives of the powers in London to recognize Belgium as an independent and neutral state. In July 1831, Prince Leopold of Saxe-Coburg (r. 1831–1865), who had connections to the British royal family and had married the daughter of Louis Philippe, became king of the Belgians. The Convention of 1839 guaranteed Belgian neutrality, which remained an article of faith in European international relations for almost a century.

Both Belgium and Serbia gained independence in 1830, and ironically, diplomatic crises involving both nations led to World War I. The assassination of an Austrian archduke by a Serbian nationalist in Sarajevo in 1914 triggered the war, and Germany's violation of Belgian neutrality brought Britain into it.

The Great Reform Bill in Britain (1832)

In Great Britain, the revolutionary year of 1830 saw the election of a House of Commons that debated the first major bill to reform Parliament. The death of George IV (r. 1820–1830) and the accession of William IV (r. 1830–1837) required the calling of a parliamentary election, held in the summer of 1830. Historians once believed the July revolution in France influenced voting in Britain, but close analysis of the time and character of individual county and borough elections has shown otherwise. The passage of the Great Reform Bill, which became law in 1832, was the result of a series of events different from those that occurred on the Continent. In Britain, the forces of conservatism and reform accommodated each other.

Political and Economic Reform Several factors contributed to this spirit of compromise. First, the commercial and industrial class was larger in Britain than in other countries. No government could ignore their economic interests without damaging British prosperity. Second, Britain's liberal Whig aristocrats, who regarded themselves as the protectors of constitutional liberty, had a long tradition of favoring moderate reforms that would make revolutionary changes unnecessary. Early Whig sympathy for the French Revolution reduced their influence. After 1815, however, they reentered the political arena. Finally, British law, tradition, and public opinion all showed a strong respect for civil liberties.

In 1820, the year after the passage of the notorious Six Acts, Lord Liverpool shrewdly reshaped his cabinet. Although they were conservatives, the new members of the government also believed it had to accommodate itself to the changing social and economic life of the nation. They favored greater economic freedom and repealed the Combination Acts that had prohibited labor organizations.

Catholic Emancipation Act English determination to maintain the union with Ireland brought about another key reform. England's relationship to Ireland was similar to that of Russia to Poland or Austria to its several national groups. In 1800, fearful that Irish nationalists might again rebel as they had in 1798 and perhaps turn Ireland into a base for a French invasion, William Pitt the Younger had persuaded Parliament to pass the Act of Union between Ireland and England. Ireland now sent a hundred members to the House of Commons. Only Protestant Irishmen, however, could be elected to represent their overwhelmingly Roman Catholic nation.

During the 1820s, under the leadership of Daniel O'Connell (1775–1847), Irish nationalists organized the Catholic Association to agitate for Catholic emancipation. In 1828, O'Connell secured his own election to Parliament, where he could not legally take his seat. The duke of Wellington, who was now prime minister, realized that henceforth Ireland might elect an overwhelmingly Catholic delegation. If they were not seated, civil war might erupt across the Irish Sea. Consequently, in 1829, Wellington and Robert Peel steered the Catholic Emancipation Act through Parliament. Roman

Beginning in the 1820s Daniel O'Connell revolutionized the organization of Irish politics. He created a grass-roots organization and collected funds to finance Irish nationalist activities. He was also known as one of the great public speakers of his generation.

Catholics could now become members of Parliament. This measure, together with the repeal in 1828 of restrictions against Protestant nonconformists, ended the Anglican monopoly on British political life.

Catholic emancipation was a liberal measure passed for the conservative purpose of preserving order in Ireland. It included a provision raising the property qualification to vote in Ireland, so that only the wealthier Irish could vote. Nonetheless, this measure alienated many of Wellington's Anglican Tory supporters in the House of Commons. The election of 1830 returned many supporters of parliamentary reform to Parliament. Even some Tories supported reform, because they thought only a corrupt House of Commons could have passed Catholic emancipation. The Tories, consequently, were badly divided, and the Wellington ministry soon fell. King William IV then turned to the leader of the Whigs, Earl Grey (1764–1845), to form a government.

Legislating Change The Whig ministry presented the House of Commons with a major reform bill that had two broad goals. The first was to replace "rotten boroughs," or boroughs that had few voters, with representatives for the previously unrepresented manufacturing districts and cities. Second, the number of voters in England and Wales was to be increased by about 50 percent through a series of new franchises. In 1831, the House of Commons narrowly defeated the bill. Grey called for a new election and won a majority in favor of the bill. The House of Commons passed the reform bill, but the House of Lords rejected it. Mass meetings were held throughout the country. Riots broke out in several cities. Finally, William IV agreed to create enough new peers to give a third reform bill a majority in the House of Lords. Under this pressure, the measure became law in 1832.

The **Great Reform Bill** expanded the size of the English electorate, but it was not a democratic measure. It increased the number of voters by more than 200,000, or almost 50 percent, but it kept a property qualification for the franchise. (Gender was also a qualification. No thought was given to enfranchising women.) Some members of the working class actually lost the right to vote because certain old franchise rights were abolished. New urban boroughs were created to allow the growing cities to have a voice in the House of Commons. Yet the passage of the reform act did not, as was once thought, constitute the triumph of middle-class interests in England: For every new urban electoral district, a new rural district was also drawn, and the aristocracy was expected to dominate rural elections. What the bill permitted was a wider variety of property to be represented in the House of Commons.

The success of the reform bill reconciled previously unrepresented property owners and economic interests to the political institutions of the country. The act laid the groundwork for further orderly reforms of the church, municipal government, and commercial policy.

EVENTS ASSOCIATED WITH LIBERAL REFORM AND REVOLUTION

1824	Charles X becomes king of France
1825	Decembrist Revolt in Russia
1828	Repeal of restrictions against British Protestant nonconformists
1829	Catholic Emancipation Act passed in Great Britain; Ottoman Sultan grants independence to Serbia
1830 (July 9)	News of French colonial conquest in Algeria reaches Paris
1830 (July 25)	Charles X issues the Four Ordinances
1830 (August 2)	Charles X abdicates; Louis Philippe proclaimed king
1830 (August 25)	Belgian revolution
1830 (November 29)	Polish revolution
1832	Organic Statute makes Poland an integral part of Russian Empire
1832	Great Reform Bill passed in Great Britain

By admitting into the political forum people who sought change and giving them access to the legislative process, it made revolution in Britain unnecessary. Great Britain thus maintained its traditional institutions of government while allowing an increasingly diverse group of people to influence them.

In Perspective

Through the Congress System, the major powers had responded to pressures on the Vienna Settlement without going to war against each other or allowing any state or group of states to annex territory. In the fifteen years between the conclusion of the Congress of Vienna and the Revolution of 1830 in France, no revolutionary disturbance had succeeded in Europe except for the Greek revolt that broke out in 1821. In Russia, the Decembrist Revolt of 1825 failed almost before it had begun. The only truly successful revolutionary activity during these years occurred in Latin America, where wars of independence ended Spain's and Portugal's centuries-old colonial domination.

Nonetheless, during the 1820s, liberal political ideas and some liberal political figures began to make inroads into the otherwise conservative domestic order. In 1830, revolution and reform again began to move across Europe. The French replaced the Bourbons with a more liberal monarchy. Belgium also achieved independence under a liberal government. Perhaps most importantly, Britain moved slowly toward a more liberal position. During the 1820s, Britain had become unenthusiastic about a political role that placed it in opposition to all change. For its own commercial reasons, it favored independence for Latin America. Popular pressures at home led the British aristocratic leadership to enact a moderate reform bill in 1832. Thereafter, Britain would be viewed as the leading liberal state in Europe and one that would support nationalistic causes.

REVIEW QUESTIONS

1. What is nationalism? What were the goals of nationalists? What difficulties did nationalists confront in realizing those goals? Why was nationalism a special threat to the Austrian Empire? What areas saw significant nationalist movements between 1815 and 1830? Which were successful and which unsuccessful?
2. What were the tenets of liberalism? Who were the liberals, and how did liberalism affect the political developments of the early nineteenth century? What is the relationship of liberalism to nationalism?
3. What difficulties did the conservatives in Austria, Prussia, and Russia face after the Napoleonic wars? How did they attempt to solve those difficulties at home and in international affairs? What were the aims of the Concert of Europe? How did the Congress of Vienna change international relations?
4. What were the main reasons for Creole discontent with Spanish rule, and to what extent did Enlightenment political philosophy influence the Creole leaders? Who were some of the primary leaders of Latin American independence? Why was Brazil's path to independence different from that of Spanish America?
5. What were the main provisions of the constitution of the restored monarchy in France? What did Charles X hope to accomplish? Why did revolution break out in France in 1830? What did this revolution achieve and what problems did it fail to resolve?
6. Why did Britain avoid a revolution in the early 1830s? What was the purpose of the Great Reform Bill? What did it achieve? Would you call it a "revolutionary" document?
7. By approximately 1830, how had European political ambitions and the ideas of liberalism and nationalism begun to undermine the Ottoman Empire? Which Ottoman territories were lost by that date?

SUGGESTED READINGS

B. Anderson, *Imagined Communities*, rev. ed. (2006). An influential and controversial discussion of nationalism.

M. S. Bell, *Toussaint Louverture: A Biography* (2007). An outstanding new biography.

M. Berdahl, *The Politics of the Prussian Nobility: The Development of a Conservative Ideology, 1770–1848* (1988). A major examination of German conservative outlooks.

A. Briggs, *The Making of Modern England* (1959). Classic survey of English history during the first half of the nineteenth century.

A. Craitu, *Liberalism under Siege: The Political Thought of the French Doctrinaires* (2003). An outstanding study of early nineteenth-century French liberalism.

M. F. Cross and D. Williams, eds., *French Experience from Republic to Monarchy, 1792–1824: New Dawns in Politics, Knowledge and Culture* (2000). Essays on French culture from the revolution through the restoration.

D. Dakin, *The Struggle for Greek Independence* (1973). An excellent explanation of the Greek independence question.

L. Dubois, *Avengers of the New World: The Story of the Haitian Revolution* (2004). An analytic narrative likely to replace others.

E. J. Evans, *Britain Before the Reform Act: Politics and Society, 1815–1832* (2008). Explores the forces that resisted and pressed for reform.

W. Fortescue, *Revolution and Counter-Revolution in France, 1815–1852* (2002). A helpful brief survey.

E. Gellner, *Nations and Nationalism* (1983). A classic theoretical work.

L. Greenfeld, *Nationalism: Five Roads to Modernity* (1992). A major comparative study.

R. Harvey, *Liberators: Latin America's Struggle for Independence* (2002). An excellent, lively treatment.

E. J. Hobsbawm, *Nations and Nationalism since 1780: Programme, Myth, Reality*, rev. ed. (1992). Emphasizes intellectual factors.

C. Jelavich and B. Jelavich, *The Establishment of the Balkan National States, 1804–1920* (1987). A standard survey.

G. A. Kelly, *The Humane Comedy: Constant, Tocqueville, and French Liberalism* (2007). The best introduction to the subject.

M. B. Levinger, *Enlightened Nationalism: The Transformation of Prussian Political Culture, 1806–1848* (2002). A clear and expansive overview on the most recent scholarship.

J. Lynch, *Simon Bolivar: A Life* (2006). Now the standard biography.

C. A. Macartney, *The Habsburg Empire, 1790–1918* (1971). Remains an important survey.

N. V. Riasanovsky, *Nicholas I and Official Nationality in Russia, 1825–1855* (1959). Remains a lucid discussion of the conservative ideology that made Russia the major opponent of liberalism.

J. Sheehan, *German History, 1770–1866* (1989). A long work that is now the best available survey of the subject.

A. Sked, *Metternich and Austria: An Evaluation* (2008). A thoughtful restoration of Metternich to the position of leading diplomat of his age.

A. B. Ulam, *Russia's Failed Revolutionaries* (1981). Contains a useful discussion of the Decembrists as a background for other nineteenth-century Russian revolutionary activity.

B. Wilson, *The Making of Victorian Values: Decency and Dissent in Britain: 1789–1837* (2007). A very lively overview of the cultural factors shaping early nineteenth-century British society.

For additional learning resources related to this chapter, please go to www.myhistorylab.com

myhistorylab

In 1848 Ana Ipatescu helped to lead Transylvanian revolutionaries against Russian rule. Transylvania is part of present-day Romania. The revolutions of 1848 in eastern Europe were primarily uprisings of nationalist groups. Although generally repressed in the revolutions of that year, subject nationalities would prove a source of political upheaval and unrest in the region throughout the rest of the century, ultimately providing the spark for the outbreak of World War I. The Art Archive/Picture Desk, Inc./Kobal Collection

21

Economic Advance and Social Unrest (1830–1850)

▼ **Toward an Industrial Society**
Population and Migration • Railways

▼ **The Labor Force**
The Emergence of a Wage-Labor Force • Working-Class Political Action: The Example of British Chartism

▼ **Family Structures and the Industrial Revolution**
The Family in the Early Factory System

▼ **Women in the Early Industrial Revolution**
Opportunities and Exploitation in Employment • Changing Expectations in the Working-Class Marriage

▼ **Problems of Crime and Order**
New Police Forces • Prison Reform

▼ **Classical Economics**
Malthus on Population • Ricardo on Wages • Government Policies Based on Classical Economics

▼ **Early Socialism**
Utopian Socialism • Anarchism • Marxism

▼ **1848: Year of Revolutions**
France: The Second Republic and Louis Napoleon • The Habsburg Empire: Nationalism Resisted • Italy: Republicanism Defeated • Germany: Liberalism Frustrated

▼ **In Perspective**

KEY TOPICS

- **The development of industrialism and its effects on the organization of labor and the family**
- **The changing role of women in industrial society**
- **The establishment of police forces and reform of prisons**
- **Early developments in European socialism**
- **The revolutions of 1848**

BY 1830, EUROPE was headed toward an industrial society. Only Great Britain had already attained that status, but the pounding of new machinery and the grinding of railway engines soon began to echo across much of the Continent. Yet what characterized the second quarter of the century was not the triumph of industrialism but the final protests of those economic groups who opposed it. Intellectually, the period saw the formulation of the major creeds supporting and criticizing the newly emerging society.

These were years of uncertainty for almost everyone. Even the most confident entrepreneurs knew the trade cycle could bankrupt them within weeks. For the industrial workers and the artisans, unemployment became a haunting and recurring problem. For the peasants, the question was sufficiency of food. It was a period of self-conscious transition that culminated in 1848 with a continent-wide outbreak of revolution. People knew one mode of life was passing, but no one knew what would replace it.

▼ Toward an Industrial Society

The Industrial Revolution had begun in eighteenth-century Great Britain with the advances in textile production described in Chapter 15. Natural resources, adequate capital, native technological skills, a growing food supply, a social structure that allowed considerable mobility, and strong foreign and domestic demand for goods had given Britain an edge in achieving a vast new capacity for production in manufacturing. British factories and recently invented machines allowed producers to furnish customers with a greater number of consumer products of a higher quality and for lower prices than those of any competitors. Also, the French Revolution and the wars of Napoleon had finally destroyed the French Atlantic trade and thus disrupted continental economic life for two decades. The Latin American wars of independence opened the markets of South America to British goods. In North America, both the United States and Canada demanded British products. Through its control of India, Britain commanded the markets of southern Asia. British banks similarly dominated the international financial markets.

The British textile industry was a vast worldwide economic network. For much of its supply of raw cotton, this industry depended on the labor of American slaves, although Britain itself had been trying to end the slave trade since 1807. In turn, the finished textiles were shipped all over the world along sea-lanes the British navy protected. The wealth that Britain gained through textile production and its other industries of iron making, shipbuilding, china production, and the manufacture of other finished goods was invested all over the world, but especially in the United States and Latin America. This enormous activity provided the economic foundation for British dominance of the world scene throughout the nineteenth century.

Despite their economic lag, the continental nations were beginning to make material progress. By the 1830s, in Belgium, France, and Germany, the number of steam engines in use was growing steadily. Exploitation of the coalfields of the Ruhr and the Saar basins had begun. Coke was replacing charcoal in iron and steel production.

Industrial areas on the Continent were generally less concentrated than in Britain; nor did the Continent have large manufacturing districts, such as the British Midlands. Major pockets of production, such as Lyons, Rouen, and Lille in France and Liege in Belgium, did exist in Western Europe, but most continental manufacturing still took place in the countryside. New machines were integrated into the existing domestic system. The slow pace of continental imitation of the British example meant that, at midcentury, peasants and urban artisans remained more important politically than industrial factory workers.

Population and Migration

While the process of industrialization spread, the population of Europe continued to grow on the base of the eighteenth-century population explosion. The number of people in France rose from 32.5 million in 1831 to 35.8 million in 1851. During approximately the same period, the population of Germany rose from 26.5 million to 33.5 million and that of Britain from 16.3 million to 20.8 million. More and more of the people of Europe lived in cities. By midcentury, one half of the population of England and Wales and one quarter of the population of France and Germany had become town dwellers. Eastern Europe, by contrast, remained overwhelmingly rural, with little industrial manufacturing.

The sheer numbers of human beings put considerable pressure on the physical resources of the cities. Migration from the countryside meant that existing housing, water, sewers, food supplies, and lighting were completely inadequate. Slums with indescribable filth grew, and disease, especially cholera, ravaged the population. Crime increased and became a way of life for those who could make a living in no other manner. Human misery and degradation in many early-nineteenth-century cities seemed to have no bounds.

The situation in the countryside was scarcely better. During the first half of the century, the productive use of the land remained the basic fact of life for most Europeans. The enclosures of the late eighteenth century, the land redistribution of the French Revolution, and the emancipation of serfs in Prussia and later in Austria (1848) and Russia (1861) commercialized landholding. Liberal reformers had hoped the legal revolution in ownership would transform peasants into progressive, industrious farmers. Instead, most peasants became conservative landholders without enough land to make agricultural innovations or, oftentimes, even to support themselves.

It is important to note the differing dates of rural emancipation across Europe. In England, France, and the Low Countries, persons living in the countryside could move freely between country and town. In Germany, eastern Europe, and Russia, such migration was difficult until the serfs were emancipated. Even when emancipation did occur, as throughout Germany early in the century, it did not make migration simple. So from Germany eastward, the pace of industrialization was much slower, in part because of the absence of a fluid market for free labor moving to the cities.

The specter of poor harvests still haunted Europe. The worst such experience of the century was the Irish famine of 1845 to 1847. Perhaps as many as half a million Irish peasants with no land or small plots simply starved when disease blighted the potato crop. Hundreds of thousands emigrated. (See "Encountering the Past: The Potato and the Great Hunger in Ireland.") By midcentury, the revolution in landholding led to greater agricultural production. It also resulted in a vast uprooting of people from the countryside into cities and from Europe into the rest of the world. The countryside thus provided many of the workers for the new factories, as well as people with few economic skills who slowly emigrated to cities in hope of finding work.

Railways

Industrial advance itself had also contributed to this migration. The 1830s and 1840s opened the first great age of railway building. The Stockton and Darlington Line opened in England in 1825. By 1830, another major line had been built between Manchester and Liverpool and had several hundred passengers a day. Belgium had undertaken railway construction by 1835. The first French line opened in 1832, but serious construction came only in the 1840s. Germany entered the railway age in 1835. At midcentury, Britain had 9,797 kilometers of railway, France 2,915, and Germany 5,856. (See Map 21–1.)

Map 21–1 **EUROPEAN RAILROADS IN 1850** At midcentury Britain had the most extensive rail network, and the most industrialized economy, in Europe, but rail lines were expanding rapidly in France, the German states, and Austria. Southern and eastern Europe had few railways, and the Ottoman Empire had none.

THE POTATO AND THE GREAT HUNGER IN IRELAND

ANY AGRICULTURAL ECONOMY that depends on a single product is in a precarious position. If the people that economy supports also depend on a single source of food, they also stand on the edge of catastrophe—they have nothing to fall back on if their only source of food fails. That kind of catastrophe occurred in Ireland, which was under British rule in the 1840s when the potato crop failed.

During the eighteenth century, almost half of the Irish population came to depend on the potato, which had been brought to Europe from South America in the seventeenth century, as virtually their only food. On less than one acre, an Irish peasant could raise enough potatoes to feed ten other people for a year and pay his rent (few Irish peasants owned their own land).

Before the 1840s, there had been isolated potato failures in parts of Ireland, but never a general failure. Then in l845, a mysterious blight, caused by a fungus, struck potato crops across Ireland. The potato vines withered in the fields, and potatoes in storage became moldy and inedible. Half the crop was lost. The Irish, with modest aid from the British government, survived, but in 1846 the blight reappeared and destroyed the entire crop. The crop of 1847 was better, but the blight came again in 1848.

This series of Irish potato crop failures was the worst natural disaster to strike nineteenth-century Europe. Without potatoes, Irish tenants could not pay their rent. Landlords drove starving tenants off their farms. Disease spread, and tens of thousands died.

In 1846, in response to the Irish famine, the British government repealed the tariffs on imported grain known as the Corn Laws and enacted a program of public works to employ the dispossessed, but the help was inadequate. Most economists and politicians believed government aid caused more harm than good, and the government was reluctant to provide charity. The 1847 Irish Poor Relief Act required anyone who occupied more than one quarter acre of land to enter a government-run workhouse before receiving poor relief, but the scale of the disaster overwhelmed the workhouses.

To escape the famine, soon known as The Great Hunger, many of the Irish poor emigrated, primarily to the United States and Britain itself. Much of Ireland became depopulated. The census of 1841 counted 8,197,000 people in Ireland; ten years later, death and emigration had cut the population by more than 1.5 million. By 1901, more waves of emigration had reduced it to 4,459,000. The population had still not recovered to prefamine levels at the dawn of the twenty-first century: In 2000, the combined population of the Irish Republic and British-ruled Northern Ireland was only 5,460,000. Alone among the nations of Europe, Ireland has fewer inhabitants today than it did in the nineteenth century.

Source: R. N. Salaman, *The History and Social Influence of the Potato* (Cambridge: Cambridge University Press, 1985); Cecil Woodham-Smith, *The Great Hunger: Ireland 1845–1849* (New York: Harper & Row, 1962).

Why was the failure of the potato crop such a disaster for Ireland?

How did the famine affect the Irish population?

Painter George Frederick Watts's 1850 depiction of a scene set during the Irish Potato Famine. So many people starved during the famine that workhouses could not shelter them all.

George Stephenson (1781–1848) invented the locomotive in 1814, but the "Rocket," his improved design shown here, did not win out over other competitors until 1829. In the following two decades the spread of railways transformed the economy of Western Europe. Image Works/Mary Evans Picture Library Ltd.

The railroads, plus canals and improved regular roads, meant people could leave the place of their birth more easily than ever before. The improvement in transportation also allowed cheaper and more rapid passage of raw materials and finished products.

Railways epitomized the character of the industrial economy during the second quarter of the century. They represented investment in capital goods rather than in consumer goods. Consequently, there was a shortage of consumer goods at cheap prices. This favoring of capital over consumer production was one reason the working class was often unable to purchase much for its wages. The railways in and of themselves also brought about still more industrialization. Embodying the most dramatic application of the steam engine, they sharply increased demand for iron and steel and then for a more skilled labor force. The new iron and steel capacity soon permitted the construction of ironclad ships and iron machinery rather than ships and machinery made of wood. These new capital industries led to the formation of vast industrial fortunes that would be invested in still newer enterprises. Industrialism had begun to grow on itself.

▾ The Labor Force

The composition and experience of the early nineteenth-century labor force was varied. No single description could include all the factory workers, urban artisans, domestic craftspeople, household servants, miners, countryside peddlers, farm workers, or railroad workers. Some of the workforce was reasonably well off and enjoyed steady employment and decent wages. Other workers were the "laboring poor," who held jobs, but earned little more than subsistence wages. Then there were those, such as the women and children who worked nearly naked in the mines of Wales, whose conditions of life shocked Europe when a parliamentary report in the 1840s publicized them. Furthermore, the conditions of workers varied from decade to decade and from industry to industry within any particular decade.

Although historians have traditionally emphasized the role and experience of industrial factory workers, only the textile-manufacturing industry became thoroughly mechanized and moved into the factory setting during the first half of the century. Far more of the nonrural, nonagricultural workforce consisted of skilled artisans living in cities or small towns. They were attempting to maintain the value of their skills and control over their trades in the face of changing features of production. All these working people faced possible unemployment, with little or no provision for their security. During their lives, they confronted the dissolution of many of the traditional social ties of custom and community.

The Emergence of a Wage-Labor Force

During the nineteenth century, artisans as well as factory workers eventually came to participate in a wage-labor force in which their labor became a commodity of the labor marketplace. This process has often been termed *proletarianization.* In the process of becoming wage laborers, artisans gradually lost both significant ownership of the means of production, such as tools and equipment, and of control over the conduct of their own trades. The process occurred most rapidly wherever the factory system arose displacing previous skilled labor. The factory owner provided the financial capital to construct the factory, to purchase the machinery, and to secure the raw materials. The factory workers contributed their labor for a wage. The process could also occur outside the factory setting if a new invention, such as a mechanical printing press, could do the work of several artisans within an urban or rural workshop setting.

Factory workers also had to submit to various kinds of factory discipline that was virtually always unpopular and difficult to impose. This discipline meant the demands for a smooth operation of the machinery largely determined working conditions. Closing of factory gates to late workers, fines for such lateness, dismissal for drunkenness, and public scolding of faulty laborers were attempts to create human discipline that would match the mechanical regularity of the cables, wheels, and pistons. The factory worker had no direct say about the quality of the product or its price. (See "Compare & Connect: Andrew Ure and John Ruskin Debate the Conditions of Factory Production," pages 628–629.)

For all the difficulties of workers in factory conditions, however, their economic situation was often better than that of textile workers who resisted the factory mode of production. In particular, English hand-loom weavers, who continued to work in their homes, experienced decades of declining trade and growing poverty in their failing attempt to compete with power looms.

Urban artisans in the nineteenth century entered the wage-labor force more slowly than factory workers, and machinery had little to do with the process. The emergence of factories in and of itself did not harm urban artisans. Many even prospered from the development. For example, the construction and maintenance of the new machines generated major demand for metalworkers, who consequently did well. The actual erection of factories and the expansion of cities benefited all craftspeople in the building trades, such as carpenters, roofers, joiners, and masons. The lower prices for machine-made textiles aided artisans involved in making clothing, such as tailors and hatters, by reducing the costs of their raw materials. Where the urban artisans encountered difficulty and where they found their skills and livelihood threatened was in the organization of production.

In the eighteenth century, a European town or city workplace had usually consisted of a few artisans laboring for a master. They labored first as apprentices and then as journeymen, according to established guild regulations and practices. The master owned the workshop and the larger equipment, and the apprentices and journeymen owned their tools. The journeyman could expect eventually to become a master. This guild system had allowed workers to exercise a considerable degree of control over labor recruitment and training, the pace of production, the quality of the product, and its price. The guild functioned to protect the integrity of the craft and the prosperity of the craftsmen.

In the nineteenth century, it became increasingly difficult for artisans to exercise corporate or guild direction and control over their trades. The legislation of the French Revolution had outlawed such organizations in France. Across Europe, political and economic liberals disapproved of labor and guild organizations and attempted to ban them. These thinkers believed guilds raised the price of both labor and products to the disadvantage of owners of capital and consumers.

Other destructive forces were also at work. The masters often found themselves under increased competitive pressure from larger, more heavily capitalized establishments or from the introduction of machine production into a previously craft-dominated industry. In many workshops masters began to follow a practice, known in France as *confection*, whereby goods, such as shoes, clothing, and furniture, were produced in standard sizes and styles rather than by special orders for individual customers.

This practice increased the division of labor in the workshop. Each artisan produced a smaller part of the more-or-less uniform final product. Thus, less skill was required of each artisan, and the particular skills a worker possessed became less valuable. To increase production and reduce costs, masters also tried to lower the wages they paid for piecework. Those attempts often led to work stoppages or strikes. Migrants from the countryside or small towns into the cities created, in some cases, a surplus of relatively unskilled workers. They were willing to work for lower wages or under less favorable and protected conditions than traditional artisans. This situation made it much more difficult for urban journeymen ever to hope to become masters in charge of their own workshops. Increasingly, these artisans became lifetime wage laborers whose skills were simply bought and sold in the marketplace.

Working-Class Political Action: The Example of British Chartism

By midcentury, such artisans, proud of their skills and frustrated in their social and economic expectations, became the most radical political element in the European working class. From at least the 1830s onward, these artisans took the lead in one country after another in attempting to formulate new ways to protect their social and economic interests.

By the late 1830s, many British workers linked the solution of their economic plight to a program of political reform known as **Chartism**. In 1836, William Lovett (1800–1877) and other London radical artisans formed the London Working Men's Association. In 1838, the group issued the Charter, demanding six specific reforms. The Six Points of the Charter included universal male suffrage, annual election of the House of Commons, the secret ballot, equal electoral districts, and the abolition of property qualifications for and the payment of salaries to members of the House of Commons.

For more than ten years, the Chartists, who were never tightly organized, agitated for their reforms. On three occasions the Charter was presented to Parliament, which refused to pass it. Petitions with millions of signatures were presented to the House of Commons. Strikes were called. The Chartists published a newspaper, the *Northern Star*. Feargus O'Connor (1794–1855), the most important Chartist leader, made speeches

COMPARE AND CONNECT

Andrew Ure and John Ruskin Debate the Conditions of Factory Production

THE FACTORY WAS itself as much an invention of the Industrial Revolution as were the new machines the factory often housed. The factory required a new organization of labor. It also made possible the production of vast new quantities of manufactured goods. From its inception the factory system provoked both praise and criticism. Andrew Ure saw much positive good arising from factory production whereas John Ruskin became a vehement critic. How might the women of Todmorden (see page 635) have replied to both writers?

QUESTIONS

1. **Why does Ure emphasize the willingness of workers to be employed in factories?**
2. **How does Ure portray the factory system as creating the possibility of new abundance?**
3. **How does Ruskin see the use of machinery reducing workers to a machine?**
4. **Is Ruskin's criticism of the division of labor a correct analysis or simply a well-crafted metaphorical criticism?**
5. **How might Ure have replied to Ruskin?**

I. Andrew Ure Praises the Factory System

Andrew Ure (1778–1857) was a Scottisch physician and a great proponent of the benefits of the factory system. In 1835 he published The Philosophy of Manufactures, *which went through many editions from then until late in the century. He saw factories as increasing productivity and also providing a healthier environment than agricultural work or mining.*

The term Factory, in technology, designates the combined operation of many orders of work—people, adult and young, in tending with assiduous skill a system of productive machines continuously impelled by a central power. This definition includes such organizations as cotton-mills, flax-mills, silk-mills, woolen-mills, and certain engineering works. . . . I conceive that this title, in its strictest sense, involves the idea of a vast automaton, composed of various mechanical and intellectual organs, acting in uninterrupted concert for the production of a common object, all of them being subordinated to a self-regulated moving force. . . .

In its precise acceptation, the Factory system is of recent origin, and may claim England for its birthplace. . . .

When the first water-frames for spinning cotton were erected at Cromford, in the romantic valley of the Derwent, about sixty years ago, mankind were little aware of the mighty revolution which the new system of labor was destined by Providence to achieve, not only in the structure of British society, but in the fortunes of the world at large.

Arkwright alone had the sagacity to discern, and the boldness to predict in glowing language, how vastly productive human industry would become, when no longer proportioned in its results to muscular effort, which is by its nature fitful and capricious, but when made to consist in the task of guiding the work of mechanical fingers and arms, regularly impelled with great velocity by some indefatigable physical power. . . .

In my recent tour, continued during several months, through the manufacturing districts, I have seen tens of thousands of old, young, and middle-aged of both sexes, many of them too feeble to get their daily bread by any of the former modes of industry, earning abundant food, raiment, and domestic accommodation, without perspiring at a single pore, screened meanwhile from the summer's sun and the winter's frost, in apartments more airy and salubrious than those of the metropolis, in which our legislative and fashionable aristocracies assemble. In those spacious halls the benignant power of steam summons around him his myriads of willing menials, and assigns to each the regulated task, substituting for painful muscular effort on their part, the energies of his own gigantic arm, and demanding in return only attention and dexterity to correct such little aberrations as casually occur in his workmanship. . . . Such is the factory system, replete with prodigies in mechanics and political economy, which promises, in its future growth, to become the great minister of civilization to the terraqueous globe, enabling this country, as its heart, to diffuse along with its commerce, the life-blood of science and religion to myriads of people still lying "in the region and shadow of death."

Source: Andrew Ure, *The Philosophy of Manufactures; or, An Exposition of the Scientific, Moral, and Commercial Economy of the Factory System* (London, 1835), pp. 13 ff., as quoted in Mack Walker, ed., *Metternich's Europe* (New York: Walker and Company, 1968), pp. 275–276, 278–279.

II. John Ruskin Decries the Impact of Industrial Production on Workers

The Englishman John Ruskin (1819–1900) was the foremost mid-nineteenth-century critic of art and architecture. He commenced his career interested primarily in painting and then moved to architecture. In the course of that transition he became increasingly sensitive to the working conditions of the craftsmen who constructed the buildings he studied. Over time he became a major social critic of the new industrial order. His earliest statement of social criticism occurred in a chapter entitled "The Nature of Gothic" in his 1851 book The Stones of Venice. *Here Ruskin passionately attacked the mechanical routine of work associated with industrial machinery. He also attacked the concept of increasing work through the division of labor, which had been conceptualized by Adam Smith in* The Wealth of Nations (1776). *Smith had illustrated the division of labor by describing a pin factory. Ruskin here responds to Smith's analysis.*

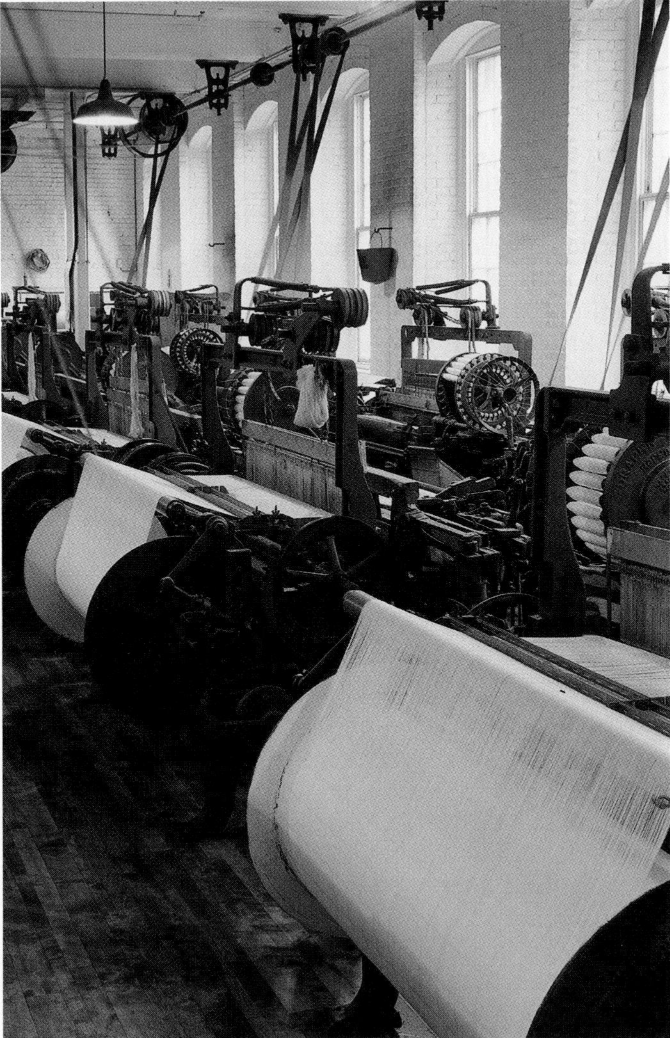

Power looms used in the mass production of textiles during the Industrial Revolution. Dorling Kindersley Medical Library/David Lyons © Dorling Kindersley. Courtesy of the Boott Cotton Mills Museum, Lowell, Massachusetts

You must either make a tool of the creature, or a man of him. You cannot make both. Men were not intended to work with the accuracy of tools, to be precise and perfect in all their actions. If you will have that precision out of them, and make their fingers measure degrees like cog-wheels, and their arms strike curves like compasses, you must unhumanize them. All the energy of their spirits must be given to make cogs and compasses of themselves. All their attention and strength must go to the accomplishment of the mean act . . . On the other hand, if you will make a man of the working creature, you cannot make a tool. Let him but begin to imagine, to think to try to do anything worth doing; and the engine-turned precision is lost at once. Out come all his roughness, all his dulness, all his incapability; shame upon shame, failure upon failure, pause after pause: but out comes the whole majesty of him also; . . .

It is verily this degradation of the operative into a machine, which, more than any other evil of the times, is leading the mass of the nations everywhere into vain, incoherent, destructive struggling for a freedom of which they cannot explain the nature to themselves. . . . It is not that men are ill read, but that they have no pleasure in the work by which they make their bread, and therefore look to wealth as the only means of pleasure. . . .

It is not, truly speaking, the labour that is divided; but the men:—Divided into mere segments of men—broken into small fragments and crumbs of life; so that all the little piece of intelligence that is left in a man is not enough to make a pin, or a nail, but exhausts itself in making the point of a pin or the head of a nail . . . . And all the evil to which that cry is urging our myriads can be met only in one way: not by teaching nor preaching, for to teach them is but to show them their misery, and to preach to them, if we do nothing more than preach, is to mock at it. It can be met only by a right understanding, on the part of all classes, of what kinds of labour are good for men, raising them, and making them happy; by a determined sacrifice of such convenience, or beauty, or cheapness as is to be got only by the degradation of the workman; and by equally determined demand for the products and results of healthy and ennobling labour.

Source: J. Ruskin, *The Stones of Venice* (New York: Lovell, Coryell, and Co., n.d.), 2, pp. 162, 164, 165–166.

In the 1830s and 1840s, the Chartists circulated petitions throughout Britain demanding political reform. Here the petitions are being taken to Parliament in a vast ceremonious procession. © Museum of London

across Britain. Despite this vast activity, Chartism as a national movement failed. Its ranks were split between those who advocated violence and those who wanted to use peaceful tactics. On the local level, however, the Chartists scored several successes and controlled the city councils in Leeds and Sheffield.

As prosperity returned after the depression of the late 1830s and early 1840s, many working people abandoned the movement. Chartists' demonstrations in 1848 fizzled. Nevertheless, Chartism was the first large-scale European working-class political movement. It had specific goals and largely working-class leadership. Eventually, several of the Six Points became law (for example, the secret ballot was enacted in 1872). Continental working-class observers saw in Chartism the kind of mass movement that workers must eventually adopt if they were to improve their situation.

▾ Family Structures and the Industrial Revolution

It is more difficult to generalize about the European working-class family structure in the age of early industrialism than under the Old Regime. Industrialism developed at different rates across the Continent, and the impact of industrialism cannot be separated from that of migration and urbanization. Furthermore, industrialism did not touch all families directly; the structures and customs of many peasant families changed little for much of the nineteenth century.

Much more is known about the relationships of the new industry to the family in Great Britain than elsewhere. Many of the British developments foreshadowed those in other countries as the factory system spread.

The Family in the Early Factory System

Contrary to what historians and other observers once believed, the adoption of new machinery and factory production did not destroy the working-class family. Before the late-eighteenth-century revolution in textile production in England, the individual family involved in textiles was the chief unit of production. The earliest textile-related inventions, such as the spinning jenny, did not change that situation. As noted in Chapter 15, the new machine was initially simply brought into the home to spin the thread. It was the mechanization of weaving that led to the major change. The father who became a machine weaver was then employed in a factory. His work was thus separated from his home. Although one should not underestimate the changes and pressures in family life that occurred when the father left for the factory, the structure of early English factories allowed the father to preserve certain of his traditional family roles as they had existed before the factory system.

In the domestic system of the family economy, the father and mother had worked with their children in textile production as a family unit. They had trained and disciplined the children within the home setting. Their home life and their economic life were largely the same. Moreover, in the home setting, the wife who worked as a spinner might have earned as much or even more than her husband. Early factory owners and supervisors permitted the father to employ his wife and children as his assistants. Thus, parental training and discipline could be transferred from the home into the early factory. In some cases, in both Britain and France, whole families would move near a new factory so that the family as a unit could work there. Despite those accommodations to family life, family members still had to face the new work discipline of the factory setting. Moreover, women assisting their husbands in the factory often did less skilled work than they had in their homes.

A major shift in this family and factory structure began in the mid-1820s in England and had been more or less completed by the mid-1830s. As spinning and weaving were put under one roof, the size of factories and of the machinery grew. These newer machines required fewer skilled operators, but many relatively unskilled attendants. This became the work of unmarried women and children. Factory owners found these workers would accept lower wages and were less likely than adult men to try to form worker organizations or unions.

Factory wages for the more skilled adult males, however, became sufficiently high to allow some fathers to remove their children from the factory and send them

THE GREAT EXHIBITION IN LONDON

THE GREAT EXHIBITION of 1851 was held in London to celebrate progress in industry and commerce achieved through the new industrial order. Its organizers invited governments and businesses from around the globe to display the products they manufactured. The organizers generally supported free trade and believed the displays would demonstrate the value of peaceful commerce.

Note the construction of the building known as the Crystal Palace. The structural iron symbolized the possibility of using new kinds of building materials. The vast quantities of glass demonstrated that a once scarce luxury good could now be produced in large quantities for everyday consumption. In the past such structures of iron and glass had been used only for small greenhouses to raise plants on aristocratic estates.

The crowds in the picture and the even larger crowds who actually attended the Great Exhibition demonstrated that, after a quarter century of social turmoil and political discontent in Europe, large numbers of people could gather peacefully in public.

The classical statues to the left were present to show that the new consumer goods industrialism made possible was compatible with an ongoing culture of elite art.

London's Crystal Palace during the International Exhibition of 1851. Victoria & Albert Museum, London, Great Britain/Art Resource, NY

To examine this image in an interactive fashion, please go to www.myhistorylab.com

myhistorylab

to school. The children who were left working in the factories as assistants were often the children of the economically depressed hand-loom weavers. The wives of the skilled operatives also usually no longer worked in the factories. So the original links of the family in the British textile factory that had existed for well over a quarter century largely disappeared. Men were supervising women and children who did not belong to their families.

Concern for Child Labor At this point in the 1830s, workers became concerned about the plight of child laborers because parents were no longer exercising discipline over their own children in the factories. The English Factory Act of 1833 forbade the employment of children under age nine, limited the workday of children aged nine to thirteen to nine hours a day, and required the factory owner to pay for two hours of education a day for these children. The effect was further to divide work and home life. The workday for adults and older teenagers remained twelve hours. Younger children often worked in relays of four or six hours. Consequently, the parental link was thoroughly broken. The education requirement began the process of removing nurturing and training from the home and family to a school, where a teacher rather than the parents was in charge of education.

After passage of the English Factory Act, many British workers demanded shorter workdays for adults. They desired to reunite, in some manner, the workday of adults with that of their children or at least to allow adults to spend more time with their children. In 1847, Parliament mandated a ten-hour workday. By present standards, this was long. At that time, however, it allowed parents and children more hours together as a domestic unit, since their relationship as a work or production unit had ceased wherever the factory system prevailed. By the mid-1840s, in the lives of industrial workers, the roles of men as breadwinners and as fathers and husbands had become distinct in the British textile industry. Furthermore, reformers' concerns about the working conditions of women in factories and in mines arose in part from the relatively new view that the place of women was in the home rather than in an industrial or even agrarian workplace.

Changing Economic Role for the Family What occurred in Britain presents a general pattern for what would happen elsewhere with the spread of industrial capitalism and public education. The European family was passing from being the chief unit of both production and consumption to becoming the chief unit of consumption alone. This development did not mean the end of the family as an economic unit. Parents and children, however, now came to depend on sharing wages often derived from several sources, rather than on sharing work in the home or factory.

Ultimately, the wage economy meant that families were less closely bound together than in the past. Because wages could be sent over long distances to parents, children might now move farther away from home. Once they moved far away, the economic link was, in time, often broken. In contrast, when a family settled in an industrial city, the wage economy might, in that or the next generation, actually discourage children from leaving home as early as they had in the past. Children could find wage employment in the same city and then live at home until they had accumulated enough savings to marry and begin their own household. That situation meant children often remained with their parents longer than in the past.

▼ Women in the Early Industrial Revolution

As noted in Chapter 15, the industrial economy ultimately produced an immense impact on the home and family life of women. First, it eventually took most productive work out of the home and allowed many families to live on the wages of the male spouse. That transformation prepared the way for a new concept of gender-determined roles in the home and in domestic life generally. Women came to be associated with domestic duties, such as housekeeping, food preparation, child rearing and nurturing, and household management, or with poorly paid, largely unskilled cottage industries. Men came to be associated almost exclusively with supporting the family. Children were raised to conform to these expected gender patterns. Previously, this domestic division of labor into separate male and female spheres had prevailed only among the relatively small middle class and the gentry. During the nineteenth century, that division came to characterize the working class as well.

Opportunities and Exploitation in Employment

Because the early Industrial Revolution had begun in textile production, women and their labor were deeply involved from the start. Although both spinning and weaving were still domestic industries, women usually worked in all stages of production. Hand spinning was virtually always a woman's task. At first, when spinning was moved into factories and involved large machines, men often displaced women. Furthermore, the higher wages male cotton-factory workers commanded allowed many married women not to work or to work only to supplement their husbands' wages.

Women in Factories With the next generation of machines in the 1820s, however, unmarried women

As textile production became increasingly automated in the nineteenth century, textile factories required fewer skilled workers and more unskilled attendants. To fill these unskilled positions, factory owners turned increasingly to unmarried women and widows, who worked for lower wages than men and were less likely to form labor organizations. Courtesy of the Library of Congress

rapidly became employed in the factories, where they often constituted the majority of workers. Their new jobs, however, often demanded fewer skills than those they had previously exercised in the home production of textiles. Women's factory work also required fewer skills than most work men did. Tending a machine required less skill than spinning or weaving or acting as forewoman. There was thus a certain paradox in the impact of the factory on women: It opened many new jobs to them but lowered the level of skills they needed to have. The supervisors of women were almost invariably men.

Moreover, almost always, the women in the factories were young, single women or widows. Upon marriage or perhaps after the birth of the first child, young women usually found their husbands earned enough money for them to leave the factory. Sometimes the factory owners, who disliked employing married women because of the likelihood of pregnancy, the influence of their husbands, and the duties of child rearing, no longer wanted them. Widows might return to factory work because they lacked their husbands' former income.

Work on the Land and in the Home In Britain and elsewhere by midcentury, industrial factory work still accounted for less than half of all employment for women. The largest group of employed women in France continued to work on the land. In England, they were domestic servants. Throughout Western Europe, domestic cottage industries, such as lace making, glove making, garment making, and other kinds of needlework, employed many women. In almost all such cases, their conditions of labor were harsh, whether they worked in their homes or in sweatshops. It cannot be overemphasized that all work by women commanded low wages and involved low skills. They had virtually no effective modes to protect themselves from exploitation. The charwoman, hired by the day to do rough house cleaning or washing, was a common sight across the Continent and symbolized the plight of working women.

The low wages of female workers in all areas of employment sometimes led them to become prostitutes to supplement their wage income. This situation prevailed across Europe throughout the century. In 1844, Louise Aston (1814–1871), a German political radical, portrayed this situation in a poem looking at the experience of a Silesian weaver as she confronts a factory owner on whom her family depends to purchase the cloth they have woven:

The factory owner has come,
And he says to me: "My darling child,
I know your people
Are living in misery and sorrow;
So if you want to lie with me
For three or four nights,
See this shiny gold coin!
It's yours immediately."[1]

Such sexual exploitation of women was hardly new to European society, but the particular pressures of the transformation of the economy from one of skilled artisans to that of unskilled factory workers made many women especially vulnerable. (See "Women Industrial Workers Explain Their Economic Situation.")

Changing Expectations in the Working-Class Marriage

Moving to cities and entering the wage economy gave women wider opportunities for marriage. Cohabitation before marriage was not uncommon. Parents had less to do with arranging marriages than in the past. Marriage now usually meant a woman would leave the workforce to live on her husband's earnings. If all went well, that arrangement might improve her situation. If the husband became ill or died, however, or if he deserted his wife, she would have to reenter the market for unskilled labor at an advanced age.

Despite these changes, many of the traditional practices associated with the family economy survived into the industrial era. As a young woman came of age, both family needs and her desire to marry still directed what she would do with her life. The most likely early occupation for a young woman was domestic service. A girl born in the country normally migrated to a nearby town or city for such employment, often living initially with a relative. As in the past, she would try to earn enough in wages to give herself a dowry, so she might marry and set up her own household. If she became a factory worker, she would probably live in a supervised dormitory. These dormitories helped attract young women to work in a factory by convincing parents their daughters would be safe.

The life of young women in the cities was more precarious than earlier. There were fewer family and community ties. There were also perhaps more available young men. These men, who worked for wages rather than in the older apprenticeship structures, were more mobile, so relationships between men and women often were more fleeting. In any case, illegitimate births increased; fewer women who became pregnant before marriage found the father willing to marry them.

Marriage in the wage industrial economy was also different in certain respects from marriage in earlier times. It still involved starting a separate household, but the structure of gender relationships within the household was different. Marriage was less an economic partnership. The husband's wages might well be able to support the entire family. The wage economy and the industrialization separating workplace from home made it difficult for women to combine domestic duties with work. When married women worked, it was usually in the nonindustrial sector of the economy. More often than not, the children rather than the wife were sent to work. This may help explain the increase in the number of births within marriages, as children in the wage economy usually were an economic asset. Married women worked outside the home only when family needs, illness, or widowhood forced them to.

In the home, working-class women were by no means idle. Their domestic duties were an essential factor in the family wage economy. If work took place elsewhere, someone had to be directly in charge of maintaining the home. Homemaking came to the fore when a life at home had to be organized separately from the place of work. Wives were concerned primarily with food and cooking, but they were also often in charge of the family's finances. The role of the mother expanded when the children still living at home became wage earners. She was now providing home support for her entire wage-earning family. She created the environment to which the family members returned after work. The longer period of home life of working children may also have increased and strengthened familial bonds of affection between those children and their hardworking homebound mothers. In all these respects, the culture of the working-class marriage and family tended to imitate the family patterns of the middle and upper classes, whose members had often accepted the view of separate gender spheres set forth by Rousseau and popularized in hundreds of novels, journals, and newspapers.

▼ Problems of Crime and Order

Throughout the nineteenth century, the political and economic elite in Europe was profoundly concerned about social order. The revolutions of the late eighteenth and early nineteenth centuries made them fearful of future disorder and threats to life and property. Industrialization and urbanization also contributed to this problem of order. Thousands of Europeans migrated from the countryside to the towns and cities. There, they often encountered poverty or unemployment and general social frustration and disappointment. Cities became

[1]As quoted in Lia Secci, "German Women Writers and the Revolution of 1848," in John C. Fout, ed., *German Women in the Nineteenth Century: A Social History* (New York: Holmes & Meier, 1984), p. 162.

WOMEN INDUSTRIAL WORKERS EXPLAIN THEIR ECONOMIC SITUATION

In 1832, there was much discussion in the British press about factory legislation. Most of that discussion concerned the employment of children, but the Examiner *newspaper suggested that factory laws should also, in time, eliminate women's employment in factories. That article provoked the following letter to the editor, composed by or on behalf of women factory workers, which stated why women needed such employment and the unattractive alternatives.*

What reasons do these women give to prove why they need to hold manufacturing jobs? What changes in production methods have led women from the home to the factory? How does the situation of these women relate to the possibility of their marrying?

Sir,

Living as we do, in the densely populated manufacturing districts of Lancashire, and most of us belonging to that class of females who earn their bread either directly or indirectly by manufactories, we have looked with no little anxiety for your opinion on the Factory Bill. . . . You are for doing away with our services in manufactories altogether. So much the better, if you had pointed out any other more eligible and practical employment for the surplus female labour, that will want other channels for a subsistence. If our competition were withdrawn, and short hours substituted, we have no doubt but the effects would be as you have stated, "not to lower wages, as the male branch of the family would be enabled to earn as much as the whole had done," but for the thousands of females who are employed in manufactories, who have no legitimate claim on any male relative for employment or support, and who have, through a variety of circumstance, been early thrown on their own resources for a livelihood, what is to become of them?

In this neighbourhood, hand-loom has been almost totally superseded by power-loom weaving, and no inconsiderable number of females, who must depend on their own exertions, or their parishes for support, have been forced, of necessity into the manufactories, from their total inability to earn a livelihood at home.

It is a lamentable fact, that, in these parts of the country, there is scarcely any other mode of employment for female industry, if we except servitude and dressmaking. Of the former of these, there is no chance of employment for one-twentieth of the candidates that would rush into the field, to say nothing of lowering the wages of our sisters of the same craft; and of the latter, galling as some of the hardships of manufactories are (of which the indelicacy of mixing with the men is not the least), yet there are few women who have been so employed, that would change conditions with the ill-used genteel little slaves, who have to lose sleep and health, in catering to the whims and frivolities of the butterflies of fashion.

We see no way of escape from starvation, but to accept the very tempting offers of the newspapers, held out as baits to us, fairly to ship ourselves off to Van Dieman's Land [Tasmania] on the very delicate errand of husband hunting, and having safely arrived at the "Land of Goshen," jump ashore, with a "Who wants me?". . .

The Female Operatives of Todmorden

From *The Examiner*, February 26, 1832, as quoted in Ivy Pinchbeck, *Women Workers and the Industrial Revolution, 1750–1850* (New York: Augustus M. Kelley, 1969), pp. 199–200.

associated with criminal activity, especially crimes against property, such as theft and arson. Throughout the first sixty years of the nineteenth century, crime appears to have increased slowly but steadily before more or less reaching a plateau.

Historians and social scientists are divided about the reasons for this rise in the crime rate. So little is known about crime in rural settings that comparisons with the cities are difficult. Moreover, crime statistics in the nineteenth century are problematic. No two

London Policeman. Professional police forces did not exist before the early nineteenth century. The London police force was created in 1828. Peter Newark's Pictures

nations kept them in the same manner. Different legal codes and systems of judicial administration were in effect in different areas of the Continent, thus giving somewhat different legal definitions of what constituted criminal activity. The result has been confusion, difficult research, and tentative conclusions.

New Police Forces

From the propertied, elite classes, two major views about containing crime and criminals emerged during the nineteenth century: better systems of police and prison reform. The result of these efforts was the triumph in Europe of the idea of a policed society in which a paid, professionally trained group of law-enforcement officers keeps order, protects property and lives, investigates crime, and apprehends offenders. These officers are distinct from the army and are charged specifically with domestic security. It is to them that the civilian population normally turns for law enforcement. A key feature of the theory of a policed society is that the visible presence of law-enforcement officers may prevent crime. These police forces, again at least in theory, did not perform a political role, although many countries often ignored that distinction. Police forces also became one of the largest groups of municipal government employees.

Professional police forces did not really exist until the early nineteenth century. They differed from one country to another in both authority and organization, but their creation proved crucial to the emergence of an orderly European society. The prefect of Paris, who was the chief administrative official of that city, set forth the principles that lay behind the founding of all of these new police units when he announced that "Safety by day and night, free traffic movement, clean streets, the supervision of and precaution against accidents, the maintenance of order in public places, the seeking out of offences and their perpetrators. . . . The municipal police is a parental police."[2]

Professional police forces appeared in Paris in 1828. The next year, the British Parliament passed legislation sponsored by Sir Robert Peel (1788–1850) that placed police on London streets. They were soon known as *bobbies* or, more disparagingly, as Peelers, after the sponsor of the legislation. Berlin deployed similar police departments after the Revolution of 1848. All of these forces were distinguished by an easily recognizable uniform. Police on the Continent carried guns; those in Britain did not.

Although citizens sometimes viewed police with suspicion, especially in Britain where many people opposed the creation of a professional police force as a threat to traditional British liberties, by the end of the century, most Europeans regarded the police as their protectors. Persons from the upper and middle classes felt police made their property more secure. Persons from the working class also frequently turned to the police to protect their lives and property and to aid them in emergencies. Of course, most people hated and feared political or secret police wherever governments, especially in Russia, created them.

Prison Reform

Before the nineteenth century, European prisons were local jails or state prisons, such as the Bastille. Governments also sent criminals to prison ships, called *hulks*. Some Mediterranean nations sentenced prisoners to naval galleys, where, chained to their benches, they rowed until they died or were eventually released. In prisons, inmates lived under wretched conditions. Men, women, and children were housed together. Persons guilty of minor offenses were left in the same room with those guilty of the most serious offenses.

Beginning in the late eighteenth century, the British government sentenced persons convicted of the most serious offenses to **transportation**. Transportation to the colony of New South Wales in Australia was regarded as an alternative to capital punishment, and the British used it until the mid-nineteenth century, when the colonies began to object. Thereafter, the British government housed long-term prisoners in public works prisons in Britain.

[2]Quoted in Clive Emsley, *Policing and Its Context, 1750–1870* (London: Macmillan, 1983), p. 58.

In many prisons, treadmills like these were the only source of exercise available to English prisoners.
Bildarchiv Preussischer Kulturbesitz

By the close of the eighteenth century and in the early nineteenth century, reformers, such as John Howard (1726–1790) and Elizabeth Fry (1780–1845) in England and Charles Lucas (1803–1889) in France, exposed the horrendous conditions in prisons and demanded change. Reform came slowly because of the expense of constructing new prisons and a lack of sympathy for criminals.

In the 1840s, however, both the French and the English undertook several bold efforts at prison reform. These efforts would appear to indicate a shift in opinion whereby crime was seen not as an assault on order or on authority but as a mark of a character fault in the criminal. Thereafter, part of the goal of imprisonment was to rehabilitate or transform the prisoner. The result of this change was the creation of exceedingly repressive prison systems designed according to the most advanced scientific modes of understanding criminals and criminal reform.

Europeans used various prison models originally established in the United States. All these experiments depended on separating prisoners from each other. One was known as the *Auburn system* after Auburn Prison in New York State. According to it, prisoners were separated from each other during the night but could associate while working during the day. The other was the *Philadelphia system*, in which prisoners were rigorously kept separated from each other at all times.

The chief characteristics of these systems were an individual cell for each prisoner and long periods of separation and silence among prisoners. The most famous example of this kind of prison in Europe was Pentonville Prison near London. There, each prisoner occupied a separate cell and was never allowed to speak to or see another prisoner. Each prisoner wore a mask when in the prison yard; in the chapel, each had a separate stall. The point of the system was to induce self-reflection in which the prisoners would think about their crimes and eventually decide to repudiate their criminal tendencies. As time passed, the system became more relaxed because the intense isolation often led to mental collapse.

In France, imprisonment became more repressive as the century passed. The French constructed prisons similar to Pentonville in the 1840s. In 1875, the French also adopted a firm, general policy of isolating inmates. France constructed sixty prisons based on this principle by 1908. Prisoners were supposed to be trained in a trade or skill while in prison so they could reemerge as reformed citizens.

The vast increase in repeat offenses led the French government in 1885, long after the British had abandoned the practice, to sentence serious repeat offenders to transportation to places such as the infamous Devil's Island off the coast of South America. Transportation was intended literally to purge the nation of its worst criminals and to ensure they would never return.

These attempts to create a police force and to reform prisons illustrate the concern about order and stability by European political and social elites that developed after the French Revolution. On the whole, their efforts succeeded. By the end of the century, an orderly society had been established, and the new police and prisons had no small role in that development.

▼ Classical Economics

Economists whose thought derived largely from Adam Smith's *The Wealth of Nations* (1776) dominated private and public discussions of industrial and commercial policy. Their ideas are often associated with the phrase *laissez-faire* (a French phrase that means roughly "let people do as they please"). Although they thought the government should perform many important functions, the classical economists favored economic growth through competitive free enterprise. They conceived of society as consisting of atomistic individuals whose competitive efforts met consumers' demands in the marketplace. They believed the mechanism of the marketplace should govern most economic decisions. They believed most government action to be mischievous and corrupt. The government should maintain a sound currency, enforce contracts, protect property, impose low tariffs and taxes, and leave the remainder of economic life to private initiative. The economists naturally assumed the state would maintain enough armed forces and naval power to protect the nation's economic structure and foreign trade. With emphasis on thrift, competition, and personal industriousness, the political economists' voice appealed to the middle classes.

Malthus on Population

The classical economists had complicated and pessimistic ideas about the working class. Thomas Malthus (1766–1834) and David Ricardo (1772–1823), probably the most influential of all these writers, suggested, in effect, that nothing could improve the condition of the working class. In 1798, Malthus published the first edition of his *Essay on the Principle of Population*. His ideas have haunted the world ever since. He contended that population must eventually outstrip the food supply. Although the human population grows geometrically, the food supply can expand only arithmetically. There was little hope of averting the disaster, in Malthus's opinion, except through late marriage, chastity, and contraception, the last of which he considered a vice. It took three quarters of a century for contraception to become a socially acceptable method of containing the population explosion.

Malthus contended that the immediate plight of the working class could only become worse. If wages were raised, the workers would simply produce more children, who would, in turn, consume both the extra wages and more food. Later in his life, Malthus suggested, in a more optimistic vein, that if the working class could be persuaded to adopt a higher standard of living, their increased wages might be spent on consumer goods rather than on begetting more children.

Ricardo on Wages

In his *Principles of Political Economy* (1817), David Ricardo transformed the concepts of Malthus into the "iron law of wages." If wages were raised, parents would have more children. They, in turn, would enter the labor market, thus expanding the number of workers and lowering wages. As wages fell, working people would produce fewer children. Wages would then rise, and the process would start all over again. Consequently, in the long run, wages would always tend toward a minimum level. These arguments simply supported employers in their natural reluctance to raise wages and also provided strong theoretical support for opposing labor unions. Journals, newspapers, and even short stories, such as Harriet Martineau's (1802–1876) series entitled *Illustrations of Political Economy*, spread the ideas of the economists to the public in the 1830s.

Government Policies Based on Classical Economics

The working classes of France and Great Britain, needless to say, resented the attitudes of the economists, but the governments embraced them. Louis Philippe (1773–1850) and his minister François Guizot (1787–1874) told the French to go forth and enrich themselves. People who simply displayed sufficient energy need not be poor. A number of the French middle class did just that. The July Monarchy (1830–1848) saw the construction of major capital-intensive projects, such as roads, canals, and railways. Little, however, was done about the poverty in the cities and the countryside.

In Germany, the middle classes made less headway. After the Napoleonic wars, however, the Prussian reformers had seen the desirability of abolishing internal tariffs that impeded economic growth. In 1834, all the major German states, except Austria, formed the ***Zollverein***, or free trading union. Classical economics had less influence in Germany because of the tradition dating from the enlightened absolutism of state direction of economic development. The German economist Friedrich List (1789–1846) argued for this approach to economic growth during the second quarter of the century.

Britain was the home of the major classical economists, and their policies were widely accepted. The utilitarian thought of Jeremy Bentham (1748–1832) increased their influence. Although **utilitarianism** did not originate with him, Bentham sought to create codes of scientific law that were founded on the principle of utility, that is, the greatest happiness for the greatest number. In his *Fragment on Government* (1776) and *The Principles of Morals and Legislation* (1789), Bentham explained the application of the principle of utility would overcome the special interests of privileged groups who prevented rational government. He regarded the existing legal and judicial systems as burdened by traditional practices that harmed the very people the law should serve. The application of reason and utility would remove the legal clutter that prevented justice from being realized. He believed the principle of utility could be applied to other areas of government administration.

Bentham gathered round him political disciples who combined his ideas with those of classical economics. In 1834, the reformed House of Commons passed a new Poor Law that followers of Bentham had prepared. This measure established a Poor Law Commission that set out to make poverty the most undesirable of all social situations. Government poor relief was to be disbursed only in workhouses. Life in the workhouse was consciously designed to be more unpleasant than life outside. Husbands and wives were separated, the food was bad, and the enforced work was distasteful. The social stigma of the workhouse was even worse. The law and its administration presupposed that people would not work because they were lazy. The laboring class, not unjustly, regarded the workhouses as new "bastilles."

MAJOR WORKS OF ECONOMIC AND POLITICAL COMMENTARY

1776	Adam Smith, *The Wealth of Nations*
1798	Thomas Malthus, *Essay on the Principle of Population*
1817	David Ricardo, *Principles of Political Economy*
1830s	Harriet Martineau, *Illustrations of Political Economy*
1839	Louis Blanc, *The Organization of Labor*
1845	Friedrich Engels, *The Condition of the Working Class in England*
1848	Karl Marx and Friedrich Engels, *The Communist Manifesto*

The second British monument to applied classical economics was the repeal of the **Corn Laws** in 1846. The Anti–Corn Law League, organized by manufacturers, had sought this goal for more than six years. The League wanted to abolish the tariffs protecting the domestic price of grain. That change would lead to lower food prices, which would then allow lower wages at no real cost to the workers. In turn, the prices on British manufactured goods could also be lowered to strengthen their competitive position in the world market.

The actual reason for Sir Robert Peel's repeal of the Corn Laws in 1846 was the Irish famine. Peel had to open British ports to foreign grain to feed the starving Irish. He realized the Corn Laws could not be reimposed. Peel accompanied the abolition measure with a program for government aid to modernize British agriculture and to make it more efficient. The repeal of the Corn Laws was the culmination of the lowering of British tariffs that had begun during the 1820s. It marked the opening of an era of free trade that continued until the twentieth century.

▼ Early Socialism

During the twentieth century, the socialist movement, in the form of either communist or social democratic political parties, constituted one of the major political forces in Europe. Less than 150 years ago, the advocates of socialism lacked any meaningful political following, and their doctrines appeared blurred and confused to most of their contemporaries. It is important to understand their early ideas and then to see (as shall be seen in later chapters) how those ideas, which for many years appeared on the margins of European political life, came to assume great importance in the late nineteenth century and beyond.

The early socialists generally applauded the new productive capacity of industrialism. They denied, however, that the free market could adequately produce and distribute goods the way the classical economists claimed. In the capitalist order, the socialists saw primarily mismanagement, low wages, misdistribution of goods, and suffering arising from the unregulated industrial system. Moreover, the socialists thought human society should be organized as a community, rather than merely as a conglomerate of atomistic, selfish individuals.

Utopian Socialism

Among the earliest people to define the social question was a group of writers whom their critics called the **utopian socialists**. They were considered utopian because their ideas were often visionary and because they frequently advocated the creation of ideal communities. They were called socialists because they questioned the structures and values of the existing capitalistic framework. In some cases, they actually deserved neither description. A significant factor in the experience of almost all of these groups was the discussion, and sometimes the practice, of radical ideas about sexuality and the family. People who might have been sympathetic to their economic concerns were profoundly unsympathetic to their views on free love and open family relationships.

Saint-Simonianism Count Claude Henri de Saint-Simon (1760–1825) was the earliest of the socialist pioneers. As a young, liberal French aristocrat, he had fought in the American Revolution. Later he welcomed the French Revolution, during which he made and lost a fortune. By the time of Napoleon's ascendancy, he had turned to a career of writing and social criticism and a concern for order.

Above all else, Saint-Simon believed modern society would require rational management. Private wealth, property, and enterprise should be subject to an administration other than that of its owners. His ideal government would have consisted of a large board of directors organizing and coordinating the activity of individuals and groups to achieve social harmony. In a sense, he was the ideological father of technocracy. Not the *redistribution* of wealth, but its *management* by experts, would alleviate the poverty and social dislocation of the age.

When Saint-Simon died in 1825, he had persuaded only a handful of people his ideas were correct. Nonetheless, Saint-Simonian societies were always centers for lively discussion of advanced social ideals. Some of the earliest debates in France over feminism took place within these societies. During the late 1820s and 1830s, the Saint-Simonians became well known for advocating sexuality outside marriage. Several of Saint-Simon's disciples also became leaders in the French railway industry during the 1850s.

Owenism The major British contributor to the early socialist tradition was Robert Owen (1771–1858), a self-made cotton manufacturer. In his early twenties, Owen

Mr Owen's Institution, New Lanark.
(Quadrille Dancing.)

Robert Owen, the Scottish industrialist and early socialist, created an ideal industrial community at New Lanark, Scotland. He believed deeply in the power of education and saw that the children of workmen received sound educations. Eileen Tweedy/Picture Desk, Inc./Kobal Collection

became a partner in one of the largest cotton factories in Britain at New Lanark, Scotland. Owen was a firm believer in the environmentalist psychology of the Enlightenment that had flowed from the thought of John Locke. If human beings were placed in the correct surroundings, they and their character could be improved. Moreover, Owen saw no incompatibility between creating a humane industrial environment and making a good profit.

At New Lanark, he put his ideas into practice. Workers were provided with good quarters. Recreational possibilities abounded, and the children received an education. There were several churches, although Owen himself was a notorious freethinker on matters of religion and sex. In the factory itself, rewards were given for good work. His plant made a fine profit. Visitors flocked from all over Europe to see what Owen had done through enlightened management.

In numerous articles and pamphlets, as well as in letters to influential people, Owen pleaded for a reorganization of industry based on his own successful model. He envisioned a series of communities shaped like parallelograms in which factory workers and farm workers might live together and produce their goods in cooperation. During the 1820s, Owen sold his New Lanark factory and then went to the United States, where he established the community of New Harmony, Indiana. When quarrels among the members led to the community's failure, he refused to give up his reformist causes. He returned to Britain, where he became the moving force behind the organization of the Grand National Union, an attempt to draw all British trade unions into a single body. It collapsed along with other labor organizations during the early 1830s.

Fourierism Charles Fourier (1772–1837) was Owen's French intellectual counterpart. He was a commercial salesperson who never succeeded in attracting the same kind of public attention as Owen. He wrote his books and articles and waited at home each day at noon, hoping to meet a patron who would undertake his program. No one ever arrived to meet him. Fourier believed the industrial order ignored the passionate side of human nature. Social discipline ignored all the pleasures that human beings naturally seek.

Fourier advocated the construction of communities, called *phalanxes*, in which liberated living would replace the boredom and dullness of industrial existence. Agrarian rather than industrial production would predominate in these communities. Sexual activity would be relatively free, and marriage was to be reserved only for later life. Fourier also urged that no person be required to perform the same kind of work for the entire day. People would be both happier and more productive if they moved from one task to another. Through his emphasis on the problem of boredom, Fourier isolated one of the key difficulties of modern economic life.

Saint-Simon, Owen, and Fourier expected some existing government to carry out their ideas. They failed to confront the political difficulties their envisioned social transformations would arouse. Other figures paid more attention to the politics of the situation. In 1839, Louis Blanc (1811–1882) published *The Organization of Labor*. Like other socialist writers, this Frenchman demanded an end to competition, but he did not seek a wholly new society. He called for political reform that would give the vote to the working class. Once so empowered, workers could use the vote to turn the political processes to their own economic advantage. A state controlled by a working-class electorate would finance workshops to employ the poor. In time, such workshops might replace private enterprise, and industry would be organized to ensure jobs. Blanc recognized the power of the state to improve life and the conditions of labor. The state itself could become the great employer of labor.

Anarchism

Other writers and activists of the 1840s, however, rejected both industry and the dominance of government. These were the **anarchists**. They are usually included in the socialist tradition, although they do not exactly fit there. Some favored programs of violence and terrorism; others were peaceful. Auguste Blanqui (1805–1881) was a major spokesperson for terror. He spent most of his adult life in jail. Seeking to abolish both capitalism and the state, Blanqui urged the development of a professional revolutionary vanguard to attack capitalist society. His ideas for the new society were vague, but in his call for professional revolutionaries, he foreshadowed Lenin.

Pierre-Joseph Proudhon (1809–1865) represented the other strain of anarchism. In his most famous work *What Is Property?* (1840), Proudhon attacked the banking system, which rarely extended credit to small-property owners or the poor. He wanted credit expanded to allow such people to engage in economic enterprise that would not involve unfair or unearned profits. Society should be organized on the basis of mutualism, which amounted to a system of small businesses and other cooperative enterprises among which there would be peaceful cooperation and exchanges of goods based on mutual recognition of the labor each area of production required. With such a social system, the state as the protector of property would be unnecessary. Later in the century, anarchists would favor a wide variety of cooperative businesses whose point was to favor the community good over that of the individual as well as to afford an essential fairness in exchange. Proudhon's ideas later influenced the French labor movement, which was generally less directly political in its activities than the labor movements in Britain and Germany.

Marxism

The mode of socialist thought that eventually exerted more influence over modern European history than any other was **Marxism**. During the late nineteenth century, its ideas permeated the major continental socialist parties. With the Bolshevik Revolution of November 1917, the communist strain of Marxist thought came to dominate the Soviet Union and, after World War II, Eastern Europe and revolutionary movements in the colonial and post-colonial world. With the collapse of the Soviet Union and of the communist governments in Eastern Europe in the last twenty years of the twentieth century, it is difficult for many people to recapture the power that Marx's political and social vision exerted over Europe and other parts of the world for more than a hundred years.

Too often, the history of European socialism has been regarded as a linear development leading naturally or necessarily to the late-nineteenth-century triumph of Marxism within the major socialist political parties. Nothing could be further from the truth. Marxist socialist ideas did eventually triumph over much, though not all, of Europe, but only through competition with other socialist formulas and largely as a result of the political situation in Germany during the last quarter of the nineteenth century. At midcentury, the ideas of Karl Marx were simply one more contribution to a heady mixture of concepts and programs criticizing the emerging industrial capitalist society. Marxism differed from its competitors in its claims to scientific accuracy, its rejection of liberal reform, its harsh criticism of other contemporary socialist platforms, and its call for revolution, though the character of that revolution was not well defined. Furthermore, Marx set the emergence of the industrial workforce in the context of a world historical development from which he drew sweeping political conclusions.

Karl Marx's socialist philosophy eventually triumphed over most alternative versions of socialism in Europe, but his monumental work became subject to varying interpretations, criticisms, and revisions that continue to this day. Library of Congress

Karl Marx (1818–1883) was born in Germany in the Prussian Rhineland. His family was Jewish, but his father had converted to Lutheranism, and Judaism played no role in his education. Marx's middle-class parents sent him to the University of Berlin, where he became deeply involved in Hegelian philosophy and radical politics. In 1842 and 1843, he edited the radical *Rhineland Gazette* (*Rheinische Zeitung*). Soon the Prussian authorities drove him from his native land. He lived as an exile, first in Paris, then in Brussels, and finally, after 1849, in London.

Partnership with Engels In 1844, Marx met Friedrich Engels (1820–1895), another young middle-class German, whose father owned a textile factory in Manchester, England. The next year Engels published *The Condition of the Working Class in England*, which presented a devastating picture of industrial life. The two men became fast friends. Late in 1847, they were asked to write a pamphlet for a newly organized and ultimately short-lived secret Communist League. *The Communist Manifesto*, published in German, appeared early in 1848. Marx, Engels, and the League had adopted the name *communist* because it was much more self-consciously radical than socialist. Communism implied the outright abolition of private property, rather than a less extensive rearrangement of society. Despite its later vast influence throughout the world, the *Manifesto*, a work of fewer than fifty pages, was at the time of its publication and for many years thereafter just one more political tract. Moreover, neither Marx nor his thought had any effect on the revolutionary events of 1848, which will be discussed more fully later in this chapter.

Sources of Marx's Ideas Marx derived the major ideas of the *Manifesto* and of his later work, including *Capital* (Vol. 1, 1867), from German Hegelianism, French utopian socialism, and British classical economics. Marx applied to concrete historical, social, and economic developments Hegel's abstract philosophical concept that thought develops from the clash of thesis and antithesis into a new intellectual synthesis. For Marx, the conflict between dominant and subordinate social groups led to the emergence of a new dominant social group. These new social relationships, in turn, generated new discontent, conflict, and development. The French utopian socialists had depicted the problems of capitalist society and had raised the issue of property redistribution. Both Hegel and Saint-Simon led Marx to see society and economic conditions as developing through historical stages. The classical economists had produced the analytical tools for an empirical, scientific examination of the industrial capitalist society.

Using the intellectual tools that Hegel, the French utopian socialists, and the British classical economists provided, Marx fashioned a philosophy that gave a special role or function to the new industrial workforce as the single most important driving force of contemporary history. Marx later explained to a friend:

> What I did that was new was to prove: (1) that the existence of classes is bound up with particular historical phases in the development of production; (2) that the class struggle necessarily leads to the dictatorship of the proletariat; (3) that this dictatorship itself only constitutes the transition to the abolition of all classes and to a classless society.[3]

In the *Communist Manifesto* and his numerous other writings, Marx equated the fate of the proletariat—that is, the new industrial labor force—with the fate of humanity itself. According to Marx, as the proletariat came to liberate itself from its bondage to the capitalist mode of industrial production, such liberation would eventually amount to the liberation of all humanity. It was this utopian vision of human emancipation, no matter how much the actual later development of the European and world economy failed to conform to Marx's predictions, that drew many people from Europe and elsewhere to embrace much of his thought and to base their political actions on their understanding of his philosophy. Besides this wider vision, however, the details of Marx's argument were also important for later nineteenth-century and twentieth-century European political life.

Revolution Through Class Conflict In the *Communist Manifesto*, Marx and Engels contended that human history must be understood rationally and as a whole. History is the record of humankind's coming to grips with physical nature to produce the goods necessary for survival. That basic productive process determines the structures, values, and ideas of a society. Historically, the organization of the means of production has always involved conflict between the classes that owned and controlled the means of production and the classes that worked for them. That necessary conflict has provided the engine for historical development; it is not an accidental by-product of mismanagement or bad intentions. Thus, piecemeal reforms cannot eliminate the social and economic evils inherent in the very structures of production. To achieve that, a radical social transformation is required. The development of capitalism will make such a revolution inevitable.

In Marx's and Engels's eyes, the class conflict that had characterized previous Western history had become simplified during the early nineteenth century into a struggle between the bourgeoisie and the proletariat, or between the middle class associated with industry and commerce, on the one hand, and the workers, on the other. The character of capitalism itself ensured the sharpening of the struggle. Capitalist production and competition would steadily increase the size of the unpropertied proletariat. Large-scale mechanical production crushed both traditional and smaller industrial producers into the ranks of the proletariat. As the business structures grew larger and larger, the competitive pressures would squeeze out smaller middle-class units. Competition among the few remaining giant concerns would lead to more intense suffering for the proletariat. The process also meant the proletariat itself would continue to expand to include more and more people. As this ever-expanding body of workers suffered increasingly from the competition among the ever-enlarging firms, Marx contended, they would eventually begin to foment revolution. Finally, they would overthrow the few remaining owners of the means of production. For a time, the workers would organize the means of production through a dictatorship of the proletariat. This would eventually give way to a propertyless and classless communist society.

This proletarian revolution was inevitable, according to Marx and Engels. The structure of capitalism required competition and consolidation of enterprise. Although the class conflict involved in the contemporary process resembled that of the past, it differed in one major respect: The struggle between the capitalistic bourgeoisie and the industrial proletariat would culminate in a wholly new society that would be free of class conflict. The victorious proletariat, by its very nature, could not be a new oppressor class: "The proletarian movement is the self-conscious, independent movement of the immense majority, in the interest of the immense majority."[4] The result of the proletarian victory would be "an association in which the free development of each is the condition for the free development of all."[5] The victory of the proletariat over the bourgeoisie would represent the culmination of human history. For the first time in human history, one group of people would not be oppressing another. (See "Karl Marx and Friedrich Engels Describe the Class Struggle," page 644.)

The economic environment of the 1840s had conditioned Marx's analysis. The decade had seen much unemployment and deprivation. During the later part of the century, however, European and American capitalism did not collapse as he had predicted, nor did the middle class become proletarianized. Rather, the industrial system benefited more and more people. Nonetheless,

[3]Albert Fried and Ronald Sanders, eds., *Socialist Thought: A Documentary History* (Garden City, NY: Anchor Doubleday, 1964), p. 295.

[4]Robert C. Tucker, ed., *The Marx-Engels Reader* (New York: W. W. Norton, 1972), p. 353.

[5]Tucker, *The Marx-Engels Reader*, p. 353.

KARL MARX AND FRIEDRICH ENGELS DESCRIBE THE CLASS STRUGGLE

The Communist Manifesto (1848) is arguably the most influential political pamphlet of modern European history. In that relatively brief document, Karl Marx and Friedrich Engels portrayed human history as developing from ancient times to the present through a series of economic class struggles. In the contemporary world, they saw the complex struggles of the past reduced to a head-on economic, political, and social clash between the bourgeoisie, or capital-owning class, and the proletariat, or workers. Both groups had emerged in the course of history. The bourgeoisie had arisen from medieval townsmen asserting their liberty against feudal landowners and then against other groups of aristocrats. In turn, as the bourgeoisie came to dominate the economy and invest their capital in modern industry, they produced the contemporary wage-labor force. Over time this labor force came to see that its interests opposed those of its economic masters. The result was to be the final class conflict of history because, as Marx and Engels argued, the proletariat, unlike any previous group seeking to establish its liberty, was so large that its victory was also the victory of humanity itself.

Whom do Marx and Engels portray as the previous enemies of the bourgeoisie? How did bourgeois economic development and dominance lead to a society based on the "cash nexus"? Why is the bourgeoisie responsible for the emergence of the proletariat? Why is the victory of the proletariat inevitable?

The history of all hitherto existing society is the history of class struggles. . . .

Our epoch, the epoch of the bourgeoisie, possesses, however, this distinctive feature: it has simplified the class antagonisms. Society as a whole is more and more splitting up into two great hostile camps, into two great classes directly facing each other: Bourgeoisie and Proletariat. . . .

Each step in the development of the bourgeoisie was accompanied by a corresponding political advance of that class. . . .

The bourgeoisie, wherever it has gotten the upper hand, has put an end to all feudal, patriarchal, idyllic relations. It has pitilessly torn asunder the motley feudal ties that bound man to his "natural superiors," and has left remaining no other nexus between man and man than naked self-interest, than callous "cash payment.". . .

The proletariat goes through various stages of development. With its birth begins its struggle with the bourgeoisie. . . .

But with the development of industry the proletariat not only increases in number; it becomes concentrated in greater masses, its strength grows, and it feels that strength more. The various interests and conditions of life within the ranks of the proletariat are more and more equalized, in proportion as machinery obliterates all distinctions of labour, and nearly everywhere reduces wages to the same low level. . . .

The bourgeoisie finds itself involved in a constant battle. . . .

Of all the classes that stand face to face with the bourgeoisie today, the proletariat alone is a really revolutionary class. . . .

All previous historical movements were movements of minorities, or in the interest of minorities. The proletarian movement is the self-conscious, independent movement of the immense majority, in the interest of the immense majority. . . .

The advance of industry, whose involuntary promoter is the bourgeoisie, replaces the isolation of the labourers, due to competition, by their revolutionary combination, due to association. The development of Modern Industry, therefore, cuts from under its feet the very foundation on which the bourgeoisie produces and appropriates products. What the bourgeoisie, therefore, produces, above all, is its own grave-diggers. Its fall and the victory of the proletariat are equally inevitable. . . .

The proletarians have nothing to lose but their chains. They have a world to win.

Karl Marx and Friedrich Engels, *The Communist Manifesto*, in Lawrence H. Simon, ed., *Karl Marx, Selected Writings* (Indianapolis: Hackett Publishing Company, Inc, 1994), pp. 158, 159, 160, 161, 165, 166–167, 168, 169, 186.

within a generation of the publication of the *Communist Manifesto*, Marxism had captured the imagination of many socialists, especially in Germany, and large segments of the working class. Marxist doctrines appeared to be based on the empirical evidence of hard economic fact. Marxism's scientific claim helped spread the ideology as science became more influential during the second half of the century. At its core, however, the attraction of the ideology was its utopian vision of ultimate human liberation, no matter how illiberal or authoritarian the governments that embraced the Marxist vision in the twentieth century were.

▼ 1848: Year of Revolutions

In 1848, a series of liberal and nationalistic revolutions erupted across the Continent. (See Map 21–2.) No single factor caused this general revolutionary groundswell; rather, similar conditions existed in several countries. Severe food shortages had prevailed since 1846. Grain and potato harvests had been poor. The famine in Ireland was simply the worst example of a more widespread situation. The commercial and industrial economy was also depressed. Unemployment was widespread. Systems of poor relief were overburdened. These

Map 21–2 **CENTERS OF REVOLUTION IN 1848–1849** The revolution that toppled the July Monarchy in Paris in 1848 soon spread to Austria and many of the German and Italian states. Yet by the end of 1849, most of these uprisings had been suppressed.

difficulties, added to the wretched living conditions in the cities, heightened the frustration and discontent of the urban artisan and laboring classes.

The dynamic force for change in 1848 originated, however, not with the working classes, but with the political liberals, who were generally drawn from the middle classes. Throughout the Continent, liberals were pushing for their program of a more representative government, civil liberty, and unregulated economic life. The repeal of the English Corn Laws and the example of peaceful agitation by the Anti–Corn Law League encouraged them. The liberals on the Continent wanted to pursue similar peaceful tactics. To put additional pressure on their governments, however, they began to appeal for the support of the urban working classes. The latter, however, wanted improved working and economic conditions, rather than a more liberal government. Moreover, their tactics were frequently violent rather than peaceful. The temporary alliance of liberals and workers in several states overthrew or severely shook the old order; then the allies began to fight each other.

Finally, outside France, nationalism was an important common factor in the uprisings. Germans, Hungarians, Italians, Czechs, and smaller national groups in eastern Europe sought to create national states that would reorganize or replace existing political entities. The Austrian Empire, as usual, was the state nationalism most profoundly endangered. At the same time, various national groups clashed with each other during these revolutions.

The immediate results of the 1848 revolutions were stunning. Never in a single year had Europe known so many major uprisings. The French monarchy fell, and other thrones were shaken. Yet the revolutions proved to be a false spring for progressive Europeans. Without exception, the revolutions failed to establish genuinely liberal or national states. The conservative order proved stronger and more resilient than anyone had expected. Moreover, the liberal middle-class political activists in each country discovered they could no longer push for political reform without also raising the social question. The liberals refused to follow political revolution with social reform and thus isolated themselves from the working classes. Once separated from potential mass support, the liberal revolutions became an easy prey for the armies of the reactionary classes.

France: The Second Republic and Louis Napoleon

As had happened twice before, the revolutionary tinder first blazed in Paris. The liberal political opponents of the corrupt regime of Louis Philippe and his minister Guizot organized a series of political banquets. They used these occasions to criticize the government and demand further admission for them and their middle-class supporters to the political process. The poor harvests of 1846 and 1847 and the resulting high food prices and unemployment brought working-class support to the liberal campaign. On February 21, 1848, the government forbade further banquets. A large one had been scheduled for the next day. On February 22, disgruntled Parisian workers paraded through the streets demanding reform and Guizot's ouster. The next morning the crowds grew, and by afternoon, Guizot had resigned. The crowds erected barricades, and numerous clashes occurred between the citizenry and the municipal guard. On February 24, 1848, Louis Philippe abdicated and fled to England.

The National Assembly and Paris Workers The liberal opposition, led by the poet Alphonse de Lamartine (1790–1869), organized a provisional government. The liberals intended to call an election for an assembly that would write a republican constitution. The various working-class groups in Paris, however, had other ideas: They wanted a social as well as a political revolution. Led by Louis Blanc, they demanded representation in the cabinet. Blanc and two other radical leaders became ministers. Under their pressure, the provisional government organized national workshops to provide work and relief for thousands of unemployed workers.

On Sunday, April 23, an election based on universal male suffrage chose the new National Assembly. The result was a legislature dominated by moderates and conservatives. In the French provinces, many people resented the Paris radicals and were frightened by their ideas. The church and the local notables still exercised considerable influence. Peasants feared that Parisian socialists would confiscate their small farms. The new conservative National Assembly had little sympathy for the expensive national workshops, which they incorrectly perceived to be socialistic.

Throughout May, government troops and the unemployed workers and artisans of Paris clashed. As a result, the assembly closed the workshops to new entrants and planned to eject many enrolled workers. By late June, barricades again appeared in Paris. On June 24, under orders from the government, General Louis Cavaignac (1802–1857), with troops drawn largely from the conservative countryside, moved to destroy the barricades and quell disturbances. During the next two days, more than four hundred people were killed. Thereafter, troops hunted down another 3,000 persons in street fighting. The drive for social revolution had ended.

Emergence of Louis Napoleon The so-called June Days confirmed the political predominance of conservative property holders in French life. They wanted a state that was safe for small property. Late in 1848, the election for president confirmed this search for social

During the February days of the French Revolution of 1848, crowds in Paris burned the throne of Louis Philippe. Bildarchiv Preussischer Kulturbesitz

order. The new president was Louis Napoleon Bonaparte (1808–1873), a nephew of the great emperor. For most of his life, he had been an adventurer living outside of France. Twice he had attempted to lead a coup against the July Monarchy. The disorder of 1848 gave him a new opportunity to enter French political life. After the corruption of Louis Philippe and the turmoil of the early months of the Second Republic, the voters turned to the name of Bonaparte as a source of stability and greatness.

The election of the "Little Napoleon" doomed the Second Republic. Louis Napoleon was dedicated to his own fame rather than to republican institutions. He was the first of the modern dictators who, by playing on unstable politics and social insecurity, changed European life. He quarreled with the National Assembly and claimed that he, rather than they, represented the will of the nation. In 1851, the assembly refused to amend the constitution to allow the president to run for reelection. Consequently, on December 2, 1851, the anniversary of the great Napoleon's victory at Austerlitz, Louis Napoleon seized power. Troops dispersed the assembly, and the president called for new elections. More than two hundred people died resisting the coup, and more than 26,000 persons were arrested throughout the country. Almost 10,000 persons who opposed the coup were transported to Algeria.

Yet, in the plebiscite of December 21, 1851, more than 7.5 million voters supported the actions of Louis Napoleon and approved a new constitution that consolidated his power. Only about 600,000 citizens dared to vote against him. A year later, in December 1852, an empire was proclaimed, and Louis Napoleon became Emperor Napoleon III. Again a plebiscite approved the action. For the second time in just over fifty years, France had turned from republicanism to Caesarism.

Frenchwomen in 1848 The years between the February Revolution of 1848 and the Napoleonic coup of 1851 saw major feminist activity by Frenchwomen. Especially in Paris, women seized the opportunity of the collapse of the July Monarchy to voice demands for reform of their social conditions. They joined the wide variety of political clubs that emerged in the wake of the revolution. Some of these clubs emphasized women's rights. Some women even tried unsuccessfully to vote in the elections of 1848. Both middle-class and working-class women were involved in these activities. The most radical group of women called themselves the Vesuvians, after the volcano in Italy. They claimed it was time for the demands of women to erupt like pent-up lava. They demanded full domestic household equality between men and women, the right of women to serve in the military, and similarity in dress for both sexes. They also conducted street demonstrations. The radical character of their demands and actions lost them the support of more moderate women.

Certain Parisian women quickly attempted to use for their own cause the liberal freedoms that suddenly had become available. They organized the *Voix des femmes (The Women's Voice)*, a daily newspaper that addressed issues of concern to women. The newspaper insisted that improving the lot of men would not necessarily improve the condition of women. They soon organized a society with the same name as the newspaper. Many of the women involved in the newspaper and society had earlier been involved in Saint-Simonian or Fourierist groups. Members of the *Voix des femmes* group were relatively conservative feminists. They cooperated with male political groups, and they urged the integrity of the family and fidelity in marriage. They furthermore warmly embraced the maternal role for women but tried to use it to raise the importance of women in society. Because motherhood and child rearing are so important to a society, they argued, women must receive better education, economic security, equal civil rights, property rights, and the rights to work and vote. The provisional government made no move to enact these rights, although some members of the assembly supported the women's groups. The emphasis on family and motherhood represented, in part, a defensive strategy to prevent conservative women and men from accusing the advocates of women's rights of seeking to destroy the family and traditional marriage.

The fate of French feminists in 1848 was similar to that of the radical workers. They were thoroughly defeated and their efforts wholly frustrated. Once the elections were held that spring, the new government expressed no sympathy for their causes. The closing of the national workshops adversely affected women workers as well as men and blocked one outlet that women had used to make their needs known. The conservative crackdown on political clubs closed another arena in which women had participated. Women were soon specifically forbidden to participate in political clubs either by themselves or with men. These repressive actions repeated what had happened to politically active Frenchwomen and their organizations in 1793.

THE REVOLUTIONARY CRISIS OF 1848 TO 1851

	1848
February 22–24	Revolution in Paris forces the abdication of Louis Philippe
February 26	National workshops established in Paris
March 3	Kossuth attacks the Habsburg domination of Hungary
March 13	Revolution in Vienna
March 15	The Habsburg emperor accepts the Hungarian March Revolution Laws in Berlin
March 18	Frederick William IV of Prussia promises a constitution; revolt against Austria in Milan
March 19	Frederick William IV is forced to salute the corpses of slain revolutionaries in Berlin
March 22	Piedmont declares war on Austria
April 23	Election of the French National Assembly
May 15	Worker protests in Paris lead the National Assembly to close the national workshops
May 17	Habsburg emperor Ferdinand flees from Vienna to Innsbruck
May 18	The Frankfurt Assembly gathers to prepare a German constitution
June 2	Pan-Slavic Congress gathers in Prague
June 17	Austrian troops suppress a Czech revolution in Prague
June 23–26	Troops of the National Assembly suppress a workers' insurrection in Paris
July 24	Austria defeats Piedmont
September 17	General Jellachich invades Hungary
October 31	Vienna falls to General Windischgraetz
November 15	Papal minister Rossi is assassinated in Rome
November 16	Revolution in Rome
November 25	Pope Pius IX flees Rome
December 2	Habsburg Emperor Ferdinand abdicates and Francis Joseph becomes emperor
December 10	Louis Napoleon is elected president of the Second French Republic
	1849
January 5	General Windischgraetz occupies Budapest
February 2	The Roman Republic is proclaimed
March 12	War is resumed between Piedmont and Austria
March 23	Piedmont is defeated, and Charles Albert abdicates the crown of Piedmont in favor of Victor Emmanuel II

March 27	The Frankfurt Parliament completes a constitution for Germany
March 28	The Frankfurt Parliament elects Frederick William IV of Prussia to be emperor of Germany
April 21	Frederick William IV of Prussia rejects the crown offered by the Frankfurt Parliament
June 18	Troops disperse the remaining members of the Frankfurt Parliament
July 3	French troops overthrow the Roman Republic
August 9–13	Austria, aided by Russian troops, defeats the Hungarians
	1851
December 2	*Coup d'état* of Louis Napoleon

At this point, women associated with the *Voix des femmes* attempted to organize workers' groups to improve the economic situation for working-class women. Two leaders of this effort, Jeanne Deroin (d. 1894) and Pauline Roland (1805–1852), were arrested, tried, and imprisoned for these activities. The former eventually left France; the latter was sent off to Algeria during the repression after the coup of Louis Napoleon. By 1852, the entire feminist movement that had sprung up in 1848 had been eradicated.

The Habsburg Empire: Nationalism Resisted

The events of February 1848 in Paris immediately reverberated throughout the Habsburg domains. The empire was susceptible to revolutionary challenge on every score. Its government rejected liberal institutions. Its borders cut across national lines. Its society perpetuated serfdom. During the 1840s, even Metternich had urged reform, but none was forthcoming. In 1848, the regime confronted rebellions in Vienna, Prague, Hungary, and Italy. The disturbances that broke out in Germany also threatened Habsburg predominance.

The Vienna Uprising The Habsburg troubles began on March 3, 1848, when Louis Kossuth (1802–1894), a Magyar nationalist and member of the Hungarian diet, attacked Austrian domination, called for the independence of Hungary, and demanded a responsible ministry under the Habsburg dynasty. Ten days later, inspired by Kossuth's speeches, students led a series of disturbances in Vienna. The army failed to restore order. Metternich resigned and fled the country. The feeble-minded Emperor Ferdinand (r. 1835–1848) promised a moderately liberal constitution. Unsatisfied, the radical students then formed democratic clubs to press the revolution further. On May 17, the emperor and the imperial court fled to Innsbruck. The government of Vienna at this point lay in the hands of a committee of more than two hundred persons concerned primarily with alleviating the economic plight of the city's workers.

What the Habsburg government most feared was not the urban rebellions but an uprising of the serfs in the countryside. Already a few serfs had invaded manor houses and burned property records. Consequently, almost immediately after the Vienna uprising, the imperial government emancipated the serfs in much of Austria. The Hungarian diet also abolished serfdom in March 1848. These actions smothered the most serious potential threat to order in the empire. The emancipated serfs now had little reason to support the revolutionary movement in the cities. These emancipations were one of the most important permanent results of the Revolutions of 1848.

The Magyar Revolt The Vienna revolt had emboldened the Hungarians. The Magyar leaders of the Hungarian March Revolution were primarily liberals supported by nobles who wanted their aristocratic liberties guaranteed against the central government in Vienna. The Hungarian diet passed the March Laws, which mandated equality of religion, jury trials, the election of the lower chamber of the diet, a relatively free press, and payment of taxes by the nobility. Emperor Ferdinand approved these measures because in the spring of 1848 he could do little else.

The Magyars also hoped to establish a separate Hungarian state within the Habsburg domains. They would exercise local autonomy while Ferdinand remained their emperor. As part of this scheme for a partially independent state, the Hungarians attempted to annex Transylvania, Croatia, and other eastern territories of the Habsburg Empire. That annexation would have brought Romanians, Croatians, and Serbs under Magyar government. These national groups resisted the drive toward Magyarization, especially the imposition on them, for the purposes of the government and administration, of the Hungarian language. The national groups whom the Hungarians were now repressing believed the Habsburgs offered them a better chance to preserve their national or ethnic identity, their languages, and their economic self-interest. In late March, the Vienna government sent Count Joseph Jellachich (1801–1859) to aid the national groups who were rebelling against the rebellious Hungarians. By early September 1848, he was invading Hungary with the support of the national groups who were resisting Magyarization. These events in Hungary represented a prime example of the clash between liberalism and nationalism. The Hungarian March Laws would have created a state that was liberal in political structure but

Louis Kossuth, a Magyar nationalist, seeking to raise troops to fight for Hungarian independence during the revolutionary disturbances of 1848. Bildarchiv Preussischer Kulturbesitz

would not have allowed autonomy to the non-Magyar peoples within its borders.

Czech Nationalism In mid-March 1848, with Vienna and Budapest in revolt, Czech nationalists demanded that the Czech provinces of Bohemia and Moravia be permitted to constitute an autonomous Slavic state within the empire similar to that just enacted in Hungary. Conflict immediately developed, however, between the Czechs and the Germans living in these regions. The Czechs summoned a congress of Slavs, including Poles, Ruthenians, Czechs, Slovaks, Croats, Slovenes, and Serbs, which met in Prague in early June. Under the leadership of Francis Palacky (1798–1876), this first Pan-Slavic Congress called for the national equality of Slavs within the Habsburg Empire. The manifesto also protested the repression of all Slavic peoples under Habsburg, Hungarian, German, and Ottoman domination. The document raised the vision of a vast east European Slavic nation or federation of Slavic states that would extend from Poland south and eastward through Ukraine and within which Russian interests would surely dominate. Although such a state never came into being, the prospect of a unified Slavic people freed from Ottoman, Habsburg, and German control was an important political factor in later European history. Russia would use **Pan-Slavism** as a tool to attempt to gain the support of nationalist minorities in eastern Europe and the Balkans and to bring pressure against both the Habsburg Empire and Germany. (See "The Pan-Slavic Congress Calls for the Liberation of Slavs.")

On June 12, the day the Pan-Slavic Congress closed, a radical insurrection broke out in Prague. General Prince Alfred Windischgraetz (1787–1862), whose wife had been killed by a stray bullet, moved his troops against the uprising. The Prague middle class was happy to see the radicals suppressed, which was finalized by June 17. The Germans in the area approved the smothering of Czech nationalism. The policy of "divide and conquer" had succeeded.

Rebellion in Northern Italy While repelling the Hungarian and Czech bids for autonomy, the Habsburg government also faced war in northern Italy. A revolt against Habsburg domination began in Milan on March 18. Five days later, the Austrian commander General Count Joseph Wenzel Radetzky (1766–1858) retreated from the city. King Charles Albert of Piedmont (r. 1831–1849), who wanted to annex Lombardy (the province of which Milan is the capital), aided the rebels. The Austrian forces fared badly until July, when

THE PAN-SLAVIC CONGRESS CALLS FOR THE LIBERATION OF SLAVS

The first Pan-Slavic Congress met in Prague in June 1848. It called for the political reorganization of the Austrian Empire and most of eastern Europe. Its calls for changes in the national standing of the various Slavic peoples would have affected the Russian, Austrian, and Ottoman Empires, as well as some of the then disunited states of Germany. The national aspirations the congress voiced would affect Europe from that time to the present. Note that the authors of the manifesto recognize that the principle of nationality, as adapted to the political life of Slavic peoples, is relatively new in 1848.

How did the authors apply the individual freedoms associated with the French Revolution to the fate of individual nations? What areas of Europe would these demands have changed? What potential differences among the Slavic peoples does the manifesto ignore or gloss over?

The Slavic Congress in Prague is something unheard-of, in Europe as well as among the Slavs themselves. For the first time since our appearance in history, we, the scattered members of a great race, have gathered in great numbers from distant lands in order to become reacquainted as brothers and to deliberate our affairs peacefully. We have understood one another not only through our beautiful language, spoken by eighty million, but also through the consonance of our hearts and the similarity of our spiritual qualities. . . .

It is not only in behalf of the individual within the state that we raise our voices and make known our demands. The nation, with all its intellectual merit, is as sacred to us as are the rights of an individual under natural law. . . .

In the belief that the powerful spiritual stream of today demands new political forms and that the state must be re-established upon altered principles, if not within new boundaries, we have suggested to the Austrian Emperor, under whose constitutional government we, the majority [of Slavic peoples] live, that he transform his imperial state into a union of equal nations. . . .

We raise our voices vigorously in behalf of our unfortunate brothers, the Poles, who were robbed of their national identity by insidious force. We call upon the governments to rectify this curse and these old onerous and hereditary sins in their administrative policy, and we trust in the compassion of all Europe. . . . We demand that the Hungarian Ministry abolish without delay the use of inhuman and coercive means toward the Slavic races in Hungary, namely the Serbs, Croats, Slovaks, and Ruthenians, and that they promptly be completely assured of their national rights. Finally, we hope that the inconsiderate policies of the Porte will no longer hinder our Slavic brothers in Turkey from strongly claiming their nationality and developing it in a natural way. If, therefore, we formally express our opposition to such despicable deeds, we do so in the confidence that we are working for the good of freedom. Freedom makes the peoples who hitherto have ruled more just and makes them understand that injustice and arrogance bring disgrace not to those who must endure it but to those who act in such a manner.

From the "Manifesto of the First Pan-Slavic Congress," trans. by Max Riedlsperger from I. I. Udalzow, *Aufzeichnungen über die Geschichte des nationalen und politischen Kampfes in Böhme im Jahre 1848* (Berlin: Rutten & Loening, 1953), pp. 223–226, as quoted in Stephen Fischer-Galati, ed., *Man, State, and Society in East European History*.

Radetzky, reinforced by new troops, defeated Piedmont and suppressed the revolt. For the time being, Austria held its position in northern Italy.

Vienna and Hungary remained to be recaptured. In midsummer, the emperor returned to the capital. A newly elected assembly was trying to write a constitution, and within the city, the radicals continued to press for concessions. The imperial government decided to reassert its control. When a new insurrection occurred in October, the imperial army bombarded Vienna and crushed the revolt. On December 2, Emperor Ferdinand, clearly too feeble to govern, abdicated in favor of his young nephew Francis Joseph (r. 1848–1916). Real power now lay with Prince Felix Schwarzenberg (1800–1852), who intended to use the army with full force.

On January 5, 1849, troops occupied Budapest. By March the triumphant Austrian forces had imposed military rule over Hungary, and the new emperor repudiated the recent constitution. The Magyar nobles attempted one last revolt. In August, Austrian troops, reinforced by 200,000 soldiers that Tsar Nicholas I of Russia (r. 1825–1855) happily furnished, finally crushed the Hungarians. Croatians and other nationalities that had resisted Magyarization welcomed the collapse of the revolt. The imperial Habsburg government survived its gravest internal challenge because of the divisions among its enemies and its own willingness to use military force with a vengeance.

Italy: Republicanism Defeated

The brief war between Piedmont and Austria in 1848 marked only the first stage of the Italian revolution. Many Italians hoped King Charles Albert of Piedmont would drive Austria from the peninsula and thus prepare the way for Italian unification. The defeat of Piedmont was a sharp disappointment to them. Liberal and nationalist hopes then shifted to the pope. Pius IX (r. 1846–1878) had a liberal reputation. He had reformed the administration of the Papal States. Nationalists believed a united Italian state might emerge under his leadership.

In Rome, however, as in other cities, political radicalism was on the rise. On November 15, 1848, a democratic radical assassinated Count Pelligrino Rossi (r. 1787–1848), the liberal minister of the Papal States. The next day, popular demonstrations forced the pope to appoint a radical ministry. Shortly thereafter, Pius IX fled to Naples for refuge. In February 1849, the radicals proclaimed the Roman Republic. Republican nationalists from all over Italy, including Giuseppe Mazzini (1805–1872) and Giuseppe Garibaldi (1807–1882), two of the most prominent, flocked to Rome. They hoped to use the new republic as a base of operations to unite the rest of Italy under a republican government.

In March 1849, radicals in Piedmont forced Charles Albert to renew the patriotic war against Austria. After the almost immediate defeat of Piedmont at the Battle of Novara, the king abdicated in favor of his son, Victor Emmanuel II (r. 1849–1878). The defeat meant the Roman Republic must defend itself alone. The troops that attacked Rome and restored the pope came from France. The French wanted to prevent the rise of a strong, unified state on their southern border. Moreover, protection of the pope was good domestic politics for the French Republic and its president, Louis Napoleon. In early June 1849, 10,000 French soldiers laid siege to Rome. By the end of the month, the Roman Republic had dissolved. Garibaldi attempted to lead an army north against Austria, but he was defeated. On July 3, Rome fell to the French forces, which stayed there to protect the pope until 1870.

Pius IX renounced his liberalism. He became one of the arch conservatives of the next quarter century. Leadership for Italian unification would have to come from another direction.

Germany: Liberalism Frustrated

The revolutionary contagion had also spread rapidly through the German states. Insurrections calling for liberal government and greater German unity erupted in Wurtemburg, Saxony, Hanover, and Bavaria where King Ludwig I (r. 1825–1848) was forced to abdicate in favor of his son. The major revolution, however, occurred in Prussia.

Revolution in Prussia By March 15, 1848, large popular disturbances had erupted in Berlin. Frederick William IV (r. 1840–1861), believing the trouble stemmed from foreign conspirators, refused to turn his troops on the Berliners. He even announced limited reforms. Nevertheless, on March 18, several citizens were killed when troops cleared a square near the palace.

The monarch was still hesitant to use his troops forcefully, and the government was divided and confused. The king called for a Prussian constituent assembly to write a constitution. The next day, as angry Berliners crowded around the palace, Frederick William IV appeared on the balcony to salute the corpses of his slain subjects. He made further concessions and implied that henceforth Prussia would helped unify Germany. For all practical purposes, the Prussian monarchy had capitulated.

Frederick William IV appointed a cabinet headed by David Hansemann (1790–1864), a widely respected moderate liberal. The Prussian constituent assembly, however, proved to be radical and democratic. As time passed, the king and his conservative supporters decided to ignore the assembly. The liberal ministry resigned and a conservative one replaced it. In April 1849, the assembly was dissolved, and the monarch proclaimed his own constitution. One of its key elements was a system of three-class voting. All adult males were allowed to vote. They voted, however, according to three classes arranged by ability to pay taxes. Thus the largest taxpayers, who constituted only about 5 percent of the population, elected one third of the Prussian Parliament. This system prevailed in Prussia until 1918. In the revised Prussian constitution of 1850, the ministry was responsible to the king alone. Moreover, the Prussian army and officer corps swore loyalty directly to the monarch.

The Frankfurt Parliament While Prussia was moving from revolution to reaction, other events were unfolding in Germany as a whole. On May 18, 1848, representatives from all the German states gathered in Saint Paul's Church in Frankfurt to revise the organization of the German Confederation. The Frankfurt Parliament intended to write a moderately liberal constitution for a united Germany. The liberal character of the Frankfurt Parliament alienated both German conservatives and the German working class. The very existence of the parliament, representing as it did a challenge to the existing political order, offended the conservatives. The Frankfurt Parliament's refusal to restore the protection the guilds had once afforded cost it the support of the industrial workers and artisans. The liberals were too attached to the concept of a free labor market to offer meaningful legislation to workers. This failure marked the beginning of a profound split between German liberals and the German working class. For the rest of the century, German conservatives would be able to play on that division.

As if to demonstrate its disaffection from workers, in September 1848, the Frankfurt Parliament called in troops of the German Confederation to suppress a radical insurrection in the city. The liberals in the parliament wanted nothing to do with workers who erected barricades and threatened the safety of property.

The Frankfurt Parliament also floundered on the issue of unification. Members differed over whether to include Austria in a united Germany. The "large German [***grossdeutsch***] solution" favored Austria's inclusion, whereas the "small German [***kleindeutsch***] solution" advocated its exclusion. The latter formula prevailed because Austria rejected the whole notion of German unification, which raised too many other nationality problems within the Habsburg domains. Consequently, the Frankfurt Parliament looked to Prussian, rather than Austrian, leadership.

On March 27, 1849, the parliament produced its constitution. Shortly thereafter, its delegates offered the crown of a united Germany to Frederick William IV of Prussia. He rejected the offer, asserting that kings ruled by the grace of God rather than by the permission of man-made constitutions. On his refusal, the Frankfurt Parliament began to dissolve. Not long afterward, troops drove off the remaining members.

German liberals never fully recovered from this defeat. The Frankfurt Parliament had alienated the artisans and the working class without gaining any compensating support from the conservatives. The liberals had proved themselves to be awkward, hesitant, unrealistic, and ultimately dependent on the armies of the monarchies. They had failed to unite Germany or to confront effectively the realities of political power in the German states. The various revolutions did manage to extend the franchise in some of the German states and to establish conservative constitutions. The gains were not negligible, but they were a far cry from the hopes of March 1848.

In Perspective

The first half of the nineteenth century witnessed unprecedented social change in Europe. The foundations of the industrial economy were laid. That emerging economy changed virtually every existing institution. Railways crossed the Continent. New consumer goods became available. Family patterns changed, as did the social and economic expectations of women. The crowding of cities presented new social and political problems. The new concern about crime and the establishment of police forces brought issues of social order to the foreground. An urban working class became one of the chief facts of both political and social life. The ebb and flow of the business cycle increased economic anxiety for workers and property owners alike.

While all these fundamental social changes took place, Europe was also experiencing continuing political strife. The turmoil of 1848 through 1850 ended the era of liberal revolution that had begun in 1789. Liberals and nationalists discovered that rational argument and small, local insurrections would not achieve their goals. The political initiative passed for a time to the conservative political groups. Henceforth, nationalists were less romantic and more hardheaded. Railways, commerce, guns, soldiers, and devious diplomacy, rather than language and cultural heritage, became the future weapons of national unification. The working class also adopted new tactics and a new organization. The era of the riot and urban insurrection was ending; in the future, workers would turn to trade unions and political parties to achieve their political and social goals.

Perhaps most importantly after 1848, the European middle class ceased to be revolutionary. It became increasingly concerned about protecting its property against radical political and social movements associated with socialism and, as the century passed, with Marxism. The middle class remained politically liberal only as long as liberalism seemed to promise economic stability and social security for its own style of life.

Finally, as will be seen more fully in the next chapter, the revolutions of 1848 also changed European conservatism. Metternich's conservative policies had not prevented the upheavals of 1848. In the following decades, European conservatives would find new ways to adapt some of the new forces of European politics to their ends. They would embrace their own forms of nationalism and even democratic structures to ensure that they remained dominant over much of Europe.

Review Questions

1. What inventions were particularly important in the development of industrialism? How did industrialism change society? Why were the years covered in this chapter so difficult for artisans? How was the European labor force transformed into a wage-labor workforce?
2. How did the industrial economy change the working-class family? What roles and duties did various family members assume? How did the role of women change in the new industrial era?
3. What were the goals of the working class in the new industrial society, and how did they differ from middle-class goals? Why did the working class and the middle class pursue different goals?
4. Why did European states create police forces in the nineteenth century? How and why did prisons change during this era?
5. How would you define socialism? What were the chief ideas of the early socialists? How did the ideas of Karl Marx differ from those of the socialists? What historical role did Marx assign to the proletariat?
6. What factors, old and new, led to the widespread outbreak of the revolutions in 1848? Were the causes in the various countries essentially the same, or did each have its own particular set of circumstances? Why did these revolutions fail throughout Europe? What roles did liberals and nationalists play in the revolutions? Why did they sometimes clash?

Suggested Readings

B. S. Anderson and J. P. Zinsser, *A History of Their Own: Women in Europe from Prehistory to the Present*, Vol. 2 (1988). A wide-ranging survey.

I. Berlin, *Karl Marx: His Life and Environment*, 4th ed. (1996). A classic introduction.

R. B. Carlisle, *The Proffered Crown: Saint-Simonianism and the Doctrine of Hope* (1987). The best treatment of the broad social doctrines of Saint-Simonianism.

J. Coffin, *The Politics of Women's Work* (1996). Examines the subject in France.

I. Deak, *The Lawful Revolution: Louis Kossuth and the Hungarians, 1848–1849* (1979). The most significant study of the topic in English.

R. J. Evans, *The Revolutions in Europe, 1848–1849: From Reform to Reaction* (2002). A series of essays by major experts.

J. F. C. Harrison, *Quest for the New Moral World: Robert Owen and the Owenites in Britain and America* (1969). The standard work.

D. I. Kertzer and M. Barbagli, eds., *Family Life in the Long Nineteenth Century, 1789–1913: The History of the European Family* (2002). Wide-ranging collection of essays.

K. Kolakowski, *Main Currents of Marxism: Its Rise, Growth, and Dissolution*, 3 vols. (1978). A classic, comprehensive survey.

D. Landes, *The Unbound Prometheus: Technological Change and Industrial Development in Western Europe from 1750 to the Present* (1969). Classic one-volume treatment of technological development in a broad social and economic context.

H. Perkin, *The Origins of Modern English Society, 1780–1880* (1969). A provocative attempt to look at the society as a whole.

J. D. Randers-Pehrson, *Germans and the Revolution of 1848–1849* (2001). An exhaustive treatment of the subject.

W. H. Sewell, Jr., *Work and Revolution in France: The Language of Labor from the Old Regime to 1848* (1980). A fine analysis of French artisans.

J. Sperber, *The European Revolution, 1841–1851* (2005). An excellent synthesis.

E. P. Thompson, *The Making of the English Working Class* (1964). A classic work.

F. Wheen, *Karl Marx: A Life* (2001). An accessible work that emphasizes the contradictions in Marx's career and personality.

D. Winch, *Riches and Poverty: An Intellectual History of Political Economy in Britain, 1750–1834* (1996). A superb survey from Adam Smith through Thomas Malthus.

THE WEST & THE WORLD

The Abolition of Slavery in the Transatlantic Economy

ONE OF THE most important developments during the age of Enlightenment and revolution was the opening of a crusade to abolish chattel slavery in the transatlantic economy. The antislavery movement constituted the greatest and most extensive achievement of liberal reformers during the eighteenth and nineteenth centuries. Indeed, it marked the first time in the history of the world that a society actually tried to abolish slavery. This achievement came as the result of the impact of Christian ethics, Enlightenment ideals, slave revolts, revolutionary wars in America and Europe, civil war in the United States, and economic dislocation in the slave economies themselves. In 1750, almost no one seriously questioned the existence of slavery, but, by 1888, the institution no longer existed in the transatlantic economy.

Chattel slavery—the ownership of one human being by another—had existed in the West as well as elsewhere in the world since ancient times and had received intellectual and religious justification throughout the history of the West. Both Plato and Aristotle provided arguments for slavery based on the assertion that persons in bondage were intended by nature to be slaves. Christian writers similarly accommodated themselves to the institution. They contended that the most harmful form of slavery was the enslavement of the soul to sin rather than the enslavement of the physical body. They also argued that genuine freedom was realized through one's relationship to God and that problems relating to the injustices of inequality would be solved in the hereafter. Christian scholastic thinkers in the Middle Ages portrayed slavery as part of the natural and necessary hierarchy of the universe.

Slavery Spreads to the Americas

Although a vast slave trade existed throughout the Mediterranean world through the end of the Middle Ages, slavery was no longer a dominant institution on the European continent or within the European economy. The European encounter with America at the end of the fifteenth century radically transformed this situation. The American continent and the West Indies presented opportunities for achieving great wealth, but a major labor shortage existed in these regions. Eventually slavery provided the means to resolve this labor shortage.

The establishment and maintenance of slavery in the transatlantic economy drew Europeans and Americans into various relationships with Africa. About the same time as the encounter with America, Europeans made contact with areas of West Africa where slavery already existed. This region became the chief source of slaves imported into the Americas. Four centuries later, during the antislavery movement, Europeans would seek to change the African economy by ending its dependence on the slave trade. Those efforts led to the penetration of Africa by European traders, missionaries, and finally colonial forces and administrators.

Although at one time or another slaves labored throughout the Americas, the system of slavery became primarily identified with the plantation economy stretching from Maryland south to Brazil, where tropical products, initially primarily sugar, were produced by slave labor. This plantation economy existed from approximately the late sixteenth through the late nineteenth centuries. The slaves on whose labor this economy was based included Native Americans enslaved within both the Spanish Empire and North America, and Africans forcibly imported into the Americas. Consequently, the slaves were virtually always of a different race from their masters. Race itself soon became part of the justification for the social hierarchy of the plantation world. In and of itself, the fact of slavery in the Americas was not unusual to the Western experience or to that of other societies in Africa or Asia. Slavery had existed at most times and places in human history. Far more unusual in the history of the West, and for that matter in the experience of all other societies that had held and continued to hold slaves, was the emergence after 1760 of an international movement to abolish chattel slavery in the transatlantic economy.

The Crusade Against Slavery

The eighteenth-century crusade against slavery originated in a profound change in the religious and intellectual outlooks on slavery among small but influential groups in both America and Europe. The entire thrust of Enlightenment reasoning to the extent that it challenged or questioned the wisdom of existing institutions gnawed away at the older defenses of slavery, most particularly the concept of an unchanging social hierarchy. Although some writers associated with the Enlightenment, including John Locke, were reluctant to question slavery and even defended it, the general Enlightenment rhetoric of equality stood in sharp contrast to the radical inequality of slavery. Montesquieu sharply satirized slavery in *The Spirit of the Laws* (1748). Similarly, the emphasis of Adam Smith in *The Wealth of Nations* (1776) on free labor and efficiency of free markets undermined defenses of slavery.

Within much eighteenth-century literature, there emerged a tendency to idealize primitive peoples living in cultures very different from those of Europe. Previously such peoples had been regarded as backward and rebellious. Now numerous writers portrayed them as embodying a lost human virtue. This expanding body of literature transformed the way many people thought about slavery and allowed some Europeans to look on African slaves in the Americas as having been betrayed and robbed of an original innocence. Additionally, much eighteenth-century European ethical thinking, as well as later romantic poetry, emphasized empathy and feeling. In such a climate, attitudes toward slavery were transformed. Once considered to be the natural and deserved result of some deficiency in slaves themselves, slavery now grew to be regarded as undeserved and unacceptable. The same kind of ethical thinking led reformers to believe that by working against slavery, for virtually the first time defined as an unmitigated evil, they would realize their own highest ethical character.

After 1807, the British Royal Navy patrolled the West African coast attempting to intercept slave-trading ships. In 1846, the British ship HMS *Albatross* captured a Spanish slave ship, the *Albañoz*, and freed the slaves. A British officer depicted the appalling conditions in the slave hold in this watercolor.
The Granger Collection, New York

Religious movements became the single most important cultural force to foster the antislavery crusade. The evangelical religious revival associated with Methodism and with other forms of Protestant preaching emphasized the conversion experience and the change of heart as a sign of having received salvation. In 1774, John Wesley, the founder of Methodism, attacked slaveholding in *Thoughts on Slavery*. Turning against slaveholding and slave trading by plantation owners and slave traders served to illustrate one clear example of such a change of heart. Some slaveholders and slave traders feared they might be endangering their own salvation by their association with the institution. John Newton, a former slave trader who underwent an evangelical conversion, wrote the hymn "Amazing Grace."

The initial religious protest against slavery originated among English Quakers, a radical Protestant religious group founded by George Fox in the seventeenth century. By the early eighteenth century, it had solidified itself into a small but relatively wealthy sect in England. Members of Quaker congregations at that time actually owned slaves in the West Indies and participated in the transatlantic slave trade. During the Seven Years' War (1756–1763), however, many Quakers experienced economic hardship. Furthermore, the war created other difficulties for the English population as a whole. Certain Quakers decided the presence of the evil of slavery in the world explained these troubles. They then sought to remove this evil from their own lives and that of their congregations and began to take action against the whole system of slavery that characterized the transatlantic economy.

Just as the slave system was a transatlantic affair, so was the crusade against it. Quakers in both Philadelphia and England soon moved against the institution. The most influential of the early antislavery writers was Anthony Benezet, a Philadelphia Quaker, whose most important publications were *Some Considerations on the Keeping of Negroes* (1754) and *A Short Account of That Part of Africa Inhabited by the Negroes* (1762). The latter work emphasized the manner in which the slave trade degraded African society itself. Benezet also drew heavily on Montesquieu. This may not be surprising because Enlightenment writers often admired the English Quakers as exemplifying a religion of tolerance and reason.

By the earliest stages of the American Revolution a small group of reformers, normally spearheaded by

Quakers, had established an antislavery network. They published pamphlets, sermons, and books on the subject. The Society for the Relief of Free Negroes Illegally Held in Bondage, the first antislavery society in the world, was founded in Philadelphia in 1775 and, when reorganized in 1784 as the Pennsylvania Abolition Society, Benjamin Franklin became its president. In 1787, the Committee for the Abolition of the Slave Trade was organized in England. In France, the Société des Amis des Noirs was founded in 1778.

The turmoil of the American Revolution and the founding of the American republic gave these groups the occasion for some of their earliest successes. Emancipation gradually, but nonetheless steadily, spread among the northern states. In 1787, the Continental Congress forbade the presence of slavery in the newly organized Northwest Territory north of the Ohio River. What is important so far as the crusade against slavery is concerned is the disappearance of slavery in approximately half of the new nation and the commitment not to extend it to an important new territory. Despite these American developments, Great Britain became and remained the center for the antislavery movement. In 1772, a decision by the chief justice affirmed that slaves brought into Great Britain could not forcibly be removed. The decision, though of less immediate importance than some thought at the time, gave further impetus to the small but growing group of antislavery reformers.

During the early 1780s, the antislavery reformers in Great Britain decided to work toward ending the slave trade rather than the institution of slavery. The horrors of the slave trade caught the public's attention in 1783 when the captain of the slave ship *Zong* threw more than 130 slaves overboard in order to collect insurance. For the reformers, attacking the trade rather than the institution appeared a less radical and a more achievable reform. To many, the slave trade appeared to be a more obvious crime than the holding of slaves, which seemed a more nearly passive act. Furthermore, attacking slavery itself involved serious issues of property rights that might alienate potential supporters of the abolition of the slave trade. The antislavery groups also believed that if the trade was ended, planters would have to treat their remaining slaves more humanely.

By the end of the 1780s, the English Quakers were joined by evangelical Christians from the Church of England to form the Society for the Abolition of the Slave Trade. The most famous of the new leaders was William Wilberforce who, for the rest of his life, fought the slave trade. Year after year, he introduced a bill to abolish the slave trade. Finally, in 1807, he saw it passed.

Slave Revolts

While the British reformers worked for the abolition of the slave trade, slaves themselves in certain areas took matters into their own hands. The largest emancipation of slaves to occur in the eighteenth century came on the island of Saint Domingue (Haiti), France's wealthiest colony, as a result of the slave revolt of 1794 led by Toussaint L'Ouverture and Jean-Jacques Dessalines. The revolt in Haiti and Haiti's eventual independence in 1804 stood as a warning to slave owners throughout the

The slave revolt on the French island of St. Domingue achieved the largest emancipation of slaves in the eighteenth century. In this print, Toussaint L'Ouverture leads the revolt. CORBIS/Bettmann

West Indies. (See Chapter 20.) There would be other slave revolts such as those in Virginia led by Gabriel Prosser in 1800 and by Nat Turner in 1831, in South Carolina led by Denmark Vesey in 1822, in British-controlled Demarra in 1823 and 1824, and in Jamaica in 1831. Each of these was brutally suppressed.

Economic Pressures

Through the conclusion of the Seven Years' War, the West Indies interest group had been one of the most powerful in the British Parliament. During the second half of the eighteenth century and beyond, new and different economic interest groups began to displace the influence of that group. Within the West Indies themselves the planters were experiencing soil exhaustion and new competition from newly tilled islands controlled by France and other new islands opened for sugar cultivation. Some older plantations were being abandoned while others operated with low profitability. Now with the new islands under cultivation there was a glut of sugar on the market, and as a consequence the price was falling.

Under these conditions some British West Indies planters, for reasons that had nothing to do with religion or humanitarianism, began to favor curtailing the slave trade. Without new slaves, French planters would lack the labor they needed to exploit their islands. During the Napoleonic Wars, the British captured a number of the valuable French islands. In order to protect the planters on the older British West Indies islands, in 1805, the British cabinet issued Orders in Council, which forbade the importation of slaves into the newly acquired French islands. By 1807, the abolition sentiment was strong enough for Parliament to pass Wilberforce's measure prohibiting slave trading from any British port.

The suppression of this trade through the navy became one of the fundamental pillars of nineteenth-century British foreign policy. Throughout the rest of the Napoleonic era the British attempted to draw allies into a policy of forbidding the slave trade. They also attempted unsuccessfully to incorporate the abolition of the slave trade into the settlement of the Congress of Vienna. In addition, the British navy maintained squadrons of ships around the coast of West Africa to halt slave traders. Although the French and Americans also patrolled the West African coast, neither was deeply committed to ending the slave trade. Nonetheless, in 1824, the American Congress made slave trading a capital offense.

The French invasion of Spain in 1808, as discussed in Chapter 21, provided the spark for the Latin American wars of independence. The leaders of these movements had been influenced by the liberal ideas of the Enlightenment and were, thus, generally predisposed to disapprove of slavery. The political groups seeking independence from Spain also sought the support of slaves by promises of emancipation. Furthermore, the newly independent nations needed good relations with Britain to support their economies, and, consequently, most of them very quickly freed their slaves to gain such support. The actual freeing of slaves was gradual and often came some years after the emancipation legislation. Despite the gradual nature of this abolition, slavery would disappear by approximately the middle of the nineteenth century from all of the newly independent nations of Latin America. The great exception was Brazil.

Abolishing Slavery in the New World

British reformers gradually recognized that the abolition of the slave trade had not actually improved the lot of slaves. In 1823, they adopted as a new goal the gradual emancipation of slaves. The chief voices calling for this change were those of William Wilberforce and Thomas Clarkson, who were active in founding the Abolition Society. The savagery with which West Indian planters put down slave revolts in 1823 and 1824 and again in 1831 strengthened the resolve of the antislavery reformers. By 1830, the reformers had abandoned the goal of gradual abolition and demanded the complete abolition of slavery. In 1833, after the passage of the Reform Bill in Great Britain, they achieved that goal when Parliament abolished the right of British subjects to hold slaves. In the British West Indies, 750,000 slaves were freed within a few years.

The other old colonial powers in the New World tended to be much slower in their own abolition of slavery. Portugal did little or nothing about slavery in Brazil, and when that nation became independent of Portugal, its new government continued slavery. Portugal ended slavery elsewhere in its American possessions in 1836; the Swedes, in 1847; the Danes, in 1848; but the Dutch not until 1863. France had witnessed a significant antislavery movement throughout the first half of the century, but slavery was not abolished in its West Indian possessions until the revolution of 1848.

During the first thirty years of the nineteenth century, the institution of slavery revived and achieved strong new footholds in the transatlantic world. These areas were the lower south of the United States for the cultivation of cotton, Brazil for the cultivation of coffee, and Cuba for the cultivation of sugar. World demand for these products made the slave system economically viable in these regions. Consequently, despite the drive to emancipation, which had succeeded in the northern states of the United States, slavery persisted in much of the Caribbean and in most of Latin America.

An antislavery movement had existed in the United States since the end of the eighteenth century, but it took on a new life in the early 1830s. The British abolition of slavery in the West Indies served as an inspiration to a new generation of American antislavery leaders, the most famous of whom was William Lloyd Garrison. He and other American abolitionists raised the question of slavery throughout the 1830s and 1840s. It was, however, the disposition of lands the United States had acquired in the Mexican War of 1847 that placed slavery at the heart of the American political debate. For over a decade the question of slavery sharply divided Americans. The election of Lincoln in 1860 brought those sectional tensions to a head, and the American Civil War erupted in the spring of 1861. In 1863, Lincoln issued the Emancipation Proclamation, which ended slavery in the combatant states. The passage of the Thirteenth Amendment to the American Constitution in 1865 abolished slavery in the United States.

The end of slavery in the United Sates left both Cuba, the most important remaining possession of the Spanish Empire in the Americas, and Brazil with slave economies. In 1868, an insurgency against Spanish colonial policy broke out in Cuba and lasted for ten years. This war disrupted much of the Cuban economy and saw some planters move toward using free labor. The Spanish forces attacked other planters by freeing their slaves. In 1870, the Spanish government passed a measure for gradual emancipation of slaves in both Cuba and Puerto Rico. In subsequent years, the sugar economy collapsed, making slavery unprofitable. Abolitionist agitation grew in Spain, and slavery was abolished in its New World colonies in 1886.

Brazil, under British pressure, had effectively ended the slave trade in 1850, but the question of the abolition of slavery was postponed for many years. In 1871, as a result of abolitionist agitation and because the Emperor Pedro II opposed slavery, a law providing for an extremely gradual abolition of slavery was passed. During the next two decades, abolitionist sentiment grew, and public figures from across the political spectrum voiced opposition to slavery. In 1888, Isabel Christiana, then regent while her father Pedro II was in Europe for medical treatment, signed a law abolishing slavery in Brazil without any form of compensation to the slave owners.

The abolition of slavery in Brazil ended a system of forced labor that had characterized the transatlantic economy for almost four hundred years. Wherever slavery had existed, however, its presence left and would continue to leave long-term consequences for the realization of equality and social justice. The end of slavery, consequently, did not end the problems that slavery created in the transatlantic world.

Africa and the End of Slavery

The transatlantic slave trade itself had adversely affected the life of Africa both through the vast loss of population over the centuries as well as through the undermining of African society through the internal slave trade. Similarly, the crusade against transatlantic slavery had drawn Europeans much more deeply into the affairs of the African continent. The various efforts by antislavery groups began to impact Africa in the first half of the nineteenth century. Their goal was to transform the African economy by substituting new peaceful trade in tropical goods for the slave trade. The reformers hoped to spread both free trade and Christianity into Africa. "Christianity and civilization" and "Christianity and commerce" were popular slogans of the day. Missionaries and traders saw themselves as natural allies in the cause.

The first effort in this direction was the resettlement of black slaves or children of black slaves into Africa. In 1787, the British established a colony of poor free blacks from Britain in Sierra Leone. The effort went badly, but a few years later former slaves once owned by British loyalists in America were settled there. Then former slaves from the Caribbean were brought to Sierra Leone. The colony became relatively successful only after 1807, when the British navy landed slaves rescued from captured slave trading ships. Sierra Leone, though quite small, became a place on the coast of West Africa where Christianity and commerce rather than the slave trade flourished. The French established a smaller experiment at Libreville in Gabon. The most famous and lasting attempt to resettle former black slaves in Africa was the establishment of Liberia by the efforts of the American Colonization Society after 1817. Liberia became an independent republic in 1847. All these efforts to move former slaves back to Africa had only modest success, but they did affect the life of West Africa.

Other antislavery reformers were less interested in establishing outposts for the settlement of former slaves than in transforming the African economy itself. In 1841, the African Civilization Society under the leadership of Thomas Fowell Buxton sent a group of paddle steamers up the Niger River in the hope of creating the basis for new trade with Africa. The goal was to establish free trade between Britain and Africa in which the manufactured goods of the former, most particularly textiles, would be exchanged for tropical agricultural goods produced by Africans. The expedition failed because most of its members died of disease. Yet the impulse to penetrate Africa for purposes of spreading trade and Christianity would continue for the rest of the century.

The antislavery movement marked the first of the intrusions of the European powers well beyond the coast of West Africa into the heart of the continent. After the American Civil War finally halted any large-scale demand for slaves from Africa, the antislavery reformers began to focus on ending the slave trade in East Africa and the Indian Ocean. This drive against slavery and the slave trade in Africa itself became one of the rationales for European interference in Africa during the second half of the nineteenth century and served as one of the foundations for the establishment of the late-century colonial empires.

The crusade against slavery in the transatlantic economy eventually touched most of the world. It radically transformed the economies and societies of both North and South America. It led to a transformation of the African economy and eventually to a significant European presence in the life of African societies. Efforts to eradicate slavery, particularly the efforts by British reformers, caused the spread of the reform movement into Asia. Slavery has not been abolished throughout the world, and antislavery societies still exist, though they receive little publicity. Yet the abolition of slavery in the transatlantic world stands as one of the most permanent achievements of the forces of eighteenth-century Enlightenment and revolution.

What were the justifications of slavery prior to the eighteenth century? What religious and intellectual developments led some Europeans and some Americans to question and criticize the institution of slavery? Why did antislavery reformers first concentrate on the abolition of the slave trade? How did both slavery and antislavery lead Americans and Europeans to become involved with Africa? How did that involvement change between approximately 1600 and 1870?

Giuseppe Garibaldi, the charismatic Italian nationalist leader, can be seen on the right urging on his troops in the rout of Neapolitan forces at Calatafimi, Sicily, in 1860. Bildarchiv Preussischer Kulturbesitz

22

The Age of Nation-States

▼ **The Crimean War (1853–1856)**
Peace Settlement and Long-Term Results

▼ **Reforms in the Ottoman Empire**

▼ **Italian Unification**
Romantic Republicans • Cavour's Policy • The New Italian State

▼ **German Unification**
Bismarck • The Franco-Prussian War and the German Empire (1870–1871)

▼ **France: From Liberal Empire to the Third Republic**
The Paris Commune • The Third Republic • The Dreyfus Affair

▼ **The Habsburg Empire**
Formation of the Dual Monarchy • Unrest of Nationalities

▼ **Russia: Emancipation and Revolutionary Stirrings**
Reforms of Alexander II • Revolutionaries

▼ **Great Britain: Toward Democracy**
The Second Reform Act (1867) • Gladstone's Great Ministry (1868–1874) • Disraeli in Office (1874–1880) • The Irish Question

▼ **In Perspective**

KEY TOPICS

- **Reforms in the Ottoman Empire**
- **The unification of Italy and Germany**
- **The shift from empire to republic in France**
- **The emergence of a dual monarchy in Austria-Hungary**
- **Reforms in Russia, including the emancipation of the serfs**
- **The emergence of Great Britain as the exemplary liberal state and its confrontation with Irish nationalists**

THE REVOLUTIONS OF 1848 collapsed in defeat for both liberalism and nationalism. In the 1850s, conservative regimes were entrenched across the Continent. Yet only a quarter century later, many of the major goals of early-nineteenth-century liberals and nationalists had been reached. Italy and Germany were each united under conservative constitutional monarchies. The Habsburg emperor accepted constitutional government and recognized the liberties of the Magyars of Hungary. In Russia, the tsar emancipated the serfs. France had become a republic. Liberalism and even democracy flourished in Great Britain. The Ottoman Empire also undertook major reforms.

Paradoxically, most of these developments occurred under conservative political leadership. War and competition with other states compelled some governments to pursue new policies at home as well as abroad. They had to find novel methods to maintain the loyalty of their subjects. Some conservative leaders preferred to carry out a popular policy on their own terms, so that they, rather than the liberals, would receive credit. Other leaders acted as they did because they had no choice.

▼ The Crimean War (1853–1856)

As has so often been true in modern European history, the impetus for change originated in war. The Crimean War (1853–1856) was rooted in the long-standing desire of Russia to extend its influence over the Ottoman Empire. Two disputes led to the conflict. First, as noted in Chapter 17, the Russians had, since the time of Catherine the Great (r. 1762–1796), been given protective oversight of Orthodox Christians in the Empire, and France had similar oversight of Roman Catholics. In 1851, yielding to French pressure, the Ottoman sultan had assigned care of certain holy places in Palestine to Roman Catholics. This decision angered the Russians and damaged Russian prestige. Second, Russia wanted to extend its control over the Ottoman provinces of Moldavia and Walachia (now in Romania). In the summer of 1853, the Russians used their right to protect Orthodox Christians in the Ottoman Empire as the pretext to occupy the two provinces. Shortly thereafter, the Ottoman Empire declared war on Russia.

Of far more significance to the great powers than the protection of Christian sites in Palestine was the fate of the weak Ottoman Empire. The Russian government envisioned the eventual breakup of the empire and hoped to extend its influence at Ottoman expense. Both France and Britain, though recognizing the difficulties of the Ottoman government and using it to their own advantage when the opportunity presented itself, opposed Russian expansion in the eastern Mediterranean, where they had extensive naval and commercial interests. The French emperor Napoleon III (r. 1852–1870) also thought an activist foreign policy would shore up domestic support for his regime.

On March 28, 1854, France and Britain declared war on Russia in alliance with the Ottomans. Much to the disappointment of Tsar Nicholas I, Austria and Prussia remained neutral. The Austrians had their own ambitions in the Balkans, and, for the moment, Prussia followed Austrian leadership.

Both sides conducted the conflict ineptly, a fact that became widely known in Western Europe because the Crimean War was the first to be covered by war correspondents and photographers. The ill-equipped and poorly commanded armies became bogged down along the Crimean coast of the Black Sea. In September 1855, after a long siege, the Russian fortress of Sevastopol finally fell to the French and British. Thereafter, both sides moved to end the war.

Peace Settlement and Long-Term Results

In March 1856, a conference in Paris concluded the Treaty of Paris. This treaty required Russia to surrender territory near the mouth of the Danube River, to recognize the neutrality of the Black Sea, and to renounce its claims to protect Orthodox Christians in the Ottoman Empire. Even before the conference, Austria had forced Russia to withdraw from Moldavia and Walachia. The image of an invincible Russia that had prevailed across Europe since the close of the Napoleonic Wars was shattered.

Also shattered was the Concert of Europe (see Chapter 20), as a means of dealing with international relations on the Continent. Following the successful repression of the 1848 uprisings, the great powers feared revolution less than they had earlier in the century, and, consequently, they displayed much less reverence for the Vienna settlement. As historian Gordon Craig put it, "After 1856, there were more powers willing to fight to overthrow the existing order than there were to take up arms to defend it."[1] As a result, for about twenty-five years after the Crimean War, European affairs were unstable, producing a period of adventurism in foreign policy. While these events reshaped Western Europe, however, the Ottoman Empire over whose fate the Crimean War had been fought undertook reforms. These need to be considered before we return to the events in Europe.

▼ Reforms in the Ottoman Empire

The short-lived Napoleonic invasion of the Ottoman province of Egypt in 1798–1799 (see Chapter 19) sparked a drive for change in the Ottoman Empire. In 1839, under pressure from imperial bureaucrats who had studied in Europe, the sultan issued a decree, called the *Hatt-i Sharif of Gülhane*, that attempted to reorganize the empire's administration and military along European lines. This decree opened what became known as the *Tanzimat* (meaning "reorganization") era of the Ottoman Empire, lasting from 1839 to 1876. The reforms, which were drawn up by administrative councils and not issued arbitrarily by the sultan, liberalized the economy, ended the practice of tax farming, and sought to eliminate corruption. The *Hatt-i Sharif* was particularly

[1] *The New Cambridge Modern History*, Vol. 10 (Cambridge: Cambridge University Press, 1967), p. 273.

A Closer LOOK

THE CRIMEAN WAR RECALLED

THE WARS OF the third quarter of the nineteenth century brought European armies once again to the foreground in European culture and art. Beginning with the Crimean War (1853–1856) and ending with those of German unification (1870), the armed forces of the various nation-states reforged European political life. Artists might record even the most difficult moments of warfare. Here, Elizabeth Thompson, Lady Butler, portrayed *Roll Call after an Engagement, Crimea*. She completed the work in 1874 two decades after the war, and Queen Victoria purchased it.

The abilities of the aristocratic officers leading the British army had been discredited, so Butler here portrays ordinary troops.

A certain nostalgia for the comradeship of soldiers even under the most difficult circumstances penetrates this scene at a time when Britain had not engaged in a major war for many years.

Lady Elizabeth Thompson Butler (1846–1933), *The Roll Call: Calling the Roll after an Engagement, Crimea* (unframed). The Royal Collection © 2005, Her Majesty Queen Elizabeth II. Photo by SC

The ill-equipment of the troops during the war had been a public scandal, and the evident suffering of these troops recalls that.

To examine this image in an interactive fashion, please go to www.myhistorylab.com

myhistorylab

remarkable for extending civic equality to Ottoman subjects regardless of their religion. Muslims, Christians, and Jews were now equal before the law. The empire also made it much easier for Muslims to enter into commercial agreements with non-Muslims, both within the empire and from abroad.

Another reform decree, called the *Hatti-i Hümayun*, was promulgated in 1856 at the close of the Crimean War. Under the influence of Britain and France, it spelled out the rights of non-Muslims more explicitly, giving them equal obligations with Muslims for military service and equal opportunity for state employment and

Ottoman reformers established a parliament in 1877, but the sultan retained most political authority. *Illustrated London News* of April 14, 1877. Mary Evans Picture Library Ltd.

admission to state schools. The decree also abolished torture and allowed foreigners to acquire some forms of property. In time, printing presses and Western-oriented schools appeared in the empire mainly via Christian missionaries, many of whom were Americans. For the first time in its long history, the Ottoman Empire actually sought to copy European legal and military institutions and the secular values flowing from liberalism.

The imperial government took these steps to gain the loyalty of its Christian subjects at a time when nationalism was making increasing inroads among them. In effect, during this reform era the Ottoman government broke down the millet system (see Chapter 13) and sought to define all its citizens as Ottoman subjects rather than as members of particular religious communities.

However, putting these reforms into practice proved difficult. In some regions of the empire, especially in Egypt and Tunis, local rulers were virtually independent of Istanbul. They carried out their own modernizing reforms, often working closely with European powers. In the capital itself, power struggles developed among courtiers, European-oriented administrators and army officers, merchants who prospered from the changes, and the *ulema*, which sought to maintain the rule of Islamic law. Because of these tensions, as well as growing nationalism in various regions, the Ottoman Empire failed to achieve genuine political strength and stability. Many Ottomans questioned the wisdom of Tanzimat and warned that replacing long-standing Islamic institutions with European ones would lead to disaster.

The Balkan wars of the late 1870s, which resulted in either the independence of, or Russian or Austrian dominance over, most of the empire's European holdings, demonstrated the inability of the Ottoman Empire to master its own destiny. (See Chapter 26.) The response to these foreign defeats resulted in greater efforts to modernize the army and the economy and to build railways and telegraphs. In 1876, reformers persuaded the sultan to proclaim an Ottoman constitution on the grounds that European political arrangements as well as technology accounted for European strength. The constitution called for a parliament consisting of an elected chamber of deputies and an appointed senate (these met for the first time in 1877) but left the sultan's power mostly intact. Nonetheless, a new sultan soon rejected even these limited steps toward constitutionalism and dismissed the parliament. In 1908, military officers carried out a revolution against the authority, though not the person, of the sultan. Another group of reformist officers, known as the *Young Turks*, came to the fore with another program to modernize the empire. They were still in charge when World War I broke out, and their decision to enter the war on the side of the Central Powers in November 1914 led to the empire's defeat and collapse. (See Chapter 26.)

One of the underlying themes of all these attempts at reform and modernization from 1839 to 1914 was the increasing secularization of the government, which sought less to question the Islamic foundations of society than to reduce the influence of the Muslim religious authorities on the state.

▼ Italian Unification

Nationalists had long wanted to unite the small, mostly absolutist principalities of the Italian peninsula into a single state. During the first half of the century, however, opinion differed about how to achieve Italian unification.

Romantic Republicans

One approach to the issue was *romantic republicanism.* After the Congress of Vienna, secret republican societies were founded throughout Italy, the most famous of which was the **Carbonari** ("charcoal burners"). They were ineffective.

After the failure of nationalist uprisings in Italy in 1831, the leadership of romantic republican nationalism passed to Giuseppe Mazzini (1805–1872). He became the most important nationalist leader in Europe and brought new fervor to the cause. He once declared, "Nationality is the role assigned by God to a people in the work of humanity. It is its mission, its task on earth, to the end that God's thought may be realized in the world."[2] In 1831, he founded the Young Italy Society to drive Austria from the peninsula and establish an Italian republic.

During the 1830s and 1840s, Mazzini and his fellow republican Giuseppe Garibaldi (1807–1882) led insurrections. Both were involved in the ill-fated Roman Republic of 1849. Throughout the 1850s, they continued to conduct what amounted to guerrilla warfare. Because both men spent much time in exile, they became well known across the Continent and in the United States.

Republican nationalism frightened moderate Italians, who wanted to rid themselves of Austrian domination but not to establish a republic. For a time, these people had hoped the papacy would sponsor unification. That solution became impossible after the experience of Pius IX with the Roman Republic in 1849. Consequently, at midcentury, "Italy" remained a geographical expression rather than a political entity.

Yet by 1860, the Italian peninsula was transformed into a nation-state under a constitutional monarchy. Count Camillo Cavour (1810–1861), the prime minister of Piedmont—not of romantic republicans—made this possible. His method was a force of arms tied to secret diplomacy. The spirit of Machiavelli must have smiled over the enterprise.

Count Camillo Cavour (1810–1861) used an opportunistic alliance with France against Austria and military interventions in the Papal States and southern Italy to secure Italian unification under King Victor Emmanuel II of Piedmont, rather than as the republic that Mazzini and Garibaldi had advocated. © Archivo Iconografico, S.A./CORBIS

Cavour's Policy

Piedmont (officially styled the Kingdom of Sardinia), in northwestern Italy, was the most independent state on the peninsula. The Congress of Vienna had restored the kingdom as a buffer between French and Austrian ambitions. As has been seen, during 1848 and 1849, King Charles Albert of Piedmont, after having promulgated a conservative constitution, twice unsuccessfully fought Austria. After the second defeat, he abdicated in favor of his son, Victor Emmanuel I (r. 1849–1878). In 1852, the new monarch chose Cavour as his prime minister.

A cunning statesman, Cavour had begun political life as a conservative but had gradually moved toward a moderately liberal position. He had made a fortune by investing in railroads, reforming agriculture on his estates, and editing a newspaper. He was deeply imbued with the ideas of the Enlightenment, classical economics, and utilitarianism. Cavour was a nationalist of a new breed who had no respect for Mazzini's ideals. A strong monarchist, Cavour rejected republicanism. Economic and material progress, not romantic ideals, required a large, unified state on the Italian peninsula.

Cavour believed that if Italians proved themselves to be efficient and economically progressive, the great powers might decide that Italy could govern itself. As premier, he promoted free trade, railway construction, expansion of credit, and agricultural improvement. He believed that such material and economic bonds, rather than fuzzy romantic yearnings, must unite the Italians. Cavour also recognized the need to capture the loyalties of those Italians who believed in other varieties of nationalism. He thus fostered the Nationalist Society, which established chapters in other Italian states to press for unification under the leadership of Piedmont. Finally, the prime minister believed only French intervention could defeat Austria and unite Italy. The accession of Napoleon III in France seemed to open the way for such aid.

[2]Quoted in William L. Langer, *Political and Social Upheaval, 1832–1852* (New York: Harper Torchbooks, 1969), p. 115.

French Sympathies Cavour used the Crimean War to bring Italy into European politics. In 1855, Piedmont sent 10,000 troops to help France and Britain capture Sebastopol. This small but significant participation in the war allowed Cavour to raise the Italian question at the Paris conference. He left Paris with no diplomatic reward, but his intelligence and political capacity had impressed everyone, especially Napoleon III. During the rest of the decade, he achieved further international respectability for Piedmont by opposing Mazzini, who was still attempting to lead nationalist uprisings. By 1858, Cavour represented a moderate liberal, monarchist alternative to both republicanism and reactionary absolutism in Italy.

Cavour bided his time. Then, in January 1858, an Italian named Felice Orsini attempted to assassinate Napoleon III. The incident heightened the emperor's interest in the Italian issue. He saw himself continuing his more famous uncle's liberation of the peninsula. He also saw Piedmont as a potential ally against Austria. In July 1858, Cavour and Napoleon III met at Plombières in southern France. Riding alone in a carriage, with the emperor at the reins, the two men plotted to provoke a war in Italy that would permit them to defeat Austria. A formal treaty in December 1858 confirmed the agreement.

War with Austria In early 1859, tension grew between Austria and Piedmont as Piedmont mobilized its army. On April 22, Austria demanded that Piedmont demobilize. That allowed Piedmont to claim that Austria was provoking a war. France intervened to aid its ally. On June 4, the Austrians were defeated at Magenta, and on June 24 at Solferino. Meanwhile, revolutions had broken out in Tuscany, Modena, Parma, and the Romagna provinces of the Papal States.

With the Austrians in retreat and the new revolutionary regimes calling for union with Piedmont, Napoleon III feared too extensive a Piedmontese victory. On July 11, he concluded peace with Austria at Villafranca. Piedmont received Lombardy, but Venetia remained under Austrian control. Cavour felt betrayed by France, but the war had driven Austria from most of northern Italy. Later that summer, Parma, Modena, Tuscany, and the Romagna voted to unite with Piedmont. (See Map 22–1.)

Garibaldi's Campaign At this point, the forces of romantic republican nationalism compelled Cavour to pursue the complete unification of northern and southern Italy. In May 1860, Garibaldi landed in Sicily with more than 1,000 troops, who had been outfitted in the north. He captured Palermo and prepared to attack the mainland. By September he controlled the city and kingdom of Naples, probably the most corrupt example of Italian absolutism. For more than two decades Garibaldi had hoped to form a republican Italy, but Cavour forestalled him. He rushed Piedmontese troops south to confront Garibaldi. On the way, they conquered the rest of the Papal States except the area around Rome, which French troops saved for the pope. Garibaldi's nationalism won out over his republicanism, and he accepted Piedmontese domination. In late 1860, Naples and Sicily voted to join the Italian kingdom. In response to the help received from France and Napoleon III's concern over the new large nation-state on his borders, Piedmont ceded Savoy and Nice, where much of the population spoke French, to France. (See "Compare & Connect: Nineteenth Century Nationalism: Two Sides," pages 668–669.)

The New Italian State

In March 1861, Victor Emmanuel II was proclaimed king of Italy. Three months later Cavour died. The new state more than ever needed his skills, because Piedmont had, in effect, not so much united Italy as conquered it. The republicans resented the treatment of Garibaldi. The clericals were appalled at the conquest of the Papal States. In the south, armed resistance against the imposition of Piedmontese-style administration continued until 1866. The economies and societies of north and south Italy were incompatible. The south was rural, poor, and backward. The north was industrializing, and its economy was increasingly linked to that of the rest of Europe. The social structures of the two regions reflected these differences, with large landholders and peasants dominant in the south and an urban working class emerging in the north.

The political framework of the united Italy could not overcome these problems. The constitution, which was that promulgated for Piedmont in 1848, provided for a conservative constitutional monarchy. Parliament consisted of two houses: a senate appointed by the king and a chamber of deputies elected on a narrow franchise. Ministers were responsible to the monarch, not to Parliament. These arrangements did not foster vigorous parliamentary life. Political leaders often simply avoided major problems. In place of efficient, progressive government, such as Cavour had brought to Piedmont, a system called *transformismo* developed. Bribery, favors, or a seat in the cabinet "transformed" political opponents into government supporters. Italian politics became a byword for corruption.

The unification was not complete. Many Italians believed other territories should be added to their nation. The most important of these were Venetia and Rome. The former was gained in 1866 in return for Italy's

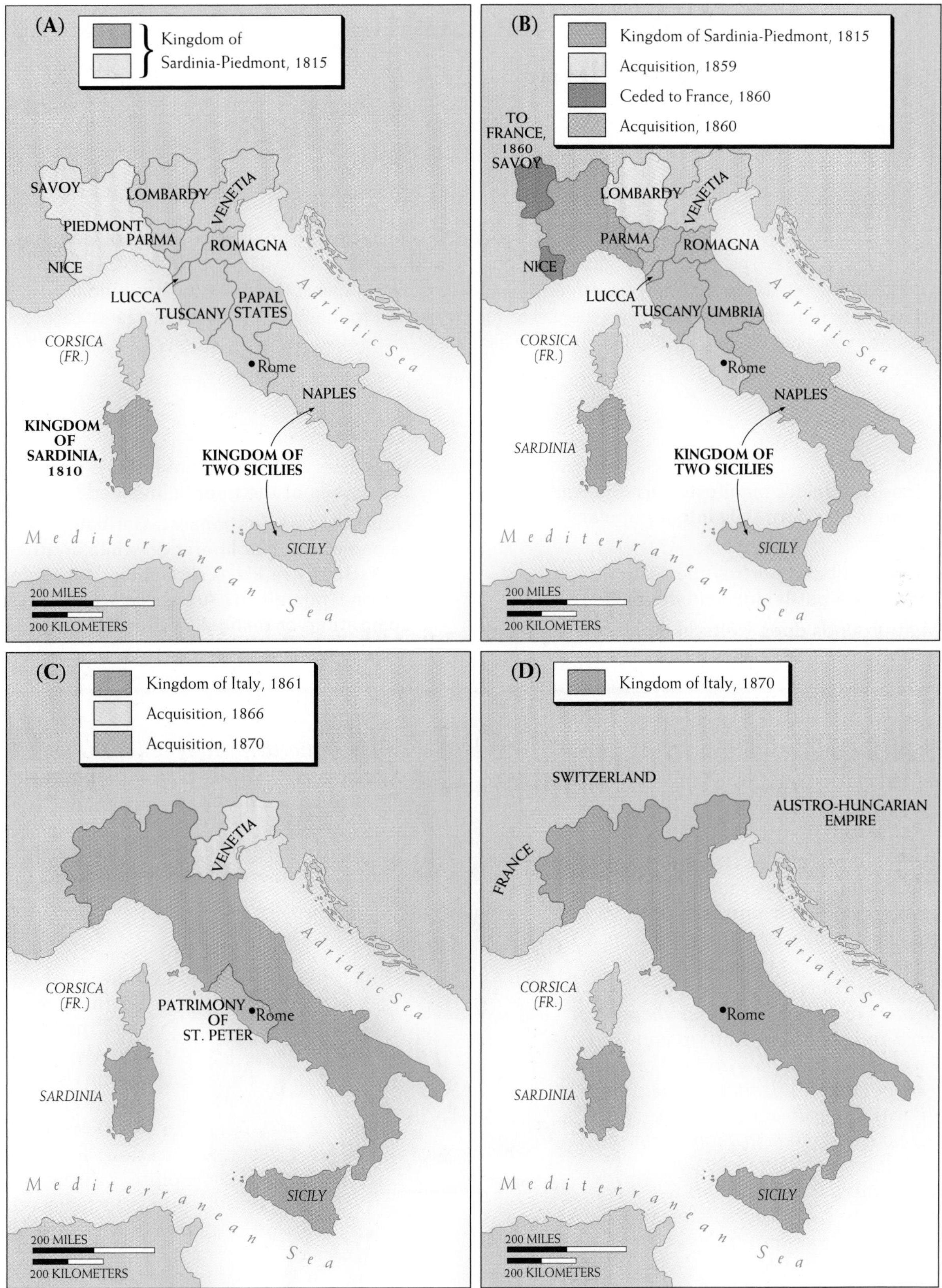

Map 22–1 **THE UNIFICATION OF ITALY** Beginning with the association of Sardinia and Piedmont by the Congress of Vienna in 1815, unification was achieved through the expansion of Piedmont between 1859 and 1870. Both Cavour's statesmanship and the campaigns of ardent nationalists played large roles.

COMPARE AND CONNECT

Nineteenth Century Nationalism: Two Sides

THE SECOND QUARTER of the nineteenth century witnessed the unification first of Italy and then of Germany. Both processes involved warfare. The Kindom of Sardina conquered and united northern Italy, and then Garibaldi led his "Red Shirts" to conquer the south. Prussia united Germany in a series of wars against Denmark, Austria, and France. These two documents illustrate different justifications for the call to military action for unifying each nation. Garibaldi presents his forces as liberators against tyranny. Treitschke makes an argument for the German annexation of Alsace and Lorraine on the grounds of national security and history.

QUESTIONS

1. **How does Garibaldi's manifesto turn the war for unification in southern Italy into a popular campaign?**
2. **How does Garibaldi portray the struggle for unification as a battle against tyranny?**
3. **On what grounds does Treitschke base the German claim to Alsace and Lorraine?**
4. **Why does Treitschke contend it is proper to ignore the wishes of the people involved?**
5. **How could one nationalist, Garibaldi, see his goal as one of popular liberation while another, Treitschke, see his as reclaiming lost regions of a national homeland? Are these two views compatible or distinctly different?**

I. Garibaldi Calls Italians to Act to Unify Their Nation

Garibaldi was the most charismatic figure in the drive for Italian unification. He was the leader of guerrilla military forces known as the Red Shirts. In May 1860 after northern Italy had been united under the Kingdom of Sardinia whose monarch was Victor Emmanuel, Garibaldi landed his force of about a thousand men in Sicily and from there they crossed into southern Italy to conquer the kingdom of Naples and make it part of a united Italian state. Garibaldi was himself a republican, but he reconciled himself to supporting Victor Emmanuel. Before leaving Sicily for the mainland, Garibaldi issued this call to arms demanding that the Italians of southern Italy rise against the kingdom of Naples. The various geographical areas he mentions were located from the south northward to Rome. The Tincino River lay in northern Italy and Garibaldi is recalling the participation of his troops in the war that unified the north.

Italians! The Sicilians are fighting against the enemies of Italy and for Italy. To help them with money, arms, and especially men, is the duty of every Italian.

Let the Marches, Umbria, Sabine, the Roman Campagna, and the Neapolitan territory rise, so as to divide the enemy's forces.

If the cities do not offer a sufficient basis for insurrection, let the more resolute throw themselves into the open country. A brave man can always find a

General Giuseppe Garibaldi (1807–1882).
Museum of the City of New York/Hulton Archive

weapon. In the name of Heaven, hearken not to the voice of those who cram themselves at well-served tables. Let us arm. Let us fight for our brothers; tomorrow we can fight for ourselves.

A handful of brave men, who have followed me in battles for our country, are advancing with me to the rescue. Italy knows them; they always appear at the hour of danger. Brave and generous companions, they have devoted their lives to their country; they will shed their last drop of blood for it, seeking no other reward than that of a pure conscience.

"Italy and Victor Emmanuel!"—that was our battle-cry when we crossed the Tincino; it will resound into the very depths of Aetna [the volcanic mountain]. As this prophetic battle-cry re-echoes from the hills of Italy to the Tarpeian Mount, the tottering thrones of tyranny will fall to pieces, and the whole country will rise like one man.

Source: "History," *The Annual Register . . . 1860* (London, 1861), p. 221 as quoted in Raymond Phineas Stearns, *Pageant of Europe: Sources and Selections from the Renaissance to the Present Day* (New York: Harcourt, Brace and Company, 1948), pp. 583–584.

II. Heinrich von Treitschke Demands the Annexation of Alsace and Lorraine

The Franco-Prussian War witnessed outbursts of extreme nationalistic rhetoric on both sides. One such voice was that of the German historian Heinrich von Treitschke (1834–1896). In a newspaper article, he demanded the annexation of Alsace and Lorraine from France. He did so even though the population of Alsace wished to remain part of France and German was not the dominant language in the region. He appealed to an earlier time when the region had been German in language and culture, and he asserted that "might makes right" to assure German domination.

The sense of justice to Germany demands the lessening of France. . . .

What is demanded by justice is, at the same time, absolutely necessary for our security. . . .

Every State must seek the guarantees of its own security in itself alone. . . .

In view of our obligation to secure the peace of the world, who will venture to object that the people of Alsace and Lorraine do not want to belong to us? The doctrine of the right of all the branches of the German race to decide on their own destinies, the plausible solution of demagogues without a fatherland, shiver to pieces in presence of the sacred necessity of these great days. These territories are ours by the right of the sword, and we shall dispose of them in virtue of a higher right—the right of the German nation, which will not permit its lost children to remain strangers to the German Empire. We Germans, who know Germany and France, know better than these unfortunates themselves what is good for the people of Alsace. . . . Against their will we shall restore them to their true selves. We have seen with joyful wonder the undying power of the moral forces of history, manifested far too frequently in the immense changes of these days, to place much confidence in the value of a mere popular disinclination. The spirit of a nation lays hold, not only of the generation which lives beside it, but of those who are before and behind it. We appeal from the mistaken wishes of the men who are there today to the wishes of those who were there before them. We appeal to all those strong German men who once stamped the seal of our German nature on the language and manners, the art and the social life of the Upper Rhine. Before the nineteenth century closes, the world will recognize that . . . we were only obeying the dictates of national honor when we made little account of the preferences of the people who live in Alsace today. . . .

At all times the subjection of a German race to France has been an unhealthy thing; today it is an offence against the reason of History—a vassalship of free men to half-educated barbarians. . . .

There is no perfect identity between the political and national frontier of any European country. Not one of the great Powers, and Germany no more than the rest of them, can ever subscribe to the principle that "language alone decides the formation of States." It would be impossible to carry that principle into effect. . . .

The German territory which we demand is ours by nature and by history. . . . In the tempests of the great Revolution the people of Alsace, like all the citizens of France, learned to forget their past. . . .

Most assuredly, the task of reuniting there the broken links between the ages is one of the heaviest that has ever been imposed upon the political forces of our nation. . . .

The people of Alsace are already beginning to doubt the invincibility of their nation, and at all events to divine the mighty growth of the German Empire. Perverse obstinacy, and a thousand French intrigues creeping in the dark, will make every step on the newly conquered soil difficult for us: but our ultimate success is certain, for on our side fights what is stronger than the lying artifices of the stranger—nature herself and the voice of common blood.

Source: From Heinrich von Treitschke, "What We Demand from France" (1870), in Heinrich von Treitschke, *Germany, France, Russia and Islam* (New York: G. P. Putnam's Sons, 1915), pp. 100, 102, 106, 109, 120, 122, 134–135, 153, 158.

alliance with Prussia in the Austro-Prussian War. French troops continued to guard Rome and the papacy until the troops were withdrawn during the Franco-Prussian War of 1870. The Italian state then annexed Rome and made it the capital. The papacy confined itself to the Vatican and remained hostile to the Italian state until the Lateran Accord of 1929. (See Chapter 27.)

By 1870, only the small province of Trent and the city of Trieste, both ruled by Austria, remained outside Italy. In and of themselves, these areas were not important, and their inhabitants were a mix of Italians, Germans, and Slavs, but they fueled the continued hostility of Italian nationalists toward Austria. The desire to liberate ***Italia irredenta***, or "unredeemed Italy," was one reason for the Italian support of the Allies against Austria and Germany during World War I.

▼ German Unification

German unification was the most important political development in Europe between 1848 and 1914. (See Map 22–2.) It transformed the balance of economic, military, and international power. Moreover, the way it was created largely determined the character of the new German state. Germany was united by the conservative army, the monarchy, and the prime minister of Prussia, who wanted to outflank Prussian liberals. A unified Germany, which two generations of German liberals had sought, was actually achieved for the most illiberal of reasons.

During the 1850s, German unification seemed remote. The political structure of the German-speaking lands was the German Confederation, which had been established at the Congress of Vienna. It was a loose federation of thirty-nine states of differing size and strength whose appointed representatives met in a central diet in Frankfurt. The two by far strongest states were Austria and Prussia. During the 1850s, Austria presided over the diet of the German Confederation. The major states continued to trade with each other through the *Zollverein* (tariff union), and railways linked their economies. Frederick William IV of Prussia had given up thoughts of unification under Prussian leadership. Austria continued to oppose any union that might lessen its influence. Liberal nation-

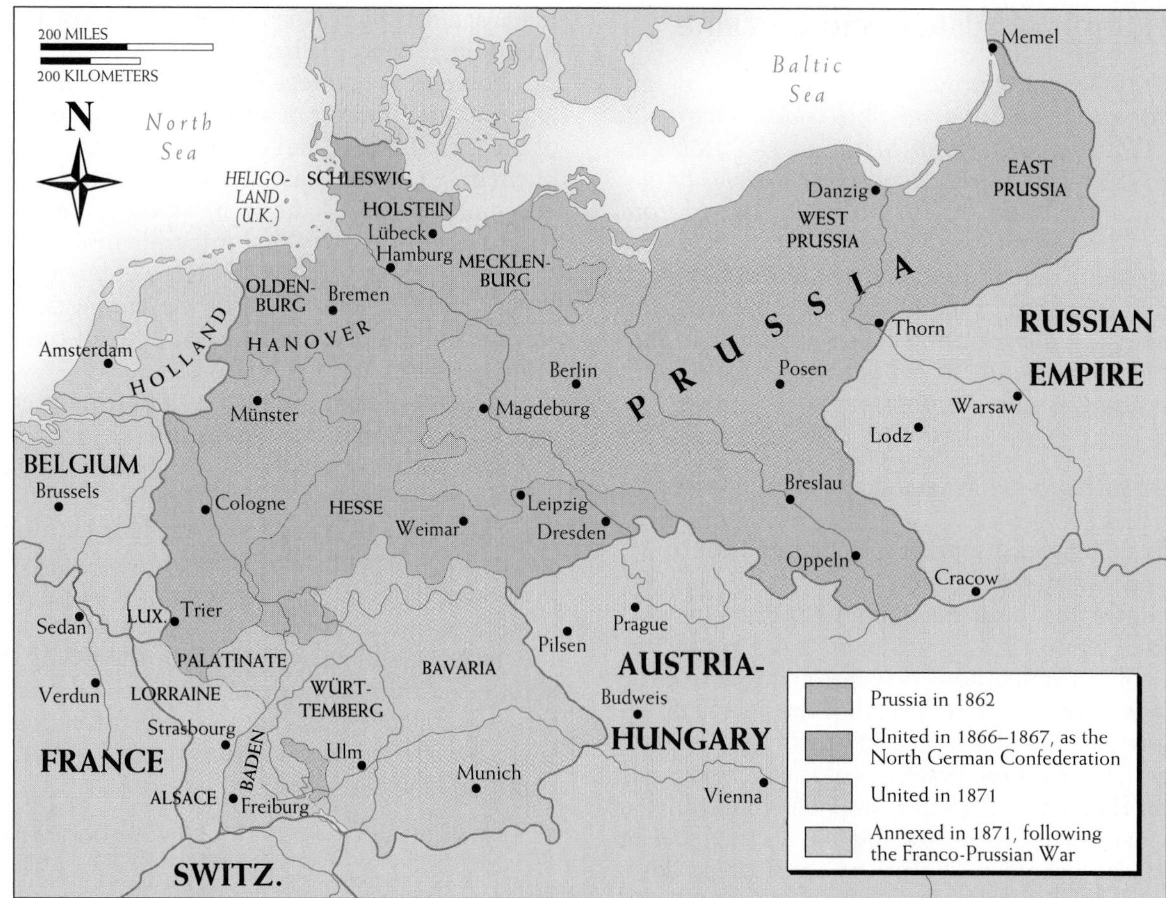

Map 22–2 **THE UNIFICATION OF GERMANY** Under Bismarck's leadership, and with the strong support of its royal house, Prussia used diplomatic and military means, on both the German and international stages, to forcibly unify the German states into a strong national entity.

alists had not recovered from the humiliations of 1848 and 1849, so they could do little or nothing for unification. What quickly overturned this static situation was a series of domestic political changes and problems within Prussia.

In 1858, Frederick William IV was adjudged insane, and his brother William assumed the regency. William I (r. 1861–1888), who became king in his own right in 1861, was less idealistic than his brother and more of a Prussian patriot. In the usual Hohenzollern tradition, his first concern was to strengthen the Prussian army. In 1860, his war minister and chief of staff proposed to enlarge the army, to increase the number of officers, and to extend the period of conscription from two to three years. The Prussian Parliament, created by the Constitution of 1850, refused to approve the necessary taxes. The liberals, who dominated the body, sought to avoid placing additional power in the hands of the monarchy. For two years, monarch and Parliament were deadlocked.

Bismarck

In September 1862, William I turned for help to the person who, more than any other single individual, shaped the next thirty years of European history: Otto von Bismarck (1815–1898). Bismarck came from Junker (noble landlord) stock. He attended a university and displayed an interest in German unification. During the 1840s, he was elected to the provincial diet, where he was so reactionary he disturbed even the king. Yet he had made his mark. From 1851 to 1859, Bismarck served as the Prussian representative to the German Confederation. Later he became Prussian ambassador to Russia and was ambassador to France when William I appointed him prime minister.

Although Bismarck entered public life as a reactionary, he had mellowed into a conservative. He opposed parliamentary government, but not a constitutionalism that preserved a strong monarchy. He understood that Prussia—and later, Germany—must have a strong industrial base. His years in Frankfurt arguing with his Austrian counterpart had hardened his Prussian patriotism. In politics, he was a pragmatist who put more trust in power and action than in ideas. As he declared in his first speech as prime minister, "Germany is not looking to Prussia's liberalism but to her power. . . . The great questions of the day will not be decided by speeches and majority decisions—that was the mistake of 1848–1849—but by iron and blood."[3] Yet this same minister, after having led Prussia into three wars, spent the next nineteen years seeking to preserve peace.

[3]Quoted in Otto Pflanze, *Bismarck and the Development of Germany: The Period of Unification: 1815–1871* (Princeton, NJ: Princeton University Press, 1963), p. 177.

Upon becoming prime minister in 1862, Bismarck immediately moved against the liberal Parliament. He contended that even without new financial levies, the Prussian constitution permitted the government to carry out its functions on the basis of previously granted taxes. Therefore, taxes could be collected and spent despite the parliamentary refusal to vote them. The army and most of the bureaucracy supported this interpretation of the constitution. In 1863, however, new elections sustained the liberal majority in the Parliament. Bismarck had to find a way to attract popular support away from the liberals and toward the monarchy and the army. He, therefore, set about uniting Germany through the conservative institutions of Prussia. In effect, Bismarck embraced the cause of German nationalism as a strategy to enable Prussian conservatives to outflank Prussian liberals.

The Danish War (1864) Bismarck's vision of a united Germany did not include all German-speaking lands. That is to say, he pursued a *kleindeutsch*, or small German, solution to unification. He intended to exclude Austria from any future united German state. This goal required complex diplomacy.

The Schleswig-Holstein problem gave Bismarck the handle for his policy. The kings of Denmark had long ruled these two northern duchies, which had never actually become part of Denmark itself. Their populations were a mixture of Germans and Danes. Holstein, where Germans predominated, belonged to the German Confederation. In 1863, the Danish Parliament moved to incorporate both duchies into Denmark. The smaller states of the German Confederation proposed an all-German war to halt this move. Bismarck, however, wanted Prussia to act alone or only in cooperation with Austria. Together, the two large states easily defeated Denmark in 1864.

The Danish defeat increased Bismarck's personal prestige and strengthened his political hand. Over the next two years, he managed to maneuver Austria into war with Prussia. In August 1865, the two powers negotiated the Convention of Gastein, which put Austria in charge of Holstein and Prussia in charge of Schleswig. Bismarck then mended other diplomatic fences. He had gained Russian sympathy in 1863 by supporting Russia's suppression of a Polish revolt, and he persuaded Napoleon III to promise neutrality in an Austro-Prussian conflict. In April 1866, Bismarck promised Italy Venetia if it attacked Austria in support of Prussia when war broke out. Now Bismarck had to provoke his war.

The Austro-Prussian War (1866) Constant Austro-Prussian tensions had arisen over the administration of Schleswig and Holstein. Bismarck ordered the Prussian forces to be as obnoxious as possible to the Austrians. On June 1, 1866, Austria appealed to the German Confederation to intervene in the dispute. Bismarck claimed that this request violated the 1864 alliance and the

The proclamation of the German Empire in the Hall of Mirrors at Versailles, January 18, 1871, after the defeat of France in the Franco-Prussian War. Kaiser Wilhelm I is standing at the top of the steps under the flags. Bismarck is in the center in a white uniform. Bildarchiv Preussischer Kulturbesitz

Convention of Gastein. The Seven Weeks' War, which resulted in the summer of 1866, led to the decisive defeat of Austria at Königgrätz in Bohemia.

The Treaty of Prague, which ended the conflict on August 23, was lenient toward Austria, which only lost Venetia, ceded as promised to Napoleon III, who in turn ceded it to Italy. Austria refused to give Venetia directly to Italy because the Austrians had crushed the Italians during the war. The treaty permanently excluded the Austrian Habsburgs from German affairs. Prussia had thus established itself as the only major power among the German states.

The North German Confederation In 1867, Prussia annexed Hanover, Hesse Kassel, Nassau, and the city of Frankfurt, all of which had all supported Austria during the war and deposed their rulers. Under Prussian leadership, all Germany north of the Main River now formed the North German Confederation. Each state retained its own local government, but all military forces were under federal control. The president of the federation was the king of Prussia, represented by his chancellor, Bismarck. A legislature consisted of two houses: a federal council, or ***Bundesrat***, composed of members appointed by the governments of the states, and a lower house, or ***Reichstag***, chosen by universal male suffrage.

Bismarck, the great conservative chancellor, unlike German liberals, actually embraced a democratic franchise because he sensed that the peasants would vote for conservatives Moreover, the *Reichstag* had little real power, because the ministers were responsible only to the monarch. The *Reichstag* could not even originate legislation. The chancellor had to propose all laws. The legislature did have the right to approve military budgets, but these were usually submitted to cover several years at a time. The constitution of the North German Confederation, which, after 1871, became the constitution of the German Empire, possessed some of the appearances, but none of the substance, of liberalism. Germany was, in effect, a military monarchy.

Bismarck's spectacular successes overwhelmed the liberal opposition in the Prussian Parliament. The liberals were split between those who prized liberalism and those who supported unification. In the end, nationalism proved more attractive. In 1866, the Prussian Parliament retroactively approved the military budget that it had rejected earlier. Bismarck had crushed the Prussian liberals by making the monarchy and the army the most popular institutions in the country. The drive toward German national unification had achieved his domestic Prussian political goal.

The Franco-Prussian War and the German Empire (1870–1871)

Bismarck now wanted to complete unification by bringing the states of southern Germany—Bavaria, Wurtemberg, Baden, and Hesse Darmstadt—into the newly established confederation. Spain gave him the excuse. In 1868, a military coup deposed the corrupt Bourbon queen of Spain, Isabella II (r. 1833–1868). To replace her, the Spaniards chose Prince Leopold of Hohenzollern-Sigmaringen, a Catholic cousin of William I of Prussia. On June 19, 1870, Leopold accepted the Spanish crown with Prussian blessings. Bismarck knew that France would object strongly to a Hohenzollern Spain.

On July 2, the Spanish government announced Leopold's acceptance, and the French reacted as expected. France sent its ambassador, Count Vincent Benedetti (1817–1900), to consult with William I, who was vacationing at Bad Ems. They discussed the matter at several meetings. On July 12, Leopold's father renounced his son's candidacy for the Spanish throne, fearing the issue would cause war between Prussia and France. William was relieved that conflict had been avoided, and he had not had to order Leopold to renounce the Spanish throne.

There the matter might have rested had it not been for the impetuosity of the French and the guile of Bismarck. On July 13, the French government instructed Benedetti to ask William for assurances he would tolerate no future Spanish candidacy for Leopold. The king refused but said he might take the question under further consideration. Later that day he sent Bismarck, who was in Berlin, a telegram reporting the substance of the meeting. The peaceful resolution of the controversy had disappointed the chancellor, who desperately wanted a war with France to complete unification. The king's telegram gave him a new opportunity to provoke war. Bismarck released an edited version of the dispatch. The revised Ems telegram made it appear that William had insulted the French ambassador. The idea was to goad France into declaring war.

The French government fell for Bismarck's bait and declared war on July 19. Napoleon III was sick and not eager for war, but his government believed victory over the North German Confederation would renew popular support for the empire. Once the conflict erupted, the southern German states, honoring treaties of 1866, joined Prussia against France, whose defeat was not long in coming. On September 1, at the Battle of Sedan, the Germans not only beat the French army but also captured Napoleon III. By late September, Paris was besieged; it finally capitulated on January 28, 1871.

GERMAN AND ITALIAN UNIFICATION

1854	Crimean War opens
1855	Cavour leads Piedmont into the war on the side of France and England
1856	Treaty of Paris concludes the Crimean War
1858 (January 14)	Attempt to assassinate Napoleon III
1858 (July 20)	Secret conference between Napoleon III and Cavour at Plombières
1859	War of Piedmont and France against Austria
1860	Garibaldi lands his forces in Sicily and invades southern Italy
1861 (March 17)	Proclamation of the Kingdom of Italy
1861 (June 6)	Death of Cavour
1862	Bismarck becomes prime minister of Prussia
1864	Danish War
1865	Convention of Gastein
1866	Austro-Prussian War
1866	Austria cedes Venetia to Italy
1867	North German Confederation formed
1870 (June 19–July 12)	Crisis over Hohenzollern candidacy for the Spanish throne
1870 (July 13)	Bismarck publishes the edited Ems dispatch
1870 (July 19)	France declares war on Prussia
1870 (September 1)	France defeated at Sedan and Napoleon III captured
1870 (September 4)	French Republic proclaimed
1870 (October 2)	Italian state annexes Rome
1871 (January 18)	Proclamation of the German Empire at Versailles
1871 (March 28–May 28)	Paris Commune
1871 (May 23)	Treaty of Frankfurt ratified between France and Germany

Ten days earlier, in the Hall of Mirrors at the Palace of Versailles, the German Empire had been proclaimed. The German princes requested William to accept the title of German emperor. The princes remained heads of their respective states within the new empire. Through the peace settlement with France, Germany annexed Alsace and part of Lorraine and forced the French to pay a large indemnity. (See "Heinrich von Treitschke Demands the Annexation of Alsace and Lorraine," page 669.)

Both the fact and the manner of German unification produced long-range effects in Europe. A powerful new state had been created in north central Europe. It was rich in natural resources and talented citizens. Militarily and economically, the German Empire would be far stronger than Prussia had been alone. The unification of Germany was also a blow to European liberalism, because the new state was a conservative creation. Conservative politics were now backed not by a weak Austria or an economically retrograde Russia, but by the strongest state on the Continent.

The two nations most immediately affected by German and Italian unification were France and Austria. The emergence of the two new unified states revealed French and Habsburg weakness. Each had to change. France returned to republican government, and the Habsburgs came to terms with their Magyar subjects.

▼ France: From Liberal Empire to the Third Republic

Historians divide the reign of Napoleon III (r. 1852–1870) into the years of the authoritarian empire and those of the liberal empire. The year of division is 1860. After the coup in December 1851, Napoleon III had controlled the legislature, censored the press, and harassed political dissidents. His support came from the army, property owners, the French Catholic Church, peasants, and businesspeople. They approved the security he ensured for property, his protection of the pope, and his economic program. French victory in the Crimean War had confirmed the emperor's popularity.

From the late 1850s onward, Napoleon III began to modify his policy. In 1860, he concluded a free-trade treaty with Britain and permitted freer debate in the legislature. By the late 1860s, he had relaxed the press laws and permitted labor unions. In 1870, he allowed the leaders of the moderates in the legislature to form a ministry, and he also agreed to a liberal constitution that made the ministers responsible to the legislature.

Napoleon III's liberal concessions sought to shore up domestic support to compensate for his failures in foreign policy. By 1860, he had lost control of the diplomacy of Italian unification. Between 1861 and 1867, he had supported a disastrous military expedition against Mexico led by Archduke Maximilian of Austria that ended in defeat and Maximilian's execution. In 1866, France had watched passively while Bismarck and Prussia reorganized German affairs. The war of 1870 against Germany had been the French government's last and most disastrous attempt to shore up its foreign policy and secure domestic popularity.

The Second Empire, but not the war, came to an inglorious end with the Battle of Sedan in September 1870. The emperor was captured and then allowed to go to England, where he died in 1873. Shortly after news of Sedan reached Paris, a republic was proclaimed and a government of national defense established. Paris itself was soon under Prussian siege, and the government moved to Bordeaux. Paris finally surrendered in January 1871, but France had been ready to sue for peace long before.

The Paris Commune

The division between the provinces and Paris became sharper after the fighting with Germany stopped. Monarchists dominated the new National Assembly elected in February. For the time being, the assembly gave executive power to Adolphe Thiers (1797–1877), who had been active in French politics since 1830. He negotiated a settlement with Prussia (the Treaty of Frankfurt), which was officially ratified on May 23.

Many Parisians, having suffered during the siege, resented what they regarded as a betrayal by the monarchist National Assembly sitting at Versailles. The Parisians elected a new municipal government, called the *Paris Commune*, which was formally proclaimed on March 28, 1871. The Commune intended to administer Paris separately from the rest of France. Radicals and socialists of all stripes participated in the Commune. In April, the National Assembly surrounded Paris with an army. On May 8, this army bombarded the city. On May 21, it broke through the city's defenses. During the next seven days, the troops killed about 20,000 inhabitants while the communards shot scores of hostages.

The Paris Commune became a legend throughout Europe. Marxists regarded it as a genuine proletarian government that the French bourgeoisie had suppressed. This interpretation is mistaken. The Commune, though of shifting composition, was dominated by petty bourgeois members. The socialism of the Commune had its roots in Blanqui's and Proudhon's anarchism rather than in Marx's concept of class conflict. The Commune wanted not a workers' state, but a nation of relatively independent, radically democratic enclaves. Its suppression thus represented not only the protection of property, but also the triumph of the centralized nation-state. Just as the armies of Piedmont and Prussia had united the small states of Italy and Germany, the army of the

French National Assembly destroyed the particularistic political tendencies of Paris and, by implication, those of any other French community.

The Third Republic

The National Assembly backed into a republican form of government against its will. Its monarchist majority was divided in loyalty between the House of Bourbon and the House of Orléans. They could have surmounted this problem, because the Bourbon claimant, the count of Chambord, had no children and agreed to accept the Orléanist heir as his successor. Chambord refused to become king, however, if France retained the revolutionary tricolor flag. Even the conservative monarchists would not return to the white flag of the Bourbons, which symbolized extreme political reaction.

While the monarchists quarreled among themselves, events marched on. By September 1873, the indemnity had been paid, and the Prussian occupation troops had withdrawn. Thiers was ousted from office because he had displayed clear republican sentiments. The monarchists wanted a more sympathetic executive. They elected as president a conservative army officer, Marshal Patrice MacMahon (1808–1893), who was expected to prepare for a monarchist restoration. In 1875, the National Assembly, still monarchist in sentiment, but unable to find a king, decided to regularize the political system. It adopted a law that provided for a Chamber of Deputies elected by universal male suffrage, a senate chosen indirectly, and a president elected by the two legislative houses. This rather simple republican system had resulted from the bickering and frustration of the monarchists.

After numerous quarrels with the Chamber of Deputies, MacMahon resigned in 1879. His departure meant that dedicated republicans controlled the national government despite lingering opposition from the church, wealthy families, and a part of the army.

The political structure of the Third Republic proved much stronger than many citizens suspected at the time. It survived challenges from persons such as General Georges Boulanger (1837–1891), who would have imposed stronger executive authority. It also survived several scandals, such as those involving sales of awards of the Legion of Honor and widespread corruption of politicians and journalists by a company that tried to construct a canal in Panama, that made its politics appear increasingly sleazy. The institutions of the republic, however, allowed new ministers to replace those whose corruption was exposed.

MAJOR DATES IN THE HISTORY OF THE THIRD FRENCH REPUBLIC

1870	Defeat by Prussia and proclamation of republic
1871	Paris Commune
1873	Prussian occupation troops depart
1873	Marshal MacMahon elected president
1875	Major political institutions of Third Republic organized
1879	MacMahon resigns as president
1894	Captain Dreyfus convicted
1906	Dreyfus's conviction set aside

The Dreyfus Affair

The greatest trauma of the Third Republic occurred over what became known as the *Dreyfus affair.* On December 22, 1894, a French military court found Captain Alfred Dreyfus (1859–1935) guilty of passing secret information to the German army. The evidence against him was flimsy and was later revealed to have been forged. Someone in the officer corps had been passing documents to the Germans, and it suited the army investigators to accuse Dreyfus, who was Jewish. After Dreyfus had been sent to Devil's Island, a notorious prison in French Guiana, however, secrets continued to flow to the German army. In 1896, a new head of French counterintelligence reexamined the Dreyfus file and found evidence of forgery. A different officer was implicated, but a military court acquitted him of all charges.

By then the affair had provoked near-hysterical public debate. The army, the French Catholic Church, political conservatives, and vehemently anti-Semitic newspapers contended that Dreyfus was guilty. Such anti-Dreyfus opinion was dominant at the beginning of the affair. In 1898, however, the novelist Émile Zola (1840–1902) published a newspaper article entitled "*J'accuse*" ("I accuse"), in which he contended that the army had denied due process to Dreyfus and had suppressed or forged evidence. Zola was convicted of libel and fled to England to avoid serving a one-year prison sentence. (See "Émile Zola Accuses the Enemies of Dreyfus of Self-Interest and Illegal Actions," page 677.)

Zola was only one of numerous liberals, radicals, and socialists who had begun to demand a new trial for Dreyfus. Although these forces of the political left had come to Dreyfus's support rather slowly, they soon realized his cause could aid their own public image. They portrayed the conservative institutions of the nation as having denied Dreyfus the rights belonging to any citizen of the republic. They also claimed, and properly so, that Dreyfus had been framed to protect the guilty persons, who were still in the army. In August 1898, further evidence of forged material came to light. The officer responsible for those forgeries committed suicide

The prosecution of Captain Alfred Dreyfus, who is shown here standing on the right at his military trial, provoked the most serious crisis of the Third Republic. © Bettman/CORBIS

in jail, but a new military trial again convicted Dreyfus. The president of France immediately pardoned him, however, and eventually, in 1906, a civilian court set aside the results of both military trials.

The Dreyfus case divided France as no issue had done since the Paris Commune. By its conclusion, the conservatives were on the defensive. They had allowed themselves to persecute an innocent person and to manufacture false evidence against him to protect themselves from disclosure. They had also embraced violent anti-Semitism. On the political left, radicals, republicans, and socialists developed an informal alliance, which outlived the Dreyfus case itself. These groups realized that the political left had to support republican institutions to achieve its goals. Nonetheless, the political, religious, and racial divisions and suspicions growing out of the Dreyfus affair continued to divide the Third Republic until France's defeat by Germany in 1940.

▼ The Habsburg Empire

After 1848, the Habsburg Empire was a problem both to itself and for the rest of Europe. An ungenerous critic remarked that a standing army of soldiers, a kneeling army of priests, and a crawling army of informers supported the empire. In the age of national states, liberal institutions, and industrialism, the Habsburg domains remained primarily dynastic, absolutist, and agrarian. The Habsburg response to the revolts of 1848–1849 had been to reassert absolutism. Emperor Francis Joseph (r. 1848–1916) was honest, conscientious, and hardworking, but unimaginative. He reacted to events but rarely commanded them.

The coronation of Francis Joseph of Hungary in 1867 is depicted in this painting. The so-called *Ausgleich*, or Compromise, of 1867 transformed the Habsburg Empire into a dual monarchy in which Austria and Hungary became almost separate states except for defense and foreign affairs. Bildarchiv der Oesterreichischen Nationalbibliothek, Wien

ÉMILE ZOLA ACCUSES THE ENEMIES OF DREYFUS OF SELF-INTEREST AND ILLEGAL ACTIONS

On January 13, 1898, Émile Zola, the leading French novelist of his day (see Chapter 24) and a strong defender of Captain Alfred Dreyfus, published perhaps the most famous newspaper article of the century in France. The format of the article was a letter to the president of the French Republic. Under a large type banner headline "J'accuse" ("I accuse"), Zola accused a series of high military officers and others of illegally and dishonestly persecuting Dreyfus. Zola knew he could possibly face charges and convictions of libel. Eventually he fled France for political refuge in England.

What are the accusations that Zola brings against Dreyfus's enemies? How does Zola see Dreyfus's enemies as protecting their own institutions and self-interest? How does Zola put his own reputation and fame on the line in defending Dreyfus?

I accuse Lt-Col du Paty de Clam of having been the diabolical agent of a miscarriage of justice (though unwittingly, I am willing to believe) and then of having defended his evil deed for the past three years through the most preposterous and most blameworthy machinations.

I accuse General Mercier of having been an accomplice, at least by weak-mindedness, to one of the most iniquitous acts of this century.

I accuse General Billot of having had in his hands undeniable proof that Dreyfus was innocent and of having suppressed it, of having committed this crime against justice and against humanity for political purposes, so that the General Staff, which had been compromised, would not lose face.

I accuse Generals de Boisdeffre and Gonse of having been accomplices to this same crime, one out of intense clerical conviction, no doubt, and the other perhaps because of the esprit de corps which makes the War Office the Holy of Holies and hence unattackable. . . .

I accuse the three handwriting experts . . . of having submitted fraudulent and deceitful reports—unless a medication examination concludes that their eyesight and their judgment were impaired.

I accuse the War Office of having conducted an abominable campaign in the press . . . in order to cover up its misdeeds and lead public opinion astray.

Finally, I accuse the first court martial of having violated the law by sentencing a defendant on the basis of documents which remained secret, and I accuse the second court martial of having covered up that illegal action, on order, by having, in its own turn, committed the judicial crime of knowingly acquitting a guilty man.

In making these accusations, I am fully aware that my action comes under Articles 30 and 31 of the law of 29 July 1881 on the press, which makes libel a punishable offence. I deliberately expose myself to that law.

As for the persons I have accused, I do not know them: I have never seen them: I feel no rancour or hatred towards them. To me, they are mere entities, mere embodiments of social malfeasance. And the action I am taking here is merely a revolutionary means to hasten the revelation of truth and justice.

. . . Let them dare to summon me before a court of law! Let the inquiry be held in broad daylight!

I am waiting.

Cinq Centimes

ERNEST VAUGHAN

L'AURORE

Littéraire, Artistique, Sociale

J'Accuse...!

LETTRE AU PRÉSIDENT DE LA RÉPUBLIQUE

Par ÉMILE ZOLA

LETTRE A M. FÉLIX FAURE

Président de la République

Monsieur le Président,

Émile Zola Letter to M. Félix Faure, President of the Republic, published in *L'Aurore*, January 13, 1898, trans. by Eleanor Levieux, in Alain Pagés, ed., *Émile Zola, The Dreyfus Affair: "J'accuse" and Other Writings* (New Haven, CT: Yale University Press, 1996), pp. 52–53.

During the 1850s, his ministers attempted to impose a centralized administration on the empire. The system amounted to a military and bureaucratic regime dominated by German-speaking Austrians. The Vienna government abolished internal tariffs in the empire. It divided Hungary, which had been so revolutionary in 1848, into military districts. The Roman Catholic Church acquired control of education. National groups, such as the Croats and Slovaks, who had supported the empire against the Hungarians, received no rewards for their loyalty. Although this system provoked resentment, it eventually floundered because of setbacks in foreign affairs.

Austrian refusal to support Russia during the Crimean War meant the new tsar Alexander II (r. 1855–1881) would no longer help preserve Habsburg rule in Hungary, as Nicholas I had done in 1849. An important external prop of Habsburg power for the past half century thus disappeared. The Austrian defeat in 1859 at the hands of France and Piedmont and the subsequent loss of territory in Italy confirmed the necessity for a new domestic policy. For seven years the emperor, the civil servants, the aristocrats, and the politicians tried to construct a viable system of government.

Formation of the Dual Monarchy

In 1860, Francis Joseph issued the October Diploma, which created a federation among the states and provinces of the empire. There were to be local diets dominated by the landed classes and a single imperial parliament. The Magyar nobility of Hungary, however, rejected the plan.

Consequently, in 1861, the emperor issued the February Patent, which set up an entirely different form of government. It established a bicameral imperial parliament, or *Reichsrat*, with an upper chamber appointed by the emperor and an indirectly elected lower chamber. Again, the Magyars refused to cooperate in a system designed to give political dominance in the empire to German-speaking Austrians. The Magyars sent no delegates to the legislature. Nevertheless, for six years, the February Patent governed the empire, and it prevailed in Austria proper until 1918. Ministers were responsible to the emperor, not the *Reichsrat*, and civil liberties were not guaranteed. Armies could be levied and taxes raised without parliamentary consent. When the *Reichsrat* was not in session, the emperor could simply rule by decree.

Meanwhile, secret negotiations between the emperor and the Magyars produced no concrete result until the Prussian defeat of Austria in the summer of 1866 and the consequent exclusion of Austria from German affairs. Francis Joseph now had to come to terms with the Magyars. The subsequent **Ausgleich**, or Compromise, of 1867 transformed the Habsburg Empire into a dual monarchy known as Austria-Hungary.

MAJOR DATES IN THE LATE-NINETEENTH-CENTURY HABSBURG EMPIRE

1848	Francis Joseph becomes emperor
1859	Defeat by France and Piedmont
1860	October Diploma
1861	February Patent
1866	Defeat by Prussia
1867	Compromise between emperor and Hungary, establishing the Dual Monarchy
1897	Ordinances giving equality of language between Germans and Czechs in Austria
1907	Universal male suffrage introduced for Austria

Francis Joseph was crowned king of Hungary in Budapest in 1867. Except for the common monarch, army, and foreign relations, Austria and Hungary became almost wholly separate states. They shared ministers of foreign affairs, defense, and finance, but the other ministers were different for each state. There were also separate parliaments. Each year, sixty parliamentary delegates from each state met to discuss mutual interests. Every ten years, Austria and Hungary renegotiated their trade relationship. This cumbersome machinery, unique in European history, reconciled the Magyars to Habsburg rule. They had achieved the free hand they had long wanted in Hungary.

Unrest of Nationalities

The Compromise of 1867 introduced two different principles of political legitimacy into the two sections of the Habsburg Empire. In Hungary, political loyalty was based on nationality because Hungary had been recognized as a distinct part of the monarchy on the basis of nationalism. In effect, Hungary was a Magyar nation under the Habsburg emperor. In the rest of the Habsburg domains, the principle of legitimacy meant dynastic loyalty to the emperor. Many of the other nationalities wished to achieve the same type of settlement that the Hungarians had won, or to govern themselves, or as time went on, to unite with fellow nationals who lived outside the empire. (See Map 22–3.)

Many of these other national groups—including the Czechs, the Ruthenians, the Romanians, and the Croatians—opposed the Compromise of 1867 that, in effect, had permitted the German-speaking Austrians and the Hungarian Magyars to dominate all other nationalities within the empire. The most vocal critics were the Czechs of Bohemia. They favored a policy of "trialism," or triple monarchy, in which the Czechs would have a position similar to that of the Hungarians. In 1871,

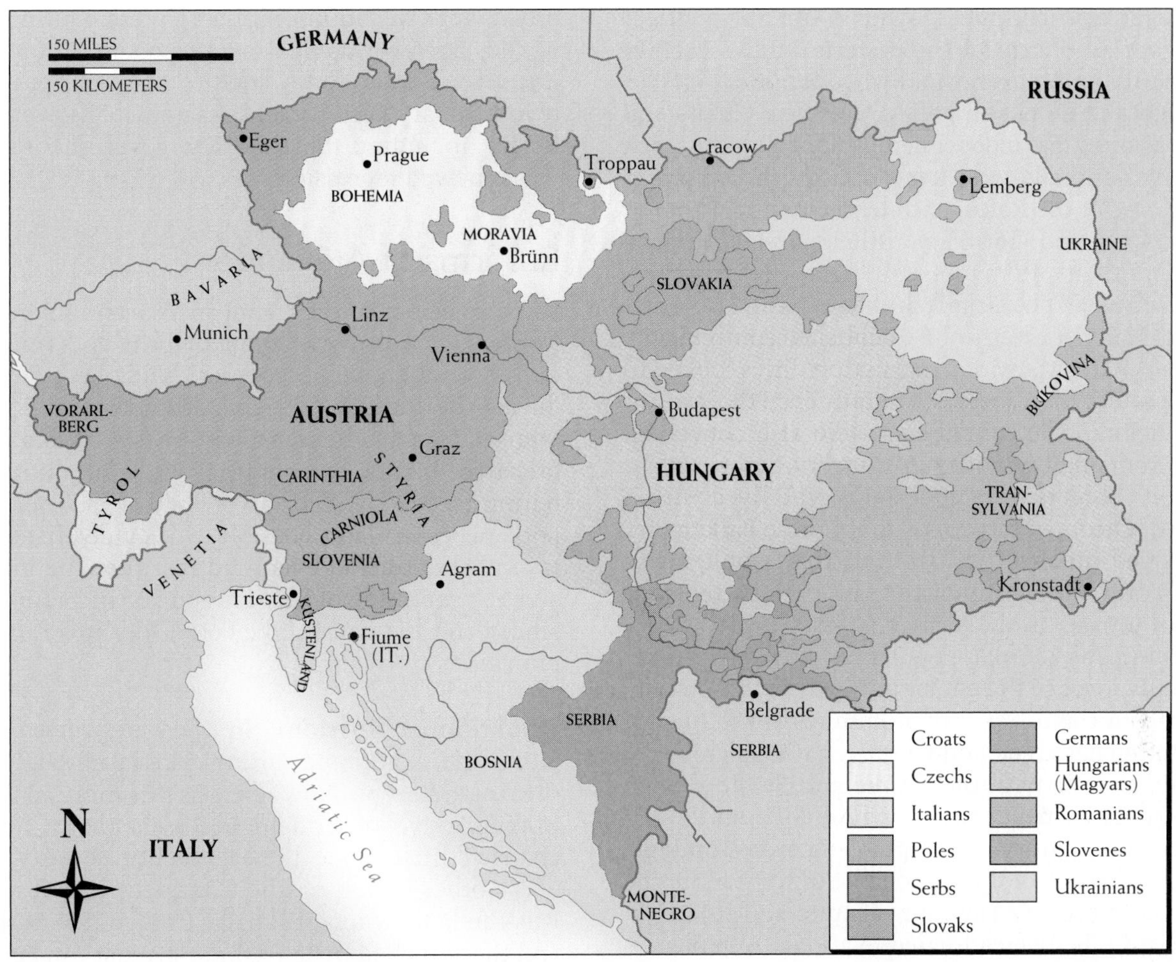

Map 22–3 **NATIONALITIES WITHIN THE HABSBURG EMPIRE** The patchwork appearance reflects the unusual problem of the numerous ethnic groups that the Habsburgs could not meld into a modern national state. Only the Magyars were recognized in 1867, leaving nationalist Czechs, Slovaks, and the others chronically dissatisfied.

Francis Joseph was willing to accept this concept. The Magyars, however, vetoed it lest they be forced to make similar concessions to their own subject nationalities. Furthermore, the Germans of Bohemia were afraid the Czech language would be imposed on them.

For more than twenty years, generous patronage and posts in the bureaucracy placated the Czechs. By the 1890s, however, Czech nationalism again became more strident. In 1897, Francis Joseph gave the Czechs and the Germans equality of language in various localities. Thereafter, the Germans in the Austrian *Reichsrat* opposed these measures by disrupting Parliament. The Czechs replied in kind. By the turn of the century, this obstructionism, which included the playing of musical instruments in the *Reichsrat*, had paralyzed parliamentary life. The emperor ruled by imperial decree through the bureaucracy. In 1907, Francis Joseph introduced universal male suffrage in Austria (but not in Hungary), but this action did not eliminate the chaos in the *Reichsrat*. In effect, by 1914, constitutionalism was a dead letter in Austria. It flourished in Hungary, but only because the Magyars relentlessly exercised political supremacy over all other competing national groups except Croatia, which was permitted considerable autonomy.

There is reason to believe nationalism became stronger during the last quarter of the nineteenth century. Language became the single most important factor in defining a nation. The expansion of education made this possible. In all countries where nationalistic groups prospered, their membership was dominated by intellectuals, students, and educated members of the middle class, all of whom were literate in the literary version of particular national languages. Furthermore, during these same years, as will be seen in Chapter 24, racial thinking became important in Europe. Racial thought maintained there was a genetic basis for ethnic and cultural groups that had hitherto been generally defined by a common history and culture. Once language and race became the ways to define an ethnic or national group, the lines between such groups became much more sharply drawn.

The unrest of the various nationalities within the Habsburg Empire not only caused internal political difficulties; it also became a major source of political instability for all of central and eastern Europe. Each of the nationality problems normally had ramifications for both foreign and domestic policy. Both the Croats and the Poles wanted an independent state in union with their fellow nationals who lived outside the empire—and in the case of the Poles, with fellow nationals in the Russian Empire and Germany. Other national groups, such as Ukrainians, Romanians, Italians, and Bosnians, saw themselves as potentially linked to Russia, Romania, Serbia, Italy, or a yet-to-be established south Slavic, or Yugoslav, state. Many of these nationalities looked to Russia to protect their interests or influence the government in Vienna. The Romanians were also concerned about the Romanian minority in Hungary. Serbia sought to expand its borders to include Serbs who lived within Habsburg or Ottoman territory. Out of these Balkan tensions emerged much of the turmoil that would spark the First World War. Many of the same ethnic tensions account for warfare in the former Yugoslavia.

The dominant German population of Austria proper was generally loyal to the emperor. A part of it, however, yearned to join the new German Empire. These Austro-Germans often hated the non-German national groups of the empire, and many of them were anti-Semites. Such attitudes would influence the young Adolf Hitler.

For the next century of European and even world history, the significance of this nationalist unrest within the late-nineteenth-century Habsburg Empire and its neighbors can hardly be overestimated. Nationality problems touched all four of the great central and eastern European empires—the German, the Russian, the Austrian, and the Ottoman. The first three had large Polish populations, and Russia, Austria, and the Ottomans had many minority groups. Each nationality regarded its own aspirations and discontents as more important than the larger good or even survival of the empires that they inhabited. The weakness of the Ottoman Empire allowed both Austria and Russia to compete in the Balkans for influence and thus further inflame nationalistic resentments. Such nationalistic stirrings affected the fate of all four empires from the 1860s through the outbreak of World War I. The government of each of these empires would be overturned during the war, and the Habsburg monarchy and the Ottoman Empire would disappear. These same unresolved problems of central and eastern European nationalism would then lead directly to World War II. They continue to fester today.

▼ Russia: Emancipation and Revolutionary Stirrings

Russia changed remarkably during the last half of the nineteenth century. The government finally addressed the long-standing problem of serfdom and undertook a broad range of administrative reforms. During the same period, however, radical revolutionary groups began to organize. These groups tried to draw the peasants into revolutionary activity and assassinated government officials, including the tsar. The government's response was renewed repression.

Reforms of Alexander II

Russia's defeat in the Crimean War and its humiliation in the Treaty of Paris compelled the government to reconsider its domestic policies. Nicholas I died in 1855 during the conflict. His son Alexander II (r. 1855–1881), who had traveled extensively in Russia and been well prepared to rule, was familiar with the difficulties the nation faced. The debacle of the war had made reform both necessary and possible. Alexander II took advantage of this turn of events to institute the most extensive restructuring of Russian society and administration since Peter the Great. Like Peter, Alexander imposed his reforms from the top.

Abolition of Serfdom In every area of economic and public life, a profound cultural gap separated Russia from the rest of Europe. Nowhere was this more apparent than in the survival of serfdom. In Russia, the institution had changed little since the eighteenth century, although every other nation on the Continent had abandoned it. Russian landowners still had a free hand with their serfs, and the serfs had little recourse against the landlords. In March 1856, at the conclusion of the Crimean War, Alexander II announced his intention to abolish serfdom. He had decided that its abolition was necessary if Russia was to remain a great power.

Serfdom was economically inefficient. There was always the threat of revolt, and the serfs forced into the

MAJOR DATES IN LATE-NINETEENTH-CENTURY RUSSIA

1855	Alexander II becomes tsar
1856	Defeat in Crimean War
1861	Serfdom abolished
1863	Suppression of Polish rebellion
1864	Reorganization of local government
1864	Reform of judicial system
1874	Military enlistment period reduced
1878	Attempted assassination of military governor of Saint Petersburg
1879	Land and Freedom splits
1881	The People's Will assassinates Alexander II
1881	Alexander III becomes tsar
1894	Nicholas II becomes tsar

army had performed poorly in the Crimean War. Moreover, nineteenth-century moral opinion condemned serfdom. Only Russia, Brazil, and certain portions of the United States among the Western nations retained such forms of involuntary servitude. For five years, government commissions wrestled over how to implement the tsar's desire. Finally, in February 1861, despite opposition from the nobility and the landlords, Alexander II ended serfdom.

The actual emancipation law was a disappointment, however, because land did not accompany freedom. Serfs immediately received the personal right to marry without their landlord's permission, as well as the rights to buy and sell property, to sue in court, and to pursue trades. What they did not receive was free title to their land. They had to pay the landlords over a period of forty-nine years for allotments of land that were frequently too small to support them. They were also charged interest during this period. The former serfs, who were now free peasant farmers, made the payments to the government, which had already reimbursed the landlords for their losses. The peasants would not receive title to the land until the debt was paid.

The procedures were so complicated and the results so limited that many serfs believed real emancipation was still to come. The redemption payments led to almost unending difficulty. Poor harvests made it impossible for many peasants to keep up with the payments, and they fell increasingly behind in their debt. The situation was not remedied until 1906, when, during the widespread revolutionary unrest following the Japanese defeat of Russia in 1905, the government grudgingly completed the process of emancipation by canceling the remaining debts.

Reform of Local Government and the Judicial System The abolition of serfdom required the reorganization of local government and the judicial system. The authority of village communes replaced that of the landlord over the peasant. The village elders settled family quarrels, imposed fines, issued internal passports that were legally required for peasants to move from one locale to another, and collected taxes. Often, also, the village commune, not individual peasants, owned the land. The nobility were given a larger role in local administration through a system of provincial and county *zemstvos*, or councils, organized in 1864. These councils were to oversee local matters, such as bridge and road repair, education, and agricultural improvement. The *zemstvos*, however, were underfunded, and many of them remained ineffective.

The flagrant inequities and abuses of the pre-emancipation judicial system could not continue. In 1864, Alexander II issued a new statute on the judiciary that for the first time introduced Western European legal principles into Russia. These included equality before the law, impartial hearings, uniform procedures, judicial independence, and trial by jury. The new system was far from perfect. The judges were not genuinely independent, and the tsar could increase as well as reduce sentences. Certain offenses, such as those involving the press, were not tried before a jury. Nonetheless, the new courts were both more efficient and less corrupt than the old system.

Military Reform The government also reformed the army. Russia possessed the largest army on the Continent, but it had floundered badly in the Crimean War. The usual period of service for a soldier was twenty-five years. Villages had to provide quotas of serfs to serve in the army. Often, recruiters simply seized serfs from their families. Once in the army, recruits rarely saw their homes again. Life in the army was harsh, even by the brutal standards of most mid-century armies. In the 1860s, the army lowered the period of service to fifteen years and relaxed discipline slightly. In 1874, the enlistment period was lowered to six years of active duty and nine years in the reserves. All males were subject to military service after the age of twenty.

Repression in Poland Alexander's reforms became more measured shortly after the Polish Rebellion of 1863. As in 1830, Polish nationalists attempted to overthrow Russian dominance. Once again the Russian army suppressed the rebellion. Alexander II then moved to Russify Poland. In 1864, he emancipated the Polish serfs to punish the politically restive Polish nobility. Russian law, language, and administration were imposed on all areas of Polish life. Henceforth, until the close of World War I, Poland was treated as merely another Russian province.

As the Polish suppression demonstrated, Alexander II was a reformer only within the limits of his own autocracy. His changes in Russian life failed to create new loyalty to, or gratitude for, the government among his subjects. The serfs felt their emancipation had been inadequate. The nobles and the wealthier educated segments of Russian society resented the tsar's persistent refusal to allow them a meaningful role in government and policymaking. Consequently, although Alexander II became known as the Tsar Liberator, he was never popular. He could be indecisive and closed minded. These characteristics became more pronounced after 1866, when an attempt was made on his life. Thereafter, Russia increasingly became a police state. This new repression fueled the activity of radical groups within Russia. Their actions, in turn, made the autocracy more reactionary.

Revolutionaries

The tsarist regime had long had its critics. One of the most prominent was Alexander Herzen (1812–1870),

Tsar Alexander II (r. 1855–1881) was assassinated on March 1, 1881. The assassins first threw a bomb that wounded several Imperial guards. When the tsar stopped his carriage to see the wounded, the assassins threw a second bomb, killing him. Bildarchiv Preussischer Kulturbesitz

who lived in exile. From London, he published a newspaper called *The Bell*, in which he set forth reformist positions. The initial reforms of Alexander II had raised great hopes among Russian students and intellectuals, but they soon became discontented with the limited character of the reforms. Drawing on the ideas of Herzen and other radicals, these students formed a revolutionary movement known as *populism*. They sought a social revolution based on the communal life of the Russian peasants. The chief radical society was called *Land and Freedom*.

In the early 1870s, hundreds of young Russian men and women took their revolutionary message into the countryside. They intended to live with the peasants, to gain their trust, and to teach them about the peasant's role in the coming revolution. The bewildered and distrustful peasants turned most of the youths over to the police. In the winter of 1877–1878, almost two hundred students were tried. Most were acquitted or given light sentences, because they had been held for months in preventive detention and because the court believed a display of mercy might lessen public sympathy for the young revolutionaries. The court even suggested the tsar might wish to pardon those students given heavier sentences. The tsar refused and let it be known he favored heavy penalties for all persons involved in revolutionary activity.

Thereafter, the revolutionaries decided the tsarist regime must be attacked directly. They adopted a policy of terrorism. In January 1878, Vera Zasulich (1849–1919) attempted to assassinate the military governor of Saint Petersburg. A jury acquitted her because the governor she had shot had a reputation for brutality. Some people also believed Zasulich had a personal rather than a political grievance against her victim. Nonetheless, the verdict further encouraged the terrorists.

In 1879, Land and Freedom split into two groups. One advocated educating the peasants, and it soon dissolved. The other, known as *The People's Will*, was dedicated to the overthrow of the autocracy. Its members decided to assassinate the tsar himself. (See "The People's Will Issues a Revolutionary Manifesto.") Several attempts failed, but on March 1, 1881, a bomb hurled by a member of The People's Will killed Alexander II. Four men and two women were sentenced to death for the deed. All of them had been willing to die for their cause. The emergence of such dedicated revolutionary opposition was as much a part of the reign of Alexander II as

THE PEOPLE'S WILL ISSUES A REVOLUTIONARY MANIFESTO

In the late 1870s, an extreme revolutionary movement appeared in Russia calling itself The People's Will. It advocated the overthrow of the tsarist government and the election of an Organizing Assembly to form a government based on popular representation. It directly embraced terrorism as a path toward its goal of the Russian people governing themselves. Members of this group assassinated Alexander II in 1881.

Which of the group's seven demands might be associated with liberalism, and which go beyond liberalism in their radical intent? Why does the group believe it must engage in terrorism as well as propaganda? Would any reforms by the Russian government have satisfied this group or dissuaded them from terrorist action?

Although we are ready to submit wholly to the popular will, we regard it as none the less our duty, as a party, to appear before the people with our program. . . . It is as follows:

1. Perpetual popular representation . . . having full power to act in all national questions.
2. General local self-government, secured by the election of all officers, and the economic independence of the people.
3. The self-controlled village commune as the economic and administrative unit.
4. Ownership of the land by the people.
5. A system of measures having for their object the turning over to the laborers of all mining works and factories.
6. Complete freedom of conscience, speech, association, public meeting, and electioneering activity.
7. The substitution of a territorial militia for the army. . . .

In view of the stated aim of the party its operations may be classified as follows:

1. Propaganda and agitation. Our propaganda has for its object the popularization, in all social classes, of the idea of a political and popular revolution as a means of social reform, as well as popularization of the party's own program. Its essential features are criticism of the existing order of things, and a statement and explanation of revolutionary methods. The aim of agitation should be to incite the people to protest as generally as possible against the present state of affairs, to demand such reforms as are in harmony with the party's purposes, and, especially, to demand the summoning of an Organizing Assembly. . . .
2. Destructive and terroristic activity. Terroristic activity consists in the destruction of the most harmful persons in the Government, the protection of the party from spies, and the punishment of official lawlessness and violence in all the more prominent and important cases in which such lawlessness and violence are manifested. The aim of such activity is to break down the prestige of Governmental power, to furnish continuous proof of the possibility of carrying on a contest with the Government, to raise in that way the revolutionary spirit of the people and inspire belief in the practicability of revolution, and, finally, to form a body suited and accustomed to warfare.

Quoted in George Kennan, *Siberia and the Exile System*, Vol. 2 (New York: The Century Co., 1891), pp. 495–499.

were his reforms. The limited character of those reforms convinced many Russians that the autocracy could never truly redirect Russian society.

The reign of Alexander III (r. 1881–1894) strengthened that pessimism. He possessed all the autocratic and repressive characteristics of his grandfather, Nicholas I, and none of the better qualities of his father, Alexander II. Some slight improvements were made to conditions in Russian factories, but Alexander III sought primarily to roll back his father's reforms. He favored the centralized bureaucracy over the *zemstvos.* He strengthened the secret police and increased censorship of the press. In effect, he confirmed all the evils that the revolutionaries saw as inherent in autocratic government. His son, Nicholas II (r. 1894–1917), would discover that autocracy could not survive the pressures of the twentieth century.

▼ Great Britain: Toward Democracy

While the continental nations became unified and struggled toward internal political restructuring, Great Britain symbolized the confident liberal state. Britain was not without its difficulties and domestic conflicts, but it seemed able to deal with them through its existing political institutions. The general prosperity of the third quarter of the century mitigated the social hostility of the 1840s. All classes shared a belief in competition and individualism. Even the leaders of trade unions during these years asked mainly to receive more of the fruits of prosperity and to have their social respectability acknowledged. Parliament itself remained an institution through which new groups and interests were absorbed into the existing political processes. In short, the British did not have to create new liberal institutions and then learn how to live within them. (See "Encountering the Past: The Arrival of Penny Postage.")

The Second Reform Act (1867)

By the early 1860s, most observers realized the franchise would again have to be expanded. The prosperity and social respectability of the working class convinced many politicians that the workers deserved the vote. Organizations such as the Reform League, led by John Bright (1811–1889), agitated for parliamentary action. In 1866, Lord Russell's Liberal ministry introduced a reform bill that a coalition of traditional Conservatives and antidemocratic Liberals defeated. Russell resigned, and the Conservative Lord Derby (1799–1869) replaced him. A surprise then occurred.

The Conservative ministry, led in the House of Commons by Benjamin Disraeli (1804–1881), introduced its own reform bill in 1867. As the debate proceeded, Disraeli accepted one amendment after another and expanded the electorate well beyond the limits the Liberals had earlier proposed. The final measure increased the number of voters from approximately 1,430,000 to 2,470,000. Britain had taken a major step toward democracy. Large numbers of male working-class voters had been admitted to the electorate.

Disraeli hoped the Conservatives would receive the gratitude of the new voters. Because reform was inevitable, it was best for the Conservatives to enjoy the credit for it. Like his contemporary Bismarck, Disraeli was prepared to embrace democracy. He thought that eventually significant portions of the working class would support Conservative candidates who were responsive to social issues. He also thought the growing suburban middle class would become more conservative. In the long run, his intuition proved correct. The Conservative Party dominated British politics in the twentieth century.

The immediate election of 1868, however, dashed Disraeli's hopes. William Gladstone (1809–1898) became the new prime minister. Gladstone had begun political life in 1833 as a strong Tory, but over the next thirty-five years, he became steadily more liberal. He had supported Robert Peel, free trade, repeal of the Corn Laws, and efficient administration. As chancellor of the exchequer (finance minister) during the 1850s and early 1860s, he had lowered taxes and government expenditures. He had also championed Italian nationalism. Yet he had opposed a new reform bill until the early 1860s. In 1866, he had been Russell's spokesperson in the House of Commons for the unsuccessful Liberal reform bill.

Gladstone's Great Ministry (1868–1874)

Gladstone's ministry of 1868 to 1874 witnessed the culmination of classical British liberalism. Those institutions that remained the preserve of the aristocracy and the Anglican church were opened to people from other classes and religious denominations. In 1870, competitive examinations for the civil service replaced patronage. In 1871, the purchase of officers' commissions in the army was abolished. The same year, Anglican religious requirements for the faculties of Oxford and Cambridge universities were removed. The Ballot Act of 1872 introduced voting by secret ballot.

The most momentous measure of Gladstone's first ministry was the Education Act of 1870. For the first time in British history, the government assumed the responsibility for establishing and running elementary schools. Previously, British education had been a task relegated to the religious denominations, which

THE ARRIVAL OF PENNY POSTAGE

WHILE THE ARMIES of the great powers were redrawing the map of Europe during the middle of the nineteenth century, new forms of administration were drawing people closer together. One of the most important of these innovations was the development of postal systems for delivering mail inexpensively. The British government took the lead.

Sending letters and newspapers through the mail had become increasingly expensive, and the British postal service ran large deficits. Other countries had similar problems. At that time the weight of the item to be mailed and the distance over which it had to be carried determined how much it cost to mail it. Furthermore, the person receiving the letter or packet, not the sender, had to pay the postage. Many officials had the privilege of franking their letters and thus paying nothing. The system encouraged resentment and schemes to avoid paying postage. Some people could not afford the postage on letters sent to them. Others put symbols on the outside of a letter, so the recipient could refuse to accept the letter but still "get the message."

Rowland Hill (1795–1879), an English reformer, proposed a simple new procedure in 1837. The price of postage would be lowered, would be uniform for most letters and newspapers regardless of distance, and would be prepaid by the sender. Franking by government officials would also end.

In 1840, the system, known as the Uniform Penny Post, began. Within two years the volume of British mail grew from approximately 75 million items to 196.5 million and, by 1849, to 329 million. The reduced cost of postage meant almost everyone could afford to send letters and postcards. It also led to a huge increase in the size of the government workforce. In Britain and most other countries, the number of postal workers was soon rivaled only by the number of soldiers and sailors.

Hill had also suggested a small, self-adhesive stamp be attached to a letter to indicate the postage had been paid. The first such stamp bore only the words POSTAGE ONE PENNY. It paid for letters up to one half ounce. A two-penny stamp was used for letters that weighed an ounce.

Other nations soon issued their own stamps. It soon became as important for governments to prevent the forging of postage stamps as currency. Consequently, stamps were printed from engraved steel plates to which small changes were made from time to time. Those changes, introduced to prevent fraud or to commemorate famous people and events, together with the sheer number of national postal systems with their own stamps, gave rise to the hobby of stamp collecting.

The rise of the modern postal system also fostered international cooperation. A treaty signed in Berne, Switzerland, in 1874, established what became the Universal Postal Union, which is still functioning. It mandates that the postage paid in the sender's nation assures delivery of a letter or package anywhere in the world.

Source: M. J. Daunton, "Rowland Hill and the Penny Post," *History Today*, August 1985; "Post, and Postal Service," *Encyclopedia Britannica*, 11th ed.

What changes did Rowland Hill introduce into the British postal service?

How did those changes affect the quantity of mail and the size of the government workforce?

With the new British postal system, the volume of mail vastly increased as did the number of postal workers involved in sorting and delivering it. Image Works/Mary Evans Picture Library Ltd.

A House of Commons Debate. William Ewart Gladstone, standing on the right, is attacking Benjamin Disraeli, who sits with legs crossed and arms folded. Gladstone served in the British Parliament from the 1830s through the 1890s. Four times the Liberal Party prime minister, he was responsible for guiding major reforms through Parliament. Disraeli, regarded as the founder of modern British conservatism, served as prime minister from 1874 to 1880. Image Works/Mary Evans Picture Library Ltd.

received small amounts of state support for the purpose. Henceforth, the government would establish schools where religious denominations had not done so.

These reforms were typically liberal. They sought to remove abuses without destroying institutions and to permit all able citizens to compete on the grounds of ability and merit. They tried to avoid the potential danger to a democratic state of an illiterate citizenry. These reforms were also a mode of state-building, because they reinforced loyalty to the nation by abolishing sources of discontent.

Disraeli in Office (1874–1880)

The liberal policy of creating popular support for the nation by extending political liberties and reforming abuses had its conservative counterpart in concern for social reform. Disraeli succeeded Gladstone as prime minister in 1874, when the election produced sharp divisions among Liberal Party voters over religion, education, and the sale of alcohol.

The two men differed on most issues. Whereas Gladstone looked to individualism, free trade, and competition to solve social problems, Disraeli believed in paternalistic legislation to protect the weak and ease class antagonisms.

Disraeli talked a better line than he produced. He had few specific programs or ideas. The significant social legislation of his ministry stemmed primarily from the efforts of his home secretary, Richard Cross (1823–1914). The Public Health Act of 1875 consolidated previous legislation on sanitation and reaffirmed the duty of the state to interfere with private property to protect health and physical well-being. Through the Artisan Dwelling Act of 1875, the government became actively involved in providing housing for the working class. That same year, in an important symbolic gesture, the Conservative majority in Parliament gave new protection to British trade unions and allowed them to raise picket lines. The Gladstone ministry, although recognizing the legality of unions, had refused such protection.

The Irish Question

In 1880, a second Gladstone ministry took office after an agricultural depression and an unpopular foreign policy undermined the Conservative government. In 1884, with Conservative cooperation, a third reform act gave the vote to most male farm workers. The major issue of the decade, however, was Ireland. From the late 1860s onward, Irish nationalists had sought to achieve **home rule** for Ireland, by which they meant Irish control of local government.

During his first ministry, Gladstone addressed the Irish question through two major pieces of legislation. In 1869, he disestablished the Church of Ireland, the Irish branch of the Anglican church. Henceforth, Irish Roman Catholics would not pay taxes to support the hated Protestant church, to which few of the Irish belonged. Second, in 1870, the Liberal ministry sponsored a land act that provided compensation to those Irish tenant farmers who were evicted and loans for those who wished to purchase their land. Throughout the 1870s, the Irish question continued to fester. Land remained the center of the agitation. Today, Irish economic development seems more complicated, and who owns the land seems less important than the methods of management and cultivation. Nevertheless, the organization of the Irish Land League in the late 1870s led to intense agitation and intimidation of landlords, who were often Protestants of English descent. The leader of the Irish movement for a just land settlement and for home rule was Charles Stewart Parnell (1846–1891). In 1881, the second Gladstone ministry passed another Irish land act that strengthened tenant rights. It was accompanied, however, by a Coercion Act to restore law and order to Ireland.

By 1885, Parnell had organized eighty-five Irish members of the House of Commons into a tightly disciplined party that often voted as a bloc. They frequently disrupted Parliament to gain attention for the cause of home rule. They bargained with the two English political parties. In the election of 1885, the Irish Party emerged holding the balance of power between the English Liberals and Conservatives. Irish support could decide which party took office. In December 1885, Gladstone announced his support of home rule for Ireland. Parnell gave his votes to a Liberal ministry. The home rule issue then split the Liberal Party. In 1886, a group known as the Liberal Unionists joined with the Conservatives to defeat home rule. Gladstone called for a new election, but the Liberals were defeated. They remained divided, and Ireland remained firmly under English administration.

The new Conservative ministry of Lord Salisbury (1830–1903) attempted to reconcile the Irish to British rule through public works and administrative reform. The policy, which was tied to further coercion, had only marginal success. In 1892, Gladstone returned to power. A second Home Rule Bill passed the House of Commons but was defeated in the House of Lords. There the Irish question stood until after the turn of the century. The Conservatives sponsored a land act in 1903 that carried out the final transfer of land to tenant ownership. Ireland became a country of small farms. In 1912, a Liberal ministry passed the third Home Rule Bill. Under the provisions of the House of Lords Act of 1911, which curbed the power of the Lords, the bill had to pass the Commons three times over the Lords' veto to become law. The third passage occurred in the summer of 1914, but the implementation of home rule was suspended for the duration of World War I.

The Irish question affected British politics in a manner not unlike that of the Austrian nationalities problem. Normal British domestic issues could not be resolved because of the political divisions Ireland created. The split of the Liberal Party proved especially harmful to the cause of further social and political reform. People who could agree about reform could not agree about Ireland, and the Irish problem seemed more important. Because the two traditional parties

MAJOR DATES IN LATE-NINETEENTH-CENTURY BRITAIN

1867	Second Reform Act
1868	Gladstone becomes prime minister
1869	Disestablishment of Church of Ireland
1870	Education Act and first Irish Land Act
1871	Purchase of army officers' commissions abolished
1871	Religious tests abolished at Oxford and Cambridge
1872	Secret Ballot Act
1874	Disraeli becomes prime minister
1875	Public Health Act and Artisan Dwelling Act
1880	Beginning of Gladstone's second ministry
1881	Second Irish Land Act and Irish Coercion Act
1884	Third Reform Act
1885	Gladstone announces support of Irish home rule
1886	Home Rule Bill defeated and Lord Salisbury becomes the Conservative prime minister
1892	Gladstone begins his third ministry; second Irish Home Rule Bill defeated
1903	Third Irish Land Act
1912	Third Irish Home Rule Bill passed
1914	Provisions of Irish Home Rule Bill suspended because of the outbreak of World War I

failed to deal with the social questions by the turn of the century, a newly organized Labour Party began to fill the vacuum.

In Perspective

Between 1850 and 1875, the major contours of the political systems that would dominate Europe until World War I had been drawn. These systems and political arrangements solved, as far as such matters can be solved, many of the political problems that had troubled Europeans during the first half of the nineteenth century. On the whole, the concept of the nation-state had triumphed. Support for governments no longer stemmed from loyalty to dynasties, but from citizen participation. Moreover, the unity of nations was now based on ethnic, cultural, linguistic, and historical bonds. The parliamentary governments of Western Europe were different from the autocracies of eastern Europe, but both political systems had been compelled to recognize the force of nationalism and the larger role of citizens in political affairs. Only Russia failed to make such concessions. In Russia the only concession to popular opinion had been the emancipation of the serfs.

Future discontent would arise primarily from the demands of labor to enter the political processes and the unsatisfied aspirations of subject nationalities. These two sources of unrest would trouble Europe for the next forty years and would eventually undermine the political structures created during the late nineteenth century.

REVIEW QUESTIONS

1. Why did the Ottoman Empire attempt to reform itself between 1839 and 1914? What was the result of these efforts?
2. Why was it so difficult to unify Italy? What groups wanted unification? Why did Cavour succeed? What did Garibaldi contribute to Italian unification?
3. How and why did Bismarck unify Germany? Why had earlier attempts failed? How did German unification affect the rest of Europe?
4. What events led to the establishment of the Third Republic in France? What were the objectives of the Paris Commune? How did the Dreyfus affair affect the Third Republic?
5. What problems did Austria share with other eastern European empires? Were they solved? Why did the Habsburgs agree to the Compromise of 1867? Was it a success?
6. What reforms did Alexander II institute in Russia? Did they solve Russia's domestic problems? Why did the abolition of serfdom not satisfy the peasants? What were the goals of *The People's Will*?
7. How did the policies of the British Liberal and Conservative parties differ between 1860 and 1890? Why was Irish home rule such a divisive issue in British politics?

SUGGESTED READINGS

V. Aksan, *Ottoman Wars, 1700–1870: An Empire Besieged* (2007). Explores the impact of war on the weakening of the Ottoman Empire.

R. Aldous, *The Lion and the Unicorn: Gladstone vs. Disraeli* (2008). An accessible volume tracing the great political rivalry of the mid-Victorian age.

I. T. Berend, *History Derailed: Central and Eastern Europe in the Long Nineteenth Century* (2003). The best one-volume treatment of the complexities of this region.

P. Bew, *Ireland: The Politics of Enmity 1789–2006* (2007). A major new, outstanding survey of the sweep of modern Irish history.

E. F. Biagini, *British Democracy and Irish Nationalism 1876–1906* (2007). Explores impact of the Irish question on British political structures themselves.

D. Blackbourn, *The Long Nineteenth Century: A History of Germany, 1780–1918* (1998). An outstanding survey.

R. Blake, *Disraeli* (1967). Remains the best biography.

J. Breuilly, *Austria, Prussia and Germany, 1806–1871* (2002). Examines the complex relations of these states leading up to German unification.

C. Clark, *Iron Kingdom: The Rise and Downfall of Prussia, 1600–1947* (2006). Now the standard survey.

M. Clark, *The Italian Risorgimento* (1998). A brief overview.

C. J. Eichner, *Surmounting the Barricades: Women in the Paris Commune* (2004). Explores the impact of women's journalism and organizing in the Commune and wider radical political tradition.

R. B. Edgerton, *Death or Glory: The Legacy of the Crimean War* (2000). Multifaceted study of a mismanaged war that transformed European politics.

B. Eklof and J. Bushnell, *Russia's Great Reforms, 1855–1881* (1994). A clear analysis.

R. Gildea, *Children of the Revolution: The French, 1799–1914* (2008). An important study of how the stresses of the French Revolution continued to be played out for the next century in French society and politics.

M. A. Hanioglu, *A Brief History of the Late Ottoman Empire* (2008). An accessible introduction.

R. Kee, *The Green Flag: A History of Irish Nationalism* (2001). A lively, accessible account.

D. Langewiesche, *Liberalism in Germany* (1999). A broad survey that is particularly good on the problems unification caused for German Liberals.

H. C. G. Matthew, *Gladstone, 1809–1898* (1998). A superb biography.

D. Moon, *Abolition of Serfdom in Russia: 1762–1907* (2001). Analysis with docments.

W. G. Moss, *Russia in the Age of Alexander II, Tolstoy and Dostoyevsky* (2002). Emphasizes the cultural background.

N. M. Naimark, *Terrorists and Social Democrats: The Russian Revolutionary Movement under Alexander III* (1983). Useful discussion of a complicated subject.

P. G. Nord, *The Republican Moment: Struggles for Democracy in Nineteenth-Century France* (1996). A major examination of nineteenth-century French political culture.

J. Parry, *The Politics of Patriotism: English Liberalism, National Identity and Europe, 1830–1886* (2006). An excellent overview of English Liberalism and how its values determined mid-Victorian relations with the Continent.

J. P. Parry, *The Rise and Fall of Liberal Government in Victorian Britain* (1994). An outstanding study.

O. Pflanze, *Bismarck and the Development of Germany*, 3 vols. (1990). A major biography and history of Germany for the period.

R. Price, *The French Second Empire: An Anatomy of Political Power* (2001). This volume along with the following title are the most comprehensive recent study.

R. Price, *People and Politics in France, 1848–1870* (2004). A clear survey.

E. Radzinsky, *Alexander II: The Last Great Tsar* (2005). An accessible biography.

L. Riall, *Garibaldi: Invention of a Hero* (2007). An exploration of a nationalist hero's reputation in his own day and later.

D. Shafer, *The Paris Commune: French Politics, Culture, and Society at the Crossroads of the Revolutionary Tradition and Revolutionary Socialism* (2005). Excellent in relating the Commune to previous and later revolutionary traditions.

A. Scirocco, *Garibaldi: Citizen of the World: A Biography* (2007). An admiring account.

A. Sked, *Decline and Fall of the Habsburg Empire 1815–1918* (2001). A major, accessible survey of a difficult subject.

D. M. Smith, *Cavour* (1984). An excellent biography.

For additional learning resources related to this chapter, please go to www.myhistorylab.com

PEARSON myhistorylab

Women Laundry Workers. Although new opportunities opened to them in the late nineteenth century, many working-class women, like these women ironing in a laundry, remained in traditional occupations. As the wine bottle suggests, alcoholism was a problem for women as well as men engaged in tedious work. The painting is by Edgar Degas (1834–1917). Réunion des Musées Nationaux/Art Resource, NY

23 The Building of European Supremacy: Society and Politics to World War I

▼ **Population Trends and Migration**

▼ **The Second Industrial Revolution**
New Industries • Economic Difficulties

▼ **The Middle Classes in Ascendancy**
Social Distinctions Within the Middle Class

▼ **Late-Nineteenth-Century Urban Life**
The Redesign of Cities • Urban Sanitation • Housing Reform and Middle-Class Values

▼ **Varieties of Late-Nineteenth-Century Women's Experiences**
Women's Social Disabilities • New Employment Patterns for Women • Working-Class Women • Poverty and Prostitution • Women of the Middle Class • The Rise of Political Feminism

▼ **Jewish Emancipation**
Differing Degrees of Citizenship • Broadened Opportunities

▼ **Labor, Socialism, and Politics to World War I**
Trade Unionism • Democracy and Political Parties • Karl Marx and the First International • Great Britain: Fabianism and Early Welfare Programs • France: "Opportunism" Rejected • Germany: Social Democrats and Revisionism • Russia: Industrial Development and the Birth of Bolshevism

▼ **In Perspective**

KEY TOPICS

- The transformation of European life by the Second Industrial Revolution
- Urban sanitation, housing reform, and the redesign of cities
- The condition of women in late-nineteenth-century Europe and the rise of political feminism
- The emancipation of the Jews
- The development of labor politics and socialism in Europe to the outbreak of World War I

THE GROWTH OF industrialism between 1860 and 1914 increased Europe's productive capacity to unprecedented and unparalleled levels. New steel mills, railways, shipyards, and chemical plants reflected an expanding supply of capital goods in the second half of the nineteenth century. By the first decade of the twentieth century, the age of the automobile, the airplane, the bicycle, the refrigerated ship, the telephone, the radio, the typewriter, and the electric light bulb had dawned. The world's economies, based on the **gold standard**, became increasingly interdependent. European manufactured goods and financial capital flowed into markets all over the globe. In turn, Europeans imported foreign raw materials and foodstuffs. Within Europe itself, the eastern and southern European countries tended to import finished goods from the west and the north and to export agricultural products.

During this half century, European political, economic, and social life assumed many of its current characteristics. Nation-states with large electorates, political parties, and centralized bureaucracies emerged. Business adopted large-scale corporate structures, and the labor force organized itself into trade unions. The number of white-collar workers increased. Western Europe became predominately urban. Socialism strongly affected the political life of all nations. The foundations of the welfare state and of vast military establishments were laid. Taxation increased accordingly.

Europe had also quietly become dependent on the resources and markets of the rest of the world. Changes in the weather in Kansas, Argentina, or New Zealand might now affect the European economy. Before World War I, however, Europe's industrial, military, and financial supremacy concealed that dependency. Many Europeans assumed their supremacy to be natural and permanent, but the twentieth century would reveal it to have been temporary.

▼ Population Trends and Migration

The proportion of Europeans in the world's total population was apparently greater around 1900—estimated at about 20 percent—than ever before or since. The number of Europeans had risen from approximately 266 million in 1850 to 401 million in 1900 and to 447 million in 1910. Thereafter, birth and death rates declined or stabilized in Europe and other developed regions, and population growth began to slow in those areas but not elsewhere. The result has been a persistent demographic differential between the developed and undeveloped world—stable or slowly growing populations in developed countries and large, rapidly growing populations in undeveloped regions—that contributes to the world's present food and resource crisis.

Europe's peoples were on the move in the latter half of the century as never before (see Map 23–1, page 692). The mid-century emancipation of peasants lessened the authority of landlords and made legal movement and migration easier. Railways, steamships, and better roads increased mobility. Cheap land and better wages accompanied economic development in Europe, North America, Latin America, and Australia, enticing people to move from regions where they had little prospect of improving their lives to regions that held or seemed to hold opportunity. In Europe itself the main migration continued to be from the countryside into urban areas. During this era, Europeans also left their own continent in record numbers. Between 1846 and 1932, more than 50 million Europeans left their homelands. The major areas to benefit from this movement were the United States, Canada, Australia, South Africa, Brazil, Algeria, and Argentina. At midcentury, most of the emigrants were from Great Britain (especially Ireland), Germany, and Scandinavia. After 1885, migration from southern and eastern Europe rose. This exodus helped relieve the social and population pressures on the Continent. The outward movement of peoples, in conjunction with Europe's economic and technological superiority, contributed heavily to the Europeanization of the world. Not since the sixteenth century had European civilization had such an impact on other cultures.

▼ The Second Industrial Revolution

During the third quarter of the nineteenth century, the gap that had long existed between British and continental economic development closed. (See Map 23–2, page 693.) The basic heavy industries of Belgium, France, and Germany expanded rapidly. In particular, the growth of the German industry was stunning. German steel production surpassed Britain's in 1893 and was nearly twice that of Britain by the outbreak of World War I. This emergence of an industrial Germany was the major fact of European economic and political life at the turn of the century.

MAJOR DATES OF THE SECOND INDUSTRIAL REVOLUTION

1856–1870	Passage of laws permitting joint stock companies: 1856, Britain; 1863, France; 1870, Prussia
1857	Bessemer process for making steel
1873	Beginning of major economic downturn
1876	Alexander Graham Bell invents the telephone
1879	Edison perfects the electric light bulb
1881	First electric power plant in Britain
1885	Gottlieb Daimler invents the internal combustion engine
1889	Daimler's first automobile
1895	Diesel engine invented
1895	Wireless telegraphy invented
1890s	First major impact of petroleum
1903	Wright brothers make first successful airplane flight
1909	Henry Ford manufactures the Model T

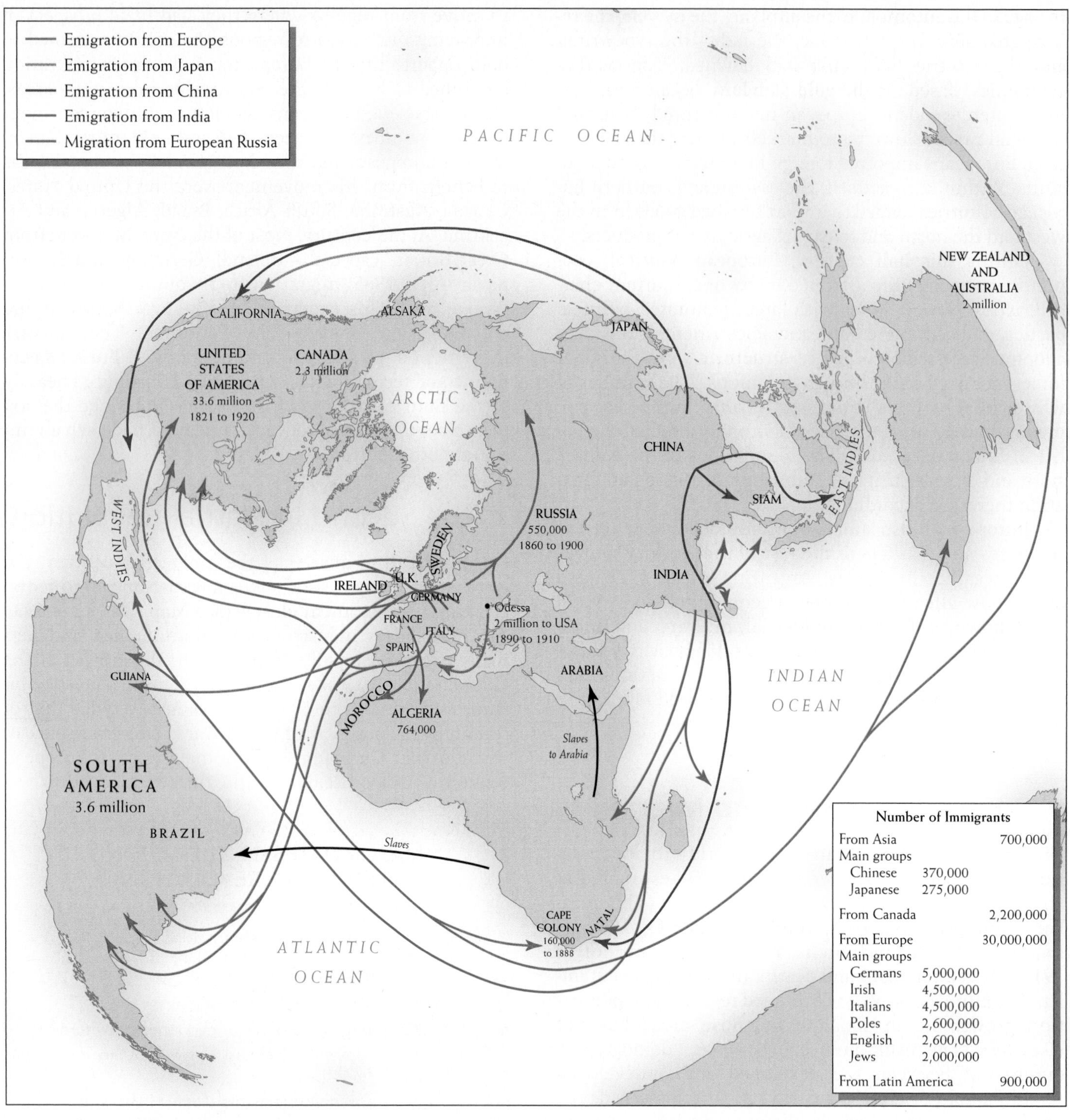

Map 23–1 **PATTERNS OF GLOBAL MIGRATION, 1840–1900** Emigration was a global process by the late nineteenth century, but more immigrants went to the United States than to every other nation combined.

New Industries

Initially, the economic expansion of the third quarter of the century involved the spread of industries similar to those pioneered earlier in Great Britain. In particular, the expansion of railway systems on the Continent spurred economic growth. Thereafter, however, wholly new industries emerged. This latter development is usually termed the ***Second Industrial Revolution***. The first Industrial Revolution was associated with textiles, steam, and iron; by contrast, the second was associated with steel, chemicals, electricity, and oil.

In the 1850s, Henry Bessemer (1830–1898), an English engineer, discovered a new process, named after

MAP EXPLORATION

Interactive map: To explore this map further, go to **www.myhistorylab.com**

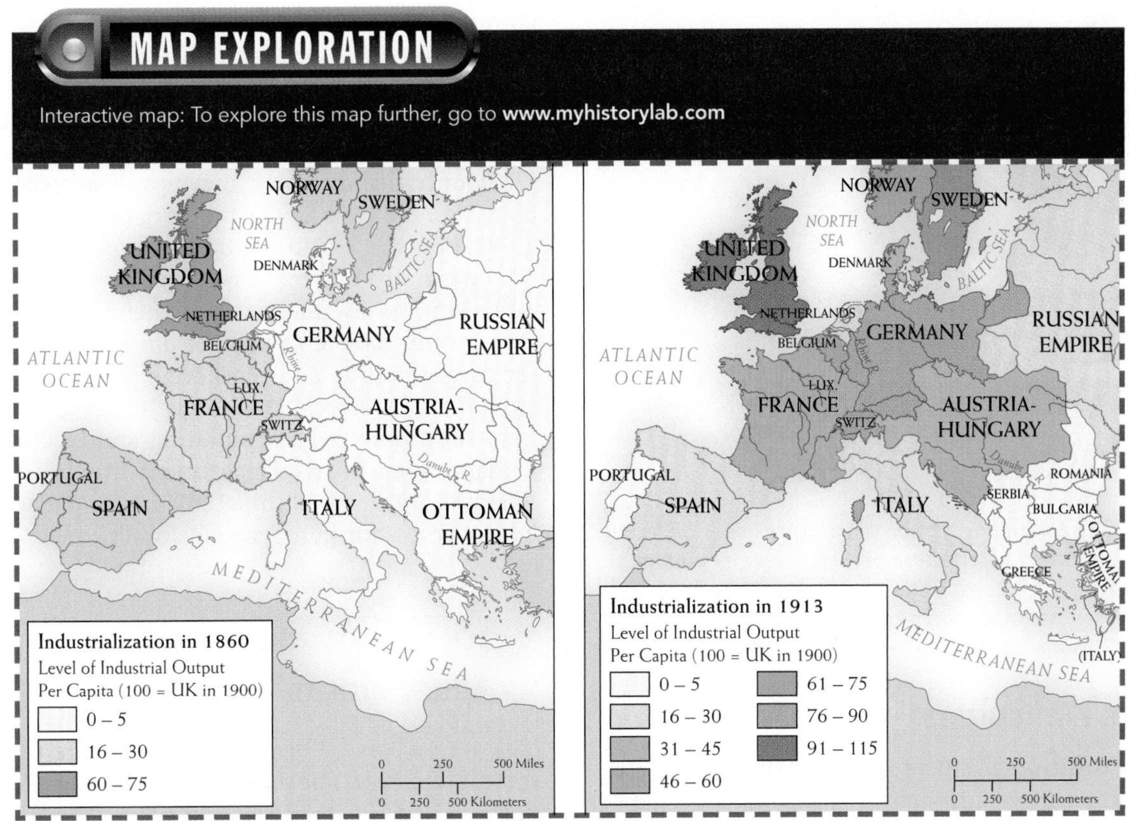

Map 23–2 **EUROPEAN INDUSTRIALIZATION, 1860–1913** In 1860 Britain was far more industrialized than other European countries. But in the following half century, industrial output rose significantly, if unevenly, across much of Western Europe, especially in the new German Empire. The Balkan states and the Ottoman Empire, however, remained economically backward.

him, for manufacturing steel cheaply in large quantities. In 1860, Great Britain, Belgium, France, and Germany combined produced 125,000 tons of steel. By 1913, the figure had risen to over 32 million tons.

The chemical industry also came of age during this period. The Solway process of alkali production replaced the older Leblanc process, allowing the recovery of more chemical by-products. The new process permitted increased production of sulfuric acid and laundry soap. New dyestuffs and plastics were also developed. Formal scientific research played an important role in this growth of the chemical industry, marking the beginning of a direct link between science and industrial development. As in so many other aspects of the Second Industrial Revolution, Germany was a leader in forging this link, fostering scientific research and education.

The most significant change for industry and, eventually, for everyday life involved the application of electrical energy to production. Electricity was the most versatile and transportable source of power ever discovered. It could be delivered almost anywhere to run either large or small machinery, making the locations of factories more flexible and factory construction more efficient. The first major public power plant was constructed in 1881 in Great Britain. Soon electric poles, lines, and generating stations dotted the European landscape. Homes began to use electric lights. Streetcar and subway systems were electrified.

In 1885, the German engineer Gottlieb Daimler (1834–1900), improving a previous prototype, invented the modern internal combustion engine. By 1889, he had mounted it on a carriage body specifically designed to incorporate a still more improved internal combustion engine, and the automobile was born. France initially took the lead in auto manufacturing, but for many years, the car remained a novelty item that only the wealthy could afford. It was the American, Henry Ford (1863–1947), who later made the automobile accessible to the masses. No single invention so transformed the mobility of large numbers of people, first through the automobile itself and then through trolleys and buses. The automobile industry, furthermore, created a vast new demand for steel and the materials that went into other auto parts and established an ever-growing demand for petroleum products that continues to this day. Then as now, Europe depended on imported supplies of oil. The major oil companies were Standard Oil of the United States, British Shell Oil, and Royal Dutch Petroleum.

458 M. FOURNIER'S "MORS."
The Winner of the Race from Paris to Berlin. 1901.

The invention and commercialization of automobiles soon led to auto races in Europe and North America. Here Henri Fournier, the winner of the 1901 Paris to Berlin Motor Car Race, sits in his winning racing car manufactured by the Paris-based auto firm of Emile and Louis Mors. Getty Images Inc.–Hulton Archive Photos

Economic Difficulties

Despite the multiplication of new industries, the second half of the nineteenth century was not a period of uninterrupted or smooth economic growth. Both industry and agriculture generally prospered from 1850 to 1873, but in the last quarter of the century, economic advance slowed. Bad weather and foreign competition put grave pressures on European agriculture and caused many European peasants to emigrate to other parts of the world.

As new farming regions developed in the United States, Canada, Argentina, Australia, and New Zealand, products from those areas challenged the market for home-produced European agricultural goods. Refrigerated ships could bring meat and dairy products to Europe from all over the world. Grain could be grown more economically on the plains of North America, Argentina, and Ukraine than it could in Western Europe, and railways and steamships made it easy and cheap to ship it across continents and oceans. These developments lowered the prices of consumer goods, but put great pressure on European agriculture.

Several large banks failed in 1873, and the rate of capital investment slowed. Some industries then entered a two-decade-long period of stagnation that many contemporaries regarded as a depression. Overall, however, the general standard of living in the industrialized nations improved in the second half of the nineteenth century. Both prices and wages, as well as profits, fell, so real wages generally held firm and even rose in some countries. Yet many workers still lived and labored in abysmal conditions. There were pockets of *unemployment* (a word that was coined during this period), and strikes and other forms of labor unrest were common. These economic difficulties fed the growth of trade unions and socialist political parties.

The new industries produced consumer goods, and expansion in consumer demand brought the economy out of stagnation by the end of the century. (See "Encountering the Past: Bicycles: Transportation, Freedom, and Sport.") Lower food prices eventually allowed all classes to spend more on consumer goods. Urbanization naturally created larger markets. People living in cities simply saw more things they wanted to buy than they would have encountered in the countryside. New forms of retailing and marketing appeared—department stores, chain stores, mail-order catalogs, and advertising—simultaneously stimulating and feeding consumer demand. (See "Paris Department Stores Expand Their Business," page 696.) Imperialism also opened new markets overseas for European consumer goods.

▼ The Middle Classes in Ascendancy

The sixty years before World War I were the age of the middle classes. The London Great Exhibition of 1851 held in the Crystal Palace displayed the products and the new material life they had forged. Thereafter, the middle classes became the arbiter of consumer taste. After the revolutions of 1848, the middle classes ceased to be a revolutionary group. Once the question of social equality and equality of property had been raised, large and small property owners across the Continent moved to protect what they possessed against demands from socialists and other working-class groups.

Social Distinctions Within the Middle Classes

The middle classes, never perfectly homogeneous, grew increasingly diverse. Their most prosperous members—the owners and managers of great businesses and banks—lived in splendor that rivaled, and sometimes exceeded, that of the aristocracy. In Britain some of them, such as W. H. Smith (1825–1891), the owner of railway newsstands, were made members of the House of Lords. The Krupp family of Germany who owned huge steel works in the Rhineland were pillars of the state and were ennobled by the German emperor and received visits from the imperial court.

Only a few hundred families gained such wealth. Beneath them were the comfortable small entrepreneurs and professional people, whose incomes permitted private homes, large quantities of furniture, pianos, pictures, books, journals, education for their children, and vacations. Also in this group were the shopkeepers, schoolteachers, librarians, and others who had either a

ENCOUNTERING THE *Past*

BICYCLES: TRANSPORTATION, FREEDOM, AND SPORT

BEFORE THE CAR came the bicycle. Bicycles were the first mass-produced, affordable machines for individual travel. Between 1880 and 1900, they took Europe and North America by storm. For the first time in history, individual men and, significantly, women had a machine that enabled them to travel on their own for work or pleasure. Bicycles had an immense impact on Western society.

The first functioning bicycles had been invented in Germany about 1817, but they were clumsy and dangerous. Made of wood, these machines lacked pedals and tires. They had to be pushed along the ground, and their riders could not control their speed. It took another eighty years for the modern bicycle to take shape. Pedals were introduced in the 1860s. Metal frames, solid rubber tires, and chain drives, which increased speed, appeared in the 1870s. In the 1880s, the ride became much smoother when John Boyd Dunlop, an Irish physician, invented the pneumatic tire, and in France, the Michelin brothers introduced the inner tube. (Before then, the ride was so rough that bicycles were sometimes called "boneshakers.") By the 1890s, the "safety bicycle" with its now familiar triangular frame and chain drive attached to the pedal and back wheel was being mass produced across Europe and North America, and men and women of the working class could afford them. By 1900, male workers of modest means across Europe were riding bicycles to work.

By increasing individual mobility, the bicycle made it easier to get to work, to hold a job farther from home, and to move about one's city or town or reach the countryside. New clothing designs, especially "bloomers," trousers worn under skirts (designed before the bicycle), permitted women to bicycle while maintaining modesty. In the 1890s, feminists like Marie Pognon in France and Susan B. Anthony in the United States hailed the "egalitarian and leveling bicycle" for the freedom it gave women.

By 1914, there were millions of cyclists across the transatlantic world. Europeans and Americans organized cycling clubs with distinctive uniforms. Some of these clubs, such as the English Clarion Cycling Clubs, the French Union Sportive du Parti Socialiste, and the German *Solidaritet*, used cycling trips to spread literature for left-wing causes. Other groups cycled for pleasure. The kinds of touring clubs that now exist for automobiles were first organized for cyclists, as were many of the early European travel guides such as the French *Guides Michelin*, which first appeared in 1900. Then as now, Michelin made tires and stood to sell more of them the more people toured the countryside.

Bicycle racing quickly became a competitive sport. The most famous professional racer in the world was Marshall Walter "Major" Taylor, an African American who raced in both the United States and Europe. Paris and other French cities built velodromes for indoor cycle racing, which was one of the official sports of the first modern Olympics in 1896. In 1903, *L'Auto*, a French sports paper, organized the first Tour de France race to increase its circulation. Six riders raced a 2,500 km-course over nineteen days.

Source: Eugen Weber, *France: Fin de Siècle* (Cambridge, MA: Harvard University Press, 1986), pp. 103–104, 195–206; Will and Terra Hanger, "Bicycles," *History Magazine*, October/November 2001.

Why did bicycles become so popular in Europe in the late nineteenth century?

What advantages did bicycles bring to women?

The bicycle helped liberate women's lives, but as this poster suggests, it also was associated with glamour and fashion. © Archivo Iconografico, S.A./CORBIS

PARIS DEPARTMENT STORES EXPAND THEIR BUSINESS

The department store in Europe and the United States became a major retailing institution in the last half of the nineteenth century. It was one of the reasons for the expansion in late-century consumer demand. This description, written by E. Levasseur in 1907, follows the growth of such stores in Paris and explains why they exerted such economic power. Note how many of their sales techniques stores still use today.

Why should French governments have favored the growth of department stores? Where did these stores stand in the process of economic production and sales? Why was the volume of sales so important? What kinds of people might have benefited from the jobs available in these stores? Why might these stores have hurt small retailers?

It was in the reign of Louis Philippe [1830–1848] that department stores for fashion goods and dresses . . . . began to be distinguished. The type was already one of other notable developments of the Second Empire; it became one of the most important ones of the Third Republic. These stores have increased in number and several of them have become extremely large. Combining in their different departments all articles of clothing, toilet articles, furniture and many other ranges of goods, it is their special object so to combine all commodities as to attract and satisfy customers who will find conveniently together an assortment of a mass of articles corresponding to all their various needs. They attract customers by permanent display, by free entry into the shops, by periodic exhibitions, by special sales, by fixed prices, and by their ability to deliver the goods purchased to customers' homes, in Paris and to the provinces. Turning themselves into direct intermediaries between the producer and the consumer, even producing sometimes some of their articles in their own workshops, buying at lowest prices because of their large orders and because they are in a position to profit from bargains, working with large sums, and selling to most of their customers for cash only, they can transmit these benefits in lowered selling prices. They can even decide to sell at a loss, as an advertisement or to get rid of out-of-date fashions.

The success of these department stores is only possible thanks to the volume of their business, and this volume needs considerable capital and a very large turnover. Now capital, having become abundant, is freely combined nowadays in large enterprises . . . . [T]he large urban agglomerations, the ease with which goods can be transported by the railways, the diffusion of some comforts to strata below the middle classes, have all favoured these developments. . . .

According to the tax records of 1891, these stores in Paris, numbering 12, employed 1,708 persons and rated their site values at 2,159,000 francs; the largest had then 542 employees. These same stores had, in 1901, 9,784 employees; one of them over 2,000 and another over 1,600; their site value was doubled.

From Sidney Pollard and Colin Holmes, *Documents of European Economic History*, Vol. 3. (London: Edward Arnold, 1972), pp. 95–96.

bit of property or a skill derived from education that provided respectable nonmanual employment.

Finally, there was a wholly new element—"white-collar workers"—who formed the lower middle class, or ***petite bourgeoisie***. They included secretaries, retail clerks, and lower-level bureaucrats in business and government. They often had working-class origins and might even belong to unions, but they had middle-class aspirations and consciously sought to distance themselves from a lower-class lifestyle. They pursued educational opportunities and chances for even the slightest career advancement for themselves and, especially, for their children. Many of them spent much of their disposable income on consumer goods, such as stylish clothing and furniture, that were distinctively middle class in appearance.

Significant tensions and social anxieties marked relations among the various middle-class groups. Small shopkeepers resented the power of the great capitalists, with their department stores and mail-order catalogs.

There is some evidence that the professions were becoming overcrowded. People who had only recently attained a middle-class lifestyle feared losing it in bad economic times. Nonetheless, in the decades immediately before World War I, the middle classes set the values and goals for most of society.

▾ Late-Nineteenth-Century Urban Life

Europe became more urbanized than ever in the latter half of the nineteenth century as migration to the cities continued. Between 1850 and 1911, urban dwellers rose from 25 to 44 percent of the population in France and from 30 to 60 percent of the population in Germany. Similar increases occurred in other Western European countries.

The rural migrants to the cities were largely uprooted from traditional social ties. They often faced poor housing, social anonymity, and, because they rarely possessed the right kinds of skills, unemployment. People from different ethnic backgrounds found themselves in proximity to one another and had difficulty mixing socially. Competition for jobs generated new varieties of political and social discontent, such as the anti-Semitism directed at the thousands of Russian Jews who had migrated to Western Europe. Indeed, much of the political anti-Semitism of the latter part of the century had its roots in the problems urban migration generated.

The Redesign of Cities

The inward urban migration placed new social and economic demands on already strained city resources and gradually transformed the patterns of urban living. National and municipal governments redesigned the central portions of many large European cities during the second half of the century. Previously, the central urban areas had been places where people from all social classes both lived and worked. From the middle of the century onward, planners transformed these districts into areas where businesses, government offices, large stores, and theaters were located, but where fewer people resided. Commerce, trade, government, and leisure activities now dominated central cities.

The New Paris The most famous and extensive transformation of a major city occurred in Paris. Like so many other European cities, Paris had expanded from the Middle Ages onward with little or no design or planning. Great public buildings and squalid hovels stood near each other. The Seine River was an open sewer. The streets were narrow, crooked, and crowded. It was impossible to cross easily from one part of the city to another either on foot or by carriage. In 1850, an accurate map of the city did not even exist. Of more concern to the government of Napoleon III (r. 1852–1870), the city's streets had for sixty years provided battlegrounds for urban insurrections that had threatened or toppled French governments on numerous occasions, most recently in 1848.

Napoleon III personally determined to redesign Paris. He appointed Baron Georges Haussmann (1809–1891), who, as prefect of the Seine from 1853 to 1870, oversaw a vast urban reconstruction program. Whole districts were destroyed to open the way for the broad boulevards and streets that became the hallmark of modern Paris. Much, though by no means all, of the purpose of this street planning was political. The wide vistas not only were beautiful, but they also allowed for the quick deployment of troops to put down riots. The eradication of the many small streets and alleys removed areas where barricades could be, and had been, erected.

The project was also political in another sense. In addition to the new boulevards, parks such as the Bois de Boulogne and major public buildings such as the Paris Opera were also constructed or completed. These projects, along with the demolition and street building, created thousands of government jobs. Many other laborers found employment in the private construction that accompanied the public works.

Further rebuilding and redesign occurred under the Third Republic after the destruction that accompanied the suppression of the Commune in 1871. Many department stores, office complexes, and largely middle-class apartment buildings were constructed. By the late 1870s, mechanical trams were operating in Paris. After much debate, construction of a subway system (the *métro*) began in 1895, long after that of London (1863). Near the close of the century, new railway stations were also erected to link the refurbished central city to the suburbs.

In 1889, the Eiffel Tower was built, originally as a temporary structure for the international trade exposition of that year. Not all the new structures of Paris bespoke the impact of middle-class commerce and the reign of iron and steel, however. Between 1873 and 1914, the Roman Catholic Church oversaw the construction of the Basilica of the Sacred Heart (*Sacré Cœur*) high atop Montmartre as an act of national penance for the sins that had supposedly led to French defeat in the Franco-Prussian War (1870–1871). Those two landmarks—the Eiffel Tower and the Basilica of the Sacred Heart—symbolized the social and political divisions between liberals and conservatives in the Third Republic.

Development of Suburbs Commercial development, railway construction, and slum clearance displaced many city dwellers and raised urban land values and rents. Consequently, both the middle classes and the working class began to seek housing elsewhere. The middle classes looked for neighborhoods removed from urban congestion. The working class looked for affordable housing.

The Eiffel Tower, shown under construction in this painting, was to become a symbol of the newly redesigned Paris and its steel structure a symbol of French industrial strength. Getty Images, Inc.—Liaison

The result, in virtually all countries, was the development of suburbs surrounding the city proper. These suburbs housed families whose breadwinners worked in the central city or in a factory located within the city limits. European suburbs, unlike those that developed in the United States, often consisted of apartment buildings or private houses built closely together with small gardens.

GROWTH OF MAJOR EUROPEAN CITIES (FIGURES IN THOUSANDS)

	1850	1880	1910
Berlin	419	1,122	2,071
Birmingham	233	437	840
Frankfurt	65	137	415
London	2,685	4,470	7,256
Madrid	281	398	600
Moscow	365	748	1,533
Paris	1,053	2,269	2,888
Rome	175	300	542
Saint Petersburg	485	877	1,962
Vienna	444	1,104	2,031
Warsaw	160	339	872

The expansion of railways with cheap workday fares and the introduction of mechanical and, later, electric tramways, as well as subways, allowed tens of thousands of workers from all classes to move daily between the city and the outlying suburbs. For hundreds of thousands of Europeans, home and work became more physically separated than ever before.

Urban Sanitation

The efforts of governments and of the increasingly conservative middle classes to maintain public order after 1848 led to a growing concern with the problems of public health and housing for the poor. A widespread feeling arose that only when the health and housing of the working class were improved would middle-class health also be secure and the political order stable.

Impact of Cholera Concerns with health and housing first manifested themselves as a result of the great cholera epidemics of the 1830s and 1840s. Unlike many other common deadly diseases of the day that touched only the poor, cholera struck all classes, and the middle class demanded a solution. Before the development of the bacterial theory of disease late in the century, physicians and sanitary reformers believed that miasmas in the air spread the infections that led to cholera and other diseases. These miasmas, which could be detected by their foul odors, were believed to arise from filth. The way to get rid of the dangerous, foul-smelling air was to clean up the cities.

During the 1840s, many physicians and some government officials began to publicize the dangerous unsanitary conditions associated with overcrowding in cities and with businesses, such as basement slaughterhouses. In 1840, Louis René Villermé (1782–1863) published his *Tableau de l'état physique et moral des ouvriers* (*Catalog of the Physical and Moral State of Workers*) about urban working-class conditions in France. In 1842, Edwin Chadwick's (1800–1890) *Report on the Sanitary Condition of the Labouring Population* shocked the English public. In Germany, Rudolf Virchow (1821–1902) published similar findings. These and various other private reports and those by public commissions closely linked the issues of wretched living conditions and public health. They also argued that sanitary reform would remove the dangers. The reports, incidentally, now provide some of the best information available about working-class living conditions in the mid-nineteenth century.

New Water and Sewer Systems The proposed solution to the health hazard was cleanliness, to be achieved through new water and sewer systems. These facilities were constructed slowly, usually first in capital cities and then much later in provincial centers. Some major urban areas did not have good water systems until after 1900. Nonetheless, the building of such systems was one of the major health and engineering achievements of the second half of the nineteenth century. The sewer system of Paris was a famous part of Haussmann's rebuilding program. In London, the construction of the Albert Embankment along the Thames involved not only large sewers discharging into the river, but gas mains and water pipes as well; all were encased in thick walls of granite and concrete, one of the new building materials of the day. Wherever these sanitary facilities were installed, the mortality rate dropped considerably—not because they prevented miasmas, but because they disposed of human waste and provided clean water free of harmful bacteria for people to drink, cook with, and bathe in.

A major feature of the reconstruction of mid-nineteenth-century Paris under the Emperor Napoleon II was a vast new sewer system to provide for drainage in the city. Sewer workmen could travel the length of the structure on small rail cars. Even today tourists still may visit parts of the mid-city Paris sewer system.
Nadar/Getty Images

MAJOR DATES RELATING TO SANITATION REFORM

1830s and 1840s	Cholera epidemics
1840	Villermé's *Catalog of the Physical and Moral State of Workers*
1842	Chadwick's *Report on the Sanitary Condition of the Labouring Population*
1848	British Public Health Act
1851	French Melun Act

Expanded Government Involvement in Public Health The concern with public health led to an expansion of governmental power on various levels. In Britain the Public Health Act of 1848, in France the Melun Act of 1851, and various laws in the still-disunited German states, as well as later legislation, introduced new restraints on private life and enterprise. This legislation allowed medical officers and building inspectors to enter homes and businesses in the name of public health. The state could condemn private property for posing health hazards. Private land could be excavated to construct the sewers and water mains required to protect the public. New building regulations restrained the activities of private contractors.

Full acceptance at the close of the century of the bacterial theory of disease associated with the discoveries of Louis Pasteur (1822–1895) in France, Robert Koch (1843–1910) in Germany, and Joseph Lister (1827–1912) in Britain increased public concern about cleanliness. Throughout Europe, issues related to the maintenance of public health and the physical well-being of the population repeatedly opened the way for new modes of government intervention in the lives of citizens.

Housing Reform and Middle-Class Values

The information about working-class living conditions the sanitary reformers revealed also led to heated debates over the housing problem. The wretched dwellings of the poor were themselves a cause of poor sanitation and thus became a newly perceived health hazard. Furthermore, the domestic arrangements of the poor, whose large families might live in a single room without any personal privacy, shocked middle-class reformers and bureaucrats. A single toilet might serve a whole block of tenements. After the revolutions of 1848, the overcrowding in housing and the social discontent that it generated were also seen to pose a political danger.

Middle-class reformers thus turned to housing reform to solve the medical, moral, and political dangers slums posed. Decent housing would foster a good home life, in turn leading to a healthy, moral, and politically stable population. As A. V. Huber, one of the early German housing reformers, declared,

> Certainly it would not be too much to say that the home is the communal embodiment of family life. Thus the purity of the dwelling is almost as important for the family as is the cleanliness of the body for the individual. Good or bad housing is a question of life and death if ever there was one.[1]

Later advocates of housing reform, such as Jules Simon (1814–1896) in France, saw good housing as leading to good family life and, ultimately, to strong patriotic feeling. It was widely believed that providing the poor and the working class with adequate, respectable, cheap housing would alleviate social and political discontent. It was also believed that the personal saving and investment that were required to own a home would lead the working class to adopt the thrifty habits of the middle classes.

Private philanthropy made the first attack on the housing problem. Companies operating on low profit margins or making low-interest loans encouraged housing for the poor. Firms such as the German Krupp Armaments concern that sought to ensure a contented, healthy, and stable workforce, constructed model housing projects and industrial communities.

By the mid-1880s, the migration into cities had made housing a political issue. Legislation in England in 1885 lowered the interest rates to construct cheap housing, and soon thereafter local governments began public housing projects. In Germany, action on housing came later in the century through the initiative of local municipalities. In 1894, France made inexpensive credit available to construct housing for the poor. None of these governments, however, adopted wide-scale housing experiments.

Nonetheless, by 1914, the housing problem had been fully recognized if not adequately addressed. The goal of housing reform across Western Europe came to be to provide homes for the members of the working class that would allow them to enjoy a family life more or less like that of the middle class. Such a home would be in the form of a detached house or an affordable city apartment with several rooms, a private entrance, and separate toilet facilities.

[1]Quoted in Nicholas Bullock and James Read, *The Movement for Housing Reform in Germany and France, 1840–1914* (Cambridge: Cambridge University Press, 1985), p. 42.

▼ Varieties of Late-Nineteenth-Century Women's Experiences

Late-nineteenth-century women and men led lives that reflected their social rank. Yet, within each rank, the experience of women was distinct from that of men. Women remained, generally speaking, economically dependent and legally inferior, whatever their social class.

Women's Social Disabilities

In the mid-nineteenth century, virtually all European women faced social and legal disabilities in three areas: property rights, family law, and education. By the close of the century, there had been some improvement in each area.

Women and Property Until the last quarter of the century in most European countries, married women could not own property in their own names, no matter what their social class. For all practical purposes, upon marriage, women lost to their husbands' control any property they owned or that they might inherit or earn by their own labor. Their legal identities were subsumed in their husbands' identities, and they had no independent standing before the law. The courts saw the theft of a woman's purse as a theft of her husband's property. Because private property and wage earning were the bases of European society, these disabilities put married women at a great disadvantage, limiting their freedom to work, to save, and to move from one location to another.

Reform of women's property rights came slowly. By 1882, Great Britain had passed the Married Woman's Property Act, which allowed married women to own property in their own right. In France, however, a married woman could not even open a savings account in her own name until 1895, and married French women did not gain possession of the wages they earned until 1907. In 1900, Germany allowed women to take jobs without their husbands' permission, but except for her wages, a German husband retained control of most of his wife's property. Similar laws prevailed elsewhere in Europe.

Family Law European family law also disadvantaged women. Legal codes required wives to "give obedience" to their husbands. The Napoleonic Code and the remnants of Roman law still in effect made women legal minors throughout Europe. Divorce was difficult everywhere for most of the century. In England before 1857, each divorce required a separate act of Parliament. Thereafter, couples could divorce, with difficulty, through the Court of Matrimonial Causes. Most nations did not permit divorce by mutual consent. French law forbade divorce between 1816 and 1884. Thereafter, the majority of nations recognized a legal cause for divorce—cruelty or injury—which had to be proven in court. In Great Britain, adultery was the usual cause for divorce, but to obtain a divorce, a woman had to prove her husband's adultery plus other offenses, whereas a man only had to prove his wife's adultery. In Germany, only adultery or serious maltreatment was recognized as reasons for divorce. Across Europe, some version of the double standard prevailed whereby husbands' extramarital sexual relations were tolerated to a much greater degree than those of wives. Everywhere, divorce required hearings in court and the presentation of legal proof, making the process expensive and more difficult for women, who did not control their own property.

The authority of husbands also extended to children. A husband could take children away from their mother and give them to someone else to rear. Only a father, in most countries, could permit his daughter to marry. In some countries, he could virtually force his daughter to marry the man of his choice. In cases of divorce and separation, courts normally awarded the husband authority over and custody of children, no matter how he had treated them previously.

The issues surrounding the sexual and reproductive rights of women that have been so widely debated recently could hardly be discussed in the nineteenth century. Until well into the twentieth century, both contraception and abortion were illegal. The law surrounding rape normally worked to the disadvantage of women. Wherever they turned with their problems—whether to physicians or lawyers—women confronted an official or legal world that men almost wholly populated and controlled.

Educational Barriers Throughout the nineteenth century, women had less access to education than men had and what was available to them was inferior to that available to men. Not surprisingly, there were many more illiterate women than men. Most women were educated only enough for the domestic lives they were expected to lead.

University and professional education remained reserved for men until at least the third quarter of the century. In Switzerland, the University of Zurich first opened its doors to women in the 1860s. The University of London admitted women for degrees in 1878. Women's colleges were founded at Cambridge during the last quarter of the century. Women could take Oxford and Cambridge university examinations but were not awarded degrees at Oxford until 1920 and at Cambridge until 1921. In France, women could not attend lectures at the Sorbonne until 1880. Just before the turn of the century, universities and medical schools in the Austrian Empire allowed women to matriculate, but Prussian universities did not admit women until after 1900. Russian women did not attend universities before 1914, but other institutions that awarded degrees were open to them. Italian universities proved themselves more open to both women students and women instructors than similar institutions elsewhere in Europe. In many countries, more foreign than native women attended university classes. This was especially the case in Zurich, where many Russian women studied for medical degrees. Many of the American women who founded or taught in the first women's colleges in the United States studied at European universities.

The absence of a system of private or public secondary education for women prevented most of them from gaining the qualifications they needed to enter a university whether or not the university prohibited them. Evidence suggests that educated, professional men feared that admitting women would overcrowd their professions. Women who attended universities and medical schools, like the young Russian women who studied medicine at Zurich, were sometimes labeled political radicals.

By the turn of the century, some men in the educated elites feared the challenge educated women posed to traditional gender roles in the home and workplace. Restricting women's access to secondary and university education helped bar them from social and economic advancement. Women would benefit only marginally from the expansion of professional employment that occurred during the late nineteenth and early twentieth centuries. Some women did enter the professions, particularly medicine, but their number remained few. Most nations refused to allow women to become lawyers until after World War I.

School teaching at the elementary level, which had come to be seen as a "female job" because of its association with the nurturing of children, became a professional haven for women. Trained at institutions designed particularly for elementary schoolteachers, usually known as normal schools, women schoolteachers at the elementary level were regarded as educated, but not as university educated. Higher education remained largely the province of men.

The few women who pioneered in the professions and on government commissions and school boards or who dispersed birth control information faced social obstacles, humiliation, and often outright bigotry. These women and their male supporters were challenging that clear separation into male and female spheres that had emerged in middle-class European social life during the

Women only gradually gained access to secondary and university education during the second half of the nineteenth century and the early twentieth century. Young women on their way to school, the subject of this 1880 English painting, would thus have been a new sight when it was painted. Sir George Clausen (RA) (1852–1944), *Schoolgirls, Haverstock Hill*, signed and dated 1880, oil on canvas, 20 1/2 × 30 3/8 in. (52 × 77.2 cm), Yale Center for British Art/Paul Mellon Collection, USA/Bridgeman Art Library (B1985.10.1). Courtesy of the Estate of Sir George Clausen

nineteenth century. Women themselves were often hesitant to support feminist causes or expanded opportunities for females because they had been so thoroughly acculturated into the recently stereotyped roles. Many women, as well as men, saw a real conflict between family responsibilities and feminism.

New Employment Patterns for Women

During the Second Industrial Revolution, two major developments affected the economic lives of women. The first was the large-scale expansion in the variety of jobs available to women outside the better-paying learned professions. The second was the withdrawal of many married women from the workforce. These two seemingly contradictory developments require explanation.

Availability of New Jobs The expansion of governmental bureaucracies, the emergence of corporations and other large businesses, and the vast growth of retail stores opened many new employment opportunities for women. The need for elementary school teachers, usually women, grew as governments adopted compulsory education laws. Technological inventions and innovations, such as the typewriter and, eventually, the telephone exchange, also fostered female employment. Women by the thousands became secretaries and clerks for governments and private businesses. Thousands more became shop assistants.

Although these jobs did open new and often better employment opportunities for women, they nonetheless required low-level skills and involved minimal training. They were occupied primarily by unmarried women or widows. Women rarely occupied more prominent positions.

Employers continued to pay women low wages, because they assumed, although they often knew better, that a woman did not need to live on what she herself earned but could expect additional financial support from her father or her husband. Consequently, a woman who did need to support herself independently could seldom find a job that paid an adequate income—or a position that paid as well as one a man who was supporting himself held.

Withdrawal from the Labor Force Most of the women filling the new service positions were young and

Women working in the London Central Telephone Exchange. The invention of the telephone opened new employment opportunities for women. Image Works/Mary Evans Picture Library Ltd.

unmarried. Upon marriage, or certainly after the birth of her first child, a woman normally withdrew from the labor force. Either she did not work or she worked at some occupation that she could pursue at home. This pattern was not new, but it had become significantly more common by the end of the nineteenth century. The kinds of industrial occupations that women had filled in the mid-nineteenth century, especially textile and garment making, were shrinking. Married or unmarried women thus had fewer opportunities for employment in those industries. Employers in offices and retail stores preferred young, unmarried women whose family responsibilities would not interfere with their work. The decline in the number of children being born also meant that fewer married women were needed to look after other women's children.

The real wages paid to male workers increased during this period, so families had a somewhat reduced need for a second income. Also, thanks to improving health conditions, men lived longer than before, so the death of their husbands was less likely to thrust wives into the workforce. The smaller size of families also lowered the need for supplementary wages. Working children stayed at home longer and continued to contribute to the family's wage pool.

Finally, the cultural dominance of the middle class established a pattern of social expectations, especially for wives. The more prosperous a working-class family became, the less involved in employment its women were supposed to be. Indeed, the less income-producing work a wife did, the more prosperous and stable the family was considered.

Yet behind these generalities stands the enormous variety of social and economic experiences late-nineteenth-century women actually encountered. As might be expected, the chief determinant of these individual experiences was social class.

Working-Class Women

Although the textile industry and garment making were much less dominant than earlier in the century, they continued to employ many women. The German clothing-making trade illustrates the kind of vulnerable economic situation that women could encounter as a result of their limited skills and the way the trade was organized. The system of manufacturing mass-made clothes of uniform sizes in Germany was designed to require minimal capital investment by manufacturers and to protect them from risk. A major manufacturer would produce clothing through what was called a *putting-out system.* The manufacturer would purchase the material and then put it out for tailoring. Usually, numerous independently owned small sweatshops or workers in their homes made the clothing. It was seldom made in a factory.

In Berlin in 1896, this system employed more than 80,000 garment workers. When business was good and demand strong, employment for these women was high. As the seasons shifted or business slackened, however, less and less work was put out, idling many of them. In effect, the workers who actually sewed the clothing carried much of the risk of the enterprise. Some women did work in clothing factories, but they, too, were subject to layoffs. Furthermore, women in the clothing trade were nearly always in positions less skilled than those of the male tailors or the middlemen who owned the workshops.

The expectation of separate social and economic spheres for men and women and the definition of women's chief work as pertaining to the home contributed mightily to the exploitation of women workers outside the home. Because their wages were regarded merely as supplementing their husbands' wages, they became particularly vulnerable to the kind of economic exploitation that characterized the German putting-out system for clothing production and similar systems elsewhere. Women were nearly always treated as casual workers everywhere in Europe.

Poverty and Prostitution

A major, but little recognized, social fact of most nineteenth-century cities was the presence of a surplus of working women who did not fit the stereotype of wife or daughter supplementing a family's income. Almost always many more women were seeking employment than there were jobs. The economic vulnerability of women and the consequent poverty many of them faced were among the chief causes of prostitution. Every major late-nineteenth-century European city had thousands of prostitutes.

Prostitution was, of course, not new. It had always been one way for poor women to find income. In the late nineteenth century, however, it was closely related to the difficulty encountered by indigent women who were trying to make their way in an overcrowded female labor force. On the Continent, prostitution was generally legalized and subject to governmental and municipal regulations that male legislatures and councils passed and male police and physicians enforced. In Britain, prostitution received only minimal regulation.

Many myths and misunderstandings have surrounded the subject of prostitution. The most recent studies of prostitution in England emphasize that most prostitutes were active on the streets for only a few years, from their late teens to about age twenty-five. Many were poor women who had recently migrated from nearby rural areas. Others were born in the towns where they became prostitutes. Certain cities—those with large army garrisons or naval bases or those, like London, with large transient populations—attracted prostitutes. Far fewer prostitutes worked in manufacturing towns, where there were more opportunities for steady employment and community life was more stable.

Women who became prostitutes usually came from families of unskilled workers and had minimal skills and education themselves. Many had been servants. They also often were orphans or came from broken homes. Contrary to many sensational late-century newspaper accounts, there were few child prostitutes. Furthermore, middle-class employers or clients rarely seduced women into prostitution, although working-class women were always potentially subject to sexual exploitation. The customers of poor working-class prostitutes were primarily working-class men.

Women of the Middle Class

A vast social gap separated poor working-class women from their middle-class counterparts. As their fathers' and husbands' incomes permitted, middle-class women participated in the vast expansion of consumerism and domestic comfort that marked the late nineteenth and the early twentieth centuries. They filled their homes with manufactured items, including clothing, china, furniture, carpets, drapery, wallpaper, and prints. They enjoyed all the improvements of sanitation and electricity. They could command the services of numerous domestic servants. They moved into the fashionable new houses being constructed in the rapidly expanding suburbs.

The Cult of Domesticity For the middle classes, the distinction between work and family, defined by gender, had become complete and constituted the model for all other social groups. Middle-class women, if at all possible, did not work. More than any other women, they became limited to the roles of wife and mother. As a result, they might enjoy great domestic luxury and comfort, but their lives, talents, ambitions, and opportunities for applying their intelligence were sharply circumscribed.

Middle-class women became, in large measure, the product of a particular understanding of social life. Home life was to be different from the life of business and the marketplace. The home was to be a private place of refuge, a view scores of women's journals across Europe set forth.

As studies of the lives of middle-class women in northern France have suggested, this image of the middle-class home and of the role of women in the home is different from the one that had existed earlier in the nineteenth century. During the first half of the century, many middle-class wives contributed directly to their husbands' business, handling accounts or correspondence. These women also frequently left the task of rearing their children to nurses and governesses. The reasons for the change during the century are not certain, but it appears that men began to insist on doing business exclusively with other men. Magazines and books for women began to praise motherhood, domesticity, religion, and charity as the proper work of women in accordance with the concept of separate spheres.

For middle-class Frenchwomen, as well as for middle-class women elsewhere, the home came to be seen as the center of virtue, children, and the respectable life. Marriages were usually arranged to benefit the family economically. Romantic marriage was viewed as a danger to social stability. Most middle-class women in northern France married by the age of twenty-one and were expected to have children soon after marriage. The first child was often born within the first year. Rearing and nurturing her children were a woman's chief tasks. Her only experience or training was for the role of dutiful daughter, wife, and mother.

Within the home, a middle-class woman largely directed the household. She oversaw virtually all domestic management and child care. She was in charge of the home as a unit of consumption, which is why so much advertising was directed toward women. All this domestic activity, however, occurred within the bounds of the approved middle-class lifestyle that set strict limits on a woman's initiative. In her conspicuous position within the home and family, a woman symbolized first her father's and then her husband's worldly success.

Department stores, such as Bon Marché in Paris, sold wide selections of consumer goods under one roof. These modern stores increased the economic pressure on small traditional merchants who specialized in selling only one kind of good. (See "Paris Department Stores Expand Their Business," page 696.)
Image Works/Mary Evans Picture Library Ltd.

Religious and Charitable Activities The cult of domesticity in France and elsewhere assigned firm religious duties to women, which the Roman Catholic Church strongly supported. Women were expected to attend Mass frequently and assure the religious instruction of their children. They were charged with observing meatless Fridays and participating in religious observances. Prayer was a major part of their daily lives. They internalized those portions of the Christian religion that stressed meekness and passivity. In other countries, religion and religious activities also became part of the expected work of women. This close association between religion and a strict domestic life for women was one reason for later tension between feminism and religious authorities.

Another important role for middle-class women was the administration of charity. Women were considered especially qualified for this work because of their presumed innate spirituality and their capacity to instill domestic and personal discipline. Middle-class women were often in charge of clubs for poor youth, societies to protect poor young women, schools for infants, and societies for visiting the poor. Women were supposed to be particularly interested in the problems of poor women, their families, and their children. Often, to receive charity from middle-class women, a recipient who was poor had to demonstrate good character. By the end of the century, middle-class women seeking to expand their spheres of activity became social workers for the church, for private charities, or for the government. These vocations were a natural extension of the roles society assigned to them.

The following obituary of a French lady who died in the late nineteenth century illustrates how these vocations and virtues received public praise for women who fulfilled them:

> The poor were the object of her affectionate interest, especially the shameful poor, the fallen people. She sought them out and helped them with perfect discretion which doubled the value of her benevolent interest. To those whom she could approach without fear of bruising their dignity, she brought, along with alms to assure their existence, consolation of the most serious sort—she raised their courage and their hopes. To others, each Sunday, she opened all the doors of her home, above all when her children were still young. In making them distribute these alms with her, she hoped to initiate them early into practices of charity. In the last years of her life, the St. Gabriel Orphanage gained her interest. Not only did she accomplish a great deal with her generosity, but she also took on the task of maintaining the clothes of her dear orphans in good order and in good repair. When she appeared in the courtyard of the establishment at recreation time, all her protégés surrounded her and lavished her with manifestations of their profound respect and affectionate gratitude.[2]

[2]Quoted in Bonnie G. Smith, *Ladies of the Leisure Class: The Bourgeoises of Northern France in the Nineteenth Century* (Princeton, NJ: Princeton University Press, 1981), pp. 147–148. Copyright © 1981 by Princeton University Press. Reprinted by permission of Princeton University Press.

As will be seen in the immediately following sections, many ideas and social forces would challenge the values this obituary celebrates, but the role for upper-middle-class women that it illustrates would dominate European life for decades to come.

Sexuality and Family Size Historians have come to realize that the world of the middle-class wife and her family was much more complicated than they once thought. Neither all wives nor their families conformed to the stereotypes. Recent studies suggest that the middle classes of the nineteenth century enjoyed sexual relations within marriage far more than was once thought. Diaries, letters, and even early medical and sociological sex surveys indicate that sexual enjoyment rather than sexual repression was fundamental to middle-class marriages. Much of the inhibition about sexuality stemmed from the dangers of childbirth, which, in an age of limited sanitation and anesthesia, were widely and rightly feared, rather than from any dislike or disapproval of sex itself.

One of the major changes in this regard during the second half of the century was the acceptance of a small family size among the middle classes. The birthrate in France dropped throughout the nineteenth century. It began to fall in England steadily from the 1870s onward. During the last decades of the century, new contraceptive devices became available, which middle-class couples used. One of the chief reasons for the apparently conscious decision of couples to limit their family size was to maintain a relatively high level of material consumption. Children had become much more expensive to rear, and at the same time, more material comforts had become available. Fewer children probably meant more attention for each of them, possibly increasing the emotional bonds between mothers and their children.

MAJOR DATES IN LATE-NINETEENTH-CENTURY AND EARLY-TWENTIETH-CENTURY WOMEN'S HISTORY

1857	Revised English divorce law
1865	University of Zurich admits women for degrees
1869	John Stuart Mill's *The Subjection of Women*
1878	University of London admits women as candidates for degrees
1882	English Married Woman's Property Act
1894	Union of German Women's Organizations founded
1901	National Council of French Women founded
1903	British Women's Social and Political Union founded
1907	Norway permits women to vote on national issues
1910	British suffragettes adopt radical tactics
1918	Vote extended to some British women
1919	Weimar constitution allows German women to vote
1920–1921	Oxford and Cambridge Universities award degrees to women
1922	French Senate defeats bill extending vote to women
1928	Britain extends vote to women on same basis as men

The Rise of Political Feminism

Plainly, liberal society and its values had neither automatically nor inevitably improved the lot of women. In particular, they did not give women the vote or access to political activity. In Catholic countries, male liberals feared that granting the vote to women would benefit political conservatives, because men thought that priests exercised undue control over women. A similar apprehension existed about the alleged influence of the Anglican clergy over women in England and Protestant pastors in parts of Germany. Consequently, anticlerical liberals often had difficulty working with feminists.

Obstacles to Achieving Equality Women also were often reluctant to support feminist causes. Political issues relating to gender were only one of several priorities for many women. Some were sensitive to their class and economic interests. Others subordinated feminist political issues to national unity and patriotism. Still others would not support particular feminist organizations because they objected to their tactics. The various social and tactical differences among women often led to sharp divisions within the feminists' own ranks. Except in England, it was often difficult for working-class and middle-class women to cooperate. Roman Catholic feminists were uncomfortable with radical secularist feminists. There were other disagreements about which goals were most important for improving women's legal and social conditions.

Although liberal society and law presented women with many obstacles, they also provided feminists with many of their intellectual and political tools. As early as 1792 in Britain, Mary Wollstonecraft (1759–1797), in *The Vindication of the Rights of Woman*, had applied the revolutionary doctrines of the rights of man to the predicament of the members of her own sex. (See Chapter 17.) John Stuart Mill (1806–1873), together with his wife, Harriet Taylor (1804–1858), extended the logic of liberal freedom to the position of women in *The Subjection of Women* (1869). The arguments for utility and efficiency so dear to middle-class liberals could be used to expose the human and social waste implicit in the inferior role assigned to women.

Furthermore, the socialist criticism of capitalist society often, though by no means always, included a harsh indictment of the social and economic position to which women had been relegated. The earliest statements in support of feminism arose from critics of the existing order who were often people who had unorthodox opinions about sexuality, family life, and property. This hardened resistance to the feminist message, especially on the Continent.

These difficulties prevented continental feminists from raising the massive public support or mounting the large demonstrations that feminists in Britain and the United States could. Everywhere in Europe, however, including Britain, the feminist cause was badly divided over both goals and tactics.

Votes for Women in Britain Europe's most advanced women's movement was in Britain. There, Millicent Fawcett (1847–1929) led the moderate National Union of Women's Suffrage Societies. She believed Parliament would grant women the vote only if it were convinced they would be respectable and responsible in their political activity. In 1908, the National Union could rally almost half a million women in London. Fawcett's husband Henry Fawcett (1833–1884) was a Liberal Party cabinet minister and economist who also supported women's suffrage. Her tactics were those of English liberals.

Emmeline Pankhurst (1858–1928) led a much more radical branch of British feminists. Pankhurst's husband, who died near the close of the century, had been active in both labor and Irish nationalist politics. Irish nationalists had developed numerous disruptive political tactics. Early labor politicians had also sometimes confronted the police over the right to hold meetings. In 1903, Pankhurst and her daughters, Christabel and Sylvia, founded the Women's Social and Political Union. For years they and their followers, known derisively as **suffragettes**, lobbied publicly and privately for extending the vote to women. By 1910, having failed to move the government, they turned to the violent tactics of arson, breaking windows, and sabotage of postal boxes. (See "Emmeline Pankhurst Defends Militant Suffragette Tactics," page 708.) They marched en masse on Parliament. The Liberal government of Prime Minister Herbert Asquith (1852–1928) imprisoned demonstrators and force-fed those who went on hunger strikes in jail. The government refused to extend the franchise. Only in 1918, and then as a result of their contribution to the war effort in World War I, did British women over age thirty receive the vote. (Men could vote at age twenty-one.)

Political Feminism on the Continent The contrast between the women's movement in Britain and those in France and Germany shows how advanced the British women's movement was. In France, when Hubertine Auclert (1848–1914) began campaigning for the vote in the 1880s, she stood virtually alone. During the 1890s, several women's organizations emerged. In 1901, the National Council of French Women (CNFF) was organized among upper-middle-class women, but it did not support the vote for women for several years. French Roman Catholic feminists such as Marie Maugeut (1844–1928) supported the franchise. Almost all French feminists, however, rejected violence. Nor were they ever able to organize mass rallies. The leaders of French feminism believed women could achieve the vote through careful legalism. In 1919, the French Chamber of Deputies passed a bill granting the vote to women, but in 1922, the French Senate defeated the bill. French women did not receive the right to vote until after World War II.

Emmeline Pankhurst (1857–1928) was frequently arrested for forcibly advocating votes for British women. Hulton Archive Photos/Getty Images Inc.

In Germany, feminist awareness and action were even more underdeveloped. German law actually forbade German women from engaging in political activity. Because no group in the German Empire enjoyed extensive political rights, women were not certain they would benefit from demanding them. Any such demand would be regarded as subversive not only of the state, but also of society.

In 1894, the Union of German Women's Organizations (BDFK) was founded. By 1902, it was supporting the right to vote. But its main concern was improving women's social conditions, increasing their access to education, and extending their right to other protections. The BDKF also tried to gain women's admittance to political or civic activity on the municipal level. Its work usually included education, child welfare, charity, and public health. The German Social Democratic Party supported women's suffrage, but the German authorities

EMMELINE PANKHURST DEFENDS MILITANT SUFFRAGETTE TACTICS

Emmeline Pankhurst (1858–1928) led the most radical wing of early twentieth-century British feminists in their demand for the vote. In 1910 she called for militant tactics against the Liberal government of Prime Minister Henry Asquith. In her autobiography of 1914 Mrs. Pankhurst explains why she undertook such tactics. These efforts failed in 1910. A partial franchise for women was enacted in Britiain in 1918. Today a statue of Mrs. Pankhurst stands not far from the Houses of Parliament.

What are Mrs. Pankhurst's assumptions about the factors that would move the British government to enact the franchise for women? Why do you think the government responded so fiercely to the attack on postal boxes? How might these tactics have backfired on the movement?

I had called upon women to join me in striking at the Government through the only thing that governments are really very much concerned about—property—and the response was immediate. Within a few days the newspapers rang with the story of the attack made on letter boxes in London, Liverpool, Birmingham, Bristol, and half a dozen other cities. In some cases the boxes, when opened by postmen, mysteriously burst into flame; in others the letters were destroyed by corrosive chemicals; in still others the addresses were rendered illegible by black fluids. Altogether it was estimated that over 5,000 letters were completely destroyed and many thousands more were delayed in transit.

It was with a deep sense of their gravity that these letter-burning protests were undertaken, but we felt that something drastic must be done in order to destroy the apathy of the men of England who view with indifference the suffering of women oppressed by unjust laws. . . .

In only a few cases were the offenders apprehended, and one of the few women arrested was a helpless cripple, a woman who could move about only in a wheeled chair. She received a sentence of eight months in the first division, and, resolutely hunger striking, was forcibly fed with unusual brutality, the prison doctor deliberately breaking one of her teeth in order to insert a gag. In spite of her disabilities and her weakness the crippled girl persisted in her hunger strike and her resistance to prison rules, and within a short time had to be released. The excessive sentences of the other pillar box destroyers resolved themselves into very short terms because of the resistance of the prisoners, every one of whom adopted the hunger strike. . . .

It was at this time, February, 1913, less than two years ago as I write these words, that militancy, as it is now generally understood by the public began—militancy in the sense of continued, destructive, guerilla warfare against the Government through injury to private property. . . . We had tried every other measure . . . and our years of work and suffering and sacrifice had taught us that the Government would not yield to right and justice . . . Now our task was to show the Government that it was expedient to yield to the women's just demands. In order to do that we had to make England and every department of English life insecure and unsafe. We had to make English law a failure and the courts farce comedy theatres; we had to discredit the Government and Parliament in the eyes of the world; we had to spoil English sports, hurt business, destroy valuable property, demoralise the world of society, shame the churches, upset the whole orderly conduct of life.

That is, we had to do as much of this guerilla warfare as the people of England would tolerate.

Emmeline Pankhurst, *My Own Story* (New York: Hearst International Library, 1914), pp. 270–271, 279–280.

and German Roman Catholics so disdained the socialists, that its support only made suffrage more suspect in their eyes. Women received the vote in Germany only in 1919, under the constitution of the Weimar Republic after the German defeat in war and revolution at home.

Throughout Europe before World War I, women demanded rights widely and vocally. Their tactics and the success they achieved, however, varied from country to country depending on political and class structures. Before World War I, only Norway (1907) allowed women to vote on national issues.

▼ Jewish Emancipation

The emancipation of European Jews from the narrow life of the ghetto into a world of equal or nearly equal citizenship and social status was a major accomplishment of political liberalism and had an enduring impact on European life. Emancipation, slow and never fully completed, began in the late eighteenth century and continued throughout the nineteenth. It moved at different paces in different countries.

Differing Degrees of Citizenship

In 1782, Joseph II, the Habsburg emperor, issued a decree that placed the Jews of his empire under more or less the same laws as Christians. In France, the National Assembly recognized Jews as French citizens in 1789. During the turmoil of the Napoleonic Wars, Jewish communities in Italy and Germany were allowed to mix on a generally equal footing with the Christian population. These steps toward political emancipation were always uncertain and were frequently limited or abrogated when rulers or governments changed. Certain freedoms were granted, only to be partially withdrawn later. Even countries that had given Jews political rights did not permit them to own land and often subjected them to discriminatory taxes. Nonetheless, during the first half of the century, Jews in Western Europe, and to a much lesser extent in central and eastern Europe, began to gain equal or more nearly equal citizenship.

In Russia, and in Poland under Russian rule, the traditional modes of prejudice and discrimination continued unabated until World War I. Russian rule treated Jews as aliens. The government undermined Jewish community life, limited the publication of Jewish books, restricted areas where Jews could live, required Jews to have internal passports to move about the country, banned Jews from many forms of state service, and excluded Jews from many institutions of higher education. The state allowed the police and right-wing nationalist groups to conduct ***pogroms***—organized riots—against Jewish neighborhoods and villages.

Broadened Opportunities

After the revolutions of 1848, European Jews saw a general improvement in their situation that lasted for several decades. In Germany, Italy, the Low Countries, and Scandinavia, Jews attained full citizenship. After 1858, Jews in Great Britain could sit in Parliament. Austria-Hungary extended full legal rights to Jews in 1867. Indeed, from about 1850 to 1880, relatively little organized or overt prejudice was expressed against Jews in Western Europe. They entered the professions and other occupations once closed to them. They participated fully in literary and cultural life. They were active in the arts and music. They became leaders in science and education. Jews intermarried freely with non-Jews as legal, secular prohibitions against such marriages were repealed during the last quarter of the century.

Outside of Russia, Jewish politicians entered cabinets and served in the highest offices of the state. Politically, Jews often were aligned with liberal parties because these groups had championed equal rights. Later in the century, especially in eastern Europe, many Jews became associated with socialist parties.

The prejudice that had been associated with Christian religious attitudes toward Jews seemed to have dissipated, although it still appeared in Russia and other parts of eastern Europe. Hundreds of thousands of European Jews migrated from these regions to Western Europe and the United States. Almost anywhere in Europe, Jews might encounter prejudice on a personal level. Yet in Western Europe, including England, France, Italy,

Because many major financial institutions of nineteenth-century Europe were owned by wealthy Jewish families, anti-Semitic political figures often blamed them for economic hard times. The most famous such family was the Rothschilds who controlled banks in several countries. The head of the London branch was Lionel Rothschild (1808–1879). He was elected to Parliament several times but was not seated because he would not take the required Christian oath. After the requirement of that oath was abolished in 1858, he sat in Parliament from 1858 to 1874. Getty Images Inc.—Hulton Archive Photos

Germany, and the Low Countries, the legalized persecution and discrimination that had so haunted Jews in the past seemed to have ended.

That newfound security began to erode during the last two decades of the nineteenth century. Anti-Semitic voices began to be heard in the 1870s, attributing the economic stagnation of the decade to Jewish bankers and financial interests. In the 1880s, organized **anti-Semitism** erupted in Germany, as it did in France at the time of the Dreyfus affair. As will be seen in the next chapter, these developments gave rise to the birth of Zionism, initially a minority movement within the Jewish community. Most Jewish leaders believed the attacks on Jewish life were merely temporary recurrences of older forms of prejudice; they felt their communities would remain safe under the liberal legal protections that had been extended during the century. That analysis would be proved disastrously wrong in the 1930s and 1940s.

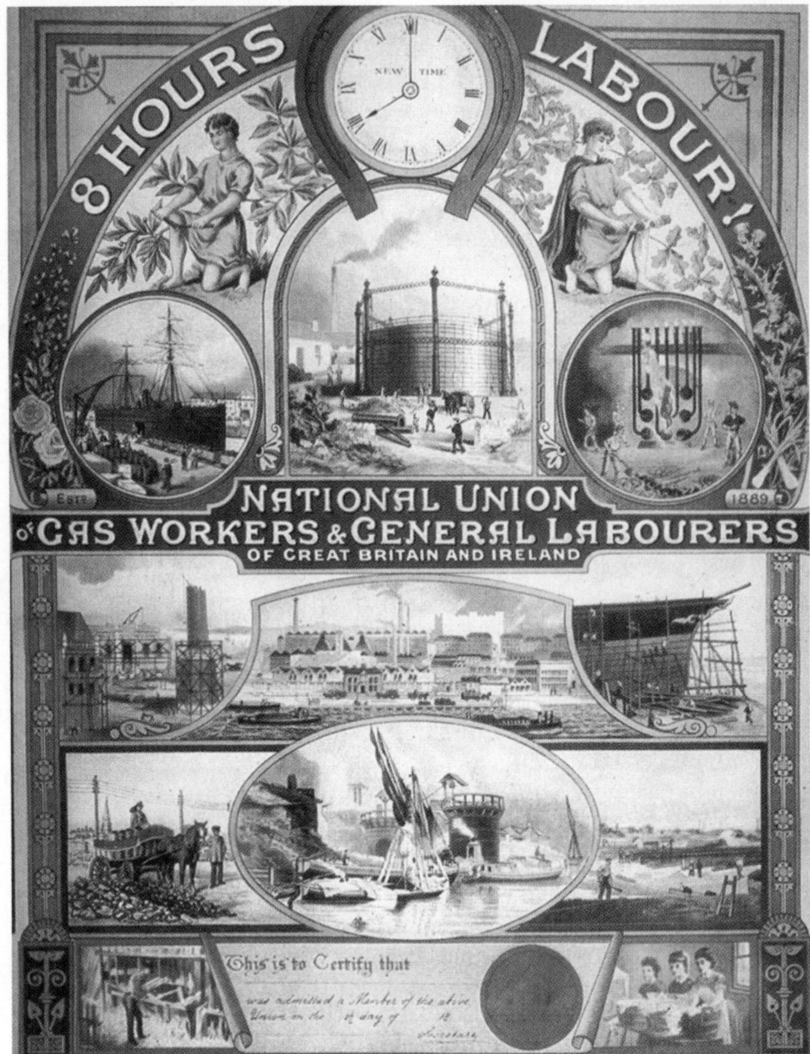

Trade unions continued to grow in late-nineteenth-century Great Britain. The effort to curb the unions eventually led to the formation of the Labour Party. The British unions often had quite elaborate membership certificates, such as this one for the National Union of Gas Workers and General Labourers of Great Britain and Ireland. The Granger Collection

▼ Labor, Socialism, and Politics to World War I

The late-century industrial expansion further changed the life of the labor force. In all industrializing continental countries, the numbers of the urban proletariat rose. The proportion of artisans and highly skilled workers declined, and for the first time, factory wage earners predominated. The number of unskilled workers in shipping, transportation, and building also grew.

Workers still had to look to themselves to improve their lot. After 1848, however, European workers stopped rioting in the streets to voice their grievances. They also stopped trying to revive the old paternal guilds and similar institutions. After midcentury, workers turned to new institutions and ideologies. Chief among these were trade unions, democratic political parties, and socialism.

Trade Unionism

Trade unionism came of age when governments extended legal protections to unions during the second half of the century. Unions became fully legal in Great Britain in 1871 and were allowed to picket in 1875. In France, Napoleon III at first used troops against strikes, but as his political power waned, he allowed weak labor associations in 1868. The Third French Republic fully legalized unions in 1884. In Germany, unions were permitted to function with little disturbance after 1890. Union participation in the political process was at first marginal. As long as the representatives of the traditional governing classes looked after labor interests, members of the working class rarely sought office themselves.

Unions directed their mid-century organizational efforts toward skilled workers and the immediate improvement of wages and working conditions. By the close of the century, industrial unions for unskilled workers were being organized. Employers intensely opposed these large unions of thousands of workers. Unions frequently had to engage in long strikes to convince employers to accept their demands. Europe suffered a rash of strikes in the decade before World War I as unions sought to keep wages in line with inflation. Despite union advances, however, and the growth of union membership (in 1910 to approximately 3 million in Britain, 2 million in Germany, and 977,000 in France), most of Europe's labor force was never unionized in this period. What the unions did represent for workers was a new collective form of association to confront economic difficulties and improve security.

Democracy and Political Parties

Except for Russia, all the major European states adopted broad-based, if not perfectly democratic, electoral systems in the late nineteenth century. Great Britain passed its second voting reform act in 1867 and its third in 1884. Bismarck brought universal male suffrage to the German Empire in 1871. The French Chamber of Deputies was democratically elected. Universal male suffrage was adopted in Switzerland in 1879, in Spain in 1890, in Belgium in 1893, in the Netherlands in 1896, and in Norway in 1898. Italy finally fell into line in 1912. The broadened franchise meant politicians could no longer ignore workers, and discontented groups could now voice their grievances and advocate their programs within the institutions of government rather than from the outside.

The advent of democracy brought organized mass political parties like those already in existence in the United States to Europe for the first time. In the liberal European states with narrow electoral bases, most voters had been people of property who knew what they had at stake in politics. Organization had been minimal. The expansion of the electorate brought into the political process many people whose level of political consciousness, awareness, and interest was low. This electorate had to be organized and taught about power and influence in the liberal democratic state.

The organized political party—with its workers, newspapers, offices, social life, and discipline—was the vehicle that mobilized the new voters. The largest single group in these mass electorates was the working class. The democratization of politics presented the socialists with opportunities and required the traditional ruling classes to vie with the socialists for the support of the new voters.

During these years, socialism as a political ideology and plan of action opposed nationalism. The problems of class were supposed to be transnational, and socialism was supposed to unite the working classes across national borders. European socialists, however, badly underestimated the emotional drawing power of nationalism. Many workers had both socialist and nationalist sympathies, which were rarely in conflict with each other. When the outbreak of war in 1914 did bring them into conflict, however, nationalist feelings prevailed.

The major question for late-century socialist parties throughout Europe was whether revolution or democratic reform would improve the life of the working class. This question sharply divided all socialist parties and especially those whose leadership adhered to the intellectual legacy of Karl Marx. The Bolshevik Revolution of November 1917 would transform socialist debates and actions and render many of the disputes of the late nineteenth and early twentieth centuries moot. During those decades, however, the dispute over whether to achieve socialism through revolution or reform sharply shaped socialist thought, party programs, and political behavior and influenced not only socialism but the larger European political arena as well.

Karl Marx and the First International

Karl Marx himself took into account the new realities that developed during the third quarter of the century. Although he continued to predict the disintegration of capitalism, his practical, public political activity reflected a different approach.

In 1864, a group of British and French trade unionists founded the International Working Men's Association. Known as the First International, its membership encompassed a vast array of radical political types, including socialists, anarchists, and Polish nationalists. In the inaugural address for the First International, Marx approved workers' and trade unions' efforts to reform the conditions of labor within the existing political and economic processes. In his private writings he often criticized such reformist activity, but these writings were not made public until near the end of the century, years after his death.

The violence involved in the rise and suppression of the Paris Commune (see Chapter 22), which Marx had declared a genuine proletarian uprising, cast a pall over socialism throughout Europe. British trade unionists, who received legal protections in 1871, wanted no connection with the events in Paris. The French authorities used the uprising to suppress socialist activity. Under these pressures, the First International held its last European congress in 1873. It soon transferred its offices to the United States, where it was dissolved in 1876.

The short-lived First International had a disproportionately great impact on the future of European socialism. Throughout the late 1860s, the organization gathered statistics, kept labor groups informed of mutual problems, provided a forum to debate socialist doctrine, and extravagantly proclaimed (and overstated) its own influence over contemporary events. From these debates and activities, Marxism emerged as the single most important strand of socialism. Marx and his supporters defeated or drove out anarchists and advocates of other forms of socialism. The apparently scientific character of Marxism made it attractive at a time when science was more influential than at any previous period in European history. Marx's thought deeply impressed German socialists, who were to establish the most powerful socialist party in Europe and became the chief vehicle for preserving and developing it. The full development of German socialism, however, also involved the influence of non-Marxist socialists in Great Britain.

Great Britain: Fabianism and Early Welfare Programs

Neither Marxism nor any other form of socialism made significant progress in Great Britain, the most advanced industrial society of the day. There trade unions grew steadily, and their members normally supported Liberal Party candidates. The "new unionism" of the late 1880s and the 1890s organized the dockworkers, the gas workers, and similar unskilled groups. In 1892, Keir Hardie (1856–1915) became the first independent working man to be elected to Parliament, but the small socialist Independent Labour Party founded a year later remained ineffective. Until 1901, labor's general political activity remained limited. In that year, however, the House of Lords, which also acts as Britain's highest court, through the Taff Vale decision, removed the legal protection previously accorded union funds. The Trades Union Congress responded by launching the Labour Party. In the election of 1906, the fledgling party sent twenty-nine members to Parliament. Their goals as trade unionists, however, did not yet include socialism. In this same period, the British labor movement became more militant. In scores of strikes before the war, workers fought for wages to meet the rising cost of living. The government took a larger role than ever before in mediating these strikes, which in 1911 and 1912 involved the railways, the docks, and the coal mines.

British socialism itself remained primarily the preserve of non-Marxist intellectuals. The **Fabian** Society, founded in 1884, was Britain's most influential socialist group. The society took its name from Q. Fabius Maximus (d. 203 B.C.E.), the Roman general whose tactics against Hannibal involved avoiding direct conflict that might lead to defeat. The name reflected the society's gradualist approach to major social reform. Its leading members were Sidney Webb (1859–1947), Beatrice Webb (1858–1943), H. G. Wells (1866–1946), Graham Wallas (1858–1932), and George Bernard Shaw (1856–1950). Many Fabians were civil servants who believed the problems of industry, the expansion of ownership, and the state direction of production could be solved and achieved gradually, peacefully, and democratically. They sought to educate the country about the rational wisdom of socialism. They were particularly interested in modes of collective ownership on the municipal level, the so-called gas-and-water socialism.

The British government and the Liberal and Conservative parties responded slowly to these pressures. In 1903, Joseph Chamberlain (1836–1914) launched his unsuccessful campaign to match foreign tariffs and to finance social reform through higher import duties. The campaign split the Conservative Party. After 1906, the Liberal Party, led by Sir Henry Campbell-Bannerman (1836–1908) and, after 1908, by Herbert Asquith, pursued a two-pronged policy. Fearful of losing seats in Parliament to the new Labour Party, they restored the former protection of the unions. Then, after 1909, with Chancellor of the Exchequer David Lloyd George (1863–1945) as its guiding light, the Liberal ministry undertook a broad program of social legislation that included establishing labor exchanges, regulating certain trades, such as tailoring and lace making, and passing the National Insurance Act of 1911, which provided unemployment benefits and health care.

Beatrice and Sidney Webb. These most influential British Fabian Socialists, shown in a photograph from the late 1920s, wrote many books on governmental and economic matters, served on special parliamentary commissions, and agitated for the enactment of socialist policies. CORBIS/Bettmann

The financing of these programs brought the Liberal majority in the House of Commons into conflict with the Conservative-dominated House of Lords. The result was the Parliament Act of 1911, which allowed the Commons to override the legislative veto of the upper chamber. The new taxes and social programs meant that in Britain, the home of nineteenth-century liberalism, the state was taking on an expanded role in the life of its citizens. The early welfare legislation was only marginally satisfactory to labor, many of whose members still thought they could gain more from the direct action of strikes.

France: "Opportunism" Rejected

French socialism was a less united and more politically factionalized movement than socialism in other countries. At the turn of the century, Jean Jaurès (1859–1914) and Jules Guesde (1845–1922) led the two major factions of French socialists. Jaurès believed socialists should cooperate with middle-class Radical ministries to ensure the enactment of needed social legislation. Guesde opposed this policy, arguing that socialists could not, with integrity, support a bourgeois cabinet they were theoretically dedicated to overthrowing. The government's response to the Dreyfus affair brought the quarrel to a head. In 1899, seeking to unite all supporters of Dreyfus, Prime Minister René Waldeck-Rousseau (1846–1904) appointed the socialist Alexander Millerand (1859–1943) to the cabinet.

The Second International had been founded in 1889 in a new effort to unify the various national socialist parties and trade unions. By 1904, the Amsterdam Congress of the Second International debated the issue of *opportunism*, as such participation by socialists in cabinets was termed. The Congress condemned opportunism in France and ordered French socialists to form a single party. Jaurès accepted the decision. Thereafter French socialists began to work together, and by 1914, the recently united Socialist Party had become the second largest group in the Chamber of Deputies. Jaurès was assassinated in 1914 in a Paris cafe at the outbreak of World War I. Thereafter in the patriotism of the war effort, French socialist leaders participated in the wartime cabinet. After the war the French socialist movement split with socialists not again serving in a French cabinet until the Popular Front Government of 1936. (See Chapter 28.)

The French labor movement, with deep roots in anarchism, was uninterested in either politics or socialism. French workers usually voted socialist, but the unions themselves, unlike those in Britain, avoided active political participation. The main labor union, Confédération Générale du Travail, founded in 1895, regarded itself as a rival to the socialist parties. Its leaders sought to improve the workers' conditions through direct action. They embraced the doctrines of **syndicalism**, which had been most persuasively expounded by Georges Sorel (1847–1922) in *Reflections on Violence* (1908). This book enshrined the general strike as a device to unite workers and gain them power. The strike tactic often conflicted with the socialist belief in aiding labor through state action. Strikes were common in France between 1905 and 1914, and the middle-class Radical ministry used troops to suppress them on more than one occasion.

Germany: Social Democrats and Revisionism

The negative judgment the Second International rendered against French socialist participation in bourgeois ministries reflected a policy of permanent hostility to nonsocialist governments that the German Social Democratic Party, or SPD, had already adopted. The organizational success of this party, more than any other single factor, kept Marxist socialism alive during the late nineteenth and early twentieth centuries.

The SDP had been founded in 1875. Its origins lay in the labor agitation of Ferdinand Lasalle (1825–1864), who wanted workers to participate in German politics. Wilhelm Liebknecht (1826–1900) and August Bebel (1840–1913), who were Marxists who opposed reformist politics, soon joined the party. Thus, from its founding, the SPD was divided between those who advocated reform and those who advocated revolution.

Bismarck's Repression of the SPD Twelve years of persecution under Bismarck forged the character of the SPD. The so-called Iron Chancellor believed socialism would undermine German politics and society. He used an assassination attempt on Emperor William I (r. 1861–1888) in 1878, in which the socialists were not involved, to steer antisocialist laws through the *Reichstag*. The measures suppressed the organization, meetings, newspapers, and other public activities of the SPD. Thereafter, to remain a socialist meant to remove oneself from the mainstream of respectable German life and possibly to lose one's job. The antisocialist legislation proved politically counterproductive. From the early 1880s onward, the SPD steadily polled more and more votes in elections to the *Reichstag*.

As simple repression failed to wean German workers from socialist loyalties, Bismarck undertook a program of social welfare legislation. In 1883, the German Empire adopted a health insurance measure. The next year the *Reichstag* enacted accident insurance legislation. Finally, in 1889, Bismarck sponsored a plan for old age and disability pensions. These programs, to which both workers and employers contributed, represented a paternalistic, conservative alternative to socialism. The state itself would organize a system of social security that did not require any change in the system of property holding or politics. Germany became the first major industrial nation to enjoy this kind of welfare program.

The Erfurt Program After forcing Bismarck's resignation mainly because of differences over foreign policy, Emperor William II (r. 1888–1918) allowed the antisocialist legislation to expire, hoping to build new political support among the working class. Even under the repressive laws, members of the SPD could sit in the *Reichstag*. With the repressive measures lifted, the party needed to decide what attitude to assume toward the German Empire.

The answer came in the Erfurt Program of 1891, formulated under the political guidance of Bebel and the ideological tutelage of Karl Kautsky (1854–1938). In good Marxist fashion, the program declared the imminent doom of capitalism and the necessity of socialist ownership of the means of production. The party intended to pursue these goals through legal political participation rather than by revolutionary activity. Kautsky argued that because capitalism by its very nature must collapse, the immediate task for socialists was to improve workers' lives rather than work for revolution, which was inevitable. So, although in theory the SPD was vehemently hostile to the German Empire, in practice the party functioned within its institutions. The SPD members of the *Reichstag* maintained clear political consciences by refusing to enter the cabinet (to which they were not invited anyway) and by refraining for many years from voting in favor of the military budget.

The Debate over Revisionism The dilemma of the SPD, however, generated the most important challenge within the socialist movement to the orthodox Marxist analysis of capitalism and the socialist revolution. The author of this socialist heresy, Eduard Bernstein (1850–1932), had lived in Britain and was familiar with the Fabians. Bernstein questioned whether Marx and his later orthodox followers, such as Kautsky, had been correct in their pessimistic appraisal of capitalism and the necessity of revolution. In *Evolutionary Socialism* (1899), Bernstein pointed to conditions that did not meet orthodox Marxists' expectations. The standard of living was rising in Europe. Stockholding was making the ownership of capitalist industry more widespread. The middle class was not falling into the ranks of the proletariat and was not identifying its problems with those of the workers. The inner contradictions of capitalism had simply not developed the way Marx had predicted. Moreover, the extension of the franchise to the working class meant that parliamentary methods might achieve revolutionary social change. For Bernstein, social reform through democratic institutions replaced revolution as the path to a humane socialist society. (See "Compare & Connect: Bernstein and Lenin Debate the Character of Tactics of European Socialism," pages, 718–719.)

Bernstein's doctrines, known as **Revisionism**, generated heated debate among German socialists, who finally condemned them. His critics argued that evolution toward social democracy might be possible in liberal, parliamentary Britain, but not in authoritarian, militaristic Germany, with its feeble *Reichstag.* Nonetheless, while still calling for revolution, the SPD pursued a course of action similar to what Bernstein advocated. Its trade union members, prospering within the German economy, did not want revolution. Its grassroots members wanted to be patriotic Germans as well as good socialists. Its leaders feared anything that might renew the persecution they had experienced under Bismarck.

Consequently, the SPD worked for electoral gains, expansion of its membership, and short-term political and social reform. It prospered and became one of the most important institutions of imperial Germany. Even middle-class Germans voted for it to oppose the illiberal institutions of the empire. In August 1914, after long debate among themselves, the SPD members of the *Reichstag* unanimously voted for the war credits that would finance Germany's participation in World War I.

Russia: Industrial Development and the Birth of Bolshevism

In the 1890s, Russia entered the industrial age and confronted many of the problems that the more advanced nations of the Continent had experienced fifty or seventy-five years earlier. Unlike those other countries, Russia had to deal with political discontent and economic development simultaneously. Russian socialism reflected that peculiar situation.

Witte's Program for Industrial Growth Tsar Alexander III (r. 1881–1894) and, after him, Nicholas II (r. 1894–1917) were determined that Russia should become an industrial power. Only by doing so, they believed, could the country maintain its position as a great power. Count Sergei Witte (1849–1915) led Russia into the industrial age. After a career in railways and other private business, he was appointed first minister of communications and then finance minister in 1892. Witte, who pursued a policy of planned economic development, protective tariffs, high taxes, putting Russia's currency on the gold standard, and efficiency in government and business, epitomized the nineteenth-century modernizer. He established a strong financial relationship with the French money market, which enabled Russia to finance its modernization program with French loans and which later led to diplomatic cooperation and an alliance between Russia and France.

Witte favored heavy industries. Between 1890 and 1904, the Russian railway system grew from 30,596 to 59,616 kilometers. The 5,000-mile-long Trans-Siberian Railroad was completed in 1903. Coal output more than tripled during the same period. Pig-iron production increased from 928,000 tons in 1890 to 4,641,000 tons in 1913. During the same period, steel production rose from 378,000 to 4,918,000 tons. Textile manufacturing continued to expand and was still the single largest industry. The factory system spread extensively.

Industrialism, however, also brought social discontent to Russia, as it had elsewhere. Landowners felt that foreign capitalists were earning too much of the profit.

The peasants saw their grain exports and tax payments finance development that did not measurably improve their lives. A small, but significant, industrial proletariat emerged. In 1900, Russia had approximately 3 million factory workers. Their working and living conditions were poor. (See "A Russian Social Investigator Describes the Condition of Children in the Moscow Tailoring Trade," page 716.) They enjoyed little state protection, and trade unions were illegal. In 1897, Witte did enact an 11.5-hour workday, but needless to say, discontent and strikes continued.

Similar social and economic problems arose in the countryside. Russian agriculture had not prospered after the emancipation of the serfs in 1861. The peasants remained burdened with redemption payments for the land they farmed, local taxes, excessive national taxes, and falling grain prices. Peasants did not own their land as individuals, but communally through the *mir*, or village. They farmed the land inefficiently through strip farming or by tilling small plots. Many free peasants with too little land to support their families had to work on large estates owned by nobles or for more prosperous peasant farmers, known as ***kulaks***. Between 1860 and 1914, the population of European Russia rose from about 50 million to around 103 million people. Land hunger and discontent spread among the peasants and sparked frequent uprisings in the countryside.

New political developments accompanied economic changes. The membership and intellectual roots of the Social Revolutionary Party, founded in 1901, reached back to the Populists of the 1870s. The new party opposed industrialism and looked to the communal life of rural Russia as a model for the future. In 1903, the Constitutional Democratic Party, or Cadets, was formed. This liberal party drew its members from those who participated in local councils called ***zemstvos***. Modeling themselves on the liberal parties of Western Europe, the Cadets wanted a constitutional monarchy under a parliamentary regime with civil liberties and economic progress.

Lenin's Early Thought and Career The situation of Russian socialists differed radically from that of socialists in other major European countries. Russia had no representative institutions and only a small working class. The compromises and accommodations achieved elsewhere were meaningless in Russia where socialists believed that in both theory and practice they must be revolutionary. The repressive policies of the tsarist regime required the Russian Social Democratic Party, founded in 1898, to function in exile. The party members greatly admired the German Social Democratic Party and adopted its Marxist ideology.

The leading late-nineteenth-century Russian Marxist was Gregory Plekhanov (1857–1918), who wrote from exile in Switzerland. At the turn of the century, his chief disciple was Vladimir Ilyich Ulyanov (1870–1924), who later took the name of Lenin. The future leader of the communist revolution was the son of a high bureaucrat. His older brother, while a student in Saint Petersburg, had become involved in radical politics; arrested for participating in a plot against Alexander III, he was executed in 1887. In 1893, Lenin moved to Saint Petersburg, where he studied law. Soon he, too, was drawn to the revolutionary groups among the factory workers. He was arrested in 1895 and exiled to Siberia. In 1900, after his release, Lenin left Russia for the West. He spent most of the next seventeen years in Switzerland.

There, Lenin became deeply involved in the disputes of the exiled Russian Social Democrats. They all considered themselves Marxists, but they differed on what a Marxist revolution would mean for primarily rural Russia and on how to structure their own party. Unlike the backward-looking Social Revolutionaries, the Social Democrats were modernizers who favored industrial development. Looking to Karl Marx's writings, most Russian Social Democrats believed Russia must develop a large proletariat before the Marxist revolution could come. They also hoped to build a mass political party like the German SPD.

Lenin dissented from both these ideas. In *What Is to Be Done?* (1902), he condemned any accommodations, such as those the German SPD practiced. He also criticized trade unionism that settled for short-term reformist gains rather than work for true revolutionary change for the working class. Lenin further rejected the concept of a mass democratic party composed of workers. Instead, he declared that revolutionary consciousness would not arise spontaneously from the working class. Rather, "people who make revolutionary activity their profession" must carry that consciousness to the workers.[3] Only a small, tightly organized elite party could possess the proper dedication to revolution and resist penetration by police spies. The guiding principle of that party should be "the strictest secrecy, the strictest selection of members, and the training of professional revolutionaries."[4] Lenin thus rejected both Kautsky's view that revolution was inevitable and Bernstein's view that democratic means could achieve revolutionary goals. Lenin substituted the small, professional, nondemocratic revolutionary party for Marx's proletariat as the instrument of revolutionary change. (See ""Compare & Connect: Bernstein and Lenin Debate the Character of Tactics of European Socialism," pages, 718–719.)

In 1903, at the London Congress of the Russian Social Democratic Party, Lenin forced a split in the party ranks. He and his followers lost many votes on questions put before the congress, but near its close they mustered a slim majority. Thereafter Lenin's faction assumed the name

[3]Quoted in Albert Fried and Ronald Sanders, eds., *Socialist Thought: A Documentary History* (Garden City, NY: Anchor Doubleday, 1964), p. 459.
[4]Fried and Sanders, *Socialist Thought*, p. 468.

A Russian Social Investigator Describes the Condition of Children in the Moscow Tailoring Trade

E.A. Oliunina was a young Russian woman who had been active among union organizers during the Revolution of 1905. Later, as a student at the Higher Women's Courses in Moscow, a school for women's postsecondary education, she began to investigate and to write about child garment workers. The clothes produced by these children might have ended up in Russian department stores that copied those in Paris, described in an earlier document in this chapter.

Why might the parents of these children have allowed them to work in these sweatshops? Why was alcoholism such a prevalent problem? Why does Oliunina regard schools as the solution to this problem?

Children begin their apprenticeship between the ages of twelve and thirteen, although one can find some ten- and eleven-year-olds working in the shops. . . .

Apprenticeship is generally very hard on children. At the beginning, they suffer enormously, particularly from the physical strain of having to do work well beyond the capacity of their years. They have to live in an environment where the level of morality is very low. Scenes of drunkenness and debauchery induce the boys to smoke and drink at an early age.

For example, in one subcontracting shop that made men's clothes, a fourteen-year-old boy worked together with twelve adults. When I visited there at four o'clock one Tuesday afternoon, the workers were half-drunk. Some were lying under the benches, others in the hallway. The boy was as drunk as the rest of them and lay there with a daredevil look on his face, dressed only in a pair of longjohns and a dirty, tattered shirt. He had been taught to drink at the age of twelve and could now keep up with the adults.

"Blue Monday" is a custom in most subcontracting shops that manufacture men's clothes. The whole workshop gets drunk, and work comes to a standstill. The apprentices do nothing but hang around. Many of the workers live in the workshop, so the boys are constantly exposed to all sorts of conversations and scenes. In one shop employing five workers and three boys, "Blue Monday" was a regular ritual. Even the owner himself is prone to alcoholic binges. In these kinds of situations, young girls are in danger of being abused by the owner or his sons. . . .

In Russia, there have been no measures taken to improve the working conditions of apprentices. As I have tried to show, the situation in workshops in no way provides apprentices with adequate training in their trade. The young workers are there only to be exploited. Merely limiting the number of apprentices would not better their position, nor would it eradicate the influx of cheap labor. An incomparably more effective solution would be to replace apprenticeship with a professional educational system and well-established safeguards for child workers. However, the only real solution to the exploitation of unpaid child labor is to introduce a minimum wage for minors.

Quoted in Victoria E. Bonnell, *The Russian Worker: Life and Labor Under the Tsarist Regime* (Berkeley: University of California Press, 1983), pp. 177, 180–181, 182–183.

Bolsheviks, meaning "majority," and the other, more moderate, democratic revolutionary faction came to be known as the **Mensheviks**, or "minority." There was, of course, a considerable public relations advantage to the name *Bolshevik.* (In 1912, the Bolsheviks organized themselves as a separate party.)

A fundamental organizational difference had existed between what in 1903 were the two chief factions of the

In this photograph taken in 1895, Lenin sits at the table among a group of other young Russian radicals from Saint Petersburg. CORBIS/Bettmann

Russian Social Democratic Party. The Mensheviks wanted a party with a mass membership, similar to the German SDP and other West European socialist parties, which would function democratically. The Bolsheviks intended the party to consist of elite professional revolutionaries who would provide centralized leadership for the working class. Lenin believed a mass party functioning in a democratic fashion would seek only to reform workers' wages, hours, and living conditions, whereas he wanted a revolution that would transform Russia.

In 1905, Lenin complemented his organizational theory with a program for revolution in Russia. In *Two Tactics of Social Democracy in the Bourgeois-Democratic Revolution*, he urged the socialist revolution to unite the proletariat and the peasantry. Lenin grasped better than any other revolutionary the profound discontent in the Russian countryside. He believed the tsarist government probably could not suppress an alliance of workers and peasants in rebellion.

Lenin's two principles—an elite party and a dual social revolution—guided later Bolshevik activity. The Bolsheviks ultimately seized power in November 1917, transforming the political landscape of the twentieth century, but they did so only after the turmoil of World War I had undermined support for the tsar and only after other political forces had already toppled the tsarist government in February 1917. Before World War I, the Bolsheviks constituted the odd man out in European socialist politics; they exerted no significant prewar influence on members of other socialist groups, who, in general, ignored them. For their part, the Bolsheviks responded by scorning the West European socialist parties that worked within their nations' political systems. Between 1900 and the outbreak of World War I, the government of Nicholas II managed to confront political upheaval more or less successfully.

The Revolution of 1905 and Its Aftermath The quarrels among the exiled Russian socialists and Lenin's doctrines had no immediate influence on events in Russia. Industrialization continued to stir resentment. In 1903, Nicholas II dismissed Witte, hoping to quell the criticism. The next year, in response to conflicts over Manchuria and Korea, Russia went to war against Japan, partly in hopes the conflict would rally public opinion to the tsar. Instead, the Russians lost the war, and the government faced an internal political crisis. The Japanese captured Port Arthur, Russia's naval base on the coast of China, early in 1905. A few days later, on January 22, a Russian Orthodox priest named Father George Gapon led several hundred workers to present a petition to the tsar to improve industrial conditions. The petioners did not know that the tsar was not even in Saint Petersburg,

COMPARE AND CONNECT

Bernstein and Lenin Debate the Character of Tactics of European Socialism

BY THE CLOSE of the nineteenth century the European Socialist movement found itself sharply divided over its future goals and tactics. On the one side some socialists, here represented by Eduard Bernstein, came to reject many of the ideas of Karl Marx, particularly that of a proletarian revolution, and embraced democratic politics as the best way to realize their goals of the improvement of the life of the working class. Others, a minority at the time, represented here by Lenin, rejected democracy and embraced the concept of violent revolution achieved by a small professional elite rather than by a spontaneous proletarian uprising. In the twentieth century after the 1917 Bolshevik Revolution in Russia, those divisions would play themselves out in an enormously hostile conflict between democratic socialist parties in Western Europe and Communists in the Soviet Union and Communist parties in Western Europe dominated by the Soviet Union. (See Chapters 26 and 27.)

QUESTIONS

1. **According to Bernstein, what specific predictions in the *Communist Manifesto* failed to materialize?**
2. **Why is the advance of democracy important to Bernstein's argument? Why does he renounce the concept of a "dictatorship of the proletariat"?**
3. **What does Lenin mean by "professional revolutionaries"? Why does Russia need such revolutionaries?**
4. **How does Lenin reconcile his antidemocratic views to the goal of aiding the working class?**
5. **How could the ideas of both Bernstein and Lenin be seen as departures from Marx's own thinking?**

I. Eduard Bernstein Urges Socialists to Embrace Democracy

Eduard Bernstein was responsible for the emergence of Revisionism within the German Social Democratic Party. He was a dedicated socialist who recognized that Marx's Communist Manifesto *(1848) had not predicted the actual future of the European working classes. Bernstein believed the capitalist system would not suddenly collapse and that socialists should change their tactics to achieve democratic political rights and pursue reform instead of revolution. (Compare this document with the passages from* The Communist Manifesto *in Chapter 21.)*

Social conditions have not developed to such an acute opposition of things and classes as is depicted in the [*Communist*] *Manifesto*. . . . The number of members of the possessing classes is today not smaller but larger. The enormous increase of social wealth is not accompanied by a decreasing number of large capitalists but by an increasing number of capitalists of all degrees. . . .

In all advanced countries we see the privileges of the capitalist bourgeoisie yielding step by step to democratic organizations. . . .

The conquest of political power by the working classes, the expropriation of capitalists, are not ends in themselves but only means for the accomplishment of certain aims and endeavours. . . .

Democracy is in principle the suppression of class government, though it is not yet the actual suppression of classes. . . . The right to vote in a democracy makes its members virtually partners in the community, and this virtual partnership must in the end lead to real partnership. . . .

Universal franchise is, from two sides, the alternative to a violent revolution. But universal suffrage is only a part of democracy, although a part which in time must draw the other parts after it as the magnet attracts to itself the scattered portions of iron. It certainly proceeds more slowly than many would wish, but in spite of that it is at work. And social democracy cannot further this work better than by taking its stand unreserved only the theory of democracy—on the ground of universal suffrage with all the consequences resulting therefrom to its tactics. . . .

Is there any sense . . . in maintaining the phrase of the 'dictatorship of the proletariot' at a time when in all possible places representatives of social democracy have placed themselves practically in the arena of Parliamentary work, have declared for the proportional representation of the people, and for direct legislation—all of which is inconsistent with a dictatorship.

The phrase is to-day so antiquated that is is only to be reconciled with reality by stripping the word dictatorship of its actual meaning and attaching to it some kind of weakened interpretation. The whole practical activity of social democracy is directed towards creating circumstances and condition which shall render possible and secure a transition (free from convulsive outbursts) of the modern social order to a higher one.

Source: From Eduard Bernstein, *Evolutionary Socialism: A Criticism and Affirmation, 1899* (New York: Schocken Books, 1961), pp. xxiv–xxv, xxix, 143–146.

II. Lenin Argues for the Necessity of a Secret and Elite Party of Professional Revolutionaries

Social democratic parties in Western Europe had mass memberships and were generally democratic organizations. In this passage from What Is to Be Done? *(1902), Lenin explains why the autocratic political conditions of Russia demanded a different kind of organization for the Russian Social Democratic Party. Lenin's ideas became the guiding principles of Bolshevik organization. Lenin departed from Marx's own thought by urging the necessity of fulminating revolution rather than waiting for it to occur as a necessary result of the collapse of capitalism.*

I assert that it is far more difficult [for government police] to unearth a dozen wise men than a hundred fools. This position I will defend, no matter how much you instigate the masses against me for my "anti-democratic" views, etc. As I have stated repeatedly, by "wise men," in connection with organization, I mean professional revolutionaries, irrespective of whether they have developed from among students or working men. I assert: (1) that no revolutionary movement can endure without a stable organization of leaders maintaining continuity; (2) that the broader the popular mass drawn spontaneously into the struggle, which forms the basis of the movement and participates in it, the more urgent the need for such an organization, and the more solid this organization must be . . .; (3) that such an organization must consist chiefly of people professionally engaged in revolutionary activity; (4) that in an autocratic state [such as Russia], the more we confine the membership of such an organization to people who are professionally engaged in revolutionary activity and who have been professionally trained in the art of combating the political police, the more difficult will it be to unearth the organization; and (5) the greater will be the number of people from the working class and from other social classes who will be able to join the movement and perform active work in it . . . .

The only serious organization principle for the active workers of our movement should be the strictest secrecy, the strictest selection of members, and the training of professional revolutionaries.

Source: From Albert Fried and Ronald Sanders, eds. *Socialist Thought: A Documentary History* (Garden City, NY: Anchor Doubleday, 1964), pp. 460, 468.

By the close of the nineteenth century, European socialists had come to doubt whether the industrial proletariat around the world, such as these workers in the United States, would or could actually bring about a revolution as predicted by Marx. Eduard Bernstein thought democratic social change would improve the lot of workers. Lenin believed an elite revolutionary party would produce such radical change. Courtesy of the Library of Congress but as they approached the Winter Palace, troops opened fire, killing approximately forty people and wounding hundreds of others. As word of this massacre spread, and large, angry crowds gathered elsewhere in the city, the military shot more people. The final death toll was approximately two hundred killed and eight hundred wounded, though at the time rumors made the numbers much larger. The day, soon known as Bloody Sunday, marked a turning point. Vast numbers of ordinary Russians came to believe they could no longer trust the tsar or his government.

During the next ten months, revolutionary disturbances spread throughout Russia. Sailors mutinied, workers went on strike, peasants revolted, and property was attacked. The uncle of Nicholas II was assassinated in Moscow. Liberal leaders of the Constitutional Democratic Party from the *zemstvos* demanded political reform. University students went on strike. Social Revolutionaries and Social Democrats agitated among urban working groups. In early October 1905, strikes broke out in Saint Petersburg, and for all practical purposes, worker groups, called **soviets**, controlled the city. Nicholas II, who had recalled Witte, issued the October Manifesto, which promised Russia a constitutional government.

Early in 1906, Nicholas II announced the creation of a representative body, the **Duma**, with two chambers. He reserved to himself, however, ministerial appointments, financial policy, and military and foreign affairs. The April elections returned a highly radical group of representatives. The tsar then replaced Witte with P. A. Stolypin (1862–1911), who had little sympathy for parliamentary government. Stolypin persuaded Nicholas to dissolve the Duma. A second assembly was elected in February 1907. Again, cooperation proved impossible, and the tsar dissolved that Duma in June. A third Duma, elected in late 1907 on the basis of a more conservative franchise, proved sufficiently pliable for the tsar and his minister. Thus, within two years of the 1905 Revolution, Nicholas II had recaptured much of the ground he had conceded.

Stolypin set about repressing rebellion, removing some causes of the revolt, and rallying property owners behind the tsarist regime. Early in 1907, special field courts-martial condemned almost 700 rebellious peasants to death. Before undertaking this repression, Stolypin, in November 1906, had canceled any redemptive payments that the peasants still owed the government from the emancipation of the serfs in 1861. He took this step to encourage peasants to assume individual proprietorship of the land they farmed and to abandon the communal system of the *mirs.* Stolypin believed farmers would be more productive working for themselves. Combined with a program to instruct peasants on how to farm more efficiently, this policy improved agricultural production. However, many peasant small-holders sold their land and joined the industrial labor force.

MAJOR DATES IN THE DEVELOPMENT OF SOCIALISM

1864	International Working Men's Association (the First International) founded
1875	German Social Democratic Party founded
1876	First International dissolved
1878	German antisocialist laws passed
1884	British Fabian Society founded
1889	Second International founded
1891	German antisocialist laws permitted to expire
1891	German Social Democratic Party's Erfurt Program
1895	French Confédération Générale du Travail founded
1899	Eduard Bernstein's *Evolutionary Socialism*
1902	The British Labour Party founded
1902	Lenin's *What Is to Be Done?*
1903	Bolshevik-Menshevik split
1904	"Opportunism" rejected at the Amsterdam Congress of the Second International

The moderate liberals who sat in the Duma approved of the new land measures. They liked the idea of competition and individual property ownership. The Constitutional Democrats wanted a more genuinely parliamentary mode of government, but they compromised out of fear of new revolutionary disturbances. Hatred of Stolypin was still widespread, however, among the country's older conservative groups, and industrial workers remained antagonistic to the tsar. In 1911, Stolypin was assassinated by a Social Revolutionary, who may have been a police agent in the pay of conservatives. Nicholas II found no worthy successor. His government simply muddled along.

Meanwhile, at court, the monk Grigory Efimovich Rasputin (1871?–1916) gained ascendancy with the tsar and his wife because of his alleged power to heal the tsar's hemophilic son Alexis, the heir to the throne, when medicine proved unable to help the boy. The undue influence of this strange, uncouth man, as well as continued social discontent and conservative resistance to any further liberal reforms, undermined the position of the tsar and his government after 1911. Once again, as in 1904, he and his ministers thought that some bold move in foreign policy might bring the regime the popular support it desperately needed.

A Closer LOOK

BLOODY SUNDAY, ST. PETERSBURG 1905

ON BLOODY SUNDAY, January 22, 1905, troops of Tsar Nicholas II fired on a peaceful procession of workers at the Winter Palace who sought to present a petition for better working and living conditions. The scene portrayed here depicts one of the enduring images of events leading to the subsequent Russian Revolutions of 1905 and 1917. It figured in at least two movies: the 1925 anti-tsarist Soviet silent film called *The Ninth of January*, and *Nicholas and Alexandra*, the lavish 1971 movie that was sympathetic to the tsar and blamed Bloody Sunday on frightened and incompetent officials. While Nicholas had not ordered the troops to fire and was not even in St. Petersburg on Bloody Sunday, the event all but destroyed any chance of reconciliation between the tsarist government and the Russian working class.

The workers are visibly defenseless in the face of the rifles being fired at them.

Although the square before the Winter Palace toward the right of the troops is large and might have allowed an escape route of sorts for the workers' procession, the troops forced the crowd into an area of narrow escape.

Bildarchiv Preussischer Kulturbesitz

The view is the one that officials in the Winter Palace, which lay behind the row of troops with rifles, would have seen.

To examine this image in an interactive fashion, please go to www.myhistorylab.com

PEARSON myhistorylab

MAJOR DATES IN TURN-OF-THE-CENTURY RUSSIAN HISTORY

1892	Witte appointed finance minister
1895	Lenin arrested and sent to Siberia
1897	11.5-hour workday established
1898	Russian Social Democratic Party founded
1900	Lenin leaves Russia for western Europe
1901	Social Revolutionary Party founded
1903	Constitutional Democratic Party (Cadets) founded
1903	Bolshevik-Menshevik split
1903	Witte dismissed
1904	Russo-Japanese War begins
1905 (January)	Japan defeats Russia
1905 (January 22)	Revolution breaks out in Saint Petersburg after Bloody Sunday
1905 (October 20)	General strike
1905 (October 26)	October Manifesto establishes constitutional government
1906 (May 10)	First Duma meets
1906 (June)	Stolypin appointed prime minister
1906 (July 21)	Dissolution of first Duma
1906 (November)	Land redemption payments canceled for peasants
1907 (March 5–16)	Second Duma seated and dismissed in June
1907	Franchise changed and a third Duma elected, which sits until 1912
1911	Stolypin assassinated by a Social Revolutionary
1912	Fourth Duma elected
1914	World War I breaks out

In Perspective

From 1860 through 1914, two apparently contradictory developments emerged in European social life. On one hand, the lifestyle of the urban middle classes became the model to which much of society aspired. The characteristics of this lifestyle included a relatively small family living in its own house or large apartment, servants, and a wife who did not earn an income. The middle classes, in general, benefited from the many material comforts that the Second Industrial Revolution had generated.

During the same period, the forces of socialism and labor unions assumed a new and major role in European political life. Their leaders demanded greater social justice and a fairer distribution of the vast quantities of consumer goods Europe was producing. Some socialists sought in one way or another to work within existing political systems. Others—particularly, those in Russia—advocated revolution. The growth in wealth and the availability of new goods and services magnified the injustices the poor suffered, and the contrast between them and the middle classes made the demands of labor and the socialists more strident. In Russia, the strains of the early stages of industrialization intensified social unrest. These strains, compounded by the humiliating defeat in a war against Japan, triggered the unsuccessful revolution of 1905.

The working class, however, was not alone in seeking change. Women, for the first time in European history, began in significant ways to demand a political role and to protest the gender inequalities embedded in law and family life. They were beginning to enter the professions and were taking a significant role in the service economy, such as the new telephone companies. These changes, as much as the demands of socialists, would, in time, raise questions about the adequacy of the much admired late-nineteenth-century middle-class lifestyle.

REVIEW QUESTIONS

1. How did the Second Industrial Revolution transform European society? What new industries developed, and which do you think had the greatest impact in the twentieth century? Why did European economic growth slacken in the second half of the nineteenth century?
2. Why were European cities redesigned during the late nineteenth century? Why were housing and health key issues for urban reform?
3. What was the status of European women in the second half of the nineteenth century? Why did they grow discontented with their lot? What factors led to change? To what extent had they improved their position by 1914? What tactics did they use to effect change? Was the emancipation of women inevitable? How did women approach their situation differently from country to country?
4. What were the major characteristics of Jewish emancipation in the nineteenth century?
5. What was the status of the European working classes in 1860? Had it improved by 1914? Why did trade unions and organized mass political parties grow? Why were the debates over "opportunism" and "revisionism" important to the Western European socialist parties?
6. What were the benefits and drawbacks of industrialization for Russia? Were the tsars wise to attempt to modernize their country, or should they have left it as it was? How did Lenin's view of socialism differ from that of the socialists in Western Europe?

SUGGESTED READINGS

A. Ascher, *P. A. Stolypin: The Search for Stability in Late Imperial Russia* (2000). A broad-ranging biography based on extensive research.

P. Birnbaum, *Jewish Destinies: Citizenship, State, and Community in Modern France* (2000). Explores the subject from the French Revolution to the present.

J. Bush, *Women Against the Vote: Female Anti-Suffragism in Britain* (2007). An important study of British women opposed to the extension of the vote to women.

T. W. Clyman and J. Vowles, *Russia through Women's Eyes: Autobiographies from Tsarist Russia* (1996). A splendid collection of relatively brief memoirs.

G. Crossick and S. Jaumain, eds., *Cathedrals of Consumption: The European Department Store, 1850–1939* (1999). Essays on the development of a new mode of distribution of consumer goods.

D. Ellenson, *After Emancipation: Jewish Religious Responses to Modernity* (2004). A volume that explores numerous examples of this response across Europe.

A. Geifman, *Thou Shalt Kill: Revolutionary Terrorism in Russia, 1894–1917* (1993). An examination of political violence in late imperial Russia.

R. F. Hamilton, *Marxism, Revisionism, and Leninism: Explication, Assessment, and Commentary* (2000). A contribution by a historically-minded sociologist.

J. Harsin, *Policing Prostitution in Nineteenth-Century Paris* (1985). A major study of this significant subject in French social history.

G. Himmelfarb, *Poverty and Compassion: The Moral Imagination of the Late Victorians* (1991). The best examination of late Victorian social thought.

E. Hobsbawm, *The Age of Empire, 1875–1914* (1987). A stimulating survey that covers cultural as well as political developments.

S. S. Holton, *Feminism and Democracy: Women's Suffrage and Reform Politics in Britain, 1900–1918* (1986). An excellent treatment of the subject.

T. Hoppen, *The Mid-Victorian Generation, 1846–1886* (1998). The most extensive treatment of the subject.

S. Kovin, *Slumming: Sexual and Social Politics in Victorian London* (2004). Explores the complexities of the extension of charity and social services in late Victorian London.

M. Malia, *Russia under Western Eyes: From the Bronze Horseman to the Lenin Mausoleum* (2000). A brilliant work on how Western intellectuals understood Russia.

E. D. Rappaport, *Shopping for Pleasure: Women in the Making of London's West End* (2001). A study of the rise of department stores in London.

H. Rogger, *Jewish Policies and Right-Wing Politics in Imperial Russia* (1986). A learned examination of Russian anti-Semitism.

M. L. Rozenblit, *The Jews of Vienna, 1867–1914: Assimilation and Identity* (1983). Covers the cultural, economic, and political life of Viennese Jews.

R. Service, *Lenin: A Biography* (2002). Based on new sources and will no doubt become the standard biography.

D. Sorkin, *The Transformation of German Jewry, 1780–1840* (1987). An examination of Jewish emancipation in Germany.

G. P. Steenson, *Not One Man! Not One Penny!: German Social Democracy, 1863–1914* (1999). An extensive survey.

N. Stone, *Europe Transformed* (1984). A sweeping survey that emphasizes the difficulties of late-nineteenth-century liberalism.

A. Thorpe, *A History of the British Labour Party* (2001). From its inception to the twenty-first century.

J. R. Walkowitz, *Prostitution and Victorian Society: Women, Class, and the State* (1980). A work of great insight and sensitivity.

For additional learning resources related to this chapter, please go to www.myhistorylab.com

PEARSON myhistorylab

Darwin's theories about the evolution of humankind from the higher primates aroused enormous controversy. This caricature shows him with a monkey's body holding a mirror to an apelike creature. National History Museum, London, UK/Bridgeman Art Library

24 The Birth of Modern European Thought

▼ **The New Reading Public**

Advances in Primary Education • Reading Material for the Mass Audience

▼ **Science at Midcentury**

Comte, Positivism, and the Prestige of Science • Darwin's Theory of Natural Selection • Science and Ethics—Social Darwinism

▼ **Christianity and the Church Under Siege**

Intellectual Skepticism • Conflict Between Church and State • Areas of Religious Revival • The Roman Catholic Church and the Modern World • Islam and Late-Nineteenth-Century European Thought

▼ **Toward a Twentieth-Century Frame of Mind**

Science: The Revolution in Physics • Literature: Realism and Naturalism • Modernism in Literature • The Coming of Modern Art • Friedrich Nietzsche and the Revolt Against Reason • The Birth of Psychoanalysis • Retreat from Rationalism in Politics • Racism • Anti-Semitism and the Birth of Zionism

▼ **Women and Modern Thought**

Antifeminism in Late-Century Thought • New Directions in Feminism

▼ **In Perspective**

KEY TOPICS

- **The dominance of science in the thought of the second half of the nineteenth century**
- **The conflict between church and state over education**
- **Islam and late-nineteenth-century European thought**
- **The effect of modernism in literature and art, psychoanalysis, and the revolution in physics on intellectual life**
- **Racism and the resurgence of anti-Semitism**
- **Late-nineteenth- and early-twentieth-century developments in feminism**

DURING THE SAME period that the modern nation-state developed and the Second Industrial Revolution laid the foundations for modern life, the ideas that marked European thought for much of the twentieth century and beyond took shape. Like previous intellectual changes, these arose from earlier patterns of thought. The Enlightenment provided late-nineteenth-century Europeans with a heritage of rationalism, toleration, cosmopolitanism, and an appreciation of science. Romanticism led them to value feelings, imagination, national identity, and the autonomy of the artistic experience.

By 1900, these strands of thought had become woven into a new fabric. Many of the traditional intellectual signposts were disappearing. Christianity had experienced the most severe intellectual attack in its history. The picture of the physical world prevailing since Newton had undergone major modification. Darwin and Freud had challenged the special place that Western thinkers had assigned to humankind. Writers began to question rationality. The humanitarian ideals of liberalism and socialism gave way to aggressive nationalism. European intellectuals were more daring than ever before, but they were also probably less certain and optimistic.

▾ The New Reading Public

The social context of intellectual life changed in the latter part of the nineteenth century. For the first time in Europe, a mass reading public came into existence as more people than ever before became drawn into the world of print culture. In 1850, about half the population of Western Europe and a much higher proportion of Russians were illiterate. That situation changed during the next half century.

Advances in Primary Education

Literacy on the Continent improved steadily from the 1860s onward as governments financed education. Hungary provided elementary education in 1868, Britain in 1870, Switzerland in 1874, Italy in 1877, and France between 1878 and 1881. The already advanced education system of Prussia was extended throughout the German Empire after 1871. By 1900, in Britain, France, Belgium, the Netherlands, Germany, and Scandinavia, approximately 85 percent or more of the people could read, but Italy, Spain, Russia, Austria-Hungary, and the Balkans still had illiteracy rates of between 30 and 60 percent.

Public education became widespread in Europe during the second half of the nineteenth century and women came to dominate the profession of school teaching, especially at the elementary level. This 1905 photograph shows English schoolchildren going through morning drills. © Hulton-Deutsch Collection/CORBIS

The new primary education in the basic skills of reading, writing, and elementary arithmetic reflected and generated social change. Both liberals and conservatives regarded such minimal training as necessary for orderly political behavior by the newly enfranchised voters. They also hoped that literacy would create a more productive labor force. This side of the educational crusade embodied the Enlightenment faith that right knowledge would lead to right action.

Literacy and its extension, however, soon became a force in its own right. The school-teaching profession grew rapidly in numbers and prestige and, as noted in Chapter 23, became a major area for the employment of women. Those people who learned to read soon discovered that much of the education that led to better jobs and political influence was still open only to those who could afford it. Having created systems of primary education, the major nations had to give further attention to secondary education by the time of World War I. In another generation, the question would become one of democratic university instruction.

Reading Material for the Mass Audience

The expanding literate population created a vast market for new reading material. The number of newspapers, books, magazines, mail-order catalogs, and libraries grew rapidly. Cheap mass-circulation newspapers, such as *Le Petit Journal* of Paris and the *Daily Mail* and *Daily Express* of London, enjoyed their first heyday. Such newspapers carried advertising that alerted readers to the new consumer products available through the Second Industrial Revolution. Other publishers produced newspapers with specialized political or religious viewpoints. The number of monthly and quarterly journals for families, women, and freethinking intellectuals increased. Probably more people with different ideas could get into print in the late nineteenth century than ever before in European history. In addition, more people could read their ideas than ever before.

Because many of the new readers were only marginally literate and still ignorant about many subjects, the books and journals catering to them were often mediocre. The cheap newspapers prospered on stories of sensational crimes and political scandal and on pages of advertising. Religious journals depended on denominational rivalry. A brisk market existed for pornography. Newspapers with editorials on the front page became major factors in the emerging mass politics. The news could be managed, but in central Europe more often by the government censor than by the publisher.

Critics pointed to the low level of public taste, but the new education, the new readers, and the myriad of new books and journals permitted a popularization of knowledge that has become a hallmark of our world. The new literacy was the intellectual parallel of the railroad and the steamship. People could leave their original intellectual surroundings because literacy is not an end in itself but leads to other skills and other knowledge.

▼ Science at Midcentury

In about 1850, Voltaire (1694–1778) would have felt at home in a general discussion of scientific concepts. The basic Newtonian picture of physical nature that he had popularized still prevailed. Scientists continued to believe that nature operates as a vast machine according to mechanical principles. At midcentury, learned persons regarded the physical world as rational, mechanical, and dependable. Experiment and observation could reveal its laws objectively. Scientific theory purportedly described physical nature as it really existed. Moreover, by 1850, science had a strong institutional life in French and German universities and in new professional societies. William Whewell of Cambridge University had invented the word "scientist" in the early 1830s, and it was in common use by the end of the century. (See "Encountering the Past: The Birth of Science Fiction.")

Comte, Positivism, and the Prestige of Science

During the early nineteenth century, science had continued to establish itself as the model for all human knowledge. The French philosopher Auguste Comte (1798–1857), a late child of the Enlightenment and a onetime follower of Saint-Simon, developed **positivism**, a philosophy of human intellectual development that culminated in science. In *The Positive Philosophy* (1830–1842), Comte argued that human thought had developed in three stages. In the first, or theological, stage, physical nature was explained in terms of the action of divinities or spirits. In the second, or metaphysical, stage, abstract principles were regarded as the operative agencies of nature. In the final, or positive stage, explanations of nature became matters of exact description of phenomena, without recourse to an unobservable operative principle.

Physical science had, in Comte's view, entered the positive stage, and similar thinking should penetrate other areas of analysis. In particular, Comte believed that positive laws of social behavior could be discovered in the same fashion as laws of physical nature. He is, thus, generally regarded as the father of sociology. Works like Comte's helped convince learned Europeans that all knowledge must resemble scientific knowledge.

THE BIRTH OF SCIENCE FICTION

DURING THE RENAISSANCE many European writers composed works about fantasy voyages to distant lands. In the seventeenth century, authors published some two hundred accounts of trips to the moon. Throughout the nineteenth century, other authors told tales of fantastic voyages into space or beneath the earth.

However, the real father of today's works of popular science fiction was Jules Verne (1828–1905). His *Five Weeks in a Balloon* (1863), a tale of a balloon trip across Africa, sold so well that a French publisher immediately gave Verne a contract to write two such stories each year for a magazine. So influential was Verne's image of the future that the United States named its first atomic submarine the *Nautilus* after the vessel the mysterious Captain Nemo commanded in Verne's *Twenty Thousand Leagues under the Sea* (1870).

Verne prided himself on his scientific veracity. He also located his stories in his own age. Readers felt they were experiencing a contemporary adventure.

Toward the turn of the century, science fiction found another master in the English novelist H. G. Wells (1866–1946), who in 1895 published *The Time Machine* in which the characters travel through time. Wells's first success was rapidly followed by *The Island of Dr. Moreau* (1896) about a mad surgeon's inhuman experiments on animals, and *The War of the Worlds* (1898) about a Martian invasion of the earth. Wells invented many of the devices, such as new stars appearing near the solar system, Martians and other planetary creatures unfriendly to humans, machinery that goes astray, and strange diseases, that would become the stock in trade for later science fiction writers.

Verne, Wells, and their many imitators published their stories in cheap illustrated magazines with mass circulations. Consequently, science fiction immediately entered popular culture. Throughout the twentieth century popular movies and television series were made based on the stories of both Verne and Wells. In 1938, when Orson Welles (1915–1985) broadcast Wells's *War of the Worlds* over the radio, many Americans actually believed Martians had landed in New Jersey. The works of Verne and Wells continue to influence the writing of science fiction.

Source: P. Nichols and J. Clute, *The Encyclopedia of Science Fiction* (New York: St. Martin's Press, 1995); Dieter Wuckel and Bruce Cassidy, *The Illustrated History of Science Fiction* (New York: Ungar, 1986); David Kyle, *A Pictorial History of Science Fiction* (London: Hamlyn, 1976).

Why is Jules Verne considered the father of modern science fiction?

What enduring plot devices did H. G. Wells introduce?

Why did science fiction become so popular?

Captain Nemo's submarine confronts a giant octopus in Verne's *Twenty Thousand Leagues under the Sea.* © Bettman/CORBIS

From the mid-nineteenth century onward, the links of science to the technology of the Second Industrial Revolution made the general European public aware of science and technology as never before. The British Fabian socialist Beatrice Webb (1858–1943) recalled this situation from her youth:

> Who will deny that the men of science were the leading British intellectuals of that period; that it was they who stood out as men of genius with international reputations; that it was they who were the self-confident militants of the period; that it was they who were routing the theologians, confounding the mystics, imposing their theories on philosophers, their inventions on capitalists, and their discoveries on medical men; whilst they were at the same time snubbing the artists, ignoring the poets, and even casting doubts on the capacity of the politicians?[1]

Her remarks would have applied in every industrialized nation in Europe. Writers spoke of a religion of science that would explain all nature without resorting to supernaturalism. Popularizers, such as Thomas Henry Huxley (1825–1895) in Britain and Ernst Haeckel (1834–1919) in Germany, worked to gain government support of scientific research and to include science in the schools and universities.

Darwin's Theory of Natural Selection

In 1859, Charles Darwin (1809–1882) published *On the Origin of Species*, which carried the mechanical interpretation of physical nature into the world of living things. The book was one of the seminal works of Western thought and earned Darwin the honor of being regarded as the "Newton of biology." Both Darwin and his book have been much misunderstood. He did not originate the concept of evolution, which had been discussed widely before he wrote. What he and Alfred Russel Wallace (1823–1913) did, working independently, was to formulate the principle of natural selection, which explained how species had changed or evolved over time. Earlier writers had believed evolution might occur; Darwin and Wallace explained how it could occur.

Drawing on Malthus, the two scientists contended that more living organisms come into existence than can survive in their environment. Those organisms with a marginal advantage in the struggle for existence live long enough to propagate. This principle of survival of the fittest Darwin called **natural selection**. It was naturalistic and mechanistic, requiring no guiding mind behind the development in organic nature. What neither Darwin nor anyone else in his day could explain was the origin of those chance variations that provided some living things with the marginal chance for survival. Only after 1900, when the work on heredity of the Austrian monk, Gregor Mendel (1822–1884), received public attention, did the mystery of those variations begin to be unraveled.

Darwin and Wallace's theory represented the triumph of naturalistic explanation, which removed the idea of purpose from organic nature. Eyes were not made for seeing according to the rational wisdom and purpose of God, but had developed mechanistically over time. Thus, the theory of evolution through natural selection not only contradicted the biblical narrative of the Creation but also undermined both the deistic argument for the existence of God from the design of the universe and the whole concept of fixity in nature or the universe at large. The world was a realm of flux. The idea that physical and organic nature might be constantly changing allowed people to believe that society, values, customs, and beliefs should also change.

In 1871, in *The Descent of Man*, Darwin applied the principle of evolution by natural selection to human beings. Darwin was hardly the first person to treat human beings as animals, but he contended that humankind's moral nature and religious sentiments, as well as its physical frame, had developed naturalistically largely in response to the requirements of survival. Neither the origin nor the character of humankind, in Darwin's view, required the existence of a god for their explanation. Not since Copernicus had removed the earth from the center of the universe had the pride of Western human beings received so sharp a blow.

Darwin's theory of evolution by natural selection was controversial from the moment *On the Origin of Species* appeared. It encountered criticism from both the religious and the scientific communities. By the end of the century, scientists widely accepted the concept of evolution, but not yet Darwin's mechanism of natural selection. The acceptance of the latter really dates from the 1920s and 1930s, when Darwin's theory was combined with modern genetics.

Science and Ethics—Social Darwinism

One area in which science came to have a new significance was social thought and ethics. Philosophers applied the concept of the struggle for survival to human social relationships. The phrase "survival of the fittest" predated Darwin and reflected the competitive outlook of classical economics. Darwin's use of the phrase gave it the prestige associated with advanced science.

The most famous advocate of evolutionary ethics was Herbert Spencer (1820–1903), a British philosopher. Spencer, a strong individualist, believed human society progresses through competition. If the weak receive too much protection, the rest of humankind is the loser. In Spencer's work, struggle against one's fellow human beings became a kind of ethical imperative. The concept could be applied to justify not aiding the poor and the

[1]Beatrice Webb, *My Apprenticeship* (London: Longmans, Green, 1926), pp. 130–131.

working class or to justify the domination of colonial peoples or to advocate aggressive competition among nations. Evolutionary ethics and similar concepts, all of which are usually termed ***Social Darwinism***, often came close to saying that "might makes right."

One of the chief opponents of such thinking was Thomas Henry Huxley, the great defender of Darwin. In 1893, Huxley declared that the physical process of evolution was at odds with human ethical development. The struggle in nature only showed how human beings should not behave. (See "Compare & Connect: The Debate over Social Darwinism," pages 730–731.) Despite Huxley's arguments, the ideas of Social Darwinism continued to influence thought and public policy on both sides of the Atlantic.

▼ Christianity and the Church Under Siege

The nineteenth century was one of the most difficult periods in the history of the organized Christian churches. Many European intellectuals left the faith. The secular, liberal nation-states attacked the influence of the church. The expansion of population and the growth of cities challenged its organizational capacity. Yet during all this turmoil, the Protestant and Catholic churches continued to draw much popular support and personal religious devotion. Furthermore, as will be seen in the next chapter, the same decades marked by skepticism among many European intellectuals saw the burgeoning of the Christian missionary movement around the globe. Nonetheless, what would in the twentieth century become the overwhelmingly secular character of European society, a development that now largely distinguishes Europe from the United States, had its roots in the changes that commenced in the late nineteenth century.

Intellectual Skepticism

The intellectual attack on Christianity challenged its historical credibility, its scientific accuracy, and its morality. The philosophes of the Enlightenment had delighted in pointing out contradictions in the Bible. The historical scholarship of the nineteenth century brought new issues to the foreground.

History In 1835, David Friedrich Strauss (1808–1874) published *The Life of Jesus*, in which he questioned whether the Bible provides any genuine historical evidence about Jesus. Strauss contended the story of Jesus is a myth that arose from the particular social and intellectual conditions of first-century Palestine. Jesus' character and life represent the aspirations of the people of that time and place, rather than events that actually occurred. Other authors also published skeptical examinations of the life of Jesus.

During the second half of the century, scholars such as Julius Wellhausen (1844–1918) in Germany, Ernst Renan (1823–1892) in France, and Matthew Arnold (1822–1888) in Great Britain contended that human authors had written and revised the books of the Bible with the problems of Jewish society and politics in mind. In the scholarship of these writers the Bible appeared not an inspired book, but one, like the Homeric epics, that had been written by normal human beings in a primitive society. This questioning of the historical validity of the Bible caused more literate men and women to lose faith in Christianity than any other single cause.

Science Science also undermined Christianity and faith in the validity of biblical narratives. This blow was particularly cruel because many eighteenth-century writers had led Christians to believe the scientific examination of nature buttressed their faith. William Paley's (1743–1805) *Natural Theology* (1802) and books by numerous scientists had enshrined that belief. The geology of Charles Lyell (1797–1875) suggested the earth is much older than the biblical records contend. By looking to natural causes to explain floods, mountains, and valleys, Lyell removed the miraculous hand of God from the physical development of the earth. Darwin's theory cast doubt on the Creation. His ideas and those of other writers suggested that the moral nature of humankind can be explained without appeal to God. Finally, anthropologists, psychologists, and sociologists proposed that religious sentiments are just one more set of natural phenomena.

Morality Other intellectuals questioned the morality of Christianity. The issue of immoral biblical stories was again raised. The morality of the Old Testament God, his cruelty and unpredictability, did not fit well with the tolerant, rational values of liberals. They also wondered about the morality of the New Testament God, who would sacrifice for his own satisfaction the only perfect being ever to walk the earth. Many of the clergy began to wonder if they could preach doctrines they felt to be immoral.

From another direction, writers like Friedrich Nietzsche (1844–1900) in Germany portrayed Christianity as a religion that glorified weakness rather than the strength life required. Christianity demanded a useless and debilitating sacrifice of the flesh and spirit, rather than heroic living and daring. Nietzsche once observed, "War and courage have accomplished more great things than love of neighbor."[2]

[2]Walter Kaufmann, ed. and trans., *The Portable Nietzsche* (New York: Viking, 1967), p. 159.

COMPARE AND CONNECT

The Debate over Social Darwinism

DURING THE LATE-nineteenth and early-twentieth centuries scientists as well as other social commentators debated the question of whether the concept of "survival of the fittest" on which Charles Darwin had based his concept of evolution by natural selection should apply to human society and the competition between nations. Some commentators, such as Herbert Spencer, had advocated generally unbridled economic competition with little or no help to the poor and others who fared badly as a result of such competition. In 1893 T. H. Huxley rejected that view. However, a few years later Karl Pearson, another distinguished British scientist who supported the idea of evolution, argued that Social Darwinism should and did govern the relationships among nations.

QUESTIONS

1. **Why does Huxley equate "social progress" with the "ethical process"?**
2. **In this passage, does Huxley present human society as part of nature or as something that may be separate from nature?**
3. **How does Pearson connect Darwin's ideas to the concept of human progress?**
4. **How might Pearson's ideas justify imperial expansion, which will be considered in the next chapter? How could these arguments foster a climate of international violence?**
5. **How might Huxley's ideas be used to support broadly beneficial social welfare programs enacted to produce national populations healthy enough to compete in the international rivalry envisioned by Pearson?**

I. T. H. Huxley Criticizes Evolutionary Ethics

T. H. Huxley (1825–1895) was a British scientist who had been among Darwin's strongest defenders. Huxley, however, became a major critic of Social Darwinism, which attempted to deduce ethical principles from evolutionary processes involving struggle in nature. Drawing a strong distinction between the cosmic process of evolution and the social process of ethical development, he argued in Evolution and Ethics *(1893) that human ethical progress occurs through combating the cosmic process.*

Men in society are undoubtedly subject to the cosmic process. As among other animals, multiplication goes on without cessation, and involves severe competition for the means of support. The struggle for existence tends to eliminate those less fitted to adapt themselves to the circumstances of their existence. The strongest, the most self-assertive, tend to tread down the weaker. But the influence of the cosmic process on the evolution of society is the greater the more rudimentary its civilization. Social progress means a checking of the cosmic process at every step and the substitution for it of another, which may be called the ethical process; the end of which is not the survival of those who may happen to be the fittest, in respect of the whole of the conditions which obtain, but of those who are ethically the best.

As I have already urged, the practice of that which is ethically best—what we call goodness or virtue—involves a course of conduct which, in all respects, is opposed to that which leads to success in the cosmic struggle for existence. In place of ruthless self-assertion it demands self-restraint; in place of thrusting aside, or treading down, all competitors, it requires that the individual shall not merely respect, but shall help his fellows; its influence is directed, not so much to the survival of the fittest, as to the fitting of as many as possible to survive. It repudiates the gladiatorial theory of existence.

It is from neglect of these plain considerations that the fanatical individualism of our time attempts to apply the analogy of cosmic nature to society. . . .

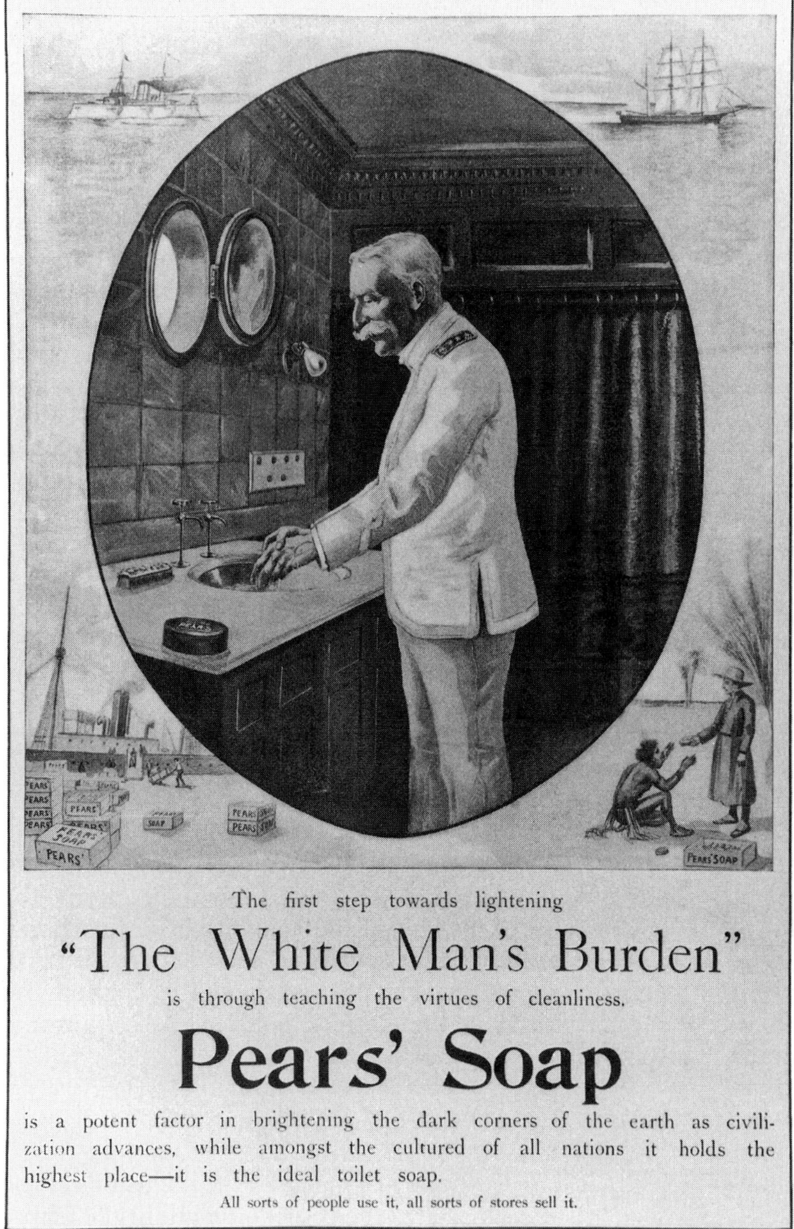

The first step towards lightening
“The White Man’s Burden”
is through teaching the virtues of cleanliness.
Pears’ Soap
is a potent factor in brightening the dark corners of the earth as civilization advances, while amongst the cultured of all nations it holds the highest place—it is the ideal toilet soap.
All sorts of people use it, all sorts of stores sell it.

Racism was often a by-product of Social Darwinist theory. At the turn of the twentieth century, racism permeated many facets of popular life. This ad for Pears' Soap caters to the racist attitudes held by many whites during this time. Library of Congress/*Colliers*, October 4, 1899

Let us understand, once for all, that the ethical progress of society depends, not on imitating the cosmic process, still less in running away from it, but in combating it.

Source: From T. H. Huxley, *Evolution and Ethics* (London: Macmillan & Co., 1893), as quoted in Franklin L. Baumer, *Main Currents of Western Thought: Readings in Western European Intellectual History from the Middle Ages to the Present*, 3rd ed., rev. (New York: Alfred A. Knopf, 1970), pp. 561–562.

II. Social Darwinism and Imperialism

T. H. Huxley's assault did not end the influence of Social Darwinism. Debates about competition among nations for trade, military superiority, and empire dominated much turn-of-the-twentieth-century political thought. The idea of biological competition became applied to nations and races and produced substantial impact on public opinion and among policymakers. In the selection that follows Karl Pearson (1857–1936), an English scientist, attempts to connect concepts from evolutionary theory—the struggle for survival and the survival of the fittest—to the development of human societies.

History shows me one way, and one way only, in which a state of civilisation has been produced, namely, the struggle of race with race, and the survival of the physically and mentally fitter race. This dependence of progress on the survival of the fitter race, terribly black as it may seem to some of you, gives the struggle for existence its redeeming features; it is the fiery crucible out of which comes the finer metal. You may hope for a time when the sword shall be turned into the ploughshare, when American and German and English traders shall no longer compete in the markets of the world for raw materials, for their food supply, when the white man and the dark shall share the soil between them, and each till it as he lists. But, believe me, when that day comes mankind will no longer progress; there will be nothing to check the fertility of inferior stock; the relentless law of heredity will not be controlled and guided by natural selection. Man will stagnate. . . . The path of progress is strewn with the wreck of nations; traces are everywhere to be seen of the hecatombs of inferior races, and of victims who found not the narrow way to the greater perfection. Yet these dead peoples are, in very truth, the stepping stones on which mankind has arisen to the higher intellectual and deeper emotional life of today.

Source: From Karl Pearson, *National Life from the Standpoint of Science*, 2nd ed. (Cambridge: Cambridge University Press, 1907), pp. 21, 26–27, 64.

These skeptical currents created a climate in which Christianity lost much of its intellectual respectability. Fewer educated people joined the clergy. Many people found they could live with little or no reference to Christianity. The secularism of everyday life proved as harmful to the faith as the direct attacks. This situation was especially prevalent in the cities, which were growing faster than the capacity of the churches to meet the challenge. Whole generations of the urban poor grew up with little or no experience of the church as an institution or of Christianity as a religious faith.

Conflict Between Church and State

The secular states of late-nineteenth-century Europe clashed with both the Protestant and the Roman Catholic churches. Liberals, including those who were religiously observant, disliked the dogma and the political privileges of the established churches. National states were often suspicious of the supranational character of the Roman Catholic Church. The primary area of conflict between the state and the churches, however, was education. Previously, most education in Europe had taken place in church schools. The churches feared that future generations would emerge from the new state-financed schools without any religious teaching. From 1870 through the turn of the century, all the major countries debated religious education.

Great Britain In Great Britain, the Education Act of 1870 provided for state-supported schools run by elected school boards, whereas earlier the government had given small grants to religious schools. The new schools were to be built in areas where the religious denominations did not provide satisfactory education. There was rivalry both between the Anglican church and the state and between the Anglican church and the Nonconformist denominations—that is, those Protestant denominations that were not part of the Church of England. All the churches opposed improvements in education because these increased the costs of church schools. In the Education Act of 1902, the government provided state support for both religious and nonreligious schools but imposed the same educational standards on each.

France The British conflict was calm compared with that in France, which had a dual system of Catholic and public schools. Under the Falloux Law of 1850, the local priest provided religious education in the public schools. The conservative French Catholic Church and the Third French Republic loathed each other. Between 1878 and 1886, a series of educational laws sponsored by Jules Ferry (1832–1893) replaced religious instruction in the public schools with civic training. The number of public schools was expanded, and members of religious orders could no longer teach in them. After the Dreyfus affair, the French Catholic Church again paid a price for its reactionary politics. The Radical government of Pierre Waldeck-Rousseau (1846–1904), drawn from pro-Dreyfus groups, suppressed the religious orders. In 1905, the Napoleonic Concordat was terminated, and church and state were separated.

Germany and the *Kulturkampf* The most extreme and violent church-state conflict occurred in Germany during the 1870s. At unification, the German Catholic hierarchy wanted freedom for the churches guaranteed in the constitution. Bismarck left the matter to the federal states, but he soon felt the Roman Catholic Church and the Catholic Center Party threatened the unity of the German Empire. In 1870 and 1871, he removed the clergy from overseeing local education in Prussia and set education under state direction. This secularization of education represented the beginning of a concerted attack on the Catholic Church in Germany.

The "May Laws" of 1873, which applied to Prussia, but not to the entire German Empire, required priests to be educated in German schools and universities and to pass state examinations. The state could veto the appointments of priests. The legislation abolished the disciplinary power of the pope and the church over the clergy and transferred it to the state. Many of the clergy refused to obey these laws, and by 1876, Bismarck had either arrested or expelled all Catholic bishops from Prussia.

In the end, Bismarck's ***Kulturkampf*** ("cultural struggle") against the Catholic Church failed. By the end of the 1870s, he abandoned his attack. He had gained state control of education and civil laws governing marriage only at the price of provoking Catholic resentment against the German state. The *Kulturkampf* was probably his greatest blunder.

Areas of Religious Revival

The German Catholic resistance to the intrusions of the secular state illustrates the continuing vitality of Christianity during this period of intellectual and political hardship for the church. In Great Britain, both the Anglican church and the Nonconformist denominations expanded and raised vast sums for new churches and schools. In Ireland, the 1870s saw a Catholic devotional revival. In France, after the defeat by Prussia, priests organized special pilgrimages to shrines for thousands of penitents who believed France had been defeated because of their sins. The cult of the miracle of Lourdes grew during these years. Churches of all denominations gave more attention to the urban poor.

In effect, the last half of the nineteenth century witnessed the final great effort to Christianize Europe. It was well organized, well led, and well financed. It failed only because the population of Europe had outstripped the resources of the churches. The vitality of the churches accounts, in part, for the intense hostility of their enemies.

A Closer LOOK

CONFLICT BETWEEN CHURCH AND STATE IN GERMANY

THE CONFLICT BETWEEN the German imperial government and the German Roman Catholic Church was among the most intense church-state encounters of the late nineteenth century. Here the tumultuous event is somewhat trivialized as Bismarck and the pope are portrayed attempting to checkmate each other.

The chess game is intended to illustrate how Bismarck sought to remove major German church leaders from public life.

Bildarchiv Preussischer Kulturbesitz

The pope has fewer and fewer pieces on the board. Those Bismarck has captured have been placed in the box on the left denoted by an indistinct German word suggesting imprisonment. The German government had sent some Catholic clergy to prison.

The chess piece in the pope's hand is called *Encyclical*, indicating the official statement that the pope could issue against the German government.

To examine this image in an interactive fashion, please go to www.myhistorylab.com

myhistorylab

The Roman Catholic Church and the Modern World

The most striking feature of Christian religious revival was the resilience of the papacy. The brief hope for a liberal pontificate from Pope Pius IX (r. 1846–1878) vanished when he fled the turmoil in Rome in November 1848. In the 1860s, embittered by the process of Italian unification, he launched a counteroffensive against liberalism. In 1864, he issued the *Syllabus of Errors*, which set the Catholic Church squarely against contemporary science, philosophy, and politics.

In 1869, the pope summoned the First Vatican Council. The next year, through the political manipulations of the pontiff and against opposition from many bishops, the council promulgated the dogma of **papal infallibility** when speaking officially on matters of faith and morals. No earlier pope had asserted such centralized authority within the church. The First Vatican Council ended in 1870, when Italian troops occupied Rome at the outbreak of the Franco-Prussian War. Thereafter the territory of the papacy was limited to the Vatican City, and the papacy made no formal accommodation to the Italian state until 1929. Pius IX and many other Roman Catholics believed the Catholic Church could sustain itself in the modern world of nation-states with large electorates only by centering the authority of the church in the papacy itself. The spiritual authority of the papacy became a substitute for its lost political and temporal authority.

Pius IX was succeeded by Leo XIII (r. 1878–1903). Leo, who was sixty-eight years old at the time of his election, sought to make accommodations to the modern age and to address its great social questions. He looked to the philosophy of Thomas Aquinas (1225–1274) to reconcile the claims of faith and reason.

Leo's most important pronouncement on public issues was the encyclical *Rerum Novarum* (1891). In that document, he defended private property, religious education, and religious control of the marriage laws, and he condemned socialism and Marxism, but he also declared that employers should treat their employees justly, pay them proper wages, and permit them to organize labor unions. The pope supported laws to protect workers and urged that modern society be organized in corporate groups that would include people from various classes who would cooperate according to Christian principles. The corporate society, based on medieval social organization, was to be an alternative to both socialism and competitive capitalism. On the basis of Leo XIII's pronouncements, democratic Catholic political parties and Catholic trade unions were founded throughout Europe. (See "Leo XIII Considers the Social Question in European Politics.")

His successor Pius X (r. 1903–1914) hoped to resist modern thought and restore traditional devotional life. Between 1903 and 1907, he condemned Catholic modernism, a movement of modern biblical criticism within the church, and in 1910 he required all priests to take an anti-Modernist oath. The struggle between Catholicism and modern thought was resumed.

Islam and Late-Nineteenth-Century European Thought

The few European thinkers who wrote about Islam in the late nineteenth century discussed it using the same scientific and naturalistic scholarly methods they applied to Christianity and Judaism. They interpreted Islam as a historical phenomenon without any reference to the supernatural, and the Qur'an received the same kind of critical historical analysis that was being directed toward the Bible. Islam, like the other great world religions, was seen as a product of a particular culture. In the works of scholars such as the influential French writer Ernest Renan, Islam was, like Judaism, a manifestation of the ancient Semitic mentality, which had given rise to a powerful monotheistic vision. Renan, and sociologists such as Max Weber, also dismissed Islam as a religion and culture incapable of developing science and closed to new ideas.

However, Renan's views were opposed in a French journal by Jamal al-din Al-Afghani (1839–1897), an Egyptian intellectual, who argued that over time Islam, which had arisen six hundred years after Christianity, would eventually produce cultures as modern as those in Europe. Al-Afghani was one of the rare Islamic writers who directly contested a European thinker.

The European racial and cultural outlooks that denigrated nonwhite peoples and their civilizations were also directed toward the Arab world. European authors who championed white racial superiority looked to India and the Aryan civilization that was supposed to have risen there and later influenced northern European life as the source of Europe's cultural superiority.

Christian missionaries reinforced these anti-Islamic attitudes. They blamed Islam for Arab economic backwardness, for mistreating women, and for condoning slavery. They also often came into conflict with Islamic religious authorities. Because the penalty for abjuring Islam is death, the missionaries made few converts among Muslims. So they turned their efforts to founding schools and hospitals, hoping these Christian foundations would eventually lead some Muslims to Christianity. Few Muslims converted, but these institutions did educate young Arabs in Western science and medicine, and many of their students became leaders in the Middle East. Eventually, as missionary families came to live for long periods of time among Arabs, they became more sympathetic to Arab political aspirations.

Within the Islamic world, and especially in the decaying Ottoman Empire, as political leaders continued to champion Western scientific education and technology, they confronted a variety of responses from religious thinkers. Some of these thinkers sought to combine modern thought with Islam. For example, the Salafi, or the salafiyya movement, believed there was no inherent contradiction between science and Islam. They believed Muhammad had wisely and properly addressed the issues of his day, and a reformed Islamic faith could do so again. The Arab world should cease imitating the West and modernize itself on the basis of a pure, restored Islamic faith. The Salafi emphasized a rational reading of the Qur'an and saw Ottoman decline as the result of Muslim religious error. This outlook, which had originally sought to reconcile Islam with the modern world, eventually led many Muslims in the twentieth century to oppose Western influence.

Other Islamic religious leaders simply rejected the West and modern thought. They included the Mahdist movement in Sudan, the Sanussiya in Libya, and the Wahhabi movement in the Arabian peninsula. Such religious-based opposition was strongest in those portions of the Middle East where the European presence was least direct, which is to say outside of Morocco, Algeria, Egypt, and Tunisia, which for all intents and purposes were under the control of Western powers by 1900, and Turkey, where Ottoman leaders had long been deeply involved with the West.

LEO XIII CONSIDERS THE SOCIAL QUESTION IN EUROPEAN POLITICS

In his 1891 encyclical Rerum Novarum, *Pope Leo XIII provided the Catholic Church's answer to secular calls for social reforms. The pope denied the socialist claim that class conflict is the natural state of affairs. He urged employers to seek just and peaceful relations with workers.*

How does Leo XIII reject the concept of class conflict? What responsibilities does he assign to the rich and to the poor? Are the responsibilities of the two classes equal? What kinds of social reform might emerge from these ideas?

The great mistake that is made in the matter now under consideration is to possess oneself of the idea that class is naturally hostile to class; that rich and poor are intended by Nature to live at war with one another. So irrational and so false is this view that the exact contrary is the truth. . . . Each requires the other; capital cannot do without labour, nor labour without capital. Mutual agreement results in pleasantness and good order; perpetual conflict necessarily produces confusion and outrage. Now, in preventing such strife as this, and in making it impossible, the efficacy of Christianity is marvelous and manifold. . . . Religion teaches the labouring man and the workman to carry out honestly and well all equitable agreements freely made; never to injure capital, or to outrage the person of an employer; never to employ violence in representing his own cause, or to engage in riot or disorder; and to have nothing to do with men of evil principles, who work upon the people with artful promises and raise hopes which usually end in disaster and in repentance when too late. Religion teaches the rich man and the employer that their work people are not their slaves; that they must respect in every man his dignity as a man and as a Christian; that labour is nothing to be ashamed of, if we listen to right reason and to Christian philosophy, but is an honourable employment, enabling a man to sustain his life in an upright and creditable way; and that it is shameful and inhuman to treat men like chattels to make money by, or to look upon them merely as so much muscle or physical power. Thus, again, Religion teaches that, as among the workman's concerns are Religion herself and things spiritual and mental, the employer is bound to see that he has time for the duties of piety; that he be not exposed to corrupting influences and dangerous occasions; and that he be not led away to neglect his home and family or to squander his wages. Then, again, the employer must never tax his work people beyond their strength, nor employ them in work unsuited to their sex or age. His great and principal obligation is to give every one that which is just.

As quoted in F. S. Nitti, *Catholic Socialism*, trans. by Mary Mackintosh (London: S. Sonnenschein, 1895), p. 409.

▼ Toward a Twentieth-Century Frame of Mind

The last quarter of the nineteenth century and the first decade of the twentieth century were the crucible of modern Western thought. Philosophers, scientists, psychologists, and artists began to portray physical reality, human nature, and society in ways different from those of the past. Their new concepts challenged the major presuppositions of mid-nineteenth-century science, rationalism, liberalism, and bourgeois morality.

Science: The Revolution in Physics

The changes in the scientific worldview originated within the scientific community itself. By the late 1870s, discontent existed over the excessive realism of mid-century science. It was thought that many scientists believed their mechanistic models, solid atoms, and absolute time and space actually described the real universe.

In 1883, Ernst Mach (1838–1916) published *The Science of Mechanics*, in which he urged that scientists consider their concepts descriptive not of the physical world, but of the sensations the scientific observer experiences. Scientists could describe only the sensations, not the physical world that underlay those sensations. In line with Mach, the French scientist Henri Poincaré (1854–1912) urged that the theories of scientists be regarded as hypothetical constructs of the human mind rather than as true descriptions of nature. In 1911, Hans Vaihinger (1852–1933) suggested the concepts of science be considered "as if" descriptions of the physical world. By World War I, few scientists believed they could portray the "truth" about physical reality. Rather, they saw themselves as recording the observations of instruments and as offering useful hypothetical or symbolic models of nature.

Marie Curie (1869–1934) and Pierre Curie (1859–1906) were two of the most important figures in the advance of physics and chemistry. Marie was born in Poland but worked in France for most of her life. She is credited with the discovery of radium, for which she was awarded the Nobel Prize in Chemistry in 1911.
The Granger Collection, New York

X Rays and Radiation Discoveries in the laboratory paralleled the philosophical challenge to nineteenth-century science. With those discoveries, the comfortable world of supposedly "complete" nineteenth-century physics vanished forever. In December 1895, Wilhelm Roentgen (1845–1923) published a paper on his discovery of X rays, a form of energy that penetrated various opaque materials. Major steps in the exploration of radioactivity followed within months of the publication of his paper.

In 1896, Henri Becquerel (1852–1908) discovered that uranium emitted a similar form of energy. The next year, J. J. Thomson (1856–1940), at Cambridge University, formulated the theory of the electron. The interior world of the atom had become a new area for human exploration. In 1902, Ernest Rutherford (1871–1937) explained the cause of radiation through the disintegration of the atoms of radioactive materials. Shortly thereafter, he speculated on the immense store of energy present in the atom.

Theories of Quantum Energy, Relativity, and Uncertainty The discovery of radioactivity and discontent with the existing mechanical models led to revolutionary theories in physics. In 1900, Max Planck (1858–1947) pioneered the articulation of the quantum theory of energy, according to which energy is a series of discrete quantities, or packets, rather than a continuous stream. In 1905, Albert Einstein (1879–1955) published his first epoch-making papers on **relativity** in which he contended that time and space exist not separately, but rather as a combined continuum. Moreover, the measurement of time and space depends on the observer as well as on the entities being measured.

In 1927, Werner Heisenberg (1901–1976) set forth his uncertainty principle, according to which the behavior of subatomic particles is a matter of statistical probability rather than of exactly determinable cause and effect. Much that had seemed unquestionable about the physical universe had now become ambiguous.

The mathematical complexity of twentieth-century physics meant science would rarely again be successfully popularized. At the same time, through applied technology and further research in chemistry, physics, and medicine, science affected daily living more than ever before. Scientists from the late nineteenth century onward became the most successful group of Western intellectuals in gaining the financial support of governments and private institutions for the pursuit of their research. They did so by relating the success of science to the economic progress, military security, and the health of their nations. Science, through research, medicine, and technological change, has thus affected modern life more significantly than any other intellectual activity.

Literature: Realism and Naturalism

Between 1850 and 1914, the moral certainties of middle-class Europeans changed no less radically than their concepts of the physical universe. The realist movement in literature portrayed the hypocrisy, brutality, and the dullness that underlay bourgeois life. The **realist** and **naturalist** writers brought scientific objectivity and observation to their work. By using the mid-century cult of science so vital to the middle class, they confronted readers with the harsh realities of life. Realism rejected the romantic idealization of nature, the poor, love, and polite society. Realist novelists portrayed the dark side of life, almost, some people thought, for its own sake.

Earlier writers, including Charles Dickens (1812–1870) and Honoré de Balzac (1799–1850), had portrayed the cruelty of industrial life and of a society based on money. Other authors, such as George Eliot (born Mary Ann Evans, 1819–1880), paid close attention to the details of her characters. These authors' work had, however, included imagination and artistry. A better morality was possible through Christian or humane values or, for Eliot, through an appreciation of humanity arising from Auguste Comte's thought.

The major figures of late-century realism examined the dreary and unseemly side of life without being certain whether a better life was possible. In good Darwinian fashion, they portrayed human beings as subject to the passions, the materialistic determinism, and the pressures of the environment like any other animals. Most of them, however, also saw society itself as perpetuating evil.

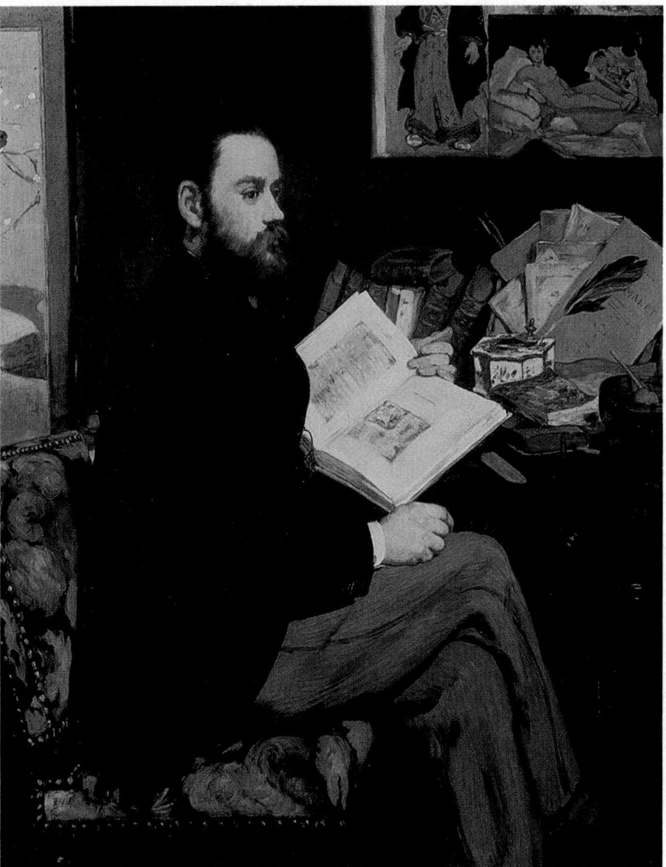

Émile Zola of France was the master of the realistic novel. *Émile Zola*, 1840–1902. Franzosischer Schriftsteller. Gemalde von Edouard Manet, 1868. Original: Paris, Louvre. Photograph: Lauros–Giraudon. © Bildarchiv Preussischer Kulturbesitz, Berlin

Flaubert and Zola

Critics have often considered Gustave Flaubert's (1821–1880) *Madame Bovary* (1857), with its story of colorless provincial life and a woman's hapless search for love in and outside of marriage, as the first genuinely realistic novel. The work portrayed life without heroism, purpose, or even civility.

The author who turned realism into a movement, however, was Emile Zola (1840–1902). He found artistic inspiration in Claude Bernard's (1813–1878) *Introduction to the Study of Experimental Medicine* (1865). Zola argued that he could write an experimental novel in which he would observe and report the characters and their actions as the scientist might relate a laboratory experiment. He once declared, "I have simply done on living bodies the work of analysis which surgeons perform on corpses."[3] He believed absolute physical and psychological determinism ruled human events in the way it did the physical world.

Between 1871 and 1893, Zola published twenty novels exploring subjects normally untouched by writers: alcoholism, prostitution, adultery, labor strife. He refused to turn his readers' thoughts away from the ugly aspects of life. Nothing in his purview received the light of hope or the aura of romance. Although critics faulted his taste and moralists condemned his subject matter, Zola enjoyed a worldwide following. As noted in Chapter 22, he took a leading role in the defense of Captain Dreyfus.

Ibsen and Shaw

The Norwegian playwright Henrik Ibsen (1828–1906) carried realism into the dramatic presentation of domestic life. He sought to strip away the illusory mask of middle-class morality. His most famous play is *A Doll's House* (1879): Its chief character, Nora, has a narrow-minded husband who cannot tolerate independence of character or thought on her part. She finally leaves him, slamming the door behind her. In *Ghosts* (1881), a respectable woman must deal with a son suffering from syphilis inherited from her husband. In *The Master Builder* (1892), an aging architect kills himself while trying to impress a young woman. Ibsen's works were controversial. He dared to attack sentimentality, the ideal of the female "angel of the house," and the cloak of respectability that hung so insecurely over the middle-class family.

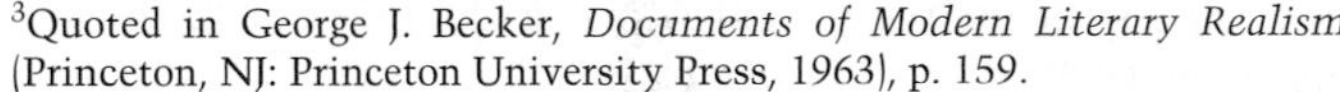

[3]Quoted in George J. Becker, *Documents of Modern Literary Realism* (Princeton, NJ: Princeton University Press, 1963), p. 159.

One of Ibsen's greatest champions was the Irish writer George Bernard Shaw (1856–1950), who spent most of his life in England. Shaw defended Ibsen's work and made his own realistic onslaught against romanticism and false respectability. In *Mrs. Warren's Profession* (1893), he dealt with prostitution. In *Arms and the Man* (1894) and *Man and Superman* (1903), he heaped scorn on the romantic ideals of love and war, and in *Androcles and the Lion* (1913), he pilloried Christianity.

Realist writers believed it their duty to portray reality and the commonplace. In dissecting what they considered the "real" world, they helped change the moral perception of the good life. They refused to let public opinion dictate what they wrote about or how they treated their subjects. By presenting their audiences with unmentionable subjects, they sought to remove the veneer of hypocrisy that had forbidden such discussion. They hoped to destroy illusions and compel the public to face reality. That change in itself seemed good. Few of the realist writers who raised these problems posed solutions to them. They often left their readers unable to sustain old values and uncertain about where to find new ones.

Modernism in Literature

From the 1870s onward throughout Europe, a new multifaceted movement, usually called **modernism**, touched all the arts. Like realism, modernism was critical of middle-class society and morality. Modernism, however, was not deeply concerned with social issues. What drove the modernists was a concern for the aesthetic or the beautiful. Across the spectrum of the arts, modernists tried to break the received forms and to create new forms. To many contemporaries, the new forms seemed formless. The English essayist Walter Pater (1839–1903) set the tone of the movement when he declared in 1877 that all art "constantly aspires to the condition of music."

Among the chief proponents of modernism in England were the members of the Bloomsbury Group, including authors Virginia Woolf (1882–1941) and Leonard Woolf (1880–1969), artists Vanessa Bell (1879–1961) and Duncan Grant (1885–1978), the historian and literary critic Lytton Strachey (1880–1932), and the economist John Maynard Keynes (1883–1946). These authors challenged the values of their Victorian forebearers. In *Eminent Victorians* (1918), Strachey used a series of biographical sketches to heap contempt on his subjects. Grant and Bell looked to the modern artists on the Continent for their models. **Keynesian economics** eventually challenged much of the structure of nineteenth-century economic theory. In both personal practice and theory, the Bloomsbury Group rejected what they regarded as the repressive sexual morality of their parents' generation.

No one charted these changing sensibilities with more eloquence than Virginia Woolf. Her novels, such as *Mrs. Dalloway* (1925) and *To the Lighthouse* (1927), portrayed individuals seeking to make their way in a world with most of the nineteenth-century social and moral certainties removed.

On the Continent, one of the major practitioners of modernism in literature was Marcel Proust (1871–1922). In his seven-volume novel *In Search of Time Past* (*A la Recherche du Temps Perdu*), published between 1913 and 1927, he adopted a stream-of-consciousness format that allowed him to explore his memories. He would concentrate on a single experience or object and then allow his mind to wander through all the thoughts and memories it evoked. In Germany, Thomas Mann (1875–1955), through a long series of novels, the most famous of which were *Buddenbrooks* (1901) and *The Magic Mountain* (1924), explored both the social experience of middle-class Germans and how they dealt with the intellectual heritage of the nineteenth century. In *Ulysses* (1922), James Joyce (1882–1941), who was born in Ireland, but spent much of his life on the Continent, transformed not only the novel, but also the structure of the paragraph.

Marcel Proust's multivolume *In Search of Time Past* (*A la Recherche du Temps Perdu*), which was published between 1913 and 1927, was one of the most significant modernist novels.

Modernism in literature arose before World War I and flourished after the war, nourished by the turmoil and social dislocation it created. The war removed many of the old political structures and social expectations. After its appalling violence, readers found themselves much less shocked by upheavals in literary forms and the moral content of novels and poetry.

The Coming of Modern Art

The last quarter of the nineteenth century witnessed a series of new departures in Western art that transformed painting and later sculpture in a revolutionary manner that has continued to the present day.

Impressionism This fundamental change in European painting arose primarily in Paris. Two major characteristics marked this new style of painting. First, instead of portraying religious, mythological, and historical themes, painters began to depict modern life itself, focusing on the social life and leisured activities of the urban middle and lower middle classes. Second, many of these artists were fascinated with light, color, and the representation through painting itself of momentary, largely unfocused, visual experience whether of social life or of landscape. Contemporaries called these paintings *impressionistic* and considered them curious and artistically shocking when they were first displayed in Paris. During the twentieth century these paintings would become the most popular works visited in both European and American art museums.

The new paintings of modern life by the impressionists, including Édouard Manet (1837–1883), Claude Monet (1840–1926), Camille Pissaro (1830–1903), Pierre-Auguste Renoir (1841–1919), and Edgar Degas (1834–1917), recorded Parisians attending cafés, dance halls, concerts, picnics, horse races, boating excursions, and beach parties. The backdrop for these works was Paris as it had been reconstructed under Napoleon III (r. 1852–1870) into a city of wide boulevards, parks, and places for middle-class leisure.

Édouard Manet (1832–1883), *A Bar at the Folies-Bergère*, 1882. Oil on canvas, 96 × 130 cm. Signed dated. Courtauld gift 1932. Courtauld Institute Gallery, London

The sites included in these paintings allowed people from different classes to mix socially while pursuing a leisure activity. One such meeting place was the Folies-Bergère, a café/concert hall where patrons could enjoy a variety of popular entertainment, including singers, musicians, dancers, gymnasts, and animal shows. Paris had many such establishments, but the Folies-Bergère was one of the largest and most expensive.

In *A Bar at the Folies-Bergère*, first displayed in 1882, Édouard Manet painted a young barmaid standing behind a table holding liquor and wine bottles and in front of a large mirror that reflects the activity occurring in front of her. (Manet actually painted this picture in his studio with a woman who worked as a barmaid posing as his model.) The table, together with its bottles, fruit, vase, and flowers, constitutes a formal still-life composition, but unlike traditional still lifes, this one shows objects of commercial consumption in a setting where leisure itself is commercially consumed. The mirror reflects the table and its contents, the music hall itself with the legs of a trapeze artist appearing in the top left corner, the audience for the performance, the back of the barmaid, and a man she is serving. Manet took great pains to paint the interior light of the hall, which appears to be coming from the newly invented electric light bulbs.

One of the great questions of the painting is the meaning and expression of the barmaid. The hubbub and restlessness of the reflected audience and the noise and excitement of the performance do not register on her face. The barmaid's expression may suggest the anonymity of so many social encounters in modern urban life. Because it was commonly assumed in Paris that many barmaids and shop girls needed to supplement their meager wages through prostitution, scholars have suggested that the woman in this painting, like the liquor and the fruit, is simply another object of commerce.

Postimpressionism By the 1880s, the impressionists had had an enormous impact on contemporary art. Their work was followed by that of younger artists who drew upon their techniques but also attempted often to relate the achievement of impressionism to earlier artistic traditions. Form and structure rather than the effort to record the impression of the moment played a major role in their work. This later group of artists has been described as ***Postimpressionists***, though they should best be understood as a continuation of the previous movement rather than a reaction against it. The chief figures associated with Postimpressionism are Georges Seurat, Paul Cézanne, Vincent Van Gogh, and Paul Gauguin.

Georges Seurat (1859–1891) was a young French painter who read extensively in contemporary scientific works about light, color, and vision. These studies led him to a technique of painting known as pointillism whereby the artist applied small dots or points of paint to the canvas. Through this laborious process he hoped to decompose colors into their basic units leaving it to the eye of the viewer to mix those dots into the desired color or shade of color. Seurat is counted among the first Postimpressionists because he saw himself bringing the new painting of modern life back into touch with earlier artistic traditions. He

Georges Seurat, *A Sunday Afternoon on the Island of La Grande Jatte*, 1884–1886. Oil on canvas. 81 3/4 × 121 1/4 in. (2.07 × 3.08 m). Helen Birch Bartlett Memorial Collection. 1926.224. Reproduction, The Art Institute of Chicago. Photograph ©, The Art Institute of Chicago. All Rights Reserved

once described his painting *A Sunday Afternoon on the Island of the Grande Jatte* (1884–1886) as "a new version of Phidias's Panathenaic procession [on the Parthenon frieze in Athens], with 'the moderns moving about . . . friezelike, stripped down to their essentials.'"[4]

Seurat also introduced implicit social commentary into the previous impressionist portrayal of leisured activity. The Grande Jatte was an island in the Seine beyond Paris where on Sundays Parisians would gather. In Seurat's painting, shadows in the foreground suggest that all is not entirely sunny for the largely middle-class afternoon crowd. The boatman smoking the pipe indicates a brooding working-class presence in the foreground of their lives. All the figures resemble the mannequins that appeared in the fashionable new Paris department stores. Except for the one child who is running, the figures appear almost mechanical, like the manufacturing processes that produced their clothing and their other domestic consumer goods. These figures, compared by one contemporary critic to lead soldiers, stand bored and perhaps puzzled by their situation of comfort, leisure, and ease.

In reaction to the impressionists' fascination with light, Paul Cézanne (1839–1906), working largely in isolation, attempted to bring form and solidity back into his paintings of still life and of the landscape of Provence. Displaying a new sensitivity to non-Western peoples and their art, Paul Gauguin (1848–1903) produced works portraying peoples living in the South Pacific. Other artists collected African masks or studied such objects in the anthropological museum in Paris. Whereas Cézanne had given artists a new way of looking at and then shaping reality, the art of Africa and of the Pacific gave artists examples of remarkable works that had no relationship to the long-standing Western artistic tradition.

Cubism The single most important new departure in early-twentieth-century Western art was *cubism*, a term first coined to describe the paintings of Pablo Picasso (1881–1973) and Georges Braque (1882–1963).

For over five hundred years, painting in the West had sought to reproduce the appearance of reality. From the time of the Renaissance, paintings functioned as a kind of window on an artistic depiction of the real world. Even the impressionists and postimpressionists essentially stood in this tradition.

Beginning in 1907, Picasso and Braque rejected the idea of a painting as constituting a window onto the real world. Rather, they saw painting as an autonomous realm of art itself with no purpose beyond itself. Braque once commented, "The painter thinks in forms and colors. The aim is not to reconstitute an anecdotal fact but to constitute a pictorial fact. . . . One does not imitate the appearance; the appearance is the result."[5] Echoing the art of ancient Egypt, medieval primitives, and Africa, Picasso and Braque represented only two dimensions in their painting. They made little or no effort to go beyond the flatness of the surface itself. They

Georges Braque, *Violin and Palette (Violon et Palette)*, 1909–1910. Autumn 1909. Oil on canvas. 91.7 × 42.8 cm (36 1/8 × 16 7/8 inches). Solomon R. Guggenheim Museum, New York, 54.1412. Photograph by Lee B. Ewing © The Solomon R. Guggenheim Foundation, New York. © 2004 Artists Rights Society (ARS), New York/ADAGP, Paris

[4]Quoted in T. J. Clark, *The Painting of Modern Life: Paris in the Art of Manet and His Followers* (Princeton, NJ: Princeton University Press, 1984), p. 266.

[5]Quoted in Max Kozloff, *Cubism/Futurism* (New York: Charterhouse, 1973), p. 11.

attempted to include at one time on a single surface as many different perspectives, angles, or views of the object painted as possible. "Reality" was the construction of their experience of multiple perceptions. The space in the paintings was literally the space of two dimensions filled with geometric shapes as well as geometric voids. The shapes stand dismantled, set in new and usually unexpected positions, communicating a sense of dislocation.

Braque's still life *Violin and Palette* (1909 and 1910) represents the cubist determination to present "a new, completely non-illusionistic and non-imitative method of depicting the visual world."[6] Various shapes seem to flow into other shapes. Portions of the violin and of the palette are recognizable, but as shapes, not as objects in and of themselves. The violin appears at one moment from a host of perspectives, but the violin has interest only in its relationship to the other shapes of color in the painting. As we move to the right of the painting, no elements reproduce a recognizable object. The painting exists as its own world and as the construction of the artist. Throughout the painting Braque is literally taking apart the violin and other objects, so that he and the viewer can analyze them. As one commentator explained in 1919 in regard to cubism, "[T]he true picture will constitute an individual object, which will possess an existence of its own apart from the subject that has inspired it."[7] The elements of the palette, the violin, and the notes of a musical score floating on folded paper tents hold interest and meaning in this painting only because they are in the painting, not because they are imitations of a violin, a palette, or a musical score.

The cubist painters sought to redirect the artistic portrayal of reality in the same manner that modernists in literature had reshaped the portrayal of social and moral experience and the new physics had reconceptualized nature itself.

Friedrich Nietzsche and the Revolt Against Reason

During the second half of the century, philosophers began to question the adequacy of rational thinking to address the human situation. No writer better exemplified this new attitude than the German philosopher Friedrich Nietzsche (1844–1900). His books remained unpopular until late in his life, when his brilliance had deteriorated into insanity. He was wholly at odds with the values of the age and attacked Christianity, democracy, nationalism, rationality, science, and progress. He sought less to change values than to probe their sources in the human character. He wanted not only to tear away the masks of respectable life, but to explore how human beings made such masks.

His first important work was *The Birth of Tragedy* (1872) in which he urged that the nonrational aspects of human nature are as important and noble as the rational characteristics. He insisted on the positive function of instinct and ecstasy in human life. To limit human activity to strictly rational behavior was to impoverish human life. In this work, Nietzsche regarded Socrates as one of the major contributors to Western decadence because of the Greek philosopher's appeal for rationality. In Nietzsche's view, the strength for the heroic life and the highest artistic achievement arises from sources beyond rationality.

In later works, such as the prose poem *Thus Spake Zarathustra* (1883), Nietzsche criticized democracy and Christianity. Both would lead only to the mediocrity of sheepish masses. He announced the death of God and proclaimed the coming of the *Overman* (Übermensch), who would embody heroism and greatness. The term was frequently interpreted as some mode of superman or super race, but such was not Nietzsche's intention. He was critical of contemporary racism and anti-Semitism. He sought a return to the heroism that he associated with Greek life in the Homeric age. He thought the values of Christianity and of bourgeois morality prevented humankind from achieving life on a heroic level.

Two of Nietzsche's most profound works are *Beyond Good and Evil* (1886) and *The Genealogy of Morals* (1887). Both are difficult books. Nietzsche sought to discover not what is good and what is evil, but the social and psychological sources of the judgment of good and evil. He declared, "There are no moral phenomena at all, but only a moral interpretation of phenomena."[8] He dared to raise the question of whether morality itself was valuable: "We need a critique of moral values; the value of these values themselves must first be called in question."[9] In Nietzsche's view, morality was a human convention that had no independent existence. For Nietzsche, this discovery liberated human beings to create life-affirming values instead. Christianity, utilitarianism, and middle-class respectability could, in good conscience, be abandoned. Human beings could create a new moral order that would glorify pride, assertiveness, and strength rather than meekness, humility, and weakness.

In his appeal to feelings and emotions and in his questioning of the adequacy of rationalism, Nietzsche drew on the Romantic tradition. The kind of creative impulse that earlier Romantics had considered the gift

[6]Edward F. Fry, *Cubism* (New York: McGraw-Hill, 1966), p. 38.

[7]Maurice Raynal, "Some Intentions of Cubism," 1919, as quoted in Fry, *Cubism*, p. 153.

[8]*The Basic Writings of Nietzsche*, ed. and trans. by Walter Kaufman (New York: The Modern Library, 1968), p. 275.

[9]Kaufman, *The Basic Writings of Nietzsche*, p. 456.

DATES OF MAJOR WORKS OF FICTION

1857	Flaubert, *Madame Bovary*
1877	Zola, *L'Assommoir*
1879	Ibsen, *A Doll's House*
1880	Zola, *Nana*
1881	Ibsen, *Ghosts*
1892	Ibsen, *The Master Builder*
1893	Shaw, *Mrs. Warren's Profession*
1894	Shaw, *Arms and the Man*
1901	Mann, *Buddenbrooks*
1903	Shaw, *Man and Superman*
1913	Shaw, *Androcles and the Lion*
1913	Proust, first volume of *In Search of Time Past*
1922	Joyce, *Ulysses*
1924	Mann, *The Magic Mountain*
1925	Woolf, *Mrs. Dalloway*
1927	Woolf, *To the Lighthouse*

In 1909 Freud and his then-devoted disciple Carl Jung visited Clark University in Worchester, Massachusetts, during Freud's only trip to the United States. Here Freud sits on the right holding a cane. Jung is sitting on the far left. Archives of the History of American Psychology—The University of Akron. Courtesy Clark University, Special Collections

of artists Nietzsche saw as the burden of all human beings. The character of the human situation that this philosophy urged on its contemporaries was that of an ever-changing flux in which nothing but change itself was permanent. Human beings had to forge from their own will and determination the values that were to exist in the world.

The Birth of Psychoanalysis

A determination to probe beneath the surface or public appearance united the major figures of late-nineteenth-century science, art, and philosophy. They sought to discern the undercurrents, tensions, and complexities that lay beneath the calm surfaces of hard atoms, respectable families, rationality, and social relationships. As a result of their theories and discoveries, educated Europeans could never again view the surface of life with complacency or even with much confidence. No intellectual development more exemplified this trend than psychoanalysis through the work of Sigmund Freud (1856–1939).

Development of Freud's Early Theories Freud was born into an Austrian Jewish family that settled in Vienna. He planned to become a lawyer but soon moved to study physiology and medicine. In 1886, he opened his medical practice in Vienna, where he lived until the Nazis drove him out in 1938. Freud conducted all his research and writing from the base of his medical practice. His earliest medical interests had been psychic disorders, to which he sought to apply the critical method of science. In late 1885, he studied in Paris with Jean-Martin Charcot (1825–1893), who used hypnosis to treat hysteria. In Vienna, he collaborated with another physician, Josef Breuer (1842–1925), and in 1895, they published *Studies in Hysteria*.

In the mid-1890s, Freud abandoned hypnosis and allowed his patients to talk freely and spontaneously about themselves. He found that they associated their particular neurotic symptoms with experiences related to earlier experiences, going back to childhood. He also noted that sexual matters were significant in his patients' problems. For a time, he thought that perhaps sexual incidents during childhood accounted for their illnesses.

By 1897, however, Freud had rejected this view. In its place he formulated a theory of infantile sexuality, according to which sexual drives and energy already exist in infants and do not simply emerge at puberty. For Freud, human beings are sexual creatures from birth through adulthood. He thus questioned in the most radical manner the concept of childhood innocence. He also portrayed the little acknowledged matter of sexuality as one of the bases of mental order and disorder.

Freud's Concern with Dreams During the same decade, Freud also examined the psychic phenomena of dreams. Romantic writers had taken dreams seriously, but few psychologists had examined them scientifically. Freud believed the seemingly irrational content of dreams must have a reasonable, scientific explanation. His research led him to reconsider the general nature of the human mind. He concluded that dreams allow unconscious wishes, desires, and drives that had been excluded from everyday conscious life to enjoy freer play in the mind. "The dream," he wrote, "is the [disguised] fulfillment of a [suppressed, repressed] wish."[10] During the waking hours, the mind represses or censors certain wishes, which are as important to the individual's psychological makeup as conscious thought is. In fact, Freud argued, unconscious drives and desires contribute to conscious behavior. Freud developed these concepts and related them to his idea of infantile sexuality in his most important book, *The Interpretation of Dreams*, published in 1900.

Freud's Later Thought In later books and essays, Freud developed a new model of the internal organization of the mind as an arena of struggle and conflict among three entities: the id, the superego, and the ego. The **id** consists of amoral, irrational, driving instincts for sexual gratification, aggression, and general physical and sensual pleasure. The superego embodies the external moral imperatives and expectations imposed on the personality by society and culture. The ego mediates between the impulses of the id and the asceticism of the superego and allows the personality to cope with the inner and outer demands of its existence. Consequently, everyday behavior displays the activity of the personality as its inner drives are partially repressed through the ego's coping with external moral expectations, as interpreted by the superego.

In his acknowledgment of the roles of instinct, will, dreams, and sexuality, Freud reflected the Romantic tradition of the nineteenth century. In other respects, however, he was a son of the Enlightenment. Like the philosophes, he was a realist who wanted human beings to live free of fear and illusions by rationally understanding themselves and their world. He saw the personalities of human beings as being determined by finite physical and mental forces in a finite world. He was hostile to religion and spoke of it as an illusion. Freud, like the writers of the eighteenth century, wished to see civilization and humane behavior prevail. More fully than those predecessors, however, he understood the immense sacrifice of instinctual drives required for rational civilized behavior. It has been a grave misreading of Freud to see him as urging humankind to thrust off all repression. He did indeed believe that excessive repression could lead to a mental disorder, but he also believed civilization and the survival of humankind required some repression of sexuality and aggression. Freud thought the sacrifice and struggle were worthwhile, but he was pessimistic about the future of civilization in the West.

Divisions in the Psychoanalytic Movement By 1910, Freud had gathered around him a small, but able, group of disciples. Several of his early followers soon moved toward theories of which the master disapproved. The most important of these dissenters was Carl Jung (1875–1961), a Swiss whom for many years Freud regarded as his most promising student. Before World War I, the two men, however, had come to a parting of the ways. Jung questioned the primacy of sexual drives in forming personality and in contributing to mental disorder. He also put less faith in reason.

Jung believed the human subconscious contains inherited memories from previous generations. These collective memories, as well as the personal experience of an individual, constitute his or her soul. Jung regarded human beings in the twentieth century as alienated from these useful collective memories. In *Modern Man in Search of a Soul* (1933) and other works, Jung tended toward mysticism and saw positive values in religion. Freud was highly critical of most of Jung's work. If Freud's thought derived primarily from the Enlightenment, Jung's was more dependent on Romanticism.

By the 1920s, the psychoanalytic movement had become even more fragmented. Nonetheless, it influenced not only psychology, but also sociology, anthropology, religious studies, and literary theory. In recent years, psychoanalysis has confronted very considerable criticism. Whether or not it survives as a model for understanding human behavior, it profoundly influenced the intellectual life of the twentieth century.

Retreat from Rationalism in Politics

Nineteenth-century liberals and socialists agreed that rational analysis could discern the problems of society and prepare solutions. These thinkers felt that, once given the vote, individuals would behave according to their rational political self-interest. Education would improve the human condition. By 1900, these views had come under attack. Political scientists and sociologists painted politics as frequently irrational. Racial theorists questioned whether rationality and education could affect human society at all.

Weber During this period, however, one major social theorist was impressed by the role of reason in human society. The German sociologist Max Weber (1864–1920) regarded the emergence of rationalism throughout society as the major development of human history. Such rationalization displayed itself in the rise of both scientific knowledge and bureaucratic organization.

Weber saw bureaucratization as the basic feature of modern social life. He used this view to oppose Marx's concept of the development of capitalism as the driving force in modern society. Bureaucratization involved the division of labor as each individual fit into a particular role in much larger organizations. Furthermore, Weber believed that in modern society people derive their own

[10]*The Basic Writings of Sigmund Freud*, trans. by A. A. Brill (New York: The Modern Library, 1938), p. 235.

self-images and sense of personal worth from their positions in these organizations.

Weber also contended—again, in contrast to Marx—that noneconomic factors might account for major developments in human history. For example, in his best known essay, *The **Protestant Ethic** and the Spirit of Capitalism* (1905), Weber traced much of the rational character of capitalist enterprise to the ascetic religious doctrines of Puritanism. The Puritans, in his opinion, worked for worldly success less for its own sake than to assure themselves that they stood among the elect of God. The theory has generated historical research and debate from its publication to the present.

Theorists of Collective Behavior In his emphasis on the individual and on the dominant role of rationality, Weber differed from many contemporary social scientists, such as Gustave LeBon (1841–1931), Émile Durkheim (1858–1917), and Georges Sorel (1847–1922) in France, Vilfredo Pareto (1848–1923) in Italy, and Graham Wallas (1858–1932) in England. LeBon was a psychologist who explored the activity of crowds and mobs. He believed that crowds behave irrationally. In *Reflections on Violence* (1908), Sorel argued that people do not pursue rationally perceived goals but are led to action by collectively shared ideals. Durkheim and Wallas became deeply interested in the necessity of shared values and activities in a society. These elements, rather than a logical analysis of the social situation, bind human beings together. Instinct, habit, and affections, instead of reason, direct human social behavior. Besides playing down the function of reason in society, all these theorists emphasized the role of collective groups in politics rather than that of the individual, formerly championed by liberals.

Racism

The same tendencies to question or even to deny the constructive activity of reason in human affairs and to sacrifice the individual to the group manifested themselves in theories of race. **Racism** had long existed in Europe. Renaissance explorers had displayed prejudice against nonwhite peoples. Since at least the eighteenth century, biologists and anthropologists had classified human beings according to the color of their skin, their language, and their stage of civilization. After late-eighteenth-century linguistic scholars observed similarities between many of the European languages and Sanskrit, they postulated the existence of an ancient race called the Aryans, who had spoken the original language from which the rest derived. During the Romantic period, writers had called the different cultures of Europe races.

The debates over slavery in the European colonies and the United States had given further opportunity for the development of racial theory. In the late nineteenth century, however, race emerged as a single dominant explanation of the history and the character of large groups of people. What transformed racial thinking at the end of the century was its association with the biological sciences. The prestige associated with biology and science in general became transferred to racial thinking, whose advocates now claimed to possess a materialistic, scientific basis for their thought. They came to claim that racial science could support a hierarchy of superior and inferior races within Europe and among the various peoples outside Europe.

Gobineau Count Arthur de Gobineau (1816–1882), a reactionary French diplomat, enunciated the first important theory of race as the major determinant of human history. In his four-volume *Essay on the Inequality of the Human Races* (1853–1854), Gobineau portrayed the troubles of Western civilization as the result of the long degeneration of the original white Aryan race. He claimed it had unwisely intermarried with the inferior yellow and black races, thus diluting the greatness and ability that originally existed in its blood. Gobineau saw no way to reverse this degeneration.

Gobineau's essay remained little known for years. However, a growing literature by anthropologists and explorers spread racial thinking. In the wake of Darwin's theory, thinkers applied the concept of survival of the fittest to races and nations. The recognition of the animal nature of humankind made the racial idea all the more persuasive.

Chamberlain At the close of the century, Houston Stewart Chamberlain (1855–1927), an Englishman who settled in Germany, drew together these strands of racial thought into the two volumes of his *Foundations of the Nineteenth Century* (1899). He championed the concept of biological determinism through race but believed that through genetics the human race could be improved and even that a superior race could be developed. (See "H. S. Chamberlain Exalts the Role of Race," page 746.)

Chamberlain was anti-Semitic. He pointed to the Jews as the major enemy of European racial regeneration. Chamberlain's book and the works on which it drew aided the spread of anti-Semitism in European political life. Also in Germany, the writings of Paul de Lagarde (1827–1891) and Julius Langbehn (1851–1907) emphasized the supposed racial and cultural dangers posed by the Jews to German national life.

Late-Century Nationalism Racial thinking was one part of a wider late-century movement toward more aggressive nationalism. Previously, nationalism had in general been a movement among European literary figures and liberals. The former had sought to develop what they regarded as the historically distinct qualities

H. S. Chamberlain Exalts the Role of Race

Houston Stewart Chamberlain's Foundations of the Nineteenth Century *(1899) was one of the most influential late-century works of racial thought. Chamberlain believed that most people in the world are racially mixed and this mixture weakens those human characteristics most needed for physical and moral strength. He also believed people who were assured of their racial purity could act with the most extreme self-confidence and arrogance. Chamberlain's views had a major influence on the Nazi Party in Germany and on others who wished to establish their alleged racial superiority for political purposes.*

What does Chamberlain mean by "Race" in this passage? How, in his view, does race, as opposed to character or environment, determine human nature? How might a nationalist use these ideas?

Nothing is so convincing as the consciousness of the possession of Race. The man who belongs to a distinct, pure race, never loses the sense of it. The guardian angel of his lineage is ever at his side, supporting him where he loses his foothold, warning him like the Socratic Daemon where he is in danger of going astray, compelling obedience, and forcing him to undertakings which, deeming them impossible, he would never have dared to attempt. Weak and erring like all that is human, a man of this stamp recognises himself, as others recognise him, by the sureness of his character, and by the fact that his actions are marked by a certain simple and peculiar greatness, which finds its explanation in his distinctly typical and super-personal qualities. Race lifts a man above himself; it endows him with extraordinary—I might almost say supernatural—powers, so entirely does it distinguish him from the individual who springs from the chaotic jumble of peoples drawn from all parts of the world: and should this man of pure origin be perchance gifted above his fellows, then the fact of Race strengthens and elevates him on every hand, and he becomes a genius towering over the rest of mankind, not because he has been thrown upon the earth like a flaming meteor by a freak of nature, but because he soars heavenward like some strong and stately tree, nourished by thousands and thousands of roots—no solitary individual, but the living sum of untold souls striving for the same goal.

From Houston Stewart Chamberlain, *Foundations of the Nineteenth Century*, Vol. 1, trans. by John Lees (London: John Lane, 1912), p. 269.

of particular national or ethnic literatures. The liberal nationalists had hoped to redraw the map of Europe to reflect ethnic boundaries. The drive for the unification of Italy and Germany had been major causes, as had been the liberation of Poland from foreign domination. The various national groups of the Habsburg Empire had also sought emancipation from Austrian domination.

From the 1870s onward, however, nationalism became a movement with mass support, well-financed organizations, and political parties. Nationalists often redefined nationality in terms of race and blood. The new nationalism opposed the internationalism of both liberalism and socialism. The ideal of nationality was used to overcome the pluralism of class, religion, and geography. The nation replaced religion for many secularized people. It sometimes became a secular religion in the hands of state schoolteachers, who were replacing the clergy as the instructors of youth. Nationalism of this aggressive, racist variety became the most powerful ideology of the early twentieth century and would reemerge after the collapse of communism in the 1990s.

Some Europeans also used racial theory to support harsh, condescending treatment of colonial peoples in the late nineteenth and early twentieth centuries. They were convinced that white Europeans were racially superior to the peoples of color whom they governed and that these peoples would always be inferior to them. Similar racial theory also informed attitudes toward peoples of color in the West itself as was the case with the inferiority ascribed to African Americans and Native Americans in the United States.

Anti-Semitism and the Birth of Zionism

Political and racial anti-Semitism, which cast such dark shadows across the twentieth century, developed, in part, from the prevailing atmosphere of racial thought and the retreat from rationality in politics. Religious anti-Semitism dated from at least the Middle Ages. Since the French Revolution, West European Jews had gradually gained entry into civil life. Popular anti-Semitism, however, survived, with the Jewish community being identified with money and banking interests. During the last third of the century, as finance capitalism changed the economic structure of Europe, many non-Jewish Europeans threatened by the changes became hostile toward the Jewish community.

Anti-Semitic Politics In Vienna, Mayor Karl Lueger (1844–1910) used anti-Semitism as a major attraction for his Christian Socialist Party. In Germany, the ultraconservative Lutheran chaplain Adolf Stoecker (1835–1909) revived anti-Semitism. The Dreyfus affair in France focused a new hatred toward the Jews.

To this ugly atmosphere, racial thought contributed the belief that no matter to what extent Jews assimilated themselves into the culture of their country, their Jewishness—and thus their alleged danger to society—would remain. For racial thinkers, the problem of race was not in the character, but in the blood of the Jew. An important Jewish response to this new, rabid outbreak of anti-Semitism was the launching in 1896 of the **Zionist** movement to found a separate Jewish state. Its founder was the Austro-Hungarian Theodor Herzl (1860–1904).

Herzl's Response The conviction in 1894 of Captain Dreyfus in France and the election of Karl Lueger in 1895 as mayor of Vienna, as well as personal experiences of discrimination, convinced Herzl that liberal politics and the institutions of the liberal state could not protect the Jews in Europe or ensure that they would be treated justly. In 1896, Herzl published *The Jewish State,* in which he called for a separate state in which all Jews might be assured of those rights and liberties that they should be enjoying in the liberal states of Europe. Furthermore, Herzl followed the tactics of late-century mass democratic politics by directing his appeal particularly to the poor Jews who lived in the ghettos of Eastern Europe and the slums of Western Europe. The original call to Zionism thus combined a rejection of the anti-Semitism of Europe and a desire to realize some of the ideals of both liberalism and socialism in a state outside Europe. (See "Herzl Calls for a Jewish State," page 748.)

Theodor Herzl's visions of a Jewish state would eventually lead to the creation of the state of Israel in 1948. BBC Hulton/CORBIS/Bettmann

▼ Women and Modern Thought

The ideas that so shook Europe from the publication of *The Origin of Species* through the opening of World War I produced, at best, mixed results for women. Within the often radically new ways of thinking about the world, views of women and their roles in society often remained remarkably unchanged.

Antifeminism in Late-Century Thought

The influence of biology on the thinking of intellectuals during the late nineteenth century and their own interest in the nonrational side of human behavior led many of them to sustain what had become stereotyped views of women. The emphasis on biology, evolution, and reproduction led intellectuals to concentrate on women's mothering role. Their interest in the nonrational led them to reassert the traditional view that feeling and the nurturing instinct are basic to women's nature. Many late-century thinkers and writers of fiction also often displayed fear and hostility toward women, portraying them

HERZL CALLS FOR A JEWISH STATE

In 1896, Theodor Herzl published his pamphlet The Jewish State. *Herzl lived in France during the turmoil and anti-Semitism associated with the Dreyfus affair. He became convinced that only the establishment of a separate state for Jews would halt the outbreaks of anti-Semitism that characterized late-nineteenth-century European political and cultural life. Following the publication of this pamphlet, Herzl began to organize the Zionist movement among Jews in both Eastern and Western Europe.*

Why does Herzl define what he calls the Jewish Question as a national question? What objections does he anticipate to the founding of a Jewish state? Why does he believe the founding of a Jewish state will be an effective move against anti-Semitism?

The idea which I develop in this pamphlet is an age-old one: the establishment of a Jewish State.

The world resounds with outcries against the Jews, and this is what awakens the dormant idea. . . .

I believe I understand anti-Semitism, a highly complex movement. I view it from the standpoint of a Jew, but without hatred or fear. I think I can discern in it the elements of vulgar sport, of common economic rivalry, of inherited prejudice, of religious intolerance—but also of a supposed need for self-defense. To my mind, the Jewish Question is neither a social nor a religious one, even though it may assume these and other guises. It is a national question, and to solve it we must first of all establish it as an international political problem which will have to be settled by the civilized nations of the world in council.

We are a people, one people.

Everywhere we have sincerely endeavored to merge with the national communities surrounding us and to preserve only the faith of our fathers. We are not permitted to do so. . . .

And will some people say that the venture is hopeless, because even if we obtain the land and the sovereignty only the poor people will go along? They are the very ones we need first! Only desperate men make good conquerors.

Will anybody say, Oh yes, if it were possible it would have been done by now?

It was not possible before. It is possible now. As recently as a hundred, even fifty years ago it would have been a dream. Today it is all real. The rich, who have an epicurean acquaintance with all technical advance, know very well what can be done with money. And this is how it will be: Precisely the poor and plain people, who have no idea of the power that man already exercises over the forces of Nature, will have the greatest faith in the new message. For they have never lost their hope of the Promised Land. . . .

Now, all this may seem to be a long-drawn-out affair. Even in the most favorable circumstances it might be many years before the founding of the State is under way. In the meantime, Jews will be ridiculed, offended, abused, whipped, plundered, and slain in a thousand different localities. But no; just as soon as we begin to implement the plan, anti-Semitism will immediately grind to a halt everywhere.

From Theodor Herzl, *The Jewish State* (New York: The Herzl Press, 1970), pp. 27, 33, 109, as quoted in William W. Hallo, David B. Ruderman, and Michael Stanislawski, eds., *Heritage: Civilization and the Jews: Source Guide* (New York: Praeger, 1984), pp. 234–235.

as creatures susceptible to overwhelming and often destructive feelings and instincts. A genuinely misogynist strain emerged in late-century fiction and painting.

Much of the biological thought that challenged religious ideas and the accepted wisdom in science actually reinforced the traditional view of women as creatures weaker and less able than men. Darwin himself held such views of women, and he expressed them directly in his scientific writings. Medical thought of the late century similarly sustained these views. Whatever social changes were to be wrought through science, significant changes in the organization of the home and the relationship between men and women were not among them.

This conservative and hostile perception of women manifested itself in several ways within the scientific community. In London in 1860, the Ethnological Society excluded women from its discussions on the grounds that the subject matter of the customs of primitive peoples was unfit for women and that women were amateurs whose presence would lower the level of the discussion. T. H. Huxley took the lead in this exclusion, as he had in a previous exclusion of women from meetings of the Geological Society. Male scientists also believed women should not discuss reproduction or other sexual matters. Huxley, in public lectures, claimed to have found scientific evidence of the inferiority of women to men. Karl Vogt (1817–1895), a leading German anthropologist, held similar views about the character of women. Darwin would repeat the ideas of both Huxley and Vogt in his *Descent of Man*. Late-Victorian anthropologists tended likewise to assign women, as well as nonwhite races, an inferior place in the human family. Still, despite their otherwise conservative views on gender, both Darwin and Huxley supported the expansion of education for women.

The position of women in Freud's thought is controversial. Many of his earliest patients, on whose histories he developed his theories, were women. Critics have claimed, nonetheless, that Freud portrayed women as incomplete human beings who might be inevitably destined to unhappy mental lives. He saw the natural destiny of women as motherhood and the rearing of sons as their greatest fulfillment.

The first psychoanalysts were trained as medical doctors, and their views of women reflected contemporary medical education, which, like much of the scientific establishment, tended to portray women as inferior. Distinguished women psychoanalysts, such as Karen Horney (1885–1952) and Melanie Klein (1882–1960), would later challenge Freud's views on women, and other writers would try to establish a psychoanalytic basis for feminism. Nonetheless, the psychoanalytic profession would remain dominated by men, as would academic psychology. Because psychology increasingly influenced child rearing and domestic relations law in the twentieth century, it, ironically, gave men a large impact in the one area of social activity that women had dominated.

The social sciences of the late nineteenth and early twentieth centuries similarly reinforced traditional gender roles. Most major theorists believed that women's role in reproduction and child rearing demanded a social position inferior to men. Auguste Comte, whose thought in this area owed much to Rousseau, portrayed women as biologically and intellectually inferior to men. Herbert Spencer, although an advocate for improving women's lot, thought they could never achieve equality with men. Émile Durkheim portrayed women as creatures of feeling and family rather than of intellect. Max Weber favored improvements in the condition of women but did not really support significant changes in their social roles or in their relationship to men. Virtually all of the early sociologists took a conservative view of marriage, the family, child rearing, and divorce.

New Directions in Feminism

The close of the century witnessed a revival of feminist thought in Europe that would grow in the twentieth century. The role of feminist writers during these years was difficult. Many women's organizations, as seen in Chapter 23, concentrated on achieving the vote for women, but feminist writers and activists raised other questions as well. Women confronted their problems as women in a variety of ways, not just by seeking the vote. Some organizations redefined ways of thinking about women and their relationships to men and society. Few of these groups were large, and their victories were rare. Nonetheless, by the early 1900s, they had defined the issues that would become more fully and successfully explored after World War II.

Sexual Morality and the Family In various nations, middle-class women began to challenge the double standard of sexual morality and the traditional male-dominated family. This often meant challenging laws about prostitution.

Between 1864 and 1886, English prostitutes were subject to the Contagious Diseases Acts. The police in certain cities with naval or military bases could require any woman identified as, or suspected of being, a prostitute to undergo an immediate internal medical examination for venereal disease. Those found to have a disease could be confined for months to locked hospitals (women's hospitals for the treatment of venereal diseases) without legal recourse. The law took no action against their male customers. Indeed, the purpose of the laws was to protect men, presumably sailors and soldiers, and not the women themselves, from infection.

These laws angered English middle-class women who believed the harsh working conditions and the poverty imposed on so many working-class women were the true causes of prostitution. They framed the issue in the context of their own efforts to prove that women are as human and rational as men and thus properly subject to equal treatment. They saw poor women being made victims of the same kind of discrimination that prevented women of their class from entering the universities and professions. The Contagious Diseases Acts assumed that women were inferior to men and treated them as less than rational human beings. The laws literally put women's bodies under the control of male customers, male physicians, and male law-enforcement personnel. They denied to poor women the freedoms that all men enjoyed in English society.

By 1869, the Ladies' National Association for the Repeal of the Contagious Diseases Acts, a distinctly middle-class organization led by Josephine Butler (1828–1906), began actively to oppose those laws. The group achieved the suspension of the acts in 1883 and their repeal in 1886. Government and police regulation of prostitution roused similar movements in other nations, which adopted the English movement as a model. In Vienna during the 1890s, the General Austrian Women's Association, led by Auguste Ficke (1833–1916), combated the legal regulation of prostitution, which would have put women under the control of police authorities. In Germany, women's groups divided between those who would have penalized prostitutes and those who saw them as victims of male society. By the turn of the century, the latter had come to dominate, although tensions between the groups would remain for some time.

The feminist groups that demanded the abolition of laws that punished prostitutes without questioning the behavior of their customers were challenging the double standard and, by extension, the traditional relationship of men and women in marriage. In their view, marriage should be a free union of equals with men and women sharing responsibility for their children. In Germany, the Mothers' Protection League (*Bund für Mutterschutz*) contended that both married and unmarried mothers required the help of the state, including leaves for pregnancy and child care. This radical group emphasized the need to rethink all sexual morality. In Sweden, Ellen Key (1849–1926), in *The Century of the Child* (1900) and *The Renaissance of Motherhood* (1914), maintained that motherhood is so crucial to society that the government, rather than husbands, should support mothers and their children.

Virtually all turn-of-the-century feminists in one way or another supported wider sexual freedom for women, often claiming it would benefit society as well as improve women's lives. Many of the early advocates of contraception had also been influenced by Social Darwinism. They hoped that limiting the number of children would allow more healthy and intelligent children to survive. Such was the outlook of Marie Stopes (1880–1958), an Englishwoman who pioneered contraception clinics in the poor districts of London.

Women Defining Their Own Lives For Josephine Butler and Auguste Ficke, as well as other continental feminists, achieving legal and social equality for women would be one step toward transforming Europe from a male-dominated society to one in which both men and women could control their own destinies. Ficke wrote, "Our final goal is therefore not the acknowledgement of rights, but the elevation of our intellectual and moral level, the development of our personality."[11] Increasingly, feminists would concentrate on freeing and developing women's personalities through better education and government financial support for women engaged in traditional social roles, whether or not they had gained the vote.

Some women also became active within socialist circles. There they argued that the socialist transformation of society should include major reforms for women. Socialist parties usually had all-male leadership. By the close of the century, most male socialist leaders, including Lenin and later Stalin, were intolerant of demands for changes in the family or greater sexual freedom for either men or women. Nonetheless, socialist writings began to include calls for improvements in the economic situation of women that were compatible with more advanced feminist ideals.

It was within literary circles, however, that feminist writers often most clearly articulated the problems that they now understood themselves to face. Distinguished

PUBLICATION DATES OF MAJOR NONFICTION WORKS

1830	Lyell, *Principles of Geology*
1830–1842	Comte, *The Positive Philosophy*
1835	Strauss, *The Life of Jesus*
1853–1854	Gobineau, *Essay on the Inequality of the Human Races*
1859	Darwin, *The Origin of Species*
1864	Pius IX, *Syllabus of Errors*
1865	Bernard, *An Introduction to the Study of Experimental Medicine*
1871	Darwin, *The Descent of Man*
1872	Nietzsche, *The Birth of Tragedy*
1883	Mach, *The Science of Mechanics*
1883	Nietzsche, *Thus Spake Zarathustra*
1891	Leo XIII, *Rerum Novarum*
1893	Huxley, *Evolution and Ethics*
1896	Herzl, *The Jewish State*
1899	Chamberlain, *The Foundations of the Nineteenth Century*
1900	Freud, *The Interpretation of Dreams*
1900	Key, *The Century of the Child*
1905	Weber, *The Protestant Ethic and the Spirit of Capitalism*
1908	Sorel, *Reflections on Violence*
1929	Woolf, *A Room of One's Own*
1933	Jung, *Modern Man in Search of a Soul*

[11]Quoted in Harriet Anderson, *Utopian Feminism: Women's Movements in Fin-de-Siècle Vienna* (New Haven, CT: Yale University Press, 1992), p. 13.

women authors were actually doing, on a more or less equal footing, something that men had always done, leading some to wonder whether simple equality was the main issue. Virginia Woolf's *A Room of One's Own* (1929) became one of the fundamental texts of twentieth-century feminist literature. In it, she meditated first on the difficulties that women of both brilliance and social standing encountered in being taken seriously as writers and intellectuals. She concluded that a woman who wishes to write requires both a room of her own, meaning a space not dominated by male institutions, and an adequate independent income. Woolf was concerned with more than asserting the right of women to participate in intellectual life, however. Establishing a new stance for feminist writers, she asked whether women, as writers, must imitate men or whether they should bring to their endeavors the separate intellectual and psychological qualities they possessed as women. As she had challenged some of the literary conventions of the traditional novel in her fiction, she challenged some of the accepted notions of feminist thought in *A Room of One's Own* and concluded that male and female writers must actually be able to think as both men and women and share the sensibilities of each. In this sense, she sought to open the whole question of gender definition. (See "Virginia Woolf Urges Women to Write," page 752.)

By World War I, feminism in Europe, fairly or not, had become associated in the popular imagination with challenges to traditional gender roles and sexual morality and with either socialism or political radicalism. So when extremely conservative political movements arose between the world wars, their leaders often emphasized traditional roles for women and traditional ideas about sexual morality. (See Chapter 27.)

Virginia Woolf charted the changing sentiments of a world with most of the nineteenth-century social and moral certainties removed. In *A Room of One's Own*, quoted in the document selection on p. 752, she also challenged some of the accepted notions of feminist thought, asking whether women writers should bring to their work any separate qualities they possessed as women, and concluding that men and women writers should strive to share each other's sensibilities. Hulton Archive Photos/Getty Images, Inc.

In Perspective

By the opening of the twentieth century, European thought had achieved contours that seem familiar to us today. Science had revolutionized thinking about nature. Physicists had transformed the traditional views of matter and energy as they probed the mysteries of the atom. Evolutionary biology had revealed that human beings are not distinct from the natural order. Many believed science would provide a new basis for ethics and morality. Christianity had experienced its most severe challenge in modern times from science, history, philosophy, and the secular national states.

Nonreligious thinkers and writers also assailed the primacy of reason. Nietzsche and Freud, in their different ways, questioned whether human beings are rational creatures at all. Weber and other social and political theorists doubted that politics could ever be entirely rational. All these developments challenged the rational values of the Enlightenment.

The racial theorists questioned whether mind and character were as important as racial characteristics allegedly carried in the blood. Racial thinking also allowed some Europeans to believe they were inherently superior to non-Europeans, Jews, and ethnic minorities in Europe itself.

Turn-of-the-century feminists demanded equal treatment for women under the law and contended that the relationship between men and women within marriage required rethinking. They set forth much of the feminist agenda for the twentieth century.

VIRGINIA WOOLF URGES WOMEN TO WRITE

In 1928, Virginia Woolf, the English novelist, delivered two papers at women's colleges at Cambridge University that became the basis for A Room of One's Own, *published a year later. There, discussing the difficulty a woman writer confronted in finding women role models, she outlined obstacles that women faced in achieving the education, the time, and the income that would allow them to write. In the passage that follows, which closes her essay, she urges women to begin to write so future women authors would have models. She then presents an image of Shakespeare's sister, who, lacking such models, had not written anything, but who, through the collective efforts of women, might in the future emerge as a great writer because she would have the literary models of the women Woolf addressed to follow and to imitate.*

How does Woolf's fiction of Shakespeare's sister establish a benchmark for women writers? What does Woolf mean by the common life through which women will need to work to become independent writers? Why does she emphasize the need for women to have both income and space if they are to become independent writers?

A thousand pens are ready to suggest what you should do and what effect you will have. My own suggestion is a little fantastic, I admit; I prefer, therefore, to put it in the form of fiction.

I told you in the course of this paper that Shakespeare had a sister; but do not look for her in Sir Sidney Lee's life of the poet. She died young—alas, she never wrote a word. She lies buried where the omnibuses now stop, opposite the Elephant and Castle [a London intersection]. Now my belief is that this poet who never wrote a word and was buried at the cross-roads still lives. She lives in you and in me, and in many other women who are not here to-night, for they are washing up the dishes and putting the children to bed. But she lives; for great poets do not die; they are continuing presences; they need only the opportunity to walk among us in the flesh. This opportunity, as I think, it is now coming within your power to give her. For my belief is that if we live another century or so—I am talking of the common life which is the real life and not of the little separate lives which we live as individuals—and have five hundred [pounds income] a year each of us and rooms of our own; if we have the habit of freedom and the courage to write exactly what we think; if we escape a little from the common sitting-room and see human beings not always in their relation to each other but in relation to reality; and the sky, too, and the trees or whatever it may be in themselves; . . . if we face the fact, for it is a fact, that there is no arm to cling to, but that we go alone and that our relation is to the world of reality and not only to the world of men and women, then the opportunity will come and the dead poet who was Shakespeare's sister will put on the body which she has so often laid down. Drawing her life from the lives of the unknown who were her forerunners, as her brother did before her, she will be born. As for her coming without that preparation, without that effort on our part, without that determination that when she is born again she shall find it possible to live and write her poetry, that we cannot expect, for that would be impossible. But I maintain that she would come if we worked for her, and that so to work, even in poverty and obscurity, is worthwhile.

From Virginia Woolf, *A Room of One's Own* (London: The Hogarth Press, 1974), pp. 170–172.

REVIEW QUESTIONS

1. Why was science dominant in the second half of the nineteenth century? How did the scientific outlook change between 1850 and 1914? What was positivism? How did Darwin and Wallace's theory of natural selection affect ethics, Christianity, and European views of human nature?
2. Why was Christianity attacked in the late nineteenth century? Why was Leo XIII regarded as a liberal pope? Why was the papacy itself so resilient?
3. Why did Europeans feel superior toward Islam? How did Islamic thinkers respond to the European challenge?
4. How did social conditions of literature change in the late nineteenth century? What was the significance of the explosion of literary matter? How did the realists undermine middle-class morality? How did literary modernism differ from realism?
5. What were the major movements associated with the rise of modern art?
6. How did Nietzsche and Freud challenge traditional morality?
7. Why were many late-nineteenth-century intellectuals afraid of and hostile to women? How did Freud view the position of women? What social and political issues affected women in the late nineteenth and early twentieth centuries? What new directions did feminism take?
8. What was the character of late-nineteenth-century racism? How did it become associated with anti-Semitism?
9. How did many ideas associated with modernism conflict with feminist goals? What were new departures in turn-of-the-century feminism?

SUGGESTED READINGS

C. Allen, *The Human Christ: The Search for the Historical Jesus* (1998). A broad survey of the issue for the past two centuries.

M. D. Biddis, *Father of Racist Ideology: The Social and Political Thought of Count Gobineau* (1970). Sets the subject in the more general context of nineteenth-century thought.

P. Bowler, *Evolution: The History of an Idea* (2003). An outstanding survey.

J. Browne, *Charles Darwin*, 2 vols. (1995, 2002). A stunning biography.

J. Burrow, *The Crisis of Reason: European Thought, 1848–1914* (2000). The best overview available.

F. J. Coppa, *The Modern Papacy since 1789* (1999). A straightforward survey.

F. J. Coppa, *Politics and Papacy in the Modern World* (2008). A broad-ranging exploration.

B. Denvir, *Post-Impressionism* (1992). A brief introduction.

T. Dixon, *The Invention of Altruism: Making Moral Meanings in Victorian Britain* (2008). An outstanding study of the changing ideas regarding social improvement in the wake of the ideas of Comte, Darwin, and Spencer.

M. Francis, *Herbert Spencer and the Invention of Modern Life* (2007). Now the standard biography.

P. Gay, *Modernism: The Lure of Heresy* (2007). A broad interdisciplinary exploration.

R. Harris, *Lourdes: Body and Soul in a Secular Age* (1999). A sensitive discussion of Lourdes in its religious and cultural contexts.

R. Helmstadter, ed., *Freedom and Religion in the Nineteenth Century* (1997). Major essays on the relationship of church and state.

J. Hodge and G. Radick, *The Cambridge Companion to Darwin* (2003). A far-ranging collection of essays with a good bibliography.

A. Hourani, *Arab Thought in the Liberal Age 1789–1939* (1967). A classic account, clearly written and accessible to the nonspecialist.

J. Köhler, *Zarathustra's Secret: The Interior Life of Friedrich Nietzsche* (2002). A controversial new biography.

W. Lacqueur, *A History of Zionism* (2003). The most extensive one-volume treatment.

M. Levenson, *The Cambridge Companion to Modernism* (1999). Excellent essays on a wide range of subjects.

B. Lightman, *Victorian Popularizers of Science: Designing Nature for New Audiences* (2007). A study that adds numerous new dimensions to the subject.

G. Makari, *Revolution in Mind: The Creation of Psychoanalysis* (2008). A major, multidimensional survey.

A. Pais, *Subtle Is the Lord: The Science and Life of Albert Einstein* (1983). The most accessible biography.

P. G. J. Pulzer, *The Rise of Political Anti-Semitism in Germany and Austria* (1989). A sound discussion of anti-Semitism and Central European politics.

F. Quinn, *The Sum of All Heresies: The Image of Islam in Western Thought* (2008). An interesting and clear overview of this important subject.

R. Rosenblum, *Cubism and 20th Century Art* (2001). A well-informed introduction.

M. Ruse and R. J. Richards, *The Cambridge Companion to the "Origin of Species"* (2008). Excellent essays based on the most recent scholarship.

C. E. Schorske, *Fin de Siècle Vienna: Politics and Culture* (1980). Classic essays on the creative intellectual climate of Vienna.

W. Smith, *Politics and the Sciences of Culture in Germany, 1840–1920* (1991). A major survey of the interaction between science and the social sciences.

F. M. Turner, *Contesting Cultural Authority: Essays in Victorian Intellectual Life* (1993). Explorations in issues relating to Victorian science and religion.

D. Vital, *A People Apart: The Jews in Europe 1789–1939* (1999). A broad and deeply researched volume.

A. N. Wilson, *God's Funeral* (1999). Explores the thinkers who contributed to religious doubt during the nineteenth and twentieth centuries.

For additional learning resources related to this chapter, please go to www.myhistorylab.com

The global British Empire dominated the nineteenth-century European imperial experience. The empire was popularized in newspapers, books, and novels, as well as in thousands of illustrations and photographs. This illustration seeks to portray the worldwide reach of the British Empire and the varied peoples whom it governed abroad and, at the same time, as seen in the caption, how it sought to build domestic pride in the imperial achievement. Similar illustrations could be found portraying the empires of France, Germany, the Netherlands, Belgium, and Russia. "Citizens of the British Empire, the Greatest Empire the world has ever known . . ." 1911, *London Illustrated News.* Mary Evans Picture Library

The British Dominions Beyond the Seas:
Natives of the Greatest Empire the World
has ever Known.
SPECIALLY PAINTED FOR "THE ILLUSTRATED LONDON NEWS"

25

The Age of Western Imperialism

▼ **The Close of the Age of Early Modern Colonization**

▼ **The Age of British Imperial Dominance**
The Imperialism of Free Trade • British Settler Colonies

▼ **India—The Jewel in the Crown of the British Empire**

▼ **The "New Imperialism," 1870–1914**

▼ **Motives for the New Imperialism**

▼ **The Partition of Africa**
Algeria, Tunisia, Morocco, and Libya • Egypt and British Strategic Concern about the Upper Nile • West Africa • The Belgian Congo • German Empire in Africa • Southern Africa

▼ **Russian Expansion in Mainland Asia**

▼ **Western Powers in Asia**
France in Asia • The United States' Actions in Asia and the Pacific • The Boxer Rebellion

▼ **Tools of Imperialism**
Steamboats • Conquest of Tropical Diseases • Firearms

▼ **The Missionary Factor**
Evangelical Protestant Missionaries • Roman Catholic Missionary Advance • Tensions Between Missionaries and Imperial Administrators • Missionaries and Indigenous Religious Movements

▼ **Science and Imperialism**
Botany • Zoology • Medicine • Anthropology

▼ **In Perspective**

KEY TOPICS

- **European imperial shift to Asia and Africa**
- **Significance of the British Empire**
- **British rule of India and resistance to it**
- **New character of late-century imperial ventures**
- **Africa partitioned**
- **Russian imperial advance into Asia**
- **Technology related to empire**
- **Religious factors in imperial ventures**
- **Scientific dimensions of imperialism**

THE HALF-CENTURY between the opening of the American Revolution and the end of the Latin American Wars of Independence (1775–1830) marked the end of the early modern era of European interaction with the wider world that had begun in the late fifteenth century. The second and third quarters of the nineteenth century witnessed the high age of the British Empire. During that time other European nations had fewer interests in the non-Western world. For a variety of reasons, this situation began to change in the 1870s, however, with the dawn of the period historians call the **New Imperialism**. For the next half-century, until the outbreak of World War I in 1914, European powers brought much of the world under their dominance and direct control. During this period the United States and Japan also first appeared as major players on the world stage.

The word ***imperialism*** is now used so loosely in political debate that it has almost lost meaning. To analyze events in the nineteenth century, it may be useful to define imperialism as "the policy of extending a nation's authority by territorial acquisition or by establishing economic and political hegemony over other nations."[1] That definition seems to apply equally well to ancient Egypt and Mesopotamia and to European domination in the nineteenth century, but the latter case had new elements. Previous imperialisms had either seized land and settled it with the conqueror's people or established trading centers to exploit the resources of the dominated area. Nineteenth-century Western imperialism did not abandon these methods, but it introduced new ones. Moreover, modern Western imperial powers benefited from the advanced economies and technologies that they had developed since the late eighteenth century.

Nonetheless, as we shall see, the age of modern imperialism and the interactions of Western nations with other parts of the world displayed many of the themes we have discussed in this book. The challenges of governing and administering empire brought to the fore constitutional issues. The technology that enabled Europeans to build empires displayed the impact of scientific knowledge on Western society and industry and Westerners' ability to use that knowledge to dominate other parts of the world. The activities of missionaries and their frequent conflict with colonial administrators reflected the struggles that had long disturbed church-state relations in their home countries. The criticism of imperial ventures by some Westerners manifested the critical spirit that has informed so much of the Western experience.

The legacies of nineteenth-century Western imperialism still affect our world today. The emergence of independent states in Asia and Africa from former colonies after World War II, the Vietnam War, the establishment of Communism in China, the rise and fall of apartheid in South Africa, and the turbulence in the Middle East all flow directly from the imperial encounters of the nineteenth and early twentieth centuries. So does much of the present-day economic structure and agricultural production of the non-Western world. Furthermore, the current tensions between Christian churches of the northern and southern hemispheres would not exist if missionaries had not planted new Christian communities in Africa and Asia during the nineteenth century. The existence of Canada, Australia, and New Zealand as self-governing nations is also the result of nineteenth-century British imperial policy. Consequently, the subjects discussed in this chapter are important for understanding both the political rivalries among European nations that led to World War I and the world in which we find ourselves today.

[1]*American Heritage Dictionary of the English Language,* 3rd ed. (New York: Houghton Mifflin, 1993), p. 681.

▼ The Close of the Age of Early Modern Colonization

The era of early modern European expansion that lasted from the late fifteenth to the late eighteenth centuries had witnessed the encounter, conquest, settlement, and exploitation of the American continents by the Spanish, Portuguese, French, and English, the establishment of modest trading posts by European countries in Africa and Asia, Dutch dominance in the East Indies (modern Indonesia), and British domination of India. During these three centuries, the European powers had largely conducted their colonial rivalries within the context of the mercantilist economic assumptions we discussed in Chapter 16. Each empire was, at least in theory and largely in fact, closed to the commerce of other nations. Furthermore, in the Americas, from New England to the Caribbean and then throughout Latin America, slavery was a major fact of economic life with most slaves imported from Africa.

Early European colonial rivalry had occurred primarily within the transatlantic world. By the early eighteenth century, the following patterns of European domination prevailed in the Americas. The Spanish Empire extended from California and Texas to Argentina. The Spanish also claimed Florida. Portugal controlled Brazil. The Dutch, French, Spanish, and British exploited the rich sugar islands of the Caribbean. France loosely controlled the Saint Lawrence and Mississippi River Valleys and the upper Atlantic coast. The British had settled the Atlantic coast from Maine to Georgia.

Between the mid-eighteenth and the early nineteenth centuries, a vast political transformation occurred in these regions. The French lost their North American empire to the British. The American Revolution drove the British from their Atlantic coastal colonies, which became the United States. But thousands of American loyalists fled to Canada, which developed a closer relationship with Britain. Warfare shifted the ownership of the Caribbean islands from one country to another with Haiti by 1804 establishing its independence from France. (See Chapter 20.) In 1803, Napoleon sold the vast Louisiana Territory to the United States. In the 1820s Latin America shook off Spanish and Portuguese control. Except for Canada, the Caribbean islands, and a few toeholds on the coasts of Central and South America, European rule in the Americas had ended. The Monroe Doctrine, which the United States announced in 1823 and the British navy enforced, closed the Americas to European colonialism.

The most striking result of these events was the collapse of Spain, Portugal, and France as significant colonial powers. Although Spain retained Cuba, Puerto Rico, Guam, and the Philippines until 1898 and Portugal had colonies in Africa until the 1970s and in Asia until 1999, neither country would ever again be a major colonial or European power. France, by contrast, remained a great European power and by 1914, it again controlled a vast overseas empire, second in size and population only to Britain's.

In contrast to early modern European empires, slavery was absent from those of the nineteenth century. In 1807 Britain had banned the slave trade and had abolished slavery itself in its own colonies in 1833–1834. (See "The West and the World: The Abolition of Slavery in the Transatlantic Economy," page 655.) Thereafter, the British navy worked to close down the slave trade of other nations (and often used this self-imposed moral duty as an excuse to interfere with foreign shipping). Consequently, although economic inequality and forced labor were common in the European empires of the late nineteenth century, the institution of slavery, which had been the chief characteristic of the earlier imperial transatlantic plantation economies, had disappeared. Africa would play a different role in modern imperialism than it had when it had served as the chief source of slaves for the Americas.

Roman Catholicism had been the driving religious influence among the early modern transatlantic empires. Almost from the moment Europeans first reached the Americas in the 1490s, Catholic priests, friars, and nuns had worked relentlessly to convert the indigenous peoples of the Caribbean, Latin America, and French Canada. These regions remain overwhelming Catholic. The largely Protestant settlers of the British colonies had been religiously zealous, but their missionary impulse was less strong, and there were fewer indigenous people along the Atlantic seaboard for them to convert. By contrast, during the nineteenth century, evangelical Protestants from Britain and the societies that backed them set the pace for missionary enterprises that other Western nations imitated, including those that sponsored Roman Catholic missions.

▼ The Age of British Imperial Dominance

During the first half of the nineteenth century, no one doubted that Great Britain was the single power that could exert its influence virtually around the world. During this half century, Britain fostered the settlements that became the nations of Canada, Australia, and New Zealand and expanded its control of India. The early nineteenth-century British Empire also included smaller colonies and islands in the Caribbean and the Pacific and Indian Oceans. However, until the 1860s and 1870s, except in India and western Canada, Britain did not seek additional territory. Rather, it extended its influence through what historians call the **Imperialism of Free Trade**.

The Imperialism of Free Trade

Nineteenth-century British imperial economic ideas differed sharply from the mercantilist doctrines that had dominated previous centuries. Mercantile economic doctrine had asserted that a nation measured its wealth in terms of the amount of gold and silver it amassed and that the amount of trade was finite: If one nation's trade increased, another nation's trade had to decrease. But in the 1770s, economic thinkers such as Adam Smith (see Chapter 17) argued that empires would best prosper by abandoning closed imperial systems in favor of free trade, that is, by fostering the exchange of goods across borders and oceans with minimal government regulation and tariff barriers. Free traders argued that this would allow trade to grow upon itself—that the amount of trade was potentially infinite—and would assure consumers the lowest prices. This outlook still dominates economic theory in the West and provides the theoretical foundation for economic globalism.

As a result of the productive energies that the Industrial Revolution of the late eighteenth and early nineteenth centuries unleashed, Britain became "the workshop of the world." It could and did produce more manufactured goods than its population could absorb on its own. Britain was also able to produce those goods, especially consumer goods such as textiles, more cheaply than anyone else. To dominate a foreign market, British merchants needed only the ability to trade without government interference in the form of tariffs, subsidies, or price controls. Until at least the 1870s, free trade alone allowed Britain to dominate economically one region of the world after another without the need to establish a formal colonial administration.

Although nineteenth-century liberals believed that free trade fostered peace, it could and did lead to warfare. The most important example of this concerned the opium trade between British merchants operating out of India and their potential Chinese customers. China had never

Armed Chinese junks were no match for British warships during the first Opium War. The war ended in 1842 with the Treaty of Nanjing. Picture Desk, Inc./Kobal Collection

been an extensive market for Western goods. Nonetheless, Europeans and Americans wanted to import Chinese goods, especially tea, silk, and porcelain, in large quantities. With the Chinese uninterested in buying Western manufactured goods, British merchants looked for another product to sell to the Chinese market. They found it in the opium produced in India. The Chinese government resisted the import of opium to prevent addiction among its people. (See "A Chinese Official Appeals to Queen Victoria to Halt the Opium Trade," page 758.)

Between 1839 and 1842 and again between 1856 and 1860, the British went to war to impose a free trade in opium on China. At the conclusion of the first of these Opium Wars, the British gained control of Hong Kong, and forced the Chinese to allow Christian missionaries to operate in China, to open various ports to British merchants who remained subject to British rather than Chinese law, and to pay substantial reparations. During the Second Opium War, Britain in alliance with France forced the Chinese to allow foreign envoys to establish embassies in Beijing, to open more ports and areas to foreign trade, and to permit Christian missionaries to operate even more freely in China. What the Chinese had learned and other nations witnessed was that the British were prepared to enforce free trade and their merchants' access to foreign markets even if the products those merchants sold poisoned buyers.

British Settler Colonies

During the early nineteenth century, Britain oversaw the settlement and economic development of three regions that had come under its domination in the eighteenth century: Canada, Australia, and New Zealand. Warfare had won Canada. Captain James Cook's voyages of exploration in the 1770s established British claims to Australia and New Zealand. Australia was first settled as a colony for British convicts. Missionaries led the colonization of New Zealand. The settlement of these lands, which attracted millions of immigrants from Britain and other European nations, resembled the westward movement in the United States during the same period, including conflicts with native peoples.

The British assumed that eventually these regions would have some form of self-government and be a market for British goods. And in fact during the nineteenth century, each of these colonies did establish responsible self-government based on British law and political institutions. The British system of self-government based on an increasingly inclusive franchise was thus transferred to large parts of the world.

▼ India—The Jewel in the Crown of the British Empire

Except for Canada, nineteenth-century British colonial interest shifted from the Atlantic world to Asia and the Indian and Pacific Oceans. During the same years that Britain had lost its North American colonies (1775–1783), it had established itself as the ruler of India. Henceforth, until its independence in 1947, India was the most important part of the British Empire and provided the base for British military and economic power throughout Asia. The protection of the commercial and military routes to India would be the chief concern of British imperial strategy during the nineteenth century. Other nations, particularly Russia, believed they could threaten Britain by bringing military pressure to bear on India. As we shall see later in the chapter, Britain largely became involved in Africa in the late nineteenth century to protect India.

Control of India meant that Britain had to dominate and govern not a land of settler-farmers, most of whom had emigrated from Britain and shared British values, but rather a vast heterogeneous nonwhite population with numerous political allegiances, complex economic and social conditions, and non-Western religions, particularly Islam and Hinduism. (British India encompassed what is today India, Pakistan, and Bangladesh.)

A CHINESE OFFICIAL APPEALS TO QUEEN VICTORIA TO HALT THE OPIUM TRADE

In 1839 the emperor of China became deeply concerned about the illegal opium trade between his country and British merchants, who are termed "barbarians," meaning foreigners, in the letter. He designated one of his officials to investigate the trade in Canton and to take steps to halt it. Among other things, this official, Lin Tse-hsü, wrote a strongly worded letter to Queen Victoria, the British monarch, whom he addressed late in the letter as "O King." He noted that all Chinese exports including tea, rhubarb, and woolens benefited the people who received them and did no harm. He appealed to the queen's conscience to halt the opium trade. He also indicated the new penalties that would be imposed on Chinese subjects and foreign merchants who engaged in the trade while appealing to those merchants not to risk the penalties. The letter produced no success for China because except for opium the country needed few products that the British could trade with them. Late in 1839 the British under the guise of enforcing free trade undertook what became known as the First Opium War, defeated China, and imposed a treaty that permitted opium to enter China.

How does Lin Tse-hsü appeal to the mutual Chinese and British recognition of the harm posed by opium? How might the penalties imposed by China serve to frighten off British merchants? How did British naval technology make China easily victimized by Britain? How does the opium trade of the middle of the nineteenth century compare with the international drug trafficking of the early twentieth century?

. . . after a long period of commercial intercourse, there appear among the crowd of barbarians [that is, foreigners trading in China] both good persons and bad, unevenly. Consequently there are those who smuggle opium to seduce the Chinese people and so cause the spread of the poison to all provinces . . . His Majesty the Emperor, upon hearing of this, is in a towering rage. . . .

The wealth of China is used to profit the barbarians. . . . By what right do they then in return use the poisonous drug to injure the Chinese people? . . . Let us ask, where is your conscience? I have heard that smoking of opium is very strictly forbidden by your country; that is because the harm caused by opium is clearly understood. Since it is not permitted to do harm to your own country, then even less should you let it be passed on to the harm of other countries—how much less to China! Of all that China exports to foreign countries, there is not a single thing which is not beneficial to people. . . .

Even if you do not sell opium, you still have this threefold profit. How can you bear to go further, selling products injurious to others in order to fulfill your insatiable desire? . . .

Now we have set up regulations governing the Chinese people. He who sells opium shall receive the death penalty and he who smokes it also the death penalty . . . . [I]n the new regulations, in regard to those barbarians who bring opium to China, the penalty is fixed at decapitation or strangulations. This is what is called getting rid of a harmful thing on behalf of mankind. . . .

The barbarian merchants of your country, if they wish to do business for a prolonged period, are required to obey our statutes respectfully and to cut off permanently the source of opium. They must by no means try to test the effectiveness of the law with their lives. May you, O King, check your wicked and sift your vicious people before they come to China, in order to guarantee the peace of your nation . . . to let the two countries enjoy together the blessings of peace.

Lin Tse-hsü to Queen Victoria, summer 1839, as quoted in Ssu-yu Teng and John K. Fairbank, *China's Response to the West: A Documentary Survey, 1839–1923* (Cambridge, MA: Harvard University Press, 1954), pp. 24–27.

In theory until 1857, India was still ruled by the Mughal Empire, which had governed the region since the 1500s. But that empire was only a shadow of its former self. Local rulers, called nawabs or maharajahs, paid little attention to the Mughal emperor who still resided in Delhi, the old imperial capital.

Initially the British achieved their domination of India through the East India Company, which was a private company of merchants chartered by Parliament in 1600. In the late eighteenth and early nineteenth centuries, the Company expanded its authority across India by warfare and negotiation. In some cases its armies, which were composed mostly of Indian troops led by British officers and paid from taxes the Company collected, defeated rulers who resisted it and seized their territory. In others, it supported one Indian ruler against another. If an Indian prince died without clear heirs or lost control of his state, the Company might annex it. By the 1830s, British control over India was essentially complete. The willingness of Indians to defer to British authority rather than accept the dominance of other Indians made British rule possible. Like the Romans, the British had perfected the imperial art of dividing and conquering (see Map 25–1).

The rationale for British rule in India changed over time. The East India Company essentially saw India as a place to make money through economic exploitation. By the early nineteenth century, while still hoping to make India profitable, the British saw themselves as bringing wise administration to a subcontinent where local authority was in disarray. In 1813, Parliament permitted British Christian missionaries to work in India. Their presence meant that for the first time Britons would challenge the religious customs of Indian Hindus and Muslims. Some British administrators began to cooperate with missionaries to bring the "enlightenment" of Western values to India. For example, the British prohibited the practice of *suttee* (Hindu widows burning themselves to death on their husband's funeral pyres). English became the official administrative language of India. (See "T. B. Macaulay Prescribes English for Indian Education," page 760.) These and other intrusions suggested that British administrators believed they could raise India to what they considered to be a higher rung on the ladder of civilization. In their own colonial empire, the French would later call this belief in the spread of Western values "the civilizing mission."

In 1857, however, India witnessed the most extensive resistance against any European power that occurred in the nineteenth century. The sepoy rebellion or mutiny (Indian troops were called sepoys) was all the more frightening to the British because it occurred within the Indian Army itself. The precipitating cause of the mutiny was the Company's introduction of new cartridges for its soldiers' muskets that the sepoys believed (falsely, the cartridges were in fact coated with vegetable oil) were lubricated with pork or beef fat. Soldiers had to bite off the

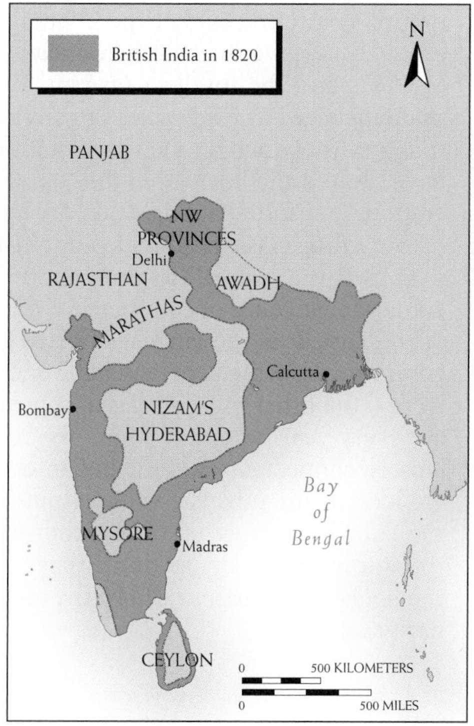

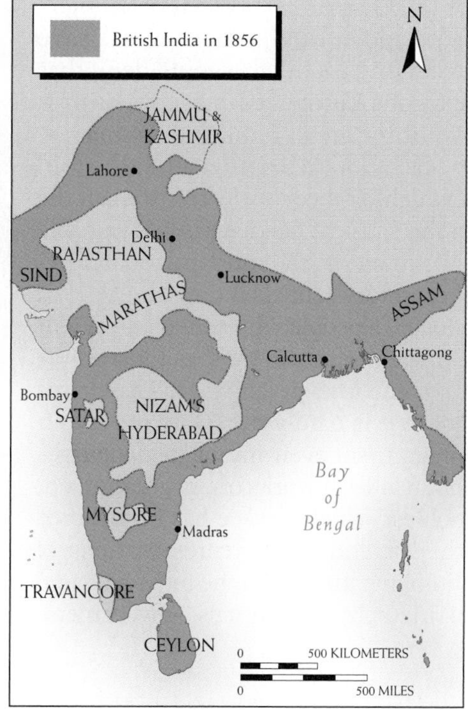

Map 25–1 **BRITISH INDIA, 1820 AND 1856.**

T. B. MACAULAY PRESCRIBES ENGLISH FOR INDIAN EDUCATION

Between 1834 and 1838, Thomas Babington Macaulay (1800–1859), best known as a Victorian historian, served on the governing council of the East Indian Company in India. In 1835 the council debated whether the education of the upper levels of Indian society should continue to be in Sanskrit or switched to English. Macaulay vigorously defended the adoption of English. His arguments reveal the sense of immense cultural superiority felt by many of the British in India. His statements also reveal contempt for Asian literature and learning. Macaulay's views carried the day. One of the ironies of the adoption of the English language throughout India is that it later gave Indian nationalists who came from many parts of the subcontinent a common language in their resistance to British rule.

Macaulay as a member of the British Parliament in 1832 had defended the Great Reform Bill (see Chapter 20) on the grounds that Parliament must make political accommodations to the rising social groups in Great Britain that had attained greater education and commercial prosperity. In his discussion of Indian education it would appear that he doubts whether the people of India can rise on their own without the introduction of Western ideas, literature, and learning. Hence, Macaulay appears liberal in the British context and much less liberal as colonial administrator in India.

How does Macaulay defend the utility of English as a language for education and how does he demean Sanskrit? What are the uses he ascribes to English in colonial India? How does he associate English with the extension of British influence throughout Asia and the Pacific?

I am quite ready to take the Oriental learning at the valuation of the Orientalists [Western scholars of Asian languages and culture] themselves. I have never found one among them who could deny that a single shelf of a good European library was worth the whole native literature of India and Arabia. . . .

It is, . . . no exaggeration to say, that all the historical information which has been collected from all the books written in the Sanskrit language is less valuable than what may be found in the most paltry abridgements used at preparatory schools in England. . . .

We have to educate a people who cannot at present be educated by means of their mother-tongue. We must teach them some foreign language. The claims of our own language it is hardly necessary to recapitulate. It stands preeminent even among the languages of the west. It abounds with works of imagination not inferior to the noblest which Greece has bequeathed to us; . . . with just and lively representations of human life and human nature; with the most profound speculations on metaphysics, morals, government, jurisprudence, and trade; with full and correct information respecting every experimental science which tends to preserve the health, to increase the comfort, or to expand the intellect of man. Whoever knows that language has ready access to all the vast intellectual wealth, which all the wisest nations of the earth have created and hoarded in the course of ninety generations. . . . In India, English is the language spoken by the ruling class. It is spoken by the higher class of natives at the seats of Government. It is likely to become the language of commerce throughout the seas of the East. It is the language of two great European communities which are rising, the one in the south of Africa, the other in Australasia; communities which are every year becoming more important, and more closely connected with our Indian empire. Whether we look at the intrinsic value of our literature, or at the particular situation of this country, we shall see the strongest reason to think that . . . the English tongue is that which would be the most useful to our native subjects.

From Thomas Babington Macaulay, "Minute of 2 February 1835 on Indian Education," Macaulay, *Prose and Poetry*, selected by G. M. Young (Cambridge, MA: Harvard University Press, 1957), pp. 721–724, 729.

end of the cartridge to use it. This would have offended both Muslims, for whom the pig was unclean, and Hindus, to whom the cow was sacred. Some Indian troops feared that the British wanted to use the religious pollution that biting pork- and beef-coated cartridges would have caused to force them to convert to Christianity. There was also simmering anger over the way the Company treated native rulers and with the Company's policy of paying British troops more than it paid Indians.

With support from native rulers, the British harshly suppressed the rebels. Their tactics became even more ruthless after sepoys massacred British women and children. Tens of thousands of Indians and more than 10,000 Britons were killed. By June 1858, the British were firmly back in control.

The immediate British political response to the mutiny was passage of the Government of India Act in 1858, which transferred political authority from the East India Company to the British Crown. Many company officials became British Crown administrators. The British also restrained their efforts to change India or to move it "toward civilization." Instead, the British administration sought to refrain from interfering with Indian religion and became distrustful of missionary efforts to convert Indians to Christianity. The British also worked more closely with Indian rulers. One third of India remained under the rule of Indian princes who swore allegiance to the British Crown and were "advised" by British officials. More British troops were also stationed in India, and Indian troops were not allowed artillery. Finally in 1877, Prime Minister Benjamin Disraeli pushed through an Act of Parliament that declared Queen Victoria (r. 1837–1901) to be Empress of India.

But India remained restive. In 1885, Hindus founded the Indian National Congress with the goals of modernizing Indian life and liberalizing British policy. Muslims organized the Muslim League in 1887, which for a time cooperated with the National Congress, but eventually sought an independent Muslim state. After World War I, the Indian nationalist movement grew stronger, in part because of British blunders, but more because Indian leaders pursued effective strategies, which we will discuss in Chapter 29.

▼ The "New Imperialism," 1870–1914

Whereas in the first three quarters of the nineteenth century Britain had largely dominated the world stage, between 1870 and 1914 other Western powers undertook colonial ventures with remarkable results. During this

The mutinous sepoy cavalry attacking a British infantry division at the Battle of Cawnpore in 1857. Although the uprising was suppressed, it was not easily forgotten. In its aftermath the British reorganized the government of India. The Granger Collection, New York

half-century, Western nations including the United States and Japan, which had industrialized and modernized its government and armed forces along Western lines between the 1860s and the 1880s, achieved unprecedented influence and control over the rest of the world and provoked intense colonial rivalries with each other. Between 1870 and 1900, Western states spread their control over some 10 million square miles and 150 million people—about one fifth of the world's land area and one tenth of its population. During this period, imperial expansion went forward with great speed, and empire was regarded as necessary for a great power. Because of the numerous actors, the speed, the extent, and the many nations involved, contemporaries at the time and historians have regarded this era as constituting a "New Imperialism" that was different from the imperialism of the early nineteenth century. Like other sweeping terms we have discussed in previous chapters, the New Imperialism is a term of convenience that covered many diverse and even conflicting actions, ideas, and activities.

Why were the imperial encounters of this era perceived to be "new"? First, they were more intentionally imperial and involved direct political and administrative control of non-Westerners by the Western powers. That is to say, in general, except for Western influence over China and European and American economic dominance in Latin America, free-trade imperialism and informal empire were abandoned. In their place arose a variety of devices for formal empire or imperial control through **protectorates** and **spheres of influence**. In a protectorate a Western nation placed officials in a foreign state to oversee its government without formally assuming responsibility for administration. In other instances, a European state, the United States, or Japan established "spheres of influence" in which it received special commercial and legal privileges in part of an Asian or African state without direct political involvement. These late-century imperial changes encompassed the British Crown taking over direct administration of India, the British establishing a protectorate over Egypt, the establishment of direct French rule in Vietnam, the division of Africa into colonies ruled by half a dozen European powers, the division of Persia (Iran) into Russian- and British-dominated zones, Japanese annexation of Korea and Taiwan, and the United States annexing Hawaii and taking control of the Philippines from Spain.

Second, the New Imperialism occurred over a relatively brief period and involved an unprecedented number of nations. In addition to the older imperial powers—Britain, France, Russia, the Netherlands, Spain, and Portugal—the newly united Germany and Italy and the Belgian monarchy, which had only existed since 1830, sought to achieve empires as did the United States and Japan.

Third, virtually none of the numerous imperial ventures of this era involved significant numbers of immi-

President Theodore Roosevelt at the controls of a steam shovel during construction of the Panama Canal in 1906. The Panama Canal serves as an example of U.S. imperialist ventures in the Western Hemisphere. Library of Congress grants as settlers. Rather in one way or another over a few decades, Westerners came to govern directly or indirectly vast numbers of non-European peoples. Fourth, during these decades Europeans at home and in colonial settings exhibited a cultural confidence and racial arrogance that marked a departure from previous eras when many persons associated with European empires esteemed indigenous cultures or assumed that these cultures could be raised on the ladder of civilization. (See "Social Darwinism and Imperialism," page 731.) Fifth, despite its worldwide scope and especially the establishment of French rule in Indochina, the New Imperialism focused to an unprecedented degree on Africa with the European powers partitioning Africa among themselves. The boundaries they established still determine Africa's political divisions.

Two other points should be noted about the New Imperialism. First, the actual number of Westerners involved in carrying it out was relatively small. Except for soldiers and sailors, only a few thousand administrators, merchants, and missionaries were associated with empire. Second, the empires created by the New Imperialism were short-lived. In most places they lasted less than a century, much less long than the earlier European empires, which had endured for more than three centuries.

▼ Motives for the New Imperialism

Because the New Imperialism cast such a long shadow over colonial peoples during the twentieth century and beyond, historians and politicians have fiercely debated its character and motives. These disputes have often reflected and still reflect debates over the relationship of the West to the non-Western world. The debates also embody the capacity for self-criticism and self-questioning that has marked Western civilization since the ancient Greeks.

Until the mid-twentieth century, the predominant interpretation of the motives for the New Imperialism was economic. This view originated in a book entitled *Imperialism: A Study* published in 1902 by the English economist and journalist J. A. Hobson (1858–1940). Hobson had opposed Britain's conquest of the Dutch-speaking, white-ruled Afrikaner republics in South Africa during the Boer War (1899–1902), which he blamed on the influence of capitalists and bankers. He saw the same influences behind the imperialist ambitions of other European states. According to Hobson, capitalist economies overproduced, which caused manufacturers, bankers, and financiers to press governments into imperial ventures to provide new markets for their excess goods and capital. Hobson declared, "Thus we reach the conclusion that Imperialism is the endeavor of our great controllers of industry to broaden the channel for the flow of their surplus weal by seeking foreign markets and foreign investments to take off the goods and capital they cannot sell or use at home."[2] Hobson, who was a radical, but not a Marxist critic of capitalism, believed that European economies should be restructured to make imperialism as he understood it unnecessary.

In 1916 Lenin adopted and modified Hobson's ideas in his book *Imperialism: The Highest Stage of Capitalism*. There Lenin maintained, "Imperialism is the monopoly stage of capitalism," the last stage of a dying system.[3] He argued that competition inevitably eliminates inefficient capitalists and therefore leads to monopoly. Powerful industrial and financial capitalists soon run out of profitable investments in their own countries and persuade their governments to gain colonies in "less developed" countries. Here they can find higher profits, new markets for their products, and safe sources of raw materials. For Lenin, as we saw in Chapter 23, capitalism could not be reformed. Revolution was needed. Lenin's concept of imperialism after the Russian Revolution of 1917 became dogma in the Soviet Bloc and influenced the thinking of Marxist historians in Western countries for about fifty years.

Hobson and Lenin presumed that something inherent in the economic and political character of capitalist states caused them to undertake imperial ventures. Each writer developed a broad theory about the New Imperialism that was based on their need to support their own political agenda—opposition to the Boer War for Hobson and the necessity for revolution for Lenin. In fact, however, the New Imperialism flowed from literally thousands of individual decisions that Western governments, administrators working in the colonies, military commanders, and leaders and ordinary people in the imperial territories took. It was easier for commentators like Hobson and Lenin to devise broad economic theories about imperialism than to examine the thousands of facts and decisions that affected each case.

The history of the Western imperial advance, as we will see in subsequent sections of this chapter, does not support the theories of Hobson and Lenin. European powers did invest considerable capital abroad and did seek markets, but not in a way that fits the Hobson-Lenin model. Britain, for example, made heavier investments abroad before 1875, when it was not actively acquiring new colonies than during the next two decades when it was expanding its empire. Only a small percentage of British and European overseas investments,

[2] J. A. Hobson, *Imperialism: A Study* (London: James Nisbet, 1902), p. 85, as quoted in H. L. Wesseling, *The European Colonial Empires* (London: Longman, 2004), p. 129.

[3] V. I. Lenin, *Imperialism, the Highest Stage of Capitalism* (New York: International Publishers, 1939), p. 88.

moreover, went to their new colonies. Most capital went into other European countries or to older, well-established states like the United States and Argentina and to the settler colonies of Canada, Australia, and New Zealand. Even when Western countries did invest in new colonies, they often did not invest in their own colonies.

The facts are equally discouraging for those who try to explain the New Imperialism by emphasizing the need for markets and raw materials. While some European businesspeople and politicians hoped that colonial expansion would cure the great depression of 1873 to 1896, few colonies were important markets for the great imperial nations. All these states were forced to rely on areas that they did not control as sources of vital raw materials. It is not even clear that control of the new colonies was particularly profitable, though Britain, to be sure, benefited greatly from its rule of India, a rule, however, established long before the New Imperialism. Nevertheless, as one of the leading students of the subject has said, "No one can determine whether the accounts of empire ultimately closed with a favorable cash balance."[4] That is true of the European imperial nations collectively, but it is certain that for some of them, like Italy and Germany, empire was a losing proposition. Some individuals (such as King Leopold II of the Belgians in the Congo) and companies, of course, made great profits from particular colonial ventures, but such people and firms were rarely able to influence national policy. Economics certainly played a part, but a full understanding of the New Imperialism requires a search for other motives.

At the time, advocates of imperialism justified it in various ways. Some, embracing what the French called the "**civilizing mission**," argued that the European nations had a duty to bring the benefits of their higher culture and superior civilization to "backward" peoples. Religious groups demanded that Western governments support Christian missionaries politically and even militarily. Some politicians and diplomats supported imperialism as a tool of social policy. In Germany, for instance, conservative nationalists hoped that imperial expansion would deflect public interest away from demands for social reform. Yet Germany acquired few colonies, and such considerations played little, if any, role in its colonial policy. In Britain, Joseph Chamberlain (1836–1914), the colonial secretary from 1895 to 1903, argued for the empire as a source of profit and economic security that would finance a great program of domestic reform, but he made these arguments well after Britain had acquired most of its empire. Another apparently plausible justification for imperialism was that colonies would attract a European country's surplus population. But most continental European emigrants went to the Americas and Australia, areas their home countries did not control.

[4]D. K. Fieldhouse, *The Colonial Empires* (New York: Delacorte, 1966), p. 393.

It is now clear that many motives beyond economic ones influenced the imperial policies of each of the major European nations. Three stand out.

First, after 1870, many political leaders came to believe that the possession of colonies or of imperial influence was an important and even necessary characteristic of a great European power. Here they were clearly following the British example. By the 1880s French politicians believed that colonies could compensate for France's loss of prestige and territory in the Franco-Prussian War of 1870–1871. Similar motives drove Russia's advance into Asia following its defeat in the Crimean War (1854–1856). As a result, vast French and Russian empires were created. Two newly created European states also embraced imperial ventures: Italy believed it must secure colonies to prove that it was a great power but did so with only modest success; Germany created a more significant, if short-lived, empire. The United States at the time of the Spanish-American War in 1898 also came to believe that possession of colonies was essential to its world status. So did Japan, which became a major imperial power in Asia, acquiring Taiwan in 1895 after defeating China and annexing the independent kingdom of Korea in 1910.

Second, much of the territorial acquisitions associated with the New Imperialism as well as subsequent Western involvement in the Middle East arose in direct response to the power vacuums that the decay of the Ottoman Empire created (see Chapter 22). In European diplomacy this became known as the Eastern Question. The Ottoman Empire at its height in the seventeenth century had extended from Algeria to the Balkans, Mesopotamia, and the Arabian Peninsula. Throughout the nineteenth century, however, the Ottoman government in Istanbul slowly but steadily lost province after province to Western powers or nationalist revolts. Ottoman decay gave rise to grave and long-lasting problems. The demise of Ottoman authority in the Balkans created the conflicts that provided the immediate cause for the outbreak of World War I, and the turmoil that has characterized much of the Middle East since 1945 originated in the collapse of Ottoman power in that area. The painfully slow collapse of the Ottoman Empire also brought the West into an unprecedented encounter with Islam.

Similar weakness in the Qing dynasty in China would both cause and permit Western intrusions there to assure access to Chinese markets and resources and to protect foreign nationals working in China, including missionaries. Mutual rivalries, however, prevented the imperial powers from carving up China into actual colonies until Japan attempted to conquer the country in the 1930s (see Chapter 28).

Third, the geo-political assumptions of European statesmen led them to deeper and deeper involvements from the eastern Mediterranean to Africa. European powers often intruded into other regions of the world to

A Closer LOOK

THE FRENCH IN MOROCCO

MANY IMPERIALISTS—EUROPEAN, American, and Asian—claimed altruistic motives for their acquisition of colonies. The French, especially, have always taken pride in bringing "French civilization" to the lands France ruled. This cover of a magazine appeared in November 1911, the year when the French decision to extend and tighten their control of Morocco sparked an international crisis. It is a good example of how France justified its colonial empire as a "*mission civilitrice*," a vocation to bring civilization to "backward" peoples.

Le Petit Journal

SUPPLÉMENT ILLUSTRÉ

DIMANCHE 19 NOVEMBRE 1911

LA FRANCE VA POUVOIR PORTER LIBREMENT AU MAROC LA CIVILISATION LA RICHESSE ET LA PAIX

The illustration reveals the arrogance of such imperial pretensions. In the top right-hand corner, a French officer in a pith helmet gives orders to a saluting African soldier.

The central figure on the cover is a shining Marianne, the symbol of the French Republic, carrying a horn of plenty from which gold coins spill out. Marianne is far larger than the Moroccans, who look at her in wonder and admiration at the benefits that French rule will bring.

The message at the bottom of the page says, "France will be able to freely bring civilization, prosperity, and peace" to Morocco.

The Granger Collection, New York

To examine this image in an interactive fashion, please go to www.myhistorylab.com

myhistorylab

protect what they regarded as their strategic interest and then had to decide what to do with those regions when faced with the necessity of administering them.

One final comment should be made about the motives for the New Imperialism. Western governments often found themselves reacting to events on the spot rather than determining an action in advance. In one region after another, a colonial administrator, military commander, group of missionaries, or business concern would act without prior authorization from the governments in Europe. This then created a situation to which those governments had to respond and often led to greater involvement in an area than European governments had ever wanted or intended. (See "Compare & Connect: Two Views of Turn-of-the-Twentieth-Century Imperial Expansion.," pages 766–767.)

COMPARE AND CONNECT

Two Views of Turn-of-the-Twentieth-Century Imperial Expansion

THROUGHOUT THE AGE of the most active European expansion, political and popular opinion was divided over whether imperialism was desirable and morally right for the major European powers. Gustav Schmoller, a German political economist, sets forth the argument in favor of imperial expansion about 1900; four years later the French socialist novelist Antole France attacked imperialism.

QUESTIONS

1. **What are the characteristics that Schmoller ascribes to other contemporary imperial powers?**
2. **What are the benefits Schmoller sees arising from colonies?**
3. **Why does France equate imperialism with barbarism?**
4. **Why does France believe that virtually no benefits result from imperialism?**
5. **How could writers looking at the European imperial enterprise come to such different conclusions about it? What values inform the views of each writer?**

I. Gustav Schmoller Makes the Case for German Imperial Expansion

Gustav Schmoller (1838–1917) was a highly respected German economist and active political figure who served in the Prussian Privy Council and as a member of the Upper Chamber in the Prussian Diet. He was a strong German nationalist. In this lecture from around the turn of the century Schmoller presents Germany as surrounded on the world scene by aggressive imperial powers. He argues that Germany must imitate them and create its own strong navy and overseas empire. Note the importance he attached to the victory of the United States in the Spanish-American War and the manner in which he portrays Spain as an unsuccessful imperial power.

In various States, arrogant, reckless, cold-blooded daring bullies, men who possess the morals of a captain of pirates . . . push themselves more and more forward into the Government. . . . We must not forget that it is in the freest States, England and North America, where the tendencies of conquest, Imperial schemes, and hatred against new economic competitors are growing up amongst the masses. The leaders of these agitations are great speculators, who have the morals of a pirate, and who are at the same time party leaders and Ministers of State. . . . The conquest of Cuba and the Philippines by the United States alters their political and economical basis. Their tendency to exclude Europe from the North and South American markets must needs lead to new great conflicts. . . . These bullies, these pirates and speculators *à la* Cecil Rhodes, act like poison within their State. They buy the press, corrupt ministers and the aristocracy, and bring on wars for the benefit of a bankrupt company or for the gain of filthy lucre. . . . We mean to extend our trade and industries far enough to enable us to live and sustain a growing population. We mean to defend our colonies, and, if possible, to acquire somewhere agricultural colonies. We mean to prevent extravagant mercantilism everywhere, and to prevent the division of the earth among the three world powers, which would exclude all other countries and destroy their trade. In order to attain this modest gain we require to-day so badly a large fleet. The German Empire must become the centre of a coalition of States, chiefly in order to be able to hold the balance in the death-struggle between Russia and England, but that is only possible if we possess a stronger fleet than that of today. . . . We must wish that at any price a German country, peopled by twenty to thirty million Germans, should grow up in Southern Brazil. Without the possibility of energetic proceedings on the part of Germany our future over there is threatened. . . . We do not mean to press for an economic alliance with Holland, but if the Dutch are wise, if they do not want to lose their colonies someday, as Spain did, they will hasten to seek our alliance.

Source: Gustav Schmoller lecture of about 1900 quoted in J. Ellis Barker, *Modern Germany: Her Political and Economic Problems, Her Foreign and Domestic Policy, Her Ambitions, and the Causes of Her Success*, 2nd ed. (London: Smith, Elder, & Co., 1907), pp. 139–140.

II. Antole France Denounces Imperialism

Antole France (1844–1924) was a famous late-century French novelist who was also active in the French socialist movement. Many socialists across Europe criticized the imperial ventures of their governments. In this passage France provides both a moral and a utilitarian critique of French imperialism around the world. He associates it with ambitious military figures, greedy businessmen, and corrupt politicians. He also contends that it brings nothing of value to France. Critiques of similar character appeared among other liberal, socialist, and radical politicians and political commentators across Europe and also in the United States. Criticism of imperialism of this character would continue until the close of the colonial age during the last quarter of the twentieth century. Notice that like Schmoller, France sees imperialism as something now characterizing all the major powers.

Arrival in Saigon of Paul Beau (1857–1927), governor general of Indo-China 1902–1907, from "Le Petit Journal," November 1902. Private Collection/The Bridgeman Art Library International

Imperialism is the most recent form of barbarism, the end of the line for civilization. I do not distinguish between the two terms—imperialism and barbarism—for they mean the same thing.

We Frenchmen, a thrifty people, who see to it that we have no more children than we are able to support easily, careful of adventuring into foreign lands, we Frenchmen who hardly ever leave our own gardens, for what in the world do we need colonies? What can we do with them? What are the benefits for us? It has cost France much in lives and money so that the Congo, Cochinchina, Annam, Tonkin, Guinea, and Madagascar may be able to buy cotton from Manchester, liquors from Danzig, and wine from Hamburg. For the last seventy years France has attacked and persecuted the Arabs so that Algeria might be inhabited by Italians and Spaniards!

The French people get nothing from the colonial lands of Africa and Asia. But their government finds it profitable. Through colonial conquest the military people get promotions, pensions, and awards, in addition to the glory gained by quelling the natives. Shipowners, army contractors, and shady politicians prosper. The ignorant mob is flattered because it believes that an overseas empire will make the British and Germans green with envy.

Will this colonial madness never end? I know well that nations are not reasonable. Considering their composition, it would be strange, indeed, if they were. But sometimes they know instinctively what is bad for them. Through long and bitter experience they will come to see the mistakes they have made. And, one day, they will realize that colonies bring only danger and ruin.

Source: Anotole France, "The Colonial Folly," (1904), as quoted in Louis L. Snyder, *The Imperialism Reader: Documents and Readings on Modern Expansionism* (New York: D. Van Nostrand Company, Inc., 1962), pp. 155–156.

▼ The Partition of Africa

For almost fifty years inter-European rivalries played out in regions far away from Europe itself and nowhere more intensely than in Africa. During the so-called "Scramble for Africa," which occurred between the late 1870s and about 1912, the European powers sought to maximize their strategic control of African territory, markets, and raw materials. Motivated by intense competition, the imperial powers eventually divided almost all the continent among themselves (see Map 25–2). The short- and long-term consequences were complex and in most cases devastating for the Africans. Among the long-term effects was that European control forcibly integrated largely agrarian African societies into the modern world industrial economy. In the process, new forms of agrarian production, market economies, social organizations, political structures, and religious allegiances emerged that would form the basis for the postcolonial African nations (see Map 25–3, page 770).

The European partition of Africa was not based on a universal policy, and each power acquired and administered its new possessions in different ways. Their goals, however, were the same: to gain control, or at least dominance, through diplomacy or force and then either to place Europeans directly in charge of administering the territories or to compel local rulers to accept European "advisers" who would exercise real authority.

Algeria, Tunisia, Morocco, and Libya

France left the Congress of Vienna in 1815 with only a few small colonies and trading posts. For a time French popular opinion seems to have resisted further colonial ventures. Then in 1830, as we saw in Chapter 20, the government of Charles X (r. 1824–1830), literally in its last days, launched a military expedition against Algiers. Following the Revolution of 1830, which deposed Charles, France did not pull back from Algeria. French governments saw Algeria's fertile coastal regions as providing the land for a settler colony. By 1871 more than 275,000 French settlers were living there. Over the decades, France pushed beyond the coast into the Sahara Desert where its forces established their authority over various nomadic Muslim peoples. The French came to regard Algeria as an integral part of France, and the European inhabitants there were French citizens who elected representatives to the parliament in Paris. Civilian French officials administered the coastal districts of Algeria, where most of the Europeans lived, as if they were part of France itself. Algeria was the most important portion of the French Empire, and it was the part of Africa that a European nation most fully and directly ruled.

In 1881–1882, the French also established a protectorate over Tunisia, which was nominally a province of the Ottoman Empire, and then between 1901 and 1912, set up another protectorate in Morocco. In both Tunisia and Morocco, the French retained the local rulers as puppet monarchs.

Italy, having failed to conquer Ethiopia in 1896, seized Libya from Turkey in 1911–1912, establishing its most important colony. These French and Italian colonial advances in North Africa demonstrated the profound weakness of the Ottoman Empire. Thus, by the outbreak of World War I, all of North Africa lay under some form of European control. In each of these cases a Western power dominated a largely Muslim population.

Egypt and British Strategic Concern about the Upper Nile

Egypt, the richest and most populous region of North Africa, came under European domination as a result of political stagnation and economic collapse. Like Tunisia, Egypt was a semi-independent province of the Ottoman Empire under the hereditary rule of a Muslim dynasty. After the failed Napoleonic invasion in 1798, the Khedives, as these rulers were titled, had tried to modernize Egypt by building new harbors, roads, and a modern army. Egypt also sought to expand its rule into the Sudan. To pay for these projects, the Khedives borrowed money from European creditors. To earn the money to repay these loans, they forced farmers to plant cash crops, particularly cotton, which could be sold on the international market. This proved a mixed blessing. When cotton prices were high, for example, during the American Civil War (1861–1865), which cut off supplies of cotton from the southern states to British and French mills, the Egyptian economy boomed, and government revenues soared. When cotton prices fell, as they did after the Civil War, so did Egyptian revenue. Ultimately, the Egyptian government became utterly dependent on European creditors for new loans at exorbitant rates of interest. The construction of the Suez Canal was the final blow to Egypt's finances.

The Suez Canal was opened in 1869. Built by French engineers with European capital, it was one of the most remarkable engineering feats of the day. The canal connected the Mediterranean to the Red Sea, which meant that ships from Europe no longer had to sail around Africa to reach Asia. In particular, the canal reduced the shipping distance from India to Britain from about 12,000 miles to 7,000 miles. The canal increased the speed of international contacts and, by reducing shipping costs, made many goods on the world market more affordable. India thus became an even more important market for British goods. Yet the tangible benefits to Egypt itself were not immediately clear. By 1875, the Khedive was bankrupt, and that year Prime Minister Benjamin Disraeli purchased the Khedive's shares in the canal to give the British government a controlling interest in its management. Egypt's

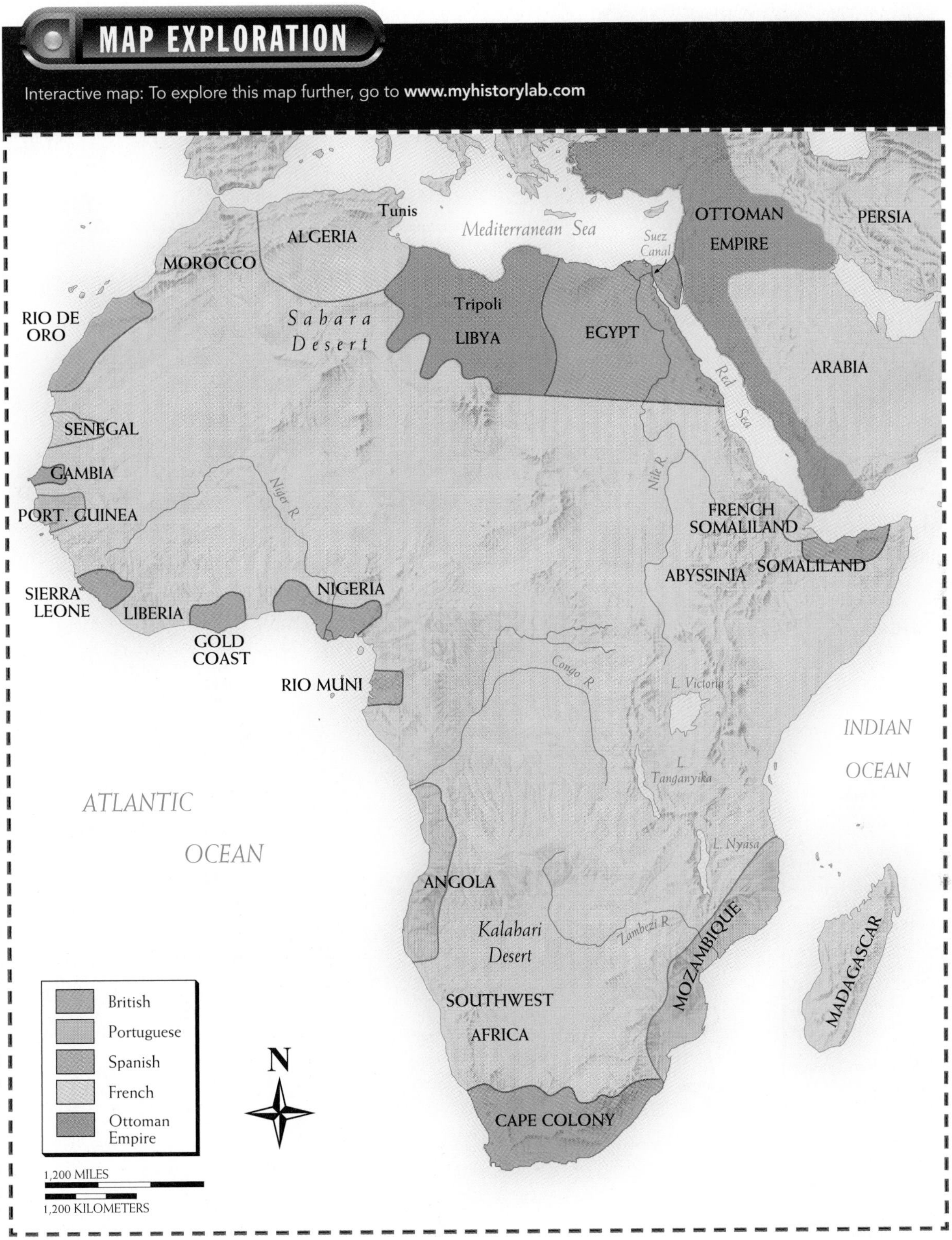

Map 25–2 **IMPERIAL EXPANSION IN AFRICA TO 1880** Until the 1880s, few European countries held colonies in Africa, mostly on its fringes.

European creditors were taking more than 50 percent of Egyptian revenue each year to repay their loans, and they forced the Egyptian government to increase taxes to raise more revenue. This provoked a nationalist rebellion, and in 1881, the Egyptian army took over the government to defend Egypt from foreign exploitation. An uncooperative, nationalist Egypt was, however, not in the interests of the European powers. So Britain in 1882 sent a fleet and army

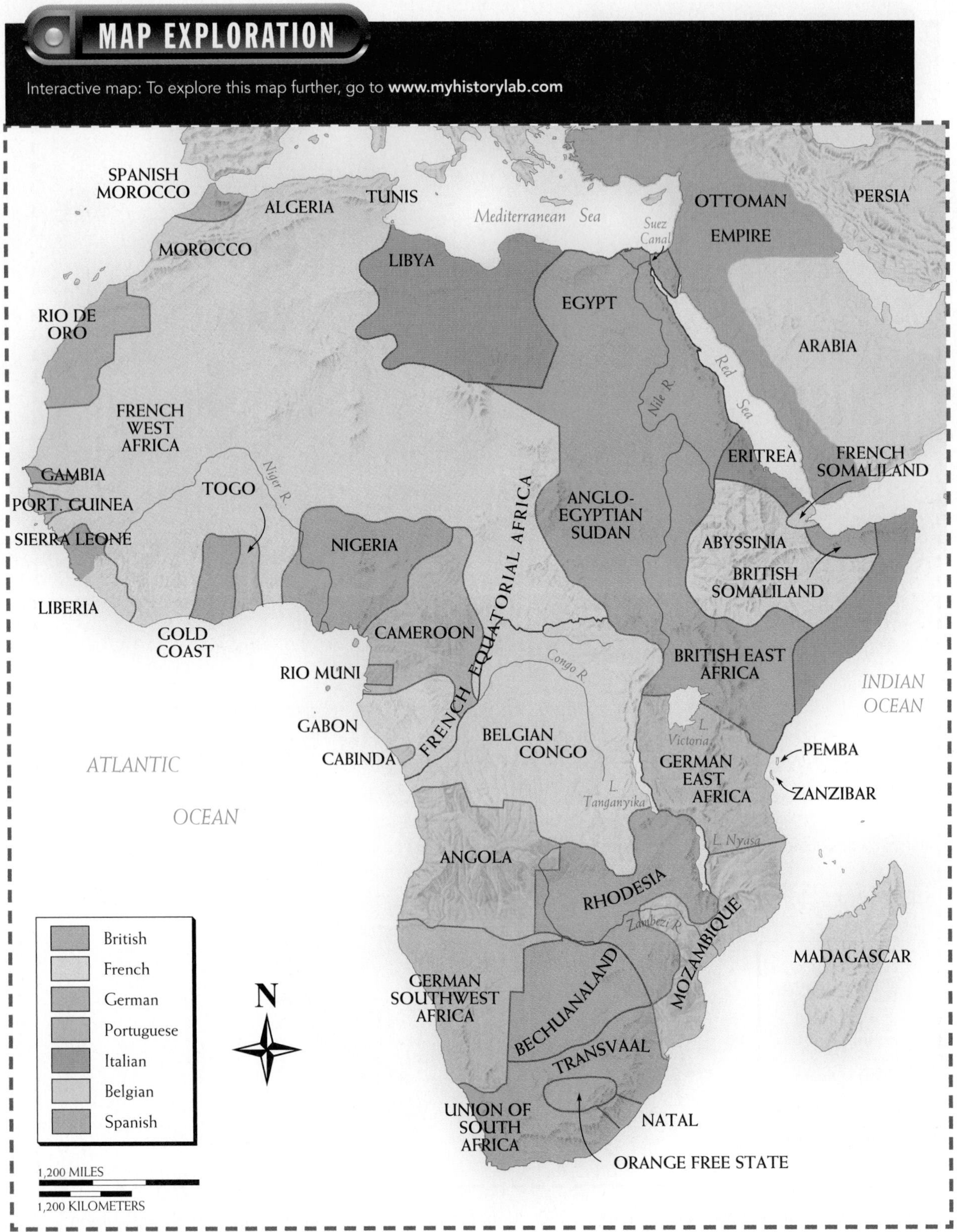

Map 25–3 **PARTITION OF AFRICA, 1880–1914** Before 1880, the European presence in Africa was largely the remains of early exploration by old imperialists and did not penetrate the heart of the continent. By 1914, the occupying powers included most large European states; only Liberia and Abyssinia (Ethiopia) remained independent.

The opening of the Suez Canal in 1869, linking Asia and Europe, was a major engineering achievement. It also became a major international waterway, reducing the distance from London to Bombay by half. Bibliothèque des Arts Decoratifs, Paris, France/The Bridgeman Art Library International

to Egypt that easily defeated the Egyptians and established seventy years of British supremacy in the country. A European power was thus drawn into the Middle East as never before.

Egypt was never an official part of the British Empire. The Khedives, who became kings after Egypt severed its ties with Turkey during the First World War, continued to reign, but a small number of British officials dominated the Egyptian administration. The British used their experience "advising" the Indian princes to run Egypt behind the façade of the Khedive's government.

Britain's primary goal in Egypt was political and military stability. Egypt had to repay its debts, and Britain was to retain control of the Suez Canal. The British built a naval base at Alexandria and installed a large garrison in Cairo. They established municipal governments that were responsible for taxation and public services and further expanded cotton cultivation. They also prevented the Egyptians from establishing a textile industry that would compete with Britain's own mills.

Economically, this meant that while the Egyptian economy grew and tax revenues increased, per capita income actually declined among Egyptians, most of whom were peasants who owned little or no land. Politically, it led to the growth of Egyptian nationalism, to Islamic militancy, and to demands that the British leave Egypt. Egyptian Islamic militants, organized into the Muslim Brotherhood in the late 1920s, would provide many of the anti-Western ideas that inspire radical Islam today.

The British occupation of Egypt quickly drew Britain even deeper into Africa along the Nile. Control of the upper Nile had been understood to be essential to the security of Egypt since ancient times. The collapse of the Khedive's authority in Cairo in 1881 had led to a similar collapse of Egyptian authority in the Sudan. In 1883 Muhammad Ahmad, a radical Muslim leader who claimed to be the Mahdi, a Muslim messiah, annihilated an Egyptian expeditionary force led by British officers. The British then sent General Charles Gordon to the Sudan, but Gordon, a hero in Britain, was killed in 1885 when the Mahdi's forces captured Khartoum, the Sudan's capital. The Mahdi himself died shortly thereafter, but his followers established a strict Islamic state. The Sudan remained in turmoil until 1898 when an Anglo-Egyptian army under General Sir Herbert, later Lord, Kitchener (1850–1916) conquered it in a remarkably violent campaign during which 11,000 Sudanese troops were killed and 16,000 were wounded by modern weaponry in a single battle at Omdurman. The British lost only 48 men in the battle. (See "Winston Churchill Reports on the Power of Modern Weaponry," page 772.) The number of casualties at

WINSTON CHURCHILL REPORTS ON THE POWER OF MODERN WEAPONRY AGAINST AN AFRICAN ARMY

In 1898 an army of approximately 25,000 British and Egyptian troops led by General Sir Horatio Kitchener invaded the Sudan to reassert British control against the forces of Abdallah al-Taashi, a Muslim religious leader, whose troops were called dervishes. The British and Egyptians were armed with modern rifles, machine guns, and artillery and were accompanied by gunboats on the Nile River. The dervishes also had guns, but they were less advanced technologically. One of the largest battles in colonial history occurred on September 2, 1898, at Omdurman, near Khartoum, the capital of Sudan. The dervish force consisted of approximately 50,000 well-disciplined troops and cavalry. Within hours, however, they were routed because of the fire-power advantage enjoyed by the British and Egyptian troops. Winston Churchill, who was serving in a cavalry regiment, later described the battle in a book on the war. Historians now believe more than 11,000 dervish troops died that day and approximately 16,000 were wounded while British casualties amounted to around 48 dead and fewer than 400 wounded. Observers at the time, as well as historians later, believed Kitchener used greater force and caused far more deaths and casualties than were necessary.

How does Churchill indicate his respect for the courage of the Dervish forces? Why might the kind of warfare made possible by advanced weapons be termed "industrial warfare"? How does Churchill convey the fearfulness of this battle?

Great clouds of smoke appeared all along the front of the British and Soudanese brigades. One after another four batteries opened on the enemy at a range of about 3,000 yards. The sound of the cannonade rolled up to us on the ridge, and was re-echoed by the hills. Above the heads of the moving masses shells began to burst, dotting the air with smoke-balls and the ground with bodies. But a nearer tragedy impended. The 'White Flags' were nearly over the crest. In another minute they would become visible to the batteries. Did they realise what would come to meet them? . . . It was a matter of machinery. . . . In a few seconds swift destruction would rush on these brave men. . . . Forthwith the gunboats . . . and other guns . . . opened on them. . . . The white banners toppled over in all directions. . . . It was a terrible sight, for as yet they had not hurt us at all, and it seemed an unfair advantage to strike thus cruelly when they could not reply. . . .

The infantry fired steadily and stolidly, without hurry or excitement, for the enemy were far away and the officers careful. . . . The empty cartridge-cases, tinkling to the ground, formed a small but growing heap beside each man. And all the time out on the plain on the other side bullets were shearing through flesh, smashing and splintering bone; blood spouted from terrible wounds; valiant men were struggling on through a hell of whistling metal, exploding shells, and spurting dust—suffering, despairing, dying. . . .

. . . at the critical moment the gunboat arrived on the scene and began suddenly to blaze and flame from Maxim guns, quick-firing guns, and rifles. The range was short; the effect tremendous. The terrible machine, floating gracefully on the waters—a beautiful white devil—wreathed itself in smoke. . . .

. . . the great Dervish army, who had advanced at sunrise in hope and courage, fled in utter rout, pursued by the Egyptian cavalry, harried by the 21st Lancers, and leaving more than 9,000 warriors dead and even greater numbers wounded behind them.

Thus ended the battle of Omdurman—the most signal triumph ever gained by the arms of science over barbarians.

Winston Spencer Churchill, *The River War: An Historical Account of the Reconquest of the Soudan*, F. Rhodes, ed., new rev. ed. (London: Longmans, Green, and Co., 1902), p. 272–273, 274, 279, 300.

Omdurman would not be matched in a single day until European armies turned modern weapons upon each other during World War I.

The British determination to secure the upper Nile and the Sudan led to one of the major crises of the imperial age. Although the French had refused to participate when British forces invaded Egypt in 1882, they retained large investments there and still hoped to influence Egyptian affairs by controlling the upper Nile. In the summer of 1898, a small French military force from West Africa reached the upper Nile at an unimportant location called Fashoda. As Kitchener's forces moved south, he confronted the French. War seemed possible until Paris ordered the French to withdraw. Instead of fighting, France and Britain eventually resolved their imperial rivalries. France acquiesced in Britain's domination of Egypt, and Britain agreed to support French ambitions in Morocco. The peaceful resolution of the Fashoda incident and other imperial disputes was essential to the formation of the loose alliance called the Anglo-French Entente in 1904 and to the two countries fighting as allies in World War I.

West Africa

France could surrender hope of dominating Egypt because it already controlled much of sub-Saharan Africa. West Africa, in particular, was a key area for French imperialism. In 1895 French West Africa included 12 million inhabitants and was eight times larger than France itself.

The British had four West African colonies: Sierra Leone, which was originally a home for freed slaves, Gambia, the Gold Coast (now Ghana), and Nigeria, the largest and most populous black African colony that any European power possessed. British slavers had worked on the Nigerian coast during the eighteenth century, and Britain had moved steadily into the Nigerian interior since the 1840s, seeking to establish trade and acquire tropical products, especially palm oil and cotton. The British annexed the port of Lagos in 1861. Various British trading companies operated on the Niger River with the Royal Niger Company, the most important of them, founded in 1886. Over time the British established protectorates over the Muslim emirates in northern Nigeria and direct control over other areas. In 1914,

The battle of Omdurman, fought on September 2, 1898 and described in the Churchill feature on page 772, demonstrated the capacity of European forces armed with the most modern weapons—in this case, a British army composed of British, Egyptian, and Sudanese troops, commanded by Major General Sir Horatio Kitchener—to decimate a vast Sudanese force armed with less advanced weapons. In the battle, which occurred near Khartoum, the British encircled the Sudanese forces. Approximately 10,000 African warriors were killed, while British losses numbered forty-eight men. Contrary to the image on this contemporary print, the British forces wore khaki rather than red uniforms. Picture Desk, Inc./Kobal Collection they combined all these territories into a single administrative unit, which they called the colony of Nigeria. To prevent indigenous resistance, British officials ran the country through local rulers, a policy known as indirect rule. Nigeria also became one of the most successful regions for British missionaries and has one of the largest Christian populations in Africa.

The Belgian Congo

Perhaps the most remarkable story in the European scramble for Africa was the acquisition of the Belgian Congo. In the 1880s, the lands drained by the vast Congo River and its tributaries became the personal property of King Leopold II of Belgium (r. 1865–1909). As a young monarch, he had become determined that Belgium, despite its small territory, must acquire colonies. No doubt he was inspired by the great commercial wealth that the neighboring Netherlands had accumulated from its long history of trade and empire in the East Indies.

The Belgian government, however, had no interest in colonies. So despite being a constitutional monarch, Leopold used his own wealth and political guile to realize his colonial ambitions. He did so under the guise of humanitarian concern for Africans. In 1876, he gathered explorers, geographers, and antislavery reformers in Brussels and formed the International African Association. He then recruited the English-born journalist and explorer Henry Morton Stanley (1841–1904) to undertake an expedition into the Congo. Stanley had previously made a great reputation by crossing Africa from east to west. Between 1879 and 1884, he explored the Congo and on Leopold's behalf made "treaties" with African rulers who had no idea what they were signing. Leopold then won diplomatic recognition for those treaties and for his own allegedly humanitarian efforts in the region, first from the United States and then in 1884–1885 from a conference in Berlin to allocate African territory among the European powers (see next section). The larger, stronger European states, particularly France, Britain, and Germany, were willing to let Leopold govern the Congo to keep one another out. Leopold, thus, personally became the ruler of an African domain that was over seventy times the size of Belgium.

Although Leopold cultivated the image of a humanitarian ruler by sponsoring antislavery conferences and manipulating public relations, his goal in the Congo was brutal economic exploitation. Leopold's administrators used slave labor, intimidation, torture, mutilation, and mass murder to extract rubber and ivory from what became known as the Congo Free State. Eventually, beginning with the African-American reporter George Washington Williams (1849–1891) and culminating with an international outcry led by the English journal-

Ivory was a prized possession used for decorative purposes and jewelry. Caravan with Ivory, French Congo, (now the Republic of the Congo). Robert Visser (1882-1894). c. 1890–1900, postcard, collotype. Publisher unknown, c. 1900. Postcard 1912. Image No. EEPA 1985-140792. Eliot Elisofon Photographic Archives. National Museum of African Art, Smithsonian Institution ist E. D. Morel (1873–1924) and the diplomat Roger Casement (1864–1916), Leopold's crimes were exposed, and he formally turned the Congo over to Belgium in 1908, the year before he died.

The cruelties in the Congo, which became the basis for Joseph Conrad's classic novel *Heart of Darkness* (1902), were recorded in photographs, eyewitness accounts, and newspaper articles and by an official Belgian commission. The most responsible historical estimates suggest that Leopold's exploitation halved the population of the Congo in about thirty years. Millions of Africans were murdered or died from overwork, starvation, and disease.

German Empire in Africa

The German chancellor Otto von Bismarck appears to have pursued an imperial policy, however briefly, from coldly political motives and with only modest enthusiasm. Bismarck had initially been dismissive of colonial ventures. By the mid- 1880s, however, he had changed his mind. In 1884 and 1885, Germany declared protectorates over South-West Africa (today the country of Namibia), Togoland, and the Cameroons in West Africa, and Tanganyika in East Africa. None of these places was particularly valuable or strategically important. Bismarck acquired colonies chiefly to improve Germany's diplomatic position in Europe and to divert France into colonial expansion and away from hostility to Germany. He also used German colonial activities in Africa to pressure the British to be reasonable about European affairs.

Bismarck had used Leopold II's efforts in the Congo to call the Berlin Conference in 1884 (not to be confused with the Congress of Berlin, which sought to settle the Eastern Question in 1879). At the Berlin Conference the major European powers decided on what amounted to the formal partition of Africa. The diplomatic representatives sat in a room where a large map of Africa hung on a wall and divided up their interests in the continent. By 1890 almost all the continent had been parceled out. Great powers and small ones expanded into areas neither profitable nor strategic for reasons that were less calculating and rational than Bismarck's.

Germany's proved to be the shortest lived of any of the European colonial ventures. German imperialism involved few Germans and produced no significant economic returns. At the end of World War I, the Allies stripped Germany of its colonial holdings. This meant that Germany was the only major West European state not drawn into the struggles of decolonization after World War II. But the German entry into the arena of imperial competition did contribute to the tensions that led to World War I (see Chapter 26). (See "Gustav Scholler Makes the Case for German Imperial Expansion," page 766.)

Genocide in South-West Africa The German Empire lasted for only about three decades, but in that time German administrators carried out a major atrocity against indigenous peoples in German South-West Africa. The Germans had occupied the region because the British were not interested in it and because parts of it appeared suitable for settlement. As German administrators seized more land and used natives as virtual slave labor, resistance mounted, and German settlers were killed

In 1904 the Herero people in the colony revolted, and the Germans decided to take severe action. They announced that the Hereros had to leave their land, and the German commander General Lothar von Trotha authorized the killing of all male Hereros and driving their women and children into the desert. (See "General von Trotha Demands that the Herero People Leave Their Land," page 776.) Hereo prisoners were placed in concentration camps where the death rates from disease were high although the Germans ran the camps with meticulous bureaucratic attention to detail. A United Nations report in 1985 concluded that by the time the Germans suppressed the revolt in 1908 80 percent of the Herero population had died.

Southern Africa

Except for coastal Algeria, only South Africa had attracted large numbers of European settlers. The Dutch had begun to settle there in the mid-1600s. By 1800, Cape Town had become an important port for ships on their way to Asia. During the Napoleonic Wars the British captured Cape Town from the Dutch. Soon thereafter, British settlers began to arrive, and British economic and cultural influence soon predominated on the Cape. Even though the British abolished slavery throughout the empire in 1834, African workers at the Cape remained subject to strict discriminatory legislation.

Not unsurprisingly, the Dutch resented British control. During the 1830s and 1840s, the Boers or Afrikaners, as the descendants of the Dutch were known, undertook the **Great Trek** during which they moved north and east of the Cape. This migration became the key moment in the forging of Afrikaner national consciousness. They founded states outside British control that would become Natal, Transvaal, and the Orange Free State. During the Great Trek the Boers also fought the Zulu people, who were themselves building an empire over other Africans. In 1843 the British annexed Natal, but the other two Boer republics remained independent.

In 1886 gold was discovered in the Transvaal, and 50,000 miners rushed to Johannesburg. There were now more non-Boer white settlers in the Transvaal than Boers, but the government refused to allow non-Boers

GENERAL VON TROTHA DEMANDS THAT THE HERERO PEOPLE LEAVE THEIR LAND

In 1904 Germany moved to repress the Herero people of South-West Africa who were resisting German rule. General Lothar von Trotha was in charge of the campaign. During his war against the Herero, he issued the following proclamation, which displays the outlook that led him and his troops to undertake a campaign of genocide against the Herero. The campaign had already, through warfare, disease, and forcing women and children into the desert, killed many Herero.

How does this proclamation indicate frustration at the incapacity of the Germans to control the Herero? How might this proclamation support the charge of genocide? What assumptions about racial superiority might lie behind this proclamation?

I, the great general of the German soldiers, send this letter to the Herero people. Herero are no longer German subjects. They have murdered, stolen, cut off the ears, and noses and other body parts from wounded soldiers, and now out of cowardice refuse to fight. I say to the people: anyone delivering a captain to one of my stations as a prisoner will receive one thousand [German] marks. . . . The Herero people must leave this land. If they do not, I will force them to do so by using the great gun [artillery]. Within the German border every male Herero, armed or unarmed, with or without cattle, will be shot to death. I will not longer receive women or children but will drive them back to their people or have them shot. These are my words to the Herero people.

General Lothar von Trotha, Proclamation of October 2, 1904 as quoted in Isabel V. Hull, *Absolute Destruction: Military Culture and the Practices of War in Imperial Germany* (Ithaca, NY: Cornell University Press, 2005), p. 56.

the right to vote. In 1895, Cecil Rhodes (1853–1902), prime minister of the Cape Colony, supported a conspiracy to install a British government in the Transvaal. The conspiracy failed and Rhodes was forced to resign, but tensions mounted between Britain and the Boers. In 1899 war broke out. Although the British finally won this Boer War in 1902, they were surprised by the strength of Boer resistance. When the Boers resorted to guerilla tactics, the British gathered Boer women and children into what they called **concentration camps** where many died from disease and exposure. (In the 1890s, the Spanish had also set up such camps when seeking to suppress a rebellion in Cuba.)

In 1910, the British combined the colonies in South Africa into a confederation whose constitution guaranteed the rule of the European minority over the majority black and nonwhite population. Africans and people of mixed race whom the British referred to as "colored" were forbidden to own land, denied the right to vote, and excluded from positions of power. To preserve their political power and economic privileges, the white elite of South Africa eventually enforced a policy of racial **apartheid**—"separateness"—that turned the country into a totally segregated land until the 1990s. The result was decades of oppression, racial tensions, and economic exploitation.

▼ Russian Expansion in Mainland Asia

The British presence in India was intimately related to Russian expansion across mainland Asia in the nineteenth century, which eventually brought huge territories and millions of people of a variety of ethnicities and religions under tsarist rule. This expansion of Russian imperialism is one of the chief sources of the ethnic tensions that exist today in the Russian Federation and in particular between that Federation and Chechnya and other parts of the Caucasus.

During the early eighteenth century, the tsars had consolidated their control around the Baltic Sea. Catherine the Great (r. 1762–1796) had gained much of southern Ukraine and opened the regions around the Black Sea to Russian control at the cost of Ottoman influence. The partitions of Poland had extended Russian authority toward the west (see Chapter 17). During the nine-

Diamond mining in South Africa took off in the late 1860s. By 1880 Kimberly, the biggest mine in the region, had 30,000 people, second only to Cape Town. Whites, such as these diamond sorters, monopolized the well-paid, skilled jobs. National Archives of South Africa

EXPANSION OF EUROPEAN POWER AND THE NEW IMPERIALISM

1869	Suez Canal completed
1875	Britain gains control of the Suez Canal
1879–1884	Leopold II establishes his personal rule in the Congo
1882	France controls Tunisia
1880s	Britain establishes protectorate over Egypt
1884–1885	Germany establishes protectorate over Southwest Africa (Namibia), Togoland, the Cameroons, and East Africa (Tanzania)
1895	Japan seizes Taiwan from China
1898	Spanish-American War: United States acquires Puerto Rico, Philippines, and Guam, annexes Hawaiian Islands, and establishes virtual protectorate over Cuba
1899	United States proposes Open Door Policy in Far East
1899–1902	Boer War in South Africa
1908	Belgium takes over the Congo from Leopold II
1905–1912	France establishes protectorate over Morocco
1910	Japan annexes Korea
1912	Italy conquers Libya from Turkey

teenth century the Russian government would look to the east where no major state could oppose its advance and where the weakness of the Ottoman Empire and China worked to Russian advantage.

Even during the eighteenth century, the tsarist government had ruled extremely diverse groups of people who were not Russian by language, religion, or cultural heritage. The Russians had generally approached these peoples in a pragmatic way, tolerating their religions and recognizing their social elites. What the Russian government sought was those elites' loyalty to the tsar rather than conformity to Russian language, the Orthodox Church, or Russian culture.

Beginning in the late eighteenth century, however, the tsarist government began to regard the nomadic societies or communities who lived in the mountainous regions to the south and east as "inorodtsy," meaning foreign. Moreover, the government drew upon the Enlightenment four-stage theory of social development, discussed in Chapter 17, to distinguish sedentary peoples as superior to those who lived as hunters, gatherers, fishermen, or nomads. One of the purposes thereafter of Russian expansion was, like that of early Victorian British administrators in India, to raise these people on the ladder of civilization. Russian governors would henceforth rarely, if ever, consider conquered peoples to be their social or cultural equals.

The nineteenth century saw Russia extend its authority in three distinct areas of mainland Asia. The first was in the Transcaucasus. This expansion came at the cost of Persia and the Ottoman Empire both of which by nineteenth-century standards had become weak states. The tsarist government presented these conquests as moves to protect Christian Georgians and Armenians from Muslim rule. But it never securely incorporated these regions into the Russian Empire because their aristocratic elites were not willing to be co-opted. By the late nineteenth century, nationalistic unrest was rising among Georgians, Armenians, and Azerbaijainis.

The Russians were also only modestly successful in subjagating the Muslim peoples living in the Caucasus regions of Chechnya, Dagestan, and Circassia. Between 1817 and 1865, the Russians had to fight a brutal guerilla war in these areas led by Imam Shamil (1797–1871). Once the Russian government had suppressed this resistance, it pursued its usual policy of seeking to gain the support of local aristocrats by recognizing their privileges and not disturbing their religion. Again this policy was only partially successful, and, as already noted, Chechen resistance to the new Russian Federation would arise in the late twentieth century.

The second prong of Russian imperial advance occurred in the vast steppes of Central Asia where various nomadic peoples lived. The most important of these were Kazakhs who remained nomadic even under Russian rule until Stalin forced them onto collective farms in the 1930s (see Chapter 27).

The final area of Russian imperial conquest occurred in southern Middle Asia from the 1860s to the 1880s. (See "The Russian Foreign Minister Explains the Imperatives of Expansion into Asia," page 000.) This is the region of present-day Uzbekistan, Turkistan, and the areas bordering Afghanistan, all of which are primarily Muslim. Here the Russians established protectorates under the nominal authority of the local rulers known as khans. Expansion in this area followed Russia's defeat in the Crimean War and sought to demonstrate that Russia could still exert imperial influence in Asia and counter the British presence in India. The Russian-British rivalry over these regions, particularly over Afghanistan, became known in journalism and fiction as "the Great Game." It sometimes brought Russia and Britain to the edge of war until the early twentieth century when both powers became concerned about German influence in the Ottoman Empire. The Anglo-Russian Convention of 1907 ended their Central Asian rivalry and gave each power spheres of influence in Persia. Like the settlement of colonial claims between Britain and France, the end of this particular imperial contest also opened the way for Britain and Russia to become allies against Germany during World War I.

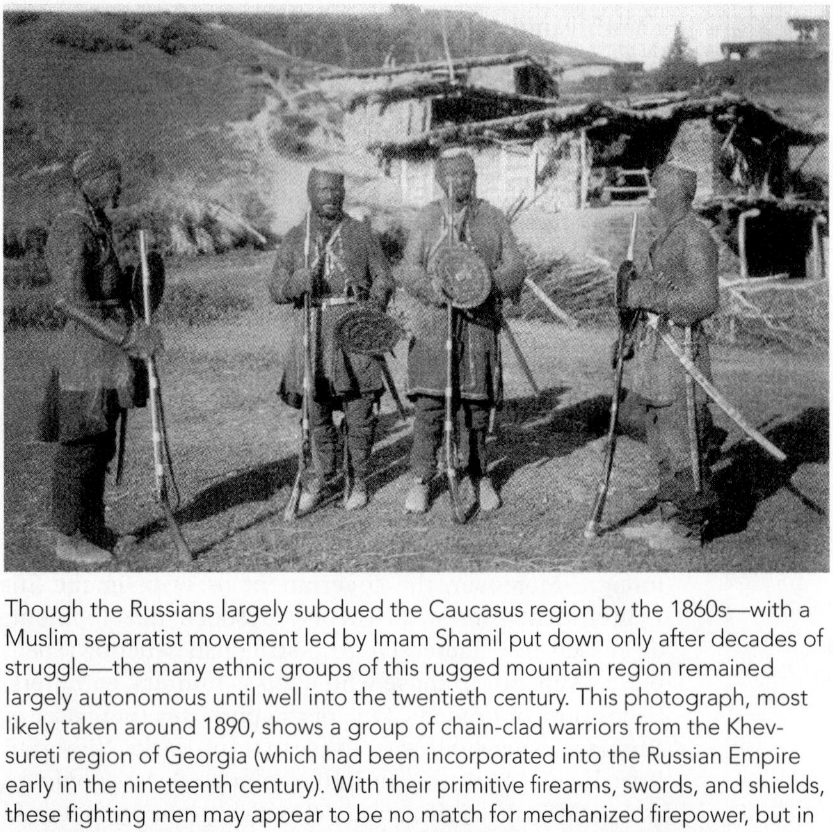

Though the Russians largely subdued the Caucasus region by the 1860s—with a Muslim separatist movement led by Imam Shamil put down only after decades of struggle—the many ethnic groups of this rugged mountain region remained largely autonomous until well into the twentieth century. This photograph, most likely taken around 1890, shows a group of chain-clad warriors from the Khevsureti region of Georgia (which had been incorporated into the Russian Empire early in the nineteenth century). With their primitive firearms, swords, and shields, these fighting men may appear to be no match for mechanized firepower, but in reality the people of this region remained largely free of governmental authority until well into the twentieth century. Courtesy of the Library of Congress

▼ Western Powers in Asia

France in Asia

While merchants had established the British interest in India and South Asia, French interest in Indochina arose because of the activity of Roman Catholic missionaries. The French domain in Indochina eventually consisted of Vietnam, Cambodia, and Laos.

French missionaries had been active in Vietnam as early as the seventeenth century. However, with papal support, they gained ground in Indochina and elsewhere in Asia in the 1830s and 1840s. Persecution soon followed. In 1856, Napoleon III (r. 1852–1870), whose troops protected the Pope in Rome and whose wife was a fervent Roman Catholic, sent forces to Vietnam to protect the missionaries and give France a base from which the French navy could operate in the Far East and French commerce could expand in Asia. By 1862, French forces controlled Saigon and the area around it. By the 1880s,

THE RUSSIAN FOREIGN MINISTER EXPLAINS THE IMPERATIVES OF EXPANSION IN ASIA

Prince Alexander M. Gorchakov (1798–1883) served as Russian foreign minister from 1856 to 1882. This was the period in which Russia conquered most of Central Asia. In this passage he justifies those conquests by asserting a Russian civilizing mission and strategic concerns. Note how he emphasizes what he regards as the superior civilization of Russia over the Asians it seeks to conquer.

How does Gorchakov equate semi-savage states with potential disorder? Why does he believe civilized states must move against the semi-savage states? How does he emphasize Russia's status as a great power by associating its problems and reasons for imperial conquest with those of other colonial nations?

The situation of Russia in Middle Asia is that of all civilized states which come into contact with semi-savage and itinerant ethnic groups without a structured social organization. In such a case the interest in the security of one's borders and in trade relations always makes it imperative that the civilized state should have a certain authority over its neighbors, who as a result of their wild and impetuous customs are very disconcerting. Initially it is a matter of containing their attacks and raids. In order to stop them, one is usually compelled to subjugate the adjoining ethnic groups more or less directly. Once this has been achieved, their manners become less unruly, though they in turn are now subjected to attacks by more distant tribes. The state is duty-bound to protect them against such raids, and punish the others for their deeds. From this springs the necessity of further protracted periodic expeditions against an enemy who, on account of his social order, cannot be caught. . . . For this reason the state has to decide between two alternatives. Either it must give up this unceasing work and surrender its border to continual disorder . . . or it must penetrate further and further into the wild lands . . . This has been the fate of all states which have come up against this kind of situation. The United States in America, France in Africa, Holland in its colonies, Britain in eastern India—all were drawn less by ambition and more by necessity along this path forwards on which it is very difficult to stop once one has started.

Prince Alexander M. Gorchakov as quoted in Andreas Kappeller, *The Russian Empire: A Multiethnic History*, Alfred Clayton, tr. (Llondon: Longman, 2001), p. 194.

France controlled all of Vietnam and had made Cambodia a protectorate. In 1896, Laos also became a French protectorate. Missionary work continued throughout Indochina, especially in Vietnam where Catholics became and remain a significant minority.

The United States Actions in Asia and the Pacific

In 1853, a United States naval squadron under Commodore Matthew C. Perry (1794–1858) arrived in Japanese waters to open Japanese markets to American goods. In 1867, American interest in the Pacific again manifested itself when the United States bought Alaska from Russia. For the next twenty-five years, the United States assumed a fairly passive role in foreign affairs, but it had established its presence in the Pacific.

Cuba's revolt against Spain in the 1890s ended this passivity and provided the impetus for the creation of an American empire. Sympathy for the Cuban cause, investments on the island, the desire for Cuban sugar, and concern over Cuba's strategic importance all helped drive the United States to fight Spain.

Victory in the brief Spanish-American War of 1898 brought the United States an informal protectorate over Cuba, and the annexation of Puerto Rico ended four hundred years of Spanish rule in the Western Hemisphere.

The United States also forced Spain to sell it the Philippines and Guam, while Germany bought the other Spanish islands in the Pacific. The United States and Germany divided Samoa between them. In 1898 the United States also annexed Hawaii, five years after an American-backed coup had overthrown the native Hawaiian monarchy. This burst of activity made the United States an imperial power. This status was confirmed when President Theodore Roosevelt sent an American fleet around the world between 1907 and 1909 and when the U.S.-built Panama Canal opened in 1914.

The Boxer Rebellion

By the close of the nineteenth century, Western powers had forced the Chinese government to give them privileged status in Chinese markets. With the backing of their governments, Christian missionaries were operating in much of China. The Qing Dynasty, which had ruled China since 1644, was in a state of near collapse, and its decay both enabled Western penetration and was exacerbated by it.

The United States feared that the European powers and Japan would soon carve up China and close its lucrative markets and investment opportunities to American interests. In 1899, to prevent this, the United States proposed the Open Door Policy, which was designed to prevent formal foreign annexations of Chinese territory and to allow businesspeople from all nations to trade in China on equal terms. Although all the powers except Russia eventually agreed to this policy in principle, they nonetheless carved out spheres of influence in China, and France, Britain, Germany, and Russia established naval bases on the Chinese coast (see Map 25–4).

Although the Qing government was too feeble to resist Western bullying, hatred of foreigners and resentment at their presence were strong. From late 1899 through the autumn of 1901, a Chinese group called The Righteous and Harmonious Society of Fists, better known in the West as the Boxers, attempted to resist the Western incursions. The Boxers, who were supported by a faction at the Qing court, hated missionaries whom they saw as agents of the imperial powers and killed thousands of their Chinese converts.

For the imperial powers, the key moment in the Boxer Rebellion was the attacks on the foreign diplomatic missions in Beijing, which lasted off and on for three months in 1900 until an international army occupied the Chinese capital in August 1900. For the second time in less than half a century, Western troops had

In 1900, an international force composed of troops drawn from Austria-Hungary, the French Third Republic, the German Empire, Italy, Japan, Russia, the United Kingdom, and the United States invaded China to put down the Boxer Rebellion, which had endangered Western missionaries and Western interests in China. In August 1900 these forces occupied Beijing. This contemporary print presents the image of a romanticized heroic assault by these foreign troops. Courtesy of the Library of Congress

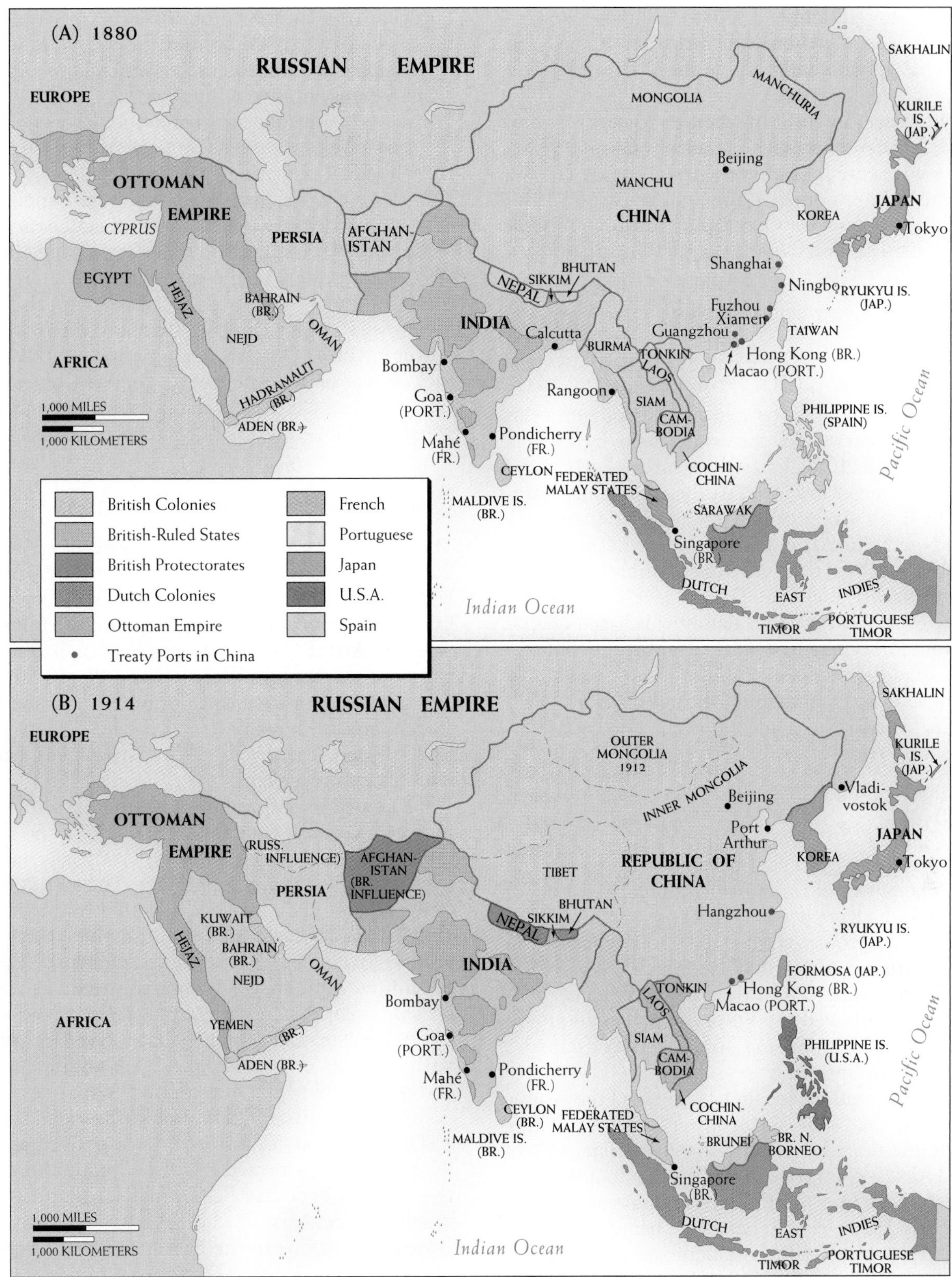

Map 25–4 **ASIA, 1880–1914** As in Africa, the decades before World War I saw imperialism spread widely and rapidly in Asia. Two new powers, Japan and the United States, joined the British, French, and Dutch in extending control both to islands and to the mainland and in exploiting an enfeebled China.

seized Beijing. In September 1901, the Chinese government agreed to execute officials who had helped the Boxers and pay large reparations to the Western powers and Japan.

The suppression of the Boxer Rebellion had demonstrated that even without formal empire Western powers could freely intervene in China. It set the stage for the collapse of the Qing dynasty in 1912 and opened China to decades of internal turmoil, foreign invasion, civil war, and eventually in 1949 a Communist Revolution.

▼ Tools of Imperialism

The domination that Europe and peoples of European descent came to exert over the entire globe by 1900 is extraordinary. It had not existed a century earlier and would not exist a century later. At the time many Europeans as well as Americans who worked their way across the North American continent in what many regarded as manifest destiny saw this domination as evidence of cultural or racial superiority (see Chapter 24). In fact, however, Western domination was based on distinct and temporary technological advantages, what one historian called the "tools of empire."[5] These tools gave Westerners the capacity to conquer and dominate vast areas of the world. (See "Encountering the Past: Submarine Cables.")

Steamboats

Europeans had long possessed naval superiority on the high seas. The power of those navies and of commercial sailing vessels had supported the early modern European empires and protected their trade routes across the Atlantic and around Africa into the Indian Ocean. That naval superiority persisted in the early nineteenth century, but it only allowed the European navies to attack and control coastal cities and strategic islands in the Indian and Pacific Oceans.

Robert Fulton, an American, had invented the steamboat in 1807. By the 1830s, steam power enabled warships to penetrate the inland rivers and shallow coastal waters of Asia and Africa, giving rise to the projection of Western power that became known as "gunboat diplomacy."

By the late 1820s, steamboats were being constructed of iron. In the 1830s, a British merchant sailed up the Niger River in West Africa on a well-armed iron steamship. In the nineteenth century, such boats carried European goods and European arms to assure trade in those goods up rivers around the world. It was almost impossible for local rulers and officials to defend themselves against iron warships.

Western steamboats were particularly effective along the vast rivers of Asia. The presence of gunboats on a river beside a city usually assured European merchants, and, especially for many decades, British merchants, access to the local markets. Iron steamboats, including some of the largest built to that date, assured British success against China in the first Opium War. The most famous of these new iron warships was the *Nemesis*, which was 184 feet long and employed two sixty-horsepower engines. This single ship armed with cannon and rockets was able to silence the guns of Chinese forts and sink wooden Chinese warships with impunity. French warships enjoyed similar advantages in Indochina.

Conquest of Tropical Diseases

Tropical diseases often proved more of an obstacle to European conquest than African or Asian armed forces. For centuries diseases, especially malaria, had prevented Europeans from penetrating deep into the forests of sub-Saharan Africa. Deaths were even high among Europeans in the trading bases on the West African coast. Often as many as one third to one half of the European traders and soldiers stationed in these posts would die from disease each year. West Africa was called "the white man's graveyard."

To move inland and increase their profits from commerce, especially after the formal end of the slave trade in the early nineteenth century, Europeans had to find a way around the malaria problem. The solution was quinine. French chemists had isolated quinine from cinchona bark as early as 1820. Slowly Western doctors began to recognize its medicinal qualities. The triumph of quinine came in 1854 when a British steamship, the *Pleiad*, under the command of a captain who was also a physician, steamed up the Niger River in West Africa with all of its crew and passengers taking quinine pills and returned with no loss of life.

Quinine pills made possible the rapid exploration and eventual partition of Africa. Moreover, the demand for quinine transformed its area of production. Originally cinchona bark had been grown in Peru. By the late nineteenth century, its chief regions of cultivation were Dutch plantations in the East Indies and British plantations in India.

Firearms

During the nineteenth century vast and momentous changes occurred in the technology of Western firearms. These changes gave Western nations an overwhelming advantage over non-Western peoples.

[5]Daniel Headrick, *Tools of Empire: Technology and European Imperialism in the Nineteenth Century* (New York: Oxford University Press, 1981). The author wishes to acknowledge his indebtedness to Headrick's scholarship in this section.

SUBMARINE CABLES

UNDER WATER TELEGRAPHIC cables were among the important inventions of the mid-nineteenth century utilizing then new electrical technology. Submarine cables amazed people of that era and the early twentieth century much as the Internet does today. These cables also allowed for unprecedented international communication.

The first submarine cable was laid between Great Britain and France in 1850, and the first transatlantic cable was installed successfully in 1866. Thereafter to a remarkable extent, made evident by the accompanying world map of the early twentieth century, the imperial strategic, military concerns of the British government determined the pattern of the installation of these cables of the Eastern Associated Telegraph Companies founded in 1872. It was a case of imperial expansion determining the application of an exciting new technology using electricity The route of the original Eastern cable of 1872 traced the coast of Western Europe, then across the Mediterranean through the Red Sea into the Indian Ocean to India, then overland in India, then eastward underwater to northern Australia and Hong Kong. By 1922, as seen in the map, cables linked all the areas of the British Empire acquired in the previous half century as well as the important markets for British trade in Latin America. The company oversaw approximately 130, 000 miles of cable. These submarine cables thus reflected late nineteenth-century British imperial expansion and also provided essential communication allowing the empire to function economically, politically, and militarily.

In 1922 the Eastern Associated Telegraph Companies of Great Britain published a celebratory fiftieth anniversary volume. It opened by declaring, "On the world's oceans, surrounded by forests of vegetation, faintly reflected in the waving seaweeds of shallow shores, amidst the haunts of creatures which never see the light of the sun, where the skeletons of the wrecked ships of to-day and yesterday loom like phantom far and near, lie the great submarine ropes with which man has encircled the earth. Through the dark underworld of the sea, across submerged continents, and over valleys, plains and mountains, trodden in an ageless past by the forerunners of mankind, these electrified ropes carry the messages of man to man." Eastern Associated Telegraph described their cables as "the nervous system of the civilized world" and boasted "There is hardly any spot in the more developed parts of the British Empire and of the world which cannot speedily be reached by a message marked 'via Eastern.'"

Source: *Fifty Years of "Via Eastern": A Souvenir and Record of the Celebrations in Connection with the Jubilee of the Eastern Associated Telegraph Companies MXMXII* (privately printed, 1922), pp. 13, 16.

The rifle was improved, so that bullets would spin more rapidly and move in a straighter direction. Early in the century Thomas Shaw invented the percussion cap for bullets. Unlike the earlier flintlock rifles, the percussion caps could easily be used in wet weather. The design of bullets themselves changed to allow greater speed and precision. By the mid-1850s, the British had adopted the Enfield rifle, which incorporated all the new technologies and was manufactured with interchangeable parts. These guns were accurate at several hundred yards. The invention of the breechloader in the 1860s brought still greater distance and precision in firepower for both rifles and artillery. Later in the century smokeless gunpowder and repeating mechanisms further enhanced accuracy and firepower.

All these technological changes were incorporated into the development of the machine gun. By 1900, the machine gun had become arguably the single most important weapon in colonial warfare and accounted for the deaths of tens of thousands of non-European peoples. Europeans also used dum-dum bullets, which exploded inside a wound, against native peoples when they would not use them against other Europeans.

Repeatedly in late-century colonial military campaigns, native peoples' guns, when they had any, were no match for European weapons. European nations also attempted to prevent new kinds of guns from being sold in Africa or other parts of the imperial world. A relatively small European force armed with the new rifles, cannon, and machine guns could overcome local armies that vastly outnumbered them. Such weaponry permitted Kitchener's overwhelming victory in the Sudan in 1898. Often Europeans ascribed their victories to their supposedly advanced civilization or racial superiority rather than recognizing that they owed their triumphs to superior firepower.

When African and Asian states did secure advanced weapons, they could either defeat European armies or carry out prolonged resistance. For example, in 1896, an Ethiopian army armed in part with modern rifles purchased from the French annihilated an invading Italian force at the Battle of Aduwa.

▼ The Missionary Factor

The modern Western missionary movement, which continues to the present day, originated in Great Britain in the late eighteenth century as a direct outgrowth of the rise of evangelical Christianity. Evangelicalism, which influenced Protestant communities from Central Europe to the United States, emphasized the authority of the Bible, the importance of a personal conversion experience, and the duty to spread the Gospel. Many Evangelicals were also concerned to prepare the world for the Second Coming of Jesus by carrying the message of Christian redemption to peoples who had not heard it. British Evangelicals first looked to unchurched groups in their own nation as the primary field for bearing Christian witness, but by the close of the eighteenth century, in a largely new departure for Protestants, small groups of Evangelicals began to be active in the non-Western world. Roman Catholics later copied these early Protestant missionary efforts. The result of this widespread nineteenth-century missionary campaign was the establishment of large Christian communities in Africa and Asia, which today thrive and continue to expand.

The Maxim was the first wholly portable machine gun, pictured here with its American-born inventor Hiram Stevens Maxim (1840–1916), who became a British citizen. Technological superiority in weaponry and naval ships accounted in large measure for the success of Western imperialism in the nineteenth century.

Evangelical Protestant Missionaries

The chief moving forces in the British missionary movement were the Baptist Missionary Society, the London Missionary Society, the Edinburgh and Glasgow Missionary Societies, and the Church [of England] Missionary Society, all founded in the 1790s. American Protestant missionary societies soon followed. One of the most influential publications urging missionary work was the Baptist William Carey's *An Enquiry into the Obligations of Christians, to use Means for the Conversion of the Heathen* (1792), which made the then novel argument that British Christians must carry their faith to non-Western peoples overseas. A year after publishing his tract, Carey himself went to India. He and others of his persuasion believed they dwelled in a providential moment of history for the expansion of Christianity. This coincided with the consolidation of British control of India and the opening of what would become a century of unprecedented imperial expansion. Initially the missionary societies, who often competed with each other along denominational lines, floundered and attracted little support, but by the mid-1820s, they were firmly established and growing enterprises. By 1900, British missionary societies employed approximately 10,000 missionaries.

German Protestants also embraced the missionary impulse. The earliest German societies such as the Leipzig Mission, founded in 1836, devoted their efforts to India. The Rhenish Missionary Society, founded 1828, established itself in East Africa and supported German colonial claims there in the 1880s. As early as 1833, the Berlin Missionary Society sent missionaries to South Africa; by 1869, it was also working in China.

Roman Catholic Missionary Advance

The nineteenth-century French Roman Catholic missionary effort was also enormous. It reflected the resurgence of the Catholic Church in France in the decades following the French Revolution and Napoleon. The Society for the Propagation of the Faith, the largest French missionary society, was founded in 1822. By the 1860s, it had over a million members. Its earliest missionaries went to China and Vietnam. Over time, however, French Catholic missionaries worked on every continent, including the islands of the Pacific. The White Fathers, so named because of their flowing white robes, were founded in 1868 to send missionaries to Africa, including Muslim North Africa.

Tensions Between Missionaries and Imperial Administrators

The mission societies and their missionaries had a complex relationship with their home governments. Missionary work did not necessarily support imperial missions. Missionaries from both Europe and America often settled in regions their governments did not control, and missionary societies often employed missionaries who came from a country other than the one sponsoring their mission. Nonetheless, the missionaries did develop many links with Western governments. The

Women played a prominent role as teachers in the Western foreign missionary effort. Miss Emily Hartwell was a turn-of-the-century, American-born Protestant missionary to the Foochow Mission in Fuzhou Shi, China. Here, in a photo from the missionary magazine *Light and Life*, she is pictured with one of her Bible classes composed of Chinese women. Her letters home spoke of the disadvantages of women in Chinese culture. Courtesy of the Library of Congress

British missionary movement often saw the expansion of the British Empire as opening the way for the spread of the Gospel. They saw the spread of Western commerce as both financially beneficial for missions and as opening up new areas for the missionary enterprise. During the Opium Wars, for example, the missionary societies demanded that the British government negotiate access for missionaries as well as traders and merchandise into China. Missionaries and advocates of free trade imperialism thus could have a mutually supportive relationship. This relationship softened toward the close of the century when the missionary societies defined themselves more strictly in terms of the spiritual mission of bearing witness to the Gospel.

Colonial administrators frequently resisted the introduction of missionaries into their territories for fear the missionaries would prove a destabilizing force as they challenged traditional religions and cultural values. Merchants and colonial governors often were not deeply concerned about changing the culture of local peoples. Missionaries might defend the rights of native peoples against official imperial policy or commercial interests' efforts to increase their profits. In the settlement colonies missionaries often clashed with the settlers who wanted to prevent native peoples from gaining the skills that would enable them to compete with whites. Colonial officials were also concerned about conflicts between Christian converts from different denominations. Some missionaries tried to change the modes of worship that an earlier generation of missionaries had introduced and persecuted converts who refused to conform. Furthermore, missionaries frequently educated persons from the lower levels of society who might resent colonial rule and the authority of native elites. The Christian vision of equality before God could, though it did not always, undermine the hierarchies of colonial authority. As one historian has commented, in India ". . . there were always prominent missionaries prepared to challenge or ignore the imperial system and their own ecclesiastical authorities."[6]

But even when colonial officials disliked them, missionaries nonetheless provided much of the educational infrastructure of imperialism particularly in India. At the village level their schools provided instruction in the local languages and English. Some of these schools received government financial support and hence became part of the administrative system. Missionaries also established institutions of higher education, including Serampore College (1818), Bishops College (1824) in Calcutta, and Forman Christian College (1865) in Lahore. Later in the century, missionaries founded women's colleges. These colleges trained primarily members of the Indian elite, both Hindu and Muslim. Instruction was invariably in English because the elites realized that knowing English was essential to their status in imperial India. As missionary groups became more directly associated with education, the number of women missionaries in India grew, and by the early twentieth century, most missionaries there were women.

The relationship of French Roman Catholic missionaries to imperialism was complicated because the governments of the Third Republic in France were usually anticlerical after the 1870s. Yet although the republican government often clashed with the Catholic Church in France, it frequently supported missionary activity abroad as a way of extending French national interests. For example, France remained the official protector of Roman Catholics in the Ottoman Empire even after the French government broke diplomatic ties with the Vatican in 1905. In some cases the government in Paris or local colonial administrators encouraged French missionary activity to make native peoples sympathetic to French rule or to block the advance of other European powers. By teaching the French language, French missionaries also made it easier for French commercial interests to operate in a territory.

By 1900, approximately 58,000 French priests, religious brothers, and nuns were involved in the missionary enterprise. Like their British and German counterparts, French missionaries also often experienced tense relations with colonial administrators. Sometimes the colonial government pressed the civilizing mission through secular physicians, teachers, and agricultural consultants to counter the religious influence of missionaries. At the same time, however, the success of the French Catholic missionary effort meant that colonial officials in Vietnam and parts of Africa and the Pacific had to deal with large numbers of native Roman Catholics who supported and admired the missionaries. Yet by the early twentieth century, French missionaries increasingly saw their role not only as winning converts but also as molding native cultures in the image of France. As one historian has written, "Spreading civilization, which missionaries had long considered simply a fortunate by-product of evangelizing, came to the fore in Catholic propaganda as the movement's chief goal. From the 1890s forward, missionary publications increasingly chronicled the lives and tribulations of missionaries committed not only to God but also to the *patrie* [the French fatherland] and a specifically French civilizing mission."[7]

However sympathetic missionaries might become to indigenous peoples, they remained spokespersons for Western civilization. Because missionaries wished to convert indigenous peoples to Western Christianity, they implicitly shared with colonial officials the general

[6]Robert Frykenberg, "Christian Missions and the Raj," in Norman Ehternington, ed., *Missions and Empire* (New York: Oxford University Press, 2005), p. 129.

[7]J. P. Daughton, *Empire Divided: Religion, Republicanism, and the Making of French Colonialism, 1880–1914* (New York: Oxford University Press, 2006), p. 18.

cultural assumption of the superiority of things Western. Yet the very concern to bring Christian truth to non-Christian groups meant that Western missionaries had to engage native cultures in ways that colonial administrators did not. Missionaries had to learn local languages to translate the Bible and in doing so probably preserved some languages from extinction. They often needed to understand indigenous customs before seeking to change them. Some missionaries thus became amateur anthropologists. Nonetheless, even when missionaries were not formal agents of empire, they introduced Western cultural values, manners, and outlooks. While colonial governments might be associated with more advanced military and transportation technology, missionaries might be associated with more advanced medicine or agriculture in the hospitals and mission stations they ran. And missionaries, like colonial officials, generally assumed that native peoples were inferior to Westerners. While a few missionaries by 1900 believed that Christians and persons of other religions could learn from each other, most missionaries, regarded non-Christians simply as heathens. That outlook, like the attitudes of secular administrators, generated its own sets of reactions.

Missionaries and Indigenous Religious Movements

Just as the presence of colonial administrations during the nineteenth century gave rise to various nationalist movements or movements that promoted the rights and interests of native peoples, the missionary activities gave rise to Asian and African religious movements that challenged the dominance of Western missionaries. The founding of new African and Asian Christian churches occurred as a result of the rejection of the racial and cultural assumptions of Western missionaries and as a means of reconciling Christianity with longstanding cultural practices, such as polygamy in Africa. The most important fact about the independent churches of Africa was that their leaders were African. For example, in 1888 David Brown Vincent established the Native Baptist Church in Lagos, Nigeria, after leaving the American-founded Baptist Church there. Not long thereafter, in South Africa Mangena Makone broke with the Methodists to found the Ethiopian Church. In Kenya, Christian members of the Kikuyu tribe split with the Church of Scotland Mission. In the early twentieth century, Christian Pentecostal groups arose among African Christians, as did other churches associated with gifts of healing or prophecy. These independent religious movements are the roots from which has sprung the current divide between Christian Churches of the northern and southern hemispheres that we will discuss more fully in Chapter 30.

In summary, how may one describe the interrelationship of the missionary movement and colonialism? First, it was dynamic and changed during the nineteenth century as missionary goals and sensibilities changed from one generation to another. Second, the missionary movement spawned an enormous amount of printed publicity in the form of newspaper and journal articles, missionary society publications, and missionary narratives and autobiographies. These materials publicized the vision of empire and raised interest in the West about the non-Western world. They also strongly influenced popular culture at a time when the churches were more influential than they are today, especially in Europe. Third, the missionary societies and the churches with which they were associated became skilled at pressuring their governments. Initially they directed their efforts toward permitting and protecting missionary activities. By the early twentieth century, however, many missionaries were supporting native peoples in their opposition to colonial authorities. Fourth, the religious effects of the missions were a two-way street. While Westerners brought Christianity to Africa and Asia, by 1900, non-Western Christians were beginning to move Christianity away from its dominance by Europeans and Americans. This process is still going on today. Finally, the missionary movement of the nineteenth century made Christianity a genuinely worldwide religion for the first time. The spread of Christianity like the development of self-government in the British settler colonies, was thus one of the major elements of the extension of Western civilization around the globe.

▾ Science and Imperialism

The early modern European encounter with the non-Western world from the fifteenth-century voyages of discovery onward had been associated with the expansion of natural knowledge. The same would be true of Western imperialism in the nineteenth and early twentieth centuries. Commencing in 1768, Captain James Cook (1728–1779) had undertaken his famous voyages to the South Pacific under the patronage of the Royal Society of London to observe the transit of the planet Venus. Sir Joseph Banks (1744–1820), later president of the Royal Society, went with him to collect specimens of plants and animals unknown in Europe. Other British, French, and Spanish naval expeditions also carried scientists with their crews. Scientific societies often cooperated with military forces to carry out their research. For example, dozens of French scholars accompanied Napoleon's invasion of Egypt in 1798.

Geography was an expanding scientific discipline in the nineteenth century. Explorers wrote of their discoveries and adventures in Africa and Asia. Some explorers, such as the Scottish Presbyterian David Livingstone (1813–1873) and the French Jesuit Armand David (1829–1900), were also missionaries. Explorers portrayed themselves as pioneers who opened wild and savage spaces for commerce, religion, and ultimately civilization. Consequently, scientific and geographical societies generally supported their nations' imperialist goals and saw their research as benefiting from it. Scientific institutes, especially astronomical observatories, were set up in colonies. Moreover, the colonial administrations employed large numbers of engineers who planned and oversaw the construction of railways, roads, bridges, harbors, dams, and telegraph lines throughout the European empires. Geologists working for governments and private companies surveyed the mineral resources of newly acquired empires. As one British historian put it, "Natural scientists formed . . . [an] important . . . category of professional 'collaborators': an interest group central to the weaving of Africa, Asia, and the Americans into the fabric of national life."[8]

Kew Garden near London was the center of a vast network of botanical research. Joseph Dalton Hooker, its director, persuaded collectors from around the world to send specimens to Kew. Tropical plants were grown in its greenhouse, where British citizens could visit the grounds and see the plants that populated the far regions of the British empire. This photo shows Kew Palace, located in Kew Garden. Dorling Kindersley © Jamie Marshall

Four areas of scientific research deserve particular mention because they demonstrate how imperialism could filter into the wider European culture and capture the imagination of domestic audiences who never set foot outside Europe. These are botany, zoology, medicine, and anthropology.

Botany

Botany was the nineteenth-century colonial science par excellence, reflecting and nurturing the vast expansion of agriculture around the globe. This expansion brought millions of acres of new land under cultivation in the Americas, Australia, New Zealand, and Algeria. Colonial officials and Western investors also forced or induced colonial peoples, mainly in the tropics, to grow cash crops, such as coffee, sugar, tea, rubber, jute, cotton, bananas, and cocoa, for export to Europe.

European botanists were intensely interested in the plants they might discover abroad. Their interest ranged from the discovery of previously unknown specimens through the development of new crops that would improve agriculture. Changes in taste, like the spread of tea and coffee drinking, and in technology, like the demand for rubber for bicycle and motorcar tires, could create demands for colonial agricultural products. Gutta-percha, a latex from trees in southeast Asia, came to fulfill a host of uses from insulating electrical wires to providing material for flooring. Palm oil from West Africa was used in cooking, industrial lubrication, soaps, and cosmetics.

British colonies almost invariably had a large botanical garden to develop useful plants. The Royal Botanical Garden at Kew, near London, was the hub in a vast network of imperial gardens dedicated to the advancement of agriculture.

Gardens such as Kew and the *Jardin des Plantes* in Paris also allowed the general public to encounter a soft and inviting side of empire. Visitors could experience different parts of the empire in a pleasant setting as they strolled along flowerbeds, under trees, or through greenhouses. These great gardens made empire appear benign and far removed from the difficulties of its administration, the oppression of its indigenous peoples, or the havoc that empire may have wreaked on the peasant farmers of faraway places. These gardens and the new products and foods that Europeans and Americans consumed persuaded them that empire was part of the general progress of the age, which they associated with science.

[8]Richard Drayton, *Nature's Government: Science, Imperial Britain, and the 'Improvement' of the World* (New Haven, CT: Yale University Press, 2000), p. 171.

The gardens with their research staffs also were devices for transforming economies. The same spirit of agricultural improvement that had begun in Britain in the eighteenth century was carried throughout the empire. Botanists worked as economic innovators to achieve intercontinental transfers of plants to secure products for their home countries and to develop colonial economies. In India, the British pushed farmers to grow cotton, hemp, tea, and cinchona trees. French botanists helped change the agricultural economy of Algeria from producing grain, which France already had in abundance, to growing wine grapes, fruit, and olives, which had ready markets in France.

One of the most important contributions British botanists made was to introduce rubber trees to British colonies. Until the 1890s the British had had to import rubber from wild trees that grew in the Amazon jungles of Brazil and Peru. To get around this expensive monopoly, British botanists in 1876 smuggled seeds from these wild trees to Kew where plants were grown for the eventual production of rubber in British tropical colonies. By the early twentieth century, British Malaya in southeast Asia had become a major producer of rubber, as did parts of the Gold Coast colony in Africa. The French and Dutch then created rubber plantations in Indochina and the East Indies. As a result, the market for wild South American rubber all but collapsed, ruining the economy of the Amazon.

As plant commodities fell in value in one part of the British Empire, British administrators and merchants would contact Kew Garden for suggestions of other profitable crops. The botanists thus profited from empire by establishing themselves as the experts for the economic development of colonies after they had been annexed or after the crops that had once supported them were no longer profitable. Planters associations in the European colonies also established their own experimental stations to improve existing crops or develop new ones for cultivation.

Zoology

In the eighteenth century some European monarchs, such as the Habsburg emperors in Vienna and the French kings in Paris, had established collections of exotic animals. In the nineteenth century zoos and zoological gardens were founded in major European and American cities. These zoos displayed animals from around the world that expeditions acquired from the regions that European imperialism was penetrating.

Other scientists would collect specimens of animals, particularly birds, which they killed and brought back from the colonies to Europe to be placed in natural history museums. These museums became increasingly popular in the late nineteenth century.

Medicine

Medical science was an integral part of the imperial enterprise on several different levels. As already noted, Westerners had to overcome various tropical diseases, especially malaria, that prevented them from surviving in the tropics. But Western medicine also became a fundamental feature of the civilizing mission of colonial administrators and missionaries, many of whom were physicians. The spread of Western medicine justified colonial rule and helped win converts. The primary diseases that Western doctors sought to battle in the tropical colonies were yellow fever, sleeping sickness, small pox, hookworm, and leprosy.

Missionaries had pioneered the introduction of Western medicine into the colonial setting. They presented themselves as people who sought to heal both body and soul. Some missionaries thought they could convert native peoples to Christianity by first demonstrating the power of Western medicine. In Africa various forms of surgery and the removal of cataracts, which restored sight, became powerful tools of conversion.

Physicians and medical researchers sought to win government financial support by demonstrating that modern medicine could cure the endemic diseases that ravaged colonial peoples. Among the most influential colonial medical institutions were the Pasteur Institutes, named after Louis Pasteur (1822–1895), the French scientist who had found a cure for rabies and other diseases. The first overseas Pasteur Institute was founded in Saigon in 1891; others followed across the French Empire.

One of the most famous cases of a cure for a tropical disease that followed an imperial involvement was the conquest of yellow fever. After U.S. forces occupied Cuba in 1898, a yellow fever epidemic struck Havana and hundreds of American troops died. The Surgeon General of the United States sent a medical commission headed by Dr. Walter Reed to Cuba to address the problem. A Cuban physician, Carlos Finley persuaded Reed to look to an insect source for the disease. Experiments convinced Reed that yellow fever was mosquito borne. Steps were taken to eradicate mosquitoes in Havana, and the epidemic ceased. The conquest of yellow fever opened the way for the later construction of the Panama Canal during which etymologists protected workers from mosquito bites.

In general in the colonial world, Western science became a vehicle for what is often termed cultural imperialism. Medical advances allowed Western penetration of the tropics and then underpinned Western cultural and political domination. European medical institutions controlled research in the colonies. Westerners seldom had respect for Asian and African medical personnel no matter how well they were trained. Yet there is no question that Western medicine either eradicated or lessened the impact of diseases that had ravaged the non-Western world for centuries and, especially in the twentieth century, extended the lifespan and physical well being of colonial or former colonial peoples.

Anthropology

Almost immediately from Christopher Columbus's first encounter with the Americas in 1492, European observers began to record and analyze the character of the non-European peoples they confronted and conquered. This interest never ceased, but in the late nineteenth century, the study of non-Western peoples became associated with the science of anthropology.

Anthropological societies were founded in Paris (1859), London (1863), and Berlin (1870). The leaders of these new societies were convinced of the multiple origins of the races of humankind (a theory termed polygenesis) and of the inherent inequality of races. The concept of multiple origins had originated earlier in the nineteenth century in the United States where it had been an argument in defense of slavery. Polygenesis was one of many scientific theories that supported a hierarchy of unequal races at the top of which Westerners always placed the white races.

Many anthropologists believed that such factors as skull type determined human character, another idea originating the United States. Paul Broca (1824–1880), a French physician who specialized in the brain, measured the skulls of human beings from different races and assigned them intellectual capacity on the basis of brain size. Other European and American scientists followed his lead. Anthropologists who studied colonial societies carried these ideas with them.

Anthropology as a social science infused with racial thinking (see Chapter 24) had become organized in Western Europe on the eve of the Scramble for Africa. Anthropologists from then through the Second World War rode the wave of imperial enthusiasm. They worked closely with colonial administrations and encouraged expeditions to explore Africa. Even anthropologists who opposed colonialism cooperated with colonial administrators once the colonial empires had been created. Moreover, whatever their private doubts about racial theory may have been, anthropologists eagerly sought university professorships in the colonies and government funding for research on the grounds that their research supported colonialism. In fact, however, colonial officials rarely sought anthropologists' advice. Instead, anthropologists influenced imperial policies through their books, lectures, and university classes. European and American readers and students were invariably told that non-Western peoples were inferior, that their economies were underdeveloped, that their societies were corrupt, decadent, or primitive, and that their religions were dangerous and false. All this proved the need for Western administration and control.

Many of these same attitudes informed the creation of the great anthropological museums in Europe and the United States. The most famous of these was and remains the Museum of Mankind (Musée de l'Homme) in Paris, which began in 1878 as a Museum of Ethnography. But one of the most remarkable is the Royal Museum for Central Africa that Leopold II established in 1897 in Brussels to showcase his Congolese empire. Leopold's museum had begun earlier that year as an exhibit at a World's Fair that also boasted an African village on its grounds with more than fifty Africans living in it. These museums, which were very popular, often presented artifacts of

Peoples from colonized nations were transported to various world's fairs and similar exhibitions during the late nineteenth and early twentieth centuries. They constituted living exhibitions, where they were expected to portray "native customs" or the like. Here at the St. Louis World's Fair of 1904 African Pygmies demonstrated beheading. In this and other similar examples, native peoples were frequently presented in demeaning roles that filled the expectations of spectators to see "exotic" behavior. Such performances and exhibitions served to convince the Western spectators of the superiority of their civilization over that of the peoples living in the colonized world. Courtesy of the Library of Congress

African and Asian culture that explorers or other travelers or researchers had brought home. These exhibitions, like the botanical gardens, zoos and museums of natural history, introduced Western audiences to what they considered to be the exotic features and otherness of non-Western peoples and cultures.

The idea of museums or zoos to display exotic creatures was also extended to human beings in both Europe and the United States. Showmen such as the American P. T. Barnum would exhibit Africans, Asians, and Native Americans. Carl Hagenbeck, a German, brought Polynesians, Sudanese, and Inuits from Canada to live in" native villages" in the Hamburg Zoo. In the thirty years before World War I, the Paris zoo staged over twenty-five such exhibitions. At World's Fairs, millions of Europeans and Americans paid to view native peoples. As late as 1958 the Brussels World's Fair, like that of Leopold II sixty years earlier, boasted a village of Congolese people.

In Perspective

Western imperialism during the nineteenth and early twentieth centuries reshaped the world in ways that still affect us today. The productive capacity, military superiority, and technological prowess first of the European powers and later of the United States allowed those nations to dominate the world as they had never been able to do before. That dominance would last for about a century. Western influence arose from decades of free-trade imperialism in the early nineteenth century that was marked in general by the absence of formal imperial government except for Britain in India and its settler colonies. The New Imperialism began in the 1870s largely as a result of the political changes that had occurred in Europe since the 1850s—the defeat of Russia in the Crimean War, the unification of Italy and Germany, and the defeat of France by Germany in 1870—that upset the balance of power and heightened tensions and competition among the great powers who increasingly sought to reassure themselves and assert their power by expanding into the non-Western world. The New Imperialism thus involved the creation of formal empires as a sign of great power status, the protection of what were seen as vital geo-political interests, an assertion of white racial superiority, and the partition of Africa. All these ideas and events led the European powers into overseas imperial rivalries that contributed to the tensions resulting in the outbreak of World War I in 1914.

Western imperialism found many supporters. Manufacturers and merchants sought markets for their goods and sources of tropical raw materials. Missionaries sought to evangelize the parts of Africa and Asia previously closed to Christianity. Scientists saw the imperial mission as creating networks for research and a new appreciation of their own efforts as supporters of their national governments. Army and navy officers looked to colonial wars as avenues for professional advancement.

For over a century, from the 1830s to the 1940s, the peoples of the non-Western world found themselves generally acted upon by foreign political, economic, and military forces that they could not effectively resist. Many of these non-Western peoples sought to work with Westerners for their own advantage. Indeed, the Western colonial empires could not have functioned without African and Asian collaborators. By the outbreak of World War I, however, discontent was stirring throughout the colonial world, and the leaders of the post–World War II movement for decolonization and independence had begun to emerge.

Review Questions

1. How did European imperial interests shift geographically in the nineteenth century? How was free trade related to the expansion of European influence around the globe?
2. What was the New Imperialism? How was it different from free-trade imperialism? Why was Britain the dominant world power until the late nineteenth century? What were the Opium Wars?
3. How did the British come to dominate India? What were the causes of the Indian rebellion of 1857? How did British rule in India change after the rebellion? Why was India so important to Britain?
4. What were the motives of the New Imperialism? To what extent was the New Imperialism related to the capitalist search for higher profits and new markets? How did colonial officials and businesspeople influence the growth of colonial empires?
5. Why was Algeria the most important part of the French Empire? What parts of the Ottoman Empire fell under European rule between the 1880s and 1914? Why did Britain come to dominate Egypt? Why did Germany and Italy acquire colonies? Why did Leopold II build an empire in the Congo? What was the Scramble for Africa?
6. How did France gain control of Indochina? How did the United States become an imperial power? Where did Russia expand in mainland Asia? What were the consequences of Western imperialism in China?
7. What were the "tools of imperialism"? Why was quinine so important for the spread of empires? What technological improvements enabled Western powers to dominate so much of the non-Western world? Why were the new colonial empires so short-lived?
8. Why did Western missionary efforts expand in the nineteenth century? Why was the relationship between Western missionaries and colonial officials so complicated? Why did Africans want to found their own churches? How has the spread of

Christianity in the non-Western world affected the Christian churches?

9. How did Westerners justify imperialism? What was the civilizing mission? What sciences were most associated with the New Imperialism? What role did racism play in the New Imperialism?

SUGGESTED READINGS

M. Adas, *Machines as the Measure of Men: Science, Technology, and Ideologies of Western Dominance* (1989). The best single volume on racial thinking and technological advances as forming ideologies of European colonial dominance.

R. Aldrich, *Greater France: A History of French Overseas Expansion* (1996). Remains the best overview.

C. Bayly, *Imperial Meridian: The British Empire and the World: 1780–1830* (1989). Places the British expansion in India into larger imperial contexts.

D. Brower, *Turkestan and the Fate of the Russian Empire* (2003). A concise treatment of a case study in Russian imperialism in Asia.

A. Burton, *Burdens of History: British Feminists, Indian Women, and Imperial Culture, 1865–1915* (1994). Explores the relationship of women in Britain's Indian empire.

A. Conklin, *A Mission to Civilize: The Republican Idea of Empire in France and West Africa, 1895–1930* (2000). An in-depth analysis of a case history of the civilizing mission.

F. Cooper and A. L. Stoler, eds., *Tensions of Empire: Colonial Cultures in a Bourgeois World* (1997). Explores difficulties of accommodating ideas and realities of empire to domestic middle-class values and outlooks.

J. Cox, *Imperial Fault Lines: Christianity and Colonial Power in India, 1818–1940* (2002). The best treatment of British missionaries in India.

J. P. Daughton, *An Empire Divided: Religion, Republicanism, and the Making of French Colonialism, 1880–1914* (2008). A superb discussion of the interaction of religion, empire, and domestic French politics.

N. P. Dirks, *The Scandal of Empire: India and the Creation of Imperial Britain* (2006). An elegant study of the interaction of British political sensibilities and the emergence of the British Empire in India.

R. Drayton, *Nature's Government: Science, Imperial Britain, and the "Improvement"of the World* (2000). The best volume on the relationship of science and imperialism.

M. H. Edney, *Mapping an Empire: The Geograhical Constuction of British India, 1765–1843* (1997). Discusses how the science of cartography contributed to the British domination of India.

N. Etherington, ed., *Missions and Empire* (2005). An excellent collection of essays.

D. Headrick, *The Tools of Empire: Technology and European Imperialism in the Nineteenth Century* (1981). Remains an important work of analysis.

A. Hochschild, *King Leopold's Ghost: A Study of Greed, Terror, and Heroism in Colonial Africa* (1999). A well-informed account of a tragedy.

I. Hull, *Absolute Destruction: Military Culture and the Practices of War in Imperial Germany* (2006). Excellent account of destructive German actions in East Africa.

R. Hyam, *Britain's Imperial Century 1815–1914: A Study of Empire and Expansion* (2002). The single best one-volume analysis.

T. Jeal, *Livingstone* (2001). This and the following title recount the lives of the two persons most associated in the popular mind with the exploration of Africa.

T. Jeal, *Stanley: The Impossible Life of Africa's Greatest Explorer* (2008).

A. Kappeller, *The Russian Empire: A Multiethnic History* (2001). A straigtforward overview that is very clear on the concepts behind Russian expansionist policy.

D. C. Lievan, *The Russian Empire and Its Rivals* (2001). Explores the imperial side of Russian government.

K. E. Meyer and S. B. Brysa, *Tournament of Shadows: The Great Game and the Race for Empire in Central Asia* (1999). A lively account of the conflict between Great Britain and Russia.

W. J. Mommsen, *Theories of Imperialism* (1980). A study of the debate on the meaning of imperialism.

M. A. Osborne, *Nature, the Exotic, and the Science of French Colonialism* (1994). Explores the impact of French horticultural gardens and imperialism.

L. Pyenson, *Civilizing Mission: Exact Sciences and French Overseas Expansion, 1830–1940* (1993). A major work of the history of both science and imperialism.

B. Porter, *The Absent-Minded Imperialists: Empire, Society, and Culture in Britain* (2006). Discusses the relatively few people actually involved in British imperialism and how imperialism often had a low profile in the British Isles.

B. Porter, *The Lion's Share: A Short History of British Imperialism, 1850–2004* (2004). A lively narrative.

R. Robinson, J. Gallagher, and A. Denny, *Africa and the Victorians: The Official Mind of Imperialism* (2000). A classic analysis that continues to bear rereading.

P. J. Tuck, *French Catholic Missionaries and the Politics of Imperialism in Vietnam, 1857–1914* (1987). Includes both narrative and documents.

H. L. Wesseling, *Divide and Rule: The Partition of Africa, 1889–1914* (1996). A clear narrative and analysis of a complicated topic.

H. L. Wesseling, *The European Colonial Empires: 1815–1919* (2004). The best recent overview of the entire nineteenth-century European colonial ventures.

E. R. Wolf, *Europe and the People Without History* (1990). A classic, highly critical account.

A. Zimmerman, *Anthropology and Antihumanism in Imperial Germany* (2001). Discusses the manner in which anthropology in conjunction with imperialism challenged humanistic ideas in German intellectual life.

THE WEST & THE WORLD

Imperialism: Ancient and Modern

THE CONCEPT OF "empire" does not win favor today, and the word *imperialism*, derived from it, has carried an increasingly pejorative meaning since it was coined in the nineteenth century. Both words imply forcible domination by a nation or a state that exploits an alien people for its own benefit. Although, in our time, the charge of imperialism arises whenever a large and powerful nation influences weaker ones, exertion of influence alone is not imperialism. To be true to historical experience, one nation's actions toward another are imperialistic only if the dominant nation exerts both political and military control over the weaker one. In that sense, the last great empire in the modern world was the conglomeration of republics and ostensibly independent satellite states dominated by Russia prior to the USSR's collapse, but the Russians and the other imperial powers after World War II took no public pride in their domination. In our day, ruling an "empire" or engaging in "imperialism" is generally considered among the worst acts a nation can commit.

Such views are rare, perhaps unique, in the history of civilization. A major source for this opinion is the Christian religious tradition, especially parts of the New Testament that deprecate power and worldly glory and praise humility. In fact, Christianity was not hostile to power and empire for it took control of the Roman Empire in the fourth century C.E. and has lived comfortably with "empire" until our own century. The rise of democracy and nationalism in the last two centuries may have been more influential in changing attitudes toward imperialism, because these movements exalt the freedom and autonomy of a people. Perhaps the modern disdain for empire building has its principal origins in the extraordinary horror of modern warfare and the historical knowledge that competition for empire has often led to war.

If, however, we are to understand the widespread experience of empire throughout history, we must be alert to the great gap that separates the views of most people throughout history from our current opinions. The earliest empires go back more than 4000 years to the valleys of the Nile and the Tigris-Euphrates, and empires arose later in China, Japan, India, Iran, and Central and South America, among other areas. Typically, they were led by rulers who were believed to be gods or the representatives of gods, or at least were godlike in their ability to rule over many people. To their own people they brought wealth and prosperity, power, and reflected glory, all considered highly desirable. No one appears to have questioned the propriety of conquering another people and taking their lands, property, and persons to benefit the conquerors. Empire seemed to be part of the order of things—good for the rulers, usually bad for the ruled.

The Greeks: Ambiguities of Power

In most respects, the Greeks resembled other ancient peoples in their attitudes toward power, conquest, empire, and the benefits that came with them. Their Olympian gods held sway over earth, heaven, and the underworld because of victorious wars over other deities, and they gloried in their rule. The heroes in the epic poems that formed the Greek system of values won glory and honor through battle, conquest, and rule over other people. They viewed the world as a place of intense competition in which victory and domination, which brought fame and glory, were the highest goals, whereas defeat and subordination brought ignominy and shame.

When the legendary world of aristocratic heroes gave way to the world of city-states (*poleis*), competition was elevated from contests among individuals, households, and clans to contests and wars among *poleis*. In 416 B.C.E., more than a decade after the death of Pericles (c. 490–429 B.C.E.), Athenian spokesmen explained to some Melian officials their view of international relations: "Of the gods we believe, and of men we know, that by a necessity of their nature they always rule wherever they have the power."[1] Although their language was shockingly blunt, it reflected the views of most Greeks.

Yet this was also a dramatic presentation of the morally problematic status of the Athenian Empire. The Athenians' harsh statement would have struck a sympathetic chord among the Greeks. They appreciated power and the security and glory it can bring, but their own historical experience was different from that of other ancient nations. Their culture had been shaped by small autonomous, independent city-states, and they considered freedom natural for people raised in such an environment. Citizens, they believed, should be free in their persons, free to maintain their own constitutions, laws,

[1]Thucydides 5.105

and customs, and their city-states should be free to conduct their own foreign relations and to compete for power and glory. The free, autonomous *polis*, they thought, was greater than the mightiest powers in the world, and the sixth-century B.C.E. poet Phocylides was prepared to compare it to the great Assyrian Empire: "A little *polis* living orderly in a high place is greater than block-headed Nineveh" (Fragment 5).

When *poleis* fought one another, the victor typically took control of a piece of borderland that was usually the source of the dispute. They did not normally enslave the defeated enemy or annex and occupy its land. In these matters, as in many others, the Greeks distinguished themselves from alien peoples who did not speak Greek and were not shaped by the Greek cultural tradition. These people were called barbarians, *barbaroi*, because their speech sounded to the Greeks like "bar bar." Because they had not been raised as people in free communities but lived as subjects to a ruler, they were, it seemed, slaves by nature. To the Greeks, then, dominating and enslaving such people was perfectly acceptable. Greeks, however, viewed themselves as naturally free, as they demonstrated by creating and living in the free institutions of the *polis*. To rule over such people, to deny them their freedom and autonomy, would be wrong—so the Greeks thought, but they did not always act accordingly. The early Spartans, for instance, had changed the status of the conquered Greeks of Laconia and Messenia to *Helots*, or slaves of the state.

The Greeks shared still another belief that interfered with the comfortable acceptance of great power and empire: They thought any good thing amassed by humans to excess, beyond moderation, eventually led to *hubris*, a condition of wanton violence arising from arrogant pride in one's greatness. Those overcome by hubris were thought to have overstepped the limits established for human beings, to have shown contempt for the gods and, thereby, to have incurred *nemesis*, or divine anger and retribution. The great example to the Greeks of the fifth century B.C.E. of the workings of hubris and nemesis was the fate of Xerxes (r. 486–465 B.C.E.), Great King of the Persian Empire. His power became so great, it filled him with a blind arrogance that led him to try to extend his rule over the Greek mainland and thus brought disaster to himself and his people. When, therefore, the Athenians undertook the leadership of a Greek alliance after the Persian War, and that leadership brought them wealth and power and, in fact, turned into what was frankly acknowledged to be an empire, their response was ambiguous and contradictory. These developments were a source of pride and gratification, but also of embarrassment and, to some Athenians, shame.

The Macedonian conquest of the Greek city-states in 338 B.C.E. marked a return to an older attitude toward empire. Alexander the Great (r. 340–323 B.C.E.) conquered the vast Persian Empire, itself the successor of empires that had stretched from the Nile to the Indus valley. The death of Alexander led to its division and eventual absorption by the emergent Roman Empire by the second century B.C.E.

The ancient world was fascinated by the clash of empires that marked its history. The Romans created the grandest of the ancient empires, but they knew theirs had been preceded by others. On the walls of the House of the Faun in Pompeii, there resides an ancient mosaic depicting the Battle of Issus (333 B.C.E.), when the Macedonian Alexander the Great defeated the Persian Empire ruled by Darius III. Alexander appears on the left of the mosaic and Darius appears on his chariot. The mosaic, based on a still more ancient lost painting, probably dates from the second century B.C.E. and was rediscovered in 1831.
Art Resource, NY

The Romans: A Theory of Empire

The Romans had fewer hesitations about the desirability of imperial power than the Greeks. Their culture, which arose from a world of farmers accustomed to hard work, deprivation, and subordination to authority, venerated the military virtues. Roman society valued power, glory, and the responsibilities

The Ottoman Turks began to overrun the Balkans in the mid-1300s. In 1526, Sultan Suleyman the Magnificent destroyed a Hungarian army at the Battle of Mohacs. The Ottoman Empire ruled most of the Balkans until the late nineteenth century. Suleyman I the Magnificent (1494-1566). Sultan Suleyman at the Battles of Mahocs (detail). Lokman, The Military Campaigns of Suleyman the Magnificent. Hunername manuscript. Ottoman dynasty, Istanbul. Topkapi Palace Museum, Istanbul, Turkey. Bridgeman-Giraudon/Art Resource, NY.

of leadership, even domination, without embarrassment. In time, the Romans formulated a theory of empire that claimed Roman rule brought great advantages to its subjects: prosperity, justice, the rule of law, and, most valuable of all, peace. In the words of their great epic poet Virgil (70–19 B.C.E.), it was the Roman practice "to humble the arrogant and be sparing to their subjects."[2] These claims had considerable foundation, and the Romans could not have ruled so vast an empire with a relatively small army for more than half a millennium if their subjects had not enjoyed these benefits. Some of the conquered had a different viewpoint, however. As one British chieftain put it in the first century C.E.: "They make a wilderness and call it peace."[3]

[2]Virgil *Aeneid* 6.850

[3]Tacitus *Agricola* 30

Muslims, Mongols, and Ottomans

The rise of Islam in the seventh century C.E. produced a new kind of empire that derived its energy from religious zeal. Bursting out of Arabia, the Muslim armies swiftly gained control of most of the territory held by the old Persian Empire, North Africa, and Spain.

In the twelfth and thirteenth centuries, the great Mongol Empire, at its height, dominated Eurasia from the Pacific to central Europe, ruling Russia for more than two centuries. As in most ancient empires, the Mongols demanded taxes and military service from the conquered. They also imposed their rule over the mighty and long-standing Chinese Empire, parts of India, and much of the Islamic world before their power declined.

Still another great empire that spanned Europe and Asia was that of the Ottomans, a Turkish people, originally from central Asia. In the fourteenth century, they established a kingdom in Anatolia (Asia Minor) and soon conquered the ancient Byzantine Empire, seizing Constantinople in 1453. In the next century, the Ottoman Empire dominated southeastern Europe, the Black Sea, North Africa from Morocco to Egypt, Palestine, Syria and Arabia, Mesopotamia and Iraq, and Kurdistan and Georgia in the Caucasus. As late as 1683, Ottoman armies threatened to take Vienna and push into western Europe. Over the next two centuries, however, Ottoman power declined as the European national states grew stronger. Russia, in particular, inflicted defeats that left Turkey in the late nineteenth century, "the sick man of Europe."

European Expansion

Europe, divided first by feudalism, then by the emergence of multiple nascent national states, had been the victim of Islamic imperial expansion during the Middle Ages, first at the hands of the Arabs, then the Turks. The crusades had produced small and transitory conquests. It was only in the late 1400s that Europeans began the economic and political expansion that culminated in their command of much of the planet by 1900. The first phase of European expansion involved the "discovery," exploration, conquest, exploitation, and settlement of the Americas. It was made possible by important developments in naval and military technology, the dynamism inherent in early commercial and financial capitalism, and the freedom to compete for wealth and power unleashed by the division into separate states.

Spain and Portugal took the lead, founding empires in Central and South America, sometimes conquering existing empires ruled by native peoples. In Central America, the Aztecs exacted labor and taxes from their subject peoples, using some of them as human sacrifices. In the Andes, the Incas ruled a great empire that also required military service and forced labor from its subjects. Both Native American empires were overthrown by Spain, which then established a vast American empire whose resources, especially gold and silver, formed the basis of the great Spanish Empire in Europe. Portugal exploited the agricultural and mineral riches of Brazil using slaves imported from Africa.

The seventeenth century saw the establishment of European trading posts and then colonies on the Indian subcontinent and in the East Indies, chiefly by the Dutch, British, and French. In North America, Spain held Mexico, Florida, and California. Of more lasting significance were French and British settlements in Canada and what was to become the United States. The British colonies, especially, represented a special kind of European overseas settlement in which concern for commerce was less important than the acquisition of land for farming.

The wars of the eighteenth century ultimately cleared North America and India of French competition, leaving both as British monopolies and important bases of what would become a worldwide British Empire. The largest and most populous empire in the history of the world, it included colonies of one sort or another on all the inhabited continents; "the sun," as the saying went, "never set on the British Empire." Whether European colonialism was profitable for the imperial powers is still controversial, but Great Britain certainly benefited more than the others. Unlike most colonial powers, the British imported great quantities of natural resources from their colonies and carried on a high percentage of their trade with them. Even more singular, the British Empire included such self-governing areas as Canada, Australia, New Zealand, and South Africa, ruled by emigrants from Britain who remained loyal to the mother country and were willing to assist it in wartime. "The jewel in Britain's imperial crown," as another saying went, "was India." With a population of some 300 million, it contained perhaps 80 percent of the empire's subjects and provided much of the imperial profit.

At the height of its power in the mid-ninteenth century, it is remarkable how little money and effort Britain needed to spend to maintain these desired conditions. The cost of its armed services, including its great navy, during these years was only about 2 to 3 percent of its gross national product—a low figure compared with other nations, and incredibly low considering Britain's status as the world's greatest empire. The British army was the smallest among the European powers: By 1880 it numbered fewer than a quarter of a million men—less than half the size of France's and barely a quarter of Russia's.

France returned to its imperial pursuits after its defeat in the Napoleonic Wars, especially in North Africa and Southeast Asia, and in the last quarter of the century, Germany and Italy joined the competition for colonies. The latter part of the century brought the European partition of Africa and the establishment of European economic and political power throughout Asia. Modernized Japan, too, became a colonial power, modeling itself on the imperialist policies of the European powers. (See Chapter 26.)

By the next century, European dominance had created a single global economy and had made events in any corner of the world significant thousands of miles away. The possession of colonies became part of the definition of a great power, and the competition for colonies helped bring on World War I.

European imperialism ultimately rested on the willingness to use force. When anti-British agitation mounted in India after World War I, General Reginald Dyer's troops fired on unarmed Indian demonstrators at Amritsar. More than three hundred Indians were killed. UPI/CORBIS/Bettmann

Toward Decolonization

The weakening of the European colonial powers in World War II began the process of decolonization. The economic value of most colonies had proved to be much smaller than anticipated, and the colonial powers lacked both the capacity and the incentive to restore their former rule. Nationalist movements in the old colonies, moreover, would make such attempts costly and unpleasant. These movements flourished under the banner of national self-determination, self-government, and independence, ideas that came from and were cherished by the European colonial powers themselves. The example of Nazi Germany, moreover, had discredited theories of racial superiority that had justified much of European imperial rule. For European imperialism the handwriting was on the wall, although some colonial powers held on more fiercely than others. The French, for instance, fought at great cost—but in vain—to retain Algeria and Indochina. By the 1970s, a postcolonial world had emerged, and the concept of empire had become unclean. (See Chapter 29.)

What were the major ancient attitudes toward imperialism? What are the major modern attitudes? How do you account for the differences? What justifications and explanations have modern people used in connection with imperialism? Which do you think are the most important? Do you think ancient and modern reasons for imperialism are fundamentally different?

World War I produced unprecedented destruction and loss of life. Rather than a war of rapid movement, much combat occurred along stationary trenches dug in both Western and Eastern Europe. Here, Austro-Hungarian troops fight from trenches on the eastern front wearing gas masks. The use of poison gas was one of the innovations of the war and was generally condemned after the war. National Archives and Records Administration

26

Alliances, War, and a Troubled Peace

▼ **Emergence of the German Empire and the Alliance Systems (1873–1890)**
Bismarck's Leadership • Forging the Triple Entente (1890–1907)

▼ **World War I**
The Road to War (1908–1914) • Sarajevo and the Outbreak of War (June–August 1914) • Strategies and Stalemate: 1914–1917

▼ **The Russian Revolution**
The Provisional Government • Lenin and the Bolsheviks • The Communist Dictatorship

▼ **The End of World War I**
Germany's Last Offensive • The Armistice • The End of the Ottoman Empire

▼ **The Settlement at Paris**
Obstacles the Peacemakers Faced • The Peace • World War I and Colonial Empires • Evaluating the Peace

▼ **In Perspective**

KEY TOPICS

- **The formation of alliances and the search for strategic advantage among Europe's major powers**
- **The origins and course of World War I**
- **The Russian Revolution**
- **The peace treaties ending World War I**
- **Impact of World War I on the European colonial empires**

IN THE SUMMER of 1914, the Archduke Francis Ferdinand, heir to the throne of Austria-Hungry, was assassinated in Sarajevo, Bosnia. This act of political violence set off a crisis that concluded with the outbreak of a European war that eventually became a worldwide conflict involving numerous colonies of the European imperial powers and the United States of America. Originally known as the Great War, the First World War witnessed unprecedented loss of life and destruction of property. The war constituted the defining event of the twentieth century from which followed revolution first in Russia and later in Germany and Austria. The Ottoman Empire would also collapse. Thereafter from that time to the present day the vast semicircle of territories commencing in Germany in central Europe then passing through eastern Europe and the Balkans into Turkey and then across northeastern Africa into the Arab peninsula has for almost a century witnessed violent shifts in political power and political ideologies.

Moreover, the deeply flawed peace settlement that ended the First World War planted the seeds of ongoing European international tension, economic dislocation, and conflict. That settlement treated Germany harshly though presumably no more harshly than Germany would have treated its foes if it had been victorious. Despite the severity of the settlement toward Germany, the new international system failed to provide realistic and effective safeguards against a return to power of a vengeful Germany. The withdrawal of the United States into a disdainful isolation from world affairs further destroyed the basis for keeping the peace on which the hopes of Britain and France relied. The economic consequences of the peace settlement produced domestic economic problems that played into the hands of extreme political parties that wished to overturn the post–World War I peace settlement.

The First World War, which produced these extensive ongoing destructive results, originated in the domestic unrest among subject nationalities on the continent and the imperial rivalries among the great powers that built up in the decades after the unification of Germany and Italy. The ferocity of the conflict was the result of the modern armament of European nations made possible by the second Industrial Revolution. The conflict reached its worldwide extent because of the empires created by European states in the nineteenth century and the rise to status of a great power by the United States.

For over two decades after 1871 European diplomats and political leaders through various alliances had been able to contain and resolve those domestic and international tensions while Europe prospered and exerted vast global influence. After 1890, however, Europe witnessed a series of international crises that might have but did not lead to war. It also witnessed important diplomatic realignments. Then in the summer of 1914 the crisis in the Balkans following the assassination of heir to the throne of Austria-Hungry erupted into a conflict of previously unimaginable extent, destruction, and political upheaval that lasted until 1918.

▼ Emergence of the German Empire and the Alliance Systems (1873–1890)

Prussia's victories over Austria and France and its creation of a large, powerful German Empire in 1871 revolutionized European diplomacy. A vast new political unit had united the majority of Germans to form a nation of great and growing population, wealth, industrial capacity, and military power. Its sudden appearance created new problems and upset the balance of power that the Congress of Vienna had forged. Britain and Russia retained their positions, although the Crimean War had weakened the latter.

Austria, however, had been severely weakened, and the forces of nationalism threatened it with disintegration. The Franco-Prussian War and the German annexation of Alsace-Lorraine badly damaged French power and prestige. The French were afraid of their powerful new neighbor as well as resentful of their defeat, their loss of territory, and the loss of France's traditional position as the dominant Western European power.

Bismarck's Leadership

Until 1890, Bismarck continued to guide German policy. After 1871, he insisted Germany was a satisfied power and wanted no further territorial gains, and he meant it. He wanted to avoid a new war that might undo his achievement. He tried to assuage French resentment by pursuing friendly relations and by supporting French colonial aspirations. He also prepared for the worst. If France could not be conciliated, it must be isolated. Bismarck sought to prevent an alliance between France and any other European power—especially Austria or Russia—that would threaten Germany with a war on two fronts.

War in the Balkans Bismarck's first move was to establish the Three Emperors' League in 1873. The League brought together the three great conservative empires of Germany, Austria, and Russia. The league soon collapsed over Austro-Russian rivalry in the Balkans that arose from the Russo-Turkish War that broke out in 1877. The tottering Ottoman Empire was held together chiefly because the European powers could not agree about how to partition it. Ottoman weakness encouraged Serbia and Montenegro to come to the aid of their fellow Slavs in Bosnia and Herzegovina when they revolted against Turkish rule. Soon the rebellion spread to Bulgaria.

Then Russia entered the fray and turned it into a major international crisis. The Russians hoped to pursue their traditional policy of expansion at Ottoman expense and especially to achieve their most cherished goal: control of Constantinople and the Dardanelles. Russian intervention also reflected the influence of the Pan-Slavic movement, which sought to unite all the Slavic peoples, even those under Austrian or Ottoman rule, under the protection of Holy Mother Russia.

The Ottoman Empire was soon forced to sue for peace. The Treaty of San Stefano of March 1878 was a Russian triumph. The Slavic states in the Balkans were freed of Ottoman rule, and Russia itself obtained territory and a large monetary indemnity. The settlement, however, alarmed the other great powers. Austria feared that the Slavic victory and the increase in Russian influence in the Balkans would threaten its own Balkan provinces. The British were alarmed both by the effect of the Russian victory on the European balance of power and by the possibility of Russian control of the Dardanelles, which would make Russia a Mediterranean power and threaten Britain's control of the Suez Canal. Disraeli was determined to resist, and British public opinion supported him. A music-hall song that became popular gave the language a new word for super patriotism: *jingoism*.

We don't want to fight,
But by jingo if we do,
We've got the men,
We've got the ships,
We've got the money too!
The Russians will not have Constantinople!

The Congress of Berlin Britain and Austria forced Russia to agree to an international conference at which the other great powers would review the provisions of San Stefano. The resulting Congress of Berlin met in June and July 1878 under the presidency of Bismarck. The choice of site and presiding officer were a clear recognition of Germany's new importance and of Bismarck's claim that Germany wanted no new territory and sought to preserve the peace.

Bismarck referred to himself as an "honest broker," and the title was justified. He wanted to avoid a war between Russia and Austria into which he feared Germany would be drawn with nothing to gain and much to lose. From the collapsing Ottoman Empire, he wanted nothing. "The Eastern Question," he said, "is not worth the healthy bones of a single Pomeranian musketeer."[1]

The decisions of the congress were a blow to Russian ambitions. Bulgaria, a Russian client, was reduced in size by two thirds and deprived of access to the Aegean Sea. Austria-Hungary was given Bosnia and Herzegovina to "occupy and administer," although those provinces remained formally under Ottoman rule. Britain received Cyprus, and France was encouraged to occupy Tunisia. These territories were compensation for the gains that Russia was permitted to keep. Germany asked for nothing, but still earned Russian resentment. The Russians believed they had saved Prussia in 1807 from complete destruction by Napoleon and had expected German gratitude. They were bitterly disappointed, and the Three Emperors' League was dead.

The Berlin settlement also annoyed the Balkan states. Romania wanted Bessarabia, which Russia kept; Bulgaria wanted the borders of the Treaty of San Stefano; and Greece wanted more Ottoman territory. The major trouble spot, however, was in the south Slavic states of Serbia and Montenegro. They resented the Austrian occupation of Bosnia and Herzegovina, as did many of the natives of those provinces. The south Slavic question, no less than the estrangement between Russia and Germany, was a threat to the peace of Europe.

[1]Quoted in Hajo Holborn, *A History of Modern Germany, 1840–1945* (New York: Knopf, 1969), p. 239.

German Alliances with Russia and Austria For the moment, Bismarck could ignore the Balkans, but he could not ignore the breach in his eastern alliance system. With Russia alienated, he concluded a secret treaty with Austria in 1879. This Dual Alliance provided that Germany and Austria would come to each other's aid if Russia attacked either of them. If another country attacked one of them, each promised at least to maintain neutrality.

The treaty was for five years and was renewed regularly until 1918. As the anchor of German policy, it was criticized at the time, and in retrospect, some have considered it an error. It appeared to tie German fortunes to those of the troubled Austro-Hungarian Empire and thus to borrow trouble for Germany. That is, Germany was much more likely to be drawn into aiding Austria-Hungary than the reverse. In addition, by isolating the Russians, the Dual Alliance pushed them to seek alliances in the West.

Bismarck was fully aware of these dangers but discounted them with good reason. He personally never allowed the alliance to drag Germany into Austria's Balkan quarrels. As he put it, in any alliance there is a horse and a rider, and he meant Germany to be the rider. He made it clear to the Austrians that the alliance was purely defensive and Germany would never be a party to an attack on Russia. "For us," he said, "Balkan questions can never be a motive for war."

Bismarck believed that monarchical, reactionary Russia would not seek an alliance either with republican, revolutionary France or with increasingly democratic Britain. In fact, he expected the Austro-German negotiations to frighten Russia into seeking closer relations with Germany, and he was right. By 1881, he had renewed the Three Emperors' League on a firmer basis. The three powers promised to maintain friendly neutrality in case a fourth power attacked any of them. Other clauses included the right of Austria to annex Bosnia-Herzegovina whenever it wished and the support of all three powers for closing the Dardanelles to all nations in case of war.

The agreement allayed German fears of a Russian-French alliance and Russian fears of a combination of Austria and Britain against it, of Britain's fleet sailing into the Black Sea, and of a hostile combination of Germany and Austria. Most importantly, the agreement reduced the tension in the Balkans between Austria and Russia.

The Triple Alliance In 1882, Italy, ambitious for colonial expansion and angered by the French occupation of Tunisia, asked to join the Dual Alliance. The provisions of its entry were defensive and directed against France. Bismarck's policy was now a complete success. He was allied with three of the great powers and friendly with the other, Great Britain, which held aloof from all alliances. France was isolated and no threat. Bismarck's diplomacy was a great achievement, but an even greater challenge was to maintain this complicated system of secret alliances in the face of the continuing rivalries among Germany's allies. Despite a war in 1885 between Serbia and Bulgaria that again estranged Austria and Russia, Bismarck succeeded.

Although the Three Emperors' League lapsed, the Triple Alliance (Germany, Austria, and Italy) was renewed for another five years. To restore German relations with Russia, Bismarck negotiated the Reinsurance Treaty of 1887, in which both powers promised to remain neutral if either was attacked. All seemed smooth, but a change in the German monarchy upset Bismarck's arrangements. (See "Bismarck Explains His Foreign Policy," page 802.)

In 1888, William II (r. 1888–1918) came to the German throne. He was twenty-nine years old, ambitious, and impetuous. He was imperious by temperament and believed he ruled by divine right. An injury at birth had left him with a withered left arm. He compensated for this disability with vigorous exercise, a military bearing, and an often embarrassingly bombastic rhetoric.

Like many Germans of his generation, William II was filled with a sense of Germany's destiny as the leading power of Europe. He wanted recognition of at least equality with Britain, the land of his mother and of his grandmother, Queen Victoria. To achieve a "place in the sun," he and his contemporaries wanted a navy and colonies like Britain's. These aims, of course, ran counter to Bismarck's limited continental policy. When William argued for a navy as a defense against a British landing in North Germany, Bismarck replied, "If the British should land on our soil, I should have them arrested." This was only one example of the great distance between the young emperor, or kaiser, and his chancellor. In 1890, William used a disagreement over domestic policy to dismiss Bismarck.

As long as Bismarck held power, Germany was secure, and the great European powers remained at peace. Although he made mistakes, there was much to admire in his understanding and management of international relations in the hard world of reality. He had a clear and limited idea of his nation's goals. He resisted pressures for further expansion with few and insignificant exceptions. He understood and used the full range of diplomatic weapons: appeasement and deterrence, threats and promises, secrecy and openness. He understood the needs and hopes of other countries and, where possible, tried to help them satisfy their needs or used those countries to his own advantage. His system of alliances created a stalemate in the Balkans and ensured German security.

During Bismarck's time, Germany was a force for European peace and was increasingly understood to be so. This position would not, of course, have been possible without its great military power. It also required, however, the leadership of a statesman who was willing and able to exercise restraint and who understood what his country needed and what was possible.

Bismarck and the young Kaiser William II meet in 1888. The two disagreed over many issues, and in 1890 William dismissed the aged chancellor. German Information Center

Forging the Triple Entente (1890–1907)

Franco-Russian Alliance Almost immediately after Bismarck's retirement, his system of alliances collapsed. His successor was General Leo von Caprivi (1831–1899), who had once asked, "What kind of jackass will dare to be Bismarck's successor?" Caprivi refused the Russian request to renew the Reinsurance Treaty, in part because he felt incompetent to continue Bismarck's complicated policy and in part because he wished to draw Germany closer to Britain, but Britain remained aloof, and Russia was alienated.

Even Bismarck had assumed that ideological differences would prevent a Franco-Russian alliance. Political isolation and the need for foreign capital, however, drove the Russians toward France. The French, who were even more isolated, encouraged their investors to pour capital into Russia if such investment would help produce security against Germany. In 1894, France and Russia signed a defensive alliance against Germany.

BISMARCK EXPLAINS HIS FOREIGN POLICY

Otto von Bismarck, chancellor of the new German Empire, guided German foreign policy in the years from its establishment of the empire in 1871 until his dismissal from office in 1890. In that period and for another quarter century, Europe was free of war among the great powers. The system of alliances Bismarck took the lead in creating is often given credit for preserving that peace. The following passage from his memoirs, written in his retirement, sets forth in retrospect his intentions in creating this system.

What alliances made up Bismarck's system? How were they meant to preserve the peace? What is Bismarck's stated purpose for avoiding a war in Europe? Were there other reasons too?

The Triple Alliance which I originally sought to conclude after the peace of Frankfurt, and about which I had already sounded Vienna and St. Petersburg, from Meaux, in September 1870, was an alliance of the three emperors with the further idea of bringing into it monarchical Italy. It was designed for the struggle which, as I feared, was before us; between the two European tendencies which Napoleon called Republican and Cossack, and which I, according to our present ideas, should designate on the one side as the system of order on a monarchical basis, and on the other as the social republic to the level of which the antimonarchical development is wont to sink, either slowly or by leaps and bounds, until the conditions thus created become intolerable, and the disappointed populace are ready for a violent return to monarchical institutions in a Cæsarean form. I consider that the task of escaping from this *circulus vitiosus*, or, if possible, of sparing the present generation and their children an entrance into it, ought to be more closely incumbent on the strong existing monarchies, those monarchies which still have a vigorous life, than any rivalry over the fragments of nations which people the Balkan peninsula. If the monarchical governments have no understanding of the necessity for holding together in the interests of political and social order, but make themselves subservient to the chauvinistic impulses of their subjects, I fear that the international revolutionary and social struggles which will have to be fought out will be all the more dangerous, and take such a form that the victory on the part of monarchical order will be more difficult. Since 1871 I have sought for the most certain assurance against those struggles in the alliance of the three emperors, and also in the effort to impart to the monarchical principle in Italy a firm support in that alliance.

Otto von Bismarck, *Reflections and Reminiscences*, ed. by Theodore S. Hamerow (New York: Harper Torchbooks, 1968), pp. 236–237.

Britain and Germany Britain now became the key to the international situation. Colonial rivalries pitted the British against the Russians in Central Asia and against the French in Africa. (See Chapter 25.) Traditionally, Britain had also opposed Russian control of Constantinople and the Dardanelles and French control of the Low Countries. There was no reason to think Britain would soon become friendly to its traditional rivals or abandon its accustomed friendliness toward the Germans.

Yet within a decade of William II's accession, Germany had become the enemy in British minds. Before the turn of the century, popular British thrillers about imaginary wars portrayed the French as the invader; after the turn of the century, the enemy was usually Germany. This remarkable transformation has often been attributed to economic rivalry between Germany and Britain, in which Germany challenged and even overtook British production in various materials and markets. Certainly, Germany made such gains, and many Britons resented them. Yet the economic problem was not a serious cause of hostility, and it waned during the first decade of the century. The real problem lay in the foreign and naval policies of the German emperor and his ministers.

William II admired Britain's colonial empire and mighty fleet. At first, Germany tried to win the British over to the Triple Alliance, but when Britain clung to its "splendid isolation," German policy changed. The idea was to demonstrate Germany's worth as an ally by withdrawing support and even making trouble for Britain. This odd manner of gaining an ally reflected the kaiser's confused feelings toward Britain, which mixed dislike and jealousy with admiration. Many Germans, especially in the intellectual community, shared these feelings. Like William, they were eager for Germany to pursue a "world policy" rather than Bismarck's limited one that confined German interests to Europe. They, too, saw England as the barrier to German ambitions. Their influence in the schools, the universities, and the press guaranteed popular approval of hostility to Britain.

In Africa, the Germans blocked British attempts to build a railroad from Cape Town to Cairo. They also openly sympathized with the Boers of South Africa in their resistance to British expansion. In 1896, William congratulated Paul Kruger (1825–1904), president of the Boer Transvaal Republic, for repulsing a British raid "without having to appeal to friendly powers [i.e., Germany] for assistance." (See Chapter 25.)

In 1898, William began to realize his dream of a German navy with the passage of a naval law providing for the construction of nineteen battleships. In 1900, a second law doubled that figure. The architect of the new navy was Admiral Alfred von Tirpitz (1849–1930), who openly proclaimed that Germany's naval policy was aimed at Britain. His "risk" theory argued that Germany could build a fleet strong enough, not to defeat the British, but to do enough damage to make the British navy inferior to that of other powers like France or the United States. The theory was, in fact, absurd, because as Germany's fleet became menacing, the British would certainly build enough ships to maintain their advantage, and Britain had greater financial resources than Germany.

The naval policy, therefore, was doomed to failure. Its main results were to waste German resources and to begin a great naval race with Britain. Eventually, the threat the German navy posed so antagonized and alarmed British opinion that the British abandoned their traditional policies of avoiding alliances.

At first, however, Britain was not unduly concerned. The general hostility of world opinion during the Boer War (1899–1902), in which their great empire crushed a rebellion by South African farmers, embarrassed the British, and their isolation no longer seemed so splendid. The Germans had acted with restraint during the war. Between 1898 and 1901, Joseph Chamberlain, the colonial secretary, made several attempts to conclude an alliance with Germany. The Germans, confident that a British alliance with France or Russia was impossible, refused and held out for greater concessions.

The Entente Cordiale The first breach in Britain's isolation came in 1902, when it concluded an alliance with Japan to defend British interests in the Far East against Russia. Next, Britain abandoned its traditional antagonism toward France and in 1904 concluded a series of agreements with the French, collectively called the Entente Cordiale. It was not a formal treaty and had no military provisions, but it settled all outstanding colonial differences between the two nations. In particular, Britain gave France a free hand in Morocco in return for French recognition of British control over Egypt. The Entente Cordiale was a long step toward aligning the British with Germany's great potential enemy.

Britain's new relationship with France was surprising, but in 1904, hardly anyone believed the British whale and the Russian bear would ever come together. The Russo-Japanese War of 1904–1905 made such a development seem even less likely, because Britain was allied with Russia's enemy, but Britain had behaved with restraint, and their unexpected defeat, which also led to the Russian Revolution of 1905, humiliated the Russians. Although the revolution was put down, it weakened Russia and reduced British apprehensions about Russian power. The British also became concerned that Russia might again drift into the German orbit.

The First Moroccan Crisis At this point, Germany decided to test the new understanding between Britain and France. In March 1905, Emperor William II landed at Tangier, made a speech in favor of Moroccan independence, and by implication asserted Germany's right to participate in Morocco's destiny. This speech was a challenge to France. Germany's chancellor, Prince Bernhard von Bülow (1849–1929), intended to show France how weak it was. He also hoped to gain colonial concessions.

The Germans demanded an international conference to show their power more dramatically. The conference met in 1906 at Algeciras in Spain. Austria sided with its German ally, but Spain, which also had claims in Morocco, Italy, Russia and the United States, voted with Britain and France. The Germans had overplayed their hand, receiving trivial concessions, and the French position in Morocco was confirmed. German bullying had, moreover, driven Britain and France closer together. In the face of the threat of a German attack on France, Sir Edward Grey (1862–1933), the British foreign secretary, without making a firm commitment, authorized conversations between the British and French general staffs. Their agreements became morally binding as the years passed. By 1914, French and British military and naval plans were so mutually dependent that the two countries were effectively, if not formally, allies.

British Agreement with Russia Britain's fear of Germany's growing naval power, its concern over German ambitions in the Near East (as represented by the German-sponsored plan to build a railroad from Berlin to Baghdad), and its closer relations with France made it desirable for Britain to become more friendly with France's ally, Russia. With French support, in 1907 the British concluded an agreement with Russia much like the Entente Cordiale with France. It settled Russo-British quarrels in Central Asia and opened the door for wider cooperation. The Triple Entente, an informal, but powerful, association of Britain, France, and Russia, was now ranged against the Triple Alliance. Italy was an unreliable ally, however, which meant two great land powers and Great Britain encircled Germany and Austria-Hungary.

William II and his ministers had turned Bismarck's nightmare of the prospect of a two-front war with France and Russia into a reality. They had made it more horrible by adding Britain to their foes. The equilibrium that Bismarck had worked so hard to achieve was destroyed. Britain would no longer support Austria in restraining Russian ambitions in the Balkans. Germany, increasingly alarmed by a sense of being encircled, was less willing to restrain the Austrians for fear of alienating them, too. In the Dual Alliance of Germany and Austria, the rider was now less clear.

Bismarck had built his alliance system to maintain peace, but the new alliance increased the risk of war and made the Balkans a likely spot for it to break out. Bismarck's diplomacy had left France isolated and impotent. The new arrangement associated France with the two greatest powers in Europe besides Germany. The Germans could rely only on Austria, and Austria's troubles made it less likely to provide aid than to need it.

▼ World War I

The Road to War (1908–1914)

The weak Ottoman Empire still controlled the central strip of the Balkan Peninsula running west from Constantinople to the Adriatic. North and south of it were the independent states of Romania, Serbia, Montenegro, and Greece, as well as Bulgaria, technically still part of the empire, but legally autonomous and practically independent. The Austro-Hungarian Empire included Croatia and Slovenia and, since 1878, had "occupied and administered" Bosnia and Herzegovina.

Except for the Greeks and the Romanians, most of the inhabitants of the Balkans spoke variants of the same Slavic language and felt a cultural and historical kinship with one another. For centuries Austrians, Hungarians, or Turks had ruled them, and the nationalism that characterized late-nineteenth-century Europe made many of them eager for independence. The more radical among them longed for a union of the south Slavic, or Yugoslav, peoples in a single nation. They looked to independent Serbia as the center of the new nation and hoped to detach all the Slavic provinces (especially Bosnia, which bordered on Serbia) from Austria. Serbia believed its destiny was to unite the Slavs at the expense of Austria, as Piedmont had united the Italians and Prussia the Germans.

In 1908, a group of modernizing reformers called the Young Turks seized power in the Ottoman Empire. Their actions threatened to breathe new life into the empire and to interfere with the plans of the European jackals to pounce on the Ottoman corpse. These events brought on the first of a series of Balkan crises that would eventually lead to war.

The Bosnian Crisis In 1908, the Austrian and Russian governments decided to act quickly before Turkey became strong enough to resist. They struck a bargain in which Russia agreed to support the Austrian annexation of Bosnia and Herzegovina in return for Austrian backing for opening the Dardanelles to Russian warships.

Austria, however, declared the annexation before the Russians could act. The British and French, eager for the favor of the Young Turks, refused to agree to the Russian demand to open the Dardanelles. The Russians were humiliated and furious, but too weak to do anything but protest. The Austrian annexation of Bosnia enraged Russia's "little brothers," the Serbs.

Germany had not been warned in advance of Austria's plans and was unhappy because the action threatened their relations with Russia and Turkey. Germany felt so dependent on the Dual Alliance, however, that it nevertheless assured Austria of its support. Austria had been given a free hand, and to some extent, Vienna was now making German policy. It was a dangerous precedent. Also, the failure of Britain and France to support Russia strained the Triple Entente. This made it harder for them to oppose Russian interests in the future if they were to keep Russian friendship.

The Second Moroccan Crisis The second Moroccan crisis, in 1911, emphasized the French and British need for mutual support. When France sent an army to Morocco, Germany took the opportunity to "protect German interests" there as a means to extort colonial concessions in the French Congo. To add force to their demands, the Germans sent the gunboat *Panther* to the Moroccan port of Agadir, purportedly to protect German citizens there. Once again, as in 1905, the Germans went too far. The *Panther*'s visit to Agadir provoked a strong reaction in Britain. For some time Anglo-German relations had been growing worse, chiefly because the naval race had intensified. In 1907, Germany had built its first dreadnought, a new type of battleship that Britain had launched in 1906. In 1908, Germany had passed still another naval law that accelerated the challenge to British naval supremacy.

These actions threatened Britain's security. Britain had to increase taxes to pay for new armaments just when its liberal government was launching its expensive program of social legislation. Negotiations failed to persuade William II and Tirpitz to slow down naval construction.

In this atmosphere, the British heard of the *Panther*'s arrival in Morocco. They wrongly believed the Germans meant to turn Agadir into a naval base on the Atlantic. The crisis passed when France yielded some insignificant bits of the Congo and Germany recognized the French protectorate over Morocco. Britain drew closer to France. The British made plans to send an expeditionary force to defend France in case Germany attacked, and the British and French navies agreed to cooperate. Without any formal treaty, the German naval construction and the Agadir crisis had turned the Entente Cordiale into a de facto alliance. If Germany attacked France, Britain must defend the French, for its own security was inextricably tied up with that of France.

War in the Balkans The second Moroccan crisis also provoked another crisis in the Balkans. Italy sought to gain colonies and to take its place among the great powers. It wanted Libya, which, though worth little before the discovery of oil in the 1950s, was at least available. Italy feared that the recognition of the French protectorate in Morocco would encourage France to move into Libya also. So, in 1911, Italy attacked the Ottoman Empire to preempt the French, and forced Turkey to cede Libya and the Dodecanese Islands in the Aegean. The Italian victory encouraged the Balkan states to try their luck. In 1912, Bulgaria, Greece, Montenegro, and Serbia jointly attacked the Ottoman Empire and won easily. (See Map 26–1.) After this First Balkan War, the victors fell out among themselves over the division of Macedonia, and in 1913 a Second Balkan War erupted. This time, Turkey and Romania joined Serbia and Greece against Bulgaria and stripped away much of what the Bulgarians had gained in 1878 and 1912.

After the First Balkan War, the alarmed Austrians were determined to limit Serbian gains and especially to prevent the Serbs from gaining a port on the Adriatic. This policy meant keeping Serbia out of Albania, but the Russians backed the Serbs, and tensions mounted. An international conference sponsored by Britain in early 1913 resolved the dispute in Austria's favor and called for an independent principality of Albania. Austria, however, felt humiliated by the public airing of Serbian demands, and the Serbs defied the powers and continued to occupy parts of Albania. Finally, in October 1913, Austria issued an ultimatum, and Serbia withdrew its forces from Albania.

During this crisis, many officials in Austria had wanted an all-out attack on Serbia to remove its threat to the empire once and for all. Emperor Francis Joseph and the heir to the throne, Archduke Francis Ferdinand, had resisted those demands. At the same time, Pan-Slavic sentiment in Russia pressed Tsar Nicholas II to take a firm stand, but Russia once again let Austria have its way with Serbia. Throughout the crisis, Britain, France, Italy, and Germany restrained their allies, although each worried about appearing to be too reluctant to help its friends.

The lessons learned from this crisis of 1913 influenced behavior in the final crisis in 1914. As in 1908, the Russians had been embarrassed by their passivity, and their allies were more reluctant to restrain them again. The Austrians were embarrassed by the results of accepting an international conference and were determined not to do it again. They had gotten better results from threatening to use force; they and their German allies did not miss the lesson.

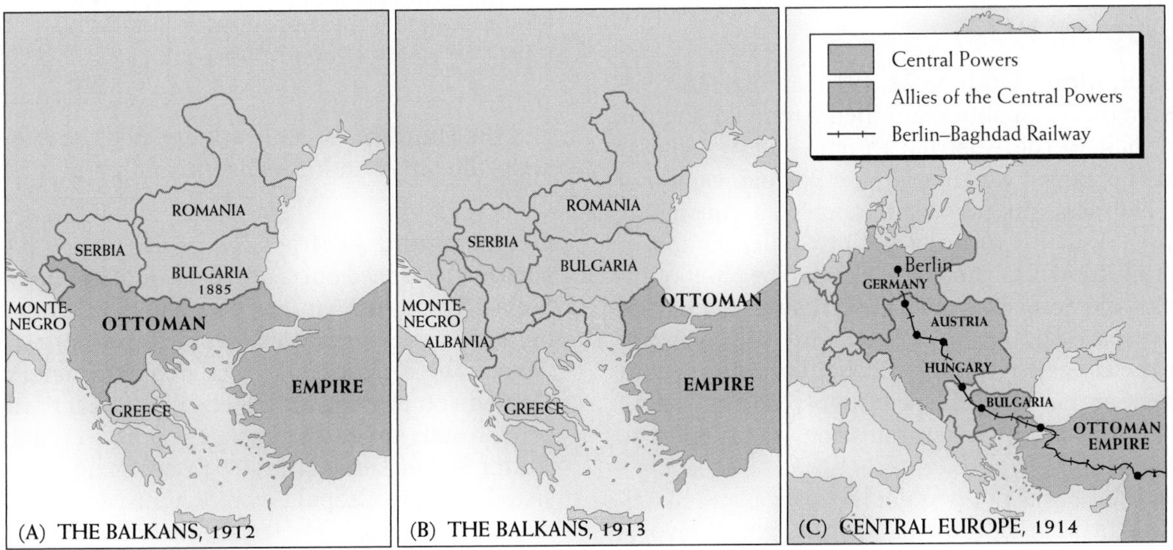

Map 26–1 **THE BALKANS, 1912–1913** Two maps show the Balkans (a) before and (b) after the two Balkan wars; note the Ottoman retreat. In (c), we see the geographical relationship of the Central Powers and their Bulgarian and Turkish allies.

THE COMING OF WORLD WAR I

1871	The end of the Franco-Prussian War; creation of the German Empire; German annexation of Alsace-Lorraine
1873	The Three Emperors' League (Germany, Russia, and Austria-Hungary)
1875	The Russo-Turkish War
1878	The Congress of Berlin
1879	The Dual Alliance between Germany and Austria
1881	The Three Emperors' League is renewed
1882	Italy joins Germany and Austria in the Triple Alliance
1888	William II becomes the German emperor
1890	Bismarck is dismissed
1894	The Franco-Russian alliance
1898	Germany begins to build a battleship navy
1899–1902	Boer War
1902	The British alliance with Japan
1904	The Entente Cordiale between Britain and France
1904–1905	The Russo-Japanese War
1905–1906	The first Moroccan crisis
1907	The British agreement with Russia
1908–1909	The Bosnian crisis
1911	The second Moroccan crisis
1911	Italy attacks Turkey
1912–1913	The First and Second Balkan Wars
1914	Outbreak of World War I

Above: The Austrian archduke Francis Ferdinand and his wife in Sarajevo on June 28, 1914. Later in the day the royal couple was assassinated by young revolutionaries trained and supplied in Serbia, igniting the crisis that led to World War I. Below: Moments after the assassination the Austrian police captured one of the assassins. Brown Brothers

Sarajevo and the Outbreak of War (June–August 1914)

The Assassination On June 28, 1914, a nineteen-year-old Serbian nationalist shot and killed Archduke Francis Ferdinand, heir to the Austrian throne, and his wife as they drove in an open car through the Bosnian capital of Sarajevo. The assassin was a member of a conspiracy hatched by a political terrorist society called Union or Death, better known as the Black Hand. The chief of intelligence of the Serbian army's general staff had helped plan and prepare the crime. Though his role was not known at the time, it was generally believed throughout Europe that Serbian officials were involved. The glee of the Serbian press after the assassination lent support to that belief.

The archduke was not popular in Austria, and his funeral evoked little grief. He had been known to favor a form of federal government for Austria that would have raised the status of the Slavs in the empire. This position alienated the conservatives among the Habsburg officials and the Hungarians. It also threatened the radical nationalists' dream of an independent south Slav state.

Germany and Austria's Response News of the assassination produced outrage everywhere in Europe except in Serbia. To those Austrians who had long favored an attack on Serbia, the opportunity seemed irresistible, but it was never easy for the Dual Monarchy to make a decision. Conrad von Hotzendorf (1852–1925), chief of the Austrian general staff, urged an attack, as he had often done before. Count Stefan Tisza (1861–1918), speaking for Hungary, resisted. Count Leopold von Berchtold (1863–1942), the Austro-Hungarian foreign minister, felt the need for strong action, but he knew German support would be required in the likely event that Russia should intervene to protect Serbia. Moreover, nothing could be done without

Tisza's approval, and only German support could persuade the Hungarians to accept a war. The question of peace or war against Serbia, therefore, had to be answered in Berlin.

William II and Chancellor Theobald von Bethmann-Hollweg (1856–1921) readily promised German support for an attack on Serbia. It has often been said that they gave the Austrians a "blank check," but their message was more specific than that. They urged the Austrians to move swiftly while the other powers were still angry at Serbia. They also made the Austrians feel they would view a failure to act as evidence of Austria-Hungary's weakness and uselessness as an ally. Therefore, the Austrians never wavered in their determination to make war on Serbia. They hoped, with the protection of Germany, to fight Serbia alone, but they were prepared to risk a general European conflict. The Germans also knew they risked a general war, but they too hoped to "localize" the fight between Austria and Serbia.

Some scholars believe Germany had long been plotting war, and some even think a specific plan for war in 1914 was set in motion as early as 1912. The vast body of evidence on the crisis of 1914, however, gives little support to such notions. The German leaders plainly reacted to a crisis they had not foreseen and just as plainly made decisions in response to events. The decision to support Austria, however, made war difficult, if not impossible, to avoid. The emperor and chancellor made that decision without significant consulting of either their military or diplomatic advisers.

William II reacted violently to the assassination. He was moved by his friendship for the archduke and by outrage at an attack on royalty. A different provocation would probably not have moved him so much. Bethmann-Hollweg was less emotional, but under severe pressure. To resist the decision would have meant flatly opposing the emperor. The German army suspected the chancellor of being soft. It would have been difficult for him to take a conciliatory position. Important military leaders, especially General Helmut von Moltke (1848–1916), Chief of the General Staff since 1906, had come to believe that the growing power of Russia threatened Germany. Moltke repeatedly spoke of the need for a decisive war against Russia, and its allies if necessary, "the sooner the better." His influence would be important at key moments in the crisis.

Bethmann-Hollweg, like many other Germans, also feared for the future. Russia was recovering its strength and would reach a military peak in 1917. The Triple Entente was growing closer and more powerful, and Germany's only reliable ally was Austria. The chancellor recognized the danger of supporting Austria, but he believed it to be even more dangerous to withhold that support. If Austria did not crush Serbia, it might collapse before the onslaught of Slavic nationalism backed by Russia. If Germany did not defend its ally, the Austrians might look elsewhere for help. His policy was one of calculated risk.

Unfortunately, the calculations proved to be incorrect. Bethmann-Hollweg hoped the Austrians would strike swiftly and present the powers with a fait accompli while the outrage of the assassination was still fresh, and he hoped German support would deter Russia. Failing that, he was prepared for a continental war against France and Russia. This policy, though, depended on British neutrality, and the German chancellor convinced himself the British would stand aloof.

The Austrians, however, were slow to act. They did not even deliver their deliberately unacceptable ultimatum to Serbia until July 23, when the general hostility toward Serbia had begun to subside. Serbia further embarrassed the Austrians by returning so soft and conciliatory an answer that even the mercurial German emperor thought it removed all reason for war, but the Austrians were determined not to turn back. (See "Compare & Connect: The Outbreak of World War I," pages 808–810.) On July 28, they declared war on Serbia, even though the army would not be ready to attack until mid-August.

The Triple Entente's Response The Russians, previously so often forced to back off, responded angrily to the Austrian demands on Serbia. The most conservative elements of the Russian government feared that war would lead to revolution, as it had in 1905, but nationalists, Pan-Slavs, and most of the politically conscious classes in general demanded action. The government responded by ordering partial mobilization, against Austria only. This policy was militarily impossible, but its intention was to put diplomatic pressure on Austria to refrain from attacking Serbia.

Mobilization of any kind, however, was a dangerous weapon because it was generally understood to be equivalent to an act of war. In fact, only Germany's war plan made mobilization the first and irrevocable start of a war. It required a quick victory in the west before the Russians were ready to act. Even partial Russian mobilization seemed to jeopardize this plan and put Germany in great danger. From this point on, the general staff pressed for German mobilization and war. Their claim of military necessity soon became irresistible.

France and Britain were not eager for war. France's president and prime minister were on their way back from a long-planned state visit to Russia when the crisis flared on July 23. The Austrians had, in fact, delivered their ultimatum to the Serbs precisely when these two men would be at sea. Had they been in Paris, they might have tried to restrain the Russians. In their absence and without consulting his government, the French ambassador to Russia gave the Russians the same assurances of support that Germany had given Austria. The British worked hard to resolve the crisis by traditional means: a conference of the powers. Austria, still smarting from its humiliation after the London Conference of 1913, would not hear of it. The Germans privately supported the Austrians but publicly took on a conciliatory tone to placate the British.

COMPARE AND CONNECT

The Outbreak of World War I

IN THE CENTURY between the Congress of Vienna and the events at Sarajevo, Europe had overcome one crisis after another without recourse to a major war. Yet the assassination of the Archduke Francis Ferdinand, heir to the Austro-Hungarian Empire, in a Bosnian town on June 28, 1914, produced a crisis that led to a general and catastrophic war. It is interesting to focus attention on the crisis of July 1914 and to trace the steps that turned a Balkan incident into a major disaster. Austria's ultimatum to Serbia and the answer of the Serbians were critical events in bringing on the war.

QUESTIONS

1. **Which of the demands were the most difficult for the Serbians to meet?**
2. **Why did the Austrians fix so short a time for response?**
3. **Which demands did the Serbians fail to grant? Why?**
4. **Was the Austrian immediate declaration of war justified?**

I. The Austrian Ultimatum

On the afternoon of July 23, after an investigation of the assassination of the Archduke Franz Ferdinand at Sarajevo, the Austrians presented a list of demands to Serbia, and the Serbs were given forty-eight hours to reply. The Austrian ambassador to Belgrade was instructed to leave the country and break off diplomatic relations unless the demands were met without reservations. The Serbians knew that some officials of the Serbian government took part in the plot.

The results brought out by the inquiry no longer permit the Imperial and Royal Government to maintain the attitude of patient tolerance which it has observed for years toward those agitations which center at Belgrade and are spread thence into the territories of the Monarchy. Instead, these results impose upon the Imperial and Royal Government the obligation to put an end to those intrigues, which constitute a standing menace to the peace of the Monarchy.

In order to attain this end, the Imperial and Royal Government finds itself compelled to demand that the Serbian Government give official assurance that it will condemn the propaganda directed against Austria-Hungary, that is to say, the whole body of the efforts whose ultimate object it is to separate from the Monarchy territories that belong to it; and that it will obligate itself to suppress with all the means at its command this criminal and terroristic propaganda. . . .

1. to suppress every publication which shall incite to hatred and contempt the Monarchy, and the general tendency of which shall be directed against the territorial integrity of the latter;
2. to proceed at once to the dissolution of the Narodna Odbrana, [a Serbian nationalist propaganda and paramilitary organization] confiscate all of its means of propaganda, and in the same manner to proceed against the other unions and associations in Serbia which occupy themselves with propaganda against Austria-Hungary; the Royal Government will take such measures as are necessary to make sure that the dissolved associations may not continue their activities under other names in other forms;
3. to eliminate without delay from public instruction in Serbia, everything, whether connected with the teaching corps or with the methods of teaching, that serves or may serve to nourish the propaganda against Austria-Hungary;
4. to remove from the military and administrative service in general all officers and officials who have been guilty of carrying on the propaganda against Austria-Hungary, whose names the Imperial and Royal Government reserve the right to make known to the Royal Government. . .;

5. to agree to the cooperation in Serbia of the organs of the Imperial Royal Government in the suppression of the subversive movement directed against the integrity of the Monarchy;
6. to institute a judicial inquiry against every participant in the conspiracy of the twenty-eighth of June who may be found in Serbian territory; the organs of the Imperial and Royal Government delegated for this purpose will take part in the proceedings held for this purpose;
7. to undertake with all haste the arrest of Major Voislav Tankositch and of; one Milan Ciganovitch, a Serbian official, who have been compromised the results of the inquiry. . .;
10. to inform the Imperial and Royal Government without delay of the execution of the measures comprised in the foregoing points.

The Imperial and Royal Government awaits the reply of the Royal Government by Saturday, the twenty-fifth instant, at 6 P.M., at the latest.

Source: "The Austrian Ultimatum," in *Outbreak of the World War*, German documents collected by Karl Kautsky and ed. by Max Montgelas and Walther Schucking, trans. by the Carnegie Endowment for International Peace. Division of International Law, Supplement I (1924), (New York: Oxford University Press, 1924), pp. 604–605.

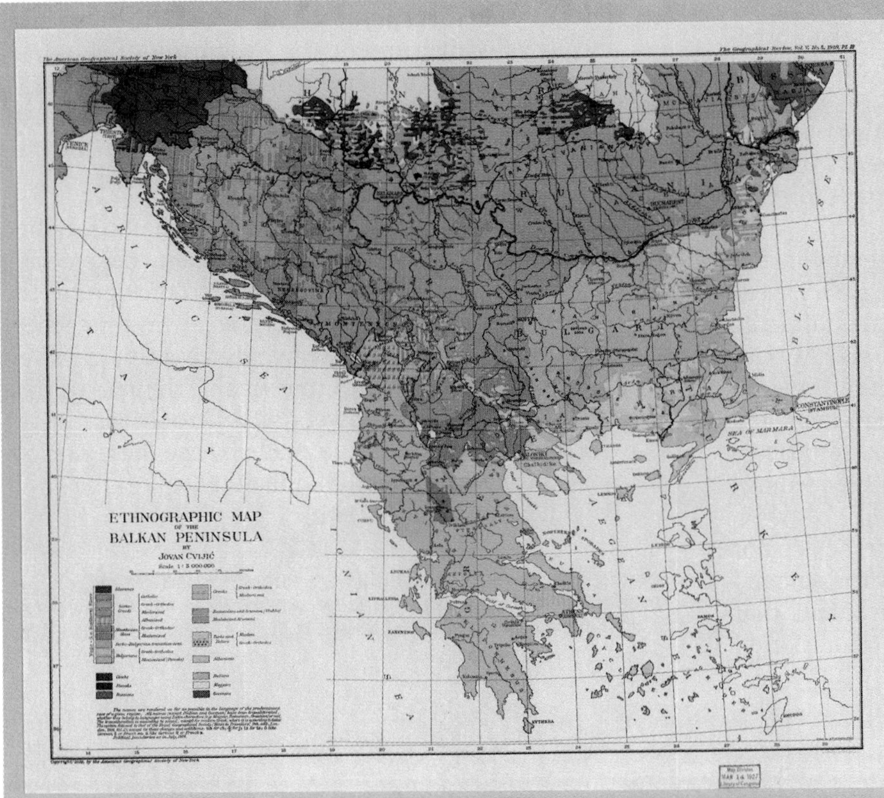

This ethnographic map of the Balkan peninsula, made by a Serbian nationalist named Jovan Cvijićin in 1918, served as inspiration for the campaign of ethnic cleansing that would devastate the region once known as Yugoslavia. Library of Congress

II. The Serbian Response

The reply of the Serbians was remarkably reasonable. In his first reaction to it the German Kaiser said: "After reading over the Serbian reply, which I received this morning, I am convinced that on the whole the wishes of the Danube Monarchy have been acceded to. The few reservations that Serbia makes in regard to individual points could, according to my opinion, be settled by negotiation. But it contains the announcement orbi et urbi of a capitulation of the most humiliating kind, and as a result, every cause for war falls to the ground." *But it was not unconditional acceptance of the ultimatum.*

The royal Servian government have received the communication of the Imperial and Royal Government of the 10th instant, and are convinced that their reply will remove any misunderstanding which may threaten to impair the good neighbourly relations between the Austro-Hungarian Monarchy and the Kingdom of Servia. . . .

The Royal Government have been pained and surprised at the statements, according to which members of the Kingdom of Servia are supposed to have participated in the preparations for the crime committed at Serajevo; the Royal Government expected to be invited to collaborate in an investigation of all that concerns this crime, and they were ready, in order to prove the entire correctness of their attitude, to take measures against any persons concerning whom representations were made to them. Falling in, therefore, with the desire of the Imperial and Royal Government, they are prepared to hand over for trial any Servian subject, without regard to his situation or rank, of whose complicity in the crime of Serajevo proofs are forthcoming, and more especially they undertake to cause to be published on the first page of the] "Journal officiel," on the date of the 13th (26th) July, the following declaration:

The Royal Government of Servia condemn all propaganda which may be directed against Austria-Hungary, that is to say, all such tendencies as aim at ultimately detaching from the Austro-Hungarian Monarchy territories which form part thereof and they sincerely deplore the baneful consequences of these criminal movements. The Royal Government regret that, according to the communication from the Imperial and Royal Government, certain Servian

(continued)

officers and officials should have taken part in the above-mentioned propaganda and thus compromised the good neighbourly relations to which the Royal Servian Government was solemnly engaged by the declaration of the 31st March, 1909, which declaration disapproves and repudiates all idea or attempt at interference with the destiny of the inhabitants of any part whatsoever of Austria-Hungary, and they consider it their duty formally to warn the officers, officials, and entire population of the kingdom that henceforth they will take the most rigorous steps against all such persons as are guilty of such acts, to prevent and to repress which they will use their utmost endeavour. . . .

The Royal Government further undertake:—

1. To introduce at the first regular convocation of the Skuptchina a provision into the press law providing for the most severe punishment of incitement to hatred or contempt of the Austro-Hungarian Monarchy, and for taking action against any publication the general tendency of which is directed against the territorial integrity of Austria-Hungary. . . .
2. The Royal Government will accept the demand of the Imperial and Royal Government, and will dissolve the "Narodna Odbrana" Society and every other society which may be directing its efforts against Austria-Hungary.
3. The Royal Servian Government undertake to remove without delay from their public educational establishments in Servia all that serves or could serve to foment propaganda against Austria-Hungary, whenever the Imperial and Royal Government furnish them with facts and proofs of this propaganda.
4. The Royal Government also agree to remove from military service all such persons as the judicial enquiry may have proved to be guilty of acts directed against the integrity of the territory of the Austro-Hungarian Monarchy, and they expect the Imperial and Royal Government to communicate to them at a later date the names and the acts of these officers and officials for the purposes of the proceedings which are to be taken against them.
5. The Royal Government must confess that they do not clearly grasp the meaning or the scope of the demand made by the Imperial and Royal Government that Servia shall undertake to accept the collaboration of the organs of the Imperial and Royal Government upon their territory, but they declare that they will admit such collaboration as agrees with the principle of international law, with criminal procedure, and with good neighbourly relations.
6. It goes without saying that the Royal Governmen consider it their duty to open an enquiry against all such persons as are, or eventually may be, implicated in the plot of the 15th June, and who happen to be within the territory of the kingdom. As regards the participation in this enquiry of Austro-Hungarian agents or authorities appointed for this purpose by the Imperial and Royal Government, the Royal Government cannot accept such an arrangement, as it would be a violation of the Constitution and of the law of criminal procedure; nevertheless, in concrete cases communications as to the results of the investigation in question might be given to the Austro-Hungarian agents.
7. The Royal Government proceeded, on the very evening of the delivery of the note, to arrest Commandant Voislav Tankossitch. As regards Milan Ziganovitch, who is a subject of the Austro-Hungarian Monarchy and who, up to the 15th June was employed (on probation) by the directorate of railways, it has not yet been possible to arrest him. . . .
10. The Royal Government will inform the Imperial and Royal Government the execution of the measures comprised under the above heads, in so far as this has not already been done by the present note, as soon as each measure has been ordered and carried out.

If the Imperial and Royal Government are not satisfied with this reply, the Servian Government, considering that it is not to the common interest to precipitate the solution of this question, are ready, as always, to accept a pacific understanding, either by referring this question to the decision of the International Tribunal of The Hague, or to the Great Powers which took part in the drawing up of the declaration made by the Servian Government on the 18th (31st) March 1909.

Belgrade, July 12 (25), 1914

Source: "Serbia's Answer to Ultimatum," from *British Diplomatic Correspondence in Collected Diplomatic Documents Relating to the Outbreak of the European War*, No. 39 (London: H.M. Stationery Office, 1915), pp. 31–37.

Soon, however, Bethmann-Hollweg realized what he should have known from the first: If Germany attacked France, Britain must fight. Until July 30, his public appeals to Austria for restraint were a sham. Thereafter, he sincerely tried to persuade the Austrians to negotiate and avoid a general war, but it was too late. The Austrians could not turn back without losing their own self-respect and the respect of the Germans.

On July 30, Austria ordered mobilization against Russia. Bethmann-Hollweg resisted the enormous pressure to mobilize, not because he hoped to avoid war, but because he wanted Russia to mobilize against Germany first and appear to be the aggressor. Only in that way could he win the support of the German nation for war, especially the backing of pacifist Social Democrats. His luck was good for a change. The news of Russian general mobilization came only minutes before Germany would have mobilized in any case. Germany then declared war on Russia on August 1. The **Schlieffen Plan** went into effect. The Germans occupied Luxembourg on August 2 and invaded Belgium, which resisted, on August 3—the same day Germany declared war on France. The invasion of Belgium violated the treaty of 1839 in which the British had joined the other powers in guaranteeing Belgian neutrality. This factor undermined sentiment in Britain for neutrality and united the nation against Germany, which then invaded France. On August 4, Britain declared war on Germany.

The Great War had begun. As Sir Edward Grey, the British foreign secretary, put it, the lights were going out all over Europe. They would come on again, but Europe would never be the same.

Although debate on the causes of the war continues, the most common opinion today is that German ambitions for a higher place in the international order under the new kaiser William II led to a new challenge to the status quo. German bullying resulted in a series of crises that led to the final crisis in July 1914, when Germany supported—indeed, pushed—its only reliable ally Austria into a war against Serbia that touched off the world war.

The deeper causes of that war are seen to be Germany's new ambitions to become a world power like Great Britain and to become the dominant power on the European continent. Germany's decision to build a battleship navy threatened Britain's interests and security. In response, the British launched an expensive and unwelcome naval race to maintain their superiority at sea and abandoned their cherished "splendid isolation" and long-standing competitions with France and Russia. In an unprecedented reversal of policy, they made an alliance with Japan and agreements with France and Russia to form the "Triple Entente," which grew from a set of colonial accords to an informal, but visible, check on German ambitions. This new international configuration alarmed Germany, which complained that jealous and hostile forces were "encircling" it. The Germans feared the growing power of the country's enemies, but Germany did not seriously attempt to ease the tension. Instead, a new arms race ensued, and Germany assumed a rigid stance in the final crisis that ended in war.

Strategies and Stalemate: 1914–1917

Throughout Europe, jubilation greeted the outbreak of war. No general war had been fought since Napoleon, and few understood the horrors of modern warfare. The dominant memory was of Bismarck's swift and decisive campaigns, in which the costs and casualties were light and the rewards great. After years of crises and resentments, war came as a release of tension. The popular press had increased public awareness of, and interest in, foreign affairs and had fanned the flames of patriotism. The prospect of war moved even a rational man of science like Sigmund Freud to say, "My whole libido goes out to Austria-Hungary."

Both sides expected to take the offensive, force a battle on favorable ground, and win a quick victory. The Triple Entente powers—or the Allies, as they called themselves—held superiority in numbers and financial resources, as well as command of the sea. (See Figure 26–1, page 812.) Germany and Austria, the Central Powers, had the advantages of possessing internal lines of communication and having launched their attack first.

Germany's war plan was based on ideas developed by Count Alfred von Schlieffen (1833–1913), chief of the German general staff from 1891 to 1906. (See Map 26–2.) It aimed to outflank the French frontier defenses

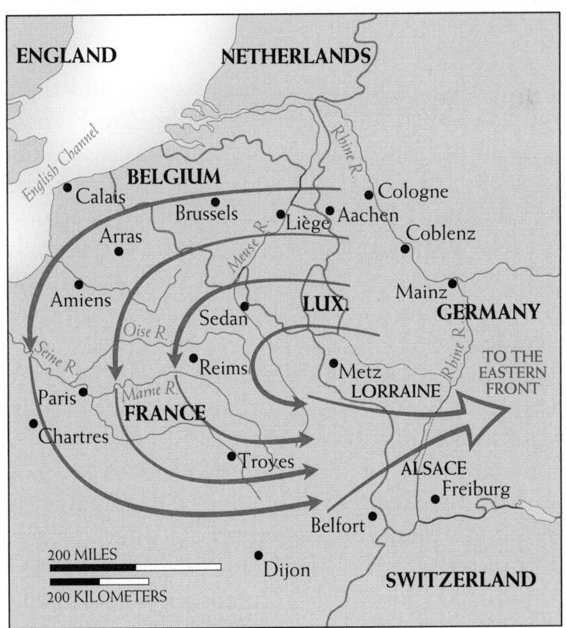

Map 26–2 **THE SCHLIEFFEN PLAN OF 1905** Germany's grand strategy for quickly winning the war against France in 1914 is shown by the wheeling arrows on the map. In the original plan, the crushing blows at France were to be followed by the release of troops for use against Russia on Germany's eastern front. The plan, however, was not adequately implemented, and the war on the western front became a long contest in place.

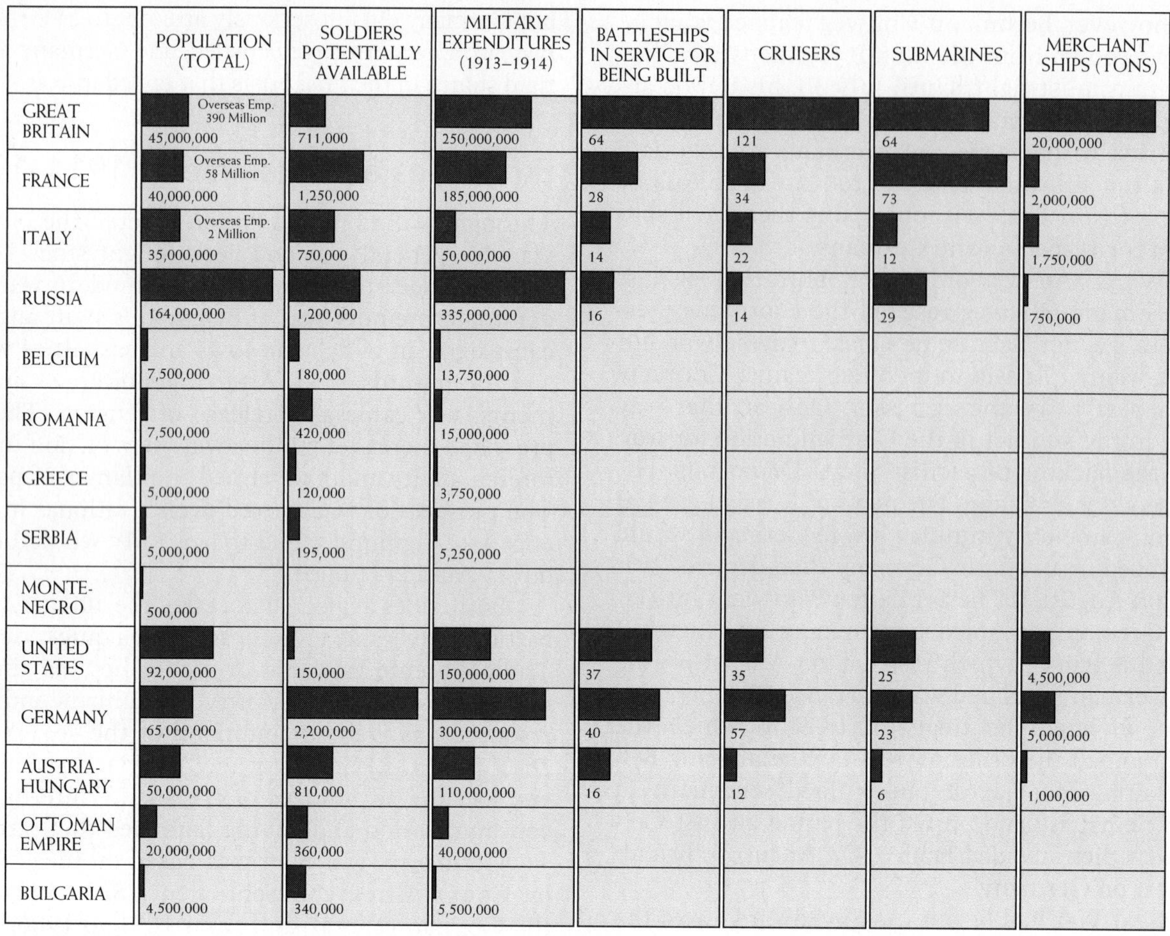

POPULATION (TOTAL)
SOLDIERS POTENTIALLY AVAILABLE
MILITARY EXPENDITURES (1913–1914)
BATTLESHIPS IN SERVICE OR BEING BUILT
CRUISERS
SUBMARINES
MERCHANT SHIPS (TONS)
GREAT BRITAIN
Overseas Emp. 390 Million
45,000,000
711,000
250,000,000
64
121
64
20,000,000
FRANCE
Overseas Emp. 58 Million
40,000,000
1,250,000
185,000,000
28
34
73
2,000,000
ITALY
Overseas Emp. 2 Million
35,000,000
750,000
50,000,000
14
22
12
1,750,000
RUSSIA
164,000,000
1,200,000
335,000,000
16
14
29
750,000
BELGIUM
7,500,000
180,000
13,750,000
ROMANIA
7,500,000
420,000
15,000,000
GREECE
5,000,000
120,000
3,750,000
SERBIA
5,000,000
195,000
5,250,000
MONTE-NEGRO
500,000
UNITED STATES
92,000,000
150,000
150,000,000
37
35
25
4,500,000
GERMANY
65,000,000
2,200,000
300,000,000
40
57
23
5,000,000
AUSTRIA-HUNGARY
50,000,000
810,000
110,000,000
16
12
6
1,000,000
OTTOMAN EMPIRE
20,000,000
360,000
40,000,000
BULGARIA
4,500,000
340,000
5,500,000

Figure 26–1 Relative strengths of the combatants in World War I.

by sweeping through Belgium to the Channel and then wheeling to the south and east to envelop the French and crush them against the German fortresses in Lorraine. The secret of success lay in making the right wing of the advancing German army immensely strong and deliberately weakening the left opposite the French frontier. The weakness of the left was meant to draw the French into attacking the wrong place while the war was decided on the German right. In the east, the Germans planned to stand on the defensive against Russia until France had been crushed, a task they thought would take only six weeks.

The apparent risk, besides the violation of Belgian neutrality and the consequent alienation of Britain, lay in weakening the German defenses against a direct attack across the frontier. The strength of German fortresses and the superior firepower of German howitzers made that risk more theoretical than real. The true danger was that the German striking force on the right through Belgium would not be powerful enough to make the swift progress vital to success. The execution of the plan fell to Count Helmuth von Moltke, the nephew of Bismarck's most effective general. Moltke added divisions to the left wing and even weakened the Russian front for the same purpose. For reasons still debated, the plan failed by a narrow margin.

The War in the West The French had also put their faith in the offensive, but with less reason than the Germans. They underestimated the numbers and effectiveness of the German reserves and overestimated what the courage and spirit of their own troops could achieve. Courage and spirit could not defeat machine guns and heavy artillery. The French offensive on Germany's western frontier failed totally. This defeat probably was preferable to a partial success, because it released troops for use against the main German army. As a result, the French and the British were able to stop the German advance on Paris at the Battle of the Marne in September 1914. (See Map 26–3, and Map 26–4, page 814.)

Thereafter, the nature of the war in the west became one of position instead of movement. Both sides dug in behind a wall of trenches protected by barbed wire that stretched from the North Sea to Switzerland. Strategically placed machine-gun nests made assaults difficult and dangerous. Both sides, nonetheless, attempted

Map 26–3 **World War I in Europe** Despite the importance of military action in the Far East, in the Arab world, and at sea, the main theaters of activity in World War I were in the European areas.

Map 26–4 **THE WESTERN FRONT, 1914–1918** This map shows the crucial western front in detail.

massive attacks preceded by artillery bombardments of unprecedented and horrible force and duration. Still, the defense was always able to recover and to bring up reserves fast enough to prevent a breakthrough.

Assaults that cost hundreds of thousands of lives produced advances of only hundreds of yards. Even poison gas proved ineffective. In 1916, the British introduced the tank, which eventually proved to be the answer to the machine gun. The Allied command was slow to understand this, however, and until the end of the war, defense was supreme. For three years after its establishment, the western front moved only a few miles in either direction.

The War in the East In the east, the war began auspiciously for the Allies. The Russians advanced into Austrian territory and inflicted heavy casualties, but Russian incompetence and German energy soon reversed the situation. A junior German officer, Erich Ludendorff (1865–1937), under the command of the elderly general Paul von Hindenburg (1847–1934), destroyed or captured an entire Russian army at the Battle of Tannenberg and defeated another one at the Masurian Lakes. In 1915, the Central Powers pressed their advantage in the east and drove into the Baltic states and Russian Poland, inflicting more than 2 million casualties in a single year.

As the battle lines hardened, both sides sought new allies. Turkey (because of its hostility to Russia) and Bulgaria (the enemy of Serbia) joined the Central Powers. Both sides bid for Italian support with promises of the spoils of victory. Because the Austrians held what the Italians wanted most, the Allies could promise more. In a secret treaty of 1915, they agreed to deliver to Italy after victory most of *Italia irredenta* (i.e., the South Tyrol, Trieste, and some of the Dalmatian Islands), plus colonies in Africa and a share of the Turkish Empire. By the spring of 1915, Italy was engaging Austrian armies. The Italian campaign weakened Austria and diverted some German troops, but the Italian alliance never produced significant results. Romania joined the Allies in 1916 but was quickly defeated and driven from the war.

In the Far East, Japan honored its alliance with Britain and entered the war. The Japanese quickly overran the German colonies in China and the Pacific and used the opportunity to put pressure on China. Both sides also appealed to nationalistic sentiment in areas the enemy held. The Germans supported nationalist movements among the Irish, the Flemings in Belgium, and the Poles and Ukrainians under Russian rule. They even tried to persuade the Turks to lead a Muslim uprising against the British in Egypt and India, and against the French and Italians in North Africa. The Allies made the same appeals with greater success. They sponsored movements of national autonomy for the Czechs, the Slovaks, the south Slavs, and againt the Poles who were under Austrian rule. They also favored a movement of Arab independence from Turkey. Guided by Colonel T. E. Lawrence (1888–1935), this last scheme proved especially successful later in the war.

In 1915, the Allies tried to break the deadlock on the western front by going around it. The idea came chiefly from Winston Churchill (1874–1965), first lord of the British admiralty. He proposed to attack the Dardanelles and capture Constantinople. This policy supposedly would knock Turkey from the war, bring help to the Balkan front, and ease communications with Russia. The plan was daring, but promising, and in its original form, it presented little risk. British naval superiority and the element of surprise might force the straits and capture Constantinople by purely naval action. Even if the scheme failed, the fleet could just sail away.

The success of Churchill's plan depended on timing, speed, and daring leadership, but all of these were lacking. Worse, the execution of the attack was inept and overly cautious. Troops were landed, and as Turkish

British tanks moving toward the Battle of Cambrai in Flanders late in 1917. Tanks were impervious to machine-gun fire. Had they been used in great numbers, they might have broken the stalemate in the west. Bildarchiv Preussischer Kulturbesitz

resistance continued, the Allied commitment increased. Before the campaign was abandoned, the Allies lost almost 150,000 men and diverted three times that number from more useful occupations.

Return to the West Both sides turned back to the west in 1916. General Erich von Falkenhayn (1861–1922), who had succeeded Moltke in September 1914, attacked the French stronghold of Verdun. His plan was not to break through the French line, but to inflict enormous casualties on the French, who would have to defend Verdun against superior firepower from several directions. He, too, underestimated the superiority of the defense. The French held Verdun with comparatively few men and inflicted almost as many casualties as they suffered. The commander of Verdun, Henri Pétain (1856–1951), became a national hero, and "They shall not pass" became a slogan of national defiance.

The Allies tried to end the impasse by launching a major offensive along the River Somme in July. Aided by a Russian attack in the east that drew off some German strength and by an enormous artillery bombardment, they hoped at last to break through. Once again, the defense was superior. Enormous casualties on both sides brought no result. The war on land dragged on with no end in sight.

The War at Sea As the war continued, control of the sea became more important. The British ignored the distinction between war supplies (which were contraband according to international law) and food or other peaceful cargo (which was not subject to seizure). They imposed a strict blockade meant to starve out the enemy, regardless of international law. The Germans responded with submarine warfare meant to destroy British shipping and starve the British. They declared the waters around the British Isles a war zone, where even neutral ships would not be safe. Both policies were unwelcome to neutrals, and especially to the United States, which conducted extensive trade in the Atlantic. Yet the sinking of neutral ships by German submarines was both more dramatic and more offensive than the British blockade.

In May 1915, a German submarine torpedoed the British liner *Lusitania*. Among the 1,200 who drowned were 118 Americans. President Woodrow Wilson (1856–1924) warned Germany that a repetition would have grave consequences; the Germans desisted for the time being, rather than further anger the United States. This development gave the Allies a considerable advantage. The German fleet that had cost so much money and had caused so much trouble played no significant part in the war. The only major battle it

A Closer LOOK

THE DEVELOPMENT OF THE ARMORED TANK

WARFARE FREQUENTLY PROVES a source of technological innovation. Such was true of World War I, which witnessed the development of numerous new weapons. Among the most important of these was the tank—an armored vehicle using a caterpillar track rather than wheels for transport. The caterpillar track had been invented in Great Britain but was then purchased by the American Holt tractor company, which devised a caterpillar tractor in the first decade of the century to cultivate areas with either wet or loose earth where a wheeled vehicle would sink into the ground. During World War I the British modified the caterpillar tractor by introducing a heavily armored closed compartment for a crew armed with machine guns. These early slow-moving tanks could drive over trenches, small hills, and rough terrain and through mud and thus bring mobility to the combat zones where trench warfare had made any kind of effective assault on enemy troops difficult. The tank was used primarily by Britain, France, and the United States in relatively small numbers in World War I, but later rapidly moving tanks became one of the major weapons of later twentieth-century warfare.

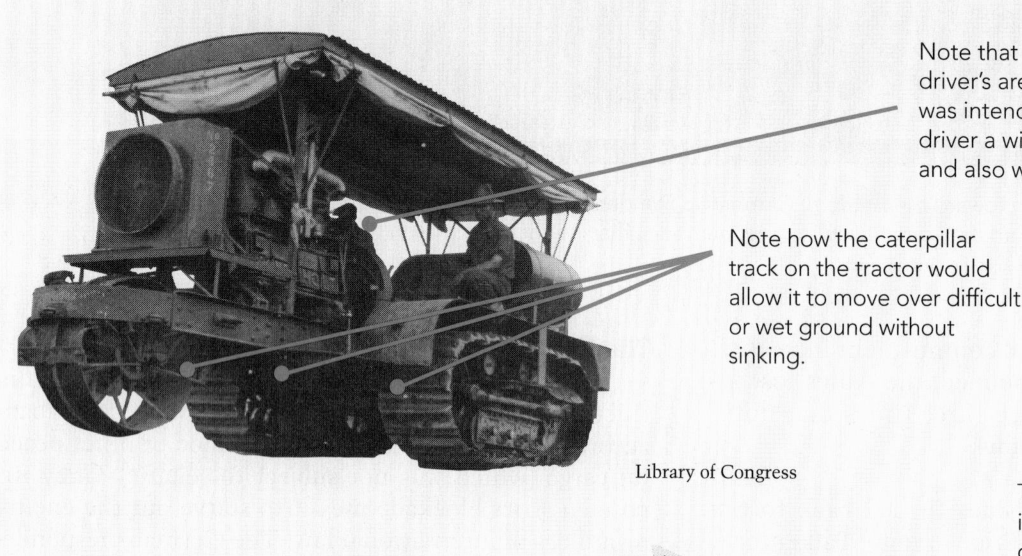

Note that the design of the driver's area of the tractor was intended to allow the driver a wide area of vision and also was fully exposed.

Note how the caterpillar track on the tractor would allow it to move over difficult or wet ground without sinking.

Library of Congress

The armament of the tank was intended to protect the tank crew from small arms fire while the opening on the top permitted the mounting of a machine gun.

The interior of the tank allowed for a small crew working in an extremely hot climate with little or no chance for escape if the tank was hit by a large artillery round or became bogged down in enemy territory.

To examine this image in an interactive fashion, please go to www.myhistorylab.com

Dorling Kindersley Media Library/Andy Crawford/Dorling Kindersley © Imperial War Museum, London

The use of poison gas (by both sides) during the First World War and its dreadful effects—blinding, asphyxiation, burned lungs—came to symbolize the horrors of modern war. This painting shows a group of British soldiers being guided to the rear after they were blinded by mustard gas on the western front. John Singer Sargent (1856–1925), *Gassed*, an Oil Study. Private Collection. 1918–1919. Imperial War Museum, London. Negative Number Q1460

fought was at Jutland in 1916. The battle resulted in a standoff and confirmed British domination of the surface of the sea.

America Enters the War In December 1916, President Woodrow Wilson intervened to try to bring about a negotiated peace. Neither side, however, was willing to renounce war aims that its opponent found acceptable. The war seemed likely to continue until one or both sides reached exhaustion.

Two events early in 1917 changed the situation radically. On February 1, the Germans announced the resumption of unrestricted submarine warfare, which led the United States to break off diplomatic relations. On April 6, the United States declared war on Germany. One of the deterrents to an earlier American intervention had been the presence of the autocratic tsarist Russia among the Allies. Wilson could conceive of the war only as an idealistic crusade "to make the world safe for democracy." That problem was resolved in March 1917 by a revolution in Russia that overthrew the tsarist government.

▾ The Russian Revolution

Many unexpected consequences flowed from World War I reshaping both Europe and the rest of the world in ways that virtually no one could have anticipated in 1910. For the rest of European history in the twentieth century no such unexpected event produced so many long-term results as the revolution that occurred in Russia in 1917. That revolution changed the course of the war and the future course of Europe by setting a Communist government in charge of a major European state and empire.

The Russian Revolution of 1917, which ultimately produced impacts over the years around the globe, went through two distinct stages. In March of that year the government of Tsar Nicholas II collapsed in the wake of popular demonstrations against the war, its casualties, and the economic and social conditions flowing from Russian participation in the conflict. Then in November a second unforeseen event occurred. The previously largely obscure and ignored Bolshevik Party led by Lenin (see Chapter 23) seized power from the provisional government. The Bolsheviks would quickly take Russia out of the war and then proceed to establish their own domestic Communist Party dictatorship.

No political faction planned or led the March Revolution in Russia. It was the result of the collapse of the monarchy's ability to govern. Although public opinion in Russia had strongly supported the country's entry into the war, the conflict overtaxed Russia's resources and the efficiency of the tsarist government.

Nicholas II was weak and incompetent and suspected of being under the domination of his German wife and the insidious peasant faith healer Rasputin, whom a group of Russian noblemen assassinated in 1916. Military and domestic failures produced massive casualties, widespread hunger, strikes by workers, and disorganization in the army. The peasant discontent that had plagued the countryside before 1914 did not subside during the conflict. In 1915, the tsar took personal command of the armies on the German front, which kept him away from the capital. In his absence, corrupt and

Petrograd munitions workers demonstrating in 1917. Ria-Novosti/Sovfoto/Eastfoto

incompetent ministers increasingly discredited the government even in the eyes of conservative monarchists. All political factions in the Duma, Russia's parliament, were discontented.

The Provisional Government

In early March 1917, strikes and worker demonstrations erupted in Petrograd, as Saint Petersburg had been renamed. The ill-disciplined troops in the city refused to fire on the demonstrators. (See "The Outbreak of the Russian Revolution.") The tsar abdicated on March 15. The government of Russia fell into the hands of members of the Duma, who soon formed a provisional government composed chiefly of Constitutional Democrats (Cadets) with Western sympathies.

At the same time, the various socialist groups, including both Social Revolutionaries and Social Democrats of the Menshevik wing, began to organize soviets, councils of workers and soldiers. Initially, they allowed the provisional government to function without actually supporting it. As relatively orthodox Marxists, the Mensheviks believed that Russia had to have a bourgeois stage of development before it could have a revolution of the proletariat. They were willing to work temporarily with the Constitutional Democrats in a liberal regime, but they became estranged when the Cadets failed to control the army or to purge "reactionaries" from the government.

In this climate, the provisional government decided to remain loyal to Russia's alliances and continue the war. The provisional government thus accepted tsarist foreign policy and associated itself with the main source of domestic suffering and discontent. The collapse of the last Russian offensive in the summer of 1917 sealed its fate. Disillusionment with the war, shortages of food and other necessities at home, and the peasants' demands for land reform undermined the government. This occurred even after the moderate socialist Alexander Kerensky (1881–1970) became prime minister. Moreover, discipline in the army had disintegrated.

THE OUTBREAK OF THE RUSSIAN REVOLUTION

The Russian Revolution of March 1917 started with a series of ill-organized demonstrations in Petrograd. These actions and the ineffectuality of the government's response are described in the memoirs of Maurice Paléologue (1859–1944), the French ambassador.

What elements contributing to the success of the March Revolution emerge from this selection? Why might the army have been unreliable? Why did the two ambassadors think a new ministry should be appointed? What were the grievances of the revolutionaries? Why is there no discussion of the leaders of the revolution? What role did the emperor (tsar) play in these events?

MONDAY, MARCH 12, 1917

At half-past eight this morning, just as I finished dressing, I heard a strange and prolonged din which seemed to come from the Alexander Bridge. I looked out: there was no one on the bridge, which usually presents such a busy scene. But, almost immediately, a disorderly mob carrying red flags appeared at the end which is on the right bank of the Neva, and a regiment came towards it from the opposite side. It looked as if there would be a violent collision, but on the contrary the two bodies coalesced. The army was fraternizing with revolt.

Shortly afterwards, someone came to tell me that the Volhynian regiment of the Guard had mutinied during the night, killed its officers and was parading the city, calling on the people to take part in the revolution and trying to win over the troops who still remain loyal.

At ten o'clock there was a sharp burst of firing, and flames could be seen rising somewhere on the Liteïny Prospekt which is quite close to the embassy. Then silence. Accompanied by my military attaché, Lieutenant-Colonel Lavergne, I went out to see what was happening. Frightened inhabitants were scattering through the streets. There was indescribable confusion at the corner of the Liteïny. Soldiers were helping civilians to erect a barricade. Flames mounted from the Law Courts. The gates of the arsenal burst open with a crash. Suddenly the crack of machine-gun fire split the air: it was the regulars who had just taken up position near the Nevsky Prospekt. The revolutionaries replied. I had seen enough to have no doubt as to what was coming. Under a hail of bullets I returned to the embassy with Lavergne who had walked calmly and slowly to the hottest corner out of sheer bravado.

About half-past eleven I went to the Ministry for Foreign Affairs, picking up Buchanan [the British ambassador to Russia] on the way.

I told Pokrovski [the Russian foreign minister] everything I had just witnessed.

"So it's even more serious than I thought," he said.

But he preserved unruffled composure, flavoured with a touch of skepticism, when he told me of the steps on which the ministers had decided during the night:

"The sitting of the Duma has been prorogued to April and we have sent a telegram to the Emperor, begging him to return at once. With the exception of M. Protopopov [the Minister of the Interior, in charge of the police], my colleagues and I all thought that a dictatorship should be established without delay; it would be conferred upon some general whose prestige with the army is pretty high, General Russky for example."

I argued that, judging by what I saw this morning, the loyalty of the army was already too heavily shaken for our hopes of salvation to be based on the use of the "strong hand," and that the immediate appointment of a ministry inspiring confidence in the Duma seemed to me more essential than ever, as there is not a moment to lose. I reminded Pokrovski that in 1789, 1830, and 1848, three French dynasties were overthrown because they were too late in realizing the significance and strength of the movement against them. I added that in such a grave crisis the representative of allied France had a right to give the Imperial Government advice on a matter of internal politics.

Buchanan endorsed my opinion.

Pokrovski replied that he personally shared our views, but that the presence of Protopopov in the Council of Ministers paralyzed action of any kind.

I asked him:

"Is there no one who can open the Emperor's eyes to the real situation?"

He heaved a despairing sigh.

"The Emperor is blind!"

Deep grief was writ large on the face of the honest man and good citizen whose uprightness, patriotism and disinterestedness I can never sufficiently extol.

From Maurice Paléologue, *An Ambassador's Memoirs* (London: Doubleday & Company, Inc., and Hutchinson Publishing Group, Ltd., 1924), pp. 221–225.

AN EYEWITNESS ACCOUNT OF THE BOLSHEVIKS' SEIZURE OF POWER

John Reed was an American newspaperman who was in Russia during the Revolution of 1917, an enthusiastic convert to Communism, a supporter of the Bolsheviks, and an ardent admirer of Lenin. In the following selections from his account of the Bolshevik revolution he described Lenin's qualities and the part Lenin played in overthrowing the provisional government.

What was the provisional government? How did it come into being? Why was it under pressure in November 1917? Which groups were vying for power? What program gave gave victory to the Bolsheviks?

THURSDAY, OCT. 26/NOV. 8

The Congress was to meet at one o'clock, and long since the great meeting-hall had filled, but by seven there was yet no sign of the presidium. . . . The Bolshevik and Left Social Revolutionary factions were in session in their own rooms. All the livelong afternoon Lenin and Trotzky had fought against compromise. A considerable part of the Bolsheviki were in favour of giving way so far as to create a joint all-Socialist government. "We can't hold on!" they cried. "Too much is against us. We haven't got the men. We will be isolated, and the whole thing will fall." So Kameniev, Riazanov and others.

But Lenin, with Trotzky beside him, stood firm as a rock. "Let the compromisers accept our programme and they can come in! We won't give way an inch. If there are comrades here who haven't the courage and the will to dare what we dare, let him leave with the rest of the cowards and conciliators! Backed by the workers and soldiers we shall go on."

At five minutes past seven came word from the left Socialist Revolutionaries to say that they would remain in the Military Revolutionary Committee. "See!" said Lenin, "They are following.". . .

It was just 8:40 when a thundering wave of cheers announced the entrance of the presidium with Lenin—great Lenin—among them. A short, stocky figure, with a big head set down in his

Lenin and the Bolsheviks

Ever since April, the Bolshevik wing of the Social Democratic Party had been working against the provisional government. The Germans, in their most successful attempt at subversion, had rushed the brilliant Bolshevik leader V. I. Lenin (1870–1924) in a sealed train from his exile in Switzerland across Germany to Petrograd. They hoped he would cause trouble for the revolutionary government.

Lenin saw the opportunity to achieve the political alliance of workers and peasants he had discussed before the war. In speech after speech, he hammered away on the theme of peace, bread, and land. The Bolsheviks demanded that all political power go to the soviets, which they controlled. The failure of the summer offensive encouraged them to attempt a coup, but the effort was a failure. Lenin fled to Finland, and his chief collaborator, Leon Trotsky (1879–1940), was imprisoned.

The failure of a right-wing countercoup gave the Bolsheviks another chance. Trotsky, released from prison, led the powerful Petrograd soviet. Lenin returned in October, insisted to his doubting colleagues that the time was ripe to take power, and by the extraordinary force of his personality persuaded them to act. Trotsky organized the coup that took place on November 6 and concluded with an armed assault on the provisional government. The Bolsheviks, almost as much to their own astonishment as to that of the rest of the world, had come to rule Russia. (See "An Eyewitness Account of the Bolsheviks' Seizure of Power.")

The Communist Dictatorship

The victors moved to fulfill their promises and to assure their own security. The provisional government had decreed an election for late November to select a Constituent Assembly. The Social Revolutionaries won a large majority over the Bolsheviks. When the assembly gathered in Janu-

shoulders, bald and bulging. Little eyes, a snubbish nose, wide, generous mouth, and heavy chin; clean-shaven now, but already beginning to bristle with the well-known beard of his past and future. Dressed in shabby clothes, his trousers much too long for him. Unimpressive, to be the idol of a mob, loved and revered as perhaps few leaders in history have been. A strange popular leader—a leader purely by virtue of intellect; colourless, humourless, uncompromising and detached, without picturesque idiosyncrasies—but with the power of explaining profound ideas in simple terms, of analysing a concrete situation. And combined with shrewdness, the greatest intellectual audacity.

. . .

Other speakers followed, apparently without any order. A delegate of the coal-miners of the Don Basin called upon the Congress to take measures against Kaledin, who might cut off coal and food from the capital. Several soldiers just arrived from the Front brought the enthusiastic greetings of their regiments.

. . . Now Lenin, gripping the edge of the reading stand, letting his little winking eyes travel over the crowd as he stood there waiting, apparently oblivious to the long-rolling ovation, which lasted several minutes. When it finished, he said simply, "We shall now proceed to construct the Socialist order!" Again that overwhelming human roar.

"The first thing is the adoption of practical measures to realise peace. . . . We shall offer peace to the peoples of all the belligerent countries upon the basis of the Soviet terms—no annexations, no indemnities, and the right of self-determination of peoples. At the same time, according to our promise, we shall publish and repudiate the secret treaties. . . . The question of War and Peace is so clear that I think that I may, without preamble, read the project of a Proclamation to the Peoples of All the Belligerent Countries . . . ."

His great mouth, seeming to smile, opened wide as he spoke; his voice was hoarse—not unpleasantly so, but as if it had hardened that way after years and years of speaking—and went on monotonously, with the effect of being able to go on forever. . . . For emphasis he bent forward slightly. No gestures. And before him, a thousand simple faces looking up in intent adoration . . . .

It was exactly 10:35 when Kameniev asked all in favour of the proclamation to hold up their cards. One delegate dared to raise his hand against, but the sudden sharp outburst around him brought it swiftly down. . . . Unanimous.

At two o'clock the Land Decree was put to vote, with only one against and the peasant delegates were wild with joy. . . . So plunged the Bolsheviki ahead, irresistible, over-riding hesitation and opposition—the only people in Russia who had a definite programme of action while the others talked for eight long months. . . .

From John Reed, *Ten Days That Shook the World* (New York: Boni and Liveright, 1919), pp. 123–129.

ary, it met for only a day before the Red Army, controlled by the Bolsheviks, dispersed it. All other political parties also ceased to function in any meaningful fashion. In November and January, the Bolshevik government nationalized the land and turned it over to its peasant proprietors. Factory workers were put in charge of their plants. The state seized banks and repudiated the debt of the tsarist government. Property of the church reverted to the state.

The Bolshevik government also took Russia out of the war, which they believed benefited only capitalism. They signed an armistice with Germany in December 1917 and in March 1918 accepted the Treaty of Brest-Litovsk, by which Russia yielded Poland, Finland, the Baltic states, and Ukraine. Some territory in the Transcaucasus region went to Turkey. The Bolsheviks also agreed to pay a heavy war indemnity.

These terms were a high price to pay for peace, but Lenin had no choice. Russia was incapable of renewing the war effort, and the Bolsheviks needed time to impose their rule. Moreover, Lenin believed that the war and the Russian example would soon lead to communist revolutions across Europe.

The new Bolshevik government met major domestic resistance. Civil war erupted between Red Russians, who supported the revolution, and **White Russians**, who opposed it. In the summer of 1918, the Bolsheviks murdered the tsar and his family. Loyal army officers continued to fight the revolution and received aid from Allied armies. Under the leadership of Trotsky, however, the Red Army eventually overcame the domestic opposition. By 1921, Lenin and his supporters were in firm control.

▼ The End of World War I

The collapse of Russia and the Treaty of Brest-Litovsk were the zenith of German success. The Germans controlled eastern Europe and its resources, especially food, and by 1918 they were free to concentrate their forces on the western front. These developments would probably have been decisive without American intervention. Still, American troops would not arrive in significant numbers for about a year, and both sides tried to win the war in 1917.

An Allied attempt to break through in the west failed disastrously. Losses were heavy and the French army mutinied. The Austrians, supported by the Germans, defeated the Italians at Caporetto and threatened to overrun northern Italy, until they were checked with the aid of Allied troops. The deadlock continued, but time was running out for the Central Powers.

Germany's Last Offensive

In March 1918, the Germans decided to gamble everything on one last offensive. (This decision was taken chiefly by Ludendorff, second in command to Hindenburg, but the real leader of the army.) The German army reached the Marne again but got no farther. They had no more reserves, and the entire nation was exhausted. In contrast, the arrival of American troops in ever-increasing numbers bolstered the Allies. An Allied counteroffensive proved irresistible. As the exhausted Austrians collapsed in Italy, and Bulgaria and Turkey dropped out of the war, the German high command knew the end was imminent.

Ludendorff was determined to make peace before the German army was thoroughly defeated in the field and to make civilians responsible for ending the war. For some time, he had been the effective ruler of Germany under the aegis of the emperor. He now allowed a new government to be established on democratic principles and to seek peace immediately. The new government, under Prince Max of Baden, asked for peace on the basis of the **Fourteen Points** that President Wilson had declared as the American war aims. These were idealistic principles, including self-determination for nationalities, open diplomacy, freedom of the seas, disarmament, and the establishment of the League of Nations to keep the peace. Wilson insisted he would deal only with a democratic German government because he wanted to be sure he was dealing with the German people and not merely their rulers.

MAJOR CAMPAIGNS AND EVENTS OF WORLD WAR I

August 1914	Germans attack in West
August–September	First Battle of the Marne
1914	Battles of Tannenberg and the Masurian Lakes
April 1915	British land at Gallipoli, start of Dardanelles campaign
May 1915	Germans sink British ship *Lusitania*
February 1916	Germans attack Verdun
May–June 1916	Battle of Jutland
February 1917	Germans declare unrestricted submarine warfare
March 1917	Russian Revolution
April 1917	United States enters war
November 1917	Bolsheviks seize power in Russia
March 1918	Treaty of Brest-Litovsk
March 1918	German offensive in the West
November 1918	Armistice

The Armistice

The disintegration of the German army forced William II to abdicate on November 9, 1918. The majority branch of the Social Democratic Party proclaimed a republic to prevent their radical Leninist wing from setting up a soviet government. Two days later, this republican, socialist-led government signed the armistice that ended the war by accepting German defeat. The German people were, in general, unaware their army had been defeated and was crumbling. No foreign soldier stood on German soil. Many Germans expected a negotiated and mild settlement. The real peace was different and embittered the Germans. Many of them came to believe Germany had not been defeated but had been tricked by the enemy and betrayed—even stabbed in the back—by republicans and socialists at home.

The victors rejoiced, but they also had much to mourn. The casualties on all sides came to about 10 million dead and twice as many wounded. The economic and financial resources of the European states were badly strained. The victorious Allies, formerly creditors to the world, became debtors to the new American colossus, which the calamities of war had barely touched.

The Great War, as contemporaries called it, the First World War to those who lived through its horrible offspring, lasted more than four years, doing terrible damage. Battle casualties alone counted more than 4 million dead and 8.3 million wounded among the Central Powers and 5.4 million dead and 7 million wounded from their opponents, and millions of civilians died from the war and causes arising from it. Among the casualties also were the German, Austro-Hungarian, Russian, and Turkish Empires. The American intervention in 1917 thrust the United States into European affairs with a vengeance, and the collapse of the Russian autocracy brought the Bolshevik revolution and the reality of a great communist state. Disappointment, resentment, and economic dislocations caused by the war brought various forms of fascism to Italy, Germany, and other countries. The comfortable nineteenth-century assumptions of inevitable progress based on reason, science and technology, indi-

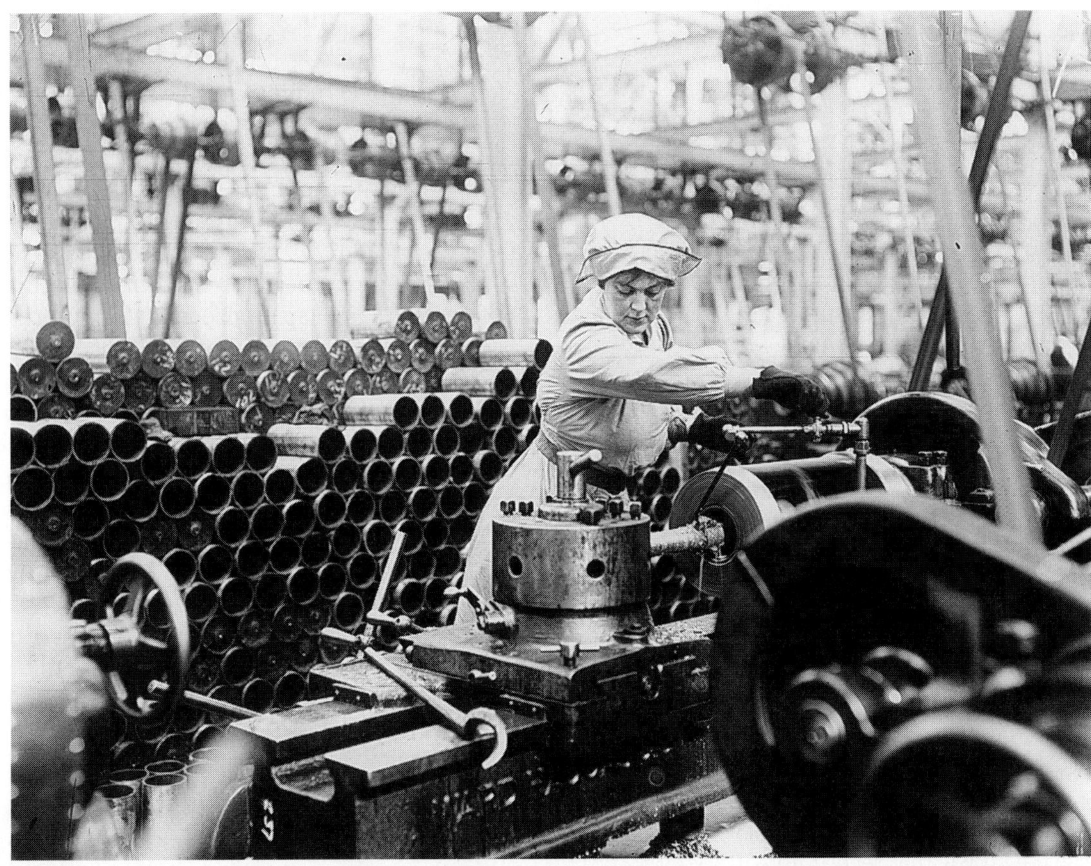

Women munitions workers in England. World War I demanded more from the civilian populations than had previous wars, resulting in important social changes. The demands of the munitions industries and a shortage of men (so many of whom were in uniform) brought many women out of traditional roles at home and into factories and other war-related work. Getty Images Inc.—Hulton Archive Photos

vidual freedom, democracy, and free enterprise gave way in many places to cynicism, nihilism, dictatorship, statism, official racism, and class warfare. It is widely agreed that the First World War was the mother of the Second and to most of the horrors of the rest of the century.

These kinds of changes affected the colonial peoples the European powers ruled, and overseas empires would never again be as secure as they had seemed before the war. Europe was no longer the center of the world, free to interfere when it wished or to ignore the rest of the world if it chose. The memory of that war lived on to shake the nerve of the victorious Western powers as they faced the new conditions of the postwar world.

The End of the Ottoman Empire

The First World War witnessed the end of the German, Austrian, and Russian Empires in the heart of Europe. The conflict also brought about the collapse of the Ottoman Empire, the ramifications of which also persist to the present day.

At the outbreak of World War I in August 1914, the Ottoman Empire was neutral, but many military officers, the so-called Young Turks who had taken control of the Ottoman government in 1909, were pro-German. After hesitating for three months, the Turks decided to enter the war on the German side in November 1914. This decision ultimately brought about the end of the Ottoman Empire. Early victories gave way to defeat after defeat at the hands of the Russians and the British, the latter assisted by Arabs from the Arabian peninsula and neighboring lands, most notably Hussein (1856–1931), *sherif* (ruler or emir) of Mecca, the city of Muhammad. The British drove the Ottomans out of Palestine and advanced deep into Mesopotamia, as far north as the oil fields of Mosul in modern Iraq. By October 30, 1918, Turkey was out of the war. In November, an Allied fleet sailed into the harbor of Constantinople and landed troops who occupied the city. The Ottoman government was helpless.

The peace treaty signed in Paris in 1920 between Turkey and the Allies dismembered the Ottoman Empire, placing large parts of it, particularly the areas Arabs inhabited, under the control of Britain and France. In Mesopotamia the British created the state of Iraq, which, along with Palestine, became British mandates. Syria and

The Allies promoted Arab efforts to secure independence from Turkey in an effort to remove Turkey from the war. Delegates to the peace conference of 1919 in Paris included British colonel T. E. Lawrence, who helped lead the rebellion, and representatives from the Middle Eastern region. Prince Feisal, the third son of King Hussein, stands in the foreground of this picture; Colonel T. E. Lawrence is in the middle row, second from the right; and Brigadier General Nuri Pasha Said of Baghdad is second from the left. CORBIS/Bettmann

Lebanon became French mandates. (**Mandates** were territories that were legally administered under the auspices of the League of Nations but were in effect ruled as colonies.) A Greek invasion of the Turkish homeland in Anatolia in 1919 provoked a nationalist reaction, bringing the young general Mustafa Kemal (1881–1938), who later took the name Ataturk, meaning "Father of the Turks," to power. He drove the Greeks out of Anatolia and compelled the victorious powers to make a new arrangement sealed by the treaty of Lausanne in 1923. Ataturk abolished the Ottoman sultanate and deposed the last caliph. The new Republic of Turkey abandoned most of the old Ottoman Empire but became fully independent of control by the European powers and sovereign in its Anatolian homeland. Under Ataturk and his successors, Turkey, although its population was overwhelmingly Muslim, became a secular state and a force for stability in the region.

The Arab portions of the old empire, however, were a different story. Divided into a collection of artificial states that had no historical reality, governed or dominated as client regimes by the British and French, they were relatively quiet during the 1920s and 1930s. The weakening of Britain and France during and after the Second World War, however, and their subsequent abandonment of control in the Middle East would create problems in the latter part of the century.

▼ The Settlement at Paris

The representatives of the victorious states gathered at Versailles and other Parisian suburbs in the first half of 1919. Wilson speaking for the United States, David Lloyd George (1863–1945) for Britain, Georges Clemenceau (1841–1929) for France, and Vittorio Emanuele Orlando (1860–1952) for Italy made up the Big Four. Japan also had an important part in the discussions. The diplomats who met in Paris had a far more difficult task than those who had sat at Vienna a century earlier. Both groups attempted to restore order to the world after long and costly wars. At the earlier conference, however, Metternich and his associates could confine their thoughts to Europe. France had acknowledged defeat and was willing to take part in and uphold the Vienna settlement. The diplomats at Vienna were not much affected by public opinion, and they could draw the new map of Europe along practical lines determined by the realities of power and softened by compromise.

Ataturk (1881–1938), the father of the Turkish Republic, sought to modernize his country by forcing Turks to adopt Western ways, including the Latin alphabet. Here he is shown teaching the alphabet as president in 1928. Turkish Cultural Office

"The Big Four" attending the Paris peace conference in 1919: Vittorio Orlande, premier of Italy; David Lloyd George, prime minister of Great Britain; Georges Clemenceau, premier of France; and Woodrow Wilson, president of the United States (left to right.). National Archives and Records Administration

Obstacles the Peacemakers Faced

The negotiators at Paris in 1919 were less fortunate. They represented constitutional, generally democratic governments, and public opinion had become a mighty force. Though there were secret sessions, the conference often worked in the full glare of publicity. Nationalism had become almost a secular religion, and Europe's many ethnic groups could not be relied on to remain quiet while the great powers distributed them on the map. Moreover, propaganda and especially the intervention of Woodrow Wilson had transformed World War I into a moral crusade to achieve a peace that would be just as well as secure. (See "Encountering the Past: War Propaganda and the Movies, page 826.") The Fourteen Points set forth the right of nationalities to self-determination as an absolute value, but in fact no one could draw the map of Europe to match ethnic groups perfectly with their homelands. All these elements made compromise difficult.

Wilson's idealism, moreover, came into conflict with the more practical war aims of the victorious powers and with many of the secret treaties that had been made before and during the war. The British and French people had been told that Germany would be made to pay for the war. Russia had been promised control of Constantinople in return for recognizing the French claim to Alsace-Lorraine and British control of Egypt. Romania had been promised Transylvania at the expense of Hungary.

Some of the agreements contradicted others. Italy and Serbia had competing claims in the Adriatic. During the war, the British had encouraged Arab hopes of an independent Arab state carved out of the Ottoman Empire. Those plans, however, contradicted the Balfour Declaration (1917), in which the British seemed to accept Zionist ideology and to promise the Jews a national home in Palestine. Both of these plans conflicted with an Anglo-French agreement to divide the Near East between themselves.

The continuing national goals of the victors presented further obstacles to an idealistic "peace without victors." France was painfully conscious of its numerical inferiority to Germany and of the low birthrate that

WAR PROPAGANDA AND THE MOVIES: CHARLIE CHAPLIN

THE VAST SCOPE of the First World War required support. As the war stretched on and its costs increased, all the competing nations intensified propaganda campaigns to justify the huge expenditure of lives and resources. Sometimes this took the form of painting the enemy in brutal and lurid colors to provoke hatred, and sometimes it took the form of sympathetic images of patriotism and sacrifice for a noble cause. These efforts, sponsored both by government and private agencies, saturated the lives of everyone—men, women, and even children—while the war lasted.

At first, most of the propaganda came in the form of writing—newspaper articles and pamphlets, justifying the war and demonizing the enemy. Soon, however, verbal efforts gave way to more emotionally powerful visual devices such as posters, cartoons, and caricatures. By the middle of the war, however, the relatively new medium of film became the most powerful weapon of propaganda. Graphically and dramatically, movies showed the enemy as either horrible or ridiculous and one's own soldiers and people as brave and noble. Such images could reach rich and poor, literate and illiterate, young and old, with great emotional effect.

Charlie Chaplin in *Shoulder Arms.* © Sunset Boulevard/ Corbis Sygma

Both sides produced films that became enormously popular, but none more so than those Charlie Chaplin (1889–1977) did for the Allies. Born in England, he came to America as a vaudeville star in 1914 and was already famous when the war broke out. His tragicomic character, the tramp, in many variations, had universal appeal. His wartime films had amazing effects: They helped sell great quantities of Liberty Bonds (which the American government used to help pay for its involvement in the war), raised the morale of civilians, and even eased the miseries of shell-shocked soldiers.

Chaplin's 1918 movie *Shoulder Arms* was his greatest wartime success. It gave a comic picture of the difficulties of basic training for American recruits and portrays the Germans as bumbling fools. In the film, Chaplin's character, exhausted by the rigors of drilling, falls asleep. He wakes up at the front, where he deceives the enemy by pretending to be a tree, captures first a German unit and finally the kaiser, all by himself.

The Germans, too, soon learned the propaganda value of films, which were more completely in the hands of the government than those made in the Allied states. The German army made comedies, melodramas, and newsreels and showed them both to the troops and the civilian public. The German government thought movies so important that even during the freezing, brutal winter of 1917–1918 when fuel supplies were at a premium, it gave movie theaters special priority to use coal and electricity, but there was no German Charlie Chaplin.

What were the purposes of propaganda in the war? What were the advantages of using movies in the war effort?

would keep it inferior. So France was naturally eager to weaken Germany permanently and preserve French superiority. Italy continued to seek *Italia irredenta*, Britain looked to its imperial interests, and Japan pursued its own advantage in Asia. The United States insisted on freedom of the seas, which favored American commerce, and on its right to maintain the Monroe Doctrine.

Finally, the peacemakers of 1919 faced a world still in turmoil. The greatest immediate threat appeared to be the spread of Bolshevism. While civil war distracted Lenin and his colleagues, the Allies landed small armies in Russia to help overthrow the Bolshevik regime. The revolution seemed likely to spread as communist governments were established in Bavaria and Hungary. A communist uprising led by the "Spartacus group" had to be suppressed in Berlin. The worried Allies even allowed an army of German volunteers to fight the Bolsheviks in the Baltic states.

Fear of the spread of communism affected the diplomats at Versailles, but it was far from dominant. The Germans played on such fears to get better terms, but the Allies, especially the French, would not hear of it. Fear of Germany remained the chief concern for France. More traditional and more immediate interests governed the policies of the other Allies.

The Peace

The Paris settlement consisted of five separate treaties between the victors and the defeated powers. Formal sessions began on January 18, 1919, and the last treaty was signed on August 10, 1920. (See Map 26–5, page 828.) Wilson arrived in Europe to unprecedented popular acclaim. Liberals and idealists expected a new kind of international order achieved in a new and better way, but they were soon disillusioned. "Open covenants openly arrived at" soon gave way to closed sessions in which Wilson, Clemenceau, and Lloyd George made arrangements that seemed cynical to outsiders.

The notion of "a peace without victors" became a mockery when the Soviet Union (as Russia was now called) and Germany were excluded from the peace conference. The Germans were simply presented with a treaty and compelled to accept it, fully justified in their complaint that the treaty had been dictated, not negotiated. The principle of national self-determination was violated many times and was unavoidable. Still, their exclusion from decisions angered the diplomats from the small nations. The undeserved adulation accorded Wilson on his arrival gradually turned into equally undeserved scorn. He had not abandoned his ideals lightly but had merely given way to the irresistible force of reality.

The League of Nations Wilson could make unpalatable concessions without abandoning his ideals because he put great faith in a new instrument for peace and justice: the **League of Nations**. Its covenant was an essential part of the peace treaty. The league was to be not an international government, but a body of sovereign states that agreed to pursue common policies and to consult in the common interest, especially when war threatened. The members promised to submit differences among themselves to arbitration, an international court, or the League Council. Refusal to abide by the results would justify economic sanctions and even military intervention by the league. The league was unlikely to be effective, however, because it had no armed forces at its disposal. Furthermore, any action required the unanimous consent of its council, consisting permanently of Britain, France, Italy, the United States, and Japan, as well as four other states that had temporary seats. The Covenant of the League bound its members to "respect and preserve" the territorial integrity of all its members; this was generally seen as a device to ensure the security of the victorious powers. The exclusion of Germany and the Soviet Union from the League Assembly further undermined its claim to evenhandedness.

Members of the League of Nations remained fully sovereign and continued to pursue their national interests. Only Wilson put much faith in the league's future ability to produce peace and justice. To get the other states to agree to the league, he approved territorial settlements that violated his own principles.

Germany In the West, the main territorial issue was the fate of Germany. Although a united Germany was less than fifty years old, no one seems to have thought of undoing Bismarck's work and dividing the country into its component parts. The French wanted to set the Rhineland up as a separate buffer state, but Lloyd George and Wilson would not permit it. Still, they could not ignore France's need for protection against a resurgent Germany. France received Alsace-Lorraine and the right to work the coal mines of the Saar for fifteen years. Germany west of the Rhine and fifty kilometers east of it was to be a demilitarized zone. Allied troops could stay on the west bank for fifteen years.

The treaty also provided that Britain and the United States would help France if Germany attacked it. Such an attack was made more unlikely by the permanent disarmament of Germany. Its army was limited to 100,000 men on long-term service, its fleet was reduced to a coastal defense force, and it was forbidden to have warplanes, submarines, tanks, heavy artillery, or poison gas. As long as these provisions were observed, France would be safe.

The East The settlement in the East reflected the collapse of the great defeated empires that had ruled it for centuries. Germany lost part of Silesia, and East Prussia

Map 26–5 **WORLD WAR I PEACE SETTLEMENT IN EUROPE AND THE MIDDLE EAST** The map of central and eastern Europe, as well as that of the Middle East, underwent drastic revision after World War I. The enormous territorial losses suffered by Germany, Austria-Hungary, the Ottoman Empire, Bulgaria, and Russia were the other side of the coin represented by gains for France, Italy, Greece, and Romania and by the appearance or reappearance of at least eight new independent states from Finland in the north to Yugoslavia in the south. The mandate system for former Ottoman territories outside Turkey proper laid foundations for several new, mostly Arab, states in the Middle East. In Africa, the mandate system placed the former German colonies under British, French, and South African rule. (See Map 25–3, page 770.)

was cut off from the rest of Germany by a corridor carved out to give the revived state of Poland access to the sea. The Austro-Hungarian Empire disappeared entirely, giving way to five small successor states. Most of its German-speaking people were gathered in the Republic of Austria, cut off from the Germans of Bohemia and forbidden to unite with Germany.

The Magyars were left with the much-reduced kingdom of Hungary. The Czechs of Bohemia and Moravia joined with the Slovaks and Ruthenians to the east to form Czechoslovakia, and this new state included several million unhappy Germans plus Poles, Magyars, and Ukrainians. The southern Slavs were united in the Kingdom of Serbs, Croats, and Slovenes, or Yugoslavia. Italy gained Trentino, which included tens of thousands of German speakers, and the port of Trieste. Romania was enlarged by receiving Transylvania from Hungary and Bessarabia from Russia. Bulgaria lost territory to Greece and Yugoslavia. Russia lost vast territories in the west. Finland, Estonia, Latvia, and Lithuania became independent states, and most of Poland was carved out of formerly Russian soil.

Reparations Perhaps the most debated part of the peace settlement dealt with **reparations** for the damage Germany did during the war. Before the armistice, the Germans promised to pay compensation "for all damages done to the civilian population of the Allies and their property." The Americans judged the amount would be between $15 billion and $25 billion and that Germany would be able to pay that amount. France and Britain, however, who worried about repaying their war debts to the United States, were eager to have Germany pay the full cost of the war, including pensions to survivors and dependents.

There was a general agreement that Germany could not afford to pay such a huge sum, whatever it might be, and the conference did not specify an amount. In the meantime, Germany was to pay $5 billion annually until 1921. At that time, a final figure would be set, which Germany would have to pay in thirty years. The French did not regret the outcome. Either Germany would pay and be bled into impotence, or Germany would refuse to pay and French intervention would be warranted.

To justify these huge reparation payments, the Allies inserted the notorious **war guilt clause** (Clause 231) into the treaty:

> The Allied and Associated Governments affirm, and Germany accepts, the responsibility of Germany and her allies for causing all the loss and damage to which the Allied and Associated Governments and their nationals have been subjected as a consequence of the war imposed upon them by aggression of Germany and her allies.

The Germans, of course, did not believe they were solely responsible for the war and bitterly resented the charge. They had lost territories containing badly needed natural resources. Yet they were presented with an astronomical and apparently unlimited reparations bill. To add insult to injury, they were required to admit to a war guilt they did not feel.

Finally, to heap insult upon insult, they were required to accept the entire treaty as the victors wrote it, without negotiation. Germany's prime minister Philipp Scheidmann (1865–1939) spoke of the treaty as the imprisonment of the German people and asked, "What hand would not wither that binds itself and us in these fetters?" There was no choice, however. The Social Democrats and the Catholic Center Party formed a new government, and their representatives signed the treaty. These parties formed the backbone of the Weimar government that ruled Germany until 1933. They never overcame the stigma of having accepted the Treaty of Versailles.

World War I and Colonial Empires

The First World War and the peace settlement introduced numerous changes and transformations into the European colonial world.

Redistribution of Colonies into Mandates The rivalries over empire that had predated the outbreak of the war and that had contributed so mightily to prewar tensions continued throughout the conflict. Through secret treaties of 1915 the Allies planned for the eventual dismemberment of the German Empire and the distribution of its colonies to allied victors. The German government had similarly envisioned taking colonial spoils had it won the conflict. In effect, the war had opened the possibility for whoever won it to expand their empires at the cost of the defeated powers. As a result, the single most important imperial consequence of World War I was Germany being stripped of its colonies and the Ottoman Empire of regions it had formerly governed.

The Covenant of the League of Nations established mandates within these former colonies and regions. These mandates located in the Middle East, Africa, and the Pacific were placed under the "tutelage" of one of the great powers under League of Nations supervision and encouraged to advance toward independence. Britain and France became the chief mandate administrators and were consequently drawn more deeply into new regions of the world, most particularly, the Middle East. In effect, the mandates became colonies of the administering powers. Some mandates, most notably Iraq, became independent between the wars. Other mandates became independent often with considerable conflict from the closing years of World War II through the third quarter of the twentieth century. These latter mandates included Palestine, Syria, Lebanon, Transjordan, Tanganyka, Kamerun, Southwest Africa, and German New Guinea to mention only some of the major areas.

Colonial Participation Colonial peoples themselves had played a significant role in the First World War. Germany itself did not call upon troops from its colonies. The war led Britain and France, however, to view their empires in new ways as sources of military as well as economic support. The French government recruited tens of thousands of Algerians into its armed forces and over 150,000 West Africans. It is estimated that more than 2.5 million British colonial troops participated in the war. More than 1.25 million Indian troops were involved either directly in combat or as laborers working for cheap wages. Canada, Australia, New Zealand, and South Africa sent hundreds of thousands of troops into the war and experienced very significant losses. The presence of so many non-European troops on the European continent even before the arrival of U.S. troops was one of the factors that made the war a genuinely world conflict. Both colonial troops of color and United States troops of color encountered significant racial prejudice in Europe.

What Europeans had learned from the wartime experience was the value of their colonies in terms of troops to be recruited and natural resources to be devoted to the war effort, and they tended to seek ways to draw them into closer relations. In this respect, the years after the war were in some respects the period of most extensive direct colonial involvement by Great Britain and France and the ongoing desire for empire on the part of Italy. When the Second World War broke out, both nations would encounter much more nationalist resistance that after the war would culminate in decolonization. (See Chapter 29.)

Impact of the Peace Settlement on Future Colonial Relations Many native colonial leaders in Africa and Asia had supported the allied war effort in the hope that their peoples would be rewarded with greater independence and better economic relations with Europe. Wilson's Fourteen Points and his emphasis on self-determination had also contributed to raising such expectations. These hopes were dashed at the peace conference and in the years thereafter. Numerous later leaders of anticolonial nationalist movements were either in Paris at the time of the conference or closely followed its events. These colonial leaders had hoped they might be allowed to put their case for independence or major administrative reform before the conference, and they had been denied that opportunity. Their disappointment led them over the years to reject engagement with the existing international order and to move in various new directions of disruptive and ultimately successful national anticolonialism.

The European powers themselves had directly contributed to these developments in another fashion. They had sought to stir nationalist uprisings in the lands of their opponents. Here the most significant effort took place among Arab peoples governed by the Ottoman Empire, which had sided with Germany. The British led Arab nationalist groups to believe that they might achieve independence in the wake of an allied victory. T. E. Lawrence, later known popularly as Lawrence of Arabia, led much of this effort on behalf of the British. For their part the Germans had attempted to stir unrest in northern Africa.

A glance at the new map of the post–World War I world could give the impression that the old imperial nations, especially Britain and France, were more powerful than ever, but that impression would be superficial and misleading. The great Western European powers had paid an enormous price in lives, money, and will for their victory in the war. Colonial peoples pressed for the rights that the West proclaimed as universal but denied to their colonies, and some influential minorities in the countries that ruled those colonies sympathized with colonial aspirations for independence. Tension between colonies and their ruling nations was a cause of serious instability in the world the Paris treaties of 1919 created.

Evaluating the Peace

Few peace settlements have undergone more severe attacks than the one negotiated in Paris in 1919. It was natural that the defeated powers should object to it, but the peace soon came under bitter criticism in the victorious countries as well. Many of the French objected that the treaty tied French security to promises of aid from the unreliable Anglo-Saxon countries. In England and the United States, a wave of bitter criticism arose in liberal quarters because the treaty seemed to violate the idealistic and liberal aims that the Western leaders had professed.

It was not a peace without victors. It did not put an end to imperialism but attempted to promote the national interests of the winning nations. It violated the principles of national self-determination by leaving significant pockets of minorities outside the borders of their national homelands.

The Economic Consequences of the Peace The most influential economic critic of the treaty was John Maynard Keynes (1883–1946), a brilliant British economist who took part in the peace conference. He resigned in disgust when he saw the direction it was taking. His book *The Economic Consequences of the Peace* (1920) was a scathing attack, especially on reparations and the other economic aspects of the peace. It was also a skillful assault on the negotiators and particularly on Wilson, whom Keynes depicted as a fool and a hypocrite. Keynes argued that the Treaty of Versailles was both immoral and unworkable. He called it a Carthaginian peace, referring to Rome's destruction of Carthage after the Third Punic War. He argued that such a peace would bring economic ruin and war to Europe unless it was repudiated.

Keynes's argument had a great effect on the British, who were already suspicious of France and glad of an excuse to withdraw from continental affairs. The decent and respectable position came to be one that supported revision of the treaty in favor of Germany. In the United States, the book fed the traditional tendency toward isolationism and gave powerful weapons to Wilson's enemies. Wilson's own political mistakes helped prevent American ratification of the treaty. Thus, America was out of the League of Nations and not bound to defend France. Britain, therefore, was also free from its obligation to France. France was left to protect itself without adequate means to do so for long.

Many of the attacks on the Treaty of Versailles are unjustified. It was not a Carthaginian peace. Germany was neither dismembered nor ruined. Reparations could be and were scaled down. Until the great world depression of the 1930s, the Germans recovered prosperity. Complaints against the peace should also be measured against the peace that the victorious Germans had imposed on Russia at Brest-Litovsk and their plans for a European settlement if they had won. Both were far more severe than anything enacted at Versailles. The attempt to achieve self-determination for nationalities was less than perfect, but it was the best effort Europe had ever made to do so.

Divisive New Boundaries and Tariff Walls The peace, nevertheless, was unsatisfactory in important ways. The elimination of the Austro-Hungarian Empire, however inevitable, created serious problems. Economically, it was disastrous. New borders and tariff walls separated raw materials from manufacturing areas and producers from their markets. In hard times, this separation created friction and hostility that aggravated other quarrels the peace treaties also created. Poland contained unhappy German, Lithuanian, and Ukrainian minorities, and Czechoslovakia and Yugoslavia were collections of nationalities that did not find it easy to live together. Territorial disputes in Eastern Europe promoted further tension.

Moreover, the peace rested on a victory that Germany did not admit. The Germans felt cheated rather than defeated. The high moral principles the Allies proclaimed undercut the validity of the peace, for it plainly fell far short of those principles.

Failure to Accept Reality Finally, the great weakness of the peace was its failure to accept reality. Germany and Russia must inevitably play an important part in European affairs, yet the settlement and the League of Nations excluded them. Given the many discontented parties, the peace was not self-enforcing, yet no satisfactory machinery to enforce it was established. The League of Nations was never a serious force for this purpose. It was left to France, with no guarantee of support from Britain and no hope of help from the United States, to defend the new arrangements. Finland, the Baltic states, Poland, Romania, Czechoslovakia, and Yugoslavia were expected to be a barrier to the westward expansion of Russian communism and to help deter a revival of German power. Most of these states, however, would have to rely on France in case of danger, and France was simply not strong enough to protect them if Germany revived.

The tragedy of the Treaty of Versailles was that it was neither conciliatory enough to remove the desire for revision, even at the cost of war, nor harsh enough to make another war impossible. The only hope for a lasting peace was that Germany would remain disarmed while the more obnoxious clauses of the peace treaty were revised. Such a policy required continued attention to the problem, unity among the victors, and farsighted leadership; but none of these was consistently present during the next two decades.

In Perspective

The unification of Germany in 1871 transformed the European international order. For twenty years a series of alliances and an ongoing process of shrewd negotiation on the part of Bismarck had brought a fragile stability to European diplomatic relations. In years after Bismarck was forced from office in 1890, Kaiser Wilhelm and the German military pursued expansively aggressive policies that destabilized European diplomatic relations. Germany became overly dependent upon its alliance with Austria. Britain, France, and Russia by the first decade of the twentieth century had come to forge the very kind of friendly diplomatic understandings that Bismarck had sought to avoid.

The first fifteen years of the twentieth century saw a number of European diplomatic crises related to imperial concerns and rivalries in the Balkan Peninsula. These crises increased distrust between Germany and other European powers and worked to cement the understandings among Britain, France, and Russia. The assassination of Archduke Francis Ferdinand in the summer of 1914 sparked a Balkans crisis that could not be contained. The initial conflict between Serbia and Austria-Hungry soon drew in Russia in support of the former and Germany in support of the latter. Thereafter, the other alliances and understandings of mutual support came into play. The war plans of the various powers quickly led to the most extensive war Europe had experienced in a century.

Other unexpected transformative events followed the military stalemate. In March 1917 revolution overthrew the tsarist government of Russia. The next month the United States entered the war. In November 1917 the Bolsheviks seized power in Russia and rapidly withdrew Russia from the conflict. By November 1918 Germany surrendered. In both Germany and Austria-Hungry the governments that had led their nations into the war had collapsed.

At the Paris Peace Conference of 1919 the victorious allies redrew the map of Europe, rearranged much of the European colonial world, established the League of Nations, and imposed a war guilt clause and high reparations on Germany. The United States refused to ratify the treaty and for two decades largely withdrew from European affairs. The peace settlement itself planted the seeds of ongoing resentment and nationalist unrest in Europe.

REVIEW QUESTIONS

1. What role in the world did Bismarck envisage for the new Germany after 1871? How successful was he in carrying out his vision? Was he wise to tie Germany to Austria-Hungary?
2. Why and in what stages did Britain abandon its policy of "splendid isolation" at the turn of the century? Were the policies it pursued instead wise ones, or should Britain have followed a different course altogether?
3. How did developments in the Balkans lead to the outbreak of World War I? What was the role of Serbia? Of Austria? Of Russia? What was the aim of German policy in July 1914? Did Germany want a general war?
4. Why did Germany lose World War I? Could Germany have won, or was victory never a possibility? What were the benefits of Versailles to Europe, and what were its drawbacks? Was the settlement too harsh or too conciliatory? Could it have secured lasting peace in Europe? How might it have been improved?
5. Why did Lenin succeed in establishing Bolshevik rule in Russia? What role did Trotsky play? Was it wise policy for Lenin to take Russia out of the war?
6. How had imperialism contributed to pre–World War I rivalries? How did the war and the peace settlement change European colonialism and plant seeds for further colonial discontent?

SUGGESTED READINGS

L. Albertini, *The Origins of the War of 1914*, 3 vols. (1952, 1957). Discursive, but invaluable.

V. R. Berghahn, *Germany and the Approach of War in 1914* (1973). Stresses the importance of Germany's naval program.

S. B. Fay, *The Origins of the World War*, 2 vols. (1928). The best and most influential of the revisionist accounts.

N. Ferguson, *The Pity of War* (1999). An analytic study of the First World War with controversial interpretations, especially of why it began and why it ended.

O. Figes, *A People's Tragedy: The Russian Revolution: 1891–1924* (1998). The best recent analytic narrrataive.

F. Fischer, *Germany's Aims in the First World War* (1967). An influential interpretation that stirred an enormous controversy by emphasizing Germany's role in bringing on the war.

D. Fromkin, *Europe's Last Summer: Who Started the Great War in 1914?* (2004). A lively and readable account of the outbreak of the war based on the latest scholarship.

D. Fromkin, *A Peace to End All Peace: The Fall of the Ottoman Empire and the Creation of the Modern Middle East* (1989). A well-informed narrative of a complicated process.

R. F. Hamilton and H. H. Herwig, *The Origins of World War I* (2003). An extensive collection of recent essays examining the subject from a number of differing perspectives.

H. Herwig, *The First World War: Germany and Austria, 1914–18* (1997). A fine study of the war from the losers' perspective.

J. N. Horne, *Labour at War: France and Britain, 1914–1918* (1991). Examines a major issue on the home fronts.

J. Joll, *The Origins of the First World War* (2006). Most recent revision of a classic study.

J. Keegan, *The First World War* (1999). A vivid and readable narrative.

P. Kennedy, *The Rise of the Anglo-German Antagonism, 1860–1914* (1980). An unusual and thorough analysis of the political, economic, and cultural roots of important diplomatic developments.

D. C. B. Lieven, *Russia and the Origins of the First World War* (1983). A good account of the forces that shaped Russian policy.

M. Macmillan, *Paris 1919: Six Months That Changed the World* (2003). The most extensive recent treatment.

Erez Manela, *The Wilsonian Moment: Self Determination and the International Origins of Anticolonial Nationalism* (2007). A major exploration of how Wilson's foreign policy at Versailles raised colonial expectations and revolts in Egypt, India, China, and Korea.

A. Mombauer, *The Origins of the First World War: Controversies and Consensus* (2002). A discussion and evaluation of historians' shifting views regarding the responsibility for the outbreak of the war.

Z. Steiner, *Britain and the Origins of the First World War* (2003). A perceptive and informed account of British foreign policy before the war.

D. Stevenson, *Cataclysm: The First World War as Political Tragedy* (2004). Analyzes the bankruptcy of reason that precipitated the war and kept it going.

N. Stone, *The Eastern Front 1917–1917* (2004). A study of the often neglected region of the war.

H. Strachan, *The First World War* (2004). A one-volume version of the massive three-volume magisterial account now underway.

S. R. Williamson, Jr., *Austria-Hungary and the Origins of the First World War* (1991). A valuable study of a complex subject.

For additional learning resources related to this chapter, please go to www.myhistorylab.com

PEARSON myhistorylab

This poster shows an idealized Soviet collective farm on which tractors owned by the state have replaced peasant labor. In reality, collectivization provoked fierce resistance and caused famines in which millions of peasants died. Poster concerning the first Five Year Plan with a photograph of Joseph Stalin (1879–1953), "At the end of the Plan, the basis of collectivisation must be completed," 1932 (colour litho.) by Klutchis (fl. 1932). Deutsches Plakat Museum, Essen, Germany/Archives Charmet/The Bridgeman Art Library

27

The Interwar Years: The Challenge of Dictators and Depression

▼ **After Versailles: Demands for Revision and Enforcement**

▼ **Toward the Great Depression in Europe**

Financial Tailspin • Problems in Agricultural Commodities • Depression and Government Policy in Britain and France

▼ **The Soviet Experiment**

War Communism • The New Economic Policy • The Third International • Stalin versus Trotsky • The Decision for Rapid Industrialization • The Collectivization of Agriculture • The Purges

▼ **The Fascist Experiment in Italy**

The Rise of Mussolini • The Fascists in Power

▼ **German Democracy and Dictatorship**

The Weimar Republic • Depression and Political Deadlock • Hitler Comes to Power • Hitler's Consolidation of Power • Anti-Semitism and the Police State • Racial Ideology and the Lives of Women • Nazi Economic Policy

▼ **Trials of the Successor States in Eastern Europe**

Economic and Ethnic Pressures • Poland: Democracy to Military Rule • Czechoslovakia: A Viable Democratic Experiment • Hungary: Turn to Authoritarianism • Austria: Political Turmoil and Nazi Occupation • Southeastern Europe: Royal Dictatorships

▼ **In Perspective**

KEY TOPICS

- Economic and political disorder in the aftermath of World War I
- Financial collapse and depression in Europe
- Britain and France face the Great Depression
- Soviet Communist consolidation under Lenin
- Stalin's forced industrialism, agricultural collectivization, and purges in the Soviet Communist Party and army
- Mussolini and the Fascist seizure of power in Italy
- Failure of the German Weimar Republic
- The Nazi seizure of power and the establishment of a police state and racial laws in Germany
- The development of authoritarian governments in most of the successor states of the Habsburg Empire

DURING THE TWO decades that followed the Paris settlement, Europe saw bold experiments in politics and economic life. Two broad sets of factors accounted for these experiments. First, the war, the Russian Revolution, and the peace treaty had transformed the political face of Europe. New political regimes had emerged in the wake of the collapse of the monarchies of Germany, Austria-Hungary, and Russia. These were the Weimar Republic in Germany, a host of successor states to the Austro-Hungarian and Russian Empires, and the Communist Soviet Union. In Great Britain, most of Ireland established itself as, in effect, an independent nation. These new governments immediately faced the problems of postwar reconstruction, economic dislocation, and nationalistic resentment. Most of these nations also included large groups who questioned the legitimacy of their governments. All the governments and societies of both Western and Eastern Europe believed themselves profoundly threatened by the Soviet Union. The Russian Revolution was thus a pivotal factor in the rise of right-wing and fascist dictators, who often justified their power on the basis of their firm opposition to the "Red Menace" and to the growing popularity of socialism and communism in many European countries during the economic crisis of the 1930s.

Second, beginning in the early twenties, economic dislocations that led to the economic downturn that became known as the Great Depression began to spread across the world. The economic troubles were caused by financial turmoil in the industrialized nations and a collapse of commodity prices that hurt the economies of the countries that exported raw materials. Faced with political instability and economic crisis, governments contrived various responses. The Great Depression itself, which began in 1929, was the most severe downturn capitalist economies had ever experienced. High unemployment, low production, financial instability, and shrinking trade arrived and would not depart. Business and political leaders despaired over the market's seeming inability to resolve the crisis. Marxists and, indeed, many other observers thought the final downfall of capitalism was at hand.

European voters looked for new ways out of the doldrums, and politicians sought to escape the pressures that the Depression had brought on them. One result of the fight for economic security was the establishment of the Nazi dictatorship in Germany. Another was the piecemeal construction of what became known as the mixed economy; that is, governments became directly involved in making economic decisions alongside business and labor. In both cases, most of the political and economic guidelines of nineteenth-century liberalism were abandoned, and so were decency and civility in political life. Authoritarianism and aggression were not the inescapable destiny of Europe. They emerged from the failure to secure alternative modes of democratic political life and stable international relations and from the inability to achieve long-term economic prosperity.

▼ After Versailles: Demands for Revision and Enforcement

The Paris settlement fostered both resentments and discontent. Those resentments counted among the chief political factors in Europe for the next two decades. Germany had been humiliated. The arrangements for reparations led to endless haggling over payments. Many national groups in the successor states of the Austro-Hungarian Empire felt that their rights to self-determination had been violated or ignored. There were strident demands for further border adjustments because significant national minorities, particularly Germans and Magyars, resided outside the national boundaries drawn in Paris. On the other side, the victorious powers, especially France, often believed that the provisions of the treaties were being inadequately enforced. Consequently, throughout the 1920s and into the 1930s, demands either to revise or to enforce the Paris treaties contributed to domestic political turmoil across the Continent. Many political figures were willing to fish in these troubled international waters for a large catch of domestic votes.

▼ Toward the Great Depression in Europe

Along with the move toward political experimentation and the demands for revision of the new international order, there was a widespread yearning to return to the economic prosperity of the prewar years. After 1918, however, it was impossible to restore in the economic realm what American president Warren Harding (1865–1923) would term *normalcy*. During the Great War, Europeans had turned the military and industrial power that they had created during the previous century against themselves. What had been "normal" in economic and social life before 1914 could not be reestablished.

The casualties from the war numbered in the millions. (See Table 27–1.) This represented not only a waste of human life and talent, but also the loss of producers and consumers.

Three factors originating in the 1920s combined to bring about the intense severity and the extended length of the **Great Depression**. First, a financial crisis stemmed directly from the war and the peace settlement. To this was added a crisis in the production and distribution of goods in the world market. These two problems became intertwined in 1929, and in Europe they reached the breaking point in 1931. Finally, both of these difficulties became worse than they might have been because no major Western European coun-

TABLE 27–1 TOTAL CASUALTIES IN THE FIRST WORLD WAR

Country	Dead	Wounded	Total Killed as a Percentage of Population
France	1,398,000	2,000,000	3.4
Belgium	38,000	44,700	0.5
Italy	578,000	947,000	1.6
British Empire	921,000	2,090,000	1.7
Romania	250,000	120,000	3.3
Serbia	278,000	133,000	5.7
Greece	26,000	21,000	0.5
Russia	1,811,000	1,450,000	1.1
Bulgaria	88,000	152,000	1.9
Germany	2,037,000	4,207,000	3.0
Austria-Hungary	1,100,000	3,620,000	1.9
Turkey	804,000	400,000	3.7
United States	114,000	206,000	0.1

Source: Niall Ferguson, *The Pity of War* (New York: Basic Books, 1998).

try or the United States provided strong, responsible economic leadership that might have resulted in some form of cooperation to face the challenge of the Depression.

The French invasion of the German Ruhr (1923) began a crisis that brought strikes and rampant inflation in Germany. Here French troops have commandeered a German locomotive during one of the strikes. UPI/CORBIS/Bettmann

Financial Tailspin

As one of the chief victors in the war, France was determined to collect reparations from Germany for the destruction the war had caused in northern France. The United States was no less determined that its allies repay the money it had lent them during the war. The European allies also owed debts to each other. German reparations were to provide the means of repaying all these debts. Most of the money that the Allies collected from each other also went to the United States.

The quest for payment of German reparations caused one of the major diplomatic crises of the 1920s; that crisis itself resulted in further economic upheaval. In early 1923 the Allies—France in particular—declared Germany to be in technical default of its reparation payments. On January 11, to ensure receipt of the hard-won reparations, French and Belgian troops occupied the Ruhr mining and manufacturing district. The **Weimar Republic** ordered passive resistance that amounted to a general strike in Germany's largest industrial region. Confronted with this tactic, the French sent technicians and engineers to run the German mines and railroads. France got its way. The Germans paid, but its victory cost France dearly. The British were alienated by the French heavy-handedness and took no part in the occupation. Britain became more suspicious of France and more sympathetic to Germany. The cost of the Ruhr occupation, moreover, vastly increased French as well as German inflation and damaged the French economy.

The political and economic turmoil of the Ruhr invasion led to international attempts to ease the German payment of reparations. At the same time, American investment capital was pouring into Europe. However, by 1928 this investment decreased as American money became diverted into the booming New York stock market. The crash of Wall Street in October 1929—the result of virtually unregulated financial speculation—saw the loss of large amounts of money. Credit sharply contracted in the United States as numerous banks failed. Thereafter, little American capital was available for investment in Europe.

As American credit for Europe began to run out, a major financial crisis struck the Continent. In May 1931 the Kreditanstalt bank in Austria collapsed. The Kreditanstalt was a primary financial institution for much of central and eastern Europe. Its collapse put severe pressure on the German banking system, which was saved only through government guarantees. As the

German difficulties increased, U.S. president Herbert Hoover (1874–1964) announced in June 1931 a one-year moratorium on all payments of international debts. The Hoover moratorium was a prelude to the end of reparations. The Lausanne Conference in the summer of 1932 brought, in effect, the era of reparations to a close. The next year the debts owed to the United States were settled either through small token payments or simply through default.

Problems in Agricultural Commodities

In the 1920s the market demand for European goods shrank leaving much of the Continent's productive capacity idle or underused. This problem originated both within and outside Europe. In both instances the difficulty arose from agriculture. Better methods of farming, improved strains of wheat, expanded acreage under the plow, and more extensive transport facilities vastly increased the quantity of grain farmers around the world produced. World wheat prices fell to record lows. Although this helped consumers, it decreased the income of European farmers. At the same time, higher industrial wages raised the cost of the industrial goods that farmers or peasants used. Consequently, they had great difficulty paying off their mortgages and loans for normal operating costs. These problems were especially acute in central and eastern Europe and increased farmers' disillusionment with liberal politics. German farmers, for example, would become prime supporters of the National Socialist Workers Party (Nazis).

Outside Europe similar problems affected other producers of agricultural commodities. The prices they received for their products plummeted. Government-held reserves of raw materials reached record levels. This glut of major world commodities involved wheat, sugar, coffee, rubber, wool, and lard. The people who produced these goods in underdeveloped nations could no longer make enough money to buy goods from industrial Europe. As world credit collapsed, the economic position of these commodity producers worsened. Commodity production had simply outstripped world demand.

The results of the collapse in the agricultural sector of the world economy and the financial turmoil were stagnation and depression for European industry. Coal, iron, and textiles had depended largely on international markets. Unemployment spread from these industries to those producing consumer goods. Persistent unemployment in Great Britain and, to a lesser extent, in Germany during the 1920s had created "soft" domestic markets. The policies of reduced spending with which the governments confronted the Depression further weakened domestic demand. By the early 1930s the Depression was feeding on itself.

Depression and Government Policy in Britain and France

The Depression did not mean absolute economic decline or total unemployment. But the economic downturn spread potential as well as actual insecurity. People in nearly all walks of life feared the loss of their economic security. The Depression also frustrated normal social and economic expectations. Even the employed often seemed to make no progress; and their anxieties created a major source of discontent.

The governments of the late 1920s and the early 1930s were not well suited in either structure or ideology to confront these problems. The electorates demanded action. The governments' responses depended largely on the severity of the Depression in a particular country and on the self-confidence of the nation's political system.

Great Britain and France, which because of their vast empires commanded very large economies, undertook moderate political experiments. In 1924 the Labour Party in Great Britain established itself as a viable governing party by forming a short-lived government. It again formed a ministry in 1929. Under the pressure of the Depression and at the urging of King George V (r. 1910–1936), the Labour prime minister Ramsay MacDonald (1866–1937) organized a National Government, which was a coalition of the Labour, Conservative, and Liberal Parties. It remained in power until 1935, when a Conservative ministry led by Stanley Baldwin (1867–1947) replaced it. (See "John Maynard Keynes Calls for Government Investment to Create Employment.")

The 1920s also saw the establishment of an independent Irish state. On Easter Monday in April 1916, a nationalist uprising occurred in Dublin, the only rebellion of a national group against any government engaged in World War I. The British suppressed the uprising but made martyrs of its leaders by executing several of them. Leadership of the nationalist cause quickly shifted from the Irish Party in Parliament to the extremist **Sinn Fein**, or "Ourselves Alone," movement. In the election of 1918, Sinn Fein won all but four of the Irish parliamentary seats outside Ulster. They refused to go to the Parliament at Westminster. Instead, they constituted themselves into a *Dail Eireann*, or Irish Parliament. On January 21, 1919, they declared Irish independence. Thereafter a civil war broke out between the military wing of Sinn Fein, which became the Irish Republican Army (IRA), and the British army. The conflict ended with a treaty in December 1921, which established the Irish Free State as one of the dominions in the British Commonwealth. The six, predominately Protestant, counties of Ulster, or Northern Ireland, were permitted to remain part of what was now called the United Kingdom of Great Britain and Northern Ireland,

JOHN MAYNARD KEYNES CALLS FOR GOVERNMENT INVESTMENT TO CREATE EMPLOYMENT

Since at least the late nineteenth century, European social critics had questioned whether capitalistic economies could function without major crises that resulted in unemployment and other social disruptions. Virtually all economists, however, believed that given enough time capitalistic economies would correct themselves. Consequently, when the Great Depression struck the worldwide economy, the governments of Western Europe and the United States initially undertook relatively modest actions to address it. They were doing what most economists at the time advocated. Socialists, of course, had long advocated government intervention. In 1936, however, John Maynard Keynes, a prominent British economist, published The General Theory of Employment, Interest and Money. *Keynes, who was not a socialist, believed that the Great Depression demonstrated that economic crises could be so severe that private investment would simply not take place and thus could not generate new economic activity that would revive employment and lift the economy out of depression. In the passage below, Keynes explains that although he believes in individual initiative, there are times it will not occur. Under those conditions he calls for the "socialisation of investment," which was his term for government spending to spark new economic activity that would expand employment. In the second paragraph, he argues that the role of such government investment or spending is to provide employment for those workers whom the private economy cannot employ. Keynes's book did not influence many policies during the Great Depression, but after World War II, many Western governments devised economic policies along the lines he advocated.*

Why does Keynes believe the private economy will not always provide sufficient employment? Why does he call government spending the "socialisation of investment"? How much of his argument is analytical? How much political?

In some respects the foregoing theory is moderately conservative in its implications. For whilst it indicates the vital importance of establishing certain central controls in matters which are now left in the main to individual initiative, there are wide fields of activity which are unaffected. The State will have to exercise a guiding influence on the propensity to consume partly through its scheme of taxation, partly by fixing the rate of interest, and partly, perhaps, in other ways. Furthermore, it seems unlikely that the influence of banking policy on the rate of interest will be sufficient by itself to determine an optimum rate of investment. I conceive, therefore, that a somewhat comprehensive socialisation of investment will prove the only means of securing an approximation to full employment; though this need not exclude all manner of compromises and of devices by which public authority will co-operate with private initiative. But beyond this, no obvious case is made out for a system of State Socialism which would embrace most of the economic life of the community. It is not the ownership of the instruments of production which it is important for the State to assume. If the State is able to determine the aggregate amount of resources devoted to augmenting the instruments and the basic rate of reward to those who own them, it will have accomplished all that is necessary. . . .

To put the matter concretely, I see no reason to suppose that the existing system seriously misemploys the factors of production which are in use. There are, of course, errors of foresight; but these would not be avoided by centralizing decisions. When 9,000,000 men are employed out of 10,000,000 willing and able to work, there is no evidence that the labour of these 9,000,000 men is misdirected. The complaint against the present system is not that these 9,000,000 men ought to be employed on different tasks, but that tasks should be available for the remaining 10,000,000 men. It is in determining the volume, not the direction, of actual employment that the existing system has broken down.

John Maynard Keynes, *The General Theory of Employment, Interest and Money* (London: Macmillan & Co., Ltd., 1960), p. 379.

with provisions for home rule. In the 1920s and 1930s, the Free State gradually severed its ties to Britain. It remained neutral during World War II and declared itself an independent republic in 1949.

The most important French interwar political experiment was the **Popular Front** Ministry, which came to office in 1936. It was composed of Socialists, Radicals, and Communists—the first time that Socialists and Communists had cooperated in a ministry. They did so because they feared right-wing political groups in France and saw the threat of such regimes elsewhere in Europe. Despite fierce resistance from business and conservative groups, the Popular Front enacted major social and economic reforms, including the forty-hour week, paid vacations for workers, and compulsory arbitration of labor disputes. But its parliamentary support gradually faded until its final collapse in October 1938.

The political changes in Britain and France were essentially of domestic significance. But the political experiments of the 1920s and 1930s that reshaped world history and civilization involved the establishment of a Soviet government in Russia, a Fascist regime in Italy, and a Nazi dictatorship in Germany.

▼ The Soviet Experiment

The consolidation of the Bolshevik Revolution in Russia established the most extensive and durable of all twentieth-century authoritarian governments. The Communist Party of the Soviet Union retained power from 1917 until the end of 1991, and its presence influenced the political history of Europe and much of the rest of the world, as did no other single factor. Unlike the Italian Fascists or the German National Socialists, the Bolsheviks seized power violently through revolution. For several years they confronted civil war, and their leaders long felt insecure about their hold on the country. The Communist Party was neither a mass party nor a nationalistic one. Its early membership rarely exceeded more than 1 percent of the Russian population. The Bolsheviks confronted a much less industrialized economy than that in Italy or Germany. They believed in and practiced the collectivization of economic life. The Marxist-Leninist ideology had vastly more international appeal than the nationalism of the Fascists and the racism of the Nazis. Communism was an exportable commodity. The Communists regarded their government and their revolution not as part of the national history of Russia, but as epoch-making events in the history of the world and the development of humanity. (See "Compare & Connect: The Soviets and the Nazis Confront the Issues of Women and the Family," pages 858–859.) Fear of communism and determination to stop its spread became one of the leading political forces in Western Europe and the United States for most of the rest of the century. Policies flowing from that opposition would influence European and American relationships with much of the rest of the world.

War Communism

Within the Soviet Union the Red Army under the organizational genius of Leon Trotsky (1879–1940) had suppressed internal and foreign military opposition to the new government during the civil war that raged from 1918 to 1920. Within months of the revolution, a new secret police, known as *Cheka*, appeared. Throughout the civil war Lenin (1870–1924) had declared that the Bolshevik Party, as the vanguard of the revolution, was imposing the dictatorship of the proletariat. Political and economic administration became highly centralized. All major decisions flowed from the top in a nondemocratic manner. Under the economic policy of **War Communism**, the revolutionary government confiscated and then operated the banks, the transport facilities, and heavy industry. The state also forcibly requisitioned grain and shipped it from the countryside to feed the army and the urban workers. The Bolsheviks used the need to fight the civil war as justification for suppressing any resistance to these economic policies.

War Communism helped the Red Army defeat its opponents. The revolution had survived and triumphed. The policy, however, generated domestic opposition to the Bolsheviks, who in 1920 numbered only about 600,000. The alliance of workers and peasants forged in 1917 by the Bolsheviks' slogan of "Peace, Bread, and Land" had begun to dissolve. Many Russians were no longer willing to make the sacrifices demanded by the central party bureaucrats. In 1920 and 1921, serious strikes occurred. Peasants were discontented and resisted the requisition of grain. In March 1921, the sailors mutinied at the Kronstadt naval base on the Baltic. The Red Army crushed the rebellion with grave loss of life. Each of these acts of opposition suggested that the proletariat itself was opposing the dictatorship of the proletariat. Also, by late 1920 it had become clear that revolution was not going to sweep across the rest of Europe. For the time being the Soviet Union would constitute a vast island of revolutionary socialism in the larger sea of world capitalism.

The New Economic Policy

Under these difficult conditions Lenin made a strategic retreat. In March 1921, following the Kronstadt mutiny, he outlined the **New Economic Policy**, or NEP. Apart from what he termed "the commanding heights" of banking, heavy industry, transportation, and international commerce, considerable private economic enterprise was allowed. In particular, peasants could farm for

Anxiety over the spread of the Bolshevik revolution was a fundamental factor of European politics during the 1920s and 1930s. Images like this Soviet portrait of Lenin as a heroic revolutionary conjured fears among people in the rest of Europe of a political force determined to overturn their social, political, and economic institutions. Bildarchiv Preussischer Kulturbesitz

a profit. They would pay taxes like other citizens, but they could sell their surplus grain on the open market. The NEP was consistent with Lenin's earlier conviction that the Russian peasantry held the key to the success of the revolution. After 1921 the countryside did become more stable, and a secure food supply seemed assured for the cities. Similar free enterprise flourished within light industry and the domestic retail trade. By 1927 industrial production had reached its 1913 level. The revolution seemed to have transformed Russia into a land of small farms and privately owned shops and businesses.

The Third International

The onset and consolidation of the Bolshevik revolution in Russia was a transforming event for the history of socialism as well as for Russia and international affairs. The revolution stunned West European socialists. In the West, before the war, as discussed in Chapter 23, social democratic parties had regarded the Russian Bolsheviks as eccentric, politically marginal Marxist extremists. The Bolshevik victory forced West European social democrats to rethink their position within the world of international socialism. For their part, the Bolsheviks intended to establish themselves as the international leaders of Marxism and regarded reformist social democrats as enemies and rivals.

In 1919, the Soviet communists founded the Third International of the European socialist movement, better known as the *Comintern*. The Comintern worked to make the Bolshevik model of socialism, as Lenin had developed it, the rule for all socialist parties outside the Soviet Union. In 1920, the Comintern imposed its Twenty-one Conditions on any socialist party that wished to join it. These conditions included acknowledging Moscow's leadership, rejecting reformist or revisionist socialism, repudiating previous socialist leaders, and adopting the Communist Party name. In effect, the Comintern sought to destroy democratic socialism, which it accused of having betrayed the working class through reform policies and parliamentary accommodation.

The decision whether to accept these conditions split every major European socialist party. As a result, separate communist and social democratic parties emerged in most countries and they fought each other more intensely than they fought either capitalism or conservative political parties. Their fierce conflict was one of the fundamental features of the interwar European political landscape.

These Comintern polices and the resulting divisions of the socialist parties directly affected the rise of the fascists and the Nazis in Western Europe. It is difficult to overestimate the fears that Soviet political rhetoric and Communist Party activity aroused in Europe during the 1920s and 1930s. Conservative and right-wing political groups manipulated and exaggerated these fears. The presence of separate communist parties in Western Europe meant that right-wing politicians always had a convenient target they could justly accuse of seeking to overthrow the government and to impose Soviet-style political, social, and economic systems in their nations. Furthermore, right-wing politicians also accused the democratic socialists of supporting policies that might facilitate a communist takeover. The divisions between Communists and democratic socialists also meant that right-wing political movements rarely had to confront a united left.

Stalin versus Trotsky

The NEP had caused sharp disputes within the Politburo, the highest governing committee of the Communist Party. The partial return to capitalism seemed to some members nothing less than a betrayal of sound Marxist principles. These frictions increased as Lenin's firm hand disappeared. In 1922 he suffered a stroke and never again dominated party affairs; in 1924 he died. In the ensuing power vacuum, an intense struggle for leadership of the party commenced. Two factions emerged. One was led by Trotsky; the other by Joseph Stalin (1879–1953), who had become general secretary of the party in 1922. Shortly before his death Lenin had criticized both men. He was especially harsh toward Stalin. However, as general secretary Stalin's base of power lay with the party membership and with the daily management of party affairs, he was able to withstand the posthumous criticism of Lenin.

Each faction wanted to control the party and thus also the state, but the struggle was fought over the question of Russia's path toward industrialization and the future of the Communist revolutionary movement. Trotsky, speaking for what became known as the left wing, urged rapid industrialization and looked to voluntary collectivization of farming by poor peasants as a means of increasing agricultural production. He further argued that the revolution in Russia could succeed only if new revolutions took place elsewhere. Russia needed the skills and wealth of other nations to build its own economy. As Trotsky's influence within the party began to wane, he also demanded that party members be permitted to criticize the policies of the government and the party. Trotsky, however, was a latecomer to the advocacy of open discussion. When he had controlled the Red Army, he had been a harsh and unflinching disciplinarian.

A right-wing faction opposed Trotsky. Although its chief ideological voice was that of Nikolai Bukharin (1888–1938), the editor of *Pravda*, the official party paper, Stalin was its true political manipulator. In the mid-1920s this group pressed for the continuation of Lenin's NEP and relatively slow industrialization.

Stalin was the ultimate victor in these intraparty rivalries. Unlike the other early Bolshevik leaders, he had not spent a long exile in Western Europe. He was much less an intellectual and internationalist. He was also much more brutal. His handling of various recalcitrant national groups within Russia after the revolution had shocked even Lenin. Stalin's power lay in his command of bureaucratic and administrative methods. He was neither a brilliant writer nor an effective public speaker; however, he mastered the crucial, if dull, details of party structure, including admission, promotion, and rewards. That mastery meant that he could draw on the support of the lower levels of the party apparatus when he clashed with other leaders.

In the mid-1920s Stalin supported Bukharin's position on economic development. In 1924 he also enunciated, in opposition to Trotsky, the doctrine of "socialism in one country." He urged that socialism could be achieved in Russia alone. Russian success did not depend on the fate of the revolution elsewhere. Stalin thus nationalized the previously international scope of the Marxist revolution. He cunningly used the apparatus of the party and his control over its Central Committee to edge out Trotsky and his supporters. By 1927 Trotsky had been removed from all his offices, ousted from the party, and exiled to Siberia. In 1929 he was expelled from Russia and eventually moved to Mexico, where he was murdered in 1940 by one of Stalin's agents. With the removal of Trotsky, Stalin was firmly in control of the Soviet state. It remained to be seen what "socialism in one country" would mean in practice.

The Decision for Rapid Industrialization

In 1927 the Party Congress decided to push for rapid industrialization. As implemented through what has been termed "industrialization by political mobilization," this policy marked a sharp departure from the NEP and a rejection of the pockets of relatively free-market operations within the larger Soviet economy.[1]

Stalin's goal was to have the Soviet Union overtake the productive capacity of its enemies, the capitalist nations. This policy required the rapid construction of heavy industries, such as iron, steel, and machine tool making, building electricity-generating stations, and manufacturing tractors. Stalin's organizational vehicle for industrialization was a series of five-year plans, starting in 1928. The State Planning Commission, or *Gosplan*, set goals for production in every area of economic life and attempted to organize the economy to meet them. The task of coordinating all facets of production was immensely complicated. Deliveries of materials from mines or factories had to be assured before the next unit could carry out its part of the plan. Enormous economic disruption occurred as the *Gosplan* built power plants and steel mills and increased the output of mines. The plans consistently favored capital projects over the production of consumer goods. The number of centralized agencies and ministries involved in planning soared, and they often competed with each other.

The rapid expansion of the industrial base created the first genuinely large factory labor force in what had been Russia. Workers were recruited from the countryside and from the urban unemployed. New cities and industrial districts in existing cities arose. Most workers were crowded into shoddy buildings with inadequate sanitation, living space, and nourishment. Their lives were as bad as or worse than anything Marx and Engels had decried in the nineteenth century.

The government and the Communist Party undertook a vast program of propaganda to sell the five-year

[1]Vladimir Andrle, *A Social History of Twentieth-Century Russia* (London: Arnold, 1994), p. 161.

Magnitogorsk was a city that became a monument to Stalin's drive toward rapid industrialization. Located in the Ural Mountains near a vast supply of iron ore, the city became the site of major iron and steel production. It was one of the new industrial cities founded under the Five Year Plans designed to challenge the capitalist production of the Western nations. National Archives and Records Administration

plans to the Russian people and to elicit their cooperation. The government boasted of the sheer size of the plants and new towns being constructed. Such propaganda was necessary because most industrial workers were displaced peasants who had never worked in a factory and often resisted industrial discipline. The party appealed to the idealism of the young in proclaiming its goals of rapidly modernizing the nation. Workers, such as a legendary coal miner named Stakhanov, who exceeded their assigned goals received rewards and publicity.

The results were impressive. Soviet industrial production rose approximately 400 percent between 1928 and 1940. Industries that had never existed in Russia challenged their foreign counterparts. Hundreds of thousands of people populated new industrial cities. The social and human cost of this effort had, however, been appalling.

The Collectivization of Agriculture

Agricultural productivity had always been a core problem for the emerging Soviet economy. Under the NEP the government purchased a certain amount of grain at prices it set itself. The rest of the grain was then supposed to be sold at market prices, which were higher than the government-set prices. Many peasant farmers of all degrees of wealth tried to circumvent this system, often by keeping grain off the market in hopes that its price would rise. The scarcity of consumer goods available for purchase in the countryside also encouraged hoarding. With little to buy from what they earned by selling their grain, farmers had little incentive to sell it. Instead, many of them preferred to hoard grain, so that they could sell it in the future when they hoped more consumer goods would be available for them to purchase. The Soviet government, however, needed the grain immediately to feed its expanding urban workforce and to pay for imports from abroad. In 1928 and 1929, as a result of peasants hoarding their grains for better prices, the Soviet government confronted shortfalls of grain on the market and the prospect of food shortages in the cities and social unrest.

Stalin therefore decided to reverse the agricultural policies of the NEP. Toward the end of the 1920s, Soviet economists and party officials devised an explanation for the difficulties they confronted in the agricultural sector. First, they asserted that the traditional peasant holdings were too small to produce enough grain to meet the country's needs. Second, they claimed that a class-enemy was responsible for the hoarding and for what they regarded as speculation in the grain trade. This enemy was the group of relatively prosperous peasants, known as *kulaks*, who numbered somewhat less than 5 percent of the rural population and were often the most productive and efficient farmers. On the basis of these ideas, Stalin decided that Soviet agriculture must be collectivized to produce enough grain for domestic food and foreign export. **Collectivization**—the replacement of private peasant farms with huge state-run and state-owned farms called collectives—would also put the Communist Party firmly in control of the farm sector of the economy and free up peasant labor to work in the expanding industrial sector. To carry out this policy, Stalin portrayed the *kulak*s as the fundamental cause of the agricultural problems.

Party officials with troops at their command carried out the initial campaign of dekulakization and collectivization. Usually they would seek first to remove *kulaks* from a village while confiscating their land and would then attempt to coerce the remaining peasants into organizing a collective farm. Enormous turmoil and violence resulted. In March 1930, Stalin called a brief halt to the process, justifying the slowdown on the grounds of "dizziness from success." After the harvest of that year had been secured, however, the drive to collectivize the farms was renewed with vehemence.

Peasants determined to keep their land, often with women in the lead, had sabotaged collectivization by slaughtering millions of livestock between 1929 and 1933. Peasants who resisted were killed outright. Others starved to death on their own farms when all the grain that they had produced was seized. Over 2 million peasants were forcibly removed from their homes and deported to distant areas of the Soviet Union or to prison camps where many died from disease, exposure, and malnutrition. Even if they survived that ordeal, they then had to patch together some kind of life as industrial workers or miners in Siberia or another inhospitable province. Their children were treated as class-enemies and political traitors. Much of the violence of collectivization occurred in Ukraine, where Stalin used the process not only to restructure agricultural production but also to crush any vestiges of Ukrainian nationalism, and many millions of lives were lost as a result.

During the drive toward collectivization, the Communist Party also targeted priests of the Russian Orthodox Church. The Party, atheistic in its ideology, had always opposed religion, but only with collectivization were many rural priests attacked and churches closed or vandalized. Between 1926 and 1937, the number of priests recorded in the Soviet census dropped by more than one half. Rabbis, Catholic priests, Protestant ministers, and mullahs received the same harsh treatment.

By 1937, over 90 percent of Soviet grain production had been collectivized. The violent transformation of Soviet agriculture meant producers on collective farms could no longer decide what crops to produce or how much to sell them for. The government organized Motor-Tractor Stations that supplied the seed and equipment for several collective farms in a region and oversaw the collection and sale of grain. The heads of these stations were Party political operatives, and they determined what payments the farmers eventually received for the grain they had produced. Alongside the state-run collective farms, by the mid-1930s, the government allowed farmers small household plots to grow fruit and vegetables for their families and for local sale. These plots became an important part of Soviet agriculture because peasants tended them so carefully and productively.

Stalin used intimidation and propaganda to support his drive to collectivize Soviet agriculture. Communist Party agitators led groups of peasants such as these to demand the seizure of the farms worked by the better-off and more successful farmers known as *kulaks*. AP/Wide World Photos

At the cost of millions of peasant lives, Stalin and the Communist Party had won the battle of the grain fields, but they had not solved the problem of producing enough food. That difficulty would plague the Soviet Union until its collapse in 1991 and remains a problem for its successor states.

The Purges

In 1933, with turmoil in the countryside and economic dislocation caused by industrialization, Stalin and others in the central Soviet bureaucracy began to fear they were losing control of the country and the party apparatus and that effective rivals to their power and policies might emerge. These apprehensions were largely a figment of Stalin's own paranoia and lust for power, but they resulted in the **Great Purges**, which remain one of the most mysterious and horrendous political events of the twentieth century. Few observers understood the purges at the time, and despite the recent opening of Soviet archives, they have still not been fully comprehended, either inside or outside the former Soviet Union.

The pretext for the onset of the purges was the assassination on December 1, 1934, of Sergei Kirov (1888–1934), the popular party chief of Leningrad and a member of the Politburo. In the wake of the shooting, thousands of people were arrested, and still more were expelled from the party and sent to labor camps. At the time, many thought that opponents of the regime had murdered Kirov, and Stalin routinely accused those whom he attacked of complicity in the crime. Today, many scholars believe that Stalin himself authorized Kirov's assassination because he was afraid of him. The available documentary evidence does not allow us to know for sure whether Stalin was involved, but he quickly used Kirov's death for his own purposes. Under Stalin, the Soviet Communist Party had already shown it could punish dissent within its ranks. The debates of the 1920s within the party and the expulsion of Trotsky had established a clear precedent for exercising firm discipline, and in the confusion surrounding the implementation of the five-year plans, persons accused of sabotage and disloyalty had been executed. The purges, however, went far beyond any of these precedents.

The purges that took place immediately after Kirov's death were just the beginning of a larger and longer process. Between 1936 and 1938, a series of spectacular show trials were held in Moscow. Former high Soviet leaders, including members of the Politburo, such as Bukharin, publicly confessed to political crimes and were convicted and executed. It is still not certain why they made their palpably false confessions, although this seems to have been the kind of ritual confession of faults and shortcomings that had long characterized internal Communist Party life. They had also been interrogated under the most difficult conditions, including torture, and feared for their families' lives. (Stalin regularly arrested the wives, children, siblings, and in-laws of "traitors" and had them shot or sent to die in labor camps.) Other lower-level party members were tried in private and shot. Hundreds of thousands, perhaps millions, of ordinary Soviet citizens received no trial at all and were either executed or deported to slave labor camps where many died. Within the party itself, thousands of members were expelled, and applicants for membership were removed from the rolls. After the civilian party members and leaders had been purged, the prosecutors turned against the government bureaucracy and the Soviet army and navy, convicting and executing thousands of officials and officers, including heroes of the civil war. The exact number of executions, imprisonments, interrogations, and expulsions is unknown, but it ran well into the millions. While the purges went on, no one in the Soviet Union, except Stalin himself, was safe.

The rational explanations of the purges—to the extent that mass murder can ever be rationally explained—probably lie in two directions. First, over the several years the purges lasted, different portions of the party leadership moved against others. Initially, Stalin and the central Moscow leadership used the purges to settle old scores and to discipline and gain more control over lower levels of the party in the far-flung regions of the Soviet Union. In addition to increasing Stalin's authority, these central bureaucratic groups wanted to eliminate any opposition to their own positions or policies. By 1937, however, Stalin seems to have become distrustful of the central party elite, his own supporters, and began to find or pretend to find enemies within its ranks. Moreover, by that date, local communist groups were allowed to designate their own victims with little direction from Moscow. Thereafter, a self-destructive cascade of accusations, imprisonments, and executions occurred throughout the party and within its highest levels. The Communist Party leadership at all levels appeared to be consuming itself in an atmosphere of terror for its own sake. This situation has been termed "centrally authorized chaos."[2]

Second, no matter how much tension and rivalry there were among the different levels and regions of the Communist Party, Stalin's primary motive in the purges was almost certainly fear for his own power and a ruthless determination to preserve and increase it. He and the deputies whom he allowed to survive the purges personally selected certain victims and determined the fate of their families. In effect, the purges created a new Communist Party that was absolutely subservient and loyal to Stalin. The "old Bolsheviks" of the October Revolution in 1917 were among his earliest targets. They and others active in the first years of the revolution knew how far Stalin had moved from Lenin's policies.

[2]J. Arch Getty and Oleg V. Naumov, *The Road to Terror: Stalin and the Self-Destruction of the Bolsheviks, 1932–1939,* trans. by Benjamin Sher (New Haven, CT: Yale University Press, 1999), p. 583.

By the mid-1930s, Stalin's purges had eliminated many leaders and other members from the Soviet Communist Party. This photograph of a meeting of a party congress in 1936 shows a number of the surviving leaders with Stalin, who sits fourth from the right in the front row. To his left is Vyacheslav Molotov, longtime foreign minister. The first person on the left in the front row is Nikita Khruschev, who headed the Soviet Union in the late 1950s and early 1960s. Itar-Tass/Sovfoto/Eastfoto

New, younger recruits replaced the party members who were executed or expelled. The newcomers knew little about old Russia or the ideals of the original Bolsheviks. They had not been loyal to Lenin, Trotsky, Bukharin, or any other Soviet leader except Stalin himself.

The internal difficulties collectivization and industrialization and his worries about internal opposition caused led Stalin to make an important shift in foreign policy. In 1934, he began to fear the nation might be left isolated against aggression by Nazi Germany. The Soviet Union was not yet strong enough to withstand such an attack. So that year he ordered the Comintern to permit communist parties in other countries to cooperate with noncommunist parties against Nazism and fascism. This reversed the Comintern policy Lenin established as part of the Twenty-One Conditions in 1919. The new Stalinist policy allowed the Popular Front Government in France to come to power.

▼ The Fascist Experiment in Italy

The first authoritarian political experiment in Western Europe that arose in part from fears of the spread of bolshevism beyond the Soviet Union occurred in Italy. The general term *fascist*, which has been used to describe the various right-wing dictatorships that arose between the wars, was derived from the Italian Fascist movement of Benito Mussolini (1883–1945).

While scholars still dispute the exact meaning of ***fascism*** as a political term, the governments regarded as fascist were antidemocratic, anti-Marxist, antiparliamentary, and frequently anti-Semitic. They hoped to hold back the spread of bolshevism, which seemed a real threat at the time. They sought a world that would be safe for the middle class, small businesses, owners of moderate amounts of property, and small farmers. The fascist regimes rejected the political inheritance of the French Revolution and of nineteenth-century liberalism. (See "Mussolini Heaps Contempt on Political Liberalism.") Their adherents believed that normal parliamentary politics and parties sacrificed national honor and greatness to petty party disputes. They wanted to overcome the class conflict of Marxism and the party conflict of liberalism by consolidating the various groups and classes within the nation for great national purposes. As Mussolini declared in 1931, "The fascist conception of the state is all-embracing, and outside of the state no human or spiritual values can exist, let alone be desirable."[3] Fascist governments were usually single-party dictatorships characterized by terrorism

[3]Quoted in Denis Mack Smith, *Italy: A Modern History* (Ann Arbor: University of Michigan Press, 1959), p. 412.

MUSSOLINI HEAPS CONTEMPT ON POLITICAL LIBERALISM

The political tactics of the Italian Fascists wholly disregarded the liberal belief in the rule of law and the consent of the governed. In 1923 Mussolini explained why the Fascists so hated and repudiated these liberal principles. Note his emphasis on the idea of the twentieth century as a new historical epoch requiring a new kind of politics and his undisguised praise of force in politics.

Who would be some nineteenth-century liberal political leaders included in Mussolini's attack? Why might Mussolini's audience have been receptive to these views? What events or developments within liberal states allowed Mussolini to portray liberalism as so corrupt and powerless?

Liberalism is not the last word, nor does it represent the definitive formula on the subject of the art of government. . . . Liberalism is the product and the technique of the nineteenth century. . . . It does not follow that the Liberal scheme of government, good for the nineteenth century, for a century, that is, dominated by two such phenomena as the growth of capitalism and the strengthening of the sentiment of nationalism, should be adapted to the twentieth century, which announces itself already with characteristics sufficiently different from those that marked the preceding century. . . .

I challenge Liberal gentlemen to tell if ever in history there has been a government that was based solely on popular consent and that renounced all use of force whatsoever. A government so constructed there has never been and never will be. Consent is an ever-changing thing like the shifting sand on the sea coast, it can never be permanent: It can never be complete. . . . If it be accepted as an axiom that any system of government whatever creates malcontents, how are you going to prevent this discontent from overflowing and constituting a menace to the stability of the State? You will prevent it by force. By the assembling of the greatest force possible. By the inexorable use of this force whenever it is necessary. Take away from any government whatsoever force—and by force is meant physical, armed force—and leave it only its immortal principles, and that government will be at the mercy of the first organized group that decides to overthrow it. Fascism now throws these lifeless theories out to rot. . . . The truth evident now to all who are not warped by [liberal] dogmatism is that men have tired of liberty. They have made an orgy of it. Liberty is today no longer the chaste and austere virgin for whom the generations of the first half of the last century fought and died. For the gallant, restless and bitter youth who face the dawn of a new history there are other words that exercise a far greater fascination, and those words are: order, hierarchy, discipline. . . .

Know then, once and for all, that Fascism knows no idols and worships no fetishes. It has already stepped over, and if it be necessary it will turn tranquilly and step again over, the more or less putrescent corpse of the Goddess of Liberty.

From Benito Mussolini, "Force and Consent" (1923), as trans. in Jonathan F. Scott and Alexander Baltzly, eds., *Readings in European History Since 1814* (New York: F. S. Crofts, 1931), pp. 680–682.

against and police surveillance of both opponents and the general citizenry. These dictatorships were rooted in the base of mass political parties.

The Rise of Mussolini

The Italian *Fasci di Combattimento* ("Band of Combat") was founded in 1919 in Milan. Most of its members were war veterans who felt that the sacrifices Italy had made in World War I had been in vain. They resented Italy's failure to gain the city of Fiume, toward the northern end of the Adriatic Sea, and other territories at the Paris conference. They feared socialism, inflation, and labor unrest.

Their leader or ***Duce***, Benito Mussolini, was the son of a blacksmith. After having been a schoolteacher and a day laborer, he became active in Italian Socialist politics and by 1912 had become editor of the socialist newspaper *Avanti*. In 1914 Mussolini broke with the Socialists and supported Italian entry into the war on the side of the Allies. His interventionist position lost him the editorship of *Avanti*. He then established his own paper, *Il Popolo d'Italia*. Later he served in the army and was wounded. In 1919 Mussolini was just another Italian politician. His *Fasci* organization was one of many small political groups in a country characterized by such entities. As a politician, Mussolini was an opportunist par excellence. He could change his ideas and principles to suit every new occasion. Action for him was always more important than thought or rational justification. His one real rule was political survival.

Postwar Italian politics was a muddle. During the war the Italian Parliament had virtually ceased to function. Ministers had ruled by decree. However, many Italians were dissatisfied with the parliamentary system as it then existed. They felt that Italy had emerged from the war as less than a victorious nation, had not been treated as a great power at the peace conference, and had not received the rewards it deserved. The main spokesman for this discontent was the extreme nationalist writer Gabriele D'Annunzio (1863–1938). In 1919 he captured Fiume with a force of patriotic Italians. The Italian army, enforcing the terms of the Versailles Treaty, eventually drove him out. D'Annunzio had provided the example of the political use of a nongovernmental military force. Removing him from Fiume made the parliamentary ministry seem unpatriotic.

Between 1919 and 1921 Italy was also wracked by social turmoil. Numerous industrial strikes occurred, and workers occupied factories. Peasants seized uncultivated land from large estates. Parliamentary and constitutional government seemed incapable of dealing with this unrest. The Socialist Party had captured a plurality of seats in the Chamber of Deputies in 1919. A new Catholic Popular Party had also done well. Both appealed to the working and agrarian classes. However, neither party would cooperate with the other, and parliamentary deadlock resulted. Under these conditions, many Italians honestly—and still others conveniently—believed that a Communist revolution might break out.

Initially, Mussolini was uncertain which way the political winds were blowing. He first supported the factory occupations and land seizures. Never one to be concerned with consistency, however, he soon reversed himself. He had discovered that many upper- and middle-class Italians who were hurt by inflation and who feared the loss of their property had no sympathy for the workers or the peasants. They wanted order rather than some vague social justice that might harm their own interests. Consequently, Mussolini and his Fascists took direct action in the face of the government's inaction. They formed local squads who terrorized Socialists. They attacked strikers and farm workers and protected strikebreakers. Conservative land and factory owners were grateful to the terrorists. The officers of the law simply ignored these crimes. By early 1922 the Fascists controlled local government in many parts of northern Italy.

In 1921 Mussolini and thirty-four of his followers had been elected to the Chamber of Deputies. Their importance grew as the local Fascists gained more direct power. The Fascist movement now had hundreds of thousands of supporters. In October 1922 the Fascists, dressed in their characteristic black shirts, began a march on Rome. Intimidated, King Victor Emmanuel III (r. 1900–1946) refused to authorize using the army against the marchers. No other single decision so ensured a Fascist seizure of power. The cabinet resigned in protest. On October 29 the monarch telegraphed Mussolini in Milan and asked him to become prime minister. The next day Mussolini arrived in Rome by sleeping car and, as head of the government, greeted his followers when they entered the city.

Technically, Mussolini had come into office by legal means. The monarch did have the power to appoint the prime minister. Mussolini, however, had no majority in the Chamber of Deputies. Behind the legal façade of his assumption of power lay months of terrorist disruption and intimidation and the threat of the Fascists' October march.

Benito Mussolini became famous for bombastic public speeches delivered in settings surrounded by his Fascist followers and military supporters. AP Wide World Photos

The Fascists in Power

Mussolini had not really expected to be appointed prime minister. He moved cautiously to consolidate his power. He succeeded because of the impotence of his rivals, his effective use of his office, his power over the masses, and his sheer ruthlessness. On November 23, 1922, the king and Parliament granted Mussolini dictatorial authority for one year to bring order to the lower levels of the government. Wherever possible, Mussolini appointed Fascists to office. Late in 1924, at Mussolini's behest, Parliament changed the election law. Previously parties had been represented in the Chamber of Deputies in proportion to the popular vote cast for them. According to the new election law, the party that gained the largest popular vote (with a minimum of at least 25 percent) received two thirds of the seats in the chamber. Coalition government, with all its compromises and hesitations, would no longer be necessary. In the election of 1924 the Fascists won a great victory and complete control of the Chamber of Deputies. They used that majority to end legitimate parliamentary life. A series of laws passed in 1925 and 1926 permitted Mussolini, in effect, to rule by decree. In 1926 all other political parties were dissolved, and Italy was transformed into a single-party, dictatorial state.

The Italian dictator made one important domestic departure that brought him significant political dividends. Through the Lateran Accord he signed with the Vatican in February 1929, the Roman Catholic Church and the Italian state made peace with each other. Ever since the armies of Italian unification had seized papal lands in the 1860s, the church had been hostile to the state. The popes had virtually secluded themselves in the Vatican after 1870. The agreement of 1929 recognized the pope as the temporal ruler of the mini-state of Vatican City. The Italian government agreed to pay an indemnity to the papacy for confiscated land. The state also recognized Catholicism as the religion of the nation, exempted church property from taxes, and allowed church law to govern marriage. The Lateran Accord brought further respectability to Mussolini's authoritarian regime.

▼ German Democracy and Dictatorship

The Weimar Republic

The Weimar Republic was born from the defeat of the imperial army, the revolution of 1918 against the Hohenzollerns, and the hopes of German Liberals and Social Democrats. Its name derived from the city in which its constitution was written and promulgated in August 1919. While the constitution was being debated, the republic, headed by the Social Democrats, accepted the humiliating terms of the Versailles Treaty. Although its officials had signed only under the threat of an Allied invasion, the republic was nevertheless permanently associated with the national disgrace and the economic burdens of the treaty. Throughout the 1920s the government of the republic was required to fulfill the economic and military provisions imposed by the Paris settlement. It became all too easy for nationalists and military figures whose policies had brought on the tragedy and defeat of the war to blame the young republic and the Socialists for the results of the conflict. In Germany, more than in other countries, the desire to revise the treaty was closely related to a desire to change the mode of domestic government.

The Weimar Constitution was a highly enlightened document. It guaranteed civil liberties and provided for direct election, by universal suffrage, of the *Reichstag* and the president. It also, however, contained crucial structural flaws that eventually allowed it to be overthrown. Seats in the *Reichstag* were allotted according to a complicated system of proportional representation. This made it relatively easy for small political parties to gain seats and resulted in shifting party combinations that led to eleven governments in thirteen years. Ministers were technically responsible to the *Reichstag*, but the president appointed and removed the chancellor, the head of the cabinet. Perhaps most important, Article 48 allowed the president, in an emergency, to rule by decree. The constitution thus permitted the possibility of presidential dictatorship.

The new government suffered major and minor humiliations as well as considerable economic instability. In March 1920 the right-wing Kapp Putsch, or armed insurrection, erupted in Berlin. Led by a conservative civil servant and supported by army officers, the attempted coup failed, but only after government officials had fled the city and workers had carried out a general strike. In the same month, strikes took place in the Ruhr mining district. The government sent in troops. Such extremism from both the left and the right would haunt the republic for all its days. In May 1921 the Allies presented a reparations bill for 132 billion gold marks. The German Republican government accepted this preposterous demand only after new Allied threats of occupation. Throughout the early 1920s there were numerous assassinations or attempted assassinations of important Republican leaders. Violence was the hallmark of the first five years of the republic.

Invasion of the Ruhr and Inflation Inflation brought on the major crisis of this period. The financing of the war and continued postwar deficit spending generated an immense rise in prices. Consequently, the value of German currency fell. By early 1921 the German mark traded against the American dollar at a ratio of 64 to 1, compared with a ratio of 4.2 to 1 in 1914. The German financial community contended that the value of the currency could not be stabilized until the reparations issue had been solved. In the meantime, the printing presses kept pouring forth paper money, which was used to redeem government bonds as they fell due.

The French invasion of the Ruhr in January 1923, to secure the payment of reparations, and the German response of passive economic resistance produced cataclysmic inflation. The Weimar government paid subsidies to the Ruhr labor force, who had laid down their tools. Unemployment soon spread from the Ruhr to other parts of the country, creating a new drain on the treasury and also reducing tax revenues. The printing presses by this point had difficulty providing enough paper currency to keep up with the daily rise in prices. Money was literally not worth the paper it was printed on. Stores were unwilling to exchange goods for the worthless currency, and farmers withheld produce from the market.

The moral and social values of thrift and prudence were thoroughly undermined. Middle-class savings, pensions, and insurance policies were wiped out, as were investments in government bonds. Simultaneously, debts and mortgages could not be paid off. Speculators in land, real estate, and industry made fortunes. Union contracts generally allowed workers to keep up with rising prices. Thus inflation was not a disaster for everyone. To the middle and lower middle classes, however, the inflation was another trauma coming hard on the heels of the military defeat and the peace treaty. Only when the social and economic upheaval of these months is grasped can one understand the German desire for order and security at almost any cost.

In 1923, Germany suffered from cataclysmic inflation. Paper money became worthless and people used it as fuel for kitchen stoves. Library of Congress

Hitler's Early Career Late in 1923 Adolf Hitler (1889–1945) made his first significant appearance on the German political scene. The son of a minor Austrian customs official, he had gone to Vienna, where his hopes of gaining admission to an elite art school were soon dashed. He lived off money sent by his widowed mother and later off his Austrian orphan's allowance. He also painted postcards for further income and later found work as a day laborer. In Vienna he encountered Mayor Karl Lueger's (1844–1910) Christian Socialist Party, which prospered on an ideology of anti-Semitism and from the social anxieties of the lower middle class. Hitler absorbed the rabid German nationalism and extreme anti-Semitism that flourished in Vienna. He came to hate Marxism, which he associated with Jews. During World War I Hitler fought in the German army, was wounded, rose to the rank of corporal, and won the Iron Cross for bravery. The war gave him his first sense of purpose.

After the conflict, Hitler settled in Munich, and during the two years after the war firmly and frequently voiced anti-Semitism as a fundamental part of his political outlook. He soon became associated with a small nationalistic, anti-Semitic political party that in 1920 adopted the name of National Socialist German Workers Party, better known simply as the **Nazis**. In the same year the group began to parade under a red-and-white banner with a black swastika. It issued a platform, or program, of Twenty-Five Points. Among other things, this platform called for the repudiation of the Versailles Treaty, the unification of Austria and Germany, the exclusion of Jews from German citizenship, agrarian reform, the prohibition of land speculation, the confiscation of war profits, state administration of the giant cartels, and the replacement of department stores with small retail shops. Originally the Nazis had called for a broad program of nationalization of industry in an attempt to compete directly with the Marxist political parties for the vote of the workers. As the tactic failed, the Nazis redefined the meaning of the word *socialist* in the party name, so that it suggested a nationalistic outlook. In 1922, Hitler said

> Whoever is prepared to make the national cause his own to such an extent that he knows no higher ideal than the welfare of his nation; whoever has understood our great national anthem, *Deutschland, Deutschland, über Alles* ["Germany, Germany, over All"], to mean that nothing in the wide world surpasses in his eyes this Germany, people and land, land and people—that man is a Socialist.[4]

[4]Alan Bullock, *Hitler: A Study in Tyranny*, rev. ed. (New York: Harper & Row, 1964), p. 76.

This definition, of course, had nothing to do with traditional German socialism. The "socialism" that Hitler and the Nazis had in mind was not state ownership of the means of production, but the subordination of all economic enterprise to the welfare of the nation. It often implied protection for small economic enterprises. Increasingly, the Nazis discovered their party appealed to virtually any economic group that was at risk and under pressure. They often tailored their messages to the particular local problems these groups confronted in different parts of Germany. The Nazis also found considerable support among war veterans, who faced economic and social displacement in Weimar society.

Soon after the promulgation of the Twenty-Five Points, the storm troopers, or **SA** *(Sturm Abteilung)*, were organized under the leadership of Captain Ernst Roehm (1887–1934). It was a paramilitary organization that initially provided its members with food and uniforms and, later in the decade, with wages. In the mid-1920s the SA adopted its famous brown-shirted uniform. The storm troopers were the chief Nazi instrument for terror and intimidation before the party controlled the government. They were a law unto themselves. The organization constituted a means of preserving military discipline and values outside the small army permitted by the Paris settlement. The existence of such a private party army and of a similar one run by the Communists was a sign of the potential for violence in the Weimar Republic and the widespread contempt for the law and the institutions of the republic.

The social and economic turmoil following the French occupation of the Ruhr and the German inflation gave the fledgling party an opportunity for direct action against the Weimar Republic, which seemed incapable of providing military or economic security. By this time, because of his immense oratorical skills and organizational abilities, Hitler personally dominated the Nazi Party. As he established his dominance within the party, he clearly had the model of Mussolini in mind and spoke of the Italian dictator's accomplishments in glowing terms. Both men recruited from disillusioned veterans of the World War. Both adopted paramilitary modes of organization. Both disparaged liberal politics as incapable of achieving great national ends and righting the wrongs of the peace settlement. Both exalted the principle of obedience to the heroic leader. In late 1923, with the memory of Mussolini's march on Rome still fresh, Hitler attempted to seize power by force.

On November 9, 1923, Hitler and a band of followers, accompanied by General Erich Ludendorff (1865–1937), attempted an unsuccessful putsch from a beer hall in Munich. When the local authorities crushed the rising, sixteen Nazis were killed. Hitler and Ludendorff were arrested and tried for treason. The general was acquitted. Hitler used the trial to make himself into a national figure. He condemned the republic, the Versailles Treaty, the Jews, and the weakened condition of his adopted country. He was convicted and sentenced to five years in prison. He actually spent only a few months in jail before being paroled. During this time, he dictated ***Mein Kampf*** ("My Struggle"), from which he eventually made a good deal of money. In this book, not taken seriously enough at the time, he outlined key political views from which he never swerved, including a fierce racial anti-Semitism, opposition to Bolshevism, which he associated with Jews, and a conviction that Germany must expand eastward into Poland and Ukraine to achieve greater "living space." Such expansion assumed the resurgence of German military might. In effect, Hitler transferred the foreign policy goals and racial outlooks previously associated with German overseas imperialism to the politics of central and eastern Europe. The natural targets of implementing these ideas would be Jews, the successor states of eastern Europe, the Soviet Union, and any groups within Germany that opposed Hitler's vision of national unity and purpose. In the mid-1920s, most observers discounted the likelihood of any German political party's carrying out such policies.

During his imprisonment, Hitler reached two other decisions. First, it appears that this was the moment when he came to see himself as the leader who could transform Germany from a position of weakness to strength. Second, he decided that he and the party must

During a Nazi Party rally in Nuremberg in 1927, Adolf Hitler stops his motorcade to receive the applause of the surrounding crowd. In the late 1920s, the Nazi movement was only one of many bringing strife to the Weimar Republic. Heinrich Hoffman/Bildarchiv Preussischer Kulturbesitz

pursue power by legal means, but as Hitler emerged from his imprisonment, he was still a regional politician (albeit one who was transforming himself into a national figure).

The Stresemann Years The officials of the republic were attempting to repair the damage from the inflation. Gustav Stresemann (1878–1929) was responsible primarily for reconstruction of the republic and for its achievement of a sense of self-confidence. Stresemann abandoned the policy of passive resistance in the Ruhr. The country simply could not afford it. Then, with the aid of banker Hjalmar Schacht (1877–1970), he introduced a new German currency. The rate of exchange was 1 trillion of the old German marks for one new Rentenmark. Stresemann also moved against challenges from both the left and the right. He supported the crushing of both Hitler's abortive putsch and smaller Communist disturbances. In late November 1923, after four months as chancellor, he resigned to become foreign minister, a post he held until his death in 1929. In that office he continued to influence the affairs of the republic.

In 1924 the Weimar Republic and the Allies renegotiated the reparation payments. The Dawes Plan lowered the annual payments and allowed them to fluctuate according to the fortunes of the German economy. The last French troops left the Ruhr in 1925. (See Map 27–1.) The same year, Field Marshal Paul von Hindenburg (1847–1934), a military hero and a conservative monarchist, was elected president of the republic. He governed in strict accordance with the constitution, but his election suggested that German politics had become more conservative. Conservative Germans seemed reconciled to the republic. This conservatism was in line with the prosperity of the latter 1920s. Foreign capital flowed into Germany, and employment, which had been poor throughout most of the postwar years, improved smartly. Giant industrial combines spread. The prosperity helped to establish broader acceptance and appreciation of the republic.

In foreign affairs, Stresemann pursued a conciliatory course. He fulfilled the provisions of the Versailles Treaty even as he attempted to revise it by diplomacy. He was willing to accept the settlement in the west but was a determined, if sometimes secret, revisionist in the east. He aimed to recover German-speaking territories lost to Poland and Czechoslovakia and possibly to unite with Austria, chiefly by diplomatic means. The first step, however, was to achieve respectability and economic recovery. That goal required a policy of accommodation and "fulfillment," for the moment at least.

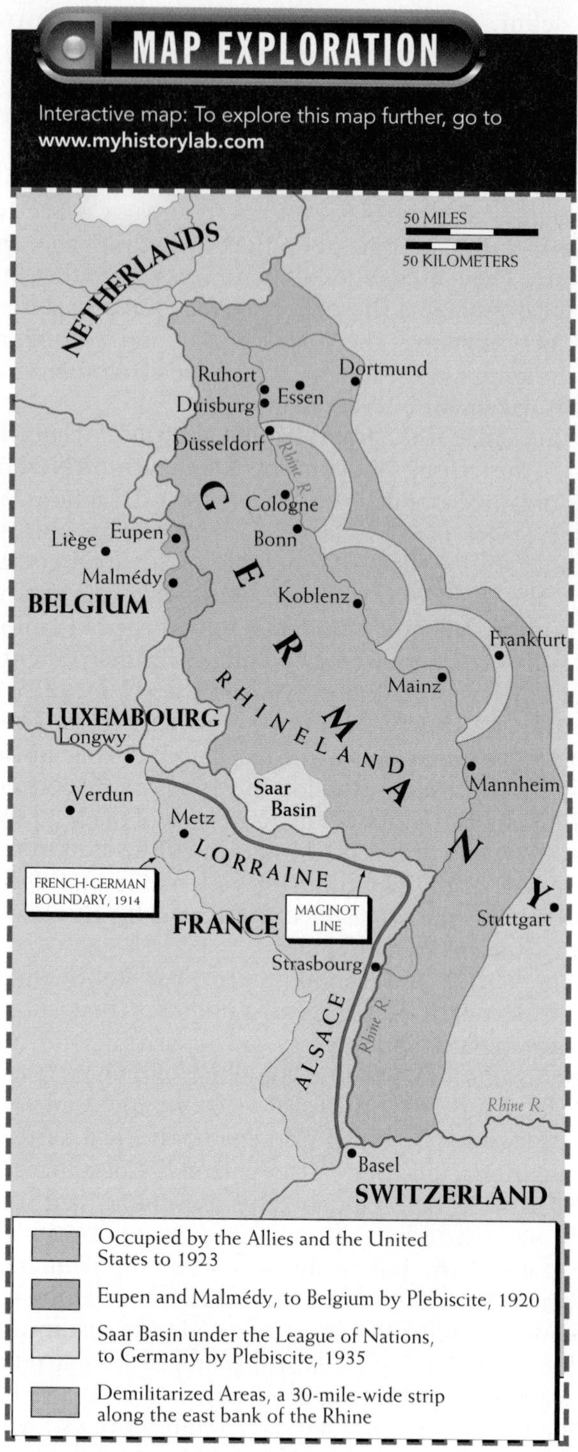

Map 27–1 **GERMANY'S WESTERN FRONTIER** The French-Belgian-German border area between the two world wars was sensitive. Despite efforts to restrain tensions, there were persistent difficulties related to the Ruhr, Rhineland, Saar, and Eupen-Malmédy regions that required strong defenses.

Locarno These developments gave rise to the Locarno Agreements of October 1925. The spirit of conciliation led foreign ministers Austen Chamberlain (1863–1937) for Britain and Aristide Briand (1862–1932) for France to accept Stresemann's proposal for a fresh start. France and Germany both accepted the western frontier established at Versailles as legitimate. Britain and Italy agreed to intervene against the aggressor if either side violated the frontier or if Germany sent troops into the demilitarized Rhineland. Significantly, no such agreement was made about Germany's eastern frontier, but the Germans made treaties of arbitration with Poland and Czechoslovakia, and France strengthened its ties with those countries. France supported German membership in the League of Nations and agreed to withdraw its occupation troops from the Rhineland in 1930, five years earlier than specified at Versailles.

Germany was pleased to have achieved respectability and a guarantee against another Ruhr occupation, as well as the possibility of revision in the east. Britain enjoyed playing a more evenhanded role. Italy was glad to be recognized as a great power. The French were happy, too, because the Germans voluntarily accepted the permanence of their western frontier, which was also guaranteed by Britain and Italy, and France maintained its alliances in the east.

The Locarno Agreements brought new hope to Europe. Germany's entry into the League of Nations was greeted with enthusiasm. Chamberlain, Briand, and Stresemann all received the Nobel Peace Prize in 1925 and 1926. The spirit of Locarno was carried even further when the leading European states, Japan, and the United States signed the Kellogg-Briand Pact in 1928, renouncing "war as an instrument of national policy." The joy and optimism were not justified. France had merely recognized its inability to coerce Germany without help. Britain had shown its unwillingness to uphold the settlement in the east. Austen Chamberlain declared that no British government ever would "risk the bones of a British grenadier" for the Polish Corridor. Germany was not reconciled to the eastern settlement. It maintained clandestine military connections with the Soviet Union and planned to continue to press for revision.

In both France and Germany, moreover, the conciliatory politicians represented only a part of the nation. In Germany especially, most people continued to reject Versailles and regarded Locarno as only an extension of it. When the Dawes Plan ran out in 1929 it was replaced by the Young Plan, which lowered the reparation payments, put a term on how long they must be made, and removed Germany entirely from outside supervision and control. The intensity of the outcry in Germany against the continuation of any reparations showed how far the Germans were from accepting their situation. Despite these problems, war was by no means inevitable. Europe, aided by American loans, was returning to prosperity. German leaders like Stresemann would certainly have continued to press for change, but there is little reason to think that they would have resorted to force, much less to a general war. Continued prosperity and diplomatic success might have won the loyalty of the German people for the Weimar Republic and moderate revisionism, but the Great Depression of the 1930s brought new forces to power.

Depression and Political Deadlock

The outflow of foreign, and especially American, capital from Germany that began in 1928 undermined the economic prosperity of the Weimar Republic. The resulting economic crisis brought parliamentary government to a halt. In 1928 a coalition of center parties and the Social Democrats governed. All went reasonably well until the Depression struck. Then the coalition partners differed sharply on economic policy. The Social Democrats refused to reduce social and unemployment insurance. The more conservative parties, remembering the inflation of 1923, insisted on a balanced budget. The coalition dissolved in March 1930. To resolve the parliamentary deadlock in the *Reichstag*, President von Hindenburg appointed Heinrich Brüning (1885–1970) as chancellor. Lacking a majority in the *Reichstag*, the new chancellor governed through emergency presidential decrees, as authorized by Article 48 of the constitution. Party divisions prevented the *Reichstag* from overriding the decrees. The Weimar Republic had become a presidential dictatorship.

German unemployment rose from 2,258,000 in March 1930 to over 6,000,000 in March 1932. There had been persistent unemployment during the 1920s, but nothing of such magnitude or duration. The economic downturn and the parliamentary deadlock worked to the advantage of the more extreme political parties. In the election of 1928 the Nazis had won only 12 seats in the *Reichstag*, and the Communists had won 54 seats. Two years later, after the election of 1930, the Nazis held 107 seats and the Communists 77.

The power of the Nazis in the streets was also on the rise. The unemployment fed thousands of men into the storm troopers, which had 100,000 members in 1930 and almost 1 million in 1933. The SA freely and viciously attacked Communists and Social Democrats. For the Nazis, politics meant the capture of power through terror and intimidation as well as through elections. Decency and civility in political life vanished. Nazi rallies resembled secular religious revivals. The Nazis paraded through the streets and the countryside. They gained powerful supporters and sympathizers among businessmen, military officers, and newspaper owners. Some intellectuals were also sympathetic. The Nazis transformed this discipline and enthusiasm born of economic despair and nationalistic frustration into impressive electoral results.

Hitler Comes to Power

For two years Brüning continued to govern with the backing of Hindenburg. The economy did not improve, and the political situation deteriorated. In 1932 the eighty-three-year-old president stood for reelection. Hitler ran against him and forced a runoff. The Nazi leader garnered 30.1 percent of the vote in the first election and 36.8 percent in the second. Although Hindenburg was returned to office, the vote convinced him that Brüning had lost the confidence of conservative German voters. In May 1932 he dismissed Brüning and appointed Franz von Papen (1878–1969) in his place. The new chancellor was one of a small group of extremely conservative advisers on whom the aged Hindenburg had become dependent. Others included the president's son and several generals. With the continued paralysis in the *Reichstag*, their influence over the president amounted to control of the government. Consequently, the crucial decisions of the next several months were made by only a handful of people.

Papen and the circle around the president wanted to draw the Nazis into cooperation with them without giving Hitler effective power. The government needed the popular support on the right that only the Nazis seemed able to generate. The Hindenburg circle decided to convince Hitler that the Nazis could not come to power on their own. Papen removed the ban on Nazi meetings that Brüning had imposed and then called a *Reichstag* election for July 1932. The Nazis won 230 seats and polled 37.2 percent of the vote. Hitler would only enter the Cabinet if he were made chancellor. Hindenburg refused. Another election was called in November, partly to wear down the Nazis' financial resources. The Nazis won only 196 seats, and their percentage of the popular vote dipped to 33.1 percent. The advisers around Hindenburg still refused to appoint Hitler to office.

In early December 1932 Papen resigned, and General Kurt von Schleicher (1882–1934) became chancellor. People were now afraid of civil war between the extreme left and the far right. Schleicher decided to try and fashion a broad-based coalition of conservative groups and trade unionists. The prospect of such a coalition, including groups from the political left, frightened the Hindenburg circle even more than the prospect of Hitler. They did not trust Schleicher's motives, which have never been clear. Consequently, they persuaded Hindenburg to appoint Hitler chancellor. To control him and to see that he did little mischief, Papen was named vice chancellor, and other traditional conservatives were appointed to the Cabinet. On January 30, 1933, Adolf Hitler became the chancellor of Germany.

It is important to emphasize that this outcome had not been inevitable. As his most distinguished biographer has observed, "Hitler's rise from humble beginnings to 'seize' power by 'triumph of the will' was the stuff of Nazi legend. In fact, political miscalculation by those with regular access to the corridors of power rather than any actions on the part of the Nazi leader played a larger role in placing him in the Chancellor's seat."[5] Hitler did not come to office on the tide of history, but through the blunders of conservative German politicians who hated the Weimar Republic and its rejection of traditional German political elites and who feared the domestic political turmoil the Depression had spawned.

Like Mussolini, Hitler had, however, technically become head of the government by legal means. All the proper legal forms and procedures had been observed. As a result, the civil service, the courts, and the other agencies of the government could support him in good conscience. He had forged a rigidly disciplined party structure and had mastered the techniques of mass politics and propaganda. (See "Encountering the Past: Cinema of the Political Left and Right.") He understood how to touch the raw social and political nerves of the electorate. His support appears to have come from across the social spectrum and not, as historians once thought, just from the lower middle class. Pockets of resistance appeared among Roman Catholic voters in the countryside and small towns. Otherwise, support for Hitler was particularly strong among groups such as farmers, war veterans, and the young, whom the insecurity of the 1920s and the Depression of the early 1930s had badly hurt. Hitler promised them security against communists and socialists, effective government in place of the petty politics of the other parties, and a strong, restored, purposeful Germany.

German big business once received much of the blame for the rise of Hitler. There is little evidence, however, that business contributions made any crucial difference to the Nazis' success or failure. Hitler's supporters were frequently suspicious of big business and capitalism. They wanted a simpler world, one in which small property would be safe from both socialism and big business. These people supported Hitler and the Nazis rather than the Social Democrats because the latter were not sufficiently nationalistic. The Nazis won out over other conservative nationalistic parties because, unlike those conservatives, the Nazis did address social insecurities.

Hitler's Consolidation of Power

Once in office, Hitler consolidated his control with almost lightning speed. This process had three facets: the capture of full legal authority, the crushing of alternative political groups, and the purging of rivals within the Nazi Party itself. On February 27, 1933, a mentally ill Dutch Communist set fire to the *Reichstag* building in Berlin. The Nazis quickly turned the incident to their own advantage by claiming that the fire proved the existence of an immediate Communist threat against the government. To the public, it seemed plausible that the Communists might attempt some action against the state now that the Nazis were in power. Under Article 48, Hitler issued an Emergency Decree suspending civil liberties and proceeded to arrest Communists or alleged Communists. This decree remained in force as long as Hitler ruled Germany.

[5]Ian Kershaw, *Hitler 1889–1936: Hubris* (New York: W. W. Norton & Company, 1999), p. 424.

CINEMA OF THE POLITICAL LEFT AND RIGHT

BEFORE THE INVENTION of television, the cinema was the most powerful cultural vehicle for political regimes to project their power. Film directors of genius were drawn to the authoritarian governments of both the left and the right, and the films they made for these regimes, especially those of Soviet Russia and Nazi Germany, still impress moviegoers.

During the 1920s, the Soviet Union promoted the cinema as a propaganda tool. The greatest Soviet film director was Sergei Eisenstein (1898–1948). His most famous film, *The Battleship Potemkin*, which critics regard as one of the most important films of all time, depicts a mutiny on a warship during the Russian revolution of 1905. In *Potemkin*, Eisenstein portrayed the working class itself as the hero of both the film and, true to Marxist doctrine, of history itself.

As Stalin gained more and more power from the mid-1920s onward, he imposed rigid censorship on the arts. To work in the Soviet Union, Eisenstein had to make films that pleased Stalin, and this he did. However, such was Eisenstein's genius that he also made two movies that many film scholars consider masterpieces: *Alexander Nevsky*, which depicts the victory of a medieval Russian prince over invading Germans, and *Ivan the Terrible*, which some see, in its depiction of the sixteenth-century despotic tsar whom Stalin admired, as Eisenstein's surrender to Stalin and others as a portrayal of tyranny.

Leni Riefenstahl (1902–2003) was by the early 1930s the most skilled documentary filmmaker in Germany and perhaps the world—an extraordinary accomplishment for a woman in a field dominated by men. Adolf Hitler asked her to make a documentary extolling the Third Reich after the Nazis took power in 1933. The results were *Triumph of the Will* (1934), about a Nazi Party rally, and *Olympia* (1938), about the Olympic Games held in Berlin in 1936. Both films display innovative, dramatically effective cinematic techniques and also the skilled political theatricality of the Nazi regime. These films dazzled audiences and are still shown in film classes as major works of twentieth-century cinematic art. Yet despite her artistry, Riefenstahl became marked—no matter how much she protested that she was a "pure" artist—as a producer of Nazi propaganda films. No American film studio would distribute her films to U.S. audiences.

After the defeat of Germany in 1945, Riefenstahl was imprisoned by the Allies under their de-Nazification program before being released in 1949. Thereafter, she attempted to rescue her career as a filmmaker, but the Nazi taint proved indelible. Instead, she became a noted photographer, especially of underwater photography. To the end or her life, Riefenstahl defends her films for the Third Reich as art, not propaganda.

Why were the Soviet and Nazi regimes so interested in the cinema?

How did Leni Riefenstahl's films of Hitler and Nazi rallies affect her later career?

Leni Riefenstahl filming the 1936 Olympic Games in Berlin with Hitler on the reviewing stand.

The *Reichstag* fire in 1933 provided Hitler with an excuse to consolidate his power. Bildarchiv Preussischer Kulturbesitz

In early March another *Reichstag* election took place. The Nazis still received only 43.9 percent of the vote. However, the arrest of the newly elected Communist deputies and the political fear aroused by the fire meant that Hitler could control the *Reichstag*. On March 23, 1933, the *Reichstag* passed an Enabling Act that permitted Hitler to rule by decree. Thereafter, there were no legal limits on his exercise of power. The Weimar Constitution was never formally repealed or amended. It had simply been supplanted by the February Emergency Decree and the March Enabling Act, which together made the constitution a dead letter.

Perhaps better than anyone else, Hitler understood that he and his party had not inevitably come to power. His potential opponents had been divided between 1929 and 1933. He intended to prevent them from regrouping. In a series of complex moves, Hitler outlawed or undermined various German institutions that might have served as rallying points for opposition. In early May 1933 the offices, banks, and newspapers of the free trade unions were seized, and their leaders arrested. The Nazi Party itself, rather than any government agency, undertook this action. In late June and early July, the other German political parties were outlawed. By July 14, 1933, the National Socialists were the only legal party in Germany. During the same months the Nazis had taken control of the governments of the individual federal states in Germany. By the close of 1933, all major institutions of potential opposition had been eliminated.

The final element in Hitler's personal consolidation of power involved the Nazi Party itself. By late 1933 the SA consisted of approximately 1 million active members and a larger number of reserves. The commander of this party army was Ernst Roehm, a possible rival to Hitler himself. The German army officer corps, on whom Hitler depended to rebuild the national army, was jealous of the SA. Consequently, to protect his own position and to shore up support with the regular army, on June 30, 1934, Hitler ordered the murder of key SA officers, including Roehm. Others killed between June 30 and July 2 included former chancellor von Schleicher and his wife. The exact number of purged victims is unknown, but it has been estimated to have exceeded one hundred. The German army, which was the only institution in the nation that might have prevented the murders, did nothing. A month later, on August 2, 1934, President Hindenburg died. Thereafter, the offices of chancellor and president were combined. Hitler was now the ***Führer***, or sole ruler of Germany and of the Nazi Party.

Anti-Semitism and the Police State

Terror and intimidation had helped propel the Nazis to office. As Hitler consolidated his power, he oversaw the organization of a police state. The chief vehicle of police surveillance was the **SS** (*Schutzstaffel*), or security units, commanded by Heinrich Himmler (1900–1945). This group had originated in the mid-1920s as a bodyguard for Hitler and had become a more elite paramilitary organization than the larger SA. In 1933 the SS had approximately 52,000 members. It was the instrument that carried out the blood purges of the party in 1934. By 1936 Himmler had become head of all police matters in Germany.

Attack on Jewish Economic Life The police character of the Nazi regime was all-pervasive, but the people who most consistently experienced its terror were the

Soon after seizing power, the Nazi government began harassing German Jewish businesses. Non-Jewish German citizens were urged not to buy merchandise from shops owned by Jews. Art Resource/Bildarchiv Preussischer Kulturbesitz

German Jews. Anti-Semitism had been a key plank of the Nazi program—anti-Semitism based on biological racial theories stemming from late-nineteenth-century thought rather than from religious discrimination. Before World War II the Nazi attack on the Jews went through three stages of increasing intensity. In 1933, shortly after assuming power, the Nazis excluded Jews from the civil service. For a time they also attempted to enforce boycotts of Jewish shops and businesses. The boycotts won relatively little public support.

Racial Legislation Then in 1935, a series of measures known as the Nuremberg Laws robbed German Jews of their citizenship. The professions and the major occupations were closed to those defined as Jews. Marriage and sexual intercourse between Jews and non-Jews were prohibited. Legal exclusion and humiliation of the Jews became the order of the day. The definition of who was a Jew in this law was both confusing and complex because the Nazis could not produce regulations based solely on a racial concept. The Nazi legal definitions of who was a Jew took into account the number of Jewish parents or grandparents, as well as whether a person practiced Judaisim. All persons with at least three Jewish grandparents were defined as Jews, but persons with two Jewish grandparents were considered Jewish only if they practiced Judaism, or if they were married to a Jew, or if they had been born to a marriage with one Jewish parent, or if they had been born out of wedlock with one Jewish parent.

Kristallnacht The persecution of the Jews increased again in 1938. Business careers were forbidden. In November 1938, under orders from the Nazi Party, thousands of Jewish stores and synagogues were burned or otherwise destroyed. The Jewish community itself had to pay for the damage that occurred on this ***Kristallnacht*** ("Night of Smashed Glass") because the government confiscated the insurance money. In many other ways, large and petty, the German Jews were harassed. This persecution allowed the Nazis to inculcate the rest of the population with the concept of a master race of pure German "Aryans" and also to display their own contempt for civil liberties. (See "An American Diplomat Witnesses *Kristallnacht* in Lepizig," page 856.)

The Final Solution After the war broke out, Hitler decided in 1942 to destroy the Jews in Europe. It is thought that over 6 million Jews, mostly from eastern European nations, died as a result of that staggering decision, unprecedented in its scope and implementation. This subject will be more fully treated in the next chapter.

Racial Ideology and the Lives of Women

Hitler and other Nazis were less interested in increasing the national population, which was Mussolini's policy in Italy, than in producing racially pure Germans. In their role as mothers, German women had the special task of preserving racial purity and giving birth to pure Germans who were healthy in mind and body. According to this view, women were to breed strong sons and daughters for the German nation. Nazi journalists often compared the role of women in childbirth to that of men in battle. Each served the state in particular social and gender roles. In both cases, the good of the nation was more important than that of the individual. (See "Compare & Connect: The Soviets and the Nazis Confront the Issues of Women and the Family," pages 858–859.)

Nazi racial ideology focused on women as the carriers and bearers of both the desired and undesired races. Nazi policy favored motherhood only for those whom its adherents regarded as racially fit for it. As early as late 1933, the government raised the issue of what kind of persons were fit to bear children for the nation. This policy disapproved of fostering motherhood among those people Nazi racism condemned—particularly the

AN AMERICAN DIPLOMAT WITNESSES *KRISTALLNACHT* IN LEIPZIG

A key event in the Nazi attack on Jews in Germany occurred on November 9 and 10, 1938, during nights of destructive terror known as Kristallnacht. *David Buffum, the American consul in Leipzig, wrote an extensive report of what happened in that city. In addition to providing the information in the passage that follows, he observed that most German citizens seemed stunned by what had occurred and deeply disapproved of it, but as his observations of the events in the Leipzig Zoo indicate, Germans were intimidated by the Nazi tactics. Buffum also reported that many German Jews came to the American consulate to find aid for emigration or help in locating husbands and sons taken to concentration camps. Both the United States and the nations of Western Europe admitted only limited numbers of Jewish refugees from Germany and, later, from Nazi-occupied Europe. Compare the events recorded in this document with the predictions that Alexis de Tocqueville made to Count Arthur de Gobineau about what might happen when racial thinking affected mass politics. (See Chapter 24.)*

Why did the Nazis claim that the destruction of life and property in Leipzig and other German cities arose from spontaneous actions? How did the Nazi perpetrators of *Kristallnacht* intimidate Jewish citizens? What aid that was available to other German citizens was denied to Jews during these destructive events? Why did other German citizens not oppose the Nazi actions against the Jews?

At 3 A.M. on 10 November 1938 was unleashed a barrage of Nazi ferocity that has had no equal hitherto in Germany. . . .

Jewish shop windows by the hundreds were systematically and wantonly smashed throughout the entire city at a loss estimated at several millions of marks. . . . According to reliable testimony, the debacle was executed by SS men and Stormtroopers not in uniform, each group having been provided with hammers, axes, crowbars and incendiary bombs.

Three synagogues in Leipzig were fired simultaneously by incendiary bombs and all sacred objects and records desecrated or destroyed, in most cases hurled through the windows and burned in the streets. . . . All the synagogues were irreparably gutted by flames. . . . One of the largest clothing stores in the heart of the city was destroyed by flames from incendiary bombs, only the charred walls and gutted roof having been left standing. As was the case with the synagogues, no attempts on the part of the fire brigade were made to extinguish the fire. . . . It is extremely difficult to believe, but the owners of the clothing store were actually charged with setting the fire and on that basis were dragged from their beds at 6 A.M. and clapped into prison.

Tactics which closely approached the ghoulish took place at the Jewish cemetery where the temple was fired together with a building occupied by caretakers, tombstones uprooted and graves violated. . . .

Ferocious as was the violation of property, the most hideous phase of the so-called 'spontaneous' action has been the wholesale arrest and transportation to concentration camps of male German Jews between the ages of sixteen and sixty, as well as Jewish men without citizenship. . . . Having demolished dwellings and hurled most of the movable effects onto the streets, the insatiably sadistic perpetrators threw many of the trembling inmates into a small stream that flows through the Zoological Park, commanding horrified spectators to spit at them, defile them with mud and jeer at their plight. The latter incident has been repeatedly corroborated by German witnesses who were nauseated in telling the tale. The slightest manifestation of sympathy evoked a positive fury on the part of the perpetrators, and the crowd was powerless to do anything but turn horror-stricken eyes from the scene of abuse, or leave the vicinity. These tactics were carried out . . . without police intervention and they were applied to men, women, and children.

From *Nazism, 1919–1945: A Documentary Reader*, Vol. 2, *State, Economy and Society, 1933–39*, ed. by J. Noakes and G. Pridham, new ed. 2000, pp. 361–362. Reprinted by permission of University of Exeter Press.

Jews, but also Slavs and Gypsies. During the mass executions of Jews in the Holocaust, Jewish women were specifically targeted for death, in part to prevent them from bearing a new generation.

Nazi theorists also discriminated between the healthy and unhealthy, the desirable and undesirable, in the German population itself. The government sought to prevent "undesirables" from reproducing, a policy that led to both the sterilization and death of many women, often because of an alleged mental "degeneracy." Some pregnant women were forced to have abortions. The Nazis' population policy was, in effect, one of selective breeding, or antenatalism, that profoundly affected the lives of women.

To support motherhood among those whom they believed should have children, the Nazis provided loans to encourage early marriage, tax breaks for families with children, and child allowances. In this respect, Nazi legislation resembled that passed elsewhere in Europe during the decade. The subsidies and other family payments were sent to husbands rather than wives, to make married fatherhood seem preferable to bachelorhood. Furthermore, these policies were administered on the premise that only racially and physically desirable children received support.

Although Nazi ideology emphasized motherhood, in 1930 the party vowed to protect the jobs of working women, and the number of women working in Germany rose steadily under the Nazi regime. The Nazis recognized that in the midst of the Depression many women needed to work, but the party urged them to pursue employment that was "natural" to their character as women. Such employment included agricultural labor, teaching, nursing, social service, and domestic service. The Nazis also intended women to be educators of the young. In that role, whether as mothers or as members of the serving professions, women became special protectors of German cultural values. Through cooking, dress, music, and stories, mothers were to instill a love for the nation in their children. As consumers for the home, women were to support German-owned shops, buy German-made goods, and boycott Jewish merchants.

Nazi Economic Policy

Besides consolidating political authority and pursuing anti-Semitic policies, Hitler still had to confront the Great Depression. German unemployment had helped propel him to power. The Nazis attacked this problem with a success that astonished and frightened Europe. By 1936, while the rest of the European economy remained stagnant, the specter of unemployment and other difficulties associated with the Great Depression no longer haunted Germany.

As far as the economic crisis was concerned, Hitler had become the most effective political leader in Europe. This success was perhaps the most important reason

MAJOR POLITICAL EVENTS OF THE 1920s AND 1930s

1919 (August)	Constitution of the Weimar Republic promulgated
1920	Kapp Putsch in Berlin
1921 (March)	Kronstadt mutiny leads Lenin to initiate his New Economic Policy
1922 (October)	Fascist march on Rome leads to Mussolini's assumption of power
1923 (January)	France invades the Ruhr
1923 (November)	Hitler's Beer Hall Putsch
1924	Death of Lenin
1925	Locarno Agreements
1928	Kellogg-Briand Pact; first Five-Year Plan launched in USSR
1929 (January)	Trotsky expelled from USSR
1929 (February)	Lateran Accord between the Vatican and the Italian state
1929 (October)	New York stock market crash
1929 (November)	Bukharin expelled from his offices in the Soviet Union; Stalin's central position thus affirmed
1930 (March)	Brüning government begins in Germany
	Stalin calls for moderation in his policy of agricultural collectivization because of "dizziness from success"
1930 (September)	Nazis capture 107 seats in German *Reichstag*
1931 (August)	National Government formed in Britain
1932 (March 13)	Hindenburg defeats Hitler for German presidency
1932 (May 31)	Franz von Papen forms German Cabinet
1932 (July 31)	German *Reichstag* election
1932 (November 6)	German *Reichstag* election
1932 (December 2)	Kurt von Schleicher forms German cabinet
1933 (January 30)	Hitler made German chancellor
1933 (February 27)	*Reichstag* fire
1932 (March 5)	*Reichstag* election
1932 (March 23)	Enabling Act consolidates Nazi power
1934 (June 30)	Blood purge of the Nazi Party
1934 (August 2)	Death of Hindenburg
1934 (December 1)	Assassination of Kirov leads to the beginning of Stalin's purges
1936 (May)	Popular Front government in France
1936 (July–August)	Most famous of public purge trials in Russia

COMPARE AND CONNECT

The Soviets and the Nazis Confront the Issues of Women and the Family

BOTH THE SOVIET and Nazi dictatorships intruded deeply into the private lives of their citizens. Some Communist writers in the Soviet Union imagined utopian changes to traditional family life and traditional roles for women. In Germany the state imposed policies on women that would make their roles of wives and mothers serve the larger political and ideological goals of the Nazi Party. Different and opposed as were these policies of the two dictatorships, both challenged the social roles of women that were emerging in Western Europe and in the United States.

QUESTIONS

1. **Why did Kollontai see the restructuring of the family as essential to the establishment of a new kind of Communist society? Would these changes make people loyal to that society?**
2. **What changes in society does the kind of economic independence Kollontai seeks for women presuppose? What might childhood be like in this society?**
3. **What are the social tasks Hitler assigns to women? How does he attempt to subordinate the lives of women to the supremacy of the state?**
4. **Why does Hitler associate the emancipation of women with Jews and intellectuals?**
5. **Why was the present and future role of women such an important topic for both the Communist and the Nazi governments?**

I. A Communist Woman Demands a New Family Life

While Lenin sought to consolidate the Bolshevik Revolution against internal and external enemies, there existed within the young Soviet Union a vast utopian impulse to change and reform virtually every social institution that had existed before the revolution or those Communists associated with capitalist society. Alexandra Kollontai (1872–1952) was a spokesperson of the extreme political left within the early Soviet Union. There had been much speculation on how the end of bourgeois society might change the structure of the family and the position of women. In this passage written in 1920, Kollontai states one of the most radically utopian visions of this change. During the years immediately after the revolution, extreme rumors circulated in both Europe and America about sexual and family experimentation in the Soviet Union. Statements such as this fostered such rumors. Kollontai herself later became a supporter of Stalin and a Soviet diplomat.

There is no escaping the fact: the old type of family has seen its day. It is not the fault of the Communist State, it is the result of the changed conditions of life. The family is ceasing to be a necessity of the State, as it was in the past; on the contrary, it is worse than useless, since it needlessly holds back the female workers from more productive and far more serious work. . . . But on the ruins of the former family we shall soon see a new form rising which will involve altogether different relations between men and women, and which will be a union of affection and comradeship, a union of two equal members of the Communist society, both of them free, both of them independent, both of them workers. No more domestic "servitude" of women. No more inequality within the family. No more fear on the part of the woman lest she remain without support or aid with little ones in her arms if her husband should desert her. The woman in the Communist city no longer depends on her husband but on her work. It is not her husband but her robust arms which will support her. There will be no more anxiety as to the fate of her children. The State of the Workers will assume responsibility for these. Marriage will be purified of all its material elements, of all money calculations, which constitute a hideous blemish on family life in our days. . . .

The woman who is called upon to struggle in the great cause of the liberation of the workers—such a woman should know that in the new State there will be no more room for such petty divisions as were formerly understood: "These are my own children, to them I owe all my maternal solicitude, all my affection; those are your children, my neighbour's children; I am not concerned with them. I have enough to do with my own." Henceforth the worker-mother, who is conscious of her social function, will rise to a point where she no longer differentiates between yours and mine; she must remember that there are henceforth only our children, those of the Communist State, the common possession of all the workers.

The Worker's State has need of a new form of relation between the sexes. The narrow and exclusive affection of the mother for her own children must expand until it embraces all the children of the great proletarian family. In place of the indissoluble marriage based on the servitude of woman, we shall see rise the free union, fortified by the love and mutual respect of the two members of the Workers' State, equal in their rights and in their obligations. In place of the individual and egotistic family there will arise a great universal family of workers, in which all the workers, men and women, will be, above all, workers, comrades.

Source: From Alexandra Kollontai, *Communism and the Family*, as reprinted in Rudolf Schlesinger, ed. and trans., *The Family in the USSR* (London: Routledge and Kegan Paul, 1949), pp. 67–69. Reprinted by permission.

This Soviet poster illustrates the role of women in communist society as key players in industrial and agricultural development and progress. This differs greatly from the traditional role assigned to women in Nazi ideology. Corbis/Bettmann © Swim Inc./CORBIS

II. Hitler Rejects the Emancipation of Women

According to Nazi ideology, women's place was in the home producing and rearing children and supporting their husbands. In this speech, Hitler urges this view of the role of women. He uses anti-Semitism to discredit those writers who had urged the emancipation of women from their traditional roles and occupations. Hitler returns here to the "separate spheres" concept of the relationship of men and women. His traditional view of women was directed against views that were associated with the Soviet experiment during the interwar years. Contrast this Nazi outlook on women and the family with the Bolshevik position described by Alexandra Kollontai in the previous document. Ironically, once World War II began, the Nazi leadership demanded that women leave the home and work in factories to support the war effort.

The slogan "Emancipation of women" was invented by Jewish intellectuals and its content was formed by the same spirit. In the really good times of German life the German woman had no need to emancipate herself. She possessed exactly what nature had necessarily given her to administer and preserve; just as the man in his good times had no need to fear that he would be ousted from his position in relation to the woman. . . .

If the man's world is said to be the State, his struggle, his readiness to devote his powers to the service of the community, then it may perhaps be said that the woman's is a smaller world. For her world is her husband, her family, her children, and her home. But what would become of the greater world if there were no one to tend and care for the smaller one? How could the greater world survive if there were no one to make the cares of the smaller world the content of their lives? No, the greater world is built on the foundation of this smaller world. This great world cannot survive if the smaller world is not stable. Providence has entrusted to the woman the cares of that world which is her very own, and only on the basis of this smaller world can the man's world be formed and built up. The two worlds are not antagonistic. They complement each other, they belong together just as man and woman belong together.

We do not consider it correct for the woman to interfere in the world of the man, in his main sphere. We consider it natural if these two worlds remain distinct. To the one belongs the strength of feeling, the strength of the soul. To the other belongs the strength of vision, of toughness, of decision, and of the willingness to act. In the one case this strength demands the willingness of the woman to risk her life to preserve this important cell and to multiply it, and in the other case it demands from the man the readiness to safeguard life. . . .

So our women's movement is for us not something which inscribes on its banner as its programme the fight against men, but something which has as its programme the common fight together with men. For the new National Socialist national community acquires a firm basis precisely because we have gained the trust of millions of women as fanatical fellow-combatants, women who have fought for the common life in the service of the common task of preserving life. . . .

Whereas previously the programmes of the liberal, intellectualist women's movements contained many points, the programme of our National Socialist Women's movement has in reality but one single point, and that point is the child, that tiny creature which must be born and grow strong and which alone gives meaning to the whole life-struggle.

Source: From J. Noakes and G. Pridham, eds., *Nazism, 1919–1945*, Vol. 2, *State, Economy and Society, 1933–39: A Documentary Reader*, Exeter Studies in History No. 8 (University of Exeter Press, 1984), pp. 449–450.

A Closer LOOK

THE NAZI PARTY RALLY

YOUNG WOMEN WERE enthusiastic supporters among the crowd extending the Nazi salute in a 1938 rally.

The Nazi Party had used what later became the ever-present Swastika (or hooked cross) symbol since 1920. Hitler himself claimed to have chosen the symbol, which he and other Nazis associated with an allegedly racially pure Aryan past. In fact, many cultures had used the Swastika as a symbol. The Nazis adopted the Swastika as the German national flag in 1935.

Nazi rallies were intended to generate nationalistic group solidarity that would demonstrate that whatever other divisions might exist in the nation, loyalty to the Nazi Party and to the nation would be more important than any other group loyalty.

The image in the photo illustrates the gender divisions Nazi ideology fostered. Men were portrayed as defenders of the homeland. Women were to pursue traditional domestic roles and to bear children for the nation.

Bildarchiv Preussischer Kulturbesitz

To examine this image in an interactive fashion, please go to www.myhistorylab.com

myhistorylab

Germans supported his tyrannical regime. The Nazi success against the Great Depression gave the regime credibility. Behind the direction of both business and labor stood the Nazi terror and police. The Nazi economic experiment proved that, by sacrificing all political and civil liberty, destroying a free trade-union movement, limiting the private exercise of capital, and ignoring consumer satisfaction, a government could achieve full employment to prepare for war and aggression.

Nazi economic policies supported private property and private capitalism but subordinated all significant economic enterprise and decisions about prices and investment to the goals of the state. Hitler reversed the deflationary policy of the cabinets that had preceded him. He instituted a massive program of public works and vast military spending. From the earliest years of the Nazi regime government spending and other economic policies served to pursue the cause of rearmament. The government built canals, reclaimed land, and constructed an extensive highway system with clear military uses. It also sent unemployed workers back to farms if they had originally come from them. Other laborers were not permitted to change jobs without official permission.

In 1935, the renunciation of the military provisions of the Versailles treaty led to open rearmament and military expansion with little opposition, as explained in Chapter 28. These measures essentially restored full employment. In 1936, Hitler instructed Hermann Göring (1893–1946), who had headed the air force since 1933, to undertake a four-year plan to prepare the army and the economy for war. The government determined that Germany must be economically self-sufficient. Armaments received top priority. This economic program satisfied both the yearning for social and economic security and the desire for national fulfillment.

With the crushing of the trade unions in 1933, strikes became illegal. There was no genuine collective bargaining. The government handled labor disputes through compulsory arbitration. It also required workers and employers to participate in the Labor Front, an organization intended to demonstrate that class conflict had ended. The Labor Front sponsored a "Strength Through Joy" program that provided vacations and other forms of recreation for workers and farmers.

▼ Trials of the Successor States in Eastern Europe

It had been an article of faith among nineteenth-century liberals sympathetic to nationalism that only good could flow from the demise of Austria-Hungary, the restoration of Poland, and the establishment of nation-states throughout eastern Europe. These new states were to embody the principle of national self-determination and to provide a buffer against the westward spread of Bolshevism. They were, however, in trouble from the beginning.

Economic and Ethnic Pressures

All the new states faced immense postwar economic difficulties. None of them possessed the kind of strong economy that nation-states such as France and Germany had developed in the nineteenth century. Indeed, political independence disrupted the previous economic relationships that each of them had developed as part of one of the prewar empires. None of the new states was financially independent; except for Czechoslovakia, all of them depended on foreign loans to finance economic development. Nationalistic antagonisms often prevented these states from trading with each other, and as a consequence, most became highly dependent on trade with Germany. The successor states of eastern Europe were poor and overwhelmingly rural nations in an industrialized world. The Depression hit them especially hard, because they had to import finished goods for which they paid with agricultural exports whose value was falling sharply.

Finally, throughout eastern Europe, the collapse of the old German, Russian, and Austrian empires allowed various ethnic groups—large and small—to pursue nationalistic goals unchecked by any great power or central political authority. The major social and political groups in these countries were generally unwilling to make compromises lest they undermine their nationalist identity and independence. Each state included minority groups that wanted to be independent or to become part of a different nation in the region. Again, except for Czechoslovakia, all these states succumbed to some form of domestic authoritarian government.

Poland: Democracy to Military Rule

The nation whose postwar fortunes probably most disappointed liberal Europeans was Poland. For more than a hundred years, the country had been erased from the map. (See Chapter 17.) An independent Poland had been one of Woodrow Wilson's Fourteen Points. When the country was restored in 1919, nationalism proved an insufficient bond to overcome political disagreements stemming from class differences, diverse economic interests, and regionalism. Furthermore, large Ukrainian, Jewish, Lithuanian, and German minorities distrusted the Polish government and resented attempts to force them to adopt Polish culture. The new Poland had been constructed from portions governed by Germany, Russia, and Austria for over a century. Each of those regions of partitioned Poland had different administrative systems and laws, different economies, and different degrees of experience with electoral institutions. A host of small political parties bedeviled the new Polish Parliament, and the executive was weak. In 1926, Marshal Josef Pilsudski (1867–1935) carried out a military coup. Thereafter, he ruled, in effect, personally until his death, when the government passed into the hands of a group of his military followers. The government became increasingly anti-Semitic, and non-Polish minorities suffered various forms of discrimination.

Czechoslovakia: A Viable Democratic Experiment

Only one central European successor state escaped the fate of self-imposed authoritarian government. Czechoslovakia possessed a strong industrial base, a substantial middle class, and a tradition of liberal values. During the war, Czechs and Slovaks had cooperated to aid the Allies. They had learned to work together and generally to trust each other. After the war, the new government had broken up large estates in favor of small peasant holdings. In the person of Thomas Masaryk (1850–1937), the nation possessed a gifted leader of immense integrity and fairness. The country had a real chance of becoming a viable modern nation-state.

There were, however, tensions between the Czechs and the Slovaks, who were poorer and more rural. Moreover, other non-Czech national groups, including Poles, Magyars, Ukrainians, and especially the Germans of the Sudetenland, which the Paris settlement had placed within Czech borders, resented being part of Czechoslovakia. The parliamentary regime might have been able to work through these problems, but extreme German nationalists in the Sudetenland looked to Hitler, who wanted to expand into eastern Europe, for help. In 1938, at Munich, the great powers first divided liberal Czechoslovakia to appease Hitler's aggressive instincts and then watched passively in early 1939 as he occupied much of the country, gave parts to Poland and Hungary, and manipulated a Slovak puppet state.

Hungary: Turn to Authoritarianism

Hungary was one of the defeated powers of World War I. In that defeat, it achieved its long-desired separation from Austria, but at a high political and economic price. In Hungary during 1919, Bela Kun (1885–1937), a communist, established a short-lived Hungarian Soviet Republic, which received socialist support. The Allies authorized an invasion by Romanian troops to remove the communist danger. The Hungarian landowners then established Admiral Miklós Horthy (1868–1957) as regent for the Habsburg monarch who could not return to his throne—a position Horthy held until 1944. After the collapse of the Kun government, thousands of Hungarians were either executed or imprisoned. It was, in part, in reaction to Kun's cooperation with socialists that Lenin ordered the Comintern to reject such cooperation in the future. Kun himself fled to Russia where Stalin later had him killed.

The Hungarians also deeply resented the territory Hungary had lost in the Paris settlement. The largely agrarian Hungarian economy suffered from a general stagnation. During the 1920s, the effective ruler of Hungary was Count Stephen Bethlen (1874–1947). He presided over a government that was parliamentary in form, but aristocratic in character. In 1932, he was succeeded by General Julius Gömbös (1886–1936), who pursued anti-Semitic policies and rigged elections. No matter how the popular vote turned out, the Gömbös party controlled Parliament. After his death in 1936, anti-Semitism lingered in Hungarian politics.

Austria: Political Turmoil and Nazi Occupation

Austria's situation was little better than that of the other successor states. A quarter of the 8 million Austrians lived in Vienna. Viable economic life was almost impossible, and the Paris settlement forbade union with Germany. Throughout the 1920s, the leftist Social Democrats and the conservative Christian Socialists contended for power. Both groups employed small armies to terrorize their opponents and to impress their followers.

In 1933, the Christian Socialist Engelbert Dollfuss (1892–1934) became chancellor. He tried to steer a course between the Austrian Social Democrats and the German Nazis, who had surfaced in Austria. In 1934, he outlawed all political parties except the Christian Socialists, the agrarians, and the paramilitary groups that composed his own Fatherland Front. He used troops against the Social Democrats but was murdered later that year during an unsuccessful Nazi coup. His successor, Kurt von Schuschnigg (1897–1977), presided over Austria until Hitler annexed it in 1938.

Southeastern Europe: Royal Dictatorships

In southeastern Europe, revision of the arrangements in the Paris settlement was less of an issue. Parliamentary government floundered there nevertheless. Yugoslavia had been founded by the Corfu Agreement of 1917 and was known as the Kingdom of the Serbs, Croats, and Slovenes until 1929. Throughout the interwar period, the Serbs dominated the government and were opposed by the Croats. The two groups clashed violently, but the Serbs had the advantage of having had an independent state with an army prior to World War I, whereas the Croats and Slovenes had been part of the Austro-Hungarian Empire. The Croats generally were Roman Catholic, better educated, and accustomed to reasonably incorrupt government administration. The Serbs were Orthodox, less well educated, and considered corrupt administrators by the Croats. Furthermore, although each group predominated in certain areas of the country, each had isolated enclaves in other parts of the nation. Bosnia-Herzegovina, in addition to Serbs and Croats, had a significant Muslim population. The Slovenes, Muslims, Albanians, and other small national groups often played the Serbs and the Croats against each other. All the political parties except the small Communist Party represented a particular ethnic group rather than the nation of Yugoslavia. The violent clash of nationalities eventually led to a royal dictatorship in 1929 under King Alexander I (r. 1921–1934), himself a

Serb. He outlawed political parties and jailed popular politicians. Alexander was assassinated in 1934, but the authoritarian government continued under a regency for his son.

Other royal dictatorships were imposed elsewhere in the Balkans: in Romania by King Carol II (r. 1930–1940) and in Bulgaria by King Boris III (r. 1918–1943). They regarded their own illiberal regimes as preventing the seizure of power by more extreme antiparliamentary movements and as quieting the discontent of the varied nationalities within their borders. In Greece, the parliamentary monarchy floundered amid military coups and calls for a republic. In 1936, General John Metaxas (1871–1941) instituted a dictatorship under King George II (r. 1935–1947) that, for the time being, ended parliamentary life in Greece.

In Perspective

By the mid-1930s, dictators of the right and the left had established themselves across much of Europe. Political tyranny was hardly new to Europe, but several factors combined to give these rulers unique characteristics. They drew their immediate support from well-organized political parties. Except for the Bolsheviks, these were mass parties. The roots of support for the dictators lay in nationalism, the social and economic frustration of the Great Depression, and political ideologies that promised to transform the social and political order. As long as the new rulers seemed successful, they did not lack support. Many citizens believed these leaders had ended the pettiness of everyday politics.

After coming to power, the dictators possessed a practical monopoly over mass communications. Through armies, police forces, and party discipline, they also monopolized terror and coercive power. They could propagandize large populations and compel people to obey them and their followers. Finally, as a result of the second Industrial Revolution, they commanded a vast amount of technology and a capacity for immense destruction. Earlier rulers in Europe may have shared the ruthless ambitions of Hitler, Mussolini, and Stalin, but they had lacked the ready implements of physical force to impose their wills.

Mass political support, the monopoly of police and military power, and technological capacity meant the dictators of the 1930s held more extensive sway over their nations than any other group of rulers who had ever governed on the Continent. Soon the issue would become whether they would be able to maintain peace among themselves and with their democratic neighbors.

Review Questions

1. What caused the Great Depression? Why was it more severe and why did it last longer than previous economic downturns? Could it have been avoided?
2. How did Stalin achieve supreme power in the Soviet Union? Why did he decide that Russia had to industrialize rapidly? Why did this require the collectivization of agriculture? Was the policy a success? How did it affect the Russian people? Why did Stalin carry out the great purges?
3. Why was Italy dissatisfied and unstable after World War I? How did Mussolini achieve power? What were the characteristics of the Fascist state?
4. Why did the Weimar Republic collapse in Germany? How did Hitler come to power? Which groups in Germany supported Hitler and why were they pro-Nazi? How did he consolidate his power? Why was anti-Semitism central to Nazi policy?
5. What characteristics did the authoritarian regimes in the Soviet Union, Italy, and Germany have in common? What role did terror play in each?
6. Why did liberal democracy fail in the successor states of Eastern Europe?

Suggested Readings

L. Ahamed, *Lords of Finance: The Bankers Who Broke the World* (2009). A lively narrative of the banking collapse leading to the Great Depression.

W. S. Allen, *The Nazi Seizure of Power: The Experience of a Single German Town, 1930–1935*, rev. ed. (1984). A classic treatment of Nazism in a microcosmic setting.

A. Applebaum, *Gulag: A History* (2003). A superbly readable account of Stalin's system of persecution and resulting prison camps.

I. T. Berend, *Decades of Crisis: Central and Eastern Europe before World War II* (2001). The best recent survey of the subject.

R. J. Bosworth, *Mussolini* (2002). A major new biography.

R. J. B. Bosworth, *Mussolini's Italy: Life Under the Fascist Dictatorship, 1915–1945* (2007). A broad-based study of both fascist politics and the impact of those politics on Italian life.

M. Burleigh and W. Wipperman, *The Racial State: Germany 1933–1945* (1991). Emphasizes the manner in which racial theory influenced numerous areas of policy.

I. Deutscher, *The Prophet Armed* (1954), *The Prophet Unarmed* (1959), and *The Prophet Outcast* (1963). Remains the major biography of Trotsky.

B. A. Engel and A. Posadskaya-Vanderbeck, *A Revolution of Their Own: Voices of Women in Soviet History* (1998). Long interviews and autobiographical recollections by women who lived through the Soviet era.

R. Evans, *The Coming of the Third Reich* (2004) and *The Third Reich in Power, 1933–1939* (2005). A superb narrative.

F. Furet, *The Passing of an Illusion: The Idea of Communism in the Twentieth Century* (1995). A brilliant account of how communism shaped politics and thought outside the Soviet Union.

G. Feldman, *The Great Disorder: Politics, Economics, and Society in the German Inflation, 1914–1924* (1993). The best work on the subject.

S. Fitzpatrick, *Stalin's Peasants: Resistance and Survival in the Russian Village After Collectivization* (1994). A pioneering study.

R. Gellately, *Lenin, Stalin, and Hitler: The Age of Social Catastrophe* (2007). A major new study of the Soviet and Nazi dictatorships.

R. Gellately and N. Stoltzfus, *Social Outsiders in Nazi Germany* (2001). Important essays on Nazi treatment of groups the party regarded as undesirables.

J. A. Getty and O. V. Naumov, *The Road to Terror: Stalin and the Self-Destruction of the Bolsheviks, 1932–1939* (1999). A remarkable collection of documents and commentary on Stalin's purges.

R. Hamilton, *Who Voted for Hitler?* (1982). An examination of voting patterns and sources of Nazi support.

J. Jackson, *The Popular Front in France: Defending Democracy, 1934–1938* (1988). An extensive treatment.

P. Kenez, *The Birth of the Propaganda State: Soviet Methods of Mass Mobilization, 1917–1929* (1985). An examination of the manner in which the Communist government inculcated popular support.

B. Kent, *The Spoils of War: The Politics, Economics, and Diplomacy of Reparations, 1918–1932* (1993). A comprehensive account of the intricacies of the reparations problem of the 1920s.

I. Kershaw, *Hitler*, 2 vols. (2001). Replaces all previous biographies.

C. Kindleberger, *The World in Depression, 1929–1939* (1986). A classic, accessible analysis.

B. Lincoln, *Red Victory: A History of the Russian Civil War* (1989). An excellent narrative account.

M. McAuley, *Bread and Justice: State and Society in Petrograd, 1917–1922* (1991). A study that examines the impact of the Russian Revolution and Leninist policies on a major Russian city.

R. McKibbin, *Classes and Cultures: England, 1918–1951* (2000). Viewing the era through the lens of class.

R. Pipes, *The Unknown Lenin: From the Secret Archives* (1996). A collection of previously unpublished documents that indicated the repressive character of Lenin's government.

P. Pulzer, *Jews and the German State: The Political History of a Minority, 1848–1933* (1992). A detailed history by a major historian of European minorities.

R. Service, *Stalin: A Biography* (2005). The strongest of a host of recent biographical studies.

J. Stephenson, *Women in Nazi Germany* (2001). Analysis with documents.

A. Tooze, *The Wages of Destruction: The Making and Breaking of the Nazi Economy* (2006). A wide-ranging, accessible study of the politics and ideology behind Nazi economic policy.

E. Weber, *The Hollow Years: France in the 1930s* (1995). Examines France between the wars.

L. Yahil, *The Holocaust: The Fate of European Jewry, 1932–1945* (1990). A major study of this fundamental subject in twentieth-century history.

In August 1945, the United States exploded atomic bombs on the Japanese cities of Hiroshima and Nagasaki. A week later Japan surrendered. Without the bombs the United States would almost certainly have had to invade Japan, and tens of thousands of Americans would have been killed. Still, the decision to use the bomb remains controversial. © CORBIS

28

World War II

▼ **Again the Road to War (1933–1939)**

Hitler's Goals • Italy Attacks Ethiopia • Remilitarization of the Rhineland • The Spanish Civil War • Austria and Czechoslovakia • Munich • The Nazi-Soviet Pact

▼ **World War II (1939–1945)**

The German Conquest of Europe • The Battle of Britain • The German Attack on Russia • Hitler's Plans for Europe • Japan and the United States Enter the War • The Tide Turns • The Defeat of Nazi Germany • Fall of the Japanese Empire • The Cost of War

▼ **Racism and the Holocaust**

The Destruction of the Polish Jewish Community • Polish Anti-Semitism Between the Wars • The Nazi Assault on the Jews of Poland • Explanations of the Holocaust

▼ **The Domestic Fronts**

Germany: From Apparent Victory to Defeat • France: Defeat, Collaboration, and Resistance • Great Britain: Organization for Victory • The Soviet Union: "The Great Patriotic War"

▼ **Preparations for Peace**

The Atlantic Charter • Tehran: Agreement on a Second Front • Yalta • Potsdam

▼ **In Perspective**

KEY TOPICS

- **The origins of World War II**
- **The course of the war**
- **Racism and the Holocaust**
- **The impact of the war on the people of Europe**
- **Relationships among the victorious allies and the preparations for peace**

THE MORE IDEALISTIC survivors of World War I, especially in the United States and Great Britain, thought of it as "the war to end all wars" and a war "to make the world safe for democracy." Only thus could they justify the slaughter, expense, and upheaval of that terrible conflict. How appalled they would have been had they known that only twenty years after the peace treaties a second great war would break out, more global than the first. In this war, the democracies would be fighting for their lives against militaristic, nationalistic, authoritarian, and totalitarian states in Europe and Asia, and they would be allied with the communist Soviet Union in the struggle. The defeat of the militarists and dictators would not bring the peace they longed for, but the Cold War, in which the European states would become powers of the second class, subordinate to two new superpowers, partially or fully non-European: the Soviet Union and the United States.

▾ Again the Road to War (1933–1939)

World War I and the Versailles treaty had only a marginal relationship to the world depression of the 1930s. In Germany, however, where the reparations settlement had contributed to the vast inflation of 1923, economic and social discontent focused on the Versailles settlement as the cause of all ills. Throughout the late 1920s, Adolf Hitler and the Nazi Party denounced Versailles as the source of all of Germany's troubles. The economic woes of the early 1930s seemed to bear them out. Nationalism and attention to the social question, along with party discipline, had been the sources of Nazi success. They continued to influence Hitler's foreign policy after he became chancellor in January 1933. Moreover, the Nazi destruction of the Weimar constitution and of political opposition meant that Hitler himself totally dominated German foreign policy. Consequently, it is important to know what his goals were and how he planned to achieve them.

Hitler's Goals

From the first expression of his goals in a book written in jail, *Mein Kampf (My Struggle)*, to his last days in the underground bunker in Berlin where he killed himself, Hitler's racial theories and goals were at the center of his thought. He meant to go far beyond Germany's 1914 boundaries, which were the limit of the vision of his predecessors. He meant to bring the entire German people—the *Volk*—understood as a racial group, together into a single nation.

The new Germany would include all the Germanic parts of the old Habsburg Empire, including Austria. This virile and growing nation would need more space to live, or ***Lebensraum***, that would be taken from the Slavs, who, according to Nazi theory, were a lesser race, fit only for servitude. The removal of the Jews, another inferior race according to Nazi theory, would purify the new Germany. The plans required the conquest of Poland and Ukraine as the primary areas for German settlement and for providing badly needed food. Neither *Mein Kampf* nor later statements of policy were blueprints for action. Rather, Hitler was a brilliant improviser who exploited opportunities as they arose. He never lost sight of his goal, however, which would almost certainly require a major war. (See "Hitler Describes His Goals in Foreign Policy.")

Germany Rearms When Hitler came to power, Germany was far too weak to permit a direct approach to reach his aims. The first problem he set out to resolve was to shake off the fetters of Versailles and to make Germany a formidable military power. In October 1933, Germany withdrew from an international disarmament conference and also from the League of Nations. Hitler argued that because the other powers had not disarmed as they had promised, it was wrong to keep Germany helpless. These acts alarmed the French but were merely symbolic. In January 1934, Germany signed a nonaggression pact with Poland that was of greater concern to France, for it undermined France's chief means of containing the Germans. At last, in March 1935, Hitler formally renounced the disarmament provisions of the Versailles treaty with the formation of a German air force, and soon he reinstated conscription, which aimed at an army of half a million men.

The League of Nations Fails Growing evidence that the League of Nations could not keep the peace and that collective security was a myth made Hitler's path easier. In September 1931, Japan occupied Manchuria. China appealed to the League of Nations. The league dispatched a commission under a British diplomat, the earl of Lytton (1876–1951). The *Lytton Report* condemned the Japanese for resorting to force, but the powers were unwilling to impose sanctions. Japan withdrew from the League and kept control of Manchuria.

When Hitler announced his decision to rearm Germany, the League formally condemned that action, but it took no steps to prevent it. France and Britain felt unable to object forcefully because they had not carried out their own promises to disarm. Instead, they met with Mussolini in June 1935 to form the so-called Stresa Front, promising to use force to maintain the status quo in Europe. This show of unity was short-lived, however. Britain, desperate to maintain superiority at sea, violated the spirit of the Stresa accords and sacrificed French security needs to make a separate naval agreement with Hitler. The pact allowed him to rebuild the German fleet to 35 percent of the British navy. Hitler had taken a major step toward his goal without provoking serious opposition. Italy's expansionist ambitions in Africa, however, soon brought it into conflict with the Western powers.

Italy Attacks Ethiopia

In October 1935, Mussolini, using a border incident as an excuse, attacked Ethiopia. This attack made the impotence of the League of Nations and the timidity of the Allies clear. Mussolini's purposes were to avenge a humiliating defeat that the Italians had suffered in Ethiopia in 1896, to restore Roman imperial glory, and, perhaps, to distract Italian public opinion from domestic problems.

France and Britain were eager to appease Mussolini to offset the growing power of Germany. They were prepared to allow him the substance of conquest if he would maintain Ethiopia's formal independence. For Mussolini, however, the form was more important than the substance. His attack outraged opinion in the West, and the French and British governments were forced to at least appear to resist.

HITLER DESCRIBES HIS GOALS IN FOREIGN POLICY

From his early career, Hitler had certain long-term general views and goals. They were set forth in his Mein Kampf (My Struggle), *which appeared in 1925 and called for uniting the German* Volk *(people), more land for the Germans, and contempt for such "races" as Slavs and Jews. Here are some of Hitler's views about land.*

On what basic principle is Hitler's policy founded? How does he justify his plans for expansion? Why is he hostile to France and Russia? Why does Hitler claim every man has a right to own farmland? Was that a practical goal for Germany in the 1930s? Could Hitler have achieved his goals without a major war?

The National Socialist movement must strive to eliminate the disproportion between our population and our area—viewing this latter as a source of food as well as a basis for power politics—between our historical past and the hopelessness of our present impotence....

The demand for restoration of the frontiers of 1914 is a political absurdity of such proportions and consequences as to make it seem a crime—quite aside from the fact that the Reich's frontiers in 1914 were anything but logical. For in reality they were neither complete in the sense of embracing the people of German nationality, nor sensible with regard to geomilitary expediency....

As opposed to this, we National Socialists must hold unflinchingly to our aim in foreign policy, namely, to secure for the German people the land and soil to which they are entitled on this earth....

The soil on which some day German generations of peasants can beget powerful sons will sanction the investment of the sons of today, and will some day acquit the responsible statesmen of blood-guilt and sacrifice of the people, even if they are persecuted by their contemporaries....

Much as all of us today recognize the necessity of a reckoning with France, it would remain ineffectual in the long run if it represented the whole of our aim in foreign policy. It can and will achieve meaning only if it offers the rear cover for an enlargement of our people's living space in Europe....

If we speak of soil in Europe today, we can primarily have in mind only Russia and her vassal border states....

See to it that the strength of our nation is founded, not on colonies, but on the soil of our European homeland. Never regard the Reich as secure unless for centuries to come it can give every scion of our people his own parcel of soil. Never forget that the most sacred right on this earth is a man's right to have earth to till with his own hands, and the most sacred sacrifice the blood that a man sheds for this earth.

The League of Nations condemned Italian aggression and, for the first time, voted economic sanctions. It imposed an arms embargo that limited loans and credits to, and imports from, Italy. To avoid alienating Mussolini, however, Britain and France refused to embargo oil, the one economic sanction that could have prevented Italian victory. Even more important, Britain allowed Italian troops and munitions to reach Ethiopia through the Suez Canal. The results of this policy were disastrous. The League of Nations and collective security were discredited, and Mussolini was alienated. He now turned to Germany, and by November 1, 1936, he spoke publicly of a Rome-Berlin **Axis**.

Remilitarization of the Rhineland

The Ethiopian affair also convinced Hitler that the Western powers were too timid to oppose him forcefully. On March 7, 1936, he took his greatest risk yet, sending a small armed force into the demilitarized Rhineland. This was a breach not only of the Versailles treaty, but also of the Locarno Agreements of 1925—agreements Germany had made voluntarily. It also removed a crucial element of French security. France and Britain had every right to resist, and the French especially had a claim to retain the only element of security left to them after the failure of the Allies to guarantee France's defense. Yet neither

This poster supports General Francisco Franco's Nationalists in the bloody Spanish Civil War, which lasted almost three years and claimed hundreds of thousands of lives. Courtesy of the Library of Congress

power did anything but register a feeble protest with the League of Nations. British opinion would not permit support for France, and the French would not act alone. Internal division and a military doctrine that stressed defense and shunned the offensive paralyzed them. A growing pacifism further weakened both countries.

In retrospect, the Allies lost a great opportunity in the Rhineland to stop Hitler before he became a serious menace. The failure of his gamble, taken against his generals' advice, might have led to his overthrow; at the least, it would have made German expansion to the east dangerous if not impossible. Nor is there reason to doubt that the French army could easily have routed the tiny German force in the Rhineland. As the German general Alfred Jodl (1890–1946) said some years later, "The French covering army would have blown us to bits."[1]

A Germany that was rapidly rearming and had a defensible western frontier presented a completely new problem to the Western powers. Their response was the policy of **appeasement**, based on the assumption that Germany had real grievances and that Hitler's goals were limited and ultimately acceptable. They set out to negotiate and make concessions before a crisis could lead to war.

Behind this approach was the universal dread of another war. Memories of the horrors of the last war were still vivid, and the prospect of aerial bombardment made the thought of a new war even more terrifying. A firmer policy, moreover, would have required rapid rearmament. British leaders especially were reluctant to pursue this path because of the expense and the widespread belief that the arms race had been a major cause of the last war. As Germany armed, the French huddled behind their newly constructed defensive wall, the Maginot Line, and the British hoped for the best.

The Spanish Civil War

The Spanish Civil War, which broke out in July 1936, made the new European alignment that found the Western democracies on one side and the fascist states on the other clearer. (See Map 28–1.) In 1931, the monarchy had collapsed, and Spain became a democratic republic. The new government followed a program of moderate reform that antagonized landowners, the Catholic Church, nationalists, and conservatives without satisfying the demands of peasants, workers, Catalán separatists, or radicals. Elections in February 1936 brought to power a Spanish Popular Front government ranging from republicans of the left to communists and anarchists. The losers, especially the Falangists, the Spanish fascists, would not accept defeat at the polls. In July, General Francisco Franco (1892–1975) led an army from Spanish Morocco against the republic.

Thus began the Spanish Civil War, which lasted almost three years, cost hundreds of thousands of lives, and provided a training ground for World War II. Germany and Italy supported Franco with troops, airplanes,

[1]Quoted in W. L. Shirer, *The Collapse of the Third Republic* (New York: Simon & Schuster, 1969), p. 281.

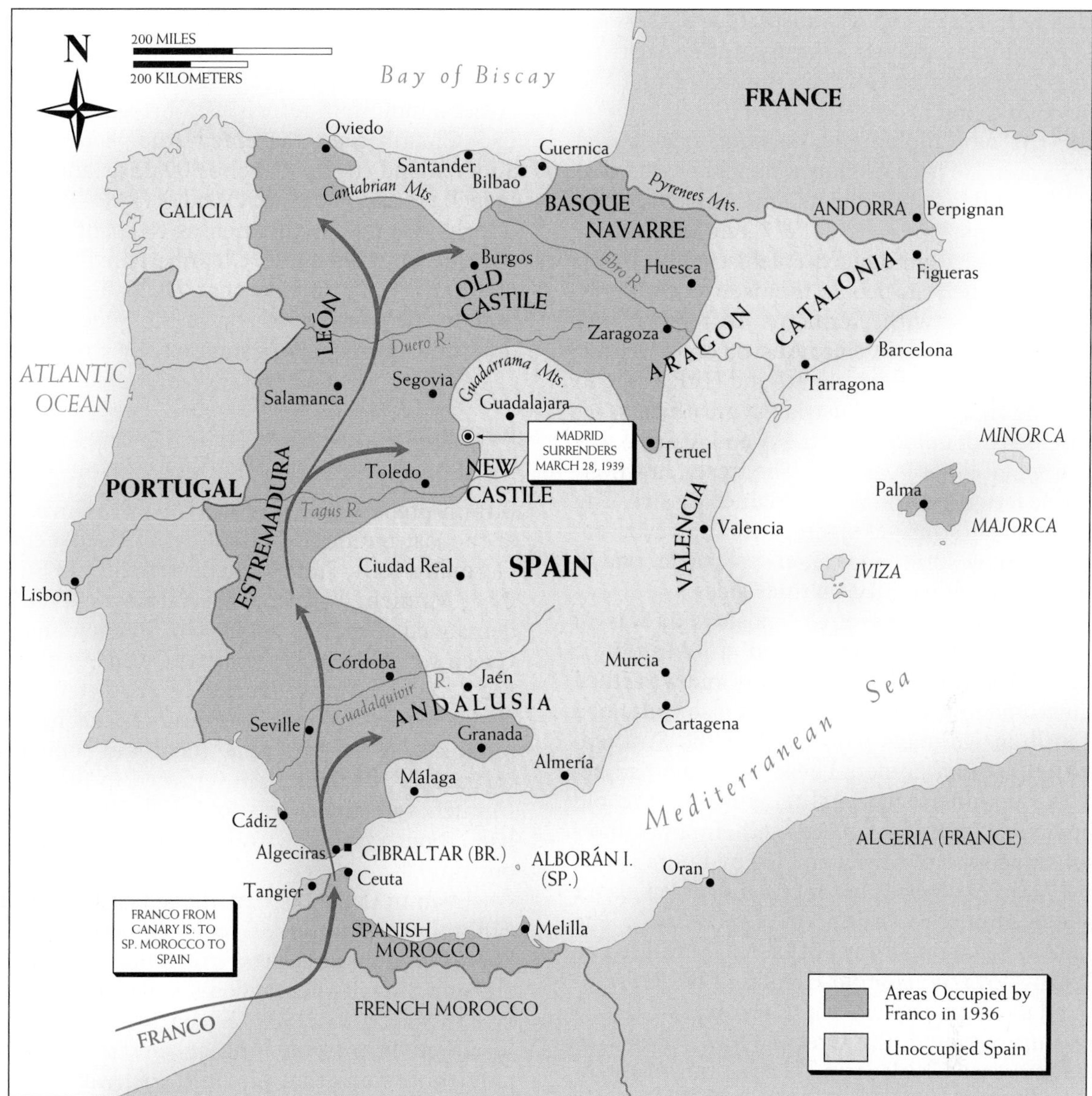

Map 28–1 **THE SPANISH CIVIL WAR, 1936–1939** The purple area on the map shows the large portion of Spain quickly overrun by Franco's insurgent armies during the first year of the war. In the next two years, progress came more slowly for the fascists as the war became a kind of international rehearsal for the coming World War II. Madrid's fall to Franco in the spring of 1939 had been preceded by that of Barcelona a few weeks earlier.

and supplies. The Soviet Union sent equipment and advisers to the republicans. Liberals and leftists from Europe and America volunteered to fight in the republican ranks against fascism.

The civil war, fought on blatantly ideological lines, profoundly affected world politics. It brought Germany and Italy closer together, leading to the Rome-Berlin Axis Pact in 1936. Japan joined the Axis powers in the Anti-Comintern Pact, ostensibly directed against international communism, but really a new and powerful diplomatic alliance. Western Europe, especially France, had a great interest in preventing Spain from falling into the hands of a fascist regime closely allied with Germany and Italy. Appeasement reigned, however. Although international law permitted the sale of weapons and munitions to the legitimate republican government, France and Britain forbade the export of war materials to either side, and the United States passed new neutrality legislation to the same end. When Barcelona fell to Franco early in 1939, the fascists had won effective control of Spain.

Austria and Czechoslovakia

Hitler made good use of his new friendship with Mussolini. He had always planned to annex his native Austria. In 1934, the Nazi Party in Austria assassinated the prime minister and tried to seize power. Mussolini had not yet allied with Hitler and was suspicious of German intentions. He quickly moved an army to the Austrian border, thus preventing German intervention and causing the coup to fail.

In 1938, the new diplomatic situation encouraged Hitler to try again. He perhaps hoped to achieve his goal by propaganda, bullying, and threats, but Austrian chancellor Kurt von Schuschnigg (1897–1977) refused to be intimidated. Schuschnigg announced a plebiscite for March 13, in which the Austrian people themselves could decide whether to unite with Germany. To forestall the plebiscite, Hitler sent his army into Austria on March 12. To his relief, Mussolini did not object, and Hitler rode to Vienna amid the cheers of his Austrian sympathizers.

The ***Anschluss***, or union of Germany and Austria, was another clear violation of Versailles. The treaty, however, was now a dead letter, and the West remained passive. The *Anschluss* had great strategic significance, however, because Germany now surrounded Czechoslovakia, one of the bulwarks of French security, on three sides.

In fact, the very existence of Czechoslovakia was an affront to Hitler. It was democratic and pro-Western; it had been created partly to check Germany and was allied both to France and to the Soviet Union. It also contained about 3.5 million Germans who lived in the Sudetenland, near the German border. These Germans had belonged to the dominant nationality group in the old Austro-Hungarian Empire and resented their new minority position. Supported by Hitler and led by Konrad Henlein (1898–1945), they made ever-increasing demands for privileges and autonomy within the Czech state. The Czechs made concessions, but Hitler really wanted to destroy Czechoslovakia. He told Henlein, "We must always demand so much that we can never be satisfied."[2]

As pressure mounted, the Czechs grew nervous. In May 1938, they received false rumors of an imminent attack by Germany and mobilized their army. The French, British, and Russians all warned they would support the Czechs. Hitler, who had not planned an attack at that time, was forced to publicly deny any designs on Czechoslovakia. The humiliation infuriated him, and he planned a military attack on the Czechs. The affair stiffened Czech resistance, but it frightened the French and British. The French, as had become the rule, deferred to British leadership. The British prime minister Neville Chamberlain (1869–1940) was determined not to allow Britain to go to war again. He pressed the Czechs to make concessions to Germany, but no concession was enough.

On September 12, 1938, Hitler made a provocative speech at the Nuremberg Nazi Party rally. His rhetoric led to rioting in the Sudetenland, and the Czechs declared martial law. German intervention seemed imminent. Chamberlain, aged sixty-nine, who had never flown before, made three flights to Germany between September 15 and September 29 in an attempt to appease Hitler at Czech expense and thus to avoid war. At Hitler's mountain retreat, Berchtesgaden, on September 15, Chamberlain accepted the separation of the Sudetenland from Czechoslovakia, and he and the French premier, Edouard Daladier (1884–1970), forced the Czechs to agree by threatening to abandon them if they did not. A week later, Chamberlain flew yet again to Germany, only to find that Hitler had raised his demands. He wanted cession of the Sudetenland in three days and immediate occupation by the German army.

Munich

Chamberlain returned to England, and France and Britain prepared for war. At Chamberlain's request and at the last moment, Mussolini proposed a conference of Germany, Italy, France, and Britain. It met on September 29 at Munich. Hitler received almost everything he had demanded. (See Map 28–2.) The Sudetenland, the key to Czech security, became part of Germany, thus depriving the Czechs of any chance of self-defense. In return, Hitler agreed to spare the rest of Czechoslovakia. He promised, "I have no more territorial demands to make in Europe." Chamberlain returned to England with the Munich agreement and told a cheering crowd that he had brought "peace with honour. I believe it is peace for our time."

Even in the short run, the appeasement of Hitler at Munich was a failure. Czechoslovakia did not survive. Soon Poland and Hungary tore more territory from it, and the Slovaks demanded a state of their own. Finally, on March 15, 1939, Hitler broke his promise and occupied Prague, putting an end to the Czech state and to illusions that his only goal was to restore Germans to the Reich. Defenders of the appeasers have argued that their policy bought valuable time in which the West could prepare for war, but the appeasers themselves, who thought they were achieving peace, did not make that argument, nor does the evidence support it.

If the French and the British had been willing to attack Germany from the west while the Czechs fought in their own defense, their efforts might have been successful. High officers in the German army were opposed to Hitler's risky policies and might have overthrown him. Even failing such developments, a war begun in October 1938 would have forced Hitler to fight without the friendly neutrality and material assistance of the Soviet Union—and without the resources of Eastern Europe that became available to him as a result of appeasement and Soviet cooperation. If, moreover, the West ever had a chance of concluding an alliance with the Soviet Union against Hitler, the exclusion of the Russians from Munich and the appeasement policy

[2]Quoted in Alan Bullock, *Hitler, a Study in Tyranny* (New York: Harper & Row, 1962), p. 443.

MAP EXPLORATION

Interactive map: To explore this map further, go to www.myhistorylab.com

Map 28–2 **PARTITIONS OF CZECHOSLOVAKIA AND POLAND, 1938–1939** The immediate background of World War II is found in the complex international drama unfolding on Germany's eastern frontier in 1938 and 1939. Germany's expansion inevitably meant the victimization of Austria, Czechoslovakia, and Poland. With the failure of the Western powers' appeasement policy and the signing of a German-Soviet pact, the stage for the war was set.

helped destroy it. Munich remains an example of short-sighted policy that helped bring on war in disadvantageous circumstances because of the very fear of war and the failure to prepare for it. (See "Compare & Connect: The Munich Settlement," pages 872–873.)

Hitler's occupation of Prague discredited appeasement in Britain. In the summer of 1939, a Gallup poll showed that three quarters of the British public believed it was worth a war to stop Hitler. Though Chamberlain himself had not lost all faith in his policy, he felt he had to respond to public opinion, and he responded to excess.

Poland was the next target of German expansion. In the spring of 1939, the Germans put pressure on Poland to restore the formerly German city of Danzig and to allow a railroad and a highway through the Polish Corridor to connect East Prussia with the rest of Germany. When the Poles would not yield, the usual propaganda campaign began, and the pressure mounted. On March 31, Chamberlain announced a Franco-British guarantee of Polish independence. Hitler appears to have expected to fight a war with Poland, but not with the Western allies, for he did not take their guarantee seriously. He had come to hold their leaders in contempt. He knew both countries were unprepared for war and that large segments of their populations opposed fighting for Poland.

Moreover, France and Britain had no means to get effective help to the Poles. The French, still dominated by the defensive mentality of the Maginot Line, had no intention of attacking Germany. The only way to defend Poland was to bring Russia into the alliance against Hitler, but a Russian alliance posed many problems. Each side was profoundly suspicious of the other. The French and the British were hostile to communism, and since Stalin's purge of the Red Army, they were skeptical of the

COMPARE AND CONNECT

The Munich Settlement

ON SEPTEMBER 29–30, 1938, Germany's dictator Adolf Hitler met with the British prime minister Neville Chamberlain, Italy's dictator Benito Mussolini, and France's prime minister Edouard Daladier to settle the fate of Czechoslovakia. The Czechs were not permitted to take part. It was the height of the Western democracies' effort to appease the dictators and resulted in the partition of Czechoslovakia, and the region called the Sudetenland was handed over to Germany, leaving the Czechs without a viable defense. Although Hitler promised to stop there, he took over the rest of the country without firing a shot on March 15, 1939. The following documents present opposite views on the achievement at Munich.

QUESTIONS

1. **Why did Chamberlain think the meeting at Munich was a success for Britain?**
2. **How would he defend his policy of appeasement?**
3. **What were Churchill's objections to the Munich agreement?**
4. **What critique would he make of the appeasement policy?**
5. **Who do you think was right? Why?**

I. Chamberlain's Evaluation

The following is an account of Chamberlain's return to England the day after the conference. He was greeted like a hero at the airport by a big crowd. Later that day he stood outside Number 10 Downing Street where again he read from the document and declared that he had brought back "peace with honour. I believe it is peace for our time."

Various shots of Mrs Chamberlain waving and shaking hands with crowds around Downing Street who are offering their support. M/S as Chamberlain's aeroplane finishes its return journey after the conference, taxis and comes to a stop at Heston. M/S of newsreel cameras filming his return from a roof at the aerodrome. M/S as Chamberlain emerges smiling from the door of a British Airways aeroplane to the cheers of the crowd. He shakes hands with a man waiting for him. L/S of crowds watching.

C/U as he makes a speech on the airfield—"The settlement of the Czech problem, which has now been achieved, is, in my view only the prelude to a larger settlement in which all Europe may find peace" (people cheer at this). "This morning I had another talk with the German Chancellor Herr Hitler and here is the paper which bears his name upon it as well as mine" (he holds paper up and waves it about, people cheer again). "Some of you perhaps have already heard what it contains, but I would just like to read it to you." (He reads—'We, the German Fuhrer and Chancellor and the British Prime Minister, have had a further meeting today and are agreed in recognising that the question of Anglo-German relations is of the first importance for the two countries, and for Europe. We regard the agreement signed last night and the Anglo-German naval agreement, as symbolic of the desire of our two peoples never to go to war with one another again' (everyone cheers) 'We are resolved that the method of consultation shall be the method adopted' (lots of "hear hears") 'to deal with any other questions that may concern our two countries, and we are determined to continue our efforts to remove possible sources of difference and thus to contribute to assure the peace of Europe.'" Everyone cheers and someone shouts "three cheers for Chamberlain" which they all do as he walks away and gets into the car. Everyone waves as he drives away.

Various shots as his car drives through the crowds to Buckingham Palace, people wave as he passes. M/S as King George VI and Queen Elizabeth (later the Queen Mother) come out onto the balcony of the palace with Neville Chamberlain and his wife. L/S as they wave and crowds wave back. L/S of cars and people blocking the street outside the palace.

Source: British Pathe.com Peace Four Power Conference 983.14.

II. Churchill's Response to Munich

In the parliamentary debate that followed the Munich conference at the end of September 1938, Winston Churchill was one of the few critics of what had been accomplished. In the following selections from his speech, he expresses his concerns.

I will begin by saying what everybody would like to ignore or forget but which must nevertheless be stated, namely, that we have sustained a total and unmitigated defeat, and that France has suffered even more than we have . . . .

We really must not waste time after all this long debate upon the difference between the positions reached at Berchtesgaden, at Godesberg and at Munich. They can be very simply epitomized if the House will permit me to vary the metaphor. One pound was demanded at the pistol's point. When it was given, £2 were demanded at the pistol's point. Finally, the dictator consented to take £1 17s. 6d. and the rest in promises of good will for the future. . . .

All is over. Silent, mournful, abandoned, broken, Czechoslovakia recedes into the darkness. She has suffered in every respect by her association with the Western democracies and with the League of Nations, of which she has always been an obedient servant. . . .

We have been reduced in these five years from a position of security so overwhelming and so unchallengeable that we never cared to think about it. We have been reduced from a position where the very word "war" was considered one which could be used only by persons qualifying for a lunatic asylum. We have been reduced from a position of safety and power—power to do good, power to be generous to a beaten foe, power to make terms with Germany, power to give her proper redress for her grievances, power to stop her arming if we chose, power to take any step in strength or mercy or justice which we thought right—reduced in five years from a position safe and unchallenged to where we stand now. . . .

The responsibility must rest with those who have had the undisputed control of our political affairs. They neither prevented Germany from rearming, nor did they rearm ourselves in time. They quarreled with Italy without saving Ethiopia. They exploited and discredited the vast institution of the League of Nations and they neglected to make alliances and combinations which might have repaired previous errors, and thus they left us in the hour of trial without adequate national defense or effective international security. . . .

We are in the presence of a disaster of the first magnitude which has befallen Great Britain and France. Do not let us blind ourselves to that. It must now be accepted that all the countries of Central and Eastern Europe will make the best terms they can with the triumphant Nazi power. The system of alliances in Central Europe upon which France has relied for her safety has been swept away, and I can see no means by which it can be reconstituted. The road down the Danube Valley to the Black Sea, the road which leads as far as Turkey, has been opened.

Source: "Churchill's Response to Munich" from *Blood, Sweat, and Tears* by Winston S. Churchill (New York: G.P. Putnam's Sons, 1941), pp. 55–56, 58, 60–61.

Agreement at Munich. On September 29–30, 1938, Hitler met with the leaders of Britain and France at Munich to decide the fate of Czechoslovakia. The Allied leaders abandoned the small democratic nation in a vain attempt to appease Hitler and avoid war. From left to right in the foreground: British Prime Minister Neville Chamberlain, French Prime Minister Edouard Daladier, Adolf Hitler, Benito Mussolini, and Italian Minister of Foreign Affairs (and Mussolini's son-in-law), Count Ciano. National Archives and Records Administration military value of a Russian alliance. Besides, the Russians could not help Poland without being given the right to enter Poland and Romania. Both nations, suspicious of Russian intentions—and with good reason—refused to grant these rights. As a result, Western negotiations for an alliance with Russia made little progress.

The Nazi-Soviet Pact

The Russians had at least equally good reason to hesitate. They resented being left out of the Munich agreement. The low priority that the West gave to negotiations with Russia, compared with the urgency with which Britain and France dealt with Hitler, annoyed them. The Russians feared, rightly, that the Western powers meant them to bear the burden of the war against Germany. As a result, they opened negotiations with Hitler, and on August 23, 1939, the world was shocked to learn of a Nazi-Soviet nonaggression pact.

The secret provisions of the pact, which were easily guessed and soon carried out, divided Poland between the two powers and allowed Russia to occupy the Baltic states and to take Bessarabia from Romania. The most bitter ideological enemies had become allies. Communist parties in the West changed their line overnight from ardently advocating resistance to Hitler to a policy of peace and quiet. Ideology gave way to political and military reality. The West offered the Russians immediate danger without much prospect of gain. Hitler offered Stalin short-term gain without immediate danger. There could be little doubt about Stalin's decision.

The Nazi-Soviet pact sealed the fate of Poland, and the Franco-British commitment guaranteed a general war. On September 1, 1939, the Germans invaded Poland. Two days later, Britain and France declared war on Germany. World War II had begun.

▼ World War II (1939–1945)

World War II was truly global. Fighting took place in Europe, North Africa, and Asia, on the Atlantic and the Pacific Oceans, and in the northern and southern hemispheres. The demand for the fullest exploitation of material and human resources for increased production, the use of blockades, and the intensive bombing of civilian targets made the war of 1939 even more "total"—that is, comprehensive and intense—than that of 1914.

The German Conquest of Europe

The German attack on Poland produced swift success. The new style of "lightning warfare," or ***blitzkrieg***, employed fast-moving, massed armored columns supported by airpower. The Poles had few planes and fewer tanks, and their defense soon collapsed. The speed of the German victory astonished the Russians, who hastened to collect their share of the booty before Hitler could deprive them of it.

On September 17, Russia invaded Poland from the east, dividing the country with the Germans. The Red Army then occupied the encircled Baltic countries. By July 1940, Estonia, Latvia, and Lithuania had become puppet republics within the Soviet Union. In June 1940, the Russians forced Romania to cede Bessarabia. In November 1939, the Russians invaded Finland, but the Finns resisted fiercely for six months. Although they were finally worn down and compelled to yield territory and bases to Russia, the Finns remained independent. Russian expansionism and the poor performance of the Red Army in Finland may well have encouraged Hitler to invade the Soviet Union in June 1941, just twenty-two months after the 1939 treaty.

Until the spring of 1940, the western front was quiet. The French remained behind the Maginot Line while Hitler and Stalin swallowed Poland and the Baltic states. Britain rearmed hastily, and the British navy blockaded

THE COMING OF WORLD WAR II

1919 (June)	The Versailles Treaty
1923 (January)	France occupies the Ruhr
1925 (October)	The Locarno Agreements
1931 (Spring)	Onset of the Great Depression in Europe
1931 (September)	Japan occupies Manchuria
1933 (January)	Hitler comes to power
1933 (October)	Germany withdraws from the League of Nations
1935 (March)	Hitler renounces disarmament, starts an air force, and begins conscription
1935 (October)	Mussolini attacks Ethiopia
1936 (March)	Germany reoccupies and remilitarizes the Rhineland
1936 (July)	Outbreak of the Spanish Civil War
1936 (October)	Formation of the Rome-Berlin Axis
1938 (March)	*Anschluss* with Austria
1938 (September)	The Munich conference and the partition of Czechoslovakia
1939 (March)	Hitler occupies Prague; France and Great Britain guarantee Polish independence
1939 (August)	The Nazi-Soviet pact
1939 (September 1)	Germany invades Poland
1939 (September 3)	Britain and France declare war on Germany

Adolf Hitler receives news of Marshal Pétain's request for an armistice following the fall of Paris in June 1940. National Archives and Records Administration

Germany. Cynics in the West called it the phony war, or *Sitzkrieg*, but Hitler shattered the stillness in the spring of 1940. In April, without warning and with swift success, the Germans invaded Denmark and Norway. Hitler's northern front was secure, and he now had both air and naval bases closer to Britain. A month later, a combined land and air attack struck Belgium, the Netherlands, and Luxembourg. German airpower and armored divisions were irresistible. The Dutch surrendered in a few days; the Belgians, though aided by the French and the British, gave up less than two weeks later.

The British and French armies in Belgium were forced to flee to the English Channel to seek escape on the beaches of Dunkirk. The heroic efforts of hundreds of Britons manning small boats saved more than 200,000 British and 100,000 French soldiers. Casualties, however, were high, and valuable equipment was abandoned.

The Maginot Line ran from Switzerland to the Belgian frontier. Until 1936, the French had expected the Belgians to continue the fortifications along their German border. After Hitler remilitarized the Rhineland without opposition, the Belgians lost faith in their French alliance and proclaimed their neutrality, leaving the Maginot Line exposed on its left flank. Hitler's swift advance through Belgium, therefore, circumvented France's main line of defense.

The French army, poorly and hesitantly led by aged generals who did not understand how to use tanks and planes, collapsed. Mussolini, eager to claim the spoils of victory when he thought it was safe to do so, invaded southern France on June 10. Less than a week later, the new French government, under the ancient hero of Verdun, Marshal Henri Philippe Pétain (1856–1951), asked for an armistice. In two months Hitler had accomplished what Germany had failed to achieve in four years of bitter fighting in the previous war.

The Battle of Britain

The fall of France left Britain isolated, and Hitler expected the British to come to terms. He was prepared to allow Britain to retain its empire in return for a free hand for Germany on the Continent. The British had never been willing to accept such an arrangement and had fought the long and difficult war against Napoleon to prevent a single power from dominating the Continent. If there was any chance the British would consider such terms, it disappeared when Winston Churchill (1874–1965) replaced Chamberlain as prime minister in May 1940.

Churchill had been an early and forceful critic of Hitler, the Nazis, and the policy of appeasement. He was a descendant and biographer of the duke of Marlborough

(1650–1722), who had fought Louis XIV in the eighteenth century. Churchill's sense of history, his feeling for British greatness, and his hatred of tyranny and love of freedom made him reject any compromise with Hitler. His skill as a speaker and a writer enabled him to inspire the British people with his own courage and determination and to undertake what seemed a hopeless fight. Hitler and his allies, including the Soviet Union, controlled all of Europe. Japan was having its way in Asia. The United States was neutral, dominated by isolationist sentiment, and determined to avoid involvement outside the western hemisphere.

One of Churchill's greatest achievements was establishing a close relationship with the American president Franklin D. Roosevelt (1882–1945). Roosevelt found ways to help the British despite strong political opposition. In 1940 and 1941, before the United States was at war, America sent military supplies, traded badly needed warships for leases on British naval bases, and even convoyed ships across the Atlantic to help the British survive.

As weeks passed and Britain remained defiant, Hitler was forced to contemplate an invasion, and that required control of the air. The first strikes by the German air force (***Luftwaffe***), directed against the airfields and fighter planes in southeast England, began in August 1940. If these attacks had continued, Germany might have gained control of the air and, with it, the chance of a successful invasion.

In early September, however, seeking revenge for some British bombing raids on German cities, the *Luftwaffe* switched its main attacks to London. For two months, it bombed London every night. Much of the city was destroyed, and about 15,000 people were killed. The theories of victory through airpower alone, however, proved false. Casualties were much fewer than expected, and morale was not shattered. In fact, the bombings united the British people and made them more resolute.

In August 1941, President Franklin Roosevelt and Prime Minister Winston Churchill met at sea and agreed on a broad program of liberal peace aims, called the Atlantic Charter, in the spirit of Woodrow Wilson's Fourteen Points (see page 897). The Granger Collection

The Royal Air Force (RAF) inflicted heavy losses on the *Luftwaffe*. Aided by the newly developed radar and excellent communications, the British Spitfire and Hurricane fighter planes destroyed more than twice as many enemy planes as the RAF lost. Hitler had lost the Battle of Britain in the air and was forced to abandon his plans for invasion.

The German Attack on Russia

The defeat of Russia and the conquest of the Ukraine to provide *Lebensraum*, or "living space," for the German people had always been a major goal for Hitler. Even before the assault on Britain, he had informed his staff of his intention to attack Russia as soon as conditions were favorable. In December 1940, even while the bombing of England continued, he ordered his generals to prepare to invade Russia by May 15, 1941. (See Map 28–3.) He apparently thought a *blitzkrieg* victory in the east would also destroy the British hope of resistance.

Operation Barbarossa, the code name for the invasion of Russia, was aimed to destroy Russia before winter could set in. Success depended, in part, on an early start, but here Hitler's Italian alliance proved costly. Mussolini was jealous of Hitler's success and annoyed by how the German dictator had treated him. His invasion of France was a fiasco, even though the Germans were simultaneously crushing the main French forces. Hitler did not allow Mussolini to annex French territory in Europe or North Africa. Mussolini instead attacked the British in Egypt and drove them back some sixty miles. Encouraged by this success, he also invaded Greece from his base in Albania (which he had seized in 1939). As he told his son-in-law, Count Ciano: "Hitler always faces me with a fait accompli. This time I am going to pay him back in his own coin. He will find out in the newspapers that I have occupied Greece."[3]

In North Africa, however, the British counterattacked and invaded Libya. The Greeks themselves pushed into Albania. In March 1941, the British sent help to the Greeks, and Hitler was forced to divert his attention to the Balkans and Africa. General Erwin Rommel (1891–1944), later to earn the title of "Desert Fox," went to Africa and soon drove the British back into Egypt. In the Balkans, the German army swiftly occupied Yugoslavia and crushed Greek resistance. The price, however, was a delay of six weeks. The diversion Mussolini's vanity caused proved to be costly the following winter in the Russian campaign.

Operation Barbarossa was launched against Russia on June 22, 1941, and it almost succeeded. Despite their

[3]Quoted in Gordon Wright, *The Ordeal of Total War, 1939–1945* (New York: Harper & Row, 1968), pp. 35–36.

Map 28–3 **AXIS EUROPE, 1941** On the eve of the German invasion of the Soviet Union, the Germany-Italy Axis bestrode most of Western Europe by annexation, occupation, or alliance—from Norway and Finland in the north to Greece in the south and from Poland to France. Britain, the Soviets, a number of insurgent groups, and, finally, America, had before them the long struggle of conquering this Axis "fortress Europe."

deep suspicion of Germany (and the excuse apologists for the Soviet Union later offered that the Nazi-Soviet pact was meant to give Russia time to prepare), the Russians were taken quite by surprise. Stalin appears to have panicked. He had not fortified his frontier, nor did he order his troops to withdraw when attacked. In the first two days, the Germans destroyed 2,000 Russian planes on the ground. By November, the German army stood at the gates of Leningrad, on the outskirts of Moscow, and on the Don River. Of the 4.5 million troops with which the Russians had begun the fighting, they had lost 2.5 million; of their 15,000 tanks, only 700 were left. Moscow was in panic, and a German victory seemed imminent.

Yet the Germans could not deliver the final blow. In August, they delayed their advance while Hitler decided strategy. The German general staff wanted to take Moscow before winter. This plan probably would have brought victory. Unlike in Napoleon's time, Moscow was the hub of the Russian transportation system. Hitler, however, diverted a significant force to the south. By the time he was ready to return to the offensive near

Moscow, it was too late. Winter devastated the German army, which was not equipped to face it.

Given precious time, Stalin restored order and built defenses for the city. Even more importantly, troops arrived from Siberia, where they had been placed to check a possible Japanese attack. In November and December, the Russians counterattacked. The *blitzkrieg* had turned into a war of attrition, and the Germans began to have nightmares of duplicating Napoleon's retreat.

Hitler's Plans for Europe

Hitler often spoke of the "new order" that he meant to impose after he had established his **Third Reich** (empire) throughout Europe. The first two German empires were those of Charlemagne in the ninth century and Bismarck in the nineteenth. Hitler predicted that his own would last for a thousand years. If his organization of Germany before the war is a proper guide, he had no single plan of government but relied on intuition and pragmatism. His organization of a conquered Europe had the same patchwork characteristics. Some conquered territory was annexed to Germany, some was not annexed but administered directly by German officials, and other lands were nominally autonomous but ruled by puppet governments.

Hitler's regime was probably unmatched in history for carefully planned terror and inhumanity. His plan of giving *Lebensraum* to the Germans was to be accomplished at the expense of people he deemed to be inferior. Hitler established colonies of Germans in parts of Poland, driving the local people from their land and employing them as cheap, virtually slave labor. He had similar plans on an even greater scale for Russia. The Russians would be driven back to Central Asia and Siberia. Frontier colonies of German war veterans would keep them in check while Germans settled European Russia.

Hitler's long-range plans included germanization as well as colonization. In lands people racially akin to the Germans inhabited, like the Scandinavian countries, the Netherlands, and Switzerland, the German nation would absorb the natives. Such peoples would be reeducated and purged of dissenting elements, but there would be little or no colonization. Hitler even had plans to adopt selected people from the lesser races into the master race. For example, the Nazis planned to bring half a million Ukrainian girls to Germany as servants and find German husbands for them.

Hitler regarded the conquered lands as a source of plunder. From Eastern Europe, he removed everything useful, including entire industries. In Russia and Poland, the Germans simply confiscated the land itself. In the West, the conquered countries had to support the occupying army at a rate several times above the real cost. The Germans used the profits to buy up everything desirable, stripping the conquered peoples of most necessities. The Nazis were frank about their policies. One of Hitler's high officials said, "Whether nations live in prosperity or starve to death interests me only insofar as we need them as slaves for our culture."[4]

Japan and the United States Enter the War

The American government was pro-British. The assistance that Roosevelt gave Britain would have justified a German declaration of war. Hitler, however, held back. The U.S. government might not have overcome isolationist sentiment and entered the war in the Atlantic if war had not been thrust on America in the Pacific.

Since the Japanese conquest of Manchuria in 1931, American policy toward Japan had been suspicious and unfriendly. The outbreak of the war in Europe emboldened the Japanese to accelerate their drive to dominate Asia. They allied themselves with Germany and Italy, made a treaty of neutrality with the Soviet Union, and forced defeated France to give them bases in Indochina. They also continued their war in China and planned to gain control of Malaya and the East Indies (Indonesia) at the expense of beleaguered Britain and the conquered Netherlands. The only barrier to Japanese expansion was the United States.

The Americans had temporized, unwilling to cut off vital supplies of oil and other materials for fear of provoking a Japanese attack on Southeast Asia and the East Indies. The Japanese occupation of Indochina in July 1941 changed that policy, which had already begun to stiffen. The United States froze Japanese assets and cut off oil supplies; the British and Dutch did the same. Japanese plans for expansion could not continue without the conquest of the Indonesian oil fields and Malayan rubber and tin.

In October, a war faction led by General Hideki Tojo (1885–1948) took power in Japan and decided to risk a war rather than yield. On Sunday morning, December 7, 1941, while Japanese representatives were in Washington to discuss a settlement, Japan launched an air attack on Pearl Harbor, Hawaii, the chief American naval base in the Pacific. The technique was similar to the one Japan had used against the Russian fleet at Port Arthur in 1904, and it caught the Americans equally by surprise. The attack destroyed much of the American fleet and many airplanes. The American capacity to wage war in the Pacific was negated for the time being. The next day, the United States and Britain declared war on Japan. Three days later, Germany and Italy declared war on the United States.

[4]Quoted in Wright, *The Ordeal of Total War*, p. 117.

The successful Japanese attack on the American base at Pearl Harbor in Hawaii on December 7, 1941, together with simultaneous attacks on other Pacific bases, brought the United States into war against the Axis powers. This picture shows the battleships USS *West Virginia* and USS *Tennessee* in flames as a small boat rescues a man from the water. U.S. Army Photo

The Tide Turns

The potential power of the United States was enormous, but America was ill prepared for war. The army was tiny, inexperienced, and poorly supplied. American industry was not ready for war. The Japanese swiftly captured Guam, Wake Island, and the Philippine Islands. By the spring of 1942, they had conquered Hong Kong, Malaya, Burma, and the Dutch East Indies. They controlled the southwest Pacific as far as New Guinea and were poised for an attack on Australia. It seemed that nothing could stop them.

In 1942, the Germans also advanced deeper into Russia, while in Africa Rommel drove the British back into Egypt until they stopped him at El Alamein, only seventy miles from Alexandria. Relations between the democracies and their Soviet ally were not close. German submarine warfare was threatening British supplies. The Allies were being thrown back on every front, and the future looked bleak.

The first good news for the Allied cause in the Pacific came in the spring of 1942. A naval battle in the Coral Sea sank many Japanese ships and gave security to Australia. A month later, the United States defeated the Japanese in a fierce air and naval battle off Midway Island. This victory blunted the chance of another assault on Hawaii and did enough damage to halt the Japanese advance. Soon American marines landed on Guadalcanal in the Solomon Islands and began to reverse the momentum of the war. The war in the Pacific was far from over, but the check to Japan allowed the Allies to concentrate their efforts on Europe.

More than twenty nations located all over the world were opposed to the Axis powers. The main combatants, however, were Great Britain, the Soviet Union, and the United States. The two Western democracies

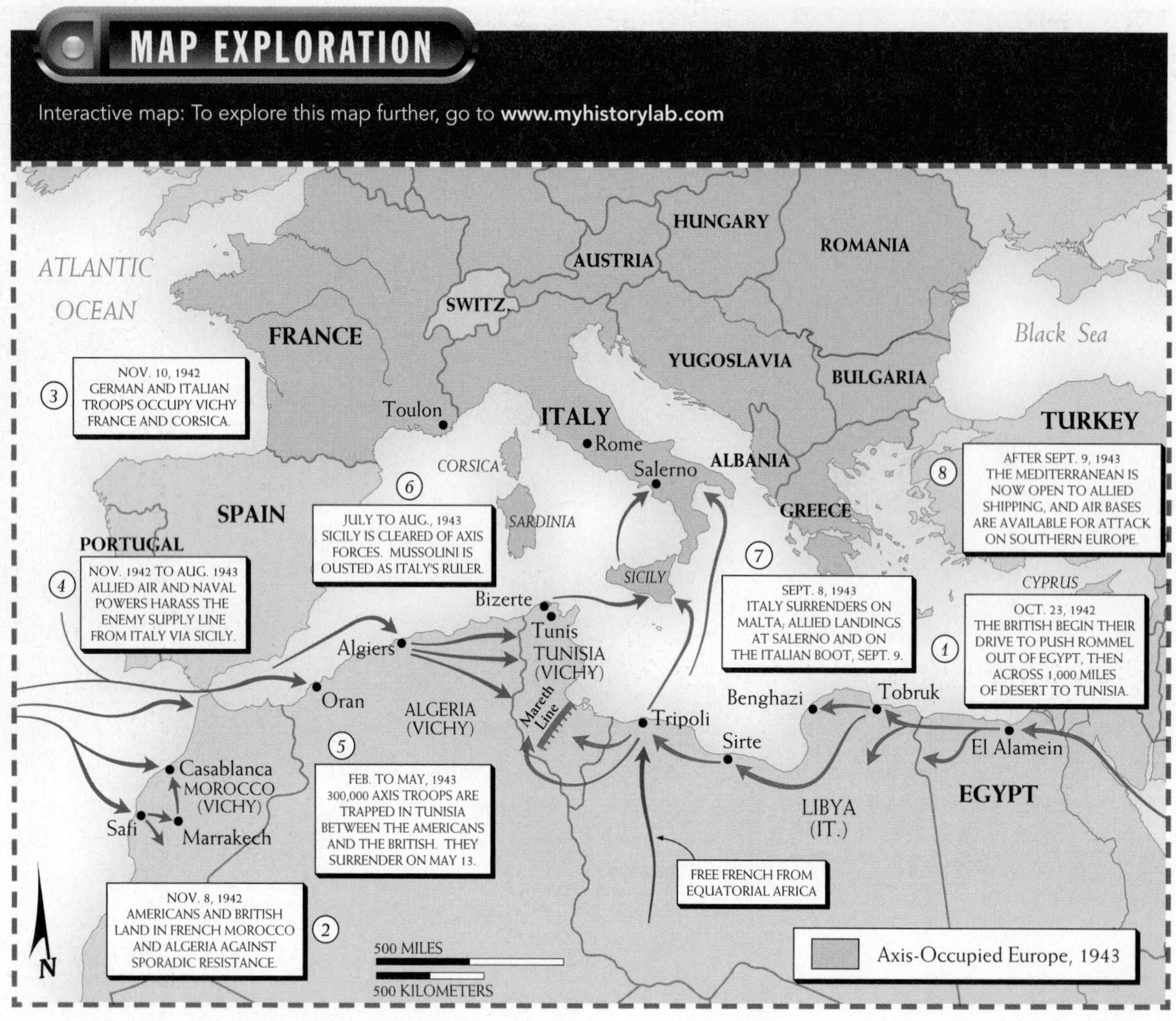
MAP EXPLORATION
Interactive map: To explore this map further, go to www.myhistorylab.com
ATLANTIC OCEAN
FRANCE
SWITZ.
AUSTRIA
HUNGARY
ROMANIA
YUGOSLAVIA
BULGARIA
Black Sea
TURKEY
ITALY
Toulon
Rome
Salerno
ALBANIA
GREECE
CORSICA
SARDINIA
SICILY
SPAIN
PORTUGAL
CYPRUS
③ NOV. 10, 1942 GERMAN AND ITALIAN TROOPS OCCUPY VICHY FRANCE AND CORSICA.
④ NOV. 1942 TO AUG. 1943 ALLIED AIR AND NAVAL POWERS HARASS THE ENEMY SUPPLY LINE FROM ITALY VIA SICILY.
⑥ JULY TO AUG., 1943 SICILY IS CLEARED OF AXIS FORCES. MUSSOLINI IS OUSTED AS ITALY'S RULER.
⑦ SEPT. 8, 1943 ITALY SURRENDERS ON MALTA; ALLIED LANDINGS AT SALERNO AND ON THE ITALIAN BOOT, SEPT. 9.
⑧ AFTER SEPT. 9, 1943 THE MEDITERRANEAN IS NOW OPEN TO ALLIED SHIPPING, AND AIR BASES ARE AVAILABLE FOR ATTACK ON SOUTHERN EUROPE.
① OCT. 23, 1942 THE BRITISH BEGIN THEIR DRIVE TO PUSH ROMMEL OUT OF EGYPT, THEN ACROSS 1,000 MILES OF DESERT TO TUNISIA.
Bizerte
Tunis
TUNISIA (VICHY)
Algiers
Oran
ALGERIA (VICHY)
Mareth Line
Tripoli
Benghazi
Tobruk
Sirte
El Alamein
EGYPT
LIBYA (IT.)
Casablanca
MOROCCO (VICHY)
Safi
Marrakech
⑤ FEB. TO MAY, 1943 300,000 AXIS TROOPS ARE TRAPPED IN TUNISIA BETWEEN THE AMERICANS AND THE BRITISH. THEY SURRENDER ON MAY 13.
FREE FRENCH FROM EQUATORIAL AFRICA
NOV. 8, 1942 AMERICANS AND BRITISH LAND IN FRENCH MOROCCO AND ALGERIA AGAINST SPORADIC RESISTANCE. ②
500 MILES
500 KILOMETERS
N
Axis-Occupied Europe, 1943

Map 28–4 **NORTH AFRICAN CAMPAIGNS, 1942–1945** Control of North Africa would give the Allies access to Europe from the south. The map illustrates this theater of the war from Morocco to Egypt and the Suez Canal.

cooperated to an unprecedented degree, but suspicion between them and the Soviet Union continued. The Russians accepted all the aid they could get. Nevertheless, they did not trust their allies, complained of inadequate help, and demanded that the democracies open a "second front" on the mainland of Europe.

In 1942, American preparation and production were inadequate to invade Europe. German submarines made it dangerous to ship the vast numbers of troops such an invasion needed across the Atlantic. Not until 1944 were conditions right for the invasion, but in the meantime other developments forecast the doom of the Axis. (See "Encountering the Past: Rosie the Riveter and American Women in the War Effort.")

Allied Landings in Africa, Sicily, and Italy In November 1942, an Allied force landed in French North Africa. (See Map 28–4.) Even before that landing, after stopping Rommel at El Alamein, British field marshal Bernard Montgomery (1887–1976) had begun a drive to the west. Now, the Americans pushed eastward through Morocco and Algeria. The two armies caught the German army between them in Tunisia and crushed it. The Allies now controlled the Mediterranean and could attack southern Europe.

In July and August 1943, the Allies took Sicily. A coup toppled Mussolini, but the Germans occupied Italy. The Allies landed in Italy, and Marshal Pietro Badoglio (1871–1956), the leader of the new Italian government, declared war on Germany. Churchill had spoken of Italy as the "soft underbelly" of the Axis, but the Germans there resisted fiercely. Still, the need to defend Italy weakened the Germans on other fronts.

Battle of Stalingrad The Russian campaign became especially demanding. In the summer of 1942, the Germans resumed the offensive on all fronts but were unable to get far except in the south. (See Map 28–5, page 882.) Their goal was the oil fields near the Caspian Sea. Stalingrad, on the Volga, was a key point on the flank of the German army in the south. Hitler was determined to take the city, and Stalin was equally

ROSIE THE RIVETER AND AMERICAN WOMEN IN THE WAR EFFORT

THE INDUCTION OF millions of men into the armed forces created a demand for new workers, especially in the defense industries. In response, millions of women entered the labor force, some of them taking jobs in defense plants to do work only men usually did. Economic pressures caused by the Great Depression of the 1930s had already brought many more women into the workforce than had been common before. Most came from poor families and worked in white-collar jobs to support themselves or to help their families eke out a living. Even so, the heavy burden of housework and the widespread hostility to women working outside the home kept most women at home.

America's entry into the war changed things quickly. The need for vast amounts of equipment to wage the war called for and attracted new groups to seek work in the many enlarged and new factories. African Americans from the south came to northern and western cities to seek well-paying jobs, and women, too, came forward in greater numbers than ever before. Prejudices of various kinds had kept them from many opportunities, but the needs of war were too important. In October 1942, President Roosevelt made the new situation clear: "In some communities employers dislike to hire women. In others they are reluctant to hire Negroes. We can no longer afford to indulge such prejudice."

Many women changed jobs to work in the defense industries; others entered the workforce for the first time, lured less by wages than by patriotism. Their brothers and boyfriends were risking their lives for their country and its ideals of freedom and democracy. They were eager to do their part to support them, to be, in the words of a current song, the woman "behind the man behind the gun." Another popular song, "Rosie the Riveter," told of a young woman working in an aircraft factory to provide protection for her boyfriend in the Marines. Rosie became one of the best known symbols of the war effort when she appeared on the cover of the *Saturday Evening Post* in a painting by Norman Rockwell. With her rivet gun on her lap she stamps on a copy of Hitler's *Mein Kampf*, the hated symbol of the evil enemy.

How did the war change women's place in American society?

What attitudes did it need to overcome?

Rosie the Riveter was one of the best known symbols of the U.S. war effort in World War II.

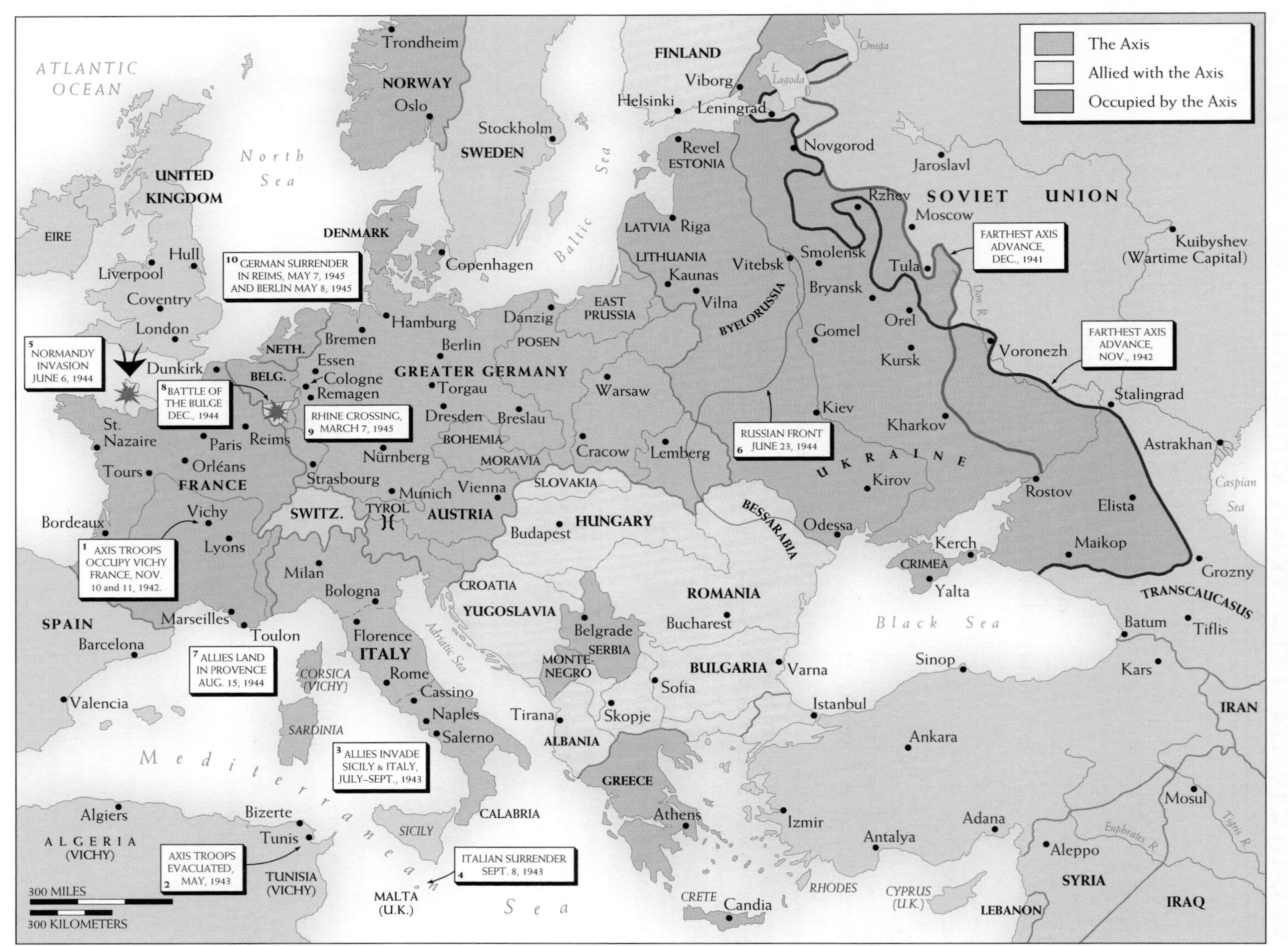

Map 28–5 **Defeat of the Axis in Europe, 1942–1945** Here are some of the major steps in the progress toward Allied victory against Axis Europe. From the south through Italy, the west through France, and the east through Russia, the Allies gradually conquered the Continent to bring the war in Europe to a close.

In the battle of Stalingrad, Russian troops contested every street and building. Although the city was all but destroyed in the fighting and Russian casualties were enormous, the German army in the east never recovered from the defeat it suffered there. Hulton Archives/Getty Images, Inc.

determined to hold it. The Battle of Stalingrad raged for months with unexampled ferocity. The Russians lost more men in this one battle than the Americans lost in combat during the entire war, but their heroic defense prevailed. Because Hitler again overruled his generals and would not allow a retreat, he lost an entire German army at Stalingrad.

Stalingrad marked the turning point of the Russian campaign. Thereafter, the Americans provided material help. Even more importantly, increased production from their own industry allowed the Russians to gain and keep the offensive. As the Germans' resources dwindled, the Russians inexorably advanced westward.

Strategic Bombing In 1943, the Allies also gained ground in production and logistics. The industrial might of the United States began to come into full force, and new technology and tactics reduced the submarine menace.

In the same year, the American and British air forces began a series of massive bombardments of Germany by night and day. The Americans were more committed to the theory of "precision bombing" of military and industrial targets vital to the enemy war effort, so they flew the day missions. The British considered precision bombing impossible and therefore useless. They preferred indiscriminate "area bombing," which they could do at night, to destroy the morale of the German people. Neither kind of bombing had much effect on the war until 1944, when the Americans introduced long-range fighters that could protect the bombers and allow accurate missions by day.

By 1945, the Allies could bomb at will. Concentrated attacks on industrial targets, especially communication centers and oil refineries, did extensive damage and helped shorten the war. Terror bombing continued, too, with no useful result. The bombardment of Dresden in February 1945 was especially savage and destructive. It was much debated within the British government and has raised moral questions since. Whatever else it accomplished, the aerial war over Germany took a heavy toll of the German air force and diverted German resources from other military purposes.

The Defeat of Nazi Germany

On June 6, 1944 ("D-Day"), American, British, and Canadian troops landed in force on the coast of Normandy. The "second front" was opened. General Dwight D. Eisenhower (1890–1969), the commander of the Allied armies, faced a difficult problem. The European coast was heavily fortified. Amphibious assaults, moreover, are especially vulnerable to wind and weather. Success depended on meticulous planning, heavy bombing, and feints to mask the point of attack. The German defense was strong, but the Allies established a beachhead and then broke out of it. In mid-August, the Allies also landed in southern France. By the beginning of September, France had been liberated.

The Battle of the Bulge All went smoothly until December, when the Germans launched a counterattack in Belgium and Luxembourg through the Ardennes Forest. Because the Germans pushed forward into the Allied line, this was called the Battle of the Bulge. Although the Allies suffered heavy losses, the Bulge was the last gasp for the Germans in the West. The Allies crossed the Rhine in March 1945, and German resistance crumbled. This time there could be no doubt the Germans had lost the war on the battlefield.

The Capture of Berlin In the east, the Russians swept forward no less swiftly, despite fierce German resistance. By March 1945, they were near Berlin. Because the Allies insisted on unconditional surrender, the Germans fought on until May. Hitler committed suicide in an underground bunker in Berlin on April 30, 1945. The Russians occupied Berlin by agreement with their Western allies. The Third Reich lasted only a dozen years instead of the thousand Hitler had predicted.

American soldiers land at Omaha Beach in Normandy on D-Day, June 6, 1944. Courtesy of the Library of Congress

Fall of the Japanese Empire

The war in Europe ended on May 8, 1945, and by then, victory over Japan was also in sight. The original Japanese attack on the United States had been a calculated risk against the odds. Japan was inherently weaker than the United States. The longer the war lasted, the more American superiority in industrial production and population counted.

Americans Recapture the Pacific Islands In 1943, the American forces, still small in number, began a campaign of "island hopping." They did not try to recapture every Pacific island the Japanese held but selected major bases and strategic sites along the enemy supply line. (See Map 28–6.) Starting from the Solomon Islands, they moved northeast toward Japan itself. By June 1944, they had reached the Mariana Islands, usable as bases to bomb the Japanese in the Philippines, China, and Japan itself.

In October of the same year, the Americans recaptured most of the Philippines and drove the Japanese fleet back into its home waters. In 1945, Iwo Jima and Okinawa fell, despite fierce Japanese resistance that included kamikaze attacks, suicide missions in which pilots deliberately flew their explosive-filled planes into American warships. From these new bases, closer to Japan, the Americans launched a terrible wave of bombings that destroyed Japanese industry and disabled the Japanese navy. Still the Japanese government, dominated by a military clique, refused to surrender.

Confronted with Japan's determination, the Americans made plans for a frontal assault on the Japanese homeland. They calculated it might cost a million American casualties and even greater losses for the Japanese. At this point, science and technology presented the Americans with another choice.

The Atomic Bomb Since early in the war, a secret program had been in progress. Its staff, many of whom were exiles from Hitler's Europe, was working to use atomic energy for military purposes. On August 6, 1945, an American plane dropped an atomic bomb on the Japanese city of Hiroshima. The city was destroyed, and more than 70,000 of its 200,000 residents were killed. Two days later, the Soviet Union declared war on Japan and invaded Manchuria. The next day, a

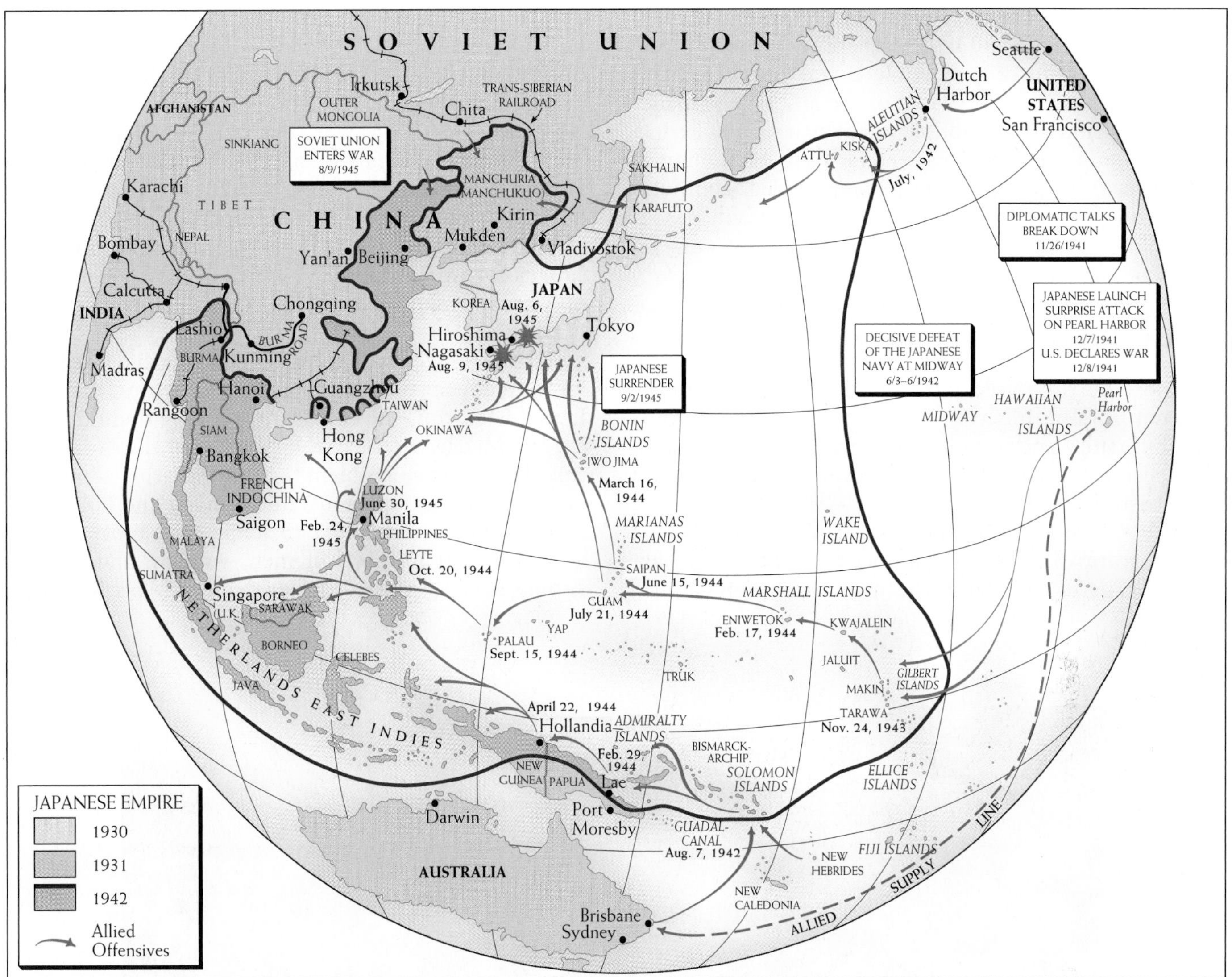

Map 28–6 **WORLD WAR II IN THE PACIFIC** As in Europe, the Pacific war involved Allied recapture of areas that had been quickly taken earlier by the enemy. The enormous area represented by the map shows the initial expansion of Japanese holdings to cover half the Pacific and its islands, as well as huge sections of eastern Asia, and the long struggle to push the Japanese back to their homeland and defeat them by the summer of 1945.

second atomic bomb hit Nagasaki. Even then, the Japanese cabinet was prepared to face an invasion rather than give up.

The unprecedented intervention of Emperor Hirohito (r. 1926–1989) finally forced the government to surrender on August 14 on the condition that Japan retain the emperor. Although the Allies had continued to insist on unconditional surrender, President Harry S. Truman (1884–1972), who had come to office on April 12, 1945, on the death of Franklin D. Roosevelt, accepted the condition. Peace was formally signed aboard the USS *Missouri* in Tokyo Bay on September 2, 1945.

Revulsion at the use of atomic bombs, as well as hindsight arising from the Cold War, have made the decision to use the bomb against Japanese cities controversial. Some have suggested the bombings were unnecessary to win the war and their main purpose was to frighten the Russians into a more cooperative attitude after the war. Others have emphasized the bureaucratic, almost automatic nature of the decision, once it had been decided to develop the bomb. To the decision makers and their contemporaries, however, matters were simpler. The bomb was a way to end the war swiftly and save American lives. The decision to use it was conscious, not automatic, and required no ulterior motive.

The Cost of War

World War II was the most terrible war in history. Military deaths are estimated at some 15 million, and at least as many civilians were killed. If we include deaths linked indirectly to the war, from disease, hunger, and other causes, the number of victims might reach 40 million. Most of Europe and large parts of Asia were devastated. Yet the end of so terrible a war brought little opportunity to relax. The dawn of the atomic age made people conscious that another major war might extinguish humanity. Everything depended on concluding a stable peace, but even as the fighting ended, conflicts among the victors made the prospects of a lasting peace doubtful.

▼ Racism and the Holocaust

The most horrible aspect of the Nazi rule in Europe arose not from military or economic necessity but from the inhumanity and brutality inherent in Hitler's racial doctrines. These were applied to several groups of people in Eastern Europe.

Hitler considered the Slavs *Untermenschen*, subhuman creatures like beasts who need not be treated as people. In parts of Poland, the upper and professional classes were entirely removed—jailed, deported, or killed. Schools and churches were closed. The Nazis limited marriage to keep down the Polish birthrate and imposed harsh living conditions.

In Russia, things were even worse. Hitler spoke of his Russian campaign as a war of extermination. Heinrich Himmler (1900–1945), head of Hitler's elite SS formations, planned to eliminate 30 million Slavs to make room for Germans; he formed extermination squads for this purpose. Six million Russian prisoners of war and deported civilians may have died under Nazi rule.

Hitler, however, had envisioned a special fate for the Jews. He meant to make all Europe *Judenrein*, or "free of Jews." For a time, he considered sending them to the island of Madagascar. Later, he arrived at the "final solution of the Jewish problem"—extermination. The Nazis built extermination camps in Germany and Poland and used the latest technology to achieve the most efficient means to kill millions of men, women, and children simply because they were Jews. (See "Mass Murder at

World War II resulted in the near-total destruction of the Jews of Europe, victims of the Holocaust spawned by Hitler's racial theories of the superiority and inferiority of particular ethnic groups. Hitler placed special emphasis on the need to exterminate the Jews, to whom he attributed particular wickedness. This picture shows Hungarian Jewish women, after "disinfection" and head shaving, marching to the concentration or death camp at Auschwitz-Birkenau, Poland. Library of Congress/Photo by Bernhard Walter; source: National Archives and Records Administration

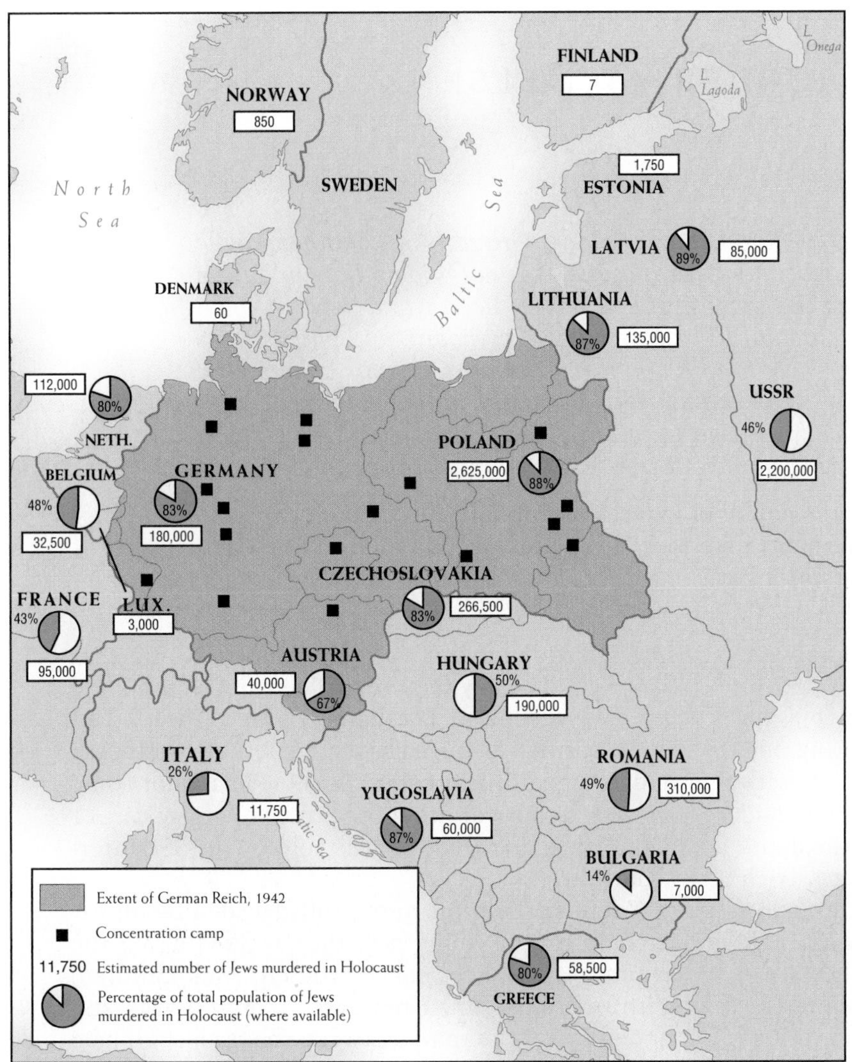

Map 28–7 **THE HOLOCAUST** The Nazi policy of ethnic cleansing—targeting Jews, Gypsies, political dissidents, and "social deviants"—began with imprisoning them in concentration camps, but by 1943 the *Endlösung*, or Final Solution, called for the systematic extermination of "undersirables."

Belsen," pages 888–889.) The most extensive destruction occurred in Eastern Europe and Russia, but the Nazis and their collaborators in occupied areas of Western Europe, including France, the Netherlands, Italy, and Belgium, also deported Jews from these nations to almost certain death in the east. Before the war was over, perhaps 6 million Jews had died in what has come to be called the **Holocaust**. Only about a million European Jews remained alive, most of them in pitiable condition. (See Map 28–7.)

It is difficult to comprehend the massive Nazi effort to eradicate the Jews of Europe. This destruction took different forms in different regions of the Continent. To explore this central event of twentieth-century European history, we examine the fate of the Polish Jewish community, which before the Second World War was the largest in Europe, consisting of 10 percent of Poland's population.

The Destruction of the Polish Jewish Community

A large Jewish community had dwelled within Poland for centuries, often in a climate of religious and cultural anti-Semitism. As a result of this anti-Semitism, Polish Jews had long lived in their own villages and later in their own urban neighborhoods. After the late-eighteenth-century partitions of Poland and the Congress of Vienna, most of Poland came under Russian rule. Through the policy of Official Nationalism (see Chapter 21), the nineteenth-century tsars identified loyalty to their government with membership in the Russian Orthodox Church. Other Christian groups, such as Lutherans and Roman Catholics, were often treated with suspicion. Jews were treated worse and were subject to a wide variety of discriminatory legislation. Polish Jews did not experience any of the forms of Jewish emancipation that occurred in Western Europe. (See Chapter 24.)

Language, food, dress, and place of residence as well as religion distinguished Jews from the rest of the Polish population, almost all of whom were Roman Catholics. Hebrew was the Polish Jews' chief written language, and Yiddish their primary spoken language. Many Jews, particularly older ones, wore distinctive dress. They ate food different from that of most Poles. Many Polish Jews also moved to cities, and Jews were regarded as an urban people in a predominantly rural nation. Moreover, Jews were among the poorest people in Poland, often working as self-employed merchants, peddlers, and craftspeople, or in industries, such as textiles, clothing, and paper, that other Poles identified as Jewish-dominated. Few Polish Jews belonged to trade unions. These conditions made them vulnerable during the economic turmoil of the 1920s and especially of the 1930s.

Polish Anti-Semitism Between the Wars

After the restoration of Poland following World War I, Polish leaders were divided about the role of Jews in Polish national life. Jozef Pilsudski (1867–1935), who dominated the interwar era, favored including Jews within the civic definition of the nation, and the constitution allowed Jews to participate in political life. After Pilsudski's death, political groups that equated citizenship with Polish ethnicity and embraced anti-Semitism came to the fore. Their ideology, no less than that of tsarist Russian Orthodoxy, defined Jews as outside the Polish nation.

MASS MURDER AT BELSEN

Hitler's calculated plan to wipe out Europe's Jews, along with millions of other people he considered undesirable for racial and other reasons, was not widely known during the war. Care was taken to keep the mass murders secret. Even when news of them leaked out, many people were reluctant to believe what they heard, and participants in the crimes were naturally not eager to talk about them. Kurt Gerstein, a colonel in the SS, was part of the apparatus of extermination. However, unlike most people involved and at great risk to himself, he tried to tell the world what was taking place. The following is an account of what he saw at the death camp at Belsen in 1942.

What were the reasons for Hitler's policy of exterminating millions of men, women, and children? Why did many Germans take part in the process? Why did so conscientious a man as Colonel Gerstein not resist?

A train arrived from Lemberg [Lvov]. There were forty-five cars containing 6,700 people, 1,450 of whom were already dead. Through the gratings on the windows, children could be seen peering out, terribly pale and frightened, their eyes filled with mortal dread . . . The train entered the station, and two hundred Ukrainians wrenched open the doors and drove the people out of the carriages with their leather whips. Instructions came through a large loudspeaker telling them to remove all their clothing, artificial limbs, glasses, etc. They were to hand over all objects of value at the counter . . . Shoes were to be carefully tied together, for otherwise no one would ever again have been able to find shoes belonging to each other in a pile that was a good eighty feet high. Then the women and girls were sent to the barber who, with two or three strokes of his scissors, cut off all their hair and dropped it into potato sacks. "That's for some special purpose or other on U-Boats, for packing or something like that," I was told by an SS-Unterscharfuhrer . . .

Then the column moved off. Headed by an extremely pretty young girl, they walked along the avenue, all naked, men, women, and children, with artificial limbs removed. I myself was stationed up on the ramp between the [gas] chambers with Captain Wirth.

No matter which political outlook dominated, discrimination against Jews existed throughout the culture and politics of interwar Poland. During those years, the Polish government, supported by spokesmen for the Polish Roman Catholic Church, pursued policies that were anti-Semitic. The Polish government nationalized the matches, salt, tobacco, and alcohol industries and then enacted legislation that discriminated against hiring Jews for these government monopolies. Other laws made it difficult for Jews to observe the Sabbath while keeping their jobs. Regulations requiring businesses to be closed on Sunday meant Jewish shops had to close two days of the week. By the late 1930s, as ethnic nationalism became stronger, the government required businesses to display their owners' names prominently, which made it easy for people to avoid Jewish shops. Because Jews were excluded from the civil service, they moved into law and medicine, which provoked further resentment.

The path of assimilation into the larger culture that many European Jewish leaders had advocated during the nineteenth century hit a dead end in Poland because many Poles refused to regard even secular, assimilated Jews as fellow Poles. Nonetheless, many Jews attempted to embrace the social practices, dress, and language of the Polish majority without actually expecting to be considered Polish. They saw themselves as moving from a traditional style of life to a more modern and Polish one. Jewish newspapers and other magazines began to be published in Polish. Jews took advantage of their right to political participation, but they were divided into different factions and could not agree on how to defend Jewish life and culture in Poland. These divisions made the Jews of Poland more vulnerable when the Second World War broke out in 1939.

Whatever active anti-Semitism existed in Poland before the German invasion of 1939, it was the Nazis who tried to destroy the Polish Jewish community and

Mothers with babies at their breasts came up, hesitated, and entered the chambers of death. At the corner stood a burly SS man with a priest-like voice. "Nothing at all is going to happen to you!" he told the poor wretches. "All you have to do when you get into the chambers is to breathe in deeply. That stretches the lungs. Inhaling is necessary to prevent disease and epidemics." When asked what would be done with them, he replied: "Well, of course, the men will have to work building houses and roads, but the women won't need to work. They can do housework or help in the kitchen, but only if they want to." For some of these poor creatures, this was a small ray of hope that was enough to make them walk the few steps to the chambers without resistance. Most of them knew what was going on. The smell told them what their fate was to be. They went up the small flight of steps and saw everything. Mothers with their babies clasped to their breasts, small children, adults, men, women, all naked; they hesitated, but they entered the chambers of death, thrust forward by the others behind them or by the leather whips of the SS [Storm Troopers]. Most went in without a word . . . Many were saying prayers. I prayed with them. I pressed myself into a corner and cried aloud to my God and theirs. How gladly I should have gone into the chambers with them; how gladly I should have died with them. Then they would have found an SS officer in uniform in their gas chambers; they would have believed it was an accident and the story would have been buried and forgotten. But I could not do that yet. First, I had to make known what I had seen here. The chambers were filling up. Fill them up well—that was Captain Wirth's order. The people were treading on each other's feet. There were 700–800 of them in an area of 270 square feet, in 1,590 cubic feet of space. The SS crushed them together as tightly as they possibly could. The doors closed. Meanwhile, the rest waited out in the open, all naked. "It's done exactly the same way in winter," I was told. "But they may catch their death!" I said. "That's what they're here for," an SS man said . . . The Diesel exhaust gases were intended to kill those unfortunates. But the engine was not working . . . The people in the gas chambers waited, in vain. I heard them weeping, sobbing . . . After 2 hours and 49 minutes, measured by my stop watch, the Diesel started. Up to that moment, men and women had been shut up alive in those four chambers, four times 750 people in four times 1,590 cubic feet of space. Another twenty-five minutes dragged by. Many of those inside were already dead. They could be seen through the small window when the electric light went on for a moment and lit up the inside of the chamber. After twenty-eight minutes, few were left alive. At the end of thirty-two minutes, all were dead.

Jewish communities elsewhere in Europe that fell under German control. In that respect, the Holocaust constitutes an event driven by German policy within the larger event of the Second World War.

The Nazi Assault on the Jews of Poland

The joint German-Soviet invasion of Poland brought millions of Jews under either German or Soviet authority. By conquering Poland, the Nazi government could carry out the destruction of Jewish communities to an extent far beyond anything possible in Germany itself. From the Nazi standpoint, the destruction of the Polish Jewish community held special importance. Polish Jewry was large and had produced many religious, cultural, and political leaders. It also constituted the single most important source for Jewish emigration beyond Eastern Europe. For the Nazis, Poland was the chief breeding ground for world Jewry.

By late autumn 1939, the Germans had begun to move against Polish Jews. The Nazi government first thought it might herd virtually all the Jews of occupied Europe into the Lublin region of Poland. By early 1940, the Nazis decided to move as many Jews as possible into ghettos, where they would be separated from the rest of the Polish population. The largest ghettos were Lodz and Warsaw, each of which had populations of several hundred thousand. The Nazis moved Jews from all over Poland and, eventually, other occupied regions by rail into these ghettos and then sealed them off with police guards and walls. Jewish councils, which were torn between responsibility to their communities and the need to respond to German orders, administered the ghettos. The Nazis confiscated and sold the personal property and businesses of the Jews who were herded into the ghettos. Jewish laborers were sent out to work as contract labor while their families remained in the ghettos. By 1941, the Polish Jews had lost their civic standing and property. They had been located in segregated communities within Poland where disease was rampant and the food supply meager. Approximately 20 percent of the population of both the Lodz and Warsaw ghettos died of disease and malnourishment.

The German invasion of the Soviet Union in June 1941 made the situation of Jews in Poland even worse. The advancing German forces killed tens of thousands of Jews in the Soviet Union during 1941 and hundreds of thousands more the next year. Bolsheviks and Jews became conflated in German thinking and propaganda. During the second half of 1941, the Nazi government decided to exterminate the Jews of Europe. From late 1941 through 1944, the Germans transported Jews from the ghettos by rail to death camps in Poland, including Kulmhof, Belzen, Sobibor, Treblinka, Birkenau, and Auschwitz. One or more of the camps were in operation from 1941 to 1944, with Auschwitz being the last closed. In these camps, Jews were systematically killed in gas chambers.

By 1945, approximately 90 percent of the pre-1939 Jewish population of Poland had been destroyed. The tiny minority of Polish Jews who had survived faced bitter anti-Semitism under the postwar Soviet-dominated government. Many immigrated to Israel, leaving only a few thousand Jews within the borders of a nation where they had numbered in the millions and where they had created a rich religious, cultural, and political community. The largest Jewish community in Europe had virtually ceased to exist.

Explanations of the Holocaust

As interest in the Holocaust has grown since the 1960s, so has debate about its character and meaning. Was it a unique event of unprecedented and unparalleled evil, or was it one specific instance of a more general human wickedness that has found expression throughout history? Are its roots to be found in flaws in human nature as a whole, or are they unique to the experience of the West or, perhaps, to the German people? Some scholars point to the horrible mass murders committed in the twentieth century by communist regimes under Stalin in the Soviet Union and under Mao in China, each of which killed many more people than did Hitler, as evidence of the more general character of the phenomenon. Others argue that the Holocaust was unique because its goal was the annihilation of a whole people, from infants to the aged, just because of who they were. Some focus on the wickedness personified by Hitler, who was driven by his fixation on the myth of Jewish power and evil.

Perhaps we should think of the problem from the standpoint of two questions: Why were the Jews the main target of Hitler's policy of extermination? How was it possible to carry out such a vast mass murder? Surely, an essential part of an answer to the first question is the persistence of anti-Semitism in Christianity and Western culture, from the Church Fathers to Luther and to the teachings of churches in modern times. Some would combine this religious and historical anti-Semitism with the coming of the Enlightenment and the social sciences, which gave rise to pseudoscientific racial theories that lent a new twist to the old hatred of the Jews. Pseudoscientific racism appears to have been the most powerful influence on Hitler, but it could not have found widespread support without deeply rooted religious and social anti-Semitism.

For example, in at least one instance in Poland, Poles turned against their Jewish neighbors in outbursts of localized anti-Semitic violence. In July 1941, in the town of Jedwabne, in northeast Poland, non-Jewish Poles killed approximately 1,600 of their Jewish fellow townspeople. This horrendous incident suggests that although the Nazis carried out most of the atrocities against the Jews, a climate of either indifference or outright support existed in Poland as well as in other parts of Nazi-occupied Europe. Yet it must also be noted that between 1942 and 1945 the Council for Aid to Jews in Occupied Poland, known as ZEGOTA and sponsored by the Polish government in exile, protected and aided the escape of many thousands of Polish Jews.

MAJOR CAMPAIGNS AND EVENTS OF WORLD WAR II

September 1939	Germany and the Soviet Union invade Poland
November 1939	The Soviet Union invades Finland
April 1940	Germany invades Denmark and Norway
May 1940	Germany invades Belgium, the Netherlands, Luxembourg, and France
June 1940	Fall of France
August 1940	Battle of Britain begins
June 1941	Germany invades the Soviet Union
July 1941	Japan takes Indochina
December 1941	Japan attacks Pearl Harbor; United States enters war against Axis powers
June 1942	Battle of Midway Island
November 1942	Battle of Stalingrad begins
July–August 1943	Allies take Sicily, land in Italy
June 1944	Allies land in Normandy
May 1945	Germany surrenders
August 1945	Atomic bombs dropped on Hiroshima and Nagasaki
September 1945	Japan formally surrenders

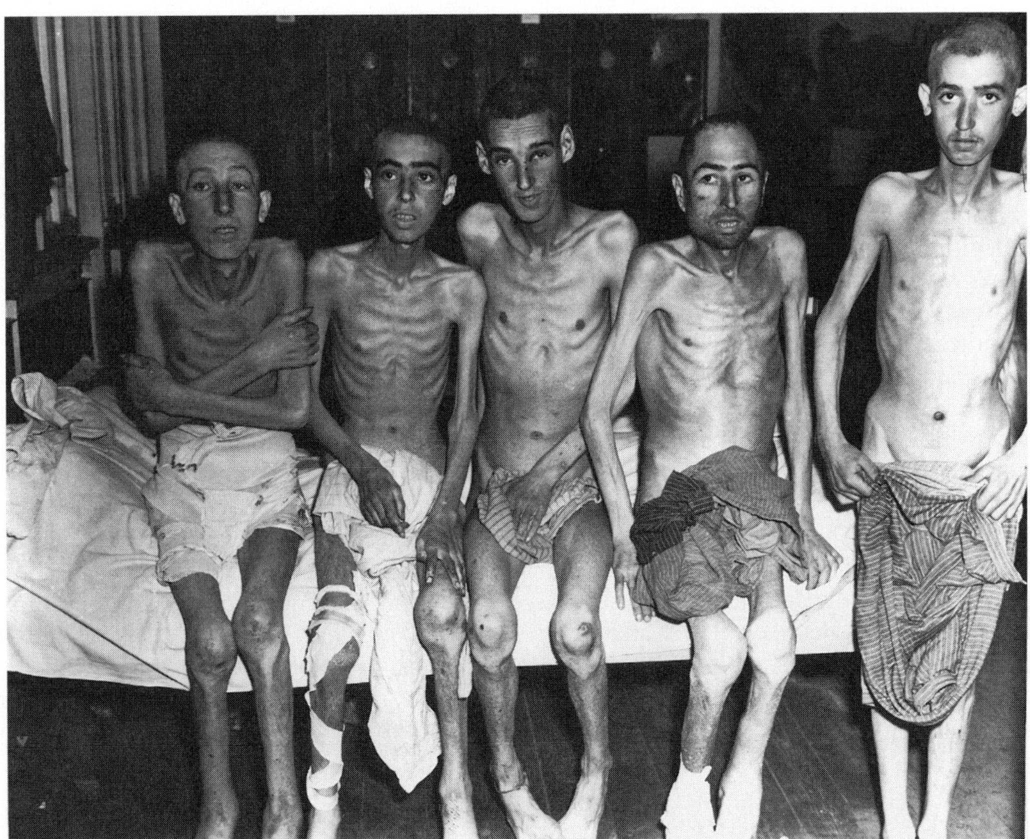

Male inmates, emaciated and freezing, at a German concentration camp in 1945. Library of Congress

As to how it was possible to murder 6 million people, part of the answer must lie in the parochial nationalism that arose during and after the French Revolution. For many people, nationalism divided the world into one's fellow nationals and all others. It encouraged, excused, and even justified terrible and violent acts performed on behalf of one's homeland. Another part of the answer may derive from the utopian visions also unleashed by some Enlightenment writers, who promised to achieve perfect societies through social engineering, regardless of the human cost. To this were added the scientific and technological advances that gave the modern state new power to command its people, to persuade them to obey by controlling the media of propaganda, and to enforce its will with efficient brutality. All of these permitted the creation of a totalitarian state that, for the first time in history, could conduct mass murder on the scale of the Holocaust.

These questions and their possible answers are but suggestions meant to encourage further and deeper thought in what will surely be a continuing debate among scholars and the general public. World War II was unmatched in cruelty in modern times. When Stalin's armies conquered Poland and entered Germany, they raped, pillaged, and deported millions to the east. The British and American bombing of Germany killed thousands of civilians, and the atomic bombs dropped on Japan killed and maimed tens of thousands more. The bombings, however, were thought of as acts of war that would help defeat the enemy. Stalin's atrocities were not widely known in the West at the time or even today.

The victorious Western allies were shocked by what they saw when they came on the Nazi extermination camps and their pitiful survivors. Little wonder it was that they were convinced the effort to resist the Nazis and all the pain it had cost were well worth it.

▼ The Domestic Fronts

World War II represented an effort at total war by all the belligerents. Never in European or world history had so many men and women and such resources been devoted to military effort. One result was the carnage that occurred during the fighting. Another was an unprecedented organization of civilians on the home fronts. Each domestic effort and experience was different, but few escaped the impact of the conflict. Everywhere there were shortages, propaganda campaigns, and new political developments.

Germany: From Apparent Victory to Defeat

Hitler had expected to defeat all his enemies by rapid strokes, or *blitzkriegs*. Such campaigns would have required little change in Germany's society and economy. During the first two years of the war, in fact, Hitler demanded few sacrifices from the German people. Spending on domestic projects continued, and food was plentiful; the economy was not on a full wartime footing. Germany's failure to quickly overwhelm the Soviet Union changed everything. Food was no longer available from the east in needed quantities, Germany had to mobilize for total war, and the government demanded major sacrifices.

A great expansion of the army and of military production began in 1942. As minister for armaments and munitions, Albert Speer (1905–1981) directed the economy, and Germany met its military needs. The government sought the cooperation of major German businesses to increase wartime production. Between 1942 and late 1944, the output of military products tripled. As the war went on, more men were drafted from industry into the army, and military production suffered.

As the manufacture of armaments replaced the production of consumer goods, shortages of everyday products became serious. Prices and wages were controlled, but the standard of living of German workers fell. Food rationing began in April 1942, and shortages were severe until the Nazi government seized more food from occupied Europe. To preserve their own home front, the Nazis passed on the suffering to their defeated neighbors.

By 1943, labor shortages became severe. The Nazis required German teenagers and retired men to work in the factories, and many women joined them. To achieve total mobilization, the Germans closed retail businesses, raised the age of eligibility of women for compulsory service, shifted non-German domestic workers to wartime industry, moved artists and entertainers into military service, closed theaters, and reduced such basic public services as mail and railways. Finally, the Nazis compelled thousands of non-Germans to do forced labor in Germany.

Hitler assigned women a special place in the war effort. The celebration of motherhood continued, with an emphasis on women who were the mothers of important military figures. Films portrayed ordinary women who became brave and patriotic during the war and remained

Bombing of Cologne. The Allied campaign of aerial bombardment did terrible damage to German cities. This photograph shows the devastation it delivered to the city of Cologne on the Rhine. United States Signal Corps

faithful to their husbands who were at the front. Women were shown as mothers and wives who sent their sons and husbands off to war. The government pictured other wartime activities of women as the natural fulfillment of their maternal roles. As air-raid wardens, they protected their families; as factory workers in munitions plants, they aided their sons on the front lines. Women working on farms were providing for their soldier sons and husbands; as housewives, they were helping to win the war by conserving food. Finally, by their faithful chastity, German women were protecting racial purity. They were not to marry or to have sex with non-Germans. During the war domestic political propaganda went beyond what occurred in other countries. Hitler and other Germans genuinely believed that weak domestic support had led to Germany's defeat in World War I; they were determined not to let this happen again. Nazi propaganda blamed the outbreak of the war on the British and the Jews and its prolongation on Germany's opponents. It also stressed the power of Germany and the inferiority of its foes.

Propaganda minister Josef Goebbels (1897–1945) used both radio and films to boost the Nazi cause. Movies of the collapse of Poland, Belgium, Holland, and France showed German military might. Throughout the conquered territories, the Nazis used the same mass media to frighten inhabitants about the possible consequences of an Allied victory. Later in the war, Goebbels broadcast exaggerated claims of Nazi victories. As the German armies were checked on the battlefield, especially in Russia, propaganda became a substitute for victory. To stiffen German resolve, propaganda now aimed to frighten Germans about the consequences of defeat.

After May 1943, when the Allies began their major bombing offensive over Germany, the German people had much to fear. The bombing devastated one German city after another but did not undermine German morale. The bombing may even have increased German resistance by seeming to confirm the regime's propaganda about the ruthlessness of Germany's opponents.

World War II increased the power of the Nazi Party in Germany. Every area of the economy and society came under the direct influence or control of the party. The Nazis were determined that they, rather than the traditionally honored German officer corps, would profit from the new authority the war effort was giving to the central government. There was virtually no serious opposition to Hitler or his ministers. In July 1944, a group of army officers attempted to assassinate Hitler; the effort failed, and there was little popular support for this act.

The war brought great changes to Germany, but what transformed the country most was the experience of physical destruction, invasion, and occupation. Hitler and the Nazis had brought Germany to such a complete and disastrous defeat that only a new kind of state with new political structures could emerge.

France: Defeat, Collaboration, and Resistance

The terms of the 1940 armistice between France, under Pétain, and Germany, signed June 22, allowed the Germans to occupy more than half of France, including the Atlantic and English Channel coasts. To prevent the French from continuing the fight from North Africa, and even more to prevent them from turning their fleet over to Britain, Hitler left southern France unoccupied until November 1942. Marshal Pétain set up a dictatorial regime at the resort city of Vichy and collaborated with the Germans in hopes of preserving as much autonomy as possible.

Some of the collaborators believed the Germans were sure to win the war and wanted to be on the victorious side. A few sympathized with Nazi ideas and plans. Many conservatives regarded the French defeat as a judgment on what they saw as the corrupt, secularized, liberal Third Republic. Most of the French were not active collaborators but were demoralized by defeat and German power.

Many conservatives and extreme rightists saw in the Vichy government a way to reshape the French national character and to halt the decadence they associated with political and religious liberalism. The Roman Catholic clergy, which had lost power and influence under the Third Republic, gained status under Vichy. The church supported Pétain, and his government restored religious instruction in the state schools and increased financial support for Catholic schools. Vichy adopted the church's views on the importance of family and spiritual values. The government made divorce difficult and forbade it entirely during the first three years of marriage. The state encouraged and subsidized large families.

The Vichy regime also encouraged an intense, chauvinistic nationalism. It exploited prejudice against foreigners working in France and fostered resentment even against French men and women whom it regarded as not genuinely "French," especially French Jews. Anti-Semitism was not new in France, as the Dreyfus affair had demonstrated. Even before Germany undertook Hitler's "final solution" in 1942, the French had begun to remove Jews from positions of influence in government, education, and publishing. In 1941, the Germans began to intern Jews living in occupied France; soon they murdered individual Jews and imposed large fines collectively on the Jews of the occupied zone. In the spring of 1942, they began to deport Jews from France—ultimately more than 60,000—to the extermination camps of Eastern Europe. The Vichy government had no part in these decisions, but it made no protest, and its own anti-Semitic policies made the whole process easier to carry out.

Some French men and women, notably General Charles de Gaulle (1890–1969), fled to Britain after the defeat of France. There they organized the French

A Closer LOOK

THE VICHY REGIME IN FRANCE

AFTER THEIR SURPRISINGLY swift conquest of France in 1940, the Germans ruled one part of it directly from Paris, leaving the rest unoccupied until 1942, but firmly under the control of a collaborationist French government under Marshal Henri Philippe Pétain (1856–1951; see Map 28–3, page 877). This regime, based in the city of Vichy, pursued a reactionary policy, turning away from the democratic ways of the defeated Third Republic. The "Propaganda Centers of the National Revolution" published the poster shown in the photo. "The National Revolution" was the name the Vichy regime gave to its program to remake France.

The house on the left, representing the Third Republic, carries the name "France and Company," which implies that the Third Republic was run like a corrupt business firm. It tilts precariously on shaky supports: egoism, radicalism, capitalism, communism, Jewry, antimilitarism, parliament, and disorder. These, in turn, rest on what Vichy considered the Republic's basic flaws: laziness, demagogy, and internationalism instead of French patriotism.

The house on the right represents the Vichy government. Its name is "France," pure and simple. It sits, safe, strong, neat, and orderly, on solid columns: school, craftsmanship, the peasantry, and the military. These rest on equally firm bases: discipline, order, thrift, and courage. Underlying all are the three basic values—work, family, and fatherland—which Vichy made its national slogan to replace the liberty, equality, and fraternity that had been the motto of French republican regimes since the French Revolution.

Philippe Noyer, *Révolution nationale*. Bibliothèque de Documentation International Contemporane.

To examine this image in an interactive fashion, please go to www.myhistorylab.com

myhistorylab

National Committee of Liberation, or "Free French." Until the end of 1942, the Vichy government controlled French North Africa and the navy, but the Free French began operating in Central Africa. From London, they broadcast hope and defiance to their compatriots in France. Serious internal resistance to the German occupiers and the Vichy government, however, began to develop only late in 1942. The Germans tried to force young people in occupied France to work in German factories; some of them joined the Resistance, but the number of all the resisters was small. Fear of German retaliation deterred many. Others disliked the violence that resistance to a powerful ruthless nation inevitably entailed. As long as it appeared the Germans would win the war, moreover, resistance seemed imprudent and futile. For these reasons, the organized Resistance never attracted more than 5 percent of the adult French population.

By early 1944, the tide of battle had shifted. The Allies seemed sure to win, and the Vichy government would clearly not survive; only then did a large-scale active movement of resistance assert itself. General de Gaulle spoke confidently for Free France from his base in London and urged the French people to resist their conquerors and the German lackeys in the Vichy government. Within France, Resistance groups joined forces to plan for a better day. From Algiers on August 9, 1944, the Committee of National Liberation declared the authority of Vichy illegitimate. French soldiers joined in the liberation of Paris and established a government for Free France. On October 21, 1945, France voted to end the Third Republic and adopted a new constitution as the basis of the Fourth Republic. The French people had experienced defeat, disgrace, deprivation, and suffering. Hostility and quarrels over who had done what during the occupation and under Vichy divided them for decades.

Great Britain: Organization for Victory

On May 22, 1940, the British Parliament gave the government emergency powers. Together with others already in effect, this measure allowed the government to institute compulsory military service, rationing, and economic controls.

To deal with the crisis, all British political parties joined in a national government under Winston Churchill. Churchill and the British war cabinet moved as quickly as possible to mobilize the nation. Perhaps the most pressing immediate need was to produce airplanes to fight the Germans in the Battle of Britain. Lord Beaverbrook (1879–1964), one of Britain's most important newspaper publishers, led this effort. The demand for more planes and other armaments inspired a campaign to reclaim scrap metal. Wrought-iron fences, kitchen pots and pans, and every conceivable metal object were collected for the war effort. This was only one successful example of the many ways the civilian population enthusiastically engaged in the struggle.

By the end of 1941, British production had already surpassed Germany's. To meet the heavy demands on the labor force, factory hours were extended, and many women joined the workforce. Unemployment disappeared, and the working classes had more money to spend than they had enjoyed for many years. To avoid inflation caused by increased demand for an inadequate supply of consumer goods, savings were encouraged, and taxes were raised to absorb the excess purchasing power.

The "blitz" air attacks in 1940–1941 were the most immediate and dramatic experience of the war for the British people. The German air raids killed thousands of people and left many others homeless. Once the bombing began, many families removed their children to the countryside. Ironically, the rescue effort improved the standard of living of many of the children, for the government paid for their food and medication. The government issued gas masks to thousands of city dwellers, who were frequently compelled to take shelter from the bombs in the London subways.

After the spring of 1941, Hitler needed most of his air force on the Russian front, but the bombing of Britain continued, killing more than 30,000 people by the end of the war. Terrible as it was, this toll was much smaller than the number of Germans Allied bombing killed. In England, as in Germany, however, the bombing may have made people more determined.

The British made many sacrifices. Transportation facilities were strained simply from carrying enough coal to heat homes and run factories. Food and clothing for civilians were scarce and strictly rationed. Every scrap of land was farmed, increasing the productive portion by almost 4 million acres. Gasoline was scarce, and private vehicles almost vanished.

The British established their own propaganda machine to influence the Continent. The British Broadcasting Company (BBC) sent programs to every country in Europe in the local language to encourage resistance to the Nazis. At home, the government used the radio to unify the nation. Soldiers at the front heard the same programs their families did at home. The most famous program, second only to Churchill's speeches, was *It's That Man Again*, a humorous broadcast filled with imaginary figures that the entire nation came to treasure.

Strangely, for the broad mass of the population, the standard of living improved during the war. The general health of the nation also improved, for reasons that are still not clear. These improvements should not be exaggerated, but they did occur, and many connected them with the active involvement of the government in the economy and in the lives of the citizens. This wartime

Fires destroy a commercial dock in London, England, during the German air raids. Despite many casualties and widespread devastation, the German bombing of London did not break British morale or prevent the city from functioning. British Information Services

experience may have contributed to the Labour Party's victory in 1945; many feared a return to Conservative Party rule would also mean a return to the economic problems and unemployment of the 1930s.

The Soviet Union: "The Great Patriotic War"

The war against Germany came as a great surprise to Stalin and the Soviet Union. The German attack violated the 1939 pact with Hitler and put the government of the Soviet Union on the defensive militarily and politically. It showed the failure of Stalin's foreign policy and the ineptness of his preparation for war. He claimed the pact had given the nation an extra year and a half to prepare for war, but this was clearly a lame and implausible excuse in light of the ease of Germany's early victories. Within days, German troops occupied much of the western Soviet Union. The communist government feared that Soviet citizens in the occupied zones—many of whom were not ethnic Russians—might welcome the Germans as liberators. The Stalinist regime had harshly oppressed these Soviet citizens.

No nation suffered more during World War II than the Soviet Union. Perhaps as many as 16 million people were killed, and vast numbers of Soviet troops were taken prisoner. Hundreds of cities and towns and well over half of the industrial and transportation facilities of the country were devastated. From 1942, thousands of Soviet prisoners worked in German factories as forced labor. The Germans also seized grain, mineral resources, and oil from the Soviet Union.

Stalin conducted the war as the virtual chief of the armed forces, and the State Committee for Defense provided strong central coordination. In the decade before the war, Stalin had already made the Soviet Union a highly centralized state; he had tried to manage the entire economy from Moscow through the five-year plans, the collectivization of agriculture, and the purges. The country was thus already on what amounted to a wartime footing long before the conflict erupted. When the war began, millions of citizens entered the army, but the army itself did not grow in influence at the expense of the state and the Communist Party—that is, of Stalin. He was suspicious of the generals, though he had presumably eliminated officers of doubtful loyalty in the purges of the late 1930s. As the war continued, however, the army gained more freedom of action, and eventually the generals were no longer subservient to party commissars. The power of Stalin and the nature of Soviet government and society, however, still sharply limited the army.

Soviet propaganda was different from that of other nations. Because the Soviet government distrusted the loyalty of its citizens, it confiscated radios to prevent the people from listening to German or British propaganda. In cities, the government broadcast to the people over loudspeakers in place of radios. During the war, Soviet propaganda emphasized Russian patriotism rather than traditional Marxist themes that stressed class conflict. The struggle against the Germans was called "The Great Patriotic War."

The regime republished great Russian novels of the past and printed more than half a million copies of Tolstoy's *War and Peace*, which was set during Napoleon's invasion of Russia, during the siege of Leningrad (Saint Petersburg). Authors wrote straightforward propaganda fostering hatred of the Germans. Serge Eisenstein (1898–1948), the great filmmaker (see "Encountering the Past," Chapter 27), produced a vast epic entitled *Ivan the Terrible*, which glorified this brutal sixteenth-century tsar. Composers wrote music to evoke heroic emotions. The most important of these was Dimitri Shostakovich's (1906–1975) *Leningrad Symphony*.

The pressure of war led Stalin to make peace with the Russian Orthodox Church, and the Patriarch of Moscow urged resistance to the Germans. Stalin hoped this new policy would increase his support at home and in Eastern Europe, where the Orthodox Church predominated.

Within occupied portions of the western Soviet Union, an active resistance movement harassed the Germans. The swiftness of the German invasion had stranded thousands of Soviet troops behind German lines. Some escaped and carried on guerrilla warfare behind enemy lines. Stalin supported partisan forces in lands the enemy held for two reasons: He wanted to cause as much difficulty as possible for the Germans, and Soviet-sponsored resistance reminded the peasants that the Soviet government had not disappeared. Stalin feared the peasants' hatred of the communist government and collectivization might lead them to collaborate with the invaders. When the Soviet army moved westward, it incorporated the partisans into the regular army.

As its armies reclaimed the occupied areas and then moved across Eastern and Central Europe, the Soviet Union established itself as a world power second only to the United States. Stalin had entered the war a reluctant belligerent, but he emerged a major victor. In that respect, the war and the extraordinary patriotic effort and sacrifice it generated consolidated the power of Stalin and the party more effectively than the political and social policies of the previous decade.

▼ Preparations for Peace

The split between the Soviet Union and its wartime allies should cause no surprise. As the self-proclaimed center of world communism, the Soviet Union was openly dedicated to the overthrow of the capitalist nations. The Soviets muted this message, however, when the occasion demanded. On the other side, the Western allies were no less open about their hostility to communism and its chief purveyor, the Soviet Union. Although they had been friendly to the early stages of the 1917 Russian Revolution, they had intervened to try to overthrow the Bolshevik regime during the resulting civil war. The United States did not grant formal recognition to the USSR until 1933. The Western powers' exclusion of the Soviets from the Munich conference and Stalin's pact with Hitler did nothing to improve relations between them during the war.

Nonetheless, the need to cooperate against a common enemy and strenuous propaganda efforts helped improve Western feeling toward the Soviet ally. Still, Stalin remained suspicious and critical of the Western war effort, and Churchill was determined to contain the Soviet advance into Europe. Roosevelt perhaps had been more hopeful that the Allies could continue to work together after the war, but even he was losing faith by 1945. Differences in historical development and ideology, as well as traditional conflicts over political power and influence, soon dashed hopes of a mutually satisfactory peace settlement and continued cooperation to uphold it.

The Atlantic Charter

In August 1941, even before the Americans were at war, Roosevelt and Churchill met on a ship off Newfoundland and agreed to the Atlantic Charter. This broad set of principles in the spirit of Wilson's Fourteen Points provided a theoretical basis for the peace they sought. When Russia and the United States joined Britain in the war, the three powers entered a purely military alliance in January 1942, leaving all political questions aside. The first political conference was the meeting of foreign ministers in Moscow in October 1943. The ministers reaffirmed earlier agreements to fight on until the enemy surrendered unconditionally and to continue cooperating after the war in a united-nations organization.

Tehran: Agreement on a Second Front

The first meeting of the leaders of the "Big Three" (the USSR, Britain, and the United States) took place at Tehran, the capital of Iran, in 1943. Western promises to open a second front in France the next summer (1944) and

NEGOTIATIONS AMONG THE ALLIES

August 1941	Churchill and Roosevelt meet off Newfoundland to sign Atlantic Charter
October 1943	American, British, and Soviet foreign ministers meet in Moscow
November 1943	Churchill, Roosevelt, and Stalin meet at Tehran
October 1944	Churchill meets with Stalin in Moscow
February 1945	Churchill, Roosevelt, and Stalin meet at Yalta
July 1945	Attlee, Stalin, and Truman meet at Potsdam

Stalin's agreement to fight Japan when Germany was defeated created an atmosphere of goodwill in which to discuss a postwar settlement. Stalin wanted to retain what he had gained in his pact with Hitler and to dismember Germany. Roosevelt and Churchill were conciliatory but made no firm commitments.

The most important decision was the one that chose Europe's west coast as the main point of attack instead of the Mediterranean. That meant, in retrospect, that Soviet forces would occupy Eastern Europe and control its destiny. At Tehran in 1943, the Western allies did not foresee this clearly, for the Russians were still fighting deep within their own frontiers, and military considerations were paramount.

Churchill and Stalin By 1944, the situation had changed. In August, Soviet armies were before Warsaw, which had revolted against the Germans in expectation of liberation, but the Russians halted and turned south into the Balkans, allowing the Germans to annihilate the Poles. The Russians gained control of Romania, Bulgaria, and Hungary, advances that centuries of expansionist tsars had only dreamed of achieving. Alarmed by these developments, Churchill went to Moscow and met with Stalin in October. They agreed to share power in the Balkans on the basis of Soviet predominance in Romania and Bulgaria, Western predominance in Greece, and equality of influence in Yugoslavia and Hungary. These agreements were not enforceable without American approval, and the Americans were hostile to such un-Wilsonian devices as "spheres of influence."

Germany The three powers easily agreed on Germany—its disarmament, de-Nazification, and division into four zones of occupation by France and the Big Three. Churchill, however, began to balk at Stalin's demand for $20 billion in reparations as well as forced labor from all the zones, with Russia to get half of everything. These matters festered and caused dissension in the future.

Map 28–8 **YALTA TO THE SURRENDER** "The Big Three"—Roosevelt, Churchill, and Stalin—met at Yalta in the Crimea in February 1945. At the meeting, concessions were made to Stalin concerning the settlement of Eastern Europe because Roosevelt was eager to bring the Russians into the Pacific war as soon as possible. This map shows the positions held by the victors when Germany surrendered.

Eastern Europe The settlement of Eastern Europe was equally thorny. Everyone agreed the Soviet Union deserved to have friendly neighboring governments, but the West insisted they also be autonomous and democratic. The Western leaders, particularly Churchill, were not eager to see Russia dominate Eastern Europe. They were also, especially Roosevelt, committed to democracy and self-determination.

Stalin, however, knew that independent, freely elected governments in Poland, Hungary, and Romania would not be friendly to Russia. He had already established a puppet government in Poland in competition with the Polish government-in-exile in London. Under pressure from the Western leaders, however, he agreed to include some Poles friendly to the West in it. He also signed a Declaration on Liberated Europe, promising self-determination and free democratic elections.

Stalin may have been eager to avoid conflict before the war with Germany was over. He was always afraid

In February 1945, Churchill, Roosevelt, and Stalin met at Yalta in the Crimea to plan for the organization of Europe after the end of the war. The Big Three are seated. Standing behind President Roosevelt is Admiral William D. Leahy. Behind the prime minister are Admiral Sir Andrew Cunningham and Air Marshal Portal. U.S. Army Photograph

the Allies would make a separate peace with Germany and betray him, and he probably thought it worth endorsing some hollow principles as the price of continued harmony. In any case, he wasted little time violating these agreements.

Yalta

The next meeting of the Big Three was at Yalta in Crimea in February 1945. The Western armies had not yet crossed the Rhine, but the Soviet army was within a hundred miles of Berlin. (See Map 28–8.) The war with Japan continued, and no atomic explosion had yet taken place. Roosevelt, faced with a prospective invasion of Japan and heavy losses, was eager to bring the Russians into the Pacific war as soon as possible. As a true Wilsonian, he also suspected Churchill's determination to maintain the British Empire and Britain's colonial advantages. The Americans thought Churchill's plan to set up British spheres of influence in Europe would encourage the Russians to do the same and would lead to friction and war. To encourage Russian participation in the war against Japan, Roosevelt and Churchill made extensive concessions to Russia, ceding the Soviets Sakhalin and the Kurile Islands, and accommodating some of their desires in Korea and in Manchuria.

Again in the tradition of Wilson, Roosevelt emphasized a united-nations organization: "Through the United Nations, he hoped to achieve a self-enforcing peace settlement that would not require American troops, as well as an open world without spheres of influence in which American enterprise could work freely."[5] Soviet agreement on these points seemed worth concessions elsewhere.

Potsdam

The Big Three met for the last time in the Berlin suburb of Potsdam in July 1945. Much had changed since the previous conference. Germany had been defeated, and news of the successful explosion of an atomic weapon reached the American president during the meetings. The cast of characters was also different: President Truman re-

[5]Robert O. Paxton, *Europe in the Twentieth Century* (New York: Harcourt Brace Jovanovich, 1975), p. 487.

placed the deceased Roosevelt, and Clement Attlee (1883–1967), leader of the Labour Party that had just won a general election, replaced Churchill as Britain's spokesperson during the conference. Previous agreements were reaffirmed, but progress on undecided questions was slow.

Russia's western frontier was moved far into what had been Poland and included most of German East Prussia. In compensation, Poland was allowed "temporary administration" over the rest of East Prussia and Germany east of the Oder-Neisse River, a condition that became permanent. In effect, Poland was moved about a hundred miles west, at the expense of Germany, to accommodate the Soviet Union. The Allies agreed to divide Germany into occupation zones until the final peace treaty was signed. Germany remained divided until 1990.

A Council of Foreign Ministers was established to draft peace treaties for Germany's allies. Growing disagreements made the job difficult, and Italy, Romania, Hungary, Bulgaria, and Finland did not sign treaties until February 1947. The Russians were dissatisfied with the treaty that the United States made with Japan in 1951 and signed their own agreements with the Japanese in 1956. These disagreements were foreshadowed at Potsdam.

In Perspective

The second great war of the twentieth century (1939–1945) grew out of the unsatisfactory resolution of the first. In retrospect, the two wars appear to some people to be one continuous conflict, a kind of twentieth-century "Thirty Years' War," with two main periods of fighting separated by an uneasy truce. To others, that point of view oversimplifies by implying the second war was the inevitable result of the first and its inadequate peace treaties. The latter opinion seems more sound, for, whatever the flaws of the treaties of Paris, the world suffered an even more terrible war than the first because of failures of judgment and will by the victorious democratic powers.

Between the two wars, the United States, which had become the wealthiest and potentially the strongest nation in the world, disarmed almost entirely and withdrew into a shortsighted and foolish isolation. Therefore, it played no important part in restraining the angry and ambitious dictators who brought on the war. Britain and France refused to face the threat the Axis powers posed until the most deadly war in history was required to put it down. If the victorious democracies had remained strong, responsible, and realistic, they could have remedied whatever injustices or mistakes arose from the treaties without endangering the peace.

The second war itself was so plainly a world war that little need be said to indicate its global character. If the Japanese occupation of Manchuria in 1931 was not technically a part of that war, it was a significant precursor. Moreover, there were Italy's attack on the African nation of Ethiopia in 1935, the Italian, German, and Soviet interventions in the Spanish Civil War (1936–1939), and Japan's attack on China in 1937. These acts revealed that aggressive forces were on the march around the globe and the defenders of the world order lacked the will to stop them. The formation of the Axis incorporating Germany, Italy, and Japan guaranteed that when the war came, it would be fought around the world.

There were fighting and suffering in Asia, Africa, the Pacific islands, and Europe, and men and women from all the inhabited continents took part in them. The use of atomic weapons brought the frightful struggle to a close. Still, what are called conventional weapons did almost all the damage; their level of destructiveness threatened the survival of civilization, even without the use of atomic or nuclear devices.

The Second World War ended not with unsatisfactory peace treaties, but with no treaty at all in the European arena, where the war had begun. The world quickly split into two unfriendly camps: the western, led by the United States, and the eastern, led by the Soviet Union. This division, among other things, hastened the liberation of former colonial territories. The bargaining power of the new nations that emerged from them was temporarily increased as the two rival superpowers tried to gain their friendship or allegiance. It became customary to refer to these nations as "the Third World," or "developing countries," with the former Soviet Union and the United States and their respective allies being the first two. Time has shown that the differences among Third World nations are so great that the term is all but meaningless.

The surprising treatment the defeated powers of the Second World War received was also largely the result of the emergence of the Cold War. Instead of holding them back, the Western powers installed democratic governments in Italy, West Germany, and Japan, took them into the Western alliances designed to contain communism, and helped them recover economically. All three are now among the richest nations in the world.

REVIEW QUESTIONS

1. What were Hitler's foreign policy aims? Was he bent on conquest, or did he simply want to return Germany to its 1914 boundaries?
2. Why did Britain and France adopt a policy of appeasement in the 1930s? Did the West buy valuable time to rearm at Munich in 1938?
3. How was Hitler able to defeat France so easily in 1940? Why did the air war against Britain fail? Why did Hitler invade Russia? Could the invasion have succeeded?

4. Why did Japan attack the United States at Pearl Harbor? How important was American intervention in the war? Why did the United States drop atomic bombs on Japan? Was President Truman right to use the bombs?
5. How did experiences on the domestic front in Britain differ from those in Germany and France? What impact did "The Great Patriotic War" have on the people of the Soviet Union?
6. What was Hitler's "final solution" to the Jewish question? Why did he want to eliminate Slavs as well? To what extent can it be said the Holocaust was the defining event of the twentieth century?

SUGGESTED READINGS

O. Bartov, *Mirrors of Destruction: War, Genocide, and Modern Identity* (2000). Remarkably penetrating essays.

A. Beevor, *The Spanish Civil War* (2001). Particularly strong on the political issues.

R. S. Botwinick, *A History of the Holocaust*, 2nd ed. (2002). A brief, but useful account of the causes, character, and results of the Holocaust.

C. Browning, *The Origins of the Final Solution: The Evolution of the Nazi Jewish Policy* (2004). The story of how Hitler's policy developed from discrimination to annihilation.

W. S. Churchill, *The Second World War*, 6 vols. (1948–1954). The memoirs of the great British leader.

A. Crozier, *The Causes of the Second World War* (1997). An examination of what brought on the war.

J. C. Fest, *Hitler* (2002). Probably the best Hitler biography.

R. B. Frank, *Downfall: The End of the Imperial Japanese Empire* (1998). A thorough, well-documented account of the last months of the Japanese Empire and why it surrendered.

J. L. Gaddis, *We Now Know: Rethinking Cold War History* (1998). A fine account of the early Cold War using new evidence emerging since the collapse of the Soviet Union.

J. L. Gaddis, P. H. Gordon, and E. May eds., *Cold War Statesmen Confront the Bomb: Nuclear Diplomacy since 1945* (1999). Essays on the effect of atomic and nuclear weapons on diplomacy since World War II.

M. Gilbert, *The Holocaust: A History of the Jews of Europe during the Second World War* (1985). The best and most comprehensive treatment.

M. Hastings, *The Second World War: A World in Flames* (2004). A fine account by a leading student of contemporary warfare.

A. Iriye, *Pearl Harbor and the Coming of the Pacific War* (1999). Essays on how the Pacific war came about, including a selection of documents.

J. Keegan, *The Second World War* (1990). A lively and penetrating account by a master military historian.

W. F. Kimball, *Forged in War: Roosevelt, Churchill, and the Second World War* (1998). A study of the collaboration between the two great leaders of the West.

M. Knox, *Common Destiny, Dictatorship, Foreign Policy, and War in Fascist Italy and Nazi Germany* (2000). A brilliant comparison between the two dictatorships.

M. Knox, *Mussolini Unleashed* (1982). An outstanding study of fascist Italy in World War II.

S. Marks, *The Illusion of Peace* (1976). A good discussion of European international relations in the 1920s and early 1930s.

W. Murray, *The Change in the European Balance of Power 1938–1939* (1984). A brilliant study of the relationship among strategy, foreign policy, economics, and domestic politics.

W. Murray and A. R. Millett, *A War to Be Won: Fighting the Second World War* (2000). A splendid account of military operations.

P. Neville, *Hitler and Appeasement: The British Attempt to Prevent the Second World War* (2005). A defense of the British appeasers of Hitler.

R. Overy, *Why the Allies Won* (1997). An analysis of the reasons for the Allied victory with emphasis on technology.

N. Rich, *Hitler's War Aims*, 2 vols. (1973–1974). The best study of the subject in English.

D. Vital, *A People Apart: The Jews in Europe, 1789–1939* (1999). A major survey with excellent discussions of the interwar period.

R. Wade, *The Russian Revolution, 1917* (2000). A fine account that includes political and social history.

G. L. Weinberg, *A World at Arms: A Global History of World War II* (1994). An excellent narrative.

For additional learning resources related to this chapter, please go to www.myhistorylab.com

myhistorylab

A statue of Queen Victoria is removed from the front of the Supreme Court building in Georgetown, former capital of the British colony of Guyana, in February 1970, in preparation for the transition to independence. Decolonization represented as dramatic a transition in world political relations as had the establishment of European empires in the nineteenth-century Victorian age.

29 The Cold War Era, Decolonization, and the Emergence of a New Europe

▼ **The Emergence of the Cold War**
Containment in American Foreign Policy • Soviet Domination of Eastern Europe • The Postwar Division of Germany • NATO and the Warsaw Pact • The Creation of the State of Israel • The Korean War

▼ **The Khrushchev Era in the Soviet Union**
Khrushchev's Domestic Policies • The Three Crises of 1956

▼ **Later Cold War Confrontations**
The Berlin Wall • The Cuban Missile Crisis

▼ **The Brezhenev Era**
1968: The Invasion of Czechoslovakia • The United States and Détente • The Invasion of Afghanistan • Communism and Solidarity in Poland • Relations with the Reagan Administration

▼ **Decolonization: The European Retreat from Empire**
Major Areas of Colonial Withdrawal • India • Further British Retreat from Empire

▼ **The Turmoil of French Decolonization**
France and Algeria • France and Vietnam • Vietnam Drawn into the Cold War • Direct United States Involvement

▼ **The Collapse of European Communism**
Gorbachev Attempts to Reform the Soviet Union • 1989: Revolution in Eastern Europe • The Collapse of the Soviet Union • The Yeltsin Decade

▼ **The Collapse of Yugoslavia and Civil War**

▼ **Putin and the Resurgence of Russia**

▼ **The Rise of Radical Political Islamism**
Arab Nationalism • The Iranian Revolution • Afghanistan and Radical Islamism

▼ **A Transformed West**

▼ **In Perspective**

KEY TOPICS

- **The origins of the Cold War and the division of Europe into Eastern and Western blocs following World War II**
- **Major moments of Cold War tensions**
- **Decolonization and the conflicts in Korea and Vietnam**
- **Polish protests against Soviet domination of Eastern Europe**
- ***Perestroika* and *glasnost* in the Soviet Union**
- **The collapse of communism in Eastern Europe and the Soviet Union**
- **The civil war in Yugoslavia**
- **The rise of radical political Islamism**

SINCE THE END of World War II in 1945, two often interrelated sets of fundamental, international political relationships have shaped the experience of Europe, the United States, and the wider global community. These were the **Cold War** between the United States and the Soviet Union and the long process of **decolonization**, whereby the peoples of those regions of the world formally or informally dominated by European nations and later by the United States have rejected that domination.

From the end of World War II in 1945 until the collapse of communist regimes in Eastern Europe between 1989 and 1991, the Soviet Union and the United States—two nuclear-armed superpowers—confronted each other in a simmering conflict known as the **Cold War**. While it lasted, this conflict dominated global politics and threatened the peace of Europe, which stood divided between the U.S.-dominated North Atlantic Treaty Organization (NATO) and the Soviet-dominated Warsaw Pact.

Decolonization very rapidly became enmeshed with the Cold War. As the nations of Europe retreated from empire, the rivalry between the two superpowers expanded into a contest for dominance in the postcolonial world. Superpower intervention aggravated local conflicts on every continent. In its efforts to limit communism, the United States became embroiled in bitter wars in Korea and Vietnam. The struggle between Israel and the Arab nations likewise became an arena of superpower conflict.

In the almost two decades since the collapse of the Soviet Union, the United States has remained the world's single superpower. It has become symbolically identified as embodying the political, economic, and cultural values of modern Western civilization. In this role, it has replaced Europe as the object of anti-Western resistance. One of the numerous results of this new situation is the clash between the United States and radical political Islamism. The result has been the terrorist attacks on the United States on September 11, 2001, and the subsequent American intervention in Afghanistan and Iraq.

One way to think of the past sixty years is to see the history of Western civilization as entering a new global era. Europe and later the United States had been active across the world scene since the end of the fifteenth century. Europe had created formal and informal regions of empire by the early twentieth century. However, commencing strongly in the 1930s and continuing to the present day, those once colonially dominated areas of the world have actively impacted upon the international relations and domestic politics of many European nations and of the United States rather than remaining regions largely subject to Western economic, political, and military influence. The give and take of political, economic, military, and cultural power has become far more reciprocal between the West and the rest of the global community.

▼ The Emergence of the Cold War

The tense relationship between the United States and the Soviet Union began in the closing months of World War II. Some scholars attribute the hardening of the atmosphere between the two countries to Harry Truman's assumption of the presidency in April 1945, after the death of the more sympathetic Franklin Roosevelt, and to the American possession of an effective atomic bomb. Evidence suggests, however, that Truman was trying to carry Roosevelt's policies forward and that Soviet actions in Eastern Europe had begun to distress Roosevelt himself. Some have also argued that Truman did not use the atomic bomb to try to keep Russia out of the Pacific. On the contrary, he worked hard to ensure Russian intervention against Japan in 1945. In part, the coldness between the Allies arose from the mutual feeling that each had violated previous agreements. The Russians were plainly asserting permanent control of Poland and Romania under puppet communist governments. The United States was taking a harder line about German reparation payments to the Soviet Union.

In retrospect, however, and as more information emerges from the previously closed Soviet archives, it appears unlikely that friendlier styles on either side could have avoided a split that arose from basic differences of ideology and interest. The Soviet Union's attempt to extend its control westward into central Europe and the Balkans and southward into the Middle East continued the general thrust of the foreign policy of tsarist Russia. Britain had traditionally tried to restrain Russian expansion into these areas, and the United States inherited that task as Britain's power waned.

The Americans made no attempt to roll back Soviet power where it existed at the close of World War II. (See Map 29–1, page 904.) At the time, American military forces were the greatest in U.S. history, American industrial power was unmatched in the world, and atomic weapons were an American monopoly. In less than a year from the war's end, the Americans had reduced their forces in Europe from 3.5 million to 500,000. The speed of the withdrawal reflected domestic pressure to "get the boys home" but was also fully in accord with America's peacetime plans and goals, which included support for self-determination, autonomy, and democracy in the political sphere, and free trade, freedom of the seas, no barriers to investment, and an Open Door policy in the economic sphere. These goals reflected American principles and served American interests well. As the strongest, richest nation in the world—the one with the greatest industrial base and the strongest currency—the United States would benefit handsomely from an international order based on such goals.

Although postwar American hostility to colonial empires created tensions with France and Britain, the main conflict lay with the Soviet Union. The growth in France

Map 29–1 **TERRITORIAL CHANGES IN EUROPE AFTER WORLD WAR II** The map shows the shifts in territory that followed the defeat of the Axis. No treaty of peace formally ended the war with Germany.

and Italy of large popular communist parties taking orders from Moscow led the Americans to believe that Stalin was engaged in a worldwide plot to subvert capitalism and democracy. From the Soviet perspective, extending the borders of the USSR and dominating the formerly independent successor states of Eastern Europe would provide needed security and compensate for the fearful losses the Soviet people had endured in the war. The Soviets could thus see American resistance to their expansion as a threat to their security and their legitimate aims. They considered American objections to Soviet actions in Poland and other states as an effort to undermine regimes friendly to Russia and to encircle the Soviet Union with hostile neighbors. The Soviets could also use this point of view to justify their own attempts to overthrow regimes friendly to the United States in Western Europe and elsewhere.

Evidence of the new mood of postwar hostility between the former allies was soon apparent. In February 1946, both Stalin and his foreign minister, Vyacheslav Molotov (1890–1986), publicly spoke of the Western democracies as enemies. A month later, Churchill gave a speech in Fulton, Missouri, in which he declared that an "Iron Curtain" had descended on Europe, dividing a free and democratic West from an East under totalitarian rule. He warned against communist subversion and urged Western unity and strength against the new menace. In this atmosphere, difficulties grew.

Containment in American Foreign Policy

The resistance of Americans and Western Europeans to what they increasingly perceived as Soviet intransigence and communist plans for subversion and expansion took a clearer form in 1947. The American policy became known as one of **containment**, the purpose of which was to resist the extension of Soviet expansion and influence in the expectation that eventually the Soviet Union would collapse from internal pressures and the burdens of its foreign oppression. This strategy, which American policymakers devised in the late 1940s, would direct the broad outlines of American foreign policy for the next four decades, until the Soviet Union did collapse from exactly such pressures. Containment marked a major departure in American foreign policy and transformed the international situation during the second half of the twentieth century. The execution of the policy led the United States to enter overseas alliances, to make formal and informal commitments of support to regimes around the world it perceived as being anticommunist, to undertake enormous military expenditures, and to send large amounts of money abroad. In all these respects, the United States assumed unprecedented long-term foreign policy responsibilities. The United States thus became a permanent player in European international relations and in areas of the world where only European nations had been involved earlier in the century. (See "Compare & Connect: The Soviet Union and the United States Draw the Lines of the Cold War," pages 906–907.)

The Truman Doctrine Since 1944, civil war had been raging in Greece between the royalist government restored by Britain and insurgents supported by the communist countries, chiefly Yugoslavia. In 1947, Britain informed the United States it could no longer financially support its Greek allies. On March 12, President Truman asked Congress to provide funds to support Greece and Turkey, which was then under Soviet pressure to yield control of the Dardanelles, and Congress complied. In a speech to Congress that gave these actions much broader significance, the president set forth what came to be called the Truman Doctrine. He advocated a policy of support for "free people who are resisting attempted subjugation by armed minorities or by outside pressures," by implication, anywhere in the world.

The Marshall Plan American aid to Greece and Turkey took the form of military equipment and advisers. For Western Europe, where postwar poverty and hunger fueled the menacing growth of communist parties, the Americans devised the European Recovery Program. Named the **Marshall Plan** after George C. Marshall (1880–1959), the secretary of state who introduced it, this program provided broad economic aid to European states on the sole condition that they work together for their mutual benefit. The Soviet Union and its satellites were invited to participate. Finland and Czechoslovakia were willing to do so, and Poland and Hungary showed interest. The Soviets, however, forbade them to take part.

The Marshall Plan restored prosperity to Western Europe and set the stage for Europe's unprecedented postwar economic growth. In addition to the vast program of American economic aid, the strong Christian Democratic movement that dominated the politics of Italy, France, and West Germany worked to keep communist influence at bay outside the Soviet sphere in Eastern Europe.

Following the declaration of the Truman Doctrine and the announcement of the Marshall Plan, the Soviet Union defined a new era of conflict between the United States and itself. (See "Compare & Connect: The Soviet Union and the United States Draw the Lines of the Cold War," pages 906–907.)

Soviet Domination of Eastern Europe

The Soviet determination to control Eastern Europe had both historical and ideological roots. Western European powers had invaded Russia twice in the nineteenth century (under Napoleon in 1812 and during the Crimean War of 1854–1856) and already twice more in the twentieth century. Tsarist Russia had governed most of Poland from the 1790s to 1915 and had intervened at the request of the Austrian Empire to put down the Hungarian revolution in 1849. Russia's interests in Turkey and the lands around the Black Sea were similarly longstanding. Given this history and the Soviet Union's extraordinary losses in World War II, it is not surprising that Soviet leaders sought to use their Eastern European satellites as a buffer against future invasions.

Stalin may have seen containment as a renewed Western attempt to isolate and encircle the USSR. In Eastern

President Harry Truman greets Secretary of State George Marshall returning from Europe. Truman and Marshall were the architects of American foreign policy during the early years of the Cold War. Hulton Archive Photos/Getty Images, Inc.

COMPARE AND CONNECT

The Soviet Union and the United States Draw the Lines of the Cold War

BETWEEN 1945 AND 1950 the lines of tensions between the United States and the Soviet Union that became known as the Cold War were drawn. Each country quickly came to define the other as its principal enemy on the world scene. These two documents illustrate the manner in which each nation set its conflict with the other into a larger framework of ideological and political rivalry. Much of the rhetoric of these two documents would characterize the Cold War from its inception until the collapse of the Soviet Union.

QUESTIONS

1. **How did the Cominform use the terms "democratic" and "imperialist" to its advantage?**
2. **Why did it see the Marshall Plan as an act of aggression?**
3. **How did the National Security Council characterize Soviet policy?**
4. **What were the goals of containment?**
5. **Why did the Council urge that the Soviet Union always be given opportunity to save face and to back down with dignity?**
6. **How does each document indicate that both the Soviet Union and the United States regarded their tensions and conflict as part of a wider global political scene?**

I. The Cominform Defines Conflict between the Soviet Union and the United States

In 1947, under the leadership of the Soviet Union, the leaders of the Soviet and East European Communist Parties formed the Communist Information Bureau, which became known as the Cominform. It was organized in the wake of the Truman Doctrine and Marshall Plan. In September 1947, the Communist Parties constituting the Cominform issued a statement that set forth their view of the emerging conflict between the Soviet bloc and the United States. In doing so, they not only attacked the United States, but also the democratic socialist parties of Western Europe that the Soviet Union had seen as an enemy since the days of Lenin.

Fundamental changes have taken place in the international situation as a result of the Second World War and in the post-war period.

These changes are characterized by a new disposition of the basic political forces operating in the world arena, by a change in the relations among the victor states in the Second World War, and their realignment.

. . . The Soviet Union and the other democratic countries regarded as their basic war aims the restoration and consolidation of democratic order in Europe, the eradication of fascism and the prevention of the possibility of new aggression on the part of Germany, and the establishment of a lasting all-round cooperation among the nations of Europe. The United States of America, and Britain in agreement with them, set themselves another aim in the war: to rid themselves of competitors on the markets (Germany and Japan and to establish their dominant position. . . .

Thus two camps were formed—the imperialist and anti-democratic camp having as its basic aim the establishment of world domination of American imperialism and the smashing of democracy, and the anti-imperialist and democratic camp having as its basic aim the undermining of imperialism, the consolidation of democracy, and the eradication of the remnants of fascism. . . .

. . . the imperialist camp and its leading force, the United States, are displaying particularly aggressive activity. . . .The Truman-Marshall Plan is only a constituent part . . . of the general plan for the policy of global expansion pursued by the United States in all parts of the World. . . .

To frustrate the plan of imperialist aggression the efforts of all the democratic anti-imperialist forces of Europe are necessary. The right-wing Socialists are traitors to this cause. . . . and primarily the French Socialists and the British Labourites . . . by their servility and sycophancy are helping American capital to achieve its aims, provoking it to resort to extortion and impelling their own countries on to a path of vassal-like dependence on the United States of America.

This imposes a special task on the Communist Parties. They must take into their hands the banner of defense of the national independence and sovereignty of their countries. . . .

The principle danger for the working class today lies in underestimating their own strength and overestimating the strength of the imperialist camp.

Source: United States Senate, 81st Congress, 1st Session, Document No. 48, *North Atlantic Treaty: Documents Relating to the North Atlantic Treaty* (Washington, DC: U. S. Government Printing Office, 1949), pp. 117–120 as quoted in Katharine J. Lualdi, *Sources of the Making of the West: Peoples and Culture* (Boston: Bedford/St. Martin's, 2009), 2, pp. 248–250.

The Allied airlift in action during the Berlin Blockade. Every day for almost a year Western planes supplied the city until Stalin lifted the blockade in May 1949. Art Resource/Bildarchiv Preussischer Kulturbesitz

The design, therefore, calls for the complete subversion or forcible destruction of the machinery of government and structure of society in the countries of the non-Soviet world and their replacement by an apparatus and structure subservient to and controlled from the Kremlin. . . .

Our overall policy at the present time may be described as one designed to foster a world environment in which the American system can survive and flourish. It therefore rejects the concept of isolation and affirms the necessity of our positive participation in the world community.

This broad intention embraces two subsidiary policies. One is a policy which we would probably pursue even if there were no Soviet threat. It is a policy of attempting to develop a healthy international community. The other is the policy of "containing" the Soviet system. . . .

As for the policy of "containment," it is one which seeks by all means short of war to (1) block further expansion of Soviet power, (2) expose the falsities of Soviet pretensions, (3) induce a retraction of the Kremlin's control and influence, and (4) in general, so foster the seeds of destruction within the Soviet system that the Kremlin is brought at least to the point of modifying its behavior to conform to generally accepted international standards. . . .

One of the most important ingredients of power is military strength. . . . Without superior aggregate military strength . . . a policy of "containment"—which is in effect a policy of calculated and gradual coercion—is no more than a policy of bluff.

At the same time, it is essential to the successful conduct of a policy of "containment" that we always leave open the possibility of negotiation with the USSR . . .

In "containment" it is desirable to exert pressure in a fashion which will avoid so far as possible directly challenging Soviet prestige, to keep open the possibility for the USSR to retreat before pressure with a minimum loss of face and to secure political advantage from the failure of the Kremlin to yield or take advantage of the openings we leave it.

Source: National Security Council, Paper Number 68, *Foreign Relations of the United States* (Washington, DC: U.S. Government Printing Office, 1977), Sections: III, IV, VI. as cited on www.seattleu.edu/artsci/history/us1945/docs/nsc68-1.htm

II. The United States National Security Council Proposes to Contain the Soviet Union

In response to the domination of Eastern Europe by Communist Parties dominated by the Soviet Union and the occupation of these nations by Soviet troops, the United States government in 1950 adopted a policy of "containment" of the Soviet Union. This policy had been debated for many months and had for all practical purposes been in effect since the declaration of the Truman Doctrine in 1947. It was formally set forth after a period of implementation in what became known as the National Security Council Paper 68, arguably the most important statement of American foreign policy of the mid-twentieth century. The paper presented the Soviet Union as a nation determined to pursue an expansionist foreign policy and ideological struggle and as a long-term solution to that challenge proposed a policy of containing the influence of the Soviet Union diplomatically and militarily.

The fundamental design of those who control the Soviet Union and the international communist movement is to retain and solidify their absolute power, first in the Soviet Union and second in the areas now under their control. . . .

MAJOR DATES OF EARLY COLD WAR YEARS

1945	Yalta Conference
1945	Founding of the United Nations
1946	Churchill's Iron Curtain speech
1947 (March)	Truman Doctrine regarding Greece and Turkey
1947 (June)	Announcement of Marshall Plan
1948	Communist takeover in Czechoslovakia
1948	Communist takeover in Hungary
1948–1949	Berlin blockade
1949	NATO founded
1949	East and West Germany emerge as separate states
1950–1953	Korean conflict
1955	Warsaw Pact founded

Europe, the Soviet Union found numerous supporters among those segments of the population who had opposed the various right-wing movements in those countries before the war and who had fought the Nazis during the war. In the autumn of 1947, Stalin called a meeting in Warsaw of all communist parties from around the globe. There they organized the Communist Information Bureau (Cominform), a revival of the old Comintern, dedicated to spreading revolutionary communism throughout the world. In Western Europe the establishment of the Cominform officially ended the era of the popular front during which communists had cooperated with noncommunist parties. Hard-liners who supported the Soviet line on every issue replaced communist leaders in the West who favored collaboration and reform.

In February 1948, in Prague, Stalin gave a brutal display of his new policy of bringing the governments of Eastern Europe under direct Soviet control. The communists expelled the democratic members of what had been a coalition government and murdered Jan Masaryk (1886–1948), the foreign minister and son of the founder of Czechoslovakia, Thomas Masaryk. President Edvard Beneš (1884–1948) was forced to resign, and Czechoslovakia was brought fully under Soviet rule. There and elsewhere in Eastern Europe, it was clear there would be no multiparty political system.

During the late 1940s, the Soviet Union required the other subject governments in Eastern Europe to impose Stalinist policies, including one-party political systems, close military cooperation with the Soviet Union, the collectivization of agriculture, Communist Party domination of education, and attacks on the churches. Longtime Communist Party officials were purged and condemned in show trials like those that had taken place in Moscow during the late 1930s. The catalyst for this harsh tightening probably was the success of Marshal Josip (Broz) Tito (1892–1980), the leader of communist Yugoslavia, in freeing his country from Soviet domination. Stalin wanted to prevent other Eastern European states from following the Yugoslav example.

The Postwar Division of Germany

Soviet actions, especially those in Czechoslovakia, increased the determination of the United States to go ahead with its own arrangements in Germany.

Disagreements over Germany During the war, the Allies had never decided how to treat Germany after its defeat. At first they all agreed it should be dismembered, but they differed on how. By the time of Yalta, Churchill had come to fear Russian control of Eastern and central Europe and began to oppose dismemberment.

The Allies also differed on economic policy. The Russians swiftly dismantled German industry in the eastern zone, but the Americans acted differently in the western zone. They concluded that if they followed the Soviet policy, the United States would have to support Germany economically for the foreseeable future. It would also cause chaos and open the way for communism. They preferred, therefore, to try to make Germany self-sufficient, and this meant restoring, rather than destroying, its industrial capacity. To the Soviets, the restoration of a powerful industrial Germany, even in the western zone only, was frightening. The same difference of approach hampered agreement on reparations. The Soviets claimed the right to the industrial equipment in all the zones, and the Americans resisted their demands.

Berlin Blockade When the Western powers agreed to go forward with a separate constitution for the western sectors of Germany in February 1948, the Soviets walked out of the joint Allied Control Commission. In the summer of that year, the Western powers issued a new currency in their zone. All four powers governed Berlin, though it was well within the Soviet zone. The Soviets feared the new currency, which was circulating in Berlin at better rates than their own currency. They chose to seal the city off by closing all railroads and highways that led from Berlin to West Germany. Their purpose was to drive the Western powers out of Berlin.

The Western allies responded to the Berlin blockade by airlifting supplies to the city for almost a year. In May 1949, the Russians were forced to reopen access to Berlin. The incident, however, was decisive. It increased tensions and suspicions between the opponents and hastened the separation of Germany into two states. West Germany formally became the German Federal Republic in September 1949, and the eastern region became the German Democratic Republic a month later. Ironically, Germany had been dismembered in a way no one had planned or expected. The two Germanys and the di-

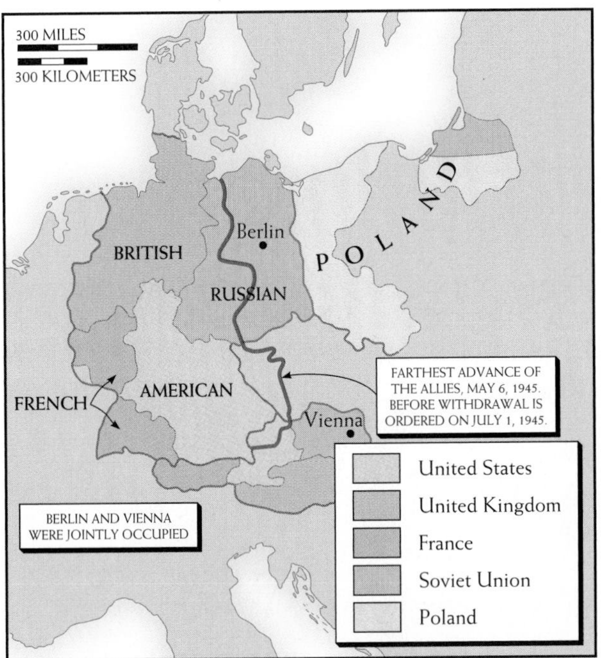

Map 29–2 **OCCUPIED GERMANY AND AUSTRIA** At the war's end, defeated Germany, including Austria, was occupied by the victorious Allies in the several zones shown here. Austria, by prompt agreement, was reestablished as an independent, neutral state, no longer occupied. The German zones hardened into an "East" Germany (the former Soviet zone) and a "West" Germany (the former British, French, and American zones). Berlin, within the Soviet zone, was similarly divided.

vided city of Berlin, isolated within East Germany, would remain central fixtures in the geopolitics of the Cold War until 1989. (See Map 29–2.)

NATO and the Warsaw Pact

Meanwhile, the nations of Western Europe had been drawing closer together. The Marshall Plan encouraged international cooperation. In March 1948, Belgium, the Netherlands, Luxembourg, France, and Britain signed the Treaty of Brussels, providing for cooperation in economic and military matters. In April 1949, these nations joined with Italy, Denmark, Norway, Portugal, and Iceland to sign a treaty with Canada and the United States that formed the North Atlantic Treaty Organization (NATO), which committed its members to mutual assistance if any of them was attacked. The NATO treaty transformed the West into a bloc. A few years later, West Germany, Greece, and Turkey joined the alliance. For the first time in history, the United States was committed to defend allies outside the western hemisphere.

A series of bilateral treaties providing for close ties and mutual assistance in case of attack governed Soviet relations with the states of Eastern Europe. In 1949, these states formed the Council of Mutual Assistance (COMECON) to integrate their economies. Unlike the NATO states, the Soviets directly dominated the Eastern alliance system through local communist parties controlled from Moscow and the presence of the Red Army. The Warsaw Pact of May 1955, which included Albania, Bulgaria, Czechoslovakia, East Germany, Hungary, Poland, Romania, and the Soviet Union, gave formal recognition to this system. Europe was divided into two unfriendly blocs. The Cold War had taken firm shape in Europe. (See Map 29–3, page 910.)

The strategic interests of the United States and the Soviet Union would not, however, permit the Cold War to be limited to the European continent. Major flash points would erupt around the world during the decades that followed, particularly in the Middle East and Asia. The establishment of a communist government in Cuba after 1959 would bring the conflict to the American hemisphere as well. In each case, the Cold War rivalry transformed what might otherwise have been regional conflicts into superpower strategic concerns.

The Creation of the State of Israel

One of the areas of ongoing regional conflict that became a major point of Cold War rivalry was the Middle East. Following World War I, Great Britain had exercised the chief political influence in the region under various mandates from the League of Nations. After World War II, both the Zionist movement, which sought to establish an independent Jewish state, and Arab nationalists, who sought to achieve self-determination, challenged British authority and influence.

British Balfour Declaration The modern state of Israel was the achievement of the world Zionist movement, founded in 1897 by Theodor Herzl (see Chapter 24) and later led by Chaim Weizmann (1874–1952). In 1917, during World War I, Arthur Balfour (1846–1930), the British foreign secretary, declared that Britain favored establishing a national home for the Jewish people in Palestine, which was then under Ottoman rule. Between the wars, thousands of Jews, mainly from Europe, immigrated to what had become British-ruled Palestine. During this period, the *Yishuv*, or Jewish community in Palestine, developed its own political parties, press, labor unions, and educational system. Arabs already living in Palestine considered the Jewish settlers intruders, and violent conflicts ensued. The British tried, but failed, to mediate these clashes.

This situation might have prevailed longer, except for the outbreak of World War II and Hitler's attempt to exterminate the Jews of Europe. The Nazi persecution united Jews throughout the world behind the Zionist ideal of a Jewish state in Palestine, and it touched the conscience of the United States and other Western powers. It seemed morally right to do something for the Jewish refugees from Nazi concentration camps.

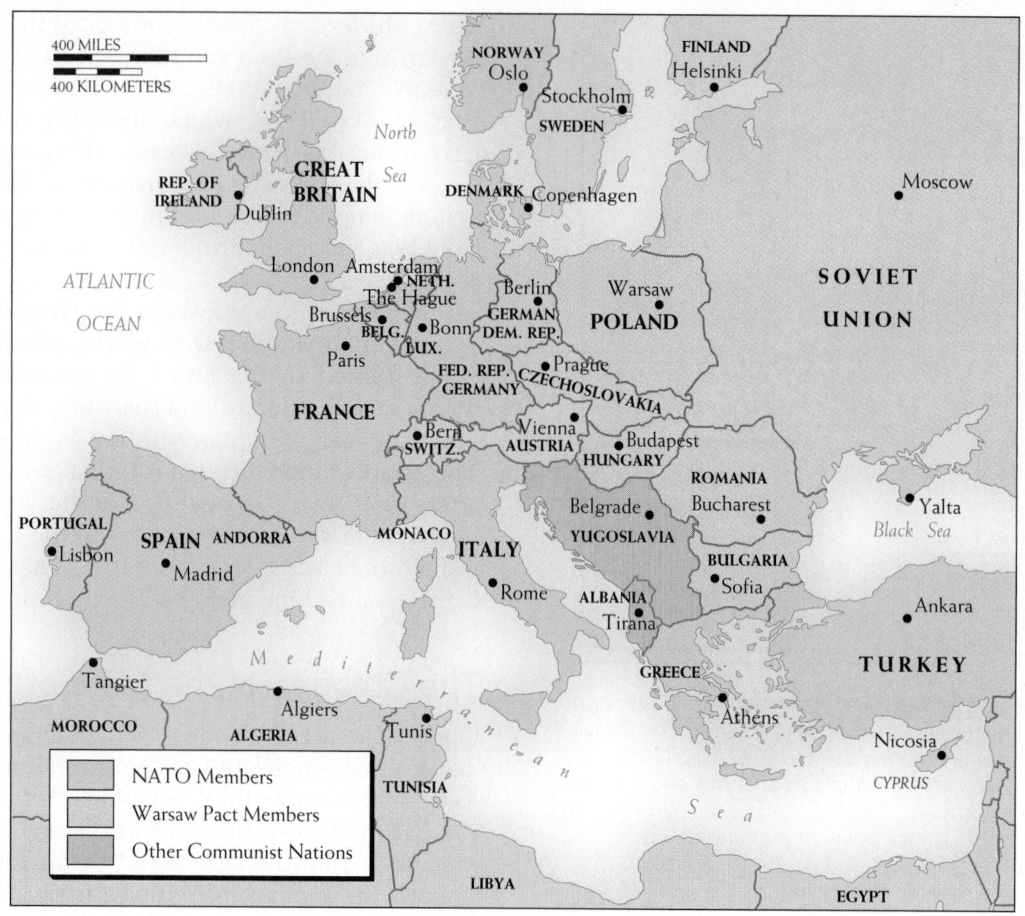

Map 29–3 **MAJOR COLD WAR EUROPEAN ALLIANCE SYSTEMS** The North Atlantic Treaty Organization, which includes both Canada and the United States, stretches as far east as Turkey. By contrast, the Warsaw Pact nations were the contiguous Communist states of Eastern Europe, with the Soviet Union, of course, as the dominant member.

The U.N. Resolution In 1947, the British turned over to the United Nations the problem of the relationship of Arabs and Jews in Palestine. That same year, the United Nations passed a resolution dividing the territory into two states, one Jewish and one Arab. The Arabs in Palestine and the surrounding Arab states resisted this resolution. Not unnaturally, they resented the influx of new settlers. Many Palestinian Arabs were displaced and became refugees themselves.

Israel Declares Independence In May 1948, the British officially withdrew from Palestine, and the Yishuv declared the independence of a new Jewish state called *Israel* on May 14. Two days later, the United States, through the personal intervention of President Truman, recognized the new nation, whose first prime minister was David Ben-Gurion (1886–1973). Almost immediately, Lebanon, Syria, Jordan, Egypt, and Iraq invaded Israel. The fighting continued throughout 1948 and 1949. By the end of its war of independence against the Arabs, Israel had expanded its borders beyond the limits the United Nations had originally set forth. Jerusalem was divided between Jordan and Israel. By 1949, Israel had secured its existence, but not the acceptance of its Arab neighbors. As long as Egypt, Jordan, Syria, Lebanon, Iraq, and Saudi Arabia, to name those nations closest, withheld diplomatic recognition from Israel, the peace was only an armed truce. (See Map 29–4.)

The Arab-Israeli conflict would inevitably draw in the superpowers. The dispute directly involved Europe because many of the citizens of Israel had emigrated from there, and Europe, like the United States, was highly dependent on oil from Arab countries. Furthermore, both the United States and the Soviet Union believed they had major strategic and economic interests in the region.

By 1949, the United States had established itself as a firm ally of Israel. Gradually, the Soviet Union began to furnish aid to the Arab nations. The bipolar tensions that had settled over Europe were thus transferred to the Middle East. Furthermore, the existence of the state of Israel would become one of the major points of contention

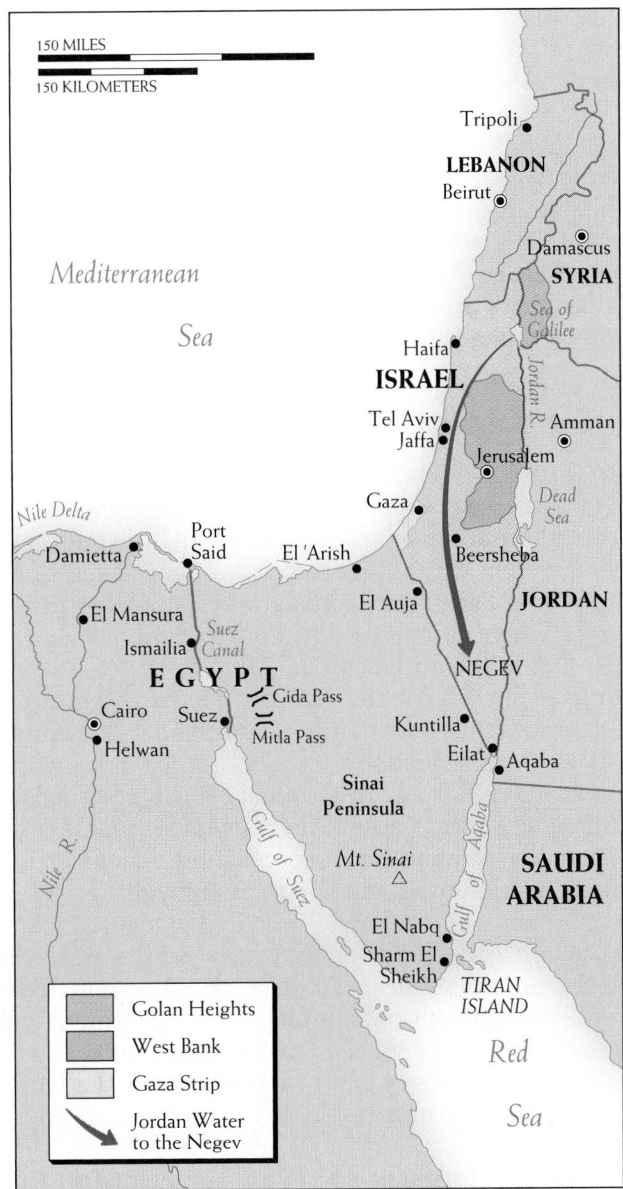

Map 29–4 **ISRAEL AND ITS NEIGHBORS IN 1949** The territories gained by Israel in 1949 did not secure peace in the region. In fact, the disposition of those lands and the Arab refugees who live there has constituted the core of the region's unresolved problems to the present day.

between the United States and the governments of the various Arab states and later one of the chief complaints of radical political Islamists against the United States.

The Korean War

While early stages of the Cold War took place in Europe and the Arab-Israeli conflict developed in the Middle East, the United States confronted armed aggression in Asia. As part of a UN police action, it intervened militarily in Korea, following the same principle of containment that directed its actions in Europe.

Between 1910 and 1945, Japan, as an Asian colonial power, had occupied and exploited the formerly independent kingdom of Korea, but at the close of World War II, the United States and the Soviet Union expelled the Japanese and divided Korea into two parts along the thirty-eighth parallel of latitude. Korea was supposed to be reunited. By 1948, however, two separate states had emerged: the Democratic People's Republic of Korea in the north, supported by the Soviet Union, and the Republic of Korea in the south, supported by the United States.

In late June 1950, after border clashes, North Korea invaded South Korea across the thirty-eighth parallel. The United States intervened, at first unilaterally and then under the authority of a UN resolution. Great Britain, Turkey, Australia, and other countries sent token forces. The Korean police action was technically a UN-sponsored venture to halt aggression. (It had been made possible when Stalin ordered the Soviet ambassador to boycott the United Nations when the key vote was taken.) For the United States, the point of the Korean conflict was to contain the spread and halt the aggression of communism.

Late in 1950, the Chinese, responding to the approach of UN forces near their border, sent troops to support North Korea. The American forces had to retreat. The U.S. policymakers believed, mistakenly, that the Chinese, who, since 1949, had been under the communist government of Mao Zedong (1893–1976), were simply Soviet puppets. Accordingly, the Americans viewed the movement of Chinese troops into Korea as another example of communist pressure against a noncommunist state, similar to what had previously happened in Europe. Today it is clear that Mao disliked Stalin and that tension existed between Moscow and the People's Republic of China, but that was little understood at the time.

On June 16, 1953, the Eisenhower administration concluded an armistice ending the Korean War and restoring the border near the thirty-eighth parallel. (See Map 29–5, page 912.) Thousands of American troops, however, are still stationed in Korea. The United States seemed to have successfully applied the lessons of the Cold War it had learned in Europe to Asia. The Korean War confirmed the American government's faith in containment. It also transformed the Cold War into a global rivalry that ranged well beyond Europe.

The formation of NATO and the Korean conflict capped the first round of the Cold War. In 1953, Stalin's death and the armistice in Korea fostered hopes that international tensions might ease. In early 1955, Soviet occupation forces left Austria after that nation accepted neutral status. Later that year, the leaders of France, Great Britain, the Soviet Union, and the United States held a summit conference in Geneva. Nuclear weapons

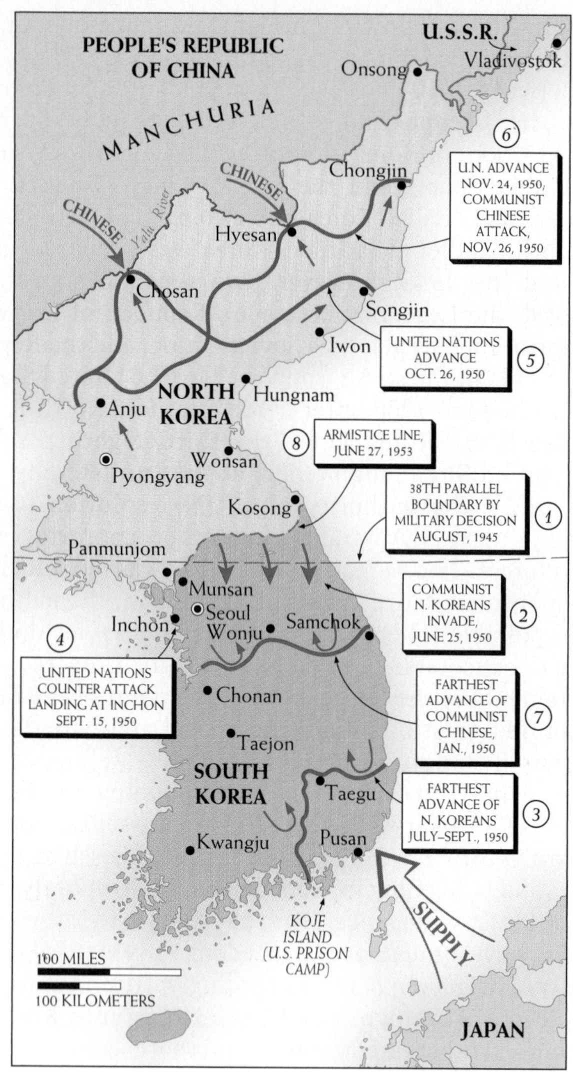

Map 29–5 **KOREA, 1950–1953** This map indicates the major developments in the bitter three-year struggle that followed the North Korean invasion of South Korea in 1950.

and the future of a divided Germany were the chief items on the agenda. Despite public displays of friendliness, the meeting produced few substantial agreements, and the Cold War soon resumed.

▼ The Khrushchev Era in the Soviet Union

No other nation had suffered greater losses or more deprivation during World War II than the Soviet Union. Many Russians had hoped the end of the war would signal a reduction in the scope of the police state and a redirection of the economy away from heavy industry to consumer products. They were disappointed. Stalin did little or nothing to modify the character of the regime he had created. If anything, his determination to centralize his authority and a desire to undertake a new wave of internal purges continued until his death on March 6, 1953.

For a time, no single leader replaced Stalin. Rather, the *presidium* (the renamed Politburo) pursued a policy of collective leadership. Gradually, however, power and influence began to devolve on Nikita Khrushchev (1894–1971), who had been named party secretary in 1953. Three years later, he became premier. Khrushchev's rise ended collective leadership, but he never commanded the extraordinary powers of Stalin.

Khrushchev's Domestic Policies

The Khrushchev era, which lasted until the autumn of 1964, witnessed a retreat from Stalinism, though not from authoritarianism. Khrushchev sought to reform the Soviet system but to maintain the dominance of the Communist Party. Intellectuals were somewhat freer to express their opinions. Although Boris Pasternak (1890–1960), the author of *Dr. Zhivago* (1957), was not permitted to receive the Nobel prize for literature in 1958, another dissident author, Aleksandr Solzhenitsyn (b. 1918), could publish *One Day in the Life of Ivan Denisovich* (1963), a grim account of life in a Soviet labor camp under Stalin. Khrushchev also made modest efforts to meet the demand for more consumer goods and decentralize economic planning. In agriculture, he removed many of the more restrictive regulations on private cultivation and sought to expand the area available for growing wheat. At first, this program led to record grain production, but inappropriate farming techniques soon reduced yields. The Soviet Union had to import vast quantities of grain each year from the United States and other countries.

The Secret Speech of 1956 In February 1956, Khrushchev made an extraordinary departure from expected practice by directly attacking the policies of the Stalin years. At the Twentieth Congress of the Com-

MAJOR DATES OF THE EARLY KHRUSHCHEV ERA

1953	Death of Stalin
1955	Austria established as a neutral state
1955	Geneva summit
1956 (February)	Khrushchev's secret speech denouncing Stalin
1956 (Autumn)	Polish crisis
1956 (October)	Suez crisis
1956 (October)	Hungarian uprising
1957	*Sputnik* launched

KHRUSHCHEV DENOUNCES THE CRIMES OF STALIN: THE SECRET SPEECH

In 1956, Khrushchev denounced Stalin in a secret speech to the Party Congress. The New York Times *published a text of that speech, smuggled from Russia.*

What specific actions by Stalin did Khrushchev denounce? Why does Khrushchev pay so much attention to Stalin's creation of the concept of an "enemy of the people"? Why does Khrushchev distinguish between the actions of Stalin and those of Lenin?

Stalin acted not through persuasion, explanation, and patient cooperation with people, but by imposing his concepts and demanding absolute submission to his opinion. Whoever opposed this concept or tried to prove his viewpoint and the correctness of his position was doomed to removal from the leading collective [group] and to subsequent moral and physical annihilation. . . .

Stalin originated the concept of "enemy of the people." This term automatically rendered it unnecessary that the ideological errors of a man or men engaged in a controversy be proved; this term made possible the usage of the most cruel repression violating all norms of revolutionary legality, against anyone who in any way disagreed with Stalin, against those who were only suspected of hostile intent, against those who had bad reputations.

This concept "enemy of the people" actually eliminated the possibility of any kind of ideological fight or the making of one's views known on this or that issue, even those of a practical character. In the main, and in actuality, the only proof of guilt used, against all norms of current legal science, was the "confession" of the accused himself; and, as a subsequent probing proved, "confessions" were acquired through physical pressures against the accused. . . .

Lenin used severe methods only in the most necessary cases, when the exploiting classes were still in existence and were vigorously opposing the revolution, when the struggle for survival was decidedly assuming the sharpest forms, even including civil war.

Stalin, on the other hand, used extreme methods and mass repressions at a time when the revolution was already victorious, when the Soviet State was strengthened, when the exploiting classes were already liquidated and Socialist relations were rooted solidly in all phases of national economy, when our party was politically consolidated and had strengthened itself both numerically and ideologically. It is clear that here Stalin showed in a whole series of cases his intolerance, his brutality and his abuse of power. Instead of proving his political correctness and mobilizing the masses, he often chose the path of repression and physical annihilation, not only against actual enemies, but also against individuals who had not committed any crimes against the party and the Soviet Government.

munist Party, Khrushchev gave a secret speech (later published outside the Soviet Union) in which he denounced Stalin and his crimes against socialist justice during the purges of the 1930s. The speech stunned party circles, but it also opened the way for genuine, if limited, internal criticism of the Soviet government and for many of the changes in intellectual and economic life cited earlier. Gradually, Khrushchev removed the strongest supporters of Stalinist policies from the presidium. By 1958, all of Stalin's former supporters were gone, and none had been executed. (See "Khrushchev Denounces the Crimes of Stalin: The Secret Speech.")

Khrushchev's speech, however, had repercussions well beyond the borders of the Soviet Union. Communist leaders in Eastern Europe took it as a signal that they could govern with greater leeway than before and retreat from Stalinist policies. Indeed, Khrushchev's speech was simply the first of a number of extraordinary events in 1956.

The Three Crises of 1956

The Suez Intervention In July 1956, President Gamal Abdel Nasser (1918–1970) of Egypt nationalized the Suez Canal. Great Britain and France who had controlled the private company that had run the canal feared that this action would close the canal to their supplies of oil in the Persian Gulf. In October 1956, war broke out between Egypt and Israel. The British and French seized the opportunity to intervene militarily; however, the United States refused to support their action. The Soviet Union protested vehemently. The Anglo-French forces had to be withdrawn, and Egypt retained control of the canal.

The Suez intervention proved that without the support of the United States the nations of Western Europe could no longer impose their will on the rest of the world. It also appeared that the United States and the Soviet Union had restrained their allies from undertaking actions that might have resulted in a wider conflict. The fact that neither of the superpowers wanted war constrained both Egypt and the Anglo-French forces.

Polish Efforts Toward Independent Action The autumn of 1956 also saw important developments in Eastern Europe that demonstrated similar limitations on independent action among the Soviet bloc nations. When the prime minister of Poland died, the Polish Communist Party leaders refused to replace him with Moscow's nominee, despite considerable pressure from the Soviets. In the end, Wladyslaw Gomulka (1905–1982) emerged as the new Communist leader of Poland. He was the choice of the Poles, and he proved acceptable to the Soviets because he promised continued economic and military cooperation, and particularly because he continued Polish membership in the Warsaw Pact. Within those limits he halted the collectivization of Polish agriculture and improved relations with the Polish Roman Catholic Church.

The Hungarian Uprising Hungary provided the third trouble spot for the Soviet Union. In late October, demonstrations of sympathy for the Poles in Budapest led to street fighting. The Hungarian communists installed a new ministry headed by former premier Imre Nagy (1896–1958). Nagy was a Communist who sought a more independent position for Hungary. He went much further in his demands than Gomulka and directly appealed for political support from noncommunist groups in Hungary. Nagy called for the removal of Soviet troops and the ultimate neutralization of Hungary. He even called for Hungarian withdrawal from the Warsaw Pact. These demands were wholly unacceptable to the Soviet Union. In early November, Soviet troops invaded Hungary; deposed Nagy, who was later executed; and imposed Janos Kadar (1912–1989) as premier.

The events of 1956 in the Middle East and Eastern Europe solidified the position of the United States and the Soviet Union as superpowers. In different ways and to differing degrees, the two superpowers had demonstrated this new political reality to their allies. The nations of Western Europe would be able to make independent policy among themselves within Europe but were generally curtailed from independent action on the broader international scene. For approximately twenty-five years, the nations of Eastern Europe would be permitted virtually no autonomous actions in either the domestic or the international sphere.

▼ Later Cold War Confrontations

After 1956, the Soviet Union began to talk about "peaceful coexistence" with the United States. With the 1957 launch of *Sputnik*, the first satellite to orbit the earth, the Soviet Union appeared to have achieved an enormous technological superiority over the West. In 1958, the two countries began negotiations toward limiting the testing of nuclear weapons. By 1959, tensions had relaxed sufficiently for Western leaders to visit Moscow and for Khrushchev to tour the United States. A summit meeting was scheduled for May 1960, and President Eisenhower was to go to Moscow.

Just before the Paris Summit Conference, the Soviet Union shot down an American U-2 aircraft that was flying reconnaissance over Soviet territory. Khrushchev demanded an apology from Eisenhower for this air surveillance. Eisenhower accepted full responsibility for the surveillance policy but refused to apologize publicly. Khrushchev then refused to take part in the summit conference, just as the participants arrived in the French capital. The conference, as well as Eisenhower's proposed trip to the Soviet Union, was thus aborted.

The Soviets did not scuttle the summit meeting on the eve of its opening simply because of the American spy flights. They had long been aware of these flights and had other reasons for protesting them when they did. By 1960, the communist world itself had split between the Soviets and the Chinese, who were portraying the Russians as lacking revolutionary zeal. Destroying the summit was, in part, a way to demonstrate the Soviet Union's hard-line attitude toward the capitalist world.

The Berlin Wall

The aborted Paris conference opened the most difficult period of the Cold War. In 1961, the new U.S. president, John F. Kennedy (1917–1963), and Premier Khrushchev met in Vienna with inconclusive results.

Throughout 1961, thousands of refugees from East Germany crossed the border into West Berlin. This outflow of people embarrassed East Germany, hurt its economy, and demonstrated the Soviet Union's inability to control Eastern Europe. Consequently, in August 1961, the East Germans, with Soviet support, erected a concrete wall along the border between East and West Berlin, separating the two parts of the city. Despite speeches and symbolic support from the West, the wall halted the flow of refugees and brought the U.S. commitment to West Germany into doubt.

The Cuban Missile Crisis

The most dangerous days of the Cold War occurred during the Cuban missile crisis of 1962. This event represented another facet of the globalization of the Cold War, on this occasion, into the Americas. Cuba lies less than 100 miles off the Florida coast, and the United States had dominated the island since the Spanish-American War in 1898. In 1957, Fidel Castro (b. 1926) launched an insurgency in Cuba, which toppled the dictatorship of Flugencio Batista (1901–1973) on New Year's Day of 1959. Thereafter Castro established a communist government, and Cuba became an ally of the Soviet Union. These events caused enormous concern within the United States.

MAJOR DATES OF LATER COLD WAR YEARS

1959	Khrushchev's visit to the United States
1960	Failed Paris Summit
1961	East Germany erects Berlin Wall
1962	Cuban missile crisis
1963	Test Ban Treaty between Soviet Union and the United States
1964	Khrushchev falls from power
1968	Soviet invasion of Czechoslovakia
1972	Strategic Arms Limitation Treaty

In 1962, the Soviet Union secretly began to place nuclear missiles in Cuba. In response, the American government, under President Kennedy, blockaded Cuba, halted the shipment of new missiles, and demanded the removal of existing installations. After a tense week, during which nuclear war seemed a real possibility, the Soviets backed down, and the crisis ended. This adventurism in foreign policy undermined Khrushchev's credibility in the ruling circles of the Soviet Union and caused other non-European communist regimes to question the Soviet commitment to their security and survival. It also increased the influence of the People's Republic of China in communist circles and convinced

During the Cuban missile crisis of 1962, the American ambassador to the United Nations displayed photographs to persuade the world of the threat to the United States less than one hundred miles from its own shores. © CORBIS

Soviet military leaders of the need to strengthen their forces, so that they would be as strong as, or stronger than, those of the United States in any future confrontation.

If the Cuban missile crisis had led to war, the United States could have launched missiles over Europe or from European bases into the Soviet Union. The crisis thus threatened Europe directly, but it was the last major Cold War confrontation to do so. In 1963, the United States and the Soviet Union concluded a nuclear test ban treaty. This agreement marked the beginning of a lessening in the overt tensions between the two powers.

▼ The Brezhenev Era

By 1964, many in the Soviet Communist Party had concluded that Khrushchev had tried to do too much too soon and had done it poorly. On October 16, 1964, Khrushchev was forced to resign. He was replaced by Alexei Kosygin (1904–1980) as premier and Leonid Brezhnev (1906–1982) as party secretary. Brezhnev eventually emerged as the dominant figure.

1968: The Invasion of Czechoslovakia

In 1968, during what became known as the Prague Spring, the government of Czechoslovakia, under Alexander Dubcek (1921–1992), began to experiment with a more liberal communism. Dubcek expanded freedom of discussion and other intellectual rights at a time when the Soviet Union was suppressing them. In the summer of 1968, the Soviet government and its allies in the Warsaw Pact sent troops into Czechoslovakia and replaced Dubcek with communist leaders more to its own liking.

At the time of the invasion, Soviet party chairman Brezhnev, in what came to be termed the *Brezhnev Doctrine*, declared the right of the Soviet Union to interfere in the domestic politics of other communist countries. Whereas the Truman Doctrine of 1947 had supported democratic governments and offered help to resist further communist penetration in Europe, the Brezhnev Doctrine of 1968 sought to sustain the communist governments of Eastern Europe and prevent any liberalization in the region. No further direct Soviet interventions occurred in Eastern Europe after 1968, yet the invasion of Czechoslovakia showed that any attempt at a greater liberalization could trigger Soviet military repression.

In the summer of 1968, Soviet tanks rolled into Czechoslovakia, ending that country's experiment in liberalized communism. This picture shows defiant flag-waving Czechs on a truck rolling past a Soviet tank in the immediate aftermath of the invasion. Hulton Archive Photos/Getty Images, Inc.

The United States and Détente

Foreign policy under Brezhnev combined attempts to reach an accommodation with the United States with continued efforts to expand Soviet influence and maintain Soviet leadership of the communist movement.

Although the Soviet Union sided with North Vietnam in its war with the United States, which is discussed later in this chapter, Soviet support was restrained. Under President Richard Nixon (1969–1974), the United States began a policy of détente with the Soviet Union, and the two countries concluded agreements on trade and on reducing strategic arms. Despite these agreements, Soviet spending on defense, and particularly on its navy, grew, damaging the consumer sectors of the economy.

During Gerald Ford's presidency (1974–1977), both the United States and the Soviet Union along with other European nations signed the Helsinki Accords. The accords recognized the Soviet sphere of influence in Eastern Europe, but they also recognized the human rights of the signers' citizens, which every government, including the Soviet Union, agreed to protect. President Jimmy Carter (1977–1981), a strong advocate of human rights, sought to induce the Soviet Union to comply with this commitment, a policy that cooled relations between the two countries.

Throughout this period of détente, in addition to its military presence in Eastern Europe, the Soviet Union pursued an activist foreign policy around the world. During the 1970s, it financed Cuban military intervention in Angola, Mozambique, and Ethiopia. Soviet funds flowed to the Sandinista forces in Nicaragua and to Vietnam, which permitted the Soviets to use naval bases after North Vietnam conquered the south in 1975. The Soviet Union also provided funds and weapons to various Arab governments for use against Israel.

Each of these actions represented either Soviet support for what it viewed as its own strategic interests or an attempt to weaken the interests of the United States. Even more importantly, following its backing down in the Cuban missile crisis, the Soviet government was determined to build up its military forces. By the early 1980s, the Soviet Union possessed the largest armed force in the world and had achieved virtual nuclear parity with the United States.

The Invasion of Afghanistan

It was at this moment of great military strength in 1979 that the Brezhnev government decided to invade Afghanistan, a strategic decision of enormous long-range consequences for the future of the Soviet Union as well as the United States. Although the Soviet Union already had a presence in Afghanistan, the Brezhnev government, for reasons that remain unclear, determined to send in troops to ensure its influence in central Asia and to install a puppet Afghan government.

The invasion brought a sharp response from the United States. The U.S. Senate refused to ratify a second Strategic Arms Limitation agreement that President Carter had signed earlier that year. The United States also embargoed grain shipments to the Soviet Union, boycotted the 1980 Olympic Games in Moscow, and sent aid to the Afghan rebels through various third parties, as did Pakistan, Saudi Arabia, and other Islamic nations. The U.S. Central Intelligence Agency became directly involved with the Afghan resistance forces, some of whom were radical Muslims. China, which felt threatened by the invasion, also helped the rebels.

Eventually, the Soviet forces bogged down in Afghanistan and could not defeat their guerrilla enemies. The Afghans killed approximately 2,000 Soviet troops a year and inflicted many other casualties. The morale and prestige of the Soviet army plummeted. At first, few Soviets knew about the problems in Afghanistan, but during the 1980s, the military failure became common knowledge in the Soviet Union. Although the Afghan war did not make daily headline news in the Western press, it sapped Soviet strength for ten years and demoralized the Soviet Union not unlike the way the Vietnam conflict did the United States.

Communism and Solidarity in Poland

Events in Poland commencing in 1980—a time when the Soviet government was becoming increasingly rigidified and involved in Afghanistan—challenged both the authority of the Polish Communist Party and the influence of the Soviet Union.

After the events of late 1956, when the Polish Communist Party had accommodated itself to Soviet domination, chronic economic mismanagement and persistent shortages of food and consumer goods plagued Poland for twenty-five years. In 1978, the election of Karol Wojtyla, cardinal archbishop of Kraków, as Pope John Paul II (d. 2005) proved important for Polish resistance to communist control and Soviet domination. An outspoken Polish opponent of communism now occupied a position of authority and enormous public visibility well beyond the reach of Soviet or communist control. The new pope visited his homeland in 1979 and received a tumultuous welcome.

In July 1980, the Polish government raised meat prices, leading to hundreds of protest strikes across the country. On August 14, workers occupied the Lenin shipyard at Gdansk on the Baltic coast. The strike soon spread to other shipyards, transport facilities, and factories connected with the shipbuilding industry. The strikers, led by Lech Walesa (b. 1944), refused to negotiate through any of the government-controlled unions. The Gdansk strike ended on August 31 after the government promised the workers the right to organize an in-

MAJOR DATES OF THE BREZHNEV ERA

1974	Solzhenitsyn expelled
1975	Helsinki Accords
1979	Soviet invasion of Afghanistan
1980	U.S. Olympic Games boycott
1981	Martial law declared in Poland in response to Solidarity
1982	Death of Brezhnev

dependent union called Solidarity. In September, the head of the Polish Communist Party was replaced, the Polish courts recognized Solidarity as an independent union, and the state-controlled radio broadcast a Roman Catholic mass for the first time in thirty years.

The summer of 1981 saw events that were no less remarkable occur within the Polish Communist Party itself. For the first time in any European communist state, secret elections for the party congress were permitted with real choices among the candidates. A single party continued to govern Poland, but for the time being, the party congress permitted real debate within its ranks.

This extraordinary Polish experiment, however, ended abruptly. In 1981, General Wojciech Jaruzelski (b. 1923) became head of the Polish Communist Party, and the army imposed martial law in December. The leaders of Solidarity were arrested. The Polish military acted to preserve its own position and perhaps to prevent a Soviet invasion similar to the one in Czechoslovakia in 1968. Martial law remained in effect until late in 1983, but the Polish Communist Party could not solve Poland's major economic problems.

Relations with the Reagan Administration

Early in the administration of President Ronald Reagan (1981–1989), the United States relaxed its grain embargo on the Soviet Union and placed less emphasis on human rights. At the same time, however, Reagan intensified Cold War rhetoric, famously describing the Soviet Union as an "evil empire." More importantly, the Reagan administration increased U.S. military spending, slowed arms limitation negotiations, deployed a new missile system in Europe, and proposed the Strategic Defense Initiative (dubbed "Star Wars" by the press), involving a high-technology space-based defense against nuclear attack. The Star Wars proposal, although controversial in the United States, was a major issue in later arms control negotiations with the Soviet Union. Star Wars and the Reagan defense spending forced the Soviet Union to increase its own defense spending when it could ill afford to do so and contributed to the economic problems that helped bring about its collapse. Yet even during Reagan's first term (1981–1985), no major transformation of the Soviet Union seemed to be in the offing.

Meanwhile throughout these four decades of the Cold War between the United States and the Soviet Union, extraordinary events had been occurring in Africa and Asia.

▼ Decolonization: The European Retreat from Empire

The transformation of much of Africa and Asia from colonial domains into independent nations was the most remarkable global political event of the second half of the twentieth century. The numbers of people involved alone reveals the magnitude of the change. At the founding of the United Nations in 1945, approximately one third of the population of the world was subject to the government of colonial powers. Since that time, more than eighty of those then non-self-governing territories have been admitted to UN membership as independent states. (See Map 29–6.)

During the interwar years the European colonial powers had confronted a variety of revolts or nationalist movements, which they had been able to contain either by military force or modest reforms. The war itself and the opportunities it provided to indigenous nationalist movements within Africa, Asia, and the Middle East transformed the situation. World War II drew the military forces of the colonial powers back to Europe. The Japanese overran European possessions in East Asia and demonstrated thus that the European presence there might not be permanent. After the dislocations of the war came the immediate postwar European economic collapse, which left the European colonial powers less able to afford to maintain their military and administrative positions abroad. Consequently, in less than a century after the great nineteenth-century drive toward empire, European imperialists found themselves in retreat around the globe.

The liberal-democratic war aims of the Allies had also undermined colonialism. It was difficult to fight against tyranny in Europe while maintaining colonial dominance abroad. The United States, and in particular Franklin Roosevelt, opposed the continuation of the colonial empires. This policy was, in part, a matter of principle, but it also recognized that both the political and economic interests of the United States were more likely to prosper in a decolonized world. The founding of the United Nations also assured the presence of an international body opposed to colonialism.

The Cold War complicated the process of decolonization. Both the United States and the Soviet Union opposed the old colonial empires, but both also worried about the potential alignment of the new nations and moved to create spheres of influence and, in some cases, alliances with the newly independent states. Certain

MAP EXPLORATION

Interactive map: To explore this map further, go to **www.myhistorylab.com**

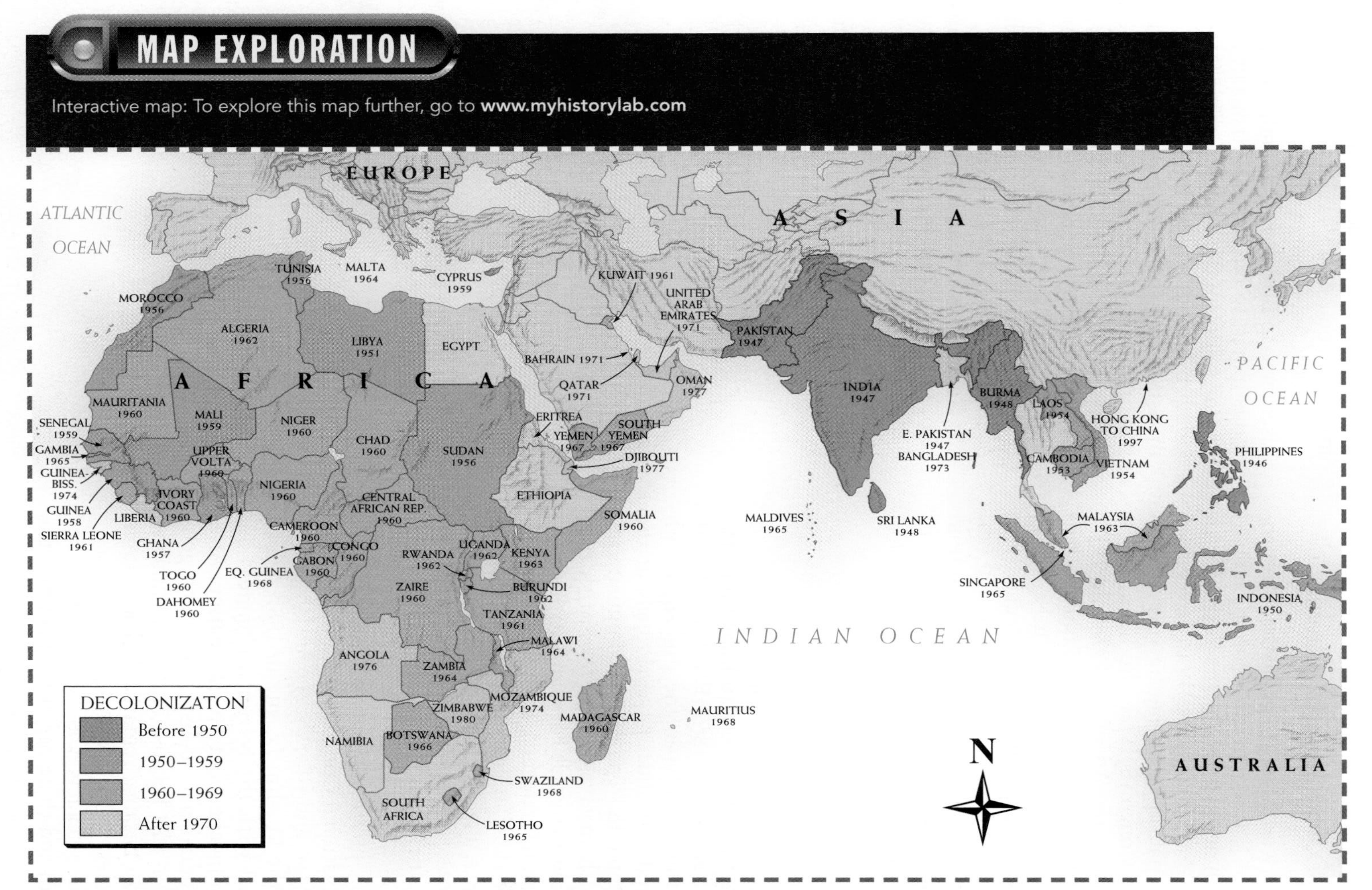

Map 29–6 **Decolonization Since World War II** The Western powers' rapid retreat from imperialism after World War II is graphically shown on this outline map covering half the globe—from West Africa to the southwest Pacific.

nations, such as India, fiercely pursued policies of neutrality in hopes of receiving aid and support from both sides.

Major Areas of Colonial Withdrawal

Decolonization was a worldwide event lasting throughout the second half of the twentieth century and beyond. It involved such dramatic moments as the Dutch being forced from the East Indies in 1949 to be replaced by the independent nation of Indonesia, the Belgian withdrawal from the Congo in 1960, the liberation of Portuguese Mozambique and Angola in 1974 and 1975, and the end of all-white rule in Rhodesia (Zimbabwe) in 1979 and most remarkably in South Africa in 1994.

Each of these events was important, especially to the peoples involved, but the two largest colonial empires were the British and the French. Their retreat from empire produced the most far-reaching repercussions not only in former colonial nations, but in both Europe and the United States as well.

India

No anticolonial movement so gripped the imagination of the Western world as that carried out in India under the leadership of Mohandas Gandhi (1869–1948). The British had solidified their rule of India in the mid-eighteenth century extending and consolidating it throughout the nineteenth. (See Chapter 25.) The British administration required the Indians themselves to pay for British rule. India supplied the raw materials for the British cotton mills. Other British policies pushed many Indians to migrate to British possessions in East Asia, Africa, and the Caribbean. For decades, the religious, ethnic, linguistic, and political divisions among Indians permitted the British to dominate the country through a divide-and-rule strategy.

As early as 1885, politically active Hindu Indians founded the Indian National Congress with the goals of modernizing Indian life and liberalizing British policy. Muslims organized the Muslim League in 1887, which for a time cooperated with the National Congress but eventually sought an independent Muslim nation. After World War I, the Indian nationalist movement grew steadily in strength, in part because of British blunders, but more importantly because remarkable leaders pursued effective strategies.

Chief among these leaders was Gandhi, who had studied law in Britain and there began to encounter the ideas of liberal Western thinkers, including the American Henry David Thoreau (1817–1862) from whom he learned the concept of passive resistance. After being called to the bar in London in 1891, he returned briefly to India and then in 1893 went to South Africa where for over twenty years he worked on behalf of Indian immigrants. During those years he continued to read widely and became convinced of the power of passive resistance. Gandhi returned to India in 1915 and soon distinguished himself as a leader of Indian nationalism by his insistence on religious toleration. From the 1920s to the mid-1940s, he inspired a growing movement of passive resistance to British rule in India. In 1930, he lead a famous march to break the British salt monopoly by collecting salt from the sea. He was repeatedly arrested and jailed by the British authorities. To embarrass the British during these imprisonments and to gain worldwide publicity, he undertook long protest fasts during which he nearly died. In 1942, during World War II, Gandhi called on the British Government to leave India. In 1947, the British Labor government, weary of the incessant agitation and uncertain of its ability to maintain control in India, decided to do so.

Gandhi became and remains the most famous anticolonial leader of the twentieth century. His career demonstrates how such a leader could use ideas taken from the West against colonial regimes. His use of passive resistance became a model for Dr. Martin

Ghandi led India from colonialism to independence. Part of his appeal was the simplicity of his life and dress. CORBIS/Bettmann

GANDHI EXPLAINS HIS DOCTRINE OF NONVIOLENCE

The most famous device Indian nationalists used against British colonial rule in India was Gandhi's doctrine of nonviolence. He had come to believe in its power during his years in South Africa. Gandhi wrote this description of the meaning of nonviolence during World War II. Yet even while enunciating its meaning, he refused to associate himself with nonviolence in international relations. This reluctance may have stemmed from his recognition that the war against the Axis powers was a war against Nazi racism and Japanese imperialism, both of which were dangerous for colonial peoples of color.

Why does Gandhi see nonviolence as evidence of strength? How does he refrain from extending nonviolence to external relations? How was Gandhi's doctrine transferable to other political movements, such as the American civil rights struggle?

I do believe that, where there is only a choice between cowardice and violence, I would advise violence. . . .

But I believe that non-violence is infinitely superior to violence, forgiveness is more manly than punishment. . . .

Non-violence is the law of our species as violence is the law of the brute. The spirit lies dormant in the brute, and he knows no law but that of physical might. The dignity of man requires obedience to a higher law—to the strength of the spirit.

I have therefore ventured to place before India the ancient law of self-sacrifice. . . .

Non-violence in its dynamic condition means conscious suffering. It does not mean meek submission to the will of the evil-doer, but it means the pitting of one's whole soul against the will of the tyrant. Working under this law of our being, it is possible for a single individual to defy the whole might of an unjust empire to save his honour, his religion, his soul, and lay the foundation for that empire's fall or its regeneration. . . .

I have not the capacity for preaching universal non-violence to the country. I preach, therefore, non-violence restricted strictly for the purpose of winning our freedom and therefore perhaps for preaching the regulation of international relations by non-violent means. But my incapacity must not be mistaken for that of the doctrine of non-violence. I see it with my intellect in all its effulgence. My heart grasps it. But I have not yet the attainments of preaching universal non-violence with effect. . . .

I do justify entire non-violence, and consider it possible in relation between man and man and nation and nation; but it is not "a resignation from all fighting against wickedness." On the contrary, the non-violence of my conception is a more active, more real fighting against wickedness than retaliation whose very nature is to increase wickedness. I contemplate a mental, and therefore a moral, opposition to immoralities. I seek entirely to blunt the edge of the tyrant's sword, not by putting up against it a sharper-edged weapon, but by disappointing his expectations that I should be offering physical resistance. . . .

Non-violence, therefore, presupposes ability to strike. It is a conscious deliberate restraint put upon one's desire for vengeance.

Luther King, Jr. (1929–1968) during the civil rights movement in the United States during the late 1950s and 1960s. (See "Gandhi Explains His Doctrine of Nonviolence.")

Gandhi and the Congress Party succeeded in forcing the British from India. However, they did not succeed in creating a single nation. Parallel to Gandhi's drive for an India characterized by diverse religions living in mutual toleration, the Muslim League led by Ali Jinnah (1876–1948) sought a distinctly Muslim state. What occurred in 1947 as the British left India was a partition of the country into the states of India and Pakistan. Intense sectarian warfare and hundreds of thousands of deaths marked the partition. A Hindu extremist assassinated Gandhi himself in 1948. It should also be noted that despite partition a vast Muslim population remained in India. Pakistan was initially a nation of two parts separated geographically by hundreds of miles of Indian territory. In 1971, East Pakistan broke away to become independent Bangladesh. As will be seen later in this chapter, the founding of Pakistan would be important for the emergence of political Islamism.

The partition of India and Pakistan illustrates an often-neglected factor in the process of decolonization. In many colonial regions, the retreat of the colonial powers opened the way for new or renewed conflicts among different ethnic and religious groups within the former colonial empires. For example, since partition, India and Pakistan have disputed the ownership of Kashmir in repeated armed clashes. Another example is the conflict over the former Portuguese colony of East Timor whose people have asserted a right to independence against the government of Indonesia, which occupied it for twenty years after Portugal withdrew in 1975.

Further British Retreat from Empire

The British surrender of India marked the beginning of a long, steady retreat from empire. Generally speaking, the British accepted the loss of empire as inevitable. British decolonization sought first to maintain whatever links were economically and politically possible without conflict. Indeed, during the 1940s and 1950s, the British undertook various development programs in their remaining Asian, African, and Caribbean colonies. These investments paradoxically made the British government and public more aware of the actual costs of empire and may have led both to accept more easily the end of empire. Second, throughout decolonization the British hoped to oversee the creation of institutions in their former colonies that would assure representative self-government once they had departed.

In 1948, Burma and Sri Lanka (formerly Ceylon) became independent. As already observed, the formation of the state of Israel and Arab nationalist movements forced Britain to withdraw from Palestine. During the 1950s, the British tried, belatedly, to prepare their tropical colonies for self-government. Ghana (formerly the Gold Coast) and Nigeria—which became self-governing in 1957 and 1960, respectively—were the major examples of planned decolonization. In other areas, such as Cyprus, Kenya, and Aden (now part of Yemen), the British withdrew under the pressure of militant nationalist movements. In many areas, violence between the British and the forces demanding independence hastened this retreat.

The development of these former colonies in the second half of the twentieth century has followed two distinct paths. In general, political instability and poverty have characterized the history of the independent states in Africa. By contrast, Asia has been an area of overall political stability and remarkable economic growth, challenging the economies of both the United States and Western Europe.

▼ The Turmoil of French Decolonization

Although the British retreat from empire involved violence, at no point did the British "make a stand." Moreover, many groups in Britain, including the leadership of the Labour Party, had long been critical of colonialism. Such was not the case with France. Having been defeated by the Nazis and then liberated by the allied forces, France believed it must reassert its position as a great power. This determination led it into two disastrous attempts to maintain its colonial empire, in Algeria and Vietnam. As will be seen, the situation in Vietnam, because of the intervention of the United States, drew French decolonization directly into the tensions of the Cold War.

France and Algeria

France had conquered the pirate's nest of Algiers in 1830 as Charles X (r. 1824–1830) futilely hoped the invasion would increase support for his monarchy. (See Chapter 20.) In late 1848, the French government made Algeria an integral part of France, establishing three administrative departments that were administered like those in France itself. Over the decades, as France consolidated and extended its position in Algeria, French soldiers and hundreds of thousands of Europeans from France and other Mediterranean countries settled there, primarily in the cities and on small farms. By the close of World War I, approximately 20 percent of the population was of European descent. Collectively these immigrants were termed the *pieds noirs* (meaning "black feet," a derogatory term). The voting structure was set up to give the French settlers as large a voice as the majority Arab Muslim population. The further one moved toward the south away from the coast and into the Sahara Desert, the greater the influence of the French military. Algerian Muslims were not given posts in the administration. Shortly after World War I, the French extended the rights of full French citizenship to Algerian Muslims who had fought in the war, who were literate in French, or who owned land, but this rewarded only a few thousand of them.

During World War II, the forces of Free France dominated Algeria after 1942 while the Vichy regime still governed metropolitan France. The Free French government did little to change the colonial status quo. Moreover, in May 1945, during celebrations of the Allied victory in World War II, a violent clash broke out at Sétif between Muslims and French settlers. Matters rapidly got out of hand, and people on both sides were killed, but the French repressed the Muslims with a considerable loss of life. The Muslims of Algeria saw this incident the same way the Russian working classes viewed Bloody Sunday in 1905. (See Chapter 23.) It robbed the French administration of legitimacy and marked the beginning of conscious Algerian nationalism. Thereafter, many Algerian Muslims supported independence. To placate Muslim opinion, in 1947, the French established a structure for limited political representation of the Muslim population and undertook economic reforms. Not unsurprisingly, these steps proved ineffective.

Algerian nationalists soon founded the National Liberation Front (FLN). In late 1954, insurrections and soon open civil war broke out in Algeria as the FLN undertook highly effective guerrilla warfare. The government of the Fourth French Republic that had been founded in 1945 adamantly declared Algeria an integral part of France and refused to compromise with the insurgents. Thereafter a war lasting until 1962 ground on between the Algerian nationalists and the French. Both sides committed atrocities; hundreds of thousands of Algerians were killed. The war divided France itself with many French citizens, often of left-wing political opinion, objecting to the war, and the French military, still smarting from its defeats in World War II and in Indochina, determined to fight on. The presence of more than 1 million European settlers in Algeria, who saw any settlement with the nationalists as a betrayal, exacerbated the situation. The French government itself became paralyzed and lost control of the army. There was fear of civil war in France itself or of a military takeover. In Algeria, violence was spreading.

In the midst of this turmoil, General Charles de Gaulle (1890–1970), who had led the Free French forces during World War II and had briefly governed France immediately after the war, reentered French political life largely at the urging of the military. His condition for taking office was the end of the Fourth Republic and the promulgation of a new constitution, which enhanced the power of the president and created the Fifth Republic. The voters ratified this, and de Gaulle became president of France in December 1958. He then undertook a long strategic retreat from Algeria. The process was neither peaceful nor easy. In 1961, for example, it looked as if a group of officers known as the OAS (Organisation Armée Secrète) would attempt a coup in Paris. There were bombings, murders, and attempts on de Gaulle's life. In 1962, however, de Gaulle held a referendum in Algeria on independence, which passed overwhelmingly. Algeria became independent on July 3, 1962.

Once the FLN took over Algeria under the presidency of Mohammed Ben Bella (b. 1919), however, a second factor came into play in French domestic life. Hundreds of thousands of *pied noirs* settlers fled Algeria for France as did many Muslims who had supported the French and

In 1959, Charles de Gaulle as president of the French Republic visited Algiers to great acclaim from its European inhabitants, known as *colons*. By 1962, however, he had sponsored a referendum that led to Algerian independence and the flight of most of those people. Loomis Dean/Getty Images, Inc.

had good cause to fear reprisals. (Thousands of pro-French Muslims who did not flee were massacred.) The emigration of this latter group marked the beginning of a large, and largely unwelcome, Muslim population in France.

France and Vietnam

One of the reasons for the strong French stand against Algerian independence had been the loss of its south Asian empire in Indochina just before the Algerian insurrection broke out in 1954. Whereas the Algerian drive toward independence essentially involved only France and the populations of Algeria, the Indochina problem eventually drew the United States into war in Vietnam.

In its push for empire, France had occupied Indochina (which contained Laos, Cambodia, and Vietnam) between 1857 and 1893. By 1930, Ho Chi Minh (1892–1969) had turned a nationalist movement against French colonial rule into the Indochina Communist Party, which the French, for a time, succeeded in suppressing. World War II, however, provided new opportunities for Ho Chi Minh and other nationalists as they fought both the Japanese who occupied Indochina in 1941 and the pro-Vichy French colonial administration that collaborated with the Japanese until 1945. The war thus established Ho Chi Minh as a major anticolonial, nationalist leader. He was a communist to be sure, but he had achieved his position in Vietnam during the war without the support of Chinese or Soviet communists.

In September 1945, Ho Chi Minh declared the independence of Vietnam under the Viet Minh, a coalition of nationalists that the communists soon dominated. By 1947, a full-fledged civil war had erupted in Vietnam. (Cambodia and, to a lesser extent, Laos remained quiescent under pro-French or neutralist monarchies.)

Until 1949, the United States displayed minimal concern about the Indochina war. The establishment of the Communist People's Republic of China that year dramatically changed the U.S. outlook. The United States now saw the French colonial war against Ho Chi Minh as an integral part of the Cold War conflict. The U.S. support for France in southeast Asia also served to gain French support for the establishment of NATO. Even though the United States supported the French effort in Vietnam financially, it was not prepared, despite divisions among policymakers, to intervene militarily. In the spring of 1954, during an international conference in Geneva on the future of Vietnam, the French military stronghold of Dien Bien Phu fell to Viet Minh forces after a prolonged siege. France lost the will to continue the struggle, which had become increasingly unpopular with the French people.

By late June, a complicated and unsatisfactory peace accord divided Vietnam at the seventeenth parallel of latitude. North of the parallel, centered in Hanoi, the Viet Minh were in charge; below it, centered in Saigon, the French were in charge. This was to be a temporary border. By 1956, elections were to be held to reunify the country. In effect, the conference attempted to transform a military conflict into a political one.

Vietnam Drawn into the Cold War

Unhappy with these arrangements, the United States, in September 1954, formed the Southeast Asia Treaty Organization (SEATO), a collective security agreement that somewhat resembled the European NATO alliance, but without the integration of military forces or inclusion of all states in the region. Its membership consisted of the United States, Great Britain, France, Australia, New Zealand, Thailand, Pakistan, and the Philippines.

By 1955, American policymakers had begun to think about Indochina, and particularly Vietnam, largely in terms of the Korean example. The U.S. government assumed, incorrectly, that, like the government of North Korea, the government in North Vietnam was basically a communist puppet of the Soviets and the Chinese. That same year, French troops began to withdraw from South Vietnam. As they left, the various Vietnamese political groups began to fight for power among themselves.

The United States stepped into the turmoil in Vietnam with military and economic aid. Among the Vietnamese politicians, it chose to support was Ngo Dinh Diem (1901–1963), a strong noncommunist nationalist who had not collaborated with the French. Because the United States had been publicly and deeply committed

MAJOR DATES IN THE VIETNAM CONFLICT

1945	Ho Chi Minh proclaims Vietnamese independence from French rule
1947–1954	War between France and Vietnam
1950	U.S. financial aid to France
1954	Geneva conference on Southeast Asia opens
1954	French defeat at Dien Bien Phu
1954	Southeast Asia Treaty Organization (SEATO) founded
1955	Diem establishes Republic of Vietnam in the south
1960	Founding of National Liberation Front to overthrow the Diem government
1961	Six hundred American troops and advisers in Vietnam
1963	Diem overthrown and assassinated
1964	Gulf of Tonkin Resolution
1965	Major U.S. troop commitment
1969	Nixon announces policy of Vietnamization
1973	Cease-fire announced
1975	Saigon falls to North Vietnamese troops

to the French, however, Vietnamese nationalists would view any government it supported with suspicion. In October 1955, Diem established a Republic of Vietnam in the territory for which the Geneva conference had made France responsible. Diem announced that the Geneva agreements would not bind his newly established government and that elections would not be held in 1956. The American government, which had not signed the Geneva documents, supported his position.

In 1960, the National Liberation Front was founded, with the goals of overthrowing Diem, unifying the country, reforming the economy, and ousting the Americans. It was anticolonial, nationalist, and communist. Its military arm was called the Viet Cong and was aided by the government of North Vietnam. Diem, a Roman Catholic, also faced mounting criticism from Buddhists and the army. His response to these pressures was further repression and dependence on an ever-smaller group of advisers.

Direct United States Involvement

The Eisenhower and Kennedy administrations continued to support Diem while demanding reforms in his government. The American military presence grew from about 600 advisers in early 1961 to more than 16,000 troops in late 1963. The political situation in Vietnam became increasingly unstable. On November 1, 1963, an army coup in which the United States was deeply involved overthrew and murdered Diem. The United States hoped a new government in South Vietnam would generate popular support. Thereafter, the United States sought to find a leader who could fulfill that hope. It finally settled on Nguyen Van Thieu (1923–2001), who governed South Vietnam from 1966 to 1975.

President Kennedy was assassinated on November 22, 1963. His successor, Lyndon Johnson (1963–1969), vastly expanded the commitment to South Vietnam. In August 1964, after an attack on an American ship in the Gulf of Tonkin, Johnson authorized the first bombing of North Vietnam. In February 1965, major bombing attacks began. They continued, with only brief pauses, until early in 1973. The land war grew until more than 500,000 Americans were stationed in South Vietnam.

In 1969, President Richard Nixon began a policy known as *Vietnamization*, which involved the gradual withdrawal of American troops from Vietnam while the South Vietnamese army took over the full military

U.S. troops engaged in combat in Vietnam. At the war's peak, more than 500,000 American troops were stationed in South Vietnam. The United States struggled in Vietnam for more than a decade, seriously threatening its commitment to Western Europe. U.S. Army Photo

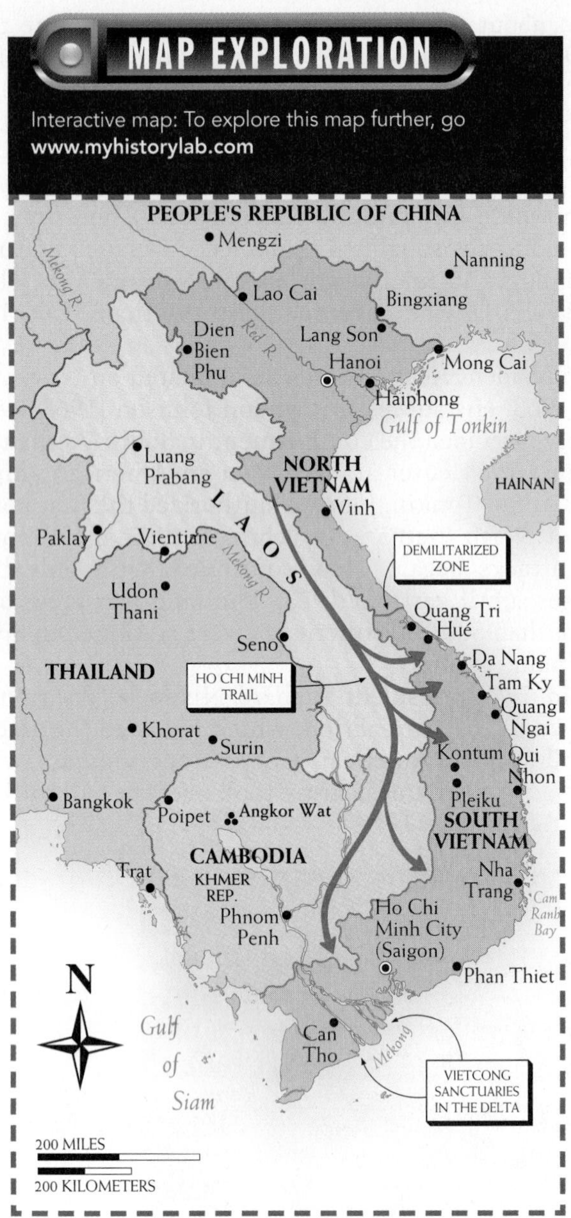

Map 29–7 **VIETNAM AND ITS SOUTHEAST ASIAN NEIGHBORS** The map identifies important locations associated with the war in Vietnam.

effort. Peace negotiations had begun in Paris in the spring of 1968, but a cease-fire was not finally arranged until January 1973. American troops left South Vietnam, and North Vietnam released its American prisoners of war. In early 1975, an evacuation of South Vietnamese troops from the northern part of their country turned into a rout when they were attacked by the North Vietnamese. On April 30, 1975, Saigon (renamed Ho Chi Minh City) fell to the Viet Cong and the North Vietnamese army. Vietnam was finally united. (See Map 29–7.)

The U.S. intervention in Vietnam, which grew out of a power vacuum left by French decolonization, affected the entire Western world. For a decade after the Cuban missile crisis, Vietnam largely diverted the attention of the United States from Europe. American prestige suffered, and the U.S. policy in Southeast Asia made many Europeans question the wisdom of the American government and its commitment to Western Europe. Many young Europeans and many people in the former colonial world as well as many Americans came to regard the United States not as a protector of liberty, but as an ambitious, aggressive, and cruel power trying to keep colonialism alive after the end of the colonial era. Within the United States, the Vietnam conflict produced enormous divisions and debates over American involvement in the rest of the world that persist to the present day.

▼ The Collapse of European Communism

The withdrawal of Soviet influence from Eastern Europe and the internal collapse of the Soviet Union are the most important European historical events of the second half of the twentieth century. They had virtually no parallel in modern European history. All of the other major governments that had disappeared in Europe earlier in the century had fallen either as the result of domestic revolution brought on by military defeat, as happened in tsarist Russia, Germany, and Austria after World War I and Italy during World War II, or military defeat followed by military occupation, as was the case with Germany after 1945 and the Third Republic in France in 1940. By contrast, the Soviet Union essentially imploded and then divided into separate successor states. There was no foreign invasion, no military defeat, and no internal revolution. Many of the factors leading to the Soviet collapse remain murky, but here is a relatively clear narrative of what occurred.

Under Brezhnev, who governed from 1964 to 1982, the Soviet government became markedly more repressive at home, suggesting a return to Stalinist policies. In 1974, the government expelled Aleksandr Solzhenitsyn. It also began to harass Jewish citizens, creating bureaucratic obstacles for those who wanted to emigrate to Israel. This internal repression gave rise to a dissident movement. Certain Soviet citizens dared to criticize the regime in public and accused the government of violating the human rights provision of the 1975 Helsinki Accords. The dissidents included prominent citizens, such as the Nobel Prize–winning physicist Andrei Sakharov (1921–1989). The Soviet government responded with further repression, placing some opponents in psychiatric hospitals and others under what amounted to house arrest. During the same period the structures of

President Ronald Reagan and Premier Mikhail Gorbachev confer at a summit meeting in December 1987. AP Wide World Photos

the Communist Party became both rigidified and corrupt, which increasingly demoralized younger Soviet bureaucrats and party members.

Gorbachev Attempts to Reform the Soviet Union

Although economic stagnation, party corruption, and the lingering Afghan war had long been undermining Soviet authority, what brought these forces to a head and began the dramatic collapse of the Soviet Empire was the accession to power of Mikhail S. Gorbachev (b. 1931) in 1985 after both of Brezhnev's two immediate successors, Yuri Andropov (1914–1984) and Konstantin Chernenko (1911–1985), died within thirteen months of each other. In what proved to be the last great attempt to reform the Soviet system, Gorbachev immediately began the most remarkable changes that the Soviet Union had witnessed since the 1920s. These reforms loosed forces that, within seven years, would force him to retire from office and would end both communist rule and the Soviet Union as it had existed since the Bolshevik revolution of 1917. (See "Encountering the Past: Rock Music and Political Protest," page 928.)

Economic *Perestroika* Gorbachev's primary goal was to revive the Russian economy to raise the country's standard of living. Initially, he and his supporters, most of whom he had appointed himself, challenged traditional party and bureaucratic management of the Soviet government and economy. Under the policy of ***perestroika***, or "restructuring," they reduced the size and importance of the centralized economic ministries.

During these same years, Gorbachev confronted significant labor discontent. A major strike by coal miners occurred in July 1989 in Siberia. Gorbachev had to settle their grievances quickly, because the economy desperately needed their output. He promised them better wages and wider political liberties.

By early 1990, in a clear abandonment of traditional Marxist ideology, Gorbachev began to advocate private ownership of property and liberalization of the economy toward free market mechanisms. Despite many organizational changes, the Soviet economy remained stagnate and even declined. The failure of Gorbachev's economic policies affected his political policies. To some extent, he pursued bold political reform because he failed to achieve economic progress.

Glasnost Gorbachev allowed an extraordinary public discussion and criticism of Soviet history and Soviet

ROCK MUSIC AND POLITICAL PROTEST

ROCK MUSIC, WHICH epitomizes popular culture throughout the Western world, was a form of entertainment with a loud antiestablishment political message. Rock originated in the United States in the 1950s with African-American musicians and working-class and country music singers. By the early 1960s, rock also included folk singers who used their music to champion the civil rights movement and protest the war in Vietnam.

European rock groups both embraced and transformed American rock music. The most spectacularly successful European group was the Beatles. Though sporting long hair and attracting the politically active young, the Beatles' lyrics were more laid back than political.

During the 1970s, in both the United States and Europe, punk rock groups, with provocative names such as the Sex Pistols, became popular. Punk rock was deeply antiestablishment, but Western society, which was increasingly pluralistic, took punk rock in its stride.

In Eastern Europe and the Soviet Union, however, punk rock was literally revolutionary. There the ever-more radical rock music of the 1970s and 1980s became a major vehicle for social and political criticism. In the face of communist cultural conformity, rock stars symbolized daring and personal heroism. Lyrics openly criticized communist governments, as in this example from "Get Out of Control," sung at a rock concert in Leningrad (now St. Petersburg) in 1986:

We were watched from the days of kindergarten.
Some nice men and kind women
Beat us up. They chose the most painful places
And treated us like animals on the farm.
So we grew up like a disciplined herd.
We sing what they want and live how they want
And we look at them downside up, as if we're
trapped.
We just watch how they hit us
Get out of control!
Get out of control!
And sing what you want
And not just what is allowed
We have a right to yell![1]

This song became popular throughout Eastern Europe. It revealed how alienated the youth of the region had become from the official culture of the communist regimes. Rock music expressed and helped spread the disaffection that contributed to the collapse of communism throughout Eastern Europe at the end of the 1980s.

How did rock music evolve into an antiestablishment form of entertainment?

Why was rock considered subversive in the Eastern bloc nations?

The Russian rock group Dynamic performs in Moscow in 1987. R. Podemi/TASS/Sovfoto/Eastfoto

[1]Quoted in Artemy Troitsky, *Back in the USSR: The True Story of Rock in Russia* (Boston: Faber & Faber, 1987), p. 127, as cited in Sabrina P. Ramet, ed., *Social Currents in Eastern Europe: The Sources and Meaning of the Great Transformation* (Durham, NC: Duke University Press, 1991), p. 239.

Communist Party policy. This development was termed ***glasnost***, or openness. The contributions to Soviet history of such figures from the 1920s and 1930s as Nikolai Bukharin, whom Stalin had executed in 1938, received official public recognition. Workers were permitted to criticize party officials and the economic plans of the party and the government. Censorship was relaxed and free expression encouraged. Dissidents were released from prison. In the summer of 1988, Gorbachev presided over a party congress that witnessed full debates.

Gorbachev soon applied *perestroika* to the political arena. In 1988, a new constitution permitted openly contested elections. After real political campaigning—a new experience for the Soviet Union—the Congress of People's Deputies was elected in 1989. One of the new members of the congress was Andrei Sakharov, the dissident physicist whom Brezhnev had persecuted. After lively debate, the Supreme Soviet, another elected body—although one the Communist Party dominated—formally elected Gorbachev president in 1989.

The policy of open discussion allowed national minorities within the Soviet Union to demand political autonomy. Throughout its history, the Soviet Union had remained a vast empire of subject peoples. The tsars had conquered some of those groups, Stalin had incorporated others, such as the Baltic states, into the Soviet Union. *Glasnost* quickly brought to the foreground the discontent of all such peoples, no matter how or when they had been subjugated. Gorbachev proved inept in addressing these ethnic complaints. He badly underestimated the unrest that internal national discontent could generate.

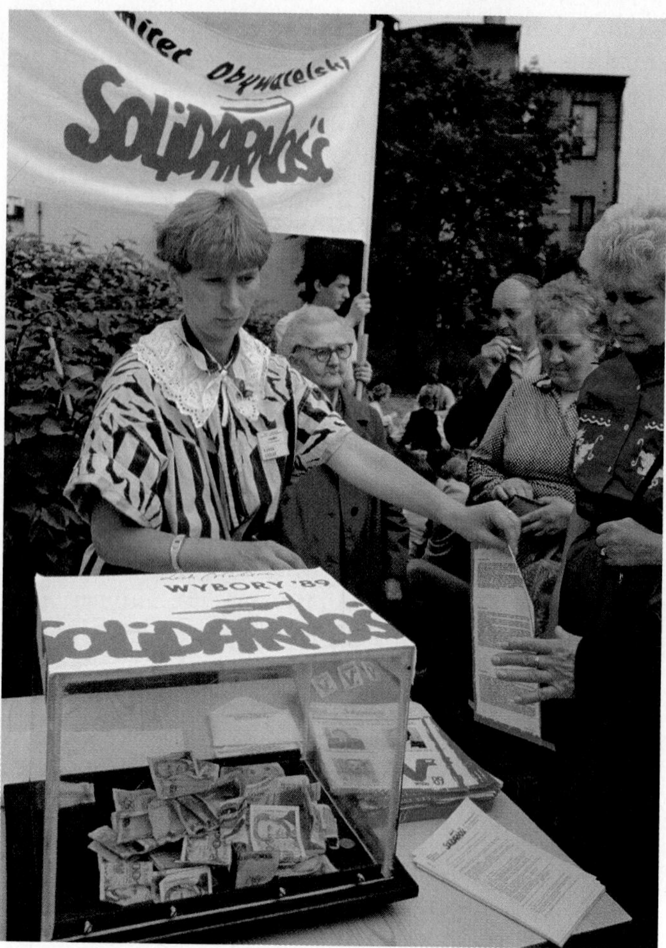

The Polish trade union "Solidarity" in 1989 successfully forced the Polish communist government to hold free elections. In June of that year Solidarity, whose members here are collecting funds for their campaign, won overwhelmingly. Bernard Bisson/CORBIS/Bettmann

1989: Revolution in Eastern Europe

Solidarity Reemerges in Poland In the early 1980s, Poland's government relaxed martial law, and it eventually released all the Solidarity prisoners, although Jaruzelski remained president. In 1988, new strikes surprised even the leaders of Solidarity. This time, the communist government could not reimpose control. After consultations between the government and Solidarity, the union was legalized. Lech Walesa again took center stage, as a kind of mediator between the government and the more independent elements of the trade union movement he had founded.

Jaruzelski began some political reforms with the tacit consent of the Soviet Union. He promised free elections to a parliament with increased powers. When elections were held in 1989, the communists lost overwhelmingly to Solidarity candidates. Late in the summer, Jaruzelski, unable to find a communist who could forge a majority coalition in Parliament, turned to Solidarity and appointed the first noncommunist prime minister of Poland since 1945. Gorbachev expressly approved the appointment.

Toward Hungarian Independence Throughout 1989, as these events unfolded within Poland, one Soviet-dominated state after another in Eastern Europe moved toward independence. Early in the year, the Hungarian government opened its border with Austria, permitting free travel between the two countries. This breach in the Iron Curtain immediately led thousands of East Germans to move through Hungary and Austria to West Germany. In May, Janos Kadar, who had been installed after the Soviet intervention in 1956, was stripped of his position as president of the Hungarian Communist Party. Thousands of Hungarians gave an honorary burial to the body of Imre Nagy, whom Kadar had executed in 1958. The Hungarian Communist Party changed its name to the Socialist Party, permitted other parties to engage openly in politics, and promised free elections by October.

German Reunification In the autumn of 1989, popular demonstrations erupted in East German cities. Adding to the pressure, Gorbachev told the leaders of the East German Communist Party that the Soviet

Union would not use force to support them. With startling swiftness, the East German government resigned, making way for a younger generation of communist leaders who remained in office for only a few weeks. In November 1989, in one of the most emotional moments in European history since 1945, the government of East Germany ordered the opening of the Berlin Wall. That week, tens of thousands of East Berliners crossed into West Berlin to celebrate, to visit their families, and to shop with money the West German government gave them. Shortly thereafter, free travel began between East and West Germany. (See Map 29–8.)

Within days of these dramatic events, West Germany and the other Western nations faced the issue of German reunification. Helmut Kohl (b. 1930), the chancellor of West Germany, became the leading force in moving toward full unification. Late in 1989, the European Economic Community accepted, in principle, the unification of Germany. By February 1990, some form of reunification had become a foregone conclusion, accepted by the United States, the Soviet Union, Great Britain, and France.

The Velvet Revolution in Czechoslovakia Revolution in Czechoslovakia rapidly followed the breach of the Berlin Wall. The popular new Czech leader who led the forces against the party was Václav Havel (b. 1936), a playwright of international standing whom the communist government had imprisoned. In December 1989, the tottering communist government, together with the Soviet Union and other Warsaw Pact states, acknowledged that the invasion of 1968 had been a mistake. Shortly thereafter, Havel's group, known as Civic Forum, forced Gustav Husak (b. 1913), who had been president of Czechoslovakia since 1968, to resign. On December 28, 1989, Alexander Dubcek became chairman of the Parliament, and the next day, Havel was elected president.

Violent Revolution in Romania The only revolution of 1989 that involved significant violence occurred in Romania. There, in mid-December, the forces of President Nicolae Ceausescu (1918–1989), who had governed without opposition since 1965, fired on crowds that were protesting conditions in the country. By December 22, Bucharest was in full revolt. Ceausescu and his wife attempted to flee, but were captured, secretly tried, and shot on December 25.

The Soviet Stance on Revolutionary Developments None of the revolutions of 1989 could have taken place unless the Soviet Union had refused to intervene militarily, in contrast to 1956 and 1968. As events unfolded, it became clear that Gorbachev would not rescue the old-line communist governments and party leaderships in Eastern Europe. In October 1989, he formally renounced the Brezhnev Doctrine. For the first time since the end of World War II, Eastern Europeans could shape their own political destiny without the fear of Soviet military intervention. Once they realized the Soviets would not act, thousands of ordinary citizens took to the streets to denounce Communist Party domination and assert their desire for democracy. The major question facing the Soviet Union became the peaceful withdrawal of its troops from Eastern Europe. The haphazard nature of that withdrawal and the general poverty to which those troops returned were other factors undermining the Soviet armed forces.

The peaceful character of most of these revolutions was not inevitable. It may, in part, have resulted from the shock with which much of the world responded to the violent repression of pro-democracy protesters in Beijing's Tiananmen Square by the People's Republic of China in May 1989. The Communist Party officials of Eastern Europe and the Soviet Union clearly decided in 1989 that they could not offend world opinion with a similar attack on democratic demonstrators.

The Collapse of the Soviet Union

Gorbachev clearly believed, as his behavior toward Eastern Europe in 1989 showed, that the Soviet Union could no longer afford to support communist governments in that region or intervene to uphold their authority while seeking to restructure its own economy. He also had concluded that the Communist Party in the Soviet Union must restructure itself and its relationship to the Soviet state and society.

Renunciation of Communist Political Monopoly In early 1990, Gorbachev formally proposed to the Central Committee of the Soviet Communist Party that the party abandon its monopoly of power. After intense debate, the committee abandoned the Leninist position that only a single elite party could act as the vanguard of the revolution and forge a new Soviet society.

New Political Forces Gorbachev confronted challenges from three major political forces by 1990. One consisted of those groups—considered conservative in the Soviet context—whose members wanted to preserve the influence of the Communist Party and the Soviet army. The country's economic stagnation and political and social turmoil deeply disturbed them. They appeared to control significant groups in the economy and society. During late 1990 and early 1991, Gorbachev, who himself seems to have been disturbed by the nation's turmoil, began to appoint members of these factions to key positions in the government. In other words, he seemed to be making a strategic retreat.

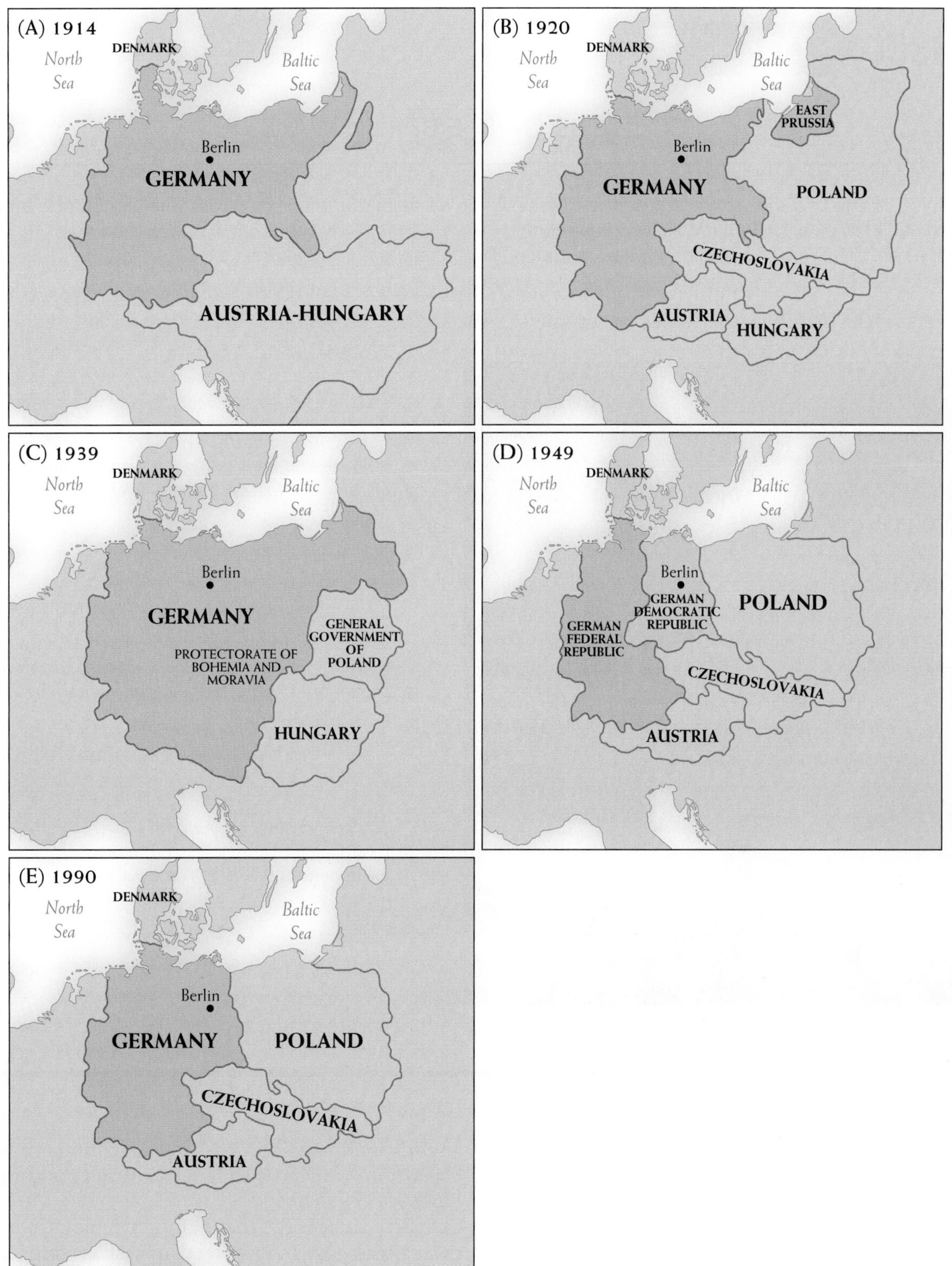

Map 29–8 **THE BORDERS OF GERMANY IN THE TWENTIETH CENTURY** Map A shows the borders of imperial Germany at the outbreak of World War I. Map B shows the borders of Germany after the Versailles peace settlement. Map C shows the borders of Germany after Hitler's invasion of the Rhineland, the Anschluss with Austria, the Munich Pact, the invasion of Czechoslovakia, and the invasion of Poland. Map D illustrates the division of Germany into the German Federal Republic (West Germany) and the German Democratic Republic (East Germany) in the aftermath of World War II. Map E illustrates the borders of Germany after reunification in 1990.

A Closer LOOK

COLLAPSE OF THE BERLIN WALL

NO SINGLE STRUCTURE so illustrated the divisions of the Cold War as the Berlin Wall, which was erected in 1961. The most symbolic moment in the collapse of communism across Eastern Europe came in November 1989 when that wall was breached.

R. Bossu/Sygma/CORBIS

The sight of hundreds of Germans standing on top of the wall would have been unthinkable just days before. Armed East German and Soviet guards had for over a quarter century prevented Germans from crossing the wall except at a few heavily guarded checkpoints.

English graffiti had been placed on the wall to ensure that an international television audience, which was largely English-speaking, would understand the aspirations of those people who wanted the wall to come down.

The overwhelmingly youthful crowd indicates the repudiation by the new generation of Germans and Europeans of the Cold War divisions.

To examine this image in an interactive fashion, please go to www.myhistorylab.com

PEARSON myhistorylab

Gorbachev initiated these moves because he was now facing opposition from a second group—those who wanted much more extensive and rapid change. Their leading spokesman was Boris Yeltsin (1931–2007). He and his supporters wanted to move quickly to a market economy and a more democratic government. Like Gorbachev, Yeltsin had risen through the ranks of the Communist Party and had then become disillusioned with its policies. Throughout the late 1980s, he had been critical of Gorbachev. In 1990, he was elected president of the Russian Republic, the largest and most important of the Soviet Union's constituent republics. In the new political climate, that position gave him a firm political base from which to challenge Gorbachev's authority and increase his own.

The third force that came into play from 1989 onward was growing regional unrest in some of the republics of the Soviet Union. These republics had experienced considerable discontent in the past, but the military and the Communist Party had always managed to repress it. Initially, the greatest unrest came from the three Baltic republics of Estonia, Latvia, and Lithuania, which had been independent states until 1940 when the Soviet Union had occupied

MAJOR EVENTS IN THE REVOLUTIONS OF 1989

January 11	Independent parties permitted in Hungary
April 5	Solidarity legalized in Poland and free elections accepted by government
May 2	Hungary dismantles barriers along its borders
May 8	Janos Kadar removed from office in Hungary
May 17	Polish government recognizes Roman Catholic Church
June 4	Solidarity victory in Polish parliamentary elections
July 25	Solidarity asked to join coalition government
August 24	Solidarity member appointed premier in Poland
October 18	Erich Honecker removed from office in East Germany
October 23	Hungary proclaims itself a republic
October 25	Gorbachev renounces Brezhnev Doctrine
November 9	Berlin Wall opened
November 17	Large antigovernment demonstration in Czechoslovakia crushed by police
November 19	Czechoslovak opposition groups organize into Civic Forum and demand resignation of communist leaders responsible for 1968 invasion
November 24	Czechoslovak communist leadership resigns
December 1	New Czechoslovak communist leaders denounce 1968 invasion; Soviet Union and Warsaw Pact express regret over 1968 invasion
December 3	Czechoslovak government announces ministry with noncommunist members
December 16–17	Massacre of civilians in Timisoara, Romania
December 22	Ceausescu government overthrown in Romania with many casualties
December 25	Announcement of Ceausescu's execution
December 28	Alexander Dubcek elected chairman of Czechoslovak Parliament
December 29	Václav Havel elected president of Czechoslovakia

them in accord with secret provisions of the Soviet-German nonaggression pact of 1939. That pact with Nazi Germany provided the only seemingly legal basis for the Soviet Union's continued control. In these republics, many local communist leaders began to see themselves as national leaders rather than as party stalwarts.

During 1989 and 1990, the parliaments of the Baltic republics tried to decrease Soviet control, and Lithuania actually declared independence. Gorbachev used military force to resist these moves. Discontent also arose in the Soviet Islamic republics in Central Asia and the Caucasus. Riots broke out in Azerbaijan and Tajikistan, where the army was used as a police force against Soviet citizens. Throughout 1990 and 1991, Gorbachev sought to negotiate new constitutional arrangements between the republics and the central government. His failure to effect such arrangements may have been the single most important reason for the rapid collapse of the Soviet Union.

The August 1991 Coup The turning point in all of these events came in August 1991, when the conservative forces that Gorbachev had brought into the government attempted a coup. Troops occupied Moscow, and Gorbachev was placed under house arrest while on vacation in Crimea. The forces of political and economic reaction—led by people who, at the time, were associated with Gorbachev—had at last tried to seize control. The day of the coup, Boris Yeltsin climbed on a tank in front of the Russian Parliament building to denounce the coup and ask the world for help to maintain the Soviet Union's movement toward democracy.

Within two days, the coup collapsed. Gorbachev returned to Moscow, but in humiliation, having been victimized by the groups to whom he had turned for support. One of the largest public demonstrations in Russian history—perhaps even the largest—celebrated the failure of the coup in Moscow. From that point on, Yeltsin steadily became the dominant political figure in the nation. The Communist Party, compromised by its participation in the coup, collapsed as a political force. The constitutional arrangements between the central government and the individual republics were revised. In December 1991, the Soviet Union ceased to exist, Gorbachev left office, and the Commonwealth of Independent States came into being. (See Map 29–9, page 934.)

The collapse of European communism in the Soviet Union and throughout Eastern Europe has closed the era in which Marxism dominated European socialism that began in the 1870s with the German socialists' adoption of Marxist thought. The Bolshevik victory in the Russian Revolution seemed to validate Marxism, and the policies of Lenin and Stalin sought to extend it around the world. Now the Soviet Union and the communist governments of Eastern Europe—heirs to the Bolshevik revolution—have vanished, and the economies they built have collapsed. As a result, Marxist socialism has been discredited, and socialism in general may find itself on the defensive in the future.

Map 29–9 **THE COMMONWEALTH OF INDEPENDENT STATES** In December 1991, the Soviet Union broke up into its fifteen constituent republics. Eleven of these were loosely joined in the Commonwealth of Independent States. Also shown is the autonomous region of Chechnya, which has waged two bloody wars with Russia in the last decade. Because the borders of Soviet republics were drawn not so much as to promote stability but instability among the many ethnic groups of the Soviet Union, long-simmering disputes flared up once the empire collapsed. The many conflicts Georgia has faced since it regained its independence in 1991 are representative: It fought unsuccessful wars in the early 1990s to keep the breakaway regions of Abkhazia and South Ossetia, both of whose populations were heavily non-Georgian, under its control. In August 2008, when Georgia attempted to reassert its sovereignty over South Ossetia after Russian provocation, it was quickly repulsed by a massive invasion from Russia that resulted in hundreds of fatalities and billions of dollars of damage.

The Yeltsin Decade

Boris Yeltsin emerged as the strongest leader within the new commonwealth. As president of Russia, he was head of the largest and most powerful of the new states. His popularity was high both in Russia and in the commonwealth in 1992, but within a year, he faced serious economic and political problems. The Russian Parliament, most of whom were former communists, opposed Yeltsin personally and his policies of economic and political reform. Relations between the president and Parliament reached an impasse, crippling the government. In September 1993, Yeltsin suspended Parliament, which responded by deposing him. Parliament leaders tried to incite popular uprisings against Yeltsin in Moscow. The military, however, backed Yeltsin, and he surrounded the Parliament building with troops and tanks. On October 4, 1993, after pro-Parliament rioters rampaged through Moscow, Yeltsin ordered the tanks to attack the Parliament building, crushing the opposition.

These actions consolidated Yeltsin's authority. The major Western powers, deeply concerned by the turmoil

A Chechen fighter points his rifle at the head of a Russian prisoner of war outside the Chechen capital Grozny in August 1996. Mindaugas Kulbis/AP Wide World Photos

in Russia, supported him. In December 1993, Russians voted for a new Parliament and approved a new constitution. By 1994, the central government found itself at war in the Islamic province of Chechnya in the Caucasus. Under Yeltsin, Russian forces held off a rebel victory, but the war reached no clear conclusion.

During the mid-1990s, to dismantle the Soviet state and economy, former state-owned industries were privatized. This complicated process involved much corruption and opportunism by individuals determined to profit from the emerging economic organization. One result was the creation of a small group of enormously wealthy individuals, whom the press dubbed "the oligarchs." While these people amassed vast wealth, the general Russian economy remained stagnant. In 1998, Russia defaulted on its international debt payments. Political assassinations occurred and have continued to the present time. The economic downturn contributed to further political unrest. In the face of these problems and in declining health, Yeltsin resigned the presidency in a dramatic gesture just as the new century opened. His hand-picked successor was Vladimir Putin (b. 1952), a relatively unknown figure at the time. Putin would lead the Russian Federation in new economic and political directions. Before considering Putin's role, it is necessary to examine the events that occurred during the 1990s in southeastern Europe.

▼ The Collapse of Yugoslavia and Civil War

Yugoslavia was created after World War I. Its borders included seven major national groups—Serbs, Croats, Slovenes, Montenegrins, Macedonians, Bosnians, and Albanians—among whom there have been ethnic disputes for centuries. The Croats and Slovenes are Roman Catholic and use the Latin alphabet. The Serbs, Montenegrins, and Macedonians are Eastern Orthodox and use the Cyrillic alphabet. The Bosnians and Albanians are mostly Muslims. Most members of each group reside in a region with which they are associated historically—Serbia, Croatia, Slovenia, Montenegro, Macedonia, Bosnia-Herzegovina, and Kosovo—and these regions constituted individual republics or autonomous areas within Yugoslavia. Many Serbs, however, lived outside Serbia proper.

Tito (1892–1980) had acted independently of Stalin in the late 1940s and pursued his own foreign policy. To mute ethnic differences, he encouraged a cult of personality around himself and instituted complex political power sharing among these different groups. After his death, economic difficulties undermined the authority of the central government, and Yugoslavia gradually dissolved into civil war.

THE BREAKUP OF YUGOSLAVIA

June 1991	Slovenia declares independence; Croatia declares independence
September 1991	Macedonia declares independence
April 1992	War erupts in Bosnia and Herzegovina after Muslims and Croats vote for independence
April 1992	Serbia and Montenegro proclaim a new Federal Republic of Yugoslavia
November 1995	Peace agreement reached in Dayton, Ohio
March 1998	War breaks out in Kosovo, a province of Serbia
March 1999	NATO bombing of Serbia begins
February 2008	Kosovo declares independence

In the late 1980s, the old ethnic differences came to the foreground again in Yugoslav politics. Nationalist leaders—most notably Slobodan Milosevic (b. 1941–2006) in Serbia and Franjo Tudjman (b. 1922) in Croatia—gained authority. The Serbs contended that Serbia did not exercise sufficient influence in Yugoslavia and that Serbs living in Yugoslavia but outside Serbia encountered systematic discrimination, especially from Croats and Albanians. Ethnic tension and violence resulted. During the summer of 1990, in the wake of the changes in the former Soviet bloc nations, Slovenia and Croatia declared independence from the central Yugoslav government, and several European nations, including, most importantly, Germany, immediately granted them recognition. The full European community soon did likewise.

From this point on, violence escalated. Serbia—concerned about Serbs living in Croatia and about the loss of lands and resources there—was determined to maintain a unitary Yugoslav state that it would dominate. Croatia was equally determined to secure independence. Croatian Serbs demanded safeguards against discrimination and violence, providing the Serbian army with a pretext to move against Croatia. By June 1991, full-fledged war had erupted between the two republics. Serbia accused Croatia of reviving fascism; Croatia accused Serbia of maintaining a Stalinist regime. At its core, however, the conflict was ethnic; as such, it highlights the potential for violent ethnic conflict within the former Soviet Union.

The conflict took a new turn in 1992 when Croatian and Serbian forces determined to divide Bosnia-Herzegovina. The Muslims in Bosnia—who had lived alongside Serbs and Croats for generations—soon became crushed between the opposing forces. The Serbs in particular, pursuing a policy called "ethnic cleansing," a euphemism redolent of some of the worst horrors of World War II, killed or forcibly removed many Bosnian Muslims.

Destruction of Sarajevo. An elderly parishioner walks through the ruins of St. Mary's Roman Catholic Church in Sarajevo. The church was destroyed by Serb shelling in May 1992.
Reuters/CORBIS/ Bettmann

More than any other single event, the unremitting bombardment of Sarajevo, the capital of Bosnia-Herzegovina, brought the violence of the Yugoslav civil war to the attention of the world. The United Nations attempted unsuccessfully to mediate the conflict and imposed sanctions that had little effect. Early in 1994, however, a shell exploded in the marketplace in Sarajevo, killing dozens of people. Thereafter, NATO forced the Serbs to withdraw their artillery from around Sarajevo.

The events of the civil war came to a head in 1995 when NATO forces carried out strategic air strikes. Later that year, under the leadership of the United States, the leaders of the warring forces negotiated a peace agreement in Dayton, Ohio. The agreement was of great complexity but recognized an independent Bosnia. NATO troops, including those from the United States, have enforced the terms of the agreement.

Toward the end of the 1990s, Serbian aggression against ethnic Albanians in the province of Kosovo again drew NATO into Yugoslav affairs. For months, through television and other media, the world watched the Serbian military deport Albanians from Kosovo where Albanians constituted a majority of the population. The tactics closely resembled those the Serbs previously used in Bosnia. There were many casualties, atrocities, and deaths. Early in 1999, NATO again carried out an air campaign and sent troops into Kosovo to safeguard the ethnic Albanians. This air campaign was the largest military action in Europe since the close of World War II. In 2000, a revolution overthrew Slobodan Milosevic. The new Yugoslav government turned the former leader over to the International War Crimes Tribunal at the Hague; however, Milosevic died in 2006 before his trial reached completion.

The disintegration of the former Yugoslavia took still another important turn in February 2008 when Kosovo with its Albanian majority population declared its independence from Serbia. The United States, a majority of the nations composing the European Union, and all Kosovo's neighbors except Serbia have recognized the independence of Kosovo. The Russian Federation, a longtime supporter of Serbia, immediately and strongly condemned the independence of Kosovo. The issue of Kosovo's independence, as will be seen in the next section, led to Russian military actions in the region of the Black Sea later in 2008.

▼ Putin and the Resurgence of Russia

Vladimir Putin, who had become president of the Russian Federation in 2000, immediately moved to establish his position as a national and nationalistic leader of the federation. He vigorously renewed the war against the rebels in Chechnya, which resulted in heavy casualties and enormous destruction there, but also strengthened Putin's political support in Russia itself. The ongoing Chechen war spawned one of the major acts of recent terrorism in Russia. In September 2003, a group of Chechens captured an elementary school in Beslan, a community in the Russian republic of North Ossetia (in the north Caucasus) on the opening day of the term. Approximately 1,200 students, teachers, and parents were held hostage for several days. When government troops stormed the school, approximately 330 of the hostages were killed. By the middle of the decade, however, Russian forces had clearly established the upper hand over the Chechen rebels and the drive toward independence was firmly checked at a very high cost in lives on both sides.

In the wake of the Chechen war and as part of his determination that the central government will dominate Russia's economy and political life, Putin has sought to diminish local autonomy and centralize power in his own hands. The central government has also moved against leading oligarchs and other businessmen with some being imprisoned. Putin used the attacks on these enormously wealthy and economically powerful figures to generate support from the broad Russian public who regard the oligarchs as thieves and one of the causes of the economic hardship of the 1990s. Putin also imprisoned political critics and opponents as well as moving against independent newspapers and television stations.

During Putin's presidency the Russian economy genuinely began to improve. Foreign debts were paid. The Russian ruble came to be regarded as a serious currency. Many more consumer goods were available. Much of this relative prosperity was the result of the oil resources available to the Russian Federation and the rising price of oil on the world market. Under Putin a clear trade-off occurred between political freedom and economic and political stability. In 2008 Putin left the elected presidency at the end of his second four-year term, turning the office over to his own handpicked successor Dmitri Medvedev (b. 1965). At the same time, however, Putin assumed the office of prime minister and clearly remained the chief political figure in the country.

Putin both as president and now prime minister has been determined to use the nation's economic recovery and new wealth to allow Russia to reassert its position as a major power on both the regional and world scene. After the terrorist attacks on the United States in September 2001, Putin supported the American assault on Afghanistan, largely because the Russian government was afraid that Islamic extremism would spread beyond Chechnya to other regions in Russia and to the largely Muslim nations that bordered Russia in Central Asia and the Caucasus. This period of cooperation proved short-lived. Putin became one of the leading voices against the American-led invasion of Iraq and has continued to criticize American policy in the region. Putin has also been sharply critical of the ongoing expansion of NATO, which has embraced nations directly bordering the Russian Federation. His government continued to attempt to exert influence in various new nations, such as the former Soviet republics of Ukraine and Georgia, that came into existence with the collapse of the former Soviet Union. (See "Vladimir Putin Outlines a Vision of the Russian Future.")

This determination to assert Russian domination over recently independent nations once part of the former Soviet Union dramatically displayed itself in August 2008. That month troops of the Russian Federation invaded the republic of Georgia. What had provoked this attack was Georgia's having shortly before sent troops into South Ossetia. Russian troops first drove the Georgians out of South Ossetia, and then continued into Georgia itself. South Ossetia itself a part of the former Soviet Union, had been divided into regions dominated by Russia and Georgia. Georgia sought to assert further influence only to be immediately and overwhelmingly blocked by Russian forces. Russia eventually withdrew after a cease-fire but had succeeded in demonstrating its power in the region and in creating potential instability in postwar Georgia.

The Russian invasion of Georgia marked a new departure in post–Soviet Russian foreign policy and a resurgence of Russian international influence following the collapse of the Soviet Union nearly twenty years earlier. During that period both the European Union and NATO had moved to expand their memberships by expanding into Eastern Europe and into regions previously dominated by or part of the former Soviet Union. The Russian Federation found itself compelled to watch over these expansions without being able to stop them or otherwise significantly influence them. Discussions had taken place about the possibility of bringing both Ukraine and Georgia into NATO. The United States had indicated support for such inclusion. Putin and other leaders of the Russian Federation had witnessed the manner in which various regions of the former Yugoslavia, most recently Kosovo in February 2008, had broken away from Serbia and established their own independence. The Russia Federation feared the example of Kosovo and the international recognition its independence had achieved might serve as a pattern for potential break-away regions in the Russian Federation. It also feared encirclement by NATO member nations where the United States might

The aftermath of an attack by a Russian warplane on an apartment block in Gori, Georgia, during the conflict in South Ossetia in August 2008. Here a Georgian man cradles the body of a relative killed during the bombing, which killed at least five people. © Gleb Garanich/Reuters/America LLC

VLADIMIR PUTIN OUTLINES A VISION OF THE RUSSIAN FUTURE

Vladimir Putin served as president of the Russian Federation from 1998 to 2008 when he moved to the office of prime minister. In one of his last presidential speeches he outlined his view of a democratic Russian future as well as his concerns about the relationship of the Russian Federation to NATO. His speech embraced a strong rhetoric of democracy but at the same time placed very considerable limits on the kind of activity and criticism that democratic parties might exercise. Note that he made no provision about who might decide if they were behaving in a fashion dangerous to the national interest. In his own time in office he imprisoned numerous political opponents. Also note his concerns about the future place in the world of the Russian Federation and his strong commitment to expansion of its military defense capacities.

How does Putin seem to embrace democratic reform? What are the limits that he places on democratic activity? How might those limits lead to government interference with the activity of political parties? What are Putin's concerns regarding NATO and the place of the Russian Federation in world affairs?

The desire of millions of our citizens for individual freedom and social justice is what defines the future of Russia's political system. The democratic state should become an effective instrument for civil society's self-organization. . . .

Russia's future political system will be centered on several large political parties that will have to work hard to maintain or affirm their leading positions, be open to change and broaden their dialogue with the voters.

Political parties must not forget their immense responsibility for Russia's future, for the nation's unity and for our country's stable development.

No matter how fierce the political battles and no matter how irreconcilable the differences between parties might be, they are never worth so much as to bring the country to the brink of chaos.

Irresponsible demagogy and attempts to divide society and use foreign help or intervention in domestic political struggles are not only immoral but are illegal. They belittle our people's dignity and undermine our democratic state. . . .

No matter what their differences, all of the different public forces in the country should act in accordance with one simple but essential principle: do nothing that would damage the interests of Russia and its citizens and act only for Russia's good, act in its national interests and in the interest of the prosperity and security of all its people. . . .

It is now clear that the world has entered a new spiral in the arms race. This does not depend on us and it is not we who began it. . . .

NATO itself is expanding and is bringing its military infrastructure ever closer to our borders. We have closed our bases in Cuba and Vietnam, but what have we got in return? New American bases in Romania and Bulgaria, and a new missile defense system with plans to install components of this system in Poland and the Czech Republic soon it seems. . . .

We are effectively being forced into a situation where we have to take measures in response, where we have no choice but to make the necessary decisions. . . .

Russia has a response to these new challenges and it always will. Russia will begin production of new types of weapons over these coming years, the quality of which is just as good and in some cases even surpasses those of other countries.

Validmir Putin, Speech at Expanded Meeting of the State Council on Russia's Development Strategy through 2020, February 8, 2008, President of Russia, Official Web Portal, www.kremlin.ru/eng/text/speeches/2008/02/08/1137_type82912type82913_159643.shtml

locate military bases. The action taken against Georgia served to demonstrate the ability of the Russian Federation to take military action on its borders and to give warning to other nations in the region of its capacity to intervene. At the same time the absence of any effective resistance to Russian actions in Georgia from either the United States or the European Union nations raised doubts about the capacity of either to influence events in the region of the Black Sea. Therefore, though the Russian incursion into Georgia was relatively brief, it demonstrated that the classic issues of European great power politics remain alive in the new Europe. Moreover, the action also demonstrated Russian willingness to take advantage of American involvement in Iraq and Afghanistan to reassert its potential authority in those regions it has dominated since the wars of Catherine the Great in the eighteenth century.

In late 2008 another question suddenly confronted Russia. As one element in the worldwide financial crisis commodity prices dropped sharply. These included the price of oil on the world market. It remains to be seen whether Russia will be able to maintain its economic growth and political resurgence in the face of dropping income from the sale of oil, which has financed its new international influence during the past decade.

▾ The Rise of Radical Political Islamism

On September 11, 2001, Islamic terrorists attacked the United States, crashing hijacked civilian domestic aircraft into the twin towers of the World Trade Center in New York City, the Pentagon in Washington, DC, and a Pennsylvania field with a vast loss of life and property. These events and those flowing from them not only transformed American foreign policy toward the Middle East but have also changed European relations with the United States.

In retrospect, we can see that those attacks were the result of forces that had been affecting not only the United States but the Western world as well for at least a half century. The end of the Cold War has been succeeded by a new political world in which both the United States and the nations of Europe, including the Russian Federation, are endangered by terrorist attacks from nongovernmental or non-state-based organizations. These groups are guided by ideologies in the Islamic world that have filled a political and ideological vacuum left by the end of the Cold War.

Radical Islamism is the term scholars use to describe an interpretation of Islam that came to have a significant impact in the Muslim world during the decades of decolonization. It is only one—and by no means the most popular—interpretation of Islam. The ideas informing radical Islamism extend back to the 1930s and resistance to British rule in Egypt, but for many years, those had little impact on the politics of the Middle East.

Arab Nationalism

Radical Islamism arose primarily in reaction to the secular Arab nationalism that developed in countries like Egypt and Syria in the 1920s and 1930s. Although Arab and other Middle Eastern nationalists, like nineteenth-century modernizers in the Ottoman Empire, believed that the path to independence and strength lay in adopting the technology and imitating the political institutions of the West, these advocates of radical Islam wanted to reject Western ideas and create a society based on a rigorous interpretation of Islam and its teachings. (See Chapter 22.)

In the wake of World War II, many of the foremost leaders of Arab nationalism against Western direct and indirect dominance, such as Gamal Abdul Nasser of Egypt, were sympathetic to socialism or to the Soviet Union. Because socialism and communism were Western ideologies, left-leaning Arab nationalism was no less Western in its orientation than were nationalists friendly to the United States. Moreover, Soviet communism was overtly atheistic and hence doubly offensive to devout Arab Muslims.

Nationalism forged by nondemocratic Middle Eastern governments, usually traditional monarchies or authoritarian regimes dominated by the military, brought different results to the various Arab nations. Oil made Saudi Arabia wealthy and powerful and the small Gulf states, such as Kuwait, rich but not powerful. Other states, such as Jordan, Syria, and Egypt, which lacked oil, remained burdened by large impoverished populations.

Arab governments defining themselves according to the values of nationalism worked out arrangements with local Muslim authorities. For example, the Saudi royal family turned over its educational system to adherents of a rigorist, puritanical form of Islam called *Wahhabism* while modernizing the country's infrastructure. The Egyptian government attempted to play different Islamic groups off against one another. These governments retained the support of prosperous, devout middle-class Muslims while doing little about the plight of the poor. In general, Muslim religious leaders were hostile to the Soviet Union and its influence in the Islamic world.

The Iranian Revolution

The Iranian Revolution of 1979 transformed the Middle East. The Ayatollah Ruhollah Khomeini (1902–1989) managed to unite both the middle and lower classes of a major Middle Eastern nation to overthrow a repressive but a modernizing government that had long cooperated with the United States. For the first time, a religiously dominated government defining itself and its mission in distinctly Islamic, as well as nationalistic, terms took control of a major state. Iran's revolutionary government was a theocracy; that is, there was no separation of religion and government or, in European terms, of church and state. The Iranian constitution gave the clergy, acting on behalf of God, the final say in all matters.

By challenging the Westernization of Iranian society, the Iranian Revolution shocked the world. It also challenged the largely secular presuppositions of Arab nationalists in states such as Egypt, Saudi Arabia, and Algeria that had failed to satisfy the needs of their own underclasses. In the mid-twentieth century, Arabs and other Middle Eastern peoples had turned to nationalism in reaction against European colonial powers. Those who grew up under nationalist leadership and still found themselves politically and economically disadvantaged, however, reacted against nationalism. The Iranian Revolution, which many thought would spread throughout the Islamic world, attracted them.

The Iranian Revolution both embodied and emboldened the forces of what is commonly called Islamic *fundamentalism*, but it is more correctly termed Islamic or Muslim *reformism*. This is the belief that a reformed or pure Islam must be established in the contemporary world. Most adherents of this point of view would emphasize personal piety and religious practice. However, a minority wish to see their states strictly governed the way Iran purports to be by Islamic law or the Shari'a. In fact, the Iranian clergy made numerous compromises to the practical demands of everyday government and the oil industry, but their public message to the world was that Iran is a strict Islamic state hostile to the West in general and the United States—"the Great Satan"—in particular. The Iranian Revolution also opposed the state of Israel on both religious and nationalistic grounds.

The conservative Arab governments feared the Iranian Revolution would challenge their legitimacy. They consequently began to pay much more attention to their own religious authorities and cracked down on radical reformist or fundamentalist Muslims. In Egypt, such actions followed the assassination in 1981 of President Anwar Sadat (b. 1918) by a member of the Muslim Brotherhood.

Afghanistan and Radical Islamism

The Russian invasion of Afghanistan of 1979, discussed earlier in this chapter, introduced a major new component into this already complicated picture, illustrating the convergence of Cold War and Islamist politics. The Soviet Union sought to impose a communist, and hence both Western and atheist, government in Afghanistan. Muslim religious authorities declared *jihad*, literally meaning "a struggle" but commonly interpreted as a religious war, against the Soviet Union. The Afghan resistance to the Soviets thus became simultaneously nationalistic, universalistic, and religious.

Thousands of Muslims, mostly fundamentalist in outlook, arrived in Afghanistan from across the Islamic world to oust the Soviets and their Afghan puppets. Conservative Arab states and the United States supported this effort, which succeeded when all Soviet forces withdrew in 1989. The conservative Arab states saw the Afghan war as an opportunity both to resist Soviet influence and to divert the energies of their own religious extremists. The United States saw the Afghan war as another round in the Cold War. The militant Muslim fundamentalists saw it as a religious struggle against an impious Western power.

The Taliban and Al Qaeda The Soviet withdrawal created a power vacuum in Afghanistan that lasted almost a decade. By 1998, however, rigorist Muslims known as the *Taliban* had seized control of the country. They imposed their own version of Islamic law, which involved strict regimentation of women and public executions, floggings, and mutilations for criminal, religious, and moral offenses. The Taliban also allowed groups of Muslim terrorists known as *Al Qaeda*, which means "Base," to establish training camps in their country. The terrorists who attacked the United States on September 11, 2001, came from these camps.

The ideology of these groups had emerged over several decades from different regions of the Islamic world but had been inculcated in Pakistan. The Pakistani government had long assigned considerable control over education to Islamic schools, or *madrasas*, that taught reformed Islam, rejection of liberal and nationalist secular values, intolerance toward non-Muslims, repudiation of Western culture, hostility to Israel, and hatred of the United States.

***Jihad* Against the United States** Once the *jihad* against the Soviet Union had succeeded, radical Muslims, largely educated in these Pakistani schools, turned their attention to the United States, the other great Western power. The event that brought about this redirection was the Persian Gulf War of 1991. The occasion for that conflict was the invasion of Kuwait by Iraq, under Saddam Hussein (1937–2006). The conservative Arab governments, most importantly Saudi Arabia, not only supported the United States but also permitted it to construct military bases on their territory. Islamic extremists who had fought in Afghanistan, one of whom was Osama Bin Laden (b. 1957), saw the establishment of U.S. bases in Saudi Arabia, which was the home of the prophet Muhammad and contains Islam's two holiest cities, Mecca and Medina, as a new invasion by Western Crusaders. The bases added a new grievance to the already long list of radical Muslim complaints against the United States.

The United States became a target because of its secular public morality, its international wealth and power, its military strength, its ongoing support for Israel, and its adherence to the UN sanctions imposed on Iraq after the Gulf War. Certain Muslim religious authorities declared a

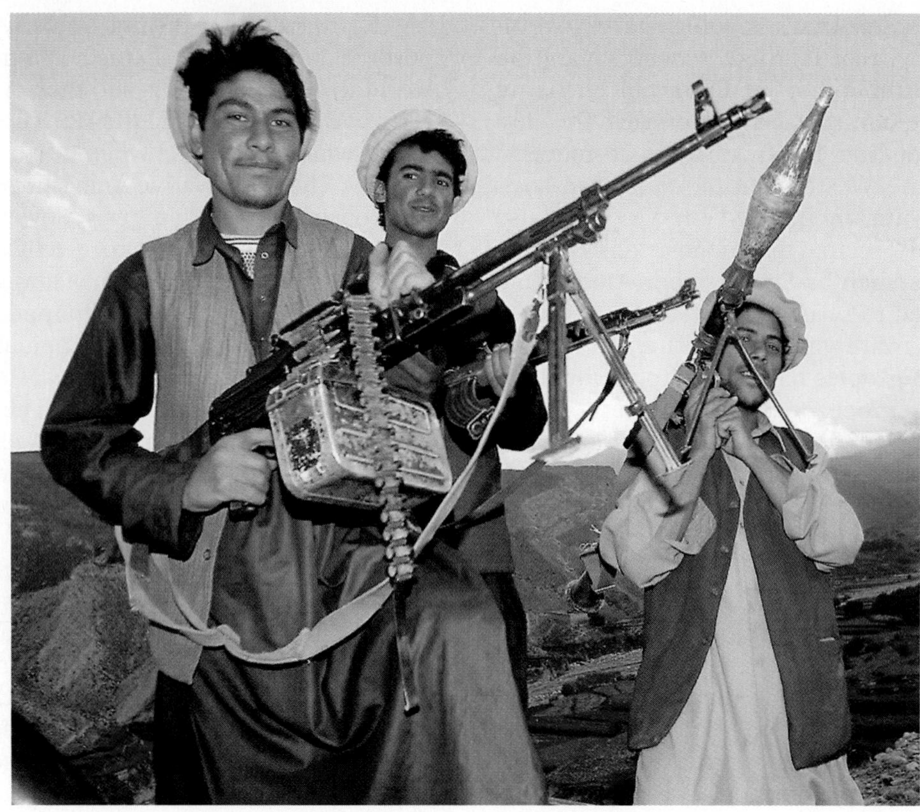

Taliban fighters brandish machine guns and rocket launchers near the Tora Bora mountains in Afghanistan, the site of a major battle with U.S. forces in late 2001. Knut Mueller/Das Fotoarchiv/Peter Arnold, Inc.

jihad against the United States, thus transforming opposition to American policies and culture into a religious war. Through the 1990s, terrorists attacks were directed against targets in or associated with the United States. These included bombings of the World Trade Center in New York City in 1993, of a U.S. army barracks in Saudi Arabia in 1996, of U.S. embassies in East Africa in 1998, and of the USS *Cole* in the Yemeni port of Aden in 2000. These attacks resulted in a considerable loss of life.

▾ A Transformed West

The attacks on the United States on September 11, 2001, transformed and redirected American foreign policy into what the administration of President George W. Bush (b. 1946) termed "a war on terrorism." In late 2001, the United States attacked the Taliban government of Afghanistan, rapidly overthrowing it. The defeat of the Taliban destroyed Al Qaeda's Afghan bases but not its leadership, which survived, although it was dispersed and remains in hiding. By 2008 there was evidence that the Taliban had regrouped and again become active.

Following the Afghan campaign, the Bush administration set forth a policy of preemptive strikes and intervention against potential enemies of the United States. The administration argued that the danger of weapons of mass destruction developed by governments such as that of Iraq falling into the hands of international terrorist organizations posed so severe a danger to the security of the United States that the nation could not wait to respond to an attack but must take preemptive action. This argument, which aroused controversy both at home and abroad, marked a major departure from previous United States foreign policy. It is a direct result of the attacks on the United States that occurred on September 11.

In 2002, the Bush administration turned its attention to Saddam Hussein's government in Iraq. Since the defeat of Iraq in 1991 by an international coalition led by the United States, Saddam Hussein, contrary to widespread expectations, had remained in power and had continued to oppress his own people. Throughout the 1990s, the Iraqi government had also resisted the work of United Nations inspectors charged with discovering and destroying weapons of mass destruction found in Iraq or facilities capable of manufacturing such weapons. The Iraqis eventually expelled the United Nations inspectors in 1998, and the United Nations was unable to reinsert them for almost five years.

The United States government adopted a policy of regime change in Iraq during the last years of the Clinton administration (1993—2001) though it did little to carry out that policy. In the wake of the September 11, 2001, attacks, however, the Bush administration determined to overthrow Saddam Hussein and remove any threat from supposed Iraqi weapons of mass destruction. In late 2002 and early 2003, the United States and British governments sought to obtain passage of United Nations Security Council resolutions that would require Iraq to disarm on its own or to be disarmed by military force. These efforts failed. France and Russia threatened to veto the measure, and a majority of the Security Council voted against it. Nonetheless, the United States and Great Britain, backed by token forces or other support from over thirty other nations, invaded Iraq in late March 2003. After three weeks of fighting, the Iraqi army and with it the government of Saddam Hussein collapsed. The announced goals of the invasion, in addition to toppling the Iraqi regime, were to destroy Iraq's capacity to manufacture or deploy weapons of mass destruction and to bring consensual government to the Iraqi people. The latter goal has remained elusive as Iraq has been violently split by deadly internal political conflict.

The invasion of Iraq was undertaken in the face of considerable opposition from France, Germany, and Russia. It also provoked large antiwar demonstrations in the United States and throughout the world. Both the war and the diplomatic difficulties preceding it disrupted the long-standing Atlantic alliance. Moreover, French and German opposition to the war created strains within Europe and particularly within NATO and the European Union, as other European governments either strongly supported or opposed the United States and Britain. As a result, the war in Iraq marked a new and divisive era in relations between the United States and Europe, and between the United States and the rest of the world.

Once the invasion of Iraq had been carried out and the occupation commenced, Al Qaeda terrorists struck in Europe itself. On March 11, 2004, at least 190 people were killed in train bombings in Madrid, Spain. The terrorist attack occurred just before the Spanish election. The Spanish government, which had supported the American invasion of Iraq, unexpectedly lost the election. The new government then soon withdrew Spanish troops from Iraq. The Madrid bombings were the largest act of terrorism against civilians in Europe since World War II. The attack demonstrated that terrorist attacks can directly influence European political processes.

The Iraq war and the bloody insurgency that followed generated enormous controversy. The coalition forces found no weapons of mass destruction in Iraq. Government commissions in the United States and Britain have criticized the intelligence information used to justify the invasion. In 2004, however, President Bush was reelected. In March 2005, thousands of Iraqis braved threats to vote in the first meaningful election held in Iraq since the 1950s; later in October 2005 they would vote to ratify a new constitution. In 2006 Saddam Hussein was tried and executed for crimes against humanity. Meanwhile in May 2005, the British government of Prime Minister Tony Blair was also reelected, though with a much reduced parliamentary majority. However, on July 7, 2005, terrorist bombings struck the London bus and subway system with a considerable loss of life. Once more, as in Spain, terrorism struck a major European city. The British government, unlike the Spanish, continued to retain its armed forces in Iraq.

The Iraq war, which has witnessed the death of more than 4,000 American troops and thousands of Iraqis, continued to cause controversy in the United States and between the United States and its NATO allies. However, in early 2007 the Bush administration increased the number of troops committed to Iraq. The purpose of the increase in troops, called "the surge" in the press, was to bring about greater internal stability in the country and most particularly in Baghdad. Over the months the level of violence did subside. By 2008 the United States under the Bush administration and the Iraq government were negotiating the future status of American troops in Iraq with the goal of significantly reducing their numbers in upcoming years. Somewhat surprisingly, issues of the economy more than those of Middle East involvement dominated the 2008 U.S. presidential campaign. Early in 2009 after assuming the presidency, President Barack Obama undertook a policy to establish an orderly withdrawal of most American combat troops from Iraq by the late summer of 2010.

In Perspective

In 1900, the major European nations dominated the world. Their wealth in terms of manufacturing, investment banking, and consumer demand profoundly influenced the lives of millions of people on every continent. Their military power, particularly their navies, and their colonial administrators controlled most of Africa and much of Asia. Many Europeans were emigrating, especially to the Americas. Wherever Europeans traveled or governed, they could expect that people on other continents would look to Europe as a model for industrial development, accumulation of wealth, and high culture in the arts and sciences. It was the apex of the European era that began at the close of the fifteenth century. In 1900, almost no one could have predicted the enormous human tragedies that would occur in Europe during the next half century or the retreat from world dominance

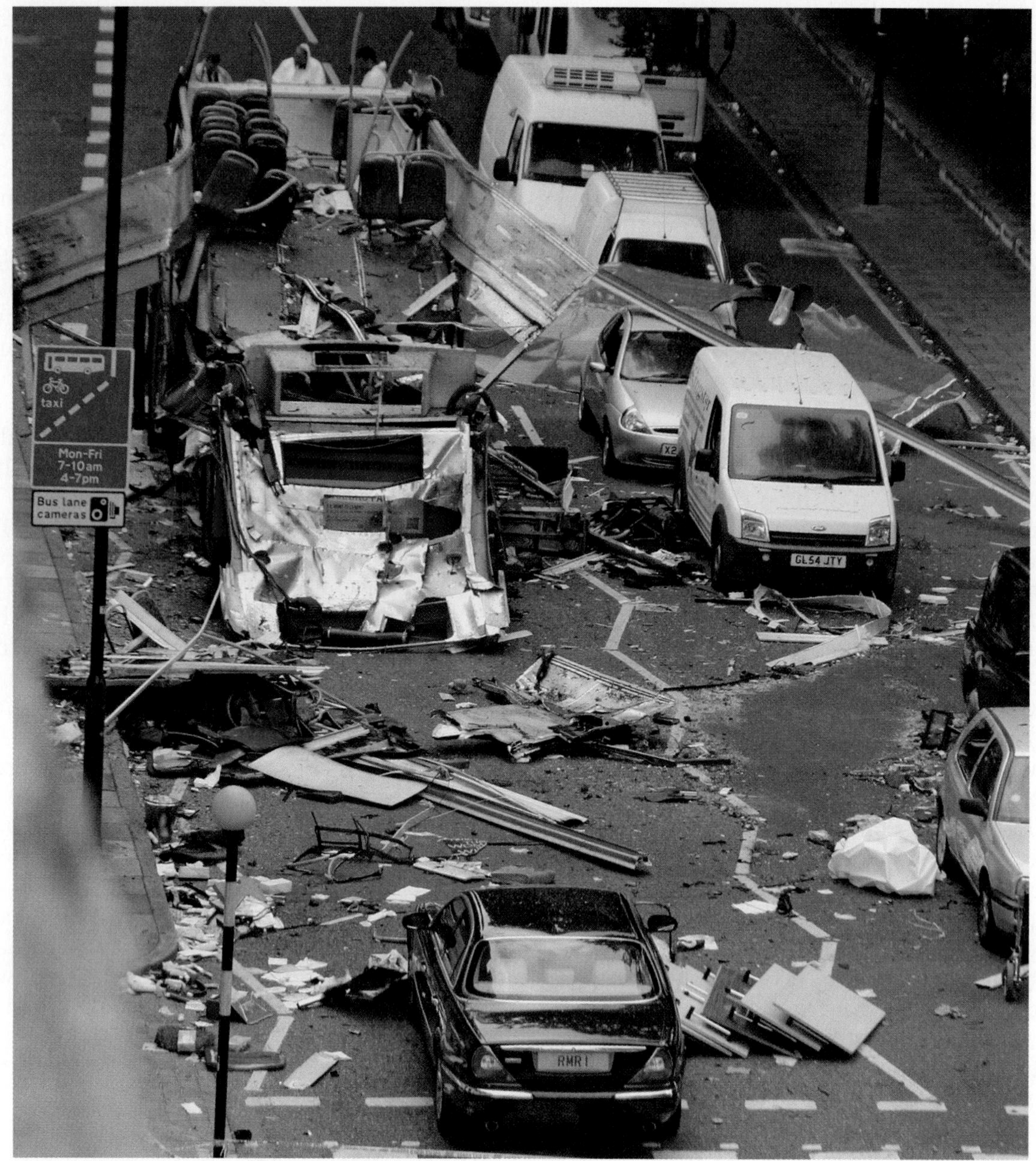

On July 7, 2005, a series of bombs rocked the London transport system with the loss of over fifty lives. This photo shows the remains of a London bus on which a suicide bomber took more than a dozen lives near Russell Square, London. Sion Touhig/CORBIS/Bettmann

that would mark the European experience during the rest of the twentieth century.

World War II resulted in the political collapse of Europe. In the wake of the war, the United States and the Soviet Union emerged as two superpowers, both of them equipped with nuclear weapons. From that time until the collapse of the Soviet Union in 1991, the U.S.–Soviet rivalry dominated world affairs. Local flash points became regions for rivalry and conflict between the two nuclear powers.

While the Cold War profoundly influenced international relations, the process of decolonization spread around the globe. One nation after another in Africa and Asia became free of direct European colonial rule. Scores of new nations emerged. Both the Soviet Union and the United States frequently filled the political, economic, and military vacuum the departure of the European colonial rulers left. This situation led each nation into major military interventions—the United States in Vietnam and the Soviet Union in Afghanistan—that had significant domestic consequences in each nation.

By the middle of the 1980s, the economy and political structures of the Soviet Union could no longer bear the burden of the Cold War. The effort to reform Soviet structures Mikhail Gorbachev commenced concluded with the surrender of political monopoly by the Soviet Communist Party. Simultaneously the Soviet Union retreated from Eastern Europe, and the states that the Soviet-controlled Communist Party formerly dominated achieved independence. By 1991, the Soviet Union had collapsed internally. The loosely structured Confederation of Independent States replaced it. Many former Soviet republics became completely independent states, some of which were hostile to Russia.

Since the collapse of the Soviet Union, the United States has remained the single superpower. Just after the turn of the new century, the United States suffered a major and unprecedented terrorist attack on its soil. Thereafter, the United States responded with unprecedented intervention in the Middle East. The political structures of that region were themselves the result of the decisions the Western powers took after World War I at the Versailles peace conference in 1919. In that regard, the conflict between the United States and many groups in the Middle East, most prominently radical political Islamists, represents one more chapter in the long, unfolding twentieth-century story of the global interaction between regions of the world European power once dominated and the West. The ongoing ramifications of decolonization have continued in the wake of the end of the Cold War.

Review Questions

1. How did the United States and the Soviet Union come to dominate Europe after 1945? How would you define the policy of *containment*? In what areas of the world did the United States specifically try to contain Soviet power from 1945 to 1982? Why were 1956 and 1962 crucial years in the Cold War?
2. How did Khrushchev's policies and reforms change the Soviet state after the repression of Stalin? Why did many people consider Khrushchev reckless?
3. Why did the nations of Europe give up their empires? How did World War II affect the movement toward decolonization? How did Gandhi lead India toward independence? How did French decolonization policies differ from Britain's? How did the United States become involved in Vietnam?
4. What internal political pressures did the Soviet Union experience in the 1970s and early 1980s? What steps did the Soviet government take to repress those protests? What role did Gorbachev's attempted reforms play in the collapse of the Soviet Union? What were the major events in Eastern Europe—particularly Poland—that contributed to the collapse of communism? What are the major domestic challenges to the new Confederation of Independent States?
5. Was the former Yugoslavia a national state? Why did it break apart and slide into civil war? How did the West respond to this crisis?
6. What were the major difficulties that the Russian Federation faced in the 1990s and beyond? How did the policies of Yeltsin and Putin address them? How has Putin attempted to preside over a resurgence of Russian great power influence? How do his goals in part reflect concern over the example of the political disintegration of Yugoslavia?
7. How did the American response to the attacks of September 11, 2001, divide the NATO alliance? Why do some European nations feel able to dissent from the U.S. position in the Middle East when they rarely did so during the Cold War?
8. What were the major causes for the rise of radical political Islamism? In what ways is the present U.S. intervention in the Middle East a result of decolonization and in what ways are other factors at work?

Suggested Readings

A. Ahmed, *Discovering Islam. Making Sense of Muslim History and Society*, rev. ed. (2003). An excellent and readable overview of Islamic–Western relations.

C. Bayly, *Forgotten Wars: Freedom and Revolution in Southeast Asia* (2007). An important volume on decolonization by a master historian of the region.

R. Betts, *France and Decolonization* (1991). Explores the complexities of the French case.

A. Brown, *The Gorbachev Factor* (1996). Reflections by a thoughtful observer.

C. Elkins, *Imperial Reckoning: The Untold Story of Britain's Gulag in Kenya* (2005). A study of the violence involved in Britain's eventual departure from Kenya.

M. Ellman and V. Kontorovich, *The Disintegration of the Soviet Economic System* (1992). An overview of the economic strains in the Soviet Union during the 1980s.

G. Fuller, *The Future of Political Islam* (2003). A good overview of Islamist ideology by a former CIA staff member.

J. L. Gaddis, *The United States and the Origins of the Cold War, 1941–1947* (1992). A major discussion.

M. Glenny, *The Balkans, 1804–1999: Nationalism, War and the Great Powers* (1999). A lively narrative by a well-informed journalist.

M. I. Goldman, *Petrostate: Putin, Power, and the New Russia* (2008). A thoughtful, but critical analysis.

D. Halberstam, *The Coldest Winter: America and the Korean War* (2007). A superb narrative by a gifted journalist.

W. Hitchcock, *Struggle for Europe: The Turbulent History of a Divided Continent, 1945–2002* (2003). The best overall narrative now available.

A. Horne, *A Savage War of Peace: Algeria 1954–1962* (1987). A now dated but still classic narrative.

R. Hyam, *Britain's Declining Empire: The Road to Decolonization, 1918–1968* (2007). The best one-volume treatment.

T. Judah, *The Serbs: History, Myth and the Destruction of Yugoslavia* (1997). A clear overview of a complex event.

J. Keay, *Sowing the Wind: The Seeds of Conflict in the Middle East* (2003). A thoughtful account.

N. R. Keddie, *Modern Iran: Roots and Results of Revolution* (2003). Chapters 6 to 12 focus on Iran from 1941 through the 1978 revolution.

J. Keep, *Last of the Empires: A History of the Soviet Union, 1945–1991* (1995) (2007). An outstanding one-volume survey.

G. Kepel, *Jihad: The Trail of Political Islam* (2002). An extensive treatment by a leading French scholar.

Y. Khan, *The Great Partition: The Making of India and Pakistan* (2008). An important recent study of a difficult issue.

P. Khanna, *The Second World: Empires and Influence in the New Global Order* (2008). A volume that seeks to provide a broad global analysis of recent events.

W. R. Louis, *Ends of British Imperialism: The Scramble for Empire, Suez, and Decolonization* (2007). A major study that captures the intensity and passions of the events.

R. Mann, *A Grand Delusion: America's Descent into Vietnam* (2001). The best recent narrative.

K. E. Meyer and S. B. Brysac, *Kingmakers: The Invention of the Modern Middle East* (2008). A lively narrative of the past two centuries of British and then American influence in the Middle East.

D. E. Murphy, S. A. Kondrashev, and G. Bailey, *Battleground Berlin: CIA vs. KGB in the Cold War* (1997). One of the best of a vast literature on Cold War espionage.

W. E. Odom, *The Collapse of the Soviet Military* (1999). A study more wide ranging than the title suggests.

M. Oren, *Power, Faith, and Fantasy: America in the Middle East: 1776 to the Present* (2007). A thoughtful, balanced analysis.

B. Parekh, *Gandhi: A Very Short Introduction* (2001). A useful introduction to Gandhi's ideas.

T. R. Reid, *The United States of Europe: The New Superpower and the End of American Supremacy* (2004). A journalist's exploration of the impact of the European Union on American policy.

T. Shepard, *The Invention of Decolonization: The Algerian War and the Remaking of France* (2008). Explores the impact of the Algerian War on French politics.

L. Shevtsova, *Russia—Lost in Transition: The Yeltsin and Putin Legacies* (2007). A major analysis and meditation on the past two decades.

J. Springhall, *Decolonization since 1945: The Collapse of European Empires* (2001). Systematic treatment of each major former colony.

B. Stanley, *Missions, Nationalism, and the End of Empire* (2003). Discusses the often ignored role of Christian missions and decolonization.

M. Thomas, *The French Empire Between the Wars: Imperialism, Politics and Society* (2005). Useful background to postwar decolonization.

M. Viorst, *In the Shadow of the Prophet: The Struggle for the Soul of Islam* (2001). Explores the divisions in contemporary Islam.

L. Wright, *The Looming Tower: Al Qaeda and the Road to 9/11* (2007). A compelling narrative.

The most important accomplishment of the European Community was the launching on January 1, 1999, of the Euro, a single monetary unit that replaced the national currencies of most of its member nations. In Frankfurt, Germany, people crowded around a symbol of the new currency. The world financial crisis that commenced in 2008 has placed many internal pressures on the European Community and upon its currency. AP Wide World Photos

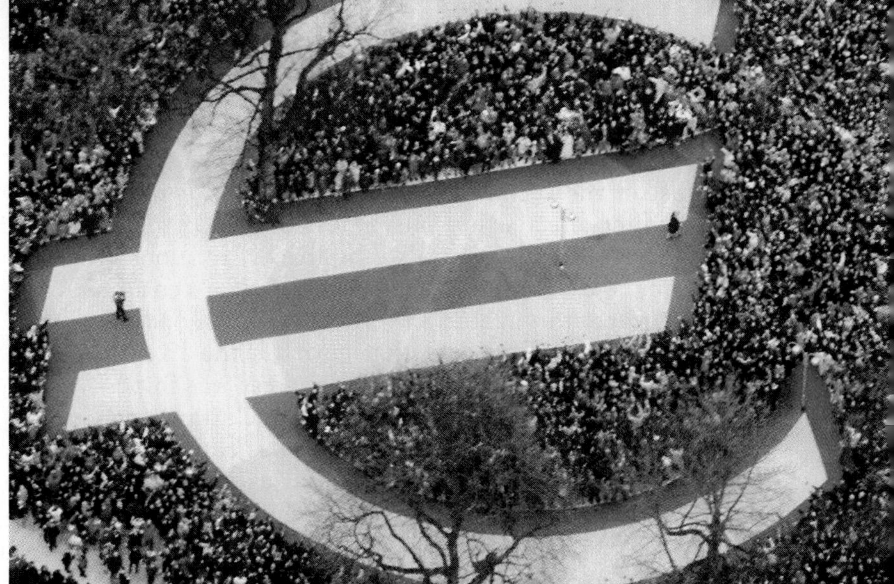

30

The West at the Dawn of the Twenty-First Century

▼ **The Twentieth-Century Movement of Peoples**
Displacement Through War • External and Internal Migration • The New Muslim Population • European Population Trends

▼ **Toward a Welfare State Society**
Christian Democratic Parties • The Creation of Welfare States • Resistance to the Expansion of the Welfare State

▼ **New Patterns in Work and Expectations of Women**
Feminism • More Married Women in the Workforce • New Work Patterns • Women in the New Eastern Europe

▼ **Transformations in Knowledge and Culture**
Communism and Western Europe • Existentialism • Expansion of the University Population and Student Rebellion • The Americanization of Europe • A Consumer Society • Environmentalism

▼ **Art Since World War II**
Cultural Divisions and the Cold War • Memory of the Holocaust

▼ **The Christian Heritage**
Neo-Orthodoxy • Liberal Theology • Roman Catholic Reform

▼ **Late-Twentieth-Century Technology: The Arrival of the Computer**
The Demand for Calculating Machines • Early Computer Technology • The Development of Desktop Computers

▼ **The Challenges of European Unification**
Postwar Cooperation • The European Economic Community • The European Union • Discord over the Union

▼ **New American Leadership and Financial Crisis**

▼ **In Perspective**

KEY TOPICS

- **Migration in twentieth-century Europe**
- **Europe's Muslim minority**
- **Changing status and role of women in Europe**
- **New cultural forces and the continuing influence of Christianity**
- **The impact of computer technology**
- **The movement toward the European Union**

THE COLD WAR defined the life of the West during most of the second half of the twentieth century. This conflict affected not only political developments and military alliances, but also the lives of millions of Europeans and Americans. For almost half a century, the easy travel throughout the world that many people take for granted today and that enriches the lives of thousands of American students every year was impossible. Vast areas were closed off. The Iron Curtain separated families. Most of Eastern Europe was cut off from the material and technological as well as cultural advances that marked the second half of the century.

Yet despite these problems, European society, especially in the West, changed remarkably after World War II, as did, of course, the United States. Western Europe enjoyed unprecedented prosperity, peace, and technological advances. During the same years Europe also took unprecedented steps toward economic cooperation and political union.

▼ The Twentieth-Century Movement of Peoples

In the twentieth century, the movement of peoples transformed European society and the character of many European communities. The Soviet communists' forced removal of Russian peasants and the Nazis' deportations and execution of European Jews were only the most dramatic examples of this development. The Second World War and the subsequent economic transformation of the Continent brought further extensive migrations. The most pervasive trend in this movement of peoples was the continuing shift from the countryside to the cities. Today, except for Albania, at least one third of the population of every European nation lives in large cities. In Western Europe, city dwellers are approximately 75 percent of the population.

Other vast forced movements of peoples by governments, however, were little discussed during the Cold War. During the century, millions of Germans, Hungarians, Poles, Ukrainians, Bulgarians, Serbs, Finns, Chechens, Armenians, Greeks, Turks, Balts, and Bosnian Muslims were displaced.

These forced displacements transformed parts of Europe. Stalin literally moved whole nationalities from one area of the Soviet Union to another and killed millions of people in the process. The Nazis first displaced the Jews and then sought to exterminate them. Throughout Eastern Europe, cities that once had large Jewish populations and a vibrant Jewish religious and cultural life lost any Jewish presence. The displacement of Germans from Eastern Europe back into Germany immediately after World War II transformed cities that had been German into places almost wholly populated by Czechs, Poles, or Russians. For example, the present Polish city of Gdansk was once the German city of Danzig, and today's Russian city of Kaliningrad had been the German Königsberg before 1945.

Displacement Through War

World War II created a vast refugee problem. An estimated 46 million people were displaced in central and Eastern Europe and the Soviet Union alone between 1938 and 1948. Many cities in Germany and in central and Eastern Europe had been bombed or overrun by invading armies. The Nazis had moved hundreds of thousands of foreign workers into Germany as slave laborers. Millions more were prisoners of war. Some of these people returned to their homeland willingly; others, particularly Soviet prisoners fearful of being executed by Stalin, had to be forced to go back, and many were executed. Hundreds of thousands of Baltic, Polish, and Yugoslav prisoners found asylum in Western Europe.

Changes in political borders after the war also uprooted many people. For example, Poland, Czechoslovakia, and Hungary forcibly expelled millions of ethnic Germans from their territories to Germany. This transfer of over 12 million Germans in effect "solved" the problem of German minorities living outside of Germany's national boundaries that had been one of Hitler's excuses for aggression against neighboring countries. In another case of forced migration, hundreds of thousands of Poles were transferred to within Poland's new borders from territory the Soviet Union annexed. Other minorities, such as Ukrainians in Poland and Italians on the Yugoslav coast, were driven into their ethnic homelands. As one historian has commented, "War, violence, and massive social dislocation turned Versailles's dream of national homogeneity into realities."[1]

External and Internal Migration

Between 1945 and 1960, approximately half a million Europeans left Europe each year. This was the largest outward migration since the 1920s, when around 700,000 persons had left annually. In the second half of the nineteenth century, most immigrants were from rural areas. After World War II, they often included educated city dwellers. Immediately after the war, some governments encouraged migration because they were afraid that, as in the 1930s, their economies would not be able to provide adequate employment for all their citizens.

Decolonization in the postwar period led many European colonials to return to Europe from overseas. The most dramatic example of this phenomenon was the more than one million French colonials who moved to

[1]Mark Mazower, *Dark Continent: Europe's Twentieth Century* (New York: Knopf, 1999), p. 218.

France after the end of the Algerian war in 1962 (see Chapter 29). Britons returned from parts of the British Empire; Dutch returned from Indonesia in the late 1940s; Belgians from the Congo in the 1960s; and Portuguese from Mozambique and Angola in the 1970s.

Decolonization also led non-European inhabitants of the former colonies to migrate to Europe. Great Britain, for example, received thousands of immigrants from its former colonies in the Caribbean, Africa, and the Indian subcontinent. France received many immigrants from its empire in Africa, Indochina, and the Arab world. This influx has proved to be a long-term source of social tension and conflict. In Britain, racial tensions were high during the 1980s. France faced similar difficulties, which contributed to the emergence of the National Front, an extreme right-wing group led by Jean-Marie Le Pen (b. 1928) that sought to exploit the resentment many working-class voters felt toward North African immigrants. In 2002, Le Pen won enough votes to become one of the two candidates in the run-off election for the French presidency, although he lost overwhelmingly to Jacques Chirac (b. 1932) in the final ballot. Similar pressures have arisen in Germany, Austria, Italy, the Netherlands, and even Denmark. Such tension did not result only from immigration from Africa and Asia; internal European migration—from the Balkans, Turkey, and the former Soviet Union, often of people in search of jobs—also changed the social and economic face of the Continent and led to a backlash. In recent years, internal immigration within the European Union has seen the movement of significant numbers of people. However, the growing Muslim presence in Europe has produced some of the most serious ethnic and political tensions.

The New Muslim Population

As recounted earlier in this textbook, well into the twentieth century the European relationship with most of the Muslim world was at arm's length or colonialist. Muslims from the Ottoman Empire, the greatest Muslim state, rarely traveled in Europe, and few Europeans traveled in the empire. Europeans encountered Muslims mainly as subjects, in colonies, such as Algeria, Egypt, the Indian subcontinent, sub-Saharan Africa, and the East Indies. In all these regions from at least the mid-nineteenth century onward, Christian missionaries often clashed with Muslim religious teachers.

At the same time, most Europeans, except for a few communities in the Balkans and the former Soviet Empire, regarded themselves and their national cultures as either Christian or secular. Indeed, until recently most Europeans paid little direct attention to Islam as a domestic matter.

That indifference began to change in the 1960s and had dissolved by the end of the twentieth century as a sizable Muslim population settled in Europe. This highly diverse immigrant community had become an issue in Europe even before the events of September 11, 2001.

The immigration of Muslims into Europe, and particularly Western Europe, arose from two chief sources: European economic growth and decolonization. As the economies of Western Europe began to recover in the quarter century after World War II, a labor shortage developed. To fill this demand, Western Europe imported laborers, many of whom came from Muslim nations. For example, Turkish "guest workers" were invited to move to West Germany—on a temporary basis, it was presumed—in the 1960s, and Britain welcomed Pakistanis. The aftermath of decolonization and the quest for a better life led Muslims from East Africa and the Indian subcontinent to settle in Great Britain. The Algerian war brought many Muslims to France. Today there are approximately 1.3 million Muslims in Great Britain, 3.2 million in Germany, and 4.2 million in France. Smaller but still significant numbers have settled in Italy, Spain, Sweden, Denmark, and the Netherlands, nations that previously had had generally homogeneous populations.

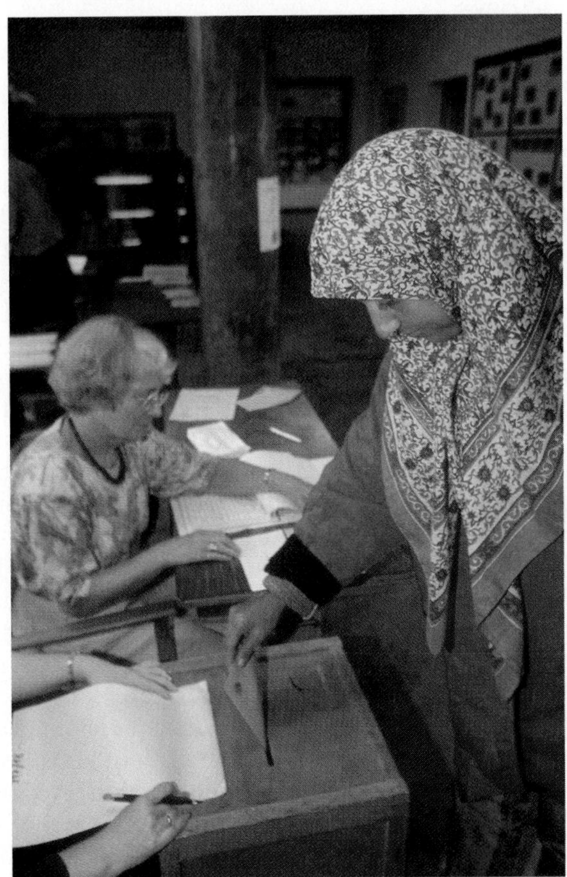

A Muslim woman wearing a traditional headscarf in Hamburg, Germany votes in the Bundestag elections. The presence of foreign-born Muslims whose labor is necessary for the prosperity of the European economy is an important issue in contemporary Europe. Many of these Muslims live in self-contained communities. Peter Arnold, Inc.

These Muslim immigrant communities share certain social and religious characteristics. Originally, many Muslims came to Europe expecting they would eventually return to their homes, an expectation their host countries shared. Neither the immigrants nor the host nations gave much thought to assimilation. Moreover, except for Great Britain, where all immigrants from the Commonwealth may vote immediately upon settling there, European governments made it difficult for Muslim, or any other, immigrants to take part in civic life. Unlike the United States, few European countries had any experience dealing with large-scale immigration. The Muslim communities have, therefore, generally remained unassimilated and self-contained. This apartness has provided internal community support for Muslim immigrants but has also prevented them from fully engaging with the societies in which they live. Many of their children have not learned European languages well, and Muslim women tend to remain confined to their homes.

Yet the world around these communities has changed. Many of the largely unskilled jobs that the immigrants originally filled have disappeared. Most of the Muslim immigrants to Europe, unlike many who have settled in the United States and Canada, were neither highly skilled nor professionally educated. As a result, they and their adult children who may have grown up in Europe find it difficult to get jobs in the modern service economy. Furthermore, as European economic growth has slowed, European Muslims have become the target of politicians, such as Le Pen in France, who seek to blame the immigrants for a host of problems from crime to unemployment.

The radicalization of parts of the Islamic world has also touched the Muslim communities in Europe. Although Turkish Muslims living in Germany come from a nation that has been secularized since the 1920s and thus tend to be less religiously observant than Pakistani Muslims dwelling in Great Britain, Muslims from both countries have been involved in radical Islamic groups, and some belonged to organizations involved in the September 11, 2001, attacks on the United States. The July 7, 2005, suicide bombings in London were carried out by four young Muslims, three of whom had been born in the United Kingdom and one in Jamaica. By contrast, the French government has exerted more control over its Muslim population. However, that policy appeared to have failed badly when in the autumn of 2005 immigrant youth, largely Muslim, carried out riots in various parts of France. These were the most serious civil disturbances in France since 1968. Subsequent riots have occurred in Paris. There have also been sharp disputes in France over attempts by the government to forbide young Muslim women from wearing headscarves while attending secular government schools.

Nonetheless, European Muslims are not a homogeneous group. They come from different countries, have different class backgrounds, and espouse different Islamic traditions. Many European Muslims and Muslim clerics disagree strongly with each other. At the same time, these Muslim communities, so often now marked by deep poverty and unemployment, have become a major concern for European social workers, who disagree among themselves about how their governments should respond to them. What has become clear, however, is that European governments cannot regard their Muslim populations as passive communities; rather European governments and societies must engage them as a permanent fact in the life of early twenty-first-century Europe.

European Population Trends

During the past quarter century, the population of Europe, measured in terms of the European birthrate, has stabilized in a manner that has deeply disturbed many observers. Europeans are having so few children that they are no longer replacing themselves. Whereas in the 1950s European women on average bore 2.1 children, that rate fell to 1.9 in the 1980s and to 1.4 at present, which is below the replacement level. In Mediterranean countries, such as Greece, Spain, and Italy, the rate is even lower. This situation stands in stark contrast to the growth in population in the United States during the past decade when the birthrate reached approximately 2.1. If the current rates more or less hold, by the middle of this century, the United States will have more people than Europe for the first time in history.

There is no consensus on why the European birthrate has declined. One reason often cited is that women are postponing having children until later in their childbearing years. Nonetheless, in response to public opinion, governments have been trying to limit immigration into Europe at a time when it may need new workers.

This falling birthrate means that Europe will face the prospect of an aging population. The energy and drive that youth can provide may shift to the other side of the Atlantic. An aging population is unlikely to give rise to economic innovation. The internal European market, now larger than the internal American market, will shrink. In contrast to the late nineteenth century (see Chapter 23), Europe itself will have fewer Europeans, and Europe's share of the world's population will also decline. Part of Europe's influence on the world in the nineteenth and early twentieth centuries was simply a consequence of the size of its population.

▾ Toward a Welfare State Society

During the decades spanning the Cold War, the U.S. involvement in Vietnam, and the Soviet domination of Eastern Europe, the nations of Western Europe achieved unprecedented economic prosperity and maintained or inaugurated independent, liberal democratic governments. Most of them also confronted problems associated with decolonization and with maintaining economic growth.

The end of the Second World War saw vast constitutional changes in much of Western Europe, except for Portugal and Spain, which remained dictatorships until the mid-1970s. Before or during the war, Germany, Austria, Italy, and France had experienced authoritarian governments. The construction of stable, liberal, democratic political frameworks became a major goal of their postwar political leaders, as well as of the United States. All concerned recognized that the earlier political structures in those nations had failed to resist the rise of right-wing, antidemocratic movements. The Great Depression had shown that democracy requires a social and economic base, as well as a political structure. Most Europeans came to believe that government ought to ensure economic prosperity and social security. Success at doing so, they hoped, would stave off the kind of turmoil that had brought on tyranny and war and could lead to communism.

Christian Democratic Parties

Except for the British Labour Party, the vehicles of the new postwar politics were not, as might have been expected, the democratic socialist parties. Outside Scandinavia, those parties generally did not prosper after the onset of the Cold War. Both communists and conservatives opposed them. Rather, various Christian democratic parties, usually leading coalition governments, introduced the new policies.

These parties were a major new feature of postwar politics. They were largely Roman Catholic in leadership and membership. Catholic parties had existed in Europe since the late nineteenth century. Until the 1930s, however, they had been conservative and had protected the social, political, and educational interests of the church. They had traditionally opposed communism but proposed few positive programs of their own. The postwar Christian democratic parties of Germany, France, Austria, and Italy, however, were progressive and welcomed non-Catholic members. Democracy, social reform, economic growth, and anticommunism were their hallmarks.

The events of the war years largely determined the political leadership of the postwar decade. On the Continent, those groups and parties, including communist parties, that had been active in the resistance against Nazism and fascism held an initial advantage. After 1947, however, in a policy the United States naturally favored, communists were systematically excluded from Western European governments.

The most immediate postwar domestic problems included not only those the physical damage of the conflict created, but often also those that had existed in 1939. The war, however, opened new opportunities to solve those prewar difficulties.

The Creation of Welfare States

The Great Depression, the rise of authoritarian states in the wake of economic dislocation and mass unemployment, and World War II, which involved more people in a war effort than ever before, changed how many Europeans thought about social welfare. Governments began to spend more on social welfare than they did on the military. This reallocation of funds was a reaction to the state violence of the first half of the century and was possible because the NATO defense umbrella, which the United States primarily staffed and funded, protected Western Europe.

The modern European welfare state was broadly similar across the Continent. Before World War II, except in Scandinavia, the two basic models for social legislation were the German and the British. Bismarck had introduced social insurance in Germany during the 1880s to undermine the German Social Democratic Party. In effect, the imperial German government provided workers with social insurance and thus some sense of social security while denying them significant political participation. In early-twentieth-century Britain, where all classes had access to the political system, social insurance was targeted toward the poor. In both the German and British systems, workers were insured only against the risks from disease, injury on the job, and old age. Unemployment was assumed to be only a short-term problem and often one that workers brought on themselves. People higher up in the social structure could look out for themselves and did not need government help.

After World War II, the concept emerged that social insurance against predictable risks was a social right and should be available to all citizens. In Britain, William B. Beveridge (1879–1963) famously set forth this concept in 1942. Paradoxically, making coverage universal, as Beveridge recommended, appealed to conservatives as well as socialists. If medical care, old-age pensions, and other benefits were available to all, they would not become a device to redistribute income from one part of the population to another.

The first major European nation to begin to create a welfare state was Britain, in 1945 to 1951 under the Labour Party ministry of Clement Attlee (1883–1967). The most important element of this early legislation was the creation of the National Health Service. France and Germany did not adopt similar health care legislation until the 1970s, because their governments initially refused to make coverage universal.

The spread of welfare legislation (including unemployment insurance) within Western Europe was related to both the Cold War and domestic political and economic policy. The communist states of Eastern Europe were promising their people social security as well as full employment. The capitalist states came to believe they had to provide similar security for their people, but, in fact, the social security of the communist states was often more rhetoric than reality.

Resistance to the Expansion of the Welfare State

Western European attitudes toward the welfare state have reflected three periods that have marked economic life since the end of the war. The first period was one of reconstruction from 1945 through the early 1950s. It was followed by the second period—almost twenty-five years of generally steady and expanding economic growth. The third period brought first an era of inflation in the late 1970s and then one of relatively low growth and high unemployment from the 1990s to the present. During each of the first two periods, a general conviction existed, based on Keynesian economics, that the foundation of economic policy was government involvement in a mixed economy. From the late 1970s, more people came to believe the market should be allowed to regulate itself and that government should be less involved in, though not completely withdraw from, the economy.

Margaret Thatcher, a shopkeeper's daughter who became the first female prime minister of Great Britain, served in that office from May 1979 through November 1990. Known as the "Iron Lady" of British politics, she led the Conservative Party to three electoral victories and carried out extensive restructuring of the British government and economy. AP Wide World Photos

The most influential political figure in reasserting the importance of markets and resisting the power of labor unions was Margaret Thatcher (b. 1925) of the British Conservative Party who served as prime minister from 1979 to 1990. She cut taxes and sought to curb inflation. She and her party were determined to roll back many of the socialist policies that Britain had enacted since the war. Her administration privatized many industries that Labour Party governments had nationalized. She also curbed the power of the trade unions in a series of bitter and often violent confrontations. Her goal was to make the British economy more efficient and competitive. Although her administration roused enormous controversy, she was able to push these policies through Parliament. Furthermore, over time the British Labour Party under the leadership of Tony Blair (b. 1953) itself largely came to accept what was at the time known as the Thatcher Revolution. (See "Compare & Connect: Margaret Thatcher and Tony Blair Debate the Government Social Responsibility for Welfare," pages 954–955.)

While Thatcher redirected the British economy, the government-furnished welfare services now found across continental Europe began to encounter resistance. The funding on which they are based assumed a growing population and low unemployment. As the proportion of the population consuming the services of the welfare state—the sick, the injured, the unemployed, and the elderly—increases relative to the number of able-bodied workers who pay for them, the costs of those services have risen.

The leveling off of population growth in Europe discussed in the previous section has thus imperiled the benefits of the welfare state, which Europeans have come to take for granted. Furthermore, during the past two decades, significant levels of unemployment in major Western European nations have increased welfare payments. The low fertility rates across the Continent mean the next working generation will have fewer people to support the retired elderly population. Middle-class taxpayers have also become reluctant to support existing systems.

The general growth of confidence in the ability of market forces rather than government intervention to sustain social cohesion has also spread in the past twenty-five years and has raised questions about the existing welfare structures. Governments across the

Continent, including those normally associated with left-of-center politics, such as the British Labour Party and the German Social Democratic Party, have limited further growth of the welfare state and have reduced benefits. In that respect, Europeans in the next few decades may look at the second half of the twentieth century as the Golden Age of welfare states and may find their own societies dealing with social welfare differently.

Simone de Beauvoir, here with her companion, the philosopher Jean-Paul Sartre, was the major feminist writer in postwar Europe.
Keystone_Paris/Getty Images Inc./Hulton Archive Photos

▼ New Patterns in Work and Expectations of Women

Since World War II, the work patterns and social expectations of European women have changed enormously. In all social ranks, women have begun to assume larger economic and political roles. More women have entered the "learned professions," and more are filling major managerial positions than ever before in European history. Yet certain more or less traditional patterns continue to describe the position of women in both family and economic life. Despite enormous gains during the second half of the twentieth century, and despite the collapse of those authoritarian governments whose social policies inhibited women from advancing into the mainstream of society, gender inequality remained a major characteristic of the social life of Europe at the opening of the twenty-first century.

Feminism

Since World War II, European feminism, although less highly organized than in America, has set forth a new agenda. The most influential postwar work on women's issues was Simone de Beauvoir's (1908–1986) *The Second Sex*, published in 1949. In that work, de Beauvoir explored the difference being a woman had made in her life. (See "Simone de Beauvoir Urges Economic Freedom for Women," page 956.) She was part of the French intellectual establishment and thus wrote from a privileged position. Nonetheless, she and other European feminists argued that, at all levels, European women experienced distinct social and economic disadvantages. Divorce and family laws, for example, favored men. European feminists also called attention to the social problems that women faced, including spousal abuse.

In contrast to earlier feminism, recent feminism has been less a political movement pressing for specific rights than a social movement offering a broader critique of European culture. Several new feminist journals appeared during the 1970s, many of which are still published: *Courage*, *Emma—Magazine by Women for Women*, and *Spare Rib*. A statement in *Spare Rib*, an English magazine, captures the spirit of these publications:

> *Spare Rib* aims to reflect women's lives in all their diverse situations so that they can recognize themselves in its pages. This is done by making the magazine a vehicle for their writing and their images. Most of all, *Spare Rib* aims to bring women together and support them in taking control of their lives.[2]

This emphasis on women controlling their own lives may be the most important element of recent European feminism. Whereas in the past feminists sought and, in significant measure, gained legal and civil equality with men, they are now pursuing personal independence and issues that are particular to women. In this sense, feminism is an important manifestation of the critical tradition in Western culture.

More Married Women in the Workforce

One of the patterns that seemed firmly established in 1900 has reversed itself. The number of married women in the workforce has risen sharply. Both middle-class and working-class married women have

[2]Quoted in Bonnie S. Anderson and Judith P. Zinsser, *A History of Their Own: Women in Europe from Prehistory to the Present*, Vol. 2 (New York: Harper Perennial, 1988), p. 412.

Margaret Thatcher and Tony Blair Debate Government's Social Responsibility for Welfare

TOWARD THE CLOSE of the twentieth century and the turn of the twenty-first century many of the assumptions that had informed the creation of mid-twentieth-century European welfare states came under criticism and redefinition. Nowhere was the debate sharper than in the United Kingdom where the modern welfare state had essentially been invented through social policies enacted in the aftermath of World War II. Margaret Thatcher's government raised serious questions about the role of government in society. By the turn of the century even the British Labour Party led by Tony Blair had come to modify its own understanding of government social responsibility.

QUESTIONS

1. **How and why does Thatcher contend that there is no such thing as society? How does she emphasize the reciprocal character of social relationships?**
2. **How does Thatcher argue in favor of personal and private charity to aid persons in need? Does she criticize all government aid to citizens?**
3. **How is it clear in Blair's speech that he is trying to lead a traditional party of the left toward a new understanding of government social responsibility?**
4. **What does Blair portray as duties of government? How does he seek to mesh government help for individuals with still assigning responsibility to the individuals receiving that help?**
5. **Though Thatcher and Blair differ in their views of policy, what social and political values do they share despite those differences?**

I. Margaret Thatcher Asserts the Need for Individual Responsibility

No single European political figure so challenged and criticized the assumptions of the welfare state and of state intervention in general than Margaret Thatcher, British prime minister from 1979 to 1990. Known as the "Iron Lady," Mrs. Thatcher repeatedly demanded that people take individual responsibility rather than rely on state-sponsored support. Yet her administration did not dismantle the key structures of the British welfare state. The discussion below is from an interview by Mrs. Thatcher in October 1987.

I think we have gone through a period when too many children and people have been given to understand "I have a problem, it is the Government's job to cope with it!" or "I have a problem, I will go and get a grant to cope with it!" "I am homeless, the Government must house me!" and so they are casting their problems on society and who is society? There is no such thing! There are individual men and women . . . there are families and no government can do anything except through people and people look to themselves first. It is our duty to look after ourselves and then also to help look after our neighbour and life is a reciprocal business and people have got the entitlements too much in mind without the obligations, because there is no such thing as an entitlement unless someone has first met an obligation and it is, I think, one of the tragedies in which many of the benefits we give, which were meant to reassure people that if they were sick or ill there was a safety net and there was help, that many of the benefits which were meant to help people who were unfortunate—"It is all right. We joined together and we have these insurance schemes to look after it." That was the objective . . . But it went too far. If children have a problem, it is society that is at fault. There is no such thing as society. There is a living tapestry of men and women and people and the beauty of that tapestry and the quality of our lives will depend upon how much each of us is prepared to take responsibility for ourselves and each of us prepared to turn round and help by our own efforts those who are unfortunate.

Source: This extract derives from a transcript of the original interview rather than the published text. Reprinted with permission from margaretthatcher.org, the official Web site of the Margaret Thatcher Foundation.

II. Tony Blair Seeks to Redefine the British Welfare State

Tony Blair (b. 1953) served as Labour Party prime minister of the United Kingdom from 1997 to 2007. During his time in office he championed what he termed "New Labour" and sought to redefine the British welfare state while still preserving many of its most basic outlines. In June 2002, he outlined his new understanding of the character of the welfare state and its role in promoting individual responsibility. In many respects his view of welfare and government social responsibility had been influenced by Margaret Thatcher's attack on earlier understandings of welfare and government social responsibility.

Despite the ongoing debate among political leaders on the merits of government programs in Britain, these programs continue to be popular. This 1998 celebration commemorates fifty years of the British National Health Service (NHS). © Tim Graham/Corbis Sygma

In welfare, for too long, the right had let social division and chronic unemployment grow; the left argued for rights but were weak on responsibilities. We believe passionately in giving people the chance to get off benefit and into work. . . .

It's right for them, for the country, for society. But with the chance, comes a responsibility on the individual—to take the chance, to make something of their lives and use their ability and potential to the full. . . .

We must give the unemployed youth the skills to find a job; give the single mother the childcare she needs to go out and work; give the middle-aged man on a disability benefit the support and confidence to go back into the office.

And we must not only lift people out of poverty. We must transform their horizons, aspirations and hopes as well—through helping people get the skills they need for better jobs, and through giving them chances to save and build up a nest egg.

Only in this way will we drive up social mobility, the great force for equality in dynamic market economies.

To do all that, ours has to be an enabling welfare state—one which helps people to help themselves. . . .

Government has a responsibility to provide real opportunities for individuals to gain skills and to get into work that pays. But individuals also have a responsibility to grasp those opportunities.

We are now seeing the beginnings of a sea-change in how people view our welfare state. There is growing public support for a welfare state that tackles poverty at its source; that gets people into work; that offers people hope—in exchange for a commitment to help themselves. . . .

This is a welfare state which reflects all our responsibilities: the responsibility we have to engage actively with the jobless to provide them with opportunities; their responsibility to engage actively with us and take those opportunities. . . .

All of our reforms have the same underlying principles—opportunity, fairness and mutual responsibility. We want to give people the chance to fulfill their potential. We want to raise people's expectations and their self-belief, by giving them the tools to help themselves.

Source: Tony Blair, June 10, 2002, as made available at www.guardian.co.uk/society/2002/jun/10/socialexclusion.politics1

SIMONE DE BEAUVOIR URGES ECONOMIC FREEDOM FOR WOMEN

Simone de Beauvoir was the most important feminist voice of mid-twentieth-century Europe. In The Second Sex, *published in France in 1949, she explored the experience of women coming of age in a world of ideas, institutions, and social expectations shaped historically by men. Much of the book discusses the psychological strategies that modern European women had developed to deal with their status as "the second sex." Toward the end of her book, de Beauvoir argues that economic freedom and advancement for women are fundamental to their personal fulfillment.*

Why does de Beauvoir argue that economic freedom for women must accompany their achievement of civic rights? Why does the example of the small number of professional women illustrate issues for European women in general? How does she indicate that even professional women must overcome a culture in which the experience of women is fundamentally different from that of men? Do de Beauvoir's comments seem relevant for women at the opening of the twenty-first century? What similarities do you see to the views of Priscilla Wakefield (Chapter 15) and Mary Wollstonecraft (Chapter 17)?

According to French law, obedience is no longer included among the duties of a wife, and each woman citizen has the right to vote; but these civil liberties remain theoretical as long as they are unaccompanied by economic freedom. . . . It is through gainful employment that woman has traversed most of the distance that separated her from the male; and nothing else can guarantee her liberty in practice. Once she ceases to be a parasite, the system based on her dependence crumbles; between her and the universe there is no longer any need for a masculine mediator. . . .

When she is productive, active, she regains her transcendence; in her projects she concretely affirms her status as subject; in connection with the aims she pursues, with the money and the rights she takes possession of, she makes trial of and senses her responsibility. . . .

There are . . . a fairly large number of privileged women who find in their professions a means of economic and social autonomy. These come to mind when one considers woman's possibilities and her future . . . [E]ven though they constitute as yet only a minority; they continue to be the subject of debate between feminists and antifeminists. The latter assert that the emancipated women of today succeed in doing nothing of importance in the world and that furthermore they have difficulty in achieving their own inner equilibrium. The former exaggerate the results obtained by professional women and are blind to their inner confusion. There is no good reason . . . to say they are on the wrong road; and still it is certain that they are not tranquilly installed in their new realm: as yet they are only halfway there. The woman who is economically emancipated from man is not for all that in a moral, social, and psychological situation identical with that of man. The way she carried on her profession and her devotion to it depends on the context supplied by the total pattern of her life. For when she begins her adult life she does not have behind her the same past as does a boy; she is not viewed by society in the same way; the universe presents itself to her in a different perspective. The fact of being a woman today poses peculiar problems for an independent human individual.

sought jobs outside the home. Because of the low birthrate in the 1930s, few young single women were employed in the years just after World War II. Married women entered the job market to replace them. Some factories changed their work shifts to accommodate the needs of married women. Consumer conveniences and improvements in health care also made it easier for married women to enter the workforce by reducing the demands child care made on their time. At the same time, all surveys indicate that the need to provide care for their children is the most important difficulty women face in the workplace. This situation is a main reason why so many women remain in part-time employment.

In the twentieth century, children were no longer expected to contribute substantially to family income. They now spend more than a decade in compulsory education. When families need more income than one worker can provide, both parents work, bringing many married women with children into the workforce. Such financial necessity led many married women back to work. Evidence also suggests that married women began to work to escape the boredom of housework and to enjoy the companionship of other adult workers.

New Work Patterns

The work pattern of European women has been far more consistent in the twentieth century than it had been in the nineteenth. Single women enter the workforce after their schooling and continue to work after marriage. They may stop working to care for their young children, but they return to work when the children begin school. Several factors created this new pattern, but women's increasing life expectancy is one of the most important.

When women died relatively young, child rearing filled a large proportion of their lives. As a longer life span has shortened that proportion, women throughout the West are seeking ways to lead satisfying lives after their children have grown. Decisions about when to have children and how many have also shaped the late-twentieth-century work pattern for women. Many women have begun to limit the number of children they bear or to forgo childbearing and child rearing altogether. The age at which women have decided to bear children has risen, to the early twenties in Eastern Europe and to the late twenties in Western Europe. In urban areas, women have fewer children and have them later in life than rural women do. These various personal decisions leave many years free to develop careers and stay in the workforce.

Women in the New Eastern Europe

Many paradoxes surround the situation of Eastern European women now that communists no longer govern the region. Under communism, women generally enjoyed social equality, as well as a broad spectrum of government-financed benefits. Most women (normally well over 50 percent) worked in these societies, both because they could and because they were expected to. No significant women's movements existed, however, because communist governments regarded them with suspicion, as they did all independent associations.

The new governments of the region are free but have shown little concern with women's issues. Indeed, the economic difficulties the new governments face may endanger their funding of health and welfare programs that benefit women and children. For example, a free market economy may limit the extensive maternity benefits to which Eastern European women were previously entitled. Moreover, the high proportion of women in the workforce could leave them more vulnerable than men to the region's economic troubles. Women may be laid off before men and hired later than men for lower pay.

▼ Transformations in Knowledge and Culture

Knowledge and culture in Europe were rapidly transformed in the twentieth century. Institutions of higher education enrolled a larger and more diverse student body, making knowledge more widely available than ever before. Also, movements such as existentialism challenged traditional intellectual attitudes. Environmental concerns also raised new issues. Throughout this ferment, representatives of the Christian faith tried to keep their religion relevant.

Communism and Western Europe

Until the final decade of the twentieth century, Western Europe had large, organized communist parties, as well as groups of intellectuals sympathetic to communism. After the Bolshevik victory in the Russian Revolution and the subsequent civil war, the Western European socialist movement divided into independent democratic socialist parties and Soviet-dominated communist parties that followed the dictates of the Third International. In the 1920s and 1930s, those two groups fought each other with only rare moments of cooperation, such as that achieved during the French Popular Front in 1936.

The Intellectuals During the 1930s, as liberal democracies floundered in the face of the Great Depression and as right-wing regimes spread across the Continent, many people saw communism as a vehicle for protecting humane and even liberal values. European university students were often affiliated with the Communist Party. They and older intellectuals visited the Soviet Union and praised what they saw as Stalin's achievements. Some of these intellectuals may not have known of Stalin's terror. Others simply closed their eyes to it, believing humane ends might come from inhumane methods. Still others defended Stalinist terror. During the late 1920s and the 1930s, communism became a substitute religion for some Europeans. One group of former communists, writing after World War II, described their attraction toward, and later disillusionment with, communism in a book entitled *The God That Failed* (1949).

Four events proved crucial to the intellectuals' disillusionment: the great Soviet public purge trials of the late 1930s, the Spanish Civil War (1936–1939), the Nazi-Soviet pact of 1939, and the Soviet invasion of Hungary in 1956. Arthur Koestler's (1905–1983) novel *Darkness at Noon* (1940) recorded a former communist's view of the purges. George Orwell (1903–1950), who had never been a communist, but who had sympathized with the party, expressed his disappointment with Stalin's policy in Spain in *Homage to Catalonia* (1938). The Nazi-Soviet pact destroyed Stalin's image as an opponent of fascism. Other intellectuals, such as the French philosopher Jean-Paul Sartre (1905–1980), continued to believe in the Soviet Union during and after the war, but the Hungarian Revolution cooled their ardor. The Soviet-led invasion of Czechoslovakia in 1968 simply confirmed a general disillusionment with Soviet policies by even left-wing Western European intellectuals.

Yet disillusionment with the Soviet Union or with Stalin did not always mean disillusionment with Marxism or with radical socialist criticisms of European society. Some writers and social critics looked to the establishment of alternative communist governments based on non-Soviet models. During the decade after World War II, Yugoslavia provided such an example. Beginning in the late 1950s, radical students and a few intellectuals found inspiration in the Chinese Revolution. Other groups hoped a European Marxist system would develop. Among the more important contributors to this non-Soviet tradition was the Italian communist Antonio Gramsci (1891–1937), especially in his work *Letters from Prison* (published posthumously in 1947). The thinking of such non-Soviet communists became important to Western European communist parties, such as the Italian Communist Party, that hoped to gain office democratically.

George Orwell (1903–1950), shown here with his son, was an English writer of socialist sympathies who wrote major works opposing Stalin and communist authoritarianism. Felix H. Man/Bildarchiv Preussischer Kulturbesitz

Another way to accommodate Marxism within mid-twentieth-century European thought was to redefine the basic message of Marx himself. During the 1930s, many of Marx's previously unprinted essays were published. These books and articles, written before the *Communist Manifesto* of 1848, are abstract and philosophical. They make the "young Marx" appear to belong more nearly to the humanist than to the revolutionary tradition of European thought. Since World War II, works such as *Philosophic Manuscripts* of 1844 and *German Ideology* have been widely read. Today, many people are more familiar with them than with the *Manifesto* or *Capital*. They allowed some people to consider themselves sympathetic to Marxism without also seeing themselves as revolutionaries or supporters of the Soviet Union. With the collapse of the communist governments of Eastern Europe and the Soviet Union, what influence Marxism will continue to have on European intellectual life in the future is unclear.

Existentialism

The intellectual movement that perhaps best captured the predicament and mood of mid-twentieth-century European culture was **existentialism**. Like the modern Western mind in general, existentialism, which has been termed the "philosophy of Europe in the twentieth century," was badly divided; most of the philosophers associated with it disagreed with each other on major issues. The movement represented, in part, a continuation of the revolt against reason that began in the nineteenth century.

Roots in Nietzsche and Kierkegaard Friedrich Nietzsche (1844–1900), discussed in Chapter 24, was a major forerunner of existentialism. Another was the Danish writer Søren Kierkegaard (1813–1855), who received little attention until after World War I. Kierkegaard was a rebel against both Hegelian philosophy and Danish Lutheranism. In works such as *Fear and Trembling* (1843), *Either/Or* (1843), and *Concluding Unscientific Postscript* (1846), he maintained that the truth of Christianity could be grasped only in the lives of those who faced extreme situations, not in creeds, doctrines, and church structures.

Kierkegaard also criticized Hegelian philosophy and, by implication, all academic rational philosophy. Philosophy's failure, he felt, was the attempt to contain life and human experience within abstract categories. Kierkegaard spurned this faith in the power of mere reason. "The conclusions of passion," he declared, "are the only reliable ones."[3]

The intellectual and ethical crisis of World War I brought Kierkegaard's thought to the foreground and also created new interest in Nietzsche's critique of reason. The war led many people to doubt whether human beings were actually in control of their own destiny. Its destructiveness challenged faith in human rationality and improvement. Indeed, the war's most terrible weapons—poison gas, machine guns, submarines, high explosives—were the products of rational technology. The pride in rational human achievement that had characterized nineteenth-century European civilization lay in ruins. The sunny faith in rational human development and advancement had not withstood the horror of war.

Questioning of Rationalism Existentialist thought thrived in this climate and received further support from the trauma of World War II. The major existential writers included the Germans Martin Heidegger (1889–1976) and Karl Jaspers (1883–1969) and the French Jean-Paul Sartre (1905–1980) and Albert Camus (1913–1960). Their books are often difficult or obscure. Although they frequently disagreed with each other, they all, in one way or another, questioned the primacy of reason and scientific understanding as ways to come to grips with the human situation. Heidegger, a philosopher deeply compromised by his association with the Nazis, argued, "Thinking only begins at the point where we have come to know that Reason, glorified for centuries, is the most obstinate adversary of thinking."[4]

The Romantic writers of the early nineteenth century had also questioned the primacy of reason, but their criticisms were much less radical than those of the existentialists. The Romantics emphasized the imagination and intuition, but the existentialists dwelled primarily on the extremes of human experience. Death, fear, and anxiety provided their themes. The titles of their works illustrate their sense of foreboding and alienation: *Being and Time* (1927), by Heidegger; *Nausea* (1938) and *Being and Nothingness* (1943), by Sartre; *The Stranger* (1942) and *The Plague* (1947), by Camus. The touchstone of philosophic truth became the experience of the individual under extreme conditions.

According to the existentialists, human beings are compelled to formulate their own ethical values and cannot depend on traditional religion, rational philosophy, intuition, or social customs for ethical guidance. The opportunity and need to define values endow humans with a dreadful freedom.

The existentialists were largely protesting against a world in which reason, technology, and politics produced war and genocide. Their thought reflected the uncertainty of social institutions and ethical values in the era of the two world wars. Since the 1950s, however, their works and ideas have found their way into university curriculums around the world, making them objects of study, if not the source of intellectual ferment they had been. They continue to be discussed in philosophy and literature classes, but their popularity has receded.

European intellectuals were attracted to communism and existentialism before and just after World War II, but in the 1960s, the turmoil over Vietnam and the youth rebellion brought other intellectual and social issues to the fore. Even before the collapse of communism, these had begun to redirect European intellectual interests.

[3]Quoted in Walter Kaufman, ed., *Existentialism from Dostoyevsky to Sartre* (Cleveland, OH: World Publishing Company, 1962), p. 18.

[4]Quoted in William Barrett, *Irrational Man* (Garden City, NY: Doubleday, 1962), p. 20.

SARTRE DISCUSSES HIS EXISTENTIALISM

Jean-Paul Sartre, dramatist, novelist, and philosopher, was the most important French existentialist. In the first paragraph of this 1946 statement, Sartre asserted that all human beings must experience a sense of anguish or the most extreme anxiety when undertaking a major commitment. That anguish arises because, consciously or unconsciously, they are deciding whether all human beings should make the same decision. In the second paragraph, Sartre argued that the existence or nonexistence of God would make no difference in human affairs. Humankind must discover the character of its own situation by itself.

How might the experiences of fascism in Europe and the fall of France to the Nazis have led Sartre to emphasize the need of human beings to choose? Why does Sartre believe existentialism must be related to atheism? Why did Sartre regard existentialism as optimistic?

The existentialist frankly states that man is in anguish. His meaning is as follows—When a man commits himself to anything, fully realizing that he is not only choosing what he will be, but is thereby at the same time a legislator deciding for the whole of mankind—in such a moment a man cannot escape from the sense of complete and profound responsibility. There are many, indeed, who show no such anxiety. But we affirm that they are merely disguising their anguish or are in flight from it. Certainly, many people think that in what they are doing they commit no one but themselves to anything: and if you ask them, "What would happen if everyone did so?," they shrug their shoulders and reply, "Everyone does not do so." But in truth, one ought always to ask oneself what would happen if everyone did as one is doing; nor can one escape from that disturbing thought except by a kind of self-deception. The man who lies in self-excuse, by saying, "Everyone will not do it" must be ill at ease in his conscience, for the act of lying implies the universal value which it denies. By its very disguise his anguish reveals itself.

Existentialism is nothing else but an attempt to draw the full conclusions from a consistently atheistic position. Its intention is not in the least that of plunging men into despair. And if by despair one means—as the Christians do—any attitude of unbelief, the despair of the existentialist is something different. Existentialism is not atheist in the sense that it would exhaust itself in demonstration of the nonexistence of God. It declares, rather, that even if God existed that would make no difference from its point of view. Not that we believe God does exist, but we think that the real problem is not that of His existence; what man needs is to find himself again and to understand that nothing can save him from himself, not even a valid proof of the existence of God. In this sense existentialism is optimistic. It is a doctrine of action, and it is only by self-deception, by confusing their own despair with ours that Christians can describe us as without hope.

From Jean-Paul Sartre, *Existentialism and Humanism* trans. by Philip Mairet (London: Methuen), in Walter Kaufman, ed., *Existentialism from Dos toyevsky to Sartre* (New York: Meridian Books, 1956), pp. 292, 310–311.

Expansion of the University Population and Student Rebellion

As rapid changes in communications technology vastly expanded access to information, more Europeans received some form of university education. In 1900, only a few thousand people were enrolled in universities in any major European country. By 2000, that figure had risen to hundreds of thousands, although university education is still less common in Europe than in the United States. Higher education is now available to people from a variety of social and economic backgrounds, and, for the first time, to women.

One of the most striking and unexpected results of this rising post–World War II population of students and intellectuals was the student rebellion of the 1960s. This development is still not well understood. Student uprisings began in the early 1960s in the United States and grew with opposition to the war in Vietnam. The student rebellion then spread into Europe and other parts of the world. It was almost always associated with a radical political critique of the United States, although Eastern European students resented the Soviet Union even more. The movement was generally antimilitarist. Students also questioned middle-class values and traditional sexual mores and family life.

The student movement peaked in 1968, when American students demonstrated forcibly against U.S. involvement in Vietnam. In the same year, students at the Sorbonne in Paris almost brought down the government of Charles de Gaulle, and in Czechoslovakia, students were in the forefront of the liberal socialist experiment. These protests failed to have an immediate effect on the policies of the governments at which they were directed. The United States stayed in Vietnam until 1973, de Gaulle remained president of France for another year, and the Soviets suppressed the Czech experiment.

By the early 1970s, the era of student rebellion seemed to have passed. Students remained active in European movements against nuclear weapons and particularly against the placement of American nuclear weapons in Germany and elsewhere in Europe. From the mid-1970s, however, although often remaining political radicals, they generally abandoned the disruptive protests that had marked the 1960s.

The Americanization of Europe

During the past half century, through the Marshall Plan, the leadership of NATO, the stationing of huge military bases, student exchanges, popular culture, and tourism, the United States has exerted enormous influence on Europe, especially Western Europe. The word *Americanization*, an often pejorative term in European publications, refers, in part, to this economic and military influence, but also to concerns about cultural loss. Many Europeans feel that American popular entertainment, companies, and business methods threaten to extinguish Europe's unique qualities. Many American firms now have European branches. Large American corporations, such as McDonald's, Starbucks, Apple computers, and the Gap, have outlets in European cities from Dublin to Moscow. American liquor companies

In 1968 a student rebellion in Paris threatened to bring down the government of Charles de Gaulle. This was only one example of the explosion of student activity that rocked the West in the late 1960s. © Bettmann/CORBIS

and distilleries now sell their goods in Europe. Casual American clothing, such as blue jeans and baseball caps, is ubiquitous in Europe. Shopping centers and supermarkets, first pioneered in America, are displacing neighborhood markets in European cities. American television programs, movies, computer games, and rock and rap music are readily available. Furthermore, as Europe moves toward greater economic cooperation, English has become the common language of business, technology, and even some academic fields—and it is American English, not British. (See "Encountering, the Past: Toys from Europe Conquer the United States.")

A Consumer Society

Although European economies came under pressure during the 1990s and experienced high levels of unemployment, the consumer sector has expanded to an extraordinary degree during most of the last half century.

The consumer orientation of the Western European economy emerged as one of the most important characteristics differentiating it from Eastern Europe. Those differences produced political results. In the Soviet Union and the nations it dominated in Eastern Europe, economic planning overwhelmingly favored capital investment and military production. These nations produced inadequate food for their people and few consumer goods. Long lines for staples, such as food and clothing, were common. Automobiles were a luxury. Housing was inadequate. Consumer goods were shoddy.

By contrast, by the early 1950s, Western Europeans enjoyed an excellent food supply that has continued to improve. Also, in a sign of the strength of Western Europe's economy, if not the healthfulness of its diet, fast-food outlets have multiplied.

Western Europe has enjoyed a similar expansion of consumer goods and services. Automobile ownership has soared. Refrigerators, washing machines, electric ranges, televisions, microwaves, videocassette recorders, cameras, computers, CD players, DVD players, and other electronic consumer items are taken for granted. Like their American counterparts, Western Europeans now have a whole gamut of products, such as disposable diapers and prepared baby foods, to help them raise children. They take foreign vacations year round, prompting the expansion of ski resorts in the Alps and beach resorts on the Mediterranean.

This vast expansion of consumerism, which, as we noted in Chapter 15, began in the eighteenth century, became a defining characteristic of Western Europe in the late twentieth century. It stood in marked contrast to the consumer shortages in Eastern Europe. Yet through even the limited number of radios, televisions, movies, and videos available to them, people in the East grew increasingly aware of the discrepancy between their lifestyle and that of the West. They associated Western consumerism with democratic governments, free societies, and economic policies that favored the free market and limited government planning. Thus, the expansion of consumerism in the West, which many intellectuals and moralists deplored, helped generate the discontent that brought down communism in Eastern Europe and the Soviet Union.

Environmentalism

After World War II, shortages of consumer goods created a demand that fueled postwar economic reconstruction and growth into the 1950s and 1960s. In those expansive times, public debate about the ethics of economic expansion and efficiency and their effects on the environment was muted. Concerns about pollution began to grow in the 1970s, and by the 1980s, environmentalists had developed real political clout. Among the most important environmental groups were the German Greens. The Greens formed a political party in 1979 that immediately became an electoral force. During these same years, concern for environmental issues, such as global warming and the pollution of water and the atmosphere, commanded the attention of governments outside Europe and of the United Nations.

Several developments lay behind this new concern for the environment. The Arab oil embargo of 1973 to 1974 pressed home two messages to the industrialized West: Natural resources are limited, and foreign, potentially hostile, countries control critical resources. By the 1970s, too, the environmental consequences of three decades of economic expansion were becoming increasingly apparent. Fish were dying in the Thames River in England. Industrial pollution was destroying life in the Rhine River between Germany and France. Acid rain was killing trees from Sweden to Germany. Finally, long-standing worries about nuclear weapons merged with concerns about their environmental effects, strengthening antinuclear groups and generating opposition to the placement of nuclear weapons in Europe.

The German **Green movement** originated among radical student groups in the late 1960s. Like them, it was anticapitalist, blaming business or pollution. The Greens and other European environmental groups were also strongly antinuclear. Unlike the students of the 1960s, the Greens avoided violence and mass demonstrations, seeking instead to become a significant political presence through the electoral process.

The 1986 disaster at the Chernobyl nuclear reactor in the Soviet Union heightened concern about

ENCOUNTERING THE *Past*

TOYS FROM EUROPE CONQUER THE UNITED STATES

TODAY MANY EUROPEANS criticize what they term *Americanization*—the intrusion of popular American products and restaurant chains onto the European scene. Yet over the past half century one European toy—LEGO building blocks manufactured in Denmark—has shaped the experience of childhood for many children in the United States and the rest of the world, entering their lives and imaginations no less powerfully than the cartoon figures associated with the American Disney Corporation.

In 1932, in the midst of the depression, Ole Kirk Christiansen opened a small business in Billund, Denmark, that manufactured household goods and wooden toys. The toys sold so well that two years later the firm renamed itself LEGO from the Danish *LEg GOdt* meaning "Play well." The company remained small, producing only wooden toys, until 1947 when it began to make molded plastic toys. It only sold its products in Denmark.

In 1955, LEGO introduced LEGO Bricks—plastic building blocks of the familiar stud-and-tube type—that it sold in sets under the name LEGO System of Play. That system, which the firm patented in 1958, allowed children to combine LEGO Bricks in an almost endless number of ways, limited only by their own imaginations and that of their parents. The company also extended its market across and began to sell in the United States in 1961.

Thereafter, the success of LEGO as a toy and as a company fed on itself. The company added many new features to the original concept of interlocking building blocks. For example, wheels enabled children to use LEGO kits to build their own trucks, trains, and similar mobile toys.

In 1968, the LEGO Company, no doubt following the example of the Disney Corporation in the United States, opened an amusement park in Billund in which the rides were designed to look like huge LEGO toys. By the end of the century, LEGO had opened similar parks in England, the United States, and Germany.

However, the company remained focused on making toys for children. It designed new toys, such as plastic figures with human heads to ride in LEGO vehicles, and whole LEGO villages, castles, and pirate ships. By the 1990s, LEGO had become the largest toy manufacturer in Europe and a part of modern culture. Museums displayed LEGO products and art built from LEGO blocks. Contests were held to construct the largest or most unusual LEGO structures. In 1999, *Fortune* magazine included the LEGO brick among the "Products of the Century," and in 2002, LEGO persuaded European and American management consultants that working with LEGO blocks would help business executives think more clearly about corporate planning. Perhaps most astonishing is that during a half century of tumultuous change, children around the world have continued to play with these little pieces of plastic.

Source: Factual information derived from the official LEGO Group Web site: www.lego.com/eng/info/history

How has LEGO been an example of the European penetration of popular culture around the world?

Why has the influence of LEGO on children's toys been less controversial than the appearance of American fast-food chains in Europe?

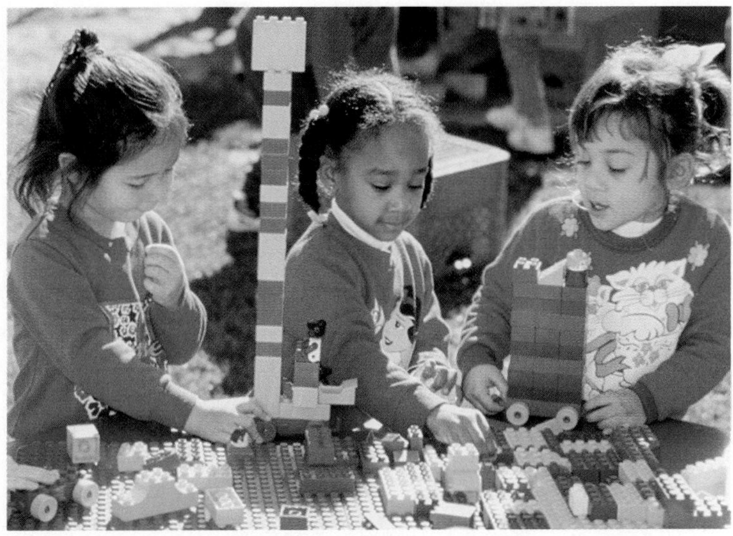

Children across the world play with LEGO toys. Tom Prettyman/PhotoEdit

environmental issues and raised questions that no European government could ignore. The Soviet government had to confront casualties at the site and relocate tens of thousands of people. Radioactive fallout spread across Europe. Environmentalists had always contended that their issues transcended national borders. The Chernobyl fire proved them right.

After Chernobyl, European governments, East and West, began to respond to environmental concerns. Some observers believe the environment may become a major political issue across the Continent. In Western Europe, environmental groups command many votes. Economic and political integration opens the possibility of transnational cooperation on environmental matters. As the European Economic Community solidifies, it and its member nations will likely impose more environmental regulations on business and industry. The nations of Eastern Europe have been forced to face the cleanup of vast areas of industrial development polluted during the communist era and to try to combine environmental protection with economic growth.

▼ Art Since World War II

It is impossible to cover even briefly the expansive and varied world of Western art since the end of World War II. However, we can note how both the Cold War and the memory of the horrors of the Second World War influenced Western art.

Cultural Divisions and the Cold War

Although they may seem like products from different centuries, the Soviet painter Tatjiana Yablonskaya's (b. 1917) sun-strewn *Bread* (1949) and the American Jackson Pollock's (1912–1956) dizzyingly abstract *One* (Number 31, 1950) were painted only one year apart. The stark differences between these two works mirror the cultural divisions of the early Cold War.

Bread, measuring over six feet high and twelve feet wide, is a monumental example of socialist realism. Established, on Stalin's orders, as the official doctrine of Soviet art and literature in 1934, socialist realism sought to create optimistic and easily intelligible scenes of a bold socialist future, in which prosperity and solidarity would reign. Manual laborers and prominent historical and political figures were painted in a traditional and often rigid figurative manner. Under Soviet control after World War II, socialist realism became the dominant artistic model throughout Eastern Europe, only waning when Nikita Khrushchev liberalized Soviet cultural policy in the late 1950s.

The looping skeins of paint in *One* (Number 31, 1950) may seem completely different from the kind of "realistic" propaganda visible in *Bread*, but Pollock's painting is in fact a central document of postwar American cultural life. Flinging paint from sticks and brushes onto his floor-bound canvas, Pollock freed his lines from representing any figure or outline. The result, in *One* (Number 31, 1950), which is over eight feet high and seventeen feet wide, is a writhing tangle of pure visual

Tatjiana Yablonskaya, *Bread*, 1949. Ria Novosti/Sovfoto/Eastfoto

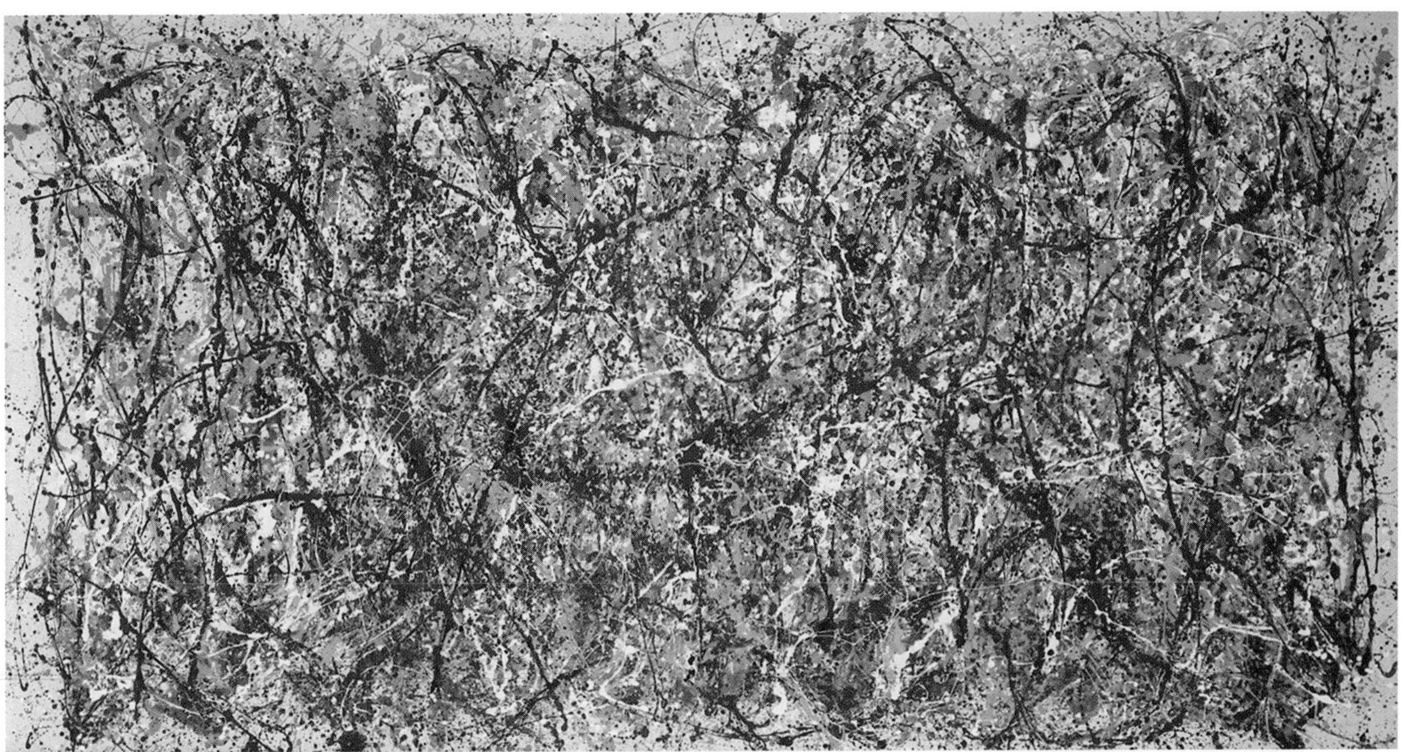

Jackson Pollock, *One* (Number 31, 1950). Oil and enamel on unprimed canvas, 8 ft. 10 in. × 17 ft. 5 5/8 in. (269.5 × 530.8 cm). The Museum of Modern Art/Licensed by Scala-Art Resource, NY. Sidney and Harriet Janis Collection Fund (by exchange). Photograph © 2000 The Museum of Modern Art, New York. 00007.68. © 2004 The Pollock-Krasner Foundation/Artists Rights Society (ARS), New York

energy. In the politically charged atmosphere of the early Cold War, critics saw Pollock's exuberant "drip" paintings as the embodiment of American cultural freedom and celebrated the Wyoming-born Pollock as a kind of artist cowboy.

Lurking behind such interpretations was the awareness that the Soviets had imposed socialist realism on Eastern Europe and the Nazis had persecuted avant-garde artists. As skeptical as many viewers might have been about the merits of abstract art (*Time* magazine, for instance, dismissed Pollock as "Jack the dripper" in 1947), many people in the West saw it as the antithesis of socialist, realist totalitarianism.

Indeed, New York City—not Paris—emerged as the international center of modern art after World War II, a position it retains today. As the home of growing collections of twentieth-century art and dozens of European artists who had fled from the Nazis, New York became a fertile training ground for young artists such as Pollock. Just as American political and economic structures became models for the postwar redevelopment of Western Europe, so did American cultural developments. By the time Pollock's first posthumous retrospective toured Europe in 1958, much European painting resembled an elegant imitation of his frenetic lines.

Yablonskaya and Pollock together illustrate the two central poles of twentieth-century art: realism and abstraction. Although artistic style is no longer as closely associated with political programs as it once was, these two poles still frame the work of countless artists today.

Memory of the Holocaust

The British sculptor Rachel Whiteread (b. 1963) is one of the leading artists of today's Europe. Her work illustrates how European art is breaking out of the modernist contours that were set at the beginning of the twentieth century. On one hand, Whiteread's art returns to what seem like familiar forms; on the other, it forces us to view these forms in ways that are as new to us as cubism was to the public in its day.

Whiteread's work is associated with minimalism in contemporary art. This movement, which originated in architecture and interior design, seeks to remove from the object being portrayed as many features as possible while retaining the object's form and the viewer's interest. Minimalist art aims to be as understated as possible. In Whiteread's hands, the minimal becomes the austere, and her work often exudes melancholy and loss.

Whiteread began her career by focusing on objects from everyday life. She would make a plaster cast of an object's interior space. Initially her subjects were small—a hot water bottle, a piece of furniture, or the space under a chair. In 1993, however, she made a cast of the interior space of an entire house that was about

Rachel Whiteread's *Nameless Library* in Vienna commemorates the thousands of Austrian Jews killed in the Nazi Holocaust. © Reuters NewMedia Inc./CORBIS

to be torn down in London. She left the work untitled, but it became known as *House*. It presents interior space as solid but temporary, subject to the passage of time. Like many of Whiteread's subjects, the object that has been molded—in this case the demolished house—no longer exists, and even the sculpture itself will eventually disappear. *House* stood on the site for only two and a half months before being razed, like the actual house itself, as part of an urban redevelopment plan.

Whiteread's most important public work, and one designed to endure, is *Nameless Library*, the Judenplatz Holocaust Memorial in Vienna, which commemorates the deaths of 65,000 Austrian Jews under the Nazis. This memorial, which resembles a vast haunting tomb, is cast in concrete and embodies the outline of books whose spines are turned inward, thus remaining forever unread and as unopenable as the library's huge concrete doors are. Whiteread has said the molded, unopened books, which have been compared to the ghost of a library, symbolize the loss both of Jewish contributions to culture and of Jewish lives in the Holocaust.

▼ The Christian Heritage

In most ways, Christianity in Europe has continued to be as hard-pressed during the twentieth century as it had been in the late nineteenth. Material prosperity, political ideologies, environmentalism, gender politics, and simple indifference have replaced religious faith for many people. Still, despite the loss of much of their popular support and legal privileges and the low rates of church attendance, the European Christian churches continue to exercise social and political influence. In Germany, the churches were one of the few major institutions that the Nazis did not wholly subdue. Lutheran clergy, such as Martin Niemöller (1892–1984) and Dietrich Bonhoeffer (1906–1945), were leaders of the opposition to Hitler. After the war, in Poland and elsewhere in Eastern Europe, the Roman Catholic Church opposed communism.

In Western Europe, religious affiliation provided much of the initial basis for the Christian Democratic parties. The churches have also raised critical questions about colonialism, nuclear weapons, human rights, war, and other issues. Consequently, even in this most secular of ages, Christian churches have influenced state and society.

Neo-Orthodoxy

Liberal theologians of the nineteenth century often softened the concept of sin and portrayed human nature as close to the divine. The horror of World War I destroyed that optimistic faith. Many Europeans felt that evil had stalked the Continent.

The most important Christian response to World War I appeared in the theology of Karl Barth (1886–1968). In 1919, this Swiss pastor published *A Commentary on the Epistle to the Romans*, which reemphasized the transcendence of God and the dependence of humankind on the divine. Barth portrayed God as wholly other than, and different from, humankind. In a sense, Barth was returning to the Reformation theology of Luther, but the work of Kierkegaard had profoundly influenced his reading of the reformer. Like the Danish writer, Barth regarded the lived experience of men and women as the best testimony to the truth of Luther's theology. Those extreme moments of life Kierkegaard described provided the basis for a knowledge of humanity's need for God.

This view challenged much nineteenth-century writing about human nature. Barth's theology, which came to be known as neo-Orthodoxy, proved influential throughout the West in the wake of new disasters and suffering.

Liberal Theology

Neo-Orthodoxy did not, however, sweep away liberal theology, which had a strong advocate in Paul Tillich (1886–1965). This German-American theologian tended to regard religion as a human, rather than a divine, phenomenon. Whereas Barth saw God as dwelling outside humankind, Tillich believed that evidence of the divine had to be sought in human nature and human culture.

Other liberal theologians, such as Rudolf Bultmann (1884–1976), continued to work on the problems of naturalism and supernaturalism that had troubled earlier writers. Bultmann's major writing took place before World War II but was popularized after the war by the Anglican bishop John Robinson in *Honest to God* (1963). Another liberal Christian writer from Britain, C. S. Lewis (1878–1963), attracted millions of readers during and after World War II. This layman and scholar of medieval literature often expressed his thoughts on theology in the form of letters and short stories. His most famous work is *The Screwtape Letters* (1942). In recent years, however, European religious thought has produced few major Protestant voices.

Roman Catholic Reform

Among Christian denominations, the most significant postwar changes have been in the Roman Catholic Church. Pope John XXIII (r. 1958–1963) initiated these changes, the most extensive in Catholicism for more than a century and, some would say, since the Council of Trent in the sixteenth century. In 1959, Pope John summoned the Twenty-First Ecumenical Council (the Emperor Constantine had called the first council in the fourth century), which came to be called Vatican II. The council finished its work in 1965 under John's successor, Pope Paul VI (r. 1963–1978). Among many changes in Catholic liturgy the council introduced, Mass was now celebrated in the vernacular languages rather than in Latin. The council also encouraged freer relations with other Christian denominations, fostered a new spirit toward Judaism, and gave more power to bishops. In recognition of the growing importance to the church of the world outside Europe and North America, Pope Paul appointed several cardinals from the former colonial nations, transforming the church into a truly world body.

In contrast to these liberal changes, however, Pope Paul and his successors have firmly upheld the celibacy of priests, maintained the church's prohibition on contraception and abortion, and opposed moves to open the priesthood to women. The church's unyielding stand on clerical celibacy has caused many men to leave the priesthood and many men and women to leave religious orders. The laity has widely ignored the prohibition on contraception.

John Paul II, the former Karol Wojtyla, archbishop of Kraków in Poland, was elected in 1978 after the death of John Paul I, whose reign lasted only thirty-four days. The youngest pope since Pius IX (r. 1846–1878), John Paul II (1920–2005) pursued a three-pronged policy during his long pontificate. First, he maintained traditionalist doctrine, stressing the authority of the papacy and attempting to limit doctrinal and liturgical experimentation.

Second, taking a firm stand against communism, he supported the spirit of freedom in Eastern Europe that brought down the communist regimes. As a cardinal in Poland, he had clashed with the communist government. After his election, he visited Poland, lending support to Solidarity. His Polish origins helped make him an important factor in the popular resistance to Eastern Europe's communist governments that developed during the 1980s. He thus opened a new chapter in the relationship between church and state in modern Europe.

Third, John Paul II encouraged the growth of the church in the non-Western world, stressing the need for social justice, but limiting the political activity of priests. The pope's concern for the expansion of Roman

Throughout his pontificate John Paul II continued a close relationship with his native Poland to which he made several visits. The earliest of these was important in demonstrating the authority of the church against Polish communist authorities. Shown here in his Polish visit of June 1999, the pope would celebrate mass before several hundred thousand Poles after the collapse of communism that had occurred a decade earlier. AP Wide World Photos

Catholicism beyond Europe and North America recognized and encouraged what appears to be a transformation in Christianity as a world religion. Whereas in Europe Christian observance whether Roman Catholic, Protestant, or Orthodox had declined sharply during the twentieth century, Christianity has grown rapidly and fervently in Africa and Latin America. Observers estimate that within a few years, over half of the world's Christians will live in those two continents. Recognizing these changes, John Paul II created more cardinals from non-Western nations.

John Paul II died in 2005. His successor was his closest collaborator, the German Cardinal Joseph Ratzinger (b. 1927), who took the name Benedict XVI. The new pope has followed his predecessor in his rigorous defense of orthodoxy. He has pursued what many regard as a more meditative pontificate. However, in September 2006 he delivered a speech in which he quoted a medieval writer criticizing Islam. The speech evoked considerable criticism in Europe and provoked riots in parts of the Islamic world. Since that event, Pope Benedict has sought to take numerous steps to initiate Christian-Muslim dialogue. He has also championed the role of religious freedom for Christians and other religiously observant peoples living in the midst of secular societies. (See "Pope Benedict XVI Calls for the Recognition of Religious Freedom as a Human Right," page 969.)

▼ Late-Twentieth-Century Technology: The Arrival of the Computer

During the twentieth century, technology crossed international borders the way popular culture did. As with other areas of European life and society, American technology had an unprecedented impact on the Continent, whether in the guise of the first airplanes or Henry Ford's method of producing affordable automobiles. It seems certain, however, that no single American technological achievement of the twentieth century will so influence Western life on both sides of the Atlantic, as well as throughout the rest of the world, as the computer.

POPE BENEDICT XVI CALLS FOR THE RECOGNITION OF RELIGIOUS FREEDOM AS A HUMAN RIGHT

On April 18, 2008, Pope Benedict XVI addressed the United Nations General Assembly in New York City. In the course of a wide-ranging speech the Pope paid special attention to religious freedom as a fundamental human right. He particularly defended religious freedom when its exercise stands in tension or conflict with the values of a surrounding secular society or other surrounding majority values.

How did Pope Benedict XVI define religious freedom as a human right? How did he portray the relationship of the exercise of religious freedom to secular values and secular social institutions? How did he relate religious freedom to human betterment?

Human rights . . . must include the right to religious freedom, understood as the expression of a dimension that is at once individual and communitarian—a vision that brings out the unity of the person while clearly distinguishing between the dimension of the citizen and that of the believer. The activity of the United Nations in recent years has ensured that public debate gives space to viewpoints inspired by a religious vision in all its dimensions, including ritual, worship, education, dissemination of information and the freedom to profess and choose religion. It is inconceivable, then, that believers should have to suppress a part of themselves—their faith—in order to be active citizens. It should never be necessary to deny God in order to enjoy one's rights.

The rights associated with religion are all the more in need of protection if they are considered to clash with a prevailing secular ideology or with majority religious positions of an exclusive nature. The full guarantee of religious liberty cannot be limited to the free exercise of worship, but has to give due consideration to the public dimension of religion, and hence to the possibility of believers playing their part in building the social order. . . .

Refusal to recognize the contribution to society that is rooted in the religious dimension and in the quest for the Absolute—by its nature, expressing communion between persons—would effectively privilege an individualistic approach, and would fragment the unity of the person. . . .

The United Nations remains a privileged setting in which the [Roman Catholic] Church is committed to contributing her experience "of humanity," developed over the centuries among peoples of every race and culture, and placing it at the disposal of all members of the international community. This experience and activity, directed towards attaining freedom for every believer, seeks also to increase the protection given to the rights of the person.

Those rights are grounded and shaped by the transcendent nature of the person, which permits men and women to pursue their journey of faith and their search for God in this world. Recognition of this dimension must be strengthened if we are to sustain humanity's hope for a better world and if we are to create the conditions for peace, development, cooperation, and guarantee of rights for future generations.

Pope Benedict XVI's Address to the United Nations General Assembly, April 18, 2008, as reproduced on the Vatican City Web site: www.vatican.va/holy_father/benedict_xvi/speeches/2008/april/documents/hf_ben-xvi_spe_20080418_un-visit_en.html

The Demand for Calculating Machines

Beginning in the seventeenth century, thinkers associated with the scientific revolution—most famously, the French mathematician and philosopher Blaise Pascal (1623–1662)—attempted to construct machines that would carry out mathematical calculations that human beings would find essentially impossible because of the tedium and the amount of time they involved. Starting in the late nineteenth century, the governments of the consolidating nation-states of Europe and of the United States confronted new administrative tasks that involved collecting and organizing vast amounts of data about national censuses, tax collection, economic statistics, and the administration of pensions and welfare legislation. During the same years, private businesses sought calculating machinery to handle and organize growing amounts of economic and business data. Such machines became technologically possible through the development of complex circuitry for electricity, the most versatile mode of energy in human history. Moreover, inventions that were dependent on electricity, including the telephone, the telegraph, underwater cables, and the wireless, created a new communications industry that in and of itself also required the organization of large databases of customer information to deliver their services. By the late 1920s, companies like National Cash Register, Remington Rand, and International Business Machines Corporation (IBM) had begun to manufacture such business machinery.

Early Computer Technology

As has happened so often in history, warfare was the chief catalyst of change. After World War I and during World War II, the major powers developed new weapons that required exact mathematical ballistic calculations to effectively strike targets with bombs delivered by aircraft or long-range guns.

The first machine genuinely recognizable as a modern digital computer was the Electronic Numerical Integrator and Computer (**ENIAC**), built and designed at Moore Laboratories of the University of Pennsylvania and put into use by the U.S. Army in 1946 for ballistics calculation. The ENIAC was an enormous piece of equipment with 40 panels, 1,500 electric relays, and 18,000 vacuum tubes. It also used thousands of punch cards, and a separate tabulator had to print the data from them. Further computer engineering occurred at the Institute for Advanced Research in Princeton, New Jersey, in laboratories at the Massachusetts Institute of Technology, and in other laboratories the U.S. government and private businesses, especially IBM, ran. The other primary sites for computer development were laboratories in Britain.

The Development of Desktop Computers

During the 1950s, however, the transistor revolutionized electronics, permitting a miniaturization of circuitry that made vacuum tubes obsolete and allowed

The earliest computers were very large. Here in a 1946 photograph J. Presper Eckert and J. W. Mauchly stand by the Electronic Numerical Integrator and Computer (ENIAC), which was dedicated at the University of Pennsylvania Moore School of Electrical Engineering. CORBIS/Bettmann

computers to become smaller. Yet computers still had to be programmed with difficult computer languages by persons expertly trained to use them.

By the late 1960s, however, two innovations transformed computing technology. First, control of the computer was transferred to a bitmap covering the screen of a computer monitor. The mouse, invented in 1964, eased the movement of the cursor around the computer screen. Second, engineers at the Intel Corporation—then a California start-up company—invented the microchip, which became the heart of all future computers.

The bitmap on the screen, operated through the mouse, in effect embedded complicated computer language in the machine, hidden from the user, who simply manipulated images on the screen with the mouse. Almost anyone could thus learn to operate computers. At the same time, the tiny microchip, itself a miniature computer or microprocessor, permitted computer technology to abandon the mainframe and move to still smaller computers. At the Xerox Corporation, engineers devised a small computer using a mouse, but the machine never achieved commercial success. By 1982, IBM had produced a small personal computer but temporarily lost the race for commercialization to a then small company called Apple Computer Corporation. The design features originally developed at Xerox informed the ideas of the Apple engineers, who, in early 1984, produced a small, highly accessible, commercially successful computer, known as the Macintosh, that would fit on a desktop in the home or office. IBM soon adopted the Apple concept with different engineering and marketing approaches and manufactured a product called the Personal Computer, or PC. By the mid-1980s, for a relatively modest cost (and one that has continued to drop), individuals had available for their own personal use in their offices or homes computers with far more power than the old mainframes. The Apple Macintosh and the IBM PC transformed computers into objects of everyday life and, in doing so, began to transform everyday life itself. Nonetheless, the chief contemporary users of computers remain governments followed by the telephone industry, banking and finance, automobile operation, and airline reservation systems.

Despite the potential democratizing character of computer technology, the computer revolution has also introduced new concepts of "haves" and "have-nots" to societies around the world. Computers, whatever their possible shortcomings, enable their users to do things that nonusers cannot do. Whether in poor school districts in the United States or in poor countries of the former Soviet bloc, students who graduate without computer skills will have difficulty making their way in the world's rapidly computerizing economy. Some commentators also fear that boys are more likely than girls to receive technological training in computers. Nations whose governments and businesses become networked into the world of computers will prosper more fully than those whose access to computer technology is deficient. In that regard, the possession of computers and the ability to use them will probably determine future economic competition, just as they have determined recent military competition.

▼ The Challenges of European Unification

The unprecedented steps toward economic cooperation and unity Western European nations took during the second half of the twentieth century were the single most important European success story of that era. The process originated from American encouragement in response to the Soviet domination of Eastern Europe and from the Western European states' own sense that they lacked effective political and economic power. Furthermore, leaders in France and Germany who recoiled from the disastrous peace that followed World War I were determined that something different would arise from the political collapse of Europe after World War II. They understood that cooperation, rather than revenge, must inform the future of Europe.

Postwar Cooperation

The mid-twentieth-century Western European movement toward unity could have occurred in at least three ways: politically, militarily, or economically. Economic cooperation, unlike military and political cooperation, involved little or no immediate loss of sovereignty by the participating nations. Furthermore, it brought material benefits to all the states involved, increasing popular support for their governments. Moreover, the administration of the Marshall Plan and the organization of NATO gave the countries involved new experience in working with each other and demonstrated the productivity and efficiency that mutual cooperation could achieve.

The first effort toward economic cooperation was the formation of the European Coal and Steel Community in 1951 by France, West Germany, Italy, and the Benelux countries (Belgium, the Netherlands, and Luxembourg). The community both benefited from and contributed to the immense growth of material production in Western Europe during this period. Its success reduced the suspicions of government and business groups about coordination and economic integration.

A Closer LOOK

THE COPENHAGEN OPERA HOUSE

THE NEW OPERA House opened in Copenhagen, Denmark in 2005. The structure has come to symbolize free enterprise in the European Union because its full cost was covered by private, rather than government, funding.

The construction of the Copenhagen Opera House reclaimed areas of decaying dockland in the city. In this respect, it symbolizes similar projects that have been undertaken in other major European ports where docks have been relocated in the late twentieth century.

Henning Larson, a Dane, was the architect. His design, however, has been criticized for being subtly commercial because some observers see the opera house as resembling the grill of an automobile.

AP Wide World Photos

To examine this image in an interactive fashion, please go to www.myhistorylab.com

PEARSON myhistorylab

The European Economic Community

It took more than the prosperity of the European Coal and Steel Community to draw European leaders toward further unity, however. The unsuccessful Suez intervention of 1956 and the resulting diplomatic isolation of France and Britain persuaded many Europeans that only by acting together could they significantly influence the United States and the Soviet Union or control their own national and regional destinies. So, in 1957, through the Treaty of Rome, the six members of the Coal and Steel Community agreed to form a new organization: the **European Economic Community (EEC)**. The members of the Common Market, as the EEC was soon known, envisioned more than a free-trade union. They sought to achieve the eventual elimination of tariffs, a free flow of capital and labor, and similar wage and social benefits in all their countries.

The Common Market achieved stunning success during its early years. By 1968, well ahead of schedule, the six members had abolished all tariffs among themselves. Trade and labor migration among the members grew steadily. Moreover, nonmember states began to copy the EEC and, later, to seek to join it. In 1959, Britain, Denmark, Norway, Sweden, Switzerland, Austria, and Portugal formed the European Free Trade Area. By 1961, however, Britain had decided to join the Common Market. Twice, in 1963 and 1967, President Charles de Gaulle of France vetoed British membership. He argued that Britain was too closely tied to the United States to support the EEC wholeheartedly. Finally, in 1973, Great Britain, Ireland, and Denmark became members. Throughout the late 1970s, however, and into the 1980s, momentum for expanding EEC membership slowed. Norway and Sweden, with relatively strong economies, declined to join. Although in 1982, Spain, Portugal, and Greece applied for membership and were eventually admitted, sharp disagreements and a sense of stagnation within the EEC continued.

The European Union

In 1988, the leaders of the EEC reached an important decision. By 1992, the EEC was to be a virtual free-trade zone with no trade barriers or other restrictive trade policies among its members. In 1991, the Treaty of Maastricht made a series of specific proposals that led to a unified EEC currency (the Euro) and a strong central bank. The treaty was submitted to referendums in several European states. Denmark initially rejected it, and it passed only narrowly in France and Great Britain, making clear that it needed wider popular support. When the treaty finally took effect in November 1993, the EEC was renamed the **European Union**. Throughout the 1990s, the Union's influence grew. Its most notable achievement was the launching in early 1999 of the **Euro**, which by 2002 had become the common currency in twelve of the member nations.

In May 2004, the European Union added ten new nations, raising the total number of members to twenty-five. (See Map 30–1.) Membership in the European Union indicated that a nation had achieved economic

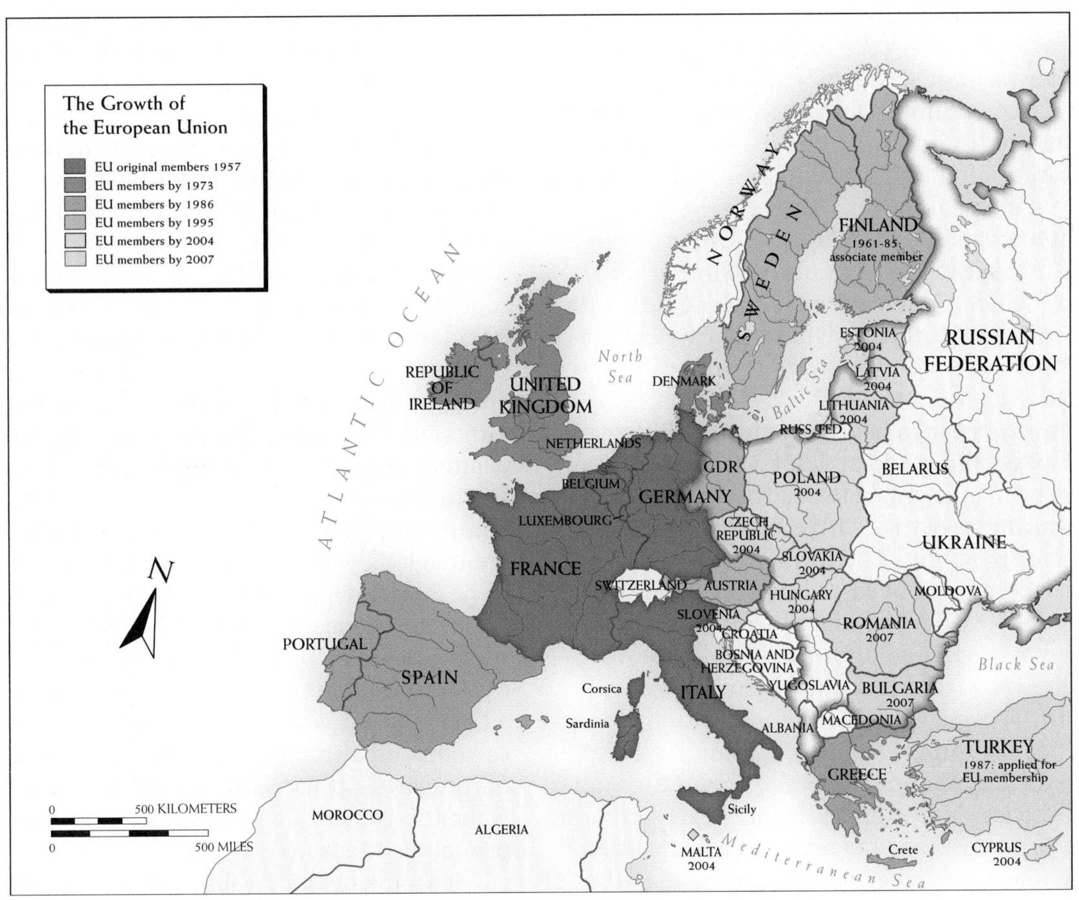

Map 30–1 **THE GROWTH OF THE EUROPEAN UNION** This map traces the growth of membership in the European Union from its founding in 1957 through the introduction of its newest members in 2007. Note that Turkey, though having applied for membership, has not yet been admitted.

stability and genuinely democratic institutions. Nonetheless, several of the new members states from the former Soviet bloc are relatively poor and will require much economic support from the Union.

Discord over the Union

The 2004 expansion of the European Union may mark for some time the high point of European integration. During that year the leaders of the member nations adopted a new constitutional treaty for the Union. This treaty, generally known as the European Constitution, was a long, detailed, and highly complicated document involving a bill of rights and complex economic and political agreements among all the member states. It would have transferred considerable decision-making authority from the governments of the individual states to the central institutions of the European Union, many of which are located in Brussels, Luxembourg, and Strasbourg. To become effective, all the member states had to ratify the constitution either by their parliaments or through national referendums.

To the surprise of many in the European elite, in the spring of 2005, referendums held in France and the Netherlands heavily defeated the new constitutional treaty. Britain, where support for further European integration was lukewarm at best, immediately postponed holding its own referendum. Public opinion in other nations also soured on the constitutional treaty. Furthermore, immediately after these events, discord erupted over the Union's internal budget. These events marked an unprecedented crisis for the European Union and for the project of European integration. A similar crisis erupted in 2008 when a referendum in Ireland failed to support changes in the European Union that would create shared institutions of foreign policy formulation and military policy.

Several factors appear to have brought the European Union to this pass. First, for at least the past fifteen years, a gap has been growing between the European political elites who have led the drive toward unity and the European voting public. The former have either ignored the latter or have moved the project along with only narrow majorities. Second, the general Western European economy has stagnated for the last decade with relatively high rates of unemployment, especially among the young. Voting against the constitution was a way to voice discontent with this situation. Third, many of the smaller member states of the European Union have felt that France and Germany have either ignored them or taken them for granted. Fourth, some nations have come to believe that they were placed at an economic disadvantage when the Euro replaced their former national currencies because the rates of exchange were unfairly calculated. Fifth, many people in

A woman stands between a "yes" and a "no" campaign poster in reference to France's referendum on the EU constitution in a street of Rennes, western France, Friday May 27, 2005, two days before the vote. AP Wide World Photos

the various states, large and small, have become increasingly reluctant to cede national sovereignty and the authority to make economic decisions to the bureaucracy in Brussels. Britain, for example, would like to see less economic regulation. France, on the other hand, is loath to see the European Union gain the power to revise the French labor code with its extensive protections and benefits for workers.

Finally, another large issue has informed the internal skeptics of the current European Union. Over the past several years, the leaders of the major member states have grown more favorable to the eventual admission of Turkey as a member state. If Turkey were admitted, Europe would have to integrate into the Union a state whose population is larger and much poorer than that of any other member state. This would place enormous social and economic burdens on the other states. Furthermore, although the Turkish government has long been seen as adamantly secular, the Turkish people are overwhelmingly Muslim. This "Islamic factor" has become increasingly controversial among those Europeans who, whether they are religiously observant or not, believe European culture to be Christian, and among those secular Europeans who are deeply concerned about the political, economic, and social implications of the Continent's already significant Muslim population. These tensions grew after 2005 when a Danish newspaper published self-consciously irreverent cartoons insulting the Prophet Muhammad. Riots broke out in parts of the Islamic world and in subsequent years Danish businesses and embassies abroad became targets of Islamic attacks.

It seems inconceivable that the effort to unify in Europe will either halt or be reversed. At the present time, however, it also seems certain that all future developments will move much more slowly and will require in-

AN ENGLISH BUSINESS EDITOR CALLS FOR EUROPE TO TAKE CHARGE OF ITS ECONOMIC FUTURE

Richard Lofthouse is the editor of CNBC European Business, *a magazine devoted to contemporary economic and business life. Educated in both Great Britain and the United States, Lofthouse brings a personal global perspective to his analysis. In the summer of 2008 he observed the tendency of Europeans to see their economic life as driven by global forces outside their control. In the face of such challenges, he called upon his readers to recall their cultural heritage and to embrace a spirit of entrepreneurship.*

Why are the challenges facing Europe and the West today international and global in contrast to the domestic political challenges of the third quarter of the twentieth century? What are the forces outside Europe impacting its economic life? What are the cultural qualities to which Lofthouse seeks to rally his readers?

In 1968, rioting across the US followed the assassination of Martin Luther King, while in France students and workers hoped to oust Charles de Gaulle's government. Broadly speaking these tumultuous events concerned generational conflict over prevailing values within the societies where the riots broke out. Forty years later, all the images of civil disobedience such as French fisherman dumping their catches and British hauliers blocking roads illustrate self-interest triggered by global forces rather than local ones, such as rising fuel and food prices.

If globalisation is a bus trip, then, Europe appears to have been steadily reduced in status from driver to conductor to helpless passenger. Almost none of the big issues currently shaping its future are European. In the past six months fear has intensified over China's economic rise and India has become the most seductive destination for entrepreneurial retailers. Most European banks have lost at least half of their value due to wildly misguided risk assessment in the US while most of the rise in the oil price reflects non-Western supply and demand habits.

One might paint Europe as the hapless victim of globalisation. Consideration of energy security suggests that the crunch will worsen as natural gas supplies evaporate (as if high oil prices weren't enough to keep you awake at night). Meanwhile, analysis of the future of retailing suggests that online retailing is set to soar, not least because even Americans are driving less in a bid to keep fuel costs down. Malls might have only just opened their doors in some emerging markets but in the West they face an uncertain future. The aviation industry believes that if oil remains at $135 a barrel, the world's airlines will lose $6.1bn this year.

It seems as if every business model in town is in the process of being wrecked by OPEC, or China's soaring resource demands, or greedy bankers; in reply, citizens protest that Congress or the European Union Commissioner or big oil companies should fix it and really, you know, it *is* someone else's fault. But that's not our view. In fact, it might be worth remembering Einstein's credo that "the significant problems we have cannot be solved at the same level of thinking with which we created them." This fragment is the basis of most of the entrepreneurship espoused in this publication, and it opens the door to creative solutions to problems that are invariably both global and local.

Europe has a leadership role to play in globalization, providing not just technological solutions to pressing problems such as climate change but perhaps more importantly offering a deep heritage of cultural intelligence and humanity arising from its eighteenth century Enlightenment.

There are hopeful signs to which one may point. A telemetry company is helping hauliers to cut their fuel consumption; an electric car project, backed by both Israel's government and Renault-Nissan, may herald the end of the internal combustion engine as we know it, and a book called *WASTEnomics* bristles with private sector solutions to excessive waste, the product of our extraordinary affluence.

Amended version of editorial published by Richard Lofthouse in *CNBC European Business* (39) (July–August 2008), p. 6. Published with the permission of the author.

creasingly complicated negotiations. Moreover, the future of the European Union has become enmeshed in often bitter and divisive debates within the member states over social policies, the future of their economies, and what role the state should play in economic affairs.

▼ New American Leadership and Financial Crisis

Much of the first decade of the twenty-first century witnessed considerable strain between the new post–Soviet Union Europe and the United States. As noted in Chapter 29, the immediate European reaction to the attacks on the United State on September 11, 2001, were sympathetic. The events leading up to the U.S. Iraq invasion in 2003 and the violence occurring since that invasion caused considerable strain between the United States and Europe, especially in terms of popular opinion. Europeans through their press and to some extent through their governments voiced much criticism over what they regarded as United States unilateral action in its foreign policy.

Three events in 2008 may have begun to change this situation and possibly to lessen those tensions. The first was the Russian invasion of Georgia discussed in Chapter 29. The United States and the European Union agreed in condemning that action. Second, the American presidential election of 2008 saw the strong victory of Barack Obama, the Democratic Party candidate. Obama is the first African American to be elected to the presidency. He ran on a platform critical of the Iraq invasion and American unilateralism. Even though he also voiced strong support for the war in Afghanistan, Obama has generated enormous popular support across Europe. Indeed during the campaign he gave a speech in Berlin that drew a crowd of tens of thousands. Obama's victory in the presidential election and the expansion of Democratic Party majorities in Congress appear to have persuaded at least for the moment many Europeans that their assumptions about American culture were incorrect and that a new era of American foreign and domestic policy is at hand. Only time, of course, can tell whether this change in European public opinion is of a lasting character.

Barack Obama shakes hands with supporters in Berlin, Germany, on July 24, 2008, following a speech he gave before a crowd of tens of thousands at the Victory Column in Tiergarten Park. Reuters/Jim Young/Landov Media

Third, during the second half of 2008 a major international financial crisis potentially of the dimensions of that of the 1930s overwhelmed the American, transatlantic, and world economies. The crisis originated in the United States mortgage market where numerous major banks found themselves holding mortgages which could not be paid. Several major financial institutions in the United States failed as did some banks in Europe. The United States and some European governments intervened deeply in areas of the economy where they had previously generally refrained from intervening. Stock markets around the world lost a third or more of their value. The interconnectedness of world markets demonstrated itself as never before with financial panic displaying itself around the globe.

The financial crisis and its broad fallout even more than the wars in Iraq and Afghanistan will be the major issues confronting the new Obama administration. The financial problems even more than matters of traditional and foreign policy may for the next several years determine the relationship of the United States and Europe and hence the role of the West in the world.

In Perspective

The twentieth century was the most destructive in human history. The wars of the first half of the century killed millions of Europeans and disrupted the fabric of European society. The Bolsheviks, Fascists, and National Socialists sought to remake whole societies according to utopian visions that resulted in repression and death on a massive scale and drove millions of Europeans from their ancestral homes.

With the defeat of National Socialism and Fascism, society in Western Europe developed along more peaceful lines with a powerful economic and cultural influence coming from the United States. Migration and the economic growth of the second half of the century reshaped the society of many Western nations. Welfare systems provided an extensive social safety net. The role and opportunities for women in society expanded. More and more Europeans across the Continent attended universities. The end of Soviet domination began a process in which Eastern Europe increasingly came to participate in the affluence of the West with its myriad consumer goods.

By the close of the century, Europe, like much of the rest of the world, had entered a new technological revolution through the computer and advances in medical care. Economic growth slowed in the 1990s, but most of Europe outside the former communist-dominated regions continued to enjoy some of the highest standards of living in the world, under liberal democratic governments.

The efforts to unify Europe have transformed the Continent and the everyday lives of its citizens. The future of the European Union, however, now stands at a crossroads. The advancing financial crisis will only place new demands on the Union.

Review Questions

1. How did migration affect twentieth-century European social life? What internal and external forces led to migration?
2. In what specific ways was Europe Americanized in the second half of the twentieth century? How do you explain the trend toward a consumer society?
3. How has Islamic migration into Europe affected social tensions on the continent? How did the migration come about? What are incidents occurring in Europe that have raised resentment within the Islamic world?
4. How did women's social and economic roles change in the second half of the twentieth century? What changes and problems have women faced since the fall of communism in Eastern Europe?
5. How did the pursuit and diffusion of knowledge change in the twentieth century? What have been the effects of the communications revolutions? Has Western intellectual life become more unified or less so? Why?
6. What did Nietzsche and Kierkegaard contribute to existentialism? How was existentialism a response to the crises of the twentieth century?
7. What were the technological steps in the emergence of the computer? What changes will computers bring in the next decade?
8. What were the major steps in the emergence of the European Union? Why is the Union now facing a crisis?

Suggested Readings

G. Ambrosius and W. H. Hubbard, *A Social and Economic History of Twentieth-Century Europe* (1989). An excellent one-volume treatment of the subject.

B. S. Anderson and J. P. Zinsser, *A History of Their Own: Women in Europe from Prehistory to the Present*, Vol. 2 (1988). A broad-ranging survey.

G. Bock and P. Thane, eds., *Maternity and Gender Politics: Women and the Rise of the European Welfare States, 1880s–1950s* (1991). Explores the emergence of welfare legislation.

E. Bramwell, *Ecology in the 20th Century: A History* (1989). Traces the environmental movement to its late-nineteenth-century origins.

P. E. Ceruzzi, *A History of Modern Computing* (2003). A comprehensive survey.

S. Collinson, *Beyond Borders: West European Migration Policy and the 21st Century* (1993). Explores a major contemporary European social issue.

R. Crossman, ed., *The God That Failed* (1949). Classic essays by former communist intellectuals.

D. Dinan, *Europe Recast: A History of the European Union* (2004). A major overview.

C. Fink, P. Gasert, and D. Junker, *1968: The World Transformed* (1998). The best collection of essays on a momentous year.

B. Graham, *Modern Europe: Place, Culture, Identity* (1998). Thoughtful essays on the future of Europe by a group of geographers.

H. S. Hughes, *Sophisticated Rebels: The Political Culture of European Dissent, 1968–1987* (1988). Thoughtful essays on recent cultural critics.

P. Jenkins, *Mrs. Thatcher's Revolution: The Ending of the Socialist Era* (1988). The best work on the subject.

P. Jenkins, *The Next Christendom: The Coming of Global Christianity* (2002). A provocative analysis.

T. Judt, *Past Imperfect: French Intellectuals, 1944–1956* (1992). An important study of French intellectuals and communism.

T. Judt, *Pastwar: A History of Europe since 1945* (2005). The most recent authoritative overview.

R. Maltby, ed., *Passing Parade: A History of Popular Culture in the Twentieth Century* (1989). Essays on a topic just beginning to receive scholarly attention.

R. Marrus, *The Unwanted: European Refugees in the 20th Century* (1985). An important work on a disturbing subject.

D. Meyer, *Sex and Power: The Rise of Women in America, Russia, Sweden, and Italy* (1987). A lively, useful survey.

N. Naimark, *Fires of Hatred: Ethnic Cleansing in Twentieth-Century Europe* (2002). A remarkably sensitive treatment of a tragic subject.

M. Poster, *Existential Marxism in Postwar France* (1975). An excellent and clear work.

H. Rowley, *Tête-á-Tête: Simone de Beauvoir and Jean-Paul Sartre* (2005). A highly critical joint biography.

S. Strasser, C. McGovern, and M. Judt, *Getting and Spending: European and American Consumer Societies in the Twentieth Century* (1998). An extensive collection of comparative essays.

F. Thebaud, ed., *A History of Women in the West*, Vol. 5: *Toward a Cultural Identity in the Twentieth Century* (1994). A collection of wide-ranging essays of the highest quality.

For additional learning resources related to this chapter, please go to www.myhistorylab.com

Energy and the Modern World

NO SINGLE TECHNOLOGICAL factor so determines the social relationships and standard of living of human beings as energy. The more energy a society can command for each of its members, the stronger and more influential it will be. Throughout recorded human history, those societies that have found ways to improve their access to sources of energy, and have then efficiently applied the energy, have dominated both their immediate environments and much of the world beyond. Indeed, the possession of, or the lack of, efficient, inexpensive sources of energy in large measure determines which nations will be wealthy and which will be poor.

Animals, Wind, and Water

For civilization to advance technologically, energy had to be applied to tasks. The earliest source of such energy was animal power, which was used all over the world except among the peoples on the American continent prior to the arrival of the Europeans. Oxen, water buffalo, and horses were the major draft animals. Of these, horses were the most efficient.

Throughout the world until the eighteenth century, however, wind and water furnished most of the energy for machinery. Sailing ships had been used since ancient times for travel, fishing, and the transport of goods. The wind also worked mills that pumped water and ground grain. Waterwheels proved to be highly flexible machines and by the eighteenth century constituted the major sources of mechanical power in Europe and much of the rest of the world. But wind and water were uncertain sources of energy. The wind could cease; drought could dry up streams. Water-powered machinery had to be located near the stream furnishing the water. Consequently, most of the mills employing such machinery were located in the countryside.

Until the eighteenth century, sailing ships were powered by wind alone. In this fourteenth-century manuscript illustration, sailors navigate with the help of an astrolabe. Ms Fr 2810 f. 188 Navigators using an astrolable in the Indian Ocean (vellum) by Boucicaut Master (fl. 1390-1430) (and workshop) Livre des Merveilles du Monde (c. 1410-12). Bibliothèque Nationale, Paris, France/Bridgeman Art Library International

Although animals, wind, and water provided energy for relatively complicated machines capable of manufacturing and transporting high-quality goods, the economic and political transformations that have driven the history of the world for the past two and a half centuries could only have occurred through a qualitative as well as quantitative leap in the manner in which human beings commanded energy. The twin sources of this world-transforming energy have been fossil fuels and electricity.

Until the second half of the eighteenth century, fossil fuels—coal, petroleum, and, to a lesser extent, natural gas—contributed only a small portion of human energy requirements. Their use as meaningful sources of energy required a series of inventions that allowed the energy of heat to be changed into mechanical energy.

Steam Power and the Age of Coal

Although peoples living near coal deposits had used it as a household fuel for a very long time, only the invention of the steam engine, patented by James Watt in 1769, established a major industrial demand for coal. The steam engine first permitted the pumping of water from coal mines to increase production. But as the industrial uses for the steam engine grew, the invention itself drove the demand for greater quantities of coal as fuel.

Coal-fueled steam power changed the face of human society during the nineteenth century and continues to provide the energy for the most powerful turbogenerators at the dawn of the twenty-first century. Steam-powered machines could be made larger and more flexible than those powered by wind or water, and as long as coal was available, they could run steadily day and night. Steam engines, in contrast to waterwheels, were transportable. Factories could be moved away from streams in the countryside to urban areas where a ready workforce existed. And goods produced in factories powered by steam engines could be carried around the world by steam-powered locomotives and ships. Those expanding markets in turn called forth more steam-powered factories and even greater use of coal. Furthermore, steam-powered factories could also produce military weapons that could be placed on steam-powered naval vessels constructed of iron and steel in vast coal-fueled blast furnaces. When Theodore Roosevelt sent the U.S. fleet around the world, it was a testimony to the power of coal and steam as well as to the power of the American navy.

The age of steam was the age of coal. The nations possessing large coal deposits dominated much nineteenth-century economic life as the nations that possess oil reserves dominate much contemporary economic life. For many decades, Great Britain dominated the world's production and delivery of coal, which was transported over the entire world. Its domination was challenged only in the late nineteenth century as the United States and later Russia and China began to produce vast quantities of the fuel. Coal remained the chief fuel for the United States until after World War I and for Western Europe until after World War II. It remains the chief fuel for China.

Coal generated a rising standard of living in Europe and the expansion of European and later American power, but coal also generated a number of social problems. The most shocking conditions of exploited labor occurred in coal mines, where parliamentary reports of the 1840s described and illustrated half-clad women and children drawing coal carts from the depths of the mines to the surface. Throughout the nineteenth and twentieth centuries, thousands of miners died in mining disasters. Work in the mines injured the health of miners, as did the pollution sent into the atmosphere by coal fires from both factories and homes. By the early twentieth century, observers had begun to note the damage to the environment caused by strip mining of coal and the later abandonment of the regions.

The Internal Combustion Engine: The Age of Oil

As with coal, the impact of petroleum, the second major fossil fuel, also depended on the invention of machinery to use it. Originally, the use for oil was limited to kerosene, the fuel used for lighting around much of the world by 1900. It was upon the world demand for lamp oil that John D. Rockefeller founded the Standard Oil Company. The invention of the internal combustion engine in 1882 by Rudolf Daimler and the diesel engine in 1892 by Rudolf Diesel transformed the demand for oil. Toward the close of the nineteenth century, extensive oil production had begun in the United States, with Russia, Romania, Sumatra, Mexico, Iran, and Venezuela starting to tap their own oil resources before World War I.

Just as the steam engine had spurred the expansion of the coal industry, the internal combustion engine drove the oil industry. Fuel oil would begin to replace coal, not so much because it was cheaper but rather because it was more efficient, easier to store and transport, and cleaner to burn. Initially, fuel oil tended to be used in those countries where it could be produced relatively near the point of use. Until the end of World War II, the United States was the primary world producer and user of oil. As fuel for the internal combustion engine, oil became the driving force of automobiles, locomotives, airplanes, ships, factory machinery, and electric generators. It revolutionized agricultural machinery and world food production, but as a fuel for transportation, it fostered a social transformation over much of the world.

Until 1924, Henry Ford had disdained national advertising for his cars. But as General Motors gained a competitive edge by making yearly changes in style and technology, Ford was forced to pay more attention to advertising. This ad was directed at "Mrs. Consumer," combining appeals to both female independence and motherly duties. Ford Motor Company

Starting in the United States and then spreading elsewhere, owning an automobile introduced a new mobility factor into social relationships. People could move easily across long distances to join a new community or to start a new job. Inexpensive gasoline for cars and public transport buses permitted the development of suburbs ever farther removed from traditional urban centers. In turn, retailing moved away from city centers to shopping malls. At the same time, wherever the mechanization of farming through improved farm machinery took place, there usually followed a movement of people from farming communities to urban areas.

Electricity Increases the Demand for Oil

The manufacture of automobiles and other forms of transport using the internal combustion or diesel engine was central to all modern industrial life. As those industries expanded, so did the construction of extensive road systems. These in turn created new demands for fuel oil.

But the greatest demand for fuel oil arose from the application of electricity to the needs of everyday life. Electricity proved to be the most flexible and versatile source of energy for the twentieth century, and its generation provided the single greatest source of demand for both coal and oil. Electricity generation would also employ new modes of water power in the forms of hydroelectric generators.

The scientific basis for the production of electric energy was Michael Faraday's study of electromagnetic induction. In 1831, he demonstrated that mechanical energy under the proper conditions could be converted into electric energy. Even more important, the reverse was also true. Electricity could be generated in one location and applied far away wherever electrical lines could be extended. The applications of electrical power have appeared to be restricted only by the limitations of the inventive imagination.

During the second half of the nineteenth century, a whole host of inventors, such as Thomas Alva Edison, worked through the production and application of electrical power to service large regions. Electricity found applications across the spectrum of human society, actions, and enterprises. Access to electricity in the course of the twentieth century became the key factor for an improved standard of living. A fundamental moment in the decision by Japan to modernize during the late nineteenth century was the construction of the Tokyo Electric Light Company in 1888. The extension of electrical lines into the American countryside was one of the major accomplishments of Franklin Roosevelt's New Deal. Electrical power transformed the workplace, but even more strikingly it transformed homes. Without access to electrical power, domestic households could not make use of any of the growing array of labor-saving appliances such as electric washing machines, electric irons, electric stoves, and electric vacuum cleaners. Electric lights brightened whole cities. Electricity replaced both coal and oil as the source of power for many locomotives; it powered public tram systems and opened the way for the telegraph, the telephone, the wireless, the motion picture camera, and television. It planted the seeds for the computer revolution in communication and information. Electricity allowed manufacturing plants and office complexes to be built wherever electric lines could be carried. Indeed, the spread of access to electrical power has been the single best indication of economic advancement for any nation or region.

Yet within this era of ever-expanding electrification, coal and oil—the fundamental fossil fuels—would still provide the underpinnings of the world's energy. In fact, more oil and coal are used to generate electricity than for any other single purpose. Throughout the twentieth century, the demand for these fuels led to the refinement of their production techniques to permit the extraction of coal from ever-deeper seams and the strip mining of it from regions where previously it would have been economically unproductive to do so. The effort to discover, extract, and transport oil would have major consequences for the world's physical and geopolitical environment far into the twentieth century.

Oil and Global Politics in the Twentieth Century

As the twentieth century began, the United States was by far the largest producer and exporter of petroleum. Yet by the 1920s, the American government began to worry about running out of oil. So, too, did the British, who depended on imported oil for all of their military and industrial needs. During the 1920s and 1930s, both governments encouraged oil companies to forge agreements for the drilling and export of oil from the Middle East. These arrangements fit into the pattern of formal and informal colonialism that still characterized the interwar period.

After World War II, Western Europe, the Soviet Union, and the nations of the Warsaw Pact began to turn from coal to oil as the basis for economic growth. (Japan followed this course during the 1960s.) By 1947, the United States had begun to import more oil than it produced. These two developments—a new dependence on oil by the industrialized nations and the expanded search for oil by the West—formed the basis for the new role that the nations of the Middle East would play in the world economy as the chief oil exporters. Simultaneously, as the world's industrialized economies were growing dependent on Middle East oil production, nationalistic leaders in that region were denouncing former colonial domination and rejecting relationships with the West and with Israel, a country that received strong political support from the United States and Western Europe. The stage was thus set for oil to play a new role in the geopolitical conflicts of the Cold War era.

Playing a major role in those conflicts was the Organization of Petroleum Exporting Nations (OPEC), founded in 1960. Regardless of their differences, OPEC members were united in two things: First, they deeply resented former colonial control of their oil supplies, and second, they were determined that their own governments, not foreign oil companies, would control those vital resources. (Mexico had brought its own petroleum industry under state control before World War II.) In 1973, during the Yom Kippur War, OPEC acted, sharply raising oil prices to nations whose govern-

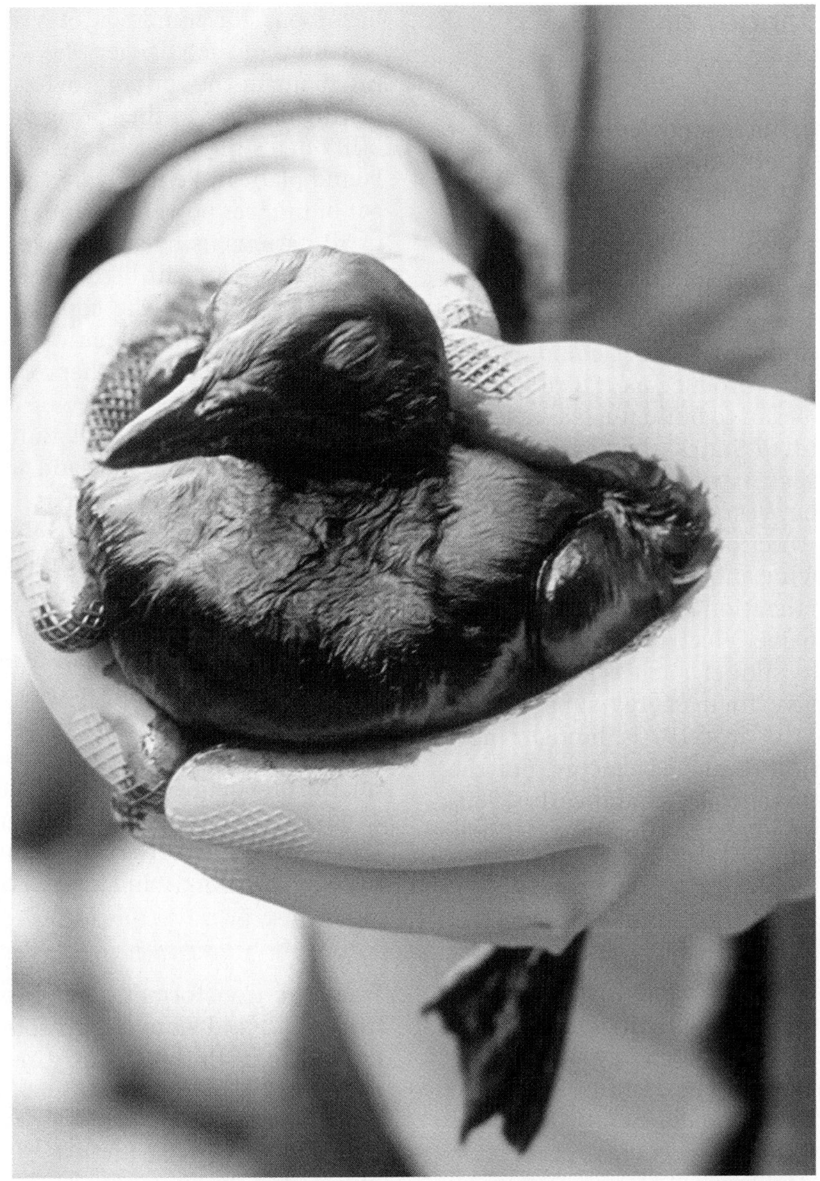

In 1989, when a supertanker spilled 35,000 tons of crude oil into Alaska's Prince William Sound, rescue workers struggled to save the lives of seabirds and animals. Nevertheless, thousands died. Ron Levy/Global Image Group

ments supported Israel. The action caused severe economic consequences in the West and spurred new efforts to develop local oil reserves in politically safe locations such as in the North Sea. OPEC would attempt similar actions on other occasions, most successfully in 1979. In that year, a revolution in Iran overthrew the government, which had long been supported by the United States. OPEC cut off oil shipments to the West, causing severe dislocations. Concerns about securing oil supplies in the West were again sparked by the Persian Gulf War and other political tensions in the region.

In addition to the political problems associated with Middle East oil production, the industrial world's reliance on oil has had severe environmental consequences. Generally, when the United States dominated oil production, the oil refineries were located near the source of oil production. As the exploitation of oil reserves moved to the Middle East and then later in the century to Alaska and to the North Sea, oil refineries became separated from the drilling locations. Crude oil was shipped to refineries on enormous tankers. More than once, these supertankers have hit shoals or gone aground, causing large oil spills, calamitous to both animals and humans.

The Promise and Danger of Nuclear Energy

Following World War II, nuclear power became a new source for the generation of electrical energy. The power of the atom, first released in the 1940s for military purposes, held the promise of virtually infinite quantities of energy. The world would no longer be dependent on finite supplies of fossil fuel located in politically tense regions of the world. The generation of such energy, however, required the most complex sets of machinery ever devised to produce electrical energy. France and Great Britain began to build nuclear reactors in the 1950s with the United States, the Soviet Union, and various other European nations following in the 1960s. Nations outside the West, such as India and Pakistan, looked to the construction of nuclear power stations as a means of moving more rapidly toward the achievements of industrialization and a rising standard of living through extensive electrification. Nations with limited supplies of fossil fuel, such as Japan, hoped nuclear energy would solve their energy supply problem. The oil shock of the mid-1970s brought new enthusiasm to the adoption of nuclear energy, but the economic downturn of the late 1970s and early 1980s slowed the construction of nuclear-generating stations. The construction of breeder reactors, which would produce their own fuel in the process of generating electrical energy, seemed to promise a world liberated from dependence on a finite supply of fossil fuels. Furthermore, unlike coal and oil, which have many uses besides that of fuel, uranium had no other economic use. The workers in the field of atomic energy were scientists and engineers rather than the kind of industrial labor force that produced coal and oil.

Yet the technology of nuclear energy production proved to be exceedingly dangerous. The atomic reactors produced spent radioactive waste that would remain hazardous for hundreds of years. After many years of warnings of such danger, the Chernobyl nuclear generating plant in the former Soviet Union caused enormous, lasting damage in the spring of 1986. In 1979, the possibility of a similar disaster had occurred at the Three Mile Island plant in Pennsylvania. Both the promise and danger of nuclear power continue to inform the political life of all nations using such power. It is wholly unclear, for example, what will be done with the radioactive spent fuel. Furthermore, the construction of nuclear generating plants has allowed nations that lack atomic weapons to train scientists and other experts who might be able to use that knowledge to develop atomic weapons. Whereas in the United States and Europe the military uses of atomic power came first and were followed by peaceful energy uses, the reverse has been the case in nations such as India and Pakistan. Despite its initial promise, nuclear power has contributed far less to energy production than we originally imagined.

The problem of energy remains with us in the new century. Environmental pollution and all the issues surrounding the nuclear generation of energy will demand increasing attention and expenditure of public funds. Similarly, the political pressures and tensions surrounding the oil supplies of the Middle East will not disappear, as advanced nations seek to secure and protect energy reserves while the nations that possess those reserves seek to secure a rising standard of living for themselves.

Trace the transformation of energy used in the West from wind and water to petroleum. How did coal transform both the industry and the military power of the West? How did inventions, such as the internal combustion engine, change the demands on sources of energy? Why did the rise of electrical power increase the need for petroleum? What opportunities and dangers has nuclear energy posed?

GLOSSARY

absolutism Term applied to strong centralized continental monarchies that attempted to make royal power dominant over aristocracies and other regional authorities.

Acropolis (ACK-row-po-lis) The religious and civic center of Athens. It is the site of the Parthenon.

Act of Supremacy The declaration by Parliament in 1534 that Henry VIII, not the pope, was the head of the church in England.

agape (AG-a-pay) Meaning "love feast." A common meal that was part of the central ritual of early Christian worship.

agora (AG-o-rah) The Greek marketplace and civic center. It was the heart of the social life of the *polis.*

Agricultural Revolution The innovations in farm production that began in the eighteenth century and led to a scientific and mechanized agriculture.

Albigensians (Al-bi-GEN-see-uns) Thirteenth-century advocates of a dualist religion. They took their name from the city of Albi in southern France. Also called *Cathars.*

Anabaptists Protestants who insisted that only adult baptism conformed to Scripture.

anarchism The theory that government and social institutions are oppressive and unnecessary and society should be based on voluntary cooperation among individuals.

Anschluss (AHN-shluz) Meaning "union." The annexation of Austria by Germany in March 1938.

anti-Semitism Prejudice, hostility, or legal discrimination against Jews.

apartheid (a-PAR-tid) An official policy of segregation, assignment of peoples to distinct regions, and other forms of social, political, and economic discrimination based on race associated primarily with South Africa.

apostolic primacy The doctrine that the popes are the direct successors to the Apostle Peter and as such heads of the church.

Apostolic Succession The Christian doctrine that the powers given by Jesus to his original disciples have been handed down from bishop to bishop through ordination.

appeasement The Anglo-French policy of making concessions to Germany in the 1930s to avoid a crisis that would lead to war. It assumed that Germany had real grievances and Hitler's aims were limited and ultimately acceptable.

Areopagus The governing council of Athens, originally open only to the nobility. It was named after the hill on which it met.

arete (AH-ray-tay) Manliness, courage, and the excellence appropriate to a hero. It was considered the highest virtue of Homeric society.

Arianism (AIR-ee-an-ism) The belief formulated by Arius of Alexandria (ca. 280–336 C.E.) that Jesus was a created being, neither fully man nor fully God, but something in between. It did away with the doctrine of the Trinity.

aristocratic resurgence Term applied to the eighteenth-century aristocratic efforts to resist the expanding power of European monarchies.

Asia Minor Modern Turkey. Also called *Anatolia.*

assignats (as-seen-YAHNTS) Government bonds based on the value of confiscated church lands issued during the early French Revolution.

Atomists School of ancient Greek philosophy founded in the fifth century B.C.E. by Leucippus of Miletus and Democritus of Abdera. It held that the world consists of innumerable, tiny, solid, indivisible, and unchangeable particles called *atoms.*

Attica (AT-tick-a) The region of Greece where Athens is located.

Augsburg (AWGS-berg) **Confession** The definitive statement of Lutheran belief made in 1530.

Augustus (AW-gust-us) The title given to Octavian in 27 B.C.E. and borne thereafter by all Roman emperors. It was a semireligious title that implied veneration, majesty, and holiness.

Ausgleich (AWS-glike) Meaning "compromise." The agreement between the Habsburg emperor and the Hungarians to give Hungary considerable administrative autonomy in 1867. It created the Dual Monarchy, or Austria-Hungary.

autocracy (AW-to-kra-see) Government in which the ruler has absolute power.

Axis The alliance between Nazi Germany and fascist Italy. Also called the *Pact of Steel.*

banalities Exactions that the lord of a manor could make on his tenants.

baroque (bah-ROWK) A style of art marked by heavy and dramatic ornamentation and curved rather than straight lines that flourished between 1550 and 1750. It was especially associated with the Catholic Counter-Reformation.

Beguines (bi-GEENS) Lay sisterhoods not bound by the rules of a religious order.

benefice Church offices granted by the ruler of a state or the pope to an individual. It also meant *fief* in the Middle Ages.

bishop Originally a person elected by early Christian congregations to lead them in worship and supervise their funds. In time, bishops became the religious and even political authorities for Christian communities within large geographical areas.

Black Death The bubonic plague that killed millions of Europeans in the fourteenth century.

blitzkrieg (BLITZ-kreeg) Meaning "lightning war." The German tactic early in World War II of employing fast-moving, massed armored columns supported by airpower to overwhelm the enemy.

Bolsheviks Meaning the "majority." Term Lenin applied to his faction of the Russian Social Democratic Party. It became the Communist Party of the Soviet Union after the Russian Revolution.

bourgeois A French word used as an adjective describing something associated with the middle class or as a noun to describe a middle-class person.

boyars The Russian nobility.

Bronze Age The name given to the earliest civilized era, c. 4000 to 1000 B.C.E. The term reflects the importance of the metal bronze, a mixture of tin and copper, for the peoples of this age for use as weapons and tools.

Bundesrat (BUHN-dees-raht) The upper house of the German federal parliament whose members are appointed by the various state governments.

Caesaropapism (SEE-zer-o-PAY-pi-zim) The direct involvement of the ruler in religious doctrine and practice as if he were the head of the church as well as the state.

cahiers de doléances (KAH-hee-ay de dough-LAY-ahnce) Meaning "lists of grievances." Petitions for reforms submitted to the French crown when the Estates General met in 1789.

caliphate (KAH-li-fate) The true line of succession to Muhammad.

capital goods Machines and tools used to produce other goods.

Carbonari (car-buh-NAH-ree) Meaning "charcoal burners." The most famous of the secret republican societies seeking to unify Italy in the 1820s.

categorical imperative According to Emmanuel Kant (1724–1804), the internal sense of moral duty or awareness possessed by all human beings.

catholic Meaning "universal." The body of belief held by most Christians enshrined within the church.

Catholic Emancipation The grant of full political rights to Roman Catholics in Britain in 1829.

censor Official of the Roman republic charged with conducting the census and compiling the lists of citizens and members of the Senate. They could expel senators for financial or moral reasons. Two censors were elected every five years.

Chartism The first large-scale European working-class political movement. It sought political reforms that would favor the interests of skilled British workers in the 1830s and 1840s.

chiaroscuro (kyar-eh-SKEW-row) The use of shading to enhance naturalness in painting and drawing.

civic humanism Education designed to promote humanist leadership of political and cultural life.

civilization A form of human culture marked by urbanism, metallurgy, and writing.

civilizing mission The concept that Western nations could bring advanced science and economic development to non-Western parts of the world that justified imperial administration.

clientage (KLI-ent-age) The custom in ancient Rome whereby men became supporters of more powerful men in return for legal and physical protection and economic benefits.

Cold War The ideological and geographical struggle between the United States and its allies and the USSR and its allies that began after World War II and lasted until the dissolution of the USSR in 1989.

collectivization The bedrock of Stalinist agriculture, which forced Russian peasants to give up their private farms and work as members of collectives, large agricultural units controlled by the state.

coloni (CO-loan-ee) Farmers or sharecroppers on the estates of wealthy Romans.

Commonwealthmen British political writers whose radical republican ideas influenced the American revolutionaries.

concentration camps Camps first established by Great Britain in South Africa during the Boer War to incarcerate noncombatant civilians; later, camps established for political prisoners and other persons deemed dangerous to the state in the Soviet Union and Nazi Germany. The term is now primarily associated with the camps established by the Nazis during the Holocaust.

Concert of Europe Term applied to the European great powers acting together (in "concert") to resolve international disputes between 1815 and the 1850s.

conciliar theory The argument that General Councils were superior in authority to the pope and represented the whole body of the faithful.

condottieri (con-da-TEE-AIR-ee) Military brokers who furnished mercenary forces to the Italian states during the Renaissance.

congregationalist A congregationalist puts a group or assembly above any one individual and prefers an ecclesiastical polity that allows each congregation to be autonomous, or self-governing.

Congress System A series of international meetings among the European great powers to promote mutual cooperation between 1818 and 1822.

conquistadores (kahn-KWIS-teh-door-hez) Meaning "conquerors." The Spanish conquerors of the New World.

conservatism Support for the established order in church and state. In the nineteenth century, it implied support for legitimate monarchies, landed aristocracies, and established churches. Conservatives favored only gradual, or "organic," change.

Consulate French government dominated by Napoleon from 1799 to 1804.

consuls (CON-suls) The two chief magistrates of the Roman state.

Consumer Revolution The vast increase in both the desire and the possibility of consuming goods and services that began in the early eighteenth century and created the demand for sustaining the Industrial Revolution.

containment The U.S. policy during the Cold War of resisting Soviet expansion and influence in the expectation that the USSR would eventually collapse.

Convention French radical legislative body from 1792 to 1794.

Corn Laws British tariffs on imported grain that protected the price of grain grown within the British Isles.

corvée (cor-VAY) A French labor tax requiring peasants to work on roads, bridges, and canals.

Council of Nicaea (NIGH-see-a) The council of Christian bishops at Nicaea in 325 C.E. that formulated the Nicene Creed, a statement of Christian belief that rejected Arianism in favor of the doctrine that Christ is both fully human and fully divine.

Counter-Reformation The sixteenth-century reform movement in the Roman Catholic Church in reaction to the Protestant Reformation.

coup d'état (COO DAY-ta) The sudden violent overthrow of a government by its own army.

creed A brief statement of faith to which true Christians should adhere.

Creoles (KRAY-ol-ez) Persons of Spanish descent born in the Spanish colonies.

Crusades Religious wars directed by the church against infidels and heretics.

culture The ways of living built up by a group and passed on from one generation to another.

cuneiform (Q-nee-i-form) A writing system invented by the Sumerians that used a wedge-shaped stylus, or pointed tool, to write on wet clay tablets that were then baked or dried (*cuneus* means "wedge" in Latin). The writing was also cut into stone.

Curia (CURE-ee-a) The papal government.

Cynic (SIN-ick) **School** A fourth-century philosophical movement that ridiculed all religious observances and turned away from involvement in the affairs of the *polis*. Its most famous exemplar was Diogenes of Sinope (ca. 400–325 B.C.E.).

deacon Meaning "those who serve." In early Christian congregations, deacons assisted the presbyters, or elders.

decolonization The process of European retreat of colonial empires following World War II.

deism A belief in a rational God who had created the universe but then allowed it to function without his interference according to the mechanisms of nature and a belief in rewards and punishments after death for human action.

Delian (DEE-li-an) **League** An alliance of Greek states under the leadership of Athens that was formed in 478–477 B.C.E. to resist the Persians. In time the league was transformed into the Athenian Empire.

deme (DEEM) A small town in Attica or a ward in Athens that became the basic unit of Athenian civic life under the democratic reforms of Clisthenes in 508 B.C.E.

demesne (di-MAIN) The part of a manor that was cultivated directly for the lord of the manor.

divine right of kings The theory that monarchs are appointed by and answerable only to God.

Domesday (DOOMS-day) ***Book*** A detailed survey of the wealth of England undertaken by William the Conqueror between 1080 and 1086.

domestic system of textile production Method of producing textiles in which agents furnished raw materials to households whose members spun them into thread and then wove cloth, which the agents then sold as finished products.

Donatism The heresy that taught the efficacy of the sacraments depended on the moral character of the clergy who administered them.

Duce (DO-chay) Meaning "leader." Mussolini's title as head of the Fascist Party.

Duma (DOO-ma) The Russian parliament, after the revolution of 1905.

electors Nine German princes who had the right to elect the Holy Roman Emperor.

émigrés (em-ee-GRAYS) French aristocrats who fled France during the Revolution.

empiricism (em-PEER-ih-cism) The use of experiment and observation derived from sensory evidence to construct scientific theory or philosophy of knowledge.

enclosure The consolidation or fencing in of common lands by British landlords to increase production and achieve greater commercial profits. It also involved the reclamation of waste land and the consolidation of strips into block fields.

encomienda (en-co-mee-EN-da) The grant by the Spanish crown to a colonist of the labor of a specific number of Indians for a set period of time.

ENIAC The Electronic Numerical Integrator and Computer. The first genuine modern digital computer, developed in the 1940s.

Enlightenment The eighteenth-century movement led by the *philosophes* that held that change and reform were both desirable through the application of reason and science.

Epicureans (EP-i-cure-ee-ans) School of philosophy founded by Epicurus of Athens (342–271 B.C.E.). It sought to liberate people from fear of death and the supernatural by teaching that the gods took no interest in human affairs and that true happiness consisted in pleasure, which was defined as the absence of pain. This could be achieved by attaining *ataraxia*, freedom from trouble, pain, and responsibility by withdrawing from business and public life.

equestrians (EE-quest-ree-ans) Literally "cavalrymen" or "knights." In the earliest years of the Roman Republic those who could afford to serve as mounted warriors. The equestrians evolved into a social rank of well-to-do businessmen and middle-ranking officials. Many of them supported the Gracchi.

Estates General The medieval French parliament. It consisted of three separate groups, or "estates": clergy, nobility, and commoners. It last met in 1789 at the outbreak of the French Revolution.

Etruscans (EE-trus-cans) A people of central Italy who exerted the most powerful external influence on the early Romans. Etruscan kings ruled Rome until 509 B.C.E.

Eucharist (YOU-ka-rist) Meaning "thanksgiving." The celebration of the Lord's Supper. Considered the central ritual of worship by most Christians. Also called *Holy Communion.*

Euro The common currency created by the EEC in the late 1990s.

European Economic Community (EEC) The economic association formed by France, Germany, Italy, Belgium, the Netherlands, and Luxembourg in 1957. Also known as the *Common Market.*

European Union The new name given to the EEC in 1993. It included most of the states of Western Europe.

excommunication Denial by the church of the right to receive the sacraments.

existentialism The post–World War II Western philosophy that holds human beings are totally responsible for their acts and that this responsibility causes them dread and anguish.

Fabians British socialists in the late nineteenth and early twentieth centuries who sought to achieve socialism through gradual, peaceful, and democratic means.

family economy The basic structure of production and consumption in preindustrial Europe.

fascism Political movements that tend to be antidemocratic, anti-Marxist, antiparliamentary, and often anti-Semitic. Fascists were invariably nationalists and exhalted the nation over the individual. They supported the interests of the middle class and rejected the ideas of the French Revolution and nineteenth-century liberalism. The first fascist regime was founded by Benito Mussolini (1883–1945) in Italy in the 1920s.

fealty An oath of loyalty by a vassal to a lord, promising to perform specified services.

feudal (FEW-dull) **society** The social, political, military, and economic system that prevailed in the Middle Ages and beyond in some parts of Europe.

fief Land granted to a vassal in exchange for services, usually military.

foederati (FAY-der-ah-tee) Barbarian tribes enlisted as special allies of the Roman Empire.

Fourteen Points President Woodrow Wilson's (1856–1924) idealistic war aims.

Fronde (FROHND) A series of rebellions against royal authority in France between 1649 and 1652.

Führer (FYOOR-er) Meaning "leader." The title taken by Hitler when he became dictator of Germany.

gabelle (gah-BELL) The royal tax on salt in France.

Gaul (GAWL) Modern France.

German Confederation Association of German states established at the Congress of Vienna that replaced the Holy Roman Empire from 1815 to 1866.

ghetto Separate communities in which Jews were required by law to live.

glasnost (GLAZ-nohst) Meaning "openness." The policy initiated by Mikhail Gorbachev (MEEK-hail GORE-buh-choff) in the 1980s of permitting open criticism of the policies of the Soviet Communist Party.

Glorious Revolution The largely peaceful replacement of James II by William and Mary as English monarchs in 1688. It marked the beginning of constitutional monarchy in Britain.

gold standard A monetary system in which the value of a unit of a nation's currency is related to a fixed amount of gold.

Golden Bull The agreement in 1356 to establish a seven-member electoral college of German princes to choose the Holy Roman Emperor.

Great Depression A prolonged worldwide economic downturn that began in 1929 with the collapse of the New York Stock Exchange.

Great Purges The imprisonment and execution of millions of Soviet citizens by Stalin between 1934 and 1939.

Great Reform Bill (1832) A limited reform of the British House of Commons and an expansion of the electorate to include a wider variety of the propertied classes. It laid the groundwork for further orderly reforms within the British constitutional system.

Great Schism The appearance of two and at times three rival popes between 1378 and 1415.

Great Trek The migration by Boer (Dutch) farmers during the 1830s and 1840s from regions around Cape Town into the eastern and northeastern regions of South Africa that ultimately resulted in the founding of the Orange Free State and Transvaal.

Green movement A political environmentalist movement that began in West Germany in the 1970s and spread to a number of other Western nations.

grossdeutsch (gross-DOYCH) Meaning "great German." The argument that the German-speaking portions of the Habsburg Empire should be included in a united Germany.

guild An association of merchants or craftsmen that offered protection to its members and set rules for their work and products.

hacienda (ha-SEE-hen-da) A large landed estate in Spanish America.

Hegira (HEJ-ear-a) The flight of Muhammad and his followers from Mecca to Medina in 622 C.E. It marks the beginning of the Islamic calendar.

heliocentric (HE-li-o-cen-trick) **theory** The theory, now universally accepted, that the earth and the other planets revolve around the sun. First proposed by Aristarchos of Samos (310–230 B.C.E.). Its opposite, the geocentric theory, which was dominant until the sixteenth century C.E., held that the sun and the planets revolved around the earth.

Helots (HELL-ots) Hereditary Spartan serfs.

heretic (HAIR-i-tick) A person whose beliefs were contrary to those of the Catholic Church.

hieroglyphics (HI-er-o-gli-phicks) The complicated writing script of ancient Egypt. It combined picture writing with pictographs and sound signs. Hieroglyph means "sacred carvings" in Greek.

Holocaust The Nazi extermination of millions of European Jews between 1940 and 1945. Also called the "final solution to the Jewish problem."

Holy Roman Empire The revival of the old Roman Empire, based mainly in Germany and northern Italy, that endured from 870 to 1806.

home rule The advocacy of a large measure of administrative autonomy for Ireland within the British Empire between the 1880s and 1914.

Homo sapiens (HO-mo say-pee-ans) The scientific name for human beings, from the Latin words meaning "Wise man." *Homo sapiens* emerged some 200,000 years ago.

honestiores (HON-est-ee-or-ez) The Roman term formalized from the beginning of the third century C.E. to denote the privileged classes: senators, equestrians, the municipal aristocracy, and soldiers.

***hoplite* phalanx** (FAY-lanks) The basic unit of Greek warfare in which infantrymen fought in close order, shield to shield, usually eight ranks deep. The phalanx perfectly suited the farmer-soldier-citizen who was the backbone of the *polis*.

hubris (WHO-bris) Arrogance brought on by excessive wealth or good fortune. The Greeks believed it led to moral blindness and divine vengeance.

Huguenots (HYOU-gu-nots) French Calvinists.

humanism The study of the Latin and Greek classics and of the Church Fathers both for their own sake and to promote a rebirth of ancient norms and values.

humanitas (HEW-man-i-tas) The Roman name for a liberal arts education.

humiliores (HEW-mi-lee-orez) The Roman term formalized at the beginning of the third century C.E. for the lower classes.

Hussites (HUS-Its) Followers of John Huss (d. 1415) who questioned Catholic teachings about the Eucharist.

Iconoclasm (i-KON-o-kla-zoom) A heresy in Eastern Christianity that sought to ban the veneration of sacred images, or icons.

id, ego, superego The three entities in Sigmund Freud's model of the internal organization of the human mind. The id consists of the amoral, irrational instincts for self-gratification. The superego embodies the external morality imposed on the personality by society. The ego mediates between the two and allows the personality to cope with the internal and external demands of its existence.

***Iliad* (ILL-ee-ad) and the *Odyssey* (O-dis-see), The** Epic poems by Homer about the "Dark Age" heroes of Greece who fought at Troy. The poems were written down in the eighth century B.C.E. after centuries of being sung by bards.

imperator (IM-per-a-tor) Under the Roman Republic, it was the title given to a victorious general. Under Augustus and his successors, it became the title of the ruler of Rome meaning "emperor."

imperialism The extension of a nation's authority over other nations or areas through conquest or political or economic hegemony.

Imperialism of Free Trade The advance of European economic and political interests in the nineteenth century by demanding that non-European nations allow European nations, most particularly Great Britain, to introduce their manufactured goods freely into all nations or to introduce other goods, such as opium into China, that allowed those nations to establish economic influence and to determine the terms of trade.

imperium (IM-pear-ee-um) In ancient Rome, the right to issue commands and to enforce them by fines, arrests, and even corporal and capital punishment.

indulgence Remission of the temporal penalty of punishment in purgatory that remained after sins had been forgiven.

Industrial Revolution Mechanization of the European economy that began in Britain in the second half of the eighteenth century.

Inquisition A tribunal created by the Catholic Church in the mid-twelfth century to detect and punish heresy.

insulae (IN-sul-lay) Meaning "islands." The multistoried apartment buildings of Rome in which most of the inhabitants of the city lived.

Intolerable Acts Measures passed by the British Parliament in 1774 to punish the colony of Massachusetts and strengthen Britain's authority in the colonies. The laws provoked colonial opposition, which led immediately to the American Revolution.

investiture controversy The medieval conflict between the church and lay rulers over who would control bishops and abbots, symbolized by the ceremony of "investing" them with the symbols of their authority.

Ionia (I-o-knee-a) The part of western Asia Minor heavily colonized by the Greeks.

Islam (IZ-lahm) Meaning "submission." The religion founded by the prophet Muhammad.

Italia irredenta (ee-TAHL-ee-a ir-REH-dent-a) Meaning "unredeemed Italy." Italian-speaking areas that had been left under Austrian rule at the time of the unification of Italy.

Jacobins (JACK-uh-bins) The radical republican party during the French Revolution that displaced the Girondins.

Jacquerie (jah-KREE) Revolt of the French peasantry.

Jansenism A seventeenth-century movement within the Catholic Church that taught that human beings were so corrupted by original sin that they could do nothing good nor secure their own salvation without divine grace. (It was opposed to the Jesuits.)

Judah (JEW-da) The southern Israelite kingdom established after the death of Solomon in the tenth century B.C.E.

Julian Calendar The reform of the calendar by Julius Caesar in 46 B.C.E. It remained in use throughout Europe until the sixteenth century and in Russia until the Russian Revolution in 1917.

July Monarchy The French regime set up after the overthrow of the Bourbons in July 1830.

Junkers (YOONG-kerz) The noble landlords of Prussia.

jus gentium (YUZ GEN-tee-um) Meaning "law of peoples." The body of Roman law that dealt with foreigners.

jus naturale (YUZ NAH-tu-rah-lay) Meaning "natural law." The Stoic concept of a world ruled by divine reason.

Ka'ba (KAH-bah) A black meteorite in the city of Mecca that became Islam's holiest shrine.

Keynesian economics The theory of John Maynard Keynes (CANES) (1883–1946) that governments could spend their economies out of a depression by running deficits to encourage employment and stimulate the production and consumption of goods.

kleindeutsch (kline-DOYCH) Meaning "small German." The argument that the German-speaking portions of the Habsburg Empire should be excluded from a united Germany.

Kristallnacht (KRIS-tahl-NAHKT) Meaning "crystal night" because of the broken glass that littered German streets after the looting and destruction of Jewish homes, businesses, and synagogues across Germany on the orders of the Nazi Party in November 1938.

kulaks (koo-LAKS) Prosperous Russian peasant farmers.

Kulturkampf (cool-TOOR-cahmff) Meaning the "battle for culture." The conflict between the Roman Catholic Church and the government of the German Empire in the 1870s.

laissez-faire (lay-ZAY-faire) French phrase meaning "allow to do." In economics the doctrine of minimal government interference in the working of the economy.

Late Antiquity The multicultural period between the end of the ancient world and the birth of the Middle Ages, 250–800 C.E.

latifundia (LAT-ee-fun-dee-a) Large plantations for growing cash crops owned by wealthy Romans.

Latium (LAT-ee-um) The region of Italy in which Rome is located. Its inhabitants were called *Latins*.

League of Nations The association of sovereign states set up after World War I to pursue common policies and avert international aggression.

Lebensraum (LAY-benz-rauhm) Meaning "living space." The Nazi plan to colonize and exploit the Slavic areas of Eastern Europe for the benefit of Germany.

levée en masse (le-VAY en MASS) The French revolutionary conscription (1792) of all males into the army and the harnessing of the economy for war production.

liberal arts The medieval university program that consisted of the *trivium* (TRI-vee-um): grammar, rhetoric, and logic, and the *quadrivium* (qua-DRI-vee-um): arithmetic, geometry, astronomy, and music.

liberalism In the nineteenth century, support for representative government dominated by the propertied classes and minimal government interference in the economy.

Logos (LOW-goz) Divine reason, or fire, which according to the Stoics was the guiding principle in nature. Every human had a spark of this divinity, which returned to the eternal divine spirit after death.

Lollards (LALL-erds) Followers of John Wycliffe (d. 1384) who questioned the supremacy and privileges of the pope and the church hierarchy.

Lower Egypt The Nile delta.

Luftwaffe (LUFT-vaff-uh) The German air force in World War II.

Magna Carta (MAG-nuh CAR-tuh) The "Great Charter" limiting royal power that the English nobility forced King John to sign in 1215.

Magna Graecia (MAG-nah GRAY-see-a) Meaning "Great Greece" in Latin, it was the name given by the Romans to southern Italy and Sicily because there were so many Greek colonies in the region.

Magyars (MAH-jars) The majority ethnic group in Hungary.

Mandates The assigning of the former German colonies and Turkish territories in the Middle East to Britain, France, Japan, Belgium, Australia, and South Africa as de facto colonies under the vague supervision of the League of Nations with the hope that the territories would someday advance to independence.

mannerism A style of art in the mid- to late-sixteenth century that permitted artists to express their own "manner" or feelings in contrast to the symmetry and simplicity of the art of the High Renaissance.

manor Village farms owned by a lord.

Marshall Plan The U.S. program named after Secretary of State George C. Marshall of providing economic aid to Europe after World War II.

Marxism The theory of Karl Marx (1818–1883) and Friedrich Engels (FREE-drick ENG-ulz) (1820–1895) that history is the result of class conflict, which will end in the inevitable triumph of the industrial proletariat over the bourgeoisie and the abolition of private property and social class.

Mein Kampf (MINE KAHMFF) Meaning *My Struggle*. Hitler's statement of his political program, published in 1924.

Mensheviks Meaning the "minority." Term Lenin applied to the majority moderate faction of the Russian Social Democratic Party opposed to him and the Bolsheviks.

mercantilism Term used to describe close government control of the economy that sought to maximize exports and accumulate as much precious metals as possible to enable the state to defend its economic and political interests.

Mesopotamia (MEZ-o-po-tay-me-a) Modern Iraq. The land between the Tigris and Euphrates Rivers where the first civilization appeared around 3000 B.C.E.

Messiah (MESS-eye-a) The redeemer whose coming Jews believed would establish the kingdom of God on earth. Christians considered Jesus to be the Messiah (*Christ* means Messiah in Greek).

Methodism An English religious movement begun by John Wesley (1703–1791) that stressed inward, heartfelt religion and the possibility of attaining Christian perfection in this life.

millets Administrative units of the Ottoman Empire that were not geographic but consisted of ethnic or religious minorities to whom particular laws and regulations applied.

Minoans (MIN-o-ans) The Bronze Age civilization that arose in Crete in the third and second millennia B.C.E.

missi dominici (MISS-ee dough-MIN-ee-chee) Meaning "the envoys of the ruler." Royal overseers of the king's law in the Carolingian Empire.

mobilization The placing of a country's military forces on a war footing.

modernism The movement in the arts and literature in the late nineteenth and early twentieth centuries to create new aesthetic forms and to elevate the aesthetic experience of a work of art above the attempt to portray reality as accurately as possible.

moldboard plow A heavy plow introduced in the Middle Ages that cut deep into the soil.

monasticism A movement in the Christian church that arose first in the East in the third and fourth centuries C.E. in which first individual hermits and later organized communities of men and women (monks and nuns) separated themselves from the world to lead lives in imitation of Christ. In the West the Rule of St. Benedict (c. 480–547) became the dominant form of monasticism.

Monophysite (ma-NO-fiz-it) Adherent of the theory that Jesus had only one nature.

monotheism The worship of one universal God.

Mycenaean (MY-cen-a-an) The Bronze Age civilization of mainland Greece that was centered at Mycenae.

"mystery" religions The cults of Isis, Mithra, and Osiris, which promised salvation to those initiated into the secret or "mystery" of their rites. These cults competed with Christianity in the Roman Empire.

nationalism The belief that one is part of a nation, defined as a community with its own language, traditions, customs, and history that distinguish it from other nations and make it the primary focus of a person's loyalty and sense of identity.

natural selection The theory originating with Darwin that organisms evolve through a struggle for existence in which those that have a marginal advantage live long enough to propagate their kind.

naturalism The attempt to portray nature and human life without sentimentality.

Nazis The German Nationalist Socialist Party.

Neolithic (NEE-o-lith-ick) **Revolution** The shift beginning 10,000 years ago from hunter-gatherer societies to settled communities of farmers and artisans. Also called the Age of Agriculture, it witnessed the invention of farming, the domestication of plants and animals, and the development of technologies such as pottery and weaving. The earliest Neolithic societies appeared in the Near East about 8000 B.C.E. "Neolithic" comes from the Greek words for "new stone."

Neoplatonism (KNEE-o-play-ton-ism) A religious philosophy that tried to combine mysticism with classical and rationalist speculation. Its chief formulator was Plotinus (205–270 C.E.).

New Economic Policy (NEP) A limited revival of capitalism, especially in light industry and agriculture, introduced by Lenin in 1921 to repair the damage inflicted on the Russian economy by the Civil War and war communism.

New Imperialism The extension in the late nineteenth and early twentieth centuries of Western political and economic dominance to Asia, the Middle East, and Africa.

nomes Regions or provinces of ancient Egypt governed by officials called *nomarchs*.

oikos (OI-cos) The Greek household, always headed by a male.

Old Believers Those members of the Russian Orthodox Church who refused to accept the reforms of the seventeenth century regarding church texts and ritual.

Old Regime Term applied to the pattern of social, political, and economic relationships and institutions that existed in Europe before the French Revolution.

optimates (OP-tee-ma-tes) Meaning "the best men." Roman politicians who supported the traditional role of the Senate.

orthodox Meaning "holding the right opinions." Applied to the doctrines of the Catholic Church.

Ottoman Empire The imperial Turkish state centered in Constantinople that ruled large parts of the Balkans, North Africa, and the Middle East until 1918.

Paleolithic (PAY-lee-o-lith-ick) **Age, The** The earliest period when stone tools were used, from about 1,000,000 to 10,000 B.C.E. From the Greek meaning "old stone."

Panhellenic (PAN-hell-en-ick) ("all-Greek") The sense of cultural identity that all Greeks felt in common with each other.

Pan-Slavism The movement to create a nation or federation that would embrace all the Slavic peoples of Eastern Europe.

papal infallibility The doctrine that the pope is infallible when pronouncing officially in his capacity as head of the church on matters of faith and morals, enumerated by the First Vatican Council in 1870.

Papal States Territory in central Italy ruled by the pope until 1870.

parlements (par-luh-MAHNS) French regional courts dominated by hereditary nobility. The most important was the *Parlement* of Paris, which claimed the right to register royal decrees before they could become law.

parliamentary monarchy The form of limited or constitutional monarchy set up in Britain after the Glorious Revolution of 1689 in which the monarch was subject to the law and ruled by the consent of parliament.

patricians (PA-tri-she-ans) The hereditary upper class of early Republican Rome.

Peloponnesian (PELL-o-po-knees-ee-an) **Wars** The protracted struggle between Athens and Sparta to dominate Greece between 465 and Athens's final defeat in 404 B.C.E.

Peloponnesus (PELL-o-po-knee-sus) The southern peninsula of Greece where Sparta was located.

peninsulares (pen-in-SUE-la-rez) Persons born in Spain who settled in the Spanish colonies.

perestroika (pare-ess-TROY-ka) Meaning "restructuring." The attempt in the 1980s to reform the Soviet government and economy.

petite bourgeoisie (peh-TEET BOOSH-schwa-zee) The lower middle class.

pharaoh (FAY-row) The god-kings of ancient Egypt. The term originally meant "great house" or palace.

Pharisees (FAIR-i-sees) The group that was most strict in its adherence to Jewish law.

philosophes (fee-lou-SOPHS) The eighteenth-century writers and critics who forged the new attitudes favorable to change. They sought to apply reason and common sense to the institutions and societies of their day.

Phoenicians (FA-nee-shi-ans) The ancient inhabitants of modern Lebanon. A trading people, they established colonies throughout the Mediterranean.

physiocrats Eighteenth-century French thinkers who attacked the mercantilist regulation of the economy, advocated a limited economic role for government, and believed that all economic production depended on sound agriculture.

plantation economy The economic system stretching between Chesapeake Bay and Brazil that produced crops, especially sugar, cotton, and tobacco, using slave labor on large estates.

Platonism Philosophy of Plato that posits preexistent Ideal Forms of which all earthly things are imperfect models.

plebeians (PLEB-bee-ans) The hereditary lower class of early Republican Rome.

plenitude of power The teaching that the popes have power over all other bishops of the church.

pogroms (PO-grohms) Organized riots against Jews in the Russian Empire.

polis (PO-lis) (plural, *poleis*) The basic Greek political unit. Usually, but incompletely, translated as "city-state," the Greeks thought of the *polis* as a community of citizens theoretically descended from a common ancestor.

politique Ruler or person in a position of power who puts the success and well-being of his or her state above all else.

polygyny (po-LIJ-eh-nee) The practice of having two or more wives or concubines at the same time.

polytheism (PAH-lee-thee-ism) The worship of many gods.

pontifex maximus (PON-ti-feks MAK-suh-muss) Meaning "supreme priest." The chief priest of ancient Rome. The title was later assumed by the popes.

Popular Front A government of all left-wing parties that took power in France in 1936 to enact social and economic reforms.

populares (PO-pew-lar-es) Roman politicians who sought to pursue a political career based on the support of the people rather than just the aristocracy.

positivism The philosophy of Auguste Comte that science is the final, or positive, stage of human intellectual development because it involves exact descriptions of phenomena, without recourse to unobservable operative principles, such as gods or spirits.

postimpressionism A term used to describe European painting that followed impressionism; the term actually applies to several styles of art all of which to some extent derived from impression or stood in reaction to impressionism.

Pragmatic Sanction The legal basis negotiated by the Emperor Charles VI (r. 1711–1740) for the Habsburg succession through his daughter Maria Theresa (r. 1740–1780).

predestination The doctrine that God had foreordained all souls to salvation (the "elect") or damnation. It was especially associated with Calvinism.

presbyter (PRESS-bi-ter) Meaning "elder." A person who directed the affairs of early Christian congregations.

Presbyterians Scottish Calvinists and English Protestants who advocated a national church composed of semiautonomous congregations governed by "presbyteries."

proconsulship (PRO-con-sul-ship) In Republican Rome, the extension of a consul's imperium beyond the end of his term of office to allow him to continue to command an army in the field.

protectorate (pro-TEC-tor-ate) A non-Western territory administered by a Western nation without formal conquest or annexation, usually a de facto colony.

Protestant Ethic The theory propounded by Max Weber in 1904 that the religious confidence and self-disciplined activism that were supposedly associated with Protestantism produced an ethic that stimulated the spirit of emergent capitalism.

Ptolemaic (tow-LEM-a-ick) **System** The pre-Copernican explanation of the universe, with the earth at the center of the universe, originated in the ancient world.

Punic (PEW-nick) **Wars** Three wars between Rome and Carthage for dominance of the western Mediterranean that were fought from 264 B.C.E. to 146 B.C.E.

Puritans English Protestants who sought to "purify" the Church of England of any vestiges of Catholicism.

Qur'an (kuh-RAN) Meaning "a reciting." The Islamic bible, which Muslims believe God revealed to the prophet Muhammad.

racism The pseudoscientific theory that biological features of race determine human character and worth.

realism The style of art and literature that seeks to depict the physical world and human life with scientific objectivity and detached observation.

Reformation The sixteenth-century religious movement that sought to reform the Roman Catholic Church and led to the establishment of Protestantism.

regular clergy Monks and nuns who belong to religious orders.

Reichstag (RIKES-stahg) The German parliament, which existed in various forms, until 1945.

Reign of Terror The period between the summer of 1793 and the end of July 1794 when the French revolutionary state used extensive executions and violence to defend the Revolution and suppress its alleged internal enemies.

relativity The scientific theory associated with Einstein that time and space exist not separately but as a combined continuum whose measurement depends as much on the observer as on the entities that are being measured.

Renaissance The revival of ancient learning and the supplanting of traditional religious beliefs by new secular and scientific values that began in Italy in the fourteenth and fifteenth centuries.

reparations The requirement incorporated into the Versailles Treaty that Germany should pay for the cost of World War I.

revisionism The advocacy among nineteenth-century German socialists of achieving a humane socialist society through the evolution of democratic institutions, not revolution.

robot (ROW-boht) The amount of labor landowners demanded from peasants in the Habsburg Monarchy before 1848.

Romanitas (row-MAN-ee-tas) Meaning "Roman-ness." The spread of the Roman way of life and the sense of identifying with Rome across the Roman Empire.

romanticism A reaction in early-nineteenth-century literature, philosophy, and religion against what many considered the excessive rationality and scientific narrowness of the Enlightenment.

SA The Nazi parliamentary forces, or storm troopers.

sans-culottes (SAHN coo-LOTS) Meaning "without knee-breeches." The lower-middle classes and artisans of Paris during the French Revolution.

Schlieffen (SHLEE-fun) **Plan** Germany's plan for achieving a quick victory in the West at the outbreak of World War I by invading France through Belgium and Luxembourg.

Scholasticism Method of study based on logic and dialectic that dominated the medieval schools. It assumed that truth already existed; students had only to organize, elucidate, and defend knowledge learned from authoritative texts, especially those of Aristotle and the Church Fathers.

scientific induction Scientific method in which generalizations are derived from data gained from empirical observations.

scientific revolution The sweeping change in the scientific view of the universe that occurred in the sixteenth and seventeenth centuries. The new scientific concepts and the method of their construction became the standard for assessing the validity of knowledge in the West.

scutage Monetary payments by a vassal to a lord in place of the required military service.

second industrial revolution The emergence of new industries and the spread of industrialization from Britain to other countries, especially Germany and the United States, in the second half of the nineteenth century.

secular clergy Parish clergy who did not belong to a religious order.

seigneur (sane-YOUR) A noble French landlord.

Sejm (SHEM) The legislative assembly of the Polish nobility.

serfs Peasants tied to the land they tilled.

Shi'a (SHE-ah) The minority of Muslims who trace their beliefs from the caliph Ali who was assassinated in 661 C.E.

Sinn Fein (SHIN FAHN) Meaning "ourselves alone." An Irish political movement founded in 1905 that advocated complete political separation from Britain.

Social Darwinism The application of Darwin's concept of "the survival of the fittest" to explain evolution in nature to human social relationships.

Sophists (SO-fists) Professional teachers who emerged in Greece in the mid–fifth century B.C.E. who were paid to teach techniques of rhetoric, dialectic, and argumentation.

soviets Workers and soldiers councils formed in Russia during the Revolution.

spheres of influence A region, city, or territory where a non-Western nation exercised informal administrative influence through economic, diplomatic, or military advisors.

spinning jenny A machine invented in England by James Hargreaves around 1765 to mass-produce thread.

SS The chief security units of the Nazi state.

Stoics (STOW-icks) A philosophical school founded by Zeno of Citium (335–263 B.C.E.) that taught that humans could only be happy with natural law. Human misery was caused by passion, which was a disease of the soul. The wise sought *apatheia*, freedom from passion.

studia humanitatis (STEW-dee-a hew-MAHN-ee tah-tis) During the Renaissance, a liberal arts program of study that embraced grammar, rhetoric, poetry, history, philosophy, and politics.

Sturm und Drang (SHTURM und DRAHNG) Meaning "storm and stress." A movement in German romantic literature and philosophy that emphasized feeling and emotion.

suffragettes British women who lobbied and agitated for the right to vote in the early twentieth century.

Sunna (SOON-ah) Meaning "tradition." The dominant Islamic group.

Sunnis Those who follow the "tradition" (sunna) of the Prophet Muhammad. They are the dominant movement within Islam to which the vast majority of Muslims adhere.

symposium (SIM-po-see-um) The carefully organized drinking party that was the center of Greek aristocratic social life. It featured games, songs, poetry, and even philosophical disputation.

syncretism (SIN-cret-ism) The intermingling of different religions to form an amalgam that contained elements from each.

syndicalism French labor movement that sought to improve workers' conditions through direct action, especially general strikes.

Table of Ranks An official hierarchy established by Peter the Great in imperial Russia that equated a person's social position and privileges with his rank in the state bureaucracy or army.

tabula rasa (tah-BOO-lah RAH-sah) Meaning a "blank page." The philosophical belief associated with John Locke that human beings enter the world with totally unformed characters that are completely shaped by experience.

taille (TIE) The direct tax on the French peasantry.

ten lost tribes The Israelites who were scattered and lost to history when the northern kingdom of Israel fell to the Assyrians in 722 B.C.E.

tertiaries (TER-she-air-ees) Laypeople affiliated with the monastic life who took vows of poverty, chastity, and obedience but remained in the world.

tetrarchy (TET-rar-key) Diocletian's (r. 306–337 C.E.) system for ruling the Roman Empire by four men with power divided territorially.

Thermidorian Reaction The reaction against the radicalism of the French Revolution that began in July 1794. Associated with the end of terror and establishment of the Directory.

thesis, antithesis, and synthesis G. W. F. Hegel's (HAY-gle) (1770–1831) concept of how ideas develop. The *thesis* is a dominant set of ideas. It is challenged by a set of conflicting ideas, the *antithesis*. From the clash of these ideas, a new pattern of thought, the *synthesis*, emerges and eventually becomes the new thesis.

Third Estate The branch of the French Estates General representing all of the kingdom outside the nobility and the clergy.

Third Reich (RIKE) Hitler's regime in Germany, which lasted from 1933 to 1945.

Thirty-Nine Articles (1563) The official statement of the beliefs of the Church of England. They established a moderate form of Protestantism.

three-field system A medieval innovation that increased the amount of land under cultivation by leaving only one third fallow in a given year.

transportation The British policy from the late eighteenth to the mid–nineteenth centuries of shipping persons convicted of the most serious offenses to Australia as an alternative to capital punishment.

transubstantiation The doctrine that the entire substances of the bread and wine are changed in the Eucharist into the body and blood of Christ.

tribunes (TRIB-unes) Roman officials who had to be plebeians and were elected by the plebeian assembly to protect plebeians from the arbitrary power of the magistrates.

ulema (oo-LEE-mah) Meaning "persons with correct knowledge." The Islamic scholarly elite who served a social function similar to the Christian clergy.

Upper Egypt The part of Egypt that runs from the delta to the Sudanese border.

utilitarianism The theory associated with Jeremy Bentham (1748–1832) that the principle of utility, defined as the greatest good for the greatest number of people, should be applied to government, the economy, and the judicial system.

utopian socialism Early-nineteenth-century theories that sought to replace the existing capitalist structure and values with visionary solutions or ideal communities.

vassal A person granted an estate or cash payments in return for accepting the obligation to render services to a lord.

vernacular The everyday language spoken by the people as opposed to Latin.

vingtième (VEN-tee-em) Meaning "one twentieth." A tax on income in France before the Revolution.

Vulgate The Latin translation of the Bible by Jerome (348–420 C.E.) that became the standard bible used by the Catholic Church.

Waldensians (wahl-DEN-see-ens) Medieval heretics who advocated biblical simplicity in reaction to the worldliness of the church.

war communism The economic policy adopted by the Bolsheviks during the Russian Civil War to seize the banks, heavy industry, railroads, and grain.

war guilt clause Clause 231 of the Versailles Treaty, which assigned responsibility for World War I solely to Germany.

water frame A water-powered device invented by Richard Arkwright to produce a more durable cotton fabric. It led to the shift in the production of cotton textiles from households to factories.

Weimar (Why-mar) **Republic** The German democratic regime that existed between the end of World War I and Hitler's coming to power in 1933.

White Russians Those Russians who opposed the Bolsheviks (the "Reds") in the Russian Civil War of 1918–1921.

zemstvos (ZEMPST-vohs) Local governments set up in the Russian Empire in 1864.

Zionism The movement to create a Jewish state in Palestine (the Biblical Zion).

Zollverein (TZOL-fuh-rine) A free-trade union established among the major German states in 1834.

INDEX

Italic page numbers refer to illustrations

A

Aachen, 189, *189,* 191, 195
Abbasids, 182
Abbey of Cluny, *205*
Abelard, Peter, 244–245, 246–247
Abolition Society, 657
Abortion
  Cathars and, 214
  in Roman Empire, 141
  19th century, 701
  20th century, 967
Abraham, 27, 28, 30
Absolutism (Enlightenment), 517–527
Absolutism (Hobbes), *415,* 415–416
Abu Bakr, *170,* 182
Abu Hamid Al-Ghazali, 181
Abu Simbel, 18
Academy of Experiments, 418
Academy of Plato, 83, 91–92
Achaemenid empire, *24*
Achilles, 38
Acrocorinth, 39
Acropolis, 39, *67,* *76,* *77,* *82*
Act of Settlement (1701), 380
Act of Succession (1534), 332
Act of Union (1707), 380
Act of Union (1798), 619
Actium, Battle of, 127, 130, *131*
Acton, Lord, 595
Acts of Supremacy (1534, 1559), 303, 332, 357
Acts of Uniformity (1549, 1552, 1559), 332, 333, 357
Adages (Erasmus), 302
Adam, 245, 247, *247*
Addison, Joseph, 494, 499
Address to the Christian Nobility of the German Nation (Luther), 315, 320
Aden, 922
Admonition to Peace, An (Luther), 322
Adrian IV, Pope, 221
Adrianople, Battle of, 156, 172
Adrianople, Treaty of, 608
Advancement of Learning, The (Bacon), 412
Aegean area, map of in the Bronze Age, *37*
Aegina, 54, 63
Aegospotami, Battle of, 74
Aemilius Lepidus, 125, 126
Aeneid (Vergil), 134, *134*
Aeschylus, 70, 76
Afghanistan
  radical Islamism and, 941–942
  Soviet invasion of, 917, 935–936
Africa
  decolonization, *902,* 922–924
  imperialism and, 768–776, *769*
  partition of, *770*
  slavery, 303, 463, 469–472, *470,* 659–660
  World War II, 880
Africa (Petrarch), 285
African Colonization Society, 659
Africanus (Publius Cornelius Scipio), 108, 285
Afrikaners, 775
Afterlife, Egyptian, 20–21, *21*
Agadir crisis, 804–805
Against the Robbing and Murdering Peasants (Luther), 322
Agamemnon, 38
Agamemnon (Aeschylus), 70
Agape, 147
Agesilaus, 75
Agon, 39
Agora, 40, 47, *77,* 92
Agrarian aristocracy, 98
Agricola, Rudolf, 302
Agriculture
  in the Americas, 309
  Athenian, 47
  Black Death and, 258, 260, 262
  Carolingian manor, 198–199
  collectivization, *833,* 841–843, *842*
  Egyptian, 4–5
  enclosures replace open fields, 444–445
  exchange between Americas and Europe, 489–491
  gardens, 286
  Greek, ancient, 47, 49–50
  Greek, classical, 72
  latifundia, 113, 115, 116
  manors and serfdom in the Middle Ages, 234–236
  moldboard plow, 199
  Neolithic Age, 3–4
  Paleolithic Age, 3
  Revolution, 443–445
  Roman, 113, 115, 116–117, 139, 141
  in the 1920s, 841–842
  18th century, 437–439, 443–445
  three-field system, 199, 235
Agrippa, 126, 127, *131,* 143
Agrippina, 142
Ahasuerus, King, *523*
Ahhiyawa, 22
Ahmad, Muhammad, 771
Ahmose, 18
Ahriman, 26
Ahura Mazda, 25, 26
Aix-la-Chapelle, Treaty of (1668), 384
Aix-la-Chapelle, Treaty of (1748), 479
Akhenaten, 20
Akkad, 7
Akkadians/Akkade, 6
Al-Afghani Jamal al-din, 734
Al Qaeda, 941, 942, 943
Al-Razi, 183
Alaric, 172
Alba, Duke of, 355–356, 360
Albanians, collapse of Yugoslavia and civil war, 937
Albañoz (ship), 656
Alberti, Leon Battista, 289
Albigensians (Cathars), 214
Albrecht of Mainz, 319
Albrecht of Wallenstein, 367, 368
Alcaeus, 53, *53*
Alcibiades, 74, 81
Alciun of York, 191–192
Aleksei, King of Russia, 397
Aleksei, son of Peter the Great, 398, 399
Alemaeonids, 48
Alemanni, 149, 156
Alencon, Duke of, 356
Alexander I, King of Yugoslavia, 862–863
Alexander I, Tsar of Russia, 566, 571, 574, 576, 606, 607, 614, 615
Alexander II, Pope, 206
Alexander II, Tsar of Russia, 678, 680–682, *682*
Alexander III, Pope, 217, 221
Alexander III, Tsar of Russia, 684, 714, 715
Alexander Nevsky, 853
Alexander the Great (Alexander III), 7, 15, 19, 87, 88, 90, 93, 166, *167,* 169, 794, *794*
  campaigns (map) of, *89*
  successors, 90–91
Alexander V, Pope, 276
Alexander VI, Pope, 295–297
Alexandria, 93, 126, 127
Alexandria Eschate, 90
Alexius I Comnenus, 178, 207
Alfonso of Sicily, Duke, 295
Alfred the Great, 216
Algarotti, Francesco, 421
Algeria, French in, 618, *671,* 768, 922–924
Algiers, 617, *617*
Ali, *170*
Ali, caliph, 179
Alimenta, 139
Allodial, 198
Almagest (Ptolemy), 409
Alsace, 669, 674
Alsace-Lorraine, 799, 827
Alvarado, Pedro de, *307*
Amasis painter, *76*
Ambrose, Bishop of Milan, 159
American Colonization Society, 659
American Holt Company, *816*
American Revolution
  crisis and independence, 482–483
  events in England, 484–486
  impact of, 486–487
  key events/dates, 485
  political ideas of Americans, 483–484
  resistance to British taxation, 481–482, *483*
Americanization of Europe, 961–962
Americas
  1763 map of, 482
  agriculture and animals, 309
  Catholic church in Spanish, 307–308
  discovery of, 303–305
  diseases introduced, 305, 307, 469, *489,* 489–490
  economy of exploitation, 308–309
  European expansion, 796
  French-British rivalry, 465
  mining, 308–309, *469*
  slavery in, 309, 463, 469–473, *470,* 655
  Spanish colonial system, 465–469
  Spanish exploration of, 305–307
Amiens, Treaty of (1802), 564
Ammianus Marcellinus, 157
Amorites, 7, 18
Amphipolis, 74, 86
Amsterdam, 373, *373*
Amun, 20
Amunemhet I, 18
Amunhotep IV, 20
Anabaptists, 326–327, 330, 346
Anacreon of Teos, 53
Anarchism, 641
Anatolia, 796, 824
Anatomy Lesson of Dr. Tulp, The (Tulp), *407*
Anaxagoras of Clazomenae, 77
Andean civilization, *305,* 305–307
Androcles and the Lion (Shaw), 738
Andromeda, 80
Andropov, Yuri, 927
Angevin (Anjouan) (English-French) Empire, 216
Angilbert, 191
Angles, 172
Anglicanism/Anglican Church, 357, 374, 378, 380, 732
Anglo-Russian Convention (1907), 778
Angola, 920
Animal sacrifice, 10
Animals, domestication of, 3, 979
Animals as energy source, 979
Anna, Empress of Russia, 437, 524
Annals of Agriculture (Young), 444
Annates, 211, 272
Anne, Queen of England, 380
Anne of Bohemia, 274
Anne of Britanny, 296
Anne of Cleves, 332
Anne of Saxony, 354
Anschluss, 870
Anthony, St., *317*
Anthony, Susan B., 695
Anthony of Egypt, 184
Anthropology, 790
Anti-Comintern Pact, 869
Anti-Corn Law League, 639, 646
Anti-Semitism, 697, *709,* 710, 848–849, 854–856, *855,* 886–891, 893
  Dreyfus affair, 675–676, *676,* 677, 710, 747, 893
  holocaust, *886,* 886–887, *887,* 890–891, *891*
Antigonus I, 90
Antioch, 148, 208
Antiochus III, 108–109
Antislavery societies, 655–657
Antisthenes, 81–82
Antitrinitarians, 327
Antoninus Pius, 136
Antony, Mark, 112, 124, 126–127, *131,* 133
Apartheid, 776
Aphrodite, 50
Apollo, 24, 50, 51, 52, *86,* 135
Apology (1580), 356
Apostolic Succession, 147
Apoxyomenos, 80
Appeasement policy, 868
Appert, Nicholas, 567, *567*
Apple Computer Corporation, 971
Aquinas, Thomas, 215, 221, 243, 335, 337, 339, 341, 415, 734
Ara Pacis (Altar of Peace), *131,* 135
Arab-Israeli conflict, 910–911
Arab nationalism, 940
Arabian Nights, The, 183, 588
Aragon, 275
Arameans, 22
Arawak, 305
Arcesilaus, 92
Arch of Constantine, *154*
Arch of Titus, *138*
Archimedes, *93,* 94
Architecture
  Assyrians, *23*
  Baroque, 346, *347*

Architecture *(cont.)*
Byzantine, *176*
Egyptian pyramids, 17, *17*
French, 225
Gothic, 224–225, *225*, 584, *584*
Greek, classical, *66, 69*, 76, *77*, 80, *81, 82*
Greek, Hellenistic, *61, 86, 91*, 93
Mesopotamian, 8
Minoan, *36*
Mycenaean, 35–36, *36*
pyramids, 7, *17*
Roman, *97, 129, 131*, 134–135, 143, *154, 189*
Romanesque, 224–225, *225*
20th century, *972*
Versailles, *383*, 431
Archons/archonship, 46, 47, 65, 76
Areopagus, 46, 63, *77*
Ares, 50*Arete*, 38–39
Arginusae, Battle of, 72
Argos, 63, 75, 86
Arianism, 159, 173
Aristagoras, 54
Aristarchus of Samos, 94
Aristobulus, 93
Aristocracy. *See also* Social classes/society
in Athens, 46
French Revolution and, 530–531
Greek, archaic, 49–50
Homeric society, 38
medieval nobles, 196, 198, 228–232
resurgence, 437
Roman patricians, 101, 121
18th century, 435–437, *436*, 455, 457
urban, 455
Aristocratic resurgence, 437
Aristogeiton, *48*
Aristophanes, 70, 76, 78–79
Aristotle, 71, 84, 86, 91, 164, 244, 409, 415, 655
Constitution of the Athenians, 84
polis and, 39, 84
views of, 84, 86, 94, 244
Arius of Alexandria, 159
Arkwright, Richard, 451
Arminius, 131
Arms and the Man (Shaw), 738
Arndt, Ernest Moritz, 572–573
Arnold, Matthew, 729
Arouet, Francois Marie. *See* Voltaire
Arras, Union of, 356
Ars Amatoria (Ovid), 134
Art/artisans, *452*, 457–458
abstractism, 964–965
Akkadian, 6
Assyrian, *23*
Baroque, 346, *347, 407*, 428–429, 431
Byzantine, *177, 179, 186*
Carolingian, *193*
cave paintings, 3
cubism, *741*, 741–742
Dutch, *407*
Dwelling Act (1875), 686
Egyptian, 19, *20*, 20–21, *21*
Etruscan, *99*
German, Weimar Republic, 853
Greek, ancient, *33*, 34, *35*
Greek, classical, *65, 66, 69, 76*, 76–77
Greek, Hellenistic, *61, 91*, 93, *112*
Greek pottery, 34, *49, 51, 53, 57*, *76*
history painting, *518, 520*
impressionism, *739*, 739–740
Islamic, *181*
Mesopotamian, *1, 8, 10*
Middle Ages, *211, 218, 224, 227*, *231, 234, 260, 277*
minimalist movement, 965, *966*
modernism, *739*, 739–742, *740*, *741*
Mycenaean, 35–36
neoclassicism, 514, *514*, 516–517
Neolithic Age, *4*
Paleolithic Age, 3
Persian, *25*, 26–27
post-impressionism, *740*, 740–741
Reformation, *313, 317, 318, 319*, *321, 331*
religious, *170, 271, 313*
religious wars, *345, 355, 367*
Renaissance, *281, 284, 286*, 289, 291, *292*, 292–293, *300*
Roman, *99, 100, 107, 111, 112*, *116, 122, 129, 131*, 134–135, *135, 136, 138*, 142–143, *146*, *151, 154, 160, 167*
romanticism, 582–584, *583*
Scientific Revolution, *407, 411*, *426*
social realism, 964–965
Spartan, 35
18th century, *433, 440*, 441, *452*, *457*, 457–458, *459*
19th century, *625*, 739–742
Artaxerxes II, 74
Artemis, 50
Artemisium, 56, 58, 80, *83*
Artevelde, Jacob van, 265
Articles of Confederation, 486
Artisan Dwelling Act (1875), 686
Artois, Count of, 546, *605*, 606, 617
Aryans, 166, 745
Asia, imperialism in, 776–782, *781*
Asia Minor, 36, 74
Aspasia, 70
Asquith, Herbert, 707, 708, 712
Assembly of Notables, 531–532, 533
Assembly of the Clergy, 532
Assignats, 545, *545*
Assur, 22
Assyria/Assyrians, 2, 7, 15, 22–23, 166–167, 168
Aston, Louise, 633
Astrology
Babylonian, 23, 111
Mesopotamian, 10, *10*
Astronomy
Brahe, 410
Copernicus, 94, 408–410, *409*, 425
Delambre, 544
Galileo, *410*, 410–411, 421, 424, 425
Greek, Hellenistic, 94
Kepler, 410
Newton, *411*, 411–412
Ptoelmaic system, 409
women, work of, 421
Atahualpa, 307
Ataraxia, 92
Ataturk, 824, *824*
Aten, 20
Athanasius, 159, 184
Athena, 50, 57, *65, 82, 91*
Athenian Constitution (Aristotle), 84
Athens,
Cimon, 63
Clisthenes and development of democracy, 48–49
Delian League, 62–63
fall of, 74
government, 46–47
invasion by Philip II, 87
Ionian rebellion and, 54
key events/dates, 49, 65
map of, *77*
Peloponnesian War, First, 63–64
Peloponnesian War, Great, 73–74, 78
Pisistratus the tyrant, 47
Second Athenian Confederation, 75
Solon, reforms of, 47
Sparta and, 34, 48, 63, 64, 75
Thirty Tyrants rule, 74
tyrannies, 43–44
women, 67, 70–71
Athletics, Greek, 50, 51
Atlantic Charter, *876*, 897
Atlantic economy, 463, 470–478
Atomic bomb, *865*, 884–885
Atomists, 77, 92
Attalus, King, 118
Attic tragedy, 76
Attica, 46, *46*, 73
Attila the Hun, 172
Attlee, Clement, 900, 951
Atum (Re), sun god, 20
Auburn Prison/system, 637
Auclert, Hubertine, 707
Auerstädt, Battle of (1806), 566
Augsburg
Diet of (1530), 329, 350
League of (1686), 388, 390
peace of (1555), 321, 330, 346, 356, 364, 367, 368, 370
Augsburg Confession, 329
Augustine, St. (Bishop of Hippo), 161, 233, 244, 285, 384, 425
Order of the Hermits of, 316
Augustinus (Jansen), 384, 388
Augustulus, Romulus, 172
Augustus (Octavius), 118, 126–127, *129*, 134
Age of Augustus, 133–135
Augustan principate, 130–132
Aurelian, 152
Aurelius, Marcus, 136, *136*, 139, 149
Ausculta fili, 269
Ausgleich, *676*, 678
Austerlitz, Battle of (1805), 566, 570
Austria. *See also* Habsburg empire
alliances with England and Russia against France, 566
aristocracy of 18th century, 435
Congress of Vienna (1815), 574–577, *575, 577*, 594
Dual Alliance, 800
Hitler's annexation of, 850, 869–870
Joseph II, 519, 520–524
key events/dates, 394
Napoleon and, 562, 563, 566, 570–571
peasant rebellion, 438, 521–522
Piedmont war with, 650, 652, 665, 666
Quadruple Alliance, 574, 576
in the 1920s, 862
serfs in, 437
Three Emperors' League (1873), 799–800
Triple Alliance, 800–801
World War I and, 806–809, 822
Austria-Hungary
breakup of, 829
formation of, 678, 679
Triple Alliance, 800–801
World War I, *820*
Austrian Succession, war of (1740-1748), 478–479, 521
Austro-Prussian War (1866), 671–672, *672*
Autocracy, 153–154
Automobile, invention of, 693, *694*, 981, *981*
Avars, 177, 189
Averröes (ibn-Rushd), 183
Avesta, 26
Avicenna (ibn-Sina), 183, *262*
Avignon papacy, 272–273
Axis Europe, *877, 882*
Ayacucho, Battle of (1824), 613
Azerbaijan, 933
Aztecs, 305, 306, *307*, 796

B

Babeuf, Gracchus, 558
Babington, Anthony, 362
Babington plot, 362
Babylonia/Babylonians, 2, 7, 11–13, 28, 167
neo-, 14, 23
Babylonian Captivity, 28, 274
Babylonian Captivity of the Church, The (Luther), 320
Babylonian Story of the Flood, 12–13, 29
Bacchus, 111
Bacon, Francis, 376, 412–414, *413*, 425
Baden, Max of, 822
Badoglio, Pietro, 880
Baghdad, 182
Bailly, Jean-Sylvain, *535*
Bakewell, Robert, 444
Baldwin, Stanley, 836
Baldwin of Bouillon, 208
Balfour, Arthur, 909
Balfour Declaration (1917), 825, 909
Balkans. *See also* World War I
Congress of Berlin, 800
map of, *805, 809*
war in, 664, 799–800, 805
Ball, John, 265
Ballot Act (1872), 684
Balzac, Honoré de, 737
Banalities, 235, 437
Bands of Jesus, 556
Bangladesh, 922
Banks, Joseph, 787
Baptist Missionary Society, 784
Bar at the Folies-Bergère, A (Manet), *739*, 740
Barbarian invasions, Roman Empire and, 149, 155–156, 172
Bardi, 284
Barnabites, 333
Barnum, P.T., 791
Baroque architecture/art, 346, *347*, *407*, 428–429, 431
Barth, Karl, 967
Basel, Council of (1431–1449), 274, 276, 324
Basel, treaties of (1795), 558
Basil the Great, 184
Basilica of the Sacred Heart, 697
Bastille, fall of, *529*, 534–535
Bathing, 456
Batista, Flugencio, 915
Battle of Cawnpore, *761*
Battle of Omdurman, 771–772, *773*
Battle of the Nations, 574
Battleship Potemkin, The, 853
Batu Khan, 279
Bavaria/Bavarians, 203, 364
Bay of Sluys, 265
Bayeaux Tapestry, 231
BBC, 895
Beaulieu, peace of (1576), 350
Beauvoir, Simone de, 953, *953*, 956
Beaverbrook, lord, 895
Bebel, August, 713, 714

Beccaria, Cesare, 505
Becket, Thomas à, 217, *218*, 219
Becquerel, Henri, 736
Beghards, 214
Beguines, 214, 215, 233
Behaim, Martin, 305, *306*
Behaim, Paul, *337*
Being and Nothingness (Sartre), 959
Being and Time (Heidegger), 959
Belgian Congo, 774–775, 920
Belgium
  independence for, 618–619
  World War I and, 811, 812, *812*
  World War II, 875
Bell, The, 682
Bell, Vanessa, 738
Belorussian Jews, 458, 469
Belsen, 888–889
Ben Bella, Mohammed, 923
Ben-Gurion, David, 910
Benedetti, Vincent, 673
Benedict of Nursia, 184, 185, 204
Benedict XI, Pope, 272
Benedict XII, Pope, 272–273
Benedict XVI, Pope (Joseph Ratzinger), 968, 969
Benedictines, 184, 185, 233
  Cluny reform movement, 204–206, 232
Benefices, 188, 196, 198, 267, 315
Benes, Edvard, 908
Benezet, Anthony, 656
Bentham, Jeremy, 639
Berchtold, Leopold von, 806
Berengar of Friuli, 203
Berlin
  Blockade, 883, *907*
  Congress of (1878), 800
  Decrees, 566
  18th century, 453
  Wall, 914–915, 930, *932*
  World War II, 883
Berlin Academy of Science, 418
Berlin Conference (1884), 775
Berlin Missionary Society, 785
Bernadotte, French marshal, 571
Bernard, Claude, 737
Bernard of Chartres, 242
Bernard of Clairvaux, 208
Bernart de Ventadorn, 217
Bernini, Gian Lorenzo, 346, 431, *431*
Bernstein, Eduard, 714, 718, *719*
Berri, Duke of, 606
Bessarabia, 874
Bessemer, Henry, 692–693
Bessus, 90
Bethlen, Stephen, 862
Bethmann-Hollweg, Theobald von, 807, 811
Beukelsz, Jan, 327
Beveridge, William B., 951
Beyle, Henri, 579
Beyond Good and Evil (Nietzsche), 742
Beza, Theodore, 338, 348, 350, 351
Bible
  Coverdale, 332
  Great, 332
  Gutenberg, 301, *301*
  King James, 379
  printing, 254, 301, *301*
  Vulgate, 161, 289, 302
Bibliothèque orientale (Oriental Library), 502
Bicycles, 695, *695*
Biel, Gabriel, 316
Bill of Rights (England), 380
Bin Laden, Osama, 941
Birth control
  Cathars and, 214
  Reformation and, 339, 341
  Roman Empire, 141
  18th century, 442
  19th century, 633, 701, 703
Birth of Tragedy, The (Nietzsche), 742
Bishops College, 786
Bismarck, Otto von, 671–673, *672,* 732, *733,* 775, 799–801, *801,* *802,* 951
Black Death
  new conflicts and opportunities, 262
  preconditions and causes, 258
  remedies, 258
  social and economic effects from, 260–262
  spread of, *259*
Black Hand, 806
Black Legend, 307
Black Shirt March, 846
Blair, Tony, 943, 952, 954–955
Blanc, Louis, 641, 646
Blanqui, Auguste, 641
Blitzkrieg, 874
Bloch, Marc, 196, 235
Blood, Council of, 355
Bloody Sunday, 720, *721*
Bloomsbury Group, 738
Blücher, Marshal von, 576
Boccaccio, Giovanni, 258, 282, 287
Bodin, Jean, 297
Boeotia, 58, 63, 74
Boer War (1899-1902), 763, 803
Boers, 775
Boethius, 244
Bohemia, 274, 393
  peasant rebellions in, 438
  Thirty Years' War (1618-1648), 365–367
Boleyn, Anne, 303, 331, 332, 357
Bolívar, Simón, 613, *613*
Bologna, Concordat of, 296
Bologna, University of, 240–242
Bolsheviks/Bolshevism, 714–722, 817, 820–821, 827, 838, 839
Bonaventure, St., 215, 221, 337
Bondage of the Will, The (Luther), 291
Bonhoeffer, Dietrich, 966
Boniface VIII, Pope, 207, 267–271, *269,* 272, 330
Boniface (Wynfrith), St., 188, 189
Book of Chants, 179
Book of Common Prayer (Cranmer), 332, 333, 357, 377, 378
Book of Esther, *523*
Book of Sports, 375
Book of the Courtier (Castiglione), 287
Book of the Dead, 20, *21*
Book of Three Virtues, The (Christine de Pisan), 287, *288*
Borgia, Cesare, 295, 296, 297
Borgia, Lucrezia, 295
Boris III, King of Bulgaria, 863
Borodino, Battle of, 574
Bosnia
  collapse of Yugoslavia and civil war, 936–937
  crisis of 1908, 804
  in the 1920s, 862
Bosnia-Herzegovina, 862, 936
Bossuet, Jacques-Bénigne, 382, 386
Boston Massacre, 482
Botany, 788–789
Bothwell, Earl of, 362
Boucher, Francois, 514, 516
Boulanger, Georges, 675
Boulton, Matthew, 451
Bourbons, 348, 466–467, 562, 563, 570, 574–575, *605,* 605–606, 612
Bourgeois, 457
Bouvines, Battle of (1214), 218, 220
Boxer Rebellion, 780, *780,* 782
Boyars, 278, 398, 401
Bracciolini, Poggio, 289
Bradao, João, *300*
Brahe, Tycho, 410
Brandeburg-Prussia, *395*
Braque, Georges, *741,* 741–742
Brasidas, 74
Brazil
  independence for, 614
  slavery in, 470, *471,* 659
Bread (Yablonskaya), 964, *964*
Brest-Litovsk, Treaty of (1918), 821
Bretez, Louis, *447*
Brétigny-Calais, peace of (1360), 265
Breuer, Josef, 743
Breughel, Pieter the Elder, 231, *231*
Brezhnev, Leonid, 916–918, 926
Brezhnev Doctrine, 916, 930
Briand, Aristide, 850–851
Briconnet, Guillaume, 303
Brienne, étienne Charles Loménie de, 532
Bright, John, 684
Britain. *See also* England
  African colonies, 757, 773
  Battle of, 875–876
  British Emancipation Act, 619
  Chartism, 627, 629–630, *630*
  conflict between church and state, 732
  Crimean War (1853-1856), 662
  decolonization, 920–921
  Disraeli, Benjamin, 684, 686, *686,* 761, 768
  in Egypt, 768–773
  Fabianism and early welfare programs, 712–713
  general strike of 1929, 836
  Gladstone, 684, *686,* 686–687
  Great Depression in, 836, 838
  Great Reform Bill of 1832, 619–620, 760
  imperialism and, *754,* 756–757, 796
  Industrial Revolution in, 449
  Irish problem, 595, 687
  key events/dates, 687, 857
  Liverpool's ministry and unrest, 602, 605
  National Government, 836
  Peterloo Massacre and Six Acts, 605
  in the 1920s, 732, 836
  Second Reform Act (1867), 684
  19th century, 623, 630, 632
  Triple Entente (1890-1907), 801–804
  welfare state, 951–955
  World War I and, 804, 805, 811–817, *815, 817,* 824–829
  World War II and, 875–876, 895–896, *896*
British Conservative Party, 712, 952
British Labour Party, 712, 836, 952
British Settler Colonies, 757, 787
Broca, Paul, 790
Bronze Age, 4, 164, xxxv
  Crete and Greek, 34–35
Brookes (ship), *475*
Brothers of the Common Life, 301, 315
Bruni, Leonardo, 285, 289
Brüning, Heinrich, 851, 852
Brunswick, Duke of, 547
Brussels, Treaty of (1948), 909
Brussels, Union of, 356
Brutus, Marcus Junius, 123, *125,* 126, 328, 333
Bubonic plague. *See* Black Death
Bucer, Martin, 325, 333
BucKingham, Duke of, 374
Buddenbrooks (Mann), 738
Buddhist Scriptures, 254
Budé, Guillaume, 303
Buffum, David, 856
Bukharin, Nikolai, 840, 843, 844, 929
Bulgaria
  in the 1920s, 863
  World War I, 800, 829
Bulgars, 177
Bulge, Battle of (1945), 883
Bullinger, Heinrich, 325
Bülow, Bernhard von, 803
Bultmann, Rudolf, 967
Bundesrat, 672
Bunker Hill, Battle of, 483
Burckhardt, Jacob, 282, 285
Burgundians, 172, 187, 265, 298
Burials/funeral customs
  Egyptian pyramids, 17, *17*
  Etruscan, 98, *99*
  Mesopotamian, 9
  Paleolithic, 3
  Roman, *99*
  tholos tombs, 35
Burke, Edmund, 548–549, 550, 600
Burma, 879, 922
Burschenschaften, 601–602, *602*
Bush, George W., 942, 943
Bute, Earl of, 481, 484
Butler, Josephine, 750
Buxton, Thomas Fowell, 659
Byron, Lord, 581, 608, *609*
Byzantine Empire, 171
  art, *176, 179, 186*
  cities, 175–176
  eastern influence, 178
  Justinian, age of, 174–176
  law, 176
  map of, *175*
  periods of, 173–174
  religion, 177
  Roman Empire and, 154, 156

C

Cadets (Constitutional Democratic Party), 715, 720, 818
Caesar, Cornelia, 121
Caesar, Julia, 122
Caesar, Julius, 121–126, *122,* 133
Caesaropapism, 187
Cahiers de doléances, 534
Calais, 265, 357
Calas, Jean, 499
Calderón de la Barca, Pedro, 341
Calendar
  Julian, 122
  Mesopotamian, *9, 10*
Caligula (Gaius), 135
Caliphate, 179
Calixtus II, Pope, 207
Calonne, Charles Alexandre de, 531, 532
Calpernius Bibulus, M., 121
Calvin, John, 303, 327–329, *328,* 333, 335, 338, 346, 348, 350, 358
Calvinism, 327–330, 346, 372
  in France, 346, 348, 364
  Thirty Years' War (1618-1648), 364–368
Cambodia, 924
Cambrai, Battle of, *815*
Cambyses, 24–25, 54
Campania, 99
Campbell-Bannerman, Henry, 712
Campo Formio, Treaty of (1797), 562, 564

Campus Martius, 135
Camus, Albert, 959
Canaanites, 27
Candide (Voltaire), 498
Cannae, 108
Cannibals, 310
Canning, George, 607–608
Canon of Medicine (Avicenna), *262*
Canons Regular, 233
Canterbury Cathedral, *218,* 219
Canterbury Tales, The (Chaucer), 218, 219
Canute, 216
Cape of Good Hope, 305
Cape Town, 775
Capet, Hugh, 218, 220
Capetian dynasty, 218, 220, 262
Capital (Marx), 642, 958
Capital punishment, *275*
Capitularies, 191
Caprivi, Leo von, 801
Capuchins, 333
Caracalla, 143
Caravaggio, Michelangelo, 428–429
Carbonari, 665
Carey, William, 785
Carlos, Don, 353
Carlowitz, Treaty of (1699), 404
Carlsbad Decrees, 602, 603
Carlyle, Thomas, 590
Carneades, 92
Carnot, Lazare, 551
Carol II, King of Romania, 863
Carolingian minuscule, 192
Carolingians, 188
  art, *193*
  breakup of empire, 192–196
  Charlemagne, 171, 187, 189–192, *190, 193*
  key events/dates, 196
  manor life, 198–199
  marriage, 248
  religion, 188–189, 199
  Renaissance, 191–192
Carrhae, 122
Carter, Jimmy, 917
Carthage, 27, 111
  Rome and, 105–109
Carthusians, 233
Cartwright, Edmund, 451
Cartwright, John, 486, 605
Cartwright, Thomas, 360
Caryatids, *82*
Casa de Contratación (House of Trade), 466
Casement, Roger, 775
Cassian, John, 184
Cassiodorus, 244
Cassius, Longinus, Garius, 123, 126
Castellio, Sebastian, 346, 358
Castiglione, Baldassare, 287
Castile, 299
Castlereagh, Viscount (Robert Stewart), 574, *575,* 576, 601, 606, 607
Castro, Fidel, 915
Catal Höyük, 3
Cateau-Cambrésis, Treaty of (1559), 348
Categorical imperative, 579
Cathars (Albigensians), 214, 267
Cathedral of St. James Santiago de Compostela, *225*
Cathedral schools, 242
Catherine I, of Russia, 524
Catherine II (the Great), 437, 458, 517, 519, 524–526, *525, 526,* 527, 549, 562, 662, 776
Catherine of Aragon, 299, 330, 331
Catholic Center Party, 732, 829
Catholic Emancipation Act, 619
Catholic League, 350, 351, 364–365
Catholicism
  church in Spanish America, 307–308
  emergence of, 148
  James II and renewal fear of a Catholic England, 379–380
  reform, 333–335
  revival of, in the Middle Ages, 204–215
  in Roman Empire, 145, 147–148
  Rome as a center for the early church, 148
  19th century attack on, 732
Catiline, 121, 133
Cato, Marcus Porcius (Cato the Elder), 109, 111, 114, 121
Cato Street Company, 605
Cato the Younger, *100*
Cato's Letters (Gordon), 483
Catullus, 133, 142
Caucasus, 776
Cavaignac, Louis, 646
Cavaliers, 378
Cavendish, Margaret, 419, *419,* 420, 421
Cavour, Camillo, *665,* 665–666
Cawnpore, Battle, *761*
Ceausescu, Nicolae, 930
Cecil, William, 357, 362
Celestine V, Pope, 267, 269
Celtis, Conrad, 302
Censor, 102
Censorship, 255
Centuriate assembly, 102
Century of the Child, The (Key), 750
Cerularius, Michael, 187
Cervantes Saavedra, Miguel de, 341–342
Cezanne, Paul, 740, 741
Chadwick, Edwin, 699
Chaeronea, Battle of, 87
Chalcedon, Council of (451), 184, 186
Chaldeans, 111
Chamber of Deputies, 606, 617, 618, 675, 711, 846, 847
Chamber of Peers, 606
Chamberlain, Austen, 850, 851
Chamberlain, Houston Stewart, 745, 746
Chamberlain, Joseph, 712, 764, 803
Chamberlain, Neville, 870–871, 872, *873,* 875
Chambord, Count de, 618, 675
Chapelier Law (1791), 541
Chaplin, Charlie, 826, *826*
Charcot, Jean-Martin, 743
Chariot racing, 146
Charioteer of Delphi, 86
Charlemagne, 171, 187, 189–192, *190, 193,* 211
Charles Albert of Piedmont, 650, 652, 665
Charles I, King of England, 377–378, *378,* 431
Charles I, King of Spain, 299, 311, 319, *320*
Charles II, King of England, 378–379, 380, 416
Charles II, King of Spain, 390
Charles III, King of Spain, 466, 467
Charles IV, Holy Roman Emperor, 300
Charles IV, King of France, 263
Charles IX, King of France, 348, 349
Charles of Anjou, King of Sicily, 220, 267
Charles the Bald, 192, 194
Charles the Bold, 298
Charles V, Holy Roman Emperor (Charles I of Spain), 194, 256, 282, 297, 319, 320, 330, 331, 333, 334, 346, 348, 352, 353, 521
Charles V, King of France, 274, 287
Charles VI, King of Austria, 394–395, 398, 400
Charles VI, King of France, 394
Charles VII, King of France, 265, 266
Charles VIII, King of France, 295, 296
Charles X, King of France, *605,* 617–618, 768, 922
Charles XII, King of Sweden, 398
Charles XIV, King of Sweden, 571
Charmides, 81
Charter (England), 627
Charter (French), 606
Charter of the Nobility, 437, 525
Chartism, 627, 629–630, *630*
Chartres, 242
Chateaubriand, Francois René de, 587, 588
Châtelet, Emilie du, 421, 497
Chattel slavery, 14, 72, 655
Chaucer, Geoffrey, 217–218, 219
Chaumont, Treaty of (1814), 574
Chechen war, 937
Chechnya, 776, 778, 935, *935,* 937
Cheka, 838
Chemical industry, 693
Cheops (Khufu), 17
Chephren (Khafre), 17, *17*
Chernenko, Konstantin, 927
Chernobyl disaster, 962, 964
Chiaroscuro, 292
Child labor, 19th century, 632, 716
Childbirth
  dangers in 18th century, 42
  in 19th century, 706
Childe Harold's Pilgrimage (Byron), 581
Childeric III, 188–189
Children
  family economy of 18th century and, 440, 442–443
  laborers, 442, 630, 632
  in the Middle Ages, 231, 248–250, *249*
  Neolithic, 3
  Reformation and, 341
  Roman, 100
  Spartan, 45
  19th century, 632, 716
  wet nursing, 341
Children's Games (Breughel), 231, *231*
Chile, 613
Ch'in dynasty, 167, *168*
China. *See also* People's Republic of China
  Boxer Rebellion, 780, *780,* 782
  Ch'in dynasty, 167, *168*
  Chou dynasty, 167
  Great Wall of China, 167, *168*
  imperialism and, 756, 758, 764
  invention of printing, 252–254, *253*
  North Korea and, 911
  Shang dynasty, 252
  Sung dynasty, 254
  Tang dynasty, 252
Chios, 64
Chirac, Jacques, 949
Cholera, 698–699
Chosroes, 177
Chou dynasty, 167
Chrétien de Troyes, 217
Christian Democratic parties, 905, 951
Christian II, King of Denmark, 329
Christian III, King of Denmark, 329
Christian IV, King of Denmark, 367
Christian Socialist Party, 747, 848, 862
Christianity, 2. *See also* Roman Catholicism
  Arianism, 159
  Byzantine Empire, 156, 177
  Catholicism, emergence of, 148
  Caucasus, 776
  Charlemagne, 189, 191
  Chechnya, 776, 778
  Cinchona bark, 782
  Circassia 778
  Council of Nicaea, 159, 173, 190
  division of, into Eastern (Byzantine) and Western (Roman Catholic), 186–187
  Enlightenment criticism of, 499–501
  Jesus of Nazareth, 28, 145, *147,* 159
  in Middle Ages, early, 183–187
  in Middle Ages, high, 210–215
  in Middle Ages, late, 267–277
  monastic culture, 183–184
  organization/terms of, 147
  papal primacy, doctrine of, 184–186
  Paul of Tarsus, 145, 147
  persecutions, 147–148, 150–151, 158–159
  rise of in Roman empire, 130, 145, 147, 150–151, *151,* 156–159, *158*
  slaves conversion to, 477
  as a state religion in Rome, 148, 159, *160*
  20th century, 966–968
  19th century attack on, 729, 732
  writers, 160–161
Christianity Not Mysterious (Toland), 498
Christiansen, Ole Kirk, 963
Christina of Sweden, Queen, *414,* 419
Christine de Pisan, 287, *288*
Chrysippus, 92
Chrysoloras, Manuel, 285, 287
Chrysostom, John, 180
Church of England, 499, 586
Church [of England] Missionary Society, 784
Church of Scotland Mission, 787
Churchill, John, 391
Churchill, Winston, 772, 814, 875–876, *876,* 880, 895, 897, 898–899, *899,* 900, 904, 908
Ciano, Count, 873, 876
Cicero, 80, 113, 121, 133, 285
Cimbri, 119
Cimmerians, 167
Cimon, 63
Cinchona bark, 782
Cinema, Nazi and Soviet use of, 853
Cinna, 120
Ciompi Revolt (1378), 284
Circassia, 778
Circus Maximus, 146
Cistercians, 214, 233
Cities/towns. *See also under name of*
  Byzantine, 175–176
  chartering of, 236
  growth of, in 18th century, 453–458
  growth of, in 19th century, 697–698
  housing reform, 700
  Kings and, 239
  medieval, 239
  Mesopotamian, 4
  Middle Ages, 236–239, 260
  polis, 39–40, 46, 58–59, 73, 78, 599, 793–794

redesign of, 455, 697–698
sanitation in, 456, 698–699
Sumerian, 5–9
19th century (late), 697–700, *698*
urban riots, 458
urban social classes, 455–458
City of God, The (Augustine), 161
City-states
Etruscan, 99
Italian, *283,* 283–285, 295
Sumerian, 7
City-states, Greek
Athens, 46–49
polis, 39–40, 46, 58–59, 73, 78
Sparta, 44–45
Civic Forum, 930
Civic humanism, 282, 289
Civil Code (1804), 564
Civil Constitution of the Clergy, 545
Civil Service Commission (Prussia), 519
Civilization, early
Assyrians, 2, 7, 15, 22–23
birth of, 1–2
Bronze Age, 4–5
defined, 1–2, 4
Egyptian, 2, 14–22
Hittites, 2, *16,* 18, 22
Kassites, *16,* 22
Mesopotamian, 2, 5–14
Mitannians, 22
Neo-Babylonians, 2, 14
Palestine, 27, *27*
Persian, 23–27
Civilization of the Renaissance in Italy (Burckhardt), 282
Civilizing mission, 764
Clarendon Code, 378
Clarkson, Thomas, 658
Claudius, 135, 142, 148
Claudius II Gothicus, 152
Clemenceau, Georges, 824, *825,* 827
Clement II, Pope, 205
Clement III, Pope, 207
Clement V, Pope, 272
Clement VI, Pope, 272, 273, 318
Clement VII, Pope, 274–275, 331
Clement VIII, Pope, 282, 297, 331, 351
Clement XI, Pope, 388
Cleomenes I, 48
Cleon, 73, 74, 76
Cleopatra, 15, 90, 126, 127
Clergy
Carolingian, 199
Civil Constitution of the Clergy, 545
Enlightenment and, 498
French Revolution and, 545
in the Middle Ages, 204–206, 232–234
secular *versus* regular, 204, 232–233
witchcraft and role of, 428, 429
Clericis laicos, 269
Clermont, Council of (1095), 207
Clientage, 100–101
Clisthenes, 48–49, 63
Clive, Robert, 465, 480, *481*
Clodia, 141
Clovis, 187
Cluny reform movement, 204–206, 232
Clytemnestra, *39,* 70
Cnossus, 34, 35, 36
Coal, 980
Cobbett, William, 605
Code (Corpus Juris Civilis) (Justinian), 176, 241
Code of Hammurabi, 7, *11,* 14, 30
Coercion Act (1817), 605
Coercion Act (1881), 687
Coeur, Jacques, 298
Coffeehouses, 494–495, 496, *496*
Colbert, Jean-Baptiste, 384, *418*
Cold War
Afghanistan, Soviet invasion of, 917
Berlin blockage, *907,* 908–909
Berlin Wall, 914–915, 930, *932*
Brezhnev era, 916–918
collapse of European communism, 926–935
containment policy, 904–905, 907
Cuban missile crisis, *915,* 915–916
Czechoslovakia, invasion of, 908, 916, *916*
decolonization, 918–922
détente, policy of, 917
emergence of, 903–905
European alliance systems, *910*
Germany, division of, 908–909, *909*
Gorbachev, 927, *927,* 929
Hungarian uprising, 914
key events/dates, 908, 915
Khrushchev era, 912–913
Korean War (1950-1953), 911, *912*
NATO and Warsaw Pact, 903, 909, 914
Paris Summit Conference, 914
Polish autonomy, 914
Polish Solidarity, 917–918
relations with Reagan administration, 918
Soviet assertion of domination of eastern Europe, 905, 908
State of Israel, creation of, 909–910
Suez crisis, 914
Vietnam and, 924–295
western Europe during, 914–916
Coleridge, Samuel Taylor, 579, 581
Colet, John, 303
Coligny, Gaspard de, 348–349
Collectivization, *833,* 841–843, *842*
College of Cardinals, 205, 206, 267
Colloquies (Erasmus), 302
Cologne, *892*
Coloni, 139, 141, 156, 234
Colonnas, 269
Colosseum, 143
Columbian Exchange, 489–491
Columbus, Christopher, 299, 305, 309, 375, 413, 471, 489, *490,* 790
Combination Acts (1799), 602, 619
COMECON (Council of Mutual Assistance), 909
Comedies
Greek Middle Comedy, 80
Greek New Comedy, 80
Greek Old Comedy, 76, 78
Cominform (Communist Information Bureau), 906–908
Comintern (Third International), 839, 844
Commentary on the Epistle to the Romans (Barth), 967
Commerce
gold and spice trade, 303–304
medieval trade routes, *237*
merchants, rise of in the Middle Ages, 236–238
Spanish Casa de Contratación (House of Trade) and Council of the Indies, 466
Committee for the Abolition of the Slave Trade, 657
Committee of General Security, 551
Committee of Public Safety, 551, 553, *553,* 555–556
Commodus, 136, 149, 152
Common Market, 972–973
Common Sense (Paine), 483
Commonwealth of Independent States, 933, *934*
Commonwealthmen, 483, 484
Communism
collapse of European, 926–935
intellectuals, 958–960
in Poland, 916, 917
in Soviet Union, 820–821, 838–844
use of term, 642
in Western Europe, 957–960
Communism and the Family (Kollontai), 858–859
Communist League, 642
Communist Manifesto, The (Marx and Engels), 643–645, 718, 958
Communist party, in the Soviet Union, 838, 842–843, 930
Compagnie des Index, 465
Complutensian Polygot Bible (Jiménez de Cisneros), 303
Compromise, 355
Compromise of 1867, *676,* 678
Computers, 968–971
Comte, Auguste, 726, 749
Concentration camps, 776
Concerning Germany (de Staël), 580
Concert of Europe, 606, 662
Conciliar theory, 276
Concluding Unscientific Postscript (Kierkegaard), 959
Concord, Battle of, 483
Concordance of Discordant Canons (Gratian), 241
Concordat of Bologna (1516), 296
Concordat of Worms (1122), 207, 221
Condition of the WorKing Class in England, The (Engels), 642
Condottieri, 284
Confection, 627
Confédération Générale du Travail, 713
Confederation of the Rhine, 564
Confessions (Augustine), 161
Confucian Classics, 254
Confucian Scriptures, 252
Congregationalists, 360
Congress of Berlin (1878), 800
Congress of Vienna (1815), 574–577, *575, 577,* 593, 594, 601, 658, *667,* 768
Congress system, 606
Conquistadores, 308
Conrad, Joseph, 775
Conservatism
in Belgium, 618–619
in Britain, 619–620
congress system, 606
in France, 617–618
in Greece, 608
in Latin America, 608–614
in Russia, 614–616
in Serbia, 608
in Spain, 607
19th century, 600–606
Conspiracy of Amboise, 348
Conspiracy of Equals, 558
Constable, John, 582, *583*
Constance, Council of (1414-1417), 274, 276, 320
Constance, peace of (1183), 222
Constant, Benjamin, 598, 599
Constantine of Russia (brother to Alexander II), 615, 616
Constantine of Russia (Grand Duke), 616
Constantine the Great, 130, 153, 154, *154,* 159, 171, 289
Constantinople, 173, 174, *503,* 814
Council of (381), 184
Crusades and, 178, 211
fall of, 174, 279
formation of, 154, 156
growth of, 171–172
Constantius, 152
Constantius II, 155
Constitution of 1791, 539
Constitution of the Athenians (Pseudo-Xenophon), 68, 84
Constitution of the Year III, 557, 558
Constitution of the Year VIII, 563
Constitutional Convention (1787), 484
Constitutional Democratic Party. *See* Cadets
Constitutions of Clarendon, 217
Consulate in France (1799-1804), 563–564
Consuls, Roman, 101–102
Consumerism, 448–449, 694, 962
Contagious Disease Acts (1864, 1886), 749
Contarini, Caspar, 335
Continental Congress, 483, 657
Continental System, 566, *568*
Conventicle Act (1593), 360
Convention (French), 547, 551, 553, 555–556, 558, 619
Convention of Gastein (1865), 671–672
Convention of Westminister (1756), 479
Conversations on the Plurality of Worlds (Fontenelle), 421
Cook, James, 757, 787
Cooper, Anthony Ashley, 416
Copenhagen Opera House, *972*
Copernicus, Nicholaus, 94, 408–410, *409,* 425
Copyright laws, 254–255
Corcyra, 43, 73
Cordoba, 183
Corfu Agreement (1917), 862
Corinth, 43, 73, 74, 75
League of, 87
Corinthian War, 75
Corn Law (1815), 602, 625, 639, 646
Cornwallis, Lord, 483, *483*
Coromantee, 476
Corpus Juris Civilis (Body of the Civil Law) (Justinian), 176, 241
Corsica, 106, 107
Cort, Henry, 452
Cortés, 297, 607
Cortés, Hernán, 306
Corvée, 437, *438*
Cottage industries, 453
Council for Aid to Jews in Occupied Poland (ZEGOTA), 890
Council of Basel (1431-1449), 274, 276, 324
Council of Blood, 355
Council of Chalcedon (451), 184, 186
Council of Clermont (1095), 207
Council of Constance (1414-1417), 274, 276, 320
Council of Constantinople (381), 184
Council of Elders, 557
Council of Ferrara-Florence, 287
Council of Five Hundred, 557, 558
Council of Foreign Ministers, 900
Council of Lyons (1274), 267
Council of Nicaea, Second (787), 190
Council of Nicaea (325), 159, 173
Council of Pisa (1409-1410), 276

Council of Regency, 300, 319
Council of Ten, 283
Council of the Indies, 466
Council of Trent (1545-1563), 334–335, 346, 355, 364, 384, 421
Council of Troubles, 355
Counter-Reformation, 333–335, 346
Counterblast to Tobacco (James I), 376
Courage (journal), 953
Court of Justice, 300
Court of Matrimonial Causes, 701
Court of Star Chamber, 300
Courtly love, 217, 230, 245, 286
Craig, Gordon, 662
Cranach the Elder, Lucas, *319*
Cranmer, Thomas, 331, 332, 333, 357
Crassus, Marcus Licinius, 120–122, 125
Cratinus, 76
Creation stories, 29
Crécy, Battle of (1346), 265
Creoles, 309, 467, 612, 614
Crime, industrialization and, 634–638
Crimean War (1853-1856), 662, *663*, 764
Critias, 78, 81
Critique of Practical Reason, The (Kant), 579
Critique of Pure Reason, The (Kant), 579
Crito (Plato), 81
Croatia/Croatians
  collapse of Yugoslavia and civil war, 936–937
  Compromise of 1867, 678
  Habsburg, 393
  in the 1920s, 862–863
Croesus, King, 23–24, 53, 79
Cromwell, Oliver, 346, 378, *378*
Cromwell, Thomas, 331, 332
Crosby, Alfred, 489
Cross, Richard, 686
Crown of Saint Stephen, 521
Crucifixion (Grunewald), *313*
Crusades, 232
  in the East, 214
  First, 178, 207–208, 212
  Fourth, 178, 211
  in France, 214
  key events/dates, 208
  map of, *209*
  motivations for, 208–209, 211
  Romanticism and, 588
  Second, 208
  Third, 209, 212, 213
Crystal Palace, *631*, 694
Cuauhtemoc, 306
Cuba
  missile crisis, *915*, 915–916
  slavery in, 659
  Spanish-American War (1898), 764, 779
Cubism, *741*, 741–742
Cult of domesticity, 704
Cult of the Supreme Being, 555, 556, 557, *557*
Cultural relativism, 510
Culture
  defined, 2
  mideastern, 28–30
Cunaxa, Battle of, 74
Cuneiform, 9
Cunitz, Mary, 421
Curia, 272, 274
Curiate assembly, 100
Curie, Marie, *736*
Curie, Pierre, *736*
Cuzco, 307
Cvijicin, Jovan, *809*
Cybele, 111
Cylon, 46
Cynics, 81, 83, 92
Cyprus, 92, 922
Cyril, 177
Cyrillic alphabet, 177
Cyrus the Great, 23–24, 54, 74, 79, 88
Czechoslovakia
  collapse of communism, 916, 930
  Compromise of 1867, 678
  formation of, 829
  Hitler's occupation of, 870
  partition of, *871*, 872–873
  revolution of 1848, 650
  in the 1920s, 861–862
  Soviet invasion of, 908, 916, *916*, 958
  under Soviet rule, 908

D

D-Day, 883, *884*
Dagestan, 778
Dacia, 139
Dail Eireann, 836
Daimler, Gottlieb, 693
Daimler, Rudolf, 980
Daladier, Edouard, 870, 872, *873*
D'Albert, Jeanne, 348
D'Albret, Charlotte, 296
D'Alembert, Jean le Rond, 495, 498, 504, 512
Damascus, 182
Damascus I, Pope, 184
d'Angoulême, Marguerite, 303
Danish War (1864), 671
D'Annunzio, Gabriele, 846
Dante Alighieri, 285, 287, 409
Danton, Jacques, 555
Daoist Scriptures, 254
Darius, King, 24–26, *25*, *167*
Darius II, 74
Darius III, 88, 90, *794*
Darkness at Noon (Koestler), 958
Darnley, Lord, 362
Darwin, Charles, *724*, 728, 730, 748, 749
d'Aubigne, Francoise, *388*
David, *27*, 28
David, Armand, 788
David, Jacques-Louis, 517, 518, *535*, *565*
David (Michelangelo), 292
Dawes Plan, 850
Day of the Barricades, 350
De-Christianization (French), 554
De Gaulle, Charles, 893, 895, 923, *923*, 961, 973
De Legibus (Cicero), 133
de Montcalm, Louis Joseph, 480
De Rerum Natura (On the Nature of the World) (Lucretius), 133
De Vries, Jan, 455
Death, Middle Ages images of, *260*, 261
Debt peonage, 309
Debt slavery, 14
Decameron (Boccaccio), 258, 282, 287
Decembrist revolt of 1825, 614–616, *616*
Decius, 158
Declaration of Independence (1776), 483
Declaration of Indulgence (1672), 379
Declaration of Indulgence (1687), 379
Declaration of Pillnitz, 546
Declaration of the Rights of Man and Citizen, 537–538, 541, 542–543, 545, 595, 606
Declaration of the Rights of Woman, 541, 543, 554
Declaratory Act, 482
Decline and Fall of the Roman Empire, The (Gibbon), 550
Decolonization, *797*, *902*, 903, 918–924, *919*, 948–949
Decretum (Gratian), 241
Decurions, 175
Defender of Peace (Marsilius of Padua), 272
Defense of Liberty Against Tyrants (Mornay), 350
Defense of the Orthodox Faith in the Holy Trinity Against the Monstrous Errors of Michael Servetus of Spain (Calvin), 358
Degas, Edgar, 739
Deism, 498–499
Delacroix, Eugène, *593*
Delambre, Jean-Baptiste, 544
Delian League, 61, 62–63
Delos, 62
Delphi, Oracle of, 50, 52–53
Deme, 48
Demesne, 198
Demeter, 50, 73
Democracy
  Athenian, 48–49, 65–69
  in the 19th century, 711, 718
Democritus of Abdera, 77, 133
Demosthenes, 31, 87
Denmark
  Lutheranism, 329
  Reformation in, 329
  Thirty Years' War (1619-1648), 367
  World War II, 909
Department stores, 696, *705*
Depression. *See* Great Depression
Derby, lord, 684
Deroin, Jeanne, 649
Descartes, René, 414, *414*, 418, 419, 422
Descent of Man, The (Darwin), 728, 749
Description of a New World, Called the Blazing World (Cavendish), 421
Description of Egypt (Napoleon), 591
Desiderius, 189
Dessalines, Jean-Jacques, 612, 657
Devil's Island, 638, 675
Devshirme, 401, *402*
d'Herbelot, Barthélemy, 502
Dhimmis, 401
D'Holbach, Baron, 500
Dialectic, 244
Dialogue on the Two Chief World Systems (Galileo), 425
Diamond mining, *777*
Diamond Sutra, *253*
Dias, Bartholomew, 305
Dickens, Charles, 737
Dictatus Papae, 206
Diderot, Denis, 495, 504, *504*, 509, 510, 512, 517
Diem, Ngo Dinh. *See* Ngo Dinh Diem
Dien Bien Phu, 924
Diesel, Rudolf, 980
Diet of Augsburg (1530), 329, 350
Diet of Speyer (1526), 321
Diet of Vesteras (1527), 330
Diet of Worms (1521), 314, 319–320
Digest (Justinian), 176
Dimitriv of Moscow, 279
Dio Cassius, 124, 148
Diocletian, 130, 143, 152–153, *154*, 158–159, 171, lix
Diogenes, 83
Dionysius I, 83
Dionysius II, 83
Dionysius the Areopagite, 289
Dionysus, 47, 53, 71, 76, *76*, 111
Diplomatic Revolution of 1756, 479–480
Directory, establishment of French, 557–558
Discourse on Method (Descartes), 414, 418, 422
Discourse on the Moral Effects of the Arts and Sciences (Rousseau), 508
Discourse on the Origin of Inequality (Rousseau), 508
Diseases, conquest of tropical, 782
Disraeli, Benjamin, 684, 686, *686*, 761, 768, 800
Divination, *10*, 98
Divine Comedy (Dante), 287, 409
Divine rights of Kings, 374, 382, 386, 617
Divorce
  Athenian, 67
  Egyptian, 11
  Mesopotamian, 14
  Muslim, 178–179, *181*
  Napoleonic Code and, 564
  Reformation and, 338
  Roman, 100, 132
  19th century, 701
  Thermidorian Reaction and, 557
Djoser, 17
Dollfuss, Engelbert, 862
Doll's House (Ibsen), 737
Dom Pedro, 614
Dom Pedro II, 614
Domesday Book, 216
Domestic system, 450
Dominic, St., 215
Dominicans, 208, 214–215, *215*, 232, 233
Domitian, 135, 136, 142
Domus, 142
Don John of Austria, 353, 356, 360
Don Juan (Byron), 581
Don Quixote (Cervantes), 342
Donatello, 292
Donation of Constantine, 189, 289, 302
Donatism, 274
Donatus, 244
Dorians, 36
d'Orleans, Philippe, 514
Doryphoros of Polycleitus, 80
Dover, Treaty of (1670), 379, 384
Dr. Zhivago (Pasternak), 912
Draco, 46
Drake, Francis, 360
Drama
  classical Greek, 80
  English, 361
Dreyfus, Alfred, 675–676, *676*, 677, 747
Dreyfus affair, 675–676, *676*, 677, 710, 747, 893
Drusus, M. Livius, 119
Dual Alliance, 800
Dubcek, Alexander, 916, 930
Dubois, Pierre, 272
Duma, 720, 818
Dumouriez, general, 548, 552
Dunhuang Caves, *253*
Dunlop, John Boyd, 695
Dupleix, Joseph, 465
Dupont de Nemours, Pierre, 505
Duran, Diego, *307*
Durant, Ariel, 165
Durant, Will, 165

Dürer, Albrecht, 210, 290, *291, 300,* 323, *323*
Durkheim, Emile, 745, 749
Dutch, in Americas, 464
Dutch East Indies Company, 373, *373*
Dyarchy, 136
Dyer, Reginald, *797*

E

Early Dynastic period, 6, 17
East India Company, 465, 480, 481, 482, 759
East Timor, 922
Eastern Associated Telegraph Companies, 783
Eastern Catholicism
  division of Christianity into Eastern (Byzantine) and Western (Roman Catholic), 186–187
Eastern question, 764
Ebla, 6
Ecbatana, 23
Ecclesiastical History (Eusebius of Caesarea), 161
Ecclesiastical reservation, 364
Eck, John, 319
Eckert, J. Presper, *970*
Eclogues (Bucolics) (Vergil), 134
Economic Consequences of the Peace, The (Keynes), 830
Economy. *See also* Great Depression
  Black Death, impact of, 260, 262
  consumer, 448–449, 694, 962
  Crusades and, 208–209, 211
  Enlightenment and, 505–507, 520
  explorations, impact of, 308–309
  family, 439–443
  financial crisis of 2008, 977
  four stage theory, 505, 507
  French Revolution and, 541, 545
  future for Europe, 975
  imperialism and, 756–757
  inflation of 1923, 847–848, *848*
  key events/dates, 687
  Keynesian economics, 738
  laissez-faire, 505, 638
  liberal goals, 598–599
  major works, 639
  mercantilist, 464–465, 505
  Nazi, 857, 860–861
  in the Netherlands, 372–373
  New Economic Policy, 838–839
  perestroika, 927
  plantation, 463
  post World War I, 834–836, 849
  post World War II, 948–949
  Roman Empire, 149, 152
  second industrial revolution and, 694
  slave, 473, 655
  19th century classical, 638–639, 691–694
  World War I and, 830–831
Edessa, 208
Edict of Chateaubriand, 348
Edict of Fontainebleau, 348
Edict of Maximum Prices (301), 154
Edict of Nantes (1598), 351–352, 381, 388, 390
Edict of Restitution (1629), 367
Edict of Toleration, 159
Edinburgh, Treaty of (1560), 362
Edinburgh and Glasgow Missionary Societies, 784
Edison, Thomas Alva, 982
Education
  Carolingian, 192
  cathedral schools, 242
  Hellenistic, 111, 113
  humanism, 287, 301
  Middle Ages, universities in, 239–245, *241*
  Reformation and, 336–338
  Roman, 111–113
  Rousseau and, 578–579
  Scholasticism, 221, 244
  Spartan, 45
  Sumerian, 9
  in the 19th century, 701–702, *702,* 725–726, 760
  20th century expansion of universities and student rebellions, 959–961, *961*
  of women (in Middle Ages), 245
  of women (Roman), 113
  of women (19th century), 701–702, *702*
Education Act (1870), 684, 732
Education Act (1902), 732
Education of the Orator (Quintilian), 287
Edward I, King of England, 268, 269, 330
Edward III, King of England, 263, *263,* 265
Edward IV, King of England, 299
Edward the Confessor, 215
Edward VI, King of England, 332–333, 356
Egmont, Count of, 354
Egypt, *5*
  ancient civilization, 2, 14–22
  Arab-Israeli conflict, 910–911
  British in, 768–773
  key events/dates, 7
  language and literature, 19
  major periods in ancient history, *17*
  Middle Kingdom, 18
  Napoleon in, 562, *590,* 590–591
  New Kingdom, 18–19
  Old Kingdom, 16–17
  religion, 19–20
  Romans in, 15, 131
  slavery, 21–22
  Suez crisis, 914
  Third Dynasty, 6–7
  Upper *versus* Lower, 14–15
  women in, 21
  World War II, 876, 879, *880*
Eiffel Tower, 697, *698*
Einhard, 191
Einstein, Albert, 736
Eisenhower, Dwight D., 883, 911, 914, 925
Eisenstein, Sergei, 853, 897
Either/Or (Kierkegaard), 959
El Alamein, 879, 880
El Greco, 292
Elamites, 7, 25, 29
Eleanor of Aquitaine, 216–217
Electricity, 693, 981–982
Electronic Numerical Integrator and Computer, 970, *970*
Elegances of the Latin Language (Valla), 289
Elements (Euclid), 94
Elements of the Philosophy of Newton (Voltaire), 497
Eliot, George, 737
Elizabeth I, Queen of England, 300, 332, 333, 346, 355, 357, *359,* 360, *360,* 362, 374
Elizabeth of Russia, 480, 524
Elizabeth of York, 299
Emancipation Act (1861), 681
Emancipation Proclamation, 478, 659
émigrés, 545–546, 547, 562
Emilie (Rousseau), 512, 513, 515, 578
Eminent Victorians (Strachey), 738
Emma-Magazine by Women for Women (journal), 953
Empedocles of Acragas, 77
Empiricism, 412–414
Employment
  Chartism, 627, 629–630, *630*
  family of 18th century, 441–442, 444–445
  Industrial Revolution in 18th century and, 448–449
  Industrial Revolution in 19th century and, 626–627, 630, 632
  of women in the 18th century, 441–442
  of women in the 19th century, 632–634, 635, 702–703
  of women in the 20th century, 953, 957
Enabling Act (1933), 854
Encomienda, 309
Encyclical, *733*
Encyclopedia, The (Diderot), 504, *504,* 510, 511, 512
Energy, modern world and, 979–984
Enfield rifle, 784
Engels, Friedrich, 642, 644
Enghien, Duke of, 563
England. *See also* Britain
  agriculture in, 444
  alliances with Austria and Russia against France, 566
  American Revolution, 481–484
  in Americas, 464, 465–466, 481–482
  aristocracy of 18th century, 435
  Austrian Succession, war of (1740-1748), 478–479
  enclosures replaces open fields, 444–445
  following American Revolution, 486–487
  game laws, 439
  Hastings, Battle of (1066), 216, *216*
  humanism in, 303
  Hundred Years' War, 262–267
  Industrial Revolution, 449
  key events/dates, 485
  Magna Carta (1215), 209, 218, 224
  Middle Ages (high) in, 215–218
  peasant rebellions in, 260, 438–439
  Quadruple Alliance, 574, 576
  Reformation in, 330–333
  Reformation Parliament, 331–332
  relations with Spain, 356–362
  revival of monarchy, 299–300, 378–379
  romantic literature, 579, 581
  social reform, 519
  suppression of reforms, following French Revolution, 549
  toleration and political stability, 493–494
  War of Jenkins's Ear, 478, 608
  William the Conqueror, 215–216, 231
England, seventeenth century
  Age of Walpole, *380,* 380–381
  Charles I, 377–378, *378*
  Charles II and restoration of the monarchy, 378–379
  civil war, 377–378
  compared with France, 374
  Cromwell, 378, *378*
  Glorious Revolution, 379–380
  James I, 374–375, 377
  James II, 379–380
  key events/dates, 379
  Long Parliament, 377–378
  parliamentary monarchy, 374
English Factory Act (1833), 632
Enheduanna, 7
ENIAC, 970, *970*
Enlightened absolutism, 493, 517–527
Enlightenment. *See also under name of author or work*
  absolutism in, 517–527
  defined, 493, 497
  Encyclopedia, The, 504, *504,* 510, 512
  formative influences on, 493–495
  major works of, 511
  philosophes, 495–498, 507–510
  print culture, impact of, 493, *494,* 494–495
  religion and, 498–504
  society and, 504–507
  women and, 511–514
Enniius, 133
Enquiry into the Obligations of Christians, to use Means for the Conversion of the Heathen, An (Carey), 785
Entente Cordiale, 803
Entertainment
  Byzantine, 175
  Greek symposium and games, 50, 51
  medieval courtly love, 230, *232*
  medieval sportsmen/warriors, 228, *229,* 230–231
  Roman, *110, 134, 138,* 146, *146,* 150
  theater, 17th century, 361
  troubadours, 217, 230
Environmentalism, 962, 964
Epaminondas, 75
Ephialtes, 63
Ephors, 45, 63
Epic of Gilgamesh, 12, *13*
Epicureans, 92
Epicurus, 92, 133
Epidamnus, 73
Epidaurus, *81*
Epikleros, 70
Episteme, 83
Equestrians, 118
Erasmus, Desiderius, 291, 296, 302, 303, 315, 320, 324, 338
Eratosthenes, 94, *94*
Erechtheum, *67, 82*
Eretria, 54
Erfurt Program, 713–714
Erik the Red, 195
Escorial, 353
Essay Concerning Human Understanding, An (Locke), 417, 493
Essay on the Inequality of the Human Races (Gobineau), 745
Essay on the Principles of Population (Malthus), 638
Estates General, French, 263, 530, 532
  becomes the National Assembly, 532–534
  formation of, 265
  Louis XIV calls, into session, 297
  Louis XVI calls, into session, 532
Esterhazy, Prince, 435
Estonia, 829, 932
Ethelred II, 216
Ethics and science, 728–729
Ethics (Spinoza), 501
Ethiopia, 917
  Italy attacks, 866–867, 900
Ethiopian Church, 787

Ethnic cleansing, *731,* 936
Etruscans, 98–99, *99*
Eubulus, 87
Eucharist, 147
Euclid, 94, 244
Eupolis, 76
Euripides, 70, 71, 76, 80
Euro, *947,* 973
Europe. *See also under name of country*
in 1714, *390*
expansion, 796–797
territorial changes after World War II, *904*
European Coal and Steel Community, 971
European Coalition, 574
European Constitution, 974, *974*
European Economic Community (EEC), 930, *947,* 972–973
European Free Trade Area, 973
European Union, *973,* 973–976
Eurymedon River, 63
Eusebius of Caesarea, 161
Evangelical Protestant Missionaries, 784
Evangelicalism, 784–785
Evans, Mary Ann (George Eliot), 737
Eve, 245, 247, *247*
Evolution and Ethics (Huxley), 730–731
Evolutionary Socialism (Bernstein), 714
Execrabilis, 276
Executions, 455
Existentialism, 959–960
Explorations, 303–305
map of, *304*
Exquemelin, Alexander, 467
Exsurge Domine, 320

F

Fabianism, 712–713
Fabius Maximus, Quintus, 108, 712
Factories, 465, 626–629, 635
Falangists, 868
Falkenhayn, Erich von, 815
Falloux Law (1850), 732
Family
Athenian, 67, 70
cult of domesticity, 704–705
economy, 439–443
Homeric society, 38
Nazi Germany, 859
Reformation and, 339–341
Roman, 100, 109, 142
Soviet Union, 858–859, *859*
Spartan, 45
18th century, 439–443
19th century, 630, 632, 634, 640, 648, 749
20th century, 953, 957
Famine in Ireland, 491, 624, 625
Fanaticism, or Mohammed the Prophet (Voltaire), 502
Faraday, Michael, 982
Farel, Guillaume, 328
Farnese of Parma, Alexander, 356
Fascism, in Italy, 844–847
Fashoda incident, 773
Fasti (Ovid), 134
Fatima, *170*
Faunus, 112, *112*
Faust (Goethe), 582
Fawcett, Millicent, 707
Fealty, 198
Fear and Trembling (Kierkegaard), 959
February Patent, 678
Feisal, Prince, *824*
Feltre, Vittorino da, 287
Feminism
antifeminism in late 19th century, 747–749
in France (1848), 647–649
obstacles to equality, 706–707
rise of political, 706–709
sexual morality and the family, 706, 749–751
19th century, 706–709, 747–751
20th century, 953, 956
voting rights, *707,* 707–708, 750
Ferdinand, Francis (Archduke of Austria), 798, 806, *806,* 808
Ferdinand I, Emperor, 352
Ferdinand II, Holy Roman Emperor, 365–366, 367, *367*
Ferdinand of Aragon, 295, 296, 298–299, 330, 341
Ferdinand of Austria, 649, 652
Ferdinand VII, King of Spain, 607, 612, 614
Ferrara-Florence, Council of (1439), 287
Ferry, Jules, 732
Festival of the Supreme Being, *557*
Feudal society
fiefs, 188, 198
loyalty, divided, 199–200
origins of, 196, 198
use of term, 196
vassalage, 196, 198, 199
Fichte, J.G., 587
Ficino, Marsilio, 287
Ficke, Auguste, 750
Fiefs, 188, 198
Filioque, 186–187
Final Act (1820), 602
Finland, 829, 874
Finley, Carlos, 789
Firearms, 782, 784
First Blast of the Trumpet Against the Terrible Regiment of Women (Knox), 350, 362
First Coalition, 551
First Continental Congress, 483
First Crusade, 178, 207–208, 212
First Intermediate Period, 18
First International, 711
First Macedonian War, 108
First Messenian War, 44
First Peloponnesian War, 63–64
First Punic War, 106–107, *107*
First Treatise of Government (Locke), 417
First Triumvirate, 121
First Vatican Council, 733
Fisher, John, 332
FitzGerald, Edward, 588
Five Weeks in a Balloon (Verne), *727*
Flagellants, *257,* 258
Flamininus, 108–109
Flanders, 220, 263
Flaubert, Gustave, 737
Flavian dynasty, 136
Flavius Josephus, *138*
Fleury, Cardinal, 392, 479
Flood Tablet (Table XI), *13*
Florence
Black Death in, 261
Renaissance in, 283–284, *284,* 295
Florentine Platonic Academy, 287, 289
Flota system, 466
Folies-Bergère, 740
Fontenelle, Bernard de, 421
Food, introduction of canned, 567
Ford, Gerald, 917
Ford, Henry, 693, *981*
Forman Christian College, 786
Foundations of the Nineteenth Century (Chamberlain), 745
Four Articles of Prague, 276
Four Books of the Sentences (Lombard), 245
Four Ordinances, 617
Four-stage theory of economics, 505, 507
Fourier, Charles, 641
Fournier, Henri, *694*
Fourteen Points, 822, 825
Fourth Crusade, 178, 211
Fourth Lateran Council (1215), 214
Fox, Charles James, 485
Fox, George, 656
Fragment on Government (Bentham), 639
Fragonard, Jean-Honoré, 516
France. *See also* French Revolution
African colonies, 773
agriculture, 445, 446–447
American Revolution and, 483
in Americas, 464, 465–466
aristocracy of 18th century, 435
Austrian Succession, war of (1740-1748), 478–479
Bourbon restoration, 348, 466–467, 562, 570, 574–575, *605,* 605–606, 612
Capetian dynasty, 218, 220
conflict between church and state, 732
Consulate in France (1799-1804), 563–564
Crimean War (1853-1856), 662
Crusades in, 214, 221
decolonization, 922–924
Dreyfus affair, 675–676, *676,* 677, 710, 747, 893
Fourth Republic, 923
Franco-Prussian War (1870-1871), 673–674
Great Depression in, 836, 838
humanism in, 303
Hundred Years' War, 262–267
imperialism and, 765, 778–779, 796
Indochina and, 924
invasions of Italy (1494-1527), 295–297
Jews in, 709–710
map of, in 1789, *540*
Middle Ages (high) in, 220–221
in Morocco, *765,* 768
Napoleon's empire, 564–567
Paris Commune, 674–675, 711
peasants in, 260, 265, 437, *438*
politics in 19th century, 713
religious wars in, 346–352
revival of monarchy in, 298
revolution of 1830, 617–618, 768
revolution of 1848, *645,* 646–649
Ruhr, invasion of, 835, *835,* 847–848
in the 1920s, 850–851
Second Republic, 646–649
18th century, 446–447, *536*
Third Republic, 675
Thirty Years' War (1618-1648), 368
Triple Entente (1890-1907), 801–804
war with Ottoman Turks, 320–321
World War I and, *812,* 812– 814, 815, 823–825, *828*
World War II and, 875, *875,* 893–895
France, Antole, 767
France, seventeenth century
absolute monarchy, 381–382, 391–392
compared with England, 374
economy of, 381–382
Edict of Nantes, revocation of, 352, 388, 389
Jansenists, suppression of, 384–385, 388
key events/dates, 384
King of divine right, 382, 386
Louis XIII and Richelieu, 352, 381
Louis XIV and Mazarin, 381
military, 384
Netherlands invasion of, 372
Nine Years' War, 388, 390
Versailles, 382, *383,* 539
War of Devolution, 384
War of Spanish succession, *390,* 390–391
Francis I, King of France, 282, 292, 296, 303, 319, 346
Francis I, King of Prussia, 571
Francis I of Austria, 566
Francis II, King of France, 348, 362
Francis II of Austria, 547, 566
Francis Joseph, Emperor of Austria, 652, 676, *676,* 678–679
Francis of Assisi, St., 215, 269, 333
Franciscans, 208, 214–215, *215,* 232, 233, 269
Franck, Sebastian, 327, 338
Franco, Francisco, *868,* 868–869
Franco-Gallia (Hotman), 350
Franco-Prussian War (1870-1871), 669–670, 673–674, 764
Franco-Russian Alliance, 801
Franconia, 203
Frankfurt, Treaty of (1871), 674
Frankfurt Parliament, 653
Franklin, Benjamin, 483, 517, 657
Franks, 149, 156, 171–173, 182, 185, 187–189
Frederick, John, 329, 330
Frederick I, King of Denmark, 329
Frederick I, King of Prussia, 397
Frederick I Barbarossa, Holy Roman Emperor, 209, 221–222, 240
Frederick II, Holy Roman Emperor, 220, 222–224, 267, 395
Frederick II (the Great), King of Prussia, 395, 397, 435, 478, 479, 480, 497, 519–520, *520,* 526, 527, 531, 549
Frederick III, Holy Roman Emperor, 261, 327, 364–365
Frederick IV, Holy Roman Emperor, 365
Frederick the Wise, 319
Frederick V, Holy Roman Emperor, 366–367
Frederick William, Great Elector, 261, 395–396
Frederick William I, King of Prussia, 397
Frederick William II, King of Prussia, 546, 549
Frederick William III, King of Prussia, 261, 570, 601
Frederick William IV, King of Prussia, 652, 653, 671
Free French, 895, 922, 923
Freedom of a Christian (Luther), 320
Freeman, 198, 200
Freemasons, 495
French Academy of Science, 418, *418*
French and Indian War (1756-1763), 479
French National Committee of Liberation, 895
French Revolution
chronology of, 559
Europe during, 548–549
monarch pre-, 530–532

Paris Commune, 547, 556
reconstruction of France, 539–546
Reign of Terror, 549–555
religion and, 554
resistance to taxation, 530–532
revolution of 1789, 532–538
second revolution, 546–548
Thermidorian reaction, 555–556
Freud, Sigmund, *743,* 743–744, 749, 811
Friars, 214
Friedrich, Caspar David, 584, *585*
Froment, Antoine, 328
Fronde, 381, 385
Fry, Elizabeth, 637
Fugger, house of, 311, 319, 352
Fulbert, Bishop, 242
Fulton, Robert, 782
Funeral Oration (Pericles), 68–69, 70
Fütterer, Katharina, *300*

G

Gainsborough, Thomas, *436*
Gaius (Caligula), 135
Gaius Gracchus, 118
Galen, 250
Galerius, 152, 159
Galileo Galilei, *410,* 410–411, 421, 424, 425
Gallican liberties, 273, 384, 388
Gallienus, 152
Gama, Vasco da, 305
Gandhi, Mohandas, *920,* 920–921
Gapon, George, 717
Garibaldi, Giuseppe, 652, *661,* 665, 666, *668,* 668–669
Garrison, William Lloyd, 659
Gastein, Convention of (1865), 671
Gatherers, 3
Gauguin, Paul, 740, 741
Gaul/Gauls
Cisalpine, 99, 122
invasion of Italy, 104
Narbonese, 122
Gay, Peter, 497
Gdansk, 948
strike at, 917–918
Gelasius I, Pope, 185
Genealogy of Morals, The (Nietzsche), 742
General Austrian Women's Association, 750
General Motors, *981*
General Theory of Employment, Interest, and Money (Keynes), 837
Geneva, Reformation in, 328–329
Genevan Academy, 338
Genius of Christianity (Chateaubriand), 587
Genoa, 283
Genocide, 775
Genocide in South-West Africa, 775
Genoese, 211
Geocentrism, *202,* 409
Geoffrin, Marie-Thérèse, *492,* 511
Geography, 787–788
George, Kara, 608
George I, King of England, 380
George II, King of England, 479, 863
George III, King of England, 481, 483, 484–486, 531
George IV, King of England, 619
George V, King of England, 836
Georgia (country), invasion of by Russian Federation, 938, *938,* 940
Georgics (Vergil), 134
Gerbert, 242
German Confederation, 601, 602, 603, 653, 669
German Democratic Republic (East Germany), 908
German Federal Republic (West Germany), 908
German Ideology, 958
Germanic tribes
Alemanni, 149, 156
fall of Roman Empire and, 172–173
Franks, 149, 156, 171–173, 182, 185, 187–189
Goths, 149, 155–156, 172
Lombards, 182, 186, 188, 189
migrations, 172, *173*
Ostrogoths, 155, 172
Roman Empire and, 155
Visigoths, 155–156, 172, 176, 187
Germany. *See also* Hitler; Holy Roman Empire; Nazis
African colonies, 775
after 1815, *575*
alliances with Russia and Austria, 800
Austro-Prussian War (1866), 671–672, *672*
Berlin blockade, *907*
Berlin Wall, 914–915, 930, *932*
Bismarck's leadership, 799–801
borders of, in the 20th century, *931*
conflict between church and state, 732, *733*
Congress of Vienna (1815), 574–577, *575, 577,* 594
Danish War (1864), 671
division into East and West, 908–909, *909*
Dual Alliance, 800
Franco-Prussian War (1870-1871), 673–674
Great Depression in, 851
Hohenstaufen Empire, 221–225
humanism in, 302
imperialism and, 766–767
map of, *363, 575*
medieval, 203–204
Napoleon and, 566, 574, 604
nationalism in, 568–570, 604
Ottonian Kings, 203
rearmament of, 866, 870
Reformation in, 316–324
reparations for World War I, 829, 835–836, 847
revolutions of 1848, *645,* 652–653
romantic literature, 581–582
Social Democratic Party (SDP) formation and revisionism, 713–714
student nationalism and Carlsbad Decrees, 601–602
Thirty Years' War, *363,* 363–364, 365–368
Three Emperors' League, 799–800
Triple Alliance, 800–801
Triple Entente, 801–804
unification of (1848-1914), *670,* 670–674
unification of East and West, 929–930, *931*
Weimar Republic, 835, 847–851
western frontier, *850*
World War I and, 806–809, 815, 822, 827, *828,* 847
World War II and effects on, 876–878, 892–893, 898
Gerstein, Kurt, 888–889
Ghana, 922
Ghengis Khan, *278,* 279
Ghent, 265, 356
Ghettos, Jewish, 458–459
Ghibelline, 283
Ghosts (Ibsen), 737
Gibbon, Edward, 161–162, 495, 500, 503
Giles of Rome, 270
Gilgamesh, 9, 11, 12
Giotto, 292
Girondists, 546–548, 551, 552
Giza pyramid, 17, *17*
Gladstone, William, 684, *686,* 686–687
Glasnost, 927–928
Glorious Revolution, 379–380
Gobineau, Arthur de, 745, 856
God that Failed, The, 958
Godfrey of Bouillon, 208
Godwinsson, Harold, 215
Goebbels, Josef, 893
Goethe, Johann Wolfgang von, 582
Gold Coast, slave trade, 473
Golden Bull, 300
Golden Horde, 279
Gömbös, Julius, 862
Gomorrah, 30
Gomulka, Wladyslaw, 914
Gorbachev, Mikhail S., 927, *927,* 929–933
Gorchakov, Alexander M., 779
Gordon, Charles, 771
Gordon, George (1751-1793), 458
Gordon, George (1788-1824). *See* Byron, Lord
Gordon, Thomas, 483
Gordon riots, 458
Göring, Hermann, 861
Gosplan, 840
Gothic architecture, 224–225, *225,* 584, *584*
Goths, 149, 155–156
Gouges, Olympe de, 541, 543, 554
Government
absolute monarchy in France, 374, 381–382
absolutionism (Enlightenment), 517–527
absolutionism (Hobbes), *415,* 415–416
absolutionism *versus* parliamentary monarchy, 374
Athenian, 46–49, 65–67, 75
Charles II and restoration of the monarchy, 378–379
counts of Charlemagne, 191
divine right of Kings, 374, 382, 386, 617
Egyptian, 17
Etruscan, 98
feudal, 186, 198–199
Franks, 187–188
Great Depression and, 836–838
Hittites, 22
Homeric, 38
key events/dates, 648–649
Long Parliament, 377–378
Macedonian, 87–88
medieval, 238–239, 278
monarchy in northern Europe, revival of, 297–301, lxvi
Persian, 25–26
Roman, early, 99–100
Rome, Republic, 121–125
Spartan, 45
Sumerian, 7
in 19th century, 708
tyrants of ancient Greece, 43–44
Goya, Francisco de, 573, *573*
Gracchus, Gaius, 118
Gracchus, Tiberius, *115,* 116–119
Grammaticus, 111
Gramsci, Antonio, 958
Grand Alliance, 390
Grand Army of Napoleon, 574
Grand National Union, 641
Grandi, 283
Granicus River, Battle of, 88
Grant, Duncan, 738
Granvelle, Cardinal, 353–354
Gratian, 241
Great Britain. *See* Britain
Great Depression
in Britain, 836, 838
factors leading to, 834–836
in France, 836, 838
major dates, 857
Nazi and, 851
Great Exhibition, *631,* 694
Great Fear, 537
Great Game, 778
Great Northern War, 398, 400–401
Great Peloponnesian War, 73–74, 78
Great Purges, 843–844
Great Reform Bill of 1832, 619–620, 760
Great Schism (1378-1417), 187, 274–276
Great Sphinx, 17, *17*
Great Trek, 775
Great Wall of China, 167, *168*
Grebel, Conrad, 326–327
Greece
imperialism and ancient, 794
revolution of 1821, 608
in the 1920s, 863
Truman Doctrine, 904–905
World War I, 805, *812, 828*
World War II, 765
Greece, ancient
agriculture, 47, 49–50
Athens, 46–49
Bronze Age, 34–36
chronology, *43*
colonization, *42,* 42–43
expansion of, 40–44
government, 38
Homer, age of, 38–39
hoplite phalanx, 40, 43, 47, *57,* 65, 169
Ionians, 54
Magna Graecia, 42
map of, *16, 42*
middle ages, 37–39
migrations, 37–38
Minoans, 34–35
Mycenaeans, *16,* 34, 35–36
Persian wars, 25, 54–58, *55*
poetry, 53
polis, 39–40, 46, 48, 58–59, 78
religion, 34, 50, 52–53
society, 45, 49–50
Sparta, 44–45
tyrants, 43–44
women, 39
Greece, classical
agriculture, 72
architecture and sculpture, *66, 69,* 76, *77,* 80, *81, 82, 83*
Athenian democracy, 65–69
Athenian empire, 64, *64*
Athens, fall of, 74
Attic tragedy, 76
Cimon, 63
culture of, 75–86
defined, 75
Delian League, 61, 62–63
division of, 63–64
drama, 80
historical literature, 79–80
map of, *62*
Old Comedy, 76, 78
Peloponnesian War, First, 63–64
Peloponnesian War, Great, 73–74, 78
philosophy, 76–78

Greece, classical *(cont.)*
religion, 72–73
slavery, 71–72
Sparta, hegemony of, 74–75
Thebes, hegemony of, 75
women, 67, 70–71, 85
Greece, Hellenistic
Alexander the Great, 88–90
Alexander the Great, successors to, 90–91
architecture and sculpture, *61, 86, 91,* 93
education, 111, 113
literature, 93
Macedonian conquest, 86–88
mathematics and science, 93–94
philosophy, 91–93
Roman conquest of, 108–109
use of term, 86
Greek League, 57
Greek thoughts, influence of, 30–31
Green movement, *962*
Greens (German), 962
Gregory I (the Great), Pope, 186, 192
Gregory IX, Pope, 214, 215
Gregory VII, Pope, 203, 206–207
Gregory X, Pope, 267
Gregory XI, Pope, 274
Gregory XII, Pope, 276
Gregory XIII, Pope, 122, 349
Grenville, George, 481
Grey, Earl, 620
Grey, Edward, 803, 811
Grey, Jane, 356, 357
Grimm, Jakob, 588
Grimm, Wilhelm, 588
Grocyn, William, 303
Gros, Antoine, *590*
Grounds of National Philosophy (Cavendish), 420
Grunewald, Matthias, *313*
Guadalcanal, 879
Guam, 879
Guayaquil, 613
Gudea, 6
Guelf, 283
Guesde, Jules, 713
Guicciardini, Francesco, 289, 296
Guilds, 627
in France, 541
medieval, 238–239, 262
Reformation and, 314
18th century, 458
Guises, 348–350, 356
Guizot, Francois, 638, 646
Gunboat diplomacy, 782
Gustavus Adolphus II, King of Sweden, 367–368
Gustavus Vasa, King of Sweden, 329
Gutenberg, Johann, 253, 301, *301*
Gymnastics in Germany, 604

H

Habsburg Empire, *277,* 393, 466, 521
Austrian Succession, war of, 478–479
formation of dual monarchy, 678
key events/dates, 678
nationalities within, 601, 678–680, *679*
peasants/serfs in, 438, 521–522
revolution of 1848, 649–650, *650*
18th century, 393–395, *394*
unrest of nationalities, 678–680
Habsburg-Valois wars, 296, 348
Habubah Kabirah, 6
Hacienda, 309
Hacienda economy, 309
Hadrian, 136, 139, 143
Haeckel, Ernst, 728
Hagenbeck, Carl, 791
Hagia Sophia, 176, *176,* 187
Haiti
Revolution, 477, 610, *610,* 612, *657,* 657–658
Hall of Mirrors, 431, *672,* 674
Haman the Agagite, *523*
Hamilcar Barca, 107
Hamlet (Shakespeare), 342
Hammer of Witches (Krämer & Sprenger), 429
Hammurabi, Code of, 7, *11,* 14, 30
Hampton Court Conference, 374
Hannibal, 107–108, 712
Hanoverian dynasty, 380
Hans Holbein the Younger, *331*
Hansemann, David, 652
Hardenberg, Prince von, 570
Hardie, Keir, 712
Harding, Warren, 834
Hargreaves, James, 450, *451*
Harmodius, *48*
Hartwell, Emily, *785*
Harun-al-Rashid, 191
Harvey, William, 415
Hasdrubal, 107
Hastings, Battle of (1066), 216, *216*
Hathaway, Anne, 342
Hatshepsut, 21
Hatti-i Hümayun, 663
Hatti-i Sharif of Gülhane, 662
Hattusas, 22
Haussmann, Georges, 697
Havel, Václav, 930
Hawkins, John, 360
Heart of Darkness (Conrad), 775
Hebrews, 24, 30
Hedio, Caspar, 325
Hegel, G.W.F., 588, 589, 600, 642, 643
Hegira, 178
Heidegger, Martin, 959
Heisenberg, Werner, 736
Hektemoroi, 72
Helena, 80
Heliocentric theory, 94, 409
Heliopolis, 20
Hellenistic Greece. *See* Greece, Hellenistic
Hellespont, 25, 54, 63, 74
Heloise, 245, 246–247
Helots, 44, 63, 72, 794
Helsinki Accords, 917, 926
Henlein, Konrad, 870
Henry I, King of England, 216
Henry I (the Fowler), King of Germany, 203
Henry II, King of England, 216–217, 219, 230
Henry II, King of France, 228, 348, 350
Henry III, Holy Roman Emperor, 205
Henry III, King of England, 220, 268
Henry III, King of France, 350
Henry IV, Holy Roman Emperor, 205, 206–207
Henry IV, King of France (Henry of Navarre), 348, 349, 350–352, *352,* 374, 381, 384, *605*
Henry the Lion, Duke of Saxony, 221, 222
Henry the Navigator, 303
Henry V, Holy Roman Emperor, 207
Henry V, King of England, 265
Henry VI, Holy Roman Emperor, 209, 222–223
Henry VI, King of England, 265, 299
Henry VII, King of England, 239, 297, 299, 331
Henry VIII, King of England, 299, 330–332, *331,* 356, 357, 360
Hephaestus, 50
Hera, 50
Heracleitus, 165
Heracles, 86
Heraclidae, 36
Heraclides of Pontus, 94
Heraclitus, 76
Heraclius, 177
Herder, Johann Gottfried, 509, 510, 579, 587–588, 589
Herders, 3
Herero people, 775, *776*
Hermandad, 299
Hermes, 50, 73
of Praxiteles, 80
Hermopolis, 20
Herodotus, 23, 56, 79
Herrmann (Arminius), 131
Herzegovina, 804
Herzen, Alexander, 681–682
Herzl, Theodor, 747, *747,* 748, 909
Hesiod, 49, 50, 134
Hestia, 50
Hetaira, 70
Hevelius, Elisabeth, 421
Hevelius, Johannes, 421
Hidalgo y Costilla, Miguel, 613–614
Hiero, 106
Hieroglyphics, 19, 35
Higglers, 439
Hill, Rowland, 685
Himmler, Heinrich, 854, 886
Hindenburg, Paul von, 815, 822, 850, 851–852, 854
Hipparchus, 48, *48,* 94
Hippias, 47, 48, *48,* 54
Hippocrates of Cos, 31, 80
Hippodamus of Miletus, 93, 250
Hippodrome, 175
Hirohito, Emperor of Japan, 885
Hiroshima, *865,* 884
History of Ancient Art (Winckelmann), 516
History of Rome (Livy), 134, 160
History of the Peloponnesian War (Thucydides), 74, 79, 415
History of the Russian Empire under Peter the Great (Voltaire), 517
History of the Saracens (Ockley), 502
History of the Two Indies (Raynal), 510
Hitler, Adolf, *873, 875,* 883. *See also* Nazis
early career, 848–851, *849*
goals of, 866
plans for Europe, 869–874, 878
remilitarization of Rhineland, 867–868
Richstag fire, 852
rise to power, 851–854, *853*
women, role of, 855, 857, 859–860
Hittites, 2, *16,* 18
HMS Albatross (ship), *656*
Ho Chi Minh, 924
Hobbes, Thomas, *415,* 415–416, 418
Hobson, J.A., 763
Hogarth, William, 455
Hohenstaufen Empire, lxxv
Frederick I Barbarossa, 221–222
Frederick II, 220, 223–224
Henry VI, 222–223
map of, *222*
Otto IV, 223
Hohenzollerns, 392, 395–397, 673
Holland, 390–391, 618
Holocaust, *886,* 886–887, *887,* 890–891, *891,* 965–966, *966*
Holstein, 671
Holy Alliance (1815), *575,* 576, 607
Holy Club, 586
Holy Land, 207
Holy League (1511), 296
Holy Roman Empire
formation of, 190
medieval, 203, 220–225
revival of monarchy in, 300–301
Thirty Years' War (1618-1648), 365–367, *366*
Holy Synod, 401
Homage to Catalonia (Orwell), 958
Homer, 34, 36, 38, 111, 134, 164, 171
Homo sapiens, 2
Honest to God (Robinson), *967*
Hong Kong, 879
Hooker, Joseph Dalton, *788*
Hooper, John, 357
Hoover, Herbert, 836
Hoplite phalanx, 40, 43, 47, *57,* 65, 169
Horace, 126, 133, 134
Horemheb, 18, 20
Horney, Karen, 749
Horse, introduction to Americas, 490
Horthy, Miklós, 862
Hospitallers, 212
Hotman, Francois, 350
Hotzendorf, Conrad von, 806
Houdon, Jean-Antoine, *497, 508,* 517
House of Commons, 377–378, 484, 485, 712
House of Hanover, 380, 391
House of Lancaster, 299
House of Lords, 378, 687, 694, 712
House of York, 299
House (Whiteread), 966
Houses of Parliament (British), 583
Housing
Artisan Dwelling Art (1875), 686
Neolithic Age, 3
reforms in 19th century, 700
Roman apartments, 142
slums, 697
Howard, Catherine, 332
Howard, John, 637
Huber, A.V., 700
Hubertusburg, Treaty of (1763), 480
Hubris, 52–63, 794
Hufton, Olwen, 442
Hugo, Victor, 579
Huguenots, 346, 348–350, 388, 499
Hugues, Besancon, 346
Huizinga, Johan, 281
Humanism, 282, 285–289, 302–303, 337
Humanitas, 111, 285
Humans
gods and, 29–30
nature and, 29
Humans, early
Bronze Age, 4
Neolithic Age, 3–4
Paleolithic Age, 2–3
Humbert, Cardinal, 206
Humbertus, Cardinal, 187
Hume, David, 447, 495, 499–500
Hundred Days, 576–577
Hundred Years' War, 218, 298
causes of, 263, 265
conclusion of, 265–267
French defeat, 265
key events/dates, 266
map of, *264*
Hungary/Hungarians, 203

aristocracy of 18th century, 435
Austria-Hungary, formation of, 678, 679
collapse of communism, 929
Habsburg, 393, 649–650
Magyars, 195, *195*, 393, 479, 521, 524, 600, 649–650, 678, 829, 862
in the 1920s, 862
under Soviet control, 905, 909
uprising of 1956, 914
World War I, 806, 807, *812*, 825
Huns, 155, 156, 157, 172
Hunt, Henry "Orator," 605
Hurrians, 7, 22
Husak, Gustav, 930
Huss, John, 255, *273*, 273–274, 320
Hussein, Saddam, 941, 942, 943
Hussein of Mecca, 823, *824*
Hussites, 273–274, 276, 315
Hutten, Ulrich von, 302
Huxley, Thomas Henry, 728, 729, 730–731, 749
Hyksos, 18, 166

I

IBM, 970, 971
Ibn-Maymum (Maimonides), 183
Ibn-Rushd (Averröes), 183
Ibn-Sina (Avicenna), 183, *262*
Ibsen, Henrik, 737
Iconoclasm, *186*, 187
Idealism, German, 687
Ignatius of Loyola, 333–334, 337
Iliad (Homer), 36, 38, 164, 171
Illuminated manuscripts, *193*
Illustrations of Political Economy (Martineau), 638
Imitation of Christ (Kempis), 315
Imperator, 130, 135
Imperial Hall, 514, *516*
Imperialism. *See also* New Imperialism
defined, 755, 793
European, 796
Greeks and, 794
Muslims, Mongols, and Ottomans and, 795–796
Romans and, 107–108, 794–795
science and, 787–791
Tools of, 782
Imperialism: A Study (Hobson), 763
Imperialism: The Highest Stage of Capitalism (Lenin), 763
Imperialism of free trade, 756–757
Imperium, 99, 101, 103, 108, 120
Imperium maius, 130
Impositions, 374
Impressionism, *739*, 739–740
In Search of Time Past (A la Recherche du temps perdu) (Proust), 738, *738*
Incas, 305, 307, 796
Index of Forbidden Books, 256, 302
India, 465
British in, 757–761, *759*, 920–922
decolonization, 920–921
Indian, use of term, 305, 308
Indian National Congress, 761, 920–921
Indigenous religious movements, 787
Indirect rule, 774
Indochina, 924
Indochina Communist Party, 924
Indonesia, 920
Indulgences, 208, 272, 315, 318–319
Industrial Revolution, 18th century
consumption of consumer goods, *448*, 448–449
defined, 448
in England, 449
iron production, 452
steam engine, 451
textile production, 449–451
women, impact on, *448*, 452–453
Industrial Revolution, 19th century
1848 revolutions, 645–653
crime and order, 634–638
economy, 638–639
employment, 626–630
family structures, 630, 632
key events/dates, 648–649, 691
map of, *645*, *693*
new industries, 692–693
population and migration, 623–624
railways, 624, *624*, 626, *626*
second, 691–694
socialism, 639–645
women in, 632–634
Infanticide, 249, 430
Ingres, Jean, *561*
Innocent III, Pope, 211, 214, 218, 223, 242, 267, 269
Innocent IV, Pope, 224
Innocent VIII, Pope, 429
Innocent X, Pope, 388
Innocent XI, Pope, 389
Inquiry into Human Nature (Hume), 499
Inquiry into the Nature and Causes of the Wealth of Nations (Smith), 505, 506, 509
Inquisition, 214
French, 221, 355
Spanish, 299
Institutes (Justinian), 176
Institutes of the Christian Religion (Calvin), 328, 329
Insula of Febiala, 142
Insulae, 142
Intel Corporation, 971
Intellectuals, communism and, 958–960
Intendants, 466
Intermediate Period, 18
Internal combustion engine, 693, 980
International African Association, 774
International Business Machines Corporation, 970, 971
International WorKing Men's Association, 711
Interpretations of Dreams, The (Freud), 744
Intolerable Acts, 482
Introduction to the Study of Experimental Medicine (Bernard), 737
Investiture struggle, 203, 206–207
Ionia/Ionians, 25, 54, 62
Ipatescu, Ana, *622*
Iphigenia in Tauris, 80
Iran, revolution of 1979, 940–941
Iraq
coalition war against, 943
formation of, 829
invasion of Kuwait, 941
Ireland
British and the Irish problem, 595, 687
Catholic Emancipation Act, 619
Charles I and, 377
Cromwell and, 378, *378*
famine of 1845-1847, 491, 624, 625
Free State, 836, 838
Home Rule Bill, 687, 838
Irish Free State, 836, 838
Irish Land League, 687
Irish Poor Relief Act (1847), 625
Irish Republican Army (IRA), 836
Irnerius, 176, 241
Iron
discovery of, 22
production in the 18th century, 452
Iron Age, 22
Iron Curtain, 904
Irrigation in early civilizations, 4–5
Isabel Christiana, 659
Isabella II, Queen of Spain, 303, 330, 341, 673
Isabella of Castile, 297, 298–299, 350, 466
Isagoras, 48
Isidore of Miletus, 250
Isin, 7
Islam/Islamic, 2. *See also* Muslims
Byzantine Empire and, 178–183
disputes and diversity, 179
empires, 182, *182*
Enlightenment and, 502–504
fundamentalism, 941
imperialism and, 795–796
late-19th century, 734
Muhammad, 178–179, 502, 503, 588–589, 734
reformism, 941
rise of, 178–183
rise of radical political, 940–942
Romanticism and, 588–591
view by world, 588–591, *590*
Western debt to, 182–183
Island of Dr. Moreau, The (Wells), *727*
Isocrates, 86, 87
Israel, *27*, 28
Arab-Israeli conflict, 910–911
creation of the state of, 909, 910
Israelites (Hebrews), 2, 24, 27–28, 30. *See also* Jews; Judaism
key events/dates, 28
Issus, Battle of, 88, *794*
Isthmus of Corinth, 50
Italia irredenta, 670, 814
Italy
attack on Ethiopia, 866–867
city-states, *283*, 283–285
fascism, 844–847
Frederick I Barbarossa, 221–222, 240
French invasions of (1494-1527), 295–297
Gallic invasion of, 104
Hohenstaufen Empire, 221–222
humanism, 282, 285–289
prehistoric, 98, *98*
Renaissance, 282–295, *284*, *286*
revolution of 1848, *645*, 650, 652
Roman conquest of, 103–105
Roman war against, 119
Triple Alliance, 800–801
unification of, 664–670, *667*
World War I and, 805, 814–815, 825, 827, 829
World War II and, 880
It's That Man Again, 895
Iturbide, Augustín, 614
Ivan III/Ivan the Great, 279
Ivan IV, the Terrible, 397
Ivan the Terrible, 853, 897
Ivan V, 397
Ivan VI, of Russia, 524
Ivo, St., 242
Ivory, *774*

J

Jacobins, 546, 548, 552, 553–554, 556, 563
Jacquerie, 260, 265
Jacques Bonhomme, 265
Jahn, Friedrich Ludwig, 604
James, 145
James Edward, the Stuart pretender, 380
James I, King of England, 362, 374–375, 431
James II, King of England, 379–380
James V, King of Scotland, 362
James VI, King of Scotland, 362, 374
Jamestown, 470
Janissaries, 402
Jansen, Cornelius, 384, 388
Jansenists, 335, 384–385, 388, 425
January Edict, 348
Japan
imperialism and, 762
in Manchuria, 878
Russo-Japanese War (1904-1905), 803
World War I and, 815, 824, 827
World War II and, 878–879, 885–886
Jardin des Plantes, 788
Jaruzelski, Wojciech, 918, 929
Jaspers, Karl, 959
Jaurès, Jean, 713
Jefferson, Thomas, 517
Jellachich, Joseph, 649
Jena, Battle of (1806), 568
Jenkins, Robert, 478
Jenkins's Ear, war of (1739), 478, 608
Jericho
fortress walls of, 165, *165*
Neolithic Age, 3
Jerome, 160, 184
Jerome, brother to Napoleon, 569
Jerome of Prague, 274
Jerusalem
Crusades and, 207
Jerusalem: or, On Ecclesiastical Power and Judaism (Mendelsohn), 502
Jesuits, 333–334, 357, 365, 384, 425
Jesus of Nazareth, 28, 145, *147*, 159
Jewish State, The (Herzl), 747, 748
Jews
anti-Semitism, *709*, 710, 745, 746, 747–748, 848–849, 854–856, *855*, 886–891, 893
Belorussian, 458, 469
Black Death and, 258
in Byzantine Empire, 186, 208
court, 459
crusades and, 208
Enlightenment and, 501–502
holocaust, *886*, 886–887, *887*, 890–891, *891*, 965–966, *966*
in the Middle Ages, 239, *240*
pogroms, 208, 258, 709
Roman, 139, 145, 186
in Spain, 299
18th century, 458–459
19th century, 709–710
Jihad, 941, 942
Jiménez de Cisneros, Francisco, 299, 303
Jinnah, Ali, 921
Joan of Arc, 265–266, *266*, 268, 298
Joanna the Mad, 299
João VI, King of Brazil, 614
Jodl, Alfred, 868
John, King of England, 211, 218, 220, 239
John George I, of Saxony, 367, 368
John II (the Good), King of France, 265

John III Sobieski, King of Poland, 392, *393*
John of Austria, Don, 353
John of Paris, 270–272
John Paul I, 967
John Paul II, Pope (Karol Wojtyla), 425, 917, 967–968, *968*
John VIII, Pope, 194
John XII, Pope, 203–204
John XXII, Pope (1316-1347), 272–273
John XXIII, Pope (1958), 967
John XXIII, Pope (1410-1415), 276
Johnson, Lyndon, 925
Johnson, Samuel, 494
Joinville, Treaty of (1584), 356
Joseph, brother to Napoleon, 570
Joseph I, of Austria, 394
Joseph II, of Austria, 519, 520–524, 527, 531, 709
Josephine de Beauharnais, 571
Josephinism, 521
Joyce, James, 738
Judah, 24, 28
Judaism, 2, 27, 157
Judith of Bavaria, 192
Jugurtha, King of Numidia, 119
Jugurthine War (111), 119, 133
Julia, daughter of Augustus, 132, 142
Julian the Apostate, 155, 159
Julius Excluded from Heaven (Erasmus), 296
Julius II, Pope, 292, 296, 318, 331
July Monarchy (France), 618, 638
July Revolution, 617–618
Jung, Carl, *743,* 743–744
Junkers, 395–397, 435, 570
Juntas, 612, 613
Jus gentium (law of peoples), 133
Jus naturale (natural law), 133
Justification by faith, 316, 318
Justinian, Emperor, 83, 171, 174–176, 186
Juvenal, 142, 144

K

Ka'ba, 178
Kadar, Janos, 914, 929
Kadesh, 22
Kamose, 18
Kant, Immanuel, 495, 501, 509, 510, 520, 568, 579
Kapp Putsch, 847
Kappel, Battles of (1529 and 1531), 325
Karnak, 20
Kashmir, 922
Kassites, *16,* 22
Kaunitz, Wenzel Anton, 480
Kautsky, Karl, 714
Kay, James, 450
Kazakhs, 778
Kellogg-Briand Pact (1928), 851
Kemal, Mustafa. *See* Ataturk
Kempis, Thomas à, 315
Kennedy, John F., 914, 915, 925
Kenya, 922
Kepler, Johannes, 410, 412
Kerensky, Alexander, 818
Kew Garden, 788, *788,* 789
Key, Ellen, 750
Keynes, John Maynard, 738, 830, 837
Khafre (Chephren), 17, *17*
Kharjites, 179
Khedives, 768, 771
Khosro I, King, 171
Khrushchev, Nikita, *844,* 913–914, 915, 916, 964
Khufu (Cheops), 17
Kierkegaard, Soren, 959, 967
Kiev, 278, 279
Kikongo, 476
Kikuyu tribe, 787
King, Martin Luther, Jr., 920–921
King Lear (Othello), 342
King Lear (Shakespeare), 342
King Tut, *1*
Kingdom of Kongo, 473
Kingdom of the Serfs, Croats, and Slovenes, 829, 862
Kirch, Gottfried, 421
Kirov, Sergei, 843
Kish, 6
Kitchener, Herbert, 771, 772, 773, *773*
Klein, Melanie, 749
Knighthood, 230
Knights of the Round Table, 217
Knights Templars, 208, 212, 239, 272
Knox, John, 350, 357, 362
Koch, Robert, 699
Koestler, Arthur, 958
Kohl, Helmut, 930
Kollontai, Alexandra, 858–859
Komeini (Khymayni), Ruhollah, 940–941
Korean War (1950-1953), 911, *912*
Kosciuszko, Tadeusz, 49
Kosovo, 937
Kossuth, Louis, 649, *650*
Kosygin, Alexei, 916
Kotzebue, August von, 602, *602,* 603
Krämer, Heinrich, 429
Kreditanstalt, 835
Kristallnacht, 855, 856
Kristeller, Paul O., 285
Kruger, Paul, 803
Krupp family, 694
Kuchuk-Kainardji, Treaty of (1774), 526, 562
Kulaks, 715, 841–842, *842*
Kulikov Meadow, Battle of, 279
Kulturkampf, 732
Kun, Bela, 862
Kutuzov, Mikhail, 574
Kuwait, 940, 941
Kyd, Thomas, 342

L

Labor. *See also* Employment
  child, 632, 716
  factory workers in 19th century, 626–627, 632–633, *633,* 635
  post World War I, 834
  unions, *710,* 710–711
  of women, *448,* 632–634, *633,* 703–704, *704*
Labor Front, 861
Labour Party (British), 712, 836
Lacombe, Claire, 553
Lade, 54
Ladies' National Association for the Repeal of the Contagious Diseases Act, 750
Lafayette, Marquis de, 535
Lagarde, Paul de, 745
Lagash, 6
Laibach, congress of (1821), 607
Laissez-faire economics, 505, 638
Lamartine, Alphonse de, 646
Lancaster, House of, 299
Land and Freedom, 682
Langbehn, Julius, 745
Language(s), 2. *See also under type of*
  Aramaic, 22, 25
  Egyptian, 19
  Italic, 98
  nationalism and, 594–595
  Semitic, 22
  of slaves, 476–477
  Sumerian, 6
Laocoön, *91*
Laos, 924
Larsa, 7
Larson, Henning, *972*
Las Casas, Bartolomé de, 307, *308*
Lasalle, Ferdinand, 713
Last Judgment (Michelangelo), *294*
Late Antiquity, 171
Lateran Accord (1929), 670, 847
Latifundia, 113, 115, 166
Latimer, Hugh, 357
Latin America. *See also under name of country*
  early exploration of, 303–307, 463–465
  map of, *611*
  viceroyalties in, 466, *468*
  wars of independence, 608–614
Latin League, 104
Latins/Latium, 98, 99, 104
Latvia, 829, 932
Laud, William, 377
Lausanne Conference, 836
Law
  Athenian, 46–47
  Byzantium Empire, 176
  Code of Hammurabi, 7, *11,* 14, 30
  Corpus Juris Civilis (Body of Civil Law) (Justinian), 176, 241
  Draconian, 46
  Enlightenment and, 505
  Licinian-Sextian, 102
  Magna Carta (1215), 209, 218, 224
  mallus under Charlemagne, 191
  Napoleonic Code, 564, 598, 700
  papacy, 272
  revival of Roman, in Middle Ages, 221
  Roman, 100–101, 133, 172
  19th century and family, 700–701
  Twelve Tables, 102, 111
Law, John, 391, *391*
Law of 22 Prairial, 555, 556
Lawrence, T.E., 815, *824,* 830
Le Pen, Jean-Marie, 949
League of Augsburg (1686), 388, 390
League of Corinth, 87
League of Nations, 822, 824, 827, 831, 851, 866, 867
League of Venice, 295, 296
LeBon, Gustave, 745
Lechfeld, 203
Lectures on Dramatic Art and Literature (Schlegel), 579
Lectures on the Philosophy of History (Hegel), 588
Lefèvre d'Etaples, Jacques, 303
Legislative Assembly, 539, 541, 546–547
Legnano, Battle of, 222
LEGO Co., 963
Leif Erikson, 195
Leipzig, Battle of, 574, 602
Leipzig Mission, 785
Lelio, 327
LeNain, Louis, 431
Lenin, Vladimir Ilyich Ulyanov, 715, 716, *716,* 719–720, 763, 817, 820, 821–822, 838–840, *839*
Leningrad Symphony (Shostakovich), 897
Leo I, Pope, 184, 185
Leo III, Emperor, 177, 187, 190
Leo III, Pope, 187, 190, 211
Leo IX, Pope, 205
Leo X, Pope, 297, 318, 319, 320, 330
Leo XIII, Pope, 734, 735
Léon, Pauline, 547, 553
Leonardo da Vinci, 292, *293*
Leonidas, King, 57, 58
Leopold I, of Austria, 390, 393–394, 397
Leopold II, of Austria, 524, 546
Leopold II, of Belgium, 774, 775, 790
Leopold of Hohenzollern, 673
Leopold of Saxe-Coburg, 619
Leotychidas, 58
Lepanto, Battle of (1571), 353, 360, 403
Lepidus, M. Aemilius, 125, 126
Leptis Magna, *139*
Lesbos, 64
Lespinasse, Julie de, 511
Lessing, Gotthold, 495, 499, 502, 568
Letter Concerning Toleration (Locke), 417, 499
Letter to the Grand Duchess Christina (Galileo), 421, 424
Letters from Prison (Gramsci), 958
Letters of Obscure Men, 302
Letters on a Regicide Peace (Burke), 550
Letters on Sunspots (Galileo), 410
Letters on the English (Voltaire), 497
Letters to the Ancient Dead (Petrarch), 285
Leucippus of Miletus, 77
Leuctra, Battle of, 75
Levasseur, E., 696
Levée en masse, 551, 558
Leviathan (Hobbes), 415, *415,* 418
Lewis, C.S., 967
Lexington, Battle of, 483
Liberal theology, 967
Liberal Unionists, 687
Liberalism
  early nineteenth century, 595, 598–600
  economic goals, 598–599
  political goals, 595, 598
  relationship to nationalism, 600
Liberia, 659
Liberty Leading the People (Delacroix), *593*
Liberum veto, 392, 549
Libri Carolini, 190
Libya, 876
  French in, 768
Licinian-Sextian Laws, 102
Lictors, 101, 103, *103*
Liebknecht, Wilhelm, 713
Life of Jesus, The (Strauss), 729
"Life of the Prophet," 170
Lin Tse-hsü, 758
Linacre, Thomas, 303
Lincoln, Abraham, 659
Lindau Gospels, 193
Linear A and B, 35, 36
List, Friedrich, 639
Lister, Joseph, 699
Literature. *See also under name of work or author*
  Attic tragedy, 76
  Babylonian, 9
  Christian writers, 160–161
  courtly love/troubadours, 217, 230
  Egyptian, 19, *19*
  fiction, *743*
  Greek, ancient, 53, 56–57
  Greek, classical, 71, 76, 79–80
  Greek, Hellenistic, 93
  Homeric, 38, 49
  humanism, 285–289, 302–303
  for the mass audience in the 19th century, 725–726
  medieval illuminated manuscripts, 193
  Mesopotamian, 9

modernism, 738–739
nonfiction works, 750
Old Comedy, 76, 78
print culture, impact of, 493, *494,* 494–495
realism and naturalism, 737–739
Reformation and, 341–343
Roman, 113, 133–135, 142–143, 160–161
romantic, 579–582
science fiction, 727
Sumerian, 6, *9*
Lithuania, 829, 932, 933
Liverpool, Lord, 602, 619
Lives of Illustrious Men (Petrarch), 285
Livestock
exchange between Americas and Europe, 490–491
Livia, wife of Augustus, *129,* 135, 142
Livingstone, David, 788
Livius Andronicus, 109
Livy, 15, 105, 134, 160, 285, 517
Lloyd George, David, 712, 824, *825,* 827
Locarno Agreement (1925), 850–851, 867
Locke, John, 380, 386, 387, *416,* 416–418, 483, 493, 499, 508, 641
Lodi, Treaty of (1454-1455), 295
Lodz, 889, 890
Lofthouse, Richard, 975
Logos, 92
Lollards, 273–274
Lombard, Peter, 245, 337, 338
Lombards, 182, 186, 188, 189
London
terrorist attacks on, 943, *944*
18th century, 449, 453, 455
World War II, 876
London, treaties of (1827, 1830), 608
London Corresponding Society, 549
London Foundling Hospital, 443
London Missionary Society, 784
London WorKing Men's Association, 627
Long Parliament, 377–378
Longinus, Gaius Cassius, 123, 126
Lorenzo the Magnificent, 284, 297
Lorraine, 669, 674
Lothar, 192, 194
Lothar II, 194
Lotharingia, 194, 203
Louis I, Prince of Condé, 348–349
Louis II, Emperor, 194
Louis III, King of France, 381
Louis IV, Holy Roman Emperor, 272, 274
Louis IX, King of France, 220–221, 235, 267, 269, 350
Louis of Nassau, 349, 354, 355
Louis Philippe, King of France, 618, 638, 646, *647*
Louis the German, King of Bavaria, 192
Louis the Pious, 192, 194
Louis VI (the Fat), King of France, 220
Louis VII, King of France, 217, 220, 221
Louis VIII, King of France, 214, 221
Louis XI, King of France, 295
Louis XII, King of France, 295–296
Louis XIII, King of France, *383,* 384
Louis XIV, King of France, 352, 372, 374, 379, 380, *381,* 381–390, 391, 396, *418,* 431, 491, 514, 530, 876
Louis XV, King of France, 391, 479, 511, 514, 516, 517, 530, 531
Louis XVI, King of France, 516, 517, *530,* 530–532, 534–535, *536,* 537, 539, 541, 545–549, *546, 548,* 600, 605
Louis XVII, King of France, 605
Louis XVIII, King of France, *605,* 605–606, 617
Lourdes, 732
L'Ouverture, Francois-Dominique Toussaint, 610, *610,* 612, 657, *657*
Lovett, William, 627
Lucas, Charles, 637
Lucien, 566
Lucinde (Schlegel), 581
Lucretius, 133
Ludendorff, Erich, 815, 822, 849
Ludwig II, King of Bavaria, 583, *584,* 652
Lueger, Karl, 747, 848
Luftwaffe, 876
Lullubi, *6*
Luneville, Treaty of (1801), 563
Lupercalia, 111, 125
Lusitania, 815
Luther, Martin, 256, 291, 302, 303, 314, 315, 316–324, *318, 324,* 335, 338, 350
Lutheranism, 341, 346
expansion of, 327–329
Thirty Years' War (1618-1648), 364–368
Lützen, Battle of (1632), 368
Luxembourg, 909
Lyceum, 84, 91
Lydia, 53
Lyell, Charles, 729
Lyons, Council of (1274), 267
Lyrical Ballards (Wordsworth and Coleridge), 581
Lysander, 74
Lysippus, 80
Lysistrata (Aristophanes), 78–79
Lytton, Earl of, 866
Lytton Report, 866

M

Maastricht, Treaty of (1991), 973
Macaulay, Thomas Babington, 760
Macbeth (Shakespeare), 342
MacDonald, Ramsay, 836
Macedon/Macedonians
Cimon and, 63
collapse of Yugoslavia and civil war, 935–936
government of Greece, 87–88
invasion of Greece, 87
Philip II, 86–88
Philip V, 108–109
rise of, *88*
Roman conquest of, 74, 108–109, 169
Macedonian Wars, 108–109
Mach, Ernest, 735
Machiavelli, Niccoló, 289, 296–297, *297*
Machine gun, 784, *784*
Macintosh computer, 971
MacMahon, Marshal, 675
Madame Bovary (Flaubert), 737
Madrid, terrorist attack on, 934
Maecenas, 126, 133, 134
Maenads, 53, *76*
Magellan, Ferdinand, 305
Magic Mountain, The (Mann), 738
Maginot Line, 868, 875
Magna Carta (1215), 209, 218, 224
Magna Graecia, 42
Magnitogorsk, *841*
Magyars (Hungarians), 195, *195,* 393, 479, 521, 524, 600, 649–650, 678, 829, 862
Mahdist movement, 734
Maimonides, Moses (ibn Maymun), 183
Maintenon, Madame de, 388, *388*
Maize, 491
Malaria, 782
Malaya, 879
Mallus, 191
Malthus, Thomas, 638, 728
Mamai, St., *151*
Mamertines, 106
Man and Superman (Shaw), 738
Mandates, 824, 829
Manet, Edward, 739–740
Mangena Makone, 787
Mani, 157–158
Manichaeism, 157–158
Mann, Thomas, 738
Mannerism, 292
Manors
Carolingian, 198–199
medieval, 234–236
Mansi, 198
Mantinea, Battle of, 75
Manumission, 113
Manzikert, 178
Mao Tse-tung, 911
Marathon, 54, xliv
Marburg Colloquy, 325
Marcel, Etienne, 265
March Laws (Hungary), 649
Marcus Agrippa, 126, *131*
Marcus Antonius, 112, 125
Marcus Aurelius, 136, *136,* 139, 148–149
Mardonius, 58
Marduk, 24, 29
Margaret of Parma, 353
Marguerite of Valois, 349
Maria Theresa, 394, 395, 478–479, *479,* 480, 519, 521, 522–523
Marian exiles, 357
Marie, Countess of Champagne, 217
Marie, Henrietta, 375
Marie Antoinette, 531, 534, 541, 546, 547, 549, *554,* 555
Marie Louise, 571
Marie Thérèse, 384
Marignano, Battle of, 296, 324
Marius, 119–120
Mark Antony, 112, 124, 126–127, *131,* 133
Marlborough, Duke of, 875
Marlowe, Christopher, 342
Marne, Battle of (1914), 812
Marriage
Athenian, 39, 67
Carolingian, 248
Christian, 180
Homeric, 38
medieval, 248
Mesopotamian, 14
Muslim, 181
in Nazi Germany, 886
Reformation and, 338, 339
Roman, 100
in the Soviet Union, 858–859
Spartan, 45
18th century, 440, 441, 442
20th century, 953, 957
19th century worKing-class, 634, 703, 705
Married Woman's Property Act (1882), 700
Mars the Avenger, 135
Marshall, George C., 905, *905*
Marshall Plan, 905, 961
Marsilius of Padua, 258, 272, 274, 297
Martel, Charles, 182, 188
Martin of Tours, 184, 192
Martin V, Pope, 276
Martineau, Harriet, 638
Marx, Karl, *642,* 642–645, 711, 718, *719,* 933
Marxism, 642–645, 711–713, 715, 718, 744, 933, 958
Mary I, Queen of England, 330, 333, 350, 356–357, *357, 359,* 372, 379
Mary II, Queen of England, 380
Mary of Guise, 350, 362
Mary Stuart, Queen of Scots, 348, 357, 360, 362, 374
Mary Tudor. *See* Mary I
Masaccio, Donatello, 292
Masaryk, Jan, 908
Masaryk, Thomas, 862, 908
Massachusetts Bay Colony, 374
Master Builder, The (Ibsen), 737
Masurian Lakes, Battle of (1914), 815
Mathematical Principles of Natural Philosophy (Newton), 411
Mathematics
Greek, Hellenistic, 93–94
Mesopotamian, *9*
metric system, 544
Sumerians, *9*
Matthys, Jan, 327
Mauchly, J.W., *970*
Mauguet, Marie, 707
Maupeou, René, 530–531
Maurice, St., *210*
Maurice of Saxony, 330, 354, 356
Max of Baden, Prince, 822
Maxim, Hiram Stevens, *784*
"Maxim" machine gun, *784*
Maximian, 152
Maximilian I, Habsburg Emperor, 295, 296, 298, 299, 300, 319
Maximilian of Austria, 574
Maximilian of Bavaria, 364–365, 367
Maximum Prices, Edict of (301), 154
May Laws, 732
Mazarin, Cardinal, 381
Mazzini, Giuseppe, 596–597, 652, 665
Mecca, 178, 941
Medea (Euripides), 70, 71
Medes, 23, 26
Medici, Cosimo de', 284, 287
Medici, Lorenzo de', 261, 297
Medici, Piero de', 295
Medicine, 789–790
medieval, 261, 262, *262*
Médicis, Catherine de, 348–349, *349,* 350, 356
Medina, 178, 941
Medina-Sidonia, Duke of, 362
Meditations (Descartes), 414
Medvedev, Dmitri, 937
Megara/Megarians, 63, 74
Megenberg, Konrad von, *202*
Mein Kampt (My Struggle) (Hitler), 849, 866, 867
Melanchthon, Philip, 337, 338
Melun Act (1851), 699
Memnon, 88
Memorial to the Peasants' Revolt (Dürer), 323
Memphis, 16
Menander, 80
Mendel, Gregor, 728
Mendelsohn, Moses, 501, 502, 520
Mendoza, Bernadino de, 362

Menes, 15
Menexenus (Plato), 70
Menkaure (Mycerinus), 17
Mennonites, 327
Mensheviks, 716–717, 818
Mentenegro, World War I and, *812*
Mercantile empires, 464–465
Mercantilism, 464–465, 505
Merchants
  in the Middle Ages, 236–238
  Renaissance, 282–283
Merneptah, 18
Merovingians, 187–188
Mersen, Treaty of (870), *194*
Mesoamerica, 305–307
Mesopotamia, 4, *5*
  civilization, 2, 5–14
  government, 7
  key events/dates, 7
  religion, 9–13
  slavery, 14
  society, 14
  Sumer/Sumerians, 2, 5–14
  writing and mathematics, 9
Messalina, wife of Claudius, 142
Messana, 106
Messenia, 44
Mesta, 299
Metamorphoses (Ovid), 134
Metaxas, John, 863
Métayer system of farming, 446–447
Methodism, 586–587, 656
Methodius, 177
Metric system, 544
Metternich, Klemens von, 574, 601, *601,* 603, 607, 649, 824
Mexico, Aztecs in, 305, 306, *307*
Michelangelo Buonarroti, 292, *294*
Middle Ages, early
  Byzantine Empire, 173–178
  Carolingian kingdom, breakup of, 192, 194
  Charlemagne, 187, 189–192
  Christendom, division of, 186–187
  Christian church, developing, 183
  cooking, 197
  feudal society, 196–200
  Franks, 171–173, 182, 185, 187–189
  Germanic migrations, 172, *173*
  Islam/Islamic world, 178–183, *182*
  key events/dates, 188
  major political and religious developments, 188
  monastic culture, 183–184, 188
  papal primacy, doctrine of, 184–186
  Roman Empire, fall of, 171–172
Middle Ages, high
  Catholic Church, revival of, 204–215
  Cluny reform movement, 204–206, 232
  Crusades, 207–211, *209*
  England in, 215–218
  Fourth Lateran Council, 214
  France in, 218–221
  Germany and Italy in, 221–225
  Innocent III, 211, 214, 218, 223
  investiture struggle, 206–207
  key events/dates, 223
  Otto I and revival of the empire, 203–204
  universities, 239–245
Middle Ages, late
  Avignon papacy, 272–273
  Black Death, 257–262
  Boniface VIII and Philip the Fair, 268–271, 272
  church during, 267–277
  Great Schism and Conciliar movement, 274–276
  Hundred Years' War, 262–267
  key events/dates, 266
  Russia during, 278–279
  13th century papacy, 267
Middle Ages, society in
  children, 231, 248–250, *249*
  clergy, 232–234
  courtly love, 230
  government, 238–239
  Jews in Christian society, 239, *240*
  knighthood, 230
  merchants, 236–238
  nobles, 196, 198, 228–232
  peasants/serfs, 198–199, *227, 234,* 234–236, 260
  schools and universities, 239–245
  sportsmen, 230
  towns and townspeople, 236–239
  warriors, 228, *229,* 230
  women, *245,* 245–248
Middle class
  19th century, 694, 696–697
  18th century urban, 455, 457
  women in 19th century, 700–701
Middle East, beliefs in ancient humans and gods, law, and justice, 29–30, 31
  humans and nature, 29
Middle East, romanticism and the, 588–591
Middle Kingdom, 18
Midway Island, 879
Midwives, 430, *430,* 442
Migrations
  ancient Greek, 37–38
  displacement through war, 948
  Germanic, 172, *173*
  19th century, 623–624, 691, *692*
  20th century, 948–950
Milan, 171, 285, 289, 295
Milan, Duchy of, 283, 285, 289
Milan Decree (1807), 566
Miletus, 54, 70
Military/weaponry
  Assyrian, 22, 166
  atomic bombs, *865,* 884–885
  British naval supremacy in, 564, 757
  catapults, 166
  cavalry, mounted, 166–167, *167*
  chariot and bow, 166
  Etruscan, 99
  fortress walls, *165,* 165–166
  French, in the mid-1600s, 384
  Greek, ancient, 52
  Greek *versus* Persian ways, 48
  Hittites, 22
  hoplite phalanx, 40, 43, 47, *57,* 65, 169
  iron-welding warriors, 167–168
  longbow in Hundred Years' War, 263
  Macedonian, 87
  medieval, 228–230
  Mitannians, *16,* 22
  Napoleonic, 563, 566, 572–573
  New Model Army, Cromwell's, *378*
  Persian, 26, 167
  poison gas, *798, 817*
  Roman, 99, 149, 152, 154, 167
  Roman legions, 169
  royal armies, 298
  Russian, 681
  shields and the phalanx, 168–169
  Spartan, 41, 45
  tanks, introduction of, *816*
  trench warfare, 812, *816*
  trireme warfare, *52,* 269
  vassalage of the Middle Ages, 186, 198, 199
  war, causes of, 157–158
  World War I, *815,* 816, *816*
  World War II, 880, 881, 883, 884–885
Militia Ordinance, 378
Mill, Harriet Taylor, 706
Mill, John Stuart, 706
Millerand, Alexander, 713
Millets, 401
Milos, 608
Milosevic, Slobodan, 936, 937
Miltiades, 54, 63, 79
Milvian Bridge, Battle of, 156
Mining
  in the Americas, 308–309
  in classical Greece, 72
Minoans, .34–35
Minos, 34
Mirandola, Pico della, 287, 289, 290, *291*
Missi dominici, 191
Missionaries
  modern Western, 784–787
Mississippi Bubble, 391
Mississippi Company, 391
Mita, 309
Mitannians, *16,* 22
Mithridates the Great, King of Pontus, 119–120
Moctezuma II, 306
Modern Devotion, 315
Modern Man in Search of a Soul (Jung), 744
Modernism
  Catholic, 733–734
  literature and art, 738–742, *739, 740, 741*
Mohacs, Battle of, *795*
Molotov, Vyacheslav, *844,* 904
Moltke, Helmut von, 807, 812
Mona Lisa (Leonardo da Vinci), 292
Monarchies
  absolute, in France, 298, 374, 381–382
  absolute, in Spain, 298–299
  medieval towns and Kings, 239
  in northern Europe, revival of, 297–301
  papacy, 211
  parliamentary, in England, 374
Monastic culture. *See also under name of order*
  Cluny reform movement, 204–206, 232
  Frank, 188
  in the Middle Ages, early, 183–184
  in the Middle Ages, high, 204–206
  revival of, in the 15th century, 333
  society of, in the Middle Ages, 232–233
Monet, Claude, 739
Mongols, 279, 795–796
Monophysitism, 182, 186
Monotheism, 28
Monroe Doctrine (1823), 607, 756
Montagu, Mary Wortley, 503
Montaigne, Michel de, 310, 346
Montenegrins, collapse of Yugoslavia and civil war, 936–938
Montesquieu, Charles de Secondat, 495, 503, 507, 511, 531, 656
Montfort, Simon de, 214
Montgomery, Bernard, 880
Montmorency-Chatillon family, 348
Moors, 299
Moravia/Moravians, 177, 438, 586
More, Thomas, 303, 330, 332
Morel, E.D., 775
Morelos y Pavón, José María, 613–614
Mornay, Philippe du Plessis, 350
Moro, Ludovico i, 295, 296
Morocco
  crises in, 803, 804–805
  French in, *765,* 768
  World War II, 880
Moscow in the Middle Ages, 279
Moses, 28, 30
Mothers' Protection League, 750
Mountain (Jacobins), 548, 551
Mozambique, 917, 920
Mrs. Dalloway (Woolf), 738
Mrs. Warren's Profession (Shaw), 738
Mughal Empire,759
Muhammad, *170,* 178–179, 502, 503, 588–589, 734
Mummification, 21
Munich agreement, 870–874, *873*
Municipalities, 136–137
Münster, 327
Müntzer, Thomas, 327
Museum of Mankind, 790
Music, *179*
Muslim Brotherhood, 941
Muslim League, 761, 920–921
Muslims, *169,* 171, 177, 178, 922–923. *See also* Islam/Islamic
  Byzantine Empire and, 177, 189, 195
  immigration and population changes, *949,* 949–950
  use of term, 178
Mussollini, Benito, 844–847, *846,* 849, 866–867, 869–870, 872, *873,* 875, 876, 880
Muthu, Sankar, 509
Mycale, Battle of, 58
Mycenae, 35, *36*
Mycenaeans, *16,* 34, 38, 168
  culture, 35–36
  Dorian invasion, 36
  rise and fall, 36

N

Naevius, 133
Nagasaki, *865,* 885
Nagy, Imre, 914, 929
Nameless Library (Whiteread), 966, *966*
Nantes, Edict of (1598), 351–352, 381, 388, 389
Napier, William, 572
Naples, Renaissance, 283, 289, 295
Napoleon Bonaparte (Napoleon I), 544, 558, *561, 566,* 569, 604, 612
  Consulate in France (1799-1804), 563–564
  Continental System, 566, *568*
  coronation of, 565, *565*
  empire (1804-1814), 564–567, *571,* 578
  European response to, 568–574
  Hundred Days, 576–577
  Middle East and, *590,* 590–591
  rise of, 562–563
  Roman Catholicism and, 563–564
Napoleon II, *699*
Napoleon III (Louis Napoleon Bonaparte), King of France, 646–647, 652, 662, 665, 666, 671, 672, 673, 674, 697, 710, 739, 778
Napoleonic Code, 564, 598, 700
Napoleonic Concordat, 732

Naram-Sin, 6, *6*
Narva, Battle of (1700), 398
Nasser, Gamal Abdel, 914, 940
Nathan the Wise (Lessing), 499, 502
National Assembly, 538, 542–543, 610, 646, 674–675
  Estates General becomes the, 532–534
National Cash Register, 970
National Constituent Assembly, 534–535, 537, 539, 541, 545, 558
National Council of French Women, 707
National Front, 949
National Government (British), 836
National Guard (French), 535, 547
National Health Service (Britain), 951, *955*
National Insurance Act (1911), 712
National Liberation Front, 923, 925
National Socialists. *See* Nazis
National Union of Gas Workers and General Labourers of Great Britain and Ireland, *710*
National Union of Women's Suffrage Societies, 707
Nationalism
  Arab, 940
  emergence of, 594–595
  in Germany, 568–570, 604
  meaning of, 596–597
  racism and, 745–747
  relationship to liberalism, 600
  romantic views of, 579–581
  student, 601–602, *602*
Nationalist Society, 665
Nationhood, 595
Native Americans, diseases introduced to, 305, 307, 469, *489*, 489–490
Native Baptist Church, 787
NATO (North Atlantic Treaty Organization), 903, 924, 937, 938, 939, 943, 971
  formation of, 909
Natural philosophy, 408
Natural selection, *724*, 728–729
Natural Theology (Paley), 729
Naturalism, in literature, 583–584, 737–739
Nature
  and the sublime, 583–584
Nature as mechanism, 412
Nausea (Sartre), 959
Navarre, 299
Naxos, 54
Nazis, 836
  -Soviet pact, 874, 958
  annexation of Austria, 850, 869–870
  assault on Jews of Poland, 889–890
  attack on Soviet Union, 876–878
  displacement of people, 948
  economic policy, 857, 860–861
  formation of, 848–849
  Great Depression and, 851
  Hitler comes to power, 851–854
  Holocaust, *886*, 886–887, *887*, 890–891, *891*
  internal party purges, 854
  occupation of Czechoslovakia, 870, 872–873
  occupation of Poland, 871, 874
  partition of Poland, *871*
  police state and anti-Semitism, 854–856
  Reichstag fire, 852, *854*
  role of women, 855, 857, 859, 860
Near East, ancient
  Assyrians, 22–23
  Hittites, 2, *16*, 22
  Kassites, *16*, 22
  key events/dates, 26
  map of, *5*, *16*
Mitannians, *16*
  Neo-Babylonians, 14, 23
Nearchus, 93
Nebuchadnezzar, 23, 24
Nebuchadnezzar II, 28
Necker, Jacques, 531, 532, 534, 580
Nefertiti, 20
Nelson, Horatio, 562, 564
Nemesis (warship), 782
Nemo, captain, *727*
Neo-Babylonians, 14, 23
Neo-Hittite states, 22
Neo-Orthodoxy, 967
Neoclassicism, 514, *514*, 516–517
Neolithic Age, 3–4, 166
Neolithic Revolution, 3–4
Neolocalism, 440
Neoplatonism, 159, 410
Nero, 135, 142, 148, 150
Nerva, 136, 139
Netherlands
  agriculture in, 444
  Louis XIV, invasion of, 372, 384
  Philip II and revolt in, 353–356, *354*
  17th-18th century, 372–373
  World War II, 878
Neumann, Balthasar, 514
Neuschwanstein, castle of, 583, *584*
New Astronomy, The (Kepler), 410
New Atlantis (Bacon), 412
New Economic Policy (NEP), 838–839
New Imperialism
  defined, 755, 761–762
  key events/dates, 777
  missionary factor, 784–787
  motives for, 763–765
  tools of, 782–784
New Kingdom, 18–19
New Rome, 156, 171
New Spain, 466, 613–614
New York City as center of art, 965
Newburn, Battle of (1640), 377
Newcomen, Thomas, 451
Newspapers, 19th century, 726
Newton, Isaac, *411*, 411–412, 427, 493, 497, 498
Newton, John, 656
Newtonianism for Ladies (Algarotti), 421
Ngo Dinh Diem, 924–925
Nguyen Van Thieu, 925
Nicaea, Council of, Second, 190
Nicaea, Council of (325), 159, 173
Nicaragua, 917
Nicene-Constantinopolitan Creed, 186
Nicene Creed, 159, 173, 190
Nicholas I, Pope, 194
Nicholas I, Tsar of Russia, 615–616, *616*, 652, 662, 678, 680
Nicholas II, Pope, 194, 205, 206
Nicholas II, Tsar of Russia, 684, 714, 717, 720, *721*, 805, 817
Nicholas of Cusa, 315
Nicholas V, Pope, 289
Nicias, 72, 73
  peace of, 74
Nicolaus of Damascus, 124–125
Niemöller, Martin, 966
Nietzsche, Friedrich, 729, 742–743, 959
Nigeria, 773–774, 922
Nijmwegen, peace of (1678 and 1679), 384, 388
Nika Revolt, 174
Nile Valley, 2, 14
Nimrud, 22
Nine Years' War, 388, 390
Ninety-five Theses, 602
Ninevah, 22, 23
Nippur, 6
Nixon, Richard, 917, 925
Noah, 13, 30
Nobiles, 103
Nobility. *See* Aristocracy
Nogaret, Guillaume de, 272
Nomarch, 17
Nomes, 17
Nonsuch, Treaty of (1585), 360
Normandy, 883, *884*
Normans (Vikings), 195, *195*, *196*, 206, 216, 265
North, Lord, 482, 484, 485
North Africa
  imperialism and, 768
  World War II, 876, 880, *880*, 893, 895
North Atlantic Treaty Organization. *See* NATO
North Briton, The (Wikes), 484
North German Confederation, 672
Northern Ireland, formation of, 836
Northern Society, 615
Northern Star, 627
Norway, 909
Novara, Battle of, 296, 652
Novellae (New Things) (Justinian), 176
Novum Organum (Bacon), 412, *413*
Nubia/Nubians, 2, 18
Nuclear energy, 984
Numidia, 119
Nuns/nunneries, 233, 248, 336, 338–339
Nuremberg Laws, 855
Nuri Pasha Said, *824*
Nystad, peace of (1721), 398

O

OAS (Organisation Armée Secrète), 923
Oates, Titus, 379
Oath of the Horatii (David), 517, 518
Obama, Barack, 934, 976, *976*
Oberman, Heiko, 281
Obrenovitch, Milos, 608
Observations upon Experimental Philosophy (Cavendish), 420
Ockley, Simon, 502
O'Connell, Daniel, 619, *619*
O'Connor, Feargus, 627
Octavian (Augustus Octavius), 19, 118, 126–127, *129*, 134
  Age of Augustus, 133–135
  Augustan principate, 130–132
October Diploma, 678
October Manifesto, 683, 720
Odes (Horace), 134
Odo, St., 204
Odo of Bayeaux, 231
Odoacer, 172
Odysseus, 38, 39
Odyssey (Homer), 36, 38, 109
Official Nationality, 615–616
Offray de la Mettrie, Julien, 500
O'Higgins, Bernado, 613
Oikos, 70
Oil, 693, 980–983, *981*, *983*
Old Comedy, 76, 78
Old Custom House Quay, *463*
Old Kingdom, 16–17
Old Regime, 434, 484, 514
Oliunina, E.A., 716
Olympia, 50, 853
Olympian gods, 50
Olympic games, 51, 853
Olympic games, in Berlin (1936), 853, *853*
Omdurman, Battle of, 772, *773*
On Christian Doctrine (Augustine), 244
On Christian Education (Augustine), 161
On Crimes and Punishment (Beccaria), 505
On Divine and Secular Learning (Cassiodorus), 244
On Ecclesiastical Power (Giles of Rome), 270
On Floating Bodies (Archimedes), *93*
On Heroes and Hero-Worship (Carlyle), 590
On Improving the Studies of the Young (Melanchthon), 337
On the Morals That Befit a Free Man (Vergerio), 287
On the Origin of Species (Darwin), 728, 747
On the Revolutions of the Heavenly Spheres (Copernicus), 408, 409, 425
On the Right of Magistrates over Their Subjects (Beza), 350
On the Trinity (Augustine), 161
One Day in the Life of Ivan Denisovich (Solzhenitsyn), 912
One (Number 31, 1950) (Pollock), 964–965, *965*
OPEC, 982–983
Open Door Policy, 780
Open Letter Concerning the Hard Book Against the Peasants, An (Luther), 323
Operation Barbarossa, 876
Opet, 20
Opium wars, 757, *757*, 758
Oppenheimer, Samuel, 459
Opportunism, 713
Optimates, 118
Oration on the Dignity of Man (Pico della Mirandola), 289, 290, *291*
Oratorians, 333
Orders in Council, 658
Organic Articles (1802), 564
Organic Statute, 616
Organization of Labor, The (Blanc), 641
Organization of Petroleum Exporting Nations (OPEC), 982–983
Orlando, Vittorio Emanuele, 824, *825*
Orléans, 266
Orléans, Duke of, 391
Orpheus/Orphic cult, 53
Orsini, Felice, 666
Orwell, George, 958, *958*
Osiris, 21, *21*, 145
Ossetia, 938, *938*
Ostrogoths, 155, 172
Othello (Shakespeare), 342
Otto I, Holy Roman Emperor, 194, 203–204, 205
Otto I, King of Greece, 608
Otto II, Holy Roman Emperor, 203, 204
Otto III, Holy Roman Emperor, 203, 204
Otto IV, Holy Roman Emperor, 220, 223
Ottoman Empire, 469, *503*, 503–504, 608
  creation of modern Near East, 823–824

Ottoman Empire,l *(cont.)*
  Crimean War (1853-1856), 662
  end of expansion, 403–404
  imperialism and, 764, *795,* 795–796
  invasion by Russia, 525–526
  reforms in, 662–664, *664*
  religious toleration, 401–403
  role of the Ulama, 402–403
  Russo-Turkish War, 799
  serfs in, 437–438
  in 17th century, *403*
  World War I, 823–824
Ottoman Turks, 174, 178, 320, 503–504, 525, *795,* 795–796
ötzi, 4, *4*
Overman (Nietzsche), 742
Ovid, 134, 141
Owen, Robert, *640,* 640–641

P

Pachomius, 184
Pacification of Ghent, 356
Paine, Thomas, 483, 549
Pakistan, 921, 922, 941
Palace of Popes, 273
Palacky, Francis, 650
Palaeologus, Michael, 267
Palatinate, 327, 364
Paleolithic Age, 2–3, 164
Paléologue, Maurice, *819*
Paleologus, Michael, 211
Palestine
  ancient, 27, *27*
  Jewish emigration to, 909
Palestrina, Giovanni Perluigi da, 333
Paley, William, 729
Pallium, 211
Palmer, Robert, 521
Palmerston, Lord, 619
Pan, 112, *112*
Pan-Slavic Congress, 650, 651
Panaetius, 111
Panama Canal, *762*
Panhellenic, 43
Pankhurst, Emmeline, 707, *707,* 708
Pantheon (Paris), 517, *517*
Pantheon (Rome), 143
Panther (warship), 804–805
Papacy. *See also under name of Pope*
  Avignon, 272–273
  Boniface VIII and Philip the Fair, 268–271, *272*
  College of Cardinals, 205, 206, 267
  doctrine of papal primacy, 184–186
  formation of, 184–186
  Fourth Lateran Council, 214
  Great Schism and Conciliar movement, 274–276
  independence of, 206
  investiture struggle, 206–207, 221
  monarchy, 211
  taxes and revenues, 211, 267
  thirteenth century, 267
Papal infallibility, 733
Papal primacy, doctrine of, 184–186
Papal States, 276
  formation of, 189
  Otto I and, 203
  Renaissance, 295, 296, 297
Papen, Franz von, 852
Paraguay, 613
Pareto, Vilfredo, 745
Paris
  Paris Commune, 547, 556, 674–675, 711
  settlement of World War I in, 824–831, *828,* 834
  18th century, *447,* 453
  19th century, 697
Paris, Treaty of (1259), 220
Paris, Treaty of (1763), 481, 484
Paris, Treaty of (1783), 483
Paris, Treaty of (1856), 662
Paris, University of, *242,* 242–243
Paris Commune, 547, 556, 674–675, 711
Paris Foundling Hospital, 443
Paris Summit Conference, 914
Parker, Matthew, 357
Parlement of Paris, 382, 493, 497, 530, 532, 533
Parlement/parlements, 382, 391–392, 458, 507, 530–532
Parleying, 216
Parliament
  American Revolution and reform for, 484–485, 486
  Charles I and, *377,* 377–378
  James I and, 374
  James II and, 379–380
  Long, 377–378
  Reformation, 331–332
  Short, 377
  18th century, 437, 439
Parliament Act (1911), 712, 761
Parmenides of Elea, 76
Parnell, Charles Stewart, 687
Parr, Catherine, 332
Parthenon, *67*
Parthia/Parthians, 122, 126, 139, 149
Pascal, Blaise, 425, 502, 969
Pasha, Ali, 353
Pasion, 72
Passau, Peace of (1552), 330
Pasternak, Boris, 912
Pasteur, Louis, 699, 789
Patel the Elder, Pierre, *383*
Pater, Walter, 738
Patricians, 101, 128
Patroclus, 38, 39
Paul, Tsar of Russia, 614
Paul III, Pope, 334–335
Paul IV, Pope, 333
Paul of Tarsus, 145, 147
Paul VI, Pope, 967
Pausanias, 58, 74
Pavia, Battle of (1525), 346
Pazzi family, 284
Peace of Augsburg (1555), 321, 330, 346, 356, 364, 367, 368, 370
Peace of Beauleiu (1576), 350
Peace of Brétigny-Calais (1360), 265
Peace of Constance (1183), 222
Peace of God, 205
Peace of Nijmwegen (1678 and 1679), 384, 388
Peace of Passau (1552), 330
Peace of Prague (1635), 368
Peace of Ryswick (1697), 390
Peace of Saint-Germain-en-Laye, 349
Pearl Harbor, 878, *879*
Pearson, Karl, 730, 731
Peasants/serfs
  abolition and serfdom in Russia, 680–681
  in France, 260, 437, *438*
  Helots, 44, 63, 72
  in the Middle Ages, 198–199, *227, 234,* 234–236, 260, 265
  Pugachev Rebellion (1773-1775), 438, *438,* 527
  rebellions of 1762 and 1769, 438
  revolt of 1381, 260, 274
  revolt of 1524-1525, *321,* 321–323
  revolt of 1358 *(Jacquerie),* 260, 265
  in 18th century, 438–439
Pedro I, Emperor of Brazil, 614
Pedro II, Emperor of Brazil, 614, 659
Peel, Robert, 619, 636, 639, 684
Pelopidas, 75
Peloponnesian League, *44,* 45, 63, 73
Peloponnesian War, *52*
  First, 63–64
  Great, 73–74, 78
Peloponnesus, 36, 44, *44*
Penelope, 38, 39
Peninsulares, 309, 466–467, 612
Pennsylvania Abolition Society, 657
Penny, Edward, *481*
Pensées (Pascal), 425, 502
Pentonville Prison, 637
People's Republic of China. *See also* China
  Tiananmen Square, 930
People's Will, 682, 683
Pepin, King of Aquitaine, 192
Pepin, son of Charlemagne, 191
Pepin I, 188
Pepin II, 188
Pepin III, 188
Percussion cap, 784
Perestroika, 927
Pergamum, 118
Pericles, 63–64, 65, 67, *67, 69,* 69–70, 73, 76, 793
Peripatos, 84
Perpetual Edict (1577), 356
Perrenot, Antoine, 353
Perry, Matthew C., 779
Persephone, 73
Persepolis, 26, 90
Perseus, King of Macedon, 109, 110
Persia/Persian wars. *See also* Iran
  Alexander the Great conquest of, 88–90, *89*
  Byzantine Empire and, 177
  chronology of, 58
  Delian League, 61, 62–63
  empire, 23–27
  Greek wars against, 25
  Ionian rebellion, 25, 54
  Peloponnesian War, Great, *52,* 73–74, 78
  rise of, 25
  Sparta and, 74
  war in Greece, 54–58, *57*
Persian Gulf War (1991), 941
Persian Letters, The (Montesquieu), 503, 507, 511
Personal computer, 970–971
Peru, 466, 613
  Incas in, 307, 310, 796
Peruzzi, 284
Pestel, 615
Pétain, Henri Philippe, 815, 875, *875,* 893, 894
Peter, 148
Peter I (the Great), Tsar of Russia, *371,* 397–398, 404, 436, 524, *526*
Peter II, Tsar of Russia, 524
Peter III, Tsar of Russia, 437, 480, 524
Peterloo Massacre, 605
Peter's pence, 211
Petite bourgeoisie, 696
Petition of Right, 377
Petrarch, Francesco, 285, 287
Petrograd, *818*
Pfefferkorn, 302
Phalanx, 40, 169, 641
Pharaohs, 16
Pharisees, 145
Phenomenology of Mind, The (Hegel), 588
Phidias, *33,* 741
Philadelphia system, 637
Philip, Archduke, *299*
Philip I, King of Macedon, 62, 84
Philip II, King of Macedon, 86–88, 169
Philip II, King of Spain, *346,* 348, 349, 350, 352–356, 357, 358, 362
Philip II (Augustus), King of France, 209, 211, 218, 220, 223, 242
Philip IV (the Fair), King of France, 207, 221, 263, 268–269, 271
Philip of Anjou, 390
Philip of Hesse, Landgrave, 325, 329, 330, 354
Philip V, King of Macedonia, 108–109
Philip V, King of Spain, 390, 391
Philip VI, King of France, 263, *263,* 466
Philippine Islands, 879, 884
Phillips, Thomas, 474
Philosophes, 495, 497–498, 507–510
Philosophia Christi (Erasmus), 302
Philosophic Manuscripts, 958
Philosophical Dictionary (Voltaire), 500
Philosophy. *See also under name of author or work*
  absolutism (Hobbes), *415,* 415–416
  empiricism (Bacon), 412–414, *413,* 425
  Enlightenment, 495–498
  Greek, classical, 76–77, 80–86
  Greek, Hellenistic, 91–93
  liberty and toleration, 416–418
  rational deduction (Descartes), 414, *414*
  Scholastic and theology *versus,* 244–245
  19th century, 742–743
Philosophy, Greek (classical)
  Aristotle, 84, 86
  Plato, 83–84, 85, 287, 289
  Socrates, 80–81
  Sophists, 77–78, 81
Philosophy, Hellenistic
  Epicureans, 92
  Stoics, 92–93
Philosophy of Manufactures, The (Ure), 628
Philoxelus of Emtrea, *167*
Phocis, 87
Phocylides, 40
Phoenicians, 27, 106
Phratries, 39, 46
Physico-theology, 427
Physics in late-19th century, 735–736
Physiocrats, 505
Pi Scheng, 253
Picasso, Pablo, 741
Pico della Mirandola, 287, 289, 290, *291*
Piedmont, 650, 652, 665, 666
Pietro Carafa, Gian, 333
Pilgrimage to Isle of Cithera (Watteau), 516
Pilgrimages, 219
Pilsudski, Marshal Josef, 861, 887
Pindar, 51
Piracy, 466, 467
Piraeus, 54
Pisa, 283, 295
Pisa, Council of (1409-1410), 276
Pisan, Christine de, 287, *288*
Pisistratus, 47

Pissaro, Camille, 739
Pitt, William (the Elder), 480, 481, 484
Pitt, William (the Younger), 485, 549, 564, *566*, 619
Pius, Antoninus, 136
Pius II, Pope, 276
Pius IX, Pope, 652, 665, 733–734
Pius V, Pope, 360
Pius VI, Pope, 545, 563
Pius VII, Pope, 563–564
Pius X, Pope, 734
Pizarro, Francisco, 307, 491
Plague, The (Camus), 959
Planck, Max, 736
Plantagenet dynasty, 216
Plantation economy, 463
Plants
  exchange between Americas and Europe, 491
Plassey, Battle of (1757), 480, *481*
Plataea, 58
Plato, 34, 45, 53, 70, 80, 81, 83–84, 85, 86, 164, 287, 289, 655
Platonism, 289
Plebeians, 101–102
  key events/dates, 102
Pleid (ship), 782
Plekhanov, Gregory, 715
Plenitude of power, 267
Pliny the Younger, 150–151, 287
Plotinus, 159, 287
Plutarch, 110, 117, 287
Plymouth Colony, 374
Pnyx, *77*
Podestà, 284
Pognon, Marie, 695
Poincarè, Henri, 736
Pointillism, 740
Poitiers, Battle of (732), 182, 188
Poitiers, Battle of (1356), 265
Poland
  aristocracy of 18th century, 435
  autonomy, 914
  destruction of Polish Jewish communities, 887
  Jews in, 459, *459*, 887–890
  Nicholas I as ruler of, 616
  occupation of, in World War II, 871, 874
  partition of (1939), *871*, 871–872
  partitions of (1772, 1793, 1795), 526, *527*, 549
  Reformation in, 330
  Russian repression in, 616, 681
  in the 1920s, 861
  Solidarity, 917–918, 929, *929*
  18th century, 392–393, 435
Polar Sea, The (Friedrich), 584, *585*
Police forces, 19th century formation of, 636, *636*
Polignac, Prince de, 617
Polis, 46, 48, 58–59, 73, 78, 794
  Aristotle and, 39, 84
  crisis of, 80–81
  Cynics and, 83
  development of, 34, 39–40
  downfall of, 80, 91
  hoplite phalanx, 40, 43, 47, *57*, 65, 169
  importance of, 40
  Plato and, 83–84
  Socrates and, 81
Polish Communist Party, 914, 917–918
Polish Patriots, 549
Polish Rebellion (1830), 681
Politburo, 843, 912
Political parties, 19th century, 711
Political Registrar (Cobbett), 605
Politics
  key events and dates, 857
Politiques, 346
Pollock, Jackson, 964–965, *965*
Polo, Marco, 305, *306*
Poltava, Battle of, 398
Polybius, 10, 111
Polygenesis, 790
Polytheists, 50
Polyzalus, *86*
Pompadour, Madame de, 511, 514
Pompeii, 140, *167*
Pompey, Gnaeus, 120–121, 122
Pont du Gard, *97*
Pontifex maximus, 111, 185
Pontius Pilate, 145
Poor Law, 602, 639
Pope, Alexander, 495
Popish Plot, 379
Popolo grosso, 283
Popolo minuto, 284
Popular assembly, 65
Popular Front, 713, 838, 957
Populares, 118, 121
Population
  expansion in the 11th century, 236
  expansion in the 18th century, 445, 453, 455
  expansion in the 19th century, 623–624, 691
  growth in the 16th century, 352–353
  Malthus on, 638
  20th century, in Europe, 950
  trends in the 20th century, 950
Populism, 682
Porcia, *100*
Porphyry, 289
Portobello, 466
Portugal
  in the Americas, 469, 796
  exploration by, 303–305, *304*
Poseidon, 50, 51, 80, *82*
Positive Philosophy, The (Comte), 725
Positivism, 726
Post-impressionism, *740*, 740–741
Postal system
  British, 685, *685*
  Persian, 25
Potato, 491
Potemaic Dynasty, 15
Potosí, 308, 352, *469*
Potsdam Conference (1945), 899–900
Poverty
  18th century, 455
  19th century, 704
Praemonstratensians, 233
Praetors, 101–102, 133
Pragmatic Sanction of Bourges, 273, 316, 394, 478
Prague, peace of (1635), 368
Prague, Treaty of (1866), 672
Prague, University of, 274
Pravda, 840
Preacherships, 316
Predestination doctrine, 328–329, 498
Prelude, The (Wordsworth), 581
Presbyterians, 360, 374, 377–378, 379
Pressburg, Treaty of, 564
Prester, John, 305
Priestley, Joseph, 549
Prince, The (Machiavelli), 297
Prince of the World, The, 260
Princeps, 130, 131, 133, 136
Principia Mathematica (Newton), 411, 421
Principles of Morals and Legislation, The (Bentham), 639
Principles of Political Economy (Ricardo), 638
Print culture, Enlightenment and, 493, *494*, 494–495
Printing press, *255*, 301
  block, 252, 253
  invention of, in China and Europe, 252–256, *253*, *255*, 301, *301*
  movable type, 252–253
Priscian, 244
Prison reform, 19th century, 636–638, *637*
Proclus, 287
Proconsulship, 101
Procopius, 174
Proletarianization, 626–627, 643, *719*
Propertius, Sextus, 134
Prosser, Gabriel, 658
Prostitution
  19th century, 633–634, 704, 749–750
Protagoras of Abdera, 31
Protectorates, 762
Protestant Ethic and the Spirit of Capitalism (Weber), 745
Protestant Reformation
  abuses of clergy, 314–316
  Anabaptists, 326–327
  Calvin and Genevan, 327–329, *328*
  Charles V, election of, 319
  consolidation of, 329–330
  criticisms of the church, 314–316
  in Denmark, 329
  education and, 336–338
  in England, 330–333
  family life and, 339–341
  how it spread, 321
  indulgences, attack on, 318–319
  indulgences, sale of, 315
  key events/dates, 332, 335
  literature and, 341–343
  Luther and German, 316–324
  Modern Devotion, 315
  political conflict and, 314
  social significance of, 335–339
  in Sweden, 329–330
  in Switzerland, *324*, 324–325
  women and, 338–339
Protestant Resistance theory, 350
Protestants, 784
Proudhon, Pierre-Joseph, 641
Proust, Michael, 738, *738*
Prussia
  aristocracy of 18th century, 435–436
  army, 466
  Austrian Succession, war of (1740-1748), 478–479, 521
  Austro-Prussian War (1866), 671–672, *672*
  Congress of Vienna (1815), 574–577, *575*, *577*, 601, 606
  defeat of reforms, 601
  Franco-Prussian War (1870-1871), 673–674
  Frederick II (the Great), 395, 397, 435, 478, 479, 480, 497, 519–520, *520*, 526, 527, 531, 549
  Frederick William, the Great Elector, 261, 395–396
  Frederick William I, 397
  Hohenzollerns and, 395–397
  Napoleon and, 566
  Quadruple Alliance, 574, 576
  revolution of 1848, 652–653
  serfs in, 445, 568
  social reforms in, 570, 601
  17th-18th centuries, *394*, 395–397, 435, 437
Prussian Civil Service Commission, 519
Psychoanalysis, 743–744
Ptah, 20
Ptolemaic Dynasty, 15, 90
Ptolemaic system, 409
Ptolemy I, 90, 93, 409
Ptolemy of Alexandria, 15, 94, 244, 287
Ptolemy Philadelphus, 105
Public Health Act (1848), 699
Public Health Act (1875), 686
Public opinion, 495
Publius Casca, 125
Publius Fannius Synistor, *116*
Pugachev, Emelyan, 438, *438*
Pugachev Rebellion (1773-1775), 438, *438*, 527
Punic Wars
  First, 106–107, *107*
  key events/dates, 107
  Second, 107–108
Puritanism/Puritans, 360, 374, 375, 377–378, 745
Putin, Vladimir, 935, 937–940
Putting-out system, 449–450, 703
Pydna, Battle of, 109, 110
Pylos, 35, 36
Pyramids, 17, *17*
Pyrenees, Treaty of the (1659), 368
Pyrrho of Elis, 92
Pyrrhus, King of Epirus, 105
Pythian games, *86*, 87
Pythokritos, *61*

Q

Qing dynasty, 780, 782
Quadruple Alliance, 574, 576, 606
Quaestors, 101
Quakers, 656–657
Quebec, *462*, 480
Quebec Act, 482
Quesnay, Francois, 505
Quetzalcoatl, 306
Quinine, 782
Quintilian, 287
Quintus Fabius Maximus, 108*Qur'an*, 178, 179, 180, 502, 734

R

Racine, Jean, 579
Racism
  anti-Semitism, *709*, 710, 745, 746, 747–748, 848–849, 854–856, *855*, 886–891, 893
  Chamberlain, views of, 745, 746
  ethnic cleansing, *731*, 936
  Gobineau, views of, 745
  Holocaust and, *886*, 886–887, *887*, 890–891, *891*
  late-19th century nationalism and, 745–747
Radetzky, Joseph Wenzel, 650–651
Radical Islamism, 940–942
Radio
  BBC, 895
  used for political propaganda, 893
Railways, 624, *624*, 626, *626*, 692
Rain, Steam and Speed-The Great Western Railway (Turner), 584, *585*
Ramessides, 18
Ramses I, 18
Ramses II, 18
Raphael, 292, *292*

Rasputin, Grigory Efimovich, 720, 817
Rastatt, Treaty of (1714), 393
Rastislav, Duke, 177
Ravenna, 172
Ray, John, 427
Raymond, Julian, 542
Raynal, G.T., 510
Razi, al- (Rhazes), 183
Re, sun god, 29
Reagan, Ronald, 918, *927*
Realism, in literature, 737–739
Red Army, 821, 838, 874
Reed, John, 820
Reed, Walter, 789
Reflections on the Revolution in France (Burke), 548, 550
Reflections on Violence (Sorel), 713, 745
Reform League, 684
Reformation. *See also* Protestant Reformation
 Catholic reform and Counter-Reformation, 333–335
 Council of Trent (1545-1563), 334–335, 346, 355, 364, 384, 421
 key events/dates, 332, 353
 in Poland, 330
Reformation Parliament, 331–332
Reichsrat, 678–679
Reichstag, 300, 672, 713, 714, 847
 fire, 852, *854*
Reign of Terror, 549–555
Reinsurance, Treaty of (1887), 801
Relativity, theory of, 736
Religion. *See also* Protestant Reformation; Reformation; type of
 Aztec, 306
 Babylonian, 23
 Byzantine Empire, 177
 Carolingian, 188–189, 199
 conflict between church and state, 732
 divisions about 1600, 364, *365*
 Egyptian, 19–20
 Enlightenment and, 498–504
 Etruscan, 98–99
 Greece, classical, 72–73
 Greek, ancient, 34, 50, 52–53
 of the Israelites, 28
 key events/dates, 217
 map of, *334*
 Mesopotamian, 9, *10*, 11
 Ottoman Empire, 401–403
 Paleolithic Age, 2–3
 Persian, 26
 popular movements of, 314–316
 Roman Empire, 132, 145, 147–151, 156–158
 Roman Republic, 109–111
 Romanticism and, 584, 586–587
 Scientific Revolution and, 421–427
 of slaves, 477, 478
 Sumerian, 9, 11
 20th century, 966–968
 in 15th century, 336
 in 16th century, 336
 19th century attack on, 729, 732
 19th century women and, 705–706
Religion within the Limits of Reason (Kant), 501
Religious wars. *See also* Crusades
 background of, 345–346
 in England, 356–362
 in France, 346–352
 key events/dates, 353
 in Spain, 352–353
 Thirty Years' War, 363–368
Rembrandt van Rijn, 346, *407*
Remington Rand, 970
Renaissance
 art, *281, 284, 286,* 289, *291, 292,* 292–293, *293*
 Carolingian, 191–192
 city-states, *283,* 283–285
 humanism, 282, 285–289, 302–303
 in Italy, 282–295, *284*
 key events/dates, 294
 northern, 301–303
 slavery, 294–295
Renaissance of Motherhood, The (Key), 750
Renan, Ernest, 734
Renoir, Pierre-Auguste, 739
Repartimiento, 309
Report on the Sanitary Condition of the Labouring Population (Chadwick), 699
Republic of Virtue, 553
Republic (Plato), 85
Requesens, Don Luis de, 356
Rerum Novarum, 734, 735
Response to Luther (More), 330
Restitution, Edict of (1629), 367
Reuchlin, Johann, 302, 315
Reuchlin affair, 302
Revisionism, 714
Rheims, 242
Rhenish Missionary Society, 785
Rhetoric, 111
Rhineland, remilitarization of, 867–868
Rhineland Gazette (Rheinische Zeitung), 642
Rhodes, Cecil, 776
Rhodesia, 920
Ricardo, David, 638
Richard II, King of England, 265, 274, 299
Richard III, King of England, 216, 299
Richard III (Shakespeare), 299
Richard the Lion-Hearted, King of England, 209, 218, 222
Richelieu, Cardinal, 352, 367–368, 381
Richenthal, Ulrich von, *273*
Riefenstahl, Leni, 853, *853*
Rigaud, Hyacinthe, *381*
Righteous and Harmonious Society of Fists, 780
Rights of Man, The (Paine), 549
Rime of the Ancient Mariner, The (Coleridge), 581
Río de la Plata, 466, 612–613
Riots, 18th century, 458
Robert Andrews and His Wife (Gainsborough), *436*
Robertson, William, 498
Robespierre, Maximilien, 553, *553,* 554, 555, *557*
Robinson, John, 967
Rock music, *928*
Rockefeller, John D., 980
Rockwell, Norman, 881
Rococo art style, 514, *514,* 516–517
Roehm, Ernst, 849, 854
Roentgen, Wilhelm, 736
Roland, Cardinal, 221
Roland, Pauline, 649
Roll Call: Calling the Roll after an Engagement, The, Crimea (Thompson), *663*
Romagna, 295
Roman Catholicism, 346, 587, 951. *See also* Catholicism; Christianity; Papacy
 Baroque art and, 346, *347,* 428–429, 431
 Cluny reform movement, 204–206, 232
 division of Christianity into Eastern (Byzantine) and Western (Roman Catholic), 186–187
 French Revolution and, 541, 545
 investiture struggle, 206–207, 221
 Joseph II, 521
 key events/dates, 217
 missionaries, 785
 modern world and, 733–734
 Napoleon and, 563–564
 revival of, in the Middle Ages, 204–215
 in Spanish America, 307–308
 20th century, 967–968
 Thirty Years' War, 364–365, 367–368
Roman Empire
 administration, 130–131, 136, 139
 agriculture, 139, 141
 architecture/art, *97, 129, 131,* 134–135, 143
 army and defense, 131–132, 172
 Augustan principate, 130–132
 Augustus, age of, 133–135
 barbarian invasions, 149, 155–156, 172
 Byzantine Empire and, 154
 Christianity, 145, 147, 150–151, *151,* 159–160, *160*
 Cicero, 133
 civil disorder, 152
 Constantine and, 153–154, 171
 decline and fall of, 161–162, 171–173
 Diocletian, 152–153, 158–159, 171
 division of the empire, *153,* 155–156
 economic problems, 149, 151–152
 emperors/rulers, 135–136, *155*
 entertainment, *110, 134, 138,* 146, *146,* 150
 foreign policy, 139
 fourth century reorganization, 152–156
 imperial power, 794–795
 imperial Rome, 135–145, 794–795
 Jews in, 139, 145
 law, 133, 172
 life in, 142
 literature/poetry, 133–135, 142–143, 160–161
 maps of, *132, 137, 155*
 persecution in, 147–148, 150–151, 158–159
 religion and morality, 132
 Roman legions, 169
 social classes, 143–145
 social order, 152
 third century, 148–149
 women, 141–142
Roman Forum, 135
Romance of the Rose, 245
Romanesque architecture, 224–225, *225*
Romania
 collapse of communism, 930
 Compromise of 1867, 678
 in the 1920s, 863
 World War I, 800, 804–805, *812,* 814, 829
 World War II, 874
Romanitas, 136
Romanov, Michael, 397
Romanov dynasty, 392, 397
Romantic Republicanism, 664–665
Romanticism, 562, 577–578
 Islam, Middle East and, 588–591
 literature, 579–582, 959
 nationalism and history, view of, 587–591
 questioning of reason, 576–579
Rome, Republic
 Caesar, 121–126, *122*
 Carthage and, 105–109
 centuriate assembly, 102
 Cicero, 121
 conquests, effects of, 105, 108–109, 116
 constitution, 101–103
 consuls, 101–102
 Crassus, 120–122
 education, 111–113
 expansion in Mediterranean, *106*
 fall of, 120–127
 First Triumvirate, 121
 Gracchi, 116–119
 Hellenistic World, conquest of, 108–109
 Italy, conquest of, 103–105
 key events/dates, 104, 108, 126
 land ownership, 116–118
 map of late, *115, 123, 143, 153*
 Marius and Sulla, 119–120
 Octavius, 117
 Pompey, 120–121, 122
 Punic Wars, 106–108
 religion, 109–111
 Second Triumvirate, 126–127
 Senate and assembly, 99, 102
 slavery, 113, 115, 139, 141, 161
 Struggle of the Orders, 102–104
 Twelve Tables, 102, 111
 war against the Italian allies, 119
 women, 100, 114
Rome, royal
 clientage, 100–102
 family, 100
 government, 99–100
 patricians and plebeians, 101–102
 women, 100
Rome, Treaty of (1957), 972
Rome-Berlin Axis Pact (1936), 867, 869
Romeo and Juliet (Shakespeare), 342
Rommel, Erwin, 876, 879, 880
Romulus, 100
Romulus Augustulus, 172
Room of One's Own, A (Woolf), *751,* 751–752
Roosevelt, Franklin D., 876, *876,* 881, 885, 897–899, *899,* 903, 982
Roosevelt, Theodore, *762,* 780, 980
Rorbach, Jacob, *321*
Rosetta Stone, 591
Rosie the Riveter, 881
Rossi, Pelligrino, 652
Rota Romana, 267
Rothschild, Lionel, *709*
Roundheads, 378
Rousseau, Jean-Jacques, 495, 496, *508,* 508–509, 512–513, 515, 517, *517,* 538, 553, 578–579
Rovere, Giuliano della, 296
Roxane, 90
Royal African Company of London, 474
Royal Air Force (RAF), 876
Royal Museum for Central Africa, 790
Royal Niger Company, 773
Royal Society of London, 418, 422, 787
Royal Standard of Ur, *8*
Rubáiyát of Omar Kharyyám, 588
Rubber trees, 789
Rubens, Peter Paul, 346, 431

Rudolf II, Emperor, 366
Ruhr, French invasion of, 835, *835*, 847–848
Rule for Monasteries (Benedict), 184, 192, 204, 233
Ruskin, John, 629
Russell, lord, 684
Russia. *See also* Soviet Union
  Alexander I, Tsar of Russia, 566, 571, 574, 576, 606, 607, 614, 615
  Alexander II, reforms of, 680–681
  alliances with Austria and England, against France, 566
  aristocracy of 18th century, 436–437
  Bolshevism, birth of, 714–722
  Catherine II (the Great), 437, 458, 517, 519, 524–526, *526*, 527, 549, 562, 662, 776
  Congress of Vienna (1815), 574–577, *575*, *577*, 594
  Crimean War (1853-1856), 662
  Decembrist revolt of 1825, 614–616, *616*
  expansion of, 398–401, *526*
  Great Northern War, 398, 400–401
  imperialism and, 776–778
  industrial growth in 19th century, 714–715
  invasion of Poland, 526, 616
  Jews in, 458–459
  key events/dates, 400, 524, 680, 722
  medieval, 278–279
  Napoleon's invasion of, 571, 574
  navy, 398
  Peter I (the Great), *371*, 397–398, 404, 436, 524, *526*
  Quadruple Alliance, 574, 576
  resurgence of, 937–940
  revolution of 1905, 717, 720, 803
  revolution of 1917, 718, 763, 817–821
  revolutionaries, 681–684
  Romanov dynasty, 397
  serfs in, 436–439, 680–681
  St. Petersburg, founding of, 398, *400*
  streltsy and boyars, 398, 400, 401
  Three Emperors' League (1873), 799
  Triple Entente (1890-1907), 801–804
  World War I and, 805, 807, 811–812, *812*, 814–815, 822, 827
  Yeltsin decade, 934–935
Russian Federation
  Georgia, invasion of, 938, *938*, 940
  Putin in, 935, 937–940
  Yeltsin decade, 934–935
Russian Orthodox Church, 400, 615, 842, 887
Russian Republic, 932
Russo-Japanese War (1904-1905), 803
Russo-Turkish War (1875), 799
Ruthenians, 650
Rutherford, Ernest, 736
Ryswick, peace of (1697), 390

S

SA (storm troopers), 849, 851, 854
Sabines, 98
Sachs, Hans, 340
Sacrosancta, 276
Sadat, Anwar, 941
Saguntum, 107–108
Sailing ships, 979, *979*
Saint Bartholomew's Day Massacre, 349–350
Saint Domingue, 478, 542, 657, *657*
Saint-Germain-en-Laye, peace of, 349
Saint John of the Cross, 333
Saint-Simon, Claude Henri de, 640, 642, 725
Saint Teresa of Avila, 333, 431
Saisset, Bernard, 269
Sakharov, Andrei, 926
Saladin, King of Egypt and Syria, 208, 212, 213
Salafi (Salafiyya) movement, 734
Salamis, Battle of, 56, 58
Sale, George, 502
Salisbury, Lord, 687
Salisbury Cathedral, *225*
Salisbury Cathedral, from the Meadows (Constable), 582, *583*
Sallust, 133
Salutati, Coluccio, 289
Salvian, 174
Samian War, 70
Samnites, 98, 104–105
Samos, 58, 64, 70
Samothrace, Winged Victory of, *61*
San Martin, José de, 612–613
San Salvador, 305, *306*
San Stefano, Treaty of (1878), 799
Sanctuary of Asclepius, *81*
Sand, Karl, 602, *602*
Sanitation
  changing attitudes toward, 456
  in cities, 456, 698–699
Sans-culottes, 547–548, 551, 553, 555, 558, 605
Sanussiya movement, 734
Sappho, 53, *53*
Sarajevo
  collapse of Yugoslavia and civil war, *936*, 936–937
  World War I and, 806
Sardinia, 107
Sardis, 24, 54
Sargent, John Singer, *817*
Sargon, 6, 7
Sartre, Jean-Paul, *953*, 958, 959–960
Sassanians, 149, 155, 171
Satires (Horace), 134
Satrap, 25, 54
Saturnalia, 112
Savonarola, Girolamo, 295
Saxons, 172, 188, 189, 203
Saxony, 203, 368
Schacht, Hjalmar, 850
Scheidmann, Philipp, 829
Schlegel, August Wilhelm von, 579
Schlegel, Friedrich, 581
Schleicher, Kurt von, 852, 854
Schleiermacher, Friedrich, 587
Schleitheim Confession, 327
Schleswig, 671
Schlieffen, Alfred von, 811
Schlieffen Plan, *811*, 811–812
Schmalkaldic Articles, 329
Schmalkaldic League, 321, 329
Schmoller, Gustav, 766–767
Scholasticism, 221, 244, 337
Schönbrunn, Peace of, 570
Schongauer, Martin, *317*
School of Athens, The (Raphael), 292
Schuschnigg, Kurt von, 862, 870
Schwarzenberg, Felix, 652
Schwenckfeld, Caspar, 327
Science
  Comte, positivism, and the prestige of, 726, 729
  Darwin's theory of natural selection, *724*, 728–730
  ethics and, 728–729
  Greek, Hellenistic, 93–94
  imperialism and, 787–791
  late-19th century, 735–736
  mid-19th century, 726–729
Science fiction, 727
Science of Mechanics, The (Mach), 735
Sciences and the Arts, The (Stalbent), *426*
Scientific induction, 414
Scientific Revolution
  Bacon, 412–414, *413*, 425
  Brahne, 410
  Copernicus, 408–410, *409*, 425
  Descartes, 414, *414*, 422
  Galileo, *410*, 410–411, 421, 424, 425
  Hobbes, *415*, 415–416
  institutions/societies, 418–419
  Kepler, 410, 412
  Locke, *416*, 416–418
  major works of, 417
  Newton, *411*, 411–412
  Pascal, 425
  religion and, 421–427
  women and, 419–421
Scientists, use of term, 408, 726
Scipio, Publius Cornelius. *See* Africanus
Scipio Aemilianus, 109, 111
Scotland, Charles I and, 374–375
Scott, Walter, 588
Scramble for Africa, 768
Screwtape Letters, The (Lewis), 967
Scutage, 198
Scythians, 25, 167
Sea Beggars, 355, 360
Sea Peoples, 18
Second Athenian Confederation, 75
Second Coalition, 562
Second Continental Congress, 483
Second Crusade, 208
Second Estates, 532
Second Industrial Revolution, 691–694
Second Intermediate Period, 18–19
Second International, 713
Second Macedonian War, 108
Second Messenian War, 44
Second Punic War, 107–108, li
Second Reform Act (1867), 684
Second Sex, The (Beauvoir), 953, 956
Second Treatise of Government (Locke), 380, 387, 417
Second Triumvirate, 126–127
Sedan, Battle of (1870), 673, 674
Sejm, 392
Sekhmet, 29
Seleucus I, 90
Seljuk Turks, 174, 178, 207
Senate, Roman, 99, 102, 117–122, 127, 130–131, 136, 153
Sentences (Lombard), 338
Sepoy, 759
September 11, 2001 attacks, 903, 940, 942
September Massacres, 547, 554
Septimus Severus, *139*, 149, 152
Serampore College, 786
Serbia/Serbs
  collapse of Yugoslavia and civil war, 936–937
  independence (1830), 608
  in the 1920s, 862
  World War I and, *805*, 805–806, 809–810, 825
Serfs. *See* Peasants/serfs
Sertorius, 120
Servant, defined, 440
Servetus, Michael, 327, 329, 346, 358
Seurat, Georges, *740*, 740–741
Sevastopol, Battle of, 662
Seven Weeks' War, 672
Seven Years' War (1756-1763), 480–481, 524, 656
Severus, Alexander, 152
Severus, Septimius, *139*, 149, 152
Sewer system, 699, *699*
Sextus Pompey, 126
Seymour, Edward, 332
Seymour, Jane, 332
Sforza family, 284
Shaftesbury, Earl of, 379, 416
Shakespeare, William, 299, 342, 361
Shamil, Imam, 778, *778*
Shang dynasty, 165, 252
Shari'a, *181*
Shaw, George Bernard, 712, 738
Shaw, Thomas, 784
Shi'a, 179
Short Account of That Part of Africa Inhabited by the Negroes, A (Benezet), 656
Short Parliament, 377
Shostakovich, Dimitri, 897
Shoulder Arms (Chaplin), 826
Shuruppak, 6
Sicily, 74, 106–107, 115, 220, 222, 223, 880
Sierra Leone, 659
Siéyès, Abbé, 532, 563
Sigismund, Emperor, 274
Signoria, 284
Silesia, 478, 479
Simon, Jules, 700
Simonides of Cos, 53
Simons, Menno, 327
Simony, 205
Sinn Fein, 836
Siraj-ud-daulah, *481*
Sistine Chapel (Michelangelo), 292
Six Acts (1819), 605, 619
Six Articles (1539), 332
Six Points of the Charter, 627, 630
Sixtus IV, Pope, 318
Sixtus V, Pope, 350, 362
Sixty-Seven Articles, 326
Skeptics, 92
Slavery
  abolishing in the New World, 655, 658–659, 756
  in the Americas, 309, 463, *469*, 469–473, *470*, *476*, *477*, 655
  Athenian, 38
  crusade against, 655–657
  Egyptian, 21–22
  end of, in Africa, 659–660
  experience of, 473, 476–478
  Greek, ancient, 38
  Greek, classical, 71–72
  in Haiti, 477, 610, *610*, 612, *657*, 657–658
  Mesopotamian, 14
  Renaissance, 294–295, *300*
  revolts, 478, *657*, 657–658
  Roman, 113, 115, 139, 141, 161
  ships, *475*
  transatlantic economy and, 463, 473, 655
Slavs, 177, 650, 651, 829
Slovenes, 862
  collapse of Yugoslavia and civil war, 936–937
Smallpox, *489*, 490
Smith, Adam, 505, 506, 509, 629, 638, 656, 756
Smith, W.H., 694
Smoking, *376*
Snefru, 17

Social classes/society
  Amorite, 7
  aristocracy of 18th century, 435–437, *436*
  Athenian, 45
  Carolingian manor, 198–199
  clientage-patron (Roman), 100–101
  coloni, 139, 141, 156, 234
  court culture and Eleanor of Aquitaine, 216–217
  Enlightenment and, 504–507
  Etruscan, 99
  feudal, 196–200
  Greek, archaic, 49–50
  Homeric, 38–39
  Mesopotamian, 7
  middle class, 495, 497, 694, 696–698
  patricians and plebeians (Roman), 101–102, 127
  printing press, 254–256
  Renaissance, 283–284
  Roman, 100–101, 141–142, 143–145, 152
  Spartan, 45
  urban, 455–458
Social classes/society, in the Middle Ages
  clergy, 199, 232–234
  knighthood, 230
  merchants, 236–238
  nobles, 196, 198, 228–232
  peasants/serfs, 198–199, *227, 234,* 234–236, 260, 265, 274
  sportsmen/warriors, 228, 230, *299*
  women, *245,* 245–248, 704–705
Social Contract, The (Rousseau), 508, 553, 578
Social Darwinism, 728–720, 730–731, *731,* 750
Social Democratic Party (SPD), 713–714
  Austrian, 862
  German, 713–714, 829, 847
  Russian, 715, 717, 719, 820, 822
Social Revolutionary Party, 715, 820
Social science, 505
Socialism
  anarchism, 641
  in Britain, 712–713
  First International, 711
  in France, 13
  in Germany, 713–714
  key events/dates, 720
  Marxism, 642–645, 711–712, 715, 718, 744, 933, 958
  utopian, 639–641
Société des Ammis des Noirs, 657
Society for the Abolition of the Slave Trade, 657
Society for the Relief and Free Negroes Illegally Held in Bondage, 657
Society of Jesus, 333
Society of Revolutionary Republican Women, 553–554, 555
Socinianism, 327
Socrates, 70, 73, 76, 80–81
Sodom, 30
Solar cults, 20
Solidarity, 917–918, 929
Solomon, *27,* 28
Solomon Islands, 884
Solon, reforms of, 47
Solzhenitsyn, Aleksandr, 912, 926
Somaschi, 333
Some Considerations on the Keeping of Negroes (Benezet), 656
Sons of Liberty, 482
Sophists, 77–78, 81
Sophocles, 76
Sophrosynee, 52
Soranus of Ephesus, 141, 250
Sorbon, Robert de, 242
Sorbonne, 242, 701, 961
Sorel, Georges, 713, 745
Sorrows of Young Werther, The (Goethe), 582
South Africa, 763, 920
Southeast Asia Treaty Organization (SEATO), 924
Southern Society, 615
Soviet Communist Party, 839, 842–843, 930
Soviet Union. *See also* Cold War; Russia
  Afghanistan, invasion of, 917
  collapse of, 930, 932–933
  collectivization, *833,* 841–853, *842*
  Comintern (Third International), 839
  communism, 827
  coup of 1991, 933
  domination of eastern Europe, 905, 908
  family legislation, 855–857
  German attack on, 876–878
  Gorbachev, 927, *927,* 929–933
  industrialization, 840–841
  Nazi-Soviet pact, 874, 958
  New Economic Policy (NEP), 838–839
  purges, 843–844
  Stalin Soviet Union *versus* Trotsky, 839–840
  Third International, 839
  urban consumer shortages, 841
  war communism, 838
  women in, 858–859, *859*
  World War II, 858–859, *859,* 896–897
Soviets, 720
Sozzini, Faustus, 327
Spain
  American Revolution and, 483
  in Americas, 305–307, 464, 465, 612, 796
  Civil War, *868,* 868–869, *869,* 958
  colonial system, 465–468
  exploration by, 305–307, *306*
  humanism in, 303
  Napoleon and, 570, 612
  Philip II, 352–356
  relations with England (1553-1603), 356–362
  religious wars in, 352–353
  revival of monarchy in, 298–299
  revolution of 1820, 607–608
  terrorist attacks on, 934
  War of Jenkins's Ear, 478, 608
Spanish-American War (1898), 764, 779
Spanish Armada, 352, 356, 362
Spanish Fury, 356
Spanish Succession, war of (1701-1714), *390,* 390–391, 466
Spare Rib (journal), 953
Sparta
  Athens and, 34, 48, 63, 64, 75
  government, 45
  hegemony of, 74–75
  Ionian rebellion and, 54
  key events/dates, 49, 73
  Peloponnesian League, *44,* 45
  Peloponnesian War, First, 63–64
  Peloponnesian War, Great, 73–74, 78
  society, 45
Spartacus, 115, 120
Spectator, The (Addison), 494
Speeches on Religion to Its Cultured Despisers (Schleiermacher), 587
Speer, Albert, 892
Spencer, Herbert, 728, 730, 749
Speyer, Diet of (1526), 321
Spheres of influence, 762
Spinning jenny, 450, *451,* 630
Spinoza, Baruch, *501,* 501–502
Spirit of the Laws (Montesquieu), 503, 507, 511, 656
Spiritual Exercises (Ignatius of Loyola), 333–334, 337
Spiritual Franciscans, 215, 269
Spiritualists, 327
Sports, Greek, ancient/classical, 51
Sprenger, Jacob, 429
Sri Lanka, 922
SS (Schutzstaffel), 854
St. Louis World's Fair, *790*
St. Peter's Basilica, 431, *431*
St. Petersburg, 398, *400,* 453, 721
Staël, Madame de, 579, 580
Stakhanov, 841
Stalbent, Adriaen, *426*
Stalin, Joseph, 778, *833,* 839–844, *844,* 853, 877, 880–881, 896–897, 898–899, *899,* 904, 908, 913, 958
Stalingrad, Battle of (1942), 880, 883, *883*
Stamp Act, 482
Stamp Act Congress, 482, 484
Standard Histories, 254
Standard Oil Company, 693, 980
Stanley, Henry Morton, 774
Starry Messenger (Galileo), 410
Statute of Laborers, 260
Steam engine, 451, 980
Steamboats, 782
Steel industry, 692
Steele, Richard, 494
Stein, Baron von, 570
Stendhal, 579
Stephen II, Pope, 189
Stephen IX, Pope, 205
Stephenson, George, *626*
Stewart, Robert (Viscount Castlereagh), 574, *575,* 576, 601, 606, 607
Stockton and Darlington Line, 624
Stoecker, Adolf, 747
Stoics, 92–93
Stolypin, P.A., 720
Stones of Venice, The (Ruskin), 629
Stopes, Marie, 750
Storm troopers (SA), 849, 851, 854
Strachey, Lytton, 738
Strafford, Earl of, 377
Stranger, The (Camus), 959
Strategic Arms Limitation, 917
Strategic Defense Initiative (Star Wars), 918
Strauss, David Friedrich, 729
Strayer, Joseph, 202
Streltsy, 398, 400
Stresa Front, 866
Stresemann, Gustav, 850
Struggle of the Orders, 102–104
Studia humanitatis, 285, 338
Studies in Hysteria (Breuer and Freud), 743
Sturm and drang, 578
Subjection of Women, The (Mill and Taylor), 706
Sublime and nature, 583–584
Submarine cables, 783
Submission of the Clergy (1532), 331
Suburbs, development, 697–698
Sudetenland, 870, 872
Suez Canal, 768, *771*
  crisis of 1956, 914
Suffragettes, 707
Sugar, 471
  slave trade, 465, 470, 472–473
Sugar Act, 481
Sugarcane, 491
Suger, abbot of St. Denis, 220
Suleyman, sultan, *795*
Sulla, Lucius Cornelius, 119–120
Sumer/Sumerians, 2, 5–14
Summa Theologiae (Aquinas), 243
Sunday on the Grande-Jatte (Seurat), *740,* 741
Sung dynasty, 254
Sunnis, 179
Superstition, 427–428
Supreme Soviet, 929
Swabia, 203
Swastika, 860
Sweden
  Great Northern War, 398, 400–401
  Lutheranism in, 329–330
  Thirty Years' War, 367–368
Swift, Jonathan, 422, 423
Swiss Brethren, 326–327
Switzerland, Reformation in, *324,* 324–325
Syllabus of Errors, 733
Sylvester II, Pope, 242
Symposium, 50, 51
Syncretism, 157
Syphilis, 490

T

Table manners, *340*
Table of Ranks, 401, 436
Tableau de l'etat physique et moral des ouvriers (Villermé), 699
Taborites, 274
Tabula rasa, 493
Tacitus, 135, 150, 249
Taff Vale decision, 712
Taille, 260, 298, 435
Taino Indians, 305
Tajikistan, 933
Tales of the Crusades (Scott), 588
Taliban regime, 941–942, *942*
Talleyrand-Périgord, Charles Maurice de, 563, *575*
Tang dynasty, 252
Tannenberg, Battle of (1914), 815
Tanzimat, 662
Taoist Scriptures, 254
Taram-Kubi, 15
Tatar. *See* Mongols
Taylor, Harriet, 706
Taylor, Marshall Walter "Taylor," 695
Technology, 20th century, 968–971
Teerling, L.B., *360*
Tegea/Tegeans, 45
Tehran Agreement (1943), 897–899
Temple at Jerusalem, *138*
Ten Articles (1536), 332
Ten lost tribes, 28
Tencin, Claudine de, 511
Tennis Court Oath, 534, *535*
Tenochitlán, 306
Tertiaries, 215
Test Act, 379
Testament (Assisi), 215
Tetrapolitan Confession, 325
Tetrarchy, 152
Tetzel, John, *318,* 319
Teutones, 119
Textile production, 449–451, 623, 626, 627, *629*
  key events/dates, 452
Thales of Miletus, 30, 76

Thasian rebellion, 63
Thasos, 63
Thatcher, Margaret, 952, *952*, 954
Theater, 17th century, 361
Theatines, 333
Thebes, 18, 20, 74, 75, 87
Themistocles, 54, 56, 57, 58, 63, 79
Theodora, Empress, 174–175, *177*, 186
Theodore II, King of Russia, 397
Theodoric, 172
Theodosius I, 156, 159
Theodulf of Orleans, 191
Theognis of Megara, 53, 83
Theologico-Political Treatise (Spinoza), 501
Theology, Scholasticism and philosophy *versus*, 244–245
Thera, 36
Thermidorian reaction, 555–556
Thermophylae, Battle of, 55–56, 58, 109
Thessaly, 75, 87
thetes, 38, 47
Thiers, Adolphe, 674
Third Coalition, 564
Third Crusade, 209, 212, 213
Third Dynasty of Ur, 6–7
Third Estate, 532–534
Third International (Comintern), 839
Third Macedonian War, 109
Third of May, The (Goya), 573, *573*
Third Orders, 215
Third Reich, 878
Third Voyage of Gulliver's Travels (Swift), 423
Thirty-Nine Articles on Religion, 357
Thirty Tyrants rule, 74
Thirty Years' Peace (445), 64, 73
Thirty Years' War (1618-1648), 363–368
  Europe about 1600, *365*
  four periods in, 365–368
  Germany in 1648, *369*
  Holy Roman Empire in 1618, *366*
  preconditions for, 363–365
  Treaty of Westphalia, 368, 392
Thistlewood, Arthur, 605
Tholos tombs, 35
Thompson, Elizabeth (Lady Butler), *663*
Thomson, J.J., 736
Thoreau, Henry David, 920
Thoughts on Slavery (Wesley), 656
Thoughts on the Imitation of Greek Works in Painting and Sculpture (Winckelmann), 516
Thousand and One Nights, The, 588
Thrace, 74
Three Emperors' League (1873), 799–800
Three Mile Island, 984
Thucydides, 31, 43, 74, 79–80, 164, 415
Thus Spake Zarathustra (Nietzsche), 742
Thutmosis I, 21
Thutmosis II, 21
Tiananmen Square, 930
Tiberius Gracchus, 116–118, *129*, 135, 142
Tieck, Ludwig, 581
Tiepolo, Gian Battista, 514
Tillich, Paul, 967
Tilly, Johann von, 365
Tilsit, Treaty of (1807), 566, 571
Time Machine, The (Wells), *727*
Tintoretto, 292
Tirpitz, Alfred von, 803
Tisza, Stefan, 806
Tito, Josip, 908, 935
Tito, Santi di, *297*
Titus, 135, *138*
Tlaxcala, 306
To the Lighthouse (Woolf), 78
Tobacco, 376, *376*
Tocqueville, Alexis de, 856
Tojo, Hideki, 878
Tokyo Electric Light Company, 982
Toland, John, 498, 503
Toleration Act (1689), 380
Tolstoy, Leon, 897
Tools of Imperialism, 782–784
  Conquest of tropical diseases, 782
  Firearms, 782–784
  Steamboats, 782
Tories, 620
Torquemada, Tomás de, 299
Tournaments, jousting, *229*, 231
Townsend, Charles, 444, 482
Toys, 963
Trafalgar, Battle of (1805), 566
Trajan, 136, 139, 148, 150–151
Transcaucasus, 778
Transformismo, 666
Transportation and prison reform, 636
Transubstantiation, 214
Transylvania
  Habsburg, 438
  peasant rebellions in, 438, *622*
Treasure of the City of Ladies, The (Christine de Pisan), 287, *288*
Treaties. *See under name of*
Treatise on Royal and Papal Power (John of Paris), 270–271
Treatise on Tolerance (Voltaire), 499
Treitschke, Heinrich von, 669
Trenchard, John, 483
Trent, Council of (1545-1563), 334–335, 346, 355, 364, 384, 421
Tribunals, 554–555
Tribunes, 102
Tribunician sacrosanctity, 130
Trinity, 159, 187
Triple Alliance, 384, 800–801
Triple Entente (1890-1907), 801–804, 807, 811
Trireme warfare, 57, 169
Triumph of the Will, 853
Trojan Horse, *91*
Troppau, congress and protocol of (1820), 607
Trotha, Lothar von, 775, *776*
Trotsky, Leon, 820, 821, 838–840
Troubles, Council of, 355
Troy, 36
Truce of God, 205
Truman, Harry S., 885, 899, 903, 905, *905*, 910
Truman Doctrine, 904–905, 916
Ts'ia Lun, 252
Tudjman, Franjo, 936
Tudor, Henry, 299
Tull, Jethro, *443*, 444
Tulp, Nicholass, *407*
Tunisia
  French in, 768
  World War II, 880
Turgot, Robert Jacques, 446–447
Turkey, 491
  admittance into European Union, *973*, 974
  formation of, 824
  Truman Doctrine, 904–905
  in World War I, 815, 822, 823, *824*
Turkish Embassy Letters (Montagu), 503
Turks
  Ottoman, 174, 178, 320, 503–504, 525
  Seljuk, 174, 178, 207
Turner, J.M.W., 584, *585*
Turner, Nat, 658
Turnvater Jahn, 604
Tutankhamun (Tutankhaten), *1*, 18, 20
Twelve Tables, 102, 111
Twelve Years' Truce, 356
Twenty-Five Points (Nazis), 848
Twenty Thousand Leagues under the Sea (Verne), *727*
Two Sicilies, 607
Two Tactics of Social Democracy in the Bourgeois-Democratic Revolution (Lenin), 717
Two-Thirds Law, 558
Tyler, Wat, 265
Tyndale, William, 330, 332
Tyrants, ancient Greek, 43–44, 47–48, 54, 74
Tyre, 105
Tyrtaeus on the Citizen Soldier, 41

U

Ulama, 402–403
Ulema, 179, 664
Ultraroyalism, 606
Ulyanov, Vladimir Ilyrich. *See* Lenin
Ulysses (Joyce), 738
Umar, 182
Umayyads, 182
Umbrians, 98
Unam Sanctam, *269*, 272
Unemployment, 694, 836–837
Uniform Penny Post, 685
Unigenitus, 388
Union of German Women's Organization (BDFK), 707
Unions, *710*, 710–711, 861
United States. *See also* American Revolution; Cold War
  containment foreign policy, 904–905, 907
  imperialism and, 779–780
  Vietnam, 924–926, *926*
  World War I and, 815, 817, 824, 827, 830–831
  World War II, 878–879, 883, 884–885
Universal Postal Union, 685
Universities in the Middle Ages, 239–245
University of Bologna, 240–242
University of Paris, *242*, 242–243
University of Prague, 274
Ur, 6, 7, *8*, 27
Urban II, Pope, *205*, 207–208, 212
Urban IV, Pope, 267
Urban VI, Pope, 274–275
Urban VIII, Pope, 425, 431
Urbanization. *See* Cities/towns
Ure, Andrew, 628–629
Ursulines, 333
Uruguay, 613
Uruk, 5, 6, *7*, *10*
Utanapishtim, *13*, 29
Uthman, 182
Utilitarianism, 639
Utopia (More), 303
Utopian socialism, 639–641
Utrecht, Treaty of (1713), 391, 464, 466, 479
Utrecht, Union of, 356
Uvarov, 615

V

Vaihinger, Hans, 736
Valens, 156, 172
Valentinian I, 156
Valerian, 149, 158
Valla, Lorenzo, 189, 258, 289, 302
Valley of the Kings, 18
Valmy, Battle of, 547
Valois dynasty, 320
van der Weyden, Roger, *281*
Van Gogh, Vincent, 740
Vandals, 172, 176
Varennes, 546
Vassalage, 196, 198, 199, 228
Vassals, 196, 198, 199, 228
Vassy massacre, *345*, 348
Vatican City, 733, 847
Vatican II, 967
Vega, Lope de, 341
Veii, 103–104
Velvet Revolution (1989), 930
Venezuela, 613
Venice, 211, *211*, 283, 285, 295–296, 453, *597*
Verdun, Battle of (1916), 815
Verdun, Treaty of (843), 194, *194*
Vergerio, Pietro Paolo, 287
Vergil, 126, 132, 133, 134, *134*, 285
Vermuyden Cornelius, 444
Verne, Jules, *727*
Verona, congress of, 607
Verona, Guarino da, 287
Versailles, 382, *383*, 431
  Hall of Mirrors, 431, *672*, 674
Versailles, Treaty of (1920), 824–831, 846, 847, 851, 861
Vervins, Treaty of (1598), 351
Vesey, Denmark, 658
Vespasian, 135, 136
Vespucci, Amerigo, 305
Vesteras, Diet of (1527), 330
Vesuvians, 648
Viceroyalties, 466, *468*
Vichy Regime, 893, 894, 922–923
Victor Emmanuel I, King of Italy, 665
Victor Emmanuel II, King of Italy, 652, *665*, 666
Victor Emmanuel III, King of Italy, 846
Victoria, Queen of Britain, 758, 761, *902*
Vienna
  Congress of (1815), 574–577, *575*, *577*, 593, 594, 601, 658, *667*, 768
  revolution of 1848, 649
Vietnam, 924–926, *926*
Vietnamization, 925–296
Vikings (Normans), 195, *195*, *196*
Villa, 154, 156
Villermé, Louis René, 699
Vincent, David Brown, 787
Vindication of the Rights of Woman, A (Wollstonecraft), 512, 515, 706
Vingtième, 435
Violin and Palette (Braque), *741*, 742
Virchow, Rudolf, 699
Virgil, 795
Visconti family, 272, 284, 285
Visigoths, 155–156, 172, 176, 187
Vita Nuova (Dante), 287
Vitruvian Man (Leonardo da Vinci), 293
Vitruvius, Marcus Pollio, *293*
Vizier, 17
Vladimir of Kiev, 278
Vogt, Karl, 749
Voix des femmes, 648, 649
Voltaire, 421, 495, 496, *497*, 497–498, 499, 500, 502, 517, *517*, 726
Voting rights for women, *707*, 707–708, 750

Vulgate (Bible), 161, 289, 302

W

Wagram, Battle of, 570
Wahhabi movement, 734, 940
Wake Island, 879
Wakefield, Priscilla, 453, 454
Waldeck-Rousseau, René/Pierre, 713, 732
Waldensians, 214, 267, 274
Walesa, Lech, 917, 929
Wall Street crash (1929), 835
Wallace, Alfred Russel, 728
Wallas, Graham, 712, 745
Wallenstein, Albrecht of, 367, 368
Walpole, Robert, *380,* 380–381, 478, 479, 483, 484
Walsingham, Francis, 362
War and Peace (Tolstoy), 897
War Communism, 838
War guilt cause, World War I, 829
War of Austrian Succession (1740-1748), 478–479, 521
War of Devolution (1667-1668), 384
War of Jenkins's Ear, 478, 608
War of the Spanish Succession (1701-1714), *390,* 390–391, *466*
War of the Worlds (Wells), *727*
War reparations, 829, 835–836, 847
Warfare/weaponry. *See* Military/weaponry
Wars of the Roses, 299
Warsaw, 889, 890
 18th century, 453
Warsaw Pact (1955), 903, 909, 914
Warton, Thomas, 579
Washington, George, 483, *483*
Water as energy source, 979, *979*
Water-clock, *66*
Water frame, 450–451
Water system, 699
Waterloo, Battle of (1815), 547, 576
Watt, James, 451, 980
Watteau, Jean-Antoine, 514, *514,* 516
Watts, George Frederick, *625*
Wealth of Nations, The (Smith), 505, 506, 509, 629, 638, 656
Webb, Beatrice, 712, *712,* 728
Webb, Sidney, 712, *712*
Weber, Max, 734, 744–745, 749
Wedgewood, Josiah, 449
Weigel, Valentin, 346
Weimar Republic, 835, 847–851
Weizmann, Chaim, 909
Welf interregnum, 223
Welfare state, 950–955
Wellesley, Arthur (Duke of Wellington), 570, 574, 619
Wellhausen, Julius, 729
Wells, H.G., 712, 727
Welsey, Charles, 656
Wentworth, Thomas, 377
Wesley, Charles, 586
Wesley, John, *586,* 586–587, 656
Wesley, Susannah, 586
West, Benjamin, *462*
West Africa, 773–774
West Indies, 465, 472
 slavery in, 470–473, 658
Western Front, *814*
Western Missionary Movement, 784
Westminister, convention of (1756), 479
Westphalia, Treaty of (1648), 368, 392
Wet nursing, 341
What is Property? (Proudhon), 641
What is the Third Estate (Siéyés), 563
What Is to Be Done? (Lenin), 715, 719
Wheat, 491
Wheatley, Francis, *433*
Whether Heretics Should Be Punished By the Sword of the Magistrates (Castellio), 358
Whewell, William, 726
Whigs, 379, 483–484, 619
White-collar workers, 696
White Mountain, Battle of (1620), 367
White Russians, 278, 821
White Terror, 606
Whiteread, Rachel, 965–966, *966*
Whitgift, John, 360
Wilberforce, William, 657, 658
Wilhelm I, kaiser, *672*
Wilkes, John, 484
"Wilkes and Liberty," 484
Wilkinson, John, 451
William I, Emperor of Germany, 671, 673, 713
William I, King of Holland, 618
William II, Emperor of Germany, 713, 801, *801,* 802–803, 807, 822
William II, of Sicily, 222
William III, King of England, 372, 373, 379–380, 384
William IV, King of England, 619–620
William Lovell (Tieck), 581
William of Ockham, 258, 272, 274, 316
William of Orange (the Silent), 354, 355, 356, 372, 379–380
William the Conqueror, 215–216, 231
William the Pious, Duke of Aquitaine, 204
Williams, George Washington, 774
Willliam I, King of Holland, 618
Wilson, Woodrow, 815, 817, 822, 824–825, *825,* 827
Winckelmann, Johann Joachim, 516
Wind as energy source, 979
Windischgraetz, Alfred, 650
"Winged Victory of Samothrace," 61
Winkelmann, Maria, 421
Wisdom of God Manifested in His Works of Creation (Ray), 427
Witchcraft, 427–428
Witte, Sergei, 714–715, 717, 720
Wojtyla, Karol (John Paul II), 917
Wolfe, James, *462,* 480
Wollstonecraft, Mary, *512,* 512–514, 515, 706
Wolsey, Thomas, 330, 331
Women
 cult of domesticity, 704
 education of Roman, 113, 114
 educational barriers, 701–702
 Egyptian, 21
 employment patterns in 19th century, 632–633, 702–703, *703*
 Enlightenment and, 511–514
 Etruscan, *99*
 family economy of 18th century and, 441–442
 feminism, 647–649, 706–709, 747–751, 953, 956
 French (1848), 647–649
 French Revolution and, 539, *539,* 547, 553–554, 557
 Greek, ancient, 39
 Greek, classical, 67, 70–71, 85
 in Homeric society, 38
 Industrial Revolution (18th century), *433,* 452–453
 Industrial Revolution (19th century), 632–634, *633,* 635
 legal issues regarding, 700–701
 medieval, *245,* 245–248
 Mesopotamian, 3, 14
 middle class, 704–706
 as midwives, 430, *430*
 Napoleonic Code and, 564, 700
 Nazi Germany and role of, 855, 858, 859, 860, 892–893
 Paleolithic Age, 3
 Plato's view of, 85
 poverty/prostitution, 704
 property rights, 700
 Reformation and, 338–339
 Renaissance, *284,* 287, 288
 Roman, 100, 114, 141–142
 Scientific Revolution and, 419–421
 in the Soviet Union, 858–859
 Spartan, 45
 as teachers, 701, *725*
 in the 19th century, 700–709, 747, 749
 in the 20th century, *953,* 956–957
 in Utopian Republic, 85
 voting rights, *707,* 707–708, 750
 witchcraft and, 428, 429
 working-class women, 248, 632–635, *690,* 703–704
 World War I and role of, *823*
 World War II and role of, 881
Women's Social and Political Union, 707
Woolf, Leonard, 738
Woolf, Virginia, 738, *751,* 751–752
Wordsworth, William, 581
Working-class women, 248, 632–635, *690,* 703–704
Works and Days (Hesiod), 49, 134
World's Fairs, *790,* 791
World-Spirit, 589
World Trade Center, terrorist attacks on, 903, 940, 942
World War I (1914-1917)
 casualties, 822, 834, *835*
 combatants, *812*
 end of, 821–824
 in Europe, *798, 813*
 major campaigns/events, *822,* 806
 naval Battles, 815, 817
 origins of, 804–805
 propaganda, 826, 893
 Sarajevo and the outbreak of, 806–811
 settlement at Paris, 824–831, *828,* 834
 strategies and stalemate, 811–817
 U.S. enters, 817
 Western Front, *814*
World War II
 allied landings in Africa, Sicily and Italy, 880
 atomic bomb, *865,* 884–885
 Battle of Britain, 875–876
 Battle of Stalingrad, 880, 883, *883*
 Battle of the Bulge, 883
 in Britain, 875–876, 895–896, *896*
 cost of, 885–886
 defeat of Germany, 883
 defeat of Japan, 884–885
 displacement of people, 948
 events leading to, 866–872, *874*
 in France, 893–895
 German attack on Soviet Union, 876–878
 German conquest/plans for Europe, 874–875
 in Germany, 870, 892–893
 Holocaust and racism, *886,* 886–887, *887,* 890–891, *891*
 Japan enters the war, 878
 major campaigns/events, *880, 890*
 map of, *885*
 preparations for peace, 897
 in Soviet Union, 858–859, *859,* 896–897
 strategic bombing, 883
 U.S. enters the war, 878
Worms, Concordat of (1122), 207, 221
Worms, Diet of (1521), 314, 319–320
Wright, Joseph, *452*
Writing, 4
 Canaanites, 27
 Carolingian minuscule, 192
 Crete, 35
 cuneiform, 9
 Greek alphabet, 40, 177
 hieroglyphics, 19, 35
 invention of, 9
 Linear A and B, 35, 36
 Persian, 27
Wycliffe, John, 255, 273–274
Wyvil, Christopher, 485

X

X-rays, invention of, 736
Xenophanes of Colophon, 30
Xenophon, 68, 80
Xerox Corporation, 971
Xerxes, 26, 54–56, *55,* 75, 79, 794

Y

Yablonskaya, Tatjiana, 964, *964*
Yalta Conference (1945), 899, *899*
Yaroslav the Wise, 278
Yellow fever, 789
Yeltsin, Boris, 932, 933, 934–935
York, House of, 299
Yorkshire Association Movement, 485
Yorktown, Battle of, 483, *485*
Young, Arthur, 444
Young Italy Society, 665
Young Plan, 851
Young Turks, 664, 804, 823
Yugoslavia
 collapse of, and civil war, 935–937, *936*
 ethnic composition of, 935
 formation of, 829, 862
 in the 1920s, 862–863
 World War II, 876

Z

Zacharias, Pope, 188
Zama, Battle of, 108
Zara, 211
Zarathushtra, 26
Zasulich, Vera, 682
Zedong, Mao, 911
Zemstvos, 681, 684, 715
Zeno, 76, 92, 172
Zeus, 50, 51, 80
Ziggurat, 11
Zionist movement, 710, 747, 748, 909
Ziska, John, 274
Zola, Émile, 675, 677, 737
Zollverein, 638, 669
Zoology, 789
Zoroaster, 26
Zoroastrianism, 26, 157
Zurich, Reformation in, 324–325
Zurich, University of, 701
Zwingli, Ulrich, 324–325, 335

GREENLAND
(DENMARK)
U.S.
CANADA
ALEUTIAN ISLANDS
UNITED KINGDOM
IRELAND
ANDORRA
ATLANTIC
OCEAN
PORTUGAL
UNITED STATES
PACIFIC
OCEAN
MOROCCO
MEXICO
BAHAMAS
CUBA
WESTERN
SAHARA
(MOROCCO)
Tropic of Cancer
U.S.
HAITI
PUERTO RICO (U.S.)
JAMAICA
ST. KITTS AND NEVIS
ANTIGUA AND BARBUDA
DOMINICA
ST. VINCENT AND
THE GRENADINES
BARBADOS
MAURITANIA
BELIZE
HONDURAS
DOMINICAN
REPUBLIC
CAPE VERDE
SENEGAL
GAMBIA
GUINEA-BISSAU
GUINEA
SIERRA LEONE
LIBERIA
IVORY COAST
GHANA
GUATEMALA
EL SALVADOR
NICARAGUA
GRENADA
COSTA RICA
TRINIDAD AND TOBAGO
GUYANA
SURINAME
FRENCH
GUIANA
(FR)
PANAMA
VENEZUELA
COLOMBIA
Equator
GALAPAGOS
ISLANDS
(ECUADOR)
ECUADOR
CENTRAL AFRICAN REPU
SÃO TOMÉ AND PRÍ
EQUATORIAL G
PERU
BRAZIL
WESTERN
SAMOA
BOLIVIA
TONGA
PARAGUAY
Tropic of Capricorn
CHILE
ARGENTINA
URUGUAY
PACIFIC
OCEAN
ATLANTIC
OCEAN
Antarctic Circle
Arctic Cir
ICELAN